Who Was Who in America®

Who Was Who in America®
with world notables

2002-2004
Volume XV

MARQUIS
Who'sWho® 562 Central Avenue
New Providence, NJ 07974 U.S.A.

Who Was Who in America

Marquis Who's Who

Published by Marquis Who's Who LLC.

For information, contact:
   Marquis Who's Who
   562 Central Avenue
   New Providence, New Jersey 07974
   1-908-673-1001
   www.marquiswhoswho.com

International Standard Book Number   0-8379-0246-0 (17-volume set)
                                     0-8379-0247-9 (volume XV)
                                     0-8379-0248-7 (Index volume)
                                     0-8379-0249-5 (volume XV and Index volume)
International Standard Serial Number   0146-8081

Manufactured in the United States of America.

Table of Contents

Preface

Marquis Who's Who is proud to present the 2004-2005 Edition of *Who Was Who in America.* This 15ᵗʰ edition features over 3,900 profiles of individuals who had previously been profiled in *Who's Who in America* and other Marquis Who's Who publications, but who have died since the publication of the last edition of *Who Was Who in America* in August, 2002.

Among the notable Americans profiled in this volume are individuals as influential and diverse as Ronald Reagan, Marlon Brando, Katharine Hepburn, and Bob Hope. The impact of these individuals during their lifetimes was enormous and their influence is certain to live on.

Of course, not every person profiled in this volume is a household name. These pages include the profiles of doctors, lawyers, entrepreneurs, researchers, inventors, and other prominent achievers who have died in the last two years.

The biographical information included in the profiles that follow was gathered in a variety of manners. In most cases, those listed had submitted their personal biographical details during their lifetime. In many cases, though, the information was collected independently by our research and editorial staffs, which use a wide assortment of tools to gather complete, accurate, and up-to-date information.

Who Was Who in America is an important component of the Marquis Who's Who family of publications. Along with *Who's Who in America* and *Who's Who in the World*, Marquis Who's Who also publishes a number of specialized and regionalized volumes. These books include *Who's Who of American Women, Who's Who in American Law, Who's Who in Medicine and Healthcare,* and *Who's Who in the East,* to name a few.

It has been Marquis Who's Who's honor to compile this edition of *Who Was Who in America.* It is our hope that the biographical profiles can begin to do justice to the individuals memorialized on these pages.

Table of Abbreviations

The following abbreviations and symbols are frequently used in this book.

A Associate (used with academic degrees only)

AA, A.A. Associate in Arts, Associate of Arts

AAAL American Academy of Arts and Letters

AAAS American Association for the Advancement of Science

AACD American Association for Counseling and Development

AACN American Association of Critical Care Nurses

AAHA American Academy of Health Administrators

AAHP American Association of Hospital Planners

AAHPERD American Alliance for Health, Physical Education, Recreation, and Dance

AAS Associate of Applied Science

AASL American Association of School Librarians

AASPA American Association of School Personnel Administrators

AAU Amateur Athletic Union

AAUP American Association of University Professors

AAUW American Association of University Women

AB, A.B. Arts, Bachelor of

AB Alberta

ABA American Bar Association

ABC American Broadcasting Company

AC Air Corps

acad. academy, academic

acct. accountant

acctg. accounting

ACDA Arms Control and Disarmament Agency

ACHA American College of Hospital Administrators

ACLS Advanced Cardiac Life Support

ACLU American Civil Liberties Union

ACOG American College of Ob-Gyn

ACP American College of Physicians

ACS American College of Surgeons

ADA American Dental Association

a.d.c. aide-de-camp

adj. adjunct, adjutant

adj. gen. adjutant general

adm. admiral

adminstr. administrator

adminstrn. administration

adminstrv. administrative

ADN Associate's Degree in Nursing

ADP Automatic Data Processing

adv. advocate, advisory

advt. advertising

AE, A.E. Agricultural Engineer

A.E. and P. Ambassador Extraordinary and Plenipotentiary

AEC Atomic Energy Commission

aero. aeronautical, aeronautic

aerodyn. aerodynamic

AFB Air Force Base

AFL-CIO American Federation of Labor and Congress of Industrial Organizations

AFTRA American Federation of TV and Radio Artists

AFSCME American Federation of State, County and Municipal Employees

agr. agriculture

agrl. agricultural

agt. agent

AGVA American Guild of Variety Artists

agy. agency

A&I Agricultural and Industrial

AIA American Institute of Architects

AIAA American Institute of Aeronautics and Astronautics

AIChE American Institute of Chemical Engineers

AICPA American Institute of Certified Public Accountants

AID Agency for International Development

AIDS Acquired Immune Deficiency Syndrome

AIEE American Institute of Electrical Engineers

AIM American Institute of Management

AIME American Institute of Mining, Metallurgy, and Petroleum Engineers

AK Alaska

AL Alabama

ALA American Library Association

Ala. Alabama

alt. alternate

Alta. Alberta

A&M Agricultural and Mechanical

AM, A.M. Arts, Master of

Am. American, America

AMA American Medical Association

amb. ambassador

A.M.E. African Methodist Episcopal

Amtrak National Railroad Passenger Corporation

AMVETS American Veterans of World War II, Korea, Vietnam

ANA American Nurses Association

anat. anatomical

ANCC American Nurses Credentialing Center

ann. annual

ANTA American National Theatre and Academy

anthrop. anthropological

AP Associated Press

APA American Psychological Association

APGA American Personnel Guidance Association

APHA American Public Health Association

APO Army Post Office

apptd. appointed

Apr. April

apt. apartment

AR Arkansas

ARC American Red Cross

arch. architect

archeol. archeological

archtl. architectural

Ariz. Arizona

Ark. Arkansas

ArtsD, ArtsD. Arts, Doctor of

arty. artillery

AS American Samoa

AS Associate in Science

ASCAP American Society of Composers, Authors and Publishers

ASCD Association for Supervision and Curriculum Development

ASCE American Society of Civil Engineers

ASHRAE American Society of Heating, Refrigeration, and Air Conditioning Engineers

ASME American Society of Mechanical Engineers

ASNSA American Society for Nursing Service Administrators

ASPA American Society for Public Administration

ASPCA American Society for the Prevention of Cruelty to Animals

assn. association

assoc. associate

asst. assistant

ASTD American Society for Training and Development

ASTM American Society for Testing and Materials

astron. astronomical

astrophys. astrophysical

ATLA Association of Trial Lawyers of America

ATSC Air Technical Service Command

AT&T American Telephone & Telegraph Company

atty. attorney

Aug. August

AUS Army of the United States

aux. auxiliary

Ave. Avenue

AVMA American Veterinary Medical Association

AZ Arizona

AWHONN Association of Women's Health Obstetric and Neonatal Nurses

B. Bachelor

b. born

BA, B.A. Bachelor of Arts

BAgr, B.Agr. Bachelor of Agriculture

Balt. Baltimore

Bapt. Baptist

BArch, B.Arch. Bachelor of Architecture

BAS, B.A.S. Bachelor of Agricultural Science

BBA, B.B.A. Bachelor of Business Administration

BBB Better Business Bureau

BBC British Broadcasting Corporation

BC, B.C. British Columbia

BCE, B.C.E. Bachelor of Civil Engineering

BChir, B.Chir. Bachelor of Surgery

BCL, B.C.L. Bachelor of Civil Law

BCLS Basic Cardiac Life Support

BCS, B.C.S. Bachelor of Commercial Science

BD, B.D. Bachelor of Divinity

bd. board

BE, B.E. Bachelor of Education

BEE, B.E.E. Bachelor of Electrical Engineering

BFA, B.F.A. Bachelor of Fine Arts
bibl. biblical
bibliog. bibliographical
biog. biographical
biol. biological
BJ, B.J. Bachelor of Journalism
Bklyn. Brooklyn
BL, B.L. Bachelor of Letters
bldg. building
BLS, B.L.S. Bachelor of Library Science
BLS Basic Life Support
Blvd. Boulevard
BMI Broadcast Music, Inc.
BMW Bavarian Motor Works (Bayerische Motoren Werke)
bn. battalion
B.&O.R.R. Baltimore & Ohio Railroad
bot. botanical
BPE, B.P.E. Bachelor of Physical Education
BPhil, B.Phil. Bachelor of Philosophy
br. branch
BRE, B.R.E. Bachelor of Religious Education
brig. gen. brigadier general
Brit. British, Brittanica
Bros. Brothers
BS, B.S. Bachelor of Science
BSA, B.S.A. Bachelor of Agricultural Science
BSBA Bachelor of Science in Business Administration
BSChemE Bachelor of Science in Chemical Engineering
BSD, B.S.D. Bachelor of Didactic Science
BSEE Bachelor of Science in Electrical Engineering
BSN Bachelor of Science in Nursing
BST, B.S.T. Bachelor of Sacred Theology
BTh, B.Th. Bachelor of Theology
bull. bulletin
bur. bureau
bus. business
B.W.I. British West Indies

CA California
CAA Civil Aeronautics Administration
CAB Civil Aeronautics Board
CAD-CAM Computer Aided Design– Computer Aided Model
Calif. California
C.Am. Central America
Can. Canada, Canadian
CAP Civil Air Patrol
capt. captain
cardiol. cardiological
cardiovasc. cardiovascular
CARE Cooperative American Relief Everywhere
Cath. Catholic
cav. cavalry
CBC Canadian Broadcasting Company
CBI China, Burma, India Theatre of Operations
CBS Columbia Broadcasting Company
C.C. Community College
CCC Commodity Credit Corporation
CCNY City College of New York
CCRN Critical Care Registered Nurse
CCU Cardiac Care Unit
CD Civil Defense
CE, C.E. Corps of Engineers, Civil Engineer
CEN Certified Emergency Nurse
CENTO Central Treaty Organization

CEO chief executive officer
CERN European Organization of Nuclear Research
cert. certificate, certification, certified
CETA Comprehensive Employment Training Act
CFA Chartered Financial Analyst
CFL Canadian Football League
CFO chief financial officer
CFP Certified Financial Planner
ch. church
ChD, Ch.D. Doctor of Chemistry
chem. chemical
ChemE, Chem.E. Chemical Engineer
ChFC Chartered Financial Consultant
Chgo. Chicago
chirurg. chirurgical
chmn. chairman
chpt. chapter
CIA Central Intelligence Agency
Cin. Cincinnati
cir. circle, circuit
CLE Continuing Legal Education
Cleve. Cleveland
climatol. climatological
clin. clinical
clk. clerk
C.L.U. Chartered Life Underwriter
CM, C.M. Master in Surgery
CM Northern Mariana Islands
CMA Certified Medical Assistant
cmty. community
CNA Certified Nurse's Aide
CNOR Certified Nurse (Operating Room)
C.&N.W.Ry. Chicago & North Western Railway
CO Colorado
Co. Company
COF Catholic Order of Foresters
C. of C. Chamber of Commerce
col. colonel
coll. college
Colo. Colorado
com. committee
comd. commanded
comdg. commanding
comdr. commander
comdt. commandant
comm. communications
commd. commissioned
comml. commercial
commn. commission
commr. commissioner
compt. comptroller
condr. conductor
Conf. Conference
Congl. Congregational, Congressional
Conglist. Congregationalist
Conn. Connecticut
cons. consultant, consulting
consol. consolidated
constl. constitutional
constn. constitution
constrn. construction
contbd. contributed
contbg. contributing
contbn. contribution
contbr. contributor
contr. controller
Conv. Convention
COO chief operating officer
coop. cooperative
coord. coordinator
CORDS Civil Operations and Revolutionary Development Support
CORE Congress of Racial Equality

corp. corporation, corporate
corr. correspondent, corresponding, correspondence
C.&O.Ry. Chesapeake & Ohio Railway
coun. council
CPA Certified Public Accountant
CPCU Chartered Property and Casualty Underwriter
CPH, C.P.H. Certificate of Public Health
cpl. corporal
CPR Cardio-Pulmonary Resuscitation
C.P.Ry. Canadian Pacific Railway
CRT Cathode Ray Terminal
C.S. Christian Science
CSB, C.S.B. Bachelor of Christian Science
C.S.C. Civil Service Commission
CT Connecticut
ct. court
ctr. center
ctrl. central
CWS Chemical Warfare Service
C.Z. Canal Zone

D. Doctor
d. daughter
DAgr, D.Agr. Doctor of Agriculture
DAR Daughters of the American Revolution
dau. daughter
DAV Disabled American Veterans
DC, D.C. District of Columbia
DCL, D.C.L. Doctor of Civil Law
DCS, D.C.S. Doctor of Commercial Science
DD, D.D. Doctor of Divinity
DDS, D.D.S. Doctor of Dental Surgery
DE Delaware
Dec. December
dec. deceased
def. defense
Del. Delaware
del. delegate, delegation
Dem. Democrat, Democratic
DEng, D.Eng. Doctor of Engineering
denom. denomination, denominational
dep. deputy
dept. department
dermatol. dermatological
desc. descendant
devel. development, developmental
DFA, D.F.A. Doctor of Fine Arts
D.F.C. Distinguished Flying Cross
DHL, D.H.L. Doctor of Hebrew Literature
dir. director
dist. district
distbg. distributing
distbn. distribution
distbr. distributor
disting. distinguished
div. division, divinity, divorce
divsn. division
DLitt, D.Litt. Doctor of Literature
DMD, D.M.D. Doctor of Dental Medicine
DMS, D.M.S. Doctor of Medical Science
DO, D.O. Doctor of Osteopathy
docs. documents
DON Director of Nursing
DPH, D.P.H. Diploma in Public Health
DPhil, D.Phil. Doctor of Philosophy
D.R. Daughters of the Revolution
Dr. Drive, Doctor
DRE, D.R.E. Doctor of Religious Education
DrPH, Dr.P.H. Doctor of Public Health, Doctor of Public Hygiene

D.S.C. Distinguished Service Cross
DSc, D.Sc. Doctor of Science
DSChemE Doctor of Science in Chemical Engineering
D.S.M. Distinguished Service Medal
DST, D.S.T. Doctor of Sacred Theology
DTM, D.T.M. Doctor of Tropical Medicine
DVM, D.V.M. Doctor of Veterinary Medicine
DVS, D.V.S. Doctor of Veterinary Surgery

E, E. East
ea. eastern
E. and P. Extraordinary and Plenipotentiary
Eccles. Ecclesiastical
ecol. ecological
econ. economic
ECOSOC Economic and Social Council (of the UN)
ED, E.D. Doctor of Engineering
ed. educated
EdB, Ed.B. Bachelor of Education
EdD, Ed.D. Doctor of Education
edit. edition
editl. editorial
EdM, Ed.M. Master of Education
edn. education
ednl. educational
EDP Electronic Data Processing
EdS, Ed.S. Specialist in Education
EE, E.E. Electrical Engineer
E.E. and M.P. Envoy Extraordinary and Minister Plenipotentiary
EEC European Economic Community
EEG Electroencephalogram
EEO Equal Employment Opportunity
EEOC Equal Employment Opportunity Commission
E.Ger. German Democratic Republic
EKG Electrocardiogram
elec. electrical
electrochem. electrochemical
electrophys. electrophysical
elem. elementary
EM, E.M. Engineer of Mines
EMT Emergency Medical Technician
ency. encyclopedia
Eng. England
engr. engineer
engring. engineering
entomol. entomological
environ. environmental
EPA Environmental Protection Agency
epidemiol. epidemiological
Episc. Episcopalian
ERA Equal Rights Amendment
ERDA Energy Research and Development Administration
ESEA Elementary and Secondary Education Act
ESL English as Second Language
ESPN Entertainment and Sports Programming Network
ESSA Environmental Science Services Administration
ethnol. ethnological
ETO European Theatre of Operations
Evang. Evangelical
exam. examination, examining
Exch. Exchange
exec. executive
exhbn. exhibition
expdn. expedition
expn. exposition
expt. experiment

exptl. experimental
Expy. Expressway
Ext. Extension

F.A. Field Artillery
FAA Federal Aviation Administration
FAO Food and Agriculture Organization (of the UN)
FBA Federal Bar Association
FBI Federal Bureau of Investigation
FCA Farm Credit Administration
FCC Federal Communications Commission
FCDA Federal Civil Defense Administration
FDA Food and Drug Administration
FDIA Federal Deposit Insurance Administration
FDIC Federal Deposit Insurance Corporation
FE, F.E. Forest Engineer
FEA Federal Energy Administration
Feb. February
fed. federal
fedn. federation
FERC Federal Energy Regulatory Commission
fgn. foreign
FHA Federal Housing Administration
fin. financial, finance
FL Florida
Fl. Floor
Fla. Florida
FMC Federal Maritime Commission
FNP Family Nurse Practitioner
FOA Foreign Operations Administration
found. foundation
FPC Federal Power Commission
FPO Fleet Post Office
frat. fraternity
FRS Federal Reserve System
FSA Federal Security Agency
Ft. Fort
FTC Federal Trade Commission
Fwy. Freeway

G-1 (or other number) Division of General Staff
GA, Ga. Georgia
GAO General Accounting Office
gastroent. gastroenterological
GATE Gifted and Talented Educators
GATT General Agreement on Tariffs and Trade
GE General Electric Company
gen. general
geneal. genealogical
geod. geodetic
geog. geographic, geographical
geol. geological
geophys. geophysical
geriat. geriatrics
gerontol. gerontological
G.H.Q. General Headquarters
GM General Motors Corporation
GMAC General Motors Acceptance Corporation
G.N.Ry. Great Northern Railway
gov. governor
govt. government
govtl. governmental
GPO Government Printing Office
grad. graduate, graduated
GSA General Services Administration
Gt. Great
GTE General Telephone and Electric Company
GU Guam

gynecol. gynecological

HBO Home Box Office
hdqs. headquarters
HEW Department of Health, Education and Welfare
HHD, H.H.D. Doctor of Humanities
HHFA Housing and Home Finance Agency
HHS Department of Health and Human Services
HI Hawaii
hist. historical, historic
HM, H.M. Master of Humanities
HMO Health Maintenance Organization
homeo. homeopathic
hon. honorary, honorable
Ho. of Dels. House of Delegates
Ho. of Reps. House of Representatives
hort. horticultural
hosp. hospital
H.S. High School
HUD Department of Housing and Urban Development
Hwy. Highway
hydrog. hydrographic

IA Iowa
IAEA International Atomic Energy Agency
IATSE International Alliance of Theatrical and Stage Employees and Moving Picture Operators of the United States and Canada
IBM International Business Machines Corporation
IBRD International Bank for Reconstruction and Development
ICA International Cooperation Administration
ICC Interstate Commerce Commission
ICCE International Council for Computers in Education
ICU Intensive Care Unit
ID Idaho
IEEE Institute of Electrical and Electronics Engineers
IFC International Finance Corporation
IGY International Geophysical Year
IL Illinois
Ill. Illinois
illus. illustrated
ILO International Labor Organization
IMF International Monetary Fund
IN Indiana
Inc. Incorporated
Ind. Indiana
ind. independent
Indpls. Indianapolis
indsl. industrial
inf. infantry
info. information
ins. insurance
insp. inspector
insp. gen. inspector general
inst. institute
instl. institutional
instn. institution
instr. instructor
instrn. instruction
instrnl. instructional
internat. international
intro. introduction
IRE Institute of Radio Engineers
IRS Internal Revenue Service
ITT International Telephone & Telegraph Corporation

JAG Judge Advocate General
JAGC Judge Advocate General Corps
Jan. January
Jaycees Junior Chamber of Commerce
JB, J.B. Jurum Baccalaureus
JCB, J.C.B. Juris Canoni Baccalaureus
JCD, J.C.D. Juris Canonici Doctor, Juris
Civilis Doctor
JCL, J.C.L. Juris Canonici Licentiatus
JD, J.D. Juris Doctor
jg. junior grade
jour. journal
jr. junior
JSD, J.S.D. Juris Scientiae Doctor
JUD, J.U.D. Juris Utriusque Doctor
jud. judicial

Kans. Kansas
K.C. Knights of Columbus
K.P. Knights of Pythias
KS Kansas
K.T. Knight Templar
KY, Ky. Kentucky

LA, La. Louisiana
L.A. Los Angeles
lab. laboratory
L.Am. Latin America
lang. language
laryngol. laryngological
LB Labrador
LDS Latter Day Saints
LDS Church Church of Jesus Christ of
Latter Day Saints
lectr. lecturer
legis. legislation, legislative
LHD, L.H.D. Doctor of Humane Letters
L.I. Long Island
libr. librarian, library
lic. licensed, license
L.I.R.R. Long Island Railroad
lit. literature
litig. litigation
LittB, Litt.B. Bachelor of Letters
LittD, Litt.D. Doctor of Letters
LLB, LL.B. Bachelor of Laws
LLD, L.L.D. Doctor of Laws
LLM, L.L.M. Master of Laws
Ln. Lane
L.&N.R.R. Louisville & Nashville
Railroad
LPGA Ladies Professional Golf
Association
LPN Licensed Practical Nurse
LS, L.S. Library Science (in degree)
lt. lieutenant
Ltd. Limited
Luth. Lutheran
LWV League of Women Voters

M. Master
m. married
MA, M.A. Master of Arts
MA Massachusetts
MADD Mothers Against Drunk Driving
mag. magazine
MAgr, M.Agr. Master of Agriculture
maj. major
Man. Manitoba
Mar. March
MArch, M.Arch. Master in Architecture
Mass. Massachusetts
math. mathematics, mathematical
MATS Military Air Transport Service
MB, M.B. Bachelor of Medicine
MB Manitoba

MBA, M.B.A. Master of Business
Administration
MBS Mutual Broadcasting System
M.C. Medical Corps
MCE, M.C.E. Master of Civil Engineer-
ing
mcht. merchant
mcpl. municipal
MCS, M.C.S. Master of Commercial
Science
MD, M.D. Doctor of Medicine
MD, Md. Maryland
MDiv Master of Divinity
MDip, M.Dip. Master in Diplomacy
mdse. merchandise
MDV, M.D.V. Doctor of Veterinary
Medicine
ME, M.E. Mechanical Engineer
ME Maine
M.E.Ch. Methodist Episcopal Church
mech. mechanical
MEd., M.Ed. Master of Education
med. medical
MEE, M.E.E. Master of Electrical
Engineering
mem. member
meml. memorial
merc. mercantile
met. metropolitan
metall. metallurgical
MetE, Met.E. Metallurgical Engineer
meteorol. meteorological
Meth. Methodist
Mex. Mexico
MF, M.F. Master of Forestry
MFA, M.F.A. Master of Fine Arts
mfg. manufacturing
mfr. manufacturer
mgmt. management
mgr. manager
MHA, M.H.A. Master of Hospital
Administration
M.I. Military Intelligence
MI Michigan
Mich. Michigan
micros. microscopic, microscopical
mid. middle
mil. military
Milw. Milwaukee
Min. Minister
mineral. mineralogical
Minn. Minnesota
MIS Management Information Systems
Miss. Mississippi
MIT Massachusetts Institute of Technol-
ogy
mktg. marketing
ML, M.L. Master of Laws
MLA Modern Language Association
M.L.D. Magister Legnum Diplomatic
MLitt, M.Litt. Master of Literature,
Master of Letters
MLS, M.L.S. Master of Library Science
MME, M.M.E. Master of Mechanical
Engineering
MN Minnesota
mng. managing
MO, Mo. Missouri
moblzn. mobilization
Mont. Montana
MP Northern Mariana Islands
M.P. Member of Parliament
MPA Master of Public Administration
MPE, M.P.E. Master of Physical
Education
MPH, M.P.H. Master of Public Health

MPhil, M.Phil. Master of Philosophy
MPL, M.P.L. Master of Patent Law
Mpls. Minneapolis
MRE, M.R.E. Master of Religious
Education
MRI Magnetic Resonance Imaging
MS, M.S. Master of Science
MS, Ms. Mississippi
MSc, M.Sc. Master of Science
MSChemE Master of Science in Chemical
Engineering
MSEE Master of Science in Electrical
Engineering
MSF, M.S.F. Master of Science of
Forestry
MSN Master of Science in Nursing
MST, M.S.T. Master of Sacred Theology
MSW, M.S.W. Master of Social Work
MT Montana
Mt. Mount
MTO Mediterranean Theatre of Operation
MTV Music Television
mus. museum, musical
MusB, Mus.B. Bachelor of Music
MusD, Mus.D. Doctor of Music
MusM, Mus.M. Master of Music
mut. mutual
MVP Most Valuable Player
mycol. mycological

N. North
NAACOG Nurses Association of the
American College of Obstetricians and
Gynecologists
NAACP National Association for the
Advancement of Colored People
NACA National Advisory Committee for
Aeronautics
NACDL National Association of Criminal
Defense Lawyers
NACU National Association of Colleges
and Universities
NAD National Academy of Design
NAE National Academy of Engineering,
National Association of Educators
NAESP National Association of
Elementary School Principals
NAFE National Association of Female
Executives
N.Am. North America
NAM National Association of Manufacturers
NAMH National Association for Mental
Health
NAPA National Association of Performing
Artists
NARAS National Academy of Recording
Arts and Sciences
NAREB National Association of Real
Estate Boards
NARS National Archives and Record
Service
NAS National Academy of Sciences
NASA National Aeronautics and Space
Administration
NASP National Association of School
Psychologists
NASW National Association of Social
Workers
nat. national
NATAS National Academy of Television
Arts and Sciences
NATO North Atlantic Treaty Organization
NATOUSA North African Theatre of
Operations, United States Army
nav. navigation

NB, N.B. New Brunswick
NBA National Basketball Association
NBC National Broadcasting Company
NC, N.C. North Carolina
NCAA National College Athletic Association
NCCJ National Conference of Christians and Jews
ND, N.D. North Dakota
NDEA National Defense Education Act
NE Nebraska
NE, N.E. Northeast
NEA National Education Association
Nebr. Nebraska
NEH National Endowment for Humanities
neurol. neurological
Nev. Nevada
NF Newfoundland
NFL National Football League
Nfld. Newfoundland
NG National Guard
NH, N.H. New Hampshire
NHL National Hockey League
NIH National Institutes of Health
NIMH National Institute of Mental Health
NJ, N.J. New Jersey
NLRB National Labor Relations Board
NM New Mexico
N.Mex. New Mexico
No. Northern
NOAA National Oceanographic and Atmospheric Administration
NORAD North America Air Defense
Nov. November
NOW National Organization for Women
N.P.Ry. Northern Pacific Railway
nr. near
NRA National Rifle Association
NRC National Research Council
NS, N.S. Nova Scotia
NSC National Security Council
NSF National Science Foundation
NSTA National Science Teachers Association
NSW New South Wales
N.T. New Testament
NT Northwest Territories
nuc. nuclear
numis. numismatic
NV Nevada
NW, N.W. Northwest
N.W.T. Northwest Territories
NY, N.Y. New York
N.Y.C. New York City
NYU New York University
N.Z. New Zealand

OAS Organization of American States
ob-gyn obstetrics-gynecology
obs. observatory
obstet. obstetrical
occupl. occupational
oceanog. oceanographic
Oct. October
OD, O.D. Doctor of Optometry
OECD Organization for Economic Cooperation and Development
OEEC Organization of European Economic Cooperation
OEO Office of Economic Opportunity
ofcl. official
OH Ohio
OK Oklahoma
Okla. Oklahoma
ON Ontario

Ont. Ontario
oper. operating
ophthal. ophthalmological
ops. operations
OR Oregon
orch. orchestra
Oreg. Oregon
orgn. organization
orgnl. organizational
ornithol. ornithological
orthop. orthopedic
OSHA Occupational Safety and Health Administration
OSRD Office of Scientific Research and Development
OSS Office of Strategic Services
osteo. osteopathic
otol. otological
otolaryn. otolaryngological

PA, Pa. Pennsylvania
P.A. Professional Association
paleontol. paleontological
path. pathological
PBS Public Broadcasting System
P.C. Professional Corporation
PE Prince Edward Island
pediat. pediatrics
P.E.I. Prince Edward Island
PEN Poets, Playwrights, Editors, Essayists and Novelists (international association)
penol. penological
P.E.O. women's organization (full name not disclosed)
pers. personnel
pfc. private first class
PGA Professional Golfers' Association of America
PHA Public Housing Administration
pharm. pharmaceutical
PharmD, Pharm.D. Doctor of Pharmacy
PharmM, Pharm.M. Master of Pharmacy
PhB, Ph.B. Bachelor of Philosophy
PhD, Ph.D. Doctor of Philosophy
PhDChemE Doctor of Science in Chemical Engineering
PhM, Ph.M. Master of Philosophy
Phila. Philadelphia
philharm. philharmonic
philol. philological
philos. philosophical
photog. photographic
phys. physical
physiol. physiological
Pitts. Pittsburgh
Pk. Park
Pky. Parkway
Pl. Place
P.&L.E.R.R. Pittsburgh & Lake Erie Railroad
Plz. Plaza
PNP Pediatric Nurse Practitioner
P.O. Post Office
PO Box Post Office Box
polit. political
poly. polytechnic, polytechnical
PQ Province of Quebec
PR, P.R. Puerto Rico
prep. preparatory
pres. president
Presbyn. Presbyterian
presdl. presidential
prin. principal
procs. proceedings
prod. produced (play production)

prodn. production
prodr. producer
prof. professor
profl. professional
prog. progressive
propr. proprietor
pros. atty. prosecuting attorney
pro tem. pro tempore
PSRO Professional Services Review Organization
psychiat. psychiatric
psychol. psychological
PTA Parent-Teachers Association
ptnr. partner
PTO Pacific Theatre of Operations, Parent Teacher Organization
pub. publisher, publishing, published
pub. public
publ. publication
pvt. private

quar. quarterly
qm. quartermaster
Q.M.C. Quartermaster Corps
Que. Quebec

radiol. radiological
RAF Royal Air Force
RCA Radio Corporation of America
RCAF Royal Canadian Air Force
RD Rural Delivery
Rd. Road
R&D Research & Development
REA Rural Electrification Administration
rec. recording
ref. reformed
regt. regiment
regtl. regimental
rehab. rehabilitation
rels. relations
Rep. Republican
rep. representative
Res. Reserve
ret. retired
Rev. Reverend
rev. review, revised
RFC Reconstruction Finance Corporation
RFD Rural Free Delivery
rhinol. rhinological
RI, R.I. Rhode Island
RISD Rhode Island School of Design
Rlwy. Railway
Rm. Room
RN, R.N. Registered Nurse
roentgenol. roentgenological
ROTC Reserve Officers Training Corps
RR Rural Route
R.R. Railroad
rsch. research
rschr. researcher
Rt. Route

S. South
s. son
SAC Strategic Air Command
SAG Screen Actors Guild
SALT Strategic Arms Limitation Talks
S.Am. South America
san. sanitary
SAR Sons of the American Revolution
Sask. Saskatchewan
savs. savings
SB, S.B. Bachelor of Science
SBA Small Business Administration
SC, S.C. South Carolina

SCAP Supreme Command Allies Pacific
ScB, Sc.B. Bachelor of Science
SCD, S.C.D. Doctor of Commercial Science
ScD, Sc.D. Doctor of Science
sch. school
sci. science, scientific
SCLC Southern Christian Leadership Conference
SCV Sons of Confederate Veterans
SD, S.D. South Dakota
SE, S.E. Southeast
SEATO Southeast Asia Treaty Organization
SEC Securities and Exchange Commission
sec. secretary
sect. section
seismol. seismological
sem. seminary
Sept. September
s.g. senior grade
sgt. sergeant
SHAEF Supreme Headquarters Allied Expeditionary Forces
SHAPE Supreme Headquarters Allied Powers in Europe
S.I. Staten Island
S.J. Society of Jesus (Jesuit)
SJD Scientiae Juridicae Doctor
SK Saskatchewan
SM, S.M. Master of Science
SNP Society of Nursing Professionals
So. Southern
soc. society
sociol. sociological
S.P.Co. Southern Pacific Company
spkr. speaker
spl. special
splty. specialty
Sq. Square
S.R. Sons of the Revolution
sr. senior
SS Steamship
SSS Selective Service System
St. Saint, Street
sta. station
stats. statistics
statis. statistical
STB, S.T.B. Bachelor of Sacred Theology
stblzn. stabilization
STD, S.T.D. Doctor of Sacred Theology
std. standard
Ste. Suite
subs. subsidiary
SUNY State University of New York
supr. supervisor
supt. superintendent
surg. surgical
svc. service
SW, S.W. Southwest
sys. system

TAPPI Technical Association of the Pulp and Paper Industry
tb. tuberculosis

tchg. teaching
tchr. teacher
tech. technical, technology
technol. technological
tel. telephone
Tel. & Tel. Telephone & Telegraph
telecom. telecommunications
temp. temporary
Tenn. Tennessee
Ter. Territory
Ter. Terrace
TESOL Teachers of English to Speakers of Other Languages
Tex. Texas
ThD, Th.D. Doctor of Theology
theol. theological
ThM, Th.M. Master of Theology
TN Tennessee
tng. training
topog. topographical
trans. transaction, transferred
transl. translation, translated
transp. transportation
treas. treasurer
TT Trust Territory
TV television
TVA Tennessee Valley Authority
TWA Trans World Airlines
twp. township
TX Texas
typog. typographical

U. University
UAW United Auto Workers
UCLA University of California at Los Angeles
UDC United Daughters of the Confederacy
U.K. United Kingdom
UN United Nations
UNESCO United Nations Educational, Scientific and Cultural Organization
UNICEF United Nations International Children's Emergency Fund
univ. university
UNRRA United Nations Relief and Rehabilitation Administration
UPI United Press International
U.P.R.R. United Pacific Railroad
urol. urological
U.S. United States
U.S.A. United States of America
USAAF United States Army Air Force
USAF United States Air Force
USAFR United States Air Force Reserve
USAR United States Army Reserve
USCG United States Coast Guard
USCGR United States Coast Guard Reserve
USES United States Employment Service
USIA United States Information Agency
USMC United States Marine Corps
USMCR United States Marine Corps Reserve
USN United States Navy

USNG United States National Guard
USNR United States Naval Reserve
USO United Service Organizations
USPHS United States Public Health Service
USS United States Ship
USSR Union of the Soviet Socialist Republics
USTA United States Tennis Association
USV United States Volunteers
UT Utah

VA Veterans Administration
VA, Va. Virginia
vet. veteran, veterinary
VFW Veterans of Foreign Wars
VI, V.I. Virgin Islands
vice pres. vice president
vis. visiting
VISTA Volunteers in Service to America
VITA Volunteers in Technical Assistance
vocat. vocational
vol. volunteer, volume
v.p. vice president
vs. versus
VT, Vt. Vermont

W, W. West
WA Washington (state)
WAC Women's Army Corps
Wash. Washington (state)
WATS Wide Area Telecommunications Service
WAVES Women's Reserve, US Naval Reserve
WCTU Women's Christian Temperance Union
we. western
W. Ger. Germany, Federal Republic of
WHO World Health Organization
WI Wisconsin
W.I. West Indies
Wis. Wisconsin
WSB Wage Stabilization Board
WV West Virginia
W.Va. West Virginia
WWI World War I
WWII World War II
WY Wyoming
Wyo. Wyoming

YK Yukon Territory
YMCA Young Men's Christian Association
YMHA Young Men's Hebrew Association
YM & YWHA Young Men's and Young Women's Hebrew Association
yr. year
YT, Y.T. Yukon Territory
YWCA Young Women's Christian Association

zool. zoological

Alphabetical Practices

Names are arranged alphabetically according to the surnames, and under identical surnames according to the first given name. If both surname and first given name are identical, names are arranged alphabetically according to the second given name.

Surnames beginning with De, Des, Du, however capitalized or spaced, are recorded with the prefix preceding the surname and arranged alphabetically under the letter D.

Surnames beginning with Mac and Mc are arranged alphabetically under M.

Surnames beginning with Saint or St. appear after names that begin Sains, and are arranged according to the second part of the name, e.g., St. Clair before Saint Dennis.

Surnames beginning with Van, Von, or von are arranged alphabetically under the letter V.

Compound surnames are arranged according to the first member of the compound.

Many hyphenated Arabic names begin Al-, El-, or al-. These names are alphabetized according to each biographee's designation of last name. Thus Al-Bahar, Neta may be listed either under Al- or under Bahar, depending on the preference of the listee.

Also, Arabic names have a variety of possible spellings when transposed to English. Spelling of these names is always based on the practice of the biographee. Some biographees use a Western form of word order, while others prefer the Arabic word sequence.

Similarly, Asian names may have no comma between family and given names, but some biographees have chosen to add the comma. In each case, punctuation follows the preference of the biographee.

Parentheses used in connection with a name indicate which part of the full name is usually omitted in common usage. Hence, Chambers, E(lizabeth) Anne indicates that the first name, Elizabeth, is generally recorded as an initial. In such a case, the parentheses are ignored in alphabetizing and the name would be arranged as Chambers, Elizabeth Anne.

However, if the entire first name appears in parentheses, for example, Chambers, (Elizabeth) Anne, the first name is not commonly used, and the alphabetizing is therefore arranged as though the name were Chambers, Anne.

If the entire middle name is in parentheses, it is still used in alphabetical sorting. Hence, Belamy, Katherine (Lucille) would sort as Belamy, Katherine Lucille. The same occurs if the entire last name is in parentheses, e.g., (Brandenberg), Howard Keith would sort as Brandenberg, Howard Keith.

For visual clarification:

Smith, H(enry) George: Sorts as Smith, Henry George
Smith, (Henry) George: Sorts as Smith, George
Smith, Henry (George): Sorts as Smith, Henry George
(Smith), Henry George: Sorts as Smith, Henry George

Who Was Who in America®

ABADI, FRITZIE, artist, educator; b. Aleppo, Syria, Mar. 10, 1915; came to U.S., 1924; d. Matloub and Esther (Nahum) A.; m. Al Hidary, Feb. 11, 1934 (div. 1955); children: Annette Hidary, Esther Louise Friedberg (dec.); m. Lewis Ginsburg, Feb. 24, 1963. Student, Art Students League, 1947-48. Contbr. art data, Smithsonian Instn., Washington, 1980; exhibited group shows, Yeshiva U., N.Y.C., 1971-79, Whitney Mus. Am. Art, N.Y.C., Butler Art. Inst., ten one-woman shows. Recipient awards in oil painting, collage, assemblage. Mem. Am. Soc. Comtemporary Artists (pres. 1971-73, dir., advisor), Hudson River Contemporary Artists, Nat. Assn. Women Artists, Artists Equity. Democrat. Jewish. Home: New York, NY. Died May 2001.

ABADY, JOSEPHINE ROSE, theatre director, educator; b. Richmond, Va., Aug. 21, 1949; m. H. Michael Krawitz. BS cum laude, Syracuse U., 1971; MFA in Direction, Fla. State U., 1973. Dir. theatre Hampshire Coll., Amherst, Mass., 1976-79; artistic dir. Berkshire Theatre Festival, Stockbridge, Mass., 1979-87, Cleve. Play House, from 1988. Asst. stage mgr. Marcel Marceau N.E. Tour; spl. asst. Williamstown (Mass.) Theatre Fest; cons. Shakespeare Company of Lenox, Mass., Sharon (Conn.) Playhouse; Nat. Endowment for the Arts artist-in-residence U. Wash., Seattle; dir. new play series The Long Wharf Theatre, New Haven, 1985-86, assoc. dir. Manhattan Theatre Club, 1986. Dir. nat. tour I Never Sang for My Father, 1987, Off-Broadway The Boys Next Door (nominated for outer critics circle award), The March On Russia, N.Y.C., 1990, A Streetcar Named Desire, Volgofrad, Russia, 1991; producer TV premier A Raisin in the Sun, 1988. Pres. Pres.'s Commn. on Scholarship in the Arts, 1980; past head of theatre programs Hampshire Coll., Bennington Coll.; guest artist NYU, U. Washington, Smith Coll. Recipient Sawyer Falk Meml. Award. Home: Great Barrington, Mass. Died May 25, 2002.

ABDOO, RAYMOND THOMAS, preventive health consultant; b. Akron, Ohio, Sept. 28, 1944; s. Raymond A. and Florence Catherine (Haubert) A.; m. Sharon Lou Jones, Aug. 11, 1962; children: Joseph, Shari, Dianna, John, RaeLynn. Student, Sch. of Behavioral Sci., Phila., 1971, Sherwood Med. Intership Sch., St. Louis, 1972. Cert. counselor, tech. rep. Union committeeman Firestone Tire & Rubber, Akron, Ohio, 1965-67; policeman City of Akron, Akron, 1967-69; tech. med. rep. Sherwood Med., St. Louis, 1969-75; pvt. practice med. cons. Suffield, Ohio, 1975-83; pvt. practice wellness cons., 1983-87; pres., cons. Physicians Wellness, Cuyahoga Falls, Ohio, 1987-89; chmn. Physicians Wellness Programs, Cuyahoga Falls, from 1989. Mem. U.S. Admin. (pres. steering com. 1995, nat. dem. com. 1994); wellness advisor Ohio Sheriffs Assn. (analyst 1993-95); wellness advisor, mem. Buckeye Sheriffs Assn., 1993-96. Author: The Love Connections, 1976, Your Personal Experience, 1985 (Meta Physics Astro Physics award 1985), The Classic Wellness Program, 1987 (Pres. award 1993). Chmn. Concerned Citizens of Am., Cuyahoga Falls, 1990-95, pres. campaign advisor U.S. Dem. Party, Cuyahoga Falls, 1995, mem. Pub. Citizens Group, 1995. With U.S. Army, 1962-64. Mem. Fraternal Order of Police of Ohio, Inc. (wellness advisor, analyst 1994-95, booster 1992-96). Democrat. Roman Catholic. Avocations: political writer, lobbyist for preventive health, chess, golf, law enforcement research. Died June 21, 2000.

ABEL, HAROLD, psychologist, educator, academic administrator; b. N.Y.C., July 31, 1926; s. Felix N. and Jennie (Schaefer) A.; m. Iris Tash, Jan. 30, 1949; children: Lawrence William, Matthew Robert. AB, Syracuse U., 1949, MA, 1951, PhD, 1958; DLitt (hon.), Hanyang U., Republic of Korea, 1979. Tchr. mentally retarded, Syracuse and Rochester, N.Y., 1950-52; asst. instr. Syracuse U., 1952-56; assoc. prof. to prof. depts. psychology and home econs. and dir. child devel. lab. U. Nebr., 1956-65, chmn. dept. human devel., 1963-65; dir. divsn. psycho-ednl. studies, prof. edn. U. Oreg., 1965-68, assoc. dean, prof. ednl. psychology Coll. Edn., 1968-70; pres. Castleton State Coll., 1970-75, Cen. Mich. U., 1975-85, prof. psychology and ednl. adminstrn., 1985-93; pres. Walden U., Mpls., 1988-91, Grad. Sch. Am., Mpls., 1993-95; chancellor Grad. Sch. Am. (now Capella U.), Mpls., 1995-98; chair bd. dirs. Capella, from 1998. With AUS, 1945-46. Mem. AAAS, Am. Psychol. Assn., Soc. Rsch. in Child Devel., Sigma Xi, Phi Delta Kappa. Died July 10, 2002.

ABELL, PAUL IRVING, retired chemistry educator; b. Pelham, Mass., July 24, 1923; s. Max F. and Virginia (Bennett) A.; m. Phyllis Killam, July 1, 1950 (div.); children: Susan E., Erin Gallagher; m. Frances Martindale, Aug. 30, 1980; 1 child, Octavia Lucy Mawson. BS, U. N.H., 1948; PhD, U. Wis., 1951. Instr. U. R.I., Kingston, 1951-64, prof. chemistry, 1964-90, ret., 1990. Fulbright lectr., Egypt, 1965-66 Served with AUS, 1943-46. Recipient Petroleum Research Fund Internat. Research grants U. Wales, 1961-62, Petroleum Research Fund Internat. Research grants U. Bristol, 1969-70 Mem. Henty Soc., Am. Chem. Soc., Chem. Soc. London, Geochem. Soc., Explorers Club, Sigma Xi, Phi Kappa Phi. Mem. rsch. expdns. in paleontology of Omo River and Lake Rudolf regions of E. Africa sponsored by Nat. Geog. Soc., 1966. Home: West Kingston, RI. Died Jan. 12, 2004.

ABERCONWAY, BARON CHARLES MELVILLE MCLAREN, business executive; b. Apr. 16, 1913; s. 2d Baron and Christabel Aberconway; m. Deidre Knewstub, 1941 (div. 1949); 3 children; m. Ann Lindsay Bullard, 1949; 1 son. Student Eton Coll.; New Coll., Oxford. Barrister, Middle Temple, 1937; chmn. John Brown & Co. Ltd., 1953-78, pres., 1978-85; chmn. English China Clays Ltd., 1963-84, pres. 1984—; dep. chmn. Westland Aircraft Ltd., 1979-84, Sun Alliance, London Ins. Co., 1976-85; dir. Nat. Westminster Bank Ltd. Pres. Royal Hort. Soc., 1961-84; commr. gen. Internat. Garden Festival, Liverpool, Eng., 1984. Served with Brit. Army, 1939-45. Died Feb. 4, 2003.

ABRAMS, GEORGE, type designer, executive; b. Bklyn., Sept. 3, 1919; s. Morris and Millie (Rosenberg) Abrahams; m. Marion Estelle Cordes, Feb. 25, 1947 (dec. 1971); children: Jeffrey, Vicki Eisenberg, Nancy, Lauren; m. Joan Allen Walker, Aug. 26, 1983. Pres. Alphabets, Inc., N.Y.C., 1948-89, Expert Alphabets Internat. Ltd., Great Neck, N.Y., from 1996. Prof. type design, Columbia U. Tchrs. Coll., N.Y.C., 1964, Parsons, New Sch., N.Y.C., 1996, Berghs Coll., Stockholm, 1997. Creator logotype mastheads Sports Illustrated, 1954, Newsweek, 1968, Saturday Evening Post, 1965, House Beautiful Mag., 1949, Ladies Home Jour., Holiday Mag., Calif. Home Mag., Am. Home Mag., Sat. Review, The Singer Co., B. Altman Co., Reed and Barton, Ballantine, Godiva; published type designs: Abrams Venetian, Abrams Augereau, Abrams Caslon, New Face. Invited to testify U.S. Ho. of Reps. 2223 Hearings on Type Design Copyright Law Revision, 1975. With USAF, 21st Weather Liaison, 3d Armored Divsn., 1942-45, ETO. Decorated 5 Battle Stars; recipient Caen (France) Meml. Invasion Medal, 1995, hon. cert. Royal Danish Soc., Copenhagen, 1987; named hon. fellow London Soc. Typographic Design. Fellow Pierpont Morgan Libr.; Internat. Assn. Bibliophiles (France), Stockholm Typographic Guild (corr.), Assn. Typographic Internat. (A Type I), Typophiles (N.Y.), The Grolier Club (membership com. 1978—). Avocations: sports cars, rare books, ethnic sculpture, photography, fine art. Died June 7, 2001.

ABRAMS, HERBERT E. artist; b. Greenfield, Mass., Mar. 20, 1921; s. Adolph and Mathilda (Shear) A.; m. Lois Kathryn Miller, June 5, 1954; children: Kathryn Ann Abrams Bindert, William Frederick. Student, Norwich (Conn.) Art Sch., 1939-40; cert. with honors, Pratt Inst., Bklyn., 1946; studies with DuMond, Art Students' League, N.Y.C., 1948-53; LHD (hon.), Johns Hopkins U., 1997. Tchr. pvt. classes, Warren, Conn., 1953-75; instr. art U.S. Mil. Acad., West Point, N.Y., 1953-74. Prin. works include portraits of Pres. Jimmy Carter, The White House, Washington, 1983, Govs. Meskill and Grasso, Conn. State Libr. Mus., Hartford, 1974, 83, Gens. Westmoreland, Abrams and Palmer, Pentagon, Washington, 1973, 75, 76, Sen. Baker, U.S. Senate, 1985, Treasury Sec. Regan, Treasury, Washington, 1986 Alan S. Boyd, Nat. Trust for Hist. Preservation, Washington, 1989, Amb. Wilkey, Washington, 1992, Pres. George Bush, The White House, 1994, First Lady Barbara Bush, The White House, 1995, Arthur Miller, Nat. Portrait Gallery, Washington, 1999, Sen. Eastland, U.S. Senate, 2001, others; represented in permanent collection Dept. Mil. History, Washington, 1972, U.S. Mil. Acad. Mus., West Point, N.Y.; designer aircraft insignia USAF, 1942. Del. Dem. State Conv., Hartford, Conn., 1978-80; chmn. Dem. Town Commn., Warren, 1978-79. Lt. USAF, 1941-45. Mem. Artists Equity Assn., Kent Art Assn., Art Students League. Avocations: tennis, gardening, golf. Died Aug. 29, 2003.

ABRUMS, JOHN DENISE, internist; b. Trinidad, Colo., Sept. 20, 1923; s. Horatio Ely and Clara (Apfel) A.; m. Annie Louise Manning, June 15, 1947; children: Louanne C. Abrums Sargent, John Ely. BA, U. Colo., 1944; MD, U. Colo., Denver, 1947. Diplomate Am. Bd. Internal Medicine. Intern Wisc. Gen. Hosp., Madison, 1947-48; resident in internal medicine VA Hosp., Albuquerque, 1949-52, attending physician, 1956-80; mem. staff Presbyn. Hosp. Ctr., Albuquerque; cons. staff physician St. Joseph Hosp., Albuquerque, 1957-85; attending physician U. N.Mex. Hosp., Albuquerque, 1954-95; med. dir. Turquoise Lodge, Albuquerque. Cons. physician A.T. & S.F. Meml. Hosp., Albuquerque, 1957-83; clin. assoc. in medicine U. N.Mex.; mem. N.Mex. Bd. of Med. Examiners. Bd. dirs. Blue Cross/Blue Shield, 1962-76. Brig. gen. M.C., U.S. Army, ret., N.Mex. Nat. Guard. Fellow ACP (life), AMA, Am. Soc. Internal Medicine (trustee 1976-82, pres. 1983-84), N.Mex. Soc. Internal Medicine (pres. 1962-64), N.Mex. Med. Soc. (pres. 1980-81), Nat. Acads. Practice (disting. practitioner), Albuquerque and Bernalillo County Med. Assn. (bd. govs. 1959-61, chmn. pub. rels. com. 1959-61), Am. Geriatric Soc., 1992—. Brig. gen. M.C., U.S. Army, ret. Republican. Episcopalian. Home: Santa Fe, N.Mex. Died July 18, 1999.

ACHESON, ROY MALCOLM, epidemiologist, educator; b. Belfast, Ireland, Aug. 18, 1921; emigrated to U.S., 1962, naturalized, 1968; s. Malcolm King and Dorothy (Rennoldson) A.; m. Fiona Marigo O'Brien, Mar. 16, 1950 (div.); children: Malcolm O'Brien, Vincent Rennoldson, Marigo Fiona. BA, Trinity Coll., Dublin, Ireland, 1945, MA, 1949, ScD, 1962; BA, U. Oxford, Eng., 1948, MA, BM, BChir, U. Oxford, Eng., 1951, DM, 1954; MA (hon.), Yale U., 1964. Intern, then resident internal medicine Radcliffe Infirmary, Oxford, 1951-55; lectr. social medicine U. Dublin (Ireland), 1955-59; reader social and preventive medicine U. London, Eng., 1959-62; mem. faculty Yale Sch. Medicine, 1962-75, prof. epidemiology, 1964-72; fellow Jonathan Edwards Coll., 1966-75; dir. Center for Tng. in Community Medicine, London (Eng.) Sch. Hygiene and Tropical Medicine, 1972-76; prof. health services studies U. London, 1974-76; prof. community medicine U. Cambridge, Eng., 1976-88, prof. emeritus, from 1988; life fellow Churchill Coll., from 1976; R. Samuel McLaughlin vis. prof. in residence Med. Sch. McMaster U., Hamilton, Ont., Can., 1976-77. Mem. expert com. health statistics WHO, 1966; cons., tech. adviser epidemiology and med. edn. Pan-Am. Health Orgn., in Peru, Venezuela, P.R., Argentina, India and Colombia, 1964-82; cons. med. edn. AID, East Pakistan, 1963; cons. epidemiology NIH, 1963-72; mem. nat. adv. com. thrombosis Nat. Heart Inst., 1968-70; mem. epidemiology study sect. Nat. Inst. Gen. Med. Scis., 1970-72; cons. epidemiology WHO, Europe, 1973, adv. health services research, Geneva, 1978-87; mem. Gen. Med. Coun., 1979-89, exec. com., edn. com., 1979-89; mem. Gen. Dental Council, 1984-89, exec. com., 1984; gov. Action in Internat. Medicine, 1988-91. Author: History of Education in Public Health, 1991; also articles in profl. jours., chpts. in book; editor Comparability in International Epidemiology, 1965, Seminars in Community Medicine, Vol. 1, 1976, Vol. 2, 1977, Jour. Epidemiology and Community Health, 1977-89. Served with Brit. Army, 1940-45. Rockefeller traveling fellow medicine, 1955-56; Commonwealth Fund travelling fellow, 1968-69; fellow Trinity Coll., Dublin, 1957-59 Fellow Royal Coll. Physicians, (faculty of pub. health med., 1972—, v.p. 1984-87), Internat. Epidemiol. Assn. (council 1964-74, gen. sec. 1964-68, ednl. sec. 1968-74) Home: Brighton, England. Died Apr. 2, 2003.

ACKERMAN, LOUISE MAGAW, civic worker, writer; b. Topeka, July 9, 1904; d. William Glenn and Anna Mary (Shaler) Magaw; BS, Kans. State U., 1926; MA, U. Nebr., 1942; m. Grant Albert Ackerman, Dec. 27, 1926; children—Edward Shaler, Anita Louise. Free lance writer, 1930—. Mem. Nat. Soc. Daus. Colonial Wars (nat. pres. 1977-80), Daus. Am. Colonists (regent Nebr. 1970-72), DAR (past v.p. gen.), Americans of Armorial Ancestry (sec. 1976-82), Nat. Huguenot Soc. (2d v.p. 1977-81), Nebr. Writers Guild (past sec.-treas.), Nat. League Am. Pen Women, Colonial Lords in Am., Nat. Gavel Soc., Soc. Descs. of Founders of Hartford, Conn., Phi Kappa Phi. Republican. Club: Nat. Writers. Lodge: Order Eastern Star. Died Dec. 14, 1996. Home: Lincoln, Nebr.

ADAIR, CHARLES ROBERT, JR., lawyer; b. Narrows, Va., Sept. 29, 1914; s. Charles Robert and Margaret (Davis) A.; m. Lillian Adele Duffee, Sept. 19, 1942 (dec. 1993). BS, U. Ala., 1942, LLB, 1948, JD, 1969. Bar: Ala. bar 1948. Since practiced in, Dadeville; solicitor, 1955-73. Vice chmn. Ala. Securities Commn., 1969-71; mem., chmn. Ala. Jud. Compensation Commn., 1984—; v.p., bd. dirs. Dadeville Industries, Inc.; bd. dirs. Bank of Dadeville, Ala.. Chmn. Dadeville One Drive, 1960; chmn. Horseshoe Bend Regional Library, 1960-65; mem., sec. planning commn. City of Dadeville, 1965-80; hon. life mem. Bethel Vol. Fire Dept. and Rescue Service, Jackson's Gap Vol. Fire Dept. and Rescue Service; trustee Ala. Law Inst., Ala. Bar Found. Served as officer USAAF, World War II. Mem. Ala. Bar Assn. (past v.p.), Tallapoosa Bar (past pres.), 5th Cir. Bar Assn. (past pres., named Avery Country Lawyer of 1999), Farrah Law Soc., VFW, Am. Legion, East Ala. Peace Officers Assn. (hon. life), The Club, Capital City Club, Quarterback Club (past capt.), The Denny Soc., Masons, Kiwanis, Scabbard and Blade, Omicron Delta Kappa, Delta Tau Delta, Phi Alpha Delta. Presbyterian. Home: Dadeville, Ala. Died 2003.

ADAIR, WILLIAM BENJAMIN, JR., lawyer; b. Houston, Nov. 29, 1951; s. William Benjamin and Barbara (Reed) A. BS in Zoology, Tex. A. and M. U., 1973; postgrad. in medicine, U. Tex., 1973-75; JD, So. Tex. Coll., 1985. Bar: Tex. 1986, U.S. Dist. Ct. (so. dist.) Tex. 1986, U.S. Dist. Ct. (we. dist.) Tex. 1989, U.S. Ct. Appeals (5th cir.) 1990, U.S. Supreme Ct. 1991. With GATX, Houston, 1978; crude oil buyer Shell Oil Co., Houston, 1979; crude oil trader Listo Petroleum, Inc., Houston, 1980-83; assoc. Adair & Myers, Houston, 1988-96. 1st lt. USAF, 1973-77. Mem. Assn. Trial Lawyers Am., Tex. Trial Lawyers Assn. Avocation: volleyball. Home: Humble, Tex. Died Jan. 17, 2002.

ADAMS, ALGALEE POOL, college dean, art educator; b. Columbia, Mo., Nov. 6, 1919; d. William I. and Anna Ethelene (Dunning) Pool; 1 dau., Judith Dean Adams. BS in Art and English, U. Mo., 1941, MA in Art, 1951; Ed.D. in Fine Arts and Art Edn, Pa. State U., 1960; postgrad. Inst. Adminstrv. Advancement, for Women, U. Mich.; postgrad., Inst. Ednl. Mgmt., Harvard U. Tchr. art Cuba (Mo.) High Sch., 1941-42, Hickman H.S., Columbia, 1942-43; art specialist elem. schs. St. Joseph, Mo., 1943-45; tchr. art St. Clair (Mo.) H.S., 1946-49; pub. sch. art supr. Webb City, Mo., 1949-51; instr. dept. of art St. Cloud (Minn.) State U., 1951-58, asst. prof., 1958-60, assoc. prof., 1960-63, prof., 1963-64, chmn. dept. art, 1959-64; prof. art edn. Mass. Coll. Art, Boston, 1964-77, also chmn. divsn. of edn., 1967-70, dir. tchr. placement, 1964-70, dir. grad. programs in edn., 1970-77; chmn. grad. coun., 1970-74; dean Firelands Coll. Bowling Green State U., Huron, Ohio, 1977-85; owner Adams Miniature Fiber Arts, Columbia, 1989. Liaison with bus. and industry; mem. gov.'s adv. commn. on edn. in arts, 1958, 67; assoc. dir. Project Renewal Mass. State Coll. System, 1974-76; art curriculum cons. to numerous pub. schs. in, Minn., 1951-64; art cons. to Minn. Ins. Info. Ctr., 1960-62; chmn. Eastern Arts Student Conf., N.Y.C., 1968; participant Internat. Conf., Notre Dame U., 1968; field reader HEW, 1966-70 Vol. tutor state literacy program; docent Detroit Inst. Arts; mem. Columbia Cultural Affairs Commn. Recipient Artisian Status award Internat. Guild Miniature Artisians, 1991, Fellow status award, 1995, Citation of Merit for Outstanding Achievement and Meritorius Svc. to Edn. Alumni Bd. U. Mo., 1997, Disting. Svc. award Mo. Western State Coll., 2001. Mem.: Zonta. Home: Columbia, Mo. Died Sept. 13, 2002.

ADAMS, CHARLES HENRY, retired animal scientist, educator; b. Burdick, Kans., Nov. 7, 1918; s. Henry Lory and Bertha Frances (Westbrook) A.; m. Eula Mae Peters, Apr. 29, 1943 (dec. Apr. 1999); m. Beryle Irene Supple Somer Janousek, Dec. 23, 2000. BS, Kans. State U., 1941, MS, 1942; PhD, Mich. State U., 1964. Instr. Kans. State U., Manhattan, 1946-47; asst. prof. U. Nebr., Lincoln, 1947-64, assoc. prof., 1964-70, prof. animal sci., 1970-83, prof. emeritus, 1983—; asst. dean Coll. Agr., U. Nebr., Lincoln, 1973-83. Contbr. articles to profl. jours. 1st lt. AUS, 1943-46 Recipient Disting. Teaching awards Gamma Sigma Delta, 1969, U. Nebr., 1971, Am. Meat Sci. Assn., 1969, Am. Soc. Animal Sci., 1972; Disting. Svc. award U. Nebr. Lincoln Alumni Assn., 1989, Doc Elliott award, 2001; named to Nebr. Hall of Agrl. Achievement, 1990. Fellow AAAS, Am. Soc. Animal Sci.; mem. Am. Meat Sci. Assn. (R.C. Pollock award 1992), Inst. Food Technologists, Nebr. Acad. Sci., Am. Legion, VFW, Rotary, Sigma Xi, Gamma Sigma Delta, Alpha Zeta, Alpha Gamma Rho. Republican. Presbyterian. Home: Lincoln, Nebr. Died Dec. 20, 2003.

ADAMS, DIANE SCRIVENER, psychotherapist; b. Washington, Mar. 25, 1939; d. Samuel, Jr., and Elizabeth Henry (Baltz) Scrivener; B.A. in Psychology, U. N.C., 1961; M.A. in Clin. Psychology, George Washington U., 1965; postgrad. U. Hartford; m. Richard C. Adams, Nov. 21, 1970. Psychol. extern D.C. Gen. Hosp., 1963-64; tchr. emotionally disturbed children Eastern State Hosp., Williamsburg, Va., 1962-63; research psychologist, adult psychiatry br. NIMH, Bethesda, Md., 1964-65; sch. psychologist, Washington, 1965-67, Prince George's County Public Schs., Md., 1967-70; sch. psychologist health dept. New London, Conn., 1971-76; pvt. practice psychotherapist, East Lyme, Conn., 1976-86; psychol. cons. Child and Family Agy., New London, 1971-86. Mem. Am. Psychol. Assn., S.E. Conn. Women's Network, D.C. Psychol. Assn. Died July 21, 1991. Home: Washington, DC.

ADAMS, ELIE MAYNARD, philosophy educator; b. Clarkton, Va., Dec. 29, 1919; s. Wade Hampton and Bessie (Callaway) A.; m. Phyllis Margaret Stevenson, Dec. 22, 1942; children: Steven Maynard, Jill Elaine. BA, U. Richmond, 1941, MA, 1944; BD, Colgate-Rochester Div. Sch., 1944; PhD, Harvard U., 1948; LHD (hon.), Wake Forest U., 1989; HHD (hon.), U. Richmond, 1992. Teaching fellow Harvard U., 1946-47; asst. prof. philosophy Ohio U., 1947-48; asst. prof. U. N.C., 1948-53, assoc. prof., 1953-58, prof., 1958-71, Kenan prof., 1971-90, prof. emeritus, 1990—2003, chmn. dept. philosophy, 1960-65, chmn. faculty, 1976-79, former chmn. Program in Humanities for Study of Human Values. Vis. prof. U. So. Calif., 1966, SUNY-Albany, 1971, U. Calgary (Alta., Can.), 1977; adv. com. Nat. Humanities Ctr. Author: The Fundamentals of General Logic, 1954, Logic Problems, 1954, (with others) The Language of Value, 1957, Ethical Naturalism and the Modern World View, 1960, 73, Philosophy and the Modern Mind, 1975, 85, (with others) The Idea of America, 1977, The Metaphysics of Self and World, 1991; The Accountability of Religion, 1992; contbr. articles in philos. and cultural jours. and newpapers; editor: Categorical Analysis: Selected Essays of Everett W. Hall on Philosophy, Value, Knowledge and Mind, 1964, Commonsense Realism, 1966. Chmn. N.C. Humanities Council, 1980-81; gov. N.C.'s Commn. on Sci. and Tech., 1982-84. Recipient Thomas Jefferson award, 1971, Outstanding Educator of Am. award, 1971; Colgate-Rochester Grad. scholar, Harvard U., Ayer fellow, James H. Wood fellow; Spl. award N.C. Adult Edn. Assn., 1988; subject of book: Festschrift-Mind, Value, and Culture: Essays in honor of Elie Maynard Adams, 1989; E. Maynard Adams Professorship established in her honor U. N.C., Chapel Hill, 1992. Mem. Mind Assn., Am. Philos. Assn. (mem. exec. com. Eastern div. 1961-64, chmn. program com. 1965), N.C. Philos. Soc. (past pres.), So. Soc. Philosophy and Psychology (exec. council 1963-66, pres. 1968-69). Home: Chapel Hill, NC. Died Nov. 17, 2003.

ADAMS, JANE MILLER, retired psychotherapist; b. Shreveport, La., June 10, 1922; d. Charles Frederick and Lucile Elizabeth (Day) Miller; m. James Franklin Adams, June 8, 1946; 1 child, Ann Morgan Adams Williams. BA, La. State U., 1950, MSW, 1960. Bd. cert. social worker La.; bd. cert. diplomat. Am. Bd. of Examiners of Clin. Social Work, emeritus. Clin. social worker Ctrl. La. State Hosp., Pineville, 1957-62, Forest Glen Mental Health Outpatient Clinic, Pineville, 1962-64; med. social worker La. Pub. Health, Alexandria, 1964-67; adminstr., therapist Alexandria Outpatient Alcoholism Clinic, 1967-73; psychotherapist Episcopal Diocese La., Pineville, 1974-82, pvt. practice, Pineville, 1982-92. Cons. and spkr. in field. Pink lady vol. Huey P. Long Regional Hosp., Pineville, 1982-85; vol. to cons. Cmty. Mental Health Day Care Ctr., Alexandria, 1984-85; staff cons. Ctrl. La. Alcoholism Clinic, Alexandria, 1975-78; alcoholism cons. Forest Glen Mental Health Outpatient Clinic, 1975-78. Democrat. Episcopalian. Avocations: gardening, poetry. Home: Pineville, La. Died Apr. 25, 2004.

ADAMS, PERRY RONALD, former college administrator; b. Parkersburg, W.Va., Sept. 16, 1921; s. Russell Douglas and Beulah Grace (Cunningham) A.; m. Ann Mallory Gillespie, Dec. 25, 1943; children— Suzanne Adams Markwell, Sally Adams Barrios. AB, U. Ky., 1943, MA, 1948; Ed.D., U. Fla., 1965. Instr. U. Ky., 1948-53; dir. music; U. Fla., 1953-65; dean instruction Polk Jr. Coll., Winter Haven, Fla., 1965-69; provost No. Va. Community Coll., Annandale, 1969-70; pres. Paul D. Camp Community Coll., Franklin, Va., 1970-79; vice chancellor Va. Community Coll. System, Richmond, 1979—83; dean Tallahasee (Fla.) C.C., 1983—87; ret., 1986. Served with USN, 1942-47. Kellogg fellow, 1963-65 Mem. ASCD, Am. Assn. Higher Edn., Am. Vocat. Assn., Phi Mu Alpha (nat. coun.), Phi Delta Kappa, Kappa Delta Pi. Home: Tallahassee, Fla. Deceased.

ADAMS, WALTER, economist, educator; b. Vienna, Aug. 27, 1922; s. Edward and Ilona (Schildkraut) A.; m. Pauline Gordon, Aug. 23, 1943; 1 child, William James. BA magna cum laude, Bklyn. Coll., 1942; MA, Yale U., 1946, PhD, 1947; LLD (hon.), Cen. Mich. U., 1973, Mich. State U., 1979; DHL (hon.), Bklyn. Coll., 1989, No. Mich. U., 1991, Miami U., 1992. Instr. econs. Yale U., 1945-47; mem. faculty Mich. State U., East Lansing, 1947—92, pres., 1969-70, Disting. Univ. prof. econs., 1970-92; Disting. prof. econs. Trinity U., Tex., 1993—98. Mem. U.S. Atty. Gen.'s Nat. Com. for Study of Antitrust Laws, 1953—55; vis. prof. Salzburg (Austria) Seminar, 1959, 60, U. Grenoble, France, 1966, Falkenstein Seminar, Germany, 1972, U. Paris, 1982, Wake Forest U., 1983, U. Ancona, Italy, 1988, Trinity U., 1989, 1992—98. Author: (Book) Readings in Economics, 1948, Monopoly in America, 1955, From Main Street to the Left Bank, 1959, Ia the World Our Campus?, 1960, The Structure of American Industry 9th edit., 1994, The Test, 1971, The Bigness Complex, 1986, Dangerous Pursuits, 1989, Antitrust Economics on Trial, 1991, Adam Smith Goes to Moscow, 1993, The Tobacco Wars, 1998; contbr. articles to profl. jours. Mem. U.S. Adv. Commn. Internat. Ednl. and Cultural Affairs, 1961-69, NAACP. With AUS, 1943-45. Decorated Bronze Star; recipient Adam Smith Gold medal in econs., Bklyn. Coll., 1942, Disting Educator award, Mich. Assn. Governing Bd., 1969, Ford Found. fellow, 1953; named Mich. Prof. of Yr., Coun. Advancement & Support Edn., 1985; named one of Best Profs. in U.S., Rolling Stone mag., 1991. Mem. AAUP (pres. 1972-74), Am. Econ. Assn., Assn. Social Econs. (pres. 1980-81), Midwest Econ. Assn. (pres. 1979-80), Yale Club Mich., Harvard Club Cen. Mich., Delta Sigma Pi. Democrat. Home: East Lansing, Mich. Died Sept. 8, 1998.

ADAMS, WARREN SANFORD, II, retired food company executive, lawyer; b. Cleve., Sept. 4, 1910; s. Otis Howard and Hermine (Weis) A. AB, Princeton U., 1930; LL.B., Harvard U., 1934; J.S.D., NYU, 1941. Bar: N.Y. 1935. Pvt. practice, N.Y.C., 1934-40; counsel chems. div. WPB, 1941; with CPC Internat. Inc. (formerly Corn Products Co.), 1946-76, gen. counsel, 1960-72, v.p., 1962-72, sr. v.p., gen. counsel, dir., 1972-76. Bd. dirs. emeritus Washington Sq. Fund, N.Y.C.; trustee, counsel Whitehall Found., Inc. Served to lt. col. USMCR, 1942-46. Mem. ABA, The Pilgrims, English Speaking Union, Racquet and Tennis Club, Met. Opera Club, Princeton Club, Ekwanok Golf Club (Vermont), Am. Soc. of Order of St. John (knight), Royal and Ancient Golf Club (Scotland), Boodles (London), Newport Country Club (Rhode Island), The Austin Club (Texas). Episcopalian. Died Apr. 25, 2004.

ADASKIN, MURRAY, composer; b. Toronto, Ont., Can., Mar. 28, 1906; s. Samuel and Nisha (Perstnyov) A.; m. Frances James, July 16, 1931 (dec. Aug. 1988); m. Asta Dorothea Larsen, May 7, 1989. Student, Royal Conservatory Music, Toronto, Can. and Paris, Music Acad. West; student of Darius Milhaud, Aspen (Colo.) Sch. Music; LLD (hon.), U. Lethbridge, Alta., Can., 1970; DMus (hon.), Brandon U., 1972, U. Windsor, Ont., 1977, U. Victoria, B.C., 1984; LLD (hon.), U. Saskatoon, Saskatoon, 1984, Brock U., 2000. Prof. music, chair dept. U. Sask., Saskatoon, 1952-66, composer in residence, 1966-73; mem. Can. Coun., 1966-69. Violinist Toronto Symphony Orch., 10 yrs. Composer (opera) Warden of the Plains, also over 129 orchestral, chamber and solo works including Man and the Universe; commd. by CBC for Exp. 1967, premier Concerto for Orch. with Victoria Symphony, 1990, premier Rivka Golani Concerto for Solo Viola and Orch., 1991, Woodwind Quintet No. 2, 1993, String Quartet No. 2 (La Cadenza), Lafayette String Quarter, 1994, Concerto for Viola and Orch. No. 2, 1995, String Quintet (for Lafayette Quartet adn Gary Karr, bass), 1995, The Travelling Musician for Narrator/Singer and Chamber by Orch., 1997, String Quartet No. 3, I Tre Vecchi Amici, 1998, Final Composition Musica Victoria 2000; subject CBC broadcasts, 1971, 89, Sta. CJRT-FM broadcast, 1993; 5 CDs included in the Adaskin Collection.; 8 CDs of Adaskin music. Bd. dirs. Saskatoon Arts Ctr,. 1966-67. Decorated officer Order of Can., 1980; named Saskatoon Citizen of Yr., 1969; recipient Lifetime award for excellence in the arts Sask. Arts Bd., 1991; Sr. Arts fellow Can. Coun., 1960-61; Can. Coun. grantee U. Sask.; featured Can. composer Sask. Music Festival Assn., 1994. Mem. Royal Soc. Arts, Can. League Composers (founding), Saskatoon Musician's Assn. (hon. life), Toronto Musician'a Assn. (hon. life). Home: Victoria, Canada. Died May 6, 2002.

ADELMAN, BENJAMIN, author; b. Bklyn., Sept. 16, 1913; s. Barnett Jacob and Tessie (Gaffin) A.; B.S., Bklyn. Coll., 1933; m. Feb. 19, 1941; children— Saul Joseph, Jonathan Reuben. With Dept. Agr., 1936-42, Civilian Prodn. Adminstrn., 1942-43, WPA, 1945-46, Naval Research Lab., 1946-52, Office Price Stblzn., 1952-53; with FDA, Washington, 1960-70, mgmt. analyst, until 1970; mgmt. analyst EPA, Washington, 1970-73; author: (with Saul J. Adelman) Bound for the Stars, 1981; contbr. articles in Sci. Digest, Rev. Popular Astronomy, Spaceworld, Sci. American. Sci. writer Benjamin and Kitty Adelman Bibl. Archeology Fund, 1982—. Mem. Am. Astronautical Soc., Nat. Capital Astronomers, Am. Friends of Israel Exploration Soc., AIAA, Planetary Soc., Nat. Space Inst. Jewish. Home: Silver Spring, Md. Died Mar. 31, 2004.

ADKINS, EDWARD CLELAND, lawyer; b. Montgomery County, Iowa, Aug. 11, 1926; s. Esse Clarence and Elsie Mae (Cline) A.; m. Claudia Kangas, Sept. 17, 1955; children: Pamela, Philip, Paul. BS, U.S. Naval Acad., 1949; JD, U. Mich., 1957. Bar: Ohio 1957, U.S. Supreme Ct. 1961, Fla. 1963, Mich. 1965, U.S. Ct. Appeals (5th cir.) 1973, U.S. Ct. Appeals (8th cir.) 1974, U.S. Ct. Appeals (11th cir.) 1982, U.S. Ct. Appeals (3d cir.) 1991. Assoc. Arter & Hadden, Cleve., 1957-64; trial counsel Gen. Motors corp., 1964-70; ptnr. litigation Holland & Knight, PA, Tampa, Fla., from 1970. Served to capt. USNR. Mem. ABA, Fla. Bar, Mich. Bar, Palma Ceia Golf and Country Club, University Club. Deceased.

AF HALLSTROM, GUSTAV JAKOB ELIEL, teacher; b. Lappfjard, Finland, May 30, 1935; s. Jakob Rafael and Birgit (Starcke) af H.; m. Karin Sievers, Feb. 27, 1965; children— Kalle, Lotta. M.A., U. Helsingfors (Finland), 1965. Prin., The Evening Sch. of Helsingfors, 1966-72; prin. Comml. Sch. of Helsingfors, 1972-76; mng. dir. Schildts Pub. House, Helsingfors, 1977-87; tchr. Swedish Lycei parkeus Skola, Borgå, Finlan, 1987-2002. Author: Commercial Correspondence, 1973. Chmn. Svenska modersmalslararna i Finland, 1965-75, Svenska folkpartiet i sodra Helsingfors, 1977-82. Mem. Swedish Workers Inst. (pres. 1977-84). Home: Helsingfors, Finland. Deceased.

AGA KHAN, PRINCE SADRUDDIN, former United Nations official, writer; b. Paris, Jan. 17, 1933; s. Sultan Mohammed and Andree Josephine (Carron) Aga Khan; m. Nina Sheila Dyer, 1957; m. Catherine Sursock. BA, Harvard U., 1954; hon. degree, Tufts U., 1986, U. Nice, France, 1988. Cons. for Afro-Asian projects UNESCO, 1958, spl. cons. to dir.-gen., 1961. Head mission, adv. UN High Commn. Refugees, 1959-60; exec. sec. Internat. Action Com. Preservation Nubian Monuments, 1961; UN dep. high commnr. for refugees, 1962-65, high commr., 1965-77; cons. to sec.-gen. UN, 1978; chmn., founding mem. Ind. Com. on Internat. Humanitarian Issues, 1983-2003; UN coord. for econ. and humanitarian programs in Afghanistan, 1988-1990; UN relief coord. for Irag and Kuwait occupation of Kuwait, 1990-1991. Author: International Protection of Refugees, 1976; pub. Paris Rev. Decorated Knight of the British Empire; Papal Order St. Sylvester (Vatican); Order Star Nile (Sudan); Order Homayoun 1st class (Iran); comdr.'s cross with star Order Merit (Poland); comdr. Legion of Honor (France); recipient UN Human Rights award, 1978, Man for Peace award, 1989; Dag Hammarskjöld medal German UN Assn., 1979; co-recipient Olympia prize Alexander Onassis Found., 1982; named Comdr. Golden Ark, The Netherlands, 1985. Mem. Harvard Islamic Assn. (founder 1951, sec. 1952), Council Islamic Affairs (pres. 1960), Inst. Differing Civilizations, Groupe de Bellerive (a founder 1977, pres. 1977), World Wildlife Fund, Consortium Costa Smeralda (chmn.). Home: Geneva, Switzerland. Died May 12, 2003.

AGNELLI, GIOVANNI, industrial executive; b. Turin, Italy, Mar. 12, 1921; s. Edoardo and Princess Virginia Bourbon del Monte Agnelli; m. Princess Marella Caracciolo di Castagneto. LLD, U. Torino, 1943. With Fiat Co., from 1943, vice chmn. bd., 1943-66, mng. dir., 1963-66, chmn., 1966-96, hon. chmn., from 1996. Chmn. IFI Istituto Finanziario Industriale, Exor Group S.A.; chmn. Giovanni Agnelli Found. Mem. adv. bd. Bilderberg Meetings; hon. co-chmn. Coun. for the U.S. & Italy; assoc. mem. Moral and Polit. Scis. Acad. of Inst. de France; life mem. Italian Senate;

chmn. Editrice La Stampa Spa. With Italian Army, 1940-45. Decorated Cross Mil. Valour, grand cross Royal Order of the No. Star; comdr. Legion of Honor (France). Mem. Italian Stock Cos. Assn. (dir.), Turin Indsl. Assn. (dir.), Confedn. Italian Industry (mem. exec. bd.). Died Jan. 24, 2003.

AGNELLI, UMBERTO, industrialist; b. Lausanne, Switzerland, Nov. 1, 1934; s. Edoardo and Virginia Bourbon del Monte Agnelli; m. Allegra Caracciolo, 1974; three children. Law degree U. Coord. Fiat Internat., Turin, Italy, 1968-70; mng. dir. Fiat SpA, 1970-76, vice chmn, 1976-79, vice chmn., mng. dir., 1979-80, vice chmn. 1980; vice chmn. Fiat Auto SpA, 1979-80, chmn., 1980-90, 2003-04; vice chmn, mng. dir. Istituto Finanziario Industriale; chmn. IFIL, Carfin; vice chmn., bd. dirs. Giovanni Agnelli Found.; bd. dirs. Danone. Vice-chmn. Internat. Coun. for New Initiatives in East-West Coop.; co-chmn. Italy Japan Bus. Group; chmn. Internat. Vienna Coun.; mem. adv. com. Allianz Versicherungs AG; mem. European adv. com. N.Y. Stock Exchange; mem. Italian Group of Trilateral Commn. Senator of the Italian Republic, 1976-79. Decorated chevalier Legion of Honor, grand officer Order of Merit (Italian Republic). Died May 27, 2004.

AHNSTROM, DORIS NEWELL, former association executive; b. Muskegon, Mich.; d. Harry W. and Vera (Newell) Ahnstrom; B.A., Brenau Coll., 1934; postgrad. N.Y. U., 1937-38, Columbia U., 1940-41. Mem. editorial dept. N.Y. Daily News, N.Y.C., 1936-42; mng. editor Skyways Mag., N.Y.C., 1942-55; air operations editor Flight Safety Found., N.Y.C., 1955-65, dir. publs., info. and edn., 1965-68, v.p. publs. and edn., 1968-78, bd. govs., 1974-75. Mem. Aerospace Writers Assn., AIAA, Internat. Soc. Aviation Writers, Aircraft Owners and Pilots Assn., Nat. Geog. Soc., Authors League Am., Am. Helicopter Soc., Alpha Delta Theta. Republican. Christian Scientist. Author: Complete Book of Helicopters, 3d edit., 1968; Complete Book of Jets and Rockets, 2d edit., 1965. Died Dec. 31, 1991. Home: Muskegon, Mich.

AIKEN, JAMES GARFIELD, lawyer; b. Waterford Works, N.J., July 4, 1917; BS in Econs., U. Pa., 1941, JD, 1948. Home: Haddonfield, NJ. Died Jan. 14, 2001.

AIKEN, JOAN (JOAN DELANO), author; b. Rye, Sussex, Eng., Sept. 4, 1924; d. Conrad Potter and Jessie (MacDonald) A.; m. Ronald George Brown, July 7, 1945 (dec. 1955); children: John Sebastian, Elizabeth Delano; m. Julius Goldstein, Sept. 2, 1976. Staff BBC, London, 1942-43; libr. UN Info. Ctr., London, 1943-49; sub-editor, features editor Argosy mag., London, 1955-60; copywriter J. Walter Thompson, London, 1960-61. Author: (juvenile fiction) All You've Ever Wanted and Other Stories, 1953, The Kingdom and The Cave, 1960, Black Hearts in Battersea, 1964, The Whispering Mountain, 1968, Night Fall, Winterthing: A Child's Play, 1970, The Cuckoo Tree, 1971, All and More, 1971, A Harp of Fishbones and Other Stories, 1972, The Skin Spinners, 1976, The Spiral Stair, 1979, The Shadow Guests, 1980, Up The Chimney Down, 1985, Give Yourself a Fright, 1989, A Foot in the Grave, 1990, Is, 1992, A Creepy Company, 1993, numerous others, (adult fiction) The Silence of Herondale, 1964, Beware of the Boquet, 1966, The Ribs of Death, 1967, The Embroidered Sunset, 1970, Castle Barebane, 1976, Last Movement, 1977, The Smile of the Stranger, 1978, The Weeping Ash, 1980, Foul Matter, 1983, Mansfield Revisted, 1984, If I Were You, 1987, Blackground, 1989, Jane Fairfax, 1990, The Shoemaker's Boy, 1991, The Midnight Moropus, 1993, Cold Shoulder Road, 1995, A Handful of Gold, 1995, Emma Watson, 1996, The Cockatrice Boys, 1996, The Jewel Seed, 1997, Moon Cake, 1998, others; translator: The Angel Inn; : The Youngest Miss Ward, 1998, The Way to Write for Children, 1998, Dangerous Games, 1999, Lady Catherine's Necklace, 2000, In Thunder's Pocket, 2000, The Song of Mat and Ben, 2002, The Scream, 2001, Bone and Dream, 2002; : Ghostly Beasts, 2002, Midwinter Nightingale, 2003. Died Jan. 4, 2004.

AIKEN, LEWIS ROSCOE, JR., psychologist, educator; b. Bradenton, Fla., Apr. 14, 1931; s. Lewis Roscoe and Vera Irene (Hess) A.; M. Dorothy Ree Grady, Dec. 16, 1956; children: Christopher, Timothy BS, Fla. State U., Tallahassee, 1955, MA, 1956; PhD, U. N.C., 1960. Assoc. prof. psychology U. N.C., Greensboro, 1960-65; prof. Guilford Coll., Greensboro, 1966-74, Sacred Heart Coll., Belmont, N.C., 1974-76, U. Pacific, Stockton, Calif., 1977-79, Pepperdine U., Malibu, Calif., 1979. Author: General Psychology, 1969, Psychological and Educational Testing, 1971, Readings in Psychological and Educational Testing, 1973, Psychological Testing and Assessment, 1976, 11th edit., 2003, Later Life, 1978, 3rd edit., 1989, Dying, Death and Bereavement, 1985, 4th edit., 2000, Assessment of Intellectual Functioning, 1987, 2d edit., 1996, Personality Assessment Methods and Practices, 1989, 3d edit., 1999, Personality: Theories, Research and Applications, 1993, 2d edit., 2000, Aging: An Introduction to Gerontology, 1994, Rating Scales and Checklists, 1996, Assessment of Adult Personality, 1997, Questionnaires and Inventories, 1997, Human Development in Adulthood, 1998, Tests and Examinations, 1998, Human Differences, 1999, Personality: Theories, Assessment, Research and Applications, 2000, Aging and Later Life, 2001, Attitudes & Other Psychosocial Constructs, 2002, Morality and Ethics in Theory and Practice, 2004; contbr. articles to profl. jours. Sgt. USMC, 1951-54 Fla. Lewis scholar, 1949-51, Gen. scholar, 1954-56; Emory U. fellow, 1957-58, U.S. Office Edn. postdoctoral fellow, 1968-69; NAS-NRC postdoctoral resident rsch. assoc., 1963-64. Fellow APA, Am. Psychol. Soc.; mem. Am. Ednl. Rsch. Assn., Sigma Xi. Home: Monroe, NC. Died Jan. 26, 2004.

ALBINSKI, HENRY STEPHEN, academic research center director, writer; b. Chgo., Dec. 31, 1931; m. Nan Bowman Albinski, Feb. 11, 1984. BA with highest honors, UCLA, 1953, MA, 1955; PhD, U. Minn., 1959. Vis. fellow Australian Nat. U., Canberra, 1963-64; cons. Rsch. Analysis Corp., McLean, Va., 1968-70; vis. prof. U. Queensland, Brisbane, Australia, 1970; cons. Ctr. Strategic and Internat. Studies, Washington, 1972-73; vis. prof. Flinders U., Adelaide, Australia, 1974, U. Sydney, Australia, 1974-75; cons. U.S. Dept. State, Washington, 1977, 93-94; vis. fellow Australian Nat. U., 1978-79, 95; cons. U.S. Fgn. Svc. Inst., Alexandria, Va., 1980; advisor Asian agenda program The Asia Found., N.Y.C., 1982; cons. ESSO Corp., Houston, 1983-84, U.S. Dept. Def., Washington, 1984-85; vis. prof. U. Melbourne, Australia, 1985-86, Australian Def. Force Acad., Canberra, 1988-89; advisor U. Hawaii, Honolulu, 1989-91; cons. Inst. Fgn. Policy Analysis, Washington, 1991-92; prof. polit. sci. and Australian and New Zealand studies and dir. Australia-New Zealand Studies Ctr. Pa. State U., University Park, 1982-98, prof. emeritus, from 1998. Haydn Williams and Curtin Internat. Inst. fellow Curtin U., Perth, 1995-96; vis. prof. U. Western. Ont., London, Can., 1969, Australian Def. Force Acad., 1992, U. Sydney, 1999—; fellow Rsch. Inst. for Asia and the Pacific; cons. Inst. Def. Analyses, Washington, 1969, Frost & Sullivan, Syracuse, N.Y., 1983-89, Pacific Forum, Honolulu, 1984-85; rsch. counselor, 1986-91; cons. Ellen Raider Internat., N.Y.C., Deakin U. Geelong, Victoria, Australia, 1992-94; advisor Nat. Coun. Fgn. Lang. and Internat. Studies, N.Y.C., 1980, East-West Ctr., Honolulu, 1987-93, Australia-Am. Study Com. on Comprehensive Security, Honolulu, 1989-91, Inst. Internat. Edn., N.Y.C., 1991-92, Coun. Internat. Coop., E. Lansing, Mich., 1992-94; vis. fellow Australian Nat. U., 1995; cons. Interlink Internat., 1998; vis. prof., fellow Rsch. Inst. for Asia and the Pacific, U. Sydney. Author: Australian Policies and Attitudes Toward China, 1965, Politics and Foreign Policy in Australia: The Impact of Vietnam and Conscription, 1969, Canadian and Australian Politics in Comparative Prespective, 1973, Australian External Policy Under Labor: Content, Process and the National Debate, 1977, The Australian-American Security Relationship: A Regional and Transregional Perspective, 1982; (monographs) The Australian Labor Party and Aid to Parochial Schools Controversy, 1966, Australia in Southeast Asia: Interest, Capacity and Acceptability, 1970, ANZUS, The United States and Pacific Security, 1987, The Australian-American Alliance: Prospects for the 1990s, 1990; Australia's Evolving American Relationship: Interests, Processes and Prospects for Australian Influence, 1995; author and co-editor: European Political Processes: Essays and Readings, 1968, 74; author and editor: Asian Political Processes Essays and Readings, 1971, Australia and the United States: Strategic and Defence Cooperation Futures, 1993; compiler, writer introduction: The United States-Australia Alliance in an East Asian Context; contbr. 130 book chpts. and articles to profl. jours. Advisor Am.-Australian Bicentennial Found., Washington, 1984-88; cons. Australian Nat. Maritime Mus., Sydney NSW, 1988. Travel fellow Rockefeller Found., 1963-64, New Zealand-U.S. Edn. Found., 1979; fellow Hoover Instn., 1984; sr. scholar Fulbright-Hays, 1974-75, 78-79, Fulbright Travel fellow, New Zealand, 1979. Mem. Australian Studies Assn. N. Am. (charter chair 1990-91, exec. bd. overseas mem. 1986-92), Australasian Polit. Studies Assn., Australian and New Zealand Assn. Canadian Studies, Am. Assn. Univ. Profs. (past pres. Pa. State U. chpt.), Am. Polit. Sci. Assn., U.S. Naval Inst., Mid. Atlantic Conf. Can. Studies (pres. 1983-84), New Zealand Polit. Studies Assn., Brit. Australian Studies Assn., Assn. Can. Studies in U.S., Internat. Studies Assn., Inter-Univ. Australasian Polit. Studies Assn., Australian Inst. Internat Affairs, Royal U.S. Inst. (Australia), Phi Beta Kappa, Pi Sigma Alpha, Pi Kappa Delta, Pi Sigma Mu, Alpha Mu Gamma, Phi Eta Sigma, Omicron Delta Kappa. Avocation: music. Home: Gladesville, Australia. Died Apr. 6, 2003; Sydney, Australia.

ALCOCK, CHARLES BENJAMIN, materials science consultant; b. London, Oct. 24, 1923; s. Arthur Charles and Margaret (Francis) A.; m. Valerie Robinson, Aug. 20, 1949; children— Deborah Susan, Martin Charles, James Benjamin BSc, Imperial Coll., London, 1944, PhD, 1955; DSc, U. London, London, 1965. With BISRA, London, Eng., 1948-50; investigator Nuffield Research Group Royal Sch. Mines, London, Eng., 1950-53; mem. faculty metall. dept. Imperial Coll., 1953-69, lectr., 1953-61, reader, 1961-65, prof. metall. chemistry, 1965-69; prof., chmn. dept. metallurgy and materials sci. U. Toronto, Ont., Can., 1969-76, prof. emeritus, from 1986. Vis. prof. Carnegie Inst. Tech., 1961, N.C. State U., 1965, Imperial Coll., 1992—; vis. com. mem. chem. engring. div. Argonne Nat. Lab., 1977-82; chmn. Can. Nat. Com. for CODATA, 1982-88, exec. com. mem., 1988-90; Ford vis. prof. U. Pa., 1968; Freimann vis. prof. U. Notre Dame, 1986, Freimann chaired prof., 1987-94, prof. emeritus, 1994—; dir. Ctr. for Sensor Materials, U. N.D., 1987-94. Author: Thermochemical Processes, 2001. Recipient Paul Lebeau medal, 1975, Kroll medal, 1983 Fellow Royal Soc. Arts, Royal Inst. Chemistry, Royal Soc. Can., Am. Inst. Metall. Engrs. Deceased.

ALCOCK, VIVIEN (DOLORES), children's author; b. Worthing, Eng., Sept. 23, 1924; d. John Forster and Molly (Pulman) A.; m. Leon Garfield, Oct. 23, 1947; 1 child, Jane Angela. Student, Ruskin Sch. Drawing and Fine Arts, Oxford, Eng., 1940-42, Camden Arts Ctr. Artist Gestetner Ltd., London, 1947-53, mgr. employment bur., 1953-56; sec. Whittington Hosp., London, 1956-64. Writings include: The Haunting of Cassie Palmer, 1980, The Stonewalkers, 1981, The Sylvia Game (A Novel of the Supernatural), 1982, Travellers by Night, 1983 (Horn Book Honor list 1985, Notable Book of Yr. ALA 1985), Ghostly Companions: A Feast of Chilling Tales, 1984, The Cuckoo Sister, 1985 (Notable Book of Yr. ALA 1986), Wait and See, 1986, The Mysterious Mr. Ross, 1987, The Monster Garden, 1988 (Voice of Youth Advocate Best Sci. Fiction Book 1988, Notable Book of Yr. ALA 1988), The Thing in the Woods, 1989, The Trial of Anna Cotman, 1990, A Kind of Thief, 1991, The Dancing Bush, 1991, Singer to the Sea God, 1992, Othergran, 1993, The Wrecker, 1994, Face at the Window, 1994, The Red-Eared Ghosts, 1996, The Silver Egg, 1997, A Gift on a String, 1998, Ticket to Heaven, 2000. Served as ambulance driver Brit. Army, 1942-46. Mem. Authors Soc. Mem. Ch. Of Eng. Avocations: painting, patchwork, reading. Home: London, England. Died Oct. 12, 2003.

ALDRICH, BAILEY, judge; b. Boston, Apr. 23, 1907; s. Talbot and Eleanor (Little) Aldrich; m. Elizabeth Perkins, Aug. 13, 1932; children: Jonathan, David. AB, Harvard U., 1928, LLB, 1932. Bar: Mass. 1932. With Choate, Hall & Stewart, Boston, 1932—54; judge U.S. Dist. Ct. Mass., 1954—59, U.S. Ct. Appeals, 1959—64; chief judge U.S. Ct. Appeals (1st cir.), 1965—72, sr. judge, 1972—99. Mem.: Am. Acad. Arts and Scis., Am. Law Inst. Home: Boston, Mass. Died Sept. 25, 2002.

ALEXANDER, ELIZABETH POPE, hospital administrator, consultant; b. South Pittsburg, Tenn., Nov. 2, 1937; d. Franklin and Virginia Lee (Stubbs) Pope; m. John Benard Furey, Nov. 12, 1968 (div. 1970); 1 child, Stephanie Elizabeth; m. Edward George Alexander, July 26, 1975. BA, Bennett Coll., 1961; MSW, Atlanta U., 1963; postgrad., Tulane U., 1964. Group worker Orleans Neighborhood Ctrs., New Orleans, 1963-65; community organizer Anti-Poverty Agy., New Orleans, 1965-67; dir. ctr. Anti-Poverty Desire Neighborhood, New Orleans, 1967-69; specialist community relations U.S. Dept. Justice, Washington, 1970-72; coordinator fed. women's program Materiel Command U.S. Army, Alexandria, Va., 1972-75; outreach worker City of New Orleans Housing Authority, 1975-76; adminstrv. officer, coordinator employee assistance program VA Med. Ctr., New Orleans, from 1976. Cons. Alexander, Cooper and Assocs. Ltd., New Orleans, v.p. 1985—; field instr. So. U., 1983—, Tulane U., 1980-85, Xavier U., 1985—; investigator EEO. Mem. Gov.'s Adv. Council Drug Abuse, New Orleans, 1986—. Mem. Nat. Assn. Female Execs., Nat. Council Negro Women, Federally Employed Women, VA Hosp. Fed. Credit Union (supervisory chmn. 1980-85), La. Assn. Substance Abuse Counselors and Trainers (cert., sec.-treas. 1979-84). Democrat. Baptist. Avocations: playing piano, bowling, reading. Home: New Orleans, La. Deceased.

ALEXANDER, MARILYN ANNE, nurse; b. Chgo., Aug. 28, 1948; d. Edward and Lorraine L. (Milinarick) Jummrich; m. David N. Alexander, Mar. 11, 1978. Diploma with honors, Sentara Norfolk Gen. Hosp., 1988. Sec. Dept. of Navy; clin. nurse II Sentara Norfolk (Va.) Gen. Hosp. With U.S. Army, 1967, with Res. 1976-78. Home: Virginia Beach, Va. Died July 14, 2001.

ALEXANDER, STEPHEN WINTHROP, sales executive; b. Port Washington, N.Y., Apr. 18, 1941; s. Eben Roy and Mary Louise (Webb) A.; m. Marian Susan Burda, Oct. 27, 1962; children: Stephen, Kevin, Jennifer, Bryan, David, Matthew, Reagan, Christopher. BS in History, St. Louis U., 1962. With advt. sales dept. Time, N.Y.C., 1965-67, 72-76, Cleve., 1967-69, Pitts., 1969-72, Midwest sales mgr. Chgo., 1976-82, 87-89, U.S. sales mgr. N.Y.C., 1982-87; v.p. sales The Sporting News, Chgo., 1990-93; v.p. advt. sales SRDS, Wilmette, Ill., 1993-95; assoc. pub. dir. Modern Maturity and The AARP Bull., 1995-97; pub. Chgo. Home and Garden, from 1997. Bd. dirs. Better Bus. Bur., Chgo., 1987-89. Chmn. CCD program St. Mary's Ch., Lake Forest, Ill., 1980-82. Capt. USMC, 1962-65. Mem. Chgo. Advt. Club (bd. dirs. 1986-87). Roman Catholic. Avocations: family activities, golf, swimming. Home: Lake Forest, Ill. Died Mar. 18, 2002.

ALFIN-SLATER, ROSLYN BERNIECE, biochemist, nutritionist, educator; b. Bklyn., July 28, 1916; d. Sam and Lillian (Rubinsky) A.; m. Grant G. Slater, July 30, 1948. BA, Bklyn. Coll., 1936; AM, Columbia U., 1942, PhD, 1946. Asst. in charge lecture div., chemistry dept. Bklyn. Coll., 1938-43, tutor gen. inorganic chemistry, 1943, instr. inorganic chemistry, qualitative analysis, evenings 1946-48; asst. instr. inorganic chemistry, exptl. phys. chemistry, food analysis Columbia U., 1943-45; research fellow Corn Industries Research Found., 1945-46; instr. biochemistry NYU Coll. Dentistry, 1945-46; research chemist indsl. enzymes Takamine Labs., Clifton, N.J., 1946-47; research fellow Sloan Kettering Inst. Cancer Research, 1947-48; research asso. dept. biochemistry and nutrition U. So. Calif. Sch. Medicine, 1948-52, vis. asst. prof., 1952-56, vis. asso. prof., 1956-59; asso. prof. nutrition UCLA, 1959-65, prof., 1965-87, prof. biol. chemistry, 1971-87, prof. emeritus, from 1987, div. head, environ. and nutritional sci. Sch. Pub. Health, 1969-77, asst. dean acad. affairs Sch. Pub. Health, 1983-87. Mem. nutrition study sect. NIH, 1968-72; mem. com. for dietary allowances, food and nutrition bd. NRC, 1970-74, mem. nat. com., internat. union nutritional scis., 1974-77, mem. food and nutrition bd., 1975-81, vice chmn., 1978-79 Editor: Human Nutrition: A Comprehensive Treatise, 7 vols., 1979-91; contbr. to sci. books, jours.; mem. editorial bd. Jour. Nutrition, 1966-70, Advances in Lipid Research, 1970-74, Am. Jour. Clin. Nutrition, 1975-78; Assoc. editor: jour. Lipids, 1972-78, AGE, Jour. Am. Aging Assn, 1977-88, Nutrition & the M.D, 1974—, Drug-Nutrient Interactions, 1980-88. Recipient nat. merit award for outstanding achievement in pub. health Delta Omega, 1985

Fellow AAAS, Am. Heart Assn. (council on arteriosclerosis), Am. Inst. Nutrition (Osborne and Mendel award 1970, Borden award 1981); mem. N.Y. Acad. Scis., Am. Soc. Biol. Chemists, Am. Oil Chemists Soc., Am. Inst. Nutrition (treas. 1977-80), Soc. Nutrition Edn. (pres. 1978-79), Internat. Soc. Cardiology, Am. Dietetic Assn. (hon.), Sigma Xi, Phi Sigma, Iota Sigma Pi, Omicron Nu (hon.) Home: Los Angeles, Calif. Died Aug. 9, 2002.

ALIYEV, HEYDAR ALIRZA, former president of Azerbaijan; b. Nakhchyvan, Azerbaijan, May 10, 1923; m. Zarifa Aziz gizi Aliyeva (dec. 1985); 2 children: Sevil, Ilham. Diploma, Azerbaijan State U., 1957; PhD (hon.), Baku State U., 1994, Hojjat-Tapu U., Ankara, Turkey, 1994. Ofcl. of security forces and mem. Council of Ministers of Nakhchyvan Autonomous Republic, 1941-49; leading ofcl. of Ministry of Internal Affairs and Com. of State Security (KGB) of Azerbaijan S.S.R.; dep. chmn., 1964-67. Chmn. with rank of maj.-gen. 1967-69; cand. mem. Central Com. of Communist Party of Azerbaijan (CPA), 1966-69, former mem. Cen. Com., former mem. Bur., 1st sec. Central Com., 1969-82; former mem. Communist Party of Soviet Union, mem. Central Com., 1971-89, cand. mem. Politburo of Central Com. 1976-82, mem., 1982-87; dep. to USSR Supreme Soviet, 1970-74; vice chmn. Soviet of the Union, 1974; 1st dep. chmn. USSR Council of Ministers, 1982-87, chmn. bur. social devel. until 1987; chmn. Supreme Majlis, Nat. Assembly, 1990-93; dep. speaker Supreme Soviet of Azerbaijan, 1990-93; speaker Supreme Soviet, acting pres., 1993; pres. Supreme Soviet, former comdr.-in-chief Armed Forces; chmn. Supreme Meilis Nakmichevan Autonomous Republic, 1991-93, dep. sprk. Supreme Soviet Azerbaijan, 1991-93, pres. Republic Azerbaijan, 1993-2003. Recipient Order of Lenin (2), and others. Died Dec. 12, 2003.

ALLARD, ROBERT WAYNE, geneticist, educator; b. L.A., Sept. 3, 1919; s. Glenn A. and Alma A. (Roose) A.; m. Ann Catherine Wilson, June 16, 1944; children: Susan, Thomas (dec.), Jane, Gillian, Stacie. BS, U. Calif., Davis, 1941; PhD, U. Wis., 1946; ScD (hon.), U. Helsinki, 1996, U. Léon, 1997. From asst. to assoc. prof. U. Calif., Davis, 1946—, prof. genetics, 1955—. Author books; contbr. articles to profl. jours. Served to lt. USNR. Recipient Crop Sci. award Am. Soc. Agronomy, 1964, DeKalb Disting. Career award Crop Sci. Soc. Am., 1983; Guggenheim fellow, 1954, 60; Fulbright fellow, 1955 Mem. Nat. Acad. Scis., Am. Acad. Arts and Scis., Am. Soc. Naturalists (pres. 1974-75), Genetics Soc. Am. (pres. 1983-84), Am. Genetics Assn. (pres. 1989), Phi Beta Kappa, Sigma Xi, Alpha Gamma Rho, Alpha Zeta. Democrat. Unitarian Universalist. Home: Davis, Calif. Died Mar. 25, 2003.

ALLEN, CHARLES MENGEL, federal judge; b. Louisville, Nov. 22, 1916; s. Arthur Dwight and Jane (Mengel) A.; m. Betty Anne Cardwell, June 25, 1949; children: Charles Dwight, Angela M. BA, Yale U., 1941; LLB, U. Louisville, 1943. Bar: Ky. 1944. Assoc. Doolin, Helm, Stites and Wood, 1944-45; pvt. practice Louisville, 1946-47; assoc. Farnsley, Hottell and Stephenson, 1947-53; pvt. practice, 1953-55; asst. U.S. atty. Western Dist. Ky., Dept. Justice, 1955-59; ptnr. Booth, Walker & Allen, Louisville, 1959-61; circuit judge Jefferson Cir. Ct., 4th Chancery Br. Jefferson County, 1961-71; dist. judge U.S. Dist. Ct. (we. dist.) Ky., Louisville, 1971-77, chief judge, 1977-85, sr. judge, 1985-99. Named Outstanding Alumnus U. Louisville, 1984; recipient Brandeis award U. Louisville Law Sch., 1985, Thomas Hogan Meml. Found award Ky. Civil Liberties Union, 1986, Grauman award U. Louisville, 1986. Mem. ABA, Fed. Bar Assn., Ky. Bar Assn. (Judge of Yr. award 1996), Louisville Bar Assn., Nat. Ry. Hist. Soc. Avocations: tennis, trains, photography, bridge. Home: Harrods Creek, Ky. Deceased.

ALLEN, IVAN, JR., retired office products company owner; b. Atlanta, Mar. 15, 1911; s. Ivan and Irene (Beaumont) A.; m. Louise Richardson, Jan. 1, 1936; children: Inman, Beaumont. Grad., Georgia Inst. Tech., 1933; LL.D., Morris Brown Coll., Clark Coll., Atlanta U., La Grange Coll., Emory U., Davidson Coll.; D of Pub. Svc., Ga. Inst. Tech., 1996. With Ivan Allen Co., Atlanta, from 1933, pres., 1946-57, vice chmn. bd., 1957, chmn. bd., 1969-95, chmn. emeritus, 1995—2003. Dir. Equitable Life Assurance Soc. Scout, scoutmaster, area pres., regional committeeman, mem. nat. exec. bd. Boy Scouts Am.; chmn. Greater Atlanta Community Chest, 1949; Lt. col. Gov.'s Staff, 1936; treas. Ga. State Hosp. Authority, 1936; sec. exec. dept. State Ga., 1945-46; mayor of Atlanta, 1961-69; Trustee Ga. Tech. Found. Served as maj. inf. AUS, World War II. Awarded Silver Beaver; awarded Silver Antelope, Silver Buffalo; Recipient Armin Maier award Atlanta Rotary Club, 1952 Mem. Ga. Tech. Alumni Assn. (pres. 1953-54), Atlanta C. of C. (pres. 1961), Nat. Stationery and Office Equipment Assn. (dist. gov. 1938-40, pres. 1955-56), Rotary, Sigma Alpha Epsilon. Home: Atlanta, Ga. Died July 2, 2003.

ALLEN, MARION CARROLL, clergyman; b. Spartanburg, S.C., Dec. 12, 1914; s. Albert Mayfield and Caroline May (Rogers) A.; B.A., Furman U., 1937; M.Div., Yale, 1940; M.A., Kans. U., 1960; m. Eleanor Earl Burt, July 31, 1943; children— Marian, Burt, Robert, Louise. Ordained to ministry Am. Bapt. Conv., 1940, received into United Ch. of Christ; pastor Bapt. chs., Bristol, Conn., 1940-47, Beaufort, S.C., 1947-50, Clemson, S.C., 1950-56, Lawrence, Kans., 1956-76; pastor First Congregational Ch., Topeka, 1976, Central Congregational Ch., 1977-80, Pilgrim Congregational Ch., Wichita, Kans., 1980—; instr. religion Clemson U., 1951-56, instr. homiletics Central Sem., Kansas City, Kans., 1959-61, English, Kans. U., 1958, 76—. Bd. dirs. YMCA, U. Kans., 1956-60; v.p. Lawrence Friends of Music, 1968-75; sec. adv. bd. Kans. Sch. Religion, 1970-76. Mem. Topeka Ministerial Alliance, Lawrence Ministerial Alliancce, Topeka Council Chs., Consultation of Cooperating Chs. Kans., Kans. Okla. Conf. United Ch. of Christ. Clubs: Masons. Author: A Voice Not Our Own, 1963. Editor: The Springs of Learning, 1969. Editor: Serving in the Armed Forces, monthly 1972-74. Home: Lawrence, Kans.

ALLER, LAWRENCE HUGH, astronomy educator, researcher; b. Tacoma, Wash., Sept. 24, 1913; s. Leslie E. and Lena Belle (Davis) A.; m. Rosalind Duncan Hall; children— Hugh Duncan, Raymond Donald, Gwendolyn Jean AB, U. Calif, Berkeley, 1936; MA, Harvard U., 1938, PhD, 1943. Instr. physics Harvard U., Cambridge, Mass., 1942-43; research physicist radiation lab. U. Calif, Berkeley, 1943-45; asst. prof. astronomy Ind. U., Bloomington, 1945-48; assoc. prof. astronomy U. Mich., Ann Arbor, 1948-54, prof. astronomy, 1954-62, UCLA, 1962-84, prof. emeritus, 1984—; vis. prof. U. Tasmania, Hobart, Australia, 1969, U. Queensland, Brisbane, Australia, 1977-78, Australian Nat. U., Canberra, 1960-61, U. Toronto, Ont., Can., 1961-62, U. Sydney, New South Wales, Australia, 1968; guest investigator radiophysics CSIRO, Epping, New South Wales, Australia, 1968, 69, 77; vis. lectr. Raman Inst., Bangalore, India, 1978, Sch. Advanced Studies, Trieste, Italy, 1981; guest investigator Mt. Wilson Obs., Pasadena, Calif., 1949-82. Author: Atmospheres of Sun and Stars, 1953, 2d edit., 1962; Stellar Interiors, Nuclear Transformations, 1954; Gaseous Nebulae, 1956; Abundances of Elements, 1961; Atoms, Stars and Nebulae, 1971, 3d edit., 1991, Physics of Thermal Gaseous Nebulae, 1984. Editor (with Dean B. McLaughlin) Stellar Structure and Evolution, 1965; (with Barbara Middlehurst) Interstellar Medium, 1967 NSF research fellow, 1968-69, 60-61 Mem. Am. Astron. Soc. (councillor 1953-56), Internat. Astron. Union (pres. stellar-spectroscopy group 1959-64), Astron. Soc. of Pacific (bd. dirs. 1974-77), Am. Acad. Arts and Scis., Nat. Acad. Scis. Lodges: Masons. Mem. Soc. Of Friends. Avocations: travel, photography. Home: Mariposa, Calif. Died Mar. 16, 2003.

ALLEY, MARY DEAN BREWER, medical foundation executive; b. Columbia, S.C., Oct. 23, 1942; d. Barney Frank and Mary Mattie (Mathis) B.; m. George Thayer Alley. BA, Winthrop U., 1963; MA, U. S.C., 1971; EdD, U. Rochester, 1988. English tchr., dept. chmn. Irmo (S.C.) High Sch., 1963-72; sch. dir. Columbia (S.C.) Jr. Coll., 1972-74; instr. Rochester (N.Y.) Inst. of Tech., 1975-78, asst. prof. mktg. and dir. career edn., 1978-84, dir. of devel., 1984-88, Boston U., 1988-89; v.p. of devel. Elmira (N.Y.) Coll., 1989-94; corp. v.p. McLeod Health, Florence, SC, from 1994; CEO McLeod Found., Florence, SC, from 1994. Ednl. cons. ITT, Bobbs-Merrill Pub., 1974-78; pres. Organizational Devel. Assocs., 1985—. Editorial Bd. mem. Jour. of Co-operative Edn., 1981-83, book reviewer, 1982; editor Pub. The Bottom Line, 1975-77, CareerLine, 1979. Dir. women's com. Rochester Philharm. Orch., Rochester, 1976—78; dir. Women's Career Ctr., Rochester, 1980—84, Women's Ctr. The So. Tier, 1993—94; active Arnot Art Mus., 1990—94; bd. dirs. Girl Scout Coun. Pee Dee Region, Inc., from 1996, pres., from 2001; active Susan B. Anthony Rep. Women, Rochester, 1975—77; bd. dirs. S.C. Planned Giving Coun., from 1997. Named to Women's Hall of Fame, 2000; recipient Mary Mildred Sullivan award, Winthrop U., 2001. Mem. Women's Studies Adv. Coun., N.Y. State Assn. Women in Higher Edn., Co. for Advancement and Support of Edn., Women in Devel., Nat. Commn. on Planned Giving S.C. Hosp. Assn., Assn. Healthcare Philanthropy, S.C. Women in Higher Edn., Leadership S.C. Class 1998, Rotary (Florence), Kappa Delta Pi, Omicron Delta Kappa. Episcopalian. Avocations: writing, reading, theatre, travel, antiques. Home: Florence, SC. Died Feb. 26, 2002.

ALLEYNE, REGINALD HARCOURT, JR., legal educator; b. 1932; BS, Tufts U., 1954; LLB, Howard U., 1959; LLM, Columbia U., 1969. Bar: N.Mex. Law clk., judge US Ct. Appeals (DC cir.), 1959—60; rsch. asst. clk. office US Supreme Ct., 1960—61; asst. to dep. atty. gen. Washington office Atty. Gen., 1961—63; field rep. dept. contract compliance US Navy, 1963—65; atty. NLRB, Albuquerque, 1965—69; acting prof. UCLA, 1969—72; prof. adminstrv. law, 1972—96; vis. prof. Boston U., 1975; legal counsel Econ. Opportunity Bd. Bernalillo County, Albuquerque, 1966—68. Author (with Dunsford and morris): (jour.) Individuals and Unions; editor (in chief): Law Jour./Howard U. Served USN, 1954—56. Mem.: Am. Arbitration Assn. (mem. labor-mgmt. panel from 1970), Fed. Mediation and Conciliation Svc. (mem. arbitration panel 1974), Los Angeles County Employee Rels Commn. (mem. 1970—73), NY Pub. Employment Rels. Bd. (mem. panel of mediators and fact finders). Died Mar. 28, 2004.

ALMOND, GABRIEL ABRAHAM, political science educator; b. Rock Island, Ill., Jan. 12, 1911; s. David Moses and Lisa (Elson) A.; m. Maria Dorothea Kaufmann, Apr. 29, 1937; children: Richard J., Peter O., Susan J. PhB, U. Chgo., 1932, PhD, 1938. Fellow Social Sci. Rsch. Coun., 1935-36, 46; instr. polit. sci. Bklyn. Coll., 1939-42; with OWI, Washington, 1942-44, War Dept., ETO, 1945; research assoc. Yale U. Inst. Internat. Studies, 1947-49, assoc. prof. polit. sci., 1949-51, prof. polit. sci., 1959-63; assoc. prof. internat. affairs Princeton, 1951-54, prof., 1954-57, prof. politics, 1957-59; prof. polit. sci. Stanford U., 1963-76; exec. head dept. polit. sci. Stanford u., 1964-68; prof. emeritus Stanford U., 1976. Cons. Air U., 1948, Dept. State, 1950, Office Naval Rsch., 1951, Rand Corp., 1954-55, sci. adv. bd. USAF, 1960-61; vis. prof. U. Tokyo, Japan, 1962, Kiev State U., USSR, 1989; Overseas fellow Churchill Coll. U. Cambridge, 1972-73; vis. fellow Australian Nat. U., 1983. Author: The American People and Foreign Policy, 1950, The Appeals of Communism, 1954, (with others) The Struggle for Democracy in Germany, 1949, The Politics of the Developing Areas, 1960, (with Sidney Verba) The Civic Culture, 1963, (with G. Bingham Powell) Comparative Politics, 1966, Political Development, 1970, (with others) Crisis, Choice and Change, 1973, Comparative Politics Today, 1974, 80, 84, 88, 92, 96, 2000, (with G. Bingham Powell) Comparative Politics: System, Process, Policy, 1978, (with Sidney Verba and others) The Civic Culture Revisited, 1980, (with others) Progress and its Discontents, 1982, A Discipline Divided, Schools and Sects in Political Science, 1990, Comparative Politics: A Theoretical Approach, 2001, (with others) Plutocracy and Politics in New York City, 1998, European Politics Today, 1999, Ventures in Political Science, 2002. Recipient Travel and Study award Ford Found., 1962-63; fellow Center for Advanced Study in the Behavioral Scis., 1956-57; sr. fellow Nat. Endowment for Humanities, 1972-73 Fellow Am. Acad. Arts and Scis.; mem. Nat. Acad. Scis., Am. Philos. Soc., Social Sci. Rsch. Coun. (bd. dirs., chmn. com. comparative politics), Am. Polit. Sci. Assn. (pres. 1965-66, James Madison award 1981, Frank Goodnow award 1999). Home: Palo Alto, Calif. Died Dec. 25, 2002.

ALPERT, ROCHELLE DEE, lawyer; b. Detroit, July 1, 1950; d. Meyer Jack and Sarah Gertrude (Beigler) A.; m. Steven Frank Greenwald, May 26, 1974; children: Elyse M., Elliot A. BA, U. Mich., 1972, JD, 1975. Bar: Calif. 1975, U.S. Supreme Ct. 1982. Ptnr. Morrison & Foerster, San Francisco, from 1975. Active pediatric coun. U. Calif. San Francisco, 1991—, parent bd. Marin Country Day Sch., Corte Madera, Calif., 1992-93; bd. dirs. Menorah Pk. Low Income Sr. Housing, San Francisco, 1991—. Mem. ABA, San Francisco Bar Assn., Internat. Trademark Assn. Home: San Francisco, Calif. Deceased.

ALT, LUCILE BACKUS, retired English language and speech educator; b. Wagner, S.D., May 17, 1918; d. Roy and Ethel (Coburn) Backus; m. Bernard Wilson Alt, Dec. 19, 1947; children: Lee Coburn, Miles Watkins, Kurt Langdon. BA in Speech, Dakota Wesleyan U., 1939; MA in English, George Peabody U., 1947; MA in Interpersonal Comm., U. Mont., 1977. Cert. profl. parliamentarian, Am. Assn. Parliamentarians; life cert. tchr., S.D. Tchr. English and speech Gregory (S.D.) H.S., 1939-41, Letcher (S.D.) H.S., 1941-43, Mitchell (S.D.) H.S., 1943-44; part-time instr. George Peabody U., Nashville, 1946-47; tchr. English and speech Vermillion (S.D.) H.S., 1947-48; prof. speech U. Mont., Missoula, 1949-51; tchr. libr. Malta (Mont.) H.S., 1955-57; prof. English Dickinson (N.D.) State Coll., 1962-65; prof., head dept. speech Mont. Tech. Sch. Mines, Butte, 1965-75; with dept. speech Flathead Valley C.C., Kalispell, Mont., 1975-90, ret., 1990. Assoc. dir. N.D. Com. Humanities and Pub. Issues, Bismarck, 1975-80; program devel. Mont. Com. Humanities and Pub. Issues, Missoula, 1980-90. With Waves, USN, 1944-46, WWII. Mem. AAUW (hon. life, past pres. chpt.), Bus. and Profl. Women, Delta Kappa Gamma. Avocation: quilting. Home: Kalispell, Mont. Died Aug. 2, 1999.

ALTMAN, HAROLD, artist educator; b. N.Y.C., Apr. 20, 1924; Student, Art Students League, 1941-42, Cooper Union, 1941-47, New Sch. Social Rsch., 1947-49, Acad. Grande Chaumiere, Paris, 1949-52, Black Mountain Coll., N.C. Asst. prof. art N.Y. State Coll. Ceramics, Alfred U., 1952-54, U. N.C., Greensboro, 1954-56, U. Wis.-Milw., 1956-62; prof. art Pa. State U., 1962-76. Exhbns. include Mus. Modern Art, Met. Mus. Art & Whitney Mus. Art, N.Y., Art Inst., Chgo., Nat. Gallery Art, Washington; commns. include Entire print ed. Mus. Modern Art, 1960, Soc. Am. Graphic Artists, 1962, Hilton Rockfeller Hotel, 1963, Jewish Mus., N.Y., 1964; one-man shows include Martha Jackson Gallery, N.Y., 1958, Art Inst., Chgo., 1960, San Francisco Mus. Art, 1961, Sagot Le Garrec Gallery, Paris, 1968, 74, State Gallery Fine Arts, Istanbul, Turkey, 1975, among others; represented in permanent collections Boston Mus. Fine Arts, L.A. County Mus., Mus. Modern Art, N.Y.C., Whitney Mus., Bklyn. Mus., Met. Mus. Art, Milw. Art Ctr., Minn. Mus. Art, Nat. Gallery of Art, Phila. Mus. Art, San Francisco Mus. Art, Smithsonian Inst., Walker Art Ctr., Art Inst. Chgo., Cin. Mus. Art, Cleve. Mus. Art, Detroit Inst. Fine Arts, San Diego Mus. Art, Albright Knox Art Gallery, Des Moines Art Ctr., Newart Art Mus., Butler Inst. Am. Art, Ga. Mus. Art, Calif. Palace of Legion of Honor, Okla. Art Ctr., N.C. Mus. Art, Wadsworth Atheneum, Phoenix Art Ctr., Norfolk Mus., Peoria Art Ctr., Princeton U. Mus. Art, Yale U. Mus. Art, Fogg Mus. Art, Harvard U., Honolulu Acad. Art, N.Y. Pub. Libr., Libr. Congress, Pa. Acad. Art, Memphis Brooks Mus. Art, Kranner Art Mus., Decordova and Dana Mus., Univs. of Mass., Colo., Ky., Maine, Minn., Va. Wis., N.D., Nebr., Wake Forest, Ohio State, Pa. State, NYU, High Mus. Art, Atlanta, Rochester Meml. Art Gallery, Philbrook Mus. Art, Tulsa, Kalamazoo Inst. Art, Anchorage Mus. Art, Boston Pub. Libr., Victoria and Albert Mus., London, Stedellkj Mus., Amsterdam, Kunst Mus., Basel, Royal Mus. Fine Arts, Copenhagen, Bibliotheque Nat., Paris, Bibliotheque Royale, Belgium, Art Gallery Ont., Malmo Mus., Sweden, Mus. Modern Art Haifa, Israel, Mus. U. Glasgow, Scotland, Mus. Carnavalet, Paris, Art Gallery Greater Victoria, Escuela De Artes Plasticas, Mexico City. Guggenheim fellow, 1960-62, Fulbright Hayes Sr. Rsch. fellow, 1964-65, Tamarind Lithography fellow; recipient Nat. Inst. Arts & Letters award, 1963, Silver medal City of Paris; grantee Nat. Endowment for the Arts. Mem. Societe des Peintres, Graveurs, Francais, Nat. Acad. Design. Died July 28, 2003.

ALVARES, ALVITO PETER, retired pharmacology and toxicology educator; b. Bombay, Dec. 25, 1935; came to U.S., 1958, naturalized citizen, 1991; s. Amancio and Diva (Vaz) A.; m. Joy Ann Schmidt, Aug. 30, 1969; children: Christopher, Kevin. BSc., U. Bombay, 1955, BSc. in Tech., 1957; MS, U. Detroit, 1960; PhD, U. Chgo., 1966. Postdoctoral fellow U. Minn., Mpls., 1965-67; sr. rsch. biochemist Burroughs Wellcome and Co., Tuckahoe, N.Y., 1967-70; rsch. assoc. Rockefeller U., N.Y.C., 1970-71, asst. prof. pharmacology, 1971-75, assoc. prof., 1975-77, Uniformed Svcs. U., Bethesda, Md., 1977-78, prof. pharmacology and toxicology, 1978-99; ret., 1999. Sixth ann. Pfizer Lectr., Case Western Res. U., Cleve., 1983; vis. prof. Fedn. Am. Soc. for Exptl. Biology, Atlanta, 1987; vis. scientist UN Devel. Program, India, 1990, Goa (India) Med. Coll., 1992; speaker in field. Author: The Liver: Biology and Pathobiology, 1982, Principles of Drug Action, 1990; mem. editl. bd. Clin. Pharmacology and Therapeutics, 1977-99, Jour. Environ. Pathology, Toxicology and Oncology, 1977-92, Jour. Pharmacology, 1977-99, Drug Metabolism and Disposition, 1987-94; contbr. over 115 articles to profl. jours. Irma T. Hirschl scholar, Irma T. Hirschl Trust, 1974-78; recipient career development award NIH, 1975-78. Mem. AAAS, Am. Soc. for Pharmacology and Exptl. Therapeutics, Am. Soc. for Biochemistry and Molecular Biology, Am. Soc. for Clin. Pharmacology and Therapeutics, Soc. of Toxicology, N.Y. Acad. Scis. Home: Potomac, Md. Died Mar. 29, 2001.

AMAKER, NORMAN CAREY, law educator; b. N.Y.C., Jan. 15, 1935; s. Carey and Gladys Mae (Corley) A.; m. Mattie Jeanette Owens, Oct. 20, 1962; children: Alicia, Alana, Arthur. BA, Amherst (Mass.) Coll., 1956; JD, Columbia U., N.Y.C., 1959. Bar: N.Y. 1961, U.S. Supreme Ct. 1964, D.C. 1973. Atty., 1st asst. counsel NAACP Legal Def. Fund, N.Y.C., 1960-71; exec. dir. Neighborhood Legal Svcs. Program, Washington, 1971-73; gen. counsel Nat. Commn. Against Discrimination in Housing, Washington, 1973; prof. Sch. of Law Rutgers U., Newark, 1973-76, Loyola U., Chgo., from 1976. Author: Civil Liberties & Civil Rights, 1967, Civil Rights & The Reagan Administration, 1988. Pres. Chgo. Forum, 1981; mem. sch. bd. Evanston (Ill.) Twp. High Sch., 1980-87. With USAR, 1961-62. Mem. ABA, Soc. Am. Law Tchrs. (bd. dirs. 1979-86. Home: Evanston, Ill. Died June 7, 2000.

AMAREL, SAUL, computer scientist, educator; b. Thessaloniki, Greece, Feb. 16, 1928; came to U.S., 1957, naturalized, 1962; s. Albert and Sol (Pelossof) Amario; m. Marianne Kroh, Dec. 20, 1953; children: Dan, David; m. Irene Rosenberg, Oct. 13, 1990. B.Sc., Israel Inst. Tech., Haifa, 1948, Ingenieur EE, 1949; MS, Columbia, 1953, D.Eng. Sci, 1955. Sci. dep. Israel Ministry Def., 1948-52, project leader control and computer systems, 1955-57; research engr. Electronic Research Lab., Columbia, 1953-55; head computer theory research RCA Labs., Princeton, N.J., 1957-69; from prof. computer sci. to prof. emeritus Rutgers U., New Brunswick, NJ, 1969-2002, prof. emeritus, from 2002. Mem. chmn./biol. info. handling rev. com. NIH, 1971-75; mem. info. sci. adv. com. N.J. Dept. Higher Edn., 1973-76; mem. exec. and adv. coms. SUMEX-AIM, 1974-90; trustee Internat. Joint Confs. Artificial Intelligence, 1981-89, gen. chmn., 1983; mem. nat. adv. com. Bionet, 1984-87; chair Fed. Coordinating Coun. for Sci. Engring. and Tech. of Office of Sci. and Tech. Policy Subcom. on Computer R&D, 1986-87; advanced tech. adv. com. NASA, 1987-90; mem. Info. Sci. and tech. Study Group, Inst. Def. Analyses, 1987-95, com. on scis. and arts, computer and cognitive cluster Franklin Inst., 1991-95; vis. prof. computer sci. Carnegie Mellon U., 1966, vis. sr. rsch. scientist, 1985; vis. scholar Stanford U., 1979; vis. rsch. fellow SRI Internat., 1983. Mem. editl. bd. Artificial Intelligence, Internat. Jour., 1969-96, Jour. Computer Langs., 1974-85, Machine Learning Jour., 1984-94, Ency. Artificial Intelligence, 1983—, Symbolic Computation book series, 1984—; contbr. articles to sci. jours. Trustee Ramapo Coll., N.J., 1969-73, Charles Babbage Found., 1995—2002, bd. dirs., 1996-2001. Fellow IEEE, AAAS, Am. Assn. Artificial Intelligence (founding, exec. coun. 1982-86); mem. Soc. Indsl. and Applied Math., Assn. Computing Machinery, Sigma Xi. Home: Princeton, NJ. Deceased.

AMBROSE, STEPHEN EDWARD, history educator, author; b. Decatur, Ill., Jan. 10, 1936; s. Stephen Hedges and Rosepha (Trippe) A.; m. Judith Dorlester, June 6, 1957 (dec. Oct. 1966); children: Stephenie, Barry; m. Moira Buckley, Sept. 30, 1967; adopted children: Andrew, Grace, Hugh. BS, U. Wis., 1957, PhD, 1963; MA, La. State U., 1958. Asst. prof. history La. State U., New Orleans, 1960-64; assoc. prof. Johns Hopkins U., Balt., 1964-69; Ernest J. King prof. maritime history U.S. Naval War Coll., Newport, R.I., 1969-70; Dwight D. Eisenhower prof. of war and peace Kans. State U., Manhattan, 1970-71; Boyd prof. history U. New Orleans, 1971-95. Vis. prof. Univ. Coll., Dublin, Ireland, 1980-81, U. Calif., Berkeley, 1986, U.S. Army War Coll., Carlisle, Pa., 1990. Author: Halleck: Lincoln's Chief of Staff, 1962, Upton and the Army, 1964, Duty, Honor, Country: A History of West Point, 1968, The Supreme Commander, 1970, Crazy Horse and Custer, 1976, Eisenhower, Soldier, General, President-Elect, 1982, Eisenhower: The President, 1983, Pegasus Bridge, 1984, Nixon: The Education of a Politician, 1988, Nixon: The Triumph of a Politician, 1990, Eisenhower: Soldier and President, 1990, Nixon: Ruin and Recovery, 1991, Band of Brothers, 1992, D-Day: June 6, 1944, 1994, Undaunted Courage, 1996, Citizen Soldiers, 1997, Americans at War, 1997, The Victors: Eisenhower and His Boys, 1998, Comrades: Brothers, Heroes, Sons, Pals, 1999, Nothing Like It in the World: The Men Who Built the Transcontinental Rairoad 1863-1869, 2000, The Good Fight: How World War II Was Won, 2001, Wild Blue: The Men and Boys Who Flew the B-24's Over Germany 1944-45, 2001, The Mississippi and the Making of a Nation, 2002, To America: Personal Reflections of an Historian, 2002; author script for BBC-TV documentary: Eisenhower: The Commander, also numerous other TV documentaries; editor: A Wisconsin Boy in Dixie, 1961, Eisenhower and Berlin, 1945, 1967; asst. editor: The Papers of Dwight D. Eisenhower: The War Years, 5 vols., 1970, Rise to Globalism: American Foreign Policy 1938-70, 1970, 76; (with James A. Barber Jr.) the Military and American Society, 1972, Ike: Abilene to Berlin, 1973, Crazy Horse and Custer: The Parallel Lives of Two American Warriors, 1975, Ike's Spies: Eisenhower and the Espionage Establishment, 1981, (with Richard H. Immerman) Milton S. Eisenhower, 1983, Eisenhower, 2 vols., 1983-84, Eisenhower: Soldier, General of the Army, President-Elect: 1890-1952, 1983, Eisenhower: The President, 1985, Eisenhower: Soldier and President, 1990, Eisenhower and the German POWs: Facts Against Falsehood, 1992, Undaunted Courage: Meriwether Lewis, Thomas Jefferson and the Opening of the American West, 1997, Citizen Soldier, 1998. Founder, The National D-Day Museum Found., New Orleans, 1991, founder The National D-Day Museum, New Orleans, 2000-. Recipient Book of Yr. award Freedoms Found., 1984, Bob Hope award Congl. Medal Honor Soc., 1999, Nat. Humanities award, 1999. Mem. Orgn. Am. Historians, Am. Mil. Inst. Congregationalist. Achievements include founding the National D-Day Museum in New Orleans on June 6, 2000. Avocations: biking, canoeing, woodworking. Home: Bay Saint Louis, Miss. Died Oct. 13, 2002.

AMBRUSTER, JOHN REA, manufacturing executive; b. Sturgis, Mich., Aug. 27, 1931; s. John R. and Dorothy A. (Stoops) A.; m. Joyce Bok, Dec. 22, 1953; children: Sara, Jeanne, David. BA, Swarthmore Coll., 1953; MBA, U. Pa., 1955. With S.C. Johnson & Son, Inc., Racine, Wis., 1955-79, v.p., 1979-86, Johnson Worldwide Assocs., Racine, from 1986. Pres. Plastimo, S.A., Lorient, France, 1984—. Bd. dirs. Women's Resource Ctr., Racine, 1982-84. Democrat. Avocations: squash, sailing. Home: Plege, France. Deceased.

AMON, WILLIAM FREDERICK, JR., biotechnology company executive; b. Chelsea, Mass., Jan. 11, 1922; s. William Frederick and Esther H. (Rautenberg) A.; m. Barbara Marie Erlandson, Aug. 2, 1944; children— William Frederick III, Janet B., Carol J., Robert J. BS Ch.E., Northeastern U., 1943. Vice pres. new bus. ventures Borden Chem., N.Y.C., 1968-72; pres., chief exec. officer Electrospin Inc., Columbus, Ohio, 1972-76; v.p. Story Chem. Co., Muskegon, Mich., 1975-76, Cetus Corp., Emeryville, Calif., 1976-87; ret., cons. Danville, Calif., from 1987. Mem.: Soc. Indsl. Microbiology, Am. Chem. Soc. Lutheran. Achievements include being a holder of numerous patents. Died Sept. 18, 2002.

AMOROSI, TERESA, artist; b. Gioiosa Ionica, Reggio Calabria, Italy, Nov. 17, 1932; d. Natale and Marianna (Quartiere) Fazzolare; m. Nicholas A. Amorosi, Apr. 22, 1956 (dec. 1988); children: Thomas, Elizabeth, Joseph. BA, Pratt Inst., 1956. Art dir. Norcross Greeting Card Co., 1950-57; artist Charmcraft Greetings, 1957-62, Manhattan Greeting Card Co., 1978-89, Magic Moments Greeting Card Co., from 1989, Sunshine Artists, from 1990, Bernard Picture Co., 1986-87, Art Resources Internat., Ltd., 1988-90. Publ. Bernard Picture Co., 1988-90, Resources Internat. Ltd., 1988-90. Illustrator: International Mother's Book, 1980. Recipient awards Washington Square Outdoor Art Show, N.Y.C., 1976, 82, 85. Mem. Tri-County Artists L.I. (treas. 1994), Fortnightly of Rockville Ctr., (art dir. 1996). Roman Catholic. Home: Lynbrook, NY. Died 2001.

AMOS, HAROLD, retired biomedical researcher, educator; b. Pennsauken, N.J., Sept. 7, 1918; BS, Springfield Coll., 1941, PhD in Bacteriology, 1952. Rsch. fellow Harvard Med. Sch., 1953-55; instr. bacteriology Springfield Coll., Boston, 1947-48; from assoc. to asst. prof. to assoc. prof. Harvard Med. Sch., Boston, 1955-70, prof. microbiology and molecular genetics, from 1970, chmn. dept. microbiology, 1965-77, prof. emeritus, from 1988. Fulbright rsch. fellow Pasteur Inst., France, 1951-53; rsch. fellow Harvard Med. Sch., 1953-55; USPHS fellow, 1952-54, sr. rsch. fellow, 1958; mem. Nat. Cancer Adv. Bd., 1972-83; trustee Josiah Macy Found., 1973—. Recipient Fulbright Rsch. fellow, 1951-53, Pub. Welfare medal NAS, 1995. Mem. Inst. Medicine-NAS, Am. Soc. Biol. Chemists, Tissue Culture Assn., Am. Soc. Microbiology. Died Feb. 26, 2003.

AMROMIN, GEORGE DAVID, pathologist, educator; b. Gomel, USSR, Feb. 27, 1919; came to U.S., 1923, naturalized, 1929; s. David Rachmiel and Fannie (Simonoff) Amromin; m. Elaine Barbara Sabath, June 13, 1942; children— Joel, Richard, Barbara, Steven, James. B.S., Northwestern U., 1940, M.D., 1943. Diplomate Am. Bd. Pathology. Intern Michael Reese Hosp., Chgo., 1943, resident in pathology, 1946-48, asst. pathologist, 1949, asst. dir., assoc. pathologist, 1954-56; rotating gen. resident Edgewater Hosp., Chgo., 1944; practice medicine specializing in pathology, Tulare, Calif., 1950-54; clin. instr. U. Ill. Med. Sch., Chgo., 1954-56; chmn. dept. pathology City of Hope Nat. Med. Ctr., Duarte, Calif., 1956-71, chmn. dept. neuropathology and research pathology, 1971-76, mem. hon. staff, cons. neuropathologist, 1976-77, pathologist emeritus, 1976—; asst. prof. pathology Loma Linda U., Calif., 1958-70, clin. prof., 1970-77; prof. pathology U. Mo., Columbia, 1977-84, emeritus, 1984—. Author: The Pathology of Leukemia, 1968. Contbr. articles to profl. jours., chpts. to books. Pathologist, Project Hope, Ecuador, South Am., 1963, 64. Neuropathology research fellow Nat. Inst. Neurologic Diseases and Blindness, Belleview Hosp., N.Y.C., 1968. Fellow ACS, Coll. Am. Pathologists (emeritus), Am. Soc. Clin. Pathologists (emeritus); mem. Boone County Med. Soc., Mo. State Med. Soc., AMA, Am. Assn. Neuropathologists, Sigma Xi, Alpha Omega Alpha. Jewish. Avocation: painting. Home: Sierra Madre, Calif.

AN, NACK YOUNG, political scientist, educator; b. Pyongyang, Korea, Jan. 25, 1936; came to U.S., 1957; s. Joon Myong and Hyong Bok (Chung) A.; m. Rose Jungja Lee, Dec. 22, 1962; children: Millie Helen, Eunice Lee, Dorothy Claire. BA, Berea (Ky.) Coll., 1961; PhD, U. Va., 1965. Asst. prof. polit. sci. Va. Poly. Inst. and State U., Blacksburg, 1964-68, Trenton (N.J.) State U., 1968-70; prof. polit. sci. Ga. State U., Atlanta, from 1970. Author: German Politics, 1971, Power and Empowerment in Higher Education, 1978; contbr. articles to profl. jours. Bd. dirs. Asian Studies Ctr., The Heritage Found. Served to sgt. U.S. Army, 1950-53, Korea. Mem. Am. Polit. Sci. Assn., So. Polit. Sci. Assn., Omicron Delta Kappa, Pi Sigma Alpha. Presbyterian. Avocations: mountain climbing, swimming. Home: Atlanta, Ga. Died Mar. 14, 2000.

ANASTOS, ROSEMARY PARK, retired higher education educator; b. Andover, Mass., 1907; AB, Radcliffe Coll., 1928, AM, 1929; PhD, U. Cologne, Germany, 1934; 25 hon. degrees, Yale U., Columbia U., NYU, Brown U., Syracuse U., U. Notre Dame, Claremont Coll., U. Pa., Oberlin Coll., others. Prof. German, acad. dean Conn. Coll., New London, 1943-47, pres., 1947-62; pres. Barnard Coll., dean Columbia U., 1962-67; vice-chancellor UCLA, 1967-70, prof. higher edn. Grad. Sch. Edn., 1967-74, prof. emeritus, 1974—2004, prof. on recall, 1974-75. Pres. United Chpts. Phi Beta Kappa, 1970-73. Author: Das Bild von Richard Wagners Tristan und Isolde, 1935, two textbooks; contbr. articles in field; contbg. editor (former): Change mag. Former chmn. bd. visitors Def. Intelligence Coll., U.S. Dept. Def.; former trustee Robert Coll., Istanbul, Turkey, New Sch. for Social Rsch., N.Y., Danforth Found., U. Hartford, Scripps Coll., Marlborough Sch., U. Notre Dame, Carnegie Found. for Advancement of Teaching, Mt. St. Mary's Coll., L.A.; former mem. adv. coun. and chmn. rsch. com. NEH; former mem. adv. coun. Fund for Improvement of Post-secondary Edn.; former dir. Am. Coun. on Edn. Recipient Woman of Yr. award L.A. Times, 1967, Radcliffe Coll. Alumnae award, 1974, medal U.S. Dept. Def. Fellow Am. Acad. Arts and Scis. Home: Los Angeles, Calif. Died Apr. 17, 2004.

ANDELSON, ROBERT VERNON, social philosopher, educator; b. Los Angeles, Feb. 19, 1931; s. Abraham and Ada (Markson) A.; m. Bonny Orange Johnson, June 7, 1964. AA, Los Angeles City Coll., 1950; AB equivalent, U. Chgo., 1952; A.M., U. So. Calif., 1954, PhD, 1960. Exec. dir. Henry George Sch. Social Sci., San Diego Extension, Calif., 1959-62; instr. philosophy and religion Northland Coll., Wis., 1962-63; asst. prof. govt. and philosophy Northwestern State U., La., 1963-65; mem. faculty Auburn (Ala.) U., 1965—; prof. philosophy Auburn U., 1973-92, prof. emeritus, from 1992, mem. grad. faculty, 1969-92; mem., dir. Robert Schalkenbach Found., from 1986, v.p., 1998-2001, Internat. Union Land Value Taxation and Free Trade, 1986-88, pres., 1997-2001. Inaugural lectr. philosophy lecture series U. Ala. at Birmingham, 1975; mem. adj. faculty Ludwig von Mises Inst., 1983—; ordained to ministry Congregational Ch., 1959; reviewer instl. grant applications NEH, 1987; fac. assoc. Lincoln Inst. Land Policy, 1993-96. Author: Imputed Rights: An Essay in Christian Social Theory, 1971; editor, co-author: Critics of Henry George, 2d edit., 2003, Commons Without Tragedy, 1991, Land-Value Taxation Around the World, 2d edit., 1997, 3rd edit., 2000; joint author (with J.M. Dawsey) From Wasteland to Promised Land: Liberation Theology for a Post-Marxist World, 1992; mem. editl. bd. Am. Jour. Econs. and Sociology, 1969—, chmn. selection com. for editor-in-chief, 1996, mem. corp., 1999—; mem. editl. bd. The Personalist, 1975-80; contbr. articles to scholarly jours. Asst. sgt. at arms Republican Nat. Conv., 1952; mem. Lee County Rep. Exec. Com., 1967-79; trustee Henry George Found. Am., 1971-75, mem. adv. commn., 1975—. Recipient Rsch. awards Found. Social Rsch., 1959, Relm Found., 1967, 2 George Washington Honor medals Freedoms Found., 1970, 72; Disting. rsch. fellow Am. Inst. for Econ. Rsch., 1993—. Mem. So. Soc. Philosophy and Psychology, Ala. Philos. Soc. (pres. 1968-69, 78-79). Home: Auburn, Ala. Died Nov. 2003.

ANDERMAN, GEORGE GIBBS, geologist; b. Albuquerque, Oct. 17, 1926; s. George Royal and Maud Burleson (Rodney) A.; m. Joan Evans, Apr. 10, 1953; chldren: Ellen, George Taylor, Evan Rodney. BA, Princeton U., 1950, PhD, 1955. Geologist Ohio Oil (now Marathon Oil), 1952-54, Gulf Oil Corp., 1954-56; chmn. bd., pres. Anderman/Smith Operating Co., Denver, from 1957. Bd. dirs. Opera Colo., Denver, Music Assocs. of Aspen, Colo., Verde Valley Sch., Sedona, Ariz. Fellow Geol. Soc. Am.; mem. Am. Assn. Petroleum Geologists, Wyo. Geol. Soc., Ind. Petroleum Assn. Am., Ind. Petroleum Assn. of Mountain States (Wildcatter of Yr. 1992). Democrat. Episcopalian. Avocations: hunting, fishing. Home: Littleton, Colo. Deceased.

ANDERSON, BUIST MURFEE, lawyer; b. Marion, Ala., Nov. 17, 1904; s. Edward Buist and Mary Agnes (Murfee) A.; m. Dorothy Mary Crawford, Feb. 27, 1932; children: Mary Jeanne Anderson Jones, David Crawford, Dudley Buist. BS, U. Va., 1924; LL.B., Yale U., 1929. Bar: Ala. 1928, Conn. 1930, U.S. Supreme Ct. 1937. Statistician, U.S. Dept. Agr., 1924-27; atty. Conn. Gen. Life Ins. Co., 1929-39, counsel, 1939-69, v.p., 1949-69; with firm Murtha, Cullina,

Richter & Pinney, Hartford, 1969-82. Dir. Colonial Life & Accident Ins. Co., 1972-90. Editor: Legal Notes, Transactions (Soc. Actuaries), 1941-64, Vance on Insurance, 3d edit., 1951, Anderson on Life Insurance, 1991. Mem. Am. Arbitration Assn., ABA, Assn. Life Ins. Counsel (pres. 1959-60), Am. Life Conv. (chmn. legal sect. 1948) Baptist. Home: Farmington, Conn. Died Aug. 10, 2002.

ANDERSON, CARL E. newspaper reporter, editor, writer; b. Brighton, Colo., Feb. 14, 1932; s. Carl Gustus and Elizabeth Helen (Distel) A.; m. Gloria Jane Green, Aug. 21, 1954; children: Gregory, Stanley, Laurel. BA, Reed Coll., 1967. Freelance writer, Oreg., 1954-88; mng. editor, news editor Headlight-Herald, Tillamook, Oreg., from 1988. Author: (poker book) Hold 'Em Poker for Winners, 1984. Pres. Woodstock Boosters, Portland, Oreg., 1955-69; precinct chair Dem. Party, Portland, 1956-59; hwy. adviser U.S. Pres.'s Adv. Cou., Portland, 1958. Served with U.S. Army, 1952-54, Korea. Decorated Commendation for Bravery. Avocations: hiking, travel. Home: Portland, Oreg. Died Sept. 14, 2001.

ANDERSON, CAROL RUTH, retired secondary school educator; b. Conewango, N.Y., Aug. 24, 1926; d. Maynard William and Hila Martha (Kent) Phillips; m. George Boyer, Mar. 27, 1948 (div. July 1967); children: Gregory, Gail, Martha; m. Donald Anderson, Jan. 13, 1978 (div. Jan. 1981) Assoc. BS, Jamestown (N.Y.) Community Coll., 1962; BEd, U. Buffalo, 1966; MS in Edn., SUNY, Fredonia, 1971; postgrad., Ariz. State U., 1980-81. Cert. secondary tchr., N.Y., Ariz. Sec. Jamestown Metal Corp., 1957-61; sec. to judge Cattaraugus County, Little Valley, N.Y., 1961-66; bus. educator Jamestown High Sch., 1966-82, Phoenix Union High Sch. Dist., 1982-88; ret., 1988. Rep. committeewoman Cattaraugus County, 1960-62. Mem. N.Y. State Ret. Tchr.'s Assn., U. of Buffalo Alumni Assn., NEA, Jamestown High Sch. Tchrs. Club (sec., treas. 1967-82), Ariz. State Ret. Tchrs. Assn., Am. Legion, VFW, Women of Moose. Republican. Methodist. Avocations: golf, bowling, skiing, reading, gardening. Home: Lakewood, NY. Died Mar. 22, 2002.

ANDERSON, DANIEL ERWIN, philosophy educator; b. Xenia, Ohio, Nov. 4, 1928; s. Frederick Erwin and Jane Lee (Santmyer) A.; m. Virginia May Dolbeare, Jan. 6, 1953; children: Robert Bruce, Jacqueline Diane Anderson Kennedy, Alan Frederick, Susan Ellen Anderson Ward. BA, Baldwin Wallace Coll., 1957; PhD, Tulane U., 1961. From instr. to asst. prof. La. State U. in New Orleans, 1961-63; asst. prof. Washington and Jefferson Coll., Washington, Pa., 1963-64; from asst. prof. to prof. philosophy Ohio Wesleyan U., Delaware, from 1964. Author: The Masks of Dionyses, A Commentary on Plato's Symposium, 1993; contbr. articles to profl. jours. With USN, 1951-53. Recipient U.S. Steel fellowship Tulane U., 1959-61, Disting. Svc. award Ohio Philos. Assn., 1987. Mem. Am. Philos. Assn., Ohio Philos. Assn. (pres. 1969-72, chair com. on status of the profession 1973—, Disting. Svc. award 1987), Am. Inst. Archeology, Concerned Philosophers for Peace, Soc. for Lesbian and Gay Philosophy, Am. Atheists. Socialist. Avocations: flying, woodworking, making jewelry. Home: Delaware, Ohio. Deceased.

ANDERSON, DAVID WALTER, physics educator, consultant; b. Heron Lake, Minn., June 18, 1937; s. Walter Olaf and Martha Gladys (Bonnell) A.; m. Jane Louise Friedlund, Dec. 17, 1960; children: Bonnie Jean, Brian David. BS in Physics summa cum laude, Hamline U., 1959; PhD in Nuclear Physics, Iowa State U., 1965. Diplomate Am. Bd. Radiology, 1968. Postdoctoral fellow in physics Iowa State U., Ames, 1965-66; prof. U. Okla., Norman, 1966-82; prof. radiation physics U. Okla. Health Ctr., Oklahoma City, 1966-82; prof., dir. radiol. physics City of Faith Med. Ctr., Tulsa, 1982-88, Tulsa Regional Med. Ctr., from 1988. Presenter in field; advisor MS and/or PhD students, 1970-84. Author: Absorption of Ionizing Radiation, 1984; contbr. over 53 articles to profl. refereed jours. Chmn. coun. ministry McFarlin Meth. Ch., 1979, chmn. adminstrv. bd., 1978. Grantee Rsch. Corp., Am. Cancer Soc., Radiation Measurement Inc. Fellow Am. Coll. Radiology; mem. Am. Assn. Physicists in Medicine (physics com. on profl. activities 1986-90), Am. Bd. Radiology (physics examiner 1986-90), Am. Coll. Radiology, Soc. Nuclear Medicine, Phi Kappa Phi. Democrat. Achievements include responsiblity for shielding design, acceptance testing, primary data on 19 new or upgraded sites of clinical accelerators. Home: Norman, Okla. Died May 22, 2003.

ANDERSON, DUWAYNE MARLO, soil scientist, university administrator; b. Lehi, Utah, Sept. 9, 1927; s. Duwayne LeRoy and Fern Francell (Fagan) A.; m. June B. Hodgin, Apr. 2, 1980; children: Lynna Nadine, Christopher Kent, Lesleigh Leigh, Valerie Lynn, Susan Leslie, Nancy Lee. BS, Brigham Young U., 1954; PhD (Purdue Research Found. fellow), Purdue U., 1958. Prof. soil physics U. Ariz., Tucson, 1958-63; rsch. scientist, chief earth scis. br. (Cold Regions Research and Engring. Lab.), Hanover, N.H., 1963-76; chief scientist divsn. polar programs NSF, Washington, 1976-78; mem. Viking sci. team NASA, 1969-76; dean faculty natural scis. and math. SUNY Buffalo, 1978-84; assoc. provost for rsch. and grad. studies Tex. A&M U., College Station, 1984-92, prof. Coll. Geoscis., 1992-97; ret., 1997; also councilor Tex. A&M Rsch. Found., 1984-93; Pegrum lectr. SUNY, 1980; v.p. Assn. Tex. Grad. Schs., 1990-91, pres., 1991-92. Cons. NASA, 1964, NSF, 1979-81, U.S. Army Cold Regions Rsch. and Engring. Lab., Hanover, N.H.; sr. U.S. rep., Antarctica, 1976, 77; bd. dirs., exec. com. Houston Area Rsch. Ctr., 1984-89; vis. prof., lectr., cons. numerous univs. Editor: (with O.B. Andersland) Geotechnical Engineering for Cold Regions, 1978; cons. editor Soil Sci, 1965—, Cold Regions Sci. and Tech., 1978-82; contbr. numerous sci. and tech. articles to profl. jours. Bd. dirs. Ford K. Sayre Meml. Ski Coun., Hanover, 1969-71; bd. dirs. Grafton County Fish and Game Assn., 1965-76, pres., 1968-70; bd. dirs. Hanover Conservation Coun., 1970-76, v.p., 1970-73. Served in USAF, 1946-49. Recipient Sci. Achievement award Cold Regions Research and Engring. Lab., 1968; co-recipient Newcomb Cleveland award AAAS, 1976; Sec. of Army Research fellow, 1966 Fellow Geol. Soc. Am., Am. Soc. Agronomy, Soil Soc. Am.; mem. AAAS, Internat. Glaciological Soc., Am. Polar Soc., Am. Geophys. Union (spl. task force on cold regions hydrology 1974-84), Soil Sci. Soc. Am., Niagara Frontier Assn. R&D Dirs. (pres. 1983-84), Licensing Execs. Soc., NASA Teams (Viking, Skylab and Planetary Geology and Geophys. Working Group), Comet Rendevous/Asteroid Flyby Mission Team, Arctic Rsch. Consortium U.S., Sigma Xi, Sigma Gamma Epsilon, Phi Kappa Phi. Home: Hamilton, Wash. Died Oct. 4, 2002.

ANDERSON, JANET ALICE, art historian, educator; b. Washington, Mar. 29, 1934; d. John Kenneth and Alice Morgan A. BA, Pa. State U., 1956, MA, 1959; PhD, U. Mich., 1970. Instr. art history Penn Hall Jr. Coll., Chambersburg, 1960-67; prof. art history U. Wis., Whitewater, from 1968. Lectr. in field. Author: Women in Fine Art, A Bibliography, 1990, Pedro de Mena, Spanish Sculptor, 1998; contbr. articles to profl. jours. Avocation: raising arabian horses. Home: Whitewater, Wis. Died Jan. 20, 2002.

ANDERSON, JOHN MUELLER, retired philosophy educator; b. Cedar Rapids, Iowa, July 29, 1914; s. Arthur G. and Lois A. (Mueller) A.; m. Mary A. Gale, 1936 (dec.); m. Barbara C. Lax., 1970 (div.); m. Jean Sylvia Bixby, 1990. BA, U. Ill., 1935, MA 1936; PhD, U. Calif. at Berkeley, 1939. Credit mgr. retail store Sears, Roebuck & Co., New Albany, Ind., 1939-41; research engr. Elgin Nat. Watch Co., Ill., 1941-42; chief spl. project Mpls.-Honeywell Co., 1942-43, asst. to chief engr., 1943-45; lectr. math. U. Minn., 1945-46; mem. faculty Pa. State U., 1946-80, prof. philosophy, 1951-68, Evan Pugh research prof. philosophy, 1968-80, prof. emeritus, 1980—. Head dept., 1948-49, 52-55, 58-67, acting asst. dean for research, 1964, summer 1965; founder, 1st dir. Inst. Arts and Humanistic Studies, 1966-68; liberal arts editor Pa. State Studies; vis. lectr. U. Ill., summer 1965; guest prof. U. Otago, New Zealand, 1955, Free U. Berlin, Germany, 1961-62, U. Calif., Santa Cruz, 1979; cons. ops. research, computer design. Author: (with Anderson and Mandeville) Industrial Management, 1942, Calhoun Basic Documents, 1952, The Individual and the New World, 1955, (with H.W. Johnstone, Jr.) Natural Deduction, 1962, The Realm of Art, 1967, The Truth of Freedom, 1977; also articles; founding editor: Man and World, 1966—; editor: Dialogue Press, 1971—; translator: (with E.H. Freund) Heidegger: Discourse on Thinking, 1966; patentee computers. Mem. Am. Philos Assn., Western Pa. Philos. Assn., AAUP, Assn. Am. Studies, Assn. Symbolic Logic, Soc. Phenomenology and Existential Philosophy (exec. com. 1965-68), Am. Soc. for Aesthetics, Am. Math. Soc., Phi Beta Kappa, Sigma Xi, Pi Gamma Mu, Alpha Tau Omega. Home: Huntingdon, Pa. Deceased.

ANDERSON, MICHAEL P. astronaut; b. Plattsburgh, N.Y., Dec. 25, 1959; married. BSc in Physics & Astronomy, U. Wash., 1981; MSc in Physics, Creighton U., 1990. Commd. 2d lt. USAF, 1981, advanced through grades to lt. col., various assignments, 1982—86, pilot tng. Vance AFB, Okla., 1986, pilot, aircraft commdr., instr. pilot, 1991—92, instr. pilot Plattsburgh AFB, NY, 1992—95; with NASA, Houston, from 1995. With docking mission Shuttle-Mir, 1998. Decorated Def. Superior Svc. medal USAF, Meritorious Svc. medal, Achievement medal with one oak leaf cluster. Avocations: photography, chess, computers, tennis. Died Feb. 1, 2003.

ANDERSON, OWEN RAYMOND, scientific and educational organization executive; b. Chestertown, Md., Aug. 27, 1919; s. Owen Raymond and Ida Frances (Jenkins) A.; m. Ida Lois Pritts, June 8, 1946; children: Penny Pritts, Jeri Alyce. BA, Washington Coll., 1940. Tchr. Garrett County Bd. Edn., Kitzmiller, Md., 1940-41, 1946; with Nat. Geog. Soc., Washington, 1946—, div. supr., 1950, adminstrv. asst., 1952-61, asst. sec., 1961-66, assoc. sec., 1966-76, v.p., sec., 1976-80, exec. v.p., 1980-91, trustee, 1981-95, vice chmn. bd., 1984-95, trustee emeritus, from 1995. Served to capt. U.S. Army, 1941-46, 50-52, ETO, Korea. Decorated Bronze Star, Purple Heart, Combat Infantry badge; recipient Alumni Citation award Washington Coll., 1981, Grosvenor medal Nat. Geog. Soc., 1991. Mem. Am. Legion, Lambda Chi Alpha. Clubs: Alfalfa. Methodist. Home: Falls Church, Va. Died Aug. 6, 2003.

ANDERSON, ROY ARNOLD, aerospace company executive; b. Ripon, Calif., Dec. 15, 1920; s. Carl Gustav and Esther Marie (Johnson) A.; m. Betty Leona Boehme, 1948; 4 children. MBA, Stanford U., 1949. Mgr. factory acctg. Westinghouse Electric Corp., 1952-56; mgr. acctg. and fin., dir. mgmt. controls Lockheed Missiles and Space Co., 1956-65; dir. finance Lockheed Ga. Co., 1965-68; asst. treas. Lockheed Aircraft Corp. (now Lockheed-Martin Corp.), 1968-69, v.p., controller, 1969-71, sr. v.p. finance, 1971-75, vice chmn. bd. dirs., chief fin. adminstrv. officer, 1975-77, chair, CEO, 1977-85, dir., chair exec. com., 1985-88, chair emeritus, 1991—2003; chair, CEO Weingart Found., 1994-98. Chair Oversight Bd., State of Calif., 1997-98. Avocations: tennis, golf, gardening. Home: La Canada, Calif. Died Oct. 21, 2003.

ANDERSON, THOMAS JEFFERSON, publisher, public speaker, syndicated columnist; b. Nashville, Nov. 7, 1910; s. William J. and Nancy Lucas (Joseph) A.; m. Carolyn Montague Jennings, Dec. 24, 1936; 1 child, Carolyn A. Porter. BA, Vanderbilt U., 1934; LLB (hon.), Bob Jones U., 1967. Securities salesman Gray-Shillinglaw & Co., Nashville, 1934-36; salesman Nunn-Schwab Securities Co., 1936-39; mgr. unlisted securities dept. J.C. Bradford Co., 1939-43; So. sales mgr. So. Agriculturist, Nashville, 1943-47; owner, pub. So. Farm Publs., 1947-71, Farm and Ranch mag., 1953-63, Am. Way Features (nat. newspaper syndicate), Straight Talk (weekly newsletter Anderson Enterprises); radio commentator, world traveler. Author: Straight Talk, 1967, Silence Is Not Golden It's Yellow, 1973. Vice presdl. candidate Am. Party, 1972, nat. chmn., 1976-78, presdl. nominee, 1976; mem. coun. John Birch Soc., 1959-76; nat. chmn. We-the-People, 1966-72. Lt. USN, 1943-46. Recipient Liberty awards Congress of Freedom, 1964—, Pub. Address award Freedoms Found. Valley Forge, 1959-60; named Man of Yr. God and Country Rally, 1966. Mem. Am. Agrl. Editors Assn. (pres. 1954), Phi Delta Theta (pres. Tenn. Alpha chpt. 1934, province pres. 1936-39), Omicron Delta Kappa. Baptist. Died Aug. 30, 2002.

ANDERSON, VIOLET HENSON, artist, educator; b. June 8, 1931; m. Charles A. Anderson, 1953. Grad., U. Tenn., Knoxville. Tchr. art Oak Ridge (Tenn.) Sch. System, 1953-54, Andrew Jackson Elem. Sch., Nashville, 1969-79; originator, dir. Andrew Jackson Art Show, Old Hickory, Tenn., 1972-79. One-woman shows include Nashville Bd. Edn., 1972, Cookeville (Tenn.) Art Ctr., 1972, Tenn. Art Gallery, 1983, 88, Brentwood (Tenn.) Libr., 1991; exhibited in group shows at Falls Creek Falls State Park, Tenn., 1984, 86, Castner Knott Art Festival, Nashville, 1983-89, 90, Downtown Arts Gallery, Nashville, 1989, Dogwood Art Festival, Knoxville, 1993, 94, 95, Summer Lights Art Festival, Nashville, 1989, 92, 93, 94; also 1928 paintings and prints in pvt. and pub. collections in 38 states and 9 fgn. countries; work featured in Nashville Banner, Chattanooga Free Press, Knoxville News Sentinel, others. Active Girl Scouts. Named Golden Poet, World of Poetry, 1989-92; included in Best Poems of 90s and Disting. Poets of Am., 1993 Nat. Libr. Poetry, Best Poems of 95, Nat. Libr. Poetry, 1996 Best Poems. Mem. Tenn. Watercolor Soc., Tenn. Art League (past officer), Friends of Tenn. Art League (bd. dirs., 1st v.p.), Cumberland Art Soc., Tenn. Artists Assn., Artists Guild, Hendersonville, Nat. Women's Caucus for Art, Mid. Tenn. Com., Nat. Mus. of Women in the Arts (charter mem., slides and photos in libr. archives), Knoxville Arts Coun., Donelson-Hermitage C. of C., Stones River Woman's Club, Internat. Soc. Poets (charter mem.), Delta Zeta (past province alumnae dir., pres. Nashville chpt.), Alpha Delta Kappa. Home: Hermitage, Tenn. Deceased.

ANDEWELT, ROGER B. federal judge; b. Bklyn., 1946; m. Maxine Mitchnick; two children. BS, Brooklyn Coll., N.Y.C., 1967; JD Order of Coif, George Wash. Univ. Nat. Law Ctr., Washington, D.C., 1971. Judge U.S. Ct. of Federal Claims, Washington, 1987—2001. Died Aug. 7, 2001.

ANDRADE, NANCY LEE (BALL ANDRADE), realtor, jeweler; b. Seattle, Nov. 17, 1937; d. Hans Peter Marcher and Hilda Dorothy (Baisch) Middleton; m. Allan L. Andrade, Mar. 15, 1971 (div. 1980). Cert. travel agt., Cannon Bus. Coll., Honolulu, 1965; cert., Erhardt Seminar Tng., Honolulu, 1980; student, U. Hawaii, 1968-71; cert. real estate broker, Stapleton Sch. Real Estate, Honolulu, 1985. Cert. notary pub. Model Kathleen Peck Modeling Agy., Seattle, 1956-60; communications mgr. RCA Communicaions, Royal Hawaiian Hotel, Honolulu, 1960-62; TV and fashion specialist Careers Unltd., Honolulu, 1960-65; travel agt. Waters Travel, Kailua, Hawaii, from 1965; realtor assoc., property mgr. various realty firms, Honolulu, 1967-74; property mgr. Nancy Andrade Property Mgmt., Honolulu, 1974-85; realtor, broker, property mgr. Nancy Andrade Realty, Honolulu and Kaneohe, from 1985. Jeweler, goldsmith Nancy Andrade Jewelry Design, 1974—; mfg. Koala Prodns., Hawaii and Australia, 1987—, Nancy Andrade Enterprises, Honolulu and Kaneohe, 1987—. Active Waikiki Residence Assn., 1978—, Neighborhood Bd., Honolulu, 1980; mem. Save Internat. Market Pl. Com. Mem. Nat. Assn. Realtors, Nat. Notary Assn. (cert.), Small Bus. Hawaii, Honolulu Bd. Realtors, Waikiki Improvement Assn., Australian-Am. C. of C., Lani-Kailua Outdoor Circle Club, Ala Wai Plaza Club, Makani Kai Marina Yacht Club, Beta Sigma Phi (v.p. Oahu coun. 1987—, v.p. Preceptor Delta 1988—, Preceptor degree 1980, Xi Zeta Exemplar degree 1969, Internat. Order Rose degree 1976, 25 Yr. Silver Circle award 1987, Alpha Chpt. Woman of Yr. 1965, Xi Zeta Chpt. Woman of Yr. 1977). Republican. Avocations: jewelry making, boating, horseback riding. Home: Woodinville, Wash. Deceased.

ANDREASON, OVE INGMAR, automotive company executive; b. Tving, Blekinge, Sweden, Mar. 24, 1933; s. Harry Joel and Hulda Maria (Samson) A.; m. Siv Teresia Aakerblom, Jan. 19, 1957; children: Thomas Helene, Ingelia. Engr., Tech. Inst. Stockholm. Sales promotion asst. Gen. Motors Nordiska AB, Stockholm, 1959-64, dist. mgr., 1965-68, mgr. field ops., 1969-71, mgr. sales staff, 1971-73, dir. sales Handen, Sweden, from 1975, Gen. Motors, Seoul, Korea, 1973-75. Motor editor Mag. Terknikons Vaerld, Stockholm, 1958-65. Home: Tyresoe, Sweden. Deceased.

ANDRIN, ALBERT ANTAL, lawyer; b. Chgo., Dec. 2, 1928; s. Antal and Helena (Lebda) A.; m. Sally Rose Cerkleski, Apr. 6, 1963; children— Lisa, Antal, Albert. B.A., Roosevelt U., 1952; LL.B., Chgo. Kent Coll. Law, 1956.

Bar: Ill. 1956. Assoc. Axelrod, Goodman & Steiner, Chgo., 1956-61; ptnr. Levy, Andrin & Stillerman, Chgo., 1961-75, Burke, Kerwin, Towle & Andrin, Chgo., 1975-83. Served to sgt. USAF, 1946-49. Mem. ABA, Ill. Bar Assn., Chgo. Bar Assn., Motor Carrier Lawyers Assn., Mensa. Home: Glendale, Ariz. Died July 10, 2000.

ANGUIZOLA, GUSTAV (ANTONIO), historian, educator, writer, consultant; b. Panama Canal Zone, Feb. 28, 1925; naturalized, U.S., 1961; s. Antonio Anguizola Palma and Melida Guerra Gómez; children: Phillip Anthony, Jerome James (dec.). BA, Evansville Coll., 1948; MA, Ind. U., 1951, PhD, 1954; Cert., Am. Sch. Classics, Athens, Greece, 1964, Stanford U., 1975. Sr. chem. tester Allby Corp., Gary, Ind., 1956-59; dept. chmn. Morris Coll., Sumter, S.C., 1959-62; spl. asst. Panam. Games Mayor of Chgo., 1959; vis. prof. SUNY, Geneseo, summers 1961, 62; chmn. dept. Elizabeth City State Coll., N.C., 1962-63; asst. prof. Purdue U., Lafayette, Hammond, Ind., 1963-66; asst. prof. history U. Tex., Arlington, 1966-82, research prof., 1982—; assoc. prof. Chgo. State U., 1967-69. Chmn. midwest Collegiate Council UN, N.Y.C., 1962-76; cons. N.C. Bd. Edn., Raleigh, 1962-63, Hispanic Am. Hist. Rev., Austin, 1970-72, Gov. of Tex., Austin, 1980-82, Inter-Am. Security Council, Washington, 1977—; chmn. bd. The Freedom Fedn., Washington, 1982-86; mem. Minorities Commn. of Tex., 1980-82; mem. Gov. of Tex. Com., 1987—. Author: Isthmian Political Instability: 1821-76, 77, 78, Life of Philippe Bunau-Varilla, 1980, Violation of Human Rights in Panama, 1980, The Taft Convention, Research Sites Panama and Canal Zone, 1986; author: (with others) The Isthmus of Panama & Relations with U.S, Encyclopaedia Britannica, 1990 edit.; contbr. articles to profl. jours. Precinct chmn. Republican Party Tex., 1979—, election judge, 1985—; mem. Nat. Com. Rep. Party, Washington, 1982—; del. State Rep. Convention, Tex., 1978—, Nat. Rep. Conv., 1992; cons. Heritage Found., Washington, 1980—, Freedom Fedn. Recipient Hays-Mundt award U.S. Dept. State, 1953, Fulbright-Hays award, 1964, Andrew Mellon award, 1982, The Ronald Reagan Gold medal, 1982; NEH grantee Stanford U., 1975, U. Chg., 1985—; named Alumnus of Yr., Evansville U., 1984 Mem. Am. Hist. Assn., AAUP (region sec. 1982—), Tex. State Tchrs. Assn., Conf. on Latin Am. History, Pacific Coast Council Latin Am. Studies, Nat. Soc. Sci. Assn., Arlington Rep. Club, Hispanic Assembly Tex., Pres.'s Club. Roman Catholic. Home: Arlington, Tex. Deceased.

ANHALT, EDWARD, screenwriter; b. N.Y.C., Mar. 28, 1914; s. Samuel and Minnie (Aschaim) A.; m. Huguette Patenaude, July 15, 1995. Lic. marriage and family therapist institutional and pvt. practice, Los Angeles, CA. Adj. prof. comm. arts Loyola-Marymount U., Inglewood, Calif., 1968-73. Screenwriter numerous films, including Mad Woman of Chaillot, Wives and Lovers, Man in the Glass Booth, Young Lions, Jerimiah Johnson (Western Hall of Fame Ann. award), Satan Bug, Pride and the Passion, Member of the Wedding, Luther, Boston Strangler (Edgar Allan Poe ann. award Mystery Writers Am.), Panic in the Streets (Acad. award), The Sniper (Acad. award nomination), The Holcroft Covenant, In Love and War, Girls, Girls, Girls, Not as a Stranger, Sins of Rachel Cade, Young Savages, Green Ice, Girl Named Tamiko, In Enemy Country, Escape to Athena, Becket (Acad. award), Hour of the Gun; (TV) QBVII (Emmy nomination), Contract on Cherry Street, The Day That Christ Died, A Time for Killing, Madam X, Peter The Great (WGA Ann. award), The Neon Empire. Capt. USAF. Recipient Academy award, 1950, 64, nomination, 1950, 51, 64, Poe award Mystery Writers Am., Lifetime award WGA, 1976, Ann. award, 1985. Home: Marina Dl Rey, Calif. Died Sept. 15, 2000.

ANNENBERG, WALTER H. philanthropist, diplomat, editor, publisher, broadcaster; b. Milw., Mar. 13, 1908; m. Veronica Dunkelman (div.); 1 child, Wallis; m. Leonore Cohn. Ed., The Peddie Sch., Wharton Sch., U. Pa.; hon. degree, Temple U., U. Pa., U. So. Calif., U. Notre Dame, Albert Einstein Coll. Medicine, Mt. Sinai Med. Coll., Hebrew U., Jerusalem, Northwestern U., Elizabethtown Coll., Howard U., Brown U., Brandeis U.; and others. Former pres., chmn., CEO Triangle Publs., Inc., including Phila. Inquirer, Phila. Daily News, Daily Racing Form, (founder) Seventeen Mag., (founder) TV Guide; also 6 AM, FM and TV Stas.; ret., 1988; U.S. ambassador to, 1968-74; chmn., pres. Annenberg Found.; founder Annenberg Sch. Comm., Grad. Sch. U. Pa., Annenberg Sch. Comm., Grad. Sch. U. So. Calif., Annenberg/Corp. Pub. Broadcasting Math/Sci. Project. Founder, trustee Eisenhower Exchange Fellowships, Eisenhower Med. Ctr., Rancho Mirage, Calif., hon. chmn. bd. trustees; trustee Winston Churchill Travelling Fellowships; emeritus trustee Met. Mus. Art, N.Y.C., Phila. Mus. Art, U. Pa., The Peddie Sch., Hightstown, N.J.; hon. mem. bd. overseers Albert Einstein Coll. Medicine, N.Y.C.; patron Churchill Archives Ctr. at Cambridge (Eng.) Coll. Former cmdr., USN. Decorated knight comdr. Order of Brit. Empire (hon.), Legion of Honor (France), Order of Merit (Italy), Order of Crown (Italy), Order of Lion (Finland), Bencher of Mid. Temple (hon.), Old Etonian (hon.); recipient Freedom medal for pioneering TV for edni. purposes U.S. Pres. Reagan, Gold medal Pa. Soc., Linus Pauling medal for humanitarianism, George Foster Peabody award, Ralph Lowell award Corp. Pub. Broadcasting, Dwight D. Eisenhower medal for leadership and svc., Generous Am. award Town & Country Mag., Wagner medal for pub. svc. Robert F. Wagner Grad. Sch. Pub. Svc. NYU, Alumni Merit award U. Pa., William Penn award Greater Phila. C. of C., The Churchill Bell award, 1993, Nat. Arts medal NEA, 1993, Phila. award, 1994, Am. Legion award, 1994, Am. Assembly award, 1994, Arch of Peace award, 1995, George Peabody Edn. Philanthropy award, 1995, Thomas Jefferson award for outstanding pub. svc. by a pvt. citizen, 1995, Steven J. Ross/Time Warner award, 1996, World Class Philadelphians award, 1998, We the People award Nat. Constitution Ctr., 1999, Crossing the River Jordan award Pub. Edn. Network, 1999, and others; named to Wharton Sch Hall of Fame, Mag. Pub. of Yr., 1984; apptd. by Pope John II as Knight Comdr. of Order of St. Gregory the Great, 1998. Fellow Am. Acad. Arts and Scis., Royal Acad. Arts in London (hon.); mem. AP, Am. Soc. Newspaper Pub., Am. Newspaper Pub. Assn., Am. Philos. Soc. (Benjamin Franklin award 1993), Internat. Press Inst., Nat. Press Club, Inter-Am. Press Assn., Overseas Press Club, Navy League U.S., Explorers Club, White's of London, Gulph Mills Golf Club, California Club, Green Valley Country Club, L.A. Country Club, The Racquet Club, Swinley Forest Club, The Club at Morningside, Century Country Club, Locust Club, U. Pa. Faculty Club, Eldorado Country Club (hon.). Home: Wynnewood, Pa. Died Oct. 1, 2002.

ANSCHUETZ, NORBERT LEE, retired diplomat, banker; b. Leavenworth, Kans., May 16, 1915; s. Otto William and Irma (Hilpert) A.; m. Roberta Cook (dec. 1990), Mar. 13, 1943; children: Carol L., Ellen Anschuetz Lewis, Susan, Nancy Anschuetz Stahl. AB, U. Kans., 1936; LLB, Harvard U., 1939; grad., Nat. War Coll., 1957, State Dept. Sr. Seminar, 1967. Bar: Mo. 1939. Practice in, Kansas City, Mo., 1939-41; with Bur. Near Ea., S. Asian and African Affairs Dept. State, 1946-51, fgn. service officer, 1951-68; assigned successively to Washington Athens, 1951-53; counselor Bangkok, 1954-56; minister-counselor Cairo, 1958-62, Paris, 1962-64, Athens, 1964-67; rep. for Middle East and Africa First Nat. City Bank N.Y., Beirut, 1968-70; fgn. affairs rep. Citibank, N.Y.C., 1971-74; dir. Citicorp. Internat. Devel. Orgn., London, 1974-76; v.p. internat. relations Citibank, 1976-80; pres. Trans World Transactions, Inc., 1984-99. Former mem. Coun. Fgn. Rels. Lt. col. U.S. Army, 1941-46; ETO. Hon. citizen Athens, 1967 Home: Washington, DC. Died Oct. 15, 2003.

ANTONSEN, CONRAD (ROBERT MICHAEL ANTONSEN), priest, educator; b. Vallejo, Calif., May 24, 1937; s. R. Wallace and Zaira (Castagnini) A. BS, U. San Francisco, 1959; BPh, St. Albert's Coll., Oakland, Calif., 1962, MA in Philosophy, 1963, MA in Theology, 1965; Lectorate, Licentiate in Sacred Theology, Le Saulchoir-Etiolles, France, 1969; Peritus in Sacred Liturgy, Institut Catholique de Paris, 1971. Joined Dominican Order, 1960, ordained priest Roman Cath. Ch., 1966. Campus minister, instr. Dominican Coll., San Rafael, Calif., 1974-78; pastor Blessed Sacrament Parish, Seattle, 1979-85, St. Mary Magdalen Parish, Berkeley, Calif., from 1987. Instr. Dominican Sch. Philosophy and Theology, grad. Theo. Union, Berkeley, 1975—, St. Thomas U., Rome, 1986, St. Mary's Coll., Moraga, Calif., 1987; dir., preacher retreats for Dominican Sisters New Zealand, 1976; facilitator for group dynamics Religious Women in Phoenix, 1973. Mem. N.Am. Acad. Liturgy, Am. Dominican Liturgical Commn., Pastoral Coun. Archdiocese Seattle, Western Dominican Planning and Ministry Commn, Alcuin. Democrat. Deceased.

ANTUPIT, SAMUEL NATHANIEL, art director; b. West Hartford, Conn., Feb. 14, 1932; s. Louis and Sylvia (Feinberg) A.; m. Rosalie Jane Littman, Dec. 30, 1956; children: Lisa Ruth, Jennifer Carol, Stephen Michael, Peter Louis. Grad., Loomis Sch., 1950; BA in English, Yale U., 1954, BFA in Graphic Design, 1956. Asst. art dir. Harper's Bazaar mag., 1958-61, Show mag., 1961-63; asst. corp. art dir. Conde Nast Publs., 1963, Pushpin Studios, 1963-64; art. dir. Art in Am., 1963-64, N.Y. Rev. Books, 1963-81, Esquire mag., 1964-68, 77; pres. Hess and/or Antupit, designer, publs., and cons., 1968-70; lectr. pub. procedures course Harvard-Radcliffe Coll., 1965-80, Stanford U., 1984-90; propr. Cycling Frog Press, Pound Ridge, N.Y., 1961—, Antupit & Others Inc., 1971—81, Subsistence Press, 1971-81; exec. art dir. Book of the Month Club, 1977-81; v.p., dir. art and design, mem. pub. com. Harry N. Abrams, Inc., N.Y.C., 1981-97; pres. CommonPlace Books, New Canaan, Conn., from 1995. Instr. Grad. Sch. Journalism Columbia U., 2000—; trustee Hiram Halle Meml. Libr.; bd. dirs. Summit Pubs. Author: (with Terry Clifford) Cures, 1980. Served with AUS, 1956-58. Recipient Design awards Art Dirs. Club N.Y.C., 1960—, Type Dirs. Club N.Y.C., 1961—, Soc. Illustrators, 1961—, Art Dirs. Club Boston, Emmy award NATAS, 1974; Am. fellow Nat. Endowment Arts, 1989. Mem. Nat. Acad. Rec. Arts and Scis., Am. Inst. Graphic Arts (bd. dirs. 1968-72, v.p. 1970-72, 90-93, Design awards 1965—, Lifetime Achievement medal 2001), Yale U. Arts Assn. (exec. com. 1972-76), Alliance Graphique Internat., Documents of Am. Design (bd. dirs. 1983—), Century Assn., Univ. Glee Club, Small Press Ctr. (bd. advisors 1999—). Home: Pound Ridge, NY. Died Apr. 5, 2003.

APFEL, ROBERT EDMUND, mechanical engineering educator, applied physicist, research scientist; b. N.Y.C., Mar. 16, 1943; s. Mark and Anita A.; m. Nancy Howe, July 13, 1968, div. Aug. 1, 2002; children: Darren Alexander, Alison Anita. BA, Tufts U., 1964; MA, Harvard U., 1967, PhD, 1970. Postdoctoral research fellow Harvard U., 1970-71; asst. prof. mech. engring. Yale U., 1971-75, assoc. prof., 1975-81, prof., 1981—, chmn. dept., 1981-86, 92-94, chmn. Council of Engring., 1988-90, dir. external affairs engring., 1994-2000; Robert Higgin prof., chairperson mech. engring., 1991-95; prin., cons. Robert E. Apfel, Ph.D., New Haven, 1972—; pres. Apfel Enterprises, Inc., New Haven, from 1987. Co-dir. Yale Ctr. for Ultrasonics and Sonics, 1994-96. Recipient A.B. Wood Medal and Prize, Inst. Physics, 1971, Ivy award Yale and New Haven Cmty. Award, 1996, Yale Grad. Sch. Mentor Award, 2002. Fellow Acoustical Soc. Am. (Biennial award 1976, v.p. 1991-92, pres. elect 1994-95, pres. 1995-96, Silver medal 1997, Gold Medal 2002), editor Acoustics Rsch. Letters Online, ARLO); mem. ASME, Am. Phys. Soc., Am. Assn. Physics Tchrs., Sigma Xi (pres. Yale chpt. 1994—)2002. Unitarian Universalist. Home: New Haven, Conn. Died Aug. 1, 2002.

APOSTOL, NELSON C. physician, educator; b. Jan. 17, 1951; Asst. prof. medicine U. Miami, 1993-94; pvt. practice, med. dir. FPN Prime Care, Miami, 1994-97; pvt. practice, vice chief of staff Trace Regional Hosp., Houston, from 1997. Author: (with others) Current Critical Care Diagnosis and Treatment, 1995, Clinician Handbook of Preventive Services, 1994. Died July 9, 2000.

APP, JAMES LEONARD, assistant dean, deceased; b. Fairmont, Minn., Jan. 27, 1936; s. Leonard Walter and Lucia Irene (Hellbusch) A.; m. Diane Catherine Conoryea, July 5, 1957; children: Timothy, Lisa, Polly, Peter. BS, U. Minn., 1957; MS, U. Wis., 1960, PhD, 1961. Asst. prof. U. Minn., 1961-63, assoc. prof., 1963-72, prof., asst. dean, 1972-73; county extension dir. Manatee County Coop. Extension, Palmetto, Fla., 1973-75; dist. dir. U. Fla. Coop. Extension, Gainesville, 1975, asst. dean, 1975-2000; ret. Vice chmn. So. Region Extension Agrl. and Natural Resources, 1983-84, chmn., 1984-85, chmn. program planning, 1985-86; sec. So. Region Extension Cmty. Resource Devel. Com., 1986-87. Contbr. articles to profl. jours.; presenter in field. Mem. Community Leaders of Am. Recipient Spl. Accomplishments award Fla. Landscape Maintenance Assn., 1989, Innovative and Aggressive Program Support award U. Fla. Or. Hort. Extension Specialists, 1979, Davis Productivity award, 1998, Fla. Automated Network award, 1998, Small Famrs Team award, 1999; named Hon. Fla. Master Gardener U. Fla. Cooperative Extension Specialists, 1984; Computerized Producers Guides grantee, 1978, 82. Mem. Am. Men of Sci., Gamma Sigma Delta. Home: Gainesville, Fla. Died Aug. 14, 2002.

APPLEBAUM, MORTON M. rabbi; b. Toronto, Ont., Can., Aug. 25, 1911; s. Joseph and Sarah (Levit) A.; m. Eleanor Wides, June 9, 1940; children: Lois Jean Podolny, Bruce Jay (dec.). BA, U. Toronto; MHL, Hebrew Union Coll., Cin., 1940; DDiv honoris cause, Hebrew Union Coll., 1965. Ordained rabbi, 1940. Rabbi Congregation Shaarey Zedek, Lansing, Mich., 1940-43, Temple Beth El, Fint, Mich., 1943-53, Temple Israel, Akron, Ohio, 1953-79; ret. Counselor B'nai B'rith Hillel Extension, Mich. State U., 1940-43; faculty U. Akron Spl. Programs, 1969-79; tchr. adult edn. St. Paul's Episcopal Ch., Akron, 1979—; bd. trustees Union Am. Hebrew Congregations; bd. govs. Hebrew Union Coll.-Jewish Inst. Religion; exec. bd. Cen. Conf. Am. Rabbis; hon. vice chmn. Rabbinical Pension Bd.; mem. various coms. Cen. Conf. Am. Rabbis. Author: What Everyone Should Know About Judaism, 4th edit.; co-author (with Rabbi Samuel M. Silver) Sermonettes for Young People, Speak to the Children of Israel. Active in past Jewish Family Svcs., Police Pub. Rels., Child Welfare Bd. Summit County Citizens Com., Goodwill Industries, ARC, many others-;;mem. Commn. on Internat. Community Concerns. Mem. Rotary. Home: Boca Raton, Fla. Died Nov. 2, 2001.

APPLEGATE, ROYCE DWAYNE, actor, writer; b. Sand Springs, Okla., Dec. 25, 1945; s. Roy Gilbert and Opal Dorothy (McCray) A.; m. Norma Jean Hilderbrand, Dec. 18, 1964 (div. 1970); 1 child, Scott Dwayne. Student, U. Pa., 1962-66. Appeared in films including Back Roads, Alligator, Splash, Harper Valley P.T.A., Prime Time, Armed & Dangerous, From the Hip, Million $ Mystery, Rampage, Loose Shoes; appeared in TV movies including Attack on Terror, Outside Chance, Centennial, Pretty Boy Floyd, The Blue & The Grey, Walton's Mountain Thanksgiving, Tom Swift Mysteries, The Gladiator, The Celebrations Family, Stir Crazy, Police Story, Mike Hammer in Vegas, Dead Wrong, The Town Bully, Murder in Mississippi; guest star in TV series Hart to Hart, Dukes of Hazzard, CHIPS, Dallas, Palmerstown U.S.A., Vegas, Charle's Angels, Starsky and Hutch, Flamingo Road, Santa Barbara, Cassidy, Man Undercover, Hollywood Beat, Little House on the Prairie, The New F.B.I., Falcon Crest, Hill Street Blues, T.J. Hooker, Dynasty, Tales of the Unexpected, Boone, Matt Houston, Gun Shy, Different Strokes, The Investigators, Buck James, Houston Knights, Designing Women, Quantum Leap, Paradise, Twin Peaks, Evening Shade; writer TV shows Welcome Back Kotter, Hizzoner, Horshaer; writer radio show Radio Kandy-John Candy; writer feature films Loose Shoes, God Bless Grandma and Grandpa. Lt. USMC, 1962-66. Home: Los Angeles, Calif. Died Jan. 1, 2003.

APTHEKER, HERBERT, historian, lecturer; b. Bklyn., July 31, 1915; s. Benjamin and Rebecca (Komar) A.; m. Fay Aptheker, Sept. 4, 1942; 1 dau., Bettina. BS, Columbia U., 1936, A.M., 1937, PhD, 1943; PhD (hon.), Martin Luther U., Halle, Germany, 1966; DHL (hon.), U. Mass., 1996. Editor Masses and Mainstream, 1948-52, Polit. Affairs, 1952-63; dir. Am. Inst. Marxist Studies, N.Y.C., 1964-85. Prof. Hostos Community Coll., City U. N.Y., 1971-77; lectr. throughout, U.S. and Europe, 1946—2003; vis. lectr. dept. history Bryn Mawr Coll., 1969-71; vis. lectr. U. Mass., 1971-72, Yale U., 1976, U. Calif. at Berkeley Law Sch., 1978-91, U. Santa Clara, 1982-83; vis. prof. Afro-Am. studies U. Calif., Berkeley, 1984 Author: To Be Free: Studies in American Negro History, 1948, rev. edit., 1992, World of C. Wright Mills, 1960, Soul of the Republic, 1964, Negro Slave Revolts in the United States, 1939, Negro in the Civil War, 1938, Nat Turner's Slave Rebellion, 1966, Mission to Hanoi, 1966, Labor Movement in the South During Slavery, 1954, The

Truth about Hungary, 1957, The Nature of Democracy, Freedom and Revolution, 1967, History of the American People, 3 vols, 1959, 60, Essays in the History of the American Negro, rev. edit, 1964, Era of McCarthyism, 1955, Dare We Be Free?, 1960, American Foreign Policy and the Cold War, 1962, American Negro Slave Revolts, 1943; rev. edit., 1963, 93, American Civil War, 1961, Urgency of Marxist-Christian Dialogue, 1970, Afro-American History: the Modern Era, 1971, Annotated Bibliography of the Published Writings of W.E.B. DuBois, 1973, Early Years of the Republic, 1783-1793, 1976, The Unfolding Drama: Studies in U.S. History, 1979, Racism, Imperialism and Peace, 1987, Abolitionism: A Revolutionary Movement, 1989, The Literary Legacy of W.E.B. DuBois, 1989, Marxism: Demise or Renewal, 1990, Anti-Racism in U.S. History, 1992; editor: Disarmament and American Economy, 1960, One Continual Cry, 1965, Marxism and Democracy, 1964, And Why Not Every Man, 1961, Marxism and Alienation, 1965, Documentary History of the Negro People in the United States, Vols. 1-7, 1951-94, Marxism and Christianity, 1967, Autobiography of W.E.B. DuBois, 1968, The Correspondence of W.E.B. DuBois, Vol. 1, 1973, Vol. II, 1976, Vol. III, 1978, The Published Writings of W.E.B. DuBois, 40 vols, 1973-86, Education for Black People (DuBois), 1973, Prayers for Dark Folk (DuBois), 1980, Against Racism: 1887-1961 (DuBois), 1985 Ind. Peace candidate for U.S. Congress, 1966; candidate Communist party for U.S. Senate, 1976. Served to maj. F.A. AUS, 1942-46, ETO. Guggenheim fellow, 1946-47; grantee Social Sci. Research Council, 1961, Rabinowitz Found., 1965, Am. Council Learned Studies, 1974; recipient Lifetime Achievement award Columbia U., 2000. Mem. Am. Hist. Assn., Assn. Study Negro Life (History award 1939, 69) Home: Santa Cruz, Calif. Died Mar. 17, 2003.

ARCHAMBAULT, LOUIS, sculptor; b. Montreal, Que., Can., Apr. 4, 1915; s. Anthime Sergius and Annie (Michaud) A.; m. Mariette Provost, June 7, 1941; children: Aubert, Eloi, Eve, Patrice. Student, Coll. Jean-de-Brebeuf, Montreal; BA, U. Montreal, 1936; Diploma, Ecole des Beaux Arts, Montreal, 1939. Former mem. faculty Musée des Beaux-Arts, Montreal, Ecole des Beaux-Arts, Montreal, U. B.C., Vancouver, Can., U. Que., Montreal, Concordia U., Montreal. Works exhibited Internat. Sculpture Exhbn., Festival of Gt. Britain, London, 1951, 10th Triennale, Milan, Italy, 1954, 28th Biennial, Venice, 1956, 11th Triennale, Milan, 1957, Brussels Universal and Internat. Exhbn., 1958, Pitts. Internat., 1958, Internat. Exhbn. Contemporary Sculpture, Expo '67, Montreal, 11th Biennial, Middelheim, 1971, Musee des Beaux Arts, Montreal, 1993; several one-man shows in Can., France, Eng.; represented in permanent collections Nat. Gallery, Ottawa, Musée du Que., Quebec City, Musée d'art contemporain, Montreal, Musee des Beaux Arts, Montreal, Museo Internazionale della Ceramica, Faenza, Italy, Can. Imperial Bank of Commerce, Montreal, Art Gallery Ont., Toronto, Sun Life Bldg., Toronto, Upland Air Terminal, Ottawa, Place des Arts, Montreal, Malton Airport, Toronto, Scarborough Coll., Toronto, Macdonald Block, Queen's Park, Toronto, Centre D'Accueil, Longueuil, Que., Centre Hospitalier, Chateauguay, Que., Fed. Food and Drug Bldg., Longueuil, Can. Council Art Bank, Ottawa, Winnipeg Art Gallery, Justice Ct. Bldg., Quebec City, Faculté de Medicine Veterinaire U. de Montreal, also others; subject of TV documentary: Searching for Louis Archambault, 1999. Decorated officer Order Can., 1968; recipient Allied Arts medal Royal Archtl. Inst. of Can., 1958; Recipient Diplome d'honneur Can. Conf. Arts, 1982; Canadian Govt. fellow for travel in France, 1953-54; Can. Council grantee, 1959, 62, 69 Achievements include Academician Royal Canadian Acad. Arts. Died Jan. 27, 2003.

ARCHIBALD, ELEANOR J. medical/surgical nurse; b. Springfield, Mass., June 4, 1930; d. Briard Poland and Helen Sigrid (Nelson) Johnson; m. John Merritt Archibald, Oct. 5, 1951; children: Susan Belinda, Sandra Lee, Sharon Lynn, Sally Anne, John Briard. Diploma in nursing, Springfield Hosp. Sch. Nursing, 1951; student, Miami Dade Community Coll., Fla. Internat. U. RN, Fla.; cert. profl. quality assurance, health care risk mgr., Fla. PSRO rep. Palm Spring Gen. Hosp., Hialeah, Fla., nurse infection control, nursing supr., coord. quality assurance, from 1979. Mem. Nat. Assn. Quality Assurance Profls., Fla. Assn. Quality Assurance Profls., Dade County Assn. Quality Assurance Profls. Home: Malabar, Fla. Died Mar. 27, 2002.

ARLEDGE, ROONE, television executive; b. Forest Hills, N.Y., July 8, 1931; m. Gig Shaw, May 21, 1994; children: Elizabeth Ann, Susan Lee, Patricia Lu, Roone Pinckney. BA, Columbia Coll., 1952; LHD (hon.), Boston U.; LLD (hon.), Wake Forest U. Prodr. network sports, Wide World of Sports ABC-TV, 1960—61, v.p. charge sports, 1964—68; pres. ABC Sports, Monday Night Football, 1968—85, ABC News, Nightline, 1977—98; group pres. ABC News and Sports, 1985—90; exec. prodr. all ABC sports programs, including 10 Olympic games, 1968; pres. ABC News, chmn., from 1998. Bd. dirs. Coun. Fgn. Rels., ESPN, Arts & Entertainment Network, History Channel; dean's coun. Harvard U. JFK Sci. of Govt. Creator ABC's Wide World of Sports, 1961, NFL Monday Night Football, 1970, ABC's World News Tonight, Nightline, 20/20, This Week with David Brinkley, PrimeTime Live, Viewpoint, Turning Point, Capital to Capital, World News This Morning, World News Now, Day One, responsible most tech. and editl. innovations in sports coverage. Mem. Pres.'s Coun. on Physical Fitness; pres. Com. Meml. Sloan Kettering Hosp.; bd. visitors Columbia Coll.; chmn. sports com. Pres.'s Coun. on Physical Fitness; trustee Columbia U. Served U.S. Army, 1953—54. Named Man of Yr., Nat. Assn. Program Execs.; named to TV Acad. Arts and Scis. Hall of Fame, 1990, U.S. Olympic Hall of Fame, 1990, Nat. Assn. Broadcasters Hall of Fame, 1994; recipient 36 Emmy awards, 4 George Foster Peabody awards, 2 Christopher awards, Broadcast Pioneers award, Gold medal, Internat. Radio and TV Soc., 1983, Disting. Svc. to Journalism Honor medal, U. Mo., John Jay Disting. Profl. Svc. award, Columbia U., Lifetime Achievement award, TV Critics Assn., Disting. Achievement award, U. So. Calif. Journlism Assn., Founders award, Acad. TV Arts and Scis. Inst., Grand Prix Montreux TV award, Olympic Order medal, Internat. Olympic Com., Grand prize, Cannes Film Festival. Mem.: Portmarnock Golf Club (Dublin), Castle Pines Golf Club, Winged Foot Golf Club, Deepdale Golf Club, Nat. Golf Links Am., Shinnecock Hills Golf Club, Royal and Ancient Golf Club. Died Dec. 5, 2002.

ARLOOK, THEODORE DAVID, dermatologist; b. Boston, Mar. 12, 1910; s. Louis and Rebecca (Sakansky) A.; BS, U. Ind. Sch. Medicine, 1932, M.D., 1934; postgrad. dermatology U. So. Calif., 1946-47. Diplomate Am. Bd. Dermatology. Intern, Luth. Meml. Hosp., Chgo., 1934-35; resident in dermatology Indpls. Gen. Hosp., 1947-49; practice medicine specializing in dermatology, Elkhart, Ind., 1950—; mem. staff Elkhart Gen. Hosp.; assoc. mem. dermatology dept. Wishard Meml. Hosp., Indpls, 1950-86, Regenstrief Hosp., Indpls., 1987—. Pres., Temple Israel, Elkhart, 1963-64; pres. B'nai B'rith, 1955. Served to capt. M.C. AUS, 1941-46; PTO. Mem. AMA, Ind. State Med. Assn., Am. Acad. Dermatology, Elkhart County Med. Soc. (pres. 1967), Noah Worcester Dermatol. Soc. Contbr. articles to med. jours. Deceased.

ARLOW, JACOB A. psychiatrist, educator; b. N.Y.C., Sept. 3, 1912; s. Adolph A. and Ida (Feldman) A.; m. Alice Diamond (dec. 2003), Oct. 31, 1936; children: Michael Saul, Allan Joseph, Seth Martin. BS, N.Y. U., 1932, MD, 1936; Grad., N.Y. Psychoanalytic Inst., 1947. Diplomate: Am. Bd. Neurology and Psychiatry. Rotating intern Harlem Hosp., N.Y.C., 1936-38; resident neuropsychiatrist USPHS Hosp., Ellis Island, N.Y., 1938-39; resident psychiatrist Kings County Hosp., Bklyn., 1939, asst. psychiatrist mental hygiene clinic, 1941; asst. resident neurologist Montefiore Hosp., Bronx, N.Y., 1940-41, asst. neurologist, 1942-44; resident psychiatrist N.Y. State Psychiat. Inst. and Hosp., N.Y.C., 1940-41; cons. psychiatrist Pride of Judea Children's Home, Bklyn., 1940-45; pvt. practice N.Y.C., 1942-92; lectr. N.Y. Psychoanaltyic Inst., 1948-50; instr. neurology Columbia Coll. Phys. and Surg., 1942-44, instr. psychiatry psychosomatic service of psychoanalytic clinic for tng. and research, 1947-51, John B. Turner vis. prof. psychiatry, 1967-68; research asso, instr. psychiatry Presbyn. Hosp.-Columbia Med. Center, 1944-51; clin. asst. prof. psychoanalytic medicine State U. N.Y. Coll. Medicine at N.Y.C., 1952-55, clin. assoc. prof., 1955-62, clin. prof., 1962-79, NYU, N.Y.C., 1979; mem. faculty Ctr. Psychoanlytic Tng., N.Y.C.; prof. emeritus Albert Einstein Coll. Medicine, N.Y.C.; pvt. practice part-time Great Neck, NY, 1984—2004. Faculty N.Y. Psychoanalytic Inst., 1956; vis. prof. psychiatry La. State U. Sch. Medicine, 1969-70, Mt. Sinai Sch. Medicine, N.Y.C., 1972-73; vis. scholar Freud chair Hebrew U., Jerusalem, April, 1985; cons. Hillside Hosp., Glen Oaks, N.Y., 1989—. Author: Legacy of Sigmund Freud, 1956, (with Charles Brenner) Psychoanalytic Concepts and the Structural Theory, 1964, Psychoanalysis: Clinical Theory and Practice, 1991; editor: Selected Writings of Bertram D. Lewin; editor-in-chief Psychoanalytic Quar., 1970-79; mem. editl. bd. Psyche. Vice pres. Great Neck (L.I.) Coop. Sch.; trustee, sec. N.Y. Psychoanalytic Inst., 1956-59. Recipient Centennial award as Alumnus of Decade 1940-49, N.Y. State Psychiat. Inst., Heinz Hartmann award, 1980; Lenox Hill Disting. Clinicians award, 1980; Vexillarius Excellentae award Pride of Judea Mental Health Ctr., Mary Sigourney award Am. Coll. Psychoanalysts 1990, Henry Loughlin award 1991. Mem. APA, Am. Psychoanalytic Assn. (pres. 1960-61, chmn. COPE 1962-66, bd. editors jours. 1958-60, chmn. bd. profl. standards 1967-70, Jour. award 1988); mem. Internat. Soc. Study of Time (coun.), Am. Psychiat. Assn., Psychosomatic Soc., N.Y. Psychoanalytic Inst. (pres. 1966-68), Internat. Psycho-Analytic Assn. (treas., v.p. 1961-69). Died May 21, 2004.

ARMEN, MARGARET ALBERTA, screenwriter; b. Washington, Sept. 9, 1921; d. Thomas Lloyd and Florence Neilson (Buehler) Sampsell; widowed; 1 child, David Lawrence Armen. BA in English, History, UCLA, 1943. Freelance TV writer for various orgns. including Warner Bros. Studios, MGM, 20th Century Fox, Lorimar Prodns., Hollywood, Calif., from 1959. Bd. govs. TV Acad., Hollywood, 1970; bd. dirs. Writers Guild Am.-West, 1975-78. Author: Hanging of Father Miguel, 1984. Mem. Western Writers Am. Avocation: horseback riding. Home: Woodland Hills, Calif. Died Nov. 10, 2003.

ARMISTEAD, MOSS WILLIAM, III, retired newspaper executive; b. Suffolk, Va., Sept. 7, 1915; s. Moss William, Jr. and Mary Judith (Smith) A.; m. Mary Ragan Bridges, Dec. 30, 1939; 1 child, Elfleda Bridges (Mrs. Peter Huff Ring). Student, Randolph-Macon Coll., 1933-36, LittD (hon.), 1996; LLD, Washington and Lee U., 1967. Reporter Covington Virginian, 1936; reporter, state editor, utility editor, legislative corr. Roanoke (Va.) Times, 1936-42; exec. sec. to Gov. of Va. and Sec. of Commonwealth, 1946-47; asst. to pub. Times & World-News, Roanoke, 1947-51, asso. pub., 1951, v.p., pub., 1954; pres., dir. Times-World Corp.; also pub. Roanoke Times and World-News, 1954-73, chmn. bd., 1955-69; exec. v.p., dir. Landmark Communications, Inc., 1973-74, pres., dir., 1974-78, chmn. exec. com., 1978-86. Pres. Roanoke Valley Devel. Corp., 1957-59; Mem. State Bd. Welfare and Instns., 1947-51; Pres. Roanoke Community Fund, 1952, Central YMCA, 1957-58; pres. Community Hosp., Roanoke Valley, 1960-73; mem. Va. Port Authority, 1958-70. Served from pvt. to 1st lt., inf. AUS, 1942-46; capt. Va. N.G., 1947-50. Decorated Purple Heart. Mem. U.S. C. of C., Va. C. of C. (v.p.), Roanoke C. of C. (pres. 1953), Am. Newspaper Pubs. Assn. (bd. dirs. 1965-74), So. Newspaper Pubs. Assn. (pres. 1975-76), Shenandoah Club (Roanoke), Phi Kappa Sigma, Sigma Delta Chi, Alpha Kappa Psi. Home: Moneta, Va. Died July 12, 2003.

ARMSTRONG, JAMES, mayor of Torrance, Calif.; b. Aug. 8, 1928. B.A., Pepperdine Coll., 1952; M.S. U. So. Calif., 1956. Tchr. Torrance Pub. Schs., Calif., 1953—, now sr. tchr. Am. govt.; mayor City of Torrance, 1978. Mem. Torrance City Council, 1972-78. Recipient Tchr. medal Freedoms Found. at Valley Forge, 1967; Robert A. Taft fellow, 1968. Mem. NEA, Calif. Tchrs. Assn., Torrance Tchrs. Assn. (pres. 1961-62), Torrance Hist. Soc. Died Jan. 4, 2002.

ARNETT, FOSTER DEAVER, lawyer; b. Knoxville, Tenn., Nov. 28, 1920; s. Foster Greenwood and Edna (Deaver) A.; m. Jean Medlin, Mar. 3, 1951; children: Melissa Lee Arnett Campbell, Foster Jr. BA, U. Tenn., 1946; LLB, U. Va., 1948. Bar: Va. 1948, Tenn. 1948, U.S. Dist. Ct. (ea. dist.) Tenn. 1949, U.S. Ct. Appeals (6th cir.) 1954, U.S. Supreme Ct. 1958, U.S. Dist. Ct. (ea. dist.) Ky. 1978, U.S. Dist. Ct. (mid. dist.) Tenn. 1983, U.S. Dist. Ct. (ea. and we. dists.) Va. 1990. In practice, Knoxville, from 1948; ptnr. Arnett, Draper & Hagood (and predecessors), from 1954. Mem. Nat. Conf. Commrs. on Uniform State Laws, 1980-83; life mem. U.S. Ct. Appeals (6th cir.) Jud. Conf. Contbr. articles to profl. jours. Pres. Knox Children's Found., 1959-61, 75-76, East Tenn. Hearing and Speech Ctr., 1963-65, Knoxville Teen Ctr., 1969-71, Knoxville News-Sentinel Charities Inc., 1985—; v.p. Ft. Loudon Assn., 1972-75; del. Rep. Nat. Conv., 1964; bd. dirs., exec. com. Tenn. Mil. Inst., 1973-75; formerly active ARC, Am. Cancer Soc., United Fund. With AUS, 1942-46, PTO; to lt. col. USAR, ret. Decorated Silver Star, Bronze Star, Purple Heart. Fellow Am. Coll. Trial Lawyers (former chair legal ethics com., mem. atty.-client relationship com., mem. other coms.), Internat. Acad. Trial Lawyers (trustee Acad. Found. 1984-91, dean 1988-89, pres. 1992-93, mem. Found. Bd. 1983-92), Internat. Soc. Barristers, Am. Bar Found. (life), Tenn. Bar Found. (charter); mem. ATLA, ABA (mem. standing coms. on unauthorized practice of law and assn. comm., aviation and space law, state cert. legal specialist), Am. Bd. Trial Advs. (adv., charter, 1st pres. Tenn. chpt. 1985-86), Am. Inns of Ct. (charter, master of the bench emeritus Hamilton S. Burnett chpt.), Southea. Legal Found. (legal adv. bd.), Tenn. Bar Assn. (pres. 1968-69), Knoxville Bar Assn. (pres. 1959-60, Govs. award 1989), Internat. Assn. Def. Counsel (sec.-treas. 1981-84), S.E. Def. Counsel Assn. (v.p. 1966), Am. Acad. Hosp. Attys. of Am. Hosp. Assn. (charter), Tenn. Hosp. Assn., Am. Soc. Law, Medicine and Ethics, Fedn. Ins. and Corp. Counsel, Def. Rsch. Inst. (charter), U.S. Supreme Ct. Hist. Soc. (founder), Tenn. Supreme Ct. Hist. Soc. (founder), Federalist Soc., SAR, Scribes, U. Tenn. Nat. Alumni Assn. (pres. 1961-62, chmn. nat. ann. giving program 1961-63), Scabbard and Blade, Scarrabbean, Torchbearer, U. Va. Law Sch. Alumni Assn. (pres. 1991-93, nat. chmn. appeals Law Sch. Found. 1986-88), Raven Soc., 511th Parachute Infantry Regiment Assn., Civitan Club, Farmington Country Club, Charlottesville, Va.), Cherokee Country Club, LeConte Club, Univ. Club (hon.), Men's Cotillion (bd. dirs. 1960-61, 63-64, 66-68, trustee 1962—), Appalachian Club (pres. 1974-76), 511th Parachute Infantry Regiment Assn., Phi Gamma Delta, Phi Delta Phi (hon.), Omicron Delta Kappa (hon.). Presbyterian. Home: Knoxville, Tenn. Died 2000.

ARONOW, RICHARD AVERY, lawyer; b. Camden, N.J., Mar. 20, 1953; s. Martin Leon and Grace Mary (Swartz) A.; m. Laura Ann Weinberg, Oct. 16, 1988. BA, Columbia Coll., 1975; JD, U. Tex., 1978. Bar: N.Y. 1979, U.S. Dist. Ct. (ea. and so. dists.) N.Y. 1979. Dir. spl. projects Coll. Houses Inc., Austin, Tex., 1977-78; asst. corp. counsel law dept. City of N.Y., 1979-82; atty. Port Authority of N.Y. and N.J., 1982-2000; dep. chief leases divsn. law dept. Pt. Authority N.Y. and N.J., from 2001. Mem. Fed. Communications Bar Assn. (N.Y. coordinating com. 1986—), N.Y. State Bar Assn., N.Y. County Lawyers Assn. (com. City of N.Y.), Assn. of Bar of City of N.Y. (transp. com. 1986—). Home: Mahwah, NJ. Died Sept. 11, 2001.

ARONSTEIN, MARTIN JOSEPH, law educator, lawyer; b. N.Y.C., Jan. 25, 1925; s. William and Mollie (Mintz) A.; m. Sally K. Rosenau, Sept. 18, 1948 (dec.); children: Katherine Aronstein Porter, David M., James K. BE, Yale U., 1944; MBA, Harvard U., 1948; LLB, U. Pa., 1965. Bar: Pa. 1965. Bus. exec., Phila., 1948-65; assoc. firm Obermayer, Rebmann, Maxwell & Hippel, Phila., 1965-67, partner, 1968-69; assoc. prof. law U. Pa., 1969-72, prof., 1972-78; counsel firm Ballard, Spahr, Andrews & Ingersoll, Phila., 1978-80, partner, 1980-81; prof. law U. Pa., 1981-86, prof. emeritus, 1986—2003; of counsel firm Morgan, Lewis & Bockius, Phila., 1986-95. Contbr. articles to law revs.; mem. Permanent Editorial Bd. Uniform Comml. Code, 1978-80, counsel, 1980-87, counsel emeritus, 1987-2003. Served with USN, 1943-46. Mem. Am. Law Inst., ABA (reporter com. on stock certs. 1973-77, chmn. subcom. on investment securities 1982-84), Phila. Bar Assn., Order of Coif, Sigma Xi, Tau Beta Pi. Died Feb. 18, 2003.

ARRINGTON, DOROTHY ANITA COLLINS, retired real estate broker; b. Laurel, Miss., Sept. 9, 1922; d. Jeff Clay and Maude Eula (Sudduth) Collins; m. Robert Newton Arrington, Oct. 27, 1956; children: Robert William, Cynthia Anne Arrington Morris. AA, Jones County Jr. Coll., 1941; student, U. Ala., 1942-43. Assoc. realtor Town & Country Village Realtors, Houston, 1970-72, McGuirt & Co., Realtors, Houston, 1974-77, 79-81, Duffy & LaRoe, Realtors, Houston, 1978-79; owner-broker Dotty Arrington, Realtors, Houston, 1972-74; asst. sales mgr. Realmco, Inc., Houston, 1977-78; pres. Dotty Arrington, Inc., Houston, 1981-89, ret., 1989. Adult tchr. Bethel Bible Series. Mem. Daus of the King, Delphians. Republican. Episcopalian. Avocations: water sports, public speaking, piano, travel, foreign languages. Died Feb. 5, 1999.

ARTHUR, JOHN EDWARD, surgeon, educator; b. Norton, Va., Apr. 15, 1922; s. Walter Lewis and Cora Lee (Harmon) A.; m. Betty June Sanders, Aug. 12, 1950 (dec.); children: Stuart, Forrest, Charles, Bonnie; m. Pauline Mae Bailey, Nov. 1988. BS, U. Tenn., 1944, MD, 1945. With Washington U., St. Louis, 1948-49; surgeon Ohio State U. Coll. Medicine, Columbus, 1949-80, prof. otolaryngology, 1949-80, emeritus, from 1981. Served to capt. U.S. Army, 1946-48. Fellow ACS; mem. Am. Soc. Head and Neck Surgeons, Am. Branch Esophogological Soc., Am. Acad. Head and Neck Surgery. Clubs: Scioto (Columbus); Indian Creek (Miami, Fla.). Republican. Episcopalian. Avocations: golfing, fishing. Died Sept. 8, 1999.

ARUJ, ESTRELLA, fashion designer, artist; b. Cordoba, Argentina, Oct. 23, 1934; came to U.S., 1963; d. Alberto and Regina (Gaguine) A.; m. Moises Aruj, Apr. 5, 1952; children: Hector Ricardo, Alberto Silvio. Degree in fashion design, Fashion Inst. Tech., 1968, degree in buying and merchandising, 1970. Designer Herman Gowns Pvt. Collection, N.Y.C., 1963-64; fashion coord. Bonwit Teller, Westchester, N.Y., 1964-68; head designer, master patternmaker Aaron Kahmi-Kamhi Group, N.Y.C., 1968-87, Dorothea of Palm Beach, Fla., 1993-94; costume designer, prodr. Fla., from 1990, Duncan Theatro, 1995. One-woman shows at Carimor Gallery, N.Y., 1985; exhibited in group shows at Argentinean Consulate, N.Y.C., 1985, Jewells Fine Art Gallery, N.J., 1985, 86, Art in Public Places Program, Palm Beach, 1990, 92, Palm Beach C.C., 1991, Kravis Ctr., Palm Beach, 1995, Spanish Latin Am. Mus. Art, Miami, 1997, Find Art Galleria, Ft. Lauderdale, Fla., 1998, Jewish Mus., Aventura, Fla., 1999, Cornell U. Art Gallery, Ithaca, N.Y., 1999, Armory Arts Mus., 1999. Tchr. art to underprivileged children, Palm Beach County; founder cultural cmty. ctr. The Courage to Dream. Mem. Argentina Arts Orgn. (pres. 1995-96, exec. dir. bd. 1995—), Palm Beach Cultural Coun. of Arts, Orgn. Cultural Argentina (head, bd. dirs. 1992—), Ctr. for Creative Edn. (exec. com. 1994—), Nat. Women's Art Mus. (Washington), Met. Mus. (N.Y.), Sephardi Fedn. (Palm Beach), World Jewish Congress, Argentina Fla. C. of C., Spanish Am. C. of C. Jewish. Avocations: painting, swimming, reading, volunteer work, travel. Home: Lake Worth, Fla. Died Mar. 2003.

ASH, PHILIP, psychologist; b. N.Y.C., Feb. 2, 1917; s. Samuel Kieval and Estella (Feldstein) A.; m. Ruth Clyde, Sept. 16, 1945 (div. Dec. 1972); children— Peter, Sharon; m. Judith Nelson Cates, June 6, 1973; 1 stepson, Nelson E. Cates. BS in Psychology, City U. N.Y., 1938; MA in Personnel Adminstrn, Am. U., 1949; PhD in Psychology, Pa. State U., 1949. Diplomate: Indsl. Psychlogy Am. Bd. Profl. Psychology. Analyst to unit chief occupational research Dept. Labor, 1940-47; research fellow Pa. State U., 1947-49, asso. prof., 1949-52; asst. to v.p. indsl. relatons Inland Steel, 1952-68; prof. psychology U. Ill., Chgo., 1968-80, prof. emeritus, 1980—. Dir. rsch. John E. Reid Assocs., Chgo., 1969-87; v.p. rsch. Reid Psychol. Sys., 1985-87; cons. London House, Inc., Park Ridge, Ill., 1987-94; dir. Ash, Blackstone & Cates, Blacksburg, Va., 1975—. Author: Guide for Selection and Placement of Employees, 2d edit., 1977, Volunteers for Mental Health, 1973, The Legality of Preemployment Inquiries, 1989, The Construct of Employee Theft Proneness, 1991, Preparing for Retirement: Guidelines and Information Sources, 1993, also other books, monographs and articles; editor: Forensic Psychology and Disability Evaluation, 1972; editor-in-chief The Va. Psychologist, 1996-2000. Mem. public adv. com. Chgo. Commn. Human Relations, 1957-80; retirement com. Chgo. Commn. Sr. Citizens, 1960-80; chmn. Ill. Psychologist Examining Com., 1963-72. Fellow AAAS, Am. Psychol. Assn. (pres. div. indsl. psychology 1968-69, Heiser award 1999); mem. Ill. Psychol. Assn. (pres. 1963-64), Chgo. Psychol. Assn., Va. Psychol. Assn. (editor-in-chief Va. Psychologist 1996-2001, Lifetime Achievements in Psychology award 1999), Va. Applied Psychology Acad. (pres. 1992-93), Midwest Psychol. Assn., Am. Pers. and Guidance Assn., Acad. for Criminal Justice Scis., Am. Criminology Assn., Internat. Assn. Applied Psychology, Sigma Xi, Phi Beta Kappa, Psi Chi. Home: Blacksburg, Va. Died June 14, 2002.

ASHBY, HAROLD KENNETH, saxophonist; b. Kansas City, Mo., Mar. 27, 1925; s. Herbert and Anna (Lewis) A. Grad., Lincoln Jr. Coll., 1942. Saxophonist Chess Recordings Record Co., Chgo., 1952-57, Duke Ellington's Orch., 1968—75; free-lance musician N.Y.C., from 1975. Served with USN, 1943-45. Home: New York, NY. Died June 13, 2003.

ASHER, ELISE, painter, poet; b. Chgo., 1912; d. Louis E. and Alice (Wormser) A.; m. Nanno F. deGroot, 1949 (div. 1957); m. Stanley Kunitz, June 21, 1958; 1 child, Babette Becker. Student, Bradford Jr. Coll.; BS, Simmons Coll. One-woman shows at Tanager Gallery, N.Y.C., 1953, Grand Central Moderns, N.Y.C., 1958, East Hampton Gallery, 1953, Mary Harriman Gallery, Boston, 1963, Bradford Jr. Coll., Mass., 1964, The Contemporaries, N.Y.C., 1966, The Gotham Book Mart Gallery, N.Y.C., 1971, Tirca Karlis Gallery, Provincetown, Mass., 1971, Benson Gallery, Bridgehampton, N.Y., 1972, Peter M. David Gallery, Mpls., 1973, Bertha Schaefer Gallery, N.Y.C., 1973, Marsh Gallery, Richmond, Va., 1976, Washignton Woman's Art Ctr., Washington, 1976, Ingber Gallery, N.Y.C., 1979, 81, 83, 85, 87, Cherry Stone Gallery, Provincetown, 1981, Nat. Acad. Scis., Washington, 1983, William Benton Mus. Art, U. Conn., 1988; exhibited in group shows at Stable Gallery, N.Y.C., 1953, 57, The Colosseum, N.Y.C., 1959, Howard Wise Gallery, N.Y.C., 1964, Jewish Mus., N.Y.C., 1970, Hudson River Mus., N.Y.C., 1971, Storm King Art Ctr., Mountainville, N.Y., 1973, Fendrick Gallery, Washington, 1976, 77, NYU, 1977, Dayton Art Inst., 1978, Provincetown Art Assn., 1979, Michael Kohler Arts Ctr., Sheboygan, Wis., 1979, Am. Acad. Arts and Letters, N.Y.C., 1980, Fine Arts Mus. L.I., 1983, 84, numerous others; represented in permanent collections U. Calif. Art Mus., Berkeley, Rose Art Mus., Brandeis U., Waltham, Mass., Finch Coll. Art Mus., N.Y.C., Ciba-Geigy Corp., Ardsley, N.Y., First Nat. Bank Chgo., Corcoran Gallery, Washington, Crocker Nat. Bank, San Francisco, Columbia Presbyn. Hosp., N.Y.C., NYU Art Collection. Author: (poems) The Meandering Absolute, 1955, Night Train, 2002. Home: New York, NY. Died Mar. 7, 2004.

ASHFORD, ROBERT LOUIS, computer professional; b. Meridian, Miss., Sept. 8, 1938; s. Walter and Bertha (Edmonds) A.; m. Ruth L. Sypert, May 16, 1992. Student, Tougaloo Coll., 1956-58. Programmer, analyst State of Calif., San Francisco, 1964-68; programming mgr. Control Data Corp., Palo Alto, Calif., 1968-73; office tech. cons. Hewlett-Packard Co., Palo Alto, 1973-95. Mem. Legal Def. Fund: Com. of 100, N.Y.C. With U.S. Army, 1961-64. Mem. NAACP (life), Space Studies Inst., Search for Extraterrestrial Intelligence, Union Concerned Scientists, Astron. Soc. Pacific (advisor, cons. 1989—, Vol. of Yr. award 1992), Group 70 (bd. dirs. pub. rels. large amateur telescope project), Project Astro (adv. bd.). Democrat. Home: San Jose, Calif. Deceased.

ASHIHARA, YOSHINOBU, architect, educator; b. Tokyo, July 7, 1918; s. Nobuyuki and Kikuko (Fujita) A.; m. Hatsuko Takahashi, Dec. 24, 1944; children: Yukiko, Taro. BArch, U. Tokyo, 1942; MArch, Harvard U., 1953; D of Engring. in Architecture, U. Tokyo, 1961. Prin. Yoshinobu Ashihara Architect & Assocs., Tokyo, from 1956; prof. architecture U. Tokyo, 1970-79, Musashino Art U., Tokyo, 1979-89; prof. emeritus U. Tokyo and Musashino Art U., Tokyo, from 1989. Archtl. councillor Nat. Diet Libr., Tokyo; adv. com. on grant aid Ministry Fgn. Affairs, Tokyo. Prin. works include Chuo Koron Bldg. (Archtl. Inst. Japan award 1960), Komazawa Olympic Gymnasium (Archtl. Inst. Japan Spl. award 1965), SONY Bldg., Japanese Pavilion, Expo'67 (Min. of Edn. award of Arts 1968), Nat. Mus. Japanese History, Tokyo Met. Art Space. Decorated Order Commendatore (Italy), Order of Culture; named Person of Cultural Merit, 1991; recipient Golden Triangle award, U.S. Nat. Soc. Interior Designers, 1970. Fellow: AIA (hon.), Japan Inst. Architects (hon.; pres. 1980—82), Royal Australian Inst. Architects (hon.); mem.: Rsch. Inst. Dwelling Culture (pres. from 1995), Japan Assn. Artists, Craftsmen and Architects (pres. from 1988), Japan Art Acad., Archtl. Inst. Japan (hon.; pres. 1985—87), Rotary. Home: Tokyo, Japan. Died Sept. 24, 2003.

ASHJIAN, MESROB, archbishop; b. Beirut, Jan. 3, 1941; s. Nerces and Martha (Kassabian) A. Student, Armenian Theol. Sem., Antelias, Lebanon, 1957-61, Ecumenical Inst., Bossey, Switzerland, 1962-63; BA, Princeton Theol. Sem., 1964, postgrad., 1970-74, ThM, 1990. Ordained priest Armenian Apostolic Ch., 1961. Mem. faculty Armenian Theol. Sem., Antelias, Lebanon, 1961-62, 64, 65, 66-70, vice dean, 1964-65, dean, 1966-70; instr. Karen Jeppe Coll., Aleppo, Syria, 1965-66; preacher St. Gregory Ch., Aleppo, 1965-66; prelate Diocese of Armenians in Iran and India, Isfahan, Iran, 1974-77; consecrated bishop, 1977; consecrated archbishop, 1983; prelate Armenian Apostolic Ch. of Am., Eastern States and Can., N.Y.C., 1978—98. Editor: Hask monthly, 1966-70, Deghegadou, 1976-77, The Holy Week in the Armenian Church Tradition, 1978, Unpublished Papers and Works of Mesrob Taliatine, 1979, St. Nerses of Lambron, 1992, Patristics and Other Essays, 1994, Encounters, 1993, Pages from Faith and Life, 1993, The Armenian Church in America, 1995, The Catholicoi of Etchmiadzin, 1995, Remembrance and Hope, 1997. Former pres. Land and Culture Found., N.Y.C.; mem. Commn. on Faith and Order WCC; pres. Found. for the Preservation of Armenian Hist. Monuments; exec. sec. 17 Centuries of the Proclamation of Christianity as State Religion of Armenia. Decorated grand protector Order Hospitallers St. George of Carinthea Mem. Asia Soc., World Coun. Chs., Princeton Club, Icomos Club. Died Dec. 2, 2003.

ASHLEY, TED, entertainment and communications company executive; Vice chmn., dir. Warner Communications Inc., N.Y.C. Died Aug. 24, 2002.

ASHLEY, WARREN COTTON, chemist, retired; b. Yorkville, Ill., Dec. 25, 1904; s. Stephen Ferriss and Cora Marie (Cotton) A.; m. Genevieve Dorothy Silkey; children: Warren C., Jim, Elizabeth. BS, U. Ill., 1929, MS, 1930, PhD, 1935. Chemist Eastman Kodak, Rochester, N.Y., 1935, Battelle Mem. Inst., Columbus, Ohio, 1935-38, Pyroxylin Products, Chgo., 1938-63, George J. Pigner & Co., Chgo., 1963. Mem. Chgo. Soc. Coatings Tech. (pres. 1954-55, Outstanding Svc. award 1978), Cook-DuPage Beekeepers Assn. (pres. 1967-68), Kendall County (Ill.) Hist. Soc. Avocation: keeping bees. Home: Naperville, Ill. Died Mar. 29, 2004.

ATCHISON, OLIVER CROMWELL, retired accountant; b. Berkeley, Calif., Jan. 19, 1918; s. Frederick Charles and Lillie Louise (Chapman) A. Student, Am. Inst. Banking, San Francisco, 1936-38. Asst. cashier Bank Am. NT&SA, San Francisco, Oakland, Calif., 1936-41; sr. warehouse acct. Alltrans Express USA Inc., San Francisco, 1953-82; ret., 1982. Editor The Dispatcher, 1984— (silver award 1985, 86, bronze award 1986, 87). With USNR, 1941-45. Recipient silver medal Chgo. Philatelic Soc., 1989. Fellow Am. Topical Assn. (treas., editor Casey Jones R.R. unit 1984—), Am. Philatelic Soc. Avocations: gardening, collecting books and organ music records. Home: San Francisco, Calif. Died Feb. 11, 2002.

ATHERTON, ALFRED LEROY, JR., former foreign service officer; b. Pitts., Nov. 22, 1921; s. Alfred Leroy and Joan (Reed) A.; m. Betty Wylie Kittredge, May 26, 1946; children: Lynne Kittredge, Michael Anton, Reed Wylie. BS, Harvard U., 1944, MA, 1947; PhD (hon.), Muskingum Coll., 1984; spl. student econs., U. Calif. at Berkeley, 1961-62. Joined U.S. Fgn. Service, 1947, accorded rank of career amb., 1981; vice consul Stuttgart, Germany, 1947-50, Bonn, Germany, 1950-52; 2d sec. Damascus, Syria, 1953-56; consul Aleppo, Syria, 1957-58; internat. relations officer Bur. Near Eastern and South Asian Affairs, State Dept., 1959-61; consul Calcutta, India, 1962-65; dep. dir. Office Near Eastern Affairs, State Dept., 1965-66; country dir. Arab States North, State Dept., 1966-67, country dir. Israel and Arab Israel affairs, 1967-69; dep. asst. sec. Bur. Near East and South Asian Affairs, State Dept., 1970-74; asst. sec. Bur. Near East and South Asian Affairs, 1974-78, ambassador-at-large, 1978-79; amb. to Egypt Cairo, 1979-83; dir. gen. Fgn. Service, dir. personnel State Dept., 1983-85; dir. The Harkness Fellowships, 1985-91. Vis. Sol M. Linowitz prof. Hamilton Coll., 1988, 92, 94; vis. Cyrus Vance prof. Mt. Holyoke Coll., 1991; vis. prof. Birmingham So. Coll., 1992, 93, 95, 98, 2000. Trustee, The Una Chapman Cox Found., 1985-87, chmn. policy coun., 1987-88, exec. dir., 1989-98; pres. Egyptian-Am. C. of C., 1985-87; chmn. N.Y.-Cairo Sister City Com., 1986-98; mem. adv. bd. Hariri Found., 1986—; mem. nat. coun. Near East Found., 1986—; bd. dirs. U.S. New Zealand Coun., 1987—, adv. commn. on Fgn Svc. Pers. System, 1988-89; mem. adv. com. Initiative for Peace and Coop. in Middle East of Search for Common Ground, 1991—, chmn., 1992-2000. 1st lt. F.A., AUS, 1943-45, ETO. Decorated Air medal, Silver Star; recipient Career Svc. award Nat. Civil Svc. League, 1975, Pres.'s award for disting. fed. civilian svc., 1980, State Dept. Disting. Svc. award, 1985, Wilbur Carr award, 1985, Fgn. Svc. Dir. Gen.'s cup, 1988, commendation for svc. to nation in sense of Senate resolution, 1979. Mem. Am. Fgn. Svc. Assn., Coun. on Fgn. Rels., Am. Acad. Diplomacy, Middle East Inst., Washington Inst. Fgn. Affairs, Nat. Press Club, Harvard Club (Washington). Unitarian Universalist. Home: Mitchellville, Md. Died Oct. 30, 2002.

ATKINS, CHOLLY (CHARLES ATKINSON), choreographer, consultant; b. Pratt City, Ala., Sept. 30, 1913; s. Sylvan and Christene (Woods) Atkinson; m. Dorothy Lee, June 12, 1944 (div. Apr. 1962); m. Maye Ollie, June 22, 1963. Choreographer various studios, L.A., 1936-39, Apollo Theatre, N.Y.C., 1940-42; choreographer, dir., cons. Motown Records, Detroit, 1965-71. Cons. Casino Records, Inc., Las Vegas, 1985—. Choreographer (vocal groups) Gladys Knight and the Pips, Las Vegas, 1964—, The Temptations, L.A., 1965—, The O'Jays, Cleve., 1974—, The Manhattans, N.Y.C., 1985—, (mus.) Black and Blue, 1989 (Tony award best choreography 1989); dancer: (films) San Francisco, 1936, Strike Me Pink, 1937, Big Broadcast of '38, 1937, (play) Hot Mikado, 1939; dancer, singer: (mus.) Gentlemen Prefer Blondes, 1949; actor: (films) Charge of the Light Brigade, 1936, Green Pastures, 1937. With U.S. Army, 1943-45. Recipient Black Heritage Award Black Music Assn., 1988. Democrat. Baptist. Avocations: golf, hiking, swimming, videotaping. Home: Las Vegas, Nev. Died Apr. 19, 2003.

ATKINS, ROBERT C. Inventor of the Atkins Diet, physician; b. Columbus, OH, Oct. 17, 1930; m. Veronica Atkins. Grad., U. Mich., 1951; MD, Cornell U., 1955. Resident St. Luke's Hosp.; founder The Atkins Ctr. for Complementary Medicine, 1972, Atkins Nutritionals, Inc., 1989, Dr. Robert C. Atkins, 1999. Co-founder Found. for the Advancement of Innovative Medicine. Author: (self help books) Dr. Atkins' Diet Revolution, 1972, Dr. Atkins' Super Energy Diet, 1975, Dr. Atkins' Super Energy Cookbook, 1978, Dr. Atkins' Health Revolution, 1988, Dr. Atkins' New Diet Revolution, 1992, Atkins for Life, 2003; co-author (with Veronica Atkins): Dr. Atkins' Quick & Easy New Diet Cookbook, 1997, Dr. Atkins' Vita-Nutrient Solution: Nature's Answer to Drugs, 1998, Dr Atkins' Age-Defying Diet Revolution, 1999. Recipient World Org. of Alternative Medicine's Recognition of Achievement award, Nat. Health Fedn. Man of the Year. Died Apr. 17, 2003.

ATKINSON, CHARLES See ATKINS, CHOLLY

ATTERBURY, BETTY WILSON, music educator, researcher; b. L.A., Apr. 29, 1937; d. Jack Wilson and Viola Narrow; m. Robert Malcolm Atterbury, June 21, 1958; children: Christine, Carolyn, Robert. BS, SUNY, Potsdam,

1959; MS, CUNY, 1970; PhD, Northwestern U., 1982. Instr. Canon Lawrence Tchr. Tng. Coll., Lira, Uganda, 1966-68; tchr. elem. music Babylon (N.Y.) Pub. Schs., 1968-71, Mid. Country Schs., Centereach, N.Y., 1971-80; grad. asst. Northwestern U., Evanston, Ill., 1980-81; asst. prof. music Appalachian State U., Boone, N.C., 1981-85; prof. U. So. Maine, Gorham, 1985-97. Author: Mainstreaming Exceptional Children in Music, 1990; co-author: Experience of Teaching General Music, 1995; editor: Elementary Music-The Best of MEJ, 1991; contbr. articles to profl. jours. Mem. Music Educators Nat. Conf., Maine Music Educators Assn. (rsch. chmn. 1985—, pres. 1992-94, exec. v.p. 1994-96), Coll. Music Soc., Coun. for Rsch. in Music Edn. (adv. com. Bull. 1989—), Pi Kappa Lambda, Sigma Alpha Iota. Home: Windham, Maine. Died Aug. 8, 1998.

AUBURN, NORMAN PAUL, university president; b. Cin., May 22, 1905; s. Joseph and Huldah A.; m. Kathleen Montgomery, June 28, 1930 (dec. 1974); children: Ames Auburn Latta, Richard, Mark, David Bruce; m. Virginia Kirk, Jan. 4, 1977. AB, U. Cin., 1927, postgrad., 1927-28, 34-35, LLD, 1952, Parsons Coll., 1945, U. Liberia, 1959, U. Akron, 1971; DSc, U. Tulsa, 1957; LittD, Washburn U., 1961; LHD, Coll. of Wooster, 1963; DCL, Union Coll., 1979. Editor Cin. Constructor, 1928-33; asst. mgr. Asso. Gen. Contractors of Am., 1928-33; publicity mgr. Allied Constrn. Industries, 1930-33; exec. sec. U. Cin. Alumni Assn., 1933-36; editor Cin. Alumnus, 1929-36; asst. dir., asst. prof. Evening Coll., U. Cin., 1936-38; assoc. prof. U. Cin., 1938-40, acting dean, 1940-41, dean and prof., 1941-43, dean of univ. adminstrn., clk. bd. dirs., 1943-51, v.p., 1943-51, acting pres., 1949; exec. dir. U. Cin. Research Found., 1943-51; pres. U. Akron, 1951-71, pres. emeritus, cons., 1971—2003. Acting pres. Council Fin. Aid to Edn., N.Y.C., 1957-58, bd. dirs., 1957-71; spl. asst. univ. relations AID, U.S. State Dept., 1965-66, cons., 1966—2003; cons. Acad. Ednl. Devel., Inc., N.Y.C., 1965-70, sr. v.p., dir. institutional ops., 1971-89, sr. v.p., emeritus, 1989-2003; acting pres. Poly. Inst., Bklyn., 1973, Stephens Coll., Columbia, Mo., 1974-75, Cedar Crest Coll., Allentown, Pa., 1977-78, Union Coll., Schenectady, N.Y., 1978-79; acting chancellor Union U., Albany, N.Y., 1978-79; sr. v.p., provost Widener U., Chester, Pa., 1979-82; acting pres. Salem Coll., W.Va., 1982-83, Lincoln U., Jefferson City, Mo., 1987-88; spl. asst. to pres. for planning W.Va. U., Morgantown, 1983-86; chmn. Univ. Council on Edn. for Pub. Responsibility, 1965-66; dir. Great Lakes Megalopolis Research Project, 1968-74; vice chmn. Am. Council Edn., 1963-64, dir., 1969-72; bd. dirs. First Fed. Savs. and Loan Assn., Akron, 1963, chmn., 1973-2003; bd. dirs. Charter One Fin., Cleve., 1988-2003, Charter One Bank, 1988-2003, 1st Nat. Bank Akron, emeritus; hon. pres. Lane Theol. Sem., Cin., 1990-2003. Contbr. articles to ednl. jours. Bd. dirs. Akron Gen. Hosp., U. Akron Devel. Found., 1967-2003; trustee Greater Akron Musical Assn., 1967-2003; trustee, sec. Lane Theol. Sem., Cin., 1945-2003, hon. pres., 1990-2003; trustee Ohio Coll. Assn., pres., 1960-61; mem. Air Force ROTC Adv. Panel to Dept. USAF, 1960-64; mem. exec. com. Ohio Research and Devel. Bd., 1962-65; pres. Herman Muehlstein Found., 1965-2003; mem. U. Cin. Endowment Fund Assn. Recipient Bert A. Polsky Humanitarian award Akron Cmty. Found., 1997, Judge Harold K. Stubbs Emeriti award for lifetime of disting. svc. African Meth. Episcopal Ch., 2000. Fellow AAAS; mem. Assn. Am. Colls. (vice chmn. commn. coll. adminstrn. 1965-68), Am. Soc. Engring. Edn., Am. Assn. State Colls. and Univs. (chmn. com. on internat. programs 1970-71), Assn. Univ. Evening Colls. (pres. 1944), Assn. Urban Univs. (pres. 1955-56, sec.-treas. 1956-65), Newcomen Soc., Cincinnatus Soc., Summit County Hist. Soc. (trustee 1975-80), Queen City Assn., Alpha Kappa Psi, Phi Alpha Delta, Lambda Chi Alpha, Omicron Delta Kappa, Scabbard and Blade. Clubs: Rotary (pres. Cin. 1950-51, Akron 1958-59), Commonwealth (Cin.), Univ. (N.Y.C., Columbus, Ohio), City, Portage Country (Akron), Lago Mar Beach (Ft. Lauderdale, Fla.). Presbyterian. Home: Akron, Ohio. Died July 21, 2003.

AUCHINCLOSS, KENNETH, magazine editor; b. N.Y.C., July 3, 1937; s. Douglas and Eleanor (Grant) A.; m. Eleanor Muir Johnson, June 5, 1971; children: Malcolm Grant, Emily Johnson. AB, Harvard U., 1959; BA, MA (Henry fellow), Balliol Coll., Oxford (Eng.) U., 1961. Asst. to dep. asst. sec. commerce, Washington, 1962-63; exec. asst. Pres.'s spl. rep. for trade negotiations, 1963-65; asst. to trustees Inst. for Advanced Study, Princeton, N.J., 1965-66; assoc. editor Newsweek, N.Y.C., 1966-69, gen. editor, 1969-72, sr. editor, 1972, exec. editor, 1973-75, mng. editor, 1975-95, editor internat. edits., 1986-95, editor-at-large, 1996—2002, ret., from 2002. Home: New York, NY. Died Mar. 4, 2003.

AUGSTEIN, RUDOLF, publisher; b. Nov. 5, 1923; D.H.C., Bath U., 1983, U. Wuppertal, 1987, Moscow State Inst. Internat. Rels., 1999; Senator (hon.), U. Hamburg, 1988. Publisher Der Spiegel (weekly), Hamburg, from 1947. Under arrest (for alleged polit. offence), 1962-63. Author: Spiegelungen, 1964; Konrad Adenauer, 1964, Preussens Friedrich und die Deutschen, 1968, Jesus Menschensohn, 1972. Elected Bundestag, 1972, resigned, 1973. Served to lt. German Army, World War II. Named Hon. citizen Hamburg, 1994; recipient Commander's Cross of the Order of Merit of the Federal Republic of Germany, 1997, Ludwig-Börne-award, 2001. Mem. German PEN. Died Nov. 8, 2002.

AUGUST, RUDOLF See SCHLOEMANN, ERNST

AUSTERLITZ, ROBERT PAUL, linguistics educator; b. Bucharest, Romania, Dec. 13, 1923; came to U.S., 1938, naturalized, 1946; s. Otto and Rose (Zellenka) A.; m. Sylvi Nevanlinna, Mar. 21, 1953 (dec. Jan. 28, 1981); children— Monica, Paul. AB, New Sch. Social Research, 1950; MA, Columbia U., 1950, PhD, 1955; student, Finland, 1951-53, Japan, 1953-54, 56-58; PhD (hon.), U. Umeå, Sweden, 1986. Mem. faculty Columbia U., N.Y.C., 1958—, prof. linguistics and Uralic studies, 1965—, chmn. dept. linguistics, 1965-68. Vis. faculty mem. Linguistic Inst., U. Wash., Seattle, summers 1962-63, Ohio State U., 1970; vis. assoc. prof. Yale U., 1964-65; vis. prof. U. Calif., Berkeley, 1969, U. Cologne, Fed. Republic Germany, 1977, U. Hawaii, 1979, Umeå, Sweden, 1982, Helsinki, Finland, 1986; cons. map lang. families Eurasia Smithsonian Instn., 1967 Author: Ob-Ugric Metrics, 1958; Co-editor: Jour. Word, 1960-65, Readings in Linguisitics II, 1966; editor: The Scope of American Linguistics, 1975. Served with AUS, 1943-45. Decorated knight 1st class Order Lion Finland; sr. fellow Nat. Endowment for Humanities, 1971-72 Fellow Am. Acad. Arts and Scis.; mem. Linguistic Soc. Am. (life, pres. 1990), Soc. Finno-Ougrienne (hon.), Kalevala-Soc. (corr.), Am. Oriental Soc. (pres. 1981-82), Linguistic Soc. Paris, Linguistic Soc. Hungary (corr.), Rheinisch-Westfälische Akademie der Wissenschaften Düsseldorf (corr.), Academia Scientiarum Hungarica (hon.), Soc. for Finnish Lit. (corr.), Finnish Acad. Scis. (corr.) Died Sept. 9, 1994.

AUSTIN, TOM AL, engineering educator; b. Ft. Worth, Nov. 21, 1943; s. George Allen and Vaye Tom Austin; m. Loretta Ann Catlett; children: Lowell, Laura Ballard, Melissa Vander Velde, Matthew, Kathryn, Andrew. BS, Tex. Tech U., 1967, PhD, 1971; MS, Utah State U., 1969. Registered profl. engr.., Tex. Sys. engr. Tex. Water Devel. Bd., Austin, 1971—72; prof. civil engring. Iowa St. U., Ames, from 1972. Capt. USAR, 1967—78. Fellow: ASCE; mem.: Am. Soc. Engring. Edn. Avocation: painting. Home: Stanhope, Iowa. Died July 23, 2003.

AVERY, GERALD K(ENNETH), oil company executive; b. Petoskey, Mich., Aug. 14, 1953; s. Kenneth James Avery and Marilyn Fay (Stoneham) Blauman; m. Carie Sue Fowler, Aug. 26, 1978; children: Krysten, Jeremiah, Taylor. Pres. Oil Trust Corp., Benzonia, Mich., from 1983, Peninsula Oil Co., Traverse City, Mich., from 1985, Land Data Energy Group, Ltd., Benzonia, Mich., from 1988. Pres. Onshore Energy Corp., 1989. Died Jan. 22, 2001.

AVERY, WILLIAM HINCKLEY, physicist, chemist; b. Ft. Collins, Colo., July 25, 1912; s. Edgar Delano and Mabel Abbey (Gordon) A.; m. Helen Wallace Palmer, July 18, 1938; children— Christopher, Patricia (Mrs. W. Randolph Bartlett, Jr.). AB, Pomona Coll., 1933; AM, Harvard, 1935, PhD in Phys. Chemistry, 1937. Postdoctoral research asst. infrared spectroscopy Harvard, 1937-39; research chemist Shell Oil Co., St. Louis, Houston, 1939-43; head propulsion div. Allegany Ballistics Lab., Cumberland, Md., 1943-46; cons. in physics and chemistry Arthur D. Little Co., Cambridge, Mass., 1946-47; profl. staff mem. Applied Physics Lab., Johns Hopkins Univ., Laurel, Md., 1947-73, asst. dir. exploratory devel., 1973-78, dir. ocean energy programs, 1978-89, ret., 1989. Mem. various coms. DOD, NASA, NRC, Nat. Acad. Scis.; Nat. Acad. Engring., 1955—2004; mem. tech. adv. bd. panel on SST environ. research Dept. Commerce, 1971; mem. subcom. AEC, Pres.'s Energy Report, 1973 Author: Renewable Energy from the Ocean: A Guide to OTEC, 1994; contbr. articles to profl. jours. Recipient C.N. Hickman award, 1951, Presdl. certificate of merit, 1948, Naval Ordnance Devel. award, 1945, IR 100 award, 1979, Sir Alfred Egerton award, 1972, William H. Avery Propulsion Rsch. Lab. established in his honor Johns Hopkins U., 1989, renamed William H. Avery Advanced Tech. Devel. Lab., 1996. Fellow AIAA (tech. dir. 1968-71); mem. AAAS, Hydrogen Energy Assn., Am. Chem. Soc., Combustion Inst. (dir. 1960-80, Sir Alfred C. Egerton Gold medal 1971), Marine Tech. Soc., Internat. Hydrogen Energy Inst., Cosmos Club (Washington), Phi Beta Kappa. Died June 26, 2004.

AVRAMOVIC, DRAGOSLAV, banker; b. Oerid, Macedonia, Oct. 14, 1919; m. Maria Avramovic; 3 children. PhD in Econs., Belgrade U. With World Bank, 1953-78; then with UN, Geneva; gov. Nat. Bank of Yugoslavia, 1994-96. Mem. adv. group of experts on econ. problems Movement of Non-Allied Countries Geneva and Internat. Commn. on problems of peace and food, 1994—. Deceased.

AXEL, LARRY EUGENE, philosophy educator; b. Kendallville, Ind., May 13, 1946; s. Thurlow E. and Mary Josephine (Layman) A.; m. Rebecca Jane Chambers, June 23, 1968; children: Darin, Jenny, Emily. BA, Ind. Cen. U., 1968; MAR, Yale U., 1970; MA, Temple U., 1972, PhD, 1975. Prof. Purdue U., West Lafayette, Ind., from 1973, co-dir. religious studies program, from 1973, founding co-chair Jewish studies program, from 1980, chair athletic affairs, from 1990. Charter mem. Buddhist/Unitarian Universalist Exch. Group, Hakone, Japan, 1987—. Co-editor Am. Jour. Theology & Philosophy, 1980—; editor: Creative Freedom, 1982, The Size of God, 1987, God, Values, and Empiricism, 1989, New Essays in Religious Naturalism, 1991. Advisor Learning and Teaching about Japan, Lafayette, Ind., 1987—. Rockefeller Found. fellow, 1968; named Prof. of Yr., Counsel for Advancement and Support of Edn., 1987; recipient Silver medal Carnegie Found. for Advancement of Teaching, 1987. Mem. Highlands Inst. for Am. Religious Thought (exec. com. 1988—), Collegium Assn. for Liberal Religious Studies (pres. 1982-84), Ctr. for Process Studies, Nat. Inst. on Holocaust, Am. Acad. Religion, Unitarian Universalist Assn. (trustee ind. study program 1987—). Home: Frankfort, Ind. Deceased.

AXELROD, GEORGE, playwright; b. N.Y.C., June 9, 1922; s. Herman and Beatrice (Carpenter) Axelrod; m. Gloria Washburn, Feb. 28, 1942 (div. June 1954); children: Peter, Steven; m. Joan Stanton, Oct. 1954; children: Nina, Jonathan. Author (Radio and TV script writer), sketches for comedians and TV Celebrity Time series, also films, from; author: Beggar's Choice, 1947, Blackmailer, 1952, Where Am I Now-When I Need Me, 1971, Small Wonder (revue with Max Wilk), 1948, (plays) The Seven Year Itch, 1953, Will Success Spoil Rock Hunter?, 1955, (films) Bus Stop; prodr.(with Clinton Wilder): (plays) Visit to a Small Planet, 1957, Goodbye Charlie, 1959; dir.: (films) Breakfast at Tiffany's, 1959; author (produced with John Frankenheimer): (screenplays) The Manchurian Candidate, 1962, Paris When it Sizzles, 1963, How To Murder Your Wife, 1965; dir.: (plays) Once More, With Feeling, 1958; prodr.: (films) Lord Love a Duck; co-author: (films) Lord Love a Duck; dir.: (plays) Star Spangled Girl; author: (films) The Secret Life of an American Wife; dir., prodr.: (films) The Secret Life of an American Wife. Mem.: Authors League Am., Dramatists Guild. Died June 21, 2003.

BAAKLINI, ABDO ISKANDAR, educator; b. Dhourshweir, Lebanon, Mar. 7, 1938; s. Iskandar A. Baaklini and Sa'ada Ya'coub; m. Rehab Karami Baaklini, children: Farid, Iskandar. BA, Am. U., Beirut, 1960, MA, 1963; PhD, SUNY, Albany, 1972. Tchr. Govt. of Iraq, Amara, 1960-61; acad. councillor U.S. Embassy, Beirut, 1962-68; with SUNY, Albany, 1972—2003, prof., dept. public adminstrn., 1994—2003, chair, dept. public. adminstr., 1989—90; dir. Ctr. for Legis. Devel., SUNY, 1990—2003. Dir., Internat Devel. Program, 1982-90; advisor USAID, various govts. Author: Legislatures in the Middle East: Their Role During Transition to Democracy, 1999, Viable Constitutionalism and Democratic Political Stability, 1997, The Brazilian Legislature and Political System, 1992, Legislative and Political Development: Lebanon, 1842-1972, Legislative Institution Building in Brazil, Costa Rica and Lebanon, 1976; contbr. articles to profl. jours. Mem. Am. Soc. Pub. Adminstrn., Am. Polit. Sci. Assn. Home: Latham, NY. Died Nov. 11, 2003.

BABA, JASON NOBUO, lawyer; b. L.A., July 31, 1957; s. Eben Chiaki and Irene Bow Chin (Yee) B.; m. Marlene Machiko Shintaku, July 3, 1988. BA, BBA, U. Hawaii, 1980; JD, UCLA, 1983. Bar: Hawaii 1983, U.S. Dist. Ct. Hawaii 1983. Assoc. Carlsmith & Dwyer, Honolulu, 1983-86, Law Offices Kevin Chee, Honolulu, 1986-87, Bays, Deaver, Hiatt, Lung & Rose, Honolulu, from 1987. Mem. ABA, Hawaii Bar Assn., Bldg. Industry Assn., Nat. Comml. Builders Coun., Nat. Assn. Home Builders. Avocations: tennis, golf. Home: Kaneohe, Hawaii. Died Aug. 17, 2001.

BABCOCK, HORACE W. retired astronomer; b. Pasadena, Calif., Sept. 13, 1912; s. Harold Delos and Mary Geddie (Henderson) B.; children: Ann Lucille, Bruce Harold, Kenneth L. BS, Calif. Inst. Tech., 1934; PhD, U. Calif., 1938; D.Sc. (hon.), U. Newcastle-upon-Tyne (Eng.), 1965. Asst. Lick Obs., Mt. Hamilton, Calif., 1938-39; instr. Yerkes and McDonald Obs., Williams Bay, Wis., Ft. Davis, Tex., 1939-41; with Radiation Lab., MIT, 1941-42, Rocket Project, Calif. Inst. Tech., 1942-45; staff mem. Mt. Wilson and Palomar Obs., Carnegie Instn. of Washington, Calif. Inst. Tech., Pasadena, 1946-80; dir. Mt. Wilson and Palomar Obs., 1964-78. Author sci. and tech. papers in profl. jours. Recipient USN Bur. Ordnance Devel. award, 1946, Draper medal NAS, 1957, Eddington medal Royal Astron. Soc., 1958, gold medal, 1970, Bruce medal Astron. Soc. Pacific, 1969, Rank award in opto-electronics, 1993. Mem. NAS (councilor 1973-76), Royal Astron. Soc. (assoc.), Societé Royale des Sciences de Liege (corr. mem.), Am. Philos. Soc., Am. Acad. Arts and Scis., Am. Astron. Soc. (councilor 1956-58, George Ellery Hale award 1990), Astron. Soc. Pacific, Internat. Astron. Union. Home: Santa Barbara, Calif. Died Aug. 29, 2003.

BABOW, IRVING PAUL, sociologist, researcher; b. Kiev, Russia, Aug. 12, 1913; came to U.S., 1914; s. Paul Louis and Rose (Millman) B.; m. Frances Sona Silberstein, Nov. 19, 1945; 1 child, Robin Lynn Babow Rowe. BA in Social Theory, U. Calif., Berkeley, 1936, PhD in Sociology, 1954. Rsch. dir., civil rights inventory Coun. Civic Unity, San Francisco, 1954-55; lectr. social welfare U. Calif., Berkeley, 1954-63; rsch. dir. Calif. Cancer Patient Study Am. Cancer Soc. Calif. Divsn., San Francisco, 1962-63; sociologist nursing rsch. U.S. Pub. Health Svc., San Francisco, 1964; rsch. social scientist Calif. Dept. Mental Hygiene, Imola, 1965-70; prof. sociology Calif. Poly. State U., San Luis Obispo, 1971-78; ind. rsch. sociologist Mill Valley, Calif., from 1979. Rsch. dir. health & rehab. study United Cmty. Fund San Francisco, 1959-60, Alameda County mental health study Mental Health Assn. & East Bay Coun. Social Planning, Oakland, Calif., 1961. Contbr. articles to profl. jours. Med. field agent U.S. Selective Svc., San Francisco, 1942-44; mem. cons. intercultural edn. Calif. Dept. Edn. Primary Schs. Divsn., Sacramento, 1945-48. Psychiat. fellow Grad. Sch. Jewish Social Work, N.Y.C., 1936-38. Mem. NASW, Am. Sociol. Assn., Am. Assn. Suicidology. Democrat. Jewish. Avocations: travel, music, writing satire. Home: Novato, Calif. Died June 13, 2001.

BACHMAN, JOHN WALTER, clergyman, educator, author; b. Youngstown, Ohio, May 30, 1916; s. Walter Herbert and Eda (Fisher) B.; m. Elsie Schiefer, Jan. 20, 1942;

children: Charles Walter, John Frederick. AB, Capital U., Columbus, Ohio, 1937, D.D., 1957; grad., Evang. Luth. Theol. Sem., Columbus, 1940; MA, Ohio State U., 1946. Ordained to ministry Luth. Ch., 1941. Minister in, Warren, Ohio, 1941-44; instr., then asst. prof. speech and chmn. dept. Capital U., 1944-46; asso. prof. then prof. radio and chmn. dept. Baylor U., 1946-52; asso. prof. then prof. practical theology and dir. Center Communication and Arts, Union Theol. Sem., N.Y.C., 1952-64; pres. Wartburg Coll., Waverly, Iowa, 1964-74; dir. communication and mission support Am. Luth. Ch., 1974-80. Vis. lectr. Candler Sch. Theology, Emory U., Christian Theol. Sem., Indpls., Hampton Inst., Pine Hill Div. Hall, Halifax, N.S., Can., Princeton Theol. Sem., Queen's Theol. Coll., Kingston, Ont., Can., Wartburg Theol. Sem., Dubuque, Iowa, Southwestern U., Georgetown, Tex.; hon. research asso. Communication Research Centre, Univ. Coll., U. London, 1959-60; mem. adv. com. on higher edn. Midwestern Conf. on Council State Govts., 1969-70; mem. Iowa Coordinating Council for Post High Sch. Edn., 1970-74; Exec. com. Iowa Coll. Found., Iowa Assn. Pvt. Colls., 1970-74 Author: How to Use Audio-Visual Materials, 1956, The Church in the World of Radio-Television, 1960, Faith That Makes a Difference, 1983, Media-Wasteland or Wonderland, 1984; editor: (with E.M. Browne) Better Plays for Today's Churches, 1964; editorial bd.: Quar. Jour. Speech, 1960-62; contbr. to periodicals. Bd. mgrs. communication commn. Nat. Council Chs., 1953-84, chmn., 1964-67; adv. bd. Center Mass. Communication, Columbia U., 1957-62, chmn. seminar pub. communication, 1962-63; commn. pub. communication Am. Luth. Ch., 1962-72; chmn. communication task force Luth. World Fedn., 1970-72, chmn. communication com., 1973; bd. dirs. Luth. World Relief, 1977-82, Luth. Film Assos., 1975-83. Mem. Speech Assn. Am. (legis. assembly 1956-60), World Assn. Christian Broadcasting (central com. 1964-67), N. Central Assn. Colls. and Secondary Schs. (com. on research and service 1967-73, com. on liberal arts edn. 1968-73) Home: Minneapolis, Minn. Died July 7, 2003.

BACKES, WAYNE A. cooperative industrial education coordinator; b. Morristown, N.J., Apr. 29, 1942; s. William Robert and Cecelia (Shingles) B.; m. Patricia J. England, Dec. 18, 1965; children: Ronald, John. BS in Edn., Omaha U., 1964; CIE Cert., Jersey City State, 1972. Cert. tchr., Nebr., tchr., coord., N.J. Tchr., coach Hastings (Nebr.) Pub. Sch., 1964-66; tchr., coach, coord. Morris Sch. Dist., Morristown, N.J., from 1970. Mem. curriculum com. N.J. Vocat. Dept., Trenton, 1974-75, 76-77; mem. Middle States Team, Trenton, 1973-74, Teaneck, 1992, Bus. Adv. Bd., Morristown, 1970—. Mem. Jaycees, Hastings, 1965-66, Nebr., 1970-74. 1st lt. U.S. Army, 1966-69. Mem. NEA, N.J. Edn. Assn., Am. Assn. Ret. Persons, N.J. Am. Automobile Assn., N.J. Coop. Indsl. Edn. Assn., Am. Legion, N.Am. Fishing Club, Boat U.S. Avocations: fishing, boating, hunting, travel, photography, sports. Home: Whippany, NJ. Died Dec. 29, 2000.

BADER, MICHAEL HALEY, lawyer, telecommunications, broadcasting executive; b. Tacoma, Aug. 28, 1929; s. Francis William and Gertrude Mary (Haley) B.; m. Joan Marie Berry, Aug. 21, 1954; children: Michael Haley, Brian Raymond, Mary Jennifer, Margaret Patricia, Joan Kerry. LLB, George Washington U., 1952; M in Liberal Studies, Georgetown U., 1980; LHD (hon.), Marymount U., 1997. Bar: D.C. 1954, Va. 1993. Assoc. Haley, Bader & Potts, Washington, 1954-59, ptnr., 1959-2000; pres. Sta. WTID-FM, Suffolk, Va., 1980-86, Sta. WGLL-FM, Mercersburg, Pa., 1983-93, Sta. WTHU-AM, Thurmont, Md., 1988-91, Sta. WCBG-AM, Chambersburg, Pa., 1989-93; counsel Garvey, Schubert & Barer, Washington, from 2000. Mng. ptnr. Sta. WGTO-AM, Cypress Gardens, Fla., 1986-88; bd. dirs. MCI Comm. Corp., Washington. Contbr. (book) Space Law and Government, 1959, Rocketry and Space Exploration, 1963. Trustee Georgetown Visitation Prep. Sch., Washington, 1986—, William G. McGowan Meml. Fund, Inc., 1993—; chmn. bd. dirs. Georgetown Symphony Orch., Washington, 1986-95; chmn. bd. advisors St. Anselm's Abbey Sch., Washington, 1992—. Mem. ABA, D.C. Bar Assn., Fed. Comm. Bar Assn. (exec. com. 1971-74), Am. Symphony Orch. League, Knights of Malta, Palaver Club, Cosmos Club. Republican. Roman Catholic. Avocations: symphony music, orchestral activities, railroading. Home: Bethesda, Md. Died Nov. 2, 2001.

BAEZ, SILVIO A. physician, medical researcher; b. Guarambare, Paraguay, July 6, 1915; s. Ricardo Baez and Regina Acosta de Baez. BA, Nat. Coll., Asuncion, Paraguay, 1935, BS, 1936; MD, Asuncion Med. Sch., Asuncion, Paraguay, 1942; D (hon.), U. Montevideo, Montevideo, Uruguay, 1968. Instr. physiology Asuncion Med. Sch., N.Y.C., Paraguay, 1943-44, instr. surgical semeiology Inst. Surgery, 1943-44; fellow Inter-Am. Tng. Adminstrn. Cornell U. Med. Coll. Dept. Physiology, 1944-45; rsch. fellow Cornell U. Med. Coll. Dept. Medicine, 1945-49, rsch. assoc., 1948-52, asst. prof., 1952-57; asst. clin. physician Cornell Med. Coll. Endocrine Clinic Dept. Medicine, 1953-57; asst. prof. dept. anesthesiology NYU Coll. Medicine, 1957-61; prof. dpet. anesthesiology and physiology Albert Einstein Coll. Medicine Yeshiva U., 1969-85, prof. emeritus, from 1985. Fulbright vis. prof. U. Montevideo, 1968; vis. prof. Japan Soc. Promotion of Sci., 1974, U. Ky. Dept. Pharmacology, Lexington, 1974-75; cons. NSF grant applications, 1973—, NIH SCOR, 1975. Mem. editl. bd. Microvascular Rsch., 1975-79, Microcirculation, 1981—; contbr. articles to profl. jours. Mem. AAAS, Acad. Medicine and Surgery (Asuncion), Am. Heart Assn. (mem. couns. on thrombosis and basic sci.), Am. Physiology Soc., Gnotobiotic Soc., Harvey Soc., Internat. Soc. Biorheology, Microcirculatory Soc. (co-founder, chmn., mem. coun. 1966-68), N.Y. Acad. Scis., European Soc. Microcirculation, Fulbright Alumni Assn., Sigma Xi. Home: Barre, Vt. Died June 25, 2001.

BAGBY, WILLIAM RARDIN, lawyer; b. Grayson, Ky., Feb. 19, 1910; s. John Albert and Nano A. (Rardin) B.; m. Mary Carpenter, Sept. 3, 1939; 1 child, John Robert; m. Elizabeth Hinkel, Nov. 22, 1975. AB, Cornell U., 1933; JD, U. Mich., 1936; postgrad., Northwestern U., 1946-47. Bar: Ky. 1937, Ohio 1952, U.S. Tax Ct. 1948, U.S. Supreme Ct. 1950, U.S. Ct. Appeals (6th cir.) 1952. Pvt. practice, Grayson, 1937-43; atty., judge City of Grayson, 1939-43; counsel Treasury Dept., Chgo., Cleve. and Cin., 1946-54; pvt. practice Lexington, Ky., from 1954. Prof. U. Ky., 1956-57; gen. counsel Headley-Whitney Mus., 1974-84; mem. Bd. of Adjustment, Lexington-Urban County City Govt., 1965-98, chmn., 1980-98. Trustee Bagby Found. Musical Arts, N.Y.C., 1963-74; trustee, gen. counsel McDowell Cancer Found., 1979-91, pres., 1988-91. Lt. USN, 1943-46. Mem. ABA (hon. life), Am. Judicature Soc., Ky. Bar Assn. (hon. life), Fayette County Bar Assn., Lexington Club, U. Ky. Faculty Club, Rotary. Democrat. Home: Lexington, Ky. Deceased.

BAGG, THOMAS CAMPBELL, physicist; b. Phila., Oct. 28, 1917; s. Thoms Campbell and Anna Josephene (Vansant) B.; m. Elizabeth Miller, May 2, 1942; children: Patricia Bagg Cole, Carol Bagg Carpenter, Thomas Campbell III. BS in Engring., Physics, Lafayette Coll., Easton, Pa., 1939. Instrument maker dept. physics Lafayette Coll., 1935-39; lab. instr. dept. physiology U. Pa., Phila., 1939-41; jr. physicist DTM Carnegie Inst., Washington, 1941; physicist radio div. Nat. Bur. Standards, Washington, 1941-51, physicist radiometry, 1951-56, systems engr. computer div. Washington, Gaithersburg, Md., from 1956. Cons. U.S. Patent Office, Washington, 1956-88, USN, Washington, 1956-85, Nat. Libr. Medica, Bethesda, Md., 1963—, NIH, Bethesda, 1960-90. Contbr. articles to profl. jours. Recipient Bronze medal U.S. Dept. Commerce, 1987. Fellow Assn. for Info. and Image Mgmt. (Award of Merit), AAAS; mem. Soc. for Image Sci. and Tech. (bd. dirs. 1987—), Am. Phys. Soc., IEEE, Am. Soc. Info. Scientists. Republican. Episcopalian. Avocations: photography, woodworking, gardening. Home: Gaithersburg, Md. Deceased.

BAHLMAN, DUDLEY WARD RHODES, history educator; b. Cin., Mar. 19, 1923; s. William T. and Janet (Rhodes) B.; m. Jean Mitchell, Dec. 29, 1951; children: Dudley R., Anne M. BA, Yale U., 1946, MA, 1947, PhD, 1951. Instr., asst. prof. Yale U., 1951-59; asst. prof. Williams Coll., Williamstown, Mass., 1959-62, assoc. prof., 1962-67, prof., 1967-87, dean of faculty, 1968-75, Class of 1924 prof., 1976-84, J.P. Baxter 3d prof., 1984-87, chmn. dept. history, 1978-84. Author: The Moral Revolution of 1688, 1957, The Diary of Sir Edward Hamilton, 1972. Served with Med. Dept. AUS, 1943-46. Morse fellow, 1957-58; Guggenheim fellow, 1965-66 Fellow Royal Hist. Soc. Clubs: Elizabethan, Century. Home: Williamstown, Mass. Died Dec. 30, 2000.

BAILAR, BENJAMIN FRANKLIN, academic administrator, administration educator; b. Champaign, Ill., Apr. 21, 1934; s. John C. and Florence (Catherwood) B.; m. Anne Tveit, Aug. 22, 1958; children: Christina, Benjamin Franklin Jr. BA, U. Colo., 1955, DHL (hon.), 1989; MBA, Harvard, 1959; DPA (hon.), Monmouth Coll., 1976. With Continental Oil Co., Houston, 1959-62; with Am. Can Co., N.Y.C., 1962-72, v.p., 1967-72; sr. asst. postmaster gen. U.S. Postal Service, Washington, 1972-74, dep. postmaster gen., 1974-75, postmaster gen., 1975-78; exec. v.p., dir. U.S. Gypsum Co., Chgo., 1978-82; pres., chief exec. officer Scott Pub. Co., N.Y.C., 1983-85; pres. Franklin Fin. Corp., 1985-87; dean, prof. adminstrn. Jones Grad. Sch. of Adminstrn. Rice U., Houston, 1987-97. Bd. dirs. Dana Corp., Toledo, Smith Internat., Inc., Houston, Trico Marine Svcs., Inc., Houston. Mem. Chgo. Club, Tau Kappa Epsilon. Home: Lake Forest, Ill. Died Aug. 16, 2002.

BAILEY, CHARLES RICHARD, political consultant; b. Logan, Utah, Nov. 16, 1929; s. Charles Bradshaw and Laura (Merrill) B.; m. Janice Johnson, Jan. 12, 1949; children: Steven, Kenneth, Rodger. Student, Utah State Coll., 1947-50. Salesman Am. Greetings Co., Cleve., 1955-60; wage and salary analyst The Boeing Co., Seattle, 1960-69; dep. chmn. Rep. Nat. Com., Washington, 1969-80, dir. U.S. senate campaigns, 1980-81, dep. chmn., 1981-82; chmn. Bailey Polit. Consultants, Washington and Ogden, Utah, from 1982. Mem. Nat. Policy Forum Rep. Nat. Com., Washington, 1994-96; cons. Vietnam Meml. Fund, Washington, 1982; creator coll. degree program Am. Inst. Applied Politics, 1980, Utah State U., lecture series Politics=Power, 1996. Developer Sunset (Utah) city recreation programs, 1954-64; v.p. Jaycees, Sunset, 1955; mem. City Coun. Sunset, 1959, mayor, 1965. Recipient Leadership award Sunset Recreation Programs, 1961. Mem. Lds Ch. Avocation: collecting santa clauses. Home: Ogden, Utah. Died Feb. 20, 2002.

BAILLIE, CHARLES DOUGLAS, banker; b. Bklyn., Sept. 12, 1918; s. Charles Tupper and Nina (Vincent) B.; m. Helene Elizabeth Kuehn, Feb. 15, 1941 (dec. Apr. 1979); children— Barbara Ann (Mrs. John Roland Obenchain), Charles Douglas, Nancy Helene (Mrs. Michael Malke); m. Nancy Lee Anderson, Oct. 22, 1982. BSBA with distinction, Ind. U., 1940; cert. exec. program, UCLA, 1956. Pers. and credit supr. Continental Ill. Nat. Bank, Chgo., 1940-52; v.p. treas., dir. Nat. Discount Corp., South Bend, Ind., 1952-54; with United Calif. Bank, L.A., 1954-75, asst. v.p., 1955-56, v.p., 1956-68, sr. v.p., 1968-70, exec. v.p., 1970-75; v.p. Mfrs. Bank, L.A., 1975-78, sr. v.p., dir., 1978-81, Mitsui Mfrs. Bank, L.A., 1981-86, cons., 1986-89; ret., 1989. Bd. dirs. Mitsui Mfrs. Bank Found., 1981-86, San Marino Community Council, 1968-76, AID-United Givers, 1977-80, United Way Los Angeles County, 1980-86; councilman City of San Marino, 1972-76; trustee San Marino Community Ch. Served from ensign to lt. Supply Corps USNR, 1942-46. Mem. Am. Inst. Banking, UCLA Exec. Program Alumni Assn., I Men's Assn., Robert Morris Assos., Town Hall, Delta Sigma Pi, Phi Gamma Delta, Beta Gamma Sigma (dirs. table) Clubs: Rotarian, San Marino City (gov. 1979-80), San Gabriel (Calif.) Country. Died Nov. 17, 2002.

BAIRD, ROGER ALLEN, retired corporation executive; b. Canton, Ill., Mar. 14, 1914; s. Frederick R. and Ruth E. (Miller) B.; m. Evelyn F. Rittenhouse, July 29, 1939 (dec. Mar. 1988); children: Jane E., Ann R.; m. Darlene Petersen, June 15, 1990. AB, U. Chgo., 1936; JD, 1938. Bar: Ill. 1939, Wis. 1956. Assoc. later partner Kirkland, Ellis, Hodson, Chaffetz & Masters (and predecessors), Chgo., 1939-56; asst. sec., gen. atty. Kimberly Clark Corp., Neenah, Wis., 1956-59, sec., 1959-75; pres. Kimberly Clark Found., 1975-80. Mem. Wis. Govt. Com. of 25, 1963-65; adv. bd. Wis. Regional Med. Program, 1972-76; trustee Appleton Meml. Hosp., 1961-75, pres., 1966-68, chmn., 1969-75; bd. dirs. Area Health Planning Agy., 1971-80; bd. dirs. Wis. Health Policy Coun., 1976-88, vice chmn., 1980-88; bd. dirs. Nat. Coun. Aging, 1976-85, Wis. State Coun. on Econ. Edn., 1980-84, Fox Valley Cmty. Found. Com., 1985-94, v.p., 1986-89, chmn., 1989-91. With USNR, 1943-46. Mem. Ill. Bar Assn., Law Club (Chgo.), Legal Club (Chgo.), North Shore Golf Club, Crystal Downs Country Club (Frankfort Mich.), Phi Gamma Delta. Presbyterian. Home: Neenah, Wis. Deceased.

BAISLEY, CHARLES WILLIAM, lawyer; b. Peekskill, N.Y., Sept. 23, 1930; s. Charles T. and Katherine (Mahoney) B.; m. Jane Brunkow, June 15, 1957; children: Kathryne Jane, Ellen B. BS, Fordham U., 1952; JD, Tulane U., 1957; Cert., U. Barcelona, Spain. Bar: La. 1957, Calif. 1960, U.S. Supreme Ct. 1960, Tex. 1972. Atty. Humble Oil & Refinery Co., Tyler, Tex., 1957-59, L.A., 1959-64; counsel Creole Petroleum Co., Caracas, Venezuela, 1964-71; sr. negotiator Esso Exploration, Houston, 1971-74; asst. gen. counsel Creole Petroleum Co., Caracas, 1974-76; assoc. gen. counsel Esso Inter America, Coral Gables, Fla., 1976-86; sr. counsel Exxon Co. Internat., Florham Park, N.J., 1986-92, Exxon Exploration Co., Houston, 1992-95; atty. Internat. Petroleum Counsel, Sarasota, from 1995. Major USAR, 1952-54. Avocations: golf, travel. Home: Sarasota, Fla. Died Sept. 11, 2001.

BAJC, VICTOR LAWRENCE, mechanical engineer; b. Postojha, Slovenia, July 28, 1922; came to the U.S., 1925; s. Lawrence and Josephine Frances (Grzely) B.; m. Ann Elizabeth Sullivan, June 28,1 958; children: Gerald, David, Stephen, Jane. B in Mech. Engring., Ohio State U., 1949. Plant engr. Dasher Rubber & Chem. Co., Fairport Harbor, Ohio, 1949-59, v.p. mfg. and engring., 1959-61; sr. engr. B.F. Goodrich, Akron, Ohio, 1961-69, project mgr., 1969-84, ret., 1984. With U.S. Army, 1943-46. Mem. NSPE, ASME. Home: Naples, Fla. Died June 8, 2000.

BAKAL, CARL, writer, public affairs consultant, photojournalist; b. N.Y.C., Jan. 11, 1918; s. William and Esther (Tutelman) B.; m. Shirley Sesser, 1956; children: Stephanie, Emilie, Amy, Wendy. BS, CCNY, 1939; postgrad., Columbia, 1949. Advt. mgr. Fotoshop, N.Y.C., 1939-41; editor Fotoshop Almanac, 1939-41; assoc. editor, contbg. editor U.S. Camera, 1939-43; sales promotion mgr. Universal Camera Corp., 1941-43; editorial chief information control div. Mil. Govt., Germany, 1947-48; writer N.Y. Mirror, 1948-50; assoc. editor Coronet mag., N.Y.C., 1950-55; free-lance writer, photo-journalist, from 1955; editor Real, See mags., 1957-58; pub. affairs cons. U.S. Dept. Commerce, 1961-62; sr. assoc. Howard Chase Assos., N.Y.C., 1962-65; dir. mag. dept. Carl Byoir & Assocs., 1966-68; account supr. Anna M. Rosenberg Assocs., 1968-84; sr. v.p. Jack Raymond & Co., Inc., N.Y.C., 1984-86; pres. Carl Bakal Assocs., N.Y.C., 1986—2004. Guest lectr. photojournalism U. Wis., 1953 Author: Filter Manual, 1953, How to Shoot for Glamour, 1955, The Right to Bear Arms, 1966, No Right to Bear Arms, 1968, Charity U.S.A, 1979; contbr. articles and photographs to publs. including McCall's, Redbook, Life, Reader's Digest, Harper's, Town & Country, Esquire, Good Housekeeping; contbr. to Ency. Photography, 1942, Treasury of Tips for Writers, 1965, Tools of the Writer's Trade, 1990; photojournalism columnist Writers Digest.; travel editor Sylvia Porter's Personal Fin. mag., 1984-86. Served to 1st lt. AUS, 1942-46, 51-52. Recipient 1st prize Popular Photography $25,000 picture contest, 1956. Mem. Author's Guild, Violoncello Soc., P.E.N., Am. Soc. Journalists and Authors (v.p. 1968), Dutch Treat Club, Nat. Coun. for Responsible Firearms Policy (founder, v.p.). Died Mar. 18, 2004.

BAKER, ELOISE M. nursing administrator, critical care nurse; b. Aberdeen, S.D., Aug. 26, 1947; m. Everett Baker; children: Eugene, Michael, Patrick. Lic. practical nurse, Sioux Falls Sch. Practical, 1970; BA in Nursing, Augustana Coll., Sioux Falls, S.D., 1978; postgrad., S.D. State U., from 1991. RN, S.D. Staff nurse coronary ICU, St. Elizabeth Hosp., Utica, N.Y.; state nurse coronary ICU St. Joseph Hosp., Minot, N.D.; cardiology nurse North Cen. Heart Inc., Sioux Falls; staff nurse ICU, Sioux Valley Hosp., Sioux Falls, head nurse coronary ICU. Mem. Am. Orgn. Nurse Execs., S.D. Orgn. Nurse Execs. Home: Sioux Falls, SD. Died Jan. 18, 2001.

BAKER, ERNEST ERICH, lawyer; b. Schweinfurt, Germany, Feb. 16, 1947; came to U.S., 1951; s. Ernest Edwin and Lydia Anna (Schneider) B.; m. Patricia Dianne Strohm, Apr. 20, 1985. BA, U. Tenn., 1969; JD, Nashville Sch. Law, 1990. Bar: Tenn. 1990, U.S. Dist. Ct. (mid. and we. dists.) Tenn. 1992. Trial atty. Burson, Allyn & Martin, Memphis, from 1990. Mem. ABA, Tenn. Bar Assn., Memphis/Shelby County Bar Assn. Presbyterian. Avocations: hiking, writing, reading, computers. Home: Bartlett, Tenn. Died Aug. 31, 2001.

BAKER, JULIUS, musician; b. Cleve., Sept. 23, 1915; s. Max and Jeannette (Selznick) B.; m. Ruth Thorp, Mar. 28, 1961. Student, Eastman Sch. Music, Rochester, N.Y., 1932-33; diploma, Curtis Inst. Music, Phila., 1937. Mem. faculty Juilliard Sch. Music, N.Y.C., 1954—, Curtis Inst. Music, Phila. Mem. faculty Carnegie Mellon U., 1990-95. Mem. Cleve. Orch., 1937-41, 1st flutist, Pitts. Symphony, 1941-43, CBS Symphony, 1943-51, Chgo. Symphony, 1951-53, mem. Bach Aria Group, 1947-65, solo flutist N.Y. Philharm. Orch., 1965-83, solo appearances throughout U.S., Europe and Japan; rec. artist for Decca, Oxford, Vanguard, VAI and King records, Japan. Home: Brewster, NY. Died Aug. 6, 2003.

BAKER, LOUIS COOMBS WELLER, chemistry educator, researcher; b. N.Y.C., Nov. 24, 1921; s. F(rancis) Godfrey and Marion Georgina (Weller) B.; m. Violet Eva Simmons, June 28, 1964; children: William W.S., Godfrey A.S. AB, Columbia U., 1943; MS, U. Pa., 1947, PhD, 1950; LHD honoris causa, Georgetown U., 1988. Asst. instr. chemistry Towne Sci. Sch./U. Pa., Phila., 1943-50; instr. chemistry The College./U. Pa., 1945-50; assoc. in chemistry The Johnson Found./U. Pa., Phila., 1950-51; instr. Martin Coll. and Rittenhouse Coll., Phila., 1945-48; asst. prof. to assoc. prof., head inorganic divsn. Boston U., 1951-62; prof. chemistry Georgetown U., Washington, from 1962, chmn. chemistry dept., 1962-84. Co-project dir. OPRD high thermal efficiency engine project, N.Y.C. and Boundbrook, N.J., 1943-45; chmn. Internat. Symposium on Heteropoly Electrolytes, Am. Chem. Soc., 1956; chmn. Nat. Acad. Sci. Com. on Recommendations to U.S. Army for Basic Sci. Rsch., 1974-78; plenary lectr. Internat. Conf. Coordination Chemistry, Moscow, 1973; sci. mem. com. on accreditation Coll. and Univs. Middle States Assn. Coll. and Secondary Schs., sci. mem. vis. com. Ferdowsi U., Mashhad, Iran, 1974-75; spkr. Gordon Rsch. Confs., 1956, 67; cons. in field. Contbr. articles on inorganic chemistry to profl. jours.; co-inventor High Thermal Efficiency Internal Combustion Engine, 1943-45. Guggenheim fellow, 1961—; recipient Tchugaev medal in Inorganic Chemistry, USSR Acad. Scis., 1973; Vicennial Gold medal Georgetown U., 1983, Pres.'s medal Disting. Svc., 1984; grantee NSF, NIH, numerous others. Fellow Washington Acad. Scis.; mem. Am. Chem. Soc. (chmn. com. rev. inorganic papers 1957-59, councilor, bd. mgrs.), Cosmos Club (Washington), Sigma Xi (past pres. Georgetown chpt.). Mem. Soc. Of Friends. Home: South Hero, Vt. Died Apr. 15, 2003.

BAKER, WINTHROP PATTERSON, JR., broadcasting executive; b. N.Y.C., July 12, 1931; s. Winthrop Patterson and Josie Lou (Kendrick) B.; m. Elizabeth Muriel Allegret, July 30, 1955; children: Winthrop Patterson III, John Adams, Michael Kendrick. Student, Vanderbilt U., 1952; BS in Bus. Adminstrn., La. State U., 1953. Dir. Sta. WJMR-TV, New Orleans, 1954-55; producer, dir. Sta. WBRZ-TV, Baton Rouge, 1955-56; program dir. Sta. KLFY-TV, Lafayette, La., 1956-57, Sta. WMBD-TV, Peoria, Ill., 1957-60; asst. program mgr. Sta. WBZ-TV, Boston, 1960-61; program mgr. Sta. WJZ-TV, Balt., 1962-65, Sta. KYW-TV, Phila., 1965-67; asst. gen. mgr. Sta. KDKA-TV, Pitts., 1967; gen. mgr. Sta. WBZ-TV, Boston, 1968-73, v.p., 1970-73; pres. Westinghouse Broadcasting Co., N.Y.C., 1973-79, corp. v.p., dir., 1974-79; dir. TV Advt. Reps., N.Y.C., 1969-79; pres. P.M. Mag. Inc. subs. Westinghouse Broadcasting Co., 1978-79; exec. v.p., dir., gen. mgr. New Eng. TV Co., Boston, 1979-81, 82; pres. Gen. Electric Broadcasting and Cablevision Co., Fairfield, Conn., 1981-82; pres., dir., gen. mgr. Sta. WNEV-TV, Boston, 1982-84; pres. Target Two, Inc., Wilton; gen. ptnr. William Street Ptnrs., Westport, Conn. Mem. Boston Youth Activities Commn., Boston, 1970-71; adv. com. U.S. Youth Games, 1971; mem. Gov.'s Commn. on Ednl. Reorgn., 1972-73; bd. dirs., vice-chmn. Boston Community Media Com., 1970-73; bd. dirs. Intercom, Boston, 1970-73, Consumer-care Council, 1970-71; mem. adv. bd. broadcasting and communications curriculum U. Pa. Wharton Sch. Bus., 1978-79, Mercer (N.J.) Community Coll., 1978-79. Mem. Am. Advt. Fedn. (dir. 1974-79), Nat. Assn. TV Program Execs., New Eng. Broadcast Assn., Mass. Broadcasters Assn. (v.p. dir. 1970-71), Mass. Audubon Soc., De Cordova Mus., Phi Kappa Phi, Mu Sigma Rho, Phi Eta Sigma, Pi Tau Pi, Beta Gamma Sigma. Died June 7, 2003.

BALDWIN, GARZA, JR., lawyer, manufacturing company executive; b. Litchfield, Ill., Mar. 10, 1921; s. Garza and Hazel (Satterlee) B.; m. Margaret Jean Skinner, Sept. 7, 1946; children: Deborah Baldwin Lyman, Garza III, Beth Baldwin Johnson, Daniel David, Benjamin Willis. Student, Vincennes U., 1938-39; BS, Ind. U., 1942, JD with high distinction, 1948. Bar: Ind. 1948, U.S. Supreme Ct. 1956, N.C. 1959. Practiced in, Indpls., Sullivan, Ind., 1948-57; city atty. Sullivan, 1951-55; asso. counsel Olin Corp., Pisgah Forest, N.C., 1957-58, div. counsel, 1958-63, sr. counsel, 1963-69, v.p., counsel fine paper and film group, 1969, v.p. corp. group fine paper and film, 1969-71, pres. group, 1971-85, v.p. parent co., 1969-85; pres., chief exec. officer Ecusta Corp., 1985-87. Bd. mgrs. Wachovia Bank & Trust Co., Asheville, N.C., 1969-90; mem. Gov.'s Council for Econ. Devel., 1967-68, Gov.'s Efficiency Study Commn., 1973-74, N.C. Council on State Policies and Goals, 1974-78; mem. Gov.'s Bus. Council on Arts and Humanities, 1981-89; bd. dirs. N.C. Citizens for Bus. and Industry, 1970-92, v.p., 1972-73, chmn., 1974-75; bd. dirs. Ednl. Found. Commerce and Industry N.C., 1965-73, U. N.C. at Asheville Found., 1971-90, N.C. Engring. Found. Trustee Transylvania Cmty. Hosp., Brevard, N.C., 1969-83, Brevard Coll., 1978-86, St. Andrews Presbyn. Coll., Laurinburg, N.C., 1978-81, U. N.C., Asheville, 1974-77, N.C. Sch. Sci. and Math., 1985-91; chmn. bd. dirs. Mem. Mission Med. Ctr., Asheville, 1986, treas., 1989-93, bd. dirs., 1981-95; mem. adv. coun. to dean Sch. Bus. Ind. U.; mem. acad. alumni fellows Ind. U.; bd. dirs. Cmty. Found. Western N.C., 1990-96, Asheville chpt. ARC, 1990-95. Lt. (j.g.) USNR, 1942-45. Mem. ABA, Ind. Bar Assn., N.C. Bar Assn., Western Carolina Mfrs. Assn. (pres. 1962-71), N.C. Indsl. Coun. (pres. 1966-67), Am. Judicature Soc., Am. Legion, Order of Coif, Masons (32 degree), Elks, Biltmore Forest Country Club, Colleton River Country Club (Bluffton, S.C.), 1st City Club (Savannah). Republican. Presbyterian. Home: Bluffton, SC. Died Mar. 15, 2003.

BALL, ROSAMUND ANN, secondary school educator; b. Charleston, W.Va., Jan. 30, 1945; d. James Andrew and Beatrice (Smith) B. BA in Secondary Edn., Shepherd Coll., 1968. Cert. secondary edn. in history, govt., English; cert. reading specialist, Pa. Tchr. secondary edn. Chambersburg (Pa.) Area Sch. Dist., from 1969. Editor: The Obstetrical Records of Dr. A.A. Biggs, 1994, Cemetery, Death, and Miscellaneous Records from Hagerstown, Md., 1994, The Records of Rev. John Alex Adams of Sharpsburg, Md., 1994, Antietam National Cemetery Payroll Book, 1866-1867, 1994, The Letters of Thomas A. Boult, 1995, The Records of Dr. Augustin A. Biggs, vol. 1-36, 1996; author: Index to the Records of the Lutheran Churches in the Sharpsburg, Md. Area, 1989, Index to the History of Boonsboro, Md., 1991, Index to the Letters of Jacob Miller, 1995, Index for Register of Persons Who Have Died in Sharpsburg, Md. and Surrounding Neighborhoods, 1995, Index to the Atlas of Washington County, Md., 1877, 1995, Washington County, Md. Jury List, 1877, 1996. Recipient 5-Yr. Vol. Svc. award Washington County Free Libr., 1995. Mem. Huguenot Soc. Md. Democrat. Avocations: genealogical research, women's spirituality studies, cooking, cats. Home: Ivydale, W.Va. Died Feb. 21, 2001.

BALLAM, SAMUEL HUMES, JR., retired corporate director; b. Phila., Apr. 12, 1919; s. Samuel Humes and Mary (McGarvey) B.; m. Dorothy Meadowcroft (dec. 2001), May 1, 1943; children— Barbara J. Ballam Stephens, Samuel H., III AB, U. Pa., 1950; A.M.P., Harvard Bus. Sch., 1959. Fin. analyst Fidelity Bank, Phila., 1936-41, 46-48, investment officer, 1948-55, asst. to pres., 1955-56, v.p. br. system, 1956-60, sr. v.p. trust dept., 1960-66, exec. v.p. comml. dept., 1966-71; pres. Fidelcor, Inc., Phila., 1971-78, chief exec. officer, 1975-78; chmn. Am. Water Works Co., Inc., 1985-88. Dir. numerous corps. Emeritus trustee U. Pa., Phila., 1970-2003; chmn. bd. dirs. Hosp. U. Pa., 1972-87; bd. dirs. Zool. Soc. Phila., Balch Inst. for Ethnic Studies, Phila., Geog. Soc. Phila., 1976-79. Capt. USAF, 1951-52. Mem.: Union League (v.p., dir.), Merion Cricket. Republican. Episcopalian. Avocations: tennis, photography. Home: Bryn Mawr, Pa. Died Nov. 13, 2003.

BALLEISEN, DONALD HERBERT, lawyer; b. Bklyn., Dec. 17, 1924; s. Leopold Lyon and Pauline (Littauer) B.; m. Carolyn Susan Kimmelfield, June 1, 1960; children: Ellen, Wendy M. Finger, Edward. AB, Princeton U., 1948; JD, Harvard U., 1951. Bar: N.Y. 1951, Ky. 1969, U.S. Supreme Ct. 1978. Assoc. Conboy Hewitt O'Brien & Boardman, N.Y.C., 1951-56, Kaye, Scholer, Fierman, Hays & Handler, N.Y.C., 1956-60; sr. atty. Am. Standard Inc., N.Y.C., 1960-62; sec., gen. counsel Penick & Ford Ltd., N.Y.C., 1962-69; ptnr. Greenebaum Doll & McDonald, Louisville, 1969-86; counsel Tilford Dobbins Alexander & Buckaway, Louisville, 1986-88; ptnr., from 1988. Trustee Lincoln Found., Louisville, 1987—, chmn. 1991—. With USN, 1944-46. Mem. ABA, Ky. Bar Assn., Louisville Bar Assn., Assn. of Bar of City of N.Y. Home: Louisville, Ky. Deceased.

BAMBARA, TONI CADE, writer, educator; b. N.Y.C., Mar. 25, 1939; BA in Theatre Arts, Queens Coll., 1959; MA in Am. Lit., CCNY, 1965; postgrad., SUNY, Buffalo; LittD (hon.), SUNY, Albany, 1990; LHD (hon.), Denison U., 1993. Family and youth case worker N.Y. Dept. Welfare, 1959-61; dir. recreation Met. Hosp. Psychiat. Divsn., 1961-62; program dir. Colony Settlement House, 1962-65; artists in resident Spellman Coll., 1978-79, Neighborhood Arts Ctr., 1975-79, Stephens Coll., 1976; instr. SEEK program City Coll., 1965-69; rsch. mentor and instr. Sch. Social Work Atlanta U., 1977, 79; asst. prof. English Rutgers U., 1969-74; instr. Scribe Video Ctr., Phila., from 1986. Arts cons. The Black Arts South Conf., 1981, Ga. State Arts Coun., 1976, 81, N.Y. State Arts Coun., 1974, NEA, 1980; humanities cons. Emory U. Inst. Lang. Arts, 1980, N.Y. Inst. for Human Svcs. Tng., 1978, N.J. Dept. Corrections, 1974; vis. prof. Afro-Am. Studies, Duke U., 1975, Atlanta U., 1977; writer, lectr. storyteller, cons. in lit., cinema, prodn., and curricula; mem. adv. bd. Black Cinemateque, Atlanta, Nat. Black Programming Consortium, Ohio, Internat. Black Cinema, Berlin/N.Y., Essence Mag.; writer, narrator for Louis Massiahs series on Dr. W.E.B. DuBois, Scribe Prodns., 1993; narrator John Akumfrah's documentary Seven Songs of Malcolm, Black Film Audio Collective, 1993, Nadine Patterson documentary on Anna Russell Jone, Patterson Prodns., 1993, others; writer various workshops; lectr. in field. Author: The Black Woman, 1970, Tales and Short Stories for Black Folk, 1971, Gorilla My Love, 1972, The Seabirds are Still Alive, 1977, The Salt Eaters, 1980 (Am. Book award The Before Columbus Found. 1981); author short stories in anthologies include Breaking the Ice, 1990, A Century of the Best Black American Stories, 1993, Before Columbus Foundation Fictions Anthology, 1992, Calling the Wind, 1993, Swords Into Plowshares: A Home Front Anthology, 1992, Daughters of Africa: An International Anthology, 1992, Confirmations, 1985, Afro-American Writers, 1983, Women Working, 1982, others; contbr. articles and short stories to profl. jours. Recipient Peter Pauper Press award in Journalism, L.I. Star, 1959, Svc. awards from Nat. Assn. Negro Bus. and Profl. Women's League, Black Child Devel. Inst., Livingston Students of Rutgers U., Harlem Triangle Tenants Assn., Kaleidoscope Summer Inst. U. Mo., Arts award Afro-Am. Heritage Collection, Ebony mag., Encore mag., Sta. WETV, George Washington Carver Disting. African-Am. Lectr. award Simpson Coll., 1979, award Langston Hughes Soc., 1981, Zora Neale Hurston Soc., 1986; grantee NEA, 1981. Home: Philadelphia, Pa. Died in 1995.

BANZER SUAREZ, HUGO, president; b. Concepción, Bolivia, May 10, 1926; Degree, Army Mil. Sch., La Paz, Bolivia, Mil. Sch. Argentine Republic, Buenos Aires, Sch. Arms Instrn., Sch. of High Command of Bolivian Army, Armored Sch. of U.S.A., Sch. of Nat. Superior Studies of Bolivia. Mil. prof.; chief high command, dep. comdr. divsn.; chief intelligence dept. Bolivian Army, comdr. mil. sch.; comdr.-in-chief Armed Forces of Bolivia; mil. attaché Embassy of Bolivia to U.S.; minister of edn. Govt. Bolivia, 1964-66; pres. Republic of Bolivia, 1971—78, 1997—2001; amb. of Bolivia Argentine Republic, 1978-97. Founder, chmn. Nat. Dem. Action Party, Bolivia, 1979, presdl. cand., 1980, 85, 89, 93, 97; pres. Polit. Coun. Patriotic Alliance, 1989. Recipient Gold medal Mayor's Office of Sucre, Bolivia, Gold medal Ret. Magistery, merit excellence medal, Guerrilleros Lanza medal, El Cóndor de los Andes award Govt. Bolivia, Army Mil. Merit medal, U.S.; decorated Govts. Argentina, Brazil, Colombia, Ecuador, Panama, Paraguay, Peru, Uruguay, Venezuela. Died May 5, 2002.

BARBERA, HENRY RAYMOND, sociology educator; b. N.Y.C., Dec. 21, 1929; PhD, Columbia U., 1971. Prof. City Coll., N.Y.C., 1971-82, U. Calif., Irvine, 1983-96. Author: Rich Nations and Poor in Peace and War, 1973, Medieval Sicily: The First Absolute State, 1994, The Military Factor in Social Change, 1998, From Provincial to Political Society, 1988, The State as Revolution, 1997; co-editor newsletter Sicilia Parra, 1980—. Mem. Am. Socio. Assn., Am. Polit. Sci. Assn., Patrons of Italian Culture (pres. 1992-97). Avocations: cooking, hiking. Home: San Marino, Calif. Died Sept. 24, 2000.

BARBIERI, FEDORA, vocalist; b. Trieste, Italy, June 4, 1919; Operatic debut as Fidalma in Cimarosa's The Secret Marriage, Teatro Comunale, Florence, Italy, 1940; appears at La Scala, Milan, 1942—, Teatro Colón, Buenos Aires, 1947—, Met. Opera House, N.Y.C., Royal Opera House, Covent Garden, London, 1950—; recordings include Aida, Il Trovatore, Requiem, Falstaff, Maschera, La Gioconda, La Favorita, others. Scholar Teatro Lirico, 1940. Died Mar. 6, 2003.

BARCHAM, JULIUS, physician; b. N.Y.C., Nov. 1, 1914; MD, U. Lausanne, 1941. Diplomate Am. Bd. Anesthesiology. Intern Harlem Hosp., N.Y.C.; resident in anesthesiology Mt. Sinai Hosp., N.Y.C. Fellow Am. Coll. Anesthesiologists; mem. AMA, Am. Soc. Anesthesiology. Home: Tamarac, Fla. Died Feb. 26, 2002.

BARE, JOSEPH LEE, retired microbiologist; b. San Angelo, Tex., Sept. 12, 1941; s. Leslie Thompson and June Grace (Tremble) B.; m. Betty Ann Dusek, Sept. 10, 1963; children: Joseph Lee II, Michael Edward. BA in Math., U. Tex., 1969, postgrad., 1975-79. Cert. clin. microbiologist. Lab. technician Tex. Dept. Health, Austin, 1963-69, microbiologist, 1969-82, chief of environ. microbiology, 1982-95, supr. lab. cert. br., 1995-98. State milk, water, shellfish certification officer Tex. Dept. Health, Austin, 1982-98. Mem. Am. Soc. Clin. Pathologists, Tex. Assn. Milk, Food and Environ. Sanitarians, Am. Waterworks Assn. Home: Rowena, Tex. Died Sept. 3, 2001.

BAREWIN, RALPH R. chemical company executive; b. Hastings, Nebr., Nov. 19, 1915; s. Samuel Phillip and Anna Rose (Sudarsky) B.; m. Gertrude Hoffman, Dec. 3, 1939; children: Barbara Barewin Riley, Deborah Shari Barewin Mullen. BA, Roosevelt U.; M in Social Services, Jane Adams. V.p. Barco Chem. Products, Inc., Chgo., 1932-44, Bar-Win Tool Supply Co., Inc., Chgo., 1946-47; pres. Barco Chem. Products, Inc., Chgo., from 1947. Mem. U.S. SBA, Am. Tech. Soc. Home: Reston, Va. Died June 28, 2001.

BAR-ILLAN, DAVID JACOB, concert pianist; b. Haifa, Israel, Feb. 7, 1930; arrived in U.S., 1954, naturalized, 1967; s. Aaron and Zilla (Beilin) Bar-Illan; m. Beverly Slater Bar-Illan, Mar. 3, 1969; children: Kim, Daniela, Jeremy. Diploma, Juilliard Sch. Music, 1950. Artist-in-residence Coll. Conservatory Music, U. Cin., 1975. Debut Carnegie Hall, 1954, N.Y. Philharm., 1960, soloist major orchs. in Europe, Israel, U.S. and, Latin Am., 1960, recitalist throughout world. Served with Israeli Army, 1948. Recipient N.Y. Liberty medal, 1986. Died Nov. 4, 2003.

BARKER, ROBERT RANKIN, corporate executive; b. Brookline, Mass., July 12, 1915; s. James Madison and Margaret (Rankin) B.; m. Elizabeth VanDyke Shelly, Mar. 7, 1942; children: James Robertson, Ann Shelly, William

Benjamin, Margaret Welch. AB magna cum laude, Harvard U., 1936. With investment and credit analysis adv. depts. J.P. Morgan & Co., 1936-49; with Wm. A.M. Burden & Co., N.Y.C., 1949-78, gen. ptnr., 1954-78, Barker, Lee & Co., N.Y.C., from 1973. Spl. asst. to asst. sec. commerce for air U.S. Dept. Commerce, 1942-43; past chmn. adv. com. endowment mgmt. Ford Found. Past trustee Am. Geog. Soc., New Canaan Country Sch., pres., Am. Farm Sch. Thessaloniki, Greece, Silvermine Guild Artists, New Canaan Libr., Mus. Modern Art, Hudson Inst.; trustee Am. Mus. Natural History, J.M.R. Barker Found., Atlantic Salmon Fedn.; past mem. bd. overseers Harvard U., pres. Officer USNR, 1943-46. Mem. Coun. Fgn. Rels., N.Y. Social Security Analysts, Phi Beta Kappa, Anglers Club, Univ. Club, Harvard Club, Brook Club, Mill Reef Club, Tabusintac, Century Club (N.Y.C.). Home: New Canaan, Conn. Died Nov. 8, 2002.

BARNATHAN, JULIUS, broadcasting company executive; b. N.Y.C., Jan. 22, 1927; s. Elias L. and Julia (Amado) B.; m. Lorraine Glogower, Jan. 13, 1952; children: Joyce Linda, Daniel Elias, Jacqueline Frances. BA, Bklyn. Coll., 1951; MA in Math. Statistics, Columbia, 1955; DSc (hon.), Gallaudet Coll., 1982. Actuarial asst. Nat. Council for Compensation Ins., 1951-52; dir. media research, statis. analyst Kenyon & Eckhardt, 1952-54; with ABC, 1954—, dir. research, 1957-59, v.p., 1959, v.p. affiliated stas., 1959-62, pres. owned TV stas., 1962, v.p., gen. mgr. TV network, 1962-65, v.p. broadcast ops. and engring., 1965-76; pres. broadcast ops. and engring. Capital Cities/ABC Inc (formerly ABC), 1976-89, sr. v.p. tech. and strategic planning, 1989-92; TV cons., from 1992. Pres. Bklyn. Coll. Bur. Econ. Research, 1949-50. Broadcast engr. for 9 Olympic Games (Emmy awards 1968, 72, 76, 84, 88; award ATAS, 1995). Served with USNR, 1944-46. Recipient Spl. Commendation award Soc. Motion Picture and TV Engrs., 1978, Engring. award Nat. Assn. Broadcasters, 1982, Trustees award for devel. of Closed Captioned for the Hearing Impaired Nat. Acad. TV Arts and Scis., 1994, TV Emmy Contbns. to TV Tech., 1994, Lifetime Achievement award, 1995; named to Broadcast and Cable Hall of Fame, 1994. Mem. NATAS (internat. coun., Spl. award 1994), Nat. Captioning Inst. (bd. dirs.), N.Am. Nat. Broadcasters Assn. (v.p.), Phi Beta Kappa, Pi Mu Epsilon. Home: Roslyn, NY. Died Dec. 1, 1997.

BARNES, EMILY ANN COODY, retired community health nurse; b. Bleckley County, Ga., Jan. 30, 1928; d. Rufus W. and Beulah Katherine (Simmons) Coody; m. Robert O. Barnes Jr., May 10, 1952 (dec.); children: Cynthia Ann Barnes Hutchins, Robert Woody. Diploma, St. Joseph's Sch. of Nursing, Savannah, Ga., 1951; student, Mid. Ga. Coll., 1957, Ga. Southwestern Coll., 1978. Head nurse Carl Vinson Med. Ctr., Dublin, Ga.; from sr. to lead nurse South Cen. Health Dist., Dublin, ret.; owner Cindy's Place for Ladies Apparel, Cochran, Ga. Home: Cochran, Ga. Died June 1, 2000.

BARNES, LINDA ERNESTINE, automotive company executive, consultant; b. Cleve., Jan. 18, 1951; d. Frank and Helen Ernestine (White) Roberts; m. Wallace Marvin Barnes Jr., Aug. 14, 1976; 1 child, Courtney Ernestine. Student, Fisk U., 1969-71, Cugahoga Community Coll., 1971-73; BA in psychology, Kent State U., 1975. Mgr. W.M.B. Assocs., Cleve., from 1975, LTM Auto Clinic, Cleve., from 1975. Mgr. Marco Assocs. Architects and Engrs., Cleve., 1976-79; field underwriter N.Y. Life, Cleve., 1978-81; ins. cons. Protected Home Mutual, Cleve., 1981-85. Vol. YWCA; active Underwriters Polit. Action Com. Recipient Vol. award Cleve. Bd. Edn., 1986. Mem. Millionaires Club, Delta Sigma Theta. Republican. Avocations: swimming, tennis, golf. Home: Cleveland, Ohio. Deceased.

BARNES, RAMONA, state legislator; b. Pikeville, Tenn., July 7, 1938; d. Ellison Wheeler; m. Larry Barnes, 1960; children: Randall, Michael, Michelle. Attended, Mich. State Coll., Waipahu C.C., Hawaii. Pres. Arctic Rsch. Cons. Internat.; mem. Alaska Ho. of Reps., 1978—2000, speaker, 1993—2000. Majority leader, spkr. pro tem, 1983-84; minority whip, 1991-92; minority leader, 1992; former chmn. judiciary com.; former mem. numerous coms. Mem. sch. bd. City of Elmendorf, Alaska, 1973-76; mem. adv. sch. bd. City of Anchorage, Alaska, 1975-76, now precinct committeewoman; del. Alaska Rep. State Conv., 1976, 78. Recipient Appreciation award Alaska Peace Ofcl. Assn., 1982, Appreciation cert. Anchorage Cmty. Mental Health Svcs., 1983-85, Am. Outstanding Legislator award Am. Exch. Coun., 1984; named Legislator of Yr., Alaska Sportsmen's Coun. and Nat. Wildlife Fedn., 1980, 81. Mem. Anchorage Rep. Women's Club, Nat. Fedn. Rep. Women, Navy League, Bus. and Profl. Women's Club, Am. Legis. Exch. Coun., Nat. Order Women Legislators. Mem. Ch. of Christ. Home: Anchorage, Alaska. Died Nov. 26, 2003.

BARNES, WALTER CARLYLE, JR., retired surgeon, medical director; b. Rutherford, N.C., May 25, 1922; s. Walter Carlyle and Mildred Elizabeth (Piehoff) B.; m. Pauline Ruth Lehman, May 25, 1948; children: Walter III, Abigail. BS, U. N.C., 1944; MD, Temple U., 1948. Diplomate Am. Bd. Surgery, Am. Coll. Surgery. Rotating intern Watts Hosp., U. N.C., Durham, 1948-49; resident in surgery Erlanger Regional Med. Ctr., Chattanooga, 1949-54; Horsley fellow St. Elizabeth Hosp., Richmond, Va., 1954-55; chief surgeon Southern Clinic, Texarkana, Ark., 1955-88; med. dir. St. Michael Hosp., Texarkana, 1988-92, ret., 1993. Contbr. articles to profl. jours. Pres. Tex. Regional Arts and Humanities Coun., Texarkana, 1987-88, Caddo coun. Boy Scouts Am., 1978; gov. bd. Texarkana Coll., 1984—. With U.S. Army, 1951-53, PTO. Fellow ACS, Southwestern Surg. Soc. (vice councilor 1970), Tex. Surg. Soc.; mem. AMA, Tex. Med. Assn. (mem. bd. councilors 1960-70), Royal Acad. Medicine, Rotary. Methodist. Avocations: hunting, gardening. Home: Texarkana, Tex. Died Mar. 27, 2001.

BARNES, ZANE EDISON, communications company executive; b. Marietta, Ohio, Dec. 2, 1921; s. Emmett A. and Frances (Canfield) B.; children: Frances, Zane Edison, Shelley Barnes Donaho; m. Lu L. Millis, Sept. 1990. BS, Marietta Coll., 1947, LLD (hon.), 1985, Okla. Christian Coll., 1980, Washington U., St. Louis, 1990. With Ohio Bell Telephone Co., 1941-60, asst. v.p. exec. ops., 1961-63, gen. plant mgr., 1963-64, v.p. pers., 1965-67; with engring. dept. AT&T, N.Y.C., 1960-61; v.p., gen. mgr. Pacific N.W. Bell Telephone Co., Portland, 1964-65, v.p. ops. Seattle, 1967-70, pres., 1970-73, Southwestern Bell Telephone Co., St. Louis, 1973-74, pres., chief exec. officer, 1974-86; chmn. bd., pres., CEO SBC Comm. Inc., St. Louis, 1983-88, chmn. bd., CEO, 1988-89; ret., 1990. Dir. emeritus SBC Comm. Inc. Life assoc. trustee Marietta Coll.; mem. vets. affairs adv. bd. The Stars and Stripes. Recipient Americanism award Anti-Defamation League of B'nai B'rith, 1980, Man of Yr. award St. Louis Globe-Dems., 1981, Levee Stone award Downtown St. Louis, Inc., 1984, Man of Yr. award St. Louis Variety Club, 1985, Search award William Greenleaf Eliot Soc. of Washington U., 1985, Leadership award St. Louis PRIDE orgn., 1988 Died Jan. 9, 2004.

BARNETT, HENRY LEWIS, pediatrician, medical educator; b. Detroit, June 25, 1914; s. Lewis and Florence (Marx) B.; m. Shirley Blanchard, Oct. 19, 1940; children— Judith Florence, Martin David. Student, Dartmouth Coll., 1931-32; BS, MD, Washington U., St. Louis, 1938; DSc (hon.), Yeshiva U., 1995. Instr. dept. pediatrics Washington U. Sch. Medicine, 1941-43; asst. prof. dept. pediatrics Cornell U. Med. Coll., 1946-50; asso. prof., 1950-55; prof., chmn. dept. pediatrics Albert Einstein Coll. Medicine, 1955-72, asso. dean clin. affairs, 1970-72, Univ. prof., 1972-81, prof. emeritus, 1981—; dir. pediatric service Bronx Municipal Hosp. Center, 1955-64; dir. Internat. Study Kidney Disease in Children, 1967-81; med. dir. Children's Aid Soc., 1981-97. Cons. Appleton-Century-Crofts, 1981-83; Mem. WHO Infant Metabolism Team to, Netherlands and Sweden, 1950, WHO Sci. Group Pediatric Rsch., 1967; adv. bd. Internat. Pediatric Assn., 1969-74; cons. Cento Meeting Pediatric Edn. and Family Planning, Ankara, Turkey, 1972, Nat.Inst. Child Health and Human Devel., 1974-85; mem. bd. on maternal, child, and family health rsch. NRC, 1974-82; mem. coun. Found. for Child Devel., 1966—; chmn. med. adv. bd. Am. Council for Emigrees in Professions, 1974-83; trustee, mem. med. adv. com. Children's Aid Soc., 1977-81; Felton Bequests vis. prof. Royal Children's Hosp., Melbourne, Australia, 1978; cons. Asian Study Renal Disease in Children, 1978-81 Contbr. articles to profl. jours.; Editor: Pediatrics, 13th-17th edits. Served to capt. M.C. AUS, 1943-46. Recipient Trustee award Children's Aid Soc., 1992, Charles Loring Brace Disting. Svc. medal, 1999. Fellow Am. Acad. Pediatrics (E. Mead Johnson award 1949, Kidney award 1992); mem. N.Y. Acad. Sci., Inst. Medicine NAS, AAAS, Soc. Pediatric Rsch. (pres. 1959-60), Soc. Exptl. Biology and Medicine, Harvey Soc., Am. Pediatric Soc. (pres. 1981-82, John Howland award and medal 1984), Am. Soc. Clin. Investigation, Assn. Am. Physicians, Am. Soc. Nephrology (John P. Peters award 1988), Brit. Pediatric Soc. (hon.), Am. Physiol. Soc., N.Y. Acad. Medicine, Nat. Turkish Pediatric Assn. (hon.), Societe Francaise de Pediatre (corr.), Royal Coll. Pediatrics and Child Health (hon.), Sigma Xi, Alpha Omega Alpha. Home: New York, NY. Deceased.

BARON, HAZEN JAY, dental scientist; b. Detroit, Mar. 12, 1934; s. Hazen Cornelius and Lauretta (Schoenfeld) B.; m. Julie Christine Enders, Nov. 26, 1953; children: Hazen Lawrence, Melvin Philip. BS, Wayne State U., 1954; DDS, Northwestern U., 1958, PhD, 1968. Pvt. practice gen. dentistry, Waukegan, Ill., 1959-62; lctr. Northwestern Dental Sch., Chgo., 1962-64; asst. dir. Warner Lambert Co., Morris Plains, N.J., 1964-69, dir., 1969-80, Johnson and Johnson, New Brunswick, N.J., 1980-87, v.p., 1987-91; freelance cons. Morristown, from 1991-. Mgt. bd. Johnson and Johnson, New Brunswick, 1987-89; trustee advisor Am. Fund Dental Health, Chgo., 1988-90; vis. com. Northwestern Dental Sch., Chgo., 1987-91. Editor: Tri-County Dental Soc., 1965-69; co-author: Oral Pathology, 1965; contrb. articles to profl. jours. Rsch. fellow NIH, 1959-62. Fellow Am. Acad. Oral Pathology; mem. Am. Acad. Periodontology, Internat. Assn. for Dental Rsch. Died Aug. 2, 2001.

BARON, JUDSON RICHARD, aerospace educator; b. N.Y.C., July 28, 1924; s. Louis and Leah (Berzin) B.; m. Selma Francine Wasserman, Sept. 4, 1949; children— Jason Roberts, Jeffrey Scott. B.Aero. Engring., NYU, 1947; SM, MIT, 1948, ScD, 1956. Registered profl. engr., Mass. Stress analyst Chance Vought Aircraft Co., 1947; mem. research staff MIT, 1948-54, research asst., 1954-56, mem. faculty, 1957—89, prof. aeros. and astronautics, 1957-89, prof. emeritus, sr. lectr., 1989-2000; cons. in field, 1957—2003. Mem. Air Force Sci. Adv. Bd., 1987-91. With AUS, 1943-46. Decorated Bronze Star; recipient Exceptional Civilian Svc. award. Dept. Air Force, 1991. Fellow AIAA (assoc. editor jour. 1989-96), Sigma Xi, Tau Beta Pi, Gamma Alpha Rho. Home: Lexington, Mass. Died Oct. 6, 2003.

BARON, NICHOLAS BRZOVIC, psychologist, educator, art appraiser; b. Braslewitz, Austria, Sept. 16, 1911; m. Katherine Baron, 1964; 1 child. BTh, Theological Coll., Srem Karlowitz, 1938; PhD, U. Marburg, Germany, 1947. Pvt. practice, from 1949; founder Jan Hus U., Scottsdale, Ariz., 1969, pres., prof. psychology, counselor, from 1972. Lectr. parapsychology, art and humanity; rebuilder destroyed churches and monasteries, 1949—. V.p., counselor Morning Star Found., 1975—, New Age Found., 1975—; supporter numerous charitable orgns. including Asian Relief Inc., Omaha Home for Boys and St. Labre Indian Sch. Named Serbian Ortodox Patriarch, Belgrade, 1976, Mitropolitain of Zagreb, 1976, Serbian Bishop, Karlovac, 1974. Mem. Am. Art Soc. (bd. dirs. 1972), Idaho Archaeologist, Congrl. Club. Avocations: callisthenics, swimming, exploring Indian culture in Ariz. and Mex. Home: Scottsdale, Ariz. Died Nov. 7, 1999.

BARR, JAMES C. property management executive; b. Tex., Aug. 6, 1915; s. James E. and Gladys (Perry) B.; m. Wanda J. Stockton, Oct. 1938; children: James C. Jr. and Linda Lee Barr Zahn. Draftman Lauritzen Makin Planning Mill, Ft. Worth, 1935-36; teller First Nat. Bank, Ft. Worth, 1936-42; ind. gen. contractor Ft. Worth, 1946-65; pres. Island Mgmt. Corp., Port Aransas, Tex., from 1965, Mustang Investment Corp., Port Aransas, from 1965. Cons. Beachhead Condominium, Port Aransas, 1989-94, Sea Isle Village, Port Aransas, 1990-94. Mayor City of Port Aransas, 1988-94; chmn. Nueces County Pk. Bd., 1967-88; mem. Port Aransas Planning Commn., 1975-77. 1st lt. USAF, 1942-46. Recipient Hospitality award State of Tex., 1986; award recipient Nueces County Sheriff's Dept., 1992, Tex. Alcohol Beverage Commn., 1992; named hon. fleet admiral Tex. State Hwy. Dept., 1993. Mem. Port Aransas C. of C. (pres. 1985-87), Rotary (Paul Harris fellow). Methodist. Avocation: fishing. Home: Port Aransas, Tex. Deceased.

BARRATT, RAYMOND WILLIAM, biologist, educator; b. Holyoke, Mass., May 4, 1920; s. George A. and Elizabeth (Bretschneider) B.; m. Helen Ruggles, July 1943 (div. 1968); children: Marguerite E., William R.; m. Barbara H. Kellerup, Oct. 16, 1971. B.Sc., Rutgers U., 1941; M.Sc., U. N.H., 1943; PhD, Yale, 1948; MA (hon.), Dartmouth, 1958. Asst. plant pathology and horticulture U. N.H., 1943-44; rsch. assoc., asst. plant pathologist Conn. Agrl. Expt. Sta., 1944-45; rsch. assoc. biology Stanford (Calif.) U., 1948-53, rsch. biologist, acting asst. prof., 1953-54; mem. faculty Dartmouth Coll., 1954-70, prof. botany, 1958-62, prof. biology, 1962-70, chmn. dept., 1965-69, lectr. microbiology Med. Sch., 1962-70; prof. biology Humboldt State U., 1970-92, dean sci., 1970-84. Mem. vis. staff Vt. Environ. Center, Ripton, summers 1970, 71; dir. Fungal Genetics Stock Ctr., 1970-85. Mem. Hanover Sch. Bd., 1964-68; mem. Dresden (N.H.) Sch. Bd., 1964-68, chmn., 1968. Mem. Genetics Soc. Am. (chmn. com. maintenance genetic stocks 1964-68), Sigma Xi, Alpha Zeta, Phi Sigma, Kappa Sigma. Achievements include research on microbial genetics. Home: Arcata, Calif. Died Dec. 26, 2002.

BARRINGER, PHILIP E. retired government official; b. Haverford, Pa., Oct. 2, 1916; s. D. Moreau and Margaret (Bennett) B.; m. Sophia F. Hazard, Aug. 10, 1946 (dec. Apr. 1979); children: Thomas H., C. Frances, Paul M.; m. Bettyanne Rusen, Oct. 15, 1988. Student, Heidelberg (Germany) Coll., 1934; AB cum laude in European History, Princeton U., 1938; LL.B., U. Pa., 1948; grad., Nat. War Coll., 1952. Bar: Pa. 1949. U.S. sec. Legal Directorate, Allied Control Council for Germany, 1945-46; with Office Sec. Def., 1949-64; dep. dir. European region Office Asst. Sec. for internat. security affairs, 1956-64; attaché, politico-mil. affairs Am. embassy, London, Eng., 1964-66; dep. dir. Near East and South Asia region Office Asst. Sec. Def. for internat. security affairs, Washington, 1966-67; dir. fgn. mil. rights Dept. Def., 1967-99; ret., 1999. Mem. numerous U.S. dels.; dir. emeritus Barringer Crater Co., Flagstaff, Ariz. Pres. Alexandria (Va.) Civic Orch., 1950-52; co-founder, mem. Cleveland Park Chamber Music Group, 1955—; trustee All Souls Unitarian Ch., Washington, 1964, 67-70, chmn., 1969-70; del. to Unitarian-Universalist Gen. Assemblies, 1968-80, Internat. Assn. for Religious Freedom meetings, 1975, 84, 87. Mem. Pa. N.G., 1937-40; served to lt. col. AUS, 1941-46, ETO. Decorated Army Commendation medal; recipient Meritorious Civilian Svc. medal Sec. Def., 1975, 81, Disting. Civilian Svc. award, 1989, 99; Meritorious Exec. award Sr. Exec. Svc., 1990. Mem. Am. Soc. Internat. Law, Internat. Inst. Strategic Studies (London), Am. Hiking Soc. (bd. dirs. 1988-94), Cosmos Club, Princeton Club, Cleveland Park Club, Potomac Appalachian Trail Club (pres. 1990-91), Appalachian Trail Conf. (bd. mgrs. 1991-97). Home: Washington, DC. Died Jan. 11, 2004.

BARRISKILL, MAUDANNE KIDD, primary school educator; b. Balt., Apr. 2, 1932; d. John Graydon and Maudine (Adams) Kidd; m. Peter Herbert Barriskill, Nov. 30, 1957; children: John, Michael. BA, So. Meth. U., 1954; student early childhood edn., Old Dominion U., 1970; student, Katharine Gibbs Sch., N.Y.C., 1954-55, Juilliard Sch. Music, 1948-50. Exec. sec., copywriter trainee J. Walter Thompson Advt. Agy., N.Y.C., 1955-59; founder Maude Barry Interior Design, Virginia Beach, 1970-73; founder, dir. The Home Sch., Virginia Beach, from 1975. Tchr. Ea. Shore Chapel Presch., Virginia Beach, 1970-75, Montessori Child Devel. Ctr., Virginia Beach. Author children's books and workbooks. Tchr. Sunday sch. Home: Virginia Beach, Va. Deceased.

BARRON, ALMEN L. microbiologist, department chairman; b. Toronto, Ont., Can., Jan. 19, 1926; came to U.S., 1954, naturalized, 1963; s. Max and Bena (Sussman) B.; m. Shirley Brovender, Sept. 14, 1949; 1 child, Joshua Charles. BSA, Ont. Agrl. Coll., U. Toronto, 1948, MSA, 1949; PhD, Queen's U., Kingston, Ont., 1953. Mem. faculty SUNY, Buffalo, 1954-74, prof. microbiology, 1968-74; dir. Erie

County (N.Y.) Virology Lab., 1968-74; prof. microbiology, chmn. dept. microbiology and immunology U. Ark. Med. Sci., Little Rock, 1974-91, prof. emeritus, from 1991. Cons. Little Rock VA Med. Ctr., 1974-91; vis. prof. Hadassah Med. Sch., Hebrew U., Jerusalem, 1972, Kaohsiung Med. Coll. (Taiwan), 1982 Co-editor: Microbiology: Basic Principles and Clinical Applications, 1983; editor: Microbiology of Chlamydia, 1988. Recipient Commonwealth Fund travel award, 1964, Golden Apple award Student AMA, 1975, 77, Disting. Faculty award Ark. Caduceus Club, 1990; Fulbright rsch. scholar Israel, 1964. Mem. Am. Acad. Microbiology (emeritus 1991—), Am. Soc. Microbiology (pres. South Central br. 1980), Infectious Diseases Soc. Am. (emeritus 1991—), Am. Assn. Immunologists. Achievements include research on Chlamydia organisms. Home: Little Rock, Ark. Died Nov. 16, 2004.

BARRON, ROBERT V. actor, writer, director; b. Charleston, W. Va., Dec. 26, 1932; s. Raymond John and Opal Edith (Estep) B.; m. Dayna Pearson, Dec. 23, 1979. BA in Theatre Arts, UCLA, 1976. Freelance actor, writer, Hollywood, Calif., from 1963; exec. dir. Saban Entertainment, Burbank, Calif., from 1986; pres. Tolucafilm Prodn. Assocs., N. Hollywood, Calif., from 1985. Dir. Granada Theatre, Granada Hills, Calif., 1981-82, Sportsman's Lodge Dinner Theatre, Studio City, Calif., 1982. Actor over 30 films including: Bill & Ted's Excellent Adventure, The Disorderlies, Fever Pitch, Honkytonk Man, The Supernaturals, Eating Raoul, The Private Eyes, A Minor Miracle, Daddy's Boys, The Road Hustlers; over 50 TV shows including L.A. Law, Night Court, Alien Nation, Judd for the Defense, etc.; writer, actor: Bonanza, 1963-71; The Wild Wild West, 1965, Tammy, 1966; writer, dir: Samurai Pizza Cats, Hallo Spencer, Adventures of Tom Sawyer, Tales of Little Women, Peter Pan, Pinnochio, others. With U.S. Army, 1952-54. Mem. SAG, AFTRA, Writers Guild of Am., Actors Equity Assn. Avocations: photography, music, rsch., horseman, animal trainer, reading, video games. Home: Salinas, Calif. Died Dec. 1, 2000.

BARRUS, PAUL WELLS, priest, deceased; b. Winterset, Iowa, June 29, 1902; s. Charles and Daisy May (Clopton) B. BA with honors, Drake U., 1933, MA, 1936; PhD, State U. Iowa, 1949. Ordained priest Roman Catholic Ch., 1978; cert. tchr., Iowa. Tchr. pub. schs., Ia., 1926-36; asst. prof. Drake U., Des Moines, 1937-42; instr. Iowa State U., Ames, 1943-45; prof., chmn. dept. English East Tex. State U., Commerce, 1949-76; priest Commerce, 1978-83, Grand Prairie, Tex., 1983-90, Richardson, Tex., from 1990. Author: Levels of Consciousness, 1988. Served with U.S. Army, 1942-43. Mem. Phi Beta Kappa, Kappa Delta Pi, Eta Sigma Phi, Phi Sigma Iota. Avocation: writing. Home: Plano, Tex. Deceased.

BARRY, A. L. church official; b. Woodbine, Iowa, Aug. 4, 1931; s. Thomas A. and Helen Barry; m. Jean Heim, Aug. 24, 1952; children: Kristin Becker, Beth Miko, Keith. Student, Bethany Luth. Coll., 1951, Concordia Theol. Sem., Luth. Sem., 1956; ThM, Luther Northwestern Sem., 1968; DD, Concordia Theological Sem., 1986. Pastor Pilgrim Luth., Mpls., 1956-60, St. John & Peace, Claremont, Minn., 1960-62, Trinity, Trimont, Minn., 1962-67; mission and stewardship counselor Iowa Dist. West, Ft. Dodge, 1967-75; exec. sec. bd. for missions Luth. Ch.-Mo. Synod, St. Louis, 1975-77; exec. for missions Iowa Dist. East, Cedar Rapids, 1977-82, pres., 1982-92, Luth. Ch.-Mo. Synod, St. Louis, from 1992. Active world missionaries, overseas ptnr. chs. in 28 countries. Author numerous stewardship, mission and evangelism booklets and materials for congregations. Home: Merritt Island, Fla. Deceased.

BARTHEL, CAROL ANNE, mental health nurse; b. St. Johns, Mich., Mar. 8, 1948; d. Willard Elsworth and Oneta (Crawford) B. Diploma in nursing, Hurley Sch. Nursing, Flint, Mich., 1973; BA in Religion, Alma (Mich.) Coll., 1970; MA in edn., U. Mich., 1976, BSN magna cum laude, 1980, MS in Nursing, 1989; postgrad., Wayne State U., Detroit, from 1991. RN, Mich. Charge nurse med. and oper. rm. Owosso (Mich.) Meml. Hosp.; instr. psychiat. mental health nursing Hurley Med. Ctr. Sch. Nursing, Flint, clin. nurse specialist in psychiatry, McLaren Regional Med. Ctr., Flint. Adj. lectr. Hurley Sch. Nursing; preceptor BSN program, bd. govs. U. Mich., Flint; cons. U. Mich. Continuing Edn. in Nursing, Flint campus; tutor Mich. League Nursing. Mem. Mental Health Resource Nurses Orgn. (v.p., sec., mem. adv. bd.), Am. Holistic Nurses Assn., Mish. Assn. of Suicidology, Sigma Theta Tau (Rho chpt.), Beta Beta Beta. Home: Ovid, Mich. Died Feb. 15, 2001.

BARTLE, ROBERT GARDNER, retired mathematics educator; b. Kansas City, Mo., Nov. 20, 1927; s. Glenn Gardner and Wanda (Mittank) B.; m. Doris Marie Sponenberg (div.), Oct. 6, 1951; children: James, John; m. Carolyn June Bloemker, Apr. 1, 1982 BA with highest honors, Swarthmore Coll., 1947; S.M., U. Chgo., 1948, PhD, 1951. Postdoctoral fellow Yale U., New Haven, 1951-52, instr., 1952-55; from asst. prof. to prof. math. U. Ill., Urbana, 1955-90, prof. emeritus, 1990—2003; prof. math Ea. Mich. U., Ypsilanti, 1990-97. Author: The Elements of Real Analysis, 1964, Introduction to Real Analysis, 1982; Exec. editor Math. Revs., 1976-78, 1986-90; mem. editorial bds. various math. jours.; contbr. articles to profl. jours. and books. Mem. Am. Math. Soc., Math. Assn. Am., London Math. Soc. Home: Ann Arbor, Mich. Died Sept. 18, 2003.

BARTLEY, ROBERT LEROY, newspaper editor; b. Marshall, Minn., Oct. 12, 1937; s. Theodore French and Iva Mae (Radach) B.; m. Edith Jean Lillie, Dec. 29, 1960; children: Edith Elizabeth, Susan Lillie, Katherine French. BS, Iowa State U., 1959; MS, U. Wis., 1962; LLD (hon.), Macalester Coll., 1982, Babson Coll., 1987; HHD (hon.), Adelphi U., 1992. Reporter Grinnell (Iowa) Herald-Register, 1959-60; staff reporter Wall Street Jour., Chgo., 1962-63, Phila., 1963-64, editorial writer N.Y.C., 1964-70, Washington, 1970-71, editor editorial page N.Y.C., 1972-78, editor, from 1979, v.p., from 1983, Dow Jones. With Asian Wall Street Jour., Wall Street Jour. Europe, WSJ.com, Opinionjournal.com, others. Author: The Seven Fat Years: And How to Do It Again, 1992. Trustee emeritus Mayo Found. Served to 2d lt. USAR, 1960. Recipient Overseas Press Club citation, 1977, Gerald Loeb award, 1979, Pulitzer prize for editorial writing, 1980 Mem. Am. Soc. Newspaper Editors, Soc. Profl. Journalists, Nat. Conf. Editl. Writers, Am. Polit. Sci. Assn., Coun. on Fgn. Rels., Heights Casino Club. Home: Brooklyn, NY. Died Dec. 10, 2003.

BARTOL, ANGELA, banker; b. Garfield Twp., Mich., Dec. 18, 1923; d. Anton and Antonia (Zgonc) Laurich; m. Frank J. Bartol June 24, 1944 (dec. 1986); children: Marcia A. Bartol Heath, Jon R. Student, Cloverland Community Coll., Escanaba, Mich., 1942, Mich. State U., 1970. Clk. U.S. Postal Svc., Trenary, Mich., 1941-42; book-keeper Alger County Creamery, Treanary, Mich., 1942-45; with Trenary State Bank, from 1949; asst. v.p. ops. 1st Nat. Bank & Trust Co., Marquette, Mich., from 1991, sr. teller, 1993. Ins. agt., asst. sec.-treas. Trenary Agy. Inc., 1970-88. Sec. Limestone Twp. Sch. Dist., Traunik, Mich., 1948-73; treas. altar soc. St. Rita's Ch., eucharistic minister choir. Mem. Trenary Lioness Club. Democrat. Roman Catholic. Avocations: coin collecting, stamp collecting, photography, reading, kniiting. Home: Traunik, Mich. Died Nov. 3, 2000.

BARTON, JO ANN, elementary school educator; b. Dearborn, Mo., Sept. 29, 1932; d. John David and Madonna Ann (Sherwood) Noble; m. Chester L. Barton, Aug. 12, 1956; children: Jo Lynn Huwe, Allen D. BS, Northwest Mo. State U., 1957. Tchr. North Platte Sch. Dist., Dearborn, Mo., Gower (Mo.) Sch. Dist., St. Joseph (Mo.) Sch. Dist.; tchr. gifted and talented Mid-Buchanan Sch., Faucett, Mo. Pres. Mid-Buchanan PTA; sec., treas, mem. welfare com. Mid-Buchanan CTA; rev. com. Mid-Buchanan Career Ladder. Home: Agency, Mo. Died Nov. 14, 2000.

BARTON, PETER RICHARD, communications executive; b. Washington, Apr. 6, 1951; m. Laura Perry. BA, Columbia U., 1971, MS, 1972; postgrad., Harvard U., 1979, MBA, 1982. Dept. sec. to gov. State of N.Y., 1975-80; sr. v.p. Tele-Communications Inc., Englewood, Colo., 1982-86; pres. Cable Value Network, Mpls., 1986-88; sr. v.p. Tele-Communications Inc., Englewood, CO, 1988-90; pres. Liberty Media Corp, 1990-97, Barton and Assocs., 1997—2002. Died Sept. 8, 2002.

BARTON, ROBERT KENNETH, obstetrician/gynecologist; b. Fountain City, Ind., Feb. 23, 1922; MD, U. Cin., 1948. Diplomate Am. Bd. Ob-Gyn. Rotating intern, then resident in ob-gyn U.S. Naval Hosp., Bethesda, Md., 1948-50, resident in ob-gyn Chelsea, 1952-53, San Diego, 1953-54; fellow in pathology Free Hosp. for Women, Brookline, Mass., 1953; ret. Fellow ACOG, ACS; mem. AMA. Home: Washington, DC. Died May 28, 2000.

BARTON, RUSSELL WILLIAM, psychiatrist, author; b. London, Apr. 21, 1923; s. Charles William and Muriel Marguerite (Hart) B.; m. Katherine Grizel Maitland-Makgill-Crichton, July 24, 1954; children: Karen Elizabeth, Sarah Muriel. M.B., BS, U. London, 1949; MD, SUNY, NY, 1990. Diplomate Am. Bd. Neurology and Psychiatry; lic. MD, N.Y. House physician, registrar, psychiat. registrar Westminster Hosp., London, 1948-53; registrar Maudsley Hosp., London, 1953-56; physician supt. Severalls Hosp., Colchester, Eng., 1960-71; dir. Rochester (N.Y.) Psychiat. Center, 1970-77, dir. residency tng., 1970-74. Cons. psychiatrist WHO, 1964, Minn. Dept. Pub. Welfare, 1965; dir. edn. Pilgrim State Hosp., Brentwood, N.Y., 1969, 70; clin. prof. psychiatry N.Y. Sch. Psychiatry, N.Y.C., 1968—; assoc. clin. prof. U. Rochester, 1971—; mem. select coms. mental hosps., med. edn., psychogeriatrics Ministry Health, London, 1963-66. Author: Institutional Neurosis, 1959, 3d edit., 1976, transl. Greek, French, German, Spanish, Dutch, Italian, Japanese, Science and Psychiatry, 1963, A Short Practice of Clinical Psychiatry, 1975, Diabetes Insipidus and Obsessional Neurosis, 1986, The Dissolution of the Mental Hospitals, 1996, (proceedings 10th World Congress of Psychiatry, Madrid) Antibiotic Psychosis, 1996. Served with Brit. Red Cross, 1945, Belsen Concentration Camp; with Royal Navy, 1948-50. Fellow Royal Coll. Physicians (Can.), Royal Coll. Psychiatrists, Royal Soc. Medicine (life), Am. Psychiat. Assn. (life), A.C.P.; mem. Royal Coll. Physicians (London), Osler Soc., Royal Soc. Lit., Soc. Authors, Players' Club (London). Home: Rochester, NY. Died June 11, 2002.

BARTON, WALTER EARL, psychiatrist; b. Oak Park, Ill., July 29, 1906; s. Alfred John and Bertha Marion (Kalish) B.; m. Elsa Viola Benson, July 2, 1932 (dec. June 1989); children: John A. (dec.), Gail M., Paul B. BS, U. Ill., 1928; MD, U. Ill., Chgo., 1931, DSc (hon.), 1975. Diplomate Am. Bd. Psychiatry and Neurology. Resident and all posts to acting supt. Worcester (Mass.) State Hosp., 1931-42; fellow in neurology Queen Sq., London, 1938; supt. Boston State Hosp., 1945-63; med. dir. Am. Psychiat. Assn., Washington, 1963-74; dir., pres. Am. Bd. of Psychiatry, Evanston, Ill., 1962-70; clin. prof. Boston U. Med. Sch., 1952-96; prof.

Dartmouth Med. Sch., Hanover, N.H., from 1974; cons. staff Mary Hitchcock Meml. Hosp., Hanover, from 1974. Cons. Sibley, Washington, NIMH, Rockville, Md., 1963-64; bd. trustees Joint Commn. Mental Illness, Washington, 1956-61; editorial bd. Adminstrn. and Policy in Mental Health Social Psychiat. and Hosp. and Community Psychiatry, 1972—. Author: Administration in Psychiatry, 1962, History and Influence, 1987, (with Gail Barton) Mental Health Administration, 1983, Ethics and Law in Mental Health Administration, 1983; contbr. over 175 articles to profl. pubs. and 10 books publ. Bd. dirs. Worchester (Mass.) Child Guidance Clinic, 1940, YMCA, 1940, Inst. of Pastorial Ch., Washington, 1941; mem. Coun. of Religion and Health, Boston, 1941. Lt. col. U.S. Army Med. Corps, 1942-46. Recipient Nolan D.C. Lewis award N.J. Psychiat. Inst., 1962, Salmon medal N.Y. Acad. of Medicine, 1974. Fellow (life) AMA, ACP, Am. Psychiat. Assn. (pres. 1961-62, med. dir. 1963-74, administrv. psychiatry com. 1983, disting. svc. award 1973), Am. Coll. of Psychiatrist,(E.B. Bowis award 1970), Am. Coll. Mental Health Administrn. (pres. 1980-81), Kiwanis, Cosmos. Republican. Congregationalist. Home: Windsor, Vt. Died Jan. 26, 1999.

BARTOW, JOAN M. developmental disabilities nurse; b. Madison, Wis., Oct. 5, 1952; d. Lawrence A. and Jane L. (Meekma) Michaelis; m. Randy E. Bartow, Sept. 17, 1988. Diploma, Meth. Hosp. Sch. Nursing, Madison, 1973. Head nurse ARC Blood Svcs., Madison, 1974-89; staff nurse Cen. Wis. Ctr., Madison, from 1989. Home: Sun Prairie, Wis. Deceased.

BASTIAN, ROBERT EDWARD, computer engineer, consultant; b. Bklyn, Dec. 13, 1937; s. Thomas Phillip and Edyth Virginia (Adams) B.; m. Joanna Antoinette Boario, Feb. 13, 1958; children: Robert Joseph, Randall Patrick, Cynthia Marie, Ronald David. BS in Engring., U. Md., 1965. Dir. mgmt. info. svcs. Washington (D.C.) Hosp. Ctr., 1958-66; software engr. Comress Inc., Washington, 1966-75, Fed. Computer Performance Evaluation & Simulation Ctr., Washington, 1975-81; cons. Integrated Microcomputer Systems, Inc., Rockville, Md., from 1983; pres. RebTech Data Systems, Inc, Bowie, Md., from 1986. Inventor: (Software) Scert Simulator, 1970, Resource Driver Program, 1977; author: (book) TSP Guide to Source Selection, 1977. With U.S. Army, 1955-58. Mem. Assn. Inst. for the Certification of Computer Profls. (cert. data processor1980, systems profl. 1985), Assn. for Computing Machinery, KC (3rd degree). Democrat. Roman Catholic. Avocation: creating crossword puzzles. Home: Bowie, Md. Died Oct. 24, 2001.

BATES, ALAN (ARTHUR BATES), actor; b. Derbyshire, Eng., Feb. 17, 1934; s. Harold Arthur and Florence Mary (Wheatcroft) B.; m. Victoria Ward, May 1970 (dec. June 1992); 2 sons (twins, 1 dec.). Student, Royal Acad. Dramatic Art, London. Appeared in stage prodns. including Hamlet, London, Butley, London and N.Y.C. (Antoinette Perry award for Best Actor 1973, Drama League N.Y. award), Poor Richard, N.Y.C., Merry Wives of Windsor and Richard III, Stratford, Ont., Taming of the Shrew, Stratford-on-Avon, Eng., 1973, Life Class, 1974, Otherwise Engaged, 1975 (variety club awards), The Seagull, 1976, Stage Struck, 1979-80, A Patriot for Me, London and L.A., 1983, One for the Road, Victoria Station, 1984, The Dance of Death, 1985, Yonadab, Nat. Theatre, 1986, (with Patrick Garland) Down Cemetery Road, 1986, Melon, 1987, Ivanov, Much Ado About Nothing, 1989, Stages, Nat. Theatre 1992-93, The Showman, London, 1993, Antony & Cleopatra, Stratford-on-Avon, 1999; films include The Fixer (Oscar award nomination), Women in Love, The Three Sisters, A Day in the Death of Joe Egg, The Go-Between, Second Best, Impossible Object, In Celebration, Royal Flash, An Unmarried Woman, The Shout, The Rose, Nijinsky, Quartet, The Return of the Soldier, 1982, The Wicked Lady, 1983, Duet for One, 1986, A Prayer for the Dying, 1987, We Think the World of You, 1988, Force Majeur, 1988, Mr. Frost, 1989, Dr. M., 1989, Hamlet, 1990, Shuttlecock, 1991, Losing Track, 1991, Silent Tongue, 1992, St. Patrick, 1999; TV shows include The Collection, 1977, The Mayor of Casterbridge, 1978, Very Like a Whale, The Trespasser, 1981, A Voyage Round My Father, 1982, An Englishman Abroad, 1985 (Brit. Acad. Film & TV Arts award, Ace award Nat. Cable TV Acad.), Separate Tables, 1983 (Ace award Nat. Cable TV Acad.), Dr. Fischer of Geneva, 1984, One for the Road, 1985, Pack of Lies, 1987, The Dog It Was That Died, 1988, 102 Boulevard Haussmann, 1990, Secret Friends, 1991, Unnatural Pursuits, 1992, Hard Times, 1994, Oliver's Travels, 1994, Nicholas' Gift, 1997, Love in a Cold Climate, 2000, The Unexpected Man, N.Y., 2000, Salem Witch Trials, U.S., 2001, Bertie and Elizabeth, U.K., 2001, Dorian Gray Theatre Royal, Windsor, Yvonne Arnaud Theatre, Guildford, U.K., 2001, The Prince and the Pauper, 2001; (film) The Grotesque, 1995, The Cherry Orchard, 1998, St. Patrick, 1999, Gosford Park, U.K., 2001, Sum of All Fears, U.S., 2001, Mothman Prophecies, Evelyn, Ireland, 2002, (TV) Arabian Nights, In the Beginning, The Prince & the Pauper, (U.S. TV film narration) The Arabian Nights, 1999, (British TV series narration) The Spying Game, 1999, (theater) The Master Builder, London, 1995, Ont., 1996, Simply Disconnected, 1996, Fortune's Fool, 1996, Life Support, 1997, Fortune's Fool, Music Box Theatre, N.Y.C., 2002; (radio) Art, Murder in Paris, Man and Boy, 1998. Served with RAF. Recipient Clarence Derwent award, Evening Std. award, 1972. Home: London, England. Died Dec. 27, 2003.

BATSCHA, ROBERT MICHAEL, museum executive; b. Rochester, N.Y., June 24, 1945; s. Theodor and Margaretha Batscha; 1 child, Eric T.G. BA, Queens Coll., 1967; M in Internat. Affairs, Columbia U., 1969, PhD in Internat.

Relations, 1972. Sr. cons. OECD, Paris, 1972-76; assoc. prof. Queens Coll., N.Y.C., 1968-72, 75-81; adj. assoc. prof. Columbia U., N.Y.C., 1980-81; pres. Mus. of TV and Radio, N.Y.C., 1981—2003. Chmn. faculty seminar in communication, Columbia U., 1977-85; pres. Population Resource Ctr., N.Y.C., 1976-81, bd. dirs.; with Ctr. for Communication, N.Y.C., 1979-2003; bd. dirs. Queens Coll. Author: Foreign Affairs News and the Broadcast Journalist, 1975, Dissemination of Social Science Research to Policy Makers, 1976. Bd. dirs. New Yorkers for Children, 1999. Mem. Century Assn. (N.Y.C.). Avocations: reading, horseback riding, travel. Home: New York, NY. Died July 4, 2003.

BAUM, DWIGHT CROUSE, investment banking executive; b. Syracuse, N.Y., Nov. 21, 1912; s. Dwight James and Katharine Lucia (Crouse) B.; m. Hildagarde Engelhardt, Jan. 17, 1942 (dec. Apr. 1999); children: Dwight J., John E. E.E., Cornell U., 1936; MBA, Harvard U., 1938. Chartered fin. analyst. Asst. to v.p. Mine Safety Appliance Co., Pitts., 1938-40; armament supply officer Brit. Air Commn., Washington, 1940-46; asst. to partner Eastman Dillon & Co., Los Angeles, 1946-47; v.p. 1st Calif. Co., Los Angeles, 1947-56; gen. partner Eastman Dillon Union Securities & Co., Los Angeles, 1956-71, sr. v.p., 1971-72, also dir., 1972-80; sr. v.p. Blyth Eastman Dillon & Co., Inc., adv. dir., 1980-83; sr. v.p. Paine Webber Inc, 1980—2002. Trustee Alice Lloyd Coll.; bd. dirs. Planned Parenthood-World Population, Los Angeles Decorated Order Brit. Empire Mem. Nat. Assn. Securities Dealers (bd. govs. 1976-79), Los Angeles Soc. Fin. Analysts, IEEE, Pacific Stock Exch., Inc. (vice chmn. 1980-82), Phi Delta Theta. Clubs: Calif. (Los Angeles), Bond (Los Angeles). Home: Pasadena, Calif. Died June 19, 2002.

BAUMAN, GEORGE DUNCAN, former newspaper publisher; b. Humboldt, Iowa, Apr. 12, 1912; s. Peter William and Mae (Duncan) B.; m. Nora Kathleen Kelly, May 21, 1938 (dec. Feb. 13, 1990); m. Lucy H. Hume, Dec. 18, 1991. Student, Loyola U., Chgo., 1930—35; JD, Washington U., St. Louis, 1948; LittD (hon.), Central Meth. Coll.; LLD (hon.), Maryville Coll.; LHD (hon.), Mo. Valley Coll., 1981, St. Louis Rabbinical Coll., 1981. Reporter Chgo. Herald Examiner, 1931-39; archtl. rep. Pratt & Lambert, Inc., St. Louis, 1939-43; reporter, rewriter, asst. city editor St. Louis Globe-Democrat, 1943-51, pers. mgr., 1951-59, bus. mgr., 1959-67, pub., 1967-84. Adv. dir. Boatmen's Bank St. Louis, 1978-84. Mem. voting membership bd. Blue Shield, 1968—77; mem. lay adv. bd. St. Vincent's Hosp., 1952—75; mem. nat. citizen's adv. com. Assn. Am. Med. Colls., 1975—84; mem. lay adv. bd. DePaul Cmty. Health Ctr., 1975—87; adv. bd. St. Louis Med. Soc., 1975—90; mem. exec. bd. St. Louis coun. Boy Scouts Am., 1967—86; mem. Pres.'s coun. St. Louis U., 1968—88; bd. visitors Mo. Mil. Acad., 1970—78; v.p. Policemen and Firemen Fund, 1968—78; pres. Health and Welfare Coun. Met. St. Louis, 1965—67; sec. Bd. Election Commrs., St. Louis, 1957—61; pres. Child Ctr. Our Lady of Grace, 1965—68, v.p. Jr. Achievement Mississippi Valley, 1968, pres., 1978—80; mem. Conv. and Visitors Bur. of Greater St. Louis, 1968—77, v.p., 1974, pres., 0975—1976, Dismas House, 1968; exec. com. Mo. Bapt. Hosp., from 1974, from 1974, treas., 1978—79, sec., from 1979, vice-chmn., 1981—84; trustee Jefferson Nat. Expansion Meml. Assn., 1968—84; trustee Mo. Pub. Expenditure Survey, 1968—89; trustee Freedoms Found. at Valley Forge, 1968—75, David Ranken Jr. Tech. Inst, from 1969, Nat. Jewish Hosp. and Rsch. Ctr., 1970—87, Laclede Sch. Law, 1981—98, chmn., 1986—98; state chmn. Mo. Com. for Employer Support Guard and Res., 1982—90; chmn. Rejis Commn., 1983—2001; mem. adv. bd. Newman Chapel, 1964—89, pres., 1968, Policemen and Firemen Fund, St. Louis, 1968, 1976—78; trustee Mo. Bapt. Hosp., from 1970; bd. dirs. Boys Clubs Am., 1969—83, St. Louis YMCA, 1967—72, BBB, 1968—72; pres. St. Vincent's Hosp., 1957—58; bd. dirs. St. Louis City Welfare Commn., 1967—70, St. Louis Mcpl. Theatre Assn., from 1968, St. Louis Symphony Soc., 1968—86, Arts and Edn. Coun., 1972—83, Policemen and Firemen Fund, St. Louis, 1966—92, United Way Greater St. Louis, 1964—84, mem. exec. com., 1964; bd. dirs. Health and Welfare Coun. Met. St. Louis, 1960—70, Catholic Charities, 0967—1981, pres., 1969—70; bd. dirs. Child Ctr. Our Lady of Grace, 1965—80, Jr. Achievement Mississippi Valley, 1953—74, nat. bd. dirs., 1979—84; bd. dirs. Dismas House, 1964—73, Human Life Found., 1973—81, Downtown St. Louis, Inc., 1977—83. Decorated Knight of Malta; recipient Silver Beaver award, 1978, Disting. Alumnus citation Washington U., 1972, Bus. Leader of Yr. award Religious Heritage Am., 1973, citation Loyola U. Alumni Assn., 1973, Right Arm of St. Louis award St. Louis Regional Commerce and Growth Assn., 1980, Silver Crown award St. Louis Rabbinical Coll., 1983, Dept. Def. medal for Disting. Pub. Svc., 1983, Com. for Support of the Guard and Reserve Seals award, 1999, Disting. Communal Svc. award B'nai Brith, 1983, St. Louis Dem. Man of Yr. award, 1984, Pres.'s award Loyola Acad., 1989; named to Loyola U. Athletic Hall of Fame, 1976. Mem. ABA, Newspaper Pers. Rels. Assn. (past pres.), Mo. C. of C. (dir. 1969-74), St. Louis C. of C. (exec. com. 1969-73, dir. 1969-73), Mo. Acad. Squires, Round Table (exec. com. 1975-84, v.p., treas. 1975-76, pres. 1977-79), Mo. Bar Assn., Bar Assn. St. Louis, Advt. Club of St. Louis (gov. 1972-75), Bogey Club (pres. 1980-82), St. Louis Club, Media Club (dir. 1968-84). Home: Saint Louis, Mo. Died Apr. 14, 2003.

BAUMGARTNER, RUDOLF, violinist, conductor; b. Zurich, Switzerland, Sept. 14, 1917; Student, U. Zurich, Zurich Conservatory; studies with, Stefi Geyer, Carl Flesch, Wolfgang Schneiderhan. Dir. Lucerne (Switzerland) Conservatory of Music, from 1960, Lucerne Festival, from 1968. Numerous appearances as a violin soloist and in chamber music ensembles; co-founder (with Wolfgang Schneiderhan) Lucerne Festival Strings, 1956, dir.; recordings on various labels. Died Mar. 22, 2002.

BAXTER, GRAHAM R. management consultant, behavioral scientist; b. Rockhampton, Queensland, Australia, June 21, 1940; came to U.S., 1969; s. Donald William and Jean (Fraser) B. BS, U. Queensland; MBA, U. New South Wales, Australia; PhD, U. Pitts. Supt. Imperial Chem. Industry, 1964; salesman Shell Oil Co., 1965-68; fin. officer Gulf Oil Corp., 1969-71; adminstr. U. Pitts., 1971-80. Recipient John Storey Meml. Prize for Excellence, U. New S. Wales, 1969. Mem. Australian Inst. Mgmt. (assoc.), Am. Soc. Tng. and Devel., Engrs. Soc. Clubs: Duquesne (Pitts.); University (Australia). Home: Pittsburgh, Pa. Deceased.

BAXTER, HARRY STEVENS, lawyer; b. Ashburn, Ga., Aug. 25, 1915; s. James Hubert and Anna (Stevens) B.; m. Edith Ann Teasley, Apr. 4, 1943; children: Anna Katherine Baxter Worley (dec.), Nancy Julia. AB summa cum laude, U. Ga., 1936, LL.B. summa cum laude, 1939; postgrad., Yale U., 1939-40. Bar: Ga. 1941. Instr. U. Ga. Law Sch., Athens, 1941; assoc. Smith Kilpatrick Cody Rogers & McClatchey, Atlanta, 1942-51; ptnr. Kilpatrick & Cody, Atlanta, 1951-86, of counsel, from 1986. Mem. State Bd. Bar Examiners Ga., 1960-66; chmn. State Bd. Bar Examiners, 1961-66; mem. Ga. Jud Qualifications Commn., 1979-86, chmn., 1984-86. Pres. Atlanta Community Chest, 1963; mem. bd. visitors U. Ga. Law Sch., 1965-68, chmn., 1965-66, chmn. alumni adv. com. on reorgn., 1963-64; chmn. chancellor's alumni adv. com. on selection of pres. U. Ga., 1966-67; gen. co-chmn. Joint Ga. Tech.-Ga. Devel. Fund, 1967; trustee U. Ga. Found., chmn., 1973-76; former William E. Honey Found., St. Joseph's Hosp., Atlanta, 1976-84. Served with AUS, 1942-45. Recipient Disting. Alumnus award U. Ga. Law Sch., 1967 Fellow Am. Bar Found.; mem. ABA, Ga. Bar Assn., Atlanta Bar Assn., Am. Law Inst., Atlanta C. of C. (dir. 1959-62), Atlanta Legal Aid Soc. (pres. 1956-57), Phi Beta Kappa, Phi Beta Kappa Assocs., Phi Kappa Phi, Omicron Delta Kappa, Phi Delta Phi Clubs: Capital City (pres. 1965-67), Lawyers (pres. 1958-59), Piedmont Driving, Commerce, University Yacht. Home: Atlanta, Ga. Deceased.

BAYLESS, RAYMOND GORDON, artist, writer, parapsychologist; b. Oakland, Calif., Feb. 13, 1920; Author: The Enigma of the Poltergeist, 1967, Animal Ghosts, 1970, The Other Side of Death, 1971, Experiences of a Psychical Researcher, 1972, Apparitions and Survival of Death, 1973, Voices from Beyond, 1976; co-author: Phone Calls from the Dead, 1979, The Case of Life After Death, 1981; contbr. articles to profl. jours., publs.; artist represented in permanent collections, including U.S. Dept. Air Force, U.S. Dept. Navy, U.S. Dept. State, Art in Embassies Program, Embassy Port Louis Mauretius Island, Nat. Air and Space Mus., Internat. Aerospace Hall of Fame, San Diego, Kern Oil and Refining Co., Long Beach, Calif., Bank of Am., San Francisco, Weingart Found., L.A., Permanent Civil War Exhibit, Naval Hist. Ctr., D.C., Washington Navy Mus., Washington Navy Yard, U.S. Naval Acad., Annapolis, Md.; various paintings displayed in The Pentagon, Washington, 1974-76, 75-88, 91-98; exhibited in Air Force Art Collection, Pentagon, Washington, Vandenberg Air Force Base, Calif., Artists in Calif. 1786-1940, Haddad's Fine Arts, Inc., Anaheim Calif., U.S. Air Force Fine Art Series, Washington; illustrator 6 book jackets Arkham House Pubs. Inc. Mem. Parapsychol. Assn. Died May 25, 2004.

BAZELON, IRWIN ALLEN, composer; b. Evanston, Ill., June 4, 1922; s. Roy and Jeanette (Green) B.; m. Cecile Gray, Feb. 5, 1960. BA, DePaul U., 1944, MA, 1945; postgrad., Mills Coll., 1946-48. Composer, N.Y.C., 1950-75. Lectr. various colls. and univs. Author: Knowing the Score...Notes on Film Music; compositions include De-Tonations, Fusions; commissioned by Koussevitsky Found., New Orleans Symphony, Kansas City Philharm., Am. Brass Quintet, Boehm Woodwind Quintet, Nat. Endowment for the Arts, Ford Found. Mem. ASCAP. Avocation: horse racing. Home: New York, NY. Deceased.

BAZERMAN, STEVEN HOWARD, lawyer; b. N.Y.C., Dec. 12, 1940; s. Solomon and Miriam (Kirschenberg) B.; m. Christina Ann Gray, Aug. 28, 1981 (div. June 1988); m. Beverly Andree, Sept. 9, 2000. BS in Math., BS in Engring., U. Mich., 1962; JD, Georgetown U., 1966. Bar: D.C. 1967, N.Y. 1968, U.S. Dist. Ct. (so. dist.) N.Y. 1970, U.S. Dist. Ct. (ea. dist.) N.Y. 1973, U.S. Claims Ct. 1976, U.S. Ct. Appeals (2d cir.) 1978, U.S. Cts. Customs and Patents Appeals 1981-82, U.S. Ct. Appeals (fed. cir.) 1982. Assoc. Arthur, Dry & Kalish, N.Y.C., 1967-80, Offner & Kuhn, N.Y.C., 1980-83; ptnr., head litigation dept. Kuhn, Muller & Bazerman, N.Y.C., 1983-87; ptnr. Moore, Berson, Lifflander, Eisenberg & Mewhinney, N.Y.C., 1987-88; of counsel Lerner, David, Littenberg, Krumholz & Mentlik, Westfield, N.J., 1988, Sutton, Basseches, Magidoff & Amaral, N.Y.C., 1988-90, Graham, Campaign & McCarthy P.C., N.Y.C., 1990-96, Bazerman & Drangel, P.C., N.Y.C., 1996—2003. Governing counsel Community Law Offices Legal Aid Soc., N.Y.C., 1974-83, treas., 1979-82. Co-author: Guide to Registering Trademarks, 1999-2003; contbr. articles to profl. jours. Vol. counsel community law offices Legal Aid Soc., N.Y.C., 1974-82, treas., 1979-82. Mem. Assn. of Bar of City of N.Y., Am. Intellectual Property Law Assn., N.Y. Patent, Trademark & Copyright Law Assn. Jewish. Avocation: horses. Home: New York, NY. Died Dec. 19, 2003.

BAZINAS, GEORGE T. accountant; b. Boston, Oct. 14, 1929; s. Theodore Bazinas and Condilo Gianakos. Acctg. cert., U. Wis., 1975; ALB cum laude, Harvard U., 1987. Forms designer BayBank, Waltham, Mass., 1968-94. Mem. alumni com. Harvard U. With U.S. Army, 1951-53, Korea. Recipient merit award Norfolk County Trust Co., Dedham, Mass., 1980. Fellow Harvard Club Boston. Democrat. Greek Orthodox. Avocations: amateur radio, stamp collecting/philately. Home: Boston, Mass. Died Mar. 24, 2001.

BEACH, EDWARD LATIMER, writer, retired naval officer; b. N.Y.C., Apr. 20, 1918; s. Edward Latimer and Alice (Fouché) B.; m. Ingrid Schenck, June 4, 1944; children: Inga, Edward A., Hugh S., Ingrid A. BSEE, U.S. Naval Acad., 1939; M.Internat. Affairs, George Washington U., 1963; ScD (hon.), Am. Internat. U., 1961; LLD (hon.), Bridgeport (Conn.) U., 1963. Commd. USN, 1939, advanced through grades to capt., 1956, ret., 1966; comdr. during 1st submerged circumnavigation of world USS Triton, 1960; prof. U.S. Naval War Coll., Newport, R.I., 1967-69; sec., staff dir. U.S. Sen. Rep. Policy Com., Washington, 1969-77; adminstrv. asst. to Senator Jeremiah Denton, 1980-81. Author: Submarine!, 1952, Run Silent, Run Deep, 1955 (Nat. Book award, 1956), Around the World Submerged, 1962, The Wreck of the Memphis, 1966, Dust on the Sea, 1972, Cold is the Sea, 1978, The United States Navy: 200 Years, 1986, Scapegoats!, 1995, Salt and Steel, 1999, others; co-author: Naval Terms Dictionary, 3rd edit., 1971, 4th edit., 1979, 5th edit., 1987—88, Keepers of the Sea, 1983, From Annapolis to Scapa Flow, 2002; contbr. articles to profl. jours. Naval aide to U.S. Pres., 1953-57. Decorated Navy Cross, others; recipient Mahan award U.S. Navy League, 1980, 2000, Theodore and Franklin D. Roosevelt award for history and lit., Am. Philos. Soc. Magellanic Premium award, Samuel Eliot Morison award USS Constn. Mus., Theodore Roosevelt Disting. Svc. medal Theodore Roosevelt Assn., Naval Order of the U.S. Rear Admiral Samuel Eliot Morison award for Naval Lit. Mem. Cosmos Club (Washington), Met. Club (N.Y.C.). Avocations: ship models, plumbing, electricity. Home: Washington, DC. Died Dec. 1, 2002.

BEACH, ROBERT CLAY, secondary school educator; b. Meat Camp, N.C., Feb. 4, 1935; s. Justin Andrew and Alma Hazel (Bryan) B.; m. Nancy Kay Boserman, Oct. 24, 1958; children: Robert C., Lena K., Brian, Rhonda S., Belinda R., Russell. BS, W.Va. U., 1962. Profl. cert. 9-12. Tchr. Berkely Springs (W.Va.) H.S., 1959-61; tchr. sci. agrl. sci. and agrl. math. Clay-Battelle H.S., Blacksville, W.Va., from 1961. Dir. Monongalia Gen. Hosp. Emergency Med. Svcs., 1990—; del. So. Regional Edn. Bd., Lexington, Ky., 1993. Mem. Polit. Subdivsn. Com., 1990, 91, 92, 93, 94, 95; chmn. Sub-Com. on Spl. Edn., 1993-95, House Com. on Agr., 1993-95; mem. W.Va. House Dels., 1990—. Recipient Hon. State degree W.Va. Assn. Future Farmers Am., 1994. Mem. ASCD, NEA, Nat. Vocat. Agr. Tchrs. Assn. (Tchr. of Tchrs. 1977), W.Va. Vocat. Assn., W.Va. Agr. Tchrs. Assn., Monongalia Edn. Assn. (v.p. 1988-89). Democrat. Methodist. Avocations: reading, writing, photography, farming, family. Died April, 1998.

BEALLES, MARY JO, elementary school educator; b. Butler, Pa., Oct. 23, 1940; d. Kennety LeRoy and Mary Elizabeth (McDowell) Wolfgang; m. Alex W. Bealles, Aug. 18, 1962 (div. 1974); 1 child, Alexander. BS in Edn., Indiana U. of Pa., 1962. Cert. elem. tchr., Pa. 6th grade tchr. Butler Area Schs., 1961-62, Baden (Pa.) Economy Schs., 1963-65; 5th grade tchr. Armstrong County Schs., Elderton, Pa., 1962-63; 4th grade tchr. Ctr. Tep. Sch., Butler, from 1969. V.p. bd. devel. Butler County Symphony, 1991. Mem. NEA, DAR, Pa. Edn. Assn., Butler Edn. Assn. Republican. Avocations: golf, reading, bridge. Home: Butler, Pa. Died Sept. 20, 2001.

BEAN, RUSSELL OWEN, accountant, comptroller; b. West Palm Beach, Fla., Feb. 14, 1948; s. Harold Earle and Sibyl (Pool) B.; m. Joyce Dillingham, July 26, 1968; 1 child, Robert Edward. A.A., Palm Beach Jr. Coll., 1967; B.A., Fla. Atlantic U., 1969. Office mgr. Al Packer Ford, West Palm Beach, Fla., 1973-77; comptroller Schumacher Buick, West Palm Beach, 1977-94, corp. sec., 1977-94. Avocation: computer programming. Died Aug. 2, 1994. Home: West Palm Beach, Fla.

BEAN, WILLIAM JAMES, federal agency administrator; b. Pocatello, Idaho, Mar. 24, 1933; s. James Lynch and Katye (Archer) B.; m. Laurine Elizabeth Campbell, Jan. 22, 1964. BA, N.Mex. Western Coll., 1958; MS, Tex. Tech. U., 1960, PhD, 1967. Rehab. program specialist Rehab. Svcs. Adminstrn., U.S. Dept. Edn., Washington, 1967-83, regional commr. Seattle, 1983-93. Home: Las Cruces, N.Mex. Died Mar. 11, 2000.

BEARDMORE, DOROTHY, state education official; b. Chgo. m. William Beardmore; 2 children. BA, Cornell U. Cert. due process spl. edn. hearing officer Mich. Dept. Edn. Mem. bd. edn. Rochester Cmty. Schs., 1967—75, mem. Bd. Edn. Oakland County Schs., Oakland County Intermediate Sch. Dist., 1974—84; mem. State Bd. Edn., Lansing, Mich., from 1984, pres., 1990—92, from 1999. Chair study Nat. Assn. State Bds. Edn., 1988, chair study group on edn. governance, 1995-96, chair study on social issues and the role for schs., 1999, bd. dirs. representing 12 midwestern states, chair by-laws com.; apptd. by gov. Midwestern Higher Edn. Com.; at-large del. Southeast Mich. Coun. Govts.; chmn. Health Schs. Network. Mem. Rep. Women's Forum. Recipient Disting. Svc. award Mich. Assn. Career

Edn., 1989, Svc. award Phi Delta Kappa, 1989, Can Doer award Sci. and Tech. Quest Honor Roll, 1991, Spirit of Independence award Oakland-Macomb Counties Ctr. for Ind. Living, 1991, Paul Harris fellow Rotary Internat., 1989, Edn. Leadership award Mich. Elem. and Mid. Sch. Prins. Assn., 1995; inducted into Mich. Edn. Hall of Fame, 1996. Mem. Delta Kappa Gamma (hon.). Deceased.

BEAUDRY, DONALD ARTHUR, lawyer; b. Ludlow, Mass., Oct. 16, 1929; s. Arthur C. and Grace (Boilard) B.; m. Ann M. Peeples, Dec. 18, 1956; children: Patricia, Thomas, David, Michelle, Diane, Roberta. BA, AIC, 1952; JD, Boston U., 1956. Bar: Mass. 1957, U.S. Dist. Ct. Mass. 1957, U.S. Ct. Appeals (1st cir.) 1957. Ptnr. Beaudry & Marsella, Springfield, Mass., 1960-63, Ely & King, Springfield, Mass., from 1963. Adj. faculty Western New England Coll. Sch. Law, Springfield, 1972-76, 88. With USN, 1956-58. Home: East Longmeadow, Mass. Died Apr. 20, 2000.

BEAUPEURT, JOSEPH EUGENE, design engineer; b. St. Joseph, Mo., Jan. 23, 1912; s. Joseph Eugene and Nora (Smith) B.; m. Helene Frances Alexander, Aug. 2, 1941; children: Sharon Lynn, Debra Jo Beau-Schantz, Edward Lee. Student aircraft design, Finlay Engring. Sch., Kansas City, Mo., 1940-41; student modern bus., Alexander Hamilton U., N.Y.C., 1947-48; cert. in mech. engring., I.C.S., Scranton, Pa., 1952; postgrad., Wichita U., 1953. Registered profl. engr., Kans. Display artist Plymouth Clothing Co., St. Joseph, 1935-37, Lee's Studio, St. Joseph, 1937-40; design engr., engring. supr. Boeing Co., Wichita, 1941-57, human factors chief, 1957-69, product devel. engr., 1969-72; chief engr. S.V. Tool Co., Newton, Kans., 1973-74; pvt. practice Manitou Springs, Colo., 1976-83; pvt. practice, Safford, Ariz., 1983-91. Prin. investigator, sponsor Office Naval Res., Washington, 1959-68. Election judge City of Manitou Springs, 1977-82; trustee Unity Ch., Wichita, 1956-59, pres. bd. trustees, 1959-60. Republican. Avocations: landscape painting, writing newspaper articles. Home: Helena, Mont. Deceased.

BECHHOEFER, BERNHARD GOLDMAN, lawyer; b. St. Paul, Jan. 24, 1904; s. Charles and Helen (Goldman) B.; m. Estelle Scharfeld, Nov. 28, 1929; children: Charles, Arthur S., William B. AB magna cum laude, Harvard U., 1925, JD, 1928; cert., Nat. War Coll., 1949. Bar: D.C. 1953, Minn. 1929, U.S. Dist. Ct. Minn. 1929, U.S. Dist. Ct. D.C. 1953. Asst. Mass. Crime Survey, Cambridge, 1928-29; ptnr. St. Paul Law Firm, 1929-42; fgn. affairs officer State Dept., Washington, 1942-58; ptnr. various law firms, Washington, 1958-82; counsel Conner & Wetterhahn, Washington, from 1982. Rschr. Brookings Inst., Washington, 1959-62, Hopkins Sch. Advanced Internat. Studies, Washington, 1962-68. Author: Postwar Negotiations Arms Control, 1961; contbr. articles to profl. jours. Mem. ABA (chmn. atomic energy com.), Cosmos Club, Internat. Club (Washington). Republican. Jewish. Home: Washington, DC. Died: Oct., 1998.

BECHTEL, JEAN PATRICIA, elementary school educator; b. Balt., July 4, 1934; d. Joseph Quintella and Victora Rita (Lombardi) Vittello; m. Maynard Levere Bechtel, May 25, 1958; children: Barry, Tamara Bechtel Townsend, Lauren Townsend, Maynard G., Celia Rainer. BA, Mary Washington Coll., 1973; student, U. Va., George Washington U., Trinity Coll. Cert. tchr. Md., Va., Pa. Tchr. St. Margaret Mary, Harrisburg, Pa., 1958-59, King George (Va.) Schs., 1973-79, Caroline County (Va.) Schs., 1979-80, Charles County (Md.) Schs., 1980-84, Annunciation of Blessed Virgin Mary, McSherrystown, Pa., from 1987. Coord. individualized math. system King George, 1974-79; coach Olympics of the Mind, Charles County, 1982-83, Md. County champions, 1983, Nat. Competition, 1983, asst. moderator student activity coun., 1989—, sci. club moderator, 1990—; developer Rsch. Explore and Discover in Sci. Vol., bd. dirs. Strawberry Hill Nature Preserve, Fairfield, Pa., 1988—. Mem. NSTA, Nat. Sci. Resource Ctr., Pa. Sci. Tchrs. Assn., Diocese of Harrisburg for Sci. Curriculum (coord. for sci. 1991—). Roman Catholic. Avocations: travel, cooking, drama, classical music, space exploration. Home: Hanover, Pa. Died Aug. 29, 2000.

BECK, CONRAD, composer; b. Lohn, Schauffhausen, Switzerland, June 16, 1901; m. Friedel Ehrsam, 1941; 2 children. Student, Konservatorium, Zürich; studied with Ibert, Honegger, Roussel, Paris, 1923-32. Prin. works include Der Tod zu Basel, Die Sonnenfinsternis, Elegie, seven symponies, concertos, two oratorios, cantatas, chamber music, other symphonic works. Recipient Ludwig Spohr prize City of Brunswick, Composers prize Assn. Swiss Composers, Kunstpreis, City of Basel; named Comdr. Order Cultural Merit, 1973. Avocation: mountaineering. Died: Oct. 31, 1989.

BECK, DOROTHY FAHS, social researcher; b. N.Y.C.; d. Charles Harvey and Sophia (Lyon) Fahs; m. Hubert Park Beck, Aug. 20, 1930 (dec. Jan. 1989); 1 child, Brenda E.F. AB, U. N.C., 1928; MA, U. Chgo., 1932; PhD (Gilder fellow), Columbia U., 1944, postdoctoral study, 1955-56. Am.-German Student Exch. fellow, Fed. Republic Germany, 1928-29. Dir. econ. rsch. ADA, 1929-32; social worker Emergency Relief Adminstrn. N.J., 1933-34, statistician, 1934-35; statistician U.S. Office Edn., 1935-36; assoc. social economist U.S. Cen. Statis. Bd., 1936-38; rsch. supr., author Am. Coll. Dentists, 1940-42; statistician Am. Heart Assn., 1947-53, Cornell U. Med. Coll., 1951-53; asst. prof. biostats. Am. U. Beirut, 1954: dir. rsch. Family Svc. Am., N.Y.C., 1956-81, dir. study counselor attitudes and feelings, 1982-87, evaluation rsch. cons., 1982-87. Co-founder, Fahs-Beck Fund for Rsch. and Experimentation; donor-adviser The N.Y. Community Trust, 1986—. Fellow Am. Sociol. Assn.; mem. Acad. Cert. Social Workers, Am. Assn. Marriage and Family Therapy (affiliate), Nat. Coun. Family Rels., Groves Conf., Am. Statis. Assn., Nat. Assn. Social Workers, Soc. Study Social Problems, Am. Pub. Health Assn., Phi Beta Kappa. Unitarian-Universalist. Author: Patterns in Use of Family Agency Service, 1962, Marriage and the Family Under Challenge, 1976, New Treatment Modalities, 1978, Counselor Characteristics: How They Affect Outcomes, 1988; co-author: Costs of Dental Care Under Specific Clinical Conditions, 1943, Myocardial Infarction, 1954, Clients' Progress within Five Interviews, 1970, How to Conduct a Client Follow-Up Study, 1974, 2d enlarged edit., 1980, Progress on Family Problems, 1973. Died May 5, 2000. Home: Kennett Square, Pa.

BECK, EARL RAY, historian, educator; b. Junction City, Ohio, Sept. 8, 1916; s. Ernest Ray and Mary Frances (Helser) B.; m. Marjorie Culbertson, Nov. 7, 1944 (dec. Feb. 1995); children: Ann, Mary Sue. AB, Capital U., 1937; MA, Ohio State U., 1939, PhD, 1942. Instr. Capital U., 1942-43, Ohio State U., 1946-49; asst. prof. Fla. State U., Tallahassee, 1949-52, assoc. prof., 1952-60, prof. history, 1960-89, chmn. dept. history, 1967-72, chmn. grad. studies, 1982-87; prof. emeritus, from 1989. Summer vis. prof. La. State U., 1955, Tulane U., 1959, Duke U., 1966 Author: Verdict on Schacht, 1956, The Death of the Prussian Republic, 1959, Contemporary Civilization I, 1959, On Teaching History in Colleges and Universities, 1966, Germany Rediscovers America, 1968, A Time of Triumph and of Sorrow: Spanish Politics During the Reign of Alfonso XII, 1874-1885, 1979, Under the Bombs: the German Home Front, 1942-1945, 1986, 99, European Homefronts, 1939-45, 1993, 98. Served with AUS, 1946-49. Mem. So. Hist. Assn. (chmn. European history sect. 1983-84), German Studies Assn. Presbyterian. Home: Jacksonville, Fla. Deceased.

BECK, JOHN ROLAND, environmental consultant; b. Las Vegas, Nev., Feb. 26, 1929; s. Roland L. and Betty L. (Shrock) B.; m. Doris A. Olson, Feb. 9, 1951; children: Elizabeth J., Thomas R., Patricia L., John William. BS, Okla. A&M U., 1950; MS, Okla. State U., 1957; postgrad., U. Tex., 1954, George Washington U., 1965. Registered sanitarian, Ohio, Ariz.; cert. wildlife biologist. Wildlife rschr. King Ranch, Kingsville, Tex., 1950-51; faculty U. Tenn.-Inst. Human Physiology, Martin, 1954-55; rsch. biologist FWS, USDI, Grangeville, Idaho, 1955-57; ctr. dir. Job Corps, OEO, Indiahoma, Okla., 1965-67; supr. animal control biology FWS, USDI, 1953-69; operating v.p. Bio-Svc. Corp., Troy, Mich., 1969-78; pres. Biol. Environ. Cons. Svc. Ltd., Prescott, Ariz., 1981-85; spl. asst. USDA - APHIS, Washington, 1986-87; prin. cons. Biol. Environ. Cons. Svc. Inc., Phoenix, 1978-93. Faculty assoc. Ariz. State U., Tempe, 1980-89; expert witness in bus. evaluations, 1979-98; expert witness in pesticide litigations, 1989-94; participant fin. seminars, 1980-85. Sr. author: Managing Service for Success, 1987, 2d edit., 1991; columnist mo. column on pest control in 2 mags., 1980-88; referee Internat. Health Related Jour., 1999—; contbr. articles to profl. jours. Active Humboldt Unified Sch. Bd., Yavapai County, Ariz., 2000—02; life mem. Rep. Nat. Com., from 1993; active Rep. Senatorial Inner Cir., 1994—99, Rep. Presdl. Roundtable, 1995—97, Nat. Rep. Congrl. Commn., from 2000, Bus. Adv. Coun.; active Rep. Presdl. Roundtable, from 2001. Capt. USAR, 1950—62. Named Rep. of Yr., Nat. Rep. Congrl. Commn., 2001; recipient Gold medal, at. Rep. Congrl. Commn., 2002. Fellow Royal Soc. Health, N.Y. Explorers Soc.; mem. ASTM (chmn. pesticide com. 1979-81, chmn. vertebrate pesticides 1994-2000), Rotary (dist. treas. 1997-99), Wildlife Soc., Sigma Xi. Republican. Baptist. Avocations: botany studies, ornithology, mammalogy. Died Feb. 7, 2003.

BECKHARD, HERBERT, architect; b. N.Y.C., Jan. 28, 1926; s. Julius and Erna (Sinn) B.; m. Eleanor Sabesin, Nov. 4, 1951; children: Susan, Karen, Thomas, Jane. BS with honors, Pa. State U., 1949; MFA, Princeton U., 1950. Draftsman, assoc., ptnr. Marcel Breuer & Assocs.— Archs., N.Y.C., 1951-83; former ptnr. Beckhard, Richlan & Assocs., N.Y.C. Guest lectr. Syracuse U., N.Y. Inst. Tech., U. N.Mex., Ill. Inst. Tech., Pa. State U. Subject of book: Architecture without Rules—The Houses of M. Breuer and H. Beckhard (D. Masello), 1993; prin. works include IBM Bldg., Boca Raton, Fla., U. Mass. Campus Ctr., Amherst, Philip Morris mfg. facility, Charlotte, N.C., Internat. Fin. Ctr., Jersey City, Cornell U. Sch. Indsl. Labor Rels., Ithaca, N.Y., Pa. State U. new rsch. ctr., University Park, Franklin Twp. Tech. Ctr., N.J., Pineles Nursing Home, Hackensack, N.J., Drew Meth. Ch., Pt. Jervis, N.Y., Temple Emeth, Teaneck, N.J., Housing Police Precinct, N.Y.C., office bldg. complex, Englewood Cliffs, N.J., Somerset, N.J. Lt. (j.g.) USNR, 1944-46, PTO. Recipient Disting. Alumnus award Pa. State U., 1974, Alumni fellow, 1982; IBM fellow Aspen Design Conf., 1983. Fellow AIA (AIA nat. honor awards for St. Francis de Sales Ch., Muskegon, Mich., Koerfer House, Ascona, Switzerland, HUD and HEW hdqrs. bldgs., Washington, Archtl. Record Houses 11 times), NAD (awards). Avocations: photography; tennis. Avocations: photography, tennis (Ea. and nat. rankings). Home: Glen Cove, NY. Died Sept. 11, 2003.

BECKMAN, ARNOLD ORVILLE, analytical instrument manufacturing company executive; b. Cullom, Ill., Apr. 10, 1900; s. George W. and Elizabeth E. (Jewkes) B.; m. Mabel S. Meinzer, June 10, 1925; children: Gloria Patricia, Arnold Stone. BSChemE, U. Ill., 1922, MS, 1923; PhD, Calif. Inst. Tech., 1928; DSc (hon.), Chapman Coll., 1965, Whittier Coll., 1971, Clarkson U., 1989, Rockefeller U., 1992, Scripps Rsch. Inst., 1994; LLD (hon.), U. Calif., Riverside, 1966, Loyola U., L.A., 1969, U. Ill., 1982, Pepperdine U., 1977, Ill. Wesleyan U., 1991; DHL (hon.), Calif. State U., Fullerton, 1984, Ill. State U., 1990. Rsch. assoc. Bell Tel. Labs., NYC, 1924-26; chem. faculty Calif. Inst. Tech., 1928—40; v.p. Nat. Tech. Lab., Pasadena, Calif., 1935-39, pres., 1939-40, Helipot Corp., 1944-58, Arnold O. Beckman, Inc., South Pasadena, Calif., 1946-58; founder Beckman Instruments, Inc. (now Beckman Coulter Inc.), Fullerton, Calif., 1935, chmn., 1940-65, chmn. emeritus, 1988—2004; vice chmn. SmithKline Beckman Corp., 1984-86. Bd. dirs. Security Pacific Nat. Bank, 1956-72, adv. dir., 1972-75; bd. dirs. Continental Airlines, 1956-71, adv. dir., 1971-73; bd. dirs. So. Calif. Edison, 1957-72. Author articles in field; inventor; patentee in field. Mem. Pres.'s Air Quality Bd., 1970-74; chmn. System Devel. Found., 1970-88; chmn. bd. trustees emeritus Calif. Inst. Tech.; hon. trustee Calif. Mus. Found.; bd. overseers House Ear Inst.; trustee Scripps Clinic and Rsch. Found.; bd. dirs. Hoag Meml. Hosp.; co-founder, chmn. emeritus, bd. dirs. Beckman Laser Inst. and Med. Clinic; mem. bd. overseers U. Calif., Irvine; founder, chmn. emeritus, bd. dirs. Arnold and Mabel Beckman Found, 1977. With USMC, 1918-19. Benjamin Franklin fellow Royal Soc. Arts; named to Nat. Inventors Hall of Fame, 1987; recipient Nat. Medal Tech., 1988, Presdl. Citizens medal, 1989, Nat. Medal of Sci., 1989, Order of Lincoln award State of Ill., 1991, Bower award for Bus. Leadership, 1992, Public Welfare Medal, NAS, 1999, Lifetime Achievement award, Nat. Inventor's Hall of Fame, 2004. Fellow Assn. Clin. Scientists; mem. NAM, AAAS, Am. Acad. Arts and Scis., L.A. C. of C. (bd. dir. 1954-58, pres. 1956), Calif. C. of C. (dir., pres. 1967-68), Nat. Acad. Engring. (Disting. Honoree, 1986, Founders Award, 1987), Am. Inst. Chemists (Gold medal 1987), Instrument Soc. Am. (pres. 1952), Am. Chem. Soc., Social Sci. Rsch. Coun., Am. Assn. Clin. Chemistry (hon.), Newcomen Soc., Auto Club So. Calif. (bd. dirs. 1965-73, hon. dir. 1973—), Sigma Xi, Delta Upsilon, Alpha Chi Sigma, Phi Lambda Upsilon. Clubs: Newport Harbor Yacht, Pacific. Died May 18, 2004.

BECKMANN, ROBERT DEAN, JR., real estate broker; b. Indpls., Oct. 12, 1941; m. Cynthia Stebbing, Nov. 27, 1965 (div. Mar. 1975). BA Polit. Sci. cum laude, Hanover Coll., 1963; MA Polit. Sci. cum laude, Georgetown U., 1965. Polit. writer UPI, Washington, 1964-65; exec. dir. Greater Indpls. Rep. Fin. Com., 1965-68; adminstrv. asst. mayor office Richard G. Lugar, Indpls., 1968-72; exec. dir. Greater Indpls. Progress Com., 1972-73; broker F.C. Tucker Co., Inc., Indpls., 1973-93; broker, cons., from 1993. Reporter, polit. writer UPI, Washington, 1964-66; producer, writer, on-air host PBS Channel 20 Indiana Arts, Indpls., 1982-88. Bd. dirs. Riley Area Revitalization Program, Indpls., Metro Indpls. Pub. Broadcasting, Inc., Greater Indpls. Progress Com., Dance Kaleidoscope, Ind. Advocates for Arts; local organizing com. mem. Pan Am. Games, 1987; chmn. Pan Am. Arts Festival, 1987; chmn. bd. Festival Music Soc., 1972-74, Indpls. Art League, 1987-88; bd. dirs. Arts Coun. Indpls., pres., 1988-90; bd. dirs. Ind. Repertory Theatre, treas., 1974-75, 86-87. Recipient Alumni Achievement award Hanover Coll., 1971, Arti award Arts Coun. Indpls., 1990. Mem. Nat. Assn. Realtors, Ind. Assn. Realtors, Metro. Indpls. Bd. Realtors, Penrod Soc. (bd. dirs.). Presbyterian. Avocations: art collecting, real estate investing and development, painting/collage, acting/singing. Died Sept. 26, 2001.

BEDELL, ARCHIE WILLIAM, family physician, educator; b. Detroit, Sept. 22, 1938; s. Archie Arnold and Mary (Barson) B.; m. Linda Suzanne Boos, Apr. 15, 1952; children: Robert, Marty, Jim, Amy. BS, Detroit Inst. Tech., 1961; MS in Biology, U. Detroit, 1963; MS in Human Anatomy, Wayne State U., 1964, PhD, 1967, MD, 1970. Diplomate Am. Bd. Family Practice. Med. intern Bon Secours Hosp., Grosse Point, Mich., 1969-71, Holden fellow, 1969-71, dir. inpatient tng. Grosse Pointe, Mich., 1971-73, founding dir. family practice residency, 1974-88; founding chmn. dept. family practice Henry Ford Hosp., Detroit, 1988-91, founding dir. family practice residency program, 1988-91; pvt. family practice Grosse Pointe, Mich., 1991-95; chmn., family practice Macomb Hosp., Warren, Mich., 1994; dir. family practice residency, dir. med. edn. Mercy Hosp., Toledo, 1995-2000, dir., from 2000. Trustee Detroit Inst. Tech., 1974-78; merit project bd. mem. Family Health Found. Am. Acad. Family Physicians, Kansas City, Mo., 1982; founding chmn. emeritus family practice Henry Ford Hosp., Detroit, 1988-91; chmn. bd. Mich. Health Coun., Lansing, 1996—; prof. family medicine Med. Coll. Ohio. Recipient Holden award Sisters of Bon Secour, Grosse Pointe, 1969, 71, Semmes award, 1970. Mem. Mich. Acad. Family Physicians (chmn. risk mgmt. 1980-90, bd. dirs. 1978-99), Ohio Acad. Family Physicians (dir. family practice residencies 1996-97), Mich. Health Coun. (chmn. bd. dirs. 1996-98). Methodist. Avocations: duck carving, golfing, hunting, fishing. Died Mar. 13, 2001.

BEDIKIAN, ARMAND E. retired anesthesiologist; b. Newark, 1931; MD, Temple U., 1957. Intern Pa. Grad. Hosp., 1957-58; resident Columbia-Presbyn. Med. Ctr., 1958-60; dir. dept. anesthesiology Bayshore Cmty. Hosp., Holmdel, N.J., 1972-96; ret., 1996. Mem. AMA, Am. Soc. Anesthesiologists, Internat. Anesthesia Rsch. Soc. Home: Holmdel, NJ. Deceased.

BEEDLE, LYNN SIMPSON, civil engineering educator; b. Orland, Calif., Dec. 7, 1917; s. Granville L. and Carol (Simpson) B.; m. Ella Marie Grimes, Oct. 20, 1946; children: Lynn, Helen, Jonathan, David, Edward. BS, U. Calif., 1941; MS, Lehigh U., 1949, PhD, 1952. Cert. U.S. Postgraduate Sch., Annapolis, 1942. With Todd-Calif. Shipbldg. Corp., Richmond, Calif., 1941; instr. Postgrad. Sch., U.S.

Naval Acad., 1941-42; officer-in-charge Underwater Explosions Research div. Norfolk Naval Shipyard, Va., 1942-47; dir. Lehigh U. Fritz Engring. Lab., Bethlehem, Pa., 1960-84; prof. civil engring. Lehigh U., 1958-77, Univ. Disting. prof., 1978—88, prof. emeritus, 1988—2003, dir. High-Rise Inst., 1983-89. Coord., chair Fazlur Rahman Khan, 1983—2001. Author: Plastic Design of Steel Frames, 1958, (with others) Structural Steel Design, 2d edit., 1974, Tall Buildings of the World, 1987; editor-in-chief: Planning and Design of Tall Buildings, 5 vols., 1978-81, Recent Developments in Tall Buildings, 1983, Advances in Tall Buildings, 1986, High-Rise Buildings-Recent Progress, 1986, Second Century of the Skyscraper, 1988, Tall Buildings: 2000 and Beyond, 1990, Cast-in-Place Concrete in Tall Building Design and Construction, 1992, Cladding, 1992, Building Design for Handicapped and Aged Persons, 1992, Fire Safety in Tall Buildings, 1992, Semi-Rigid Connections in Steel Frames, 1992, Cold-Formed Steel in Tall Buildings, 1993, Structural Systems for Tall Buildings, 1995, Architecture of Tall Buildings, 1995, Habitat and the High-Rise, 2 vols., 1995, Tall Building Structures--A World View, 1996, Structural, Design, Codes and Special Building Projects, 1997, (with others) 100 of the World's Tallest Buildings, 1998; contbr. (with others) articles to profl. jours. Served with USNR, 1941-47. Recipient Robinson award Lehigh U., 1952, Hillman award, Lehigh U. 1973, Silver medal Am. Welding Soc., 1957, Lynn S. Beedle Disting. Civil Environ. Engring. award, Lehigh U., 2003, Regional Tech. Mfg. award Am. Iron and Steel Inst., 1958, Constrn. award Engring. News Record, 1965, 73, Engr. of Yr. award Lehigh Valley sect. NSPE, 1977, Internat. Contbns. award Japan Soc. Civil Engrs., 1994, John Fritz medal by various profl. engring. assns., 1994; named Acad. Specialist U. Jordan, 1987, Bangladesh U. Engring. and Tech., 1988, one of 125 top people since 1874 who has contributed most to the constrn. industry Engring. News-Record, 1999. Fellow: ASCE (hon.; bd. dirs. 1974—77, bd. dis. Lehigh Valley sect. 1979—82, past chmn. structural sivsn. exec. com., past mem. rsch. com., Rsch. prize 1956, E.E. Howard award 1963, Shortridge Hardesty award 1993, OPAL award for lifetime achievement in mgmt. 2002), Royal Soc. Arts; mem.: AIA (liaison mem. regional and urban design com. 1973—76), Coun. Tall Bldgs. and Urban Habitat (dir. 1976—99, dir. emeritus from 1999, chmn. 1970—76, Lynn S. Beedle award 2002), Fritz Engring. Rsch. Soc., Nat. Acad. Engring., Structural Stability Rsch. Coun. (life; exec. com. from 1947, chmn. 1966—70, dir. 1970—93, dir. emeritus from 1993, Lifetime Achievement award 2000, Lynn S. Beedle award 2001), Internat. Assn. Bridge and Structural Engring. (hon.), Am. Inst. Steel Constrn. (T.R. Higgins Lectureship award 1973, Spl. Citation award 1991, Lifetime Achievement award 2000, Geerhardt Haaijer Edn. award 2003), Welding Rsch. Coun. (Disting. Engring. Alumnus award 2000). Presbyterian (elder). Home: Hellertown, Pa. Died Oct. 30, 2003.

BEEVERS, HARRY, biologist, educator; b. Shildon, Eng., Jan. 10, 1924; came to U.S., 1950, naturalized, 1958; s. Norman and Olive (Ayre) B.; m. Jean Sykes, Nov. 19, 1949; 1 child, Michael BSc, U. Durham, Eng., 1945, PhD, 1947; DSc, Purdue U., 1972, U. Newcastle-on-Tyne, 1974, Nagoya U., 1986. Rsch. fellow Oxford U., England, 1946-50; asst. to prof. Purdue U., West Lafayette, Ind., 1950-69; prof. biology U. Calif., Santa Cruz, 1969-90, prof. emeritus, 1990—2004. Fellow Crown Coll. U. Calif., Santa Cruz, 1969— Author: Respiratory Metabolism in Plants, 1961; contbr. articles to profl. jours. Recipient von Humboldt Sr. Scientist award, 1987. Mem. NAS, Am. Soc. Plant Physiologists (Stephen Hales award 1970, pres. 1960, Barnes award 1999), Am. Soc. Biol. Chemists, Am. Acad. Arts and Scis., Accademia Nazionale dei Lincei, Deutsche Botanische Gesselschaft (hon.), Academia Europaea (fgn.), Bayerische Akademie der Wissenschaften (corr.). Home: Carmel, Calif. Died Apr. 14, 2004.

BEGGS, DAVID WALKER, dermatologist; b. East Orange, N.J., Apr. 21, 1929; s. Charles Wendell and Edith Elizabeth (Walker) B.; A.B., Centre Coll. of Ky., 1951; M.D., Jefferson Med. Sch., 1955; m. Evelyn Ann Stout, Aug. 21, 1953; children— Daniel L., Ann E. Intern, Muhlenburg Hosp., Plainfield, N.J., 1955-56; resident in dermatology Jefferson Med. Sch. Hosp., Phila., 1963-65, U. Pa. Med. Sch., Phila., 1965-66; indsl. physician Am. Cyanamid Co., Bound Brook, N.J., 1959-63; practice medicine specializing in dermatology, Red Bank, N.J., 1966—; assoc. dermatologist Riverview Hosp., Red Bank, 1966—, Monmouth Med. Center, Long Branch, N.J., 1966— . Clk. of vestry Ch. of Holy Communion, Fair Haven, N.J., 1967-71. Served with USNR, 1957-59. Ross V. Patterson fellow, 1964-65. Mem. N.J. Dermatol. Soc., Am. Acad. Dermatology, Monmouth County Med. Soc., N.J. Med. Soc., Hahnemann Med. Sch., Am. Physicians Art Assn. Republican. Episcopalian. Club: Early Am. Coppers. Died May 24, 1995. Home: Fair Haven, NJ.

BEGLARIAN, GRANT, foundation executive, composer, consultant; b. Tiflis, Republic of Georgia, Dec. 1, 1927; came to U.S., 1947, naturalized, 1954; s. Boghos and Arax (Boghosian) B.; m. Joyce Heeney, Sept. 2, 1950; children: Eve, Spencer. B.M., U. Mich., 1950, M.Mus., 1952, D.MA; univ. Regents creative arts fellow, 1958. Ford Found. composer in residence Cleveland Heights (Ohio) Schs., 1959-60; editor Prentice Hall Inc., 1960-61; pres. Music Book Assocs., N.Y.C.; also field rep. and project dir. Ford Found., 1961-68; dean, prof. music Sch. Performing Arts, U. So. Calif., 1969-82; pres. Nat. Found. for Advancement of Arts, 1982-91. Lectr. and cons. in arts and edn.; adv. for arts in state and nation, pub. and pvt. sectors; mem. music coun. Yale U., 1974-76; mem. music adv. coun. Princeton U.; mem. panel Inst. Internat. Edn., NEA; founding prin. The Group, N.Y., 1991—; sr. adv. Am. Mus., Giverny, France, 1992-94, Fund for Arts and Culture Ctrl. and Ea. Europe, 1993—; Nat. Guild Cmty. Schs. for Arts, 1994-96; bd. dirs. Think Quest Partnerships, Advance Network and Svcs., 1996—. Compositions include String Quartet, 1947, Violin Sonata, 1949, Cello Sonata, 1952, Divertimento for Orchestra, 1957, Nurse's Song; for chorus and orch., 1960, Sinfonia for Orch., 1961, A Hymn for Our Times; for multiple bands, 1967, Fables...for Cellist and Actor, 1971, Diversions, 1973, Sinfonia for Strings, 1974, To Manitou!, 1976, Elegy for Cellist, 1979, Partita for Orch., 1986. Served with U.S. Army, 1952-54. Recipient Gershwin award Meml. Found., 1959, Grammy award, 1996; Ford Found. grantee, 1959, 62, 68 Mem. ASCAP (ann. award com. 1965-85), Am. String Tchrs. Assn. (Disting. Svc. award 1992), Internat. Coun. Fine Arts Dean (pres. 1980-82), Am. Music Ctr., Coll. Music Soc., Nat. Ad Hoc Forum of Film/Video Schs., Arts Edn. Consultancy in U.S., Gt. Britain, USSR, Eastern Europe, Israel, Mex., Japan, Iran, Century Assn. (N.Y.). Mem. Armenian Apostolic Ch. Died July 5, 2002.

BEHREND, WILLIAM LOUIS, electrical engineer; b. Wisconsin Rapids, Wis., Jan. 11, 1923; s. Albert and Eva Mae (Barney) B.; m. Manet Louise Whitrock, July 7, 1945; children: Jane Louise, Ann Behrend Luther. BS in Elec. Engring., U. Wis., 1946, MS, 1947. Research engr. David Sarnoff Research Ctr., RCA, 1947-64; advanced devel. engr. comml. systems div. RCA, Meadows Lands, Pa., 1964-66, prelimanary design and systems analyst, 1966-84; ret., 1984; cons. engr., 1984-90. Contbr. articles on elec. engring. to profl. jours.; patentee in field. Served with USNR, 1944-46. Recipient RCA David Sarnoff Rsch Ctr. Outstanding Rsch. award, 1956, 59, 63, RCA Comml. Systems Div. Outstanding Contbns. to Product Tech. award, 1974. Fellow IEEE (Scott Helt award 1971); mem. N.Y. Acad. Scis., Sigma Xi Died Apr. 11, 2003.

BEHRENDT, THOMAS A. lawyer; b. N.Y.C., Nov. 16, 1952; s. Gerhard Max and Ann Cecile (Shenkman) B.; m. Maureen V. Wasik, Dec. 21, 1993. BA, Union Coll., 1982; JD, Golden Gate U., 1995. Sr. atty. Mental Hygiene Legal Svc., Mineola, NY, 1982-93; legal dir. Conn. Legal Rights Project, Inc., Middletown, Conn., from 1993. Adv. council Conn. Protection and Adv. for Individuals with Mental Illness, Hartford, Conn., 1996—. Mem. Nat. Lawyers Guild, Natl. Assn. for Rights Protection and Adv. (treas. 1995—). Died June 13, 2001.

BEILSTEIN, HENRY RICHARD, microbiologist, educator; b. Phila., Dec. 2, 1920; s. Henry Nicholas and Anna Elizabeth (Binder) B.; m. Grace Alta Marple, June 8, 1946; children: Janet Lee Bittner, Richard Alan (dec.), David Richard. BS in Bacteriology, Phila. Coll., 1943, MS in Microbiology, 1961, PhD in Microbiology, 1970. Registered microbiologist Nat. Registry Microbiologists, registered specialist microbiologist. Analytical chemist Merck Sharp & Dohme, Glenolden, Pa., 1943-45; biol. processor, sr. microbiologist Pub. Health Labs., City of Phila., 1945-61; asst. dir. pub. health lab. Health Dept., City of Phila., 1961-70; dir. Pub. Health Labs., Phila., 1970-78; dir. MLT program Manor Coll., Jenkintown, Pa., 1978-86; assoc. prof. microbiology and immunology Temple U. Sch. Podiatric Medicine, Phila., 1974—79; adj. assoc. prof. microbiology and immunology Temple U. Sch. Medicine, Phila. Adj. prof. biology Beaver Coll., Glenside, Pa., 1986-91; assoc. prof. dept. microbiology MCP/Hahnemann Med. Coll., 1970-79, former adj. assoc. prof. microbiology and immunology; adj. faculty microbiology Montgomery County C.C., Pa. State U., Abington, Gwynedd-Mercy Coll., Gwynedd, Pa. Co-author: (book chpt.) Current Diagnosis, 1974, 77 (cassette tapes) Topics in Clinical microbiology, 1972; co-author publ. on microbiology of gonorrhea, pub. by Am. Soc. Microbiology; contbr. articles and reports to profl. publs. Bd. dirs., former chmn. Child Evangelism Fellowship of Phila., Child Evangelism Fellowship, State of Pa., Harrisburg, 1992. Recipient Legion of Honor award Chapel of 4 Chaplains, 1978, Scientist of the Year, Am. Soc. Microbiology (ea. Pa. br.), 2001. Fellow APHA, Am. Acad. Microbiology Christian Med. and Dental Soc. (exec. coun., pres. 1982-84); mem. Am. Sci. Affiliation, Am. Soc. for Microbiology (bd. dirs. Ea. Pa. br., pres. 1981-83, Scientist of Yr. Ea. Pa. br. 2001). Avocations: music, photography, stamp collecting, bible study and teaching, travel. Home: Philadelphia, Pa. Died July 10, 2004.

BELIN, GASPARD D'ANDELOT, retired lawyer; b. Scranton, Pa., May 30, 1918; s. Gaspard d'Andelot and Margery (Jenks) B.; m. Harriet Lowell Bundy, Oct. 11, 1941; children: Harriet Lowell Belin Winkelman, Constance Belin Gibb, Richard, Margaretta Belin, Alletta Belin Farmer. BA, Yale U., 1939, LL.B., 1946. Bar: Mass. 1947. With firm Choate, Hall & Stewart, Boston, 1947-62, ptnr., 1955-62, 65-90. Gen. counsel Dept. Treasury, 1962-65. Past pres. Yale U. Coun., Cambridge Civic Assn.; trustee Mus. Sci.; past v.p. Boston Athenaeum; former dir. Mus. Trustee Assn.; past trustee Brigham & Women's Hosp.; past city councillor Cambridge. Capt. AUS, 1942-45, ETO. Recipient Yale medal, 1998. Fellow Am. Acad. Arts and Scis.; mem. ABA, Boston Bar Assn., Am. Law Inst. Episcopalian. Home: Lexington, Mass. Died 2003.

BELK, GENE DENTON, company executive; b. Dallas, Dec. 27, 1938; s. Eugene Franklin and Frances Powel (Denton) B.; m. Mary Schug, Dec. 27, 1963. BS in Edn., U. Tex., 1966, MA, 1969; PhD in Zoology, Ariz. State U., 1974. Tchr. biology Johnston High Sch., Austin, Tex., 1969; tchr. sci. biology Guam Pub. Sch. System, Agana, 1970-71; vis. asst. prof. zoology Ariz. State U., Tempe, 1974-75; pres., chief exec. officer Brackenridge Stables, Inc., San Antonio, from 1975; adj. prof. Our Lady of the Lake U., San Antonio, from 1978. Specialist group chmn. inland waters crustacea Species Survival Commn., Internat. Union for Conservation of Nature. Editor: Internat. Symposium on Euphyllopod Crustacea, 1991, 95; contbr. over 50 articles to sci. jours. With U.S. Army, 1961-63. Recipient Wilks award Southwestern Assn. of Naturalists, 1968, R.M. Harris award Ariz.-Nev. Acad. of Scis., 1977. Mem. Am. Soc. Zoologists, Southwestern Assn. Naturalists, Tex. Acad. Sci., Ariz.-Nev. Acad. Sci., Sigma Xi, AAAS, The Crustacean Soc. (treas. 1986—). Avocations: horseback riding, photography, camping, nature study. Home: San Antonio, Tex. Died Apr. 18, 2001.

BELL, BERNARD RAYMOND, economist; b. Phila., Jan. 9, 1912; s. Louis and Frances Rose (Mayerson) B.; m. Jackie Hunter, Aug. 6, 1938 (dec. 1977); children: Wendy, Carolyn; m. Judith Isabelle Blom, May 9, 1980. BA, U. Pa., 1931; cert., U. Paris, 1932; cert. in social work, U. Pa., 1935. Rsch. asst. Yale U., New Haven, 1935; economist, soil conservation svc. USDA, Albuquerque, 1935-39, economist bur. agrl. econs. Berkeley, Calif., 1939-41, Washington, 1941-42; dir. div. econ. analysis Office of Coord. Inter-Am. Affairs, Washington, 1942-45; economist U.S. Strategic Bombing Survey Office of Sec. of War, London, Washington, Fed. Republic Germany, 1945-46; chief economist U.S. Export-Import Bank, Washington, 1946-53; ptnr., economist Gass, Bell & Assocs., Jerusalem, Washington, 1955-59; dir. econ. adv. staff Office of Prime Min. Govt. of Israel, Jerusalem, 1953-55; ptnr., chmn. bd. dirs. Surveys and Rsch. Corp., Washington, 1959-65; dir. India mission World Bank, Washington, 1964-66, dep. dir. projects dept., 1966-68, dir. resident staff in Indonesia, 1968-72, v.p. East Africa, 1972-74, v.p. East Asia and Pacific, 1974-77. Cons. economist Govt. Indonesia, World Bank, Internat. Fin. Corp., Washington, 1977-93. Bd. dirs. Housing Devel. Fin. Corp., Bombay, 1980-89, Assuransi Jiwa Dharmala Manulife, Jakarta, 1987-92, Pt. Pepan Sejahtera, Jakarta, 1975-89; trustee Pub. Adminstrv. Svc., 1978—. Recipient Bintang Mahaputra Adipradana award, Govt. of Indonesia, 1981. Avocations: tennis, music. Deceased.

BELL, MILO C. marine engineer; b. 1905; BS, U. Wash., 1923. Mem. staff Wash. Dept. Fisheries, 1930-33, 35-43, from instr. to prof., 1940-75; prof. emeritus U. Wash., from 1975; prin. Milo Bell Cons., from 1990. Cons. Wash. Dept. Fisheries, 1951-57, various U.S. power cos. 1957—, Wash. Water Rsch. Ctr., 1968-69; mem. Internat. Pac Salmon Fisheries Commn., 1943-51. Mem. Nat. Acad. Engrs. Home: Bodega Bay, Calif. Deceased.

BELL, NORA KIZER, college president; b. July 25, 1941; m. David A. Bell; children: Caroline, Elizabeth B. Lafitte, Thomas P. AB in Philosophy magna cum laude, Randolph-Macon Woman's Coll., Lynchburg, Va.; MA, U. S.C.; PhD, U. N.C. From asst. prof. to assoc. prof. dept. philosophy U. S.C., Columbia, 1977-89, adj. prof. Sch. Pub. Health, 1979-93, adj. prof. Dept. Medicine, 1985-93, ethicist-in-residence Sch. Medicine, 1985-93, chair dept. philosophy, 1987-92, mem. grad. faculty, genetic counseling program Sch. Medicine, 1989-93, prof. dept. philosophy, 1989-93, dir. Ctr. for Bioethics, 1992-93; prof. dept. philosophy U. North Tex., Denton, 1993-97, dean Coll. Arts and Scis., 1993-97; pres. Wesleyan Coll., Macon, Ga., 1997—2002, Hollins Coll., Roanoke, Va., 2002—04. Bd. dirs. SunTrust Bank, 1999. Former mem. editl. bd. U. North Tex. Press, Internat. Jour. AID Edn. and Prevention; contbr. numerous articles to profl. jours.; presenter in field. Bd. dirs. Ctrl. Ga. Girl Scout Coun., 1997, Ga. Health Decisions, 1997, Nat. Assn. Schs. and colls. United Meth. ch. 1998, Commn. on Colls., Southern Assn. Coll. adn Schs., 1999, FIHE, 1998,Ga. Women of Achievement, 1997, Coun. Colls. Arts and Scis.; trustee Columbia (S.C.) Coll. for Women, 1994-98; mem. S.C. Commn. on Aging, 1989-93; co-founder S.C. Health Decisions. University fellow U. N.C. 1975, Nat. Endowment for the Humanities Summer Rsch. fellow 1980, fellow 1985, S.C. Woman of Yr., 1992; Ord. of the Palmetto, 1993. Mem. Macon History Club, Macon Rotary Club, Mortar Board, Sigma Xi, Tau Alpha Pi, Omicron Delta Kappa, Phi Beta Kappa, Phi Kappa Phi. Died Jan. 24, 2004.

BELL, RAYMOND MARTIN, retired physics educator; b. Weatherly, Pa., Mar. 21, 1907; s. Frank T. and Marion E. (Seibert) B.; m. Lillian Mae Kelly, Mar. 28, 1942; children: Carol A., Martha J., Edward F. AB, Dickinson Coll., 1928; AM, Syracuse U., 1930; PhD, Pa. State U., 1937; ScD (hon.), Washington and Jefferson Coll., 1976. Prof. physics Washington (Pa.) and Jefferson Coll., 1937-75; ret., 1975. Author numerous books on physics, astronomy, history, and genealogy, including Ancestry of Richard Nixon, 1972, Ancestry of Samuel Clemens (grandfather of Mark Twain), 1984; contbr. numerous articles to profl. jours. Fellow Am. Soc. Genealogists, Geneal. Soc. Pa.; mem. AAUP, Phi Beta Kappa, Sigma Xi. Republican. Methodist. Avocations: radio, television, genealogy. Home: Coralville, Iowa. Died Apr. 12, 1999.

BELL, RICHARD QUENTIN, psychologist, educator; b. Logan, Utah, Feb. 10, 1919; s. George A. and Ruth (Moench) B.; m. Alice M. Bottoms (div. 1975); children: Linda, Sylvia, Richard Jr.; m. Dolores A. Garis, Sept. 27, 1992. AB, U. Mo., 1940, MA; PhD, Stanford U., 1941. Clin. psychologist Nat. Inst. Mental Health, Bethesda, Md., 1951-53, chief sect. on infant devel., 1953-66, chief child rsch. br., 1967-74; prof. dept. psychology U. Va., Charlottesville,

1975-89; ret. Vis. scientist dept. zoology Cambridge (Eng.) U., 1961-62. Author: Child Effects on Adults, 1977; contbr. articles to profl. jours. Maj. U.S. Army, 1946-51. Recipient Commendation medal USPHS, 1966. Fellow APA. Home: Charlottesville, Va. Died Dec. 19, 2001.

BELL, WILLIAM JACK, journalism educator; b. nr. Norcatur, Kans., Nov. 1, 1915; s. James S. and Ruth (Diefendorf) B.; m. Marjorie May Andrews, May 9, 1942 (dec. May 1991). BA, BS, Emporia (Kans.) State Tchrs. Coll., 1937, MS, 1940; PhD, U. Mo., 1949. Tchr. high sch., Colby, Kans., 1937-42; reporter-editor Colby Free Press-Tribune, 1937-42; grad. asst., instr. U. Mo. Sch. Journalism, 1946-49; asst. prof. U. Okla. Sch. Journalism, 1949-51; photographer Daily Oklahoman, Oklahoma City, summer 1951; prof. journalism, head journalism and graphic arts dept. East Tex. State U., Commerce, 1951-83, prf. emeritus, 1985. City commr. Commerce, 1960-64, 74-84, mayor pro tem, 1964-67, 74-84, mayor, 1967-70, 84-86; bd. dirs. Sulphur River Mcpl. Water Dist., 1971-72, chmn. airport adv. bd., 1971-74; mem. exec. com. NetSeO Trails coun. Boy Scouts Am., 1953-57; pres. exec. bd. Commerce Pub. Libr., 1993—. Served with USNR, 1942-45. Recipient Faculty award East Tex. State U., 1976; Named Piper prof., 1982, Disting. Alumnus, Emporia State U., 1985; named to East Tex. State U. Athletic Hall of Fame, 1989. Mem. Sports Info. Dirs., Nat. Assn. Intercollegiate Athletics (pres. 1964-67, coord. 1968-82, named to Helms Found. Hall of Fame 1970), Commerce C. of C. (bd. dirs. 1955-57, 59-62, 69-71, bd. dirs. 1995—, v.p. 1985, pres. 1987-88, named Citizen of the Decade of 1980s, 1990), Lions (pres. Commerce 1959-60, dep. dist. gov. 1962-64, sec.-treas. 1987-95, club newsletter editor 1954—, Melvin Jones fellow), Phi Delta Kappa (historian 1957-69), Sigma Delta Chi. Home: Commerce, Tex. Died Jan. 1, 2003.

BELLIS, JOHN MARVIN, psychiatrist; b. Stamford, Conn., Aug. 4, 1922; s. John Marvin and Bessie Eleanor (Clark) B.; m. Elizabeth Costenbader, 1947 (div. 1961); 1 child, James Rittenhouse; m. Inge Maria Ladenbauer, 1961 (div. Jan. 1985); children: Marvin Paul, Christopher Lukas; m. Joyce Szpunar, Dec. 28, 1985. MD, Harvard U., 1951. Diplomate Am. Bd. Psychiatry and Neurology. Intern St. Elizabeths Hosp., Washington, 1951-52, resident, 1952-53, Yale-VA, New Haven, 1953-55; coord. rsch. and tng. Conn. Dept. Mental Health, Hartford, 1955-58; pvt. practice psychiatry Greater New Haven, from 1955. Lt. (j.g.) USNR, 1943-46, PTO. Mem. AMA, Am. Psychiat. Assn., Am. Group Therapy Assn., Am. Soc. for Clin. Hypnosis, Inst. Bioenergetic Analysis (sr. trainer). Democrat. Presbyterian. Home: Hamden, Conn. Deceased.

BELLOW, GARY, lawyer, educator; b. 1935; BA, Yale U., 1957; LLB, Harvard U., 1960; LLM, Northwestern U., 1961. Bar: NY 1962, DC 1962, Calif. 1966, Mass. 1974. Dep. dir. Legal Aid Agy., Washington, 1962—65; adminstrv. dir. United Planning Orgn., Washington, 1965, dep. exec. dir., 1965—66; dep. dir. Calif. Rural Legal Assistance, Los Angeles, Calif., 1966—68; assoc. prof. U. So. Calif., 1966—68; vis. prof. Harvard U., Cambridge, Mass., 1971—72, prof. law, from 1972. Co-author (with Beatrice Moulton): (book) The Lawyering Process, 1978; co-author: (with J. Kettleson) The Mirror of Pub. Interest Ethics, 1978; co-author: (with Beatrice Moulton) Preparing and Presenting the Case, 1980, Profl. Responsibility, 1981, Clin. Studies in Law, in Looking at Law Sch., 1984. Mem.: ABA (mem. com. on legal aid and indigent defendants.), OEO, Nat. Adv. Com. on Law and Poverty (mem.), Vera Inst., Mass. Advocacy Ctr. (bd. dir.). Died Apr. 13, 2000.

BELSKY, IGOR DMITRIYEVICH, choreographer; b. Leningrad, Russia, Mar. 28, 1925; m. Lyudmila Alekseyeva; 1 child. Student, Leningrad Choreography Sch. Dancer Leningrad Kirov Theatre Opera and Ballet, 1943-63, prodr., choreographer, 1959-62, chief choreographer, 1962-66; tchr. folk character dance Leningrad Choreography Sch., 1946-73; tchr. choreography Leningrad Conservatory, from 1966; choreographer Kirov Ballet, 1973-77, prof., from 1982. With Cairo Ballet, 1977; art dir. St. Petersburg Ballet, 1979-92; pres. Vaganova Ballet Acad., St. Petersburg, 1992—. Appearances in plays, including Swan Lake, Fountain of Bakhchiserai, Romeo and Juliet, Yarushllin's Shurale, Stone Flower, Thunder Road; chief prodns. include Shores of Hope, 1959, Leningrad Symphony, 1961, Humpbacked Horse, 1963, Eleventh Symphony, 1966, The Nutcracker, 1969, Icarus, 1974. Named People's Artist of R.S.F.S.R., 1966. Died July 3, 1999.

BELTZ, WILLIAM ALBERT, publisher; b. Meriden, Conn., Aug. 24, 1929; s. Albert Henry and Marie Adelade (Heusel) B.; m. Beverly Sawyer, May 31, 1958; children—John, Jane, Kurt, Adam. AB, Tufts U., 1951. With Bur. Nat. Affairs, Inc., Washington, 1956—; assoc. editor, then exec. editor Nat. Affairs, Inc., 1965-79; pres., editor in chief Bur. Nat. Affairs, Inc., 1979-96, chief exec. officer, 1980-96; chmn. Nat. Affairs, Inc., from 1991. Bd. dirs. McArdle Printing Co., Silver Spring, Md. Trustee The Washington Opera Co., 1989-91, The Shakespeare Theater, 1991-99; Washington trustee Fed. City Coun., 1992—. Mem.: Wash. Theater Awards Soc. (dir. from 1986, pres. 1988—98), Info. Industry Assn. (dir.), The White House Corrs. Assn., Nat. Press (Washington). Democrat. Episcopalian. Home: Alexandria, Va. Died Oct. 17, 2003.

BEMMANN, KATHRYN CHIZEK, psychiatrist; b. Cato, Wis., Oct. 29, 1931; d. Frank and Celia (Cigler) Chizek; m. Irving Stewart Bemmann, May 3, 1958. BS in Medicine, Marquette U., 1953, MD, 1956. Diplomate Am. Bd. Psychiatry and Neurology. Intern St. Joseph Hosp., Milw., 1956-57; resident Assoc. Tng. Program of Milw., 1958-61; staff physician Milwaukee County Hosp. for Mental Diseases, 1957-58; staff psychiatrist Milw. Psychiat. Hosp., 1961-62; practice medicine specializing in psychiatry, victim treatment issues Waukesha, Wis., 1962-95; founder, med. dir. Women & Families Clinic, Waukesha, 1978-86. Mem. hon. staff Waukesha Meml. Hosp., 1962-95, med. dir. psychiat. unit, 1967-70; asst. clin. prof. Med. Coll. Wis. (former Marquette U. Sch. Medicine), Milw., 1964—; mem. cmty. psychiatry staff Waukesha Mental Health Sys., 1992-95. Mem. Wis. State Commn. on Status of Women, 1977-78, Women's Ctr., Inc., 1977-81, now mem. adv. bd.; mem. adv. bd. Sexual Assault Treatment Ctr., Family Hosp., Milw., 1976-78, Planned Parenthood of Wis., Waukesha, 1983-86; mem., organizer Victim Svcs. Coord. Coun., Waukesha, 1978-80; hon. chair steering com. Women Students Loan Fund Med. Coll. Wis., 1986—; active Encore-Plus Young Waukesha Breast and Cervical Cancer Screening, 1994—; mem. adv. bd. Ctr. for Breast Care, Waukesha Meml. Hosp., 1995, mem. breast cancer project team, 1993-95. Named Outstanding Woman, Coalition of Waukesha County Women's Groups, 1978; recipient Founder's award, U. Wis. Friends and Alumni, Waukesha, 1981. Fellow Am. Psychiat. Assn. (life, subcom. on edn. of psychiatrists on ethical issues 1987-91); mem. AMA, Am. Med. Women Assn. (pres. state group Women in Medicine in Wis. 1977-80, councilor of orgn. 1990-91, pres.-elect 1991-93, pres. 1993-94, immediate past pres. 1994-95, archives com. chair 1995—, cofounder breast cancer support network 1990—, Wis. state dir. 1987-91, bylaws com. chmn. 1986-87), Wis. Psychiat. Assn. (chpt. pres. 1976-77, chmn. com. on women 1977-89, chmn. ad hoc work group on edn. of psychiatrists on sexual exploitation of profls. 1985-89), State Med. Soc. of Wis. (founder com. on women physicians 1980-83), Waukesha County Med. Soc., Alpha Sigma Nu. Democrat. Home: Appleton, Wis. Died Dec. 25, 2000.

BENDINER, ELMER, writer; b. Pitts., Feb. 11, 1916; s. William and Lillian (Schwartz) B.; m. Esther Shapiro, Oct. 4, 1941; children: Winifred Bendiner Viani, Jessica. Student, CCNY, 1932-35. Editor Sci. & Medicine, Inc., N.Y., 1958-68, World-Wide Med. News Svc., N.Y., Geneva, 1968-71; writer, corr. Hosp. Practice Inc., N.Y., Geneva, 1971-75, sr. editor N.Y.C., 1975-95. Mem. Authors Guild. Author: The Bowery Man, 1961, A Time for Angels, 1975, The Virgin Diplomats, 1976, The Fall of Fortresses, 1980, The Rise and Fall of Paradise, 1983; co-author: (with Jessica Bendiner) Biographical Dictionary of Medicine, 1990; contbr. articles to Hospital Practice, MD Mag., N.Y. Times Mag., Esquire, The Nat., and more. 1st lt. USAF, 1941-45. Decorated Disting. Flying Cross, U.S. Air medal with three oak leaf clusters, Purple Heart, USAF, 1941-45. Home: Bronx, NY. Died Sept. 16, 2001.

BENFORADO, DAVID M. environmental engineer; b. N.Y.C., Nov. 17, 1925; s. Mark Joseph and Mathilde (Abraham) B.; m. Ruthann Martin, May 5, 1950; children: Mark Andrew, Marcia Ann, David Dean. BS in Chem. Engring., Columbia, 1948; student, CCNY, 1942-44. Registered profl. engr., N.Y. Engr., Skelly Oil Co., Eldorado, Kans., 1948-53; applied research engr. Walter Kidde Nuclear Labs., Garden City, N.Y., 1953-56; heat transfer specialist Trane Co., La Crosse, Wis., 1956-61; mgr. application engring. Penn Brass & Copper, Erie, Pa., 1961-65; product mgr. air pollution control equipment Air Preheater Co., Wellsville, N.Y., 1965-69; sr. environ. engring. specialist 3M, St. Paul, 1969-94. Cons. control odorous indsl. emissions; mem. com. odors from stationary and mobile sources NRC, 1978; gen. conf. chair nat. meeting Air Pollution Control Asns., 1986; cons. for subcom. on pollution prevention EPA Sci. Adv. Bd. Environ. Engring. Com., 1991. Mem. City of Woodbury (Minn.) Solid Waste Adv. Commn., 1987-95; apptd. pub. mem. Minn. Emergency Response Commn., 1991; active Boy Scouts Am., 1937—; mem. Am. Inst. Pollution Prevention, 1990-96; pres. BMD Environ. Vols., Woodbury, Minn. Fellow Air and Waste Mgmt. Assn. (dir. 1968—, pres. 1972-73, hon. mem. 1981—, chmn. gen. conf. ann. nat. meeting 1986); mem. Am. Inst. Chem. Engrs., Am. Acad. Environ. Engrs. (diplomate, trustee 1981-84, pres. 1990), Woodbury Lions Club (sec. 1970, bd. dirs. 1971—, pres. 1978). Home: Saint Paul, Minn. Died June 1, 2003.

BENINSON, JOSEPH, dermatologist; b. Bklyn., Apr. 17, 1918; s. Isadore and Ida (Kopalof) B.; m. Eleanor Stolmack, 1946 (dec. Mar. 1966); children: Maureen Elena, Ellen Lynn, Ilene Lee, Fern Alison; m. Evelyne Marte Holschauer, July 17, 1977; children: Jonathan Adam Mathew, Jennifer Alexandra. BS in Zoology, Tex. A&M, 1944, DVM, 1947; MD, U. Tex., 1951. Diplomate Am. Bd. Dermatology. Resident in dermatology U. Tex. Sch. Medicine, 1952-53, Henry Ford Hosp., 1953-55, assoc. in dermatology, from 1955; clin. assoc. prof. dept. dermatology U. Mich. Med. Sch., from 1978. Dir. Leg Ulcer Clinic, Henry Ford Hosp., Dermatology Peripheral Vascular Sect., physician advisor; lectr., speaker in field. Contbg. author to books; mem. editl. bd. Angiology, Vascular Medicine, Internat. Coll. Angiology, Jour. of Disability; contbr. over 75 articles to profl. jours. Achievements include research in the field of angiology in pressure gradient therapy. Served with USAF, 1942-46. Recipient Golden Eagle award The Coun. on Internat. Non-theatrical Events, 1979, grants NIH, 1985-86, 87-88; Nat. Pres.'s award Am. Coll. Angiology, 1989. Mem. AMA, Am. Acad. Dermatology, Soc. Investigative Dermatology, Mich. Dermatol. Soc., Am. Coll. Angiology (v.p.), Brazilian Coll. Angiology (hon.), Wayne County Med. Soc., Internat. Soc. Lymphology (Nat. Pres.'s award 1984), N.Am. Soc. Lymphology, Internat. Coll. Angiology (hon., v.p.), Henry Ford Hosp. Med. Assn. (Disting. Career award 1990). Home: Bloomfield Hills, Mich. Died Feb. 23, 2001.

BENNETT, CHARLES EDWARD, former congressman, educator; b. Canton, N.Y., Dec. 2, 1910; s. Walter James and Roberta Augusta (Broadhurst) B.; m. Jean Bennett; children: Bruce, James, Lucinda. JD, U. Fla., 1934; HHD (hon.), U. Tampa, 1950; LLD (hon.), Jacksonville U., 1972, Edward Waters Coll., 1988, U. North Fla., 1990; DSc (hon.), Maine Maritime Acad., 1989; LLD (hon.), St. Lawrence U., 1992, U. Fla., 1994. Bar: Fla. 1934. Practiced, Jacksonville, 1934-42; mem. Fla. Ho. of Reps., 1941-42, 81st-102d Congresses, 3d Fla. Dist., 1949—93, chair ethics com., mem. armed svcs. com., chmn. seapower subcom.; prof. Jacksonville (Fla.) U., 1992—2003. Author: Laudonniere and Fort Caroline, 1964, Settlement of Florida, 1968, Southernmost Battlefields of the Revolution, 1970, Three Voyages, 1974, Florida's French Revolution, 1981, Twelve on the River St. Johns, 1989; co-author: Congress and Conscience, 1970, A Quest for Glory, 1991. Capt. AUS, 1942-47; overseas in New Guinea andthe Philippines, including guerrilla fighting in Luzon. Decorated Silver Star, Bronze Star, Philippine Legion of Honor and Gold Cross, 1968, French Legion of Honor, 1976; recipient Disting. Service award Pres.'s Com. on Employment of Handicapped, 1969 Mem. DAV, Am. Legion, VFW, Fla. Bar Assn., Jacksonville Bar Assn., Jacksonville Jr. C. of C. (pres. 1939), U. Fla. Alumni Assn. (pres.) Democrat. Mem. Disciples of Christ Ch. Clubs: Masons, Lions, Rotary. Died Sept. 6, 2003.

BENNETT, DAVE, lawyer; b. Seattle, Nov. 3, 1930; s. Alvin Lowell and Jessie Lorena (Wintz) B.; m. Elizabeth Autry; children: Teresa Katherine, Rebecca Denise, David Stephen. BA, U. Tex., 1952, JD, 1954. Bar: Tex. 1954, U.S. Supreme Ct. 1967, D.C. 1970, U.S. Dist. Ct. D.C. 1970, U.S. Ct. Appeals (D.C. cir.) 1970, U.S. Dist. Ct. (we. dist.) Tex. 1987, U.S. Ct. Appeals (5th cir. 1987); cert. specialist in residential real estate law Tex. Bd. Legal Specialization, 1986. Ptnr. Kelly & Bennett, Shepherd, Tex., 1954-56; pvt. practice law Austin, Tex., 1956-59; staff atty. Fed. Nat. Mortgage Assn., Dallas, 1959-64, sr. counsel Atlanta, 1964-65, legis. counsel Washington, 1965-69, asst. gen. counsel, 1969-82; pvt. practice law Austin, from 1982. Cons. U.S. Agy. Internat. Devel., various locations, 1971-74 Mem. State Bar Tex., Travis County Bar Assn., Coll. of State Bar of Tex. Democrat. Methodist. Home: Austin, Tex. Deceased.

BENNETT, DAVID HINKLEY, lawyer; b. Portage, Wis., Sept. 18, 1928; s. Ross and Helen (Hinkley) B.; m. LaVonne Wilson, Feb. 3, 1955; children: Mark H., Todd W., John D. BBA, U. Wis., 1952, LLB, 1956. Bar: Wis. 1956, U.S. Ct. Appeals (7th cir.) 1962, U.S. Supreme Ct. 1966. Ptnr. Bennett & Bennett, Portage, from 1956. Dist. atty. Columbia County, Wis., 1959-67; regent Wis. State Univs., 1965-71. Served to 2d lt. AUS, 1953-56. Mem. Wis. Bar Assn. Lodges: Masons. Republican. Presbyterian. Home: Portage, Wis. Died Dec. 2004.

BENNETT, GERALD THOMAS, lawyer, law educator; b. Miami, Fla., June 1, 1937. BA, St. Bernard's Coll., 1958; MA, Barry Coll., 1962; JD with high honors, U. Fla., 1966. Bar: Fla. 1967, U.S. Dist. Ct. (no. and so. dists.) Fla. 1967, U.S. Ct. Appeals (5th cir.) 1967, U.S. Tax Ct. 1967, U.S. Supreme Ct. Assoc. Turner, Hendrick, Fascell and Guilford, Coral Gables, Fla., 1966-68; ptnr. Bennett, Schwartz and Schwartz, Gainesville, Fla., 1968-71; asst. prof. law U. Fla., part-time 1968-71, assoc. prof., 1971-74, prof., 1974—; mem. Gov.'s Task Force for Ct. Adminstrn., 1970-71, Spl. Fla. Supreme Ct. Adv. Com. to Revise Fla. Rules of Criminal Procedure, 1970—; cons. Spl. Counsel on Organized Crime, Office of Gov., 1973-74; mem. Citizen Rev. Bd., Alachua County Sheriff's Dept., 1973; mem. capital outlay com. City of Gainesville, 1972-73; dir. advanced trial program Nat. Inst. for Trial Advocacy, 1978-85; mem. Gov.'s Task Force for Criminal Justice Reform, 1980-82. Co-author: Organized Crime, A Desk Book for Florida Prosecutors, 1975, Criminal Justice Standards Benchbook for Special Court Judges, 1975, The Standards in the Courts, 1975, ABA Standards and Commentary on Mental Incompetance to Stand Trial, 1984; contbr. articles to law jours. Mem. 8th Jud. Cir. Bar Assn., ABA (com. on psychiatry and criminal law 1975-77), Fla. Bar Assn. (criminal rules com. 1972—), Fla. Inst. Judiciary. Died: Nov. 13, 1999.

BENNETT, HAROLD CLARK, clergyman, religious organization administrator; b. Asheville, N.C., July 30, 1924; s. Charles C. and Emily H. (Clark) B.; m. Phyllis Jean Metz, Aug. 17, 1947; children: Jeffrey Clark, John Scott, Cynthia Ann Bennett Howard. Student, Asheville Biltmore Jr. Coll., 1946, Mars Hill Coll., 1946-47; BA, Wake Forest U., 1949; postgrad., Duke U. Div. Sch., 1949-51; M.Div., So. Bapt. Theol. Sem., 1953; LL.D. (hon.), Stetson U., 1968; D.D. (hon.), Campbell U., 1982, Wake Forest U., 1985; STD (hon.), Southwest Bapt. U., 1991. Clk. FBI, Washington, 1942-43; ordained to ministry Baptist Ch., 1948; pastor Glen Royal Bapt. Ch., Wake Forest, N.C., 1948-51; chaplain Ky. State Reformatory, LaGrange, 1951-53, Ky. Woman's Prison, 1951-53; pastor Westpoint (Ky.) Bapt. Ch., 1952; asst. pastor First Bapt. Ch., Shreveport, La., 1953-55; pastor Beech St. Bapt. Ch., Texarkana, Ark., 1955-60; supt. new work Sunday Sch. Dept., Sunday Sch. bd. So. Bapt. Conv., Nashville, 1960-62; interim pastor Little West Fork Bapt. Ch., Hopkinsville, Ky., 1960, Two Rivers Bapt. Ch., Nashville, 1962; sec. met. missions home mission bd. So. Bapt. Conv., Atlanta, 1962-65; dir. missions div. Bapt. Gen. Conv. Tex., Dallas, 1965-67; exec. dir., treas. Fla. Bapt. Conv., Jacksonville, 1967-79; pres., CEO So. Bapt. Conv., Nashville, 1979-92, exec. com., pres. emeritus, 1992—2003. Vice chmn. Religion in Am. Life, 1979-91; mem. bd. incorporators Covenant Life Ins. Co., Phila., 1990-93; chmn. U.S. Ch. Leaders, 1987-89, active, 1979-83; mem. Bapt. Joint Com. on Pub. Affairs, Washington, 1979-91, Internat. Adv. Com. for World Evangelization, 1986-89; vis. prof. So. Bapt. Theol. Sem., Louisville, 1993-94; pres. N.Am Bapt. Fellowship, 1994-96, mem., 1979-97. Compiler: God's Awesome Challenge, 1980; Contbr. numerous articles to religious publs.; author: Reflections of Faith, 1983. Mem. adv. coun. Fla. State Alcoholism, 1973-78; trustee Fla. Meml. Coll., Miami, 1967-74, Am. Bible Soc., N.Y.C., 1980-2003; dir. First Am. Nat. Bank Tenn., 1987-94; mem. Nashville Literacy Task Force, Souper Bowl of Caring, Columbia, S.C., mem., 1997-2003, chmn. 1997-99; deacon First Bapt. Ch., Nashville, 1991-94, 98-2001. With A.C. USN, 1942-45. Named Ky. Col.; recipient Good Shepherd award Boy Scouts Am., 1986. Mem. Assn. Bapt. State Exec. Secs. (pres. 1978-79), Assn. Bapt. State Conv. Ch. Bond Plans (pres. 1978-79), Fla. Bapt. State Bd. Missions (exec. dir., treas., sec. 1967-79), Bapt. World Alliance (gen. coun. 1979-2000, v.p. 1990-95), Am. Bible Sioc. (trustee 1980-2003, corp. sec. 1995-96, vice-chmn. 1996-2003), Nashville C. of C. (law and justice com. 1984-93), Friends of Coll. of Judea and Samaria (bd. dirs. 2001-03). Home: Brentwood, Tenn. Died July 27, 2003.

BENNETT, LAWRENCE ALLEN, psychologist, criminal justice researcher; b. Selma, Calif, Jan. 4, 1923; s. Allen Walter and Eva Eleanor (Hall) B.; m. Beth J. Thompson, Aug. 14, 1948; children: Glenn Livingston, Yvonne Irene Solis. BA, Fresno State Coll., 1949; MA, Clarement Grad. Sch., 1954, PhD, 1968. Supervising psychologist Calif. med. facility Calif. Dept. Corrections, Vacaville, 1955-60, deptl. supr. clin. psychology Sacramento, 1960-67, chief rsch., 1967-76; dir. Ctr. for Study Crime, Delinquency and Corrections So. Ill. U., Carbondale, 1976-79; dir. Office Program Evaluation, 1979-84; dir. crime prevention and enforcement divsn. Nat. Inst. Justice, Washington, 1985-86, dir. adjudication and corrections divsn., 1987-88; criminal justice cons. Sacramento, from 1988; practice clin. psychology, 1988-99. Mem. part-time faculty U. Calif., Davis and Berkeley, 1959-76, Calif. State U., Sacramento, 1988—; mem. bd. Calif. Crime Technol. Rsch. Found., 1970-75; mem. Calif. Interdepartmental Coordinating Coun., 1967-76, chmn., 1970; bd. dir. Am. Justice Inst., Sacramento, 1970-79, 88—, v.p., 1989-90, pres., 1991-2003; project dir. San Francisco Project, 1999-2002; mem. juvenile adv. bd. State of Ill., 1977-79; mem. Calif. Blue Ribbon Commn. on Inmate Population Mgmt., 1988-90. With U.S. Army, 1942-45, 49-50. Author: (with Thomas S. Rosenbaum and Wayne R. McCollough) Counseling in Correctional Environments, 1978; contbr. articles to profl. jours. Decorated Bronze Star with oak leaf cluster. Mem. APA, Acad. Criminal Justice Scis., Am. Soc. Criminology, Am. Correctional Assn. (rsch. coun. 1992-95), Evaluation Rsch. Soc., Assn. for Correctional Rsch. and Info. Mgmt. (pres. 1989-90). Unitarian Universalist. Home: Sacramento, Calif. Died Feb. 8, 2004.

BENNETT, MARY ELLEN, health care facility surveyor; b. Bklyn., May 13, 1944; d. Leon Alfred Thompson and Ruth Earle Kamrara; m. Jonas Shepard (div.); children: Jonas A. Shepard, Stephen K. Shepard, Tslané M. Shepard; m. Julian L. Bennett (div.); 1 child, Julian L. Bennett III. ADN, Mass. Bay C.C., 1971; student, Northeastern U., Boston, 1974; MPH, Boston U., 1979; EdD, U. Mass., 1991. RN, Mass. Rsch. clin. charge nurse Harvard U. Rsch. Clin. Ctr., Boston, 1971-73; physician asst. Roxbury (Mass.) Comprehensive Cmty. Health Ctr., 1974-80; clin. coord. Northeastern U., Boston, 1978-80; adminstr., mgr. Univ. Home Health Svcs., Brookline, Mass., 1980-81; nurse cons. Elm Hill Nursing Home, Roxbury, 1982-83; field ops. supr. Mass. Dept. Pub. Health, Boston, 1988-89, health care facility surveyor, 1983-88 and from 89; chair sch. bd. Berea Seventh Day Adventist Acad., Dorchester, Mass., from 1992. Lectr. in field. Contbr. articles to profl. jours. Recipient citations and awards. Seventh-day Adventist. Avocation: singing with gospel group. Home: Peabody, Mass. Died Jan. 18, 2002.

BENNETT, ROBERT FREDERICK, lawyer, former governor; b. Kansas City, Mo., May 23, 1927; s. Otto F. and Dorothy Bess (Dodds) B.; m. Olivia Fisher, July 16, 1971; children: Robert Frederick, Virginia Lee, Cathleen Kay, Patricia Ann. AB, U. Kans., 1950, LLB, 1952, JD, 1970. Bar: Kans. 1952, Mo. 1952, U.S. Supreme Ct. 1967. Practiced in, Johnson County, Kans., 1952—; assoc. Bennett, Lytle, Wetzler, Martin & Pishny, 1952-74, 79-97; gov. State of Kans., Kans., 1975-79; assoc. Lathrop & Gage LC, from 1998. Mem. city coun. City of Prairie Village, Kans., 1955-57, mayor, 1957-65; pres. Kans. League Municipalities, 1959; mem. Kans. Senate, 1965-75, pres., 1973-75; chmn. com. on urban and rural devel. Nat. Gov.'s Conf., 1976, mem. exec. com., 1976-79; vice chmn. Rep. Gov.'s Conf., 1976-77, chmn., 1977-78. Chmn. nat. com. on child abuse and neglect Edn. Commn. of States, 1975-78; mem. bd. govs. U. Kans. Law Sch.; co-chmn. Kans. Citizens Justice Initiative Commn., 1987—. Recipient Disting. Alumni award U. Kans., 1979, Disting. Svc. citation, 1984, Fred Ellsworth Medallion award, 1990. Fellow Am. Bar Found. (life); mem. ABA, Mo. Bar Assn., Kans. Bar Assn. (past sec.-treas. exec coun.), Johnson County Bar Assn., VFW, Am. Legion, Rotary, Masons, Shriners. Deceased.

BENNINGER, FRED, communications company executive; b. Gunsburg, Germany, 1917; arrived in U.S., 1928; m. Esther Benninger; 2 children. Grad., NYU, 1937, U. So. Calif., 1941. Exec. v.p., gen. mgr. Flying Tiger Line, 1946—67; pres. Internat. Leisure Co., 1967—71; chmn., CEO MGM Grand Hotel, Las Vegas, 1971—82; chmn. Western Airlines, 1972—78; pres. Tracinda Corp., 1982—86; chmn. bd., CEO MGM Grand Inc., Beverly Hills, Calif., 1986—91; mem. bd. dirs., exec. com. MGM/UA Communications Co., Beverly Hills. Died Feb. 29, 2004.

BENO, DAVID WILLIAM, environmental protection specialist; b. Green Bay, Wis., Sept. 10, 1931; s. William Joseph and Ruth Evelyn (Witbro) B.; m. Elmarie Alden Welsch, Jan. 30, 1957 (div. July 1984); children: Deborah, David, Steven; m. Peggy LaVerne Knapp, Aug. 17, 1985. Student, Ill. Coll., 1954-55; BS, U. Wis., 1957, MS, 1964; postgrad., Loyola U., Maywood, Ill., 1969-71. Registered microbiologist in Pub. Health and Med. Lab. Bacteriologist III Wis. State Lab. of Hygiene, Madison, 1962-63; rsch. microbiologist Naval Med. Rsch. Unit #4, Great Lakes Naval Base, Ill., 1963-74; biologist U.S. Army Corps of Engrs., Chgo., 1975-79; environ. protection specialist U.S. EPA, Chgo., 1979-91; retired, 1991. Instr. Lake County Jr. Coll., Grayslake, Ill., 1976-77; environ. cons. Integrated Lakes Mgmt., Waukegan, Ill., 1990—. Contbr. numerous articles profl. jours. V.p. Wildwood (Ill.) Pk. Dist., 1978-84; treas. Wildwood Improvement Assn., 1970-78; umpire Wildwood Little League, 1975-81. Lt. comdr. USNR, 1948-91. Nominated Environ. Protector of the Year, Lake Calumet Environ. Group, Chgo., 1987. Mem. Am. Soc. for Microbiology, Assn. Mil. Surgeons of the U.S., N.Y. Acad. Scis., Retired Officers Assn. (charter mem.), The Civil War Trust (charter mem.), The Civil War Soc. (charter mem.), Lions (pres. Gagewood club 1974). Avocations: Civil War history, mil. history, coin collecting, reading, gardening. Home: Gurnee, Ill. Died Mar. 25, 2002.

BENSON, CHARLES EDWARD, aircraft company executive; b. Dubuque, Iowa, Dec. 13, 1912; s. John Alexander and Katie Martha (Butcher) B.; m. Dorothy Mae Seibert, Sept. 20, 1941 (div. Aug. 1951); m. Maxine Luella Welch, Feb. 10, 1952; children: Linda Jeanne, Thomas Charles, Carol Ann. Cert. aircraft and engine mechanic, mechanic examiner; lic. marine navigator. Ind. mechanic on heavy equipment and marine engines, 1926-37; machinist Miami (Fla.) Ship Bldg. Co., 1937-38; mechanic Eastern Airlines, Miami, 1938-41; mechanic, instr. San Antonio, 1941-46; owner, mgr. Benson Aero-Motive Co., San Antonio, 1946-48, Benson Aero-Motive Inc., San Antonio, from 1948. Designer, developer shipboard fire fighting trainer simulating on-deck aircraft crash landing, numerous others. Avocations: hunting, fishing. Home: San Antonio, Tex. Died Sept. 4, 2001.

BENSON, FRANCIS POST, corporate executive; b. Phila., Nov. 5, 1927; s. Francis Post Sr. and Isabel Katharine (Strawbridge) B.; m. Joan Eirene Moriya, June 11, 1949; children: Steven, Paul, Philip, Sandra. BS in Indsl. Engring., U. Miami, 1950. V.p. Mettler Instrument Corp., Princeton, N.J., 1959-62; dir. indsl. engring. div. ITT, N.Y.C., 1962-69; ptnr. Laird, Inc., N.Y.C., 1969-72; v.p. Gen. Instrument Corp., N.Y.C. and Taipei, Taiwan, 1972-74; pres. Univenture Corp., N.Y.C., 1974-76, Ascensores Otis De Venezuela, Caracas, Venezuela, 1976-80; mng. dir. Industrias Plasticas Trilla, Madrid, 1981-83, Cervecería Y Malteria Quilmes, Buenos Aires, 1983-87; co-owner Three Cities Rsch., Inc., N.Y.C., from 1987. Exec. v.p. bd. dirs. Gulf Coast Lubrication, Inc., Metairie, La., 1987—; pres., bd. dirs. Media Materials, Inc., Balt., 1988—. With U.S. Army, 1946-47. Mem. ASME, Nat. Soc. Profl. Engrs., Met. Club, Can. Club. Democrat. Unitarian Universalist. Avocations: martial arts, skiing. Home: New York, NY. Deceased.

BENSON, JAMES DEWAYNE, university administrator; b. Fairbury, Nebr., June 23, 1925; s. Earl Mark and Cleone Matilda (Wycoff) B.; m. Maran Schueller, May 29, 1948; children— David, Barbara, Mary, Stephen. B.Sc., Creighton U., 1949; MA, U. Iowa, 1952, PhD, 1958. Asst. prof. mktg. Iowa State U., 1952-54, 55-57; asso. prof. So. Ill. U., 1957-62, U. Iowa, 1962-70; dean Coll. Bus. Administrn., No. Ariz. U., 1970-73; dir. corp. mktg. Motorola Inc., Chgo., 1973-75; dean Coll. Bus., No. Ill. U., 1975-84, v.p. bus. affairs, 1984-86; prof. U. Wis., La Crosse, 1986-90; vol. exec. Internat. Exec. Svc. Corp., Slavjansk, Ukraine, 1994-95, vol. Bhatislava, Slovakia, from 1996. Bd. dirs. BeeLine Motor Freight Inc., Benson Color Tech., Rockford Spring Inc.; cons. Jefferson Davis and Assocs., Corn Belt Coop., Northwestern Bell Telephone Co., Motorola, Inc. Contbr. articles to profl. jours. Pres. No. Ariz. Social Welfare, 1971-73. Served to 2nd lt., AC AUS, 1943-45. Mem. Am. Mktg. Assn., Midwest Econs. Assn., Midwest Bus. Assn., Am. Assembly Collegiate Schs. Bus. (pres. Mid-continent East region), Western and Mid-Western Deans Colls. of Bus., DeKalb (Ill.) C. of C., Omicron Delta Epsilon, Beta Gamma Sigma, Phi Eta Sigma. Home: Henderson, Nev. Deceased.

BENSON, PAUL, federal judge; b. Verona, N.D., June 1, 1918; s. Edwin C. and Annie (Peterson) B.; married; children: Santal E. Manos, Polly Benson Diem, Amy Benson Rogowski, Laurel Benson Bingenheimer, Peter. BSc, U. N.D., 1942; LLB, George Washington U., 1949. Bar: N.D. 1949. Adminstrv. asst. Senator Milton R. Young, 1946-49; assoc. H.B. Spiller, Cavalier, N.D., 1949-50; mem. Shaft, Benson, Shaft and McConn, Grand Forks, N.D., 1950-71; atty. gen. State of N.D., 1954-55; chief judge U.S. Dist. Ct. N.D., Fargo, 1971-85, sr. judge, 1985—98. Chmn. Grand Forks County chpt. ARC, 1954-55; pres. congregation United Luth. Ch., Grand Forks, 1959. Lt. USNR, 1942-46. Mem. ABA, VFW, Elks. Home: North Oaks, Minn. Died Apr. 22, 2004.

BENTEL, MARIA-LUISE RAMONA AZZARONE (MRS. FREDERICK R. BENTEL), architect, educator; b. N.Y.C., June 15, 1928; d. Louis and Maria-Teresa (Massaro) Azzarone; m. Frederick R. Bentel, Aug. 16, 1952; children: Paul Louis, Peter Andreas, Maria Elisabeth. BArch, MIT, 1951; Fulbright scholar, Scuola d'Architettura, Venice, Italy, 1952-53. Registered profl. architect, Conn., N.Y., N.J., Va., Vt. registered profl. planner, N.J. Partner Bentel & Bentel (Architects), Locust Valley, N.Y., 1955—; pres. Tesstoria Realty Corp., N.Y.C., 1961—; v.p., sec.-treas. Correlated Designs, Inc., Locust Valley, 1961—; partner Cobblestone Enterprises, 1967; founding mem. Locust Valley Bus. Dist. Planning Commn., 1968—. Regional vice chair MIT Ednl. Coun.; adv. mem. MIT Coun. for the Arts; assoc. prof. architecture Sch. Architecture and Fine Arts N.Y. Inst. Tech.; mem. APD panel N.Y. State Coun. for Arts, 1985-89. Archtl. works include C.W. Post Coll. L.I. U (N.Y. State Assn. Architects award 1975, Gold Archi award L.I. Assn. Architects 1974), Hempstead Bank, Nassau Centre Office Bldg., North Shore Unitarian Sch., Plandome, N.Y., Shelter Rock Library, Searingtown, N.Y., St. Anthony's Ch., Nanuet, N.Y., Kinloch Farm, Va., Steinberg Learning Center-Woodmere (N.Y.) Acad., St. Francis de Sales Ch., Bennington, Vt., Neitlich residence, Oyster Bay Cove, N.Y., Amityville (N.Y.) Pub. Library, Jericho (N.Y.) Pub. Library, John B. Gambling residence, Lattingtown, N.Y., Glen Cove (N.Y.) Boys' Club at Lincoln House, Salten Hall, N.Y. Inst. Tech., N.Y. Coll. Osteo. Med. at N.Y. Inst. Tech., Old Westbury, Commack (N.Y.) Pub. Library, St. Mary Star of the Sea Ch., Far Rockaway, Oberlin Residence, St. Hyacinth's Ch.; Museums at Stony Brook, St. Joseph's Coll. Libr., N.Y. Inst. Tech. Libr., 1989, Simpson residence, St. Stephen's Ch., Warwick, N.Y., 1991, Pavilion Old Westbury (N.Y.); contbr. religious architecture chpt. to Time Saver Standards (De Chiara and Callender), 1973. Mem. comml. panel Am. Arbitration Assn.; bd. dirs. L.I. Soc. AIA; chmn. adv. panel on govt. bldg. projects GSA, 1976; chmn. Inst. Internat. Edn.; mem. nat. adv.-selection com. Fulbright-Hays awards, 1976-78, 80, 82; chair Locust Valley Libr. Adv. Bd., 1973-80. Named Woman Architect of Year Nassau-Suffolk County, 1976 Fellow AIA (corp. mem., chmn. design com., dir. L.I. chpt.); mem. N.Y. State Assn. Architects (chmn. design awards com.), Nat. Council Archtl. Registration Bds., MIT Alumnae Assn., MIT Alumni L.I. Home: Locust Valley, NY. Died Nov. 8, 2000.

BENTON, STEPHEN ANTHONY, media arts and sciences educator; b. San Francisco, Dec. 1, 1941; s. Frederick William and Emma Jeanne (Brun) B.; m. Jean Nosworthy Lamphier, Mar. 17, 1964; children: James Edward Brun, Julia Anne Nosworthy. BSEE, MIT, 1963; MS in Engring., Harvard U., 1965, PhD in Applied Physics, 1968. Sr. scientist Polaroid Corp., Cambridge, Mass., 1961-85; asst. prof. Harvard U., Cambridge, 1968-73; prof. MIT, Cambridge, 1982—2003, head program in media arts and scis., 1987-94, dir. Ctr. for Advanced Visual Studies, 1996—2003. Bd. dirs. Color, Inc., Portsmouth, N.H.; cons. in field. Inventor in field. Fellow Optical Soc. Am. (dir.), Internat. Soc. for Optical Engring. (dir.), Soc. for Imaging Sci. and Tech. (dir.); mem. IEEE, Holographic Display Artists and Engrs. Club (Japan). Avocations: photography, scuba diving. Home: Lincoln, Mass. Died Nov. 9, 2003.

BERDJIS, FAZLOLLAH, physicist; b. Soley, Kurdistan, Iraq, Feb. 4, 1943; came to U.S., 1982; s. Muzaffar and Monireh Berdjis; divorced; children: Vahid, Monireh. Vordiplom in Physics, Univ. Munich, 1967, diplom in Physics, 1972, D in Physics, 1978. Sci. co-worker Max-Planck Inst., Germany, 1978-82; asst. prof. physics U. Ill., Chgo., 1982-85; prof. physics and maths. Orange Coast Coll., Costa Mesa, Calif., from 1990. Vis. physicist, UCLA, 1985-90; mem. faculty U. Phoenix, 1990—; conducted seminars U. Munich, 1979, 80; reviewer Math. Revs. Contbr. articles to profl. jours. Mem. Internat. Assn. Math. Physicists, Am. Math. Soc., Am. Phys. Soc., UN Assn., Assn. for Baha'i Studies. Home: Brooklyn, NY. Died Oct. 28, 2001.

BERG, SISTER MARIE MAJELLA, retired academic administrator; b. Bklyn., July 7, 1916; d. Gustav Peter and Mary Josephine (McAuliff) B. BA, Marymount Coll., 1938; MA, Fordham U., 1948; DHL (hon.), Georgetown U., 1970, Marymount Manhattan Coll., 1983. Registrar Marymount Sch., N.Y.C., 1943-48; prof. classics, registrar Marymount Coll., N.Y.C., 1948—57; registrar Marymount Coll. of Va., Arlington, 1957-58, Marymount Coll., Tarrytown, N.Y., 1958-60; pres. Marymount U., Arlington, Va., 1960-93, chancellor, 1993—2001, pres. emerita, 2001—03. Pres. Consortium for Continuing Higher Edn. in Va., 1987-88; mem. com. Consortium of Univs. in Washington Met. Area, 1987-93, chmn., 1992-93. Contbr. five biographies to One Hundred Great Thinkers, 1965; editor Otherwords column of N.Va. Sun newspaper, Arlington, College to University: A Memoir, 1999. Bd. dirs. Internat. Hospice, 1984-96, Ballston Partnership, 1992—, Hope, SOAR, 10th Dist. Congl. Award Coun., No. Va.; vice chmn. bd. Va. Found. Ind. Colls., 1992-93; cmty. advisor Jr. League No. Va., 1992-2004; mem. Friends of TACT, 1994-2004. Recipient commendation Va. Gen. Assembly, Richmond, 1990, 93, Elizabeth Ann Seton award, 1991, Arlington Notable Women award Arlington Commn. on Status of Women, 1992, Voice and Vision award Arlington Cmty. TV Channel 33, 1993, Pro Ecclesia et Pontifice medal Holy See, 1993; elected to Va. Women's Hall of Fame, 1992; named Washingtonian of Yr., Washingtonian mag., 1990, Arlington Cmty. Hero award, 1999; named to Washington Bus. Hall of Fame, Washingtonian mag. 1998, Jr. Achievement, 1998. Roman Catholic. Avocations: sewing, crocheting, reading. Home: Tarrytown, NY. Died Apr. 5, 2004.

BERGER, ARTHUR VICTOR, music educator, composer, critic; b. N.Y.C., May 15, 1912; s. Louis Charles and Ethel (Gerstenzang) B.; m. Esther Turitz, May 25, 1937 (dec. 1960); m. Ellen Phillipsborn Tessman, Dec. 8, 1967 BS in Music, NYU, 1934; MA, Harvard U., 1936; MusD (hon.), New Eng. Conservatory, 1987; student, Longy Sch. Music, Cambridge, Mass., 1934-36, Ecole Normale de Musique, Boulanger, France, 1937-39; MusD (hon.), New Eng. Conservatory of Music, 1987. Editor Musical Mercury, 1934-37; mus. reviewer Boston Transcript, 1934-37; instr. Mills Coll., 1939-41, N. Tex. State Coll., 1941, Bklyn. Coll., 1942-43; music reviewer N.Y. Sun, 1943-46; assoc. music critic N.Y. Herald Tribune, 1946-53; mem. faculty Brandeis U., Waltham, Mass., 1953-80, Naumburg prof. music, 1962-69, Irving G. Fine prof. music, 1969-80, Irving G. Fine prof. emeritus, 1980—2003; composer-in-residence Berkshire Music Ctr., 1964. Faculty composition dept. New Eng. Conservatory of Music. Composer: Two Episodes for Piano, 1933, Quartet in C Major for Woodwinds, 1941, Partita for Piano, 1947, Intermezzo for Piano, 1948, Duo for Violin and Piano, No. 2, 1950, Duo for Cello and Piano, 1951, Polyphony for Orchestra, 1956, Chamber Music for Thirteen Players, 1956, String Quartet, 1958, Three Pieces for Two Pianos, 1961, Five Pieces for Piano, 1969, Septet, 1966, Trio for Guitar, Violin, and Piano, 1972, 5 Songs for Tenor, 1979, Trio for Violin, Cello, and Piano, 1980, Partita for Wind Quintet, 1984, Persepectives II for 15 Players, 1985, Ode to Ronsard for Soprano, 1987, Diptych, 1990, Collage III, 1992, numerous others; works recorded on New Worlds Records and CRI Labels; author: (contributer) The Book of Modern Composers, 1942, Aaron Copland, 1953, most recent edit. 1990, Culture for the Millions?: Mass Media in Modern Society, 1964, Aesthetic Analysis, 1967, Atlantic Brief Lives, 1971, Musical Mercury: Modern Music: Perspectives on Schoenberg and Stravinsky, 1972, Charles Ives Remembered: An Oral History, 1974, Reflections of an American Composer, 2002; co-founder, editor Perspectives of New Music, 1962-63, editorial bd., 1962; contbr. articles and revs. to Atlantic, Saturday Rev., Harper's Bazaar, N.Y. Rev., N.Y. Times. Recipient commns. from CBS, 1944, Dimitri Mitropoulos, 1952, Louisville Orch., 1955, Fromm Music Found., 1959, League Composers, 1951, award Nat. Inst. Arts and Letters, 1960, Naumburg Recording award, 1964, citation for string quartet N.Y. Music Critics Circle, 1962, award St. Botolph Club Arts, 1968; grantee Am. Council Learned Socs., 1936; research grantee Fulbright Found., 1960, 61 Fellow Am. Acad. Arts and Scis.; mem. Am. Composers Alliance (bd. govs. 1957-59, 63—), Am. Soc. Authors, ASCAP, Nat. Acad. Arts and Letters, Mass. Coun. on the Arts and Humanities. Home: Cambridge, Mass. Died Oct. 7, 2003.

BERGER, JEFFREY WAYNE, ophthalmologist, biophysicist; b. N.Y.C., Oct. 11, 1963; s. Jack and Eve (Meltz) B.; m. Karen Feiwus, Aug. 24, 1986; children: Adina, Tamar, Joseph. BS in Engring., Princeton U., 1985; PhD, U. Pa., 1991, MD, 1992. Diplomate Nat. Bd. Med. Examiners. Resident Mass. Eye and Ear/Harvard, Boston, 1993-96; asst. prof. Scheie Eye Inst. U. Pa., Phila., from 1996. Contbr. sci. papers to profl. publs. Recipient Resident Rsch. award Am. Soc. Lasers Surg. Med., 1995; Ronald G. Michels fellow RGM Found., 1996, Heed fellow Heed Found., 1996. Mem. Soc. Photo-Optical Instrument Engrs.-Biomed. Optics, Assn. Rsch. Vision Ophthalmology. Home: Cherry Hill, NJ. Died Jan. 25, 2001.

BERGSON, ABRAM, economist, educator; b. Balt., Apr. 21, 1914; s. Issac Burk and Sophia (Rabinovich) B.; m. Rita S. Macht, Nov. 5, 1939; children: Judith, Emily, Lucy. AB, Johns Hopkins U., 1933; PhD, Harvard U., 1940; LL.D., U. Windsor, 1979; D.H.L., Brandeis U., 1985. Instr. econs. Harvard U., 1937-38, 39-40; asst. prof. econs. U. Tex., 1940-42; economist various agys. Fed. Govt., 1942-46; mem. U.S. delgation Moscow Reparations Conf., summer, 1945; assoc. prof. econs. Columbia U., 1946-50, prof., 1950-56; prof. econs. Harvard U., 1956-71, George F. Baker prof. econs., 1971-84, prof. emeritus, 1984—2003; dir. The Russian Research Center, Harvard U., 1964-68, 77-80. Cons. Rand Corp., 1948-88. Author: Structure of Soviet Wages, 1944, Economics of Soviet Planning, 1964, Essays in Normative Economics, 1966, Planning and Productivity under Soviet Socialism, 1968, Productivity and the Social System, 1978, Welfare, Planning, and Employment, 1982, Planning and Performance in Socialist Economies, 1989; contr. to books, articles to profl. econ. jours.; co-editor: Economic Trends in the Soviet Union, 1963, The Soviet Economy: Toward the Year 2000, 1983. Mem. social sci. advisory bd. ACDA, 1966-73, chmn., 1972-73. Fellow Econometric Soc., Am. Acad. Arts and Scis., Am. Econ. Assn. (disting. fellow); mem. Nat. Acad. Scis., Am. Philos. Soc., Social Sci. Research Council (dir.-at-large 1963-69) Jewish. Died Apr. 23, 2003.

BERIO, LUCIANO, composer; b. Oneglia, Italy, Oct. 24, 1925; s. Ernesto Berio and Ada dal Fuime; m. Cathy Berberian, 1950 (dissolved 1964); 1 child; m. Susan Oyama, 1964 (dissolved 1971); 2 children; m. Talia Pecker, 1977; 2 children. Student, Liceo Classico & Conservatorio, Milan; DMus (hon.), City U., London, 1980. Founder Studio de Fonologia Musicale, Italian Radio; tchr., then prof. composition, lectr. Mills Coll., Calif.; tchr. composition, lectr. Harvard U., Cambridge, Mass.; tchr. Berkshire Music Ctr., Tanglewood, 1960; tchr. composition Dartington Summer Sch., England, 1961—62; prof. comosition Juilliard Sch. Music, N.Y.C., 1965—71. Dir. electro-acoustic sect. IRCAM, Paris, 1974—80; artistic dir. Israel Chamber Orch., 1975, Acad. Filarmonica Romana, 1976, Orch. Regionale Toscana, 1982, Maggio Musicale Fiorentino, 1984; founder, dir. Tempo Reale, Florence, Italy, from 1987. Compositions include: 5 Variazioni (Ommagio a Joyce), 1958, Circles, 1960, Visage, 1961, Epifanie, 1963, Passagio, 1962, Laborintus II, 1965, O King, 1968, Sinfonia, 1969, This Means That..., 1970, Opera, 1970, Sequenzas for solo instruments, A-ronne for eight voices, 1974—75, Coro for Chorus and Orchestra, 1975—76, La Ritirata Notturna di Madrid, 1975, Ritorno degli Snovidenia, 1977, La Vera Storia, 1978, Corale Formazioni, 1986, Ricorrenze, 1987, Concerto II, 1988, Ofanim, 1988, Canticum Novissimi Testamenti, 1989, Rendering (Schubert), 1990, Continuo, 1991. Recipient Wolf prize, 1990, Imperial Praemium prize, 1996. Died May 27, 2003.

BERKMAN, LILLIAN, foundation executive, corporation executive, art collector; b. N.Y.C. BA summa cum laude, NYU, 1942, MA summa cum laude, 1943, H.H.D. (hon.), 1976; DFA (hon.), Marquette U., 1996. Dir. pub. relations J.I. Case Co., 1957-60; pres. Gen. Alarm Corp., N.Y.C., 1965—; corp. dir., head advt. and pub. relations Am. Tractor Corp., 1948-56; dir. Allied Stores Corp., 1974-86, Mich. Nat. Corp., 1977-86, Mich. Nat. Bank, Detroit, 1977-87, Mich. Nat. Investment Corp., 1978-87, MNC-Western Leasing, 1980-87. Pres. Rojtman Found., Inc., 1967—; cultural advisor Coca Cola Co., 1978—; bd. dirs. Sterling Nat. Bank N.Y., Sterling Nat. Corp., Sterling Bancorp.; v.p., asst. to chmn. for corp. planning and devel. Associated Comm. Corp., 1988-94, vice chmn., 1990-94; v.p., asst. to chmn. long range planning Associated Group, Inc., 1995-2000. Fellow in perpetuity Met. Mus. Art, N.Y.C., 1964—; donor Rojtman Medieval Sculpture Gallery, 1964, trustee medieval art com., 1974—; mem. exec. council Inst. Fine Arts, NYC, 1972—; trustee Poly. Inst. N.Y., 1977—; nat. adv. coun. St. Petersburg (Fla.) Mus. Fine Arts, 1990—; fellow Pierpont Morgan Library, 1969—, Frick Mus., N.Y., 1980—, Nat. Council San Francisco Museums, 1985—; bd. dirs. United Cerebral Palsy Research and Ednl. Found., Inc., 1973—, Inner City Scholarship Fund, 1980—; vice chmn., dir. Salvation Army, 1986—; mem. Met. Opera Nat. Council, 1973—; overseer U. Pa. Mus., 1982—; dir. Latin Am. Arts Council, 1988—; chmn. Theban expdn. to Valley of the Kings, Egypt, 1977—; cultural advisor to Costa Rica, 1978—; chmn., bd. dirs. Associated American Artists, Inc., 1983-2000; mem. dean's adv. bd., vis. com. overseers Harvard Law Sch., 1997; bd. dirs. Met. Opera N.Y.; mem. chmn.'s coun. Met. Mus. N.Y. Recipient Highest Honor award Nat. Indsl. Advertisers Assn., 1956, Pere Marquette award Marquette U., 1966, Philippine Golden Heart Presdl. award for cultural interchange, 1976, Kairos award Marquette U., 1992, Friends of Inner-City Scholarship Fund award, 1996. Mem. Nat. Assn. Corp. Dirs., Economic Club of N.Y., Lotos Club, Univ. Club of N.Y. (mem. coun.), Harmonee Club of N.Y., Harvard Club of N.Y., Phi Beta Kappa Assocs. (bd. dirs., v.p. Middle Atlantic dist. awards com.). Home: New York, NY. Deceased.

BERLINER, JOSEPH SCHOLOM, economics educator; b. N.Y.C., Sept. 4, 1921; s. Michael and Yetta (Eisenberg) B.; m. Ann Korenbaum, Nov. 7, 1943; children: Paul, Carl, Nancy. BA, Harvard U., 1947, PhD, 1953. Mem. faculty Syracuse (N.Y.) U., 1956-63; prof. econs. Brandeis U., Waltham, Mass., 1963-85, prof. emeritus, 1985—. Author: Factory and Manager in the USSR, 1957, Economy, Society and Welfare, 1972, The Innovation Decision in Soviet Industry, 1976, Soviet Industry From Stalin to Gorbachev, 1988, The Economics of the Good Society, 1999. Social Sci. Rsch. Coun. fellow; Guggenheim Found. fellow; Kennan Inst. fellow; grantee NSF, Nat. Coun. Soviet and East European Rsch. Mem. Assn. Comparative Econ. Studies (pres. 1975-76), Am. Assn. Advancement Slavic Studies (pres. 1963-64), Am. Econ. Assn. Democrat. Jewish. Home: Cambridge, Mass. Deceased.

BERLOWE, PHYLLIS HARRIETTE, public relations counselor; b. N.Y.C. d. Louis and Rose (Jachez) Berlowe. Student, Hunter Coll., 1950-52. Account exec. Ted Sills & Co., N.Y.C., 1959-63, Harshe-Rotman & Druck, N.Y.C., 1963-65; exec. v.p. Edward Gottlieb & Assocs., N.Y.C., 1965-78; v.p. Hill & Knowlton, Inc., N.Y.C., 1972-79; v.p., group supr. Doremus & Co., N.Y.C., 1980-83, v.p., group supr., marketshare divsn., 1983-86; pres. The Berlowe Group, N.Y.C., from 1986. Named to founding roster Nat. Honor Roll of Women in Pub. Rels. No. Ill. U., 1993. Fellow Pub. Rels. Soc. Am. (citations 1976-78, 80-83, Silver Anvil 1977); mem. Counselors Acad. (chmn. 1981), Women Execs. in Pub. Rels. (pres. 1982), N.Y. Pub. Rels. Soc. (pres. 1990-91, citations 1993-95, John W. Hill award 1992). Home: New York, NY. Deceased.

BERMAN, MURIEL MALLIN, optometrist, humanities lecturer; b. Pitts. d. Samuel and Dora (Cooperman) Mallin; m. Philip I. Berman (dec. 1997), Oct. 23, 1942; children: Nancy, Nina, Steven. Student, U. Pitts., 1943, Carnegie Tech. U., 1944-45; BS, Pa. State Coll. Optometry, 1948; postgrad., U. Pitts., 1950, Muhlenberg Coll., 1954, Cedar Crest Coll., 1953, DFA (hon.), 1972; hon. degree, Hebrew U., Israel, 1982; DHL (hon.), Ursinus Coll., 1987, Lehigh U., 1991. Lic. Pa., N.J. Practice optometry, Pitts.; sec.-treas., dir. Philip and Muriel Berman Found.; underwriting mem. Lloyd's of London, 1974—94. Lectr. on travels, art, UN activities, women's status and affairs. Producer: (TV) College Speakout, 1967-77; producer, moderator: (TV) Guest Spot. Active in UNICEF, 1959-2004, ofcl. non-govtl. orgns., 1964, 74; U.S. State Dept. del. UN Internat. Women's Yr. Conf., Mexico City, 1975; mem. State Dept. Arts and Humanities Com. Nat. Commn. on Observance of Women's Yr., 1975; adv. com. U.S. Ctr. for Internat. Womens Yr., Washington; founder, donor Carnegie-Berman Coll. Art Slide Library Exchange; mem. Aspen (Colo.) Inst. Humanistic Studies, 1965, Tokyo, 1966; chmn. exhibits Great Valley council Girl Scouts U.S.A., 1966; adminstrv. head, chmn. various events Allentown Bicentennial, 1962; vice-chmn. Women for Pa. Bicentennial, 1976; co-chmn. Lehigh County Bicentennial Bell-Trek, 1976; patron Art in Embassies Program, Washington, 1965; chmn. Lehigh Valley Ednl. TV, 1966; program chmn. Fgn. Policy Assn. Lehigh County, 1965-67; treas. ann. ball Allentown Symphony, 1955; mem. art adv. com. Dieruff High Sch., Allentown, 1966; co-chmn. art. com. Episcopal Diocese Centennial Celebration, 1971; mem. Pa. Council on Status of Women, 1968-73; reappointed Pa. Gov.'s Commn. on Women, 1984; chmn. numerous art shows; mem. Art Collectors Club Am., Am. Fedn. Art, Friends of Whitney Mus., Mus. Modern Art, Mus. Primitive Art, Jewish Mus., Kemmerer Mus., Bethlehem, Pa., Univ. Mus., Phila., Archives of Am. Art, Met. Opera Guild, others; ofcl. del. Dem. Nat. Conv., 1972, 76, mem. Democratic Platform Com., 1972; former mem. Pa. Humanities Coun.; bd. dirs. Heart Assn. Pa., Allentown Art Mus. Aux., Phila. Chamber Symphony, Baum Art Sch., Lehigh County Cultural Ctr., Heart Assn. Pa., Baum Art Sch., Young Audiences, Israel Mus., Hadassah Womens Orgn.; bd. govs. Pa. State System of Higher Edn., 1986—; trustee Kutztown State Coll., 1960-66, vice-chmn. bd., 1965; trustee, sec. bd. Lehigh Community Coll.; mem. nat. bd. UN-U.S.A., 1977; trustee Pa. Council on Arts, Pa. Ballet, Smithsonian Art Council, Bonds for Israel, Hadassah (nat. bd. with portfolio), Am. Friends Hebrew U., 1984; former mem. bd. regents Internat. Ctr. for Univ. Teaching of Jewish Civilization, Israel; fine arts chmn. Women's Club; mem. com. on Prints, Drawings, & Photography Pa. Mus. Art, 1984; hon. chmn. Bucks County Coillectors Art Show; hon. bd. dirs., former trustee Phila. Mus. Art. Named Woman of Valor State of Israel, 1965; recipient Centennial citation Wilson Coll., 1969, Henrietta Szold award Allentown chpt. Hadassah, Outstanding Woman award Allentown YWCA, 1973, George Washington Honor medal Freedoms Found. at Valley Forge, 1985, Hazlett award Outstanding Svc. to Arts Pa., Outstanding Citizen award Boy Scouts Am., 1982, Myrtle Wreath award Pa. Region Hadassah, Mt. Scopus award State of Israel Bonds, 1984, Woman of Yr. award Am. Friends Hebrew U., Phila., 1984, Arts Ovation award, 1989, Cmty. Spirit award City of Allentown, 1990, Pres.' Medallion award West Chester U., 2002, Eberly award Pa. State Sys. Higher Edn., 2002, Am. Coun. Jewish Mus. award, 2003, others; hon. fellow Hebrew U., 1975. Mem. LWV, NOW, Am. Fedn. of Art., Pa. Hist. Soc. (life), Jewish Publ. Soc. Am. (former pres., chmn. bd. 1984), Disting. Daus. Pa., Art Collector's Club Am., Wellesley Club. Jewish. Avocation: american and english sculpture art. Died Apr. 13, 2004.

BERNBACH, PAUL, lawyer, investor; b. Brooklyn, Dec. 31, 1945; s. William and Evelyn (Carbone) B.; m. Therese Dorn, June 24, 1967; children: Elizabeth, Sarah, Matthew. AB, Columbia U., 1967; JD, U. Pa., 1970. Bar: N.Y. Assoc. Simpson, Thacher & Barlett, N.Y.C., 1970-79; asst. to pres., dir. acquisitions Joseph E. Seagram & Sons, Inc., N.Y.C., 1979-81; ptnr. Bernbach & Plotkin, N.Y.C., 1982—2003; dir. Doyle Dane Bernbach Internat., Inc., N.Y.C., 1982-84. Trustee Packer Collegiate Inst., Bklyn., 1983—2003, Bklyn. Mus., 1985-2003 mem. Gov.'s Real Estate Adv. Bd., adv. com. Citizen's Cultural, N.Y., 1985-2003. Mem. Heights Casino Club (Bklyn.), University Club, Order of Coif Clubs: Heights Casino (Bklyn.). Died June 14, 2003.

BERNEIS, KENNETH STANLEY, physician, educator; b. Bloomington, Ind., Dec. 25, 1951; s. hans Ludwig and Regina (Fischhoff) B.; m. Karen Lou Sachs, Nov. 23, 1975; children: Erica, Erin, Ellen, Elaina, Elyse. BS, U. Mich., 1973, MD, 1977. Diplomate Am. Bd. Family Practice; cert. geriats. Intern, resident Bronson Hosp. and Borgess Med. Ctr., 1977-80; pvt. practice Ostego, Mich., 1980—98; owner Ostego Family Physicians, 1981—97; clin. instr. Mich. State U., from 1980; preceptor Southwestern Mich. Area Health Edn. Ctr., from 1980; chief of staff Pipp Cmty. Hosp., 1985-86, vice-chief of staff, 1985-86, chief of staff, from 1986, chief ob-gyn., from 1985, chief pharmacy and therapeutics, from 1984; chief quality assurance Mirnet Rsch. Network, from 1981; pres. Med. Care Review, PLLC, from 2002. Med. dir. Bronson Healthcare Group Nursing Homes; geriatrics quality officer Borgess-Pipp; clin. cons. Borgess-Pipp Health Ctr., 1997—99; hospice bd. Wings of Hope; adj. faculty We. Mich. U., from 2001, Davenport U., from 2000; owner Med. Care Rev., PLLC, from 2003. Mem. AMA, NRA, Am. Geriatrics Soc. (cert.), Am. Acad. Family Physicians. Home: Plainwell, Mich. Died Jan. 24, 2004.

BERNSTEIN, ELLIOT LOUIS, television executive; b. N.Y.C., May 14, 1934; s. George Rubin and Renee (Horlick) B.; m. Marcy Adrienne Rosen, June 3, 1979; children: Joan, Daniel, Julie, Lisa BA, Bklyn. Coll., 1958. Writer, reporter, editor, TV producer UPI, N.Y.C., 1958-63; with ABC News, N.Y.C., 1963-66, bur. chief Saigon, 1966-67, Chgo., 1967-69; dir. news KGO TV, San Francisco, 1969-71; asst. news dir. ABC TV, N.Y.C., 1971, weekend news producer, 1972, spl. events producer, 1972-78; news producer CBS, N.Y.C., 1978. Adj. faculty Grad. Sch. Journalism, Columbia U. Producer: Sunday Morning, 1978-79, Morning News, 1979-80; exec. producer: Morning with Charles Kuralt, 1980-81; producer: Sixty Minutes, 1981-85, West 57th, 1985—; sr. producer: On the Road with Charles Kuralt, 1983—, The American Parade, 1984—, Try To Remember, 1988—, Sunday Morning, 1988—. Served with AUS, 1958. Recipient Silver Gavel, 1976, Janus award Am. Mortgage Bankers Assn., 1976, Emmy award, 1984, EDI award Nat. Easter Seals Soc., 1994, Peabody award, 1998. Mem. Writers Guild Am. East. Died Aug. 26, 2002.

BERNSTEIN, RICHARD K. physician, diabetologist; b. N.Y.C., June 17, 1934; m. Anne E. Hendon, Dec. 23, 1956; children: Julie, Laura, Jeffrey, Lili. BA in Liberal Arts and Math., Columbia U., 1954, BS in Indsl. and Mgmt. Engring., 1955, postgrad., 1959-60, 1978; MD, Albert Einstein Coll. Medicine, 1982. Diplomate Nat. Bd. Med. Examiners, Am. Acad. Wound Mgmt. Indsl. engr., data processing mgr., pers. mgr. Nat. Silver Co., N.Y.C., 1955-58; asst. to exec. v.p. Clay Adams, Inc., N.Y.C., 1958-64, dir. rsch., devel. and mktg., 1964-67; corp. sec., dir. corp. planning Nat. Silver Industries, Inc., N.Y.C., 1967-78, cons., bd. dirs., 1978-82; med. intern N.Y. Med. Coll., Valhalla, 1982-83; pvt. practice ltd. to diabetes mellitus and baryatrics Mamaroneck, N.Y., from 1983. Mem. com. on women Westchester County Med. Soc., N.Y., 1984-95; adj. instr. medicine N.Y. Med. Coll.; cons. rehab. medicine Albert Einstein Coll. Medicine; dir. Peripheral Vascular Disease Clinic Jacobi Med. Ctr. Author: Diabetes: The Glucograf Method for Normalizing Blood Sugar, 1981, Diabetes, Type II, 1990, Diabetes Solution, 1997; reviewer Diabetes Care; contbr. numerous articles to profl. jours.; patentee method for treatment of obesity. Fellow Am. Coll. Endocrinology, Am. Coll. Nutrition; mem. AMA, AAAS, IEEE (life), ASME (life), Nat. Flute Assn., Westchester Acad. Medicine, Am. Assn. Clin. Endocrinologists, Inst. Gen. Semantics, Internat. Soc. Gen. Semantics, Am. Assn. Diabetes Educators, Am. Diabetes Assn. (couns. on complications and nutritional scis.), Am. Med. Writers Assn. (exec. com. 1991—, chmn. awards com. 1991-97), Nat. Assn. Sci. Writers, Internat. Diabetes Fedn. (life), Engring. in Medicine and Biology Soc., European Assn. for Study of Diabetes, Astron. Soc. of Pacific, Amateur Astronomers Assn., Fedn. Am. Scientists, Inst. Indsl. Engrs. (life), Med. Adv. Bd. Diabetes Interview. Home: Mamaroneck, NY. Died Aug. 26, 2001.

BERREY, ROBERT WILSON, III, retired judge; b. Dec. 6, 1929; s. Robert Wilson and Elizabeth (Hudson) B.; m. Katharine Rollins Wilcoxson, Sept. 5, 1950; children: Robert Wilson IV, Mary Jane, John Lind. AB, William Jewell Coll., 1950; MA, U. S.D., 1952; LLB, Kansas City U., 1955; LLM, U. Mo., Kansas City, 1972; grad. Trial Judges Coll., U. Nev., 1972; postgrad., Ariz. State U., U. Nev. Bar: Mo. 1955, Kans. 1955. Assoc. Shugert and Thomson, 1955-56, Clark, Krings & Bredehoft, 1957-61, Terry and Welton, 1961-62; judge 4th Dist. Magistrate Ct., Jackson County, Mo., 1962-79; assoc. cir. judge 16th Cir. Ct., Jackson County, 1979-81, cir. judge, 1981-83, mem. mgmt.-exec. com., 1979-83; judge Mo. Ct. Appeals (we. dist.), Kansas City, 1983-97, chief judge, 1994, chmn. rules com., 1990-91, mem., 1993-95, conf. sec., 1992-93, mem. security com., 1992-94; ret., 1997. Mem. Supreme Ct. Com. to Draft Rules and Procedures for Mo.'s Small Claims Ct., 1976-86. Vol. legal cons. Psychiat. Receiving Ctr. Del. Atlantic Coun. Young Polit. Leaders, Oxford, Eng., 1965; Kansas City rep. to Pres.'s Nat. Conf. on Crime Control; del.-at-large White House Conf. on Aging, 1972; former pack chmn. Cub Scouts Am.; counselor, com. mem. Boy Scouts Am., sponsor Eagle Scouts; vice chmn. water fowl com. Mo. Conservation Fedn., 1968-69, chmn. water fowl com., 1971-73; v.p. Cook PTA, 1967-68; mem. cts. and judiciary com. Mo. Bar, 1969-73; mem. Midwest region adv. com. Nat. Pks. Svcs., 1973-78, chmn., 1973-78; mem. Mo. State Judicial Planning Commn., 1977; chmn. Senatorial Redistricting Com., Mo., 1991; bd. dirs., founder Kansas City Open Space Found., 1976; regional dir. Young Rep. Nat. Fedn., 1957-59, gen. counsel, 1959-61, nat. vice-chmn.; chmn. Mo. Young Rep. Fedn., 1960, nat. committeeman, 1959-60, 61-64; Mo. alt.-at-large Rep. Nat. Conv., 1960, asst. gen. counsel, 1964, del. state and dist. convs., 1960, 64, 68; bd. dirs. Naturalization Coun., Kansas City, pres., 1973—, Native Sons of Kansas City, 1987—, chmn. long-range planning com., 1992, 1st v.p., 1994, pres., 1995; trustee Kansas City Mus., 1972-73, Hyman Brand Hebrew Acad., 1983—, Woods Meml. Christian Ch., 1988—, chmn., deacon, 1988-91, elder, 1991-94, 96—, chmn. trustees, 1992—, chmn. property, 1991-97, vice chmn. bd. dirs., 1998-99, chmn. bd. dirs., 1998-99, chmn. strategic and bldg. planning com., 1995, chmn. ofcl. bd., 1998-99; mem. status coun. LEAA, 1993-96; hon. life dir. Rockhurst Coll. Mem. Mo. Bar (Disting. Svc. award 1973, agr. law com., com. coun. 1980-81), Kansas City Bar Assn., Urban League (past exec. com. dir.), SAR (registrar 1998-99), Kansas City Mus. Natural Sci. Soc. (charter), Tex. Longhorn Breeders Assn. (life), Am. Royal (bd. govs.), Am. Forestry Assn. (life), Mo. Longhorn Breeders Assn. (life), Mo. Farm Bur., Clay County Lodge (life, Mo. Marshall 1993, jr. warden 1994, sr. warden 1995, worshipful master 1995-97), Nat. Soc. SAR (law commendation medal 1995, 98), Shrine, Ararat Temple (hon. life, provost), DeMolay Legion Honor (life), Waldo Optimist Club (v.p. 1967-68), Ducks Unltd. (life, nat. trustee 1986-89, state trustee/nat. del. 1992, 94, nat. spl. projects com. 1990-95, trustee emeritus 1993, life sponsor U.S., Can., Mex., state coun. 1985—, Sportsman of Yr. 1985, Conservation Svc. award 1992, Absentee Conservation Farmer Lubbock County Soil and Water Conservation Dist. 1994), The Explorers Club, Kansas City Club, Hartwell Hunt Club (dir. 1994-97), U. Club Kansas City, J Club, William Jewell Coll., Alpha Phi Omega, Delta Theta Phi (life, Toast 1990), Pi Gamma Mu, Tau Kappa Epsilon (Hall of Fame 1986). Home: Excelsior Springs, Mo. Deceased.

BERRIE, RUSSELL, sales executive, business owner; b. N.Y.C., Mar. 18, 1933; s. Nathan and Naomi (Edleman) B.; m. Kathy Bohbot (div. Dec. 1983); children: Brett, Richard, Leslie, Scott; m. Uni Juliana Yang, Dec. 29, 1983 (div. 1991, remarried Sept. 6, 1992); children: Nicole Alanna, David Benjamin. Student, NYU, U. Fla. Toy salesman Modern Toy Co., Chgo., 1956; pvt. practice mfrs. rep. Ft. Lee, N.J., 1957-66; mfrs. rep., pres., chmn. bd. dirs. Russ Berrie & Co. Inc., Palisades Park, Oakland, N.J., from 1963. Bd. dirs. United Retail Group; lectr. in field. Holds numerous copyrights in field. Bd. overseers NYU Grad. Sch. Bus., 1986—; bd. dirs. George Rothman Inst. for Entrepreneurial Studies, Fairleigh Dickinson U.; founding mem., bd. dirs. Boys Town Jerusalem Found. Am., N.Y.C., Jewish Hosp. and Rehab. Ctr., Jersey City; trustee United Jewish Community Bergen County, River Edge, N.J., Jewish Community Ctr. on Palisades, Tenafly; founder Yeshiva U. Sch. Bus., N.Y.C.; chmn. Israeli Bus. Conf. Hebrew U., Jerusalem, 1986. Recipient Ayuda award Ayuda Toy Dr., 1984-85, Rizzuto award UNICO Nat. Italian-Am. Svc. Orgn., 1987, Gate of Jerusalem award Boys Town Jerusalem, 1987, Humanitarian award Cath. Community Svcs., 1986, Entrepreneur of Yr. award Venture Mag. and Arthur Young, 1988; named Man of Yr., Cath. Community Svcs., 1986, Entrepreneurial Leader of Yr., New Jersey Success Mag., 1989. Mem. Toy Mfrs. Am., Am. Bus. Conf. Jewish. Avocations: ballet, opera, sports. Home: Englewood, NJ. Died Dec. 25, 2002.

BERRY, RICHARD DOUGLAS, architectural educator, urban planner and designer; b. Denver, Oct. 28, 1926; s. Howard Thomas and Susie Ann (Ross) B. BA in Humanities, U. Denver, 1951; B.Arch., U. Calif-Berkeley, 1957. Assoc., project dir. Victor Gruen Assocs., Architects and Planners, Los Angeles and N.Y.C., 1957-63; mem. faculty urban planning and architecture depts. U. So. Calif., Los Angeles, 1963-75, prof. architecture, 1976-87, prof. emeritus, from 1988. Planning, programming and design cons. on new community devel. Irvine Co., Newport Beach, Calif., 1964-65, GE, 1967-68, HUD, 1973-74; cons. GE Found., 1967-68; ednl. cons. U. N.C., 1971-73; vis. prof. urban design U. Wash., Seattle, 1969; lighting deisgner, scenic artist University City Theatre, Denver, 1947-48. Served with arty. U.S. Army, 1951-53, Korea. Recipient urban design award for Downtown Cin. Renewal Plan, Progressive Architecture, 1963, rsch. achievement award for solar zoning and design Nat. Endowment for Arts, 1984; various rsch. and ednl. grants from pub. and pvt. orgns. Mem. AAAS, AAUP, Am. Inst. Cert. Planners, Am. Planning Assn., Nat. Trust for Hist. Preservation. Home: San Diego, Calif. Deceased.

BERRY, WILLIAM JAMES, III, water purification company executive; b. Durham, N.C., Mar. 7, 1950; s. William James and Rowena Meadows (Knott) B. AB, Duke U., 1972; MRP, U. N.C., 1975. Analyst N.C. Employment Security Commn., Raleigh, 1972-73; v.p. Darco Water Sys., Inc., Durham, N.C., 1974-76; water resources planner U.S. Water Resources Council, Washington, 1976-82; pres. Dracor, Inc., Durham, from 1982. Vol. Durham Arts Coun., 1988-90; pres. Forest Hills Neighborhood Assn., 1990—; bd. dirs. Stagehands (Vols. to Arts), 1989—, Durham Art Guild, Inc., 1991—; vestryman St. Philip's Ch., Durham, 1992—. Mem. Inst. Environ. Scis., N.C. Water Resources Assn., Durham C. of C. Episcopalian. Home: Durham, NC. Deceased.

BERSH, PHILIP JOSEPH, psychologist, educator; b. Phila., Sept. 9, 1921; s. Michael and Sophie (Faggen) B.; m. Jacqueline Edith Fratkin, June 8, 1952; children: Lauren Helene, Marilyn Ellen. AB, Temple U., 1944; AM, Columbia U., 1947, PhD, 1949. Lectr. Columbia U., 1948-54, research assoc., 1951-54; lectr. U. Wis., 1951; chief intelligence and electronic warfare br. Rome Air Devel. Ctr., N.Y., 1954-62; lectr. Utica Coll., Syracuse U., N.Y., 1958-60, Hamilton Coll., 1961-62; chief combat systems lab. U.S. Army Behavioral Sci. Rsch. Inst., Washington, 1962—67, assoc. dir. human performance experimentation, 1966—67; lectr. George Washington U., 1966-67; prof. psychology Temple U., Phila., 1967—2004. Vis. prof. dept. psychology Inst. Psychiatry U. London, 1979; cons. U.S. Army Research Inst. for Behavioral and Social Scis. Cons. editor: JSAS; Catalog Selected Documents in Psychology, 1976-79; mem. editorial bd. Jour. Exptl. Analysis of Behavior, 1980-83, 85-87; contbr. articles on psychology to profl. jours. Served with AUS, 1942-46, ETO. NRC postdoctoral fellow, 1950 Fellow APA, AAAS, Am. Psychol. Soc., Assn. Behavior Analysis; mem. Psychonomic Soc., Ctr. for Behavioral Studies, Ea. Psychol. Assn., Sigma Xi. Home: Bala Cynwyd, Pa. Died Apr. 2, 2004.

BERTRAM, FREDERIC AMOS, architect; b. Detroit, Oct. 15, 1937; s. Martin Terrance and Marjorie Constance (Saunders) B. Student, Ctr. for Creative Studies, Detroit, 1957-58; B.Archtl. Engring., Lawrence Inst. Tech., 1962. Registered architect, Mich., Calif., Tex., Fla.; cert. Nat. Council Arch. Rev. Bd. With Detroit City Plan Commn., 1962-63, Louis G. Redstone Assocs., 1963-65, Ziegelman and Ziegelman, 1965-68, Giffels and Rossetti, 1968-69; v.p. design Rossetti Assocs., Detroit, 1969-80, prin. in-charge Los Angeles, 1980-82; chmn. design juror awards program Delaware Valley Masonry Inst., 1978; chmn. design juror neon sign competition for students Lawrence Inst. Tech., 1978, juror design competition, 1979, Masonry Inst. Mich., 1979; lectr. in field; vis. design critic Cranbrook Acad. Art, 1977; pres. Frederic A. Bertram & Assoc., L.A., 1982-84; v.p. dir. ops. RMM Inc., Dallas, 1984-85; v.p., dir. design The Stewart Corp. Architects, Tampa, Fla., 1986-88, pvt. practice Tampa, 1991-93; architect Genesis Group Inc., Tampa, 1993-94, Wannemacher Russell Architects, St. Petersburg, Fla., from 1995. Prin. works, Alcoa Chem. and Metallurgy Bldg., Merwin, Pa. (design), United Airlines Reservation Ctr., Dearborn, Mich. (2 design), Cottonwood Condominiums, Traverse City, Mich. (2 design), Frederic A. Bertram residence, Lake Orion, Mich. (3 design), Gt. Am. Ins. Co. Office Bldg., Birmingham, Mich. (2 design), Ford Motor Land Devel. Office Bldgs., Dearborn, (design), St. John Fisher Coll., Rochester (design), Henry Ford Hosp. Ambulatory Ctr., Dearborn (3 design), Rossetti Assocs. Office Bldg., Detroit (3 design), Henry Ford Hosp. Edn. and Research, Detroit (design), Mfrs. Bank, Detroit (design), Bendix Hdqrs., Southfield, Mich. (design), Bon Secour Hosp., Grosse Pointe, Mich. (3 design), Pressure Vessel, Detroit (design), Washington Blvd Mall, Detroit (design), Monroe City Hall, Mich. (design), Tampa Internat. Airport expansion (design). Served with N.G., 1956-63. Recipient Design award Tampa YMCA-YWCO Fitness Ctr. Fellow AIA (nat. com. on design 1977-80, mem. coms. Detroit, mem. Calif. council), Engring. Soc. Detroit; mem. Tampa Bay AIA. Home: Clearwater, Fla. Died Dec. 1, 2002.

BESSE, RALPH MOORE, retired lawyer; b. Shadyside, Ohio, Nov. 23, 1905; s. Jesse Allman and Hope (Fish) B.; m. Augusta Woodward Mitchell, Apr. 28, 1934; children: Jean Elizabeth Besse Minehart, William Truman, Robert Allen. AB magna cum laude, Heidelberg Coll., 1926; JD, U. Mich., 1929; LL.D., Baldwin-Wallace Coll., 1957, Oberlin Coll., 1962, Case Inst. Tech., 1962, Western Res. U., 1963, Cleve. Marshall Law Sch., 1959; L.H.D., Wilberforce Coll., 1963, Ursuline Coll., 1970. Bar: Ohio 1930. Assoc. Squire, Sanders & Dempsey, 1929-40, ptnr., 1940-48, 70-85; with Cleve. Electric Illuminating Co., 1948-70, pres., 1960-67, chmn. bd., chief exec. officer, 1967-70; chmn. Nat. Machinery Co., 1962-90, bd. dirs., 1962-94. Author: Besse: What Can One Man Do. Contbr. articles to profl. jours. Mem. adv. bd. Ctr. for the Book, Libr. of Congress, 1979; chief U.S. Army Ordinance Cleve. Dist., 1951-62; trustee Nat. History Day, 1980, Ursuline Coll., 1963, 92, John Huntington Art and Poly. Trust, 1966-86, John Huntington Fund for Edn., 1966-86, Heidelberg Coll., 1949-80, Case Western Reserve U., 1970-76, chmn. bd. dirs., 1971-75. Recipient Cleve. medal for pub. service Cleve. C. of C., 1960, Ursula Laurus award Ursuline Coll., 1965, Eisenman award Jewish Community Fedn. Cleve., 1966, Human Relations award NCCJ, 1967, award Cleve. Bus. League, 1967, Univ. medal Case Western Res. U., 1976, Wisdom award of honor Wisdom Soc., 1979, Disting. Service award Ohio Coll. Assn., 1980, Disting. Alumni award U. Mich., 1981, James Dodman Nobel award Coun. Human Rels., 1982; named Father of Community Colls. in Ohio, 1961; elected to Ohio Found. of Ind. Colls. Hall of Fame, 2000, Ohio Found. Hall Excellence, 2000, Educator of Yr., Heidelberg Coll. Alumni, 2000; Ralph M. Besse chair in bus. established by Heidelberg Coll., 1979, Ralph M. Besse award for teaching excellence established by Cuyahoga Community Coll., 1980; numerous other awards Fellow Am. Bar Found.; mem. ABA, Ohio Bar Assn., Bar Assn. Greater Cleve. Home: Charlottesville, Va. Died Oct. 25, 2002.

BEST, HOLLIS GARBER, judge; b. Curry County, N.Mex., July 10, 1926; s. Ernest and Neely Civil (Stratton) B.; m. Kathryn Jean LaFollette, Aug. 4, 1947; children: David S., Daniel E., Laura J. Best Marks, Kathryn A. AB, Fresno State U., 1948; JD, Stanford U., 1951. Bar: Calif. 1951. Dep. dist. atty. County of Fresno, Fresno, Calif., 1951-53; ptnr. Manfredo, Best & Forbes, Fresno, 1953-63, McCormick, Barstow, Sheppard, Coyle & Best, Fresno, 1963-72; judge Calif. Superior Ct., Fresno, 1972-84; assoc. justice Calif. 5th dist. Ct. Appeals, Fresno, from 1984, presiding justice, 1990-94; magistrate judge Ea. Dist. Calif., from 1994. Mem. exec. com., Conf. State Bar Dels., Calif., 1969-71; adj. prof. law, San Joaquin Coll. Law, Fresno, 1974-84. Lt. (j.g.) USNR, 1944-46, PTO. Mem. Calif. Judges Assn. (sec.-treas. 1979-80), Calif. Judges Found. (bd. dirs. 1987-90), Fresno County Bar Assn. (pres. 1963), Rotary. Republican. Avocations: golf, reading. Home: Fresno, Calif. Died Aug. 15, 2003.

BETANZOS, RAMON JAMES, humanities educator, educator; b. Dearborn, Mich., Oct. 17, 1933; AB in Philosophy, Sacred Heart Sem. Coll., 1955; STB in Sacred Theology, The Cath. U. Am., 1959; AM in History, U. Mich., 1963, PhD in History, 1968. Ordained priest Roman Cath. Ch., 1959. Asst. prof. history and philosophy Sacred Heart Sem. Coll., Detroit, 1968-74; asst. prof. Monteith Coll., 1974-78; asst. prof. humanities Wayne State Univ., Detroit, 1978-87, assoc. prof. humanities, 1987-93, prof., from 1993, chair dept. Humanities, from 1992. Cons. Macomb County and Macomb County C. C., 1976, Prentice-Hall, 1989, Holt, Rinehart and Winston, 1989; lectr. numerous acad. seminars. Translator: (with critical introduction) Einleitung in die Geisteswissenschaften (Wilhelm Dilthey), 1988, Die Sechs Grossen Themen der Abendländischen Metaphysik (Heinz Heimsoeth), 1993; contbr. articles to profl. jours. Recipient Probus Club award, 1988; faculty rsch. grantee Wayne State U., 1987-91, grantee Earhart Found., 1989. Mem. AAUP, Wissenschaftliche Buchgesellschaft, Deutscher Akademischer Austauschdienst. Home: Pleasant Ridge, Mich. Deceased.

BEVERETT, ANDREW JACKSON, retired marketing executive; b. Midland City, Ala., Feb. 21, 1917; s. Andrew J. and Ella Levonia (Adams) B.; m. Martha Sophia Landgrebe, May 26, 1951; children: Andrew Jackson III, James Edmund, Faye A. BS, Samford U., 1940; MBA, Harvard U., 1942. With United Air Lines, Chgo., 1946-66; dir. aviation econs., sr. mktg. econ. cons. Mgmt. and Econs. Rsch., Inc., Palo Alto, Calif., 1966-71; sr. economist Stanford Rsch. Inst., Menlo Park, 1971-72; pres. Edy's on the Peninsula stores, 1973-78; real estate broker, fin. and tax cons. Saratoga, San Jose, Calif., 1979-99; ret., 1999. With USNR, 1942-46. Mem. Nat. Assn. Enrolled Agts., Nat. Assn. Realtors, Pi Gamma Mu, Phi Kappa Phi. Home: San Jose, Calif. Died Nov. 17, 2002.

BEVIS, EM OLIVIA, nursing educational consultant; b. Graceville, Fla., Mar. 20, 1932; d. James Edison and Willie (Bullock) B.; m. Julian Richard Friedman, Dec. 27, 1974; children: Esther, Sheldon. BSN, Emory U., 1955; MA, U. Chgo., 1958; EdD, U. Ga., 1990; student, U. Fla., 1950-52. Prof. nursing San Jose (Calif.) State U., 1962-73; prof. nursing, coord. Savannah grad. program Med. Coll. of Ga., Augusta, 1975-80; head dept. nursing, prof. Ga. So. U., Stateboro, 1980-85, adj. prof. rsch., from 1985. Cons. in nursing edn. Mem. Nat. League for Nursing, ANA, Nightingale Soc., Am. Acad. Nursing, Sigma Theta Tau, Pi Lambda Theta, Kappa Delta Pi. Died July 20, 2000.

BEYER, JANICE MARY, management educator; b. Milw., May 1, 1934; d. Elmer Raymond and Elizabeth Helen (Schmidt) B.; m. Thomas M. Lodahl, Sept. 4, 1954 (div. 1974); children: Claire Lodahl Budge, Andrea Lodahl Henneman; m. Harrison M. Trice, Oct. 12, 1974 (div. 1990). MusB, U. Wis., 1955; MS, Cornell U., 1970, PhD, 1973. Asst. prof. SUNY, Buffalo, 1973-78, assoc. prof., 1978-81, prof., 1981-86, NYU, N.Y.C., 1986 88; prof. dept. mgmt. U. Tex., Austin, from 1988, Rebecca L. Gale regents prof. bus., 1988; dir. Ctr. for Orgn. Rsch., from 1992. David T. McLaughlin vis. prof. The Amos Tuck Sch., Dartmouth Coll., 1994. Co-author: Implementing Change, 1978, Cultures of Work Organizations, 1993; editorial bd. Adminstrv. Sci. Quar., 1974-84, 1992—, Acad. Mgmt. Jour., 1981-84, editor, 1985-87; editorial bd. Acad. Mgmt. Exec., 1987-89, Jour. of Orgnl. Behavior, 1990—, Jour. of Socio-Econs., 1989—. Recipient Mark Keller award Jour. Alcohol Studies, 1985. Fellow Acad. Mgmt. (pres. 1990-91), Internat. Fedn. Scholarly Assn. of Mgmt. (pres elect 1991-92, pres. 1993—); mem. Soc. Advancement Socio-Econs. (exec. coun. 1989-92), Am. Sociol. Assn., Ea. Acad. Mgmt. (bd. dirs. 1983-86). Avocation: tennis. Home: Princeton, NJ. Died June 20, 2001.

BIALA, JANICE, artist; b. Biala, Grodno, Russia, Oct. 18, 1903; d. Chaim and Esther (Singer) Tworkovsky; m. Daniel Brustlein, July 1942. Student, Art Students League, N.Y., 1923. Solo and group exhbns. throughout U.S. and Europe; represented in permanent collections Whitney Mus., Phillips Collection, Washington, Mus. Lausanne, Switzerland, Princeton (N.J.) Mus., Newark Mus., Musée de Grenoble, France, Musée d'Ingres, Montabar, France. Decorated officer des Arts et Lettres (France). Deceased.

BIANCHI, PETER VIERI, artist; b. Kenosha, Wis., Oct. 18, 1920; s. Abramo and Maria Bianchi; m. Elizabeth Ann Thomas, Sept. 17, 1981. Student, Mizen Acad. Art, Chgo., 1939-41, Chgo. Acad. Art, 1945, Am. Acad. Art, Chgo., 1946-49. Apprentice artist Haddon Sundblom, Johnson & White Art Studio, Chgo., 1949-51; staff artist Nat. Geographic Soc., Nat. Geographic Mag., Washington, 1959-73; fine artist Kenosha, 1951-59, Silver Spring, Md., from 1974. Maj. oil paintings include Archangel Raphael (gold medals for religious order), The Madonna of the Airways, The Dead Sea Scrolls, Anazi Indian Collection, Hannibal, Greece, Rome collection, Our Lady of Emmitsburg, Am. Indian religious and western subjects, portraiture of people of note; exhibits religious and Am. Indian hist. art on West coast. Home: Greenbelt, Md. Died Jan. 3, 2001.

BIANCHI, UGO DONATO, archbishop; b. Pennabilli, Italy, Feb. 10, 1930; Ordained priest to Roman Cath. ch., 1954. Consecrated bishop, 1977; archbishop City of Urbino, Urbania and Sant' Angelo, Italy, from 1977. Died 1999.

BICK, DAVID GREER, healthcare executive; b. Toledo, June 29, 1953; s. James D. and Carol Jean (Hermann) B.; m. Cynthia Brightfield; children from previous marriage: Jennifer Kelly, Jesse Quinn, Matthew Adam, Wylie Christine; stepchildren: Alec, Christopher. BE, U. Toledo, 1975; cert. health cons., Purdue U., 1981. Dir. sales Blue Cross, Toledo, 1981-82; v.p. mktg. Blue Cross/Blue Shield Cen. N.Y., Syracuse, 1983; exec. dir. Preview-Health Benefits Mgmt. of Ohio, Toledo, 1984-87; chief mktg. exec. HMO Health Ohio Blue Cross and Blue Shield of Ohio, 1984-87, v.p. sales and support svcs., mut. health svcs., 1988; v.p. sales and mktg. FHP, Inc., 1989-95; v.p. gov. programs Blue Cross Blue Shield of Tex., from 1995. Mem. steering com. Medicare/Medicaid. Author: (poetry) Paupers and Profiteers, Proud Words on a Dusty Shelf. Mem. People's Med. Soc., Hastings Ctr.-Inst. and Soc. of Ethics and Life, Am. Coll. of Healthcare Execs., Alliance Healthcare Strategy, Tex. Assn. Health Plan, Nat. Inst. Health Care Mgmt., Acad. for Healthcare Mgmt., U.S. Tennis Assn. (competition com., mktg. com., champs com.), U. Toledo Alumni Assn., Boilermaker Club (Purdue). Roman Catholic. Avocations: photography, golf, tennis. Home: Allen, Tex. Deceased.

BICKS, ROBERT ALAN, lawyer; b. N.Y.C., May 27, 1927; s. Alexander and Henrietta (Isaacson) B.; m. Patricia Hughes, Apr. 14, 1956; children: Michael, Peter, James, Sarah. BA magna cum laude, Yale U., 1949, LLB, 1952. Bar: N.Y. 1952, D.C. 1959, U.S. Supreme Ct. 1959. Clk. to judge N.Y. Ct. Appeals, N.Y.C., 1952-53; exec. sec. com. to study antitrust laws Office of U.S. Atty. Gen., Washington, 1953-54; legal asst. to head antitrust div. U.S. Dept. Justice, Washington, 1954-59, asst. atty. gen. antitrust div., 1960-61; ptnr. Breed, Abbott & Morgan, N.Y.C., from 1961. Bd. dirs. Ideal Basic Industries, Inc., Denver. Comments editor Yale U. Law Jour. Named one of 10 Outstanding Young Men in Am. Jaycees, 1960. Mem. ABA, Fed. Bar Assn., N.Y. State Bar Assn., Assn. of Bar of City of N.Y., Am. Judicature Soc., Phi Beta Kappa. Avocation: yacht racing. Home: New York, NY. Died Dec. 25, 2002.

BIDDLE, GARY JAMES, manufacturing executive; b. Tiffin, Ohio, Nov. 9, 1938; s. Harold J. and Virginia (Lang) B.; m. Jeanne Castelluccio, May 9, 1981; children: Amanda J., Gregg G. AA, Rider Coll., 1971, BS in Commerce, 1975. Various staff positions Am. Standard, Inc., Tiffin, 1957-66, mfg. cons. N.Y.C., 1966-69, mgr. product control Trenton, N.J., 1969-73, dir. mgmt. info. systems Piscataway, N.J., 1973-83, staff v.p. mgmt. info. systems N.Y.C., 1983-86, v.p. info. systems, from 1986. Mem.: Union League (N.Y.C.). Avocations: golf, skiing. Home: Belle Mead, NJ. Deceased.

BIDLACK, RUSSELL EUGENE, librarian, educator, former dean; b. Manilla, Iowa, May 25, 1920; s. Harold Stanley and Mabel (Thompson) B.; m. Melva Helen Sparks, June 13, 1942; children: Stanley Alden, Martha Sue, Christopher Joel, Harold Wilford. BA with honors, Simpson Coll., 1947, Litt.D. (hon.), 1976; AB in L.S. with honors, U. Mich., 1948, A.M. in L.S, 1949, A.M. in History, 1950, PhD (L.S.), 1954. Instr. library sci. U. Mich., 1951-56, asst. prof., 1956-60, assoc. prof., 1960-65, prof., 1965-85, dean Sch. Library Sci., 1969-85, prof. and dean emeritus, 1985—. Author: The City Library of Detroit, 1817-1837, 1955, Letters Home, the Story of Ann Arbor's Forty-Niners, 1960, John Allen and the Founding of Ann Arbor, 1962, The Yankee Meets the Frenchman, 1965, The ALA Accreditation Process, 1977, Ann Arbor's First Lady, Events in the Life of Ann I. Allen, 1998. Served to master sgt. AUS, 1941-46. Recipient Beta Phi Mu award for distinguished service to edn. for librarianship, 1977; Melvil Dewey medal creative profl. achievement, 1979; Joseph W. Lippincott award for disting. service to librarianship, 1983 Mem. ALA (chmn. subcom. to rewrite Standards accreditation 1969-72, chmn. com. 1974-76, chmn. Melvil Dewey award jury 1973-74, chmn. Am. Library History Roundtable 1973-74, mem. council 1972-76, chmn. nominating com. 1980-81), Mich. Library Assn. (pres. tech. services sect.), Assn. Library and Info. Sci. Edn. (chmn. deans and dirs. group 1978-79), Mich. Hist. Soc. Home: Ann Arbor, Mich. Deceased.

BIEDERMAN, DONALD ELLIS, lawyer; b. N.Y.C., Aug. 23, 1934; s. William and Sophye (Groll) B.; m. Marna M. Leerburger, Dec. 22, 1962; children: Charles Jefferson, Melissa Anne. AB, Cornell U., 1955; JD, Harvard U., 1958; LLM in Taxation, NYU, 1970. Bar: N.Y. 1959, U.S. Dist. Ct. (so. dist.) N.Y. 1967, Calif. 1977. Assoc. Hale, Russell & Stentzel, N.Y.C., 1962-66; asst. corp. counsel City of N.Y., 1966-68; assoc. Delson & Gordon, N.Y.C., 1968-69; ptnr. Roe, Carman, Clerke, Berkman & Berkman, Jamaica, N.Y., 1969-72; gen. atty. CBS Records, N.Y.C., 1972-76; sr. v.p. legal affairs and adminstrn. ABC Records, L.A., 1977-79; ptnr. Mitchell, Silberberg & Knupp, L.A., 1979-83; exec. v.p., gen. counsel Warner/Chappell Music Inc., L.A., 1983-99, cons., from 2000. Adj. prof. Sch. Law Southwestern U., L.A., 1982-2000, prof. law, dir. entertainment and media law inst., 2000—, Pepperdine U., Malibu, Calif., 1985-87, Loyola Marymount U., L.A., 1992; lectr. Anderson Sch. Mgmt. UCLA, 1993, U. So. Calif. Law Ctr., 1995-97. Editor: Legal and Business Problems of the Music Industry, 1980; co-author: Law and Business of the Entertainment Industries, 1987, 2nd edit., 1991, 3d edit., 1995, 4th edit., 2001. Bd. dirs. Calif. Chamber Symphony Soc., L.A., 1981-92; dir. Entertainment Law Inst. U. So. Calif., 1993-2000. 1st lt. U.S. Army, 1959. Recipient Hon. Gold Record, Recording Industry Assn. Am., 1974, Trendsetter award Billboard mag., 1976, Gold Triangle award Am. Acad. Dermatology, 1999; named Entertainment Lawyer of Yr., Beverly Hills Bar Assn., 2000. Mem. N.Y. Bar Assn., Calif. Bar Assn., Riviera Country Club, Cornell Club. Democrat. Jewish. Avocations: golf, skiing, travel, reading. don. Home: Los Angeles, Calif. Died Aug. 8, 2002.

BIENVENU, ROBERT CHARLES, lawyer; b. Milw., Dec. 3, 1922; s. Harold John and Nellie (Davidson) B.; AB, U. Calif., Berkeley, 1947; JD, U. Pacific, 1953. Bar: Calif. 1954. m. Martha Beard, Mar. 28, 1945 (dec. 1969); children: Susan Krestan, Nancy Simas, John; m. Joyce Marlene Holley, Aug. 13, 1971. State parole officer Dept. Corrections, Sacramento, 1947-54; mem. Hoover, Lacy & Bienvenu, Modesto, Calif., 1954-66; pvt. practice, 1966—. Pres., Stanislaus County Sch. Bds. Assn., 1968-69; mem. Modesto City Schs. Bd. Edn., 1961-81; mem. Calif. Rep. Cen.Com. 1960-70; bd. dirs. Modesto Symphony Orch., 1966-72, Retarded Children's Soc. Stanislaus County, 1965-70, Am. Cancer Soc., 1955-60. With AUS, 1942-45. Mem. ABA, State Bar Calif., Stanislaus County Bar Assn., Am. Trial Lawyers Assn. Home: Modesto, Calif. Deceased.

BIERN, ROBERT OSCAR, cardiologist; b. Huntington, W.Va., Dec. 21, 1932; BA, Princeton U., 1954; MD, Johns Hopkins U., 1958. Diplomate Am. Bd. Internal Medicine, Am. Bd. Cardiovasc. Disease. Intern U. Va. Hosps., 1958-59; resident in medicine Cin. Gen. Hosp., 1960-61; resident in cardiology U. Va. Hosps., 1961-62; fellow in cardiology Johns Hopkins Hosp., Balt., 1964-66; staff cardiologist Anne Arundel Med. Ctr., Annapolis, Md., from 1966. Asst. prof. Johns Hopkins U. Died Aug. 7, 1999.

BIERNACKI-PORAY, WLAD OTTON, architect; b. Lwow, Poland, June 9, 1924; s. Roman Alexander and Ewa Valeria (Biernacki) P.; m. Zofia Maria Balicki, Aug. 15, 1947; children: Krystyna Cora, Teresa Nora, Marek Victor. BA, U. Rome, 1948; MA, Univ Coll., London, 1950. Registered architect, U.S., U.K., Can., Poland. Chief designer, ptnr. Howard T. Fisher Assoc., N.Y.C., 1954-55; prin. Biernacki-Poray & Assocs., N.Y.C. and Montclair, N.J., 1955—; pres. Mike Poray & Assocs. Engring. Ltd., Nigeria; chmn. Poray, Peter & Assocs. Ltd., London; pres. Am. Biotech. Corp., Montclair, 1975—. Prin. works include: U.S. Fed. Office Bldg., Newark, 1968, Pediatric Inst. and Med. Acad., Krakow, Poland. Bd. dirs. Albert Schweitzer Fellowship, N.Y.C., 1975—, pres. Am. Rsch. Hosp., N.Y.C., 1960—. Lt. Arty., 1939-45, ETO, NATOUSA. Mem. Interplan Assn. Engrs. (pres. 1966-80), Am. Tower Assn. (pres. 1970—), AIA, Knight of Souvereign Order of St. John, Order of St. John of Jerusalem, Knight of Malta. Roman Catholic.Deceased. Home: Montclair, NJ.

BILHARTZ, LYMAN EMERSON, medical educator, physician; b. Dallas, Feb. 27, 1953; s. Harrell Louis and Jesse Joy (Coleman) B.; m. Janet Elizabeth Leonard, Dec. 30, 1972; children: Jacob Lyman, Tess Marie, Nathaniel James. Student, U. Tex., 1971-74, MD, 1978. Diplomate Am. Bd. Internal Medicine, Am. Bd. Gastroenterology. Resident in internal medicine U. Calif., San Francisco, 1978-81, chief resident in internal medicine, 1981-82; gastroenterology fellow Southwestern Med. Sch., Dallas, 1982-86, prof. medicine, 1986—2004. Attending physician Parkland Meml. Hosp., Dallas, 1986-2004; pres. SW Med. Sch. Faculty Senate, 1993. Ordained elder Northridge Presbyn. Ch., Dallas. Fellow ACP; mem. Am. Gastroent. Assn. (rsch. scholar 1987), Alpha Omega Alpha (former sec.). Avocations: sailing, birdwatching, sacred choral music. Home: Dallas, Tex. Died May 24, 2004.

BILLER, MORRIS (MOE BILLER), former union executive; b. N.Y.C., Nov. 5, 1915; m. Anne Fiefer, Aug. 24, 1940 (dec. 1978), Colee Farris, (div.); children: Michael, Steven. Student, Bklyn. Coll., 1936-38, CCNY, 1946. With U.S. Postal Svc., 1937-92; active Am. Postal Workers Union, Washington, 1937—2001, N.E. regional coord., 1972-80, pres., 1980—2001, pres. emeritus, 2001—03; gen. pres. Manhattan-Bronx Postal Union (N.Y. Metro Area Postal Union), 1959-80. Mem. exec. coun. AFL-CIO; bd. dirs. Union Labor Life Ins., Co.; exec. v.p. pub. employee dept. AFL-CIO; pub. mem. fed. adv. council occupational safety and health Dept. Labor. Bd. dirs. Assn. Children with Retarded Mental Devel., United Way Internat.; adv. bd. Cornell U. Trade Union Women Studies Program; adv. council Empire State Coll.; nat. bd. dirs., fed. thrift adv. council A. Philip Randolph Inst.; nat. labor chairperson March of Dimes Telethon; v.p., Muscular Dystrophy Assn. With AUS, 1943-45, ETO. Recipient Disting. Service award N.Y.C. Central Labor Council, 1977; recipient Community Service award N.Y.C. Central Labor Council, 1979, Spirit of Life award City of Hope, 1982, Walter P. Reuther Meml. award Ams. for Democratic Action, 1982 Mem. Combined Fed. Campaign (exec. com.), N.Y.C. Central Labor Council (exec. bd dirs.), Central Labor Council (bd. dirs. central rehab.), Coalition Labor Union Women, Postal, Telegraph and Telephone Internat. (mem. exec. com.), NAACP, A. Philip Randolph Inst. Home: New York, NY. Died Sept. 5, 2003.

BILLINGHAM, RUPERT EVERETT, zoologist, educator; b. Warminster, Eng., Oct. 15, 1921; s. Albert E. and Helen (Green) B.; m. Jean Mary Morpeth, Mar. 29, 1951; children: John David, Peter Jeremy, Elizabeth Anne. BA, Oriel Coll., Oxford, Eng., 1943, MA, 1947, DPhil, 1950, DSc, 1957; DSc (hon.), Trinity Coll., 1965, U. Pa., 1992. Lectr. zoology U. Birmingham, Eng., 1947-51; research fellow Brit. Empire Cancer Campaign; hon. research asso. dept. zoology Univ. Coll., London, 1951-57; mem. Wistar Inst.; Wistar prof. zoology U. Pa., Phila., 1957-65; prof., chmn. dept. med. genetics, dir. Henry Phipps Inst., U. Pa. Med. Sch., 1965-71; prof., chmn. dept. cell biology and anatomy U. Tex. Health Sci. Center at Dallas, 1971-86, prof. emeritus, from 1990. Mem. allergy and immunology study sect. NIH, 1959-62; mem. transplantation immunology com. Nat. Inst. Allergy and Infectious Diseases, NIH, 1968-70, 71-73, mem. council, 1980-83; mem. sci. adv. bd. St. Jude Children's Research Hosp., Memphis, 1965-70; mem. sci. adv. com. Mass. Gen. Hosp., 1976-79 Contbr. articles to profl. jours.; Editorial bd.: Transplantation, 1980-82; adv. editorial bd.: Placenta, 1980-85; adv. editor: Jour. Exptl. Medicine, 1963-84; assoc. editor: Am. Jour. Reproductive Immunology, 1981-86, Jour. Immunology, 1964-72, Cellular Immunology, 1970-86, Jour. Exptl. Zoology, 1976-80; hon. editorial bd.: Developmental and Comparative Immunology, 1977-80. Served to lt. Royal Navy, 1942-46. Recipient Alvarenga prize Coll. Physicians, Phila., 1963, hon. award Soc. Plastic Surgeons, 1964, Fred Lyman Adair award Am. Gynecol. Soc., 1971, Medawar Transplantation award, 1994. Fellow Royal Soc. (London), N.Y. Acad. Scis., Am. Acad. Arts and Scis.; mem. Am. Assn. Immunologists, Transplantation Soc. (pres. 1974-76), Am. Assn. Transplant Surgeons (hon.), Internat. Soc. Immunology of Reprodn. (pres. 1983-86), British Transplantation Soc. (hon. 1988). Home: Vineyard Haven, Mass. Died Nov. 16, 2002.

BILLINGSLEY, CHARLES EDWARD, retired transportation company executive; b. DeQueen, Ark., Sept. 2, 1933; s. James Glazebrook and Malcolm Elizabeth (Rice) B.; m. Gloria Ann Smith, Sept. 4, 1954; children: Charles M. (dec.), Mark E., Barbara A. BA, U. Okla., 1955, MA, 1960. CPA, Okla. Various mgmt. positions GE, 1959-66; supr. budgets and analysis Pa. R.R., Chgo., 1966-68; contr. ea. region Pa. Cen. R.R., Indpls., 1968; mgr. budgetary adminstrn. Ebasco Industries, N.Y.C., 1968-69; asst. contr. Union Pacific Corp., N.Y.C., 1969-70, Omaha, 1970-88, contr. Bethlehem, Pa., 1988-90, v.p., contr., 1990-95; sr. v.p. Union Pacific Corp., Bethelehem, Pa., 1995-97. Mem. acctg. adv. com. U. Nebr., Omaha, 1980-83, adv. coun. Coll. Bus., Kans. State U., Manhattan, 1983-87, profl. acctg. coun. U. Iowa, Iowa City, 1985-88, bd. visitors Sch. Acctg., U. Okla., Norman, 1990—. Capt. U.S. Army, 1957. Recipient John P. Begley Disting. Svc. award Creighton U., 1989, John D. DeVries

Svc. award Iowa State U., 1989, Outstanding Contbn. award U. Iowa, 1990; named Beta Alpha Psi Acct. of Yr. for Industry, 1993. Mem. AICPA, Okla. Soc. CPAs, Am. Acctg. Assn., Inst. Internal Auditors (bd. dirs. 1980-85, chmn. audit com. 1985), Fin. Execs. Inst., Plaza Club, Delta Tau Delta. Republican. Methodist. Home: San Antonio, Tex. Died Sept. 10, 2001.

BILLS, ROBERT E(DGAR), emeritus psychology educator; b. Nutley, N.J., Dec. 15, 1916; s. Willis Minard and Leah Catherine (Condit) B.; m. Annie Tarleton Carley, Dec. 22, 1944; children: Mary Ann Bills Niles, Leah Catherine Bills Hawkins. BS, Western Ky. U., 1938; MA, U. Ky., 1946; EdD, Columbia U., 1948. Tchr. sci. Breathitt County (Ky.) Bd. Edn., 1938-42; tchr. Anchorage Bd. Edn. (Ky.), 1943-44, prin., 1944-45; critic tchr. sci. U. Ky. Coll. Edn., 1945-46; faculty Coll. Arts and Scis., 1948-52, chmn. div. biol. scis., 1950-51, assoc. prof., 1952-56; prof. psychology, chmn. dept. Auburn U., 1956-61; prof. ednl. psychology U. Ala., 1961-69, rsch. prof. edn., 1969-70, rsch. prof. emeritus, from 1979, asst. dean rsch., 1961-63; interim dean Coll. Edn., 1963-65, dean, 1965-69, dean emeritus, from 1979. Mem. coun. psychol. resources of S. Regional Edn. Bd., 1953-56; chmn. Ky. Bd. Examiners Psychologists, 1954-56; vis. prof. U. Fla., 1953, 54, Mich. State U., 1956, U. Wash., 1963; lectr. in field. Author: Education for Intelligence or Failure?, 1982; contbr. chpts. to books, articles in field to profl. jours. Bd. dirs. Southeastern Ednl. Corp., 1966-67; sec. Ala. Coalition for Better Edn., 1969-70, pres., 1971-72. Served with U.S. Army, 1943-44; with USCG Aux., 1982-99. Recipient Ednl. Press Assn. award for distinguished contbn. to ednl. journalism, 1982. Fellow APA (sec.-treas. divsn. 1963-66), Mid-South Edn. Rsch. Assn. (v.p. 1978, pres. 1979), ASCD (dir. 1962-64), U.S. Coast Guard Aux. (mem. nat. staff 1989-98), Sigma Xi, Kappa Delta Pi, Psi Chi, Phi Delta Kappa. Home: Tuscaloosa, Ala. Died Sept. 30.

BINDER, FREDERICK MOORE, college president; b. Atlantic City, N.J., Nov. 18, 1920; s. Paul Reginald and Kathryn (Moore) B.; m. Grace Irene Brandt, May 27, 1943; children: Janet Binder Houts, Roberta Lynn. BA, Ursinus Coll., 1942, LL.D. (hon.), 1960; MA, U. Pa., 1948, PhD, 1955; Litt.D. (hon.), Wagner Coll, 1964; L.H.D. (hon.), Rider coll., 1967, Hartwick Coll., 1985; Pd.D. (hon.), Susquehanna U., 1969. Tchr. Somerville (N.J.) High Sch., 1946; asst. registrar Temple U., 1946-47, dept. history, 1947-55; dean, asso. prof. history Thiel Coll., 1955-57, acad. v.p. prof. history, 1957-59, acting pres., 1959, pres. Hartwick Coll., 1959-69; assoc. commr. for higher edn. N.Y. State Edn. Dept., 1969-70; pres. Whittier Coll. (Calif.), 1970-75, Juniata Coll., Huntingdon, Pa., 1975-86; lectr. in Am. diplomatic history U. Leeds, Eng., 1986-87; pres. Fgn. Policy Rsch. Inst., Phila., 1989-90. Mem. N.Y. State Regents Exams. Bd., 1962-68; Fulbright lectr., Yugoslavia, 1967-68 Author: Serbian Assignment, 1971, Coal Age Empire, 1974; Contbr. book revs. and articles to profl. publs. Chmn. Ind. Coll. Funds. Am., 1966-67; bd. dirs. S.W. Mus., 1970-75, trustee Fox Hosp., Oneonta, N.Y., 1965—; mem. Pa. State Bd. Edn., 1983-88, Pa. state bd. Am. Cancer Soc., 1985-86. Lt. (j.g.) USNR, 1942-45; lt. comdr. Res. Recipient Newcomen award for contbn. to cause of material history Newcomen Soc. in N.Am., 1955; hon. fellow Humberside Coll. of Higher Edn., Hull, Eng., 1986. Mem. Am. Assn. Univ. Adminstrs. (v.p. 1981-83), Newcomen Soc., Pa. Acad. Deans (chmn. 1959), Hist. Soc. Pa., Empire State Found. for Ind. Liberal Arts Colls. (chmn. 1962-63), Cosmos Club, Alpha Chi Rho (nat. scholarship officer 1957-59) Episcopalian. Died Jan. 28, 2004.

BING, RALPH SOL, advertising executive; b. Cleve., May 21, 1917; s. Sol Ralph and Helen (Einstein) B.; m. Barbara Cohen, Nov. 8, 1953; children: Aleta, Ralph Sam. Student, U. Ill., 1936-37; cert., John Huntington Poly., Cleve., 1939, Kent State U., 1966. Advt. copywriter The May Co., Cleve., 1938-41; advt. mgr. The Heights Press (now named Sun Newspapers), Cleve., 1941-42; ptnr. Bing and Haas Advt., Cleve., 1946-51; pres. Ralph Bing Advt. Co., Cleve., from 1951, Mktg. Assocs., Beachwood, Ohio, 1975-79; owner Ralph Bing Advt. Cons., San Diego, 1980-87. Combat corr. 82nd Airborne div., The Stars and Stripes. Author: Smoke Dreams, 1950, History of the Temple, 1950; contbr. numerous articles to profl. jours., also radio and TV commls. Councilman City of Beachwood, 1965-79; pres. grouping of municipalities Coun. of Couns., Cleve., 1978-79; mem. Rancho Bernardo (Calif.) Pub. Utilities Commn., 1983-85; chmn. Community Alert Program Rancho Bernardo, 1986; mem., corr. sec., mem. exec. bd. Rancho Bernardo Community Coun., 1993—; v.p. North County Interfaith Coun., 1996-97; bd. dirs. Ctr. for Humane Edn. for So. Calif., 1995-97. Recipient Outstanding Citizen award Beachwood Civi League, 1980, Outstanding Service award United Appeal, 1950, 51, Appreciation plaque Ohio Bar Assn., 1975; Ralph S. Bing Days named in his honor Beachwood City Council, 1979, 80. Mem. Family Svc. Assn. (hon. life), Rancho Bernardo Press Club (exec. bd. 1991—, v.p. 1994-95, pres. 1996), Woodcrafts Club, Masons. Republican. Avocations: dogs, community activites, volunteer work. Died Aug. 25, 2001.

BINNION, JOHN EDWARD, education educator; b. Paris, Tex., July 14, 1918; s. Roy Cecil and Johnnie Mary (Garner) B.; m. Doris Lee Campbell, Mar. 30, 1945; children: Margaret Ann, John Edward II, Mary Virginia, Dianna Lee. AA, Chaffey Coll., Ontario, Calif., 1936; BBA, U. Tex., 1945; MA, N.Mex. Highlands U., 1951; EdD, Okla. State U., 1953; MBA, U. Denver, 1972. CPA, Okla., Tex.; cert. adminstrv. mgr. Acct. D&B Emsco Mfg. Co., Dallas, 1945-46; acct., office mgr. Lumber Dealer's Supply Co., Long Beach, Calif., 1946-47; tchr. Sawyer (Kans.) H.S., 1947-50; asst. prof. bus. edn. and bus. adminstrn., supr. USAF clk.-typist program N.Mex. Highlands U., 1950-52; assoc. prof. bus. edn. and acctg. Southwestern State U., Weatherford, Okla., 1953-55; prof. bus. edn., chmn. dept. U. Denver, 1955-65; prof. bus. edn. charge grad. program bus. edn. Tex. Tech. U., Lubbock, 1965-68; nat. dir. edn., edn. divsn Lear Siegler, Inc., 1968-72; prof., chmn. dept. bus. edn. Cleve. State U., 1972-79, prof. acctg., 1979-81; assoc. dean James J. Nance Coll. Bus. Adminstrn., 1980-81, prof. emeritus, 1981—2002. Pres. Tex. Ednl. and Adminstrv. Mgmt. Systems, Crowell, Tex., 1981—2002; textbook cons. U.S. Armed Forces Inst., 1955-68; test coordinator, profl. standards program Nat. Assn. Ednl. Secs., 1965-69; mem. Policies Commn. Bus. and Econ. Edn., 1962-66; commr. Accrediting Commn. Assn. Ind. Colls. and Schs., 1963-69; mem. Colo. Adv. Com. Bus. Edn., 1955-65, U.S. Office Edn. Adv. Council Insured Loans to Vocat. Students, 1966-69; cons. Acad. Ednl. Devel., 1965-67, Ednl. Testing Service; chmn. mgmt. com. Inst. Certifying Secs., 1970-73. Author: Equipment Standards for Business Classrooms, 1954, Selected Authorities in Business Education, 1965; co-author: College Accounting for Secretaries, 1971; editor Western Bus. Rev, 1958-62, Colo. Study Guides for Bus. Edn, 1957-65, Purple Heart Mag., 1980-85; contbr. articles to profl. jours. Chmn. Foard County Dem. Com., 1982-88, 1996-2002. Capt. AUS, 1940-44; lt. col. Colo. State Guard. Recipient Purple Heart and decorations for valor, Vets. Small Bus. Advocate of Yr. award U.S. Small Bus. Adminstrn., 1993; named to Ohio Vets. Hall of Fame, 1996. Mem. AICPA, Tex. Soc. CPAs, Okla. Soc. CPAs, Adminstrv. Mgmt. Soc. (Diamond Merit award 1976), Mountain Plains Bus. Edn. Assn. (pres. 1964-65), Nat. Bus. Edn. Assn., Nat. Assn. Bus. Tchr. Edn. (nat. sec. 1957-59), Assn. Ind. Colls. and Schs. (recipient award of merit Accrediting Commn. 1978), Svc. Corps Retired Execs. (SCORE), Mil. Order Purple Heart (nat. comdr. 1973-74, pres. svc. found. 1988-92, chmn. bd. 1992-95), Rotary, Delta Pi Epsilon (nat. treas. 1958-61, nat. exec. sec. 1962-66), Beta Gamma Sigma, Pi Omega Pi, Phi Beta Lambda, Alpha Kappa Psi, Beta Alpha Psi, Kappa Kappa Psi, Delta Tau Delta, Phi Delta Kappa. Democrat. Methodist. Home: Boise, Idaho. Died June 14, 2002.

BINNS, WALTER GORDON, JR., investment management executive; b. Richmond, Va., June 8, 1929; s. Walter Gordon and Virginia Belle (Matheny) B.; m. Alberta Louise Fry, Apr. 1, 1972; 1 child, Amanda; 1 stepdau., Clarissa AB, Coll. William and Mary, 1949, AM, Harvard U., 1951; MBA, NYU, 1959. Trainee Chase Nat. Bank, N.Y.C., 1953-54; with GM, N.Y.C., 1954-94, asst. treas., 1974-82, chief investment funds officer, 1982-94, v.p., 1986-94; pres., CEO GM Investment Mgmt. Corp., 1990-94. Bd. dirs. Options Clearing Corp., Inc., Equity Fund Latin Am., Commonwealth Equity Fund; investment adv. com. N.Y. State Common Retirement Fund, 1987-94; mem. pension mgrs. adv. com. N.Y. Stock Exch., 1988-94; mem. Gov. Cuomo's Task Force on Pension Fund Investment, 1988-89; mem. adv. com. Pension Benefit Guaranty Corp., 1991-95; mem. adv. com., bd. Chgo. Mercantile Exch., 1988-97, Chgo. Bd. Trade, 1992-93, Commodity Futures Trading Commn., 1992-94; mem. investment adv. com. Va. Retirement Systems, 1994—, Barings/ING Pvt. Equity Ptnrs., 1996—, SUN Asset Mgmt. Ltd., 1997—; mem. fiduciary panel Prudential Ins. Co., 1994-95. Trustee ARC Retirement System, 1987-90, Citizens Budget Commn., N.Y.C., 1982-94, Endowment Assn., Coll. William and Mary, Med. Coll. Va. Found., Maymont Found., Nat. Coun. Econ. Edn., 1982-94, Futures Ind. Assn., 1988-90; bd. dirs. Alcoholism Coun. Greater N.Y., 1982-92; bd. dirs. Cmty. Fund. of Bronxville, Eastchester Tuckahoe, Inc., 1986-92, Friends of Libr. Coll. William and Mary Coll., 1991-97, Fin. Execs. Rsch. Found., 1988-91, Christian Children's Fund, Nat. Coun. on Alcoholism and Drug Dependence, Vellore Christian Med. Coll. & Hosp. Bd.; founder, interim chmn. Friends of Higher Edn. Va., 1997—. Mem. Fin. Execs. Inst. (chmn. com. on employee benefits 1977-80, com. on investment of employee benefit assets 1985-88, treas. 1991-93), Bronxville Field Club, Harvard Club (N.Y.C.), Grolier Club, Commonwealth Club, Westwood Racquet Club, N.Y. Athletic Club, Phi Beta Kappa, Beta Gamma Sigma. Home: Richmond, Va. Died Apr. 2002.

BISIEWICZ, ALAN WALTER, insurance executive, social work consultant; b. Springfield, Mass., Jan. 27, 1951; s. Fred and Eleanor Ann (Innarelli) B.; m. Susan Patricia Duffy; 1 child, Zachary. BA, Amherst Coll., 1973; MSW, Smith Coll., 1978. Sch. adjustment counselor Northampton (Mass.) Pub. Schs., 1978-81; psychiatric social worker Community Care Mental Health Ctr., Springfield, 1981-82; asst. prof. psychiatry U. Mass. Med. Sch., Northampton, 1982-83; dir. employee assistance program Mass. Mut. Life Ins. Co., Springfield, from 1983. Bd. dirs. Pioneer Valley Consumer Counseling Service, Springfield; cons. Osborn (Mass.) Clinic, 1983—. Mem. Nat. Assn. Social Workers, Am. Assn. Profl. Hypnotherapists, Assn. Labor/Mgmt., Adminstrs. and Cons. on Alcoholism. Roman Catholic. Avocations: tennis, swimming, squash, bicycling. Home: Amherst, Mass. Died Dec. 6, 2001.

BISIG, CHARLES JOSEPH, surgeon; b. Louisville, July 9, 1953; MD, U. Louisville. Diplomate Am. Bd. Surgery. Intern Charity Hosp., New Orleans, 1979-80; resident in gen. surgery Tulane U., New Orleans, 1980-82, U. Louisville, 1982-85; staff Humana Audubon Hosp., Louisville. Fellow ACS; mem. AMA, Ky. Med. Assn., Jefferson County Med. Assn. Died June 18, 1999.

BISK, ANATOLE See BOSQUET, ALAIN

BITKER, MARJORIE MARKS (MRS. BRUNO VOLTAIRE BITKER), writer, editor; b. N.Y.C., Feb. 9, 1901; d. Cecil Alexander and Rachel (Fox) Marks; A.B. magna cum laude (Caroline Duror Meml. fellow), Barnard Coll., 1921; M.A., Columbia U., 1922; m. James C. Jacobson, 1922 (div. 1942); children— Emilie J. Jacobi, Margaret J. Strange, Elizabeth J. Reiss; m. 2d, John C. Mayer, Oct. 24, 1942 (dec. June 1945); m. 3d, Bruno Voltaire Bitker, Oct. 10, 1957 (dec. 1984). Free lance writer, 1922—; editor Farrar Straus, N.Y.C., 1946-47, G.P. Putnam's Sons, N.Y.C., 1947-53, David McKay Co., N.Y.C., 1953-55; now editorial cons., book reviewer, feature writer. Lectr., Hunter Coll., Coll. City N.Y., 1949-53; Women's Chair for Humanistic Studies, Marquette U., 1972-73. Mem. pres.'s council Alverno Coll., 1975-77; bd. visitors U. Wis., 1962-68; alumnae trustee Barnard Coll., 1964-68, Barnard-in-Milw.; co-founder, past pres., hon. bd. dirs. in perpetuity Bookfellows: Friends Wis. Libraries. Recipient Barnard Alumnae Recognition award, 1978. Mem. AAUW, Women's Nat. Book Assn., Bookfellows Milw. (pres. 1971-73, dir.), Phi Beta Kappa. Author: (novels) Gold of Evening, 1975, A Different Flame, 1976; contbr. articles, and book revs. to mags. and newspapers.

BJORNSON, MARIA, theatrical designer; Theatrical designer, London, from 1971. Designer (mus.) over one hundred prodns. including: The Phantom of the Opera (Antoinette Perry awards for best scenic design and best costume design 1988, Drama Desk award for Best Set and Costume 1988), Follies (Drama Mag. Designer of Yr.), Aspects of Love (Drama Mag. Designer of Yr.), (operas) Janacek Cycle (Prague Silver medal design), Cosi Fan Tutte, Mahagonny, Figaro, Carmen, Valkyrie, Toussaint L'Ouverture, Donnerstag Aus Licht, Tales of Hoffmann, Rosenkavalier (theatre) Blue Angel, Measure for Measure, Lulu, Camille, A Midsummer's Night Dream, Hamlet, The Tempest, Hedda Gabler, Katya Kasanova, 1994, Sleeping Beauty, 1994, The Rise and Fall of the City of Mahagonny, 1995. Recipient Designer's Designer Great Britain Observer Mag., 1989. Died Dec. 13, 2002.

BLACK, EUGENE ROBERT, writer, investment banker; b. July 19, 1924; married; 3 children. BA, Yale U., 1945; BLitt, Oxford (Eng.) U., 1948. Asst. to fin. v.p. Am. Express Co., N.Y., 1949-52; gen. mgr. Inter-Americana de Financiamentos e Investimentos SA, Brazil, 1952-55; gen. ptnr. Lazard Freres & Co., N.Y., 1955-79; spl. asst. to sec. for econ. devel. Dept. of Interior, Washington, 1980-81. Dir. Repertory Theatre of Lincoln Ctr., Am. Shakespeare Festival Theatre, Stratford, Conn. Playwright 15 off-Broadway, regional and comty. prodns. including Immortal Beloved, The Possessor, Tribulation, Peter and Alexis, The Big Alabama Wonder, The Monument, Going Away, (polit. trilogy) Camelot Lost, The Confrontation, The Driving Dream; also 4 novels, screenplays and children's stories. Bd. dirs. Lincoln Ctr. Repertory Co., Am. Shakespeare Theater, N.Y.C. Cultural Coun.; chmn. bd. dirs. Circle in the Square Theater; chmn. Mayor's Report on the N.Y. Theater, City of N.Y. Mayor's Cultural Com. With USMC. Mem. Fgn. Policy Assn. (dir.), Coun. for Latin Am. (dir.), Investment Banking Assn. (dir. fgn. investment com.). Home: Palm Beach, Fla. Died Apr. 24, 2000.

BLACKWELL, LUCIEN E. congressman; b. Whitsett, Pa., Aug. 1, 1931; Pres. Internat. Longshoren's Union, Local 1332, 1973—91; former chmn. Phila. Gas Commn.; Pa state rep., 1973—75; city councilman, 1974—91; mem. 102-103 Congresses from 2d dist. Pa., Washington, 1991—95; mem. budget com.; mem. pub. works and transp. com. Vice chmn. econ. devel. sub. Pub. Works and Transp. With U.S. Army. Died Jan. 24, 2003.

BLAIR, BEATRICE, priest; b. Boskon, Mass., Dec. 22, 1929; d. Montgomery and Virginia (Mason) B.; m. Harper Sibley, Feb. 19, 1949 (div. 1969); children: Elizabeth, Harper, Montgomery Blair, John Durbin; m. John Robbins, Aug. 3, 1975. BA, SUNY, N.Y.C., 1978; MDiv, Gen. Theol. Sem., N.Y.C., 1978. Ordained priest, 1978. Coord. Planned Parenthood, N.Y.C., 1972-73; exec. dir. Nat. Abortion Rights Action League, N.Y.C., 1974-75; assoc. rector Ch. of the Heavenly Rest, N.Y.C., 1978-85, St. Marks Ch. in the Bowery, N.Y.C., 1985-90; assoc. priest Calvary 1st George's Ch., N.Y.C., 1990-94 and from 94; interim vicar St. George's Ch., N.Y.C., 1994. Mem. Nat. Abortion Rights Action League (chair 1978-81), N.Y. State Nat. Abortion Rights Action League (chair 1984-88), N.Y. Met. Religious Coalition for Abortion Rights (pres. 1985—). Democrat. Episcopalian. Deceased.

BLAIR, ROBERT NOEL, artist; b. Buffalo, Aug. 12, 1912; s. Charles Francis and Grace Ethylin (McGonegal) B.; m. Jeannette Kenney, Aug. 8, 1943; children: Jeanne Elizabeth (dec.), David Francis, Bruce Allen. Student, Albright Art Sch., 1931, Sch. Mus. Fine Arts, 1931-33, Art Inst. Buffalo, 1937, U. Buffalo, 1951. Painted Western N.Y., No. Vt. subjects, 1933-43; instr. Art. Inst. Buffalo, 1939-42, dir., 1945-49; instr. Buffalo Mus. Sci., 1939-42, U. Buffalo, 1952. Contbg. author: Water Colorists at Work, 1972; contbr. painting of Vt. in color to Vermont Life Mag., spring 1988, watercolor to Met. Mus. books, 1991; one-man shows Buffalo, 1937-41, 45, 53, N.Y.C., 1938-41, 53, 62, Albright Art Gallery, Buffalo, 1942, 54-55, U. Ala., 1944, others, paintings exhibited Internat. Water Color Exhibit. Bklyn., Art Inst., Chgo., exhbns. Nat. Gallery, Washington, Fleming Mus., Vt., State U. Coll., Buffalo, 1966, Burchfield Art Ctr., State U. Coll., Buffalo, 1985, Burchfield-Pemney Art Ctr., 2000, others; painter murals, Fifth area Chapel, Fort Mc-

Clellan, Ala., 1943, Post Hosp., 1944, Bethlehem Steel Plant, Lackawanna, 1947, Olean (N.Y.) House, Unitarian Ch., East Aurora, N.Y., Lake View Hotel, Lake View, New York, works in permanent collection, Nat. Mus. History and Art, Taiwan, Niagara U., Colgate U., Met. Mus., N.Y.C., Munson Williams Proctor Inst., Utica, Dubuque and Bryn Mawr art assos., Butler Art Inst., Ford Motor Co., U. State N.Y., 100 paintings and drawings of World War II in Burchfield Art Ctr., SUNY, Buffalo, 1986; 42 paintings and 2 drawings of the Battle of the Bulge and Army glider action included in U.S. Army art collection. Served with AUS, 1942-45. Awarded water color prize Western N.Y. exhibit, 1940-44, 1947-51; Guggenheim fellow, 1946-51; Silver and Gold medals Buffalo Soc. Artists, 1947, 50; Ala. Water Color Soc., 1947; water color prize Art Inst. Chgo., 1948; watercolor prize N.Y. State Exhbn., 1950; Waugh prize Buffalo Soc. Artists Ann., 1951, 54; gold medal, 1955, 57-68; silver medal, 1956, 62, 69; water color prize 2d Spring Art Exhibit, Buffalo, 1957; 1st watercolor prize Youngstown (Ohio) Nat., 1953; 1st watercolor prize Western N.Y. Exhbn., 1963; 1st watercolor prize Chautaqua Nat. Exhibit, 1963; watercolor prize Balt. Water Color Club, 1954; Buffalo Soc. Artists ann. painting prize, 1958, 62-65, 70; watercolor prize, 1959; gold medal, 1972; Silvermine Guild watercolor prize, 1958; drawing prize Indsl. Niagara Art Exhbn.; 1st painting prize Cooperstown N.Y. Nat. Exhbn., 1970, water color prize, 1989; 1st Watercolor prize White Mountain Art Festival, Sholow, Ariz., 1970; watercolor prize Chautauqua Nat. Exhbn., 1972; Watercolor award West Tex. Watercolor Nat., 1985 others. Mem. Am. Water Color Soc., Patteran Soc., Buffalo Soc. Artists. Died June 15, 2003.

BLAKE, ROBERT FREDERICK, media relations and broadcast executive; b. N.Y.C., Oct. 20, 1915; s. Joseph Everett and Vivian (Parker) B. Student, pub. and pvt. schs., N.Y.C. Motion picture editor The New Yorker Mag., N.Y.C., 1937-39; continuity editor WOR, N.Y.C., 1939-41; dir. publicity WOR/WWOR-TV, N.Y.C., 1945-50; owned station div. NBC, N.Y.C., 1951-53; dir. press info. CBS TV Network, Hollywood, Calif., 1954-60; dir. pub. info. Group W (Westinghouse Broadcasting Co.), N.Y.C., 1960-74; dir. pub. relations WPIX, Inc., N.Y.C., 1974-80; dir. press info. CBS Cable Div., N.Y.C., 1980-83; pres. pub. relations/TV prodn. Robert Blake Enterprises, Inc., Bridgehampton, N.Y., from 1983. Contbr. articles to Stars and Stripes, and Yank Mag. Served with USAF, 1941-45, ETO. Decorated Bronze Star. Mem. Media Rels. Cons. 1988—, Overseas Press Club. Died May 13, 2001.

BLANK, BLANCHE DAVIS, political science educator; b. N.Y.C. d. Joseph B. and Mathilda (Markendorff) Davis; m. Joseph S. Blank, Jr., Oct. 10, 1945; children: Laura, Barbara, Alice. BA, Hunter Coll., 1944; MA Univ. fellow, Maxwell Sch., Syracuse U., 1945; PhD, Columbia U., 1951. Lectr., City Coll., 1946-49, New Sch. Social Research, 1951-52; instr. Hunter Coll., CUNY, 1956-59, asst. prof., 1960-62, assoc. prof., 1963-67, prof. polit. sci., 1968-77, dean div. social scis., 1972-77, dir. grad. studies, 1967-68, acting pres., 1993—95; academic v.p. Yeshiva U., 1977-81, prof., 1981—93. Vis. prof. Sarah Lawrence Coll., 1969-70; cons. Coll.-Fed. Agy. Internship Program, 1966-71; dir. Mayor's Task Force on City Personnel, 1965-66; mem. Chancellor's Com. on Status of Women, CUNY, 1972, Charter Revision Study Group, 1972; founder, co-chmn. Inst. Trial Judges, 1973-87; mem. Commn. on Higher Edn., Middle States Assn., 1987-93. Author books and articles on Am. govt., polit. parties and pub. adminstrn. Bd. dirs. Pub. Interest Pub. Relations, 1976-83, Fund for Peace; mem. Democratic County Com., Greenburgh, 1956-64; chmn. Greenville Dem. Com., 1960-64; mem. women's com. Muskie Presdl. Campaign, 1972, Udall; trustee Coll. New Rochelle, 1987-93. Recipient Shuster Faculty awards, 1961, 72; N.Y. Legis. grantee, 1964; Univ. research grantee, 1965; NSF research grantee, 1966 Mem. AAUP, Am. Polit. Sci. Assn., Am. Soc. Pub. Adminstrn., ACLU (free speech com.), Common Cause (gov. bd. N.Y. State 1975-77, commr.). Died Dec. 19, 2003.

BLEIBERG, GERTRUDE TIEFENBRUN, artist; b. N.Y.C., Mar. 11, 1921; d. Samuel and Anna (Gross) T.; m. Donald Joseph Bleiberg (wid.); children: Diana Jacobson, Deborah Jacobson, Victoria Zatkin, Wendy Maybaum. BE, UCLA, 1941; Gen. Secondary Tchg. Credential, U. So. Calif., L.A., 1942; BFA, San Francisco Art Inst., 1975, MFA, 1977. Tchr. Quincy (Calif.) H.S., 1942-44; substitute tchr. Palo Alto Unified Sch. Dist., 1966-75; co-owner Pluma Indsl. Hosp., Quincy, 1944-59; artist Palo Alto, from 1977. One-woman shows include Bridge Gallery, San Francisco, 1980, Monterey Peninsula Mus. of Art, Calif., 1982, San Jose Mus. of Art, Calif., 1983, Print Club, Phila., 1986, City of Palo Alto, Calif., 1986, Wenninger Gallery, Boston, 1988, Elizabeth S. Fine Mus., San Francisco, 1988, Branner Spangenberg Gallery, Palo Alto, 1989, Jennifer Pauls Gallery, Sacramento, 1986, 90, Richard Sumner Gallery, Palo Alto, 1994, San Francisco Mus. of Art Rental Gallery, 1996; retrospective San Francisco Mus. of Art Rental Gallery, 1996, Palo Alto Cultural Ctr., 1996, Koret Gallery, Palo Alto, 1996, Stanford Faculty Club, Stanford (Calif.) U., 1996; group exhbns. include Richard Hansen Fine Arts Gallery, Fresno, 1988, Pajaro Valley Art Coun., Art Mus. of Santa Cruz, 1988, Stanford U. Faculty Club, 1989, 96, Palo Alto Cultural Ctr., 1989, 96, Bank of Am., Raychem; numerous others; pub. collections include Rutgers Archives Coll., N.J., San Jose Mus. of Art; work pub. in numerous catalogues and publs. Mem. AAUW, Women's Caucus of Art (Lifetime Achievement award 1992-93), Soroptimist. Democrat. Home: Oakland, Calif. Died Aug. 10, 2001.

BLINN, LORENA VIRGINIA, natural sciences educator; b. East Chicago, Ind., Sept. 8, 1939; d. Ralph Hastings and Edith (Harwell) Stoops; m. Gerald H. Martin, Aug. 21, 1971 (div. May 1982); children: Matthew Christopher, Elizabeth Ashley; m. Walter Craig Blinn, May 18, 1985. BS in Pre-Med./Chemistry, U. Ga., 1961, MS in Zoology/Sci. Edn., 1964; PhD in Sci. Edn./Geology, Mich. State U., 1971. Biology tchr. McIntyre Park Sr. High Sch., Thomasville, Ga., 1961-62; instr. dept. natural sci. Mich. State U., East Lansing, 1964-71, asst. prof., 1971-80, assoc. prof., 1980-85, prof., 1985-89, prof. Ctr. Integrative Studies Gen. Sci., Coll. Natural Sci., from 1989. Vis. prof. contemporary biology Inst. Techs. MARA, Shah Alam, Malaysia, 1986-87. Co-editor: Natural Science Lab Manual, 1976; contbr. articles to profl. jours. Founder, pres. Friends of Historic Williamstown (Mich.), 1974; founder Williamston Mine Reclamation Com., 1982; sec. bd. dirs. Capital Area Wildlife Rehab. Assn., Lansing, Mich., 1989—. Nominee for Nat. Prof. of Yr., Coun. for Advancment and Support of Edn., 1992, 93. Mem. Nat. Sci. Tchrs. Assn., AAAS. Avocations: archeology, travel, nature, geology, history. Home: Williamston, Mich. Deceased.

BLOCH, FEDERICO, airline executive; b. San Salvador, El Salvador, Feb. 22, 1954; s. Max and Carmen (Macias) B.; m. Jacqueline Laffite, Jan. 24, 1981; children: Eric, David. BS and MS in Indsl. Engring., Stanford U., 1975; MBA, Harvard U., 1979. Exec. v.p. TACA Internat. Airlines, San Salvador, 1981-91, pres., CEO, 1992—2004. Bd. dirs. Sherwin-Williams, San Salvador, La Migueleña, S.A., San Salvador, Inv. Universales, S.A., San Salvador, Latin Pass. Bd. dirs. Habitat, San Salvador, 1990-92, Found. for Social and Econ. Devel., San Salvador; founding mem. Higher Sch. Edn., San Salvador, U. José Matías Delgado, San Salvador. Mem. L.Am. Airlines Assn. (pres.), Young Pres. Orgn. (chmn.), Am. C. of C. (bd. dirs., San Salvador C. of C. (bd. dirs.). Home: San Salvador, El Salvador. Died Apr. 26, 2004.

BLOK, JOSEPH, surgeon; b. Amsterdam, Mar. 24, 1930; MD, Free U. Amsterdam, 1956. Diplomate Am. Bd. Surgeon. Intern Jewish Gen. Hosp., Montreal, 1957-58; resident in surgery Queen Mary VA Hosp., Montreal, 1959-60, resident in pathology, 1960-64; fellow in vasc. surgery Brookdale Hosp., Bklyn., 1964-65, 65-66; attending surgeon, vasc. surgeon Brookdale Hosp. Med. Ctr., Bklyn., from 1966. Fellow Am. Coll. Anesthesia, Am. Coll. Surgeons. Home: Lynbrook, NY. Died Jun. 5, 1999.

BLOK, VICTOR RUVIM, physicist; b. Kishenev, Moldova, USSR, Sept. 8, 1945; came to U.S., 1987; s. Ruvim Semion and Sara Benjamen (Cohen) B.; m. Natalie Yuri Smorodina, Sept. 5, 1970; children: Sergey, Roman. MS in Electronics, Moscow Inst. Physics & Tech., USSR, 1968; PhD in Physics, Novosibirsk Inst. Chem. Kinetics, USSR, 1978. Rsch. scientist Photolithographic Lab., Moscow, 1968-74; grad. studies Moscow U., Moscow, 1974-78; rsch. scientist Quantum Electronics Lab., Moscow, 1978-82, Chemical Catalysts Lab., Moscow, 1982-85, Med. Software Labs., Moscow, 1985-87; prof. U. Md., Balt., 1988-89; former pres. Applied Science Rsch. Lab., Balt. Contbr. articles to Physica, Solid State Comms., Jour. Optical Soc. Am., Optical Comms., Phys. Rev.; former editor-in-chief Vestnik Mag., Balt. Founder, mem. The Trust Group, Moscow, 1982-83; pres. Friendship and Dialog Group, Dolgoprudny, USSR, 1983-87. Died May 25, 2004.

BLONSTON, GARY LEE, journalist; b. Cleve., May 14, 1942; s. Edward Preston and Billie Marguerite (Bass) V.; children: R. Scott, Nancy L. BS in Journalism, Northwestern U., 1963, MS in Journalism, 1964. Reporter Miami (Fla.) Herald, 1964-66; reporter, asst. city editor, Washington corr., Sunday editor, exec. news editor Detroit Free Press, 1966-80, exec. news editor, 1980-81, nat. corr., 1981-87, San Jose Mercury News, 1987-89, Knight-Ridder Newspapers, Bethesda, Md., from 1990. Recipient Scripps-Howard Meeman award for excellence in environ. reporting, 1970, Disting. Community Service award Nat. Urban Coalition, 1982 Home: San Jose, Calif. Died Apr. 4, 1999.

BLOOMER, WILLIAM ERNEST, thoracic and cardiovascular surgeon, educator; b. Denver, Dec. 20, 1916; s. Charles Ernest and Jane Winifred (French) B.; m. Cornelia Huntington Day, Oct. 29, 1959; children: Lianne French, William Ernest, Robert Day, Charles Campbell. BS, Stanford U., 1938; MD, Yale U., 1942. Diplomate Am. Bd. Surgery, Bd. Thoracic Surgery; lic. Calif., Conn., Washington. Intern in surg. svc. Stanford (Calif.) U. Hosp., 1942-43; fellow in thoracic surgery Yale U. Sch. Med., 1946-47; asst. resident in surgery New Haven (Conn.) Hosp., 1947-48, resident in thoracic surgery, 1949-50, assoc. resident in gen. surgery, 1950-51; vol. fellow dept. surgery Lahey Clinic, Boston, 1951; chief resident in surgery New Haven (Conn.) Hosp., 1952; fellow, rsch. asst. in cardiovasc. surgery Yale U. Sch. Med., 1952, instr. surgery, 1953-54, asst. prof. surgery, 1954-59; clin. asst. prof. surgery U. So. Calif., 1959-61; assoc. prof. in residence UCLA, 1961-66; chief thoracic and cardiovasc. surgery L.A. County Harbor Gen. Hosp., 1961-66; assoc. clin. prof. surgery UCLA Sch. Medicine, from 1961; ptnr. pvt. practice cardiac thoracic and vascular surgery St. Vincent's Hosp., L.A., 1959-60; ptnr. pvt. practice thoracic and cardiovasc. surgery Hosp. of Good Samaritan, L.A., 1960-61; ptnr. pvt. practice Long Beach, Calif., 1966-69; pvt. practice thoracic and cardiovasc. surgery, from 1969. Mem. courtesy staff Long Beach Cmty. Hosp., St. Mary Med. Ctr. Long Beach, Downey Cmty. Hosp., Hosp. of the Good Samaritan L.A., dir. pro tem hyperbaric rsch. and therapy unit, 1966-67; mem. attending staff Harbor Gen. hosp., Torrance, Calif.; mem. provisional courtesy staff Drs. Hosp. of Lakewood; mem. hon. staff UCLA Med. Ctr. Thoracic and Cariovasc. Surgery; active hon. staff Long Beach meml. Med. Ctr., chief thoracic and cariovasc. surgery sect., 1978-81, 84-85; travelling fellow Rockefeller Found. visit med. schs., S. Am., 1958. Contbr. numerous articles to profl. jours. Served to maj. U.S. Army Med. Corps., 1943-46, ETO. Mem. AMA, ACS, Am. Coll. Cardiology, Internat. Cardiovasc. Soc., Am. Assn. Thoracic Surgery, Am. Coll. Chest Physicians, Am. Thoracic Soc., Calif. Med. Assn., Soc. Thoracic Surgeons, Soc. Vascular Surgery, New Eng. Surg. Soc., L.A. Acad. Medicine, L.A.. County Med. Assn., L.A. Surg. Soc., Long Beach Surg. Soc., Sigma Xi. Home: Pasadena, Calif. Died Jan. 15, 2001.

BLOUNT, WINTON MALCOLM, JR., retired manufacturing company executive; b. Union Springs, Ala., Feb. 1, 1921; s. Winton Malcolm and Clara B. (Chalker) B.; m. Carolyn Self Blount, Dec. 22, 1981; children: Winton Malcolm III, Thomas A., S. Roberts, Katherine Blount Miles, Joseph W. Student, U. Ala., 1939-41; LHD (hon.), Judson Coll., 1967, Amherst Coll., 1990; HHD (hon.), Huntingdon Coll., 1969; LLD, Birmingham-So. Coll., 1969; DCL, U. Ala., 1969, DSci., 1971; D in Pub. Svc., Seattle-Pacific Coll., 1971; PhD (hon.), Rhodes Coll., Samford U., Washington and Jefferson Coll., Troy State U.; DCS (hon.), St. John's U., 1983. Pres., chmn. bd. Blount Bros. Corp., Montgomery, Ala., 1946-68; postmaster gen. U.S. Washington, 1969-71; chmn. exec. com. Blount, Inc., Montgomery, Ala., from 1973, chmn. bd., CEO, 1974-90, 91-93, chmn. bd., 1990-91 and from 93. Mem. Pres.'s Cabinet, Washington, 1969-71. Chmn. Ala. Citizens for Eisenhower, 1952; Southeastern dir. Nixon-Lodge, 1959-60; bd. dirs. United Appeals Montgomery; bd. dirs. Montgomery YMCA, also life mem.; former trustee So. Rsch. Inst.; trustee Rhodes Coll., former chmn. bd.; trustee emeritus U. Ala.; bd. visitors Air U., Maxwell AFB, Ala., 1971-73; mem. adv. coun. U.S. Army Aviation Mus., Ft. Rucker, Ala.; trustee So. Ctr. Internat. Studies. With USAAF, 1942-45. Named One of 4 Outstanding Young Men Ala., 1956, Man of Yr., Montgomery, 1961, Citizen of Yr., Montgomery Advertiser, 1987; recipient citation for disting. svc. City of Montgomery, 1966, Ct. Honor award Montgomery Exch. Club, 1968, Nat. Brotherhood award NCCJ, 1970, Silver Quill award Am. Bus. Press, 1971, Charles Frankel prize NEH, 1991, Disting. Svc. to Arts award Nat. Govs. Assn., 1992, Disting. Svc. award Rhodes Coll., 1993. Mem. Am. Mgmt. Assns. (trustee), Bus. Coun., Conf. Bd., NAM (Golden Knight Mgmt. award Ala. coun. 1962), Am. Enterprise Inst., U.S. C. of C. (nat. pres. 1968), Ala. C. of C. (pres. 1962-65), Newcomen Soc. N.Am., Rotary. Home: Montgomery, Ala. Died Oct. 24, 2002.

BLUE, DONALD SHERWOOD, lawyer; b. Danville, Pa., Jan. 17, 1956; s. Samuel Bruce and Ellen Grace (Salsbury) B.; m. Catherine Anne Mahoney, Oct. 4, 1980; children: Mairead, Pierce. BA in Govt., Shippensburg State Coll., 1977; JD magna cum lauda, U. Pitts., 1980. Bar: Pa. 1980, U.S. Dist. Ct. (we. dist.) Pa. 1980. Assoc. Kirkpatrick & Lockhart, Pitts., 1980-82, Pepper, Hamilton & Scheetz, Harrisburg, Pa., 1982-85; gen. atty. Koppers Co. Inc., Pitts., 1985-86; assoc. Reed, Smith, Shaw & McClay, Pitts., 1986-89; ptnr. Doepken, Keerican & Weiss, Pitts., from 1989. Mem. Order of Coif. Clubs: Pitts. Athletic Assn., Fox Chapel Yacht. Republican. Episcopalian. Home: Westwood, NJ. Died May 30, 2001.

BLUM, JOHN ALAN, urologist, educator; b. Bklyn., Feb. 2, 1933; s. Louis J. and Pauline (Kushner) B.; m. Debra Merlin Ackerman, June 30, 1957; children: Louis Jeffrey, Alfred Merlin, Jacqueline. AB, Dartmouth, 1954; MD, NYU, 1958; MS, U. Minn., 1965. Diplomate Am. Bd. Urology. Intern, U. Minn. Hosp., Mpls., 1958-59, resident, 1959-64; practice medicine, specializing in urology, Chgo., 1964-66, Mpls., 1966-67, San Diego, 1969—; chmn. dept. urology Mt. Sinai Hosp., Chgo., 1965-66; asst. prof. urology U. Minn., Mpls., 1967; assoc. clin. prof. urology U. Calif., San Diego, 1969—; chief of staff Hillside Hosp., San Diego, 1989-92; chmn. dept. surgery, div. urology Mercy Hosp., San Diego, 1991-93; mem. staff Scripps Hosp., La Jolla, Calif., 1969—; adj. assoc. prof. uro-pathology Uniform Svcs. U. of Health Sci., Behtesda, Md., 1988—. Bd. dirs. Vietnam Vet. Leadership Program. Capt. USNR, 1967-93, Vietnam, ret. 1993. Fellow ACS; mem. Am., Calif. med. assns., Am. Urol. Assn., San Diego Urol. Soc. (pres. 1991-93), San Diego Surg. Soc. (pres. 1977), Phi Beta Kappa, Sigma Xi, Alpha Omega Alpha, San Diego Yacht Club. Research in devel. of silicone rubber for urinary tract. Died Nov. 30, 1999.

BLUMBERG, DONALD FREED, management consultant; b. Phila., Jan. 30, 1935; s. Harry and Sara (Freed) Blumberg; m. Judith Blumberg, June 16, 1960; children: Michael, Susan. BA, U. Pa., 1952, BEE, 1957, MBA, 1958, postgrad., 1963. Sr. planner IBM Corp., 1960—61; dir. planning and rsch. svc. Pa. Rsch. Assocs., 1962—65; dir. ops. rsch. and long range planning Philco Ford Corp., 1965—68; mgr. mgmt. sci. div. Sci. Mgmt. Corp., 1968; v.p. Computer Scis. Corp., 1969; pres., CEO D.F. Blumberg & Assocs., Inc., Ft. Washington, Pa., 1969; chmn. Blumberg Shaw Cons., Ltd., London, London, 1988. Instr. U. Pa.; lectr. Am. Mgmt. Assn., Temple U., 1993—94; mem. Upper Dublin Twp. Govt. Study Commn., 1974—75; acting prin. dep. asst. sec. def. U.S. Dept. Def., 1975. Author: Managing Service As A Strategic Profit Center, Managing Service Using CRM Technology (award McGraw Hill); contbr. over 450 articles in field to profl. jours. Mem. bd. dirs. U. Pa. Engring. Sch.; pres. Enclave High Rise Condominium. Served to 1st lt. U.S. Army, 1959—60. Mem.: IEEE, Ops.

Rsch. Soc. Am., Inst. Mgmt. Scis., Assn. for Svc. Mgrs. (Del. Valley chpt. chair), Inst. Dirs. Democrat. Jewish. Home: Dresher, Pa. Died May 29, 2004.

BLUMENTHAL, FRITZ, printmaker, painter; b. Mainz, Germany, June 16, 1913; came to U.S., 1938, naturalized, 1944; s. Albert and Recha (Feibelmann) B.; m. Marianne Leiter, Mar. 31, 1947; children: John Frederick, Stephanie Ann. Student, U. Frankfort, Germany, 1931, U. Freiburg, 1932, U. Wurzburg, 1932-36; MD, U. Bern, Switzerland, 1937. One-man shows: Albany Inst. History and Art, N.Y., 1952, Gutenberg Mus., Mainz, 1964, Kunstverein, Ulm, W.Ger., 1965, Kenneth Taylor Gallery, Nantucket, Mass., 1965, others; group shows: Audubon Artists, N.Y.C., 1945, Print Club Phila., 1960-72, Herbert E. Feist Gallery, N.Y.C., 1972, Pratt Graphic Ctr., 1974-77, U. Del. invitational: Disting, Mid-Atlantic Artists, 1980, Weintraub Gallery, N.Y.C., 1984, The Mt. Aramah Exhibition: The Art of Rockland and Orange, Arden, N.Y., 1986, Sragow Gallery, N.Y.C., 1988, Nat. Mus. Am. Art, Washington, 1988-89, 97, McNay Art Inst., San Antonio, 1989, Bibliothèque Nationale, Paris, 1992, Mus. Fine Arts, Boston, 1990-91, others; represented in permanent collections: Met. Mus. Art, N.Y.C., Nat. Gallery of Art, Washington, Nat. Mus. Am. Art, Washington, Smithsonian Instn., Washington, Stedelijk Mus. Amsterdam, Netherlands, Victoria and Albert Mus., London, Yale U. Art Gallery, Nat. Pinacothek, Athens, Greece, Bklyn. Mus., Mus. and Library, Lincoln Ctr., N.Y. Public Library, Mus. Modern Art, N.Y.C., Mus. Fine Arts, Boston, Bündner Kunstmuseum, Chur, Switzerland, Bibliothèque Nationale, Paris, The Israel Mus., Jerusalem, Tel Aviv Mus. Art, Morgan Guarantee Trust Co., N.Y.C., Gutenberg Mus., Mainz, Fed. Republic Germany, Kunstverein, Ulm, Fed. Republic Germany, St. Louis Art Mus., Mus. de les Arts Grafiques Barcelona, Spain, Mus. Nacional d'Art de Catalunya, Barcelona, Fogg Mus. Art, Harvard U., Cambridge, Mass., Staatliche Graphische Sammlung, Munich, Germany, Staatsgalerie Moderner Kunst, Munich, Herbert F. Johnson Mus. Art Cornell U., The Minn. Inst. Arts, Meml. Art Gallery U. Rochester, others; commns. include 48 program cover designs for Greater Middletown Arts Coun. and N.Y. State Coun. on Arts; author poetry pub. literary mags., analyzed in Deutsche Exilliteratur seit 1933 vol. 2, 1989; subject of books Das Neue Mainz: Fritz Blumenthal (Werner Spanner), 1964, The Art of Monoprint (La Liberté and Mogelon), 1974, others. Recipient First Prize in Painting Nantucket Art Assn., Mass., 1961. Home: Middletown, NY. Died June 4, 2002.

BOBRIN, GEORGE MARTIN, lawyer; b. Phila., Aug. 10, 1910; s. Ellis and Celia (Sklar) B.; m. Estelle Lambert; children: Yale R., Irwin A., Brenda I. Glickman. BA, Rutgers U., Camden, 1956; JD, Temple U., 1959. Owner, operator Bobrin's Furniture, Camden, N.J., 1943-52; ptnr. Weinsten & Bobrin, Phila., 1960-70, Bobrin, Shore & Newman, Phila., from 1971. Mem. Phila. Bar Assn. (arbitration com. 1983), Am. Arbitrators Assn. Home: Monmouth Jct, NJ. Deceased.

BOCKELMAN, JOHN RICHARD, lawyer; b. Chgo., Aug. 8, 1925; s. Carl August and Mary (Ritchie) B. Student, U. Wis., 1943-44, Northwestern U., 1944-45, Harvard U., 1945, U. Hawaii, 1946; BSBA, Northwestern U., 1946; MA in Econs., U. Chgo., 1949, JD, 1951. Bar: Ill. 1951. Atty.-advisor Chgo. ops. office AEC, 1951-52; asso. firm Schradzke, Gould & Ratner, Chgo., 1952-57, Brown, Dashow & Langeluttig, Chgo., 1957-59, Antonow & Weissbourd, Chgo., 1959-61; partner firm Burton, Isaacs, Bockelman & Miller, Chgo., 1961-69; pvt. practice Chgo., 1970—. Prof. bus. law Ill. Inst. Tech., Chgo., 1950-82; lectr. econs. DePaul U., Chgo., 1952-53; bd. dirs., sec. Arlington Engring. Co.; bd. dirs., v.p., Universal Distbrs., Inc. Pres. 1212 Lake Shore Dr. Condo Assn., Chgo., Near North Assn. of Condo Pres., Chgo. Served with USNR, 1943-46. Mem. ABA, Ill. Bar Assn., Chgo. Bar Assn., Cath. Lawyers Guild Chgo., Lake Point Tower Club, Barclay Ltd. Club, Whitehall Club, Internat. Club, Anvil Club (East Dundee, Ill.), Univ. Club (San Diego), Tavern Club (Chgo.), Phi Delta Theta. Deceased.

BODDIE, BENJAMIN F. advertising agency executive; b. Kingstree, S.C., Apr. 25, 1925; s. William W. and Helen (Scott) B.; m. Alberta Brandon, Mar. 23, 1950; children: Benjamin C., Julie Boddie Neilson, David T., Sally Boddie Raybourn. BA, U. S.C., 1949. Writer News and Courier, Charleston, S.C., 1949-50; account dir. McCann-Erickson, Inc., Houston, 1951-60, mgr. New Orleans, 1960-61; operating mgr. McCann-Erickson-Hakuhodo, Tokyo, 1966-70; v.p. corp. communications Williams Cos., Tulsa, 1970-83; pres. Ben Boddie Advt., Tulsa, from 1983. Mng. ptnr. Sta. KOKI-TV, Tulsa, 1982-89. Chmn. fin. com. Okla. Rep. Party, 1977. Lt. USN, 1950-51, Korea. Chmn. fin. com. Okla. Rep. Com., 1977. Lt. USN, 1950-51, Korea. Mem. Tulsa Press Club (pres. 1982-83). Republican. Episcopalian. Died Jan. 19, 2001.

BODIN, JEROME I. pharmaceutical company executive, pharmaceutical chemist; b. N.Y.C., July 2, 1930; s. Sam and Martha (Warshofsky) B.; m. Jacqueline Sandra Kurlansky; children: Michelle Beth, Philip Louis. BS, Columbia U., 1952, MS, 1954; PhD, U. Wis., 1958. Cert. pharmacist, N.Y. Research analyst Pfizer, Inc., Bklyn., 1958-61; dir. Drug Standards Lab., Washington, 1962-63; chemist FDA, Washington, 1963-64; assoc. dir., pharmaceutical chemist Carter-Wallace, Inc., Cranbury, N.J., from 1964. Author: (with others) Pharmaceutical Analysis, 1961; contbr. articles to profl. jours. Trustee Citizens Organized for Med. Planning, Inc., East Windsor, N.J., 1971-74; chmn. East Windsor Bd. Health, 1972-74; mem. East Windsor Planning Bd., 1986, East Windsor Twp. Council, 1987. Fellow Am. Found. Pharm. Edn.; mem. Am. Chem. Soc., Am. Assn. Pharm. Scientists, Exch. Club Greater Princeton (bd. dirs. 1994—), Sigma Xi. Clubs: Democratic (East Windsor) (treas.). Lodges: Lions, B'nai B'rith. Democrat. Jewish. Home: Hightstown, NJ. Died Feb. 2, 2004.

BOEKER, PAUL HAROLD, non-profit organization official, diplomat; b. St. Louis, May 2, 1938; s. Victor W. and Marie Dorothy (Bernthal) B.; m. Margaret Macon Campbell; children: Michelle Renee, Kent Elliott, Katherine Madison. AB magna cum laude, Dartmouth Coll., 1960; postgrad., Princeton U., 1961; MA in Econs., U. Mich., 1967. Joined Dept. State, 1961; vice consul Duesseldorf, Germany, 1962-63; 2d sec. Am. Embassy, Bogotá, Colombia, 1964-66; mem. White House Task Force on Internat. Devel., 1969; dir. Office Devel. Fin., Dept. State, 1970; 1st sec. Am. Embassy, Bonn, Germany, 1971-73; mem. policy planning staff Dept. State, 1974, dep. asst. sec. state for internat. fin. and devel., 1975, sr. dep. asst. sec. state for econ. and bus. affairs, 1976; ambassador to Bolivia, 1977-80; dir. Fgn. Service Inst., Washington, 1980—83; mem. Sec.'s Planning Council, Washington, 1983-84; ambassador to Jordan, 1984-87; pres. Inst. of the Ams., U. Calif., San Diego, 1998—2003; exec. advisor Wirless Facilities Inc., 1997—2003. Author: Lost Illusions: Latin America's Struggle for Democracy; editor: Latin America's Turnaround, 1993. Recipient Arthur S. Fleming award for outstanding young people in fed. service, 1976, Presdl. Disting. Service award, 1985, 87. Mem. Am. Acad. Diplomacy, Coun. on Fgn. Rels. Died Mar. 29, 2003.

BOGDANOV, NIKITA ALEXEEVICH, geology educator; b. Astrakhan, Russia, July 23, 1931; s. Alexey Alexeevich and Irina Vladimirovna (Butkevich) B.; m. Olga Andreevna Dmitrieva, Oct. 6, 1971; children: Vladimir, Alexandr. Student, Moscow Geol. Prospecting Inst., 1954; cand. sci., Geol. Inst. of USSR Acad. Sci., 1962, DSc, 1972. Jr. scientist to sr. scientist dept. tectonics and geology Ocean Geol. Inst. USSR Acad. Sci., 1954-78; head dept. oceanic lithosphere, dep. dir., dir. Inst. Lithosphere, Russian Acad. Sci., from 1978; prof. Moscow U., from 1990. Mem. coun. of dirs. Circum-Pacific Coun. for Energy and Mineral Resources, Houston, 1980—; mem. steering com. Internat. Geol. Congress, 1984—. Author: Stratigraphy and Geological Correlation, 1992—, Izvestiya AN SSSR, 1984-91, Island Arcs; mem. editorial bd. Interperiodica Jour.; contbr. more than 200 articles to profl. jours., chpts. to books. Recipient Internat. Spendiarov prize in geology, 1984. Mem. Russian Acad. Scis., Australian Geol. Soc. (hon.). Home: Moscow, Russia. Died Dec. 14, 2002.

BOGGS, ROBERT WAYNE, human services administrator, consultant; b. St. Helena, Calif., Sept. 17, 1941; s. Wayne Cress Boggs and Ann Isham Stevenson; m. Donna J. Ferguson, Nov. 24, 1967, children: Jacquelin, Ryan. BS, Fresno State U., 1964; PhD, U. Calif., Davis, 1970. Bd. cert. nutritionist. Staff mem. Procter & Gamble, Cin., 1970-73, sect. head, 1973-76, assoc. dir., 1976-83, dir., 1983-99; cons. RWB Mgmt. Sys., Cin., from 1999. Author: (book) Transforming Clinical Development Performance Through Benchmarking and Metrics, 2001. Exec. sec. Procter Found., from 1982; mem. pharm. sci. bd. U. Cin., from 1987, mem. adv. bd., 1991—94; pres. Glendale Youth Sports, 1989; mem. athletic bd. St. Xavier H.S., 1991—93; mem. adv. bd. Cin. Classics, 1995; CFO Village of Glendale, from 2001; sr. warden Christ Ch. Glendale, 1988; bd. dirs. Cin. Riverhawks, from 1997. Mem.: Drug Info. Assn., Nutrition Today Soc., Am. Inst. Nutrition (mem. adv. bd. 1988—91). Avocations: soccer, equestrian events, John Deere tractor restoration. Died Jan. 16, 2003.

BOGORAD, LAWRENCE, biologist, educator; b. Tashkent, USSR, Aug. 29, 1921; came to U.S., 1922; s. Boris and Florence (Bernard) B.; m. Rosalyn G. Sagen, June 29, 1943; children— Leonard Paul, Kiki M. Lee. BS, U. Chgo., 1942, PhD, 1949. Instr. botany U. Chgo., 1948-51, asst. prof. dept. botany, 1953-57, assoc. prof., 1957-61, prof., 1961-67; prof. biology Harvard U., Cambridge, Mass., 1967-92, chmn. dept. biology, 1974-76, dir. Maria Moors Cabot Found., 1976-87, Maria Moors Cabot prof. biology, 1980-92, prof. emeritus, 1992—2003. Vis. investigator Rockefeller Inst., N.Y.C., 1951-53; com. on sci. and pub. policy NAS, 1977-81; com. on sci. engring. and pub. policy NAS-NAE-IOM1990-92; mem. Assembly of Life Scis., NRC, Space Studies Bd., 1995-98; joint coun. on food and agrl. scis. Dept. Agr., 1978-82. Assoc. editor Bot. Gazette, 1958; mem. editl. com. Ann. Rev. Plant Physiology, 1963-67, Ann. Rev. Cell Biology, 1984-88; mem. editl. bd. Plant Physiology, 1965-66, Biochimica Biophysica Acta, 1967-69, Jour. Cell Biology, 1967-70, Jour. Applied and Molecular Genetics, 1981-85, Plant Molecular Biology, 1981-85, Plant Cell Reports, 1981-85; editor, chmn. editl. bd. Proc. Nat. Acad. Scis., 1991-95. Served with AUS, 1943-46. Merck fellow, 1951-53; Fulbright fellow, 1960; recipient Career Rsch. award NIH, 1963 Fellow Am. Acad. Arts and Scis.; mem. NAS (chmn. botany sect. 1974-77, mem. coun. 1989-92, editor procs., chmn. editl. bd. Procs. 1991-95), AAAS (bd. dirs. 1982-86, pres. 1986-87, chmn. bd. 1987), Am. Philos. Soc., Am. Soc. Biol. Chemistry, Am. Soc. Cell Biology, Am. Soc. Plant Physiologists (pres. 1968-69, Stephen Hales award 1982), Royal Danish Acad. Scis. and Letters (fgn.), Soc. Devel. Biology (pres. 1984). Home: Lexington, Mass. Died Dec. 28, 2003.

BOHANON, LUTHER L. federal judge; b. Ft. Smith, Ark., Aug. 9, 1901; s. William Joseph and Artelia (Campbell) B.; m. Marie Swatek, July 17, 1933; 1 son, Richard L. LLB, U. Okla., 1927; LLD (hon.), Oklahoma City U., 1991. Bar: Okla. 1927, U.S. Supreme Ct. 1937. Gen. practice law, Seminole, Okla. and Oklahoma City, 1927-61; judge U.S. Dist. Ct. Okla. (no., ea., and we. dists.), 1961-74, sr. judge, 1974—. Mem. platform com. Democratic Nat. Conv., 1940. Served to maj. USAAF, 1942-45. Recipient citations and awards including citation from Okla. Senate and Ho. of Reps., 1979, Okla. County Bar Assn. and Jour. Record award, 1987, Humanitarian award NCCJ, 1991; Luther Bohanon Am. Inn of Ct. named in his honor Am. Inn of Ct. XXIII/U. Okla., 1991. Mem. U.S. Dist. Judges Assn. (10th cir.), Fed. Judges Assn., Okla. Bar Assn., Oklahoma County Bar Assn., Oklahoma City C. of C., Sigma Nu, Phi Alpha Delta. Clubs: Mason (Shriner, 32 deg.), K.T, Jester, Kiwanis, Com.of 100, Men's Dinner Club. Methodist. Died July 18, 2003.

BOL, DOUGLAS JOHN, minister, psychologist, religious broadcaster; b. Grand Haven, Mich., July 31, 1935; s. J. Edward and Jean B. (Putnam) B.; m. Marylin Seman, July 31, 1954; children: Gary Douglas, Julie Ann. LLB, LaSalle Extension U., 1960; BBA, Western Mich. U., 1963; BD cum laude, Grand Rapids Bapt. Theol. Sem., 1966, MDiv, 1970; MEd, U. Ariz., 1972, EdD, 1973. Ordained to ministry Gen. Assn. Regular Bapt. Chs., 1966. Pastor Eastview Bapt. Ch., Tucson, 1970-73; psychologist, pastoral counselor Tucson, from 1970. Speaker, dir. radio broadcast Psychology in the Bible, Tucson, 1973-82; host Let's Talk radio broadcast, 1982-85, cable TV series Insight for Happiness, 1985—; clin. psychologist serving on med. staff of 9 hosps. in city of Tucson. Bd. dirs., pres. Inst. Family Living, 1970—. With U.S. Army, 1966-70, Res. USANG, 1970-91. Mem. APA, Ariz. Psychological Assn., So. Ariz. Psychological Assn. Home: Tucson, Ariz. Died May 10, 2001.

BOLTON, ROBERT HARVEY, banker; b. Alexandria, La., June 19, 1908; s. James Wade and Mary (Calderwood) B.; m. Elsie Elizabeth McLundie (dec. Mar. 1987); children: Robert Harvey Jr., Elizabeth McLundie (Mrs. Robert Conery Hassinger), Mary Calderwood (Mrs. James Kelly Jennings Jr.); m. Abigail Crow Goodwin. BS, U. Pa., 1930. With credit dept. Guaranty Trust Co., N.Y.C., 1930-32; asst. cashier Rapides Bank & Trust Co., Alexandria, 1932-36, cashier, 1936-43, v.p., 1943-47, exec. v.p., 1947-56, pres., 1956-86, chmn., 1986-90, sr. chmn., from 1990, also bd. dirs. Bd. dirs. New Orleans br. Fed. Res. Bank Atlanta., 1979-81, First Commerce Corp., New Orleans; nat. bd. dirs. Robert Morris Assocs., 1943-45; La. rep. to Conf. State Bank Suprs., 1964-71. Mem. La. State U. Found., Pineville, devel. bd., Pres.'s club, bd. dirs. James C. Bolton Libr., Alexandria; fin. steering com. Attakapas coun. Boy Scouts Am., 1971-84; chmn. Rapides Parish chpt. ARC, 1943, Alexandria Little Theatre, 1942; hon. chmn. La. Coll. Quality Edge Dr. '95; bd. dirs. Rapides United Givers, Indsl. Devel. Bd. Ctrl. La.; mem. exec. com. Ctrl. Cities Devel. Com., Coun. for Better La., 1970—, Bus. and Indsl. Devel. Corp. La., 1971-73; mem. La. Bapt. Conv. Fedn. Bd., 1994-95; deacon Emmanuel Bapt. Ch., chmn. fin. com., chmn. Every Mem. Canvass, 1937-74; mem. citizen's adv. com. La. Spl. Edn. Ctr., La. Pub. Broadcasting; chmn., mem. St. Francis Cabrini Hosp. Found. Bd.; mem. Pub. Affairs Rsch. Coun. Recipient Disting. Svc. award Jr. C. of C., 1943, Humanitarian of Yr. award Arthritis Found., 1990, Disting. Svc. award La. N.G., Disting. Citizen award Boy Scouts Am., 1991, Outstanding Citizen award YWCA, 1992, Disting. Svc. award Trustees La. Coll., 1993, Rapides Arts and Humanities Cultural Advocate award, 1994. Mem. VFW, Am. Bankers Assn. (pres. state bank divsn. 1955), Mortgage Bankers Assn. (mem. Washington com. 1962-74), La. Bankers Assn. (pres. 1980, mem. legis. study com. 1950—, fed. affairs com. 1971—, Lifetime Achievement award 2000). Died July 15, 2003.

BONHAM, ROBERT LOGAN, life insurance agent; b. Denver, Oct. 24, 1927; s. Robert Lamb and Natalie (Logan) B.; m. Judith Tobey, Apr. 22, 1960; stepchildren: Gregory, Daryl Louise. BA in Econs., Lehigh U., 1950; B in Fgn. Trade, Am. Grad. Sch. Internat. Mgmt., 1957. CLU. Asst. gen. adjuster Gen. Adjustment Co., Inc., N.Y.C., 1950-54; auditing mgr. 1st Nat. Bank Boston, Rio de Janeiro, 1959-60; asst. contr. South P.R. Sugar Corp., Ensenada, P.R., 1960-64; v.p., treas. Propane Gas of P.R., San Juan, 1964-65; exec. v.p. Allegro Corp., San Juan, 1965-66; v.p., bus. mgr. Volkswagen Interamericana S.A., San Juan, 1966-67; career agt. Mowy Fin. Svcs., San Juan, from 1967. Fellow Life Underwriter Tng. Coun.; mem. Am. Soc. CLU and ChFC (v.p., bd. dirs. San Juan chpt. 1983—), Toastmasters (founding bd. dirs. San Juan chpt. 1973-80), Rotary. Avocations: golf, salt water sailing. Home: San Juan, PR. Deceased.

BONIME, WALTER RAYMOND, psychiatrist, psychoanalyst, educator; b. Monteville, Conn., July 12, 1909; s. Ellis and Rebecca (Strongin) B.; m. Mary McGovern, Dec. 7, 1940 (div. 1953); children: Karen, Stephen; m. Florence Cummings, Sept. 5, 1953; stepchildren: Frank Cummings, Norma Lovins; children: Karen, Stephen. BA, U. Wis., 1933; MD, Columbia U., 1938. Intern Sinai Hosp., Balt., 1938-39; resident Cen. Islip State Hosp., L.I., N.Y., 1939-41; pvt. practice, N.Y.C., from 1941. Clin. prof. psychiatry N.Y. Med. Coll., Valhalla, 1947—; tng. analyst Dept. Psychiatry, Inst. of Psychoanalysis of N.Y. Med. Coll. Author: (with Florence Bonime) The Clinical Use of Dreams, 1962; author: Collaborative Psychoanalysis, 1989. Passed asst. surgeon USPHS, 1943-46. Fellow Am. Psychiat. Assn., Am. Acad. Psychoanalysis (charter, editorial bd. jour. 1973—); mem. Soc. Med. Psychoanalysts (pres. 1963-64). Died Oct. 24, 2001.

BONK, ARNOLD ELI, dentist, consultant; b. Bklyn., Aug. 6, 1951; s. Jacob and Bernice Bonk; m. Helen Bonk, Aug. 29, 1972; children: Allison, Jason. BS, Bklyn. Coll., 1972; DMD, Tufts U., 1975. Resident Mt. Sinai Hosp., N.Y.C., 1975-76; pvt. practice Brookline, Mass., 1976-77, Boston, 1977-85, N.Y.C., from 1986. Cons. Univ. Patents, Inc., Westport, Conn., 1985—, Howmedica/Pfizer, N.Y.C., 1988—; pres. Dental Techs., Westport, 1985-86. Fellow Acad. Gen. Dentistry; mem. ADA, Met. Dental Soc. (sec. 1982-85), 1st Dist. Dental Soc. (peer rev. com. 1987—), Alpha Omega. Home: Fairfield, Conn. Died Dec. 3, 2001.

BONNER, THOMAS NEVILLE, history and higher education educator; b. Rochester, N.Y., May 28, 1923; s. John Neville and Mary (McGowan) B.; children by previous marriage: Phillip Lynn, Diana Joan; m. Sylvia M. Firnhaber, Dec. 28, 1984. AB, U. Rochester, 1947, MA, 1948; PhD, Northwestern U., 1952; LLD, U. N.H., 1974, U. Mich., 1979. Acad. dean William Woods Coll., 1951-54; prof. history, chmn. dept. social sci. U. Omaha, 1955-62; Fulbright lectr. U. Mainz, Germany, 1954-55; prof., head history dept. U. of Cin., 1963-68, v.p. acad. affairs, provost, 1967-71; pres. U. N.H., Durham, 1971-74, Union Coll.; chancellor Union U., Schenectady, 1974-78; pres. Wayne State U., Detroit, 1978-82, disting. prof. history and higher edn., 1983-97; vis. scholar Ariz. State U., Tempe, 1997—2003. Vis. prof. U. Freiburg, Fed. Republic Germany, 1982-83. Author: Medicine in Chicago, 1957, 91, The Kansas Doctor, 1959; (with others) The Contemporary World, 1960, Our Recent Past, 1963, American Doctors and German Universities, 1963, 87, To the Ends of the Earth: Woman's Search for Education in Medicine, 1992, Becoming a Physician: Medical Education in Great Britain, France, Germany and the United States, 1750-1945, 1995, Iconoclast: Abraham Flexner and a Life in Learning, 2002; editor, translator: Journey Through the Rocky Mountains, 1959. Democratic candidate for Congress, 1962; legis. aide to Senator McGovern, 1962-63. Served with Radio Intelligence Corps AUS, 1942-46, ETO. Guggenheim fellow, 1958-59, 64-65 Mem. Am. Hist. Assn., Orgn. Am. Historians, Am. Assn. for History Medicine, Phi Beta Kappa, Pi Gamma Mu, Phi Alpha Theta. Home: Scottsdale, Ariz. Died Sept. 2, 2003.

BOOKOUT, JOHN G. insurance company executive; Chmn. bd. dirs. Woodmen of World Life Ins. Soc., Omaha. Died July 18, 2003.

BOONE, DOROTHY MAE, county official; b. Gordon, Nebr. d. C.H. and Ethel Mae (Lewis) Perkins; m. M.H. Boone Oct. 2, 1943 (dec. Sept. 1954). AA, Iowa Western Community Coll., Council Bluffs, 1977; grad., Am. Legion Officers Sch., Indpls., 1973. Notary pub., Iowa. Nat. VA accredited svc. rep. Office Gen. Counsel, Washington, from 1976; exec. sec., adminstrv. asst., adminstrv. sec. Pottawattamie County Veterans' Affairs Commn., Council Bluffs, Iowa; dir. Veteran Affairs Commn., Pottawattamie County, 1987-92; profl. svc. officer DAV, from 1989; mem. local bd. SSS, Washington, from 1980; mem., chair Harrison, Shelby and Pottawattamie counties Shelby and Pottawattamie counties SSS, from 1981; med. com. Dept. Vets. Affairs Med. Ctr., Omaha, from 1997. Mem. med. commn. bd. VA Hosp., Omaha, 1997—. Recipient Cert. of Appreciation Kiwanis, 1985, VA Nat. Svc. Officers award, 1960, SSS, 1991, commendation DAV, 1987, County Svc. award Nat. VA, 1986, 92, Rep. Congl. Order Liberty, 1993, Internat. Order Merit award, 1994, Rep. Nat. Congl. Order of Freedom, 1995, Citizen of Yr. award His Royal Highness Kevin Prince Regent Hutt River Province Principality, 1995, Rep. Congl. Order of Freedom award Newt Gingrich, Spkr. of House, 1995, Cert. of Appreciation Ams. for Sr. Citizens in U.S.A., 1995; Citizen of Yr. Prince Kevin Prince Regent, 1995, Citizen of Royal Proclamation, 1995, John Phillips award, 1998, Actiones Nostros award Father Domenic, L.A., 1999, Anglea Dei award, 1999, Agimus Tibi Gratias, 1999. Home: Council Bluffs, Iowa. Deceased.

BOORSTIN, DANIEL JOSEPH, historian, lecturer, educator, author, editor; b. Atlanta, Ga., Oct. 1, 1914; s. Samuel and Dora (Olsan) Boorstin; m. Ruth Carolyn Frankel, Apr. 9, 1941; children: Paul Terry, Jonathan, David West. AB summa cum laude, Harvard U., 1934; postgrad., Inner Temple, London, 1934—37; BA with honors, Oxford U., 1936, BCL with honors, 1937; JSD, Yale U., 1940; LittD (hon.), Cambridge U., 1967; LLD (hon.), Harvard U., 1993; other hon. degrees. Cert.: Inner Temple (barrister-at-law) 1937, bar: Mass. 1942. Instr., tutor history and lit. Harvard and Radcliffe Coll., 1938—42; lectr. legal history Harvard Law Sch., 1939—42; asst. prof. history Swarthmore Coll., 1942—44; from asst. prof. to prof. Am. history U. Chgo., 1944—69, Preston and Sterling Morton disting. svc. prof., 1964—69; Walgreen lectr. Am. instns., 1952; dir. Nat. Mus. History and Tech., Smithsonian Instn., Washington, 1969—73, sr. historian, 1973—75; libr. of Congress Libr. of Congress, 1975—87, libr. of Congress emeritus, from 1987. Vis. lectr. U. Rome, 1950—51, Kyoto U., Japan, 1957; cons. social sci. rsch. ctr. U. P.R., 1955; lectr. in field; 1st incumbent of chair Am. history U. Paris, 1961—62; prof. U. Cambridge, 1964—65; sr. fellow Huntington Libr., 1969; mem. Commn. on Critical Choices for Ams., 1973—77; mem. Indo-Am. joint subcommn. edn. and culture Dept. State, 1974—81; mem. Japan-U.S. Friendship Commn., 1978—84; mem. Am. Revolution Bicentennial Commn.; sr. atty. office lend lease adminstrn. Dept. Justice, Washington; fellow Trinity Coll., 1964—65; mem. task force on exploration NASA, 1989. Author: The Mysterious Science of the Law, 1941, 1996, Delaware Cases, 1792-1830, 1943, The Lost World of Thomas Jefferson, 1948, The Genius of American Politics, 1953, The Americans: The Colonial Experience, 1958 (Bancroft award, 1959), America and the Image of Europe, 1960, The Image or What Happened to the American Dream, 1962, The Americans: The National Experience, 1965 (Francis Parkman prize, 1966), The Landmark History of the American People, 1968, 1987, The Decline of Radicalism, 1969, The Sociology of the Absurd, 1970, The Americans: The Democrtic Experience, 1973 (Pulitzer prize, 1974, Dexter prize, 1974), Democracy and Its Discontents, 1974, The Exploring Spirit, 1976, The Republic of Technology, 1978; author: (with Brooks M. Kelley) A History of the Untied States, 1981, 1991; author: The Discoverers, 1983 (Watson-Davis prize History of Sci. Soc., 1986), 1991, Hidden History, 1987, The Creators, 1992, Cleopatra's Nose, 1994, The Daniel J. Boorstin Reader, 1995, The Seekers, 1998, Daniel J. Boorstin: A Comprehensive and Selectively Annotated Bibliography, 2000; editor: An American Primer, 1966, American Civilization, 1972, Am. History, Ency. Britannica, 1951—55; mem. bd. editors:, from 1981; contbr. articles and book revs. to various publs. Trustee Colonial Williamsburg, Kennedy Ctr., Cafaritz Found., Woodrow Wilson Ctr., Thomas Gilcrease Mus.; mem. bd. visitors USAF Acad., 1968—70. Named to, Japanese Order of Sacred Treasure, 1st class, Grand Officer, Portugal, Legion of Honor, France, Order of Cultural Merit, Belgium; recipient Younger prize, 1936, Charles Frankel prize, NEH, 1989, Nat. Book award, Nat. Book Award Com., 1989, numerous others; scholar Rhodes scholar, Balliol Coll., Oxford U., 1936. Fellow: Royal Hist. Soc. (corr.), Am. Geog. Soc. (hon.); mem.: Colonial Soc. Mass., Orgn. Am. Historians, Am. Studies Assn. (pres. 1969—71), Am. Antiquarian Soc., Am. Philos. Soc. (Thomas Jefferson medal 1999), Am. Acad. Arts and Scis., Elizabethan Club (Yale U. chpt.), Nat. Press Club, Internat. House Japan, Cosmos Club, Phi Beta Kappa (Disting. Svc. to Humanities award 1988). Jewish. Home: Washington, DC. Died Feb. 28, 2004.

BOOTH, TAYLOR LOCKWOOD, computer science and engineering educator; b. Middletown, Conn., Sept. 22, 1933; s. George Robert and Della (Bell) B.; m. Aline Loyzim, Jan. 1, 1955; children: Laurine, Michael, Shari. BS, U. Conn., 1955; MS (Fortesque fellow 1955-56), 1956, PhD, 1962. Systems engr. Westinghouse Electric Corp., Balt., 1956-59; instr. U. Conn., Storrs, 1959-63, asst. prof., 1963-67, asso. prof., 1967-69, prof. computer sci. and elec. engring., 1969—, chmn. dept., 1972-77, 79-85; dir. Computer Applications and Research Ctr., from 1985. Cons. computer sci. and engring. to various firms, 1962—; mem. Computing Scis. Accreditation Bd., 1984—, pres., 1984-85; mem. Engring. Accreditation Commn., 1985— Author: Sequential Machines and Automata Theory, 1967, Digital Networks and Computer Systems, 1972, 2d edit., 1978, Computer Engineering: Hardware and Software Design, 1984, Computing: Fundamentals and Applications, 1974. Fellow IEEE (Centennial medal 1984); mem. IEEE Computer Soc. (sec. 1981-82, 1st v.p. 1982—, v.p. for edn. 1982-83), Assn. Computing Machinery, Conn. Acad. Sci. and Engring., Am. Soc. Engring. Edn. (Frederick Emmons Terman award 1972), Sigma Xi. Home: Mansfield Center, Conn. Died 1986.

BOREL, ARMAND, mathematics educator; b. Chaux-de-Fonds, Switzerland, May 21, 1923; m. Gabrielle Pittet, May 8, 1952; children: Dominique, Anne-Christine. Master Mathematics, Federal Inst. Tech., Zurich, Switzerland., 1947; Dr. Degree, U. Paris, 1952; PhD (hon.), U. Geneva, 1972. Asst. Federal Inst. Tech., Zurich, 1947-49, prof., 1955-57, 83-86; attaché de Recherches French Nat. Center Sci. Research, Paris, 1949-50; acting prof. algebra U. Geneva, Switzerland, 1950-52; mem. Inst. Advanced Study, Princeton, 1952-54, prof., 1957-93, prof. emeritus, 1993—2003. Vis. prof. U. Chgo., 1954-55, 76, MIT, 1958, 69, Tata Inst. Fundamental Rsch. Bombay, 1961, 68, 83, 90, 92, 95, 99, 2002, U. Paris, 1964, U. Calif., Berkeley, 1975, Yale U., 1978, U. Hong Kong, 1999, 2000, 01. Recipient Brouwer medal Dutch Math. Soc., 1978, Balzan prize, 1992. Mem. NAS, Acad. Arts and Sci., Am. Philos. Soc. (fgn.), Finnish Acad. Scis. and Letters (fgn.), French Acad. Scis. (fgn.), Academia Europaea (fgn.), European Acad. Scis., Am. Math. Soc. (Leroy P. Steele prize 1991), Swiss Math. Soc., French Math. Soc. Died Aug. 11, 2003.

BOREL, JACQUES, writer; b. Paris, Dec. 17, 1925; s. Pierre and Lucie (Dubee) B.; m. Christiane Idrac, Sept. 25, 1948; children: Denis, Anne, Helene, Claude, Claire. Licence des Lettres, Sorbonne, U. Paris, 1948, Maitrise Lettres, 1949. Cert. tchr., France. Tchr., Lycee Blaise Pascal, Clermont-Ferrand, France, 1952-54. Tchr. Lycee Paul Lapie, Courbevoie, France, 1954-56, Lycee Rodin, Paris, 1956-67; lit. adviser Editions Gallimard, Paris, 1969-75, Editions Balland, Paris, 1979-82; cultural attaché French Embassy, Belgium, 1984-86; vis. prof. Middlebury Coll. (Vt.), summer 1966, U. Hawaii, Honolulu, 1968-69, Portland State U. (Oreg.), summer 1967, U. Calif.-Irvine, fall 1969, U. Calif.-Riverside, fall 1980, NYU, N.Y.C., 1983. Author: (novels) L'Adoration (The Bond), 1965, Le Retour, 1970, Histoire de mes Vieux Habits, 1979, Petite Histoire de mes Reves, 1981, L'Attente, La Clôture, 1989, Le Déferlement, 1993, L'Aveu Différé, 1997, La Mort de Maximilien Lepage, 2001, (diary) La Depossession, 1973, Journal de la Mémoire, 1994, (essays) Marcel Proust, 1972, Commentaires, 1974, Poesie et Nostalgie, 1979, Un Voyage Ordinaire, 1975, Paroles Écrites, Commemorations, 1990, Propos sur l'Autobiographie, 1994, L'Effacement, 1998, Sur Les Poètes, 1998, Ombres et Dieux, 2001, (poems) Sur Les Murs Du Temps, 1990, playwright Tata ou de L'education, 1967, translator James Joyce's Collected Poems, 1967; editor Verlaine's Complete Works, 1958, 1962, 1972. Decorated officier Ordre Nat. Des Arts et Lettres; recipient prix Goncourt, Academie Goncourt, Paris, 1965, Grand pri Soc. des Gens de Lettres pour l'Ensemble de l'Oeuvre, 1994. Mem. PEN Club. Home: Bures-sur-Yvette, France. Died Sept. 25, 2002.

BORG, ANITA, computer scientist; b. Oak Park, Ill., Jan. 17, 1949; d. Carl Edwin and Beverly May (Borg) Naffz. BA, NYU, N.Y.C., 1973, MS, 1976, PhD, 1981. Asst. prof. N.Y. Inst. Tech., N.Y.C., 1978-80; sr. sys. designer Auragen Systems Corp., Ft. Lee, N.J., 1982-85; fault tolerant sys. cons. Nixdorf Computer, Paderborn, Germany, 1985-86; mem. rsch. staff Digital Equipment Corp., Palo Alto, Calif., 1986-97, Xerox Palo Alto Rsch. Ctr., Palo Alto, from 1997; pres. Inst. Women and Tech., Palo Alto, from 1997. Presdl. appointee Congl. Commn. on Advancement of Women and Minorities in Sci. Enring. and Tech. Co-inventor method for acquiring address traces, 1993. Founder Systers Internet, 1987, Grace Hopper Celebration of Women in Computing, Washington, 1994. Recipient World of Today and Tomorrow award Santa Clara County Girl Scouts, 1994, Pioneer award Electronic Frontier Found., 1995, Augusta Ada Lovelace award Assn. Women in Computing, 1995; inductee Women in Tech. Internat. Hall of Fame, 1998. Fellow Assn. Computing Machinery (coun. mem. 1991-95); mem. IEEE Computer Soc., Computing Rsch. Assn. (bd. dirs. 1994—). Avocations: flying, hiking, gardening, mountain biking, travel. Home: Los Altos, Calif. Died Apr. 5, 2003.

BORNMANN, CARL MALCOLM, lawyer; b. Somerville, N.J., Aug. 13, 1936; s. John Carl Bornmann and Dorothy Louise (Balliet) Capparelli; children: Carl, Gregory, Melissa. BS, Ohio U., 1958; JD with distinction, Ind. U., 1961; MA, Columbia U., 1989. Bar: Ind. 1961, N.Y. 1962, U.S. Dist. Ct. (so. and ea. dists.) N.Y. 1962, U.S. Ct. Appeals (2d cir.) 1962, U.S. Supreme Ct. 1965. Assoc. Cahill, Gordon, Reindel & Ohl, N.Y.C., 1961-69; ptnr. Cahill, Gordon & Reindel, N.Y.C., from 1970. Dir. Residents for the Future of Briarcliff Manor, 1994-96; del. USSR People to People Internat., 1990. Mem. ABA (bus. law sect.), N.Y. State Bar Assn., Japan Soc. of N.Y.C., Collier County (Fla.) Bar Assn. (assoc.), Order of Coif. Home: Kinnelon, NJ. Died, 1999.

BORST, LYLE BENJAMIN, physicist, researcher; b. Chgo., Nov. 24, 1912; s. George William and Jean Carothers (Beveridge) B.; m. Barbara Mayer, Aug. 19, 1939; children: John Benjamin, Stephen Lyle, Frances Elizabeth. AB, U. Ill., 1936, A.M., 1937; PhD, U. Chgo., 1941. Instr. U. Chgo., 1940-41, rsch. assoc. metall. lab., 1941-43; sr. physicist Clinton Labs., Oak Ridge, 1943-46; (both labs. working on atomic bomb project); asst. prof. dept. chemistry MIT, Cambridge, 1946; chmn. dept. reactor sci. and engring. Brookhaven Nat. Lab., 1946-51; prof. physics U. Utah, 1951; chmn. dept. physics Coll. Engring NYU, 1954-61; prof. physics SUNY, Buffalo, 1961-83, prof. emeritus, from 1983; master Clifford Furnas Coll., 1969-74. Author: Megalithic Software, Part I: England, Part II: Europe and the Near East, Part IIIa: Japan Studies of Prehistoric Science. Fellow AAAS, Am. Phys. Soc.; mem. ACLU (nat. bd. 1958-62, chmn. Niagra Frontier chpt. 1967-69), Phi Beta Kappa, Tau Beta Pi, Sigma Pi Sigma. Achievements include design and operation of Brookhaven reactor; research on sub-critical power reactors. Home: Buffalo, NY. Died July 30, 2002.

BORTHWICK, BRUCE MAYNARD, retired political scientist; b. Port Jefferson, NY, May 2, 1938; s. George and Helen Maynard Borthwick; m. Doris Ann Esch, Apr. 20, 1963; children: Andrew Eliot, Philip Vernon, Hannah Laura. BA in Polit. Sci., Syracuse U., 1959; MA in Nr. Ea. Studies, U. Mich., 1960, PhD in Polit. Sci., 1965. Cert. Certificat d'Etudes Francaises, Premier Degre Alliance Francaise, Paris, 2001. Lectr. polit. sci. Georgetown U., Washington, 1964—65; prof. polit. sci. Albion (Mich.) Coll., 1965—2000; fgn. expert, instr. of english China Inst. of Mining, Xuzhou, 1984—85; vis. prof. U. Mich., Ann Arbor, 1990; ret. Coord. Arabic speaking acad. immersion program U. Jordan, Amman, 1993; participant Fulbright Seminar Abroad, Pakistan, 1987, Expt. in Internat. Living, Cairo, 1961. Author: (textbook) Comparative Politics of the Middle East; contbr. articles to profl. jours. Pres. Albion Br., NAACP, 1999—2000; mem. Sister City Com., Albion - Noisy-le-Roi, France, 2000—02; sec. Citizens to Beautify Albion; pres. Albion Non-Profit Housing Corp., 1975—77; session mem. First Presbyn. Ch., Albion, 1986—91. Fellow Ctr. for Mid. Ea. Studies, U. Tex., Austin, 1977, Fulbright Seminar Abroad, U.S. Dept. of Edn. and U.S. Edn. Found. in Pakistan, 1987, Program for Inter-Institutional Collaboration in Area Studies, U. Mich., 1990, USIA, Ctr. for Arabic Study Abroad, 1994, Sr. Rsch., Am. Ctr. of Oriental Rsch., Amman, Jordan, 1998, 2002; grantee East Asia Faculty Devel. grant, Gt. Lakes Colleges Assn., 1975, Mid. Ea. Polit. Systems at U. of Tex., NEH, 1977, Andrew W. Mellon grant for faculty devel., Albion Coll., 1980. Mem.: Mid. East Studies Assn. (assoc.; selection com. for the dissertation award in the social sciences 1982), Ctr. for Mid. Ea. Studies U. Chgo. (assoc.), Mich. Conf. for Polit. Scientists (assoc.; pres. 1990), Brit. Soc. for Mid. Ea. Studies (assoc.). Presbyterian. Achievements include research in the Islamic sermon as a channel of political communication; privatization and private sector participation in the Jordanian water sector; water in Israeli-Jordanian relations. Avocations: travel, international exchange, Chinese cooking, bicycling, canoeing. Home: Albion, Mich. Died Nov. 16, 2002.

BOSQUET, ALAIN (ANATOLE BISK), poet, writer, critic; b. Odessa, Russia, Mar. 28, 1919; Alexander and Berthe (Turiansky) Bisk; m. Norma E. Caplan, 1954. Ed.,

Free U. Brussels, Sorbonne, U. Paris. Mng. editor La Voix de France, N.Y.C., N.Y., 1942; With Allied Control Coun., Berlin, from 1945; with Dept. State, Berlin, to 1951. Literary art critic various dailies and revs.; prof. French lit. Brandeis U., 1958-59; prof. Am. lit. U. Lyons (France), 1960-61; pres. Acad. Mallarme, 1994-97, hon. pres., 1997—; mem. juries Theophraste-Renaudot, pres. Max Jacob Jury, 1993—. Author books of poetry: Langue morte (prix Guillaume Apollinaire 1952), 1951; Quel royaume oublié, 1955; Premier Testament (prix Sainte-Beuve 1957); Deuxième Testament (prix Max Jacob 1959); Mâître objet, 1962; Quatre Testaments et autres poemes (grand prix de Poésie de l'Académie Française 1967), Le livre du doute et de la grâce, 1977; Poèmes, Un (1945-1967), 1979, Poèmes Deux (1970-1974), 1982; Sonnets pour une Fin de Siècle, 1980; Un Jour Après La Vie, 1984, Le Tourment de Dieu, 1987 (Prix Chateaubriand), Bourreaux et acrobates, 1989 (Grand prix for poetry City of Paris 1989, Jules Supervielle prize 1990), Demain Sans Moi, 1994, God's Torment, 1994, La Fable Et Le Fouet (Aphorisms), 1995, No More Me, 1995, Je Ne Suis Pas un Poete d'eau Douce, 1996; (essays) Saint-John Perse, 1953; Emily Dickinson, 1957; Walt Whitman, 1959; Anthologie de la poésie américaine, 1956, many others; 35 jeunes poètes americaine, 1961; Verbe et vertige (on contemporary poetry) (prix Fémina-Vecaresco 1962), 1961; Entretiens avec Salvador Dali, 1967; La Mémoire ou l'oubli, 1990, (memoirs) Les fruits de l'an dernier, 1996, La Russie en lambeaux, 1991, Un Amour Par Téléphone (Marlene Dietrich), 1992; (novels); Un besoin de malheur, 1963;; La confession mexicaine (prix Interallié), 1965; Les tigres de papier, 1968; Les bonnes intentions, 1975; Une mere russe, 1978 (Grand Prix for novels of French Acad.); Jean-Louis Trabart; Médecin, 1981; L'enfant que tu etais, 1982 (Prix Marcel Proust); Ni Guerre Ni Paix, 1983; Les Fêtes Cruelles, 1984, Lettre à mon père qui aurait eu cent ans (Prix Saint-Simon) 1987, Les Solitudes (trilogy) 1992 (prix for French lang. 1992); Les Trente Premières Années, 1993, Georges Et Arnold, Arnold Et Georges, 1995, A Russian Mother, 1996, Portrait d'un milliardaire malheureux, 1997, Un parc, une femme, quelques mensonges, 1997; (short stories) Un homme pour un autre, 1985, Le Métier D'Otage, 1989, Comme un Refus De La Planetè, 1989; (plays) Un détenu à Auschwitz, 1991. Served with Belgian and French armies, 1940, U.S. Army, 1942-45. Mem. Royal Acad. Lang. and Lit. Belgium, Acad. Letters Que. (hon.), European Acad. Poetry Luxembourg (pres. 1996—). Home: Paris, France. Died Mar. 17, 1998.

BOTHWELL, DORR, artist; b. San Francisco, May 3, 1902; d. John Stuart and Florence Isabel (Hodgson) B. Student, Calif. Sch. Fine Arts, Rudolph Schaeffer Sch. Design, U. Oreg. Painter, Tau, Manu'a, Am. Samoa, 1928-29, 1930-31, 49-51, 89, 1960-61, 89, 1966-67, 1974, 1982, 1985, 1987; instr. Calif. Sch. Fine Arts, San Francisco, 1945-58, San Francisco Art Inst., 1959-60, Rudolph Schaeffer Sch. Design, 1960-61, Mendocino (Calif.) Art Ctr., 1962-93, San Francisco Art Inst., 1961. Instr. Sonoma State Coll., summer 1964, U. Calif. Ext., Mendocino Art Ctr., 1965-71, 90; faculty Ansel Adams Yosemite Workshop, 1964-77, Victor (Colo.) Sch. Photography, 1979. Exhibitor, West Coast exhbns., 1927—, 3d biennial São Paulo, Brazil, Pitts. Internat., 1952, 55, Art: U.S.A., 1958, Bklyn. Mus., 1976, Mendocino (Calif.) Art Ctr., 1992; one-man shows include De Young Meml. Mus., San Francisco, 1957, 63; retrospective exhbn. Bay Window Gallery, Mendocino, 1985, Spl. Anniversary exhbn. 1986-87, Tobey Moss Gallery, L.A., 1989, 91, 93, Bothwell Studio, Mendocino, Calif., 1989, Mendocino Art Ctr., 1992, Gallery Mendocino, 1994-95; travelling exhbn. Oakland (Calif.) Mus., 1995, UCLA Mus., Westwood, 1995, Logan (Utah) Art Mus., 1995; works in permanent collection, San Diego Gallery Fine Art, Crocker Gallery, Sacramento, San Francisco Mus. Art, Whitney Mus. Am. Art, Bklyn. Mus., Mus. Modern Art, Fogg Mus., Met. Mus., Victoria and Albert Mus., London, Brit. Mus., London, Bibliothèque Nationale, Paris, France, Worcester (Mass.) Art Mus., Cleve. Mus. Art, Boston Mus. Art, Oakland (Calif.) Mus., DeYoung Mus., San Francisco, L.A. County Mus., 1994, Oakland Mus., 1995, Gene Autry Mus., L.A., 1995, Palms (Calif.) Art Guild, 1996; author: Notan: The Principle of Dark-Light Design, 1968, 2d edit., 1976, Danish edit., 1977, 3d edit., 1991, On The Edge of America: California Modernist Art, 1996. Recipient 1st prize, 4th ann. exhbn. San Francisco Soc. Women Artists, 1929; Pres.'s purchase prize, 1941; Leisser-Farnham award 7th ann. exhbn. San Diego Art Guild, 1932; hon. mention 7th ann. exhbn. So. Calif. Artists, 1933; spl. prize 9th ann. exhbn., 1937; Artists Fund prize ann. exhbn. drawings and prints San Francisco Art Assn., 1943; hon. mention 2d spring ann. Calif. Palace Legion of Honor, San Francisco, 1947; purchase prize 2d nat. print ann. Bklyn. Mus., 1948; 1st prize 9th ann. Nat. Serigraph Soc., N.Y.C., 1948; grantee Pollock-Krasner Found., 1998. Home: Apache Junction, Ariz. Deceased.

BOUDEWYNS, TIMOTHY MICHAEL, federal judge; b. Des Moines, Iowa; s. Robert M. and Florence E. (Blackmer) Boudewyns; m. Linda Louise Askins; children: Philip Matthew, Rebecca Lyn Asher. Graduate in Polit. Sci, Calif. State U., Sacramento, 1970; JD, U. Kansas Law Sch., 1974; ML in Labor Law, U. Mo. at Kansas City Law Sch., 1981. Bar: (US Supreme Ct., US Ct. Appeals for the First Circuit, US Ct. Mil. Appeals, Dist. Ct. of So. Dist. Iowa, and Supreme Cts. RI and Iowa.). Apptd. magistrate judge US Dist. Ct. R.I., 1991—97. Joined USAF, 1964—70, served in Vietnam, mil. judge Judge Advocate Gen. Corps USN, ret. navy comdr., 1991. Decorated Navy Commendation medal, Vietnam Meritorious Unit Citation (Gallantry Cross medal); recipient Air Force Unit award. Died Nov. 27, 1997.

BOUDRA, DOUGLAS BRYANT, professor, researcher; b. Russelville, Ark., May 1, 1950; s. Odie Abner and Ruby Elizabeth (Bryant) B. AB in Physics, Washington U., St. Louis, 1972; MS in Atmospheric Sci., U. Mich., 1974, PhD in Atmospheric Sci., 1977. Intern in meteorology Nat. Weather Svc., Indpls., summer 1972; with U. Miami, Fla., 1978-80, assoc. prof. rsch., 1987-88, assoc. prof., from 1988. Contbr. articles to profl. jours. Coord. blood drive marine sch. U. Miami, 1983—, solicitor United Way, 1984, 87. NSF rsch. grantee, 1979—. Mem. Am. Meteorol. Soc., Am. Geophys. Union, Oceanography Soc. (chartered). Democrat. Avocations: guitar, singing, tennis, volleyball, dance. Home: Hollywood, Fla. Deceased.

BOUGHTON, JAMES KENNETH, instrument engineer, educator; b. Akron, Ohio, Mar. 22, 1922; s. James Arthur and Louise (Smith) B.; student U. Akron, 1940-42; B.S. in Elec. Engring., Ill. Inst. Tech., 1944; M.S., Lamar Coll. Tech., 1968; Ph.D. Columbia Pacific U.; m. Evelyn Frances Robottom, Feb. 10, 1945; children; Steven Kent, Susan Lynn, Lisa Jean, Jeffrey Leigh (dec.). With Goodyear Tire and Rubber Co., 1942-77, machine designer, Akron, 1951, atomic supt. elec. and instrument maintenance, 1953-60, mgr. engring., Beaumont, Tex., 1960-77; sr. instrument engr. Stubbs Overbeck & Assocs., Beaumont, 1977-86; sec.-treas. Westbury Mgmt. Group, Inc., 1983-88; founder, pres. Boughton Enterprises Cons. Engrs., 1989—; assoc. prof. Lamar U., Beaumont, 1977-90; ptnr. Vantec Inc., Cons. Engrs., 1974; instr. U. Akron, 1947-49. Mem. cultural affairs com. Lamar U., 1968-70; active Beaumont Symphony, Lamar Philharm. Orch. Served to lt. comdr. USNR, 1942-45, 51-53; PTO. Recipient Goodyear Patent award, 1974. Registered profl. engr., Ohio. Mem. IEEE (life, sr.), Beaumont C. of C. Republican. Episcopalian (sr. warden 1970-71). Patentee tire bldg. machines, prodn. counters and controls. Died Apr. 7, 1994. Home: Sour Lake, Tex.

BOURCIER, JOHN PAUL, state supreme court justice; b. Providence, Mar. 27, 1927; s. Louis J. and Lydia E. (Garceau) B.; m. Norma M. DiLuglio, Aug. 20, 1951; children: Carol Bourcier Fargnoli, Norma J. Bourcier Bucci. BA, Brown U., 1950; LLB, Vanderbilt U., 1953. Bar: U.S. Dist. Ct. R.I. 1955, U.S. Ct. Appeals 1956, U.S. Immigration Svc. 1956, U.S. Ct. Mil. Appeals 1958, U.S. Tax Ct. 1960, U.S. Army Bd. Rev. 1965, U.S. Dist. Ct. Fla. 1965, N.H. 1965, Va. 1965. Trial atty. Bourcier & Bordieri, Providence, 1953-74; assoc. justice R.I. Superior Ct., Providence, 1974-95; justice R.I. Supreme Ct., Providence, from 1995. Chair Supreme Ct. Com. on Future of R.I. Cts.; invited judiciary panelist Rev. of Supreme Ct. Cases, 1987-92; lectr. in field; instr. Roger Williams Coll., 1982-95; guest lectr. Brown U., 1979-95, Bryant Coll., 1990-93, R.I. C.C., 1989-90; lectr. R.I. Fire Marshalls Arson Seminars, 1989—, New Eng. Fire Marshalls Arson Seminars, 1990-95; chmn. Superior Ct. Jury Trial Instrn. Rev. Com., mem. Civil Rules Rev. Com., others. Asst. editor Vanderbilt Law Rev., 1951-53. With USN, 1944-46. Named for life Assoc. Justice R.I. Supreme Ct. by Gov. Lincoln Almond, 1995—; inducted LaSalle Acad. Hall of Fame, 1998. Died Aug. 15, 2002.

BOURNE, MEL, production designer, art director; b. Newark, N.Y., 1923; s. Max and Frieda B.; children: Timothy, Tristan, Travis. BS, Purdue Univ., 1945; attended, Yale Sch. of Drama, 1945-48. Art dir.: (films) That Night, 1957, (with George Jenkins) The Miracle Worker, 1962, Annie Hall, 1977, The Greek Tycoon, 1978, (TV movie) The Silence, 1975, The Quinns, 1977, (TV spl.) The Mike Wallace Profiles, 1981; prodn. designer: (theatre) The Male Animal, Seagulls over Sorrento, The Millionairess, End as a Man, Carousel, (films) Interiors, 1978 (Academy award nomination best art direction 1978), Nunzio, 1978, Manhattan, 1979, Luna, 1979, Windows, 1980, Stardust Memories, 1980, Thief, 1981, A Midsummer Night's Sex Comedy, 1982, Still of the Night, 1982, Zelig, 1983, Broadway Danny Rose, 1984, The Natural, 1984 (Academy award nomination best art direction 1984), F/X, 1986, Manhunter, 1986, Fatal Attraction, 1987, Cocktail, 1988, The Accused, 1988, Rude Awakening, 1989, Reversal of Fortune, 1990, Man Trouble, 1992, Indecent Proposal, 1993, Angie, 1994, (TV series) Howdy Doody, 1947-60, We, The People, 1948-49, Believe It or Not, 1949-50, The Aldrich Family, 1949-53, The Goldbergs, 1949-54, The Roberta Quinlan Show, 1949-51, The Lux Video Theatre, 1950-54, Kojak, 1972, (TV pilots) Miami Vice, 1985, Equal Justice, 1990; prodn. designer, actor: (films) The Fisher King, 1991 (Academy award nomination best art direction 1991). Died Jan. 14, 2003.

BOUWSMA, WILLIAM JAMES, history educator; b. Ann Arbor, Mich., Nov. 22, 1923; s. Oets Kolk and Gertrude (DeVries) B.; m. Beverly Jean Hancock, July 9, 1944; children: John Roger, Philip Hancock, Paul Joseph, Sarah Elizabeth. AB, Harvard U., 1943, MA, 1947, PhD, 1950. Instr. to assoc. prof. U. Ill., 1950-56; asso. prof. history U. Calif., 1956-61, prof., 1961-68, chmn. dept., 1966-67, vice chancellor for acad. affairs, 1967-69; prof. history Harvard U., 1969-71; Sather prof. history U. Calif., Berkeley, 1971-91, Sather prof. emeritus, 1991—2004, chmn. dept., 1981-83, faculty lectr., 1975. Author: Concordia Mundi: Career and Thought of Guillaume Postel, 1957, Venice and the Defense of Renaissance Liberty, 1968, Culture of Renaissance Humanism, 1973, John Calvin. a Sixteenth-Century Portrait, 1987, A Usable Past, 1990, The Waning of the Renaissance 1550-1640, 2000. Bd. trustees Nat. Humanities Ctr., Meeter Ctr. Calvin Studies, Ch. Div. Sch. of Pacific. Served with AUS, 1943-46. Fulbright fellow, 1959-60; Guggenheim fellow, 1960; Behavioral Sci. Center fellow, 1963-64; Nat. Humanities Inst. fellow, 1976-77; Mellon sr. fellow Nat. Humanities Ctr., 1983-85 Fellow Am. Acad. Arts and Scis.; mem. Am. Hist. Assn. (pres. 1978, Nancy Lyman Roelker award 1992), Am. Philos. Soc., Renaissance Soc. Am. (council), Am. Soc. Reformation Research (pres. 1963), Soc. Italian Hist. Studies (pres. 1973-75) Home: Berkeley, Calif. Died Mar. 2, 2004.

BOWDEN, LEWIS WESLEY, management consultant; b. Broken Arrow, Okla., Sept. 23, 1924; s. Lewis Wesley and Pearl Edith (Lawrence) B.; m. Rolande Meyer, June 26, 1946 (div. Oct. 1954); m. Ljerka Nada Sobotincic, May 19, 1956; children: Allen Hugh, Moira Tatiana. AB, Yale U., 1947; postgrad., Columbia U., 1950. Researcher Dept. of State, Washington, 1950-52, fgn. service officer, 1952-78; econ. counselor U.S. Embassy, Moscow, 1970-73; dep. asst. sec. U.S. Dept. Commerce, Washington, 1973-74, U.S. Dept. Treasury, Washington, 1974-78; mng. dir. Parsons Saudi Arabia, Jeddah, 1979-82; pres. Curved Hill Mgmt. Co., Bethesda, Md., 1982-99. Cons. U.S. Treasury, Washington, 1982, 83, 84; assoc. Bldg. Devel. Counsel, Washington, 1983-84. Served to lt. USN, 1943-46, PTO. Recipient Superior Honor award Dept. of State, 1974. Mem. Am. Fgn. Service Assn. Clubs: Mory's (New Haven). Republican. Avocations: opera, tennis, inventions. Home: Bethesda, Md. Died Feb. 16, 1999.

BOWER, PAUL GEORGE, lawyer; b. Chgo., Apr. 21, 1933; s. Chester L. and Retha (Dausmann) B.; m. Elreen L. Thurlow, June 23, 1962; children: Stephanie, Julienne, Aimee. BA, Rice U., 1955; postgrad., Calif. Inst. Tech., 1959-60; LL.B., Stanford U., 1963. Bar: Calif. 1964, U.S. Sureme Ct. 1969. Assoc. Gibson, Dunn & Grutcher, Los Angeles, 1963-67, ptnr., 1970—93. Asst. dir. Nat. Adv. Com. Civil Disorder, 1967-68; spl. asst. to dep. atty. gen. U.S. Dept. Justice, 1968-69, consumer counsel, 1969; bd. dirs. Legal Aid Found.; former trustee Sierra Club Legal Def. Fund; mem. legal svcs. Trust Fund Commn., 1990-93, chair, 1993-94; dep. gen. counsel Webster Commn., 1992. With U.S. Army, 1956-59. Mem. Calif. Bar Assn., L.A. County Bar Assn., Beverly Hills Bar Assn., Order of Coif. Democrat. Died Dec. 31, 2003.

BOWER, RODNEY A. labor union official; b. Buffalo, May 5, 1937; s. Bertram L. and Marion H. B.; m. Betty Jo Anderson, 1949; 3 children. Former mem. Internat. Fedn. Profl. and Tech. Engrs., Silver Springs, Md., pres., 1972—88, pres. local 13, 1953-54, exec. sec., 1954-56, 60-68, exec. v.p., 1968-72, pres. gen. electric locals council, 1957-59, sec.-treas., 1955-57, internat. v.p. Atlantic area, 1964-70. Died Mar. 22, 2004.

BOWERS, JOHN ZIMMERMAN, physician, scientist, educator; b. Catonsville, Md., Aug. 27, 1913; s. John Culler and Adelaide (Schuman) B.; children: John C., Mary I., David W.; m. Akiko Kobayashi, Apr. 17, 1970. BS, Gettysburg Coll., 1933, Sc.D. (hon.), 1958, MD, U. Md., 1938, Sc.D., 1959; L.H.D., Woman's Med. Coll., 1967; Docteur Honoris Causa, Universite d'Aix-Marseille, France, 1976; D.Sc., Morehouse Coll., 1985. Intern, resident Univ. Hosp., Balt., 1938-41; Harvard fellow in pathology New Eng. Deconess Hosp., Boston, 1943-44; fellow in tropical medicine U.S. Naval Med. Sch., Bethesda, Md., 1944; dep. dir. AEC, Washington, 1947-50; asst. prof. dept. medicine Johns Hopkins U., Balt., 1948-50; dir. Radioactive Isotope Lab., Balt., 1950; dir., rsch. fellow Crocker Radiation Lab. U. Calif., Berkeley, 1950; prof., dean Coll. Medicine radiobio. lab., med. cons. AEC, U. Utah, 1950-55; dean, prof. medicine Med. Sch. U. Wis., 1955-62; pres. Macy Found., N.Y.C., 1965-80. Cons. Ford Found., India, 1952-59, WHO, 1963-69, UNESCO, 1968, adv. com. Radiation Effects Rsch. Found. of NAS, 1982, N.Y. Acad. Scis., 1967; mem. adv. com. The Pres.'s Health Resources, 1958-61; cons. to surgeon gen. USAF, 1959-64; mem. adv. com. for sci. publs. USPHS, 1962-66; vis. prof. Kyoto (Japan) U. Med. Sch., 1962-64, U. Philippines, 1962; mem. staff Rockefeller Found., 1964-65, cons., 1978-84; mem. adv. com. history of life scis. NIH, 1970-74; mem. exec. com. Nutrition Found., 1972, also trustee; adj. prof. N.Y. Med. Coll., 1980; bd. visitors Air U., Montgomery, Ala., 1959-62. Author: Medical Education in Japan, From Chinese Medicine to Western Medicine, 1965, Western Medical Pioneers in Feudal Japan, 1970, Doctor on Desima, 1970, Western Medicine in a Chinese Palace, 1972, National Health Services, 1973, An Introduction to American Medicine, 1975, When the Twain Meet: The Rise of Western Medicine in Japan, 1980, The Radiation Effects Research Foundation, Hiroshima - It's Origin and Growth, 1985, The History of the U.S. Atomic Bomb Casualty Commission, NAS, 1983; editor, chmn. editl. bd. Jour. Med. Edn., 1956-62; mem. bd. assoc. editors Jour. History of Med. and Allied Scis., 1974; co-author, editor: Advances in American Medicine - Essays at Bicentennial American Medicine, 1975; mem. editl. bd. Grants mag., 1978; contbr. articles to profl. jours. Mem. exec. com. Western Interstate Com. for Higher Edn., 1952-55; mem. adv. com. for med. and pub. health Kellogg Found., 1955-64; mem. bd. overseers Morehouse Coll. Med. Sch., 1976-79; mem. bd. med. acad. adv. com. Chinese U. Hong Kong, 1976—, mem. com. Am. Cancer Soc., 1977-80; trustee Gettysburg Coll., 1977-79, East Asian History Scis. Found., 1980—, Giovanni Lorenzini Found., Inc., 1980—; mem. Com. de Patronage Med. D'Afrique Noire, 1978—; mem. adv. coun. Am. Trust for Brit. Libr., 1980—. Served as comdr. USNR, 1941-45. Decorated Legion of Merit for Combat, Purple Heart, 1944; recipient Order of the Legion of Honor (France), 1975, Order of the Rising Sun (Japan), 1982; Alan Gregg travel scholar China Med. Bd., 1962-63; Andrew Wellington Cordier fellow Columbia U. Sch. Internat. Affairs, 1977. Fellow ACP; mem. AMA (coun. on med. edn. in hosps. 1958-63), Am. Assn. for History of Medicine,

Assn. Am. Med. Colls. (v.p. 1952, exec. coun. 1953-59), Am. Osler Soc., Internat. Acad. History Medicine (sec.-treas. 1975), Japan Soc. for Med. Edn. (hon.), Indian Assn. Advancement Med. Edn. (hon.), Coun. Fgn. Rels., Century Assn., Asia Soc., Am. Soc. French Legion Honor, Med. Alumni Assn. U. Md., Union Club, Univ. Club, Cosmos, Alpha Omega Alpha, Nat. Honor Med. Soc. (pres. 1968-78). Home: Lakewood, NJ. Deceased.

BOWLIN, EVE SALLEE, retired ob-gyn nurse practioner; b. San Jacinto, Calif., Nov. 16, 1913; d. Joseph and Theda (Bergman) Sallee; widow; children: Chad, Barbara, McKim, Jonathan (dec.). LVN, Mt. San Jacinto Coll., 1967; diploma in nursing, Loma Linda U., 1970; teaching credential, San Bernardino State Coll., 1976; RNP, U. Calif., San Francisco, 1977. Lic. vocat. nurse, Calif. Tchr. English to fgn.-born students Coachella Valley Sch. Dist., Thermal, Calif.; pub. health nurse Riverside County Health Dept., Indio, Calif., ob.-gyn. nurse; rural health clinic prenatal care provider El Progreso del Desierto, Coachella, Calif., 1981-90; gynecologic nurse Ribton Wade, M.D., 1990-94; ret., 1998. Vol. Liga Flying Drs. of Mercy; vol. counselor Peer Counseling Program. Mem. So. Calif. Pub. Health Assn. (charter), LaQuinta Soroptimist Internat. (recipient svc. awards), Toastmasters. Home: Indio, Calif. Died Sept. 3, 2000.

BOWLING, JOYCE BLANKENCHIP, retired critical care nurse; b. White Deer, Tex., Nov. 17, 1932; d. Roy Lee and Myrtle Dove (Milhoan) Blankenchip; m. J.C. Bowling, July 24, 1952. Diploma, Northwest Tex. Sch. Nursing, 1953; AS, Amarillo Coll., 1953; BSN, West Tex. State U., 1983. RN, Tex.; cert. med.-surg. nursing, gerontology, nursing adminstrn. AACN; cert. emergency nurse. Staff nurse emergency rm. Parkland Hosp., Dallas, 1960-62; staff nurse Meth. Hosp., Dallas, 1962-68; staff nurse medicine, then head nurse CCU St. Paul Hosp., Dallas, 1969-73; charge nurse, supr. Southwestern Dialysis Ctr., Dallas, 1973-74; dir. nurses Caruth Rehab. Inst., Dallas, 1974-75; staff nurse VA Med. Ctr., Dallas, 1976-79, Amarillo, Tex., 1979-85, head nurse surg. unit, 1985-88, clin. coord., 1988-96, ret., 1996. Mem. AACN (cert.), Emergency Nurses Assn. (cert.), Tex. Nurses Assn., Am. Heart Assn., Nat. Kidney Found., Am. Cancer Soc., Sigma Theta Tau. Avocations: reading, needlework, travel, fishing. Home: Webbers Falls, Okla. Died Nov. 27, 2000.

BOWNES, HUGH HENRY, judge; b. N.Y.C., Mar. 10, 1920; s. Hugh Gray and Margaret (Henry) Bownes; m. Irja C. Martikainen, Dec. 30, 1944 (dec. Jan. 1991); m. Mary Davis, July 12, 1992. BA, Columbia U., 1941, LLB, 1948. Bar: N.H. 1948. Since practiced in, Laconia; ptnr. firm Nighswander, Lord & Bownes, 1951—66; assoc. justice N.H. Superior Ct., 1966—68; judge U.S. Dist. Ct. N.H., Concord, 1968—77, U.S. Ct. Appeals (1st cir.), 1977—90, sr. judge, 1990—2003. Chmn. Laconia chpt. ARC, 1951—52; pres. bd. Laconia Hosp. Assn., 1963—64; mem. Laconia City Coun., 1953—57; chmn. Laconia Dem. Com., 1954—57; mayor Laconia, 1963—65; mem. Dem. Nat. Com. for N.H., 1963—66. Maj. USMC, 1941—46. Decorated Silver Star, Purple Heart. Mem.: ABA, Belknap County Bar Assn. (pres. 1965—67), N.H. Bar Assn., Am. Law Inst., Laconia C. of C. (past pres.), Lions Club (past pres. Laconia). Home: Branford, Conn. Died Nov. 5, 2003.

BOYCE, GERALD G. b. Embarrass, Wis., Dec. 29, 1925; s. Charles William and Selma (Van Norman) B.; m. Kathryn Davis; 1 son, Charles William II. BS, Wis. State U.; M.F.A., U. Iowa, 1950; postgrad., Americano Guatemaletco Instituto, Ind. U., U. Ill., Oxford (Eng.) U., 1979, Brit. Mus., Courtauld Inst., London. Prof. art history U. Indpls., 1950-88, prof. emeritus, from 1988, chmn. art dept., 1950-88; lectr. art history DePauw U., 1968-84; tchr. Fresno State Coll., Wabash Coll., DePauw U., Ind. U. Tchr. St. John's U., N.Y.C., 1989; cons. Ind. Bell Telephone Co., 1967-70, U.S. Post Office Dept., 1972, Smithsonian Instn.; mem. Gov.'s Commn. on the Arts. One-man retrospective show Swope Art Mus., Terre Haute, Ind., 1993; exhibited in group shows L.A. County Mus., San Francisco Mus. Art, Art Inst. Chgo., 1954, Mus. Modern Art, N.Y.C., 1956, Corcoran Gallery Art, Washington, 1971, Mus. Contemporary Crafts, N.Y.C.; represented in permanent collections Ball State U., DePauw U., Earlham Coll., Evansville Coll., St. John's U., Marquis Inc., Ind. State U., Minot Coll., S.D., Wabash Coll., U. Iowa, Swope Art Mus., Rose-Hulman Inst. Tech. Served with USAAF, World War II. Mem. Nat. Coll. Art Conf., Am. Crafts Council (sec. N. Central region 1962-66), Coll. Art Assn., Midwest Coll. Art Assn., Nat. Art Adminstrs. Conf., Ethnographic Arts Soc. (exec. com.), Assn. of Gravestone Studies. Methodist. Home: Morgantown, Ind. Died Dec. 15, 1999.

BOYCE, GERARD ROBERT, lawyer, accountant; b. Bridgeton, N.J., Sept. 7, 1954; s. Raymond Gerard Fannon and Joan Marie Carguil; adopted by Lester William Boyce. BS, Fairleigh Dickinson U., 1976; JD, Seton Hall U., 1983; LLM, NYU, 1987. Bar: N.J. 1983, N.Y. 1987, U.S. Dist. Ct. N.J. 1983, U.S. Dist. Ct. N.Y. 1987, U.S. Tax Ct. 1989. Acct. Granet & Granet CPA's, Union, N.J., 1976-78; mgr. Allied Corp., Morristown, N.J., 1978-84; assoc. Barrett Smith Schapiro Simon & Armstrong, N.Y.C., 1984-85; internat. tax counsel Jos. E. Seagram & Sons, Inc., N.Y.C., 1985-86; assoc. Milbank Tweed Hadley & McCloy, N.Y.C., 1986-92; ptnr. Brown Raysman & Millstein, N.Y.C., from 1992. Mem. ABA, Am. Inst. CPA, N.Y. State Bar Assn., Assn. of Bar of City of N.Y. Home: Franklin Lakes, NJ. Died June 4, 2001.

BOYD, JAMES BURDETTE, farmer; b. Holly Bluff, Miss., Aug. 1, 1937; s. James Ansel and Annie (Grean) B.; m. Walter Joy Koonce, Aug. 24, 1959; children: Paige, Alison, Laura. BS, U. So. Miss., 1959. Coach, tchr. math, sci. Lumberton High Sch., Miss., 1959-60; co-founder, pres. Holly Bluff Gin Co., Miss., from 1975; pres. Boyd Seed Co., Holly Bluff, from 1982, Roanoke Farms, Holly Bluff, from 1960. Bd. dirs. Yazoo Valley Oil Mill, Jackson, Miss., Deer Creek Compress, Rolling, Fork, Miss., Silver Creek Drainage Commn., 1975-80. Pres. Holly Bluff Sch. Bd., 1969—; mem. sch. bd. Sharkey Acad., Rolling Fork, 1970-79. Mem. Seed Improvement Assn., Farm Bur., Soil & Water Conservation Com., Yazoo Country Club. Republican. Presbyterian. Avocations: golf, tennis. Home: Jackson, Miss. Deceased.

BOYER, HAROLD EDWIN, oral and maxillofacial surgery educator; b. Reading, Pa., Aug. 9, 1925; m. E. Kathryn Boyer, Aug. 1, 1948 (div); children: Bonnie, Brian; m. Mary Margaret Black, Mar. 23, 1991. Student, Lebanon Valley Coll.; DDS, U. Pa., 1952, MSc, 1958. Diplomate Am. Bd. Oral and Maxillofacial Surgery. Prof. oral and maxillofacial surgery U. Louisville Sch. Dentistry, from 1958, chmn. oral surgery, 1959-69, asst., then assoc. dean, 1959-69, dean, 1969-72, v.p. health affairs, 1972-82, chmn. dept. oral and maxillofacial surgery, 1983-86, adminstr. health scis., from 1969, responsible for devel. and constrn. Health Sci. Ctr., 1960-82. Contbr. articles to dental jours., including Dental Clinics N.Am., Jour. Oral and Maxillofacial Surgeons, Current Therapy in Dentistry. Active Louisville chpt. Am. Cancer Soc., 1978-82, Louisville chpt. Am. Heart Assn., 1982. With U.S. Army, 1943-46. Recipient Disting. Svc. award U. Pa., 1996. Fellow Am. Coll. Dentistry, Internat. Coll. Dentistry. Home: Louisville, Ky. Died Apr. 6, 2002.

BOYETT, DOROTHY ELEANOR ANDERSON, dietitian, educator; b. Bear Lake Township, Mich., Oct. 17, 1915; d. Carl Emil and Julia (Johnson) Anderson; widowed; children: Marilyn Boyett Annan, John M. Jr., Carl E. BS, Mich. State U., 1937; Tchg. Cert., Fla. So. Coll., 1967; MA in Tchg., Rollins Coll., 1971. Cert. dietitian, Am. Dietetic Assn. Civil svc. dietitian Sta. Hosp., Ft. Bragg, N.C., 1939-43; chief dietitian, chief instr. Army Hosp., Ft. Bragg, N.C., 1943-45; kindergarten tchr. 1st Meth. Ch., Clermont, Fla., 1959-67; hosp. dietitian Southlake Meml. Hosp., Clermont, Fla., 1967-69, consulting dietitian, 1969-70; tchr. Clermont Elem. Sch., 1967-80. Charter mem. Nat. Mus. Women in Arts, Washington, 1986-87; gallery chmn. Southlake Art League, Clermont, 1985-86, corr. sec., 1986-97. Capt. U.S. Army Med. Corp, 1943-45. Mem. Clermont C. of C. (Gem of the Hills award, 1995). Avocations: poetry-prose writing, pastel artist. Home: Clermont, Fla. Died Oct. 17, 2001.

BOYLE, EDWARD J., SR., federal judge; m. Edith Boyle, Jan. 29, 1936; two children. Student U. Richmond Sch. of Law, 1934; LLB Loyola U., 1935. ptnr. Boyle, Lozes & Zinser, New Orleans; pvt. practice, 1936-62; ptnr. Christenson & Boyle, New Orleans, 1937-38; asst. U.S. Atty., U.S. Dist. Ct. (ea. dist.) La., New Orleans, 1945-48; ptnr. Sehrt & Boyle, New Orleans, 1962-66; ptnr. Sehrt, Boyle & Wheeler, New Orleans; judge U.S. Dist. Ct. (ea. dist.) La., until 1981, sr. judge, 1981—. Died July 24, 2002.

BOZORTH, SQUIRE NEWLAND, lawyer; b. Portland, Oreg., Oct. 25, 1935; s. Squire Smith and Ethel Elizabeth (Newland) B.; m. Louise Crosby Mathews, Aug. 9, 1967; children: Squire Mathews, Caroline Rutgers. BS, U. Oreg., 1958; LLB, NYU, 1961. Bar: N.Y. 1961. Assoc. Milbank, Tweed, Hadley & McCloy, N.Y.C., 1961-70, ptnr., 1970-95, cons. ptnr., from 1995. Assoc. counsel Rockefeller U., 1973-83. Bd. dirs., exec. com., v.p. Fedn. Protestant Welfare Agys., 1970-89; bd. dirs. The Hess Found., 1988-99, The Hurricane Allen St. Lucia Rebuilding Fund, 1988-99; pres. bd. trustees Scarsdale Pub. Libr., 1991-93; trustee Marilyn M. Simpson Charitable Trusts; trustee, exec. com. The Parks Coun., 1991-94, Internat. House, 1991-94, Diocese of N.Y., Episcopal Ch., 1995-98, 2001—; dir., v.p. Dillon Fund; trustee Cathedral St. John the Divine, 1999—. Mem. N.Y. State Bar Assn. (exec. com. internat. law sect., chmn. internat. estate and trust law com. 1990-93), N.Y. Law Inst. (exec. com.), Century Assn., Phi Beta Kappa. Episcopalian. Home: New York, NY. Deceased.

BRADEN, SAMUEL EDWARD, economics educator; b. Hoihow, Hainan, China, June 6, 1914; s. Samuel Ray and Mary (Altman) B.; m. Beth Black, 1937; children: Mary Beth, Stephen, John, David. AB, U. Okla., 1932; MA, U. Wis., 1935, PhD, 1941; LL.D. hon., Ill. State U., 1976, Ind. U., 1983. Instr. to prof. Ind. U., 1937-67; assoc. dean Coll. Arts and Sci., 1954-59, v.p., 1959-67; pres. Ill. State U., 1967-70; chmn. div. bus. and econs. Ind. U. S.E., 1970-80. Mem. exec. com. Council Internat. Ednl. Exchange, N.Y., 1967-83; exec. dir. Ind. Conf. Higher Edn., 1963-67; sr. economist Combined Raw Materials Bd., Washington, 1942-43 Author: (with C.L. Christenson, others) Economics, Principles and Problems, 1946, (with G.A. Steiner, others) Economic Problems of the War; Contbr. articles to ednl. publs. Bd. overseers St. Meinrad Sem.; mem. bd. Hughes Group, Inc.; bus. economist Shaw Internat. Inc.; mem. bd. Christian edn. Presbyn. Ch. Fulbright sr. research fellow U.K., 1949-50 Mem. Am., Midwest econ. assns., Am. Finance Assn., Phi Beta Kappa. Home: Bloomington, Ind. Died Aug. 13, 2003.

BRADLEY, JEFF(REY MARK), arts critic; b. Springfield, Mass., Jan. 9, 1944; s. Richard Gerald and Helen Virginia (Breglio) B. Student, Brown U. Reporter Springfield Union, 1965-69; western Mass. corr. AP, 1969-72, fgn. corr., 1972-83, bur. chief Beijing, 1983-86, Toronto, Ont., Can., 1986-88; arts critic-at-large Denver Post, from 1989. Knight journalism fellow Stanford U., 1988-89; lectr. on music and opera U. of Denver, Ctrl. City Opera, Colo. Symphony Orch., Denver, 1990-99. Co-author: Denver, Confluence of the Arts, 1995. Recipient Bell award Nat. Assn. Mental Health, 1969. Deceased.

BRADSHAW, CARL JOHN, investor, lawyer, consultant; b. Oelwein, Iowa, Nov. 1, 1930; s. Carl John and Lorraine Lillian (Thiele) B.; m. Katsuko Anno, Nov. 5, 1954; children: Carla K., Arthur Herbert, Vincent Marcus. BS, U. Minn., 1952, JD, 1957; LLM, U. Mich., 1958; MJur, Keio U., Tokyo, 1962. Bar: Minn. 1960, U.S. Supreme Ct., 1981, Calif. 1985. Assoc. Graham, James & Rolph, Tokyo, 1961-63; assoc. prof. law U. Wash., Seattle, 1963-64; sr. v.p. Oak Industries, Inc., Crystal Lake, Ill., 1964-84, dir. internat. ops., 1964-70, dir. corp. devel., 1970-72, pres. communications group, 1972-78, chief legal officer, 1979-84; counsel Seki & Jarvis, L.A., 1985-87, Bell, Boyd & Lloyd, L.A., 1987; prin. The Pacific Law Group, L.A., Tokyo and Palo Alto, Calif., from 1987, The Asian Mktg. Group, Torrance, Calif., from 1992. Participant Japanese-Am. program for cooperation in legal studies, 1957-61. Contbr. articles to legal and bus. jours Bd. dirs. Japan-Am. Soc., Chgo., 1966-72; bd. dirs., fin. dir. San Diego Symphony Orch. Assn., 1980-81. Served to lt. (j.g.) USN, 1952-55 Fulbright scholar, 1958-59, Ford Found. scholar, 1960-61. Fellow Radio Club Am.; mem. Minn. Bar Assn., Calif. Bar Assn., Am. Soc. Internat. Law, Internat. Fiscal Assn., Regency Club, Order of Coif. Avocations: reading, bible study. Home: San Diego, Calif. Died Mar. 2003.

BRADY, FRANK BENTON, retired technical society executive; b. Pomeroy, Ohio, June 1, 1914; s. Charles Wesley and Julia Bessie (Cross) B.; m. Lucille Marie Svitzer, Feb. 3, 1950; children: Susan Erika, John Benton (dec.), Alan Gibson. Student, U. Cin., 1933-39. Registered profl. engr., D.C. Radio engring. asst. Crosley Radio Corp., Cin., 1933-39; radio engr. Aircraft Radio Lab., Dayton, Ohio, 1939-46; flight projects engr. Air Transport Assn., Washington, 1946-55, dir. nat. airspace systems engring., 1976-79; jr. ptnr. Mills Petticord & Mills Architects and Engrs., Washington, 1955-57; sr. staff cons. Singer Co.-Gen. Precision, Washington, 1957-74; aviation cons. Washington, 1974-76; exec. dir. The Inst. of Navigation, Washington, 1979-90; ret., 1990. Author: A Singular View-The Art of Seeing with One Eye, 1972, (with others) (textbook) Avionics Navigation Systems, 1968; patentee in field. Trustee Cosmos Club Found., 1970—, USN Sailing Found., Annapolis, Md., 1987—. Recipient Medal of Freedom War Dept., 1946, citation Radio Tech. Commn. Aeronautics, 1963, 92. Fellow IEEE (life; guest editor Proc. spl. issue Instrument Landing 1959, Global Navigation 1983), Inst. Navigation; mem. Cosmos Club, New Providence Club, Naval Acad. Sailing Squadron Annapolis. Avocations: sailing, writing, restoration of nautical and scientific antiques. Died Feb. 4, 2003.

BRADY, WALLACE ANTHONY, judge; b. Portage City, Wis., Oct. 20, 1921; s. Charles H. and Ella (Riley) B.; m. Mary Elizabeth Garvin, June 9, 1949; children: Patricia, Charles, Steven, Timothy, John. BA, U. Wis., 1943, LLB, 1947. Bar: Wis. 1947. Pvt. practice, Elroy, Wis., 1947-79; circuit court judge State of Wis., Mauston, 1980-99. Lt. USN, 1943-45. Mem. Wis. Bar Assn., Juneau City Bar Assn., Rotary. Roman Catholic. Home: Elroy, Wis. Died May 30, 1999.

BRADY, WILLIAM WEBB, lawyer; b. Elgin, Ill., Nov. 9, 1914; s. William H. and Helen (Webb) B.; m. Barbara Frances Rosewater, Sept. 28, 1940; children: Barbara Brady Bostwick, Nancy Brady Shafer, Katherine A., Margaret Brady Safford. BCom, Northwestern U., 1936, JD, 1940; LHD (hon.), Judson Coll., 1979. Bar: Ill. 1940, U.S. Tax Ct. 1940; CPA, Ill. Acct. Arthur Andersen & Co., Chgo., 1936-37; assoc. Mayer, Meyer, Austrian & Platt, Chgo., 1940-41; atty. Office Price Adminstrn., Chgo., 1941-43; ptnr. Gromer & Brady, Elgin, Ill., 1946-50, Brady, McQueen, Martin, Collins & Jensen, predecessors, Elgin, from 1952; pvt. practice Elgin, 1950-51. Mem. faculty Sch. Law Northwestern U., Chgo., 1939-79; spl. asst. atty. gen. State of Ill., 1969-76; lectr. on taxes throughout U.S. and Can. Bd. editors Ill. Law Rev., 1939-40; contbr. articles to legal jours., chpts. to books. A founder, past pres. Elgin Coun. of Chs.; pres. Elgin United Community Fund, 1963-65; chmn. bd. trustees Judson Coll., 1962-67; trustee No. Bapt. Theol. Sem., Oak Brook, Ill., 1962—, Bapt. Theol. Union, 1975-85; former trustee, deacon, moderator lst Bapt. Ch., Elgin; mem. adv. bd. St. Joseph Hosp., 1971—; pres., 1972-82, also co-chmn. fund-raising campaign. Recipient Disting. Service award Elgin Cosmopolitan Club, 1970, Greater Elgin Area YMCA, 1987, Republican of Yr. award Elgin Twp. Rep. Orgn., 1975, Citizen of Yr., United Way Elgin, 1978, Willis A Reed Humanitarian award, 1987. Fellow Am. Bar Found., Am. Coll. Probate Counsel, Ill. Bar Assn. Fellows; mem. ABA, Ill. Bar Assn., Kane County Bar Assn. (Community Service award 1987), Elgin Bar Assn., Am. Judicature Soc., Elgin Country Club, Union League Chgo., Masons, Elks, Rotary (pres. Elgin 1954-55). Avocations: reading, boating. Home: Elgin, Ill. Deceased.

BRAGENZER, JUNE ANNA RUTH GRIMM, retired community health nurse; b. Detroit, July 21, 1923; d. Arthur John and Ruth Irene (Hamilton) Voss; m Ernest W. Grimm (dec. 1982); children: Betty Gondeck West, Cheryl Davis, Peggy Toth, Linda; m. Fred C. Bragenzer, June 30, 1985. Diploma, Evang. Deaconess Hosp., 1944; BSN, U. Mich.,

1980; postgrad., Wayne State U., 1974, 75, 78-79, U. Mich., 1980-81. RN, Mich. Charge nurse Dana Corp., Riverview, Mich., 1969-70; supervisory care nurse Enrico Fermi II/Detroit Edison, Monroe, Mich., 1970-76; relief nurse McCords Stamping Plant, Wyandotte, Mich., 1983-86, ret., 1986. With N.C., U.S. Army, 1943-44. Mem. ANA, Am. Assn. Occupational Health Nurses (cert. specialist), Mich. Assn. Occupational Health Nurses, Sigma Theta Tau. Home: Flat Rock, Mich. Died June 11, 1999.

BRAIDWOOD, LINDA SCHREIBER, archaeologist; b. Grand Rapids, Mich., Oct. 9, 1909; d. F. Robert and Mathilde (Neumann) Schreiber; m. Robert J. Braidwood, Jan. 4, 1937; children: Gretel, Douglas. Student, Wellesley Coll., 1927-28, U. Munich, 1928-29; AB, U. Mich., 1932; MA, U. Chgo., 1943. Field asst. Syrian expdn., Oriental Inst. U. Chgo., 1937-47, prehist. project field asst. Oriental Inst., from 1947, Oriental Inst. assoc., from 1947, instr. home study dept., 1957-63. Author: Digging Beyond the Tigris, 1953; co-author: Excavations in the Plain of Antioch I, 1960, Prehistoric Archeology Along The Zagros Flanks, 1983; contbr. articles and revs. to profl. jours.; mem. adv. bd. jour. Archaeology, 1952-67. Fulbright rsch. fellow, Turkey, 1963-64 Died Jan. 15, 2003.

BRAIDWOOD, ROBERT JOHN, archaeologist, educator; b. Detroit, July 29, 1907; s. Walter J. and Rhea (Nimmo) B.; m. Linda Schreiber, 1937; children: Gretel, Douglas. AB, U. Mich., 1932, AM, 1933; PhD, U. Chgo., 1942; ScD (hon.), U. Ind., 1971; Docteur (hon.), U. Sorbonne, Paris, 1975; LittD (hon.), U. Rome, 1984. Archeol. field work, Iraq, Syria, Iran, Turkey, 1930—; faculty Oriental Inst., U. Chgo., 1933—, prof. Old World prehistory, 1954-76, prof. emeritus, 1976—; faculty U. Chgo., 1940—, prof. dept. anthropology, 1954-76, now emeritus. Vis. prof. Istanbul U., 1963-64. Recipient Frydell medal Soc. for Am. Archaeology, 1995. Fellow NAS, Am. Acad. Arts and Scis., Am. Philos. Soc., Soc. Antiquaries (London) (hon.); mem. Am. Anthrop. Assn. (exec. bd. 1962-64, disting. lectr. 1971), Internat. Union Pre-and-Protohistoric Scis. (former U.S. del. permanent council), Conf. Asian Archaeology-New Delhi (found. mem.); corr. mem. Deutsche Archaologische Institut, Académie des Inscriptions et Belles Lettres, Institut de France, Göteborgs Kungl. Vetenskaps och Vitterhets Samhalle, Istituto Italiano di Preistoria e Protostoria, Jysk Arkaeologist Selskab, Österreichsche Akademie der Wissenschaft. Died Jan. 15, 2003.

BRAKE, EDWARD THOMAS, entertainer, college administrator; b. Springfield, Mo., June 16, 1942; s. Elbridge Thomas and Geraldine Frances (Gallagher) B. BS in Edn., Diploma in Voice, SW Mo. State U., 1964; studies with Marjorie Lawrence, 1964-66; MS in Edn., So. Ill. U., 1966. Dean students Bethany Coll., Lindsborg, Kans., 1966-70; dir. fin. aid. Trenton (N.J.) State Coll., 1970-76; dean admissions Phila. Coll. Performing Arts, 1976-86; exec. dir. enrollment and admissions N.C. Sch. of the Arts, Winston-Salem, from 1986. Actor/singer Starlight Theatre, Kansas City, Mo., 1964-68. Performed as soloist Phila. Orch./Phila. Boys Choir, 1978, singer Bob Hope China Spl., Bejing, 1978; performer with Duke Ellington, on tour, 1973. Judge Miss. Md. Pageant, 1978, Phila. pageants, 1976-83, various others; v.p., bd. dirs. Phila. Boys Choir, life mem.; mem. Singing City Choir, Phila., 1972-79, Piedmont Chamber Singers, Winston-Salem, N.C., 1986-90, bd. dirs. 1988-90. Avocations: photography, reading, the arts. Deceased.

BRAKHAGE, JAMES STANLEY, filmmaker, educator; b. Kansas City, Mo., Jan. 14, 1933; s. Ludwig and Clara (Dubberstein) B.; m. Mary Jane Collom, Dec. 28, 1957 (div. 1987); children: Myrrena, Crystal, Neowyn, Bearthm, Rarc; m. Marilyn Jull, Mar. 30, 1989; children: Anton, Vaughn. PhD, San Francisco Art Inst., 1981; PhD (hon.), Calif. Arts, 1994, Bard Coll., 2000. Lectr. Sch. Art Inst. Chgo., 1969-81; prof. U. Colo., Boulder, 1981; mem. Filmmakers Coop., N.Y.C., Canyon Cinema Coop., San Francisco, London Filmmakers Coop., Can. Filmmakers' Distbn. Ctr., Toronto, Lightcone, Paris, France. Faculty lectr. U. Colo., 1990-91. Films include Interim, 1952, Desistfilm, 1954, Anticipation of the Night, 1958, Window Water Baby Moving, 1959, The Dead, 1960, Blue Moses, 1962, Mothlight, 1963, Dog Star Man, 1964, Songs in 8mm, 1964-69, Scenes from Under Childhood, 1967-70, The Weir Falcon Saga, 1970, The Act of Seeing with One's Own Eyes, 1971, The Riddle of Lumen, 1972, Sincerity and Duplicity, 1973-80, The Text of Light, 1974, Desert, 1976, The Governor, 1977, Burial Path, 1978, Nightmare Series, 1978, Creation, 1979, Made Manifest, 1980, Salome, 1980, Murder Psalm, 1980, Roman Numeral Series, 1979-81, the Arabic series, 1980-82, Unconscious London Strata, 1982, Tortured Dust, 1984, The Egyptian Series, 1984, The Loom, 1986, Nightmusic, 1986, The Dante Quartet, 1987, Faust, parts I-IV, 1987-89, Marilyn's Window, 1988, Visions in Meditation, 1989-90, City Streaming, 1989, Glaze of Cathexis, 1990, Babylonian Series, 1989-90, Passage Through: A Ritual, 1990, A Child's Garden and the Serious Sea, 1991, Delicacies of Molten Horror Synapse, 1991, Christ Mass Sex Dance, 1991, Crack Glass Eulogy, 1992, (For Marilyn), 1992, Boulder Blues and Pearls and, 1993, Interpolations 1-5, 1992, Blossom Gift Favor, The Harrowing, Tryst Haunt, Study in Color and Black and White, Stellar, Autumnal, 1993, Three Homerics, 1993, Naughts, Chartres Series, Ephemeral Solidity, Elementary Phrases, Black Ice, First Hymn to the Night—Novalis, 1994, The Mammals of Victoria, 1994, Paranoia Corridor, 1994, Cannot Exist, 1995, Cannot Not Exist, 1995, I Take These Truths, We Hold These, and I, 1995, In Consideration of Pompeii, 1995, Earthen Aerie, 1995, Spring Cycle, 1995, The Lost Films, 1995, b Series, 1995, Last Hymn to the Night - Novalis, 1995, Preludes 1-24, 1995, 96, The Fur of Home, 1996, Beautiful Funerals, 1996, Polite Madness, 1996, Sexual Saga, 1996, The Lost Films, 1996, Commingled Containers, 1997, Shockingly Hot, 1997, Yggdrasill Whose Roots Are Stars in the Human Mind, 1997, Selfsong/Deathsong, 1997, "..." Reels 1-5, 1998, The Birds of Paradise, 1998, The Lion and the Zebra Make God's Raw Jewels, 1998, The Earth Song of the Cricket, 1998, Cricket Requiem, 1998, Worm and Web Love, 1999, Persian Series 1-5, 1999, Moilsome Toilsome, 1999, The Dark Tower, 1999, Cloud Chamber, 1999, The God of Day Had Gone Down Upon Him, 2000, Water for Maya, 2000, Persian Series 6-12, 2000, Rounds, 2000, Jesus Trilogy and Coda, 2001, Persian Series 13-18, 2001, Dance, 2001, Occam's Thread, 2001, Lovesong, 2001, Lovesong 2, 2001, Microgarden, 2001, Max, 2002, Panels For The Walls of Heaven, 2002, more; retrospectives Mus. Modern ARt, 1971, 77, 95, 2001; author: Metaphors on Vision, 1963, A Moving Picture Giving and Taking Book, 1971, The Brakhage Lectures, 1972, Seen, 1975, Film Biographies, 1977, Brakhage Scrapbook, 1982, Film at Wits End, 1989, Phillip Taaffee: A Conversation with Stan Brakhage, 1998, The Essential Brakhage, 2001. Recipient Brussels Worlds Fair Protest award, 1958, Brandeis citation, 1973, Colo. Gov.'s award for arts and humanities, 1974, Jimmy Ryan Morris Meml. Found. award, 1979, Telluride Film Festival medallion, 1981, Maya Deren award Am. Film Inst., 1986, medal U. Colo., 1988, Outstanding Achievement award Denver Internat. Film Festival, 1988, MacDowell medal, 1989, Libr. Congress Nat. Film Registry, 1992, Anthology Film Archives honor, 1993, The Colo. 100 Cert. of Recognition, 1993, Disting. Prof. award U. Colo., 1994; retrospective Mus. Modern Art, 1995; grantee Avon Found., 1965-69, NEA, 1974-75, 77, 80, 83, 88, U. Colo. Coun. Rsch. and Creative Work, 1983, Rocky Mountain Film Ctr., 1985; Rockefeller fellow, 1967-69, Guggenheim fellow, 1978. Democrat. Home: Boulder, Colo. Died Mar. 9, 2003.

BRAMSON, BERENICE LOUISE, soprano, teacher; b. Omaha, Nebr., May 29, 1929; d. Harry Lazarus and Irene (Schiffer) Sommer.; m. Alan Lewis Bramson, Sept. 10, 10, 1950; children: Barbara E. Bramson Dodge, Steven S. Grad. high sch., Omaha, Nebr. Co-dir. The Center for Music in Westchester, Westchester, N.Y., from 1980; founder, dir. The Sch. for Singers, Katonah, N.Y., from 1981. Guest instr. Skidmore Coll., SUNY Binghamton, Cornell U. Opera appearances: Vancouver Opera Assn., N.Y. Grand Opera, Bklyn. Opera Soc.; soloist with: Denver Symphony, Buffalo Philharmonic, Wichita Symphony, Amarillo Symphony, Caramoor Festival Orchestra, Goldman Band, New Orchestra of Westchester, Chappaqua (N.Y.) Orchestra and others; solo appearances Weill Hall at Carnegie Hall, Merkin Hall, Alice Tully Hall, Town Hall, N.Y.C. and others; premiered music of American composers; recordings: Gemini Hall "Women's Work", 1975 and others. Home: Katonah, NY. Deceased.

BRANCH, CHARLES HENDRIX, non-profit public service agency executive; b. Chgo., Mar. 30, 1926; s. Harold Francis and Margaret (Brokaw) B.; m. Marguerite Ann Hendrix, June 24, 1950; children: Laura Hendrix, Steven Hendrix, Patricia Allison. BA, U. Wis., 1949. Reporter Kansas City (Mo.) Star, 1944, 45; asst. editor Wis. Alumnus, Madison, 1947-49; mgr. publicity, book editor Abingdon Press, Nashville, 1949-53; various creative and exec. positions with advt. agencies, Nashville, Cin., Columbus, Memphis, 1953-90; founder, pres. Charles Branch & Assocs., Inc., Memphis, 1991-96. Adj. journalism prof. Memphis State U., 1964-67, 90-91. Humor columnist Memphis Press-Scimitar, 1971; prodr., host Talks with Authors WYPL-TV, Memphis, 1996—; lectr. Nat. Planned Giving Inst., 1969-89; freelance writer, Memphis; contbr. articles to popular mags. Area pub. rels. Muscular Dystrophy Assn., 1972-77, Radio Free Europe, 1965-72; trustee Memphis and Shelby County Pub. Libr. and Info. Ctr., 1979-87, pres. bd., 1982-87; bd. dirs. Lewis Sr. Citizens Ctr., 1974-80, Crimestoppers, 1989-91, Theatre Memphis, 1980-89, v.p. 1987-91; mem. Tenn. Coun. Human Rels., 1961-69. 1st lt. USAAF, 1944-45, U.S. Army, 1950-52. Mem. Pub. Rels. Soc. Am. (bd. dirs. 1985-93, pres. 1991, Lifetime Achievement award 1998). Home: Memphis, Tenn. Died Dec. 9, 2002.

BRANDO, MARLON, JR., actor; b. Omaha, Apr. 3, 1924; s. Marlon and Dorothy Pennebaker (Myers) B.; m. Anna Kashfi, 1957 (div. 1959); 1 son, Christian; m. Movita Brando (div.); Miko, Rebecca; m. Tarita Teriipaia (div.); Simon, Cheyenne (dec. 1995); children, Ninna Priscilla, Stefano. Student, Shattuck Mil. Acad., 1939-41; student The Method, New Sch. for Soc. Rsch., Actors' Studio. Actor: N.Y. plays, including I Remember Mama, 1944, Candida, 1946, Streetcar Named Desire, 1947; motion pictures include The Men, 1950, Streetcar Named Desire, 1951, Viva Zapata, 1952 (Best Actor, Cannes Internat. Film Festival), Julius Caesar, 1953, The Wild One, 1953, Desirée, 1954, On the Waterfront, 1954 (Acad. award for best actor), Guys and Dolls, 1955, Teahouse of the August Moon, 1956, Sayonara, 1957, The Young Lions, 1958, The Fugitive Kind, 1960, One Eyed Jacks (also dir.) 1960, Mutiny on the Bounty, 1962, The Ugly American, 1963, Bedtime Story, 1964, The Saboteur, 1965, The Chase, 1966, The Appaloosa, 1966, A Countess from Hong Kong, Reflections in A Golden Eye, 1967, Candy, The Godfather, 1972 (Acad. award for best actor), Last Tango in Paris, 1972, Missouri Breaks, 1976, Superman, 1978, Apocalypse Now, 1979, The Formula, 1980, A Dry White Season, 1989, The Freshman, 1990, Jericho, Christopher Columbus: The Discovery, 1992, Don Juan DeMarco, 1995, The Island of Dr. Moreau, 1996, The Brave, 1997, Free Money, 1998, The Score, 2001, Apocalypse Now Redux, 2001; TV appearance in Roots: The Next Generations, 1979; author: (with Robert Lindsey) Brando: Songs My Mother Taught Me, 1994. Died July 1, 2004.

BRANDSTETTER, ROBERT DANIEL, physician, educator; b. N.Y.C., Feb. 27, 1947; s. Christian Gotlieb and Muriel Viola (Edington) B.; m. Veronica Ann Seipel, July 2, 1967 (div. Jan. 1980); children: William, Daniel, Jennifer, Karen; m. Deanne Elizabeth Sachs, Mar. 6, 1982; children: Elizabeth, Kathleyn. BA, Lehman Coll., 1974; MD, Albert Einstein Med. Coll., 1977. Intern N.Y. Hospital -Cornell Univ. Med. Coll., 1977-78, resident, 1978-80; pulmonary fellowship Mass. Gen. Hosp. Harvard Med. Sch., 1980-82; research fellow in medicine Harvard Med. Sch., 1980-82; asst. prof. clin. medicine N.Y. Med. Coll., 1982-84, assoc. prof. clin. medicine, 1984-90, prof. clin. medicine, from 1990. Asst. dir. of medicine New Rochelle (N.Y.) Hosp. med. Ctr., 1982-90, dir. of medicine, 1990—, assoc. program dir. in medicine, 1982-90, program dir. in internal medicine, 1990; cons. sci. sect. Nat. Enquire, 1986-90. Author: Pulmonary Medicine-Problems in Primary Care, 1989; editor N.Y. State Jour. of medicine, 1989-90; contbr. articles to profl. publs. Mem. Am. Mus. Natural History, N.Y., 1980, Stamford (Conn.) Mus. Nature Ctr., 1980, Roxbury Community Assn., Stamford, 1984, North Stamford (Conn.) Assn., 1984. With USN, 1965-69, Morocco. Recipient Jonas E. Salk award for med. studies Mayor of N.Y.C., 1974, Disting. William Hammond award for svcs. N.Y. State Med. Soc., 1990. Fellow ACP, Am. Coll. Chest Physicians, Am. Coll. Critical Care; mem. AMA, Program Dirs. in Medicine of Am., Am. Thoracic Soc., New Rochelle Softball League, Phi Beta Kappa. Republican. Roman Catholic. Avocations: photography, softball. Home: Greenwich, Conn. Died Oct. 18, 1999.

BRANSFORD, MALLORY WATKINS, music minister; b. Williamsburg, W.Va., Mar. 9, 1912; s. Wesley Henry and Martha (Fox) B.; m. Helen Elizabeth Zahn, Aug. 4, 1937; children: Marcia Ruth, Robert Wesley. MusB, Oberlin Coll., 1934; MusM, Butler U., 1936, B Music Edn., 1946; PhD in Edn., Walden U., 1976. Minister music Central Ave United Meth. Ch., 1944-46, Roberts Park United Meth. Ch., 1942-44; minister music, dir. children's music Zion Evang. United Ch. of Christ, Indpls., from 1946. Chmn. organ dept. Butler U., Indpls., 1948—; music specialist Indpls. Pub. Schs., 1944-79. Author: Teaching and Learning Guide, 1976; (recordings) Choral and Organ Favorites, 1976, Sounds of Zion, 1984. Recipient Disting. Svc. award Ind. Music Educator's Assn., 1979, Caleb B. Smith medal of honor DeMolay Legion of honor, Grand Lodge Ind., 1984. Mem. Am. Guild Organists (dean 1953-55), Nat. Assn. Keyboard Artists, Columbia Club (Indpls.), Masons (organist Supreme coun. 1976—), Scottish Rite (33d degree), Phi Mu Alpha Sinfonia. Home: Indianapolis, Ind. Died Aug. 21, 2001.

BRASS, PHILLIP, obstetrician-gynecologist; b. Wilkes-Barre, Pa., June 9, 1925; MD, Duke U., 1952. Diplomate Am. Bd. Ob-Gyn. Intern Kings County Med. Ctr., Bklyn., 1952-53; resident Gorgas Hosp., Panama City, Panama, 1960-61; resident in ob-gyn. Md. Gen. Hosp., Balt., 1961-63; cons. staff ob-gyn. South Miami Hosp., Bapt. Hosp., Miami; staff Kenoal Regional Hosp., Miami, Parkway Regional Med. Ctr. East and West, North Miami Beach, Fla. Fellow ACOG; mem. Am. Fertility Soc. Died Feb. 18, 2002.

BRATTON, MARY JO, history educator; b. Matoaka, W.Va., July 18, 1926; d. Thomas Josiah and Mary Irene (McKinstry) Jackson; divorced; children: Katherine, Jess, Jackson. BA, Montreat Coll., 1948; BS, Va. Poly. Inst., 1949; MA, U. N.C., 1966, PhD, 1969. Rsch. assoc. Med. Coll. Va., Richmond, 1950-53; instr. U. N.C., Chapel Hill, 1963-67; asst. prof. E. Carolina U., Greenville, N.C., 1967-73, assoc. prof., 1974-82, prof., from 1982, univ. historian, from 1980; chair dept. history East Carolina U., Greenville, N.C., from 1992. Author: East Carolina University, 1986, Greenville: Heart of the East, 1990; contbr. articles to profl. jours. NEH fellow, 1974, 76. Mem. So. Hist. Assn., So. Assn. for Women Historians, Assn. Historians in N.C. Home: Greenville, NC. Deceased.

BRAY, ABSALOM FRANCIS, JR., lawyer; b. San Francisco, Nov. 24, 1918; s. Absalom Francis and Leila Elizabeth (Veale) E.; m. Lorraine Cerena Paule, June 25, 1949; children: Oliver, Brian, Margot. BA, Stanford U., 1940; JD, U. So. Calif., 1949. Bar: Calif. 1949, U.S. Supreme Ct. 1960. Sr. ptnr. Bray & Baldin and successive firms to Bray & Bray, Martinez, Calif., from 1949, now pres. Founder, bd. dirs. John Muir Nat. Bank, Martinez. Chmn. Martinez Recreation Commn., 1949-54; chmn. nat. bd. dirs. Camp Fire Girls, 1959-61, 69-71; pres. Contra Costa County (Calif.) Devel. Assn., 1959-60, Contra Costa County Hist. Soc., 1995-97. Lt. USNR, 1942-46. Mem. State Bar Calif. (chmn. adoption com. 1955-56), Martinez His. Soc. (pres. 1984), Mohn Muir Meml. Assn. (pres. 1989-92), Navy League U.S. (pres. Contra Costsons, Rotary (pres. Martinez 1970-71). Home: Martinez, Calif. Deceased.

BRAY, DAVID MAURICE, academic dean; b. Abilene, Tex., Feb. 21, 1941; s. Andrew Maurice and Mauress Laneyl (Brown) B.; m. Louise Hardin, Aug. 22, 1964; children: Louisa, Andrew. BA, So. Meth. U., 1963; postgrad., Oxford (Eng.) U., 1963-64, U. Md., 1964-66. With Office Mgmt. and Budget, Exec. Office of Pres., Washington, 1965-76, asst. chief econ. affairs internat. programs div., 1969-73, dep. assoc. dir. for econs. and govt., 1973-76; spl. asst. for econ. affairs to dir. CIA, Washington, 1973; assoc. v.p. bus. and fin. Med. Ctr., U. Chgo., 1976-78, assoc. v.p. adminstrn. and exec. dir. hosps. and clinics, 1978-82; dean for fin. and adminstrn. Med. Sch. Harvard U., Boston, 1982-89, exec. dean for adminstrn. Med. Sch., 1989—98. Bd. dirs. South Shore Bank, Chgo., Chi Systems Inc., Ann Arbor, Mich.; chmn. Vin Fen Corp. Prin. Ctr. for Excellence in Govt.; bd. dirs. Boston Ballet Sch. Mem. Am. Econs. Assn., Am. Assn. Med. Colls., Am. Coll. Healthcare Execs., Internat. Health Econs. & Mgmt. Inst., Council Teaching Hosps., Am. Hosp. Assn., Ill. Hosp. Assn. Methodist. Home: Shrewsbury, Vt. Died Jan. 22, 2004.

BRAY, PIERCE, business consultant; b. Chgo., Jan. 16, 1924; s. Harold A. and Margaret (Maclennan) B.; m. Maud Dorothy Minto, May 14, 1955; children— Margaret Dorothy, William Harold, Andrew Pierce. BA, U. Chgo., 1948, MBA, 1949. Fin. analyst Ford Motor Co., Dearborn, Mich., 1949-55; cons. Booz, Allen & Hamilton, Chgo. and Manila, Philippines, 1955-58; mgr. pricing, then corp. controller Cummins Engine Co., Columbus, Ind., 1958-66; v.p. fin. Weatherhead Co., Cleve., 1966-67; from v.p. to dir. Mid-Continent Tel. Corp. (now ALLTEL Corp.), Hudson, Ohio, 1967—76, dir., 1976—85; chmn. various subs. Mid-Continent Telephone Corp. (now ALLTEL Corp.), Hudson, Ohio. Instr. fin. and econs. U. Detroit, 1952-54; chmn. investor relations com. U.S. Telephone Assn., 1974-85; chmn. exec. com. Inst. Public Utilities, 1981-83. Trustee Beech Brook, Cleve., Ohio, 1972-96, life trustee, 1996—, treas., 1976-79, pres., 1979-81; bd. dirs. Breckenridge Village Retirement Cmty., 1991-2001, chmn. fin. com. 1995-2001; trustee Ohio Presbyn. Retirement Svcs., 1996-2001; chmn. fin. com., 1999-2001; chmn. safety com. Walloon Lake Assn., 1995-2000. With AUS, 1943-46. Mem. Fin. Execs. Inst. (bd. dirs. 1993-96), Cleve. Treasurers Club, Union Club Cleve., Walloon (Mich.) Yacht Club (chmn. bd. 1980-81, 85-86, 93-2003, commodore 1981-82, 87-88, bd. dirs., sec. 1988-2003), Ohio Masters Swim Club (hon., trustee 1985-92, 96-98, 2001-, sec. 1989-93), Lake Erie Local Masters Swim Com. (chmn. 1992-96), Delta Upsilon. Presbyterian. Avocations: competitive swimming, sailing, volunteer and church activities. Died Aug. 11, 2003.

BREATHITT, EDWARD THOMPSON, JR., lawyer, railroad executive; b. Hopkinsville, Ky., Nov. 26, 1924; s. Edward Thompson Sr. and Mary Josephine (Wallace) B.; m. Lucy Alexander Breathitt; children: Mary Frances, Linda Key, Susan Holleman, Edward Thompson III. BS in Commerce, U. Ky., 1947, LLB, 1950, JD, 1970, LLD (hon.), 1965, U. Marshall, 1966, U. Ky., 1967. Bar: Ky. 1950, U.S. Supreme Ct. 1974. Ptnr. Trimble, Soyars & Breathitt, Hopkinsville, 1960-62; gov. State of Ky., Frankfort, 1963-67; ptnr. Trimble, Soyars & Breathitt, Hopkinsville, 1968-72; v.p. Southern Ry. Co., Washington, 1972-82, Norfolk Southern Corp., Washington, 1982-86, sr. v.p., 1986-92; with Wyatt Tarrent & Combs Law firm, Lexington, Ky., 1992—2003. Mem. adv. bd. Am. Security Bank, Washington, 1987-90; mem. Ky. Econ. Devel. Corp., 1979-2003; chmn. bd. trustees U. Ky., 1992-99. Mem. legis. State of Ky., Frankfort, 1952-56; chmn. and pres. Commn. on Rural Property, Washington, 1965-67; pres. Commn. to Fulfill These Rights, Washington, 1965-67. With USAAF, 1942-45. Named Conservationist of Yr. Nat. Wildlife Fedn. and Outdoor Life Mag., 1966; recipient Conservationist award U.S. Dept. of Interior, 1967, Lincoln Key award for Civil Rights, 1966. Fellow U. Ky.; mem. Ky. Bar Assn., D.C. Bar Assn., Chevy Chase Club, Pendenis Club. Democrat. Methodist. Avocations: fishing, hunting, golf, tennis, hiking. Home: Lexington, Ky. Died Oct. 14, 2003.

BREDSDORFF, ELIAS LUNN, writer; b. Roskilde, Denmark, Jan. 15, 1912; Student, U. London, 1934; Cand. mag., Copenhagen U., 1938, Dr.phil., 1964. Tchr. lit. and English Vordingborg (Denmark) Tng. Coll., 1939-43; organizer Frit Danmark, 1943-45, editor newspaper, 1945-46; Queen Alexandra lectr. Danish Univ. Coll. U. London, 1946-49; lectr. Danish Cambridge (Eng.) U., 1949-60, reader and head dept. Scandinavian studies, 1960-79. Author: D.H. Lawrence: Et Forsoeg paa en politisk Analyse, 1937, Corsaren, 1941 (expanded version pub. as Goldschmidts "Corsaren" med en udfoerlig redegoerelse for striden mellem Soeren Kierkegaard og "Corsaren" 1962), John Steinbeck, 1943, Danish Literature in English Translation: A Bibliography, 1950, (with others) An Introduction to Scandinavian Literature, from the Earliest time to Our Day, 1951, H.C. Andersen og Charles Dickens: Et Venskab og dets oploesning, 1951, H.C. Andersen og England, 1952, Hans Christian Andersen, 1805-2nd April-1855, 1955, Danish: An Elementary Grammar and Reader, 1956, Drama i Syrakus, 1956, Kinas Vej: Samtaler og rejseindtryk, 1957, Bag Ibsen's maske: To imaginaere interviews med Henrik Ibsen, 1962, Henrik Pontoppidan og Georg Brandes, 2 vols., 1964, Literatura i obschestvo Skandinavii, 1971, Kommer det os ved?, 1971, Den store nordiske krig om seksualmoralen, 1973, Hans Christian Andersen, 1975, Fra Andersen til Scherfig, 1978, Nonsens og bonsens, 1978, Kjeld Abells Billedkunst, 1979, Revolutionaer humanisme, 1982, Min egen Kurs, 1983, Mit engelske liv, 1984, H.C. Andersen: Mennesket og Digteren, 1985; editor: Sir Edmund William Gosse, Correspondence with Scandinavian Writers, 1960, Kjeld Abell, Synskhedens Gave: Prosa og vers, 1962, En bog om Mogens Fog, 1991, Aerkedansk-12 Essays fra Glaenoe, 1992; Kjeld Abell Et Brevportrait, 1993, H.C. Andersen og Georg Brandes, 1994, Medmennesker og Modmennesker, 1994, Syndebukken, En bog om, Oscar Wilde, 1999, Højskolebarnet, 2000; author introduction, supr. translations Contemporary Danish Plays: An Anthology, 1955, author notes, supr. translations Contemporary Danish Prose: An Anthology, 1968; (with C.E. Bay) Henrik Pontoppidauns Breve I-II, 1998; contbr.to Chambers' Ency., Cassell's Ency. of Literature, Ency. Americana, Penguin Compantions to World Literature; editor. Fellow Peterhouse, Cambridge, 1963-79. Fellow Royal Danish Acad. Sci. and Letters. Home: Copenhagen, Denmark. Died Aug. 8, 2002.

BREINES, SIMON, retired architect; b. Bklyn., Apr. 4, 1906; s. Louis and Anna (Backrack) B.; m. Nettie Weissman (dec. 2001), 1935; children: Paul, Joseph. B.Arch., Pratt Inst., 1941. Partner Pomerance & Breines, N.Y.C. Adviser Gen. Services Adminstrn.; bd. dirs. Fine Arts Fedn. of N.Y., N.Y. Landmarks Conservancy.; Mem. Citizens Union, Community Service Soc., Parks Assn., all N.Y.C.; architect mem. Art Commn. City N.Y., 1971-74. Architect for: pub. bldgs. including Grand Concourse Pub. Library, Bronx, N.Y.C., Lexington Sch. for Deaf, Rose F. Kennedy Research Center, Albert Einstein Coll. of Medicine, New Campus, State U. N.Y. at Brockport, New Coll. Dentistry, N.Y. U. Cons. Housing Assistance Adminstrn; Author: Architecture and Furniture of Alvar Aalto, 1942, (with John Dean) The Book of Houses, 1946, (with William Dean) The Pedestrian Revolution: Streets Without Cars, 1976; Contbr.: chpt. to USSR: A Concise Handbook, 1947, Small Urban Spaces, 1969. Arnold W. Brunner scholar N.Y. chpt. AIA, 1947, 66; Recipient Bard award City Club N.Y., 1967 Fellow AIA (honor award 1967) Home: Scarsdale, NY. Died Sept. 16, 2003.

BRENNER-WORMSER, EVELYN ROZELLA, mental health nurse; b. L.A., Apr. 3, 1929; d. Frank R. and Anne Louise (Kessler) Brenner; m. Joseph J. Wormser, Nov. 19, 1955; children: Alan, Deborah Anne, Lisa Michelle. RN, Bapt. Meml. Hosp. Sch. Nursing, San Antonio, 1949; BSN, Incarnate Word Coll., San Antonio, 1954; MSN, Tex. Woman's Coll., Denton, 1971; postgrad., U. Tex., Austin, 1981-84. Staff/charge nurse nursery Rober B. Green Hosp., San Antonio, 1949-50; staff/charge nurse obstetrics Brook Army Hosp., San Antonio, 1950-53; charge nurse pediatrics Santa Rosa Hosp., San Antonio, 1953-54; instr. Bapt. Meml. Sch. Nursing, San Antonio, 1954-56, La Leche League, 1967-70, Dallas Assn. Parent Edn., 1967-70, Tex. Woman's U. Sch. Nursing, Denton, 1971, El Centro Sch. Nursing, Dallas, 1971-72; pvt. practice mental health nursing Dallas, from 1972. Instr., asst. prof. and specialist U. Tex., Arlington, 1974-87; cons. in field; lectr. in field. Contbr. articles to profl. jours. NIMH grantee, 1971—. Mem. Am. Nurses Assn., Tex. Nurses Assn., Nat. League Nursing, Am. Orthopsychiatric Assn. (fellow), Dist. 4 Psych/Mental Health Conf. Group (chmn. 1987-89), Sigma Theta Tau. Home: Dallas, Tex. Deceased.

BRENT, JOAN MARCELLA, nurse; b. N.Y.C., Nov. 27, 1934; d. John W. and Naomi (McClain) Hogan; m. Richard Louis Brent; children: Roger, Tracy, Kenneth, Richard. Grad. in Nursing, N.Y. Med. Coll., 1956. RN. Nurse emergency room Flower-5th Ave Hosp., N.Y.C., 1956-57; staff nurse USPHS Hosp., Staten Island, N.Y., 1957-58; nurse Richard L. Brent, M.D., East Lyme, Conn., from 1978. Trustee St. Bernard High Sch., Vacasville, Conn., 1976-87, chmn., 1985-87; nurse ARC, New London, Conn., 1971-82, instr., 1975-82, bd. dirs.state bd. bllod services program, Farmington, 1976-80; mem. adv. bd. dirs. Cath. Charity, New London, 1972—; bd. dirs. Big Bros./Big Sisters, New London. Recipient Service award ARC, 1982, Bernard award St. Bernard High Sch., 1987. Mem.: USCG Acad. Officers Wives (pres. 1975-76); Thames River Garden (pres. 1984-86); St. Matthias Ladies (pres. 1973-74). Roman Catholic. Home: Niantic, Conn. Deceased.

BRETT, PHILIP, conductor, music educator; b. Edwinstowe, Eng., Oct. 17, 1937; came to U.S., 1966; s. George Wilfred and Ida Ellen (Buxton) B. BA, King's Coll., 1958, MusB, 1961, MA, 1962, PhD, 1965. Fellow King's Coll., Cambridge, Eng., 1963-66; asst. lectr. Cambridge U., 1963-66; from asst. prof. to assoc. prof. music U. Calif., Berkeley, 1966-78, prof., 1978—91, chmn., 1988-90; prof. U. Calif, Riverside, 1991—2001, U. Calif., L.A., 2001—02. Chorus master Philharm. Baroque Orch., San Francisco, 1987-91 Contbr. of various scholarly works including Consort Songs, 1967, Word-Setting in the Songs of Byrd, 1971-72, Benjamin Britten, Peter Grimes, 1983, Britten's Dream, in Musicology and Difference, 1993, Musicality, Essentialism, and the Closet, 1994, Eros and Orientalism in Britten's Operas, in Queering the Pitch, 1994; Text, Context and the Early Music Editor, in Authenticity and Early Music, 1988; editor Collected Works of William Byrd, Consort Songs for Voice and Viols, 1970, The Byrd Edition: Madrigals, Songs and Canons, 1976, The Masses, 1981, Gradualia I: The Marian Masses, 1990, Gradualia I: All Saints and Corpus Christi, 1991, Gradualia I: Other Feasts and Devotions, 1993, Gradualia II: Christmas to Easter, 1997. Recipient Grammy nomination, 1991. Mem. Am. Musicol. Soc. (bd. dirs. 1984-86), Royal Mus. Assn. Home: Riverside, Calif. Died Oct. 16, 2002.

BREWER, MICHAEL ANDREW, osteopath; b. Alva., Okla., Oct. 17, 1956; s. Charles Lilburn and Juanita (Frieze) B.; m. Kayla Dee Lakin, June 5, 1982; children: Michael Todd, Elizabeth Aryn, Sarah Michelle. BS, N.W. Okla. State U., 1978; DO, Okla. Coll. Osteo. Med., 1982. Pvt. practice, Alva, 1983-86; physician, owner Hominy (Okla.) Med. Clinic, 1986-90; physician Jay (Okla.) Community Clinic, 1990-91, med. dir., from 1991. Med. examiner Woods County, Osage County, Delaware County, Okla. Mem. Am. Osteo. Assn., Osage County Osteo. Soc. (v.p. 1989-90). Republican. Methodist. Avocations: boating, camping, ornithology, icthyology. Home: Grove, Okla. Died Oct. 23, 2001.

BRINKHOUS, KENNETH MERLE, retired pathologist, educator; b. Clayton County, Iowa, May 29, 1908; s. William and Ida (Voss) Brinkhous; m. Frances E. Benton, Sept. 5, 1936; children: William Kenneth, John Robert. Student, U.S. Mil. Acad., 9125; AB, U. Iowa, 1929, MD, 1932; DSc, U. Chgo., 1967, U. N.C., 1995. Asst. in pathology U. Iowa, 1932—33, instr., 1933—35, assoc. in pathology, 1935—37, asst. prof., 1937—45, assoc. prof., 1945—46; prof. pathology U. N.C., Chapel Hill, 1946—61, alumni distinguished prof., 1961—80, emeritus, 1980—93. Mem. Nat. Adv. Heart and Lung Coun., 1969—74; chmn. med. adv. coun. Nat. Hemophilia Found., 1954—73; sec. gen. Internat. Com. Hemostasis and Thrombosis, 1966—78. Bd. editors Perspectives in Biol. Medicine, from 1968; editor: Archives Pathology and Lab. Medicine, 1974—83, Yearbook Pathology Clin. Pathology, 1980—91. From capt. to lt. col. M.C. U.S. Army, 1941—46, col. Med. Res. Corps U.S. Army, from 1946. Co-recipient Ward Burdick award, Am. Soc. Clin. Pathologists, 1941, 1963; named H.P. Smith lectr., 1974; recipient O. Max Gardner award, 1961, N.C. award, 1969, Internat. Heart Rsch. award, 1969, Murray Thelin award, Nat. Hemophilia Found., 1972, Disting. Achievement award, Modern Medicine, 1973, Maude Abbott award, Internat. Acad. Pathology, 1985, Disting. Svc. award, AMA, 1986, 50th Yr. Rsch. award, NIH, 1992, Landsteiner award, Am. Assn. Blood Banks, 1994. Mem.: Acad. Clin. Lab. Physicians and Scientists (Cotlove award 1991), Assn. Pathology Chmn. (Disting. Svc. award 1989), Univs. Assoc. Rsch. and Edn. Pathology (pres. 1964—68), Fedn. Am. Socs. Exptl. Biology (pres. 1966—67), Am. Soc. Exptl. Pathology (pres. 1965—66), Am. Assn. Pathologists and Bacteriologists (sec.-treas. 1968—71, pres. 1973, Gold-headed Cane award 1981), Internat. Soc. Thrombosis and Haemostasis (pres. 1971, Robert P. Grant award 1985), Assn. Am. Physicians, Am. Acad. Arts and Scis., Inst. Medicine, Nat. Acad. Scis. Home: Chapel Hill, NC. Died Dec. 11, 2000.

BRINKLEY, DAVID MCCLURE, news commentator; b. Wilmington, N.C., July 10, 1920; s. William Graham and Mary (West) B.; m. Ann Fischer, Oct. 11, 1946; children: Alan, Joel, John; m. Susan Adolph, June 10, 1972; 1 child, Alexis. Reporter Wilmington (N.C.) Star-News, 1938-41; reporter, bur. mgr. United Press Assns., various So. cities, 1941-43; news writer, broadcaster radio and TV NBC, Washington, from 1943, Washington corr., 1951-81; anchorman ABC This Week, 1981-97; ret., 1997. Recipient duPont award, Peabody award, Sch. Bell award, Pres. Medal of Freedom, 1992, other journalism awards. Died June 11, 2003.

BRINTON, DILWORTH CARLOS, underwriter; b. Victor, Idaho, Nov. 2, 1917; s. Van B. and Vida D. (Driggs) B.; m. Pearl Randall, May 2, 1946; children: Dilworth Carlos Jr., Barbara Nelson, Robert W., Richard R., Ann Despain. BSBA, U. Ariz., 1940; postgrad., U. Calif., Berkeley, 1943. CLU. Life underwriter N.Y. Life Ins. Co., Mesa, Ariz., from 1946. Contbr. articles to profl. jours. Pres., bd. dirs. Ariz. State Hosp. Bd., 1952-57. Staff sgt. U.S. Army, 1943-46. Mem. Nat. Assn. Life Underwriters (officer), Million Dollar Round Table, Ariz. Assn. Life Underwriters (pres., bd. dirs. 1967, Outstanding Life Underwriter 1982), Tri-City Life Underwriters (founding pres. Mesa chpt. 1972). Republian. Ch. of Jesus Christ Latter-day Saints. Home: Mesa, Ariz. Died July 19, 1999.

BRITTENHAM, RAYMOND LEE, investment company executive; b. Moscow, Feb. 8, 1916; s. Edward Arthur and Marietta (Wemple) B.; m. Mary Ann Stanard, Nov. 3, 1956; children: Edward C., Carol. AB, Principia Coll., Elsah, Ill., 1936; postgrad., Kaiser Wilhelm U., Berlin, Germany, 1937; LLB, Harvard U., 1940. Bar: Ill. 1940, N.Y. 1946. Assoc. Pope & Ballard, Chgo., 1940-42, Mitchell Carroll, N.Y.C., 1947-56; v.p., gen. counsel ITT and subs., 1962-68, sr. v.p. law, counsel, 1968-80, dir., 1965-80; with Lazard Freres & Co., N.Y.C., 1980-89; pres. Spanish Inst., 1980-82, vice chmn., 1982-90. Maj. AUS, 1942-46. Decorated Bronze Star medal; Croix de Guerre France and Belgium; chevalier Ordre de Leopold Belgium). Mem. ABA, Coun. Fgn. Rels., University Club (N.Y.C.). Home: New York, NY. Deceased.

BROBST, ROBERT ARTHUR, chemical engineer; b. Oskaloosa, Iowa, June 8, 1922; s. Barton Hamerick and Ella (McMillen) B.; m. Anne Frances Pfleger, June 14, 1947; children: Robert Barton, Paula Kathleen Brobst Pennington. Student, Iowa State U., 1940-42, BS in Chem. Engring., 1948; student, U. Notre Dame, 1942-43. Chem. engr. Thompson Soya Products, Hiawatha, Kans., 1948-51; rsch. engr. Midwest Rsch. Inst., Kansas City, Mo., 1951-54; devel. engr. Huron Milling Co., Harbor Beach, Mich., 1954-58; devel. supr. Hercules Inc., Harbor Beach, 1958-62, with, 1962-77, plant mgr., 1977-84; ret. Chemistry tchr. Highland (Kans.) Jr. Coll., 1948-50; math. tchr. Mich. Dept. Vocat. Edn., Harbor Beach, 1959-62. Patentee starch derivative films. Pres. Harbor Beach Bd. Edn., 1960-88; mem. Harbor Beach Planning Commn., 1978-85; bd. dirs. Grice Hist. Soc., 1986—. 2d lt. USMCR, 1942-46, CBI, 1st lt. USMC, 1950-52, Korea. Mem. Cen. States Youth Exch. (corr. 1983—), Mid-Mich. NAIC (bd. dirs. 1989—), Huron County C. of C. (treas. 1990—, bd. dirs. 1988—), Harbor Beach C. of C. (exec. sec. 1986—, Person of Distinction 1989), Dist. 631 Youth Exch. (treas. 1985—), Rotary (pres. Harbor Beach chpt. 1975-76, Paul Harris fellow 1984, Svc. PolioPlus 1988), Mich. Chosin Few (sec.-treas. 1991-92). Avocations: world travel, photography, computers, genealogy. Home: Harbor Beach, Mich. Deceased.

BROCK, RAYMOND THEODORE, counselor, educator; b. Skiatook, Okla., Feb. 20, 1927; s. Clarence C. and Hazel M. (Boyer) B.; m. Lynita Corinne Kennemer, Sept. 2, 1949; children: Cynthia L., Andrea J., Robert C. BA, Phillips U., 1949, BS, 1950; MA, U. Tulsa, 1953, EdD, 1972. Lic. counselor, Okla. Prin. Nigeria Bible Inst., Umuahia, West Africa, 1953-55; asst. prof. Southwestern Coll., Waxahachie, Tex., 1956-59; editor div. fgn. missions Assemblies of God, Springfield, Mo., 1959-62; adminstr. Oakview Convalescent Hosp., Glendora, Calif., 1962-64, Foothill Christian Sch., Glendora, 1964-65; assoc. pastor Oak Cliff Assembly of God, Dallas, 1965-66; chmn. behavioral scis. Evangel Coll., Springfield, 1966-85; assoc. prof. psychiatry and behavioral medicine Oral Roberts Sch. Medicine, Tulsa, 1985-89; counselor Inst. for Christian Living, Tulsa, 1985-91, also bd. dirs., chmn., 1985-91; min. edn. Carbondale Assembly of God, Tulsa, 1986-92. Cons. Eurasia Teen Challenge, Wiesbaden, Germany, 1978—, Trinity Christian Ctr., Singapore, 1984—, Nat. Teen Challenge, Springfield, Mo., 1994—. Author: The Christ-Centered Family, 1977, Dating and Waiting for Marriage, 1978, The Emotional Side of Men, 1983, The Holy Spirit and Counseling, vol. I, 1985, editor The Holy Spirit and Counseling, vol. II, 1988. Mem. adv. bd. Pk. Cen. Hosp., Springfield, 1972-76. U.S. Dept. Health Edn. & Welfare grantee, 1966-68. Mem. ACA, APA, Am. Assn. for Marriage and Family Therapy, Christian Assn. for Psychol. Studies. Avocations: writing, traveling. Home: Tulsa, Okla. Died Oct. 2, 2001.

BROCKHOUSE, BERTRAM NEVILLE, physicist, retired educator; b. Lethbridge, Alta., Can., July 15, 1918; s. Israel Bertram and Mable Emily (Neville) Brockhouse; m. Doris Isobel Mary Miller, May 22, 1948; children: Ann, Gordon, Ian, James, Alice Elizabeth, Charles. BA, U. B.C., 1947; MA, U. Toronto, 1948, PhD, 1950; DSc (hon.), U. Waterloo, 1969, McMaster U., 1984, U. Toronto, 1995, U. B.C., Can., 1996; Doctor of Laws (hon.), Dalhousie U., 1996; D Arts and Scis (hon.), U Lethbridge, 1997. Research officer Atomic Energy of Can., Ltd., Chalk River, 1950—59, br. head, neutron physics, 1960—62; chmn. dept. physics McMaster U., 1967—70, prof. physics, 1962—84, prof. emeritus, 1984—2003. Contbr. sci. articles on neutron physics and condensed matter physics to profl. jours. Served Royal Can. Navy Vol. Res., 1939—45. Recipient Centennial medal of Can., 1967, Queen's Jubilee medal, 1977, Order of Can., 1982, Companion, 1995, Duddell medal and prize, Inst. Physics and Phys.Soc., 1963, Nobel prize in Physics, 1994; fellow Guggenheim, 1970—71; grantee NRC of Can., 1962—78. Mem.: Royal Swedish Acad. Scis. (fgn. mem. from 1984), Am. Acad. Arts and Scis. (hon. fgn. mem.), Am. Phys. Soc. (Buckley prize 1962), Can. Assn. Physicists (achievement in physics 1967), Royal Soc. London, Royal Soc. Can. (Tory Medal 1973). Roman Catholic. Home: Mount Hope, Canada. Died Oct. 13, 2003.

BROCKMAN, HAROLD WILLIAM, mathematics educator; b. Sidney, Ohio, Mar. 31, 1922, s. William H. and Margaret (Klindworth) B.; m. Lorraine L. Loufman, Dec. 18, 1954; 1 child, Sally Ann. BE, Capital U., 1948; MA, Ohio State U., 1950, PhD, 1962. Prof. math. Capital U., Columbus, Ohio, 1949-92, prof. emeritus, from 1992. Editor Ohio Jour. Sch. Math., 1976-88. 1st lt. U.S. Army, 1942-46. Mem. Am. Math. Soc., Math. Assn. Am., Nat. Coun. Tchrs. of Math., Sch. Sci. and Math. Assn., Ohio Coun. Tchrs. of Math. Lutheran. Home: Columbus, Ohio. Deceased.

BRODHEAD, QUITA, artist; Spkr. in field. One woman shows at Salon d'Autonne, Paris, also 8 in N.Y., 7 in Phila.; exhibited in group show at Creuse Gallery, Paris, Chez Barbier, Paris; retrospective Pa. Acad. Fine Arts Sch. gallery; represented in permanent collections at Pa. Acad. Fine Arts, Phila. Art Mus., Del. Art Mus., Wilmington, N.J. State Mus., Trenton, Munson-Williams-Proctor, Ithaca, N.Y., Bryn Mawr (Pa.) Coll. Libr., Woodmere Mus., Phila., Westerdahl Collection C.I. Spain, Ashville (N.C.) Art Mus., Museo des Bellas Artes, Tenerefe, Spain, State Mus. Pa.; retrospective exhibit Hollis Taggart Gallery, N.Y.C., 2001, Phila. Mus. Am. Art, 2001; included in Jane Piper and Her Circle, Pa. State Mus., Harrisburg, 2000—; also pvt. collections. Past bd. fellows Acad. Fine Arts, Pa.; chmn. exhbn. com. Nat. Exhibits of Blind Artists. Recipient numerous awards for excellence in art; fellow Va. Ctr. for Creative Arts, Pa. fellow Percy M. Owens Meml. award. Mem. Artists Equity, Mus. Modern Art N.Y.C., Phila. Mus. Art, Woodmere Art Mus. Phila., Pa. Acad. Fine Arts. Died Sept. 4, 2002.

BRODIE, SHELDON J. physician; b. N.Y.C., Apr. 10, 1926; s. Barnet and Mildred (Maidman) B.; m. Charlotte Kaplan, Dec. 18, 1954; children: Martha Jane, Barnett. BS, L.I. U., 1946; MD, U. Lausanne, Switzerland, 1952; postgrad. med. degree, NYU, 1959. Diplomate Am. Bd. Dermatology, 1961. Intern Kings County Hosp., N.Y.C., 1953-54, resident specializing in Dermatology, 1954; base dermatologist Camp Lejeune, N.C., 1955-56; chief dermatology St. Albans Naval Hosp., N.Y.C., 1956; attending dermatologist NYU Hosp., N.Y.C., 1960—2003; prof. clin. dermatology NYU Med. Sch., 1961—2003. Dermatologist Bellevue Med. Ctr., Vets. Adminstrn. Hosp., N.Y.C., Mid Island Hosp., Beth Page N.Y. Author: (with others) Archives of Dermatology, Yearbook of Dermatology. Served to lt. M.C., U.S. Navy, 1954-56. Fellow Am. Acad. Dermatology. Home: Boca Raton, Fla. Died Oct. 29, 2003.

BRODSKY, JACK GERARD, independent film producer; b. N.Y.C., July 3, 1932; s. Aaron and Shirley (Palatnick) B.; m. Dorothy Chaika, Nov. 26, 1958; children: Richard, Peter. Grad., Shipman Sch. Journalism, 1951. Mem. staff N.Y. Times, 1951-56; v.p. advt.-publicity Filmways Inc., N.Y.C., 1962-64; v.p. Rastar Prodns., Columbia Pictures, N.Y.C., 1967-69; v.p. advt. and publicity Columbia Pictures, Burbank, Calif., 1976-79; ind. motion picture producer, 1969-76; exec. v.p. prodn. Big Stick Prodns., Burbank, 1979-83; exec. v.p. advt., publicity, promotion 20th Century-Fox Film Corp., Beverly Hills, Calif., 1983-85; ind. producer Burbank Studios, 1985—. Producer: motion pictures Little Murders, 1971, Summer Wishes, Winter Dreams, 1973; exec. producer: motion pictures Everything You Always Wanted To Know About Sex, 1973; co-producer: Romancing the Stone, 1983; The Jewel of the Nile, 1985; co-author: The Cleopatra Papers, 1963. Served to cpl. U.S. Army, 1952-54, ETO. Home: Sherman Oaks, Calif. Died Feb. 18, 2003.

BROGREN, PAUL A. retired insurance company executive; b. Muskegon, Mich., Feb. 26, 1914; s. Oscar Lawrence and Nellie Jane (Snell) B.; m. Bertha Nancy Peterson, Dec. 4, 1940 (dec. July 1969); children: William P., Susan J., Thomas P., John P., Daniel P., Paul A. Jr.; m. Judith G. Weber, Dec. 31, 1967 (dec. 1988). Student, Muskegon Jr. Coll., 1934; BA in Bus. Adminstrn., George Washington U., 1937. From gen. foreman to supt. Continental Aviation Corp., 1942-45; treas. Assoc. Risk Mgmt., 1967-74; factory mgr. Continental Motors Corp., Muskegon, 1946-60; pres. Chaddock, Winter & Alberts, Muskegon, 1960-98; ret., 1998. Treas. Whitehall Dist. Sch. Bd., Whitehall, Mich., 1957-66; trustee Muskegon Intermediate Sch. Dist., 1967-70; mem., trustee diaconate bd. First Bapt. Ch., 1991—. Mem. Old Times Baseball Assn. (v.p. bd. dirs. 1970, pres.), Muskegon Torch Club (pres. 1973-74), Muskegon Shrine Club (pres. 1968). Republican. Baptist. Avocations: baseball, football, basketball, golf, ministry. Home: Muskegon, Mich. Died Apr. 24, 2000.

BRONSON, CHARLES (CHARLES BUCHINSKY), actor; b. Ehrenfeld, Pa., Nov. 3, 1921; m. Harriet Tendler (div.); 2 children; m. Jill Ireland, 1969 (dec.); 1 child, Zuleika; 2 stepchildren. Appeared in films You're in the Navy Now, 1951, Red Skies of Montana, 1952, Pat and Mike, 1952, House of Wax, 1953, Drumbeat, 1954, Vera Cruz, 1954, Jubal, 1956, Machine Gun Kelly, 1958, Never So Few, 1959, The Magnificent Seven, 1960, A Thunder of Drums, 1961, Lonely Are the Brave, 1962, The Great Escape, 1963, The Battle of the Bulge, 1965, The Sandpiper, 1965, This Property is Condemned, 1966, The Dirty Dozen, 1967, Adieu, L'Ami, Once Upon a Time in the West, 1969, Rider in the Rain, 1970, You Can't Win Them All, 1970, Someone Behind the Door, 1971, Chato's Land, 1971, Red Sun, 1972, The Valachi Papers, 1972, The Mechanic, 1972, Pancho Villa, The Stone Killer, 1973, Death Wish, 1974, Breakout, 1975, Mr. Majestyk, Hard Times, Breakheart Pass, 1976, St. Ives, 1976, Chino, 1976, From Noon Till Three, 1976, Telefon, 1977, Love and Bullets, 1979, Cabo Blanco, 1979, Borderline, 1980, The White Buffalo, Death Hunt, 1981, Death Wish II, 1982, The Evil that Men Do, 1984, Death Wish III, 1985, Murphy's Law, 1986, Assassination, 1987, Messenger of Death, 1988, Kinjite, 1989, The Indian Runner, 1991, Death Wish, V, 1993, Dead to Rights, 1995; TV appearances include Redigo, Man With a Camera, The Travels of Jamie McPheeters, Twilight Zone, The Big Valley, The FBI, Raid on Entebbe, The Line-Up, The Legend of Jesse James, Act of Vengeance, 1986, Yes Virgina, There is a Santa Claus, 1991, The Sea Wolf, 1993; (TV movie) Family of Cops, 1995, Breach of Faith: Family of Cops II, 1997. Served with AUS, 1943-46. Died Aug. 30, 2003.

BROOKS, DONALD LEE, civil engineering and scientific consulting firm executive; b. Boston, 1956; s. Douglas Lee and Elizabeth Brooks; m. Terry O'Sullivan, 1987 (div. 1989); m. Jill Blondin, 1991; children: Nathan Donald, Kylie Elizabeth. BA in Environ. Biology, Earlham Coll., Richmond, Ind., 1979; postgrad., U.Ariz., 1984. Registered profl. engr., Ariz.; diplomate Am. Coll. Forensic Examiners. Field biologist/vegetation mgr. Colo. River Projects Ariz. State U. Ctr. for Environ. Studies, 1980-81; rsch. asst. dept. watershed mgmt. U. Ariz., Tucson, 1982-84; subdivsn. engr., devel. divsn. mgr. Pima County Dept. Transp. & Flood Control Dist., Tucson, 1984-89; mgr. water resources Anderson-Passarelli, Tucson, 1989; v.p. URBAN Engring., Tucson, 1989-92; project mgr. Johnson-Brittain Assocs., Tucson, 1992; client mgr. David Evans & Assocs., Tucson, 1992-93; pres., prin. engr. ICON Cons. USA, Inc., Tucson, from 1993; prin. engr., environ. scientist Total Infrastructure Solutions LLC, Tucson, from 1998. Hydraulic engr., cons. Devel. Alternatives Inc./U.S. Agy. Internat. Devel., Cochabamba, Bolivia, 1993. Contbr. articles to profl. jours. Bd. dirs. Saguaro Credit Union, 1998, Mem. ASCE, Am. Inst. Hydrology (profl. hydrologist), Ariz. Floodplain Mgmt. Assn. (Outstanding Svc. award 1990-91), Assn. State Floodplain Mgrs., Am. Water Resources Assn., So. Ariz. Home Builders Assn., Adventure Club N.Am., Rocks & Ropes Tucson, Cliffhanger Soc. (v.p.). Mem. Soc. Friends. Avocations: rock climbing, skiing, electronic music, motorcycling. Home: Tucson, Ariz. Deceased.

BROOKS, HARVEY, physics educator; b. Cleve., Aug. 5, 1915; married, 1945; 4 children. AB, Yale U., 1937; PhD, Harvard U., 1940; DSc (hon.), Yale U., 1962, Union Coll., 1962, Harvard U., 1963, Kenyon Coll., 1963, Brown U., 1964. Mem. staff underwater sound lab. Harvard U., 1942-45; asst. dir. ord rsch. lab. Pa. State U., 1945; rsch. assoc. rsch. lab., assoc. lab. head. Knolls Atomic Power Lab. Gen. Electric Co., 1946-50; prof. applied physics Harvard U., Cambridge, Mass., 1950-86, prof. tech. and pub. policy, 1975-86, dean divsn. engring. and applied physics, 1957-75, Benjamin Peirce emeritus prof. tech. and pub. policy, from 1986, Gordon McKay emeritus prof. applied physics, 1986—2004. Chmn. com. undersea warfare NRC, 1957-63, chmn. commn. soc. tech. sys., 1975-78; mem. adv. com. reactor safeguards, programs and policies AEC, 1958; chmn. solid state adv. panel Office Naval Rsch.; mem. Pres.'s Sci. Adv. Com., 1959-64, Nat. Sci. Bd., 1962-74; mem. adv. com. sci. and technol. devel. UN, 1987-91. Author one book and numerous tech. publs.; editor-in-chief Jour. Physics and Chem. Solids, 1956-80. Recipient E.O. Lawrence award Am. Engring. Soc., 1960; Guggenheim fellow, 1956-57. Fellow AAAS (Philip Hauge Abelson award 1993), Am. Phys. Soc. (Forum award 1993); mem. NAS (sr. mem. inst. medicine, chmn. com. sci. and pub. policy 1966-72), Nat. Acad. Engring., Am. Philos. Soc., Am. Acad. Arts and Sci. (pres. 1970-75). Achievements include research on solid state physics, underwater sound, nuclear reactors, and science policy. Home: Cambridge, Mass. Died May 28, 2004.

BROOKS, HERBERT PAUL, hockey coach; b. St. Paul, Aug. 5, 1937; s. Herbert David and Pauline E. (Johnson) B.; m. Patricia Diane Brooks, Sept. 27, 1965; children: Daniel, Kelly. BA, U. Minn., 1962. Coach U. Minn., Mpls., 1972-79, U.S. Olympic Team, 1979-80, N.Y. Rangers, N.Y.C., 1981-85, St. Cloud (Minn.) State U., 1986-87, Minn. North Stars, Mpls., 1987-88, N.J. Devils, 1992-93; salesman Jostens, Mpls., 1985-86; coach Pitts. Penguins, 1999—2000. Inducted into U.S. Hockey Hall of Fame, 1990. Home: Saint Paul, Minn. Died Aug. 11, 2003.

BROOKS, MARTIN G. lawyer; b. Phila., Jan. 16, 1941; s. Charles Brooks and Betty Potter; previous marriage to Linda Jo Brooks; m. Carol Ann Brooks, Nov. 30, 1992; children: Cheryl Diane Brooks Moranville, Ruth Michelle Brooks Giahi. BBA, U. Miami, 1966, JD, 1969. Bar: Fla. 1969, U.S. Dist. Ct. (so. dist.) Fla. 1970, U.S. Supreme Ct. 1976, U.S. Ct. Appeals (5th cir.) 1977, U.S. Ct. Appeals (11th cir.) 1995; cert. mediator, Fla. Staff acct. Alfred Grodin CPA, 1963-66, Ralph Beardon CPA, 1966-67; contr. Am. Fiberglass Boat Corp., 1967-69; dir., contr., sec./treas., house counsel Am. Urban Devel. Corp., 1969-75; atty. Savitt Kotzen Riskin & France, 1975-76; pvt. practice Hollywood, Fla., from 1977. Guardian ad litem 17th Jud. Cir. Broward County, Fla., 1989—; del. All Bar Conf. for Bar Pres., 1989-90; vice-chmn. sect. F 17th jud. cir. Fla. Bar Grievance Com., 1991-92, chmn.,, 1992-93. With USAF, 1958-62. Mem. ABA, Broward County Bar Assn., Acad. Fla. Trial Lawyers, Fla. Acad. Profl. Mediators Inc., South Broward Bar Assn. (v.p. 1988-89, pres. 1989-90), Assn. Broward County Mediators, Internat. Law Soc., Phi Delta Phi. Avocation: model train collecting. Home: Pmbk Pines, Fla. Died June 8, 2001.

BROSS, STEWARD, JR., lawyer; b. Lancaster, Pa., Oct. 25, 1922; s. Steward Richard and Katherine Mauk (Hoover) B.; m. Isabel Florence Kenney, May 10, 1943; 1 dau., Donna Isabel Bross Campagna. Student, McGill U., Montreal, Can., 1940-42; LLB, Columbia U., 1948. Bar: N.Y. 1948. Pvt. practice, N.Y.C.; ptnr. Cravath, Swaine & Moore, 1958-92, ret., 1992; adv. com. fgn. direct investment program Office of Sec. Dept. Commerce, 1969; adv. com. regulations Office Fgn. Direct Investment, 1968 70. Regent, trustee emeritus The Cathedral Ch. of St. John the Divine, N.Y.C.; warden emeritus Trinity Ch., N.Y.C. Served as officer Canadian Navy, 1942-45. Mem. ABA, N.Y. State Bar Assn., Assn. of Bar of City of N.Y., Pilgrims U.S., Econ. Club N.Y., Union Club, Rockefeller Center Club, Links Club, Univ. Club N.Y. Home: New York, NY. Died 2003.

BROUWER, MARK NICHOLAS, retired publisher, newspaper; b. Lynden, Wash., June 19, 1913; s. Jacob George and Kate (Prakken) B.; m. Cornelia Ella Stryker, July 7, 1937; 1 child, Margaret Lee. AB, Hope Coll., 1935; MA, U. Mich., 1941. Asst. pub. State Jour., Lansing, Mich., 1948-57; editor, pub. Willard (Ohio) Times, 1957-80, Crestline (Ohio) Advocate, 1984-99; ret., 1999. Editor, pub. Reading (Mich.) Hustler, 1942-57; pres. Ohio Newspapers Assn., Columbus, 1978-79. Mem. U.S. Power Squadrons, Crestline Area C. of C. (pres. 1986), Sandusky Sailing Club, Sandusky Yacht Club. Presbyterian. Avocations: golf, sailing, music, reading. Home: Cleveland Hts, Ohio. Died Feb. 12, 1999.

BROWN, BURNELL ROLAND, JR., anesthesiology educator, biomedical researcher; b. Dallas, May 9, 1933; s. Burnell R. Sr. and Josephine Elizabeth Brown; m. Helen Diane Guilbault, Dec. 24, 1959; children: Monica, Michelle, Gregory, Philip. BS, Springhill Coll., 1954; MD, Tulane U., 1958; PhD in Pharmacology, U. Tex., 1969. Diplomate Am. Bd. Anesthesiology. Asst. prof. medicine U. Tex., Dallas, 1968-69, Harvard U., Boston, 1969-71; prof. anesthesiology U. Ariz., Tucson, from 1971. Head FDA Com. on Anesthetic and Respiratory Drugs, 1977-79. Editor Anesthesiology Journal, 1973-82; contbr. articles to profl. jours. Served to capt. U.S. Army, 1959-62. Named Plenary Speaker World Congress Anesthesiologists, Manila, Philipines, 1983. Mem. Assn. Univ. Anesthetists (pres. 1980-82). Republican. Roman Catholic. Avocations: astronomy, jogging, music. Home: Tucson, Ariz. Deceased.

BROWN, CHARLES NELSON, physicist; b. Victoria, Can., June 3, 1941; came to U.S., 1963; s. Ronald Nelson and Jessie Evelyn (Jones) B.; m. Mary Katherine Ehmann, Mar. 27, 1967; children: Christopher Nelson, Susan Louise Kerby. BSc, U. British Columbia, Vancouver, Can., 1963; AM, U. Rochester, 1966, PhD, 1968. Rsch. fellow Harvard U., Cambridge, Mass., 1968-71, rsch. asst. prof., 1971-74; staff scientist Fermi Nat. Accelerator Lab., Batavia, Ill., from 1974. Vis. prof. U. Wash., Seattle, 1979; adj. prof. No. Ill. U., DeKalb, 1988-91; vis. scientist NSF, Washington, 1992-93. Alderman 4th Ward, City of Geneva, Ill., 1987-92, 96—; sec. Kane County Pub. Bldg. Commn., 1988—. Woodrow

Wilson fellow, 1963, Kodak grad. fellow, 1965, lectr. fellow Japan Soc. for Phys. Sci., 1983. Fellow Am. Phys. Soc. Achievements include discovery of the fifth quark. Home: Geneva, Ill. Died Feb. 8, 2002.

BROWN, DAVID M. astronaut; b. Arlington, Va., Apr. 16, 1956; s. Paul and Dorothy Brown. BSc in Biology, Coll. William & Mary, 1978; MD, Ea. Va. U., 1982. Intern Med. U. S.C., 1982—84; commd. lt. USAF, 1984, advanced through grades to capt.; dir. med. svc. Navy Br. Hosp., Adak, Alaska, 1984—88; pilot tng. USAF, 1988—90, various assignments, 1990—92; served on USS Independence, 1992—95; astronaut NASA, Houston, from 1996. Varsity gymnist Coll. of William & Mary, Va., 1974—78. Performer: Circus Kingdom. Decorated Meritorious Svc. medal USAF; named Navy Operational Flight Surgeon of Yr., 1986. Fellow: Aerospace Med. Assn. (assoc.); mem.: Internat. Assn. Military Flight Surgeon Pilots (pres.), Soc. USN Flight Surgeons. Avocations: flying, bicycling, touring. Died Feb. 1, 2003.

BROWN, DEE ALEXANDER, author; b. La., 1908; s. Daniel Alexander and Lulu (Cranford) B.; m. Sara B. Stroud, Aug. 1, 1934; children— James Mitchell, Linda. BS, George Washington U., 1937; MS, U. Ill., 1951. Librarian Dept. Agr., Washington, 1934-42, Aberdeen Proving Ground, Md., 1945-48; agrl. librarian U. Ill. at Urbana, 1948-72, prof., 1962-75. On-camera narrator The Wild West, 1993, The Real West series, 1993-95, others. Author: Wave High the Banner, 1942, reprint, 1999, Grierson's Raid, 1954, Yellowhorse, 1956, Cavalry Scout, 1957, The Gentle Tamers: Women of the Old Wild West, 1958, The Bold Cavaliers, 1959, They Went Thataway, 1960, (with M.F. Schmitt) Fighting Indians of the West, 1948, Trail Driving Days, 1952, The Settler's West, 1955, Fort Phil Kearny, 1962, The Galvanized Yankees, 1963, Showdown at Little Big Horn, 1964, The Girl from Fort Wicked, 1964, The Year of the Century, 1966, Action at Beecher Island, 1967, Bury My Heart at Wounded Knee, 1971, Andrew Jackson and the Battle of New Orleans, 1972, The Westerners, 1974, Hear That Lonesome Whistle Blow: Railroads in the West, 1977, 2d edit., 2001, Tepee Tales, 1979, Creek Mary's Blood, 1980, The American Spa, 1982, Killdeer Mountain, 1983, Conspiracy of Knaves, 1987, Wondrous Times on the Frontier, 1991, When the Century Was Young, 1993, The American West, 1994, (with Mort Künstler) Images of the Old West, 1996, Best of the West, 1998, The Way to Bright Star, 1998, Civil War Anthology, 1998; on-camera narrator: The Wild West, 1993, The Real West, 1993-95, other documentaries of the Am. West; contbr.: Growing Up Western, 1990; editor: Agricultural History, 1956-58, Pawnee, Blackfoot and Cheyenne, 1961. Served with AUS, 1942-45. Recipient A.L.A. Clarence Day award, 1971, Christopher award, 1971, Illinoisian of Yr., Ill. News Broadcasters Assn., 1972, W.W.A. Golden Saddleman award, 1984. Mem. Authors Guild, Soc. Am. Historians, Western Writers Am., Beta Phi Mu. Home: Little Rock, Ark. Died Dec. 12, 2002.

BROWN, FRED ELMORE, investment executive; b. Muskogee, Okla., July 20, 1913; s. Fred E. and Alice (Washington) B.; m. Margaret Ann Gillham, Nov. 15, 1941 (dec.); 1 child, Frederick Elmore; m. Enid Sillcox Darlington, Dec. 22, 1977. BS, U. Okla., 1934; MBA, Harvard U., 1936; LHD (hon.), U. Okla., 1994. Sr. ptnr. J. & W. Seligman & Co., 1955-81; chmn., chief exec. officer J. & W. Seligman & Co. Inc., 1981-89, sr. advisor, dir., 1989-93, cons., dir., 1994-2000, cons., from 2000. Dir. emeritus Seligman Funds, Tri-Continental Corp. Trustee Adirondack Cmty. Trust, Lake Placid Edn. Found., Lake Placid Ctr. for the Arts; sr. mem. adv. com. Coll. Bus. Adminstrn., U. Okla.; bd. dirs. Bizzell Libr. Soc.; dir. Lake Placid Horse Show Assn. Lt. col. OQMG AUS, 1942-46. Decorated Legion of Merit; recipient Disting. Svc. citation, 1982, Regents Alumni award U. Okla., 1985; Arthur Barto Adams fellow, 1993; inducted Okla. Hall of Fame, 1982; Fred E. Brown chair in bus. named in his honor, Coll. Bus. Adminstrn., U. Okla. Mem. Union Club, Beta Theta Pi, Beta Gamma Sigma. Episcopalian. Home: Lake Placid, NY. Died Aug. 30, 2002.

BROWN, HARRY DEARMAN, corporate executive; b. Monroe, La., Mar. 5, 1925; s. Harry DeArman and Dollie Taylor (Cornett) B.; m. Luella Charlotte Christianson, Jan. 11, 1949; children: Ralph Walter, Lawrence Christianson. BSEE, La. Tech., 1948. Cert. flight instr. glider. Field engr. Schlumberger Well Svcs., Houma, La., 1948-51; dist. mgr. Schlumberger Surenco, Anaco, Venezuela, 1951-56, div. mgr., 1956-57; tech. asst. to pres. Mid. and Far East Schlumberger Overseas, Houston, 1957-58; interpretation and sales mgr. South and Cen. Am. Schlumberger Surenco, Caracas, Venezuela, 1959-67, div. mgr. Western Venezuela Lake Maracaibo, Venezuela, 1967-71; field tech. equipment coord. worldwide Schlumberger Limited, Houston, 1971-76; internat. coord. worldwide Schlumberger Tech. Svcs., Houston, 1976-84; pres. Brown Advisors Inc., Houston, from 1984. Cons. lectr. Nat. Oil Cos., S.Am. and Mid. East, U. Houston, 1994—; rsch. engr. Maurer Engring. Inc.; cons. logging engr. Transworld Oil, Houston; mktg. dir. Ludlam & Assocs. Editor: The Log Analysis mag., 1983-85; contbr. tech. articles to workbooks and profl. socs. Pres., v.p., chmn. com. Woodshire Civic Club, Houston, 1984—. Sgt. U.S. Army, 1943-46. Decorated Two Bronze Stars. Mem. Am. Assn. Petroleum Geologists, Soc. Petroleum Engrs. (sect. chmn. 1965, 69, 70, worldwide logging chmn. 1985), Soc. Profl. Well Log Analyst (v.p. tech. 1981-82, v.p. pubs. 1983-85, pres. Houston 1979-80, gen. chmn. annual meeting 1986, v.p. Houston 1994—, Medal of Honor, 1991), Houston Geol. Soc. (emeritus), Nat. Orgn. Mfg. and Dels. Soc., Am. Petroleum Inst., Am. Legion. Republican. Methodist. Avocations: tennis, soaring, cycling, bridge. Deceased.

BROWN, HERMIONE KOPP, lawyer; b. Syracuse, N.Y., Sept. 29, 1915; d. Harold H. and Frances (Burger) Kopp; m. Louis M. Brown, May 30, 1937 (dec. Sept. 1996); children— Lawrence D., Marshall J., Harold A. BA, Wellesley Coll., 1934; LLB, U. So. Calif., 1947. Bar: Calif. 1947. Story analyst 20th Century-Fox Film Corp., 1935-42; assoc. Gang, Kopp & Tyre, Los Angeles, 1947-52; ptnr. to sr. ptnr. Gang, Tyre, Ramer & Brown, Inc., Los Angeles, from 1952. Lectr. copyright and entertainment law U. So. Calif. Law Sch., 1974-77. Contbr. to profl. publs. Fellow Am. Coll. Trust and Estate Coun.; mem. Calif. Bar Assn. (chair probate law cons. group nd. legal specialization 1977-82, trust and probate law sect., exec. com. 1983-86, advisor 1986-89), L.A. Copyright Soc. (pres. 1979-80), Order of Coif, Phi Beta Kappa. Avocations: literature, theatre, music. Home: Beverly Hills, Calif. Died Sept. 23, 2003.

BROWN, IONA, violinist, orchestra director; b. Salisbury, Wiltshire, England, Jan. 7, 1941; Studied with Hugh Maguire, London, Remy Principe, Rome, Henryk Szeryng, France. Violinist Nat. Youth Orch. of Gt. Britain, 1955-60, Philharmonia Orch. of London, 1963-66; former violinist Acad of St. Martin in the Fields, concertmaster, dir.; artistic dir. Norwegian Chamber Orch., Oslo; prin. guest dir. L.A. Chamber Orch., 1987-91; former prin. guest dir. City of Birmingham Symphony Orch., England. Died June 5, 2004.

BROWN, JAMES ISAAC, rhetoric educator; b. Tarkio, Mo., Dec. 15, 1908; s. John Vallance and Ada (Moore) B.; m. Ruth Bernice Sam, Sept. 19, 1942; children: Katherine Ada, Susan Phyllis. BA, Tarkio Coll., 1930, D.H.L. (hon.), 1976; MA, U. Chgo., 1933; PhD, U. Colo., 1949; D.H.L. (hon.), U. Minnesota, 2002. Instr. English Monmouth Coll., 1933-34; faculty U. Minn., from 1934, successively instr., asst. prof., assoc. prof., 1934-77, prof. rhetoric, 1954-77, acting chief rhetoric, 1947-48. Instr. English, Yavapai Coll., 1982-84; vis. lectr. U. Colo., summers 1950, 52, 54, U. Utah, summer 1955; staff mem. Effective Communication in Industry Course, summer 1954, 55; instituted Reading Efficiency Program in Industry, summers 1957, 58; conf. leader Mgmt. Clinic, Hot Springs, Va., 1956; communications cons. Minn. Mining & Mfg. and Caterpillar Tractor Cos., 1964 Author: Efficient Reading, 1952, (with G. Robert Carlsen) Brown-Carlsen Listening Comprehension Test, 1954, Lex-o-Gram, 1954, (with Eugene S. Wright) Minnesota Efficient Reading Tachistolide Series, Minnesota Clerical Training Tachistoslide Series and Minnesota Timing Series, 1955, Revision of Nelson Denny Reading Test, 1960, (with Rachel Salisbury) Building a Better Vocabulary, 1959, Explorations in College Reading, 1959, Exercise Manual for Explorations in College Reading, 1959, (with George Sanderlin) Effective Writing and Reading, 1962, Pyramid, 1963, Programmed Vocabulary (TV edit., coll. edit. and high sch. edn.), 1964, 3d edit., 1980, Guide to Effective Reading, 1966, (with O.M. Haugh) College English Placement Test, 1969, Acceleread System, 1970, also the visual-linguistic basic reading series, 1966—, Efficient Reading, Revised Form A, 1971, Revised Form B, 1976, 6th edit., 1984, 7th edit., 1993, 8th edit., 1997, Forms C and D, Nelson-Denny Reading Test, 1973; Forms E and F, Nelson-Denny Reading Test, 1981, Forms G and H, 1992; Reading Power, 1975, alt. edit., 1978, 2d edit., 1983, 3d edit., 1987, 4th edit., 1991, 5th edit., 1995 (with Vivian V. Fishco), 6th edit., 2001, Better Spelling, 1971, 2d edit., 1978, 3d edit, 1985, 4th edit., 1991, 5th edit., 1996, Word Power, 1982, EyeSCAN, 1999; mem. adv. bd., cons. ednl. edit. Reader's Digest, 1957; courses ednl. TV Success thru Better Spelling; tapes Putting Words to Work, for U.S. Dept. Edn.; cons. editor Jour. Internat. Listening Assn., 1986. Mem. visitor bd. Embry-Riddle Aeronautical U., Ariz., 1996—. Served with AUS, 1943-45, ETO. Recipient Tarkio Coll. Student Assn. Hall of Fame Award, 1965, Certificate of Merit in recognition outstanding ind. study course Efficient Reading Nat. Extension Assn., 1972, award of merit Gamma Sigma Delta, 1977, Winston Churchill Medal of Wisdom, 1988, Eisenhower Am. Achievement Honor award, 1989; named to Listening Hall of Fame, 1980. Mem. AAUP, Internat. Platform Assn., Nat. Council Tchrs. English, Nat. Soc. Study Communication (exec. sec. 1951, chmn. com. on reading comprehension 1951-63, pres.), Internat. Reading Assn., Conf. Coll. Composition and Communication, Speech Assn. Am., Am. Council Edn., Yavapai Symphony Assn. (pres. 1988-91), Phi Delta Kappa. Episcopalian (vestry mem. 1982-86, sr. warden 1984-86). Home: Eureka, Calif. Died Nov. 28, 2002.

BROWN, JESSE, former federal official; b. Detroit, Mar. 27, 1944; married; 2 children. Grad. with honors, Chgo. City Coll.; student, Roosevelt U., Cath. U. Am. Nat. svc. officer Disabled Am. Vets., Chgo., 1967-72, supr. nat. svc. staff and nat. appeals staff Washington, chief of claims nat. svc. and legis. hdqrs., dep. nat. svc. dir., exec. asst. to nat. adjutant, exec. dir., 1989-93; sec. Dept. Vets. Affairs, Washington, 1993-97. V.p. Mayor's Com. on Employment of Handicapped, Chgo. With USMC, 1963-65. Decorated Purple Heart, Vietnam Svc. Medal, republic of Vietnam Campaign medal. Mem. AMVETS, DAV, VFW, Am. Legion, Marine Corps League, Mil. Order Purple Heart, Polish Legion Am. Vets., U.S.A. Ret. Enlisted Assn., Jewish War Vets., Vietnam Vets. Am. Inc. Died Aug. 15, 2002.

BROWN, SIR JOHN (GILBERT NEWTON), retired publisher; b. July 7, 1916; s. John and Molly B.; m. Virginia Braddell; 3 children. Ed, Lancing Coll., Hertford Coll; MA in Zoology, Oxford U. With Bombay br. Oxford Univ. Press, 1937-40, 46-49, sales mgr., 1949-56, pub., 1956-80. Chmn. Univ. Bookshops Ltd., Oxford; dir. Book Tokens Ltd., Willshaw Booksellers Ltd., Manchester, Eng.; chmn. B.H. Blackwell Ltd., dir. Blackwell Group Ltd., 1980-87; pres. Pubs. Assn., 1963-65; mem. nat. libraries com. EDC for Newspapers, Printing and Pub. Industry, 1967-70; mem. Adv. Com. Sci. and Tech. Info., 1969-73; mem. communication adv. com. U.K. nat. com. UNESCO; asst. treas. Royal Lit. Fund; bd. dirs. Brit. Library, 1973-79; mem. Royal Soc. Sci. Info.; past mem. bd. Brit. Council. Commd. Royal Arty., 1941, served, 41-46, Japanese prisoner of war, 1942-45. Professorial fellow Hertford Coll., Oxford U., 1974-80. Died Mar. 3, 2003.

BROWN, KENT LOUIS, SR., surgeon; b. Westfield, N.Y., Mar. 15, 1916; s. Louis J. and Emma (Kent) B.; m. Elizabeth Myers, June 26, 1940; children: Karen Elizabeth Johnson, Kent Louis Jr., David S., Garry Myers. BS, Cornell U., 1938; MD, SUNY, Buffalo, 1942; postgrad., Case Western Res. Med. Sch. Diplomate Am. Bd. Surgery. Rotating intern St. Luke's Hosp., Cleve., 1942-43, asst. resident surgery, 1946-49, chief resident surgeon, 1949-50, pres. staff, 1961-62; now hon. mem. active staff, past pres. staff St. Vincent Charity Hosp., Cleve.; mem. staff Westfield Meml. Hosp., from 1989. Bd. dirs. Westfield Meml. Hosp., 1977—, med. dir.; emeritus asst. clin. prof. Case-Western Res. U. Med. Sch., Cleve.; elected to Bd. of Health, Chatauqua, N.Y. Author: Medical Problems and the Law, The Medical Witness, A Medical History of Westfield, N.Y., 1992.; past editor: The Cleve. Physician; editor: Medicine in Cleveland and Cuyahoga County: 1810-1976; contbr. articles to profl. jours. Bd. dirs. Fredonia Chamber Players; pres. bd. trustees Cleve. Med. Libr., 1972, also past trustee; past pres. med. cons. City of Cleve. Safety Dept.; mem. Patterson Libr. Bd., Westfield, N.Y., 1986—, pres. bd. trustees, 1991-92; chmn. bd. trustees Westfield Presbyn. Ch., 1984-87; past trustee Cleve. br. Am. Cancer Soc., Cuyahoga County. Served with USN, 1942-46, PTO. Fellow ACS (past mem. trauma com.); mem. AMA, Ohio State Med. Assn., Am. Assn. Surgery of Trauma, Cleve. Acad. Medicine, Chautauqua County Med. Soc., Westfield C. of C., Am. Legion, VFW, Buffalo Acad. Medicine; named Paul Harris Fell. by Westfield Mayville Rotary Club for outstanding contrib. to the Westfield Comm. Fellow ACS; mem. AMA, Ohio State Med. Assn., Am. Assn. Surgery of Trauma, Cleve. Acad. Medicine, Chautauqua County Med. Soc., Westfield C. of C., Am. Legion, VFW, Buffalo Acad. Medicine. Clubs: Aesculapian Soc. Cleve. (past pres.), Innominatum Soc. (past pres.), Pasteur (past pres.), Medical Arts (past pres.), Union. Lodges: Kiwanis (past pres.). Republican. Died Apr. 30, 1999.

BROWN, MATTHEW, lawyer; b. N.Y.C., Mar. 26, 1905; s. Jack Goddard and Pauline B. (Roth) B.; m. Edna Goodrich, Nov. 8, 1932; 1 child, Patricia Brown Specter. BS, NYU, 1925; LLB, Harvard U., 1928; LLD (hon.), Suffolk U., 1983. Bar: Mass. 1928, U.S. Supreme Ct. 1935. Sr. ptnr. Brown, Rudnick, Freed & Gesmer, Boston, 1940-88, counsel, from 1988; spl. justice Boston Mcpl. Ct., 1962-72. Chmn. Boston Broadcasters, 1972-81. Selectman Town of Brookline, Mass., 1953-64; trustee New Eng. Aquarium, Boston, 1981-88; mem. Nat. Jewish Coalition, Boston, 1984, Holocaust Meml. Coun., Washington; bd. dirs. Palm Beach Fellowship of Christians and Jews, Palm Beach Civic League. Fellow Brandeis U., Waltham, Mass., 1985 (hon.). Mem. ABA, Mass. Bar Assn., Boston Bar Assn., Am. Jewish Com. (hon. v.p.), Combined Jewish Philanthropies (hon. trustee, life), Belmont Country Club. Died Sept. 2003.

BROWN, PAUL BRADLEY, architect; b. Lake City, Minn., Apr. 20, 1912; s. Clark William and Belle (Patton) B.; m. Betty V. Padou, Dec. 29, 1945 (dec. May 1989); children: Barry, Bennett, Bradley. AB, Oberlin Coll., 1933; B.Arch., U. Mich., 1936. Draftsman Hugh Keyes (Architet), Detroit, 1936-37; designer I.M. Lewis (Architect), Detroit, 1937-39, Harley Ellington Assos. Inc., Detroit, 1939-48, project architect, 1948-55, prin., 1955-70; exec. partner Harley Ellington Pierce Yee & Assos., 1970-82. Pres. Birmingham (Mich.) Planning Commn., 1956-58; pres. Forum for Detroit Area Met. Goals, 1962-67. Served with USNR, 1943-45. Fellow AIA (pres. Detroit chpt. 1961-63, Gold medal Detroit chpt.), Engring. Soc. Detroit (Gold medal); mem. Mich. Soc. Architects (dir. 1964-65) Home: Woodbridge, Va. Died Aug. 17, 2002.

BROWN, RICHARD ARTHUR, political consultant; b. N.Y.C., Oct. 22, 1918; s. Benjamin Brown and Ruth (Halper) Sachs; m. Vivian Neilson; 1 child, Jennifer Jo. Student, CUNY, 1936-40, NYU Law Sch, 1946-47. Exec. dir. Clearing House for Youth Groups, N.Y.C., 1940; assoc. program dir. Anti Defamation League Bnai Brith, N.Y.C., 1947-51; asst. dir. Bonds for Israel, N.Y.C., 1951-52; state orgn. dir. Vol. for Stevenson, N.Y.C., 1952; polit. columnist N.Y. Post, N.Y.C., 1955; pub. rel. dir. Stevenson for Pres., N.Y.C., 1955-56; exec. dir. Com. for Dem. Voters, N.Y.C., 1959-65; adminstrv. asst. Rep. James H. Scheuer, M.C., Washington, 1965-71; former pres. Richard A. Brown Cons., Washington. Coord. N.Y. State Festival, Washington; former treas. Rangel for Congress, Washington; former dir. N.Y. Congl. Tour, Washington; cons. A.A.R.P., Washington, 1984-87. Contbr. articles on vets. orgn. to Ency. Britannica, 1947-53. Former Chmn. N.Y. Found. for Sr. Citizens, N.Y.C.; founder Lexington Dem. Club, N.Y.C., 1949; N.Y. State founder Am. for Dem. Action, 1948. With U.S. Army, 1941-45. Democrat. Jewish. Avocations: reading, travel, golf. Home: Washington, DC. Died Feb. 13, 2004.

BROWN, ROBERT THORSON, retired forest ecology educator, researcher; b. Rochester, Minn., Sept. 29, 1923; s. Lloyd Kent and Alma Idso Brown; m. Viola Jarvenpaa, Sept. 1, 1953; children: Linda Anne, Cynthia Ellen, Lisa Linnea, Erik Thorson. BSChE, U. Wis., 1947, BS in Botany, 1948, MS in Botany, 1949, PhD in Botany, 1951. Prof. Mich. Technol. U., Houghton, 1951-83, Tianjin (China) Inst. Tech., 1992-93. Fulbright prof. Helsinki (Finland) U., 1971-72, Cukurova U., Adana, Turkey, 1980-81, U. West Indies, St. Augustine, Trinidad, 1986-87; USAID prof., Gorakhpur (India) U., 1968; lectr. Soviet Acad. Sci., Kiev, 1972. Contbr. numerous articles to profl. jours., including Ecology, Forest Sci., Soil Pollution, Acta Forestalia Fennica, Water, Air & Soil Pollution, others. Mem. sch. bd., Houghton, 1962-65; pres. Mich. Tech Credit Union, Houghton, 1962-68. Recipient medal of Forestry, Finnish Forestry Soc., 1979. Fellow: AAAS; mem.: Sigma Xi. Democrat. Presbyterian. Avocations: photography, gardening. Home: Houghton, Mich. Died Aug. 25, 2002.

BROWN, THOMAS WILLIAM, osteopathic physician, obstetrician, gynecologist; b. Detroit, Oct. 10, 1946; s. William Floyd and Dorothy Fern (Skitch) Brown; m. Debra Lynne Dawson, Sept 29, 1984; children: Stephen Michael, Scott William. BA, Western Mich. U., 1968; DO, Coll. Osteopathic Medicine, Des Moines, Iowa, 1972. Diplomate Am. Bd. Ob.-Gynecologists. Chief ob.-gyn. USAF Hosp., Clovis, N. Mex., 1980-82; physician pvt. practice, Fairfield, Calif., 1982-90; staff physician Kaiser Permanente, Vallejo, Calif., from 1990. Mem. Am. Coll. Ob.-Gyn., Solano County Med. Soc., Rosicrucian Order, AMORC. Avocations: tennis, reading. Home: Fairfield, Calif. Died Sept. 8, 2001.

BROWN, WILLIAM FRANK, small business owner; b. Warren, Ohio, July 6, 1930; s. Stephen John and Mary Brown; m. Florence Charlotte MacFarlane, Sept. 3, 1956; children: Viktoria Ann, Erik Stephen, Kerri Elizabeth. Student, Hiram Coll., 1949—50; BS in Pharmacy, Purdue U., 1953. Pharmacist Boyer Pharmacy, Columbus, Ohio, 1953—57; sales rep. Geigy Pharms., Ardsley, NY, 1957—59, dist. mgr. Summit, NY, 1959—66, regional mgr., 1966—75, mgr. pharmacy rels., 1975—81; owner Minor Chord Music Store, Acton, Mass., from 1981. Named Ky. Col. Unitarian Universalist. Avocation: violin. Home: Carlisle, Mass. Died Mar. 17, 2001.

BROWNING, JOHN, pianist; b. Denver, May 23, 1933; s. John and Esther (Green) B. Student, Occidental Coll., D.Mus. (hon.), 1975; student, Juilliard Sch. Music; D.Mus. (hon.), Ithaca Coll.; student, Lee Pattison, Calif., Rosina Lhevinne, N.Y.C. Debut, Denver, 1943; N.Y.C. debut N.Y. Philharmonic Orch. at Carnegie Hall, 1956; appearances with numerous orchs., U.S., Europe, Mexico, Russia, Eng.; recitalist; pianist: for world premiere performance Samuel Barber's First Piano Concerto with Boston Symphony Orch; pianist with Cleve. Orch. on Dept. State tour to USSR, 1965; rep., Am. govt. World's Fair, Brussels, 1968, instr. master classes, Northwestern U., 1975-80, Manhattan Sch. Music, 1980-86, Juilliard Sch., 1986—2003; rec. artist. Served with U.S. Army. Recipient Jr. award KFI-Hollywood Bowl Young Artists Competition, 1945, Steinway Centennial award Nat. Fedn. Music Clubs, 1954, Edgar M. Leventritt award, 1955, Queen Elisabeth Internat. Concours award, 1956; Lhevinne Meml. scholar; recipient Grammy award Best Instrumental Soloist with Orch., 1992, Grammy award Best Instrumental Soloist (without Orch.) for Barber: The Complete Solo Piano Music, 1994. Mem. Pi Kappa Lambda. Home: New York, NY. Died Jan. 26, 2003.

BROWNING, NORMA LEE (MRS. RUSSELL JOYNER OGG), journalist; b. Spickard, Mo., Nov. 24, 1914; d. Howard R. and Grace (Kennedy) B.; m. Russell Joyner Ogg, June 12, 1938. AB, B.J., U. Mo., 1937; MA in English, Radcliffe Coll., 1938. Reporter Los Angeles Herald-Express, 1942-43; with Chgo. Tribune, from 1944, Hollywood columnist, 1966-75. Vis. lectr. creative writing, editorial cons., mem. nat. adv. bd. Interlochen Arts Acad., Northwood Inst. Author: City Girl in the Country, 1955, Joe Maddy of Interlochen, 1963, (with W. Clement Stone) The Other Side of the Mind, 1965, The Psychic World of Peter Hurkos, 1970, (with Louella Dirksen) The Honorable Mr. Marigold, 1972, (with Ann Miller) Miller's High Life, 1972, Peter Hurkos: I Have Many Lives, 1976, Omarr: Astrology and the Man, 1977, (with George Masters) The Masters Way to Beauty, 1977, (with Russell Ogg) He Saw A Hummingbird, 1978, (with Florence Lowell) Be A Guest At Your Own Party, 1980, Face-Lifts: Everything You Always Wanted to Know, 1981, Joe Maddy Of Interlochen: Portrait of A Legend, 1991; Contbr. articles to nat. mags. Recipient E.S. Beck award Chgo Tribune. Mem. Theta Sigma Phi, Kappa Tau Alpha. Died June 11, 2001; Calif.

BROYHILL, ROY FRANKLIN, manufacturing executive; b. Sioux City, Iowa, June 20, 1919; s. George Franklin and Effie (Motes) B.; BBA, U. Nebr., 1940; m. Arline W. Stewart, Jan. 30, 1943; children: Lynn Diann (dec.), Craig G., Kent Bryan, Bryce Alan. Trainee mgr. Montgomery Ward Co., 1940; semi-sr. acct. L. H. Keightley, 1941-42; chief accountant Army Exchange Service, Sioux City, 1942-46; chmn. Broyhill Co., 1946-88, dir., 1988—; pres., dir. Star Printing & Pub. Co., South Sioux City, 1949-94, ret. 1994, chmn., bd. dir., 1994—; pres. Broyhill Corp., 1953-92, dir. 1992—, chmn., 1953—; v.p. Broyhill Mfg. Co., 1978-87, pres., 1953-92, dir., 1992—; pres., chmn. bd. Broyhill Inc., 1996; ret. dir. 1st Nat. Bank, Sioux City. Mem. U.S.A. Exec. Res.; past mem. Nebr. dist. adv. council SBA. Mayor of Dakota City, 1951-53; mem. Nebr. Republican Central Com., 1954-56. Past mem. local sch. bd. Trustee U. Nebr. Found. Served with AUS, 1940-41. Recipient Citation, Nebr. Gov., 1996. Mem. Farm Equipment Mfrs. Assn. (past dir., pres. 1971-72), Atokad Racing Assn. (past dir.), N.A.M., U.S., South Sioux City chambers commerce, Nebr. C. of C. (dir. 1972-73), Alumni Assn. U. Nebr. (past dir.), Trustee Found. U. Nebr., Am. Legion (life), Beta Theta Pi, Alpha Kappa Psi. Presbyn. (elder). Clubs: U. Nebr. Chancellor's. Lodges: Masons (Shrine). Died OCt. 4, 1999. Home: Pickstown, SD.

BRUCE, DAVID STEWART, biology educator; b. Amherst, Ohio, Sept. 17, 1939; s. George Stewart and Carolyn Mary (Guild) B.; m. Janet Sue Foltz, Aug. 19, 1961; children: Rob Stewart, Scot David. BA, BS in Edn., Taylor U., 1962; MS, Purdue U., 1965, PhD, 1968. Vis. asst. prof. biology Purdue U., West Lafayette, Ind., 1968; from asst. to assoc. prof. Seattle Pacific Coll., 1968-74; assoc. prof. Wheaton (Ill.) Coll., 1974-78, prof., from 1978, acting chmn. biology dept., 1989-90, coord. sci. div., 1991-92, 96. Dir. Wheaton Coll. Sci. Sta., Rapid City, S.D., 1988-89, 90-91, co-dir., 1991-92, 93-95, 97. Contbr. articles to sci. publs. NSF equipment grantee, 1972-74; Burroughs-Wellcome Fund Rsch. Travel fellow, 1980; rsch. grantee Dr. Scholl Found., 1987, 88, 89. Fellow Am. Sci. Affiliation; mem. AAAS, Am. Physiol. Soc. (participant profl. rsch. confs., chmn. tchg. sect. 1993-96), Sigma Xi. Avocations: spelunking, photography, basketball. Home: Wheaton, Ill. Deceased.

BRUCE, ROBERT A. cardiologist, educator; b. Somerville, Mass., Nov. 20, 1916; s. Robert S. and Mabel P. (Peterson) B.; m. Eleanor H., Nov. 22, 1940; children: Robert H., Nancy F. (dec.), Peter M., Scott A. BS, Boston U., 1938; MS, U. Rochester, 1940, MD with honors, 1943. Asst. prof., head of cardiology dept. U. Wash., Seattle, 1953-54, assoc. prof., 1954-59, prof., 1959-70, co-dir., 1970-81, prof. emeritus, 1981—2004. Cardiology cons. Social Security Disability Program, Seattle, 1983-88. Former mem. bd. trustees Horizon House, Seattle. Fellow Am. Coll. Cardiologists. Home: Seattle, Wash. Died Feb. 12, 2004.

BRUCE, ROBERT LEE, education educator; b. Gordon, Nebr., Apr. 14, 1925; s. Arthur Logan and Ruth Alice (Auker) B.; m. Charlotte Ann Rieke, June 7, 1949; children: Thomas Robert, Ann Lynn (dec.). BS, U. Nebr., 1949; MS, Cornell U., 1951, PhD, 1962. County ext. agt. U. Nebr. Ext., Stapleton, 1949-50; pubs. editor U. Md., College Park, 1952-55, asst. state leader, agrl. ext., 1955-61; asst. prof., assoc., to prof. ext. edn. Cornell U., Ithaca, N.Y., from 1961. Vis. prof. Reading (Eng.) U., 1967-68, 89-90, U. Saskatchewan, 1975, U. Pertanian Malaysia, Serdang, 1982-83, U. B.C., Vancouver, 1983. Contbr. articles to profl. jours., ext. publs., book chpts. in field. Mem. County Bd. Reps., Tompkins County, N.Y., 1970-75; trustee Tompkins-Cortland Community Coll., Dryden, N.Y., 1980 . Sgt. U.S. Army, 1943-46, ETO. Fellowship Adult Edn., Fund for Adult Edn., Cornell U., 1957-58. Mem. AAAS, Adult Edn. Rsch. Conf. (steering com. 1970-72), Can. Assn. Adult Edn. Avocations: photography, graphics, painting. Home: Ithaca, NY. Deceased.

BRUCH, FRANCES BALLARD, medical/surgical and oncological nurse; b. Pleasant Shade, Tenn., June 18, 1925; d. Albert Fred and Tennie (Hackett) Ballard; m. Donald Judson Bruch, Aug. 22, 1957; children: Rebecca, Donald Judson Jr., Beverly, Allan. BSN, Memphis State U., 1980; BPS, Univ. Coll., Memphis, 1978. Med.-surg. and oncological staff nurse St. Francis Hosp., Memphis; med.-surg. staff nurse Meth. Hosp., Memphis; health care coord. Mid South Found. for Med. Care, Memphis. Mem. Sigma Theta Tau, Phi Kappa Phi. Home: Eads, Tenn. Died May 1, 2001.

BRUCKER, WILBER MARION, retired lawyer; b. Saginaw, Mich., Apr. 13, 1926; s. Wilber Marion and Clara (Hantel) B.; m. Doris Ann Shover, June 23, 1951; children: Barbara Ann, Wilber Marion, Paul Bradford. Student, Wayne State U., 1943; AB, Princeton U., 1949; JD, U. Mich., 1952. Bar: Mich. 1953. Assoc. Clark, Klein, Brucker & Waples, Detroit, 1952-58; pvt. practice Detroit, 1958-61; ptnr. Brucker & Brucker, Detroit, 1961-67, McInally, Rockwell & Brucker, Detroit, 1968-78, McInally, Brucker, Newcombe, Wilke and DeBona, Detroit, 1978-86; pres. Alliance Fin. Corp., 1986-89; sr. legal counsel Riley and Roumell, Detroit, 1990-96; dir. Bank of Dearborn, Mich., 1970-89, Alliance Fin. Corp., 1982-89; ret. Legal counsel Econ. Club Detroit, 1968-86; arbitrator Am. Arbitration Assn., 1965-79; bd. dirs. Cmty. Bank Dearborn. Bd. govs. Wayne State U., Detroit, 1967-78, chmn. bd. govs., 1972; pres. bd. trustees Arnold Home, 1968-96; mem. Witanagamote, 1956—, Centurions, 1977-96, Woodworkers, 1991—; mem. bd. canvassers City of Grosse Pointe Farms, Mich., 1972-74; pres. Grosse Pointe Sr. Mens Club, 1998-99. Mem. ABA, Mich. Bar Assn., Country Club of Detroit, Masons. Home: Grosse Pointe Farms, Mich. Died Nov. 9, 2003.

BRUNER, CHARLOTTE HUGHES, French language educator; b. Urbana, Ill., May 8, 1917; d. Charles Hughes and Nell Converse (Bomar) Johnston; m. David Kincaid Bruner, July 16, 1939; children: Nell Kincaid Bruner Sedransk, Charles Hughes. BA, U. Ill., 1938; MA, Columbia U., 1939. Tchr. French Iowa State U., 1942-44, 55—, prof., 1980-87, prof. emeritus, from 1987; instr. U. Ill., 1944-45. Writer, dir. radio series, 1974, 79, 80-86; editor: Unwinding Threads: Writing by Women in Africa, 1983, The Heinemann Book of African Women's Writing, 1993; consulting editor for Africa: The Feminist Companion to Literature in English, 1990; contbr. articles to profl. jours. Named to Iowa Women's Hall of Fame, 1997. Mem. MLA, African Lit. Assn. (vice chmn. 1978-79), Am. Tchrs. French, Coll. Lang. Assn., Phi Beta Kappa, Phi Kappa Phi, Phi Sigma Iota, Pi Delta Pi. Home: Ames, Iowa. Died Dec. 4, 1999.

BRYAN, DOROTHY JEAN, artist; b. Bowling Green, Ohio, Aug. 27, 1924; d. Howard Thomas and Rae (Beauchamp) Uber; m. Ashel Gano Bryan; children: Rebecca Bryan Bergert, David A. Bryan, Katherine Bryan Hollingsworth. Grad. high sch., Bowling Green. Pres. Medici Circle, Bowling Green State U.; com. mem. Arts Unltd., Friends of Music. Exhibited in group shows at Bowling Green State U., 1st Nat. Bank-Toledo, Mid-Am. Bank, Bowling Green, Art Expo, Toledo Mus. Area Artist Show, Toledo Mus. Collectors Corner, State House, Columbus. Com. mem. Heritage 1976, Bowling Green, 1975-75, Heritage 2000, Bowling Green, 1995—, Ohio Arts Coun. for Art Program, 1995-96, Aesthetic Devel. Ctr., 1995-96. Named Hon. Alumnus Bowling Green State U., 1987; recipient Outstanding Citizen City of Bowling Green, 1995, Govs. award for the Arts State of Ohio, 1994, Outstanding Philanthropist, 1994. Republican. Avocation: golf. Home: Bowling Green, Ohio. Died Feb. 15, 2001.

BRYAN, SISTER MARY GERARD, health science facility administrator; b. Bklyn., May 28, 1933; d. Vincent Edward and Teresa (Minola) B. Diploma, Bklyn. Hosp. Sch. Nursing, 1955; BS in Nursing, DePaul U., 1962, MS in Nursing, 1968. RN, Ill.; cert. nursing home adminstr., N.Y. Staff nurse Bklyn. Hosp., 1955, St. Charles Hosp., Pt. Jefferson, L.I., 1955-56; with Resurrection Health Care Corp., Chgo., 1956-58 and from 60; exec. v.p., chief operating officer Resurrection Hosp., 1963-89; exec. dir. Resurrection Ministries of N.Y., from 1990. Mem. Am. Coll. Hosp. Execs. Roman Catholic. Home: Chicago, Ill. Deceased.

BRYANT, BARBARA C. social worker; b. Providence, May 26, 1925; d. Willis Edgar and Bertha Ellen (Melanson) Chandler; m. Robert Charles Bryant; children: Stephen, Douglas, Marjorie. BA, Bates Coll., 1947; MSW, Simmons Coll., 1950. Diplomate Am. Bd. Edn. Social worker Family Svcs., Ypsilanti, Mich.; social worker Cambridge (Mass.) Schs.; pvt. practice; social worker Winchester (Mass.) Hosp. Home: Winchester, Mass. Died June 11, 2001.

BRYANT, FELICE, songwriter, vocalist; b. Milw., Aug. 7, 1925; m. Boudleaux Bryant, 1945 (dec. 1987); children: Dane, Del. With Tannen Music, Acuff-Rose Publs.; co-founder Showcase Music, from 1954; founder House of Bryant, from 1967. Violinist Atlanta Symphony, Hank Penny's Band, Mack & Sandy's Traveling Tent Show. Songwriter Baltimore, Bye Bye Love, Come Live with Me, Country Boy, Have a Good Time, Problems, Take a Message to Mary, Wake Up, Little Susie, I'm Little But I'm Loud, Country Gentleman, How's The World Treating You, Bird Dog, All I Have to Do Is Dream, Love Hurts, Rocky Top, Bessie the Heifer, Waitress, Waitress, Out Behind the Barn, It's a Lovely, Lovely World, Just Wait Till I Get You Alone, Hey, Joe, Back Up, Buddy, Have a Good Time, Christmas Can't Be Far Away, I've Been Thinking, Hawkeye, I'm the Richest Man in the World, We Could, Living in My Heart, He Wears My Ring, Mexico, many others. Inducted into National Songwriters Hall of Fame, 1986, Country Music Hall of Fame, 1991. Died Apr. 22, 2003.

BRYANT, MARY ELIZABETH, theatrical press agent; b. Apopka, Fla., Oct. 17; d. Theodore Alfred Bryant and Mabel Elizabeth (Eddy) Bryant-Decker. AB, U. Miami, 1953. Press and pub. rels. agt. Never Too Late, 1962, She Loves Me, 1963, Flora, The Red Menace, 1965, Superman, 1966, Cabaret, 1966, Zorba, 1968, Company, 1970, Follies, 1971, Night Music, 1973, The Visit, 1973, Love for Love, 1974, Pacific Overtures, 1976, Side by Side by Sondheim, 1977, On the Twentieth Century, 1978, Sweeney Todd, 1979, Evita, 1980, Merrily We Roll Along, 1981, A Doll's Life, 1982, Grind, 1985, Roza, 1987, Grandchild of Kings, 1992, Kiss of the Spider Woman, 1993, Show Boat, 1994, Barrymore, 1997, Candide, 1997, Ragtime, 1997. Mem. Assn. Theatrical Press Agts. and Mgrs. Home: New York, NY. Died Feb. 22, 2004.

BRZUSTOWICZ, RICHARD JOHN, neurosurgeon, educator; b. Bklyn., Dec. 19, 1917; s. John B. and Victoria Eleanor (Szutarska) B.; m. Alice Lorraine Cinq-Mars, May 30, 1945; children: Richard John, Thaddeus P., Victoria, Barbara, John, Teresa, Krystyna, Mary. BS, CCNY, 1938; MD, SUNY, 1942; MS in Neurol. Surgery, U. Minn., 1951. Diplomate: Am. Bd. Psychiatry and Neurology, Am. Bd. Neurol. Surgery. Intern Bklyn. Hosp., 1942-43, asst. resident in surgery, 1947-48; resident in pathology Kings County Hosp., Bklyn., 1946-47; fellow in neurol. surgery Mayo Found., U. Minn.-Rochester, 1948-51; practice medicine specializing in neurol. surgery Rochester, N.Y., 1951—; asst. prof. anatomy U. Rochester Sch. Medicine and Dentistry, 1961-68, clin. sr. instr. neurol. surgery, 1962-71, clin. asst. prof., 1971—; chmn. dept. neuroscis., div. neurol. surgery St. Mary's Hosp., Rochester, 1951-83, pres. med. adv. bd., 1972-75; cons. in neurosurgery to various hosps., 1951—. Vol. physician St. Mary's Hosp., Rochester, 1987—; mem. adv. bd. mil. pers. supplies com. on helmets NRC, 1972-78. Assoc. editor Bull. Polish Med. Sci. and History, 1963-67; mem. editorial bd. Bull. of the Monroe County Med. Soc., 1957-79, chmn., 1967-73, editor, 1976-79; contbr. articles on neurology to med. jours. Mem. parents adv. coun. U. Rochester, 1966-69, adv. bd. Alliance Coll., Cambridge Springs, Pa., 1967-70; sec. med. adv. bd. St. Mary's Hosp., Rochester, 1970-72, pres. med. adv. bd. and med. and dental staff, 1972-75, med. adv. bd., 1975-82; served to capt. U.S. Army, 1943-46. Recipient Vincentian award St. Mary's Hosp., 1989. Mem. N.Y. State Med. Soc., Monroe County Med. Soc. (editor bull. 1967-73, 76-79), Am. Assn. Neurol. Surgeons, N.Y. State Neurosurg. Soc., Rochester Acad. Medicine (Paine prize 1952, award of merit 1988), Am. Acad. Neurology, Am. Assn. Med. Systems and Informatics, Congress Neurol. Surgeons, Catholic Physicians Guild (pres. 1956-57, 86-87), Cath. Medical Assn., Nat. Med. and Dental Assn., Polish Inst. Arts and Scis. (med. sect.), Am. Med. Writers Assn., AMA, N.Y. Acad. Scis., AAAS, Am. Heritage Soc., Polish Med. Alliance, Polish Am. Hist. Assn., Am. Physicians Art Assn., Alumni Assn. Mayo Found., Am. Philatelic Soc., Polonus Philatelic Soc., Sigma Xi. Roman Catholic. Home: Rochester, NY. Died Feb. 8, 2003.

BUCHINSKY, CHARLES See BRONSON, CHARLES

BUCK, ANNE MARIE, library director, consultant; b. Birmingham, Ala., Apr. 12, 1939; d. Blaine Alexander and Marie Reynolds (McGeorge) Davis; m. Evan Buck, June 17, 1961 (div. Apr. 1977); children: Susan Elizabeth Buck Rentko, Stephen Edward. BA, Wellesley (Mass.) Coll., 1961; MLS, U. Ky., 1977. Bus. mgr. Charleston (W.Va.) Chamber Music Soc., 1972-74; dir. Dunbar (W.Va.) Pub. Libr., 1974-76; tech. reference libr. AT&T Bell Labs., Naperville, Ill., 1977-79, group supr. libr. Reading, Pa., 1979-83, group supr. support svcs. North Andover, Mass., 1983; dir. libr. network Bell Communications Rsch. (Bellcore), Morristown, N.J., 1983-89, dir. human resources planning Livingston, N.J., 1989-91; univ. libr. N.J. Inst. Tech., Newark, 1991-95, Calif. Inst. of Tech., Pasadena, from 1995. Adj. prof. Rutgers U., New Brunswick, N.J., 1989-90; instr. U. Wis., Madison, 1988-90; v.p. Engring. Info. Found., N.Y.C., 1994—; mem. Engring. Info. Inc. (bd. dirs.), Castle-Point-on-the-Hudson, Hoboken, N.J., 1988-98; spkr. profl. assn. confs., 1982—; libr. cons. North Port (Fla.) Area Libr., 1990-91; co-chair Caltech Conf. on Scholarly Comm., 1997. Mem. editorial adv. bd. Highsmith Press, 1991-97; contbr. articles to profl. jours. Sect. mgr. United Way of Morris County, Cedar Knolls, N.J., 1984-95; advisor Family Svc. Transitions Coun., Morristown, 1987-90; mem. local svcs. and programs com. San Gabriel Valley (Calif.) United Way, 1998-2000; libr. trustee Lisle (Ill.) Pub. Libr. Dist., 1978-80; bd. dirs. Kanawha County Bicentennial Commn., Charleston, W.Va., 1974-76; personnel com., denominational affairs com., Neighborhood Ch., Pasadena, Calif., 1996-2002; mem. Carnegie Mellon U. Librs. adv. bd., 1999—. Recipient Vol.'s Gold award United Way, 1991, Disting. Alumna award U. Ky. Sch. Libr. and Info. Sci., 1996. Mem. ALA (Grolier Nat. Libr. Week grantee 1975), Am. Soc. Info. Sci. and Tech. (chpt. chmn. 1987-89, Chpt. of Yr. award 1988, treas. 1992-95, chair Cretsos Leadership Award jury 1999-2001), Conf. Bd. Inc. (chmn. info. svcs. adv. coun. 1987-89), Spl. Libr. Assn., Am. Soc. Engring. Edn., Archons of Colophon, Indsl. Tech. Info. Mgrs. Group, Women in Engring. Programs and Advocates Network, Wellesley Coll. Alumni Assn. (class rep. 1986-91), N.J. Wellesley Club (regional chmn. 1986-89, corr. sec. 1994-95), Pasadena Wellesley Club (program chmn. 1999-2002), Rotary, Beta Phi Mu. Unitarian Universalist. Avocations: choral singing, travel, photography. Home: Pasadena, Calif. Died Apr. 2, 2003.

BUCK, RICHARD FORDE, physicist; b. Enterprise, Kans., Dec. 8, 1921; s. Charles Fay and Ruth (Scott) N.; m. Harriet J. Ojers, June 4, 1944; children: David R., Janet H., Paul S., Bryan T., Neal A., Daniel C. BS in Physics, U. Kans., 1943; MS in Physics, Okla. State U., 1955. Registered profl. engr., Okla. Cereal chemist Flour Mills Am., Kansas City, Mo., 1940-41; application engr. Tung-Sol Lamp Works, Newark, N.J., 1946-48; from instr. to assoc. prof. physics Okla. State U., Stillwater, 1948-76, assoc. prof. tech., 1976-84, prof. emeritus, from 1984. From engr. to lab. dir. Rsch. Found. Electronics Lab., Stillwater, 1948-76; dir. electronics lab. div. engring., tech. and architecture, Stillwater, 1976-84; cons. to USAF, NASA, various comml. mfrs. in aerospace industry, 1954-84. Founder, life bd. mem. Sheltered Workshop for Payne County, Okla., 1969—; past pres., life bd. mem. Stillwater Group Homes, 1980—; past chmn. bd. 1st Christian Ch., Stillwater, 1950—. 1st lt. U.S. Army, 1942-46, ETO. Republican. Home: Stillwater, Okla. Died Aug. 15, 2000.

BUDGE, HAMER HAROLD, mutual fund company executive; b. Pocatello, Idaho, Nov. 21, 1910; m. Jeanne Keithly, Aug. 30, 1941; 1 dau., Kathleen. Student, Coll. of Idaho, 1928-30; AB, Stanford U., 1933; LLB, U. Idaho, 1936. Bar: Idaho 1936. Pvt. practice, Boise, 1936-42, 46-51; mem. U.S. Ho.of Reps. from 2nd Idaho dist., 1951—61; dist. judge Boise, 1961-64; commr. SEC, 1964-69, chmn., 1969-71; pres., chmn. Investors Mut., Inc., Investors Stock Fund, Inc., Investors Selective Fund, Inc., Investors Variable Payment Fund, Inc., IDS New Dimensions Fund, Inc., IDS Progressive Fund, Inc., IDS Growth Fund, Inc., IDS Bond Fund, Inc., IDS Cash Met Fund Inc., Mpls., 1971-78; also bd. dirs., 1971-86. Mem. Idaho Legislature, 1939, 41, 49, majority floor leader; mem. 82d-86th Congresses from 2d Dist. Idaho, mem. rules, appropriations and interior coms.; Bd. dirs. Salvation Army. Served to lt. comdr. USNR, 1942-45. Mem. Am., Idaho bar assns., Sigma Alpha Epsilon. Republican. Mem. Ch. of Jesus Christ of Latter-day Saints. Clubs: Burning Tree. Home: Scottsdale, Ariz. Died July 22, 2003.

BUEHNER, DONALD FRANCIS, family physician; b. Mt. Vernon, Ind., Sept. 11, 1918; s. Sylvester Henry and Anna (Engelhart) B.; m. Lucille Margaret Kollker, Dec. 31, 1941 (dec. May 1973); children: Donald C., Timothy K, Rebecca Buehner Conley, Lucinda Buehner Barkley, Nicholas J.; m. Jeanne McPherson Knight, Nov. 12, 1976. AB, Wabash Coll., 1941; MD, St. Louis U., 1950. Diplomate Am. Bd. Family Physicians. Intern Protestant Deaconess Hosp., Evansville, Ind., 1950-51; practice family medicine Evansville, from 1951; mem. staff St. Mary's Med. Ctr., pres. staff, 1959. Pres. Med. Arts Bldg., Inc., Evansville. Served with AUS, 1942-45. Fellow Am. Acad. Family Physcians; mem. AMA (Physicians Recognition award), Ind. Med. Assn., Ind. Acad. Family Physicians (1st dist. pres. 1968), Beta Theta Pi. Clubs: Rolling Hills Country (Newburgh, Ind.). Roman Catholic. Avocation: golf. Home: Evansville, Ind. Deceased.

BUFFET, BERNARD, painter; b. Paris, July 10, 1928; s. Charles Buffet and Blanche-Emma Colombe; m. Annabelle Schwob, 1958; 3 children. Student, Lycée Carnot, Ecole Nat. Supéeure Beau Ar. Shows: ann. exhbn. Galerie Drouant-David, 1949-56, Galerie David & Garnier, 1957-67, Galerie Maurice Garnier, 1968—; retrospective exhbns., Paris, 1958, Berlin, 1958, Belgium, 1959, Tokyo, 1963, Musée d'Unterlinden, 1969, Wierger Deurne, Holland, 1977, Musée Postal, Paris, 1978, Zurich, Switzerland, 1983, Toulouse, France, 1985, Musée Pouchkine, Moscou, Musée de l'Ermitage, Saint Pétersbourg, 1991, Château de Chenonceau et Musée Gustave Courbet, Ornans, 1993. Documenta Halle, Kassel, 1994; Bernard Buffet Museum, Japan, 1973—; illustrator books, engraver, lithographer and state designer; mem. Acad. des Beaux-Arts, 1974—. Decorated officer Légion d'honneur; officier Ordre des Arts et des Lettres; recipient grand prix de la Critique, 1948. Died Oct. 4, 1999.

BUFFKINS, ARCHIE LEE, television executive; b. Memphis, Mar. 30, 1934; s. John and Ada (Stittiams) B.; div.; 1 child, LeRachel Harombe. BS, Jackson State U., 1956; MA, Columbia, 1961, EdD, 1963; postgrad. research, Harvard U., summer 1972; postgrad. study, July 1994; postgrad. research, Oxford U., summer 1972, U. Amsterdam, summer 1972, Tel-Aviv U., 1973-74, U. Maine, 1970-71, Chgo. Conservatory, summer 1956. Instr. div. band music Ft. Ord (Calif.) Mil. Band Sch., 1957-58; instr., chmn. div. humanities Morristown (Tenn.) Coll., 1958-59; asst. prof., dir. freshman studies, div. fine arts Jackson (Miss.) State U., 1960-61; assoc. prof., head dept. music Ky. State U., Frankfort, 1963-66; prof., dir. grad. research in music, dept. music and fine arts Tex. So. U., Houston, 1966-68; prof., chmn. dept. music R.I. Coll., Providence, 1968-70; exec. asst. to chancellor U. Maine Eight-Campus System, Portland, 1970-71; chancellor U. Md., Eastern Shore, Princess Anne, 1971-75; asst. dean grad. studies U. Md. (College Park Campus), 1975-79; pres. Nat. Commn. on Cultural Diversity, Kennedy Center, 1979-85, dir. Office Cultural Diversity, 1985-93; cons. prodr. Kennedy Ctr., 1992-93; sr. v.p. broadcasting Md. Pub. TV, Owings Mills, from 1993, interim pres., CEO, 1995-97, sr. v.p. strategic devel., rsch., 1997-99; v.p. corp. affairs Sinclair Broadcast Group, Inc., Cockeysville, MD, 1999-2001; pres. Legacy of Learning-Corp., Baltimore, from 2001. Commr. higher edn. Afro-Am. Edn. Assn. in R.I., 1968-71; dir. Conf. on Black Students and Higher Edn. in R.I., R.I. Coll., 1969, Conf. on Higher Edn. and Urban Setting, Boston, 1969, Md. Pub. Broadcasting Commn., 1986-93; coordinator Conf. on Afro-Am. Studies and High Sch. Curriculum, U. Maine, 1971; chmn. Nat. Black Think Tank, 1976; pres. John F. Kennedy Center Nat. Commn. on Blacks in the Arts; Chief adminstr. Free Urban Edn. Center, Houston, 1966-68; dir. Acad. Tutorial Inst. in Black Community of Houston, 1966-68, Black Fine Arts Festival, 1966; exec. dir. Eastern div. Council on Afro-Am. Studies, Boston, 1968-71; chmn. exptl. curriculum com. Gov.'s Sch. for Gifted in Arts, Providence, 1968, bd. dirs., 1969-70; chmn. ednl. policy com., bd. dirs. Nat. Sch. Vol. Program, Inc., N.Y.C., 1968-70; chmn. edn. task force (Portland Model Cities Project), 1970-71; founder, dir. Center for Exptl. Studies in Higher Edn. Adminstrn., Portland, 1970-71; sr. adviser Nat. Accrediting Assn. for Afro-Am. Programs, N.Y.C., 1968-71; mem. U.S. Nat. Adv. Council on Adult Edn., 1974-79; chmn. Nat. Task Force on Adult Edn. and Urban Policy, 1977, Nat. Black Music Colloquium and Competition, 1978, Md. Black Congress on Higher Edn.; coordinator Black Higher Edn. Caucus of U. Md. System; chmn. Nat. Task Force on Urban Policy and Adult Edn.; chmn. exec. council Regional Research and Clearinghouse Network on Minorities and Grad. Edn.; chmn. Inter-Instnl. Task Force on Pluralism, 1990-95; mem. Gov. Info. Tech. Bd., Md., 1995—; appt. by Md. Gov. to Md. Commn. for Celebration 2000, 1997, bd. dirs. Safe Waterways in Md. Foundn. (SWIM), 2000—. Producer: Tribute to Historically Black Colls. and Univs, 1980, White House/Kennedy Center Jazz Salute to Lionel Hampton, White House Phase I, Kennedy Center Concert Hall Phase II, 1981; appeared with, Monterey Symphony Orch., Bach Festival Orch., Columbia U. Orch., Riverside Symphony Orch., Waukegan Community Orch., Tchrs. Coll. Concert Wind Ensemble, Ft. Ord Symphonic Concert Band, San Jose Woodwind Ensemble, Memphis String and Woodwind Chamber Ensemble.; co-producer: television series Tell It Like It Is, Community Service Television Project, Houston, 1967; Author: An Intellectual Approach to Musical Understanding, 1965, Philosophical Thoughts of a University Scholar, 1973, Arts Advocacy: The Economic Impact of the Arts in an Age of Austerity, Parts I and II; mem. bd. advisers, bd. dirs.: Urban Concerns mag; contbr. articles to profl. jours.; Composer: The Night Is Dark, 1967, Trio in A Minor, 1967, Mass, 1967, Integrity: Tone Poem for String Orchestra, 1968, Symphony For Tomorrow, 1969, Melodies For A Soprano, 1969, String Quartet No. 2, 1972, Sonata For Violin and Piano, 1972, Suite For Violin and Piano, 1972, Sonatina for Violin and Piano (for Sanford Allen), 1980, others. Bd. dirs. Eastern Shore Heart Assn., Salisbury, Md., R.I. Council on Arts, R.I. Philharmonic Orch., Internat. Econ. Devel. Corp., 1969-70, Afro-Art Center, Inc., 1968-70, Maine Savs. Bank, Center for Experiments in Higher Edn., Houston, 1967-70; trustee Peninsula Gen. Hosp., Salisbury, Md., 1970-76, Portland Symphony Orch., 1968-70; mem. exec. bd. Afro-Am. Soc., N.Y.C., 1966-70, New Eng. States Coll. Assn. Music Faculties, Plymouth, N.H., 1968-70, Delmarva council Boy Scouts Am., Wilmington, Del., 1970-76; mem. corp. bd. Edn. Devel. Center, Inc., Newton, Mass., 1970-72, Peoples Savs. Bank & Trust, Providence, 1968-70; mem. exec. bd. Nat. Christian Leadership Conf. for Israel, 1970-75; mem. Nat. Arts Evaluation Panel for Minority Programs, 1970-80; bd. dirs. Afro-Am. Museums Assn., Washington, 1980-95; mem. adv. bd. D.C. Youth Chorale Assn., 1981—, Prince George's Performing Arts, 1987-95; mem. nat. task force on anti-Semitic incidents Anti-Defamation League, N.Y.C., 1980-81; mem. nat. steering com. Martin Luther King Holiday, Washington, 1980-95; mem. planning com. Nat. Black Coll. Day, 1981—; mem. Com. for a Free World, N.Y.C., 1981—, The Jazz Philharmonic Orch., 1987—; mem. exec. com. Coalition for Strategic Stability in Middle East, Washington, 1981—; Am. chmn. FUBA: South African Sch. of the Arts, 1986; bd. trustees Md. Citizens for Arts, 1995; bd. dirs. Gordon Ctr. for Performing Arts at Jewish Cmty. Ctr., 1994—; dist. chmn. Balt. Trailblazers-Boy Scouts Am., 1994-99, bd. dirs. Balt. coun., 2000—; trustee St. Mary's Coll. Md., 2000—. Served with U.S. Army, 1956-58. Recipient Young Classical Musician award Memphis Music Soc., 1952; Black Intellectual Leadership award Houston, 1967; Disting. Alumni award Jackson State U., 1973; Nat. Cultural Recognition award Tuskegee, Ala., 1981; named to Mid-Eastern Athletic Conf. Hall of Fame Durham, N.C., 1981 Mem. Md. Assn. for Higher Edn. (chmn. panel adminstrv. affairs 1973), Mid. States Assn. Colls. and Secondary Schs. (evaluation bd. 1972-96), Am. Coun. on Edn., Nat. Assn. State Univs. and Land-Grant Colls., NAACP (exec. bd. Prince George's chpt. 1979-86, chmn. edn. com. 1980-86, Md. edn. com. 1985-87). Home: College Park, Md. Deceased.

BULL, A. VIVIEN, foreign language educator; b. Torquay, Eng., Nov. 25, 1921; came to U.S., 1946; d. Reginald Bennett and Clarice (Lord) Seaton; m. Malcolm Stirling Bull, July 8, 1944 (dec. May 1967); children: Tony, Christopher, Pamela, Julian, Nicholas, Dana. BA in French, Cambridge U., Eng., 1942; MA in French, U. N.Mex., 1973, PhD in French and Latin, 1976. Lectr. Calif. State U., San Bernardino, 1976-80, asst. prof., 1980-83, assoc. prof., 1983-86, prof. dept. fgn. langs., from 1986. Author: A Vous de Choisir, 2d rev. edit., 1985. Danforth fellow Danford Assocs., 1979. Mem. Modern and Classical Langs. Assn. So. Calif. (jour. editor 1978-85), Calif. Classical Assn. (jour. co-editor 1983—), Soc. for 18th Century Studies, Western Soc. for 18th Century Studies, South-Cen. Soc. for 18th Century Studies. Clubs: Tennis (Albuquerque) (bd. dirs. 1957-60). Episcopalian. Avocation: travel. Home: Albuquerque, N.Mex. Deceased.

BULLOCK, J(AMES) ROBERT, judge; b. Provo, Utah, Dec. 16, 1916; s. James A. and Norma (Poulton) B.; m. Ethel Hogge, Aug. 29, 1949; children: James Robert Jr., C. Scott, David A., Steven H. BS, Utah State U., 1938; JD with honors, George Washington U., 1942. Bar: U.S. Ct. Appeals (D.C. cir.) 1942, Utah 1946, Colo. 1946, U.S. Supreme Ct. 1969. Ptnr. Aldrich, Bullock & Nelson, Provo, 1950-73; judge 4th Dist. Ct. Utah, 1973-85; sr. judge Dist. Cts. Utah, from 1985, chmn. bd. sr. judges, 1988-92. Mem. Utah Jud. Coun., 1973-83, chief judge, 1981-83. Mem. Utah State Ho. of Reps., 1963-67; mem. Utah Constn. Revision Commn., 1969-76, vice chmn., 1974-76. Comdr. USN, 1941-46, ETO, PTO. Mem. ABA, Utah Bar Assn. (pres. 1972-73, Judge of the Yr. 1983), Am. Inns of Ct. (charter), Riverside Country Club, Rotary (pres. 1958-59), Order of Coif, Phi Delta Phi. Avocation: golf. Deceased.

BUNIM, MARY-ELLIS, television producer; b. Northampton, Mass., July 9, 1946; d. Frank Roberts and Roslyn Dena (LaMontagne) Paxton; m. Robert Eric Bunim, Jan. 31, 1971 (div. 2000); 1 dau., Juliana. Pres. Bunim-Murray Prodns., L.A., 1988—2004. Exec. prodr. series Search for Tomorrow, CBS-TV, 1976-81, As the World Turns, CBS-TV, 1981-84, Santa Barbara, NBC-TV, 1984-86, syndicated Crime Diaries, ABC-TV series Loving, 1989-90, FBC series American Families, 1990; co-creator, exec. prodr. MTV series The Real World, 1992-2004, Road Rules, 1995-2004, Real World, Road Rates Challence, 1999—, Making the Band, 2000—, NBC spl. Friends and Lovers, 1994, NBC spl. High School Reunion: Class of '86, 1996, (ABC pilot) Catch Me If You Can, 1998, (ABC pilot) Detroit Receiving, 1999, (CBS movie) Personally Yours, 2000, Fox's Love Cruise, 2001, Fox's Girl Next Door: The Search For A Playboy Playmate, 2002, syndicated series Starting Over, 2003—, (feature film) The REal Cancun, 2003, (VH1 series) Born to Diva, 2003. Died Jan. 29, 2004.

BUNJA, ALEX R. nurse anesthetist; b. Johnstown, Pa., Feb. 17, 1924; s. Michael and Mary (Horania) B. Diploma, Pa. Hosp. Sch. Nursing, Phila., 1949, Grad. Hosp. U. Pa., 1956; AA, Golden West Coll., Huntington Beach, Calif., 1982. Cert. nurse anesthetist. Anesthetist Fresno (Calif.) Anesthesia Group; pvt. practice as nurse anesthetist Calif. Vol. local chpt. ARC; singer ch. choir. Served to sgt. U.S. Army, PTO. Mem. Am. Assn. Nurse Anesthetists. Home: Northridge, Calif. Died July 4, 2001.

BURACK, SYLVIA KAMERMAN, retired editor, publisher; b. Dec. 16, 1916; d. Abraham and Augusta (Chermak) Kamerman; m. Abraham S. Burack, Nov. 28, 1940 (dec.); children: Elizabeth Biller Burack Chapman, Susan Burack Finer, Ellen J.B. Burack Toker. BA magna cum laude, Smith Coll., 1938; LittD (hon.), Boston U., 1985. Editor, pub. (plays) The Drama Mag. for Young People, 1978-99, The Writer Mag., 1978-1999; ret., 1999. Editor: Little Plays for Little Players, 1952, Blue Ribbon Plays for Girls, 1955, Blue Ribbon Plays for Graduation, 1957, A Treasury of Christmas Plays, 1958; Children's Plays from Favorite Stories, 1959, Fifty Plays for Junior Actors, 1966, Fifty Plays for Holidays, 1969, Dramatized Folk Tales of the World, 1971, On Stage for Christmas, 1978, Christmas Play Favorites for Young People, 1982, Holiday Plays Round the Year, 1983, Plays of Black Americans, 1987, 88, Patriotic and Historical Plays for Young People, 1987, Plays from Favorite Folk Tales, 1987, The Big Book of Comedies, 1989, The Big Book of Christmas Plays, 1988, The Big Book of Holiday Plays, 1990, The Big Book of Folktale Plays, 1991, Plays of Great Achievers, 1992, The Big Book of Dramatized Classics, 1993, The Big Book of Large-Cast Plays, 1995, The Big Book of Skits, 1996, 30 Plays from Favorite Stories, 1997, (adult) Writing the Short Short Story, 1942, Book Reviewing, 1978, The Writer's Handbook, 2000 and annually, Writing and Selling Fillers, Light Verse, and Short Humor, 1982, Writing and Selling the Romance Novel, 1983, Writing Mystery and Crime Fiction, 1985, How to Write and Sell Mystery Fiction, 1990, How to Write and Sell Your Article, Writing for Children and Young Adults, 2000. Mem. Brookline Sch. Com., 1949-69, Mass. Bd. Higher Edn., 1973-75; fellow Mass. Hist. Soc. Libr.; trustee Mass. State Coll. Sys., 1971-75, chmn., 1974-75; trustee U. Mass., 1975-81, Max C. Rosenfeld Scholarship Fund; mem. PEN Am. Ctr. Recipient Distin. Svc. award Brookline Rotary Club, 1973, Freedom Found. award, 1988, Smith Coll. medal, 1995, Raven award Mystery Writers Am., 1998; Sylvia K. Burack Libr., Brookline H.S. named in her honor. Mem. Nat. Book Critics Cir., LWV, Friends of Libr. at Boston U. (pres. 1981-83, bd. dirs. 1991—), English-Speaking Union (bd. dirs. Boston br. 1994-98), Phi Beta Kappa. Home: Brookline, Mass. Died Feb. 14, 2003.

BURCHETT, LOWELL ALAN, science association administrator, consultant; b. Seiling, Okla., Sept. 19, 1933; s. Leslie Dean and Elda Faith (Perkins) B.; m. Lois Merlene Link, Sept. 1, 1951; children: Delores, Clyde, Daryl, Joyce, Tina. BS in Agrl. Edn., Okla. State U., 1956; MS in Agronomy, Kans. State U., 1970. Tchr. vocat.-agr. Highland (Kans.) Rural High Sch., 1956-60; agrl. agt. Doniphan County, Troy, Kans., 1960-61, Jackson County, Holton, Kans., 1961-65; supt. North Cen. Kans. Experiment Fields Kans. Agrl. Experiment Sta., Belleville, 1965-73; exec. dir. Kans. Crop Improvement Assn., Manhattan, from 1973. Trustee, advisor Manhattan Christian Coll., 1965—; cons. Am. White Wheat Producers Assn., Atchison, Kans., 1987—. Contbr. articles to Farm Jour., Solutions mag., Furrow mag., Agri-Fin.; author, co-author articles to Jour. of Applied Seed Prodn., Cropsci., Agronomy Jour.; editor Seed Source, KSDI Newsletter, 1973-91. Del. Kans. Com. of Farm Orgns., Topeka, 1973-91. Capt. inf. U.S. Army, 1956-68. Mem. Am. Soc. Agronomy, Crop Sci. Soc. Am., Sigma Xi. Republican. Mem. Christian Ch. Achievements include research in conservation tillage programs for grain sorghum. Died Dec. 13, 2001.

BURCKHALTER, JOSEPH HAROLD, chemistry educator; b. Columbia, S.C., Oct. 9, 1912; s. Edward Wilson Burckhalter and Elizabeth Belle Strain; m. Virginia Ruth Feikert, July 10, 1943 (div. Mar. 1989); children: David Liggett, Robert Edward, Jane Ellen; m. Julia Riddick Johnston, Oct. 7, 1989. BS in Chemistry, U. S.C., 1934; MS in Chemistry, U. Ill., 1938; PhD in Chemistry, U. Mich., 1942. Sr. rsch. chemist Parke, Davis & Co., Detroit, 1942-47; assoc. prof., pharm. chemistry U. Kans., Lawrence, 1947-50, prof., chmn. pharm. chemistry, 1950-60; Fulbright prof. Tuebingen U., Germany, 1955-56; prof., chmn. medicinal chemistry U. Mich., Ann Arbor, 1960-83; prof. pharm. chemistry Nat. Def. Med. Ctr., Taiwan, 1974-75; rsch. prof., med. chemistry Fla. Inst. Technology, Melbourne, 1983; ret., 1983. Cons. NIH, Bethesda, Md., 1956-82, Parke, Davis & Co., Detroit, 1947-60, The Upjohn Co., Kalamazoo, 1960-70. Author: (book) Essentials of Medicinal Chemistry, 1976; patentee in field. Inducted into Nat. Inventors Hall of Fame, Akron, Ohio, 1995; recipient Am. Innovator award U.S. Patent and Trademark Office, Washington, 1995, Disting. Alumni awards U. S.C., U. Ill., 1997, 99; decorated Order of Palmetto, S.C., 1996. Mem. Am. Pharm. Assn. Found. (recipient First Rsch. Achievement award med. chemistry 1962), Am. Chem. Soc. Achievements include patents for fluorescent antibody labeling agents, FITC and RITC; research in marketing synthetic drugs made with formaldehyde. Avocations: reading, tennis, bridge, dance, crossword puzzles. Home: Melbourne, Fla. Died May 9, 2004.

BURDITT, GEORGE MILLER, JR., lawyer; b. Chgo., Sept. 21, 1922; s. George Miller and Flora Winifred (Hardie) B.; m. Barbara Helen Stenger, Feb. 17, 1945 (dec. Feb. 2001); children: Betsey Burditt Blessing, George M., Deborah, Barbara Burditt Perry. BA, Harvard U., 1944, LLB, 1948. Bar: Ill. 1949, D.C. 1981, U.S. Dist. Ct. (no. dist.) Ill. 1952, U.S. Ct. Appeals (7th cir.) 1961, U.S. Ct. Appeals (D.C. cir.) 1962, U.S. Ct. Appeals (4th cir.) 1974, U.S. Supreme Ct. 1974, U.S. Ct. Appeals (2d cir.) 1978, U.S. Ct. Appeals (8th cir.) 1988. With law dept. Swift & Co., Chgo., 1948-54; ptnr. Chadwell & Kayser and predecessors, Chgo., 1955-69, Burditt and Radzius, Chgo., 1969-98, Bell, Boyd and Lloyd, Chgo., from 1998. Adj. prof. Northwestern U. Sch. Law, 1967-97; gen. counsel Food and Drug Law Inst.; dir. Gerber Products, 1973-93. Contbr. articles to profl. jours. Mem. Ill. State Ho. of Reps., 1965-72, asst. majority leader, 1971-72; Rep. candidate U.S. Senate, 1974. 2d lt. USAAF, 1943-45. Named Outstanding Legislator, Better Govt. Assn., 1969, 71; recipient Presdl. award Cook County Bar Assn., 1981, Defender of Justice award Nat. Conf. Christians & Jews, 1992; named to Ill. Basketball Hall of Fame, 2000, LTHS Hall of Fame, 2000. Mem. ABA, Ill. State Bar Assn., D.C. Bar Assn., Chgo. Bar Assn. (pres. 1980-81), N.Y. Bar Assn., Fed. Bar Assn., Met. Bar Leaders Caucus (pres. 1981-82), Harvard Law Sch. Assn. (pres. 1988-90), Harvard Law Soc. Ill. (pres. 1980-81), Union League Club, Econ. Club, Mid-Day Club, Crystal Downs Country Club, Law Club Chgo. (pres. 1980-81). Home: Chicago, Ill. Deceased.

BURELLI RIVAS, MIGUEL ANGEL, Venezuelan government official; b. July 8, 1922; Student, U. de Los Andes, Bogotá, U. Ctrl. de Venezuela y de Ecuador, U. Nat. de Bogotá, U. de Madrid, U. di Firenze. Pre-seminary prof. polit. sociology, chief prof. mining and agrarian legislation Faculty of Law, U. de Los Andes, Bogotá; chief prof. humanities I and II Faculty of Civil Engring., dir. univ. culture, founder sch. of humanities, founder-dir. univ. revs., bibliotheca, universitas emeritensis; polit. dir. Ministry of the Interior; dir.- gen. Ministry of Fgn. Affairs; mem. Venezualan Supreme Electoral Coun., 1961; min. of justice Govt. of Venezuela, 1964-65, amb. to Columbia, 1965-67, amb. to U.K., 1967-69, amb. to U.S., 1974-76, min. of fgn. affairs, 1994—99. Died Oct. 22, 2003.

BURG, ANTON BEHME, chemist, retired educator; b. Dallas City, Ill., Oct. 18, 1904; s. Frank Winchester and Sadie Quinton (Hornby) B. BS, U. Chgo., 1927, MS, 1928, PhD, 1931. Researcher Kimberley-Clark Co., Neenah, Wis., 1928-29; rsch. asst. U. Chgo., 1929-31, instr., 1931-39; from asst. prof. to prof. U. So. Calif., L.A., 1939-74, dept. head, 1940-50, prof. emeritus, 1974—2003. Cons. in field. Contbr. numerous articles to profl. jours. Fellow AAAS; mem. Am. Chem. Soc. (Mallinckrodt award Tolman medal 1969), AAUP, Sigma Xi, Phi Beta Kappa. Home: Los Angeles, Calif. Died Nov. 19, 2003.

BURG, H. PETER, financial executive; b. Akron; BS, MBA, U. Akron; postgrad., Harvard U. Fin. analyst trainee Ohio Edison, assoc. fin. analyst, econ. analyst, dir. fin. studies, treas., 1974, v.p., 1985, sr. v.p., CFO, 1989, FirstEnergy Corp., pres., COO, 1998-99, pres. & CEO, 1999-00; chmn. & CEO FirstEnergy Corp, Akron, OH, from 2000. Interim pres. Pa. Power, 1994-95; pres. Ohio Edison, The Illuminating Co., Toledo Edison Co.; mem. fin. com. Edison Elec. Inst.; bd. dirs. Energy Ins. Mutual, Key Bank. Bd. dirs. Summit County chpt. ARC; past pres. U. Akron Alumni Assn.; past bd. dirs. Akron Child Guidance Ctr.; active various coms. United Way. Died Jan. 13, 2004.

BURGESS, MYRTLE MARIE, retired lawyer; b. Brainerd, Minn., May 3, 1921; d. Charles Dana and Mary Elzaida (Thayer) Burgess. BA, San Francisco State U., 1947; JD, Hastings Coll. Law, 1950. Bar: Calif. 1951. Pvt. practice law, San Francisco, 1951-52, Reedley, Calif., 1952—; judge pro tem Fresno County Superior Ct., 1974-77; now owner/operator Hotel Burgess. Bd. dirs. Reedley Indsl. Site Devel. Found., 1970-81; dir., 2d v.p. Kings Canyon unit Calif. Republican Assembly, 1973-75; pres., bd. dirs. Sierra Community Concert Assn., Reedley council Girl Scouts U.S.A., 1955-56, Fresno Cmty. Concert Assn., 1995—; commr. Fresno City-County Commn. Status of Women; bd. dirs., treas. Reedley Downtown Assn., 1983—; bd. dirs. Kinship Program, 1988; bd. dirs., sec. Kings View Found., bd. dirs. Calif. Hotel Motel Assn., 1993—. Recipient award for remodeling and preservation of old bldg. Fresno Hist. Soc., 1975, others. Mem. ABA, Calif. Bar Assn., Fresno County Bar Assn., World Jurist Assn., Am. Trial Lawyers, Reedley C. of C. (bd. dirs. 1958-63, 87-91, Woman of Yr. 1971, Athenian award 1988). Republican. Presbyterian. Clubs: Bus. and Profl. Women's (pres.). Lodge: Order Eastern Star. Deceased.

BURKE, B. MEREDITH, population researcher, writer, bioethicist; b. L.A., Feb. 14, 1947; d. Louis Harold and Sylvia (Roseman) Goldberg. BA in econs., UCLA, 1967; MA in econs., U. So. Calif., 1971; MA, U. Pa., 1973, PhD, 1979. Cons. economist 1st Nat. Bank Boston, 1971-72, World Bank, Washington, 1974, Maseru, Lesotho, 1981; instr. internat. stats. program U.S. Census Bur., Washington, 1977; project dir. United Mine Workers Health and Retirement Funds, Washington, 1977-78; dir. Population Ctr. Nat. Coun. on Aging, Washington, 1980-81; cons. economist Electric Power Rsch. Inst., Calif., 1984-85; rsch. assoc. Stanford Med. Sch., Palo Alto, Calif., 1986; coord. health mgmt. tng. San Jose State U., 1993; coord. mgmt. info. Family Planning Internat. Asst., N.Y.C., 1988-90; coord. health mgmt. tng. San Diego State U., 1987. Med. ethics com. L.A. County Bar Assn., 1988; vis. scholar The Hoover Inst., Stanford U., 1996—97; founder, dir. Lariam Action-U.S.A., 1996—2000; sr. fellow Negative Population Growth, Washington, 1998—2000, Californians for Population Stabilization, from 2001; spkr. and writer in field. Co-author: (book) Prenatal Testing: A Sociological Perspective, 1994, (with Gavin Jones) The Demographic Obstacle to the Attainment of Educational Goals in the Republic of Korea, 1969; opinion writer: The Wall Street Jour., Newsweek, The N.Y. Times, numerous others; contbr. articles and reports to profl. jours. Pres. Nat. Women's Polit. Caucus, San Diego, 1987—88; vice chmn. allocation com. United Way Santa Clara County, Calif., 1984; chair Maternal Child and Adolescent Health Adv. Bd., San Mateo County, Calif., 1986—87; bd. dirs. Girls Club San Diego, 1987—88. Mem.: Sociologists for Women in Soc., Population Assn. Am., Mensa. Democrat. Avocations: writing fiction, jazz singing, photography, matchmaking. Died Dec. 10, 2002.

BURKE, HAROLD DEVERE, retired purchasing specialist; b. Sturgis, Mich., May 2, 1922; s. Oscar and Harriet (Iler) B.; m. Polly L. Fuess, Nov. 27, 1943; children: Virginia Sue Batt, John Robert. Student, Argubright Bus. Coll., Battlecreek, Mich., 1938-40, W.Va. Wesleyan Coll., 1942-43. Purchasing mgr. Kirsch Co., Sturgis, 1940-82. Pres. Southwestern Mich. Purchasing Mgmt., Kalamazoo, 1982, dir. nat. affairs, 1983; fed. sch. rep. St. Joseph County Intermediate Sch., Centreville, Mich., 1984, State of Mich., 1985. Pres. sch. bd. Sturgis Pub. Schs., 1968-72, St. Joseph County Intermediate, 1972-90. Lt. col. USAF, 1942-46, Italy. Decorated Air medal with three clusters, USAF. Mem. Knights of Pythias (supreme chancellor internat. 1988-90, grand chancellor for state 1962-63), Masons, Elks (trustee 1982), Am. Legion (past comdr. 1978), VFW. Republican. Home: White Pigeon, Mich. Deceased.

BURKE, MARY THOMAS, educator; b. Westport, County Mayo, Ireland, Nov. 28, 1928; d. Thomas J. and Anne (McGuire) B. BA, Belmont (N.C.) Abbey Coll., 1962; MA, Georgetown U., 1965; PhD, U. N.C., Chapel Hill, 1968. Elem. tchr. St Patrick's Sch., Charlotte, N.C., 1950-51, St Agnes Sch., Greenport, N.Y., 1951-54; tchr. Charlotte (N.C.) Cath. High Sch., 1954-64; academic dean Sacred Heart Coll., Belmont, N.C., 1967-70; assoc. prof. U. N.C., Charlotte, 1970-75, prof., chmn. human svcs. dept., 1975-99, prof., coord. grad. counseling program, from 1996. Chmn. State Adv. Coun. on Pupil Pers. Svcs., 1972—76; mem. faculty Marshall U., Charlotte, 1999. Co-editor: (with Judith Miranti) Ethical and Value Issues in Counseling, 1992, Counseling: The Spiritual Dimension, 1995. Bd. dirs. McKlenburg chpt. and state divsn. Am. Cancer Soc., 1977-83, treas., 1983-86, crusade chmn., 1986; chairperson United Way, U. N.C., Charlotte, 1974; bd. dirs. St. Joseph Hosp. and St. Joseph's Health Svcs., Asheville, Selwyn Life Ctr., Charlotte, 1986-90; bd. dirs. Nat. Bus. Forms, Greeneville, Tenn., 1973—, asst. sec., treas. bd. dirs., 1975-92, sec., treas., 1992—; trustee Belmont Abbey Coll., 1994—, chair acad. com., mem. exec. com., 1996—; mem. legacy giving bd. United Way of Ctrl. Carolinas, 2000—. Recipient Anti-Defamation award, B'nai B'rith Women, 1978, Ray Thompson Human Rels. award, N.C. Assn. for Non-White Concerns, 1978, WBT Woman of Yr. award, 1979, Ella Stephen Barret Leadership award, 1983, AWO Good of Soc. award, Am. Cancer Soc., 1981, Leadership award, 1988, Faculty Svc. award, Gen. Alumni Assn. U. N.C., 1994, Silver Medalian Humanitarian award, Nat. Conf. Christians and Jews, 1995, Meritorious award, Assn. for Spiritual Ethical and Religious Values in Counseling, 1995, named Excellence in Tchg. award finalist, Nations Bank, 1995, Tchr. Excellence award, 1996, Cal Francis Beatty Humanitarian award, 1997, Counselor of Yr. award, Am. Counseling Assn., 1998, Devoted Svc. award, Metrolina AIDS Project, 2001, Humanitarian award, ECO Found., 2002. Mem. AACD (human rights com. 1992-93), N.C. Pers. and Guidance Assn. (exec. com. 1973-90, editl. bd. jours. 1975-78, pres. Metrolina chpt. 1973-74, state pres.-elect 1980-81, pres. 1981-82, leadership award 1983), N.C. Guidance Assn. (program com. 1974-75), Nat. Cath. Guidance Assn. (state rep. 1974-79), N.C. Assn. Religious and Value Issues in Counseling (chairperson 1974, pres. 1985-86, 93-94, bd. dirs. 1986-94), N.C. Assn. Counselors Educators and Suprs. (pres. 1997—), Am. Pers. and Guidance Assn., Am. Counselor Educators and Suprs. Assn., Assn. Religious Values in Counseling, N.C. Assn. Group Work, N.C. Mental Health Assn., N.C. Sch. Counselors Assn. (Counselor Educator of Yr. award 1975), So. Assn. Counselor Educators and Suprs., Assn. for Religious Values in Counseling (bd. dirs. Metrolina AIDS Project 1989-90, pres. bd., 1990-92, pres.-elect 1989-90, pres. 1990-91, treas. 2000—, Pres.' award 1992), Coun. Accreditation of Counseling and Related Edn. Programs (bd. dirs. 1993—, vice chair 1994-96, chair 1996-2000, ACA liaison to Nat. Bd. Cert. Counselors 1994-97), Phi Delta Kappa, Delta Kappa Gamma, Chi Sigma Iota (pres. 1997-98, Leadership award 1998), Mu Tau Beta (Devoted Svc. award 1994). Deceased.

BURKHARDT, PETER JON, corporate professional; b. Charleston, W.Va., Aug. 19, 1957; s. Orion Percy and Bonita Louis (Huskamp) B.; m. Joanne Frances Cesar, May 2,3 1981 (div. 1989); children: Jason Peter, Alysia Nicole; m. Linda Swain Hilburt, Dec. 28, 1991. Student, S.E. Mo. State U., 1976-77; BA, Ariz. State U., 1980. Coll. rep. Anheuser-Busch Inc., Tempe, Ariz., 1977-80; mgmt. trainee Calgon Corp., St. Louis, 1980, new product researcher, 1980-81; gen. mgr. Tri-Distributors Inc., Lexington, N.C., 1981-83, pres., from 1983. Bd. dirs. Branch Bank & Trust, Lexington, 1984—, N.C. Malt Beverage Inst., Raleigh, N.C., 1987—. Bd. pres. United Way of Davidson County, Lexington, 1984—; bd. dirs. Davidson Alcoholic Care Inc., Lexington, 1984-85, Davidson County Domestic Violence Inc., Lexington, 1987—, Family Life Ctr., Lexington, 1987—, Davidson County Family & Youth Violence Counseling, 1990—. Recipient Gold Wholesaler award Anheuser-Busch Inc., 1984, Ambassador Wholesaler award, 1985, 86, 87, 88, 89, 90, N.C. Wholesaler of the Yr. award, 1989. Mem. Internat. Mgmt. Council, N.C. Beer Wholesalers Assn., nat. Beer Wholesalers Assn., Willow Creek Country, Sapona Country, Elks. Republican. Roman Catholic. Avocations: golf, camping, water skiing, snow skiing. Home: Seattle, Wash. Died Nov. 27, 2000.

BURKOWSKY, MITCHELL ROY, speech and language pathology educator; b. Cooperstown, N.Y., Aug. 11, 1931; s. Edward and Fannie (Gertz) B.; m. Diane Francine Benowitz, June 24, 1956; children: Ruth, Joel, Rena. BA, SUNY, Albany, 1952; PhD, Wayne State U., 1960. Asst. prof. Detroit Inst. Tech., 1959-61; asst. prof., clin. dir. U. N.D., Grand Forks, 1961-65; postdoctoral resident Med. Ctr. U. Fla., Gainesville, 1965-66; asst. prof. Syracuse (N.Y.) U., 1966-72; from assoc. prof. to disting. svc. prof. SUNY, Fredonia, from 1972. Cons. VA Med. Ctr., Buffalo, 1983-92. Author: Teaching American Pronunciation to Foreign Students, 1969; author, editor: Parents' and Teachers' Guide to the Care of Autistic Children, 1970, Orientation to Language and Learning Disorders, 1973; co-author: Contemporary Voice Therapy-Children and Adults, 1987. Mem., pres., bd. visitors N.J. Adam Devel. Ctr., Perrysburg, N.Y., 1978-95. With U.S. Army, 1952-54. Mem. Soc. Preservation and Encouragement of Barbershop Quartet Singing in Am. (office holder), Jamestown Area Swim Ofcls. Avocations: singing, gardening, cooking, antiqueing. Home: Fredonia, NY. Died Mar. 9, 2000.

BURNETT, ANGELA, lawyer; b. Phila., Dec. 19, 1955; d. Thomas Louis and Cassandra Beth (Walker) B. BS, Howard U., 1977; MS, George Washington U., 1979; JD, Georgetown U., 1986. Bar: D.C. 1987. Dictationist, news asst. Reuters, Ltd., Washington, 1977-79; lectr. Howard U., Washington, 1979-80; dir. community affairs Sta. WTTG-TV, Washington, 1980-82; govt. affairs editor Titsch Communications, Washington, 1982-83; policy analyst Nat. Telecommunications and Info. Adminstrn., Washington, 1983-86; atty. FCC, Washington, 1987-90; asst. gen. counsel Info. Industry Assn., Washington, from 1990. Bd. dirs. Big Sisters Met. Washington, 1981-84, Am. Lung Assn., 1987—. Mem. Fed. Comms. Bar Assn., Women's Bar Assn., Am. Women in Radio and TV, Nat. Black Media Coalition. Unitarian Universalist. Home: Washington, DC. Deceased.

BURNETT, HENRY BOWEN, JR., advertising executive; b. Summit, N.J., July 11, 1930; s. Henry Bowen Sr. and Alicia Louella (Broughton) B.; m. Louisa Dawson Patterson, July 12, 1953 (div. 1963); children: Whiteley, Alicia Adams, William Nicholas; m. Gretchen Elna Fall, July 10, 1968. AB in Fine Arts, Harvard U., 1952. Copywriter Dickie-Raymond Inc., Boston, 1957-65, account supr. N.Y.C., 1965-66, dir. spl. projects Boston, 1966-67, creative dir., v.p., dir. west coast ops. L.A., 1969-70; freelance direct mail copywriter Calif., from 1970. V.p., dir., editor Forum Communications Corp., Santa Barbara, Calif., 1971-82. Inventor word game Phlounder; contbr. articles to profl. jours. Adv. bd. mem. Humanitas Internat., Menlo Park, Calif. 1980—; bd. dirs. Nuclear Age Peace Found., Santa Barbara, 1987—. With U.S. Army, 1952-54. Recipient Sweepstakes award Am. Advt. Fed., San Francisco, 1971, Gold awards Folio Mag., Direct Mktg. awards, N.Y.C. 1981, 1985, 1987. Mem. Direct Mktg. Assn. (Gold Mail Box award), Direct Mktg. Creative Guild, Harvard Club of N.Y.C., Am. Philatelic Soc. Democrat. Avocation: stamp collecting/philately. Home: Santa Barbara, Calif. Deceased.

BURNETT, JERROLD J. engineering executive; b. Mt. Pleasant, Tex., May 31, 1931; s. Jerrold J. and Dove Glen (Hamilton) B.; m. Jann Eiland, Jan. 25, 1953; children: James Haynes, Jill. ASEE, U. Tex., Arlington, 1951; BA, Tex. A&M U., 1953; MS, Tex A&M U., Kingsville, 1958; PhD, U. Okla., 1966. Registered profl. engr., Colo. Equipment engr. Southwestern Bell Telephone, Dallas, 1955-57; asst. instr. Tex. A&M U., Kingsville, 1957-58; instr. U. Dallas, 1958-59; rsch. scientist N.Mex. Inst. Mining and Tech., Socorro, 1959-61; assoc. prof., head dept. Northwestern Okla. State U., Alva, 1961-64; program mgr. NSF, Washington, 1977-78; prof. Colo. Sch. Mines, Golden, 1966-86, prof. emeritus, from 1986; mgr. measurement standards lab. King Fahd U. of Petroleum and Minerals, Dhahran, Saudi Arabia, 1989-95. Cons. to industry and govt.; chmn. bd. dirs. The Diversity, Denver, 1973-86. Author numerous sci. and engring. articles. USPHS fellow, 1964-66. Mem. Soc. Am. Mil. Engrs. (bd. dirs.), Colo. Sci. Suprs. Assn. (hon. life), Sigma Xi, Sigma Pi Sigma. Avocations: photography, travel. Died July 21, 2001.

BURNHILL, MICHAEL SETH, obstetrician-gynecologist; b. Bklyn., Mar. 7, 1928; BA, Syracuse U., 1949; MD, U. Vt. Coll. Medicine, 1953. Diplomate Am. Bd. Obstetricians & Gynecologists. Intern New Eng. Med. Ctr. Hosps., Boston, 1953-54; resident ob-gyn. Mt. Sinai Hosp., N.Y.C., 1956-60; hosp. appt. RW Johnson U. Hosp., New Brunswick, N.Y., from 1979; v.p. med. affairs Planned Parenthood Fedn. Am., Inc., N.Y.C., from 1995. Peer reviewer Internat. Jour. Gyn. and Obstets., Obstets. and Gyn., Am. Jour. Obstets. and Gyn. Lt. comdr. USNR, 1956-65. Fellow ACOG; mem. Am. Fertility Soc., Assn. Reproductive Health Profls., Nat. Abortion Fedn. Home: Fort Lauderdale, Fla. Died Aug. 4, 2000.

BURNS, CLARENCE HENRY, mayor of Baltimore; b. Balt., Sept. 13, 1918; s. Clarence Henry Sr. and Selena (Green) B.; m. Edith Phillips, Nov. 5, 1939; 1 child, Cheryl. Mcpl. employee City of Balt., 1949-71; mem., com. chmn. Balt. City Council, 1971-82, v.p., 1977-82, pres., 1982-87; mayor City of Balt., from 1987. V.p. Balt. Legal Aid Bur., 1969-71; chmn. East Balt. Community Orgn., 1971-82; mem. Balt. Met. Area Regional Planning Council, 1982-87; mem. Gov.'s Chesapeake Bay Critical Areas Com., Annapolis, Md., 1984-87. Chmn. exec. bd. Eastside Dem. Orgn., Balt., 1967-87; gen. vice chmn. United Fund Greater Balt. Area, 1974-75; bd. dirs. United Way of Cen. Md.; alt. del. Dem. Nat. Conv., 1976, del., 1980, 84. Served as sgt. USAF, 1943-46. Recipient Community Service award Cen. Md. com. of Sickle Cell Anemia Inc., 1984, Contbns. to Black Econ. Devel. award The Hub Orgn., Balt., 1985, Harry Bard Disting. Citizenship award Community Coll. Balt., 1987, Andrew White medal Loyola Coll., Balt., 1987. Mem. Nat. League Cities, U.S. Conf. Mayors, Am. Legion. Lodges: Optimists, Elks. Democrat. Roman Catholic. Avocations: jazz, family. Home: Baltimore, Md. Died Jan. 12, 2003.

BURRESS, JAMES E. shopping center building executive; b. Tronton, Tenn., June 22, 1924; s. Vernon Ashley and Winnie (Burkett) B.; m. Tiz Sisk, Apr. 21, 1971 (div.); 1 child, Lisa Bell; m. Caroline Singleton; 1 child, James B. BS, Union U., Jaskson, Tenn.; MA, U. Tenn.; Dr. Bus. Adminstrn. (hon., Lambuth Coll., Jackson, Tenn., 1958. Mgr. station Tri-State Bus. Line, Jackson, Tenn., 1958-63; gen. passenger agent So. Bus Line, Alexander, La., 1963-70, v.p. ops., 1970-74; cons. Nat. Cons. Co., Atlanta, 1974-78, v.p. charge operator Jackson, Tenn., 1978-81, pres. br. office, 1981-86, cons. shopping ctr., 1986-88, sr. cons., 1988-89; retired, cons., from 1989. Dir. Tenn. Realty Bd., Nashville, 1987-89; examiner Tenn. Realty Offices, 1988—. Editor: Jackson Realtor, 1988 (distinguished award 1988); co-author: Tennesse Realtor Manual, 1988, asst. editor, 1988. With U.S. Army, 1942. Mem. Trenton C. of C. (pres.), Lions Internat. (man of the yr. 1982), Trenton Lions, Milton Club (dir. 1986-89). Democrat. Baptist. Avocations: golf, boating, travel, fishing. Home: Trenton, Tenn. Deceased.

BURROUGHS, ROBERT CLARK, theatre educator, designer; b. Milw., Mar. 1, 1920; s. S. Dillon and Matta (Smith) B.; m. Patricia Yvon Genematas, Dec. 29, 1951; children: Robert Clark II, Christopher Dillon. BA, Hanover Coll., 1943; MA, Iowa U., 1947; postgrad., Cornell U., 1951-53. Art dir. Tucson Children's Theatre, 1950-70; prof. drama U. Ariz., Tucson, 1947—93, head dept. drama, 1978—93. Chmn. theatre program Nat. Music Camp, Interlochen, Mich., 1958-78; guest dir. Ariz. Theatre Co., Tucson, 1969, 74, 75. Exhibited in group show titled Design Reflections, 1974-75; dir. Imperial Players, Cripple Creek, Colo., 1968-81. Narrator Ann. San Xavier Festival, Tucson, 1958-86; designer Tucson Festival Soc., 1950-54; bd. dirs. Jr. League Children's Series, Tucson, 1952-54, Tucson Med. Ctr. Fund Raiser, 1968. Served to sgt. U.S. Army, 1943-46. Recipient Directing and Design prize Am. Coll. Theatre Festival, 1969, Citation of Merit, Am. Coll. Theatre Festival, 1977; Research grantee U. Ariz. Found., Eng., 1986, Humanities Grants Com., 1986. Mem. Ariz. Theatre Assn., Dramatist Guild Inc., Assn. Communications Adminstrs., Am. Theatre Assn., Ariz. Alliance for Arts Edn. Democrat. Methodist. Avocations: swimming, travel, reading. Home: Tucson, Ariz. Died Sept. 21, 2003.

BURROWS, PAUL A. consumer products executive; Various sr. mgmt. positions Broadway Stores, chief info. officer, 1993-96, Coldwell Banker Corp., L.A.; sr. v.p., chief info. officer ShopKo Stores, Inc., Green Bay, Wis., from 1997. Died Oct. 1, 2003.

BURRUS, W. SPEIGHT, accountant, consultant; b. Engelhard, N.C., Nov. 8, 1937; s. Claud W. and Helene (Gibbs) B.; divorced; children: Kevin Speight, Sabrina Lynn, Charles Swindell, John Korbin. BBA, East Carolina U., 1960. CPA, Va., N.C. Pvt. practice acctg., Chesterfield, Va., 1964-74, Engelhard, from 1974, Pinehurst, N.C. Dir. Elizabeth City (N.C.) Area C. of C., 1972-75, Elizabeth City United Way, 1974-75; pres. Elizabeth City Boys Club, 1975-76. Named Boss of Yr. Bus. and Profl. Womens' Club Elizabeth City, 1978-79. Fellow Am. Inst. CPA's, N.C. Assn. CPA's (bd. dirs. 1978-80, pres. Albemarle-Outer Banks chpt. 1978-79); mem. Pinehurst Bus. Guild. Lodges: Rotary (bd. dirs., treas. Pinehurst club 1985—). Republican. Episcopalian. Avocations: golf, swimming, hunting, fishing. Home: Pinehurst, NC. Deceased.

BURTON, CHARLES HENNING, lawyer; b. Washington, Nov. 25, 1915; s. Charles Henry and Bessie R. (Harrell) B.; m. Mary Sheppard, Sept. 6, 1941; children: Nancy Leigh Burton Wysling, Susan C. Burton Roberts, Mary Ellen Burton Graves, Charles S. Attended, George Washington U., 1937-41; LLB, Am. U., 1936, LLM, 1937. Bar: DC 1936, Md. 1957. Gen. counsel D.C. Unemployment Compensation Bd., 1938-42; mem. firm MacCracken & O'Rourke, Washington, 1946-50; mem. Law Offices Robert Ash, Washington, 1950-56; gen. partner Bauersfeld, Burton, Hendricks and Vanderhoff, Bethesda, Md., from 1956. Ltd. ptnr. A.W.S. Assocs., S & H Assocs.; pres., dir. North Shore Corp., Links, Inc., Charles H. Burton, P.A.; dir. Mattos, Inc., Sisk Mailing Svc. Inc., Sisk Fulfillment, Inc.; gen. counsel Bapt. World Alliance, McLean, Va., 1958, Calvary Bapt. Ch., 1950. Bd. dirs. Jovius Found., Mustard Seed Found., F.W. Harris Found. for Personal Evangelism; trustee Kendall Mission Fund; v.p. Cen. Union Mission; nat. chmn. World Peace Through Law of World Jurist Assn. Comdr. USNR, 1942-46. Fellow Am. Bar Found.; mem. Am. Bar Assn. (editor Young Lawyer 1946-48, nat. sec. Jr. Bar 1949, nat. vice-chmn. 1950, nat. chmn. 1951, ho. of dels. 1952-59), Sigma Chi, Sigma Nu Phi. Clubs: Montgomery County Country. Home: Germantown, Md. Died Dec. 23, 2003.

BURTON, HOWARD ALAN, software engineer; b. Bklyn., May 9, 1951; s. Lawrence and Esther Pearl (Sconduto) B.; m. Rosemary Condino, Sept. 17, 1986. MA, SUNY, Stony Brook, 1974; PhD, St. Louis U., 1978. Rsch. assoc. Md. Psychiat. Rsch. Ctr., U. Md. at Balt. Med. Sch., 1978-81; pres., dir. Syncom, Inc., St. Louis, 1982-84, Synclastic Communications, Inc., Balt., from 1982. Cons. Logicon, Inc., Washington, 1985-88, Gould Ocean Systems Divsn., Balt., 1988, Martin Marietta Ocean Systems Ops., Balt., 1988-89, MCA, Va., 1989-92, Westinghouse ESG, Balt., 1992—. Mem. AAAS, Soc. Neurosci. Home: Annapolis, Md. Died Aug. 22, 2001.

BUSCH, DAVID BRUCE, radiation pathologist; b. Pitts., July 25, 1953; s. Joseph Sherman and Barbara Joy (Ehrman) B. AB, U. Calif., Berkeley, 1974, MA, 1976, PhD, 1980; MD, U. Miami, 1982. Diplomate Am. Bd. of Pathology. Pathology resident U. Wis., Madison, 1982-86; radiation pathologist Armed Forces Inst. of Pathology, Washington, from 1986. Registrar radiation pathology registry Am. Registry of Pathology, Washington, 1986—; diagnostician DNA repair disorders. Contbr. articles to profl. jours. Mem. AAAS, Am. Chem. Soc., Environ. Mutagen Soc. Libertarian. Jewish. Avocations: cycling, science fiction reading, star trek, hiking, rock music. Home: Takoma Park, Md. Died Apr. 12, 2002.

BUSCH, PAUL L. engineering executive; BS in Humanities and Engring., BSCE, MS in Sanitary Engring., MIT. Registered profl. engr. N.Y. Vis. prof. U. N.C.; mentor to M Engring. program Cornell U.; mem. adv. coun. Sch. of Civil and Environ. Engring., U. Cornell, others; mem. NRC Water Sci. and Tch. Bd., NRC com. to rev. Met. Washington Water Supply Study; provider expert testimony USEPA hearings and to Ho. of Reps. Com. on Pub. Works; mem. NRC Bd. Environ. Studies and Toxicology; mem. EPA's Nat. Adv. Coun. for Environ. Policy and Technology; trustee-at-large Bd. of Control of the Water Environment Fedn.; mem. Constrn. Industry Round Table; mem. sci. adv. bd. Strategic Environ. R&D Program, 1998—. Past pres. Am. Acad. Environ. Engrs. Designated AAEE Kappe Disting. Lectr., 1990; recipient Gordon Maskew Fair award 1991. Mem. AAAS, ASCE (Freese prize 1998), Am. Water Works Assn., Water Environ. Fedn., Am. Chem. Soc., N.Y. Acad. Sci., Nat. Acad. Engring. Died July, 1999.

BUSHNELL, GEORGE EDWARD, JR., lawyer; b. Detroit, Nov. 15, 1924; s. George E. and Ida Mary (Bland) B.; children: George Edward III, Christopher Gilbert Whelden, Robina McLeod Bushnell Hogan. Mil. student, U. Kans., 1943; BA, Amherst Coll., 1948; LLB, U. Mich., 1951; LLD, Detroit Coll. Law, 1995. Bar: Mich. 1951, D.C. 1980, U.S. Dist. Ct. (ea. dist.) Mich. 1951, U.S. Dist. Ct. (we. dist.) Mich. 1971, U.S. Ct. Appeals (6th cir.) 1955, U.S. Ct. Appeals (fed. cir.) 1995, U.S. Ct. Appeals for the Armed Forces 1995, U.S. Supreme Ct. 1971, U.S. Ct. Internat. Trade 1995. From assoc. to sr. ptnr. Miller, Canfield, Paddock and Stone, Detroit, 1953-77, of counsel, 1989-2001; sr. ptnr. Bushnell, Gage, Doctoroff & Reizen, Southfield, Mich., 1977-89. Commr. Mich. Jud. Tenure Commn., 1969-83, chmn., 1978-80; pres. State Bar Mich., 1975-76; bd. dirs. Nat. Jud. Coll., 1985-89; mem. Mich. Atty. Discipline Bd., 1990-96; lectr. in field. Elder Grosse Pointe Meml. Ch.; moderator Detroit Presbytery, United Presbyn. Ch. U.S.A., 1972, pres. program agy. bd., 1972-76; bd. dirs. Econ. Devel. Corp. of Detroit, 1976—, Econ. Growth Corp. of Detroit, 1978-96, Tax Increment Fin. Authority, Detroit, 1984—, Econ. Devel. Authority, Detroit, 1988-98, Mich. Partnership to Prevent Gun Violence, 1995—, pres.-elect, 1999-2000; bd. trustees New Detroit, Inc., 1972—, chmn., 1974-75. Served with USAR, 1942-56. Decorated Bronze Star, Army Commendation medal. Mem. NAACP (life, co-chmn. fight for freedom fund dinner 1968), ABA (ho. of dels. 1976—, chmn. ho. of dels. 1988-90. pres.-elect 1993-94, pres. 1994-95, past pres. 1995-96, others, Trial Attys. of Am. (pres. 1971-89), State Bar Mich. bd. of bar commrs. 1970-76, pres. 1975-76, John Hensel award for svcs. to the arts 1990, Roberts P. Hudson award for spl. svcs. to the bar and the people of Mich., 1979, 85, Cooley Law Sch. Louis A. Smith (disting. jurist award 1995), Detroit Bar Assn. (bd. dirs. 1958-65, pres. 1964-65, past pres. com. 1980—, bench & bar award for svc. to the judicial sys., the legal profession and the cmty. 1989), Nat. Conf. of Bar Pres. (pres. 1984-85), 6th Jud. Cir. Conf. (life), Am. Law Inst., Am. Arbitration Assn. (bd. dirs. 1970-82), Am. Coll. Trial Lawyers, Am. Bar Found. (life), Am. Judicature Soc. (bd. dirs. 1977-82), Can. Bar Assn. (hon.), Internat. Soc. Barristers, Fed. Bar Assn., Masons (33 deg.), Met. Club (N.Y.C.) Phi Delta Phi, Psi Upsilon. Democrat. Died Aug. 7, 2002.

BUSSE, EWALD WILLIAM, psychiatrist, educator; b. St. Louis, Aug. 18, 1917; s. Frederick Ewald and Emily Louise (Stroh) B.; m. Ortrude Helen Schnaedelbach, July 18, 1941; children: Ortrude Susan Busse White, Barbara Ann, Ewald Richard, Deborah Emily Busse Bragg. AB, Westminster Coll., 1938, ScD (hon.), 1960; MD, Washington U., St. Louis, 1942. Diplomate Am. Bd. Psychiatry and Neurology, Am. Bd. Qualification in Clin. Neurophysiology. Intern St. Louis City Hosp., 1942; resident in neuropsychiatry and psychiatry McCloskey Gen. Hosp., Temple, Tex., 1943-46, Colo. Psychiat. Hosp., Denver, 1946-48; faculty, head dept. psychosomatic medicine U. Colo., Denver, 1950-53; prof. Duke U. Med. Ctr., Durham, N.C., 1953-65, J.P. Gibbons prof. psychiatry, 1965-87, chmn. dept., 1953-74, dir. Ctr. for Study Aging, 1957-70, assoc. provost, dean Sch. Medicine, 1974-82, dean emeritus, 1982—2004; pres., CEO N.C. Inst. Medicine, 1987-94, pres. emeritus, 1994—2004. Mem. coun. Nat. Inst. on Aging, Bethesda, Md., 1979-83; chmn. geriat. and gerontology adv. com. VA, 1981-86 Author, editor: Behavior and Adaptation in Late Life, 1969, 2d edit., 1977, Handbook of Geriatric Psychiatry, 1980, 2d edit., 1994, Part II, Vol. II-Psychiatry Update, 1983, The Duke Longitudinal Studies, 1985, Aging: The Universal Human Experience, 1987, Geriatric Psychiatry, 1989, (textbook) Geriatric Psychiatry, 1996; author: Cerebral Manifestations of Cardiac Dysrhythmias, 1979. Mem. N.C. State Commn.

on Care of Elderly, Raleigh, 1968-73; mem. Durham County Commn. in Mental Health, 1971-74; pres. biomed. rsch. panel White Ho. Conf. on Aging, 1975-76, sect. chmn. del., 1978-81; mem. sci. adv. bd. Alliance for Aging Rsch., 1986-2004; bd. dirs. Greater Durham United Way, 1987-92. Maj. U.S. Army, 1943-46. Recipient Brookdale Found. award, 1982, Alumni Achievement award Westminster Coll., 1984, Disting. Alumni award Washington U., 1992, Pioneer award Govs. Commn. on Reduction of Infant Mortality, 1993, Alumni Achievement award Washington U., 2002, Field Svc. award Internat. PM, 2003; Busse Bldg. named in his honor Duke U., 1985; Busse Internat. Rsch. award endowed, 1990; Ewald Busse award created in his honor N.C. Dept. Human Resources, 1990; Busse Lecture endowment, 1995. Fellow Am. Psychiat. Assn. (pres. 1971-72, chmn. ethics com. 1981-85, Jack Weinberg Meml. award, Warren Williams award 1987, Disting. Svc. award 1988), Am. Geriat. Soc. (pres. 1975-76 Allen Thewlis award), Gerontol. Soc. Am. (pres. 1967-68, Freeman award), ACP (Menninger award 1971), Southeastern Med. Dental Soc. (pres. 1978-80); mem. Internat. Assn. Gerontology (pres. 1983-89, Sandoz prize 1983), World Psychiat. Assn. (ethics com.), N.Y. Acad. Medicine (Salmon award 1980). Clubs: Hope Valley; Beech Mountain (N.C.). Lodges: Rotary/Durham, Order of the Long Leaf Pine (gov. N.C. chpt. 2002); Masons. pres., 1972-73. hon. mem., 2002. Gov. N.Y. Ordin at 7th Long Land Pine, 2002. Home: Durham, NC. Died Mar. 7, 2004.

BUSSMANN, CHARLES HAINES, publisher; b. Pitts., Mar. 9, 1924; s. Amos George and Ann (Haines) B. Student, Colgate U., 1946. With Pit & Quarry Publs., Inc., 1946-63, v.p., 1957-63, dir., 1960-63; pres., dir. Compass Publs., Inc., Arlington, Va., 1963-1999. Bd. dirs., trustee Harbor Branch Oceanographic Instn., Inc., Harbor Branch Instn., Inc. Served with USAAF, 1942-43. Fellow Marine Tech. Soc. (hon.); Mem. Indsl. Marketers Cleve. (past bd. dirs.), Am. Bus. Press, Marine Tech. Soc., Am. Oceanographic Orgn., Advt. Club Cleve., T.F. Club Cleve. (past pres.), Theta Chi. Deceased.

BUTLER, LILLIAN CATHERINE, biochemistry educator; b. Chgo., Dec. 1, 1919; d. William Joseph and Lillian Eleanor (Kennedy) B. BS, U. Ill., 1941; MS in Biochemistry, U. Tex., 1945; PhD in Nutrition, U. Calif.-Berkeley, 1953. Assoc. prof. U. Ill., Champaign/Urbana, 1956-58; vis. scientist NIH, Endocrinology Sect., Bethesda, Md., 1958-60; rsch. biochemist and supr. VA Hosp., Diabetes Rsch. Unit, Birmingham, Ala., 1960-63; assoc. prof. rsch. Coll. Medicine, U. Ala., Birmingham, 1963-66; assoc. prof. nutrition U Md., College Park, 1967-78; ret. Author/editor: Nutrition from Infancy Through the Geriatric, 1976; contbr. articles to profl. jours. Nat. Inst. Cancer postdoctoral fellow, 1953-55, Nat. Inst. Arthritis and Metabolic Diseases fellow, 1949-53. Mem. Am. Chem. Soc., Am. Inst. Nutrition, Ariz. Watercolor Guild, Sigma Xi, Iota Sigma Pi, Sigma Delta Epsilon. Avocations: piano, watercolor painting. Home: Tucson, Ariz. Deceased.

BUTLER, RICHARD COLBURN, banker, lawyer; b. Little Rock, Jan. 1, 1910; s. R. Colburn and Edna (Clok) B.; m. Gertrude Remmel, Mar. 7, 1936; 1 son, Richard Colburn. Student, Little Rock Jr. Coll., 1929; AB, U. Ark., 1931, LLD (hon.), 1986, Hendrix Coll., 1981. Bar: Ark. 1933, U.S. Supreme Ct. 1943. Gen. practice law, Little Rock, 1933-63; partner firm House, Holmes, Butler & Jewell, 1941-63; pres., chmn. bd. Comml. Nat. Bank Little Rock, 1963-80, sr. chmn., 1980-81. Pres., dir. Ark. Nat. Stockyards Co., 1958-78, First Ark. Devel. Fin. Corp.; chmn., dir. Little Rock Abstract Co., 1971-81; chmn. Peoples Savs. & Loan Assn., Little Rock, 1980-84; dir. Kin-Ark Corp., Tulsa, 1972-91, 94—. Bd. dirs., treas. Heifer Project Internat., 1986-91; pres. Maumelle Gardens, Inc., 1968—; mem. United Meth. Found., 1964—, chmn. bd. dirs., 1981-84; pres. bd. trustees Little Rock U., 1961-63; bd. dirs. Little Rock Boys Club, pres., 1960; bd. dirs. Heifer Internat. Found., 1991—; nat. assoc. for Ark. Boys Clubs America, 1964-74; mem. Pillars Club, United Way Pulaski County; trustee Hendrix Coll., Conway, Ark., 1969-81; trustee Heifer Internat. Found., 1993—; founder Butler Arboretum, Little Rock, Butler Ctr. at Little Rock public library. Maj. USAAF, 1942-46, CBI. Decorated Bronze Star. Mem. ABA, Ark. Bar Assn., Am. Judicature Soc., Am. Hemerocallis Soc., Am. Iris Soc. Found. (life, regional v.p. 1960-61), Iris Found. (pres. 1995—, bd. dirs.), Bookfellows (pres. 1961), Little Rock C. of C. (pres. 1952), Am. Daffodil Soc. (bd. dirs. 1987-90), Nat. Trust for Historic Preservation, U. Ark.-Little Rock Heritage Assn. (founding mem.), Little Rock Country Club, Little Rock XV Club, U. Ark. Chancellor's Club, Union League (Chgo.), Kiwanis. Methodist (chmn. bd. trustees 1960-82). Home: Little Rock, Ark. Died Sept. 13, 1999.

BUTTS, VIRGINIA, corporate public relations executive; b. Chgo. BA, U. Chgo. Writer Dave Garroway radio show NBC, N.Y.C., 1953; writer, producer, talent Sta. WBBM-TV, Chgo.; midwest dir. pub. relations for mags. Time, Fortune, Life and Sports Illustrated, Time Inc., 1956-63; dir. pub. relations Chgo. Sun Times and Chgo. Daily News, 1963-74, v.p. pub. relations Field Enterprises Inc., Chgo., 1974-84; v.p. pub. rels. The Field Corp., 1984-90; pub. rels. counsel Marshall Field V, Chgo., from 1991. Pub. affairs com. Art Inst. Chgo., exec. prodn. assoc., 1985; instr. TV Columbia Coll. Contbr. Lesly's Public Relations Handbook, 1978, 83, World Book Ency. Recipient Clarion award Women in Communications, Inc., 1975-76, Businesswoman of the Yr. award Lewis U., 1976. Mem. Pub. Rels. Soc. Am. (nat. bd. ethics 1987-93), Publicity Club Chgo. (Golden Trumpet award 1968-69, 75-76, 80), Nat. Acad. TV Arts and Scis., The Chgo. Network. Achievements include the Lion at Lincoln Park Zoo named for her public relations work; late Milton Caniff's character in Steve Canyon Comic Strip named for her; for work in the film Continental Divide "the producer wishes to thank Virginia Butts and the editors and staff of the Chicago Sun-Times for their generous cooperation and assistance in the filming of this motion picture.". Died Feb. 2, 2003.

BUZZELLI, MICHAEL JOHN, critical care nurse; b. Hibbing, Minn., Aug. 5, 1954; s. Evarist A. and Beverly A. Buzzelli; m. Janice Buzzelli; children: Kimberly, Laura, Beverly. BSN, U. N.D., 1976; MA, Webster U., 1993. Staff nurse ICU U.S. Army, Washington, 1978-81, asst. head nurse ICU Seoul, Korea, 1981-82, Ft. Ord, Calif., 1982-86, instr. practical nurses Ft. Sam Houston, Tex., 1986-90; head nurse surg. ICU Brooke Army Med. Ctr., 1990-91; chief nurse 41st Combat Support Hosp., Ft. Sam Houston, 1991-94; chief mobilization edn. tng. & security Ft. Wainwright, Alaska, 1994-98; ret. U.S. Army, 1998; staff devel. and human resources Hudson (Ohio) Elms, Hudson, Ohio, from 1999. Contbr. articles to profl. jours. Lt. Col. U.S. Army, 1977-98. Recipient Expert Field Med. Badge, Meritorious Svc. Medal. Mem. AACN, 38th Parallel Nurses Assn., Nat. League Nursing. Home: Richfield, Ohio. Died Nov. 30, 2001.

BYE, RANULPH DEBAYEUX, artist, author; b. Princeton, NJ, June 17, 1916; s. Arthur Edwin and Mary C. (Heldring) B.; m. Mary DuBois McCarty, May 24, 1941 (div. 1981); children: Dennis L., Barbara D., Stephen G., Catherine M.; m. Glenna C. Lange, Oct. 16, 1983. Diploma, Phila. Mus. Sch. Indsl. Art, 1938; student, Art Students League, N.Y.C., 1940-41; D Pub. Svc. (hon.), Bucks County C.C., Newtown, Pa., 1994. Assoc. prof. painting Moore Coll. Art, Phila., 1949-79. Condr. watercolor workshop in Eng. and Ireland, 1987, Maine Coast Art Workshop, 1990. One-man shows include Newman Galleries, Phila, Hahn Gallery, Phila., Woodmere Art Mus., Chestnut Hill, Phila., 2002; retrospective at Woodmere Art Mus., 2002; group shows Am. Watercolor Soc., Allied Artists, NYC, NAD, Phila. Waercolor Club; represented in permanent collections Smithsonian Instn., Davenport, Iowa, Mcpl. Art Gallery, Reading, Pa., James A. Michener Art Mus., Doylestown, Pa., Pub. Mus., Temple U. Sch. Pharmacy, Phila., Munson, Williams Proctor Inst., Utica, NY, Mus. Fine Arts, Boston, William Penn Mus., Harrisburg, Pa.; author, illustrator: The Vanishing Depot, 1973, rev. edit., 1983, 3d edit., 1994, Ranulph Bye's Bucks County, 1989, Ranulph Bye's Collection of Old Firehouses, 2000; author: (with Margaret Bye Richie) Victorian Sketchbook, Painting Buildings in Watercolor, 1994. Served with U.S. Army, 1942-45. Recipient numerous awards including Gold medal Nat. Arts Club, 1963, Nat. Arts Club Award, 1988, Newman Galleries award, Mems.' Show award NJ Water Color Soc., 1991, 3d award with merit Pa. Watercolor Soc., Keystone medal and award, 1996, Patrons Purchase award Watercolor U.A.S., Springfield, Mo., 1997, Salmagundi members' medal, 1999. Mem. NAD (nat. academician 1994, cert. of merit, Adolph and Clara Obrig prize 1993), Am. Watercolor Soc. (6 awards 1964-92, Dolphin fellow 1985), Phila. Watercolor Club (Franklin Mint award 1988, 90, Savoir Faire prize 1993), Allied Artists Am. (Strathmore award 1986, Henry Gasser Meml. award 1989), Nat. Acad. N.Y., Salmagundi Club (34 awards 1958-2003), Phila. Water Color Soc. (disting.). Mem. Soc. Of Friends. Home: Mechanicsville, Pa. Died Nov. 19, 2003.

BYNUM, JULIA REBECCA BRANYON, elementary educator; b. Fayette, Ala., Jan. 21, 1948; d. Thomas Aaron Sr. and Edna Josephine (Madden) Branyon; m. William Michael Hopkins, Apr. 3, 1971 (dec. Aug. 1972); stepchildren: Lena Faye, Othelia Marie, William Carl; 1 child, Julia Michele; m. Thomas Homer Bynum, July 18, 1975; stepchildren: Thomas Tyrone, Michael Daren; 1 child, Amanda Paige. BA, Samford U., 1970; MA, U. Ala., 1974, AA cert., 1977. Cert. elem. sch. tchr., Ala. Elem. tchr. Muscogee County Bd. Edn., Columbus, Ga., 1970-71, Fayette (Ala.) County Bd. Edn., from 1974. Mem. UDC, Fayette, 1973—, Fayette Music Study Club, 1986—, reporter, 1987-88. Mem. NEA, Ala. Edn. Assn., Fayette County Edn. Assn., Alpha Delta Kappa (pres. Rho chpt. 1984-86, altruistic chmn. Ala. chpt. 1987-88, cen. dist. chmn. 1988—). Baptist. Avocations: music, calligraphy, cooking, interior decorating, house designs. Home: Fayette, Ala. Deceased.

BYRD, OTTO LEE (MIKE BYRD), minister; b. Pekin, Ill., Dec. 23, 1946; s. Luther Nathaniel and Betty Marie (Swingle) B.; m. Janet Faye Smith, June 11, 1966; children: Creighton Malachi, Ryland Micah. MS, Western Ill. U., 1972; MDiv, Denver Sem., 1977; EdD, U. No. Colo., 1979; DMinistry, Fuller Theol. Sem., 1988. Ordained to ministry Evangel. Free Ch. Am., 1976. Guidance dir. Sciota (Ill.) Northwestern High Sch., 1972-74; youth minister South Suburban Christian Ch., Littleton, Colo., 1975-76; pastor, sr. pastor Mountain View Evangel. Free Ch., Greeley, Colo., 1977-82; sr. pastor Community Bible Ch., San Bernardino, Calif., from 1982. V.p. Chinese for Christ Theol. Sem., Rosemead, Calif., 1985—. Contbr. articles to mags. With U.S. Army, 1965-68, Vietnam. Bd. dirs. Leadership Renewal Ctr., Inc., Yucaipa, Calif., 1989—, Samaritan Emergency Shelter, San Bernardino, Calif., 1990—. Mem. Internat. Leadership Council. Republican. Avocations: hiking, camping, reading. Home: Greeley, Colo. Deceased.

CADWELL, FRANCHELLIE MARGARET, advertising agency executive, writer; b. Hamilton, Bermuda, Apr. 23, 1933; came to U.S., 1938; d. Margaret (Roulston) C.. BS, Cornell U., 1955; MBA, NYU. Pres. Cadwell Davis Ptnrs., N.Y.C., 1975—2002. Author: The Un-Supermarkets, 1969. Mem. Pres. Coun. Cornell Women; bd. dirs. N.Y. Humane Soc.; bd. govs. N.Y. Arthritis Found., N.Y.C.; bd. mem. Nat. Parks; mem. Pres.'s Com. Employment of People with Disabilities. Recipient Nat. Humanitarian award, YWCA award, Entrepreneurial award Women Bus. Owners of N.Y., 1983, Girl Scouts USA award. Mem. Advt. Women N.Y., Fashion Group, Cosmetic Toiletry and Fragrance Assn., Non-Prescription Drug Mfrs., Women in Comm. (Matrix award 1980). Home: New York, NY. Died May 25, 2003.

CADY, EDWIN HARRISON, English language educator, author; b. Old Tappan, N.J., Nov. 9, 1917; s. Edwin Laird and Ethel Sprague (Harrison) C.; m. Norma Woodard, Aug. 31, 1939; children: Frances (Mrs. Edward Hitchcock, dec.), Elizabeth (Mrs. Larry Saler). AB, Ohio Wesleyan U., 1939, LittD (hon.), 1964; MA, U. Cin., 1940; PhD, U. Wis., 1943; LittD (hon.), Oklahoma City U., 1967; LHD (hon.), Georgetown U., 1989. Instr. English U. Wis., 1945, Ohio State U., 1946; from asst. prof. to prof. Syracuse U., 1946-59; Rudy prof. English Ind. U., 1959-73; prof. English Duke U., 1973-87, Andrew W. Mellon prof. humanities, 1975-87, prof. emeritus, from 1987. Vis. prof. Am. lit., Uppsala and Stockholm, Sweden, 1951-52 Author: The Gentleman in America, 1949, The Road to Realism: The Early Years, 1837-1885, of William Dean Howells, 1956, The Realist at War: The Mature Years, 1885-1920, of William Dean Howells, 1958, Stephen Crane, 1962, rev. edit., 1980, John Woolman: The Mind of the Quaker Saint, 1965, The Light of Common Day, 1971, The Big Game: College Sports and American Life, 1979, Young Howells and John Brown, 1985. Editor: (with H.H. Clark) Whittier on Writers and Writing, 1950, Literature of the Early Republic, 1950, rev. edit, 1969, (with L. Ahnebrink) An Anthology of American Literature, 1953, (with L.G. Wells) Stephen Crane's Love Letters to Nellie Crouse, 1954, (with F.J. Hoffman and R.H. Pearce) The Growth of American Literature, 1956, W.D. Howells, The Rise of Silas Lapham, 1957, Corwin K. Linson, My Stephen Crane, 1958, (with D.L. Frazier) The War of the Critics Over William Dean Howells, 1962, W.D. Howells, The Shadow of a Dream and An Imperative Duty, 1962, William Cooper Howells, Recollections of Life in Ohio, 1963, The American Poets, 1800-1900, 1966, (with D.F. Hiatt) W.D. Howells, Literary Friends and Acquaintance, 1968, Nathaniel Hawthorne, The Scarlet Letter, 1969, W.D. Howells as Critic, 1973, (with C. Anderson and L. Budd) Toward a New American Literary History: Essays in Honor of Arlin Turner, 1980, (with N.W. Cady) Critical Essays on W.D. Howells, 1866-1920, 1983, A Modern Instance, 1984; (with Louis J. Budd) On Whitman: The Best from American Literature, On Mark Twain: The Best from American Literature, 1987, On Emerson: The Best from American Literature, On Melville: The Best from American Literature, 1988, On Faulkner: The Best from American Literature, 1989, On Dickinson: The Best from American Literature, 1989, On Hawthorne: The Best from American Literature, 1990, On Henry James: The Best from American Literature, 1990, On Robert Frost: The Best from American Literature, 1991, On Humor: The Best from American Literature, 1991, On Howells: The Best From American Literature, 1993, On Poe: The Best From American Literature, 1993, W.D. Howells, Pebbles, Monochromes, and Other Modern Poems, 1891-1916, 2000; gen. editor: A Selected Edition of W.D. Howells, 1966-68; assoc. editor: Am. Lit. mag, 1973—; chmn. bd. editors, 1979-86, mng. editor, 1986-87. Mem. exec. com. Center Am. Editions, 1964-68; mem. U.S. Nat. Commn. for UNESCO, 1969-71. Served with Am. Field Service, 1943-44, Italy; with USNR, 1945. Recipient citation Ohio Wesleyan U., 1991; Guggenheim fellow, 1953-54, 75-76 Mem. MLA (chmn. Am. lit. sect. 1979, Jay B. Hubbell medal Am. lit. sect. 1990), Guild Scholars, Am. Antiquarian Soc., Phi Beta Kappa, Omicron Delta Kappa, Phi Gamma Delta. Episcopalian. Home: Olney, Ill. Died Aug. 30, 2003.

CAFIERO, EUGENE ANTHONY, manufacturing executive; b. N.Y.C., June 13, 1926; s. Anthony and Frances (Lauricell) C. BA, Dartmouth Coll., 1946; MS, MIT, 1961; DSc (hon.), Wittenburgh U., 1976. Pres. Chrysler Corp., Highland Park, Mich., 1975-78, vice-chmn., 1978-79; pres. DeLorean Motor Corp., N.Y.C., 1979-81; pres., chief exec. officer Keene Corp., N.Y.C., 1982-86; chmn., pres., CEO KDI Corp., N.Y.C., 1986-93; former chmn. NBC On Site Media, N.Y.C. Chmn. Voltarc Tech., Inc. Lt. (j.g.) USNR, 1944-47. Named Internat. Exec. of Yr. Thunderbird Sch., Phoenix, 1977; Sloan fellow MIT, 1959. Died Dec. 8, 2003.

CAHILL, JOSEPH T. former university president; b. Phila., June 1, 1919; Student, Mary Immaculate Sem.; MA, St. John's U., 1950; LL.D., Niagara U., 1967; Litt.D., China Acad., 1969; LL.D., Nat. Chengchi U., Taipei, Taiwan, 1971, St. Mary's U., San Antonio, 1973; L.H.D., Mercy Coll., 1974. Ordained priest Roman Catholic. Ch. order of Congregation of Mission, 1946. Former dir. students, mem. faculty St. Joseph's Coll., pres., superior, 1962-64; prof. history Niagara U., Niagara Falls, N.Y., 1953-56, dir. dramatics, 1953-56, moderator athletics, 1956-58, dean Grad. Sch. and Sch. Edn., 1958-59, acad. v.p., dean Coll. Arts and Scis., 1959-62, pres., 1964-65, St. John's U., Jamaica, N.Y., 1965-89, pres. emeritus, disting. prof. of history, 1989—2003. Died Sept. 27, 2003.

CAHN, JEAN CAMPER, lawyer; b. Balt., May 26, 1935; d. John Emory Touissant and Florine (Thompson) C.; m. Edgar S. Cahn, 1957; children: Jonathan Daniel, Reuben Camper. BA cum laude, Swarthmore Coll., 1957; JD, Yale U., 1961. Bar: Conn. 1961, D.C. 1963, U.S. Ct. Appeals

(D.C. cir.) 1964, U.S. Supreme Ct. 1964. Assoc. gen. counsel New Haven Redevel. Agy., 1961-63; internat. atty. Office Legal Adv. Dept. of State, Washington, 1963-65, internat. atty. Office Econ. Opportunity, 1964-65; pvt. practice D.C., 1965-68; co-founder, co-dean, prof. Antioch Sch. Law, Washington, 1971-80; of counsel Fernandez, Caubi, Fernandez, Aguilar, Cancio and Berenguer, Miami, Fla., from 1986. Bd. dirs., founder Urban Law Inst., Nat. Legal Svc. Program; adj. prof. Howard U., 1965-68; vis. prof. George Washington U., 1968-71; disting. vis. prof. Middlebury Coll., 1984, London Sch. Econs.; lectr. Yale Law Sch., 1962-63; cons. in field. Contbr. articles to profl. jours. Recipient Jefferson award, 1969, 70, 71, 76, Bronze award Info. Film Producers Am., 1979, Chris plaque 27th Ann. Columbus Film Festival, 1979, Key to City, New Orleans, 1968; Minna Shaughnessy fellow, 1981-82. Mem. ABA, Nat. Bar Assn., D.C. Bar Assn., Conn. Bar Assn., Nat. Legal Aid and Defenders Assn., Nat. Assn. Black Women Attys., Sigma Gamma Rho. Jewish. Home: Miami, Fla. Deceased.

CALABRESI, PAUL, oncologist, educator, pharmacologist; b. Milan, Apr. 5, 1930; U.S. citizen; married, Cellia Treadway; three children. BA, Yale U., 1951, MD, 1955; MD (hon.), U. Genova (Italy), 1996. Diplomate Am. Bd. Internal Medicine (sec.-treas. 1982-84). Intern Harvard Med. Svc., Boston City Hosp., 1955—56, asst. resident, 1958—59; project assoc. U. Wis., 1956—58; from instr. to assoc. prof. medicine and pharmacology Yale U., 1960—68; prof. med. sci. Brown U., 1968—83, chmn. dept. medicine, 1974—93, prof., chmn. emeritus, 1993—2003; clin. prof. pharmacology Coll. Pharmacy, U. R.I., Kingston, 1977—2003; former prof. pharmacology R.I. Hosp. Field investigator Nat. Cancer Inst., NIH, 1956—60, mem. cancer chemotherapy collaborative program rev. com., 1965—66, bd. sci. counselors, 1983—88; mem. Pharmacol.-Toxicol. Rev. Com., Nat. Inst. Genetic Med. Sci., 1967—70, exptl. therapeutic study sect., 1972—76, chmn., 1975—76; rsch. fellow dept. medicine Yale U., 1959—60, head divsn. clin. pharmacology and chemotherapy, dir. clin. pharmacol. rsch. ctr., 1965—67; vis. scientist U. Lausanne, Switzerland, 1966—67; physician-in-chief, chmn. dept. medicine Roger Williams Gen. Hosp., Providence, 1968—91, v.p. acad. affairs, 1977—91; mem. rsch. coun. and drug rsch. bd. NAS, 1968—75; mem. sci. group on evaluation and testign of drugs for mutagenicity, principles and problems WHO, 1971; cons. Study Group Hycanthone, 1971; counselor Environ. Mutagen Soc., 1971—74; chief medicine Women and Infants Hosp. R.I., 1974—80; cons. Miriam Hosp., Meml. Hosp., Providence VA Med. Ctr., R.I. Hosp.; former cons. St. Joseph's Hosp.; former mem. Sci. and Pub. Affairs Com., Am. Assn. Cancer Rsch.; mem. Nat. Cancer Adv. Bd., Nat. Cancer Inst., from 1991, chmn., 1991—94, mem. pres.'s cancer panel, from 1995; former dir. divsn. clin. pharmacology R.I. Hosp.; former dir. Brown-Tufts Cancer Ctr.; vis. prof. numerous univs. Fellow Eleanor Roosevelt Internat. Cancer fellow, Am. Cancer Soc., 1966—67; scholar Burroughs Wellcome scholar clin. pharmacology, 1964—68. Master: ACP (sci. program com. 1975—78, clin. pharmacol. com. 1977—82, chmn. 1978—82); mem.: Am. Soc. Clin. Pharmacology and Therapeutics (38th Oscar B. Hunter Meml. award 1995), Am. Cancer Soc. (St. George medal 1996), Am. Assn. Clin. Rsch., Am. Fedn. Clin. Rsch., Am. Soc. Clin. Oncology (pres. 1969—70), Am. Soc. Pharmacology and Exptl. Therapeutics, Am. Soc. Hematology, Inst. Medicine-NAS. Died Oct. 25, 2003.

CALL, OSBORNE JAY, retail executive; b. Afton, Wyo., June 4, 1941; s. Osborne and Janice C.; m. Tamra Compton, Dec. 16, 1977; children— Thad, Crystal. Student, Ricks Coll., Rexburg, Idaho, Brigham Young U., Provo, Utah. Engaged in petroleum mktg., 1960-68; v.p. Caribou Four Corners, Afton, 1964-68; pres. Flying J Inc. (retail and wholesale gasoline and real estate devel. co.), Brigham City, Utah, 1968—. Dir. No. div. First Security Bank, Brigham City. Died Mar. 15, 2003.

CALLAHAN, FLORENCE MARY, administrative assistant; b. Teaneck, N.J., Aug. 27, 1936; d. Walter and Florence (Collins) C. BA in Journalism and Polit. Sci., NYU, 1975. Sec. CBS, Inc., N.Y.C., 1968-72, exec. sec., 1972-88, adminstrv. asst., from 1988. Contbr. articles to newsletters; corr. articles on town meetings. Vol. Presdl. and Congrl. campaigns, N.Y., N.J., 1975—. Mem. Women in Communications, Soc. Profl. Journalists. Home: New Milford, NJ. Died Oct. 27, 1995.

CALLNER, BRUCE WARREN, lawyer; b. Camden, N.J., Sept. 20, 1948; s. Phillip David and Miriam June (Caplan) C.; m. Janet Adams, Apr. 25, 1970 (div. Dec. 1982); children: David, Michelle; m. Kathy Lynne Portnoy, Mar. 9, 1983; 1 child, Samantha. BS in Psychology, Western Mich. U., 1970; JD, U. Notre Dame, 1974. Bar: Ga. 1974, U.S. Dist. Ct. (no. dist.) Ga. 1975, U.S. Ct. Appeals (5th cir.) 1975, U.S. Ct. Appeals (11th cir.) 1981. Ptnr. Nall & Miller, Atlanta, 1974-81, Alembik, Fine & Callner, P.A., Atlanta, from 1981. Lectr. law Emory U., Atlanta. Author: Georgia Domestic Relations Casefinder, 1990, 2d edit., 1996. Vol. numerous legal orgns. Mem. ABA (family law and litigation sects.). Ga. Bar Assn. (family law and litigation sects.), Atlanta Bar Assn. (family law, litigation and sects., speaker's bur.); fellow Am. Acad. Matrimonial Lawyers, Nat. Council Family Relations, Southeastern Council Family Relations, NOW, Assn. Family Conciliation Cts. Democrat. Jewish. Home: Decatur, Ga. Died Jan. 17, 2001.

CAMP, MAX WAYNE, music educator; b. Arab, Ala., July 4, 1935; s. Roy Hubert and Alice Mellie (Cox) C. Mus.B., U. Ala., 1957; Mus.M., Peabody Coll., Vanderbilt U., 1965; D.M.E., Okla. U., 1977. Teaching assoc. Snead Coll., Boaz, Ala., 1965-67, Athens (Ala.) Coll., 1967-68; Disting. prof. emeritus U. S.C., Columbia, 1970—; dir. Camp Sch. of Music, Huntsville, Ala., 1957-70; tchr. master classes and piano workshops; rsch. fellow U. Düsseldorf Sch. of Medicine Dept. of Neurology, 1988, 89. Mem. Music Tchrs. Nat. Assn., S.C. Music Tchrs. Assn., Pi Kappa Lambda, Phi Mu Alpha. Author: Developing Piano Performance: A Teaching Philosophy, 1981; Guidelines for Developing Piano Performance, Books I and II, 1985; Teaching Piano: The Synthesis of Mind, Ear and Body, 1992; contbr. articles to profl. jours. Died March 21, 1996. Home: Columbia, SC.

CAMPANELLI, PAULINE EBLE, artist; b. N.Y.C., Jan. 25, 1943; d. Joseph and Dorothy Eble; m. Dan Campanelli, May 24, 1969. Grad., Ridgewood Sch. of Art, 1964; student, Art Students League, 1965-67. Fine arts pub. N.Y. Graphic Soc. Exhibited in group shows including Am. Art Gallery, Greenwich, Conn., Temple U., Lever House; represented in pub., corp. and pvt. collections throughout U.S.; author: Wheel of the Year, 1989, Ancient Ways, 1991, Circles, Groves and Sanctuaries, 1992, Rites of Passage, 1994, Halloween Collectibles, 1995, Art of Pauline and Dan Campanelli, 1995, Romantic Valentines, 1996, Holiday Collectibles, 1997; art work and home featured in Colonial Homes, Country Living, Country Almanac, Country Collectibles. Avocations: artist, historian, naturalist. Home: Phillipsburg, NJ. Deceased.

CANAVAN, BERNARD, retired pharmaceuticals executive, physician; b. Valleyfield, Fife, Scotland, 1936; s. Thomas and Helen (Toner) C.; m. Margaret Reid, Dec. 26, 1957; 1 child, Helen. B in Medicine, BChir, Univ. Edinburgh, Scotland, 1960. Licentiate Med. Council Can. Intern St. Joseph's Hosp., London, Ont., Can., 1960-61; general practice medicine Toronto, Ont., Can., 1961-69; med. dir. Wyeth Ltd. Can., Toronto, 1969-70, pres., 1970-75; exec. asst. to pres. Wyeth Internat. Ltd., Phila., 1975, group v.p., 1975-78, exec. v.p., 1978-80, pres., 1980-84, Wyeth Labs., Phila., 1984-87; chmn. Wyeth-Ayerst Labs., Phila., 1987-90; exec. v.p. Am. Home Products Corp., N.Y.C., 1987-90; pres. Am. Home Products, N.Y.C., from 1990. Trustee Sch. Nursing U. Pa.; bd. dirs. Bryn Mawr Hosp. Mem.: Phila. Country. Roman Catholic. Avocations: art collecting, golf, music. Home: Jupiter, Fla. Died Aug. 13, 2002.

CANDER, LEON, retired physician; b. Phila., Oct. 7, 1926; s. Joseph Harry and Anna (Glick) C.; m. Geraldine Piontkowski, Dec. 11, 1954; children, Alan Drew, Harris Scott. MD, Temple U., 1951. Rsch. fellow in physiology Grad. Sch. Medicine, U. Pa., 1952-56; resident in medicine Beth Israel Hosp., Boston, 1956-58; asst. in medicine Harvard U. Med. Sch., Boston, 1957-58; sr. instr. medicine Tufts U. Med. Sch., Boston, 1958-60; asst. prof. medicine Hahnemann Med. Coll., Phila., 1960-63, assoc. prof., 1963-66; prof., chmn. dept. physiology and medicine U. Tex. Med. Sch., San Antonio, 1966-72; chmn. dept. medicine, dir. med. edn. Daroff div. Albert Einstein Med. Ctr., Phila., 1972-80; prof. medicine Jefferson Med. Coll., Phila., 1972-89; head sect. of chest diseases, dir. med. edn. Daroff div. Albert Einstein Med. Ctr., Phila., 1980-88; clin. prof. medicine Hahnemann Med. Coll., Phila., 1985—2002; head sect. of chest diseases Mt. Sinai Hosp., Phila., 1988-96, ret., 2002. Mem. Nat. Adv. Coun. on Black Lung; nat. cons. U.S. Dept. Labor Black Lung Program, 1978—. Soc. Editor: (with J. H. Moyer) Aging of the Lung, 1963. Research fellow Nat. Acad. Scis., 1954-55 Fellow ACP; mem. Am. Thoracic Soc., Am. Physiol. Soc. Home: Wynnewood, Pa. Died Sept. 19, 2003.

CANN, JOHN RUSWEILER, biophysics educator; b. Bethlehem, Pa., Dec. 11, 1920; s. John Henry and Anna (Rusweiler) C.; m. Minerva Elda Butz, Sept. 7, 1946; children: Susan Austin, Richard L., David C. BS in Chemistry, Moravian Coll., 1942; MS in Chemistry, Lehigh U., 1943; MA in Chemistry, Princeton U., 1945, PhD in Phys. Chemistry, 1946. Rsch. assoc. Cornell U., Ithaca, N.Y., 1947; from rsch. fellow to sr. rsch. fellow Calif. Inst. Tech., Pasadena, 1947-50; from asst. prof. to assoc. prof. biophysics U. Colo. Med. Ctr., Denver, 1951-63; USPHS spl. rsch. fellow Carlsberg Found. Biol. Inst., Copenhagen, 1961-62; prof. biophysics U. Colo. Med. Ctr., Denver, 1963-91, emeritus prof., from 1991. Adj. prof. biochemistry Kans. State U., Manhattan, 1987-91; mem. adv. panel molecular biology div. of biol. and med. sci. NSF, 1967-70. Mem. editl. bd. Jour. Biol. Chemistry, 1982, 88-93, 95—, Archives of Biochemistry and Biophysics, 1980-95, Internat. Jour. Peptide and Protein Rsch., 1978-88; co-author: (with D.W. Talmadge) The Chemistry of Immunity in Health and Disease, 1961; author: Interacting Macromolecules: The Theory and Practice of Their Electrophoresis, Ultracentrifugation and Chromatography, 1970; contbr. articles to profl. jours.; reviewer manuscripts for sci. jours. Recipient John Amos Comenius Alumni award Moravian Coll., 1968, Med. Alumni award U. Colo., Denver, 1976; rsch. support grantee NIH, 1952-91. Fellow AAAS; mem. Am. Chem. Soc., Am. Soc. Biochem. Molecular Biologists, Biophysics Soc., Sigma Xi (past pres. U. Colo. chpt.). Achievements include use of circular dichroism, fluorometry and nuclear magnetic resonance in research in solution conformation of peptides and their interactions with lipids and other biological molecules; and research in electrophoresis, isoelectric focusing, sedimentation and chromatography of reacting systems, and electrophoresis of protein-DNA complexes. Home: Longmont, Colo. Died Aug. 25, 2001.

CANNON, CAROLYN R. occupational health nurse; b. Ashland, Pa., Aug. 26, 1938; d. Lester L. and Roberta (May) Hummel; m. Patrick F. Cannon, May 16, 1964; children: Shawn P., Patricia L., Jennifer C. AS, Pa. State U., Ashland, 1956; diploma in nursing, Ashland State Hosp., 1959. RN, Pa.; cert. occupational health nurse. Oper. rm. nurse Phila. Gen. Hosp., Phila. VA Hosp.; critical care nurse Med. Pers. Pool, Phila.; occupational health nurse, product liability assoc. SmithKline Beecham Corp., Phila. Mem. AACCN (S.E. PA chpt.), Am. Assn. Occupational Health Nurses, Northeast Occupational Health Nurses Assn., Pa. Occupational Health Nurses Assn., Phila. Occupational Health Nurses Assn. Home: Philadelphia, Pa. Died Nov. 7, 2000.

CANTALUPO, JAMES RICHARD, restaurant company executive; b. Oak Park, Ill., Nov. 14, 1943; s. James Francis and Eileen Patricia (Goggin) C.; m. Jo Ann Lucero, June 16, 1973; children: Christine, Jeffrey. BS in Acctg., U. Ill.-Champaign, 1966. C.P.A., Ill. Staff acct. Arthur Young & Co., Chgo., 1966-71, mgr., 1971-74; controller McDonald's Corp., Oak Brook, Ill., 1974-75, sr. v.p., controller, 1981-85, sr. v.p., zone mgr., 1985-87, pres. McDonald's Internat., 1987—97, CEO, 1991—2004, chmn., 2003—04. Bd. dirs. Sears, Roebuck and Co., Rohm and Haas Co., Ill. Tool Works, Inc. Treas. McDonald Polit.. Action Com., Oak Brook, 1979-85; chmn., dir. Nat. Multiple Sclerosis Soc., Chgo.-No. Ill. chpt.; trustee Ronald McDonald House Charities Mem. Chgo. Coun. Fgn. Rels. (bd. dirs.), Am. Inst. C.P.A.'s, Ill. Soc. C.P.A.'s, Inst. Corp. Controllers Roman Catholic. Died Apr. 19, 2004.

CARBERRY, JAMES JOHN, chemical engineer, educator; b. Bklyn., Sept. 13, 1925; s. James Thomas and Alice (McConnin) C.; m. Judith Ann Bower, Sept. 12, 1959 (div.); children: Alison Ann, Maura O'Malley; m. Margaret V. Bruggner, Sept. 24, 1974. BS, U. Notre Dame, 1950, MS, 1951; DEng, Yale U., 1957. Process engr. E.I. duPont de Nemours & Co., Gibbstown, N.J., 1951-53, sr. rsch. engr. Wilmington, Del., 1957-61; tchg. and rsch. fellow Yale U., 1953-57; prof. chem. engring. U. Notre Dame (Ind.), 1961-99, prof. emeritus chem. engring., from 1999. Mem. U.S.-Soviet working com. chem. catalysis; cons. in field. Author: Chemical and Catalytic Reaction Engineering, 1976; editor: Catalysis Revs., 1974-90. Mem. adv. coun. chem. engring. dept. Princeton U., 1980-88. With USNR, 1944-46. Recipient award for advancement pure and applied sci. Yale Engring. Assn., 1968; NSF fellow Cambridge U. (Eng.), 1965-66; Fulbright-Hays sr. scholar, Italy, 1973-74; Kelley lectr. Purdue U., 1978; Richard King Mellon fellow, Sir Winston Churchill fellow Cambridge U., 1979-82; vis. fellow Clare Hall Coll., Cambridge U., 1987; vis. chaired prof. Politecnico di Milano, Italy, 1987; life fellow Clare Hall, Cambridge U., 1988; Gruppo Attivitá Verdiane, Roncole verdi, 1987—. Fellow Royal Soc. Arts (London), N.Y. Acad. Scis., Am. Inst. Chemists; mem. NAE, Am. Chem. Soc. (Murphree award indsl. and engring. chemistry 1993), Am. Inst. Chem. Engrs. (R.H. Wilhelm award in chem. reaction engring. 1976, Autoclave Engrs. award 1988, William H. Walker award 1989), AICHE, Nat. Acad. Engring., Yale Alumni Assn. (rep.), Yale Engring. Assn., Lucrezia Borgia Soc., Sigma Xi, Fellowship of Cath. Scholars, Yale Club (N.Y.C.). Deceased.

CARBONE, WALTER EGIDIO, chemical engineer; b. N.Y.C., June 8, 1914; s. Francis N. and Lucy M. (Pollina) C.; m. Eleanor M. McDevitt, Apr. 3, 1943 (dec. Apr. 1979); 1 child, Janet F. Carbone Johnson; m. Mary L. Coram, Feb. 13, 1981. Degree in mech. engring., Stevens Inst Technologie, 1935; MSChemE, Columbia U., 1958. Registered profl. engr., N.Y., Md., Fla. Design engr. Semet-Solvay Engring. Corp., N.Y.C., 1935-39; plant engr. Semet-Solvay divsn. Allied Chem. Corp., Ashland, Ky., 1939-40, engring. and sales positions Wilputte Coke Oven divsn., 1940-52, contract engr., project mgr., sales mgr., 1952-63, dir. sales, 1963-67, v.p. sales, 1967-70; exec. v.p. Wilputte Corp., 1970-79, sr. cons., 1979-80, pres., 1980-82; ind. cons. Towson, Md., from 1982. Spkr. in field. Contbr. articles to profl. publs. Fellow AIChE; mem. Am. Arbitration Assn., Assn. Iron and Steel Engrs., Am. Chem. Soc., Ea. States Blast Furnace and Coke Oven Assn., Western States Blast Furnace and Coke Plant Assn., Tau Beta Pi. Republican. Roman Catholic. Avocations: photography, electronics, high fidelity equipment, reading, travel. Home: Luthvle Timon, Md. Died June 7, 2000.

CAREY, JAMES C., JR., plastic surgeon; b. Chgo., 1932; MD, Northwestern U., 1957. Intern Cook County Hosp., Chgo., 1957-58, resident in gen. surgery, 1958-63; plastic surgeon U. Mo., Kansas City, 1980-82; now plastic surgeon Twin Cities Cmty. Hosp., Templeton, Calif. Deceased.

CAREY, RAYMOND GIDDENS, JR., lawyer; b. Evansville, Ind., Apr. 12, 1944; s. Raymond Giddens Sr. and Faye Vivian (Kingsbury) C.; m. Virginia Rea (div. Dec. 1981); children: Kimberly Rea, Jason Rea; m. Julie Duncan Davis, Aug. 19, 1989. AB, Williams Coll., 1966; JD, U. Colo., 1969. Bar: Colo. 1969, U.S. Dist. Ct. Colo. 1969. Assoc. Sheldon, Nordmark & Bayer, Denver, 1969-71; ptnr. Bayer, Carey & McGee, Denver, from 1971. Bd. dirs. Geneva Glen Camps, Inc., Indian Hills, Colo., Ctr. Policy Rsch., Inc., Denver; instr. program for advanced profl. devel. U. Denver, 1977-80. Mem. Second Jud. Dist. Nom. Com., Denver, 1977-82. Fellow Am. Acad. Matrimonial Lawyers; mem. ABA, Colo. Bar Assn. (bd. govs. 1982-84, 87-89, Family Law Coun. 1980—), Denver Bar Assn., Law Club Denver (pres. 1984-85), Denver Athletic Club. Home: Denver, Colo. Deceased.

CARLISLE, SUSAN GOODMAN, academic administrator, educator; b. Phila., Dec. 28, 1932; d. Nathan G. and Julia (Nusbaum) Goodman; m. Robert B. Carlisle, Aug. 31, 1954; children: R. Bruce Jr., Julia Ellen, Christopher Goodman. BA, Cornell U., 1954; MA, Boston U., 1960. Asst. to assoc. prof. English SUNY, Canton, 1965-82; lectr. Tufts U., Medford, Mass., 1978-79 and from 81, curriculum coord. Decision Making Ctr., 1981-91, co-dir. Ctr. Tchg. and Advising, from 1993. Editor: Environmental Decision Making, 1991; contbr. articles, poems, book chpts. to profl. jours., mags. Nat. scholar Cornell U., Ithaca, N.Y., 1950-54. Mem. AAUP, Environ. Design Rsch. Assn., Phi Beta Kappa, Phi Kappa Phi. Democrat. Avocations: culture and environment studies, writing poetry, ornithology, travel. Home: Medford, Mass. Died Mar. 5, 2000.

CARLOS, ANDREW C. beverage distribution executive; CFO Nat. Distbg., Atlanta. Died Sept. 1999.

CARLOS, MICHAEL C. wine, spirits and linen service wholesale executive; b. 1927; Chmn. bd., dir., co-CEO Nat. Distbg. Co., Inc., Atlanta. Died Dec. 14, 2002.

CARLSON, LOREN MERLE, political science educator; b. Mitchell, SD, Nov. 2, 1923; s. Clarence A. and Edna M. (Rosenquist) C.; m. Verona Gladys Hole, Dec. 21, 1950; children: Catherine Ann, Bradley Reed, Nancy Jewel. BA, Yankton Coll., 1948; MA, U. Wis., 1952; JD, George Washington U., 1961. Bar: S.D. 1961, U.S. Supreme Ct. 1976. Asst. dir. Govt. Rsch. Bur., U. S.D., 1949-51; orgn. and methods examiner Dept. State, Washington, 1951-52; asst. dir. legis. rsch. State of S.D., 1953-55, dir., 1955-59, budget officer, 1963-68; rsch. asst. to U.S. Senator from S.D., 1959-60, adminstrv. asst., 1960-63; dir. statewide ednl. svcs. U. S.D., Vermillion, 1968-74, dean continuing edn., 1974, 1976—87, from assoc. prof. to prof. polit. sci., 1968—89, emeritus prof. polit. sci., from 1989; admin. asst. to US Rep. from SD, 1975—76; hwy. laws study dir. U. S.D. Law Sch., Vermillion, 1963; mng. editor U. S.D. Press, 1985-89, sr. editor, 1989-93. Chmn. Model Rural Devel. Commn., Dist. II, State of SD, 1972-74; chmn. Region VII Planning Commn. on Criminal Justice, S.D., 1969-74; vice-chmn. South East Coun. of Govts., 1989-90, chmn., 1993-97. Author: (with W.O. Farber and T.C. Geary) Government of South Dakota, 1979; contbr. articles profl. publs. Mem. Vermillion City Coun., 1980-90, 91-92, pres. 1982-90; mem. S.D. Humanities Found., 1989-97; mem. Vermillion Home Rule Task Force, 2002-03; bd. dirs. Vermillion Devel. Co., pres., 1987; mem. Vermillion Golf Course/Rsch. Market Analysis Study Rev. Com., 1993-94; mem. Vermillion Facilities Task Force, 1996-97; Rep. candidate State House of Reps., 1986; hon. life trustee U. S.D. Found., 1998. Named Outstanding Young Man Pierre Jaycees, 1959 Fellow: Nat. Univ. Continuing Edn. Assn.; mem.: Farber Found. (exec. bd. dirs. 1993—2001), Nat. Meml. Mt. Rushmore Soc., Spirit Mound Trust (v.p. 1984—2003), S.D. City Mgr. Assn. (hon.), Karl Mundt Found., S.D. Adult Edn. Assn. (chmn. 1973—74), ASPA, Pi Kappa Delta, Pi Sigma Alpha. Republican. Lutheran. Home: Vermillion, SD. Died Jan. 26, 2004.

CARMICHAEL, VIRGIL WESLY, mining, civil and geological engineer, former coal company executive; b. Pickering, Mo., Apr. 26, 1919; s. Ava Abraham and Rosevelt (Murphy) Carmichael; m. Emma Margaret Freeman, Apr. 1, 1939 (dec.); m. Colleen Fern Wadsworth, Oct. 29, 1951; children: Bonnie Rae, Peggy Ellen, Jacki Ann. BS, U. Idaho, 1951, MS, 1956; PhD, Columbia Pacific U., San Rafael, Calif., 1980. Registered profl. engr. Asst. geologist Day Mines, Wallace, Idaho, 1950; mining engr. De Anza Engring. Co., Troy, Idaho, Santa Fe, 1950-52; hwy. engring. asst. N.Mex. Hwy. Dept., Santa Fe, 1952-53; asst. engr. U. Idaho, 1953-56; minerals analyst Idaho Bur. Mines, 1953-56; mining engr. No. Pacific Ry. Co., St. Paul, 1956-67; geologist N.Am. Coal Corp., Cleve., 1967-69, asst. v.p. engring., 1969-74, corp. v.p., head exploration dept., 1974-84; travel host Satrom Travel and Tour, Bismarck, N.D., 1988-92. Advisor photogeology People to People "Hard Rock" Minerals Del. to China, 1981; leader People to People Coal Mechanization Del. to China, 1982; advisor photogeology Carbocol, Columbia, 1984—85; mem. Bismarck Scottish Rite Children's Hearing Impairment Bd., 1991—97, from 2000. Asst. chief distbr. Emergency Mgmt. Fuel Resources N.D., 1968—92; bd. dirs., chmn. fund dr. Bismarck-Mandan Orch. Assn., 1979—83; 1st v.p., bd. dirs., chmn. fund drive Bismarck Arts and Galleries Assn., 1982—86; mem. and spl. advisor (Minerals) Nat. Def. Exec. Res., from 1983; mem. Fed. Emergency Mgmt. Agy., from 1983; life mem. adv. bd. Bismarck Salvation Army, from 1988, chmn., 1993—95; sci. rsch. bd. N.D. Acad. Sci. Found., 1986—91. Finalist J. C. Penney Golden Rule award, 1996; recipient A award for sci. writing, Sigma Gamma Epsilon. Mem.: N.D. Acad. Sci., N.Y. Acad. Sci., Am. Inst. Profl. Geologists (past pres. local chpt.), Breezy Shores Resort and Beach Club (bd. dirs. from 1986), Scottish Rite (Royal Order of Scotland), Kiwanis Internat. (Minndaks Dist. awards), Kiwanis (past pres., disting. lt. gov., disting. chmn. internat. found. 1991—2000, pres. adv. com., Tablet of Honor), York Rite (grand comdr. N.D. Commandery 2001—02, grand high priest from 2002, Knight Templar Cross of Honor, Knight of York Cross of Honor), Masons (trustee 1998—2001, past master, trustee 1987—92, N.D. Masonic Found. 1987—92, 1994—99, chmn. 1990—92, 1997—99, Mason of the Yr. Bismarck lodge 1992, Gen. Grand Masters award, Cryptic Mason award, Crytptic Mason Med. Rsch. Found., Scottish Rite, Knight Comdr. Cross of Honor, Royal Order of Scotland, 33d degree), Am. Legion (life), Elks (life). Republican. Home: Bismarck, ND. Died Apr. 5, 2003.

CARNEVALE, ANTHONY, judge; b. Providence, R.I. m. Audrey. BS, R.I. Coll., 1972; MEd, Providence Coll., 1976; JD, Suffolk U., 1984. Commd. Air Nat. Guard, 1970; mem. R.I. Ho. of Reps., 1977-88; judge R.I. Supreme Ct., from 1988. Mem. R.I. Bar Assn., R.I. Trial Judges Assn. Deceased.

CARNEY, DENNIS JOSEPH, former steel company executive, consulting company executive; b. Charleroi, Pa., Mar. 19, 1921; s. Walter Augustus and Ann (Nandor) C.; m. Virginia M. Horvath, June 12, 1943 (dec. Jan. 1984); children— Colleen A., Dennis Joseph, Glenn P., Lynn C., Dianne V. BS in Metallurgy, Pa. State U., 1942; Sc.D., Mass. Inst. Tech., 1949. With U.S. Steel Corp., Pitts., 1942-74, gen. supt., 1963-65, v.p. long range planning, 1965-68, v.p. applied research, 1968-72, v.p. research, 1972-74; v.p. ops. Wheeling-Pitts. Steel Corp., 1974-75, exec. v.p., dir., 1975-76, pres., 1976-85, chief operating officer, 1976-77, chief exec. officer, 1977-85, chmn. bd., 1978-85; ret., 1985; pres. Intra-Continental Cons. Co, Fort Lauderdale, Fla., 1985—. Author: (with others) Gases in Metals, 1956. Bd. dirs. Wheeling (W.Va.) Coll. Served to lt. (j.g.) USNR, 1943-46. Fellow Am. Soc. Metals (Grossmann award Pitts. chpt. 1959, trustee 1972—); mem. Am., Brit., Internat. iron and steel insts., Am. Inst. Mining, Metall. and Petroleum Engrs. (McKune award 1951, Benjamin F. Fairless award 1978), Am. Iron and Steel Engrs., Sigma Xi, Tau Beta Pi, Sigma Nu. Clubs: South Hills Country (Pitts.), Duquesne (Pitts.) (dir.); Laurel Valley Country, Fox Chapel Country. Died June 15, 2003.

CARPENTER, ALLAN, writer, editor, publisher; b. Waterloo, Iowa, May 11, 1917; s. John Alex and Theodosia (Smith) C. BA, U. No. Iowa, 1938. Founder, editor, publisher Tchrs. Digest mag., 1940-48; dir. pub. relations Popular Mechanics mag., 1943-62; founder, 1962, since pres. Carpenter Pub. House, Inc., Chgo.; founder Infordata Internat. Inc., 1970-89, chmn. bd., dir., 1970-89; partner, editor Index to U.S. Govt. Periodicals, 1972-90; ret. Historian of Cook County, 1999. Author over 231 nonfiction books including Between Two Rivers, Iowa Year By Year, 1940, 3d edit., 1997, 52 vol. Enchantment of America state series, 52 vol. New Enchantment of America, Enchantment of Africa, 38 vol. Enchantment of Latin America, 20 vol. Illinois, Land of Lincoln, 1968, All About the U.S.A., 1986, 7 vol. The Mighty Warriors, 1987, 4 vol. Encyclopedia of the Midwest, 1988, Encyclopedia of the Central West, 1990, Encyclopedia of the Far West, 1990, Facts About the Cities, 1992, 2d rev. edit., 1996, World Almanac of the U.S.A., 1993, 3rd rev. edit., 1999, Between Two Rivers Iowa Year By Year, 3rd rev. edit., 1999; creator, editor 16 vol. Popular Mechanics Home Handyman Ency., 1962; founder, pub. Index to Readers Digest, 1980-90, Index to Alternative Health Periodicals. Pres., chmn. Chgo. Businessmen's Symphony Orch., 1942-65, prin. string bass sect.; founder, 1954; since pres. Music Council Met. Chgo.; prin. bass violist non-profl. symphony orchs. Recipient Lifetime Achievement award, U. No. Iowa, 1988. Mem. Soc. Wilson Descendants, Inc. (pres. 1955-93, chmn. 1994, founder James "Tama Jim" Wilson award), Ill. St. Andrews Soc. (life), Arts Club Chgo. Died May 11, 2003.

CARPENTER, NAN COOKE, English language educator; b. Louisa County, Va., July 29, 1912; s. Charles Richard and Nan (Cooke) C. B in music, Hollins Coll., 1937; MA in musicology, U. N.C., 1941; MA in Eng., Yale U., 1945, PhD in music history, 1948. Music tchr. Blair Jr. High Sch., Norfolk, Va., 1935-40; Eng. prof. U. Mont., Missoula, 1948-63, Southern Ill. U., Carbondale, 1963-64; music prof. Syracuse (N.Y.) U., 1964-65; Eng. prof. Ga. Southwestern Coll., Americus, 1965-66, U. Ga., Athens, 1966-70, comp. lit. prof., 1970-80, chmn. comp. lit. dept., 1975-80. Author: Rabelais and Music, 1954, Music in the Medieval and Renaissance Universities, 1958, John Skelton, 1969, A Quiver of Quizzez for Quidnuncs, 1985. Officer Athens Humane Soc., 1968-99; reader, pianist Recording for Blind, Athens, 1968-99. Fellow ASLS, 1954-55. Home: Thomasville, Ga. Died May 14, 1999.

CARR, SUSAN PRICE, lawyer; b. New Rochelle, N.Y., Feb. 16, 1946; d. Lewis Bruce and Dorislee (Kadis) C.; m. Kenneth David Burrows, June 22, 1967 (div.); m. Anthony M. Radice, Nov. 24, 1986; 1 child, Julia Price. BA, Vassar Coll., 1967; MA, NYU, 1972; JD, Columbia U., 1972. Bar: N.Y. 1973, U.S. Dist. Ct. (so. and ea. dists.) N.Y. 1973, U.S. Ct. Appeals (2nd cir.) 1975, U.S. Ct. Appeals (D.C. cir.) 1977, U.S. Supreme Ct. 1977. Law clk. U.S. Dist. Ct. (ea. dist.) N.Y., Bklyn., 1972-73; litigation assoc. Paul, Weiss, Rifkind, Wharton & Garrison, N.Y.C., 1973-81; litigation counsel Time Warner Inc. (formerly Warner Communications Inc.), N.Y.C., from 1981. Articles editor Columbia Law Rev., 1971-72. Harlan Fiske Stone scholar, 1971-72. Mem. Assn. of Bar of City of N.Y. (com. on entertainment and sports law 1987-89), Fed. Bar Coun. (trustee 1984-91, v.p. 1991—). Home: New York, NY. Deceased.

CARREÑO, RICHARD DENNIS, writer; b. N.Y.C., Jan. 28, 1946; s. Ralph Joseph and Marion (Berman) C.; m. Nancy Dickinson Brown, Aug. 7, 1971; children: Abigail, Justin, Hunter IV. BA, U. Mass., 1978. Asst. city editor Telegram and Gazette, Worcester, Mass., 1971-78; reader ombudsman The News, Southbridge, Mass., 1978-79; corr. Boston Globe, 1978-80; writer Writers Clearinghouse, Quinebaug, Conn., from 1978. Farmer Rambles Farm, Fabyan, 1978—. Republican. Episcopalian. Avocation: horsemanship. Home: North Grosvenordale, Conn. Deceased.

CARRO, JORGE LUIS, law educator, consultant; b. Havana, Cuba, Nov. 27, 1924; arrived in USA, 1967, naturalized, 1973; s. Luis and Maria G. (Gonzalez) Carro; m. Edy Jimenez; 1 child, Edy C. BA, Havana Inst., 1945; JD, U. Havana, 1950; MLS, Kans. State Tchr. Coll., 1969. Bar: Havana, Cuba 1950. Practice, Havana, Cuba, 1950—57; legal cons. Swiss embassy, Havana, Cuba, 1963—67; legal adv. Apostolic Nuncio, Havana, Cuba, 1963—67; asst. libr. U. Wis., Milw., 1969, asst. libr., instr. Whitewater, 1969—72; libr., asst. prof. Ohio No. U., 1972—75; assoc. prof., 1975—76; assoc. prof. law, libr. U. Cin., 1976—78; acting dean, 1978—79; prof., libr., 1979—86; prof., from 1986. Author: (novels) Govt. Regulation of Bus. Ethics, 1981—82; contbr. articles books revs. to profl. jour. Mem.: Cin. Bar Assn., ABA. Republican. Roman Catholic. Deceased.

CARROLL, AILEEN, retired librarian; b. Mason, Wis., Aug. 7, 1914; d. John P. and Mary (Noonan) C. BA, De Paul U., 1938; MA, Northwestern U., 1940; MLS, Rosary Coll., 1965. Tchr. Chgo. Pub. Schs., 1940-52; systems media dir., libr. organizer Cook County Pub. Schs., from 1952. Author and pub. of children's poetry. Vol. St. Vincent's Orphanage, Chgo., Sacred Heart Home for the Aged, Chgo. Recipient scholarship AAUW, 1991. Mem. AAUW (Western Springs, Ill.), LWV, Rep. Club of Oak Park, Art Group of Western Springs. Home: Western Springs, Ill. Died Dec. 10, 2001.

CARROLL, JOHN BISSELL, psychologist, educator; b. Hartford, Conn., June 5, 1916; s. William James and Helen M. (Bissell) C.; m. Mary Elizabeth Searle, Sept. 6, 1941 (dec. Oct. 6, 2001); 1 child, Melissa (Mrs. F. Stuart Chapin III). BA, Wesleyan U., 1937; PhD, U. Minn., 1941; AM (hon.), Harvard U., 1953; ScD (hon.), U. Minn., 1986. Instr. Mt. Holyoke Coll., 1940-42, Ind. U., 1942-43; lectr. U. Chgo., 1943-44; research psychologist Dept. Army, 1946-49; asst. prof. Harvard Grad. Sch. Edn., 1949-53, asso. prof., 1953-57, prof. edn., 1957-62, prof. ednl. psychology, 1962-67; sr. research psychologist Ednl. Testing Service, Princeton, N.J., 1967-74; prof. psychology U. N.C., Chapel Hill, 1974-82, prof. emeritus, 1982—. Mem. com. aptitude examiners Coll. Entrance Exam. Bd., 1952-65, commn. tests, 1967-70; adv. com. on new ednl. media U.S. Office Edn., 1961-64 Author: The Study of Language, 1953, Modern Language Aptitude Test, 1958, Language and Thought, 1964, Human Cognitive Abilities, 1993; editor: Language, Thought and Reality, 1956, Toward a Literate Society, 1975, Perspectives on School Learning: Selected Writings, 1985; contbr. articles to profl. jours. Served to lt. (j.g.) USNR, 1944-46. Recipient E.L. Thorndike award for disting. svc. to ednl. psychology, 1970, Diamond Jubilee medal Inst. of Linguists, 1970, award Am. Ednl. Rsch. Assn., 1979, Ednl. Testing Svc. award for disting. svc. to measurement, 1980, Nat. Conf. on Rsch. in English award for disting. rsch., 1990, Lewis M. Terman/Maude A. Merrill award for disting. lifetime contbn. to study of human cognitive abilities, 1994, Saul B. Sells award Soc. Multivariate Exptl. Psychology, 1994, E.F. Lindquist award Am. Ednl. Rsch. Assn., 1997, Lifetime Contbn. award divsn. 5 Am. Psychol. Assn., 1997, Gold medal award for life achievement Am. Psychol. Found., 2002; named to Reading Hall of Fame, 1977. Fellow APA, Am. Psychol. Soc. (James McKeen Cattell fellow award 1998); mem. Psychometric Soc. (pres. 1960-62), Linguistic Soc. Am., Nat. Acad. Edn. (v.p. 1977-81). Home: Fairbanks, Alaska. Died July 1, 2003.

CARROLL, JOHN MOORE, retired electrical engineer; b. Butte, Mont., Oct. 27, 1911; s. William Craig and Harriet Lane (McKay) C.; m. Kathleen McClintock, Apr. 18, 1938 (div. 1964); children: Susan, William; m. Virginia Lee Roberts, Dec. 31, 1966; stepchildren: Thomas Gilbert, Rodney Gilbert, Gary Gilbert. Student, Oreg. State U., 1931; BA in Engring., N.W. Schs., 1958. Elec. supt. Harvey Aluminum Co., The Dalles, Oreg., 1957-62; sr. elec. engr. Aetron-Blume-Atkinson, Stanford, Calif., 1962-66, Bechtel Power Corp., San Francisco, 1968-75; sr. cost engr., contract adminstr. Burns & Roe, Inc., Paramus, N.J., 1975-79; sr. elec. engr. J.A. Jones, Inc., Hanford, Wash., 1979-88; cons., elec. estimator Kennewick, Wash., 1988-90; ret., 1990. Elec. estimator Tempest Co., Omaha, 1985; elec. engr. Metcalf & Eddy, Inc., Long Beach, Calif., 1987. Stephens Min. Presbyn. Ch., 1993. Capt. U.S. Army, 1942-46, PTO. Decorated Bronze Star. Mem. Nat. Soc. Profl. Engrs., IEEE, Am. Assn. Cost Engrs., Am. Arbitration Assn., Masons, Shriners. Republican. Avocation: amateur radio. Deceased.

CARSON, GORDON BLOOM, retired engineering executive; b. High Bridge, NJ, Aug. 1, 1911; s. Whitfield R. and Emily (Bloom) C.; m. Beth Lacy, June 19, 1937 (dec. Mar. 1998); children: Richard Whitfield (dec. Oct. 2002), Emily Elizabeth (Mrs. Lee A. Duffus), Alice Lacy (Mrs. William P. Allman), Jeanne Helen (Mrs. Michael J. Gable). BSMechE, Case Inst. Tech., 1931, D Engring., 1957; MS, Yale U., 1932, ME, 1938; LLD, Rio Grande Coll., 1973. With Western Electric Co., 1930; instr. mech. engring. Case Inst. Tech., 1932-37, asst. prof., 1937-40, asso. prof. indsl. engring. charge indsl. div., 1940-44; with Am. Shipbldg. Co., 1936; patent litigation, 1937; research engr., dir. research Cleve. Automatic Machine Co., 1939-44; asst. to gen. mgr. Selby Shoe Co., 1944, mgr. engring., 1945-49, sec. of corp., 1949-53; sec., dir. Pyrrole Products Co., 1948-53; dean engring. Ohio State U., Columbus, 1953-58, v.p. bus. and finance, treas., 1958-71; dir. Engring. Exptl. Sta., 1953-58, Accuray Corp., 1960-82, Cardinal Funds, Inc., 1962-98; exec. v.p. Albion (Mich.) Coll., 1971-76, exec. cons., 1976-77; asst. to chancellor, dir. fin. Northwood Inst., 1977-82; v.p. Mich. Molecular Inst., 1982-88; prin. Whitfield Robert Assocs., from 1988. Mem. adj. faculty Northwood U., from

1984; exec. cons. DeVos Grad. Sch. Mgmt., 1977—83. Editor: The Production Handbook, 1958; cons. editor, 1972—; Author of tech. papers engring. subjects. Trustee White Cross Hosp. Assn., 1960-71; bd. dirs. Orton Found., 1953-58, Cardinal Funds, 1966-98; bd. dirs. Goodwill Industries, 1959-67, 1st v.p., 1963-64; v.p. Ohio State U. Rsch. Found., 1958-71; v.p., chmn. adv. coun. Ctr. for Automation and Soc., U. Ga., 1969-71; chmn. tool and die com. 5th Regional War Labor Bd., 1943-45; chmn. Ohio state adv. com. for sci., tech. and specialized personnel SSS, 1965-70; pres. Larkin Parking Condo Assn., Inc., 1992—. Fellow ASME, AAAS, Inst. Indsl. Engrs. (pres. 1957-58); mem. Columbus Soc. Fin. Analysts (pres. 1974-75), Fin. Analysts Fedn. (bd. dirs. 1964-65), C. of C. (bd. dirs., treas. 1952-53), Am. Soc. Engring. Edn., Assn. Univs. for Rsch. in Astronomy (bd. dirs. 1958-71), Midwestern Univs. Rsch. Assn. (bd. dirs. 1958-71), U.S. Naval Inst., Nat. Soc. Profl. Engrs. (life), Romophos, Sphinx, Rotary (Paul Harris fellow), Sigma Xi (fin. com. 1975-89, nat. treas. 1979-89), Masons (32 deg.), Tau Beta Pi, Zeta Psi, Phi Eta Sigma, Alpha Pi Mu, Omicron Delta Epsilon. Home: Midland, Mich. Died Aug. 3, 2003.

CARSON, LUCIAN JOSEPH, lawyer; b. Portland, Oreg., Aug. 10, 1939; s. Joseph Kirtley and Myrtle (Cradick) C.; m. Sally Lindsey Hunt, May 17, 1969; children: Edward Lucian, Joseph Andrew. BA in Polit. Sci., Portland State U., 1962; JD, Willamette U., Salem, Oreg., 1969. Bar: Oreg. 1969, U.S. Dist. Ct. Oreg. 1973, U.S. Tax Ct. 1971. Clk. Oreg. Tax Ct., Salem, 1969-70; assoc. Davies, Biggs, Strayer, Stoel & Boley, Portland, 1970-72; ptnr. Carson & Duncan, Hillsboro, Oreg., 1972-73, Douglas, Carson, Dickey & Lynch, P.C., Salem, from 1973. Bd. dirs. Consumer Credit Counseling, Salem, 1980—, Salem Pub. Library Found., 1988—. With security agy., U.S. Army, 1962-65. Mem. ABA, Oreg. Bar Assn. Episcopalian. Home: Salem, Oreg. Deceased.

CARTER, ANNE COHEN, physician, educator; b. N.Y.C., Nov. 27, 1919; d. Arthur Joseph and Nellie (Zuckerman) Cohen; m. Charles Edward Carter, 1945 (div.); m. William Benjamin Heller, Nov. 4, 1947 (dec.); children: James Albert, Susan Klee. BA, Wellesley Coll., 1941; MD, Cornell U., 1944. Diplomate Am. Bd. Internal Medicine. Intern Bellevue Hosp., N.Y.C., 1944-45; resident in medicine N.Y. Hosp., N.Y.C., 1945-46; instr. in medicine Cornell U. Med. Coll., N.Y.C., 1948-52, asst. prof. medicine, 1952-55; rsch. fellow Russell Sage Inst. Pathology, N.Y.C., 1951-55; asst. prof. medicine SUNY-Downstate Med. Ctr., Bklyn., 1955-58, assoc. prof. medicine, 1958-68, chief div. endocrinology, 1958-92, prof. medicine, 1958-82; vis. scientist Bronx VA Hosp., Lab. Dr. Solomon A. Berson, Bronx, 1963-64; prof. medicine N.Y. Med. Coll., Valhalla, 1982-97, prof. emeritus, from 1997. Vis. prof. medicine SUNY Health Sci. Ctr., Bklyn., 1982-95, prof. emeritus, 1997; asst. physician N.Y. Hosp., 1945-47, physician, 1947-55, asst. attending physician, 1953-55; asst. vis. physician Kings County Hosp. Ctr., Bklyn., 1955-59, vis. physician, 1959-72, active attending physician, 1972-84, cons., 1984-95; rsch. assoc. Jewish Chronic Disease Hosp., Bklyn., 1957-67; attending physician State U. Hosp., Bklyn., 1967-84, cons., 1984-95; cons. Bklyn. VA Hosp., 1971-84; attending physician Westchester County Med. Ctr., Valhalla, 1982-97; dir. ambulatory cancer detection svcs., 1982-97; attending physician St. Agnes Hosp., 1993-97. Contbr. chpts. to books, articles to profl. jours. Bd. dirs. Am. Cancer Soc., Inc., N.Y.C., 1977—, Westchester div., 1985-91; trustee Wellesley Coll., 1971-89, trustee emerita, 1989—; trustee Dana Hall Sch., Wellesley, 1990-98. Recipient Pub. Edn. award Am. Cancer Soc., Westchester div., 1988, Alumna Achievement award Dana Hall Sch., Wellesley, Mass., 1990, Alumnae Achievement award Wellesley Coll., 1994, Gender Equity award Am. Women's Med. Assn., 1995, Pres. award Am. Cancer Soc. Westchester Divsn., 1997. Fellow AAAS, Westchester Acad. Medicine; mem. Am. Soc. Clin. Oncology, Am. Med. Assn., Endocrine Soc. (chmn. awards com. 1989-90), Soc. Exptl. Biology and Medicine, Am. Soc. Internal Medicine, Women's Med. Assn. N.Y.C. (v.p. 1990-92, fin. asst. fund treas. 1983 , pres. 1992), Women's Med. Assn. Westchester (pres. 1988-90), AAUP, Am. Diabetes Assn., Am. Fedn. Clin. Research, Am. Med. Women's Assn., Inc., (dir. N.Y. State 1991-99, Pres. Recognition award 1993), Am. Soc. Bone and Mineral Rsch., Assn. Community Cancer Ctrs., Assn. Women in Sci., Assn. Women in Sci. Ednl. Found. (bd. dirs. 1982-99), Harvey Soc., Internat. Soc. Preventive Oncology, Internat. Soc. Psychoneuroendocrinology, Nat. Hospice Orgn., Inc., N.Y. Acad. Sci., N.Y. Acad. Medicine, N.Y. State Med. Soc., N.Y. State Soc. Internal Medicine, Westchester County Med. Soc., N.Y. Met. Breast Cancer Group Inc., Cosmopolitan Club, Sigma Xi. Democrat. Jewish. Avocations: travel, photography, cooking. Home: New York, NY. Deceased.

CARTER, BENNETT LESTER (BENNY CARTER), musician, composer, conductor; b. N.Y.C., Aug. 8, 1907; LHD (hon.), Princeton U., 1974. Condr. workshops Baldwin Wallace Coll., Princeton, Yale, Cornell U., Duke U., from 1970; vis. lectr. Princeton U., 1973, 77, mem. adv. coun. music dept., from 1976; mem. music adv. panel NEA, 1976-79; artist in residence Rutgers U., 1986. Early career as alto saxophonist, clarinetist, trumpeter, arranger with various bands including Charlie Johnson, Fletcher Henderson, Chick Webb, Horace Henderson, 1925-32; leader own band, 1932-35, 38-46; toured Europe, 1935-38, Japan, 1978-79, 81, 83, 87; arranger BBC studio orch., 1936-38; composer, condr. music for movies including Stormy Weather, 1943, As Thousands Cheer, 1943, Panic in the Streets, 1950, Snows of Kilimanjaro, 1952, The Five Pennies, 1959, Guns of Navarone, 1961, A Man Called Adam, 1966, Buck and the Preacher, 1972, Cosmic Eye, 1985; appeared motion picture Snows of Kilimanjaro, 1952; rec. star, then free-lance artist, swing arranger; music dir., arranger for various singers, background music TV shows; albums include: Benny Carter French RCA, Ridin' In Rhythm, 1933, Benny Carter, Swingin' at Maida Vale, Django Reinhardt & The American Jazz Greats, Benny Carter, 1983 & 1946, Complete Benny Carter on Keynote, Jazz Giant, 1957, Further Definitions, 1961, The Benny Carter 4—Montreux '77, Wonderland, A Gentleman and His Music, Central City Sketches, 1987, In the Mood For Swing, 1987, Over the Rainbow, 1989, All That Jazz, 1990, All Of Me, 1991, Cosmopolite: The Oscar Peterson Verve Sessions, 1994, Elegy in Blue, 1994, Best of Benny Carter, 1995, The King, 1996, New Jazz Sounds: The Urbane Section, 1996, Three Jazz Giants, 1996. Recipient Silver award Esquire, 1943, Gold award, 1946, Bicentennial Nat. Music award Am. Music Conf., 1976, Golden Score award Am. Assn. Music Arrangers, 1980, Grammy Lifetime Achievement award, 1987, Bird trophy, The Hague, 1987, Songwriters Guild Aggie award, 1988, Down Beat Internat. Critics Poll award, 1989, Down Beat Mag. composer award, 1990, Down Beat Mat. arranger award, 1990, Grammy awd. for Harlem Renaissance Suite, 1992. Died July 12, 2003.

CARTER, GERALD EMMETT, retired archbishop; b. Montreal, Que., Can., Mar. 1, 1912; s. Thomas Joseph and Mary (Kelty) Carter. BTh, Grand Sem. Montreal, 1936; BA, U. Montreal, 1933, MA, 1940, PhD, 1947, LTh, 1950; DHL, Duquesne U., 1963; LLD (hon.), U. Western Ont., 1966, Concordia U., 1976, U. Windsor, 1977, McGill U., Montreal, 1980, Notre Dame (Ind.) U., 1981, St. Francis Xavier U., 1998; LittD, St. Mary's U., Halifax, 1980, Pontificial Inst., 1995; D of Sacred Letters (hon.), U. St. Michael's Coll., 1998; LLD (hon.), Assumption U., 1999. Ordained priest Roman Cath. Ch., 1937. Founder, prin., prof. St. Joseph Tchrs. Coll., Montreal, 1939—61; chaplain Newman Club, McGill U., 1941—56; charter mem., 1st pres. Thomas More Inst. Adult Edn., Montreal, 1945—61; mem. Montreal Cath. Sch. Commn., 1948—61; hon. canon Cathedral Basilica Montreal, 1952—61; aux. bishop London and titular bishop Altiburo, 1961; bishop of, 1964—78; archbishop of Toronto, 1978—90; elevated to cardinal, 1979; ret., 1990. Chmn. Episcopal Commn. Liturgy Can., 1966—73, Internat. Com. for English in the Liturgy, 1971; mem. Consilium of Liturgy, Rome, 1965, Sacred Congregation for Divine Worship, 1970; appointee Econ. Affairs Coun. of Holy See, 1981; v.p. Cath. Conf. Ont., 1971—73, Can. Cath. Conf., 1973; pres. Can. Conf. Cath. Bishops, 1975; coun. mem. Synod of Bishops, 1977. Author: The Catholic Public Schools of Quebec, 1957, Psychology and the Cross, 1959, The Modern Challenge to Religious Education, 1961, A Shepherd Speaks, 1981. Decorated companion Order of Can. Roman Catholic. Died Apr. 6, 2003.

CARTER, NELL, actress, singer; b. Birmingham, Ala., Sept. 13, 1948; d. Horace L. and Edna (M.) Hardy; m. Georg Krynicki, 1982 (div. 1992); children: Tracey, Joshua Bernard, Daniel. Student, Bill Russells Sch. Drama, 1970-73. Numerous radio and TV appearances in Ala.; numerous club appearances and concerts including Los Angeles Philharm; appeared in play and film: Hair; appeared in: films Modern Problems, 1981, Back Roads, 1981, The Grass Harp, 1995, The Crazysitter, 1995, The Proprietor, 1996, Fakin' Da Funk, 1997, Special Delivery, 1999; TV appearances include: Baryshnikov on Broadway, The Big Show, Christmas in Washington, Nell Carter, Never Too Old to Dream; star: TV series Gimme a Break, 1981-87, You Take the Kids, 1990-91, Hangin' with Mr. Cooper, 1993-94; TV movie Cindy, 1978, Final Shot: The Hank Gathers Story, 1992, Maid For Each Other, 1992; theatrical appearances include: Dude; Don't Bother Me, I Can't Cope; Jesus Christ Superstar; Bury the Dead; Rhapsody in Gershwin; Blues is a Woman; Black Broadway; Ain't Misbehavin', Fakin' Da Funk, 1997. Recipient Tony award; OBIE award; Drama Desk award; Soho News award for Ain't Misbehavin. Mem. AFTRA, SAG, Equity, NAACP (life). Jewish. Died Jan. 23, 2003.

CARTER, VICTOR M. private investor; b. Rostov-on-Don, Russia, Aug. 21, 1910; s. Mark and Fanya (Rudnick) C.; m. Adrea Zucker, July 15, 1928; 1 dau., Fanya. Dir., 1st Interstate Bank, Nat. Lumber, Ampal-Am. Israel Corp.; mem. exec. com. IDB Bankholding Co.; v.p., dir. So. Calif. Theatre Assn. Past pres. United Way, City of Hope, Japan Am. Soc., Japanese Philharmonic Soc. Bd. dirs. Fedn. Jewish Welfare Orgns., World Affairs Council, Century City Cultural Commn.; hon. chmn. bd. Israel Devel. Corp., CLAL (Israel) Ltd. (exec. com.), Teva Pharm.; bd. govs. Jewish Agy., Inc. Democrat. Mem. Masons, B'nai B'rith, Hillcrest Country Club. Home: Los Angeles, Calif. Died Mar. 27, 2004.

CASALS-ARIET, JORDI, physician; b. Viladrau, Girona, Spain, May 15, 1911; came to U.S., 1936, naturalized, 1946; s. Martin and Margarida (Ariet) Casals-A.; m. Ellen Evelyn Brock, Dec. 6, 1941; 1 dau., Christina. B.Ciencias, Instituto Nacional, Barcelona, Spain, 1928; Licenciado en Medicina y Cirurgia con Grado, U. Barcelona, 1934. Intern Med. Sch. Hosp., Barcelona, 1934-36; research asso. Cornell U. Med. Coll., N.Y.C., 1936-38; asso. Rockefeller Inst. Med. Research, N.Y.C., 1938-52; mem. staff Rockefeller Found., N.Y.C., 1952-74; prof. epidemiology Yale U., 1964-81, prof. emeritus, 1981—2004; vis. prof. dept. neurology Mt. Sinai Sch. Medicine, N.Y.C., 1981-84, professorial lectr. dept. neurology, 1984—2004. Contbr. articles to profl. jours. Served with Spanish Army, 1933. Recipient Kimble Methodology award Am. Pub. Health Assn., 1969 Fellow Am. Soc. Tropical Medicine and Hygiene (Taylor award 1968), Royal Soc. Tropical Medicine and Hygiene (hon.); mem. Soc. Exptl. Biology and Medicine, Harvey Soc., AAAS, N.Y. Acad. Medicine, N.Y. Acad. Scis., French Soc. Microbiology (hon.), Internat. Com. on Taxonomy of Viruses (life). Home: New York, NY. Died Feb. 10, 2004.

CASEY, ALBERT VINCENT, business policy educator, retired business executive; b. Boston, Feb. 28, 1920; s. John Joseph and Norine (Doyle) C.; m. Eleanor Anne Welch, Aug. 25, 1945 (dec. 1989); children: Peter Andrew, Judith Anne. SB, Harvard, 1943, MBA, 1948. With S.P. Ry., 1948-61, asst. v.p., asst. treas., 1953-61; v.p., treas. Ry. Express Agy., N.Y.C., 1961-63; v.p. finance Times-Mirror Co., Los Angeles, 1963-64, exec. v.p., dir., 1964-66, pres., mem. exec. com., 1966-74; chmn. bd., pres. Am. Airlines, 1974-80, chmn. bd., 1980-85; U.S. Postmaster General, 1986; disting. prof. bus. policy Edwin L. Cox Sch. Bus., So. Meth. U., Dallas, 1986-88; chmn., chief exec. officer First Republic Bank Corp., Dallas, 1988-89; pres., chief exec. officer Resolution Trust Corp., 1991-93; disting. exec. in res. Cox Sch. Bus. So. Meth. U., Dallas. Bd. dirs. MAG Aerospace Industries, Clark/Bardes; chmn. Nat. Drugs Don't Work Partnership. Author (autobiography): Casey's Law: If something can go right it should, 1997. 1st lt. AUS, 1942-46. Mem.: Dallas Country, Bohemian, Eldorado Country (Indian Wells, Calif.), Met. (Washington), Marrakesh (Palm Desert, Calif.). Died July 10, 2004.

CASH, JOHNNY, entertainer; b. Kingsland, Ark., Feb. 26, 1932; s. Ray and Carrie (Rivers) C.; m. Vivian Liberto, 1954, div. 1966, children: Rosanne, Kathleen, Cindy, Tara; June Carter (dec. 2003), Mar. 1, 1968; 1 child, John Carter. H.H.D., Gardner-Webb Coll., 1971, Nat. U., San Diego, 1975, L.H.D. (hon.), 1976. Pres. House of Cash, Inc., Song of Cash, Inc.; v.p. Family of Man Music, Inc. Mem. adv. com. Peace Corps, Country Music Assn., John Edwards Meml. Found. Profl. composer, also, rec. artist; TV performer: the Johnny Cash Show, 1969-71; Author: (autobiography) Man in Black, 1975, (novel) Man in White, 1986; composer documentary rec. The True West; subject of documentary films Johnny Cash, the Man, His World, His Music; actor: (films), Door to Door Maniac, 1961, Night Rider, 1962, A Gunfight, 1971, The Gospel Road, 1973, All My Friends Are Cowboys, 1998; actor: (TV movies) Colombo: Swan Song, 1974, Thaddeus Rose and Eddie, 1978, Where Have All the Children Gone, 1980, The Pride of Jesse Hallam, 1981, Murder in Coweta County, 1983, The Baron and the Kid, 1984, North and South (mini series), 1985, Last Days of Frank and Jesse James, 1986, Stagecoach, 1986, Davy Crockett: Rainbow in the Thunder, 1988; actor: (TV appearances): The Spade Cooley Show, 1958, The Rebel, The Tennessee Ernie Ford Show, 1960, This Is Tom Jones, Sesame Street, Hee Haw, The Andy Williams Show, 1969, Beat-Club, 1972, Little House on the Prarie, 1976, The Muppet Show, 1980, Saturday Night Live, 1982, Dr. Quinn, Medicine Woman, 1993, 1994, 1997, Renegade, 1996, The Simpsons (voice only), 1997; albums include: Johnny Cash and His Hot and Blue Guitar, 1957, Johnny Cash Sings the Songs That Made Him Famous, 1958, The Fabulous Johnny Cash, 1959, Hymns by Johnny Cash, 1959, Songs of Our Soil, 1959, Greatest Johnny Cash, 1959, Johnny Cash Sings Hank Williams, 1959, Ride This Train, 1960, Now There Was A Song, 1960, Now, Here's Johnny Cash, 1961, Hymns from the Heart, 1962, The Sound of Johnny Cash, 1962, All Aboard the Blue Train, 1962, Blood, Sweat, and Tears, 1963, Ring of Fire, 1963, The Christmas Spirit, 1963, Keep on the Sunny Side, 1964, I Walk the Line, 1964, The Original Sun Sound of Johnny Cash, 1964, Bitter Tears: Ballads of the American Indian, 1964, Orange Blossom Special, 1965, Ballads of the True West, 1965, Mean as Hell, 1965, Everybody Loves a Nut, 1966, Happiness is You, 1966, Johnny Cash & June Carter, 1967, Johnny Cash's Greatest Hits, 1967, Carryin' on with Cash and Carter, 1967, From Sea to Shining Sea, 1968, At Folsom Prison, 1969, The Holy Land, 1968, At San Quentin, 1969, Johnny Cash, 1969, Original Golden Hits, Vol. I, 1969, Original Golden Hits, Vol. II, 1969, Story Songs of the Trains and Rivers, 1969, Got Rhythmn, 1969, The Blue Train, 1970, The Walls of a Prison, 1970, Sunday Down South, 1970, Showtime, 1970, Hello, I'm Johnny Cash, 1970, The Singing Storyteller, 1970, The World of Johnny Cash, 1970, Johnny Cash Sings I Walk the Line, 1970, Man in Black, 1971, Understand Your Man, 1971, Original Golden Hits, Vol. III, 1971, A Thing Called Love, 1972, Give My Love to Rose, 1972, America, 1972, The Johnny Cash Songbook, 1972, Christmas: The Johnny Cash Family, 1972, The Gospel Road, 1973, Any Old Wind That Blows, 1973, The Fabulous Johnny Cash, 1973, Johnny Cash and His Woman, 1973, Sunday Morning Coming Down, 1973, Ballads of the American Indians, Ragged Old Flag, 1974, Five Feet High and Rising, 1974, The Junkie and Juicehead Minus Me, 1974, Johnny Cash Sings Precious Memories, 1975, The Children's Album, 1975, John R. Cash, 1975, Johnny Cash at Osteraker Prison, 1975, Look at Them Beans, 1975, Strawberry Cake, 1975, One Piece at a Time, 1976, Destination Victoria Station, 1976, The Last Gunfighter Ballad, 1977, The Rambler, 1977, I Would Like to See You again, 1978, Gone Girl, 1978, Johnny Cash-Silver, 1979, A Believer Sings the Truth, 1979, Rockabilly Blues, 1980, Classic Christmas, 1980, The Baron, 1981,, Encore, 1981, The Surviivors, 1982, The Adventures of Johnny Cash, 1982, Songs of Love and Life, 1983, I believe, 1984, Highwayman, 1985, Rainbow, 1986, Believe in Him, 1986, Johnny Cash is Coming to Town, 1987, Water From the Wells of Home, 1988, JOhnny Cash: Patriot, 1990, Boom Chicka Boom, 1990, Mystery of Life, 1991, Johnny Cash: American Recordings, 1994, Highwaymen (with Willie Nelson, Kris Kristofferson, Waylon Jennings), 1995, Unchained, 1996, Johnny Cash: The Hits, 1996, VH1 Storytellers with Willie Nelson, 1998, Just as I am, 1999, Johnny Cash and June Carter Cash: It's All in the Family, 1999, Love God Murder, 2000, Super Hits, 2000, American III: Solitary Man, 2000, Essential Johnny Cash, 2002, American IV: The Man Comes Around, 2002; TV documentary film Johnny Cash at San Quentin; promotional film United Way of America, 1972; co-writer, producer narrator: film The Gospel Road, 1972, Tennessee Nights, 1989, Return to the Promised Land, 1993, Radio Star - die AFN - Story, 1994. Hon. com. mem. Israel's 25th Anniversary. Served with USAF. Recipient No. 1 Hit Song award for Tennessee Flat Top Box, Country Music Assn., 1988, Golden Boot award, 1990, Grammy Living Legend award, 1993, Contempory Folk Album Grammy American Recordings, 1995; named to Country Music Hall of Fame, 1980, to Songwriter's Hall of Fame, 1984, to Rock-n-Roll Hall of Fame, 1992; Grammie Lifetime Achievement Award, 1999. Achievements include having over 53 million albums sold. Died Sept. 12, 2003.

CASH, JUNE CARTER, singer; b. Maces Springs, Va., June 23, 1929; d. Ezra and Maybelle (Addington) Carter; m. John R. Cash; children: Rebecca Carlene, Rozanna Lea, John Carter. Student, Neighborhood Playhouse Sch. Dramatics, 1955-56; HHD (hon.), Nat. U., San Diego, 1977. Singer with Carter Family, 1939-43, with Carter Sisters (and mother), after 1943; performed on Sta. XERF, Del Rio Tex., Sta. KWTO, Springfield, Mo.; mem. Grand Ole Opry, Sta. WSM, Nashville; TV appearances include John Davidson Show, Tennessee Ernie Show, Johnny Cash Show, others; films include: Thaddeus, Rose and Eddie, Country Music Holiday; TV movies: Stage Coach, Murder Coweta Country, The Baron, The Last Days of Frank and Jessie James, Keep on The Sunny Side, Appalachian Pride, Gospel Road, Country Music Caravan, Road to Nashville, Tennessee Jamboree, Gospel Road; TV spl. The Best of The Carter Family; songs recorded include: Baby It's Cold Outside, Music Music Music, Love Oh Crazy Love, Let Me Go Lover, Leftover Loving, Press On; contbr. to album Johnny Cash is Coming to Town, 1987; author: Among My Klediments, 1979, From the Heart, 1986, Mother Maybelle's Cookbook, 1989; co-author: Ring of Fire; appeared in film The Apostle, 1997. Recipient Grammy for Best Traditional Folk Album of Yr., 2000. Died May 15, 2003.

CASPER, DAVID J. chef; b. Milw., May 27, 1956; s. James T. and Eileen (McGee) C. AOS, Culinary Inst. Am., Hyde Park, N.Y., 1978. Chef garde manger Rancho Bernardo Inn, San Diego, 1979-80; sous chef Northwood Club, Dallas, 1980; kitchen mgr. Wonderful World Cooking, Dallas, 1980-81; pvt. chef Am. Petroleum Ptnrs., Dallas, 1981-82; exec. chef Christoffers, Dallas, 1982-85, Cynthia Michaels Inc., Dallas, from 1985. Mem. Nat. Assn. Catering Execs. Home: Milwaukee, Wis. Deceased.

CASPI, ELIAHU, chemist; b. Warsaw, June 10, 1913; came to U.S., 1950; s. Jacob and Rose (Goldberg) Silberschatz; m. Sara Kelrich, May 8, 1948; 1 child, Daniel. Mag.Sc. in Chemistry, U. Warsaw, 1939; PhD, Clark U., 1955. Staff scientist Standard Inst. of Israel, Tel-Aviv, 1943-50; scientist Worcester Found. for Exptl. Biology, Shrewsbury, Mass., 1951-57, staff scientist, 1957-62, sr. scientist, 1962-71, prin. scientist, 1971-91, prin. scientist emeritus, from 1992. Mem. sci. adv. bd. Worcester Found. for Exptl. Biology, 1969-79; vis. prof. Tel Aviv U., 1969, Ben Gurion U., 1977, Louis Pasteur U., Strasbourg, France, 1980-81; Lady Davis vis. prof. Hebrew U., 1978. With Hagana Def. Force, 1943-48, Israel Def. Force, 1948-50. Recipient Career Devel. award Nat. Cancer Inst., Disting. Accomplishment award Am. Chem. Soc. Mem. AAAS, Am. Chem. Soc., Chem. Soc., Am. Soc. for Biochemistry and Molecular Biology, Phytochem. Soc. N.Am., Worcester Com. on Fgn. Rels. Achievements include research in non-oxidative biosynthesis of triterpenes; steric course of hydroxylation at primary carbon atoms; steric mode of incorporation of C-2, 4 and 5 hydrogen atoms of MVA into steroids and protosterols; biosynthesis of hormones and plant steroids. Home: Worcester, Mass. Died May 13, 2001.

CASSEL, RUSSELL NAPOLEON, retired clinical research psychologist; b. Harrisburg, Pa., Dec. 18, 1911; s. Herman I. and Sallie (Hummer) C.; m. Lan Dam, Oct. 5, 1964; children— Louis A., Angelica V., Gary R., Lynn V., Gail J., Sallie M., Susie L. Student Pa. State U., 1929-32; B.S., Millersville State Coll., 1937; M.Ed., Pa. State U., 1939; D.Ed., U. So. Calif., 1949; grad. Air War Coll., 1963-65. Diplomate Am. Bd. Profl. Psychology. Tchr. rural sch., North Twp., Pa., 1935-38; tchr. Dauphin (Pa.) Jr. High Sch., 1938-40; personnel cons. U.S. Army Air Force, 1940-46; prof. ednl. psychology U. San Diego, 1949-51; research psychologist U.S. Air Force, San Antonio, 1951-57; sch. psychologist Phoenix Schs., 1957-59; dir. pupil personnel services Lompoc Unified Schs., Calif., 1959-61; cons. to schs. Dept. State, Viet-Nam also Liberia, 1961-67; prof. ednl. psychology U. Wis.-Milw., 1967-74; editor Project Innovation, Chula Vista, Calif., 1969—. Contbr. articles to profl. jours.; author books in field, psychol. tests, computerized programs. Served to col. USAF, 1951-57. Fellow Am. Psychol. Assn., Assn. Correctional Psychology (past pres.), San Diego Computer Soc. (past pres.), Phi Delta Kappa. Republican. Lutheran. Home: Chula Vista, Calif. Died May 18, 2004.

CATES, NELIA BARLETTA DE, diplomat of Dominican Republic; b. Santo Domingo, Dominican Republic, Dec. 21, 1932; d. Amadeo and Nelia (Ricart) Barletta; m. Miguel Morales Abreu, Oct. 29, 1953 (div. 1961); m. John Martin Cates, Nov. 19, 1976. Ed. in Argentina, Cuba and U.S.A.; diploma, Duchesne Coll., 1950. Cultural attache Embassy of Dominican Republic, London, 1975-85, amb., permanent rep. to Internat. Maritime Orgn., 1985-94; pres. Companía Editorial El Mundo S.A., La Habana, Cuba, from 1994. Mem. Maritime Orgn., 1985-86. Died Aug. 24, 2002.

CATHCART, DAVID ARTHUR, lawyer; b. Pasadena, Calif., June 1, 1940; s. Arthur James and Martelle C.; m. Janet Eileen Farley, June 19, 1973; children: Sarah Emily, Rebecca Eileen. BA with great distinction, Stanford U., 1961; MA, Harvard U., 1966, LLB cum laude, 1967. Bar: Calif. 1968, U.S. Dist. Ct. (ctrl. dist.) Calif. 1969, U.S. Dist. Ct. (so. and no. dists.) 1975, U.S. Dist. Ct. (ea. dist.) 1979, U.S. Ct. Appeals (9th cir.) 1975, U.S. Supreme Ct. 1979. Assoc. Gibson, Dunn & Crutcher LLP, L.A., 1968-70, 72-75, ptnr., from 1975. Legis. asst. U.S. Senate, Washington, 1971-72; mem. NLRB Adv. Com., 1994-98. Editor-in-chief: Employment Discrimination Law Five-Year Cumulative Supplement, 1989, Employment-At-Will: A 1989 State-By-State Survey, 1990; co-author: California Employment Litigation Practice Guide, 2001; contbr. chpts. to legal texts, articles to profl. jours. Bd. dirs. Western Ctr. on Law and Poverty, LA, 1985-88, U.S.-South Africa Leadership Devel. Program, 1992—, Employers Group, 2000-03. Woodrow Wilson fellow, 1961-62, Danforth fellow, 1961-64. Fellow Coll. of Labor and Employment Lawyers; mem. ABA (mem. coun. 1997—, mgmt. co-chmn. equal employment opportunity law com., 1994-96, sect. labor and employment law, co-chmn. employment and labor rels. law com., 1985-88, litig. sect., class action task force 2002-03), LA County Bar Assn. (chmn. labor and employment law sect. 1991-92), Am. Employment Law Coun. (chmn. 1993—), Chancery Club, City Club on Bunker Hill, Harvard Club NYC, Phi Beta Kappa. Died Sept. 30, 2003.

CATRAMBONE, JOSEPH ANTHONY, data processing executive; b. Chgo., Sept. 21, 1924; s. Nicola F. and Theresa C.; m. Thelma M. Evans, Dec. 29, 1951; children: Nicola, Christina, Catherine, Dawn, Joseph, Christopher, Laura, Mary, Arthur, Theresa, Noel, Eugene. BS, St. Benedicts Coll., 1947; MA, U. Maine, 1953. Asst. dir. lab for applied scis. U. Chgo., 1958-62; sr. system analyst Service Bur. Corp., Chgo., 1962-64; ops. research analyst Ill. Inst. Tech., Chgo., 1964-66; sr. research engr. Northrup Aircraft Corp., Chgo., 1966-68; dir. adminstrv. data processing U. Ill., Chgo., 1968-72, asst. to v.p., 1972-75, asst. v.p., 1975-79, assoc. v.p., 1979-83; v.p. info. systems Loyola U. Chgo., from 1983. Sr. math. U. Chgo. Inst. System Research, 1953-57; head coach Damar (Kans.) High Sch., 1947-50. Ensign USN, 1943-46. Mem. Assn. Computing Machinery, Profl. Assn. for Computing and Info. Tech. in Higher Edn. (bd. dirs., v.p. 1979-80, pres. 1980-81), Coll. and Univ. Computer Users (pres. 1983-84, bd. dirs.). Home: Chicago, Ill. Deceased.

CAUFIELD, MARY ELIZABETH, community health nurse; b. Bklyn., July 26, 1936; d. William J. and Rita A. (Walsh) C. RN, St. Vincent's Hosp., N.Y.C., 1957; BS, St. John's U., Bklyn., 1960; MS, U. Pa., 1966. Staff nurse, asst. head nurse St. Vincent's Hosp., N.Y.C., 1957-60; nursing instr. med.-surg. St. John's Episcopal Hosp. Sch. Nursing, Bklyn., 1960-62; pub. health nurse N.Y.C. Dept. Health, 1962-65; asst. supr. Vis. Nurse Assn. Bklyn., 1966-69, supr., 1969-75, adminstr., 1975-87, dir. patients svcs.-ops., from 1987. Mem. ANA, Nat. League Nursing, APHA, Pub. Health Assn. N.Y.C., Nurses House, Home Care Assn. N.Y. State. Home: Brooklyn, NY. Deceased.

CECIL, ROBERT SALISBURY, telecommunications company executive; b. Manila, Philippines, May 28, 1935; came to U.S., 1941; s. Robert Edgar and Susan Elizabeth (Jurika) C.; m. Louise Nuttal Millholland, Nov. 30, 1963; children: Scott Douglass, James Hilliard; m. Patricia Louise Fisher, July 14, 1997; 1 child, Robert Scott. BSEE, U.S. Naval Acad., 1956; MBA, Harvard U., 1962. Commd. 2d lt. USAF, 1956, advanced through grades to 1st lt., 1958, ret., 1960; dir. govt. programs IBM, Washington, 1976-77; corp. v.p. mktg. Motorola Inc., Schaumburg, Ill., 1977-84; pres. Cellular Group Lin Broadcasting, N.Y.C., 1984-91; chmn. Plantronics, Inc., Santa Cruz, Calif., from 1992. Bd. dirs. Q Media, Xantrex, CW Saskfund III, Ltd. Mem. Lyford Cay Club, Vancouver Lawn Tennis and Badminton Club, Rotary Internat. Republican. Episcopalian. Home: Whistler, Canada. Deceased.

CHAIT, HELEN SPORN, lawyer; b. N.Y.C., Jan. 6, 1914; d. Jacob Samuel and Bertha (Lax) Sporn; m. Frederick Chait, Sept. 22, 1938 (wid. 1988). BA, Barnard Coll., 1933; LLB, Columbia U., 1938. Bar: N.Y. 1938, Pa. 1953. Asst. to reporter for property restatement Am. Law Inst., N.Y.C., 1938-41; rev. atty. N.Y. State Labor Relations Bd., N.Y.C., 1941-42; office of gen. counsel Bd. of Econ. Warfare, Washington, 1942-43; assoc. Root, Clark, Buckner and Ballantine, N.Y.C., 1943-46, Cleary, Gottlieb, Friendly and Hamilton, N.Y.C., 1946-51; house counsel N.W. Levin (investment mgr.), N.Y.C., 1951-53; dep. city solicitor, chief counsellor Law Dept. City of Phila., 1953-59; chmn. Phila. Tax Rev. Bd., 1960-66; ptnr. Goodis, Greenfield, Narin and Mann, Phila., 1966-71, Narin and Chait, Phila., 1971-89; of counsel Krekstein, Wolfson & Krekstein, Phila., from 1989. Trustee, sec. bd., exec. com., Phila. Coll. of Art (now U. of the Arts), 1970--;trustee, sec. bd. Phila. Gen. Hosp. Research Fund, 1966-76. Mem. ABA, Phila. Bar Assn. (chmn. local govt. com. 1965), Locust Club. Home: Philadelphia, Pa. Deceased.

CHAIT, WILLIAM, librarian, consultant; b. N.Y.C., Dec. 5, 1915; s. Max and Mollie (Miller) C.; m. Beatrice L. Faigelman, June 13, 1937; 1 son, Edward Martin. BA, Bklyn. Coll., 1934; B.L.S., Pratt Inst., 1935; MS in L.S, Columbia U., 1938. Library asst., br. librarian Bklyn. Pub. Library, 1935-45; service command librarian 2d Service Command AUS, 1945-46; chief in- service tng., personnel control Milw. Pub. Library, 1946-48; dir. Kalamazoo Pub. Library, 1948-56, Dayton and Montgomery County Pub. Library, 1956-78, dir. emeritus, 1979—. Mem. Library Cons., Inc. Pres. Kalamazoo Council Social Agys., 1954-55, Dayton City Beautiful Com., 1968-69; treas. Montgomery County Hist. Soc., 1968-69; trustee On-Line Computer Library Center, 1974-85, treas., 1976-79. Fulbright lectr. library sci. U. Tehran, 1969-70 Mem. Pub. Library Assn. (pres. 1964-65), ALA (treas. 1976-80, council 1981-85, chmn. personnel adminstrn. sect. 1958-60), Mich. Library Assn. (pres. 1955-56), Ohio Library Assn. (pres. 1964-65), S.C. Library Assn. Home: Hilton Head Island, SC. Deceased.

CHALL, JEANNE STERNLICHT, psychologist, educator; b. Shendishov, Poland, Jan. 1, 1921; came to U.S., 1927:; d. Hyman and Eva (Kreinik) Sternlicht; m. Leo P. Chall, June 8, 1946 (div. 1964). BBA cum laude, CCNY, 1941; MA, Ohio State U., 1947, PhD, 1952; MA (hon.), Harvard, 1965; HLD, Lesley Coll., 1972. Rsch. asst. Ohio State U., Columbus, 1945-47, rsch. assoc., instr., 1947-49; instr. CCNY, 1950-52, asst. prof., 1952-62, assoc. prof., 1962-65, prof., 1965; vis. assoc. prof. Harvard U. Grad. Sch. Edn., Cambridge, Mass., 1963, prof., 1965-91, prof. emeritus, 1991. Readability cons., 1950—; faculty summer sessions Tchrs. Coll., Columbia U., N.Y.C., 1958, 60-61; mem. Nat. Com. on Dyslexia and Related Reading Disorders, 1968-69, steering com. Project Literacy, U.S. Office Edn.; sec.-treas. Nat. Conf. on Rsch. in English, 1962, v.p. 1964-65, pres. 1965. Author: Readability: Research and Application, 1958, Learning to Read: The Great Debate, 1967, updated edit., 1983, 3d edit., 1996; co-author: (with Dale) A Formula for Predicting Readability, 1948, Readability Revisited: The New Dale-Challl Formula, 1995; (with Roswell) Diagnostic Test of Word Analysis Skills, 1956, 59, 78, 96, Diagnostic Assessments of Reading with Trial Teaching Strategies, 1992, Stages of Reading Development, 1983, 2d edit., 1996, Creating Successful Readers: A Practical Guide to Testing and Teaching at All Levels, 1994, Reading Difficulties: Effective Mehods for Successful Teaching, 1999; (with Jacobs and Baldwin) The Reading Crisis: Why Poor Children Fall Behind, 1990, (with Conard) Should Textbooks Challenge Students? The Case for Easier or Harder Books, 1991; (with Roswell, Fletcher, Richmond) Teaching Children to Read: A Step by Step Guide for Volunteer Tutors, 1998; (with Bissex, Conard, Harris-Sharples) Qualitative Assessment of Text Difficulty, 1996; (with Popp) Teaching and Assessing Phonics, 1996; contbr. articles to profl. jours. Recipient Andre Favat award Mass. Coun. Tchrs. Eng., 1979, Am. Ednl. Rsch. Assn. award, 1982, 86, Edward L. Thorndike award APA, 1982, Disting. Rsch. award Nat. Conf. on Rsch. in English, 1993, Samuel T. Orton award Internat. Dyslexia Assn., 1996, Internat. Acad. Edn. award, 1997; named to the Reading Hall of Fame, 1979, Nat. Acad. Edn., 1979. Fellow APA; mem. Nat. Assn. Remedial Teaching (chmn. program com. 1955), Nat. Reading Coun., Internat. Reading Assn. (dir. 1961-65, chmn. pre-conf. inst. 1959-61, membership com. 1958-60, Citation of Merit 1979), Am. Ednl. Rsch. Assn., Nat. Soc. for Study of Edn. (dir. 1972-78), Phi Delta Kappa. Home: Cambridge, Mass. Deceased.

CHAMBERLAIN, CHARLES ERNEST, lawyer, former congressman; b. Ingham County, Mich., July 22, 1917; s. Orson W. and Clara Adella (DaFoe) C.; m. Charlotte Mary Craney, Dec. 2, 1943; children: Charlotte Ellen, Christine Clark, Charles Ernest, Jr. BS in Commerce, U. Va., 1941, LL.B., 1949. Bar: Va. bar 1949, Mich. bar 1949, also D.C. bar 1949. Pvt. practice of law, Lansing, Mich., 1950—; asst. pros. Ingham County, 1950; city atty. East Lansing, 1953-54; legal counsel Mich. Senate Judiciary Com., 1953-54; pros. atty. Ingham County, 1955-56; mem. 85th-93d congresses from 6th Dist. Mich., mem. ways and means com.; ptnr. firm Webster, Chamberlain & Bean, Washington, 1975—. Served as officer USCG, World War II. Mem. Am., Mich., Va., D.C. bar assns., SAR. Republican. Home: Waterford, Va. Died Nov. 29, 2002.

CHAMBERS, DAVID L. retired adult educator; b. Picton, Ont., Can., Apr. 28, 1920; s. David Lyall and Ruth (Farrington) C.; m. Patricia Anne Chambers; children: Katherine Anne, David William, Sharon Patricia, Michelle Laverne, Scott Alexander. Diploma, Rochester Inst. Tech., 1965. Tool and die maker Xerox Corp., Webster, N.Y., foreman indsl. components, ret., tchr. machine use, adult evening classes; now ret. With U.S. Army, 1939-43 WW II. Home: Rochester, NY. Died Nov. 10, 2001.

CHANDLER, LARRY DONALD, software engineer; b. Mansfield, Ohio, June 19, 1948; s. Joseph and Marie (Brown) C. BS in Computer Info. Sci., Ohio State U., 1971. Programmer Sperry Corp., Eagan, Minn., 1974-98. Contbr. articles to profl. jours. Capt. U.S. Army, 1971-74. Mem. Assn. Computer Machinery, Computer Soc. of IEEE, Math. Assn. Am., Armed Forces Communication Electronics Assn. Republican. Avocations: reading, cycling. Home: Nashua, NH. Died Feb. 11, 1999.

CHANTILIS, PETER S. lawyer, mediator; b. Chgo., Apr. 15, 1934; s. Samuel A. and Rose P. Chantilis; children: Samuel, Stephanie Chantilis Bray. BBA, So. Meth. U., 1955,

LLB, 1957. Ptnr. Coffee and Chantilis, 1957-62, Coffee, Coffee and Chantilis, 1962-77; sole practitioner, 1977-83; atty. The Law Offices of Chantilis and Morgan, 1983-87; ptnr. Chantilis & Brousseau, 1987-92; sole practitioner Dallas, from 1992. Adj. prof. So. Meth. U. Sch. Law, 1992; lectr. in field. Author materials in field. Dir. Dallas Jazz Orch., 1992; chmn. Park Cities Sesquicentennial Com., 1982-86; parish coun. rec. sec. Holy Trinity Greek Orthodox Ch., 1988-90; city commr. City of University Park; mem. adv. bd. dirs. Cmtys. Found. Tex.; pres. Cotton Bowl Coun. Fellow Tex. Bar Found.; mem. ABA, Internat. Bar Assn., Dallas Bar Assn., Soc. Profls. in Dispute Resolution, Am. Acd. Atty.-Mediators (exec. dir. 1992), Assn. of Atty.-Mediators, Inc., Am. Arbitration Assn. (panel of arbitrators), Nat. Speakers Assn., North Tex. Speakers Assn., Alpha Tau Omega. Deceased.

CHAPANIS, ALPHONSE, human factors engineer, ergonomist; b. Meriden, Conn., Mar. 17, 1917; s. Anicatas and Mary (Barkevich) Chapanis; m. Marion Amelia Rowe, Sept. 23, 1941 (div. 1960); children: Roger, Linda Chapanis Fox; m. Natalia Potanin, Mar. 25, 1960 (div. 1987); m. Vivian Woodward, Nov. 24, 2001. BA, U. Conn., 1937; MA, Yale U., 1942, PhD, 1943; DSc, U. Conn., 1998. Cert. Human Factors Profl. Prof. psychology The Johns Hopkins U., Balt., 1946-82; prof. emeritus, from 1999; pres. Alphonse Chapanis, PhD, P.A., Balt., 1974-99. Mem. tech. staff Bell Labs., Murray Hill, N.J., 1953-54; mem. adv. panel USAF Office Sci. Rsch., Washington, 1956-59; mem. com. on human factors NRC, Washington, 1980-85; liaison scientist Office Naval Rsch., Am. Embassy, London, 1960-61; cons. IBM, Yorktown Heights, N.Y. and Bethesda, Md., 1960-95, Loral Fed. Sys., Bethesda, 1995-96. Author: Research Techniques in Human Engineering, 1959, Man-Machine Engineering, 1965, Human Factors in Systems Engineering, 1996, The Chapanis Chronicles; 50 Years of Human Factors Research, Education, and Design, 1999; co-author: Applied Experimental Psychology, 1949; editor: Ethnic Variables in Human Factors Engineering, 1975; co-editor: Human Engineering Guide to Equipment Design, 1963; contbr. over 175 articles to profl. jours. Capt. USAAF, 1943-46. Recipient Disting. Contbn. for Applications in Psychology award APA, 1978, Outstanding Sci. Contbn. to Psychology, Md. Psychol. Assn., 1981, Outstanding Achievement in Behavioral and Social Sci. award Wash. Acad. Sci., 1997. Fellow AAAS, Soc. Engrng. Psychologists (Franklin V. Taylor award 1963), Human Factors and Ergonomics Soc. (Paul W. Fitts award 1973, Pres.' Disting. Svc. award 1987), Ergonomics Soc. (hon.), Internat. Ergonomics Assn. (Outstanding Contbn. award 1982). Achievements include patent (with others) on Correlation of Seismic Signals. Home: Baltimore, Md. Died Oct. 4, 2002.

CHAPLIN, GEORGE, newspaper editor; b. Columbia, S.C., Apr. 28, 1914; s. Morris and Netty (Brown) C.; m. Esta Lillian Solomon, Jan. 26, 1937 (dec. Jan. 2001); children: Stephen Michael, Jerry Gay. BS, Clemson Coll., 1935; Nieman fellow, Harvard U., 1940-41; HHD (hon.), Clemson U., 1989; LHD (hon.), Hawaii Loa Coll., 1990. Reporter, later city editor Greenville (S.C.) Piedmont, 1935-42; mng. editor Camden (N.J.) Courier-Post, 1946-47, San Diego Jour., 1948-49; mng. editor, then editor New Orleans Item, 1949-58; asso. editor Honolulu Advertiser, 1958-59, editor in chief, 1959-86, editor at large, from 1986. Mem. selection com. Jefferson fellowships East-West Ctr.; chmn. Gov.'s Conf. on Year 2000, 1970; chmn. Hawaii Commn. on Year 2000, 1971-74; co-chmn. Conf. on Alt. Econ. Futures for Hawaii, 1973-75; charter mem. Goals for Hawaii, 1979-81; alt. U.S. rep. South Pacific Commn., 1978-81; chmn. search com. for pres. U. Hawaii, 1983; chmn. Hawaii Gov.'s Adv. Coun. on Fgn. Lang. and Internat. Studies, 1983-94; rep. of World Press Freedom Com. on missions to Sri Lanka, Hong Kong, Singapore, 1987. Editor, officer-in-charge: Mid-Pacific edit. Stars and Stripes World War II; editor: (with Glenn Paige) Hawaii 2000, 1973, Presstime in Paradise: The Life and Times of the Honolulu Advertiser 1856-1995, 1998. Bd. dirs. U. Hawaii Rsch. Corp., 1970-72, Inst. for Religion and Social Change, Hawaii Jewish Welfare Fund, Charleston Christian-Jewish Coun.; mem. bd. govs. East-West Ctr., Honolulu, 1980-89, chmn., 1983-89; mem. bd. govs. Pacific Health Rsch. Inst., 1984-90, 93-97, pres., 1995-96; bd. govs. Straub Med. Found., 1989-98, Hawaii Pub. Schs. Found., 1986-87; trustee Clarence T. C. Ching Found., 1986-95; mem. Temple K.K. Beth Elohim; Am. media chmn. U.S.-Japan Conf. on Cultural and Ednl. Interchange, 1978-86; co-founder, v.p. Coalition for Drug-Free Hawaii, 1987-90; panelist ABA Conf., 1989; mem. Civilian Adv. Group, U.S. Army, Hawaii, 1985-95; co-chair Hawaii State Commn. on Judicial Salaries, 1995-98. Capt. AUS, 1942-46. Decorated Star Solidarity (Italy), Order Rising Sun (Japan), Prime Minister's medal (Israel); recipient citations Overseas Press Club, 1961, 72, Headliners award, 1962, John Hancock award, 1972, 74, Distinguished Alumni award Clemson U., 1974, E.W. Scripps award Scripps-Howard Found., 1976, Champion Media award for Econ. Understanding, 1981, Judah Magnes Gold medal Hebrew U. Jerusalem, 1987, Herbert Harley award Am. Judicature Soc., 1991, Regents medal of distinction U. Hawaii, 1998; inductee Honolulu Press Club Hall of Fame, 1987. Mem. Honolulu Symphony Soc., Pacific and Asian Affairs Council (dir.), Internat. Press Inst., Am. Soc. Newspaper Editors (dir., treas. 1973, sec. 1974, v.p. 1975, pres. 1976), Friends of East-West Ctr., Harbour Club. Home: Mc Lean, Va. Died Feb. 17, 2003.

CHARGAFF, ERWIN, biochemistry educator emeritus, writer; b. Austria, Aug. 11, 1905; came to U.S., 1928, naturalized, 1940; s. Hermann and Rosa C.; m. Vera Broido; 1 son, Thomas. Dr. phil., U. Vienna, 1928; Dr. phil. h.c, U. Basel, 1976; Sc.D. (hon.), Columbia U., 1976. Research fellow Yale U., 1928-30; asst. U. Berlin, Germany, 1930-33; research assoc. Inst. Pasteur, Paris, France, 1933-34; faculty Columbia U., 1935—, prof. biochemistry, 1952-74, prof. emeritus, 1974—, chmn. dept. biochemistry, 1970-74. Vis. prof., Sweden, 1949, Japan, 1958, Brazil, 1959; vis. prof. Coll. de France, 1965, Naples, Palermo, Cornell, 1966, Stazione Zoologica, Naples, 1969. Author: Essays on Nucleic Acids, 1963, Voices in the Labyrinth, 1977, Heraclitean Fire, 1978, Das Feuer des Heraklit, 1979, Unbegreifliches Geheimnis, 1980, Bemerkungen, 1981, Warnungstafeln, 1982, Kritik der Zukunft, 1983, Zeugenschaft, 1985, Serious Questions, 1986, Abscheu vor der Weltgeschichte, 1988, Alphabetische Anschlaege, 1989, Vorlaeufiges Ende, 1990, Vermächtnis, 1992, Ueber das Lebendige, 1993, Armes Amerika: Arme Welt, 1994, Ein zweites Leben, 1995, Die Ausicht vom 13. Stock, 1998, Ernste Fragen, other lit. work in English and German; contbr. numerous articles to profl. jours.; editor: the Nucleic Acids, 3 vols., 1955, 60. Recipient Pasteur medal, 1949, award, Soc. Biol. Chemistry, Paris, 1961, Neuberg medal, Am. Soc. European Chemists, 1958, Bertner Found. award, Houston, 1965, C.L. Ma, C.L. Mayer prize, French Acad. Scis., 1963, Dr. H.P. Heineken prize, Netherlands Acad. Scis., Gregor-Mendel medal, Leopoldina, 1973, Nat. medal of Sci., 1975, medal, N.Y. Acad. Medicine, Disting. Svc. award, Columbia U., 1982, Johan-Heinrich Merck prize, German Acad. Land. and Lit., 1984, Lit. prize, City of Vienna, 1994, Gold medal, 2001; fellow Guggenheim, 1949, 1958. Fellow Am. Acad. Arts and Scis.; mem. Nat. Acad. Scis., Am. Philos. Soc.; fgn. mem. Royal Swedish Physiographic Soc., German Acad. Scis. Leopoldina. Home: New York, NY. Died June 20, 2002.

CHARLES, RAY (RAY CHARLES ROBINSON), musician, singer, composer; b. Albany, Ga., Sept. 23, 1930; s. Bailey and Areatha Robinson; 9 children. Student music at sch. for blind, St. Augustine, Fla. TV appearances Ray Charles' 50 Years in Music, Uh-Huh!, 1991; TV advertising, from 1992. Musician: played with bands in south, organized trio, played on TV in Seattle, formed own band, 1954; musician: (rec. artist) Atlantic Records, 1952—59, ABC-Paramount, 1959—65, Tangerine Records, 1965—73, Crossover Records Co., from 1973; musician: numerous TV, concert appearances, (albums) Message from the People, Volcanic Action of My Soul, Renaissance, Porgy and Bess, Brother Ray is At It Again, Rockin' With Ray, Friendship, Do I Ever Cross Your Mind, The Genius After Hours, From the Pages of My Mind, 1986, Just Between Us, 1988, Greatest Country and Western Hits, 1988, Genius + Soul = Jazz, 1991, (with Willie Nelson) Seven Spanish Angels and Other Hits, Goin' Down Slow, The Real Ray Charles, 1986, Wish You Were Here Tonight, Would You Believe, 1990, (with Milt Jackson) Soul Brothers Soul Meeting, 1989, Birth of a Legend, 1992, The Session Vol. 2, 1992, My World, 1993, Blues and Jazz, 1994, Strong Love Affair, 1996, and others; performer: sang in We Are the World, 1985; appeard in films : Blues for Lovers, 1966; Blues Brothers, 1980; Limit Up, 1989; Spy Hard, 1996. Established (Ray Charles) Robinson Foundation. Named number 1 male singer, 16th Internat. Jazz Critics Poll, 1968, into the Rock and Roll Hall of Fame, 1986, 1986; named to Playboy Jazz and Pop Hall of Fame, Songwriters Hall of Fame; recipient New Star award down beat Critics poll, 1958, 1961—64, Image award, NAACP, 12 Grammy awards, Grammy Lifetime Achievement award, 1987, best soul/R & B artist, Down Beat critics poll, 1984, hon. life chmn. Rhythm and Blues Hall of Fame, gold records include Ray Charles' Greatest Hits, 1962, Modern Sounds in Country and Western Music, Vol. 1 1962, Vol. 2, 1963, Ray Charles: A Man and His Soul, 1967, Leadership awd., NAFEO, 1991, Lifetime Achievement award, Ebony Mag., 1993. Died June 10, 2004.

CHARNEY, JONATHAN ISA, law educator, lawyer; b. NYC, Oct. 29, 1943; s. Wolfe R. and Rita Dorothy (Greenfield) Charney; m. Sharon Renee Lehman, June 12, 1966; children: Tamar, Adam, Noah. BA, NYU, 1965; JD, U. Wis., 1968. Bar: Wis. 1968, Tenn 1974, NY 1980, US Supreme Ct. 1971. Atty., Land and Natural Resources div. Dept. Justice, Washington, 1968—71; atty., chief marine resources sect., 1972; asst. prof. law Vanderbilt U., Nashville, 1972—75; assoc. prof., from 1978. Cons. in field; vis. prof. U. Pa., 1989. Contbr. articles profl. jour. Mem.: Order of Coif, Internat. Boundary Rsch. Unit (mem. bd. adv. from 1993), Assn. Am. Law Sch. (chmn. internat. law sect. 1985), Am. Jour. Internat. Law (bd. editors from 1986, editor in chief from 1998), Am. Soc. Internat. Law (exec. council 1982—85, v.p. 1994—96), Am. Law Inst., Coun. Fgn. Rels., Am. Br. Internat. Law Assn. (chair com. on formation of internat. law 1986—90), ABA (chair internat. law sect. internat. ct. com. 1988—89, dep. vice chair sect. on internat. law, pub. internat. law div. 1988—90), Wis. Law Rev. (bd. editors 1966—68), Ocean Develop. and Internat. Law (bd. editors from 1985, editor in chief from 1998), Marine Policy Ctr. (sr. advisors com. 1987—96, chair 1991—96), Woods Hole Oceanographic Inst. Deceased.

CHASE, MERRILL WALLACE, immunologist, educator; b. Providence, Sept. 17, 1905; s. John Whitman and Bertha H. (Wallace) C.; m. Edith Steele Bowen, Sept. 5, 1931 (dec. 1961); children: Nancy Steele (Mrs. William W. Cowles), John Wallace, Susan Elizabeth (dec. 1985); m. Cynthia Hambury Pierce, July 8, 1961 (dec. Apr. 1997). AB, Brown U., 1927, ScM, 1929, PhD, 1931, ScD honoris causa, 1977, Rockefeller U., 1988; MD honoris causa, U. Münster, Fed. Republic Germany, 1974. Instr. biology Brown U., 1931-32; staff mem. Rockefeller Inst. Med. Research, 1932-79; prof. immunology and microbiology, head lab. immunology and hypersensitivity Rockefeller U., 1956-79. Med. adv. council Profl. Ednl. and Research Task Force, Asthma and Allergy Found. Am., 1955-83. Editor: (with C.A. Williams) Methods in Immunology and Immunochemistry, Vol. 1, 1967, Vol. 11, 1968, Vol. III, 1970, vols. IV, 1977, and V, 1976. Fellow Am. Acad. Allergy (hon., Disting. Svc. award 1969), Am. Coll. Allergists (hon.), Am. Acad. Arts and Scis.; mem. AAAS, Am. Assn. Immunologists (pres. 1956-57), Am. Soc. Microbiology (program chmn. 1959-61), Harvey Soc., N.Y. Acad. Scis., N.Y. Allergy Soc. (hon.), Nat. Acad. Sci. Republican. Universalist-Unitarian. Achievements include special research in hypersensitivity to simple chemical allergens, studies Kveim antigen in sarcoidosis, studies tuberculins and mycobacterial antigens. Home: New York, NY. Died Jan. 5, 2004.

CHASE, WILLIAM HOWARD, public policy consultant, editor; b. Omaha, Jan. 30, 1910; s. Charles Herbert and Pauline (Kottal) C.; m. Elizabeth Coykendall, Oct. 25, 1935; children: Anne Coykendall, Alison Howard, Thomas Howard. AB, U. Iowa, 1932; postgrad., London Sch. Econs., 1932-33, Harvard U., 1934-36; PhD (hon.), Dong-Guk U., Seoul, Korea, 1968. Instr. internat. relations Harvard U., 1935-36; editl. editor Register & Tribune, Des Moines, 1936-38; exec. Am. Retail Fedn., Washington, 1939-40; editor Whaley-Eaton Letter, Washington, 1941; dir. pub. services Gen. Mills, Mpls., 1941-45; dir. pub. relations Gen. Foods, N.Y.C., 1945-52; v.p., gen. exec. McCann-Erickson; pres. Communications Counselors, Inc., Howard Chase Assocs., 1959-68; chmn. Council Mgmt. Change, Inc., 1965—; pub. Innovation and Mgmt. of Change Letter, 1965-76; v.p. Am. Can Co., Greenwich, Conn., 1970-75, asst. to chmn., 1970-75; pres. Howard Chase Enterprises, Inc., 1974—; prof. Grad. Sch. Bus. Adminstrn., U. Conn., 1974-82, Poly. Inst. N.Y., 1975-78; editor Corp. Pub. Issues, 1976—. Asst. to sec. commerce, asst. dir. Office Def. Moblzn., 1950-51; mem. dental adv. com. NIH, 1962-65; mem. nat. com. on cmty. health HEW, 1965—; info. policy cons. Pres.'s Food for Peace Coun.; mem. Exec. Res. USIA. Author: By any Other Name, Issue Management: Origins of the Future, 1984. Trustee Wellesley Coll., 1948-60; bd. dirs. Stamford Mus., 1977-89, Mannes Coll. Music North Conway Inst.; vice chmn. Nat. Citizens for Eisenhower campaign, 1952. Recipient Profl. Proficiency award Pub. Rels. Soc. Am., 1948, 81, 82, Nat. Pub. Rels. Achievement award Ball State U., 1991; named One of Ten Distinguished Young Men of Year U.S. Jr. C. of C., 1943; named to Arthur W. Page Soc. Hall of Fame, 1989. Mem. N.Y. Council Fgn. Relations, Acad. Polit. Sci., Pub. Relations Soc. Am. (past pres.), Issues Mgmt. Assn. (founder, chmn. 1989), Phi Beta Kappa, Alpha Tau Omega. Clubs: Landmark (Stamford, Conn.); Harvard (N.Y.C.); Metropolitan (Washington). Home: Stamford, Conn. Died Aug. 19, 2003.

CHAWLA, KALPANA, astronaut; b. Karnal, India; BS in Aeronautical Engrng., Punjab Engrng. Coll., India, 1982; MS in Aerospace Engrng., U. Tex., 1984; PhD in Aerospace Engrng., U. Colo., 1988. With NASA Ames Rsch. Ctr., 1988; v.p., rsch. scientist Overset Methods, Inc., Los Altos, Calif., 1993-94; astronaut NASA Lyndon B. Johnson Space Ctr., Houston, from 1994, with astronaut office EVA/Robotics and Computer Brs., mission specialist on STS-87, 1997. Avocations: flying, hiking, backpacking, reading. Died Feb. 1, 2003.

CHENG, DAVID HONG, mechanical engineering educator; b. I-Shing, China, Apr. 19, 1920; came to U.S., 1945, naturalized, 1956; s. Tze Kuen (dec. Sept. 2002) and Tseng Sun (Sheng) C.; m. Lorraine Hui-Lan Yang, Sept. 4, 1949; children: Kenneth, Gloria. MS, U. Minn., 1947, PhD; William Richmond Peters, Jr. fellow, Columbia U., 1950; LHD (hon.), William Paterson U. N.J., 1997. Instr. Rutgers U., 1949-50; structural engr. Ammann & Whitney, N.Y.C., 1950-52; sr. engr. M.W. Kellogg Co., N.Y.C., 1952-55; lectr. CCNY, 1955, asst. prof. civil engrng., 1955-58, assoc. prof., 1959-65, prof., 1966-86, dir. grad. studies and exec. officer Ph.D. programs in engrng., 1977-78, dean engrng., 1979-86. Cons. M.W. Kellogg Co., Inst. Def. Analyses, N.Y.C. Transp. Adminstrn., ASME; pres. Techtran Inc., 1986; dir., v.p. China-Am. Tech. Corp., 1995— Author: Nuclei of Strain in the Semi-infinite Solid, 1961, Analysis of Piping Flexibility and Components, 1973, On Lao Tzu, 2000, A New Interpretation of Lao Tzu's Thought (in Chinese), 2000. Trustee governing bd. William Paterson Coll. N.J., 1990-97, William Paterson U., 1997-99. Recipient 125th Anniversary medal Coll. City N.Y., 1973; Am. Soc. Engrng. Edn.-NASA Faculty fellow, 1964-65; hon. rsch. fellow Harvard U., 1967; William Peterson Univ. Main Libr. renamed David and Lorraine Cheng Libr. Mem. ASCE, ASME, Chinese Inst. Engrs. (Achievement award 1984), Sigma Xi, Tau Beta Pi (Outstanding Tchr. award 1972), Chi Epsilon, Phi Tau Phi. Died Sept. 14, 2002.

CHERASKIN, EMANUEL, physician, dentist; b. Phila., June 9, 1916; m. Caroline Elwood, Sept. 23, 1944; 1 child, Lisa. AB, U. Ala., Tuscaloosa, 1939, MA, 1941; DMD, U. Ala., Birmingham, 1952; MD, U. Cin., 1943. Intern Hartford (Conn.) Mcpl. Hosp., 1943-44; resident St. Mary's Hosp., Evansville, Ind., 1946-47; pvt. practice Moundville, Ala., 1947-48; instr. in anatomy Med. Coll. Ala., Birmingham, 1948-50, asst. prof. physiology, 1950-52; assoc. prof., chmn. dept. oral medicine U. Ala. Sch. Dentistry, Birmingham, 1952-56, dir. postgrad. studies, 1956-57, prof., chmn. divsn. oral surgery and oral medicine, 1956-62, prof., chmn. dept. oral medicine, 1962-79, prof. emeritus, from 1979. Active staff mem. U. Ala. Hosps., 1957-79; cons. Predictive Medicine Program, Hollywood, Calif., 1965-67, So. Acad. Clin. Nutrition, 1965-70, So. Calif. Acad. Nutritional Rsch., 1967-70, Ohio Acad. Clin. Nutrition, 1968-71, N.E. Acad.

Clin. Nutrition, 1970-75, McDonagh Med. Ctr., Inc., 1981-86, Olive W. Garvey Ctr. for Improvement of Human Functioning, 1981—, BioNutrionics, 1984-85; mem. adv. bd. Health Optimizing Inst., 1988—. Author: Vitamin C...Who Needs It?, 1993, Health and Happiness, 1989, The Vitamin C. Controversy: Questions and Answers, 1988, Human Health and Homeostasis, 1999; co-author numerous books; contbr. articles to profl. jours. and chpts. to books; mem. several editl. bds. of profl. jours. Capt. U.S. Army, 1944-46. Mem. Birmingham Dist. Dental Soc., Ala. State Med. Soc., AMA, Am. Acad. Oral Medicine (life), Am. Geriatrics Soc., Am. Dental Assn. (life), Am. Holistic Med. Assn. Home: Birmingham, Ala. Died Aug. 3, 2001.

CHERNOW, JAY HOWARD, music industry executive; b. N.Y.C., Dec. 3, 1935; s. Meyer and Gertrude (Simon) C.; m. Eileen Phyllis Messing; children: Michael, Laurie Beth. Tech. degree, RCA Insts., N.Y.C., 1955. Technician N.Y.C. Dept. Hospitals, 1955-58; prodn. mgr. Am. Litho-Craft, N.Y.C., 1958-64; mktg. dir. Mic-Tone Printing Corp., N.Y.C., 1964-72, San Juan Music Group, N.Y.C., 1972-84, pres., from 1984; pres. bd. dirs. Tring Internat., U.K., from 1984. Mem. B'nai B'rith, Odd Fellows. Jewish. Home: Manalapan, NJ. Deceased.

CHESTON, GEORGE MORRIS, lawyer; b. Phila., Aug. 18, 1917; s. Radcliffe and Sydney (Ellis) C.; m. Winifred Dodge Seyburn, May 5, 1955; 1 dau., Sydney. AB, Harvard U., 1939, LL.B., 1947. Bar: Pa. 1947. Since practiced in, Phila.; atty. firm Ballard, Spahr. Andrews & Ingersoll, Phila., 1947-52; farmer Georgetown, S.C., 1968-94. Treas. Nat. Citizens for Eisenhower, 1955-56 Pres. Phila. Soc. for Svcs. to Children, 1959-69; trustee United Fund, Phila., 1958-69; bd. dirs. Phila. Zool. Soc., 1977-86, Saratoga Performing Arts, Am. Fedn. Arts; trustee Phila. Mus. Art, 1962—, pres., 1968-76, Nat. Mus. of Racing. Served to comdr. USNR, 1941-46, PTO. Home: Philadelphia, Pa. Died Oct. 15, 2003.

CHI, MICHAEL RAY, civil and mechanical engineer, educator; b. Tianjin, Hobei, Republic of China, Jan. 9, 1925; came to U.S., 1947; s. Houran and Naikon (Sun) C.; m. Lotta Chia Jui Li, June 15, 1957; children: Loretta Elizabeth, Maxwell Michael. BSCE, U. Tianjin, 1946; MS, La. State U., 1949; DSc, George Washington U., 1969. Registered profl. engr., D.C., Va. Rsch. engr. Nat. Bur. Standards, Washington, 1953-58; prof. engring. Cath. U. Am., Washington, 1958-87, emeritus prof., 1987—2004; former chief engr. Chi Assocs. Inc., Arlington, Va. Rsch. engr. Fed. Hwy. Adminstrn., Washington, 1967-69; phys. scientist Nat. Hwy. Traffic Safety Adminstrn., 1972-73; gen. chmn. Southeastern Conf. Mechanics, 1972-73. Author: Theory of Prestressed Concrete, 1963; editor: Development of Theoretical and Applied Mechanics, 1974, Vehicle Handling and Crash Symposium, 1974, International Symposium on Slurry Wall as Permanent Transportation Structures, 1978. Convenor Orgn. Chinese-Ams., No. Va., 1975, vice chmn. Chinese Ams. for Reagan Bush, Va., 1979; del. Va. Rep. Conv., Norfolk, 1980. Recipient Alumni Achievement award George Washington U. Alumni Assn., 1986. Fellow Nat. Soc. Forensic Engrs., ASME (Washington sect. chmn. 1974-75), Washington Acad. Scis.; mem. D.C. Soc. Profl. Engrs. (pres. 1986-87, Outstanding Svc. award 1988), Cosmos Club. Roman Catholic. Home: Arlington, Va. Died June 29, 2004.

CHIAT, JAY, retired advertising agency executive; b. N.Y.C., Oct. 26, 1931; s. Sam and Min (Kretchmer) C.; children: Debra, Marc, Elyse. BS, Rutgers U. Prodn. asst. NBC, New York, 1953-54; mgr. of recruit advertising Aero-Jet General Corp., Sacramento & Azusa, Calif., 1956-57; v.p. & dir. Leland Oliver Co., Santa Ana, Calif., 1957-62; founder, pres. Chiat & Associates, Inc., 1963-68; chmn. bd., CEO Chiat Day Inc. Advertising, Venice, Calif., 1968-96. Served with USAF, 1956-57. Died Apr. 23, 2002.

CHRISMAN, O. DONALD, orthopedic surgeon, physical anthropologist; b. Springfield, Mo., Sept. 16, 1917; s. Oscar Day and Katherine (Ramsey) C.; m. Miriam Usher, Nov. 29, 1943; children: Nicholas Ramsey, David Abbott. BS in Biochemistry, Harvard U., 1938, MD, 1942; MA in Anthropology, U. Mass., Amherst, 1988. Diplomate Am. Bd. Orthop. Surgery. Intern Boston City Hosp., 1942-43; resident in orthop. Johns Hopkins Hosp., Balt., 1947-49; orthop. instr. Johns Hopkins Med. Sch., Balt., 1948-49; chief orthop. Cooley Dickenson Hosp., Northampton, Mass., 1950-84; assoc. prof hygiene Amherst (Mass.) Coll., 1950-70; orthop. rsch. assoc. Yale Med. Sch., New Haven, Conn., 1955-57, from asst. prof. to prof. orthop., 1957-93, orthop. lectr., from 1994; rsch. assoc. in anthropology U. Mass., Amherst, from 1988. Author: The OsteoArthritis Cascade: The Function of Aspirin, 1972 (Kappa Delta award 1992); also articles including The Role of Trauma in Arthritis (Nichols Andry award 1981); orthop. editor Arthritis and Rheumatism Anns.; assoc. editor Clin. Orthop., 1960—; asst. editor Jour. Bone and Joint Surgery, 1965-72. Coord. for Crippled Children Groups and Clinics, Cerebral Palsy, Polio, etc., Western Mass., 1952—. Lt. Navy Med. Corps, 1943-46. Grantee NIH, 1960s, 70s, Arthritis Found., 1950's, Sterling-Winthrop, 1950's, 70's, Upjohn, 1970s and 80s. Mem. Am. Orthop. Rsch. Soc. (pres. 1966-67), Assn. Bone and Joint Surgeons (pres. 1973-74), New Eng. Orthop. Soc. (pres. 1970-72). Democrat. Episcopalian. Avocations: forensic physical anthropology, archaeology, mountain climbing, skiing, gardening. Home: Bedford, Mass. Died Aug. 31, 2002.

CHRISTIAN, GEORGE EASTLAND, political consultant; b. Austin, Tex., Jan. 1, 1927; s. George Eastl and Ruby (Scott) C.; m. Elizabeth Anne Brown, July 30, 1950 (dec. 1957); m. Jo Anne Martin, June 20, 1959; children—Elizabeth, Susan, George Scott, Robert Bruce, John, Brian. B. Journalism, U. Tex. Sports editor Temple (Tex.) Daily Telegram, 1949; corr. Internat. News Service, 1949-56; asst. to Senator Price Daniel, Washington, 1956, to Gov. Price Daniel, Austin, 1957-63, to Gov. John Connally, Austin, 1963-66; press sec., spl. asst. to Pres. Johnson, Washington, 1966-69; pres. George Christian, Inc. Author: The President Steps Down. Chmn. Headliners Found.; mem. Tex. Hist. Commn.; bd. dirs. Scott & White Meml. Hosp., U. Tex. Communication Found., McDonald Obs.; vice chmn. Lyndon B. Johnson Found. Served with USMC, 1944-46. Recipient Tex. award for hist. preservation; named Disting. Alumnus U. Tex. Mem. Sigma Delta Chi. Clubs: Austin, Metropolitan, Headliners (Austin). Democrat. Episcopalian. Home: Austin, Tex. Died Nov. 27, 2002.

CHRISTOPHER, WILFORD SCOTT, public relations consultant; b. Enid, Okla., Feb. 8, 1916; s. W. Scott and Mary Elizabeth (Heaton) C.; m. Marjorie Lois Lester, Dec. 30, 1941; 1 son, Scott Douglas. BA, Phillips U., 1938; MA, U. Iowa, 1941. Cert. chamber exec. Asst. prof. speech Phillips U., 1939, assoc. prof. sociology, 1940-42; clin. psychologist US Med. Adminstrn., 1942-44; chief VA Guidance Ctr U. Miami (Fla.), 1944-45; pub. relations dir. Miami (Fla.) C. of C., 1946-51; gen. mgr. Greater Tampa C. of C., 1951-64, exec. v.p., 1964-76, pres., 1976-78; dir. community relations U. Tampa, Fla., 1978-81; pres. W. Scott Christopher & Assos. (public relations), 1981-96. Spl. asst. to chmn. Nat. Exec. Svcs. Corp., N.Y.C., 1980-82, Tampa, Fla.; mem. tech.-occupation adv. com. Hillsborough Jr. Coll., 1969-76, chmn. advanced mgmt. curriculum com., 1958-59; mem. Adv. Group on Continuing Edn. for Urban Leadership, 1967-68; mem. internat. com. C. of C. U.S., 1972-75, sr. adv. coun., 1978—, dir., 1976-78, chmn. nat. adv. coun. urban devel. 1959-60). Author Tampa's People With a Purpose, 1993; contbr. C. of C. Adminstrn. Bd. dirs. Tampa Philharm. Orch. Assn., Tampa Oral Sch. for Deaf, 1971-74; trustee U. South Fla. Found., 1959-65, 87-88, H.B. Plant Mus., 1979-82; mem. pres.'s adv. bd. U. South Fla., 1975-78, mem. pres.'s coun., 1978—; mem. exec. com. Fla. Eye Inst., U. South Fla. Coll. Medicine, 1982-90, bd. dirs., mem. exec. com. Suncoast Gerontology Ctr., 1986-96; v.p. Fla. Found. Eye Rsch.; trustee, mem. exec. com. U. Tampa, 1977-78, mem. bd. fellows, 1974, chmn. bd. fellows, 1976-77, sec.-treas., 1981-82; trustee Berkeley Prep. Sch., 1963-71, v.p., 1967-71. With USAF, 1942-44. Named Tampa Citizen of Year, 1972, Tampa Humanitarian of Year, 1973; elected Phillips U. Hall of Fame, 1988. Mem. Fla. C. of C. Execs. Assn. (pres. 1954), Southeastern Inst. C. of C. Execs. (pres. 1956), So. Assn. C. of C. Execs. (pres. 1972), Inst. Orgn. Mgmt. (bd. regents 1975-77), Am. C. of C. Execs. (sec.-treas., v.p. 1960, pres. 1961-62, chmn. nat. panel on exec. certification 1966) Clubs: Tampa Exchange (pres. 1956), Executive (past pres.), University (dir.), Tampa Yacht and Country, Ye Mystic Krewe of Gasparilla. Home: Tampa, Fla. Died Dec. 2, 1999.

CHURCHILL, ALLEN DELOS, lawyer; b. Sioux Falls, S.D., June 5, 1921; s. Edward Delos and Iva Edna (Allen) Churchill; m. Melva Fein, Jan. 16, 1925; 1 child, Victoria Ann. BA, Washington U., St. Louis, 1948; JD, Washington U., 1950. Bar: Mo. 1950, U.S. Dist. Ct. (ea. dist.) Mo. 1950, Ill. 1965, U.S. Dist. Ct. (so. and ctrl. dists.) Ill. 1965, U.S. Ct. Appeals (7th cir.) 1974. Trial atty. Mo. Pacific R.R., St. Louis, 1950—62; solo practice St. Louis, 1962—65, Belleville, Ill., 1965—67; ptnr. Dunham, Boman, Leskera & Churchill, Belleville, 1967—77, Churchill, Nester & McDonnell, Belleville, 1977—85, Churchill & McDonnell, Belleville, 1985—90, Churchill, McDonnell & Hatch, Belleville, 1990—97, Brown & Assocs., Belleville, 1997—99, Heyl Royston, Voelker & Allen, Belleville, from 2000. With AC U.S. Army, 1942—45. Fellow: Am. Bd. Trial Advocates (advocate), Ill. Bar Found., Internat. Soc. Barristers, Am. Coll. Trial Lawyers; mem.: St. Clair County Bar Assn. (pres. 1974—75), St. Louis Met. Bar Assn., Mo. Bar Assn., Ill. State Bar Assn., Media Club. Deceased.

CIHLAR, CHRISTINE CAROL, academic director public affairs; b. Milw., Feb. 25, 1948; d. Peter Joseph and Sylvia (Sunstrom) C.; m. Frederick L. Rippy Jr., July 25, 1981. BA, Luther Coll., 1970. Advt. mgr. Gazette Press, Glenwood Springs, Colo., 1970-71; prodn. mgr. Eitzen Typesetting, Denver, 1971-72; asst. editor Colo. Leader, Denver, 1971-72; dir. pub. info. Luther Coll., Decorah, Iowa, 1972-78; proprietor, founder The Emporium, Decorah, 1975-77; regional sales rep. food svc. div. Hormel Co., Charlotte, N.C., 1978-80; asst. to pres. St. Mary's Coll. Md., St. Mary's City, 1980-84, dir. pub. affairs, from 1984. Editor: Luther Mag., 1972-78, Luther Collage, 1974-78, Coll. Chips, 1968-69, St. Mary's In The News, 1984—; contbr. articles and essays to local publs. Pres. Four Seasons Homeowners Assn., Charlotte, 1979-80; bd. dirs. United Way St. Mary's County Inc., Lexington Park, Md., v.p., 1984-88, pres., 1988-93; bd. dirs. Hospice of St. Mary's Inc., Leonardtown, Md., 1984-90; treas. Good Shepherd Luth. Ch., Charlotte, 1979-80. Mem. AAUW, Pub. Rels. Soc. Am., Coun. for Advancement and Support of Edn. (forum for instl. advancement 1972—), Edn. Writers Assn., Am. Numismatic Assn., Rotary. Democrat. Home: California, Md. Deceased.

CILLIE, PETRUS JOHANNES, retired publishing company executive, journalism educator; b. Stellenbosch, South Africa, Jan. 18, 1917; s. Gabriel Gideon and Maria Elizabeth (Van Niekerk) C.; m. Elizabeth Frederika Bester, Aug. 13, 1936; children: Maria Elizabeth Cillie De Vries, Angelique Maryn Cillie Edwards. BSc, Stellenbosch U., 1935, DLitt (hon.), 1975. Reporter Die Burger, Afrikaans daily, Cape Town, South Africa, 1935-38, subeditor, 1938-44, asst. editor, 1944-54, editor, 1954-77; prof. journalism Stellenbosch U., 1977-83, lectr. extraordinary, 1983-85, mem. univ. council, 1984-92; chmn. Nasionale Pers, Cape Town, 1977-92. Author books of essays. Recipient Markus Viljoen medal Akademie Vir Wetenskap En Kuns, 1979, D.F. Malan medal, 1985; decorated Order for Meritorious Service (Gold), 1988; recipient M.S. Louw award A. Handelsinstituut, 1992. Mem. National Party. Mem. Dutch Reformed Ch., Died 1999. Home: Cape Town, South Africa.

CIRILLO, VINCENT A. judge; b. Ardmore, Pa., Dec. 19, 1927; s. Francesco and Victoria Cirillo; m. Beatrice D'Orazio; children: Vicnent A. Jr., Gregory F., Victoria A. BA cum laude, Villanova U., 1951; JD, Temple U., 1955. Bar: Pa. 1956, U.S. Dist. Ct. (ea. dist.) Pa. 1957, U.S. Ct. Appeals (3d cir.) 1960, U.S. Sureme Ct. 1963. Law clk. to Presiding Judge Harold G. Knight, 1955-58; asst. dist. atty. Motgomery County, Pa., 1958-62; pvt. practice Norristown, Pa., 1963-70; judge Ct. of Common Please, Pa., 1971-82, Superior Ct. Pa., 1981-91 and from 91, pres. judge, 1986, judge, 1986-91. Lectr. in field. Contbr. articles to profl. jours. Asst. Solicitor Montgomery County, Pa.; former commr. Lower Merion Twp., Motgomery County; mem. awards jury Valley Forge Freedoms Found., 1966, nat. coun. trustees; bd. dirs. Montgomery Coutny Boys Club; exec. bd. Norristown Police Athletic League; mem. Supreme Ct.'s Adv. Com. on Appellate Ct. Rules, 1985-86. With U.S. Army, Korea. Recipient Legion of Honor award Chapel of Four Chaplains, 1985, Cert. of Appreciaton, Pa. State Police, 1978, Optimist Club City Line, 1959; named Man of Yr., Catholic War Vets, 1974-75. Mem. ABA, State Jud. Assn. ABA, Am. Judicature Soc., Am. Inst. Italian Culture, Pa. Bar Assn., Pa. Conf. State Trial Judges, Pa. Bar Assn. (ho. of dels.), Phila. Bar Assn. (appellate ct. rules com.), Montgomery County Bar Assn., Internat. Juvenile Officers Assn., Justinian Soc., Gen. Alumni Assn. Temple U. (bd. dirs.), Am. Legion, Camp Rainbow (bd. dirs.), KC, Catholic War Vets, Lions, Norristown Exch. Club, Plymouth Coutnry Club, Bala Country Club, Optimist, Sons of Italy, Phi Alpha Delta. Home: Narberth, Pa. Deceased.

CITRON, DAVID SANFORD, physician; b. Atlanta, Jan. 8, 1920; s. Morris and Ida (Levine) Citron; m. Doris Berman, Feb. 14, 1946; children: Michael, Dennis, Lynn, Steven. AB, U.N.C.-Chapel Hill, 1941, cert. in medicine, 1943; MD, Washington U., St. Louis, 1944. Lic. physician N.C., diplomate Am. Bd. Internal Medicine, Am. Bd. Family Practice. Intern Barnes Hosp., St. Louis, 1944—45; resident USPHS Hosp., Kirkwood, Mo., 1946—49, Boston, 1949—52; practice internal medicne Charlotte, NC, 1952—73; dir. family practice residency Charlotte Meml. Hosp. & Med. Ctr., 1973—84, dir. med. edn., 1984—87. Mem. N.C. Bd. Med. Examiners, 1974—81, 1984—87; bd. dirs. Nat. Bd. Med. Examiners, 1981—95. With USPHS, 1946—52. Recipient Disting. Svc. award, U. N.C. Sch. Medicine, 1975. Fellow: ACP; mem.: Mecklenburg County Med. Soc. (pres. 1972—73), N.C. Med. Soc., AMA, Inst. of Medicine/NAS. Democrat. Jewish. Died June 24, 2003.

CLARK, LAUREL BLAIR SALTON, astronaut; b. Ames, Iowa, Mar. 10, 1961; d. Robert Salton and R.J.C. Brown; m. Jonathan B. Clark; 1 child. BSc in Zoology, U. Wis., 1983, MD, 1987. Diplomate Nat. Bd. Med. Examiners, lic. Wis. Commd. lt. USN, advanced through grades to capt., with diving medicine dept., 1987; intern Naval Hosp., Bethesda, Md., 1987—88; navy undersea med. officer tng. Naval Undersea Med. Inst., Groton, Conn.; radiation health officer, undersea med. officer USN; med. dept. head Submarine Squadron Fourteen, Holy Loch, Scotland; tng. Naval Aerospace Med. Inst., Pensacola, Fla.; naval flight surgeon USMC Night Attack Harrier Squadron; group flight surgeon Marine Aircraft Group; flight surgeon Naval Flight Officer advanced tng. squadron, Pensacola; with NASA, Houston, 1996—97, mission specialist, 1997—2000, mem. crew STS-107, from 2000. Decorated 3 Commendation medals USN, Nat. Def. medal, Overseas Svc. ribbon. Mem.: Soc. U.S. Naval Flight Surgeons, Aerospace Med. Assn. Avocations: scuba diving, hiking, camping, bicycling, parachuting. Died Feb. 1, 2003.

CLARK, RUSSELL GENTRY, retired federal judge; b. Myrtle, Mo., July 27, 1925; s. William B. and Grace Frances (Jenkins) C.; m. Jerry Elaine Burrows, Apr. 30, 1959; children: Vincent A., Viki F. LLB, U. Mo., 1952. Bar: Mo. 1952. Mem. firm Woolsey, Fisher, Clark, Whiteaker & Stenger, Springfield, Mo., 1952-77; judge U.S. Dist. Ct. (we. dist.) Mo., Kansas City, 1977-91, sr. judge, 1991-2000; ret., 2000. 2d lt. U.S. Army, 1944-46. Fellow Am. Bar Found.; mem. ABA, Internat. Platform Soc., Mo. Bar Assn. (continuing legal edn. com. 1969), Greene County Bar Assn. (dir. 1968-71), Kiwanis (past pres. Springfield chpt.). Clubs: Kiwanis (past pres. Springfield chpt.). Democrat. Methodist. Home: Springfield, Mo. Died Apr. 17, 2003.

CLARK, SYLVIA MARGARET, healthcare service administrator; b. St. Anthony, Idaho, Oct. 4, 1937; d. Paul James and Jennie (Dorrance) Shank; m. Paul Wilson Clark, July 14, 1958 (div. 1981); children: Geoffrey Wilson, Courtney Anne. Nursing diploma, Johns Hopkins Hosp., Balt., 1958; BA in Healthcare Mgmt., Antioch U. West, 1983; midwifery tng., Queen Charlotte's Maternity Hosp., London, 1977. RN, Colo.; cert. nurse midwife, nurse practitioner. Nurse for pvt. physician, Monroeville, Pa., 1963-65; clin. supr. Planned Parenthood Rocky Mtns., Colorado Springs, Colo., 1967-70; area adminstr. Denver, 1970-74; program devel. con. Aurora, Colo., 1978-80; dir. tng. and edn., 1980-81; assoc. dir., 1981-86; exec. dir., 1986—2003;

adminstrv. asst. Family Planning Assn., London, 1974-75; nursing sister Marie Stopes Well Woman Health Ctr., London, 1977-78. Mem. editorial bd. Jour. Ob-Gyn and Neonatal Nursing, 1981-84; contbr. articles to profl. jours. Mem. ANA, APHA, Am. Coll. Nurse Midwives, Nat. Assn. Nurse Practitioners Reproductive Health (pres. 1980-83), Assn. Reproductive Health Profls., Alliance Profl. Women, Rotary, Women's Forum Colo. Avocations: horses, hypnosis, environmental protection. Home: Monument, Colo. Died Jan. 12, 2004.

CLARK, WILLIAM D. lawyer, educator; b. Lansing, Mich., Nov. 30, 1938; AB, Lansing C.C., 1963; BA, Mich. State U., 1965; MBA, Calif. Pacific U., 1970; JD, Cooley U., 1975; LLD (hon.), Pacific U., 1983. Bar: Fla. 1983, Mich. 1977, U.S. Tax Ct. 1978, U.S. Supreme Ct. 1980. Adminstrv. asst. to Gov. State Mich., Lansing, 1960-61; cons. Sci. Mgmt. Coun., Ann Arbor, Mich., 1965-67; dir. plant ops. Woodard Mfg. Corp., Owosso, Mich., 1967-70; dep. supt. bus. and legal affairs Ingham Intermediate Sch. Dist., Mason, Mich., 1970-79; prof. law Sch. Law Cooley U., Lansing, 1979-86; prof. bus. Manatee C.C., Venice, Fla., 1986-94; pvt. practice Venice, Fla., from 1994. Mem. select com. for conformance review Assn. Sch. Bus. Ofcls. (cert. of conformance, 1974, 75, 76). Author: Managing the Florida Condominium, 1988, Landlord/Tenant Rights in Florida, 1993, Florida Landlord & Tenant Desk Manual, 1994, Managing the Florida Homeowners' Association, 1995, Board Service for the Florida Community Association, 1995, Managing the Florida Mobile Home Park, 1995, Florida Construction Liens, 1996; co-author: Financial and Managerial Accounting for Elementary and Secondary School Systems, 1979, Government Accounting and Financial Reporting, 1979. Home: Venice, Fla. Died Mar. 27, 2001.

CLARKE, ALLEN BRUCE, mathematics educator, retired academic administrator; b. Saskatoon, Sask., Can., Sept. 8, 1927; came to U.S., 1947, naturalized, 1953; s. Arthur Roy and Florence (Clarke) C.; m. Florence Myres, Sept. 14, 1949; children— David John, Richard Neil, Deborah Lynn. BA with Honours, U. Sask., 1947; M.Sc., Brown U., 1949, PhD, 1951. From instr. to prof. U. Mich., 1951-67; Fulbright lectr. U. Turku and U. Abo, Finland, 1959-60; prof., chmn. dept. math. Western Mich. U., Kalamazoo, 1967-78, dean Coll. Arts and Sci., 1978-88, assoc. v.p., 1988-90, provost, 1990-91. Cons., lectr. probability and random processes. Author: Elementary Statistics, 1961; (with R.L. Disney) Probability and Random Processes for Engineers and Scientists, 1970, Probability and Random Processes, 1985; contbr. articles to profl. jours. Mem. Math. Assn. Am. (sect. chmn. 1969-70), Inst. Math. Statistics, ACLU. Home: Portage, Mich. Died Nov. 26, 1999.

CLARKE, J. CALVITT, JR., retired federal judge; b. Harrisburg, Pa., Aug. 9, 1920; s. Joseph Calvitt and Helen Caroline (Mattson) C.; m. Mary Jane Cromer, Feb. 1, 1943 (dec.1985); children: Joseph Calvitt III, Martha Tiffany; m. Betty Ann Holladay, May 29, 1986. BS in Commerce, JD, U. Va., 1945. Bar: Va. 1944. Practiced in, Richmond, Va., 1944-74; partner firm Bowles, Anderson, Boyd, Clarke & Herod, 1944-60; firm Sands Anderson, Marks and Clarke, 1960-74; judge U.S. Dist. Ct. (ea. dist.) Va., 1975-91, sr. judge, 1991—99. Mem. 4th Circuit Judicial Conf., 1963; hon. consul for Republic of Bolivia, 1959-75 Chmn. Citizen's Advisory Com. on Joint Water System for Henrico and Hanover counties, Va., 1968-69; mem. Mayor's Freedom Train Com., 1948-50; del. Young Republican Nat. Conv., Salt Lake City, 1949, Boston, 1951; chmn. Richmond (Va.) Republican Com., 1952-54; candidate for Congress, 1954; chmn. Va. 3d Dist. Rep. Com., 1955-58, 74-75, Va. State Rep. Conv., 1958—; co-founder Young Rep. Fedn. of Va., 1950, nat. committeeman, 1950-54, chmn., 1955; chmn. 3d dist. Speakers Bur., Nixon-Lodge campaign, 1960, mem. fin. com., 1960-74; chmn. Henrico County Republican Com., 1956-58; fin. chmn. 1956; pres. Couples Sunday Sch. class Second Presbyn. Ch., Richmond, Va., 1948-50, mem. bd. deacons, 1948-61, elder, 1964-99, 1st Presbyn. Ch., Virginia Beach, 1999—; bd. dirs. Family Service Children's Aid Soc., 1948-61, Gambles Hill Community Center, 1950-60, Christian Children's Fund, Inc., 1960-67, Children, Inc., 1967-75, Norfolk Forum, 1978-83; mem. bd. of chancellors Internat. Consular Acad., 1965-75; trustee Henrico County Pub. Library, chmn., 1971-73. Fellow Va. Law Found.; mem. Va. State Bar (mem. 3rd dist. com. 1967-70, chmn. 1969-70), Richmond Bar Assn., Norfolk-Portsmouth Bar Assn., Va. Bar Assn., Thomas Jefferson Soc. of Alumni U. Va. Lile Law Soc., McGuires U. Sch. Alumni (pres. 1995-96), Am. Judicature Soc., ABA, Va. Bar Assn. (vice chmn. com. on cooperation with fgn. bars 1960-61), Richmond Jr. C. of C. (dir. 1946-50), Windmill Point Yacht Club, Westwood Racquet Club (pres. 1961-62), Commonwealth Club, Delta Theta Phi. Died May 6, 2004.

CLARKE, OSCAR WITHERS, physician; b. Petersburg, Va., Jan. 29, 1919; s. Oscar Withers and Mary (Reese) C.; m. Susan Frances King, June 18, 1949; children— Susan Frances, Mary Elizabeth, Jennifer Ann BS, Randolph Macon Coll., 1941; MD, Med. Coll. Va., 1944. Intern Boston City Hosp., 1944-45; resident internal medicine Med. Coll. Va., 1945-46, 48-49, fellow in cardiology, 1949-50; pvt. practice specializing in internal medicine and cardiology Gallipolis Holzer Med. Ctr., Ohio, 1950—; pres., bd. dirs. Holzer Clinic Inc., 1981-89. Bd. dirs. Ohio Valley Devel. Co., Gallipolis, Cmty. Improvement Corp.; pres. Ohio State Med. Bd.; chmn. Ohio Med. Edn. and Rsch. Found., Commn. Heart Attack Alert Program NIH, 1995-96; pres. Gallipolis City Bd. Helath, 1955—, Gallia County Heart Coun., 1955—. Contbr. articles to med. jours. V.p. Tri-State Regional coun. Boy Scouts Am., 1957; pres. Tri-State Community Concert Assn., 1957-59; trustee Med. Meml. Found., Holzer Hosp. Found. Capt. M.C., AUS, 1946-48, ETO Recipient John Stewart Bryant pathology award Med. Coll. Va., 1943. Fellow ACP (Laurate award 1997), Royal Soc. Medicine; mem. AMA (chmn. coun. on ethics and jud. affairs 1991—), Am. Heart Assn., Gallia County Med. Soc. (pres. 1953), Cen. Ohio Heart Assn. (Merit medal 1960, trustee), Ohio Med. Assn. (pres. 1973-74, Disting. Svc. citation 1988, Physician of Century 1996), Am. Soc. Internal Medicine (Disting. Internist award 1992), Alpha Omega Alpha, Sigma Zeta, Chi Beta Phi. Clubs: Rotary (pres. 1953-54). Presbyterian. Home: Greeley, Colo. Died Aug. 16, 1999.

CLARKE, RICHARD ALAN, electric and gas utility company executive, lawyer; b. San Francisco, May 18, 1930; s. Chauncey Frederick and Carolyn (Shannon) C.; m. Mary Dell Fisher, Feb. 5, 1955; children: Suzanne, Nancy C. Stephen, Douglas Alan. AB Polit. Sci. cum laude, U. Calif., Berkeley, 1952, JD, 1955. Bar: Calif. 1955. Pres. Pacific Gas and Electric Co., San Francisco, 1985-86, chmn. bd., CEO, 1986-94, chmn. bd., 1994-95; ptnr. Rockwell, Fulkerson and Clarke, San Rafael, Calif., 1960-69. Past mem. Bus. Coun.; bd. dirs. Potlatch Corp., CNF TransInc. Former mem. Pres.'s Coun. on Environ. quality; past trustee Berkeley Found.; past trustee, past adv. bd. Walter A. Haas Sch. Bus. and Boalt Hall Sch. Law, U. Calif., Berkeley; former chmn. adv. bd. Ctr. for Orgnl. and Human Resource Effectiveness, U. Calif., Berkeley; former co-chair U. Calif. Regents Outreach Adv. Bd.; former chair Bay Area Econ. Coun.; bd. dirs., past chmn. Bay Area Coun.; former bd. dirs. Nature Conservancy of Calif. Mem.: San Francisco C. of C. (past dir., v.p. econ. devel.). Home: San Rafael, Calif. Died Dec. 14, 2002.

CLAUSEN, BRENDA G. legal assistant; b. Denison, Iowa, Mar. 30, 1969; d. Ronald G. and Marjorie A. (Bandow) Clausen. BA, Buena Vista Coll., 1991; student U. Iowa, from 1995; student, U. Iowa, from 1995. Asst. food and beverage mgr. Dakota Dunes C.C., SD, 1991—92; catering dir. Marriott Corp., Storm Lake, Iowa, 1992—95. Scholar, U. Iowa, from 1995. Mem.: AAUW, ATLA (assoc.), ABA (assoc.). Democrat. United Church Of Christ. Avocation: golf. Home: Adel, Iowa. Died Aug. 13, 2001.

CLAYTON, ROBERT HUGH, pharmacist, consultant; b. Gilmer, Tex., Aug. 22, 1957; s. Robert Franklin and Reita Joyce (Willtrout) C.; m. Deborah Lynn Taylor, May 17, 1980; children: Charlton Franklin, Brianne Elizabeth, Robert Patrick. Student, Kilgore (Tex.) Jr. Coll., 1975-76, 77, U. Tex., 1977-78; BS in Pharmacy, U. Houston, 1981. Staff pharmacist Eckerd Drugs, Bryan, Tex., 1981-84, chief pharmacist College Station, Tex., 1984, Twin City Pharmacy, Bryan, 1984-89, The Pharmacy Shop, Bryan, from 1989. Bd. dirs., v.p. Better Bus. Bur., 1991-92. Mem. Am. Pharm. Assn., Tex. Pharm. Assn. (vice chmn. sect. cons. pharmacists 1986-87), Brazo Valley Pharm. Assn. (v.p. 1984-85, pres. 1985-87, 89, sec. 1988), Nat. Assn. Retail Druggists, Brazos Valley Diabetic Assn., Am. Assn. Diabetes Educators. Avocations: camping, water skiing, cycling. Home: College Station, Tex. Deceased.

CLEARY, JOHN WASHINGTON, lawyer; b. Milw., Feb. 22, 1911; s. Peter A. and Mathilda A. (Borning) C.; m. Alice M. Shinners, Jan. 15, 1938; children: Terrence P., Mary E., Peter J., Margaret A., John T., Catherine A. JD, Marquette U., 1933. Bar: Wis. 1933. Since practiced in Milw.; partner Erbstoeszer, Cleary & Misey, 1936-82, Fiorenza & Hayes, 1982—. Sec. Hopkins Savs. & Loan Assn., Milw., 1936-65, pres., 1965—; faculty Savs. and Loan Inst., Milw., 1961-63 Vice chmn. Milw. Commn. Community Relations, 1959-63; savs. and loan commr., Wis., 1963-65; mem. pres.'s senate Marquette U., 1977—; bd. dirs. Greater Milw. chpt. ARC, pres., 1961-63; trustee Marquette U. High Sch.; gov. nat. ARC. Mem. Wis. Legis. Council, Milw. Savs. and Loan Council (pres. 1948-50), Wis. Savs. and Loan League (pres. 1954-55), U.S. Savs. and Loan League (dir. 1962-63) Home: Milwaukee, Wis. Died Feb. 12, 2003.

CLEMENTS, WOODROW WILSON, beverage company executive; b. Tuscaloosa, Ala., July 30, 1914; s. William Houston and Martha (Christian) C.; m. Eloise Davis, Mar. 20, 1937; 1 son, Wayne Wilson.; m. Virginia Thomas, 1982. Student, Howard Coll., Birmingham, Ala., 1932-33, U. Ala., 1933-35, L.H.D. (hon.), 1974. Began as route salesman advancing to sales mgr. Dr Pepper Bottling Co., Tusculoosa, 1935-42; with Dr Pepper Co., 1942—, successively dist. mgr., sales promotion mgr., asst. mgr. bottler service, gen. sales mgr., 1942-49, 49-51, v.p., gen. sales mgr., 1951-58, v.p. mktg., 1958-67, exec. v.p., dir., 1967-68, pres., 1969-80, chief exec. officer, 1970-86, chmn., 1974-86, chmn. emeritus, from 1986. Past dir. Council Opportunities Selling; exec. council Internat. and Comparative Law Center; mem. Cotton Bowl Council; gen. chmn. Dallas Salute to Vietnam Vets., 1973; devel. council Tex. Sports Hall of Fame; adv. council Nat. Alliance Businessmen, Council Religious Heritage Am., Salvation Army; mem. alumni council Pres.'s Cabinet U. Ala.; trustee Dallas Hist. Soc, 1987—; bd. visitors U. Ala. Coll. Commerce and Bus. Adminstrn.; past bd. dirs. North Tex. Commn., Dallas Council World Affairs, Dallas Civic Opera, Dallas Citizens' Council; bd. dirs. Boy Scouts Am., Better Bus. Bur. Met. Dallas; trustee Council on Opportunities in Selling; chmn. bd. govs. Jr. Achievement Dallas; vice chmn. Dallas County Community Coll. Dist. Found., 1988-89; active space bus. roundtable North Tex. Recipient Mktg. Man of Decade award Am. Mktg. Assn., 1970, Golden Plate award Am. Acad. Achievement, 1970, George Washington certificate Freedoms Found. at Valley Forge, 1975, Entrepreneur of Yr. award So. Meth. U. Sch. Bus., 1975, Beverage Industry Man of Yr. award Beverage Industry publ., 1976, Chief Exec. Officer of Yr. in Beverage Industry award Fin. World, 1977, Horatio Alger award, 1980, Disting. Am. award Nat. Football Hall of Fame, 1980; named Beverage World Hall of Fame, 1982; inducted into U. Ala. Bus. Hall of Fame, 1988. Mem. Sales and Marketing Execs. Internat. (regional v.p., pres. 1968-69, chmn. bd. 1969-70, Distng. Salesman award 1972), Dallas Personnel Assn. (dir.), S.W. Sales Execs. Council (pres., named Distng. Sales Exec. 1969), Grocery Mfrs. Am. (past dir.), Dallas Sales Exec. Club (pres. 1957), Dallas C. of C. (dir.), Horatio Alger Assn. (pres. 1987—). Clubs: Dallas Country, University, Chaparral, City, Tower. Lodges: Rotary. Baptist. Died Oct. 3, 2002.

CLEVELAND, RICHARD JOSEPH, surgeon; b. Taunton, Mass., Mar. 29, 1932; s. Richard J. and Grace (Dunphy) C.; children: Richard Jay, Melissa, Janice. BS, Tufts U., 1954; MD, Med. Coll. Va., 1960. Diplomate Am. Bd. Thoracic Surgery (bd. dirs. 1988—), Am. Bd. Surgery. Intern Yale U. Med. Ctr., New Haven, Conn., 1960-61; resident gen., thoracic surg. Med. Coll. Va., 1961-66, instr. thoracic and cardiac surgery, 1966; prof. surgery Tufts U. Med Sch, from 1972, chmn. dept., from 1975; exec. sec., treasurer Am. Bd. Thoracic Surgery, Evanston, Il. Asst. prof. surgery UCLA, 1967-70; chief cardiovascualr surgery Harbor Gen. Hosp., Torrance, Calif., 1970-72; dir. surgery svcs., chmn. dept. gen. surgery New Eng. Med. Ctr., 1975— Mem. Res. Rev. Com. for Thoracic Surgery, 1980-85; dir. ABTS, 1979-87, chmn. 1987-89. Lt. (j.g.) USN, 1954-56. Mem. ACS, AMA, Am. Surg. Assn., Am. Assn. Thoracic Surgery, Soc. Univ. Surgeons, Soc. Vascular Surgery, Soc. Thoracic Surgeons, Internat. Cardiovascular Soc., Am. Coll. Cardiology, Am. Coll. Chest Physicians, Internat. Soc. Surgery, Thoracic Surgery Dirs. Assn., Pan Pacific Surg. Assn., New Eng. Surg. Soc., Boston Surg. Soc., Alpha Omega Alpha. Died June 11, 2002.

CLINE, JAMES EDWARD, transportation research analyst, chemist; b. Glens Falls, N.Y., Nov. 13, 1913; s. Max and Ella (Aronson) C.; m. Ethel Rhoda Ellis, Aug. 17, 1937; children: Harvey Ellis, Maryanne, Harold Michael. AB, Cornell U., 1934; AM, Harvard U., 1935, PhD, 1937. Asst. in photochemistry Harvard U., Cambridge, Mass., 1937-41; chemist TVA, Wilson Dam, Ala., 1941-45; chief rsch. chemist Beason Co., Boston, 1945-48; project leader MIT, Cambridge, 1948-52; engrng. specialist Sylvania Electric, Woburn, Waltham, Mass., 1952-58, 62-64; engrng. group leader Raytheon Mfg. Co., Newton, Mass., 1958-61; staff scientist Kearfott Semiconductor Corp., Newton, 1961-62; electronics researcher NASA, Cambridge, 1964-70; ops. rsch. analyst U.S. Dept. Transp., RSPA, Transp. Systems Ctr., Cambridge, from 1970. Contbr. articles to profl. jours. Mem. John Harvard Soc., Phi Kappa Phi. Deceased.

CLINGAN, FOREST MELROSE, historian; b. Fresno, Calif., June 1, 1918; s. William Melrose and Sara Lorena (Brewer) C.; m. Helen Elizabeth Gates, Apr. 5, 1942; 1 child, Susan Elizabeth. BA, Fresno State U., 1940; BS, Calif. Inst. Tech., Pasadena, 1942; MS, Rensselaer Poly. Inst., 1946. Commd. U.S. Navy, 1942, advanced through grades capt., ret. 1974; historian Dunlap, Calif., from 1974. Author: Oak to Pine to Timberline, 1985. Episcopalian. Died Feb. 3, 2001.

CLINTON, LESLIE LYNCH, personal property appraiser, consultant, educator; b. Biddeford, Maine, May 28, 1950; d. Thomas Francis and Agnes Boyd (Murdoch) Lynch; m. John Frampton Bryson III, Mar. 1975 (dec. 1978); m. Stephen Clinton, Feb. 1979 (div. 1987). BA, Goucher Coll., 1973. Retail mgr. Phila. region Bonwit Teller, 1973-78; freelance graphic artist advt. Phila., 1978-81; with purchasing MCI Corp., Pleasantville, N.J., 1981-82; freelance appraiser, cons. Pleasantville, from 1981; mktg. study analyst DCI Corp., Elkins Park, Pa., 1982-83; advt. dir. Fine Arts Co., Phila., 1984-88; mktg. dir. Freeman/Fine Arts Co., Phila., 1988-94. Cons. Slosberg Auctioneers, Phila., 1994—; staff educator, cons. Rinker Enterprises, Inc., Emmaus, Pa., 1994—. Contbg. author: Valuation Strategies in Divorce, 1993. Past chair Jr. League vols. Woodmere Art Mus., Chestnut Hill, Pa., 1990-91; active Preservation Coalition, Phila., 1992—, Found. Architecture, Phila., 1992—, Jr. League, 1988-93; benefit organizer Ctr. City Residents Assn., Phila., 1992, 93. Mem. Appraisers Assn. Am. (cert.), Am. Soc. Notaries, Am. Soc. Appraisers (sr., bd. dirs. 1993—, mem. admissions bd. 1994—), Textile Arts Soc., Victorian Soc. (treas. Phila. chpt. 1990-92, bd. dirs. 1990—, sec. membership 1992-94). Avocations: golfing, auctions, writing art reviews, computer art. Died June 19, 1999.

CLONEY, WILLIAM THOMAS, JR., international marathon consultant; b. Boston, Oct. 29, 1911; s. William T. and Elizabeth Anne (McLaughlin) C.; m. Arline Patricia Lynch, June 29, 1937; children: Mary E. (Mrs. William D. Benjes, Jr.), Kathleen (Mrs. N. Phillips Dodge III), Martha (Mrs. W. Brooke Hamilton, Jr.) (dec.), William Thomas (killed in action). AB, Harvard U., 1933, student Grad. Sch. Edn., 1934-35. With Boston Herald, 1930-53; sports editor Boston Post, 1953-56; jr. master Roxbury Latin Sch., 1935- 36; instr. to assoc. prof. English and journalism Northeastern U., 1937-53; pub. relations counsel, 1956-59; asst. to pres. Keystone Custodian Funds, 1956-62, v.p., 1962-78. Pres. Boston Athletic Assn.; dir. Boston Marathon, 1946-82; pres. emeritus Assn. Internat. Marathons Inc., 1982— Author: The Story of a New England Industrialist, James Lorin Richards, 1952; also mag. articles. Sec. Sholley Found. Inc., 1956—. Served to lt. col. AUS, 1942-46. Home: Duxbury, Mass. Died Jan. 16, 2003.

COALE, ANSLEY JOHNSON, economics educator; b. Balt., Nov. 14, 1917; s. James Johnson and Nellie Ansley (Johnson) C.; m. Sarah Hamilton Campbell, Oct. 18, 1941; children: Ansley Johnson, Robert Campbell. BA, Princeton U., 1939, MA, 1941, PhD, 1947; D (hon.), U. Louvain, Belgium, 1979; D.honoris causa, U. Liege, Belgium, 1983; LL.D. (hon.), U. Pa., 1983; DHL (hon.), Princeton (N.J.) U., 1994. Research asst. Office Population Research, Princeton, 1941-42; instr. elec. communications M.I.T., 1943-44; sec. com. social implications atomic energy Social Sci. Research Council, 1946-47; faculty Princeton, 1947-86, prof. econs., 1959-86; dir. Princeton (Office Population Research), 1959-75. Vis. prof. demography U. Calif., Berkeley, 1987; U.S. rep. UN Population Commn., 1961-67; Social Sci. Research Council-Nat. Sci. Research Council fellow Inst. Advanced Study, 1947-49; chmn. com. on population and demography Nat. Acad. Scis., 1977-82; fellow Ctr. Advanced Study Behavioral Scis., 1982-83 Author: The Problems of Reducing Vulnerability to Atomic Bombs, 1947, (with Edgar M. Hoover) Population Growth and Economic Development in Low Income Countries, 1958, (with Melvin Zelnik) New Estimates of Population and Births in the United States, 1963, (with Paul Demeny) Regional Model Life Tables and Stable Populations, 1966, The Growth and Structure of Human Populations, 1972, (with B. Anderson and E. Härm) Human Fertility in Russia Since the Nineteenth Century, 1979, (with S. Watkins et al) The Decline of Fertility In Europe, 1986; also articles. Served with USNR, 1942-46. Recipient Mindel Sheps prize in math. demography, 1974, Irene Taeuber prize in population rsch., 1988. Fellow AAAS, Am. Statis. Assn., Brit. Acad. (corr.); mem. Population Assn. Am. (pres. 1967-68), Am. Econ. Assn., Am. Philos. Soc., Internat. Population Union (pres. 1977-81), Am. Acad. Arts and Scis., Nat. Acad. Scis., The Royal Acad. Home: Newtown, Pa. Died Nov. 5, 2002.

COBURN, JAMES, actor; b. Laurel, Nebr., Aug. 31, 1928; children: James IV, Lisa; m. Paula Murad, Oct. 22, 1993. BA, L.A. City Coll. Owner Panpiper Prodns., Hollywood, Calif Appeared in movies Ride Lonesome, 1959, Face of A Fugitive, 1959, The Magnificent Seven, 1960, Hell Is For Heroes, 1962, The Great Escape, 1963, Charade, 1964, The Americanization of Emily, 1964, Major Dundee, 1965, Our Man Flint, 1966, What Did You Do in the War, Daddy?, 1966, In Like Flint, 1967, Pat Garrett and Billy the Kid, 1973, The Last of Sheila, 1973, Bite the Bullet, 1975, Hard Times, 1975, Sky Riders, 1976, The Last Hard Men, 1976, Midway, 1976, The Muppet Movie, 1979, Fire Power, 1979, Cross of Iron, 1977, Golden Girl, 1979, Loving Couples, 1980, The Baltimore Bullet, 1980, High Risk, 1981, Looker, 1981, Martin's Day, 1985, Death of a Soldier, 1986, Young Guns II, 1990, Hudson Hawk, 1991, The Player, 1992, (narrator) Hugh Hefner: Once Upon a Time, 1992, Sister Act 2, 1993, Maverick, 1994, Eraser, 1996, Nutty Professor, 1996, Skeletons, 1996, The Disappearance of Kevin Johnson, 1996, Ben Johnson: Third Cowboy on the Right, 1996, Affliction, 1997, Keys to Tulsa, 1997, Payback, 1999, Atticus, 1999, The Good Doctor, 2000, Proximity, 2001, Yellow Bird, 2001, The Man From Elysian Fields, 2001, Monsters Inc (voice), 2001, Snow Dogs, 2002, American Gun, 2002; TV mini-series The Dain Curse, 1978, Malibu, 1983, Draw, 1984; TV films The Dain Curse, 1978, Malibu, 1983, Draw!, 1984, Sins of the Father, 1985, Crash Landing: The Rescue of Flight 232, 1992, The Hit List, 1993, Greyhounds, 1994, The Set Up, 1995, Ray Alexander: A Menu for Murder, 1995, The Avenging Angel, 1995, The Cherokee Kid, 1996, The Second Civil War, 1997, Mr. Murder, 1998, Atticus, 1999, Noah's Ark, 1999, Missing Pieces, 2000, Walter and Henry, 2001; producer The President's Analyst, 1967, Waterhole No. 3, 1967; writer Circle of Iron, 1979; numerous TV guest appearances including Perry Mason, Profiler. Won Best Supporting Actor, American Academy Awards, Affliction, 1999. Died Nov. 18, 2002.

COBURN, SEYMOUR KAY, corrosion consultant; b. Chgo., Dec. 21, 1917; s. Henry and Kate (Brownstein) C.; children: Karen, Kenneth, Monica, Valerie, Marshall. BS in Organic Chemistry, U. Chgo., 1940; MS in Organic Chemistry, Ill. Inst. Tech., Chgo., 1951. Chemist Synthetical Labs., Chgo., 1934-36; rsch. chemist Miner Lab. divsn. A.D. Little, Chgo., 1940-44, Lever Bros., Chgo., 1944-50; chem. lab. chief Assoc. Am. R.R., Chgo., 1950-59; assoc. rsch. cons. U.S. Steel Corp., Pitts., 1959-83; pres. Corrosion Cons., Inc., Pitts., from 1983. Author and editor: Atmospheric Factors-Corrosion of Engineering Metals, 1978, Corrosion Protection Steel Piles, 1981, Corrosion: Source Book, 1984. Mem. ASTM (chmn. com.), Am. Soc. Metals, Am. Chem. Soc., Nat. Assn. Corrosion Engrs. (chmn. com.). Jewish. Achievements include research in litigation and fire protective coating fields. Home: Pittsburgh, Pa. Died Jan. 4, 2001.

CODD, EDGAR FRANK, computer scientist; b. Portland, Eng., Aug. 19, 1923; div.; 4 children. BA, MA, Oxford (Eng.) U., 1948; MS, U. Mich., 1963, PhD in Comm. Sci.), 1965. Program mathematician IBM, N.Y.C., 1949-53; head Multiprogramming Systems, 1959-61; mgr. Can Guided Missile Program, 1953-57; cons., 1961-85; chief scientist E.F. Codd & Assocs., Miami, Fla., 1985 92, prin., from 1992. Rsch. U. Mich., 1964-65. Fellow IEEE, Brit. Computer Soc., Assn. Computing Machinery (Turing award 1981); mem. Am. Acad. Arts & Scis., Sigma Xi. Home: Miami, Fla. Died Apr. 18, 2003.

COE, NANCY PATRICIA, artist; b. San Jose, Calif., Apr. 4, 1934; d. Henry Sutcliffe and Pearle (Hersey) C. BA in Art, Leland Stanford Jr. U., Calif., 1956. Bd. dirs. Moral Dimentions, Santa Clara, Calif.; lectr. in field. One-woman shows include Reno Little Theater, 1960, Washoe Hosp., Reno, 1962, Villa Montalvo, Saratoga, Calif., 1964, 68, Triton Mus. Art, Santa Clara, 1966, 91, San Jose City Coll., 1969, The Villages Adult Cmty., San Jose, 1982-83; exhiited in group shows at Intown Art and Gallery, Bangor, Maine, 1997. Tchr. how to draw a face to children of Santa Clara County, San Jose, 1966-74; active San Jose Mus. Art, 1987—, Fine Art Mus., San Francisco, 1987-97, Holocaust Mus. Recipient 1st award Nev. Artists Assn., 1960. Mem. Nat. League Am. Cen. Women, Women in the Arts. Roman Catholic. Home: San Jose, Calif. Deceased.

COETZEE, ARTHUR O. academic administrator; Provost Andrews U., Berrien Springs, Mich. Deceased.

COFFEY, JOHN JOSEPH, lawyer; b. Darby, Pa., Dec. 1, 1936; s. William F. and Helen (Bolder) C.; m. Laura Marie Torchia, Sept. 20, 1958; children: John Jr., Christopher, Timothy, Andrew. BS, Villanova U., 1958; JD, Temple U., 1967. Bar: Pa., U.S. Dist. Ct. (ea. dist.) Pa., U.S. Ct. Appeals (3rd cir.). Ptnr. Marshall, Dennehey, Warner, Coleman and Goggin, Phila. Capt. USNR, 1958-84. Died Apr. 14, 2004.

COFFEY, WILLIAM MICHAEL, lawyer; b. Racine, Wis., Aug. 16, 1932; s. Raymond Richard and Catherine Cecilia (Costello) C.; m. Nancy Jane Shuford, June 15, 1957; children— Patrick, Peggy, Michael, Jane. B.S., U. Wis., 1959, LL.B., 1961. Bar: Wis. 1961, U.S. Dist. Ct. (ea. dist.) Wis., U.S. Supreme Ct., U.S. Ct. Appeals (7th cir.). Atty., SEC, Chgo., 1961-63; asst. U.S. Atty., Chgo. and Milw., 1963-65; ptnr. Shellow, Shellow & Coffey, Milw., 1966-69, Coffey, Murray & Coffey, Milw., 1970-75, Coffey & Coffey, Milw., 1975-81, Coffey, Coffey & Geraghty, Milw., 1981—; lectr. U. Wis. Law Sch.-Madison, 1975—. Co-author: Defense of Criminal Cases in Wisconsin. Served with U.S. Army, 1952-54; Korea. Fellow Am. Coll. Trial Lawyers; mem. ABA (mem. task force on standards of criminal justice), Nat. Assn. Criminal Def. Lawyers, State Bar Wis. (bd. govs. 1981-82), State Pub. Defenders (bd. dirs., 1977-79). Died 1988. Home: Milwaukee, Wis.

COFFIELD, MARY ELEANOR, speech clinician, educator; b. Ft. Smith, Ark., July 28, 1921; d. Willard M. and Edith Isabel (Stemmons) C. Student, No. Ariz. State U., 1941-42; BE, Cen. Mo. State U., 1948; MA in Speech Pathology, U. Denver, 1960. Lic. speech pathologist, Mo. Tchr. music pvt. kindergarten, Carthage, Mo., 1940-41; tchr. Columbian Elem. Sch., Carthage, 1943-47; fellowship tchr. Lab. Sch. Cen. Mo., Warrensburg, 1947-48; elem. tchr. Roswell (N.Mex.) Schs., 1948-49, Kansas City (Mo.) Sch., 1949-50; speech clinician Carthage Schs., 156-59, 60-86. Editor Jasper County Jour., 1983—. Pres. Rep. Women, Carthage, Carthage Social Agys.; hon. mem. United Presbyn. Ch., mem. choir, commn. synod; treas. McCune-Brooks Hosp. Aux.; mem. Presbytery Com., Profl. Devel. and Support Com., Presbytery Nominating Com.; moderator, enabler Gathering of Presbyn. Women in Carthage; mem. com. planning World Day of Prayer, Jasper County Sheltered Facilities Bd.; past pres., v.p., sec. Jasper County Crisis Intervention Bd.; past sec.-treas. Hard of Hearing Parents and Friends Group; instr. home nursing, chmn. water safety, staff aide ARC; pres. Friends of Libr., 1994-99. Named Citizen of Yr. Carthage Lions, 1985, Richard M. Webster Citizen of the Yr., Carthage C. of C., 1999, Grand Marshall, Carthage Christmas Parade, 2000; recipient citation Future Farmers Am., 1985, Recognition Outstanding Svc. award Region V Coun. Devel. Disabilities, 1989, Richard M. Webster Citizen of Yr. award Carthage C. of C., 1999, Years of Svc. award Stones Throw Theatre, 2000. Mem. AAUW (pres., Woman of Distinction 1990), Internat. Platform Assn., Coun. Exceptional Children (state treas. 1969, 89, Merit award 1982, Mo. Tchr. of Yr. 1986, Nat. Tchr. of Yr. 1987, participant ann. meeting 1992, 93, 94), Am. Speech and Hearing Assn. (life), Mo. Assn. Social Welfare (life, chmn. state membership), Four State Stroke Club (sec. 1975—), Joplin Area Assn. Retarded Citizens (pres. 1978-81, 87-89, bd. dirs.), Carthage Tchrs. (Outstanding Ret. Mem.), Jasper County Hist. Soc., Ret. Tchrs. Assn. (pres. 1992-98). Avocations: photography, singing, collecting angels, bells, elephants. Died May 28, 2002.

COFFIN, DAVID ROBBINS, art historian, educator; b. N.Y.C., Mar. 20, 1918; s. H. Errol and Lois (Robbins) C.; m. Nancy Merritt Nesbit, June 10, 1947; children— Elizabeth, David Tristram, Lois, Peter. AB, Princeton, 1940, M.F.A., 1947, PhD, 1954; postgrad., Yale U., 1940-41. Instr. fine arts U. Mich., 1947-49; lectr. art and archaeology Princeton, 1949-54, asst. prof., 1954-56, assoc. prof., 1956-60, prof. art and archaeology, 1960-66, Marquand prof. art and archaeology, 1966-70, Howard Crosby Butler Meml. prof. history architecture, 1970-88, prof. emeritus, 1988—2003, chmn. dept. art and archaeology, 1964-70; editor-in-chief Art Bull., 1959-62. Kress prof. CASVA Nat. Gallery Art, 1995-96. Author: Villa d'Este at Tivoli, 1960, The Villa in the Life of Renaissance Rome, 1979, Gardens and Gardening in Papal Rome, 1991, The English Garden: Meditation and Memorial, 1994, Princeton University's Graduate College, 2000; editor: The Italian Garden, 1st Dumbarton Oaks Colloquium on History of Landscape Architecture, 1972. Recipient Howard R. Marraro book award Am. Cath. Hist. Assn., 1979; Fulbright research award to Italy, 1951-52; McCosh Faculty fellow, also Am. Council of Learned Socs. fellow, 1963-64; Guggenheim Meml. Found. fellow, 1972-73; recipient Alice Davis Hitchcock book award Soc. Archtl. Historians, 1960; Howard T. Behrman award for disting. achievement in humanities, 1982 Mem. Coll. Art Assn. Am. (dir. 1957-61), Soc. Archtl. Historians (dir. 1968-70, treas. 1970-71), Renaissance Soc., Phi Beta Kappa. Home: Princeton, NJ. Died Oct. 14, 2003.

COFONE, JOSEPH A. obstetrician/gynecologist; b. Providence, R.I., 1930; MD, U. Bologna, 1957. Diplomate Am. Bd. Obstetrics & Gynecology. Intern St. Joseph's Hosp., Providence, 1957-58; resident in obstetrics M. Hague Maternity Hosp., Jersey City, 1958-59, Carney-St. Margaret's Hosp., Boston, 1960-63; fellow Tufts U., Boston, 1962; staff Women-Infants Hosp., Providence, St. Joseph Hosp., North Providence. Clin. asst. prof. ob/gyn. Brown U. Med. Sch., Providence. Mem. Am. Coll. Gynecology & Obstetrics, Northeastern Obstetric & Gynecol. Soc., R.I. Med. Soc. Home: Johnston, RI. Died June 21, 1999.

COGNATA, JOSEPH ANTHONY, retired football commissioner; b. Ashtabula, Ohio, Feb. 11, 1946; s. Joseph and Ella Jane (Dispense) C.; m. Betty Jean Jacobs, Dec. 17, 1978; children: Joseph Anthony Jr., Susan, Diana, Christina. Student, Kent State U., 1964-66. Sales rep. Endicott Buick, Pompano Beach, Fla., 1977-80; sales mgr. Fla. Chrysler Plymouth, West Palm Beach, Fla., 1980-82; owner, CEO So. States Football Club, Tequesta, Fla., 1982-85; backfield/spl. teams coach San Jose (Calif.) Bandits Minor League Football Sys., 1987-90, asst. head coach Calif. Outlaws, 1990-91; asst. to dir. football ops. Profl. Spring Football League, Meadowlands, N.J., 1991-92; co-founder Golden West Football League, Sacramento, 1991-97; commr. West Coast Amateur Football League, Mountain View, Calif., 1992-97; pres., CEO, commr. Pacific Western Football Alliance, Sacramento, 1992-97; pres. CEO U.S. Amateur Football Fedn., 1994-97; ret., 1997. Pres., CEO West Coast Football Conf., 1994-95. Author: Complete Football Playbook, 1969. Lutheran. Avocations: reading, sporting events, concerts, theater, dog. Died June 20, 2000.

COHN, BERNARD SAMUEL, anthropologist, historian, educator; b. Bklyn., May 13, 1928; s. Nathan and Blanche (Herc) C.; m. Rella Israly, Mar. 19, 1950; children: Jenny Miriam, Abigail Catherine, Jacob Israly, Naomi Juliet. BA, U. Wis., 1949; PhD (Social Sci. Research Council fellow), Cornell U., Ithaca, N.Y., 1954. Research assoc., asst. prof. anthropology U. Chgo., 1956-58, vis. asst. prof. history, 1959-60, prof. anthropology and South Asian history, 1964-95, prof. emeritus, 1995—2003, chmn. dept. anthropology, 1969-72. Assoc. prof., chmn. dept. anthropology U. Rochester, 1960-64; vis. prof. history U. Mich., 1967, 79, NYU, 1982, Calif. Inst. Tech., 1987, research fellow Australian Nat. U., 1979, 82; chmn. joint com. on South Asia Social Sci. Research Council-Am. Council Learned Socs., 1983-88; spkr. in field. Assoc. editor: Jour. Asian Studies, 1962-65; editorial bd.: Comparative Studies in Society and History, 1966—, Jour. Peasant Studies; co-author: (with Milton B. Singer) Structure and Change in Indian Society; author: India: The Social Anthropology of a Civilization, 1971, An Anthropologist among the Historians and Other Essays, 1987, Colonialism and Its Forms of Knowledge the British in India, 1996, India: The Social Anthropology of a Civilization, 2000. Served with AUS, 1954-56. Rockefeller Found. fellow, 1957-59; Am. Council Learned Socs. fellow, 1962; Guggenheim fellow, 1964; fellow Center Advanced Study Behavioral Scis., 1967-68; Fellow Am. Inst. Indian Studies, 1975; NEH fellow, 1982-83 Fellow AAAS; mem. Assn. Asian Studies (chmn. S. Asia com. 1962-64), Am. Anthrop. Assn., Am. Ethnological Soc. (exec. bd. 1969-72) Home: Chicago, Ill. Died Nov. 25, 2003.

COHN, JAN KADETSKY, American literature and American studies educator; b. Cambridge, Mass., Aug. 9, 1933; d. Allan Robert and Beatrice (Goldberg) Kadetsky; m. Donald S. Solomon, Feb. 6, 1955 (div. 1968); children: Cathy Rebecca, David Seth; m. William Henry Cohn, Mar. 9, 1969. BA, Wellesley Coll., 1955; MA, U. Toledo, 1961; PhD, U. Mich., 1964. From instr. to asst. prof. U. Toledo, 1964-68; assoc. prof. U. Wis., Whitewater, 1968-70, Carnegie Mellon U., Pitts., 1970-79; prof., dept. chair George Mason U., Fairfax, Va., 1979-87; dean faculty Trinity Coll., Hartford, Conn., 1987-94, G. Keith Funston prof. Am. lit. and Am. studies, 1994—2004. Cons. in field. Author: The Palace or the Poorhouse, 1979, Improbable Fiction, 1980, Romance and the Erotics of Property, 1988, Creating America, 1989, The Saturday Evening Post (covers), 1995; editor: Henry James, The Portrait of a Lady, 2001. Bd. dirs. Nat. Bldg. Mus., Washington, 1987-91; trustee Norman Rockwell Mus., Sturbridge, Mass., 1997; exec. bd. dirs. Conn. Pub. Broadcasting, Hartford, 1988-92. Fellow Am. Coun. Learned Socs., 1972, NEH, 1972-73. Mem. Modern Language Assn., Popular Culture Assn., Am. Culture Assn., Am. Studies Assn., Phi Kappa Phi. Democrat. Jewish. Died July 1, 2004.

COHN, ROBERT, financial planning company executive; b. Phila., June 1, 1922; s. Louis and Dora (Filderman) C.; m. Selma Eita Tarnoff, Mar. 18, 1944; children: Lawrence Jay, Cheryl Barbara. DVM, Middlesex U., 1945. Registered investment adviser. Ptnr. Standard Merchandising Co., Phila., 1946-69; chief exec. officer Supreme Mdse. Co., Phila., 1970-83, Asset Planning Assocs., Wyndmoor, Pa., 1984-85; pres. SKC Fin. Planners, Inc., Willow Grove, Pa., 1985—2003. Mem. adj. faculty Coll. Fin. Planning, Denver; speaker to profl. meetings, confs. and seminars. Contbg. author Practical Fin. Planning mag., 1988. Recipient award of appreciation Coll. Fin. Planning. Mem. Inst. Cert. Fin. Planners (cert., founder, bd. dirs. Delaware Valley chpt. 1986), Nat. Assn. Personal Fin. Advisors, Registry Fin. Planning Practitioners. Jewish. Avocations: gardening, bridge. Home: Glenside, Pa. Died Jan. 30, 2004.

COLBURN, RICHARD DUNTON, business executive; b. Carpentersville, Ill., June 24, 1911; s. Cary R. and Daisy (Dunton) C.; children: Richard Whiting, Carol Dunton, Keith Whiting, Christine Isabel, David Dunton, McKee Dunton, Daisy Dunton, Franklin Anthony. Student, Antioch Coll., 1929-33. Pres. Consol. Foundries Mfg. Corp. (and predecessors), 1944-64. Underwriting mem. Lloyds of London. Died June 3, 2004.

COLE, BENJAMIN RICHASON, publishing executive; b. Indpls., July 10, 1916; s. Almon Theodore and Maude (Richason) Cole; m. Alice Louise Porteous, Sept. 11, 1937 (dec. 1982); children: Alan Andrew, Amy Alice, Benjamin Richason; m. Kathleen Gibbs Martin, Feb. 12, 1983. Student, Butler U., 1934-35, Ind. State Tchrs. Coll., 1938, Am. Press Inst. of Columbia, 1948. Reporter Terre Haute (Ind.) Tribune-Star Pub. Co., 1938-40; Reporter Terre Haute Star, 1940-44; with Indpls. Star, 1944-86, statehouse reporter, 1945-48, asst. city editor, 1948, city editor, 1948-49, Washington Corr., 1949-86; corr. Arizona Republic, Phoenix, 1955-86. Mem.: Soc. Profl. Journalists (named to Washington Hall of Fame 1981, Ind. Hall of Fame 1989), Press Club Indpls., Nat. Press Club, Gridiron Club, Cosmos Club, Masons. Presbyterian. Home: Arlington, Va. Died Dec. 22, 2002.

COLE, HELEN, state legislator; b. Tishomingo, Okla., July 13, 1922; m. John Cole; 2 children. Former mayor, Moore, Okla., mem. Okla. Ho. of Reps., 37-39th sessions; mem. Okla. Senate, 1984-96; appointee Ethics Com., Chief Justice, 1998. Died Apr. 7, 2004.

COLE, JANET See HUNTER, KIM

COLE, JOHN EMERY, III, acoustical consultant; b. Upper Darby, Pa., May 20, 1942; s. John Emery Jr. and Ethel Marie (Denkhaus) C.; m. Judith Ann Parker, June 28, 1968; children: John Alexander, Stephen Parker. BSME, Drexel U., 1965; ScM, Brown U., 1967, PhD, 1970. Assoc. prof. mech. engring. Tufts U., Medford, Mass., 1970-77; prin. scientist Cambridge (Mass.) Acoustical Assocs., 1977-99. Mem. ASME, Acoustical Soc. Am., Sigma Xi. Unitarian-Universalist. Home: Lexington, Mass. Died Feb. 13, 1999.

COLE, SALLY ANN, critical care nurse; b. Phila., Jan. 9, 1940; d. William Joseph and Sara Erma (Jones) C.; m. Daniel Cesarini, Feb. 18, 1955 (div. Dec. 1966); children: Daniel Lee, Robert Harold, Richard Dale. Grad., North Montgomery County Area Vocational Tech. Sch., Lansdale, Pa., 1969; ASN, Univ. State N.Y., Albany, 1989. RN, Fla. Nurse North Penn Hosp., Lansdale, 1969-73; LPN St. Petersburg (Fla.) Gen. Hosp., 1974-89, ICU nurse, 1974-95, RN, 1989-95. RN, Fla.; cert. ACLS, Am. Heart Assn. Recipient Best Bedside Nursing Care award North Montgomery County Nursing Assn., 1969. Fellow AACN. Republican. Avocations: camping, canoeing, biking, travel, cooking. Home: Saint Petersburg, Fla. Died Apr. 10, 2002.

COLEMAN, NEIL LLOYD, geologist, researcher; b. Belvidere, Ill., Sept. 3, 1930; s. Lloyd Otis and Alice Katherine (Green) C.; m. Gwyneth Jane Davies, Dec. 29, 1952. BA, Cornell Coll., 1952; MS, U. Chgo., 1957, PhD, 1960. Geologist USDA/Nat. Sedimentation Lab., Oxford, Miss., 1959-69; rsch. unit leader USDA/Nat. Sedementation Lab., Oxford, Miss., 1969-81, lab. dir., 1981-88, geologist, from 1988. Adj. assoc. prof. civil engring. U. Miss., Oxford, 1961—, Memphis State U., 1989-90, Clemson U., 1990—. Contbr. articles to Jour. Hydraulic Rsch., Water Resources Rsch.; contbr. over 50 articles to profl. jours. With U.S. Army, 1953-54, Korea. Mem. Am. Geophys. Union, Internat. Assn. Hydraulic Rsch. (Harold J. Schoemaker award 1983), N.Y. Acad. Sci., Miss. Acad. Sci. Achievements include introduction of basis of current two-layer theory of suspended sediment concentration, of hypothesis that the Karman coefficient in turbulent flows is invariant under sediment suspension; first demonstration of time-variation of the Darcy-Weisbach resistance coefficient in unsteady stream flows. Home: Oxford, Miss. Deceased.

COLLETT, FARRELL REUBEN, art educator; b. Bennington, Idaho, Nov. 13, 1907; s. Charles Merrill and Mary Elnora (Munk) C.; m. Martha Howard Collett, July 9, 1940; children: Collett, Michael Farrell, Howard Merrill. AB, Brigham Young U., 1932, MA, 1946; HHD, Weber State Coll., 1977; PhD in Humanities (hon.), Weber State U., 1976. Cert. tchr., Utah. Art tchr. Provo (Utah) High Sch., 1933-38, Ogden (Utah) High Sch., 1938-39, Weber State U., Ogden, 1939-76, prof. emeritus, from 1976. Art tchr. Brigham Young U., Provo, 1954; prof. art Utah State U., U. Calgary, 1966-67; illustrator Caru Art Svc., N.Y.C., 1955-57; freelance illustrator, graphic designer, N.Y.C., L.A., San Francisco, Chgo. Dir. Utah State Inst. Fine Arts, Salt Lake City, 1962-64. Lt. Comdr. USNR, 1942-46. Recipient Dixon Meml. award, 1973, nat., Best of Show purchase award Dixie Coll. State-Wide Invitational Art Show, 1996; state and local art awards; Weber State U. art bldg. dedicated as F. R. Collett Art Bldg. & Gallery, 1982, 6th Ann. Gov.'s Art award State of Utah, 1994, Ohio Valley Art League award of Merit, 1994; named Disting. Utahn, UK/Utah Centennial Yr. Festival, 1996. Mem. Soc. Animal Artists, Color Country Art Assn. Mem. Lds Ch. Avocations: reading, music, sports, golf, fishing. Home: Saint George, Utah. Died Mar. 14, 2000.

COLLIER, LUCILLE ANN See MILLER, ANN

COLLINS, JANET FAY, retired dancer, dance educator, choreographer; b. New Orleans, Mar. 2, 1917; Student, L.A. City Coll., L.A. Art Ctr. Sch.; studied dance with, Adolph Bolm, Carmelita Maracci, Mia Slavenska; student ballet, San Francisco Sch. Ballet; studied Hebrew music with, composer Ernest Bloch. Tchr. Sch. Am. Ballet, 1949-52; faculty Marymount Manhattan Coll., 1958, Manhattanville Coll. of Sacred Heart, Purchase, N.Y., 1959. Keynote spkr. 8th Internat. Conf. of Blacks in Dance, 1995 Prin. dancer L.A. mus. theater prodns. Run Little Chillun, 1940, The Mikado in Swing, 1940; dancer with Lester Horn Co., Katherine Dunham Co.; choreographer numerous works including Genesis, 1965, Canticle of the Elements, 1974; painter religious subjects. Vol. tchr. St. Joseph's Sch. for Deaf, Bronx, 1957. Julius Rosenwald fellow, 1945, Donaldson award for best dancer on Broadway, 1951, Merit award Mademoiselle mag., 1950; named The Most Outstanding Debutante of the Season, Dance mag., 1949, Young Woman of the Yr., 1950 Home: Kirkland, Wash. Died May 28, 2003.

COLLINS, WINIFRED QUICK (MRS. HOWARD LYMAN COLLINS), organizational executive, retired navy officer; b. Great Falls, Mont.; m. Howard Lyman Collins (dec.). BS, U. So. Calif., 1935; grad. Harvard-Radcliffe Program in Bus. Adminstrn., 1938; MA, Stanford U., 1952. Commd. ensign U.S. Navy, 1942, advanced through grades to capt. 1957; personnel dir. Midshipman's Sch., Smith Coll., 1942-43; chief Naval Personnel for Women, 1957-62; ret.; nat. v.p. U.S. Navy League, 1964-70, nat. dir. and chmn. nat. awards com., 1964-95; chmn. newsletter com. Nat. Navy League, 1995—; nat. dir. Ret. Officers Assn.; former cons. HEW; former trustee Helping Hand Found.; former mem. Sec. Navy's Bd. Advs. and Tng. Naval Pers.; dir. CPC Internat., Inc., 1977-84, chmn. employee investment com., mem. audit, exec. compensation and exec. coms.; bd. dirs. Leadership Found.; trustee U.S. Naval Acad. Found., 1977—. Author: More Than a Uniform-A Navy Woman in a Navy Man's World, 1997. 1st v.p. Republican Women of D.C. Decorated Legion of Merit, Bronze Star, Sec. Navy Commendation medal; recipient Navy's Disting. Civilian Pub. Svc. award, 1971, 77, Disting. Svc. award Navy League of U.S., 1973, Hall of Fame award Nat. Navy League, 1990, Lone Sailor award U.S. Navy Meml. Found., 1997, Disting. Pub. Svc. award Sec. of Navy, 1997, USN Meml. award, 1997; named to Hall of Fame Internat. Bus. and Profl. Women's Assn., 1994. Mem. VFW, Am. Legion, Nat. Navy League (life), Retired Officers Assn., Harvard Grad. Bus. Sch. Washington Club (past dir.), Army Navy Town Club, Army Navy Country Club, Capital Spkrs. Club, Chevy Chase Club, Welcome to Washington Internat. Club. Died May 1999.

COLON, ALEX, actor; b. Patillas, P.R., Jan. 26, 1941; came to U.S., 1951; s. Dionicio and Lucia (Santiago) C.; divorced; 1 child, Naii Luz. Actor films including The Hospital, The Supercops, The Taking of Pelham 1-2-3, The Mighty Quinn, Red Scorpion, Invasion U.S.A., Death of an Angel, Deal of the Century, TV films Women of San Quentin, Centennial, Raid on Entebbe, The Law, Hustling, others; TV appearances include (series) Cagney & Lacey, Scarecrow & Mrs. King, Hill St. Blues, Quincy, Rockford Files, Quantum Leap, Matlock, Hunter, Kojak, Police Story, Police Woman, others; appeared on Broadway in The Gingerbread Lady, off-Broadway in Each Day Dies With Sleep. Home: Studio City, Calif. Deceased.

COLTON, FRANK BENJAMIN, retired chemist; b. Bialystok, Poland, Mar. 3, 1923; came to U.S., 1934, naturalized, 1934; s. Rubin and Fanny (Rosenblat) C.; m. Adele Heller, Mar. 24, 1950; children: Francine, Sharon, Laura, Sandra BS, Northwestern U., 1945, MA, 1946; PhD, U. Chgo., 1949. Research fellow Mayo Clinic, Rochester, Minn., 1949-51; with G.D. Searle & Co., Chgo., 1951-86, asst. dir. chem. research, 1961-70, research advisor, 1970-86. Contbr. articles to profl. jours. Pioneer in organic and steroid chemistries. Patentee first oral contraceptive Recipient Discovery medal for first oral contraceptive Nat. Assn. Mfrs., 1965, Profl. Achievement award U. Chgo., 1978, Achievement award Indsl. Research Inst., 1978; inducted in Nat. Inventors Hall of Fame, 1988. Mem. Am. Chem. Soc., Chgo. Chemists Club. Home: Phoenix, Ariz. Died Nov. 25, 2003.

COLWIN, ARTHUR LENTZ, biologist, educator; b. Sydney, Australia, Jan. 26, 1911; came to U.S., 1936, naturalized, 1942; m. Laura North Hunter, June 15, 1940. B.Sc., McGill U., 1933, M.Sc., 1934, PhD (NRC Can. fellow), 1935-36; Moyse Travelling fellow, Cambridge (Eng.) U., 1934-35; Seessel fellow, Yale, 1936-37, Royal Soc. Can. fellow, 1937-38. Mem. faculty Queens Coll., 1940-73, prof., 1957-73, prof. emeritus, 1973—2003; adj. prof. Rosenstiel Sch. Marine and Atmospheric Sci., U. Miami, Fla., 1973—. Fulbright research fellow Tokyo U., 1953-54; vis. scientist Nat. Inst. Med. Research, London, Eng., 1960 Mem. editorial bd. Jour. Exptl. Zoology, 1964-68, Jour. Morphology, 1964-68, Biol. Bull, 1969-73, Am. Zoologist, 1970-75; contbr. articles to profl. jours. Trustee Marine Biol. Lab., Woods Hole, Mass., 1962-72. Served to capt. USAAF, 1943-46. Fellow N.Y. Acad. Scis., AAAS; mem. Internat. Inst. Developmental Biology, Internat. Soc. Cell Biology, Am. Soc. Zoologists, Soc. Study Devel. and Growth, Soc. for Study of Reprodn., Electron Microscope Soc. Am. Asso. Achievements include spl. research fertilization, devel. biology, cell contacts and assn., membrane structure and behavior. Home: Miami, Fla. Died Nov. 1, 2003.

COMBS, EARL BURNS, architect; b. Richmond, Va., Feb. 13, 1931; s. Earl Burns and Opal (Earnest) C. BArch, Cornell U., 1954, M in Regional Planning, 1959. Project designer Perkins and Will, White Plains, N.Y., 1954-57; teaching asst. Cornell U., Ithaca, N.Y., 1957-58; Fulbright fellow architecture U. Rome, 1958-59; designer Ballard, Todd and Snibbe, N.Y.C., 1960-61, Space Design Group, N.Y.C., 1961-63; pvt. practice archtl. design, from 1963; pvt. practice architecture, from 1967. Vis. critic Cornell U. Coll. Architecture, 1957. Contbr. articles to profl. jours. Recipient Award for House Design, Archtl. Record, 1971. Mem. AIA (landmarks preservation com. 1968-69), Gargoyle Soc. Deceased.

COMBS, HARRY BENJAMIN, aircraft company executive; b. Denver, Jan. 27, 1913; s. Albert Henry and Mildred (Berger) C.; m. Virginia Prout, Feb. 28, 1956; children: Harry Benjamin, Anthony, Clara (Mrs. Christopher Moore). BS, Yale, 1935; postgrad., Colo. U., 1927-38. Salesman Pan Am. Airways, N.Y.C., 1935-37; with Bosworth Chaunte-Loughridge & Co. (investment bankers), Denver, 1937-39; owner, pres. Combs Aircraft, Inc., Denver, 1939-66; adviser Gates Aviation & Combs Aircraft, Inc., Denver, 1966-72; pres., dir. Gates Learjet Corp., Wichita, Kans., 1971—82. Author: Kill Devil Hill, Secret of the Wright Brothers (Aviation Writers Assn. writing award for best non-fiction book 1979). Colo. dir. CD, 1951-54; mem. Yale Scholarship Com., 1951, Yale Alumni Bd., 1962, Project Beacon Com., 1961, Colo. Water Pollution Bd., 1965-72; mem. Colo. Game and Fish Commn., 1965-72, chmn., 1971. Served to 1st lt. USAAF, 1944-45. Mem. Nat. Air Trade Assn. (Colo. chmn. 1946-49), Gen. Aviation and Mfg. Assn. (dir.), Aviation Man of Yr. award 1974), Soc. Free Space Floaters, Conquistadores del Cielo, Lafayette Flying Corps (hon.), Delta Psi. Clubs: Denver, Denver Country, Arlberg Ski (Denver); Wings, Yale, New York; Nat. Aviation (Washington); Mach II, OX 5. Home: Denver, Colo. Died Dec. 23, 2003.

COMBS, MAXINE SOLOW, English language educator; b. Dallas, June 14, 1937; d. Eugene Maxwell and Sayd Frances Solow; m. Edouard Gauthier; m. 2d Bruce Combs; children: Bella, Wayne; m. 3d Martin Bernstein, Feb. 20, 1992. BA, Mills Coll., 1958; MA, Wayne State U., 1961; PhD, U. Oreg., 1968. Instr. English Idaho State U., Pocatello, 1963-65; lectr. English Lane C.C., Eugene, Oreg., 1966-69, Am. U., Washington, 1970-74; asst. prof. English George Mason U., Fairfax, Va., 1979-88; instr. English Howard U., Washington, 1988-89; asst. prof. English U. of D.C., Washington, 1972-77, 81-88 and from 90. Author: (chapbook of poems) Swimming out of the Collective Unconscious, 1988, (chapbook of stories) Foam of Perilous Seas, 1989 (Slough Press Fiction award), (short stories and novella) Handbook of the Strange, 1995. Home: Washington, DC. Died Feb. 18, 2002.

COMSTOCK, WALTER, biologist, educator; b. Chgo., Sept. 29, 1946; s. George and Una (Feldman) C.; m. Mary Beth Lederer, Dec. 28, 1968; two children. BS, Coll. Emporia, 1970. Tchr. Kenton County Schs., Erlanger, Ky., 1970-71; tchr. biology Forest Hills Schs., Cin., 1971-99, ret., 2000. Co-editor: Biology: A Molecular Approach, 1989. Coach Acad. Quiz team, 1989-2000. Avocations: wood turning, wood sculpting. Home: Milford, Ohio. Died Oct. 3, 2000.

CONABLE, BARBER B., JR., international agency administrator; b. Warsaw, N.Y., Nov. 2, 1922; s. Barber B. and Agnes G. (Gouinlock) C.; m. Charlotte Williams, Sept. 13, 1952; 4 children. AB, Cornell U., 1942, LLB, 1948. Bar: N.Y. 1948. Pvt. practice law, Buffalo, 1948-50, Batavia, NY, 1952-64; U.S. senator from N.Y., 1963-64; mem. 89th-98th congresses from 30th N.Y. dist., 1965-85, Pres. Reagan's Commn. on Def. Mgmt., from 1985; prof. U. Rochester, NY, 1985-86; pres. World Bank, Washington, 1986—91. Sr. fellow, Am. Enterprise Inst., 1985. Editor: Cornell U. Law Quar., 1947-48. Mem. sr. adv. com. Kennedy Inst. Politics; trustee U.S. Capitol Hist. Soc., Mus. Am. Indian. Served with USMCR, 1942-46, 50-51. Mem.: Rotary (pres. Batavia chpt.). Republican. Home: Alexander, NY. Died Nov. 30, 2003.

CONAN, ROBERT JAMES, JR., chemistry educator, consultant; b. Syracuse, N.Y., Oct. 30, 1924; s. Robert James and Helen M. (O'Brien) C. BS, Syracuse U., 1945, MS, 1947; PhD, Fordham U., 1950. Instr. Fordham U., N.Y.C., 1947-49; asst. prof. Le Moyne Coll., Syracuse, 1949-54, assoc. prof., 1954-58, prof. chemistry, 1958-89, prof. emeritus, from 1990. Cons. Carrier Corp., Syracuse, 1949-63, Owl Wire and Cable Co., Oneida, N.Y., 1952-62, Edison Audio Archives, Syracuse, 1972-86; rschr. U. Stockholm, Sweden, 1953, Swiss Fed. Inst. Tech., 1967, U. South Fla., 1988-90; mem. com. Onondaga Lake Sci. Coun., Syracuse, 1964-65; vis. prof. U. South Fla., 1991-2001. Contbr. over 50 articles to profl. jours. Recipient Plaque award Le Moyne Coll., 1989. Mem. Am. Chem. Soc. (chmn. Syracuse sect. 1958, 72, nat. councillor 1982-85, Unique Plaque Svc. award 1989, Spl. 50 Yr. Pin, life mem.), Tech. Club Syracuse (pres. 1981-82, plaque award). Republican. Roman Catholic. Avocations: music, irish genealogy. Died Nov. 8, 2002.

CONGAR, YVES CARDINAL, archbishop; b. Sepan, France, 1904; Created and proclaimed cardinal, 1994. Died 1995.

CONGER, CLEMENT ELLIS, foreign service officer, curator; b. Rockingham, Va., Oct. 15, 1912; s. Clement E. and Hallie (Ramsay) C.; m. Lianne Hopkins, May 29, 1948;

children— William Ramsay, Jay Alden, Shelley Louise. Grad., Strayer Coll., George Washington U., 1933-34, Adj. Gen. Officer Candidate Sch., Ft. Washington Md., 1943; DHL, Coll. William and Mary, 1977. Asst. finance examiner PWA, 1933-34; officer mgr., corr. Chgo. Tribune, Washington, 1934-41; office mgr. U.S. Rubber Co., Washington, 1941-42, pub. relations asst. N.Y.C., 1946-47; staff asst., asst. exec. dir. asst. sec. state for occupied areas Dept. State, 1947-49; staff asst., asst. exec. dir. Bur. German Affairs, 1949-54, asst. chief protocol, 1955-57, dep. chief protocol, 1958-61; spl. asst. to dir., exec. sec. ACDA State Dept., Washington, 1962-69; dep. chief protocol, 1969-70; curator Diplomatic Reception Rooms State Dept., 1961-92, White House curator, 1970-86; curator Blair House, 1976-92. Chmn. Fine Arts Ctr. Dept. State, 1961-92; sr. cons. Christie's Manson and Woods, 1992-95; lectr. on diplomatic reception rooms Dept. of State and White House.; former advisor White House Preservation Fund; mem. Com. for Preservation White House; mem. Com. Disting. Ams. for Mt. Vernon; former vice chmn. Com. on Gov.'s Mansion, Richmond, Va.; chmn. pres.'s house refurbishing com. Coll. William and Mary; v.p. Lee-Jackson Found.; chmn. Va. Trust for Historic Preservation; mem. Collectors Circle Nat. Gallery Art; mem. H.F. du Pont Collectors Circle, Winterthur Mus.; former mem. Winston Churchill Travelling Fellowship Found. Contbr. articles, illustrations to various publs. radio, TV programs. Mem. Nat. Adv. Com. on Monuments and Sites; former mem. The Woodlawn Plantation Found.; mem. adv. com. Mount Vernon, acquisitions com. Supreme Ct. Hist. Soc.; bd. dirs. Decatur House, Nat. Trust for Hist. Preservation, Tudor Pl., Dumbarton House; v.p. Lee-Jackson Found.; trustee Canterbury Cathedral Trust in Am.; advisor Gunston Hall Plantation; hist. preservation advisor Com. for Preservation Treasury Bldg.; former vestryman, sr. warden Hist. Christ Ch., Alexandria, Va.; mem. devel. bd., former trustee Washington Nat. Cathedral. Maj. AUS, 1942-46; asst. sec. combined civil affairs com. Combined Chiefs Staff. Recipient Thomas Jefferson award Am. Soc. Interior Designers, 1978; Gold medal of honor Nat. Arts Club, 1980; Disting. Svc. award and medal Dept. State, 1981; Swan Ball award, 1985, Ann Pamela Cunningham award Mary Washington Coll., 1986, Award of Excellence, Decorative Arts Trust, 1987, Sr. Exec. Svc. award for disting. performance Dept. State U.S. Govt., Henry Francis DuPont award and gold medal Winterthur, 1992, Sec. of State's disting. gold medal, 1992, others. Mem. SAR, Soc. Cin., Chevaliers de Tastevin, Internat. Orgn. Experts (hon.), Assn. Diplomatic Studies (bd. dirs.), Raleigh Tavern Soc., Colonial Williamsburg Va. Found., Nat. Cathedral Assn., Gulf Stream Bath & Tennis Club (Del Ray Beach, Fla.), Met. Club (Wash.), Chevy Chase Club (Wash.). Episcopalian. Home: Delray Beach, Fla. Died Jan. 11, 2004.

CONIGLIO, JOHN GIGLIO, biochemistry educator; b. Tampa, Fla., July 21, 1919; s. Giuseppe and Maria (Giuseppe) C.; m. Carmen Sylvia Moreno, Dec. 27, 1942; children: JOhn William, Robert Freeman, David Martin. BS in Chemistry, Furman U., 1940; PhD in Biochemistry, Vanderbilt U., 1949. Tchr. high sch., Kershaw, S.C., 1940-41; supr. Ordnance Dept., Childersburg, Ala., 1942-43; chemist E.I. duPont, Childersburg, 1943-44; supr. Tenn. Eastman Corp., Oak Ridge, 1944-45; predoctoral fellow Atomic Energy Commn., 1949-50, postdoctoral fellow, 1950-51; from instr. to prof. dept. biochemistry Vanderbilt U., Nashville, 1951-90, prof. emeritus dept. biochemistry, from 1990. Cons. LIPID Rsch. Group, Va. Hosp., Nashville, 1961-65; ad hoc cons. various rsch. orgns., 1970-90; com. mem. FASEB Com. on Edn., Bethesda, Md., 1985-89; mem. adv. com. Med. Div. Oak Ridge Assn. Univ., Tenn., 1970-74. Contbr. articles to profl. jours.; assoc. editor LIPIDS, 1969—, Nutrition Rev., 1984-94. Spl. Rsch. fellow USPHS, 1961-62; rsch. grantee USPHS, others, 1951-90. Achievements include various rsch. findings in lipid metabolism and in lipid chemistry and metabolism of male reproductive tissue. Home: Nashville, Tenn. Died Feb. 26, 2001.

CONLEY, JOHN JOSEPH, otolaryngologist; b. Carnegie, Pa., 1912; MD, U. Pitts., 1937. Intern Mercy Hosp., Pitts., 1937-38; resident Kings County Hosp., Bklyn., 1938-41. Recipient Disting. Svc. award AMA, 1992. Home: New York, NY. Died Sept. 21, 1999.

CONN, HADLEY LEWIS, JR., physician, educator; b. Danville, Ind., May 6, 1921; s. Hadley L. and Fyrne (Holtsclaw) C.; m. Betty Jean Aubertin, Sept. 18, 1946; children: Eric Hadley, Jeffrey Wood, Thomas Brian, Andrew Randall, Lisabeth Ann Hayes. BA, U. Ind., 1942, MD, 1944; MS (hon.), U. Pa., 1972. Assoc. scientist Brookhaven Nat. Lab., N.Y., 1953-55; asst. prof. U. Pa. Sch. Medicine, Phila., 1956-59, assoc. prof., 1959-64, prof. medicine, 1964-72; dir. Clin. Research Center Hosp. of U. Pa. Sch. Medicine, 1970-72; chmn. dept. medicine Presbyn.-U. Pa. Med. Center, Phila., 1964-69. Vis. prof. medicine Am. U. Beirut, 1969-70; chmn. dept. medicine Univ. Medicine and Dentistry N.J.-Rutgers Med. Sch., Piscataway, 1972-83, dir. Cardiovascular Inst., 1982-91, prof. medicine, chmn. emeritus, 1992. Author: Myocardial Cell, 1966, Cardiac and Vascular Disease, 1971, Platelets, Prostaglandins and Lipids, 1980, Health and Obesity, 1983. Sec. Nat. Bd. Med. Examiners, 1962-65; bd. govs. Am. Heart Assn., 1969-72; pres. Heart Assn. S.E. Pa., 1967, Detweiler Found., 1973-85. Served to capt. M.C., AUS, 1946-48. Mem. ACP, Am. Coll. Cardiology (trustee 1963-69), AMA, Am. Soc. Clin. Investigation, Am. Clin. and Climatological Soc., Assn. Univ. Cardiologists, Am. Phys. Soc., Assn. Profs. Medicine, Phi Beta Kappa, Alpha Omega Alpha. Clubs: Rittenhouse; Merion Cricket (Phila.). Republican. Home: Princeton, NJ. Deceased.

CONN, LEWIS MORTON, business publications executive director; b. Louisville, Nov. 16, 1915; s. Harry F. and Tessie (Friedman) C.; m. Irene Fox, July 26, 1940; children: Peter, Deborah, Paul. BA, U. Louisville, 1937. Pub. Jefferson Reporter, Louisville, 1953-75; pres. Greater Ky. Pubs., Inc., Shelbyville, Ky., 1966-68; pub. Ky. Bus. Ledger, Louisville, Ky., 1975-81; exec. dir. Assn. of Area Bus. Publs., Louisville; Annapolis, Md., from 1981; pres. Area Bus. Databank, Inc., Louisville, 1983-85. Chmn. Better Bus. Bur. Served with U.S. Army, 1943-45, PTO. Avocations: power boating, travel. Home: Falls Church, Va. Deceased.

CONNALLY, ERNEST ALLEN, retired federal agency administrator; b. Groesbeck, Tex., Nov. 15, 1921; s. Ernest Lackey and Pauline (Allen) C.; m. Janice Muriel Wegner, Aug. 28, 1951; children: Mary Allen, John Arnold Student, Rice U., 1939-40, U. Tex., 1940-42, U. Florence, Italy, 1947; BArch, U. Tex., 1950; MA, Harvard U., 1952, PhD, 1955. Asst. prof. architecture Miami U., Oxford, Ohio, 1952-55; assoc. prof. Washington U., St. Louis, 1955-57, vis. prof., 1962; assoc. prof. U. Ill., Urbana, 1957-61, prof., 1961-67; assoc. Ctr. for Advanced Study, 1966-67; asst. dir. Nat. Park Svc., U.S. Dept. Interior, Washington, 1967-72, assoc. dir., 1972-78; chief appeals officer cultural resources Nat. Park Service, Dept. Interior, Washington, 1982-92; assoc. dir. Heritage Conservation and Recreation Service, 1978-79. Cons. restoration hist. bldgs., 1952—; cons. UNESCO, Nepal, 1968, mem. working group for Sukhotai Hist. Park, Thailand, 1982-88; sec.-treas, U.S. com. Internat. Coun. on Monuments and Sites, 1969-73, chmn., 1973-75, sec.-gen., ICOMOS, Paris, 1975-81; Fulbright prof. U. Melbourne, Australia, 1963; U.S. del. UNESCO Conf. on Cultural Property, 1968; U.S. rep. Internat. Conf. on Rec. Hist. Monuments, Prague, Czechoslovakia, 1969; U.S. del., v.p. Gen. Assembly, Internat. Centre for Study of Preservation and Restoration of Cultural Property, Rome, 1971, 77, mem. exec. bd., 1971-75; mem. U.S.-USSR Joint Working Group on Urban Environ., 1973-81; bd. dirs. Pa. Ave. Devel. Corp., Washington, 1974-78; charter mem. Sr. Exec. Svc. of U.S.A., 1979. Author: Printed Books on Architecture, 1485-1805, 1960; also articles in jours., encys.; important works include restoration of Louis Bolduc house, 1956-57, Bolduc-LeMeilleur house, St. Genevieve, Mo., 1967 Maj. USAAF, 1942-46, lt. col. Res., 1956-58. Decorated Officier Ordre des Arts et des Lettres, France, 1986; recipient Research award Am. Philos. Soc., 1957, Disting. Service award Dept. Interior, 1978, Crowninshield award Nat. Trust Hist. Preservation, 1980, AIA Presdl. citation, 1990; named Membre d'Honneur ICOMOS, 1981, Trustee of Am., 1986, recipient Prix Gazzola, 1996. Mem. AIA (hon.), SAR, Soc. Archtl. Historians (past bd. dirs.), Nat. Trust for Hist. Preservation (past trustee), Fulbright Assn., Nat. Pks. and Conservation Assn., Assn. for Preservation Va. Antiquities, Gargoyle, Cosmos Club, Harvard Club (Washington), Alpha Rho Chi, Tau Sigma Delta, Phi Kappa Phi. Episcopalian. Home: Alexandria, Va. Died Dec. 23, 1999.

CONNELL, JOHN M. mechanical engineer; b. Decauter, Ill., Aug. 22, 1938; s. Frank S. and Emily (Dostelak) C.; m. Nadine Mary Broom, June 15, 1962; 1 child, Kathleen. BS in Mech. Engring., Valpraiso U., 1960. Application engring. mgr. Parker Hannatin Corp., Des Plaines, Ill., 1967-85; chief engr. B & H Machine Inc., Minerva, Ohio, from 1985. Republican. Roman Catholic. Avocation: golfing. Died Sept. 16, 2001.

CONNIFF, RAY, musician, composer, conductor; b. Attleboro, Mass., Nov. 6, 1916; s. John Lawrence and Maude (Angela) Conniff; m. Emily Jo Ann Imhof, Feb. 14, 1938; children: James Lawrence, Jo Ann Patricia; m. Ann Marie Engberg, Aug. 23, 1947; 1 foster child, Richard J. Bibo; m. Vera Schmidheiny, Aug. 24, 1968; 1 child, Tamara Allegra. Student, Juilliard Sch. Music; studied with Tom Timothy, Sol Kaplan, Hugo Friedhofer. Music editor Hollywood Reporter. Musician (trombone player, arranger): Bunny Berigan, Bob Crosby, Artie Shaw, Harry James Orch.; arranger, composer, condr., rec. artist: Columbia Records; musician: (albums) Here We Come A-Caroling, 1986, Concert in Rhythm, Vol. 1, 1987, Rhapsody in Rhythm, 1988, Invisible Tears, 1994, Speak to Me of Love, 1994, Friendly Persuasion, 1994. Died Oct. 12, 2002.

CONNOLLY, THOMAS EDMUND, humanities educator; BS, Fordham U., 1939; MA, U. Chgo., 1947, PhD, 1951. Lectr. English Loyola U., Chgo., 1947-50; instr. English U. Idaho, Moscow, 1950-51; asst. prof. English Creighton U., Omaha, 1951-53, U. Buffalo (N.Y.), 1953-59, assoc. prof., 1959-64; prof. English SUNY, Buffalo, 1964-87, dir. MA in humanities program, 1978-81, prof. emeritus, from 1987. Vis. prof. English and Am. Lit. U. Coll., Dublin. Ireland, 1966-67; acting provost faculty arts and letters SUNY, 1970-71; mem. adv. bd. The Irish Tradition, Global Village, N.Y.C., 1988-90; bd. overseers Mellen U. Turks & Caicos Islands, 1998—; presenter in field. Author: The Personal Library of James Joyce, 1955, James Joyce's Scribbledehobble, 1961, (with Selig Adler) From Ararat to Suburbia, 1960, Swinburne's Theory of Poetry, 1964, James Joyce Exhibition: A Catalogue, 1978, Faulkner's World, 1988, A Neo-Aristotelian and Joycean Theory of Poetic Forms, 1995, James Joyce's Books, Portraits, Manuscripts, Notebooks, Typescripts, Page Proofs, Together with Critical Essays about Some of His Works, 1997, Essays on Fiction: Dickens, Melville, Hawthorne and Faulkner, 1999; editor: Joyce's Portrait, 1962, Nathaniel Hawthorne: Young Goodman Brown, 1968, Hawthorne's Scarlet Letter, 1970. Summer Rsch. fellow, 1963. Mem. AAUP, MLA, James Joyce Found. Avocations: golf, gardening. Home: Agoura Hills, Calif. Deceased.

CONOLE, CLEMENT VINCENT, business administrator; b. Binghamton, N.Y., Sept. 29, 1908; s. P.J. and Briget (Halleran) C.; m. Marjorie Anable, Sept. 26, 1931; children: Barbara McElroy, Marjorie A. Hargrave, Richard C., Jacalyn Harman. BSCE, Clarkson Coll. Tech., Potsdam, N.Y., 1931; postgrad., Cornell U., NYU, Yale U.; MBA, Fla. Atlantic U. Licensed profl engr. and land surveyor, N.Y., Pa. Engr. City of Binghamton, also N.Y. State, 1930-32; ptnr. Richmeyer, Harding and Conole, 1932-33; engr. Dept. of Interior, 1933-35; dist. dir. Fed. Works Adminstrn.; dist. supt. N.Y. Unemployment Ins. Div., 1936-37; asst. state indsl. commr. Binghamton and Rochester, N.Y., 1937-39; dep. indsl. commr. State of N.Y., 1939-43; dir. indsl. bur. C. of C. Bd. of Trade of Phila., 1943-44, operating mgr., 1945-46, exec. v.p., 1946-52; also editor, pub. Greater Phila. mag., 1945-50; v.p. Bankers Securities Corp., 1952-55; pres. Mcpl. Publs., Inc., 1947-50; pub. relations cons. Phila.-Balt. Stock Exchange, 1947-52; chmn. bd., pres., dir. Hearn Dept. Stores, Inc., N.Y.C., 1952-54; dir., chmn. bd. James McCutcheon & Co., 1956-57; ptnr. Franklin D. Roosevelt Jr., 1954-59; chmn. bd., dir. Bus. Supplies Corp. Am., Skytop, Pa., 1962-65; chmn. bd. dir., pres. Tabulating Card Co., Inc., Princeton, N.J., 1955-62; chmn. bd. dir. Am. Bus. Mgmt. Co., 1955-62, Whiting Paper Co., Inc., 1959-62, Sky Meadow Farms, Inc., 1965-68; prof. adminstrn. Fla. Atlantic U., 1972-74; chmn. bd. trustees, pres. Am. Coll. Adminstrs. Execs. Mgrs., Laguna Hills, Calif.; dean Grad. Sch. Adminstrn. Coll. of Boca Raton, Fla. Exec. head mgmt. engring. divsn. S.D. Leidesdorf & Co., 1954-55; dir. City Stores Corp., City Stores Mer. Co., Inc., City Splty. Stores Co., Inc., Oppenheim Collins & Co., Franklin Simon Co., N.Y.C., R.H. White Co., Boston, Wise Smith & Co., Hartford, Conn. Mem. Broome County Planning Commn., 1936-38, Pa. War Manpower Commn.; chmn. War. Emergency Bd. N.Y. State, 1941; industry mem. appeals com. Nat. War Labor Bd., 1943-45; cons. HOLC and FHA, 1936-39; chmn. Armed Forces Regional Council, Pa. and Del., 1950-52; mem. adv. com. 2d Army, 4th Naval Dist.; pres. 175th Anniversary of the Signing of the Declaration of Independence, 1951; pres. Phila. Conv. and Visitors Bur., 1953; chmn. United Com. Fund, Princeton; apptd. mem. State Commn. to reorgn. Govt. City N.Y., 1953; apptd. mem. Mayor's Adv. Council, chmn. com. on city mgmt. and adminstrn., 1954; Citizens Com. to Keep N.Y. Clean, 1955, Citizens Com. on Cts., 1955; pres. Quiet City Campaign, 1956; vice chmn., sec. Phila. Parking Authority.; trustee William Shelton Harrison Found., Hun School, Princeton, N.J., Clarkson Coll. of Tech. Named Adm., Flagship Fleet, Am. Airlines, 1942, to Honorable Order of Ky. Colonels, 1950, Amb., TWA, 1957 Mem. Am. Mgmt. Assn., Am. Inst. Mgmt. (pres. coun., charter mem. adv. bd.), Nat. Retail Rsch. Inst. (bd. dirs.), Bronx Bd. Trade (bd. dirs. 1954-64), Ave. of Americas Assn. (bd. dirs. 1952-55), Soc. for Advancement Mgmt., Nat. Assn. Cost Accts., Commerce and industry Assn. N.Y. (treas., bd. dirs., exec. com. 1954-58), Lambda Iota (pres.), Delta Upsilon (trustee), Midday Club (Phila.), Phila. Country Club, Lake Placid Club, Skytop Club, Merion Cricket Club, Racquet Club, Poor Richard Club, Pen and Pencil Club, Economic Club, Union League, Nat. Golf Links Am., Uptown Club, Springdale Golf Club, Rotary, Nassau Club, Laguna Hills Golf Club, Pinehurst Country Club, Royal Palm Yacht and Country Club (gov.), Mission Viejo Country Club, El Niguel Country Club, P.G.A. Nat. Golf Club, Calif. Club, Phi Beta Lambda. Deceased.

CONRAD, HELEN BOTT, organization executive; b. Triadelphia, W.Va., Dec. 21, 1918; d. Carl J. and Catherine (Wagner) Bott; widow; children: Carol Conrad Stickel, Joan Conrad Wildpret, Cinday Conrad Peters. Student, Elliot Sch. Bus., Wheeling, W.Va., 1937-38. Sec. Wheeling Steel and Wheeling Pitts. Steel Corp., 1940-71; ret., 1971; membership sec. Brooks Bird Club, Inc., Wheeling, from 1973, hon. mem., 1978, reservationist, from 1982, adminstr., from 1985. Home: Triadelphia, W.Va. Deceased.

CONRAD, JOSEPH LAWRENCE, Slavic language educator; b. Kansas City, Mo., June 26, 1933; s. Lawrence Herman and Marguerite (Smith) C.; divorced; children: Belinda, Karla, Allan. BA, U. Kans., 1955; PhD, U. Tex., 1961. From instr. to asst. prof. Fla. State U., Tallahassee, 1959-62; from asst. prof. to assoc. prof. U. Tex., Austin, 1962-66; assoc. prof. U. Kans., Lawrence, 1966—70, prof., 1970—2003. Author book; contbr. numerous articles to profl. jours. Grantee Inst. Internat. Edn., 1955-56, Internat. Rsch. and Exch. Bd., 1964-86; Fulbright Rsch. award, 1981, 83. Mem. AAAS (bd. dirs. 1994-97), Am. Assn. Tchrs. Slavic and East European Langs., Soc. Slovene Studies, others. Avocations: literature, language, folklore. Died Dec. 21, 2003.

COODLEY, EUGENE L. internist; b. L.A., Jan. 14, 1920; s. Oscar and Rae (Karot) C.; m. Gloria B. Coodley, July 11, 1946; children: Lauren, Cheryl, Gregg. BA, UCLA, 1939; MD, U. Calif., San Francisco, 1943. Diplomate Am. Bd. Internal Medicine. Chief medicine Phila. Gen. Hosp., 1967-73; prof. medicine Hahnemann U. Sch. Medicine, Phila., 1973-80, chief internal medicine, 1973-80; chief internal medicine sect. VA Med. Ctr., Long Beach, Calif., from 1985; prof. medicine V U. Calif.-Irvine Sch. Medicine, Orange, from 1980. Chief medicine Kern County Hosp., Bakersfield, Calif., 1965-67; asst. clin. prof. Calif. Coll. Medicine, Orange, 1965-67. Author: Clinical Enzymology, 1978, Geriatric Heart Disease, 1987, Odyssey of a Physician, 1995; contbr. chpts. to books. Chmn. 61st Dist. Dem. Club, L.A., 1979. Capt. M.C., U.S. Army, 1944-46, PTO. Recipient 1st prize for sci. exhibit AMA, Chgo., 1969. Fellow ACP, Am. Coll. Cardiology (3rd prize 1974). Home: Long Beach, Calif. Died Jul. 23, 1999.

COOK, CHAUNCEY WILLIAM WALLACE, retired food products company executive; b. Hugo, Okla., June 22, 1909; s. Chauncey William and Minnie Malona (Cherry) C.; m. Ethel Frances Crain, Dec. 27, 1934; children: David William, Frances Ann (Mrs. Ann C. Cole). BS, U. Tex., 1930; postgrad., Columbia U., 1930-31; LL.D., C.W. Post Coll., L.I. U., 1967, Babson Inst. Bus. Adminstrn., 1967, Iona Coll., 1968; L.H.D., Pace Coll., 1969; D.Eng., Mich. Tech. U., 1969. Prodn. engr. Procter & Gamble Co., 1931-37, plant engr., 1937-42; chief engr. Gen. Foods Corp., 1942-44; mgr. mfg. and engring. Maxwell House div. Gen. Foods Corp., Hoboken, N.J., 1944-46, prodn. mgr., 1946-51, product mgr., 1951-52, mgr. sales and advt., 1952-53, asst. gen. mgr., 1953-55, gen. mgr., 1955-59; v.p. Gen. Foods Corp., 1955-59, exec. v.p., 1959-62, pres., 1962-65, pres., chief exec. officer, 1965-66, chmn., chief exec. officer, 1966-73, chmn., pres., chief exec. officer, 1972, chmn., 1973-74, chmn. exec. com., 1974-80. Mem. Bus. Coun., 1966-2003; chmn. food sub-coun. Nat. Indsl. Pollution Control Coun., 1970-73. Trustee Com. for Econ. Devel., 1965-74, Coun. of Americas, 1965-74, The Conf. Bd., 1964-76, chmn., 1972-73; bd. dirs. Coun. Better Bus. Burs., 1970-73; mem. devel. bd. U. Tex. System, 1969-74, chmn. devel. bd., 1981-83, mem. exec. com. Chancellor's Coun. Recipient Distinguished Engring. grad. award U. Tex., 1963; Distinguished Achievement award U. Tex. Ex-Students Assn. N.Y., 1963; Distinguished Alumnus award Ex-Students Assn. U. Tex., 1965; Alumni medal Columbia U. Alumni Assn., 1969; C. Walter Nichols award N.Y. U. Grad. Sch. Bus. Adminstrn., 1972; Herbert Hoover award Am. Wholesale Grocers Assn., 1979 Mem. Tex. Philos. Soc., Pi Sigma Epsilon (hon.), Tau Beta Pi, Beta Gamma Sigma, Eta Kappa Nu, Delta Chi. Clubs: Austin, Headliners (Austin, Tex.). Died May 19, 2003.

COOK, CHRISTOPHER DIXON, communications company executive; b. Santa Monica, Calif., Sept. 14, 1942; s. Albert and Virginia (Dixon) C.; m. Elizabeth Burkman, June 18, 1966 (div. 1983); two children. BA, N.C. State U., 1964; MA, U. Va., 1966. English instr. U. N.C., Charlotte, 1966-69; acct. exec. K. Drake Assocs., Detroit, 1969-72; pub. rels. acct. supervisor, advt. acct. exec. Cochrane Chase & Co., Newport Beach, Calif., 1972-76; pres. Cook Comms. Svcs., Inc., Irvine, Calif., 1976-91, Atlanta, 1992-2000, Newport Beach, Calif., from 2000. Died May 29, 2002.

COOK, FRED JAMES, journalist, author; b. Point Pleasant, N.J., Mar. 8, 1911; s. Frederick P. and Huldah (Compton) C.; m. Julia Barbara Simpson, June 5, 1936 (dec. 1974); children: Frederick P. II, Barbara J. (Mrs. Richard Shibla); m. Irene H. Line, 1976 (dec. 1992). Litt.B., Rutgers U., 1932. Reporter Asbury Park Press, N.J., 1933-36, desk man, city editor, 1938-44; editor N.J. Courier, Toms River, 1936-37; rewriteman, feature writer N.Y. World Telegram and Sun, 1944-59; free-lance writer, 1959—2003. Author of: numerous books including The FBI Nobody Knows, 1964, The Corrupted Land, 1966, The Secret Rulers, 1966, The Plot Against the Patient, 1967, What So Proudly We Hailed, 1968, The Nightmare Decade, The Life and Times of Senator Joe McCarthy, 1971, Julia's Story, The Tragedy of an Unnecessary Death, 1976, The Great Energy Scam: Private Billions vs. Public Good, 1983, Maverick, Fifty Years of Investigative Reporting, 1984 Recipient Page One award N.Y. Newspaper Guild, 1958, 59, 60, spl. award for crusading journalism, 1980, Sidney Hillman Found. award, 1960 Mem. Authors League Am. Home: Asbury Park, NJ. Died Apr. 4, 2003.

COOK, JAMES, magazine editor, writer; b. Schenectady, N.Y., Nov. 9, 1926; s. Harold James and Ruth May (Turner) Cook; m. Claire Rose Kehrwald, Sept. 12, 1953; children: Karen Louise, Cassandra Claire. AB, Bowdoin Coll., 1947; A.M., Columbia U., 1948. Instr. English Yankton (S.D.) Coll., 1948—49, Ohio U., 1949—52; editor Popular Publs., N.Y.C., 1952—53; mng. editor Railroad mag., 1953—55; assoc., sr. editor Forbes mag., N.Y.C., 1955—76, exec. editor, 1976—92; reviewer Forbes Restaurant Guide, 1970—71; editor Forbes in Arabic, 1975—76; free lance writer, from 1992. Author: Fellow Travelers, 1999. Died Oct. 16, 2002.

COOK, JAMES FIELDER, producer, director; b. Atlanta; s. George Lindsey and Marion (Fielder) C.; children: Rebecca Eden, Lindsey Fielder. BA cum laude in English Lit., Washington and Lee U.; postgrad. Elizabethan drama, U. Birmingham, Eng.; DFA, Washington and Lee U. Exec. J. Walter Thompson (advt.); ptnr. Unit Four. Dir. Lux Video Theatre; prodr., dir. Kraft TV Theatre, Kaiser Aluminum Hour; TV prodr., dir. Am. Jewish Com; freelance dir. Studio One, Philco-Goodyear Playhouse, U.S. Steel-Goodyear Playhouse, Playhouse 90, pres. Eden Prodns., Inc.; prodr., dir. Du Pont Show of Week; TV pilot films for series Ben Casey, The 11th Hour, The Waltons, Beacon Hill; dir. motion pictures Patterns, Home is the Hero, A Big Hand for the Little Lady, How to Save a Marriage and Ruin Your Life, Prudence and the Pill, London, Eagle in a Cage, Yugoslavia, The Hideaways, Too Far to Go, Seize the Day; theatrical Broadway prodns. A Cook for Mr. General, off-Broadway prodn. Manuvers; author: original TV plays Zone Four, The Moment of the Rose, Throw Me a Rope; Recipient TV awards for: Snapfinger Creek, A Profile in Courage, Throw me a Rope, Project Immortality, A Big Deal in Lorado, Brigadoon, Teacher, Teacher, The Price, Sam Hill: Who Killed the Mysterious Mr. Foster, Goodbye Raggedy Ann, The Homecoming, The Hands of Cormac Joyce, Miracle on 34th Street, This Is the West that Was, Miles to Go Before I Sleep, Beacon Hill, The Pilot, Judge Horton and the Scottsboro Boys, Beauty and the Beast, A Love Affair: The Eleanor and Lou Gehrig Story, Too Far to Go, I Know Why the Caged Bird Sings, Gangin the Savage, Family Reunion, The Francis Farmer Story, Why Me?, (mini series) Evergreen, A Special Friendship, Sweet Talk, A Member of The Wedding. Mem. Acad. Motion Picture Arts and Scis. (bd. govs.), Dirs. Guild Am. (v.p., mem. nat. bd.). Clubs: Players (N.Y.C.), N.Y. Athletic (N.Y.C.); Riviera Country (Los Angeles). Died June 20, 2003.

COOKE, LAWRENCE HENRY, lawyer, former state chief judge; b. Monticello, N.Y., Oct. 15, 1914; s. George L. and Mary (Pond) C.; m. Alice McCormack, Nov. 25, 1939; children— Edward M., George L., II, Mary L. Cooke Opie. BS cum laude, Georgetown U., 1935; LLB, Union U., 1938, LLD (hon.), 1975, Siena Coll., 1964, N.Y. Law Sch., 1979, Bklyn. Law Sch., 1980, Pace U., 1980, N.Y. Law Sch., 1981, Syracuse U., 1985. Bar: N.Y. 1939. Pvt. practice, Monticello, 1939-53; Sullivan County judge, 1954-61; Supreme Ct. justice 3d Jud. Dist., 1962-68; assoc. justice Appellate div. 3d Dept., Albany, 1969-74; assoc. judge N.Y. State Ct. Appeals, Albany, 1975-78, chief judge, 1979-84; sr. counsel Hall, Dickler, Lawler, Kent & Friedman, N.Y.C., 1985-87, Couch, White, Brenner, Howard & Feigenbaum, Albany, N.Y., from 1987; Dist. scholar in residence Pace U. Sch. Law, N.Y., 1989-92. Arbitrator internat. law cases, 1986—; chmn. Conf. Chief Justice, 1982-83; pres. Nat. Ctr. for State Cts., 1982-83, adv. com., 1989—; chmn. N.Y. Fair Trial, Free Press Conf., 1979-84; chmn. adv. coun. Nat. Symposium on Civil Justice Issues, 1986; chmn. assocs. com. Nat. Ctr. for State Cts., 1985-86; lectr. Brookings Inst., 1984, 86; John F. Sonnett Meml. lectr. Fordham U. Law Sch., 1981; Charles Evans Hughes Meml. lectr. N.Y. County Lawyers Assn., 1981; keynote spkr. Internat. Jewish Jurists and Lawyers Conv., Jerusalem, 1981, Gender Task Force Anniversary, 1996; mem. Sen. Daniel P. Moynihan Jud. Screening Com., 1985-93; chair Gov. Pataki Jud. Screening Com., 1995-97; hon. chair State Instl. Commentary, 1996. Supr. Town of Thompson, N.Y., 1946-49; chmn. Sullivan County Bd. Suprs., 1947-48; bd. visitors Sch. Law Fordham U., 1987—; bd. dirs. State Justice Inst., 1986-88; formerly chair local dist. Boy Scouts Am., Monticello dist. ARC, Monticello March of Dimes, Sullivan County United Fund Drive, Monticello Cath. Charities Drive; hon. chair Sullivan County Assn. Retarded Citizens; former trustee Ethelbert Crawford Meml. Libr.; bd. dirs. St. Joseph's Sanatorium, Sullivan County Hist. Soc., Sullivan County Cerebral Palsy Assn; mem. edn. bd. N.Y. State Bar Found., 1985-95, State Ct. Commentary, Albany Law Sch., 1990—, Govt. Law and Policy Jour., N.Y. State Bar Assn., 1990—. Recipient Torch of Liberty award B'nai B'rith, 1967, Friend of Press award N.Y. State Soc. Newspaper Editors, 1985, 1st Amendment award Deadline Club, 1985, Seymour medal Am. Arbitration Assn., 1985, Toney Rivers Watson award Jud. Friends of Nat. Bar Assn., 1984, award of merit Am. Judges Assn., 1983, Law Day award N.Y. State Trial Lawyers' Assn., 1983, John Carroll award Georgetown U. Alumni Assn., 1982, Golda Meir Meml. award Jewish Lawyers Guild, 1983, Grange 50 yr. mem. award, 1989, Disting. Founders award N.Y. State Assn. Cmty. Dispute Resolution Ctrs., Inc., 1991, Sullivan County Cath. of Yr. award, 1993, Shields award Sullivan County, 1991, Gold medal Albany Law Sch., 1995, Nat. Ctr. for State Cts. Recognition dinner, 1995, Monticello Masons De Witt Clinton award, 1995, Gender Fairness award N.Y. State Assn. Women Judges, 1996, keynote spkr. anniversary of Gender Bias Task Force Report, 1996, Judiciary award Sullivan co-chpt. NAACP, 1996, Rosen award Orange-Sullivan Women's Bar Assn., 1996, Golden Trumpet award Firefighters Assn. State N.Y., 1997; Sullivan County courthouse renamed Lawrence H. Cooke Sullivan County Courthouse, 1997, Lawrence H. Cooke Gallery at Sullivan County Hist. Mus. dedicated in his honor, 1999; named Grand Marshal, Sullivan County Firefighter's Ann. Parade, 1998. Fellow Am. Bar Assn. Found.; mem. ABA, N.Y. State Bar Assn. (past chmn. young lawyers sect., Gold medal 1985), Assn. of Bar of City of N.Y., Albany County Bar Assn., N.Y. State Women's Bar Assn. (hon.), Sullivan County Bar Assn. (pres.), Am. Law Inst., Am. Judicature Soc. (bd. dirs. 1987-90), Nat. Ctr. for State Cts. (Disting. Svc. award 1987), Rockland County Magistrates' Assn. (Disting. Svc. award 1987); pres. Hudson Valley Vol. Fireman's Assn., 1965-66, Sullivan County Vol. Fireman's Assn., Monticello Fire Dept. Democrat. Roman Catholic. Deceased.

COOKE, THEODORE FREDERIC, JR., chemist; b. Pittsfield, Mass., Jan. 28, 1913; s. Theodore Frederic Sr. and Mabel Lavinia (Roberts) C.; m. Virginia Breed Hegamyer, Sept. 28, 1940 (dec. 1968); children: June, Frederic, Nancy, Susan; m. Barbara Ann Wilkins, June 23, 1973. BS in Chemistry, U. Mass., 1934; PhD in Chemistry, Yale U., 1937. Rsch. chemist Standard Oil Devel. Co., Linden, N.J., 1937-40, Am. Cyanamid Co., Bound Brook, N.J., 1940-42, group leader, 1945-50, asst. dir. applied rsch., 1950-60, dir. R&D, 1960-70; dir. sci. svcs. Stamford, Conn., 1970-78; dir. liaison programs Yale U., New Haven, 1978-86; dir. tech. ctr. Textile Rsch. Inst., Princeton, N.J., from 1978; v.p. R & D Chem-Tek Corp., Newton, N.C., 1986-93. Recruiter Internat. Exec. Services Corp., Stamford, 1987—. Contbr. articles to profl. jours.; patentee in field. Served to maj. U.S. Army, 1942-45. Recipient Wilbur Lucius Cross medal Yale U. Grad. Sch. Alumni Assn., 1994. Fellow Am. Inst. Chemists, N.J. Inst. Chemists (chmn. 1958-60, Honor Scroll 1972); mem. Assn. Research Dirs. (councilor 1984), Am. Chem. Soc., Am. Assn. Textile Chemists and Colorists (Olney medal 1983). Clubs: Martinsville (N.J.) Community (pres. 1958-60). Republican. Presbyterian. Avocations: archeology, tennis, skiing, gardening. Home: Stamford, Conn. Died Jan. 6, 1997.

COOPER, ARTHUR MARTIN, magazine editor; b. N.Y.C., Oct. 15, 1937; s. Benjamin Albert and Elizabeth (Sadock) Cooper; m. Amy Levin, June 9, 1979. BA, Pa. State U., 1959. Writer, reporter Harrisburg Patriot (Pa.), 1964—66; corr. Time mag., N.Y.C., 1966—67; assoc. editor Newsweek, N.Y.C., 1967—76; editor Penthouse mag., N.Y.C., 1976—77, CBS Family Weekly, N.Y.C., 1978—83; editor-in-chief Gentlemen's Quar., Conde-Nast Publs., N.Y.C., 1983—2003. Lt. (j.g.) USN, 1960—63. Recipient Profl. journalism fellow, Stanford U., 1970—71, Alumni fellow, Pa. State U., 1990. Mem.: Am. Soc. Mag. Editors (Editor of Yr. 1985). Home: New York, NY. Died June 9, 2003.

COOPER, BERNARR, communications educator; b. Bklyn., Oct. 6, 1912; s. Louis Kupperberg and Jennie (Linker) Cooper; m. Adella Shaw, June 7, 1945; children: Stephanie, Janet. AB cum laude, Wabash Coll., Crawfordsville, Ind., 1932; postgrad., U. Mich., 1945-46; PhD, Stanford U., 1956. Cert. tchr., English, Japanese. Assoc. U.S. Govt., Japan, 1946-49, chief media materials, 1949-52; tchr. H.s. Town of Belmont, Calif., 1952-57; asst. prof. U. N.Mex., Albuquerque, 1957-59; assoc. prof. media Fla. State U., Tallahassee, 1959-62; chief Bur. Mass Comm. N.Y. State Edn. Dept., Albany, 1962-82; prof. comm. and media Worcester (Mass.) State Coll., 1982-92, prof. emeritus, from 1992. Cons. to regents, adj. faculty N.Y. State Dept. Edn., SUNY, 1982-84; dir., prodr. Brit. Embassy, Tokyo, 1944-47; dir. intern program Worcester State Coll., 1982-90; acad. supr. Wang Industries, Mass., 1982-88; cons., guest lectr. Fairleigh Dickinson U., Hinds Jr. Coll., UN, Berkshire C.C., U. Miss., Stephens Coll., Ill. Audio Visual Assn., Internat. Conf. Bus. Edn., Niagara Falls City Sch. Dist., Dept. Instrn. U. Nova Scotia, SUNY, Coll. at Genesee, Coll. at Brockport, Coll. at Cortland. Author: Planning for Depth, 1970-80, Understanding Television, 1970-73, The Microphone is Yours: Radio Production-Directing (in Japanese); author, editor: ITFS, What It is - How to Plan, 1973-76; contbr. articles to profl. jours. Lt. U.S. Army, 1943-46. Grantee U.S. Govt., 1970-80, UN, 1970's. Mem. AAUP, NEA, Nat. Assn. Edn. Broadcasters (planner, tchr. 1958), Am. Soc. Pub. Adminstrn., Am. Acad. Polit. and Social Scis., Speech Comm. Assn., Nat. Adv. Coun. Fgn. Langs. for Elem. Schs., Masons (past master 1962), Phi Beta Kappa. Home: Rensselaer, NY. Died: July 22, 1999.

COOPER, J. MICHAEL, advertising executive; b. 1949; Grad., Southwest Mo. State U., 1971. CPA. With Associated Wholesale Grocers, 1971-72, Gen. Grocer Co., 1972-73, McLean Enterprises, 1973-74, Paul Mueller Co., 1974-78; pvt. practice as acct., 1978-81; with Lawrence Photo-Graphic, 1981-84, Noble & Assocs., Springfield, Mo., from 1984, now sec., CFO. Deceased.

COOPER, LAWRENCE DANIEL, auditor, accountant; b. Hannibal, Mo., July 24, 1945; s. Lawrence Milton and Mary Margaret (Bono) C. B in acctg., U. Tex., San Antonio, 1976; MBA, Webster U., 1982. Acctg. clk. Nat. Frozen Food Service, San Antonio, 1964-66; retail buyer Solo Serve Corp., San Antonio, 1970-73, retail store mgr., 1973-75; auditor Datapoint Corp., San Antonio, 1976; auditor in audit agy. USAF, San Antonio, 1976-84, auditor in commissary service Inspector Gen.'s Office, 1984-86, auditor supr. in commissary service Inspector Gen.'s Office, from 1986. Mem. exec. cadre Civilian Comptroller Career Mgmt. program, San Antonio, 1981-84. Treas. local Cath. Ch. orgn., 1981, pres., 1983. Served as sgt. USAF, 1966-70. Mem. Am. Soc. Mil. Comptrollers (v.p. 1986-87, pres. 1987—), Assn. Govt. Accts., Kelly Mgmt. Assn., Services Soc., Internat. Tng. in Communications. Democrat. Roman Catholic. Avocation: computers. Home: Spring Branch, Tex. Deceased.

COOPER, WILLIAM EUGENE, consulting engineer; b. Erie, Pa., Jan. 11, 1924; s. William Hall and Ruth E. (Dunn) C.; m. Louise I. Ferguson, June 23, 1946; children: Margaret, Glenn, Keith, Joyce, Carol. Student, Stevens Inst. Tech., 1941-43; BS, Oreg. State Coll., 1947, MS, 1948; PhD, Purdue U., 1951. Instr. Purdue U., 1948-52; cons. engr. Knolls Atomic Power Lab., GE, 1952-63; engring. mgr. Lessells and Assos., Waltham, Mass., 1963-68; sr. v.p., tech. dir. Teledyne Materials Rsch., Waltham, Mass., 1968-76; cons. engr. Teledyne Engring. Svcs., Woburn, 1976-94; staff cons. Teledyne Brown Engring., Marion, Mass., 1994-95. Contbr. articles to tech. jours. Served with AUS, 1943-46. Named Distinguished Engring. Alumnus Purdue U., 1974, named to Engring. Hall of Fame Oreg. State Coll., 1998. Mem. ASME (hon., B.F. Langer Nuclear Codes and Standards award 1978, hon. mem. boiler and pressure vessel com. 1980, v.p. codes and standards and mem. exec. com. of council 1980-81, sr. v.p. codes and standards 1981-84, Pressure Vessel and Piping medal 1983, codes and standards medal 1986), NAE, Soc. Exptl. Mechanics (Murray lectr. 1977), Am. Nat. Standards Inst. (dir. 1981-84), Sigma Xi, Pi Tau Sigma, Sigma Pi Sigma. Achievements include development of comprehensive design criteria for pressure vessels and piping in critical services. Home: Lexington, Mass. Deceased.

COORS, JOSEPH, brewery executive; b. Nov. 12, 1917; m. Anne Coors; children: Jeff, Peter, Joseph Jr., Grover, John. Grad., Cornell U., 1940. With Adolph Coors Co., Golden, Colo., v.p., from 1947, pres., 1977-85, chief oper. officer, 1982—88, vice chmn., 1975, 1982—2000. Founder, honorary trustee Heritage Found., 1972. Regent U. Colo., 1967-72. Died Mar. 15, 2003.

COOX, ALVIN DAVID, history educator; b. Rochester, N.Y., Mar. 8, 1924; s. Irving and Ruth (Werner) C.; m. Hisako Suzuki, Apr. 7, 1954; 1 child, Roy Alan. BA, NYU, 1945; MA, Harvard U., 1946, PhD, 1951. Teaching fellow Harvard U., Cambridge, Mass., 1948-49; sr. historian Johns Hopkins U., Washington, 1949-54; lectr. U. Calif. Far East Div., Tokyo, 1954-56, U. Md. Far East Div., Tokyo, 1956-64; prof. history San Diego State U., from 1964, dir. Japanese Studies, 1985-97, dir. Asian Studies, 1966-79. Scholar-diplomat in residence Dept. State, 1981; rsch. assoc. Japanese Nat. Inst. for Def. Studies, Tokyo, 1984—; vis. prof. Shiga Nat. U., Hikone-Otsu, Japan, 1954-55; historian Japanese Rsch. Div., Tokyo, 1955-57; adj. prof. U.S. Naval War Coll., San Diego, 1985—; dir. AASCU/JSI nat. summer inst. for Japan Studies, San Diego and Tokyo, 1987—. Author: Year of the Tiger, 1964, Japan: The Final Agony, 1970, Tojo, 1975, Anatomy of a Small War, 1977, Nomonhan 1939, 1985, The Unfought War, Japan 1941-42, 1992; co-editor: China and Japan, 1978, The Japanese Image, 1965-66; editor Orient/West Mag., 1958-65. Decorated Order of Rising Sun with gold rays (Japan); named outstanding prof., Calif. State Univ. System, 1973; recipient Samuel Eliot Morison award Am. Mil. Inst., 1987, Yokohama Culture Prize (Japan), 1993, nat. faculty award Phi Beta Delta, 1994; fellow Rockefeller Found., 1961-64, Japan Found., 1983-84, 90-91, NEH, 1985, Fulbright Rsch. Fellow, 1989. Mem. Assn. Calif. State Univ. Profs., Assn. Asian Studies, Internat. House Japan, Calif. Pacific Rim Commn., Am. Mil. Inst., Phi Beta Kappa (pres. Nu chpt. 1973). Avocation: writing. Home: San Diego, Calif. Died Nov. 4, 1999.

COPEK, PETER JOSEPH, humanities center director, educator; b. Chgo., May 28, 1945; s. Peter Joseph and Catherine Mary (Balchunas) C. BS, Loyola U., Chgo., 1967; MA, Northwestern U., Evanston, Ill., 1969, PhD, 1973. Asst. prof. English Oreg. State U., Corvallis, 1972-77, assoc. prof. English, from 1977, dir. ctr. for the humanities, from 1978. Contbr. articles to profl. jours. Rockefeller Found. fellow, 1975; Nat. Endowment for the Humanities grantee, 1977-82, NEH grantee, 1984-89, John Ben Snow Trust grantee, 1987. Mem. Modern Lang. Assn., Soc. for Cinema Studies. Home: Tampa, Fla. Died June 13, 2001.

COPELAN, GRACE LEIGH, retired educator; b. Mooresville, N.C., Mar. 14, 1925; d. Samuel Pou and Ada Elizabeth (Gattis) Gupton; m. Broughton Hale Copelan, Mar. 25, 1945; 1 child, Phillip Broughton. BA, U. N.C., 1966; MEd, N.C. Ctrl. U., 1980. Cert. tchr., N.C. Mgr. Grace 5 & 10 Cent Stores, Durham, N.C., 1950-55, propr. Carrboro, N.C., 1956-66, Creedmoor, N.C., 1956-66; tchr. Chapel Hill/Carrboro Schs., 1966-72, So. Christian Acad., Durham, N.C., 1972-74, Orange County Schs., Hillsborough, N.C., 1974-90; ret., 1990. Mem. Bot. Garden Found., U. N.C. Gen. Alumni Assn., Carolina Basket Makers, Redmont Rug Hookers Am. Traditional Hooking Assn. Democrat. Baptist. Home: Chapel Hill, NC. Died Dec. 26, 2000.

COPLANS, JOHN RIVERS, artist; b. London, June 24, 1920; came to U.S., 1960; s. Joseph Moses and Celia (Taneborne) C.; divorced; children: Barbara Ann, Joseph John. Student, L'academie de la grande chaumiere Paris, 1947-49. Sr. lectr. Maidstone Coll. Art, Eng., 1956-60; vis. prof. U. Calif., Berkeley, 1960-61; Disting. vis. prof. Am. U., Cairo, 1983; Koopman Disting. chair U. Hartford, Conn., 1991; dir. art gallery U. Calif. at Irvine, 1965-67; sr. curator Pasadena (Calif.) Mus. Modern Art, 1967-71; founding editor ARTFORUM Mag., San Francisco, 1962, editor in chief, N.Y.C., 1971-76; dir. Akron (Ohio) Art Mus., 1978-80; founding pub., editor Dialogue mag., Ohio, 1978-80. Exhibited paintings and photographs in one-man mus. shows Chgo. Art Inst., 1961, 81, 89, M.H. de Young Meml. Mus., San Francisco, 1963, Musée du Nouveau Monde, La Rochelle, 1986, San Francisco Mus. Modern Art, 1988, Mus. Modern Art, N.Y., 1988, Musée de la Vieille Charité, Marseille, 1989, Frankfurter Kunstverein, 1990, Mus. Boymans-van Beunigen, Rotterdam, 1990, Gulbenkian Found., Lisbon, Portugal, 1992, Centre Georges Pompidou, Paris, 1994, Ludwig Forum, Aachen, 1995, PS1 Contemporary Art Ctr., N.Y., 1997, Paco Das Artes, Sao Paulo, 1998, Scottish Nat. Gallery of Modern Art, Edinburgh, 1999, Malmö Konshall, Sweden, 1999, Inst. Cooperation Art Rsch., Paris, 1999, Liljevalchs Konsthall, Sweden, 2000; represented in collections, Met. Mus., N.Y.C., Mus. Modern Art, N.Y.C., Cleve. Mus., Art Inst. Chgo., High Mus., Atlanta, Wadsworth Atheneum, Conn., Israel Mus., Fogg Art Mus., Cambridge, Mass., Jerusalem, Mcpl. Mus., Amsterdam, Netherlands, Bibliotheque Nationale, Paris, Centre Georges Pompidou, Paris, Mus. des Beaux-Arts, Strasbourg, Victoria and Albert Mus., Musee De Art Contempaino, Que., Winnipeg Art Mus., Manitoba, Tate Gallery, London, Arts Coun. Gt. Britain, Nat. Gallery Can., Ottawa, Bklyn. Mus., Internat. Mus. Photography, Rochester, L.A. County Mus., San Francisco Mus. Modern Art, Mpls. Inst. Art, Mus. of Contemporary Art, Chgo., Whitney Mus. Am. Art, Honolulu Contemporary Mus. and Acad. of Arts, Hawaii, Mus. of Fine Art, Houston, Milw. Art Mus., Yale U. Art Gallery, New Haven, Conn., Wis., Mus. Contemporary Art, Helsinki, Boston Mus. of Fine Arts, Mus. Folkwang, Essen, Ludwed Forum, Aachen, Musée Art Modern, St. Etienne, Staatsgalerie, Stuttgart, Fed. Republic Germany, Swedish State Collection; author: Cezanne Watercolors, 1967, Serial Imagery, 1968, Andy Warhol, 1970, Roy Lichtenstein, 1972, Ellsworth Kelly, 1973, Decisions, Decisions, 1976, Weegee The Famous, 1968, A Body of Work, 1987, Provocations, 1996, A Self-Portrait, 1997; organized numerous mus. exhbns. and, articles for art mags. Served with RAF, 1938-40; served to capt. King's African Rifles, 1940-46. Recipient Frank Jewitt Mather award, 1974, Best Photography Exhbn. award Internat. Assn. Art Critics, 1998; Guggenheim fellow, 1969, 85; NEA fellow, 1975, 80, 86, 92; named Officier De L'ordre des Arts et des Lettres, Paris, 2001. Died Aug. 21, 2003.

CORAH, NORMAN LEWIS, retired dentistry educator; b. Kenmore, N.Y., July 18, 1933; s. Leo Wesley and Alice Beulah (Congdon) C.; m. Patricia Ann Laney, June 21, 1958; children: Norman Lewis Jr., Joseph Leo. BA, U. Buffalo, 1955, PhD, 1960. Instr. U. Buffalo, 1959-60; rsch. instr. Washington U., St. Louis, 1960-61, asst. prof., 1961-65; assoc. prof. SUNY, Buffalo, 1965-71, prof., 1971-96, prof. emeritus, from 1996. Editor: Origins of Abnormal Behavior, 1971; contbr. 75 articles to profl. jours. Recipient Rsch. Career Devel. award Nat. Inst. of Dental Rsch., 1969, Disting. Scientist award Internat. Assn. for Dental Rsch., 1991. Mem. AAAS, APA, Am. Assn. Dental Schs., Am. Cut Glass Assn. (ea. bd. dirs. 1990-92). Avocations: collecting glass, furniture construction, travel. Home: Buffalo, NY. Died Mar. 21, 2001.

CORBETT, JACK ELLIOTT, clergyman, retired foundation administrator, author; b. Oak Park, Ill., Nov. 27, 1920; s. Elliott Wesley and Clara Helen (Froelich) C.; m. Sarah Anne Rapp, July 1, 1945; children: Kathleen, Marjorie, Stephen. BS, Temple U., 1950; MDiv, Crozer Seminary, Chester, Pa., 1950; PhD in Internat. Rels., Am. U., 1967. Pastor Landenberg (Pa.)-Hamorton Ch., 1949-50, Comty. Meth. Ch., McHenry, Ill., 1950-58, Oregon (Ill.) Meth. Ch., 1958-61; ofcl. Bd. of Ch. and Soc. United Meth. Ch., Washington, 1961-80, Balt. Conf. United Meth. Ch., 1971—96; v.p. Pax World Fund, Portsmouth, NH, 1971—96; pres. Pax World Found., Bethesda, Md., 1971—92, hon. chmn., 1993-2001; founder Pax Internat., Washington, 2001—02. Author: Prophets on Main Street, 1964, Christians Awake, 1970, Turned On By God, 1971, Becoming A Prophetic Community, 1980. Chmn. Nat. Coalition To Ban Handguns, 1974-75. Unitarian-Univ. Peace Fellowship award, 1991, Alumni award for contbns. in internat. rels. Am. U. Sch. Internat. Svc., 1999, Founder's award Coalition to Stop Gun Violence, 1999, Ann. Achievement award Alumni Assn. Am. U., 2000. Mem. UN Assn. (bd. dirs. Washington area 1975—, v.p. 1985-89, pres. 1990-91). United Methodist. Avocations: tennis, swimming, travel. Died Mar. 18, 2003.

CORBETT, RONALD JOHN, psychotherapist; b. Detroit, Feb. 7, 1936; s. Stephen and Mildred (Mein) C.; m. Marilyn Ann Schultz, June 20, 1964; children: Theresa, Patrick, Brian. B in Philosophy, U. Detroit, 1959; MSW, Wayne State U., 1964; D of Social Work, Cath. U., 1972. Therapist Cath. Social Services, Detroit, 1964-67, exec. dir. Grand Rapids, Mich., 1975-76; asst. prof., dir. clinic U. Detroit, 1970-75; therapist Genesee County (Mich.) Social Srvices, Flint, 1976-79; psychotherapist Meredith Counseling, Farmington, Mich., from 1979. Pub. speaker seminars, tchrs.' groups, etc., Detroit, 1979—; mem. Detroit Com. Human Relations, 1970-80; cons. to Young Lawyers Orgn., Detroit, 1970-80. Author: Predicting the Employability of ADC Mothers, 1972. Served with USN, 1959-61. Mem. Nat. Assn. Social Workers (cert.), Mich. Assn. Marriage Counselors, Am. Assn. Marriage and Family Counselors, Mich. Inter-Profl. Assn., Nat. Council on Family Relations. Democrat. Roman Catholic. Avocations: sailing, woodworking, reading. Home: Novi, Mich. Deceased.

CORDASCO, MARGARET B. secondary school educator; b. Kearny, N.J., Jan. 6, 1933; d. John and Ethel Wilkie (Loy) Bolland; m. Anthony V. Cordasco, May 26, 1956; children: Alan James, Scott Edward. BA magna cum laude, Smith Coll., 1954; MA, William Paterson Coll., 1971. Cert. elem. tchr. Tchr. 3rd grade Nutley (N.J.) Bd. Edn.; tchr. 6-8 grades Pequannock (N.J.) Bd. Edn.; adj. instr. William Paterson Coll., Wayne, N.J. Mem. Nat. Count. Tchrs. Edn., Beta Chi (Pi Lambda Theta chpt., past recording sec. and v.p.). Home: Wayne, NJ. Died Jan. 8, 2002.

CORE, EDWARD K. state legislator, farmer; m. Joyce Core; children: Tony, Elizabeth Core Orts. BSc, Ohio State U.; postgrad. Antioch Coll. Farmer, Rushsylvania, Ohio; mem. Ohio Ho. of Reps. Columbus. Former commr. Logan County, Ohio; former supr. Logan Soil and Water Conservation Dist. Grantee NSF. Mem. Ohio Cattlemen's Assn., Farm Bur., Nat. Fedn. Ind. Bus., AMVETS, NRA, Elks, Sigma Phi Epsilon. Republican. Home: Rushsylvania, Ohio. Died Aug. 9, 1999.

COREY, EDWIN RAYMOND, business administration educator; b. Detroit, Dec. 27, 1919; s. Joseph Z. and Ethel Gwendolyn (Mungeer) C.; m. Joan Castleton Danner, Aug. 27, 1949 (div. Mar. 1961); m. Charlotte Worrall, Jan. 5, 1968; children: David P., Thomas C., Frederick D., Margaret W., Elizabeth Joy, Mary L. AB, Amherst Coll., 1941; MBA, Harvard U., 1943; MA and PhD, Harvard Grad. Sch. Arts & Sci., 1950. Asst. prof. bus. adminstrn. Harvard U., Boston, 1950-56, assoc. prof. bus. adminstrn., 1956-61, prof. bus. adminstrn., 1961—90, dir. research Grad. Sch. Bus., 1980-85. Bd. dirs. Norton Co., Worcester, Mass. Author: Organizational Strategy, 1971, Industrial Marketing, 1983, Procurement Management, 1975, Problems in Marketing, 1981. Served to lt. USN, 1942-46. Mem. Am. Mktg. Assn. Avocations: sailing, hiking, photography, carpentry. Home: Wellesley, Mass. Died May 28, 2004.

COREY, JEFF, actor, director, educator; b. N.Y.C., Aug. 10, 1914; s. Nathan and Mary (Peskin) C.; m. Hope Victorson, Feb. 26, 1938; children: Eve Corey Poling, Jane, Emily. Student, Feagin Sch. Drama, 1930-32, UCLA, 1955. Prof. drama Calif. State U.-Northridge, 1966-71, Chapman Coll.'s World Campus Afloat, 1973—2002; founder creative drama workshop Los Angeles Juvenile Hall, 1968. Guest lectr. U. Tex., Austin, Ball State U., Muncie, Ind., U. So. Calif., L.A.; mem. faculty Am. Film Inst.; mem. faculty grad. program dramatic writing Tisch Sch. of Art, NYU; mem. adv. coun. Calif. Edn. Theater Assn.; bd. dirs. Ojai Music Festivals Inc.; guest artist U. Ill., Bloomington. Stage actor, N.Y.C., 1932-40, appeared in Hamlet as Rosencranz with Leslie Howard, God Bless Our Bank with Ann Sothern, King Lear, In the Matter of J. Robert Oppenheimer; dir. TV films, various films, 1970—2002, profl. actors workshop, Hollywood, 1951—2002; actor numerous films including True Grit, Butch Cassidy and the Sundance Kid, Little Big Man, The Color of Night, Surviving the Game, (starring roles TV series) Helltown, Morning Star/Evening Star; contbr. articles on film, stage acting to profl., popular publs. Served with USNR, 1943-45. Recipient citation USN, 1945. Mem. Acad. Motion Picture Arts and Scis. (actors com. 1970-2002), Screen Actors Guild (dir.), Dirs. Guild Am., Actors Equity Assn. Died Aug. 16, 2002.

CORNELL, DAVID ROGER, health care executive; b. Glen Falls, N.Y., Apr. 5, 1944; s. Junius R. and Isabelle (Richardson) C.; m. Alma Files (dec. 1967); children: Kimberley Anne Farley, Kelly Elizabeth. BA, U. Vt., 1966; cert. phys. therapy, Duke U., 1967; MBA, U. S.C., 1973; PhD, Columbia Pacific U., 1986. Dir. phys. therapy Univ. Hosp., Augusta, Ga., 1970-72, adminstrv. resident, 1972; adminstrv. asst. Drs. Hosp., Augusta, 1973-74; asst. adminstr. Cypress Cmty. Hosp., Pompano Beach, Fla., 1974; assoc. adminstr. North Ridge Gen. Hosp., Ft. Lauderdale, Fla., 1975-77, adminstr., 1977-79; pres. Mont. Deaconess Med. Ctr., Great Falls, 1979-88, Western Res. Care Sys., Youngstown, Ohio, 1988-91; pres., CEO Albany (N.Y.) Med. Ctr., 1991-94; COO New England Med. Ctr., Boston, 1995-97; pres., CEO New England Med. Ctr. Internat., Boston, 1997-2000; chmn., pres., CEO Irish Hill Internat., Canfield, Ohio, from 2000. With U.S. Army, 1968-69. Fellow: Am. Coll. Health Care Execs., Am. Acad. Med. Adminstrs.; mem.: Am. Hosp. Assn. (del. 1984—91). Home: Canfield, Ohio. Died Sept. 29, 2002.

CORNELSEN, RUFUS, clergyman; b. Colony, Okla., Jan. 29, 1914; s. Isaac and Anna (Boese) C.; m. Frances Louise Deen, Aug. 4, 1946; children: Susan Kathleen Cornelsen France, David Alan, Sara Ann Cornelsen De Cubellis. AB, Southwestern State Tchrs. Coll., Weatherford, Okla., 1935; Th.B., So. Bapt. Theol. Sem., 1937; B.D., Union Theol. sem., 1939; postgrad., Columbia U., 1939-40, Lutheran Theol. Sem., 1941-42, Princeton Theol. Sem., 1948-49; Litt.D., Gettysburg Coll., 1964. Ordained to ministry United Lutheran Ch., 1942; pastor Emanuel Luth. Ch., New Brunswick, N.J., 1942-57, Luth. Student Assn., Rutgers U., 1942-57; assoc. dir. social action United Luth. Ch. Am., 1957-58, dir. social action, 1958-62, sec. for civil and econ. life Luth. Ch. in Am., 1962-65; rep. to UN, 1964-65; assoc. gen. sec. for planning and program Nat. Council Chs. of Christ in U.S., 1965-68; exec. dir. Met. Christian Council Phila., 1968-79; dir. Office of Christian-Jewish Relations, Nat. Council Chs., 1980-82; former chmn. Nat. Inst. on the Holocaust. Exec. sec. New Brunswick Council Chs., 1945-46; mem. social missions com. Luth. Synod N.Y., 1947-50; exec. bd. Luth. Synod N.J., 1950-52, mem. bd. social missions, 1950-56, pres., 1955-56; mem. commn. social responsibility United Luth. Ch., 1952-57; Luth. World Fedn. fellow study laymen's insts., Europe, 1958; mem. bd. social ministry Luth. Ch. Am., 1966-72, cons. div. mission to, N.Am., 1973-76; bd. dirs. Union Theol. Sem., 1958-76, Phila. Fellowship Commn.; past trustee Protestant Found. Students, Rutgers U.; bd. dirs. NCCJ. Contbr. articles, chpts. to religious publs. Mem. nat. coun., nat. bd. YMCA, 1967-72, mem. armed svcs. com., 1967-72; bd. govs. USO; bd. dirs. Inst. for Jewish-Christian Understanding, Muhlenberg Coll., 1990—. Mem. Urban League New Brunswick (dir. 1944-68, pres. 1946- 48), Nat. Council Chs. (rep. Latin Am. Conf. Ch. and Soc. 1962), World Council Chs. Home: Swarthmore, Pa. Died Nov. 24, 2003.

CORRADO, ALBERT GUY, allergist, immunologist, internist; b. Connellsville, Pa., Aug. 3, 1914; BA, U. Pitts., MD, 1938; LLD, Gonzaga U., 1993. Intern Mercy Hosp., Pitts., 1938-39, resident pathology, 1939-40; fellow pneumonia rsch. Mellon Inst., 1940-41; resident cardiovasc. disease Finney Gen. Hosp., Thomasville, 1943-44, resident gastroenterology, 1944-45; hon. Kadlec Med. Ctr., Richland, Wash. Fellow ACP, Am. Coll. Chest Physicians, Am. Coll. Allergy and Immunology. Home: Coraopolis, Pa. Died Feb. 22, 2001.

CORRINGTON, JOHN WILLIAM, writer, lawyer, educator; b. Memphis, Oct. 28, 1932; s. John Wesley and Viva Lillian (Shelley) C.; m. Joyce Elaine Hooper, Feb. 6, 1960; children: Shelley Elaine, John Wesley, Robert Edward Lee, Thomas Jonathan Jackson. BA, Centenary Coll., 1956; MA, Rice U., 1960; PhD, U. Sussex, Brighton, Eng., 1965; JD, Tulane U., 1975. Bar: U.S. Ct. Appeals (5th cir.), U.S. Supreme Ct. From instr. to asst. prof. La. State U., Baton Rouge, 1960-66; assoc. prof. Loyola U., New Orleans, 1966-72; assoc. Plotkin and Bradley, New Orleans, 1975-78; writer, producer Corrington Prodns., Ltd., New Orleans, Los Angeles, from 1978. Author: (poems) Where We Are, 1962, The Anatomy of Love, 1964, Mr. Clean and Other Poems, 1964, Lines to the South, 1965, (novels) And Wait for the Night, 1964, 65, 67, The Upper Hand, 1967, 68, 69, The Bombardier, 1970, 72, Shad Sentell, 1984, 86, All My Trials, 1987, (anthologies) Southern Writing in the Sixties: Fiction,

1966, Southern Writing in the Sixties: Poetry, 1967 (short fiction) The Lonesome Traveller and Other Stories, 1968, The Actes and Monuments, 1978, The Southern Reporter and Other Stories, 1981; co-author: (with Joyce H. Corrington) (screenplays) Von Richthofen and Brown, 1969 (retitled The Red Baron), The Omega Man, 1970, Boxcar Bertha, 1971, The Arena, 1972, The Battle for the Planet of the Apes, 1973, The Killer Bees, 1974, (TV episodes) Search for Tomorrow, 1978-80, Another World, 1980, Texas, 1980-81, General Hospital, 1982, Capitol, 1982-83, One Life to Live, 1984, Superior Court, 1986—, (novels) So Small a Carnival, 1986, A Project Named Desire, 1987, A Civil Death, 1987. Recipient award Nat. Endowment for the Arts, 1967, Best Am. Short Story awards, 1973, 76, 77; fellow Rice U., 1960-63. Mem. La. Bar Assn. Roman Catholic. Home: Malibu, Calif. Deceased.

CORTADA, JAMES N. mayor, former diplomat; b. N.Y.C., May 10, 1914; s. James A. and America D. (Colas) C.; m. Shirley E. Barlow, Nov. 25, 1944; children: James William, Vera Christina, Monica Elodia. BS, Havana (Cuba) Bus. Coll., 1948. Pvt. bus., 1932-42; fgn. service officer Dept. State, 1942-70; assigned successively Havana, Dept. Commerce, Washington, Barcelona, Spain, Dept. of State, Basra, Iraq, Cairo, Egypt; dep. dir., then dir. Office Near East and South Asia Regional Affairs, Dept. State, Washington, 1960-62; charge d'affaires Taiz, Yemen, 1963-64; Dept. State sr. fellow UCLA, 1964-65; dean Sch. Profl. Studies, Fgn. Service Inst., 1965-67; Am. consul gen. Barcelona, 1967-70; mayor Town of Orange, Va., 1978-82, 90-92, councilman, 1990-92. Prof. 4th Summer Univ., Principality of Andorra, 1985 Co-author: (with son James W. Cortada) U.S. Foreign Policy in the Caribbean, Cuba and Central America, 1985, Can Democracy Survive in Western Europe, 1996. Mem. Town of Orange Planning Commn., 1983-90; mem. Va. Power Customer Adv. Bd., 1990-94; chmn. Orange County Comprehensive Plan Com., 1988-90. Paul Harris fellow Rotary Found., 1994. Mem. Orange County C. of C., Orange County Hist. Soc., Royal Acad. Belles Lettres (corr., Barcelona, v.p.) Clubs: Dacor House (Washington). Lodges: Rotary. Home: Orange, Va. Died Nov. 1, 1999.

COSER, LEWIS ALFRED, sociology educator; b. Berlin, Nov. 27, 1913; came to U.S., 1941, naturalized, 1948; s. Martin and Margarete (Fehlow) C.; m. Rose Laub(dec. 1994), Aug. 25, 1942; children: Ellen Perrin, Steven. Student, Sorbonne, Paris, France, 1935-38; PhD in Sociology, Columbia U., 1954; D (hon.), Humboldt U., Berlin, 1993. Instr. U. Chgo., 1948-50; mem. faculty Brandeis U., 1951-68, prof. sociology, 1960-68; Disting. prof. SUNY, Stony Brook, 1969-87; adj. prof. sociology Boston Coll., 1987-97, Boston Univ., 1997—2003. Fellow Ctr. for Advanced Study Behavorial Scis., Stanford, Calif., 1968-69, 79-80; vis. prof. U. Calif., Berkeley, 1957-58 Author: The Functions of Social Conflict, 1956, (with B. Rosenberg) Sociological Theory, 1957, 5th edit., 1982, (with Irving Howe) The American Communist Party, 1957, 2d edit., 1962, Sociology Through Literature, 1963, rev. edit., 1971, Men of Ideas, 1965, Georg Simmel, 1965, Political Sociology, 1967, Continuities in the Study of Social Conflict, 1967, Masters of Sociological Thought, 1971, enlarged edit., 1977, Greedy Institutions, 1974, (with Kadushin and Powell) The Culture and Commerce of Publishing, 1982, Refugee Scholars in America, 1984, A Handful of Thistles, 1988; editor: Maurice Halbwachs: On Collective Memory, 1992, Everett C. Hughes: On Work Race and the Sociological Imagination, 1994. Named Disting. Prof. Emeritus, 1986. Mem. Am. Acad. Arts and Scis., ACLU, Am. Sociol. Assn. (pres. 1975-76), Ea. Sociol. Soc. (pres. 1964-65). Home: Cambridge, Mass. Died July 8, 2003.

COTTON, JOHN, poet; b. London, Mar. 7, 1925; s. Arthur Edmund and Florence (Mandy) C.; m. Peggy Midson, Dec. 1948; children: Toby, Bevis. BA with honors, U. London, 1956. Tchr. English Middlesex Edn. Authority, Eng., 1947-57; head English dept. Southall Grammar Tech. Sch., Eng., 1957-63; headmaster Highfield Comprehensive Sch., Hemel Hempstead, Eng., 1963-85. Tutor Arvon Found., Totleigh Barton, Devon, Eng., Pearse Housewriting Courses, 1985—; mem. lit. panel Eastern Arts; dep. lt. County of Hertfordshire, 1988. Writings include: (poetry) Fourteen Poems, 1967, Outside the Gates of Eden and Other Poems, 1969, Ampurias, 1969, Old Movies and Other Poems, 1971 (Publication award Arts Coun. Gt. Britain 1971), The Wilderness, 1971, Columbus on St. Dominica, 1972, Photographs, 1973, A Sycamore Press Broadsheet, 1973, British Poetry since 1965: A Selected List, 1973, Kilroy Was Here, 1974, Places, 1981, Day Books, 1981, Catullus at Sirmione, 1982, The Storyville Portraits, 1984, The Crystal Zoo, 1985, Dust, 1986, Oh Those Happy Feet!, 1986, The Poetry File, 1988, (with Fred Sedgwick) Two by Two, 1990, Here's Looking At You Kid, 1992, First Things, 1993; Oscar The Dog and Friends, 1994; editor (poetry) I am the Song, 1996; contbr. to several poetry anthologies; editor: Priapus, 1962-72, Private Libr., 1970-80; adv. editor Contemporary Poets of the English Lang. Dep. lt. County of Hertfordshire, 1989. Served Royal Navy Comandos, 1942-46, Far East. Page scholar English Speaking Union, 1975. Mem. Nat. Poetry Soc. (mem. coun., chmn. coun. 1973-75, 77, treas. 1986-89), Ver Poets (pres.), The Toddington Poetry Soc. (pres.). Died Mar. 20, 2003.

COTTRELL, MELVIN, state legislator; Student, Rutgers U. Committeeman Jackson (N.J.) Twp., 1986-91, mayor, 1988-89; mem. N.J. Gen. Assembly, Dist. 30, from 1990; asst. supt. pub. property Ocean County (N.J.). Recipient Mil. Order of Purple Heart, 1990. Mem. Jackson Elks. Republican. Died Oct. 9, 2002.

COULSON, JOHN SELDEN, retired marketing executive; b. Chgo., Aug. 14, 1915; s. Leonard Ward and Mabel (Selden) C.; m. Jane Eleanor Rinder, Nov. 28, 1943; children: Jane Greer Coulson Sherry, Nancy Allen Coulson Hobor, Ann Selden Coulson Hubbard, Sara Rinder Coulson Ellis. BA, U. Chgo., 1936; MBA, Harvard U., 1938. With Montgomery Ward & Co., Chgo., 1938-41, 45-48; sr. assoc. Joseph White & Assos., Chgo., 1948-50; rsch. supr. Leo Burnett Co., Inc., Chgo., 1950-55, mgr. rsch. dept., 1955-58, v.p. charge rsch., 1958-77; dir. Leo Burnett USA, Chgo., 1973-77; ptnr. Communications Workshop, Inc., Chgo., 1977-90, ret., 1990. Lectr. U. Chgo., 1955, 78, Northwestern U., 1960-71, Columbia Coll., 1974-76, U. Ill., 1977 Mktg. Issues editor Jour. Mktg, 1960-81; mem. editorial bd. Jour. Advt, 1971-83; mem. policy bd. Jour. Consumer Research, 1972-79; Contbr. chpts. to On Knowing the Consumer, 1966, Handbook of Modern Marketing, 1970, Cognitive and Affective Responses to Advertising, 1988. Mem. citizens bd. U. Chgo., 1969-75; bd. mgrs. Lawson YMCA, Chgo., 1970-89; bd. govs. Chgo. Heart Assn., 1980-91; mem. community adv. bd. Sta. WBEZ, Pub. Radio, Chgo., 1980—; mem. publicity com. Art Inst. Chgo., 1972-87. Lt. comdr. USNR, 1941-45. Mem. Am. Statis. Assn. (past pres. Chgo. chpt.), Am. Mktg. Assn. (past pres. Chgo. chpt., nat. v.p.), Am. Assn. for Pub. Opinion Rsch. (exec. coun. 1969-72, 78-81), U. Chgo. Alumni Assn. (pres. 1969-73, Alumni medal 1987), Univ. Club, Harvard Bus. Sch. Club Chgo. (bd. dirs. 1976-82), Psi Upsilon, Alpha Kappa Psi. Home: Evanston, Ill. Deceased.

COULTER, GARY EUGENE, art educator; b. Oberlin, Kans., Aug. 28, 1935; s. Eugene E. and Sylvia Irene (White) C.; m. Marcille Holmberg, Aug. 12, 1956 (div. Sept. 1979); children: Thomas E., Lori J., Meg R., Timothy J. BA, Ft. Hays State U., 1960, MA, 1961; MFA, U. Kans., 1963. Instr. art Hutchinson (Kans.) Pub. Schs., 1961-62; instructorship U. Kans., Lawrence, 1962-63; prof., chair art dept. Hastings (Nebr.) Coll., 1963-80; pres. Sculpture Studio and Foundry, Inc., Pueblo West, Colo., 1980-86; vis. prof. Cottey Coll., Nevada, Mo., 1986-87; dir. bronze foundry Tucumcari (N.Mex.) Area Vocat. Sch., 1987-90; prof., chair art dept. N.Mex. Highlands U., Las Vegas, 1990-91, Ft. Hays State U., Hays, from 1991. Bronze sculptures represented in numerous pub. and pvt. collections, including 18 foot bronze Somewhere, Everywhere At Nat. Meml. to Fallen Firefighters, Colorado Springs, Colo. Staff sgt. U.S. Army, 1955-58. Hon. fellow U. Wis., 1973. Mem. Nat. Art Edn. Assn., Nat. Coun. Art Adminstrs., Coll. Art Assn., Hays Art Coun. Home: Trinidad, Colo. Died Nov. 10, 2000.

COUNSILMAN, JAMES EDWARD, retired physical education educator; b. Birmingham, Ala., Dec. 28, 1920; s. Joseph Walter and Ottilia Lena (Schamburg) C.; m. Marjorie E. Scrafford, June 15, 1943; children: Cathy, James (dec.), Jill, Brian. BS, Ohio State U., 1947; MS, U. Ill., 1948; PhD, U. Iowa, 1951. Mem. phys. edn. faculty, swim coach Cortland (N.Y.) State U., 1952-57; mem. faculty Ind. U., Bloomington, 1957-90, prof. phys. edn., 1966-90, swim coach, 1957-90; pres. Counsilman Co., Inc. (film producers and publishers), 1971-90, 1971-89; ret., 1990. Author: The Science of Swimming, 1969, rev. edit., 1994, The Complete Book of Swimming, 1977, Competitive Swimming Manual, 1977. U.S. Olympic Men's Team coach, 1964, 76; founding pres. Internat. Swimming Hall of Fame, 1963. Served as bomber pilot USAAF, 1943-45. Decorated Air medal with cluster, D.F.C. Ind. swim teams have won 20 consecutive Big Ten Swimming championships, 1961-80, 83, 84, 85; 6 consecutive NCAA championships, 1968-73 Fellow Am. Coll. Sports Medicine; mem. AAHPER, Am. Swim Coaches Assn. (past pres.), Coll. Swim Coaches Assn., English Channel Swim Assn. Achievements include swimming English Channel 1978 becoming oldest Channel swimmer. Home: Bloomington, Ind. Died Jan. 4, 2004.

COX, ARCHIBALD, lawyer, educator; b. Plainfield, N.J., May 17, 1912; s. Archibald and Frances Bruen (Perkins) C.; m. Phyllis Ames, June 12, 1937; children— Sally, Archibald, Phyllis. AB, Harvard U., 1934, LL.B., 1937, LL.D. (hon.), 1975, Loyola U., Chgo., 1964, U. Cin., 1967, U. Denver, 1974, Amherst Coll., 1974, Rutgers U., 1974, Mich. State U., 1976, Wheaton Coll., 1977, Northeastern U., 1978, Clark U., 1980; L.H.D. (hon.), Hahnemann Med. Coll., 1980, U. Mass., 1981, Georgetown U., 1988. Bar: Mass. 1937. Gen. practice law Ropes, Gray, Best, Coolidge & Rugg, Boston, 1938-41; atty. Office of Solicitor Gen., U.S. Dept. Justice, 1941-43, solicitor gen., 1961-65; assoc. solicitor Dept. Labor, 1943-45; lectr. law Harvard U., 1945-46, prof. law, 1946-61, Williston prof. law, 1965-76, Carl M. Loeb U. prof., 1976-84, prof. emeritus, 1984—2004; vis. prof. Boston U., 1985-97. Spl. investigator cases Mass. Legislature, 1972; dir. Office Watergate Spl. Prosecution Force, Washington, 1973; Co-chmn. Constrn. Industry Stblzn. Com., 1951-52; chmn. Wage Stablzn. Bd., 1952 Author: Cases on Labor Law, 1948, 12th edit., 1976, 11th edit. (with Derek C. Bok, Robert Gorman and Mathew W. Finkin), 1981, Law and the National Labor Policy, 1960, (with Mark DeWolfe Howe, J.R. Wiggins) Civil Rights, the Constitution and the Courts, 1967, The Warren Court, 1968, The Role of the Supreme Court in American Government, 1976, Freedom of Expression, 1981, The Court and the Constitution, 1987. Mem. bd. overseers Harvard U., 1962-65. Mem. ABA, Am. Acad. Arts and Scis., Common Cause (chmn. 1980-92), Health Effects Inst. (chmn. 1985-2001). Home: Brooksville, Maine. Died May 29, 2004.

COX, DALLAS WENDELL, JR., lawyer; b. Mar. 10, 1943; s. Dallas Wendell Cox and Fern (Maurer) Heidbreder; m. Lynn Barbre, Aug. 2, 1969 (div. Oct. 1982); children: Dallas Barbre, Ryan Ralph. BA, U. Ill., Champaign, 1964; JD, U. Mo., 1967; MLA, Washington U., 1991, MA, 1994. Bar: U.S. Supreme Ct. 1967, Mo. 1967, U.S. Dist. Ct. Mo. 1967. Ptnr. Cox, Moffitt & Cox, St. Louis, 1967-78; pvt. practice law St. Louis, from 1978. Attendee global forum UN Conf. on Environ. and Devel., Rio de Janeiro, 1992. Editor Jour. Mo. Bar., Mo. Conservationist; contbr. articles to profl. jours. Asst. scoutmaster St. Louis area Boy Scouts Am., 1984-94; advocate Mo. Prairie Found., bd. dirs., 1993—; alderman City of Town and County, Mo., 1995- conservation commn. chmn., 1995-99. Lt. (j.g.) USNR, 1971. Mem. ATLA, Mo. Assn. Trial Lawyers (bd. govs. 1990-93), Lawyers Assn. St. Louis, Eagle Scouts Assn. (bd. dirs. 1988-91, vol. award of merit 1992), Greater Yellowstone Coalition, Windstar Found., Wilderness Soc., Nature Conservancy, Sigma Chi. Avocations: conservation, backpacking. Home: Town And Country, Mo. Deceased.

COX, J. WILLIAM, retired physician, health services administrator; b. St. Louis, Aug. 31, 1928; s. William E. and Evelyn C.; m. Anne Maczewsk, June 11, 1949; 1 child, William E. Student, Washington U., St. Louis; MD, St. Louis U., 1952, PhD, 1953. Diplomate Am. Bd. Internal Medicine. Chief rsch. labs. VA Hosps., St. Louis, 1953-54; commd. med. officer USN, 1954, advanced through grades to Vice Adm., ret., 1983; chief medicine, dir. clinics Naval Hosp., Subic Bay, Philippines, 1961-63, chief medicine, dir. rsch. Phila., 1965-69; dir. edn., tng. USN Med. Dept., Washington, 1971-77; comdg. officer Naval Regional Med. Ctr., San Diego, 1978-80; Surgeon Gen. USN, Washington, 1980-83, ret.; assoc. dir. Grad. Sch. Pub. Health San Diego State U., 1983-88; dir. Dept. Hlth. Svcs. County of San Diego, 1987-93; ret., 1994. Cons. in pub. health, profl. rels. AMA, Chgo., 1983-87. Contbr. numerous tech. reports, articles to profl. jours. Chmn. tech. adv. group San Diego County Bd. Suprs., 1986-93; chmn. spl. svcs. divsn. San Diego County coun. Boy Scouts Am., Access to Care Commn., San Diego County 1990-94, Commn. on Access to Health Care, San Diego, 1990-93. Decorated Legion of Merit; recipient Borden award for Med. Rsch., Borden Corp., St. Louis U., 1981, Svc. award Uniformed Svcs. Univ. Health Scis., Bethesda, Md. 1983, Diogenes award Pub. Rels. Soc. Am., Silver Beaver award Boy Scouts Am., 1986-90. Fellow ACP, Phila. Coll. Physicians, Am. Coll. Cardiology; mem. AMA (Spl. award for Meritorious Svc. 1983, ho. of dels. 1970-83, 86-94), Calif. Med. Assn. (ho. of dels. 1984-94), Rotary. Republican. Avocations: swimming, music. Died Nov. 2002.

COXETER, HAROLD SCOTT MACDONALD, mathematician; b. London, Feb. 9, 1907; s. Harold Samuel and Lucy (Gee) C.; m. Hendrina J. Brouwer, Aug. 20, 1936; children: Edgar, Susan Coxeter Thomas. BA, Trinity Coll., Cambridge (Eng.) U., 1929, PhD, 1931, rsch. fellow, 1931-35; hon. degrees, U. Alta., Acadia U., U. Waterloo, Trent U., U. Toronto, Carleton U., U. Giessen, McMaster U., York U. Rockefeller Found. fellow Princeton U., 1932-33, Procter fellow, 1934-35; asst. prof. math. U. Toronto, 1936-44, asso. prof., 1944-48, prof., 1948—2003. Vis. prof. numerous univs. including Columbia U., 1949, U. Amsterdam, 1966, Calif. Inst. Tech., 1977, U. Bologna, 1978 Author: Non-Euclidean Geometry, 1942, Regular Polytopes, 1948, The Real Projective Plane, 1949, Introduction to Geometry, 1961, Projective Geometry, 1964, Twelve Geometric Essays, 1968, Regular Complex Polytopes, 1974, Kaleidoscopes, 1995. Hon. fellow, Trinity Coll., Cambridge, Eng. Fellow Royal Soc. London (Sylvester medal), Royal Soc. Can. (Tory medal); mem. K. Nederlandse Akademie Wetensch. (fgn.); hon. mem. Mathematische Gesellschaft, Wiskundig Genootschap, Edinburgh and London Math. Soc., Am. Acad. Arts and Scis. (fgn. hon.), Companion of Order of Can. Home: Toronto, Canada. Died Mar. 31, 2003.

COY, WILLIAM RAYMOND, civil engineer; b. Omaha, Nov. 28, 1923; s. Vern Elmer and Edna Mae (Seymour) C.; m. Geraldine Petra Zaback, July 31, 1943; children: Carol Sue, William R. Jr., Russell B., Steven D., Marcus R. Student, Omaha Mcpl. U., 1944, 45. Registered profl. engr., N.D. Lab. technician U.S. Army CE, 1946-57; paving engr. CE, Albuquerque Dist., Roswell, N.Mex., 1958-61; chief materials testing CE Ballistic Missile Constrn., Minot and Grand Forks, N.D., 1961-65; engr.-in-charge CE Green River Dam, Campbellsville, Ky., 1965-68; chief concrete sect. CE Divsn. Lab., Omaha, 1968-78; chief materials engr. CE Missouri River Divsn., Omaha, 1978-87; assessor, constrn. tech. Nat. Inst. Stds. and Tech., Omaha, 1987-95. With USN, 1945-46. Mem. Soc. Am. Mil. Engrs., Am. Concrete Inst. Home: Bellevue, Nebr. Died Sept. 22, 2001.

CRAIG, WILLIAM WARREN, geoscience educator, researcher; b. Kansas City, Mo., Apr. 1, 1935; s. Paul Oren and Hollis Edna (Newcomer) C.; m. Patricia Mae Neal; children: Jefrey Warren, Kathleen Elizabeth, Jennifer Paulette, Andrew Neal, David Clark. BA, U. Mo., 1957, MA, 1961; PhD, U. Tex., 1968. Assoc. prof. geology N.E. Mo. State U., Kirksville, 1965-68; asst. prof. geology U. New Orleans, 1968-71, assoc. prof. geology, 1971-75, assoc. prof., chmn. dept. geology, 1976-77, prof., chmn. dept. geology, 1977-81, 90-96, prof. geology, 1981-90 and from 96. Acad. cons. La. Earth Sci. Tchrs. Assn., 1989—. Transactions editor Gulf Coast Assn. Geol. Socs., 1997. 1st lt. arty. U.S. Army, 1957-59, Korea. Recipient STAR award Nat. Sci. Tchrs. Assn., 1991, Outstanding Educator award Gulf Coast Assn. Geol. Socs., 1994, Disting. Svc. to Sci. Edn. award La. Sci. Tchrs. Assn., 1997. Fellow Geol. Soc. Am., New Orleans Geol. Soc. (sec. 1979-80, pres. 1983-84); mem. Nat. Assn. Geosci. Tchrs. (Neil Miner award 1997), Paleontol. Soc. Home: New Orleans, La. Deceased.

CRANSTON, ROBERT WALKER, JR., anesthesiologist; b. Wellsburg, W.Va., Aug. 24, 1919; MD, Albany Med. Coll., 1946. Diplomate Am. Bd. Anesthesiology. Intern Pitts. Med. Ctr., 1946-47; resident in anesthesiology Brooke Gen. Hosp., San Antonio, 1953-56; med. staff Backus Hosp., Norwich, Conn., 1965-89; ret., 1989. With U.S. Army, 1943-65. Mem. AMA, Am. Soc. Anesthesiology, Am. Coll. Anesthesiology. Home: Stuart, Fla. Died Aug. 22, 2000.

CRAWFORD, WILLIAM REX, JR., former ambassador; b. Phila., Apr. 22, 1928; s. William Rex and Dorothy (Buckley) C.; m. Celia Faulkner Clevenger, Sept. 18, 1992; 1 child from previous marriage, Sarah Lowry. BA cum laude, Harvard, 1948; MA, U. Pa., 1950. Joined U.S. Fgn. Svc., 1951-79; fgn. svc. officer Jidda, 1951-53, Venice, 1954; Arabic lang. tng., 1955-57; consul in Aden, charge d'affaires Yemen, 1957-59; officer charge Arab-Israeli affairs State Dept., 1959-64, 1964-67, Cyprus, 1968-72; amb. Yemen Arab Republic, 1972-74; amb. to Cyprus, 1974-78; prin. dep. asst. sec. state for Near Ea. and South Asian affairs, 1978-79; exec. dir. Nat. Com. to Honor 14th Centennial of Islam, 1979-82; pres. Eisenhower Exch. Fellowships, 1982-83, The Crawford Found., 1981-91. With USN, 1948-49. Recipient Dept. State Meritorious Svc. award, 1959; William A. Jump award for Disting. Fed. Svc., 1964; Woodrow Wilson fellow Princeton, 1967-68 Mem. Mid. East Inst. Clubs: Hasty Pudding Inst., Dacor. Home: Washington, DC. Died Aug. 4, 2002.

CREACH, DAVID CLEO, retired tool designer, engineering draftsman; b. Carthage, Mo., June 23, 1918; s. Benjamin Russell and Libbye Florence (McCrory) C.; m. Phyllis Stone, 1948 (div. 1955); m. Muriel Pauline Reed, 1956 (div. 1965); 1 child, Douglas Jonathan; adopted children: Margaret, Timothy Michael. A in Structural Design, SUNY, Farmingdale, 1952. Machine tool operator, Huntington Park, Calif., 1940-41, U.S. Steel, Gary, Ind., 1946-47; merchant seaman U.S. Freighters, Tankers, 1948-50; mem. surveyor crew Voohrees Engring. Co., Farmingdale, 1952-53; tool designer Douglas Aircraft Co., El Segundo, Calif., 1953-63; engring. draftsman McDonald Douglas Co., Huntington Beach, Calif., 1963-67; boiler tender Martin Bros. Lumber Mill, Portland, Oreg., 1973-79; ret., 1980. Sgt. U.S. Army Air Force, 1942-45, ETO. Avocation: sociology. Home: Eugene, Oreg. Died Oct. 18, 2001.

CREBS, P(AUL) TERENCE, lawyer; b. St. Louis, Apr. 14, 1938; s. Edward Rudd and Edith Ruth (Beppler) C.; m. Carol Ann Kring, June 17, 1961 (div. 1987); children: Paul T. Jr., Susan J.; m. Karen Charlotte Hensel, July 25, 1987. AB, Washington U., St. Louis, 1960, JD, 1962. Bar: Mo. 1962, U.S. Dist. Ct. (ea. dist.) Mo. 1962, U.S. Ct. Appeals (8th cir.) 1962, U.S. Ct. Appeals (7th cir.) 1977, U.S. Ct. Appeals (10th cir.) 1988, U.S. Dist. Ct. (so. dist.) Ill. 1989, U.S. Supreme Ct. 1990, U.S. Dist. (we. dist.) Mo., 1997. Ptnr. Fordyce & Mayne, St. Louis, 1962-76, Gallop, Johnson, Crebs & Neuman, St. Louis, 1976-81, Peper, Martin, Jensen, Maichel & Hetlage, St. Louis, 1981-87, Herzog, Crebs & McGhee, LLP, St. Louis, from 1987. Assoc. editor Washington U. Law Quar., 1961-62. Bd. dirs. North Ctrl. and South Ctrl. Regional Ctrs. for Deaf-Blind, Mpls. and Dallas, 1972-78; mem. Met. St. Louis Devel. Disability Coun., 1974-80, Presbyn. Children's Svcs., 1989-92. Mem. ABA (fin. officer coun., mem. tort and ins. practice sect. 1983-89), Internat. Assn. Def. Counsel (chair accident life and health com. 1979-80), Fedn. Ins. and Corp. Counsel (vice-chair bus. torts sect. 1990-94, vice chair life health and disability sect. 1993-94, chmn. employment litigation and civil rights sect. 1994-96, chmn. intellectual property sect. 1997—), Mo. Bar Assn., Mo. Orgn. Def. Lawyers, Bar Assn. Met. St. Louis, Trial Attys. Am. (v.p., dir. 1994—), Defense Rsch. Inst. Presbyterian. Home: Saint Louis, Mo. Died October 1999.

CRECELIUS, ROBERT ALLEN, financial consultant; b. Princeton, Ind., Apr. 10, 1927; s. Henry and Maude Muller (Miley) C.; m. Sylvia Ann Cribb, Nov. 12, 1966; children: Beth Ann, Robert Allen Jr. BS in Bus. Stats., Ind. U., 1950; postgrad., N.Y. Inst. Fin., 1967. Cert. fin. planner. Agt. gen. ins. various agys., 1950-67; account exec. Hayden, Stone Inc., 1967-69; regional mgr. Westam. Fin. Corp., Princeton, Inc., 1969-86; pres., sec., treas. Coordinated Ins. Ctr., Inc., Princeton, from 1982; sec.-treas Wealth Concepts Inc., Princeton, from 1984; regional mgr. Anchor Nat. Fin. Services Inc., Princeton, from 1986. Cons. Nat. Ctr. Fin. Edn., San Francisco, 1987—. Treas. Rep. party Fla., Miami, 1967, del. Nat. Conv., 1968; mem. Temple Christian Acad. Fin. Com., Princeton. Mem. Internat. Assn. Fin. Planners, Inst. Cert. Fin. Planners, Ind. Soc. Pub. Accts., Masons. Deceased.

CREECH, WILBUR LYMAN, retired career officer; b. Argyle, Mo., Mar. 30, 1927; s. Paul and Marie (Maloney) C.; m. Carol Ann DiDomenico, Nov. 20, 1969; 1 son, William L. Student, U. Mo., 1946-48; BS, U. Md., 1960; MS, George Washington U., 1966; postgrad., Nat. War Coll., 1966. Commd. 2d lt. U.S. Air Force, 1949; advanced through grades to gen.; fighter pilot 103 combat missions USAF, North Korea, 1950 51; pilot USAF Thunderbirds, 1953-56; comdr., leader Skyblazers, Europe aerial demo team USAF, 1956-60; dir. Fighter Weapons Sch., Nellis AFB, Nev., 1960-61; advisor to comdr. Argentine Air Force, 1962; exec., aide to comdr. Tactical Air Command, 1962-65; dep. comdr. fighter wing, 177 combat missions in F-100 fighters and asst. dep. chief staff for ops. 7th Air Force, Vietnam, 1968-69; comdr. fighter wings USAF in Europe, Spain and W.Ger., 1969-71; dep. for ops. and intelligence Air Forces Europe, 1971-74; comdr. Electronic Systems Div., Hanscom AFB, Mass., 1974-77; asst. vice chief of staff HQS Air Force, Washington, 1977-78; comdr. Tactical Air Command, Langley AFB, Va., 1978-85. Lectr., internat. mgmt. expert; cons. in field. Author: The Five Pillars of TQM, 1994. Decorated D.S.M. with three oak leaf clusters, Silver Star medal, Legion of Merit with two oak leaf clusters, D.F.C. with three oak leaf clusters, Air medal with 14 oak leaf clusters, Air Force Commendation medal with two oak leaf clusters, Army Commendation medal; Spanish Grand Cross. Died Aug. 26, 2003.

CREELMAN, MARJORIE BROER, psychologist, educator; b. Toledo, Dec. 5, 1908; d. William F. and Ethel (Griffin) Broer; m. George Douglas Creelman, June 29, 1932 (div. Dec. 1958); children: Carleton Douglas, Stewart Elliott, Katherine George Skrobela. AB, Vassar Coll., 1931; MA, Columbia U., 1932; PhD, Western Res. U., 1954. Asst. psychologist N.Y. Psychiat. Inst., N.Y.C., 1932-33, Sunny Acres Sanitorium, Cleve., 1947-48; clin. asst. dept. psychology Case Western Res. U., Cleve., 1947-49, supr. field work, dir. practicum tng. program, 1949-54; asst. to dir. parent edn. program Children's Aid Soc., Cleve., 1952-53; ptnr., sr. assoc. Creelman Assocs., Cleve., 1954-58; pvt. practice psychology Cleve., 1954-61, Washington, 1964-69; research psychologist behavioral studies St. Elizabeth's Hosp., Washington, 1963-65, dir. psycho-physiology, clin. and behavioral studies, 1965-67; dir. psychol. services Alexandria Community Mental Health Ctr., 1967-69; mem. policy and planning com. Midwest Tng. Ctr. in Human Relations, 1954-60; prof. psychology Cleve. State U., 1969-76, prof. emeritus, from 1976; pvt. practice psychology, from 1969. Mem. profl. staff Gestalt Inst. Cleve., 1969-81, hon. fellow, 1978—. Author: The Experimental Investigation of Meaning, 1965; editor: Ohio Psychologist, 1956-59; contbr. articles to profl. jours. Mem. Citizen's Adv. Bd. Case Western Res. U. Psychiat. Habilitation Ctr., 1979-81. Fellow Internat. Council Psychologists (sec. 1964-65), Am. Soc. Group Psychotherapy and Psychodrama, Ohio Psychol. Assn.; mem. Internat. Soc. Gen. Semantics (v.p. Cleve. chpt. 1950-61), Am. Acad. Psychotherapists (life, publs. com. directory editor 1963-67), Cleve. Acad. Cons. Psychologists (pres. 1957-58), Sigma Delta Epsilon, Psi Chi, Alpha Chi Omega. Clubs: Cleve. Skating. Home: Cleveland, Ohio. Deceased.

CREMEANS, FRANK A. former congressman; b. Cheshire, Ohio, Apr. 5, 1943; m. Carol; 2 d., 1 s. BFA in Edn., U. Rio Grande, 1966; M in Edn., Ohio U., 1969. Tchr. Lorain County schs., 1966-67, Gallia schs., 1968-71, asst. supt., 1976; prin. Point Pleasant Jr. H. S., 1971-72; guidance couselor Kyger Creek local sch. dists., 1972-74, supt., 1975; founder, owner, oper., pres. Cremeans Concrete & Supply Co., Inc., from 1974; mem. 104th Congress from 6th Ohio dist., 1994-96. Home: Gallipolis, Ohio. Died Jan. 2, 2003.

CREMERS, CLIFFORD JOHN, mechanical engineering educator; b. Mpls., Mar. 27, 1933; s. Christian Joseph and Marie Hildegard C.; m. Claudette May Humble, Sept. 25, 1954; children: Carla Ann, Rachel Beth, Emily Therese, Eric John, Melissa Joan. BSME, U. Minn., 1957, MSME, 1961, PhD, 1964. Rsch. fellow in mech. engring. U. Minn., 1959-61, instr. mech. engring., 1961-64; asst. prof. Ga. Inst. Tech., Atlanta, 1964-66; assoc. prof. U. Ky., Lexington, 1966-71, prof., 1971-98, chmn. dept. mech. engring., 1975-84, 94-95, prof. emeritus, 1998-99. Cons. to industry, state and fed. agys., UNESCO; vis. prof. Imperial Coll. Sci. & Tech., London, 1973; Lady Davis prof. Technion, Haifa, 1986. Contbr. articles on heat transfer to profl. jours. With USNR, 1953-55. NSF grantee, 1965, 66, 69, 71, 76, 81, 86, NASA grantee, 1967, 68, 69, 70, 71, 72, 73, 94; Trane Co. fellow U. Minn., 1959, 60. Fellow ASME (past v.p. basic engring.), AIAA (assoc.); mem. AAAS, Am. Soc. Engring. Edn., Sigma Xi. Roman Catholic. Home: Lexington, Ky. Deceased.

CRENNA, RICHARD, actor; b. L.A., Nov. 30, 1927; Attended, U. So. Calif. Owner Pendick Enterprises, 1966— Actor radio programs including Our Miss Brooks, Boy Scout Jamboree, A Date with Judy, The Great Gildersleeve; TV series Slattery's People, Our Miss Brooks, The Real McCoy's, All's Fair, 1976-77; films include Pride of St. Louis, 1952, It Grows on Trees, 1952, Red Skies Over Montana, 1952, John Goldfard, 1965, The Sand Pebbles, 1966, Made in Paris, 1966, Wait Until Dark, 1967, Please Come Home, Star, 1968, Marooned, 1969, Red Sky at Morning, 1971, Doctor's Wives, 1971, Catlow, 1971, Dirty Money, 1972, The Man Called Noon, 1973, Breakheart Pass, 1976, Death Ship, Body Heat, 1981, First Blood, 1982, Table for Fire, 1983, Summer Rental, 1985, The Flamingo Kid, 1985, Rambo First Blood Part II, 1985, Rambo III, 1988, Leviathan, 1989, Hot Shots! Part Deux, 1993, Jade, 1995, Pyromaniac's Love Story, 1995, Sabrina, 1995; TV movies include Thief, 1971, Footsteps, 1972, Centennial, 1979, The Day The Bubble Burst, 1982, Passions, 1984, The Rape of Richard Beck (Emmy award Best Actor Ltd. Series), 1985, Doubletake, 1985, A Case of Deadly Force, 1986, On Wings of Eagles, 1986, Plaza Suite, Kids Like These, 1987, Police Story: The Freeway Killings, In the Name of Love: A Texas Tragedy, 1995, Texas Grace, 1996, Race Against Time: The Search for Sarah, 1996, Deep Family Secrets, 1997, 20,000 Leagues Under the Sea, 1997; TV miniseries Internal Affairs, 1988, Stock With Each Other, 1989, Blood Brothers: The Case of the Hillside Stranglers, Murder In Black and White, 1990, Montana, 1990, Last Flight Out, 1990, Murder Times Seven, 1990, And the Sea Will Tell, 1991, Intruders, 1992, Terror on Track 9, 1992, A Place to Be Loved, 1993, The Forget-Me-Not Murders, 1994, Jonathan Stone: Threat of Innocence, 1995. Mem. Dirs. Guild Am. Died Jan. 17, 2003.

CRESPI, IRVING, public opinion and market research consultant; b. Bklyn., May 8, 1926; s. Joseph and Esther (Crespi) C.; m. Joan Striefling, Aug. 4, 1968; children: Robert Joseph, Judith Lofton. BSS., CCNY, 1945; MA, State U. Ia., 1946; PhD, New Sch. for Social Research, 1955. Instr. sociology Triple Cities Coll., Endicott, N.Y., 1948-50; instr. sociology Harpur Coll., SUNY, 1950-51, 53-55, asst. prof. sociology, 1955-56; v.p. Gallup Orgn., Inc., Princeton, N.J., 1958-70, exec. v.p., 1970-76; v.p. Mathematica Policy Rsch., 1976-77, sr. v.p., 1977-78, sr. fellow, 1978-79; v.p. Roper Orgn., 1979-81; owner Irving Crespi & Assos., Princeton, 1981-89; prof. mktg. Baruch Coll.-CUNY, 1986-88; dir. media and pub. affairs rsch. Total Rsch. Corp., 1989-91, v.p quality, 1991-94; part-time mkt. rsch. cons. Princeton, 1994—2004. Author: (with H. Mendelsohn) Polls, Television and New Politics, 1971; Pre-Election Polling: Sources of Accuracy and Error, 1988, Public Opinion, Polls and Democracy, 1989, The Public Opinion Process: How The People Speak, 1997; contbr. articles to profl. jours. Trustee Paul F. Lazarsfeld Fund, 1977-79. Served with USAF, 1951-53. Mem. Am. Assn. Pub. Opinion Rsch. (v.p. 1975-76, pres. 1976-77, chmn. standards com. 1966-68, conf. chmn. 1970, award for exceptionally disting. achievement 1997), Am. Sociol. Assn., Am. Mktg. Assn. (dir. 1970-72), World Assn. for Pub. Opinion Rsch. (v.p. 1974-76, pres. 1976-78), Market Rsch. Coun. Jewish. Home: Princeton, NJ. Died Mar. 18, 2004.

CRESS, LAWRENCE DELBERT, university dean, educator; b. Spokane, Wash., Feb. 20, 1947; s. Delbert H. and Faye E. (Miller) C.; m. Linda Fairburn, Feb. 1, 1969; 1 child, Meghan. BA, Pacific Luth. U., Tacoma, 1969; MA, U. Va., 1973, PhD, 1976. From asst. prof. to prof. history Tex. A&M U., College Station, 1976-87; prof. U. Tulsa, 1987-94; dean Coll. Liberal Arts Willamette U., Salem, Oreg., from 1994. Author: Citizen in Arms, 1982. Mem., chair Okla. Found. for Humanities, Oklahoma City, 1988-94. Home: Salem, Oreg. Died Apr. 3, 2000.

CRESS, RONALD DANEWOOD, orthopedic surgeon; b. Mexia, Tex., Dec. 29, 1927; s. Samuel Oliver and Roxie Lee (Wright) C.; m. Mary Gwendolyn Whitfield, June 4, 1950; children: Ronda Kay, Donna Berna, Samuel Edward. AS, Tarlton State U., 1950; DVM, Tex. A&M U., 1954; MD, U. Tex., 1961. Intern John Sealy Hosp., Galveston, Tex., 1961-62, orthopedic resident, 1962-66; orthopedic surgeon Orthopedic clinic of Galveston County Assn., Tex. City, from 1966. Sergeant USMC, 1947, China. Methodist. Avocations: hunting, ranching. Home: La Marque, Tex. Died Sept. 6, 2001.

CREWS, ROBERT THORNTON, medical technology educator; b. Pensacola, Fla., Oct. 12, 1933; s. Thornton and Willie R. (Shaffer) C.; m. Hester Mary Bickel, Aug. 30, 1960; children: Kenneth Bruce, Caryl Wynn Crews Knolton. BS, Auburn U., 1955, MS, 1966; med. tech. cert., Baylor U., 1956; PhD, U. So. Miss., 1980. Lic. med. technologist; registered lab. scientist. Blood bank technologist Wadley Blood Bank and Rsrch. Ctr., Dallas, 1955-56; head serology div., blood bank Mobile County Hosp., Mobile, Ala., 1956-57; med. technologist Ft. Ord (Calif.) Army Hosp. Lab., 1957-59, Salinas Valley Meml. Hosp. Lab., Salinas, Calif., 1958-59; head div. serology, clin. lab. U. Fla. Teaching Hosp. Lab., Gainesville, 1959-60; instr. med. tech. Auburn (Ala.) U., 1959-65; teaching supr. Sch. Med. Tech. St. Mary's Meml. Hosp., Knoxville, Tenn., 1965-66; adminstrv. technologist Wesley Med. Ctr., Wichita, Kans., 1966-71; chmn. dept. med. tech. U. So. Miss., Hattiesburg, 1971-81; program dir. med. tech. Austin Peay State U., Clarksville, Tenn., from 1981. Mem. rsrch. adv. panel Med. Lab. Observer; mem. rev. panel NSF, 1975, 77; mem. Middle Tenn. Area Health Edn. Coun., Murfreesboro, 1988-93; mem. adv. coun. Tenn. Area Health Edn. Coun., Nashville, 1989-94; team coord. for site visit teams Nat. Accrediting Agy. for Clin. Lab. Scis., 1989—. HEW-USPHS grantee, 1972-77, 78. Mem. Am. Soc. for Med. Tech., Tenn. Soc. for Med. Tech., Am. Soc. for Clin. Lab. Sci., Tenn. Soc. for Clin. Lab. Sci., Lambda Tau. Mem. Ch. of Christ. Home: Clarksville, Tenn. Deceased.

CRIDER, IRENE PERRITT, education educator, small business owner, consultant; b. Chatfield, Ark., Apr. 29, 1921; d. Dolphus France and Eula Allan (Springer) Perritt; m. Willis Jewel Crider, Aug. 3, 1945; 1 child, Larry Willis. BA, Bethel Coll., 1944; MA, Memphis State U., 1957; EdD, Fla. Atlantic U., 1977. Cert. elem., secondary tchr., administr., Tenn. Tchr. various schs., Tenn., 1941-57; dean girls Lake Worth (Fla.) Jr. High, 1957-65; dean women Lake Worth High Sch., 1965-73; gen. instructional supr. Palm Beach (Fla.) County Pub. Schs., 1973-75; asst. prin. Jupiter (Fla.) High Sch., 1975-76; supr. interns Fla. Atlantic U., Boca Raton, 1977-83, Palm Beach Atlantic Coll., West Palm Beach, Fla., 1982-84; cons. Paris, Tenn., 1984-87; owner, beauty sys. cons. Irene's Acad. Individual Image Improvement, from 1991. Instr. edn. Bethel Coll., McKenzie, Tenn., 1987, prof. MEd Grad. Program; cons. in field. Contbr. articles to profl. jours. Founder, bd. dirs., charter mem. Palm Beach County Kidney Assn., 1973-93; chmn. citizens action com. Fla. Ch. Women United, 1982-84. Mem. Tallahassee Theatre Guild, Women's Club Tallahassee, Tallahassee Area C. of C., Zonta (Lake Worth, pres. 1969-70), Order Ea. Star, Delta Kappa Gamma (charter pres. Beta Xi-Mu 1968-70, chmn. state com., scholarship), Phi Delta Kappa, Beta Phi

Mu. Democrat. Methodist. Avocations: gardening, reading, spectator sports, color analysis, Amera Natural nails cons. and beauty systems cons. Died Apr. 4, 2000.

CRIGHTON, DAVID GEORGE, mathematician, educator; b. Llandudno, Wales, Nov. 15, 1942; s. George Wolfe Johnston and Violet Grace (Garrison) C.; m. Mary Christine West, Mar. 2, 1969 (div. Oct. 1985); children: Benjamin Alexander, Beth Miranda; m. Johanna Veronica Hol, Sept. 6, 1986. BA, MA, U. Cambridge (Eng.), 1964; PhD, U. London, 1969; ScD, U. Cambridge, 1993; PhD (hon.), Tech U. Crete, 1999; DSc (hon.), U. Manchester Inst. Sci. Tech., 1999, Loughborough U., 1999. Prof. applied math. U. Leeds (Eng.), 1974-85, U. Cambridge, from 1986, head dept. applied math. and theol. physics, from 1991, master Jesus Coll., from 1997. Contbr. over 100 articles to sci. jours. Recipient AIAA medal, 1986, Rayleigh medal Inst. of Acoustics, U.K., 1988, Per Bruel gold medal, ASME, 1993, Gauss medal Braunschweigische Wissenschaftliche Gesellschaft, 1995, Otto Laporte award Am. Phys. Soc., 1998. Fellow Royal Soc.; mem. European Mechanics Soc. (pres.), AAAS (hon.). Home: Cambridge, England. Deceased.

CRIM, CHERYL LEIGH, nurse; b. Winchester, Va., Oct. 23, 1956; d. Victor L. and Mary (Martin) C. BS in Nursing, U. Va., 1979; postgrad., Shenandoah Coll. and Conservatory of Music, from 1987. RN. Cert. psychiatric and mental health nurse. Nurse Med. Coll. Va., Richmond, 1979-80, Henrico Doctor's Hosp., Richmond, 1980-81, Winchester (Va.) Med. Ctr., from 1981. Mem. Va. Soc. Profl. Nurses. Avocations: piano, oil painting. Home: Clear Brook, Va. Deceased.

CRIM, JOSEPH CALVIN, lawyer; b. Winfield, W.Va., Nov. 7, 1926; s. Floyd Dewitt and Stella (Sparks) C.; m. Ann Cook, July 26, 1965; children: Kim E., Joseph F., John C. BS, W.Va. U., 1947, LLB, 1950. Bar: W.Va. 1950. Supt. Columbia Gas Transmission Corp., Charleston, W.Va., 1959-67, supt. land, 1967-73, dir. land, 1973-80, sr. atty., from 1984; v.p. Appalachian Co., Worthington, Ohio, 1980-84. Served to 1st lt. U.S. Army, 1943-46, 51-53, 61-62, PTO, ETO, with Res., ret. Mem. W.Va. Bar Assn., Eastern Mineral Law Found., Am. Assn. Petroleum Landmen. Home: Charleston, W.Va. Deceased.

CRISONA, JAMES JOSEPH, retired lawyer; b. N.Y.C., Aug. 30, 1907; s. Frank and Rachel (Fantino) C.; m. Claire Peysson (dec. 1990), July 8, 1934; children: Claire Mary, Cynthia. B.C.S., N.Y.U., 1928, LL.B., 1931. Sr. partner Crisona Bros., N.Y.C., 1945-57; mem. N.Y. State Assembly, 1946; gen. counsel, dir. Hudson & Manhattan R.R., 1948-54; v.p., gen. counsel, dir. Phoenix-Campbell Corp., 1951-57; mem. N.Y. State Sen., 1955—57; pres. Boro of Queens, N.Y.C., 1957-59; supreme ct. justice State N.Y., 1959-76. Mem. Queens County Bar Assn. Lodges: K.C. Home: New York, NY. Died Sept. 4, 2003.

CROCKETT, CHARLES DABNEY, aerospace engineer, writer; b. Denver, July 29, 1924; s. James A. and Jeannette B. (Currie) C.; m. Vivian Irene O'Neill, Apr. 3, 1949; children: Carol J., Lorie D., Tamara G., Michael O. BS in Gen. Engring., Dartmouth Coll., 1947; MS in Structural Engring., U. Colo., 1955. Registered profl. engr., Ala., Colo. Chemist, metallurgist Gardner of Denver County, 1949-50; structural engr. Bur. Reclamation, Denver, 1949-50; power, pump, plants and dams Dept. Interior, Denver, 1949-50; structural engr. Bur. Reclamation, Denver, 1952-62; aerospace engr. NASA/Marshal Space Flight Ctr., Huntsville, Ala., from 1962. Contbr. articles to profl. jours. Served to col. USMC, 1942—. Recipient Presdl. Citation, Pres. USA, 1995. Mem. ASCE (sr.), AIAA, Marine Officer Assn., Naval Inst. (sr.). Home: Huntsville, Ala. Died July 17, 2001.

CROCKETT, THEO NEILL, labor union administrator; b. McKinney, Tex., Dec. 25, 1946; s. Leo Neill and Louise (Cibolski) C.; m. Betty Barry, Jan. 25, 1967 (div. July 1976); m. Elaine Odle Crockett, Aug. 15, 1976; 1 child, Emiy Louise. BA, Austin Coll., Sherman, Tex., 1969. Pres. C & C Constrn., McKinney, 1975; salesman Lone Star Co., Dallas, 1976; sales mgr. Quid Systems, Exxon, Ft. Worth, 1977; mgr. Miles Homes, McKinney, 1978; project mgr., carpenter foreman Mack Shaw, Tyler, Tex., 1981-82, T.C. Crist, Dallas, 1982-87, Midwest Woodworking, St. Louis, 1989; pres. T.N. Crockett Constrn., McKinney, from 1981, Local 429 Carpenters & Joiners Am., McKinney, from 1981. Vol. ARC, McKinney, 1989—. Mem. Am. Econs. Assn. Avocations: collecting 19th century carpenter tools, reading, classical lit., hunting, fishing. Deceased.

CRONYN, HUME, actor, writer, film director; b. London, Ont., Can., July 18, 1911; came to U.S., 1932; s. Hume Blake and Frances Amelia (Labatt) C.; m. Jessica Tandy, Sept. 27, 1942 (dec.); children: Susan Cronyn Tettemer, Christopher, Tandy. Grad., Ridley Coll., 1930; student, McGill U., 1930-31; grad., Am. Acad. Dramatic Art, 1934; LL.D. (hon.), U. Western Ont., 1974; LHD (hon.), Fordham U., 1985. Lectr. drama Am. Acad. Dramatic Arts, N.Y.C., 1938-39, Actors' Lab., Los Angeles, 1945-46; bd. govs. Stratford Festival, Can. Author: Rope (screen version), 1947, Under Capricorn (screen version), 1948, also various short stories and mag. articles; author (with Susan Cooper) play Foxfire and ABC teleplay The Dollmaker (Christopher and Writers Guild awards 1985), (autobiography) A Terrible Liar, 1991. First profl. theatre appearance, Nat. Theatre Stock Co., Washington, 1931; appeared in Hippers Holiday, N.Y.C., 1934, various plays, N.Y.C., including High Tor, Room Service, The Three Sisters, The Weak Link, Retreat to Pleasure, The Survivors (star); motion pictures include Shadow Of A Doubt, 1943, Life Boat, 1944, The Seventh Cross, 1944, The Postman Always Rings Twice, 1946, The Green Years, 1946, A Letter for Evie (star), 1945, Brute Force (star), 1947, Top O' The Morning, People Will Talk (star), 1951, Sunrise at Campobello, 1960, Cleopatra, 1963, Gaily Gaily, 1968, The Arrangement, 1968, There Was a Crooked Man, 1969, Conrack, 1974, Parallax View, 1974, Honky Tonk Freeway, 1980, The World According to Garp, 1981, Roll Over, 1981, Impulse, 1983, Brewster's Millions, 1985, Cocoon, 1985, Batteries Not Included, 1987, Cocoon: The Return, 1988, The Pelican Brief, 1993, Camilla, 1994, Marvin's Room, 1996, Alone, 1996, (animated) People, 1995; (TV movies) An African Love Story, 1996, 12 Angry Men, 1997.Sea People, 1998, Santa and Pete, 1999, Yesterday's Children, 2000, Off Season, 2001; starred in ANTA touring prodn. of Hamlet, 1949; co-starred with Jessica Tandy in ANTA touring prodn. of The Little Blue Light, Brattle Theatre, Cambridge, Mass., 1950, The Fourposter, 1951-53, Madame Will You Walk, 1953-54, The Honeys; A Day by the Sea, 1955, The Man in the Dog Suit, 1958; dir.: ANTA touring prodn. of Portrait Of A Madonna, Los Angeles, 1946, Now I Lay Me Down To Sleep, 1949-50, Hilda Crane, 1950, The Egghead, 1957, all N.Y.C.; appears in major network dramatic shows TV, including Show of the Week; TV appearances include Foxfire, A Hallmark Prodn., 1987, Day One, 1988, Age Old Friends, 1988, Broadway Bound, 1991, Christmas on Division Street, 1991, To Dance with the White Dog, 1993 (Emmy award, Lead Actor - Special, 1994); appeared in: Big Fish, Little Fish, 1961, Tyrone Guthrie Prodns., Mpls., 1963; played Polonius in Hamlet, N.Y.C., 1964; producer: Slow Dance on the Killing Ground, 1964; produced and starred: (with Jessica Tandy) comedy prodn. The Marriage (a dramatic series), 1954, Triple Play, 1958, 59; appeared title role: (with Jessica Tandy) Richard III, 1965; in: (with Jessica Tandy) Cherry Orchard, 1965; as Harpagon in: comedy prodn. The Miser, Mpls., 1965; as Tobias in A Delicate Balance, 1966, 67; as Harpagon in: revival The Miser, Mark Taper Forum, Los Angeles, 1968; as Frederick William Rolfe in: revival Hadrian VII, Stratford Nat. Theatre Co., Can., 1969, tour, 1969-70; as Capt. Queeg in: Caine Mutiny Court Martial, Los Angeles, 1971-72; appeared in: Promenade All, N.Y.C., 1972; dir., appeared in tour, 1972-73; appeared in: (with Jessica Tandy) Samuel Beckett Festival, Lincoln Center, N.Y.C., 1972; and tour Krapp's Last Tape in Samuel Beckett Festival, Toronto, Washington, other cities, 1973, (with Jessica Tandy) Noel Coward in Two Keys, 1974, tour, 1975, Many Faces of Love, 1974, 75, 76; appeared as Shylock in The Merchant of Venice; as Bottom in: (with Jessica Tandy) A Midsummer Night's Dream, Stratford (Ont., Can.) Festival, 1976; co-producer: (with Mike Nichols and star) The Gin Game (Pulitzer prize 1978), Golden Theatre, N.Y.C., 1977; tour The Gin Game, U.S., Can., Eng., USSR, 1978-79; star: tour Foxfire, Stratford (Ont.) Festival, 1980, Guthrie Theatre, Minn., 1981, Ethel Barrymore Theatre, N.Y.C., 1983; Traveler in the Dark, Am. Repertory Theatre, Loeb Drama Ctr., Cambridge, 1984; limited run of Foxfire, Ahmanson Theatre, Los Angeles, 1985; (with Jessica Tandy) The Petition, Golden Theatre, N.Y.C., 1986. Decorated Order of Canada; recipient Comodia Matinee Club award for Fourposter, 1952, Barter Theatre award for outstanding contbn. to theatre, 1961, Delia Austria medal N.Y. Drama League for Big Fish, Little Fish 1961, Antoinnette Perry (Tony) award, also Variety N.Y. Drama critics poll of performance as Polonius, 1964, 9th ann. award Am. Acad. Dramatic Art 1964, Straw Hat award for best dir. 1972, Obie award for outstanding achievement, disting. performance Krapp's Last Tape 1973, Brandeis U. Creative Arts award 1978, nominee Tony award for The Gin Game 1979, winner Los Angeles Critics award 1979, named to Theatre Hall of Fame 1974, Nat. Press Club award 1979, Commonwealth award for disting. service in dramatic arts, 1983, Humanitas Prize, 1985, Christopher Award and Writers Guild Award for Dollmaker, 1985 (with Susan Cooper), Kennedy Ctr. Honors, 1986, Alley Theatre award, 1987, Franklin Haven Sargent award Am. Acad. Dramatic Arts as disting. alumnus for quality of acting, 1988, Nat. Medal of Arts, 1990; Emmy award supporting actor Broadway Bound, 1992, Antoinette Perry Lifetime Achievement Award, 1994 (with Jessica Tandy). Emmy award Lead Actor for To Dance with White Dog, 1994. Mem. AFTRA, Screen Actors Guild, Writers Guild Am., Actors Equity Assn., Soc. Stage Dirs. and Choreographers, Dramatists Guild. Died June 15, 2003.

CROOKS, JOSEPH WILLIAM, lawyer; b. Washington, Oct. 10, 1942; s. James Alexander and Ann Michon (Kipp) C.; m. S. Jean Hayes, Sept. 11, 1965 (div. 1982); 1 child, James Lewis; m. Laurie L. Henderson, June 28, 1985; 1 child, Ryan Deaton-Crooks. BA with honors and distinction, Lehigh U., 1964; JD, George Washington U., 1967. Bar: D.C. 1968, Md. 1968, Ga. 1970, U.S. Ct. Appeals (D.C. cir.) 1968, U.S. Ct. Appeals (11th cir.) 1971, U.S. Supreme Ct. 1971. Assoc. Willey & Crooks, Washington, 1967-68, Jones, Bird & Howell, Atlanta, 1972-75, ptnr., 1975-81; asst. gen. counsel Emory U., Atlanta, 1981-82, gen. counsel, from 1982, v.p., gen. counsel, from 1993. Adj. prof. law Emory U., 1988. Chmn. bd. dirs. My Turn Now, Inc., Atlanta, 1987-89. Capt. JAGC, U.S. Army, 1968-71. Mem. ABA, Am. Law Inst., Nat. Assn. Coll. and Univ. Attys., Am. Acad. Hosp. Attys., State Bar Ga., Ga. Acad. Hosp. Attys., Order of Coif. Home: Stone Mountain, Ga. Died Jan. 18, 1999.

CROSBY, GEORGE MINER, former state legislator; b. St. Johnsbury, Vt., Nov. 24, 1916; s. Fred Morant and Susan Julia (Miner) C.; m. Gertrude Roderick, Dec. 21, 1944; children: Susan, Peter, William. Grad. pvt. sch., St. Johnsbury. Printer Cowles Press, Inc., St. Johnsbury, 1934-41; asst. advt. mgr. Caldeonian-Record newspaper, St. Johnsbury, 1946-50; sales rep. Gen. Foods Corp., St. Johnsbury, 1950-53, Lever Bros. Co., St. Johnsbury, 1953-80, French and Bean Co., St. Johnsbury, 1980-95; mem. Vt. Ho. of Reps., Montpelier, 1990-94. Elderhostel lectr. St. Johnsbury Acad. Contbr. articles to history publs. Pres. St. Johnsbury Athenaeum, 1974-76; trustee Vt. Hist. Soc., Montpelier, 1989-96; chmn. State House Adv. Bd., Montpelier, 1988-95. With USNR, 1942-46. Recipient Citizen of Yr. award St. Johnsbury C. of C., 1984, Legis. award Lyndon State Coll., 1986, Alumnni Svc. award St. Johnsbury Acad., 1989. Mem. VFW (legis. officer 1985), Am. Legion (post fin. officer 1973-74). Republican. Roman Catholic. Avocations: history, stamp and coin collecting. Home: Saint Johnsbury, Vt. Deceased.

CROSBY, JOHN O'HEA, opera general director; b. N.Y.C., July 12, 1926; s. Laurence Alden and Aileen Mary (O'Hea) C. Grad., Hotchkiss Sch., 1944; BA, Yale U., 1950, DFA (hon.), 1991; LittD (hon.), U. N.Mex., 1967; MusD (hon.), Coll. of Santa Fe, 1968, Cleve. Inst. Music, 1974; LHD (hon.), U. Denver, 1977. Pres. Manhattan Sch. Music, 1976-86 Accompanist, opera coach, condr., N.Y.C., 1951-56, founder, gen. dir., mem. conducting staff Santa Fe Opera, 1957-2000; guest condr. various opera cos. in U.S. and Can. and Europe, 1967—; condr. U.S. stage premiere Daphne, 1964, U.S. profl. premier Danae, 1982; U.S. profl. premier Friedenstag, 1988; world premiere Wuthering Heights, 1958. With inf. AUS, 1944-46, ETO. Recipient Nat. Medal of Arts, 1991, Verdienstkreuz 1st klasse Bundesrepublik, Deutschland, 1992. Roman Catholic. Died Dec. 15, 2002.

CROSBY, THOMAS F. judge; b. Long Beach, Calif., June 4, 1940; m. Patty Wichite, Nov. 20, 1982; 2 children. AB with great distinction, Stanford U., 1962; LLB, U. Calif., Berkeley, 1965; LLM, U. Va., 1988. Bar: Calif. 1966, U.S. Dist. Ct. (no. dist.) Calif. 1966, U.S. Ct. Appeals (9th cir.) 1966, U.S. Dist. Ct. (ctrl. dist.) Calif. 1977, U.S. Dist. Ct. (so. dist.) Calif. 1979; cert. in criminal law. With NLRB, 1965-66, Peace Corps, 1966-68, Orange County (Calif.) Dist. Atty.'s Office, 1968-73; ptnr. Crosby & Luesebrink, then Crosby, Garey & Bonner, Calif., 1973-81; judge Superior Ct., 1981-82; assoc. justice Calif. Ct. Appeals, Santa Ana, 1982—2001. Contbr. articles to law jours. Mem. Delta Upsilon, Phi Alpha Sigma. Died Jan. 23, 2004.

CROSS, RALPH EMERSON, retired mechanical engineer; b. Detroit, June 3, 1910; s. Milton Osgood and Helen (Heim) C.; m. Eloise Florence Fountain, June 18, 1932; children: Ralph Emerson, Carol (Mrs. Peter G. Wodtke), Dennis W. Student, MIT, 1933; D.Eng. (hon.), Lawrence Inst. Tech., 1977. V.p. Cross Co., Fraser, Mich., 1932-67, pres., gen. mgr., 1967-79, chmn., 1979-82; chmn. bd. Cross & Trecker, Bloomfield Hills, Mich., 1979-82, chmn. emeritus, dir., 1982-86; chmn. bd., CEO Intelitec Corp., Grosse Pointe Farms, Mich., 1982-89. Chmn. bd., pres. Cross Internat. A.G., Fribourg, Switzerland, 1965-68; pres. Cross Export Corp., 1972-80; spl. cons. to asst. sec. Air Force for Material, 1955-59; mem. corp. Econ. Devel. Corp. Greater Detroit, 1968-73, Mich. Blue Shield, 1969-74; mem. corp. devel. com. MIT, 1970-2003; mem. Am. Iranian Joint Bus. Coun., 1975-76; trustee Lawrence Inst. Tech., 1979-2003; pres. SME Edn. Found., 1979-84, chmn. emeritus, dir., 1984-2003. Recipient Engring. citation Am. Soc. Tool Engrs., 1956, Corp. Leadership award MIT, 1976; elected to Machine Tool Hall of Fame, 1992. Mem. NAE, Nat. Machine Tool Builders Assn. (pres. 1975), Soc. Automotive Engrs., Soc. Mfg. Engrs. (hon.), Engring. Soc. Detroit, Lochmoor Club, Quail Ridge Country Club, Delray Beach Club, Detroit Athletic Club. Home: Grosse Pointe Farms, Mich. Died June 26, 2003.

CROSS, WILLIAM REDMOND, JR., corporate director, foundation executive; b. N.Y.C., Apr. 26, 1917; s. William Redmond and Julia (Newbold) C.; m. Sally Curtiss Smith, June 14, 1958; children: William Redmond III, Pauline Cross Reeve, Frederic Newbold. Grad., Groton (Mass.) Sch., 1937; BA, Yale, 1941. With Hanover Bank, N.Y.C., 1941-43, N.Y. Trust Co., 1946-59, v.p., Safe Deposit Co. N.Y. Trust Co., 1952-59, Morgan Guaranty Trust Co., N.Y.C., 1959-79; head Midtown offices, 1962-65, sr. v.p., 1964-73, head met. div. gen. banking dept., 1967-71, sr. credit officer gen. banking div., 1971-72, sr. v.p., head corp. fin. div., 1972-73, exec. v.p., 1973-78, vice chmn. credit policy com., 1978-79; ret., 1979. Bd. dirs. Jacob and Valeria Langeloth Found., 1955—, pres., 1979-96; bd. dirs. Caramoor Center for Music and Arts, 1976-79; trustee Childrens Aid Soc., 1962-75, Chapin Sch., 1969-75, Citizens Budget Com., 1963-79, Rippowam-Cisqua Sch., Bedford, N.Y., 1974-77. Served to lt. (j.g.) USNR, 1943-46. Mem.: Yale (past dir., past treas.), Racquet and Tennis (N.Y.C.). Home: Waccabuc, NY. Died Nov. 22, 2002.

CROSSLEY, RANDOLPH ALLIN, retired corporate executive; b. Cupertino, Calif., July 10, 1904; s. John P. and Elizabeth (Hall) C.; m. Florence Pepperdine, July 23, 1928; 1 dau., Meredith (Mrs. Jack E. Young). Student, A. to Zed Coll. Prep. Sch., 1921-23, U. Calif., 1923-25; LLD honoris causa, Pepperdine U., 1990. Founder Crossley Advt., Honolulu, 1929; pres. Hawaiian Tuna Packers, Ltd., Honolulu, 1930-34, Hawaiian Fruit Packers, Ltd., 1936-54, Aloha Stamp Co., Ltd., 1954-64, Nonou Devel. Co., Ltd., Honolulu; pres., exec. officer Crossley Contracting Co., 1954-63, Crossco, Ltd., from 1964; pres., chief exec. officer Am. Pacific Group, Inc., 1967-69, chmn., chief exec. officer, 1969-72; pres. Am. Pacific Life Ins. Co. Ltd., 1967-69; chmn. Hawaii Corp., 1968-76; pres., dir. Pacific Savs. and Loan Assn., 1962-65; chmn. Medi-Fund Corp., San Francisco, 1969-76. Mem. Public Utilities Commn., 1945-47

Mem. Hawaii Ho. of Reps.; 1943-45 Constl. Conv., 1950, Hawaii Senate, 1959-64; chmn. Rep. party Hawaii, 1950-52, Rep. candidate for gov., 1966, 74, Rep. nat. committeeman from, Hawaii, 1967-69, Presdl. elector, 1972. Mem. NAM (dir. 1970-76), C. of C. Hawaii (dir. 1954-59, 71-74), Newcomen Soc., N. Am. (hon. trustee), Rancheros Visitadores (Calif.) Past trustee, treas. Kawaiahao Ch. Clubs: Outrigger Canoe (Honolulu); Bohemian (San Francisco); Pebble Beach (Calif.). Home: Pebble Beach, Calif. Died Feb. 23, 2004.

CROW, LEO ALLEN, retired plant manager; b. Vergennes, Ill., Feb. 11, 1926; s. Millard Ezra and Sophie Annalena (Hespenheider) C.; widowed; children: Darrell, Ricky, Glenda, Brenda, Stephen. Student, Ill. State U., 1944-46, U. Ill., 1945-46, Bradley U., 1950-51. Agt. U.S. Intelligence, U.S. and Europe, 1956-65; salesman Calame's Trade Ctr., Santa Clara, Calif., 1965-66; sales mgr. Pio's Motorsport, Reno, Nev., 1966-67; master mech. Arrow Group Industries, Breese, Ill., 1967-74; plant supt. Sandoval (Ill.) Zinc Co., 1974-85; sales clk. Goodwin Furniture Co., Framingham, Mass., 1986-87; sales rep. New Eng. Vinyl Co., Framingham, 1987; asst. sales mgr. Am. Aqua of New Eng., Norwood, Mass., 1987-88; ret., 1988. With U.S. Army, 1956-65. Mem. Santa Clara Valley Artist's Assn. Avocation: fine artist. Home: Bellingham, Mass. Died Aug. 6, 1999.

CROWELL, DONALD W. diversified financial services company executive, financial consultant; BA, Stanford U., 1956, MBA, 1958. Mng. ptnr., CEO Crowell, Weedon & Co., L.A., 1967—2004. Died June 20, 2004.

CROWLEY, JOHN SCHAFT, business machine executive; b. Rochester, N.Y., July 21, 1923; s. Harry Burtis and Margaret Delores (Schaft) Crowley; married; children: John, Katherine, Margaret, Sheilah. BS, U. Rochester, 1943; MBA, Harvard U., 1948. Sr. ptnr., dir. McKinsey & Co., N.Y.C., 1952—77; former exec. v.p. Xerox Corp., Stamford, Conn. Dir., pres. Am. Found. for Blind, Helen Keller Internat.; vice chmn. Ednl. Broadcasting Corp., Sta. WNET/13, N.Y.C., NY; bd. chmn. Greenwich (Conn.) Convent of Sacred Heart; mem. trustees' coun. U. Rochester. With USN, 1944—46. Mem.: Genesee Valley Club, Racquet and Tennis Club, Stanwich (Greenwich), Blind Brook (Port Chester, N.Y.), Country of Rochester Club, Econ. Club (N.Y.C.). Republican. Roman Catholic. Died Mar. 31, 2004.

CROXTON, FRED(ERICK) E(MORY), JR., retired information specialist, consultant; b. Columbus, Ohio, Oct. 14, 1923; s. Frederick Emory and Rosetta Ruth (Harpster) C.; m. Dorothy Duboise, Apr. 18, 1948 (div. 1978); m. Arlene Beekman Bilbrough, Dec. 1, 1978 (div. 1991); m. Mary Barker King, Apr. 8, 1993; children: Elizabeth C., Helen Croxton Harrand; stepchildren: Amy Bilbrough Speas, Karin Bilbrough Lertora, Kim Bilbrough Chandler, Kathleen King, Christine King Lokey, Brian King. BA, Oberlin Coll., 1944; MA, Columbia U., 1960. Tech. insp. Kellex Corp., 1944-45; sr. chem. and tech. engr. Union Carbide Nuclear Co., 1946-49; various positions Tech. Info. Svc., U.S. AEC, Oak Ridge, Tenn., 1949-53; supt. info. and records Goodyear Atomic Corp., Piketon, Ohio, 1953-62; dir. Redstone Sci. Info. Ctr., U.S. Army Missile Command, Huntsville, Ala., 1962-68; exec. v.p. Informatics Tisco, College Park, Md., 1968-70; dir. adminstrv. dept. Libr. of Congress, Washington, 1970-76, dir. reader svcs. dept., 1976-78, dir. automated systems office, 1978-85. Cons. in info. system design and mgmt., 1971-91. Contbr. articles to profl. jours. Chmn. Pike County chpt. ARC, 1959-60, Pike County Free Pub. Libr., 1957-62. With AUS, 1945-46. Mem. AAAS, Am. Chem. Soc., Imperial Lakes Golf and Racquet Club. Home: Mulberry, Fla. Died June 17, 2003.

CRUMBLEY, EDWARD EUGENE, financial planner; b. Marietta, Ohio, Sept. 13, 1942; s. Charles Gerald and Alice Ann (Danford) C.; m. Barbara Carol Collins, July 3, 1965; children: Edward Jr., Carrie A., Jason T., Jodi M. BA in Econs., Marietta Coll., 1970; MBA in Fin. Planning, Golden Gate U., 1985. CFP; Calif. ins. license. Staff mgr. Ohio Bell, Cleve., 1970-79, AT&T, Morristown, N.J., 1979-80, Pacific Telesis, San Francisco, 1980-84; registered rep. Linsco/Pvt. Ledger, San Diego, from 1985. Bd. mem. Boy Scouts Am., Rohnert Park, Calif., 1973-85; bd. mem., pres. Little League Baseball, Rohnert Park, 1979-87; pres. Cath. Youth Orgn. Basketball, Rohnert Park, 1981-87. Mem. Internat. Assn. Fin. Planning. Lutheran. Avocations: golf, tennis, softball, camping. Home: Rohnert Park, Calif. Died Aug. 17, 2000.

CRUMP, SPENCER, publishing company executive; b. San Jose, Calif., Nov. 25; s. Spencer M. and Jessie (Person) C.; m. Cynthia Fink, 1992 (div. 1999); children by previous marriage: John Spencer, Victoria Elizabeth Margaret. BA, U. So. Calif., 1960, MS in Edn, 1962, MA in Journalism, 1969. Reporter Long Beach (Calif.) Ind., 1945-49; freelance writer Long Beach, 1950-51; travel columnist, picture editor Long Beach Ind.-Press-Telegram, 1952-56; pres. Crest Industries Corp., Long Beach, 1957-58; editor suburban sects. L.A. Times, 1959-62; editl. dir. Trans-Anglo Books, L.A., 1962-73, pub., 1973-81, Zeta Pubs. Co., Corona Del Mar, Calif., from 1981. Mng. dir. Person-Crump Ranch and Investment Co. (formerly Person Properties Co.), Justiceburg, Tex., 1951—; chmn. dept. journalism Orange Coast Coll., 1966-84; chmn. bd. Zeta Internat., 1976—; cons. Queen Beach Press, 1974-87, Flying Spur Press, 1976—, So. Pacific Transp. Co., 1979-80, Interurban Press/Trans-Anglo Books, 1981-87; bd. dirs. Zeta Britain, Zeta Internat.; chmn. bd. T & S Publs. Group, Inc., Canyon Lake, Calif., 1988-89. Author: Ride the Big Red Cars, 1962, Redwoods, Iron Horses and the Pacific, 1963, Western Pacific-The Railroad That was Built Too Late, 1963, California's Spanish Missions Yesterday and Today, 1964, Black Riot in Los Angeles, 1966, Henry Huntington and the Pacific Electric, 1970, Fundamentals of Journalism, 1974, California's Spanish Missions—An Album, 1975, Suggestions for Teaching the Fundamentals of Journalism in College, 1976, The Stylebook for Newswriting, 1979, Newsgathering and Newswriting for the 1980s and Beyond, 1981, Riding the California Western Skunk R.R., 1988, Durango to Silverton by Narrow Gauge Rail, 1990, Riding the Cumbres & Toltec Railroad, 1992, Rails to the Grand Canyon, 1993, Route 66: America's First Main Street, 1994. Mem. Los Angeles County Democratic Central Com., 1961-62. Mem. Book Pubs. Assn. So. Calif., Fellowship Reconciliation, Soc. Profl. Journalists. Unitarian-Universalist. Died Oct. 30, 2002.

CULBERSON, WILLIAM LOUIS, botany educator; b. Indpls., Apr. 5, 1929; s. Louis Henry and Lucy Helene (Hellman) C.; m. Chicita Forman, Aug. 24, 1953. BS, U. Cin., 1951; Diplome d'Etudes Supérieures, U. de Paris, 1952; PhD, U. Wis., 1954. NSF postdoctoral fellow Harvard U., Cambridge, Mass., 1954-55; instr. Duke U., Durham, N.C., 1955-58, asst. prof., 1958-64, assoc. prof., 1964-70, prof., 1970-84, Hugo L. Blomquist prof., 1984-95. Vis. rsch. prof. Mus. Nat. d'Histoire Naturelle, Paris, 1980; grants dir. Stanley Smith Hort. Trust, 2000—. Author over 100 rsch. papers. Dir. Sarah P. Duke Gardens at Duke U., Durham, 1978-98. Grantee NSF, 1957-93. Mem. Am. Bryological and Lichenological Soc. (pres. 1987-89), Bot. Soc. Am. (pres. 1991-92), Am. Soc. Plant Taxonomists, Mycol. Soc. Am. Avocation: greenhouse gardening. Home: Durham, NC. Deceased.

CULBERTSON, KATHERYN CAMPBELL, lawyer; b. Tom's Creek, Va., Aug. 14, 1920; d. Robert Fugate and Mary Campbell (Leonard) C. BS, East Tenn. State U. (1940); BS in L.S, George Peabody Library Sch., 1942; JD, YMCA Night Law Sch., Nashville, 1968. Bar: Tenn. 1969. Libr. Bur. Ships Tech. Libr., U.S. Navy Dept., Washington, 1945-49, 51-53, Lincoln Elementary Sch., Kingsport, Tenn., 1949-50, 51, Regional Libr., Tenn. State Libr. and Archives, Johnson City, 1953-61; dir. extension svcs. libr. Met. Govt. Nashville and Davidson County, Tenn, 1961-71; state libr. and archivist State of Tenn., Nashville, 1972-82; pvt. practice law Nashville, 1982—2002. Mem. library com. Pres.'s Com. on Employment of Handicapped, 1966-86; Nat. Bus. and Profl. Women's Found., 1968-70; pres. Tenn. Fedn. Bus. and Profl. Women's Clubs, 1974-75 Contbg. author: Encyclopedia of Education, 1966; Editor: YMCA Alumni Assn. Bull, 1970-71. Named One of Five Women of Yr. Nashville Banner-Davidson County Bus. and Profl. Women's Club, 1979 Mem. Tenn. Bar Assn., Nashville Bar Assn., Nashville Bus. and Profl. Women's Club (past pres.), Brentwood Bus. and Profl. Women. Republican. Died July 1, 2002.

CULLISON, WILLIAM LESTER, association executive; b. Balt., Aug. 26, 1931; s. William Lester and Margaret Elizabeth (Quick) C.; m. Lorraine Stella Wirtz, Dec. 24, 1953; 1 child, Beth Lynn. BS, U.S. Merchant Marine Acad., 1953; LLB, LaSalle Extension U., Chgo., 1968; MBA, Fla. Atlantic U., 1975. 3d asst. engr. Am. Trading and Production Co., N.Y.C., 1953, 54-55; asst. dir. sci. and tech. Am. Petroleum Inst., N.Y.C., 1957-68; exec. dir. Tech. Assn. Pulp and Paper Ind., Atlanta, from 1968. Served as lt. USN, 1954-56. Mem. Am. Soc. Mechanical Engrs., Soc. Research Adminstrs. (charter), Ga. Soc. Assn. Execs. (pres. 1975-76, Cliff Clark award 1977), Am. Soc. Assn. Execs. (sec. treas. 1986-87, vice chmn. 1987-88, Key award 1985). Republican. Episcopal. Club: Peachtree Tennis (Norcross, Ga.). Lodge: Masons. Avocation: bookbinding. Died in 1999.

CULLMAN, JOAN, theatrical producer; b. Far Rockaway, NY; Grad., Bklyn. Coll. Adv. bd. dirs. Musical Theatreworks; bd. dirs. Bay Street Theatre; vice chmn. Lincoln Ctr. Theatre, Inc. Co-prodr. plays Carmelina, One Night Stand, Oh, Brother!, The Rink, Mademoiselle Colombe, Eating Raoul, Orphans, Anything Goes, Cole, Art (Tony award best play 1998). Died Mar. 18, 2004.

CULVER, FLORENCE MORROW, volunteer; b. Central Lake, Mich., Nov. 27, 1915; d. Robert Edmund Morrow and Roxana Grace Wilkinson; m. Charles Beach Culver, Oct. 1935 (dec. Sept. 1967); children: Sara Roxana, Eric Charles; m. Clair Lawrence Magoon, July 23, 1977. Student, Detroit (Mich.) Bus. Sch. Vol. group leader Recovery, Inc., Bloomfield Hills, Mich., from 1964. Prodr. United Cable TV, Channel 52 for Rochester Symphony Concerts. Pres. Huntington Woods (Mich.) Study Club, 1967-69; founder, pres. Rochester (Mich.) Symphony Guild, 1978-80, now publicity chmn., historian; pres. bd. Rochester Symphony, 1982-84, historian. Recipient spl. tribute Mich. Ho. of Reps., 1986. Democrat. Unitarian Universalist. Avocations: music, art, bridge, sailing, swimming. Home: Bellaire, Mich. Died May 17, 2000.

CUMMINGS, ROBERT EUGENE, retired counseling psychologist; b. Honolulu, Aug. 15, 1930; s. Bernard Joseph and Mary (Moran) C.; m. Margit Castle, May 16, 1973; children: Michael Robert, Caroline Marie. BA, U. Calif., 1953; MA, San Diego State U., 1962; EdD, U. Mo., 1969. Lic. Psychologist, Tenn. Psychology intern Jefferson Barracks Vets. Hosp., Columbia, Mo., 1965-66; staff psychologist Agnew State Hosp., San Jose, Calif., 1967-72; counseling psychologist Mt. Home VA Med. Ctr., Johnson City, Tenn., 1971-95; ret., 1995. With Office Vocat. Rehab., 1962-66. Author: (poem) Now and Then, (book) Poems & Sculpture, 1977; contbr. articles to profl. jours. Lt. (j.g.) USN, 1953-57, Korea. Mem. Psi Chi (hon.). Home: Johnson City, Tenn. Died Jan. 7, 1999.

CUNNINGHAM, GLENN CLARENCE, government official; b. Omaha, Sept. 10, 1912; s. George Warner and Emma (Seefus) C.; m. Janis Thelen (dec. 1987), July 25, 1941; children— Glenn Clarence, Judith, Mary, James Robert, David George, Ann Melissa. AB, U. Omaha, 1935. Mgr. Jr. C. of C., Omaha, 1937-40, pres., 1945-46; mgr. Convention Bur., Omaha C. of C., 1941, Omaha Safety Council, 1941-47; Mem. 85th-91st Congresses, 2d Nebr. dist., 1957—71; former asst. to dir. Bur. Outdoor Recreation, Dept. Interior, Washington. Fire commr., also mem. bd. edn., City of Omaha, 1947-48, mayor, 1948-54; del. Republican Nat. Conv., 1948, 52; Nebr. dir. U.S. Savs. Bond div. U.S. Treasury, 1954-56; form bd. govs. Met. Tech. Community Coll. Decorated Legion of Honor, Order of De Molay.; Named Omaha's Outstanding Young Man, 1945, Nebr. Outstanding Young Man, 1945 Mem. U. Omaha Alumni Assn., Pi Kappa Alpha. Republican. Episcopalian. Home: Omaha, Nebr. Died Dec. 18, 2003.

CUNNINGHAM, WALTER JACK, electrical engineering educator; b. Comanche, Tex., Aug. 21, 1917; s. Walter Jack and Percy Adele (Moore) C.; m. Barbara Virginia Lynch, Feb. 26, 1944; children: Lawrence Bradford, John Hartwell. AB, U. Tex., 1937, AM, 1938; PhD, Harvard U., 1947. Instr. physics and communication engring. Harvard, 1939-46; part-time research OSRD, in acoustics and electric circuits, 1939-46; asst. prof. elec. engring. Yale U., 1946-50, assoc. prof., 1950-56, prof. engring. and applied sci., 1956-81, prof. elec. engring., 1981-88, assoc. chmn. dept. engring. and applied sci., 1969-72, prof. emeritus, from 1988. Author: Introduction to Nonlinear Analysis, 1958, Engineering at Yale, 1992; bd. editors Am. Scientist, 1955-81, 83-90, Jour. Franklin Inst., 1962-75; also articles. Mem. IEEE, Acoustical Soc. Am., Sigma Xi (bd. editors, chmn. com. on publs. 1983-87). Home: Hamden, Conn. Died Jan. 7, 2004.

CURRAN, ROBERT, columnist; b. Boston, Oct. 4, 1925; s. Sylvester and Ann (Coyne) C.; m. Mary Sullivan Curran, June 14, 1952 (dec.); children: Robert Jr., Mark S., John F. BA, Cornell u., 1949. Copywriter J. Walter Thompson, N.Y.C., 1951-61; editor Fawcett Pubs., N.Y.C., 1964-65; sports publicist NBC-TV, N.Y.C., 1965-66; syndicated columnist N.Y.C., 1966-67; columnist Buffalo News, 1967—99. Staff sgt. U.S. Army, 1943-45, ETO. Recipient Best Column award in N.Y. State AP, 1971, Prin. award Freedoms Found., Valley Forge, Pa., 1972. Avocations: swimming, golf. Home: Williamsville, NY. Died Mar. 13, 2003.

CURRY, DOROTHY HONAKER, retired medical/surgical nurse and administrator; b. Hinton, W.Va., Nov. 6, 1928; d. Frank R. and Mabel S. (McGhee) Honaker; m. Frank E. Curry, Sept. 12, 1952. Diploma, St. Francis Sch. Nursing, Charleston, W.Va., 1949. RN, Fla., W.Va. Evening supr. St. Vincent's Hosp., Jacksonville, Fla.; asst. dir. nursing Summers County Hosp., Hinton; nursing supr. VA Med. Ctr., Beckley, W.Va.; ret. Mem. ANA, W.Va. Nurses Assn. Home: Hinton, W.Va. Died June 4, 2000.

CUSHING, RALPH HARVEY, chemical company executive; b. Buffalo, Nov. 3, 1922; s. Benjamin Ralph and Ella Mabel (Lukens) C.; m. Edith Elizabeth Smith, Nov. 27, 1947; children: Sharonrose, Paul Ralph. BS ChemE, Drexel U., 1952. Chem. engr. Bristol Labs., Syracuse, N.Y., 1952-60; project engr. Mobay Chem. Co., Pitts., 1960-63; sr. project engr. Gulf Research Co., Harmarville, Pa., 1963-65; sr. researcher, mgr. engring., dir. coordinated computer services, sr. cons. Enron Corp. (formerly No. Nat. Gas Co.), Omaha, 1965-86; pres. CISSCO, Inc., Omaha, from 1968. Patentee corrosion protection of pipelines; contbr. articles to profl. jours. Lay minister Meth. Ch., Pitts., 1960-63. Served to cpl. U.S. Army, 1944-46, CBI. Mem. Am. Inst. Chem. Engrs., Am. Assn. Cost Engrs., Nat. Assn. Corrosion Engrs. (corrosion specialist 1978—). Republican. Avocations: photography, computer art. Home: Omaha, Nebr. Died Mar. 2, 2001.

CUTLER, CASSIUS CHAPIN, physicist, retired educator; b. Springfield, Mass., Dec. 16, 1914; s. Paul A. and Myra B. (Chapin) C.; m. Virginia Tyler, Sept. 27, 1941; children: (Cassius) Chapin, William (Urban) (dec.), Virginia Cutler Raymond. B.Sc., Worcester Poly. Inst., 1937, D.Eng. (hon.), 1975. With Bell Telephone Labs., 1937-78, asst. dir. electronics and radio research, 1959-63, dir. electronic and computer systems research lab. Holmdel, N.J., 1963-78; prof. applied physics Stanford U., 1979-96, ret., 1997. Contbr. articles to profl. jours. Mem. 1st Ch. of Christ Scientist, Keyport, N.J., 1966-78, Menlo Park, Calif., 1979-96, reader, chmn. bd., Plainfield, N.J., 1946-66. Recipient Robert H. Goddard Disting. Alumni award Worcester Polytechnic Inst., 1982. Fellow IEEE (Edison medal 1981, Centennial medal 1984, Alexander Graham Bell medal 1991), AAAS; mem. Nat. Acad. Engring. Nat. Acad. Scis., Sigma Xi. Achievements include patents for numerous devices. Home: Waterford, Maine. Died Dec. 1, 2002.

CUTLER, JOHN CHARLES, physician, educator; b. Cleve., June 29, 1915; s. Glenn Allen and Grace Amanda (Allen) C.; m. Eliese Helene Strahl, Nov. 21, 1942. BA, Western Res. U., 1937, MD, 1941; M.P.H., Sch. Hygiene and Pub. Health, Johns Hopkins U., 1951. Diplomate: Am. Bd. Preventive Medicine and Pub. Health. Commd. asst. surgeon (lt. j.g.) USPHS, 1941, advanced through grades to asst. surgeon gen. (rear adm.), 1958; intern USPHS Hosp.,

Staten Island, N.Y., 1941; venereal disease investigations Pub. Health Svc. Venereal Disease Rsch. Lab., Stapleton, N.Y., 1943-46; venereal disease rsch. and demonstration Guatemala, 1946-48; assigned WHO, 1949-50; with venereal disease divsn. USPHS, 1951-54; program office Bur. State Svcs., 1954-57; asst. dir. Nat. Inst. Allergy and Infectious Diseases, 1958; asst. surgeon gen. for program, 1958-59; health officer Central dist. Allegheny County Health Dept., 1959-61; dep. dir. Pan Am. San. Bur., regional office for Americas WHO, 1961-68; prof. internat. health, dir. population program Grad. Sch. Public Health, U. Pitts., 1968-79, chmn. dept. health svcs. adminstrn., 1979-80, assoc. dept. chmn., prof. internat. health, 1980-85, prof. emeritus, 1985—. Pres. Family Planning Coun. Southwestern Pa., 1971-72; sec. Am. Social Health Assn., 1972-76; pres. Internat. Health Soc., 1972-73, Am. Assn. World Health, 1973-75, Assn. Voluntary Sterilization, 1977-83; sec.-treas. World Fedn. Health Agys. for Advancement Vol. Surg. Contraception, 1975-81, pres.-elect., 1981-85, pres. 1985-87. Contbr. articles to med. publs. Pres. UN Assn., Pitts., 1988-90. Fellow APHA; mem. Phi Beta Kappa. Home: Pittsburgh, Pa. Died Feb. 8, 2003.

CYRULNIK, IRWIN MICHAEL, psychologist; b. N.Y., Nov. 25, 1943; BA in Psychology, CUNY, 1965; MA in Psychology, Yeshiva U., 1967, PhD in Psychology, 1971. Lic. psychologist, N.Y. Prof. psychology Cathedral Coll., Douglaston, N.Y., 1971-88; pvt. practice, Flushing, N.Y., from 1988. Mem. APA. Home: Flushing, NY. Died Jan. 26, 2002.

CYRUS, VIRGINIA JOAN, educator; b. Snohomish, Wash., Sept. 3, 1939; d. George Stanley and Ruth Elizabeth (Brodigan) Dubuque; m. John Dennis Cyrus, June 30, 1962; children: Cynthia Joan, Liesl Jane. BA, Pomona Coll., 1961; MA, U. Wash., 1964, PhD, 1968. Instr. Maricopa County Community Coll., Phoenix, 1971-73, Cerro Coso Community Coll., Ridgecrest, Calif., 1973-74; prof. English, women's studies Rider U., Lawrenceville, N.J., from 1975. Cons. in field. Editor: Experiencing Race, Class and Gender in the United States; freelance editor for univs. and women's orgns., 1971—; contbr. articles to mags., newspapers, brochures and newsletters. Founding coord. Ariz. Women's Polit. Caucus, Phoenix, 1971-73 (Women of the Yr. award 1972); bd. dirs. Bucks County Opportunity Coun., Doylestown, Pa., 1985-90. Recipient Rhoda Freeman Recognition award N.J. Coll. and U., 1988. Mem. NOW, MLA, AAUP, Nat. Women's Studies Assn. (nat. coord. 1982-85, Disting. svc. award 1990), Women's Caucus Modern Languages, Phi Beta Kappa. Home: Southampton, Pa. Died Oct. 11, 2001.

CZARNIK, MARVIN RAY, retired aerospace engineer; b. St. Louis, Sept. 19, 1932; s. Stanley Bernard and Laura (Kramer) C.; m. Mary Ann Miller, Nov. 26, 1955; children: Kristy Kay, Carol Lee. BSEE, Washington U., St. Louis, 1954; extension student, U. Mo., 1964. Automatic flight control for aircraft McDonnell-Douglas Corp., St. Louis, 1955-60, developer guidence system Gemini space rendezvous, 1960-68, Skylab program devel., 1968-72, Space Shuttle software devel., 1972-78, mgr. software engring., 1978-89, dir. mission planning spl. programs, 1989-92; retired, 1992. Home: Deer Park, Tex. Deceased.

DACRE OF GLANTON, Baron See TREVOR-ROPER, H(UGH) R(EDWALD)

DAELHOUSEN, SCOTT GLENN, construction executive, photographer; b. Warren, Pa., Apr. 17, 1950; s. Glenn Lester and Ruth Elizabeth (Brocklehurst) D.; m. Brenda Althea Bachman, Oct. 19, 1974; children: Kim Noel, Eric Scott. BS, Pa. State U., 1972, MCE, 1977. Registered profl. engr. Pa., N.J., Fla. Field engr. Chantilly (Va.) Constrn. Corp., 1972-74, Herbert R. Imbt, Inc., State Coll., Pa., 1976-81; constrn. engr. Stone & Webster Engring. Corp., Boston, 1982-90; constrn. mgr. Gilbert Commonwealth, Inc., Reading, Pa., from 1990. Prin. author for U.S. Doe. Stone & Webster Engring. Corp., Boston, 1987-90. Photographer: (color photos) New Orleans View, 1984 (1st pl.), Camden, Maine, 1989, (2nd pl.), Christmas Lights, 1990 (2nd pl.), Cover Photo 25th Anniversary Issue, 1985; (b&w photos) NMP2, 1985, (hon. mention), NMP2, 1989 (1st pl.). Mem. Nat. Soc. Prof. Engrs., Pa. State Alumni Assn. (life), Delta Mu Sigma (v.p. 1969-70), Chi Epsilon (treas.). Baptist. Avocations: photography, swimming, scuba diving. Home: Reading, Pa. Died Feb. 9, 2002.

DAHL, CURTIS, English literature educator; b. New Haven, July 6, 1920; s. George and Elizabeth Eudora (Curtis) D.; m. Mary Huntington Kellogg, Nov. 15, 1952; children: Julia Curtis (dec.), Winthrop Huntington Kellogg. BA, Yale U., 1941, MA, 1942, PhD, 1945. Dir. fellowships, asst. to editor Dodd, Mead & Co., 1944-46; instr. English, U. Tenn., 1946-48; mem. faculty Wheaton Coll., Norton, Mass., 1948—91, prof., 1958-91, Samuel Valentine Cole prof. English lit., 1966-91, Samuel Valentine Cole prof. emeritus, 1991—2004. Vis. prof. So. Ill. U., 1964, 66, 70, U. Wash., 1967, Brown U., 1970; vis. lectr. in English Bridgewater State Coll., 1992-98. Author: Robert Montgomery Bird, 1963; editor: There She Blows: A Narrative of a Whaling Voyage, 1971, Around the World in 500 Days, 1999; contbr. articles to profl. jours. Fence-viewer Town of Norton, 1964-77, 1989-2004, selectman, 1970-73; chmn. Norton Historic Dist. Commn., 1975-87, 1990-99, Norton Hist. Commn., 1976-80. Carnegie fellow Harvard U., 1954-55; Guggenheim fellow, 1957-58; Fulbright prof. U. Oslo, 1965-66 Mem. MLA, Nat. Assn. of Scholars, Melville Soc., Boston Browning Soc., Presbyn. Hist. Soc. Republican. Home: Norton, Mass. Died Apr. 5, 2004.

DAHL, DONALD DOUGLAS, newswriter; b. Savage, Mont., Mar. 25, 1920; s. Alfred Kristian and Elsie (McDonell) D.; m. Helen Copeland, Oct. 6, 1946 (div. 1978); children: Christine Dahl, Karen McKenzie. BA, U. N.D., 1941; MS, Columbia U., 1950. Supr. Fed. Writers Project, Bismarck, N.D., 1941; extension editor U. N.H., Durham, 1946-49; reporter Journal Bulletin, Providence, 1950; correspondent United Press, Manila, The Philippines, 1951-53; copy editor, wire editor, news editor The Albuquerque Tribune, 1954-82. Lt. USNR, 1942-46, PTO. Mem. Beta Theta Pi. Presbyterian. Home: Albuquerque, N.Mex. Died Oct. 15, 1999.

DAHLSTEN, DONALD LEE, entomology educator; b. Clay Center, Nebr., Dec. 8, 1933; s. Leonard Harold and Shirley B. (Courtright) D.; m. Reva D. Wilson, Sept. 19, 1959 (div.); children: Dia Lee, Andrea; m. Janet Clair Winner, Aug. 7, 1965; stepchildren: Karen Rae, Michael Allen. BS, U. Calif., Davis, 1956; MS, U. Calif., Berkeley, 1960, PhD, 1963. Asst. prof. Los Angeles State Coll., 1962-63; asst. entomologist U. Calif., Berkeley, 1963-65, lectr., 1965-68, asst. prof., 1968-69, assoc. prof., 1969-74, prof. entomology, from 1974, chmn. divsn. Biol. Control, 1980-88;, 1990-91; chmn. dept. cons. and resource studies U. Calif., Berkeley, 1989-91, dir. lab. biol. control, 1992-94; assoc. dean instrn. and student affairs Coll. Natural Resources, U. Calif., Berkeley, 1996—2002. Vis. prof. Yale Sch. Forestry and Environ. Studies, 1980-81, Integrated Pest Mgmt. Team People's Republic China, 1980, 81.. Mem. AAAS, Am. Inst. Biol. Scis. (vis. prof., lectr. 1970-71), Entomol. Soc. Am., Entomol. Soc. Can., Soc. Am. Foresters. Home: Berkeley, Calif. Died Sept. 3, 2003.

DALEY, ARTHUR STUART, retired humanities educator; b. Osceola, N.Y., Sept. 16, 1908; s. Kieran A. and Mary (Adams) D.; m. Jean Abendroth, Aug. 29, 1942; 1 child, Arthur Stuart. AB with honors in English, Syracuse U., 1932; postgrad., Harvard U., 1932-33; PhD, Yale U., 1942. Instr. English Syracuse (N.Y.) U., 1935-37, Ind. U., 1946-47, UCLA, 1947-49; asst. prof. English U. Nev., 1949-54; prof., chmn. dept. Coe Coll., 1954-59; prof. Drake U., Des Moines, 1959-76, chmn. dept., 1959-67, coord. humanities div., 1967-75, prof. emeritus, from 1976. Co-author: Private Charity in England, 1747-57, 1938; contbr. articles, especially on Shakespeare, to profl. jours.; contbr. articles to rev. Norton crit. edit. Wuthering Heights (Emily Bronte), Shakespeare Studies XXI, The Upstart Crow XIV. Served to lt. col. AUS, 1941-46, 51-53; lt. col. AUS ret. Decorated Bronze Star; hon. grant of English armorial bearings, 1978; mem. by right Ancient and Hon. Arty. Co. Mass. Mem. MLA, Soc. Mayflower Descs., Shakespeare Assn., The Mediaeval Acad. Am., Am. Brontë Soc., Theta Alpha Phi, Sigma Nu. Home: San Diego, Calif. Died June 18, 2003.

DALLAS, DONALD EDWARD, JR., corporate executive; b. East Cleveland, Ohio, Sept. 17, 1931; s. Donald Edward and Zella Gwynn (Rogers) D.; m. Marianne Mock, May 25, 1968 (dec. 1981); children: Susan, Benjamin. BS, U. Cin., 1954; postgrad., MIT, 1958-61. Rsch. engr. Ludlow Corp., Needham Heights, Mass., 1961-63; sales rep. J. M. Huber Corp., Westwood, Mass., 1963-69, mktg. mgr. Edison, N.J., 1969-73; pres. D.E. Dallas & Assocs. Inc., Balt., Wellesley, Mass. and Freeport, Maine, from 1962; mktg. mgr. Allis-Chalmers Corp., West Allis, Wis., 1974-87; pres. Hoult Engring. & Mfg. Co., Wayland, Mass., 1987-88; mktg. mgr. Allis Mineral Systems (formerly Boliden Allis, Inc.), West Allis, Wis., 1987-92; pres., CEO Electro/Magnetic Solutions, Inc., Denver, 1992-95, Advanced Environ. Sys., Inc., South Freeport, Maine, 1995-96; vice-chmn. AES Tech. Corp., South Freeport, from 1996; pres., COO AES Technologies, Inc., South Freeport, from 1996, AEST R&D, Inc., South Freeport, from 1996. Lectr. mktg. MIT, 1988-92. Contbr. articles to profl. jours. With USNR, 1954-64. Mem. ASME, Engrs. Soc. Western Pa. Home: Framingham, Mass. Died July 5, 2000.

DALY, JOSEPH RAYMOND, advertising executive; b. N.Y.C., May 14, 1918; s. William C. and Mary (Hendrick) D.; m. Elizabeth R. Schulte, Apr. 19, 1947 (div.); children: Dorothy E., Suzanne J., Peter J., Timothy J., Mark, Andrew, Jennifer; m. Kathy Christy, Nov. 5, 1988. AB, Fordham U., 1940. With John A. Cairns (advt.), 1946-49; with DDB Needham Worldwide DDB Needham Worldwide, Inc. (formerly Doyle Dane Bernbach), N.Y.C., 1949-89; sr. v.p., mgmt. supr. DDB Needham Worldwide, Inc. (formerly Doyle Dan Bernbach Internat.), N.Y.C., 1959-69, pres., 1968-74, chmn. bd., 1974-86, chmn. exec. com., 1986-88; chmn. Vitafort Internat. Inc., N.Y.C., 1986-93. Served to lt. comdr Air Corps, USN, 1940-46, PTO. Decorated Navy Cross, Purple Heart, Air medal. Mem.: Rockefeller Ctr. Luncheon, Turf and Field (N.Y.C.); Marco Polo, Ocean Reef. Died Dec. 6, 2003.

DAMRON, MARVIN ARTHUR, principal; b. Keokuk, Iowa, Sept. 14, 1936; s. Arthur Glenn and Elizabeth Minnett (Edwards) D.; m. Patricia Ann Rickert, July 28, 1957; children: Timothy, Michael, Deborah, Patrick; foster children: Lan Tu, Cuong Quach. Student, Western Ill. U., 1954-56; BS in Agrl. Edn., U. Ill., 1958, MEd, 1963, postgrad., from 1992. Cert. secondary tchr. and adminstr., Ill. Vocat. tchr. agriculture Hamilton (Ill.) Community Schs., 1958-61; tchr. Kewanee (Ill.) Commmunity Sch. Dist. 229, 1962-67, prin. high sch., from 1967. Presentor in field. Contbr. article to pubs. Exec. officer Kewanee Drug & Alcohol Task Force, 1983—; cons. Lt. Gov.'s Com. to Serve Ill., Chgo., 1991-92; mem. Legis. Com. on Alcohol Problems, Springfield, Ill., 1992, 93; chairperson Legis. Adv. Com., Moline, Ill., 1992, 93; bd. dirs. Ill. Ch. Action on Alcohol Problems, Springfield, 1992—, Youth Svcs. Planning Bd., Henry, Rock Island and Mercer Counties, Ill. Sgt. U.S. Army, 1954-63. Grantee U.S. Dept. Edn., 1989, Lt. Gov.'s Office Ill., 1992. Mem. Nat. Assn. Secondary Sch. Prins., Ill. Prins. Assn. (state parliamentarian 1988—), Ill. Assn. Future Homemakers Am. (hon., Outstanding Svc. award 1987), Kewanee C. of C. (bd. dirs., chairperson edn. com. 1991—), Henry County Youth Svc. Bur. (bd. dirs. 1990—), Kiwanis (Legion of Honor 1991, treas. 1993), Mackinaw Valley Canoe Club, John Deere Two Cylinder Club. Methodist. Avocations: train collecting, traveling. Home: Kewanee, Ill. Died Oct. 10, 2000.

DANFORTH, FRANCES MUELLER (MRS. WILLIAM PAUL DANFORTH), civic worker; b. Austin, Tex., Mar. 23, 1914; d. Rudolph George and Laura Emma (Von Boeckmann) Mueller; B.J., U. Tex., 1935, B.A., 1936; M.S., Columbia U., 1938; m. William Paul Danforth, Aug. 16, 1942; children— William Paul, Douglas Mueller, Donald Lee. Grader dept. journalism U. Tex., Austin, 1934; asst. dir. Interscholastic League Press Bur., U. Tex., 1936-37; asst. editor Alcade, monthly alumni mag., 1936-37, 38-42; editor Star Points, nat. papers Delta Delta Delta Chgo., 1968-70; now buyer, bookkeeper Danforth's Antiques and Gifts, Austin. Pres., Austin Symphony League, 1967-68; state v.p. Tex. Women's Assn. Symphony Orchs., 1970; pres. Austin Vol. Bur., 1966-68; bd. dirs., sec. USO, 1971-72; bd. dirs. Symphony Orch. Soc.; bd. dirs., sec. Cen-Tex. chpt. ARC, pres. Altenheim, 1961-62. Mem. Women in Communications, Mortar Board (Austin alumna pres. 1978—) Delta Delta Delta, Lutheran (pres. ch. women 1972-74). Clubs: Settlement, Lawyers Wives (mem. bd., sec. 1973-74), Woman's (sec. 1972-74, v.p. 1977-79) (all Austin). Home: Austin, Tex. Deceased.

DANNEHY, JOSEPH F. state supreme court justice; Judge Conn. Circuit Ct., 1961-65; chief judge Conn. Ct. Common Pleas, 1965-68; judge Conn. Superior Ct., 1968-84; chief presiding judge Conn. Appellate Ct., 1984-85; justice Conn. Supreme Ct., Hartford, 1985-87; state referee Conn. Superior Ct., Hartford, 1987—2003. Died Dec. 16, 2003.

DANTON, JOSEPH PERIAM, librarian, educator; b. Palo Alto, Calif., July 5, 1908; s. George Henry and Annina (Periam) D. PhD, U. Chgo., 1935. Libr., assoc. prof. bibliography Temple U., Phila., 1936-46; dean Sch. Librarianship, U. Calif.-Berkeley, 1946-61, assoc. prof., 1946-47, prof., 1947-76, prof. emeritus, 1976—2002, J. Periam Danton dean, prof., 1946-76. Vis. prof. Grad. Libr. Sch., U. Chgo., 1942, Columbia, 1946; vis. lectr. U. Toronto, 1963, Univs. of Belgrade, Ljubljana, Novi Sad, Zagreb, 1965, U. B.C., 1968, 79, McGill U., 1969, U. P.R., 1970, U. Md., 1977, U. N.C., 1977, U. Tex., 1979, Hebrew U., Jerusalem, 1965, 85; Fulbright rsch. scholar, Germany, 1960-61, Austria, 1964-65; surveyor and cons. numerous libraries; UNESCO Libr. Cons., Jamaica, 1968; del. Internat. Fedn. Libr. Assns. meeting, 1939-1972; Ford Found. cons. on libraries in SE Asia (with R. C. Swank), 1963; hon. research fellow U. London, 1974-75. Author various works, 1946-99. Served as lt. USNR, 1942-45, PTO. Recipient Berkeley citation, 1976, Beta Phi Mu award, 1983; Carnegie fellow, 1933-35, Guggenheim fellow, 1971. Mem. Assn. Am. Libr. Schs. (pres. 1949-50), Internat. Fedn. Libr. Assns. (chmn. com. libr. edn. 1967-72). Democrat. Died Nov. 12, 2002.

DANZIGER, PAULA, writer; b. Washington, U.S., Aug. 18, 1944; Tchr. jr. high sch. Author: The Cat Ate My Gymsuit, 1974 (N.J. Inst. of Tech. award 1976, Mass. Children's Book award Edn. Dept. of Salem State Coll. 1979, Nene award Hawaii Assn. of School Librs. and Hawaii Libr. Assn. 1980, Children's Choice award Internat. Reading Assn. and Children's Book Coun. 1980), The Pistachio Prescription, 1978 (Children's Book of Yr. citation Child Study Assn. 1978, Mass. Children's Book award Edn. Dept. of Salem State Coll. 1979, Children's Choice award Internat. Reading Assn. and Children's Book Coun. 1979, Nene award Hawaii Assn. of School Librs. and Hawaii Libr. Assn. 1980, Ariz. Young Reader award 1983), Can You Sue Your Parents for Malpractice?, 1979 (Children's Choice award Internat. Reading Assn. and Children's Book Coun. 1980, N.J. Inst. of Tech. award 1980, Land of Enchantment award N. Mex. Libr. Assn. 1982), There's a Bat in Bunk Five, 1980 (Children's Choice award Internat. Reading Assn. and Children's Book Coun. 1981, CRABbery award Prince George's County Meml. Librs. 1982, Young Reader's medal 1984), The Divorce Express, 1982 (Children's Choice award Internat. Reading Assn. and Children's Book Coun. 1983, Parents' Choice award for lit. Parents' Choice Found. 1982, Woodward Park School Annual Book award 1983, S.C. Young Adult Book award S.C. Assn. of School Librs. 1985), It's an Aardvark-Eat-Turtle World, 1985 (Parents' Choice award for lit. Parents' Choice Found. 1985, Children's Book of Yr. citation Child Study Assn. 1985), This Place Has No Atmosphere, 1986, Remember Me to Harold Square, 1987, Everyone Else's Parents Said Yes, 1989, Make Like a Tree and Leave, 1990, Not for a Billion Gazillion Dollars, 1992, Earth to Matthew, 1992, Thames Doesn't Rhyme with James, 1994, Amber Brown Is Not a Crayon, 1994, You Can't Eat Your Chicken Pox, Amber Brown Goes Fourth, 1995, Seguiremos Siendo Amigos, 1995, Amber Brown Wants Extra Credit, Amber Brown Sees Red, 1997, Snail Mail No More, 2000, What A Trip Amber Brown, 2001, Its

Justin Time Amber Brown, 2001, Its A Fair Day Amber Brown, 2003, Get Ready for Second Grade, Amber Brown, 2003, Amber Brown Is Green With Envy, 2004. Died July 8, 2004.

D'AREZZO, KAREN WILLIAMS, science writer; b. Royal Oak, Mich., Mar. 29, 1950; d. Winston Conway and Margaret Jane (Wilcox) Williams; m. Alfred John D'Arezzo Jr., Aug. 28, 1971; children: Andrew Williams, James John, Daniel Wilkin. Student, U. Wis., 1968-71; BS in Comms., U. Tenn., 1972. Cert. editor in the life scis. Assoc. campus dir. Campus Crusade for Christ, Johnson City, Tex., 1972-74, Austin, Tex., 1974-75, Boston, 1975-77; sr. editor devel. office Trinity Coll., Chgo., 1977-81; tech. writer Oak Ridge (Tenn.) Nat. Lab., 1982-87; sr. med. writer Biotech. Svcs. Inc., Little Rock, 1990-92; cons. med. writer U. Ark. for Med. Scis., Little Rock, from 1992, sr. med. writer, 1993-94; dir. of grants and sci. publs. Ark. Cancer Rsch. Ctr., Little Rock, from 1994. Mem. Am. Med. Writers Assn. Presbyterian. Died July 27, 2000.

DARLING, RALPH CLEMENT, vascular surgeon; b. Richmond, Calif., Aug. 28, 1927; s. Ralph Clement and Ruth (Alger) D.; m. Elaine Cicma, Mar. 25, 1948; children—Cynthia, Clement, Wendy, Beth. AB, Boston U., 1949, MD cum laude, 1953. Diplomate: Am. Bd. Surgery, Am. Bd. Thoracic Surgery. Intern Mass. Gen. Hosp., 1953-54; asst. in pathology Children's Hosp., Boston, 1955; resident in surgery Children's Med. Center, Boston, 1955, cons. vascular surgery, 1969—; asst. resident, then clin. asst. surgery Mass. Gen. Hosp., 1956-59, chief vascular clinic, 1969-79, sr. vascular surgeon, 1979—. Chief resident in thoracic and cardiac surgery, asst. in surgery Baylor U. Hosp., Houston, 1959-60; mem. faculty Harvard U. Med. Sch., 1964—, asso. clin. prof. surgery, 1975—; cons. M.I.T., USPHS, USAF, Walter Reed Army Med. Center; cons. Molecular Biology, Jefferson Med. Coll., Phila. Contbr. numerous articles to med. jours. Served with USMC, 1945-46. Mem. AMA, Am. Thoracic Soc., A.C.P., Am. Fedn. Clin. Research, Mass. Med. Soc., New Eng. Cardiovascular Soc., Boston Surg. Soc., Soc. Vascular Surgery, Am. Coll. Chest Surgeons, Am. Geriatric Soc., Am. Assn. Surgery Trauma, New Eng. Surg. Soc., Internat. Cardiovascular Soc., Pan-Pacific Surg. Assn., Am. Trauma Soc. (a founder), Am. Heart Assn. (exec. council cardiovascular surgery), Assn. Advanced Med. Instrumentation, New Eng. Soc. Vascular Surgery (pres., founder 1980), Royal Soc. Medicine, Am. Surg. Assn., Soc. Internat. Chirurgie, Alpha Omega Alpha. Home: Cataumet, Mass. Died Jun. 26, 1999.

DASH, SAMUEL, lawyer, educator; b. Camden, N.J., Feb. 27, 1925; s. Joseph and Ida (Weinberg) D.; m. Sara Goldhirsh, July 14, 1946; children: Judy, Rachel. BS, Temple U., 1947; JD cum laude, Harvard, 1950; LL.D. (hon.), Fairfield (Conn.) U., 1974, Georgetown U., 1983; PS.D. (hon.), Temple U., 1978. Bar: Ill. 1950, Pa. 1952, U.S. Supreme Ct. 1955, D.C. 1978. Teaching fellow Northwestern, 1950-51; trial atty., criminal div. U.S. Dept. Justice, Washington, 1951-52; asst. dist. atty., chief appeals div. Phila., 1952-54; 1st asst. dist. atty., 1954-55; dist. atty., 1955-56; partner firm Blank and Rudenko, Phila., 1956-58, Dash & Levy, Phila., 1958-63; dir. Phila. Council Community Advancement, 1963-65; prof. law, dir. Inst. Criminal Law and Procedure Georgetown U. Law Sch., Washington, 1965—2004; chief counsel U.S. Senate select com. presdl. campaign activities (Senate Watergate com.), 1973-74; cons. Ford Found., 1958-63, Nat. Assn. Attys. Gen., 1971-73, Law Reform Com., Australia, 1977-81; spl. cons. on Cerro Maravilla investigation Senate of P.R., 1983-92; chief counsel impeachment inquiry Senate of Alaska, 1985; ethics counsel Office of Ind. Coun. in Whitewater Matter, 1994—98. Exec. dir. D.C. Jud. Conf. on Mental Disorders and the Law, 1965-70; dir. Divi Hotels, Aruba, 1980-89. Author: The Eavesdroppers, 1959, Chief Counsel, 1976; Contbr. articles to profl. jours. Mem. Human Relations Commn. Phila., 1957-65; exec. com. Community Relations Council, Phila., 1960-65; bd. dirs. Hebrew U., Jerusalem, 1975, Fedn. Jewish Agys., Phila., 1960-65, Albert Einstein Med. Center, 1962-65, Internat. League Human Rights, 1972-2004; chmn. trustees Pub. Defenders Service D.C., 1967-76. Served to 2d lt. USAAF, 1943-46, ETO. Recipient civic awards various civic orgns.; Annual award Nat. Assn. Criminal Def. Lawyers, 1959; Commendation certificate Am. Bar Assn., 1971; others.; Sr. Fulbright scholar U. Melbourne, Australia, 1977 Mem. ABA (standing com. on ethics and profl. responsibility 1984-89, chmn. criminal justice sect. 1971, chmn. spl. com. on criminal justice 1986-89, mem. spl. com. on drug crisis), Am. Law Inst., Pa. Bar Endowment (dir. nationwide investigation wiretapping 1956-59), Nat. Assn. Criminal Lawyers (pres. 1958), B'nai B'rith (Phila. regional chmn. Anti-Defamation League 1960-63, nat. commr. 1960-63) Home: Chevy Chase, Md. Died May 29, 2004.

DASHNER, DAVID PATTERSON, bank investment officer, educator; b. Waco, Tex., July 30, 1942; s. Curtis Warnell and Betty Jo (Harridine) D.; m. Judith Ann DelPezzo, Jan. 14, 1967 (div. Dec. 1982); m. Marina Antropow Cramer, Oct. 9, 1983; children: Eric Michael, Kristin Joanna; stepchildren: Tanya Cramer, Michael John Cramer. BA, Austin Coll., 1964. CLU; ChFC. Agt., sales mgr. Phoenix Mutual Life, West Orange, N.J., 1981-85; agt., trainer Met Life, Lyndhurst, N.J., 1985-86; fin. planner Benefit Security Planners, Westwood, N.J., 1986-87; fin. planner, trainer MONY Agy., Edison, N.J., 1987-89; fin. counselor CIGNA/MarinEdge, N.Y.C., 1989-93; trust, investment bus. devel. staff Marine Midland Bank, N.Y.C., from 1993. Adj. prof. CFP program Pace U., N.Y.C., 1995-98, NYU, N.Y.C., 1997, Baruch Coll., N.Y.C., 1998. Editor (newsletter) Lions Club, 1986-89; contbr. articles to profl. jours. Cub scout leader Boy Scouts Am., South Orange, N.J., 1974-80, asst. scout master, Rochelle Park, N.J., 1982-84; bd. mem. Mainstreet Montclair, N.J., 1986-89; bd. advisor New Atlantic Ind. Booksellers Assn., Phila., 1990-98. Mem. Internat. Assn. for Fin. Planning (N.Y. chpt. editor, pub. The New York Planner 1994-97, v.p. devel. 1997-98). Democrat. Presbyterian. Avocations: reading, writing, gardening, grandchildren. Home: Nutley, NJ. Died May 29, 2002.

DAVENPORT, FOUNTAIN ST. CLAIR, electronic engineer; b. Harmony, N.C., Jan. 16, 1914; s. Dennis F. and Margaret E. (Winfield) D.; m. Jane Helena Hermann, June 11, 1948 (dec. Sept. 1973); 1 child, Sylvia Jane; m. Joyce Allen Huff, Mar. 16, 1974 (dec. 1983); m. Florence Cereceda Ryan, May 19, 1985 (dec. Sept. 1997). BEE, U. Miami, 1950; postgrad., U. Balt.; MS, Fla. Inst. Tech., 1970. Engr. Bendix Aviation Corp., Towson, Md., 1951-53; project engr. Vitro Labs., Eglin AFB, Fla., 1953-55; engr. A RCA Missile Test Project, Patrick AFB, Fla., 1955-60; supr. radar engring., guided missiles range divsn. Pan Am. World Airways, Inc., Patrick AFB, 1960-65; sr. systems engr. Aerospace Svcs. Divsn., Patrick AFB, 1965-77; pvt. practice cons. engring., 1977-82; pres. Davenport Enterprises, Inc., 1982-88. Cons. N.R.C., Churchill Rsch. Range, Man., Can., 1966-67; faculty Fla. Inst. Tech., 1958-60, 62-63, mem. edn. com., 1964, adj. faculty physics and aerospace scis., 1979-85. Life mem. Friends Melbourne Libr. With USN, 1934-37, USNR, 1937-45. Mem. IEEE (life), Am. Def. Preparedness Assn. (life), Amnesty Internat., Masons (32 deg.). Home: Melbourne, Fla. Died Aug. 7, 2002.

DAVID, GUY ALBERT, electrical engineer; b. Thiais, Paris, Mar. 29, 1932; arrived in US, 1985, naturalized, 1997; s. Emile and Suzanne (Laine) D.; m. Nicole Marguerite Cossin, Apr. 16, 1955 (div. Oct. 1985); children: Gilles, Bernard, Anne, Odile; m. Evelyne Lyliane Brenner, Jan. 5, 1986. Degree in engring., U. Caen, France, 1953; MA, U. Paris, 1963, PhD, 1967. Engr. Telecomms. Radio Electriques et Telephoniques, Paris, 1955—66, head advanced studies, 1967—75, dir. mil. comm., 1975—85, Global Positioning Sys. specialist, 1978—85, Sci. Application Internat. Corp., Torrance, Calif., from 1980; dep. mgr., Global Positions Sys. specialist Magnavox, Torrance, Calif., 1985—88; dir. engring. Amcomp, Torrance, Calif., 1988—93, Global Positioning Sys. specialist, 1988—2001, sr. engr., 1993—2001; sr. systems engr., Global Positioning specialist Sci. Application Internat. Corp., Torrance, Calif., from 2001. Advisor French Civil Aviation del. Internat. Civil Aviation Orgn., Montreal, Canada, 1972; cons. European Space Agy., 1974—76; mem. NATO Indsl. Adv. Group Subgroup 5, 1976—85; corr. Internat. Radio Consultative Com., 1976—85; mem. Internat. Schiffs-Studien Orgn., 1984—85; lectr. in field. Author: (book) Radio Communications; co-author: (book) Space Communications; contbr. articles to trade and tech. jours., mags., and procs.; holder 20 patents. Decorated Chevalier de l'Ordre du Mérite; recipient Grand Prix de l'Electronique Gen. Ferrié. Mem. IEEE, Inst. Navigation, Soc. des Electriciens et des Electroniciens, Anciens de la Radio et de l'Electronique. Avocations: music, golf, bicycling. Home: Stockbridge, Ga. Died Nov. 5, 2003.

DAVIDSON, DONALD HERBERT, philosophy educator; b. Springfield, Mass., Mar. 6, 1917; s. Clarence Herbert and Grace (Anthony) D.; m. Nancy Hirschberg, Apr. 4, 1975 (dec. 1979); 1 child, by previous marriage, Elizabeth Ann; m. Marcia Cavell, July 3, 1984. BA, Harvard U., 1939, MA, 1941, PhD, 1949; DDL (hon.), LittD (hon.), Oxford U., 1995; PhD (hon.), Stockholm U., 1999. Instr. philosophy Queen's (N.Y.) Coll., 1947-50; from asst. prof. to prof. Stanford (Calif.) U., 1951-67; prof. Princeton (N.J.) U., 1967-70, chmn. dept. philosophy, 1968-70, prof., 1970-76, Rockefeller U., N.Y.C., 1970-76, U. Chgo., 1976-81, U. Calif., Berkeley, from 1981. Apptd. Willis S. and Marion Slusser prof., vis. prof. Tokyo U., 1955; Gavin David Young lectr. U. Adelaide, 1968; John Locke lectr. Oxford (Eng.) U., 1970; vis. prof. U. Sydney, 1968, U. Pitts., 1972, U. Capetown, 1980, U. Venice, 1991, U. Rome, 1993, law & philosophy NYU, 1993; John Dewey lectr. U. Minn., 1975; Matchette Found. lectr. U. Wis., 1976; Carus lectr., 1980; Hägerstrom lectr., 1980; Josè Gaos vis. lectr. U. Mex., 1980; George Eastman vis. prof. Balliol Coll., Oxford, 1984-85; Kant lectr. Stanford U., 1986; S.J. Keeling Meml. lectr. Greek philosophy Univ. Coll., U. London, 1986; Fulbright Disting. lectr., India, 1985-86; Selfridge lectr. Lehigh U., 1986; Thalheimer lectr. Johns Hopkins U., Balt., 1987, David Ross Boyd lectr. U. Okla., 1988, John Dewey lectr. Columbia U., 1989, Alfred North Whitehead lectr. Harvard U., 1990, Heisenberg lectr., Munich, 1981; Kant lectr. U. Munich, 1993, Spinoza lectr. Jerusalem U., 1993, Grambieh and Orr lectr. Dartmouth Coll., 1993, Alan Donagan meml. lectr. Notre Dame, 1994, Josep Ferrater Mora lectr., Girona Spain, 1994; Franquini chair lectr. U. Leuven, Belgium, 1994; Jean Nicod lectr. Caen & Paris, 1995; Shearman Meml. lectr. Univ. Coll., London, 1995; Hill vis. prof. U. Minn., 1997; Hermes lectr. U. Perugia, 2001; Francesco Sanches lectr. U. Lisbon, 2001. Co-Author: (with Patrick Suppes) Decision Making: An Experimental Approach, 1957; author: Essays on Actions and Events, 1980, Inquiries into Truth and Interpretation, 1983; co-editor: (with J. Hintikka) Words and Objections, 1969, (with Gilbert Harman) Semantics for Natural Language, 1970, The Logic of Grammar, 1975, Subjective, Intersubjective, Objective, 2001; mem. editl. bd. Philosophia, 1970—, Theoretical Linguistics, 1973—, Theory and Decision, 1974—, Erkenntnis, 1974—, Current Commentary in the Behavioral and Brain Sciences, 1976—. Lt. (s.g.) USNR, 1942-45, MTO. Recipient Hegel prize City of Stuttgart, Fed. Republic Germany, 1991; Teschemacher fellow in classics and philosophy, 1939-41; Rockefeller fellow in humanities, 1945-46; Rockefeller fellow for research, 1948; Ford Faculty fellow, 1953-54; Am. Council Learned Socs. fellow, 1958-59, Center Advanced Study Behavioral Scis. fellow, 1969-70, Guggenheim fellow, 1973-74, All Souls Coll. Oxford U. fellow, 1973-74, Vis. fellow Rsch. Sch. Social Scis., Australian Nat. U., 1977, Hon. Rsch. fellow Univ. Coll., London, 1978; Sherman Fairchild Disting. scholar Calif. Inst. Tech., 1989; Rsch. grant NSF, 1964-65, 68. Fellow Am. Acad. Arts and Scis., AAAS, Brit. Acad. (corr.); mem. Am. Philos Assn. (sec. Pacific Coast div. 1956-59, v.p. 1961, pres. Eastern div. 1973-74, pres. Pacific div. 1985-86), Am. Philos Soc., Institute Internacional de Philosophie, Norwegian Acad. Sci. and Letters, AAUP. Home: Berkeley, Calif. Died Aug. 30, 2003.

DAVIES, TUDOR THOMAS, federal agency administrator; b. Bridgend, Glamorgan, U.K., Sept. 3, 1938; came to U.S., 1966; s. John Glyn and Iris (Thomas) D.; m. Elaine Fitzback, June 29, 1985; children: Clive L., Lee Carole, Christine Leone. Postdoctoral fellow Dalhousie U., Halifax, Can., 1964-66; asst. prof. U. S.C., Columbia, 1966-68, assoc. prof., 1968-73; dir. Great Lakes Program EPA, Mich., 1972-75, dep. dir. Gulf Breeze Rsch. Lab., 1975-79, dir. Chesapeake Bay program, 1977-83, dir. Narragansett Rsch. Lab., 1979-83, dir. office marine and estuarine protection, 1984-91, dir. office sci. and tech., 1991—2001. Home: Springfield, Va. Died Nov. 27, 2003.

DAVIS, BRUCE HENRY, small business owner, copywriter; b. Houston, Dec. 5, 1948; s. Winston Hardie and Bette Jo (Baker) D. BJ with spl. honors, U. Tex., 1971. Copywriter Rives Dyke & Co., Houston, 1971-73; tchr. asst. U. Tex., Austin, 1973-74; copywriter Metzdorf Advt., Houston, 1974; owner, creative dir. Bruce Henry & Davis Advt., Houston, from 1974. Author: Dalhart Windberg, In the Path of the Masters, 1978, The World of Charles Frace, 1982; editor: Charles Frace-Nature's Window, 1992. Recipient Best of Show Copy award Houston Advt. Club, 1976, 8 Gold medals, 1974-81, Gold medal Art Dirs. Club of Houston, 1982. Mem. Art Dirs. Club of Houston (bd. dirs. 1976-84, pres. 1984-85). Home: Houston, Tex. Died Apr. 27, 2001.

DAVIS, CORDELIA, cardiac rehabilitation nurse; b. Knoxville, Tenn., May 17, 1944; d. Vaughn E. Sr. and Juanita B. Smith; m. Jack T. Davis, Dec. 16, 1967; 1 child, Heather LeAnn. Diploma, U. Tenn., 1966. RN, Tenn. Staff nurse cardiac rehab. U. Tenn. Meml. Hosp., Knoxville, 1966-69, asst. head nurse, 1970-76, head nurse, 1977-90, admitting office nurse, from 1990. Active ARC. Award recipient Mended Hearts. Home: Knoxville, Tenn. Died Apr. 7, 2000.

DAVIS, DONALD A. surgeon; b. Danbury, Conn., Aug. 29, 1908; MD, Columbia U., 1940. Diplomate Am. Bd. Surgery. Intern Bellevue Med. Ctr., N.Y.C., 1940-41; resident in surgery Bellevue Hosp. Ctr., N.Y.C., 1942, 46-48; pvt. practice; prof. clin. surgery NYU. Mem. Am. acad. Pediats.; mem. AMA, Ea. Surg. Soc., Internat. Surg. Soc., Pan-Pacific Surg. Assn. Home: Southbury, Conn. Died Nov. 12, 1999.

DAVIS, EDGAR KEITH, anesthesiologist; b. North Loup, Nebr., Nov. 18, 1909; MD, U. Colo., 1944. Diplomate Am. Bd. Anesthesiology. Intern St. Luke's Hosp., Denver, 1944-45; resident Colo. Med. Ctr., Denver, 1963-64. Fellow Am. Coll. Anesthesiology; mem. AMA, Am. Soc. Anesthesiologists. Home: Half Moon Bay, Calif. Died Dec. 21, 1999.

DAVIS, JAMES HORNOR, III, lawyer; b. Clarksburg, W.Va., Oct. 9, 1928; s. James Hornor II and Martha (Maxwell) D.; m. Ouida Caldwell, July 1, 1950; children—James Hornor IV, Lewis Caldwell. AB, Princeton U., 1950; LL.B., U. Va., 1953. Bar: W.Va. 1953. Ptnr. firm Preston & Davis, Charleston, 1953-65, Spilman, Thomas, Battle & Klostermeyer, Charleston, 1965-86; of counsel Campbell, Woods, Bagley, Emerson McNeer & Herndon, Charleston, from 1987. Mem. W.Va. Ho. of Dels., 1961-62, W.Va. Senate, 1963-66; pres. Dingess-Rum Properties, Inc. Hon. trustee Ea. Mineral Law Found. Served with USAF, 1953-55. Fellow ABA (life); mem. Am. Law Inst. (life), Am. Judicature Soc. (dir. 1978-81), W.Va. Jud. Coun. (chmn. 1973-81), W.Va. Bar Assn. (pres. 1985-86), Kanawha County Bar Assn., Nat. Coun. Coal Lessors (chmn. 1980—), W.Va. Mfrs. Assn. (chmn. 1973-75, hon. dir.) Democrat. Episcopalian. Home: White Sulphur Springs, W.Va. Died Mar. 4, 2004.

DAVIS, KENNETH SIDNEY, writer; b. Salina, Kans., Sept. 29, 1912; s. Charles DeForest and Lydia (Ericson) D.; m. Florence Marie Olenhouse, Feb. 19, 1937 (dec. Mar. 1987); m. Jean Stafford Dormer, July 21, 1990. BS, Kans. State U., 1934; MS, U. Wis.-Madison, 1935; Litt.D. (hon.), Assumption Coll., 1968. Reporter Daily Capital, Topeka, 1934; info. specialist Soil Conservation Service, USDA, Upper Miss. Valley region, 1935-40; editor plant newspaper Hercules Powder Co., 1942-43; war corrs. attached to SHAEF Doubleday and Co., N.Y.C., 1944; instr. journalism NYU, N.Y.C., 1945-47; spl. asst. to Milton S. Eisenhower, pres. Kans. State U. and chmn. U.S. Commn. for UNESCO, 1947-49; editor Newberry Library Bull., Newberry Library, Chgo., 1955-59; mem. personal staff Adlai E. Stevenson, Chgo., 1955-56. Author: (novels) In the Forests of the Night, 1942 (Friends of Am. Writers award 1943), The Years of the Pilgrimage, 1948, Morning in Kansas, 1952, (non-fiction) Soldier of Democracy, A Biography of Dwight Eisenhower, 1945, River on the Rampage, 1953, A Prophet in His Own

Country: The Triumphs and Defeats of Adlai E. Stevenson, 1957, The Hero: Charles A. Lindbergh and the American Dream, 1959, (with John A. Day) Water, The Mirror of Science, 1961, Experience of War: The U.S. in World War II, 1965, The Cautionary Scientists: Priestley, Lavoisier, and the Founding of Modern Chemistry, 1966, The Politics of Honor: A Biography of Adlai E. Stevenson, 1967, Eisenhower: American Hero, 1969, FDR: The Beckoning of Destiny, 1882-1928, 1972 (Soc. Am. Historians Francis Parkman prize 1973), Invincible Summer, An Intimate Portrait of the Roosevelts (based on the recollections of Marion Dickerman), 1974, Kansas: A Bicentennial History, 1976, FDR: The New York Years 1928-1933, 1985, FDR: The New Deal Years 1933-1937, 1986; FDR: Into the Storm 1937-40, 1993, FDR: The War President, 1940-1943, 1999; editor: The Paradox of Poverty in America, 1969, Arms, Industry, and America, 1971. Recipient Centennial award Kans. State U., 1963; Guggenheim fellow, 1974, 76. Fellow Soc. Am. Historians Clubs: Century (N.Y.C.). Avocations: gardening; hiking. Home: Manhattan, Kans. Died June 10, 1999.

DAVIS, MARTIN S. investment company executive; b. N.Y.C. Student, CUNY, NYU. With Samuel Goldwyn Prodns., N.Y.C., 1947-55, Allied Artists Corp., N.Y.C., 1955-58, Paramount Pictures Corp., N.Y.C., 1958-69, COO, 1966-69; sr. v.p. Paramount Communications Inc. (formerly Gulf & Western Inc.), N.Y.C., 1969-74, exec. v.p., 1974-83, chmn. exec. com., chief exec. officer, 1983-94; mng. ptnr. Wellspring Capital Mgmt. L.L.C., N.Y.C., from 1995. Bd. dirs. Nat. Amusements, Inc., parent co. Viacom, Inc. Chmn. N.Y. chpt. Nat. Multiple Sclerosis Soc., Montefiore Med. Ctr.; trustee Carnegie Hall, Thomas Jefferson Meml. Found., Inc. Died Dec., 1999.

DAVIS, MILTON WICKERS, JR., chemical engineer, educator; b. Frederick, Md., Apr. 5, 1923; s. Milton Wickers and Elizabeth Howard Griffith (Wood) D.; m. Roberta B. McIntyre, Dec. 18, 1948; 1 child, Gaither Griffith; m. Jane Crayton, May 21, 1955; 1 child, Richard Render; m. Harriett P. Ackerman, Dec. 24, 1977. B.E., Johns Hopkins U., 1943; MS, U. Calif.-Berkeley, 1949, PhD, 1951. Research asst. U. Calif. Radiation Lab., 1947-50; research engr. atomic energy div. duPont Co., Wilmington, Del., 1950-54; research supr. duPont Co. (Savannah River plant), Aiken, S.C., 1954-62; disting. chair prof. chem. engring. U. S.C., Columbia, 1962-88, disting. prof. emeritus in chem. engring., from 1988; cons. Nat. Inst. Standards and Tech. U.S. Dept. Commerce, from 1989. Contbr.: Chemical Processing of Nuclear Fuels, 1970; patentee catalyzed hydrogenation and dehydrogenation processes, 1985, catalysts for the synthesis of ammonia, 1986, extraction Cesium and Strontium from nuclear waste, 1988. Served to lt. USNR, 1943-46, PTO. Fellow Am. Inst. Chem. Engrs.; mem. Am. Chem. Soc., Md. Soc. War of 1812, Sea Pines Country Club, Sigma Xi, Delta Phi, Tau Beta Phi. Episcopalian. Died Mar. 3, 2003.

DAVIS, RAYMOND GILBERT, retired career officer, real estate developer; b. Fitzgerald, Ga., Jan. 13, 1915; s. Raymond Roy and Zelma Miranda (Tribby) D.; m. Willa Knox Heafner, Apr. 25, 1942; children: Raymond Gilbert, Jr., Gordon Miles, Willa Kay Kerr. BS in Chem. Engring. with honors, Ga. Sch. of Tech., 1938; postgrad., Marine Basic Sch., Phila., 1954, Marine Corps Sch., Quantico, Va., 1954-55, Nat. War Coll., Washington, 1959-60. Commd. 2d lt. USMC, 1938, advanced through grades to gen., 1971, served in USS Portland, 1939, exec. officer, battery comdr., 1941-42, exec. officer, 1942-43, commdg. officer, 1943-44, tactical insp. Marine Corps Schs., 1944-45, chief inf. sect. Marine Air-Inf. Sch., 1945-47, asst. chief of staff, 1947-49, insp.- instr., 1949-50, commdg. officer, 1950-51, action officer, 1951-53, asst. dir. Marine Sch. Quantico, 1955-57, asst. G-2 Washington, 1957-59; chief analysis br., mem. staff comdr. in chief U.S. Forces, Paris, 1960-63; asst. divsn. comdr. USMC, Okinawa, 1963-64, commdg. gen., 1963-64, asst. dir. pers., 1964-65, asst. chief of staff, 1965-68, dep. commdg., then commdg. gen., 1968-69, dep. edn. dir. Marine Corps Devel. and Edn. Command, 1969-70, commdg. gen., 1970-71, asst. comdt., 1971-72, ret., 1972; exec. v.p. Ga. C. of C., 1972-74; pres. RGMW, Inc., Stockbridge, Ga., from 1975. Apptd. by Pres. Bush as chmn. Korean War Vets. Meml. Adv. Bd.; chmn. Greater Atlanta Marine Corps Coordination Coun. Trustee, mem. bd. visitors Valley Forge Mil. Acad., Wayne, Pa., Marine Mil. Acad., Harlington, Tex., chmn. bd. trustees, 1991; bd. visitors Berry Coll., Mount Berry, Va., 1973-2003. Decorated Medal of Honor, Navy Cross, Disting. Svc. medal with 1 gold star, Silver Star with 1 gold star, Legion of Merit with 1 gold star, Bronze Star, Purple Heart; Nat. Order of Vietnam, 4th and 5th class, Vietnamese Cross of Gallantry with 3 palms. Mem. Retired Officers Assn. (past pres., hon. pres. for life, past pres., life bd. dirs. First marine Divsn. Assn., life mem., hon. pres., bd. dirs. Third Marine Divsn. Assn.), Am. Legion (life), Vets of Fgn. Wars (life), Marine Corps League (life), Disabled Am. Vets, (life), Korean War Vets. Assn. (pres. North Ga. chpt.). Died Sept. 3, 2003.

DAVIS, TRUE, corporate executive; b. St. Joseph, Mo., Dec. 23, 1919; s. William True and Helen (Marstella) D.; m. Virginia Bruce Motter, Jan. 24, 1948 (dec. Sept. 1969); children— William True, Bruce Motter, Lance Barrow. Student, Cornell U., 1937-40; LHD, Tarkio U., 1963; JD, Mo. Western Coll., 1979. Salesman Anchor Serum Co., St. Joseph, Mo., 1940-41, v.p., sales mgr., 1945-50, pres., 1950-60; pres., dir. Research Labs., Inc., 1952-60, Pet's Best Co., 1954-60, World Health Inst., Ltd., 1958-60, Peters Serum Co., Kansas City, 1956-60, Wilke Labs., Inc., West Plains, Mo., Wilke Labs. of Tenn., Memphis, 1956-60, Peerless Serum Co., St. Joseph, 1956-60, Med. Industries, Inc., St. Joseph, 1957-60, Gothic Advt., Inc., St. Joseph, 1956-60, Certified Labs., Inc., St. Joseph, 1956-60, Davis Estate, Inc., St. Joseph, 1958-75, Carolina Vet. Supply, Inc., Charlotte, N.C., 1956-60, Anchor Serum Co. of Ind., Inc., Indpls., 1959-60, Anchor Serum Co. N.J., Camden, 1959-60, Anchor Serum Co. Minn., So. St. Paul, 1960; chmn., dir. Chemico Labs., Inc., Miami, Fla., 1960-63; chmn. Thompson Hayward Chem. Co., Kansas City, Mo., 1961-63; pres., dir. Philips Roxane, Inc., N.Y.C., 1959-63; v.p., dir. Philips Electronics and Pharm. Industries Corp., 1959-63; U.S. exec. dir. Inter-Am. Devel. Bank, 1966-68. Ambassador to, Switzerland, 1963-65, asst. sec. treasury, 1965-68; pres., chmn. bd. dirs. Nat. Bank of Washington, 1969-73; dir. Laurel Race Course, Md. 1970-84, Tri Ltd., Bahamas, 1976-98; trustee Riviere Realty Trust, Washington, 1972-83; Chmn. U.S. Port Security Com., 1965-68, N.Y. Pier Com., 1966-68, Pub. Adv. Com. Customs Adminstrn., 1966-68; mem. Fgn. Trade Zones Bd., 1965-68; U.S. del. Internat. Maritime Coord. Orgn., London, 1966, GATT Conf. Anti-Dumping Laws, Geneva, 1966; adviser U.S. delegation to World Bank and IMF, 1966; chmn. Dept. Commerce Export Expansion Coun., 1962-63, Washington Urban Coalition, 1971-72; mem. adv. bd. dirs. Washington Mut. Investors Fund, 1971-91. Contbr. articles to trade, farm publs. Pres. Animal Health Inst., 1954-56, dir., 1946-59; mem. Nat. Serum Control Agy., 1947-58, chmn., 1954-55; exec. com. United Fund, 1960; bd. govs. Am. Royal, Kansas City, Mo., 1960-84; mem. Cornell U. Coun., 1962-68; bd. dirs. Washington Internat. Horse Show, 1975-85, pres., 1978-80, staff gov., Mo., 1949-54, 58-68, Ky., 1953-54; dir. Internat. Eye Found., Washington, 1995-98. Served to lt. USNR, 1943-45, chief test pilot Pearl Harbor. Recipient V.F.W. Outstanding Citizen award St. Joseph, 1960, St. Joseph Jr. C. of C. Boss Year award, 1960, Americanism Gold Medal, 1967, Exceptional Svc. award U.S. Treas., 1968. Mem. N.Y. Acad. Scis. (life), Am. Legion, VFW (nat. Americanization com. 1961-63, chmn. state com. 1960-63, Nat. Gold Medal for Americanization 1967, U.S. Treasury Exceptional Svc. award 1967), Coun. Am. Ambs., Mo. Acad. Squires, Metropolitan Club (Washington), Fairfax Hunt Club, Royal Yacht Club (Tasmania). Democrat. Home: Saint Joseph, Mo. Died 2003.

DAVIS, ULILLAH ELMORE, pharmacist; b. Ashland, Miss., Mar. 15, 1932; d. Hayse and Graftee (McKenzie) Elmore; m. Edward Davis, Jr., Dec. 5, 1959; children— Karen Lynn, Keith Edward. B.S. in Pharmacy, Xavier U., New Orleans, 1955. Registered pharmacist, La., Ohio. Instr. chemistry, biology, dean of women, Miss. Indsl. Coll., Holly Spring, 1956-57; asst. mgr. Shauter Drug Co., Cleve., 1958-59; staff pharmacist Highland View Hosp., Warrensville, Ohio, 1960-70, asst. dir. pharmacy, 1971-78; sr. staff pharmacist Cleve. Met. Gen. Hosp., 1979; dir. pharmacy Kenneth W. Clement Ctr., Cleve., 1980-97; SunnyAcres Skilled Nursing Facility, 1985-97; treas. Phillis Wheatley Assoc., 1985. Trustee Lee Seville Ch., 1985. Recipient Super Achievement award Highland View Hosp, 1975. Mem. Cleve. Soc. Hosp. Pharmacists, Ohio Soc. Hosp. Pharmacists, Am. Soc. Hosp. Pharmacists, Nat. Pharm. Assn., Cleve. Pharm. Assn. (sec. 1984-97, pres. 1985), Xavier Alumni Assn., Cleve. Tots and Teens (v.p. 1973-75, Super Performance award 1979), East End Settle Coop. (pres. 1975-78), NAACP, Nat. Council Negro Women, Phillis Wheatley Aux., Alpha Kappa Alpha Achievement award 1982). Democrat. Baptist. Avocations: gourmet cooking; jogging. Died Jan. 15, 1997. Home: Cleveland, Ohio.

DAVIS, VINCENT, political science educator; b. Chattanooga, May 3, 1930; married; 3 children. BA, Vanderbilt U., 1952; M.P.A., Woodrow Wilson Sch., Princeton U., 1959, MA, 1960, PhD, 1961. Mem. faculty dept. politics, research asst. Center Internat. Studies, Princeton U., 1959-61, vis. research prof., 1969-70; mem. faculty Dartmouth Coll., 1961-62; mem. faculty Grad. Sch. Internat. Studies, research asso. Social Sci. Found. U. Denver, 1962-71; Patterson prof. internat. studies U. Ky., Lexington, 1971-98, dir. Patterson Sch. Diplomacy and Internat. Commerce, 1971-93; Nimitz prof. polit. sci. U.S. Naval War Coll., 1970-71; prof. emeritus U. Ky., Lexington, from 1998. Exec. coun. Inter-Univ. Seminar Armed Forces and Soc., U. Chgo., 1972-79; chmn. civilian adv. panel Sec. Def. Com. Excellence in Mil. Edn., 1974-76; cons., lectr. in field; mem. internat. affairs fellowships com. Coun. on Fgn. Rels., N.Y.C., 1980—; adj. fellow Ctr. Strategic and Internat. Studies, Washington, 1992—; speaker NATO Conf. on Post-Soviet States of Eastern and Cen. Europe, Oslo, 1992; mem. Sec. State's Adv. Bd. on Hist. Archives and Documentation; bd. dirs. UN Assn. U.S.A., Rep. Nat. Policy Forum. Author: Postwar Defense Policy and the U.S. Navy, 1943-46, 1966, The Admirals Lobby, 1967, The Politics of Innovation, 1967, The Analysis of International Politics, 1971, Henry Kissinger and Bureaucratic Politics: A Personal Appraisal, 1979, The Post-Imperial Presidency, 1980; co-author, co-editor: Reorganizing America's Defense, 1985; also monographs, spl. reports; editor: Sage Papers in Internat. Studies, 1971-77; contbr. to profl. jours., encys. Served with USN, 1952-56; capt. Res. ret. Mem. Internat. Studies Assn. (exec. dir. 1964-71, chmn. intensive panels 1972-74, pres. 1976-77), Am. Polit. Sci. Assn., Internat. Inst. Strategic Studies. Died Mar. 28, 2003.

DAVIS, WILLIAM COLUMBUS, history educator, writer, lecturer; b. Birmingham, Ala., Aug. 28, 1910; s. William Columbus and Maude (Gray) D.; m. Mildred J. Dorman, July 24, 1948 (dec.); m. Dorothy A. Fleetwood, Feb. 14, 1987 (dec.). AB, U. Ala., 1931, MA, 1932, Harvard U., 1943, PhD, 1948. Adminstrv. positions U.S. Senate, 1933-46; asst. prof. history U. Ga., 1948-51; faculty George Washington U., 1951-66, prof. Latin Am. history and govt., 1960-66, dir. Latin Am. studies, 1952-66; prof. internat. affairs, dir. Latin Am. studies, dir. lecture program, only permanent mem. faculty Nat. War Coll., Washington, 1963-74; dir., participant numerous radio, TV programs in field. Lectr. various colls. and univs.; vis. prof. Samford U., 1983, 85. Author: The Last Conquistadores: The Spanish Intervention in Peru and Chile, 1863-1866, 1950, The Columns of Athens, 1951, Warnings from the Far South: Democracy versus Dictatorship in Uruguay, Argentina and Chile, 1995; co-author: Soviet Bloc Latin American Activities and Their Implications for United States Foreign Policy, 1960; editor: Index to the Writings on American History, 1902-1940, 1956, Am. Hist. Assn.'s Guide to Hist. Lit., 1960; contbr. articles on Latin Am. devels. to various publs Mem. Phi Beta Kappa, Pi Kappa Phi. Baptist. Home: Mc Lean, Va. Died Dec. 24, 2003.

DAVISON, ELLEN MARGARET, museum curator, educator; b. Scotland County, Mo., Sept. 16, 1929; d. Myron Barnes and Ethel Margaret (Davis) Kirkpatrick; m. Norman Delbert Korbitz, Dec. 23, 1949 (div. 1960); 1 son, Norman Delbert; m. 2d, Walter Sears Davison, May 26, 1962; 1 dau., Jane Ellen. Student Iowa Weselyan Coll., Mt. Pleasant, 1948-49; B.S. in Edn., U.S.D., 1951; postgrad. U. Mo., 1961, N.E. Mo. State U., 1970-71. Cert. tchr. Mo., Iowa, Ala., Fla., Ohio. Tchr., Garfield High Sch., Garrettsville, Ohio, 1951-52; mem. staff coop. extension service USDA, Fla. State U., Tallahassee, 1952; tchr. Jackson (Ala.) Jr. High, 1953; tchr. Ledbetter Country Day Sch., Dallas, 1959-60; mem. staff coop. extension service USDA, U. Mo., Columbia, 1960-62, extension home economist, 1965-66; sales agt. United Farm Agy., Kirksville, Mo., 1964-65; tchr. Ophelia Parrish Jr. High, Kirksville, 1967; substitute tchr. Kirksville Sch. Dist., 1980-83; curator Adair Co. Hist. Mus. and Library, Kirksville, 1981-83. Mem. United Methodist Women. Mem. Am. Econs. Assn., Mo. Home Econs. Assn. (sec.-treas. NE dist.), Extension Home Economists, NEA, PTA, Kirksville (Mo.) Tchrs. Assn., Alpha Theta Kappa Phi, Alpha Phi Sigma. Methodist. Home: Kirksville, Mo. Deceased.

DAVISON, FREDERICK CORBET, foundation executive; b. Atlanta, Sept. 3, 1929; s. Frederick Collins and Gladys (Carsley) D.; m. Dianne Castle, Sept. 3, 1952; children— Frederick Corbet, William Castle, Anne Harper. D.V.M., U. Ga., 1952; PhD, Iowa State U., 1963; H.H.D. (hon.), Presbyn. Coll., 1977; LL.D. (hon.), Mercer U., 1979; hon. degree, U. N.B., Can., 1985. Pvt. practice veterinary medicine, Marietta, Ga., 1952-58; rsch. assoc. Iowa State U., Ames, 1958-60, asst. prof., 1960-63; assoc. Inst. Atomic Research, Ames, 1960-63; asst. dir. dept. sci. activities AVMA, Chgo., 1963-64; dean sch. vet. medicine U. Ga., Athens, 1964-66; vice chancellor Univ. System Ga., 1966-67, pres., 1967-86, U. Ga., Athens, 1967-86, prof. vet. medicine, Fred C. Davison chair Sch. Vet. Medicine, 1986-88; pres., chief exec. officer Nat. Sci. Ctr. Found., Inc., Augusta, Ga., 1988—2004. Bd. dirs. EduTrek, Southeastern Tech. Ctr.; trustee Presbyn. Coll. Contbr. articles to profl. jours. Mem. NE Ga. commn. Boy Scouts Am., past pres. Area 5; hon. mem. bd. counselors Oxford Coll. Recipient Disting. Achievement award Iowa State U., 1979, Disting. Svc. award Univ. Ga., 1975, Appreciation award, 1976, Silver Beaver award and Silver Antelope award Boy Scouts Am.; named Georgian of Yr. Ga. Assn. Broadcasters, 1980. Mem. Am., Ga. vet. med. assns., Sigma Xi, Phi Kappa Phi, Sigma Alpha Epsilon, Omega Tau Sigma, Alpha Zeta, Phi Zeta, Gamma Sigma Delta. Home: Augusta, Ga. Died Apr. 28, 2004.

DAVIS WICHERN, ANNE LOGAN, medical educator; b. Rahway, N.J., Dec. 2, 1924; d. Chester Morrison and Elisabeth (Logan) D.; m. Walter Adam Wichern Jr., Mar. 24, 1956; children: Walter Adam III, Anne Logan. BA, Wellesley Coll., 1945; MD, Columbia U., 1949. Diplomate Am. Bd. Internal Medicine with subspecialty in pulmonary medicine, Nat. Bd. Med. Examiners. Intern 1st med. divsn. Bellevue Hosp., N.Y.C., 1949-50, resident chest svc. and pediatric pulmonary divsn., 1952-53, resident 1st med. divsn., 1954, 55-56, pulmonary fellow, 1955-58, asst. vis. physician, 1958-63, assoc. attending physician, 1963-69, dir. emphysema clinic, 1956—2001, asst. dir. chest svc., from 1968, dir. chest clinic, 1987-92, med. dir. respiratory therapy dept., 1976-92. Vis. fellow dept. medicine Coll. Physicians and Surgeons, Columbia U., N.Y.C., 1954-55, instr. in medicine, 1957-60, assoc. in medicine, 1960-64, asst. prof. medicine, 1964-68; physician/cons. VA Hosp., N.Y., 1972-90; assoc. prof. clin. medicine NYU Med. Ctr., 1968—; assoc. attending physician NYU Med. Ctr., 1971—; attending physician Bellevue Hosp. Ctr., N.Y.C., 1968—; asst. physician Presbyn. Hosp., N.Y., 1954-55; leader pulmonary del. to People's Republic of China, People to People Citizens Ambassador Program, 1986; mem. various task forces, cons. in field, govt. adv. coms. Manuscript reviewer jours. in field; contbr. articles to profl. publs., chpts. to books. V.p. Berwick Boys Found., 1979—, Stony Wold-Hebert Fund, Inc., 1990-93; pres. bd. trustees Nightingale Bamford Sch., 1979-83; bd. dirs. Bellevue Assn., Inc., 1979-82; mem. session Madison Ave. Presbyn. Ch., 1987-92, 93—; pres. N.Y. Lung Assn., 1977-79, N.Y. Trudeau Soc., 1973-74; mem. N.Y. Coalition to Elinimate Tuberculosis, 1991—. Grantee Dazian Found., 1954-58, Stony Wold-Herbert Fund, 1969-72. Fellow ACP; mem. Am. Thoracic Soc. (pres. 1980-81, pres. ea. sect. 1977-78, publs. com. 1980-81, Amerson lecture selection com. 1975-79, chmn. fed. appropriations com. 1981-83), Am. Lung Assn. (pres. 1989-90), Am. Clin. and Climatol. Assn., Am. Bd. Internal Medicine (pulmonary disease subspecialty bd.

1978-83), N.Y. Acad. Medicine, State Thoracic Soc. (pres. 1973-74), N.Y. State Med. Soc., N.Y. County Med. Soc., Internat. Union Against Tuberculosis and Lung Disease, William A. Briscoe Lung Club. Avocations: painting, hiking, sailing. Home: New York, NY. Died Mar. 9, 2003.

DAWN, FREDERIC SAMUEL, chemical and textile engineer; b. Shanghai, Republic of China, Nov. 24, 1916; s. Keith Frederic and Paula (Yui) D.; m. Marie Dunn; children: Robert, William, Victoria. BS in Chemistry summa cum laude, China Inst. Tech., 1936; MS in Textile Engring., U. Lowell and N.C. State U., 1938, 39; PhD in Chemistry, Nat. Inst. Tech., 1948; DSc in Chemistry with honors, China Inst. Tech., 1967. Prof. China Inst. Tech., Shanghai, 1939-49; dir. rsch. China Textile Ind., Inc., Shanghai, 1945-49; postdoctoral rsch. fellow and assoc. U. Wis., Madison, 1950-55; dir. rsch. Decar Plastic Corp., Madison, 1955-60; supervisory rsch. engr. USAF, Aeronautical Systems Div., Wright Patterson AFB, 1960-62; chief matls. rsch. lab. NASA Manned Spacecraft Ctr., Houston, 1962-76; dir. adv. matls. rsch. and devel. NASA Johnson Space Ctr., Houston, 1976-89, chief engr., sr. exec. svc. Fed. Govt., from 1989. Adv. bd. Nat. Elec. Mfrs. Assn., N.Y.C., 1956-60. Tech. adv. com. Jour. Indsl. Fabrics, 1985-87; contbr. articles to profl. jours. Bd. dirs. Houston Sister City Soc., 1970—; mem. Presdl. Task Force, Washington, 1982—; mem. bd. regents Liberty U., Lynchburg, Va., 1995—. Decorated Legion of Merit; named to Space Tech. Hall of Fame, U.S. Space Found., 1989; recipient Exceptional Engring. Achievement medal NASA, 1984, Sci. medal, 1991, Tech. award, 1991, Presdl. Medal Legion of Merit, 1994, Pioneer award Orgn. Chinese Americans, 2000, numerous awards from NASA and other govt., agy., profl. and community orgns. Fellow NSPE, AIAA, Am. Inst. Chemists; mem. Am. Chem. Soc. (sr. mem.), Phi Lambda. Achievements include research in high-temperature and flame resistant materials; development of nonflammable Beta fibers; development and design of high temperature, flame resistant and thermal/micrometeoroid protective polymeric materials and coatings for Apollo, Space Shuttle and Advanced extravehicular space suit, intravehicular flight suit, related flight equipment and spacecraft thermal protection system; patents in field. Home: Houston, Tex. Deceased.

DAWSON, MARTHA MORGAN, minister, writer; b. Anderson, Ind., Aug. 30, 1908; d. Earl R. and Elena (Hill) Morgan. Student, Colo. U.; D. in Div. Sci. (hon.), Brooks Divinity Coll., 1986. Ordained to ministry, 1982. Sales profl., owner, Denver, 1959-68; copywriter Maginot Advt. Co., Denver, 1968-71; travel host Middle East, 1971-84; instr. Brooks Divine Sci. Coll., 1979-91, Divine Sci. Sch., Washington, from 1994. Columnist: Aspire, 1978-81; contbr. articles, stories, poems to religious and gen. publs. Mem. Colo. Poetry Soc. (pres. 1977-79), Altrusa, Denver Woman's Press Club (pres. 1973-74). Died Jan. 8, 2001.

DAWSON, WILLIAM JOHNSON, JR., retired humanities and social sciences educator; b. Newark, Ohio, Oct. 7, 1925; s. William Johnson and Zora Jeddie (Glenn) D.; m. Mary Evelyn Cardwell, Sept. 8, 1948; children: Kenneth Robert, Karen Sue, Ann Elizabeth, Carol Glenn. BS, Va. Poly Inst., 1949, MS, 1950; MA, Presbyn. Sch. Christian Edn., 1962, Appalachian State U., 1966; EdD, N.C. State U., 1972. High sch. tchr. Prince Edward County Schs., Farmville, Va., 1950-52; merchandising mgr. Presbyn. Book Stores, Richmond, Va., 1953-57; asst. book editor John Knox Press, Richmond, 1957-62; religion instr. Lees-McRae Coll., Banner Elk, N.C., 1962-66; sociology instr. Rockingham Community Coll., Wentworth, N.C., 1966-72; chmn. divsn. humanities and social scis. New River C.C., Dublin, Va., 1972-83, prof. humanities and social scis., 1983-91, ret., 1992. Mem. chancellor's faculty adv. com. Va. C.C. Sys., Richmond, 1988-90. Mem. Gov.'s Adv. Bd. on Aging, Richmond, 1989-94, Pulaski County Bd. Suprs., 1983-87; chmn. bd. dirs. New River Cmty. Action, Christiansburg, Va.; vice chmn. Rural Va., Richmond, 1978-80. With U.S. Army, 1944-46, The Philippines. Mem. Phi Kappa Phi, Phi Delta Kappa. Democrat. Mem. Soc. Of Friends. Avocations: political and social svc. activities. Home: Dublin, Va. Died Jan. 2, 2002.

DAY, CHON, cartoonist; b. Chatham, N.J., Apr. 6, 1907; s. Lawrence and Nell Hunter (Van Orden) D.; m. Irene Townley, June 2, 1934; children— Clinton, Robert, Stephen. Student, Lehigh U., 1926, Art Students League, N.Y.C., 1929. Cartoons appearing in New Yorker, Saturday Evening Post, numerous other mags.; author, illustrator: I Could Be Dreaming, 1945, What Price Dory, 1955, Brother Sebastian, 1957, Brother Sebastian Carries On, 1959, Brother Sebastian at Large, 1961 (Recipient Best gag cartoonist award Nat. Cartoonists Soc. 1956, 62, 70, Best Spl. Features award 1969, named to R.I. Heritage Hall of Fame 1972). Named to R.I. Journalism Hall of Fame, 1989. Mem. Nat. Cartoonists Soc. Clubs: Lions (past pres.), Westerly Yacht. Baptist. Deceased.

DAY, LAWRENCE JAMES, artist, educator; b. Phila., Oct. 29, 1921; s. Lawrence Francis and Ethel M. (Swain) D.; m. Ruth Eileen Fine, Oct. 1, 1983. BFA, Tyler Sch. Art, Phila., 1950; BS in Edn., Temple U., 1950. Tchr. Phila. Bd. Edn., 1951, 53; prof. art Phila. Coll. Art. (now U. of the Arts), 1953-88; prof. emeritus U. of the Arts, 1988-98. One-man shows include: Dubin Gallery, Phila., 1951, 54, 55, 57, Parma Gallery, N.Y.C., 1954, 60, R.I. U., 1969, Miami U., 1973, Cin. Art Inst., 1974, Hollins Coll., 1976, Gross-McCleaf Gallery, Phila., 1975, 77, 79, 81, 82, 83, 84, 85, Rider Coll., 1985; exhibited in group shows: Pa. Acad. Fine Arts, Lehigh U., 1976, Phila. Mus. Art, 1976, Acad. Arts and Letters, N.Y.C., 1984, numerous others; retrospective exhbn. Jane Haslem Gallery, Washington, 1958-88. Bd. advisors Artist Choice Mus., N.Y.C. Recipient Hazlett Meml. award Gov. of Pa., 1982, Citation City of Phila., 1988; McDowell Found. grantee, 1978, Ingram-Merrill Found. grantee, 1984-85. Mem. Coll. Art Assn. Am., Am. Soc. Aesthetics. Democrat. Died Apr. 14, 1998. Died Apr. 14, 1998. Home: Takoma Park, Md.

DAZEY, WILLIAM BOYD, retired lawyer; b. Chgo., Sept. 23, 1915; s. Alva William and Emma Mayo (Boyd) D.; m. Dolores Ann Melton, July 20, 1959; children: Barbara Ann Dazey Lantos, William Melton, Thomas Sumner, Daniel Putnam, Johnathan Mayo. Student, U. Ill., 1933; LL.B., Cumberland U., 1935. Bar: Tex. 1940. Ptnr. firm Godard & Dazey, Texas City, 1940-58; cons. Japan UN Assn., Tokyo, 1958-60; legal advisor Japan Consul Gen., Houston, 1960-86; ptnr. Dazey & Newey, Houston, 1970-80. Served to 2d lt. U.S. Army, 1942-46. Decorated Bronze Star with oak leaf cluster, Purple Heart; Third Order Sacred Treasure (Japan). Mem. ABA, State Bar Tex., Nat. Order Battlefield Commns., Japan-Am. Soc. Houston (founder, past pres.), Am. Inst. for Internat. Steel (emeritus), Rotary, Torch Club, Phi Delta Theta. Democrat. Unitarian Universalist. Home: San Antonio, Tex. Died Nov. 13, 2002.

DEAN, DEAREST (LORENE GLOSUP), composer; b. Oct. 4, 1911; d. John Henry and Bessie Marie Donnelly Peterson; m. Eddie Dean, Sept. 11, 1931; children: Donna Lee Knorr, Edgar Glosup II. Bd. dirs. Acad. Country Music, Hollywood, 1960—62. Composer: One Has My Name, 1948, The Lonely Hours, 1970, 1501 Miles of Heaven, 1970, Walk Beside Me, 1980. Sec. ARC, Burbank, Calif., 1943. Mem.: ASCAP. Republican. Avocation: golf. Home: Westlake Vlg, Calif. Died July 12, 2002.

DEAN, FRANCIS HILL, landscape architect, educator; b. San Francisco, Oct. 1, 1922; s. John Samuel and Ethel (Hill) D.; m. Myrtle Oda Enoltt, Sept. 1, 1944 (dec. 1969); children: Gary Dean, Tamara Dean; m. Carolyn Anderson Bower, Aug. 12, 1971; stepchildren: Deborah Friou, Linda Friou, Sally Friou, George Friou. BS, U. Calif., Berkeley, 1948; M in Liberal Arts, U. So. Calif., 1984. Lic. landscape architect, Calif. Designer Eckbo, Royston & Williams, Los Angeles and San Francisco, 1948-58; prin. Eckbo, Dean & Williams, Los Angeles, San Francisco and Seattle, 1958-64; prin., v.p. Eckbo, Dean, Austin & Williams, Pasadena, San Francisco, 1964-73, EDAW Inc., Newport Beach and San Francisco, 1973-79; lectr. Calif. State Poly. U., Pomona, Calif., 1976-87, prof., 1987-89, ret., 1992; landscape cons. U. Calif.-Santa Barbara, 1972-76; mem. adv. council U. Calif. Ext. Landscape Arch. program, Irvine, 1979-87; landscape archtl. works include Riverside Mall, Calif., Santa Ana-Santiago Creek Study, 1966, Huntington Beach Cen. Pk., 1970-73, San Marcos Creek Study, 1991. Vis. lectr. U. Guelph, Ont., Can., 1981, La. State U., 1980, Osaka (Japan) U., 1973, Internat. Urban Ecosystem Symposium, Osaka, 1990. Mem. Fire Protection Task Force, Orange County, Calif., 1976-77, South Laguna Civic Assn., 1974-92, Save Elysian Park Com., L.A., 1963-67. Served to capt. USAAF, 1942-45, ETO. Recipient Profl. awards Concrete Industry, 1971, Am. Inst. Planners, 1971, Calif. Parks and Recreation Soc., 1973. Fellow Am. Soc. Landscape Architects (jury mem., local chpt., L.A., 1984, San Francisco, 1983, Seattle, 1993, Portland, 1994, L.A. Chpt. AIA, 1983, Profl. award 1972), Calif. Coun. Landscape Arcitects (honor award 1991 Richard J. Newtra award for profl. excellence 1995), Sigma Lambda Alpha (disting.). Home: Vashon, Wash. Died Apr. 29, 2003.

DEAN, RUTH J(OSEPHINE), retired French language educator; b. N.Y.C., Mar. 10, 1902; d. Amos Dean and Lovisa Vaughn (Mallory) D. BA, Wellesley Coll., 1922; BA with honors, Oxford (Eng.) U., 1924, MA, 1928, DPhil, 1938; LHD, U. Pa., 1979; DHL, Mt. Holyoke Coll., 1989. Mem. faculty Mt. Holyoke Coll., South Hadley, Mass., from 1934, Mary Lyon prof. French, from 1966, prof. emerita, from 1967. Mem. Inst. Advanced Study, Princeton, N.J., 1943-44, 50-51; lectr., vis. prof. U. Pa., Phila., 1969-75, prof. emerita, 1975—; hon. rsch. fellow Inst. Romance Studies, U. London, 1990—; br. and state pres., mem. nat. coms. AAUW, 1940-61. Co-editor The Rule of St. Benedict, 1964; contbr. articles, revs. to numerous jours. Palmer fellow AAUW, 1943-44; Guggenheim fellow, 1948-49; sr. fellow NEH, 1967-68. Fellow Medieval Acad. Am. (past coun., com. mem., v.p., pres.), Brit. Acad. (corr.); mem. MLA (exec. coun., mem. bds., coms., v.p. 1958-80), Ordre des Palmes Academiques (France). Avocations: travel, swimming, skiing. Home: New York, NY. Died Feb. 3, 2003.

DEANE, BUDDY (WINSTON JOE DEANE), retired broadcaster; b. St. Charles, Ark., Aug. 2, 1924; s. George Ballard and Estelle S. (Walton) D.; m. Helen Bernice Stephenson, July 4, 1948; children: Joellen Deane Beard, Deborah Paula, Dinah Dawn Deane Marks. Student, Kemper Mil. Sch., 1942-43, Cornell U., 1944, Northwestern U., 1946-47. Broadcaster Stas. KGHI and KXLR, Little Rock, 1945-49, Sta. WHHM, Memphis, 1949-52, Stas. WITH Radio and WJZ-TV, Balt., 1953-64; host The Buddy Deane Show, 1957—64; owner, mgr. Stas. KOTN and KFXE, Pine Bluff, Ark., 1960-83, Sta. KWEL, Midland, Tex. Former pres. Ark. Broadcasters, 1978-79; crusade chmn. Jefferson County chpt. Am. Cancer Soc., crusade chmn. state chpt., 1983-84; former bd. dirs. Pine Bluff/Jefferson County C. of C.; served as drive chmn. (twice) for United Way of Jefferson County, currently bd. dirs.; chmn., founder Freedom Fest ann. community celebration, Pine Bluff, 1989-90. Recipient Pioneer award Ark. Broadcasters, 1983, Pine Bluff All Civic Night award for Exceptional Leadership Pine Bluff-Jefferson County C. of C., Award of Exceptional Accomplishment Ark. Community Devel. Program, 1985, 90; inducted into Leadership Pine Bluff Hall of Fame, 1989; attained highest local rating in Am. for his Buddy Deane Show, WJZ-TV, Balt., 1959; named no. 1 Disc Jockey in Am. Bill Gavin Award, 1961; movie Hairspray, released 1988-89, based on Buddy Deane TV show. Mem. Kiwanis (disting. pres. Pine Bluff club, disting. lt. gov. Mo.-Ark. club, Kiwanian of Yr. Pine Bluff club, legion of merit internat. club 1991), Pine Bluff C. of C. (tourism com.), Three Rivers Audubon Soc. (chmn. edn. com., pres. 2 terms, now bd. dirs.), 50 for the Future (sr., former bd. dirs.). Methodist. Avocations: travel, bird watching, wildlife photography, reading, community activities. Home: Pine Bluff, Ark. Died July 16, 2003.

DEANGELIS, ALDO A. former state senator; b. Chgo. Hts., Ill., Mar. 25, 1931; m. Meredith Roberts; 4 children. Grad., Knox Coll., Galesburg, Ill., 1954; postgrad., U. Chgo., Govs. State U. Founder, pres. Dial Tube, 1961-65; co-founder, past pres. Vulcan Tube and Metals Co., 1969-78; mem. Ill. State Senate, 1978-96, asst. majority leader. Bd. dirs. Bank of Homewood. Bd. dirs. United Way of Chgo. Hts. Served with U.S. Army, 1954-56. Mem. C. of C., Mfrs. assn. Chgo. (dir.). Republican. Home: Naples, Fla. Died Feb. 13, 2004.

DEBUSSCHERE, DAVID ALBERT, brokerage executive, retired professional basketball player and team executive; b. Detroit, Oct. 16, 1949; s. Marcel D. and Dorothy D. DeB.; m. Gerri Warnock, 1968; children: Michelle, Peter, Dennis Grad., Detroit U., 1962. Baseball player, pitcher Chgo. White Sox, Am. League, 1962-63; basketball player, coach Detroit Pistons, NBA, 1962-68; basketball player N.Y. Knickerbockers, 1968-74, mem. world champion team, 1970, 73, former exec. v.p., dir. basketball ops.; v.p., gen. mgr. N.Y. Nets, Am. Basketball Assn., 1974-75; commr. Am. Basketball Assn., 1975-76; dir. of basketball ops. N.Y. Knicks, 1982—86; v.p. Williamson, Picket & Gross Inc., N.Y.C. Author: The Open Man: A Championship Diary, 1970. Player NBA All-Star Team, 1966-68, 70-73. Died May 14, 2003.

DE CAMP, L(YON) SPRAGUE, author; b. N.Y.C., Nov. 27, 1907; s. Lyon and Emma Beatrice (Sprague) de C.; m. Catherine Adelaide Crook, Aug. 12, 1939; children: Lyman Sprague, Gerard Beekman. BS, Calif. Inst. Tech., 1930; MS, Stevens Inst. Tech., 1933. Instr. Inventors Found., 1933-36; prin. Sch. Inventing and Patenting, Internat. Corr. Schs., 1936-37; editor Fowler-Becker Pub. Co., 1937-38; asst. editor ASME, 1938; free lance writer, 1938-42, 46—. Author: (with Willy Ley) Lands Beyond, 1953 (Internat. Fantasy award), (with Fletcher Pratt) Tales From Gavagan's Bar, 1953 (Cleve. Sci. Fiction award), An Elephant for Aristotle, 1959 (Fiction award Athenaeum of Phila.), Lest Darkness Fall, Rogue Queen, the Ancient Engineers, Great Cities of the Ancient World, Lovecraft: A Biography, Literary Swordsmen and Sorcerers, The Reluctant King, (with wife) Dark Valley Destiny, also numerous other books, articles and stories. Served from lt. to lt. comdr. USNR, 1942-46. Recipient J.R.R. Tolkien award for life work in fantasy, 1976, Grand Master Nebula award Sci. Fiction Writers Am., 1979, World Fantasy award lifetime achievement, 1984. Mem. Univ. Mus. U. Pa., History of Sci. Soc., Soc. History of Tech., Sci. Fiction Writers Am., Dallas Paleontol. Soc., Dallas Mus. Natural History, Smithsonian Assocs., Authors Guild Am., Trap Door Spiders Club, First Fandom Club. Deceased.

DECAMP, ROSEMARY SHIRLEY, actress, enamelist; b. Prescott, Ariz., Nov. 14, 1910; d. William Val and Margaret Elizabeth (Hinman) DeC.; m. John Ashton Shidler, June 28, 1941; children— Margaret, Martha, Valerie, Nita. BA, Mills Coll., 1932, M. A., 1933. Mem. faculty Mills Coll., 1932-33; State Dept. cultural grantee, tchr., Pakistan, 1963-64; participant State Dept. Tour, Pakistan, 1963-64 Appeared on radio, 1933-53, including, One Man's Family, 1933, Easy Aces, 1935, Dr. Christian, 1937-53, Hollywood Hotel, 1939, Lux Radio Theater; appeared in feature films, including Yankee Doodle Dandy, 1942, Jungle Book, 1942, Hold Back the Dawn, 1941, Rhapsody in Blue, 1944, This is the Army, 1944, Shine on Harvest Moon, 1952; appeared on TV, 1947—, including Life of Riley, 1949, Death Valley Days, 1952-77, Bob Cummings Show, 1954-58, That Girl, 1964-68, Love Boat, B.J. and the Bear, St. Elsewhere, 1986, Murder She Wrote, 1989; TV film: The Time Machine, 1978; TV miniseries Blind Ambition, 1979; films include By the Light of the Silvery Moon, So This is Love, Many Rivers to Cross, Strategic Air Command, Saturday the 14th; copper enamelist, exhibited in one-woman shows, Los Angeles Museum Sci. and Industry, 1969, Jocelyn Center, Torrance, Calif., 1969, Highland-Hollywood Blvd. Savs. & Loan Gallery, 1970; exhibited in group show, Palos Verdes Community Art Gallery, 1981; represented in pvt. collections; guest columnist: La Daily Jour, 1959-64; author children's novel: Here Duke, 1962, (with others) The Courage to Grow Old; writer, spkr. (audiocassette) Tales from Hollywood, 1991. Fine arts commr. City of Torrance, 1971-73; bd. dirs. Torrance Meml. Hosp., 1970-75. Mem. Screen Actor's Guild (dir. 1953-65) Deceased.

DECESARE, PAULA DOREEN, small business owner; b. Berlin, N.H., June 29, 1936; d. William Briry and Mildred Victoria (Sloan) Raymond; m. William Joseph DeCesare, Feb. 16, 1957; children: Jay Raymond, Mark William, Brett Patrick. Student, Jackson Coll., 1954; AA in Communication, Leland Powers Sch. Broadcasting and Speech, 1955-

57. Copy writer, salesperson Sta. WHVW Radio, Hyde Park, N.Y., 1963-67; mgr. real estate Mobile Home Park, Hudson, N.Y., from 1967; pres., sole incorporator Alice in Videoland Ltd., Kingston, N.Y., from 1983. Mgr. real estate numerous comml. holdings, 1967—; sales agt. Equitable Life Assurance, N.Y.C., 1975-77; account exec. sales Sta. WKIP Radio, Poughkeepsie, N.Y., 1977-83. Episcopalian. Avocations: nature study, travel, reading, family activities, theater. Home: Kingston, NY. Deceased.

DE COTEAU, DENIS, music director, conductor; b. N.Y.C. BA, MA in Music, NYU; studied, Mozarteum, Salzburg, Austria; MusD, Stanford U. Asst. condr. San Francisco Ballet, 1970-74, music dir., condr., from 1974; artistic advisor Stockton Symphony, from 1994. Condr. Oakland Symphony Youth Orch., 1970-79, Aichii U. Orch., Nagoya, Japan, 1982—, Tokyo City Philarm. Orch., 1989, San Francisco Conservatory of Music; prin. guest condr. Deutches Jugendorchester, 1976, 78, 80; guest condr. Nat. Music Camp Assn. Australian Youth Orch., 1980—, Oreg. Mozart Players, 1989; assoc. condr. San Francisco Symphony, 1986; music dir., condr. Flagstaff (Ariz.) Festival of Arts, 1977-83. Guest appearances with numerous dance cos. including Kansas City Ballet, State of Ala. Ballet, San Diego Ballet, Ballet West, Honolulu Ballet, and Oakland Ballet; guest condr. BBC Scottish Symphony, St. Louis Symphony, New Orleans Philharm., Tokyo City Philharm, Radio Frei Orch. (Berlin), San Francisco Symphony, Seattle Symphony, Oakland Symphony, San Francisco Chamber Orch. and others; appeared with Yomiuri Orch., Tokyo; invited condr. (recs.) Nat. Philharm. London, (concerts) Australia's Bicentennial, World Expo, Brisbane; condr. opera premiere Song of Pegasus (Marin Theatre Playhouse). Recipient Pierre Monteux Conducting Prize, 1969, Adventuresome Programming award ASCAP, 1976. Deceased.

DEERE, CYRIL THOMAS, retired computer company executive; b. Rockville, Conn., Apr. 28, 1924; s. Albert Bertram and Belle Murdie (King) D.; m. Shirley Ann Scheiner, June 2, 1945; children: Sandra Deere Leinz, Kathryn Deere Lloyd. BS, Yale U., 1948. With Lee Paper Co., Vicksburg, Mich., 1949-50, Addressograph-Multigraph Corp., Hartford, Conn. and Cleve., 1950-69; founder Data Card Corp., Minnetonka, Minn., 1969-81, v.p. mktg., 1969-75, sr. v.p., 1975-77, exec. v.p., 1977-80, pres., 1980-82, dir. plastics div., 1974-81; pres., dir. Can. Data Card Ltd., Toronto, Ont., 1974-81; chmn. bd. Data Card Internat., 1977-78;; founder, dir. Data Card Japan, 1980-81; founder, pres. Card Tech. Corp., Saddlebrook, N.J., 1983-85. Served with USMC, 1943-44. Decorated Purple Heart. Mem. Am. Nat. Stds. Inst. (1st chmn. credit card stds. com. 1968-73), Input/Output Systems Assn. (pres. 1975. Clubs: Univ. (Denver), Oak Creek Country (Sedona, Ariz.). Home: Arvada, Colo. Died Mar. 28, 2002.

DEERING, TERRY WILLIAM, state legislator; b. Du Quoin, Ill., Nov. 7, 1958; s. Ernest and Virdell Nell (Heck) D.; m. Reita Jean Peradotta, Sept. 3, 1983; children: Greyson Tyler, Clayton Burke, Allyssa Morgen. Grad. high sch., Nashville, Ill. Delivery person Lorenz Distbg. Co., Nashville, 1976-77; equipment oper. Pitts Quarry, Radom, Ill., 1977-78; machine oper. Gen. Tire & Rubber Co., Mt. Vernon, Ill., 1978-79; equipment oper. Kinkaid Stone Co., Campbell Hill, Ill., 1979; coal miner Arch of Ill., Percy, 1979-90; elected mem. Ill. Gen. Assembly, Springfield, from 1990. Village trustee Village of DuBois, Ill., 1978, village pres., 1979-90; officer Ill. Jaycees, DuBois, 1977-81. Mem. KC, Troopers Lodge. Democrat. Roman Catholic. Avocations: sports, woodworking, music, travel. Home: Nashville, Ill. Died June, 1997.

DEFAZIO, SAMUEL, software engineer, researcher; b. Pitts., Sept. 16, 1945; s. Samuel Anthony and Isabella Valentine (Bair) DeF.; m. Louise Ann Thomas, Oct. 5, 1974; 1 child, Amy Louise. BS in Math., Pa. State U., 1973; MS in Computer Sci., U. Pitts., 1980, PhD in Computer Sci., 1988. Systems engr. IBM, Poughkeepsie, N.Y., 1974-75; mgr. info. systems Gulf Oil Corp., Pitts., 1975-85; mem. sr. tech. staff Mead Data Cen., Dayton, Ohio, 1985-90; pres., chief exec. officer Software Devel. Assocs., Dayton, 1990-91; program mgr. textual data base technology Sequent Computer Systems, Inc., Dayton, Ohio, from 1991. Mem. adv. bd. Ctr. for Parallel, Distributed and Intelligence Systems, U. Pitts., 1987-90; co-chmn. com. Applied Info. Techs. Rsch. Ctr., Columbus, Ohio, 1987-90. Contbr. articles to profl. jours. Chmn. Task Force on Alternative Financing for Clear Creek Schs., Springboro, Ohio, 1988-89. Recipient best paper award Compsac 81 Conf. Com., 1981. Mem. IEEE Computer Soc., Assn. for Computing Machinery, Assn. for Computing Machinery Sigmetrics and SIGMOD Soc. Died Mar. 30, 2001.

DEGENHARDT, JOHANNES JOACHIM, archbishop; b. Jan. 31, 1926; s. Julius and Elfriede Degenhardt. Ordained in Paderborn, 1951. Student chaplain Pädagogische Hochschule, Paderborn, Bezirksdekan Hochstift, Paderborn; bishop of Paderborn, 1968; archbishop, from 1974; elevated to cardinal, 2001. Chair edn. com. Conf. German Bishops. Author: Lukas, Evangelist der Armen, 1966, Ein Segen sollt ihr sein, 1984, Ermutigung zum Glauben, 1989. Died July 25, 2002.

DE HARTOG, JAN, writer; b. Haarlem, Holland, Apr. 22, 1914; s. Arnold Hendrik and Lucretia (Meyjes) de H.; m. Lydia van Schagen, 1936 (div.); children: Arnold, Sylvia; m. Angela Wyndham-Lewis, 1946 (div.); children: Nicholas, Catherine; m. Marjorie Mein, 1961; children: Eva, Julia. Student, Amsterdam Naval Coll., 1930. Staff mem. Amsterdam Municipal Theatre, 1932-37; writer-in-residence, lectr. creative playwriting U. Houston, 1962. Author: (plays) Mist, 1938, De Ondergang van de Vrijheid, 1939 (Gt. Nat. Drama prize 1939), Skipper Next to God, 1946, This Time Tomorrow, 1947, The Fourposter, 1951 (Tony award 1952), Death of a Rat, 1956, William and Mary, 1964, (novels) The Lost Sea, 1951, Mary, 1951, The Distant Shore, 1952, The Little Ark, 1954, A Sailor's Life, 1956, The Spiral Road, 1957, The Inspector, 1960, Waters of the New World, 1961, The Artist, 1963, The Hospital, 1964, The Call of the Sea, 1966, The Captain, 1966, The Children, 1968, The Peaceable Kingdom, 1971, The Lamb's War, 1979, The Trail of the Serpent, 1983, Star of Peace, 1984, The Commodore, 1986, The Centurion, 1989, The Peculiar People, 1992, The Outer Buoy, 1994,, De Vlucht, 1999, (mus.) I Do, I Do, 1966. Captain, Netherlands Merchant Marine. Recipient Netherlands Cross of Merit; named Officier de l'Academie, France, 1952, Commandeur of Netherlands Lion by Queen Beatrix of the Netherlands, 1996. Mem. Coun. of Am. Master Mariners. Mem. Soc. Of Friends. Died Sept. 22, 2002.

DELAPORTE, JACQUES, archbishop; b. Roye-Sur-Matz, Oise, France, Oct. 11, 1926; s. Fernand and Léonie (de Saint Quentin) D. Grad., Gregorian Pontifical U., Rome; diplome, École Des Hautes Études Commerciales. Cert. civil law, theology. Diocesian chaplain, Beauvais, France, 1955-62; chaplain Paris, 1962-69; parish priest St. Jean Baptiste, Beauvais, 1969-71; arch-priest Compiègne, 1971-76; auxiliary bishop Nancy, France, 1976-80; archbishop Cambrai, France, from 1980. Pres. Commn. Épiscopale des Migrations, 1982-88, Commn. Justice et Paix, 1988—. Author: Oser L'Espérance, 1989, L'Immigration, Le Coeur et La Raison, 1990, Le Coeur du Christ icone de Dieu, 1998. Avocation: tennis. Died Nov. 21, 1999.

DELAY, DOROTHY (MRS. EDWARD NEWHOUSE), violinist, educator; b. Medicine Lodge, Kans., Mar. 31, 1917; d. Glenn Adney and Cecile (Osborn) DeLay; m. Edward Newhouse, Mar. 5, 1941; children: Jeffrey H., Alison Dinsmore. Student, Oberlin Coll., 1933-34, MusD (hon.), 1981; BA, Mich. State U., 1937; Artists diploma, Juilliard Grad. Sch. Music, 1941; DFA (hon.), Mich. State U., 1991; LHD (hon.), U. Colo., 1991; DMusic (hon.), Columbia U., 1994, Duquesne U., 1998, Brown U., 2000. Prof. violin The Juilliard Sch., N.Y.C., 1947—, Starling prof. violin, from 1987; mem. faculty Sarah Lawrence Coll., 1948-87, Meadowmount Summer Sch. Music, Westport, N.Y., 1948-70; Dorothy DeLay prof. Aspen Summer Music Sch., 1971—; Starling prof. violin U. Cin., 1974—; vis. prof. violin Phila. Coll. Performing Arts, 1977-83, New Eng. Conservatory, 1978-87, Royal Coll. Music, Eng., from 1987; condr. Master classes univs. and conservatories in U.S., Europe, Asia, Africa, Near East.; dir. DeLay Int. of the Starling Found., Juilliard Sch. Music, from 1996. Solo (chamber music performances in) U.S., Can., S.Am., 1937—46, violinist, founder Stuyvesant Trio, 1940—42; contbr. articles on violins, violinists to various encys. Decorated Order of the Sacred Treasure Japan; named to Am. Classical Music Hall of Fame, 2002; recipient Outstanding Artist-Tchr. award Am., String Tchrs. Assn., 1975, Highest Honor citation Fedn. of Music Clubs, 1983, Gov.'s award, State of Kans., 1982, Alumni Accomplishment award, Mich. State U., 1984, King Solomon award., Am.-Israel Cultural Found., 1985, Disting. Svc. award Ministry of Culture, Republic of Korea, 1991, Nat. Medal of the Arts with Presdl. Citation, 1994, Am. Eagle award Nat. Music Coun., 1995; Sanford fellow, Yale U. Fellow: Royal Coll. Music, Gt. Brit.; mem.: Mu Phi Epsilon (award of merit 1989). Home: Nyack, NY. Died Mar. 24, 2002.

DELLENBACK, JOHN RICHARD, association executive; b. Chgo., Nov. 6, 1918; s. William H. and Margaret (Albright) D.; m. Mary Jane Benedict, Sept. 10, 1948; children: Richard Ludlow, David Albright, Barbara Clare. BS in Applied Econ. Sci, Yale U., 1940; JD, U. Mich., 1949. Faculty Oreg. State U., 1949-51; partner in law with Frank J. Van Dyke, Medford, Oreg., 1952-66; mem. Oreg. Ho. of Reps., 1960-66, 90th-93d Congresses, 4th Dist. Oreg., 1967-75; dir. Peace Corps, Washington, 1975-77; pres. Christian Coll. Coalition, Washington, 1977-88, pres. emeritus, from 1988. Mem. Oreg. Bd. Bar Examiners. Moderator Oreg. Synod United Presbyn. Ch.; mem. Permanent Jud. Commn. Gen. Assembly United Presbyn. Ch.; del. Republican Nat. Conv., 1964, 68, 72; chmn. bd. dirs. World Vision U.S.; sec., bd. dirs. World Vision Internat.; bd. dirs. Bread for World; trustee Howard U. Served to lt. comdr. USNR, 1942-46. Mem. ABA, Oreg. Bar Assn., Jackson County Bar Assn., Oreg. Soc. of D.C. (pres.), Cosmos Club, Athletic Club, Phi Beta Kappa. Clubs: Cosmos (Washington); Arlington (Portland). Home: Washington, DC. Died Dec. 7, 2002.

DEL OLMO, FRANK, newspaper editor; b. L.A., May 18, 1948; s. Francisco and Margaret Rosalie (Mosqueda) D.; m. Karen Margaret King, Feb. 6, 1970 (div. Sept. 1982); 1 child, Valentina Marisol; m. Magdalena Beltran-Hernandez, Nov. 10, 1991; 1 child, Francisco Manuel. Student, UCLA, 1966-68; BS magna cum laude in Journalism, Calif. State U., Northridge, 1970. Reporter-intern L.A. Times, 1970-71, gen. assignment reporter, 1971-80, columnist, editorial bd., 1980-90, deputy editor, 1990-98, assoc. editor, 1998—2004. Instr. Chicano Studies, Calif. State U., 1970-71; contbg. editor Race Relations Reporter, Nashville, 1973-75; on-air host, writer "Ahora" Sta. KCET-TV, L.A., 1974; chief writer, rschr. KNBC, 1975; bd. contbrs., freelance reporter Nuestro Mag., 1976-81; program co-dir. Summer Program Minority Journalists, 1990, faculty mem. 1979, vis. faculty mem. 1978, 80-83, 85, 89; vis. profl. Dow-Jones Newspaper Fund U. So. Calif. Sch. Journalism, 1975, bd. dirs. Numerous lectrs., presentations at colls., univs. Named Senior Faculty of Summer Program Minority Journalists Inst. Journalism Edn.; recipient Emmy award, 1976, Sigma Delta Chi Achievement award, 1982, Profl. Achievement award UCLA Alumni, 1990, Pulitzer Prize, 1984; Neiman fellowship Harvard U., 1987-88. Died Feb. 19, 2004.

DEL RE, ROBERT, civil engineer; b. N.Y.C., June 3, 1930; s. Nicholas and Virginia (Higginbotham) Del Re; m. Joyce Maley, Aug. 20, 1971 (dec. Oct. 4, 2001). BS, Marietta Coll., 1952, BS in Petroleum Engring., 1973. Engr. Greeley & Hansen, Chgo., 1957-71, assoc., 1971-83; cons. Camp Dresser & McKee Inc., Cambridge, Mass., 1983—, constrn. cons., Tampa, Fla. Patron Tampa Bay Art Ctr., mem. Morning Star Sch. Bd. Served with C.E.C., USNR, 1952-55. Registered profl. engr., Calif. Mem. ASCE (com. contract adminstrn., chmn. task com. on resident engr., mem. steering com. constrn. industry dispute avoidance and resolution task force, Fla. West Coast br. Engr. of Yr. 1986), Am. Acad. Environ. Engrs. (diplomate), Nat. Soc. Profl. Engrs., Fla. Engring. Soc., Fla. Pollution Control Assn., Soc. Am. Mil. Engrs., Am. Arbitration Assn., Earthquake Engring. Research Inst., Inter-Am. Assn. San. Engrs., Am. Water Works Assn., Tampa Hist. Soc., Tampa Preservation, Pi Epsilon Tau, Alpha Tau Omega. Clubs: University (Chgo. and Tampa). Contbr. articles to profl. jours. Home: Tampa, Fla. Deceased.

DEMANES, FLOYD A. lawyer, arbitrator, mediator, consultant; b. Kewanee, Ill., Nov. 20, 1921; s. James and Mary (Mikwee) D.; m. Eve Douquet, June 1, 1947 (div. July, 1985); children: David Jeffrey, Mark Scott. Student Econs., U. Ill., 1939-43, JD, 1949. Bar: Ill. 1950, Calif. 1960. Assoc. Murphy, Pearson and O'Connor, Chgo., 1950; pvt. practice Peoria, 1950-59; pub. defender Peoria County, Ill., 1956-59; chief trial counsel So. Pacific R.R. Cos., San Francisco, 1959-61; pvt. practice San Bruno, Calif., 1961-66, Burlingame, Calif., from 1966. Judge pro tem San Mateo Superior Ct., 1972-91; former rating atty. for Martindale-Hubbell over 25 yrs., numerous mediations and arbitrations. Contbr. articles to profl. jours.; frequent lectr. and speaker to bar assn. meetings in U.S. and Can. Capt. U.S. Army, 1943-46 ETO. Decorated Bronze Star medal; named Lawyer of Yr. U. Ill., 1975. Mem. ABA, ATLA (aviation law com. 1970-72, chmn environ law sect 1970-72, bd. govs. 1979-80), Ill. Bar Assn., Peoria County Bar Assn. (ethics com.), Calif. Bar Assn. (com. on fed. cts. 1973, del to state bar conv. 1963-64), San Mateo County Bar Assn. (past mem. bench and bar com., ethics com.), North San Mateo County Bar Assn. (past mem., pres. ethics com.), World Jurist Assn., Lawyer Pilots Bar Assn., Am. Bd. Profl. Liability Attys., Nat. Bd. Trial Advocacy, Internat. Soc. Air Safety Investigators (life), Air Travelers' Assn. (nat. adv. bd.), Profl. Airman's Assn. (pres. 1971), Calif. Trial Lawyers Assn. (bd. govs. 1965—, chmn. aviation law sect. 1968-72, environ. problems com. 1970-72, pres. 1973-74), San Mateo County Trial Lawyers Assn. (founder, pres. 1967-68, bd. dirs. 1963-65), North San Mateo County Bar Assn. (pres.1965). Republican. Episcopalian. Avocations: fly fishing, scuba diving, hunting. Home: Dublin, Calif. Died June 25, 2001.

DEMARCHI, ERNEST NICHOLAS, retired aerospace executive; b. Lafferty, Ohio, May 31, 1939; s. Ernest Constante and Lena Marie (Cireddu) D.; m. Carolyn Marie Tracz, 1960; children: Daniel Ernest, John David, Deborah Marie; m. Sharon Titherley, 1996. BME, Ohio State U., 1962; MS in Engring., UCLA, 1969. Registered profl. engr., Ohio; registered profl. cert. mgr. Exec. N.Am. Aviation/Rockwell/Boeing, 1962—2002; ret., 2002. Mem. Apollo, Skylab and Apollo-Soyuz missions design team in electronic and elec. systems, mem. mission support team for all Apollo and Skylab manned missions, 1962-74, mem. Space Shuttle design team charge elec. systems equipment, 1974-77, in charge Orbiter Data Processing System, 1977-81, in charge Orbiter Ku Band Communication and Radar System, 1981-85, in charge orbitor elec. power distbr., displays, controls, data processing, 1984-87, in charge space based interceptor flt. exper., 1987-88, kinetic energy systems, 1988-90, ground based interceptor program, 1990-97, dep. program mgr. Nat. Missile Def. Program, 1997-2000, assoc. dep. program mgr. Space Shuttle Program, 2000-02. Recipient Apollo Achievement award NASA, 1969, Apollo 13 Sustained Excellent Achievement Snoopy award, 1971, Exceptional Svc. award Rockwell Internat., 1972, Outstanding Contbn. award, 1976, NASA ALT award, 1979, Shuttle Astronaut Snoopy award, 1982, Pub. Svc. Group Achievement award NASA, 1982, Rockwell Pres.'s award, 1983, 87. Mem. AIAA, ASME, Nat. Mgmt. Assn., Assn. U.S. Army, Varsity O Alumni Assn. Died June 28, 2003.

DEMARCO, ROLAND R. foundation executive; b. Mt. Morris, N.Y., July 21, 1910; s. Marion and Mary (Scalzette) DeM.; m. Lydia Hees, June 23, 1934; children: Richard, Ronald, Lynn Diploma, Geneseo State Tchrs. Coll., 1930; BS, N.Y. State Coll. Tchrs., 1934; AM, Columbia U., 1937, PhD, 1942; student, U. Munich, Germany, 1937, Shrivenham Am. U., Eng., 1945; postgrad., Officers Candidate Sch., 1944, Air Intelligence Sch., 1944; LLD, Chungang U., Seoul, Korea, 1959; DLitt, Sung Kyun Kwan U., Seoul, 1969; D.Litt., Hanyang U., Seoul, 1974. Instr. Gowanda Pub. Schs., 1930-34; dir. social studies East Islip H.S., N.Y., 1934-38; instr. social scis. Coll. Charleston, 1939, Columbia U., 1939-40; staff mem. Air Intelligence Sch., 1944-45; vis. prof. Columbia U., 1946-47; prof. history, head dept. social scis. Ala. State Tchrs. Coll., 1940-46, pres. dept., dean, 1949, from adminstrv. head to pres., 1949-52; pres. Finch Coll., 1952-70, pres. emeritus, cons., 1970-75; chmn., CEO Internat. Human Assistance Programs, Inc., N.Y.C., 1973-82, hon. chmn., 1982-84, 85-96, pres., CEO, 1984-85; head history dept. Finch Jr. Coll., 1947-49. Curriculum cons. Jackson County Schs., Ala., 1940-43; mem. Nat. Adv. Coun. Edn. Disadvantaged Children, 1971-73; exec. vice chmn., chmn. ednl. adv. com. Am.-Korea Found., 1953-64, pres., 1964-68, 71-73, hon. chmn., 1968-71, chmn., chief exec. officer, 1973-75. Author: The Italianization of African Natives, 1943, The Comeback Country, Vol. I: Light of the East, an Insight into Korea, 1972. Contbr. articles to profl. jours. Founder Fathers of Am.-Korean Found., 1952; trustee Allen Stevenson Sch. Boys, pres., 1956-58; bd. dirs., treas. Council Higher Edn. Instns., N.Y.C.; pres. All Am. Open Karate Championships, 1965-80, Karate Championships North Am., 1967-80; v.p. World Taekwan Do Fedn., 1973-82; trustee Universidad Politecnica de P.R., San Juan, 1974-85; bd. dirs. Am. Behavioral Scis., 1967-80; color commentator ABC-TV Wide World of Sports for Billiard Championship Match, 1962. Served to 1st lt. USAAF, 1943-46 Decorated Order Cultural Merit Nat. medal (Korea); named hon. citizen of Seoul, 1964, knight officer Order of Merit (Italy); recipient Disting. Alumni award, SUNY, 1969, Coll. Arts and Sci. at Geneseo, 1971, Profl. Achievement award, Geneseo Alumni Assn., 2001. Home: Rochester, NY. Died Mar. 21, 2003.

DEMBO, LAWRENCE SANFORD, English educator; b. Troy, N.Y., Dec. 3, 1929; s. Irving and Mildred (Spiwak) D.; m. Royce Benderson, Mar. 15, 1953. BA, Syracuse U., 1951; MA, Columbia, 1952; PhD, Cornell U., 1955. Instr. English Cornell U., 1959-60; asst. prof. UCLA, 1960-65; Fulbright lectr. Montpellier, France, 1963-64; prof. English U. Wis., Madison, 1965-90, prof. emeritus, from 1990. Author: Hart Crane's Sanskrit Charge, A Study of the Bridge, 1960, The Confucian Odes of Ezra Pound, A Critical Appraisal, 1963, Conceptions of Reality in Modern American Poetry, 1966, The Monological Jew, A Literary Study, 1988, Detotalized Totalities: Synthesis and Disintegration in Naturalist, Existential, and Socialist Fiction, 1989; editor: Nabokov, The Man and His Work, 1967, Criticism, Speculative and Analytical Essays, 1968; co-editor: The Contemporary Writer: Interviews with Sixteen Novelists and Poets, 1972, Doris Lessing, Critical Studies, 1974, Directions for Criticism, 1977, Interviews with Contemporary Writers, Second Series, 1972-82, 83; editor in chief: Contemporary Literature, 1966-90; mem. editorial bd. Am. Lit., 1973 76; author poetry/contbr. regional jours. Served to lt. USNR, 1955-65. Guggenheim fellow, 1968-69; Am. Council Learned Socs. fellow, 1977-78 Home: Middleton, Wis. Died Dec. 5, 2003.

DEMBSKI, JANUSZ, historian, librarian; b. Gokańcz, Sept. 22, 1929; s. Franciszek and Matylda (Graclik) D.; m. Krystyna Dyzert, Mar. 8, 1958; children: Katarzyna, Magdalena. BA, U. Poznań, Poland, 1953; MA, U. Warsaw, Poland, 1955. Asst. prof. U. Poznań, 1955-56; libr. U. Libr., Posnań, 1956-62; dir. The Raczyński Libr., Posnań, from 1962. Bd. mem. Wieniawski Mus. Soc., Poznań, 1964—. Author: Bibliografia-Kultury Poznania 1945-1989, 1990, Bibliografia-Historii Poznania, 1995. Recipient Propagating of Culture award Prime Min., 1978, City award Mayor of Poznań, 1983. Mem. Polish Soc. Librs. Avocations: car, gardening, collecting bronze medals. Home: Poznań, Poland. Died Jan. 16, 1997.

DEMING, FREDERICK LEWIS, banker; b. Des Moines, Sept. 12, 1912; s. Fred Kemp and Erva Pearl (Smyres) D.; m. Corinne Inez Wilson, Feb. 4, 1935; children: Frederick Wilson, Richard Louis. AB, Washington U., St. Louis, 1934, MA, 1935, PhD, 1941. Mgr. research dept to 1st v.p. Fed. Res. Bank, St. Louis, 1941-57, pres. Mpls., 1957-65; undersec. for monetary affairs U.S. Dept. Treasury, Washington, 1965-69; gen. ptnr. Lazard Freres & Co., N.Y.C., 1969-71; pres. Nat. City Bancorp., Mpls., 1971-82. Trustee Washington U., 1966—2003; trustee Macalester Coll., 1959—2003, Endowment Fund, ARC, Washington, 1965-86. Mem.: Cosmos Club, Met. Club, Mpls. Club. Democrat. Home: Sanibel, Fla. Died Aug. 21, 2003.

DEMLING, JOSEPH ANTHONY, technical publications supervisor, writing and editing consultant; b. Denver, Mar. 30, 1936; s. Francis Charles Demling and Mary Frances (Kempter) Moss; m. Janice Louise Laub, Aug. 15, 1965 (div. Mar. 12, 1987); children: Joseph Adam, Jennifer Annette, James Andrew. AEE, Colo. Tech. Inst., 1960. Electronics technician Hathaway Instruments, Denver, 1960-61; sr. tech. writer Cushing and Nevell, Denver, 1961-62; tech. publs. engr. Martin Marietta Corp., Denver, 1962-66; writing dept. supr. Tech. Graphics Inc., Denver, 1966-68; sr. writer, editor Honeywell Inc., Littleton, Colo., 1968-79, supr. tech. publs., from 1979. Writing cons. Tech. Documentation Assocs., Denver, 1975-78. Writer and editor numerous tech. articles. Served as cpl. USMC, 1954-57. Mem. Mensa (columnist Matrix Mag. of Denver chpt.), Intertel. (contbr. articles to jour.). Avocations: chess, four-wheeling, running, weight training, reading. Home: Littleton, Colo. Deceased.

DEMUZIO, VINCE THOMAS, state legislator; b. Gillespie, Ill., May 7, 1941; s. Vince and Catherine McKnight (Murphy) D.; m. Deanna Joan Clemonds, June 23, 1962; children: Bradley, Stephanie. BA, Sangamon State U.; MA, U. Ill., Springfield, 1996; JD (hon.), Lewis and Clark C.C. Investigator Office of Sec. of State, Springfield, Ill.; exec. dir. Ill. Valley Econ. Devel. Corp., Carlinville; mem. Ill. State Senate, Springfield, 1974—2004, asst. majority leader, 1983-92, asst. minority leader, 1992—2003, majority leader, 2003—04. State ctrl. committeeman 20th Congl. Dist., Springfield, 1982-2002; state chmn. Ill. Dem. Ctrl. Com., 1986-90; precinct committeeman Macoupin County Dem. Ctrl. Com., Carlinville, 1992-2004, chmn., 1992-2004. Named Friend of Agriculture Ill. Extension Adviser's Assn., 1993, Legislator of Yr. Ill. Edn. Assn., 1976; recipient Ill. Agriculture award Ill. Assn. Vocat. Agriculture Tchrs., 1993. Mem. K. of C., Elks. Roman Catholic. Avocations: historical, biographical and political reading. Home: Carlinville, Ill. Died Apr. 27, 2004.

DENNETT, WILSON PAGE, accountant; b. Exeter, N.H., Apr. 27, 1928; s. Francis Card and Eva Mae (Benson) D.; m. Margaret Esther Denham, Dec. 26, 1952; children: Dorothy Dennett Schmidt, Susan Dennett Engle, James Wilson, David Charles. A of Acctg., Burdett Coll., 1949; BBA in Acctg., Northeastern U., 1955. CPA. Clk., acct. Jenney Mfg. Co., Boston, 1950-51; staff acct., auditor U.S. Smelting, Refining & Mfg. Co., Boston, 1952-59; sole practice CPA Hampton, N.H., 1960-84; sr. ptnr. Dennett and Dennett, CPA's, Hampton, from 1985. Auditor Seacoast Vis. Nurse Assn., Hampton, 1962-67. Treas. Town of Hampton, 1969—, Hampton Sch. Dist., 1959—, Hampton River Boat Club, 1968—; past deacon, auditor 1st Congl. Ch., Hampton. Mem. Nat. Soc. Pub. Accts., Am. Inst. of CPA's, N.H. Soc. of CPA's, State of N.H. Bd. of Accountancy CPA, Portsmouth (N.H.) Power Squadron, Hampton Beach C. of C. (bd. dirs.), Govt. Fin. Officers Assn., Hampton JC's (1st treas. 1961-63). Lodges: Rotary (pres. Hampton club 1972-73), Shriners (bd. dirs. Portsmouth club), Order of Ea. Star. Republican. Avocations: boating, ballroom dancing, coin collecting/numismatics. Home: Hampton, NH. Deceased.

DENNIS, WALTER DECOSTER, suffragan bishop; b. Washington, Aug. 23, 1932; BA, Va. State Coll., 1952; MA, NYU, 1953; M.Div., Gen. Theol. Sem., 1958, D.D. (honoris causa), 1980, Interdenominational Theol. Ctr.-Absalom Jones Theol. Inst., 1977; L.H.D. (hon.), Va. State U., 1983, Episcopal Sem. of S.W., 1983. Ordained deacon Protestant Episcopal Ch., 1956, ordained priest, 1958, ordained suffragan bishop, 1979. Curate St. Phillip's Ch., Bklyn., 1956; asst. min. Cathedral Ch. of St. John the Divine, N.Y.C., 1956-60, canon residentiary, 1965-79; vicar St. Cyprian's Ch., Hampton, Va., 1960-65; suffragan bishop of N.Y., 1979-99. Adj. asst. prof. Am. history and constl. law Hampton Inst., 1961-65; adj. prof. Christian ethics Gen. Theol. Sem., 1975-79; lectr. U. of South Div. Sch., Sewanee, Tenn., 1974-75; mem. Nat. Task Force on Hunger, Episc. Ch., 1975-76; mem. adv. bd. Episc. Ch.'s Teaching Series: Ethics, 1975-99; convenor Black Caucus Diocese of N.Y., 1976-77; served as Diocese examining chaplain; mem. religious liberty com. Nat. Coun. Chs.; rsch. fellow Episc. Theol. Sem. of SW, 1978; N.Y. dep. Gen. Conv., 1979; mem. numerous coms. Diocese of N.Y.; adminstr. numerous programs for Cathedral Ch. of St. John the Divine; chmn. standing commn. Constn. and Canons; mem. Joint nominating com. for election of presiding bishop; mem. Standing Commn. on Structure of the Ch., 1995—; v.p. Province II, 1996—, mem. coun. of advice to presiding bishop, 1996—. Author: (booklets) Puerto Rican Neighbors, 1958, Mexican American Neighbors, 1960; contbg. author: (chpt.) On the Battle Lines, 1962; contbr. articles to profl. jours. Bd. dirs. Manhattanville Cmty. Ctr., Inc., Abortion Repeal Assn., Assn. For Study of Abortion, Inst. for Study of Human Resources, Homosexual Cmty. Counselling Ctr., Nat. Orgn. for Reform of Marijuana Laws, N.Y. Tng. Sch. for Deaconesses, Soc. Juvenile Justice and Sex Info. and Edn. Counsel of U.S., Planned Parenthood Fedn. of Am., Lenox Hill Hosp. Mem. Union Black Episcopalians, Guild of St. Ives (founder, sec.). Died Mar. 30, 2003.

DENSEN-GERBER, JUDIANNE, psychiatrist, lawyer, educator; b. N.Y.C., Nov. 13, 1934; d. Gustave A. and Beatrice D.; m. Michael M. Baden, June 14, 1958; children: Trissa Austin Baden, Judson Michael, Lindsey Robert Baden, Sarah Densen Baden AB cum laude, Bryn Mawr Coll., 1956; LLB, Columbia U., 1959, JD, 1969; MD, NYU, 1963. Bar: N.Y. 1961. Rotating intern French Hosp., N.Y.C., 1963-64; resident psychiatry Bellevue Hosp., N.Y.C., 1964-65, Met. Hosp., N.Y.C., 1965-67; ethics com. Park City Hosp., Bridgeport, Conn., 1988-93; mem. core staff Addiction Services Agy., N.Y.C., 1966-67; founder Odyssey House (psychiat. residence for rehab. narcotics addicts), N.Y.C., Mich., Maine, N.H., Utah, La., Australia, N.Z., 1967, from clin. dir. to pres. bd., 1967-82, exec. dir., 1967-74; pres., founder, CEO Odyssey Inst. Am., 1974-82; pres. Odyssey Inst. Australia, 1977-86, Odyssey Inst. Internat., Inc., 1978—2003; chair Odyssey Inst. Corp. Conn., 1974—2003; attending physician Gracie Sq. Hosp., N.Y.C., 1982-93, Park City Hosp., Bridgeport, Conn., 1985-93; mem. ethics com. Bridgeport Hosp., 1985—2000, attending physician, 1985—2000, Northwest Gen. Hosp., Detroit, 1985-86; active staff St. Vincent's Hosp., Bridgeport, 1987-2000; courtesy staff Norwalk Hosp., 1993—2000. Assoc. vis. prof. law U. Utah Law Sch., 1973-75; adj. prof. law N.Y. Law Sch., 1973-76; chairperson plenary session drug abuse Am. Acad. Forensic Scis., 1972, sec. psychiatry sect., 1973, chmn. sect., 1974-2003; founder, 1973, since pres. Inst. Women's Wrongs; founder, since pres. Odyssey Inst. (health care for socially disadvantaged), 1974-80; bd. dirs. Simpson St. Devel. Assn., An Extraordinary Event (One to One for Mental Retardation), Bridge House; mem. Nat. Adv. Commn. Criminal Justice Standards and Goals, 1971-74, Pres.'s Commn. on White House Fellows, 1972-76; mem. drug experience adv. com. HEW, 1973-76; v.p. psychiat. sect. Internat. Forensic Medicine Conf., Budapest, 1967; pres. N.Y. Council Alcoholism, 1978-2003; co-chair com. on reproductive rights vs. best interest of the child Mich. State Senate, 1984-86; trustee Nat. Forensic Ctr., Princeton, N.J., 1985-2003, keynote speaker nat. conf., 1988, lectr., 1988; speaker Conf. for Multiple Personality Disorder, Chgo., 1985-2003; cons. to Mich. State Legislature to draft legislation on The Best Interests of the Child vs. the New Reproductive Techs., 1986; amicus curiae brief in Mary Beth Whitehead appeal Surrogate Mothering, 1987; sr. non-govt. psychiatrist L'Ambiance Plaza disaster, Bridgeport, 1987; guest lectr. narcotics addiction NYU Sch. Medicine, also Sch. Law.; in field dir. Daitch Shopwell, Inc.; cons. substance abuse Insight Inc., Flint, Mich., 1987-88; guest speaker Cornell U., 1989, Internat. Hypnosis Soc. of Yale, 1989, Cumberland Law Sch., 1989, Sacred Heart U., 1994; founder, CEO, pres. The Family Maintenance Health Orgn., LLC; guest speaker Nat. Ctr. Forensic Scis. Author: (with Trissa Austin Baden) Drugs, Sex, Parents and You, 1972, We Mainline Dreams, The Odyssey House Story, 1973, Walk in My Shoes, 1976; (with David Sandberg) The Role of Child Abuse in Delinquency and Juvenile Court Decision-Making, 1984, Chronic Acting-Out Students and Child Abuse: A Handbook for Intervention, 1986, Shortened Forms: A Manual for Teachers On; (with John Dugan) Issues in Law and Psychiatry, 1988; contbr. articles to profl. jours.; editor: Jour. Corrective and Social Psychiatry, 1975; co-developer, co-inventor virocidal surface cleaner against AIDS, 1988 Mem. N.Y.C. Crime Control Commn., 1975-79, Gov.'s Task Force on Crime Control, Albany, N.Y., 1977-79, N.Y. State Crime Control Planning Bd., 1975-79; del. White House Conf. on Youth, 1971; bd. dirs. Nat. Coalition for Children's Justice, 1975-2003, Am. Soc. for Prevention of Cruelty to Children, 1979-2003, Mary E. Walker Found., 1978; psychiat. cons. Good Shepherd Home for Girls, 1989-90. Recipient Woman of Achievement award AAUW, 1970; Myrtle Wreath award Hadassah, 1970; B'nai B'rith Woman of Greatness award, 1971; Otty award for service to N.Y.C. Our Town Newspaper, 1977; named Dame of White Cross Australia, #1 Dame of Malta, Ky. Col., N.Y. State Hon. Fire Chief. Fellow Am. Coll. Legal Medicine (Congl. cert. merit 1990, #2 Rep. gold medal, 2002); mem. AMA, Conn. State Soc., Fairfield County Med. Soc., Soc. Med. Jurisprudence, Therapeutic Communities Am. (founding mem., 1st v.p. 1975-2003), Am. Acad. Psychiatry and Law (mem. AIDS ad hoc com 1988-2003), Am. Psychiat. Assn., Women's Forum N.Y. (founding mem.), Nat. Women's Forum, Internat. Women's Forum, Internat. Soc. Multiple Personality and Dissociative States, Conn. Med. Assn., Am. Orthopsychiat. Assn., ABA, N.Y. State Bar Assn., N.Y. County Women's Bar Assn., N.Y. Assn. Vol. Agys. Narcotics Addiction and Substance Abuse (dir. 1968-2003), Am. Psychiat. Assn., N.Y. Med. Assn., Post Traumatic Stress Syndrome Soc., Fairfield County Med. Soc. (physicians health subcom. 1986-92), Congl. Physicians Advisory Coun. (hon. chmn) 2001-2003, Congl. Bus. Commn. (hon. chmn) 2001-2003, Womens City Club N.Y.C. Republican. Unitarian Universalist. Died May 11, 2003.

DENTON, ELWOOD VALENTINE, economist; b. Peoria, Ill., Feb. 14, 1912; s. George Washington and Nina (Brown) D.; m. Sara Reinartz, Sept. 17, 1938; 1 child, Edwood Valentine, II. B.S. in Bus., Miami U., Oxford, Ohio, 1934; M.B.A., Case Western Res. U., 1948; diploma Stonier Grad. Sch. Banking Rutgers U., 1955. Statistician, Armco Steel Corp., Middletown, Ohio, 1935-40; econ. analyst, asst. cashier Fed. Res. Bank, Cleve., 1940-59; adminstr. Central Nat. Bank, Cleve., 1960-65; v.p. Nat. Bank of Jackson (Mich.), 1965-69; salary adminstr. Consumers Power Co., Jackson, 1969-71, corp. economist, 1971-77, ret., 1977; econ. cons. Downtown Devel. Authority, Jackson, 1978-79; mem. Jackson Ofcls. Compensation Commn., 1971-79; chmn. Council on Econ. Edn. for Mich., 1976-77; mem. advisory coun. on econ. edn. Olivet Coll., 1971-78; mem. Chgo. Economists Group, Fed. Res. Bank Chgo., 1971-77; 1st v.p., sec., dir. 1st Walnut Creek Mut., Rossmoor-Walnut Creek, Calif., 1987-88; pres. Family Svc. Assn. Jackson County (Mich.); dir., sec. Golden Rain Found., 1984-87, chair audit com., 1989-92; Rossmoor-Walnut Creek, 1985-87. Lt. commdr. Supply Corps, USNR, 1942-45. Decorated Navy Commendation ribbon. Mem. Nat. Assn. Bus. Economists, Econ. Soc. Mich. (governing bd. 1973-79, treas. 1977-79), Family Service Assn. Cleve. (life), Phi Beta Kappa, Beta Theta Pi. Republican. Lutheran. Club: Kiwanis (pres. Bay Village, Ohio, club 1963-64). Author: What Is a Social Worker Worth?, 1957. Home: Vienna, Va. Died Nov. 26, 2002.

DEPPER, ESTELLE M. lawyer; b. Oakland, Calif., May 13, 1942; d. Martin S. and Estelle D. Depper. BA, U. Calif., Berkeley, 1964, JD, 1967. Bar: Calif. 1967. V.p., mng. sr. counsel Wells Fargo Bank, San Francisco, 1982-98; sole practitioner San Francisco, from 1998. Author: California Trust Administration, 1998. Bd. dirs. Holy Names H.S., Oakland, 1996—. Mem. ABA (chair com. on adminstrn. and distbn. of trusts 1989-93), Calif. State Bar (exec. com. for estate planning sect. 1979-81), San Francisco Bar Assn. (chair probate and trust law sect. 1979-80), Alameda County Bar Assn. Home: Oakland, Calif. Deceased.

DE SEIFE, RODOLPHE J.A. law educator; b. Alexandria, Egypt, Aug. 8, 1925; came to U.S. 1946; s. Rodolphe H. and Hermine (v. Droesel) de S.; m. Gloria B. Vasta, Mar. 25, 1948; children: Alix Clotilde, Gabrielle Hermine, Suzanne Aimée, Rodolphe Charles. AB with honors, Coll. de la Ste. Famille, Cairo, Egypt, 1943; postgrad., Columbia U., 1947-48; JD, Cath. U. Am., 1955; LLM, George Washington U., 1965. Bar: D.C. 1955, U.S. Supreme Ct. 1958, U.S. Ct. Appeals (4th cir.) 1961, Md. 1971, U.S. Ct. Appeals (7th cir.) 1977, Ill. 1990. Mgr. tariffs and schedules Air France, N.Y.C., 1948-51; air transport examiner Civil Aeronautics Bd., Washington, 1951-55; litigation atty. Antitrust div. U.S. Dept. Justice, Washington, 1955-57; assoc. Baker, McKenzie & Hightower, Washington, 1957-58; of counsel Simpson, Thacher and Bartlett, Washington, 1960-62, Paris, 1958-72;

asst. prof. law W.Va. U., 1973-75; dir. W. Va. Resources Ctr., 1973-75; prof. law No. Ill. U., De Kalb, from 1975. Faculty Nat. Jud. Coll., Reno, Nev., 1985—; cons. U.S. Dept. Labor, Washington, 1981-94; mem. alternative dispute resolution coord. com. Ill. Supreme Ct., 1990—; cons. minority U.S. Senate Fgn. Rels. Commn., 1988; cons. alternative com. Ill. Supreme Ct., 1990—; gen. counsel Société Amèricaine de Philosophie de Langue Francaise, 1989—. Author: Solving Disputes Through Commercial Arbitration, 1987, Law for the Tourist, 1956, An Introduction to the Shar'ia (The Law of Islam), 1994, (practice guide) Domke on Arbitration, 1986; editor/translator: China Comes of Age, 1971; contbr. articles to profl. jours. Founder, bd. dirs., gen. counsel United Community Nat. Bank, Washington, 1964-65; charter mem. Washington Legal Found. Acad. Adv. Bd., 1986—; cons. U.S. Senate Subcom. on Constn., 1985-86; vol. atty. Legal Aid Soc., Washington, 1955-58. Lt. col. U.S. Army Res. ret. Recipient Silver Medal City of Toulon, France, 1987, Raoul Follereau award, Cairo, 1941. Mem. ABA (Gold Key award Am. Law Students Assn. 1955), Am. Arbitration Assn., D.C. Bar Assn., Md. Bar Assn., Arab Am. Bar Assn. of Ill. (bd. dirs. 1994—), Scribes, German Am. Law Assn., Delta Theta Phi (Gold Key scholar 1954). Clubs: Nat. Lawyers (Washington), Officers (Bolling Field AFB, Washington). Republican. Roman Catholic. Home: Bethesda, Md. Deceased.

DE SHAZOR, ASHLEY DUNN, business consultant; b. Blackstone, Va., May 28, 1919; s. Francis Bertram and Carrie Lee (Joyner) DeS.; m. Margot Joy Best, Sept. 18, 1943 (dec. June 1966); children: Margot Joy DeShazor Brydon, Nancy De Shazor Bourke, Linda De Shazor Dunlosky; m. Shirley Dean Laffey, June 1, 1968; 1 son, Dean Laffey. BSBA, U. Richmond, Va., 1941. With Sears, Roebuck & Co., also pres. Sears, Roebuck de Colombia, 1941-63; with Montgomery Ward & Co., Chgo., 1963-80, procurement asst. to v.p. and gen. mdse. mgr., 1963-65, v.p., corp. credit mgr., 1966-80. Bd. dirs. Montgomery Ward Credit Corp., Signature Fin./Mktg. Inc., Montgomery Ward Auto Club, Jefferson Stores, Inc. Trustee, exec. com. Nat. Found. Consumer Credit; bd. govs. Credit Rsch. Ctr. and Privacy Rsch. Ctr., Purdue U.; trustee Farm Found.; bd. assocs. U. Richmond, 1972-80; mem. Fulbright grant selection com. for Colombia; mem. Ill. Electronic Funds Transfer Study Commn. Lt. comdr. USNR, ret., 1958. Mem. Nat. Retail Mchts. Assn. (bd. dirs., past chmn. credit mgmt. divsn.), Acad. Polit. Sci. (life), The Retired Officers Assn. (life), U.S. Naval Inst. (life), Rotary Club (Scottsdale, Ariz.), Paradise Valley Country Club (Ariz.), Sigma Alpha Epsilon. Presbyterian. Home: Paradise Valley, Ariz. Died Aug. 19, 2002.

DETARNOWSKY, NIXON, forensic safety engineer; b. Chgo., Oct. 29, 1913; s. George and Bertha Duffield (Nixon) deT.; m. Althea Jean Murphy, (wid. Oct. 1952); children: Althea Oakley, Kristin Carrol; m. Jean Burwell Moore; children: Nixon Alexander, Anne Travis. BS, Harvard U., 1935. Cert. Indsl. Safety Engring., Ill. Safety inspector Shipways and Plate Shop, Fed. Shipbuilding and Dry Dock Co., 1943-44; safety supr. Western Electric Co., Manhattan, N.Y., 1944-46; safety engr. The F&M Schaefer Brewing Co., 1946-59, corp. mgr., safety and med. svcs., 1960-71; sr. cons. Risk Adminstrn. Svcs., 1971-72; mgr., safety, health and med. group Am. Nat. Standards Inst., 1972-78; cons. forensic safety engring., from 1971. Treas. Pilot Knob (N.Y.) Assn., 1984—, Pilot Knob Vol. Fire Fighters Asn., 1983—. Active church choir, Harrisena Community Ch., Queensbury, N.Y. Mem. Safety Execs. of N.Y. (pres. 1958), Veterans of Safety (pres. Met. chpt. 1961), Standards Engring. Soc., Am. Soc. Safety Engrs. (pres. Met. chpt. 1956, adminstr., cons. div., 1983-85). Home: Kattskill Bay, NY. Died June 5, 2000.

DETRA, RALPH WILLIAM, research laboratory administrator; b. Thompsontown, Pa., Mar. 23, 1925; s. Ralph Emerson and Sara Jane (Portzline) D.; m. Charlesanna Francis Eberly, June 21, 1947; children: Stephen William, David Eberly. BS in Mech. Engring., Cornell U., 1946, MS of Aero. Engring., 1951; DSc of Tech., Eidgenossische Technische Hochschule, Zurich, Switzerland, 1953. Supr. aerodynamic research, aviation gas turbine div. Westinghouse Corp., Kansas City, Mo., 1953-55; v.p. missile programs Avco Systems Div., Wilmington, Mass., 1960-66, v.p. gen. mgr., 1966-71; prin. research scientist Avco Everett (Mass.) Research Labs. Inc., 1955-59, v.p. fossil energy tech., 1972-81, exec. v.p., gen. mgr., 1981-84, pres., 1984-90; ret. Avco Rsch. Lab., Everett, Mass., 1990. Pres. Tyco Labs. Inc., Waltham, Mass., 1971-72. Author papers in field. Lt. (j.g.) USN, 1943-47. Fellow NRC, 1951-52. Mem. Sigma Xi, Tau Beta Pi. Republican. Episcopalian. Avocation: woodworking. Home: Gloucester, Mass. Died June 30, 1997.

DEUSCHLE, KURT WALTER, physician, educator; b. Kongen, Germany, Mar. 14, 1923; came to U.S., 1924, naturalized, 1949; s. John and Marie (Schaefer) D.; m. Jeanne Magagna, 1975; children by previous marriage— Kurt J., Sally, James. BS cum laude, Kent State U., 1944; MD, U. Mich., 1948. Intern Colo. Gen. Hosp., Denver, 1948-49; resident medicine, fellow oncology Upstate Med. Ctr. SUNY, Syracuse, 1950-52; resident U.S.P.H.S. Navajo Indian Reservation, Ft. Defiance, Ariz., 1953; instr. medicine Upstate Med. Ctr. SUNY, Syracuse, 1954-55; asst. prof. pub. health and preventive medicine Cornell Med. Coll., 1955-60; prof., chmn. dept. community medicine U. Ky., 1960-68; Ethel H. Wise prof., chmn. and dir. dept. community medicine Mt. Sinai Sch. of Medicine, CUNY, 1968-90, prof. emeritus, from 1990; prof. emeritus, disting. svc. prof. Mt. Sinai Hosp., from 1993; Ethel H. Wise chmn. emeritus Mt Sinai Sch. of Medicine, CUNY, from 1993, Disting. Svc. prof. dept. community medicine, from 1993, Ethel H. Wise chmn. emeritus. Merrimon lectr. U. N.C., Chapel Hill, 1975; mem. N.Y.C. Bd. Health, 1982-89; vis. prof. U. Lagos, Nigeria, 1977, Chinese Med. Assn., People's Republic China, 1986; mem. Tb control adv. com. Center Disease Control Dept. HEW; cons. manpower intelligence NIH; mem. Inst. Medicine of Nat. Acad. Scis., Washington; mem. rural health systems del. to China, 1978; mem. Nat. Adv. Environ. Health Scis. Coun. NIH, 1982-86; sr. advisor Report of U.S. Preventive Services Task Force, The Guide to Clinical Preventive Servcies, HHS, 1989; mem. com. pub. health N.Y. Acad. Medicine, 1983—, N.Y. State Council on Grad. Med. Edn., 1987—, adv. com. Am. Ba. Family Practice, 1986—. Author: (with J. Adair) The People's Health: Anthropology and Medicine in a Navajo Community, 1970, rev. and expanded edit., 1988; Contbr. to: (ed. John Norman) Medicine in the Ghetto, 1969, Community Medicine: Teaching, Research and Health Care, (ed. Lathem and Newberry), 1970. Served with AUS, 1943-46. Recipient Award of Honor, Mayor of N.Y.C., 1989, Jacobi award Associated Alumni Mt. Sinai Med. Ctr., 1989, Alexander Richman Commemorative award Mt. Sinai Med. Ctr., 1991; Duncan Clark award Assn. Tchrs. Preventive Medicine, 1990; Commonwealth Fund sr. health fellow, 1966-67 Fellow AAAS, Am. Coll. Preventive Medicine (past pres., Disting. Svc. award 1975); mem. Am. Pub. Health Assn. (award for excellence in domestic health 1975), Alpha Omega Alpha. Home: New York, NY. Died Feb. 10, 2003.

DEVANEY, JOHN FRANCIS, magazine editor, writer; b. N.Y.C., Mar. 15, 1926; s. John and Delia (McGowan) D.; m. Barbara Teeny Masciocchi, Apr. 16, 1955; children: John, Luke. BS, NYU, 1949. Sports editor Parade mag., N.Y.C., 1956-62, Fawcett Publs., N.Y.C., 1962-70, CBS Publs., N.Y.C., 1976-79; editor Sport mag., N.Y.C., 1979-82, CBS-Women's Day Sports, N.Y.C., 1982-85, Harris Golf Mags., N.Y.C., from 1986. Adj. lectr. Fordham U., 1980—. Author: Horse's Mouth, 1986, Bo Jackson: Man for All Seasons, 1988, Ronald Reagan, President, 1990, Break 100 in 21 Days, 1991; editor: Memories Mag., 1991-92. With AUS, 1944-46, ETO. Mem. PEN. Roman Catholic. Avocations: jazz, swing. Home: New York, NY. Deceased.

DEVINE, CHARLES JOSEPH, JR., urologist, educator; b. Norfolk, Va., Feb. 23, 1923; s. Charles Joseph and Julia Vera (Campbell) D.; m. Rae Lou Ellis, Sept. 30, 1950; children— Charles Joseph III, Paul E., Jane C., David C., Rachel A. BA, Washington and Lee U., 1943; MD, George Washington U., 1947; DSc (hon.), Ea. Va. Med. Sch., 1994. Diplomate: Am. Bd. Urology, Nat. Bd. Med. Examiners. Intern Brady Inst., Johns Hopkins Hosp., 1947-48; fellow in urology Cleve. Clinic, 1948-50; resident in urology U.S. Naval Hosp., Phila., 1951; with Devine Fiveash Urology, Ltd., Norfolk, Va., 1952-91, pres., 1975-84; chief urology Med. Center Hosps., 1979-80. Pres. med. staff Norfolk Gen. Hosp., 1970; chmn. surgery dept. DePaul Hosp., 1965-66; chief of urology Children's Hosp. of King's Daus., 1977-85; clin. coord. for urology Eastern Va. Med. Sch., 1973-75, prof. urology, 1975-94, chmn. dept., 1975-89, emeritus prof., 1994—; dir. Devine Ctr. for Genito-urinary Reconstruction, Sentara Norfolk Gen. Hosp., 1991—; mem. Project Hope, Alexandria, Egypt, 1977; Royal Australasian Coll., Surgeons Found. lectr., 1982, condr. symposia; vis. prof. univs. Co-editor: Urology in Practice, 1978; mem. editorial bd. Jour. Urology, 1978-89, Weekly Updates in Urology, 1978—; contbr. numerous articles to profl. jours., chpts. in books. Served to lt. M.C. USNR, 1950-52. Fellow ACS (pres. Va. chpt. 1967), Am. Acad. Pediats., Am. Soc. Plastic and Reconstructive Surgeons (assoc.); mem. AMA, AAAS, Med. Soc. Va., Norfolk Acad. Medicine, Am. Urol. Assn. (hon.) (Disting. Contbn. award 1993, Ramon Griteras award 1997, others), Va. Urol. Soc. (pres. 1968), Tidewater Urol. Assn., Societe Internationale d'Urologie, Am. Assn. Genitourinary Surgeons, Soc. Pediat. Urology, Soc. Univ. Urologists, Genitourinary Reconstructive Surgeons (founding pres. 1987-88), Seaboard Med. Soc., N.Y. Acad. Scis., Alpha Tau Omega, Nu Sigma Nu. Clubs: Norfolk Yacht and Country (Norfolk), U.S. Sailing. Roman Catholic. Home: Norfolk, Va. Died Feb. 12, 1999.

DEVISÉ, PIERRE ROMAIN, city planner, educator; b. Brussels, July 27, 1924; came to U.S., 1935, naturalized, 1958; s. Victor Pierre and Madeleine (Cupers) DeV.; m. Margaret Ahern, Nov. 17, 1978; children: Peter Charles, Daniel Romain. BA, U. Chgo., 1945, MA, 1958; PhD, U. Ill., 1985. Chancellor Belgian Consul, Chgo., 1945-47, comml. attache, 1947-56, Belgian Consulate Gen., Chgo.; planning dir. Hyde Park-Kenwood Conf., 1956-57; research planner Northeastern Ill. Planning Commn., 1958-60; sr. planner Chgo. City Planning Dept., 1961-63; asst. dir. Hosp. Planning Council for Met. Chgo., 1964-70, Ill. Regional Med. Program, 1971-73; prof. urban scis. U. Ill., 1973-81; prof. pub. adminstrn. Roosevelt U., Chgo., 1982—89. Lectr. De Paul U., 1962; vis. lectr. U. Mich., 1966, U. Hawaii, 1968, U. Ill., 1969, 70, U. Iowa, 1971, U. Chgo., 1972; prin. investigator Chgo. Regional Hosp. Study, 1966; exec. dir. Chgo. Commn. to Study Conv. Week Disorders, 1968-70; cons. Chgo. Commn. on Human Relations, 1966, Chgo. Model Cities Program, 1968, Cook County Council Govts., 1968, Comprehensive Health Planning, Inc., 1971; Census Bur., 1973, U.S. Senate Health Subcom., 1974, HEW, 1975, Ho. Ways and Means Com., 1975, Senate Banking Com., 1976. Author: monographs including Suburban Factbook, 1960, Social Geography of Metropolitan Chicago, 1960, Chicago's People, Jobs and Homes, 1963, Chicago's Widening Color Gap, 1967, Chicago's Apartheid Hospital System, 1968, Chicago, 1971, Ready for Another Fire, 1971, Misused and Misplaced Hospitals and Doctors, 1973, Chicago's Future, 1976, Chicago: Transformations of an Urban System, 1976, Chicago in the Year 2000, 1978; Descent From the Summit, 1985 Mem. Am. Statist. Assn., Chgo. Assn. Commerce and Industry, Am. Soc. Pub. Adminstrn., Am. Pub. Health Assn., Assn. Am. Geographers, Nat. Council Geog. Edn., Planned Parenthood Assn. Chgo., Old Town Boys Club. Clubs: City (Chgo.). Home: Chicago, Ill. Died May 26, 2004.

DEVLIN, GAIL E. insurance company executive; Sr. v.p. fin., dir. investor rels. The Chubb Corp., Warren, N.J. Died 2001.

DE WEERDT, MARK MURRAY, retired judge; b. Cologne, Germany, May 6, 1928; arrived in Can., 1949. s. Hendrik Eugen and Ina Dunbar (Murray) de W.; m. Linda Anne Alden Hadwen, Mar. 31, 1956; children: Simon André, Murray Hadwen, David Lockhart, Charles Dunbar. MA, Glasgow (Scotland) U., 1949; LLB, B.C. U., 1955. Cert. barrister and solicitor, B.C. 1956, N.W.T. 1958. Assoc. solicitor Cross & O'Grady, Victoria, B.C., 1956-57; adv. coun. Can. Dept. Justice, Ottawa, 1957-58; Crown Atty. Yellowknife, N.W.T., 1958-63; sr. counsel Can. Dept. Justice, Vancouver, 1976-79, gen. counsel and dir., 1979-81; sr. ptnr. deWeerdt, Searle, Finall et al., Yellowknife, N.W.T., 1958-71; magistrate and juvenile ct. judge N.W.T. Magistrate's Ct., Yellowknife, N.W.T., 1971-73; gen. solicitor Ins. Corp. B.C., Vancouver, 1974-76; justice N.W.T and Yukon Supreme Cts., Yellowknife & Whitehorse, 1981-96, Supreme Ct. of B.C., 1996-97, N.W.T and Yukon Cts. of Appeal, 1981-97, Ct. Martial Appeal Ct. of Can., 1995-97; ret., 1997; dep. judge Supreme Ct. N.W.T., 1996-97 and from 97, Nunavut Supreme Ct., from 1999. Mem. Pension Appeals Bd. under Can. Pension Plan, 1999—; chair jud. coun. N.W.T., Yellowknife, 1981-96; dir. Canadian Judges' Conf., 1982-89; alternating mem. Can. Judicial Coun., 1985-7, 89-91, 93-95. Author profl. papers. Vice-chmn. Yellowknife Sch. Dist. #1, 1964-68. Apptd. Queen's Coun., Can., 1968; recipient Commr.'s award for pub. svc. at highest level, 1997. Mem. Can. Bar Assn., Can. Inst. Adminstrn. Justice (life), N.W.T. Bar Assn. (pres. 1967-71), MacKenzie River and N.W.T. Progressive Conservative Assn. (pres. 1959-71). Avocations: reading, walking. Home: Vancouver, Canada. Died 2003.

DEWEY, DAVID LAWRENCE, banker, business consultant, author; b. Roswell, N.Mex., Feb. 13, 1952; s. Joseph J. Tydlaska and Dortha C. Dunlap. Student, Am. Inst. Banking, Dallas, 1973-75; BSJ in Pub., Market and Fiction Writing, Writers Inst. Am., Mamaroneck, N.Y., 1981; AA in Bus., N.Mex. State U., Alamogordo, 1985; cert. in computer ops., Banking Coll., Orlando, 1987; BA, grad. Western States Sch. Banking, U. N.Mex., 1991. Ops. officer 1st Nat. Bank Alamogordo, 1971-77, v.p. ops. and info. systems, 1985-91; bus. mgmt. cons. Quik-Key Systems Inc., Alamogordo, 1978-84, chmn. bd. Atlanta, 1978-84, Alamogordo, 1978-84; bus. mgr. Grindell & Rollins Ins. Inc., Alamogordo, 1984-85. Bus. cons., 1977—; owner, mgr. 3 cos., Alamogordo, 1978-84; bd. dirs. BDP Am., Miami. Author: Revelations, 1994; freelance contbr. articles to newspapers; syndicated columnist; composer: You Walked Away with My Heart, 1978. Mem. President's Adv. Council, 1984-87. Mem. Broadcast Music Corp., Writers Guild Am. Avocations: writing articles, novels, short stories, reading, swimming, travel. Home: Alamogordo, N.Mex. Deceased.

DEWEY, MICHAEL LAWRENCE, secondary school educator; b. Madison, Wis., Apr. 7, 1955; s. Lawrence And Lois (Rasmussen) D.; m. Tina Brieschke, June 20, 1981; child Alexander. MusB, U. Wis., 1978, Am. Conservatory, Chgo., 1981; MusM, U. Wis., 1982. Cert. K-12 tchr. instrumental music. Band dir. Madison Area Catholic Band Program, 1978-79; orch. dir. Crystal Lake (Ill.) High Sch., 1979-80; teaching asst. U. Wis., Madison, Wis., 1981-82; orch. dir. Madison Met. Sch., 1982-83, Middleton (Wis.) Cross Plains Sch., from 1983. Dir. Flambeau Chamber Players, Madison, 1985—, clarinetist Symphony Orch., Beloit, Wis., 1988—, Capital City Band, Madison, 1970—; condr. Summer Music Clinic, Madison, 1989—, Middleton Civic Orch., 1984—; organist Salem United Ch. of Christ, Verona, Wis., 1989—; clarinetist, asst. condr. VFW Band, Madison, 1968-73, 81—. Mem. Madison Musicians Assn., Middleton Edn. Assn., Wis. Sch. Music Assn. Lutheran. Avocations: travel, fishing, music, wine. Home: Middleton, Wis. Died June 21, 2001.

DEWHURST, WILLIAM GEORGE, psychiatrist, educator, research director; b. Frosterley, Durham, Eng., Nov. 21, 1926; came to Can., 1969; s. William and Elspeth Leslie (Begg) D.; m. Margaret Dransfield, Sept. 17, 1960; children— Timothy Andrew, Susan Jane BA, Oxford U., Eng., 1947, B.M., B.Ch., 1950; MA, Oxford U., 1961; D.P.M. with distinction, London U., 1961. House physician, surgeon London Hosp., 1950-52, jr. registrar, registrar, 1954-58; registrar, sr. registrar Maudsley Hosp., London, 1958-62, cons. physician, 1965-69; lectr. Inst. Psychiatry, London, 1962-64, sr. lectr., 1965-69; assoc. prof. psychiatry U. Alta., Edmonton, Can., 1969-72, prof., 1972-92, prof. emeritus, from 1992, Hon. prof. pharmacy and pharm. scis., 1979-97, chmn. dept. psychiatry, 1975-90, dir. emeritus neurochem. rsch. unit, from 1990, hon. prof. oncology, 1983-97, chmn. med. staff adv. bd., 1988-90. Mem. Atty. Gen. Alta. Bd. Rev., 1991, N.W.T. Bd. Rev., 1992-98, 95 Yukon Bd. Rev., 1994-98; pres.'s coun. U. Alta. Hosps., 1988-90, quality improvement coun., 1988-90, ethics consultative com., 1984-88, planning com. Vision 2000, 1985-

87, hos ps.' planning com. and joint conf. com., 1971, 80, 87-90; cons. psychiatrist Royal Alexandra Hosp., Edmonton, Edmonton Gen. Hosp., Alberta Hosp., Ponoka, Ponoka Gen. Hosp.; chmn. med. coun. Can. Test Com., 1977-79, Royal Coll. Text Com. in Psychiatry, 1971-80, examiner, 1975-83. Co-editor: Neurobiology of Trace Amines, 1984, Pharmacotherapy of Affective Disorders, 1985; also conf. procs. Referee Nature, Can. Psychiat. Assn. Jour., Brit. Jour. Psychiatry; mem. editorial bd. Neuropsychobiology, Psychiat. Jour. U. Ottawa. Contbr. over 100 articles to profl. jours. Chmn. Edmonton Psychiat. Svcs. Steering Com., 1977-80; chmn. Edmonton Psychiat. Svcs. Planning Com., 1985-90; mem. Provincial Mental Health Adv. Coun., 1973-79, Mental Health Rsch. Com., 1973, Edmonton Bd. Health, 1974-76; Can. Psychiat. Rsch. Found., 1985— (also bd. dirs.); bd. dirs. Friends of Schizophrenics, 1980—, Alta., 1988; grant referee Health & Welfare Can., Med. Rsch. Coun. Can., Ont. Mental Health Found., Man. Health Rsch. Coun., B.C. Health Rsch. Found. Capt. Royal Army M.C., 1952-54. Fellow Can. Coll. Neuropsychopharmacology (pres. 1982-84, Coll. medal 1993), Am. Psychopathol. Assn., Am. Coll. Psychiatrists, Am. Psychiat. Assn., Royal Coll. Psychiatrist; mem. AAAS, Alta. Psychiat. Assn. (pres. 1973-74), Can. Psychiat. Assn. (pres. 1983-84), Alta Coll. Physicians and Surgeons, Alta. Med. Assn. (nominating coun. 1992-93, health issues coun. 1994-98, co-chmn. task force on drug info., 1996-98), Child and Adolescent Assn. (bd. dirs., v.p. 1992, pres. 1994-98), Assn. for Acad. Psychiatry, Brit. Med. Assn. (Alta. rev. bd. 1991—), Faculty Club. Anglican. Avocations: music, hockey, football, chess, athletics. Home: Edmonton, Canada. Died Apr. 28, 2001.

DEWOLFE, GEORGE FULTON, lawyer; b. Oak Park, Ill., Jan. 22, 1949; s. John Chauncey and Dorothy Sinclair (Fulton) DeW. A.B., Yale U., 1971; LL.B., U. Toronto, Ont., Can., 1974. Bar: Ill. 1975, U.S. Dist. Ct. (no. dist.) Ill. 1975, U.S. Dist. Ct. (ea dist.) Wis. 1976, U.S. Ct. Appeals (7th cir.) 1980, N.Y. 1983, U.S. Supreme Ct. 1985. Assoc. DeWolfe, Poynton & Stevens, Chgo., 1975-80, ptnr., 1980—; legal adviser Brit. Consulate Gen., Chgo., 1984—; gen. counsel Suburban Hosp., Hinsdale, Ill., 1984—; adj. prof. law DePaul U., 1985—; mem. adv. bd. Health Law Inst., DePaul U., 1986—; spl. counsel City of Evanston, Ill., 1988. Assoc. editor U. Toronto Faculty of Law Rev., 1973-74, Hospital Law, 1986—; gen. editor Health Law, 1987. Bd. dirs., sec. St. Leonard's House of Episc. Diocese of Chgo., 1975-83, Chgo. AIDS Symposium Found., 1987; mem. Chgo. Area AIDS Task Force, 1987—. Mem. ABA, Ill. Bar Assn., Chgo. Bar Assn. (cert. appreciation 1983-84), Ill. Assn. Hosp. Attys., Nat. Health Lawyers Assn., Am. Soc. Law and Medicine, Am. Acad. Hosp. Attys. Club: University (Chgo.), Yale (Chgo.). Died 1989. Home: Chicago, Ill.

DEYNEKA, PETER, JR., religious organization executive; b. Chgo., Sept. 13, 1931; s. Peter and Vera (Demidovich) D.; m. Anita Marson, June 15, 1968. BA in Bibl. Lit., Wheaton Coll., 1953; MDiv, No. Bapt. Sem., 1957; Doctorate (hon.), No. Bapt. Seminary, 1996. Missionary Slavic Gospel Assn., Ecuador, Argentina, 1961-63, asst. dir., 1966-74, pres. Wheaton, Ill., 1975-91; dir. Russian Bible Inst., Buenos Aires, 1962-63; missionary, chaplain U.S. Army Seoul, Republic of Korea, 1963-65. Elder Coll. Ch., Wheaton, 1983-85; guest lectr. Fuller Theol. Sem., 1984, Grad. Sch., Wheaton Coll., 1984; pres. Russian Ministries, Wheaton, 1991—; guest spkr. TV and radio programs; cons. on religion in USSR and Eastern Europe, Billy Graham Assn., Trans World Radio, others. Co-author: Christians in the Shadow of the Kremlin, 1974, Peter Dynamite, 1975, A Song in Siberia, 1977. Mem. Interdenominational Fgn. Mission Assn. (bd. dirs.), S.Am. Crusades (bd. dirs.), Soc. for Study Religion and Communism (bd. dirs. 1979-81), Romanian Missionary Soc. (bd. dirs.), Soc. for Ctrl. Asian Nationalities (coun. advisors), The Commission (1992—). Home: Wheaton, Ill. Died Dec. 23, 2000.

DEYOUNG, EDWIN LAWSON, chemistry educator; b. Milw., Jan. 14, 1929; s. Henry Chung and Lillien (Lawson) DeY.; m. Eloise Ann Cunningham, July 6, 1956. BS, U. Louisville, 1952, MS, 1953; PhD, U. Ill., 1956. Rschr. Standard Oil Co., Whiting, Ind., 1956-60; dir. rsch. RBP Chem. Co., Milw., 1960-62; rschr. Unival Products, Des Plaines, Ill., 1962-68; prof. chemistry Chgo. City Colls., 1968-99. Contbr. articles to profl. publs. Cpl. U.S. Army, 1946-49. Fellow Am. Inst. Chemists. Achievements include 24 patents in field. Home: Chicago, Ill. Died Jan. 21, 1999.

DIAMOND, IRENE (IRENE DIAMOND), foundation administrator; b. Pitts., May 7, 1910; d. Horace and Leah (Grekin) Levine; m. Aaron Diamond, 1942 (dec.); 1 child, Jean. Ed., Pitts. Pub. Schs.; LHD (hon.), City Coll., CUNY, 1989, The Juilliard Sch., 1992; LLD (hon.), Queens Coll., CUNY, 1990, New Sch. Social Rsch., N.Y.C., 1994, Rockefeller U., 1997. Asst. editor story div. Warner Bros., Hollywood, Calif., 1934-35, editor, 1937-40; supr. dept. lit. Leland Hayward, Hollywood, 1935-37; editor story and talent div. Samuel Goldwyn-MGM, Hollywood and N.Y.C., 1940-41; editor story div., head talent div. Hal Wallis-Paramount Pictures, Hollywood and N.Y.C., 1941-70; pres., bd. dirs. Aaron Diamond Found., Inc., N.Y.C., 1986-96, Irene Diamond Fund, N.Y.C., from 1996. Bd. dirs. Aaron Diamond AIDS Rsch. Ctr., 1989—. Recipient Pres.'s medal Bank St. Coll., 1989, Liberty award Lambda Legal Def. and Edn. Fund, 1990, Disting. Community Svc. award United Hosp. Fund, 1990, medal Correctional Assn. of N.Y./Osborne Assn., 1990, Sybil C. Simon Disting. Patron award Arts and Bus. Coun., 1994, Disting. Grantmaker award Coun. on Founds., 1998, Brooke Astor award for outstanding contbns. to advancement of sci. Rockefeller U., 1999, Nat. Medal of Arts, Pres. Clinton, 1999. Mem. Film Soc. of Lincoln Ctr., Young Concert Artists, Human Rights Watch. Died Jan. 21, 2003.

DIAMOND, RICHARD EDWARD, publisher; b. S.I., N.Y., May 24, 1932; s. Joseph H. and Gertrude (Newhouse) D.; m. Alice W. Blach, July 27, 1963; children: Caroline Harrison, Alison, Richard Edward. Student, Cornell U., 1953; LHD (hon)., Wagner Coll., 1991. With S.I. Advance, 1953—2004; publisher, 1979—2004. Bd. dirs. Newspaper Advt. Bur. Trustee. S.I. Acad., 1967-89, pres. bd. dirs., 1977-87; bd. dirs. S.I. Hosp., 1978-88. Recipient Disting. Citizens award Wagner Coll., S.I., 1976 Mem. Am. Newspapers Pubs. Assn., Newspaper Assn. Am. (bd. dirs.). Jewish. Home: Staten Island, NY. Died Feb. 12, 2004.

DI BIASI, ELEANOR S. nurse, educator; b. N.Y.C., June 6, 1954; d. John Gerald and Joan Ann (De Martinis) Stapleton; divorced; children: Noré, Noël Grace. AAS in Nursing, Coll. S.I., 1975; BA in Psychology, CUNY, S.I., 1977; BSN, Wagner Coll., 1982, MSN, 1989; PhD in Nursing, Adelphi I., 1995. Lic. RN, N.Y., N.J. Head nurse South Beach Psychiat. Ctr., S.I., 1975-77; staff nurse Victory Meml. Hosp., Bklyn., 1978-80; adj. faculty Wagner Coll., S.I., 1988-94; faculty Columbia U. Sch. Nursing, N.Y.C., 1996; adj. prof., coursework Masters level thesis advisor Seton Hall U. Coll. Nursing, N.J., 1997; adj. prof. N.J. City Sch. Nursing, 2000; pvt. practice mental healthcare provider, from 1995. Cons., contact person Endometriosis Assn., Milw., 1994—. Rsch. dir.: (book) Health Care Trajectory, 1999; contbr. rsch. articles to profl. jours. Mem. N.Y. State Nurses Assn., Sigma Theta Tau. Avocations: boating, designing and making clothing, home decorating. Died July 6, 2002.

DICKERSON, GORDON EDWIN, animal geneticist, biologist; b. La Grande, Oreg., Jan. 30, 1912; s. Malcolm Gordon and Olive (Merrifield) D.; m. Myra Elizabeth Warren, Sept. 11, 1933; children: Alfred Gordon, Malcolm John, Davis Warren, Dean Ames. BS, Mich. State U., 1933; MS, U. Wis., 1934, PhD, 1937. Instr. U. Wis., Madison, 1935-41; geneticist Bur. Animal Industries USDA, Ames, Iowa, 1941-47; prof. animal sci. U. Mo., Columbia, 1947-52; geneticist, dir. rsch. Kimber Farms, Inc., Fremont, Calif., 1952-65; geneticist rsch. br. Can. Agriculture, Ottowa, Ont., Can., 1965-67; prof. animal sci. U. Nebr., Lincoln, 1967-87; rsch. geneticist U.S. Meat Animal Rsch. Ctr., Agrl. Rsch. Svc., USDA, Lincoln, 1967-87, collaborator, from 1987. Editor: Proceedings 3rd World Congress on Genetic Applied Livestock Production, 1987; contbr. articles to profl. jours. V.p. Mayor's Com. on Internat. Friendship, Lincoln, 1968—; pres. UN Assn., Lincoln, 1989-92. Named to Agrl. Rsch. Svc. Hall of Fame, 1990. Fellow AAAS, Am. Soc. Animal Sci. (breeding and genetics award 1970, Morrison award 1978); mem. Am. Dairy Sci. Assn., Genetics Soc. Am., Am. Genetics Assn., World Poultry Assn., Brit. Soc. Animal Production, U. Nebr. Emeritus Assn. (pres. 1988-89), Poultry Sci. Assn., Sigma Xi (pres. U. Nebr. chpt. 1987-88), Gamma Sigma Delta (Internat. Disting. Svc. Agr. award 1990). Republican. Presbyterian. Home: Lincoln, Nebr. Deceased.

DICKSON, DAVID WATSON DALY, retired college president; b. Portland, Maine, Feb. 16, 1919; s. David Augustus and Mary Margaret (Daly) D.; m. Vera Mae Allen, Aug. 5, 1951 (dec. July 1979); children: David Augustus II, Deborah Anne, Deirdre Elizabeth; m. Barbara Childs Mickey, Feb. 14, 1981; children: Robert Warren, Sharon Marlissa. AB, Bowdoin Coll., 1941, LHD (hon.), 1974; MA, Harvard U., 1942, PhD, 1949; LHD (hon.), Bloomfield Coll., 1983; DLitt (hon.), Montclair State Coll., 1989. Instr. to assoc. prof. English Mich. State U., 1948-63; prof., head English dept. No. Mich. U., Marquette, 1963-66; dean No. Mich. U. (Sch. Arts and Sci.), 1966-67, v.p. acad. affairs, 1967-68; provost, v.p. acad. affairs, prof. English Fed. City Coll., Washington, 1968-69; prof. English, asst. to pres. State U. N.Y. at Stony Brook, 1969-72, dean continuing and developing edn., prof. English, 1972-73; pres. Montclair State Coll., Upper Montclair, N.J., 1973-84, pres. emeritus, 1989, Disting. Service prof., 1984-88, prof. emeritus, 1989. Cons. Nat. Found. for Humanities, 1969-71, Mott Found., 1973-74; speaker in field. Author: An Isolate of Isolates, 1995; contbr. articles to profl. jours. Chmn. lt. com. Mich. Coun. Arts, 1963-68; bd. dirs. Nat. Com. on Future of State Colls. and Univs.; trustee Montclair Art Mus., North Essex Devel. and Action Coun., Bloomfield Coll., 1984-89; bd. overseers Bowdoin Coll., 1966-75, trustee, 1975-82; mem. policy bd. Project Change; mem. Bd. Commn. on Higher Edn. Mid. States Assn. Colls. and Secondary Schs., 1978-84; pres. Flagler County Auditorium, 1992-93. 1st lt. AUS, 1943-46. Recipient Disting. Teaching award Mich. State U., 1952; Disting. Educator award Bowdoin Coll., 1971; Austrian Cross of Honor for Letters and Arts; Rosenwald fellow, 1942-43; Smith Mundt fellow Syrian Nat. U. Damascus, 1958 59 Mem. MLA, Milton Soc., Am. Assn. State Colls. and Univs. (chmn. com. on undergrad. studies), Am. Assn. Colls. (commn. on liberal learning), Phi Beta Kappa, Omega Psi Phi, Sigma Psi Phi, Phi Kappa Phi, Rotary. Roman Catholic. Home: Palm Coast, Fla. Died Dec. 17, 2003.

DICOVSKY, CARLOS JOSE, physician; b. Rosario, Argentina, July 18, 1934; s. Elias Dicovsky; children: Sonia, Claudio. Med. diplomate, Rosario, 1959. Intern Sherbrooke (Que., Can.) Hosp.; resident Queen Mary Vets. Hosp., Montreal, Que., Can., Montreal Heart Inst., St. Vincent Charity Hosp., Cleve.; physician, dir. Cardiac Clinic, Paterson, N.J., from 1976. Author: The Auricular Electrocardiogram, Principios de Hemodinamia, Principios de Ecocardiografia y Doppler. Fellow Am. Coll. Cardiology; mem. Argentine Am. Med. Soc. (past pres. 1991-94). Avocation: boating. Home: Fort Lee, NJ. Died Oct. 26, 2000.

DIEHL, WILLIAM HENRY S. civil engineer; b. Washington, Dec. 14, 1930; s. John Richard Wilmot and Consuelo (Seggerman) D.; m. F. Wietske Hoogland, Sept. 7, 1968 (dec. Oct. 1993). BS in Civil Engring., Stanford (Calif.) U., 1952; MS, U. Tex., 1959; diploma in hydraulic engr., Internat. Inst. Hydraulic and Sanitary Engring., Delft, The Netherlands, 1960, diploma in sanitary engring., 1976. Registered profl. engr., Tex. Civil engr. Lance Engrs., Inc., El Paso, 1954-56, Tex. Hwy. Dept., El Paso, 1956-58, Morrison-Knudsen, San Francisco, 1961, Fed. Power Commn., Washington, 1962-76, Fed. Energy Regulatory Commn., Washington, from 1985; hydraulic engr. U.S. Geol. Survey, Austin, Tex., 1958-59; sr. civil engr. Haskoning Engrs., Nijmegen, The Netherlands, 1977-80. Mem. Internat. Niagara Working Com., Buffalo, N.Y., 1972-76. 1st lt. U.S. Army, 1952-54, Korea. Mem. ASCE, U.S. Com. Large Dams, Am. Legion. Roman Catholic. Home: Clinton, Md. Deceased.

DIJKSTRA, EDSGER WYBE, computer science educator, mathematician; b. Rotterdam, The Netherlands, May 11, 1930; came to U.S., 1984; s. Douwe Wijbe and Brechtje Cornelia (Kluyver) D.; m. Maria Cornelia Debets, Apr. 23, 1957; children: Marcus Joost, Femke Elisabeth, Rutger Michael. Candidaats degree, U. Leyden, The Netherlands, 1951; doctoral degree, U. Leyden, 1956; PhD, U. Amsterdam, 1959; DSc (hon.), Queen's U. Belfast, No. Ireland, 1976, Athens U. Econs and Bus., 2001. Staff mem. Math. Centre, Amsterdam, The Netherlands, 1952-62; prof. math. Tech. U., Eindhoven, The Netherlands, 1962-73; rsch. fellow Burroughs Corp., Nuenen, The Netherlands, 1973-84; prof., Schlumberger Centennial chair in computer sci. U. Tex., Austin, 1984-99, prof. emeritus, from 1999. Editor Acta Informatica. Disting. fellow Brit. Computer Soc.; mem. Royal Netherlands Acad. Arts and Scis., Am. Acad. Arts and Scis. (hon. fgn.), Assn. for Computing Machinery (Turing award 1972) Home: Austin, Tex. Died Aug. 5, 2002.

DILL, JOEL STANDISH WESLEY, neuropsychologist; b. St. Mary's, Ohio, Sept. 20, 1940; s. Joel Wesley and Virginia Muriel (Frey) D.; m. Janet Marie Gress, Aug. 23, 1969; children: Darin Wesley, Sarah Gress. BA, Capital U., 1962; MA, Wittenberg U., 1967; EdD, Ball State U., 1970. Prof. Ball State U., England, Fed. Rep. Germany, 1970-71, U. Evansville (Ind.), 1971-89; dir. Community Rehab. Svcs. Evansville, 1989-90; neuropsychologist Tri State Rehab. Hosp., Evansville, from 1990; owner, psychologist Ednl. Enrichment Ctr., Evansville, from 1987. Vocat. cons., U.S. Dept. H.E.W., Evansville, Paducah, Ky., 1983—. Lutheran. Avocations: basketball, softball, baseball. Home: Evansville, Ind. Died Feb. 26, 2001.

DILLON, BARBARA LADENE, professional speaker, writer; b. Oklahoma City, Dec. 9, 1935; d. Leonard Paul and Ora Belle (Rogers) B.; m. Donald Dean Dillon, Mar. 21, 1954; children: Timothy Scott, Lisa Colleen. Student, Ctrl. State U., Edmond, Okla., 1960-64; B of Liberal Studies, U. Okla., 1977-79. Legis. lobbyist Okla. Tchrs. Wives, Oklahoma City, 1964-65; civil servant USAF, 1965, various office assignments, 1966-79; logistics officer Tinker AFB, Oklahoma City, 1979-81, prodn. mgmt. specialist, 1981-90, ret., 1990; pres. multimedia co. Prairie Tales, Norman, Okla., from 1995. Zig ziglar facilitator Tinker Mgmt. Assn., Tinker AFB, 1984-86; chair fund-raising E-3 divsn., Tinker AFB, 1988-90; guest lectr. Sch. Architecture U. Okla., 1993. Author: (with Donald Dean Dillon) Affirmations for a Successful Life (Or Things Your Momma Should Have Told You), 1995. Sponsor area K-3 Toastmasters Clubs, Tinker AFB, 1977-90; com. mem. constitution, deacon First Christian Ch., 1976; councilwoman City Coun. Edmond, Okla., 1969-73; bd. dirs. Hill Burton Hosp. Funds, Oklahoma City, 1973-74; trust fund mem. Edmond Utility Trust, 1972-73; deacon First Presbyn. Ch., Edmond, 1969-73. Tinker Mgmt. Assn. scholar, 1977, 78. Mem. Oklahoma City Profl. Spkrs. Toastmasters Club (pres. 1990), Look Who's Talking Toastmasters (mentor 1990, sec., treas. 1991-92), Sooner Toastmasters (sec., treas. 1991-92, Outstanding Toastmaster 1994), 3001 Toastmasters (pres., Outstanding Toastmaster 1984), Toastmasters Internat. Okla. (lt. gov. edn. and tng. 1991-92, adminstrv. lt. gov. 1990-91, gov. Dist. 16 1992-93, Disting. Dist. award 1993, Disting. Toastmaster 1984, and recipient of The Disting. Toastmasters award, 1997, Able Bronze and Silver award 1990, Outstanding Area Gov. Dist. 16), Tinker Mgmt. Club (4th v.p. 1984), Okla. Territorial Tellers, Oklahoma City Boomer Storytellers (pres. 1995-96, edn. v.p. 1994-95). Democrat. Southern Baptist. Avocations: water aerobics, fly fishing, water colorist, reading, bluegrass music, beethoven. Died Mar. 1, 2001.

DILLON, BRENDAN, Irish ambassador to Vatican; b. Dublin, Ireland, Nov. 30, 1924; s. William and Pauline (Kerrigan) D.; m. Alice O'Keefe, July 29, 1949; children—Justin, Piers, Jarlath, Geraldine, Gregory. Student Blackrock Coll., Dublin; B.A., M.A., Univ. Coll., U. Dublin. Counsellor Embassy of Ireland, Brussels, 1964-68; chief of protocol Dept. Fgn. Affairs Ireland, Dublin, 1968-70, asst. sec., 1972-73; ambassador of Ireland to Denmark, 1970-72; permanent rep. of Ireland to European Communities, Brussels, 1973-81; ambassador of Ireland to France, Paris, 1981-86, to vatican, Rome, 1986—; permanent rep. of

Ireland to OECD, Paris, 1981-86; permanent del. of Ireland to UNESCO, Paris, 1981-86. Decorated Grand Cross, Order Leopold II (Belgium), Grand Cross, Order of Merit (Luxembourg). Deceased.

DILLON, CLARENCE DOUGLAS, retired investment company executive; b. Geneva, Aug. 21, 1909; s. Clarence and Anne McE. (Douglass) D.; m. Phyllis C. Ellsworth, Mar. 10, 1931 (dec.); children: Phyllis Ellsworth (Mrs. Phyllis Collins), Joan Douglas (Duchesse de Mouchy); m. Susan S. Sage, Jan. 1, 1983. Grad., Groton Sch., 1927; AB, Harvard U., 1931, LL.D., 1959, NYU, 1956, Lafayette Coll., 1957, U. Hartford, 1958, Columbia U., 1959, Williams Coll., 1960, Rutgers U., 1961, Princeton U., 1961, U. Pa., 1962, Middlebury Coll., 1963; LL.D (hon.), Bradley U., 1964, Washington U., St. Louis, 1970; LL.D., Tufts U., 1982, Marymount Manhattan Coll, 1984. Mem. N.Y. Stock Exchange, 1931-36; dir. U.S. & Foreign Securities Corp. and U.S. & Internat. Securities Corp., 1937-53; pres. U.S. & Fgn. Securities Corp. and U.S. & Internat. Securities Corp., 1947-53, pres., dir., 1967-71, chmn. bd., 1971-84. Dir. Dillon, Read & Co., Inc., 1938-53, chmn. bd., 1946-53, chmn. exec. com., dir., 1971-81; ambassador to France, 1953-57; under sec. of state for econ. affairs Dept. State, 1958-59, under sec. of state, 1959-61, sec. of treasury, 1961-65 Life trustee NY Presbyn. Hosp.; trustee emeritus Pierpont Morgan Libr.; Pres. Met. Mus. Art, N.Y.C., 1970—78; chmn., 1978—83; chmn. Rockefeller Found., 1972—75; chmn. Brookings Instn., 1970—76; pres. bd. overseers Harvard Coll., 1968—72; chmn. Internat. Coun. MOMA, 1969—70. Ensign to lt. comdr. USNR, 1941—45. Decorated Air medal, Legion of Merit, Presdl. medal of freedom. Mem. Soc. Colonial Wars N.Y., Soc. of Cincinnati. Clubs: Racquet and Tennis, Knickerbocker, Links, Century, Pilgrims (N.Y.C.); Metropolitan (Washington). Died Jan. 10, 2003.

DIMITER, ALEXANDER SERGE, chemical company executive; b. Russia, Oct. 8, 1920; came to U.S., 1949. s. Alexander Dimitry and Alexandra S. (Ox-Povich) D. MS, U. Eng. Sci., Sofia, Bulgaria, 1943; PhD, Brown Forrest Acad., Sussex, Eng., 1967. Reg. profl. engr. Chief chemist Oleo Bros. Doneff, Varna, Bulgaria, 1943-45; technical dir. Ind. Mitsomphonou, Athens, Greece, 1945-49; v.p. research LLD Chemical, Inc., N.Y.C., 1950-53; chief cons. Morgan Laminating, N.Y.C., from 1953; v.p. research Dimiter Emulsion & Chemical Co., Poughkeepsie, N.Y., 1958-62, pres., from 1962. Cons. Qutronic Corp., N.Y.C., 1952-62, Morgan Laminating, Inc., 1953—, mgmt. adv. panel Chemical Week, McGraw-Hill, N.Y.C., 1979. Mem. Assn. Russian-Am. Engrs. in U.S.A., Soc. Mfg. Engrs. (sr.). Avocations: sailing, boating. Deceased.

DINCE, ROBERT REUBEN, financial consultant; b. N.Y.C., Dec. 27, 1924; s. Robert R. and Irene (Hess) D.; m. Miriam Konuitz, May 23, 1947; 1 child, Anna Crosby. BS, Rutgers U., 1945; MA, U. Calif., L.A., 1950; Phd, Cornell U., 1960. Prof. dept. fin. U. Ga., Athens, 1953-87, ret., 1987. Dep. comptroller of the currency U.S. Treasury, Washington, 1975-78. Deceased.

DINH, THANH KIM, chemical engineer; b. Vietnam, Jan. 2, 1954; came to U.S., 1980; s. Vuong Van Dinh and Xoan Thi Nguyen. BSChemE, U. Nebr., 1984, MSChemE, 1985. Registered profl. engr., Tex. Rsch. engr., pilot plant supr. Burzynski Rsch. Inst., Stafford, Tex., 1987-90; process engr. W.R. Grace - Nitroparafins Plant, Deer Park, Tex., 1990-92; process engr., supr. engring. Schenectady Internat., Freeport, Tex., from 1993. Mem. AIChE, Tau Beta Pi, Pi Mu Epsilon, Phi Lambda Upsilon. Achievements include development of a Fortran code to solve a system of boundary valued ordinary differential equations using multiple shooting technique with hybrid method; mathematical model for kinetic parameter recovery for cellulose pyrolysis with radiant heating. Home: Houston, Tex. Died Nov. 16, 2000.

DIPALMA, CARLO, cinematographer; b. Rome, Apr. 17, 1925; Cinematographer: (films) Lata mancia, 1956,L'Impiegato, 1960, Long Night in 1943, 1960, The Assassin, 1965, Divorce Italian Style, 1962, Leoni al sole, 1961, Terrible Sheriff, 1962, Three Fables of Love, 1962, Omicron, 1963, Liola, 1963, Love in Four Dimensions, 1965, The Red Desert, 1965, the Naked Horns, 1964, The Three Faces, 1965, Cemetery of the Living Dead, 1965, A Question of Honour, 1965, Blow Up, 1966, The Queens, 1966, For Love and Gold, 1966, I Married You for Fun, 1967, Girl with a Pistol, 1968, The Bitch Wants Blood, 1968, On My Way to the Crusades, I Met a Girl Who..., 1969, The Appointment, 1969, Help Me My Love, 1969, Drama of Jealousy, 1970, The Couples, 1970, The Pacifist, 1970, Nini Tirabuscio, 1970, Noi donne siamo fatte cosi, 1971, Together, 1981, The Tragedy of a Ridiculous Man, 1982, Identification of a Woman, 1982, The Black Stallion Returns, 1983, Gabriela, 1984, Hannah and Her Sisters, 1986, Off Beat, 1986, The Secret of My Success, 1987, September, 1987, Radio Days, 1987, Alice, 1990, Shadows and Fog, 1992, Husbands and Wives, 1992, Manhattan Murder Mystery, 1993, Bullets Over Broadway, 1994, The Monster, 1996, Mighty Aphrodite, 1995, Everyone Says I Love your, 1996, Deconstructing Harry, 1997, Another World Is Possible, 2001; (TV Movies) La Clemenza di Tito, 1980 Don't Drink the Water, 1994; Dir.: (films) Teresa the Thief, 1972, Blonde in Black Leather, 1975, Mimi Bluette...fiore del mio giardino, 1977, L Addio a Enrico Berlinguer, 1984. Died July 9, 2004.

DI TELLA, GUIDO, former Argentinean government official; b. Buenos Aires, June 12, 1931; Degree in Indsl. Engring., U. Buenos Aires, 1955; PhD in Economics, MIT, 1959. Prof. economics U. Buenos Aires, 1962-76, 83, dir. Inst. Econ. and Social Rsch., 1965-66; prof. economics Cath. U., Buenos Aires, 1981; assoc. mem. St. Antony's Coll., U. Oxford, 1976; dir. Inst. Torcuato Di Tella, 1958; chmn. Fondo Nacional de las Arts, 1974-75; sec. of state for coordination and econ. programming, 1975-76; nat. congressman Justicialista Party, Province of Buenos Aires, 1980-89; Argentine Extraordinary, Plenipotentiary Amb. to White House U.S.A., 1986-89; min. def., 1991; min. fgn. affairs, internat. trade and worship, 1991—99. Author: Las Etapas del Desarrollo Economico Argentino, 1962, Los Ciclos Economicos Argentinos, 1973, La Estrategia del Desarrollo Indirecto, 1973, Peron-Peron, 1982; co-editor: Economics in the Long View, Vols. I, II and III, 1982, The Political Economy of Argentina 1880-1945, 1986, Argentina, Australia and Canada, 1987, Inflation, Stabilization, 1988, Argentina Between the Great Powers 1939-46, 1983, The Political Economy of Argentina 1946-83, 1989. Died Dec. 31, 2001.

DIVONE, LOUIS VINCENT, aerospace engineer, educator, federal official, author; b. NYC, July 24, 1934; s. Dominic and Christina Agnes (Cassa) D.; m. Judene Frances Smith, Aug. 10, 1968. B in Aero. Engring., Poly. Inst. Bklyn., 1955; MS, MIT, 1956. Mem. tech. staff Jet Propulsion Lab. Calif. Inst. Tech., 1956—67, 1969—72; program mgr. NASA, 1962—63; cons. Dept. Transp., 1968—69; dir. wind energy sys. NSF, 1973—74; dir. Wind Energy Tech. Divsn. Dept. Energy, Washington, 1977—83, dir. Office Solar Elec. Techs., 1982—84, 1986—90, assoc. dep. asst. sec. Transp. Tech., 1990—91, assoc. dep. asst. sec. for Bldgs. Tech., 1992—94, acting dep. asst. sec. bldg. techs., 1994—95, acting dep. asst. sec. bldg. tech., state and cmty. programs, 1996, assoc. dep. asst. sec. for indsl. techs., 1997—99; pvt. cons. Washington, from 2000. Spl. asst. to dir. market planning and rsch. Grumman Aerospace Corp., 1984-85; professorial lectr. George Washington U., 1976-84; cons. Wind Energy Working Group, UN, 1979-81; chmn. wind energy exec. com. Internat. Energy Agy., 1978-82. Co-editor Energy series Inst. Elec. Engrs., 1990-2000; contbr. papers to profl. symposia; patentee variable area rocket nozzle, self-attaching fluid coupling. Recipient Apollo Achievment award NASA, 1970, Spl. Achievement award ERDA, 1976, Pres.'s Exec. Exch. Program appointment, 1984-85, Disting. Career Svc. award DOE, 1999. Fellow: AAAS, AIAA (assoc.); mem.: Sr. Exec. Assn., Seaplane Pilots Assn., Va. Aero. Hist. Soc., Smithsonian Assn., Antique Airplane Assn., Cessna 180 Owners Club, Tau Beta Pi, Sigma Xi. Home: Oakton, Va. Died May 9, 2004.

DIXON, DOROTHY BEATRICE, former school administrator; b. Albert Lea, Minn., June 1, 1921; d. Peter Bernard and Elsie Leonora (Sybilrud) Hoidale; m. James George Dixon, Jr., Aug. 14, 1941; children: Richard, Paula, Paul, James III, Peter, Deborah. Student, Biola Coll., La Mirada, Calif., 1941-43. Founder, dir. Grace Brethren Christian Schs., Temple Hills, Md., 1965-86, dir. Clinton and Calvert, Md., from 1986, also cons., from 1987, dir. emeritus. Speaker banquets, retreats. Author: (Bible studies series) Pleasing Him, 1951, His Own, 1961, Hidden Beauty, 1973, How Mature?, 1987. Republican. Mem. Grace Brethren Ch. Home: Boynton Beach, Fla. Deceased.

DIXON, JAMES GEORGE, JR., minister, headmaster; b. Wichita, Kans., Feb. 3, 1922; s. James George and Lena Mae (Wertz) D.; m. Dorothy Beatrice Hoidale, Aug. 14, 1941 (dec. June 1991); children: Richard, Paul, Paula, James III, Peter, Deborah. Grad. cum laude, Biola Coll., 1944; BD cum laude, Grace Theol Sem., 1947, MDiv, 1949; BA, Wooster Coll., 1949. Ordained to ministry Grace Brethren Ch., 1947. Pastor Sunnymede Brethren Ch., South Bend, Ind., 1944-47, W. 10th St. Brethren Ch., Ashland, Ohio, 1947-51, 1st Brethren Ch., Washington, 1951-61, Grace Brethren Ch. Greater Washington, Temple Hills, Md. and Washington, from 1961. Pres. Christian Edn. and Sunday Sch. Bd., 1951-81; dir. Grace Theol. Sem., Winona Lake, Ind., 1951-68; cons. Gospel Light Publs., Calif., 1961-65. Named Pastor of Yr., Fellowship Grace Brethren Chs. Mins., 1988. Republican. Home: Boynton Beach, Fla. Deceased.

DIXON, LORRAINE, city official; b. Chgo., June 18, 1950; BS in Secondary Edn., Chgo. State U., 1972. Alderman, ward 8, Chgo., from 1991. Chmn. Com. on Budget and Govt. Ops., 1994—; pres. pro-tempore Chgo. City Coun.; bd. dirs. Open Hands Chgo. and Jackson Park Hosp. Mem. United Negro Coll. Fund, Cook County Dem. Women, Ill. Majority Women's Caucus, Operation PUSH, 87th St. C. of C. (bd. dirs.). Died June 29, 2001.

DIXON, MARY AGNES, secondary school educator; b. Lewisburg, W.Va., June 14, 1949; d. Harry F. and Alice (Hayes) Shields; m. Donald R. Dixon, Apr. 21, 1973; children: Darin H., David F. BS in Edn., Concord Coll., 1971; MS, W.Va. U., 1983. Cert. tchr., Va. Tchr. English Greenbrier East High Sch., Lewisburg, W.Va., 1972-73, Botetourt Intermediate Sch., Fincastle, Va., 1973-75; tchr. English and speech Lewisburg Jr. High Sch., 1975-83; tchr. English McLane Jr. High Sch., Brandon, Fla., 1983-84; tchr. English and speech Alleghany High Sch., Covington, Va., from 1985. Home: Covington, Va. Died Sept. 7, 2000.

DODD, ROBERT BRUCE, physician, educator; b. Fairbury, Nebr., Apr. 12, 1921; s. Cyrus Milo and Blanche (Kohl) D.; m. Mary Elinor Karll, Dec. 30, 1949; children: Hollyce Ann (Mrs. Thomas Gregory Rose), Robert Bruce, David Karll. Student, U. Chgo., 1939-41; MD, U. Nebr., 1945. Intern Research and Edn. Hosps. U. Ill., 1945-46; dir. anesthesia Columbia Hosp., Milw., 1948-49; trainee in anesthesia Mass. Gen. Hosp., 1950-51, asst. anesthetist, 1951; practice medicine specializing in anesthesiology Milw., 1948-49, Dallas, 1951-53, Balt., 1953-56, St. Louis, 1956-69, Springfield, Ill., 1969-87; instr., assoc. prof. anesthesiology Southwestern Med. Sch. U. Tex., Dallas, 1951-53; prof., head dept. anesthesia Sch. Medicine U. Md., 1953-56; Henry E. Mallinckrodt prof. anesthesiology, head div. anesthesiology Sch. Medicine, Washington U., 1956-69; anesthesiologist-in-chief Barnes Hosp., 1956-68; cons. VA Hosps., Dallas, McKinney, Tex., 1951-53, USPHS Hosp., Balt., 1955-56, VA Hosp., St. Louis City Hosps., 1956-69; clin. prof. anesthesiology So. Ill. U. Sch. Medicine, 1969-83 and from 87, prof., head dept. anesthesiology, 1983-87; anesthesiologist Meml. Hosp., Springfield, 1969-87, head dept. anesthesia, 1975-85. Author: Diethyl Ether, 1962. Contbr. articles to profl. jours. Served with M.C. AUS, 1946-48. Mem. AMA, Am. Soc. Anesthesiologists (2d v.p. 1967-68), Ill. Soc. Anesthesiologists (1st speaker ho. dels., pres., Disting. Service award 1986), St. Louis Soc. Anesthesiologists (past pres.), Internat. Anesthesia Research Soc., Assn. U. Anesthetists (past treas.), Sangamon County Med. Soc., So. Med. Assn. (past sect. chmn.), Alpha Omega Alpha Home: Dallas, Tex. Died Nov. 18, 1999.

DODSON, ANN GAY, artist, horticulturist; b. Hall County, Apr. 22, 1912; d. Homer Tillman and Nancy MeLinda (Black) Phagad; m. William Gay, July 10, 1936 (div. Sept. 1940); 1 child, William Dale Gay; m. Clarence Dodson, June 29, 1947. AS in Art, Brenau Coll., 1933. Advisor Friend of the State Bot. Garden of Ga., Athens, 1970—, fundraiser 1970; The Garden Club of Ga., Inc., Athens, 1993—, Am. Sumter County Hist. Trust, Americus, Ga., 1986—; overall chmn. for decorating the White Ho. Pres. Jimmy Carter's Inauguation, Washington, 1977; overall chmn. decorations Carter Presdl. Ctr. 1986; horticulture chmn. Americus-Sumter County Hist. Dedication Preservation, 1987. Award of Honor Nat. Coun. of State Garden, 1995, Cert. of Appreciation Ga. Soc. of Clubs, DAR, 1995, Award of Honor Deep South Region NCSGC, 1995. Mem. The Garden Club of Ga., Inc. (bd. dirs. 1969—), DAR (regent), The State Bot. Garden of Ga. (advisor 1970—), Am. Sumter County Hist. Trust (charter mem. 1971—), Plains Nat. Hist. Preservation Trust Inc., Am Camellia Soc. Democrat. Baptist. Avocation: flower arranging. Home: Jefferson, Ga. Died Sept. 23, 1999.

DODSON, JOHN PAUL, tax executive; b. Memphis, Nov. 1, 1938; BS in Acctg., U. Tenn., 1970; MBA, Middle Tenn. State U., 1972. Acct. Sandoz Pharms., Hanover, N.J., 1960-66; tax acct. Genesco, Inc., Nashville, Tenn., 1966-72; acctg. instr. Mid. Tenn. State U., Murfreesboro, 1972-74; tax mgr. excise Weyerhaeuser Co., Tacoma, 1974-91; sr. mgr. tax Ernst & Young, Seattle, 1991-92; tax refund auditor Bogle & Gates, Seattle, from 1993. With USN, 1956-59. Mem. Inst. Mgmt. Accts., Inst. Property Taxation (cert. sales tax mem.), Evergreen Maltese Club (bd. dirs. 1985-92). Home: Hermitage, Tenn. Died Sept. 28, 2000.

DODSON, OSCAR HENRY, numismatist, museum consultant; b. Houston, Jan. 3, 1905; s. Dennis S. and Maggie (Sisk) D.; m. Pauline Wellbrock, Dec. 17, 1932; 1 child, John Dennis. BS, U.S. Naval Acad., 1927; grad., U.S. Naval Postgrad. Sch., 1936; MA in Russian History, U. Ill., 1953. Commd. ensign USN, 1927, advanced through grades to rear adm., 1957; moblzn. planning officer Bur. Naval Personnel, 1945-48; comdg. officer U.S.S. Thomas Jefferson, 1949-50; prof. naval sci., comdr. Naval ROTC unit U. Ill., 1950-53; comdr. Landing Ship Flotilla, Atlantic Fleet, 1954-55; chief staff U.S. Naval mission to Greece, 1955-56, 1st Naval Dist., Boston, 1956-57; ret., 1957; asst. prof. history U. Ill., 1957-59; dir. Money Mus., Nat. Bank Detroit, 1959-65, World Heritage Mus., U. Ill., Urbana, 1966-73, now dir. emeritus; acting dir. Champaign County Hist. Mus., 1980-81. Mem. numis. adv. com. Smithsonian Instn., 1946; mem. Ann. Assay Commn., 1948, U. Ill. Found. Pres.'s Council, U.S. Naval Acad. Found.; visited numis. socs. under auspices State Dept., USSR, Finland, Poland, Austria, Denmark, 1959 Author: Money Tells the Story, 1962; contbg. editor Coinage Mag., 1973-87; contbr. articles to profl. and numis. jours. Decorated Silver Star. Fellow Am. Numis. Soc., Explorer's Club; mem. SAR, Am. Numis. Assn. (life, Farran Zerbe award 1968, bd. govs. 1950-55, pres. 1957-61), Am. Mil. Inst., Archaeol. Inst. Am., U. Ill. Alumni Assn. (Loyalty award 1966), U.S. Naval Acad. Alumni Assn., Rotary (pres. Champaign chpt. 1972-73), N.Y. Yacht Club, Army-Navy Club, Washington, Champaign Country Club. Deceased.

D'OENCH, RUSSELL GRACE, JR., publishing consultant; b. N.Y.C., Feb. 16, 1927; s. Russell Grace and Dorothie (Sharp) D'O.; m. Ellen Gates, Sept. 10, 1949; children: Peter, Ellen, Russell Grace III. LittD (hon.), Wilcox Coll. Nursing, 1993. Reporter Berkshire Eagle, Pittsfield, Mass., 1947-52; pub., editor Sunnyvale (Calif.) Standard, 1952-56; pres. Sagamore Press, Inc., N.Y.C., 1956-58; editor, chmn. bd. dirs. Middletown (Conn.) Press, 1959-91; chmn. Dormers Corp., Middletown, from 1992. Mem. Middletown adv. bd. Conn. Nat. Bank, chmn., 1982-86; vis. lectr. Wesleyan U., 1967-71; corporator Farmers and Mechanics Bank, Middletown, 1960-93; bd. dirs. Conn. Acad. for Edn. in Math., Sci. and Tech., 1995-2001, Middlesex County Cmty. Found.; chmn. Middletown, 1994-2000. Contbg. author: Read All About It. Chmn. bd. dirs. Wilcox Coll. Nursing, 1991-94; mem. trustees coun. Conn. Conf. Ind. Colls., 1992-94; bd. dirs. Goodspeed Opera Found., 1972-2001, Conn. Pub. Expenditure Coun., 1965-67, 89-93; past bd. dirs. Conn. Student Loan Found., Conn. Humanities Coun.,

Middlesex Meml. Hosp., Conn. Hosp. Assn.; bd. dirs. Govs. for Higher Edn., 1983-88, chmn., 1983-85; pres. Middletown Found. for Arts, 1984-2002; active Commn. to Study Higher Edn., Conn. Gov.'s Commn. on Higher Edn. and Economy; past chmn. Conn. Joint Com. on Ednl. Tech.; past chmn., dir. Middlesex Hosp.; chmn., dir. Conn. Regional Med. Program. Mem. Am. Soc. Newspaper Editors, New Eng. Soc. Newspaper Editors (past pres., dir.), Sigma Delta Chi (Conn. chpt., past sec.). Home: Middletown, Conn. Died Nov. 24, 2002.

DOERR, HARRIET, writer; b. Apr. 8, 1910; m. Albert E. Doerr, 1930 (dec.); children: Michael, Martha Doerr Toppin BA, Stanford U., 1977. Author: Stones for Ibarra, 1984 (Am. Book award for first work of fiction 1984, Bay Area Reviewers fiction award 1985, P.E.N. Los Angeles fiction award 1985, Commonwealth Club of Calif. gold medal for fiction 1985), Under an Aztec Sun, 1990, Consider This, Señora, 1993, The Tiger in the Grass, 1995. Recipient Transatlantic Rev.-Henfield Found. award, 1982, Am. Acad. and Inst. of Arts and Letters Harold D. Vursell Meml. award, 1985; Wallace Stegner fellow, 1980-81; Nat. Endowment for Arts grantee, 1983. Home: Pasadena, Calif. Died Nov. 24, 2002.

DOHENY, JAMES JEROME, chemistry consultant; b. Effingham, Ill., June 22, 1906; s. James J. and Julia A. (Willenberg) D. BSChE, Ill. Inst. Tech., 1927, MSChE, 1932. Instr. chemistry, math. Chgo. schs., 1927-34, 37-41; with alcohol tax unit U.S. Treas. Dept, Chgo., 1935-37; convention mgr. Am. Chem. Soc., Washington, 1946-50, exec. sec. expn. mgr. Chgo. sect., 1950-71; cons. meetings and expn. Chgo., from 1971. Hon. del. Ausstellungs-Tagung fuer Chemisches Apparatewesen, Frankfurt, Fed. Republic Germany, 1961—. Lt. U.S. Army, 1942-46. Recipient merit award Chgo. Assn. Tech. Soc., 1984, disting. svc. award Chgo. sect. ACS, 1984. Fellow AAAS; mem. Nat. Assn. Exposition Mgrs. (hon.). Home: Elmwood Park, Ill. Died Oct. 31, 2000.

DOHERTY, JOHN F. priest; b. Jersey City, Dec. 22, 1925; s. Patrick J. and Catherine Ann (O'Brien) D. MA in Philosophy, Berchmans Coll., 1950; MA in Theology, Woodstock Coll., 1956, STL in Theology, 1957; PhD in Sociology, Fordham U., 1963. Ordained priest Roman Cath. Ch. Proc. sociology Ateneo de Manila (Philippines) Coll., 1963-80, v.p. for acad. affairs, 1964-71; dir. rsch. East Asian Pastoral Inst., 1965-71; pastor U. Hawaii, from 1981. Author: Interlocking Directories in Phil. Inst., 1979, Sociology of Religion, 1968, Change in Religions and Social Attitudes,1 964, Philippine Urban Poor, 1985; contbr. articles to profl. jours. Trustee St. Francis Med. Ctr., Honolulu, 1987—, Inst. Philippino Culture, Manila, 1978-80, Asian Inst. Mgmt., Manila., 1965-68; chair bd. dirs. Alger Found., Honolulu, 1989—; bd. dirs., chair Aina Jupaa O'Maili Homeless Project, Honolulu, 1985—. Mem. Am. Sociol. Assn., Soc. for Sci. Study Religion, Internat. Assn. for History of Religion, Phi Beta Kappa, Delta Sigma Tau. Home: Honolulu, Hawaii. Deceased.

DOLAN, WILLIAM DAVID, JR., physician; b. Westerly, R.I., Apr. 30, 1913; s. William David and Mary E. (Dunn) D.; m. Christine Shea, Nov. 25, 1942; children— William David, III, Mary Anne, John Patrick. BS, U. R.I., 1935; MD, Georgetown U., 1942; D.Sc. (hon.), Marymount U., 1975, Georgetown U., 1983. Intern Georgetown U. Hosp., 1942-43, resident, 1943-45; practice medicine specializing in pathology Arlington, Va., 1947-95; dir. pathology Arlington Hosp., 1947-95. Pres. med. staff Arlington Hosp., 1982-87, trustee; asst. dean sch. medicine affairs at Arlington Hosp. Georgetown U., clin. prof. dept. pathology. Council to dean Georgetown U., 1977—. Served to maj., M.C. AUS, 1942-47. Recipient Distinguished Service to Pathology award Am. Soc. Clin. Pathologists and Coll. Am. Pathologists, 1976, The Brent award Diocese of Arlington, 1989. Mem. AMA (council on sci. affairs, chmn. 1985), So. Med. Assn., Med. Soc. Va. and D.C., Arlington County Med. Soc. (past pres.), Am. Cancer Soc. (bd. dirs.), Am. Soc. Clin. Pathologists (past pres., disting. svc. award honoring Israel Davidsohn 1991), Am. Blood Commn. (past pres.), Coll. Am. Pathologists, Internat. Acad. Pathology, Va. Soc. for Pathology, Arlington County C. of C. (past dir.), Am. Registry of Pathology (pres. 1991-93), Alpha Omega Alpha. Clubs: Washington Golf and Country. Roman Catholic. Home: Arlington, Va. Died June 4, 1999.

DOLIN, JOEL DAVID, electronics executive, engineer; b. N.Y.C., Jan. 10, 1932; s. Irving and Carrie (Schwartz) D.; m. Lea Sharon Pruitt, June 14, 1969; children: Jennifer Lea, Claudia Martine. BA, Columbia Coll., 1953, BS, 1954, MS, 1955. Project adminstr. Loral Electronics, N.Y.C., 1958-59; engr. Ampex Corp., Redwood City, Calif., 1959-60; systems engr. McCarthy Assn., Menlo Park, Calif., 1960-62; pres. Leasametric, Foster City, Calif., 1962-80. Pres. Target Fin. Corp., Foster City, 1981—. Served to lt. (j.g.) USN, 1955-58. Republican. Jewish. Home: Burlingame, Calif. Died May 4, 2000.

DOMAN, NICHOLAS RICHARD, lawyer; b. Budapest, Hungary, Apr. 10, 1913; s. Odon and Irene (Parkany) D.; m. Katharine Huntington Bigelow, 1951 (dec.); children: Daniel Bigelow, Alexander Macdonald; m. Judith Nicely Perrin, 1992. Student, London Sch. Econs., 1932; MA in Law, U. Colo., 1935; JD, U. Budapest, 1936; postgrad., Geneva Sch. Internat. Studies, 1937. Bar: D.C. 1947, N.Y. 1948, U.S. Supreme Ct 1948. Mem. research faculty U. Chgo., 1939-40; lectr. Rotary Internat. Inst., Chgo., 1940-41, 46-47; asst. prof. govt. and econs. Coll. William and Mary, 1941-42; asst. to U.S. Chief Prosecutor Nuremberg Trial, 1945-46; practice law N.Y.C. and Washington, 1948—2002. Adj. prof. Sch. Law, NYU, 1959-77; founder Nicholas R. Doman Soc. Internat. Law U. Colo., 1967; symposium leader on internat. transactions Am. Law Inst.-ABA, Am. Soc. Internat. Law, World Peace Through Law; v.p., dir., gen. counsel Assn. to Unite the Democracies, Washington; panelist, commentator on internat. politics for TV and radio. Author: The Coming Age of World Control, 1942; Contbr. articles to profl. jours., popular publs. Trustee Pitzer Coll., 1975—. Served to 1st lt. AUS, 1942-45, Italy. Recipient George Washington award, 1979; Norlin award U. Colo., 1980 Mem. Internat. Law Assn. (exec. com. 1965—, hon. v.p. U.S. br.), Am. Law Inst. (life), Internat. Bar Assn., Union Internationale des Avocats, Order Coif (hon.), Shelter Island Yacht Club, Gardiner's Bay Country Club, Univ. Club (N.Y.C.). Home: Shelter Island, NY. Died Jan. 26, 2004.

DONALDSON, JEFF RICHARDSON, visual artist, educator; b. Pine Bluff, Ark., Dec. 15, 1942; s. Sidney Frank and Clementine Frances (Richardson) D.; children: Jameela Kaneeka, Tarik Jeff. BA, Ark. State Coll., 1954; MS, Inst. of Design, Ill. Inst. Tech., 1963; PhD, Northwestern U., 1974. Chmn. art dept. Marshall High Sch., Chgo., 1958-65; asst. prof. art Northeastern U., Chgo., 1965-69; lectr. Northwestern U., Evanston, Ill., 1969-70; prof., chmn. dept. art, art gallery dir. Howard U., Washington, 1970-76, assoc. dean Coll. Fine Arts, 1985-91, acting dean Coll. Fine Arts, 1991-92, dean Coll. Fine Arts, 1992—98. Art cons. Student Non-Violent Coordinating Com., 1963-66, CORE, Chgo., 1962-63; organizer, contbg. artist Wall of Respect, Chgo., 1967; founder Africobra Artists Guild, 1968; chmn. N. Am. zone, 2d World Black and African Festival of Arts and Culture, Lagos, Nigeria, 1975; advisor art assessment div. IRS, Washington, 1976; cons. Nat. Endowment for Humanities; v.p. internat. festival com., U.S. and Can.; FESTAC 77. (recipient first prize for painting, Art and Soul Competition, Chgo. 1968, first prize award, Black Expressions Competition, Chgo. 1969); Editor: Ill. Art Edn. Yearbook, 1969; Contbr. articles to mags. Bd. dirs. Nat. Center for Afro-Am. Artists, Boston; mem. adv. bd. Studio Mus. in Harlem, 1970-74; former mem. corp. bd. Children's Hosp., Washington; former mem. D.C. Art Commn. Served with AUS, 1955-57. Ford Found. fellow, 1967-68; Northwestern U. fellow, 1968-69 Home: Washington, DC. Died Feb. 29, 2004.

DONALDSON, ROBERT MACARTNEY, JR., physician; b. Hubbardston, Mass., Aug. 1, 1927; s. Robert Macartney and Helen Mildred (Morrow) D.; m. Priscilla Hurd, Sept. 1, 1950; children: Robert M., John H.; m. Phyllis Bodel, Jan. 14, 1974; m. Ellen Garvey, Jan. 5, 1986 BS, Yale U., 1949; MD, Boston U., 1952. Diplomate Am. Bd. Internal Medicine (bd. govs. 1984-90). Intern Montreal (Que., Can.) Gen. Hosp., 1952-53; resident Boston VA Hosp., 1955-57; fellow in gastroenterology Peter Bent Brigham Hosp., Boston, 1957-59; instr. Harvard U. Med. Sch., 1957-59; asst. prof. medicine Boston U., Med. Sch., 1959-64, prof., chief gastroenterology, 1967-73; assoc. prof. U. Wis. Med. Sch., 1964-67; prof. medicine, dept. internal medicine Yale U. Med. Sch., 1973-97, dep. dean, 1987-91; acting dean, 1991-92. Chmn. adv. bd. Nat. Center Ulcer Research and Edn., 1975-88; chmn. adv. tng. grant com. NIH, 1967-73; chmn. adv. research com. VA, 1968-71. Editor: Jour. Gastroenterology, 1970-77; contbr. chpts. med. textbooks. Served with USNR, 1953-55. Recipient Clin. Investigator award VA, 1959-64; spl. fellow NIH, 1957-59; named Disting. VA Physician, 1995-97. Master ACP; mem. Am. Gastroenterol. Assn. (pres. 1979-80), Am. Fedn. Clin. Research, Am. Soc. Clin. Investigation, Assn. Am. Physicians. Home: Guilford, Conn. Died July 8, 2003.

DONEGAN, CAROLYN MAY, artist; b. Rochester, N.Y., July 4, 1937; d. Lawrence Alexander and Madeline May (Doud) Heslip; m. William Eugene Donegan, Jan. 30, 1960; children: David Loring, Christine Ann, Bradley Lawrence. Sculptor Arts Reach, Rochester, N.Y., from 1990. Prin. works include sculptures, Coping Series at Strong Meml. Hosp., U. Rochester Med. Ctr., Pain Treatment Ctr., Cancer Action. Mem. Arts for Greater Rochester. Avocations: theatre, Scrabble. Home: West Henrietta, NY. Deceased.

DONNELLY, MARIAN CARD, art historian, educator; b. Evanston, Ill., Sept. 12, 1923; d. Harold S. and Ethel (Gates) Card; m. Russell J. Donnelly, Jan. 21, 1956; 1 child, James Armstrong. AB summa cum laude, Oberlin Coll., 1946, MA, 1948; PhD, Yale U., 1956. Instr. fine arts Upsala Coll., 1948-50; art librarian U. Rochester, 1951-53; research asso. decorative arts Art Inst., Chgo., 1956-57; vis. lectr. U. Chgo., 1965; asst. prof. dept. art history U. Oreg., Eugene, 1966-68, asso. prof., 1969-73, prof., 1973-81, prof. emeritus, 1981-99. Participant Attingham (Eng.) Summer Sch., 1972, 75; vis. research scholar in art history U. Copenhagen, 1972; lectr. U. Oreg. Center for Internat. Music, Stuttgart, Germany, 1972 Author: The New England Meeting Houses of the Seventeenth Century, 1968, A Short History of Observatories, 1973, Architecture in the Scandinavian Countries, 1992, Oregon Bach Festival 1970-94, 1994, A History, Society of Architectural Historians, 1998; contbr. articles to profl. jours. Bd. dirs.-at-large Oreg. Bach Festival. Am. Council Learned Socs. grantee, 1959-60 Fellow Royal Soc. Arts (London); mem. Archeol. Inst. Am., Nat. Trust for Scotland, Soc. for Preservation of New England Antiquities, Soc. Archtl. Historians (bd. dirs. 1964-67, 78-81, assoc. editor newsletter 1966-72, 2nd v.p. 1972-74, 1st v.p. 1974-76, pres. 1976-78, gen. chmn. Bicentennial programs 1975-76), Phi Beta Kappa. Home: Eugene, Oreg. Died Nov. 15, 1999.

DONOVAN, ROBERT JOHN, retired journalist; b. Buffalo, Aug. 21, 1912; s. Michael J. and Katherine (Sullivan) D.; m. Martha Fisher, May 9, 1941 (dec.); children: Patricia, Peter, Amy; m. Gerry Van der Heuvel, Mar. 17, 1978. Litt.D. (hon.), Am. Internat. Coll., 1962, Stonehill Coll., 1983. Mem. staff Buffalo Courier-Express, 1933-37; with N.Y. Herald Tribune, 1937-63, on European edit., 1945, mem. Washington bur., 1947-63, chief Washington bur., 1957-63, L.A. Times, 1963-70; assoc. editor Los Angeles Times, Los Angeles, 1970-77; fellow Woodrow Wilson Internat. Center for Scholars, 1978-79; sr. fellow Woodrow Wilson Sch. Pub. and Internat. Affairs, Princeton, N.J., 1979-80; Ferris prof. journalism Princeton U., 1980-81. Guest scholar Woodrow Wilson Internat. Ctr. for Scholars, 1990-91. Author: The Assassins, 1955, Eisenhower: The Inside Story, 1956, (with Joseph W. Martin, Jr.) My First Fifty Years in Politics, 1960, PT 109: John F. Kennedy in World War II, 1961, The Future of the Republican Party, 1964, Conflict and Crisis: The Presidency of Harry S Truman, 1945-48, 1977, Tumultuous Years: The Presidency of Harry S Truman, 1949-53, 1982, Nemesis: Truman and Johnson in the Coils of War in Asia, 1984, The Second Victory: The Marshall Plan and the Postwar Revival of Europe, 1987, Confidential Secretary: Ann Whitman's Twenty Years with Eisenhower and Rockefeller, 1988, (with Ray Scherer) Unsilent Revolution: Television News and American Public Life, 1948-1991, 1992, Boxing The Kangaroo: A Reporter's Memoir, 2000; also mag. articles. Served AUS, World War II; staff Stars and Stripes in Paris. Mem. White House Corrs. Assn. (pres. 1954), Gridiron Club, Army-Navy Country Club, Isla del Sol Yacht and Country Club. Home: Saint Petersburg, Fla. Died Aug. 8, 2003.

DOOB, JOSEPH LEO, mathematician, educator; b. Cin., Feb. 27, 1910; s. Leo and Mollie (Doerfler) Doob; m. Elsie Haviland Field, June 26, 1931 (dec. Jan. 1991); children: Stephen, Peter, Deborah. BA, Harvard U., 1930, MA, 1931, PhD, 1932; DSc (hon.), U. Ill., 1981. Faculty U. Ill., Urbana, 1935—78, successively assoc., asst. prof., assoc. prof., 1935—45, prof. math., 1945—78, emeritus prof., 1978—2004. Recipient Nat. medal of sci., 1979. Mem.: NAS, Acad. Scis. (Paris) (fgn., assoc.), Am. Acad. Arts and Scis. Home: Urbana, Ill. Died June 7, 2004.

DOOLIN, LAWRENCE E. microbiologist; b. Ottumwa, Ind., Aug. 22, 1927; s. John Green and Georgia (Ferguson) D.; m. Alice Hobbs Doolin, July 6, 1968. BS, Wayne State U., 1959, MS, 1962, PhD, 1966. Rsch. assoc. Albert Einstein Med. Ctr., Phila., 1966-68; rsch. scientist Eli Lilly & Co., Indpls., 1969-99. Contbr. articles to profl. jours.; patentee in field. Fellow AAAS, Am. Soc. Microbiology, Ind. Soc. Microbiology (editor 1972-74); mem. Nat. Orgn. Profl. Advancement Black Chemists and Chem. Engrs. (pres. 1988-90), NAACP, Bachelor Benedict Club (sec. 1988-90). Baptist. Avocations: photography, coin collector, chrystal collector. Home: Indianapolis, Ind. Died Mar. 28, 1999.

DORST, JOHN PHILLIPS, physician, radiology and pediatrics educator; b. Cin., July 8, 1926; s. Stanley Elwood and Mary (Conway) D.; m. Marcia Louise Kinney, June 17, 1950; children: Stanley Kinney, N. Heather, John Radcliffe, Margaret. Student, Princeton U., 1944, 47-48, U. Cin., 1946, Pomona Coll., 1948-49; MD, Cornell U., 1953. Rotating intern U. Iowa Hosps., 1953-54; resident in pathology Northwestern Hosp., Mpls., 1954; resident in radiology VA Hosp., Mpls., 1955, State U. Iowa Hosps., 1955-58; fellow in pediatric radiology U. Cin. Coll. Medicine, 1958-59, from asst. prof. to assoc. prof. radiology, also from instr. to asst. prof. pediatrics, 1959-66; mem. faculty Johns Hopkins Med. Sch., from 1966, assoc. prof. radiology, 1966-70, prof. radiology, 1970-95, assoc. prof. pediatrics, 1967-78, prof. pediatrics, 1978-95; radiologist Johns Hopkins Hosp., from 1966; prof. emeritus pediatrics, radiology Johns Hopkins Med. Sch., Balt., from 1995. Vis. lectr. Armed Forces Inst. Pathology, 1968-87; cons. NIH, 1969-87, Francis Scott Key Med. Ctr. (formerly Balt. City Hosp.), 1971-94, Kennedy-Krieger Inst. (formerly John F. Kennedy Inst.), Balt., 1972—. Mem. adv. editorial bd. Radiology, 1973-90. With U.S. Army, 1944-46. Fellow Am. Coll. Radiology; mem. Radiol. Soc. N.Am., Am. Roentgen Ray Soc., Soc. Pediatric Radiology (sec.-treas. 1973-76, pres. 1977-78), Md. Radiology Soc., Sigma Xi, Alpha Omega Alpha. Home: Columbia, Md. Deceased.

DOUGHERTY, ROBERT JAMES, safety consultant; b. Bartlesville, Okla., Aug. 31, 1923; s. Charles Francis and Isabelle Frances (Meder) D.; m. Margaret Rita Cullen, Nov. 27, 1946 (div. 1974); children: Robert Jr., Kathleen, Deborah, Dennis, Laurie, Maureen; m. Frances Munoz Tart, Oct. 1, 1974; stepchildren: Robert, Sheila, George, Amanda, James Tart. Student, St. Charles Seminary, Carthagena, Ohio, 1941-44. Cert. safety profl. Corp. safety dir. Stearns Roger Corp., Denver, 1953-69; civil svc. safety officer U.S. Bur. Mines, Denver, 1969-70; safety mgr. U.S. Army Adv. Team, Vietnam, 1970-73, U.S. Civil Svc., Fort Sam Houston, Tex., 1973-83; safety cons., advisor San Antonio, from 1983. Mem. Colo. Dept. Edn. ad hoc com. safety edn. curriculum, 1966; guest speaker Nat. and Internat. Safety Confs. Contbr. articles to profl. jours. Vice chmn. Alamo Field Fed. Health and Safety Coun., San Antonio, 1980; mem. sch. bd. dist. 50, Westminster, Colo., 1969-70; mem. gov.'s hwy. safety commn., Denver, 1968-75; group safety officer maj. Civil Air Patrol, Denver. Decorated Medal of Honor (1st class, Vietnam), Medal for U.S.A. Civil Svc. in Vietnam. Mem. Am. Soc. Safety Engrs. (regional v.p., bd. dirs. 1960-62, past pres. Colo. chpt.), Vets. Safety Internat.

(bd. dirs. 1964-65, regional v.p. 1964-65), Nat. Safety Coun. (past safety program cons., past editor Constrn. newsletter), Colo. Soc. Engrs. (life). Died Aug. 5, 2001.

DOUGLAS, DAVID WILLIAM, biomedical engineer; b. Honolulu, Aug. 12, 1924; s. Charles Eugene and Letitia (Phillips) D.; m. Ruth Laura Cochran, June 15, 1948; children: Leonard, Bruce, Donna. Cert. in Electronics, U.S. Navy; BA, Pomona Coll., 1948; postgrad., U. So. Calif., 1948-50; MSEE, U. Mo., 1969, PhD, 1971. Sr. project engr. Amelco, Inc., 1955-58; chief engr. Biophys. Rsch., Calif., 1958-59; sr. rsch. engr. Spacelabs, Inc., 1959-61; sr. rsch. scientist Cavitron Corp., 1975-77; staff scientist Mistogen Med., Oakland, Calif., 1979; pres. Douglas Sci. Products, Inc., Lenexa, Kans., from 1979. Cons. biomed. engr., 1961—; cons. Bendix-Pacific, North Hollywood, Calif., Electro-Optical Systems, Pasadena, Calif., Statham Instruments, L.A., Cavitron Corp., N.Y.C. and Anaheim, Calif., Puritan-Bennett Corp., Kansas City, Parker-McCrory Mfg., Kansas City, 1985-87, Med. Devices, Internat., Toronto, Ont., Can., 1986-88, others; asst. prof. biomed. engring., elec. engring., cardiology, surgery, U. Mo., Columbia, 1971-75; rsch. assoc. Mo. Regional Med. Program, 1967-72; biomed. cons. VA. Patentee in field; contbr. to tech. publs. Mem. IEEE (sr.), Assn. Advancement of Med. Instrumentation, Masons, Phi Beta Kappa, Sigma Xi. Died Sept. 5, 2000.

DOUGLASS, MALCOLM PAUL, social studies educator; b. Pullman, Wash., Aug. 18, 1923; s. Aubrey Augustus and Mary Evelyn D.; m. Enid Hart; children: Malcolm Paul Jr., John Aubrey, Susan Douglass. BA, Pomona Coll., 1947; MA, Columbia U., 1948; EdD, Stanford U., 1954. Tchr. Sacramento City Schs., 1947-50; prin. San Lorenzo (Calif.) Sch. Dist., 1950-54; prof. Claremont (Calif.) Grad. U., 1954-94, prof. emeritus, from 1994. Cons. various govtl. and sch. entities, 1954-; dir. Ctr. Ednl. Studies Claremont Grad. U., 1971-89, dir. Claremont Reading Conf., 1959-89, adv. bd. George G. Stone Ctr. for Children's Books, 1966-89; dir. ann. conf. Claremont Reading Conf., 1959-89. Author: Social Studies: From Theory to Practice in Elementary Education, 1967, Reading in Education: A Broader View, 1973, Learning to Read: The Quest for Meaning, 1989, The History, Psychology, and Pedagogy of Geography, 1998; assoc. editor: Tchr. Edn. Quar.; contbr. articles to profl. jours. Bd. trustees Oakwood Sch., North Hollywood, Calif., 1983-89, Wildlife Game Search Found., Winston, Oreg., 1981-2001. With inf. U.S. Army, ETO, 1943-46. Mem. Nat. Coun. Geographic Edn., John Dewey Soc., Soc. for the Study of Curriculum History. Home: Claremont, Calif. Died Dec. 2003.

DOUGLASS, RICHARD H. educator, reserve police officer, retired naval reserve officer; b. Dubuque, Iowa, Nov. 13, 1933; s. Millard Horace and Olive Lola (Smith) D.; m. Kathleen Naoma Lilley, July 14, 1964; children: Michael Derald, Kathleen Elizabeth. AA, John Muir Jr. Coll., 1953; BA, U. Calif., Santa Barbara, 1955; MA, U. So. Calif., 1965; gen. secondary credential, U. Calif., Santa Barbara, 1956; post cert., Pasadena Police Acad., 1972. Tchr. Duarte (Calif.) Unified Sch. Dist., from 1959; foreign language dept. chairperson Duarte (Calif.) High Sch., 1966-78; tchr. Citrus Community Coll., Glendora, Calif., from 1983. Advisor yearbook Halconado, 1962; advisor, editor yearbooks Upward Bound III, Upward Bound IV, 1980-81. Instr. Boy Scouts Am., 1972-83. Served to sr. chief quartermaster USNR, 1952-86. NDEA scholar U. So. Calif., 1965; scholar Nat. Endowment Humanities, 1973; recipient Cert. of Appreciation, City of Pasadena, 1975—, City of Duarte Community Svc. award, Svc to Youth, 1988, Calif. Assemblyman Richard Mountjoy Svc. Youth award, 1988, Calif State Senator Newton Russell Svc. award, 1988, PTSA Golden Apple award Svc. to Youth, 1989; named Hon. Counselor U.S. Military Acad., West Point, N.Y., 1983. Mem. MLA, Calif. Fgn. Lang. Tchrs. Assn., Naval Enlisted Res. Assns. (life), U. So. Calif. Alumni Assn. (life alumnus), Duarte Unified Edn. Assn. (pres. 1964-65, negotiator 1969-79, Appreciation cert. 1978), Duarte High Sch. Key Club (advisor 1985—, Lambda Chi Alpha. Democrat. Avocations: stamp collecting, fine books collector, walking, travel. Home: Arcadia, Calif. Deceased.

DOW, ROBERT STONE, neurologist; b. Colo., Jan. 4, 1908; s. Simon Stone and Mary Edna (Sisson) D.; m. Margaret Willetta Leever, July 9, 1934; children: Margreita, Barbara. BS, Linfield Coll., 1929; MA, MD, U. Oreg., Portland, 1934, PhD, 1935; DSc (hon.), Linfield Coll., 1963. Diplomate Am. Bd. Neurology. From asst. prof. to assoc. prof. Anatomy U. Oreg., Portland, 1939-46, clin. instr. Nuerology, 1940-46, asst. clin. prof. Neurology, 1946-52, assoc. clin. prof. Neurology, 1952-66, clin. prof. Neurology, 1966; intern Wis. Gen. Hosp., Madison, 1935-36. Fellow Dept. of Physiology Yale U., New Haven, 1936-37; adj. prof. Northwestern Coll. of Law, Lewis and Clark Coll., 1986-88. Co-author (book) Physiology & Pathology of Cerebellum, 1958. Fellow Belgium-Am. Found., 1937-38, Rockefeller Inst., 1938-39; recipient Disting. Svc. award Western Inst. on Epilipsy, 1979, Ann. Svc. award Multnomah County med. Soc., 1978, Aubney R. Watzek award Lewis and Clark Coll., 1986, Discovery award Med. Rsch. Found. of Oreg., 1988; named Alumnus Of Yr. Linfield Coll., 1982. Fellow Am. Acad. of Neurology; mem. ACP, AMA, Am. Assn. of Anatomists, Am. EEG Soc. (pres. 1958), Am. Neurolog. Soc., Am. Physiol. Soc., Am. Assn. Neurolog. Surgeons, Am. Epilespy Soc. (pres. 1965), Oreg. Med. Assn., Soc. of Neurosci., Sigma Xi, Alpha Omega Alpha, Univ. Club. Republican. Avocation: reading. Home: Portland, Oreg. Deceased.

DOWIYOGO, BERNARD, Nauruan government official; b. Feb. 14, 1946; Student, Australian Nat. U. Mem. parliament Govt. of Nauru, from 1973, pres., 1976-78, 89-95, min. justice, 1983-89, min. health and edn., 1989, min. civil aviation, 1992-95, min. island devel. and industry, 1992-95, min. external affairs, 1992-95, min. public svc., 1992-95. Chmn. Bank of Nauru, 1985—. Sec. Nauru Gen. Hosp.; gen. mgr. Nauru Coop. Soc. Died Mar. 9, 2003.

DOWLEY, FRANCIS HOTHAM, art history educator; b. N.Y.C., Dec. 13, 1915; s. Francis Dwight and Helen Agnes (Blackburne) D. BA in Philosophy, Princeton U., 1936; MA in Philosophy, U. Chgo., 1941, PhD, 1953. Instr. U. Chgo., 1949-53, asst. prof. art history, 1953-58, assoc. prof., 1959-73, prof. to prof. emeritus, 1974—2003. Contbr. research publs. in art history. Served to lt. (j.g.) USN, 1943-46, Japan. Grantee Am. Council Learned Socs., Paris, 1947-48 Mem. Am. Soc. Eighteenth Century Studies (chmn. com. Best Article Prize 1972-75), Coll. Art Assn., Societe de L'Histoire de l'Art Francais, Art Inst. Chgo. Clubs: Quadrangle (Chgo.). Roman Catholic. Home: Chicago, Ill. Died Dec. 5, 2003.

DOWNING, ROBERT JAMES, artist; b. Hamilton, Ont., Can., Aug. 1, 1935; s. Albert James and Dora Florence (Figgins) D.; m. Miriana Kaludjerovic, Sept. 27, 1980; children by previous marriage: Sara Lynn, Michael John. Police constable City of Hamilton, 1957-60. Lectr. U. Toronto, 1967-68; part-time lectr. Fanshawe Coll. Art and Tech., 1969-71, Ont. Coll. Art and Design, 1971-73, 81-82, Banff Ctr. Sch. Fine Art, 1974, Calif. State U., Long Beach, 1974-78, La Salle, Singapore, 1987-88; vis. lectr. Sheridan Coll., Art's Sake, Ont. Coll. Art and Design, Toronto, 1979-80; art program dir. Appleby Coll., Oakville, 1973; prepared, implemented visual and tactile awareness program for secondary sch. art and design tchrs. Molepolole Coll. Edn., Botswana, 1985-86; artist-in-residence Dynamics Graphics Project, U. Toronto, 1997-99. One-man shows include Dunkelman Gallery, Toronto, Can., 1963, Galerie Agnes Lefort, Montreal, Can., 1968, Whitechapel Art Gallery, London, 1969, York U. Art Gallery, Toronto, 1970, Gallery House Sol, Georgetown, 1971, Robert McLaughlin Gallery, Oshawa, 1972, U. Alta., Can., 1973, Cultural Resources Ctr., Huntington Beach, Calif., 1978, Coll. Pk., Toronto, 1981, A Room in the Artist's Home, Toronto, 1985, Art Gallery Hamilton, 1992, The Japan Found., Toronto, 1997; group exhbns. include Mil. Hdqrs. Bldg., Ottawa, 1956, John Pace Gallery, Laguna Beach, Calif., 1964, Ont. Arts Coun., 1967, Nat. Gallery Can., 1967, Rothmans Art Gallery, 1968, Montreal Mus. Fine Arts, 1968, Richard DeMarco Gallery, Scotland, 1969, middelheim Pk., Belgium, 1971, Arts Coun. Gt. Brit., 1971, Ont. Soc. Artists, 1972, Winnipeg Art Gallery, 1972, Burnaby Art Gallery, B.C., 1973, Centennial Gallery and Libr., Oakville, Ont., 1973, Long Beach Mus. Art, 1976, Smithsonian Inst., 1978, Pollock Gallery, Toronto, 1978, David Mirvish Gallery, Toronto, 1979, Koffler Ctr., Toronto, 1981, Nat. Gallery Botswana, 1986, Singapore Sci. Ctr., 1988; commns. include Jan Wallace Archtl. Offices, Laguna Beach, Calif., 1964, U. Toronto Med. Scis. Bldg., 1967, Mohawk Coll. Art and Tech., Hamilton, 1968, U. Waterloo Student Svds. Bldg., 1971, Sheraton Conv. Ctr., Toronto, 1972, Valley Bank Nev., Las Vegas, 1975, United Gas Pipe Line Co., Houston, 1976, Jefferson Shopping Mall, Louisville, 1978, Westinghouse Can. Ltd., Toronto, 1981, Esso Singapore Pte. Ltd., 1987, Singapore Sci. Ctr., 1988; completed CD Rom of life's work, 1999; represented in pub. collections. Nat. Gallery Can., Art Gallery Ont., U. Western Ont., Agnes Etherington Art Ctr., Ont. Sci. Ctr., Govt. of Ont., Singapore Nat. Theatre Trust, Can. Confedn. Ctr. Cultural rep. Texaco Can., Inc., 1980-81. Photographer with Royal Can. Navy, 1952-57. Served with Royal Can. Navy, 1952—57. Recipient Ont. Arts Coun. award, 1967, 78, 79, Can. Coun. award, 1967-71, 79, 85. Mem. Can. Artists Rep. (founder 1967), Sculpture Soc. Can., Ont. Soc. Artists (exec. coun. 1979-80), Royal Can. Acad. Arts. Died July 22, 2003.

DRABKIN, HARRY PINKUS, lawyer; b. Sonora, Calif., Apr. 4, 1936; s. Israel and Anna (Saul) D.; m. Mary Goldstein, Dec. 19, 1964; children: Roger Sherman, Andrew Scott, Ruth. BA, San Francisco State Coll., 1960, gen. secondary credential, 1961; JD, Lincoln U., 1969. Bar: Calif. 1970, U.S. Ct. Appeals (9th cir.) 1970, U.S. Dist. Ct. (no. and ea. dists.) Calif. 1970, U.S. Dist. Ct. (cen. dist.) Calif. 1973, U.S. Dist. Ct. (so. dist.) Calif. 1977, U.S. Supreme Ct. 1993. Dep. counsel counsel Stanislaus County Counsel, Modesto, Calif., 1970-98, ret., 1998. Chmn. probate and mental health sect. County Counsels Assn., 1985-88. Pres. Congregation Beth Shalom of Modesto, 1971-73, 88-90, 92-93. Specialist 4th class U.S. Army Airborne, 1956-58. Jewish. Deceased.

DRAHMANN, BROTHER THEODORE ROBERT, education educator; b. Perham, Minn., June 7, 1926; s. Vincent Henry Drahmann and Louise Cecile Speiser. BS in History, St. Mary's Coll., Winona, Wis., 1949, DEd (hon.), 1981; M in Social and Indsl. Relations, Loyola U., Chgo., 1956; degree in edn. adminstrn., Coll. St. Thomas, St. Paul, 1974. Joined Cath. order Bros. of the Christian Schs. Tchr. De La Salle High Sch., Chgo., 1949-56, prin., 1956-62; counselor St. Mary's Coll., 1963-66; prin. Cretin High Sch., St. Paul, 1966-70; supr. schs. Christian Bros., St. Paul, 1970-72; supt. schs. Archdiocese of St. Paul/Mpls., 1972-78; dir. grad. studies Coll. St. Thomas, 1978-80; pres. Christian Bros. U., Memphis, 1980-93; dir. edn. Christian Bros. Conf., Landover, Md., 1993-98; prof. edn. St. Mary's U. of Minn., Mpls., Minn., from 1998. Mem. U.S. Cath. Conf. Com. on Edn., Washington, 1993-99; mem. adv. com. Coun. Am. Pvt. Edn., Washington, 1993-98; mem. Chief Adminstrs. Cath. Edn., 1993—; exec. dir. Lasallian Assn. Univs. and Colls., 1993-98. Author: (manual) Catholic School Principal-Outline for Action, 1980, rev. 1989, (brochure) Governance & Administration in Catholic Schools, 1985. Trustee St. Mary's Coll., 1972-81, Lewis U., Romeoville, Ill., 1982-93, Coll. Santa Fe, 1995-2002, De La Salle Inst., 1995-2002; charter mem. Hall of Fame, Sch. Edn., U. St. Thomas, 2001—. Named Disting. Grad. Coll. St. Thomas, 1984, Oustanding Tennessean Gov. of Tenn., Nashville, 1988, Most Influential Cath. Educator for Past 25 Yrs., Today's Cath. Tchr. jour., 1997. Mem. Nat. Cath. Ednl. Assn. (Outstanding Educator of Yr. award 1985, bd. dirs. 1986-94), Assn. Cath. Colls. and Univs. (bd. dirs. 1985-94), NCCJ (chmn. bd. Memphis chpt. 1980-93, Humanitarian award 1990), Econ. Club of Memphis (bd. dirs. 1988-93), Rotary (bd. dirs. Memphis club 1984-89, pres. 1987-88), KC, Mil. and Hospitaller Order St. Lazarus Jerusalem (knight comdr. 1991—, Martyrs of Memphis award 1994), Pi Gamma Mu, Alpha Kappa Delta, Delta Epsilon Sigma. Avocations: reading, swimming. Home: Saint Paul, Minn. Died 2002.

DRAKE, CHARLENE, city comptroller; b. Chgo., Aug. 8, 1952; d. Charles LeRoy and Catherine (Watson) D. BS, No. Ill. U., 1974. Exec. sec. Village of Robbins, Ill., 1974-77, asst. treas., 1978-81; jr. acct. Wilson & Gills, CPA, Chgo., 1977-78; adminstrv. asst. Modern Health and Rapid Therapy, Inc., Markham, Ill., 1981-83; comptroller City of Harvey, Ill., from 1983. Mem. Pride of Robbins Temple, 1978—; bd. dirs. Robbins Community Ctr., treas., 1975-81; bd. dirs. Robbins Pub. Library Dist., 1976-80, United Way of Robbins, 1980—; charter mem. Community Woman Interested in Drug Edn.-W.I.D.E., 1987—. Named one of Outstanding Young Women Am., 1981. Mem. Ill. Mcpl. Treasurers Assn. (bd. dirs. 1986-88), Mcpl. Tresurers Assn. of U.S. and Can., No. Ill. U. Black Alumni Assn. (treas. 1984-88), Robbins Alumni Assn. (pres. 1987-88, numerous other offices 1980—, Service award 1981-82), Nat. Assn. for Female Execs., Zeta Phi Beta, Zeta Tau Zeta (numerous regional and state offices 1972—, numerous awards 1981, 86, Zeta of Yr. 1987). Democrat. Baptist. Avocations: bowling, tennis, reading, traveling. Home: Harvey, Ill. Deceased.

DRAKE, STANLEY ALBERT, cartoonist; b. Bklyn., Nov. 9, 1921; s. Albert Edward and Josephine (Seaburry) D.; m. Elaine Moller, Dec. 6, 1976. Student, Art Students League, N.Y.C., 1938-39. Comml. artist, N.Y.C., 1947-53; creator comic strip The Heart of Juliet Jones, from 1953. Illustrator: Golf Digest mag. 1969—, The Touch System for Better Golf (Bob Toski), 1970; artist for Kelly Green (Leonard Starr); adventure series Dargaud, Neuilly-Sur-Seine, France, 1980—, art work done on comic strip Blondie for Dean Young, 1984. With U.S. Army, 1942-46. Mem. Nat. Cartoonists Soc. (Story Strip Cartoonist of Yr. award 1969, 70, 72), Artists and Writers Assn. (pres.). Died Mar. 10, 1997.

DRAPER, VERDEN ROLLAND, accountant, educator; b. St. Louis, Feb. 23, 1916; s. Neal McLain and Florence (Meyers) D.; m. Eileen Ogden, Aug. 18, 1940; children: Mallen, Eileen Ann, Cynthia, Patti, Verden. BS, Washington U., St. Louis, 1938. With Price Waterhouse & Co. (C.P.A.s), St. Louis, 1938-51, Tulsa, 1951-55, Pitts., 1955-60, Buffalo, 1960—. Mem. faculty Washington U., St. Louis U., U. Tulsa. Author: (with Robert H. Irving) Accounting Practices in the Petroleum Industry, 1958; contbr. articles profl. publs. Former pres. Better Bus. Bur. Western N.Y. Served with USNR, World War II. Mem. Am. Inst. C.P.A.s Mo., Okla., Pa., N.Y. State socs. C.P.A.s, Am. Accounting Assn., Buffalo Area C. of C. (treas., dir.), Beta Gamma Sigma, Omicron Delta Kappa, Delta Sigma Pi (Alumnae award 1938), Alpha Kappa Psi (hon.), Theta Xi. Clubs: Buffalo Country (past treas., gov.), Buffalo. Presbyterian. Home: Naples, Fla. Deceased.

DRAPER, WILLIAM FRANKLIN, artist, portrait and landscape painter; b. Hopedale, Mass., Dec. 24, 1912; s. Clare Hill and Matilda Grace (Engman) D.; m. Barbara Cagiati, Oct. 7, 1944 (div. 1969); children: William Franklin, Francesca Cagiati Draper Linke (dec.), Margaret Joy Draper Starr. Student, Pomfret (Conn.) Sch., 1927-31, Harvard U., 1931-33, NAD, 1933-34, Grande Chaumiere, Paris, 1935, Art Students League, N.Y.C., 1937. Instr. Art Students League N.Y., 1965-74. Exhibited Nat. Gallery, Washington, Met. Mus., Nat. Portrait Gallery, NAD, Chgo. Art Inst., Inst. Modern Art, Mus. Fine Arts, Boston, Nat. Gallery, London, Wally Findlay Galleries, N.Y.C., 1990, Palm Beach, Fla., 1991; works include 3 murals, Bancroft Hall, U.S. Naval Acad.; portraits of numerous pub. figures including Pres. John F. Kennedy, Pres. Richard M. Nixon, King Faisal and King Saud of Saudi Arabia, Paul Mellon, Gov. John Waihee of Hawaii, Gov. Charles S. Robb of Va., Mayor John V. Lindsay of N.Y.C., Senator Harry F. Byrd of Va., John D. Rockefeller, Thomas Watson and John Opel, chief exec. officers of IBM, Robert C. Wilburn for Carnegie Inst., Dr. Lewis Thomas, Gov. Harry Hughes of Md., Shah of Iran, Dr. Charles Mayo, Terence Cardinal Cooke, Leon Cardinal Suenens, John Cardinal Krol, Mrs. Norman Chandler, Margaret Clapp, Mildred McAfee Horton, Mrs. John J. Louis, Mrs. August Belmont, Ilka Chase, Celeste Holm, Mrs. Endicott Peabody, Mrs. Walter H. Annenberg, Amb. Walter H. Annenberg, Winton Blount, David Rockefeller; represented in permanent collections including Chrysler, Boston Mus. Sci., Nat. Racing Mus., Saratoga, Yale Ctr. for Brit. Art, Nat. Gallery Art, Washington, Nat. Portrait Gallery, Washington, Carnegie Inst., others; one-man shows include N.Y.C., Boston, St. Louis, Palm Beach, Atlanta. Served as lt. comdr., ofcl. combat artist USNR, 1942-46. Decorated

Bronze Star; Gold medal, Portrait Society of America, 1999. Mem. Century Assn., Harvard Club, Knickerbocker Club, Lotus Club. Home: New York, NY. Died Oct. 26, 2003.

DRENNAN, F. RICHARD, lawyer; b. Washington, Jan. 16, 1922; s. Richard Patrick and Margaret Gertrude (Murray) D.; m. Marion Virginia Shea, Aug. 9, 1951; children: Richard, Peter, Paul, Mary Susan, John. BS, Va. Poly. Inst., 1947; JD, Boston Coll., 1950. Bar: Mass. 1951, U.S. Dist. Ct. Mass. 1955. Pvt. practice law, Pittsfield, Mass., from 1951. From spl. asst. atty. gen. to asst. dist. atty. Commonwealth of Mass., 1970-79. Author articles. Bd. dirs. Auto Club Berkshire County, Pittsfield, 1969—. Lt. U.S. Army, 1943-46, Italy. Named to Medford (Mass.) H.S. Sports Hall of Fame, 1989. Mem. Berkshire County Bar Assn., Eagles (chmn. bd. trustees), Am. Legion, KC. Roman Catholic. Avocations: golf, reading, travel, spectator sports. Home: Pittsfield, Mass. Died Apr. 22, 2002.

DRESSNER, HOWARD ROY, foundation executive, lawyer; b. N.Y.C., Feb. 14, 1919; s. Sol and Anna (Gross) D.; m. Sonia Segoda, Apr. 6, 1942; 1 son, Robert. BS, N.Y. U., 1940; LL.B., Columbia U., 1948. With N.Y. U., 1948-64; successively instr. pub. speaking, asst. prof. pub. speaking, asst. v.p. devel.; dir. Albert Gallatin Assos., 1956-65; asst. to v.p. domestic programs Ford Found., 1964-67, sec. found., 1967-71, sec., gen. counsel found., 1971-76, v.p., gen. counsel, sec. found., 1976-84; counsel Shereff, Friedman, Hoffman & Goodman, 1984-90; pres. N.Y. Nonprofit Com., 1984-91. Author: Essays in Bewilderment, 1998; co-author: Business Writing. Candidate for N.Y. State Assembly, 1966; active Nonprofit Com., 1984—. Served to maj. AUS, World War II. Decorated Bronze Star medal. Home: New York, NY. Died Dec. 31, 2002.

DREXLER, FRED, insurance executive; b. Oakland, Calif., Nov. 17, 1915; s. Frederic I. and Jessie (Day) D.; m. Martha Jane Cunningham, Dec. 26, 1936 (dec. June 1987); children: Kenneth, Roger Cunningham, Martha Drexler Lynn. AB, U. Redlands, 1936; JD, Golden Gate U., 1947, LL.D., 1971. Bar: Calif. 1947. Editor Mill Valley (Calif.) Record, 1936-42; employee relations Marinship Corp., 1942-45; office mgr. Bechtel Corp., 1945-46; asst. to pres. Indsl. Indemnity Co., San Francisco, 1946-48, asst. sec., 1948-51, sec., 1951-56, sr. v.p., sec., 1956-67, exec. v.p., sec., 1967-68, pres., 1968-70, chmn. bd., chief exec. officer, 1970-76, chmn. exec. com., 1976-78, dir., 1957-86. Dir. Crum & Forster, 1970-83, Montgomery St. Income Securities, Inc. (dir. 1977, chmn. bd. 1988-91); mem. Calif. Workmen's Compensation Study Commn., 1963-65; founder Calif. Workers Compensation Inst., 1964, pres., 1971-74, honoree testimonial dinner, 1985; pres. Pacific Ins. and Surety Conf., 1967-68 Pres. Marin (Calif.) United Fund, 1956; exec. bd. Marin coun. Boy Scouts Am., 1948-69, adv. bd., 1970—, mem. nat. exec. bd., 1973-87; trustee Marin Country Day Sch., 1960-62, United Bay Area Crusade, 1955-73; trustee Golden Gate U., 1957—, chmn. bd., 1968-70; bd. dirs. San Francisco Bay Area Coun., 1972-76, Buck Inst. for Age Rsch., 1989—; trustee Pacific Presbyn. Med. Ctr., 1974-91; chmn. bd. Inst. Philos. Rsch., 1978-95, trustee, 1973-95; trustee World Affairs Coun. No. Calif., 1973-79, Calif. Pacific Med. Ctr., 1991—. Recipient Silver Beaver, Silver Antelope awards Boy Scouts Am. Mem. Calif. Bar Assn. Clubs: Bankers (San Francisco) (pres. 1976-78), Bohemian (San Francisco), Pacific Union (San Francisco). Baptist. Home: San Francisco, Calif. Died Dec. 3.

DRINNAN, ALAN JOHN, oral pathologist; b. Bristol, Eng., Apr. 6, 1932; came to U.S., 1962, naturalized, 1970; s. Leslie Cyril and Doris May (Porter) D.; m. Marguerite G. Bondolfi, Apr. 4, 1956; children: Michael James, Julia Mary. B.D.S., Bristol U., 1954, M.B.Ch.B., 1962; D.D.S., SUNY, 1964. Tutor oral surgery Bristol U., Eng., 1957-58; asst. prof. SUNY-Buffalo, 1964-68, assoc. prof., 1968-71, prof. dept. oral medicine, chmn., 1971-94, disting. prof., 1994—2000, disting. prof. emeritus, from 2000. Contbr. articles to numerous publs. Served to capt. Royal Army Dental Corps Brit. Army, 1955-57. Fulbright sr. scholar U. Melbourne, Australia, 1981 Mem. ADA, Am. Acad. Oral Pathology (pres.), Internat. Assn. Dental Research, Internat. Assn. Oral Pathologists (pres.). Home: Buffalo, NY. Died Jan. 8, 2004.

DRUMMOND, LEWIS A. seminary president, minister; b. Dixon, Ill. s. Wendall Addison and Elsie Lottie (Newbury) D.; m. Betty Rae Love. AB in English, Samford U., 1950; BD in N.T., Southwestern Bapt. Theol. Sem., Ft. Worth, 1955; ThM in Philosophy, Southwestern Bapt. Theol. Sem., 1958; PhD, U. London, 1963; postdoctoral studies, Oxford (Eng.) U. Ordained to ministry Bapt. Ch. Pastor New Bethel Bapt. Ch., Columbiana, Ala., 1949-50, 8th Ave. Bapt. Ch., Ft. Worth, 1951-53, 1st Bapt. Ch., Granbury, Tex., 1953-56, Glen Iris Bapt. Ch., Birmingham, Ala., 1956-61, 9th and O Bapt. Ch., Louisville, 1964-68; chair evangelism and practical theology Spurgeon's Theol. Coll., Oxford U., London, 1968-73; Billy Graham prof. evangelism, dir. Billy Graham Ctr. So. Bapt. Theol. Sem., Louisville, 1973-88; pres. Southeastern Bapt. Theol. Sem., Wake Forest, NC, 1988—92. Prof.-at-large U. Zagreb, Yugoslavia; assoc. evangelist Billy Graham Evangelistic Team, Poland, Australia; mem. faculty Billy Graham Sch. Evangelism; lectr. Southwestern Bapt. Theol. Sem., Ft. Worth, Golden Gate Bapt. Theol. Sem., San Francisco, New Orleans Bapt. Theol. Sem., Luther Rice Theol. Sem., St. Petersburg, Fla., Hong Kong Bapt. Theol. Sem., Philippine Bapt. Theol. Sem., Baguio, East Germany Bapt. Theol. Sem., Boukow, German Dem. Republic, Yugoslavia Bapt. Theol. Sem., Novi Sad, Poland Bapt. Theol. Sem., Warsaw, West Australia Bapt. Theol. Sem., Perth, Sydney (Australia) Bapt. Theol. Sem., Guatemala Bapt. Theol. Sem., Carfif (Wales) Bapt. Theol. Sem., Scottish Bapt. Theol. Sem., Glasgow, Trinity Evang. Div. Sch., Deerfield, Ill., Asbury Theol. Sem., Wilmore, Ky., Samford U., Birmingham, Mobile (Ala.) Coll., Carson-Newman Coll., Jefferson City, Tenn., U. Sydney, Union U., Jackson, Tenn., Miss. Coll., Clinton, Okla. Bapt. U., Shawnee, Campbellsville (Ky.) Bapt. Coll., Wheaton (Ill.) Coll., S.W. Bapt. U., Bolivar, Mo., Wingate (N.C.) Bapt. Coll., Campbell Coll., Buies Creek, N.C., Fla. Bapt. Theol. Coll., Graceville. Author: Evangelism: The Counter-Revolution, 1972, Life Can Be Real, 1974, Leading Your Church in Evangelism, 1976, The Awakening That Must Come, 1979, Witnessing for God to Men, 1980, The Revived Life, 1981, Charles G. Finney: The Birth of Modern Evangelism, 1982, The Life and Ministry of Charles G. Finney, 1984, If My People Will...I Will, 1985, The People of God in Ministry, 1985, How to Answer a Skeptic, 1986; also articles in Christianity Today, Bapt. Theol. Quar.; editor: What the Bible Says, 1974, Here They Stand: Sermons from Eastern Europe, 1976. With U.S. Army Air Corps, World War II. Mem. Bapt. World Alliance (com. on evangelism and edn.), Royal Inst. Philos., Evang. Philos. Soc., Acad. Profs. Evangelism (pres. 1978-80). Died Jan. 4, 2004.

DRYER, RICHARD EDWARD, rabbi; b. N.Y.C., Nov. 29, 1930; s. Oscar Albert and Anna (Frankl) D.; m. Arlene Terry Gottlieb, Dec. 25, 1955; 1 child, Deborah. BA, CCNY, 1951; BHL, Hebrew Union Coll., 1954, MAHL, 1957, DD (hon.), 1982. Ordained rabbi, 1957. Commd. 2d lt. U.S. Army, 1957, advanced through grades to col., 1979, chaplain various locations, 1957-87, ret., 1987; rabbi Temple Mizpah, Abilene, Tex., 1987-90, Temple Beth Emeth, Sherman, Tex., from 1990; faculty Tex. Luth. Coll., Seguin, from 1992. Chmn. armed svcs. com. San Antonio Jewish Community Ctr., 1988—, chmn. Judaic practices com., 1989—. Mem. allocations panel United Way, San Antonio, 1987—. Recipient Four Chaplains award B'nai B'rith, N.Y.C., 1965, Medal of Merit, Jewish War Vets. USA, Atlantic City, N.J., 1966; named Chaplain of Yr., Assn. Jewish Chaplains of Armed Forces, 1986; decorated Legion of Merit, Bronze Star. Mem. Cen. Conf. Am. Rabbis (bd. dirs. 1979-80), Kallah of Tex. Rabbis (pres. 1989-90), Am. Acad. Religion. Home: San Antonio, Tex. Died June 4, 2001.

DUBE, LEROY S. state legislator; b. Haverhill, Mass., Aug. 14, 1908; m. Agnes G. Dube. Student, Burdett Coll., 1926, U. Mass., U. N.H. Chmn. Bd. Selectmen; del. Rep. Constl. Conv.; town auditor, mem. Budget Com.; mem. State Seacoast Water Commn.; N.H. state rep. Dist. 9, Dist. 16, from 1994; mem. constnl. and statutory rev. com. N.H. Ho. of Reps. Dist. mgr. Elec. Utilities. Trustee Trust Funds; mem. Red Cross Fund Drs.; notary pub.; active Boy Scouts Am., Mass. Heart Assn., former dir. Mem. Assn. N.H. Assessors (past exec. dir.), Nat. Coun. Rep., Lone Tree Coun. (past pres.), Rotary Club (past dir.). Died July 14, 1997.

DUBNICK, BERNARD, retired pharmaceutical company administrator; b. Bklyn., May 29, 1928; s. Jacob Joseph and Lena Bella (Slotkoff) D.; m. Maxine Audrey France, Aug. 31, 1952 (dec. Mar 1963); children: Joshua, Jeffrey Robert; m. Selma Lydia Blumenthal, July 3, 1966. BS, CCNY, 1949; PhD, U. Ill., 1953. Scientist Warner-Lambert, Morris Plains, N.J., 1953-55, sr. scientist, 1955-62, sr. rsch. assoc., 1962-72, dept. head pharmacodynamics, 1972-77; dir. biochem. pharmacology Warner Lambert/Parke Davis, Ann Arbor, Mich., 1977; dir. CV-CNS rsch. sect. med. rsch. divsn. Am. Cyanamid Co., Pearl River, N.Y., 1977-94, ret., 1994; founder, v.p. Theragem, Inc., Old Tappan, from 1994. Chair Biochem. Pharmacology Disc Group, N.Y.C., 1973-74. Author: (with others) Immunopharmacology, 1975, Search for New Drugs, 1978; chpt. co-editor: Psychopharmacology, Third Generation of Progress, 1987. Bd. dirs. Family Svc. West Essex, Essex County, N.J., 1972-73, pres., 1974-75; mem. Family Orgn. Mid-Bergen Mental Health Ctr., Paramus, N.J., 1983; mem. Bergen Co. Mental health bd., 2002—. Fellow AAAS, N.Y. Acad. Scis. (chair biochem. sect. 1974-75); mem. Am. Soc. Pharmacology & Exptl. Therapeutics (pharmacology in industry subcom. 1978-80), Am. Chem. Soc. (treas. North Jersey sect. 1960-62). Democrat. Jewish. Home: Old Tappan, NJ. Died Oct. 7, 2002.

DUBOW, ARTHUR MYRON, investor, lawyer; b. Chgo., Sept. 18, 1933; s. David and Matilda (Polster) D.; m. Isabella Goodrich Breckinridge, Mar. 2, 1962 (div. Dec. 1983); children: Charles Stewart, Alexandra Breckinridge; m. Barbara J. Shattuck, Dec. 27, 1986. AB, Harvard U., 1954, LLB, 1957. Bar: N.Y. 1962. Assoc. firm Webster Sheffield Fleischmann Hitchcock & Chrystie, N.Y.C., 1960-64; v.p., dir. Back Bay-Orient Enterprises, Inc., Boston, 1965-68, pres., 1968-76; pres., dir. Bayorient Holding Corp., Boston, 1969-76; pres. Korea Capital Corp., N.Y.C., 1968-76, Fortune Capital Ltd., Boston, 1979-84; pres., dir. Boston Co. Energy Advisers, 1981-85; chmn. Instl. Shareholder Svcs., 1989-91. Pres. Fourth Estate, Inc., 1990-96; bd. dirs. Sulpetro Can. Ltd., Calgary, Alta., 1966-76, Dallas, 1973-76, chmn. exec. com., 1974-76; bd. dir. Castle Convertible Fund, Inc., Spectra Fund, Inc., Alger Funds, Coolidge Investment Corp., Herald Prodns., Inc.; fellow Ctr. for Internat. Affairs Harvard U., 1976-77. Mem. mgmt. com. Parenting mag., 1986-90. Mem. vis. com. dept. visual and environ. studies, dept. East Asian langs. and civilizations Ctr. for Sci. and Internat. Affairs, Harvard U., 1971-87; bd. dirs. Inst. Ednl. Leadership, 1982-89, Sabre Found., 1980-96, Thomas Jefferson Forum, 1986-92; chmn. bd. dirs. Potomac Assocs., Inc., Washington, 1975-95; mem. nat. adv. com. on accreditation and instl. eligibility U.S. Dept. Edn., 1982-86; co-chmn. New Am. Filmmakers' Series, Whitney Mus. Am. Art, N.Y.C., 1970-76; mem. adv. bd. Sch. Advanced Internat. Studies, 1980-88; trustee Arthur Dubow Found. With U.S. Army, 1957-59. Mem.: Harvard of N.Y. and Somerset; Tavern (Boston). Home: Wainscott, NY. Died Dec. 3, 1999.

DUDLEY, ROBERT THANE, electronics executive; b. Burlington, Kans., Mar. 16, 1916; s. John Vern and Mabel (Hill) D.; m. M. Edythe Cooper, Feb. 25, 1942; 1 child, Debra Clair. AA, U. Tenn., Martin, 1936; BS in Bus. Law, U. Tenn., 1940. Adminstrv. asst. Tenn. State Legislature, Nashville, 1941-42; dist. mgr. Sterling Electric Co., Memphis, 1946-50, Ft. Worth Steel Co., Chgo., 1950-55; sales mgr. Imperial Electric Co., Akron, Ohio, 1955-59, Fincor div. Incom Internat. Inc., York, Pa., 1960-67; chief exec. officer Electrol Co., Inc., York, from 1964. Adv. com. York Vocat. Tech. Sch. Served to 1st lt. USAF, 1942-46. Mem. Ind. Mgmt. Club, York, Mfrs. Assn. York, Inc., York C. of C. (Small Businessman Yr. 1984, Ben Franklin Parternership award 1983). Clubs: Viking Amateur Athletic (York). Democrat. Presbyterian. Avocations: travel, reading, hiking, sports. Home: York, Pa. Died Apr. 14, 1999.

DUECKER, STEVEN ECKMANN, health facility administrator; b. Ft. Morgan, Colo., Oct. 26, 1954; s. John Fred Jr. and Mary Helen (Eckmann) D.; m. Nancy Elizabeth Mills, May 31, 1980; 1 child, Lacy Elizabeth. BBA, U. Cin., 1978, M in Health Adminstrn., 1984. Acct. plant cost Procter and Gamble Co., Cin., 1979-80, acct. fixed assets, 1980-81, acct. product cost, 1981-82; staff planner Good Samaritan Hosp., Cin., 1983-85, planning assoc., 1985; chief oper. officer Mercy Shared Svcs., Inc., Cin., from 1986. Mem. Greenhills Vol. Fire Dept. and Life Squad, 1977-84; CPR instr. ARC, 1979; advisor U. Cin. Career Resource Ctr., 1985; sec., treas., bd. dirs. La Valle Sch., 1988—. Mem. Greater Cin. Alliance for Hosp. Planning, Tri-State Hosp. Adminstrs. Forum, Ohio Hosp. Assn., Am. Hosp. Assn. (mem. hosp. planning sect.), Am. Coll. Hosp. Execs. Avocations: golf, tennis. Home: Cincinnati, Ohio. Deceased.

DUFFIN, RICHARD JAMES, mathematician, educator; b. Chgo., Oct. 13, 1909; s. Daniel and Mary (Curran) D.; m. Carolyn Jeanne Hartman, July 19, 1947; children— Virginia Mae, Martha Jane. BS in Engring., U. Ill., 1932, PhD in Physics, 1935. Teaching asst. physics U. Ill., 1935, assoc. math., 1941-42; instr. math. Purdue U., 1936-41; physicist terrestrial magnetism Carnegie Instn. Wash., 1942-46; faculty Carnegie-Mellon U., 1946—, prof. math., 1948-70, Univ. prof. math. scis., 1970—. Vis. prof. Purdue U., 1949, Inst. Advanced Studies, Dublin, Ireland, 1959; dir. spl. research applied math. Duke, 1958; distinguished vis. prof. engring. U. State N.Y. at Stony Brook, 1967; disting. vis. prof. math. Tex. A. and M. U., 1968; cons. in field, 1956— Co-author: Geometric Programming, 1967; Mem. editorial bds. jours. in field. Recipient von Neumann theory prize Ops. Research Soc. Am., 1982 Mem. Nat. Acad. Scis., Am. Acad. Arts and Scis., Am. Math. Soc., Soc. Indsl. and Applied Math. (nat. lectr. 1961, 64, 76), Nat. Philosophy Soc., Sigma Xi (Monie A. Ferst award 1984), Tau Beta Pi, Triangle. Home: Pittsburgh, Pa. Died October 29, 1996.

DUFFY, ROBERT TOWNSEND, retired aerospace engineer; b. Guyencourt, Del., Dec. 29, 1926; s. Edward Reese and Alice Ann (Brabson) D.; m. Joyce Irene Wright, Dec. 17, 1960; children: Lynn Launa, Brian Edward, Patricia Lee, Bruce Townsend. Cert. engring., Spartan Sch. Aero., Tulsa, Okla., 1948; BME, U. Va., 1956. Profl. engr., Va. Mech. design engr. Goodyear Aircraft Corp., Akron, Ohio, 1949-50, flight test engr., 1950-52; wind tunnel test engr. NACA, Wallops Island, Langley Field, Va., 1952-58; engr. project and ops. mgmt. br. Wallops Sta. NASA, Wallops Island, 1958-64, asst. head ops. div. Wallops Sta., 1964-68, dir. ops. Wallops Flight Ctr., 1968-80; head ops. div. NASA-GSFC Wallops Flight Facility, Wallops Island, 1980-90; dep. dir. suborbital projects and ops. NASA GSFC/WFF, Wallops Island, 1990-93. Mem. chancellor's adv. com. for airway sci. program, U. Md. Ea. Shore, Princess Anne, 1988-93. Bd. dirs. Opportunity Skyway of Eastern Shore, 1992—. With USN, 1945-46, PTO. Mem. AIAA, Masons. Republican. Presbyterian. Avocations: music, gardening, fishing, reading. Home: Pocomoke City, Md. Died Apr. 3, 2001.

DUGAN, CHARLES FRANCIS, II, lawyer; b. Ann Arbor, Mich., Aug. 8, 1939; s. Charles F. and Mary (Minton) D.; m. Janice C. Prior, June 11, 1961; children: Heather, Stephanie, Suzanne, Kathleen. B.A., Miami U., Oxford, Ohio, 1960; J.D., U. Mich., 1963. Bar: Ohio 1963. Assoc., Vorys, Sater, Seymour & Pease, Columbus, Ohio, 1963-69, ptnr., 1970-91; bd. dirs., sec. Buckeye Fin. Corp., 88 Fund, Inc., Ohio Inst. Fin., Columbus, 1974-90, TEAM Am. Corp., 1992—; co-chmn. enforcement adv. com. Ohio Securities div., Columbus, 1980-91; lectr. in field. Contbr. articles to profl. jours. Trustee, sec. Nat. Ch. Residences of Worthington, 1972—; pres. Seal of Ohio council Girl Scouts Am., 1976-79.; music dir. Berlin Presbyn. Ch., Del. County, Ohio, 1987—. Mem. Columbus Bar Assn. (securities law com.), Ohio State Bar Assn. (corp. law com.), ABA (fed. regulation of securities com.).

DUHAMEL, RONALD J. Canadian government official; Min. vet. affairs, sec. of state Govt. of Can., Ottawa, Ont. Died Oct. 2.

DUKE, PAUL ROBERT, lawyer; b. Phila., Mar. 1, 1929; s. Robert James and Sara Mary (Dougherty) D.; m. Cecilia Mary McCann, Aug. 8, 1953; children: Paul R. Jr., Michael

C., Thomas J., Kathleen M., Kevin E., Robert James III, Mary Beth, John P. AB magna cum laude, St. Joseph's U., 1950; LLB cum laude, U. Pa., 1953. Bar: Pa. 1954, D.C. 1976. Law clk. to presiding justice Pa. Supreme Ct., 1955-56; asst. solicitor Pa. R.R., Phila., 1956-59, asst. gen. solicitor, 1959-65; asst. gen. counsel Pa. Cen. Transp. Co., Phila., 1965-71, gen. reorgn. counsel, 1971-73, gen. counsel, 1973-75, v.p. law, 1975-76; ptnr. Covington & Burling, Washington, 1976-99. Mem. Del. County Rep. Exec. Com., Pa., 1960-64; Del. County Home Rule Study Commn., 1973-76. Served to 1st lt. Med. Service Corps., AUS, 1953-55. Mem. D.C. Bar Assn., Phila. Bar Assn. Roman Catholic. Home: Rockville, Md. Died Nov. 22, 2003.

DUNCAN, CHARLES TIGNOR, lawyer; b. Washington, Oct. 31, 1924; s. Robert Todd and Nancy Gladys (Jackson) D.; m. Dorothy Adelena Thrasher, July 31, 1947 (dec. Dec. 1972); 1 child, Charles Todd; m. Pamela Jo Thurber, Aug. 10, 1996. BA, Dartmouth Coll., 1947; JD, Harvard U., 1950; LLD (hon.), Dartmouth Coll., 1986; LLD (hon.), Howard U., 2004. Bar: N.Y. 1951, D.C. 1953, U.S. Supreme Ct. 1954, Md. 1955. Assoc. Rosenman, Goldmark, Colin & Kaye, N.Y.C., 1950-53; partner Reeves, Robinson & Duncan, Washington, 1953-60; prin. asst. U.S. atty. Washington, 1961-65; gen. counsel U.S. Equal Employment Opportunity Commn., Washington, 1965-66; corp. counsel D.C., D.C., 1966-70; acting dir. pub. safety, 1969; partner Epstein, Friedman, Duncan & Medalie, Washington, 1970-74; dean, prof. law Sch. Law Howard U., 1974-78; ptnr. Peabody, Lambert & Meyers, Washington, 1978-84, Reid & Priest, Washington, 1984-90, sr. counsel, 1990-94; mem. Iran-U.S. Claims Tribunal, The Hague, 1994—2000. Trustee Northfield Mt. Hermon Sch., 1980—90, chmn., 1987—90; sr. dir. NAACP Legal Def. and Edn. Fund. With USNR, 1944—46. Recipient numerous career awards including Disting. Svc. award D.C. Bar, 1974, William J. Brennan, Jr. award D.C. Bar, 2001, Resolution 564 citation for legal career of 50 yrs., Senate of Md., 2002, Thurgood Marshall Brown v. Bd. Edn. award, Thurgood Marshall Ctr. Trust, Inc., 2004. Fellow Am. Bar Found. (life); mem. ABA, Nat. Bar Assn., D.C. Bar Unified (Pub. Service award 1974, pres. 1973-74), Phi Beta Kappa, Alpha Phi Alpha, Sigma Pi Phi, Delta Theta Phi. Lodges: Masons (32 deg.). Democrat. Achievements include being an active participant in preparation and presentation of sch. desegregation cases before U.S. Supreme Ct., 1953-55. Home: Annapolis, Md. Died May 4, 2004.

DUNCAN, JOHN MALVIN, minister; b. Plainview, Tex., Aug. 29, 1934; s. Malvin Eural and Velma (Thompson) D. Banker, 1959-69; with McGavack Miller Fin. & Ins., 1973-87; min. Help Open People's Eyes (H.O.P.E.) Ministries, Plainview, Tex., from 1987. Served with U.S. Army, 1959-69. Deceased.

DUNCAN, POPE ALEXANDER, college administrator; b. Glasgow, Ky., Sept. 8, 1920; s. Pope Alexander and Mabel (Roberts) D.; m. Margaret Flexer, June 30, 1943; children—Mary Margaret Jones, Annie Laurie Kelly, Katherine Maxwell Aimone. BS, U. Ga., 1940, MS, 1941; Th.M., So. Bapt. Theol. Sem., 1944, PhD, 1947; postgrad., U. Zurich, 1960-61; LLD (hon.), Rollins Coll., 1987; LittD (hon.), Limestone Coll., 1987; LLD (hon.), Stetson U., 1987; EdD (hon.), Alderson-Broaddus Coll., 1994; LLD (hon.), William Jewell Coll., 1999. Instr. physics U. Ga., 1940-41; fellow So. Bapt. Theol. Sem., 1944-45; dir. religious activities Mercer U., 1945-46, Roberts prof. ch. history, 1948-49; prof. religion Stetson U., 1946-48, 49-53; prof. ch. history Southeastern Bapt. Theol. Sem., 1953-63; dean Brunswick Coll., 1964; pres. South Ga. Coll., Douglas, 1964-68; v.p. Ga. So. U., Statesboro, 1968-71, pres., 1971-77, Stetson U., DeLand, Fla., 1977-87, chancellor, 1987—2002, chancellor emeritus, 2002—03. Author: Our Baptist Story, 1958, The Pilgrimage of Christianity, 1965, Hanserd Knollys, 1965, Memoirs, 2002 Pres. Wake Forest Civic Club, 1959-60, Ga. Assn. Colls., 1968-69; pres. Coastal Empire council Boy Scouts Am., 1973-74; chmn. council of presidents So. Consortium for Internat. Edn., Inc., 1974-75; mem. commn. on colls. So. Assn. Colls. and Schs., 1978-82; bd. dirs. Fla. Endowment for Humanities, 1978; chmn. pres.'s council Ind. Colls. and Univs. Fla., 1982-84; chmn. Fla. Ind. Colls. Fund, 1980-81; mem. exec. com. So. Univ. Conf., 1981-85. Mem. Am. Hist. Assn., Am. Soc. Ch. History, Douglas Coffee County C. of C. (dir. 1966-68), DeLand (Fla.) C. of C. (dir. 1978-81), Nat. Assn. Ind. Colls. and Univs. (dir. 1979-83), Fla. Assn. Colls. and Univs. (bd. dirs. 1978-85, v.p. 1981-82, pres. 1982-83, Disting. Service award 1987), Nat. Collegiate Athletic Assn. (pres.'s commn. 1985-87), Assn. So. Bapt. Colls. and Schs. (pres. 1980-81), Assn. Ch. Related Colls. and Univs. of the South (pres. 1984-85), Phi Beta Kappa, Omicron Delta Kappa, Phi Kappa Phi, Phi Delta Kappa, Kappa Delta Pi, Pi Mu Epsilon, Phi Eta Sigma, Sigma Phi Sigma. Lodges: Rotary (dir. 1965-66, 70-72, pres. 1967-68). Democrat. Baptist. Home: Deland, Fla. Died Dec. 18, 2003.

DUNLAP, GEORGE WILLIAM, banker; b. Rock Hill, S.C., Sept. 7, 1912; s. Herbert M. and Mary Joe (Witherspoon) D.; m. Ann Myddleton, June 24, 1939; 1 child, Ann Sheperd Williams. BA, Presbyn. Coll., 1935. Asst. sec. treas. Victoria Cotton Mill, Rock Hill, 1935-42; pres. Canada Dry Bottling Co., Rock Hill, 1947-56; pres., gen. mgr. Home Fed. Savs. Bank, Rock Hill, from 1956. Bd. dirs. Investors Title Ins. Co., Chapel Hill, N.C.; bd. dirs. S.C. League of Savs., Columbia, S.C.; trustee Winthrop Coll., Rock Hill, 1980—. Mem. Winthrop Coll. found. Served to maj. U.S. Army, 1942-46. Named Man of Yr., Am. Legion, 1985. Mem. U.S. C. of C. Lodges: Rotary (pres. 1949). Presbyterian. Avocations: golf, boating. Home: Rock Hill, SC. Deceased.

DUNLAP, MARY CYNTHIA, law consultant, educator; b. Napa, Calif., May 25, 1948; d. Frank Leslie and Betty Marion (McBean) D.; life ptnr. Maureen C. Mason. BA with honors, U. Calif., Berkeley, 1968, JD, 1971. Bar: Calif. 1972, U.S. Dist. Ct. (no. dist.) Calif. 1972, U.S. Ct. Appeals (9th cir.) 1972, U.S. Supreme Ct., 1975. Co-founder, atty. Equal Rights Rights Advocates, Inc., San Francisco, 1973-78; pvt. practice San Francisco, 1980-90; pub. interest law cons., from 1995; dir. Office of Citizen Complaints City of San Francisco, from 1996. Vis. law prof. U. Tex. Law Sch., Austin, 1979; mem. adj. law faculty Golden Gate U. Law Sci., San Francisco, 1980-95, Stanford (Calif.) Law Sch., 1988-93, Hastings Coll. Law, San Francisco, 1990-93, U. Mich. Law Sch., Ann Arbor, 1994; bd. mem. BALIF, San Francisco, 1987-90; dir. summer program NEH, San Francisco, 1980. Co-editor: Violence Against Women, 1997; contbr. articles to law jours. Bd. mem. San Francisco AIDS Found., 1983-85; nat. co-chair March for Lesbian & Gay Rights on Dem. Conv., San Francisco, 1984. Mem. ACLU No. Calif. (bd. mem. 1978), Calif. Women Lawyers (founding bd. mem. 1976-77), Coalition for Civil Rights. Democrat. Avocations: art (printmaking, collage, painting), amateur ornithology. Home: San Francisco, Calif. Died Jan. 17, 2003.

DUNLAP, WILLIAM PETRIE, psychologist, educator; b. Boston, Mar. 14, 1941; s. Charles E. and Lorna (Alfred) D.; m. Janis Lundy, Aug. 11, 1968 (div. Apr., 1983); children: Stephan J., Susan E., Anne M. BS, Tulane U., 1963, MS, 1967, PhD, 1969. Asst. prof. Tulane U., New Orleans, 1969-74, assoc. prof., 1974-82, prof., from 1982. Mem. editorial bd. Jour. Applied Psychology, 1992—, Jour. Gen. Psychology, 1986—; contbr. over 150 articles to profl. jours., chpts. to books, 1969—. Home: Metairie, La. Died Feb. 28, 2002.

DUNLOP, JOHN THOMAS, economics educator, former secretary of labor; b. Placerville, Calif., July 5, 1914; s. John W. and Antonia (Forni) D.; m. Dorothy Webb, July 6, 1937; children: John Barrett, Beverly Claire, Thomas Frederick. AB, U. Calif., 1935, PhD, 1939; LLD, U. Chgo., 1968, U. Pa., 1976, Harvard U., 1987. Acting instr. Stanford U., 1936-37; instr. Harvard U., 1938-45, assoc. prof. econs., 1945-50, prof. econs., 1950-85, Lamont U. prof., 1970-85, dean faculty arts and scis., 1970-73; Served as vice chmn. Boston Regional War Labor Bd., 1944-45; chmn. Nat. Joint Bd. for Settlement of Jurisdictional Disputes in bldg. and constrn. industry, 1948-57. Cons. Office Econ. Stabilization, 1945-47, NLRB, 1948-52, Atomic Energy Labor Panel, 1948-53; mem. bd. inquiry Bituminous Coal Industry, 1950; pub. mem. ESB, 1950-52; mem. Emergency Bds. 109, 130, 167; mem. Presdl. R.R. Commn., 1960-62, Missile Sites Labor Commn., 1961-67, Pres.'s EEOC, 1964-65; impartial chmn. Constrn. Industry Joint Conf., 1959-68; dir. Cost of Living Coun., 1973-74; sec. labor, 1975-76; chmn. Mass. joint com. Mcpl. Police and Fire, 1977-2003; chmn. Pay Adv. Com., 1979-80, Social Security Coun., 1989-91; chmn. Future Worker/Mgmt. Rels. Com., 1993-95, Mass. Blue Ribbon Commn. on Older Workers, 1997-2000, Att. Gen. internat. adv. com., 1997-2000, Foster G. McGaw prize com., 1986-2003. Author: Wage Determination under Trade Unions, 1944, Collective Bargaining: Principles and Cases, 1949, 2d edit., 1953, Industrial Relations Systems, 1958, 2d edit., 1993, (with D.C. Bok) Labor and the American Community, 1970, The Lessons of Wage and Price Controls, 1977, Business and Public Policy, 1980, Dispute Resolution: Negotiation and Consensus Building, 1984, The Management of Labor Unions, 1990, (with A.M. Zack) Mediation and Arbitration of Employment Disputes, 1997, (with others) A Stitch in Time, 1999; editor Wertheim Series in Industrial Relations, 1945—. Named to Nat. Housing Hall of Fame; recipient Murray, Meany, Green award AFL-CIO, 1987, gold medal award Nat. Policy Assn., 2000. Mem. Am. Acad. Arts and Scis., Am. Philos. Soc., Inst. Medicine (life), Nat. Acad. Arbitrators, Nat. Acad. Human Resources. Died Oct. 2, 2003.

DUNN, JOHN THORNTON, endocrinologist, educator; b. Washington, Oct. 27, 1932; s. William LeRoy and Thelma (Brumfield) D.; m. Ann M. Davis, June 30, 1962; children: Catherine, Margaret, Robert. AB, Princeton U., 1954; MD, Duke U., 1958. Intern N.Y. Hosp., N.Y.C., 1958-59; resident U. Utah, Salt Lake City, 1959-61; rsch. fellow in thyroid studies Mass. Gen. Hosp. and Harvard U., Boston, 1961-62, 63-64; rsch. fellow in biochemistry Med. Sch. Harvard U., Boston, 1964-66; asst. prof. endocrinology U. Va., Charlottesville, 1966-70, assoc. prof., 1970-76, prof., assoc. chmn. dept. medicine, 1976-97. Cons. UNICEF, WHO, WB, etc., 1970-2004 Contbr. numerous articles to sci. and profl. jours. Recipient Career Devel. award NIH, 1971-76. Mem. Am. Thyroid Assn., Internat. Coun. in Control of Iodine Deficient Diseases (exec. dir. 2001-04, editor 1986-2004), Endocrine Soc., Am. Soc. Molecular Biology and Biochemistry, Assn. Am. Physicians. Home: Charlottesville, Va. Died Apr. 9, 2004.

DUNN, PARKER SOUTHERLAND, retired chemical company consultant; b. Portsmouth, Ohio, Aug. 25, 1910; s. Joseph Sidney and Florence (Bowen) D.; m. Mayde Smith, July 15, 1939 (dec. May 1996); children: Joseph Smith, Dwight James. B.Chem. Engring., Ohio State U., 1930; MS, MIT, 1931. Tech. asst. Mead Corp., Chillicothe, Ohio, 1930-32; foreman Columbia Southern Corp., Barberton, Ohio, 1932-33, asst. plant supt. Corpus Christi, Tex., 1934-38, tech. dir., 1938-41; research dir. Potash Co. Am., Carlsbad, N.Mex., 1941-46, resident mgr., 1946-51; asst. v.p. Am. Potash & Chem. Corp., Trona, Calif., 1951-52, v.p., 1952-55, Los Angeles, 1955-63, dir., 1958-71, pres., 1963-69, chmn. bd., 1969-71; v.p. Kerr McGee Corp., 1968-73, cons., 1975-90. V.p. Kerr McGee Nuclear Corp., 1974-75; v.p., dir. Am. Lithium Chems. Co., 1959-64, San Antonio Chem. Co., 1957-75 Recipient Benjamin Garver Lamme engring. medal Ohio State U., 1966 Mem. Am. Inst. Chem. Engrs., AIME Anglican. Home: Soquel, Calif. Died Feb. 27, 2003.

DUNN, RALPH, former state legislator; b. Pinckneyville, Ill., Feb. 28, 1914; m. Ellen Dunn; 4 children. Grad., Pinckneyville Cmty. H.S., 1933. Real estate investor; mem. from 115th dist. Ill. Ho. of Reps., 1973-85; mem. Ill. State Senate, 1985-97. Mem. higher edn. com., appropriations II com., elem. and secondary edn. com., others. Del. 6th Constnl. Conv., 1969-70. Died May 3, 2004.

DUNNAVANT, ANTHONY LEROY, religion educator; b. Hagerstown, Md., June 23, 1954; s. Ezra LeRoy and Edith Etta (Higgins) D.; m. Nancy Ruth Gragson, May 24, 1975; children: Erin Edith, Bridget Renee, Caitlin Paige, Tara Johanna. BA, Fairmont State Coll., 1974; MA, W.Va. U., 1976; MDiv, Vanderbilt U., 1979, MA, 1981, PhD, 1984. Ordained to ministry Christian Ch. (Disciples of Christ), 1980. Min. First Christian Ch., Mannington, W.Va., 1972-74, Dolls Run Christian Ch., Core, W.Va., 1974-75, First Christian Ch., Guthrie, Ky., 1976-84; assoc. prof. ch. history Lexington (Ky.) Theol. Sem., from 1987. Author: Central Christian Church, 1991; contbg. author: Case Study of Mainstream Protestantism, 1991; contbr. articles to profl. jours. Recipient postdoctoral scholarship Ctr. for Congregational Edn., Lilly Endowment, 1985-86. Mem. AAUP, Am. Acad. Religion, Assn. for the Sociology of Religion, Assn. of Profs. and Researchers in Religious Edn., Disciples of Christ Hist. Soc. Home: Lexington, Ky. Died Feb. 8, 2001.

DUNNE, JOHN GREGORY, writer; b. Hartford, Conn., May 25, 1932; s. Richard Edwin and Dorothy (Burns) D.; m. Joan Didion, Jan. 30, 1964; 1 child, Quintana Roo. AB, Princeton U., 1954. Writer, editor Time mag., N.Y.C. Columnist: New West, Saturday Evening Post, 1967-69, Esquire, 1976-77, 1986-87; author: books, including: Delano: The Story of the California Grape Strike, 1967, The Studio, 1969, Vegas: A Memoir of a Dark Season, 1974, True Confessions, 1977, Quintana and Friends, 1978, Dutch Shea, Jr., 1982, The Red White and Blue, 1987, Harp, 1989, Crooning, 1990, Playland, 1994, Monster: Living Off the Big Screen, 1997, Nothing Lost, 2004; (with Joan Didion) screenplay Panic in Needle Park, 1971, Play It As It Lays, 1973, A Star is Born, 1976, True Confessions, 1981, Hills Like White Elephants, 1991, Broken Trust, 1995, Up Close & Personal, 1996; contbr. articles to mags., including New Yorker, New York Rev. Served with U.S. Army, 1954-56. Home: New York, NY. Died Dec. 30, 2003.

DURBIN, ENOCH JOB, aeronautical engineering educator; b. N.Y.C., Sept. 6, 1922; s. David and Ida (Deutsch) D.; m. Marilyn Lehman, Sept. 15, 1945; 3 children. BS, CCNY, 1943; MS, Rensselaer Poly. Inst., 1947. Rsch. scientist NACA, Langley, Va., 1947-51; sr. mem. tech. staff N. Am. Aviation, Downey, Calif., 1951-54; prof. aero-mech. sci. Princeton U., 1957—93, prof. emeritus, 1993—2003, dir. instrumentation and control lab., 1954—2003; founder, dir. Ctr. Alt. Fueling of Combustion Engines, U. B.C., 1980-82; chmn. steering com. Nat. Ctr. Alt. Transp. Fuels, 1989—2003; founder, dir. Entrepreneural Ctr. Princeton U., 1993—2003. Cons. European and U.S. auto industry. Author: Methane-fuel for the Future, 1982; gen. editor, contbg. author: Flight Test Manual, 1964; patentee in field including natural gas storage system and traveling spark ignition system. Mem. Princeton Borough Council, 1965-68; pres. Unitarian Ch. Princeton, 1975-77. Served with U.S. Army, 1943-46. Fellow AAAS, Instrument Soc. Am.; mem. Internat. Symposium on Automotive Tech. and Automation, Sigma Xi. Home: Princeton, NJ. Died May 27, 2003.

DURHAM, JAMES MICHAEL, SR., marketing professional, retired military officer; b. Shreveport, La., May 27, 1937; s. Judson Burney and Edith Eloise (Whittington) D.; m. Constance Manuela Alvarez, June 4, 1960; children: Jennifer Paige Esperanza Kessler, James Michael Jr., Christopher Jon, David Bradley, Matthew Craig. BS in Math., Centenary Coll. of La., 1959; MSME, N.Mex. State U., 1963; MS in Sys. Mgmt., U. So. Calif., 1981; MBA, Mich. State U., 1988. Commd. 2d lt. U.S. Army, 1959, advanced through grades to col., 1979, mgmt. analyst Army Office Chief of Staff, 1972-74; command and staff positions 3d Infantry Div. U.S. Army, Wurzburg, Germany, 1974-77; student U.S. Army War Coll., Carlisle Barracks, Pa., 1977-78; product mgr. U.S. Army Tank-Automotive Materiel Readiness Command, Warren, Mich., 1978-80; commander Mainz Army Depot, Mainz, Germany, 1980-83; exec. officer to deputy commanding gen. U.S. Army Devel. and Readiness Command, Alexandria, Va., 1983; program mgr., tactical vehicles U.S. Army Tank-Automotive Command, Warren, Mich., 1984-86; ret. U.S. Army Tank Automotive Command, Warren, Mich., 1986; dir. tank automotive programs Cypress Internat., Troy, Mich., 1986-89; v.p. govt. business Cummins Engine Co., Inc., Columbus, Ind., 1989-92, v.p. govt. products, 1992-95, ret., 1995; pres. Cummins Mil. Sys. Co., Inc., Columbus, 1992-93, JD Interests Inc., Farnham, Va., from 1995; v.p. mktg. and bus. devel. Lear Siegler Svcs., Inc., Annapolis, Md., 2002. Guest lectr. Wayne State U. Chmn. Bartholomew County Solid Waste Mgmt. Dist. Citizens Adv. Com., 1991-95, Bartholomew County Solid Waste Mgmt. Authority, 1993-95, Bartholomew County Landfill Site Selection Com., 1993; co-chmn. Project Water, Columbus, 1990-95; chmn. bd. dirs. Am. Youth Activities Assn., Mainz, Germany, 1980-83, pres. Am.

Youth Activities Assn., Kitzingen, Germany, 1975-77; bd. dirs. Indpls. Mus. Art-Columbus Gallery, 1995; chmn. devel. com. Richmond County (Va.) Habitat for Humanity, 1996-2002, bd. dirs., 1997-2002, v.p., 1998, pres., 1999-2001; trustee No. Neck chpt. Assn. for the Preservation of Va. Antiquities, 1999, vice dir., 2000-01, dir., 2001-2002. Decorated Legion of Merit with oak leaf cluster, Bronze Star, Vietnam campaign medal with 60 device, Vietnamese Cross of Gallantry with palm. Mem.: ASME, Hist. Soc. No. Neck of Va. (bd. dirs. 1998—2002), U.S. Army Ordnance Corps Assn., Ret. Officers Assn. (sec. Potomac chpt. 1997—98, dir. 1999—2001), Soc. Automotive Engrs., Soc. Mfg. Engrs., Assn. U.S. Army, Nat. Def. Indsl. Assn. (exec. bd. tank and automotive sys. divsn. from 1991, steering com. combat vehicle sys. divsn. from 1988, chmn. 1991—95, steering com. tactical vehicle sys. sect. 1986—95, Silver medal 2000). Republican. Avocation: reading. Home: Farnham, Va. Died Jan. 22, 2004.

DURRIE, ROBERT PAUL, SR., real estate broker; b. Laurel, Nebr., May 17, 1921; s. Harry K. and Selma A. D.; m. Mary A. Stephenson, Aug. 14, 1944; children: Mary Lynn, Daniel S., Robert P. Jr. BS, U. Nebr., 1948. Salesman Magee's Inc., Lincoln, Nebr., 1940-47, dept. mgr., 1947-54, buyer, v.p., 1955-68, mdse. mgr., v.p., 1968-76, pres., 1976-83; real estate agt. Harrington Assocs., Lincoln, 1985-99. Trustee U. Nebr. Found., 1980-99, Byron Meml. Hosp., 1970-99, chmn. bd., 1980-84. Trustee Westminster Presbyn. Ch. Found., 1970-80. Served to capt. U.S. Army, 1942-47, ETO. Mem. Rotary Club 14, Lincoln Country Club, Nat. Bd. Realtors, Lincoln Bd. Realtors, Phi Gamma Delta. Republican. Avocations: spectator sports, golf, reading. Home: Lincoln, Nebr. Died Aug. 4, 1999.

DURYEA, PERRY BELMONT, JR., former state legislator, business executive; b. East Hampton, N.Y., Oct. 18, 1921; s. Perry Belmont and Jane (Stewart) D.; m. Elizabeth Ann Weed, Apr. 4, 1944; children— Lynn, Perry Belmont III; m. Marie Therese Hanratty, Feb. 7, 1991. BA, Colgate U., 1942; LL.D., Dowling Coll., 1963, Southampton Coll., 1968; L.H.D. (hon.), Sienna Coll., 1972; LLD (hon.), Colgate U., 1993. Mem. N.Y. State Assembly, 1960-78, minority leader, 1966-68, speaker of assembly, 1969-74, minority leader, 1975-78; former chmn. Perry B. Duryea and Son, Inc., Montauk, NY. Vice chmn. Beker Industries, Greenwich, Conn., 1979-86, pres., 1986-88; former chmn. L.I. Comml. Bank. Del. Rep. Nat. Conv., 1972, 76. Served to lt. comdr. USN, 1943-46. Recipient Disting. Alumni award Colgate U., 1972; Pres.'s Disting. Service award SUNY, Buffalo, 1972 Mem.: Masons. Presbyterian. Home: Montauk, NY. Died Jan. 11, 2004.

DURYEE, WILLIAM RANKIN, retired cell physiology educator, consultant; b. Saranac Lake, N.Y., Nov. 11, 1905; s. George Van Waganen and Margaret Van Nest (Smith) D.; m. June 30, 1931 (dec. Jan. 1983); 1 child, Sanford Huntington. BA in Biology, Yale U., 1927, PhD in Zoology and Anatomy, 1933. Instr. Northwestern U., Evanston, Ill., 1937-40; chief med. publs. Office Surgeon Gen., Washington, 1944-45; with NRC, Washington, 1945-46; sr. fellow Nat. Cancer Inst., NIH, Bethesda, Md., 1948-55; head cell physiology unit WCI, Bethesda, 1950-55; prof. cell physiology George Washington U., Washington, 1955-60, rsch. prof. pathology, 1960-70, prof. emeritus, from 1971; cons. biology rsch. Arlington, Va., from 1979. Invited lectr. U. Pa. Bicentennial Conf., Phila., 1941; mem. sci. adv. coun. Damon Runyon Meml. Fund, N.Y.C., 1961-68; profl. assoc. com. on growth NRC, 1946-48; guest investigator U. Copenhagen, 1984-85, U. Munich, 1985. Mem. editl. bd. Jour. Nat. Cancer Inst.; contbr. articles to sci. jours., including Biol. Bull, Sci., Anat. Record, Annals N.Y. Acad. Sci.; made first films of living genes. Maj. Med. Adminstrv. Corps, U.S. Army, 1939-45. Fellow N.Y. Acad. Scis. (hon.); mem. AAAS (coun. 1958-64), Am. Inst. Biol. Scis. (co-founder, governing bd. 1953-57), Royal Soc. Medicine (affiliate, London), Am. Soc. Physiology, Biophysics Soc. (charter), Washington Acad. Medicine, Philos. Soc. Washington, Cosmos Club (chmn. libr. com.). Episcopalian. Achievements include performed first microdissection on the human egg, first isolation of living chromosomes from amphibian eggs, a first dissection of nucleoli, first radioautographs of single cells; discovered gene loops and circular DNA strands; made first films of living genes. Home: Watertown, NY. Died Dec. 19, 2000.

DUSH, DAVID MICHAEL, psychologist, researcher; b. St. Johns, Mich., Dec. 27, 1953; s. George E. and Hellen Marie (Fabus) D.; m. Billie R. Hothem, Jan. 2, 1982; children: Elayna Hothem, Erin Marie. BS, Mich. State U., 1976; MA, U. Man., Winnipeg, Can., 1978; PhD, Kent State U., 1981. Asst. prof. Drake U., Des Moines, 1981-84; adj. asst. prof. Cen. Mich. U., Mt. Pleasant, 1984—2003; former program evaluator Midland-Gladwin (Mich.) Ctr. Mental Health; former pres. Health Scis. Corp., Sanford, Mich.; former editor The Hospice Jour., Midland. Cons., advisor various hospices, orgns., and corps.; former pub. Mature Health mag., Sanford. Contbr. articles to profl. jours. Mem. Am. Psychol. Assn., Midwestern Psychol. Assn., Nat. Hospice Orgn., Mich. Hospice Assn. (chmn. research and evaluation com. 1986-88), Soc. Behavioral Medicine. Home: Sanford, Mich. Died Nov. 20, 2003.

DUTY, ROBERT CLIFFORD, chemistry educator; b. Morrison, Ill., Sept. 28, 1931; s. Frank Sulvester and Edna Lucile (Gregory) D.; m. Royce LaVerne Riley, Aug. 17, 1958; children: Dianna Michelle, David Michael. BS in Chemistry, U. Ill., 1953; MEd in Adminstrn., Midwestern U., Wichita Falls, Tex., 1956; PhD in Chemistry, U. Iowa, 1961. Chemist Exxon Petroleum Co., Baton Rouge, 1960-61; prof. chemistry Western State Coll., Gunnison, Colo., 1961-63, Ill. State U., Normal, 1963-87; lectr. chemistry Baylor U., Waco, Tex., from 1989. 1st lt. USAF, 1957. Grantee Dept. Energy, 1977-79, 1982-85, Baylor U., 1992=93, 93-94. Mem. AAAS, Am. Chem. Soc. (sec.-treas. Heart of Tex. sect. 1992—), Sigma Xi (sec.-treas. Baylor U. club 1992—). Avocations: fishing, hunting, golfing. Home: Waco, Tex. Died June 7, 2000.

DYBA, JOHANNES FELIX, bishop; b. Berlin, Sept. 15, 1929; s. Felix Nikolaus and Johanna (Bruell) D. LLD, U. Heidelberg, Germany, 1954; D in Canon Law, Pontifical Lateran U., Rome, 1962. Head German desk Secretariat of State, Vatican City, 1966-68; diplomatic rep. Holy See, Buenos Aires, 1968, The Hague, The Netherlands, 1969-72, Kinshasa, Zaire, 1972-74, Cairo, Egypt, 1975-77; under sec. Pontifical Coun. Justice & Peace, Rome, 1977-79; archbishop apostolic del. and pro-nuncio Holy See, Monrovia, Liberia, 1979-83; bishop of Fulda Cath. Ch., Fulda, Germany, from 1983, bishop for German Armed Forces Bonn, Germany, from 1990. Contbr. articles to profl. jours. Named Officer of Oranje Order, The Queen of the Netherlands, 1972; recipient Grand Cross of Merit, The Pres. of Germany, 1994. Mem. Cartellverband. Avocations: stamp collecting/philately, cartophily. Home: Fulda, Germany. Deceased.

DYER, JOHN MARTIN, lawyer, marketing educator; b. St. Louis, Feb. 27, 1920; s. George L. and Katharine (Dobson) D.; m. Emily Ramsay Young, Aug. 9, 1947; children: Katherine, Susan, Patricia Ann, Theresa, Carolyn. AB, St. Louis U., 1941; MBA, U. Pa., 1953; JD, U. Miami, Fla., 1967. Bar: Fla. 1951, U.S. Supreme Ct. 1966. Practiced in, Miami, from 1951; prof. mktg. U. Miami, 1958-59, prof., from 1969, acting chmn. dept. mktg., 1968-69, chmn. mktg. dept., 1982-84; adj. prof. Fla. Atlantic U., Boca Raton, 1995, St. Thomas U., Miami, Fla., from 1996. Speaker, cons. in field; dir. Atlas Sewing Ctrs. Inc., 1960; vis. prof. U. Del., 1969, 70, Disting. vis. prof., 1969; lectr. Universidad Nacional, Leon, Nicaragua, 1959; Disting. vis. prof. San Francisco State U., summer 1975; mem. adv. bd. Internat. Bank of Miami, 1971-75; dir. U.S. Govt. Securities Fund, Inc., Fla. Mut. Ins. Co.; mem. Fla. Dist. Export Council, 1971, 73-75, 76-77, 81-99; dir. subcom. for Latin Am. U.S. Senate Interstate and Fgn. Commerce Com. Staff, 1960; mem. Southeastern World Trade Group, U.S. Dept. Commerce, 1957; trustee Ctr. for Internat. Bus., Dallas, 1976—; ednl. cons. Nat. Assn. Credit Mgmt., S. Fla., 1977; editor conf. reports, program dir. various internat. trade seminars; dir. Rayne Internat., Inc., Pinnacle Fund, Fla.; editorial cons. Internat. Round Table Journal, 1988; bd. dirs. Internat. Mktg. Inst. Sports, 1988; appointed by U.S. Sec. Commerce to Fla. Dist. Export Coun., 1992; bd. dirs. Destination Sun Airways, Starwood Furniture Mfr., Inc., 1994; adj. prof. Fla. Atlantic U., 1991, Thomas U., Miami. Contbg. author: Marketing in Latin America, 1960; author: United States-Latin American Trade and Financial Relations, 1961, (with F. C. Dyer) Export Financing, 1963, Bureaucracy vs. Creativity: The Dilemma of Modern Leadership, 1965, The Enjoyment of Management, 1971, Guidelines to Operating in Latin America, 1970, International Finance Law and Marketing, 1976, 4th edit., 1980; contbr. (with F. C. Dyer) articles, revs. to profl. jours.; cons. editor: (with F. C. Dyer) Industria Turistica, 1972—; contbg. editor: (with F. C. Dyer) Wall Street Rev. of Books; cons. editor: Internat. Round Table Jour. 1986—. Spkr. platform com. Nat. Rep. Conv., 1968; mem. Fla. dist. export coun. U.S. Dept. Commerce/U.S. sec. of Commerce; bd. dirs. Goodwill Industries, Inc., Miami, 1977—, mem. adv. bd., 1978—, Destination Sun Airlines, 1992—; mem. internat. trade com. City of Miami; hon. advisor World Trade Coun. Palm Beach County, 1982. Named hon. vice consul Govt. Guatamala, 1959; recipient Phi Sigma Phi award for achievement in fgn. commerce, Propeller Club U.S., 1954, Forum on Finance award, Am. Securities Assn., 1954, Bus. Week plaque, U. Miami, 1972, Iron Arrow award, 1970, cert. of appreciation, student chpt. Alpha Kappa Phi, 1971, First Pres's. award, Am. Grad. Sch. Internat. Mgmt., 1975, Gold Key, City of Coral Gables, Fla., 1980, Met.-Dade County cert. of appreciation, 1980, Internat. Mktg. award, Fla. Exporters and Importers Assn., 1983, Dyer Internat. Scholarship award, U. Miami, 1989, Internat. award, Ill. Def. Coun., 1994, Hall of Fame award, World Trade Ctr., Miami, 1996; fellow N.Y. Stock Exchange Faculty, 1954. Mem.: Fla. Internat. Devel. Adv. Coun., Am. Arbitration Assn., Internat. Exec. Svc. Corps, Assn. Edn. Internat. Bus., Am. Fgn. Law Assn., Fla. Bar Assn., Fed. Bar Assn., Acad. Mktg. Scis., Fla. Coun. Internat. Devel. (hon.), Am. Inst. Fgn. Trade (assoc.), Caribbean C. of C. (bd. dirs. 1991—92, 1992—93, sr. dir. strategy group 1991), Phi Alpha Delta, Alpha Kappa Psi, Lambda Chi Alpha, Beta Gamma Sigma. Home: Miami, Fla. Died May 22, 2003.

EADES, JAMES BEVERLY, JR., aeronautical engineer; b. Bluefield, W.Va., July 22, 1923, s. James Beverly and Harriet Beulah (Smith) E.; m. Sara M. Porterfield, Dec. 20, 1950; children: Sara Leslie, Beverly Anne, James Christian. Student, Bluefield Coll., 1940-42; BS in Aero. Engring., Va. Poly. Inst., 1944, MS in Applied Mechanics, 1949, PhD, 1958. Registered profl. engr., Va., W.Va.; lic. real estate agt. Asst. prof. aero. engring. Va. Poly. Inst., Blacksburg, 1947-50, asst. prof., research assoc. aero. engring., 1953-58, prof. aero. engring., 1958-60, 60-67, head aerospace engring., 1961-67; aero. research scientist NACA, Langley Research Center, Langley Field, Va., 1958, 59, Naval Ordnance Lab., Silver Spring, Md., 1960, 63-69; research assoc. NAS, Goddard Space Flight Center, NASA, Greenbelt, Md., 1967-69; sr. scientist Analytical Mechanics Assocs., Inc., Seabrook, Md., 1969-77; sr. staff scientist Bus. and Technol. Systems, Inc., Seabrook, 1977-79, prin. scientist, 1979-81; v.p., prin. scientist Engring. and Sci. Assocs., Inc., Rockville, Md., 1981-93; cons., sr. scientist Analytical Mechanics Assocs., Inc., Hampton, Va., 1990-94; real estate sales person Realty Investments Corp., Kensington, Md., from 1974; real estate sales and cons., from 1993. Dir. Conf. Lunar Explorations, 1962; instr. engring. sect. Naval Officer Candidate Sch., Newport, RI, 1951—85. Asst. exec. editor: Celestial Mechanics Jour., 1969-75. Served to lt. USNR, World War II, 1951-53, Korea; comdr. Ret. Res. Assoc. fellow AIAA (chmn. Blue Ridge sect. 1964, profl. edn. com. 1969-75); mem. Celestial Mechanics Inst. (v.p.), Am. Astronautics Soc., Va. Acad. Sci. (sec. engring. sect. 1961, chmn. sect. 1962, mem. council, chmn. space sci. and tech. sect. 1968), Sigma Xi, Sigma Gamma Tau, Tau Beta Pi. Clubs: Mason. Home: Silver Spring, Md. Died Dec. 14, 2003.

EADS, M. ADELA, state senator; b. Bklyn., Mar. 2, 1920; Ed., Sweet Briar Coll. Mem. Conn. Ho. of Reps., Hartford, 1978-80, Conn. Senate, Hartford, 1980—2000. Senate minority leader serving on legis. mgmt. com., exec. nominations com.; senate pres. pro tempore, 1995, 96; mem. exec. nominations, co-chair select com. children, Senate Rep. leader, select com. children's regulations review; mem. adv. bd. New Milford Bank & Trust Co., Glenholm Devereux Sch., Susan B. Anthony Project. Trustee Marvelwood Sch., Kent, Conn.; bd. dirs. Drugs Don't Work, Easter Seals; mem. Conn. Bd. Edn., 1972-76. Mem. Nat. Orgn. Women Legislators, Conn. Orgn. Women Legislators. Home: Kent, Conn. Died July 8, 2003.

EARLY, JAMES MICHAEL, electronics research consultant; b. Syracuse, N.Y., July 25, 1922; s. Frank J. and Rhoda Gray Early; m. Mary Agnes Valentine, Dec. 28, 1948; children: Mary Beth Early Dehler, Kathleen, Joan Early Farrell, Rhoda Early Alexander, Maureen Early Mathews, Rosemary Early, James, Margot Early. BS, N.Y. Coll. Forestry, Syracuse, N.Y., 1943; MS, Ohio State U., 1948, PhD, 1951. Instr., research assoc. Ohio State U., Columbus, 1946-51; dir. lab. Bell Telephone Labs., Murray Hill, N.J., 1951-64, Allentown, Pa., 1964-69; dir. research and devel. Fairchild Semicondr. Corp., Palo Alto, Calif., 1969-83, sci. advisor, 1983-86; research cons., 1987—2004. Contbr. over 20 papers to profl. jours. Served with U.S. Army, 1943-45. Fellow AAAS, IEEE (numerous coms., John Fritz Medal bd. of award); mem. IEEE Electron Device Soc. (J.J. Ebers award 1979), Am. Phys. Soc. Roman Catholic. Achievements include 14 patents; discovery of Space Charge Layer Widening effect (now called Early effect); invention of the high frequency bipolar transistor and intrinsic barrier transistor; developer of Telstar solar cells and transistors, of sealed junction beam lead integrated circuits; design theory of bipolar transistors; definition of fundamental speed-power limits in junction devices; first commercial use of ion implanter in semiconductor devices; first use of buried channel charge coupled devices, of traveling wave charge-coupled detectors, of high speed ECL and advanced CMOS; procurement of first practical commercial electron beam machine for maskmaking; proposing fastest bipolar circuit. Died Jan. 12, 2004.

EASLEY, LOYCE ANNA, painter; b. Weatherford, Okla., June 28, 1918; d. Thomas Webster and Anna Laura (Sanders) Rogers; m. Mack Easley, Nov. 17, 1939; children: June Elizabeth, Roger. BFA, U. Okla., 1943; postgrad., 1947-49; student, Art Students League, N.Y.C., 1977; postgrad., Santa Fe Inst. Fine Arts, 1985. Tchr. Pub. Sch., Okmulgee, Okla., 1946-47, Hobbs, N.Mex., 1947-49; tchr. painting N.Mex. Jr. Coll., Hobbs, 1965-80; tchr. Art Workshops in N.Mex., Okla., Wyoming. Numerous one-woman shows and group exhbns. in mus., univs. and galleries, including Gov.'s Gallery, Santa Fe, Selected Artists, N.Y.C., Roswell (N.Mex.) Mus., N.Mex. State U., Las Cruces, West Tex. Mus., Tex. Tech U., Lubbock; represented in permanent collections USAF Acad., Colorado Springs, Colo., Roswell Mus., Carlsbad (N.Mex.) Mus., Coll. Santa Fe, N.Mex. Supreme Ct, also other pvt. and pub. collections; featured in S.W. Art and Santa Fe mag., 1981, 82. Named Disting. Former Student, U. Okla. Art Sch., 1963; nominated for Gov's. award in Art, N.Mex., 1988. Mem. N.Mex. Artists Equity (lifetime mem. 1963). Democrat. Presbyterian. Home: Albuquerque, N.Mex. Died Jan. 20, 2002.

EASTERBROOK, JAMES ARTHUR, psychology educator; b. East Baudette, Minn., Apr. 10, 1923; s. William James and Bertha Lillian (Amorde) E.; m. Margaret Pamela Edith Evans, Nov. 19, 1944; children: Christine, Anthony, Pamela, Laurence, Margaret. BA with honors, Queen's U., Kingston, Ont., Can., 1949, MA (J. McBeth Milligan fellow), 1954; PhD, U. London, 1963. Mem. Canadian Def. Research Sci. Service, Churchill, Man., Edmonton, Alta., Halifax, N.S., 1950-57; research psychologist Burden Neurol. Inst., Bristol, Eng., 1959-61; mem. faculty medicine U. Alta. at Edmonton, 1961-67; prof. psychology U. N.B. at Fredericton, 1967-88, prof. emeritus, from 1990; mem. N.B. Bd. Examiners in Psychology, 1973-79, chmn., 1978-79. Served with RCAF, 1941-45. Mem. Brit. Psychol. Soc. (life), Coll. Psychologists New Brunswick (life). Home: Charters Settlement, Canada. Died Mar. 10, 2003.

EASTMAN, JOHN RICHARD, retired manufacturing company executive; b. Ottawa, Ohio, Sept. 28, 1917; s. Herbert Parrett and Marie (Brown) E.; m. Hope Ruth, June 12, 1943; 1 child, Janet Ruth. BA, Ohio State U., Columbus, 1939, LL.B., 1941. Bar: Ohio 1941. With firm Eastman, Stichter, Smith & Bergman, Toledo, 1941-42, 46-75, ptnr.,

1950-75; sr. v.p., gen. counsel Sheller-Globe Corp., Toledo, 1975-77, pres., 1977-82, vice chmn., 1982-86. Lectr. Coll. Law, U. Toledo, 1954-55 Bd. dirs. United Way, 1978-82, 84-87. Served with USNR, 1942-46. Decorated Purple Heart. Mem. ABA., Ohio Bar Assn., Lucas County Bar Assn. (pres. 1960), Toledo Bar Assn. (exec. com. 1963-69), Am. Judicature Soc., Internat. Assn. Ins. Counsel, Am. Coll. Trial Lawyers, Toledo C. of C. (chmn. 1985-86). Clubs: Toledo, Toledo Country, Belmont Country. Home: Toledo, Ohio. Deceased.

EASTMAN, THOMAS GEORGE, investment management executive; b. L.A., July 28, 1946; s. George Lockwood and Louisa (Forrester) E.; m. Terry Beckley, Aug. 20, 1972; children: Timothy, David. AB, Stanford U., 1968; MBA, Harvard U., 1970. Analyst Systech Fin. Corp., Walnut Creek, Calif., 1971-72; v.p. for acquisitions Coldwell Banker, L.A., 1972-79; sr. v.p. The Boston Co. Real Estate Counsel, Boston, 1979-81; exec. dir., co-chmn. Aldrich, Eastman & Waltch, Boston, 1981-96; founder Forrester Capital LLC, Boston, from 1997. Bd. dirs. Bedford Property Investors, Inc. Mem. Urban Land Inst., The Counsellors of Real Estate, Nat. Assn. Real Estate Investment Mgrs. (past chmn.) Home: Weston, Mass. Died, no date given.

EATHERTON, LARRY EUGENE, pharmacist, consultant; b. Burwell, Nebr., Mar. 8, 1932; s. William W. and Fern M. (Shafer) E.; m. Shirley J. Lysinger, Aug. 23, 1953 (div. July 1981); children: Jeffry A., Melinda S. (dec.), Sarah Jane (dec.); m. Nelrita J. Lydia, Aug. 1, 1981. BS in Pharmacy, U. Nebr., 1954. Cert. emergency med. technician. Pharmacist Warren Drug Co., Beatrice, Nebr., 1956-58, Macy Drug, Ft. Morgan, Colo., 1958-60; pharmacist, owner, mgr. Akron (Colo.) Drug, from 1960. Cons. pharmacist Washington County Pub. Hosp., Akron, 1962—. Vol. Washington County Ambulance Svc., 1982-89. 1st lt. U.S. Army, 1954-56, Korea. Mem. Colo. Pharmacal Assn. (bd. dirs. 1984—, pres. 1989—), Akron C. of C. (pres. 1962-65, 88), Masons, Elks. Republican. Avocations: raising registered quarter horses, golf. Home: Las Animas, Colo. Died Mar. 9, 2002.

EBAN, ABBA, Israeli government official; b. Cape Town, South Africa, Feb. 2, 1915; s. Abram and Alida (Solomon) E.; ed. U. Cambridge (Eng.); Hon. Dr., NYU, Boston U., U. Md., U. Cin., Temple U., others; m. Susan Ambache, 1947; 1 son, 1 dau. Liaison Officer Allied Hdqrs with Jewish Population in Jerusalem, 1940; chief instr. Middle East Arab Centre in Jerusalem; joined service of Jewish Agy., 1946; liaison officer with UN Spl. Com. on Palestine, 1947, rep. provisional Govt. of Israel to UN, 1948, permanent rep., 1949-59; amb.r to U.S., 1950-59; minister without portfolio, 1959-60; minister of edn., 1960-63; dep. prime minister, 1963-66; minister of fgn. affairs, 1966-74; mem. Knesset, 1959—; chmn. com. security and fgn. affairs, 1984—; vis. prof. Columbia U., 1974; mem. Inst. Advanced Study, Princeton U., 1978; pres. Weizmann Inst. Sch., 1958-66. Fellow World Acad. Arts and Scis., Am. Acad. Arts and Scis., Am. Acad. Polit. Sci. Author: The Modern Literary Movement in Egypt, 1944; Maze of Justice, 1946; Voice of Israel, 1957; Tide of Nationalism, 1959; My People, 1968; My Country, 1972; Abba Eban: An Autobiography, 1977; The New Diplomacy, 1983, Heritage: Civilization and the Jews, 1984, Personal Witness, 1990. Home: Herzliya, Israel. Died Nov. 17, 2002.

EBBITT, WILMA ROBB, English educator; b. Moose, Sask., Can., June 29, 1918; came to U.S., 1940; d. William Alexander and Annie (Archer) Robb; m. David Rodney Ebbitt, Dec. 28, 1942. PhD, Brown U., 1943; LLD (hon.), U. Regina, 1988. With dept. English U. Chgo., 1945-68; lectr. U. Colo., 1968-69; prof. English Pa. State U., 1974-88, prof. emeritus. Vis. prof. English U. tex., Austin, 1973-74. Home: Newport, RI. Died Sept. 17, 2000.

EBERLY, RUSSELL ALBERT, lawyer, manufacturing company executive; b. Dover, Ohio, July 27, 1922; s. Herbert Lamoyne and Meta Charlotte (Bimeler) E.; B.S., Washington and Jefferson Coll., 1944; J.D., Akron U., 1950; m. Jean McWilliams Fisher, Jan. 19, 1946; children— Ann Eberly Calvert, James Allen. Bar: Ohio 1950, Pa. 1977. Patent atty. B.F. Goodrich Co., Akron, 1946-52; with PPG Industries, Inc., 1952, asst. patent counsel, then corp. patent counsel, Pitts., 1970-77, corp. counsel, 1977-78, v.p. law, 1978-79, v.p., gen. counsel, 1979—1996; dir. PPG Industries Found. Mem. devel. council Washington and Jefferson Coll., 1979, trustee, 1981. Served with USNR, 1943-46. Mem. ABA, Am. Patent Law Assn., Assn. Gen. Counsel, Patent Law Assn. Pitts. Republican. Methodist. Clubs: Duquesne (Pitts.); South Hills Country. Died Dec. 22, 1996.

EBSEN, BUDDY (CHRISTIAN EBSEN JR.), actor, dancer; b. Belleville, Ill., Apr. 2, 1908; m. Dorothy Ebsen; children: Elizabeth, Alix, Susannah, Cathy, Bonnie, Kiersten, Dustin. Chief exec. officer Polynesian Concept, Inc. Broadway debut as dancer in Ziegfeld prodn. Whoopie, 1928; dance team with sister Vilma Ebsen in nightclubs and musicals including Flying Colors, 1932; appeared in plays The Male Animal, Our Town, The Best Man, 1987; author play Champagne General; film appearances include Broadway Melody of 1936, Captain January, 1936, The Girl of the Golden West, 1938, Thunder in God's Country, 1951, Night People, 1954, Between Heaven and Hell, 1956, Breadfast at Tiffany's, 1961, The Interns, 1962, Mail Order Bride, 1964, The One and Only Genuine Original Family Band, 1968, The Beverly Hillbillies, 1993; TV movies include Stone Fox, 1986, The Daughters of Joshua Cabe, 1972, Terror at 37,000 Feet, 1972, Tom Sawyer, 1973, Leave Yesterday Behind, 1978, Fire on the Mountain, 1981, Working Tra$h, 1990; star TV series: Davy Crockett, 1954-55, Northwest Passage, 1958-59, The Beverly Hillbillies, 1962-71, Matt Houston, 1986, Barnaby Jones, 1973-79; other TV appearances include Broadway TV Theatre, The Twilight Zone, Gunsmoke, Maverick, Hawaii Five-O; (mini-series) The Bastard, 1978; songwriter; author: The Other Side of Oz, 1994, Kelly's Quest, 2001. With USCG, World War II. Mem. AFTRA. Died July 6, 2003.

ECHOLS, JAMES FRANKLIN, small business owner; b. Adel, Ga., June 26, 1932; s. James Brown and Cleo (Futch) E.; m. Eloise Purvis, May 3, 1953; 1 child, James F. Jr. Honor grad., Gordon Mil. Coll., Barnesville, Ga., 1949. Salesman Echols & Son Jewelers, Tifton, Ga., 1949-65, owner, from 1965. Chmn. Downtown Tifton Devel. Authority, 1986—, Tifton Main St. Bd., 1988—. Recipient Disting. Service award, Tifton Jaycees, 1965. Mem. Ga. Retail Jewelers Assn. (pres. 1964-65), Ga. Retail Assn. (chm. bd., Atlanta, 1988—), Spring Hill Country Club (pres. 1986-87), Elks. Baptist. Avocations: golf, writing, civic activities. Home: Tifton, Ga. Deceased.

ECHOLS, MARY LOUISE BROWN, elementary school educator, secondary school educator; b. Milligan, Fla., Nov. 13, 1906; d. Edward Reese and Barbara Alabama Brown; m. Louie Samuel Echols Jr., June 18, 1932 (dec. Oct. 1984); 1 child, Louie Samuel III. AB, cert. in spoken English, Fla. State Coll. for Women, 1928; MEd, U. Fla., 1953, postgrad. Cert. elem. tchr., English tchr., biology tchr., sci. tchrs., Fla. (life); cert. jr. coll. instr. Tchr. Greenville (Fla.) H.S., 1928-29, Madison (Fla.) H.S., 1929-30, Dixie County H.S., Cross City, Fla., 1930-37, 41-43, Gainesville (Fla.) H.S., 1951-66; agronomist technician U. Fla., Gainesville, 1946; coord. lang. arts Alachua County Sch. Bd., Gainesville, 1966-67, reading specialist, 1967-68, 1969-71; reading coord., 1971-72; ret. Alachua County Sch. Bd., Gainesville, 1972. Mem. leadership res. pool Bd. Pub. Instruction, Gainesville, 1969—; compiler curriculum guide 7-12 lang. arts Alachua County Sch. Bd., Gainesville, 1966; mem. team teaching unit; del. White House Conf. Edn. Vol. hospice Light Up a Life, Gainesville, 1989-90; active Friends of Libr. Alachua County; contbr., active Matheson Hist. Ctr., Gainesville. Recipient Fifty Yrs. Membership cert. Fla. Fedn. Women's Clubs, 1995. Mem. AAUW (telephone com.), Alachua County Ret. Tchrs., Fla. Ret. Educators, Gainesville Woman's Club, Nat. Ret. Tchrs. Assn., Gainesville Garden Club (assoc.), Matheson Hist. Soc., Fla. State U. Emeritus Club, Phi Kappa Phi, Delta Kappa Gamma. Democrat. Methodist. Avocations: world travel, bridge, sewing, doll collecting, writing short stories. Home: Gainesville, Fla. Deceased.

ECKER, PEDER KALOIDES, former judge; b. Sioux City, Iowa, Oct. 21, 1929; s. Peder Kornelius and Amalia Helena (Kaloides) E.; m. Marjorie Mae, Feb. 14, 1990; children: Diane Jankord, Debra Maniaci, Dorothy Ann Dupper, Dawn Nelson, Donna. BS in Polit. Sci., U. S.D., 1954, JD, 1955. Bar: S.D. 1955, Nebr. 1958, U.S. Dist. Ct. S.D. 1960. Ptnr., Dana, Golden, Moore & Rasmussen, Sioux Falls, S.D., 1959-77; judge U.S. Bankruptcy Ct., Sioux Falls, 1969-94, ret., 1994; sole practice, Sioux Falls, 1977-79; U.S. magistrate Dist. S.D., Sioux Falls, 1977-79; founding dir., chmn. bd. Sun Bank of S.D., Sioux Falls, 1974-79; party chmn. Democrat Minnehaha County, 1965-68; state chmn. South Dakota Democratic Party, 1968-69. Served with U.S. Army, 1948-49, to capt. Res., 1962-68. Recipient Achievement award ABA, 1965. Mem. Am. Bankruptcy Inst., 2d Cir.Bar Assn., Nat. Conf. Bankruptcy Judges (past bd. govs.), S.D. Young Lawyers Assn. (past pres.), S.D. Bar Assn. (bd. commrs. 1965-68), Comml. Law League, S.D. Trial Lawyers Assn. Presbyterian. Lodges: Masons, El Riad Shrine, El Riad Clowns. Home: Sioux Falls, SD. Died Jan. 30, 2002.

ECKERT, ERNST R. G. mechanical engineering educator; b. Prague, Czech Republic, Sept. 13, 1904; came to U.S., 1945, naturalized, 1955; s. Georg and Margarete (Pfrogner) E.; m. Josefine Binder, Jan. 30, 1931; children: Rosemarie Christa Eckert Kohler, Elke, Karin Eckert Winter, Dieter. Diploma Ing., German Inst. Tech., Prague, 1927, Dr.Ing., 1931; Dr. habil., Inst. Technology, Danzig, 1938; Dozent, Inst. of Technol., Braunschweig, Germany, 1940; hon. doctorates, Inst. Tech., Munich, 1968, Purdue U., 1968, U. Manchester, Eng., 1968, U. Notre Dame, 1970, Poly. Inst. Romania, Jassy, 1973, U. Minn., 1995, Czech Republic, 1999. Chief engr., lectr. Inst. Technology, Danzig, 1934-38; sect. chief thermodynamics Aero. Research Inst., Braunschweig, 1938-45; prof., dir. Inst. Technology, Prague, 1943-45; cons. USAF, 1945-49, Lewis Flight Propulsion Lab., NASA, 1949-51; prof. mech. engring. dept. U. Minn., 1951-73, dir. thermodynamics and heat transfer and of heat transfer lab., 1955-73, regents' prof. emeritus mech. engring., 1973—2004, ret. Former vis. prof. Purdue U.; former cons. Gen. Electric Co., Trane Co.; U.S. rep. aerodynamics panel Internat. Com. Flame Radiation Author: (with Drake) Introduction to the Transfer of Heat and Mass, 1950, 2d edit., 1959, Heat and Mass Transfer, (translated by J.F. Gross), 1963; others in German, Russian, and Chinese, (with Goldstein) Measurement Techniques in Heat Transfer, 1970, 2d edit., 1976, (with Drake) Analysis of Heat and Mass Transfer, 1972; Chmn. hon. editorial adv. bd. Internat. Jour. Heat and Mass Transfer; former editor: Thermal Scis. series, Wadsworth Pub. Co., Belmont, Cal.; editor: Thermo and Fluid Dynamics; co-chmn. adv. editorial bd.: Heat Transfer-Japanese Research; co-editor: Energy Developments in Japan; chmn. hon. editorial adv. bd.: Letters in Heat and Mass Transfer; editorial adv. bd.: Numerical Heat Transfer; contbr. articles to sci. mags. Mem. Nat. Commn. Fire Prevention and Control, 1970-73. Recipient Max Jacob Meml. award, 1961, Disting. Teaching award U. Minn., 1965, award Western Electric Fund, 1965, gold medal French Inst. Energy and Fuel, 1967, Vincent Bendix award, 1972, Alexander von Humboldt U.S. sr. scientist award, 1980, A.V. Luikov medal, 1979, Aircraft Gas Turbine Tech. award, 1994, gold medal Czech Acad. Sci., 1994, Founders award Nat. Acad. of Engring., 1995; rsch. fellow Japan Soc. Promotion Sci., 1982. Fellow N.Y. Acad. Scis., AIAA; mem. ASME (hon.), NAE (Gold medal and Founders award 1995), Wissenschaftliche Gesellschaft für Luft und Raumfahrt, Sigma Xi, Pi Tau Sigma, Tau Beta Pi. Home: West Saint Paul, Minn. Died July 8, 2004.

ECKERT, ROGER E(ARL), chemical engineering educator; b. Lakewood, Ohio, Aug. 8, 1926; s. Elmer George and Elsie V. (Schwede) E.; children: Roger Earl, Rhonda Carol, Robyn Claire. BS, Princeton U., 1948; MS, U. Ill., 1949, PhD, 1951. Process devel. engr., indsl. and biochems. dept. E.I. duPont de Nemours & Co., Inc., Wilmington, Del., 1951-64, math. cons., 1956-60, sr. research engr., engring. research lab. and elastomers chems. dept., 1960-64; assoc. prof. Purdue U., West Lafayette, Ind., 1964-73; asst. head Sch. Chem. Engring., 1970-75, prof. chem. engring., 1973—. Vis. prof. U. Colo., 1971, U. Wis., 1981; Am. Soc. Engring. Edn.-NASA faculty fellow Case Western Res. U. and Lewis Research Center, 1966-67 Contbr. tech. articles to profl. jours. Served with U.S. Army, 1946-47. Mem. Am. Inst. Chem. Engrs., Phi Beta Kappa, Sigma Xi, Phi Lambda Upsilon, Pi Mu Epsilon, Alpha Chi Sigma. Presbyterian. Home: West Lafayette, Ind. Deceased.

EDDE, HOWARD JASPER, retired engineering executive; b. Page City, Kans., Dec. 14, 1937; s. Gilbert Herman and Jennie (Foulke) E.; m. Marilyn Ann Scheleen, Sept. 9, 1961; children: Michael, Heather, Sonja. BS, Kans. State U., 1959; MS, U. Kans., 1961; PhD, U. Tex., 1967. Registered profl. engr. Wash., Oreg., Pa., Ariz. Project engr. State of Kans. Dept. Highways, Topeka, 1959-60, Nat. Coun. for Air and Stream Improvement, Baton Rouge, La., 1961-64, regional engr. Balt., 1967-70; project engr. Roy F. Weston Co., West Chester, Pa., 1966-67; v.p. EKONO OY, Helsinki, Finland, 1970-74; pres. Howard Edde, Inc., Bellevue, Wash., 1974-96. Affiliate prof. U. Wash., Seattle, 1972-92; lectr. Johns Hopkins U., Balt., 1967-70; mem. contractor selection com. EPA, 1985—; prof. Seattle U., 1987-89, chmn. civil engring. adv. bd., 1986-90; numerous speaking engagements. Author: (textbooks) Environmental Control for Pulp and Paper Mills, 1984, Environmental Aspects of Pulping Operations and Their Wastewater Implications, 1989; contbr. over 65 articles on energy conservation and environ. control to profl. jours. Fellow ASCE (chmn. Tech. Coun. on Cold Climate Engring. awards coms. 1988-90, various coms.); mem. TAPPI (chmn. wastewater treatment com. 1978-81, process energy use subcom. 1984, Best Paper award-gen. category 1991); Water Environment Fedn. (various coms.), Nat. Sci. and Engring. Rsch. Coun. Can., Am. Bd. Engring. and Tech., Inc. Republican. Lutheran. Avocations: skiing, sailing. Home: Bellevue, Wash. Deceased.

EDELMANN, OTTO KARL, music educator; b. Vienna, Feb. 5, 1917; s. Wenzel and Maria (Krystufek) E.; widowed; m. Ilse-Maria Straub, Apr. 13, 1960; children: Elisabeth, Peter-Alexander, Paul-Armin. Diploma, Univ. Music, Vienna, 1938. Mem. States-Theater, Gera, Germany, 1938, Nuremburg, Germany, 1939, Staatsoper Vienna, 1948-78. Author: Ein Meistersinger aus Wien, 1987; appeared in opera houses throughout world, including Met. Opera, N.Y.C., Opera House, Rio de Janeiro; appeared on numerous opera records. Served with German mil., 1940-47, prisoner of war, USSR. Recipient Order of Daneborg (Denmark) 1962; Cross of Honor Republic of Austria, Cross of Sci. and Arts Republic of Austria, Medal of Gold City of Vienna, 1987. Avocations: boxing, painting. Died May 14, 2003.

EDELSON, SIDNEY, astronomer; b. N.Y.C., Aug. 24, 1916; s. Benjamin and Sarah (Rubin) E.; m. Erny Margaret Andersen, May 9, 1947. BA, Bklyn. Coll., 1938; MA, NYU, 1949, Georgetown U., 1953, PhD, 1961. Mathematician U.S. Naval Obs., Washington, 1948-55; astronomer U.S. Naval Rsch. Lab., Washington, 1955-64; physicist NASA Ames Rsch. Ctr., Moffet Field, Calif., 1964-72; solar physicist U. Graz, Austria, 1972-75. Panel mem. U.S. Civil Svc. Examiner for Scientific and Tech. Pers., Potomac River Naval Command, 1962-64; with China Waterways Transport, 1946-48. Contbr. articles to profl. jours. including Astrophysical Jour., Astronomical Jour., Nature, Solar Physics. Lt. comdr. USN, 1941-46, ETO, PTO, China. Recipient Spl. Breast Order of Yun Hui for meritorious svc., China, 1947. Mem. Rsch. Soc. of Am., U.S. Naval Inst. (assoc.), Am. Astron. Soc. Home: Santa Barbara, Calif. Died Mar. 24, 2002.

EDELSON, STUART MICHAEL, artist, sculptor; b. N.Y.C., July 3, 1944; s. Samuel and Eve (Popow) E. Adj. lectr. Franklin & Marshall Coll., Lancaster, Pa., 1978, Lehigh U., Bethlehem, Pa., 1981, Lehman Coll., N.Y.C., 1983. One man shows include Franklin & Marshall Coll., 1978, Lehigh U., 1981; exhibited in group shows at Alonzo Gallery, N.Y.C., 1972-79, Bklyn. Mus., 1982, Pace U., N.Y.C., 1984, Foxworth Gallery, N.Y.C., 1984-86, Cork Gallery-Lincoln Ctr., N.Y.C., 1985, Toulouse Lautrec Mus., Albi, France, 1986, Arcadia Gallery, N.Y.C., 1987; author: Egypt-Mania, 1983, Black Glass-A Sea Myth, 1986. Mem. Author's Guild. Democrat. Jewish. Avocations: swimming, touring ancient sites. Home: New York, NY. Deceased.

EDEN, LEE SMYTHE, broadcasting executive; b. Memphis, Sept. 13, 1937; s. Lee S. and Helen (Harris) E.; m. Ann Wheaton Graff, Apr. 6, 1974; children: Elizabeth Graff, Kate Smythe; 1 dau. from previous marriage, Meredith Napier. AB, Columbia Coll., 1959. Account exec. Fuller, Smith & Ross, N.Y.C., 1959-61; editor Transporter, Orleans, France, 1961-63; copywriter Liller, Neal, Battle & Lindsey, Atlanta, 1963-64; dir. rsch./sales promotion WAGA-TV, Atlanta, 1964-65, WCAV-TV, Phila., 1965-67; TV/radio mgmt. cons. McHugh & Hoffman, Birmingham, Mich., 1967-69; asst. to chmn. Post-Newsweek Stas., Washington, 1969-71; program dir. sta. WPLG-TV, Miami, Fla., 1971-73; exec. v.p. Telcom Assocs., N.Y.C., 1973-74; v.p. Corinthian Broadcasting, N.Y.C., 1974-80; chmn., pres., chief exec. officer TVS TV Network, N.Y.C., 1980-85; pres., chief exec. officer TVS, Inc., Hilton Head Island, S.C., from 1980, People's Choice Cable TV Network, Westport, CT, 1985-86; pres. Multi Market TV Syndication, 1986-87, Eden Communications, from 1986, Sea Marsh TV, from 1987. Served with U.S. Army, 1961-63. Mem. City Tavern Club of Washington, South Beach Racquet Club. Republican. Episcopalian. Home: Hilton Head Island, SC. Died Nov. 14, 1999.

EDER, HOWARD ABRAM, physician, education educator; b. Milw., Sept. 23, 1917; s. Samuel and Rebecca (Abram) Eder; m. Barbara Straus, July 15, 1954 (dec. Nov. 1997); children: Rebecca, Susan, Michael. AB, U. Wis., 1938; MD, Harvard U., 1942, MPH, 1945; MD (hon.), U. Linkoping, Sweden. Intern Peter Bent Brigham Hosp., Boston, 1942—43, asst. resident, 1943—44; research fellow in medicine Harvard Med. Sch., 1943—44, research fellow in biochemistry, 1945—46; asst. in medicine, asst. physician Rockefeller U. Hosp., 1946—50; asst. prof. medicine Cornell U. Med. Coll., N.Y.C., 1950—53; mem. staff Nat. Heart Inst., Bethesda, Md., 1953—55; assoc. prof. medicine State U. N.Y., Downstate Med. Coll., Bklyn., 1955—57, Albert Einstein Coll. Medicine, 1957—60, prof., 1960—88, prof. emeritus, 1989—2004. Chmn. lipid metabolism adv. com. Nat. Heart, Lung and Blood Inst., 1978—80, mem. bd. sci. counselors, 1986—90, chmn., 1989—90; mem. diabetes and heart disease rev. panel NIH, 1995—96. Editl. bd. Am. Jour. Physiology, 1968—71, 1979—82, Jour. Lipid Rsch., from 1964, Am. Jour. Medicine, 1976—80. Mem.: Am. Diabetes Assn., Am. Heart Assn. (mem. coun. on arteriosclerosis, Disting. Accomplishment award 1985, Spl. Recognition award 1993), Am. Physiol. Soc., Am. Soc. Biol. Chemists, Am. Soc. Clin. Investigation, Assn. Am. Physicians, Inst. Medicine NAS, Interurban Clin. Club (pres. 1971—72), Alpha Omega Alpha, Phi Beta Kappa. Home: Bronx, NY. Died Jan. 15, 2004.

EDLEY, CHRISTOPHER FAIRFIELD, association executive; b. Charleston, W. Va., Jan. 1, 1928; s. Phillip and Helen (Penn) E.; m. Zaida Coles, Sept. 2, 1950; children: Christopher F., Judith Coles. AB, Howard U., 1949; LL.B., Harvard U., 1953; LL.D., Swarthmore Coll., 1976; L.H.D., Rust Coll., 1975. Bar: Mass. 1953, Pa. 1954. Asst. dist. atty., Phila., 1954-56; ptnr. Moore, Lightfoot and Edley, 1956-60; chief adminstrn. justice div. U.S. Commn. Civil Rights, 1960; regional counsel Fed. Housing and Home Fin. (now HUD), 1961-63; program officer in charge govt. and law Ford Found., 1963-73; pres. United Negro Coll. Fund., Inc., 1973—91. Dir. Am. Airlines., A & P Co. Active numerous civic and charitable orgns. including bd. dirs. The Congl. Award, Internat. House, NAACP, Legal Def. Fund, Center Nat. Policy Rev., Citizens Research Found., Nat. Com. Against Discrimination in Housing, Nat. Adv. Council Minorities in Engring.; mem. vis. com. Harvard Law Sch., 1972-78; trustee Nat. Partnership to Prevent Drug and Alcohol Abuse. Served with U.S. Army, 1946-47, 50-51. Recipient Howard U. Alumni award, 1959, Disting. Service award Phila. Commn. Human Relations, 1966; Outstanding Achievement award Ohio State U., 1977; named Humanitarian Father of Year, 1974, numerous others. Mem. Am., Nat., Mass., Pa. bar assns., Assn. Bar City N.Y. Home: New Rochelle, NY. Died May 5, 2003.

EDMUNDS, ROBERT THOMAS, retired surgeon; b. Toledo, Sept. 14, 1924; s. Marion Kenneth and Frances Ethel (McCauley) E.; widowed, 1983; children: Nancy, Priscilla, Elizabeth, Cynthia, Robert. BA, Harvard U., 1947; MD, Columbia U., 1951. Diplomate Am. Bd. Surgery. Intern St. Luke's Hosp., N.Y.C., 1951-52, asst. resident surgery, 1952-55, resident surgery, 1955-56, attending surgeon, 1956-78; clin. prof. surgery Columbia Coll. Physicians and Surgeons, N.Y.C., 1966-78; mini-residency in occupational medicine Inst. Environ. Health U. Cin. Coll Medicine, 1983; med. dir. U.S. Steel Corp., Pitts., 1978-89, ret., 1989. Prin. investigator Cen. Oncology Group, Madison, Wis., 1956-70. Contbr. articles to profl. jours. Lt. (j.g.) USNR, 1942-46. Fellow ACS; mem. Union Club. Republican. Congregationalist. Achievements include enhancement of vision in albino children by use of contact lenses with opaque sclerae. Home: Danbury, Conn. Deceased.

EDSALL, JOHN TILESTON, biological chemistry educator; b. Phila., Nov. 3, 1902; s. David Linn and Margaret Harding (Tileston) E.; m. Margaret Dunham, May 1, 1929 (dec. 1987); children— James Lawrence Dunham (dec.), David Tileston, Nicholas Cranford AB, Harvard U., 1923, MD, 1928; postgrad., Cambridge U., Eng., 1924-26; D.Sc. (hon.), U. Chgo., Western Res. U., U. Mich., N.Y. Med. Coll.; D.Phil. (hon.), U. Göteborg, Sweden, 1972. With Harvard U., Cambridge, Mass., 1928—, asst. prof. biol. chemistry, 1932-38, assoc. prof., 1938-51, prof., 1951-73, emeritus, 1973—. John Simon Guggenheim Meml. Found. fellow Calif. Inst. Tech., 1940-41, Harvard U., 1954-56; Fulbright lectr. U. Cambridge, 1952, U. Tokyo, 1964; vis. prof. Coll. de France, Paris, 1955; pres. 6th Internat. Congress Biochemistry, N.Y.C., 1964; vis. prof. UCLA, 1977; vis. lectr. Australian Nat. U., Canberra, 1970 Author: (with E.J. Cohn) Proteins, Amino Acids and Peptides, 1943, (with J. Wyman) Biophysical Chemistry, 1958, (with H. Gutfreund) Biothermodynamics, 1983; editor: (with F.M. Richards, C.B. Anfinsen, D.S. Eisenberg and others) Advances in Protein Chemistry, Vols. 1-47, 1944-95, 1995, Jour. Biol. Chemistry, 1958-67; (with D. Bearman) Archival Sources for the History of Biochemistry and Molecular Biology, 1980; chmn. editl. bd. Procs. NAS, 1968-72; chmn. survey of sources The History of Biochemistry and Molecular Biology, 1975-80; contbr. articles to profl. jours. Recipient Passano Found. award, 1966; scholar Fogarty Internat. Ctr. NIH, Bethesda, Md., 1970-71 Mem. Am. Philos. Soc., Nat. Acad. Scis., Am. Chem. Soc. (sec. div. biol. chemistry 1946-48, chmn. 1948-49, Willard Gibbs medal Chgo. sect. 1972), Am. Soc. Biol. Chemists (pres. 1957-58), Am. Acad. Arts and Scis. (rep. on U.S. Nat. Commn. for UNESCO 1950-56), AAAS (mem. com. on sci. freedom and responsibility 1976-82, chmn. 1979-81, Philip Hauge Abelson award 1989), Deutsche Akademie der Naturforscher, European Molecular Biology Orgn. (assoc.), Royal Danish Acad. Scis., Royal Swedish Acad. Scis. Home: Cambridge, Mass. Died June 12, 2002.

EDWARDS, CHARLES GARLAND, minister, counselor, health educator; b. Muncie, Ind., Sept. 25, 1926; s. Lowell Adelbert and Josephine Thelma (Cunnington) E.; m. June Elizabeth Day, Aug. 4, 1946; children: James Joseph, Robert Jan. BA, Andrews U., 1946; MS in Pub. Health, Loma Linda (Calif.) U., 1975; PhD, Newport (Calif.) U., 1981. Pastor, evangelist Ind. Conf. of Seventh Day Adventists, 1946-54, Ky., Tenn. Seventh Day Adventists, 1954-63, So. New England Seventh Day Adventists, 1963-64; evnagelist, youth and public rels. dir. Upper Columbia Seventh Day Adventists, Spokane, Wash., 1964-68; youth dir. Northern Calif. Seventh Day Adventists, Oakland, 1968-71, health and pub. rels. Pleasant Hills, 1971-85; pastor Upper Columbia Seventh Day Adventists, Wentachee, Wash., from 1985. Author: A Bold One for God., 1978, Stress, 1980, Wacifundo and the Whirlwind, 1994, One Pilgrim's Progress Through the Twentieth Century, 1996. Bd. mem. Friendship Ctr., Wenatchee, 1985—, Habitat for Humanity, 1992—; pres. Cooperating Christian Chs. of the Wenatchee Valley, 1990-94. Mem. Riverview Kiwanis (pres. 1971-72, award 1972). Deceased.

EDWARDS, EDWARD ALLEN, retired vascular surgeon, anatomist; b. East Lyme, Conn., July 29, 1906; s. Max and Nellie (Gordon) E.; m. Elizabeth Betsy Borwick, May 31, 1931; children: Alicia Betsy, Frederic Thomas. MD, Tufts U., 1928. Diplomate Am. Bd. Surgery. Surg. intern Boston City Hosp., 1928-31; resident in obstetrics Lying-In Hosp., Boston, 1931; rsch. fellow in pathology Med. Examiner's Office, Boston, 1931; rsch. fellow in anatomy Harvard Med. Sch., Boston, 1931-34; surg. practice vascular disease Boston, 1931-77; clin. prof. anatomy Harvard Med. Sch., Boston, 1934-67, clin. prof. anatomy emeritus, from 1973; assoc. in surgery Peter Bent Brigham Hosp., Boston, 1950-69, surgeon, 1969-73, surgeon emeritus, from 1973; chief rehab. Boston Ou-Patient Clinic VA, 1977-86. Mem. physician-in-residence program VA Hosp., 1972-74. Author: Thrombosis in Arteriosclerosis Lower Extremities, 1950, (with others) Operative Anatomy of Thorax, 1972, Operative Anatomy Abdomen and Pelvis, 1975; contbr. chpts. to med. texts and numerous articles to sci. jours. Pres. New Eng. Soc. Vascular Surgery, Boston, 1982-83. Maj. Med. Corps AUS, 1942-45. Fellow ACS; mem. New Eng. Surg. Soc., Am. Assn. Anatomists, Am. Heart Assn. (mem. adv. bd. sect. on circulation). Achievements include research in radiography of blood vessels, orientation of venous valves and their destruction by thrombophlebitis, dynamics after arterial stenosis, application of physical methods to clinical study vascular disease, spectrophotometry of living skin. Home: Boston, Mass. Died Mar. 17, 1999.

EDWARDS, JOAN ANNETTE, elementary art educator; b. Dayton, Ohio, Sept. 16, 1945; d. Austin David and Delphine Edwards; children: Allen Stephen Ashcraft, Rhonda Ashcraft Snyder. AA, Enterprise (Ala.) State Jr. Coll., 1982; BFA, Fla. Atlantic U., Boca Raton, 1986; MEd, Columbus (Ga.) State U., 1997. Cert. art educator, Ga. Tchr. art Muscogee County Sch. Dist., Columbus, Ga., from 1992. Exhibited in juried art exhibit at Memphis Arts Festival, 1997, 98, Ctrl. Wyo. Coll., Riverton, 1998, 99. Recipient Silver award Decatur (Ga.) Arts Alliance Visual Arts Exhbn., 1997. Home: Columbus, Ga. Died Feb. 5, 2002.

EDWARDS, WAYNE A. school administrator, religious studies educator; b. Putnam, Conn., Dec. 26, 1934; s. Dorian Arthur and Celia Evangeline (Gallup) E.; m. Esther Sylvia Balwit, June 4, 1955; children: Valerie, Kevin, Karen, Lynette. BA in Psychology and Sociology, Ea. Nazarene Coll., 1959; MEd in Edn. and Reading, Holy Names Coll., 1974; postgrad., Western Evang. Sem., 1995-96. Teaching asst. Ea. Nazarene Coll., Wollaston, Mass., 1957-59; educator Oakland (Calif.) Pub. Schs., 1959-77; cons. NEA, Burlingamee, Calif., 1976-77; exec. v.p. Ednl. Svcs., Inc., Oakland, 1965-72; owner, adminstr. Wayne Edwards Learning Ctrs., Walnut Creek, Calif., 1972-92; Bibl. counselor trainer McMinnville, from 1992; adminstr. Valley Christian Sch., McMinnville, 1995-97. Vice chmn. retirement com. Calif. Tchrs. Assn., Oakland, 1975-77; ednl. cons., 1993—. Author: (seminar program) Learning for Keeps, 1987. Dir. West Contra Costa PTA Coun., Richmond, Calif., 1968-72; dir., v.p., pres. Pinole (Calif.) C. of C., 1977-85; founding dir., counselor, educator Shepherd's Way Drug Rehab., San Pablo, Calif., 1989-91. Scholar Calif. Assn. Neurologically Handicapped Children, 1974. Mem. Nat. Released Time Edn. Assn. (western dir. 1988-96, pres. 1993-94), Calif. Released Time Edn. Assn. (founding pres. 1982-89, bd. dirs., tchr. trainer 1989-92), Coun. Exceptional Children, El Sobrante C. of C., Gideons Internat. (various offices 1960-67). Avocations: reading, rafting, bible studies. Home: Mcminnville, Oreg. Died June 23, 2000.

EDWARDSON, JOHN RICHARD, retired agronomist; b. Kansas City, Mo., Apr. 17, 1923; s. George Edward and Louise Marie (Sundstrom) E.; m. Betty Jo Cook, Aug. 24, 1948 (dec.); children: George, Elizabeth, Sarah; m. Mickie Newbill, Dec. 26, 1969. BS in Agr., Tex. A&M U., 1948, MS in Agronomy, 1949; PhD in Biology, Harvard U., 1954. Asst. agronomist U. Fla., Gainesville, 1953-60, assoc. agronomist, 1960-66, agronomist, 1966-97; ret., 1997. Author: Some Properties of the Potato Virus Y Group, 1974; co-author: Viruses Infecting Legumes, CRC Handbook, 1991; contbr. articles to Am. Jour. Botany, 1966. Staff sgt. U.S. Army, 1943-45, ETO. Fellow AAAS, Am. Phytopathol. Soc. (Ruth Allen award 1992). Democrat. Achievements include research in describing the structure of potyvirus-induced cylindrical inclusions, using cylindrical inclusions for classification of potyviruses, using cylindrical inclusions in diagnosing infections induced by potyviruses. Home: Gainesville, Fla. Died 2003.

EFORO, JOHN FRANCIS, financial officer; b. N.Y.C., June 30, 1930; s. John J. and Rose (Lo Trionti) E.; m. Tina Liggio, Dec. 23, 1956; children— Joanne, Carla, John C. BA in Econs, CCNY, 1952; postgrad., Am. Inst. Banking, 1953-55. Asst. v.p. ops. Nat. Bank of N.Am., N.Y.C., 1958-69; v.p., comptroller United Mut. Savs. Bank, N.Y.C., 1969-82; officer, dir. Joint Computer Ctr., Inc., N.Y.C., 1974-82; sr. v.p., chief fin. officer State of N.Y. Mortgage Agy., 1982-94, N.Y. State Fin. Agy., 1993-94, N.Y. State Med. Care Facilities Fin. Agy., 1993-94; cons., from 1994. Died Aug. 17, 2002.

EGAN, WILLIAM FRANKLIN, III, marketing professional; b. Phila., Pa., May 19, 1931; s. William F. and Katherine Bennett (MacFarlane) E. AB in Economics, Cornell U., 1953; MBA in Mktg., U. of Miami, 1957. Asst. grocery merchandiser Kroger Company, Memphis, Tenn., 1957-58; adv. sales prom., pr[]. dir. Integrity Natl. Life Ins. Co., Phila., Pa., 1958-59; pres. Walter S. Chittick Co., Phila., Pa., 1959-75, Chittick Egan Advt., Bala Cynwyd, Pa., Egan Advt., Wayne, Pa., from 1980-, Direct Mktg. Mgmt. Cons., Pa., from 1980-. Dir. Caples Award DMCG, N.Y.C., 1981-84, pres. Dir. Mktg. Mgmt. Co., 1987, Dir. Reserve Officers Asso., Colorado Spg., 1954-55., Lt., QMC 1953-55. Recipient Benny award, Phila. Direct Mktg. Assn., Silver Mailbox, Direct Mktg. Assn., N.Y., Neographic award, Graphic Arts Assn. of Greater Phila., Creative Excellence, DMA, N.Y. Mem. Assn. of Direct Mktg. Agencies (pres. 1977-79), Direct Mktg. Assn., Phila. Direct Mktg. Assn., Direct Mktg. Creative Guild, Overbrook Golf Club, OC Yacht Club. Republican. Christian Science. Died Jan. 20, 2002.

EGAR, JOSEPH MICHAEL, mathematics educator; b. Jacksonville, Fla., Feb. 2, 1930; s. Michael Bartholdi and Angie (Keane) E.; m. Margaret Mae Wells, Nov. 23, 1961; children: Michael, Rebecca, Patrick, John. BS in Engring., U. Okla., 1952, postgrad., 1960; PhD in Geophysics, Tex. A&M U., 1959. From instr. to asst. prof. Tex. A&M U., College Station, 1955-59; assoc. prof. math. Ball State U., Muncie, Ind., 1960-63, U. Akron, Ohio, 1963-66, Cleve. State U., from 1966. Sr. lectr. Hatfield (Eng.) Poly., 1974-75; hon. rsch. fellow Birmingham (Eng.) U., 1980. Mem. Math. Assn. Am., Mathematicians for Ednl. Reform. Home: Cleveland Hts, Ohio. Deceased.

EGER, FELIX MARTIN, physics educator; b. Lwów, Poland, May 31, 1936; came to U.S., 1947; s. Arnold and Sonja (Krutjanska) E.; m. Judith Kirshner, Oct. 15, 1971. BS, MIT, 1958; PhD in Physics, Brandeis U., 1963. Postdoctoral appointee Lawrence Livermore (Calif.) Lab., 1965-67; sr. rsch. assoc. Ctr. for History of Philosophy of Sci., Boston U., 1974-75; from assoc. prof. to prof. Physics Coll. S.I. CUNY, Staten Island, from 1976. Bd. editors Sci. and Edn., Dordrecht, The Netherlands, 1991—; contbr. articles to sci. publs. Mem. Am. Phys. Soc., Philosophy of Sci. Assn., Soc. Lit. and Sci., Philosophy of Edn. Soc. Home: Groton, NY. Died Mar. 24, 2002.

EGGER, ROSCOE LYNN, JR., consultant, former IRS commissioner; b. Jackson, Mich., Sept. 19, 1920; s. Roscoe L. and Harriette L. (Youngs) E.; m. Betty Slattery; children: Gabrielle Egger Shaykin, Antoinette Egger Taylor. BA, Ind. U., 1942; LLB, George Washington U., 1950. With GAO, 1946-48; pvt. practice acctg., 1948-50; pvt. practice law, 1956-81; founder Office of Govt. Svcs., 1956-81; with Office of Govt. Service, Price Waterhouse, 1981-86; commr. IRS, Washington, 1981-86. Mem. Commn. on Adminstrv. Rev. Ho. of Reps.; chmn. bd. Nat. Cathedral Sch. for Girls, 1974-76; chmn. bd. dirs. Wolf Trap Assocs.; bd. dirs. C. of C. U.S.A., 1973-79, Chesapeake Bay Maritime Mus. With U.S. Army, 1943-46. Mem. ABA, AICPA, D.C. Bar Assn. Clubs: Met. (Washington), Country Club of Green Valley, Ariz. Republican. Episcopalian. Home: Green Valley, Ariz. Died Oct. 14, 1999.

EHRLICH, PAUL, chemist, educator; b. Vienna, Feb. 26, 1923; came to U.S., 1940, naturalized, 1944; s. Jacob and Irma (Hutter) E.; m. Celia Lesley, Apr. 16, 1949; children— Daniel, James, Catherine, Margot, Paul R. BS, Queens Coll.,

1944; MS, U. Wis., 1948, PhD, 1951. Phys. chemist Nat. Bur. Standards, Washington, 1951-53; postdoctoral fellow Harvard, 1953-54; research chemist, scientist Monsanto Co., Springfield, Mass. and St. Louis, 1955-67; asso. prof., prof. SUNY, Buffalo, 1967-91, prof. emeritus, from 1991. Adj. prof. U. Mass., Amherst, 1992—99. Mem. editl. bd. Jour. Macromolecular Sci, 1966-81; contbr. articles to profl. jours. Served with AUS, 1944-46. Rsch. grantee NSF, 1968, 72, 75, 77, 79, 86, 89, 92. Mem. AAAS, Am. Chem. Soc., Am. Phys. Soc. Home: Lebanon, NH. Died Feb. 18, 2003.

EHRMAN, JOACHIM BENEDICT, mathematics educator; b. Nuremberg, Germany, Nov. 12, 1929; emigrated to U.S., 1938, naturalized, 1943; s. Fritz Sally and Ilse (Benedict) E.; m. Gloria Jeanette Gould, Jan. 24, 1961; 1 son, Carl David. AB, U. Pa., 1948; A.M., Princeton, 1949, PhD, 1954. Research physicist N.Am. Aviation, Inc., Downey, Calif., 1951-53; instr. physics Yale, 1954-55; research physicist U.S. Naval Research Lab., Washington, 1955-68; prof. dept. applied math. U. Western Ont., Can., 1968—. Asso. prof. physics George Washington U., 1956-57; lectr. U. Md., 1963-64; vis. research staff Plasma Physics Lab., Princeton, 1975-76 Contbr. profl. jours. Mem. Phi Beta Kappa. Jewish. Home: London, Canada. Died Apr. 18, 2004.

EIDE, CRAIG DONALD, accountant; b. Mpls., May 13, 1949; s. Lloyd Norman and Donna Mae (Mickelson) E.; m. Linda Ann Briggs, Dec. 17, 1971; children: Eric, Elliott. BS, USCG Acad., 1971; MBA, U. Chgo., 1976. CPA, Wash. Commd. ensign USCG, various, 1971, advanced through grades to lt. various locations, 1974; staff acct. Coopers & Lybrand, Portland, Maine, 1977-79; sr. acct. Baumgartner, Kueckelhan, Seattle, 1979-81; controller Northwest Steel Rolling Mills, Seattle, 1981-84, Trade Products Inc., Lynnwood, Wash., 1984-87, v.p. fin., from 1987. Mem. Wash. Soc. CPA's. Democrat. Lutheran. Home: Seattle, Wash. Died Mar. 29, 2001.

EISELE, MILTON DOUGLAS, viticulturist; b. N.Y.C., Apr. 2, 1910; s. Charles Francis and Helen Agnes (Dolan) E.; B.A., U. Calif.-Berkeley, 1933; grad. San Francisco Stock Exch. Inst., 1938; m. Barbara Lois Morgan, July 26, 1941; children: Helen Frances Eisele Osthimer, Barbara Glennis, William Douglas. Investment cashier Wells Fargo Bank, San Francisco, 1934-39; coordinator cement sales Permanente Corp., 1940-41, constrn. supt., 1941-43; mgr. refractory div. Kaiser Aluminum, 1943-47, mgr. regional sales, Chgo., 1947-50, mgr. foil div., 1950-55, mgr. prodn., 1955-60, mgr. market and prodn. devel., 1960-65, mgr. investments, 1966-71; ret., 1971; former owner, operator Eisele Vineyards, Napa Valley, Calif., 1969-89. Dir., former pres. Napa Valley Found., 1981-85; bd. dirs., past chmn. Vintage Hall, Inc., 1973-85; bd. dirs., pres. Napa Valley Heritage Fund, 1973—; past pres., bd. dirs. Upper Napa Valley Assocs., 1976-80; mem. adv. coun. Napa County Land Trust, 1976-79; mem. Napa County Grand Jury, 1988-89, hon. co-chmn. 150th anny. planting first grapes. Mem. Am. Soc. Enologists, Napa Valley Grape Growers Assn. (dir.), Calif. Assn. Wine Grape Growers (dir., former sec., chmn. 1986-87), Calif. Vintage Wine Soc. (bd. dirs., pres. 1994—), Agrl. Coun. of Napa County, Wine and Winegrape Mktg. Order State of Calif. (dir. 1984), Napa Valley Growers and Vinters (chmn. bd. dirs., mktg. and promotion com. 1985—), Marin County Wine & Food Soc., Kappa Alpha Order. Republican. Episcopalian (vestryman, sr. warden 1966-69). Deceased.

EISENPREIS, ALFRED, communications and marketing executive; b. Vienna, June 16, 1924; came to U.S., 1939, naturalized, 1942; s. Siegmund and Claire (Silberman-Günsberg) E.; 1 child, Steven. AB, St. Thomas Coll., 1943; MA, N.Y. Sch. Social Research, 1974; cert., Army Staff Coll., 1983, Nat. Def. U., 2000; PhD, Union Inst. U., 1999. Exec. Pomeroy's Inc. (dept. store), Wilkes-Barre, Pa., 1943-57; with Allied Stores Corp., N.Y.C., 1957-74, v.p. planning and research, 1963-69, v.p. mktg., 1970-74; adminstr. Econ. Devel. Adminstrn. City of N.Y., 1974-76; v.p. Newspaper Advt. Bur., 1977-86, sr. v.p., 1986-91; pres. Eisenpreis & Co., Ltd. Cons., N.Y.C., from 1991; editl. dir. Retail Ad-Week, N.Y.C., 1992-95; dir. Henchy & Assocs., N.Y.C., 1982-86; v.p. City Innovation, 1992-95, vice chmn., dir., 1995-2000; pres. Cmty. Action Network, 1996-98, vice chmn., 1998-99. Cons. N.Y. C. of C., Econ. Devel. Coun. N.Y.C., 1976; adj. prof. Grad. Sch. Mgmt. and Urban Professions, New Sch. Social Research, 1975-82, mem. adv. coms. on manpower and tourism programs, 1975-82, bd. overseers Grad. Sch. Mgmt. and Urban Professions, 1984-87; mem. policy com. City of N.Y., 1974-76; pres. N.Y.C. Indsl. Devel. Corp., 1974-76; mem. Port Devel. Coun. N.Y., 1974-76; vice chmn. Interagy. Rail Com., 1975; steering com. Westside Hwy., 1974-76; chmn. Retail Rsch. Inst., 1963-68; mem. com. dept. store statistics Fed. Res. System, 1960-65; chmn. adv. com. Ctr. Econ. Projections, Nat. Planning Assn., 1963-68; mem. dept. urban rsch. Nat. Acad. Scis., 1964-69; cons. U.S. Dept. Commerce, 1965-69; dir. Greater Jamaica Devel. Com., 1965-68; trustee Fed. Statis. Users Conf., 1965-67, N.Y. Met. Regional Statis. Ctr., 1965-67; mem. Census Adv. Com., 1966-68, 72-74; mem. nat. mktg. adv. com. U.S. Dept. Commerce, 1968-72; cons. Office of Emergency Preparedness-Fed. Emergency Mgmt. Agy., 1966-82; mem. Nat. Def. Exec. Res., 1966—, Fed. Emergency Mgmt. Agy. Res., 1990—, Nat. Mgmt. Coun. Mktg. Edn., chmn., 1972-81; mem. Nat. Bus. Coun. on Consumer Interests, 1972-73; mem. local candidates com. Citizens Union, 1995—. Author: The Changing Consumer, 1961, Organization for Multi-Unit Stores, 1962, Evaluation of Retail Store Location Research, 1965, Retail Marketing, 1981, Print Advertising for Shopping Centers, 1993. Trustee Wilkes U., Wilkes Barre, Pa., 1968-74, Reece Sch., N.Y.C., 1968-72; dir. Jewish Publs. Soc., 1992-97, mem. nat. coun., 2002—; trustee, exec. com. Union Am. Hebrew Congregations, 1970-81, trustee, 1992-98; trustee French and Polyclinic Med. Sch. and Health Ctr., N.Y.C., 1972-73, Pub. Devel. Corp., 1974-76, Emanu-El Congregation, N.Y.C., 1971—, treas., 1985—; chmn. Libr. Explorers Club, 1998—; bd. dirs. N.Y.C. Conv. Ctr., 1974-76, N.Y.C. Conv. and Visitors Bur., 1974-76, Nat. Coun. for Urban Econ. Devel., 1975-76, Nat. Found. Jewish Culture, 1974—, treas., 1977-86, v.p., 1986-88, mem. exec. com., 1992-93, life trustee, 1998—; adv. com. N.Y. Pub. Libr., 1968-74; mem. exec. com. N.Y.C. chpt. Am. Jewish Com., v.p., 1984-86, bd. dirs., 1975—; mem. adv. com. Inst. Internat. Edn., N.Y.C., 1974-78; mem. N.Y.C. Jewish Cmty. Rels. Coun., 1976-78; mem. pres.'s coun. Sch. Social Work, NYU, 1977-80; v.p. Joyce Theater Found., N.Y.C., 1980-84; exec. com. Am. Jewish Hist. Assn., 1983-85; sr. v.p. Mothers/Fathers Day Coun., 1986-96; exec. com., bd. dirs. Cancer Rsch. and Treatment Fund, 1987—; mem. exec. com. Promesa Found., N.Y.C., 1995-2000; mem. adv. bd. The Skirball Ctr., 2000—. Recipient I.M. Lubin award New Sch., 1974, Trustees award Internat. Coun. Shopping Ctrs., 1991; named to Retail Advt. Hall of Fame, 1989; resident fellow Explorers Club, 1997—; vis. scholar N.Y. Acad. Scis., 2000—. Fellow Royal Geog. Soc.; mem. Forecasters Club N.Y. (hon. life mem., pres. 1973-74), Am. Statis. Assn., Am. Hist. Assn., Am. Econ. Assn., Am. Polit. Sci. Assn., Nat. Retail Mchts. Assn. (bd. dir. 1963-72, exec. com. 1968-72, v.p. 1970, Silver Plaque award 1966), U. Club Libr. Assocs. (chmn. 1983-90), Am. Retail Fedn. (dir., exec. com. 1968-72), Retail Advt. Conf. (bd. dir. 1987-91), N.Y. Acad. Scis., Nat. Assn. Scholars, Retail Mktg. Soc. (hon., life), Internat. Newspaper Advt. and Mktg. Execs. (hon. life), Regional Plan Assn. N.Y.C. (com. 2d regional plan), Archaeol. Inst. Am. (bd. trustees 1997-2002, chmn. Archaeology mag. 1999-2002, exec. com. 2000-02, chmn. nominating com. 2000-02), Explorer's Club, Grolier Club, Univ. Club, Dutch Treat Club, Lansdowne Club (London), East India Devonshire Club (London). Home: New York, NY. Died Mar. 27, 2003.

EISNER, JACK P. writer; b. Warsaw, Nov. 15, 1926; came to U.S., 1949; s. Aron and Janet Zlatka (Szteiman) E.; m. Helen, 1950 (div. 1973); m. Sara Joanna, 1988; children: Shirley, Philip, Arnold. MA, Emory U., 1954. Founder, pres. Warsaw Ghetto Resistance Orgn., N.Y.C., from 1962, Holocause Meml. Found., N.Y.C., Chgo., from 1978. Author: The Survivor, 1981. Mem. World Congress Holocaust Survivors (founder, pres.). Home: New York, NY. Died Aug. 24, 2003.

ELDRIDGE, PATRICIA DARLENE, social services administrator; b. Mpls., June 11, 1937; BA, Augsburg Coll., 1959; MSW, U. Minn., 1961. Cert. social worker; lic. clin. social worker; cert. diplomate social worker. Caseworker Travelers Aid Soc., Mpls., 1959-63, supr., 1961-63; caseworker Luth. Social Svcs., Mpls., 1963-65, intake supr., 1965-68, casework supr. unmarried parents, 1968-73, dir. adoption/child care, from 1973. Home: Minneapolis, Minn. Died Oct. 24, 2000.

ELIKANN, LAWRENCE S. (LARRY ELIKANN), television and film director; b. N.Y.C., July 4, 1923; s. Harry and Sadye (Trause) E.; m. Corinne Corky Schuman; Dec. 6, 1947; children— JoAnne Jarrin, Jill Barad. BA, Bklyn. Coll., 1943; E.E., Walter Harvey Coll., 1948. Tech. dir. NBC-TV, N.Y.C., 1948-64; comml. dir. VPI-TV, N.Y.C., 1964-66, Filmex-TV, N.Y.C., 1966-68, Plus two TV, N.Y.C., 1968-70. Dir. mini-series Last Flight Out, The Great L.A. Earthquake, The Big One, The Inconvenient Woman, Fever, Story Lady, One Against the Wind, Bonds of Love, I Know My First Name is Steven, Hands of a Stranger, Kiss of a Killer, God Bless the Child, Out of Darkness, Menendez—A Killing in Beverly Hills, Tecumseh—The Last Warrior, A Mother's Prayer, Blue River, "Unexpected Family", Lies He Told. Mem. Mus. Contemporary Art of L.A., L.A. County Mus.; mem. rsch. coun. Scripps Clinic and Rsch. Found. With Signal Corps, U.S. Army, 1943-46. Recipient Emmy award, 1978-79, 89, Golden Globe award, 1989, 91, 94, Christopher award 1973-76, 77, 78-79, 91, Chgo. Internat. Film Festival award 1977, Internat. Film and TV Festival of N.Y. award, 1977, Dir. of Yr. award Am. Ctrs. for Children, 1978; Humanitas prize, 1988, 94, 96. Mem. NATAS (gov. 1961-63), Dirs. Guild Am., Am. film Inst., Nat. Hist. Preservation Soc., Smithsonian Inst., Scripps Inst. (bd. dirs.), Acad. TV Arts and Scis. Died Feb. 4, 2004.

ELLENBOGEN, CHARLES, internist; b. Winston-Salem, N.C., Feb. 10, 1939; s. Edward and Adele (Wilinsky) E.; divorced; children: Daniel, Jennie. SB, U. Chgo., 1960, MD, 1964. Intern USAF Med. Ctr., Lackland AFB, Tex., 1965-66, medicine resident, 1966-68, fellow infectious diseases, 1968-70; dir. internal medicine, lt. col. 483 USAF Hosp., Cam Rahn Bay, 1970-71; chief infectious disease USAF Med. Ctr., Lackland AFB, 1971-77; assoc. prof., vice-chmn. medicine U. Mo., Kansas City, 1977-80; dir. internal medicine Fayetteville (N.C.) Area Health Edn. Ctr., 1980-96; med. dir. primary care network Cape Fear Valley Health Sys., from 1997. Author: FAHEC Clinical Manual, 1990, 91; contbr. over 20 articles to profl. jours. Recipient Sustaining Membership award Air Force Assn., 1983, Commendation medal USAF, 1987. Fellow ACP, Infectious Disease Soc. Am.; mem. AMA, Cumberland County Med. Soc., N.C. Med. Soc. Avocations: U.S. civil war history, modern history, bicycling. Home: Fayetteville, NC. Died Oct. 9, 1999.

ELLIOTT, HOLLY HALL, retired rehabilitation therapist, counselor; b. L.A., Jan. 20, 1920; d. Wilford Raymond and Adnee (Wright) Hall; m. James Wagner Elliott, May 7, 1944(dec. Dec. 1968); children: James Paul, Dennis Hall, Mark Andrew. BA in Music, U. Calif., L.A., 1941; MS in Counseling, Sacramento (Calif.) State U., 1970. Counselor, therapist U. Calif., San Francisco, 1970-80; instr. San Francisco State U., 1980-85; rsch., writing Laugley Porter Psychiat. Inst., San Francisco, 1985-92, retired, 1992. Adv. com. Calif. State Dept. Rehab., Sacramento, 1980-84; cons. in field; lectr. in field. Author: Mental Health Assessment of Deaf Clients, 1987, Mental Health Assessment Special Conditions, 1989; contbr. articles to profl. jours. Pres. El Dorado County Bd. Edn., Placerville, Calif., 1962-68, Deaf Svcs. Network, San Francisco, 1978-85. Mem. Nat. Com. Devel. Deaf Ministries United Methodist Ch. (gen. conf.), United Methodist Congress of the Deaf (bd. dirs., pres. 1982-88), Assn. Late Deafened Adults (I. King Jordan award 1994), Deaf Svcs. North (pres. 1974-85, Bridge award 1984), Delta Kappa Gamma (hon.). Democrat. Avocations: research, writing, disability access for churches. Home: Portland, Oreg. Deceased.

ELLIOTT, IVAN A., JR., lawyer; b. Carmi, Ill., Oct. 31, 1923; s. Ivan A. and Malen (Stinson) E.; m. Lauralynn Parkerson, Sept. 17, 1950; children: Cynthia Ann, Rebecca Sue Griffin, Marjorie Kay, Martin. BA, U. Ill., 1948, LLD, 1950. Bar: Ill. 1950, U.S. Dist. Ct. (so. dist.) Ill. 1954, U.S. Ct. Appeals (7th cir.) 1959, U.S. Supreme Ct. 1967. Ptnr., pres. Conger & Elliott, P.C. and predecessor firm Conger & Elliott, Carmi, from 1952. Chmn. bd. dirs. 1st Nat. Bank, Carmi, 1993-96; bd. dirs. Tecumseh Internat. Corp., Carmi Area Indsl. Corp., Carmi Times Pub. Co., v.p. 1966-74, White County Abstract Co., pres. 1966—; asst. atty. gen. State of Ill., 1961-68; atty. City of Carmi, 1960-61; bd. dirs. Ill. Inst. for Continuing Legal Edn., 1989—, exec. com. 1997. Author: Revovable Trusts in Ill., 1997; contbr. articles to profl. jours. Mem. Ednl. Service Region Study Commn., 1979; gen. counsel Presbytery Southern Ill., 1965-71, 72-76, 79-97, trustee, 1962-65, 72-76, 79-97, pres. bd. trustees, 1972-76, 79-97, State Us. Civil Service System, 1968-97, chmn. 1969-78, 81-97, Bd. Higher Edn., 1973-77; moderator Presbytery Southeastern Ill., 1982-83; trustee So. Ill. U., 1967-97, chmn. 1973-77, Police Pension Fund City of Carmi, 1957—, pres. 1957—; bd. dirs. Southern Ill. U. Found., 1968—, exec. com., 1970-97, McKinely Found. at U. Ill., 1954-71. Served to lt. col. U.S. Army, 1942-46, 50-52, ETO. Recipient Kathryn G. Hansen award U.S. Civil Service System Ill., 1972; Disting. Svc. award Southern Ill. Univ., 1994, Addis E. Hall award Ill. Inst. for Continuing Legal Edn., 1995. Fellow Am. Coll. Probate Counsel; mem. ABA, Ill. Bar Assn. (com. on publs. 1979-88, chmn. 1986-87, sec. exec. com. legal edn. 1955-57, subcom. merchantability of title real estate sect., various others), White County Bar Assn. (sec. 1960-64), Southeastern Ill. Bar Assn., Fedn. Local Bar Assn. Ill. (pres. so. div. 5th dist. 1965-66), Am. Judicature Soc., Am. Law Inst., Ill. Inst. for Continuing Edn. (bd. dirs. 1986—), VFW, Am. Legion (post judge adv. 1957—), Ill. Oil and Gas Assn., Wabash Valley Assn., Carmi C. of C. (pres. 1955-56, Outstanding Citizen of Yr. award 1981), Golden Key, Order of Coif, Phi Beta Kappa, Phi Kappa Phi, Phi Alpha Delta, Sigma Phi Epsilon. Lodges: Kiwanis (pres. Carmi 1957, sec. 1953-56), Elks. Democrat. Home: Carmi, Ill. Died May 28, 2000.

ELLIS, ELIZABETH MUELLER, psychologist; b. Milw. d. Louis John Jr. and Jean (Cunliffe) Mueller; m. Walter Healy, Jr., Jan. 9, 1943; m. Daniel Mortimer Friedman, Oct. 18, 1975; children: Elizabeth Rizzi, Jonathan, Benjamin, Nancy McElligott. BA, U. Chgo., 1949; MA, George Washington U., 1963; PhD, U. Md., 1972. Cert. group psychotherapist. Consulting sch. psychologist Potomac (Md.) Sch., 1962-63; staff psychologist Alexandria (Va.) Mental Health Ctr., 1963-70; cons. Cmty. Psychiatric Clinic, Bethesda, Md., 1972-84; pvt. practice Washington, from 1980; supr. staff Affiliated Cmty. Counselors, Rockville, Md., 1988-89; counselor Family Life Ctr., Columbia, Md., 1989-91. Adj. prof. child psychology Trinity Coll., Washington, 1974; cons. Prince George's County Drug Abuse Program, Md., 1973. Editor: Psychology & Life, 1949. Fellow Md. Psych. Assn.; mem. APA, Am. Group Psychotherpy Assn., Psi Chi. Home: Washington, DC. Died June 1, 2002.

ELLIS, LOREN BURRELL, paint company executive; b. Nampa, Idaho, Apr. 15, 1952; s. Abram Burrell and Marjorie Joyce (Draper) E.; m. Carmen Maria Loera; 1 child, Lorenna Lee. Student, N.W. Nazarene Coll., 1971-73, Boise State U., 1977-79. Store mgr. Caldwell (Idaho) Paint & Glass, 1979-80, State Paint & Glass, Boise, Idaho, 1980-82; pres. Ponderosa Paint Mfg., Inc. (formerly Mountain States Paint Mfg. Co.), Boise, from 1982. Bd. dirs. Treasure Valley Bank, Fruitland, Idaho. Co-founder Paint Your Heart Out, community svc. event, Boise, 1984; mem. adv. bd. Boise Salvation Army, 1985—; mem. president's community adv. bd. N.W. Nazarene Coll., Nampa, 1986—. Recipient Community Svc. award City of Boise, 1985. Mem. Color Guild Assocs., Rotary. Republican. Nazarene. Home: Nampa, Idaho. Died July 26, 1999.

ELLISTON, LARRY JOE, financial executive; b. Monterey Park, Calif., June 11, 1951; s. Robert Eugene and June Rose (Berard) E.; m. Peggy Lynn Gordon, Aug. 5, 1978; children: Rachel, Michael, Melanie, Jennifer. Grad., San Juan High Sch., 1969. Wealth and asset mgr. Elliston & Assocs., Wealth and Asset Mgmt., Tustin, Calif. Instr. Calif. Inst. Internat. Bus. and Econs., Beverly Hills, 1991. Editor: Series 7 Study Guide, 1991-92. Precinct capt. Rep. Party, Sacramento, 1980; scoutmaster, chair troop com., chair pack com., asst. scoutmaster, Webelo den leader, Boy Scouts Am., 1979-92. Mem. Lds Ch. Deceased.

ELLSWORTH, RALPH EUGENE, retired librarian; b. Forest City, Iowa, Sept. 22, 1907; s. Wallace Henry and Helma C. (Gorenson) E.; m. Theda Chapman, Aug. 1931; children: Peter C., John David. AB, Oberlin Coll., 1929; BS, Case Western Res. U., 1931; PhD, U. Chgo., 1937; LHD, Case Western Reserve, Oberlin, 1956, 1987. Libr. Adam State Coll., Alamosa, Colo., 1931-34; dir. of librs. U. Colo., Boulder, 1937-44; 58-72, U. Iowa, Iowa City, 1944-58. Cons. on more than 200 projects including work in 6 fgn. countries; mem. of ALA com. that wrote Libr. Bill of Rights. Author: numerous books including The Economics of Book Storage, 1969, Planning Manual for Academic Library Buildings, 1973, Ellsworth on Ellsworth: an Autobiography, 1983; contbr. articles to profl. jours. Recipient Brett Meml. scholarship, 1931, U. Chgo. fellowship, 1937, Denver Pub. Libr. Nell Scott Meml. award, 1972. Mem. ALA (life), Colo. Libr. Assn. (pres. 1932, 59, 70), Assn. Reference Librs. (pres. 1952, 60). Democrat. Avocation: trout fishing. Home: Boulder, Colo. Died Nov. 12, 2000.

ELMAN, PHILIP, lawyer; b. Paterson, N.J., Mar. 14, 1918; s. Jacob and Anne (Nirenberg) E.; m. Ella M. Shalit, Dec. 21, 1947; children: Joseph, Peter, Anthony. AB, CCNY, 1936; LL.B., Harvard U., 1939. Bar: N.Y. 1940, D.C. 1948. Law clk. to Judge Magruder, U.S. Ct. Appeals, Boston, 1939-40; atty. FCC, 1940-41; law clk. to Supreme Ct. Justice Frankfurter, 1941-43; asst. chmn. Office Fgn. Econ. Coordination, State Dept., 1943-44; asst. to solicitor gen. U.S., 1944-61; legal adviser Mil. Govt. U.S., Berlin, 1945-46; commr. FTC, 1961-70; of counsel Wald, Harkrader & Ross, 1971-84; vol. mediator D.C. Superior Ct., U.S. Ct. Appeals (D.C. cir.), 1985-93. Prof. law Georgetown U. Law Ctr., Washington, 1970-76, adj. prof., 1984-93, U. Hawaii, Honolulu, 1982-92. Editor: Of Law and Men (papers of Felix Frankfurter), 1956; mem. staff: Harvard Law Rev. Recipient Rockefeller Pub. Service award, 1967 Mem. Am. Law Inst., Phi Beta Kappa. Home: Chevy Chase, Md. Died Nov. 30, 1999.

ELTON, ROBERT LOUIS, radiation oncology therapist, college official; b. Salt Lake City, May 19, 1946; s. Louis Earl and Illa Lynn (Page) E. BS, Brigham Young U., 1972; cert. in radiologic tech., Latter-day Saints Hosp., Salt Lake City, 1974. Dir. clin. edn. Weber State Coll. Allied Health Sci.; therapist oncology Provo, Utah, from 1981; mgr. oncology dept. Utah Valley Regional Med. Ctr., Provo, from 1983. Tchr. Am. Cancer Soc., 1988—. With U.S. Army, 1971-76. Recipient Dept. Mgr. Excellence award Utah Valley Med. Ctr., 1985. Mem. Am. Registry Radiologic Technologists, Am. Soc. Radiologic Technologists, Utah Soc. Radiologic Technologists, Intermountain Soc. Artists, Radiation Therapy Soc. Utah (pres. 1984-85). Republican. Mem. Lds Ch. Avocations: art, horse training and showing, hunting, fishing. Home: Lindon, Utah. Died May 12, 2001.

ELTON, WILLIAM R. English literature educator, poet; b. N.Y.C., Aug. 15, 1921; s. William and Mollie Elton. AB, Bklyn. Coll., 1941; MA, U. Cin., 1942; PhD, Ohio State U., 1957. Asst. Ohio State U., 1942-45, instr., 1945-46, Brown U., Providence, 1946-50, NYU, 1950-51; vis. asst. prof. English U. Conn., 1952-53; asst. prof. Ohio State U., 1953-55; asst. prof. to prof. U. Calif., Riverside, 1955-69; vis. prof. Columbia U., 1969; prof. English lit. CUNY, from 1969. 1st vis. Mellon prof. Inst. for Advanced Study, Princeton, 1984-85; bd. dirs. Shakespeare Inst. of N.Y.; lectr. Lincoln Coll., Oxford, Eng., 1951, U. Paris VII, Ecole Normale Supérieure, 1990; Fulbright lectr., India, 1960, New Coll., Oxford, 1990; cons. in field. Author: Guide to the New Criticism, 5th edit., 1953, King Lear and the Gods, 1966, 2d edit., 1988, Shakespeare's Ulysses and die Frage des Wertes, 1968, Wittgenstein's Trousers: Poems, 1991, Shakespeare's World: Renaissance Intellectual Contexts, 1979, Shakespeares: Troilus and Cressida and the Inns of Court Revels, 2000, others; founding editor Shakespearean International Yearbook; editor: Shakespearean Research and Opportunities, 1965—, A Bibliography of Shakespeare's Timon of Athens, 1971, others; adv. editor Shakespeare Studies, 1965—; founder, co-editor Poetry N.Y., 1985—; cons. editor Jour. History of Ideas, 1981—; contbr. numerous articles to profl. jours., chpts. to books. Recipient numerous fellowships, grants from various orgns. including CUNY Research Found., 1984-85, 85-86, Huntington Library, 1988. Mem. MLA, Renaissance Soc. Am., Malone Soc., Internat. Soc. for Neoplatonic Studies, Shakespeare Assn. Am., Soc. for Renaissance Studies (Eng.), PEN Club, English Inst., Am. Philol. Assn., Soc. for Ancient Greek Philosophy, Internat. Assn. Profs. of English. Died Aug. 18, 2000.

ELY, JOHN HART, lawyer, former university dean; b. N.Y.C., Dec. 3, 1938; s. John H. and Martha Foster (Coyle) E.; children: John Duff, Robert Allan Duff, m. Gisela Cardonne, 2002. AB summa cum laude, Princeton U., 1960; LL.B. magna cum laude, Yale U., 1963, MA (hon.), 1971, Harvard U., 1973; LLD, U. San Diego, 1988, Ill. Inst. Tech., 1991. Bar: D.C. 1965, Calif. 1967. Atty. Warren Commn., 1964; law clk. to Chief Justice Warren, 1964-65; Fulbright scholar London Sch. Econs., 1965-66; atty. Defenders, Inc., San Diego, 1966-68; asso. prof., then prof. law Yale U. Law Sch., 1968-73; prof. Harvard U. Law Sch., 1973-1982, Ralph S. Tyler, Jr. prof. constl. law, 1981-1982; Richard E. Lang prof. law Stanford U. Law Sch., Calif., 1982-87, dean, 1982-87; Robert E. Paradise prof. Stanford (Calif.) U. Law Sch., 1987-96; Richard A. Hausler prof. U. Miami (Fla.) Law Sch., 1996—2003. Gen. counsel U.S. Dept. Transp., 1975-76 Author: Democracy and Distrust, 1980, War and Responsibility, 1993, On Constitutional Ground, 1996. Served with USAR, 1963-69. Fellow Woodrow WIlson Internat. Ctr. scholars (1978-79), Am. Acad. Arts and Scis., Coun. on Fgn. Rels. Home: Coconut Grove, Fla. Died Oct. 25, 2003.

ENDLER, NORMAN SOLOMON, psychology educator; b. Montreal, Que., Can., May 2, 1931; m. Beatrice Kerdman, June 26, 1955; children— Mark, Marla. B.Sc., McGill U., 1953, M.Sc., 1954; PhD, U. Ill., 1958. Registered psychologist, Ont., Can. Psychologist Pa. State U., 1958-60; lectr. psychology York U., Downsview, Ont., 1960-62, asst. prof., 1962-65, assoc. prof., 1965-68, prof., 1968-95, Disting. rsch. prof., from 1995. Cons. Toronto East Gen. Hosp., 1964-84, Clarke Inst., Toronto, 1972-81; vis. scholar Oxford (Eng.) U., 1993. Author: Holiday of Darkness, 1982, rev., 1990, (with E.J. Shipton, F.D. Kemper) Maturing in a Changing World, 1971, (with D. Magnusson) Interactional Psychology and Personality, 1976, (with L.R. Boulter, H. Osser) Contemporary Issues in Developmental Psychology, 1976, (with D. Magnusson) Personality at the Crossroads: Current Issues in Interactional Psychology, 1977, (with J. McV. Hunt) Personality and the Behavioral Disorders, 2d edit., 1984, (with E. Persad) Electroconvulsive Therapy: The Myths and the Realities, 1988, (with C.D. McCann) Depression: New Directions in Research, Theory, and Practice, 1999 (2nd edit.), (with J.D.A. Parker) Coping Inventory for Stressful Situations, 1990, 2d edit., 1999, (with J.M. Edwards, R. Vitelli) Endler Multidimensional Anxiety Scales, 1991, (with M. Zeidner) Handbook of Coping: Theory, Research & Applications, 1996, (with J.D.A. Parker) Coping with Health Injuries and Problems Scale, 2000, (with G.L. Flett) EMAS-Social Anxiety Scales, 2002. Recipient Can. Silver Jubilee medal, 1978; grantee Ont. Mental Health Assn., 1968-74, Can. Coun., 1969-78, Social Scis. and Humanities Rsch. Coun., 1979-80, 91—; Killam Rsch. fellow Can. Coun., 1987-89. Fellow Am. Psychol. Assn., Can. Psychol. Assn. (D.O. Hebb award for disting. contbn. to psychology as a sci. 1997), Ont. Psychol. Assn., Royal Soc. Can. (Innis-Gerin medal 1997). Home: Toronto, Canada. Died May 7, 2003.

ENGEL, GEORGE LIBMAN, psychiatrist, internist, educator; b. N.Y.C., Dec. 10, 1913; BA, Dartmouth Coll., 1934; MD, Johns Hopkins U., 1938; MD (h.c.), U. Bern, Switzerland, 1980; ScD (h.c.), Med. Coll. Ohio, 1986. Rotating intern Mt.Sinai Hosp., N.Y.C., 1938-41, fellow in medicine Peter Bent Brigham Hosp., Boston, 1941-42; instr. and asst. prof. medicine and psychiatry U. Cin. Coll. Medicine, 1942-46; asst. prof., assoc. prof., prof. medicine and psychiatry U. Rochester Sch. Medicine and Dentistry, N.Y., 1946-84, prof. emeritus psychiatry and medicine, 1984—. Lectr., vis. prof. numerous socs., hosps. and univs., 1959—, including U. Minn., U. Chgo., Albert Einstein Coll. Medicine, Columbia U., Univ. Coll. Hosp., London, SUNY-Bklyn., U. Pa., Albany Med. Coll., Monash U., Melbourne, Australia, U. Ariz., Mt. Sinai Hosp. and Med. Sch., U. Rochester Med. Center Alumni Assn., Tufts U., U. Calif.-San Francisco, U. Western Ont., London, Can., U. Mo., Case West Res. U., Temple U., U. So. Calif., U. Sask., Saskatoon, Can., SUNY-Syracuse, U. Ala., Johns Hopkins U., U. Colo., Beth Israel Med. Ctr., U. Ill., Urbana, Med. U. S.C., Mt. Sinai Med. Ctr., Milw., U. W. Va., Emory U., Brown U., N.Y. Med. Coll.; sci. adv. bd. Helen Dowling Inst. Biopsychosocial Medicine, Erasmus U., Rotterdam, Holland. Author: Fainting, 1950, 2d edit., 1962, Psychological Development in Health and Disease, 1962 (transl. into German, Japanese, Italian), (with W.L. Morgan) The Clinical Approach to the Patient, 1969 (transl. into Spanish, Italian and German), Interviewing the Patient, 1973; mem., former mem. editorial bd. Advances in Psychosomatic Medicine, Family Systesms Med., Jour. AMA, 1973-77, Jour. Psychiat. Research, Perspectives in Biology and Medicine, Psychoanalysis and Contemporary Thought, Psychosomatic Medicine; assoc. editor. Cin. Jour. Medicine; contbr. over 300 articles on psychosomatic medicine, internal medicine, EEG, clin. neurology, psychiatry, psychoanalysis, human devel. and med. edn. to profl. publs. Recipient Jacobi medal Mt. Sinai Hosp. and Med. Sch. Alumni Assn., 1972, gold medal U. Rochester Med. Ctr. Alumni Assn., 1972, student senate citation U. Rochester Sch. Medicine and Dentistry, 1983, exec. com. resolution, 1983, Albion O. bernstein Med. award Med. Soc. State of N.Y., 1989. Fellow AAAS; mem. Inst. Medicine NAS (sr.), Am. Coll. Psychoanalysts (charter), Am. Psychiat. Assn. (life; Vestermark award 1979, Presdl. citation 1988), Am. Psychoanalytic Assn., Am. Psychopathol. Assn., Am. Psychosomatic Soc. (pres. 1954), Am. Soc. for Clin. Investigation (emeritus), Assn. Am. Physicians, Chgo. Psychoanlytic Soc., Cin. Acad. Medicine, Internat. Soc. for Psychosomatic Medicine (founding mem.), N.Y. Acad. Scis., Rochester Acad. Medicine (award of merit 1976, Albert David Kaiser award 1988), Soc. Psychosomatic Research (London) (hon.), Western N.Y. Psychoanalytic Soc. (pres. 1969-71), Arbeitsgemeinschaft für Bio-Psycho-Sociale Medezin (Switzerland; hon.). Home: Rochester, NY. Died Nov. 26, 1999.

ENGLISH, JOHN F. lawyer; b. Bklyn., Apr. 21, 1926; s. Thomas and Anne E. (Daley) English; m. Regina Schneider, 1979; 1 child, Danette. BA, Iona Coll., 1952; JD, Fordham U., 1955. Ptnr. Suozzi, English & Klein, P.C., Mineola, NY, from 1961. Mem. Dem. Nat. Com., 1968—72, gen. counsel, 1972—73; sec. Nassau County (N.Y.) Dem. Com., 1953, chmn. com., 1958—69. With USN, 1943—47. Recipient Disting. Svc. award, LI Daily Press, 1963. Mem.: NCCJ, Nassau County Bar Assn., United Cerebral Palsy LI, Friends of Mercy Hosp., Legal Aid Soc. Nassau County. Roman Catholic. Died 1987.

ENNIS, HALLIE JANE, ambulatory services administrator; b. Chelsea, Okla., Oct. 19, 1937; d. Kenneth Arden and Josephine (Williams) Atkins; m. David P. Ennis, Sept. 12, 1966. G.N., St. John's, Tulsa, 1958. Head nurse ICU Physician's Hosp., Plattsburgh, N.Y., 1964-66; head nurse post anesthesia care unit Bapt. Med. Ctr., Oklahoma City, 1966-74, head nurse anesthesia, post anesthesia care unit, ASU, 1974-80, dir. surg. svcs., 1980-90, exec. assoc. ambulatory svcs., from 1990. Contbr. articles to profl. publs. 1st lt. USAF, 1962-64. Named Outstanding Woman of Okla., Bus. and Profl. Women, Okla., 1982. Mem. Okla. Soc. Post Anesthesia Nurses (pres. 1974-76, Award of Merit 1985), Am. Soc. Post Anesthesia Nurses (founding dir. 1980—, pres. 1981-82), Am. Bd. Post Anesthesia Nurse Certification (pres. 1983-87), Am. Orgn. Nurse Execs., A.O.R.N. Avocations: reading, golf, travel. Home: Oklahoma City, Okla. Died Feb. 9, 2002.

ENSMINGER, AUDREY HELEN, writer, publishing company executive; b. Winnipeg, Manitoba, Can., Dec. 30, 1919; d. Ernest William and Helen Myra (Greaves) Watts; m. M.E. Ensminger,June 11, 1941; children: John Jacob, Janet Aileen (dec.). BSc, U. Manitoba, 1940; attended, U. Minn., Twin Cities, 1940-41; MSc, Wash. State U., 1943. Dietitian Wash. State U., Pullman, 1944-46; v.p. Ensminger Pub. Co., Pegus Press, Inc. Trustee Agrisvcs. Found., Clovis, Calif., 1962—. Co-author: China: The Impossible Dream, 1973; sr. author: Foods and Nutrition Encyclopedia, 1994; author: The Concise Encyclopedia of Food and Nutrition, 1995. Recipient Humanitarian award Acad. Dentistry Internat., 1987, Disting. Svc. award AMA, 1993, Hon. Mention Am. Med. Writer's Assn., 1995; Marion Eugene Ensminger and Audrey Helen Ensminger Internat. Rm. dedicated Iowa State U., 1998, M.E. and Audrey H. Ensminger Pavilion dedicated at Wash. State U., 2003. Republican. Avocation: music. Home: Sun City, Ariz. Died Jan. 28, 2004.

EPSTEIN, HERBERT M. anesthesiologist, retired educator; b. Newburgh, N.Y., Jan. 21, 1925; s. Charles and Rose (Shafer) E.; m. Sylvia Epstein, Sept. 7, 1947; children: Susan Gersh, Peter. MD, U. Rochester, 1949. Diplomate Am. Bd. Anesthesiology. Intern Grace-New Haven Cmty. Hosp., 1949-50; resident in anesthesiology Hartford (Conn.) Hosp., 1952-54; attending anesthesiologist Evanston (Ill.) Hosp., 1954-96, chmn. dept. anesthesiology, 1970-90, pres. profl. staff, 1987, emeritus anesthesiologist. Prof. emeritus anesthesiology Northwestern U. Med. Sch., Chgo.; cons. exec. svc. corp. Chgo., 1996—. Bd. dirs. Evanston Hosp., 1985, 95. Lt. M.C. USNR, 1950-52. Fellow Am. Coll. Anesthesiology; mem. AMA, Am. Soc. Anesthesiologists, Exec. Svc. Club (Chgo.), Yale Club. Home: Glencoe, Ill. Died Sept. 25, 2000.

ERB, RONALD LOUIS, data processing executive; b. Rapid City, S.D.., May 12, 1935; s. William David Louis and Lydia (Reiman) E.; m. Nelda Mae Nichtern, Nov. 30, 1957 (div. Jan. 1985); children: Scott David, Ronnell Rae, Kerry Lynn. Computer operator Twin City Fed. Savs. and Loan Assn., Mpls., 1957-60; mgr. data processing Data Inc., Sioux Falls, 1960-62, v.p., 1963-66, pres. Sioux City, Iowa, from 1966, Mid Am. Computer Service and Supply Inc., Sioux Falls, from 1975, Wager Pro, Inc., Sioux Falls, from 1989. Served with U.S. Navy, 1955-57. Home: Sioux Falls, SD. Deceased.

ERICSON, HAROLD LOUIS, communications executive; b. Hector, Minn., Dec. 11, 1909; s. Alfred Louis and Mabel (Grover) E.; m. Ella Louise Benson, Aug. 6, 1931 (div. 1968); children: Charles, James, Rolfe; m. Lillian Leiferman, June 5, 1968. BA, Cornell Coll., Mt. Vernon, Iowa, 1936. Pres. Minn. Ctrl. Telephone Co., Hector, 1952-68, N.Am. Commun. Corp., Mpls., 1968-70, Frontier Telephone Co., Mpls., 1970-73, Cencom Corp., Rushford, Minn., 1973-75, chmn. bd., 1975-77; pres. Hecto Co., Castle Rock, Minn., from 1970, Futures Found., Castle Rock, from 1980. Cons. telephone engr., 1955-75. Author: Handbook for Survival, 1989; co-author: Principles of Noise Control in Aircraft, 1945. Mem. Acoustical Soc. Am., Rotary (pres. 1992-93). Achievements include patent for instrument for gliders. Home: Castle Rock, Minn. Deceased.

ERIVIN, ELVIA MAYE, elementary school educator; b. Okmulgee, Okla., Oct. 7, 1935; d. Homer Jr. and Mary Ellen (Dixon) Morgan; m. John Bruce Erivin, May 31, 1958; children: Anita Mignon, Jonathan Boris. BS, Langston (Okla.) U., 1958; MS, Ft. Hays State U., Hays, Kans., 1989. Cert. tchr., elem. adminstr., Okla., Kans. With dietary dept. U. Okla. Med. Ctr., Oklahoma City, 1959-61; tchr. Anadarko (Okla.) Pub. Schs., 1964-70, Unified Sch. Dist. 480, Liberal, Kans., from 1971. Tutor Seward County Community Coll., Liberal, 1986—. Vice pres. Action Against Drugs, Liberal, 1989—. Recipient edn. svc. award Coun. for Progressive Action, Liberal, 1985; Johnson O'Malley grantee Anadarko Pub. Schs., 1967. Mem. NEA, Nat. Assn. for Edn. Young Children, Kans. Assn. for Edn. Young Children, Liberal Edn. Assn. (meeeting and conf. team 1987-89, cert. of appreciation 1989), AAUW (chmn. women issues and women's work/women's worth Liberal 1987—, cert. of appreciation 1989), Washington Sch. PTA (life). Democrat. Baptist. Avocations: cooking, sewing, hiking, boating, fishing. Home: Liberal, Kans. Died Jan. 19, 2002.

ERNSBERGER, FRED MARTIN, retired materials scientist; b. Ada, Ohio, Sept. 20, 1919; 4 children. AB, Ohio Northern U., 1941; PhD in Phys. Chemistry, Ohio State U., 1946. Shift foreman WYE Beta Lab, Oak Ridge, Tenn., 1944-45; rsch. chemist U.S. Naval Ordnance Test Sta., 1947-54, S.W. Rsch. Inst., San Antonio, Tex., 1954-56,

Mellon Inst. of Indsl. Rsch., 1957; rsch. chemist Glass Rsch. Ctr. PPG Industries, Inc., 1958-82; ret., 1982. Adj. prof. dept. material sci. and engring. U. Fla., Gainesville, 1982—; Teltech cons., 1982-2001. Recipient IR-100 award, 1981, Scholes award, 1989. Fellow Am. Ceramic Soc. (Frank Forrest award 1964, Toledo Glass and Ceramic award 1970, G.W. Morey award 1974, Albert Victor Bleininger award 1993); mem. Am. Chem. Soc., Am. Ceramic Soc. Achievements include research in surface chemistry, surface structure, mechanical properties of glass and glass-ceramics, chemistry of float glass. Died Jan. 5, 2003.

ERSLEV, ALLAN JACOB, physician, educator; b. Copenhagen, Apr. 20, 1919; came to U.S., 1946, naturalized, 1949; s. Aage Holger and Anina (Henriques) E.; m. Elisabeth Curtis Lewis, Dec. 21, 1947; children: Wendy, Carole Elisa, Eric Allan, Barbara Kim. MD, U. Copenhagen, 1945; DSc (honoris causa), Jefferson Med. Coll., 1989. Intern Copenhagen County Hosp., 1945-46; research fellow Meml. Hosp., Sloan Kettering Found., N.Y.C., 1946-48; intern, resident, research fellow Yale Sch. Medicine, 1948-53; assoc., asst. prof. medicine Thorndike Lab., Harvard Med. Sch., 1955-59; assoc. prof. medicine Jefferson Med. Coll., Phila., 1959-63, Cardeza research prof., dir. Cardeza Found., 1963-85, Disting. prof., 1985-89, Disting. prof. emeritus, 1989—2003, vice chmn. for rsch. dept. internal medicine, 1992-93. Served as lt. Danish Army, 1943-45, as capt. U.S. Army, 1953-55 Recipient Hagedorn award Denmark 1991; Damon Runyon fellow, 1951-52; Guggenheim fellow, 1967-68 Mem. Am. Soc. Hematology, Internat. Soc. Hematology, Assn. Am. Physicians, Am. Soc. Clin. Investigation, Interurban Clin. Club Spl. research in control of red cell prodn. Home: Haverford, Pa. Died Nov. 12, 2003.

ESGRO, JOSEPH JOHN, surgeon; b. New Brunswick, N.J., Sept. 22, 1957; MD, U. Medicine and Dentistry N.J., Newark, 1983. Diplomate Am. Bd. Surgery. Resident in gen. surgery Maine Med. Ctr., Portland, 1983-88; fellow in surg. oncology M.D. Anderson Cancer Ctr., Houston, 1988-90; staff Orlando (Fla.) Regional Med. Ctr. Mem. ACS, AMA, Soc. Am. Gastrointestinal Endoscopic Surgeons, Soc. Surg. Oncology. Home: Orlando, Fla. Died Nov. 14, 1999.

ESPELAGE, HOWARD JOHN, retired police chief; b. Cin., June 14, 1929; s. Frank and Erma M. (Woefle) E.; m. Joan F. Espelage, May 2, 1953; children: David, Terry, Sandra. BS in Criminal Justice magna cum laude, U. Cin., 1974. Police capt. City of Cin. Police Dept., 1952-82; asst. police chief Green Twp., Cin., 1982-87; police chief City of Loveland, Ohio, 1988-95. With USN, 1946-49, 50-51. Fellow FOP; mem. VFW. Avocations: fishing, boating, hunting. Home: Cincinnati, Ohio. Died Feb. 4, 2002.

ESPY, WILLARD RICHARDSON, author; b. Olympia, Wash., Dec. 11, 1910; s. Harry Albert and Helen Medora (Richardson) E.; m. Ann A. Hathaway, 1933; 1 child, Ian Alden; m. Hilda S. Cole, 1940; children: Mona Margaret, Freddy Medora, Joanna Page, Cassin Richardson, Jefferson Taylor (dec.); m. Louise J. Manheim, 1962. BA, U. Redlands, 1930; student, U. Paris, Sorbonne, 1930-31. Reporter Tulare (Calif.) Times, 1932, Brawley (Calif.) News, 1932; asst. editor World Tomorrow, N.Y.C., 1933-35; copy editor L'Agence Havas, 1937-40; mgr. promotion and pub. rels. Reader's Digest, 1941-57; producer, interviewer radio program Personalities in Print, 1957-58; creative advt. dir. Famous Artists Schs., 1958-63; publisher Charter Books, 1963-66; pub. relations cons. N.Y.C., 1963-75; panelist Harper Dict. Contemporary Usage, 1976, 83. Contbg. editor: Harvard Mag, 1978-85, Writer's Digest, 1985-92; author: Bold New Program, 1951, The Game of Words, 1972, An Almanac of Words at Play, 1975, Oysterville: Roads to Grandpa's Village, 1977, The Life and Works of Mr. Anonymous, 1977, O Thou Improper, Thou Uncommon Noun, 1978, Say It My Way, 1980, Another Almanac of Words at Play, 1980, Have a Word on Me, 1981, Espygrams, 1982, A Children's Almanac of Words at Play, 1982, Word Puzzles, 1983, The Garden of Eloquence, 1983, Words to Rhyme With, 1986, The Word's Gotten Out, 1989, Omak Me Yours Tonight, 1993, Skulduggery on Shoalwater Bay, 1998, A New Almanac of Words at Play, 1999; contbr. articles to periodicals. Recipient Gov.'s award for contbn. to cultural life of Wash., 1973, 76; Capt. Robert Gray medal Wash. State Hist. Soc., 1979 Mem. PEN, Nat. Book Critics' Circle, Authors Guild. Clubs: Century Assn., Dutch Treat, Book Table, Coffee House (N.Y.C.). Home: New York, NY. Died Feb. 25, 1999.

ESTES, JOSEPH RICHARD, pastor; b. Louisville, Apr. 24, 1925; s. Emmet Floyd and Anna Grace (Harman) E.; m. Helen Frances Trout, June 3, 1948; children: Ann Katherine, Joseph R. Jr., David Timothy, Mark Allen, J. Philip. BA, Georgetown Coll., 1948; BD, So. Bapt. Sem., 1951, PhD, 1957; postgrad., U. Basel, U. Zurich, Switzerland, 1960-63. Ordained to ministry, Bapt. Ch., 1946. Instr. So. Bapt. Theol. Sem., Louisville, 1952-57; pastor 1st Bapt. Ch., Bowling Green, Ky., 1956-60; prof. Bapt. Theol. Sem., Zurich, 1960-63, Ky. So. Coll. (now U. Louisville), 1963-65; dept. dir. Home Mission Bd., So. Bapt. Conv., Atlanta, 1965-70; pastor 1st Bapt. Ch., DeLand, Fla., 1970-76; prof. Spanish Bapt. Sem., Madrid, 1976-77; pastor Emmanuel Ch., Madrid, 1976-77, Beechwood Bapt. Ch., Louisville, from 1977. Bd. dirs. Ky. Bapt. Conv., Middletown, 1956-60. Author: The Christian in the World, 1970; author booklets on world religions. Counsellor Boy Scouts Am., Crestwood, Ky., 1953-56; bd. dirs. Girls Clubs Am., Bowling Green, 1956-60; pres. Civitan Club Louisville, 1979-80, bd. dirs., 1980-84. 2d lt. USAAF, 1944-45. Mem. Masons, Scottish Rite. Democrat. Avocations: golf, travel, reading. Home: Warsaw, Ky. Died Mar. 14, 1999.

ESTES, JOSEPH WORTH, physician, medical history educator; b. Lexington, Ky., May 10, 1934; s. Joseph Alvie and Betsy (Worth) E.; m. Cynthia Waggoner, June 20, 1959. AB, Harvard U., 1955; MA, Boston U., 1963, MD, 1964. Intern Mass. Gen. Hosp., Boston, 1964-65; fellow Univ. Hosp., Boston, 1965-66, Hosp. for Sick Children, London, 1966-67; asst. prof. Sch. of Medicine Boston U., 1967-72, assoc. prof. Sch. of Medicine, 1972-81, prof. history of pharmacology Sch. of Medicine, from 1981. Author: Hall Jackson & The Purple Foxglove, 1979, The Medical Skills of Ancient Egypt, 1989, Dictionary of Protopharmacology, 1990, (with others) The Changing Humors of Portsmouth, 1986; co-editor: Medicine in Colonial Massachusetts, 1620-1820, 1980. Pres. Mass. Libr. Trustees Assn., 1973-77; vice chair Mass. Gov.'s Conf. on Librs., 1973-81. With U.S. Army, 1955-57, CBI. Mem. Am. Assn. for the History of Medicine (sec., treas. 1989—). Home: Westwood, Mass. Died Oct. 22, 2000.

ESTKA BERDING, JEAN THERESA, fund raiser; b. Chgo., Dec. 18, 1923; d. Joseph and Clementine (Pielaszkiewicz) Estka. Grad. high sch., Chgo. Rivetor Lockheed, Calif., 1944; field rep. Fund Raiser Meml. for Women in Mil. Svc. of Am., Washington, from 1988. Good will amb. Munich, Fed. Republic of Germany, 1965, hosp. vol. VA Hosp. Hines, Maywood, Ill., 1963-66, With U.S. Army M.C., 1944-45. Beautification award Skokie (Ill.) C. of C., 1987. Mem. VFW (bd. dirs. #3854 1963-66), Lincolnwood Lang. Bank (translator 1988—), Real Fussball Club. Roman Catholic. Avocations: travel, gardening, language, archery, reading. Home: Skokie, Ill. Deceased.

ESTLE, THOMAS LEO, physicist, researcher; b. Columbus Junction, Iowa, Jan. 8, 1931; s. Vincent Lambert and Ruby Jean (O'Neill) E.; m. Arlene Ruth Poggemiller, Oct. 10, 1953; children: Mark David, Ann Elizabeth, Laura Kay, Karen Ruth. BA, Rice Inst. (now U.), 1953; MS, U. Ill., 1954, PhD, 1957. Mem. tech. staff Tex. Instruments, Inc., Dallas, 1958-62, br. mgr., 1962-66, sr. rsch. physicist, 1966-67; physics dept. chair Rice U., Houston, 1982-86, prof. physics, 1967-96, prof. emeritus, from 1996. Chair solid state physics and material sci. com. Los Alamos Meson Physics Facility, 1978-80; mem. subcom. on Muon Sources, Nat. Rsch. Coun., 1982-84. Author: The Physical Principles of Electron Paramagnetic Resonance, 1973, Quantum States of Atoms, Molecules and Solids, 1976, Understanding More Quantum Physics, 1991, (with others) Hydrogen in Semiconductors, 1991, Optical Properties of Ions in Solids, 1975; contbr. articles to profl. jours. Rsch. grantee NSF, 1969-99, Robert A. Welch Found., 1981-95, Rsch. Corp., 1980. Fellow: Am. Phys. Soc. Achievements include research on solid state physics. Home: Houston, Tex. Died Aug. 18, 2002.

ETHEREDGE, FOREST DEROYCE, former state senator, former university administrator; b. Dallas, Oct. 21, 1929; s. Gilbert Wybert and Theta Erlene (Tate) E.; m. Joan Mary Horan, Apr. 30, 1955; children: Forest William, John Bede, Mary Faith, Brian Thomas, Regina Ann. BS, Va. Poly. Inst. and State U., 1951; MS, U. Ill., 1953; postgrad., Northwestern U., 1953-55; PhD, Loyola U., Chgo., 1968. Mem. faculty City Colls. Chgo., 1955-65, chmn. phys. sci. dept., 1963-65; dean instrn. Rock Valley Coll., 1965-67, v.p., 1966-67; pres. McHenry County Coll., 1967-70, Waubonsee Community Coll., 1970-81; Ill. state senator Ill. State Senate, 1981-93, higher edn. com., 1981-91, mem. intergovtl. coop. commn., 1982-91, co-chmn. legis. info. system, 1983-93, minority spokesman appropriations I com., 1986-93; prof. pub. adminstrn. Aurora (Ill.) U., 1991-2001, dean Sch. of Bus. and Profl. Studies, 1994-99, dean emeritus, from 1999. Author: School Boards and the Ballot Box, 1989. Bd. dirs. Ill. Math. and Sci. Acad. Mem.: Rotary (pres. Aurora chpt. 1978-79). Republican. Roman Catholic. Home: Aurora, Ill. Died June 26, 2004.

ETIM, BARBARA ANN, English educator; b. Dec. 23, 1942; d. Daniel and Hazel Mae (Quaintance) Craig; divorced; children: Ann, Jennifer, Linda. BS in Edn., U. Wis., Milw., 1971. Postal clk. U.S. Post Office, Milw., 1964-66; English tchr. Milw. Pub. Schs., from 1971. Tutor Laubach Literacy Ctr., Milw., 1980; Sunday sch. tchr. St. Nicholas Ch., Milw., 1980, 91. Mem. Nat. Coun. Tchrs. of English. Roman Catholic. Home: Milwaukee, Wis. Deceased.

ETKIND, EFIM GRIGORIEVICH, educator, author; b. St. Petersburg, Russia, Feb. 26, 1918; s. Grigori Etkind and Polina Spivak; m. Katherine Zvorykina, 1940; 2 children; m. Elke Liebs, 1994. Cand. Philol.Sc., Leningrad. U., 1947, D of Philol. Scis., 1965; Docteur d'Etat, Sorbonne, U. Paris, 1975; Dr honoris causa, U. Geneva, 1999. Tchr. Faculty Romance Langs. Leningrad Pedagogical Inst., 1952-74. Degrees and title of prof. removed, expelled from USSR Union of Writers for def. of various poets, 1974; left USSR, 1974; now mem. faculty U. de Paris X, 1986, prof. emeritus, 1986-92; prof. univs. Geneva, Lausanne, Venezia, Cologne, Jerusalem, Helsinki, Harvard, Eugene, Oreg., Columbus, Ohio, Barcelona, Spain, Praha, Middlebury Coll., Vienna, Russian Sch. Norwich, U. Vt. Author: Poetry and Translation, 1963, Bertolt Brecht, 1971, Russian Poet-Translators from Trediakovsky to Pushkin, 1973, The Substance of Verse and the Problems of the Theory of Translation, 1974, Notes of a non-Conspirator, 1977, Form as Content, 1977, Un art en crise (Essai d'une poétique de la traduction poétique), 1981, Poésie Russe, Anthology 18th-20th Centuries, 1983, Russische Lyrik von der Oktoberrevolution bis zur Gegenwart, Versuch einer Darstellung, 1985, Symmetry in the Poems of Pushkin, 1988, 323 Epigrams of Soviet-Russia, 1988, Inside (about Russian poetry of 20th century), 1996, The Interior Person and the Exterior Speaking (about the Russian novel), 1997; translator: The Little Freedom (transls. German poetry of 5 centuries) (E. Etkind), 1998. Served with Soviet Army, World War II. Decorated chevalier Palmes Académiques (France); fellow Wissenschaftskolleg Zu Berlin, 1996-97. Mem. Bavarian Acad. Fine Arts (corr.), Acad. Sci. and Lit. Mainz (corr.), German Acad. Lang. and Poetry (corr.), Acad. Human Scis. (St. Petersburg). Home: Puteaux, France. Died Nov. 2, 1999.

ETTER, RUSSELL FORREST, artist, retired; b. Grosse Pointe, Mich., Aug. 15, 1933; s. Forrest James and Margaret Susanna (Motznik) E. BFA, Wayne State U., 1955. Graphic artist Macmillan Co., N.Y.C., 1957-58; editl. layout artist Am. Craft Coun., N.Y.C., 1958-60, 66; asst. to pres. Aaron Burns Inc., N.Y.C., 1960-65; art dir. McGraw-Hill, N.Y.C., 1966-72; graphic designer Arnold Saks Assocs., N.Y.C., 1972-95. Avocation: travel. Home: Poughquag, NY. Died May 15, 2002.

ETTINGER, MORT, marketing educator; b. Chelsea, Mass., May 6, 1924; s. Louis Edward and Rose (Rosnitsky) E.; m. Charlotte Kahn, Nov. 12, 1950; children: Linda Joyce (dec.), Steven Alan, Jonathan Mark. BA, U. Maine, 1949; MS in Retailing, NYU, 1950. V.p. sales Ship n' Shore, Aston, Pa., 1972-77, sr. v.p. internat., 1977-78; sr. v.p. Ship'n Shore, Aston, Pa., 1978-80; v.p. J.G. Hook, Phila., 1980-82; pres. Ettinger Enterprises, Lynn, Mass., 1982-86; prof. Suffolk U., Boston, 1986-87, Salem (Mass.) State Coll., 1986-99, chairperson mktg. dept., 1987-97. Pres. The Exec. Woman, The Boston Collection. Mem. Dem. Town Com., Marblehead, Mass., 1987-99; hon. ambassador-at-large Govt. of Guam. With USN, 1943-46, PTO. Fellow Acad. Mktg. Sci.; mem. Am. Collegiate Retailing Assn., Am. Mktg. Assn. (exec. v.p. Boston chpt. 1994-95), World Comm. Assn., Sr. Exec. Inner Cir. (all coll. com. 1994-96, 97-99), VFW, Masons, Shriners, Alpha Mu Alpha, Mu Kappa Tau, Delta Mu Delta (hon.). Democrat. Jewish. Home: Wellesley Hls, Mass. Died Feb. 23, 1999.

ETZWILER, DONNELL DENCIL, pediatrician, researcher; b. Mansfield, Ohio, Mar. 29, 1927; s. Donnell Seymour and Berniece Jean (Meek) Etzwiler; m. Helen Brown Beard, Mar. 3, 1989; children from previous marriage: Nancy, Lisa, Diane, David. BA cum laude, Ind. U., 1950; MD, Yale U., 1953. Intern dept. pediat. Sch. Medicine Yale U., New Haven, 1953—54; resident dept. pediat. N.Y. Hosp. Cornell Med. Sch., N.Y.C., 1954—55, instr. pediat. N.Y. Hosp., 1956—57; mem. faculty Clin. Inst. Med. Sch. U. Minn., Mpls., 1957—74, clin. instr., asst. clin. prof. pediat., 1974—84, clin. prof. dept. pediat., 1985—99, clin. prof. dept. family practice and cmty. medicine, 1990—99, clin. prof. emeritus pediat. and family practice, from 1999; pediatrician Park-Nicollet Med. Ctr., 1957—96; founder, pres., chief med. officer Internat. Diabetes Ctr., 1967—96, pres. emeritus, from 1996. Instr. Project Hope, Trujillo, Peru, 1962; mem. Nat. Commn. on Diabetes, 1975—77; chmn. WHO Collaborating Ctr. for Diabetes, 1988—94; dir. WHO Diabetes Collaborating Ctr. in Diabetes Edn., Transl. & Computer Tech., chmn., from 1988; co-dir. Internat. Diabetes Programme, Russia, 1994; mem. exec. com. Compass Project, 1988—96, pres., 1998—2000. Author: Education and Management of the Patient with Diabetes Mellitus, 1967, 3d edit.; editor: Learning to Live With Diabetes (in Russian), 1985, 2d edit., 1991; co-editor: Staged Diabetes Management, 1992, 2000, Manyo de la Diabetes por Elapas, 2000; contbr. articles to profl. jours. Chmn. Med. and Sci. adv. bd., 1998—99; bd. dirs., pres. Compass Project, from 1998; bd. dirs. Minn. Soc. for the Blind, 1977—85, Diabetes Edn. and Rsch. Found., 1985—88, Chronimed, 1988—98. With USNR, WWII. Recipient Good Neighbor award, Sta. WCCO, 1977, 1985, Park Nicollet Med. Ctr. Cmty. award, 1987, Park Nicollet Med. Found. Rsch. award, 1991, Educator award, 1993, Cir. of Leadership award, Am. Diabetes Assn., 1997, Shotwell award, 2000; fellow, NIH, 1955—56. Fellow: All India Inst. Diabetes; mem.: AMA, European Assn. for Study of Diabetes, Internat. Soc. Pediat. and Adolescent Diabetes, Minn. Med. Assn., Am. Acad. Pediat., Inst. Medicine of NAS (med. dir. Minn. affiliate 1959—84, bd. dirs.), Am. Assn. Diabetes Educators (hon.), Am. Dietetic Assn. (hon.; pres. 1976—77, Disting. Svc. Youth award 1976, Banting medal 1977, Becton-Dickinson award 1978, Upjohn Educator award 1983, Med. Alley Honor award 1988, Russian award for peace 1994), Am. Pub. Health Assn., Am. Group Practice Assn., Soc. Pub. Health Educators, Internat. Diabetes Fedn. (v.p. 1976—85, exec. com. 1978—85, dir. 1978—85, bd. mgmt. 1978—85, chmn. internat. com. juvenile diabetes 1978—85). Congregationalist. Home: Minneapolis, Minn. Deceased.

EULAU, HEINZ, political scientist, educator; b. Offenbach, Germany, Oct. 14, 1915; s. Arthur and Martha (Spier) E.; m. Cleo Mishkin, June 8, 1946; children— Lauren, Peter. AB, U. Calif. at Berkeley, 1937, MA, 1938, PhD, 1941. Research asso. Library of Congress, 1941-42; sr. analyst Spl. War Policies Unit, Dept. Justice, 1942-44; asst. editor New Republic, 1944-47; from asst. prof. to prof. Antioch Coll., 1947-57; prof. polit. sci. Stanford U., 1958-86, William Bennett Munro prof., 1973-86, prof. emeritus, 1986—2004. Vis. legis. research prof. U. Calif. at Berkeley, 1961-62; vis. prof. Inst. Advanced Studies, Vienna, Austria, 1964-65; vis. prof. Erasmus U., Rotterdam, Netherlands, 1985; mem. behavioral sci. div. NRC, 1969-73; bd. overseers, chmn. Nat. Election Studies, 1977-84; former assoc. dir. Inter-Univ.

Consortium for Polit. and Social Research. Author: Class and Party in the Eisenhower Years, 1962, The Legislative System, 1962, Journeys in Politics, 1963, The Behavioral Persuasion in Politics, 1963, Micro-Macro Political Analysis, 1969, Labyrinths of Democracy, 1973, Technology and Civility, 1977, The Politics of Representation, 1978, Politics, Self, and Society, 1986, Crossroads of Social Science, 1989, Micro-Macro Dilemmas in Political Science, 1996, The Politics of Academic Culture, 1998. Fund Advancement Edn. fellow, 1951-52; Center Advanced Study Behavioral Scis. fellow, 1957-58; Guggenheim Found. fellow, 1979-80 Fellow AAAS, Am. Acad. Arts and Scis.; mem. Am. Polit. Sci. Assn. (pres. 1971-72) Home: Palo Alto, Calif. Died Jan. 18, 2004.

EULE, JULIAN NATHAN, law educator; b. Kew Gardens, N.Y., Sept. 23, 1949; s. Leo Eule and Hanna (Gruenbaum) Minkin; m. Carole Lynn Rubin, Aug. 8, 1971; children: Lisa, Brian. BA, SUNY, Stony Brook, 1970; JD, Cornell U., 1973; LLM, Harvard U., 1977. Bar: N.Y. 1974, U.S. Ct. Appeals (2d cir.) 1974, U.S. Supreme Ct. 1977, U.S. Ct. Appeals (3d cir.) 1980, Pa. 1981, U.S. Ct. Appeals (9th and D.C. cirs.) 1984. Assoc. Shearman & Sterling, N.Y.C., 1973-74; law clk. U.S. Dist. Ct. (so. dist.) N.Y., 1974; spl. legal counsel Gov. of Conn., Hartford, 1974-75; law clk. U.S. Ct. Appeals (2d cir.), N.Y.C., 1975-76; asst. prof. law Temple U., Phila., 1977-80, assoc. prof., 1980-82, prof. law, 1982-84, counsel to dean Law Sch., 1983-84; prof. law UCLA, from 1984, assoc. dean, 1992-95. Vis. prof. Hebrew U., Jerusalem, 1977. Mem. gov.'s task force on off-shore oil State of Conn., 1974; hearing examiner EEOC, Washington, 1979-80, Pa. Bd. Med. and Edn. Licensure, 1980-82; cons. Calif. Com. Bar Examiners, San Francisco, 1985. Mem. Order of Coif. Deceased.

EVANS, DONALD LEROY, real estate company executive; b. Madison, Wis., Apr. 22, 1933; s. LeRoy E. and Pearl U. Evans. BS, U. Wis., 1959, MS, 1964. Staff appraiser Am. Appraisal Group, Milw., 1959-64; founder, chmn. D.L. Evans, Inc., Madison, from 1964. Co-founder U. Wis. Real Estate Alumni Assn., 1979. Dir. U. Wis. Found.; trustee U. Wis. Rsch. Park. Gunnery sgt. U.S. Army, 1953-55, Korea. Mem. Am. Soc. Appraisers (sr.; pres. 1968; Appreciation award 1968), Am. Soc. Real Estate Counselors, Am. Inst. Real Estate Appraisers (pres. 1972; Appreciation award 1972), Madison Bd. Realtors (bd. dirs. 1974-76; Appreciation award 1976). Lodges: Rotary. Republican. Lutheran. Home: Madison, Wis. Died Sept. 28, 2000.

EVANS, EARL ALISON, JR., retired biochemist; b. Balt., Mar. 11, 1910; s. Earl Alison and Florence (Lewis) E.; 1 adopted child, David Lasswell. Student, Balt. Poly. Inst., 1922-26; B.Sc., Johns Hopkins, 1931; PhD, Columbia, 1936. Research asst. pharmacology Johns Hopkins Med. Sch., 1931-32, asst. lab. endocrine research, 1932-34, univ. fellow biochemistry Columbia, 1934-36; instr. biochemistry U. Chgo., 1937-39, asst. prof., 1939-41, asso. prof. biochemistry, acting chmn. dept., 1941-42; on leave, 1947-48; prof., 1942—; chmn. dept. biochemistry 1942-72. Fellow Rockefeller Found. U. Sheffield, Eng., 1939-40; chief sci. officer Am. embassy, London, 1947-48; del. Vatican Acad. Sci., 1948; cons. to sec. state, 1951-53; mem. bd. sci. counselors Nat. Inst. Arthritis and Metabolic Diseases, NIH, 1960-63; mem. div. med. scis. NRC, 1962-65; chmn. postdoctoral fellowships Nat. Acad. Sci.-NRC, 1963-65; mem. divisional com. biol. and med. scis. NSF, 1963-66; Harvey Soc. lectureship, 1942; nat. lectureship Am. Chem. Soc., 1945; Pan Am. lectureship, 1948. Author: Biochemistry of Bacterial Viruses, 1952, (with others) Biological Symposia V, 1941, Symposium on Respiratory Enzymes, 1942; Editor: (with others) Biological Action of the Vitamins, 1942; Contbr. (with others) articles to sci. jours. Adv. bd. Am. Found. Continuing Edn. Fellow All Souls Coll., Oxford U., 1969; Fellow Pierpont Morgan Library; Soc. Scholars Johns Hopkins U.; Recipient Gold Key U. Chgo. Sch. Medicine Alumni Assn. Fellow AAAS; mem. Am. Chem. Soc. (Eli Lilly prize in biol. chemistry 1942), Am. Soc. Biol. Chemists (treas. 1943-44), Biochem. Soc. (Gt. Britain), Am. Soc. Bacteriologists, Asociacion Quimica Argentina, Sigma Xi, Tau Beta Pi. Clubs: Univ. (Chgo.), Racquet (Chgo.); Travellers (London). Episcopalian. Home: Chicago, Ill. Deceased.

EVANS, FRANCIS COPE, retired ecologist; b. Phila., Dec. 2, 1914; s. Edward Wyatt and Jacqueline Pascal (Morris) E.; m. Rachel Worthington Brooks, June 12, 1942; children—Kenneth Richardson, Katharine Cope, Edward Wyatt II, Rachel Howe. BS, Haverford Coll., 1936; D.Phil. (Rhodes scholar), Oxford U., 1939; Claypole fellow, U. Calif., Berkeley, 1939-40. Research asst. Hooper Found., San Francisco, 1939-41; jr. zoologist U. Calif., Davis, 1941-43; instr., asst. prof. Haverford (Pa.) Coll., 1943-48, acting dean, 1944; asst. prof., assoc. prof. U. Mich., Ann Arbor, 1948-59, prof., assoc. dir. E.S. George Res., 1959-82, prof. emeritus, from 1982. Editor publs.: Mus. Zoology, Ann Arbor, 1968-78; Contbr. sci. articles to profl. jours. Recipient Painton award Cooper Ornithol. Soc., 1963; Guggenheim fellow, 1962-63; Erskine fellow U. Canterbury, Christchurch, N.Z., 1976-77 Fellow AAAS; mem. Ecol. Soc. Am. (pres. 1983, Disting. Service award 1987), Brit. Ecol. Soc., Am. Soc. Naturalists, Soc. for Study Evolution. Mem. Soc. Of Friends. Home: Ann Arbor, Mich. Died Aug. 16, 2002.

EVANS, JANE, marketing executive; b. Hannibal, Mo., July 26, 1944; d. L. Terrell Evans and Katherine (Rosser) Pierce; m. George Sheer, June 17, 1970; 1 child, Jonathan BA, Vanderbilt U., 1965; postgrad., L'Universite d'Aix Marseille. Pres. I. Miller, N.Y.C., 1970-73; v.p. internat. mktg. Genesco, N.Y.C., 1973-74; pres. Butterick Vogue Patterns, N.Y.C., 1974-77; v.p. adminstrn. and corp. devel. Fingerhut, Mpls., 1977-79; exec. v.p. fashion Gen. Mills, Inc., N.Y.C., 1979-84; pres., chief exec. officer Monet Jewelers, N.Y.C., 1984-87; gen. ptnr. Montgomery Consumer Fund, San Francisco, 1987-89; pres., chief exec. officer Inter Pacific Retail Group, San Francisco, 1989-91; former v.p., gen. mgr. Home and Personel Svcs.-US West, Phoenix; former COO Gamut Interactive; former CEO Opnix Internet Technologies. Bd. dir. Equitable Life Assurance Soc., Philip Morris, N.Y.C., Catalyst, N.Y.C., Edison Bros. Stores, Inc. Bd. dirs. Open Hand, San Francisco. Recipient award Women's Equity Action League, 1982; Entrepreneurial Woman award Women Bus. Owners N.Y.C., 1982; named Corp. Am.'s Top Woman Exec., Savvy Mag., 1983, Fin. Woman of Yr., Fin. Women's Assn., 1986; named one of Ten Most Wanted Mgrs., Fortune Mag., 1986. Mem. Young Pres. Orgn., Com. of 200, Fashion Group N.Y., Women's Forum, Fashion Inst. Tech. (bd. dirs.). Avocations: golf, tennis, gourmet cooking, piano. Home: Paradise Vly, Ariz. Died Nov. 16, 2003.

EVANS, JOHN F. lawyer; b. Athens, May 8, 1941; s. Raymond Louis Evans and Augusta (Farnham) Larson; m. Margaret Alice McClendon, July 10, 1957; children: Deborah Jean, John Clayton, Timothy Courtney. BA, U. N.C., 1964, LLB, 1966. Bar: N.C. 1966, D.C. 1968, Fla. 1977, U.S. Dist. Ct. (so. dist.) Fla. 1979, U.S. Dist. Ct. (no. dist.) Fla. 1980, U.S. Ct. Appeals (5th cir.) 1980, U.S. Ct. Appeals (11th cir.) 1984. Law clk. U.S. Dist. Ct. (ea. dist.), Clinton, N.C., 1966-68; asst. U.S. atty. D.C., Washington, 1968-75; spl. atty. U.S. Dept. Justice Miami (Fla.) Strike Force, 1975-79; ptnr. Zuckerman, Spaeder, Taylor & Evans, Miami, from 1979. Mem. ABA, Fed. Bar Assn. Deceased.

EVANS, ROGER LYNWOOD, scientist, patent liaison; b. Ipswich, Suffolk, Eng., June 25, 1928; came to U.S., 1953; s. Evelyn Jesse and Ethel Jane (Woods) E.; m. Jane Adelaide Baird, Nov. 24, 1954 (div. 1976); children: Robert Malcolm Baird, Roderick Lawrence Woods, Alison Clare; m. Wendy Dorothy Grove, Apr. 11, 1977. BA in Natural Sci., Oxford (Eng.) U., 1953, MA, 1955, DPhil in Natural Sci., 1958; MS in Inorganic Chemistry, U. Minn., 1955. With chem. and radiopharm. R & D dept. 3M Co., St. Paul., 1958-77, patent liaison, 1977-91; developer intellectual property initiative, tech. devel. dept., 1992-93; cons. 3M, 1993-99. Originator 3M Richard G. Drew Creativity Award, 1970, program cons., 1995—. Founder, editor Newsletter of the Tech. Forum, 1971-93; inventor, writer, producer series of videos on intellectual property topics. Mem., chmn. Mendota Heights Planning Commn., 1962-68, Sunfish Lake Planning Commn., 1968-84, Dakota County Planning Commn., Minn., 1965-72. 2d lt. Brit. Army, 1946-49, Eng. Anglican. Avocations: photography, amateur opera singer, travel, writing. Died Feb. 1, 2003.

EVERETT, CLIFTON WHITE, lawyer; b. Robersonville, N.C., Sept. 12, 1917; s. Ruben Samuel and Ruby Bell (Brown) E.; m. Marjorie Louise Whitehurst; children—Clifton White, Janet Everett Davis, Amy Everett Constantino. B.A. magna cum laude, Wake Forest U., 1938, J.D. magna cum laude, 1940. Bar: N.C. 1940, U.S. Dist. Ct. (ea. dist.) N.C. 1940. Sr. ptnr. Everett, Everett, Warren & Harper, Greenville, N.C.; dir., gen. counsel Home Fed. Savs. & Loan Assn. Ea. N.C., Greenville, 1978—. Mayor, Town of Bethel, N.C., 1955-61; chmn. bd. trustees Pitt Community Coll., 1978—; chmn. conf. bd. trustees N.C. Conf., United Methodist Ch., 1980-84. Mem. ABA (del.), Am. Counsel and Jud. Merit Selection Com., N.C. State Bar (pres. 1983-84), N.C. Bar Assn. (bd. govs. 1970-74), Pitt County Bar Assn. (pres. 1947). Democrat. Methodist. Lodges: Masons, Shriners, Rotary. Died Feb. 25, 1989.

EVERS, NELLE DWYER, critical care nurse; b. Collbran, Colo., Dec. 27, 1910; d. Arthur Roy and Maude Lodema (Edwards) Dwyer; m. John Henry Evers, Oct. 22, 1933 (dec.); children: Yvonne, John, Robert, James, Kayren, Sherryl. Student, Western State Coll., Gunnison, Colo., 1929; AS, Mesa Coll., 1964. RN, Colo. Nurse Alzheimer's unit Family Health West, Fruita, Colo. Home: Fruita, Colo. Died Feb. 6, 2002.

EWALT, H. WARD, optometrist; b. Pitts., Feb. 2, 1907; s. Harry W. and Carrie I. (Brown) E.; m. Sara E. Long, Dec. 27, 1984. BS, Ohio State U.; grad. cert. in aniseikonia, Dartmouth Coll., 1940; DOS (hon.), So. Coll. Optometry, Ill. Coll. Optometry; DSc (hon.), Pa. Coll. Optometry. Pvt. practice optometry, Pitts. Mem. summer sch. faculty dept. psychology Pa. State U., 1943-44; lectr. in field.; chmn. Tri-State Conf. on Vision and Reading, 1957-82; founder optometric extension program Mid. Atlantic Congress; 1st optometric cons. Office of Surgeon Gen. of U.S. Army, 1950-70; mem. nat. adv. coun. on health professions ednl. assistance NIH/Dept. HEW, 1967-71; chmn. Internat. Conf. on Visual Sci., 1968. Editor: Manual of Optometric Tests and Requirements; author numerous monographs, papers in field. Founder Dracomtra Players; former bd. dirs. Drama League Pitts.; chmn. Pine Twp. Planning Commn., 1962-75; chmn. bldg. com. Salem united Meth. Ch.,1 963, chmn. adminstrv. bd., 1972-75; trustee Wildermuth Found., 1974, pres., 1979—; pres. Tine Twp. Civic Assn., 1956, Pine Twp. Sch. Bd., 1958. Recipient Disting. Svc. award Jaycees, 1971, Grant Honors, Nat. Eye Rsch. Found., 1971; named Optometrist of Yr. Western Pa. Optometric Soc. and Pa. Optometric Assn., 1979. Fellow AAAS, Am. Acad. Optometry, Internat. Acad. Preventative Medicine (hon.); mem. Am. Optometric Assn. (chmn. 1945-51, mem. coun. on edn. and profl. guidance 1938-51, 1st chmn. com. on practice mgmt., chmn. contact lens com., mem. long term planning com., sec.-treas. 1955-61, pres. 1962-63, Apollo award 1965, trustee), Am. Optometric Found. (life), Internat. Reading Assn., Optometric Hist. Soc., Internat. Optic League (exec. com. 1962), Survey Commn. of Optometry, Internat. Nat. Acads. of Practice, Air Line Passengers Assn., Ohio State U. Alumni Assn. (life, mem. alumni adv. bd. 1968-76, chmn. 1976, Centennial award 1970, past pres.), Audubon Soc., Masons, Kiwanis, Phi Kappa Alpha, Epsilon Phi Epsilon, Omega Delta, Beta Sigma Kappa (Gold medal 1951). Home: Cranberry Township, Pa. Deceased.

EYER, JERRY CARL, psychologist; b. Atlantic City, N.J., Nov. 16, 1945; s. Lester Emory and Alma Pearl (Schirmer) E.; m. Lynne Helen Hesla, Nov. 13, 1982. BA in Psychology, Alma Coll., 1968; MA in Psychology, Mich. State U., 1972, PhD in Psychology, 1974. Lic. psychologist, Ala., Okla., S.D. Instr. Mich. State U., East Lansing, 1974-75, Lansing (Mich.) Community Coll., 1973-75; asst. prof., assoc. prof. Huron (S.D.) Coll., 1975-77; unit psychologist S.D. Devel. Ctr., Redfield, 1977-82, dir. edn. Custer, S.D., 1982-87; program dir. W.D. Partlow Devel. Ctr., Tuscaloosa, Ala., 1987-88; dir. psychol. svcs. Okla. Devel. Disabilities Svc. Div., Tulsa, 1989-91. Chief exec. officer Eyer and Assocs., Hominy, Okla., 1991—; USPHS trainee, 1968-72. Mem. Am. Psychol. Assn., Am. Psychol. Soc., Am. Assn. Mental Retardation, Assn. Behavior Analysis, Okla. Psychol. Assn. Home: Tulsa, Okla. Died Dec. 30, 2000.

FAGIOLO, VINCENZO CARDINAL, archbishop; b. Segni, Italy, Feb. 5, 1918; Ordained priest Roman Cath. Ch., 1943. Prelate auditor Roman Rota, 1967-71; ordained archbishop Chieti-Vasto, 1971; sec. Congregation Insts. Consecrated Life & Socs. Consecrated Life, 1984-90; pres. Pontificial Coun. for the Interpretation of Legislative Texts, Rome, 1991-94; created and proclaimed cardinal, 1994; pres. disciplinary commn. Roman Curia, from 1990. Died Sept. 22, 2000.

FAIRBANK, WILMA CANNON, author; b. Cambridge, Mass., Apr. 23, 1909; d. Walter Bradford and Cornelia (James) Cannon; m. John King Fairbank, June 29, 1932; children: Holly, Laura. BA magna cum laude, Radcliffe Coll., 1931. Pvt. painting, Peking, China, 1932-35, Cambridge, 1936-41; officer U.S. State Dept. Divsn. Cultural Rels., 1942-45; chief cultural officer U.S. Embassy China, Chungking, Nanking, 1945-47. Author: Adventures in Retrieval, 1972, America's Cultural Experiment in China, 1976, Liang and Lin: Partners in Exploring China's Architectural Past, 1994; editor: A Pictorial History of Chinese Architecture, 1984. Home: Cambridge, Mass. Died Apr. 4, 2002.

FALCKE, CAJ OLOF, econometrician, United Nations senior official; b. Helsinki, Finland, Mar. 2, 1941; came to U.S., 1967; s. Boris S. and Gretel L. (Örn) F.; m. Liisa T. Ylkänen, Oct. 30, 1964; children: GiGi M., Tania L. MSc, U. Helsinki, 1966, LSc, 1970, PhD, 1982; M in City Planning, U. Calif., Berkeley, 1969. Teaching and rsch. asst. U. Calif., 1968-69; economist Finnish Broadcasting Co., Helsinki, 1969-72; assoc. expert ILO, Manila, 1972-73; prin., chief economist David M. Dornbusch & Co., Inc., San Francisco, 1973-83; chief methodology unit sectoral studies br. UN Indsl. Devel. Orgn., Vienna, Austria, 1983-88, sr. economist, from 1988. Tech. adviser UN, Kuala Lumpur, Malaysia, 1975-76; sr. economist Louis Berger Internat., Inc., Kenya, Nairobi, 1982; cons. World Bank, Washington, 1976, 81. Author: Water Quality and Property Prices, 1982; contbr. numerous articles to profl. jours. U.S. Govt. grantee, 1967-68, Fulbright grantee, 1967-69; Kone Found. fellow, 1971, 72; Cultural Fund Finland scholar, 1981. Mem. Am. Econ. Assn., UN Indsl. Devel. Orgn. Ski Club (v.p. 1984-85, pres. 1985-90), N.Y. Acad. Scis. Democrat. Avocations: skiing, squash, photography, gastronomy, languages. Home: Albany, Calif. Died June 5, 2001.

FALK, LEE HARRISON, performing arts executive, cartoonist; b. St. Louis; s. Benjamin and Eleanor (Allina) F.; m. Elizabeth Moxley, Dec. 31, 1976; children: Valerie, Diane, Conley. BA, U. Ill. Pres. Provincetown (Mass.) Acad. of Arts, 1964-72, Truro (Mass.) Center for Arts at Castle Hill, 1979-82. Creator comic strips Mandrake the Magician, 1934—, The Phantom, 1936—; author: (plays) Passionate Congressman, 1945, Winkelberg (with Ben Hecht), 1960, Eris, 1965, Home at Six, 1965, (with Alan Cranston) The Big Story, 1940, (musicals) Mandrake, 1974, (with John LaTouche) Happy Dollar, 1950; prodr., dir. summer theatres, 1940-60 With Office War Info., Washington, 1942-43; with AUS, 1944-45. Recipient Life-Time Achievement awards: Adamsen, Stockholm, 1986, Lucca, City of Rome, 1984, Inkpot, San Diego, 1989, Haxtur award, Ovieto, Spain, 1989—, Salon award, Barcelona, Spain, 1990 Great Eastern award, N.Y.C. and Goteborg, Sweden, 1990. Mem. Nat. Cartoonist Soc. (Silver T-Square award 1986, Lee Falk Day 1994, St. Louis), Features Coun. (bd. dirs.), charter mem., New Dramatists Guild, Players Club (N.Y.C., bd. dirs., chmn. admissions com. 1991—, lifetime dir. 1998), Century Club (N.Y.C.), Dutch Treat Club (N.Y.C.). Died: March 13, 1999.

FALKNER, FRANK TARDREW, physician, educator; b. Hale, Eng., Oct. 27, 1918; arrived in U.S., 1956, naturalized, 1963; s. Ernest and Ethel (Letten) Falkner; m. June Dixon, Jan. 1948; 2 children. MD, Cambridge U., 1945. Diplomate Am. Bd. Clin. Nutrition. Intern London Hosp., 1945; resident Guys Hosp., London, 1947—48, Children's Hosp., Cin., 1948—50; practice medicine specializing in pediat. England, 1948—56, 1948—56, Louisville, 1956—70, Yellow Springs, Ohio, 1971—79; chmn. dept. pediat. U. Louisville, 1963—70; dir. Fels Rsch. Inst., Yellow Springs, 1971—79; Fels prof. pediat., prof. obstetrics and gynecology U. Cin. Coll. Medicine, 1979—79; prof. child and family health U. Mich., 1979—81; prof. and chmn. maternal and child health U. Calif., Berkeley, 1981—89, prof. pediat. San Francisco, 1981—89, prof. emeritus Berkeley, from 1989. Editor-in-chief International Child Health, syndicated columnist on children's and young people's health; contbr. articles to profl. jours. Recipient Fellowship to Am. Meml. Hosp. created in his name, 2000. Fellow: Royal Coll. Pediat. and Child Health, Am. Acad. Pediat.; mem.: French Pediatric Soc., Inst. Medicine NAS (sr.), Am. Pediatric Soc. Home: San Francisco, Calif. Died Aug. 21, 2003.

FALLON, JOHN JOSEPH, lawyer; b. New Rochelle, N.Y., Feb. 2, 1923; s. Francis X. and Beatrice (Hume) F.; m. Ethel Mary Schwartz, Dec. 27, 1948; children: Michael Brian, Kevin Christopher, Moira Anne, Mary Patricia, John Hume. AB, U. Notre Dame, 1948; JD, Cornell U., 1951. Bar: Mo., Kans. 1951. Assoc. Stinson, Mag, Thomson, McEvers and Fizzell, Kansas City, Mo., 1951-54; ptnr. Fallon Guffey and Jenkins and predecessors, Kansas City, Mo., 1955-69; counsel Popham, Conway, Sweeny, Fremont & Bundschu, Kansas City, Mo., 1970-78; ptnr. Fallon & Sappington and predecessors, Kansas City, Mo., 1979-94, Kutak Rock, Kansas City, 1995—; founding pres. Nat. Cath. Reporter Pub. Co., 1964-68. Pres. Mo. C. of C., 1967-69; trustee Avila Coll., 1982-86; mem. Jackson County Bond Adv. Com., 1967-72; co-chmn. Mo. Lawyer's Com. for Re-election Pres., 1972. With AUS. Decorated Bronze Star, Purple Heart. Died Feb. 21, 1996. Home: Shawnee Mission, Kans.

FANDEL, MICHAEL RALPH, publishing company executive, educator; b. San Diego, Mar. 12, 1955; s. Ralph Jr. and Mary Teresa (Crowley) F. BS in Bus., San Francisco State U., 1984; MS in Indsl. Rels., U. Wis., 1987. Dept. mgr. Union Bank, San Francisco, 1979-84; pers. mgr. Jardine Ins. Brokers, Inc., San Francisco, 1984-85, Lunar Radiation Corp., Madison, Wis., 1986-88; internat. compensation analyst Bank Am., San Francisco, 1988-89; mgr. human resources Ziff-Davis Pub. Co., Foster City, Calif., from 1989. Instr. U. Calif.-Berkeley Extension, Menlo Prk, 1990—. Mem. Indsl. Rels. Rsch. Inst., No. Calif. Human Resources Coun. Democrat. Roman Catholic. Avocation: travel. Deceased.

FARLEY, DENNIS, land use planner and zoning administrator; b. Lodi, Calif., Feb. 6, 1944; s. James and Agnes LuLu (Boardman) F.; m. Brit Tordis Hansen Farley, Aug. 19, 1967; children: Tor Brian, John Eric, Shawn Leif. AA in Constrn. Tech., Santa Monica Technology, Santa Monica, 1970; BS in City & Regional Planning, Calif. Polytechnic State U., San Luis Obispo, 1973. Planner Huerfano Las Animas Area Coun. Gouts, Trinidad, Calif., 1973-75; house designer Mesterhus Stavanger A.L., Stavanger, Norway, 1975-77; jr. planner Kern County, Calif., Bakersfield, Calif., 1978; planner Uinta County Lincoln-Uinta Assn. Govts., Kemmerer, Wyo., 1978-81; planning dir. Uinta County, Evanston, Wyo., 1981-93; planning & zoning adminstr. McPherson County, Kans., from 1993. Adv. mem. Sch. Dist. No. 1 Needs Assessment Com., Evanston, 1979-80; mem. bd. dirs. Better Environment and River Project, 1987-93; dir. emergency mgmt. Uinta County, Wyo., 1988-91; vice chmn. Local Environ. Protection Com., 1993—; mem. SBDA Housing Task Force, 1996—. With U.S. Army, 1965-67. Mem. Am. Planning Assn., Kans. Assn. County Planning & Zoning Officials, Kiwanis. Republican. Avocations: gardening, landscaping, woodworking, home remodeling, fishing. Home: Mcpherson, Kans. Died May 16, 2000.

FARLEY, JENNIE TIFFANY TOWLE, industrial and labor relations educator; b. Fanwood, N.J., Nov. 2, 1932; d. Howard Albert and Dorothy Jan (Van Wagner) Towle; m. Donald Thorn Farley Jr., June 16, 1956; children: Claire Hamlin, Anne Tiffany, Peter Towle. BA, Cornell U., 1954, MS, 1969, PhD, 1970. Editl. staff Mademoiselle and Seventeen, N.Y.C., 1954-56; freelance writer Eng., Sweden, Peru, 1956-67; lectr., rsch. assoc., adj. asst. prof. Cornell U., Ithaca, N.Y., 1970-72, dir. women's studies, 1972-76; from asst. prof. to assoc. prof. Cornell U. Sch. Indsl. and Labor Rels., Ithaca, N.Y., 1976-89, prof., from 1989. Exec. bd. dirs. women's studies program Cornell U. Sch. Indsl. and Labor Rels., 1970—; vis. prof. Ctr. for Women Scholars and Rsch. on Women Uppsala U., Sweden, 1985-86; trustee Cornell U., 1988-92. Author: Affirmative Action and the Woman Worker, 1979, Academic Women and Employment Discrimination, 1982; editor: Sex Discrimination in Higher Education, 1982, The Woman in Management, 1983, Women Workers in Fifteen Countries, 1985. Recipient Corinne Galvn award Tompkins County Human Rights Commn., 1987. Mem. AAUP, AAUW (pres. Ithaca chpt. 1980-82), NOW (Unsung Heroine award 1991), Sociologists for Women in Soc., Cornell Women's of Tompkins Country Club. Home: Ithaca, NY. Died June 19, 2002.

FARRELL, LAURENCE F. aerospace executive; b. Jersey City, Apr. 26, 1927; s. Edward A. and Maude M. (Gibney) F.; married; 1 child, Ellyn M. BS, Seton Hall U., 1950, MBA, 1953; JD, Fordham U., 1952; Fgn. Service, Georgetown U., 1970. Dir. customer relations Internat. Telephone & Telegraph Corp., N.Y.C. and Washington, 1952-71; exec. dir. Nat. Investor Relations Inst., Washington, 1973-82; pres., chief exec. officer The Farrell Group, Washington, 1971-83; dir. govt. relations Sabreliner Corp., St. Louis, from 1983. Bd. dirs. Nat. Sports Found., Washington; cons. Control Data Corp., Mpls., 1974-80, LTV Corp., Dallas, 1973-81. Del. Rep. Assembly Com. Va., Richmond, 1978; pres. McLean (Va.) Citizens Assn., Fairfax, 1982-84. Served to sgt. U.S. Army, 1945-47. Mem.: Congressional Country (Washington); Kiawah Country (Charleston, S.C.). Home: Charlotte, NC. Deceased.

FARRELL, PETER SNOW, musician, retired educator; b. Greensboro, N.C., Sept. 13, 1924; s. Charles Anderson and Anne Patricia (McKaughan) F.; m. Miriam Louise Mellott, Apr. 21, 1946; children: David Gerard, Jeffrey Bernard. MusB, U. Rochester, 1948, MusM, 1954, artists diploma, 1953. Prof. music U. Ill., Champaign-Urbana, 1954-72; prof. U. Calif., San Diego, 1972-91, prof. emeritus, from 1991. Prin. cellist Columbus Philharm. Orch., 1948-49, San Diego Symphony Orch., 1969, La Jolla Symphony Orch., 1998—; profl. performing artist cello and viola da gamba, 1946—. Performer festivals in U.S., Germany, Poland, France, Eng.; contbr. articles and revs. to profl. jours. With U.S. Army, 1943-46, PTO. Mem. Viola da Gamba Soc. Am. (bd. dirs. 1956-60), San Diego Early Music Soc. (mem. adv. bd.), U. Calif. San Diego Emeriti Assn. (pres. 1995-96). Avocations: hiking, cross-country skiing. Home: San Diego, Calif. Died Jan. 26, 2002.

FARROW, ROBERT CONVERSE, health care administrator; b. Greensville, S.C., Dec. 8, 1936; s. Willie and Azzle (Knuckles) F.; m. Violet Alice Brockenbrough, July 7, 1962; children: Robert Wayne, Trina Lynn Farrow-Ware. BA, Bklyn. Coll., 1970; MA, NYU, 1974; MPH, Columbia U., 1982. Cert. Am. Coll. Health Care Adminstrs.; cert. sch. counselor; cert. nursing home adminstr. Sch. counselor Salem (N.J.) Bd. Edn., 1970-71; asst. adminstr. Victory Lake Nursing Ctr., Hyde Park, N.Y., 1971-87, adminstr., from 1987. Mem. Dutchess County Bd. Coop. Edn., Poughkeepsie, N.Y., 1974-83, Hospice, Poughkeepsie, 1986-89. With U.S. Army, 1960-64. Recipient Summer Excellence award U.S. Dept. Labor Summer Youth Employment, 1979, Gentleman Distinction award The Bykota Club, 1990. Mem. APHA, Am. Coll. Health Care Execs., Am. Coll. Health Care Adminstrs. (pres. N.Y. chpt. 1989-91), Nat. Notary Assn., Rotary Internat. Home: Hendersonvlle, Tenn. Died Feb. 24, 2001.

FAST, HOWARD MELVIN, author; b. N.Y.C., Nov. 11, 1914; s. Barney and Ida (Miller) F.; m. Betty Cohen, June 6, 1937 (dec. 1994); children: Rachel Ann, Jonathan; m. Mercedes O'Connor, June 17, 1999. Student, NAD, 1933. Began writing, 1932; Army film project, 1944; European corr. Esquire and Coronet mags., 1945; mem. staff Office of War Info., 1942-44, chief newswriter, originator Voice of Am., 1982-83. Emmy award for The Ambassador, Benjamin Franklin 1974; author: (novels) Two Valleys, 1932, Strange Yesterday, 1933, The Children, 1936, Place in the City, 1937, Conceived in Liberty, 1939; biography Haym Salomon, 1941; The Romance of a People, 1941; (novel) The Last Frontier, 1941; (biography) Baden Powell, 1941; (novel) Tail Hunter, 1942, The Unvanquished, 1942; (biography) Goethals and the Panama Canal, 1942; The Picture Book History of the Jews, 1942; (novel) Citizen Tom Paine, 1943, Freedom Road, 1944; The Incredible Tito, 1944; The American: A Middle Western Legend, 1946; Never Forget: The Story of the Warsaw Ghetto, 1946; Intellectuals in the Fight for Peace, 1949; Peekskill, U.S.A., 1951; (novel) Spartacus, 1952; The Last Supper, and Other Stories, 1955; The Naked God, 1957; Moses, Prince of Egypt, 1958; The Howard Fast Reader, 1960; The Edge of Tomorrow, 1961; Tony and the Wonderful Door, 1968, The Crossing, 1971; General Zapped an Angel, 1971, Last Frontier, 1971; The Hessian, 1972 (Notable Book citation ALA 1972); My Glorious Brothers, 1972, A Touch of Infinity, 1973, The Art of Zen Meditation, 1977, The Magic Door, 1980, Time and the Riddle: Thirty-One Zen Stories, 1981, The Call of Fife and Drum: Three Novels of the Revolution, 1987, (under name E.V. Cunningham) Sylvia, 1960, Phyllis, 1962, Alice, 1963, Shirley, 1963, Lydia, 1964, Penelope, 1965, Helen, 1966, Margie, 1966, Sally, 1967, Samantha, 1967, Cynthia, 1968, The Assassin Who Gave Up His Gun, 1969, Millie, 1973, The Case of the One Penny Orange, 1977, The Case of the Russian Diplomat, 1978, The Case of the Poisoned Eclairs, 1979, The Case of the Sliding Pool, 1981, The Case of the Kidnapped Angel, 1982, The Case of the Murdered Mackenzie, 1984, The Case of the Angry Actress, 1984, The Wabash Factor, 1986; (as Walter Ericson) Fallen Angel, 1951; (plays) The Hammer, 1950, Thirty Pieces of Silver, 1954, George Washington and the Water Witch, 1956, David and Paula, 1982; Editor: Selected Works of Paine, 1945, Collection of Short Stories: Patrick Henry and the Frigate's Keel, 1945, Best Short Stories of Theodore Dreiser, 1947, Under the Name of Howard Fast, The American (biography of Peter Altgeld, former gov. of Ill.), 1946, Carkton, 1947, My Glorious Brothers, 1948, Departure, 1949, Literature and Reality, 1949, The Proud and the Free, 1950, The Passion of Sacco and Vanzetti, 1953, Silas Timberman, 1954, The Story of Lola Gregg: The Winston Affair, 1959, April Morning, 1961, Power, 1962, The Crossing; (play) Agrippa's Daughter, 1964, The Hill; (drama), 1963, Torquemada, 1966, The Hunter and the Trap, 1967, The Jews, 1968, The Hessian, 1970, The Immigrants, 1977, Second Generation, 1978, The Establishment, 1979, The Legacy, 1981, Max, 1982, The Outsider, (play) The Novelist, 1986, The Immigrant's Daughter; (novel), 1985, (play) Citizen Tom Paine, 1986; (novel) Dinner Party, 1987, The Pledge, 1988, (newspaper column), Greenwich Time, 1981, The Confession of Joe Cullen, 1989, (autobiography) Being Red, 1990, War and Peace, Collection of Essays, 1992, (novel) The Trial of Abigail Goodman, 7 Days in June, The Bridge Builder's Story, 1995, An Independent Woman, 1997, Redemption, 1999; columnist N.Y. Observer, 1989-92, Greenwich Time, 1992-2000, Stamford Advocate, 1992, Barbara Lavette, 1998, (novel) Greenwich, 2000. Mem. World Peace Council, 1950-55; Am. Labor Party Congl. candidate 23d Dist., N.Y., 1952. Recipient Breadloaf Literary award, 1937, Schomburg award for race relations, 1944, Literary Lion award N.Y. Public Library, 1945, Newspaper Guild racial equality award, 1947, Jewish Book Council annual award, 1947, Peace Prize USSR, 1954, Secondary Education annual book award, 1962, Emmy award Nat. Acad. TV Arts and Scis., 1976, Peabody award, 2001. Mem. Century Club, N.Y.C. Jewish. Died Mar. 12, 2003.

FAUL, GEORGE JOHNSON, former college president; b. Santa Ana, Calif., Oct. 11, 1918; s. George William and Esther Francis (Johnson) F.; m. June Patricia Lynch, Dec. 22, 1949; children: Robert M., Alison. Student, Santa Ana Jr. Coll., 1936-38; AB, Stanford U., 1941, MA, 1947, EdD, 1954; HHD (hon.), Monterey Inst. Internat. Studies, 1980. Counselor Visalia Coll., 1947, Stanford U., 1947-48; dir. guidance Coll. of the Sequoias, 1948-50; dean student pers. Contra Costa Coll., 1950-58, pres., 1958-64; pres., supt. Monterey (Calif.) Peninsula Coll., 1964-80, pres. emeritus, 1980—2003. Lectr. U. Calif., Stanford U.; former mem. ednl. adv. bd. Sci. Rsch. Assocs. Mem. exec. com., chmn. Richmond Park and Recreation Commn., 1958-64, hon. life mem. Calif. PTA; pres. Cmty. Welfare Coun., West Contra Costa County, 1960-62; bd. dirs., charter mem. Serviceman's Oppurtunity Coll.; bd. dirs. Monterey Peninsula Cmty. Chest, Cmty. Theatre of Carmel, Bach Festival, Monterey Jazz Festival, Alcoholism Coun. of Monterey Peninsula, USO, Friends of Photography, Monterey History and Art Assn., past pres. Monterey Penisula Mus. of Art, Monterey Peninsula Coll. Found.; v.p. Carmel Heritage, Casa Amesti Found.; bd. govs., treas. Monterey Peninsula Found., mem. adv. bd.; founder, former exec. dir. Monterey County Cultural Commn. Lt. cmdr. USNR, 1942-47. bd. dir. Calif. Jr. Coll. Assn. bd. dir. Western Assn. Offices and Coll. bd. dir. Calif. Jr. Coll. Assn. bd. dir. Western Assn. Offices and Coll. Recipient Santa Ana Coll. Alumni Achievement award, 1968. Mem. Disabled Am. Vets. (life), Stanford U. Alumni Assn. (life), Pacific Biol. Lab. Club, Delta Upsilon. Home: Carmel, Calif. Died Mar. 29, 2003.

FAULKNER, HENRY, III, automotive executive; b. 1949; m. Susan Price. With Henry Faulkner Inc., Phila., 1970-81; CEO Faulkner Orgn., Trevose, Pa., from 1981. Died Apr. 28, 2003.

FAUST, A. DONOVAN, retired communications executive; b. Indpls., May 31, 1919; s. Glenn L. and Lela Vivien (Smith) F.; m. Barbara Lou Wilson, Aug. 4, 1951; 1 child, Thomas. Student, Taylor U., 1936-37, Purdue U., 1937-39. Broadcasting performer, producer, exec., 1939-54; gen. mgr. Sta. WJRT-TV, Flint, Mich., 1954-65; with Gen. Electric Broadcasting Co., 1966-82; v.p., gen. mgr. WNGE-TV, Nashville, 1966-70, KOA-TV, Denver, 1970-71; v.p. sta. ops. Gen. Electric Broadcasting Co., 1971-74, pres., 1979-82; v.p., gen. mgr. Gen. Electric Cablevision Corp., Schenectady, 1974-78, pres., 1979-82. Chmn. Evansville Cable TV, Ind.; dir. Tau Epsilon Music, Inc., N.Y.C., Tomorrow Program Syndication, Inc., N.Y.C. Bd. dirs. Com. of Sponsors, Flint Coll. and Cultural Devel., 1958-65, United Way Middle Tenn., 1968-70, 78-84, YMCA, Flint, Mich., 1958-64, Nashville, 1967-70, Denver, 1971-73, Nashville Better Bus. Bur., 1968-70, 78-80, Svc. Corps. of Ret. Execs., Opportunities Industrialization Ctr., 1984-90, Sr. Citizens, Inc., 1986-92, Sr. Citizens Endowment; mem. Mich. Gov.'s Coun. on Traffic Safety, 1962-64, Colo. Gov.'s Task Force on Jobs for Vets., 1972-73. Named Newsmaker of Tomorrow Time Mag.-Pitts. C. of C., 1953 Mem. Nat. Assn. Broadcasters (mem. radio code bd. 1967-70), UHF TV Assn. (v.p., dir. 1953-54), ABC-TV Network Affiliates Assn. (bd. govs. 1966-70), Soc. TV Pioneers. Home: Nashville, Tenn. Died Dec. 13, 1999.

FAVORS, MALACHI, jazz musician, bassist; b. Chgo., Aug. 22, 1937; Played with Roscoe Mitchell Group, 1963, with Muhal Richard Abrams', 1960's, Assn. Advancement of Creative Musician Big Band, 1965, Joseph Jarman, Roscoe Mitchell and later Lester Bowie and Don Moye, now known as Art Ensemble of Chgo., (with Fontella Bass), 1995, performed in France, 1969-71; recs. include Reese and the Smooth Ones, Message to Our folks, People in Sorrow, Tutankhamun, Fanfare for the Warriors, Nice Guys, The Third Decade, recitals (with Art Ensemble of Chicago) Ancient to the Future, 1987, Naked, 1988, Express, 1989, (with Amabutho) Soweto, 1990; appeared at Ann Arbor Blues and Jazz Festival, 1972, Chgo. Jazz Festival, 1980, others. Died Jan. 27, 2004.

FAY, MARY SMITH, genealogist; b. Burnt Prairie, Ill., Aug. 27, 1915; d. William Logan and Mary Myrtle (Hunsinger) S.; m. Charles Hemphill Fay, Sept. 4, 1969 (dec.). BS, U. Ill., 1936, MS, 1937. Cert. genealogist. Tchr. math and gen. scis. Crossville (Ill.) High Sch., 1937-38; hosp. adminstr. U. Mich., Ann Arbor, 1939-45, Monmouth Meml. Hosp., Long Branch, N.J., 1945-47; supr., tech. info., exploration and prodn. Rsch. Lab. Shell Oil Co., Houston, 1948-69; freelance genealogist, from 1969. Author: War of 1812 Veterans in Texas, 1979 (1st prize Tex. State Geneal. Soc. 1980), rev. 1994, Edwin Fay of Vermont and Alabama 1794-1876: His Origins from 1656 and his Descendants to 1987, 1988. Mem. nat. bd. Med. Coll. Pa., Phila., 1989—; bd. dirs. Houston Pub. Libr., 1997—; 2d v.p. Clayton Libr. Friends, 2000—. Fellow Tex. State Geneal. Soc., Am. Soc. Genealogists; mem. DAR (former regent, Ann Poage chpt.),

Colonial Dames of Am. (chpt. VIII), Daus. Am. Colonists (Daniel Braman chpt.), U.S. Daus. 1812 (hon. nat. v.p.), Tex. Navy (hon. admiral). Episcopalian. Home: Houston, Tex. Died July 7, 2000.

FAY, PETER WARD, history educator; b. Paris, Dec. 3, 1924; s. Willis Ward and Joan (Peters) F.; m. Phyllis Ford, 1950 (div. 1955); 1 dau., Jennifer; m. Mariette Robertson, Dec. 21, 1957; children: Todor, Lisa, Jonathan, Benjamin. BA, Harvard U., 1947, PhD, 1954; BA, Oxford U., 1949. Instr. Williams Coll., 1951-55; asst. prof. history Calif. Inst. Tech., 1955-60, assoc. prof., 1960-70, prof. history, 1970-97, prof. emeritus, 1997—2004. Author: Opium War 1840-42, 1975, The Forgotten Army: India's Armed Struggle for Independence, 1942-45, 1993. Served with AUS, 1943-46. Rhodes scholar, 1947 Mem. Am. Hist. Assn., Assn. for Asian Studies Clubs: Signet Soc. Democrat. Home: Sierra Madre, Calif. Died Jan. 18, 2004.

FEASTER, DOROTHEA VIVIEENE, parks and recreation talent director; b. N.Y.C., Mar. 22, 1954; d. Claude Walter and Marion Henrietta (Stoney) F.; 1 child, Taiysha Mone Brown. Student, CCNY, 1971-73, Coll. New Rochelle and Coll. Laguardia, 1978-90. Dir. Bronx (N.Y.) Fiscal Pks. and Recreation, 1983-90, Bronx (N.Y.) Pks. and Recreations Talent Network, from 1990. Treas. women's com. Pks. and Recreation, 1989—. Avocations: handball, paddleball, tennis, billiards, board games. Home: Bronx, NY. Deceased.

FEATHERS, ELIZABETH KELLOGG, retired secondary education educator; b. Kuliang, Fujian, China, Aug. 17, 1920; came to U.S., 1927; d. Edwin Dwight and Alice Rogers (Ropes) Kellogg; m. Joseph John Feathers, July 16, 1943; children: John Edwin, Alice Irene, James Kellogg, Joseph Marvin, Jesse Roger, Jeffrey Mark. Car, Pacific U., 1941; postgrad., U. Wash., 1954; tchr. cert., Lewis Clark State Coll., Lewiston, Idaho, 1968. Tchr. English Clatskanie (Oreg.) H.S., 1941-43; substitute tchr. Tucson (Ariz.) H.S., 1944; tchr., prin. Lexington (Oreg.) H.S., 1947-48; substitute tchr. Seattle Pub. Schs., 1954-56; postmaster replacement U.S. Postal Svc., Spalding, Idaho, 1973-96. Spkr. in field. Author, editor: 50th Anniversary of Congregational Presbyterian Church, 1989; contbr. articles to newspapers. Treas. Congl. Presbyn. Ch., Lewiston, Idaho, 1976-91; registrar, chief judge primary and gen. elections, Spalding; den mother, leader Boy Scouts and Girl Scouts, Seattle, Dillon, Mont. and Lewiston, 1954-76. Mem. PEO (sec., treas., chaplain, 50-yr. membership honor), Sacajawea Study Club. Democrat. Mem. United Ch. of Christ. Avocations: stamp collecting, reading, camping, travel, history. Home: Seattle, Wash. Died Nov. 29, 2000.

FECHTEL, EDWARD RAY, retired lawyer, educator; b. Pocatello, Idaho, Apr. 20, 1926; s. Edward Joseph and Frances Lucille (Myers) F.; m. Jewell Reagan, Apr. 7, 1950 (div.); children: Scot Gerald, Mark Edward, Kim; m. 2d Mary K. Milligan, Dec. 1983. BA in Bus., Idaho State U., 1949; JD, U. Oreg., 1967; MBA in Fin., 1968. Bar: Oreg. 1967, U.S. Dist. Ct. Oreg. 1967, U.S. Tax Ct. 1967, U.S. Ct. Appeals (9th cir.) 1968, U.S. Ct. Appeals (11th cir.) 1985, U.S. Ct. Appeals (10th cir.) 1986, U.S. Ct. Appeals (8th cir.) 1987, U.S. Supreme Ct. 1988. Sales rep. Genesco, 1950-59; gen. mdse. mgr. Fargo Wilson Wells Co., Pocatello, 1960-64; ptnr. Husband, Johnson & Fechtel, Eugene, Oreg., 1967-83, Ray Fechtel, P.C., 1984-96, ret., 1997; prof. bus. law U. Oreg.; lectr. Oreg. State Bar. Bd. dirs. Legal Aid Soc., Lane County, Oreg., Oreg. Citizens for Fair Land Planning. With USN, 1944-46. Mem. ABA, ATLA, Oreg. State Bar Assn., Phi Alpha Delta. Republican. Home: Eugene, Oreg. Died June 9, 2001.

FEEHAN, THOMAS, lawyer; b. Joliet, Ill., Mar. 1, 1926; m. Beverly Ann Long, Nov. 21, 1953; children: Colleen, Kathleen, Thomas, Brian, Kevin. BS, Loyola U., Chgo., 1949, JD, 1953. Bar: Ill. 1953, U.S. Dist. Ct. (no. and so. dists.) Ill. 1956. Pres. Thomas, Wallace, Feehan, Baron & Kaplan, Joliet, from 1956. Chmn. Will County Rep. Cen. Com., 1964-78; mem. Ill. State Toll Hwy. Commn., Oak Brook, 1974-78; pres. Boys Club Joliet, 1974. Served as ensign USN, 1944-46. Fellow Ill. Bar Found.; mem. ABA, Ill. Bar Assn., Ill County Bar Assn. (pres. 1980, 82), Assn. Trial Lawyers Am., Joliet C. of C. (pres. 1974). Clubs: Union League (Chgo.). Republican. Roman Catholic. Home: Joliet, Ill. Died Sept. 8, 2000.

FEHRER, CATHERINE, French language educator, art historian; b. Munich, Feb. 8, 1912; came to U.S., 1914; d. Oscar and Mabel (Vanderbilt) F. AB, Vassor Coll., 1934; MA, Bryn Mawr Coll., 1935, PhD, 1942. Instr. modern lang. Murray (Ky.) State Tchrs. Coll., 1941-43; asst. prof. modern lang. Western Coll. for Women, Oxford, Ohio, 1943-45; asst. prof. French Wilson Coll., Chambersburg, Pa., 1945-47, Wilkes Coll., Wilkes-Barre, Pa., 1947-48, Suffolk U., Boston, 1948, assoc. prof. French, prof. French, chmn. modern lang. dept., prof. emeritus, from 1977; rsch. art history Julian Acad., Paris, from 1981. Contbr. articles to profl. jours. Hon. trustee Florence Griswold Mus. Mem. Coll. Club (pres. 1975-78). Home: New Haven, Conn. Died May 23, 2001.

FEINBERG, JOEL, philosophy educator; b. Detroit, Oct. 19, 1926; s. Abraham J. and Marion (Tahl) F.; m. Betty Grey Sowers, May 29, 1955; children— Melissa, Benjamin. Student, U. Ill., 1944-45; BA, U. Mich., 1949, MA, 1951, PhD, 1957. Instr. philosophy Brown U., 1955-57, asst. prof., 1957-62, Princeton U., 1962-64, assoc. prof., 1964-66; prof. U. Calif. at Los Angeles, 1966-67; prof. philosophy Rockefeller U., N.Y.C., 1967-77, U. Ariz., 1977—94. Author: Doing and Deserving, 1970, Social Philosophy, 1973, Rights, Justice and the Bounds of Liberty, 1980, Harm to Others, 1984, Offense to Others, 1985, Harm to Self, 1986, Harmless Wrongdoing, 1988, Freedom and Fulfillment, 1992, Freedom and Fulfillment, 1992; contbg. author: Philosophy in America, 1965, Educational Judgments, 1973, Philosophy and Environmental Crisis, 1974; editor: Reason and Responsibility, 1965, Moral Concepts, 1969, The Problem of Abortion, 1973, Philosophy of Law, 1975. Served with AUS, 1944-46. Fellow Ctr. for Advanced Study in Behavioral Scis., 1960-61, liberal arts fellow in law and philosophy Harvard Law Sch., 1963-64, Guggenheim Found. fellow, 1974-75, Rockefeller Found. fellow, 1981-82, resident fellow Rockefeller Found. Study and Conf. Ctr., Bellagio, Italy, 1989; Fullbright lectr., Kyoto, Japan, 1987. Fellow Am. Acad. Arts and Scis., Am. Philos. Assn. (v.p. Pacific div. 1980-81, pres. 1981-82, chmn. nat. bd. officers 1986-89); mem. Am. Soc. Polit. and Legal Philosophy (program chmn. 1963, sec.-treas. 1971-72, pres. 1989-92). Home: Austin, Tex. Died Mar. 29, 2004.

FEINN, BARBARA ANN, economist; b. Waterbury, Conn., Feb. 16, 1925; d. David Harris and Dora (Brandvein) F.; m. Steven L. Wissig, Jan. 10, 1991. AB magna cum laude, Smith Coll., 1946; MA (univ. scholar), Yale U., 1947, PhD (univ. fellow), 1952; cert., Oxford (Eng.) U., 1949. Rsch. economist First Nat. City Bank, N.Y.C., 1953-54; assoc. economist Office Messrs. Rockefeller, N.Y.C., 1954-61; asst. to dir. N.Y. State Office for Regional Devel., N.Y.C., 1961-62; cons. economist Nelson A. Rockefeller, N.Y.C., 1963-64; pvt. cons., 1965-68; sr. coun. economist N.Y. State Coun. Econ. Advisers, N.Y.C., 1969-72; chief economist Office S.C. Gov., Columbia, 1972-74, State of S.C., 1974-92; mem. bd. econ. advisors, 1976-88; sec. bd. econ. advisors, 1986-88; exec. dir. bd. econ. advisors, 1988-92; econ. cons., from 1993. Adj. prof. bus. adminstrn. U. S.C., Columbia, 1972-74; ofcl. participant White House Conf. on Balanced Nat. Growth and Econ. Devel., 1978; del. meetings on nat. balanced growth Nat. Govs. Assn., Leesburg, Va., 1977; mem. S.C. Gov.'s Task Force on the Economy, 1980-84; mem. productivity measurement com. S.C. Coun. on Productivity, 1981-84. Dir. Smith Coll. Alumnae Fund Program, N.Y.C., 1965-66, mem. spl. gifts com., 1971, class v.p., 1986-91, class treas., 1991-96, 96—; del. assembly Assn. Yale Alumni, 1983-86, 91-94. Recipient Wilbur Lucius Cross medal Yale U., 1987. Mem. Am. Econ. Assn., Nat. Assn. Bus. Econs., Downtown Economists Luncheon Group, Carolinas Econ. Assn., Phi Beta Kappa. Clubs: Yale (N.Y.C. and cen. S.C.); Summit, Wildewood (Columbia, S.C.), Woodcreek (Columbia), The Faculty (Columbia), Smith Coll. (Columbia). Contbr. articles to profl. jours. Home: Columbia, SC. Deceased.

FEINSILVER, DAVID B. psychiatrist; b. Boston, Nov. 11, 1939; s. Oscar and Goldie (Gans) F.; m. Miriam Hoffman, Apr. 21, 1963; children: Ethan Joshua, Marissa Leah. BA, Brandeis U., 1961; MD, Tufts U., 1965. Intern Mt. Zion Hosp., San Francisco; resident Yale U., New Haven, Conn.; Grant program coord. NIMH, Chevy Chase, Md., 1969-71; staff psychiatrist Chestnut Lodge Hosp., Rockville, Md., 1971-99. Editor: Towards a Comprehensive Model for Schizophrenic Disorders, 1986. Avocation: photography. Home: Washington, DC. Died Feb. 23, 1999.

FELDMAN, ROBERT GEORGE, neurologist, medical educator; b. Cin., Apr. 27, 1933; s. Jacob and Katie (Green) F.; m. Gail Poliner, Dec. 25, 1960; children— John, Elise. BA, U. Cin., 1954, MD, 1958. Diplomate Am. Bd. Psychiatry and Neurology, Am. Bd. Electroencephalography. Research asst. pharmacology U. Cin., 1949-54; jr. pharmacologist William S. Merrell Co., Reading, Ohio, 1951-56; fellow Nat. Assn. Mental Health, UCLA, 1957; intern Los Angeles County Hosp., 1958-59; resident neurology Yale-New Haven Med. Center, 1959-63, W. Haven VA Hosp., 1961; fellow metabolic diseases Yale Med. Sch., 1961-62; USPHS spl. fellow, 1962-63; practice medicine, specializing in neurology, 1963—2003; neurologist-in-chief Boston Med. Ctr. (formerly Univ. Hosp., Boston City Hosp.), 1969-99; co-investigator Environ. Hazards Ctr., Boston VA Med. Ctr., 1995—2003; chief neurology VA Med. Ctr., Boston, 1968-97. Mem. staff Beth Israel Hosp.; vis. fellow Montreal Neurol. Inst., 1962, Mayo Clinic and Found., Rochester, Minn., 1962; asso. electroencephalographer Yale-New Haven Med. Center, 1962-63; mem. faculty Harvard Med. Sch., 1963-2003, lectr., 1968-2003; lectr. Sch. Public Health, 1978-2003; mem. faculty Boston U. Sch. Medicine, 1963-2003, prof. neurology, 1970-2003, chmn. dept., 1969-99, prof. pharmacology, 1977-2003, dir. occupl. environ. neurology program, 1984-2003, chmn. emeritus, 1999-2003; prof. environ. health Boston U. Sch. Pub. Health chief neurology svcs. Boston VA hosps., 1968-97; mem. nat field adv. group Neurology VA, 1972-75; mem. sci. coun. Com. to Combat Huntington's Disease, 1972-75; chmn. Zone 1 Profl. Standards Rev. Orgn., 1973-78; mem. profl. adv. bd. Epilepsy Found., 1976-85; mem. coun. sci. advisors Nat. Inst. Occupational Safety and Health, 1984-90. Editor-in-chief Jour. Club Neurology, 1982-85; contbg. editor Am. Jour. Indsl. Medicine, 1980-2003; mem. editl. bd. Jour. Clin. Neuropharmacology, 1986-2003, editor sect. on neurotoxicology, 1996-2001; mem. editl. bd. Jour. Occupl. Rehab., 1991-2003, Neurology Forum, 1990-95, others; author book; editor 3 books; contbr. articles and abstracts to profl. jours. Bd. dirs. Postgrad. Med. Inst., 1973; bd. dirs. Norfolk County Med. Soc.; v.p. Mass. Med. Soc., 1973. Named Jameson-Parkinson hon. lectr., Soc. Occupl. Medicine, London, 2001; recipient Robbins award for excellence in tchg., 1987, Metcalf award for excellence in tchg., 1995, Fred Springer award, Am. Parkinson's Disease Assn., 2002. Fellow: Royal Acad. Medicine, Am. Acad. Neurology (councillor 1979—84, v.p. 1989—91); mem.: APHA, AMA, Nat. Acad. Scis. (cons.), Boston U. Med. Ctr. Med. Dental Staff (pres. 1994—95), World Fedn. Neurology (chair neurotoxicology sci. group 2000—02), Am. Parkinson Disease Assn. Ctr. Advanced Rsch. (dir. 1993—2003), Assn. Am. Med. Colls. (rep. to coun. of acad. socs. 1991—96), Mass. Med. Soc., Am. Heart Assn. (fellow stroke coun.), Am. Med. EEG Assn., Ea. EEG Soc., Am. Neurol. Assn. (2d v.p. 1992—93), Am. Acad. Toxicology, Boston Soc. Psychiatry and Neurology (pres. 1972—73), Am. Assn. Electromygraphy and Electrodiagnosis (cert.), Am. Epilepsy Soc. Home: Braintree, Mass. Died Aug. 7, 2003.

FELLER, DAVID E. law educator, arbitrator; b. 1916; AB, Harvard U., 1938, LLB, 1941. Bar: Mass. 1941, D.C. 1942. Lectr. law and econs. U. Chgo., 1941—42; atty. U.S. Dept. Justice, Washington, 1946—48; assoc. gen. counsel CIO, Washington, 1949—53, United Steelworkers, Washington, 1949—60; gen. counsel ind. union dept. AFL-CIO, 1961—66, United Steelworkers, 1961—65; ptnr. Goldberg, Feller & Bredhoff, Washington, 1955—60, Feller, Bredhoff & Anker, 1961—65, Feller & Anker, 1965—67; John H. Boalt prof. emeritus U. Calif.-Berkeley Sch. Law. Editor Harvard Law Rev. Bd. dirs. NAACP Legal def. and Edn. Fund, 1960—97; pres. Coun. U. Calif. Faculty Assns., 1973—89. Mem.: ABA (sec. labor law sect. 1972—73), Fed. Mediation and Conciliation Roster of Arbitrators, Nat. Acad. Arbitrators (v.p. 1985—87), Phi Beta Kappa. Home: Berkeley, Calif. Died Feb. 10, 2003.

FELTON, JEAN SPENCER, physician; b. Oakland, Calif., Apr. 27, 1911; s. Herman and Tess (Davidson) F.; m. Janet E. Birnbaum, June 27, 1937 (dec.); children: Gary, Keith, Robin; m. Suzanne E. Colvin, Sept. 2, 1990. AB, Stanford U., 1931, MD, 1935. Diplomate: Am. Bd. Preventive Medicine, Am. Bd. Indsl. Hygiene. Intern Mt. Zion Hosp., San Francisco, 1934-35, resident in surgery, 1935-36, Dante Hosp., San Francisco, 1936-38; practice medicine San Francisco, 1938-40; guest lectr. indsl. sociology U. Tenn. at Knoxville, 1946-53; med. dir. Oak Ridge Nat. Lab., 1946-53; cons. dept. medicine, prof. dept. preventive medicine, pub. health U. Okla. Med. Sch., 1953-58; cons. indsl. hygiene Okla. State Dept. Health, 1953-58; past cons. VA, St. Louis area; prof. occupational health U. Calif. Schs. Medicine and Pub. Health, Los Angeles, 1958-68; dir. occupational health service Dept. Personnel, County Los Angeles, 1968-74; med. dir. occupational health Naval Regional Med. Center, Long Beach, Calif., 1974-78; clin. prof. community medicine U. So. Calif., 1968-82, clin. prof. emeritus, 1982—; clin. prof. medicine U. Calif., Irvine, 1975—. Cons. occupational health NASA, USN, VA, AEC, USPHS, Social Security Adminstrn., 1955-62; Fellow through Distinction faculty occupational medicine Royal Coll. Physicians, London, 1997—. Author: (with A. H. Katz) Health and Community, 1965, Man, Medicine, and Work, 1965, Occupational Medical Management, 1990; bd. dirs. Excerpta Medica, Sect. XXXV, The Netherlands; mem. editl. panel Occupational Medicine, London, 1994—; contbr. articles to med. jours. Past mem. youth svc. com. Oak Ridge Welfare Coun., 1946-53; past mem. Tenn. Commn. on Childen, Welfare Svcs. Dept.; chmn., mem. adv. bd. Oak Ridge; past mem. Gov.'s Com. on Utilization Physically Handicapped Pres.'s Com. on Employment People with Disabilities, 1947-94. Lt. col. M.C., 1940-46. Decorated Army Commendation Ribbon, 1946; recipient Citation for Excellence in Med. Authorship by Am. Assn. Indsl. Physicians and Surgeons, 1948; Knudsen award Indsl. Med. Assn., 1968; Physician of Yr. award Calif. Gov.'s Com. on Employment of Handicapped, 1979; Physician of Yr. award Pres.'s Com. on Employment of Handicapped, 1979 Fellow Am. Coll. Preventive Medicine (pres. 1966-67), Am. Acad. Occupational Medicine, Am. Occupational Med. Assn. (Meritorious Svc. award 1965, Health Achievement in Industry award 1983), Am. Pub. Health Assn., Collegium Ramazzini (coun. of fellows 1994—); mem. AMA (sec., vice chmn. sect. preventive and indsl. medicine and pub. health 1949-53, chmn. sect. 1953), Am. Indsl. Hygiene Assn., Nat. Rehab. Assn. So. Calif. (dir.), So. Calif. Ind. Hygiene Assn. (past pres.), Am. Coll. Occupational Medicine (Robert A. Kehoe award 1989), New Eng. Occupational Med. Assn. (Harriet F. Hardy award 1989), Soc. Occupational Medicine (hon.). Unitarian Universalist. Achievements include preparing standard operating procedure of U.S. Army indsl. med. program at San Francisco Port of Embarkation (adopted by the U.S. Army Chief of Transp. for use by all Ports of Embarkation). Died 2003.

FELTS, WILLIAM ROBERT, JR., physician; b. Judsonia, Ark., Apr. 24, 1923; s. Wylie Robert and Willie Etidorpha (Lewis) Felts; m. Jeanne E. Kennedy, Feb. 17, 1954 (div. 1971); children: William R. III, Thomas Wylie, Samuel Clay, Melissa Jeanne; m. Lila Mitchell Dudley, Feb. 14, 1987 (dec. Feb. 1993). BS, U. Ark., 1944, MD, 1946. Intern Garfield Meml. Hosp., Washington, 1946—47; resident in medicine Gallinger Mcpl. Hosp., Washington, 1949—51, George Washington U. Hosp., 1951—53, trainee in rehab. (rheumatology), 1955—57; asst. chief arthritis rsch. unit VA Hosp., Washington, 1953—54, adj. asst. chief, 1954—58, chief, 1958—62; cons. in rheumatology U.S. Naval Hosp., Bethesda, Md., 1959—70; mem. faculty dept. medicine George Washington U., instr., 1957—59, asst. prof., 1959—62, assoc. prof., 1962—80, prof., 1980—93, prof. emeritus, from 1993, dir. divsn. rheumatology, 1970—79, mem. univ. faculty senate exec. com., 1991—93. Mem. Nat. Commn. on Arthritis and Related Musculoskeletal Diseases, 1975—76, Nat. Arthritis adv. bd., 1977—80, 1990—93; mem. nat. com. on health policy Project Hope, 1977; mem. steering com. Health Policy Agenda for Am. People,

1982—87; mem. Nat. Com. Vital and Health Stats., 1983—87, 1988—91; mem. adv. com. on disabilities White House Conf. on Aging, 1995; mem. D.C. Health Planning Adv. Com., 1969—72, WHO Task Force on Rheumatology in Developing Countries, 1982, 84, U.S. Del. to 10th Revision Conf. Internat. Classification of Diseases; chmn. med. adv. com. D.C. chpt. Arthritis Found., 1963—85, vice chmn. of chpt. bd. dirs., 1983—94, chmn., 1992—96; bd. dirs. Symposium on Computer Applications in Med. Care, 1980—88, pres.-elect, 1982—83, pres., 1983—84; cons. health affairs and mem. profl. adv. bd. Control Data Corp., 1976—83, Nat. Ctr. for Health Stats., 1991—93. Contbr. articles to profl. jours. in field in med. socioecons.; editl. adv. bd., cons. internal medicine Current Procedural Terminology, 3d edit., 1972—73, editl. adv. bd. Internal Medicine News, 1976—93. Bd. dirs. Nat. Capital Med. Found., 1979—84, pres., 1980—81. Served with U.S. Army, 1947—49. Recipient Disting. Svc. award, AMA, 1996. Master: Am. Coll. Rheumatology; fellow: Am. Coll. Med. Informatics; mem.: AMA (coun. on legis. 1980—90, chmn. 1985—87, chmn. editl. adv. panel CPT-4 1980—92), Med. Assn. South Africa (lectr. 1995, 1996), Internat. League Against Rheumatism (chmn. subcom. on classification and nomenclature 1982—94, mem. epidemiology com. 1989—93), Rheumatism Soc. D.C. (pres. 1963—64), So. Med. Assn. (sec. sect. internal medicine 1978—79, vice chmn. 1979—80, chmn. 1980—81, assoc. councilor 1979—81, 1985—86), D.C. Soc. Internal Medicine (exec. coun. 1975—78), D.C. Med. Soc. (chmn. legis. com. 1972—76, 1976—78), Inst. Medicine NAS, Am. Soc. Internal Medicine (dir. 1968—78, pres. 1976—77), Nat. Acad. Practice in Medicine (chmn. 1991—93), Nat. Acads. of Practice (pres. 1993—96), Kappa Sigma, Phi Chi, Alpha Epsilon Delta. Republican. Baptist. Deceased.

FENDLER, OSCAR, lawyer; b. Blytheville, Ark., Mar. 22, 1909; s. Alfred and Rae (Sattler) F.; m. Patricia Shane, Oct. 26, 1946; children: Tilden P. Wright III (stepson), Frances Shane. BA, U. Ark., 1930; LL.B., Harvard, 1933. Bar: Ark. bar 1933. Practice in, Blytheville, 1933-41, 46—. Spl. justice Ark. Supreme Ct., 1965; Mem. Ark. Jud. Council, 1959- 60; pres. Conf. Local Bar Assn., 1958-60; pres. bd. dirs. Ark. Law Rev., 1961-67; mem. Ark. Bd. Pardons and Paroles, 1970-71 Mem. Miss. County Democratic Central Com., 1948—. Served with USNR, 1941-45. Fellow Am. Coll. Trust and Estate Counsel, Am. Bar Found.; mem. ABA (chmn. gen. practice sect. 1966-67, mem. council sect. gen. practice 1964—, ho. dels. 1968-80, mem. com. edn. about Communism 1966-70, com. legal aid and indigent defendants 1970-73, chmn. com. law lists 1973-76, Founders award 1992), Ark. Bar Assn. (chmn. exec. com. 1956-57, pres. 1962-63), Am. Judicature Soc. (dir. 1964-68), Scribes, Nat. Conf. Bar Presidents (exec. council 1963-65), Blytheville C. of C. (past v.p., dir.), Navy League, Am. Legion. Clubs: Blytheville Rotary (past pres.). Died Dec. 23, 2002.

FERGUSON, DONALD GUFFEY, radiologist; b. West Newton, Pa., July 19, 1923; s. Rutherford Hayes and Beulah Cristabel (Guffey) F.; m. Anne Benedict Gallagher, MAr. 4, 1961. BS, U. Pitts., 1944, MD, 1946. Diplomate Am. Bd. Radiology, Am. Bd. Nuclear Medicine. Intern S. Side Hosp., Pitts., 1946-47; resident in radiology and radiation therapy Meml. Sloan-Kettering, N.Y.C., 1950-52; staff radiologist Thomas Jefferson U. Hosp., Phila., 1952-55; attending radiologist Mercy Hosp., Pitts., 1955-57; sr. staff S. Side Hosp., Pitts., from 1957, St. Clair Meml. Hosp., Pitts., from 1957; clin. asst. prof. radiology U. Pitts., from 1956. With M.C., U.S. Army, 1948-50. Am. Cancer Soc. fellow. Fellow Am. Coll. Radiology (dist. councilor 1972-78, pres. Pa. chpt. 1979-80); mem. Soc. Nuclear Medicine (chpt. pres. 1957-58), Pitts. Roentgen Soc. (pres. 1967-68), Am. Med. Assn. (ho. of dels. 1987-99), Pa. Med. Soc. (pres. 1992-93), Radiol. Soc. N.Am., Am. Roentgen Ray Soc., Orgn. State Med. Assn. Pres. (pres. 1998-99), Allegheny County Med. Soc., Masons. Presbyterian. Home: Canonsburg, Pa. Deceased.

FERGUSON, JOHN MARSHALL, retired federal judge; b. Marion, Ill., Oct. 14, 1921; s. John Marshall and Vessie (Widdows) F.; m. Jeanne Harmon, Sept. 23, 1950; children: Marcia Ferguson Velde, Mark Harmon, John Scott, Mary Sue Holley. Student, So. Ill. U., 1939-41, S.E. Mo. Tchrs. Coll., 1941; LLB, JD, Washington U., St. Louis, 1948. Bar: Ill. 1949, U.S. Ct. Appeals (7th cir.) 1956, U.S. Supreme Ct. 1960. Asst. mgr. I.W. Rogers Theaters, Inc., Anna, Ill., 1934-42; atty. U.S. Fidelity & Guaranty Co., St. Louis, 1948-51; assoc. Baker, Kagy & Wagner, East St. Louis, Ill., 1951-56, ptnr., 1956-59, Wagner, Conner, Ferguson, Bertrand & Baker, East St. Louis and Belleville, Ill., 1959-72; magistrate judge U.S. Dist. Ct. (so. dist.) Ill., 1990-94. Pres. bd. Arch Aircraft, Inc., 1966-68; disciplinary commr. Ill. Supreme Ct., 1957-90, mem. joint com. on revision disciplinary rules, 1972-74; mem. hearing bd. Ill. Registration and Disciplinary Commn., 1974-90; pres. 1st Dist. Fedn. Bar Assns. Precinct committeeman Stookey Twp., St. Clair County (Ill.) Republican Com., 1958-62; Bd. dirs., v.p. East St. Louis chpt. ARC. Capt. AUS, 1942-45. Mem. ABA, Ill. Bar Assn. (prof. responsibility com. 1975-86, chmn. 1983-84), St. Clair County Bar Assn., 7th Fed. Cir. Bar Assn. (bd. govs.), Ill. Club (govs., pres. 1966-67), East St. Louis City Club (pres. 1960-61), Ill. Club (gov. pres. 1966-67), St. Clair Country Club (Belleville, pres. 1972-73), Masons, Elks, Delta Theta Phi. Home: Belleville, Ill. Died Mar. 2003.

FERGUSON, PAMELA ANDERSON, mathematics educator, educational administrator; b. Berwyn, Ill., May 5, 1943; d. Clarence Oscar and Ruth Anne (Stroner) Anderson; m. Donald Roger Ferguson, Dec. 18, 1965; children: Keith, Amanda. BA, Wellesley Coll., 1965; MS, U. Chgo., 1966, PhD, 1969. Asst. prof. Northwestern U., Evanston, Ill., 1969—70, U. Miami, Coral Gables, Fla., 1972—77, assoc. prof., 1978—81, prof. math., 1981—91, dir. honors program, 1985—87, assoc. provost, dean Grad. Sch., 1987—91; pres. Grinnell Coll., Iowa, 1991—97, prof. math., 1991—2003, Breid McFarland prof. of sci., 2003—04. Mem. Nat. Sci. Bd., 1998—2004; vis. com. phys. scis. divsn. U. Chgo., from 1996. Contbr. articles to profl. jours. Mem. Iowa Rsch. Coun., 1993—97. Grantee NSF grantee. Mem.: Am. Women in Math., Am. Math. Soc., Wellesley Club, Phi Beta Kappa, Omicron Delta Chi, Sigma Xi. Lutheran. Avocations: hiking, reading, skiing. Home: Des Moines, Iowa. Died Apr. 24, 2004.

FERGUSON, RONALD THOMAS, writer; b. N.Y.C., May 3, 1933; s. Thomas Robert and Eleanor Lillian (Jonasson) F.; m. Faith Ann Casebolt, Dec. 28, 1964; children: Elizabeth, Karen, Thomas. BA in History and French, SUNY, Albany, 1954; MA in European History, Pa. State U., 1961; PhD in European and Asian History, U. Minn., 1970. Temp. instr. history Pa. State U., University Park, 1957-59; head dept. history Atlantic Highlands (N.J.) H.S., 1958-59; instr. history Ithaca (N.Y.) Coll., 1961-63; sr. tchg. asst., supr. history 1-2-3 program U. Minn., Mpls., 1963-65; acting assoc. prof. history U. Hawaii Manoa, Honolulu, 1966-69; prof. history Indiana (Pa.) U., 1969-88; writer Indiana, Pa., from 1988. Author: Blood and Fire: Contribution Policies of French Armies in Germany, 1667-1715, 1970. With U.S. Army, 1955-57. Fulbright rsch. scholar French Army Archives, 1965-66. Mem. Aircraft Owners and Pilots Assn., Air Force Assn. (life), USN Inst., Polit. Sci. Assn. Lutheran. Avocations: locksmith, french-german-swedish linguist. Home: Indiana, Pa. Deceased.

FERGUSON, WILKIE D., JR., federal judge; b. 1938; m. Betty J. Tucker; 2 children. BS, Fla. A & M Univ., 1960; JD, Howard U., 1968; LHD (hon.), Fla. Meml. Coll., 1993. Acct. Ford-Philco Corp., 1963-65; staff atty. Legal Svcs. of Greater Miami, Inc., Brownsville, Fla., 1968-70; pvt. practice McCrary, Ferguson & Lee, Miami, Fla., 1970-73; judge Fla. Cir. Ct. for 11th Cir., 1976-80; judge industrial claims, 1977-78; judge Fla. Ct. Appeals for 3d Dist., 1980-93, U.S. Dist Ct. (so. dist.) Fla., from 1993. Staff atty. Dade County Sch. Bd., 1972-73; mem. jury instructions com. Supreme Ct. Governing bd. Pub. TV, WPBT: vol. United Way Dade County (Outstanding Vol. Svc. award, 1987). With U.S. Army, 1960-64, capt. USAR, 1964-68. Fla. A & M Univ. scholar, 1956, Howard U. scholar, 1965; Reginald Heber Smith fellow U. Pa., 1968; recipient Disting. Svc. award Am. Soc. Pub. Adminstrn., 1973, Achiever of the Yr. award Achievers Club Greater Miami, 1977, Outstanding Jurist award NBA, 1992, Recognition for Excellence in Pub. Svc. award King of Clubs, 1993, Outstanding Alumni award Howard U. Sch. Law, 1999, William H. Hastie award Jud. Coun.-Nat. Bar Assn., 2000. Mem. ABA, Nat. Bar Assn. (Exemplary Judicial Svc. award, 1984, Thurgood Marshall Achievement award, 1986), Dade County Bar Assn., No. Dade Bar Assn., Fla. Bar Assn., Am. Inns of Ct., Fla. A & M Univ. Alumni Assn., Alpha Phi Alpha (Community Svc. award, 1977), Phi Alpha Delta. Died June 9, 2003.

FERON, JAMES MARTIN, newspaperman; b. Woodside, N.Y., June 23, 1928; s. James J. and Flora (Trostler) F.; m. Jeanne Margaret Clare, Feb. 28, 1953; children: Robert, Michael, Andrew, Margaret. BA, Marietta Coll., 1950; MS, Columbia U., 1955. With N.Y. Times, 1952—91; beginning as copy boy, successively news clk., radio news writer, gen. assignment N.Y. area corr. UN, 1959-61, 1961-65, 1965-70, 1970-73, 1973. Assoc. in journalism Columbia U. Grad. Sch. Journalism, 1978. Contbr. to: Ency. Year Book, 1963-66. Served with Signal Corps AUS, 1948-50. Pulitzer travelling fellow, 1955 Died June 19, 2004.

FERRE, LUIS A. political organization administrator; b. Feb. 17, 1904; m. Tiody de Jesus, 1980. BA, MIT, 1924, MA, 1925; LLD (hon.), Harvard U., Amherst Coll.; LHD (hon.), NYU; D in Internat. Law (hon.), Fla. Internat. U.; D in Music, New Eng. Conservatory Music. Pres., CEO PR Cement Co., Inc.; mem. P.R. House Repr, 1953—56; gov. Puerto Rico, 1969-72; senator P.R. Legis., 1976-85; pres. Senate, 1977—80; chmn. P.R. Rep. Party, from 1975. Sr. adv. UN Edn., Scientific and Cultural Orgn., 1982-83; mem. Rep. Nat. Com.; del. Rep. Nat. Conv., 1968, 72, 76, 80, 84. Contbr. articles to profl. jours. Decorated Knight of the Holy Sepulchre Pope John XXIII, 1959, Order of Vasa, 1963. Fellow ASME, Am. Soc. Arts and Scis., Elks, Met. Opera; mem. AIA. Died Oct. 21, 2003.

FERRI, ROGER CESARE, architect, artist; b. N.Y.C., Dec. 13, 1949; s. Atelio Roger and Marion (Bosser) F. BArch, Pratt Inst., 1972; postgrad., Art Student's League, 1978-81. Registered architect, N.Y., N.J., Pa., Fla., Conn., Mass. Maine, Ohio, La. Prin. Roger Ferri Architect, N.Y.C., 1977-84 and from 86; v.p., design prin. Welton Becket Assocs., N.Y.C., 1984-86. Adj. asst. prof. Columbia U., N.Y.C., 1983-84. Recipient award of excellence for residential design Archtl. Record, l982, 87; N.Y. State Coun. Arts archtl. fellow, l979; grantee SOM Found., l980. Mem. Archtl. League of N.Y., AIA, Mcpl. Arts Soc. of N.Y., Am. Assn. of Mus., Royal Soc. of the Arts. Avocations: swimming, sailing, classical music. Home: New York, NY. Deceased.

FERRIS, FREDERICK JOSEPH, gerontologist, social worker; b. Troy, N.Y., June 2, 1920; s. John and Amelia (Deeb) F.; m. Ellen J. Walsh, June 12, 1965. BA cum laude, SUNY, Albany, 1942; MS, Columbia U., 1949, DSW, 1968. Head social studies dept. Heatly H.S., Green Island, N.Y., 1946-47; sec. info. svc. Greater N.Y. Fund, N.Y.C., 1949-51; exec. sec. N. Met. div. United Community Svcs., Boston, 1951-53, mem. rsch. div. com., 1953-57; dir. community orgn., asst. prof. Boston Coll. Sch. Social Work, 1953-57; dean, prof. Nat. Cath. Sch. Social Svc. Cath. U. Am., Washington, 1960-69, mem. adv. com. Gerontology Conf., 1985-91; with AARP-Nat. Ret. Tchrs. Assn., Washington, coord. White House Conf. on Aging, 1970-72; dir. planning and rsch. dept. and adminstr. Andrus Found., 1970-86. Adv. assoc. prof. Fordham U. Sch. Social Svc., 1957-60; lectr. Adelphi U., Rutgers U., 1959-60; social planning cons. Am. Found. for Blind, 1958-59; proposal reviewer NSF; cons. Inst. Community Studies, United Way Am., 1970, Psychiat. Inst. Found.; del. White House Conf. on Aging, 1971, resource person, 1981; tech. rev. panel Nat. Coun. on Aging; mem. commn. on svcs. to aging Archdiocese of Washington, 1971-76; vice chmn. Joint Legis. Com., Boston, 1954-57. Book reviewer Social Thought. Mem. exec. com. Nat. Vol. Orgns. for Ind. Living for the Aging, 1972—74, 1977—82; mem. commn. on aging Cath. Charities U.S.A., from 1972, chmn., 1978—84; bd. dirs. Social Svc. Exch., Boston, 1955—57, Child Welfare League Am., 1966—70, Cath. Internat. Union Social Svc., 1967—72, Christ Child Soc., Washington, 1967—73; treas., bd. dirs. Nat. Conf. Cath. Charities, Archdiocese of Washington, 1976—83; chmn. Washington com. 13th Internat. Conf. Schs. Social Work, 1965—66; active Montgomer County Commn. Aging, 1987—93, mem. pub. policy com., 1st & 2d vice chmn., 1988—92, mem. exec. com., planning com., chmn., 1992—93, nominating com., chmn. econ. security com., 1988—90; mem. Am. Task Force for Lebanon; bd. dirs. Montgomery County Dept. Social Svcs., 1994—2001; mem. parish coun. Ch. of the Annuciation, Washintton, 1968—70, chair ch. and cmty. com., chair task force on self-study, chair nominating com., mem. nominating com., mem. task force self study. Capt. U.S. Army, 1942—46, maj USAR. Recipient Lasker Doctoral fellowship Columbia U., 1957-58, Pres.'s Centennial medal Cath. U. of Am., 1988, Outstanding Citizenship award Albany County LWV, 1942. Mem. Nat. Assn. Social Workers (chpt. treas. 1956-57, task force on svcs. to aging 1973-75), Mass. Conf. Social Work (dir., chmn. nominating com. 1956-57), Alumni Assn. Columbia U. Sch. Social Work (chpt. chmn. 1954-55, dir. 1956-59), United Comty. Funds and Couns. Am. (nat. adv. com. health and welfare svcs. 1955-57, coun. planning execs. 1957-59), Nat. Assn. Hearing and Speech Agy. (nat. tng. adv. com. 1963-70), Acad. Cert. Social Workers, Coun. Social Work Edn. (deans adv. com. fed. welfare agys. 1962-64, 66-68, ho. of dels. 1977-86, adv. bd. gerontol. content in social work edn. 1983-86), So. Gerontol. Soc. (dir. 1981-86), Am. Soc. on Aging, Assn. Gerontology in Higher Edn. (com. interorganizational rels., program com., Disting. Svc. Recognition award 1995), Gerontol. Soc., John Carroll Soc., Univ. Club Washington. Home: Washington, DC. Died Oct. 13, 2002.

FESHBACH, HERMAN, physicist, researcher; b. N.Y.C., Feb. 2, 1917; s. David and Ida (Lapiner) Feshbach; m. Sylvia Harris, Jan. 28, 1940; children: Carolyn Barbara, Theodore Philip, Mark Frederick. BS, CCNY, 1937; PhD, MIT, 1942; DSc (hon.), Lowell Tech. Inst., 1975; degree (hon.), U. Lowell, 1974, U. Torino, Italy, 2000. Tutor CCNY, 1937—38; instr. MIT, Cambridge, 1941—45, asst. prof., 1945—47, assoc. prof., 1947—55, prof., 1955—87, Cecil and Ida Green prof. physics, 1976—83, inst. prof., 1983—87, inst. prof. emeritus, from 1987, dir. Ctr. for Theoretical Physics, 1967—73, head dept. physics, 1973—83. Cons. AEC; chmn. nuc. sci. adv. com. Dept. Energy and NSF, 1979—82. Author (with P.M. Morse): Methods of Theoretical Physics, 1953; author: (with A. deShalit) Theoretical Nuclear Physics, Nuclear Structure, 1974; author: Theoretical Nuclear Physics: Nuclear Reactions, 1992; editor: Annals of Physics; contbr. articles to profl. jours. Associated Univs., Inc., 1974—87, 1990—96; hon. trustee, from 1966. Recipient Harris medal, CCNY, 1977, Nat. med. of Sci., 1987; fellow John Simon Guggenheim Meml. Found., 1954—55, Ford, CERN, Geneva, 1962—63. Mem.: AAAS (chmn. physics sect. 1987—88), NRC, NAS, Internat. Union Pure and Applied Physics (chmn. nuc. physics sect. 1984—90), Am. Acad. Arts and Scis. (v.p. Class I 1973—76, pres. 1982—86), Am. Phys. Soc. (divisional councillor 1974—78, exec. com. 1974—78, v.p. 1979—80, pres. 1980—81). Home: Minneapolis, Minn. Died Dec. 22, 2000.

FEUER, LEWIS S. sociologist, educator, philosopher; b. N.Y.C., Dec. 7, 1912; s. Joseph and Fannie (Weidner) F.; m. Kathryn Jean Beliveau, Oct. 13, 1946; 1 child, Robin Kathryn (Mrs. Miller). BS, CCNY, 1931; A.M., Harvard U., 1932, PhD, 1935; L.H.D. h.c., Hebrew Union Coll., 1986. Asst. in philosophy Harvard, 1935-37; instr. philosophy Coll. City N.Y., 1939-42; faculty Vassar Coll., 1946-51, U. Vt., 1951-57; prof. philosophy and social sci. U. Calif. at Berkeley, 1957-66; prof. sociology U. Toronto, 1966-76; Univ. prof. sociology and govt. U. Va., Charlottesville, 1976-83, Univ. prof emeritus. Hugo A. Wolfsohn Meml. lectr. U. Melbourne, La Trobe and Monash, Australia, 1986; cons. Radio Liberty, Fgn. Service Inst., Internat. Communication Agy., 1970— Author: Psychoanalysis and Ethics, 1955, Spinoza and the Rise of Liberalism, 1958, The Scientific Intellectual, 1963. rept. new introduction, 1992, The Conflict of Generations, 1969, Marx and the Intellectuals, 1969, Einstein and the Generations of Science, 1974, Ideology and the Ideologists, 1975, The Case of the Revolutionist's Daughter, 1983, Imperialism and the Anti-imperialist Mind, 1986, Jews in the Origins of Modern Science and Bacon's Scientific Utopia, 1987; contbr. Autobiographical Essay to Philosophy, History and Social Action, 1988; editor Marx and Engels, Basic Writings on Politics and Philosophy, 1959 (transls. into French, Italian, Spanish, Hebrew, Japanese, Portuguese, German.). Served with AUS, 1942-46. Ford fellow for Advancement of Edn., 1954-55; exchange scholar Inst. Philosophy, Soviet Acad. Sci., Moscow, USSR, 1963; recipient Bowdoin medal Harvard, 1935 Mem. Am. Sociol. Assn., Am. Philos. Assn., Am. Polit. Sci. Assn., Am. Jewish Hist. Soc. (Leo Wasserman award 1982), Assn. for Jewish Studies, Univ. Ctrs. for Rational Alternatives (pres. 1986—), Cambridge Union U. Tchrs. (sec. 1935-37), AAUP (pres. Vt. chpt. 1955-56), Authors Guild, Phi Beta Kappa. Research, numerous publs. Home: Waban, Mass. Died Nov. 24, 2002.

FIEDLER, LESLIE AARON, English educator, actor, author; b. Newark, Mar. 8, 1917; s. Jacob J. and Lillian (Rosenstrauch) F.; m. Margaret Ann Shipley, Oct. 7, 1939 (div. 1972); children: Kurt, Eric, Michael, Deborah, Jenny, Miriam; m. Sally Andersen, 1973; stepchildren: Soren Andersen, Eric Charles Andersen. BA, NYU, 1938; MA, U. Wis., 1939, PhD, 1941; postgrad., Harvard U., 1946-47. Mem. faculty U. Mont., 1941-64, from instr. to assoc. prof. English, 1941-53, prof., 1953-64, chmn. dept. English, 1954-56; prof. SUNY, Buffalo, from 1965. Vis. prof. U. Rome, 1951-52, U. Bologna and Ca Foscari U., Italy, 1952-53, Princeton (N.J.) U., 1956-57, Athens U., 1961-62, U. Sussex, Eng., 1967-68, U. Paris, 1970-71; jr. fellow Ind. U. Sch. Letters, 1951—; assoc. Calhoun fellow Yale U., New Haven, 1969—. Author: (with others) Leaves of Grass: 100 Years After, 1955, An End to Innocence, 1955, The Art of the Essay, 1959, rev. edit., 1969, The Image of the Jew in American Fiction, 1959, Love and Death in the American Novel, 1960, rev. edit., 1966, No. In Thunder, 1960; (with J. Vinocur) The Continuing Debate, 1964; Waiting for the End, 1964, Back to China, 1965, Waiting for the End, 1964, Back to China, 1965; (with others) The Girl in the Black Raincoat, 1966; The Last Jew in America, 1966, The Return of the Vanishing American, 1967, Nude Croquet and Other Stories, 1969, Being Busted, 1970, Collected Essays, 1971, The Stranger in Shakespeare, 1972, The Messengers Will Come No More, 1974, In Dreams Awake, 1975, Freaks, 1977, A Fiedler Reader, 1977, The Inadvertent Epic, 1979, Olaf Stapledon, 1982, What Was Literature?, 1982, Fiedler on the Roof, 1991, Love and Death in the American Novel, 1993, Freaks, 1993, (collected essays) Stranger in a Strange Land, 1994, Tyranny of the Normal, 1996, A New Fiedler Reader, 1999, Introduction to the Star Rover, 1999, (short stories) Pull Down Vanity, 1962; (novel) The Second Stone, 1963; (film) When I Am King; editor: (with others) Master of Ballantrae, 1951; (with S. Weil) Waiting for God, 1952; Poems of Whitman, 1959; (with Arthur Zeiger) O Brave New World, 1967; assoc. editor: Ramparts, 1959-65; contbg. editor: Am. Judaism; lit. editor: Running Man, 1967-69; contbr. short stories, poems and articles to jours. U.S. and abroad. Lt. (j.g.) USNR, 1942-46. Rockefeller fellow in humanities, 1946-47, Fulbright fellow, 1951-53, Kenyon rev. fellow in criticism, 1956-57, Guggenheim fellow, 1970-71; recipient Furioso prize for Poetry, 1951, Nat. Inst. Arts and Letters award, 1957, grant-in-aid Am. Coun. Learned Socs., 1960, 61; Christian Gauss lectr., 1956; recipient Ivan Sandroff award for lifetime contbn. to Am. arts and letters Nat. Book Critic Cir., 1998, PEN Ctr. USA West award for body of work, 1999, Mem. MLA (Hubbell medal), AAUP, English Inst., Am. Acad. and Inst. Arts and Letters (dept. lit.), Dante Soc. Am., PEN, Phi Beta Kappa. Died Jan. 29, 2003.

FIELD, SELMA G. public relations professional; b. Jan. 31, 1925; BS, SUNY, Albany, 1946. Dir. public relations Cmty. Gen. Hosp., Harris, NY, from 1960; pres. Field Assocs., Ltd., Monticello, NY, from 1960. Co-Author: (books) Publicity Manual For Libraries, Publicity Manual For Law Enforcement, Promoting and Marketing Your Craft, How To Get Rich With OPN. Chair Coll. Coun. SUNY, New Paltz, N.Y., 1985-97, pres. Casa Ct. Appointed Special Advocates, Monticello, N.Y., 1994-98, vice-pres. Literacy Vols. of Am., 1990—, vice-pres. Monticello Ctrl. Sch. Bd. Edn., 1962-72. Died Dec. 19, 2001.

FILBY, PERCY WILLIAM, library consultant; b. Cambridge, Eng., Dec. 10, 1911; came to U.S., 1957, naturalized, 1960; s. William Lusher and Florence Ada (Stanton) F.; m. Nancie Elizabeth Giddens (div. 1957); children: Ann Veronica Filby Chesworth, Jane Vanessa Johnson, Roderick, Guy; m. Vera Ruth Weakliem, 1957. Student, Cambridge U. Librarian Cambridge U., 1930-37, dir. sci. library, 1937-40; sec. to Sir James Frazer, 1934-39; crytographer, head German Dip. sect. Bletchley, 1940-45; sr. researcher, archivist Brit. Fgn. Office, 1946-57; asst. dir. Peabody Inst., Balt., 1957-65; librarian, asst. dir. Md. Hist. Soc., Balt., 1965-72, dir., 1972-78, ret., 1978; library cons., 1978—. Cons. on rare books, calligraphy; appraiser rare books and manuscripts. Author: Cambridge Papers, 1936, Calligraphy and Handwriting in America, 1710-1962, 1963, (with others) Two Thousand Years of Calligraphy, 1965, American and British Genealogy and Heraldry, 1970, 3d edit., 1983, supplement, 1986, (with others) Star Spangled Books, 1972, Who's Who in Genealogy and Heraldry, 1981, 2d edit., 1990, Passenger Lists Bibliography, 1538-1900, 1981, 2d edit., 1988, (with others) Passenger and Immigration Lists Index, 13 vols., 1981, 82, supplements, 1983—, Philadelphia Naturalizations, 1982, Bibliography of American County Histories, 1985, 2d printing 1987, Directory of American and Canadian Libraries with Genealogy and Local History Collections, 1988, (with others) Germans to America, 1850—, vols. 1-56, Italians to America, 1980-87, vols. 1-13. Mem. Ellis Island Restoration Commn. Served to capt. Intelligence Corps. Brit. Army, 1940-46, cryptographer, Bletchley, Eng., 1940-46. Recipient Genealogy award RASD History Sect., 1993, Filby prize 2000. Fellow Soc. Genealogists (London), Nat. Geneal. Soc., Manuscript Soc. (pres. 1976-78); mem. ALA (Mudge citation for disting. reference librarianship 1989), Spl. Libraries Assn. (pres. Balt. chpt. 1961-62), Soc. Scribes (v.p.), Soc. for Italic Handwriting, Soc. Am. Archivists, Typophiles, Balt. Bibliophiles (pres. 1963-65, 89-91), Am. Antiquarian Soc., Bibliog. Soc. Am. (coun. 1978-82), Grolier Club (N.Y.C.), Am. Soc. Genealogists (cert. appreciation 2000). Home: Savage, Md. Died Nov. 2, 2002.

FINBY, NATHANIEL, radiologist, educator; b. N.Y.C., May 31, 1917; BA, Johns Hopkins U., 1938, MD, 1942. Diplomate Am. Bd. Radiology. Intern Grasslands Hosp., Valhalla, N.Y., 1942-43; resident in radiology N.Y. Hosp., 1952-54; prof. emeritus Columbia U. Coll. Phys. and Surg., N.Y.C., from 1982. Fellow Am. Coll. Radiology; mem. AMA, Radiol. Soc. N.Am. Home: Vero Beach, Fla. Died Sept. 30, 1999.

FINE, ALBERT SAMUEL, educator; b. Phila., Oct. 24, 1923; s. Max and Sylvia (Lerner) F.; m. Selma Joyce Skolnick, Mar. 29, 1959; 1 child, Martin. BA, Bklyn. Coll., 1950, MA, 1953; PhD, NYU, 1970. Rsch. chemist VA Hosp., Bklyn., 1956-70, chief dental rsch. N.Y.C., 1970-88; assoc. prof. histology, cell biology and peridontics NYU Coll. Dentistry, N.Y.C., from 1970. With U.S. Army, 1942-46, ETO. Mem. Am. Chem. Soc., Am. Inst. Biol. Sci., Sigma Xi. Home: Brooklyn, NY. Died June 14, 2002.

FINE, WILLIAM IRWIN, real estate developer; b. St. Paul, May 26, 1928; s. Adolph and Ida (Cohen) F.; m. Bianca M. Fine, Apr. 10, 1994. BLS, U. Minn., 1949, LLB, 1950. Bar: Minn. 1950, Tex. 1950. Asst. dist. atty. Dallas County, 1950-52; judge adv. gen. USAF, Keesler AFB, Miss., 1952-53; ptnr., founder Fine, Simon & Schneider, Mpls., 1953-69; pres., co-founder Fine Properties Corp., Chgo., 1969-71; mng. gen. ptnr., co-founder Fine Assocs., Mpls., from 1972; co-founder VISTA Sci., Inc., 1991, DYUAR, Inc., 1992. Advisor Inst. Tech. U. Minn., Mpls., 1987—. Trustee Sci. Mus. Minn., St. Paul, 1989-94; co-founder/co-chmn. William I. Fine Theoretical Physics Inst. U. Minn., 1987; charter mem. indsl. liaison com. Materials Rsch. Lab. U. Chgo., 1993-97. Mem. AAAS, Am. Inst. Physics. Home: Minneapolis, Minn. Died May 18, 2002.

FINEMAN, MARK ELLIOTT, journalist; b. Chgo., Aug. 3, 1952; s. Sidney and Juanita (Herman) F. BA, Syracuse U., 1974. Assoc. editor Suburban Week sect. Chgo. Sun-Times and Daily News, 1974-78; spl. projects writer Call-Chronicle Newspapers, Allentown, Pa., 1978-81; staff writer Phila. Inquirer, 1981-82, Asia corr., 1982-86; bur. chief, Manila Los Angeles Times, 1986-89, bur. chief, Philippines, India, Cyprus & Mexico City, 1989—2003. Recipient Amos Tuck award for econ. reporting Dartmouth Coll., 1980, 81, cert. of excellence Overseas Press Club, U.S.A., 1985, George Polk award for fgn. reporting L.I. U, 1985, Disting. Writing award Am. Soc. Newspaper Editors, 1987, Overseas Press Club citation for excellence, 1987. Died Sept. 24, 2003.

FINLEY, HAROLD MARSHALL, investment banker; b. McConnelsville, Ohio, Feb. 24, 1916; s. Harry Marshall and Kate (Cotton) F.; m. Jean Rowley, Sept. 19, 1943; 1 child, Robert W. BS cum laude, Northwestern U., 1933; BD cum laude, Chgo. Theol. Sem., 1944; postgrad., U. Chgo., 1949; LLD, Lincoln Meml. U., 1975; DHL, Lakeland Coll., 1990; LLD, Lewis U., 1995; DHL, Muskingum Coll., 1997. Vice pres. Chgo. Title and Trust Co., 1963-76; sr. v.p. Burton J. Vincent, Chesley & Co., Chgo., 1976-84, Prescott, Ball & Turben, Chgo., 1984-92, Kemper Securities, 1992-94; 1st v.p. Howe Barnes Investments, Chgo., 1994-99. Author: Everybody's Guide to the Stock Market, 1956, 59, 65, 68, The Logical Approach to Successful Investing, 1971; columnist Market Trends, Chgo. Today, 1961-74, Chgo. Tribune, 1974-81. Trustee Chgo. Boys and Girls Club; active Lockport Twp. H.S. Bd. Edn., 1961-64; trustee Alice Lloyd Coll., Chgo. Theol. Sem., Kobe Coll., Lewis U.; trustee Lincoln Meml. U., chmn., 1981-99; trustee Scholl Coll. Podiatric Medicine, 1986-96, Sci. and Arts Acad., 1994-99; treas. Ill. Humane Soc., 1986-99. Mem. Investment Analysts Soc. Chgo., Chartered Fin. Analysts, Transp. Securities Club Chgo., Delta Sigma Pi. Clubs: Univ. (Chgo.), Rotary (Chgo.) (pres. 1978-79). Congregationalist. Home: Lockport, Ill. Died Dec. 14, 1999.

FINNEGAN, MARY ELIZABETH O'DONNELL, classicist, educator; b. Lubec, Maine, Sept. 24, 1907; d. Edward Eugene and Mary Rysam (Sleight) O'Donnell; m. Reynold Edward Finnegan, Oct. 23, 1929 (dec. Jan. 1974); children: Maureen F. Landrigan, Edward William, Reynold Joseph. BA cum laude, Coll. New Rochelle, 1927; MA, Tufts U., 1980; PhD in Humanities, Fla. State U., 1991; DHL (hon.), U. System N.H., 1983. Tchr. Latin and French Lancaster (N.H.) Acad., 1927-29, 1932-33; tchr. social studies Berlin (N.H.) High Sch., 1943-46, tchr. English and fgn. langs., 1958-72, head langs. dept., 1970-72; tchr. English Gorham (N.H.) High Sch., 1946-58; tutor Tufts U., Medford, Mass., 1978-79; teaching asst. Fla. State U., Tallahassee, 1982-85; adj. prof. U. System N.H., Berlin, from 1976, prof. emeritus, from 1991; vis. asst. prof. Dartmouth Coll., Hanover, N.H., 1987-88. Sch. vol., Gorham, N.H., summers 1976—; dir. ednl. workshops North Country Edn. Found.; lectr. CANE Inst., 1993. Contbr. book reviews to profl. jours.; contbr. articles to profl. jour. Mem. AAUW (Gift honoree 1985, Life Mem. award 1992), Am. Classical League (lectr. 1978, 89, 91), Classical Assn. New Eng. (mem. exec. bd., recipient Beach Barlow award 1982), N.H. Classical Assn. (bd. dirs. 1965-80), Ret. Tchrs. Assn., Berlin Bus. and Profl. Women Assn. (Women of Achievement award 1981), Nat. Fedn. Women's Clubs, Coll. New Rochelle Alumnae Assn. (alumnae coun. 1982, medalist), Eta Sigma Phi, Kappa Gamma Pi (alumnae coun. Coll. New Rochelle 1974—). Democrat. Roman Catholic. Avocations: volunteerism, family history. Home: Berlin, NH. Deceased.

FINOGENOV, PAVEL VASILYEVICH, Soviet government official; b. 1919. Grad. Leningrad Mil.-Mech. Inst., 1953.former mem. CPSU; various posts including dir. of a plant, 1941-60; dep. dir. Soviet of Nat. Economy, Vladimir, 1960-65; USSR dep. minister, 1965-73, 1st dep. minister, 1973-79, minister of def. industry, 1979—89; mem. Supreme Soviet. Died Jan. 22, 2004.

FIOL-MATTA, LYNN, composition and language educator; b. San Juan, P.R., Dec. 22, 1955; d. Juan R. and Emma (Matta Mendez) Fiol Bigas. BA, U. P.R., 1977; MA, NYU, 1989. Vis. instr. Manhattan Coll., Bronx, N.Y. Mem. NCTE, ASCD. Home: Long Island City, NY. Died Nov. 6, 2000.

FIORE, ERIC EMANUEL, experimental test pilot; b. N.Y.C., Aug. 10, 1957; s. A. Christopher and Judith R. (Ullman) F.; m. Carol A. Mayer, May 30, 1980; children: Tia J., Robin R. BS in Aerospace Engring. summa cum laude, St. Louis U., Cahokia, Ill., 1982; grad. flight test engr., Nat. Test Pilot Sch., Mojave, Calif., 1992. Lic. airline transport pilot, FAA. Test pilot Fairchild Aircraft Inc., San Antonio, 1991-94; engring. test pilot Cessna Aircraft Co., Wichita, Kans., from 1994. Capt. USAF, 1983-91. Decorated Nat. Def. Svc. medal, Combat Readiness medal, Air Force Commendation medal with oak leaf cluster; named Disting. Grad., USAF Pilot Tng., Sheppard AFB, Tex., 1984, USAF Officer Tng. Sch., Lackland AFB, TEx., 1983. Mem. AIAA, Soc. Exptl. Test Pilots, Order of Daedalians. Home: Loveland, Colo. Died Nov. 15, 2000.

FISCH, CHARLES, physician, educator; b. Nesterov (Zolkiew), Poland, May 11, 1921; s. Leon and Janette (Deutscher) F.; m. June Spiegal, May 23, 1943; children: Jonathan, Gary, Bruce. AB, Ind. U., 1942, MD, 1944; MD (hon.), U. Utrecht, The Netherlands, 1983. Diplomate Am. Bd. Internal Medicine, Am. Bd. Cardiovasc. Medicine (mem. 1977-82). Intern St. Vincent's Hosp., Indpls., 1945; resident in internal medicine VA Hosp., Indpls., 1948-50; fellow gastroenterology Marion County Gen. Hosp., Indpls., 1950-51, fellow in cardiology, 1951-53; asst. prof. medicine Ind. U. Med. Sch., 1953-59, assoc. prof., 1959-63, prof., 1963—90, disting. prof., 1975, dir. cardiovasc. divsn., 1963 90, disting. prof. emeritus, 1990—2002; dir. Krannert Inst. Cardiology, 1953-90. Mem. cardio-renal adv. com. HEW-FDA, 1973-77; Connor lectr. Am. Heart Assn., 1980; chmn. manpower rev. com. Nat. Heart, Lung and Blood Inst., 1985-89; Charles Fisch chair in cardiology Ind. U. Author: Electrocardiography of Arrythmias, 1989; co-editor Digitalis, 1969, Cardiac Electrophysiology and Arrythmias, 1991, Electrophysiology of Clinical Arrythmias, 2000; contbr. articles to med. jours.; former mem. editorial bd. Am. Heart Jour., Am. Jour. Electrocardiology, Coeur et Medicine Interne, 1970—, Am. Jour. Medicine, 1973, Circulation, Am. Jour. Cardiology; assoc. editor Am. Jour. Cardiology. Capt. M.C. AUS, 1946-48. Recipient James Herrick award Am. Heart Assn. Fellow ACP, Am. Coll. Cardiology (pres. 1975-77, dir., chmn. publ. com. 1988-94, Gifted Tchr. award 1993), World Congress Cardiology (v.p. 1986); mem. Am. Fedn. Clin. Rsch., Ctrl. Soc. Clin. Rsch., Am. Physiol. Soc., Assn. Univ. Cardiologists, Assn. Am. Physicians, N.Am. Soc. for Pacing and Electrophysiology (Dist. Tchr. award 1994). Home: Indianapolis, Ind. Died June 24, 2002.

FISCHER, JOHN ALBERT, surgeon, retired; b. Dobbs Ferry, N.Y., Aug. 15, 1920; MD, Albany Med. Coll., 1947. Diplomate Am. Bd. Surgery. Intern Union Meml. Hosp., Balt., 1947-48, resident in surgery, 1948-49, Perry Point (Md.) VA Hosp., 1949-53; ret., 1985. Mem. staff Union Hosp. Cecil County, Elkton, Md.; cons. VA Med. Ctr., Perry Point; mem. courtesy staff Med. Ctr. Dela., Wilmington, 1954-87; chief surgery Union Hosp., 1957-85; assoc. program Md. Sch. Medicine, 1994. Fellow ACS; mem. AMA. Home: Potomac, Md. Died Mar. 23, 2001.

FISCHOFF, EPHRAIM, humanities educator, sociologist, social worker; b. N.Y.C., Oct. 2, 1904; s. Aaron and Betty (Gunsberg) F.; m. Marion Judson, Dec. 28, 1943; children: Aronel, Gabriel and Raphael (twins), Michael, Bettina, Daniel. AB, CCNY, 1924; MHL, Jewish Inst. Religion, 1928; DSocial Sci., New Sch. Social Research, 1942; DD, Hebrew Union Coll., 1982. Ordained rabbi, 1928. Ministry, religious edn. group work, 1928-42; lectr. sociology Pa. State U., 1935-36; lectr. Jewish Tchrs. Sem., N.Y., 1937-42; editorial cons. World Jewish Congress, 1941-45; lectr New Sch. Social Research, N.Y.C., 1942-51, Hunter Coll. (CCNY), 1942-46; asst. editor Jour. Legal and Polit. Sci., 1943-45; acting exec. dir. Conf. Jewish Relations, 1946; head dept. sociology Am. Internat. Coll., Springfield, Mass., 1946-54; lectr. Hartford Sem. Found., 1953-54; dir. B'nai B'rith Hillel Found. (U. Calif.-Berkeley), 1954-55, B'nai B'rith Hillel Found. (Yale U.), 1955-58; prof. humanities and social sci., dir. honors program Lynchburg Coll., Va., 1960-69; prof. sociology, anthropology and Am. Studies U. Wis.-Stevens Point, 1969-76; prof. social welfare Sangamon State U., Springfield, Ill., 1976, univ. prof. humanities, 1977-83, prof. emeritus, 1983—. Vis. prof. Hollins Coll. U. Va., 1965-67, Sir George Williams U. Montreal, 1970; lectr. So. Ill. Sch. Medicine, 1979-81, lectr., sr. cons., vis. prof. in med. humanities, 1982-84; clin. prof. dept. internal medicine, vis. prof.dept. surgery, 1984—; lectr. in humanities Lincoln Library, Springfield, Ill., 1978-90. Author: William Beaumont, Elizabeth Blackwell, Oliver Wendell Holmes, Sir William Osler, Pearson Mus. Monograph Series, 1981-82; trans., editor: (M. Hirschfeld) Sexual History of the World War; translator: (Max Weber) Sociology of Religion, 1963; contbr.: Great Thinkers of the Twentieth Century, 1963, Contemporary Jewish Thought, A Reader, 1963, Economy and Society, 1968; contbr., dept. editor: Encyclopaedia Judaica, 1967-68; editorial cons. From War to Peace Series, Inst. Jewish Affairs, World Jewish Congress, 1944-48. Mem. exec. bd. ARC; mem. exec. bd. Pres.'s Com. Physically Handicapped, NCCJ; active Park Ridge Ctr. Fellow Am. Sociol. Assn. Fellow Soc. for Applied Anthropology; mem. Nat. Assn. Social Workers (charter mem.), Acad. Cert. Social Workers, Am. Philos. Assn., Am. Studies Assn., Am. Acad. Polit. and Social Scis., Central Conf. Am. Rabbis, Soc. for Pschol. Study Social Issues; mem. Hist. Sci. Soc., Am. Soc. for History of Medicine, Soc. Sci. Study Religion, Am. Acad. Religion, Soc. Health Human Values, Hastings Ctr., Gerontol. Soc. Am., Am. Jewish Hist. Soc., Jewish Law Assn., Abraham Lincoln Assn., Société Européenne de Culture, Internat. Sociol. Assn., Soc. for Lit. and Sci., Ill. State Hist. Soc., Nat. Humanities Faculty, H.G. Wells Soc., Assn. for Sociology Religion, Amnesty Internat., Alpha Omega Alpha (hon.) Lodges: B'nai Brith. Home: Fort Wayne, Ind. Deceased.

FISH, RICHARD WAYNE, chemistry educator; b. Gowrie, Iowa, Aug. 27, 1934; s. Albert Lawrence and Myrtle Lulu (Carr) F.; m. Madeleine Paula Fischer, June 14, 1964; children: Brian Charles, Daniel Mark. BS in Chemistry, Iowa State U., 1956; PhD in Organic Chemistry, Mich. State U., 1960. Research chemist Chevron Research subs. Standard Oil Co. Calif., Richmond, Calif., 1960-61; research assoc. Brandeis U., Waltham, Mass., 1961-63; NSF postdoctoral fellow U. Calif., Berkeley, 1963-64; mem. faculty Calif. State U., Sacramento, from 1964, prof. chemistry, 1970. Recipient research award Calif State U., Sacramento, 1968-69, Meritorious Performance Incentive award, Calif. State U., Sacramento, 1985. Mem. Am. Chem. Soc. (chmn. Sacramento sect. 1982-83), Sigma Xi. Democrat. Home: Sacramento, Calif. Died Nov. 28, 2001.

FISHER, CHARLES PAGE, JR., consulting geotechnical engineer; b. Richmond, Va., Sept. 24, 1921; s. Charles Page and Annie Laura (Wright) F.; m. Joyce Mayo Isom, Dec. 23, 1972. BSC.E., U. Va., 1949; S.M., Harvard U., 1950; PhD, N.C. State U., 1962. Registered profl. engr., Md., Va., N.C., S.C., Tenn. Instr. to assoc. prof. civil engring. N.C. State U., Raleigh, 1955-69; pres. Geotech. Engring. Co., Research Triangle Park, N.C., 1963-78; prin. C. Page Fisher Cons. Engr., Durham, N.C., 1978—; corp. sec. Troxler Electronics Labs., Research Triangle Park, N.C., 1961—. Served with USN, 1941-45. Fellow Am. Cons. Engrs. Council, ASCE; mem. ASTM, Nat. Soc. Profl. Engrs., Am. Arbitration Assn., Internat. Soc. Soil Mechanics and Found. Engring., Cons. Engrs. Council N.C. Home: Hurdle Mills, NC. Died Dec. 1, 2001.

FISHER, CHESTER LEWIS, JR., retired lawyer; b. Maplewood, N.J., May 30, 1911; s. Chester Lewis and Katherine Barton (Riddle) F.; m. Grace Annette Tainsh, Nov. 23, 1943; children: Chester Lewis III, Jane Alison Swiggett. Grad., Mercersburg Acad., 1929; AB, Princeton U., 1933; JD, Cornell U., 1936. Bar: N.Y. 1937, P.I. 1945, N.J. 1947, U.S. Supreme Ct 1972. Instr. phys. edn. Cornell U., 1933-36; practiced law N.Y.C., 1936-39; atty. Met. Life Ins. Co., 1939-57, asst. v.p., asst. to pres. and chmn., 1957-60, 3d v.p., 1960-63, 2d v.p., 1963-65, v.p., 1965-76. Village trustee Briarcliff Manor, N.Y., 1969-71, mayor, 1971-77. Served from 1st lt. to col. USAAF, 1940-46. Decorated Legion of Merit. Mem. Assn. Life Ins. Counsel (past pres.), SAR. Episcopalian. Home: Williamsburg, Va. Died May 21, 2002.

FISHER, JON HERBERT, chemical company executive; b. Wheeling, W. Va., May 14, 1947; s. Herbert Austin and Mary Melissa (Lewis) F.; m. Sarah May Lewis, Dec. 3, 1966; children: Jon Jeffrey, Matthew Austin. Student Ohio U., 1965-67; MBA, Case Western Res. U., 1982. With Harshaw Chem. Co., Cleve., 1970-83, mgr., 1976-80, bus. mgr., 1980-81, dir., 1981-83; with Harshaw Filtrol, Cleve., 1983-88, v.p., 1983-85, v.p., gen. mgr., 1985-88; v.p., bus. dir. Engelhard Corp.,, Edison, N.J., 1988—; dir. Harshaw Chem. BV, DeMeern, Holland, Harshaw Murata, Kobe, Japan, Harshaw Juarez, Mexico City, Harshaw Chem. Ltd., Daventry, Eng. Asst. scoutmaster Boy Scouts Am., Geneva, Ohio, 1971—; mem. United Way Regional Com., Greater Cleve. Growth Assn., Intrasci. Research Found., Republican Nat. Com. Recipient Honorable Order Ky. Col. Mem. Dry Color Mfrs. Assn. (bd. dirs., 1st v.p., pres.), Chem. Market Research Assn., Cleve. Com. on Fgn. Relations, Case Western Reserve U. Alumni Assn., Browns Backers Assn. Club: Madison Country. Avocations: golf, 18th century antiques, photography, traveling. Died Feb. 11, 1996. Home: Madison, Ohio.

FISHER, LINDA GIVIN, artist; b. July 7, 1956; BFA, Moore Coll. Art, 1978. Artist Foltz/Wessinger Advt., Lancaster, Pa., 1979-80, Millersville (Pa.) U., 1985-95, Lancaster Design & Art, Inc., 1980-85, Ampersand Design, Talmage, Pa., from 1985. Died Mar. 5, 2001.

FISHER, SHIRLEY IDA A. photography and humanities educator; b. Cleve., Aug. 7, 1935; d. E. and I. (Morley) F. BFA, Ohio U., 1957, MFA, 1959; postgrad., U. Calif., Berkeley, from 1964, U. Calif., Santa Cruz, from 1964. Instr. Detroit Community Ctr., 1960-63; med. photographer Ford Hosp., Detroit, 1961-63; comml. photographer Detroit, 1960-63; photo producer San Jose State U., 1963-70, prof. photography, 1966-67; prof. digital photography and humanities, coord. dept. De Anza Coll., Cupertino, Calif., 1967-99, founder digital photography dept., 1985-99. Photojournalist to Mexican, Puerto Rican and Costa Rican dept. tourism; photographer in over 67 countries; owner Hispanic and Anglo Publs., San Jose, 1986—, World Images Photography, Cupertino, 1963—; 1st invited Am. photographer to Ecuador. Work in internat. mus., embassies, bi-nat. ctrs. and pvt. collections; author, editor: Argentine and Chilean Photo, 1984, Cinco de Mayo en San Jose, 1987; author/editor/photographer: El Dia de Las Muertos, 1999; author/editor/photographer, The Sea, 2000; editor: Self Reflections, 1987. Am. participant USIS serving in Ecuador, Uruguay, Chile, Bolivia, Venezuela, Brazil, Argentina, 1981-86. Mem. Soc. Photog. Edn., Sister Cities San Jose (Calif.), Friends of Photography, Peninsula Advt. Photographers Assn., Bookies Art Caucas, Adobe Users Group, Phi Theta Kappa, Kappa Alpha Mu. Avocations: travel, writing, photographic exhibiting, theme projects, private photo classes, metaphysics. Died Oct. 2.

FISK, TREVOR ANTHONY, university officer; b. Ammanford, Wales, U.K., May 8, 1943; came to U.S., 1978; s. Sidney Harold and Eira (Davies) F.; m. Pamela Mary Cherry, Aug. 3, 1968; children: Eliot, Lloyd, Sloan, Amanda. BS in Econs., London Sch. of Econs., 1964; SM in Mgmt., MIT, 1976. Dir. mktg. Nat. Extension Coll., Cambridge, U.K., 1964-66; asst. to gen. sec. Nat. Union of Tchrs., London, 1965-66; sec., v.p. Nat. Union of Students, London, 1966-68, pres., 1968-69; various positions Brit. Steel Corp., London, 1969-78; v.p. mktg. and planning Cooper Hosp. U. Med. Ctr., Camden, N.J., 1978-85; assoc. v.p. mktg. and planning Thomas Jefferson U., Phila., 1985-90, v.p. external rels., from 1990. Cons. Am. Coll. of Radiology, Reston, Va., 1987—, O.E.C.D., Paris, 1968-69, Mobil Oil, London and N.Y.C., 1968-69; lectr. Wharton Sch. of Bus. Adminstrn. U. of Pa., 1984—; adj. asst. prof. Robert Wood Johnson Med. Sch., 1983—; mem. editorial bd. Jour. of Health Care Mktg., 1989—, Jour. of Strategic Healthcare Mgmt., 1983—. Co-author: Marketing and Nursing, 1989; author: Advertising Health Services, 1986; contbr. more than 20 articles to profl. jours. Mem. mktg. com. Am. Cancer Soc., Phila., 1985-86; dir. S.J. C. of C., 1979-85; trustee various colls.; councillor London Borough of Hounslow, 1971-75. Mem. Acad. Health Svcs. Mktg. (treas. 1991-92, bd. dirs. 1990-93). Avocations: circuit tng., tennis, antique maps, poetry. Home: Haddonfield, NJ. Deceased.

FITCH, HOWARD MERCER, lawyer, labor arbitrator, travelogue exhibitor and producer; b. Jeffersonville, Ind., Dec. 23, 1909; s. J. Howard and Kate Orvis (Girdler) F.; m. Jane Rogers McCaw, Dec. 25, 1930 (dec. 1983); children: Catherine Mercer Druitt, Jane Rogers Butterworth; m. Nancy Dolt Langley, Apr. 28, 1984. B.M.E., U. Ky., 1930, MS, 1936, M.E., 1939; JD magna cum laude, U. Louisville, 1942. Bar: Ky. 1942, Ill. 1954, U.S. Patent Office 1943; registered profl. engr., Ky. Engr. Western Electric Co., Kearney, N.J., 1930-32; joined Am. Air Filter Co. Inc., 1936, served as sales engr., prodn. mgr., mgr. legal and patent dept., asst. to exec. v.p., 1950-53, mgr. Herman Nelson div., 1953-58, v.p., 1954-72, dir. ops., 1958-63; practice law Louisville, from 1942; ptnr. Hunt & Fitch, 1945-58; labor arbitrator, 1973-88; ret., 1988. Patentee in field. Mem. nat. com. Atlantic Union Com.; mem. Louisville Labor-Mgmt. Com.; bd. dirs. Louisville Urban League, Louisville Better Bus. Bur., Consumers Adv. Council. Mem. AMA, ABA, ASME, ASHRAE, Am. Arbitration Assn. (panel of arbitrators, ret. 1988), Nat. Acad. Arbitrators, Ky. Bar Assn., Louisville Bar Assn., Louisville C. of C., Assoc. Industries Quad Cities (past pres.), Am. Soc. Human Resources Adminstrn., Louisville Pers. Assn., Hon. Order Ky. Cols., SAR, Exec. Club (bd. dirs.), Filson Club, Univ. Club, Pendennis Club, Arts Club (past pres.), Ky. Soc. Natural History, Louisville Photog. Soc., English Speaking Union, Internat. Soc. Poets. Episcopalian. Deceased.

FITZGERALD, THOMAS ROLLINS, university administrator; b. Washington, Feb. 23, 1922; s. Thomas Rollins and Bessie (Sheehy) F. BA, Woodstock (Md.) Coll., 1945, MA, 1948; S.T.L., Facultes St. Albert de Louvain, Belgium, 1953; PhD, U. Chgo., 1957. Joined Soc. of Jesus, 1939; ordained priest Roman Cath. Ch., 1952; instr. classics Novitiate St. Isaac Jogues, Wernersville, Pa., 1957-58, dean studies, asst. prof. classics, 1958-64; dean Coll. Arts and Scis., Georgetown U., 1964-66, acad. v.p., 1966-73; pres. Fairfield (Conn.) U., 1973-79, St. Louis U., 1979-87; assoc. prof. fine arts and classics Loyola Coll., Balt., 1987-96, prof. emeritus, 1996—2004. Pres. Conn. Conf. Ind. Colls., 1975-77; mem. New Eng. Bd. Higher Edn., 1977-79; trustee Gonzaga H.S., Washington, 1969-74, 87-94; chmn. bd. trustees St. Peter's Coll., Jersey City, 1969-75; trustee U. Scranton, Pa., 1974-77, Boston Coll. H.S., 1976-79, Mo. Bot. Garden, 1981-87, U. Detroit, 1982-90, St. Joseph Prep. Sch., Phila., 1988-91; bd. dirs. Nat. Assn. Ind. Colls. and Univs., 1977-79, 82-85. Democrat. Died Mar. 22, 2004.

FITZPATRICK, THOMAS BERNARD, dermatologist, educator; b. Madison, Wis., Dec. 19, 1919; s. Joseph J. and Grace (Lawrence) F.; m. Beatrice Devaney, Dec. 27, 1944; children: Thomas B., Beatrice, John, L. Scott, Brian. BA with honors, U. Wis., 1941; MD, Harvard U., 1945; fellow, Mayo Found., 1948-51; PhD, U. Minn., 1952; fellow, Commonwealth Fund, Oxford, 1958-59; DSc (hon.), U. Mass., 1987, U. Rochester Med. Sch., 1996. Intern 4th (Harvard) Med. Service, Boston City Hosp., 1945-46; biochemist Army Med. Ctr., Md., 1946-48; asst. prof. dermatology U. Mich. Med. Sch., 1951-52; prof., head divsn. dermatology U. Oreg. Med. Sch., 1952-58; Edward Wigglesworth prof. dermatology Harvard Med. Sch., 1959-87, prof. emeritus, 1987—2003, head dept., 1959-90; chief dermatology svc. Mass. Gen. Hosp., Boston, 1959-87. Prosser White orator St. John's Dermatol. Soc., London, 1964; Dohi internat. exch. lectr. dermatology, Japan, 1969; spl. cons. USPHS, NIH; cons. in dermatology Brigham and Women's Hosp., Children's Hosp. Med. Ctr., Boston, 1962-2003; mem. sci. adv. bd. EPA, 1985; mem. climatic impact com., chmn. health effects NAS; pres. Dermatology Found., 1971, Internat. Pigment Cell Soc., 1978-81, Assn. Profs. Dermatology, 1983. Chief editor: Dermatology in General Medicine, 1971, 4th edit., 1993; mem. editl. bd. New Eng. Jour. Medicine, 1961-69; editor Year Book Dermatology, 1984-97, Fitzpatrick's Dermatology in General Medicine, 5th edit., 1999; columnist Boston Globe, 1984—. Capt. MC U.S. Army, 1946-48. Decorated Officer Order of Rising Gold Rays (Japan), 1986; recipient Mayo Found. Alumni Rsch. award, 1951, Stephen rothman award, gold medal, 1960, Outstanding Achievement award U. Minn. Bd. Regents, 1964, Myron Gordon award 6th Internat. Pigment Cell Conf., 1965, Disting. Svc. award Dermatology Found., 1989, award for founding Dermatology Found., U. Wis., 1983, award for discovery of PUVA photochemotherapy for psoriasis Nat. Psoriasis Found., 1993, Nat. Med. Rsch. award Nat. Health Coun., 1994, Discovery award Dermatology Found., 1997, Mentor award Am. Skin Assn., 2000, Cert. of Appreciation Internat. League of Dermatol. Socs., 2001; Established Thomas B. Fitzpatrick prof. dermatology and endowed chair Harvard U., 1987, Thomas B. Fitzpatrick profl. chair, 1990. Fellow Am. Acad. Dermatology (hon., master, past bd. dirs.); mem. NAS (mem. inst. medicine 1994), Royal Soc. Medicine (hon.), Am. Acad. Arts and Scis., Assn. Am. Physicians, Soc. Investigative Dermatology (hon., pres. 1959-60), Am. Soc. for Clin. Investigation (emeritus 1965), Brit. Assn. Dermatology (hon.), South African Dermatol. Soc. (hon.), Med. Assn. Israel Dermatol. Soc. (hon.), St. John's Hosp. Dermatol. Soc. (London, hon.) Argentina, Danish, French, Spanish, Italian, Finnish, German, Polish, Austrian, Mex. dermatol. socs. (hon.), French Soc. Dermatology and Syphiligraphy (fgn. corr.), Australasian Coll. Dermatologists, Alpha Omega Alpha. Home: Lexington, Mass. Died Aug. 16, 2003.

FJELDE, ROLF GERHARD, translator, writer, educator; b. Bklyn., Mar. 15, 1926; s. Paul and Amy (Nordstrom) F.; m. Christel Mueller, Sept. 1, 1964; children: Michele, Eric, Christopher. BA, Yale U., 1946; MA, Columbia U., 1947; postgrad., U. Copenhagen, 1952-53, U. Heidelberg, 1953, U. Oslo, 1965. Copywriter J.M. Hickerson Advt. Inc., N.Y.C., 1948-50; sr. copywriter, editorial asst. book dept. Popular Sci. and Outdoor Life Pub. Co., N.Y.C., 1950-52; part-time instr. Pratt Inst., Bklyn., 1954-56, instr., 1956-58, asst. prof., 1958-65, assoc. prof., 1965-69, prof. English and Drama, from 1969. Playwright-in-residence Eugene O'Neill Meml. Theater Found., 1966, 67, 70; tchr. drama history Juilliard Sch., N.Y.C., 1973-83. Author (poetry) Washington, 1955, The Imaged World, 1962, (plays) Washington, 1966, The Rope Walk, 1967, Rafferty One by One, 1975, The Bellini Look, 1982; translator: (works by Ibsen) Peer Gynt, 1964, 80, Four Major Plays vol. I, 1965, 92, vol. II, 1970, Complete Major Prose Plays of Ibsen, 1978; editor: Ibsen: Twentieth Century Views, 1965, Ibsen News and Comment, 1979-85; founding editor Yale Poetry Rev., 1945-49, Poetry New York, 1949-51. Decorated Royal Medal of St. Olaf (Norway), 1991; recipient Acad. Award in Lit., Am. Acad. Arts and Letters, 1993; Am.-Scandinavian Found. fellow, 1952-53, 65, Yaddo fellow in creative writing, 1952-54, Nat. Translation Ctr. fellow Ford Found., 1967-68; Hoffman Eminent scholar Fla. State U., 1995. Mem. Ibsen Soc. Am. (pres. 1979-94, founder). Died Sept. 10, 2002.

FLACK, JOE FENLEY, county and municipal official, former insurance executive; b. Menard, Tex., Feb. 23, 1921; s. Frank H. and Evelyn (Fenley) F.; m. Ann Tarry, Jan. 21, 1945; children: Kate T., Joan E., Joe Fenley. BBA with honors, U. Tex., 1943. C.P.A., Tex. Acct. Ernst & Ernst (C.P.A.s), Houston, 1946-47; with Am. Gen. Ins. Co., 1947-81, treas., 1951-81, sr. v.p., also dir., 1968-81; chief fin. officer, auditor Harris County and Port of Houston Authority, from 1981; partner John L. Wortham and Son, Houston, 1947-65. Chmn. bd., pres., treas., dir. Knickerbocker Corp.; v.p., dir. Md. Casualty Co., Maine Bonding & Casualty Co., Robert Hampson & Son, Ltd.; v.p., treas., dir. Am. Gen. Fire & Casualty Co., Nat. Standard Ins. Co., Am. Gen. Leasing & Finance Corp., Atlas Realty Co., Am. Gen. Investment Corp., Am. Gen. Realty Co.; v.p. Assurance Co. Am., Marasco Co., Inc., No. Ins. Co. N.Y.; dir. Am. Gen. Capital Corp., Am. Gen. Life, Tex., Am. Gen. Life Del. Exec. bd. Boy Scouts Am.; mayor pro-tem Bunker Hill Village, Tex., 1959-61, mayor, 1961-65; trustee, v.p. sch. bd. Spring Branch Ind. Sch. Dist., 1967-75; bd. dirs. Kappa Sigma Found., U. Tex., Houston chpt. Salvation Army; mem. exec. com. U. Tex. Health Sci. Ctr., Houston. Served to lt. USNR, 1943-45. Mem. U. Tex. Ex-Students Assn. (exec. council, regional v.p.), River Oaks Country Club. Methodist. Home: Houston, Tex. Died Feb. 22, 2001.

FLANIGAN, MICHAEL CLETUS, rhetoric and composition educator; b. Ecorse, Mich., Apr. 5, 1936; s. William Paul and Florence (Bowman) F.; m. Jeanne Marie Brosius, Sept. 19, 1987; children: Michael B., Katherine M., Timothy S., Ian T., Pippa B., Jay, Jayne, Jack. BA, Case Wesern Res. U., 1963; MA, Northwestern U., 1967, PhD, 1969. Tchr. Cleve. Bd. Edn., 1963, Euclid (Ohio) Bd. Edn., 1963-65; dir. Euclid English Demonstration Ctr., 1965-66; co-dir. Curriculum Ctr. in Composition, Evanston, Ill., 1968-70; asst.

prof. Ind. U., Bloomington, 1970-73, assoc. prof., 1973-79, dir. 1st yr. studies, 1974-81; dir. rhetoric and composition U. Okla., Norman, from 1981. Fulbright prof. Lund (Sweden) U., 1987; cons. South African Black Schs., Johannesburg, 1984; cons. scholar U. Stockholm, 1982; mem. English adv. com. Coll. Bd., 1983-87; cons. evaluator Writing Program Adminstrs., 1980—. Author: Using Media in Language Arts, 1977, Conflict, 1979, English, 1983; contbr. articles to profl. jours. Pvt. USMC, 1953-56, Korea. Mem. Nat. Coun. Tchrs. English (sec.-treas. Assembly for Rsch. 1988—, state coord. achievement awards in writing 1978-81). Avocations: hiking swimming, biking. Home: Norman, Okla. Died May 15, 2002.

FLEMING, ROBERT WRIGHT, investment banker; b. Washington, Aug. 26, 1918; s. Robert Vedder and Alice Listen (Wright) F.; m. Martha Wills Schoenfeld, Nov. 21, 1942; children: Margaret Johanna, Robert Vedder II, Bruce Wright. BA, George Washington U., 1941. Washington rep. Pan. Am. Airways, 1946-48; became v.p., sec., dir. Folger Nolan Fleming Douglas Inc., Washington, 1950, now pres., dir. Bd. dir., mem. exec. com. Acacia Mut. Life Ins. Co.; bd. dirs. Security Storage Co.; cons. dir. emeritus Riggs Nat. Bank, Washington.; dir., chmn. audit com. Medlantic Healthcare Group, Inc. (formerly Washington Healthcare Corp.); mem. Washington Bd. Trade, N.Y., Am. stock exchanges.; chmn. endowment and investment com. Washington Hosp. Center; chmn. adv. com. Pub. Svc. Commn. D.C., 1967-70 Treas. Nat. Citizens for Eisenhower Congl. Com., 1953-55; Bd. dirs., treas. Easter Seals Soc. Disabled Children and Adult's, Inc.; chmn. bd. trustees endowment fund ARC; pres. Rotary Found., 1976-78; past bd. dirs. Washington Heart Assn., D.C. chpt. A.R.C.; trustee Boys Club of Washington. Served as lt. comdr. USNR, 1941-46. Mem. Friendly Sons St. Patrick, Nat. Assn. Security Dealers (bd. govs.), Assn. Stock Exchange Firms, Investment Bankers Assn., Phila.-Balt. Exchange, Nat. Geog. Soc. (finance com.), Kappa Alpha, Omicron Delta Kappa. Clubs: Burning Tree (Bethesda, Md.); Chevy Chase (Md.); Metropolitan (Washington), Alfalfa (Washington); Pine Valley Golf (N.J.); Rehoboth Beach Country (Del.). Lodges: Rotary. Died Feb. 8, 2003.

FLEXNER, JAMES THOMAS, author; b. N.Y.C., Jan. 13, 1908; s. Simon and Helen (Thomas) F.; m. Beatrice Hudson, 1950; 1 child, Helen Hudson. Grad., Lincoln Sch. of Tchrs. Coll., Columbia U., 1925; BS magna cum laude, Harvard U., 1929; LHD, Ea. Ill. U., 1985. Reporter N.Y. Herald Tribune, 1929-31; exec. sec. Noise Abatement Commn., N.Y.C. Dept. of Health, 1931-32. Cons. Colonial Williamsburg, 1956-57, Amon Carter Mus. Western Art, 1974-75; lectr. on founding fathers, history of Am. art and civilization. Author: Doctors on Horseback: Pioneers of American Medicine, 1937, America's Old Masters, 1939, (with Simon Flexner) William Henry Welch and the Heroic Age of American Medicine, 1941, Steamboats Come True, 1944, History of American Painting, Vol. I: First Flowers of Our Wilderness: American Painting, the Colonial Period, 1947 (Life in America prize 1946), John Singleton Copley, 1947, A Short History of American Painting, 1950, The Traitor and the Spy, 1953, History of American Painting, Vol. II: The Light of Distant Skies 1760-1835, 1954, Gilbert Stuart, 1955, Mohawk Baronet: Sir William Johnson of New York, 1959, History of American Painting, Vol. III: That Wilder Image: The Native School from Thomas Cole to Winslow Homer, 1962 (Francis Parkman prize 1963), George Washington, Vol. I: The Forge of Experience 1732-1775, 1965, The World of Winslow Homer 1936-1910, 1966, George Washington, Vol. II: George Washington in the American Revolution 1775-1783, 1968, The Double Adventure of John Singleton Copley, 1969, Nineteenth Century Painting, 1970, George Washington, Vol. III: George Washington and the New Nation 1783-1793, 1970, George Washington, Vol. IV: Anguish and Farewell 1793-1799, 1972 (Nat. Book award for biography 1972), Washington: The Indispensable Man, 1974 (Christopher award 1974, Am. Book award nomination 1980), The Face of Liberty, 1975, The Young Hamilton, 1978, States Dyckman: American Loyalist, 1980, Asher B. Durand: An Engraver's and a Farmer's Art, 1983, An American Saga: The Story of Helen Thomas and Simon Flexner, 1984, Poems of the 1920s, 1991, On Desperate Seas: A Biography of Gilbert Stuart, 1995, Maverick Progress: An Autobiography, 1996, Random Harvest, Shorter Publications Down the Years, 1997; Washington biographies dramatized in CBS miniseries, 1984 (Peaody award 1984); contbr. mags. and newspapers. Trustee emeritus N.Y. Pub. Library. Libr. Congress grantee, 1945; Guggenheim fellow, 1953, 79; recipient Pulitzer Prize spl. citation, 1972, Archives Am. Art award Smithsonian Inst., 1979, Gold medal Am. Acad. Inst. Arts and Letters, 1988. Mem. PEN (pres. 1954-55, hon. v.p. 1963-66), Soc. Am. Historians (pres. 1975-77), Am. Acad. Inst. Arts and Letters (v.p. for lit. 1981-85, Gold medal 1988), Autthors League of Am., Century Assn., Phi Beta Kappa. Clubs: Century (hon.). Died Feb. 13, 2003.

FLYNN, DANIEL FRANCIS, investment company executive; b. Hartford, Conn s. Daniel C. and Frances E. (Hurley) F.; m. Barbara L. Quinn, June 12, 1965; children: Daniel C., Garrett S., Laura D. BA, Coll. of the Holy Cross, 1956; JD, U. Conn., 1962. Bar: Conn. 1962. Chmn., CEO John G. Martin Found., Farmington, from 1969; dir., chmn., CEO, pres. JCI Corp., Farmington, Conn., from 1968, Resources Mgmt. Corp., Farmington, from 1976; dir., chmn., CEO Resources Investment Co., Farmington, from 1977, RMC Realty Co., Farmington, from 1985. Former dir. Security-Conn. Life Ins. Co. Former regent, mem. exec. com. U. Hartford, former chmn. resources com., mem. com. regent mems., mem. investment com.; trustee, mem. exec. com. Horace Bushnell Mem. Hall Corp.; bd. vis. Barney Sch.; hon. life mem., bd. mgrs. Silver Hill Found., Inc., past dir., past dir. devel. com.; mem. exec. com., past pres. U. Conn. Law Sch. Found., Inc.; trustee Conn. Policy and Econ. Coun., Inc.; corporator St. Francis Hosp. and Med. Ctr.; founding trustee John G. Martin Scholarship Trust; spl. gifts chmn. United Way Hartford; former trustee Hartford Art Sch.; past pres. Westmont Residents' Assn.; mem. Pres. Coun. Coll. Holy Cross. Mem. Am. Soc. Internat. Law, Am. Judicature Soc., Am. Assn. Individual Investors, Conn. Bar Assn., Newcomen Soc. Am., Twentieth Century Club. Home: Hartford, Conn. Died Oct. 25, 2003.

FÖLDIAK, GABOR, chemistry educator; b. Budapest, Hungary, Mar. 30, 1929; s. Zsolt and Elisabeth (Gárdos) F.; m. Susan Braun (div. 1967); 1 child, Peter; m. Judith Ury, June 8, 1968; 1 child, Gregory. Diploma in chemistry, Tech. U. Budapest, 1951; MBA, U. Econs./Scis. Budapest, 1960; PhD in Chemistry, U. Veszprém, Hungary, 1960; DSc in Chemistry, Hungarian Acad. Scis., Budapest, 1966. Cert. European engring. educator. Scientist, sr. rschr. Hungarian Oil and Gas Rsch. Inst., Veszprém, Budapest, 1949-63; post-doctoral fellow Max-Planck-Inst. Strahlenchemie, Mülheim/Ruhr, Germany, 1960-63; sr. rschr., dir. gen. Inst. Isotopes Hungarian Acad. Scis., Budapest, from 1976; chmn. Inst Grad. Studies, Tech. U. Budapest, 1976-83, prof., from 1979. Vis. prof. U. Notre Dame, Ind., 1977-78, 88-89; chmn. Hungarian Bus. Acad., Budapest, 1991—; chmn. bd. trustees Ctrl. Inst. Physics, Hungarian Acad. Scis., Budapest, 1992-96. Author, editor: Radiation Chemistry of Hydrocarbons, 1981, Industrial Application of Radioisotopes, 1986; mem. editl. bd. Hungarian Chem. Jour., 1981—; contbr. articles to profl. jours. Dep. min. edn. and culture, Hungary, 1983-86. Mem. Hungarian Chem. Soc. (chmn. com. radiation chemistry 1990-99, prize 1999), Body of Hungarian Acad. Scis. (Prize Hungarian Acad. Scis. 1951). Avocation: collector crime fictions. Home: Budapest, Hungary. Deceased.

FOLEY, DANIEL PATRICK, psychology educator; b. Cin., Oct. 15, 1920; s. Daniel Patrick and Mildred Dowell (Lamborn) F. LittB in Greek, Xavier U., 1945; Licentiate in Philosophy, West Baden (Ind.) Coll., 1948, Licentiate in Sacred Theology, 1955; MA in Exptl. Psychology, Loyola U., Chgo., 1951; PhD in Clin. Psychology, Ottawa U., Ontario, Can., 1962. Lic. clin. psychologist, Ohio. Tchr. St. Ignatius High Sch., Cleve., 1950-51; dir. pub. rels. St. Xavier Sch., Cin., 1957-58; prof. psychology Xavier U., Cin., 1958-87, prof. emeritus, from 1987; pvt. practice psychology Cin., from 1962. Contbr. articles to profl. jours. Mem. Am. Psychol. Assn., Cin. Psychol. Assn. (bd. govs. 1966-67). Died Aug. 13, 2000.

FOLINSBEE, LAWRENCE JOHN, physiologist, researcher; b. Vancouver, B.C., Can., Nov. 28, 1945; came to U.S., 1963; s. John Allan and Agnes Emily (Colpitts) F.; m. Jane Elizabeth Furchner, Aug. 24, 1969; chldren: John Alan, Emily Jane. BS, U. Oreg., 1967, MS, 1969; PhD, U. Calif., Davis, 1972. Rsch. assoc. U. Calif., Davis, 1969-72; post-doctoral fellow U. Toronto, Ont., Can., 1972-74, asst. prof., 1973-74; assoc. rsch. physiologist U. Calif., Santa Barbara, 1974-84; sr. scientist ABB Environ. Svcs., Chapel Hill, N.C., 1984-90; rsch. physiologist EPA, Research Triangle Park, N.C., 1990-95; chief environ. media assessment br. Nat. Ctr. Environ. Assessment, EPA, Research Triangle Park, N.C., from 1995. Cons. Am. Petroleum Inst., Washington, 1983-84; mem. adv. bd. Electric Power Rsch. Inst., Palo Alto, Calif., 1987-93. Mem. editorial bd. Toxicology and Indsl. Health Jour., 1983-93; editor: Environmental Stress: Individual Human Adaptations, 1978; assoc. editor: Medicine and Science in Sports and Exercise; author chpts. in books; contbr. over 70 articles to profl. jours. Rsch. grantee NIH, EPA, Electric Power Rsch. Inst. Fellow Am. Coll. Sports Medicine; mem. Am. Physiol. Soc., Am. Thoracic Soc. Democrat. Episcopalian. Home: Chapel Hill, NC. Died Sept. 9, 2001.

FOLK, KATHERINE PINKSTON, English language educator, writer, journalist; b. Corsicana, Tex., Feb. 8, 1925; d. Lucian Albert and Katherine (Shell) Pinkston; m. Elmer Ellsworth Folk, Apr. 21, 1946; children: Russell Harter, David Shell, Barbara Kay Folk Nowotny. BA in Journalism, Tex. Tech. U., 1946; postgrad., U. Houston, 1960-71. Reporter Scurry County Times, Snyder, Tex., 1946; dir. advt. Dunlaps Dept. Store, Lubbock, Tex., 1946; instr. English Odessa (Tex.) Coll., 1948-53; dir. communication, editor Viva Mag. Houston Met. Ministries, 1979-80; dir. communication for continuing edn. Houston Community Coll. System, 1989-90, instr. English, from 1980. Auditor creative writing Rice U., Houston, 1966; tutor English Spring Br. Ind. Sch. Dist., Houston, 1970-75. Contbr. articles to popular mags. Ann. sponsor Odessa Coll., 1950-53; mem. Harris County Heritage Soc., Houston, 1985-91, Nat. Fedn. Rep. Women, Houston, 1987-99, literacy chair, 1999, Country Playhouse Little Theatre, 1987-96; bd. dirs. Spring Br. YWCA, Houston, 1990-91. Mem. AAUW, Jr. League Houston (patron tea rm.), Nat. Fedn. Press Women, Soc. Children's Book Writers, Romance Writers Am., Delta Delta Delta (chmn. scholarship com. 1972). Episcopalian. Avocations: writing, reading, walking, music, travel. Home: Houston, Tex. Died Sept. 13, 2001.

FOOTE, W. DAVID, comptroller; b. Great Barrington, Mass., Aug. 1, 1940; s. Wilbur Ephriam and Mable Louise (Billings) F.; m. Helen Marie Zgorliski, June 21, 1982' children: Matthew David, Amy Anne, Sarah May, Dana Jette Becker, Whitney Meredith. BSA, Bentley Coll., 1965; MBA, Northeastern U., Boston, 1971; postgrad., Harvard U., 1976. CPA, Md.; cert. mgmt. acct., cert. fin. mgr. Auditor Internat. Silver, Meriden, Conn., 1960-62; corp. account mgr. EG&G, Bedford, Mass., 1962-66; div. contr. mcCord Corp., Allentown, Pa., 1966-70, McCord Corp., Dover, N.H., 1970-75; div. v.p. material mcCord Corp., Dover, N.H., 1976-78; group contr. Excello Corp., Detroit, 1978-80, div. v.p. ops. Walled Lake, Mich., 1980-82; exec. v.p. Forest Fuels, Marlborough, N.H., 1982; group contr. Sheller Globe, Cleve., 1982-85; dir. corp. acctg. AMC, Southfield, Mich., 1985-87; mgr. acctg. transition Chrysler Corp., Highland Park, Mich., 1988; controller, chief acctg. officer Ametek, Inc., Paoli, Pa., 1989-91; founder, prin. WDF Advocacy, 1992-96; v.p. Boscobel, Inc., from 1996. Vestryman St. George's Episcopal Ch., Milford, Mich., 1986-88, sr. warden, 1987-88, chmn. bldg. com., 1987-88; bd. dirs. Expressive Therapy Concepts. Mem. AICPA, Fin. Execs. Inst., Inst. Mgmt. Accts. (com. acad. rels. exam. rev. com. 1989-90, exam. grader 1993-97), Valley Forge Inst. Mgmt. Accts. (bd. dirs.). Home: Coatesville, Pa. Died Feb. 9, 2001.

FORBES, GILBERT BURNETT, physician, educator; b. Rochester, N.Y., Nov. 9, 1915; s. Gilbert DeLeverance and Lillian Augusta (Burnett) F.; m. Grace Moehlman, July 8, 1939; children: Constance Ann (Mrs. Joseph F. Citro), Susan Young (Mrs. William A. Martin). BA, U. Rochester, 1936, MD, 1940. Intern Strong Meml. Hosp., Rochester, 1940-41; resident St. Louis Children's Hosp., 1941-43; practice medicine, specializing in pediatrics Los Alamos, 1946-47; instr. pediatrics Sch. Medicine, Washington U., St. Louis, 1943-46, asst. prof., 1947-50; prof. pediatrics, chmn. dept. Southwestern Med. Sch., Dallas, 1950-53; assoc. prof. pediatrics Sch. Medicine, U. Rochester, 1953-57, prof., 1957-68, prof. pediatrics, prof. radiation biology, 1968—2003, Alumni Disting. Service prof. pediatrics, 1978—2003, chmn. faculty council, 1969-70, acting co-chmn. dept. pediatrics, 1974-76. Cons. Nat. Inst. Child Health and Human Devel.; mem. sci. adv. com. Nutrition Found., 1963-66; mem. Nat. Council on Radiation Protection; mem. com. infant nutrition, com. dietary allowances NRC, 1960-63; vis. research fellow U. Oxford, Eng., 1970-71 Author: Human Body Composition, 1987; assoc. editor: Am. Jour. Diseases Childhood, 1964-72; chief editor, 1973-82; asso. editor: Nutrition Revs, 1961-71; editor Pediatric Nutrition Handbook, 1985; contbr. numerous articles to profl. jours. Recipient Research Career award USPHS, NIH, 1962—2003, Borden award Am. Acad. Pediatrics, 1964, Alumni award to faculty U. Rochester, 1975; Albert David Kaiser award, Rochester Acad. Medicine, 1979, Arthur Kornberg Rsch. award, 1997. Mem. AAAS, Am. Pediatric Soc. (coun., v.p. 1975-76, John Howland award 1992), Soc. Pediatric Rsch. (past pres.), Am. Acad. Pediatrics (com. on nutrition 1974-80), Monroe County Med. Soc., U. Rochester Med. Alumni Assn. (past pres., Gold medal 1982), Rotary, Sigma Xi, Alpha Omega Alpha, Theta Chi. Home: Rochester, NY. Died June 26, 2003.

FORBES, JAMES WENDELL, publishing consultant; b. Evansburg, Alta., Can., Oct. 8, 1923; s. Prescott and Annie Alvira (MacLean) F.; m. Carolyn J. Irvine, May 14, 1965; children: James Wendell Jr., Elizabeth MacLean. B in Commerce, U. B.C., 1948. Various positions, circulation dept. Time Inc., 1948-70; dir. circulation Life mag., 1962-64, adminstr. book pub. div., 1964-68; asst. planning dir. Time-Life Books, 1969; asst. to mng. dir. Time-Life Records, 1970; pub. cons. Ridgefield, Conn., 1970-99; cons. dep. pub. Guideposts mag., 1975-91. Mgr. direct response advt. Young & Rubicam Internat., Inc., 1973-74; founder Sch. Mag. Mktg., 1979; chmn. bd. Direct Mktg. Assn., 1964-65. Author newsletter On Publishing; contbr. articles to profl. jours. Bd. dirs. Peale Ctr. Christian Living, 1985-95, Insts. Religion and Health, 1986-91; incorporator Ridgefield Boys' Club, 1986-99; chmn. bd. missions Conglist. Ch., 1976, deacon, 1977, chmn. bd. deacons, 1978-79, chmn. parish rels. com., 1985-86, dir. Diocesan transitions program, Conn., 1998-99, mem. Bishop and Diocesan exec. com. program and budget, 1999. With RCAF, 1943-45. Recipient Mag. Circulation Hall of Fame award Direct Mktg. Assn., 1987, Silver Apple award Direct Mail Club N.Y., 1989, Lee C. Williams award Fulfillment Mgmt. Assn./X.Y.Z./The Circulation Mktg. Com. Mag. Pubs. Assn., 1990; elected to Direct Mktg. Assn. Hall of Fame, 1995. Mem. Literary and Sci. Exec. Assn. U. B.C. (hon.). Died July 7, 1999.

FORD, FRANKLIN LEWIS, history educator, historian; b. Waukegan, Ill., Dec. 26, 1920; s. Frank Leland and Dorothy Elsey (Lewis) F.; m. Eleanor Rose Hamm, Jan. 8, 1944; children: Stephen Joseph, John Franklin. AB, U. Minn., 1942; MA, Harvard U., 1948, PhD, 1950. Mem. faculty Bennington Coll., 1949-52; mem. faculty Harvard U., 1953-91, prof. history, 1959-91, McLean prof. ancient and modern history, 1968-91; emeritus, 1991—2003; dean faculty arts and scis. Harvard U., 1962-70, acting dean, 1973. Chmn. bd. dirs. Harvard Univ. Press, 1986-91; mem. Inst. for Advanced Study (Princeton), 1974. Author: Robe and Sword, 1953, Strasbourg in Transition, 1958, Europe, 1780-1830, 1970, rev. edit., 1989, Political Murder, 1985, French and German transl., 1990; co-editor: Traditions of Western Civilization, 1966. Served with U.S. Army and O.S.S., 1943-46. Fulbright research fellow France, 1952-53; Guggenheim fellow Germany, 1955-56; fellow Ctr. Advanced Study Behavioral Scis., 1961-62; fellow Nat. Humanities Ctr., 1983-84, 88, 89. Mem. Am. Philos. Soc., Phi Beta Kappa. Home: Lexington, Mass. Died Aug. 31, 2003.

FORD, JOSEPH FRANCIS, accounting educator; b. Phila., Mar. 16, 1919; s. John Joseph and Anne (Schneider) F.; m. Janet Bruce Weiler (dec. 2003), Apr. 18, 1942; children: Emilie Louise, Linda Jean. BS in Commerce with highest honors, Drexel Inst. Tech., 1941; MBA magna cum laude, U. Pa., 1952. CPA, Pa. With Curtis Pub. Co., 1938, Scott Paper Co., 1939, Joseph H. McGrath & Co., CPAs, Phila., 1940-41; mem. faculty Drexel U., Phila., 1946-85, prof. accounting, 1952-85, dir. M.B.A. program, 1951-66; assoc. dean Drexel U. (Coll. Bus. and Adminstrn.), 1966-73, 77-85, acting dean, 1970-71, 76-77. Author: (with others) Principles of Accounting, 1954. Vice pres. Home and Sch. Assn. Drexel Hill Sch. Served to lt. col. AUS, 1941-46, ETO. Decorated Bronze Star. Mem. Am., Pa. insts. C.P.A.s, Res. Officers Assn., Scabbard and Blade, Phi Kappa Phi, Beta Gamma Sigma, Sigma Rho. Republican. Presbyn. (pres. trustees). Home: Drexel Hill, Pa. Died Mar. 23, 2004.

FORDYCE, MARIANNE MAX, marketing executive; b. St. Louis; d. Charles Willard Max and Myrtle Anne (Davis) O'Hara. AB summa cum laude, St. Louis U., 1968, MA in Rsch. Modern European History, 1970. Client svc./copywriter Atkinson & Assocs., Inc., St. Louis, 1977-78; mgr. advt. Indsl. Engring. and Equipment Co., St. Louis, 1978-83; dir. corp. communications Snyder Gen., Dallas, 1983-88; dir. advt./mktg. Lennox Internat., Dallas, 1988-92; mem. staff Maxfield Comm., Mktg. Cons., from 1992. Recipient Gold award MultiImage Internat. Inc., 1985, Flair award of excellence Advt. Fedn. of St. Louis, 1982. Mem. Bus. Profls. Advt. Assn., Am. Advt. Fedn., Phi Beta Kappa. Avocations: reading, fine cooking, weight training. Home: Dallas, Tex. Deceased.

FORESTER, RUSSELL, artist; b. Salmon, Idaho, May 21, 1920; s. Alvin R. and Mary (Isley) Forester; m. Marie-Christine Meynet, Feb. 2, 1968; 1 child, Lynn 1 stepchild, William C. Attinger. Student, Inst. Design Chgo., 1950. Prin. Russell Forester Arch., Inc., 1948-76. One-man shows include La Jolla (Calif.) Mus. Contemporary Art, Everson Mus. Art, Syracuse, N.Y., Willard Gallery, N.Y., Galerie Maurer, Zurich, Switzerland, Track 16, L.A., 1997, Athenaeum Music & Arts Libr., La Jolla, 1999, exhibited in group shows at La Jolla Mus. Contemporary Art, Guggenheim Mus., N.Y.C., San Francisco Mus. Modern Art, Represented in permanent collections Guggenheim Mus., N.Y.C., Cedars-Sinai Med. Ctr., L.A., McCrory Corp., N.Y.C., 1st Nat. Bank Chgo. Fellow: AIA (emeritus). Died May 30, 2002.

FORKOSCH, MORRIS DAVID, retired lawyer, law educator, writer; b. N.Y.C., Feb. 26, 1908; s. Samuel and Yetta (Heimowitz) Forkosch; m. Selma Millner, Nov. 29, 1934 (dec.); children: Joel Anton, Jonathan Andrew. LLB, St. John's U., 1930, LLM, 1932; BA, N.Y.U., 1936, MA, 1938, JSD, 1946; PhD, New Sch., 1952, MSc, 1956; LLD (hon.), Woodlands U., 1978; LHD (hon.), U. Humanistic Studies, 1979. Bar: N.Y. 1931, Minn. 1956, Philippines 1946, U.S. Dist. Ct. (so. dist.) N.Y. 1932, U.S. Dist. Ct. (ea. dist.) N.Y. 1934, U.S. Supreme Ct. 1939. Sole practice, NYC, 1931—44, 1946—49, from 1972; prof. law Bklyn. Law Sch., 1949—72, chmn. dept. pub. law, 1952—72, prof. emeritus, from 1972. Vis. prof. U. San Diego Law Sch., 1972—73, U. Melbourne Sch. Law, 1975, Cardozo Law Sch., 1981—82; Fulbright sr. lectr. Taiwan, 1975—76; gen. counsel League to Champion Human Rights, 1934—41. Author: A Treatise on Labor Law, 1953, A Treatise on Labor Law rev. edit., 1965, The Polit. Philosophy of Arnold Brecht, 1954, A Treatise on Adminstrv. Law, 1956, Antitrust and the Consumer, 1956, Carmody-Forkosch N.Y. Practice 8th edit., 1963, Constl. Law 2d rev. edit., 1963, Essays in Legal History in Honor of Felix Frankfurter, 1966, Outer Space and Legal Liability, 1982; contbr. numerous articles to profl. jours. Pres. Zionist Orgn. 13, 1936—38, Am. Soc. Legal History, 1958—61. To lt. U.S. Army, 1944—46. Mem.: Assn. Bar City of N.Y. Died Aug. 16, 1999.

FORMIGONI, MAURI, artist, educator, gallery director; b. Louisville, Nov. 6, 1941; d. Maurice Vernon and Dorothy Marie (Neeld) Monihon; m. Ugo Carlo Formigoni, Sept. 15, 1965 (div. 1988); children: Gregg, Marco, Tania; m. Danijel Žuré, Jan. 27, 1992. BA, Kalamazoo Coll., 1963; postgrad., Sch. of Art Inst., Chgo., 1966-68; MA, Sangamon State U., 1972. Rsch. asst. U. Chgo., 1963-66; courtroom artist ABC-TV, Chgo., 1973; assoc. prof. visual arts U. Ill., Springfield, from 1985, gallery dir., from 1985. Part-time instr. Lincoln Land C.C., Springfield, 1972-83. Mural commd. by Ill. Dept. Rev. Commn., 1988; exhibited in solo shows at Daut Pasha Hamman Mus., Skopje, Macedonia, 1991, Artemesia Gallery, Chgo., 1994, more than 40 group exhibits. Project Completion grantee Ill. Arts Coun., 1982, Chmn.'s grantee Ill. Arts Coun., 1994, Artist's grantee Springfield Area Arts Coun., 1988; Fulbright fellow, 1990-91. Mem. Coll. Art Assn., Chgo. Artists' Coalition, Fulcrum Gallery Soho. Deceased.

FORRESTER, WILLIAM RAY, law educator, arbitrator; b. Little Rock, Jan. 14, 1911; s. William Thomas Forrester and Louise (Lucas) Brooks; m. Celine Mortee Penn, Oct. 31, 1942; children: William Ray Jr., Catherine Lucas, David Chalaron, Stephen Labarre. BA, U. Ark., 1933; JD, U. Chgo., 1935; LLD (hon.), U. Ark., 1963, Tulane U., 1992. Bar: Ill., 1936, N.Y. 1970. Trust dept. First Nat. Bank, Chgo., 1935; atty. Defrees, Buckingham, Jones & Hoffman, Chgo., 1935-40; asst. prof. to prof. law Tulane U., New Orleans, 1941-49, dean, prof. law, 1952-63, Vanderbilt U., Nashville, 1949-52, Cornell U., Ithaca, N.Y., 1963-78; prof. constitutional law U. Calif., San Francisco, from 1976. Interim chmn. U.S. Steel, Pitts., 1948, bd. arbitration U.S. Steel Workers; arbitrator Internat. Harvester, Chgo., 1949, United Auto Workers. Pub. trustee Food and Drug Law Inst., 1970-78. Mem. Nat. Acad. Arbitrators (bd. govs. 1948-51), Adminstrv. Conf. U.S. Home: San Francisco, Calif. Died Feb. 16, 2001.

FORTINBERRY, TOXIE THOMAS, real estate broker; b. Tylertown, Miss., May 15, 1908; s. Thomas Calvin and Irene (Magee) F.; m. Martha Costen, Dec. 11, 1937; children: Sylvia L., Merle I., Martha C., Toxie Ann, Sabrina S., Marjorie E., Thomas A., Mary Lu, Luther W. Student, Holmes Jr. Coll., Goodman, Miss., 1929-31, Southwestern U., Memphis, 1931-33; BBA, U. Tenn., 1955. Park dir. City of Memphis, 1933-34; salesman Nat. Life Ins. Co., Memphis, 1934-40; real estate broker Memphis, 1940-57; builder, auctioneer, appraiser Fortinberry Auction and Realty Co., Water Valley, from 1957. V.p., bd. dirs. Batesville Religious Counseling Ctr.; chmn. Yalobusha County Rep. Party, 1963; alt. del. Rep. Nat. Conv., 1972. Mem. Nat. Assn. Realtors (realtor of Yr. 1984, 85), Northwest Bd. Realtors (past pres., Realtor of Yr. 1972, 76, 78), North Cen. Bd. Realtors (pres., Realtor of Yr. 1981, 84), Nat. Farm Land Inst. (Realtor of Yr 1983), Miss. Farm Land Inst., Nat. Auctioneers Assn., Miss. Auctioneers Assn. (Past pres.), Auctioneers Guild, Nat. Assn. Rev. Appraisers, Nat. Assn. Master Appraisers, Water Valley C. of C. Clubs: Yalobusha Country. Lodges: Rotary (pres. Water Valley chpt. 1973-74), Masons, Shriners. Avocations: music, golf, travel. Home: Water Valley, Miss. Deceased.

FORWARD, ROBERT L(ULL), physicist, businessman, consultant, writer; b. Geneva, N.Y., Aug. 15, 1932; s. Robert Torrey and Mildred (Lull) F.; m. Martha Neil Dodson, Aug. 29, 1954; children— Robert Dodson, Mary Lois, Julie Elizabeth, Eve Laurel BS in Physics, U. Md., 1954, PhD, 1965; MS in Applied Physics, UCLA, 1958. With Hughes Aircraft Co., 1956-87, assoc. mgr. theoretical studies dept., 1966-67, mgr. exploratory studies dept., 1967-74; sr. scientist Hughes Research Labs., Malibu, Calif., 1974-87; owner, chief scientist Forward Unltd., Clinton, Wash., 1987—2002; ptnr., chief scientist Tethers Unlimited, 1994-97; v.p., chmn. bd. dirs., sec., treas., chief scientist Tethers Unltd., Inc., 1997—2002. Popular sci. writer and lectr. Author: (sci. fiction) Dragon's Egg, 1981, The Flight of the Dragonfly, 1983, Starquake, 1985, Rocheworld, 1986, Martian Rainbow, 1991, Timemaster, 1992, Camelot 30K, 1993, (with Julie Forward Fuller) Return to Rocheworld, 1993, Rescued from Paradise, 1995, (with Martha Dodson Forward) Marooned on Eden, 1993, Ocean under the Ice, 1994, Saturn Rukh, 1997, (nonfiction) (with Joel Davis) Mirror Matter: Pioneering Antimatter Physics, 1988, Future Magic, 1988, Indistinguishable from Magic, 1995; contbr. numerous articles to sci. jours. Capt. USAF, 1954-56. Hughes fellow, 1956-62. Fellow AIAA (assoc.), Brit. Interplanetary Soc.; mem. Am. Phys. Soc., Author's Guild, Sci.-Fiction and Fantasy Writers' Am., Sigma Xi, Sigma Pi Sigma. Died Sept. 21, 2002.

FOSTER, EUGENE LEWIS, engineering executive; b. Clinton, Mass., Oct. 9, 1922; s. George Frank and Georgie Nina (Lewis) F.; m. Mavis Estelle Howard, July 30, 1944; children— Kaye Louise, Eugene Howard, Mark Edward, Carol Anne. BSM.E., U. N.H., 1944, MS, 1951; Mech. E., M.I.T., 1953, Sc.D., 1954. Research engr. Procter and Gamble, Cin., 1946-47; instr. U. N.H., 1947-49; asst. prof. mech. engring. M.I.T., Cambridge, 1950-56; pres., chmn. Foster-Miller Assocs., Inc., Waltham, Mass., 1956-72; cons. Office of Sec. of Transp., Washington, 1972-73; chmn. Foster-Miller Assocs., 1974—; pres. UTD, Inc., Alexandria, Va., 1976-93, pres. emeritus, from 1993. Mem. U.S. nat. com. for tunneling tech. Nat. Acad. Sci., 1975-79 Author: (with W.A. Wilson) Experimental Heat Power Engineering, 1956; also articles. Mem. Recreational and Environ. Com. Fairfax County, Va., 1976-78. Served with C.E. U.S. Army, 1943-46. Mem. ASME, ASCE, N.Y. Acad. Scis., AAAS, Nat. Soc. Profl. Engrs. Home: Alton Bay, NH. Died Mar. 2, 1999.

FOSTER, JULIAN FRANCIS SHERWOOD, political science educator; b. London, July 27, 1926; came to U.S., 1953; s. George Sherwood and Norah Patrickson (Langford) F.; m. Beatrice Ingrid Joerer Lindner, Feb. 22, 1957; children— Hugh, Fiona, Jennifer. BA with first class honours, New Coll., Oxford, 1951, MA (English Speaking Union fellow, Fulbright scholar), 1955; PhD, UCLA, 1963. Asst. prof. polit. sci. U. Santa Clara, Calif., 1957-61; asst. prof. polit. sci. Calif. State U., Fullerton, 1963-65, assoc. prof., 1965-70, prof., 1970-93, chmn. faculty council, 1966-67, acad. senator, 1971-78, dept. chmn., 1978-84, chmn. acad. senate, 1986-88. Vis. prof. politics U. Durham, U.K., 1984-85; intern univ. adminstrn. Am. Council on Edn., 1967-68. Author: None Dare Call it Reason, 1964; editor, frequent contbr.: Reason: A Review of Politics, 1965-66; editor, contbr.: Protest: Student Activism in America, 1970, Politics in the United States and California, 1995. Served with Royal Navy, 1945-47. Home: Santa Ana, Calif. Died July 2002.

FOSTER, RUTH MARY, dental association administrator; b. Little Rock, Jan. 11, 1927; d. William Crosby and Frances Louise (Doering) Shaw; m. Luther A. Foster, Sept. 8, 1946 (dec. Dec. 1980); children: William Lee, Robert Lynn. Grad. high sch., Long Beach, Calif. Sr. hostess Mon's Food Host of Coast, Long Beach, 1945-46; dental asst., office mgr. Dr. Wilfred H. Allen, Opportunity, Wash., 1946-47; dental asst., bus. asst. Dr. H. Erdahl, Long Beach, 1948-50; office mgr. Dr. B.B. Blough, Spokane, Wash., 1950-52; bus. mgr. Henry G. Kolsrud, D.D.S., P.S., Spokane, from 1958, Garland Dental Bldg., Spokane, from 1958. Sustaining mem. Spokane Symphony Orch. Mem. NAFE, Nat. Assn. Dental Assts., DAV Aux., DAV Comdrs. Club, Wash. State Fedn. Bus. and Profl. Women (dir. dist. 6), Spokane's Lilac City Bus. and Profl. Women (past pres.), Nat. Alliance Mentally Ill, Wash. Alliance Mentally Ill, Internat. Platform Assn., Spokane Club, Credit Women's Breakfast Club, Dir.'s Club, Inland N.W. Zool. Soc., Pioneer Circle of Women Helping Women. Democrat. Mem. First Christian Ch. Avocations: gardening, reading, continuing education studies. Home: Spokane, Wash. Died Oct. 24, 2001.

FOUNTAIN, L. H. former congressman; b. Leggett, N.C., Apr. 23, 1913; s. Lawrence H. and Sallie (Barnes) F.; m. Christine Dail, May 14, 1942; 1 dau., Nancy Dail. AB, U. N.C., 1934, JD, 1936, LL.D. hon., 1981. Bar: N.C. 1936. Reading clk. N.C. Senate, 1936-41; mem. 83d-97th Congresses from 2d N.C. Dist., mem. fgn. affairs com., chmn. inter-govtl. relations and human relations subcom. of govt. operations com. for 28 yrs.; mem. internat. security and sci. affairs subcom., Europe and Middle East subcom. 97th Congress. Mem. U.S. del. 22d session UN Gen. Assembly, 1967, Presdl. Adv. Com. on Federalism, 1981-82; charter mem. Adv. Commn. on Intergovtl. Relations, 1959-82; former chmn. subcom. on Near Eastern Affairs of Fgn. Affairs Com.; sponsor legislation leading to 1st ind. insp. gen. in HEW, worked for establishment of insp. gens. in other fed. agys. Mem. exec. com. East Carolina council Boy Scouts Am.; State senator 4th Senatorial Dist., Gen. Assembly, 1947-52; Pres. Edgecombe Young Democratic Club, 1940; eastern organizer Young Dem. Clubs of N.C., 1941; past chmn. exec. com. 2d Congl. Dist.; elder Presbyterian Ch., unbroken Sunday sch. or Bible class attendance, 1916—; trustee St. Andrews Presbyn. Coll., N.C., 1955-71, 72-74, Nat. Presbyn. ch., Washington, 1961-64, 77-80. Served to maj. AUS, 1942-46.; lt. col. USAR (ret.). Elected Tarboro's Man of Year, 1948; recipient citation for distinguished pub. service N.C. Citizens Assn., 1971; Distinguished Service award U. N.C. Sch. Medicine, 1973; Distinguished Service award N.C. League Municipalities, 1976; Distinguished Services to Higher Edn. and Scholarly Community award Am. Assn. Univ. Presses, 1975; Leadership and Disting. Service award Assn. Fed. Investigators, 1978; Person of Yr. award Inst. Internal Auditors, 1979 Mem. N.C. Bar Assn., N.C. Farm Bur., N.C. Grange, Am. Legion. Lodges: Kiwanis (lt. gov. 6th N.C. div.). Democrat. Died Oct. 10, 2002.

FOURAKER, LAWRENCE EDWARD, retired business administration educator; b. Bryan, Tex., Oct. 28, 1923; s. Leroy L. and Laura (Broach) F.; m. Patricia Orr, June 14, 1949; children: Senter Fouraker Jones, Lawrence Anderson. BA, Tex. A.&M. Coll., 1947, MS, 1948; PhD, U. Colo., 1951; MA (hon.), Harvard U., 1963; PhD (hon.), U. Pan Americana, Mex., 1987, St. Norbert Coll., West De Pere, Wis., 1974. Instr. U. Wyo., 1948-49; from asst. prof. to prof. Pa. State U., 1951-61; mem. faculty Bus. Sch. Harvard U., Cambridge, Mass., 1961-83, prof. bus. adminstrn., 1962-82, Edsel Bryant Ford Prof., 1968-70, 80-83, dir. divsn. rsch., 1968-70, George Fisher Baker prof. bus. adminstrn., 1970-80, dean Bus. Sch., 1970-80, prof. emeritus. Author: (with S. Siegel) Bargaining and Group Decision Making, 1960, Bargaining Behavior, (with H. Bierman and R. Jaedicke) Quantitative Analysis for Business Decisions, 1961. Trustee Dana Farber Med. Inst., Mass. Gen. Hosp., 1974-80, Pine Manor Coll., Mus. Fine Arts, Boston, 1971—, pres., 1980-84; mem. Resources for the Future; mem. vis. com. Harvard U. Meml. Ch., 1980—. With AUS, 1943-46. Home: Chestnut Hill, Mass. Deceased.

FOX, ANNETTE JOY, marketing specialist; b. Pacific Grove, Calif., Mar. 8, 1951; d. Kenneth Fredrick and Emma Margaret (Courtney) Brosi; children: Amber Leigh, Heather Leigh; m. Frederick William Fox, Dec. 15, 1985. BA, Ind. U., 1977; MBA, Amber U., 1987. Tax investigator Ind. Dept. Revenue, Indpls., 1971-73; service rep. Ind. Bell, Indpls., 1973-81, Southwestern Bell, Dallas, 1981-83; account specialist AT&T Info. Systems, Dallas, 1983-84; account exec. Executone, Dallas, 1984-85; coordinator mktg. Contel, Dallas, 1985-88, product mgr. Merrifield, Va., 1988-91; mktg. staff specialist GTE, Irving, Tex., from 1991. Troop leader Girl Scouts Am., Richardson, Tex., 1985—; coach Richardson Soccer Assn., 1984-85. Mem. NAFE, Am. Mktg. Assn., U.S. Telephone Assn., Carroll High Sch. Boosters. Clubs: Toastmasters. Avocations: sailing, snow and water skiing. Home: Fort Worth, Tex. Died Aug. 9, 2000.

FOX, MAXINE RANDALL, banker; b. Yates Ctr., Kans., Feb. 18, 1924; d. Carey Holaday and Nettie Myrrl (Herder) Randall; m. Joseph Marlin Fox, Aug. 25, 1946 (dec. 1992); children: Kathryn Lynette Fox Wilz, Jonathan Randall Fox. A in Fine Arts, Colo. Woman's Coll., 1942; B Music Edn., U. Denver, 1946. Pub. sch. music. tchr. Barr Lake (Colo.), 1942-43, Independence Sch., Fort Lupton, Colo., 1943-44, Fowler Pub. Schs., Fowler, Colo., 1944-48, 1952-54; employee The Fox Ins. Agy., Fowler, Colo., 1948-55, co-owner, 1955-86; with The Fowler (Colo.) State Bank, from 1949, vice chmn. bd. dirs., from 1987. Former mem. Fowler Libr. Bd.; mem. PEO. Named woman of Yr., Eta Tau chpt. Beta Sigma Phi, 1997. Mem. AAUW, DAR, First Families Ohio, Descendants Colonial Clergy (life), Fowler Hist. Soc. (past treas.), Fowler C. of C., Friends of Libr., Fowler Women's Club, Order Ea. Star, Fowler Golf Club, Pueblo Golf and Country Club. Republican. Methodist. Avocations: genealogy, reading, fishing, gardening, bridge. Home: Fowler, Colo. Died Sept. 11, 2001.

FOX, ROBERT KRIEGBAUM, retired manufacturing executive; b. Covington, Ohio, Apr. 1, 1907; s. Ammon L. and Josephine (Kriegbaum) F.; m. Dorothy Carroll Bush, Aug. 28, 1934; children: Susan, Hannah, Robert L. AB, Ohio State U., 1929, MA, 1930, PhD, 1932. Chemistry instr. Bethany Coll., W.Va., 1932-36; mem. faculty Hiram Coll., Ohio, 1936-41; partner Fox Chem. Co., Coshocton, Ohio, 1941-45; pres. Lancaster Glass Corp., 1945-76, chmn. bd., 1976-91, Indiana Glass Co., 1956-74; v.p., treas. Lancaster Colony Corp., 1962-82. Dir. Hocking Valley Nat. Bank, 1948-77, Lancaster Colony Corp., 1962-91. Mem. Sigma Xi, Phi Lambda Upsilon. Clubs: Mason, Shriner, Rotarian. Home: Lancaster, Ohio. Deceased.

FOX, SIDNEY WALTER, chemist, educator; b. Los Angeles, Mar. 24, 1912; s. Jacob and Louise (Burmon) F.; m. Raia Joffe, Sept. 14, 1937; children: Jack Lawrence, Ronald Forrest, Thomas Oren. BA, UCLA, 1933; PhD, Calif. Inst. Tech., 1940. Technician Rockefeller Inst., 1934-35; rsch. asst. Calif. Inst. Tech., 1935-37, tchg. fellow, 1937-39; rsch. chemist Cutter Labs., 1940-41; dir. vitamin assay lab. U. Mich., 1941-42; rsch. chemist F.E. Booth Co., 1942-43; from asst. prof. to prof. chemistry Iowa State Coll., 1943-55; head chem. sect. Iowa Agrl. Expt. Sta., 1949-55; dir., prof. Oceanographic Inst., Fla. State U., 1955-61, Inst. for Space Bioscis., 1961-64, Inst. Molecular and Cellular Evolution, U. Miami, Coral Gables, Fla., 1964-89; Disting. rsch. prof. dept. plant biology So. Ill. U., Carbondale, 1989-92. Lectr. Chinese Acad. Sci., 1979, collaborator, lectr., 1986; lectr. natural genesis Pope John Paul II and Vatican Scientists, 1984, 85, 90; mem. internat. com. Evolution of Info. Processing, 1989-91; cons. AEC, 1947-55, Staley Mfg. Co., 1954-60, NASA, 1960-91, USA-USSR interacad. lectr., 1969; chmn. subcom. on nomenclature of biochemistry NRC, 1956-57; mem. adv. panel on systematic biology NSF, 1958-60; disting. rsch. scientist dept. marine sci. U. South Ala., 1993—; Plenary lectr. Trieste, Italy, 1994-95. Author: (with Joseph F. Foster) Introduction to Protein Chemistry, 1957, (with Klaus Dose) Molecular Evolution and the Origin of Life, 1972, rev. edit., 1977; editor: Origins of Prebiological Systems, 1965 (with others) The Origin of Life and Evolutionary Biochemistry, 1974; assoc. editor: (with others) Chem. Rev., 1957-58; editor: BioSystems, 1965-94, Jour. Microencapsulation, 1981-93, Individuality and Determinism, 1984; editor: Selforgn., 1986, (with Mae-Wan Ho) Evolutionary Processes and Metaphors, 1988; contbr. (with others) articles to sci. jours. Recipient honors medal and citation as outstanding scientist Fla., Fla. Acad. Scis., 1968, Iddles award, 1973, spl. recognition NASA, 1979; named Disting. Scientist of Yr., Tex. Christian U., 1968; honoree Festschrift on Molecular Evolution, 1972, Molecular Evolution and Protobiology, 1984, Symposium on Polyamino Acids, The Emergence of Life, and Industrial Applications, Am. Chem. Soc., 1994. Fellow AAAS (nominations com. 1975-76, Chautauqua lectr. 1979-82), Am. Soc. Biol. Chemists; mem. Am. Chem. Soc. (chmn. divsn. biol. chemistry 1958-59, nat. councilor 1955-58, award Fla. sect. 1974), Internat. Union Biochemistry (U.S. nat. com. 1956-59, sec. 1957-59), Internat. Soc. Study Origin of Life (co-founder, v.p. 1970-74), Am. Soc. Cell Biologists, Soc. Neurosci., Ill. Acad. Sci. (hon.), Sigma Xi. Achievements include pioneering of amino acid sequence determination in proteins, plausible theory of origins of life via laboratory experiments, discovery (with others) of amino acid precursors on the moon, production of protoorganism in laboratory following extensive characterization, production of synthetic neuron; inventor of thermal proteins synthetic living systems. Home: Mobile, Ala. Died Aug. 10, 1998.

FOX, WILLIAM RICHARD, retired physician; b. Bozeman, Mont., Oct. 12, 1915; s. William Edward Fox and Anah Grace Bump; m. Esther Viola Jorgenson, Aug. 15, 1948 (dec. 1985); 1 child, Susan Jane Fox. MD, U. Manitoba, Can., 1941. Intern St. Joseph Hosp., St. Paul, 1940-41; staff Good Samaritan Hosp, Johnson Clinic, 1941-85; pub. health officer Pierce County, 1948-85; surgeon Gt. No. Ry., 1950-70. Past pres. Rugby Econ. Devel. Assn. Recipient N.D. Physicians Community and Profl. Svc. award, 1984. Mem. Union Hills County Club (Sun City Ariz.), Mason (past master), Shriners, Elks. Avocations: golf, bowling, crafts. Home: Denver, Colo. Died July 31, 1999.

FRACKMAN, RICHARD BENOIT, investment banker; b. N.Y.C., Apr. 14, 1923; s. H. David and Ruth (Warren) F.; m. Noel Stern, July 2, 1950; 1 dau., Noel Dru Frackman Pyne. Grad., Pratt Sch. Bus., 1941; student, U. Pa., 1941-42, NYU, 1946-48, N.Y. Inst. Fin., 1962-63. Mdse. mgr. R.H. Miller Stores, Inc., N.Y.C., 1946-49; v.p., mdse. mgr. Darling Stores Corp., N.Y.C., 1949-61; stockbroker, sr. security analyst, ltd. partner Burnham & Co., N.Y.C., 1962; v.p., corp. Burnham & Co. Inc., 1972; sr. v.p. Drexel Burnham Lambert, Inc., 1972-89; mem. hearing bd. N.Y. Stock Exchange, 1978 ; ltd. ptnr. Cowen & Co., N.Y.C., 1989-98; mng. dir., from 1992; mem. exec. com. Securities Industry Assn., N.Y.C., from 1980; arbitrator NYSE, N.Y.C., from 1992; mng. dir. S.G. Cowen Securities Corp., 1998-2000, Dominick & Dominick, from 2000. Pres. Greenville Community Coun., 1967-70; vice chmn. Town of Greenburgh (N.Y.) Planning Bd., 1970-77; bd. dirs. N.Y. State Planning Fedn., 1975-78; mem. Westchester County Regional Plan Assn., 1970-92; trustee Sarah Lawrence Coll., Bronxville, N.Y., 1979-87; mem. Coun. of N.Y. State U. at Purchase, 1996—, chmn. 1998—,, Purchase Coll. Found., 1996—; mem. N.Y. State Rep. Com., 1976-82, 97—. Capt. USAAC, 1942-46. Recipient Silver Box award Greenville Community Council, 1970 Mem. N.Y. Soc. Security Analysts (sr. mem.), Fin. Analysts Fedn. Clubs: Metropolis Country (White Plains, N.Y.) (gov. 1974—, v.p. 1977-78, treas. 1979-80, pres. 1981-83); Harmonie (N.Y.C.). Home: Scarsdale, NY. Deceased.

FRADY, MARSHALL BOLTON, television journalist, author; b. Augusta, Ga., Jan. 11, 1940; s. Joseph Yates and Jean Marshall (Bolton) F.; m. Susanne Barker, Jan. 20, 1961 (div. Oct. 1966); m. Gloria Mochel, Nov. 10, 1966 (div. 1975); children: Katrina, Carson, Shannon; m. Gudrun Barbara Schunk, May 14, 1975. BA, Furman U., 1963; postgrad., U. Iowa, 1965-66. Corr. Newsweek mag., Atlanta and Los Angeles, 1966-67; staff writer Saturday Evening Post, Atlanta, 1968-69; contbg. editor Harper's mag., Atlanta, 1969-71; writer Life mag., Atlanta, 1971-73; chief corr. ABC News Closeup, N.Y.C., 1979-86; former corr. ABC-TV News Nightline. Author: Wallace, 1968, Across A Darkling Plain, 1971, Billy Graham, 1979, Southerners, 1980. Recipient Golden Eagle Council Internat. Non-Theatrical Events, 1980, 83; recipient Emmy Nat. Acad. TV Arts and Scis., 1981-82; named Disting. Alumnus Furman U., 1982; Woodrow Wilson fellow, 1963 Died Mar. 9, 2004.

FRAME, SCOTT BARNHART, surgeon; b. Portsmouth, Va., Jan. 31, 1952; s. Eldon Benjamin and Gwenevere Olivia (Barnhart) Frame; m. Joyce Ann Viola, June 7, 1986. MD, U. N.Mex., 1980, BSBA, 1974. Diplomate Am. Bd. Surgery. Resident in surgery Naval Hosp., Portsmouth, 1980-86; fellow in trauma, crit. care Tulane U., New Orleans, 1987-88; surgeon U. Tenn. Med. Ctr., Knoxville, 1990-97; assoc. prof. surgery U. Tenn., Knoxville, 1990-97; surgeon U. Cin. Med. Ctr., from 1997; assoc. prof. surgery U. Cin., from 1997. Author: (book) Retroperitoneal Trauma, 1993; editor: (book) PHTLS textbook, 1994. Mem. Am. Coll. Surgery, Am. Assn. for the Surgery of Trauma, Internat. Coll. Surgeons, Soc. Am. Gastrointestinal Endoscopic Surgery, Soc. Crit. Care Medicine. Died Mar. 14, 2001.

FRANK, JOHN PAUL, lawyer, writer; b. Appleton, Wis., Nov. 10, 1917; s. Julius Paul and Beatrice (Ullman) F.; m. Lorraine Weiss, May 11, 1944; children: John Peter, Gretchen, Karen, Andrew, Nancy. BA, U. Wis., 1938, MA, LL.B., 1940; J.S.D., Yale U., 1946; LL.D., Lawrence U., 1981; HHD, Ariz. State U., 1997. Bar: Wis. 1940, D.C. 1966, Ariz. 1954, U.S. Supreme Ct. 1954. Law clk. U.S. Supreme Ct. Justice Hugo L. Black, 1942; asst. to sec. interior, 1943; to atty. gen., 1944-45; asst. prof. law Ind. U., 1946-49; asso. prof. law Yale, 1949-54; vis. lectr. law U. Wash., 1966, U. Ariz., 1967, Ariz. State U., 1969, 72; with firm Covington & Burling, Washington, 1947, Arnold & Porter, Washington, 1948, 53; mem. firm Lewis & Roca, Phoenix, 1954—. Mem. adv. com. civil procedure Jud. Conf. U.S., 1960-70; chmn. U.S. Circuit Judge Nominating Commn.-9th Circuit Panel, South, 1977; mem. exec. com. Adv. Com. on Appellate Justice; mem. Ariz. Commn. Appellate Ct. Appointments, 1974-85; chmn. sr. adv. bd. 9th Cir. Ct. Appeals. Author: Mr. Justice Black, 1949, Cases on Constitutional Law, 1950, Cases on the Constitution, 1951, My Son's Story, 1952, Marble Palace, 1958, Lincoln as a Lawyer, 1961, Justice Daniel Dissenting, 1964, The Warren Court, 1964, American Law: The Case for Radical Reform, 1969, Clement Haynsworth, The Senate and the Supreme Court, 1991; also articles. Dem. precinct committeeman, 1956-86; counsel Ariz. Dem. Com., 1962-67, 79-99. Recipient Lewis F. Powell, Jr. award, Am. Inns of Ct. Found., 1997. Fellow Am. Bar Found.; mem. ABA, Maricopa County Bar Assn., Am. Law Inst. (coun). Died Sept. 7, 2002.

FRANK, SANDERS THALHEIMER, physician, educator; b. Middletown, Conn., May 11, 1938; s. Harry S. and Pauline (Thalheimer) F.; B.A., Amherst Coll., 1959; M.D., N.Y. Med. Coll., 1963; children: Geoffrey Brooks, Susan Kimberly, Jonathan Blair. Intern, Sinai Hosp., Balt., 1963-64; resident Wilford Hall Med. Center, San Antonio, 1965-68; pvt. practice medicine, specializing in pulmonary disease, Monterey Park, Calif., 1971-92; dir. respiratory care Garfield Hosp., Monterey Park, 1974-92, Beverly Hosp., Montebello, Calif., 1975-78; assoc. prof. medicine U. So. Calif., L.A., 1972-90; pvt. practice, Zanesville, Ohio, 1992—. Served to maj. USAF, 1964-71. Decorated USAF Commendation medal; recipient Philip Hench award for demonstrating relationship of rheumatoid arthritis to lung disease, 1968; award of merit Los Angeles County Heart Assn., 1974. Fellow Royal Soc. Medicine (London), Am. Coll. Chest Physicians, A.C.P.; mem. Am. Thoracic Soc., Calif. Thoracic Soc., Nat. Assn. Dirs. Respiratory Care, Respiratory Care Assembly Calif., Alpha Omega Alpha. Contbr. articles in field to med. jours. Recorded relationship of ear-lobe crease to coronary artery disease, 1973. Home: Pacific Palisades, Calif. Died 1997.

FRANKEL, BETTY SOPHIA, landscape designer, writer, photographer; b. N.Y.C., Mar. 26, 1923; d. Harry B. and Estelle Ruth (Weil) Schwartz; m. Richard William Frankel, Feb. 7, 1943; children: Martha F., Barbara A., Edward H. BS in Botany, U. Mich., 1944, M in Land Architecture, 1973. Tchr. sci. and math. Elmira (N.Y.) Schs., 1945-46; tchr. English and art Farmington (Mich.) Schs., 1962; asst. botanist Cranbrook Inst. of Sci., Bloomfield Hills, Mich., 1964-65; garden writer Detroit Free Press, from 1969; freelance garden and landscape designer Farmington, from 1973. Instr. gardening Schoolcraft Community Coll., Livonia, Mich., 1987—. Author: Adventures in Landscape, 1973, chpt. Natural History of Farmington, 1976. Founding mem. Farmington Hills Beautification Commn., 1966-70, 86—, Farmington Hills Pk. Commn., 1971-80. Recipient Frieda Bottom award Met. Detroit Landscape Assn., 1976. Mem. Garden Writers Assn. of Am., Federated Garden Clubs of Mich., Landscape Critics Coun., AAUW, Mich. Botanical Club, Mich. Nature Assn., Phi Kappa Phi, Phi Sigma (medal). Democrat. Jewish. Deceased.

FRANKEL, STANLEY ARTHUR, columnist, educator, business executive; b. Dayton, Ohio, Dec. 8, 1918; s. Mandel and Olive (Margolis) F.; m. Irene Baskin, Feb. 20, 1946; children: Stephen, Thomas, Nancy. BS with high honors, Northwestern U., 1940; student, Columbia U., 1940, U. Chgo., 1946-49. Reporter Chgo. News Bur., 1940; publicist CBS, 1941; asst. to pres. Esquire and Coronet mags., N.Y.C., 1946-56; pres. Esquire Club, 1956-58; with McCall Corp., N.Y.C., 1958-61, asst. to pres. and pub., 1958-61, v.p., 1959-61; v.p., dir. corporate devel. Ogden Corp., 1961-88, cons., from 1988, Manning, Selvage & Lee Pub. Relations Corp., N.Y.C., from 1987; weekly columnist This Week mag., from 1990. Dir. Michaelis Prodns., Inc., Rockwood Corp., Careful Office Service Inc., Western Calif. Canners Corp., Internat. Terminal Operating Co., Inc., Ogden Am. Corp.; adj. prof. Baruch Coll., CUNY, 1974—, Pace U., 1983—; bd. dirs. Baruch Coll. Ctr. of Mgmt., 1986—; bd. visitors PhD Program Baruch Coll., 1986—, bd. mgmt. dept. Baruch Coll., CUNY; guest lectr. NYU, 1974; mem. Pres.'s Adv. Council on Pece Corps, 1965, Pres.'s Adv. Council on Youth Opportunity.; Mem. chancellor's panel SUNY, 1970-72; mem. N.Y. State Task Force on Higher Edn., 1974-76; bd. mem., exec. com. Nat. Council Crime and Delinquency; bd. mem., vice chmn. Nat. Businessmen's Council; bd. dirs., officer Scarsdale Adult Sch.; adv. bd. Channel 14 Cable TV Sta. Author: History of 37th Division, 1947, Frankel-y Speaking About WWII In the South Pacific, 1992; columnist The Week mag., 1989—; regular guest cable TV series Frankel-y Speaking, Westchester County, N.Y., 1944—; contbr. articles to popular mags. Exec. bd. Writers for Stevenson, 1952, 56, for Kennedy, 1960, McGovern for Pres., 1972; pub. rels. dir. Stevenson-for-Pres., 1956; chmn. Writers for Senator Humphrey Vice-Presdl. campaign, 1964; exec. bd. Businessmen for Humphrey-Muskie, 1968; mem. nat. exec. com. McGovern for Pres., 1972; vice chmn. N.Y. State McGovern for Pres. Com., 1972; bd. overseers Rutgers U., 1977-80; chancellor's external rels. com. CUNY, 1977-80; bd. dirs., v.p., mem. exec. com. YMCA of Greater N.Y.; founder Pub. Rels. Bd., Inc., N.Y.C. and Chgo., Bedford Stuyvesant Project (T.R.Y.); mem. V.P.'s Task Force on Youth Unemployment, 1979-80; mem. Cable TV Adv. Coun., Scarsdale, N.Y., 1996—. Maj. AUS, 1940-46. Decorated 2 Presdl. Citations, 3 Bronze Stars; recipient Peabody award for TV Series Adlai Stevenson Reports, 1961-63; Northwestern U. Alumni Merit award, 1964 Mem. Town Club (bd. govs.), Sunningdale Country Club, Dutch Treat Club, Northwestern U. Club N.Y. (pres. 1964), Overseas Press Club, Scarsdale Town Club, Phi Beta Kappa, Phi Beta Kappa Assocs. (pres. 1983-90, trustee, disting. lectr. 1988), Phi Beta Kappa Assn. Westchester County (pres 1980—85). Died Nov. 12, 1999.

FRANKLIN, RICHARD W. retired obstetrician/gynecologist; b. Portland, Oreg., 1923; MD, U. Oreg. Health Scis. U., 1948. Diplomate Am. Bd. Ob-Gyn. Intern Emanuel Hosp., Portland, 1948-49, resident in ob-gyn., 1949-50, 52-54. Mem. AMA. Home: Gresham, Oreg. Died June 11, 1999.

FRANKO, BERNARD VINCENT, pharmacologist, educator; b. West Brownsville, Pa., June 9, 1922; m. Marie Burke, June 25, 1946; 9 children BS in Pharmacy, W.Va. U., 1954, MS in Pharmacology, 1955; PhD in Pharmacology, Med. Coll. Va., 1958. With A.H. Robins Co., Richmond, Va., 1958—, assoc. dir. pharmacology, 1968-71, 73-77, dir. pharmacologic research, 1971-73, monitor, dir. good lab. practices dept., 1978-81, mgr. research coordination and tng. sect., 1981-90, ret., 1990; asst. prof., adj. asst. prof. pharmacology Med. Coll. Va., Richmond, from 1961. Contbr. numerous articles to profl. jours. Fellow AAAS; mem. Am. Soc. Pharmacology and Exptl. Therapeutics, Soc. Exptl. Biology and Medicine. Home: Richmond, Va. Died Mar. 28, 2003.

FRAPPIER, ELIZABETH JANE, mental health center administrator; b. Bethlehem, Pa., Apr. 8, 1932; d. Claud Andrew and Sara Irene (Beckett) Fegley; m. Robert Magner Frappier; children: Robert F., Paul A., James C., Ann E., MaryJane. AAS, Moravian, Bethlehem, 1952. Asst. to city clk. City of Bethlehem, 1952-53; airline ticket agt. United Airlines, Phila., 1953-55; field rep. Am. Heart Assn., Newton, Pa., 1978-79; office mgr. Congl. Office, Langhorne, Pa., 1979-82; asst. to ctr. dir. Penndel (Pa.) Mental Health Ctr., from 1985. State committeewoman Rep. Pa., 1981—; committeewoman Bucks County Rep., Middletown Twp., 1979—; fundraising com. Queen of Universe Bldg. Fund, Middletown Twp., 1986. Mem. Bucks County Coun. Execs., 1985—. Roman Catholic. Avocations: bridge, golf, tennis. Home: Langhorne, Pa. Died Mar. 11, 2001.

FRASER, CHARLES ELBERT, real estate developer, resort, park and urban planner; b. Hinesville, Ga., June 13, 1929; s. Joseph Bacon and Pearl (Collins) F.; m. Mary Wyman Stone, Nov. 30, 1963; children: Mary Wyman Stone, Laura Lawton. Student, Presbyn. Coll., 1946-48, LL.D. (hon.), 1985; BBA, U. Ga., 1950; JD, Yale U., 1953. Bar: Ga. bar 1953. Pres. Sea Pines Plantation Co., Hilton Head Island, S.C., 1957-83, Parks Am. Inc. and Community Design Inst., Hilton Head Island, from 1983. U.S. commr. gen. for 1982 World's Fair, 1980-82; mem. space sta. adv. com. Office Tech. Assessment Contbr. articles on land use, planning, leisure, recreation to various publs. Chmn. Beaufort County Bd. Dirs., 1962-63; mem. Pres.'s Citizens Adv. Com. on Environ. Quality, 1968-69, Pres.'s Citizens Adv.

Com. on Natural Beauty and Outdoor Recreation, 1964-68; past mem. S.C. Parks, Recreation and Tourism Commn., 1967-74; chmn. Nat. Recreation and Parks Assn., 1974-76; trustee Nat. Recreation Found., 1968—, So. Ctr. Internat. Studies; bd. visitors Presbyn. Coll., 1971. Served to 2d lt. USAF, 1954-56. Recipient Certificate of Excellence in Pvt. Community Planning AIA, 1968, Citation for Excellence in Large Scale Recreational Communities, U. L.I. Mem. Am. Soc. Landscape Architects (hon.), AIA (hon.), Chief Execs. Org. Presbyterian (elder). Clubs: Metropolitan (N.Y.C.); Plantation (Hilton Head Island); Chatham (Savannah, Ga.); S.C. Golf (chmn.), S.C. Yacht. Home: Hilton Head Island, SC. Died Dec. 15, 2002.

FRASER, DAVID A. retired lawyer; b. Syracuse, N.Y., Dec. 30, 1911; s. Hector Alexander and Minnie (Salmon) F.; m. Marion Ford, Sept. 17, 1938; children: David, Robert, Frederick, Janet. BA, Hamilton Coll., 1934; JD, Cornell U., 1937. Bar: N.Y.; U.S. Ct. of Appeals (2d cir.). Ptnr. Fraser Brothers, Syracuse, N.Y., 1938-58, Coulter, Fraser, Bolton, Bird and Ventre, Syracuse, 1958-87, counsel, 1987-2000; retired. Past pres., mem. life adv. bd. Salvation Army, Syracuse, 1960—; pres. Hiscock Legal Aid Soc., Syracuse, 1969-70, Onondaga Co. Bar. Assn., 1968-69, Onondaga Co. Libr. Sys., Syracuse, 1966; dir. Syracuse C. of C., 1957-62; chmn. Greater Syracuse Safety Coun., 1963-64; chmn. libr. trustees Syracuse U., 1963-70; trustee Hamilton coll., 1969-75. Mem. N.Y. State Bar Assn., Grolier Club, Phi Beta Kappa. Republican. Epicopalian. Home: Wilmington, Del. Died Mar. 1, 2003.

FRASER, EARL DONALD, land use planner, consultant; b. Missoula, Mont., Sept. 9, 1912; s. William Issac and Grace Millie (Beeman) F.; m. Elizabeth Argento, May 16, 1942. BArch in City Planning, MIT, 1937; M in Regional Planning, Harvard U., 1939. Town planner Town Planning Bds., Milford and Peterboro, N.H., 1937-38; city planner State Planning Bds., Ala. and Miss., 1939-41; sr. planner Md. Nat. Park and Planning Commn., Silver Spring, 1942-43; planning cons. various cities, Kalamazoo, Mich., 1946-53; exec. dir. Redevel. Agy., San Bernadino, 1954-55; dir. planning Sacramento County, Sacramento, 1955-77; cons. Earl D. Fraser, Sacramento, from 1978. Dir. specific plan Am. River Pkwy., 1937; cons. gen. plan Galt, Calif., 1979-54, Jackson, Calif. 1981. Trustee Regional Hosp. Planning Coun. Sacramento, Yolo, and Placer Counties, Calif., 1956-74. Lt. USN, 1943-45. Mem. Am. Planning Assn. (various offices 1946-93), Am. Inst. Cert. Planners (various offices 1946-94), Internat. Torch Club (bd. dirs., sec.-treas. 1947-94). Avocations: hunting, fishing. Died Nov. 20, 2001.

FRAZIER, ALTON EUGENE, interior designer; b. Minden, La., Sept. 11, 1922; s. Carlton Randolph and Gertrude (Sexton) F.; m. Irene Sipple; children: Joan Marie, Dan Jay, Carol Ann, Robert Eugene, Carlton Todd; m. Jacquelyn Heller. Student, La. Tech. U., 1940-42; LLB, La. State U., 1949, JD, 1968. Bar: La. 1949; cert. interior designer, N.Y.; registered interior designer, Tex. Pvt. practice in law, Minden, 1949-60; profl. instr. Dale Carnegie Leadership, Ark., La., Tex., 1960-69; interior designer Sangers Design Studio Inc., Dallas, 1960-63, Eugene Frazier Studio, Dallas, from 1963. Dir. distbr. Alpine Air Purifiers, Dallas, 1995; independent distbr. Nikken, Inc., Dallas, 1994; instr. So. Meth. U., Dallas, 1956=59; bd. dirs. Cosmopolitan Life Ins. Co.; writer Park Cities People Newspaper, Dallas. Author: Good Taste Begins With You, 1969, Kitchens, The Miracle Room, 1979, New Fashions in Floors, 1979, Glamourize With Lighting, 1979. Patron 500 Inc., Dallas; active Dallas Mus. Fine Arts. Mem. Am. Soc. Interior Designers (profl. mem.), Allied Design Profls., Nat. Writers Assn., Smithsonian Inst., Airliner Gourmet Study Club, Primetimers Internat. Methodist. Avocations: reading, entertaining, gourmet cooking, world travel, writing. Home: Dallas, Tex. Died Mar. 2, 2001.

FRECHETTE, J. RENE, lawyer; b. Hartford, Conn., Oct. 11, 1948; s. Paul Emile and Rolande (Godbout) F.; m. Marilyn Poindexter, Jan. 8, 1977. BA summa cum laude, U. Conn., 1975; JD, U. Iowa, 1978; postgrad., Hartford U. Bar: Iowa 1978, U.S. Dist. Ct. (no. dist.) Iowa 1978, Conn. 1980, U.S. Ct. Appeals (2d cir.) 1986. Law clk. U.S. Dist. Ct. (no. dist.) Iowa, Cedar Rapids, 1978-80; assoc. Day, Berry & Howard, Hartford, 1980-86; atty. CIGNA Corp., Bloomfield, Conn., 1986-88, counsel, from 1988. Notes and comments editor Iowa Law Rev., 1977-78. Mem. Windsor (Conn.) Bd. Tax Rev., 1988-92. Mem. ABA, Conn. Bar Assn., Haartford County Bar Assn., Am. Corp. Counsel Assn. Democrat. Roman Catholic. Home: Windsor, Conn. Deceased.

FREDRICKSON, DONALD SHARP, physician, scientist; b. Canon City, Colo., Aug. 8, 1924; s. Charles Arthur and Blanche Sharp Fredrickson; m. Henrietta Priscilla Dorothea Eekhof, Sept. 5, 1950; children: Eric Henderikus, Rurik Charles. Student, U. Colo., 1942—43; BS, U. Mich., 1946, MD, 1949; MD (hon.), Karolinska Inst., Stockholm, 1977; DSc (hon.), U. Mich., 1977, Mt. Sinai Sch. Medicine, 1978, U. N.C., 1979, Georgetown U., 1981, Yeshiva U., 1981, N.J. U. Medicine and Dentistry, 1982, Med. U. S.C., 1985, George Washington U., 1985, U. Rochester, 1986. Intern Peter Bent Brigham Hosp., Boston, 1949—50; house staff mem., fellow Peter Bent Brigham and Mass. Gen. hosps., 1950—53; mem. sr. rsch. staff lab. cellular physiology and metabolism Nat. Heart and Lung Inst., Bethesda, Md., 1953—61, clin. dir. inst., 1961—66, dir. inst., 1966—68, chief molecular disease br. div. intramural research, 1966, dir. div. intramural research, 1968—74; pres. Inst. Medicine, NAS, 1974—75; dir. NIH, 1975—81; scholar-in-residence NAS, 1981—83; v.p. Howard Hughes Med. Inst., Bethesda, 1983, pres., chief exec. officer, trustee, 1984—87; scholar Nat. Libr. Medicine, from 1987. Professorial lectr. medicine George Washington U. Sch. Medicine, 1958—64; lectr. preventive medicine Georgetown U. Sch. Medicine, 1963—84; pres. DS Fredrickson Assocs., from 1987; rschr. Nat. Heart, Lung and Blood Inst., 1987—90; bd. dirs. Surmodics, Inc. Editor (with others): The Metabolic Basis of Inherited Disease, 1st-6th edit, 1989; author: The Recombinant DNA Controversy: Memoir, 2001; contbr. articles to profl. jours.; editor (with others): The Metabolic Basis of Inherited Disease, 1st-6th edits., 1989; contbr. articles to profl. jours. With U.S. Army, 1943—45. Recipient Internat. award, James F. Mitchell Found. for Med. Edn. and Rsch., 1968, Disting. Achievement award, Modern Medicine, Superior Svc. award, HEW, 1970, Disting. Svc. award, 1971, Jimenez Das award, 1971, McCollum award, Am. Soc. Clin. Nutrition/Am. Inst. Nutrition, 1971, Modanina prize, 1975, Irving Cutter medal, 1978, Gairdner Found. ann. award, 1978, Purkinje medal, Czechoslovakian Med. Soc., 1980, Fondazione Lorenzini medal, 1980, Disting. Pub. Svc. award, HHS, 1981, Disting. Svc. award, Miami Winter Symposium, 1985, Svc. to Sci. award, Arthur M. Sackler Found., 1986, Sandoz Lifetime Achievement award, 1993. Fellow: ACP (award for outstanding work in sci. as related to medicine 1976), AAAS, Am. Coll. Cardiology (gold medal 1967, Disting. Svc. award 1983), Royal Coll. Physicians (London); mem.: NAS, Med. Soc. Sweden, Assn. Am. Physicians, Harvey Soc. (hon.), Am. Soc. Clin. Investigation, Am. Philos. Soc., Am. Acad. Arts and Scis., Acad. Kingdom of Morocco, Phi Kappa Phi, Alpha Omega Alpha, Phi Beta Kappa. Died June 7, 2002.

FREE, ALFRED HENRY, clinical chemist, consultant; b. Bainbridge, Ohio, Apr. 11, 1913; s. Alfred Harry and Alice Virginia (Clymer) F.; m. Dorothy Hoffmeister, June 20, 1934 (div. Mar. 1947); children: Charles Alfred, Jane Alison, Barbara Beth; m. Helen Mae Murray, Oct. 18, 1947; children: Eric Scot, Penny Alene, Kurt Allen, James Jacob, Bonnie Anne, Nina Joann. AB, Miami U., Oxford, Ohio, 1934; MA, PhD, Case Western Res. U., 1939. Diplomate Am. Bd. Clin. Chemistry. Lab. asst. Cleve. Clinic Rsch. Found., 1934-35; tchg. fellow dept. biochemistry Sch. Medicine Case Western Res. U., Cleve., 1935-39, instr., 1939-40, sr. instr., 1940-42, assoc. prof., 1942-46; numerous sci. positions to v.p. sci. rels. Ames divsn. Miles Inc., Elkhart, Ind., 1946-78; sr. sci. cons. diagnostics divsn. Bayer Corp. (formerly Miles Inc.), Elkhart, Ind., from 1978. Bd. dirs. Nat. Com. on Clin. Lab. Standards, 1976-83. Author: (with Helen Free) Urodynamics, 1972, Urinalysis in Clinical Laboratory Practice, 1974; editor blood and body fluids Biol. Abstracts, 1940-78; contbr. over 200 articles to sci. jours. Bd. dirs. Elkhart County chpt. Am. Cancer Soc., 1972; mem. blood collection com. ARC. Recipient award for 40 yrs. outstanding med. sci. contbns. Med. Econs., 1986, Nat. Clin. Lab. Leadership award Washington G-2 Reports, 1994; named to Sci. and Engring. Hall of Fame, 1996. Fellow AAAS, Assn. Clin. Scientists (nat. pres. 1972, Diploma of Honor 1973); mem. Am. Chem. Soc. (past chmn. nat. coms., chmn. St. Joseph Valley sect. 1962-63, 75-76, Shrine award 1982, Mosher award 1984), Am. Assn. Clin. Chemistry (chmn., councilor Chgo. sect. 1974, 75-77, Svc. award 1989, Nat. Fisher Profession award 1982, nat. award outstanding contbn. in spl. rsch. area 2000), Am. Inst. Chemistry (Chgo. chpt., Honor Scroll 1967), Lions (founding mem. Elkhart club, 1st chmn. Ind. Lions Eye Bank, bd. dirs., Citizen of Yr. award Chgo. 1983, Presbyterian. Achievements include several patents on clinical laboratory methodology; development of dipstick method of urinalysis through expansion of a series of dry chemical reagents. Home: Elkhart, Ind. Died May 15, 2000.

FREEBY, WAYNE ALFRED, chemical engineer; b. Elkhart, Ind., Aug. 21, 1929; s. Wayne Leo and Luella Jane (Fishley) F.; m. Delores Jane Noffsinger, July 1, 1951; children: Steven Wayne, Linda Sue. BSChemE, Tri-State U., 1959; MSChemE, U. Idaho, 1966. Rsch. engr. Miles Labs., Elkhart, 1959-60; sr. reactor engr. Phillips Petroleum Co., Idaho Falls, Idaho, 1960-66; sr. engr. Idaho Nuclear Corp., Idaho Falls, 1966-70; supr., mgr. Allied Chem. Corp., ICP, Idaho Falls, 1970-79; mgr. Exxon Nuclear Idaho Co., Idaho Falls, 1979-80, Ford, Bacon & Davis Utah, Salt Lake City, 1980-81; mgr., supr. Bechtel Nat. Inc., San Francisco, 1981-87; staff engr. Westinghouse Idaho Nuclear Co., Idaho Falls, from 1987. Author of reports for profl. publs.; reviewer Nuclear Technology Journal, Am. Nuclear Soc., LaGrange Park, Ill., 1987-88; patentee in field. Troop leader Boy Scouts of Am., Idaho Falls, 1967-69. Corp. U.S. Army, 1952-54, Korea. Mem. Am. Nuclear Soc., Am. Inst. Chem. Engrs. (div. dir. 1984-86, div. vice chmn. 1987, div. chmn. 1988), Tam Twirlers Square Dance Club, Calif. (publicity chmn. 1984). Republican. Methodist. Avocations: sports, camping, hiking, skiing, stamp collecting. Home: Rocklin, Calif. Died Sept. 15, 2000.

FREED, MALCOLM F. gynecologist; b. Balt., Nov. 7, 1930; s. Irvin F. and Goldie R. (Miller) F.; m. Phyllis R. Frankel, Sept. 4, 1955; children: Helaine Annette Freed Seibert, Ira Jay. BS, U. Md., 1952; MD, U. Md., Balt., 1954. Diplomate Am. Bd. Ob-Gyn. Chief gynecologist North Charles Gen. Hosp., Balt., 1964-90; assoc. chief gynecology Wyman Park Assocs. Johns Hopkins Health Care Systems, Balt., from 1993. Pres. med. staff North Charles Gen. Hosp., Balt., 1982-84, pres. med. exec. com., 1984-86. Capt. U.S. Army, 1957-59. Mem. Am. Coll. Ob-Gyn., Md. Ob-Gyn. Soc., Balt. County Med. Soc. Home: Baltimore, Md. Died.

FREEDMAN, FRANK HARLAN, federal judge; b. Springfield, Mass., Dec. 15, 1924; s. Alvin Samuel and Ida Hilda (Rosenberg) F.; m. Eleanor Labinger, July 26, 1953; children: Joan Robin Goodman, Wendy Beth Greedman Mackler, Barry Alan. LL.B., Boston U., 1949, LL.M., 1950; PhD (hon.), Western New Eng. Coll., Springfield, 1970. Pvt. practice law, 1950-68; mayor City of Springfield, 1968-72; judge U.S. Dist. Ct. Mass., Springfield, 1972-86, chief judge, 1986-92; now sr. judge, from 1992. Chmn. fund raising drs. Muscular Dystrophy, Leukemia Soc.; mem. Susan Auchter Kidney Fund Raising Com.; mem. Springfield City Council, 1960-67, pres., 1962; del. Republican Nat. Conv., 1964, 68; mem. Springfield Rep. Com., 1959-72. Served with USNR, 1943-46. Greenaway Drive Elem. Sch. rededicated as Frank H. Freedman Sch., 1974; recipient Silver Shingle award for disting. service Boston U., 1984. Mem. Hampden County (Mass.) Bar Assn., Lewis Marshall Club on Jurisprudence (pres.) Jewish. Died Aug. 21, 2004.

FREEDMAN, STANLEY ARNOLD, lawyer; b. N.Y.C., Oct. 3, 1922; s. David Aaron and Ruth (Silverstein) F.; m. Martha Taintor Thomas, May 2, 1943; children: Ann. E., Lucy D., David A, Edith L. BA magna cum laude, Harvard U., 1943, JD cum laude, 1949. Bar: N.Y. 1949, Ohio 1959. Assoc. Wickes Riddell Bloomer Jacobi & McGuire, N.Y.C., 1949-55, Rosenman Goldmark Colin & Kaye, N.Y.C., 1955-58; ptnr. Smith & Schnacke, L.P.A., Dayton, Ohio, 1959-89, Thompson, Hine and Flory, Dayton, Ohio, from 1989. Mem. Ohio Continuing Legal Edn. Commn., Columbus, 1988-93, chmn., 1992-93; bd. dirs. TBC Corp., Memphis. Bd. dirs. Jobs for Grads of Dayton, Inc., 1987—, AIDS Found. Miami Valley, Dayton Philharm. Orch. Assn., 1990—. Mem. ABA, Ohio Bar Assn., Dayton Bar Assn., Assn. of Bar of City of N.Y. Democrat. Avocation: tennis. Home: Dayton, Ohio. Died April 22, 1997.

FREEDMAN, WALTER, lawyer; b. St. Louis, Oct. 30, 1914; s. Sam and Sophie (Gordon) F.; m. Maxine Weil, June 23, 1940; children— Jay W., Sandra Freedman Sabel. AB, JD, Washington U., 1937; LLM, Harvard, 1938. Bar: Mo., Ill., D.C. Atty. SEC, Washington, 1938-40, U.S. Dept. Interior, Washington, 1940-42; chief counsel Office Export Control, Foreign Econ. Adminstrn., 1942-44, dir., 1944-45; ptnr. Freedman, Levy, Kroll & Simonds (and predecessor firm), Washington, 1946-2001, Foley & Lardner, Washington, from 2001. Fairchild fellow Harvard U. Law Sch., 1937-38 Editor-in-chief: Washington U. Law Quarterly, 1936-37; Contbr. articles to profl. jours. Decorated chevalier de l'Order de la Couronne (Belgium); recipient Disting. Alumni award Washington U. Sch. Law, 1995. Mem. Am. Law Inst., ABA, Fed. Bar Assn., D.C. Bar Assn., Woodmont Country Club (bd. mgrs.), Cosmos Club, Phi Beta Kappa, Omicron Delta Kappa, Phi Sigma Alpha. Jewish (trustee temple). Home: Washington, DC. Died July 4, 2002.

FREEMAN, ORVILLE LOTHROP, lawyer, former governor of Minnesota, think tank executive; b. Mpls., May 9, 1918; s. Orville E. and Frances (Schroeder) F.; m. Jane C. Shields, May 2, 1942; children: Constance Jane, Michael Orville. BA magna cum laude, U. Minn., 194O; LL.B., 1946; LL.B. (hon.), U. Seoul, (Korea); hon. degree, Am. U., Fairleigh Dickinson U., St. Joseph's Coll. Bar: Minn. 1947. Mem. Larson, Loevinger, Lindquist and Freeman, Mpls., 1947-55; gov. Minn., 1955-61; sec. U.S. Dept. Agr., 1961-69; pres. E.D.P. Tech. Internat. Inc., 1969-70; pres., chief exec. officer Bus. Internat. Corp., N.Y.C., 1970-81, chmn. bd., 1981-84; sr. ptnr. internat. law Popham, Haik, Schnobrich, Kaufman & Doty, Ltd., Washington, 1985-95. Dir. Natomas Corp., Multinat. Agribus. Sys., Inc., Franklin Mint, Grumman Corp., Slater, Michael Foods, Mycogen Corp., San Diego; mem. faculty Salzburg (Austria) Seminar, 1974, 77; vis. scholar Hubert Humphrey Inst., U. Minn., Mpls., 1995-99. Asst. charge vets. affairs to mayor Mpls., 1945-49; chmn. Mpls. Civil Svc. Commn., 1946-49; sec. Minn. Dem. Farmer Labor Party, 1946-48, chmn., 1948-50; mem. exec. com. Japan-U.S. Bus. Adv. Coun.; chmn. India-U.S. Bus. Adv. Coun., CARESBAC, 1986-96, chmn. emeritus; mem. adv. com. Hubert Humphrey Inst.; chmn. U.S.-Nigerian Agrl. Consultative Com.; chmn. bd. dirs. World Watch Inst., 1970-96, chmn. emeritus, 1997—; pres. Agr. Coun. Am., 1985-90; chmn. bd. govs. UN Assn. U.S.A.; mem. Presdl. Commn. on World Hunger; past trustee Luth. Ch. in Am. Lt. col. USMCR, 1942-49, USMCR 1949-69. Mem. Exec. Alumni Assn., Phi Beta Kappa, Delta Sigma Rho. Home: Minneapolis, Minn. Died Feb. 20, 2003.

FREEMAN, STEPHEN ALBERT, retired foreign language educator; b. Cambridge, Mass., May 9, 1898; s. Samuel Albert and Mary Reddin (Reed) F.; m. Ruth Mildred Hayden, June 5, 1923 (dec. Aug. 9, 1983); children: Hope Mina, Caroline Marcia, Harvey Albert. AB, Harvard U., 1920, MA, 1921, PhD, 1923; LHD, U. Vt., 1950; LLD, Norwich U., 1953; LittD, Dickinson Coll., 1961; LLD, McGill U., 1966; Litt D, Middlebury Coll., 1966. Instr. French Brown U., Providence, 1923-25; prof. French Middlebury (Vt.) Coll., 1925-63, v.p., 1943-63, dir. lang. schs., 1946-70, acting pres., 1940, 42, 52; ret., 1970. Author: (book) The Middlebury College Foreign Language Schools, 1975, The Congregational Church of Middlebury, Vt., 1991; contbr. numerous articles to profl. jours. Pres. Middlebury chpt. Phi Beta Kappa, 1939-63, Am. Assn. Tchrs. French, 1940-44, Nat. Fedn. Modern Lang. Tchrs. Assns., 1948, 54, Fedn. of Alliance Française, 1959-59; moderator Ind. Dist. 4 Sch. Dist., Middlebury, 1969-85; pres. Addison County Grammar Sch. Corp., Middlebury, 1943—; trustee Porter Med. Ctr., Middlebury, 1972-85. Lt.(j.g.) USN Aviation,

1917-1918; col. mil. intelligence USAR, 1949-56. Mem. Middlebury Rotary Club (Paul Harris fellow). Republican. Avocations: gardening, photography. Home: Shelburne, Vt. Died July 10, 1999.

FREIMAN, DAVID GALLAND, pathologist, educator; b. N.Y.C., July 1, 1911; s. Leopold and Dorothy (Galland) F.; m. Ruth Schein, Sept. 2, 1949; children: Nancy, Leonard. AB, CCNY, 1930; MD, L.I. Coll. Medicine (now Downstate Med. Center SUNY), 1935; AM (hon), Harvard U., 1962. Intern, house physician Jewish Hosp. of Bklyn., 1935-36; intern Kingston Ave. Hosp. (for Contagious Disease), Bklyn., 1938; intern, resident pathology Montefiore Hosp., 1938-43; asst. pathologist Mass. Gen. Hosp., 1944-50; attending pathologist Cin. Gen. Hosp., Drake Meml. Hosp., 1952-56; pathologist-in-chief, dir. labs. Beth Israel Hosp., Boston, 1956-79, emeritus, 1979—2003, former spl. asst. to pres.; cons. pathologist VA, Hosps., Cin., Ft. Thomas, Ky., 1954-56, Boston, 1962-85; instr. pathology Med. Sch. Tufts U., 1947-48, Harvard U. Med. Sch., 1949-50, clin. prof. pathology, 1956-62, prof., 1962-84, Mallinckrodt prof. pathology, 1969-79, prof. emeritus, 1984—2003; prof. anatomy, interim chmn. dept. anatomy U. Mass. Coll. Medicine, 1985-87; asst. prof. pathology Coll. Medicine, U. Cin., 1950-52; assoc. prof. U. Cin. Coll. Medicine, 1952-56; lectr. pathology Simmons, 1962-78. Cons. pathology Cambridge Hosp., 1968-85, Uniformed Services U. Health Scis., 1974-75, Children's Hosp. Med. Center, Boston, 1977-90; mem. joint faculty Harvard-MIT, 1975-79 Mem. editorial bd. Am. Jour. Pathology, 1961-82, Circulation, 1962-67, Human Pathology, 1969-93, assoc. editor, 1979-91; mem. editorial adv. com. Atlas of Tumor Pathology, 1966-87; contbr. articles to profl. jours. Recipient Stratford prize CCNY, 1931, Alumni prize L.I. Coll. Medicine, 1935; Kirstein fellow in med. edn. Harvard U., 1971-72 Mem.: AAAS, Internat. Soc. for Haemostasis and Thrombosis, New Eng. Soc. Pathologists, Mass. Med. Soc., Am. Soc. Clin. Pathologists, Histochem. Soc., Internat. Acad. Pathology, Am. Soc. for Investigative Pathology, Alpha Omega Alpha, Sigma Xi, Phi Beta Kappa. Home: Newton, Mass. Died Dec. 10, 2003.

FREIMARCK, GEORGE STEPHEN ALFRED, educator; b. N.Y.C., May 3, 1917; s. George William and Irene Susanne (Fabricius) F.; BA, Columbia Coll., 1938; MA, Columbia U., 1942; PhD (hon.), Wentworth Inst. Tech., 1991; m. Mary Elisabeth McAvoy, Nov. 11, 1950; children: George Geoffrey, Mary Elisabeth, Catherine Carey. Grad. asst. Columbia U., 1941-42; consul, sec. diplomatic service Fgn. Service, U.S. Govt., 1945-66; with Wentworth Inst. Tech., Boston, 1966—, prof. humanities and social scis., 1967—, dean gen. studies, 1968-74, editor Context, quar. publ. Coll. Arts and Scis.; emeritus prof. humanities and social sci., 1988. Mem. parish council Our Lady Star of the Sea Ch., Marblehead, Mass., 1979-80; vol., docent in maritime history Peabody Mus. Salem (Mass.), 1988—; pres. Friends of the Abbot Pub. Libr., Marblehead, 1990-92. Served with U.S. Army, 1942-45; ETO. NEH fellow, 1979. Mem. Mass. Fedn. Tchrs. (v.p. 1982-88), Am. Fgn. Service Assn., Fgn. Service Retirees of New Eng., Acad. Polit. Sci. Clubs: John Jay Assocs. of Columbia Coll., Columbia U. Club of New Eng. (bd. dirs.), Friends of Switzerland (bd. dirs. Boston chpt.), Civic League (Marblehead), Wentworth Retirees Club (sec., treas. 1991). Author: USA, A Pictorial Survey, 1957. Home: Marblehead, Mass.

FRENCH, BERTHA DORIS, medical, surgical and geriatrics nurse; b. Augusta Center, N.Y., Jan. 18, 1911; d. Charles Madison and Tillie (Hallenbeck) F. Diploma, Faxton Hosp. Sch. Nursing, Utica, N.Y., 1933. RN, N.Y., Tex.; registered Mi Esperanza Adult Day Care Facility. Pvt. duty nurse, Brownsville, Tex.; dir. nurses Retama Manor Nursing Home, Brownsville, 1972, Valley Grande Manor Nursing Facility, Brownsville, 1973-76, PRN Home Health Agy., Brownsville; staff nurse Brownsville Med. Ctr.; relief dir. nursing svc. Village at Valley Inn, Brownsville, Brownsville Good Samaritan Ctr.; DON Ebony Lake Convalescent Ctr., 1990; nursing cons. Casa del Sol Adult Day Care Ctr., Brownsville, Harlingen, and San Benito, Tex., 1992-94; charge nurse, dir. Casa del Sol Adult Day Care Ctr. #2, Brownsville, from 1991; adv. dir. J & J Home Health Agency; asst. Mary Lou Watkins, MD, PhD, 1994-97; charge nurse Casa del Sol Day Care Ctr. #3, Brownsville, 1993-97, Tropical #2 Adult Day Care Ctr., Brownsville, from 1997; asst. dir., nurse Mi Esperanza Adult Day Care, Brownsville, from 1999. Cons. San Benito (Tex.) Adult Day Care Ctr., 1996—, Happy Hearts Adult Day Care Ctr., Brownsville; guest spkr. LVN program Tex. Southmost Coll., 1990; pvt. duty for Gladys Porter; founder Gladys Porter Zoo, 1980. Recipient Recognition award Mayor of Brownsville, 1992. Died Dec. 22, 2000.

FRENCH, RICHARD FREDERIC, retired music educator; b. Randolph, Mass., June 23, 1915; s. Herbert F. and Edith (MacGregor) F. BS, Harvard U., 1937, MA, 1939; MusD, Concordia U., 1998. Asst. prof. music Harvard U., 1947-51; dir. publs., v.p. Asso. Music Pubs., 1951-60; pres. N.Y. Pro Musica, 1959-70, dir., 1959—; Robert S. Tangeman prof. sacred music Union Theol. Sem., N.Y.C., 1961-73, adj. prof. sacred music, 1973-77; prof. music Inst. Sacred Music, Yale U., 1973-85, prof. emeritus; grad. faculty, dir. doctoral studies Julliard Sch., N.Y.C., 1985-99. Vis. prof. music Yale Sch. of Music, 1994, 96, 99. Contbr. articles to books, mags. Trustee Schola Musicae Liturgicae, Bklyn. Music Sch. Served with USAAF, 1942-45. Decorated Bronze Star. Mem. Am. Musicol. Soc., Internat. Soc. Contemporary Music (treas. U.S. sect.) Clubs: Harvard (N.Y.C.), Yale (N.Y.C.), Century Assn. (N.Y.C.). Home: Boston, Mass. Deceased.

FRIDMAN, JONATHAN DIETER, electrical engineer, physicist, consultant, educator; b. Istanbul, Turkey, Feb. 11, 1932; arrived in U.S., 1952; s. Emile and Olga (Friedmann) F.; m. Eva Jane Neumann, Mar. 29, 1960; children: Nathaniel Richard, Geoffrey Mark. BSEE, Robert Coll., Istanbul, 1952; MSEE, Purdue U., 1953; spl. student in computer control sys., Harvard U., 1956-58; postgrad. in astrophysics, Brandeis U., 1964-67. Reg. profl. engr., Mass. Rsch. asst. Sloan Sch. Mgmt. MIT, Cambridge, 1953-54; jr. R & D engr. Sigma Instruments Inc., Braintree, Mass., 1954-56; R & D engr. Rsch. Divsn. Raytheon, Waltham, Mass., 1956-58; mem. def. rsch. staff Lincoln Lab. MIT, Lexington, Mass., 1958-66; prin. rsch. scientist AVCO Rsch. Lab., Everett, Mass., 1966-68; prin. engr. Space and Info. Sys. Divsn. Raytheon, Sudbury, Mass., 1968-71, prin. engr. and tech. dir. Electro-Optics Lab., Equipment Divsn., 1971-80; lectr. continuing edn. North Eastern U., Boston, 1969-80; mem. sr. tech. staff and project leader MITRE Corp., Bedford, Mass., 1980-94; sr. lectr. U. Mass., Lowell, 1988-1997; telecomm. and networks engr. Volpe Nat. Transp. Sys. Ctr., Cambridge, Mass., from 1998. Adj. prof. computer sys. and elec. engring. dept. Boston U., 1980-88. Pres. Internat. Students Assn. Greater Boston, 1956-57, Adventures in Music, Inc., Boston, 1966-70; chmn. Sch. Needs Com., Sudbury, 1971-76; elected mem. Mass. Dem. Party Conv., Sudbury, 1994, 96, 98, 99; town com. mem. Dem. Party, Sudbury, 1991—; pres. East-West Comm. Assocs., Sudbury, 1994—. Internat. scholar Purdue U., 1952-53, Sloan Sch. scholarship MIT, 1953-54; Space Sci. fellow NASA, 1964-67. Mem. IEEE (sr., NEREM program com. chmn. 1973), Soc. Photo-Instrumentation Engrs. (N.Eng. steering com. 1996-2000). Home: Sudbury, Mass. Died Jan. 16, 2002.

FRIED, BURTON DAVID, physicist, researcher; b. Chgo., Dec. 14, 1925; s. Albert O. and Bertha (Rosenthal) F.; m. Sally Rachel Goldstein, Aug. 17, 1947; children— Joel Ethan, Jeremy Steven. BS, Ill. Inst. Tech., 1947; MS, U. Chgo., 1950, PhD, 1952. Instr. physics Ill. Inst. Tech., 1947-52; research physicist Lawrence Berkeley Lab. of U. Calif., 1952-54; sr. staff physicist TRW Systems, Los Angeles, 1954-86; dir. research lab. (Ramo-Wooldridge Computer Div.), Los Angeles, 1961-63; prof. physics UCLA, 1963—. Served with USNR, 1944-46. Fellow Am. Phys. Soc. (chmn. plasma physics div. 1978-79); mem. Sigma Xi. Achievements include research and publs. on theoretical elementary particle and plasma physics. Home: Palm Desert, Calif. Deceased.

FRIED, JOSEF, chemist, educator; b. Przemysl, Poland, July 21, 1914; came to U.S., 1938, naturalized, 1944; s. Abraham and Frieda (Fried) F.; m. Erna Werner, Sept. 18, 1939 (dec. Nov. 1986); 1 dau., Carol Frances. Student, U. Leipzig, 1934-37, U. Zurich, 1937-38; PhD, Columbia U., 1941. Eli Lilly fellow Columbia U., 1941-43; research chemist Givaudan, N.Y., 1943; head dept. antibiotics and steroids Squibb Inst. Med. Research, New Brunswick, N.J., 1944-59, dir. sect. organic chemistry, 1959-63; prof. chemistry, biochemistry and Ben May Lab. Cancer Research, U. Chgo., 1963—, Louis Block prof., 1973—84, chmn. dept. chemistry, 1977-79; prof. emeritus, 1984—2001. Mem. med. chem. study sect. NIH, 1963-67, 68-72, chmn., 1971; mem. com. arrangements Laurentian Hormone Conf., 1964-71; Knapp Meml. lectr. U. Wis., 1958 Mem. bd. editors: Jour. Organic Chemistry, 1964-69, Steroids, 1966-86, Jour. Biol. Chemistry, 1975-81, 83-88; contbr. articles to profl. jours. Recipient N.J. Patent award, 1968, Roussel prize 1992, Gregory Pincus medal, 1994. Fellow AAAS, N.Y. Acad. Scis.; mem. NAS, Am. Acad. Scis., Am. Chem. Soc. (award in medicinal chemistry 1974, Alfred Burger award in medicinal chemistry 1996), Am. Soc. Biol. Chemists, Swiss Chem. Socs., Brit. Chem. Socs., Sigma Xi. Achievements include patents in field. Home: Chicago, Ill. Died Aug. 17, 2001.

FRIED, WALTER JAY, lawyer; b. N.Y.C., May 27, 1904; s. Joseph and Flora V. (Shamberg) F.; m. Louise E. Goldman, June 8, 1934; 1 son, Michael W.; m. Brita Digby-Brown (dec. 2000), July 8, 1948. BA magna cum laude, Harvard, 1924; LL.B., Columbia U., 1928. Bar: N.Y. 1929, D.C. 1966. Practiced in, N.Y.C., 1929—79; former mem. firm, former counsel Fried, Frank, Harris, Shriver & Jacobson; mem. faculty Bklyn. Law Sch., 1931-39. Dir. Salant Corp., 1969-93. Former chmn. Am. Chess Found.; hon. trustee Guild Hall, East Hampton, N.Y., chmn., 1974-78; former trustee Southampton Hosp. Served to maj. AUS, 1942-45. Decorated Legion of Merit. Mem. Assn. Harvard Chemists, Phi Beta Kappa Clubs: Maidstone (East Hampton), Harvard (N.Y.C.), Manhattan Chess (N.Y.C.) (hon. dir.). Home: New York, NY. Died Nov. 30, 2003.

FRIEDHEIM, ERIC ARTHUR, publisher, editor; b. London, Apr. 21, 1910; s. Arthur and Madeleine (Sander) F.; m. Elizabeth Sweeney, Dec. 31, 1951 (dec. 1984); m. Edith Ann Dorsey, Apr. 14, 1990 Student, Am. U., 1928-30. Washington corr. Internat. News Service, 1931-42; combat corr. Air Force mag., 1945-46; also mng. editor Air News mag.; public relations adv. U.S. aviation industry, 1946; public relations and advance rep. Nat. Freedom Train, 1947-49; public relations dir. European Travel Commn., 1951-52; editor, pub. Travel Agt. mag., N.Y.C., 1951-88, chmn., editor in chief, 1989-2000; pub. Interline Reporter, 1957-85, El Travel Agt. International, 1979-84; assoc. publisher Palm Beach Soc., Fla., 1987-92. Travel columnist N.Y. Post, Los Angeles Times; travel adv. com. Dept. Commerce; adv. com. U.S. Travel Service, Congl. Travel and Tourism Caucus, Travel Industry Assn., Govt. Affairs Coun. Author: Fighters Up, an official history of World War II pilots in Europe, 1945, Travel Agents: From Caravans and Clippers to the Concorde. 1992, Agents of Change: The Story of Vacation-.Com. Co-sponsor with Kennedy Ctr. Performing Arts of Arthur Friedheim ann. competition for best musical works by Am. composers, 1978-85; endowed Eric Friedheim Libr. Nat. Press Club, Johns Hopkins U., Arthur Friedheim Music Libr., Peabody Inst., Eric Friedheim Quadrangle and Journalism Ctr., Am. U.; producing assoc. Country Playhouse, Westport, Conn.; endowed Friedheim Journalism Ctr. Am. U. Served as officer USAAF, 1942-45; col. USAFR; ret. Decorated Air medal; named to Travel Hall of Fame, 1980, Hall of Leaders, Travel Industry Assn., 1987; recipient Jesse Neale award Am. Bus. Press, 1984, Europa award European Travel Commn., 1986. Fellow Inst. Cert. Travel Agts.; mem. Am. Soc. Travel Agts., Soc. Am. Travel Writers (charter), Caribbean Tourist Assn., Pacific Area Travel Assn., Discover Am. Travel Orgns., Confederacione Organiziones Turisticas de la Am. Latina, World Tourism Orgn. Clubs: Nat. Press (Washington); Skal, Wings (N.Y.C.). Episcopalian. Died 2002.

FRIEDHEIM, ROBERT LYLE, political scientist, educator; b. N.Y.C., Aug. 1, 1934; s. Joseph and Blanche (Vogel) F.; m. Robin Rudolph; children: Jessica Faulkner, Amy. AB, Columbia Coll., 1955; MA, Columbia U., 1957; PhD, U. Wash., 1962. Teaching asst., predoctoral assoc. U. Wash., 1958-61; from asst. prof. to assoc. prof. polit. sci. Purdue U., 1961-66; dir. law of sea project, profl. staff mem. Ctr. for Naval Analysis, Arlington, Va., 1966-76; prof. internat. rels., assoc. dir. inst. for marine studies U. So. Calif., 1976-89, dir. sea grant program, 1980-89, dir. sch. internat. rels., 1992-96. Advisor U.S. Arctic Rsch. Commn., 1986-96; mem. adv. panel Office Tech. Assessment U.S. Congress, 1988-89; mem. internat. ocean sci. policy com. bd. ocean sci. and policy Nat. Rsch. Coun.; lectr., invited visitor Nat. Bur. Oceanography, Beijing, 1984; mem. adv. group Ocean Policy Roundtable, Woods Hole, 1983; del. Commn. of Califs., 1978-80. Editor: Jour. Ocean and Coastal Mgmt., Ocean Devel. and Internat. Law Jour.; contbr. articles to profl. jours. and chpts. to books; author: Negotiating the New Ocean Regime, 1993, The Seattle General Strike, 1964, (with others) Japan and the New Ocean Regime, 1984, Forecasting Outcomes of Multilateral Negotiations: Methodology, Vol. 1, 1977, The Navy and the Common Sea, 1972, others. Grantee NSF, 1978-80, 1977-78, 1974-75, ONR, 1978-80; CNA fellow, 1971-72. Mem. Am. Soc. Internat. Law, Internat. Studies Assn. (chair internat. orgn. sect. 1970-73, mem. adv. bd. environ. studies sect. 1989—). Avocations: reading, computers, skiing, sailing, hiking. Home: Playa Del Rey, Calif. Died Jan. 31, 2001.

FRIEDLANDER, HENRY Z. lawyer, polymer chemist; b. N.Y.C., May 18, 1925; s. Joseph and Estelle Barr (Zuckert) F.; divorced; children: Jeffrey Dean, Joel Edan. AB, Oberlin Coll., 1948; MS, U. Ill., 1949, PhD, 1952; JD, Fordham U., 1974. Bar: Conn. 1979, N.Y. 1985; U.S. Patent Office, 1975, U.S. Ct. Appeals (fed. cir.), 1979. Rsch. chemist Am. Cyanamid Co., Stamford, Conn., 1952-57; group leader AMF, Stamford, Conn., 1958-65; asst. to corp. dir. rsch. Union Carbide Corp., Tarrytown, N.Y., 1966-78; patent atty. Stauffer Chem. Co., Ardsley, N.Y., 1978-83; sr. patent atty. Lackenbach Siegel Marzullo & Aronson, Scarsdale, N.Y., from 1985. V.p., bd. dirs. 65 Main St. Corp., White Plains, N.Y., 1955-65. Author book chpts.; contbr. 40 articles on polymerization and membrane separations to profl. jours. Lay leader Stamford (Conn.) Unitarian Ch. With USN, 1944-46, PTO. Mem. Chemists Club N.Y.C. (mem. libr. com.), The Landmark Club, Am. Chem. Soc. (nat. councilor 1982-86), Am. Intellectual Property Soc., River Hills Ski Club. Republican. Unitarian Universalist. Avocations: travel, tennis, skiing. Home: Stamford, Conn. Deceased.

FRIEDMAN, ERICK, concert violinist, educator; b. Newark, N.J., Aug. 16, 1939; s. Abraham David and Lillian Edith (Herman) F. Artist tchr. N.C. Sch. for the Arts, Winston-Salem, 1973-78; artist faculty Manhattan Sch. Music, N.Y.C., 1978-83; artist-in-residence So. Meth. U., Dallas, 1983-89; prof. music Yale U., New Haven, 1989—2004. Music dir., former condr. Garrett Lakes Arts Festival; guest panelist Nat. Endowment for the Arts, Washington, 1983-88; guest juror panels various internat. competitions including Dealey Competition, Taipei Internat. Competition, Amb. in Washington, Can. Music Competitions. Performer numerous recordings RCA Red Seal, Monitor, also Kultur videocassettes; recorded Bach Double Violin Concerto with Sir Malcolm Sargent, Jascha Heifetz and New Symphony Orch. of London, 1961, Paganini Concerto, Cadenza, 1962. Nominee Grammy awards, 1963, 64; Recipient: Grammy award (Best Historical Album), 1996. Avocations: chess, drawing. Died Mar. 30, 2004.

FRIEDMAN, MARK JAY, cardiologist; b. Queens, N.Y., May 27, 1955; MD, SUNY, 1981. Diplomate Am. Bd. Internal Medicine, Am. Bd. Cardiovascular Disease. Intern Long Is. (N.Y.) Jewish Hosp., New Hyde Pk., 1981-82, resident internal medicine, 1982-84, resident medicine, 1986-87; physician; fellow cardiology Brookdale Hosp., Brooklyn, N.Y., 1984-86; physician Northshore U. Hosp., St. Francis Hosp., Winthrop U. Hosp., L.I. Jewish Hosp.; pvt. practice. Mem. Am. Coll. Cardiology, ACP, AMA, N.Y.S., Queens (N.Y.) Med. Soc. Died Mar. 13, 1999.

FRIEDMAN, MITCHELL, health sciences educator, researcher; b. Bklyn., Sept. 26, 1944; s. Philip Friedman and Betty Young; m. Ina Meredith Fixman, June 18, 1971; children: Philip Alan, Daniel Edward. MD, U. Miami, Coral Gables, 1969. Diplomate Am. Bd. Internal Medicine, Subspecialty Bd. Pulmonary Diseases, lic. physician La., N.C., Fla. Med. intern Parkland Meml. Hosp., Dallas, 1969—70; jr. asst. resident in medicine Jackson Meml. Hosp., Miami, Fla., 1970—71, sr. asst. resident in medicine, 1973—74; NIH postdoctoral fellow divsn. pulmonary diseases Mt. Sinai Med. Ctr., Miami Beach, Fla., 1974—76; asst. prof. U. N.C., Chapel Hill, 1976—92; prof. Tulane U. Health Scis. Ctr., New Orleans, from 1992. Dir. critical care dept. medicine U. N.C., 1983—90; program dir. Clinical Rsch. Curriculum award Tulane U. Med. Ctr., from 1991; chief pulmonary VA Med. Ctr., New Orleans, 1992—2001; dir. respiratory therapy Tulane U. Health Sci. Ctr., NOLA, from 1992; grant reviewer Can. Insts. Health Rsch., from 2001; mem. Asthma Mgmt. Program for Charity Hosps., State of La., from 1998, bd. dirs. La. Cancer and Lung Trust Fund, from 2000; mem. adv. bd. BattellePharma, Boehringer Ingelheim COPD Disease Mgmt. Mem. editl. bd.: Jour. COPD, E-Medicine-Medicine and Surgery, P&T, ad hoc reviewer: various jours.; contbr. over 140 articles to profl. jours. Bd. dirs. La. Cancer and Lung Trust Fund, 2001. Capt. U.S. Army Med. Corps, 1971—73. Named Edward G. Schlieder Ednl. Found. Prof. of Pulmonary Diseases, 1977; recipient Pulmonary Young Investigator award, NIH, 1978—81, numerous grants. Fellow: Am. Coll. Physicians, Am. Coll. Chest Physicians (finalist Cecile Lehman Mayer award 1977); mem.: AAAS, New Orleans Acad. Internal Medicine, Assn. Subspecialty Profs., Nat. Assn. for Med. Direction of Respiratory Care (bd. dirs. from 2001), Soc. Critical Care Medicine, Am. Thoracic Soc. (rsch. grant com. from 1997, health care policy com. from 2001), Am. Physiol. Soc., Am. Fedn. Med. Rsch., Assn. Pulmonary and Critical Care Medicine Program Dirs., Assn. for Patient Oriented Rsch., Am. Heart Assn. (coun. on cardiopulmonary and critical care from 1980), Gen. Clinical Rsch. Ctr. Program Dir.'s Assn., So. Soc. Clinical Investigation, Musser-Burch Soc., Sigma Xi, Alpha Epsilon Delta, Alpha Omega Alpha. Avocations: tennis, golf. Home: New Orleans, La. Died June 20, 2003.

FRIEDMAN, REGINIA H. obstetrician/gynecologist; b. N.Y.C., 1959; MD, Mt. Sinai Sch. Medicine, N.Y.C., 1983. Diplomate Am. Bd. Obstetrics & Gynecology. Intern St. Luke's-Roosevelt Hosp. Ctr., N.Y.C., 1983, resident in ob/gyn., 1983-87; staff ob/gyn. Morristown (N.J.) Meml. Hosp., 1997; med. dir. Planned Parenthood of Greater No. N.J., Morristown, 1994—2001. Mem. Am. Coll. Obstetrics & Gynecology, N.J. Women's Med. Assn. Home: West Orange, NJ. Died Mar. 30, 2001.

FRIEDMAN, RONALD MARVIN, cellular biologist; b. Brooklyn, N.Y., Apr. 26, 1930; s. Joseph and Helen (Plotkin) F. BS, Columbia U., 1960, postgrad. in mammalian and comparative physiology, 1961-63; MS, NYU, 1967, PhD, 1976. Predoctoral fellow Inst. Microbiology, 1968-72, NYU, 1972-76; postdoctoral fellow Dept of Molecular Biochemistry and Biophysics Yale U., 1972-75; vis. fellow Princeton U. Dept. Chemistry, 1975-82; Res. scientist N.Y. State Inst. Basic Rsch. Human Nutrition and Biochemistry, 1979-82; NIH fellow Albert Einstein Coll. Medicine Dept. of Oncology, 1981-82; sr. rsch. scientist dept. infectious diseases Harvard Med. Sch., 1982-85; adv., prof. Chulalongkorn U., Bangkok, Thailand, 1993-95; assoc. rsch. prof. Johns Hopkins U., 1996-98; rsch. scientist Roswell Park Cancer Inst., 1998-2000, Columbia Coll. Physicians and Surgeons, from 2000; prof. dept. microbiology Changmai Med. Sch., from 1999. Research fellow meml. Sloan-Kettering Cancer Center, N.Y.C.,. N.Y., 1984-85; sr.research assoc. dept. pathology Cath. Med. Ctr., 1983-84; sr. research assoc. inmolecular biology (in collaboration with the U.S. Fish and Wildlife Service) CUNY, 1985-86; research assoc. dept. immunology and biochemistry Roswell Park Meml. Inst., Buffalo, 1986-87; research assoc., infectious disease, Channing Laboratory, Harvard Medical School, Boston, 1987-88; letter addressed to Kurt Waldheim, Sec. Gen. U.N. (promoting the philosophy of human dignity and its impact on world peace is our only hope for survival), N.Y., 1987-88; asst. research prof. CCNY, 1988-89; vis. scientist in molecular biology, Lewis Thomas Labs, Princeton U.1989-1992; vis. prof. Kasetsart U. Bangkok, Thailand, 1992-94, vis. scholar Boston U. 1992-93; scientific cons. U. Rangoon, 1993—, mem. faculty, Johns Hopkins U, 1996; cons. biological scis. Govt. of Philippines; cons. to various university cellular-molecular labs, inspector of Cell Biology Research in Poland and Russia, Citizens Ambassador Program; advisor curriculum research and cell/molecular biology, lectr. cellular and molecular biology. Asst. to Sec. of Agr., 1970-71 serving as spl. liaison to Congress; conducted survey of emergency med. home call service, Bronx County, NY., 1971-72. Knights Templar fellow, 1973-87; NIH fellow, 1981-82; recip. award for meritorious service, Masonic Valley of White Plains, 1996. Mem. Nat. Inst. of Health (alumni member), Harvey Soc., Fedn. Am. Soc. for Exptl. Biology, Am. Soc. Cell Biologists, Sigma Xi. Lodges: Masons, Shriners, K.T. Achievements include proving that cancer was universal by inducing it in the lowest form of life. Home: Bronx, NY. Died Mar. 6, 2003.

FROEHLICH, JOACHIM WILLIAM, college president; b. Waterbury, Conn., June 27, 1944; s. George Thomas and Anna Catherine (Praines) F. AB, St. Anselm Coll., 1967; MA, SUNY, Buffalo, 1971; PhD, Catholic U. Am., 1977. NSF trainee SUNY, Buffalo, 1969-70; teaching asst. Cath. U., 1972-73; asst. prof. econs. St. Anselm Coll., Manchester, N.H., 1970-79, chmn. dept. econs., 1975-79, pres., 1979-89; supt. Schs. for Diocese of Manchester, 1990—91; headmaster, dir. devel. Woodside Priory sch., Portola Valley, Calif., 1991—95; pres. Loras Coll., Dubuque, Iowa, 1995—2001, Elms Coll., Chicopee, Mass., 2001—03. Mem. Am. Econ. Assn., Eastern Econ. Assn. Roman Catholic. Died Nov. 21, 2003.

FROMM, ERIKA (MRS. PAUL FROMM), clinical psychologist; b. Frankfurt, Germany, Dec. 23, 1919; came to U.S., 1938, naturalized, 1944; d. Siegfried and Clementine (Stern) Oppenheimer; m. Paul Fromm(dec. 1987), July 20, 1938; 1 child, Joan (Mrs. Greenstone)(dec. 1996). PhD magna cum laude, U. Frankfurt, 1933; postgrad. child care program, Chgo. Inst. for Psychoanalysis, 1949-51. Diplomate: Am. Bd. Examiners in Profl. Psychology, Am. Bd. Examiners Clin. Hypnosis. Rsch. assoc. dept. psychiatry U. Amsterdam, Holland, 1934-35; chief psychologist Apeldoorn State Hosp., Holland, 1935-38; rsch. asst. in psychiatry U. Chgo., 1939—40; chief psychologist Francis W. Parker Sch., Chgo., 1944-51; supervising psychologist Inst. for Juvenile Rsch., 1951-53; asst. prof. to assoc. prof. med. sch. Northwestern U., 1954-60; prof. U. Chgo., 1960-76, prof. emeritus, 1976—2003. Author: (with L.D. Hartman) Intelligence - A Dynamic Approach, 1955; (with Thomas M. French) Dream Interpretation: A New Approach, 1964 2d edit., 1986; (with Ronald E. Shor) Hypnosis: Developments in Research and New Perspectives, 1972, 2d. edit., 1979; (with Daniel P. Brown) Hypnotherapy and Hypnoanalysis, 1986; (with Daniel P. Brown) Hypnosis and Behavioral Medicine, 1987; (with Stephen Kahn) Selfhypnosis: The Chicago Paradigm, 1990; (with Michael R. Nash) Contemporary Hypnosis Research, 1992; (with Michael R. Nash) Psychoanalysis and Hypnosis, 1997;(with Stephen Kahn) Changes in the Therapist, 2000; also numerous articles in profl. jours.; mem. editl. bd. Jour. Clin. and Exptl. Psychopathology, 1951-59; clin. editor: Internat. Jour. Clin. and Exptl. Hypnosis 1968-97, editl. cons., 1998-2003; assoc. editor Bull. Brit. Soc. Exptl. and Clin. Hypnosis, 1982-90; mem. bd. cons. editors Psychoanalytic Psychology, 1982-88; mem. adv. bd. editors Imagination, Cognition and Personality: Sci. Study of COnsciousness, 1982-2003; assoc. editor Hypnos: European Jour. Hypnosis, 1996-2003. Fellow AAAS, APA (pres. divsn. 30 1972-73, Psychoanalysis award 1985, 97, Hypnosis award for Eminent Enduring Contbns. to Advancement of Profl. Hypnosis 1994); mem. Am. Orthopsychiat. Assn. (dir. 1961-63), Soc. Clin. Exptl. Hypnosis (Best Rsch. Paper award 1965, sec. 1965-67, v.p. 1971-75, pres. 1975-77, Arthur Shapiro award 1973, Best Clin. Paper award 1986, Best Book pub. in Field of Hypnosis award 1987, 91, 93), The Netherlands Soc. for Hypnosis (hon.), Am. Bd. Psychol. Hypnosis (pres. 1971-74, Rollo May award Saybrook Inst. 1997), Ill. Psychol. Assn. (coun. 1951-53, 55-57, bd. examiners 1959-62, v.p. bd. examiners 1960-61), Soc. Projective Techniques, Am. Bd. Examiners in Psychol. Hypnosis (Morton Prince award 1970), Nat. Acad. Practice Psychology (Disting. Practioner in Psychology award 1982), Am. Soc. Clin. Hypnosis (award 1997, 99), Sigma Xi. Home: Chicago, Ill. Died May 26, 2003.

FRUMKIN, ALLAN, art dealer; b. Chgo., July 5, 1926; s. Joseph and Libbie F.; m. Jean Martin; children: Robert, Peter. Ph.B., U. Chgo., 1945. Owner and dir. Allan Frumkin Gallery, Chgo., 1952-80, N.Y.C., 1959-90; pres. Frumkin/Adams Gallery, Inc., N.Y.C., 1990-95; pvt. art dealer N.Y.C., from 1995. Ida Cordelia Beam Disting. vis. prof., U. Iowa, 2000. Recipient U. Chgo. ALumni Assn. Profl. Achievement award, 1981 Died Dec. 9, 2002.

FRUSH, JAMES CARROLL, JR., real estate development company executive; b. San Francisco, Oct. 18, 1930; s. James Carroll and Edna Mae (Perry) F.; m. Patricia Anne Blake, Oct. 29, 1960 (div. 1977); children: Michael, Gloria; m. Carolyn Fetter Bell, Aug. 23, 1978; 1 child, Stephen. BA, Stanford, 1953; postgrad., U. Calif., San Francisco, 1957-58; MA, Saybrook Inst., 1981, PhD, 1985. Ptnr. James C. Frush Co., San Francisco, 1960-70; v.p., bd. dir. Retirement Residence, Inc., San Francisco, 1964-70, pres., from 1970, Nat. Retirement Residence, San Francisco, 1971-89, Casa Dorinda Corp., 1971-89, Retirement Residence Inc. Ala., Daphne, from 1995. Pres. Marin Shakespeare Festival, 1971-73, James C. Frush Found., 1972-78; adj. prof. gerontology, psychology and theology Spring Hill Coll., Mobile, Ala., 1988—; adj. prof. counseling edn. U. South Ala., Mobile. Author (with Benson Eschenbach): The Retirement Residence: An Analysis of the Architecture and Management of Life Care Housing, 1968, Self-Esteem in Older Persons Following a Heart Attack: An Exploration of Contributing Factors, 1985, Kind Hearts, Self-esteem and the Challenges of Aging, 2000; contbr. articles to profl. jours.; producer ednl. films. Bd. dirs. San Francisco Sr. Ctr., 1973-78, Found. to Assist Calif. Tchrs. Devel. Inc., 1987-89; mem. adv. bd. Christus Theol. Inst., Mobile, Ala., 1992-95; mem. ethics com. adv. bd. Westminster Village, Spanish Ft., 1994—; bd. dirs. com. affirmative aging Episc. Diocese Ctrl. Gulf Coast, 1996—. Recipient Humanities award Stanford U., 1953. Mem. Gerontol. Soc., Southeastern Psychol. Assn., Assn. for Anthropology and Gerontology, Stanford Alumni Assn., Ala. Writers Forum, RSVP (adv. bd. Mobile chpt. 1988-94), C.G. Jung Soc. of Gulf Coast (pres.), Ala. Humanities Found. Speakers Bur. (presenter 1993-94, 94-95), Gulf Coast Storyteller's Guild. Home: Daphne, Ala. Deceased.

FRY, MAXWELL JOHN, economist, educator; b. Maidenhead, Eng., Feb. 12, 1944; came to U.S., 1974; s. Thomas Maxwell and Jeanne Mary (Kislingbury) F.; m. Celia Gordon, June 17, 1972; children: Benjamin, Zoe, Jeremy, Caroline. BS, London Sch. Econs., 1965; MA, UCLA, 1966; PhD, London Sch. Econs., 1970. Lectr. Morley Coll., 1966-67; lectr. Middle East Tech. U., Ankara, Turkey, 1967-69; lectr. fin. econs. City U. London, 1969-74; prof. econs. U. Hawaii, Honolulu, 1974-81; vis. prof. Bogazici U., Istanbul, 1977-79, UCLA, 1981-85; prof. econs. U. Calif.-Irvine, 1981-89, chmn. dept., 1983-85; Tokai Bank prof. internat. fin. U. Birmingham, from 1989; dir. Bank of England Ctr. for Ctrl. Banking Studies, from 1997. Advisor to min. fin. Govt. of Afghanistan, Kabul, 1972-73, to min. State Econ. Enterprises, Turkey, 1978-79, to gov. Ctrl. Bank Bangladesh, 1984-86, to dir. Bank of Eng., 1990, to min. fin. and govt. Ctrl. Bank Mauritius, 1994-96; cons. to internat. agys., ctrl. banks, AID; vis. fellow Brasenose Coll., Oxford (Eng.) U., 1986; vis. scholar IMF, 1989-90; fellow Inst. S.E. Asian Studies, 1993; sr. Houblon-Norman fellow Bank Eng., 1997. Author: Finance and Development Planning in Turkey, 1972, The Afghan Economy, 1974, Money and Banking in Turkey, 1979, American Money and Banking, 1984, Improving Domestic Resource Mobilization through Financial Development, 1985, Money, Interest and Banking in Economic Development, 1988, 2d edit., 1995, Foreign Direct Investment in Southeast Asia: Differential Impacts, 1993, Central Banking in Developing Countries: Objectives, Activities and Independence, 1996, Emancipating the Banking System and Developing Markets for Government Debt, 1997, Payment Systems in Global Perspective, 1999; contbr. articles to profl. jours.; rsch. on ctrl. banking, monetary policy, domestic resource moblzn., fgn. debt, fgn. direct investment, and balance of payments in developing countries, European monetary union, monetary and exchange rate policies in Ea. Europe. Recipient award Brit. Social Sci. Rsch. Coun., 1971, rsch. award NSF, 1975, 83, award Econ. and Social Rsch. Coun., 1995; Fulbright scholar, 1965. Avocation: playing violin and viola. Home: Birmingham, England. Died 2000.

FRYE, JUDITH ELEEN MINOR, editor; b. Seattle; d. George Edward and Eleen G. (Hartelius) Minor; m. Vernon Lester Frye, Apr. 1, 1954. Student, UCLA, 1947-48, U. So. Calif., 1948-53. Acct., officer mgr. Colony Wholesale Liquor, Culver City, Calif., 1947-48; credit mgr. Western Distbg. Co., Culver City, Calif., 1948-53; ptnr. in restaurants Palm Springs, L.A., 1948; ptnr. in date ranch La Quinta, Calif., 1949-53; ptnr., owner Imperial Printing, Huntington Beach, Calif., 1955—2002. Editor, pub. New Era Laundry and Cleaning Lines, Huntington Beach, 1962—; registered lobbyist, Calif., 1975-84. Mem. Textile Care Allied Trade Assn., Calif. Coin-op Assn. (exec. dir. 1975-84, Cooperation award 1971, Dedicated Svc. award 1976), Nat. Automatic Laundry & Clearning Coun. (Leadership award 1972), Women Laundry & Drycleaning (past pres., Outstanding Svc. award 1977), Printing Industries Assn., Master Printers Am., Nat. Assn. Printers & Lithographers. Died Aug. 17, 2002.

FUJIKI, SUMIKO, psychiatric nurse; b. Devil's Slide, Utah, Feb. 21, 1926; d. Jusaburo and Shigeyo (Nishimura) F. Diploma, Thomas D. Dee Meml. Hosp., Ogden, Utah, 1948; AS, Weber Jr. Coll., 1948; BSN, U. Utah, 1949; MSN, Washington U., St. Louis, 1954; PhD in Cultural Found. of Edn., U. Utah, 1976. Instr., Thomas D. Dee Meml. Hosp. Sch. Nursing, 1949-52; instr. psychiat. nursing Washington U., 1953-55; asst. prof. to assoc. prof. psychiat-mental health nursing U. Utah, 1957-78, head grad. program in psychiat.-mental health nursing child psychiatry, 1957-67; vis. assoc. prof. UCLA, 1978-80; assoc. prof. nursing U. Colo., Denver, 1980—; assoc. prof. nursing U. Utah, 1967-80; mem. rev. com.; cons., visitor psychiat. nursing edn. NIMH, 1975-78; mem. Bd. Ethnic Nurses for Advancement of Health Care, 1978—; prof. Calif. State U., Bakersfield; family and marriage counselor; counselor Helpline, 1978-80. Bd. dirs. Asian Pacific Devel. Ctr., Denver, 1980-83. Mem. ANA, Nat. League Nursing (vis. nurse 1975—), Asian Human Svcs. Assn., Japanese-Am. Citizenship League (bd. dirs. Salt Lake City 1978), Sigma Theta Tau. Home: Bakersfield, Calif. Died May 29, 2001.

FUJIYAMA, WALLACE SACHIO, lawyer; b. Honolulu, Aug. 8, 1925; s. George Susumu and Cornelia (Matsumoto) F.; m. Mildred Hatsue Morita, Jan. 24, 1959; children—Rodney Michio, Susan Misao, Keith Susumu. B.A., U. Hawaii, 1950; J.D., U. Cin., 1953. Bar: Hawaii 1954. Dep. atty. gen. State of Hawaii, Honolulu, 1954-56, examiner employment relations bd., 1956-59; ptnr. Chuck & Fujiyama, 1959-74; pres. Fujiyama, Duffy & Fujiyama, Honolulu, 1974—; dir. 1st Hawaiian Bank; chmn. adv. bd. Duty Free Shoppers Ltd., 1982—, lectr. William S. Richard Sch. Law, Honolulu, 1981—. Mem. Hawaii Statehood Commn., Honolulu, 1957-59; regent U. Hawaii, 1974-82; bd. dirs. Honolulu Symphony, 1983—, Hawaii Imin Centennial Corp., 1983—; mem. Palama Settlement Exec. Campaign Com., 1981—, Stadium Authority, 1982—. Served to pvt. U.S. Army, 1944-46. Mem. Hawaii Bar Assn. (bd. bar examiners 1962-82, pres. 1973, jud. appointments com. 1975), ABA mem. ho. of dels. 1973, active com. mem.), Hawaii Trial Lawyers Assn. (pres. 1971-79), Assn. Trial Lawyers Am., Calif. Trial Lawyers Assn., Fedn. Ins. Counsel, Def. Research Inst., Am. Judicature Soc., Trial Attys. Am., Am. Bd. Trial Advocates (pres. Hawaii chpt. 1980—), Am. Inn of Ct. (bencher 1982—), Hastings Ctr. Trial and Appellate Advocacy (bd. dirs. 1977—), Order of Coif, Phi Alpha Delta. Clubs: Honolulu Internat. Country (dir., gen. counsel), Waialae Country, Plaza (bd. dirs. 1985—). Home: Honolulu, Hawaii. Deceased.

FULD, STANLEY HOWELLS, lawyer; b. N.Y.C., Aug. 23, 1903; s. Emanuel I. and Hermine (Frisch) F.; m. Florence Geringer, May 29, 1930 (dec. Feb. 1975); children: Hermine (Mrs. Maurice N. Nessen), Judith (Mrs. Frank Miller); m.

Stella F. Rapaport, Jan. 4, 1976. AB, CCNY, 1923; LLB, Columbia U., 1926, LLD, 1959, Hamilton Coll., 1949, Union Coll., 1961, Yeshiva U., 1962, N.Y. Law Sch., 1962, NYU, 1963, Jewish Theol. Sem. Am., 1964, Syracuse U., 1967; LL.D., St. John's U., 1970, CUNY, 1972. Bar: N.Y. 1926, U.S. Supreme Ct. 1933. Atty. Gilman & Unger, N.Y.C., 1926-35; counsel legal div. Nat. Recovery Adminstrn., Washington, 1935; asst. dist. atty. N.Y. County, 1935-44; atty. Hartman, Craven & Fuld, N.Y.C., 1944-46; spl. asst. atty. gen., liaison counsel, state investigations N.Y. State, 1944-45; apptd. assoc. judge Ct. of Appeals, 1946; elected for full term, beginning 1947, 61; chief judge State of N.Y. and Ct. of Appeals, 1967-73; spl. counsel firm Kaye, Scholer, Fierman, Hays & Handler, N.Y.C., from 1974; dir. Greater N.Y. Mut. Ins. Co., from 1974, Petrie Stores Corp., 1978-82. Chmn. adminstrv. bd. Jud. Conf. State N.Y., 1967-73; mem. N.Y. State Ct. Facilities Task Force, 1980-82; Chmn. N.Y. Fair Trial Free Press Conf., 1967-73, hon. chmn., 1974—; chmn. Nat. Commn. on New Technol. Uses of Copyrighted Works, 1975-78, Fellows of N.Y. Bar Found., 1978-83, Greater N.Y. Health Care and Health Facilities Commn., 1979-80 Bd. editors N.Y. Law Jour, 1976—. Commr. Nat. Hillel Commn., 1947-56; chmn. bd. visitors City Coll., CUNY, 1973-81; bd. dirs. Phi Beta Kappa Assos., 1949-80, hon. dir., 1980—; bd. visitors Columbia Law Sch., 1951—; chmn. bd. dirs. and exec. com. Jewish Theol. Sem. Am., 1966-74, mem. exec. com., bd. dirs., 1966-86, hon. bd. dirs., hon. chmn. exec. com., 1986—; pres. Inst. for Religious and Social Studies, 1974-83; trustee Beth Israel Med. Center, 1971—, Grad. Sch. of Polit. Mgmt., 1987—, Manhattan East Community Services, Inc., Nat. Ctr. Automated Info. Retrieval, 1966-81, trustee emritus, 1981—; mem. N.Y.C. Charter Revision Commn., 1982-83; chmn. Nat. News Council, 1974-76; bd. dirs. Hunter Coll. Student Social, Community and Religious Clubs Assn., 1948-90, chmn., 1974-87; bd. dirs. Empire State Report, 1974-81, Prisoners Legal Services, 1976—, Benjamin N. Cardozo Sch. Law of Yeshiva U., 1976-81, hon. dir., 1981—, Atlantic Legal Found., 1987—; mem. Judicate, 1987—; bd. govs. Daytop Village, 1978-81. Recipient Joseph M. Proskauer medal lawyers div. Fedn. Jewish Philanthropies, 1959; Cardozo award K.P., 1951; Harlan Fiske Stone award Assn. Trial Lawyers City N.Y., 1966; medal for excellence Columbia Law Sch. Alumni Assn., 1967; Gold medal for disting. svc. in the law N.Y. State Bar Assn., 1971; John Peter Zenger award N.Y. State Soc. Newspaper Editors, 1970; Gold medallion for disting. pub. svc. Nassau County Bar Assn., 1971; John H. Finley award for disting. svc. to N.Y. City Coll. Alumni Assn., 1971; award of merit Lotos Club, 1972; Earl Warren medal for disting. contbns. to humanity and civilization Jewish Theol. Sem. Am., 1972; Martin Luther King medal City Coll. N.Y., 1974; Torch of Learning award Am. Friends of Hebrew U., 1977; Stanley H. Fuld Professorship in law established at Columbia Law Sch., 1977; named to Hall of Fame Townsend Harris Hall, 1989. Fellow Acad. Am. Arts and Scis.; mem. ABA, Assn. of Bar of City of N.Y. (hon.), N.Y. State Bar Assn. (First Ann. award of Comml. and Fed. Litig. sect. 1995), Ind. Jud. Adminstrn., Am. Law Inst. (life), CCNY Alumni Assn. (v.p.), Columbia Law Alumni Assn. (bd. dirs.), Columbia Law Rev. Assn. (bd. dirs.), Columbia Law Rev. Assn. (bd. dirs. 1949-92), Order of Coif, Phi Beta Kappa. Republican. Jewish (trustee synagogue). Died July 22, 2003.

FULLER, MAURICE DELANO, JR., lawyer; b. San Francisco, Sept. 5, 1930; s. Maurice DeLano and Marie Elizabeth (Haub) F.; m. Martha Foster Hewett, June 13, 1953; children: Gwendolyn Hewitt, Katherine Hewitt, Daniel DeLano. AB with great distinction, Stanford U., 1953, JD, 1955. Bar: Calif. 1956, U.S. Dist. Ct. (no. dist.) Calif. 1956, U.S. Ct. Appeals (9th cir.) 1956, U.S. Supreme Ct. 1971. Assoc. Pillsbury, Madison & Sutro, San Francisco, 1956-63, ptnr., from 1964. Editor-in-chief Stanford Law Rev., 1954-55. Bd. visitors Stanford U. Law Sch., 1979-83, 89-91, mem. exec. com., 1979-83, chmn., 1981-82; mem. governing bd. Menlo Park (Calif.) City Sch. Dist., 1979-83; trustee Jr. Statesman Found., 1960-75. With USNR, 1950-51. Mem. ABA, Calif. Bar Assn., San Francisco Bar Assn., Order of Coif, Phi Beta Kappa. Clubs: Bohemian (sec., bd. dirs. 1979-82) (San Francisco). Republican. Home: Atherton, Calif. Died: May, 1999.

FULTON, JAMES FRANKLIN, industrial designer; b. Cin., Apr. 13, 1930; s. A. Franklin and and Martha D. (Hurst) F.; m. Mary Sherman Walbridge, Sept. 12, 1953 (div. 1975); children: Martha W., James Franklin, Jr., Laurel C. Grad., Pratt Inst., 1951. Designer Towle Silver Co., Newburyport, Mass., 1951; designer Owens-Corning Fiberglas Co., Toledo, 1952; sr. designer Harley Earl, Inc., Detroit, 1953-58; design dir., mgr. Compagnie de l'Esthetique Indsl., Paris, 1958-60; v.p., dir. product design Transp. Housing Components-Lowey,Snaith (Cons.), N.Y.C., 1960-66; pres. Fulton & Partners, Inc., N.Y.C., 1966—91. Chmn. Design History Found., Pratt/Corcoran Partnership-Del. Coll. of Art and Design; bd. dirs. Dime Savs. Bank of N.Y., Worldesign Found. Pub. Places A Jour. of Environ. Design. Chmn. bd. trustees Pratt Inst, 1992-2000. Recipient Dean's medal Pratt Inst., 1951, Contemporary Achievement award, 1967. Fellow Indsl. Designers Soc. Am. (Bronze Apple award 1991). Clubs: N.Y. Yacht, Century Assn. Patentee in field. Home: Charlestown, RI. Died Apr. 29, 2003.

FULTON, LEE DANIEL, retired obstetrician; b. 1913; MD, U. Calif., San Francisco, 1940. Diplomate Am. Bd. Ob-gyn. Intern U. Calif. Hosps., 1940-41, resident in ob-gyn., 1941-42, 46-48. Fellow Am. Coll. Ob-Gyn., Am. Coll. Surgeons; mem. AMA, Calif. Med. Assn. Home: Redding, Calif. Died Jul. 15, 1999.

FURTH, JOSEPH HERBERT, economist, retired; b. Vienna, Oct. 12, 1899; came to U.S., 1938; s. Emil Ritter and Ernestine (Kisch) von F.; m. Emma Paula Kaan, Nov. 11, 1929; children: Werner Frank, Helmut Frederick. JD, Univ. Vienna, Austria, 1921; student, Harvard U., 1938-39. Lawyer, Vienna, 1922-38; prof. econs. Lincoln U., Oxford, Pa., 1939-43; internat. economist Fed. Res. Bd., Washington, 1943-65; lectr. Catholic U., Washington, 1945-50; faculty assoc. in residence Fgn. Svc. Inst., Rosslyn, Va., 1966-72. Adj. prof. Am. Univ., Washington, 1950-66; social sci. fellow Rockefeller Found., 1931-32. Contbr. articles to profl. jours.; co-author: International Role of the Dollar, 1974. Mem. Libr. Bd., Takoma Park, Md., 1972-75. Lt. Austrian Army (artillery), 1917-18. Mem. Am. Econ. Assn. Democrat. Lutheran. Home: Chevy Chase, Md. Deceased.

FUTCHER, PALMER HOWARD, physician, educator; b. Balt., Sept. 13, 1910; s. Thomas Barnes and Gwendolen Marjorie (Howard) F.; m. Mary Viola Rightor, Nov. 21, 1942 (dec. Mar. 1985); children: Marjorie Rightor, Jane Pillow. AB, Harvard U., 1932; MD, Johns Hopkins U., 1936. Diplomate Am. Bd. Internal Medicine (exec. dir. 1967-75). Intern, then asst. resident and chief resident Johns Hopkins Hosp., 1936-39, 41; asst. resident Rockefeller Inst. Hosp., 1939-41; asst. prof. medicine Washington U., St. Louis, 1946-48; assoc. prof. medicine Johns Hopkins U., Balt., 1948-66, U. Pa., Phila., 1967-89, prof., 1989-94, asst. dean John Hopkins U. Sch. Medicine, 1959-62, dir. health svcs. med. instns., 1962-66. Physician in charge pvt. outpatient svc. Johns Hopkins Hosp., 1948-57. Author: Giants and Dwarfs, 1933; contbr. numerous articles to profl. jours. Comdr. M.C. USNR, 1941—46. Fellow Coll. Physicians Phila.; mem. Am. Soc. Clin. Investigation, Endocrine Soc., Am. Diabetes Assn., Am. Clin. and Climatol. Assn., Am. Osler Soc., World Federalist Assn., 14 West Hamilton St. Club (Balt.), Phi Beta Kappa. Democrat. Episcopalian. Avocations: tennis, golf, sailing, fishing, world peace affairs. Home: Cockeysville Hunt Valley, Md. Died Jan. 29, 2004.

GABEL, CREIGHTON, retired anthropologist, educator; b. Muskegon, Mich., Apr. 5, 1931; s. Kenneth Alonzo and Edith Myrtle (Creighton) G.; m. Jane Whitfield, Sept. 6, 1952; children: James, Anne, Molly. BA, U. Mich., 1953, MA, 1954; PhD, U. Edinburgh, Scotland, 1957. Instr. Northwestern U., 1956-58, asst. prof., 1958-63; asso. prof. Boston U., 1963 69, prof., 1969-96, prof. emeritus, from 1996; research assoc. Boston U. African Studies Center, 1963-96, chmn. anthropology dept., 1970-72, 76-79. Author: Stone Age Hunters of the Kafue, 1965, Analysis of Prehistoric Economic Patterns, 1967; editor: Man Before History, 1964; editor: Reconstructing African Culture History, 1967, Jour. Field Archaeology, 1985 95. NSF grantee, 1960-61, 66-67; Fulbright grantee, 1973; Social Sci. Research Council grantee, 1963-64 Mem. Comm. Internat. Exchange of Scholars (chmn. discipline screening com. in archaeology 1985-88) Home: Weymouth, Mass. Died Feb. 22, 2004; Vero Beach, Fla..

GABRIEL, CHARLES ALVIN, retired air force officer; b. Lincolnton, N.C., Jan. 21, 1928; s. Paul Lamont and Lettie Jane (Goodson) G.; m. Dorothy Currin Cutts, Aug. 11, 1951; children— Jane Letticia, Charles Alvin Student, Catawba Coll., Salisbury, N.C., 1944-46; BS, U.S. Mil. Acad., 1950; MS, George Washington U., 1963; grad., Indsl. Coll. Armed Forces, 1967. Commd 2d lt. U.S. Air Force, 1950, advanced through grades to gen., 1980; air officer comdg. Air Force Acad., 1956-59, Hdqrs. USAF, 1963-66; spl. asst., exec. officer to chief of staff SHAPE, 1967-70; vice comdr., comdr. 432d Tactical Reconnaissance Wing, Udorn, Thailand, 1971-72; dep. dir. ops. Hdqrs. U.S. Air Force, 1972-75; dep. chief staff ops. Tactical Air Command, Langley AFB, Va., 1975-77; dep. comdr. U.S. Forces Korea/UN Command, Korea, 1977-79; dep. chief staff for ops., plans and readiness Hdqrs. U.S. Air Force, Washington, from 1979; comdr. in chief U.S. Air Force in Europe; comdr. Allied Air Forces Central Europe, Ramstein Air Base, Fed. Republic Germany, 1980-82; chief of staff U.S. Air Force, 1982—86; ret., 1986. Bd. dirs. GEC Marconi Electronic Systems Corp., E-Systems Inc., Electronic Systems Corp., Riggs Nat. Bank Va., United Svcs. Life Ins. Corp., Jessup Group Inc.; bd. dirs., chmn. FLT Internat., JGW Assocs.; corp. adv. bd. Martin Marietta. Vice chmn., bd. advisors Citadel Coll.; bd. advisors Def. Intelligence Coll. Decorated Def. D.S.M., USN D.S.M., Legion of Merit with one bronze oak leaf cluster, D.F.C. with four bronze oak leaf clusters, Air medal with 14 oak leaf clusters, AF Commendation medal with one oak leaf cluster, Presdl. Unit citation, AF Outstanding Unit award, Republic of Korea Order of Nat. Security, Merit and Presdl. Unit citation, Korean Succession medal with two bronze stars, Vietnam Svc. medals with four bronze stars, Republic of Vietnam Gallantry Cross with Palm, UN Svc. medal, Republic of Vietnam Campaign medal, Federal Republic of German Grand Cross, Star of Armed Forces of Ecuador, Brazilian AF Order of Aero. Merit, Venezuelan AF Cross, French Legion of Honor, Pakistani 1st Class Spl. Meritorious award. Mem. Coun. Fgn. Rels. Died Sept. 4, 2003.

GABRIEL, EARL A. osteopathic physician; b. Phila., Aug. 13, 1925; s. John and Rose (Cohen) G.; m. Fredelle, Feldman, Dec. 19, 1948; children: Debra Mae, Barbara Lynn, Sheri Ann, Michael David. BS, Muhlenberg Coll., 1950; D.O., Phila. Coll. Osteo. Medicine, 1954. Gen. practice osteo. medicine, Allentown, Pa., 1955-78; chief of staff Allentown Osteo. Hosp., 1967-68, chmn. intern tng., 1956-58; prof., chmn. family practice medicine, assoc. dean clin. affairs Coll. Osteo. Medicine of Pacific, Pomona, Calif., 1978-88, assoc. dean clin. affairs for postdoctoral tng., 1983-88; med. dir. clinics, 1986-88; ret., 1988; pvt. practice gen. medicine, 1988-90, Rancho Cucamonga, Calif., 1990-94; dir. med. edn. San Bernardino (Calif.) County Med. Ctr., from 1994. Mem. Pa. Gov.'s Sci. Adv. Com. on Health Care Delivery, 1970, 71; preceptor in gen. practice Phila. Coll. Osteo. Medicine; mem. ad hoc profl. group FDA, HEW, 1976-77; mem. Pa. Profl. Services Rev. Orgn. Council, 1977 Editorial adviser Family Practice News, 1976—. Active Lehigh Valley Cancer Soc. Served with USNR and USMCR, 1943-46, PTO, CBI. Recipient cert. of honor Phila. Coll. Osteo. Medicine, 1981, Alumni Achievement award Muhlenberg Coll., 1983; elected Physicians Hall of Fame John Shankwiler Soc. Muhlenberg Coll., 1995; Shankweiler fellow, 1995. Fellow Am. Coll. Gen. Practice in Osteo. Medicine and Surgery (cert., pres. div. 1959, Disting. Svc. award, life mem. Pa. div. 1978); mem. Lehigh Valley Osteo. Soc. (pres. 1959-60), Pa. Osteo. Med. Assn. (pres. 1970, Disting. Svc. award 1975), Am. Osteo. Assn. (cert., ho. dels. 1966—, trustee 1970—, pres. 1975-76, cons. family gen. practice com. on osteo. colls. and bur. profl. edn. 1988), Osteo. Physicians and Surgeons of Calif. (trustee 1981—, pres. 1985), Calif. Bd. Osteo. Examiners, Phi Epsilon Pi (pres. 1950), Sigma Sigma Phi. Clubs: Masons, Shriners, Jester, Lions (Host Pomona), Lehigh Valley. Republican. Jewish. Died: Dec. 28, 1999.

GAINES, HOWARD CLARKE, retired lawyer; b. Washington, Sept. 6, 1909; s. Howard Wright and Ruth Adeline-Clarke Thomas Gaines; m. Audrey Allen, July 18, 1936; children: Clarke Allen, Margaret Anne. JD, Cath. U. Am., 1936. Bar: D.C. bar 1936, U.S. Supreme Ct. bar 1946, U.S. Ct. Claims bar 1947, Calif. bar 1948. Individual practice law, Washington, 1938-43, 46-47, Santa Barbara, Calif., 1948-51; asso. firm Price, Postel & Parma, Santa Barbara, 1951-54, partner, 1954-88; of counsel, 1989-94; ret., 1994. Chmn. Santa Barbara Bench and Bar Com., 1972-74 Chmn. Santa Barbara Police and Fire Commn., 1948-52; mem. adv. bd. Santa Barbara Com. on Alcoholism, 1956-67; bd. dirs. Santa Barbara Humane Soc., 1958-69, 85-92; bd. trustees Santa Barbara Botanic Garden, 1960—, v.p., 1967-69; bd. trustees Cancer Found. Santa Barbara, 1960-77; dir. Santa Barbara Mental Health Assn., 1957-59, v.p., 1959; pres. Santa Barbara Found., 1976-79, trustee, 1979—. Fellow Am. Bar Found.; mem. ABA, Bar Assn. D.C., State Bar Calif. (gov. 1969-72, v.p. 1971-72, tres. 1971-72), Santa Barbara County Bar Assn. (pres. 1957-58), Am. Judicature Soc., Santa Barbara Club. Republican. Episcopalian. Home: Santa Barbara, Calif. Died Dec. 30, 2002.

GAINES, NATALIE MALLIE, interior designer; b. Cleve. d. Harry Mallie and Anna Shiek; m. Leon Gaines, 1949 (div. 1981). Student, Pratt Inst. Design, 1934-36. Designer various women's clothing mfrs., Cleve., 1937-50; owner Natalie Gaines Interiors, Cleve., from 1950. Lectr. various orgns., Cleve., 1988—. Designer Masonic Temple lobby, Warrensville Heights, Ohio, 1970, Montefiore Home for Aged, Cleveland Heights, Ohio, 1980; contbr. articles to mags. including House Beautiful, Better Homes and Gardens and to local newspapers. Designer Lobby of Masonic Temple, Warrensville Heights, Ohio, 1970, Montefiore Home for the Aged, Cleve. Heights, 1980; lectr. various orgns., Greater Cleve., 1988--. Mem. Am. Soc. Interior Designers, Nat. Homes Fashion League. Avocations: golf, gardening, badminton, horseback riding. Died 2000.

GAITHER, GANT, sculptor; b. Hopkinsville, Ky., Aug. 1, 1917; s. Joseph Gant and Jane Eskridge (Lum) G. Student U. Mex., Mexico City, 1933-34; B.A., U. of South, 1938; postgrad. Yale Sch. Architecture, 1938-39. Owner, producer Miami Beach Playhouse, Fla., 1940-43; producer Broadway Theater, N.Y.C., 1947-56; exec. producer Paramount Pictures Corp., Hollywood, Calif., 1960-64; former artist-designer, licensor Shedrain Umbrella Co., Portland, Oreg., Lilli Ann Corp. Ladieswear, San Francisco, Bergquist Imports, Cloquet, Minn., Artex-Green Corp., Bklyn., Schreter Mens Neckwear, Balt., Art Guild Greeting Cards, Glendale, Calif. Artist-sculptor The Zoophisticates Collection, New York, Paris, Chgo., Mexico City, other locations. Author: Princess of Monaco, 1957. Author/illustrator: Sally Seal, 1964. Trustee Princess Grace Found.; bd. dirs. Baar & Beards Inc. Scarves, N.Y.C., Jewelmark Originals Ltd., N.Y.C. Served as sgt. USAF, 1943-46, PTO. Decorated Bronze Star; recipient Loews Monte-Carlo ann. bronze trophy Internat. Circus Festival, Monaco, 1984. Republican. Episcopalian. Mem. Yale Club. Home: Palm Springs, Calif. Died Feb. 16, 2004.

GALBRAITH, JOHN SEMPLE, history educator; b. Glasgow, Scotland, Nov. 10, 1916; came to U.S., 1925; naturalized, 1931; s. James M. and Mary (Marshall) G.; m. Laura Huddleston, Aug. 22, 1940; children: James M., John II., Mary P. BA, Miami U., Oxford, Ohio, 1938; MA, U. Iowa, 1939, PhD, 1943; LLD, Mount Union Coll., 1968. Prof. Brit. Empire history UCLA, 1948-64, 69-84, chmn. dept., 1954-58; chancellor U. Calif., San Diego, 1964-68, prof. history, 1984—87. Smuts vis. fellow Cambridge (Eng.) U., 1968-69. Author: The Establishment of Canadian Diplomatic Status in Washington, 1951; The Hudson's Bay Company as an Imperial Factor, 1957; Reluctant Empire, 1963; Mackinnon and East Africa, 1972; Crown and Charter, 1974; The Little Emperor, 1976. Served as officer AUS, 1943-46. Mem. AAUP, Royal Hist. Soc., Am. Hist. Assn. (pres. Pacific Coast br. 1965), Can. Hist. Assns., Soc. Am. Historians, African Studies Asns., Athenaeum Club (London), Phi Beta kappa. Home: San Diego, Calif. Died June 10, 2003.

GALVIN, THOMAS JOHN, Former information science policy educator and librarian; b. Arlington, Mass., Dec. 30, 1932; s. Thomas John and Elizabeth (Rossiter) G.; m. Marie C. Schumb, Nov. 24, 1956; 1 child, Siobhan Marie Wee. AB, Columbia U., 1954; SM, Simmons Coll., Boston, 1956; PhD, Case Western Res U., 1973. Reference libr. Boston U., 1954-56; dir. Abbot Pub. Libr., Marblehead, Mass., 1956-59; asst. dir. Simmons Coll. Libr., 1959-62; assoc. dir., prof. Sch. Libr. Sci., 1962-74; dean, prof. Sch. Libr. and Info. Sci., U. Pitts., 1974-85; exec. dir. Am. Libr. Assn., Chgo., 1985-89; prof. info. sci. and policy, dir. info. sci. doctoral program SUNY at Albany, 1989-99, prof. emeritus, 1999. Grad. fellow Case Western Res U., 1965-66; external examiner U. Ibadan, Nigeria, 1976-78; trustee Thayer Pub. Libr., Braintree, Mass., 1973-74; faculty fellow Ctr. for Tech. in Govt. SUNY, Albany. Author: Library Resource Sharing, 1977, Problems in Reference Service, 1965, Current Problems in Reference Service, 1971, The Case Method in Library Education, 1973, The On-Line Revolution in Libraries, 1978, The Structure and Governance of Library Networks, 1979, Excellence in School Media Programs, 1980, Information Technology, 1982, Priorities for Academic Libraries, 1982, Navigating the Networks, 1994, Smart IT Choices, 1996; also articles. Recipient Alumni Achievement award Simmons Coll. Sch. Libr. Sci., 1978, Disting. Alumnus award Case Western Res. U., 1979, Disting. Svc. award Pa. Libr. Assn., 1985, Ida and George Eliot prize Med. Libr. Assn., 1988, award contbr. to edn. Assn. for Libr. Info. Sci. Edn., 1993. Mem. ALA (pres. 1979-80, exec. bd., coun.; past pres. libr. edn. div., Isadore Gilbert Mudge award 1972), Assn. for Libr. and Info. Sci. Edn., Phi Beta Kappa, Beta Phi Mu. Democrat. Roman Catholic. Home: Chicago, Ill. Died Feb. 18, 2004.

GAMACHE, ALBERT, state legislator; Mem. Maine Ho. of Reps., Augusta, from 1993. Died Feb. 22, 1999.

GARAN, D. G. See GARANCE, DOMINICK

GARANCE, DOMINICK (D. G. GARAN), lawyer, author; b. Varaklani, Latvia, Oct. 14, 1912; came to U.S., 1950, naturalized, 1955; s. John and Virginia (Cakuls) Garans. LL.M., U. Riga, Latvia, 1935; J.U.D., U. Freiburg, Germany, 1945; LL.D., U. Paris, France, 1947; PhD, U. London, Eng., 1949. Bar: N.Y. 1958. Atty.-at-law, legal counsel Ministry of Welfare, Riga, 1936-42; law sec. French Mil. Govt. in Germany, Freiburg, 1945-46; documentary officer Harvard Law Sch. Internat. Program of Taxation, 1952-57; pvt. practice law N.Y.C., 1958—. Author: The Paradox of Pleasure and Relativity, 1963, Relativity for Psychology, A Causal Law for the Modern Alchemy, 1968, The Key to the Sciences of Man, 1975, Against Ourselves: Disorders from Improvements under the Organic Limitedness of Man, 1979, Our Sciences Ruled by Human Prejudice, 1987. Mem. ABA, N.Y. State Bar Assn., N.Y. State Trial Lawyers Assn., N.Y. Acad. Sci., Philosophy of Sci. Assn., Am. Assn. Advancement Sci., Lacuania. Died May 1, 2002.

GARCÉS, RAMON, journalist; b. Laredo, Tex., Dec. 15, 1925; s. Primo Mirales Garcés and Manuela Morales; m. Juanita Gil, Sept. 16, 1650; children: Alicia, Rolando, Laura Ysela. Student, U. Tex., 1946—50; degree in internat. comm., Am. U., 1980. News editor Radio KTXN, Austin, Tex., 1950—51; sports editor Laredo Times, 1951—56, city editor, 1956—61, Laredo Free Press, 1951—56; fgn. svc. officer U.S. Info. Agy., Washington, 1967—89; ind. video prodr. Garces News Bur., Reston, Va., 1989—95, freelance writer, 1995—99. Editor, pub. LULAC News League United L.Am. Citizens, Laredo, 1960—63; presdl. press aide for Pres. Lyndon B. Johnson White House, Washington, 1967—68; Spanish br. dir. Voice of Am., Washington, 1978—81; organizer press coverage and confs. for state visits of Pres. Jimmy Carter, Sec. of State Henry Kissinger and V.P. George Bush; translator for Pres. Lyndon Johnson for visit to south Tex.; translator for Pres. Renee Barrientos of Bolivia; translator for Pres. Juan Velasco Alvarado of Peru. Recipient Best Polit. Reporting award, AP, Austin, 1963, Hon. Mention Migrant Workers award, Headliners Club, Austin, 1963. Mem.: Sigma Delta Chi. Home: Austin, Tex. Died Sept. 21, 2002.

GARCIA, CELSO-RAMON, obstetrician, gynecologist, educator; b. N.Y.C., Oct. 31, 1921; s. Celso García y Ondina and Oliva (Menèndez del Valle) G.; m. Shirley Jean Stoddard, Oct. 14, 1950; children: Celso-Ramón Jr., Sarita Garcia Cole. BS, Queens Coll., 1942; MD, SUNY Downstate Med. Ctr., 1945; MA (hon.), U. Pa. Intern Norwegian Hosp., Bklyn., 1945-46; resident, rsch. fellow in gynecology Cumberland Hosp., Bklyn., 1949-50; assoc. in ob-gyn. U. P.R., San Juan, 1953-54; asst. prof. ob-gyn. Sch. Medicine and Tropical Medicine, San Juan, 1954-55; co-dir. Rock Reproductive Study Ctr.; asst. obstetrician and gynecologist Boston Lying-In Hosp.; assoc. surgeon Free Hosp. for Women, Brookline, Mass., 1955-65; sr. scientist, dir. tng. program in physiology reprodn. Worcester Found. for Exptl. Biology, Shrewsbury, Mass., 1960-62; asst. surgeon, chief Infertility Clinic, Mass. Gen. Hosp.; from asst., instr. to clin. assoc. ob-gyn. Harvard Med. Sch., 1962-65; prof. obstetrics and gynecology U. Pa., Phila., 1965-92, William Shippen, Jr. prof. human reprodn., 1970-92, William Shippen, Jr. prof emeritus, 1992—2004, dir. infertility and reproductive endocrinology and surgery, 1987-95. Extraordinary prof. U. San Luis Potosi, Mex., 1974; rapporteur com. of experts on clin. aspects oral gestogens WHO, Geneva, 1965; mem. ad hoc adv. com. contraceptive devel., contract program Nat. Inst. Child Health and Human Devel., 1971-75; original team mem. which developed clin. application of 1st FDA approved progestagen-estrogen combinations for oral contraception (the Pill); developer, dir. 1st tng. program in physiology of reprodn. in U.S.; innovator surg. approach to infertility of women; cons. Pa. Hosp., 1973-94; asst. staff Faulkner Hosp., Jamaica Plain, Boston; courtesy staff Glover Meml. Hosp., Needham, Mass., 1962-65; adv. bd. Global Alliance for Women's Health, 1995-2004. Chmn. nat. med. adv. com. Planned Parenthood World Population, 1971-74; mem. nat. adv. child and human devel. coun. Nat. Inst. Child Health and Human Devel., 1981-84. With AUS, 1943-48. Recipient Carl G. Hartman award Am. Soc. Study of Sterility, 1961, Sesquicentennial award U. Mich., 1967, MD Master Tchg. award Alumni Assn. SUNY, 1989, Recognition award APGO Wyeth-Ayerst, 1993, Frank L. Babbott award SUNY, 1995, Sci. Leadership award Global Alliance Women's Health, 2000; Sidney Graves fellow in gynecology Harvard Med. Sch., 1955. Fellow: ACOG, ACS, Coll. Physicians Phila.; mem.: AMA, Boston Obstet. Soc. (emeritus), Phila. Obstet. Soc., Am. Soc. Reproduction Medicine (bd. dirs., past pres.), Soc. Reproductive Surgeons (founding pres.), Assn. Planned Parenthood Physicians (past pres.), Fedn. Columbian Socs. Ob-Gyn. (hon.), Cuban Soc. Ob-Gyn. (hon.; in exile), Am. Physiol. Soc., Am. Gynecol. and Obstet. Soc., Am. Soc. Gynecol. Surgeons, Global Alliance Women's Health (adv. bd. from 1994, rep. to U.N. Econ. and Social Coun. 1998), Alpha Omega Alpha, Sigma Xi, Masons. Democrat. Presbyterian. Home: Merion Station, Pa. Died Feb. 1, 2004.

GARDINER, ROBERT, engineering executive; Pres. Hay & Co. Cons., Inc., Vancouver, B.C., Can. Recipient T.C. Keefer medal Can. Soc. Civil Engring., 1996. Deceased.

GARDNER, JOHN UNDERHILL, hospital administrator; b. Long Branch, N.J., Dec. 17, 1924; s. John Henry and Mercedee (Crum) G.; children from previous marriage: Sarah, John, Eve, Thomas; m. Helen A. McGowan. AB, Princeton (N.J.) U., 1949; MD, N.Y. Med. Coll., 1953; MS in Medicine, U. Minn., 1957. Diplomate Am. Bd. Internal Medicine. Pvt. practice in internal medicine, New Bedford, Mass., 1958-86; v.p. med. affairs, med. dir. St. Lukes Hosp., New Bedford, from 1986. Corporator Compass Savs. Bank, New Bedford, 1965—. Pres. bd. dirs. Salvation Army, New Bedford, 1965-66; med. advisor Boy Scouts Am., New Bedford, 1963-68. 2d lt. U.S. Army, 1943-46. Fellow ACP; mem. Masons. Avocations: blacksmithing, silversmithing, antique sales. Home: Mattapoisett, Mass. Died Mar. 31, 1999.

GARDNER, MARSHALL CLOSSON, foundation administrator, lawyer; b. Logansport, Ind., June 11, 1918; s. Harry Marshall and Alice Jane (Closson) G.; m. June Archer Haller, Jan. 5, 1946; children: David Marshall, Debra June. BS, George Washington U., 1943, MS, 1950, JD with honors, 1955. Bar: D.C. 1955, U.S. Supreme Ct. 1958. Biologist U.S. Fish and Wildlife Svc., Washington, 1942-55; trial atty. Antitrust Divsn. Dept. Justice, Washington, 1955-74; adminstrv. appeals judge Appeals Coun. Social Security Adminstrn., Arlington, Va., 1974-84; pvt. practice Washington, 1984-91; pres. Found. of the Fed. Bar Assn., Washington, from 1991. Treas., dir. Fed. Bar Bldg. Corp., Washington, 1960—. Editor Fed. Bar Jour., 1956-71; editorial notes editor, sec. George Washington U. Law Sch. Jour., 1954-55. Pres. North Four Corners Citizens Assn., Silver Spring, Md., 1954-55. Lt. USNR, 1943-46, PTO, 1950-53, Korea. Mem. Fed. Bar Assn. (nat. pres. 1965, Pres.' award 1989), George Washington U. Law Assn. (nat. pres. 1981), Washington Acad. Scis., Nat. Press Club, Washington Biologists and Field Club, Am. Legion (state comdr. D.C. 1968-69, nat. legis. commn. Indpls. 1988—), Order of Coif, Sigma Xi. Avocations: travel, stamp collecting. Home: Bowie, Md. Died Apr. 3, 2001.

GARDNER, RICHARD ALAN, psychiatrist, writer; b. Bronx, N.Y., Apr. 28, 1931; s. Irving and Amelia (Weingarten) Gardner; m. Lee Robbins, Apr. 14, 1957 (div. Nov. 1984); children: Andrew Kevin, Nancy Tara, Julie Anne; m. Patricia Lefevere, July 4, 1987 (div. Apr. 1998). AB, Columbia U., 1952; MD, SUNY Downstate Med. Ctr., 1956; cert. psychoanalysis, William A. White Psychoanalytical Inst., 1966. Diplomate Am. Bd. Psychiatry and Neurology, Am. Bd. Child Psychiatry. Intern Montefiore Hosp., N.Y.C., 1956-57, resident child psychiatry, 1959-60, 62-63; dir. child psychiatry U.S. Army Hosp., Frankfurt, Federal Republic of Germany, 1960-62; mem. attending staff Presbyn. Hosp., N.Y.C., from 1963; pvt. practice specializing in psychiatry, child psychiatry, forensic psychiatry and psychoanalysis Cresskill, NJ, from 1963; instr. child psychiatry Columbia Coll. Physicians and Surgeons, N.Y.C., 1963-70, assoc. child psychiatry, 1970-72, asst. clin. prof. child psychiatry, 1972-76, assoc. clin. prof. child psychiatry, 1976-83, clin. prof. child psychiatry, 1983—2003. Vis. prof. child psychiatry U. Louvain, Belgium, 1981—83, U. St. Petersburg, Russia, 1990—97; mem. faculty William A. White Psychoanalytic Inst., 1967—83. Author: The Child's Book About Brain Injury, 1966, The Boys and Girls Book About Divorce, 1970, Therapeutic Communication With Children: The Mutual Storytelling Technique, 1971, Dr. Gardner's Stories About the Real World, vol. I, 1972, MBD: The Family Book About Minimal Brain Dysfunction, 1973, Understanding Children: A Parent's Guide to Child Rearing, 1973, Dr. Gardner's Fairy Tales for Today's Child, 1974, Psychotherapy With Children of Divorce, 1976, The Parent's Book About Divorce, 1977, Dr. Gardner's Modern Fairy Tales, 1977, The Boys and Girls Book About Step-Families, 1981, Family Evaluation in Child Custody Litigation, 1982, Dr. Gardner's Stories About the Real World, vol. II, 1983, Separation Anxiety Disorder: Psychodynamics and Psychotherapy, 1984, Child Custody Litigation: A Guide for Parents and Mental Health Professionals, 1986, The Psychotherapeutic Techniques of Richard A. Gardner, 1986, Hyperactivity, the So-Called Attention Deficit Disorder and the Group of MBD Syndromes, 1987, The Parental Alienation Syndrome and the Differentiation Between Fabricated and Genuine Child Sex Abuse, 1987, Psychotherapy With Adolescents, 1988, Family Evaluation in Custody Mediation, Arbitration and Litigation, 1989, The Girls and Boys Book About Good and Bad Behavior, 1990, Sex Abuse Hysteria: Salem Witch Trials Revisited, 1991, The Parents Book About Divorce, 2d edit., 1991, The Parental Alienation Syndrome: A Guide for Mental Health and Legal Professionals, 1992, Self-Esteem Problems of Children: Psychodynamics and Psychotherapy, 1992, The Psychotherapeutic Techniques of Richard A. Gardner, 2d edit., 1992, True and False Accusations of Child Sex Abuse: A Guide for Legal and Mental Health Professionals, 1992, Conduct Disorders of Childhood: Psychodynamics and Psychotherapy, 1994, Protocols for the Sex Abuse Evaluation, 1995, Psychogenic Learning Disabilities: Psychodynamics and Psychotherapy, 1996, Testifying in Court: A Guide for Mental Health Professionals, 1995, Psychotherapy With Victims of Child Sexual Abuse: True, False, and Hysterical, 1996, Dream Analysis in Psychotherapy, 1996, The Parental Alienation Syndrome, 2d edit., 1998, The Utilization of the Gardner Children's Projective Battery, 1999, Therapeutic Interventions for Children With Parental Alienation Syndrome, 2001, Sex Abuse Trauma? vs. Trauma from Other Sources?, 2002; editor (in chief): Internat. Jour. Child Psychotherapy, 1972—73. Capt. USAR, 1960—62. Fellow: Am. Psychiat. Assn. (life), Am. Acad. Child and Adolescent Psychiatry, Am. Acad. Psychoanalysis. Home: Tenafly, NJ. Died May 25, 2003.

GARFINKEL, HERBERT, political science educator, university official; b. N.Y.C., June 16, 1920; s. Julius Louis and Gertrude (Goldstone) G.; m. Evelyn Epstein, Sept. 3, 1940; children— Laura, Paul. MA, U. Chgo., 1950, PhD, 1956. Instr. polit. sci. Ill. Inst. Tech., 1948-51; research asst. Nat. Opinion Research Ctr., U. Chgo., 1950-51; instr. Mich. State U., 1951-53; asst. prof. Dartmouth, 1953-59; faculty Mich. State U., East Lansing, 1959—, prof. polit. sci., 1964-73; dean James Madison Coll., 1966-73; provost, vice chancellor acad. affairs U. Nebr., Omaha, 1973-78, interim chancellor, 1977-78; v.p. acad. affairs and prof. polit. sci. U. Louisville, 1978-85, v.p. emeritus, prof. emeritus, from 1985. NATO prof. Inst. Social Studies, The Hague, Netherlands, 1965-66 Author: When Negroes March, 1959, 2d edit., 1969, (co-author) The Democratic Republic, 1966, 2d edit., 1970, The Constitution and The Legislature, 1961; contbr. articles to profl. jours. Served as officer U.S. Mcht. Marine, 1943-45. Ctr. for Advanced Study Behavioral Scis. fellow, 1958-59; research fellow Social Sci. Research Council, 1960-61 Mem. Am. Polit. Sci. Assn. Home: Peoria, Ill. Died Sept. 27, 2003.

GARLAND, JAMES BOYCE, lawyer; b. Gastonia, NC, June 16, 1920; s. Peter Woods and Kathleen (Boyce) G.; m. Elizabeth Matthews, Nov. 9, 1951 (dec.); children: Elizabeth Garland Wren, Woods Garland Potts, James Boyce Jr., Rebecca Garland Morris. BS, U. N.C., 1941, LLB, 1946. Bar: N.C. 1946, U.S. Ct. Appeals (4th cir.) 1981, U.S. Supreme Ct. 1989. Ptnr. Garland & Garland, Gastonia, 1946-59, Garland & Eck, Gastonia, 1961-62, Garland & Alala, Gastonia, 1962-80, chmn. bd. dirs., 1980-88; ptnr. Garland & Wren, 1988-93. Mem. N.C. Ho. of Reps., 1949-51; campaign chmn. United Way of Gaston County, Inc., 1988, pres., 1990; chmn. bd. trustees Lees McRae Coll., 1984-86; vice chmn. bd. trustees Gaston Coll., 1988-90; chmn., bd. visitors Lineberger Comprehensive Cancer Ctr. U. N.C., Chapel Hill, 1988-92; pres. U. N.C. Law Alumni Assn., 1971-72, U. N.C. Gen. Alumni Assn., 1973-74; vice chmn. bd. visitors U. N.C., Chapel Hill; mem. N.C. Local Govt. Commn., 1970-75, Gastonia City Coun., 1985-87; Mayor City of Gastonia, 1987-97, mayor emeritus, 2000; bd. dirs. N.C. League of Municipalities, 1992-94; commissioned 2nd Lt. Field Artillery, 1942; sec. bd. trustees U. N.C., Charlotte, 1993—; pres. Schiele Mus. Natural History and Planetarium, 1984-85. Served to capt. N.C. N.G., 1942-59, WWII. Decorated Bronze Star; named Citizen of Yr. Gastonia Civitan Club. Fellow Am. Bar Found.; mem. ABA, N.C. Bar Assn. (chmn. edn. law com., v.p. 1984-85, N.C. Soc. Cin., Gen. Practice Hall of Fame 1995), Gaston County Bar Assn. (pres.), N.C. State Bar, Gaston County C. of C. (pres. 1980-81), N.C. Jr. C. of C. (v.p. 1953-54), Gastonia Jr. C. of C. (pres. 1952-53, Disting. Svc. award 1955), Daniel Jonathan Stowe Botanical Garden (pres. 1991-96, vice chmn. bd. 1996—), Jaycees (W. Duke Kimbrell Life-time Achievement award 1998), Gaston Country Club, Biltmore Forest Country Club, Rotary (pres. 1960-61, dist. gov. 1966-67), Phi Delta Phi. Democrat. Presbyterian. Home: Gastonia, NC. Died Nov. 29, 2002.

GARRETT, PAUL WILLIAM, retired management executive; b. Harrisville, W.Va., Oct. 16, 1921; s. Grover C. and Sarah Ann (Six) G.; m. Mary Evelyn, Mar. 26, 1943; children: Robert Eugene, David Roger, Patricia Ann. AS, Salem Tech. Sch., 1948. Pres. Garrett Cons. Inc., Columbiana, Ohio, 1965-87, ret., 1987. Patentee in field. Mem. local sch. bd.; vol. Santa local children's hosp.; vol. local church. With U.S. Army, 1943-44. Mem. Masons. Avocation: golf. Home: Columbiana, Ohio. Died Apr. 9, 2000.

GARRITY, LEONA MARY, retired social worker and educator; b. Detroit, Jan. 28, 1908; d. Leo Anthony and Florence Elizabeth (Cook) Schafer; m. John Peter Garrity, Oct. 16, 1937. BA magna cum laude, Marygrove Coll., Detroit, 1930; MSW, Wayne State U., 1940; postgrad., U.

Mich., Detroit, 1950. Caseworker, case supr. Detroit Dept. Pub. Welfare, 1930-43; casework supr., acting dir. Travelers Aid Soc., Detroit, 1943-56, caseworker, 1968, Guardian Angel Home, Detroit, 1960-64. Instr. social work U. Detroit, 1943-46, Mercy Coll., Detroit, 1944-46, 50-51, 55-56, Madonna Coll., Livonia, Mich., 1967; field work instr. for grad. students Wayne State U., Detroit, 1948-49, 53-54, U. Mich. Sch. Social Work, 1953. Author: The Cook Book, 1976, (autobiography) Letter of Thanks, 1988. Vol. United Found., Detroit, 1949-56; del. United Community Svcs., Detroit, 1950-55; vice chmn. Harper Woods (Mich.) Com. on Community Svcs., 1955-59; bd. dirs. Secular Franciscans-St. Bonaventure Frat., 1937-41; v.p. Detroit Archdiocesan Coun. Cath. Women, 1953-56; bd. dirs. Father Solanus Casey Guild, Detroit, 1964-66, v.p., 1972-74. Recipient recognition award Women's Recruitment Corp., United Found., 1953, plaque Father Solanus Casey Guild, 1975. Mem. NASW, AAUP, Acad. Cert. Social Workers, Nat. Coun. Cath. Women (nat. social action com. 1951-53), Kappa Gamma Pi (pres. Detroit chpt. 1951-53). Avocations: travel, family history. Home: Saint Clair Shores, Mich. Deceased.

GART, MURRAY JOSEPH, journalist, consultant; b. Boston, Nov. 9, 1924; s. John and Frieda (Fisher) G.; m. Jeanne Brooks, Feb. 26, 1950; children: Mitchell Brooks, Marcia Anne. BA in Econs, Northeastern U., 1949, LHD (hon.), 1970. Reporter Honolulu Star-Bull., 1949-50; editor Weekly Ind. Record, Cape May County, N.J., 1950-51; reporter, city editor Wichita Beacon, 1951-53; reporter, news editor Wichita Eagle, 1953-55; bur. chief Time-Life mag. News Svc., Toronto, Can., 1955-57, Boston, 1957-59; chief Midwest corr. Time mag., 1959-61, bur. chief, 1961-64, London, 1964-66; asst. mng. editor Fortune mag., N.Y.C., 1966-69; chief of corrs. Time-Life News Svc., 1969-78; asst. mng. editor Time mag., 1972-78; editor The Washington Star, 1978-81; sr. editor Time Inc., 1981-82; assoc. Johns Hopkins Fgn. Policy Inst., Washington, 1982-84; cons. Time, Inc., 1982-89. Dir. Mid. East Inst., 1988-2004, Am. Near Ea. Refugee Aid, 1993-2004, bd. dirs. Washington Inst. Fgn. Affairs; Geopolitics of Energy, 1985-94. Editor: Cosmos Jour., 1992-95. Served with AUS, 1943-46. Recipient Best Mag. Fgn. Affairs Reporting award, Overseas Press Club, 1988. Mem. Coun. on Fgn. Rels., Cosmos Club, Northeastern U. Corp. Home: Mitchellville, Md. Died Mar. 31, 2004.

GASTON, RANDALL WALLACE, police chief; b. Lake Charles, La., Mar. 18, 1944; s. Wallace Howard and Mary Jean (Hubbs) G.; m. Linda Lou Lockwood; children: Debora Gaston Ricks, Aaron, Bryan, Allison. BS, Long Beach State Coll., 1971; MPA with honors, U. So. Calif., 1974; grad., FBI Nat. Acad., 1982. Police officer Anaheim (Calif.) Police Dept., 1965-69, police sgt., 1969-73, police lt., 1973-83, police capt., 1983-94, police chief, from 1994. Instr. Orange County (Calif.) C.C.s, 1971-94. Mem. Internat. Police Chiefs Assn., Calif. Police Chiefs Assn., Orange County Police Chiefs Assn., FBI Nat. Acad. Assocs., Kiwanis Club of Greater Anaheim (bd. dirs. 1990-95), Phi Kappa Phi. Avocations: gardening, bicycling. Deceased.

GATSKI, ROBERT LAWRENCE, retired physician; b. West Hazelton, Pa., May 27, 1919; s. Peter Paul and Estella (Schlacky) G.; m. Betty Eileen Carey, June 29, 1942; children— Robert Lawrence, Charles P., Marsha E., Mark. Student, Bucknell U., 1942-44; MD, Jefferson Med. Coll., 1948. Diplomate: Am. Bd. Psychiatry, Nat. Bd. Med. Examiners. Intern St. Josephs Hosp., Lancaster, Pa., 1948-49; resident Danville (Pa.) State Hosp., 1949-53; acting clin. dir. Gov. Bacon Health Center, Delaware City, Del., 1954-55; clin. dir. Danville (Pa.) State Hosp., 1954-55, supt., adminstr., 1955-77; ret., 1977; practice medicine specializing in psychiatry, 1977-97; med. dir. Cmty. Mental Health Clinic, Danville and Bloomsburg, Pa., 1977-97; ret., 1997. Acting supt. Retreat State Hosp., 1965-67; psychiat. cons. Geisinger Med. Ctr., Bloomsburg Hosp., Muncy (Pa.) State Indsl. Home, Eastern Fed. Penitentiary, Lewisburg, Pa. Editor Pa. Psychiat. Quar., 1959-63, cons. editor, 1963-65. Mem. coun. on stroke Susquehanna Valley Regional Med. Program, 1971-72; mem. Pa. Drug Standardization Com. Recipient Alumni award Bucknell U., 1971 Mem. AMA, Am. Psychiat. Assn., Am. Coll. Hosp. Adminstrs. Avocation: research mental disorders. Died Nov. 28, 1999.

GAUGHAN, NORBERT F. bishop; b. Pitts., May 30, 1921; s. Thomas L. and Martha (Paczkowska) G. MA, St. Vincent Coll., Latrobe, Pa., 1944; PhD, U. Pitts., 1963; LLD, Seton Hill Coll., 1963; DD (hon.), Lebanon Valley Coll., 1980. Ordained priest Roman Cath. Ch., 1945. Chancellor Diocese of Greensburg, Pa., 1960-75, vicar gen., 1970-75, aux. bishop, 1975-84; bishop Diocese of Gary, Ind., 1984—. Author: Shepherd's Pie, 1978, Troubled Catholics, 1988. Bd. dirs. Westmoreland Mus. Art, Greensburg, v.p., 1979— Avocations: photography; silkscreens. Died Oct. 1, 1999.

GAULTNEY, JOHN ORTON, life insurance agent, consultant; b. Pulaski, Tenn., Nov. 7, 1915; s. Bert Hood and Grace (Orton) G.; m. Elizabethine Mullette, Mar. 30, 1941; children: Elizabethine G. McClure, John Mullette, Walker Orton, Harlow Denny. Student, Am. Inst. Banking, 1936; diploma, Life Ins. Agy. Mgmt. Assn., 1948, Little Rock Jr. Coll., 1950; Mgmt. C.L.U. diploma, 1952; grad. sales mgmt. and mktg., Rutgers U., 1957. CLU. With N.Y. Life Ins. Co., from 1935, regional v.p., 1956-64, v.p. N.Y.C., 1964-67, v.p. in charge group sales, 1967-68, v.p. mktg., 1969-80, agt., 1980—; life ins. cons., 1981—. V.p. N.Y. Life Variable Contracts Corp., 1969-80; hon. dir. Bank of Frankewing (Tenn.), 1984— Elder Presbyn. Ch., 1952; chmn. Downtown YMCA, Atlanta, 1963-65; mem. Bd. Zoning Appeals, Bronxville, N.Y., 1970-80; mem. Nashville YMCA, 1981—; mem. pub. rels. com. Nat. Coun. YMCAs, 1965-80; mem. internat. world svc. com. YMCA, 1968-80; chmn. Vanderbilt YMCA, N.Y.C., 1974-76, bd. dirs., 1966-76; bd. dirs. Memphis YMCA, 1939-40, Little Rock YMCA, 1941-55, Atlanta YMCA, 1959-65, chmn. downtown, 1962-63; bd. dirs. Greater N.Y. YMCA, 1975-80, chmn. fund drive, 1972; dir. Internat. Assn. Y's Men's Clubs, 1936-42. Capt. inf. AUS, 1942-45, MTO. Decorated Silver Star, Bronze Star with 3 clusters, Purple Heart with 2 clusters.; recipient Devereux C. Josephs award N.Y. Life Ins. Co., 1954, Cross of Mil. Svc., UDC, 1973; named Ark. Traveler, 1955; hon. citizen Tenn., 1956; Tenn. Amb., 1981-87; Ky. col., 1963; inducted into Tenn. Ins. Hall of Fame, 2001. Mem. Am. Soc. CLUs, Tenn. Soc. CLUs, Ark. Soc. CLUs (pres. 1950-51), Nat. Assn. Life Underwriters, Heritage Found., Carnton Assn. (bd. dirs. 1981-90, pres. 1987-88), N.Y. So. Soc. (trustee 1965-80), Williamson County Hist. Soc. (pres. 1983-85), Brentwood Hist. Trust, Giles County Hist. Soc., 361st Inf. Assn. World War II (pres. 1967-70), Mass. Soc. of the Cin., SAR (N.Y. state dir. 1970-80), Soc. Colonial Wars, Descendants of Colonial Clergy, Tenn. Sons of Revolution, Assn. Preservation Tenn. Antiquities (trustee 1984-93), Tenn. Soc. in N.Y. (pres. 1971-74, trustee 1980-85), Newcomen Soc. in Am., English Speaking Union, Capital City Club (Atlanta), Nashville City Club, Victory Svcs. Club (London), Nat. Sojourners (pres. 2000-2001), Heroes of '76 (comdr. 1993-94), Sovereign Mil. Order of the Temple of Jerusalem, Rotary, Masons, Shriners, Jesters. Home: Brentwood, Tenn. Died Sept. 26, 2003.

GAY, ELISABETH FEITLER, actress; b. Vienna, Dec. 16, 1916; d. Paul and Loni (Rosenbaum) Feitler; m. Joseph Gay (dec.); children: Cathy, Paul, Jill. BA, Sarah Lawrence Coll., 1974, MFA, 1977; PhD, NYU, 1986. Head of acting co. Sara Lawrence Players, Bronxville, N.Y., 1974-79; artist in residence Westchester Schs., 1974-79; acting tchr. U. Bridgeport, Conn., 1977-79; drama therapist, acting tchr. Bellevue Hosp., N.Y.C., 1984-86; acting tchr. Sarah Lawrence Coll., 1986. Author short stories. Brownie leader Stephenson Sch., New Rochelle, 1951-53; actress Guidance Ctr., New Rochelle, 1950. Mem. AFTRA, Am. Sr. Profls. at Eckerd Coll., Actors Equity, Assn. Sr. Profls., Kappa Delta Pi. Democrat. Jewish. Avocations: play directing, theatre, movies, gardening, reading. Home: New Rochelle, NY. Died Apr. 6, 2003.

GAYLORD, EDWARD LEWIS, publishing company executive; b. Denver, May 28, 1919; s. Edward King and Inez (Kinney) G.; m. Thelma Feragen, Aug. 30, 1950; children: Christine Elizabeth, Mary Inez, Edward King II, Thelma Louise. AB, Stanford U., 1941; LLD, Oklahoma City U., Okla. Christian Coll., Pepperdine U., 1984. Chmn. Okla. Pub. Co., Oklahoma City; editor, pub. Daily Oklahoman, Oklahoma City, Okla., Sunday Oklahoman; pres. OPUBCO Resources, Inc., OPUBCO Devel. Co.; past chmn. Gaylord Entertainment, Nashville. Chmn. bd. Gayno, Inc., Colorado Springs; ptnr. Cimarron Coal Co., Denver; past chmn., bd. dirs. Broadmoor Hotel, Colorado Springs. Chmn., trustee Okla. Industries Authority; hon. chmn. bd. govs. Okla. Christian Coll.; bd. dirs. Okla. State Fair, pres., 1961-71; past chmn. bd. dirs. Nat. Cowboy and Western Heritage Mus.; past chmn. Okla. Med. Rsch. Found.; past trustee Casady Sch., Oklahoma City U. Served with AUS, 1942-46. Recipient Brotherhood award NCCJ, 1961, Humanitarian award NCCJ, 1971, Disting. Svc. award U. Okla., 1981, Golden Plate award Am. Acad. Achievement, 1985, Pathmaker of Oklahoma County award Oklahoma City/County Hist. Soc., 1996, Pres.'s award for 50 Yrs. of Svc., 4-H and Future Farmers Am., 1996, Disting. Citizen award Last Frontier Coun. Boy Scouts Am., 1996, Silver Buffalo award, 1999; Adam Smith award Hillsdale Coll. and Shavano Inst., 1996; named to Okla. Hall of Fame, 1974, Okla. Journalism Hall of Fame, 1994; first recipient Spirit of Am. award U.S. Olympic Com., 1984. Mem. Oklahoma City C. of C. (dir., past pres.), So. Newspaper Pubs. Assn. (past pres.) Congregationalist. Home: Oklahoma City, Okla. Died Apr. 27, 2003.

GEE, JERRY BROOKSHER, education educator; b. Helena, Ark., Jan. 28, 1936; s. Brooksher and Vida (Cash) G.; m. Mary Janice Eaves, Mar. 20, 1958; children: Jerry, Michael, Jason, Andrea. BMEd, U. So. Miss., 1958; MEd, Miss. State U., 1965; EdD, La. State U., 1977. Dir. bands, assoc. prof. Nicholls State U., Thibodaux, La., 1966-74, prof. edn. and adminstrn./supervision, from 1974. Testing supr. NTE, GRE, GMAT, MCAT, LSAT, Nicholls State U., Thibodaux, 1979—; presenter in field. Contbr. articles to profl. jours. Mem. Am. Ednl. Rsch. Assn. Home: Thibodaux, La. Died Sept. 12, 2001.

GEHRING, PERRY JAMES, retired toxicologist, retired chemicals executive; b. Yankton, S.D., Mar. 15, 1936; s. Rinold Lou and Bertha (Reiger) G.; m. Barbara Tennis, Aug. 8, 1959; children: Daniel, Matthew, Elizabeth, Heidi. BS, D.V.M., U. Minn., 1960, PhD in Pharmacology, 1965. Research assoc. Iowa State U., 1960-61; with Dow Chem. Co., Midland, Mich., 1965-68, 70-89, dir. toxicology, 1974-78, dir. health and environ. scis., 1978-81, v.p. agrl. chems. research and devel., dir. health and environ. sci., 1981-89; v.p. R & D Dow Agro Scis., Indpls., 1989-98. Assoc. prof. pharmacology Mich. State U., 1968—70, adj. prof., 1970—92; adj. prof. toxicology Ind. U., 1996—2001; trustee Nutrition Found., 1981; chmn. sci. adv. panel Chem. Industry Inst. Toxicology, 1976—80; mem. safe drinking water subcom. organic contaminants Nat. Acad. Scis., 1975—76, mem. nat. ctr. toxicol. rsch. rev. com., 1976—77; participant internat. meetings. Assoc. editor: Toxicology and Applied Pharmacology Jour., 1977-80; mem. editorial bds. profl. jours.; contbr. articles to profl. publs. Recipient Founders award Chem. Industry Inst. Toxicology, 1983; inducted into U. Minn. Athletic Hall of Fame, 1993; NIH fellow, 1961-65. Mem. Soc. Toxicology (pres. 1980-81, coun. 1975-77, Frank R. Blood award 1979, Merit award 1983), Internat. Union Toxicology (v.p. 1983-86, dir. 1981-83, pres. 1986-90), Am. Soc. Pharmacology and Exptl. Therapeutics, Am. Crop Protection Assn. (chmn. sci. regulatory oversight coun. 1989-93). Presbyterian (trustee 1983-86). Home: Carmel, Ind. Died Nov. 6, 2003.

GEIS, FLORENCE LINDAUER, psychology educator; b. Oakland, Calif., Apr. 3, 1933; d. Earl Sherman and Alma Frederica (Dahm) Lindauer; m. Jon Geis, 1954 (div. 1960). BA, U. Ariz., 1956; PhD, Columbia U., 1964. Rsch. assistantship Columbia U., N.Y.C., 1960-64, adj. asst. prof., summer 1964; asst. prof. psychology NYU, 1964-67, U. Del., Newark, 1967-71, assoc. prof., 1971-82, prof. psychology, from 1982. Author: Studies in Machiavellianism, 1970, Personality Research Manual, 1978, Instructor's Guide for Personality Research Manual, 1978, Seeing and Evaluating People, 1982, Research on Seeing and Evaluating People, 1983, The Organizational Woman: Power and Paradox, 1992; contbr. articles to profl. jours., chpts. to books. Grantee Nat. Inst. Edn., 1979, U. Del., 1972; recipient Heritage Rsch. award Am. Psychol. Assn., 1991, E. Arthur Trabant award Women's Equity, 1989. Mem. AAUP, AAUW, APA, NOW, Am. Psychol. Soc., Ea. Psychol. Assn. Avocation: organic gardening. Home: Landenberg, Pa. Deceased.

GEITTMANN, WILLIAM FREDERICK, retired obstetrician-gynecologist; b. Beaver Dam, Wis., 1909; MD, Northwestern U., 1935. Diplomate Am. Bd. Ob-Gyn. Intern St Luke's Hosp., Chgo., 1934-35, resident, 1936-37; pvt. practice ob-gyn. Lakeside, Mich., 1938-93. Mem. AMA, Am. Acad. Obstetrics and Gynecology, Ctrl. Assn. Obetricians and Gynecologists. Home: Lakeside, Mich. Deceased.

GELBER, JACK, playwright, director; b. Chgo., Apr. 12, 1932; s. Harold and Molly (Singer) G.; m. Carol Westenberg, Dec. 22, 1957; children: Jed, Amy. BS in Journalism, U. Ill., 1953. Adj. assoc. prof. Columbia U., N.Y.C., 1967-72, prof., 1967-72, Bklyn. Coll., 1972—2003. Author: (plays) The Connection, 1959 (Obie award 1960, Drama Desk award 1960, Variety's N.Y. Drama Critics' Poll award 1960), The Apple, 1961, Square in the Eye, 1965, The Cuban Thing, 1968, Sleep, 1972, (adapter) Barbary Shore, 1974, Jack Gelber's New Play: Rehearsal, 1976, Starters, 1982, Big Shot, 1988, Magic Valley, 1990, (novel) On Ice, 1964; dir. (plays) The Kitchen, 1966, The Cuban Thing, 1968, Indians, 1968, Kool Aid, 1971, The Chickencoop Chinaman, 1972, The Kid, 1972 (Obie award 1972), Barbary Shore, 1974, Farmyard, 1975, Hamlet, 1976, A Streetcar Named Desire, 1976, Jack Gelber's New Play: Rehearsal, 1976, Eulogy For A Small Time Thief, 1977, Seduced, 1979 (Obie award 1979), The Man and The Fly, 1981, The House of Ramon Iglesia, 1983, Night Music, 1984, Carl and the Professor, 1985, Dream of a Blacklisted Actor, 1986, Chinese Coffee, 1990, Born Guilty, 1992. Recipient Vernon Rice award for outstanding contbn. to off-Broadway, 1959-60, Directing award Village Voice, 1972-73; Guggenheim fellow, 1963-64, 66-67; Rockefeller grantee, 1972; Nat. Endowment Arts fellow, 1974; CBS fellow Yale U., 1974-75. Home: New York, NY. Died May 9, 2003.

GELLIS, SYDNEY SAUL, physician; b. Claremont, N.H., Mar. 6, 1914; s. Morris Aaron and Minnie (Bernstein) G.; m. Matilda Lichter, March 6, 1939; children: Beth Louise Gellis Crocker, Stephen E. AB magna cum laude, Harvard U., 1934; MD, Harvard Med. Sch., 1938. Diplomate Am. Acad. Pediatrics. Resident in pediatrics Yale-New Haven Hosp., 1938-39, Children's Hosp., Cin., 1939-41; chief resident in pediatrics Johns Hopkins Hosp., Balt., 1941-42; captain armed forces epidemiol. bd. M.C., epidemiology bd. U.S. Army, ETO, 1942-46; asst. prof. pediatrics Harvard Med. Sch., Boston, 1946-55; chief outpatient and emergency Children's Hosp., Boston, 1946-53; prof., chmn. pediatrics Boston U. Med. Sch., 1955-65, dean, 1963-65; pediatrician-in-chief Boston City Hosp., 1955-65; prof., chmn. dept. pediatrics Tufts U. Med. Sch., Boston, 1965-83; prof. pediatrics New Eng. Med. Ctr., Boston, from 1965, pediatrician-in-chief, 1965-83. Editor: Yearbook of Pediatrics, 1952-85, Pediatric Notes, 1977—; contbr. articles to profl. jours. Fellow Am. Acad. Pediatrics (Jacobi award 1978, lifetime Med. Edn. award, 1993); mem. Am. Pediatric Soc. (John Howland medal award 1994), Pediatric Rsch. Soc. (sec.-treas. 1946-52, pres. 1972); corr. mem. Acad. Pediatrics (France), New Zealand Pediatric Soc. Died Dec. 6, 2002.

GENOVESI, ANTHONY J. state legislator; m. Joyce Genovesi; 5 children. Grad., St. Peter's Coll.; LLB, Fordham U. State rep. Dist. 39 N.Y. State Assembly, from 1987. Adj. lectr. Baruch Coll., CUNY. Mem. Cmty. Planning Bd.; mem. Mayor's Coun. on Intergroup Rels.; dir. Dem. Assembly Campaign Com., 1980-86; Dem. State Committeeman, 39th Assembly Dist., 1975—; del. Dem. Nat. Conv., 1978, 80, 82, 84; exec. dir. N.Y. State Legis. Commn. on Econ. and Efficiency in Govt. and Commn. Pub. Mgmt. Sys., 1979-86. Mem. K.C., B'nai B'rith. Died 1998.

GENSKOW, JACK KUENNE, psychology educator; b. Milw., Mar. 19, 1936; BS, U. Wis.-Milw., 1961; MA, U. Ill., 1962, PhD, 1967. Psychologist, dir. Decatur (Ill.) Evaluation Ctr., 1965-77; research utility specialist Ill. D.V.R., Springfield, 1977-78; assoc. prof. Sangamon State U., Springfield,

1978-88, prof., from 1988; psychol. cons. Goodwill Industries, Springfield, from 1978. Chair adv. coun. Ill. Dept. Rehab. Svcs., 1983-93; co-chair Rehab. R&T Ctr. adv. coun., U. Wis.-Stout. World Rehab. Fund fellow, 1986; recipient Marlene Nelson Service award Ill. Rehab. Assn., 1977, Harold Scharper Achievement award U. Ill., 1967. Mem. ACA, Am. Psychol. Assn., Nat. Rehab. Assn. Home: Springfield, Ill. Died Dec. 20, 2000.

GENTRY, GRANT CLAYBOURNE, food retail company executive; b. Chgo., June 5, 1924; s. Grant Claybourne and Helen C. (Cooley) Gentry; m. Doris L. Helsten, Sept. 8, 1943; children: Grant, Scott. JD, DePaul U., 1949. Bar: Ill. 1949. Assoc. McKnight, McLaughton & Dunn, 1949—53; tax atty. Internat. Harvester Co., 1953—57; exec. v.p., dir. Jewel Cos., Chgo., 1957—75; pres., chief adminstrn. officer, dir. Great Atlantic & Pacific Tea Co., Montvale, NJ, 1975—78; ptnr. Adamy, Foley & Gentry, Chgo., 1978—79; chmn., CEO Pantry Pride, Inc., Ft. Lauderdale, Fla., 1979—86; dir. Borman's Inc. Bd. dirs. Loyola U. Chgo. With AUS, 1943—46. Mem.: ABA, Nat. assn. Food Chaines, Internat. Assn. Chain Stores, Big Canyon Club, Park Ridge Country Club, Blindbrook County Club. Died Mar. 4, 2004.

GERMANOTTA, DANTE J. retired sociology educator; b. Racine, Wis., Sept. 3, 1929; s. Angelo Germanotta and Madelyn Schoeller; m. Betsy Erdman, June 14, 1952; children: Beth, Paul, John, Mary. BA, North Ctrl. U., 1951; STM, Evang. Theol. Sem., 1954; PhD, Boston U., 1968. Minister United Meth. Ch., Cambridge, Mass., 1957-60; minister edn. United Ch., Walpole, Mass., 1960-65; prof. sociology Claflin Coll., Orangeburg, S.C., 1965-68, Defiance (Ohio) Coll., 1968-73, Curry Coll., Milton, Mass., 1973-89, 90-93, acting dean, 1989-90. Contbr. articles, book revs. to profl. jours. State edn. coord. NAACP, Orangeburg, 1965-68; advisor Black Student Union, Defiance, 1968-72; mem. Edn. Collaborator, Boston, 1975-80; offcl. observer U.N. Conf. on Prisoners, Havana, 1990; adv. bd. Farm Labor Organising Com., Toledo, Ohio, 1969-73, Internat. Conf. on Prison Abolition, 1983-88; sch. com. Lincoln-Sudbury H.S., Mass., 1975-81; pres. Mass. Coun. Prison Edn., Milton, 1984-93. Knapp Fund scholar U. Wis., 1947-49; recipient Disting. Svc. award S.C. NAACP, 1968. Mem. AAUP. Avocations: bee keeping, camping, piano, clarinet, travel. Died Apr. 13, 2004.

GERMER, RICHARD ELIASON, oil company executive; b. Tremonton, Utah, Aug. 12, 1946; s. Kenneth Louis and Phylis (Eliason) G.; m. Ilene Kaye Uhrich, Apr. 13, 1968; children: Kim, Kyle, Kati. BBA, Utah State U., 1972. Sr. v.p. Flying J Inc., Brigham City, Utah, from 1972, also bd. dirs.; pres. Big West Oil Co., Brigham City, from 1986, also bd. dirs. Bd. dirs. Flying J Exploration and Prodn., Billings, Mont. Republican. Avocations: skiing, tennis. Home: Centerville, Utah. Died Mar. 15, 2003.

GERRISH, HOLLIS G. confectionery company executive; b. Berwick, Maine, June 23, 1907; s. Perley G. and Grace (Guptill) G.; widowed, 1997; AB, Harvard U., 1930, postgrad. Bus. Sch., 1930-31; m. Catherine G. Ruggles, Sept. 10, 1946. With Squirrel Brand Co., mfg. confectioners, 1931—, pres., 1939-42, 46—. Bd. dirs. Middlesex-Cambridge (Mass.) Lung Assn., Cambridge YMCA, East End House; corp. mem. Cambridge Home for the Aged; trustee Lesley Coll., Cambridge; corp. mem. New Eng. Deaconess Hosp. Served as lt. comdr. USNR, 1942-46; capt. USNR. Mem. Am. Soc. Candy Technologists, Cambridge Hist. Soc., Nat. Tax Assn., Mass. Audubon Soc. Episcopalian (trustee). Clubs: Harvard, Faculty, New England Confectioners, Norfolk Trout, Flycasters, Cambridge, Economy. Lodge: Rotary. Deceased. Home: Cambridge, Mass.

GERRY, ELBRIDGE THOMAS, banker; b. N.Y.C., Nov. 22, 1908; s. Robert L. and Cornelia (Harriman) G.; m. Marjorie Kane, May 21, 1932; children: Elbridge T., Peter G., Marjorie K. AB, Harvard U., 1931. With Hanover Bank, 1931-36; with Brown Brothers Harriman & Co., N.Y.C., 1936—, ptnr., 1956-95, ltd. ptnr., from 1996. Hon. trustee Am. Mus. Natural History. Deceased.

GETTING, IVAN ALEXANDER, physicist, former aerospace company executive; b. N.Y.C., Jan. 18, 1912; s. Milan and Harriet (Almasy) G.; m. Dorothea Louise Gracy, Oct. 2, 1937 (dec. Sept. 1976); children: Nancy Louise Secker, Ivan Craig, Peter Alexander; m. Helen Avery, Jan. 9, 1977. SB, MIT, 1933; DPhil, Oxford U., 1935; DSc (hon.), Northeastern U., 1954, U. So. Calif., 1986. Jr. fellow Harvard U., Cambridge, Mass., 1935-40; mem. staff, head divsn. 8 radiation lab. MIT, Cambridge, 1940-45, assoc. prof. elec. engring., 1945-46, prof., 1946-50; asst. for devel. planning, dep. chief of staff USAF, Washington, 1950-51; v.p. engring and research Raytheon Corp., Waltham, Mass., 1951-60; pres., chief exec. officer The Aerospace Corp., El Segundo, Calif., 1960-77. Cons. USAF, USN, U.S. Army, NRC, Dept. Def., others, 1945. Contbr. articles to profl. jours.; patentee in field. Former dir., Los Angeles World Affairs Council. Fellow: IEEE, IEEE (hon.; pres. 1978), Am. Inst. Physics; mem.: Nat. Acad. Engring. (Draper award 2003), Am. Acad. Arts and Scis., Cosmos Club, L.A. Yacht Club. Died Oct. 11, 2003.

GETTY, J. PAUL, foundation executive; b. Sept. 7, 1932; s. J. Paul and Ann Rork G.; m. Gail Harris, 1956 (div.); two children; m. Talitha Pol, 1966 (wid. 1971); 1 child; m. Victoria Holdsworth, 1994. With Getty Oil Italia, 1959-70; pres. The KBE Found., Reno, from 1991. Philanthropist to Nat. Gallery, London, 1985, others; provider charitable trust to help the homeless, community projects for young offenders, the preservation of old churches, programmes to rehab. prison inmates. Avocation: watching cricket and old movies. Died Apr. 17, 2003.

GEUTHER, ROBERT OTTO, manufacturing company executive, consultant; b. Mokena, Ill., Aug. 31, 1909; s. Nicholas J. and Charlotte (Hohenstein) G.; m. Erna F. Yunker, Mar. 28, 1931; children: Anita C. Peterson (dec.), Helen R. (dec.), Janet R. Anderson, Irene H. Adams. AA, Concordia Coll., Milw., 1930. Advt. copy chief U.S. Gypsum Co., Chgo., 1931-37; news editor Building The Nat. News Review, Chgo., 1937-41; copy chief Evans Assocs. Advt. Agy., Chgo., 1941-48; exec. v.p. H.D. Hudson Mfg. Co., Chgo., 1948-79, also bd. dirs., from 1971. Pres. Bd. Edn. Pub. Schs., Mokena, 1956-65; chmn. Mokena Plan Commn., 1961-65, Mokena Zoning Bd. Appeals, 1963-65; active Luth. Ch. Charities Fund, lifetime samaritan club mem.; mem. Southwest Suburban Genealogical and Hist. Soc., Frankfort Area Hist. Soc., Concordia Hist. Inst., Internat. Luth. Laymen's League, The Nature Conservancy, Nat. Arbor Day Found., Am. Heritage Soc., Nat. Geographic Soc., Smithsonian Assocs. Recipient Merit award Luth. Child and Family Svcs., 1973. Mem. Nat. Sprayer and Duster Assn. (pres. 1971, 72), Nat. Agricultural and Mktg. Assn. (bd. dirs, 1956—), Mokena C. of C. (Citizen of the Yr., 1964), Rotary Club (pub. Com. 1980-90). Republican. Avocations: reading, writing, photography, golf, gardening. Home: Valparaiso, Ind. Deceased.

GEYELIN, PHILIP LAUSSAT, journalist; b. Devon, Pa., Feb. 27, 1923; s. Emile Camille and Cecily (Barnes) G.; m. Cecilia Sherman Parker, Jan. 28, 1950; children— Mary Sherman, Emile Camille, Philip Laussat, Cecily Parker. Grad., Episcopal Acad., Overbrook, Pa., 1940; BA, Yale, 1944. With Washington bur. A.P., 1946-47; mem. staff Wall Street Jour., 1947-66, diplomatic corr., 1960-67; former mem. editorial staff Washington Post, editor editorial page, 1968-79, former syndicated columnist. Editor-in-residence Fgn. Policy Inst., Sch. Advanced Internat. Studies, Johns Hopkins U. Author: Lyndon B. Johnson and the World, 1966. Former mem. bd. dirs. Alliance Francaise, Washington; pres. bd. trustees Georgetown Day Sch., 1971-74. Served to 1st lt. USMCR, 1943-46. Fellow Inst. Politics Harvard Sch. Govt., 1967; recipient Pulitzer prize for editorial writing, 1969 Former mem. Council on Fgn. Relations (former dir.) Clubs: Gridiron, Overseas Writers, Federal City (Washington). Home: Washington, DC. Died Jan. 9, 2004.

GHIAUROV, NICOLAI, opera singer; b. Velingrad, Bulgaria, Sept. 13, 1929; m. Zlatina Ghiaurov; 2 children. Student, Acad. Music, Sofia, Bulgaria, Moscow Conservatory. Debut at Sofia Opera House in Barber of Seville, 1955; roles include Don Basilia in The Barber of Seville, King Philip in Don Carlo, Ramfis in Aida, Varlaanin Boris Godunov; appearances in maj. opera houses include La Scala, Lyric Opera Chgo., Met. Opera, Phila. Lyric Opera, London Royal Opera, Bolshoi Opera; recordings include (with various Bulgarian orchs.) The Art of Nikolai Ghiaurov, Opera aarias & Songs, Public Performances (1966-1970), Russian Romances. Recipient 1st prize Internat. Singin Contest Paris, 1955 Died June 2, 2004.

GIANNINI, GEMMA, photographer; b. Chgo., Sept. 21, 1951; d. Armando and Maria (Raffanti) G.; m. William Edward Schultz, Jan. 28, 1978. BA, U. Ill., Chgo., 1974, M of Health Professions Edn., 1981. Research asst. U. Ill., Chgo., 1974-78, instr., 1979-80; mgr. exams Am. Soc. Clin. Pathologists, Chgo., 1980-82, dir. exams, 1983; owner Signature Photography, Elk Grove Village, Ill., from 1987. Intern Profl. Photographer's Am., Mt. Prospect, Ill., 1986; test cons. Michael Reese Hosp., Chgo., 1979. Author: articles, Evaluation & Health Profls., 1986, Med. Edn., 1981; reviewer Health Care Edn., 1979; video tape and manual, Interview skills, 1976. Instr. workshop Am. Dietetic Assn., Chgo., 1979. Mem. Advt. Photographers Am. Roman Catholic. Avocation: horsemanship. Home: Mchenry, Ill. Died May 6, 2002.

GIARD, HENRY L. radiologist; b. Haverhill, Mass., Mar. 14, 1929; s. William J. and Lea H. (Chenevert) G.; m. Tomasina S. Giard, July 3, 1954; children: Linda, Carol. BS, Tufts U., 1952, MD, 1956. Diplomate Am. Bd. Radiology. Radiologist USN, 1956-76; pvt. practice radiology. Capt. USN 1970-76. Died Dec. 19, 1999.

GIBB, MAURICE, vocalist, songwriter; b. Isle of Man, Eng., Dec. 22, 1949; s. Hugh and Barbara; m. Yvonne; children: Adam, Samantha. Performed in: (with bros. Barry and Robin as group) amateur shows The Blue Cats, Manchester, in 1950's; formed: (with bros.) The Bee Gees, 1958, One Night Only, 1998; disbanded (with bros.), 1969, reunited (with bros.), 1971; appeared in (with bros.) local clubs, Brisbane, Australia; released: (with bros.) 1st single record Three Kisses of Love, Australia, 1963; appeared on (with bros.) own weekly TV show in, Australia, in 1960's; returned to (with bros.), Eng., 1967, signed with (with bros.), NEMS Enterprises; made 1st U.S. TV appearance on: (with bros.) Am. Bandstand, 1967; former rec. group for, Robert Stigwood Orgn.; composer (with bros.); music and lyrics for film Saturday Night Fever, 1977; title song of film Grease, 1978; appeared in film; appeared in film Sergeant Pepper's Lonely Hearts Club Band, 1978; albums include Bee Gees First, 1967, Horizontal, 1968, Idea, 1968, Rare, Precious and Beautiful, Volume I, 1968, Odessa, 1969, Best of the Bee Gees, 1969, Rare, Precious and Beautiful, Volume II, 1970, Cucumber Castle, 1970, Two Years On, 1971, To Whom It May Concern, 1972, Life in a Tin Can, 1973, Best of Bee Gees, Volume II, 1973, Mr. Natural, 1974, Main Course, 1976, Children of the World, 1976, Bee Gees Gold Volume I, 1976, Odessa, 1976, Here At Last...Bee Gees...Live, 1977, Saturday Night Fever, 1977, Sergeant Pepper's Lonely Hearts Club Band, 1978, Spirits Having Flown, 1978, Bee Gees Greatest Hits, 1979, Living Eyes, E.S.P., 1987, Best of, vols. 1 and 2, 1987, High Civilization, 1991, Size Isn't Everything, 1993, To Be Or Not To Be, 1995, Still Waters, 1997. Recipient Grammy award, 1971, 78; citation of achievement BMI, 1971, 75, 76, 77; Record of Yr. award Stereo Rev., 1973; Trendsetter award Billboard, 1977; Best Movie Soundtrack award Italian Record Reviewers, 1978; Ampex Golden Reel award; numerous RIAA Gold and Platinum albums and singles, numerous gold and platinum albums and singles from various locations, including Can., South Africa, Germany, Belgium, Holland, Australia, N.Z., France, Hong Kong; Named Pop Stars of Yr. Holland, 1967, Hon. Citizens of Man. (Can.), Hon. Citizens of City of Winnipeg, 1975, Hon. Citizens State of Fla., 1978; recipient Nat. 2UE award Australia, 1966, Golden Lion award Radio Luxemburg, 1967, Carl-Allan award Eng., 1967, Valentine award Eng., 1968, Iver Novello award, 1968-69, 76-77, 77-78; inducted Rock and Roll Hall of Fame, 1997. Died Jan. 12, 2003.

GIBSON, ALTHEA, retired professional tennis player, golfer, state official; b. Silver, S.C., Aug. 25, 1927; d. Daniel and Annie B. (Washington) G.; m. William A. Darben, Oct. 17, 1965; m. Sydney Llewellyn, Apr. 11, 1983. BS, Fla. A&M Coll., 1953; D. Pub. Service (hon.), Monmouth Coll., 1980; LittD (hon.), U. N.C., Wilmington, 1987; LHD (hon.), Upsala Coll., 1989. Amateur tennis player, U.S., Europe, and S.Am., 1941-58; asst. instr. dept. health and phys. edn. Lincoln U., Jefferson City, Mo., 1953-55; made profl. tennis tour with Harlem Globetrotters, 1959; community rels. rep. Ward Baking Co., 1959; joined Ladies Profl. Golf Assn. as profl. golfer, 1963; apptd. to N.Y. State Recreation Council, 1964; staff mem. Essex County Park Commn., Newark, 1970, recreation supr., 1970-71; dir. tennis programs, profl. Valley View Racquet Club, Northvale, N.J., 1972; tennis pro Morven; athletic commr. State of N.J., Trenton, 1975. Recreation mgr. City of East Orange, N.J., 1980; mem. N.J. State Athletic Control Bd., 1986; spl. cons. Gov.'s Coun. Phys. Fitness and Sports, N.J., 1988; winner world profl. tennis championship, 1960, Wimbledon Women's Singles Championship, 1957, 58, Wimbledon Women's Doubles Championship, 1956-58, U.S. Women's Singles Championship, 1957, 58. Appeared in the movie The Horse Soldiers, 1958; author: I Always Wanted to Be Somebody, 1958. Named Woman Athlete of Yr., AP Poll, 1957-58; named to Lawn Tennis Hall of Fame and Tennis Mus., 1971, Black Athletes Hall of Fame, 1974, S.C. Hall of Fame, 1983, Fla. Sports Hall of Fame, 1984, Sports Hall of Fame of N.J., 1994. Mem. Alpha Kappa Alpha. Died Sept. 28, 2003.

GIBSON, BRIAN, film director, film producer; b. Reading, Eng., Sept. 22, 1944; s. Victoria; m. Lynn Whitfield (div.); 1 child, Grace; m. Paula Guarderas; 1 child, Raphaela. Dir. (films): Joey, 1975, (TV) Where Adam Stood, 1976, Billion Dollar Bubble, 1976, Dinner at the Sporting Club, 1978, (TV) Blue Remembered Hills, 1980, Poltergeist II: The Other Side, 1986, The Murderers Among Us: The Simon Wiesenthal Story, 1989, (TV) Drug Wars: The Camarena Story, 1990, What's Love Got to Do With It, 1993, (TV) The Josephine Baker Story, 1991 (Emmy award 1991), The Juror, 1996, Still Crazy, 1998; writer, dir. Breaking Glass, 1980. Home: Sherman Oaks, Calif. Died Jan. 4, 2004.

GIBSON, COUNT DILLON, JR., physician, educator; b. Covington, Ga., July 10, 1921; s. Count Dillon and Julia (Thompson) G.; m. Katherine Vislocky, June 10, 1950; children— Gabriella, Thomas, Alexis, George. BS, Emory U., 1942; MD, 1944. Diplomate: Am. Bd. Internal Medicine. Intern Columbia-Presbyn. Med. Center, 1944-45, asst. resident medicine, 1947-50, med. resident, 1950-51; asst. prof., asso. prof. medicine Med. Coll. Va., 1951-57; prof. preventive medicine, chmn. dept. Tufts U. Sch. Medicine, Boston, 1958-69; physician-in-chief Home Med. Service; attending physician New Eng. Med. Ctr. Hosps.; gen. dir. Tufts-Columbia Point Health Ctr.; vis. physician Boston City Hosp., to 1969; prof., chmn. dept. family, community and preventive medicine Stanford (Calif.) U., 1969-87, prof. dept. health research and policy, 1988-91, prof. emeritus, from 1991. Mem. Calif. Health Manpower Policy Commn., 1977-85; pres. SimulMed, Inc., 1997—. Contbr. articles to profl. jours. Bd. dirs. Hayward (Calif.) Vesper Hosp., 1980-85, Drew Health Found., 1988-90. Capt. M.C., AUS, 1945-47. Mem. A.C.P. Roman Catholic. Died July 23, 2002.

GIBSON, DON, country western musician; b. Shelby, N.C., Apr. 3, 1928; Writer: (songs) I Can't Stop Loving You, 1958, Oh Lonesome Me; writer, musician: (songs) Give Myself a Party, Blue Blue Day, Sea of Heartbreak, Lonesome Number One, Woman, 1972; albums include Don't Stop Loving Me, Rockin' Rollin' Gibson, The Best of Don Gibson. inducted into Country Music Hall of Fame, 2001. Died Nov. 17, 2003.

GIBSON, ELEANOR JACK (MRS. JAMES J. GIBSON), retired psychologist, educator; b. Peoria, Ill., Dec. 7, 1910; d. William A. and Isabel (Grier) Jack; m. James J. Gibson, Sept. 17, 1932; children: James J., Jean Grier. BA, Smith Coll., 1931, MA, 1933, DS (hon.), 1972; PhD, Yale U., 1938, DS (hon.), 1996, Rutgers U., 1973, Trinity Coll., 1982, Bates Coll., 1985, U. S.C., 1987, Emory U., 1990, Middlebury Coll., 1993; LHD (hon.), SUNY, Albany, 1984, Miami U., 1989. From asst. to asst. prof. Smith Coll., 1931—49; rsch. assoc. psychology Cornell U., Ithaca, NY,

1949—66, prof., from 1973, Susan Linn Sage prof. psychology, from 1972. Vis. prof. MIT, 1973, Inst. Child Devel., U. Minn., 1980; Disting. vis. prof. U. Calif., Davis, 1978; vis. scientist Salk Inst., La Jolla, Calif., 1979; vis. prof. U. Pa., 1984; Woodruff vis. prof. psychology Emory U., 1988—90. Author: Principles of Perceptual Learning and Development, 1967 (Century award); author: (with H. Levin) The Psychology of Reading, 1975; author: Odyssey in Learning and Perception, 1991; author: (with Anne Pick) Ecological Approach to Perceptual Learning and Development, 2000; author: Perceiving the Affordances: A Portrait of Two Psychologists, 2001. Recipient Wilbur Cross medal, Yale U., 1973, medal for disting. svc., Tchrs. Coll. Columbia U., 1983, Nat. medal Sci., 1992, Lifetime Achievement award, Internat. Soc. Ecol. Psychology, William James fellowship, Am. Psychol. Soc., 1989; fellow, Guggenheim Found., 1972—73, Inst. Advanced Study, Princeton, 1959—60, Inst. Advanced Study in Behavioral Scis., Stanford, Calif., 1963—64, Montgomery fellow, Dartmouth Coll., 1986. Fellow: APA (pres. divsn. 3 1977, Disting. Scientist award 1968, G. Stanley Hall award 1970, Gold medal award 1986), AAAS (divsn. chair 1983); mem.: NAS, Vt. Acad. Sci. and Engring., Am. Acad. Arts and Scis., Soc. Rsch. in Child Devel. (Disting. Sci. Contbn. award 1981), Psychonomic Soc., Nat. Acad. Edn., Soc. Exptl. Psychologists (Howard Crosby Warren medal 1977), Ea. Psychol. Assn. (pres. 1968), Italian Soc. Rsch. in Child Devel. (hon.), N.Y. Acad. Scis. (hon.), Brit. Psychol. Soc. (hon.), Sigma Xi, Phi Beta Kappa. Home: Middlebury, Vt. Died Dec. 30, 2002.

GIBSON, MARX A. b. Champaign, Ill., Dec. 24, 1940; s. Marx A. Sr. and Mildred I. (Dodge) G.; m. Marjorie Ann DeVries, Oct. 29, 1967 (dec. Apr. 1982); children: Jorie, Greg, Amy; m. Dolores Kane, Oct. 27, 1984; 1 stepchild, Keith Edward Gawla; 1 adopted child, Andrew Kpedi. Student, Govs. State U., University Park, Ill., 1965, U. Maine, 1958-61, U. Kans., 1958-61. Exec. editor Star Publs., Harvey, Ill., 1965-74; city editor The Herald-News, Joliet, Ill., 1974-80; mng. editor The Daily Jour., Kankakee, Ill., 1980-90; city editor The Herald-News, Joliet, 1990-93, mng. editor, 1993-94, gen. mgr., 1994-96; v.p. Fox Valley Press, Inc., Plainfield, Ill., from 1995. Bd. dirs. Apex Quality Impressions, Lockport, Ill.; cons. Top Gun Writers, Elwood, Ill., 1990-96. Bd. dirs., sec. St. Joseph Med. Ctr., Joliet, 1996; v.p., bd. dirs. Guardian Angel Home, Joliet, 1996. Served with USAF, 1961-65, Turkey. Named Editor of Yr., Ill. Press Assn., 1978; recipient more than 100 awards for writing. Mem. Ill. Press Found. (bd. dirs. 1994—), Kiwanis Club of Joliet (bd. dirs. 1994-96). Avocations: fishing, reading, writing, travel. Home: Manteno, Ill. Died July 9, 2000.

GIDDENS, ZELMA KIRK, broadcast executive; b. Lafayette, Ala.; d. James William and Eunice (Rice) Kirk; grad. So. Union Jr. Coll., 1932; student Auburn U., 1934-35; m. Kenneth R. Giddens, May 19, 1934; children: Annsley Giddens Green, Therese Giddens Greer, Sara Kay Glenday. With Sta. WKRG-AM, 1947-55; with Sta. WKRG-AM-FM-TV, Mobile, Ala., 1955—, vice chmn., treas., 1960—. Founder, Mus. for Women's Art, Washington; trustee, Nat. Symphony. Mem. Smithsonian Assos., Mobile C. of C., Nat. Gallery Art Circle, Friends of Kennedy Ctr., Nat. Press Club, Am. Newspaper Women's Assn. Died Sept. 26, 1994. Home: Mobile, Ala.

GIENAPP, WILLIAM EUGENE, history educator; b. Denton, Tex., Feb. 27, 1944; s. William Herman and June Beatrice (Wade) G.; m. Erica Lee Kilian, Aug. 24, 1968; children: William Kenneth, Jonathan Eric. BA, U. Calif., Berkeley, 1967, PhD, 1980; MA, Yale U., 1969. Acting. instr. U. Calif., Berkeley, 1979-80; asst. prof. U. Wyo., Laramie, 1980-85, assoc. prof., 1985-89; prof. Harvard U., Cambridge, Mass., 1989—2003. Chmn. Lincoln Prize Jury, 1997, Avery Craven Award Com., 1998; bd. advisors Lincoln Forum, Lincoln Studies Ctr., Knox Coll., 1997-2002; mem. adv. bd. Hist. Soc., 1998-2000; mem. adv. com. Abraham Lincoln Bicentennial Commn. Author: Origins of the Republican Party, 1987 (Avery Craven award, 1988); co-author: Nation of Nations, 1990, 2d edit., 1993, 3rd edit., 1997, 4th edit., 2000, Why the War Came, 1996, Nation of Nations: Concise Narrative, 1995, 3d edit., 2001, Civil War and Reconstruction, 2001, Abraham Lincoln and Civil War America, 2002, This Fiery Trial: The Speeches and Writings of Abraham Lincoln, 2002, Abraham Lincoln and Civil War America: A Biography, 2002; mem. editl. bd. Presidential Papers of Abraham Lincoln. Mem. Civil War Soc., So. Hist. Assn., Hist. Soc., Soc. Hists. Early Republic, Soc. Am. Baseball Rsch. Home: Lincoln, Mass. Died Oct. 29, 2003.

GIFFIN, HERBERT MARTIN, surgeon; b. Atlantic City, Dec. 22, 1909; s. Samuel Robert and Edith May (Boothby) G.; m. Cleda Arlene Martin, 1942 (dec. 1988); children: Claire L., Arlene E., Charles Bradford, Robert Bruce. AB, Princeton U., 1931; MD, Johns Hopkins U., 1935. Diplomate Am. Bd. Surgery. Resident in surgery U. Pa., Phila., 1935-37; fellow Mayo Grad. Sch. Mayo Grad. Sch. U. Minn., Rochester, 1937-42; first asst. in surgery Mayo Clinic, Rochester, 1940-42; surgeon Yater Clinic, Washington, from 1947, dir., chmn. bd. dirs., 1970-76. Clin. assoc. prof. surgery Georgetown U., Washington, 1960—; mem. staff George Washington U. Hosp., Washington Hosp. Ctr., Sibley Meml. Hosp.; former mem. staff Children's Hosp., Suburban Hosp., Arlington Hosp.; lectr. VA Hosp., Bethesda Naval Hosp., Walter Reed Hosp. Elder Chevy Chase Presbyn. Ch., Washington, 1952—. Lt. comdr., USN, 1942-47. Fellow ACS; mem. D.C. Med. Soc., AMA, Washington Acad. Surgery, Gen. Soc. Mayflower Descendants (surgeon gen. 1970-73), Soc. Mayflower Descendants in D.C. (surgeon 1965—). Republican. Avocations: history, geneology, hiking, farming, writing. Home: Annandale, Va. Died Dec. 23, 1999.

GIFFIN, MARY ELIZABETH, psychiatrist, educator; b. Rochester, Minn., Mar. 30, 1919; d. Herbert Ziegler and Mary Elizabeth (Nace) G. BA, Smith Coll., Northampton, Mass., 1939; MD, Johns Hopkins, 1943; MS, U. Minn., 1948. Diplomate Am. Bd. Psychiatry and Neurology. Cons. in neurology and psychiatry Mayo Clinic, Rochester, 1949-58; med. dir. Josselyn Clinic, Northfield, Ill., 1958-89; pvt. practice psychiatry Northfield, from 1989. Mem. faculty Inst. for Psychoanalysis, Chgo., 1963-89. Contbr. numerous articles to profl. jour. Mem. Ill. Psychiat. Soc., Am. Acad. Child Psychiatry. Republican. Mem. Am. Bapt. Ch. Avocation: creative writing. Home: Winnetka, Ill. Deceased.

GIFFORD, JONATHAN BERRY, architect; b. Aurora, Ill., Dec. 10, 1942; s. William Carleton and Jewel Berry G.; m. Helen Grube, Sept. 10, 1966; children: Jonathan Knell, Peter Berry. AB, Stanford U., 1964, MArch, 1966. Draftsman CSS Assocs. Architects, Palo Alto, Calif., 1966-71, assoc., 1971-78, v.p., 1978-79, pres., from 1979-. Dir. Palo Alto-Stanford Heritage, Palo Alto, 1988. Pres. Palo Alto YMCA, 1980, sr. dir., 1988--; chmn. City of Palo Alto Historic Resources Bd., 1988. Mem. AIA (bd. dirs. Santa Clara chpt.), Rotary. Avocations: fishing, gardening, swimming. Home: Palo Alto, Calif. Deceased.

GIFFORD, RAY WALLACE, JR., retired physician, educator; b. Westerville, Ohio, Aug. 13, 1923; s. Ray Wallace and Alma Marie (Wagoner) G.; m. Frances Anne Moore, Jan. 13, 1973; 1 son, George; children by previous marriage: Peggy, Cynthia, Susan. BS, Otterbein Coll., 1944, ScD (hon.), 1986; MD, Ohio State U., 1947; M.Sc., U. Minn., 1952. Diplomate: Am. Bd. Internal Medicine. Intern Colo. Gen. Hosp., Denver, 1947-48; fellow in internal medicine Mayo Clinic, Rochester, Minn., 1949-52; practice medicine specializing in hypertension and nephrology; asst. prof. medicine, cons. sect. medicine Mayo Clinic, Mayo Found., Rochester, 1953-61; staff mem. dept. hypertension and nephrology Cleve. Clinic Found., 1961-67, head dept. hypertension and nephrology, 1967-85, sr. physician dept. hypertension and nephrology, 1986-93, acting chmn. dept. hypertension and nephrology, 1991-92, cons. dept. hypertension and nephrology, 1994-99, bd. govs., 1973-78, vice chmn., 1977-78, vice chmn. div. medicine, 1978-93, chmn. regional health affairs, 1986-93, 94-98; prof. internal medicine Ohio State U. Coll. Medicine, Columbus, Ohio, 1993—2000. Asst. attending physician U.S. Congress, 1954-56; chmn. hypertension task force Intersoc. Commn. on Heart Disease Resources, 1979-81; mem. nat. high blood pressure coordinating com. Nat. Heart, Lung and Blood Inst., 1978-2004; mem. 2d, 3d, 4th, 6th and 7th, and chmn. 5th joint nat. coms. on detection, evaluation and treatment of high blood pressure, 1979-80, 83-84, 87-88, 91-92, 96-97, 2003; mem. Congl. Commn. on Drug Approval Process, 1981-82; mem. adv. com. to dir. NIH, 1982-86; mem. Joint Commn. on Accreditation of Healthcare Orgns., 1989-90; mem. Forum on Drug Devel., Inst. Medicine, 1990-94. Author (with William Manger): Pheochromocytoma, 1977, 1996, 100 Questions and Answers About Hypertension, 2001; editl. bd.: Stroke Jour., 1971—74, Am. Jour. Cardiology, 1973—78, mem. editl. bd.: Geriatrics, 1974—2002, Hypertension Rsch., 1994—99, Jour. Cardiovascular Risk, 1994—98, Jour. Geriatric Cardiology, 1994—98; contbr. numerous papers to med. jours. Mem. Rochester City Coun., 1960-61, Rep. precinct committeeman, Cleveland Heights, Ohio, 1966-70. Lt. comdr. M.C., USNR, 1954-56. Recipient Alumni Achievement award Ohio State U., 1962, Alumni Medalist award, 1989; Disting. Sci. Achievement award Otterbein Coll., 1970, Spl. Achievement award, 1992; individual achievement award high blood pressure edn. programs Nat. Heart, Lung and Blood Inst., 1989, Bristol Myers lifetime achievement award Am. Heart Assn., 1992; spl. achievement award Cleve. Clinic Alumni Assn., 1994; Ray W. Gifford, Jr. endowed chair in hypertension established at Cleve. Clinic, 1994; named to Cleve. Med. Hall of Fame, 1997. Fellow ACP (master), Am. Coll. Cardiology (bd. trustees 1969-70, gov. Ohio chpt. 1970-73), Am. Coll. Chest Physicians (chmn. com. on hypertension 1970-72, Simon Rodbard Meml. award 1982); mem. AMA (coun. on sci. affairs 1976-85, vice chmn. 1981-83, chmn. 1983-85, trustee 1986-90), Am. Heart Assn. (bd. dirs. 1969-72, chmn. stroke coun. 1970-72), Am. Soc. Clin. Pharmacology and Therapeutics (pres. 1976-77, Oscar B. Hunter Meml. award in Therapeutics 1979, Henry W. Elliott award Disting. Svc. 1995), Ctrl. Soc. Clin. Rsch., Internat. Soc. Hypertension, Interstate Postgrad. Med. Assn. (pres. 1976-77), Interam. Soc. Hypertension, Coun. on Geriatric Cardiology (bd. dirs. 1989-92), Ohio State U. Alumni Assn. (bd. dirs. 1990-95). Methodist. Home: Fountain Hills, Ariz. Died May 4, 2004.

GIKNIS, FRANCIS LAWRENCE, cardiologist, retired; b. Turners Falls, Mass., Sept. 5, 1921; MD, Tufts U., 1946. Diplomate Am. Bd. Internal Medicine. Ensign USN, 1942, advanced through grades to lt. (j.g.), 1946; intern USN Hosp., Chelsea, Mass., 1946-47, resident in internal medicine, 1947, 49-52; resident in pathology Northeastern Deacon and Children's Hosp., Boston, 1950-51; resident in cardioogy USN Hosp., San Diego, 1959-60; clin. assoc. prof. medicine Albany (N.Y.) Med. Coll.; chief cardiology Ellis Hosp., Schenectady, N.Y., 1966-72. Fellow ACP, Coun. on Clin. Cardiology, Am. Heart Assn. Home: Schenectady, NY. Died July 27, 2000.

GILB, CORINNE LATHROP, history educator; b. Lethbridge, Alta., Can., Feb. 19, 1925; d. Glen Hutchinson and Vera (Passey) Lathrop; m. Tyrell Thompson Gilb, Aug. 19, 1945 (dec. July 6, 2001); 1 child, Lesley Gilb Taplin; 1 child, Tyra. BA, U. Wash., 1946; MA, U. Calif., Berkeley, 1951, law student, 1950-53; PhD, Harvard U., 1957. History lectr. Mills Coll., Oakland, 1957-61; prof. humanities San Francisco State U., 1964-68; rsch. assoc. U. Calif., Berkeley, 1953—67; prof. history Wayne State U., Detroit, 1968-94, co-dir. Liberal Arts Urban Studies program, 1976-86; dir. planning City of Detroit, 1979-85; pres. Atherton Press, Calif., from 1997. Spl. cons. Calif. Legislature, 1963, 64; vis. scholar Hoover Instn., Stanford U., fall 1993; UN Nongovtl. Orgn. rep. Internat. Orgn. for Unification of Terminological Neologisms, 1995—. Author: (history books) Conformity of State to Federal Income Tax, 1964, Hidden Hierarchies, 1966, Toward Holistic History, 2004, The World's Earliest Cities, 2004. Guggenheim fellow, France and Yugoslavia, 1968; grantee Social Sci. Rsch. Coun. Mem. Internat. Soc. Comparative Study of Civilizations (five terms exec. coun., 1st v.p. 1995-98), No. Calif. World Affairs Coun., Commonwealth Club, Churchill Club, various acad. assns. Presbyterian. Home: Atherton, Calif. Died Jan. 20, 2003.

GILBERT, JOHN ROBERT, advertising and public relations agency executive; b. Long Beach, Calif., July 17, 1946; s. Walter E. and Marian S. Gilbert; m. Patricia R. Rector, Apr. 20, 1974; 1 child, Kent E. BA, Washington U., St. Louis, 1969. Announcer Starr Broadcasting, Kansas City, Mo., 1971-72; prime time news mgr. Greater Kansas City C. of C., 1972-74; mgr. pub. info. Mo. Pub. Svc. Co., Kansas City, 1974-80; sr. v.p. The Boasberg Co., Kansas City, 1980-90; CEO, Gilbert, Christopher & Assocs., Kansas City, 1990-95; v.p. Bernstein-Rein Advt., Kansas City, from 1995. Bd. dirs. Mo. Bank and Trust, Kansas City. Bd. govs. Am. Royal, Kansas City, 1994—. Capt. U.S. Army, 1969-71. Mem. Pub. Rels. Soc. Am., Greater Kansas City C. of C. (small bus. com. 1994—). Avocations: racing sports cars, collecting classic cars. Home: Shawnee Mission, Kans. Died 1999.

GILCHRIST, ROBERT SPENCER, retired education educator; b. Kans., Aug. 20, 1905; s. William Robert and Elizabeth (Allen) G.; m. Marjorie Hamilton Gilchrist, Sept. 1928 (div. Nov. 1944); 1 child, Norma Lou; m. Adele Ackworthy Green Gilchrist, Sept. 1, 1945; children: William, Robert, Suzanne Adele AB, No. Colo. U., 1927, MA, 1928; postgrad., NYU. Tchr. 4th, 5th grades, Severance, Colo., 1922; tchr. grades 5-9, head of 2 tchr. sch. Pritkin, Colo., 1923; tchr. social studies, math. jr. h.s., Webster Groves, Mo., 1928; dir. Big Bend Tng. Sch., jr. h.s. supr. Colo. Tchrs. Coll., Greeley, 1928; prin. Maplewood (Mo.) Jr. H.S., 1930, Lyndover (Mo.) Elem. Sch., 1930, Ben Franklin Jr. H.S., Ridgewood, N.J., 1931-35; prin., dir. secondary edn. Greeley, Colo., 1935; dir. U. Sch., prof. edn. Ohio State U., Columbus, Ohio, 1941; asst. supt. secondary edn. Mpls., 1946; assoc. supt. instrn., 1948; asst. supt. instrn. Pasadena, Calif., 1949; supt. schs. University City, Mo., 1955; dir. curriculum Edn. Rsch. Coun. Am., Cleve., 1964; dir. Mid-Continent Regional Edn. Lab., Kansas City, Mo., 1966; prof. edn., sch. adminstrn. U.S. Internat. U., San Diego, 1969-76; retired, 1976. Dir. Student Work Program Nat. Youth Adminstrn., Washington, 1941; coord. Grandpeople vol. program Westwood Elem. Sch. Poway (Calif.) Unified Sch. Dist., Gradpeople Citizen program, Twin Peaks Middle Sch., 1983; rschr. in field; developer Home, Sch. and Cmty. Teamwork for Quality Edn., 1992. Author (with others) Curriculum Development: A Humanized Approach, 1974; contbr. numerous articles to profl. jours. Mem. Am. Assn. Sch. Adminstrs. (emeritus, Disting. Svc. award in Edn. 1980). Congregationalist. Home: Chula Vista, Calif. Died Apr. 28, 2002.

GILDEN, GLEN GARTH, minister; b. Anacortes, Wash., Sept. 12, 1926; s. Glen Garth and Charlie (Brown) G.; m. Melba Vileen Osborn, Dec. 27, 1947; children: Sharon Christine Gilden Gayagas, Glen Jr., Sheryl Cathleen Gilden Jones, Ronald. BA, Whitworth Coll., 1948; MSW, Portland (Oreg.) State U., 1964. Ordained to ministry Salvation Army, 1949; registered social worker. Comdg. officer Salvation Army, Wash., Mont., Oreg., Ariz., 1949-67, divisional sec., 1967-73, dir. social svc. Hong Kong, 1973-82; asst. prin. Sch. for Officers' Tng., L.A., 1982-83; pub. rels. dir. Salvation Army, Mexico City, 1984-88, comdg. officer Riverside, Calif., from 1989. Bd. dirs. Sunday Sch. Conf., Riverside, 1990-91. Mem. NASW. Home: Sun City, Calif. Died Mar. 11, 2001.

GILELS, ZINAIDA, violinist, instructor; b. Odessa, USSR, Feb. 2, 1924; came to U.S., 1985; d. Grigori and Rosalia (Diner) G.; m. Vladimir Muravyov; 1 child, Victor. MA, Moscow State Conservatory, 1949. Prof. of violin Ctrl. Music Sch. Moscow State Conservatory, 1960-83, asst. to prof. Yankelevich, founder modern violin sch., 1960-73; mem. faculty Longy Sch. Music, Boston, from 1986, New England Conservatory, Boston, from 1989, Boston Conservatory, from 1994. Vis. prof. Inst. Musicale St. Cecilia, Portogruaro, Italy, 1986—, Kuhmo (Finland) Violin Sch. and Festival, 1987-92, Music Sch. Fiesola, Italy, 1992—, Ryoko Saski Sch. Music, Tokyo, 1994; jury mem. The Paganini Internat. Competition, Genoa, Italy, 1991. Home: Allston, Mass. Died May 7, 2000.

GILLESPIE, ROBERT HALL, retired obstetrician, gynecologist; b. Florence, S.C., Dec. 16, 1910; s. Richard Thomas and Elizabeth Leslie (Hall) G.; m. Charlotte Hazeltine Granberry, July 16, 1942; children: Jan, Miriam, Emily,

Laura. BS, Presbyn. Coll., Clinton, S.C., 1932; MD, Emory U., 1938. Diplomate Am. Bd. Ob-gyn. From intern to resident in ob-gyn. Grady Meml. Hosp., Atlanta, 1938-42; pvt. practice, 1945-80; med. cons. Soc. Against Disability, Ga., 1980-89. Fellow ACOG; mem. AMA, Med. Assn. Atlanta, South Atlantic Assn. Ob-gyn. Home: Atlanta, Ga. Died Aug. 31, 1999.

GINSBERG, HAROLD SAMUEL, retired virologist, educator; b. Daytona Beach, Fla., May 27, 1917; s. Jacob and Anne (Kalb) G.; m. Marion Reibstein, Aug. 4, 1949; children: Benjamin Langer, Peter Robert, Ann Meredith, Jane Elizabeth. AB, Duke U., 1937; MD, Tulane U., 1941, DSc (hon.), 1995, hon. degree, 1996. Resident Mallory Inst. Pathology, Boston, 1941-42; intern, asst. resident Boston City Hosp., 4th Med. Service, 1942-43; resident physician, assoc. Rockefeller Inst., 1946-51; assoc. prof. preventive medicine Western Res. U. Sch. Medicine, 1951-60; prof. microbiology, chmn. dept. U. Pa. Sch. Medicine, 1960-73, Coll. Phys. and Surg. Columbia, 1973-85, prof. microbiology and medicine, dir. section molecular pathogenesis of infection, 1986-97. Part time expert scientist NIH, Rockville, Md., 1993-99; mem. commn. acute respiratory diseases Armed Forces Epidemiological Bd., 1959-73; cons. NIH, 1959-72, 75—, Army Chem. Corps, 1962-64, NASA, 1969-73, Am. Cancer Soc., 1969-73, mem. coun. on rsch. and pers., 1976-80; v.p. Internat. Com. on Nomenclature of Viruses, 1966-75; mem. space sci. bd., chmn. panel microbiology Nat. Acad. Sci., 1973-74; chmn. microbiology exam. com. Nat. Bd. Med. Examiners, 1974-79; mem. microbiology and infectious disease com. Nat. Inst. Allergy and Infectious Disease, NIH, 1976-81, chmn., 1979-81; co-chmn. Inst. Medicine, NAS Roundtable: AIDS: Modern Approaches Vaccines and Anti-Viral Drugs, 1989-92; mem. U.S. Nat. Com. for Internat. Union of Microbiological Socs. (USNC/IUMS), Nat. Rsch. Coun., 1992-97. Contbr. textbooks; co-author: Microbiology, 1967, 4th edit., 1990, Virology, 2d edit., 1988, Vaccines 88-95, Modern Approaches to New Vaccines, Including Prevention of AIDS; mem. editorial bd. Jour. Infectious Diseases, Jour. Immunology, Jour. Exptl. Medicine, Jour. Virology and Bacteriological Revs., Jour. Acquired Immune Deficiency Syndromes; editor: Jour. Virology, 1979-84, Cancer Research, 1978-82. Served to lt. col. M.C. AUS, 1943-46. Decorated Legion of Merit; Fogarty scholar NIH, 1993-94; recipient Disting. Svc. award Coll. Physicians and Surgeons, Columbia U., 1991, Acad. medal N.Y. Acad. Medicine, 1994, Bristol-Myers Squibb award for Disting. Achievement in Infectious Disease Rsch., 1994, Outstanding Alumnus award Tulane Sch. Medicine, 1995. Fellow AAAS; mem. NAS, Inst. Medicine of NAS., Assn. Am. Physicians, Am. Acad. Microbiologists (chmn. bd. govs. 1971-72, bd. govs. 1993-99), Am. Soc. Clin. Investigation (councillor 1958-60), Am. Assn. Immunologists, Am. Soc. Microbiology (chmn. virology div. 1961-62, councillor div. 1977-81), Soc. Exptl. Biology and Medicine, Assn. Med. Sch. Microbiology Chairmen (pres. 1972-73), Harvey Soc. (pres. 1984coun. 1985-88), Cen. Soc. Clin. Research, Am. Soc. Biol. Chemists, Am. Soc. Virology (pres. 1983), Alpha Omega Alpha. Home: Bethesda, Md. Died Feb. 2, 2003.

GINSBERG, PEARL, teacher, bookkeeper; b. Bklyn., Apr. 29, 1920; d. Joseph and Anna (Ballenszweig) G. BA, NYU, 1960, MA, 1962, cert. paralegal, 1965. Bookkeeper Hudson Greeting Cards, N.Y.C., 1946-51; ward clk. Montefiore Hosp., Bronx, N.Y., 1952-55; tchr. Bd. Edn., Bronx, N.Y., 1962-85; mem. bd. edn. Dist. 11, from 1988. Recipient Humanitarian award Assn. Jewish Profls., Orange County, N.Y., 1990, Lifetime Achievement award, 1994. Mem. LWV, United Fedn. Tchrs. Democrat. Jewish. Avocations: reading, knitting, travel, bridge, walking. Home: Bronx, NY. Deceased.

GINZBERG, ELI, economist, emeritus educator, writer, foundation administrator, consultant; b. N.Y.C., Apr. 30, 1911; s. Louis and Adele (Katzenstein) Ginzberg; m. Ruth Szold, July 14, 1946 (dec. Aug. 1995); children: Abigail, Jeremy, Rachel. Student, U. Heidelberg, U. Grenoble, 1928—29; AB, Columbia U., 1931, AM, 1932, PhD, 1934, LittD, 1982, Jewish Theol. Sem., 1966; LLD, Loyola U., Chgo., 1969; LHD, Rush U., 1985; DHL, Kirksville Osteo. Sch., 1993; LLD, Phila. Coll. Osteo. Medicine, 1994; DHL, State Coll. of Optometry, N.Y., 1995; DSc, N.Y. Coll. Osteo Medicine, 1996. Faculty Columbia U., N.Y.C., from 1935, dir. rsch. econs. and group behavior, 1948—49, 1939—42, A. Barton Hepburn prof. econs. Grad. Sch. Bus., 1967—79, prof. emeritus, spl. lectr. Grad. Sch. Bus., from 1979, dir. conservation human resources project, 1950—90, dir. Eisenhower Ctr. for Conservation Human Resources, from 1990; dir. Revson Fellows Program for Future City of N.Y., from 1979. Adj. prof. health and socl. Barnard Coll., 1980—88; spl. lectr. health and soc. Sch. Pub. Health, Columbia U., from 1989; hon. faculty mem. Indsl. Coll. Armed Forces; chmn. bd. Manpower Demonstration Rsch. Corp., 1974—82, chmn. bd. emeritus, 1982—98; spl. asst. to chief statistician U.S. War Dept., 1942—44; spl. asst. to dir. hosp. divsn. U.S. War Dept. (Surgeon Gen.'s Office), 1944, dir. resources analysis divsn., 1944—46; cons. Dept. Army, 1946—70, Dept. State, 1953, 56, 1965—69, Dept. Labor, 1954—82, Dept. Def., 1964—71, Dept. Commerce, 1965—66, 1979—80, GAO, 1973—82, Exec. Office Pres., 1942; mem. med. adv. bd. to Sec. War, 1946—48; U.S. rep. 5 power Conf. Reparations for Non-Repatriable Refugees, 1946; dir. N.Y. State Hosp. Study, 1948—49; mem. Com. on Wartime Requirements for Sci. and Specialized Pers., 1942; med. cons. Hoover Commn., 1952; adviser Commn. Chronic Illness, 1950—53; mem. adv. coun. NIMH, 1959—63; chmn. com. on studies White House Conf. on Children and Youth, 1960; dir. staff studies Nat. Manpower Coun., 1951—61; chmn. Nat. Manpower Adv. Com., 1962—74, Nat. Commn. for Manpower Policy, 1974—79, Nat. Commn. for Employment Policy, 1979—82; mem. Nat. Adv. Allied Health Coun., 1968—72; mem. sci. adv. bd. USAF, 1969—73; chmn. taskforce manpower rsch. Dept. Def., 1970—71; mem. Inst. Medicine, NAS, from 1972; mem. Office of Sci. and Engring. pers. adv. com. NAS, 1984—91; advisor Internat. Inst. Mgmt. Sci. Ctr., Berlin, 1982—89; mem. ORT Acad. Adv. Coun., 1984—91, chmn., from 1991; mem. Econ. Policy Coun. UN Assn. USA, 1984—87; co-chair adv. com. Job Creation Project Nat. Com. for Full Employment, 1984—86; mem. Mayoral Commn. to Consider Future of Child Health in N.Y.C., 1987—88; mem. med. adv. bd. Hadassah-Hebrew U., 1988—97; bd. dirs. Found. Biomed. Rsch., from 1988; mem. Mayoral Commn. to Rev. Health and Hosps. Corp., 1991—92. Author: The House of Adam Smith, 1934, The Illusion of Economic Stability, 1939, Grass on the Slag Heaps: The Story of the Welsh Miners, 1942, The Unemployed, 1943, The Labor Leader, 1948, A Pattern for Hospital Care, 1949, Agenda for American Jews, 1950, Occupational Choice, 1951, The Uneducated, 1953, Psychiatry and Military Manpower Policy, 1953, What Makes an Executive, 1955, The Negro Potential, 1956, Effecting Change in Large Organizations, 1957, Human Resources, 1958, The Ineffective Soldier, 3 vols., 1959, The Nations's Children, 3 vols., 1960, Planning for Better Hospital Care, 1961, The Optimistic Tradition and American Youth, 1962, The American Worker in The Twentieth Century, 1963, The Troublesome Presence, 1964, Talent and Performance, 1964, The Negro Challenge to the Business Community, 1964, The Pluralistic Economy, 1965, Keeper of the Law: Louis Ginzberg, 1966, Life Styles of Educated Women, 1966, Educated American Women-Self-Portraits, 1966, Manpower Strategy for Developing Countries, 1967, The Middle Class Negro in the White Man's World, 1967, Manpower Strategy for the Metropolis, 1968, Business Leadership and the Negro Crisis, 1968, Men, Money and Medicine, 1969, Urban Health Services-The Case of New York, 1971, Manpower Advice for Government, 1972, New York Is Very Much Alive, 1973, Corporate Lib: Women's Challenge to Management, 1973, Federal Manpower in Transition, 1974, The Great Society: Lessons for the Future, 1974, The University Medical Center and the Metropolis, 1974, The Future of the Metropolis, 1974, The Manpower Connection: Education and Work, 1975, Jobs for Americans, 1976, The Human Economy, 1976, Regionalization and Health Policy, 1977, The Limits of Health Reform, 1977, The House of Adam Smith Revisited, 1977, Health Manpower and Health Policy, 1978, Good Jobs, Bad Jobs, No Jobs, 1979, American Jews: The Building of a Voluntary Community (in Hebrew), 1979, Employing the Unemployed, 1980, The School/Work Nexus, 1981, Technology and Employment: Concepts and Claifications, 1986, Medicine and Society, 1987, Executive Talent, 1988, Bridges to Work, 1989, Physicians, Politicians, and the Public, 1989; editor: The Delivery of Health Care: What Lies Ahead, 1982, The Coming Physician Surplus: In Search of a Public Policy, 1983, Home Health Care: Its Role in the Changing Health Services Market, 1983, Beyond Human Scale: The Large Corporation at Risk, 1985, American Medicine: The Power Shift, 1985, The U.S. Health Care System: A Look to the 1990s, 1985, Understanding Human Resources: Perspectives, People and Policy, 1985, From Health Dollars to Health Services: New York City 1965, 1986, From Physician Shortage to Patient Shortage: The Uncertain Future of Medical Practice, 1986, Medicine and Society: Clinical Decisions and Societal Values, 1987, The Skeptical Economist, 1987, Young People at Risk: Is Prevention Possible, 1988, Executive Talent:Developing Tomorrow's Leaders, 1988; : The Financing of Biomedical Research, 1989, My Brother's Keeper, 1989, Does Job Training Work: The Clients Speak Out, 1989, The Medical Triangle, 1990, Health Services Research: Key to Health Policy, 1991, The Eye of Illusion, 1993, The Economics of Medical Education, 1993, The Road to Reform: The Future of Health Care in America, 1994, Medical Gridlock and Health Reform, 1994, The Changing U.S. Labor Market, 1994, The Financing of Medical Schools in an Era of Health Reform, 1995, Tomorrows Hospitals, 1996, Improving Healthcare of the Poor: The New York City Experience, 1997, New Deal Days, 1933-34, 1998, Teaching Hospitals of its Urban Poor, 2000, The Changing Health Market Place, 2000. Dir. rsch. United Jewish Appeal, 1941; bd. govs. Hebrew U., Jerusalem, 1953—59. Fellow: AAAS, Am. Acad. Arts and Scis.; mem.: AAUP, AOA (hon.), Allen O. Whipple Surg. Soc., N.Y. Sci. Policy Assn. of N.Y. Acad. Scis., Soc. Med. Cons. to Armed Forces (assoc.), Indsl. Rels. Rsch. Assn., Am. Econ. Assn., Beta Gamma Sigma, Phi Beta Kappa. Died Dec. 12, 2002.

GIORDANO, SALVATORE, manufacturing executive; b. Bklyn., 1910; Student pub. schs., Bklyn.; DEng (hon.), Widener U., 1974. Stock clk. Frank J. Quigan, Inc., Bklyn., 1927-30, head plant prodn., 1930-34, v.p., acting chief exec. officer, 1934-42, pres., 1942-45, Fedders-Quigan Mfg. Co. (merger Frank J. Quigan, Inc.), Bklyn., 1945-52; dir. Fedders-Quigan Mfg. Co., from 1945; chmn. Fedders-Quigan Mfg. Co. (named changed to Fedders Corp. 1958), from 1952. Chmn. NYCOR, Inc., 1986—. Patentee antiaircraft ammunition clip, 1943. Trustee Widener U.; former trustee Morristown Meml. Hosp. Recipient citations Cath. Interracial Coun., United Jewish Appeal, Columbian Civic Club, Torch of Liberty award Anti-Defamation League, B'nai B'rith. Died 2003.

GIPS, ELIZABETH, radio broadcaster; b. Yonkers, N.Y., May 5, 1922; d. Jerome and Jeanne (Weis) G.; m. Paul Lansman, Sept. 1942 (div. 1965); children: Jeremy Lansman, Joel Lansman. Student, Mills Coll. Pres. BFA Jewelry Co., San Francisco, 1955-67; radio broadcaster KDNA, St. Louis, 1968-73, KZSC, Santa Cruz, Calif., 1974-83, KOMY, Watsonville, Calif., 1980-81, KKUP, Cupertino, Calif., 1980-97. Author: Scrapbook of a Haight Ashbury Pilbrim, 1994; contbr. articles to mags. Avocation: spiritual teaching and seeking. Home: Santa Cruz, Calif. Died May 27, 2001.

GIROUX, PAUL HENRY, retired music educator, musician; b. Humboldt, Ariz., May 24, 1916; s. Frank William and Adda Jenny Mae (Gilbert) G.; m. Flo Annette Carroll, Dec. 26, 1945 (dec. June 1996); 1 child, Nicki Suzette Giroux de Navarro. Student, No. Ariz. U., 1934-39, BA in Music Edn., 1947; BS in Psychology, MA in Music Edn., U. Wash., 1952. Cert. secondary tchr., Wash. Undergrad. asst. dept. music No. Ariz. U., 1935-39; music dir. Radio KTAR, Phoenix, 1939-49; cantor Temple Beth Israel, Phoenix, 1939-49; organizer band for prisoners Ariz. State Prison, from 1947; grad. asst. music and psychology U. Wash., Seattle, 1950-52; music tchr. Jefferson Jr. H.S., Olympia, Wash., 1953-55; chmn. arts divsn. Everett (Wash.) C.C., 1955-78; ret. Organizer ongoing prisoners concert band, Ariz. State Prison, 1947. Flute soloist Everett Cmty. Band, 1960-78, Nat. Champion Shrine Band, Tucson, 1978—. Condr. Everett Symphony, 1955-65; choir master Trinity Episcopal Ch., Everett, 1963-69; band master of ceremonies Sabbar Shrine, Tucson, 1979—, band flute soloist, 1979—. Capt. U.S. Army Ordnance, 1942-45. Decorated Bronze star U.S. Army, Philippines, 1945; Contemporary Music grantee Ford Found., Eastman Sch., Rochester, N.Y., 1969; Theodore Presser fellow Theodore Presser Pub., U. Wash., Seattle, 1952-53. Mem. NEA (life), Am. Fedn. Musicians (life), Music Educators Nat. Conf. (life), VFW (life), Elks (life), Masons (life), Phi Delta Kappa (emeritus), Phi Mu Alpha Sinfonia (life). Episcopalian. Achievements include undergraduate director of music for the first world-wide broadcast conducted, NBC-BBS Easter Sunrise Service, Grand Canyon, Arizona. Home: Tucson, Ariz. Died Nov. 14, 2002.

GLASGOW, JANIS MARILYN, foreign language educator; b. Wooster, Ohio, Aug. 24, 1934; d. Paul Ellsworth and Edna Helen (Smith) G. BA, Case Western Reserve U., 1956; MA, U. Wis., 1958; PhD, UCLA, 1966. Grad. teaching asst. U. Wis., Madison, 1957-58, UCLA, 1958-62; asst. prof. French San Diego State U., 1962-68, assoc. prof., 1968-80, prof. French, 1980-94; maître de confs. U. Paris VIII, 1973-74; exch. prof. French U. Nice (France), 1982; exch. prof. comparative lit. U. Nantes (France), 1985. Author: Une Esthetique de Comparaison: Balzac et George Sand, 1978; editor: George Sand: Collected Essays, 1985, Gabriel, 1988, Questions d'Art et de Littérature, 1991. Fulbright scholar, 1956-57, Robert V. Merrill Grad. scholar, 1961-62. Mem. MLA (regional del. Pacific coast 1974-75, 89-91), Am. Assn. Tchrs. French (pres. 1979-81), Am. Soc. French Acad. Palms, Mensa, Phi Beta Kappa (pres. Epsilon Assn. of Calif. 1972-73, pres. Nu chpt. of Calif. 1976-77, 88-90). Avocations: art, genealogy, travel, reading, scholarly research. Home: San Diego, Calif. Died May 2, 2001.

GLASSMAN, JEROME MARTIN, clinical pharmacologist, educator; b. Phila., Mar. 2, 1919; s. Martin K. and Dorothea (Largeman) G.; m. Justine Helena Rizinsky, June 15, 1952; children: Martin J., Lorna R., Gary J. AB, U. Pa., 1939, MA, 1942; PhD, Yale U., 1950. Research assoc. lab. applied physiology Yale U., New Haven, 1950-51; head dept. pharmacology Wyeth Labs., Phila., 1951-62; dir. biol. research USVRevlon, Yonkers, N.Y., 1962-69; dir. clin. research and pharmacology Wampole Labs., Stamford, Conn., 1969-75; dir. clin. investigation Wallace Labs., Cranbury, N.J., 1975-88; cons. to pharm. industry, from 1988. Adj. assoc. prof. pharmacology N.Y. Med. Coll., 1973-82 Contbr. articles to profl. jours.; patentee in field Scoutmaster Boy Scouts Am., 1957-62, chmn. troop com., 1976-81 Recipient Citation, U.S. Office Scientific Research and Devel. Fellow AAAS, N.Y. Acad. Scis., Am. Coll. Clin. Pharmacology, Am. Coll. Clin. Pharmacology and Chemotherapy; mem. Biometric Soc., Am. Soc. Pharmacology and Exptl. Therapeutics, Soc. Exptl. Biol. Medicine, Soc. Toxicology, Sigma Xi Died Apr. 21, 2003.

GLEASON, JOHN JAMES, theatrical lighting designer; b. Bklyn., Apr. 10, 1941; s. John James and Sue (Manzolillo) G. BA, Hunter Coll., 1963. Theatre design cons. Mummer Theatre, Oklahoma City, 1968-71, NTID, Rochester, N.Y., 1968-72, Repertory Theatre of Lincoln Ctr., N.Y.C., 1972, NYU, 1983, master tchr. design, assoc. chair Tisch Sch. of the Arts, 1972-97. Lighting designer The Great White Hope, 1968, Over Here, 1974, My Fair Lady, 1976, The Royal Family, 1976, Der Rosenkavalier, Dallas Opera, 1982, Black Angel, Off Broadway, 1982, The Survivor, Broadway, 1981, The Philadelphia Story, Lincoln Ctr. Theatre Co., Madame Butterfly, Dallas Opera, The Mikado, N.Y.C. Opera, 1984, Werther, N.Y.C. Opera, 1986, The Magic Flute, N.Y.C. Opera, 1987, Dr. Faustus, N.Y.C. Opera, 1992, Vanessa, Juilliard Opera, 1991, Fennimore & Gerda/Les Memelles de Tiresias, Juilliard Opera, 1992, 93, Puccini's Trittico, Juilliard Opera, 1985, Don Giovanni and Le Nozze di Figaro, Juilliard Opera, 1987, Die Zauberflöte, N.Y.C. Opera, 1987, King John, N.Y. Shakespeare Festival, 1988, Enrico IV, Roundabout Theatre, 1989, Jakob Lenz, N.Y. premiere The Crucible, 1988, L'Amico Fritz, 1989, Am. premiere Rothschild's Violin, 1990, Cimarosa's Le Donne Rivali, 1991, Viaggio A Reims, 1994, Incoronazione de Poppea, 1995, Love of 3 Oranges, 196, Really Rosie, Maurice Sendak Nat. Co., Monsieur Choufleuri, Lincoln Ctr., 1997, Hansel and Gretel, 1998, Il Cappello di Paglia di Firenze, 1998; author: (screenplays) Overdue, 1985, Needing You, 1985, Final Cut,

1986, Into the Dark, 1989; contbg. editor: (mag.) Lighting Dimensions, Falstaff, 1991. Recipient Annual Theatre Design award Maharam Found., N.Y.C., 1972-73; recipient Drama Critics Circle award Los Angeles, 1975 Mem. Art Students League of N.Y. (life). Home: Watsontown, Pa. Died Oct. 28, 2003.

GLEATON, CASSAUNDRA WHITE, secondary school educator; b. Bainbridge, Ga., Oct. 19, 1945; d. William Irvin and Irma (Cone) White; m. James Leon Robinson (div.); m. William Marion Gleaton; children: Hope, William. Diploma, Ga. Southwestern Coll., 1965, MS, 1980; BS, Valdosta (Ga.) State Coll., 1967. Cert. sci. edn. and reading tchr., Ga. Tchr. Dougherty County Pub. Schs., Albany, Ga., 1967-86, Gwinnett County Pub. Schs., Lawrenceville, Ga., from 1986. Mem. Ga. Assn. of Edn., NEA, PAGE, Kappa Delta Pi. Republican. Methodist. Home: Georgetown, Ga. Died Sept. 8, 2000.

GLENN, JOHN FRANKLIN, retired chemist; b. Phila., May 4, 1915; s. John F. and Marion Elizabeth (Wilkinson) G.; m. Mary Virginia Hayes, Oct. 29, 1943; children: John F. Glenn III, Lesley H. Cochran. BS in Chemistry, U. Pa., 1937; MS in Chemistry, U. Del., 1957, PhD in Chemistry, 1960. Rsch. chemist L.D. Caulk Co., Milford, Del., 1937-64, dir. rsch., 1964-68, v.p. rsch., 1968; dir. ctrl. rsch. Dentsply (formerly L.D. Caulk Co.), York, Pa., 1968-78, ret., 1978. Participant conf. on adhesive dental material, U. Ind., U. Va., 1961-65. Author: The Cutting Edge, 1976; contbr. articles to profl. jours. Lectr. in field. Mem. Del. Bd. Nursing, Dover, 1989-92; participant Gov.'s Conf. on Pub. Utilities, Pub. Transit, Dover, 1988-93; lectr., Arthritis Found., 1984—, Lt. col. U.S. Army, 1941-46, rsch., 1946-63. Mem. Am. Chem. Soc., Internat. Assn. Dental Rsch. (Souder award for dental materials rsch. 1979), Dental Materials Group (pres. 1963), Internat. Stds. Orgn. (leader dentistry com. 1968-79). Democrat. Episcopalian. Achievements include several dental materials patents. Home: Dover, Del. Died Mar. 26, 2001.

GLENN, WILLIAM WALLACE LUMPKIN, surgeon, educator; b. Asheville, N.C., Aug. 12, 1914; s. Eugene Byron and Elizabeth Elliot (Lumpkin) G.; m. Amory Potter, May 15, 1943; children: William Amory Lumpkin, Elizabeth Glenn McLellan BS, U. S.C., 1934; MD, Jefferson Med. Coll., 1938; MA (hon.), Yale U., 1962; MD (hon.), U. Cadiz, 1981. Diplomate Am. Bd. Surgery, Am. Bd. Thoracic Surgery. Intern Pa. Hosp., Phila., 1938-40; surg. resident Mass. Gen. Hosp., Boston, 1940-42, 45-46; asst. physiology Harvard Sch. Pub. Health, 1941-43; asso. surgery Jefferson Med. Coll., Phila., 1946-48; mem. faculty Yale Med. Sch., from 1948, prof. surgery, 1962-74, Charles W. Ohse prof. surgery, 1974 85, Charles W. Ohse prof. emeritus surgery, 1985—, chief cardiovascular surgery, 1948-76, sr. rsch. scientist, 1985-87; hon. staff Yale-New Haven Hosp. Cons. Surgeon Gen. Com. Environ. Medicine, 1962-64 Co-editor: Thoracic and Cardiovascular Surgery, 1962, 75, editor, 1983; co-editor: Complex Surgical Problems, 1981; mem. editorial bd. numerous jours.; cons., editor: Cardiac Pacemakers, 1964; contbr. articles to profl. jour. Mem. com. cardiovascular systems NRC, 1955-56; bd. dirs. Charles E. Culpeper Found., 1976-85. Served to maj., M.C. AUS, World War II, ETO. Mem. Am. Heart Assn. (pres. 1970-71), Internat. Soc. Surgery (v.p. U.S. sect.), Internat. Surg. Group (pres. 1964, hon. 1994), Am. Surg. Assn., ACS (chmn. Conn. adv. com. 1963-66, gov. 1967-72), Soc. Univ. Surgeons, New Eng. Surg. Soc. (pres. 1983-84), So. Surg. Assn., New Eng. Soc. Vascular Surgeons (pres. 1979-80), Am. Assn. Thoracic Surgery, Vascular Surg. Soc., Halstead Soc., Soc. Thoracic Surgeons (hon.), Morys' Assn. (New Haven), Yale Club of N.Y., Sigma Xi, Alpha Omega Alpha. Episcopalian. Home: Peterborough, NH. Died Mar. 10, 2003.

GLOSS, ELIZABETH FLORENCE, nursing educator, educator; b. N.Y.C., Dec. 2, 1935; d. Joseph and Susan (Getsy) G. Diploma, Mary Immaculate Hosp., 1956; BS, St. John's U., 1963; MEd, Columbia U., 1969, EdD, 1983. From staff nurse to head nurse, then from asst. instr. to instr. Mary Immaculate Hosp., 1956-71; coord., instr. Cath. Med. Ctr. Sch. Nursing, 1971-76; asst. prof., dept. chmn., lectr. L.I.U., C.W. Post Coll. Nursing, 1976-80; asst. prof., curriculum and clin. coord., team leader CUNY and CCNY, 1978-82; dir. nursing ctr., asst. prof. nursing SUNY, 1982-93, assoc. prof. nursing, from 1993. Guest lectr. Tchrs. Coll. Columbia U., 1982, vis. scholar, 1984-85; adj. asst. prof. nursing Regents Coll. N.Y., Adelphi U., 1984-89; cons. in field. Author: (with others) Medical Surgical Nursing: Nursing Process Approach, 1991, 94, 95; contbr. articles to profl. jours.; internat. presenter in field. Grantee USHHS, 1987-89, CUNY Rsch. Found., 1980-82, Community Grants, 1986-96. Mem. ANA, N.Y. Nurses Assn., Am. Heart Assn. Coun. Rsch. Com. (grants and rsch. for women and heart disease), Sigma Theta Tau Internat. (regional rsch. award 1992-93). Home: Mineola, NY. Died May 4, 2001.

GLOSSIP, EVA, real estate broker; b. Jamesville, Mo., Aug. 4, 1923; d. Samuel T. Gardner and Pearl Edith (Fox) G.; m. Jim Glossip, June 6, 1941; children: Marilyn Kay Glossip Noe, Susan Faye Glossip Bilyeu. Student, Draugron Bus. Coll., Springfield, Mo., Career Sch. Real Estate. Owner, mgr., sec. Gen. Merc. Bus., 1944-69; owner, mgr. Glossip Realty Co., Springfield, Mo., from 1972; committee woman North Gallaway Twp., Christian County, Mo., from 1978. Recipient cert. of excellence Nat. Statis. Research Co., Chgo., 1981. Mem. Nat. Assn. Realtors, Mo. Assn. Realtors (Million Dollar Club), Greater Springfield Bd. Realtors. Republican. Southern Baptist. Lodges: Shriners, Order Eastern Star. Died Oct. 12, 2000.

GLOSUP, LORENE See DEAN, DEAREST

GLOVER, WILLIAM HARPER, theater critic; b. N.Y.C., May 6, 1911; s. William Harper and Lily P. (Freir) G.; m. Isobel M. Cole, Oct. 26, 1936 (div. 1973); m. Virginia F. Holden, Aug. 29, 1985 LittB, Rutgers U., 1932. City editor Asbury Park (N.J.) Press, 1935-39; news editor AP newsfeatures, 1941-53, theatre writer, 1953-78; drama critic for AP, 1960-78. Contbr. to periodicals. Served to lt. (j.g.) U.S. Maritime Service, 1943-45. Mem. N.Y. Drama Critics Circle (pres.), New Drama Forum, N.Y. Acad. Scis., Phi Beta Kappa, Sigma Delta Chi. Clubs: The Players (N.Y.C.), Overseas Press (N.Y.C.); N.Y. Press. Died Dec. 20, 2002.

GLUSSMAN, BETTY BERMAN, nurse; b. N.Y.C., July 28, 1930; d. Albert A. and Helen (Westfried) Berman; children: Anne Karen, Charles. BSN, Columbia U., 1954, MEd, 1978; MSN, Adelphi U., 1974. Mem. faculty Glen-Cove (N.Y.) Hosp. Sch. Practical Nursing, 1968-72, Bronx (N.Y.) Community Coll., 1974-76, Pace U., Briarcliff, N.Y., 1976-81; mem. faculty, asst. prof. U. Miami, 1981-82; asst. prof. Fla. Internat. U., Miami, 1982-85; nurse practitioner South Shore Hosp., Miami Beach, Fla., 1985-87; nurse practitioner gerontology Miami Vets. Affairs, from 1987. Contbr. articles to profl. jours. Mem. Nurses Orgn. Vets. Affairs. Avocations: reading, writing, swimming. Deceased.

GNODTKE, CARL F. former state legislator; b. Jan. 2, 1936; m. Mary Jane Frame; children: Julie, Jacquie, Calvin, Lora, Charles (dec.). Rep. Mich. Dist. 43, 1978-92, Mich. Dist. 78, 1993-97. Commr. Berrien County, Mich., drain commr.; twp. officer; bd. dirs. Berrien County Parks and Recreation Commn., Bd. Pub. Works; mem. conservation com. Mich. Ho. Reps., recreation & environ. com., pub. health com., towns and counties com., minority vice chmn. agrl. com., vice chmn. labor com., bus. & fin. com., conservation, environ. & great lakes affairs com.; dir. Galien River Soil Conservation Dist.; bd. dirs. Berrien County Econ. Devel. Corp.; farmer. Mem. Farm Bur. Home: Sawyer, Mich. Deceased.

GOCHENOUR, EDWIN ALLEN, state senator; b. Sylacauga, Ala., Nov. 23, 1952; m. Ginger Gochenour; children: Kyle, Brandon. Student, Mercer U. Senator 27th dist. Ga. State Legislature, from 1992. Mem. interstate cooperation com., natural resources com., sci. tech. and industry com., corrections, correctional instns. and properties com. Ga. State Senate. Mem. Macon (Ga.) Water Authority, 1988-92. With USMC, 1972-74. Deceased.

GODFREY, JOHN, internist; b. New Haven, Conn., May 5, 1916; s. Charles Stafford and Dorothy (Godfrey) Wayman; m. Jean Hester Fuller, Sept. 12, 1941; children: John, Peter, Judith, Patricia, Jane. AB, Dartmouth Coll., 1938, cert., 1939; MD, Harvard U., 1941; fellow, Medicine Lahey Clinic, Boston, 1946-47. Diplomate Am. Bd. Internal Medicine. Intern Hitchcock Hosp., Hanover, N.H., 1941-43; resident Medicine Faulkner Hosp., Jamaica Plain, Mass., 1946; asst. chief medicine VA Hosp., White River Junction, Vt., 1948-51; chief medicine Olean (N.Y.) Gen. Hosp., 1958-72, chief of staff, 1972-77; ret., 1985. Contbr. articles to profl. jours. Pres. Catt. County Mental Health Bd., Little Valley, N.Y., 1948. Served to maj. MC, AUS, 1943-46, ETO. Fellow Am. Coll. Physicians; mem. AMA (Vol. Physicians in Vietnam award 1969), N.Y. State Med. Soc. Republican. Presbyterian. Avocations: orcharist, sailing, tennis, skiing, music. Home: Olean, NY. Died Nov. 20, 2001.

GODSEY, DORIS SANDQUIST, nurse; b. Concord, N.H., Mar. 7, 1921; d. Martin and Susanna Charlotta (Linnarson) Sandquist; m. Paul James Godsey, July 10, 1946 (dec. July 1988); children: Susan M., Paul J. Jr., James P. Diploma, Evangeline Booth Hosp., 1941, Mass. Gen. Hosp., 1946; BS, Ind. State U., 1949; MSN, U. Md., 1970. Nurse pvt. duty, Boston, 1941-43; head nurse Mass. Gen. Hosp., Boston, 1945-46; staff nurse pvt. duty, Terre Haute, Ind., 1946-49; cons. ARC, La Porte, Ind., 1950; faculty Beatty Meml. Hosp., Westville, Ind., 1958-61, Lancaster (Pa.) Gen. Hosp., St. Joseph Hosp., 1962-68; cons. curriculum Meml. Gen. Hosp., Elkins, W.Va., 1970-71; assoc. prof. W.Va. Wesleyan Coll., Buckhannon, 1971-83; retired W.V.a Wesleyan Coll., Buckhannon, 1983; insvc. policies, procedures La Rue D. Carter Meml. Hosp., Indpls., from 1991. Sec., treas. Mental Health Assn. Upshur County, Buckhannon, 1971-87. Mem. Sigma Theta Tau, Omicron Delta Kappa. Republican. Avocations: family, rug hooking, symphony. Home: Indianapolis, Ind. Died Apr. 10, 2000.

GOEPP, ROBERT AUGUST, dental educator, oral pathologist; b. Chgo., Nov. 3, 1930; s. Charles August and Ernestine Josephine (Mertz) G.; m. Iraida Pineiro, July 9, 1960; children— Robert C., Heidi M., Myra J. BS in Biology, Loyola U.-Chgo., 1954, D.D.S., 1957; MS in Pathology, U. Chgo., 1961, PhD in Pathology, 1967. Instr. to assoc. prof. Sch. Medicine, U. Chgo., 1961-75, prof. dentistry and pathology, 1975-96, prof. emeritus, from 1996. Med. Med. Radiation Adv. Coun. FDA, 1979-82; mem. Nat. Coun. Radiation Protection, Washington, 1976-94. Contbr. articles to profl. jours. Recipient Career Devel. award USPHS, 1970 Fellow Am. Coll. Dentists, Internat. Coll. Dentists, Am. Acad. Oral Pathology, Am. Acad. Dental Radiology (pres. 1974), Ill. Soc. Oral Pathologists (pres. 1977-78), Inst. Medicine Chgo., Odontographic Soc. Chgo. (bd. dirs., treas. 1993-99, chmn. 2001—); mem. ADA (chmn. coun. dental rsch. 1981-82). Roman Catholic. Avocations: music, piano. Home: Chicago, Ill. Died Mar. 30, 2003.

GOETZ, RAYMOND, law educator, labor arbitrator; b. Rockford, Ill., May 14, 1922; s. Fred J. and Irma W. (Rathke) G.; m. Elizabeth Morey, Apr. 24, 1951; children: Raymond, Sibyl Goetz Wescoe, Thomas, Victoria, Steven, Morey. JD, U. Chgo., 1950, MBA, 1963. Bar: Ill. 1950, Kans. 1966. Assoc. Seyfarth, Shaw, Fairweather & Geraldson, Chgo., 1950-57, ptnr., 1957-66; prof. law U. Kans., Lawrence, 1966-87, prof. emeritus, from 1987. Permanent umpire Ford Motor Co. and UAW, Detroit, 1984-89; salary arbitrator Major League Baseball, N.Y.C., 1984-91; mem. arbitration panel AT&T, Communications Workers Am., 1988-96. Trustee Village of Northfield (Ill.), 1955-57, Kans. Pub. Employees Retirement System, Topeka, 1968-76. Lt. (j.g.) USNR, 1943-47, PTO. Mem. ABA (sec. sect. labor law 1977-78, neutral co-chmn. com. on labor arbitration 1980-83), Nat. Acad. Arbitrators (bd. govs. 1992-95), Indsl. Rels. Rsch. Assn. (exec. bd. Kansas City chpt. 1968-94), Am. Arbitration Assn. (labor arbitrator 1967-96). Avocation: contemporary art. Died May 2, 2000.

GOIN, OLIVE BOWN, biologist; b. Pitts., Dec. 2, 1912; d. Charles Elmer and Anne Louise (Hay) Bown; m. Coleman Goin, June 7, 1940 (dec.); children: Lynda, Coleman Jr. AB, Wellesley Coll., 1934; MS, U. Pitts., 1936. Asst. lab. mammalogy Carnegie Mus., Pitts., 1934-40; lab. instr. to asst. prof. U. Fla., Gainesville, 1942-46; rsch. assoc. Mus. of No. Ariz., Flagstaff, 1971-80; ret. Author: World Outside My Door, 1955, Introduction to Herpetology, 1962, Comparative Vertebrate Anatomy, Man and the Natural World, 1970, Introduction to Herpetology, 2d edit., 1971, Journey Onto Land, 1974, Man and the Natural World, 2d edit., 1975 (all with C.J. Goin); (with C.J. Goin and George Zug) Introduction to Herpetology, 3rd edit., 1978; contbr. numerous articles to profl. jours. Avocations: reading, crossword puzzles. Home: Las Vegas, Nev. Died June 2, 2000.

GOLANY, GIDEON SALOMON, urban designer; b. Jan. 23, 1928; came to U.S., 1967, naturalized, 1975. s. Jacob and Rajena G.; m. Esther Klein, Jan. 10, 1956; children: Ofer, Amir. BA, Hebrew U., Jerusalem, 1956, MA, 1962, PhD, 1966; MS in Environ. Design, Technion-Israel Inst. Tech., Haifa, 1965; diploma comprehensive planning, Inst. Social Studies, The Hague, Netherlands, 1965. Lectr. architecture and town planning Technion-Israel Inst. Tech., 1963-67; lectr. city and regional planning Cornell U., 1967-68; research planner Office of Research, Resources and Devel., Cornell U., 1968; assoc. prof. urban and regional planning Coll. Architecture, Va. Poly. Inst. and State U., Blacksburg, 1968-70; vis. prof. urban and regional planning Inst. Desert Research, Ben-Gurion U. of the Negev, Beer Sheva, Israel, 1975-76; prof. urban and regional planning Pa. State U., 1970-87, research prof. urban design and planning, 1987-91, Disting. prof. urban design, from 1991, chmn. grad. program, 1971-76, dir. PhD program on Environ. Design, Div. Environ. Design and Planning, 1987-89; propr. Gideon Golany Assocs., 1987-89. Cons. in field; hon. prof. China Acad. Scis., China Acad. Mgmt. Sci., Tongji U., Shanghai, People's Republic China, Xian (People's Republic China) Inst. Metallurgy and Constrn. Engrng. Author, editor more than 27 books including: Geography of Israel, 1962, New Town Planning and Development--A World Bibliography, 1973, Strategy for New Community Development in the United States, 1975, Innovations for Future Cities, 1976, New-Town Planning: Principles and Practice, 1976, Urban Planning for Arid Zones: American Direction and Experience, 1978, Earth-Sheltered Habitat: History, Architecture and Urban Design, 1983, Design for Arid Regions, 1983, Earth-Sheltered Dwellings in Tunisia, 1988, Urban Underground Space in China, 1989, Design and Thermal Performance, 1990, Chinese Earth-Sheltered Dwellings: Indigenous Lessons for Modern Urban Design, 1992, Ethic and Urban Design, 1995, Geo-Space Urban Design, 1996, Japan's Urban Environment, 1998; co-author: New Geographic Dictionary, 2 vols., 1966; co-editor: The Contemporary New Communities Movement in the United States, 1974; editor: International Urban Growth Policies, 1978, Arid Zone Settlement Planning: Israeli Experience, 1979, Housing in Arid Lands: Design and Planning, 1980, Desert Planning: International Lessons, 1982, Design for Arid Regions, 1983, Earth Sheltered Habitat: History, Architecture, and Urban Design, 1983; also articles. Mem., founder Kibbuts Baeri, communal settlement, Negev, 1946-52. Served with Hagana, 1946-48; Served with Israeli Army, 1948-50, 56, 67. Recipient prize Com. Encouragement Towards Rsch. and Higher Studies, Histadrut, Tel-Aviv, 1963, Faculty Scholar medal Pa. State U., 1987, Faculty Research/Creative Devel. award, 1987; grantee Govt. Netherlands, 1965, NSF, 1972-74; Fulbright rsch. awards, 1982, 90-91, 95-96. Mem. Assn. Engrs. and Architects Israel, Am. Underground Space Assn., Internat. New Towns Assn., Internat. Ctr. for Arid-Semi Arid Land Studies, Assn. Arid Land Studies. Died Dec. 8, 1999.

GOLD, THOMAS, astronomer, educator; b. Vienna, May 22, 1920; s. Max and Josefine (Martin) G.; m. Merle Eleanor Tuberg, June 21, 1947; children Linda, Lucy, Tanya; m. Carvel Lee Beyer, Dec. 27, 1972; 1 dau., Lauren. BA, Cambridge (Eng.) U., 1942, MA, 1945, Sc.D., 1969; fellow, Trinity Coll., Cambridge, 1947; MA (hon.), Harvard, 1957. Lectr. physics Cambridge (Eng.) U., 1948-52; chief asst. to Astronomer Royal, Gt. Britain, 1952-56; prof. astronomy Harvard, 1958, Robert Wheeler Willson prof., 1958-59; prof. astronomy, dir. Center Radiophysics and Space Research Cornell U., 1959-81, chmn. dept., 1959-68, asst. v.p. for research, 1970-71, John L. Wetherill prof., 1971-86. Contbr. articles to profl. jours. Hon. fellow Trinity Coll., Cambridge, 1986-2004 Fellow Royal Soc. London, Am. Geophys.

Union; mem. U.S. Nat. Acad. Sci., Am. Philos. Soc., Am. Acad. Arts and Scis., Royal Astron. Soc. (Gold medal 1985; past councillor), Am. Astron. Soc. Died June 22, 2004.

GOLDBERG, JOSEPH PHILIP, government official; b. Bklyn., May 1, 1918; s. Max and Fanny (Steltzer) G.; m. Selma Takiff, Aug. 22, 1943; children: Seth M., Lise A. BSS, CCNY, 1937; MA, Columbia U., 1938, PhD, 1950. Instr. econ. history CCNY, 1937-39; high sch. tchr. N.Y.C., 1938-42; economist Bur. Labor Stats., Washington, 1942; econ. adviser Nat. War Labor Bd. and Wage Stabilization Bd., Washington, 1943-46; labor adviser Office of Housing Expediter, 1946-48, staff dir. joint congl. com., 1948; divsn. chief Bur. Labor Stats., Labor Dept., Washington, 1949-51, spl. asst. to commr. of labor stats., 1954-86, with Wage Stabilization Bd., 1951-53. Instr. Am. U., 1948-49; rsch. assoc. Harvard U., 1957, U. Mich., 1964-69, Internat. Labor Orgn. Inst. Indsl. Rels. Studies, 1973—; U.S. del. 22 Internat. Labor Orgn. maritime and internat. labor confs., 1956-85; cons. on maritime industry U.S. Dept. Labor, 1986—. Author: The Maritime Story, 1958; (with others) Collective Bargaining and Technological Change in American Transportation, Monograph on Modernization in the Maritime Industry, 1971, Productivity Bargaining in the Private Sector, 1975, The Law and Practice of Collective Bargaining, 1976, Frances Perkins, Isadore Lubin and the Bureau of Labor Statistics, 1980, The AFL and a National Bureau of Labor Statistics, 1983, The First One Hundred Years of the Bureau of Labor Statistics, 1985; contbr. articles to profl. jours. Pres. J.F. Kennedy H.S. PTA, 1968-69, New Hampshire Estates, 1956-57, trustee schs. Montgomery County, 1957-62, 86—; arbitrator, consumer protection and Health Advocacy Specialist Md. State Atty. Gen.; mediator Washington Mediation Svc., Docent-Smithsonian Inst., 1986-99. Rsch. grants Yale Fund, Harvard, U. Mich., Ford Found.; recipient Meritorious Svc. award Labor Dept., 1963, 85, Commr.'s Eminent Svc. award, 1973. Mem. AAAS, Indsl. Rels. Rsch. Assn. (pres. D.C. chpt. 1963-64, mem. nat. exec. bd. 1973-76), Am. Econ. Assn., Phi Beta Kappa. Home: Silver Spring, Md. Died Dec. 4, 2002; Silver Spring MD.

GOLDBERGER, ROBERT FRANK, academic administrator, biochemist, physician; b. N.Y.C., June 2, 1933; s. Morris Aaron and Gertrude (Felshin) G.; m. Marianne Rudolf, May 8, 1958; children: Malka, Erica, Laura. AB, Harvard U., 1954; MD, NYU, 1958. Biochemist Nat. Inst. Arthritis, Metabolism, Digestive Diseases, NIH, Bethesda, Md., 1961-66, chief sect. on biosynthesis & control, 1966-73; chief lab. of biochemistry Nat. Cancer Inst., NIH, Bethesda, 1973-79; dep. dir. for sci. NIH, Bethesda, 1979-81; v.p. for health sci. Columbia U., N.Y.C., 1981-83, provost, 1981-89, acting pres., 1987-88. Chmn. Gordon Conf. on Biol. Regulatory Mechanisms, N.H., 1973-74; pres. Found. for Advanced Edn. in the Scis., 1976-78; mem. nat. adv. council Harriman Inst. for Advanced Study of Soviet Union, N.Y., 1982—; pres. Reid Hall Inc., Columbia U., N.Y.C., 1983—. Author, co-author over 75 articles and 1 book; editor 8 vols. on molecular biology (Best Life Scis. Book award 1979). Served as asst. surgeon gen. USPHS, 1979-81. Recipient Superior Service award HEW, Bethesda, 1973, Meritorious Service medal USPHS, 1977, Soloman A. Berson award in Health Scis., NYU, 1985. Mem. Am. Soc. Biol. Chemists, Am. Soc. Cell Biology, Am. Soc. Microbiology, Biophys. Soc., Genetics Soc. Am. Died Apr. 5, 2003.

GOLDEN, DANIEL LEWIS, lawyer; b. N.Y.C., May 7, 1913; s. Louis and Rose (Rosen) G.; m. Evelyn Shayevitz, July 9, 1941 (dec.); children: Roger M., Leslie Rosemary; m. Eugenia Alice Norman, Feb. 14, 1997. BS, Lafayette Coll., 1934; LLD (hon.), 1993; JD, Rutgers U., 1938. Bar: N.J. 1939, D.C. 1976, U.S. Supreme Ct. 1957. Practice, South River, from 1940; now of counsel Greenbaum, Rowe, Smith, Ravin, Davis & Himmell LLP, Woodbridge, N.J. Active survey legal systems USSR, East Europe for State Dept. Exchanges Programs, also for ABA, N.J. Bar Assn., 1961-75. Chmn. ethics Com., 1967; mem. N.J. Gov.'s Commn. on Individual Liberty and Personal Privacy, 1977-84; bd. trustees Lafayette Coll., 1975-80. Lt. USAAF, 1942-45. Recipient Kidd hon. citation for law Lafayette Coll., 1970, Bell Disting. Svc. Alumni award, 1985; Rutgers Law award, 1971, Lawyer of Yr. N.J. Commn. on Professionalism, 1998. Fellow Am. Bar Found. (state chmn. 1985-90, nat. chmn. 1992-93), Am. Acad. Martimonial Lawyers; mem. ABA (ho. of dels. 1972-90, chmn. adv. commn. on election law), N.J. Bar Assn. (pres. 1970-71, editorial bd. N.J. Lawyer mag. 1969—), Middlesex County Bar Assn. (pres. 1960-61), Assn. Trial Lawyers Am., Trial Attys. N.J. (bd. trustees 1969—, Lifetime Achievement award 1986), N.J. Bar Found. (Medal of Honor award 1991), Pi Lambda Phi (honoree 1997). Home: Little Silver, NJ. Died Jan. 11, 2004.

GOLDHIRSH, BERNARD A. publisher; b. N.Y.C., Mar. 22, 1940; s. Leonard M. and Sylvia (Blank) G. m. Wendy Jo Goldhirst(dec. 1999), children: Elizabeth, Benjamin. BS, MIT, 1961. Pub. Sail Mag., Boston, 1967-80, Inc. Mag., Boston, 1979—2000, High Tech. Mag., Boston, 1981—87; chmn. bd. World Exec. Digest, Hong Kong, 1984-91, Univ. Seminars, Boston, 1985—2003. Mem. vis. com. MIT, 1984— Mem.: St. Butolph (Boston). Died June 29, 2003.

GOLDMAN, ARNOLD IRA, biophysicist, statistical analyst; b. Chgo., Mar. 13, 1945; s. Morton Irving and Rita Mae (Satten) G.; m. Sandra Gail Lipman, Aug. 8, 1971; children: Jennifer Lauren, Lesley Anne. MS in Radiol. Health, U. Pitts., 1968; PhD in Biophysics, Med. Coll. Va., 1974. Postdoctoral fellow Jules Stein Eye Inst., UCLA, 1974-75; staff fellow Nat. Eye Inst., NIH, Bethesda, Md., 1975-79; asst. prof. Med. Coll. Wis., Milw., 1979-82; rsch. v.p. otorhinolaryngol. and ophthal. divsn., dir. MIS Biomatrix, Inc., Ridgefield, N.J., 1983-2001. Ind. statis. cons., Milw., 1980-83. Contbr. to profl. publs. including Science. Lt. (j.g.) USPHS, 1968-70. Mem. Assn. Rsch. in Vision and Ophthalmology. Home: Suffern, NY. Died Aug. 1, 2001.

GOLDMAN, DAVID TOBIAS, federal agency administrator; b. N.Y.C., Jan. 25, 1933; s. Joseph Louis and Frances Miriam (Snyder) G.; m. Elizabeth Ann Ward, Sept. 15, 1957; children: Daniel, Jonathan, Michael, Benjamin, Joshua. BA, Bklyn. Coll., 1952; MS, Vanderbuilt U., 1954; PhD, U. Md., 1958. Chief nuclear methods Knolls Atomic Power Lab., Schenectady, N.Y., 1959-65; chief reactor theory Nat. Bur. Standards, Washington, 1965-72, dep. dir. inst. basic standards, 1972-78, assoc. dir. planning nat. measurement lab., 1978-82; exec. assoc. for tech. Dept. Commerce, Washington, 1982-85; mgr. Argonne (Ill.) area office Dept. Energy, 1985-87; asst. mgr. labs. Chgo. ops. Dept. of Energy, Argonne, 1987-90, acting mgr., 1990-92; dep. sci. advisor, 1992-93; dep. mgr. Chgo. ops., 1993-95; exec. assoc. R&D mgmt. US Dept. Energy, Washington, from 1995. Adj. prof. nuclear engring. Rensselaer Polytech. Inst., Troy, N.Y., 1959-65, U. Md., College Park, 1965-78; cons. in field. Editor: Neutron Cross Sections Technology, 1968, GE Chart of the Nuclides, 1959-68; contbr. articles to profl. jours. Chmn. Noise Control Adv. Bd., Montgomery City, Md., 1979-85. NSF fellow, 1958. Fellow Am. Phys. Soc.; mem. Am. Nat. Metric Coun. (bd. dirs. 1979-94, Achievement award 1984), ASTM (vice chmn. metric com. 1979-87, chmn. com. on rsch. and tech. planning 1991-95), Am. Nuclear Soc. (chmn. reactor physics divsn. 1964-65). Home: Bethesda, Md. Died Aug. 31, 2000.

GOLDMAN-RAKIC, PATRICIA SHOER, neuroscience educator; b. Salem, Mass., Apr. 22, 1937; AB cum laude, Vassar Coll., 1959; PhD, UCLA, 1963; AM (hon.), Yale U., 1979. USPHS predoctoral fellow dept. psychology UCLA, 1961—63, USPhS postdoctoral fellow dept. psychiatry, 1963—64; rsch. assoc. dept. animal behavior Am. Mus. Natural History, N.Y.C., 1964—65; staff fellow sect. neuropsychology NIMH, Bethesda, Md., 1965—68, rsch. physiologist Lab. Neuropsychology, 1968—78, chief sect. devel. neurobiology, 1978—79; prof. neurosci. sect. neurobiology Yale U. Sch. Medicine, New Haven, 1979—2003, joint appointment dept. psychology, 1991—96, dir. grad. studies sect. neuroanatomy, 1981—86, acting chmn. sect. neurobiology, 1986—87. USPHS postdoctoral trainee dept. psychiatry NYU, N.Y.C., 1964—65; vis. scientist MIT, Cambridge, 1974—75; Edward Sacher lectr. Columbia U., 1992; Herbert Birch meml. lectr. Internat. Neuropsychobiology Soc., 1981; Plenary lectr. Union Swiss Socs. for Exptl. Biology, 1983; Sigma Xi lectr. Brown U., 1984, SUNY Downstate Med. Sch., Bklyn., 1988; Kendon Smith meml. lectr. U. N.C., 1985, Hal Robinson disting. lectr., 92; Bernard Sachs meml. lectr. Child Neurology Soc., Memphis, 1985; Frontiers of Sci. lectr. Am. Psychiat. Assn., 1988; Sally Harrington Goldwater lectr. Barrow Neurol. Inst., Phoenix, 1990; 4th Hillarp lectr. European Neurosci. Soc., 1990; Rushton lectr. Fla. State U., 1990; Lanier lectr. U. Ill., 1991; Jock Cleghorn meml. lectr. McMaster U., 1994; mem. sci. adv. bd. Ency. Neurosci., from 1994; mem. Nat. Adv. Mental Health Coun., from 1993, numerous others; participant sems., confs., symposia and workshops throughout the world. Editor-in-chief: Cerebral Cortex, mem. adv. bd. : Advances in Neurosci., Behavioral Brain Rsch., Behavioral Neurosci., Brain Rsch., Brain Rsch. Bull., Concepts in Neurosci., Devel. Brain Rsch., Devel. Neuropsychology, Devel. Psychobiology, Exptl. Neurology, Jour. Neurosci., Progress in Brain Rsch., Trends in Neurosci., Sci., Critical Revs. in Neurobiology, Biol. Psychiatry, Neuropsychopharmacology, Jour. Comparative and Physiol. Psychology. Recipient Lieber award, Nat. Alliance for Rsch. on Schizophrenia and Depression, 1991, award, Robert T. and Claire Pasarow Found., 1993, prize in neurosci., Fyssen Found., Paris, 1990, Alden Spencer award, Columbia U., 1982, Karl Spencer Lashley prize, Am. Philos. Soc., 1996; grantee NIMH, 1980—2000. Fellow: APA (Disting. Sci. Contbn. award 1991), AAAS (John P. McGovern award 1993), N.Y. Acad. Scis., Am. Psychopath. Assn.; mem.: NAS, Inst. Medicine, Am. Acad. Arts and Scis., Internat. Brain Rsch. Orgn., Internat. Neuropsychology Symposium, Am. Anat. Assn. (Krieg Cortical Discoverer award Cajal Club 1989), Internat. Soc. for Devel. Psychobiology, Soc. for Neurosci. (councilor 1984—88, Young Investigator Award selection com. 1985—87, pres. 1989—90). Home: New Haven, Conn. Died July 31, 2003.

GOLDSMITH, WERNER, mechanical engineering educator; b. Düsseldorf, Rhineland, Germany, May 23, 1924; came to U.S., 1938; s. Siegfried and Margarethe (Grunewald) G.; m. Adrienne Kessler (div.); children: Stephen M., Andrea Jo; m. Penelope I. Alexander, Oct. 5, 1973; 1 child, Remy M. BSME, U. Tex., 1944, MSME, 1945; PhDME, U. Calif., Berkeley, 1949; doc. caus. (hon.), U. Patras, Greece, from 2002. Registered mech. and safety engr., Calif. Engr. Westinghouse Electric Co., Pitts. and Phila., 1945-47; instr. div. engring. design U. Calif., Berkeley, 1947-49, asst. prof., 1949-55, assoc. prof. dept. mech. engring., 1955-60, prof., 1960-87, prof. emeritus in active svc., 1988-97, prof. Grad. Sch., 1997—2003; mech. engr. U.S. Naval Weapons Ctr., China Lake, Calif., from 1951. Instr. math. U. Pitts., 1945-46; lectr. in engring. U. Pa., Phila., 1946-47; engring. cons. govt., industry, legal profession, Berkeley, 1953-2003; chmn. head injury com. NIH, Bethesda, Md., 1966-70; cons. Fuze div. U.S. Army, Picatinny Arsenal, N.J., 1970-76; panel mem. Nat. Rsch. Coun. Rev. Armament and Materials Disectorate of Army Rsch. Labs.; vis. prof. Technion, Haifa, Israel, Nat. Poly. U., Athens, Greece, Tokyo Inst. Tech., East China Inst. Tech., Nanjing, 1968—, T.H., Eindhoven, Holland, Inst. Su. Matériaux et Construction Mécanique, St. Ouen, France; cons. mech. engring. dept. U. Calif., San Diego, 1997-2003. Author: A History of the Department of Mechanical Engineering, University of California, Berkeley, 1997; (monograph) Impact, 1960, reprint, 2001; co-author, co-editor: Introduction to Bioengineering, 1996; contbr. over 250 articles on impact, wave propagation, rock mechanics, biomechanics, head and neck injuries, protective devices, exptl. mechs. to profl. jours.; also numerous tech. reports. Guggenheim fellow, 1953-54, Fulbright rsch. fellow U.S. Dept. State, 1974-75, 81-82, Lady Davies fellow Lady Davies Trust Fund, 1986; named Outstanding Engring. Grad. by U. Calif. Berkeley Engring. Alumni Assn., 2001, named Disting. Academician U. Tex. Coll. Engring., Austin. Fellow Am. Acad. Mechanics (spl. issue internat. jour. Impact Engring. honoring 70th birthday 1994); mem. ASME (hon., chair West Coast applied mechanics divsn. 1960, hon. mem. 1997, honoree 3-day symposium Applied Mechanics/Materials divsns. 1995), NAE, Faculty Club (Berkeley). Avocations: tournament bridge, collecting old maps, stamp collecting, classical music. Died Aug. 23, 2003.

GOLDSON, ALFRED LLOYD, oncologist, educator; BS, Hampton Inst., 1968; MD, Howard U., Washington, 1972. Diplomate Am. Bd. Therapeutic Radiology; med. lic. D.C.; cert. Ga. state med. bd. Resident in radiation therapy Howard U. Hosp., Washington, 1972-75; fellow Meml. Sloan-Kettering Cancer Ctr., N.Y.C., 1975-76; clin. instr. radiation therapy coll. medicine Howard U., 1976, from asst. prof. to assoc. prof., 1977-79, chmn. dept. radiotherapy, 1979—2004, prof., 1984. Clin. assoc. prof. radiation oncology coll. medicine Georgetown U., Washington, 1979; chmn. radiation therapy Greater Southeastern Cmty. Hosp., 1991; chmn. Howard U. Cancer Com., 1985-2004; interim dir. Howard U. Cancer Ctr., 1991, exec. com., 1979-2004; chmn. adv. bd. Howard U. Coll. Allied Health Scis. Radiation Therapy Tech., 1977-2004; appt. to Nat. Cancer Adv. Bd., 1994-2004. Contbr. articles to profl. jours. Chmn. D.C. Cancer Consortiu,; chmn. trial com. Nat. Cancer Inst., 1984-86, patient data query editl. bd., 1984-86; program com. nat. conf. Am. Cancer Soc., 1984, trustee, 1979-2004; mem. Nat. Cancer Adv. Bd., 1994-2004. Jr. Faculty Clin. fellow Am. Cancer Soc., 1977-79. Mem. Am. Soc. Therapeutic Radiology (scientific program com. 1982-85), Am. Coll. Radiology (com. radiotherapy rsch. and devel. 1982-85), Am. Soc. Clin. Onocology, Nat. Med. Assn., Radiologic Soc. North Am., Mid-Atlantic Soc. Radiation Onocologists, N.Y. Acad. Scis., Meml. Sloan-Kettering Radiation Therapy Dept. Alumni Assn. (pres. 1989). Home: Washington, DC. Died Feb. 7, 2004.

GOLDSTEIN, FRED, accountant; b. N.Y.C., Aug. 24, 1924; s. Max and Mary (Frisch) G.; m. Roslyn Weissman, Dec. 24, 1953; children: Lori Beth, Barry Mark. BBA cum laude, CCNY, 1950; MBA, NYU, 1952. CPA. Ptnr. Wertheim & Co., N.Y.C., from 1959. Lectr. Found. Acctg. Edn., N.Y.C., 1986. Pres. South Park Civic Assn., Roslyn, 1962-63, Temple Sinai Brotherhood, Roslyn, 1979-80, of Temple Sinai, 1987-89; mem. exec. bd. N.Y. Fed. Union, N.Y. State chpt. Union of Am. Hebrew Congregations. With inf. U.S. Army, WWII. Decorated Bronze Star, Purple Heart. Mem. AICPA, N.Y. State Soc. CPAs, Jewish Chautauqua Soc. (life). Jewish. Home: Roslyn, NY. Died Sept. 11, 2003.

GOLDSTEIN, PEGGY R. sculptor; b. NYC, Jan. 16, 1921; d. Francis Mortimer and Ruth (Schram) Rosenfeld; m. E. Ernest Goldstein, June 22, 1941; children: Susan Lipsitch, Daniel Frank. AB, Smith Coll., 1941; student, Art Inst. Chgo., 1941-42, Corcoran Sch. Art, 1951-52, Acad. de la Grand Chaumière, Paris, 1952-53, Atelier 17, 1953, 66-67, Acad. de Peinture Orientale, 1973-75. Tchr. Anacostia Neighborhood Mus., Smithsonian Instn., Washington, 1967-68, Am. Coll., Paris, 1976-77. One woman shows include Creative Gallery, NYC, 1951, 53, Springfield Mus. Fine Arts, Mass., 1956, SW Tex. State Coll., San Marcos, 1960, Laguna Gloria, Austin, 1956, 61, Maison du Décor, Washington, 1968, Gottesman and Ptnrs., London, 1976, Galerie Lambert, Paris, 1970, 73, 77-78, Galerie de la Cathédrale, Fribourg, 1981, Galerie Cimaise, Lausanne, 1983, Galerie Cardas, Lausanne, 1983, Galerie Valentine, Bex, 1984, Galerie Farel, Aigle, 1982, 85, Le Vieux Bourg, Denges, 1987, Galerie Motte, Geneva, 1989, Animalart, Austin Tex., 1995, Waldorf Sch. Balt., 2000; exhibited in group shows at Salon de la Jeune Sculpture, 1961, 71-76, Salon de Mai, 1970, 72-73, 77, Galerie Horizon, 1978-2000, Galerie Picpus, Montreux, 1981, Biennale of Fedn. Internat. de la Médaille, 1983, 85, 87, Création 85, Montreux, 1986, France-Chine, Marseille, 1987, Gravure, Paris, 1987, Galerie Siret, Paris, 1987-88, U. Fribourg, 1988, La Fondation Taylor, Paris, 1990, Galerie Les Hirondelles, Coppet, 1990, Bibliothèque Nat., Paris, 1992, Austin Visual Arts Assn., 1999-2000, Waldorf Sch., Baltimore, 2000; US Info. Agy. exhbns. Latin Am.; represented in permanent collections Bibliothèque Nat., Paris, Nat. Archives, Washington, Musée Jenisch, Vevey, Bibliothèque Nat., Berne, L.B.J. Libr., Austin, Tex.; also pvt. collections; executed bronze sculpture Nat. Hdqrs. Am. Camping Assn., Ind., 2 bronze mural sculptures, Austin, sculpture Andrews Elem. Sch., Austin; designer 20 medals Adminstrn. des Monnaies et Médailles, Ministère de Fin., Paris, 1973-86; illustrator: At Home After 1840, 1965; author, calligrapher: Lóng is a Dragon: Chinese Writing for Children, 1990 (Gold award Parents Choice 1991); author, calligrapher, illustrator: Hu is a Tiger, An Introduction to Chinese Writing, 1995; contbr. articles to profl. jours. Recipient Sculpture prize Soc. Washington D.C. Artists, 1954, Small Sculpture award Ball State Tchrs. Coll.,

1961, Prize UPFS Concours de Masque, 1977; Prèfecture de Paris grantee, 1971; nominated Outstanding Ptnr., Ptnrs. in Edn., Austin Adopt-a-Sch., 1995-96. Fellow Tex. Fine Art Assn., Austin Visual Arts Assn. Home: Austin, Tex. Died Aug. 9, 2003.

GOLDSTEIN, STEVEN, neurologist; b. Bronx, N.Y., June 1, 1959; BS in Chemistry, Haverford (Pa.) Coll., 1981; MD, Pa. State U., 1985. Diplomate Am. Bd. Psychiatry and Neurology. Intern Beth Israel Med. Ctr., N.Y.C., 1985-86; resident in neurology Columbia-Presbyn. Med. Ctr./Neurol. Inst., N.Y.C., 1986-88, chief resident in neurology, 1988-89; fellow in cerebrovascular disease and neurology U. Pa., Phila., 1989-90; assoc. attending neurology/staff noninvasive vascular lab Morristown (N.J.) Meml. Hosp., 1990-98, Overlook Hosp., Summit, N.J., 1990-98, Robert Wood Johnson Med. Ctr., Piscataway, N.J., 1995-98, clin. asst. prof. neurology Sch. Medicine, 1995-98; staff neurologist U. Pitts. Med. Ctr. Health Sys., 1998—2004; assoc. prof. neurology U. Pitts. Sch. Medicine, 1998—2004. Exec. com. U. Pitts. Med. Ctr. Stroke Inst., 1998-2004; spkr. Bristol-Myers, Inc., 1999-2004; course co-dir. U. Pitts. combined Neurosci. Conf., 1998-2004. Contbr. articles to profl. jours. McGill-Rhoads scholar, 1977-81; NIH grantee, 1983, Am. Heart Assn. grantee, 1984. Mem. Am. Heart Assn. (stroke coun.), Am. Soc. Neuroimaging, Am. Acad. Neurology, Phi Beta Kappa. Avocation: violist. Deceased.

GOLDSTINE, HERMAN HEINE, mathematician, association executive; b. Chgo., Sept. 13, 1913; s. Isaac Oscar and Bessie (Lipsey) Goldstine; m. Adele Katz, Sept. 15, 1941 (dec. 1964); children: Madlen, Jonathan; m. Ellen Watson, Jan. 8, 1966. BS, U. Chgo., 1933, MS, 1934, PhD, 1936; PhD honoris causa (hon.), U. Lund, Sweden, 1974; DSc (hon.), Amherst Coll., 1978, Adelphi U., 1978, Rutgers U., 1994. Rsch. asst. U. Chgo., 1937—37, instr., 1937—39, U. Mich., Ann Arbor, 1939—42, asst. prof., 1942—50; assoc. project dir. electronic computer project Inst. Advanced Study, Princeton, 1946—55, acting project dir., 1954—57, permanent mem., 1952—2004; dir. math. scis. dept. IBM Rsch., 1960—65; dir. sci. devel. IBM Data Processing Hdqrs., White Plains, 1965—67; cons. to dir. rsch. IBM, 1967—69, fellow, 1969—2004; exec. officer Am. Philos. Soc., Phila., 1984—97. Head electronic Numerical Integrator and Computer Project U.S. Army; officer in charge of sub-sta. Aberdeen Proving Grounds, U. Pa., 1942—46; cons. various govt. and mil. agys., 1946—84. Author: Author: The Computer from Pascal to vonNeumann, 1972, New and Full Moons 1001 B.C. to A.D. 1651, 1973, A History of Numerical Analysis from the 16th through the 19th century, 1977, A History of the Calculus of Variations from the 17th through the 19th Century, 1980; editor: Mathematical Papers of John I and James I Bernouilli, 1988, Die Streitschriften von Jacob und Johann Bernouilli, 1991. Bd. dirs. Nat. Constrn. Ctr., 1987—90; trustee Hampshire Coll., 1969—77, U. Pa. Press, from 1985; mem. adv. coun. history of sci. program Princeton U., 1982—87; mem. vis. com. phys. sci. divsn. U. Chgo., 1976—86; mem. com. Annenberg Rsch. Inst., 1987—91; bd. dirs. Glaucoma Svc. Found. to Prevent Blindness, from 1989. Lt. col. U.S. Army, World War II. Named to Hall of Fame, U.s. Army Ordnance Dept., 1997; recipient Alumni Achievement award, U. Chgo., 1975, Harry Goode award, Am. Fedn. Info. Processing Socs., 1979, Charter Pioneer award, IEEE, 1982, Nat. medal sci., U.S. Army, 1983, Outstanding Civilian medal, 1983, Disting. Svc. medal, 1996, Disting. Civilian Svc. medal, 1996, Herman Goldstine Fellowship in Math. Scis. IBM Rsch. renamed in honor, 1998. Mem.: NAS, Coll. Physicians Phila., Math. Assn. Am., Am. Acad. Arts and Scis., Am. Philos. Soc. (Ben Franklin medal), Am. Math. Soc., Union League, Century Assn., Phi Beta Kappa (book award in sci. 1973). Home: Bryn Mawr, Pa. Died June 16, 2004.

GOLDSTONE, JAMES, film, television and stage director; b. Los Angeles, June 8, 1931; s. Jules C. and Anita (Rosenberg) G.; m. Ruth Liebling; children: Peter, Jeffrey, Barbara. BA in English Lit., Dartmouth Coll., 1953; MA in Drama, Bennington Coll., 1959. Ind. film and TV dir., from 1958. Mem. film adv. bd. Dartmouth Coll., 1991—; vis. prof. Sch. of the Arts Grad. Film Divsn. Columbia U., 1996-97. Dir. numerous TV show episodes including Amos Burke, It's A Man's World, Death Valley Days, Bat Masterson, Outer Limits, The Man From UNCLE, Doctor Kildare, Route 66, Perry Mason, Rawhide, The Eleventh Hour, The Fugitive, The Lieutenant, The Chrysler Theater, (TV show pilots) Star Trek, The Senator, (also writer) Ironsides, (also creator) Iron Horse, (TV films) Scalplock, 1966, Shadow Over Elveron, 1967, A Clear and Present Danger, 1970 (Emmy award nomination), Cry Panic, 1974, Things in Their Season, 1974, Journey from Darkness, 1975 (Christopher award), Eric, 1975 (Internat. Film Festival award), Studs Lonigan miniseries, 1979, Kent State, 1982 (Emmy award Best Dir., Gold medal N.Y. Film Festival), Charles & Diana: A Royal Love Story, 1982, Calamity Jane, 1983, The Sun Also Rises miniseries, 1984, Dreams of Gold, 1986, Earth*Star Voyager miniseries, 1987, (feature films) Jigsaw, 1968, A Man Called Gannon, 1968, Winning, 1969, Brother John, 1971, Red Sky at Morning, 1971, The Gang That Couldn't Shoot Straight, 1972, They Only Kill Their Masters, 1973, Swashbuckler, 1976, Rollercoaster, 1977, When Time Ran Out, 1980. Pres. Bennington Area Arts Coun., 1991-95; trustee Vt. Arts Coun., 1995—; founding mem., bd. dirs. Vt. Film Commn., 1997—, pres.-elect, 1998-99. Mem. Dirs. Guild Am. (co-chmn. pres's. com. 1986—, mem. dirs. coun. nat. bd.), Writers Guild Am., Film Editors Union, Acad. TV Arts and Scis. (bd. govs. 1966-68, mem. awards adv. com., Emmy award 1981), Acad. Motion Picture Arts and Scis. (mem. dirs's. exec. com. 1985—). Home: Shaftsbury, Vt. Died Nov. 5, 1999.

GOLUB, SAMUEL JOSEPH, textile sciences consultant; b. Middleboro, Mass., July 25, 1915; s. Solomon Harry and Bessie (Caplan) G.; m. Faye Goldstein, Sept. 21, 1940; children: Shepard Carl, Joan Nancy Golub Cohen. BS, U. Mass., Amherst, 1938, MS, 1940; PhD, Harvard U., 1945. Assoc. prof. biology U. Mass., Ft. Devens, 1945-46; biology editor Webster's Dictionary, Springfield, Mass., 1946-48; asst. prof. Brandeis U., Waltham, Mass., 1949-56; sr. rsch. assoc. Fabric Rsch. Labs., Dedham, Mass., 1956-59; assoc. dir. ACH Fiber Svc., Boston, 1959-63; asst. dir. Albany Internat. Rsch. Co., Dedham, 1963-85; cons. on textile scis., Newton, Mass., from 1985. Contbr. articles to profl. jours.; patentee in textile field. Chmn. Am. Cancer Soc., Newton, 1970. Recipient Civilian Meritorious Svc. award USN, 1945; grantee Rogoff Found., 1974. Fellow Am. Inst. Chemists; mem. ASTM (hon. 1980, chmn. com. on dists. 1971-72, com. D13, 1972-78, com. on standards 1973-76, task groups 1960-85), Fiber Soc., Am. Assn. Textile Chemists and Colorists, Internat. Wool Textile Assn. (tech. rep. for U.S. 1972-78), Phi Kappa Phi. Deceased.

GOMILLION, JESSE D., JR., otolaryngologist; b. Mobile, Ala., Sept. 17, 1923; MD, U. Tex., 1947. Intern U. Tex. Hosps., 1947-48, resident, 1948-50. Mem. AMA, Am. Acad. Otllaryngology Head & Neck Surgery, So. Med. Assn. Died June 28, 1999.

GONDA, HARRY HENRIK, psychiatrist; b. Mako, Hungary, Apr. 17, 1915; came to U.S., 1949, naturalized, 1954; s. Joseph and Regina (Frankel) G.; m. Clara Turai-Lichtig, May 6, 1939; children: John Richard, Robert Dale. Baccalaureate summa cum laude, Matura Realgymnasium, Debrecen, Hungary, 1933; MD cum laude, U Debrecen, 1939. Diplomate Am. Bd. Psychiatry and Neurology; lic. physician, N.Y., Calif.; cert. mental health adminstr.; lic. sch. psychiatrist, N.Y.C. Rotating intern Univ. Hosps., Debrecen, 1940-41; resident in internal medicine Chevra Kadisha Hosp., Nagyvarad, Hungary, 1941-42; resident Neuropsychiat. Inst., U. Debrecen, 1945; fellow in child psychiatry Bklyn. Juvenile Guidance Ctr., 1959, Jewish Bd. Guardians, 1960-61; dep. dir. Suffolk Psychiat. Hosp., to 1970; med. dir. South Shore Child Guidance Ctr., Freeport, N.Y., 1970-79; staff psychiatrist South Nassau Communities Hosp., Oceanside, N.Y., 1975-80; psychiat. cons. Student Health Svc. Calif. State U., Long Beach, 1979-91; psychiat. cons. Long Beach Mental Health Ctr.-Children's Day Treatment Ctr., from 1980. Pvt. practice adult psychiatry, 1957-80, child and adolescent psychiatry, 1961-80; asst. clin. prof. psychiatry Albert Einstein Coll. Medicine, 1966-74; asst. prof. clin. psychiatry SUNY, Stony Brook, 1976-80. Fellow Am. Psychiat. Soc.; mem. Med. Soc. State of N.Y., Soc. for Adolescent Psychiatry, N.Y. State Hosps. Med. Alumni Assn. (sec. 1976-80). Home: Santa Ana, Calif. Deceased.

GOOD, ROBERT ALAN, physician, educator; b. Crosby, Minn., May 21, 1922; s. Roy Homer and Ethel Gay (Whitcomb) Good; m. Noorbibi K. Day, 1986; children from previous marriage: Robert Michael, Mark Thomas, Alan Maclyn, Margaret Eugenia, Mary Elizabeth. BA, U. Minn., 1944, MB, 1946, PhD, MD, U. Minn., 1947, DSc (hon.), 1989; MD (hon.), U. Uppsala, Sweden, 1966; DSc (hon.), NY Med. Coll., 1973, Med. Coll. Ohio, 1973, Coll. Medicine and Dentistry, NJ, 1974, Hahnemann Med. Coll., 1974, U. Chgo., 1974, St. John's U., 1977, U. Health Sci., Chgo. Med. Sch., Chgo., 1978, Miami Children's Hosp., 1986, U. Minn. Med. Sch., 1989, U. Rome, Rome. Tchg. asst. dept. anatomy U. Minn., Mpls., 1944—45; from instr. pediat. to assoc. prof. U. Minn. Med. Sch., 1950—54, Am. Legion Meml. rsch. prof. pediat., 1954—73, prof. microbiology, 1962—72, Regents prof. pediat. and microbiology, 1969—73, prof., head dept. pathology, 1970—72; intern U. Minn. Hosps., 1947, asst. resident pediat., 1948—49; pres., dir. Sloan-Kettering Inst. for Cancer Rsch., 1973—80, mem., 1973—81; prof. pathology Sloan-Kettering divsn. Grad. Sch. Med. Scis. Cornell U., 1973—81, dir., 1973—80; adj. prof., vis. physician Rockefeller U., 1973—81; prof. medicine, pediat. and pathology Cornell U. Med. Coll., 1973—81; dir. rsch. Meml. Sloan-Kettering Cancer Ctr., v.p., 1980—81; dir. rsch. Meml. Hosp. for Cancer and Allied Diseases, 1973—80, also attending physician depts. medicine and pediat.; attending pediatrician N.Y. Hosp., 1973—81; mem., head cancer rsch. program Okla. Med. Rsch. Found., 1982—85; prof. pediat., rsch. prof. medicine, Okla. Med. Rsch. Found. prof. microbiology and immunology U. Okla. Health Sci. Ctr., 1982—85; attending physician, head divsn. immunology Okla. Children's Meml. Hosp., 1982—85; attending physician in internal medicine Okla. Meml. Hosp., 1983—85; physician-in-chief All Children's Hosp., St. Petersburg, Fla., 1985—2001; prof., chmn. dept. pediat. U. South Fla., St. Petersburg, 1985—91, prof. depts. pediat., microbiology, immunology and medicine, from 1985; head allergy and clin. immunology, dept. pediat. U. South Fla./All Children's Hosp., St. Petersburg, 1985—2002, dir. allergy/immunology tng. program dept. pediat., 2003; disting. univ. prof. U. South Fla., St. Petersburg, 1989—2003. Vis. investigator Rockefeller Inst. for Med. Rsch., NYC, 1949—50, asst. physician to hosp., NY, 1949—50; attending pediatrician Hennepin County Gen. Hosp., 1950—73, cons., 1960—73; mem. Unitarian Svc. Commn. Med. Exch. Team to France, Germany, Switzerland and Czechoslovakia, 1958; cons. VA Hosp., Mpls., 1959—60; cons., sci. advisor Nat. Jewish Hosp., Denver, 1964—69, Children's Asthma Rsch. Inst. and Hosp., Denver, 1964—69; mem. study sects. USHPS, 1952—69; expert adv. panel on immunology WHO, from 1967; cons. Merck & Co., NJ, 1968—72, Nat. Cancer Inst., 1973—74; ad. hoc com. Pres.'s Sci. Adv. Coun. on Biol. and Med. Sci., 1970, Pres.'s Cancer Panel, 1972; awards com. Lyndon B. Johnson Found., 1972; adv. com. Bone Marrow Transplant Registry, from 1973; chmn. Internat. Bone Marrow Registry, 1977—79; fgn. adv. Acad. Med. Sci., China, from 1980; chmn. Fla. Gov.'s Task Force on AIDS, 1985—87, mem., 1988—94. Author numerous books, editor; contbr. articles to profl. jours. Adv. coun. Children's Hosp. Rsch. Found., Cin., 1954—58; bd. sci. advisers Jane Coffin Childs Meml. Fund Med. Rsch., 1972—74, Merck Inst. Therapeutic Rsch., 1972—76; trustee Eleanor Naylor Dana Charitable Trust, from 1982; bd. dirs. Allergy Found. Am., 1973. Fellow: AAAS, Am. Acad. Pediat. (1st hon. fellow sect. on allergy and immunology), Am. Acad. Arts and Sci., NY Acad. Sci., Acad. Multidisciplinary Rsch., Am. Coll. of Allergy and Immunology (hon. John P. McGovern Lectureship award 1993, Schering Jaros Lecture award 1993), The Philippine Pediat. Soc. (hon.), Am. Coll. Physicians (award 1993), Royal Soc. Medicine; mem.: AAUP, NAS, Internat. Bone Marrow Transplant Registry (charter), Pioneer, Am. Soc. Transplant Surgeons, Internat. Soc. Immunopharmacology (founding mem.), Western Assn. Immunologists, Transplant Soc., Internat. Soc. Exptl. Hematology (award in pioneering leadership and accomplishments 1994), Internat. Soc. Blood Transfusion, Practitioner's Soc., Detroit Surg. Assn. (McGraw medal 1969), Am. Clin. and Climatol. Assn. (Gordon Wilson Gold medal 1967), Soc. for Pediatric Rsch., Soc. for Exptl. Biology and Medicine (past pres.), Reticuloendothelial Soc. (past pres.), NAS Inst. Medicine (charter), Minn. State Med. Assn., Internat. Soc. for Transplantation Biology, Internat. Acad. Pathology, Am. Soc. Transplant Surgeons (hon.), Internat. Soc. Nephrology, Infectious Disease Soc. Am. (Squibb award 1968), Harvey Soc., Ctrl. Soc. Clin. Rsch. (past pres.), Assn. Am. Physicians, Am. Soc. Microbiology, Am. Soc. Exptl. Pathology (past pres.), Am. Soc. Clin. Investigation (past. pres.), Am. Rheumatism Assn., Northwestern Pediatric Soc., Mpls. Pediatric Soc., Am. Pediatric Soc. (John Howland award 1987), Am. Assn. Immunologists (past pres.), Am. Assn. Anatomists, Am. Fedn. Clin. Rsch., Am. Assn. History of Medicine, Phi Beta Kappa, Alpha Omega Alpha, Sigma Xi. Home: Saint Petersburg, Fla. Died June 13, 2003.

GOOD, ROBERT MCCLIVE, investment manager; b. Covington, Va., Sept. 30, 1952; s. William Fulton and Elizabeth Traynum (Vance) G.; m. Kathleen Susan Flosi, June 12, 1976; children: Andrew McClive, Hannah Elizabeth, Pamela Isabel. BA summa cum laude, Princeton U., 1974; PhD, Yale U., 1980; MSBA, MIT, 1986. Asst. prof. Brown U., Providence, R.I., 1980-83, Dartmouth Coll., Hanover, N.H., 1983-84, U. Pa., Phila., 1984-85; mng. dir. Cambridge Assocs. Inc., Boston, 1985-97; ptnr. South St. Advisors, Providence, from 1997. Mem. adv. bd. Exxel Capital, Buenos Aires, 1995—, Latin Am. Enterprise Fund, Miami, 1995-97. Author: The Sheep of His Pasture, 1982; contbr. articles to profl. jours. Fellow Am. coun. Learned Socs., Am. Schs. Oriental Rsch.; mem. Phi Beta Kappa. Home: Providence, RI. Died Apr. 5, 2002.

GOODE, WILLIAM JOSIAH, sociology educator; b. Houston, Aug. 30, 1917; s. William J. and Lillian Rosalie (Bare) G.; m. Josephine Mary Cannizzo, Dec. 22, 1938 (div. 1946); children: Brian Erich, Rachel (dec.), Barbara Nan; m. Ruth Siegel, Oct. 20, 1950 (div. 1971); 1 son, Andrew Josiah. BA, U. Tex., 1938, MA, 1939; PhD, Pa. State U., 1946; D.Sc. (hon.), Upsala U., 1970. Instr. sociology Pa. State U., 1941-43; social sci. analyst Inter-Am. Statis. Inst., 1943-44; asst. prof. Wayne State U., 1946-50; asso. research dir. Columbia U., 1950-52, asso. prof. sociology, 1952-56, prof., 1956-74, Giddings prof. sociology, 1975-77; prof. Stanford U., 1977-86, prof. emeritus, from 1986; assoc. Harvard U., 1986-92; vis. prof. Hebrew U., Jerusalem, 1992-93; rsch. assoc. sociology George Mason U. Prof. Free U. Berlin, 1954; vis. fellow Wolfson Coll., Oxford U., 1980; U.S. del. UN Conf. Aid to Tech. Undeveloped Nations, 1963; bd. dirs., sec. Social Sci. Research Council; gov., asso. dir. Bur. Applied Social Research; mem. behavioral scis. tng. com. Nat. Inst. Gen. Med. Scis., NIMH, 1966-67; vis. scholar Nat. Acad. Scis., China, 1986; vis. prof. Hebrew U., Jerusalem, 1992-93. Author: Religion Among the Primitives, 1951, Methods in Social Research, 1952, After Divorce, 1956, Struktur Der Familie, World Revolution and Family Patterns, 1963, The Family, 1964, 82, Family and Society, 1965, Dynamics of Modern Society, 1966, Explorations in Social Theory, 1973, (with L. Mitchell and F. Furstenberg) Willard Waller: On the Family, Education and War, 1970, Principles of Sociology, 1977, The Celebration of Heroes: Prestige as a Social Control Process, 1979, World Changes in Divorce Patterns, 1993; co-author: The Other Half, 1971, Social Systems and Family Patterns, 1971; editor: series Sociol, 1953; assoc. editor: Marriage and Family Living, 1956; contbr. articles to profl. jours. Served with USNR, 1944-45. Guggenheim fellow, 1965-66, 83-84; sr. scientist career grantee NIMH, 1969-74; Russell Sage Found. fellow, 1983-84; recipient MacIver award Am. Sociol. Soc., 1965, Burgess award Nat. Council Family Relations, 1969, Merit award Eastern Social Soc., 1992. Fellow Am. Acad. Arts and Scis.; mem. Am. Sociol. Soc. (exec. com., council 1959-62, pres. 1971-72), Eastern Sociol. Soc. (pres. 1959-60, exec. com. 1959-61), ACLU (dir.), Sociol. Research Assn. (exec. council, pres. 1967—) Home: Fairfax, Va. Died May 4, 2003.

GOODHUE, MARY BRIER, lawyer, former state senator; b. London, 1921; naturalized, 1942; d. Ernest and Marion H. (Hawks) Brier; m. Francis A. Goodhue, Jr., May 15, 1948 (dec. Sept. 1990); 1 child, Francis A. III. BA, Vassar Coll., 1942; LLB, U. Mich., 1944. Bar: N.Y. 1945. Assoc. Root, Clark, Buckner & Ballantine, N.Y.C., 1945-48; asst. counsel N.Y. State Crime Commn., N.Y.C., 1951-53, Moreland Commn., N.Y.C., 1953-54; mem. firm Goodhue, Arons & Neary and predecessors, Mt. Kisco, 1955—2002. Mem. N.Y. State Assembly from 93d Dist., 1975-78, N.Y. State Senate, 1979-92. N.Y. del. Nat. Women's Conf., Houston, 1977. Mem. ABA, West Bar Assn., No. Westchester Bar Assn. Home: Mount Kisco, NY. Died Mar. 24, 2004.

GOODMAN, DAVID BARRY POLIAKOFF, physician, educator; b. Lynn, Mass., June 1, 1942; s. Nathan and Eva (Poliakoff) G.; m. J. Kathleen Greenacre, 1994; children: Derek, Alex AB, Harvard Coll., 1964; MD, U. Pa., 1968, PhD, 1972. Intern dept. pathology U. Pa. Hosp., Phila., 1971-72; assoc. pediatrics and biochemistry U. Pa. Sch. Medicine, Phila., 1972-73, research asst. prof., 1973-76, assoc. prof., 1980-82, prof. pathology and lab. medicine, 1982—, dir. div. lab. medicine, 1980-83; dir. endocrinology-oncology lab., from 1984; asst. prof. internal medicine Yale U. Med. Sch., New Haven, 1976-79, assoc. prof., 1979-80. Cons. NSF, VA, Ctr. Oral Health Research, U. Pa. Contbr. numerous articles to profl. jours.; mng. editor: Metabolic Bone Disease and Related Rsch., 1981-90; editor Hormonal Regulation Epithelial Transport Ions and Water, 1981, Technology Impact: Potential Directions for Laboratory Medicine, 1984. Recipient Achievement award Upjohn Co., 1968; Roland Jackson scholar, 1964-68; Pa. Plan scholar, 1968-72 Fellow N.Y. Acad. Scis. (Lamport award 1981); mem. Acad. Clin. Lab. Physicians and Scientists, AAAS, Am. Assn. Pathologists, Am. Fedn. Clin. Research, Am. Heart Assn., Am. Physiol. Soc., Am. Soc. Bone and Mineral Research, Soc. Devel. Biology, Soc. Neurosci. Home: Wynnewood, Pa. Died Feb. 17, 2003.

GOODMAN, DONALD C. university administrator; b. Chgo., Nov. 24, 1927; s. Alexander Goodman and Freda (Mermelstein) G.; m. Martha Huggins, July 3, 1968; children: Brian and Eric (twins), Michael and Susan (twins), Elaine, Alison; stepchildren: Bruce, Adam, Mitchell. BS, U. Ill., 1949, MS, 1950, PhD, 1954. Instr. U. Pa., 1954-56; mem. faculty U. Fla., 1956-68, prof., 1963-68, chmn. dept. anatomical scis., 1965-68; co-dir. Center Neurol. Sci., 1964-68; prof. anatomy, chmn. dept. SUNY Med. Center, Syracuse, 1968-82, dean Coll. Grad. Studies, 1973-82, interim dean med. scis., 1975-76, v.p. acad. affairs, 1975-78, v.p. research and acad. affairs, 1978-82; v.p. acad. affairs East Tenn. State U., 1982; dean health related professions SUNY-Syracuse Health Scis. Ctr., 1983-95, v.p. acad. affairs, 1983-86, provost, 1986-95, interim pres., 1992. Mem. interdisciplinary studies adv. coun. Fla. Gulf Coast U., 1997. Author books and articles; editor: Brain, Behavior and Evolution. Mem. study sect. NIH. Served with AUS, 1946-48. Recipient Annual Research award Fla. chpt. Sigma Xi; fellow award Assn. Schs. Allied Health Professions, 1993. Fellow Am. Soc. Allied Health Professions; mem. Am. Assn. Anatomists (exec. com. 1978-82), Nat. Coun. Univ. Rsch. Adminstrs., Soc. Neurosci., Am. Assn. Higher Edn., Sigma Xi. Home: Punta Gorda, Fla. Deceased.

GOODMAN, EDMUND NATHAN, surgeon, pain management consultant; b. NYC, July 14, 1908; s. Benjamin Harry and Sophia (Schweisheimer) Goodman; m. Marian Powers, Mar. 9, 1950; children: Wendy, Tonne, Edmund Jr., Stacy. BS, CCNY, 2028; MD, Columbia U., 1933, MEd, DSc, 1942; postgrad., Cambridge U., 1935—36. Intern Presbyn. Hosp., NYC, 1936—38; asst. resident, then resident in surgery Columbia-Presbyn. Hosp., NYC, 1938—41, instr. in surgery, 1941, asst. clin. prof. surgery, 1950—65, assoc. clin. prof., 1965—81; attending surgeon Mt. Sinai Hosp., NYC, 1947—49; practice medicine specializing in pain mgmt. Roslyn, Roslyn, NY, 1982—96. Lt. comdr. USN, 1941—46. Mem.: ACS, Am. Bd. Surgery, NY Acad. Med., NY Surg. Soc. Died Dec. 9, 2003.

GOODRUM, RUTH ANN, elementary school educator; b. Muscatine, Iowa, Apr. 8, 1943; d. Harold W. and Elsie L. (Irwin) Boorn; m. Bryan J. Goodrum, June 15, 1968; children: Brent W., Joseph B. AA, Muscatine C.C., 1963; BA, U. No. Iowa, 1965. Cert. tchr., Iowa. Tchr. elem. grades Hubbard (Iowa) Community Sch., 1965-68, Wilton (Iowa) Community Sch., 1968-99. Contbr. articles to profl. jours. Sec. Wilton Park Bd., 1976-80; mem. Wilton Libr. Bd., 1990-99; sec. Wilton Found. Bd., 1983-99; pres. Mississippi Bend UniServ Unit, Eldridge, Iowa, 1987-88, Wahkonsa Ladies League, Wilton, 1990-99; mem. altar and rosary bd. Wilton St. Mary's Ch., 1980-99; participant Role of Women, Davenport (Iowa) Diocese, 1988-99. Mem. NEA (rep. assembly mem.), Iowa State Edn. Assn. (del. assembly 1965-99), Wilton Edn. Assn. (negotiations chair 1985-99), Wahkonsa Country Club, Bloomington Grange, Ptnrs. in Edn. (chairperson). Republican. Roman Catholic. Avocations: reading, writing, spectator sports. Home: Walton, Iowa. Died June 25, 1999.

GOODWIN, ELIZABETH CAROL, special education educator; b. Jacksonville, Fla., Aug. 14, 1946; d. Arthur Lee and Florence Mabery (Ivey) Dunnam; m. James Stanley Goodwin, May 29, 1970; 1 child, Carolyn Sue. AA, Fla. Jr. Coll., 1967; BA, U. W. Fla., 1969; MEd, U. N. Fla., 1987; postgrad., Jacksonville U., from 1991. Cert. spl. edn. tchr., Fla. Substitute tchr. Duval County Schs., Jacksonville, 1970-71, 79-87, from 1988, spl. edn. tchr., 1987-88, Twin City Bapt. Temple, Lunenberg, Mass., 1976-77, Univ. Christian Sch., Jacksonville, 1977-78; tchr. Am. and western history Victory Christian Sch., Jacksonville, 1978-79. Author: (poems) Sunshine and Daisies, 1981. Leader Awanas, Tampa, Fla., 1972-74; Sunday sch. tchr., choir tchr. local ch.; foster parent. 2d lt. U.S. Army, 1970. Scottish Rite scholar, 1976-77; named Outstanding Tchr. of Yr., Twin City Christian, 1976-77. Mem. Coun. for Exceptional Children, Duval Tchrs. United, Kappa Delta Pi. Democrat. Baptist. Avocations: sewing, crafts, gardening. Home: Jacksonville, Fla. Died Oct. 8, 2001.

GOODWIN, ELLEN PEMBERTON, marriage and family therapist; b. Columbia, S.C., Sept. 6, 1938; m. Joel Sexton Goodwin, July 9, 1960; children: Joel II, James, Charles, Mary Katherine. BSN, U. N.C., 1960; MEd, U. N.C., Greensboro, 1980, PhD, 1988. Cert. marital and family therapist, N.C. RN VA Hosp., Bklyn., 1960; pub. health nurse N.Y.C. Dept. Health, Bklyn., 1961; pvt. practice Salisbury, N.C., 1980-84; cert. marital and family therapist Ctr. for Creative Living, Salisbury, from 1984. Onicron Nu hon. scholar, 1980. Mem. Am. Assn. Marital and Family Therapist, Nat. Coun. Family Rels. Home: Salisbury, NC. Deceased.

GORBMAN, AUBREY, biologist, educator; b. Detroit, Dec. 13, 1914; s. David and Esther (Korenblit) G.; m. Genevieve D. Tapperman, Dec. 25, 1938; children— Beryl Ann, Leila Harriet, Claudia Louise, Eric Jay. AB, Wayne State U., 1935, MS, 1936; PhD, U. Calif., 1940. Research assoc. U. Calif., 1940-41; instr. zoology Wayne U., 1941-44; Jane Coffin Childs fellow in anatomy Yale, 1944-46; asst. prof. zoology Barnard Coll., Columbia, 1946-49, assoc. prof., 1949-53, prof., 1953-63, exec. officer dept. zoology, 1952-55; prof. zoology U. Wash., Seattle, 1963—85, prof. emeritus, 1985—2003, chmn. zoology dept., 1963-66; biologist Brookhaven Nat. Lab., 1952-58; Fulbright scholar College de France, Paris, 1951-52; Guggenheim fellow U. Hawaii, 1955-56; vis. prof. biochemistry Nagoya U. Japan, 1956, Tokyo U., 1960, 84; James chair in zoology St. Francis Xavier U., 1985; adj. prof. zoology U. Alta., Can., 1985—. Editor: Comparative Endocrinology; editorial bd.: Endocrinology, 1957-61; editor-in-chief: Gen. and Comparative Endocrinology. Fellow A.A.A.S., N.Y. Zool. Soc., N.Y. Acad. Sci.; mem. Endocrine Soc., Am. Inst. Biol. Scis. (governing bd. 1969-75), Am. Soc. Zoologists (pres. 1976), Soc. Exptl. Biology and Medicine, Phi Beta Kappa. Home: Seattle, Wash. Died Sept. 21, 2003.

GORDON, LEONARD VICTOR, retired psychology educator; b. Montreal, Aug. 15, 1917; came to U.S., 1936, naturalized, 1938; s. Peter Z. and Bessie Victoria (Kirsch) G.; m. Katharine Ann Burton, Nov. 30, 1946; children: John Christopher (dec.), Jeffrey Burton. BA, UCLA, 1940; MA, Ohio State U., 1947, PhD, 1950. Instr. Ohio State U., Columbus, 1947-49, rsch. assoc., 1949-50; assoc. dir. office rsch. svcs. Boston U., 1950-51; vis. asst. prof. U. N.Mex., Albuquerque, 1951-52; divsn. dir. Naval Pers. Rsch. Activity, San Diego, 1952-62; lab chief U.S. Army Pers. Rsch. Office, Washington, 1962-66; prof. ednl. psychology and stats. SUNY, Albany, 1966-87, prof. emeritus, from 1987; pres. Intertest, Guilderland, N.Y, from 1985. Disting. vis. prof. Wilford Hall U.S. Air Force Med. Ctr., Lackland AFB, Tex., 1977-79; rsch. adv. com. Office of Edn., 1969-70; advisor European Test Publishers Group, 1992—; adv. com. Ednl. Psychologist, 1973-74; grant referee NIE, 1972-73, Can. Coun., 1975-77, NSF, 1977-78; external examiner U. West Indies, 1978-81, Patna U., 1969-75, India Inst. Tech., 1977-81; lectr., cons. in field. Author: (with Ross L. Mooney) Mooney Problem Check Lists, 1950, Gordon Personal Profile, 1953, (rev. edit. 1993), 1978, Gordon Personal Inventory, 1956, (rev. edit. 1993), 1978, Global edit., 1992, Survey of Interpersonal Values, 1960, (rev. edit.), 1976, Gordon Occupational Check List, 1963, (rev. edit.), 1981, Work Environment Preference Schedule, 1973, Measurement of Interpersonal Values, 1975, (with Akio Kikuchi) Social Psychology of Values, 1975, (rev. edit. with Akio Kikuchi), 1981, Survey of Personal Values, 1967, (rev. edit.), 1984, School Environment Preference Survey, 1978; mem. editl. bd. Jour. Applied Psychology, 1971-82; contbr. articles to profl. jours. Rsch. coord. Peace Corps, Washington, 1964-65; internat. steering com. Evaluation Rsch. Soc., 1976-77. With USAAC, 1941-44. Recipient Personal commendations Dir. of the Peace Corps, 1965, Sec. of the Army, 1965. Fellow Am. Psychol. Assn., AAAS; mem. Internat. Assn. Applied Psychology, Am. Ednl. Research Assn., Nat. Council Measurement in Edn., Author's Guild. Home: Schenectady, NY. Died Aug. 11, 2003.

GORDON, THOMAS CHRISTIAN, JR., former justice; b. Richmond, Va., July 14, 1915; s. Thomas Christian and Ruth Nelson (Robins) G. BS, U. Va., 1936, LL.B., 1938. Bar: Va. bar 1937. Assoc. Parrish, Butcher & Parrish, Richmond, 1938-40; assoc., then ptnr. McGuire Woods LLP (and predecessors), Richmond, 1940-65, 72-83; justice Supreme Ct. Va., 1965-72; lectr. Law Sch., U. Va., 1970-72, Marshall-Wythe Sch. Law, 1979-81. Bd. editors: Va. Law Rev, 1937-38. Trustee, past pres. Childrens Hosp., Richmond. Served to maj. AUS, 1941-45. Fellow Am. Bar Found.; mem. Am. Bar Assn., Va. Bar Assn. (pres. 1963-64) Episcopalian (vestry, sr. warden). Home: Richmond, Va. Died May 17, 2003.

GORMAN, CLIFF, actor; b. N.Y.C. m. Gayle Stevens. Student, U. N.Mex., UCLA; BS in Edn., NYU. Mem. Jerome Robbins' Am. Theatre Lab., 1966-67. N.Y.C. appearances include Hogan's Goat, 1965, Ergo, 1968, Boys in the Band, 1968 (Obie award), Lenny, 1972-73 (Drama Desk award, Toni award), Chapter Two, 1977, Doubles, 1985; stage appearance in Social Security, 1986; film appearances in Justine, 1969, The Boys in the Band, 1970, Cops and Robbers, 1973, An Unmarried Woman, 1978, Night of the Juggler, 1979, All That Jazz, 1979, Angel, 1984, Night and the City, 1992, Hoffa, 1993, Ghost Dog, 1999; TV appearances in The Trial of the Chicago Seven, 1970, Class of 63, 1973, The Bunker, 1981, Double Take, 1985, Internal Affairs, 1988, Howard Beach, 1989, Murder in Black and White, 1990, Vestige of Honor, 1990, Murder Times Seven, 1990, Terror on Track 9, 1992, Return of Ironside, 1993, Silent Betrayal, 1994, Forget-Me-Not Murders, 1994, Down Came a Blackbird, 1995; TV shows include Law and Order, Police Story, Hawaii Five-O, Streets of San Francisco, Trapper John, Murder She Wrote, Friday the 13th-The Series, Cagney and Lacey, Spenser for Hire. Recipient La Guardia Meml. award, 1972, Show Bus. award, 1972. Mem. Honor Legion N.Y.C. Police Dept., Friends George Spelvin (life). Home: New York, NY. Died Sept. 5, 2002.

GORMAN, MARVIN, science administrator, pharmaceutical industry consultant; b. Detroit, Sept. 24, 1928; s. Meyer and Sara (Evintzky) G.; m. Sue Eisler (div. Nov. 12, 1974); children: David, Judith, Debra; m. Lura Chaney, Oct. 2, 1976. BS in Chemistry, U. Mich., 1950; PhD in Chemistry, Wayne State U., 1955. Sr. scientist Eli Lilly, Indpls., 1956-64, rsch. assoc., 1964-69, advisor, 1969-81, rsch. cons., 1981-82; v.p. infectious disease Bristol-Myers Squibb, Syracuse, N.Y., 1982-86, sr. v.p. rsch. Wallingford, Conn., 1986-88, exec. v.p., gen. mgr. Seattle, 1988-91; cons. pharm. industry Key West, Fla., from 1991; v.p. product devel. Pathogenesis Corp., Seattle, 1992-94; v.p. San Souci Enterprises, from 1993. Editor: (book) Beta-Lactam Antibiotics, 1983; contbr. over 100 articles to profl. jours.; mem. editorial bd. AntiMicrobial Agents & Chemotheraphy, 1975-80, Jour. of Antibiotics, 1975-91. Fund raiser Northwood Inst., Indpls., 1980-82; vo. exec. Internat. Exec. Svc. Corps., Stamford, Conn., 1992—. Mem. Am. Chem. Soc. (chmn. 1978), Gordon Rsch. Conf. (chmn. 1974), Am. Soc. for Microbiology, Protein Soc. Achievements include 18 patents in field; discovery and development of 2 antitumor agents, 5 cephalosporins, and 1 antiparisitic agent for veterinary use. Home: Key West, Fla. Died July 10, 2001.

GORTIKOV, STANLEY MERRILL, retired music association executive; b. Los Angeles, May 14, 1919; s. Joseph and Goldie (Harris) G.; children: Jane, James, Scott. AB, U. So. Calif., 1941. Prodn. mgr. L.K. Shapiro Co., 1949-60; dir. corp. devel. Capitol Records, Inc., 1960, sr. v.p., 1966-68, pres., 1968-69; v.p., then pres. Capitol Records Distbg. Corp., Hollywood, Calif., 1960-68; exec. v.p. Capitol Industries, Inc., 1969, pres., chief exec. officer, 1969-71; pres. Rec. Industry Assn. Am., 1972-87, chmn. bd., 1987-88. Served to lt. col. AUS, 1941-45. Decorated Bronze Star. Home: Los Angeles, Calif. Died June 24, 2004.

GOTTLIEB, PHILIP M. allergist and immunologist, internist; b. Phila., Apr. 12, 1912; MD, U. Pa., 1935. Diplomate Am. Bd. Allergy and Immunology, Am. Bd. Internal Medicine. Rotating intern Phila. Gen. Hosp., 1935-37; resident in internal medicine Mt. Sinai Hosp., N.Y.C., 1938-39; emeritus head allergy sect. dept. medicine Einstein Med. Ctr., Phila.; emeritus assoc. prof. clin. medicine Temple U., Phila. Fellow ACP, Am. Assn. Immunologists, Am. Coll. Allergy and Immunology; mem. Phila. Coll. Physicians, Alpha Omega Alpha. Home: Media, Pa. Died Apr. 18, 2002.

GOTTSCHALK, ADELE M. surgeon; b. N.Y.C., Dec. 28, 1941; d. Otto George and Ada Mae Gottschalk. BS, CUNY, 1963; MD, SUNY, Buffalo, 1967. Intern and resident surgery U. Chgo. (Ill.) Hosp. and Clinics, 1967-70; resident surgery Michael Reese Hosp., Chgo., 1970-71, U. San Diego (Calif.) Hosp., 1971-73; gen. surgeon Kaiser Hosp. Harbor City, Calif., from 1973. Home: Palos Verdes Estates, Calif. Died Sept. 22, 2001.

GOULD, LOIS, author; m. Philip Benjamin, 1959 (dec.); children: Anthony, Roger; m. Robert E. Gould. BA, Wellesley Coll. Former police reporter, feature writer L.I. Star Jour.; former exec. editor Ladies Home Jour. Contbr. articles to N.Y. Times, McCalls, Ms.; columnist N.Y. Times, 1977; author: (novels) Such Good Friends, 1970, Necessary Objects, 1972, Final Analysis, 1974, A Sea-Change, 1976, La Presidenta, 1981, Medusa's Gift, 1991, No Brakes, 1997; (non-fiction) Sensible Childbirth, 1962, So You Want to Be a Working Mother!, 1966, Subject to Change, 1988, (essays) Not Responsible for Personal Articles, 1978, (story) X: A Fabulous Child's Story, 1978. Died May 29, 2003.

GOUYON, PAUL CARDINAL, archbishop; b. Bordeaux, France, Oct. 24, 1910; s. Jean-Baptiste Louis and Jeanne (Chassaing) G.; ed. in France. Ordained priest Roman Catholic Ch., 1937, consecrated bishop, 1957; bishop of Bayonne, 1957, titular archbishop of Pessinonte, 1963, archbishop of Rennes, 1964-85, now archbishop emeritus of Rennes; elevated to Sacred Coll. Cardinals, 1969. Decorated Croix de Guerre, officer Legion of Honor, comdr. Nat. Order Merit. Mem. Pax Christi (past pres. French sect.). Author several books. Died Sept. 26, 2000.

GOWENS, VERNEETA VIOLA, journalist; b. Mar. 19, 1913; d. William and Mary Cawthorne (Fowler) Gibson; m. Albert Gowens, July 17, 1936; children: Victoria Ann Goweks Utke, Mary Ann Gowens Buer. Student, Bryant and Stratton Bus. Coll. Clk., pub. rels. worker Chgo. and Riverdale Lumber Co., 1934-45; feature writer, women's editor Tribune Publs., Harvey, Ill., 1960-62, Star-Tribune, Williams Press, Chicago Heights, Ill., 1963-78; freelance writer; script writer variety shows Ship Ahoy, 1963, Fair 'n' Square, 1964. Contbr. to Internat. Altrusan, 1974, Ch. Herald, 1977. Sunday sch. tchr., youth leader 1st Ref. Ch.,

South Holland; mem. editl. coun. Ch. Herald, Ref. Ch. in Am., 1976-82; pres. Dist. 150 PTA, 1965-66; adv. com. program in ltd. occupation tng. Thornton H.S., 1963-69; mem. South Holland Indsl. Commn., 1965-68; bd. dirs. Family Svc. and Mental Health Ctr. of South Cook County, Ill., 1974-77; mem. South Holland unit Salvation Army, 1958—; judge Internat. Teen Pageant, 1969; mem. South Holland Cmty. Chest, 1978-87; adv. bd. Thornton C.C. nursing program, 1976-83; spl. events and publicity coms. South Holland Centennial, 1994; active South Holland Diamond Jubilee, 1969, South Holland Cable Commn., 1984—, South Holland Centennial Com., 1994. Recipient award South Holland C. of C., 1970, Genoa coun. K.C., 1974, Village of South Holland, 1969, 1st pl. in contest No. Ill. U., 1974, 75, award Suburban Press Found., 1969, 1st pl. award Ill. Press Assn., 1973, Sr. Medal of Honr. award Cook County Sheriff's Dept., 1997, 50 other awards in writing. Mem. Ill. Women's Press Assn. (Woman of Yr. 1974, award 1978), Nat. Fedn. Press Women (1st pl. Sweepstakes award 1976). Home: Clarendon Hills, Ill. Deceased.

GOZ, HARRY G. actor, singer; b. St. Louis, June 23, 1932; s. Isadore and Helen (Becker) G.; m. Margaret O. Avsharian, May 3, 1958; children: Michael P., Melissa S., Geoffrey C. Student, Washington U., St. Louis, 1950-51, St. Louis Inst. Music, 1954-56. Toured with Boris Goldovsy Co. in 1959, sang in operas Don Giovanni, St. Louis, 1955, La Boheme, St. Louis, 1955; singer, actor: (Broadway shows) Bajour, 1964, Fiddler on the Roof, 1965-70, Two by Two, 1970, Prisoner of Second Ave, 1972, Born Yesterday, 1976, Hocus Pocus Dominocus, 1978, To Bury A Cousin, 1980, Ferocious Kisses, 1981, Chess, 1988, (other stage prodns.) Cafe Crown, Kiss of the Spider Woman; (films) Mommie Dearest, Bill, Bill on His Own, Marathon Man, Looking Up, Rapping, Mace, Darrow, Kennedy, (stock) over 40 appearances in musicals, comedies, dramas, operas; (TV): Search for Tomorrow, The Guiding Light, The Edge of Night, All My Children, L.A. Law, Wise Guy, The Ed Sullivan Show, Ned & Stacy, Merv Griffin Show, Law and Order, David Frost Show, Law and Order Spl. Victims Unit, 3d Watch; co-prodr.: Brother Champ (42nd St. Theatre) 1976, The Importance of Being Oscar, 1998; rep. over 1200 products and comml. campaigns TV and radio voice overs and on camera appearances. With U.S. Army, 1952-54. Home: Manhasset, NY. Died Sept. 6, 2003.

GRABEMANN, KARL W. lawyer; b. Chgo., Apr. 27, 1929; s. Karl H. and Trude (Stockram) G.; m. Mary Darr, Dec. 6, 1958; children: Robert S., Lisa D. BS, Northwestern U., 1951, JD, 1956. Bar: Ill. 1957, U.S. Supreme Ct. 1960, U.S. Ct. Appeals for D.C. 1957, U.S. Ct. Appeals for 7th Circuit 1957, U.S. Ct. Appeals for 5th Circuit 1967, U.S. Dist. Ct. for D.C. 1957, U.S. Dist. Ct. for No. Dist. Ill. 1957. Atty. NLRB, Chgo., 1956-60; ptnr. firm Turner, Hunt & Woolley, Chgo., 1960-69, Keck, Mahin & Cate, Chgo., 1969-79, McDermott, Will & Emery, Chgo., 1979-89; of counsel Murphy, Smith & Polk, Chgo., from 1990. Mem. ABA, Ill. Bar Assn., Chgo. Bar Assn. Clubs: Metropolitan (Chgo.). Republican. Died 2002.

GRABER, EDWARD ALEX, obstetrician-gynecologist, educator; b. Chgo., July 24, 1914; s. Irving D. and Grace (Davis) G.; m. Sylvia H. Hess, Nov. 24, 1938; 1 son, Fredric Jay. MD, Emory U., 1936. Diplomate: Am. Bd. Gyn. Assoc. dir. ob-gyn Lenox Hill Hosp., N.Y.C., 1972-75; attending obstetrician-gynecologist N.Y. Hosp., 1975-88; prof. ob-gyn Med. Sch. Cornell U., N.Y.C., from 1975, emeritus Med. Sch., 1988; hon. attending physician N.Y. Hosp.-Cornell Med. Ctr., N.Y.C., from 1971. Author: Gynecologic Endocrinology, 1961, (with Barber) Are The Pills Safe?, Obstetric and Gynecology Procedures, 1969, Gynecological Oncology, 1970, Surgical Disease in Pregnancy, 1974, (with G. Schaefer) Complications of Gynecological Surgery, 1982; contbr. articles to profl. jours. Fellow Am. Coll. Ob-Gyn, ACS, N.Y. Acad. Medicine (pres. ob-gyn sect. 1971-72), N.Y. Gynecol. Soc. (pres. 1972-73); mem. AMA Home: New York, NY. Died Dec. 7, 1999.

GRACE, JASON ROY, advertising agency executive; b. N.Y.C., Dec. 5, 1936; s. Jack and Mitzi (Goldstick) G.; m. Marcia Jean Bell, May 16, 1966; children: Jessica Bell, Nicholas Bell. Student, Cooper Union, 1955-56, 58-62. Art dir. Benton & Bowles Inc., N.Y.C., 1962-63, Grey Advt., N.Y.C., 1963-64; sr. v.p., creative mgmt. supr. Doyle Dane Bernbach Inc., N.Y.C., 1964-72; creative dir., exec. v.p. Gilbert, Grace & Stark, N.Y.C., 1972-75, Doyle Dane Bernbach Inc., 1975-79, exec. v.p., exec. creative dir., from 1979, vice chmn., 1981-86, chmn. bd. U.S., exec. creative dir., from 1986; chmn. bd. Grace and Rothschild. Film dir., 1970— Elected art dirs. Hall of Fame, 1986—; trustee Cooper Union, 1987—; bd. dirs. Nat. Mus. Am. History, Smithsonian Inst., 1988—. With U.S. Army, 1956-58. Recipient 8 Andy awards Advt. Club N.Y., 28 Clio awards Am. Film Festival, 5 Gold Lion awards, 3 Silver Lion awards Cannes Film Festival, 9 Gold medals Art Dirs. Club, Best TV Comml. of Last 20 Yrs. award; recipient Internat. Broadcasting award, 1980, St. Gaudens medal Cooper Union Alumni Assn., Grand Masters Lifetime Achievement award N.Y.C. Tech. Coll., 2002; 6 commls. named in Clio Hall of Fame, Outstanding Alumnus Sch. Art and Design, 1987; 4 commls. placed in permanent collection Mus. Modern Art; elected to Creative Hall of Fame, The One Club, 1994, 97; 2 commls. in Advtg. Age's 50 Best TV Commls. of All Time, 3 of Top 6 in TV Guide's List of Best 50 Commls. of All Time. Home: New York, NY. Died Feb. 26, 2003.

GRAHAM, OTTO EVERETT, JR., retired athletic director; b. Waukegan, Ill., Dec. 6, 1921; s. Otto Everett and Cordonna (Hayes) G.; m. Beverly Jean Collinge, Oct. 7, 1945; children— Duey, Sandy, David. BA, Northwestern U., 1944. Quarterback with Cleve. Browns, 1946-55; coach Coll. All-Stars vs. Nat. Football League champions, 1958-65, 69-70; athletic dir., head football coach USCG Acad., New London, Conn., 1959-66, athletic dir., 1970-85; gen. mgr., head coach Washington Redskins, 1966-68. Pres. Fellowship Christian Athletes, 1956-57; former mem. bd. dirs. Washington YMCA. Served with USNR, 1944-45; now capt. USCG, ret. Named All Am. in football and basketball, 1943, All Pro quarterback, 1951, 52, 54, 55; named to Coll. Football Hall of Fame, 1955, Pro Football Hall of Fame, 1965, NFL 75th Yr. Anniversary Team, 1994, NFL 75 Yr. All-Time Team, 1994. Home: Sarasota, Fla. Died Dec. 17, 2003.

GRAHAM, SAXON (LLOYD GRAHAM), epidemiology educator; b. Buffalo, Jan. 14, 1922; s. Lloyd S. and Kathryn (Graser) G.; m. Caroline Lee Morgan, June 19, 1948; children: Robin Porter, Saxon Parker, Morgan Graser. BA, Amherst Coll., 1943; MA, Yale U., 1949, PhD, 1951; DSc (hon.), SUNY, Buffalo, 1996. Asst. prof. Chatham Coll., Pitts., 1951-53; asst. prof. biostats. U. Pitts., 1953-56; from asst. prof. to prof. epidemiology dept. sociology and dept. social and preventive medicine SUNY, Buffalo, from 1957, chmn. dept. social and preventive medicine, 1981-91, prof. emeritus, from 1992; assoc. to prin. cancer rsch. scientist Roswell Pk. Cancer Inst., Buffalo, 1956-65, prof. SUNY div., from 1967. Mem. epidemiology and disease control sect. NIH, Bethesda, Md., 1966-70; cons. WHO, Switzerland, 1965-66; dir. demographic studies, Kabul, Afghanistan, 1970-74; chmn. adv. com. to study long-term effects of plutonium Los Alamos (N.Mex.) Nat. Lab., 1976-86; mem. coun. advisors divsn. cancer rsch., resources and ctrs. Nat. Cancer Inst., Bethesda, 1973-77, mem. bd. sci. councillor divsn. cancer prevention and control, 1982-86; mem. sci. coun. Internat. Agy. Rsch. on Cancer, Lyon, France, 1986-90. Author: American Culture, 1957; contbr. numerous articles to profl. jours. Spl. agt. Counter Intelligence Corps, U.S. Army, 1943-46, PTO. Nat. Cancer Inst. grantee, 1969-91. Fellow APHA, Am. Coll. Epidemiology, Am. Sociol. Assn.; mem. Soc. Epidemiologic Rsch. (pres. 1987-88), Am. Epidemiol. Soc., Planned Parenthood, Nat. Abortion Rights League, Orchard Park Country Club, Concord Ski Club (Ellicottville, N.Y.), Scriptores (Buffalo). Republican. Avocations: piano, oil painting, alpine skiing, golf. Home: Orchard Park, NY. Died Aug. 20, 2002.

GRAHAM, VICTOR ERNEST, French language educator; b. Calgary, Alta., Can., May 31, 1920; s. William John and Mary Ethel (Wark) G.; m. Mary Helena Faunt, Aug. 1, 1946; children: Ian Robert, Gordon Keith, Miriam Elizabeth, Ross William. BA, U. Alta., 1946; BA (Rhodes scholar), Oxford U., 1948, MA, 1952, DLitt, 1968; PhD, Columbia U., 1953. Asst. prof. French and English U. Alta. Calgary br., 1948-52, assoc. prof. French, 1952-57, prof., 1957-58, asst. to dir., 1952-58; assoc. prof. French U. Toronto, Ont., 1958-60, prof., 1960-85, chmn. grad. dept. French, 1965-67; assoc. dean U. Toronto (Sch. Grad. Studies), 1967-69; vice prin. Univ. Coll., 1969-70. Vis. prof. U. Mich., 1954-55, U. Victoria, 1980-81; mem. governing council U. Toronto, 1973-76 Author: Critical Edition of the Poetry of Philippe Desportes, 7 vols., 1958-63, The Imagery of Proust, 1966, Rymes, Pernette du Guillet, 1968, (with W. McAllister Johnson) Le Recueil des Inscriptions 1558, 1972, The Paris Entries of Charles IX and Elisabeth of Austria 1571, 1974, The Royal Tour of France by Charles IX and Catherine de'Medici (1564-1566), 1979, Bibliographie des etudes sur Marcel Proust et son oeuvre, 1976, The Art of the Chinese Snuff Bottle: The J&J Collection, 1993, (with Hugh Moss and Ka Bo Tsang) A Treasury of Chinese Stuff Bottles, Vol. 1 Jade, 1995, Vol. 2 Quartz, 1998, Vol. 3, Stones Other than JAde and Quartz, 1998, others. Columbia U. open fellow, 1948; Can. Council sr. fellow, 1963; Guggenheim fellow, 1970; Connaught sr. research fellow in humanities, 1978 Fellow Royal Soc. Can. Home: Toronto, Canada. Deceased.

GRANT, JAMES DENEALE, health care company executive; b. Washington, July 9, 1932; s. Deneale and Frances (Hoskins) G.; m. Bonnie Carol Johnson, June 14, 1955; children: Glenn James, Bruce William, Scott Stockman. BS, William and Mary Coll., 1954; MBA, Wharton Sch. U. Pa., 1956; postgrad. (Pub. Affairs fellow), Stanford U., 1963-64. Mem. staff AEC, Washington, 1956-64; v.p. Nat. Inst. Pub. Affairs, Washington, 1964-69; dep. dir. White House Conf. Food, Nutrition and Health, 1969-70; dep. commr. FDA, Washington, 1970-72; asst. to chmn. CPC Internat. Inc., Englewood Cliffs, N.J., 1972-73, v.p., 1973-86; chmn., chief exec. officer T Cell Scis., Inc., 1986-92, chmn., 1992-97. Bd. dirs. Targeted Genetics Corp.; cons. U.S. Bur. Budget, 1965-69, U.S. Civil Svc. Commn. (Office Pers. Mgmt.), 1965-69; mem., vice chmn., sec. adv. com. HHS, FDA, 1990-91. Chmn. Bergen County United Fund, 1974-75; trustee Nutrition Found., 1973-78; chmn. adv. group to sec. gen. UN Conf. on Sci. and Tech. for Devel., 1979. Recipient U.S. Govt. Career Edn. award, 1963. Mem.: Omicron Delta Kappa. Presbyterian. Home: New York, NY. Died July 2002.

GRANT, LEONARD J. theatrical executive; b. N.Y.C., June 24, 1933; s. Julius Greenblatt and Rose Greenblatt; div.; 1 child, Mark Allen (dec.). BA, CCNY, 1954. TV dir./producer Emil Mogul Advt., N.Y.C., 1954-58; spl. asst. to HRH Edward the Duke of Windsor, N.Y.C., 1955, Rudolph Haley, Spl. Counsel, Senate Crime Commn., N.Y.C., 1956; exec. producer Lawrence-Schnitzer Film Prodn., L.A., from 1958; pres. Leonard Grant & Assocs., Hollywood, from 1959, Stelen Music Pub. Co., Hollywood, 1962-75, Triplex Prodns. Inc., Hollywood, 1964-72, Tangent Prodns. Inc., Hollywood, from 1978. Creator The Establishment singing group, Hollywood, 1962-75; creator, exec. dir. Scandals night club, Hollywood, 1976-80. Producer (theater prodns.) Big Time Buck White, 1964 (Obie award 1968), The Dirtiest Show in Town, 1970, Inherit the Wind, 1990. Sgt. U.S. Army, 1951-53. Recipient Spl. Award of Appreciation, Conf. of Personal Mgrs., 1971, Spl. Resolution, City of L.A., 1979. Mem. Conf. Personal Mgrs. (v.p. 1968-71, Statuette 1971), Acad. TV Arts & Scis. Avocations: travel, music, environment. Died Apr. 15, 2001.

GRANT, NICHOLAS JOHN, metallurgy educator; b. South River, N.J., Oct. 21, 1915; s. John and Mary (Sudnik) G.; m. Anne T. Phillips, Sept. 12, 1942 (dec. Apr. 1957); children: Anne P., William D. (dec.), Nicholas P.; m. Susan Mary Cooper, Aug. 1963; children: Johnathan, Katharine. SB, Carnegie Inst. Tech., 1938; ScD, MIT, 1944. Metallurgist Bethlehem Steel Co., 1938-40; former mem. faculty MIT, former prof. metallurgy; dir. Ctr. Materials Sci. and Engring., 1968-77, former ABEX prof. advanced materials. Pres., bd. dir. N.E. Materials Lab., Inc., 1954-66; tech. dir. Investment Castings Inst.; cons. industry; bd. dir. Loomis-Sayles Mut. Fund (change name to CGM), Capital Devel. Fund, Fixed Income Fund, Kimball Physics Inc., Instron Corp., Nat. Forge Co., Memry Corp.; mem. materials com. NASA, 1958-67, research com., 1970-76; chmn. working group electrometallurgy and materials U.S.-USSR Joint Sci. and Tech. Agreement; lectr. ann. Powd Met. Fundamental Lecture, 1960; lectr. ann. Japanese Lecture, 1986. Author 1 book; editor several books; contbr. 525 articles to profl. jours., also chpts. to books; holder 35 U.S. patents, more than 40 fgn. patents. Recipient Disting. Service award Investment Castings Inst., 1956, Merit award Carnegie Mellon U., J. Wallenberg award Royal Acad. Engring. Scis., Sweden, 1978, Disting. Service award Metal Powders Ind. Fedn., 1985; N.J.G. grant named in his honor Internat. Conf., 1985; N.J.G. grad. fellowship named in his honor MIT, 1987; named hon. prof. U. Sci. and Tech., Beijing, China, 1992. Fellow Am. Soc. Metals (mem. com. radioactive waste 1986-88, N.J.G. undergrad. fellowship named in his honor 1990), AIME (ann. Krumb lectr. 1978); mem. ASTM, NAE, Am. Acad. Arts and Scis., Japan Inst. Metals (hon.), Sigma Xi, Tau Beta Pi, Theta Tau, Alpha Xi Epsilon. Home: Scituate, Mass. Died May 1, 2004.

GRAUBARD, SEYMOUR, lawyer; b. N.Y.C., Mar. 8, 1911; s. John and Edna (Kiesler) G.; m. Blanche Kazon (dec. 2003), Aug. 24, 1941; 1 child, Katherine (Mrs. William Calvin). AB, Columbia U., 1931, LL.B., 1933. Bar: N.Y. 1933. Legislative asst. to bd. aldermen, N.Y.C., 1934-35; ptnr. Joseph D. McGoldrick, N.Y.C., 1936-37; law sec. to comptroller N.Y.C., 1937-41; sec. to justice Supreme Ct. N.Y. County, 1942, 45-46; ptnr. Graubard Miller (formerly Graubard & Moskowitz), N.Y.C., 1948—85; of counsel Graubard & Miller, 1985—92. Lectr. municipal govt. N.Y. U., New Sch. Social Research, 1938-40 Co-author: Building Regulation in New York City, 1944. Mem. N.Y.C. Commn. Govtl. Operations, 1959-61, Coordinating Council Criminal Justice, 1967-70; Nat. chmn. Anti-Defamation League, B'nai B'rith, 1970-76; pres. ADL Found., 1976-80; chmn. bd. dirs. Fund for N.Y.C., to, 1978; bd. dirs. Palm Beach Civic Assn., 1996-2003. Served to maj. U.S. Army, 1942-45. Mem. Assn. Bar City N.Y. (past chmn. com. city cts.), N.Y. State Bar Assn., N.Y. County Lawyers Assn. Clubs: City (trustee past pres.), Harmonie (N.Y.C.). Home: Palm Beach, Fla. Died Oct. 29, 2003.

GRAVES, FRED HILL, retired librarian; b. Rockdale, Tex., Feb. 11, 1914; s. Fred Hill and Etta Sherman (Loper) G. BA, Southwest Tex. State Coll., San Marcos, 1935; postgrad., U. Tex., 1938, 41, U. Chgo., 1943-46; MS, Columbia U., 1954, advanced cert. in librarianship, 1973. Successively tchr. English, librarian, prin. Rockdale (Tex.) High Sch., 1935-43; asst. librarian Bemidji (Minn.) State Coll., 1943-44; acting librarian Hardin-Simmons U., 1944-45; librarian Tex. A. and I. U., Kingsville, 1945-51; asst. to dean Sch. Library Service, Columbia U., 1952-54, vis. lectr., spring terms 1968, 69, 70, 71, 72, 73, 76, Sch. Library Service, Columbia, summer terms 1979, 80, 81, 82; asst. prof. Grad. Sch. Library Service, Rutgers U., 1954-60; vis. instr. So. Conn. State Coll., New Haven, fall 1960; head librarian Cooper Union, N.Y.C., 1960-78. Editor: Tex. Library Jour, 1948-49. Mem. Jamestowne Soc., ALA, N.Y. Library Assn., N.Y. Tech. Services Librarians (exec. bd. 1960-66, pres. 1965-66) Home: Dunedin, Fla. Deceased.

GRAVES, ROBERT LAWRENCE, mathematician, educator; b. Chgo., Sept. 1, 1926; s. Lawrence Murray and Josephine (Wells) G.; m. Barbara Junette Sward, Oct. 20, 1951; children— Susan Johanna, Julia Lowell, Christine Craig, Virginia Anne. BA, Oberlin Coll., 1947; MA, Harvard U., 1948, PhD, 1952. Teaching fellow Harvard U., 1949-51; supervisory and rsch. positions Standard Oil Co., Ind., 1951-58; mem. faculty Grad. Sch. Bus. U. Chgo., 1958—2004, prof. applied math., 1965—2004, assoc. dean Grad. Sch. Bus., 1972-73, 75-81, dep. dean, 1981-85, assoc. dean for PhD studies, 1990-94, assoc. provost computing and info. systems, 1985-87, assoc. provost, 1987-90. On leave as dir. European Inst. Advanced Studies in Mgmt., Brussels, Belgium, 1973-75 Author: (with H.B. Thorelli) INTOP, The International Operations Simulation, 1964, (with L.G. Telser) Functional Analysis in Economics, 1972; editor: (with Philip Wolfe) Recent Advances in Mathematical Programming, 1963. Served to ensign USNR, 1944-46. Mem. Am. Math. Soc., Math. Assn. Am., Operations Research Soc., Inst. Mgmt. Sci. (mem. council 1971-73), Assn.

Computing Machinery (co-chmn. spl. interest group for math. programming 1961-63) Clubs: Quadrangle (U. Chgo.). Episcopalian. Home: Flossmoor, Ill. Died Mar. 2, 2004.

GRAY, CLARKE THOMAS, microbial biochemistry educator; b. Norwood, Ohio, May 7, 1919; s. Charles William and Adelaide (Clarke) G.; m. Mary Agnes Finneran, July 18, 1942; children: Eileen Ann, Charles William II. BS, Eastern Ky. State U., 1941; PhD, Ohio State U., 1949; postgrad. (Guggenheim fellow), Oxford (Eng.) U., 1959-60; MA (hon., Dartmouth Coll., 1964; DSc (hon.), Eastern Ky. U., 1988. Dir. biol. control William S. Merrell Co., Cin., 1943-45; rsch. fellow Nat. Tuberculosis Assn. Ohio State U., Columbus, 1946-48, instr. bacteriology, 1948-49; biochemist Leonard Wood Meml. Found., Boston, 1949-59; rsch. assoc. Harvard U. Med. Sch., Boston, 1949-59; assoc. prof. microbiology Dartmouth Coll. Med. Sch., Hanover, N.H., 1960, prof. microbiology, 1962-84, chmn. dept. microbiology, 1965-80, dir. molecular biology program, 1966-69, prof. microbiology emeritus, from 1984. Adj. prof. biology Dartmouth Coll., 1971-84; vis. scientist Lab. de Chimie Bacterienne, Nat. Ctr. Scientific Rsch. (CNRS), Marseilles, France, 1972. Mem. AAAS, Am. Soc. Biochemistry and Molecular Biology. Democrat. Achievements include discovery of 4 bacterial enzymes, 2 novel bacterial cytochromes, transitional states between aerobic and anaerobic life; co-discovery and proof of oxidative-phosphoryation in bacteria; metabolic studies on the mycobacteria causing tuberculosis and leprosy. Home: Hanover, NH. Died July 27, 2001.

GRAY, GEORGE, mural painter; b. Harrisburg, Pa., Dec. 23, 1907; s. George Zacharias and Anna Margaret (Barger) G. Ed., Harrisburg Tech. H.S., Phila., 1927-30, Acad. Fine Arts, Wilmington, Del., 1931-33, Art Students League, N.Y.C., Howard Pyle Sch. Illustration, Wilmington. Designer stage scenery, N.Y.C., 1926; invited to sketch scenes of army life in various forts and camps; tchr. anatomy and figure constrn. while attending art classes, Phila., Wilmington, later staff artist, U.S. Inf. Jour., U.S. Cav. Jour., Washington, N.Y. Nat. Guardsmen, Pa. N.G. Mag., mural painter patron, Gen. J. Leslie Kincaid, pres., Am. Hotels Corp., N.Y.C., 1934—; murals exhibited in hotels throughout U.S., including MacArthur of Battan, Hotel Jefferson-Clinton, Syracuse, N.Y.; Gen. George Rogers Clark, Louisville; 3 murals Hist. L.I, Suffolk County Savs. and Loan Bank, Babylon, L.I., Pony Express Nat. Meml. Mus., St. Joseph, Mo.; mural painting Brooklyn Bridge, Seamen's Ch. Inst., N.Y.C.; hist. picture map, Hotel Huntington, L.I., portraits and paintings in pvt. collections, U.S. and abroad; mil. artist, Engring. Bd., Ft. Belvoir, Va., combat artist, U.S. Coast Guard Hdqrs., Washington, originator, chmn., Navy Art Cooperation and Liaison Com. of Salmagundi Club. Founder, chmn. Coast Guard Art Program Salmagundi Club. Recipient Meritorious Pub. Svc. citation Dept. Navy, 1964; Louis E. Seley NACAL award, 1970; medal of honor Salmagundi Club, 1973; George Gray award U.S. Coast Guard, 1983 Life fellow Royal Soc. Arts (London); mem. Soc. Illustrators, Am. Mil. Inst., Am. Soc. Marine Artists, Co. Mil. Collectors and Historians, Nat. Soc. Mural Painters, Am. Vets. Soc. Artists, Am. Artists Profl. League, Nat. Hist. Soc. (founding mem.), Assn. Mil. Surgeons U.S., Navy League U.S. (Commodore Club), U.S. Naval Inst., Armed Forces Mgmt. Inst., Artists Fellowship, Arts Club (Washington), Salmagundi Club of N.Y. (originator, chmn. COGAP, Coast Guard art program of club) Died Jan. 4, 2004.

GRAY, SPALDING, actor, writer, performance artist; b. Providence, R.I., June 5, 1941; s. Rockwell and Elizabeth Gray; m. Renee Shafransky, Aug. 1991 (div. 1994); m. Kathy Russo; children: Forrest, Theo 1 stepchild, Marissa. BA, Emerson Coll., 1965. Writer/dir. (stage) Scales, 1966, Rumstick Road, 1977; writer: 47 Beds, 1981, 8x Gray, 1982, In Search of the Monkey Girl, 1982, Gray's Anatomy, 1996; writer, performer (monologues) Swimming to Cambodia, 1984, Monster in a Box, 1992, Gray's Anatomy, 1993; author: (non fiction) Three Places in Rhode Island, Sex and Death to the Age 14, Impossible Vacation, 1992; actor, in films Variety, 1983, The Communists Are Comfortable (and three other stories), 1984, The Killing Fields, 1984, Almost You, 1984, Hard Choices, 1986, Seven Minutes in Heaven, 1986, True Stories, 1986, Swimming to Cambodia, 1987, Stars and Bars, 1988, Clara's Heart, 1988, Beaches, 1988, Heavy Petting (documentary), 1989, Straight Talk, 1992, Monster in a Box, 1992, Twenty Bucks, 1993, King of the Hill, 1993, The Pickle, 1993, The Paper, 1994, Bad Company, 1995, Beyond Rangoon, 1995, Jimmy Zip, 1999, Julie Johnson, 2000, Kate & Leopold, 2001, How High, 2001, Revolution #9, 2002, The Paper Mache Chase, 2003; TV movies include The Image, 1990, To Save a Child, 1992, Zelda, 1993; TV spls. include Spalding Gray: Terrors of Pleasure, 1987. Founder (with Elizabeth Le Comte) of the Wooster Group, 1975. Died Jan. 11, 2004.

GRAZIANO, CHARLES DOMINIC, pharmacist; b. Cariati, Italy, June 28, 1920; s. Frank Dominic and Marianna (Bambace) G.; student Dowling Jr. Coll., 1939, 40; B.S. in Pharmacy, Drake U., 1943; m. Corrine Rose Comito, Feb. 5, 1950; children— Craig Frank, Charles Dominic II, Marianne, Kimberly Rose, Mark, Suzanne. Pharmacist Kings Pharmacy, Des Moines, 1946-47; partner Bauder Pharmacy, Des Moines, 1948-61, owner, 1962—. Mem. Des Moines Art Center. Served with AUS, 1943-45; ETO. Decorated Bronze Star. Named Drake U. Parent of the Year, 1983-84. Mem. Des Moines C. of C., Nat. Assn. Retail Druggists, Iowa, Polk County pharm. assns., St. Vincent de Paul Soc., Am. Pharm. Assn., Phi Delta Chi. Roman Catholic. Died Sept. 4, 1996. Home: Des Moines, Iowa.

GREEN, ADOLPH, playwright, lyricist; b. N.Y.C., Dec. 2, 1915; s. Daniel and Helen (Weiss) G.; m. Phyllis Newman, Jan. 31, 1960; children: Adam, Amanda. Student pub. schs., N.Y.C. Writer, author: (Broadway musicals with Betty Comden) On the Town, 1944-45 (Theatre World award 1944), Billion Dollar Baby, 1945, Bonanza Bound, 1947, Bells are Ringing, 1956 (Tony award nomination outstanding musical 1957), Subways are for Sleeping, 1961-62, Fade Out-Fade In, 1964, On the Twentieth Century, 1978 (Tony award best book 1978, Tony award best score 1978, Grammy award nomination 1978), A Doll's Life, 1982 (Tony award nomination best book 1983, Tony award nomination best score 1983); (stage lyrics with Betty Comden) Two on the Aisle, 1951, Wonderful Town, 1953 (Tony award outstanding musical 1953, Donaldson award 1953, N.Y. Drama Critics' Circle award best new musical 1953), Peter Pan, 1954, Say, Darling, 1958, Do Re Mi, 1960 (Grammy award nomination 1961, Tony award nomination best musical 1961), Leonard Bernstein's Theatre Songs, 1965, Hallelujah, Baby!, 1967 (Grammy award nomination 1967, Tony award best score 1968, Tony award best lyrics 1968, Tony award best musical 1968), Lorelei, 1973, By Bernstein, 1975, The Madwoman of Central Park, 1979, Diamonds, 1984-85, The Will Rogers Follies, 1991 (Tony award best original score 1991, N.Y. Drama Critics' Circle award best new musical 1991, Grammy award best musical show album 1991); (stage book with Betty Comden) Applause, 1970-72 (Tony award best musical 1970); (stage music with Betty Comden) Straws in the Wind, 1975; (plays with Betty Comden) A Party, 1958 (expanded as A Party with Betty Comden and Adolph Green; Obie award Village Voice 1959, Grammy award nomination 1959), Singin' in the Rain, 1985-86 (Tony award nomination best book 1986), Jerome Robbins' Broadway, 1989-90; (screenplays with Betty Comden) Good News, 1947, The Barkleys of Broadway, 1949, On the Town, 1949 (Screenwriters Guild award 1949), Take Me Out to the Ballgame, 1949, Singin' in the Rain, 1952 (Screenwriters Guild award 1952), The Band Wagon, 1953 (Academy Award nomination best story and screenplay 1953), It's Always Fair Weather, 1955 (Academy Award nomination best story and screenplay 1955, Screenwriters Guild award 1955), Auntie Mame, 1958, Bells are Ringing, 1960 (Screenwriters Guild award 1960, Grammy Award nomination 1960), What a Way to Go, 1964; (film music; songs) Mamushka from The Addams Family, 1991; (stage appearances) On the Town, 1944, A Party, 1958, The Cradle Will Rock, 1964, Lyrics and Lyricists, 1971, George Abbott...A Celebration, 1976, Phyllis Newman in Vamps and Rideouts, 1982, The New Yorkers, 1984, Happy Birthday, Mr. Abbott!; or, Night of 100 Years, 1987, Players Club Centennial Salute, 1989, Give My Regards to Broadway, 1991; (film appearances) Greenwich Village, 1944, Simon, 1980, My Favorite Year, 1982, Garbo Talks, 1984, Lily in Love, 1985, Funny, 1988, Je veux rentrer a la maison, 1989. Named to Songwriters Hall of Fame, 1980; Lion of the Performing Arts, New York Public Library, 1987; Kennedy Ctr. Honor, 1991. Died Oct. 24, 2002.

GREEN, CECIL HOWARD, geophysicist, consultant, educator; b. Manchester, Eng., Aug. 6, 1900; s. Charles Henry and Maggie (Howard) G.; m. Ida M. Flansburgh, Feb. 6, 1926. Student, U. B.C.; BSEE, MIT, 1923, SM, 1924; DEng., Colo. Sch. Mines, 1953; DSc, U. Tulsa, 1961, U. Sydney, Australia, 1961, U. B.C., 1964, So. Meth. U., 1967, U. Mass., 1974, Tex. Christian U., 1974; D.Sc., Oxford U., 1986; LLD, Austin Coll., 1966; D Civil Jurisprudence, U. Dallas, 1976; D Comml. Sci. (hon.), Suffolk U., 1978; D Philanthropy (hon.), Hawthorne Coll., 1987; LHD (hon.), U. So. Calif., L.A., 1990. Rsch. engr. A.C. engring. dept. GE, Schenectady, 1924-26; rsch. engr. Raytheon Mfg. Co., Cambridge, Mass., 1926-28, Fed. Telegraph Co., Palo Alto, Calif., also Newark, 1928-30; party chief Geophys. Svc. Inc., Dallas, 1930-36, supr., 1936-41, v.p., 1941-50, pres., 1950-56, chmn. bd., 1956-59, hon. chmn., 1959—; founder dir. Tex. Instruments, Inc. Hon. lectr. earth and planetary scis. MIT, 1973—; cons. prof. earth scis. Stanford U., hon. lectr. earth scis., 1983; hon. lectr. geophysics U. B.C., 1984; founder Green Coll. Oxford U., 1979, Green Ctr. Study Sci. and Soc. U. Tex. Dallas 1992, Green Coll. U. B.C., 1993. Trustee Scripps Clinic and Rsch. Found., Woods Hole Oceanographic Inst., SW Med. Found.; trustee So. Meth. U. Found. for Sci. and Engring., pres., 1964-66; trustee, past pres. St. Mark's Sch. Tex.; trustee Tex. Christian U.; trustee, mem. exec. com. Austin Coll.; membership com., life mem. corp., mem. vis. com. dept. physics, vis. com. earth and planetary scis. MIT; mem. com. earth scis. Stanford; chmn. Excellence in Edn. Found. Decorated Knight of Brit. Empire, 1991; recipient Santa Rita award U. Tex. System; with Ida Green, Linz award City of Dallas, 1974, (with Ida Green) Internat. Ednl. and Research Tribute, Nat. Acad. Scis., 1978, (with Ida Green) Pub. Welfare medal Nat. Acad. Scis., 1979, award for excellence in humanities North Dallas C. of C., 1978, citation So. Meth. U. Inst. for Study Earth and Man, 1979, Gt. Trekker award U. B.C., 1983, Hon. Lay award for disting. service AMA, 1984, Gold Plate award Am. Acad. Achievement, 1984, Freedom of City award Vancouver, B.C., Can., 1987, Philanthropist of Year awards City of Dallas, 1987, City of San Diego, 1988, (with Ida Green) Uncommon Man award Stanford U., 1988, Scientist of Year award City of San Diego, 1989, Lifetime Achievement award Reginald S. Lourie Ctr. Infants and Young Children, 1993, Nat. Philanthropist of Yr. award Nat. Assn. Fund Raising Execs., 1994, Waldo E. Smith medal Am. Geophysical Union, 1995, Lifetime Achievement award U. British Columbia, 1998; inducted into Industry Pioneer Offshore Energy Ctr. Hall of Fame, 1998. Fellow Am. Acad. Arts and Scis.; mem. AIA (hon. mem.), IEEE (hon. mem.), NAS (hon. mem.), MIT Alumni Assn. (pres. 1968-69, hon. chmn. San Diego sect. 1995), Am. Assn. Petroleum Geologists (hon. 1993), Soc. Exploration Geophysicists (hon. life mem., past pres., Kaufman medal 1966, Maurice Ewing medal 1978), Am. Assn. Petroleum Geologists (Human Needs medal 1974, hon. mem. 1993), European Assn. Exploration Geophysicists, Mex. Assn. Petroleum Geoplogists, Am. Geophys. Union (hon., Waldo E. Smith Medal, 1995), Tex. Assn. Grad. Edn. and Rsch. (hon. chmn.), Dallas Geol. Soc. (hon. life), Dallas Geophys. Soc. (hon. life), Knight of the Brit. Empire (hon. 1991), Explorers Club. Clubs: Dallas Country, Dallas Petroleum; La Jolla (Calif.) Country. Died Apr. 11, 2003.

GREEN, KEITH, physiologist; b. Nuneaton, Eng., Aug. 16, 1940; came to U.S., 1964; s. Henry and Doris Sarah (Prime) Green; m. Mary Vallance, Sept. 5, 1964; children: Kathryn Anne, John Philip Ross. BSc, U. Leicester (Eng.), 1961; PhD, U. St. Andrews (Scotland), 1964, DSc, 1984. Fellow ophthalmology Johns Hopkins U. Sch. Medicine, Balt., 1964-66, instr. ophthalmology, 1966-67, asst. prof. ophthalmology, 1967-71; assoc. prof. ophthalmology Med. Coll. Ga., Augusta, 1971-76, prof. ophthalmology, 1976-78, regents' prof., from 1978. Cosn. Xerox Corp., Rochester, N.Y., 1981-83, Paco Pharm. Svcs., Lakewood, N.J., 1987-89. Contbr. sci. papers to profl. publs. Recipient Career Devel. award NIH, 1970-74, Sr. Sci. Investigator award for rsch. to prevent blindness, 1994; Sr. Internat. fellow Fogarty Ctr. NIH, 1982-83. Mem. Internat. Soc. on Ocular Toxicology (sec.-treas. 1988-92, pres.-elect 1992-94, pres. 1994-96), Am. Acad. Ophthal. Achievements include patent on new drug to reduce intraocular pressure; expertise on marijuana effects on eye; research on corneal physiology, on ocular physiology and pharmacology, on ocular toxicology, and on membrane transport. Home: Evans, Ga. Died Nov. 22, 2001.

GREEN, RICHARD GEORGE, lawyer; b. N.Y.C., Dec. 13, 1913; s. Louis and Kate G. (Gottler) G.; m. Lynn Estelle Gold, Nov. 15, 1940 (div. 1954); m. Ruth M. Davis, July 2, 1954; children: Anna, Jennifer, Nancy, Richard Jr. BA, CUNY, 1932; LLB, Bklyn. Law Sch., 1936, JD, 1967. Bar: N.Y. 1937, U.S. Dist. Ct. (so. dist.) N.Y. 1940, U.S. Ct. Internat. Trade 1951, U.S. Ct. Appeals (2d cir.) 1951, U.S. Dist. Ct. (ea. dist.) 1964, U.S. Supreme Ct. 1967, U.S. Ct. Appeals (Fed. cir.) 1982. Asst. corp. counsel City of Long Beach, N.Y., 1937; assoc. Irving Ribman Esq., N.Y.C., 1938-39; mng. atty. Hays, St. John, Abramson & Schulman, N.Y.C., 1939-40; house counsel Newspaper PM Inc., N.Y.C., 1940-48; pvt. practice law N.Y.C., 1948-76; ptnr. Green & Hillman, N.Y.C., 1976-93; pvt. practice N.Y.C., from 1993. Adj. prof. SUNY, Stony Brook, 1974-75; lectr. Rutgers Law Sch., Newark, 1975-77, NYU Law Sch., N.Y.C., 1975-77; arbitrator Civil Ct., N.Y.C., 1980—; spec master N.Y. Supreme Ct., 1991—, Civil Ct., N.Y.C., 1994—. Editor Jour. Assn. for Psychiat. Treatment Offenders, 1963-66. Park commr. Village Lloyd Harbor, N.Y., 1969-73; pres. Cold Spring Harbor Youth Ctr., N.Y., 1969-73; chmn. bd. dirs., trustee Inst. Advancement Med. Communication, N.Y.C. and Phila., 1965-80; bd. dirs., pres. Harry Futterman Fund Inc., N.Y.C., 1950-85. 1st lt., U.S. Army, 1943-46. Mem. ABA (various coms.), Assn. Bar of City of N.Y., N.Y. County Lawyers Assn., Copyright Soc. U.S. (trustee 1982-85, 88-90, editl. bd. 1984-86), ACLU (chmn. free speech and assn. com. 1980-86), Am. Arbitration Assn. (arbitrator 1960—), Nat. Press Club (Washington). Avocations: swimming, fishing, reading. Home: New York, NY. Died Sept. 3, 2001.

GREEN, SEDGWICK WILLIAM, corporate director; b. N.Y.C., Oct. 16, 1929; s. Louis A. and Evelyn Schoenberg G.; m. Patricia Freiberg, May 29, 1966; children: Catherine Ann, Louis Matthew. AB magna cum laude, Harvard U., 1950, JD magna cum laude, 1953. Bar: N.Y., D.C. Assoc. Cleary, Gottlieb, Steen & Hamilton, N.Y.C., 1956-66; mem. N.Y. State Assembly, Albany, 1965-68; assoc. Paul, Weiss, Rifkind, Wharton & Garrison, N.Y.C., 1966-68; regional adminstr. U.S. Dept. of Housing and Urban Devel., NY, 1970—77, 1970—77, 1970—77, 1970—77; chair Federal Regional Coun., N.Y., P.R., N.J., and V.I., 1971-77; mem. of congress U.S. Ho. of Reps., Washington, 1978-93; mem. N.Y.C. Campaign Fin. Bd., 1994-2000; law clk. Judge Cary T. Washington U.S. Ct. Appeals (D.C. cir.), 1955—56. Mem. House Appropriations Com., ranking Rep. mem. VA-HUD-INd. Agys. Subcom., 1981-93, Fgn. Opers. Appropriations Subcom., 1991-92; mem. space studies bd. Nat. Rsch. Coun., 1995-2001; bd. dirs. Gen. Am. Investors Co., N.Y.C., Energy Answers Corp., Albany, ClientSoft Corp., Miami, Fla.; vice-chair N.Y.C. Housing Devel. Corp., 1994—. Contbr. articles to profl. jours. Co-chair Nat. Commn. on Severely Distressed Pub. Housing, Washington, 1991-92; chair bd. govs. N.Y. Acad. of Scis., 1999-2001; mem. Gov. Pataki's adv. com. Rivers & Estuaries Ctr. on Hudson, 2000—; trustee New Sch. Univ., N.Y.C., 1985—; treas. Assn. of the Bar of the City of N.Y., 1976-78; del. Rep. Nat. Conv., 1980, 88, 92; trustee Montefiore Med. Ctr., Am. Assembly, Citizens Housing and Planning Coun., N.Y., others; trustee, treas., Acad. Polit. Sci. 1st lt. (Jag Corp) U.S. Army, 1953-55. Recipient Congl. award Nat. Coalition for Sci. and Technology, 1982. Mem. Jewish Assn. for Svcs. for the Aged (pres. 1994-95, trustee). Republican. Jewish. Avocation: reading. Home: New York, NY. Died Oct. 14, 2002.

GREEN, SHARON JOYCE ALLIGOOD, broadcast executive; b. Kingsport, Tenn., Oct. 8, 1950; d. Lewis C. and Billie (Boggs) Alligood; m. Tony A. Green, Jan. 10, 1974 (div. July 1977); 1 child, Kevin Lewis. Student, Edmondson Bus. Coll., 1969; AB, Edmondson Jr. Coll., 1978. Sec. Sta. WTCI-TV, Chattanooga, 1970-71, traffic dir., 1971-83, program dir., 1983-89, membership devel. dir., 1990-92, Chattanooga Cable TV Co., from 1993. Grad. asst. Dale Carnegie Courses, Chattanooga, 1987-88. Mem. Nat. Soc. Fund Raising Execs., Hamilton Pl. Rotary (info. chmn. 1990-91, sec. 1991-92, bd. dirs. 1992-95). Republican. Presbyterian. Avocations: piano, racquetball, tennis, weight training. Home: Chattanooga, Tenn. Deceased.

GREENBERG, ARNOLD HARVEY, pediatrics educator, cell biologist; b. Winnipeg, Man., Can., Sept. 29, 1941; s. Samuel H. and Bertha (Segal) G.; m. Sharon Domey, 1967 (div. 1983); children: David E., Juliet R.; m. Faye L. Hellner, 1981; children: Marni L. Hellner, Rachel D. Hellner, Katherine R. Hellner. BS in Med. Genetics, MD, U. Man., 1965; PhD in Immunology, U. London, 1974. Rotating intern Winnipeg Gen. Hosp., 1965-66; jr. resident in pediatrics Winnipeg Children's Hosp., 1966-67; asst. resident in pediatrics Johns Hopkins Hosp., Balt., 1967-68, rsch. fellow in pediatric endocrinology, 1968-70; sabbatical dept. immunology Nat. Inst. for Med. Rsch., Mill Hill, London, 1978-89; sabbatical Lab. of Chemoprevention Nat. Cancer Inst./NIH, Bethesda, 1988; from asst. prof. to assoc. prof. pediatrics and immunology U. Man., Winnipeg, 1974-85, prof. pediatrics, immunology and human genetics, 1986-2000, disting. prof., from 2000; dir. Man. Inst. Cell Biology, Winnipeg, 1988-2000. Mem. dept. pediatrics exec. coun. U. Man., 1978-81, dept. pediatrics continuing med. edn. com., 1981-85, chmn. dept. pediatrics GFT exec. com., 1983-88, animal care com., 1979-89, FACS mgmt. com., 1979-89, chmn. instnl. self study rsch. com. faculty of medicine, 1989-90, dept. pediatrics promotion com., 1984-91, chmn. biology cancer course, 1986-92, chmn. dept. immunology rev. com., 1992, dept. pediatrics exec. com., 1988-92, chmn. faculty of medicine rsch. com., 1991-93, inst. and interdisciplinary rsch. group com., 1991—; mem. grants panel B Nat. Cancer Inst., 1977-82, 84-85, fellowhip panel, 1984, Terry Fox expansion programs grants panel, 1987, chmn., 1989-90, awards panel, 1990-91; adv. com. on rsch. Alberta Cancer Bd.; mem. immunology and transplantation grants panel Med. Rsch. Coun., 1986-90; med. adv. com. Children's Rsch. Found., 1980-90; lectr. WHO, Clin. Rsch. Ctr., Harrow, England, Middlesex Hosp. Med. Sch., London, Univ. Coll., London, U. Saskatchewan, Queen's U., U. Pa., Jackson Labs., Bar Harbor, Me., McGill U., U. Alberta, Can. Fed. Biol. Socs., Karolinska Inst., Stockholm, Weizmann Inst., Rehovot, Israel, Deutches Krebsforschungszentrum, Heidelberg, Germany, U. Rochester, NIH, Soc. for Behavioral Medicine, New Orleans, Bristol-Myers Co., McMaster U., Mt. Sinai Hosp. Rsch. Inst., Toronto, Nat. Inst. Med. Rsch., London, Charing Cross Rsch. Inst., London, UCLA, Salk Inst., RJR Nabisco Co., Colby-Sawyer Coll., Rutgers U., Quebec Cancer Inst., Brown U., U. Western Ontario, Ontario Cancer Inst., Hosp. for Sick Children, Toronto, Henry Ford Hosp., Detroit, Wayne State U., CIBA Found., Australian Behavioral Immunology Group, St. Vincent's Hosp., Sydney, Australia, Walter and Eliza Hall Inst. for Med. Rsch., Melbourne, Australia, NRC Biotechnology Rsch. Inst., Montreal, U. Minn., U. Toronto, Reichmann Rsch. Inst., Toronto, Basel (Switzerland) Inst. Immunology, Epilanges, Lausanne, Switzerland; also various symposiums, confs., and workshops; sabbatical with Ctr. d'Immunologie INSERM, Ctr. Nationale de Recherche Scientifique, Marseille-Luminy, 1994. Assoc. editor: Jour. Nat. Cancer Inst.; adv. bd. Cancer and Metastasis Rreviews, Cell Death and Differentiation; guest editor: Nature, Jour. Immunology, Molecular and Cellular Biology, Cancer Rsch., Molecular Carcinogenesis, Invasion and Metastasis, Immunology Letters; contbr. numerous articles to sci. jours. including Jour. Clin. Endocrinology, Jour. Pediatrics, Nature New Biology, Johns Hopkins Med. Bull., European Jour. Immunology, Nature. Recipient Am. Coll. Chest Physicians prize for student rsch., 1964, Terry Fox Career award Nat. Cancer Inst., 1982-85, Children's Hosp. Rsch. Found. Teddy award, 1991, Sr. Scientist award Sigma Xi, 1993; named Nat. Cancer Inst. Terry Fox Cancer Rsch. Scientist, 1985-99; fellow Med. Rsch. Coun., 1968-71, 71-74, Schering travel fellow, 1977, Nuffield Found. travel fellow, 1978, Dept. of External Affairs travel fellow, 1978; Med. Rsch. Coun. scholar, 1974-79, Nat. Cancer Inst. scholar, 1979-82. Mem. Am. Assn. for Cancer Rsch., Am. Assn. of Immunologists, Can. Soc. for Immunology (exec. coun. 1979-82, 89-92, Cinader award 1997), Soc. for Psychoneuroimmunology, Can. Med. Assn., Can. Inst. of Acad. Medicine, Nat. Can., assoc. editor jour. 1975—), Can. Fedn. of Biol. Studies (sci. policy com. 1979-85). Home: Winnipeg, Canada. Deceased.

GREENBERG, MORRIS, lawyer; b. Portland, Maine, Dec. 19, 1908; s. Samuel L. and Ruth (Rosen) G.; m. Sylvia Dena Goldberg, Dec. 11, 1938; children: Ruth, Barbara, Deborah, Stanley. LLB, Boston U., 1933. Bar: Maine 1933. Pres. Morstan Corp., Portland, Maine, 1963-87, Pine Tree Terr. Devel. Co., Portland, from 1953. Bd. dirs. various corps., Maine. Pres. Zionist Orgn., Maine, 1947-48; bd. dirs. Temple Beth El, Portland, 1970; mem. United Jewish Appeal, 1960—, Jewish Community Ctr., 1970—. Mem. Assn. Trial Lawyers Am., Boston U. Dean's Club; fellow Bankruptcy Inst. Avocation: collecting antiques. Home: Portland, Maine. Deceased.

GREENBLATT, MARK LEO, lawyer, urban planner; b. New Brighton, Pa., Mar. 9, 1947; s. Harry Abraham and Edna Bess (Rosenberg) G.; m. Deana Charlene Beisel, June 22, 1975. BA, Mich. State U., 1968, postgrad., 1968-69; M in City Planning, U. Pa., 1971; JD, Capital U., 1985. Bar: Ohio, 1986, U.S. Dist. Ct. (so. dist.) Ohio, 1987, Ill. 1995. Asst. acct. Harry A. Greenblatt, New Brighton, Pa., 1971-72; planner Village of Arlington Heights (Ill.) Planning Dept., 1972-75, Allen L. Kracower & Assoc., Des Plaines, Ill., 1975-76, Mid-Ohio Regional Planning Commn., Columbus, 1986-93; sole practice Columbus, 1986-93, Lincolnwood, Ill., 1995—96. Served with U.S. Army, 1971, capt. Res. Richard King Mellon fellow, 1968-69. Jewish. Home: Lincolnwood, Ill. Died July 1996.

GREENE, A(LVIN) C(ARL), author; b. Abilene, Tex., Nov. 4, 1923; s. Alvin Carl and Marie (Cole) G.; m. Betty Dozier, 1950 (dec.); children: Geoffrey, Mark, Eliot, Meredith Elizabeth; m. Judy Dalton Hyland, 1990. BA, Abilene Christian U., 1948; HLD (hon.), Austin Coll., 1992. Mem. staff Abilene Reporter-News, 1948-52, 58-60; book editor Dallas Times Herald, 1960-68, editor editorial page, 1963-65; staff U. Tex., Austin, 1968-69, 73; exec. editor Southwestern Hist. Quar., 1968-69; exec. producer Sta. KERA-TV, Dallas, 1970-71; editorial bd. KAAM, KAFM, 1979-81; narrator A.C. Greene's Historic Moments Sta. WFAA, 1982-83; commentator MacNeil/Lehrer News Hour, 1983-89; columnist Dallas Morning News, from 1983. Author: A Personal Country, 1969, new paperback edit., 1998, Living Texas, 1969, The Last Captive, 1972, Santa Claus Bank Robbery, 1972, illustrated edit., 1999, Dallas: The Deciding Years, 1973, A Christmas Tree, 1973, Views in Texas, 1974, A Place Called Dallas, 1975; (with Roger Horchow) Elephants in Your Mailbox, 1980; 50 plus Best Books on Texas, 1982, 2d edit., 1998, The Highland Park Woman, 1983, Dallas USA, 1984, Texas Sketches, 1985, Taking Heart, 1990, 900 Miles on the Butterfield Trail, 1994, Joy to the World, 1995, Christmas Memories, 1996, They are Ruining Ibiza, 1998, Sketches From the 5 States of Texas, 1998, (poems) Memory of Snow, 2001. Emeritus dir. Ctr. for Tex. Studies U. North Tex., 1993-96. With USNR, 1943-46, PTO, CBI. Recipient award NCCJ, 1964, Bookend award Tex. Book Festival, 1998; Dobie-Paisano fellow, 1968, Tex. State Hist. Com., 1994. Fellow Tex. Inst. Letters (pres. 1969-71, award 1964, 73, 88), Tex. State Hist. Assn.; mem. Writers Guild Am., Nat. Rlwy. Hist. Assn., Salado L.R. Theater. Presbyterian. Died Apr. 5, 2002.

GREENE, DAVID B. television and film director; b. Manchester, Eng., Feb. 22, 1921; Dir.: (films) The Shuttered Room, 1966, Sebastian, 1968, The Strange Affair, 1968, I Start Counting, 1969, Godspell, 1973, Gray Lady Down, 1978, Hard Country, 1981, (TV films) The People Next Door, 1970, (Emmy award), Madame Sin, 1971, The Count of Monte Cristo, 1975, Ellery Queen, 1975, Lucan, 1977, The Trial of Lee Harvey Oswald, 1977, Friendly Fire, 1979 (Emmy award), A Vacation in Hell, 1979, The Choice, 1981, World War III, 1982, Rehearsal for Murder, 1982, Take Your Best Shot, 1982, Ghost Dancing, 1983, Prototype, 1983, Sweet Revenge, 1984, Fatal Vision, 1984 (Emmy nomination), Guilty Conscience, 1985, Murder Among Friends, 1985, The Child Is Mine, 1985, Triplecross, 1986, Vanishing Act, 1986, Miles to Go, 1986, Circle of Violence: A Family Drama, 1986, The Betty Ford Story, (TV miniseries) Rich Man, Poor Man, 1976, Roots, 1979 (Emmy award), (cable miniseries) The Guardian, 1984. Mem. Dirs. Guild Am. Died Apr. 7, 2003.

GREENE-MERCIER, MARIE ZOE, sculptor; b. Madison, Wis., Mar. 31, 1911; d. Louis J.A. and Zoé (Lassagne) Mercier; m. Wesley Hammond Greene, June 21, 1937; children: Steven Hardy, Richard Stuart, Roger Hammond. AB, Radcliffe Coll., 1933; postgrad., New Bauhaus, Chgo., 1937-38. Exhibited solo shows Southwest Mo. State Coll., 1950, Argent Gallery, N.Y.C., Hohenberg Gallery, Chgo., 1951, 53, Layton Gallery, Milw., 1951, Westwinds Bookshop, Duxbury, Mass., 1951, Newton Ctr. Women's Club, 1950, Art Inst. Chgo., 1955, Chgo. Pub. Libr., 1956, Am. Inst. Archs., Chgo., 1957, Paris Galerie Duncan, 1963, Florence Galleria d'arte Arno, 1965, Rome Galleria Numero, 1966, Milan Numero, 1966, Venice Numero, 1966, S.Stefano, 1968, Milan Gian Ferrari, 1969, Trieste Centro Italo Americano, 1968, 70, Venice La Fenice, 1969, Athens, New Forms, 1970, Perpignan, Main de Fer, 1971, Rome, Artivisive, 1972, Chgo. Met. Structures Inc., 1974, Centre Noroit, Arras, France, 1977, Amerika Haus, West Berlin, 1977, Galerie Musée de Poche Paris, 1978, Maison Française, Chgo., 1979, 83, Stadt Bad Homburg v.d. Höhe, 1979, Amerika Haus, Stuttgart, 1979, Alliance Francaise de Washington, 1980, Skulpturenpark Mus., Bad Nauheim Fed. Republic Germany, 1986, Oberhessisches Mus., Giessen, Fed. Republic Germany, 1986, Galerie Loehr, Frankfurt, Fed. Republic Germany, 1991; exhibited in group shows Art Inst. Chgo., 1947, 48, 52, 55, Boson Mus. Arts, 1950, Am. Fedn. Arts, 1953, Mus. Contemporary Art, Chgo., 1968, Paris Salon d'Automne, 1962, 1971, 72, 73, 74, Salon des Beaux Arts, Salon des Independants, 1952, de la Jeune Sculpture, 1966, Salon de Mai, 1973, 74, 75, 76, 77, 78, 86, London Royal Inst. Galleries, 1954, Trieste II Exhbn. Sacred Art, 1966, Legnano, Pagani Found., 1966, 69, 70, 71, 72, Campo S. Moisé, Comunne di Venezia, 1970, 72, Florence Biennale, 1971, 1st Sculpture Triennale, Paris, 1978, UNESCO, Paris, 1979, La Found. Nat. Arts Graphiques et Plastiques, Paris, 1979, Bauhaus Archiv Mus., W. Berlin, 1979, Capitol Children's Mus., Washington, 1980-81, Kurhausgarten, Bad Homburg, 1979, 80, 81, Moholy-Nagy, New Vision for Chgo., Ill. State Mus., Springfield & Chgo., 1990, 4-town travelling show Arras, France, 1990-91, Internat. Exhibition Frankfurt Kunstmesse, Galerie Loehr, 1991, Annual Mem. Show Arts Club Chgo., 1948-94; represented in permanent collections at Roosevelt U., Radcliffe Coll., S.W. Mo. State Coll., Grinnell Coll., Randolph Macon Coll., Bauhaus-Archiv Mus., Berlin, Mus. Modern Art, Venice, Stone Container Corp., 1st Nat. Bank, Chgo., Internat. Film Bur., 1st Bapt. Ch., Chgo., Bloomington, Ind., Musée des Sables, Barcarès, France, 1971, Govt. Bldg., Homburg-Saar, 1974, C.E.S. Verlaine, Arras, France, Centre Noroit, Arras, 1978, Western Ill. U., 1979, David and Alfred Smart Gallery, U. Chgo., permanent sculptures and collages Oberhessisches Mus., Giessen, Germany, 1995—; mem. U.S. del. 9th Congress Internat. Artists Assn., UNESCO, Stuttgart, W. Germany, 1979. Recipient Silver medal and 1st prize Composition, 1968, Gold medal, grand prize modern sculpture, Cannes, Semaines Internat. de la Femme, 1969, Hors Concours, Nice, 1970, Grand prix Humanitaire de France, médaille de vermeil, ler Prix Internat. de Sculpture, Mérite Belgo-Hispanique Palmes d'Or, Festival de St. Germain-des-Prés, Paris, 1975; USIS West Berlin grantee, 1977; Stadt Bad Hamburg v.d. Höhe grantee, 1979, Mary Mildred Sullivan award Randolph-Macon Coll., 1985, The Radcliffe College Alumnae Assn. Recognition awd. for visual arts, 1998. Author: Trieste, 101 Disegni, 1969; Venezia, 101 Disegni, 1970; Salzburg, 101 Zeichnungen, 1970; Editrice Libreria Internazionale Italo Svevo Trieste, 1969; Editor: Mussa, Italo, Marie Zoe Greene-Mercier Rome, Sifra, 1968, Art Internat., 1978, Public Art New Directions, 1981, Contemporary Women Sculptors, 1986, Am. Women Sculptors, 1990; contbr. to mags. Memoir, Leonardo Magazine, 1982; Reminiscences, Harvard Crimson, 1983. Mem. Renaissance Soc. (hon. mem. U. Chgo.), Arts Club of Chgo., Artists Equity Ass. (pres., chgo. chpt. 1959-62). Home: Chicago, Ill. Deceased.

GREFE, ROLLAND EUGENE, lawyer; b. Ida County, Iowa, June 27, 1920; s. Alfred William and Zoma Corrine (Lasher) G.; m. Mary Arlene Cruikshank, June 12, 1943; 1 son, Roger Frederick. BA, Morningside Coll., 1941; JD, State U. Iowa, 1946. Bar: Iowa 1946. Assoc. Schaetzle, Williams & Stewart, Des Moines, 1946-48, Schaetzle, Swift, Austin & Stewart, Des Moines, 1948-52; ptnr. Schaetzle, Austin & Grefe (and related firms), Des Moines, 1952-60, Austin, Grefe & Sidney, Des Moines, 1960-71; sr. ptnr. Grefe & Sidney, Des Moines, 1971-95; mem. Grefe & Sidney P.L.C., from 1995. Dir. Freeman Decorating Co., 1969—, Cowles Syndicate, Inc., 1982-86; mem. bd. mgrs. Lawyers Com. Network, L.L.C., 1997-2000, chair, 1998-2000. Bd. dirs. Des Moines Area C.C., 1966-76, pres., 1967-76; bd. dirs. Westminster Presbyn. Ch. Found., 1975-89, Iowa State Bar Found., 1979-91; trustee Des Moines Water Works, 1984-99, pres., 1987, 91, 96. Lt. USNR, 1942-45. Fellow Am. Bar Found., Am. Coll. Trust and Estate Counsel; mem. ABA (ho. of dels. 1982-96, Iowa state del. 1992-93, bd. govs. 1993-96, standing com. on tech. and info. systems 1998-2001, sr. lawyers divsn. chair internet and tech. com. 2000-02), Assn. Endowment Found. Coll. (mem. pension plan adminstrn. com. 1994-2000), Polk County Bar Assn. (pres. 1971-72), Iowa State Bar Assn. (bd. govs. 1972-76, pres. 1978-79, chmn. com. on long-range planning 1979-81, Award of Merit 1982), Des Moines Estate Planners, Lincoln Inne. Clubs: Sertoma (Des Moines), Des Moines Embassy (Des Moines), Wakonda (Des Moines). Republican. Presbyterian. Home: Des Moines, Iowa. Died Feb. 14, 2004.

GREGG, DAVID PAUL, information storage media specialist; b. Los Angeles, Mar. 11, 1923; s. David D. and Ferol Adelle (Bozardt) G.; m. Donna M. Ostrom, Aug., 1959 (div. 1979); children: Daniel P., Debora N., Alicia L., Wade A. K., Thomas R., Connie J. Student, Kans. State U., 1945-47; BSEE, U. So. Calif., 1950, postgrad., 1960, Case Inst. Tech., 1956. Video engr. Ampex Corp., Redwood City, Calif., 1955-56; optical and disk sys. engr. Westrex subs. AT&T, Hollywood, Calif., 1956-60; digital magnetic tape and videodisk cons. Mincom divsn. 3M Co., West Los Angeles, Calif., 1960-61; v.p., co-founder digital magnetic tape and video disk sys. Winston Rsch. Corp., Culver City, Calif., 1961-62; pres., founder ultra high speed music tape duplicators and video disk Gauss Electrophysics, Inc., Santa Monica, Calif., 1964-67, also chmn. bd.; video disk cons. MCA/DiscoVision, Inc., Universal City, Calif., 1968-71; sys. cons. ITT Laboratorios de España, Madrid, 1969-73. Cons. Del Mar Avionics, Culver City, 1973-75, cons. laser stripchart recorder, recordable CD, 1986-91; cons. Model 757 design Boeing Comml. Aircraft, Renton, Wash., 1979-81; cons., lic. info. storage media specialist DiscoVision Assocs., Irvine, Calif., 1982—; cons. satellite infrared optics Hughes Aircraft, Culver City, 1976-78. Contbr. articles to profl. jours.; basic patentee in videodisk, optical ribbon and XUV fields. With USN, 1940-43. Mem. AAAS, Soc. Motion Picture and TV Engrs. (life), Optical Soc. Am. (sr.), European Optical Soc., Soc. Photo-Instrumentation Engrs. (sr.), Audio Engring. Soc. (sr.), Tech. Coun. of Motion Picture-TV Industry (sr.). Achievements include invention of optical disk and its derivatives, compact discs, CD-ROM, laserdisc, minidiscs, others. Died Nov. 8, 2001.

GREGORY, JAMES, retired actor; b. N.Y.C., Dec. 23, 1911; s. James Gillen and Axemia Theresa (Ekdahl) G.; m. Ann Catherine Miltner, May 25, 1944. Grad. high sch. Actor, from 1936. Actor: (summer stock prodns.) Deer Lake, Pa., 1936-37, 39, Millbrook, N.Y., 1938, Braddock Heights, Md., 1940, Buck's County Playhouse, New Hope, Pa., 1941, Ivy Tower Playhouse, Spring Lake, N.J., 1951, (Broadway shows) Key Largo, 1939, Journey to Jerusalem, 1940, In Time to Come, 1941, Dream Girl, 1945, All My Sons, 1947, Death of a Salesman, 1948-49 (played Biff on Broadway with 5 Willy Lomans), Dead Pigeon, 1954, Fragile Fox, 1955, Desperate Hours, 1956-57, (films) The Young Strangers, 1955, Al Capone Story, 1955, Gun Glory, 1956, Nightfall, 1956, The Big Caper, 1956, A Distant Trumpet, 1961, Underwater Warrior, 1962, PT-109, 1965, The Sons of Katie Elder, 1967, The Manchurian Candidate, 1967, Captain

Newman, M.D, 1967, Million Dollar Duck, 1968, Clam Bake, 1967, Secret War of Harry Frigg, 1968, Beneath the Planet of the Apes, 1970, The Hawaiians, 1970, Shoot Out, 1971, The Late Liz, 1971, $1,000,000. Duck, 1971, The Strongest Man in the World, 1974, The Main Event, 1979, Wait Til Your Mother Gets Home, 1982, X-15, Death of a Salesman, also 5 Matt Helm pictures, (TV shows) Big Valley, Bonanza, Gunsmoke, Rawhide, Playhouse 90, Climax, Alfred Hitchcock Presents, Twilight Zone, Quincy, as Inspector Luger in Barney Miller, Mr. Belvedere, 1986. Served with USNR, USMCR, 1942-45, PTO. Mem. Soc. Preservation and Encouragement Barber Shop Quartet Singing Am. Clubs: Hollywood Hackers, Golf. Home: Sedona, Ariz. Died Sept. 16, 2002.

GREGORY, NORMAN WAYNE, chemistry educator, researcher; b. Albany, Oreg., June 23, 1920; s. Arthur Donald and Edith Florence (Self) G.; m. Lillian Virginia Larson, May 21, 1943; children: Norman Wayne Jr., Martha Jean, Brian Neil. Student, Lower Columbia Jr. Coll., 1936-38; BS, U. Wash., Seattle, 1940, MS, 1941; PhD, Ohio State U., 1943. Research chemist Radiation Lab., U. Calif., Berkeley, 1944-46; instr. U. Wash., Seattle, 1946-47, asst. prof., 1947-53, assoc. prof., 1953-57, prof. chemistry, 1957-89, prof. emeritus and from 1989, chmn. dept., 1970-75. Author: Physical Chemistry, 1964; contbr. articles to profl. jours. Mem. Am. Chem. Soc. (chmn. Puget Sound sect. 1964, treas. 1962). Home: Seattle, Wash. Died May 25, 2003.

GREGORY, WILLIAM ARTHUR, neuroscientist, anatomist; b. Napoleon, Ohio, Apr. 16, 1953; s. Jess F. Jr. and Margie N. G. BS in Psychology, Ohio State U., 1975; MA in Psychology, Mich. State U., 1979, PhD in Anatomy, 1982; postgrad., Harvard U., 1988-90. Rsch. fellow Albert Einstein Coll. Med., Bronx, N.Y., 1982-85; instr. NYU Coll. Med., N.Y.C., 1985-88, Harvard Med. Sch., Boston, 1988-90; rsch. fellow Univ. Med. Dental N.J., Piscataway, 1991-93. Contbr. articles to profl. jours. Mem. Soc. for Neurosci. Democrat. Home: Gainesville, Fla. Deceased.

GRENE, DAVID, classics educator; b. Dublin; Grad., Trinity Coll., U. Dublin, 1934, MA, 1936; postgrad., U. Vienna. Instr. Harvard U., 1936; with U. Chgo., from 1937; mem. Com. on Social Thought, since 1946; now prof. emeritus. Recipient Gordon J. Laing award U. Chgo. Press, 1989. His translations of the Greek tragedies have sold nearly a million copies in 25 years. Died Sept. 10, 2002.

GRESKA, THOMAS FRANCIS, astronautical engineer; b. Providence, Mar. 26, 1940; s. Stanly S. and Pearl (Geatar) G.; m. Pam Greska (div. 1987); children: Stephanie Ann, Brian Thomas; m. Caroline Mayer, June 1, 1988. M in Engring., Calif. State U., Hayward, 1964; postgrad, El Camino Coll., 1982-84. Registered profl. engr., Calif. Design engr. Fleetwood Enterprise, Riverside, Calif., 1969-72, Fores Mfg.-Yacht, Tustin, Calif., 1973-80, Mattel Toys, Hawthorne, Calif., 1980-85; design dept. mgr. Astronautics Corp. Am., Torrance, Calif., 1986-87; project designer Condor Pacific Ind., Canoga Park, Calif., from 1987; owner, ptnr. Skywords, L.A., from 1986. Instr. astronomy El Camno Coll., 1985-87; cons. in field. With U.S. Army, 1960-64. Mem. Polaris Obs. Assn. (chmn. 1983-84), Aircraft Owners & Pilots Assn., Exptl. Aircraft Assn. Deceased.

GREVE, LUCIUS, II, metals company executive; b. St. Paul, July 23, 1915; s. Joseph and Lillian (King) G.; m. Marguerita Philippa Buller Colthurst, Aug. 31, 1940; children: Lucius Richard, Guy Robert. Salesman Electric Auto-Lite Co., Detroit, 1934-42, methods engr. Bay City, Mich., 1944-45, project engr., 1944-45, with sales dept., 1946-49; pres. L. Greve Sales Co., Bay City, from 1949. Exec. v.p. Graphic Metals Co., 1962—, dir., chmn. fin. com., 1962—; pres. Montezuma Mining Co., 1963—. Mem. Sch. Sites Com., 1952, Sch. Citizens Com., 1957; sec. Saginaw Bay Assn., 1957. Mem. U.S. Power Squadron, Saginaw Bay Yacht Club (dir. 1961, comdr. 1965, 66, chmn. nom. com. 97), Bay City Country Club, Great Lakes Crusing Club. Home: Bay City, Mich. Died Sept. 26, 2001.

GREVE, TIM, editor; b. Bergen, Norway, Feb. 20, 1926; s. Arent and Anna (Gade) G.; m. Marit Nansen, May 8, 1950; children: Kari, Anne. Magister artium, U. Oslo, 1951. Diplomat Norwegian Govt., 1950-73; dir. gen. Ministry of Fgn. Affairs, 1967-73, Norwegian Nobel Inst., Oslo, 1973-77; editor in chief Verdens Gang, Oslo, from 1978. Author books. Home: Lysaker, Norway. Died: April 27, 1986.

GRIFFIN, DONALD R(EDFIELD), zoology educator; b. Southampton, N.Y., Aug. 3, 1915; s. Henry Farrand and Mary Whitney (Redfield) G.; m. Ruth M. Castle, Sept. 6, 1941 (div. Aug. 1965); children: Nancy Griffin Jackson, Janet Griffin Abbott, Margaret, John H.; m. Jocelyn Crane, Dec. 16, 1965 (dec. Dec. 1998). BS, Harvard U., 1938, MA, 1940, PhD, 1942. Jr. fellow Harvard U., Cambridge, Mass., 1940-41, 46, rsch. assoc., 1942-45, prof., 1953-65, assoc. Mus. of Comparative Zoology, from 1989; asst. prof. Cornell U., Ithaca, N.Y., 1946-47, assoc. prof., 1947-52, prof., 1952-53, Rockefeller U., N.Y.C., 1965-86, prof. emeritus, 1986—2003, trustee, 1973-76. Vis. lectr. Princeton U., N.J., 1987-89; pres. Harry Frank Guggenheim Found., N.Y., 1979-83. Author: Listening in the Dark, 1958 (Nat. Acad. Scis. Elliot medal 1961), Echoes of Bats and Men, 1959, Animal Structure and Function, 1962, Bird Migration, 1964 (Phi Beta Kappa prize 1966), The Question of Animal Awareness, 1976, Animal Thinking, 1984, Animal Minds, 1992, rev. edit. 2001. Mem. Am. Ornithologists Union, Am. Soc. Zoologists, Am. Physiol. Soc., Ecol. Soc. Am., Am. Acad. Arts and Scis., Nat. Acad. Scis., Am. Philos. Soc., Animal Behavior Soc., Phi Beta Kappa, Sigma Xi. Home: Lexington, Mass. Died Nov. 7, 2003.

GRIFFIN, JAMES HILTON, consulting engineer; b. Elmo, Tex., July 27, 1917; s. James Linton and Katie Irene (Hilton) G.; m. Dorothy Aileen Rapsilver, June 13, 1942; children: James Edwin, Charles Danforth, Katherine Irene, John Hilton, Laura Nell, Robert Linton, Roger Dean. BS Chem. Engring., Tex. A&M U., 1938, MS Chem. Engring., 1940. Registered profl. engr., Tex. Rsch. engr. Nat. Lead Co. Baroid Divsn., Houston, 1940-41; prodn. engr. Organic Divsn. Dow Chem. Co., Freeport, Tex., 1941-42, asst. supt. prodn. control, 1942-46, supt. prodn. control Styrene Divsn., Rubber Res., Def. Plant, 1942-46; prin., CEO J.H. Griffin & Assocs., Brookshire, Tex., from 1946, Rapsilver Internat., Inc., Brookshire, from 1957. Patentee in field. Mem. Am. Inst. Chem. Engrs., NSPE, Nat. Soc. Profls. Engrs. in Pvt. Practice, AF&AM, Masons. Avocations: floriculture, hunting, travel, grandchildren. Home: Brookshire, Tex. Died June 4, 2001.

GRIFFIN, W. C. bishop; Bishop Ch. of God in Christ, Albuquerque. Deceased.

GRIFFITHS, DANIEL EDWARD, dean emeritus; b. Bridgeport, Conn., May 8, 1917; s. Frederick George and Helen (Quist) G.; m. Priscilla Tomlinson, June 22, 1946; children: Priscilla Ann Griffiths Russel, Michael Edward. EdB, Central Conn. State Coll., 1940; MEd, U. N.H., 1949; PhD, Yale, 1952. Asst. prof. edn. Colgate U., 1949-52; prof. State Coll. Tchrs., Albany, N.Y., 1952-55; dir. coop. devel. pub. sch. adminstrn., asso. coordinator ednl. research N.Y. State Dept. Edn., 1955-56; assoc. prof., then prof. edn. Columbia Tchrs. Coll., 1956-61; assoc. dean Sch. Edn. NYU, N.Y.C., 1961-65, dean Sch. Edn., Health, Nursing and Arts Professions, 1965-83, spl. asst. to chancellor, 1983-86, dean emeritus, from 1986, prof. emeritus, from 1988. Dir. devel. criteria of success in sch. adminstrn. project, coop. research br. U.S. Office Edn., 1957-61, dir. devel. taxonomies of orgnl. behavior in edn. project, 1964; dir. N.Y.C. Study Tchr. Mobility, 1963; pres. N.Y. State Tchr. Edn. Conf. Bd., 1973-83; chmn. Nat. Commn. on Excellence in Ednl. Adminstrn., 1986-88. Author: Human Relations in School Administration, 1956, Administrative Theory, 1959, Organizing Schools for Effective Education, 1962, Administrative Performance and Personality, 1962, The School Superintendent, 1967; editor: Behavioral Science and Educational Administration, 1964, Developing Taxonomies of Organizational Behavior in Education, 1969, The Dilemma of the Deanship, 1980, Administrative Theory in Transition, 1985; co-editor: Leaders for America's Schools: The Report and Papers of the National Commission on Excellence in Education Administration, 1988; chmn. editorial bd. NYU Edn. Quar., 1968-83; editor: Ednl. Adminstrn. Quar, 1975-79; editor spl. issue Ednl. Adminstrn. Quar., summer 1991; mem. editorial bd. Libr. of Edn., 1961-67, chmn., 1964-67; contbn. author or editor of over 300 articles, pamphlets and books. Pres. Sch. Bd. Greenburgh, N.Y., 1961-64. Served with USAAF, 1943-46. Recipient 1st Roald F. Campbell Lifetime Achievement award in ednl. adminstrv., 1992. Mem. Am. Ednl. Rsch. Assn., Nat. Conf. Profs. Ednl. Adminstrn., Am. Assn. Colls. Tchr. Edn. (dir. 1975-78), Assn. Colls. and Schs. of Edn. in State Univs. and Land Grant Colls. and Affiliated Pvt. Units. (exec. bd. 1972-83), Assn. Deans of Edn. in Pvt. Univs. (chmn. 1972-83), Univ. Coun. Ednl. Adminstrn., Ea. Srs. Golf Assn. (pres. 1992-94), Scarsdale Golf Club (pres. 1980), Westchester Srs. Golf Assn. (pres. 1978-80), Westchester Golf Assn. (mem. exec. com. 1993—), Kappa Delta Pi, Phi Delta Kappa. Home: Scarsdale, NY. Deceased.

GRIFFITHS, MARTHA, former lieutenant governor, lawyer; b. Pierce City, Mo., Jan. 29, 1912; m. Hicks G. Griffiths(dec. 1996) BA, U. Mo.; JD, U. Mich. Mem. Mich. Ho. of Reps., 1949-52; judge Recorders Ct., Detroit, 1953; U.S. rep. from Mich. Washington, 1955-75, lt. gov. State of Mich., 1983—91; ptnr. Griffiths & Griffiths, Detroit. Democrat. Died Apr. 22, 2003.

GRIGGS, RUTH MARIE, retired journalism educator, writer, publications consultant; b. Linton, Ind., Aug. 11, 1911; d. Roy Evans Price and Mary Blanche (Hays) P.; m. Paul Philip Griggs, Aug. 4, 1940. BS, Butler U., 1933; postgrad., U. So. Calif., 1938, Northwestern U., 1939; MA, U. Wyo., 1944. Cert. tchr. journalism, English, speech, bus. edn. Travel writer indpls. Star, 1927-37; summer reporter Worthington Times, Ind., 1928-33; journalism, speech tchr. Warren Ctrl. H.S., Indpls., 1937; tchr. bus. edn., journalism Greene Twp. H.S., South Bend, Ind., 1937-38; tchr. journalism, English, bus. edn. Howe H.S., Indpls., 1938-46; tchr. journalism Butler U., Indpls., 1946-48, evenings, 1972-76; dir. publs. Broad Ripple H.S., Indpls., 1948-77. Summer journalism workshop instr. numerous univs., 1949-80. Author: History of Broad Ripple, 1968; co-author: Handbook for High School Journalism, 1951, Teacher's Guide to High School Journalism, 1965, Marquette Memoirs, 1996, 2001. S Press Club of Ind., 1984; recipient Rabb award Women's Press Club of Ind., 1988, Disting. Alumni award Butler U. Alumni Bd., 1989. Mem. Journalism Edn. Assn. (v.p., pres. 1963-69, Towley award 1965), Women in Comm. (pres. Indpls. 1969-70, Wright award 1969, Kleinhenz award 1978), Nat. Fed. Press Women (youth projects bd. 1979-87, Recognition award 1991), Columbia Scholastic Press Assn. (life, Gold Key award 1964, Golden Crown 1975), Ind. H.S. Advisers Assn. (pres. 1972, Sengenberger award 1965), Delta Zeta (Ind. Woman of Yr. 1984). Republican. Presbyterian. Home: Indianapolis, Ind. Died Jan. 29, 2003.

GRINDSTAFF, ROY ARTHUR, minister; b. Cambridge, Ohio, Jan. 18, 1946; s. William Roy and Hazel Mae (Barrett) G.; m. Loris Marie Caudill, Sept. 3, 1966; children: Roy Arthur II, Yolonda Grace, Benjamin Caudill. BA magna cum laude, Olivet Nazarene U., 1972, MA, 1973; MDiv, Asbury Theol. Sem., 1977; PhD in Communication, Ohio State U., 1990. Ordained to ministry Internat. Ch. of Foursquare Gospel, 1969. Pastor Foursquare Gospel Ch., Bradley, Ill., 1968-73, Royal Oak (Mich.) Community Foursquare Ch., 1973-74, Sugartree Ridge Cir., United Meth. Ch., Hillsboro, Ohio, 1974-77, New Guilford United Meth. Ch. and West Carlisle Federated Ch., 1977-80; interim pastor Interim Cardington Cir., United Meth. Ch., 1982, Mt. Vernon (Ohio) Christian Missionary Allaince, 1985; prof. Mt. Vernon Bible Coll., 1977-78, 85-86; adj. faculty Cen. Ohio Tech. Coll., 1985, Mt. Vernon Nazarene Coll., 1986, 88; adminstrv. chaplain Mt. Vernon Devel. Ctr., from 1978, program coord., 1983-88, chair human rights com., from 1979, chair resident sexuality com., 1978-80 and from 89. Co-author: Chaplaincy Services, 1982. Mem. task force on ch. and handicapped Ohio Coun. Chs., 1980-83; chaplain Country Club Ctr., 1980-84; v.p. PTO, Royal Oak, 1974; mem. bus. adv. coun. Mt. Vernon Sch. Bd., 1989—. Mem. Speech Communication Assn., Religious Communication Assn., Soc. for Pentecostal Studies, Am. Acad. Religion and Study of Bibl. Lit., Knox County Ministerial Assn. (sec.-treas. 1983-85, pres. 1988-90), Ohio State Chaplains' Assn. (program com. 1988—, sec. 1991—), Theta Phi. Home: Mount Vernon, Ohio. Died Nov. 7, 2001.

GRISWOLD, IDAWEASE JOHNSON, librarian; b. Oxford, Miss., May 29, 1932; d. Willie Leonard and Ida Bernice Johnson; m. John Jr. Jewel Griswold Jr., Feb. 13, 1955; children: Gemiel Griswold Matthews, John Anthony. BA, LaSalle U., Phila., 1975; MLS, Drexel U., 1978. Cert. in libr. sci., elem. edn. Fed. employee U.S. Govt., Phila., 1955-63; sch. employee Sch. Dist. of Phila., 1966-80, tchr., libr., 1980-93; propr. Ancestors Alive Bookshop, Phila., from 1995. Vol. libr. Manna Bible Inst., Phila., 1994—. Co-author: History and Genealogy Stephen Bailey, 1982. Served with WAC, 1951-54. Recipient Excellence in Teaching award, Phila., 1990, Christian Svc. award Jones Tabernacle Ch., 1984, 89. Mem. Pa. Ret. Tchrs. Assn., Pa. Assn. Sch. Librs., Assn. Phila. Sch. Librs., African Am. Genealogy Group (local archivist 1993—), Assn. for Study of African Am. Life and History (local sec. 1992), Friends Free Libr. Phila. (sec. local br. 1980—). Democrat. Avocations: book collecting and historical documents, travel to historic sites. Home: Philadelphia, Pa. Died May 2, 2001.

GRISWOLD, MARTHA KERFOOT, social worker; b. Oklahoma City, Mar. 22, 1930; d. John Samuel III and Frances (Mann) Kerfoot; m. George Littlefield Griswold, Jan. 28, 1967. AB, Occidental Coll., 1951; MRE, U. So. Calif., 1956, postgrad., 1962. Cert. social worker. Teen dir. Toberman Settlement, San Pedro, Calif., 1954-56; social worker County of L.A., 1956-62; cons. community orgn. L.A., 1962-84; dir. LIV Disability Resources Ctr., Altadena, Calif., from 1984. Instr. Calif. State U., L.A., 1966-68, 1983-84; chair Childrens' Adv. Com. L.A. County Dept. Mental Health, 1985-86; coordinator So. Calif. Conf. on Living Long Term with Disability, 1985-87. Co-host, prodr. radio program on disability Access Unlimited, Sta. KPFK-FM, 1987—, host. prodr. cable TV program on disability issues LIVstyles, 1992—. Mem. Pasadena (Calif.) City Disability Issues Com., 1984-86, Pasadena Strategic Planning Task Force, 1985-86, commn. disability access City of Pasedena, 1990-97, commn. on diversity, 1997—; com. on aging and long-term care Region 2 United Way, L.A., chairperson, 1989-90, Pasadena Awareness: A Cmty. Effort for Disabled (PACED v.p.), 1983—. Recipient award So. Calif. Rehab. Assn., 1986, Disting. Alumna award Claremont Sch. Theology, 1996. Mem. AAUW, NASW, Californians for Disability Rights, Acad. Cert. Social Workers, Health and Social Svc. Workers with Disabilities. Congregationalist (UCC). Home: Monrovia, Calif. Died June 20, 2000.

GROENING, WILLIAM ANDREW, JR., lawyer, former chemical company executive; b. Saginaw, Mich., Nov. 20, 1912; s. William Andrew and Rose (Egloff) G.; m. Virginia Jane Gann, July 27, 1940 (dec. Aug. 1990); children: Mary R. Groening Flores, William Andrew III, Janet R. Groening Marsh, Phyllis L. Groening Beehr, Theodore J.; m. Haven Johnstone Blake, Jan. 26, 1991. BA, U. Mich., 1934, JD, 1936; LLD, Saginaw Valley State U., 1974. Bar: Mich. 1936. With legal dept. Dow Chem. Co., Midland, Mich., 1937-51, asst. gen. counsel, 1951-67, gen. counsel, 1968-77, asst. sec., 1955-71, v.p., 1971-77, mem. finance com., 1972-77; sec., dir. Dow Corning Corp., 1961-77, Kartridg-Pak Co., 1966-77. Author: The Modern Corporate Manager: Responsibility and Regulation, 1981. Mem. Regina High Sch. Bd., 1963-67; bd. arbitrators Roman Catholic Province of Mich., 1970-71; chmn. pension com. Mich. Cath. Conf., 1975-85; chmn. bd. Saginaw Valley Coll., 1963-73; charter commr. City of Midland, 1944, city councilman, 1946-52, mayor, 1950-52; trustee Willard and Martha Dow Meml. Ednl. Fund, 1949-75, pres., 1951-75; nat. chmn. U. Mich. Law Sch. Fund, 1979-80. Mem. State Bar Mich. (chmn. anti-trust law sect. 1967-68), Mich. Conf. Bar Pres. (chmn. 1952-53), ABA, Midland County Bar Assn. (past pres.), Am. Judicature Soc. (past dir., v.p., exec. com.) Clubs: KC, Midland Country, Rumson Country, Delray Beach. Home: Delray Beach, Fla. Deceased.

GROLD, L. JAMES, psychiatrist; b. L.A., May 28, 1932; s. Leo James and Evelyn (Fox) G.; m. Janis Jensen, Apr. 4, 1958; children: Eric, Kevin, Katherine. BA, Stanford U.,

1953, MD, 1956. Diplomate Am. Bd. Psychiatry and Neurology. Intern Los Angeles County Gen. Hosp., L.A., 1956-57; fellow Menninger Sch. Psychiatry, Topeka, 1957-60; pvt. practice, L.A., from 1962. Exec. dir. Resthaven Psychiat. Hosp., L.A., Calif., 1962—65; med. dir. Westwood Psychiat. Hosp., L.A., 1965—69; dir. profl. edn. Malibu Cmty. Counseling Ctr.74, 75; mem. staff L.A. PTA Child Guidance Clinic, 1962—63, Los Angeles County Hosp, 1962—71, Westwood Hosp., 1963—65, St. John's Hosp., 1969—76; asst. clin. prof. U. So. Calif., L.A., Calif., 1962—70; exec. dir., psychiat. cons. 1-800-THERAPIST; psychiat. cons. Life ADJ Team; faculty Web Ed Coll. Psychiatry; crisis and trauma cons. to corps.; cons. to attys. on criminal and civil cases, asst. in jury selection, expert witness testimony, from 1996; cons. to corps. on chem. biol. and nuclear disasters, acute stress disorder and PTSD, from 1996. Mem., assoc. editor Trauma-E; contbr. articles to med. jours. Bd. dirs. Malibu Colony Assn., 1984-88, v.p., 1987-88; chmn. Save Our Beach LEgal Fund, 1984-88; mem. vol. med. staff, mem. mental health com., psychiat. cons. Venice Family Clinic, 1990—; advisor to pres. Menninger Found., 1988-89; active USPHS Nat. Disaster Med. Assistance Team, 1993—; instr. 1996 Olympics Disaster Preparedness Tng. Capt. M.C., U.S. Army, 1960-62. Recipient cert. of commendation City of L.A., 1987, U.S. Congress, 1988, Venice Family Clinic, 1992. Fellow Am. Psychiat. Assn. (life); mem. Nat. Assn. Pvt. Psychiat. Hosps. (edn. com. 1962-69), So. Calif. Psychiat. Soc. (chmn. com. on psychiat. hosps. 1964-67, mem. membership com. 1967-68, task force on developing vol. pro bono svcs. 1991-93). Home: Marina Del Rey, Calif. Died Jan. 24, 2003.

GROSS, CHARLES MERRILL, art educator; b. Cullman, Ala., Sept. 18, 1935; s. Robert Merrill and Delma (Hesterly) G.; m. Rosalie Westbrook, Jul. 4, 1956; 1 child, Robert Mark. Diploma, Marion Mil. Inst., 1954; BFA, Atlanta Coll. Art, 1967; MFA, U. Guanajuato, Mexico, 1968. Instr. Miss. Coll., Clinton, 1968-69; prof. U. Miss., Oxford, from 1969. V.p. So. Assn. Sculptors, 1972-76. Recipient First Place award Mid-South Exhbn., 1969, others; Henry J. Toombs grantee, 1965-66. Avocation: cattle ranching. Home: Oxford, Miss. Died Feb. 14, 2002.

GROSS, HAL RAYMOND, bishop; b. Walla Walla, Wash., Jan. 15, 1914; s. John J. and Millie (Hale) G.; m. Evelyn Blythe Kerr, July 22, 1933; 1 dau., Patricia Ann Gross Simmons. Student, Oreg. State U., 1931-36; JD, Willamette U., 1939; student, Ch. Div. Sch. of Pacific, 1946, D.D., 1965. Bar: Oreg. bar 1939. Pvt. practice in, Corvallis, 1939-42; atty. Oreg. Unemployment Compensation Commn., 1942-44; ordained to ministry Episcopal Ch., 1946; pastor U. Oreg., 1946-47; rector St. Paul's Ch., Oregon City, 1947-61; archdeacon Episcopal Diocese Oreg., 1961-65; suffragan bishop Oreg., 1965-79; ret., 1979. Mem. exec. council Episcopal Ch., 1975-79; vice chmn. Ho. of Bishops, 1976-79 Trustee Ch. Div. Sch. of Pacific, 1950-55, 72-73. Mem. Oreg. Bar Assn., Phi Delta Theta. Clubs: Rotary (hon.). Democrat. Episcopalian. Home: Wilsonville, Oreg. Died Oct. 13, 2002.

GROSS, JEANNE BILGER, music educator; b. West Manchester, Ohio, June 16, 1925; d. Paul Leonard and Irene (Leas) Bilger; m. Virgil Dean, Dec. 28, 1947; children: Debra Jill, Richard Dean. B. Music Ed., Otterbein Coll., 1947; MA, Ohio State U., 1976, PhD, 1987. Cert. music educator, supr. and cons. Tchr. high sch. music vocal Worthington (Ohio) Schs., 1947-49; vocal music tchr. jr. high (7th, 8th and 9th grades) Columbus (Ohio) Pub. Schs., 1949-50; music educator Westerville (Ohio) City Sch., 1968-89. Adj. prof. grad. edn. program Nova U., Ft. Lauderdale, Fla., summer 1989. Author: Benjamin Russel Hanby, Ohio Composer Educator, 1987. Dissertation honored in Music Edn. Coun. Rsch. in Music Edn's., 1987. Mem. AAUW, Ohio Hist. Soc., Westerville Hist. Soc., Ohio Edn Assn., Westerville Edn. Assn., Music Educators Nat. Conf. Ohio Music Educators Assn. (speaker, clinician), Assn. for Supervision and Curriculum Devel. (ednl. cons. state conv.), Pi Kappa Lambda, Phi Delta Kappa, Phi Delta Gamma. Avocations: antiques, history, bicycling. Home: Westerville, Ohio. Deceased.

GROSS, PRIVA BAIDAFF, art historian, retired educator; b. Wieliczka, Poland, June 19, 1911; came to U.S., 1941, naturalized, 1955; d. Israel and Leopolda (Friedman) Baidaff; Ph.M., Jagellonian U., Cracow, Poland, 1937; postgrad. (N.Y. U. scholar 1945-47), N.Y. U. Inst. Fine Arts, 1945-48; m. Feliks Gross, July 25, 1937; 1 dau., Eva Helena Gross Friedman. Mem. faculty Queensborough Community Coll., CUNY, 1961-81, assoc. prof. art history, 1971-81, ret., 1981, co-chmn. art and music dept., 1966-68, chmn. art dept., 1968-74, dir. coll. gallery, 1968-77. SUNY grantee, 1967. Mem. AAUW (dir. 1972-76, 1980-82), Coll. Art Assn. Am., Soc. Archtl. Historians, Gallery Assn. N.Y. State (dir. 1972-73), N.Y. State Assn. Jr. Colls., AAUP, Polish Inst. Arts and Scis. Am., Council Gallery and Exhbn. Dirs. (dir. 1970-72). Contbr. articles, revs. to profl. publs; Deceased. Home: New York, NY.

GROSSMAN, JULIUS, orchestra conductor; b. Bklyn., Nov. 1, 1912; s. Meyer and Fannie (Hodes) G.; B.S., N.Y. U., 1933; m. Ruth Cassack, May 26, 1948; children— Jean, Marc. Chmn. music dept. High Sch. Performing Arts, N.Y.C., 1947-70; condr. Lena Symphony, N.Y.C., Naumburg Orch., Nat. Music Week Orch., N.Y.C.; mus. dir., condr. Julius Grossman Orch., N.Y.C., 1957—. Served with inf. U.S. Army, 1944-46. Decorated Bronze Star. Mem. Musicians Union. Home: New York, NY. Died Nov. 12, 2002.

GROVERT, ROBERT EUGENE, manufacturing executive; b. Trenton, Nebr., Jan. 7, 1921; s. Joseph Julius and Mary Edith (Gillaspie) G.; m. Doris Hedelt, Feb. 28, 1948 (dec.); children: Karen Jo, Beverly Kaye, Leslie Anne, Barbara Gaye. BS, U. Nebr., 1943. Served with U.S. Army, 1944-47; advanced through grades to col. USAF, 1962; staff officer The Pentagon, Washington, 1962-64; col. Office Sec. of Def., Washington, 1964-66; ofcl. rep. AF U.S. Embassy, Bonn, Fed. Republic of Germany, 1966-70; dir. systems analysis Socialist Republic of Vietnam, 1970-71; ret., 1971; exec. asst. to pres. Nat. Polit. Action Com. Representing U.S. Bus., Washington, 1971-74; pres. Polit. Action Com. Representing Bus. in Pa., Harrisburg, 1973-74; corp. dir. Northrop Corp., Washington, 1974-83, former v.p., sr. corp. exec. European div. Bonn. Bd. dirs. Fokker Aircraft Co., Amsterdam. Various mil. decorations, USAF and fgn. countries. Republican. Avocations: reading, music, various sports. Home: Bonn, Germany. Died Oct. 18, 2003.

GRUSH, HELEN BUTLER, educational consultant; b. Winchester, Mass., Aug. 1, 1921; d. Horace and Helen Gretchen (Avery) Butler; m. Willard Parker Grush, Aug. 29, 1942 (dec.); children: Sandra LeFlore Bergmann, Jeffrey Willard, Kimball Warren. BS, Northeastern U., 1970; MEd, Boston U., 1974. Tchr. Smith Sch., Lincoln, Mass., 1962-64; instr., author Mass. Coun. Pub. Schs., Boston, 1963-65; supr. Community Svc. Corps-Migrant, Boston, 1965-66; ednl. dir. Perceptual Edn. Rsch., Wellesley, Mass., 1966-68; asst. prof. Lesley Coll. Grad. Sch., Cambridge, Mass., 1972-80; co-founder LEAD Ednl. Resources, Lexington, Mass., 1972; author, lectr., instr. Logical Encoding and Decoding Program, 1972-85; editorial cons. Logical Encoding and Decoding Program Ednl. Resources, Bridgewater, Conn., from 1985. Mem. founding com.Pilgrim Congl. Ch., Lexington; pres. Florence Crittenden League. Mem. AAUW (bd. dirs.), Laudholm Preserve, Fla. Ctr. for the Arts, Vero Beach ARt Club. Republican. Congregationalist. Home: Westford, Mass. Died Nov. 26, 2001.

GRYTE, ROLF EDWARD, internist, allergist; b. Mpls., Mar. 8, 1945; s. Ralph Edward and Irene (Lindquist) G.; m. Barbara Lee Deems, June 8, 1971; children: David, Kirsten, Kristofer. BA, U. Minn., 1967; DO, Kirksville Coll. Osteopathic Medicine, 1971. Diplomate Am. Osteopathic Bd. Internal Medicine. Intern Kirksville (Mo.) Osteopathic Hosp., 1971-72, resident in internal medicine, 1972-75, chief resident, 1974-75, assoc. prof. internal medicine, 1975-79, 1989—; dir. Allergy and Environ. Health Clinic Kirksville Coll. Osteopathic Medicine; pvt. practice medicine specializing in internal medicine, allergy, and asthma, Kirksville, 1979-87; med. dir. inhalation therapy dept. Kirksville Osteopathic Med. Ctr., 1975-80, 1988—; med. dir. inhalation therapy dept. Grim Smith Hosp., Kirksville, 1979-87, med. dir. pulmonary rehab. program, 1983-87; chief staff Kirksville Osteopathic Med. Ctr., 1990—, bd. govs., 1990—; black lung examiner Dept. Labor, 1983-87; social security disability examiner, 1975—. Med. dir. Planned Parenthood of Northeast Mo., Kirksville, 1972-82; mem. Conservation Fedn. of Mo. Nat. Osteopathic Coll. scholar. Fellow Am. Coll. Osteopathic Internists; mem. AMA, Am. Coll. Osteopathic Allergists and Immunologists, Am. Heart Assn., Mo. Thoracic Soc., Mo. Assn. Osteopathic Physicians and Surgeons, N.E. Mo. Osteopathic Assn., Sierra Club, Sigma Sigma Phi, Psi Sigma Alpha. Republican. Lutheran. Avocation: hunting, fishing, boating., Died Sept. 11, 1999.

GUBERNICK, LISA, magazine editor; b. L.A., 1955; Degree in English, Bryn Mawr Coll., 1978. Journalist Securities Week, 1981-83, East Side Express, 1983-84, American Lawyer, 1984; sr. editor Forbes, Inc., N.Y.C., 1984-98. Author 2 books, including: Squandered Fortune: The Life and Times of Huntington Hartford, 1991, Get Hot or Go Home: Trisha Yearwood, The Making of a Nashville Star, 1993. Died Mar. 16, 2004.

GUBTA, INDRAJIT, trade association administrator; Pres. World Fedn. of Trade Unions, Prague, Czech Republic. Died Feb. 2001.

GUENETTE, ROBERT HOMER, television production executive; b. Holyoke, Mass., Jan. 12, 1935; s. Alfred Guenette and Mary (Graham) Atwell; m. Frances Gudemann, Feb. 22, 1961; 1 child, Mark David. Grad. high sch., Holyoke, Mass. Film editor various prodn. cos., N.Y.C., 1952-61; freelance news dir., producer, writer all major networks, N.Y.C., 1961-67; v.p. creative affairs Met. Broadcasting, N.Y.C., 1964; writer Seven Arts Prodns., Los Angeles, 1964; pres. Robert Guenette Prodns., N.Y.C., 1967-71; producer, dir., writer Wolper Prodns., Los Angeles, 1971-75. Dir: The Tree (also prodr.), 1969, Appointment with Destiny (also prodr.) (TV), 1971, The Mysterious Monsters, 1975, The Making of Star Wars, 1977, The Amazing World of Psychic Phenomena, 1977, SPFX: The Empire Strikes Back (also prodr.), 1980, The Man Who Saw Tomorrow (also prodr.), 1980, Great Movie Stunts: Raiders of the Lost Ark (also prodr.)(TV), 1981, Celebrate the Century (also prodr.), 1991; screenwriter: (films) William Faulkner's Mississippi (Emmy award 1964), The Defector, 1966, The Tree, 1967, They've Killed the President!, (Emmy award 1972), Mysterious Monsters, 1975, The Amazing World of Psychic Phenomena, 1977, The Man Who Saw Tomorrow, 1980, Children of the Night (TV), 1985, Power and Fear: The Hollywood Graylist, 1990, Here's Looking At You, 1991, Golf: The Greatest Game, 1993, Orson Welles: What Went Wrong, 1994; producer only: William Faulkner's Mississippi, 1965, Victory at Entebbe, 1976, Diky Hocker, 1979. Mem. Caucus for Producers, Writers and Dirs., Internat. Documentary Assn. (bd. dirs. 1980-86, pres. 1986-87), Dirs. Guild Am., Writers Guild Am., Producers Guild Am. Avocation: horse racing. Home: Venice, Calif. Died Oct. 31, 2003.

GUERARD, ALBERT JOSEPH, retired modern literature educator, writer; b. Houston, Nov. 2, 1914; s. Albert Lèon and Wilhelmina (McCartney) G.; m. Mary Maclin Bocock, July 11, 1941; children: Catherine Collot, Mary Maclin, Lucy Lundie. AB, Stanford U., 1934, PhD, 1938; AM, Harvard U., 1936. Instr. Amherst (Mass.) Coll., 1935-36; mem. faculty Harvard U., Cambridge, Mass., 1938-61, successively instr. English, asst. prof., assoc. prof., 1948-54, prof., 1954-61, Stanford (Calif.) U., 1961-85, Albert L. Guerard prof. lit., 1965-85. Author: The Past Must Alter, 1937, Robert Bridges, 1942, The Hunted, 1944, Maquisard, 1945, Joseph Conrad, 1947, Thomas Hardy, 1949, Night Journey, 1950, Andrè Gide, 1951, Conrad the Novelist, 1958, The Bystander, 1958, The Exiles, 1963, The Triumph of the Novel: Dickens, Dostoevsky, Faulkner, 1976, The Touch of Time: Myth, Memory and the Self, 1980, Christine/Annette, 1985, Gabrielle, 1992, The Hotel in the Jungle, 1996, Suspended Sentences, 1999; co-editor: The Personal Voice, 1964. Served as tech. sgt. psychol. warfare br. AUS, World War II. Recipient Paris Rev. Fiction prize, 1963, Lit. award Am. Acad. Arts and Letters, 1998; Rockefeller fellow, 1946-47; Fulbright fellow, 1950-51; Guggenheim fellow, 1956-57; Ford fellow, 1959-60; Nat. Found. Arts fellow, 1967-68; Nat. Found. Humanities fellow, 1974-75. Mem. Am. Acad. Arts and Scis., Pen Ctr. West, Phi Beta Kappa. Home: Stanford, Calif. Died Nov. 9, 2000.

GUEST, MICHAEL KURT, lawyer; b. Ypsilanti, Mich., Apr. 14, 1949; s. Elmer B. G. and Joanne R. (Pizarek) Ardery; m. Janet K. Browning, Aug. 29, 1970; children: Christine, Matthew, Andrew, Anya. AB with distinction and honors, Ind. U., 1971, JD cum laude, 1974. Bar: Ind. 1974, U.S. Dist. Ct. (so. dist.) Ind. 1974, U.S. Ct. Appeals (7th cir.) 1977, U.S. Supreme Ct. 1978. Assoc. McHale, Cook & Welch, P.C., Indpls., 1974-77, profl. mem., from 1977, shareholder, from 1981, officer, dir., from 1982. Bd. dirs. Kocolene Devel. Corp., Kocolene Mktg. Corp., Shadowood Golf, Inc., Seymour, Ind. Note editor: Ind. Law Jour., 1973-74. Bd. dirs. Christamore House, Indpls., 1984-89, pres., 1988-89; bd. dirs. Walther Cancer Inst., Indpls., 1987—, vice chmn., chmn. exec. com., 1989-97. Fellow Indpls. Bar Found., Ind. Bar Found.; mem. ABA, Ind. Bar Assn., Indpls. Bar Assn., Indpls. Athletic Club, Univ. Club, Country Club Indpls., Phi Eta Sigma, Phi Beta Kappa. Home: Indianapolis, Ind. Died Aug. 31, 1999.

GUGGENHEIM, CHARLES E. motion picture and television director/producer; b. Cin., Mar. 31, 1924; s. Jack Albert and Ruth Elizabeth (Stix) G.; m. Marion Davis Streett, June 29, 1957; children: Grace Stix, Jonathan Streett, Philip Davis. BA, U. Iowa, 1948; HHD (hon.), Washington U., St. Louis, 1978, Am. U., 1995. Prodr. Louis G. Cowan, Inc., N.Y.C., 1948-51; prodr., dir. Fund for Adult Edn., Ames, Iowa, 1951-52; acting dir. KETC Ednl. TV Commn., St. Louis, 1952-54; pres. Guggenheim Prodns., Inc., Washington, from 1955. Prodr.: (TV series) Sunday at the Zoo, 1950 (George Foster Peabody award); prodr., dir.: (films) Nine from Little Rock, 1964 (Acad. award 1964), RFK Remembered, 1968 (Acad. award 1968), Monument to the Dream, 1967 (Acad. award nomination 1968), Children Without, 1964 (Acad. award nomination 1964), The Klan: A Legacy of Hate in America, 1982 (Acad. award nomination 1983), High Schools, 1983 (Acad. award nomination 1984), The Johnstown Flood, 1989 (Acad. award 1990), A Time for Justice, 1994 (Acad. award 1995), D-Day, 1994 (Acad. award nomination 1995), The Shadow of Hate, 1995 (Acad. award nomination 1996), A Place in the Land, 1998 (Acad. award nomination 1999). Trustee Danforth Found., St. Louis, 1968—, Found. for the Nat. Archives, 1994—, White House Hist. Assn., 1998—; media dir. Stevenson Presdl. Com., 1956, Kennedy Presdl. Com., 1968, McGovern Presdl. Com., 1972, Kennedy for Pres. Com., 1980, 75 U.S. senator and gov.'s campaigns, 1955-85. With U.S. Army, 1943-46. Recipient Disting. Achievement award U. Iowa, Conservation Svc. award U.S. Dept. Interior, 1968, Inst. Honors, AIA, 1987, Eartwatch award, 1991, 99. Mem. Acad. Motion Picture Arts and Scis., Writer's Guild of Am., Cosmos Club, Univ. Club (N.Y.). Home: Washington, DC. Died Oct. 9, 2002.

GUILD, NELSON PRESCOTT, retired state education official; b. Keene, N.H., Nov. 20, 1928; s. Louis F. and Hope (Mason) Guild; m. Margaret Adele Graf, June 24, 1950; children: Douglas, Matthew(dec.). BA, U. N.H., 1953; MA, Pa. State U., 1955, PhD, 1958. Asst. prof. govt. Hamilton Coll., Clinton, N.Y., 1958-64, assoc. prof., 1964-66; dean Frostburg (Md.) State Coll., 1966-69, pres., 1969-85; interim exec. dir. bd. trustees Md. State Univs. and Colls., 1985-87. Author: (with Kenneth T. Palmer) Introduction to Politics: Essays and Readings, 1968. Served with USAF, 1946-49. Home: Frostburg, Md. Died Jan. 5, 2004.

GUILINGER, JAMES WILLIAM, state agricultural education coordinator; b. Monmouth, Ill., Jan. 26, 1930; s. Gerald Ralph and Stella Louise (BrownLee) G.; m. Carol Louise Ross, Aug. 1, 1950. BAgr, U. Ill., 1951, MEd, 1958, postgrad., 1958-75. Cert. all grade supr., Ill. Agrl. instr. Williamsfield (Ill.) Unit Dist. Schs., 1951-66; exec. sec. McDonough County Farm Bur., Macomb, Ill., 1966-67; agrl. instr. Sycamore (Ill.) Unit 427 Schs., 1967-88; customer svc. dir. Dicken Grain Corp., Sycamore, 1988-89; state agrl. edn. coord. FCAE, speaker Ill. State Bd. Edn., Rantoul, from 1989. Contbr. articles to profl. jours. Sec. Sycamore Farmers

Club Fair Bd., 1967—; active Ill. Leadership Coun. for Agrl. Edn., Rantoul, 1983—, Rep. Presdl. Task Force, Washington, 1983—, Rep. Nat. Com., Washington, 1983—; pres. DeKalb County (Ill.) Selective Svc. Bd., 1990. Recipient Cert. of Recognition, Ill. House, Senate and Gov., 1982. Mem. NEA (life), Nat. Vocat. Agr. Tchrs. Assn. (life, spkr. 1970—, pres. 1977-78), Nat. FFA Alumni Assn. (life, nat. coun. mem.-at-large 1994—, spkr. 1985—, hon. Am. FFA degree 1966, contbr. FFA Found.), Am. Vocat. Assn. (life, spkr. 1979—, pres. 1986-87, Region III Tchr. of Yr. 1981, Nat. Tchr. of Yr. 1981, Ship citation 1987), Ill. Vocat. Assn. (life, bd. dirs. 1973-75, Ill. Tchr. of Yr. 1980-81), Ill. Assn. Vocat.-Agr. Tchrs. (pres. 1973-74), Ill. FFA Alumni Assn. (sec. 1972, pres. 1989-91, hon. State FFA degree 1954). Methodist. Avocation: world war ii aircraft and military history. Home: Roseville, Ill. Died May 8, 2002.

GUIN, EMMA LOIS, primary care nurse; b. Hoke County, Jan. 29, 1931; m. Hope Gilbert and Annie Belle (Black) Autry; children: Catherine Brock, Dennis Strother, Edward Strother. RN, Presbyn. Hosp., 1951; cert. FNP, U. N.C., 1976. RN. FNP staff Scotland County Health Dept., Laurinburg, N.C.; FNP Dr. R.G. Townsend, Raeford, N.C.; pub. health nurse I Hoke County Health Dept., Raeford; staff nurse VA Hosp., Fayetteville, N.C. Recipient Cert. Merit award NCPHA, 1992. Mem. ANA (bd. dirs.). Home: Raeford, NC. Deceased.

GUMB, RAYMOND DANIEL, computer science educator, researcher; b. Atlanta; s. Albert Melvin and Rebecca (Johnson) G.; m. Mary Ann Spriegel, May 1975 (dec. Sept. 2000); children: Christopher W., Robert D., Lawrence F.; m. Albis Balza, Aug. 2002. SB, MIT, 1960; MA, Emory U., 1967; PhD, Lehigh U., 1970. Instr. and rsch. positions TRW Computers, MIT, Raytheon, Ga. Tech., 1960-67; asst. prof. philosophy Lafayette Coll., Easton, Pa., 1970-71; asst. prof., assoc. prof. computer sci. Temple U., Phila., 1971-80; prof. computer sci. Calif. State U., Northridge, 1979-84, N.Mex. Tech., Socorro, 1984-86, U. Mass., Lowell, from 1986. Author: Rule Governed Linguistic Behavior, 1972, Evolving Theories, 1979, Programming Logics, 1989; editor, author: Essays in Semantics and Epistemiology, 1983. Travel grantee Assn. for Symbolic Logic/NSF, 1979, 99; rsch. grantee Sandia Nat. Lab., 1985-86. Mem. Assn. for Symbolic Logic, Assn. for Computing Machinery, Soc. for Exact Philosophy, Am. Assn. for Artificial Intelligence, Sigma Xi. Home: North Chelmsford, Mass. Died 2002.

GUMP, RICHARD ANTHONY, SR., lawyer; b. Tulsa, Nov. 22, 1917; s. Harry Allen and Mary (Hanrahan) G.; m. Billie Louise Nail, Feb. 18, 1941; children: Marilyn Virginia Gump Stewart, Richard Anthony. BBA, U. Tex., 1939, LL.B., 1940. Bar: Tex. bar 1940. Spl. agt. FBI, 1940-45; founder, mng. ptnr. Akin, Gump, Strauss, Hauer and Feld, Dallas, 1945—2003. Mem. ABA, Dallas Bar Assn., State Bar Tex., Tex. Bar Found., Salesmanship Club Dallas, Northwood Club, Headliners Club (Austin, Tex.), Serra Club. Roman Catholic. Home: Dallas, Tex. Died June 21, 2003.

GUNN, THOM(SON) (THOMSON WILLIAM GUNN), poet, retired English educator; b. Gravesend, Eng., Aug. 29, 1929; came to U.S., 1954; s. Herbert Smith and Ann Charlotte (Thomson) G. BA, Trinity Coll., Cambridge (Eng.) U., 1953. Tchr. English, sr. lectr. U. Calif., Berkeley, 1958-66, 73-99; ret., 1999. Author: Fighting Terms, 1954, The Sense of Movement, 1957, My Sad Captains, 1961, Touch, 1967, Moly, 1971, Jack Straw's Castle and Other Poems, 1976, Selected Poems, 1979, The Passages of Joy, 1982, The Occasions of Poetry, 1982, expanded edit., 1985, The Man with Night Sweats, 1992, Shelf Life, 1993, Collected Poems, 1993, Boss Cupid, 2000. Recipient Robert Kirsch award L.A. Times, 1988, Shelley Meml. award Poetry Soc. Am., 1990, Forward 1st prize, 1992, Bay Area Book Reviewers award for poetry, 1973, 93, PEN USA West Poetry award, 1973, 93, Lenore Marshall Poetry prize, 1993, Medal of Merit for poetry Am. Acad. Arts and Letters, 1998, David Cohen prize for lit., 2003; Lila Wallace Reader's Digest grantee, 1991; MacArthur fellow, 1993. Died Apr. 25, 2004.

GUNNESS, ROBERT CHARLES, retired chemical engineer; b. Fargo, N.D., July 28, 1911; s. Christian I. and Elizabeth (Rice) G.; m. Beverly Osterberger, June 18, 1936; children: Robert Charles, Donald Austin, Beverly Anne. BS, U. Mass., Amherst, 1932; MS, MIT, 1934, D.Sc., 1936. Asst. prof. chem. engring. MIT, 1936-38; research dept. Standard Oil Co. Ind., 1938-47, mgr. research, 1947-51, asst. gen. mgr. mfg., gen. mgr. supply and transp., 1952-56, exec. v.p., 1956-65, pres., 1965-74, vice chmn., 1974-75, dir., 1953-75. Vice chmn. research and devel. bd. Dept. Def., 1951 Trustee U. Chgo., Rush-Presbyn.-St. Lukes Hosp.; life mem. Mass. Inst. Tech. Corp.; past chmn. Nat. Merit Scholarship Corp.; past pres., trustee John Crerar Library. Fellow Am. Inst. Chem. Engrs. (council 1951); mem. Nat. Acad. Engring., Am. Chem. Soc., Am. Acad. Arts and Scis., Sigma Xi, Phi Kappa Phi, Kappa Sigma. Home: Fullerton, Calif. Died Jan. 28, 2004.

GUNTHER, GERALD, lawyer, educator; b. Usingen, Germany, May 26, 1927; came to U.S., 1938, naturalized, 1944; s. Otto and Minna (Floersheim) Gutenstein; m. Barbara Kelsky, June 22, 1949; children: Daniel Jay, Andrew James. BA, Bklyn. Coll., 1949; MA, Columbia, 1950; LLB, Harvard, 1953; LLD (hon.), Ill. Inst. Tech., 1987, Bklyn. Law Sch., 1990, Bklyn. Coll. of CUNY, 1990, Duquesne U., 1995, Valparaiso U., 1996. Bar: N.Y. 1955. Law clk. Judge Learned Hand, 1953-54, Chief Justice Earl Warren, 1954-55; assoc. Cleary, Gottlieb, Friendly & Hamilton, N.Y.C., 1955-56; assoc. prof. law Columbia U., N.Y.C., 1956-59, prof., 1959-62; prof. law Stanford U., 1962-72, Wm. Nelson Cromwell prof., 1972-95, prof. emeritus, from 1995; lectr. polit. sci. Bklyn. Coll., 1949-50. Author: John Marshall's Defense of McCulloch versus Maryland, 1969, (with K.M. Sullivan) Constitutional Law, 14th edit., 2001, Learned Hand: The Man and the Judge, 1994, 95, (with K.M. Sullivan) First Amendment Law, 1999; mem. editl. bd. Found. Press, 1972—, Stanford Univ. Press, 1983-86; mem., Overseers' Com. to visit The Harvard Law Sch., 1974-80, 1995-2001; mem. adv. bd. and editl. bd. Ency. of Am. Constn., 1983-86; contbr. articles to profl. jours. Recipient Disting. Alumnus award Bklyn. Coll., 1961, Learned Hand medal for excellence in fed. jurisprudence Fed. Bar Coun., 1988, Richard J. Maloney prize for disting. contbns. to legal edn. Bklyn. Law Sch., 1990, Erwin N. Griswold Triennial prize Supreme Ct. Hist. Soc., 1995, Bernard Witkin medal State Bar Calif., 1995, Triennial award (for Hand biography) Order of the Coif, 1999; Guggenheim fellow, 1962-63; Ctr. Advanced Study in Behavioral Scis. fellow, 1969-70; Fulbright-Hays lectr. Ghana, 1970; NEH fellow, 1980-81, 85-86. Fellow AAAS; mem. Am. Philos. Soc., Am. Law Inst., Am. Hist. Assn. (mem. com. Littleton-Griswold Fund, 1968-73), U.S. Assn. Constnl. Law (bd. dirs. 1997—). Home: Stanford, Calif. Died July 30, 2002.

GUNTHER, JACOB E., III, state representative; b. Middletown, N.Y. m. Aileen Gunther; children: Jake IV, Caitlin, Mary Alice. AA, Orange County CC. Apptd. vice chair N.Y. State Legis. Commn. on Rural Resources; N.Y. state rep., 1992—2003. Elected three consecutive four yr. terms Forestburgh Town Justice; mem. N.Y. State Magistrate's Assn. Died July 9, 2003.

GURASH, JOHN THOMAS, insurance company executive; b. Oakland, Calif., Nov. 25, 1910; s. Nicholas and Katherine Restovic Gurash; 1 child, John N. Student Loyola Univ. Sch. Law, 1934. With Pacific Employers Ins. Co., 1944—53; pres., organizer Meritplan Ins. Co., 1953—59; exec. vpres. Pacific Employers Ins. Co., 1959—60, pres., 1960—68, chmn. bd., 1968—76; vpres. Ins. Co. N. Am., 1966—70; exec. vpres. INA Corp., 1968—69, dir., 1968—69, chmn., 1969—74, pres., 1969—74, CEO, 1969—74, chmn., 1974—75, CEO, 1974—75, chmn. bd., 1975, chmn. exec. comt., 1975—79; chmn. bd. CertainTeed Corp. and Saint Gobain Corp., 1978—92, chmn. emeritus, from 1992; chmn. Horace Mann Educators Corp., Springfield, Ill., 1989—96, chmn. emeritus, 1996—2003; dir. St. Gobain Corp., chmn. bd. dirs., 1991—92; trustee emeritus Occidental Col., Los Angeles; former trustee Orthopaedic Hosp., Los Angeles; dir. Weingart Found., bd. dirs. Bd. dirs. Weingart Found. Home: Pasadena, Calif. Died Oct. 21, 2003.

GURLEY, PAUL G. management executive, merger and acquisition consultant; b. Milan, Tenn., Sept. 4, 1946; s. Gordon Dee and Cecile (Parenteau) G.; m. Mary Harvey Jones, Sept. 24, 1988. BBA, Memphis State U., 1969. CPA. Asst. data processing auditor 1st Nat. Bank, Memphis, 1969-72; mgr. Cannon & Co. CPAs, Memphis, 1972-79; acct. pvt. practice, Memphis, 1979-82; dir. legis. affairs City of Memphis, 1983-92; ptnr. Mark Browder & Assocs., 1992-94; CFO Beale St. Mgmt., Memphis, from 1994. Pres. Memphis Jaycees, 1974-75; treas. Nat. Civil Rights Mus. Found., Inc., Memphis, 1992-94. Mem. AICPA, Tenn. Soc. CPA's. Roman Catholic. Avocations: photography, sports. Home: Memphis, Tenn. Died Aug. 13, 2001.

GUSHMAN, JOHN LOUIS, former corporation executive, lawyer; b. Lima, Ohio, May 29, 1912; s. Louis Alexis and Belle (Whitney) G.; m. Helen Louise Little, Sept. 11, 1937; children: Sally Gillespie, Susan Fetters, John Louis. BA, Ohio State U., 1934, JD, 1936; certificate of completion, Inst. Mgmt., Northwestern U., 1953. Bar: Ohio 1936. Practiced law with Williams, Eversman & Morgan, Toledo, 1936-47; with legal dept. and successively v.p., gen. mgr. internat. div. Owens-Ill., Inc., 1947-61; pres., chief operating officer, dir. Anchor Hocking Corp., 1961-67, pres., dir., chief exec. officer, 1967-71, chmn. bd., chief exec. officer, 1971-77, chmn. exec. com. of bd. dirs., 1977-82. Former chmn. bd. trustees Ohio State U. Served as maj. USAAF, World War II. Mem. Order of Coif, Phi Beta Kappa, Phi Delta Theta. Presbyterian. Home: Naples, Fla. Deceased.

GUSTAVSON, ERICK BRANDT, broadcast executive; b. Rockford, Ill., June 2, 1936; s. Sven Ragnar and Ruth Emelia (Johnson) Gustavson; m. Mary Janet Gustavson, Nov. 21, 1964; children: Ruth Marie, Timothy Brandt. Student, Northwestern Coll., St. Paul, 1954-56, Cuyahoga CC, Cleve., 1957-58, Loyola U., Chgo., 1962-64; LLD (hon.), Calif. Grad. Sch. Theology, 1985. Mgr. Sta. WCRF, Moody Bible Inst., Cleve., 1960-67; dir. broadcasting Moody Bible Inst., Chgo., 1968-74, v.p. devel., 1974-86; gen. mgr. Sta. KAIM-AM-FM, Billy Graham Evang. Assn., Honolulu, 1967-68; bd. dirs., exec. com. Nat. Religious Broadcasters, Morristown, NJ, 1968-89, pres., 1982-85, Parsippany, NJ, 1990—2001; exec. v.p. Trans World Radio, Chatham, NJ, 1986-90. Pres. Evang. Christian Pubs., Chgo., 1985; charter dir. Evang. Coun. Fin. Accountability, Washington, 1979—84, Washington, 1989—2001. Charter mem. Rep. Presdl. Task Force, Washington, 1980—2001; trustee Calvary Evang. Mission, 1989—2001. Recipient Chinese Culture award, Inst. Chinese Culture, N.Y.C., 1989. Mem.: Trans World Radio Internat. (chmn. 1996), Back to Bible Broadcast (trustee 1986—90). Home: Jeffersonton, Va. Died May 14, 2001.

GUSTIN, RALPH LIVINGSTON, JR., retired insurance company executive, lawyer; b. West Somerville, Mass., Mar. 7, 1918. A.B., Harvard U., 1940, LL.B., 1943, grad. advanced mgmt. program, 1960. Bar: Calif. 1947, Mass. 1953, U.S. Supreme Ct. Assoc. McCutchen, Thomas, Matthew, Griffiths & Greene, San Francisco, 1947-53; assoc. counsel John Hancock Mut. Life Ins. Co., Boston, 1953-57, 2d v.p., counsel, 1957-62, v.p., gen. solicitor, 1962-65, v.p., gen. counsel, 1965-66, sr. v.p., gen. counsel, 1967-78, exec. v.p., gen. counsel, 1979-83. Sec., bd. dirs. Mass. Bay United Fund, 1957-73; sec., bd. dirs. United Fund of Greater Boston. Mem. ABA (ho. of dels.), Mass. Bar Assn., Boston Bar Assn., Calif. State Bar, Life Ins. Counsel (pres. 1976-77), Nat. Assn. Securities Dealers (bd. govs., vice chmn. 1971-74). Home: Wellesley, Mass. Died Aug. 10, 2002.

GUTIERREZ, GERALD ANDREW, theatrical director; b. N.Y.C., Feb. 3, 1955; s. Andrew and Obdulia A. (Concheiro) G.; m. Wendy J. Wasserstein, Dec. 3, 1983 (div. Dec. 1986); children: Ginger Joy, Phyllis Kate, Edna Elizabeth. BS in Theater Arts, Juilliard Sch., 1972; postgrad., Yale U., 2000—01. Resident dir. St. Nicholas Theater, Chgo., 1977-80, Playwrights Horizons, N.Y.C., 1980-84; assoc. artistic dir. Acting Co., N.Y.C., 1986—88, artistic dir., 1988—89; assoc., artistic dir. Lincoln Ctr. Thea., N.Y.C., 1993. Co-author Sunset at Camp O'Henry, 1984; co-author play for TV Latenite, 1985; author film script A Bag of Shells, 1980; dir. plays including Three Sisters, 1975 (also prodr.), A Life in the Theatre, 1977-1978, Elegy for Young Lovers, San Francisco Opera, 1978, She Loves Me, 1980, Meetings, 1981, The Curse of an Aching Heart, 1982, Little Johnny Jones, 1982 Geniuses, 1982-1983, The Rise and Rise of Daniel Rocket, 1982, Isn't It Romantic, 1983-1984, Terra Nova, 1984, Much Ado about Nothing, 1986-1987, One Two Three Four Five, 1987-1989, Emily, 1988, The Most Happy Fella, 1991 (Connecticut Drama Critics award for best dir., LA Drama Critics award for best dir.), White Liars/Black Comedy, 1993, Playboy of the West Indies, 1993, Abe Lincoln in Illinois, 1993-1994, The Heiress, 1994 (Tony award for best dir., NY Drama Desk award for best dir., Antoinette Perry award for best dir., 1995), Dog Opera, New York Shakespeare Festival, 1995, A Delicate Balance, 1996 (Tony award for best dir., Antoinette Perry award for best dir., NY Drama Desk award for best dir., 1996), Once upon a Mattress, 1996-1997, Ivanov, 1997-1998, The Primary English Class, 1998, Honour, 1998, Ring 'round the Moon, 1999, Sail Away (musical revue), 1999, Man of La Mancha, 2000, Boys and Girls, 2002, Dinner at Eight, 2002-2003. Mem.: Players Club, Dirs. Guild, Soc. of Stage Dirs. and Choreographers, Actors Equity Assoc. Democrat. Episcopalian. Avocation: gourmet chef. Home: Brooklyn, NY. Died Dec. 30, 2003.

GUTMAN, JEREMIAH SHELDON, lawyer; b. Bklyn., Oct. 19, 1923; s. Theodore and Elsie (Edenbaum) G.; m. Marilyn Gates; children: Thea, Mara, Rebecca, Malaika. BA, CCNY, 1943; LLB, NYU, 1949. Bar: N.Y. 1949, U.S. Dist. Ct. (so. dist.) N.Y. 1951, Bd. of Immigration Appeals, 1952, U.S. Dist. Ct. (ea. dist.) N.Y. 1955, U.S. Ct. Appeals (2d cir.) 1957, Tax Ct. of U.S. 1959, Supreme Ct. of U.S., 1959, U.S. Ct. Mil. Appeals, 1961, U.S. Ct. Claims 1961, U.S. Ct. Appeals (5th cir.) 1964, U.S. Dist. Ct. (no. dist.) Miss., 1964, U.S. Dist Ct. (ea. dist.) La., 1965, U.S. Ct. Appeals (8th cir.), 1965, U.S. Ct. Appeals (10th cir.), 1966, U.S. Ct. Appeals (D.C. cir.) 1968, U.S. Dist. Ct., D.C., 1970, U.S. Ct. Appeals (3rd cir.), 1970, U.S. Ct. Appeals (4th cir.), 1971, U.S. Dist. Ct. (we. dist.) Tex., 1971, U.S. Dist. Ct. (no. dist.), N.Y., 1971, U.S. Dist. Ct. (so. dist.) Tex., 1972, U.S. Ct. Appeals (11th cir.), 1981, U.S. Dist. Ct. (we. dist.), N.Y., 1987, U.S. Ct. Appeals (1st cir.), 1989. Ptnr. Levy, Gutman, Goldberg & Kaplan, N.Y.C., 1949—2004. Co-chmn. Nat. Coalition Against Censorship, N.Y.C.; pres. Am. Israeli Civil Liberties Coalition; bd. dirs., mem. exec. com. N.Y. Civil Liberties Union, N.Y.C.; bd. dirs. ACLU, N.Y.C. With U.S. Army, 1943-46. Fellow Am. Orthopsychiat. Assn.; mem. ABA, Fed. Bar Assn., Assn. of Bar of City of N.Y., N.Y. County Bar Assn., Assn. Trial Lawyers Am. Avocation: civil liberties. Home: Hastings Hdsn, NY. Died Feb. 25, 2004.

GUTMANN, JOSEPH, art history educator; b. Wuerzburg, Unterfranken, Germany, Aug. 17, 1923; came to U.S., 1936; s. Henry and Selma (Eisemann) G.; m. Marilyn Tuckman, Oct. 8, 1953; children: David H., Sharon D. BS, Temple U., 1949; MA, NYU, 1952; PhD, Hebrew Union Coll., 1960, DD, 1984, DHL, 1999. Ordained Rabbi. Assoc. prof. art history Hebrew Union Coll., Cin., 1960-69; adj. prof. art. Univ. of Cin., 1961-68; vis. prof. art. Antioch Coll., Yellow Springs, Ohio, 1964; prof. art history Wayne State U., Detroit, 1969-89, prof. art history emeritus, from 1989. Vis. prof. art history U. Mich., Ann Arbor, 1985, Spertus Coll. Judaica, Chgo., 1989; vis. prof. religious studies U. Windsor, Ont., Can., 1990-92, U. Ctrl. Fla., Orlando, 1998-2001, cons. Spertus Mus. Chgo., Skirball Cultural Ctr., L.A., The Jewish Mus., N.Y., Yeshiva U. Mus., N.Y.; adv. bd. Internat. Survey of Jewish Monuments of CAA-SAH. Author: Juedische Zeremonialkunst, 1963, Jewish Ceremonial Art, 1964, 2d edit. 1968, Images of the Jewish Past, 1965, (with S.F. Chyet) Moses Jacob Ezekiel: Memoirs from the Baths of Diocletian, 1975, Ephraim Moses Lilien's Jerusalem, 1976, Hebrew Manuscript Painting, 1978, (with V. Mann) Danzig 1939: Treasures of a Destroyed Community, 1982, The Jewish Sanctuary, 1983, The Jewish Life Cycle, 1987, Sacred Images: Studies in Jewish Art from Antiquity to the Middle Ages, 1989; editor Beauty in Holiness: Studies in Jewish Customs and Ceremonial Art, 1970, No Graven Images: Studies in Art and the Hebrew Bible, 1971, Die Darmstaedter Pessach-Haggadah, 1972, The Dura-Europos Synagogue: A Re-Evaluation, 1973, rev. 2d edit., 1992, The

Synagogue: Studies in Origins, Archaeology and Architecture, 1975, The Temple of Solomon: Archaeological Fact and Medieval Tradition in Christian, Islamic and Jewish Art, 1976, The Image and the Word: Confrontations in Judaism, Christianity and Islam, 1977, Ancient Synagogues: The State of Research, 1981; author (monthly column) Gutmann on Art Nat. Jewish Post and Opinion, For Every Thing a Season: Proceedings of the Symposium on Jewish Ritual Art, 2002. Chmn. Community Forum Midrasha, Birmingham, Mich., 1986-88. Served as cpl. USAF, 1943-46. Recipient Faculty Recognition award Wayne State U., 1980; Gershenson Disting. Faculty fellow, 1986-88, Henry Morgenthau fellow Hebrew Union Coll., 1957-58, Meml. Found. Jewish Culture grantee 1959, 72; Am. Council of Learned Socs. grantee, N.Y., 1983, Am. Philos. Soc. grantee, Phila., 1965. Mem. Cen. Conf. Am. Rabbis, Coll. Art Assn. Jewish. Avocations: reading, painting. Home: Huntington Woods, Mich. Died Feb. 1, 2004; Farmington Hills, Mich..

GUYTON, ARTHUR CLIFTON, physician, educator; b. Oxford, Miss., Sept. 8, 1919; s. Billy Sylvester and Mary Katherine (Smallwood) G.; m. Ruth Alice Weigle, June 12, 1943; children— David, Robert, John, Steven, Catherine, Jean, Douglas, James, Thomas, Gregory. AB, U. Miss., 1939; MD, Harvard, 1943. Intern Mass. Gen. Hosp., 1943, asst. resident, 1946; acting asso. prof. physiology U. Tenn. Med. Sch., 1947; asso. prof. pharmacology U. Miss. Med. Sch., Oxford, 1947-48, prof. chmn. dept. physiology and biophysics Jackson, 1948-89, prof. emeritus, from 1989. Mem. cardiovasc. rsch. study sect. NIH, 1954-58, mem. physiology tng. com., 1958-64, chmn., 1961-64; mem. adv. coun. Nat. Heart and Lung Inst., 1971-75; mem. physiology com. Nat. Bd. Med. Examiners, 1960-64, chmn., 1962-64 Author: Function of the Human Body, 6th rev. edit., 1984, Textbook of Medical Physiology, 10th rev. edit., 2000, Circulatory Physiology: Cardiac Output and Its Regulation, rev. edit., 1973, Circulatory Physiology II: Dynamics of the Body Fluids, Circulatory Physiology III: Arterial Pressure and Hypertension, 1980; Human Physiology and Mechanisms of Disease, 7th rev. edit., 2002; contbr. articles to profl. jours.; editor Internat. Rev. Physiology. Served in med. research USN, 1944-46. Recipient commendation by Army for wartime rsch., One of 10 Outstanding Young Men of Am. award U.S. Jr. C. of C., 1951, Ida Gould award AAAS, 1959, Wiggers award Am. Physiol. Soc., 1972, ALZA award Biomed. Engring. Soc., 1972, Ross McIntyre award, 1972; Disting. Rsch. award Am. Heart Assn., 1976; Einthoven award Leiden, Holland, 1979; CIBA award for hypertension rsch. Am. Heart Assn., 1980, Merck internat. award for hypertension rsch., 1984, Sci. Achievement award AMA, 1990, ACP award, 1992. Fellow AAAS, Am. Coll. Cardiology (v.p. 1965-66); mem. Am. Heart Assn., Fedn. Am. Socs. Exptl. Biology (pres. 1975-76), Am. Physiol. Soc. (pres. 1974-75), Miss. Acad. Sci. (pres. 1963-64), So. Soc. for Clin. Rsch. (pres. 1956-57), Circulation Soc. (chmn. 1970), Miss. Heart Assn. (pres. 1955-56), Russian Acad. Natural Sci. (medal of merits 1998), Alpha Omega Alpha, Pi Kappa Pi, Sigma Alpha Epsilon, Tau Kappa Alpha, Alpha Kappa Kappa, Phi Eta Sigma, Alpha Epsilon Delta, Omicron Delta Kappa, Phi Beta Kappa. Died Apr. 3, 2003.

HAAK, HAROLD HOWARD, university president; b. Madison, Wis., June 1, 1935; s. Harold J. and Laura (Kittleson) H.; m. Betty L. Steiner, June 25, 1955; children— Alison Marie, Janet Christine. BA, U. Wis., 1957, MA, 1958; PhD, Princeton U., 1963. From asst. prof. to assoc. prof. polit. sci., pub. adminstrn. and urban studies San Diego State Coll., 1962-69, dean coll. profl. studies, prof. pub. adminstrn. and urban studies, 1969-71; acad. v.p. Calif. State U., Fresno, 1971-73, pres., 1980-91, pres. emeritus, 1991—2003, trustee prof., 1991-2000, trustee, prof., vice chancellor acad. affairs, 1992-93; v.p. U. Colo., Denver, 1973, chancellor, 1974-80; pres. Fresno Pacific U., 2000—02. Trustee William Saroyan Found., 1981-91; mem. NCAA Pres. Commn., 1987-91; bd. dirs. Fresno Econ. Devel. Corp., 1981-91, Cmty. Hosps. Ctrl. Calif., 1989-92, Pacific Luth. Theol. Sem., 1998-2002; bd. visitors Air Univ.; mem. Army adv. panel on ROTC affairs, 1988-92; vice-chair Calif. Commn. on Agr. and Higher Edn., 1993-96; pres., trustee Ctrl. Calif. br. Leukemia and Lymphoma Soc., 2002—2003; pres., bd. dirs. Armenian Agribus. Edn. Fund, 2002—2003. Recipient U. Colo. medal, 1980. Mem.: Phi Kappa Phi, Phi Beta Kappa. Home: Fresno, Calif. Died Dec. 26, 2003.

HAAS, LESTER CARL, retired architect; b. Shreveport, La., Apr. 9, 1913; s. Jacob and Hanna (Kahn) H.; m. Niki Kal, Nov. 1, 1942; children: Dale Frances, Catherine Kal (Mrs. Fred Donald Youngswick). BA, Johns Hopkins U., 1933; BArch, U. Pa., 1936; postgrad., Ecole Des Beaux-Arts, N.Y.C., 1936-37; diplome, Ecole Des Beaux-Arts, Fontainebleau, France, 1939; vis. student in residence, Am. Acad., Rome, Italy, 1940. Archtl. apprentice W. Pope Barney, Phila., 1936-39; architect Robert & Co., 1940-41; prin. Lester C. Haas, Architect, Shreveport, 1946-65; ptnr. Haas, Massey & Assocs. (architects), Shreveport, 1966-88; mng. partner TAG-The Archtl. Group, 1978-85; prin. Lester C. Haas, FAIA(E), CCS-Architect, 1989-98, ret., 1998. Co-author: weekly column Ark-La-Texture, 1967-71. Principal works include, Pioneer Bank and Trust Co., Shreveport main office and 9 br. banks, 1948-78, KTBS offices, radio and TV studios, Shreveport, 1948-76, Caddo Sch. Exceptional Children, Shreveport, 1956, also addition, 1977, La Sands Western Hills Motel, Bossier City, La., 1957, St. Pius X Sch., convent and sanctuary alterations, North Shreveport, 1962, Barksdale Officer Club, Barksdale AFB, La. Alteration and Addition, 1965, Northwestern State U. at Shreveport, 1966, Restoration and Renovation of the Strand Theatre, Shreveport, 1978-85, C-Barc Adult Workshop, Shreveport, 1970, additions, 1979, Adminstrv. Center, Caddo Parish Sch. Bd., Shreveport, 1971, Master Plan and Adminstrn. Bldg., Delgado Coll., New Orleans, 1979-81, Shreveport Chamber Pla., 1983, Caddo Parish Communications Dist. Number 1, Emergency Communication Ctr. E-911, 1988. Chmn. rev. com. N.W. La. Areawide Health Planning Council, 1973-75, pres., 1975-76; pres. Travelers Aid, 1951, Children's Service Bur., 1952, Courtyard Players Civic Theatre, 1954, ARC, 1963-65, NCCJ, 1965-69; nat. bd., 1970-73, St. Vincent Acad. Parents Club, 1966-67, Lyric Ball, 1967, Caddo Found. for Exceptional Children, 1972-74; v.p. Caddo-Bossier Assn. Retarded Citizens, 1957, United Fund, 1963-67, Caddo Found. Exceptional Children, 1967-72; adv. bd. Congregation Daughters of Cross, 1965-69; community adv. com. Jr. League, 1973-76, all Shreveport; mem. Shreveport Bldg. Bd., 1979-83; pres. Mental Health Assn. Caddo-Bossier, 1981-82; founding mem. Caddo-Bossier Assn. Retarded Citizens Found., 1997. Lt. USNR, 1942-45. Decorated Navy Commendation ribbon; recipient Merit award 2d Internat. Lighting Exposition, 1947; Ann. Brotherhood citation Shreveport chpt. NCCJ, 1974; John Stewardson Travelling scholar in architecture, 1939-40; honoree Martin Luther King Health Ctr. Christian Svc. Inst., 1991; recipient 5 CSI Regional Specification awards. Fellow AIA (pres. N.La. chpt. 1955, exec. com. Gulf States regional council 1956, pres. Shreveport chpt. 1984); mem. Constrn. Specifications Inst. (cert. constrn. specifier 1979, pres. Shreveport chpt. 1970-71, Nat. Jury Fellows 1974-76), La. Architects Assn. (rep. to Gov.'s Com. to Rewrite Fire Marshal's Act 1973, bd. dirs. 1984), Shreveport Jr. C. of C. (past v.p.), Shreveport C. of C. (bd. dirs., officer), Am. Legion, D.A.V., Tau Sigma Delta. Jewish (pres. congregation 1967, 68). Club: Greater Shreveport Racquet. Died July 24, 2003.

HABAKKUK, JOHN HROTHGAR, economic historian; b. Barry, Wales, May 13, 1915; s. Evan Guest and Anne (Bowen) H.; MA, St. John's Coll., Cambridge U., 1940; m. Mary Elizabeth Richards, Aug. 8, 1948; children: David, Alison, Kate, Lucy. Fellow, Pembroke Coll., Cambridge U., 1938-50, univ. lectr. Faculty Econs. and Politics, 1946-50; vis. prof. Harvard U., 1954-55, U. Calif., Berkeley, 1962-63; prof. econ. history, fellow All Souls Coll., Oxford U., 1950-67, fellow, 1988-2001—; prin. Jesus Coll., 1968 84, vice chancellor univ., 1973-77; pres. Univ. Coll., Swansea, 1975-84; trustee Rhodes Scholarships, 1977-86; mem. Adv. Coun. Pub. Records, 1958 70, Social Sci. Rsch. Coun., 1967-71, Royal Hist. Manuscripts Commn., 1977-85. Chmn. Oxfordshire Health Authority, 1982-84. Created knight bachelor, 1976; hon. fellow Pembroke and St. John's colls., Cambridge U., Jesus Coll., Oxford,, All Souls Coll., Oxford, Univ. Coll. Swansea, 1991. Fellow Brit. Acad.; mem. Royal Hist. Soc. (pres. 1977-80). Author: American and British Technology in the 19th Century, 1962; Population Growth and Economic Development since 1750, 1970, Marriage, Debt and the Estate System, 1994; co-editor: Economic History Review, 1950-60, Cambridge Economic History, Vol. VI, 1965. Home: Oxford, England. Died Nov. 3, 2002.

HACKETT, BUDDY, actor; b. Bklyn., Aug. 31, 1924; s. Philip and Anna (Geller) Hacker; m. Sherry Cohen, June 12, 1955; children— Sandy Zade, Ivy Julie, Lisa Jean. Ed. pub. schs., Bklyn. Theatrical appearances include: Call Me Mister, 1946, Lunatics and Lover, 1954, I Had A Ball, 1964; motion picture appearances include: Walking My Baby Back Home, 1953, Gods Little Acre, 1958, Music Man, 1962, The Wonderful World of The Brothers Grimm, 1961, All Hands on Deck, 1961, Everything's Ducky, 1961, It's a Mad, Mad, Mad, Mad World, 1962, Golden Head, 1963, Muscle Beach Party, 1964, The Love Bug, 1969, Friend to Friend, Scrooged, 1988, (voice) The Little Mermaid, 1989, Paulie, 1998; star TV series Stanley, 1956-57, Fish Police, 1992; TV, cafe and nightclub appearances throughout U.S.; recipient Donaldson award 1955, Venice Film Festival award 1961. Died June 30, 2003.

HACKL, ALPHONS J. publisher; b. Warman, Can. s. John J. and Anna (Moser) H.; m. Muriel J. Forster, Feb. 2, 1946; 1 son, John Raymond. Grad., Handelsschule, Salzburg, Austria, 1934; student, Nat. U., 1937-38, Corcoran Sch. Art, 1938-40, U. Chgo., 1941; BA, Sussex Coll. Tech., 1945; postgrad., Internat. Summer Sch., St. Peter Coll., Oxford U., 1976; JD, LaSalle U., 1991. Apprentice Funder & Mueller, printers, Salzburg, 1934-36; advt. copywriter, art dir., account exec. advt. agy. and dept. store Washington, 1936-40; founder, chmn. emeritus Colortone Press, Washington, 1946—; founder Acropolis Books, Ltd., Washington, from 1959; lectr., instr. George Washington U., 1974-78. Past mem. adv. coun. SBA; mem. adv. bd. publ. specialist program George Washington U.; adv. bd. Washington Tech. Inst.; adj. prof. LaSalle U., 1992; counselor Svc. Corps Ret. Execs. (S.C.O.R.E.), chmn. chpt. Manasota #116. Contbr. articles to profl. publs.; patentee programmed instruction device. Chmn. Met. Sch. Printing, 1972-74. Capt. AUS, 1941-45. Decorated Bronze Star; recipient George Washington Honor medal Freedoms Found., Award of Excellence Image Industry Coun. Internat. Fellow Corcoran Art Gallery; mem. Pub. Rels. Soc. Am., Assn. Am. Pubs., Nat. Press Club, Svc. Corp Ret. Execs. (chmn. chpt. # 116), Sarasota Yacht Club, Lotos Club (N.Y.C.), U.S. Power Squadron Club. Episcopalian. Home: Sarasota, Fla. Died June 8, 2004.

HADDAD, MARYLOU PHYLLIS, elementary education educator; b. Bklyn., Sept. 21, 1937; d. John Jr. and Ann Marie (Garzia) Scorsone; m. Jamil Raouf Haddad, Aug. 1, 1959; children: Ralph John, John Lawrence, James Matthew. BA magna cum laude, Hunter Coll., 1982; MA, CUNY, 1985; cert. of advanced study in ednl. comm. and tech., NYU, 1991. Tchr. N.Y.C. Bd. Edn., from 1984. Participant Comprehensive Sch. Improvement Planning Com., N.Y.C., 1985-87, Henry St. Settlements Arts in Education Program, N.Y.C., 1988-91, Henry St. Settlement Arts and Ptnrs. Program, N.Y.C., 1990, Sch. Based Mgmt. and Shared Decision Making Program, N.Y.C., 1993-95, The Bklyn. Mus. Tchr. Inst., 1995-96. Mem. AAUW, Nat. Mus. Women in Arts (charter mem.), Kappa Delta Pi. Avocations: water colors, print making. Home: Brooklyn, NY. Died May 10, 2001.

HADEN, CHARLES HAROLD, II, federal judge; b. Morgantown, W.Va., Apr. 16, 1937; s. Charles H. and Beatrice L. (Costolo) H.; m. Priscilla Ann Miller, June 2, 1956; children: Charles H., Timothy M., Amy Sue. BS, W.Va. U., 1958, JD, 1961. Ptnr. Haden & Haden, Morgantown, W.Va., 1961-69; state tax commr. W.Va., 1969-72; justice Supreme Ct. Appeals W.Va., 1972-75, chief justice, 1975; judge U.S. Dist. Ct. No. and So. Dists. W.Va., Parkersburg, 1975-82; chief judge U.S. Dist. Ct. (so. dist.) W.Va., 1982—2002; Charles H. Haden II prof. law W.Va. Coll. Law, 2004. Mem. W.Va. Ho. of Dels., 1963-64; asst. prof. Coll. Law, W.Va. U., 1967-68; mem. com. adminstrn. probation system Jud. Conf., 1979-86; mem. 4th Cir. Jud. Coun., 1986-91, 96-2000, U.S. Jud. Conf., 1997—2002, chair exec. com., 2000-02. Mem. Bd. Edn., Monongalia County, W.Va., 1967-68; bd. dirs. W.Va. U. Found., 1986-2004; past. mem. vis. coms. W.Va. U. Coll. Law & Sch. Medicine. Recipient Outstanding Alumnus award W.Va. U., 1986; named Outstanding Appellate Judge in W.Va., W.Va. Trial Lawyers Assn., 1975, Outstanding Trial Judge in W.Va., 1982, Justicia Officium, W.Va. U. Coll. of Law award; inducted into Acad. Disting. W.Va. U. Alumni, 2004. Fellow Am. Bar Found., W.Va. State Bar Found.; mem. ABA, W.Va. Bar Assn., W.Va. State Bar Assn., Am. Judicature Soc., 4th Cir. Dist. Judges Assn. (pres. 1993-95), W.Va. U. Alumni Assn. (pres. 1982-83), W.Va. U. Order of Vandalia. Died Mar. 20, 2004.

HAENSEL, VLADIMIR, chemical engineering educator; b. Freiburg, Germany, Sept. 1, 1914; arrived in U.S., 1930; s. Paul and Nina (Tugenhold) Haensel; m. Mary Mcgraw, Aug. 28, 1939 (dec. 1979); children: Mary Ann Ahlen(dec.), Kathee Webster; m. Hertha Skala, Sept. 14, 1986. BS, Northwestern U., 1935, PhD, 1941, DSc, 1957; MS, MIT, 1939; DSc (hon.), U. Wis., Milw., 1979. Rsch. chemist Universal Oil Products Co. (name changed to UOP Inc.), Des Plaines, Ill., 1937—64, v.p., dir. rsch., 1964—72, v.p. sci. and tech., 1972—79, cons., from 1979; prof. U. Mass., Amherst, from 1979, prof. emeritus. Co-author (sci. books); contbr. articles to profl. jours.; patentee in field. Recipient Chgo. Jr. C. of C. award, 1944, Precision Sci. Co. award in petrolem chemistry, 1952, Indsl. and Engring. Chemistry award, Esso Rsch. and Engr. Co., 1965, Modern Pioneers in Creative Industry award, Nat. Assn. Mfrs., 1965, Chem. Pioneer award, Am. Inst. Chemists, 1967, Perkin medal, 1967, Nat. Medal Sci., 1973, Eugene J. Houdry award in applied catalysis, 1977, Henry J. Albert award, Internat. Precious Metal Inst., 1993. Mem.: AIChE (Profl. award 1957), ACS, NAS (Svc. award in chemistry 1991), NAE (Charles Stark Draper prize 1997), Catalysis Soc, Tau Beta Pi, Phi Lambda Upsilon, Sigma Xi. Home: Amherst, Mass. Died Dec. 16, 2002.

HAGAN, WILLIAM JOHN, educational organization executive; b. St. Louis, Mar. 9, 1924; s. James Edward and Mary Eliz (Hencke) H.; m. Norma Jean McClelland, June 11, 1949; children: Kevin, Janet, Kathy, Jeanne, Patricia, William Jr. BS, Northwestern U., 1958. Sec., contr. F.E. Compton Co., Chgo., 1961-63, treas., 1963-66; admnstrv. v.p. Encyclopaedia Brittanica Edn. Corp., Chgo., 1966-68, v.p. ops., from 1969. Chmn. Boy Scouts Am. Troop #50, Deerfield, 1963-83. With USAF, World War II. Decorated Air medal; Croix de Guerre (Frnace). Mem. Assn. Cinema and Video Labs., Soc. Motion Picture and TV Engrs. Avocation: golf. Home: Deerfield, Ill. Deceased.

HAGEN, UTA THYRA, actress; b. Göttingen, Germany, June 12, 1919; came to U.S., 1926; d. Oskar F. L. and Thyra A. (Leisner) H.; m. Herbert Berghof, Jan. 25, 1957 (dec. Nov. 1990); 1 child, Leticia. DFA (hon.), Smith Coll., 1978; LHD (hon.), De Paul U., 1981, Wooster Coll., 1982; DFA (hon.), U. Wis., Madison, 2000, Pa. State U., 2000. Former tchr. acting Herbert Berghof Studio, N.Y.C., former chmn. Appeared as Ophelia, Dennis, Mass., 1937, as Nina in Sea Gull, N.Y.C., 1938, Key Largo, 1939, Vicki, 1942, Othello, 1943-45, Masterbuilder, 1947, Faust, 1947, Angel Steet, 1948, Street Car Named Desire, 1948, 50, Country Girl, 1950, G.B. Shaw's Saint Joan, 1951-52, Tovarich, City Center, 1952, In Any Language, 1952, The Deep Blue Sea, 1953, The Magic and the Loss, 1954, The Island of Goats, 1955, A Month in the Country, 1956, Good Woman of Setzuan, 1957, Who's Afraid of Virginia Woolf, 1962-64 (Antoinete Perry award 1963), The Cherry Orchard, 1968, Charlotte, 1980; also univ. tour 1981-82, Mrs. Warren's Profession, Roundabout Theatre, N.Y.C., You Never Can Tell, Circle in the Square, Mrs. Klein, Lortel Theatre, 1995-96, on tour, 1996-97, Collected Stories, Lortel Theatre, 1998-99, Six Dance Lessons in Six Weeks, Geffen Theatre, 2001; (films) The Other, 1972, The Boys from Brazil, 1978, Reversal of Fortunes, 1990; TV appearances include A Month in the Country, 1956, Out of Dust, 1959; appeared in numerous TV spls. and guest star appearances including Lou Grant, 1982, A Doctor's Story, 1984, PBS Am. Playhouse prodn. The Sunset Gang, 1991, 02, 1999, Limon: A Life Beyond Words (narrator), 2001; author: Respect for Acting, 1973, Love for Cooking, 1976, Sources, a Memoire, 1983, A Challange for the Actor, 1991; appearances include numerous roles with the H.B. Playwrights Found., 1965-98. Former chmn. bd. HB Playwrights Found. Recipient Antoinette Perry award, 1951, 63, N.Y. Drama Critics award, 1951, 63, Donaldson award for best actress, 1951, London Critics award for best actress, 1963-64 season, Outer Cir. award, Mayor's Liberty medal, 1986, Drama Legend award 1986, John Houseman award for disting. svc., 1987, Campostella award for disting. svc., 1987, Living Legacy award Women's Internat. Ctr., 1994, Lucille Lortell Lifetime Achievement award, 1995, Lortell award, 1996, Drama League Lifetime Achievement award, 1996, Obie Lifetime Achievement award 1996, Jeffry award, chgo., 1997, Antoinette Perry Lifetime Achievement award, 1999; named to Theatre Hall of Fame, 1981. Mem. Am. Acad. of Arts and Scis. Home: New York, NY. Died Jan. 14, 2004.

HAGGITT, RODGER C. pathology educator; b. Detroit, Aug. 28, 1942; s. Russell Phillip and Eldora Emma (Reynolds) H.; m. Mary Jane Dugan, May 18, 1985; children: Kathryn, Scott. Student, East Tenn. State U., 1960-63; MD, U. Tenn., 1967. Diplomate Am. Bd. Pathology, Anatomic and Clin. Pathology. Pathologist New Eng. Deaconess Hosp., Boston, 1974-77; dir. surg. pathology Bapt. Meml. Hosp., Memphis, 1977-84; dir. hosp. pathology U. Wash., Seattle, from 1984, prof. pathology, from 1984, adj. prof. medicine. Instr. pathology Harvard Med. Sch., Boston, 1974-77; clin. assoc. prof. U. Tenn., Memphis, 1977-84. Author book chapters; contbr. articles to profl. jours. Served to maj. U.S. Army, 1972-74. Recipient Disting. Teaching award U. Tenn. Coll. Medicine, 1981, Outstanding Teaching award U. Tenn. Med. Student Exec. Council, 1983. Fellow Am. Soc. Clin. Pathology (mem. coun. on anatomic pathology 1980-86, chmn. 1982-85), Coll. Am. Pathologists; mem. Gastrointestinal Pathology Soc. (pres. 1981), Am. Gastroenterol. Assn. (mem. abstract rev. com. 1985—), Alpha Omega Alpha. Home: Seattle, Wash. Died June 28, 2000.

HAGOPIAN, JOHN HARRY, hazardous materials safety management company executive, chemical engineer; b. Arlington, Mass., June 5, 1948; s. Harry and Armine (Sarian) H. BS in Chem. Engring., Tufts U., 1970, MS in Chem. Engring., 1971. Sr. cons. Arthur D. Little, Inc., Cambridge, Mass., 1972-91; chmn. bd., pres. Hazmat America Inc., Arlington, from 1991. Cons. in field. Sr. author: Emergency Action Guides, 1984-93, Handbook of Chemical Hazard Analysis Procedures, 1989 (Note 1 award 1988); contbr. chpts. to books, articles to profl. jours. Mem. edn. adv. com., hazardous materials mgmt. program Tufts U., Medford, Mass., 1989-91. Mem. Am. Inst. Chem. Engrs. Avocations: music, microcomputers, reading, movies. Home: Northborough, Mass. Died May 31, 2000.

HALABY, NAJEEB E. financier, lawyer; b. Dallas, Nov. 19, 1915; s. Najeeb Elias and Laura (Wilkins) H.; m. Doris Carlquist, Feb. 9, 1946 (div. 1977); children: Lisa (Queen Noor of Jordan), Christian, Alexa; m. Jane Allison Coates Frick, Oct. 1, 1980 (dec. 1996); m. Libby Anderson Cater, Dec. 1, 1997. AB, Stanford U., 1937; student, U. Mich. Law Sch., 1937-38; LL.B., Yale, 1940; LL.D., Allegheny Coll., 1967, Loyola U., Los Angeles, 1968, Dowling Coll., 1985, Embry Riddle & Aero. U., 1993. Bar: Calif. 1940, D.C. 1948, N.Y. 1973. Pvt. practice, L.A.; with O'Melveny & Myers, 1940-42; test pilot Lockheed Aircraft Corp., Burbank, Calif., 1942-43; fgn. affairs adviser to sec. def., 1948-53; dep. asst. sec. def., 1952-54; with L. S. Rockefeller and Bros., 1953-56; pres. Am. Tech. Corp.; sec.-treas., counsel Aerospace Corp.; faculty lectr. UCLA; dir. def. studies program; chmn. UCLA (1960 disarmament conf.); pvt. practice law Calif., 1959-61; adminstr. FAA, 1961-65; pres. Pan Am World Airways, 1968-72, chmn., chief exec. officer, 1969-72; pres. Halaby Internat. Corp., 1973—2003; chmn. Save The Children Found., 1992-98, Dulles Access Rapid Transit, Inc., 1985-98. With Nat. Ctr. for Atmospheric Rsch. Found., 1985-2002. Trustee Aspen Inst., chmn., Wolf Trap Found., (Va.), Jones Inst. Reproductive Biology, Flight Safety Found.; elected chmn. bd. visitors AOPA Flight Safety Found.; mem. adv. coun. Brookings Inst., Libr. of Congress, Smithsonian Instn., Nat. Gallery of Art, Stanford in Washington. Served as naval aviator USN World War II; asst. chief fighter sect. Naval Air Test Center Patuxent River, Md. Decorated Legion of Honor France; Order of Cedars Lebanon; medal of Independence Jordan; recipient Arthur Fleming award; Godfrey L. Cabot award; Monsanto Air Safety award; Glen Gilbert Air Traffic award, Nat. Air and Space Mus. trophy Smithsonian Instn., 1995. Fellow AIAA; mem. Soc. Exptl. Test Pilots, Corbey Ct., Coun. on Fgn. Rels. Clubs: Alibi, Metropolitan; Chevy Chase; Bohemian (San Francisco); Piping Rock (N.Y.C.), Explorers, Tower. Died July 2, 2003.

HALE, JOHN RIGBY, history educator; b. Ashford, Kent, Eng., Sept. 17, 1923; s. E. R. S. and Hilda (Birks) H.; m. Rosalind Williams, 1953; 3 children; m. 2d, Sheila Haynes, 1965; 1 son. Ed. Jesus Coll., Oxford U., Johns Hopkins U. and Harvard U.; MA, DLitt Fellow and tutor in modern history Jesus Coll., Oxford U. (Eng.), 1949-64; prof. history U. Warwick (Eng.), 1964-69; prof. Italian and history, Univ. Coll., London U., 1970-88, prof. emeritus, 1988—; vis. prof. Cornell U., 1959, U. Calif.-Berkeley, 1968-69, UCLA, 1990; chmn. Brit. Soc. for Renaissance Studies, 1973-78; pub. orator U. London, 1980-83. Trustee Nat. Gallery, London, 1973-80, chmn. bd. trustees, 1975-81; trustee Victoria and Albert Mus., London, 1983-86, The British Mus., London, 1985-93, chmn. adv. com. Govt. Art Collection, 1983-93; mem. Royal Mint Adv. Com., 1979-93, Museums and Galleries Commn., 1982-93. Author: England and the Italian Renaissance, 1954, new edit., 1996; The Italian Journal of Samuel Rogers, 1956; Machiavelli and Renaissance Italy, 1961; The Literary Works of Machiavelli, 1961; The Evolution of British Historiography, 1964; Renaissance Europe 1480-1520, 1971; Italian Renaissance Painting, 1977; Florence and the Medici: the Pattern of Control, 1977; Renaissance Fortification: Art or Engineering?, 1977; the Italian Journal of Antonio de Beatis, 1979; Renaissance War Studies, 1983, War and Society in Renaissance Europe, 1985, new edit., 1998, Artists and Warfare in the Renaissance, 1990, The Civilization of Europe in the Renaissance, 1993 (Time-Life Silver Pen award 1994, Heinemann award 1994); editor: Certain Discourses Military by Sir John Smyth, 1964; Renaissance Venice, 1973. Decorated commendatore Ordine Al Merito della Repubblica Italiana; recipient Socio Straniero, Accademia Arcadia, Rome, 1972, Knight Bachelor, 1984, Academicus exclasse (bronze award) Accademia Medicea, Florence, Italy, 1980, Bolla prize for services to Venice, 1982. Fellow British Acad., Soc. Antiquaries, Royal Soc. Lit., Accademia Nazionale dei Lincei., Died Aug. 25, 1999. Home: Twickenham, England.

HALE, KENNETH BYRON, retired law enforcement officer, educator; b. Caledonia, Mich., May 18, 1920; s. Herman and Lucille Florence (Rhead) H.; m. Erika Anna Justus, Mar. 10, 1943; children: Kenneth Byron, Thomas Gerard, Judith Eileen. BS in Police Adminstrn., Mich. State U., 1941. Agt. U.S. Secret Svc., Toledo, Ohio, Washington, 1941-42, spl. agt. Chgo. and Washington, 1945-47, Detroit, 1949-55, spl. agt. in charge Omaha and Indpls., 1955-71; adminstr., instr. Ind. Ctrl. Coll., Indpls., 1972-74; chief of police Police Dept., Indpls., 1974-75. Mem. Marion County Area Police Svcs., 1965-70; scoutmaster Boy Scouts Am., 1953-59; precinct insp. Marion County Election Bd., Indpls., 1977-99. Capt., Mil. Intelligence U.S. Army, 1942-45, 47-49 ETO. Mem. Internat. Assn. Chiefs of Police, Ind. Assn. Chiefs of Police, Police League Ind. (Officer of Yr. 1971), Assn. Former Agts. of U.S. Secret Svc. Republican. Lutheran. Avocations: bowling, fishing, genealogy. Home: Woodbridge, Va. Died Dec. 15, 2000.

HALE, SHADRACH PAYNE, real estate lawyer; b. Trenton, Ga., Jan. 13, 1912; s. Shabrach Jerome and Clara (Street) H.; m. Margaret Virginia Ashworth, Apr. 16, 1937; children: S. Jerome II, Patricia Elaine. LLB, Chattanooga Coll.Law, 1931, LLM, 1934. Bar: Ga. 1931, Tenn. 1936. Ptnr. Hale & Hale, Trenton, 1931-36, McClure, McClure & Hale(formerly McClure & McClure), Chattanooga, 1938-41, Hale & Ellis, Chattanooga, 1942-80, Hale, Hale & McInturff, Chattanooga, from 1980. Sec. Milligan-Reynolds Guaranty Title Agy., Inc., 1941—, exec. v.p., 1975, chmn. bd., chief Exec. officer, 1976—, dir., 1944—. Mem. ABA, Tenn. Bar Assn., Chattanooga Bar Assn., Sigma Delta Kappa. Prebyterian. Clubs: Chattanooga Golf and Country, Mountain City. Lodge: Kiwanis. Home: Chattanooga, Tenn. Deceased.

HALEY, JOHN HARVEY, lawyer; b. Hot Springs, Ark., May 29, 1931; s. Harvey H. and Anne (Tanner) H.; m. Cynthia Martin, Sept. 7, 1997. AB, Emory U., 1952; LLB, U. Ark., 1955. Bar: Ark. 1955, U.S. Dist. Ct. (we. dist.) Ark. 1955, U.S. Ct. Appeals (8th cir.) 1955, U.S. Supreme Ct. 1971. Clk. Ark. Supreme Ct., Little Rock, 1955-56; ptnr. Rose Law Firm, Little Rock, 1956-71, Haley, Young, Bogard & Gitchell, Little Rock, 1971-73, Laser, Sharp, Haley, Young & Boswell, Little Rock, 1973-82, Haley, Polk & Heister, Little Rock, 1982—86, Arnold, Grobmyer & Haley, Little Rock, 1986—96; owner Haley Law Firm, Little Rock, 1996—2002; of counsel Eichenbaum, Liles & Heister, Little Rock, 2002—03. Bd. dirs. North Ark. Telephone Co., Flippin, Ark.; Munro and Co., Hot Springs, Ark., Rose Creek Industries, Plaza Partnership, Talweg, LLC, Memphis; lectr. U. Ark. Law Sch., Little Rock, 1956-60, CLU instr., 1961-65; spl. counsel liquidation and rehab. Ark. Ins. Dept., 1967-71; pres. Combustion Technologies LLC, Little Rock, 1996-2003. Editor Ark. Law Rev., 1954-55. Chmn. Ark. State Bd. Correction, 1967-72, Ark. State Bd. Law Examiners, 1960-63, Election Rsch. Coun., Little Rock, 1961-64; dir. Wildwood Ctr. Performing Arts, Little Rock, 1994-99, Florence Crittenden Home, Little Rock, 1994-99; scoutmaster Second Presbyn. Ch. Troop, Little Rock, 1962-65. Methodist. Avocations: piloting, sailing, bicycling, underwater photography, skiing. Home: Little Rock, Ark. Died Dec. 4, 2003.

HALL, CHARLES FREDERICK, space scientist, government administrator; b. San Francisco, Apr. 7, 1920; s. Charles Rogers and Edna Mary (Gibson) H.; m. Constance Vivienne Andrews, Sept. 18, 1942; children— Steven R., Charles Frederick, Frank A. BS, U. Calif., Berkeley, 1942. Aero. research scientist NACA (later NASA), Moffett Field, Calif., 1942-60, mem. staff space projects, 1960-63; mgr. Pioneer Project, NASA, 1963-80. Recipient Disting. Service medal NASA, 1974, Achievement award Am. Astronautical Soc., 1974, Spl. Achievement award Nat. Civil Service League, 1976, Astronautics Engr. award Nat. Space Club, 1979; inducted into Hall of Fame NASA-AMES, 2000. Achievements include rsch., reports on performance of wings and inlets at transonic and supersonic speeds, on conical-cambered wings at transonic and supersonic speeds, 1942-60; pioneer project launched 4 solar orbiting, 2 Jupiter and 2 Venus spacecraft. Home: Los Altos, Calif. Deceased.

HALL, CONRAD L. cinematographer; b. Tahiti, 1926; s. James Norman H. Student, U. So. Calif. Early career in indsl. TV films, commls.; films include Incubus, 1961, The Wild Seed, 1965, Morituri, 1965, Harper, 1966, The Professionals, 1966, Cool Hand Luke, 1967, Divorce American Style, 1967, In Cold Blood, 1967, Hell in the Pacific, 1968, Butch Cassidy and the Sundance Kid, 1968, Tell Them Willie Boy Is Here, 1969, The Happy Ending, 1969, Fat City, 1972, Electra Glide in Blue, 1973, Smile, 1975, The Day of the Locust, 1975, Marathon Man, 1976, Black Widow, 1987, Tequila Sunrise, 1988, Class Action, 1989, Jennifer 8, 1992, Searching for Bobby Fisher, 1992 (Academy Award nominee, Best Cinematographer, 1993), Love Affair, 1994, Without Limits, 1998, A Civil Action, 1998, American Beauty, 1999, Road to Perdition, 2002 (Academy Award, Best Cinematographer, 2003). Recipient Oscar award for Butch Cassidy and the Sundance Kid, 1969, Am. Soc. of Cinematographers award, 1989. Died Jan. 4, 2003.

HALL, GARY, transplant coordinator; b. Melbourne, Victoria, Australia, Feb. 24, 1943; came to U.S., 1944; s. Scotty H. and Olive Melva (Axton) H.; m. Cheryl Diana, Feb. 12, 1972; children: Stephanie, Adam, Alexandra. Student, U. Ill., 1960-62; BS, Coll. William & Mary, 1965. Br. mgr., dist. supr. Prudential Mortgage Corp., Newport News, Va., 1965-66; br. mgr. Assocs. Fin. Svcs. Corp., Newport News, Va., 1966-69; br. mgr., exec. v.p. Wil-Var Enterprises, Inc., Norfolk, Va., 1969-77; dir. organ procurement U. Louisville, 1978-79; transplant coord. Mid-South Transplant Found., Memphis, from 1979. Contbr. articles to profl. jours. Mem. N.Am. Transplant Coords. Orgn. (Cert. merit 1985, 86, 87), Nat. Kidney Found. West Tenn. (Disting. Svc. award 1981, Pres. award 1984), Am. Liver Found., Southeastern Organ Procurement Found. (various coms.), United Network Organ Sharing. Republican. Methodist. Home: Memphis, Tenn. Died Dec. 21, 2001.

HALL, JUANITA JUSTICE, librarian; b. Olive Hill, Ky., Mar. 6, 1927; d. Lee Roye and Mary Opal (Phillips) Justice; m. John D. Hall (dec. Jan. 1994); 1 child, Diane. AB in Edn., Morehead State U., 1967, MA in Edn., 1973; MSLS, U. Ky., 1970. Libr. Camden Carroll Libr., Morehead (Ky.) State U., 1966-69, head of cataloging, from 1969. Mem. ALA. Home: Ashland, Ky. Died June 20, 2000.

HALL, PIKE, JR., lawyer; b. Shreveport, La., May 27, 1931; s. Pike and Hazel (Tucker) H.; m. Anne Oden Hall, Dec. 24, 1951; children: Brevard Hall Knight, Pike III. BA, La. State U., 1951, JD, 1953. Bar: La. 1953. Asst. city atty. City of Shreveport, 1954-58; elected mem. Caddo Prish Sch. Bd., Shreveport, 1964-70; judge 2d Cir. Ct. Appeal, Shreveport, 1971-85, chief judge, 1985-90; justice Supreme Ct. La., 1990-94; counsel Blanchard, Walker, O'Quin & Roberts, Shreveport, 1994—99. Past chmn. La. Conf. of Ct. Appeal Judges; past bd. govs., vice chmn. La. Jud. Coll.; chmn. La. Jud. Bugetary Control Bd., 1992-94. Mem. adminstrv. bd. First United Meth. Ch., Shreveport. Mem. ABA, La. State Bar Assn. (past bd. govs., past Ho. of Dels.), Shreveport Bar Assn., Order of Coif. Democrat. Avocations: golf, fishing, hunting. Home: Shreveport, La. Died Nov. 25, 1999.

HALL, RICHARD CLAYTON, retired psychologist; b. Pitts., Apr. 29, 1931; s. Clayton LeClaire and Genevieve (Gorman) H.; m. Doris Margaret Bjorkland, Aug. 26, 1963; children: Karen, Janice, Dorothy. BS in Psychology with honors, Trinity Coll., 1952; MS, U. Pitts., 1959, PhD, 1963. Rsch. psychologist Polk (Pa.) Ctr., 1963-68, dir. behavior modification programs, 1968-75, chmn. subcom. human rights for behavior mgmt. procedures, 1987-89, staff psychologist, 1989-91; ind. researcher Key West, Fla., 1975-84, Polk, Pa., 1985-95; retired, 1995. Contbr. articles to profl. jours. With U.S. Army, 1953-55. NSF Coop. Grad. fellow, 1959. Mem. Sigma Xi, Pi Gamma Mu. Democrat. Presbyterian. Avocations: soloist at ch., civic operetta groups. Died Oct. 18, 2002.

HALSEY, WILLIAM, artist, educator; b. Charleston, S.C., 1915; m. Corrie McCallum. Student U. S.C., 1932-34, Boston Mus. Sch. Fine Arts, 1935-39, U. Mex., 1939-41, DFA (hon.) Coll. Charleston, 1995. Instr. Boston Mus. Fine Arts Sch.; dir. Telfair Acad. Sch., Savannah, Ga., Gibbes Art Gallery Sch., Charleston, S.C.; artist-in-residence Castle Hill Found., Ipswich, Mass., Mus. Sch., Greenville County Mus., S.C.; instr. to asst. prof. to artist-in-residence Coll. Charleston, 1965-84. One-man shows include: Bertha Schaefer Gallery, N.Y., Berkshire Mus., Pittsfield, Mass.; Norton Gallery, West Palm Beach, Fla., Mint Mus. Art, Charlotte, N.C., Greenville County Mus. Art, Greenville, S.C., Columbia Mus. Art., S.C., SECCA, Winston-Salem, N.C., Spoleto Festival, USA, Halsey Gallery Coll. Charleston, 1995; exhibited in group shows: Met. Mus. N.Y., Boston Mus. Fine Arts, Whitney Mus. Am. Art, Mus. Modern Art, N.Y.C., Bklyn. Mus., Jewish Mus., N.Y., Chgo. Art Inst., Pasadena Art Inst., Birmingham Mus., Ringling Mus., Sarasota, Fla., Palazzo Venezia, Rome; represented in permanent collections at Balt. Mus., NAD, Nat. Collection of Am. Art, Ind. U., Ga. Mus., Greenville County Mus., Gibbes Art Gallery, Columbia Mus., S.C. State Art Commn., S.C. Nat. Bank, C&S Nat. Bank, First Fed. Savs. & Loan Assn., Springs Mills; executed mural in Berkshire Mus., Pittsfield, Mass., Balt. Hebrew Congl. Temple, Balt., Md., Beth Elohim Synagogue Tabernacle, Charleston; decorations and paintings in Dock St. Theatre, Charleston; portraits in Simons Fine Arts Ctr., Coll. of Charleston, Charleston County Court Room, Dock St. Theatre, others. Author: (with Corrie McCallum) A Travel Sketchbook, 1971, Maya Jour., 1976. James W. Paige fellow, 1939-41; Pepsi-Cola fellow, 1948; Hughes Found. fellow, 1950-51; grantee S.C. Com. for Humanities, 1982, Coll. of Charleston, 1982; fine arts gallery at Coll. of Charleston named in his honor, 1984. Died Feb. 14, 1999. Home: Charleston, SC.

HAMBURG, JOSEPH, physician, educator; b. Phila., Sept. 9, 1922; s. Thomas and Gertrude (Shulitzky) Hamburg; m. Minerva Glickman, July 10, 1949 (dec. June 6, 1983);

children: Jay, Marianne, Bonnie; m. Estelle Guttman, Aug. 25, 1985. Student, Temple U., 1938—42; MD, Hahnemann Med. Coll., 1951, ScD (hon.), 1979; LHD (hon.), Thomas Jefferson U., 1993. Diplomate Am. Bd. Family Practice. Intern Stamford (Conn.) Hosp., 1951—52; pvt. practice medicine Stamford, 1952—63; asst. prof. Coll. Medicine U. Ky., Lexington, 1963—66; dean Coll. Allied Health Professions, 1966—84, prof. medicine, community medicine and allied health edn., 1971—91, dean and prof. emeritus, from 1992. Cons. in field; pres. Ky. Peer Rev. Orgn., 1980; chmn. Nat. Coun. for Edn. Health Profls. in Health Promotion, 1986—97. Gen. editor Review of Allied Health Education, Vols. 1-5, 1972—85. Served with U.S. Army, 1942—46. Mem.: AMA, Ky. Acad. Family Practice, Am. Acad. Family Practice, Ky. Med. Assn., Inst. Medicine NAS, Am. Soc. Allied Health Profns. (pres. 1972). Home: Highland Beach, Fla. Died Sept. 20, 2002.

HAMERMESH, MORTON, physicist, researcher; b. N.Y.C., Dec. 27, 1915; s. Isador J. and Rose (Kornhauser) H.; m. Madeline Goldberg, 1941; children: Daniel S., Deborah R., Lawrence A. BS, Coll. City N.Y., 1936; PhD, N.Y.U., 1940. Instr. physics Coll. City N.Y., 1941, Stanford, 1941-43; research asso. Radio Research Lab., Harvard, 1943-46; asst. prof. physics N.Y.U., 1946-47, asso. prof., 1947-48; sr. physicist Argonne Nat. Lab., 1948-50, asso. dir. physics div., 1950-59, dir. physics div., 1959-63, assoc. lab. dir. basic research, 1963-65; prof. U. Minn., Mpls., 1965-69, 70-86, prof. emeritus, 1986—2003; head Sch. Physics and Astronomy, 1965-69, 70-73; prof. physics, chmn. dept. physics State U. N.Y., Stony Brook, 1969-70. Translator: Classical Theory of Fields (by Landau and Lifshitz), 1951; numerous papers in field. Fellow Am. Phys. Soc.; mem. Research Soc. Am. Home: Minneapolis, Minn. Died Nov. 14, 2003.

HAMILTON, GEORGE HEARD, curator; b. Pitts., June 23, 1910; s. Frank Arthur and Georgia (Heard) H.; m. Polly Wiggin, Oct. 20, 1945; children: Richard, Jennet. BA, Yale U., 1932, MA, 1934, PhD, 1942; MA, Cambridge U., 1971; Litt.D., Williams Coll., 1977. Research asso. Walters Art Gallery, Balt., 1934-36; instr. history art Yale U., 1936-43, asst. prof., 1943-47, asso. prof., 1947-56, prof., 1956-66; curator modern art Univ. Art Gallery, 1940-66; Robert Sterling Clark prof. art Williams Coll., Williamstown, Mass., 1963-64, prof. art, 1966-75, prof. emeritus, 1975—, vis. prof., 1976-85; dir. Sterling and Francine Clark Art Inst., Williamstown, 1966-77, dir. emeritus, 1977—2004. Slade Prof. fine arts Cambridge U., 1971-72; Kress prof. in residence Nat. Gallery Art, Washington, 1978-79 Author: Manet and His Critics, 1954, Art and Architecture of Russia, 1954, European Painting and Sculpture 1880-1940, 1967, (with W.C. Agee) Raymond Duchamp-Villon, 1967, 19th and 20th Century Art: Painting, Sculpture, Architecture, 1970; editor: (catalogue) Collection Société Anonyme, Yale U. Art Gallery, 1950. Trustee Mus. Modern Art; v.p., trustee Hill-Stead Mus., Farmington, Conn., 1970-82; vice chmn., trustee Joseph H. Hirshhorn Mus. and Sculpture Garden, Washington, 1971-75. Fellow Am. Acad. Arts and Scis.; mem. Coll. Art Assn. Am. (pres. 1966-68), Internat. Assn. Art Critics (pres. Am. sect. 1967-69). Home: Williamstown, Mass. Died Mar. 29, 2004.

HAMILTON, IRENE TILL, economist; b. Syracuse, N.Y., Dec. 12, 1906; d. Edward and Frances (Wehner) Hamilton. AB, Syracuse U., 1928; MA, Radcliffe Coll., 1929; PhD, Columbia U., 1937. Economist U.S. Govt., Washington, 1937-85. Home: Arlington, Va. Died Nov. 19, 2001.

HAMILTON, THOMAS STEWART, physician, hospital administrator; b. Detroit, June 19, 1911; s. J.T. Stewart and Lucy (Safford) H.; m. Amy Washburn, June 30, 1937; children: Ann Washburn Hamilton Brainerd, Barbara Hamilton Almy, Jeanne. Grad., Philips Exeter Acad., 1930; AB, Williams Coll., 1934, D.Sc. (hon.), 1969; postgrad., Harvard, 1934-36; M.B., Wayne U., 1938, MD, 1939; D.Sc. (hon.), Trinity Coll., 1962, U. Hartford, 1975. Intern, asst. resident Harper Hosp., Detroit, 1938-40; gen. practice medicine Truro, Cape Cod, Mass., 1940-41; asst. dir. Mass. Gen. Hosp., Boston, 1941-42, 45-46; dir. Newton-Wellesley Hosp., Newton Lower Falls, Mass., 1946-54; exec. dir. Hartford (Conn.) Hosp., 1954-76, pres., 1969-76, pres. emeritus, 1976—; prof. U. Conn. Sch. Medicine, 1978-86, prof. emeritus, from 1986. Dir. Phoenix Mut. L.I.C., 1962-82. Contbr. articles to profl. jours. Trustee Soc. for Savs., 1961-70, McLean Fund, 1968-89; commr. Joint Commn. Accreditation Hosps., 1960-66; mem. cancer control com. USPHS, 1964-70, mem. liaison com. on med. edn., 1969-75; regent U. Hartford, 1962-68. Served to lt. col. M.C. AUS, 1942-45. Recipient Disting. Alumnus award Wayne State U. Sch. Medicine, 1970, Disting. Pub. Svc. award Conn. Bar Assn., 1975, Gold Medal award New Eng. Hosp. Assembly, 1975, Lifetime Achievement award Coll. Health Care Execs., 1999; inducted into Modern Health Care Hall of Fame, 1999. Fellow Am. Coll. Hosp. Adminstrs. (regent New Eng. 1953-57, Gold Medal award 1971); mem. AMA (mem. internship rev. com. 1958-68), Mass. Med. Assn., Conn. Med. Assn., Hartford County Med. Assn., Assn. Am. Med. Colls. (sec.-treas. 1968-70), Coun. Tchg. Hosps. (chmn. 1970), Am. Hosp. Assn. (pres., chmn. bd. trustees 1962-63, Disting. Svc. award 1969), Conn. Hosp. Assn. (pres. 1966, Disting. Svc. award 1970), Mass. Hosp. Assn. (pres. 1951), Soc. Med. Adminstrs. (pres. 1968-70), Med. Adminstrs. Conf., Marine Hist. Soc. Clubs: Masons Island Yacht. Home: Bloomfield, Conn. Died July 29, 2002.

HAMOVITCH, WILLIAM, economist, educator, university official; b. Montreal, Que., Can., Sept. 1, 1922; came to U.S., 1946, naturalized, 1953; s. Abraham and Tillie (Weisenfeld) H.; m. Mitzi Berger, May 30, 1946 (dec. Dec. 31, 1992); children: Alan, Susan. B.Com., McGill U., 1943; M.P.A. (Adminstrn. fellow), Harvard, 1945, MA, 1946, PhD, 1949. Lectr., asst. prof. U. Buffalo, 1946-53; asst. prof., assoc. prof., prof. Queens Coll. City U. N.Y., Queens, 1953-86, chmn. dept. econs., 1965-76, provost, acad. v.p., 1976-84, acting pres., 1985; v.p. acad. affairs William Paterson Coll. N.J., Wayne, 1986-92, ret., 1992. Research scientist N.Y.C. Temp. Commn. on City Finances, 1965; Chmn. Commn. on Off-Track Betting in Nassau County, 1970 Author: Conflict and Stability in Labor Relations: A Case Study, 1952; Editor: The Federal Deficit: Fiscal Imprudence or Policy Weapon?, 1965, Monetary Policy: The Argument From Keynes' Treatise to Friedman, 1966, Employment and Occupation Projections for Nassau-Suffolk to 1985, 1968. Fellow Royal Econ. Soc.; mem. Am. Econ. Assn. Home: Brooklyn, NY. Died Apr. 20, 2003.

HAMPTON, LIONEL LEO, composer, conductor, entertainer; b. Birmingham, Ala., Apr. 12, 1908; s. Charles and Gertrude (Whitfield) H.; m. Gladys Riddle, Nov. 11, 1936 (dec.). Student, U. So. Calif., 1934; Mus.D. (hon.), Allen U., Columbia, S.C., Pepperdine U., 1975; PhD in Music (hon.), Xavier U., 1975, SUNY, 1983, U. Calif., 1984, Howard U., 1979, Glassboro State Coll., 1981, U. Liege, Belgium. Mem. Benny Goodman Quartet, 1936-40; organized band, Lionel Hampton Orch., 1940; one of first blacks to play in white band (Benny Goodman), 1930's; 1st band to feature electric bass and organ; 1st black band to play in major hotels and music halls; albums include Reunion at Newport, 1967 (1993), Sentimental Journey, 1986, Flying Home, 1991 Rhythm, Rhythm, Tempo and Swing, 1992, Flying Home, 1993, You Better Know, 1994, Just Jazz-Live At the Blue Note '91 With the Golden Men of Jazz, Dedicated to Dizz-Hampton, Slide & The Jazz Masters, 1993, Slide with Freddie Hubbard, 1994, Classics: 1937-39 with Cootie Williams, Rex Stewart, Dizzy Gillespie et al, 1991, The Complete Lionel Hampton-Vols. 1&2 1937-38, 1994, Masterpieces 10 Recorded 1937-40 & 42, 1994; composer maj. symphonic work, King David Suite, 1953. Human rights commr. City of N.Y., 1984, 85, 86; apptd. ambassador of music to UN, 1985; established Lionel Hampton Jazz Endowment Fund, 1984 Recipient Gold medal City of Paris, 1985, George Frederick Handel medallion, Ebony Mag. Lifetime Achievement Awd., 1989; voted to Playboy's Jazz and Pop All-Stars Bands, last 28 yrs.; Lionel Hampton Sch. of Music named in his honor U. Idaho, 1987; Lionel Hampton Ear Research Found. established in his honor, 1987. Mem. Alpha Phi Alpha. Clubs: Friars (N.Y.C.). Lodges: Elks (grand band master), Masons (33 deg.). Home: Allendale, NJ. Died Aug. 30, 2002.

HAND, RAYMOND W. state legislator; b. Uhrichsville, Ohio, Sept. 9, 1928; m. Carole Smiley. BS, Ohio State U., 1953, LLB, JD, 1955. Mem. Mo. Ho. of Reps., Jefferson City, from 1986. Atty., cons., St, Louis. Republican. Home: Saint Louis, Mo. Deceased.

HANE, MIKISO, history educator; b. Hollister, Calif., Jan. 16, 1922; s. Ichitaro and Hifuyo (Taoka) H.; m. Rose Michiko Kanemoto, Sept. 19, 1948; children: Laurie Shizue, Jennifer Kazuko. BA, Yale U., 1952, MA, 1953, PhD, 1957. Asst. prof. history U. Toledo, Ohio, 1959-61, Knox Coll., Galesburg, Ill., 1961-66, assoc. prof. history, 1966-72, prof. history, 1972-92, prof. emeritus, 1993—2003. Author: Japan, A Historical Survey, 1972, Peasants, Rebels and Outcasts, 1982, Emperor Hirohito and His Chief Aide, 1982; editor, translator: Reflections on the Way to the Gallows, 1988, Eastern Phoenix: Japan Since 1945, 1996, Japan, A Short History, 2000. Fulbright grantee, 1957-58, Japan Found. grantee, 1973, NEH grantee, 1979-80. Mem. Assn. for Asian Studies (bd. dirs. 1985-88), Am. Hist. Assn. (teaching div. 1980-83), Midwest Conf. on Asian Affairs (pres. 1988), Nat. Coun. on Humanities. Buddhist. Home: Galesburg, Ill. Died Dec. 8, 2003.

HANES, LEE DUNCAN, mental health facility administrator; b. Kansas City, Mo., June 2, 1927; d. Elmer Lee and Edna Beryl (Ingram) Duncan; widowed; 1 child: William Duncan. BS in Pharmacy, U. Kansas City, Mo., 1949; BS in Medicine, U. Mo., 1952; MD, U. Kans., 1954. Diplomate Am. Bd. Psychiatry and Neurology; lic. psychiatrist, Kan., Mo., N.Y. Intern St. Luke's Hosp., Kansas City, 1954-55; pvt. practice Kansas City, 1955-56; resident in psychiatry Greater Kansas City Mental Health Found., 1956-59; asst. clin. dir. Psychiat. Receiving Ctr., Kansas City, 1959-62; supervisory positions various mental health ctrs. Mo., 1962-69; asst. commr. of mental health N.Y. State Dept. of Mental Hygiene, 1969-70; dir. St. Lawrence Psychiat. Ctr., Ogdensburg, N.Y., from 1970. Mem. adv. bd. St. Lawrence County Mental Health Bd., 1970-75; mem. adv. com. Comprehensive Community Mental Health Ctr., Watertown, N.Y., 1970-90, acting dep. ops. commr. Office of Mental Health, 1983; clin. instr. pathology, 1950-52, psychiatry U. Mo., Columbia, 1959-62; asst. clin. prof. psychiatry U. Mo., Columbia, 1962-69. Author: (with R. Epps) Day Care of Psychiatric Patients, 1964; contbr. articles to profl. jours. Bd. dirs. Ogdensburg Boys Club, 1973—, Ogdensburg Bicentennial com., 1973-76, St. Lawrence County Economic Devel. Coun., 1977-81; active Augsburg Inst. Inc. for Youth and Families, 1990—; vice chmn. Ogdensburg Arts Festival, 1975; mem. community adv. bd. of Ogdensburg Correctional Facility, 1982—, regional planning adv. coun. 1989—; mem. St. John's Episcopal Ch. Vestry, 1985-88. Recipient Ogdensburg VFW citation, 1974, St. Lawrence U. North Country citation, 1976, alumni svc. award U. Mo. Med. Sch., 1993; named Hon. Parade Marshall Seaway Festival Ogdensburg C. of C., 1979. Fellow Am. Psychiat. Assn. (life), Am. Orthopsychiat. Assn. (life); mem. AMA (Physicians Recognition award 1991), Am. Group Psychotherapy Assn., Assn. of Mental Health Adminstrs., Am. Assn. Of Psychiatric Adminstrs., N.Y. State Assn. of Facility Dirs. (Exceptional Achievement award 1986), Assn. of Mental Health Adminstrs. (cert.), Zonta (hon.). Deceased.

HANKE, KARL WILLIAM, III, insurance company executive; b. Frankfurt, Fed. Republic of Germany, Feb. 16, 1958; came to U.S., 1960; s. Karl W. and Barbara R. (Favory) H.; m. Miriam Elizabeth Schubkegel, Oct. 28, 1979; children: Karl W. IV, Luke T., Audra F., Maranda E.; m. P.J. Walker, Dec. 31, 1993. Student, Western Ill. U., 1978-80. Registered fraternal ins. counselor. Laborer McGraw Edison Co., Macomb, Iowa, 1977-78; owner, operator Simrock Western Ill. U., East Iowa U., Macomb, 1979-80; dist. rep. Modern Woodmen Am., Macomb, 1980-84, dist. mgr. Peoria, Ill., 1984-86, agy. mgr., 1986-96; pres. Dayspring Fin., Blue Springs, Md., from 1996. Bd. dirs. Full Employment Coun. Greater Kansas City, 1992—. Fellow Fraternal Ins. Counselors (pres. Mo. 1993); mem. Kansas City Life Underwriters Assn. (LUPIC chmn. bd. dirs. 1993, 94), Life Underwriters Assn. (bd. dirs. 1985-86, Nat. Quality award 1985-89, Nat. Sales Achievement award 1985-89), Am. Heart Assn. Blue Springs (dir. 1988), Million Dollar Round Table, Gen. Agy. Mgrs. Assn., Blue Springs C. of C. (Blue Blazer 1986—), Kansas City C. of C. Republican. Lutheran. Avocations: music, golf. Home: Kansas City, Mo. Died Mar. 16, 2002.

HANLEY, JAMES MICHAEL, former congressman; b. Syracuse, N.Y., July 19, 1920; s. Michael Joseph and Alice (Gillick) H.; m. Rita Harrington, Aug. 12, 1950; children: Christine Mary, Peter James. LL.D. (hon.), LeMoyne Coll., Syracuse, 1967, Syracuse U., 1980. Former funeral dir., Syracuse; owner Callahan-Hanley-Mooney Funeral Home, Syracuse, 1953-84; mem. 89th-92d Congresses from 34th Dist. N.Y., 1965-73, 93d-98th Congresses from 32d Dist. N.Y., 1973-85; mem. banking, fin. and urban affairs com., post office and civil service com., small bus. com., ad hoc com. on Irish affairs. Hon. life comdr. Onondaga County Vets. Council; mem. Onondaga County Dem. Com., also campaign coordinator, 1963; trustee Coll. Environ. Sci. and Forestry, SUNY, Syracuse. Served with AUS, World War II, 1942-46. Named Humanitarian of Yr., Salvation Army, 1980; James M. Hanley Fed. Office Bldg. and Courthouse named in his honor Syracuse, 1981 Mem. Am. Legion (past post comdr.), Holy Name Soc., Ancient Order Hibernians, Regular Vets. Assn. (past N.Y. comdr.), Syracuse Police Benevolent Assn., Army and Navy Union, Order of Alhambra (past grand comdr. Navarre Caravan). Clubs: Antique Auto, All City Veterans (Syracuse). Lodges: KC (past grand knight Syracuse council, Man of Yr. 1960), Kiwanis, Elks. Home: Syracuse, NY. Died Oct. 16, 2003.

HANSON, DAVID GORDON, otolaryngologist, surgeon; b. Seattle, Nov. 16, 1943; m. Terri Dangerfield, Jan. 22, 1976. BS, Wheaton Coll., 1966; MD, U. Wash., 1970; MS, U. Minn., 1976. Intern Hennepin County Gen. Hosp., Mpls., 1971-72; resident in surgery and otolaryngology U. Minn., Mpls., 1972-76; sr. surgeon NIH, Nat. Inst. Neurol. and Communicative Disorders and Stroke, USPHS, Bethesda, Md., 1975-78; asst. prof. surgery UCLA Sch. Medicine, 1978-83, assoc. prof., vice chief divsn. head and neck surgery, 1983-89; prof., chmn. dept. otolaryngology Northwestern U. Med. Sch., Chgo., 1989—2002; chmn. otolaryngology Northwestern Meml. Hosp., Chgo., 1989—2002. Chief sect. head and neck surgery VA Med. Ctr., West Los Angeles, 1983-89. Contbr. articles to profl. jours. Served to comdr. USPHS, 1975-78. NIH grantee, 1983—. Fellow ACS, Triological Soc., Am. Laryngological Assn, Am. Broncho-Esophagol. Assn., Am. Soc. Head and Neck Surgery, Am. Acad. Otolaryngology (Award of Honor, 1985); mem. AMA. Avocations: skiing, sailing. Home: La Porte, Ind. Died July 10, 2002.

HAPPEL, STEPHEN P. university dean; b. Indpls., Aug. 18, 1944; s. Hermann Ernst and Jane Rita (Connor) H. BA, St. Meinrad (Ind.) Coll., 1966; MA, Ind. U., 1969; PhL, Higher Inst. Philosophy, Leuven, Belgium, 1973; PhD, Cath. U. Louvan, Leuven, Belgium, 1977, STD, 1979. Assoc. prof. dept. religion St. Meinrad Sch., 1978-83, Cath. U. Am., Washington, 1983-99, chair dept. religion, 1994-99, dean Sch. Religious Studies, 1999—2003. Cons. Dept. Def., Washington, 1985-87, Drexler Assocs., Annapolis, Md., 1987-89. Author: Coleridge's Religious Imagination, 1984, A Catholic Vision, 1984, Conversion and Discipleship, 1984, Metaphors for God's Time in Science and Religion, 2002. Named Flannery Prof., Gonzaga U., 1992-93, Rsch. Prof., Vatican Obs. Rsch. Group, Rome, 1989-99, Am. Coun. Learned Socs. Travel awardee, 1991. Fellow Soc. Arts Religion and Contemporary Culture; mem. MLA, Am. Acad. Religion, Cath. Theol. Soc. Am. Avocations: jogging, piano. Home: Washington, DC. Died Oct. 4, 2003.

HARDIN, GARRETT, retired biology educator; b. Dallas, Apr. 21, 1915; s. Hugh and Agnes (Garrett) H.; m. Jane Swanson, Sept. 7, 1941; children: Hyla, Peter, Sharon, David. ScB, U. Chgo., 1936; PhD, Stanford U., 1941. Staff mem. Carnegie Instn., Washington and Palo Alto, Calif., 1942-46; prof. biology U. Calif., Santa Barbara, 1946-78, prof. emeritus, 1978—2003. Author: Biology: Its Principles and Implications, 1949, 2d edit., 1966, Biology: Its Human Implications, 1949, Nature and Man's Fate, 1959, Population, Evolution and Birth Control, 1964, Birth control, 1970,

Exploring New Ethics for Survival, 1972, Stalking the Wild Taboo, 1973, Mandatory Motherhood, 1974, Managing the Commons, 1977, The Limits of Altruism, 1977, Promethean Ethics, 1980, Naked Emperors, 1982, Filters against Folly, 1985, Living Within Limits, 1993, The Ostrich Factor, 1998; (classic essay) The Tragedy of the Commons, 1968. Home: Santa Barbara, Calif. Died Sept. 14, 2003.

HARDIN, GEORGE CECIL, JR., petroleum consultant; b. Oakwood, Tex., Oct. 6, 1920; s. George Cecil and Pearl (Moore) H.; m. Virginia Howard, Nov. 21, 1942; children—George Howard, Susan. BS in Geology and Petroleum Engring, Tex. A&M U., 1941; PhD in Geology (Van Hise fellow 1941), U. Wis., 1942. Registered engr., Tex., Okla. Mining engr. Victory Fluorspar Mine, Cave In Rock, Ill., 1942; geologist U.S. Geol. Survey, 1942-45, party chief, 1944-45; geologist Carter Gragg Oil Co., Palestine, Tex., 1945-46; geologist, petroleum engr. M.T. Halbouty Cons. Firm, Houston, 1946-51; exploration and prodn. mgr. M.T. Halbouty Oil and Gas Interests, Houston, 1951-59, gen. mgr., 1959-61; exec. v.p., dir. Halbouty Alaska Oil Co., 1957-61; partner Hardin and Hardin (cons. geologists), Houston, 1961-65; mgr. oil and gas expln. Kerr-McGee Oil Ind., Inc., 1964-65; v.p. N.Am. Oil & Gas Exploration, 1965-67, v.p. oil, gas and minerals exploration, 1967-68, group v.p. exploration, 1968; v.p. Kerr-McGee, Argentina, 1967-68, Kerr-McGee Can., Ltd., 1967-68, Kerr-McGee Australia, Ltd., 1967-68; pres. Royal Resources Corp., 1968-70, Ada Oil Exploration Corp., 1970-71, Ashland Exploration Co., 1971-80; sr. v.p. Ashland Oil Inc., 1971-80; dir. Ashland Oil Can Ltd., 1976-79, Allied Bank of Tex., Houston, 1956-78, mem. exec. com., 1956-62, chmn. auditing com., 1962-65; vice-chmn., dir. Integrated Energy, Inc., 1981-83. Author articles in field. Fellow Geol. Soc. Am.; mem. Houston Geol. Soc. (pres. 1961-62), Gulf Coast Assn. Geol. Socs. (pres. 1959), Am. Assn. Petroleum Geologist (sec.-treas. 1964-66), Am. Inst. Profl. Geologists. Clubs: Petroleum (bd. dirs. 1956-58), Grandfather Country (Linville, N.C.). Home: Morrisville, NC. Deceased.

HARE, FREDERICK KENNETH, geography and environmental educator, university official; b. Wylye, Eng., Feb. 5, 1919; s. Frederick Eli and Irene (Smith) H.; m. Suzanne Alice Bates, Aug. 23, 1941 (div. 1952); 1 son, Christopher John; m. Helen Neilson Morrill, Dec. 26, 1953; children: Elissa Beatrice, Robin Gilbert. BS with 1st class honors, U. London, 1939; PhD, U. Montreal, 1950; LL.D., Queens U., 1964, U. Western Ont., 1968, Trent U., 1979, Meml. U., 1985; D.Sc., McGill U., 1969, Adelaide U., 1974, York U., 1978; DLitt, Thorneloe Coll. Laurentian U., 1983; grad. (hon. cert.), Nat. Def. Coll.; D.Sc., Toronto U., 1987, Windsor U., 1988, Guelph U., 1995. Asst. prof. geography McGill U., 1945-49, prof., chmn. dept. geography, 1950-62, prof. geography and meteorology, dean faculty arts and scis., 1962-64; dir. Arctic Meteorology Research Group, McGill Sub-Arctic Research Lab., 1954-62; prof. geography King's Coll., U. London, 1964-66; master of Birkbeck Coll., U. London, 1966-68; pres. U. B.C., Vancouver, Can., 1968-69; prof. geography and physics U. Toronto, Ont., Can., 1969-84, chmn. adv. bd. Inst. Internat. Programs, 1990-94, Univ. prof., 1976-84, univ. prof. emeritus, 1984—, dir. Inst. Environ. Studies, 1974-79; provost Trinity Coll., 1979-86; gov. Trinity Coll. Sch., 1979-86; chancellor Trent U., Peterborough, Ont., 1988-95. Dir.-gen. rsch. coordination Can. Dept. of Environment, 1972-73, sci. adviser, 1972-74; mem. NRC, Can., 1962-64; mem. Natural Environment Research Coun., U.K., 1965-68; bd. dirs. Resources for the Future, 1968-80; mem. spl. programme panel on ecoscis. NATO, 1972-75, chmn., 1974-75; mem. Can. Environ. Adv. Council, 1973-78; mem. corp. Woods Hole Oceanographic Inst., 1976-79; chmn. Canadian Climate Program Planning Bd., 1979-90; chmn. Royal Soc. Can. Commn. on Lead in the Environment, 1984-86, tech. adv. com. on R & D Atomic Energy of Can. Rsch. Ltd., 1991-95; mem. Resources for the Future, 1980—; chmn. Tech. Adv. Panel on Nuclear Safety, Ont. Hydro, 1990-94, active, 1994-99; commr. Ont. Nuclear Safety Rev., 1986-88. Author: The Restless Atmosphere, 1953, On University Freedom, 1967, (with M.K. Thomas) Climate Canada, 1974, 2d edit., 1979; author, editor: (with R.A. Bryson) Climates of North America; Contbr. (with R.A. Bryson) articles to sci. publs. Served as meteorologist Brit. Air Ministry, 1941-45; flight lt., meteorol. br. R.A.F.V.R., 1943-45, Gt. Britain. Fellow King's Coll., 1967; hon. fellow Trinity Coll. 1991—; recipient Patterson medal, 1973, Massey medal, 1974; Patron's medal Royal Geog. Soc., 1977; decorated Officer Order Can., 1978, promoted to Companion, 1987; recipient U. Toronto Alumni Faculty award, 1982, Internat. Meteorol. Orgn. Prize, 1989. Fellow AAAS, Royal Soc. Can. (Centenary medal 1982, Dawson medal 1988, Climate Inst. award 1991), Royal Meteorol. Soc. (past pres.), Royal Geog. Soc., Am. Geog. Soc. (hon. fellow), Arctic Inst. N.Am. (past chmn.), Am. Meteorol. Soc. (emeritus). Deceased.

HARGRODER, CHARLES MERLIN, retired journalist; b. Franklin, La., Sept. 5, 1926; Student, La. State U., 1943-47. Writer Baton Rouge Morning Adv., 1947-50, Monroe (La.) Morning World, 1952-53; exec. asst. to gov. State of La., Baton Rouge, 1953-56; pub. rels. sec. to Congressman Hale Boggs, U.S. Ho. of Reps., 1956-57; regional rep. Inter-Industry Hwy. Safety Com., 1957-58; writer New Orleans Times-Picayune, 1959-88, polit. writer, columnist, 1961-88. Author: Ada and the Doc, 1999. With U.S. Army, 1950-52. Mem. Theta Xi. Republican. Home: Baton Rouge, La. Died Sept. 15, 2002.

HARGROVE, THOMAS STEPHEN, choreographer, artistic director, ballet master; b. Helena, Mont., July 2, 1954; s. Harold Benjamin and Emma (Boehm) H. Student, Banff Sch. of the Fine Arts, 1973-74, Harkness House of Dance, N.Y.C., 1975; BFA, U.S. Internat. U., 1978, MFA in Classical Ballet, 1980. Resident choreographer U.S. Internat. U., San Diego, 1976-80; artistic dir. Western Ballet Theatre Co., Portland, Oreg., 1980-81; exec. producer Harman Prodns., Portland, 1981-84; prof. classical ballet, dir. dance performance Calif. State U., Chico, from 1986; classical ballet master Dept. Edn. Calif. State Summer Sch. of the Arts, Sacramento, from 1987. Guest lectr., classical ballet master Dance Dept. Calif. Inst. of the Arts, Valencia, 1987—; disting. vis. prof. Calif. State U., Fullerton; performance evaluator Nat. Endowment for the Arts, Calif. Arts Coun., Marin Found./Buck Trust, San Francisco, 1992. Mem. Internat. Inst. for Edn. Through the Arts (bd. dirs.), Black Mountain Dance Assn. (bd. dirs.). Home: Coronado, Calif. Died Mar. 9, 2002.

HARIG, CONSTANCE COLLEEN, heathcare administrator; b. Glens Falls, N.Y., Mar. 27, 1954; d. Richard B. and Charlotte I. (Sherman) Fowler; m. Michael J. Harig, June 18, 1977; children: Tracy, David. AS in Nursing, Adirondack Community Coll., 1976; BS, Loyola U., New Orleans, 1979; MS in Health Care Adminstrn., Coll. of St. Francis, Joliet, Ill., 1990. Cert. nursing home adminstr., La. Staff nurse intensive care unit Hotel Dieu Hosp., New Orleans; head nurse St. Charles Gen. Hosp., New Orleans; dir. nursing Gen. Living Ctrs., Baton Rouge, v.p. ops./nursing. Mem. LSNA, NGNA, Am. Soc. Perenteral & Enteral Nutrition. Home: Baton Rouge, La. Died Oct. 12, 2000.

HARKARVY, BENJAMIN, artistic director; Artistic dir. Royal Winnipeg (Can.) Ballet, 1957-58; artistic dir., founder The Netherlands Dance Theatre, 1959-69; artistic dir. Harkness Ballet, N.Y.C., 1969-70, Dutch Nat. Ballet, The Netherlands, 1970-71, Pa. Ballet, Phila., 1972-82; freelance choreographer various ballet cos., 1982-91; artistic dir. dance divsn. Juilliard Sch., N.Y.C., from 1992. Dir. ballet project Jacob's Pillow, 1983—89. Choreographer ballets Time Passed Summer, Recital for Cello and 8 Dancers, Cinque Madrigali, Frames. Home: New York, NY. Died 2003.

HARMON, JOHN LAFAYETTE, retired petroleum engineer; b. Hillsboro, Tex., June 24, 1929; s. John Lee and Winnie Kate (Stallings) H.; m. Lucile Gracy, Dec. 23, 1949 (div. June 1973); m. Bettye Sue McKinney, June 21, 1974; children: John C., David L., Christopher L. BS in Geology, U. Tex., 1952. Rsch. engr. Midstates Petroleum, Abilene, Tex., 1952-54; geol. engr. Kent Waddell & Co., Abilene, Tex., 1954-55, Connally Oil Co., Abilene, Tex., 1955-63; engr., owner J.L. Harmon & Assocs., Abilene, Tex., 1963-86; engr., drilling supr. Texland Petroleum, Inc., Lubbock, 1986-95. Contbr. articles to profl. jours. Mem. Soc. Petroleum Engrs. (sr., 25-yr. club). Republican. Episcopalian. Avocations: fishing, golf, photography. Home: Granbury, Tex. Died Jan. 31, 2002.

HARPER, ROBERT ALLAN, retired consulting psychologist; b. Dayton, Ohio, Apr. 25, 1915; s. Earl Paull and Mary (Belden) H.; m. Flora Mie Bridges; children: Robert Belden, John Paull. Student, U. Dayton, 1934-36; BA, Ohio State U., 1938, MA, 1939, PhD, 1942. Instr. Kent State U., 1942-43; analyst War Manpower Commn., 1943; assoc. prof. Wagner Coll., 1943-45; psychiat. social worker U.S. Army, 1945-46; asst. prof. Ohio State U., 1946-50, dir. marriage counseling clinic, 1949-50; chmn. family life dept., dir. marriage counseling service Merrill-Palmer Inst., Detroit, 1950-53; pvt. practice psychotheraphy Washington, 1953-92. Author: (with John F. Cuber) Problems of American Society, 1948, Marriage, 1949, Psychoanalysis and Psychotherapy: 36 Systems, 1959, (with Albert Ellis) Creative Marriage, 1961, A Guide to Rational Living, 1961, 75, 98, How to Stop Destroying Your Relationships, 2001, Dating, Mating, and Relating: How to Build a Healthy Relationship, 2003; (with Walter R. Stokes) 45 Levels to Sexual Understanding and Enjoyment, 1971, The New Psychotherapies, 1975; cons. editor: Jour. Sex Edn. and Therapy, Psychotherapy, Jour. Rational-Emotive Therapy, Jour. Contemporary Psychotherapy, Internat. Jour. Family Therapy Fellow Am. Psychol. Assn. (pres. div. psychotherapy 1978-79, pres. div. cons. psychology 1980-81, pres. div. humanistic psychology 1983-84, exec. bd. div. ind. practice, coun. reps. 1978-84, 90-96), Am. Assn. Marriage Counselors (sec. 1954-58, pres. 1960-62), Nat. Coun. Family Rels. (dir. 1951-55), Am. Acad. Psychotherapists (pres. 1961-63), Am. Group Psychotheraphy Assn., Eastern Psychol. Assn., D.C. Psychol. Assn. (dir. 1982-85); mem. Am. Soc. Psychologists in Pvt. Practice (exec. com.), Soc. Sci. Study Sex, Interam. Soc. Psychologists, Am. Soc. Group Psychotherapy and Psychodrama, Internat. Council Psychologists (exec. bd. 1971-74), N.Y. Acad. Scis., Internat. Soc. Gen. Semantics, Inst. Rational Living (bd.), ACLU, Washington Soc. Clin. Psychologists (exec. com.), Nat. Acads. Practice (treas. 1982-88), Phi Beta Kappa. Clubs: Cosmos. Home: Washington, DC. Died Jan. 10, 2004.

HARRIS, CHAUNCY DENNISON, geographer, educator; b. Logan, Utah, Jan. 31, 1914; s. Franklin Stewart and Estella (Spilsbury) H.; m. Edith Young, Sept. 5, 1940; 1 child, Margaret (Mrs. Philip A. Straus, Jr.). AB, Brigham Young U., 1933; BA, Oxford U., 1936, MA, 1943, DLitt, 1973; postgrad., London Sch. Econs., 1936-37; PhD, U. Chgo., 1940; DEcon (honoris causa), Catholic U., Chile, 1956; LLD (honoris causa), Ind. U., 1979; DSc (honoris causa), Bonn U., 1991, U. Wis., Milw., 1991. Instr. in geography Ind. U., 1939-41; asst. prof. geography U. Nebr., 1941-43, U. Chgo., 1943-46, assoc. prof., 1946-47, prof., 1947-84, prof. emeritus, 1984—2003, dean social scis., 1955-60, chmn. non western area programs and internat. studies, 1960-66, dir. ctr. for internat. studies, 1966-84, chmn. dept. geography, 1967-69, Samuel N. Harper Disting. Svc. prof., 1969-84, spl. asst. to pres., 1973-75, v.p. acad. resources, 1975-78. Del. Internat. Geog. Congress, Lisbon, 1949, Washington, 1952, Rio de Janeiro, 1956, Stockholm, 1960, London, 1964, New Delhi, 1968, Montreal, 1972, Moscow, 1976, Tokyo, 1980, Paris, 1984, Sydney, Australia, 1988, Washington, 1992, The Hague, 1996; v.p. Internat. Geog. Union, 1956-64, sec.-treas., 1968-76; mem. adv. com. for internat. orgns. and programs Nat. Acad. Scis., 1969-73, mem. bd. internat. orgns. and programs, 1973-76; U.S. del. 17th Gen. Conf. UNESCO, Paris, 1972; exec. com. div. behavioral scis. NRC, 1967-70; hon. cons. geography Libr. of Congress, 1974-80, mem. coun. of scholars, 1980-83, Conseil de la Bibliographie Géographique Internationale, 1986-94. Author: Cities of the Soviet Union, 1970; editor: Economic Geography of the U.S.S.R, 1949, International List of Geographical Serials, 1960, 71, 80, Annotated World List of Selected Current Geographical Serials, 1960, 64, 71, 80, Soviet Geography: Accomplishments and Tasks, 1962, Guide to Geographical Bibliographies and Reference Works in Russian or on the Soviet Union, 1975, Bibliography of Geography, Part I, Introduction to General Aids, 1976, Part 2, Regional, vol. 1, U.S., 1984, A Geographical Bibliography for American Libraries, 1985, Directory of Soviet Geographers 1946-87, 1988; contbr. Sources of Information in the Social Sciences, 1973, 86, Encyclopedia Britannica, 1989, Columbia Gazetteer of the World, 1998; contbg. editor: The Geog. Rev., 1960-73, Soviet Geography, 1987-91, Post-Soviet Geography and Economics, 1992-99; hon. editor Urban Geography, 1984-2003 contbr. articles to profl. jours. Life mem. vis. com. U. Chgo. Libr.; pres. coun. Residents Assn., Montgomery Place, Chgo., 2000-01. Recipient Alexander Csoma de Körösi Meml. medal Hungarian Geog. Soc., 1971, Lauréat d'Honneur Internat. Geog. Union, 1976; Alexander von Humboldt Gold Medal Gesellschaft für Erdkunde zu Berlin, 1978; spl. award Utah Geog. Soc., 1985; Rhodes scholar, 1934-37. Fellow Japan Soc. Promotion of Sci.; mem. Assn. Am. Geographers (sec. 1946-48, v.p. 1956, pres. 1957, Honors award 1976), Am. Geog. Soc. (coun. 1962-74, v.p. 1969-74; Cullum Geog. medal 1985), Am. Assn. Advancement Slavic Studies (pres. 1962, award for disting. contbns. 1978), Am. Acad. Arts and Scis., Social Sci. Rsch. Coun. (bd. dir. 1959-70, vice-chmn. 1963-65, exec. com. 1967-70), Internat. Coun. Sci. Unions (exec. com. 1969-76), Internat. Rsch. and Exchs. Bd. (exec. com. 1968-71), Nat. Coun. Soviet and East European Rsch. (bd. dir. 1977-83), Nat. Coun. for Geog. Edn. (Master Tchr. award 1986); hon. mem. Royal Geog. Soc. (Victoria medal 1987), Geog. Socs. Berlin, Frankfurt, Rome, Florence, Paris, Warsaw, Belgrade, Japan, Chgo. (Disting. Svc. award 1965, bd. dir. 1954-69, 82-90), Polish Acad. Scis. (fgn. mem.). Home: Chicago, Ill. Died Dec. 26, 2003.

HARRIS, ELIZABETH ANN, marketing research professional; b. Huntington, N.Y., Apr. 29, 1957; d. Gordon Israel and Sondra Roberta (Epstein) H. BA, SUNY, Albany, 1979; Diplome Etudes Universitaire Generale, U. Besancon, France, 1979; MBA in Internat. Mktg., Pa. State U., 1983. Customer svc. rep. N.Y. office Credit Industriel et Comml., 1979-80; customer svc. rep. Daval Steel, N.Y.C., 1980-81; instr. mktg. Pa. State U., University Park, 1982-83; market analyst World Trade Ctr., N.Y.C., 1983-84, Nat. Gypsum Co., Dallas, 1984-86; mgr. market rsch. Hanley-Wood, Inc., Washington, 1986-88, Domtar Gypsum, Ann Arbor, Mich., 1988-90; mktg. svc. bus. profl. Ann Arbor, 1990, Harris Solutions, Ann Arbor, 1991. Mem. NAFE, Am. Mktg. Assn. Died May 16, 2000.

HARRIS, FREDERICK PHILIP, retired philosophy educator; b. Portland, Oreg., Aug. 28, 1911; s. Philip Henry and Nellie Louise (Humpage) H.; m. Hester Almira Larson, July 15, 1943; children: Judith, Jacquelyn, Jennifer, Elizabeth, Marcia, Frederick (dec.). AB, Willamette U., 1935; MA, Columbia U., 1937, PhD, 1944; cert. in Japanese, U. Mich., 1944. Tutor Horace Mann Sch. for Boys, N.Y.C., 1935-41; instr. English Rutgers U., New Brunswick, N.J., 1941-42; psychologist Bur. Psychol. Svcs., U. Mich., Ann Arbor, 1946; assoc. prof. philosophy Case Western Res. U., Cleve., 1946-55, chmn. dept., 1948-57; headmaster Am. Sch. in Japan, Tokyo, 1957-66; prof. Oreg. State U., Corvallis, 1967-80, chmn. dept. philosophy, 1967-76. Fulbright vis. prof. faculty edn. Kyoto (Japan) U., 1955-57; prof. Rockefeller Found. Am. Studies Seminar, Doshisha U. Japan, 1956; vis. prof. U. Oreg., Eugene, summer 1950, U. Hawaii, Honolulu, summer 1966, Lewis & Clark Coll., Portland, 1966-67; dir. Oreg. Study Ctr. Waseda U., Tokyo, 1977-80; vis. prof. Grad. Sch. Commerce Waseda U., 1980, Open Coll., 1982-92; pres. Tokyo Internat. Co., 1986-92; advisor Japan Intercultural Comm. Soc., Tokyo, 1980-82. Author: The Neo-Idealist Political Theory, 1944; editor: The Teaching of Philosophy, 1950; editor Perspectives, Japan Intercultural Comm. Soc., 1981-82. Advisor Internat. Sch., Nagoya, Japan, 1963-66, Sendai Am. Sch., Japan, 1963-65; del. 1st Am.-Japan Student Conf., Aoyama Gakuin, Tokyo, 1934. Staff sgt. U.S. Army, 1942-45. Fulbright grantee Kyoto U., 1955, 56; Frederick Philip Harris Libr. named in his honor Am. Sch. in Japan, Tokyo, 1966. Mem. Am. Philos. Assn., Asiatic Soc. Japan (counselor 1986-89), Japan English Forensics Assn., Nature Conservancy, Wilderness Soc. Methodist. Avocations: swimming, hiking, mountain climbing, pottery, travel. Home: Portland, Oreg. Died Sept. 20, 2001.

HARRIS, JAMES ARTHUR, SR., school system administrator, economist, consultant; b. Portsmouth, Va., June 20, 1928; s. Ambrose Edward and Annie Eula Pitts (Lawson) H.; m. Ursula Harris, June 7, 1954; children: James A. Jr., Edmond F. AB, Va. State Univ., 1956; MA, NYU, 1959; PhD, Pacific Western U., 1983. Adj. assoc. prof. in econs. St. John's U., Jamaica, N.Y.; advisor to sr. v.p. econ. devel., dir. minority and women bus. lendinq N.Y. State Urban Devel. Corp., N.Y.C.; sr. faculty, adj. assoc. prof. mgmt. NYU, N.Y.C.; pres. Acquitech Systems, Inc., Bklyn., 1988-93; supt. Buffalo Pub. Schs., from 1996. Cons. in field; leader cons. team evaluation mission Bur. Africa programs UN Devel. Program, N.Y.C.; mem. roster cons. and tech. assistance experts UN Devel. Program, UN Indsl. Devel. Orgn., African Devel. Bank, West African Devel. Bank, World Bank, UN Ctr. for Human Settlements, UN Econ. Commn. for Africa, UN Econ. and Social Commn. for Africa, UN Econ. and Social Commn. for Asia and Pacific, Asian Devel. Bank, UN Econ. and Social Commn. for Western Asia, Internat. Fund. for Agrl. Devel., UN Conf. Trade and Devel./GATT, Internat. Trade Ctr., Geneva. Contbr. articles to profl. publs. Recipient award for teaching excellence and outstanding talent as tchr. NYU Sch. Continuing Edn., 1986, Great Tchr. award in recognition of superb accomplishment NYU Alumni Coun., 1994. Mem. Am. Econ. Assn., Nat. Econ. Assn., N.Y. Acad. Scis., Internat. Studies Assn., Internat. Polit. Sci. Assn., Assn. for Study Afro-Am. Life History, Am. Arbitration Assn. (internat. arbitration panel). Home: Brooklyn, NY. Deceased.

HARRIS, MARY PAPAJOHN, business executive; b. Athens, Greece, Dec. 3, 1939; came to U.S., 1948; d. Harry M. and Alice (Anagnostopoulos) Papajohn; m. Andreas Harris, May 1, 1965 (div. 1981); children: Konstantine Philip, Alexander Scott. B.A., Marymount Manhattan Coll., 1971; M.P.A., Columbia U., 1984; cert. Sorbonne, 1962. Asst. to mayor City of N.Y., 1966-69; pres. MRC TV Network, N.Y.C., 1969-80; exec. v.p. Clipper Internat. Products, 1980-82; with Manhattan Bank, N.Y.C., 1983; dir. corp. relations Am. Standards Testing Bur., N.Y.C., 1984—; v.p. Am. Standards Bioscis. Corp., Reading, Pa., 1984-86; v.p. Newspaper Advt. Bur., N.Y.C., 1986—. bd. dirs. Ivy Club, 1983; chair Youth Against Cancer, 1979-82. Recipient Leadership award Met. Regional Council, N.Y.C., 1978; Outstanding Service award Am. Cancer Soc., 1980. Mem. AAUW, LWV, Hellenic Am. C. of C., Council Greek Am. Affairs, N.Y. Acad. Scis. Greek Orthodox. Clubs: Princeton of N.Y., City (N.Y.C.). Home: New York, NY.

HARRIS, RICHARD (RICHARD ST. JOHN), actor; b. County Limerick, Ireland, Oct. 1, 1933; s. Ivan and Mildred (Harty) H.; m. (Joan) Elizabeth Rees Williams, Feb. 9, 1957 (div.); m. Ann Turkel (div. 1981). Attended, London Acad. Music and Dramatic Arts, 1956. Mem. Joan Littlewood's Theatre Workshop, 1956. Prodr., dir. Winter Journey, London, 1956; profl. acting debut The Quare Fellow at Theatre Royal, Stratford, Eng., 1956; performances include (stage) A View from the Bridge, London, 1956, Man, Beast and Virtue, London, 1958, The Pier, London, 1958, The Giner Man, 1959, Fings Ain't Wot They Used T' Be, 1959, The Dutch Courtesan, 1959; toured Russia and Eastern Europe in Macbeth, 1957-58; numerous tours in Camelot; (TV plays) 1956-58; (TV appearances) The Iron Harp, 1957, Victory, 1960, The Snow Goose, 1968 (Emmy award nominee), Camelot, 1982, Maigret, 1988, Abraham, 1994; (TV movies) Abraham, 1994, The Great Kindinsky, 1995, The Hunchback, 1997; (films) Alive and Kicking, 1958, Shake Hands With the Devil, 1959, The Wreck of the Mary Deare, 1959, A Terrible Beauty, 1960, The Long and the Short and the Tall, 1961, The Guns of Navarone, 1961, Mutiny on the Bounty, 1962, This Sporting Life, 1963 (Cannes Film Festival Best Actor award 1963, Acad. award nominee 1963), The Red Desert, 1964, The Three Faces fo a Woman, 1965, Major Dundee, 1965, The Heroes of Telemark, 1965, The Bible, 1966, Hawaii, 1966, Caprice, 1967, Camelot, 1967 (Golden Globe award for best actor 1968), The Molly Maguires, 1970, A Man Called Horse, 1970, Cromwell, 1970, Man in the Wilderness, 1971, The Deadly Trackers, 1973, 99 44/100 Dead, 1974, Juggernaut, 1974, Robin and Marian, 1967, Echoes of Summer, 1976 (also exec. prodr.), The Return of a Man Called Horse, 1976 (also exec. prodr.), The Cassandra Crossing, 1977, Gulliver's Travels, 1977, Orca, 1977, Golden Rendesvouz, 1977, The Wild Geese, 1978, The Ravagers, 1979, Game for Vultures, 1979, The Last Word, 1979, Tarzan, the Ape Man, 1981, Triumphs of a Man Called Horse, 1983, Highpoint, 1984, Your Ticket is No Longer Valid, Martin's Day, 1985, Mack the Knife, 1989, King of the Wind, 1990, Ruby Dreams, 1990, The Field, 1990 (Golden Globe nominee, Acad. award nominee), Patriot Games, 1992, Unforgiven, 1992, Silent Tongue, 1993, Wrestling Ernest Hemingway, 1993, This is the Sea, 1994, Savage Hearts, 1995, Cry, the Beloved Country, 1995, Trojan Eddie, 1996, Smilla's Sense of Snow, 1997, Grizzly Falls, 1999, To Walk With Lions, 1999, The Royal Way, 2000, Gladiator, 2000, Harry Potter and the Sorceror's Stone, 2001, The Pearl, 2001, The Count of Monte Cristo, 2002, Harry Potter and the Chamber of Secrets, 2002; actor, writer: (with Lindsay Anderson) The Diary of a Madman, 1963, (with Wolf Mankowitz) Bloomfield, 1971; songs recorded include McArthur Park, 1968 (Grammy award nominee), Didn't We, 1969, My Boy, 1971; albums include A Tramp Shining (Grammy award nominee), The Prophet Kahil Gibran, His Greatest Performances, MacArthur Park and His Time, Jonathan Livinston Seagull (Grammy award for best spoken word 1973); musical compositions include The Last Castle, 1976, Zach Bass Theme, 1971; author: I, In The Membership of My Days: Poems, 1973, Honor Bound: A Novel, 1982. Mem. Knights of Malta. Died Oct. 25, 2002.

HARRIS, SHELDON HOWARD, history educator; b. Bklyn., Aug. 22, 1928; s. Peter Harris and Bertha Perry; m. Sheila J. Black, Oct. 30, 1955; children: Robin L., David A. AB cum laude, Bklyn. Coll., 1949; MA, Harvard U., 1950; PhD, Columbia U., 1958. Lectr. Bklyn. Coll., 1957-58; assoc. prof. New Bedford (Mass.) Inst. Tech., 1958-63; prof. Calif. State U., Northridge, 1963-91, prof. emeritus, from 1991. Author: Paul Cuffe, 1972, Factories of Death, 1994; contbr. articles to profl. jours. Rsch. grantee various orgns. Mem. Am. Hist. Assn., Sierra Club. Avocations: walking, traveling, bird watching. Home: Granada Hills, Calif. Died 2002.

HARRISON, LOU SILVER, composer, educator; b. Portland, Oreg., May 14, 1917; Student, San Francisco State U., 1934-35, Henry Cowell and Arnold Schoenberg; DFA (hon.), Mills Coll., 1988, Calif. State U., Sacramento, 1993. Prof. music Black Mountain Coll., 1947-48, San Jose State U., Calif., 1967-80, Mills Coll., Oakland, Calif., 1980—. Am. rep. League of Asian Composers Conf., 1975. Composer Third Symphony, 1981-82, Last Symphony, 1990, Homage to Pacifica, 1991; puppet opera Young Caesar, 1970-71; Four Strict Songs (commn. from Louisville Orch.), 1955, Suite for Piano, Violin and Small Orch., 1951. Grantee Guggenheim, 1952, 54, Rockefeller, Korea, 1962-63; Fulbright sr. scholar N.Z., 1983. Mem. Nat. Acad. Arts and Letters (music mem.). Died Feb. 2, 2003.

HARRISON, WILLIAM WRIGHT, bank executive; b. Kingston, N.Y., Aug. 6, 1915; s. James Burwell and Isabella (Clarke) H.; m. Janet Phillips, Apr. 6, 1940; children: Janet P. (Mrs. Richard Rea Hinch), Susan F. (Mrs. Glassell Slaughter Fitz-Hugh Jr.), William Wright Jr. Student, U. Va., 1933-34. With Va. Nat. Bank (formerly Peoples Nat. Bank Charlottesville), 1942-81, chmn., chief exec. officer, 1969-80, dir., cons., 1980-85. Former chmn. Allied Bank Internat.; dir. Royster Co., Norfolk, Shennandoah Life Ins. Co.; chmn. Minbanc Capital Corp., Washington. Former chmn. Mcpl. Bond Commn., Norfolk; chmn. Va. Found. Ind. Colls.; bd. dirs. Gen. Hosp. Virginia Beach, pres.; bd. dirs. U. Va. Patent Found., Va. Opera, Old Dominion U. Rsch. Found., Gov.'s Commn. on Indsl. Devel.; trustee Norfolk Found., Ea. Va. Med. Sch. Found., Chrysler Mus., Norfolk; former bd. visitors U. Va.; former commr. Va. Port Authority. Mem. Norfolk C. of C. (pres. 1971) Clubs: Princess Anne Country, Harbor. Episcopalian. Home: Virginia Beach, Va. Died Mar. 28, 2001.

HARROD, HOWARD LEE, religion educator; b. Holdenville, Okla., June 9, 1932; m. Annemarie Nussbaumer; children: Lee Ann, Amy Ceil. BA, Okla. U., 1957; BD, Duke U., 1960; STM, Yale U., 1961, MA, 1963, PhD, 1965. Asst. prof. Howard U., 1964-66; assoc. prof. Drake U., 1966-68; prof. Vanderbilt U., from 1968, chair grad. dept. religion, 1972-75. Lectr. Howard U., 1964, Drake U. Div. Sch., 1966, U. Mont., 1971, Vanderbilt U., 1989. Author: Mission Among the Blackfeet, 1971, The Human Center: Moral Agency in the Social World, 1981, Renewing the World: Plains Indian Religion and Morality, 1987, Becoming and Remaining a People: Native American Religions on the Northern Plains, 1995, The Animals Came Dancing: Native American Sacred Ecology and Animal Kinship, 2000; (with others) Radical Theology: Phase Two, 1967; contbr. to: The Encyclopedia of Religion, 1987, Dictionary of Pastoral Care and Counseling, 1990, Encyclopedia of the American Indian, 1995, Harper's Dictionary of Religion, 1995; mem. editorial bd.: (series) Social World of Biblical Antiquity; newsletter editor Soc. for Study of Native Am. Religious Traditions; contbr. articles to religious jours. Scholar Drake U., 1966, NEH, 1967, Vanderbilt U., 1969, 70, 75, Am. Assn. Theol. Schs., 1971, 94; fellow Yale U., 1960-62, Rockefeller fellow, 1962-63, 88, fellow Vanderbilt U., 1981-82, 87-88, Am. Coun. Learned Socs., 1981-82. Deceased.

HART, CHARLES EDWIN, III, lawyer; b. Waterbury, Conn., Dec. 7, 1919; s. Charles Edwin Jr. and Katherine (Reed) H.; m. Janice Ruth Colburn, July 22, 1950; children: Constance Hart Walkingshaw, Katherine Wainwright, Stephanie Hart Cotton. BA, Yale U., 1941; LLB, Columbia U., 1948. Bar: N.Y. 1948, Ohio 1958, Calif. 1961. Assoc. Chadbourne & Parke, N.Y.C., 1948-56; asst. gen. counsel N.Am. Aviation, Elsegundo, Calif., 1956-67; staff v.p., assoc. gen. counsel Rockwell Internat. Corp., Elsegundo, 1967-81; of counsel Secor, Cassidy & McPartland, Waterbury, from 1981. Vice chmn. United Way Annual Fund Dr., Waterbury, 1987; dir. Mattatuck Hist. Soc., Waterbury, 1982-87; steering com. Mattatuck Mus. Capital Fund Dr., Waterbury, 1984-85; sr. warden St. Matthews Episcopal Ch., Pacific Palisades, Calif., 1964, 65, 67, 68; trustee Westlake Sch. for Girls, L.A., 1973-76; chmn. adv. coun. Episcopal Ch. Found., L.A., 1979-81; mem. alumni coun. Kent (Conn.) Sch., 1984-90. With USNR, 1941-56, PTO, ETO. Mem. ABA, Calif. State Bar Assn., Waterbury Club (dir. 1983-87), Highfield Club (Middlebury, Conn.). Republican. Episcopalian. Home: Waterbury, Conn. Deceased.

HART, CHRISTINE ROGERS, real estate broker; b. Eastland, Tex., May 13, 1925; d. Woodville Jefferson Rogers and Florence Ione (Stoker) Rogers Dimaline; m. Robert Toole Sawtelle, Aug. 31, 1947 (div. Dec. 1970); children: Roger Scott Sawtelle, Kathryn Sawtelle Scott, William Franklin Sawtelle, Suzanne Sawtelle Rawlinson; m. John Joseph Hart, Sept. 3, 1978. Student, Hockaday Jr. Coll., Dallas, 1942-43; BA in Spanish, U. Tex., 1945, BA in Music, 1971. Lic. real estate broker. Tchr. N.E. Sch. Dist., San Antonio, 1954-55; pres. Chris Sawtelle, Realtor, Austin, 1972-78; co-owner Hart Group, San Antonio. Organizer precinct Good Govt. League, San Antonio, 1948; v.p. San Antonio Bar Aux., 1952, v.p. Planned Parenthood San Antonio, 1957; mem. choir St. David's Episcopal Ch., 1956-70. Mem. Nat. Assn. Realtors, Tex. Assn. Realtors, San Antonio Bd. Realtors, Austin Bd. Realtors. Republican. Avocations: golf, tennis, piano, organ. Deceased.

HART, HORACE, graphic arts consultant; b. Rochester, N.Y., July 14, 1910; s. Leo and Ethel Mae (Steuerwald) H.; m. Joan Ruth Stein, May 30, 1934; children: Karen Gail, Nancy Joan Hart Wartow. BA, Harvard U., 1933. Pres. Leo Hart Co., Rochester, 1933-55; ptnr. Playtime House, Rochester, 1939-56; dir. printing and pub. industries div. Dept. Commerce, 1957-63; pres. Lanston Monotype Co. and Monotype Co. of Can., Ltd., Phila., 1963-66; cons. to graphic arts industry Springwater, N.Y., from 1966. Edn. adviser Nat. Printing Equipment Assn., 1966-69, tchr. Rochester Inst. Tech, 1949-50; U.S. del. Internat. Conf. Printing and Pub. Execs., Milan, 1959; chmn. U.S. del. Tripartite Tech. Meeting for Printing and Allied Trades, Geneva, 1962. Author: Bibliotheca Typographica, 1934, Printing: Industrial Giant, 1944, A Mid-Century Review of Printing in the U.S.A., 1959, Bibliography of the History of Printing, 1987. Chmn. N.Y. area Nat. Def. Exec. Res. Assn., 1972-74; trustee U. Rochester Librs. Friends; hon. mem. Gutenberg Mus., Mainz, Germany. Recipient Elmer G. Voight award Edn. Coun. Graphic Arts Industry, 1961, established Horace Hart award, 1962. Mem. Am. Inst. Graphic Arts, Wynken de Worde Soc. Eng., Tupe Dirs. Club, Nat. Press Club, The Typophiles, Printing Industry Rochester (pres. 1937-40, 42-49), Printing Industry Am. (dir. 1944-49, chmn. coms. on edn., gen. mgmt., Pres.'s Conf. 1952-56), Nat. Printing Equipment Mfrs. (dir. 1966-68), Advt. Coun. Rochester (dir. 1942-52), Graphic Arts Assn. Execs. (hon.), Direct Mail Advt. Assn. Washington (hon.), Printing Industry Washington (hon.). Republican. Jewish. Deceased.

HART, THOMAS ARTHUR, education educator; b. Buenos Aires, Aug. 18, 1905; came to U.S., 1915; s. Joseph Lancaster and Tennessee Ann (Hamilton) H.; m. Catherine Royer, Sept. 26, 1976 (dec. July 1985); m. Dorothy Elvira Carlstrom, Mar. 9, 1986; children: Roger Carlstrom, R. William Carlstrom. BS, William and Mary Coll., 1930; MS, Emory U., 1933, MA, 1937; PhD, U. Chgo., 1941. Prof. biology West Ga. Coll., Carrollton, 1933-42; fgn. service officer U.S. State Dept., various nations in Latin Am., 1945-63; prof. edn. U. Pitts., 1963-76; program asst. R. William Carlstrom and Assocs., Seattle, from 1987. Cons. ministries of edn., Bolivia, Ecuador, Paraguay, Venezuela, Brazil, 1963-77. Author: Compendium de Biologia (2 vols.), 1962; contbr. articles to profl. jours. Served to lt. col. U.S. Army, 1943-45, PTO. Mem. Sigma Xi. Democrat. Unitarian Universalist. Avocations: travel, Spanish lang., vol. community health activities. Home: Seattle, Wash. Deceased.

HARTE, JOHN JOSEPH MEAKINS, bishop; b. Springfield, Ohio, July 28, 1914; s. Charles Edward and Ruth Elizabeth (Weisenstein) H.; m. Alice Eleanor Taylor, Oct. 14, 1941; children: Victoria Ruth, Joseph Meakins Jr., Judith Alice. AB, Washington and Jefferson Coll., 1936; DD (hon.), Washington & Jefferson Coll., 1954; STM, Gen. Theol. Sem., 1939, STD (hon.), 1955, D in Ministry, 1985; DD (hon.), U. South, 1955. Ordained to ministry Episc. Ch., 1939. Rector All Saints' Ch., Miami, Okla., 1939-41; curate Trinity Ch., Tulsa, 1941-42; rector St. George's Ch., Rochester, N.Y., 1942-43, All Saints' Ch., Austin, Tex., 1943-51; chaplain Episcopal students U. Tex., Austin; dean St. Paul's Cathedral, Erie, Pa., 1951-54; suffragan bishop Dioceses of Dallas, 1954-62; bishop Diocese of Ariz., 1962-80. Bd. dirs. Citibank, Ariz., Gen. Conv. Episcopal Ch., 1952; chmn. St. Luke's Hosp., Tucson, 1962-80, St. Luke's Hosp. Med. Ctr., Phoenix, 1962-80; trustee Bloy Episcopal Sch. Theology; pres. Pacific Province, 1967-68. Author: Some Sources of Common Prayer, 1944, The Language of the Book of Common Prayer, 1945, The Title Page of the Book of Common Prayer, 1946, The Church's Name, 1958, The Elizabethan Prayer Book, 1959, The 1662 Prayer Book, 1962. Bd. dirs. Human Rights Commn. City of Phoenix, 1962-65. Named Man of Yr. NCCJ, Ariz., 1969, Anti-Defamation League, Ariz., 1975. Mem. Nat. Orgn. Episcopalians for Life (chmn., founder 1966—), Am. Legion, Beta Theta Pi. Lodges: Shriners (Imperial chaplain 1962-65), KT (Grand chaplain 1951-52), Masons. Home: Phoenix, Ariz. Died 19 Dec., 1999.

HARTH, ROBERT JAMES, performing arts executive; b. Louisville, June 13, 1956; s. Sidney and Teresa O. H.; 1 child, Jeffrey David Harth Curtis. BA in English, Northwestern U., 1977; DMusic (hon.), Cleve. Inst. Music. Assoc. mgr. Ravinia (Ill.) Festival Assn., 1977-79; v.p., gen. mgr. Los Angeles Philharm. Assn., 1979-89, Hollywood Bowl, 1979-89; pres., chief exec. officer Aspen (Colo.) Music Festival and Sch., Music Assocs. of Aspen, Inc., 1989-2001; exec., artistic dir. Carnegie Hall, 2001—04. Hon. trustee Aspen Music Festival and Sch.; trustee Am. Symphony Orch. League, bd. trustees. Mem.: Curtis Inst Music (bd. overseers), European Concert Hall Orgn. Died Jan. 30, 2004.

HARTLING, POUL, former United Nations official; b. Copenhagen, Aug. 14, 1914; s. M. and Mathilde Hartling; M.Div.; m. Elsebeth Kirkemann, 1940; 4 children. Sec. to Student Christian Movement, 1934-35; sec. to Denmark's Christian Movement of Sr. Secondary Students, 1939-43; curate of Frederiksberg Ch., 1941-45; chaplain St. Luke Found., 1945-50; prin. Zahle's Tchrs. Tng. Coll., 1950-68; mem. Folketing, 1957-60, 64-77; chmn. Liberal Party Parliamentary Group, 1965-68; mem. Nordic Council, 1964-68, pres., 1966-73, v.p., 1977; minister of Fgn. Affairs, 1968-71; prime minister, 1973-75; chmn. Liberal Party, 1973-77; UN high commr. for refugees, Geneva, 1978-85. Author: Sursum corda (History of Student Christian Movement); The Danish Church, 1964; From 17 Years in Danish Politics, 1974; I dine haender, 1977, Autobiography I-IV, 1980-85, Erik Eriksen (a biography), 1990. Died Apr. 30, 2000.

HARTZ, CARROLL JUAN, psychologist; b. Tell City, Ind., Apr. 20, 1929; s. Bernard William and Mildred Katherine (Hess) H.; m. Bettye Carol Dunville, Sept. 16, 1961; children: Benjamin Clay, John David, Nathan Alan, Laura Ann. BS, Ind. State U., 1955, MS, 1958. Cert. sch. psychologist, Ind. Indsl. edn. tchr. Madison (Ind.) High Sch., 1955-59; sch. psychologist Gary (Ind.) Pub. Schs., 1959-61, School City of Hammond (Ind.), from 1961; instr. in psychology Purdue U.-Calumet, Hammond, from 1971. Regional coord. psychol. svcs. dept. pupil pers. State Supt. Office of Ind. Dept. Pub. Instrn., Indpls., 1969-70; fellow in suicide prevention NIMH, Washington, 1970-71; mem. mental health bd. Lake County Mental Health Assn., Hammond, 1970's. Contbr. articles to profl. jours. Trainer, educator various hotlines in Lake County, Ind.; psychologist St. James Counseling & Social Svcs. Sgt. U.S. Army, 1953-55, Korea. Named to Hon. Order Ky. Cols. Commonwealth of Ky., 1981; recipient Adam Benjamin Advocacy award Lake County Mental Health Assn., 1989, Sagamore of the Wabash award Gov. Bayh of Ind., 1991. Mem. Ind. Sch. Psychologists Assn. (pres. 1970's, Nat. PTA liaison 1968-69), APA, Suicidology Am., PTA (life), Phi Delta Kappa. Democrat. Roman Catholic. Avocations: fishing, helping people. Home: Hammond, Ind. Died June 26, 2000.

HARVEY, HAROLD ELMER, retired obstetrician-gynecologist, educator; b. Fairbury, Nebr., Aug. 2, 1923; s. Harry Evans and Vera Beatrice (Peterson) H.; m. Rosemary Monson, July 10, 1949; children: Joan E., Mary K. Harvey Hoard, Harold E. Jr., James F. BS, U. Nebr., MD, 1947. Intern Cottage Hosp., Santa Barbara, Calif., 1947-48; resident ob-gyn. U. Pa. Grad. Sch. Medicine, Phila., 1948-49, U. Kans. Med. Ctr., 1951-55; chief staff Lincoln (Nebr.) Gen. Hosp., 1986-88; ret. Courtesy staff Bryan Meml. Hosp., St. Elizabeth Hosp.; clin. assoc. prof. U. Nebr. Coll. Medicine. Fellow ACS; mem. AMA, ACS, Am. Fertility Soc., Ctrl. Assn. Ob-gyn. Home: Lincoln, Nebr. Died Aug. 10, 2000.

HARVEY, ROBERT GENE, English language educator; b. Liberal, Mo., Jan. 6, 1942; s. Ernest and Ella (Hedges) H.; m. Barbara Kae Dobbins, Aug. 8, 1964; 1 child, Susan Kae Harvey Dunakey. BS in English Edn., Pittsburg (Kans.) State U., 1965, MS in English, 1969; DA in English, Ill. State U., 1983. English tchr. East Ctrl. Coll., Union, Mo., from 1969. Mem. Nat. Coun. Tchrs. of English, Am. Fedn. Tchrs., Mo. Assn. Cmty. and Jr. Colls., Phi Theta Kappa (hon.). Presbyterian. Avocation: photography. Home: Union, Mo. Died May 19, 2002.

HARWELL, EDWIN WHITLEY, judge; b. Ashland, Ala., June 4, 1929; s. William Thomas and Effie Belle (Whitley) H.; m. Olma Lillian Motes, Nov. 27, 1957. Student, Jacksonville State U., 1948-49; BS, JD, U. Ala., 1952. Bar: Ala. bar 1952. Practicing atty., 1954-71; circuit judge, 1971-77; city judge City of Oxford, 1977—; individual practice law, 1977—. Served with AUS, 1952-54. Mem. Ala. Bar Assn., Calhoun County Bar Assn. (past pres.), VFW, Ala. Mcpl. Judges Assn. (past pres.), United Comml. Travelers, Elk, Moose, Anniston Exch. (past pres.). Baptist. Home: Anniston, Ala. Died Mar. 2003.

HASLAM, CHARLES LINN, biotechnology executive, lawyer, educator; b. Birmingham, Ala., June 7, 1944; s. John Billups and Edmonia Berry (Henley) H.; m. Foley Ann Vickerman, May 30, 1981 (div. Aug. 1995); 1 child, Charles Linn. AB in Politics, Princeton U., 1965; cert., Coll. Europe, 1966; JD, Duke U., 1969. Asst. prof. Va. Poly. Inst. & State U., Blacksburg, Va., 1969-72; assoc. counsel, assoc. sec. AAUP, Washington, 1972-74; univ. counsel, adj. prof. Law Duke U., Durham, N.C., 1974-77; gen. counsel U.S. Dept. Commerce, Washington, 1977-79; pvt. practice Washington, 1980-96; chmn., CEO Krug Internat. Corp., Houston, 1996-98; pres., CEO U.S. Transgenics, Inc., Washington, from 1998. Sec. DDL Electronics, Inc., Newbury Park, Calif., 1995-96; bd. dirs., Ambry Genetics Corp. Democrat. Presbyterian. Avocation: aviation. Home: Skyland, NC. Deceased.

HATCH, DAVID LINCOLN, sociology educator; b. Belmont, Mass., Oct. 2, 1910; s. Roy Winthrop and Bertha May (Roper) H.; m. Mary Alice Gies, Aug. 24, 1940; children: Charles Winthrop, Abby (Mrs. Joel S. Cleland), Faith Winslow (Mrs. William R. Mann), Elizabeth Ann (Mrs. Terry R. Dimmery). AB, Dartmouth Coll., 1933; MA, Montclair State Coll., 1934, Harvard U., 1948, PhD, 1949. Tchr. history and social studies pub. H.S., Madison, N.J., 1934-36, Summit, N.J., 1936-37, Montclair, N.J., 1937-40; instr. sociology Conn. Coll. for Women, New London, 1942-43; vis. lectr. sociology Clark U., Worcester, Mass., 1945-46; asst. prof. sociology U. Ky., Lexington, 1946-48; assoc. prof. Syracuse (N.Y.) U., 1948-54; prof., head dept. history and sociology, dir. divsn. social sci. Madison Coll., Harrisonburg, Va., 1954-57; prof. U. S.C., Columbia, from 1957, acting chmn. dept. anthropology and sociology, 1969-70, chmn. dept., 1970-73; vis. prof. Benedict Coll., Columbia. Research cons. S.C. State Hosp., Columbia, 1962-64 Author: (with R. W. Hatch) The Story of New England, 1938, (with Mary G. Hatch) Under the Elms: Yesterday and Today, 1949; Contbr. (with Mary G. Hatch) numerous articles to profl. jours., popular mags. Mem. adv. bd. Le Domain Humain, London, Eng., 1964-76; mem. adv. council S.C. Sch. Desegregation Cons. Center, Columbia, 1968; mem. regional aging adv. com. Central Midlands Regional Planning Council, S.C. Fellow Am. Sociol. Assn. (chmn. com. on recruitment for S.C. 1964-67); mem. Soc. Sci. Study Religion, Nat. Coun. on Family Rels., Ea. Sociol. Soc., So. Sociol. Soc. (chmn. com. on teaching sociology 1958-60), S.C. Sociol. Assn. (pres. 1977-78). Home: Columbia, SC. Died July 2, 2002.

HATCHER, BALDWIN, minister, educator; b. Chgo., Aug. 27, 1953; s. Willie James and Carmelethia (Hunt) H. BA, NYU, 1976; MDiv, Union Theol. Sem., N.Y.C., 1980. Ordained to ministry Bapt. Ch., 1980. Min. Sharon Bapt. Ch., N.Y.C., 1973-77, Greater Zion Hill Bapt. Ch., N.Y.C., 1979-87; tchr. N.Y.C. Bd. Edn., 1984-99. Min. Riker's Island Ho. of Detention for Men, N.Y.C., 1975; guest lectr. NYU, 1976; adj. lectr. Bronx Community Coll., 1982-83, Mercy Coll.; chaplain Terence Cardinal Cook Hosp., N.Y.C., 1985-87; panelist Black studies program Taconic Correctional facility, Mt. Kisco, N.Y. Vol. fund raiser Assn. for Help of Retarded Children, N.Y.C., 1990-99. Nat. Fellowship Fund fellow, 1976-80; Roothbert Fund scholar, 1976; named Teacher of Yr. N.Y.C. Bd. Edn. Home: Bronx, NY. Died Aug. 1999.

HAUGAARD, NIELS, pharmacologist, educator; b. Copenhagen, Feb. 25, 1920; came to U.S., 1940, naturalized, 1952; s. Gotfred C. and Karen L. (Pedersen) H.; m. Ella Elizabeth Shwartzman, June 22, 1947 (dec. Feb. 1980); children: David Gregory, Lisa Karen; m. Dorothy Tosi, 1983; children: Gregory, Kimberly, Pamela. Student, U. Copenhagen, 1938-40; AB with honors, Swarthmore Coll., 1942; PhD in Biochemistry, U. Pa., 1949. Instr. U. Pa., Phila., 1949-52, asst. prof. rsch. medicine, 1952-54, asst. prof. pharmacology, 1954-60, assoc. prof., 1960-65, prof., 1965—87, prof. emeritus, 1987—2004, mem. Med. Coun., 1972-75, chmn. Grievance Commn., 1986; mem. cardiovascular scis. study sect. NIH, 1978-82. Sect. editor Chem. Abstracts, 1960-65; mem. editl. bd. Circulation Rsch., 1964-69, Molecular and Cellular Biochemistry, 1986-96; contbr. articles to profl. jours. Mem. Bristol Twp. (Pa.) Sch. Bd., 1957-60. Guggenheim Found. fellow, 1952; Commonwealth Found. fellow, 1965 Mem. ACLU, Am. Soc. Biol. Chemists, Am. Soc. Pharmacology and Exptl. Therapeutics (editorial bd. jour. 1965-68). Achievements include rsch. on mechanism of hormone action, oxygen toxicity, mitochondrial metabolism, bladder function and metabolism, role of lipoic acid in acetyl choline formation. Home: Narberth, Pa. Died Jan. 15, 2004.

HAUS, HERMANN ANTON, electrical engineering educator; b. Ljubljana, Slovenia, Aug. 8, 1925; arrived in U.S., 1948, naturalized, 1956; s. Otto Maxmilian and Helene (Hynek) Haus; m. Eleanor Laggis, Jan. 24, 1953; children: William Peter, Stephen Christopher, Cristina Ann, Mary Ellen. Student, Technische Hochschule, Graz, 1946—48, Technische Hochschule, Vienna, 1948; BS, Union Coll., 1949; MS, Rensselaer Poly. Inst., 1951; ScD, Mass. Inst. Tech., 1954; DSc (hon.), Union Coll., 1989, Tech. U. Vienna, Austria, 1990; DSc (hon.), U. Gent, Belgium, 1994. Asst. to assoc. prof. MIT, Cambridge, 1954—62, prof. elec. engring., 1962—73, Elihu Thomson prof. elec. engring., 1973—87, inst. prof., from 1987. Vis. prof. Technische Hochschule, Vienna, 1959—60, Tokyo Inst. Tech., 1980; vis. MacKay prof. U. Calif., Berkeley, 1968; cons. Raytheon Co., 1956—91, Lincoln Labs., from 1963; nat. acad. scis. adv. panel Radio Propagation Lab. Nat. Bur. Standards, 1965—67. Author (with R.B. Adler): Circuit Theory of Linear Noisy Networks, 1959; author: (with L.D. Smullin) Noise in Electron Devices, 1959; author: (with P. Penfield, Jr.) Electrodynamics of Moving Media, 1967, Waves and Fields in Optoelectronics, 1984; author: (with J.R. Melcher) Electromagnetic Fields and Energy, 1989, Electromagnetic Noise and Quantum Optical Measurements, 2000; author: (with Christina Manolatou) Passive Components for Dense Optical Integration, 2001; mem. editorial bd. : Jour. Applied Physics, 1960—63, Electronics Letters, 1965—73, Internat. Jour. Electronics, 1975—82. Recipient Pres.'s Nat. Medal of Sci., 1995, Ludwig Wittgenstein prize, Oesterreichische Forschungsgemeinschaft, 1997; fellow, Guggenheim, 1959—60; scholar, Fulbright, 1985. Fellow: IEEE, Am. Acad. Arts and Scis., Optical Soc. Am. (Frederic Ives medal 1994), Am. Phys. Soc.; mem.: NAE, NAS, Phi Delta Theta, Tau Beta Pi, Eta Kappa Nu, Sigma Xi. Home: Lexington, Mass. Died May 21, 2003.

HAUSCHKA, THEODORE SPAETH, biologist, researcher, educator; b. Reichenau, Austria, July 31, 1908; came to U.S., 1928, naturalized, 1937; s. Hugo and Carola (Spaeth) H.; m. Elsa Voorhees, Mar. 29, 1938; children—Stephen Denison, Peter Voorhees, Margaret Spaeth. AB, Princeton U., 1930; MS (Harrison fellow), U. Pa., 1941, PhD, 1943; Sc.D. (hon.), Bates Coll., 1984. Tchr. biology Chestnut Hill Acad., Phila., 1935-39; instr. U. Pa., 1942-43, Army specialist tng. program, 1943-44; biologist Lankenau Hosp. Research Inst., Phila., 1943-48, sr. mem., 1949-54; asso. dir. Marine Exptl. Sta., Truro, Mass., 1945-47; sr. mem. Inst. Cancer Research, Phila., 1949-54; cons. cancer research Lederle Lab., Am. Cyanamid Co., 1953-65; dir. biol. research Roswell Park Meml. Inst., Buffalo, 1954-75, cons., 1975-99; research prof. biology SUNY-Buffalo Grad. Sch., 1954-74. Mem. carcinogenesis adv. panel, cons. Nat. Cancer Inst., 1972-74. Contbr. articles to profl. jours. Trustee Med. Found. Buffalo, 1965-69. Fellow AAAS, N.Y. Acad. Sci.; mem. Am. Assn. Tissue Banks, Am. Genetic Assn., Soc. for Developmental Biology, Am. Naturalists, Soc. Exptl. Biology and Medicine, Transplantation Soc., Am. Assn. Cancer Research (v.p. 1958, pres. 1959), Sigma Xi. Died Nov. 17, 1999.

HAUSER, HARRY RAYMOND, lawyer; b. N.Y.C., July 12, 1931; s. Milton I. and Lillian (Perlman) H.; m. Deborah Marlowe, Aug. 6, 1954; children: Mark Jeffrey, Joshua Brook, Bradford John, Matthew Milton. AB, Brown U., 1953; JD, Columbia U., 1959. Bar: N.Y. 1959, Mass. 1963, Wash. 1972. Practice in, N.Y.C., 1959-61, Boston, 1962—2002; atty. Sperry Rand Corp., 1959-61, Hotel Corp. Am., N.Y.C., 1961-62, v.p., sec., gen. counsel, 1962-70; mem. firm Gadsby & Hannah, 1971—2002. Life trustee Temple Israel, Boston; pres. emeritus, dir. N. Bennett St. Sch. Mem. ABA, N.Y. State Bar Assn., Mass. Bar Assn., D.C. Bar Assn., Internat. Bar Assn. Home: Newton Upper Falls, Mass. Died Feb. 6, 2003.

HAUSPURG, ARTHUR, utilities company executive; b. N.Y.C., Aug. 27, 1925; s. Otto and Charlotte (Braul) H.; m. Catherine Dunning Mackay, July 26, 1947; children: Peter R., David A., Daniel L. BSE.E., Columbia U., 1945, MSE.E., 1947. Asst. v.p. Am. Electric Power Corp., 1968; v.p. Consol. Edison Co. N.Y. Inc., N.Y.C., 1969-73, sr. v.p., 1973-75, exec. v.p., chief operating officer, 1975, chief operating officer, 1975-81, pres., 1975—, chief exec. officer, 1981-90, chmn., 1982-90, also dir., ret., 1990. Dir. Prudential-Bache High Yield Fund Inc., Prudential-Bache High Yield Mcpls. Inc., Prudential-Bache Tax-Free Money Fund Inc., Prudential-Bache Growth Opportunity Fund Inc., Prudential-Bache Govt. Securities Trust; Bd. dirs. Com. for Econ. Devel., Regional Plan Assn., N.Y.C. Partnership, Econ. devel. Council N.Y.C., Electric Power Research Inst., Cen. Park Conservancy. Contbr. articles to profl. jours.; patentee in field. Bd. dirs. N.Y. Zool. Soc. Served with USNR, 1943-46. Fellow IEEE; mem. Nat. Acad. Engring., Council Fgn. Relations (dir.), Chamber Commerce and Industry (bd. dirs.) Home: Rye, NY. Died Feb. 19, 2003.

HAVAS, PETER, physicist, researcher; b. Budapest, Hungary, Mar. 29, 1916; came to U.S., 1941, naturalized, 1948; s. George G. and Irene (Harmos) H.; m. Helga Francis Höllering; children: Eva Catherine, Stephen Walter. Student, U. Vienna, Austria, 1937-38; Absolutorium, Technische Hochschule, Vienna, 1938; PhD, Columbia U., 1944. Rsch. fellow Institut de Physique Atomique, Lyon, France, 1938-41; lectr. in physics Columbia U., N.Y.C., 1941-45; instr. physics Cornell U., 1945-46; asst. prof. physics Lehigh U., Bethlehem, Pa., 1946-49; assoc. prof., 1949-54; prof., 1954-65; prof. physics Temple U., Phila., 1965-81; prof. emeritus, from 1981. Mem. Inst. for Advanced Study, Princeton, N.J., 1953-54, Bohr Inst., Copenhagen, 1954, Argonne Nat. Lab., 1958; vis. prof. U. Göttingen, Germany, 1973; adj. prof. physics U. Pa., 1982-88, Utah State U., 1987-90. Mem. editl. bd. Acta Phys. Austriaca, 1968-76, Jour. Math. Physics, 1975-77, KINAM (mex.) 1979-2004; mem. editl. adv. bd. The Collected Papers of Albert Einstein, 1989-91. Guggenheim fellow, 1953-54. Fellow AAAS, Am. Phys. Soc., Soc. Gen. Relativity and Gravitation (internat. com. 1980-89), Acad. Scis. at Phila. (bd. dirs. 1983-2004). Achievements include rsch. on classical and quantum theories of radiation, theory of relativity, especially equations of motion, found. problems, math. physics, history and philosophy of physics. Home: Jenkintown, Pa. Died June 26, 2004.

HAWKINS, BENJAMIN SANFORD, musician; b. Painesville, Ohio, Aug. 3, 1909; s. Marcus Earl and Annetta Edith (Hanor) H.; m. Sarah Mary Stewart, Sept. 10, 1930 (div. Jan. 1934); m. Mildred Elizabeth Smith, Oct. 21, 1935; 1 child, Benjamin Sanford Jr. Ind. banjoist, guitarist, bassist various speakeasys, radio stas., nightclubs, 1924-38; bassist, banjoist Bobbie Sherwood Orch., 1940's; bassist, vocalist Shades of Blue, 1950-55; banjo and bass overdubbing various surf music records, Los Angeles, 1955-59; ind. banjoist, entertainer various MC bases, AFBs., 1960s; leader Ben Hawkins and His Music, 1960s-70s; banjo duet with Al Chernet throughout SE Fla., from 1979. Rec. artist (album) Big Ben's Banjo, 1954; performed with numerous bandleaders including Charlie Spivak, Jack Teagarden, Lester Lanin, Meyer Davis. Served as cadet USAAF, 1942-43. Mem. Am. Fedn. Musicians, Screen Actors Guild. Democrat. Avocation: restoring antique cars and airplanes. Deceased.

HAWLEY, MICHAEL C. consumer products company executive; BA, Boston Coll. Various Gillete Co., 1961-65, gen. mgr., 1965-69, various, 1969-70, bus. devel. mgr., 1970-72, gen. mgr., 1972-76, group gen. mgr. Asia Pacific group Sydney, Australia, 1976-85, v.p. ops. svcs. Boston, 1985, copr. v.p., 1985-89, pres. Oral-B Labs., Inc. Redwood City, Calif., 1989-93, exec. v.p. internat. group Boston, 1993-95, pres., COO, 1995-99, chmn., CEO, 1999-2000; ret., 2000. Home: Boston, Mass. Died June 13, 2004.

HAWTHORNE, ROBERT M., JR., science educator, consultant; b. Akron, Ohio, Nov. 1, 1929; s. Robert M. and Elizabeth (DeFriend) H.; m. Judith Parker, Mar. 5, 1955; children: Kelvin, Christopher, David, Margaret. BS in Chemistry, Columbia U., 1956; PhD in Organic Chemistry, Rutgers U., 1963; MA in History of Sci., U. Notre Dame, 1978. Rsch. chemist Nat. Starch & Chem. Co., Plainfield, N.J., 1956-59; analytical chemist Am. Cyanamid Co., Bound Brook, N.J., 1959-60; instr. Rutgers U., New Brunswick, N.J., 1961-63; tchr. Marlboro (Vt.) Coll., 1963-68; asst. prof., then assoc. prof. North Cen. campus Purdue U., Westville, Ind., 1968-81; assoc. prof., then prof., dean of faculty Unity (Maine) Coll., 1981-91. Cons. Manley Bros., Chesterton, Ind., 1980-81; textbook cons. Holt, Rinehart & Winston, Harcourt-Brace-Jovanovich, John Wiley & Sons; cons. in field 1991—. Author: Organic Chemistry for Nonchemists, 1988, Basic Chemistry for Nonchemists; mem. bd. editors A Century of Chemistry, 1976; contbr. articles to profl. jours., chpts. to books. Fellow Am. Inst.

Chemists, Am. Chem. Soc. (sec.-treas., chmn. history of chemistry div. 1979-80, 74-77, sec. Maine sect. 1982-83, chmn. 1989-91, Green Mountain (Vt.) sect. chmn. 1996-98). Democrat. Unitarian Universalist. Home: Marlboro, Vt. Died Sept. 1, 2000.

HAWTHORNE, WILLIAM JOHN, art educator; b. Somers Point, N.J., Aug. 11, 1945; s. Harry Robert and Mary (McCracken) H.; m. Sandra Anna Birch, June 13, 1970 (div. June 1991); 1 child, William John; m. Leah Gay Trantham, Aug. 2, 1991; children: Natalie Elisabeth Blake, Amanda Lynne Cummings. AS in Bus. Adminstrn., Atlantic C.C., Mays Landing, N.J., 1970; BA in Art Edn., Glassboro State Coll., 1973, MA in Art Edn., 1977. Cert. tchr., N.J. Tchr. Mulllica Township Schs., Elwood, N.J., 1973-76, Somers Point (N.J.) Schs., from 1976. Tchr. migrant edn. Mullica and Buena Sch. Dist., Elwood, Minetola, N.J., summers 1973-76; owenr Ware Natural Rush and Cane Co. Author; Early Life on the Wading River, 1976, History of the Port Elizabeth Academy, 1977, (with others) Sociology Today, 1978. Past. mem. Batsto (N.J.) Citizens Com., 1976-79; exhibitor, donor baskets and chairs Down Jersey Folk Mus., Millville, N.J., 1995. Staff sgt. USAF, 1963-67. Grantee Hist. Cold Spring Village, N.J., 1993. Mem. Am. Legion, N.J. Edn. Assn., N.J. Art Educators Assn., Congress of N.J. Parents and Tchrs. Assn. (life). Republican. Presbyterian. Avocations: chairmaking, scrimshanding, basketmaking, pottery, writing. Home: Egg Harbor Township, NJ. Died July 2, 2001.

HAWVER, WALTER WILLIAM, journalist; b. Hudson, N.Y., Feb. 13, 1922; s. Walter William and Helen Bernadine (McAree) H.; m. Concetta Mary Grandinetti, Oct. 31, 1943; children: Marilyn Conti Pezzano Burns, Margaret Ferrara, Philip, Ann Marquis, Mary Ellis-Harden. BA, St. Michael's Coll., 1948, MA, 1950. Reporter Hudson (N.Y.) Register, 1941, 45; reporter, editor Burlington (Vt.) Daily News, 1946-52; columnist Albany (N.Y.) Knickerbocker News, 1952-63; city editor Albany (N.Y.) Times-Union, 1963-65; news dir. WTEN-TV, Albany, 1965-70, KTRK-TV, Houston, 1970-85; asst. prof. Miss. U., Oxford, 1985-89, 92, Sam Houston U., Huntsville, Tex., 1989-90. Author: Capital Cities/ABC, The Early Years 1954-1986 How the Minnow Came to Swallow the Whale, 1994. Ensign USN, 1942-48. Avocations: golf, tennis. Died June 1, 2001.

HAYES, GEORGE J. retired neurosurgeon; b. Washington, 1918; MD, Johns Hopkins U., 1943. Diplomate Am. Bd. Neurol. Surgery. Intern Johns Hopkins Hosp., 1944; fellow neurosurgery Lahey Clinic, Boston, 1944-46; chief neurosurgery svc. Walter Reed Gen. Hosp., Washington, 1947-49, 50-51, 55-66; fellow neurosurgery Duke Hosp., 1949-50; chief neurosurg. svc. Brooke Army Hosp., Ft. Sam Houston, Tex., 1953-55; dir. profl. svc. Office Svc. Gen. Dept. Army, 1966-68. Prin. dep. asst. sec. def. health & environment Office Sec. Def., 1971-74; clin. prof. neurosurgery George Washington U. Mem. ACS, Inst. Medicine-NAS, Am. Assn. Neurol. Surgeons. Died Nov. 4, 2002; m.

HAYES, WILLIAM ALOYSIUS, economics educator; b. Chgo., June 25, 1920; s. John and Stella (Ahern) H.; m. Joan Leahy, Aug. 22, 1953; children— Mary, Joseph, William, Anne, Patrick, Margaret, John, Teresa. AB, DePaul U., 1942; MA, Cath. U. Am., 1948, PhD, 1952. Instr. econs., asst. prof., asso. prof. DePaul U., Chgo., 1950-60, prof. econs., 1960—, chmn. dept., 1959-67. Exec. bd. Nat. Cath. Social Action Conf., pres., 1962; bd. dirs. Adult Edn. Centers, Chgo. Mem. Am. Econ. Assn., Cath. Econ. Assn. (exec. council, pres. 1968), AAUP, Blue Key, Beta Gamma Sigma, Pi Gamma Mu. Home: Chicago, Ill. Died 12 Oct, 1999.

HAYS, LARRY WELDON, lawyer; b. Houston, Feb. 8, 1936; s. Weldon Edgar and Clara Elizabeth (Carney) H. B.A., U. Tex., 1958; J.D., U. Houston, 1968. Bar: Tex. 1968. Asst. county atty. Harris County (Tex.), 1969-81, 83—; counsel Stewart Title Co., Houston, 1981-83. Mem. Harris County Hist. Commn. Capt. U.S. Army, 1972. Mem. Tex. Dist. and County Attys. Assn., Houston Bar Assn., Tex. State Hist. Assn., Sons Republic of Tex., Houston Club, SAR, SCV, Phi Alpha Delta. Home: Rosenberg, Tex.

HEARNE, CHARLES ELMER, JR., lawyer; b. Salisbury, Md., July 27, 1909; s. Charles Elmer Sr. and Annie (Hayman) H.; m. Anna Murrell, July 14, 1944; children: Charles E. III, Stephen M. LLB, U. Balt., 1931; student, U. Md., 1926-28. Bar: Md. 1934, U.S. Dist. Ct. Md. 1939. Ptnr. Duer, Hearne & Duer, Salisbury, 1935-42, Clark & Hearne, Salisbury, 1950-53, Hearne, Fox & Bailey, Salisbury, 1953-76, Hearne & Bailey, Salisbury, 1976-79, of counsel, from 1979. Sec. Wicomico Meml. Com., Salisbury, 1953-59; pres. Wicomico Recreation Com., Salisbury, 1946-55. Capt. U.S. Army, 1942-45. Mem. BPOE. Democrat. Methodist. Avocation: golf. Home: Salisbury, Md. Deceased.

HEARST, ROSALIE, philanthropist, foundation executive; b. Oklahoma City, Mar. 07; d. Mathis O. and Audell Bertha (Clary) Wynn; m. George Randolph Hearst, Sr., July 16, 1958. Student, Oklahoma City Coll., UCLA. Hearst rep. U.S. Senate Youth Program; pres. George Randolph Hearst Meml. Found. for Diabetic Edn.; pres. Rosalie Hearst Ednl. Found.; bd. dirs. Elvirita Lewis Found; life mem. Eisenhower Med. Ctr., Pathfinders, Tiempo de Los Ninos, Desert Hosp. Aux., Desert Press Club, Coll. of the Desert Aux., Internat. Orphans; bd. dirs. Pathfinder's Ranch Boys' Club; past bd. dirs. numerous charitable orgns.; trustee emeritus The Bob Hope Cultural Ctr.; coord. Officers' Wives Vol. Svcs. Dibble Gen. Hosp., Palo Alto; coord. Am. Women's Vol. Svcs. Sawtelle Hosp. L.A.; created Rosalie and George Hearst Fellowship in Ophthalmology U. Calif Berkeley. Named Woman of Yr. City of Hope, 1971, Disting. Woman Northwood Inst. Midland, Mich., 1988; recipient award for Lifetime Achievement in Community Service Palm Springs Women's Press Club. Home: Palm Springs, Calif. Died Oct. 22, 1999.

HEATH, PETER LAUCHLAN, philosophy educator; b. Milan, May 9, 1922; came to U.S., 1962; s. Philip George and Olga (Sinclair) H. BA with honors, Magdalen Coll., Oxford, Eng., 1942. Asst. prof. U. Edinburgh, Scotland, 1946-58; assoc. prof. U. St. Andrews, Scotland, 1958-62; prof. philosophy U. Va., Charlottesville, 1962-95, prof. emeritus, from 1995. Author/commentator: The Philosopher's Alice, 1974; editor: On the Syllogism (A. de Morgan), 1966; translator: Science of Knowledge (J.G. Fichte), 1970, System of Transcendental Idealism (F.W.J. Schelling), 1978, others. Capt. Brit. Army, 1942-46, ETO. Mem. Lewis Carroll Soc. N.Am. (pres. 1976-8). Avocations: book collecting, golfing. Home: Charlottesville, Va. Died Aug. 4, 2002.

HEATH, ROBERT GALBRAITH, neurologist, psychiatrist, former educator; b. Pitts., May 9, 1915; s. Robert Malcolm and Minnie Coleman (Galbraith) H.; m. Eleanor Bugher Wright, Sept. 7, 1940; children: Anne, Shari, Barbara, Carol, Robert Galbraith. BS, U. Pitts., 1937, MD, 1938; D.M.Sc., Columbia U., 1949; D.Sc. (hon.), Tulane U., 1985. Intern Mercy Hosp., Pitts., 1939; instr. medicine U. Pitts., 1939-40; asst., chief resident neurology Neurol. Inst., N.Y., 1940-42, asst. attending neurologist, 1946-49; psychiatrist Pa. Hosp. Nervous and Mental Diseases; also demonstrator neurology Jefferson Med. Coll., 1942-43; instr. neurology Columbia, 1946-49; attending psychoanalyst Columbia (Psychoanalytic Clinic), 1951-56; prof. Tulane U., 1949-85, emeritus prof. psychiatry and neurology, 1985—, chmn. dept. psychiatry and neurology, 1949-80. Sr. vis. physician Charity Hosp.; cons. VA Hosp., New Orleans, Southeast La. State Hosp., East La. State Hosp.; med. staff DePaul Hosp.; chief med. officer Mcht. Marine Rest Center, U.S. Marine Hosp.; chief psychiatrist U.S. Penitentiary, Lewisburg, Pa., 1943-46; pres. Inst. Mental Hygiene of New Orleans, med. dirs., 1965—; med. adviser to La. dir. SSS; USPHS (coms. psychosurgery and tng. grants); com. med. edn. Am. Psychiat. Assn.; U.S. rep. Internat. Symposium on Biol. and Clin. Aspects Central Nervous Systems, Basle, Switzerland; mem. sci. adv. bd. Am. Council on Marijuana, 1980— Author: Selective Partial Ablation of the Frontal Cortex (ed. F. A. Mettler), 1949; editor: Studies in Schizophrenia, 1954, Serological Fractions in Schizophrenia, 1963, The Role of Pleasure in Behavior, 1964; adv. bd.: Jour. Nervous and Mental Disease, 1978—; author 400 sci. papers. Recipient Mental Health award Mental Health Assn. La., 1978; Robert G. Heath M.D. chair named in his honor Tulane U., 1985, 93. Fellow Am. Coll. Neuropsychopharmacology (charter), Am. Acad. Neurology, N.Y. Acad. Medicine, ACP; mem. Am. Neurol. Assn., Am. Assn. Psychoanalytic Medicine, AMA, Soc. Research Psychosomatic Problems, Soc. Biol. Psychiatry (v.p. 1967-68, pres. 1968-69, Gold Medal award for pioneer research in field 1972, Disting. Service award 1983), Assn. Research in Nervous and Mental Disease, AAAS, Am. Acad. Psychonanalysis (trustee, Frieda Fromm-Reichman award 1974), La. Psychiat. Assn. (pres. 1960-61, award 1977), Sigma Xi. Died Sept. 21, 1999.

HEBERT, CHARLES ALEXANDRE, information broker; b. Terre Haute, Ind., Feb. 11, 1906; s. Joseph Alexandre and Mabel (Chewning) H. BA, U. N.C., 1934; MA, NYU, 1950, postgrad., from 1951. Engr. Bell Telephone Labs., N.Y.C., 1929-49; officer, lt. comdr. USN, 1941-46; asst. v.p. Engring. Rsch. Assoc., Arlington, Va., 1947-48; rsch. assoc. dept. indsl. engring. Columbia U., 1949-51; owner Rsch. Svc., N.Y.C., from 1950. Author: Carrier Telefon System, 1938, Annotated Bibliography of Audio-Visual Aids for Management Development Programs, 1958; patentee in field. Mem. Soc. Historique Acadienne. Avocation: genealogy. Home: New York, NY. Died Nov. 26, 2001.

HECHINGER, JOHN WALTER, hardware chain executive; b. Washington, Jan. 18, 1920; s. Sidney Lawrence and Sylvia (Frank) H.; m. June Ross, May 26, 1946; children— Nancy, John Walter, S. Ross, Sally. BS, Yale U., 1941. With Hechinger Co., Landover, Md., co-chmn., chief exec. officer, 1958-90, chmn., 1990—96. Chmn. D.C. City Coun., 1967-69; commr. D.C. Jud. Nominating Com., 1980-87; mem. Dem. Nat. Com., 1972-92; former rep. UN; bd. dirs. Eugene and Agnes Meyer Found., Nat. Urban Coalition, Handgun Control, Inc. With USAAF, World War II. Decorated Air medal. Jewish. Home: Washington, DC. Died Jan. 18, 2004.

HECHT, DONN, songwriter, screenwriter, agent; b. Pitts., Apr. 18, 1930; s. Matthew J. and Valeria H.; m. Rosana Aguirre Acevedo, Feb. 21, 1975; children: Donn Jr., Beverly. Creative works include: (compositions) Walking After Midnight, Snowbound, Night Train, La Mirada, Cry Not for Me, The Touch of His Hand, The Sermon On The Mount, Rock Bottom, So Dear to My Heart, Never No More, Spring is Gone, Without Your Love, Theme for Billie, I Took the Blues Out of Tomorrow, In the Country, The Battle of Chavez Ravine, Downgrade, I'm Satisfied, Poet's Love Letter, Philosophy, One-By-One, Fingerprints, Who Am I?, Ballad of the M.I.A., Old Candles, I Used to Know Her, No Matter What, Mr. Blue Jay, If I Were Your Pillow, It's Not Enough, Nothing But Love, Half Past Midnight, The Theme from the Raisin Tree, Once Upon a Star, Save a Place in Your Heart for Me, I Was Only Teasing You, Who Knows, As Long As I Have You, I Never Got Over You, More and More and More, I'll Still Be in Love with You, All Those Teardrops, I've Cried, Until, With Love Everything Will be Right, It's Funny What Love Can Do, Because I Just Can't Take It, That's What Love Means to Me, I Don't Want No Heartaches, It All Depends on You, Pills, Pills, Pills, Why Are You Leaving Me, Well That's Love, Day By Day, Zombie Woman, One Short of Living, Together, Too Much Month for the Money Blues, Sho Ya' Right, Misery, (recs.) The Patsy Cline Story, 1977, I Remember Patsy, 1978, All My Best, 1979, Unstoppable, 1982, Come Down from the Hills, 1984, The Trinity Session, 1989, The Chase, Garth Brooks, 1992-94 (No. 1 Best Seller Billboard Top Country Albums Chart), Greatest Hits (Patsy Cline), 1992-93 (No. 1 Best Seller Billboard Top Country Catalogue Albums), (motion picture soundtracks) Coalminer's Daughter, 1980, Sweet Dreams, 1986, (TV series) Wise Guy, 1989-99, Diamonds and Chicken Soup, Clear and Present Danger, Your Ring is Off My Finger (but Still Around My Heart), (song) Hawaii Five-O, Alice in Wonderland, Millenuim II, The Pretenders, Women O the Night, Theme for Celine Dion, Theme for Holiday in Spain, Hello Bed, I Guess I'll Just Be Moving On, Looking for Mr. Right; Debut album box set Prodrs. Showcase, Platinum 2000 series with co-writer Sylvia Sue Blackard: Beyond This Time And Day, Love Everlasting (And True), Take a Chance On Me, At Last I Belong, Here Comes Fun and Games, The Mystery of Love, How Did We Get Here, Heart Whispers, Desert Heart, Candle of Love, Vision of Dreams, She Has My Heart and the Key, Your First Love Will Be My Last, On the Wings of Love, Love Keeps on Singing, Two Hearts-One Love, Sweet September, She Is My Texas Star, Destiny, Sunset in Santa Fe, I Can't Get Over You ('Till I'm Out From Under Him), Let's Drink to What If, Your Heart Was Home to Me, Letter to My Heart, Pages of the Past, Light in the Window, Soulmate; contbr. articles to profl. jours. Recipient Billboard Gold Medallion (three-time recipient, two top ten, one #1), 2000, Broadcast Music Inc. Spl. Citation of Achievement award, 2000. Achievements include Achievements include having a collective career sales of approximately 24 million. Died Oct. 18, 2002.

HECKMAN, ROBERT E. anesthesiologist; b. Boston, 1925; MD, Tufts U., 1956. Diplomate Am. Bd. Anesthesiology. Intern Hitchcock Meml. Hosp., 1956-57; resident in anesthesiology Tufts-New Eng. Hosps., Boston, 1957 59; chmn. ethics com. Kent Gen. Hosp., Dover, Del., 1988-2001. Fellow Am. Coll. Anesthesiology; mem. Am. Soc. Anesthesiology, Internat. Anesthesia Rsch. soc. Deceased.

HEDRICK, WALLY BILL, artist; b. Pasadena, Calif., 1928; s. Walter Thomas and Velma Laurel (Thurman) H., m. Jay DeFeo (div.), 1 child. Student, Otis Art Inst., Los Angeles, 1947, Calif. Coll. Arts and Crafts, 1954; B.F.A., Calif. Sch. Fine Arts, 1955; MA, San Francisco State U., 1958. Instr. San Francisco State U., 1958-59, Calif. Sch. Fine Arts, 1960-64, Art Inst. San Francisco, 1964-70, San Francisco Acad. Art, 1971, San Jose State U., 1972-73, Indian Valley Coll., from 1974. Instr. summer session Art. Inst. San Francisco, 1978; instr. U. Calif., Davis, 1984, 86. One-man shows include Pasadena (Calif.) Arts Ctr., 1950, M.H. de Young Meml. Mus., San Francisco, 1955, Calif. Sch. Fine Arts, San Francisco, 1956, Oakland (Calif.) Mus., 1958, Isaacs Gallery, Toronto, Can., 1961, New Mission Gallery, San Francisco, 1963, San Francisco Art Inst., 1967, Sonoma Satte Coll., Calif., 1968, 63 Bluxome St., San Francisco, 1975, Gallery Paule Anglim, San Francisco, 1982, 84, 89, 90, Emanuel Walter Gallery, 1985, Atholl McBean Gallery, 1985, Natsoulas-Novelozo Gallery, Davis, Calif., 1989, Mills Coll. Art Gallery, 1994, Gallery Paule Anglim, 1994, Calif. Mus. of Art, 1999, Linc Real Art Gallery, San Francisco, Calif., 2002, Sonoma State U. Art Gallery, Rohnert Pk., Calif., 2002; group exhibitions include Gallery Paule Anglim, San Francisco, 1992, ACGI Gallery, Berkeley, Calif., 1993, The Crocker Mus., Sacramento, 1994, The Oakland Mus., Calif., 1994, San Francisco Art Inst., 1994, Richmond Art Ctr., Calif., 1995, San Francisco Women Artists Gallery, 1995, Whitney Mus. Am. Art, N.Y.C., 1995, Walker Art Ctr., Mpls., 1996, M.H. de Young Meml. Mus., 1996, numerous others; represented in permanent collections, Aldrich Mus. Contemporary Art, Ridgefield, Conn., Mus. Modern Art, N.Y.C., Smithsonian Instn., San Francisco Mus. Modern Art, City and County San Francisco, L.A. County Mus. Art, Laguna (Calif.) Mus., Mus. Contemporary Art, Ridgefield, Conn., Oakland Mus., Calif. State U. Sonoma, U. Calif. San Francisco. San Francisco Art Commn., San Francisco Art Inst., San Francisco Internat. Airport, Univ. Art Mus., Berkeley, Calif., Mills Coll., Oakland; represented by Gallery Paule Anglim. Served with AUS, 1950-52. Recipient Adeline Kent award, 1985, Golden Bear award Calif. State Fair, 1990, merit award, 1991, award of excellence, 1996; grantee Nat. Endowment Arts, 1962, 82, 93, Marin Arts Coun.-Bucks Found., individual artist grantee San Francisco Found., 1985-86, Adolph and Esther Gottlieb Found. grantee, 1997, Pollack-Krasner Found. grantee, 1999. Home: Bodega, Calif. Died Dec. 17, 2003.

HEILBRUN, CAROLYN GOLD, English literature educator; b. East Orange, N.J., Jan. 13, 1926; d. Archibald and Estelle (Roemer) Gold; m. James Heilbrun, Feb. 20, 1945; children: Emily, Margaret, Robert. BA, Wellesley Coll., 1947; MA, Columbia U., 1951, PhD, 1959; DHL (hon.), U. Pa., 1984, Bucknell U., 1985, Russell Sage Coll., 1987, Smith Coll., 1989, Berea Coll., 1991, New Sch. for Social Rsch., 1993, Lewis and Clark Coll., 1993, Pace U., 1996, Brown U., 1997, Lewis and Clark U., 1993, Duke U., 1998; DFA (hon.), Rivier Coll., 1986; DFA, U. St. Thomas, 1994. Instr. Bklyn. Coll., 1959-60, Columbia U., N.Y.C., 1960-62, asst. prof., 1962-67, assoc. prof., 1967-72, prof. English lit., 1972—86, Avalon Found. prof. humanities, 1986-93, prof. emeritus, 1986-93. Vis. prof. U. Calif., Santa Cruz, 1979, Princeton U., N.J., 1981, Yale Law Sch., 1989. Author: The Garnett Family, 1961, Christopher Isherwood, 1970, Towards Androgyny, 1973, Reinventing Womanhood, 1979, Writing a Woman's Life, 1988, Hamlet's Mother and Other Women, 1990, The Education of a Woman: The Life of Gloria Steinem, 1995, The Last Gift of Time: Life Beyond Sixty, 1997, When Men Were the Only Models We Had, My Teachers: Barzun, Fadiman, Trilling, 2002, Collected Stories by Amanda Cross, 1997, 12 novels as Amanda Cross, 1964—98 (Nero Wolfe award, 1981), In the Last Analysis, 1964, The James Joyce Murder, 1967, Poetic Justice, 1970, The Theban Mysteries, 1971, The Question of Max, 1971, Death in a Tenured Position, 1981, Sweet Death, Kind Death, 1984, No Word from Winnifred, 1986, A Trap for Fools, 1989, The Players Come Again, 1990, An Imperfect Spy, 1995, The Puzzled Heart, 1998. Guggenheim fellow, 1966, Rockefeller fellow, 1976, Sr. Rsch. fellow NEH, 1983; recipient Alumnae Achievement award Wellesley Coll., 1984, award of excellence Grad. Faculty of Columbia Alumni, 1984. Mem. MLA (pres. 1984, Life Achievement award 1999), Am. Acad. Arts and Scis. (elected), Mystery Writers Am. (exec. bd. 1982-84), Phi Beta Kappa Home: New York, NY. Died Oct. 9, 2003.

HEIMER, RALPH, editor; b. Vienna, Nov. 4, 1921; came to U.S., 1938; s. Oskar and Irene (Cziegler) H.; m. Caryl P. Biren, June 13, 1921 (dec. Feb. 1993); children: Robert, Paul; m. Phyllis M. Sampson, Aug. 23, 1974. BS, CCNY, 1948; MS, Columbia U., 1951, PhD, 1957. Asst. prof. Cornell Med. Coll., N.Y.C., 1956-63; assoc. prof. N.J. Coll. Medicine, Jersey City, 1963-66; prof. Thomas Jefferson U., Phila., 1967-90, prof. emeritus, from 1991; editor Allegheny U. Health Scis., Phila., from 1996. Head sci. com. Estern Pa. chpt. Arthritis Found., Phila., 1985-88. Sgt. U.S. Amy, 1942-46. NIH grantee, 1963-66, 67-83; Arthritis Found. grantee, 1963-66. Mem. Am. Assn. Immunologists, Am. Soc. for Biochemistry. Achievements include discovery of structure of sialic acid; location of rheumatoid factor in the synovium; proteoglycans in colon cancer; patent on detection of proteoglycan. Home: Philadelphia, Pa. Deceased.

HEIMLICH, RICHARD ALLEN, geologist, educator; b. Elizabeth., N.J., Aug. 8, 1932; s. Simon William and Sidnie W. (Simon) H.; m. Charlee Marcus, July 23, 1961; children: Steven A., John P. BS, Rutgers U., 1954; MS, Yale U., 1955, PhD (JD Dana scholar 1956), 1959. Mem. faculty Kent (Ohio) State U., 1961—, prof. geology, 1970—, chmn. dept., 1976-92. Author: Field Guide: Southern Great Lakes, 1977, Field Guide: The Black Hills, 1980; also papers and articles. Served with Ordnance Corps AUS, 1959-60. Grantee NSF, 1967-69, 69-71, Los Alamos Nat. Lab., 1979, 80, U.S. Dept. Edn., 1979-92. Fellow Geol. Soc. Am.; mem. Am. Inst. Profl. Geologists, No. Ohio Geol. Soc., Sigma Xi. Home: Kent, Ohio. Deceased.

HEISKELL, ANDREW, publishing executive; b. Naples, Italy, Sept. 13, 1915; s. Morgan and Ann (Hubbard) H.; m. Cornelia Scott, Nov. 12, 1937 (div.); children: Diane, Peter; m. Madeleine Carroll (div.); m. Marian Sulzberger Dryfoos, 1965. Ed. in, France; student, Harvard Bus. Sch., 1935-36; LL.D., Shaw U., 1968, Lake Erie Coll., 1969, Hofstra U., 1972, Hobart and William Smith Colls., 1973; D.Litt., Lafayette Coll., 1969. Reporter N.Y. Herald-Tribune, 1936-37; assoc. editor Life mag., 1937-39, asst. gen. mgr., 1939-42, gen. mgr., 1942-46, pub., 1946-60; v.p. Time, Inc., 1949-60, chmn. bd., 1960-69, chmn. bd., chief exec. officer, 1969-80. Bd. dirs. Book-of-the-Month Club, Inc., Vivian Beaumont Theater, Inc. Bd. dirs. People for the Am. Way, Internat. Exec. Service Corps; chmn. bd. trustees N.Y. Public Library, 1981—2003; trustee Enterprise Found., Trust for Cultural Resources of N.Y.C.; hon. trustee Brookings Instn.; bd. advisors Dumbarton Oaks Research Library and Collection; chmn. Bryant Park Restoration Corp., Pres.'s Com. on Arts and Humanities; bd. visitors Grad. Sch. and Univ. Ctr. CUNY. Fellow Harvard Coll. Clubs: Century Assn., Links, River, Harvard (N.Y.C.). Home: New York, NY. Died July 6, 2003.

HEITMANN, FREDERICK WILLIAM, bank executive, lecturer; b. Chgo., Apr. 14, 1922; s. Frederick William and Louise (Snyder) H.; m. Peggy A. Smith, Sept. 6, 1947; children: Daryl Jean Riley, Scott Keith; m. 2d Deborah Lee Drinan, Oct. 1, 1980; m. 3d, Kathleen M. Dense, May 20, 1992. BS, Northwestern U., 1943; M. in Banking, U. Wis., 1953. Vice-pres. Northwest Nat. Bank, Chgo., 1952-57, exec. v.p., 1957-63, former pres., CEO; former chmn. La Salle Northwest Nat. Bank, Chgo., also bd. dirs. Bd. dirs. La Salle Northbrook Bank, Ill., W.N. Lanne Interfinancial Inc., Northbrook; faculty mem. various univs. Chmn. State Ill. Commn. Higher Edn., 1960-65, vice-chmn., 1965-75; chmn. banking and fin. div. Ill. Crusade of Mercy, 1976. Recipient Silver Anniversary All-Am. award Sports Illus. Mag., 1967; recipient Disting. Alumnus Merit award Northwestern U., 1968; F.H.A. Pub. Housing citation Washington, 1970 Mem.: Mid-Am. (Chgo.); North Shore Country (Glenview, Ill.) (treas., dir.); Bankers; Chikaming Country (Lakeside, Mich.). Home: Northbrook, Ill. Died Apr. 30, 2004.

HEIZER, DAVID EUGENE, health information management educator; b. Sidney, Nebr., Aug. 24, 1946; s. Clifton Edwin and Verna Rose (Davison) H.; m. Bonnie Elizabeth Alsbury, Feb. 14, 1986 (div. Feb. 1996); children: Bradley John, Kurt Clifton. BS, Coll. St. Mary, 1974; MPA, U. Mo., Kansas City, 1989. Supr. Archbishop Bergen Mercy Hosp., Omaha, 1974-75; cons. pvt. practice, Omaha, 1975-77; rsch. asst. Health Info. Tech. Svcs., Omaha, 1977-79; coord. med. audit St. Joseph Hosp., Omaha, 1979-83; dir. St. Joseph (Mo.) State Hosp., 1984-93, St. Francis Hosp., Maryville, Mo., 1993-95; asst. prof. Mo. Western State Coll., 1995—. Donor Dream Factory, 1994, 95, 96. Mem. Am. Health Info. Mgmt. Assn., Mo. Health Info. Mgmt. Assn., Masons, U. Mo. Kansas City Alumni Assn. Republican. Avocations: arabian horses, swimming. Home: Cary, Ill. Died Jan. 19, 2001.

HELLER, EDGAR ELWOOD, family physician; b. Vermilion, Ohio, Mar. 23, 1922; s. Bernhardt Robert Heller and Helen Barbara Bitzer; m. Jeannette Hughes, Sept. 20, 1947; children: David Hughes, Lisl Ann (dec.) AB, Ursinus Coll., 1943; MD, Wake Forest U., 1950. Diplomate Am. Bd. Family Practice; lic. physician, Fla., Ala., Minn. Intern St. Barabas Hosp., Mpls., 1951; pvt. practice Mankato, Minn., 1953-76; student health physician Auburn (Ala.) U., 1976, Fla. State U., Tallahassee, 1976-87; physician various instns., Fla., Minn., Ala., Wis., from 1987. Acting dir. student health svcs. Fla. State U., Tallahassee, 1980-81. Lt. U.S. Army, 1951-52, Korea. Regional Cardiology fellow, 1974. Mem. AMA, Fla. State Med. Assn., Indian Rine County Med. Assn. Republican. Methodist. Avocations: swimming, golf, music performance. Home: Vero Beach, Fla. Deceased.

HELLER, PAULINE BERMAN, lawyer; b. N.Y.C., Dec. 25, 1911; d. Morris and Rose (Fried) Berman; m. Harry Heller, Aug. 29, 1934; children: Judith H. Zangwill-Fribush, Mary H. Lesser. AB magna cum laude, Hunter Coll., 1932; LLB, Columbia U., 1934. Bar: N.Y. 1935, D.C. 1953, U.S. Supreme Ct. 1962. Atty. various govt. agys. and law firms, N.Y.C. and Washington, 1934-55, 65-72; trial and appellate atty. U.S. Dept. of Justice, Washington, 1955-64; asst. gen. counsel, cons. Bd. Govs. Fed. Reserve System, Washington, 1972-73, 76-82 and from 92; of counsel Arnold & Porter, Washington, 1983-92. Author: (law books) Federal Bank Holding Company Law, 1986, revised edits., 1987, 88, 89, 90, 91, Handbook of Federal Bank Holding Company Law, 1976; contbr. articles to profl. jours; contbr. Columbia Law Rev., Columbia U. Named to Hunter Coll. Hall of Fame. Mem. Phi Beta Kappa. Avocations: travel, theater. Home: Bethesda, Md. Deceased.

HELLMUTH, GEORGE FRANCIS, architect; b. St. Louis, Oct. 5, 1907; s. George W. and Harriet M. (Fowler) H.; m. Mildred Lee Henning, May 24, 1941; children: George William, Nicholas Matthew, Mary Cleveland, Theodore Henning, Daniel Fox. BArch, Washington U., 1928, MArch, 1930; Steedman traveling fellow, 1931; diploma, Ecole des Beaux Arts, Fontainebleau, France. Founder Hellmuth, Yamasaki & Leinweber, 1949-55, Hellmuth, Obata & Kassabaum, 1955-78, HOK Internat., Inc., 1977-86; numerous offices including, St. Louis, N.Y.C., San Francisco, Dallas, Washington, Tokyo, Japan, Kuwait City, Kuwait, Berlin, Kansas City, Mo., Tampa, Fla., Los Angeles, Hong Kong and London; pres. Bald Eagle Co., Gladden, Mo.; co-founder Hellmuth Dunn Inc., Hellmuth Dunn and Co., St. Louis, from 1994. Chmn. St. Louis Landmarks and Urban Design Commn., 1950-70; co-founder Hellmuth Dunn Inc., Designers and Mfrs. of Dinner and Decorative Wares. Prin. archtl. works include: King Saud U., Riyadh, Saudi Arabia; King Khaled Internat. Airport, Riyadh; (outside U.S.) Nile Tower, Cairo, Egypt, U. West Indies, Trinidad, Spanish Honduras secondary sch. system, Am. Embassy, El Salvador, Am. embassy housing, Cairo, Canadian medium and maximum prisons, Taipei World Trade Ctr., Taiwan, Housing for Royal Saudi Naval Forces, Saudi Arabia, Military Secondary Schools, Saudi Arabia, Air Def. Command Hdqtrs. Complex, Saudi Arabia, Burgan Bank Hdtrs., Kuwait, Asoka Dev., Kuala Lumpur, Chesterton Retail Mall, U.K.; prin. archtl. works include: (U.S.) Nat. Air and Space Mus., Washington, Marion Fed. Maximum Security Prison, (Ill.), IBM Advanced systems Lab, Los Gatos, Calif., Dallas/Ft. Worth Regional Airport, U. Wis. Med. Center, Madison; Internat. Rivercenter, New Orleans; SUNY Health Scis. Complex, Buffalo, The Galleria/Post Oak Center, Houston, E.R. Squibb Co, Lawrenceville, N.J., McDonnell Planetarium, St. Louis, Dow Research and Devel. Facility, Indpls.; Commonwealth P.R. Penal System; Duke U. Med. Center, Durham, N.C.; Lubbock Regional Airport, (Tex.), Lambert-St. Louis Internat. Airport, St. Louis, D.C. Courthouse, St. Louis U. Sch. Nursing, No. Ill. U. Library, Mobil Oil Hdqtrs., Fairfax, Va., Cities Service Research Ctr., Tulsa, Marriott Corp. Hdqtrs., Bethesda, Md., McDonnell Douglas Automation Ctr., St. Louis, Moscone Conv. Ctr., San Francisco, Piers 1. 2. 3., Boston, Clark County Dentention Ctr., Las Vegas, Nev., Pillsbury Research and Devel. Facility, Mpls., Saturn Automotive Facility, Tenn., Burger King World Hdqrs., Miami, Exxon Research and Egrning. Ctr., Clinton, N.J., Incarnate Word Hosp., St. Louis, Kellogg Co. Hdqrs., Battle Creek, Mich., Fleet Ctr., Providence, Phillips Point, West Palm Beach, Fla., Sohio Corp. Hdqrs., Cleve., Lincoln Tower, Miami, 2000 Pennsylvania Ave., Washington, Providence Park, Fairfax, Va., Tower One, Houston, Griffin Tower, Dallas, ARCO Tower, Denver, Levi's Plaza, San Francisco, Southwestern Bell Telephone Hdqrs., St. Louis, Met. Life Bldg., St. Louis, Burger King Hdqrs., Miami, Fla., Saturn Automotive Facility, Tenn., Living World Edn. Ctr., St. Louis Zoo, BP Hdqrs, London, U. Ala.-Birmingham Hosp., Univ. Hosp. at St. Louis U., Mo., Saint Louis Galleria Expansion, 801 Grand Office Bldg., Des Moines, Moore Bus. Forms Hdqrs., Lake Forest, Ill., The Fla. Aquarium, Tampa, Fed. Reserve Bank Mpls., Fed. Reserve Bank Cleve., Jacobs Field, Cleve., Oriole Park at Camden Yards, Balt., NYU Replacement Hosp., N.Y.C., Northwestern Meml. Replacement Hosp., Chgo., U.S. EPA Environ. Rsch. Facility, Research Triangle Park, N.C., Thomas F. Eagleton U.S. Courthouse, St. Louis, Exxon Corp. World Hdqs., Irving, Tex., Huangpu Dist. Master Plan, Shanghai, Hongkong Stadium, Victoria, Hong Kong, Fukuoka (Japan) Internat. Airport Terminal, Sendai (Japan) Internat. Airport Terminal, many other indsl. and bus. corporate hdqrs., research centers. Designated knight Sovereign Mil. Order of Malta in U.S.A. Fellow AIA (First Honor award 1956). Home: Carmel, Calif. Died Nov. 5, 1999.

HELMHOLZ, AUGUST CARL, physicist, educator emeritus; b. Evanston, Ill., May 24, 1915; s. Henry F. and Isabel G. (Lindsay) H.; m. Elizabeth J. Little, July 30, 1938; children: Charlotte C.K. Colby, George L., Frederic V., Edith H. Roth. AB, Harvard Coll., 1936; student, Cambridge U., 1936-37; PhD, U. Calif., Berkeley, 1940; Sc.D. (hon.), U. Strathclyde, 1979. Instr. physics U. Calif.-Berkeley, 1940-43, asst. prof., 1943-48, assoc. prof., 1948-51, prof., 1951-80, emeritus, 1980—2003, chmn. dept., 1955-62; former rsch. physicist Lawrence Berkeley Lab. Mem. Vis. Scientist Program, 1966-71; governing bd. Am. Inst. Physics, 1964-67. Recipient Citation U. Calif., Berkeley, 1980; Berkeley fellow, 1988—, Guggenheim fellow, 1962-63. Fellow Am. Phys. Soc.; mem. AAAS, Am. Assn. Physics Tchrs., AAUP, Phi Beta Kappa, Sigma Xi. Home: Lafayette, Calif. Died Oct. 29, 2003.

HELMS, MARY ANN, critical care nurse, consultant; b. Compton, Calif., Jan. 7, 1935; d. Raymond Whitfield and Amanda Zelpha (Hancock) Spencer; m. Willard Ford Helms, Mar. 15, 1958; children: Michael steven, Steven Allen. AA in Nursing, El Camino Coll., 1971; BSN, Calif. State U., L.A., 1976; MA in Mgmt., St. Mary's Coll., 1978; MSN, Ariz. State U., 1985; PhD in Health Svc. Adminstrn., Columbia Pacific U., 1993. RN; cert. clin. specialist, health care quality. Med. sec., bookkeeper Palm Springs (Calif.) Med. Clinic, 1956-61; office mgr. William R. Stevens Ins. Agy., Santa Ana, Calif., 1961-63, I.J. Weinrot & Son Ins. Agy., L.A., 1963-67; staff nurse VA Hosp., 1971, Kaiser Found. Hosp., Harbor City, Calif., 1971-76; supr., coord. pediat. Maricopa County Gen. Hosp., Phoenix, 1976-80; critical care nurse Phoenix Bapt. Hosp., 1980-81, critical care mgr., 1981-89, clin. nurse specialist, 1989-95, critical care cons., 1986-95, nursing cons., 1986-99. Mem. ANA, AAAS, Am. Cons's. League, Am. Statis. Assn., N.Y. Acad. Sci., Smithsonian Instn., Phoenix Zoo, Phoenix Art Mus., Calif. State U. Alumni Assn., KAET Pub. Broadcasting Sys., Ariz. Nurses Assn., Ariz. State U. Alumni Assn., Columbia Pacific U. Alumni Assn., Phi Kappa Phi, Alpha Gamma Sigma, Sigma Theta Tau. Episcopalian. Achievements include research on effects of noise pollution on physical and mental health of citizenry, phenylketonuria testing in Los Angeles, measurement of attitudes toward children in pediatric nurses, nursing practice, physiological changes with back massage, incidence of prolonged Q-T interval in critically ill patients, incidence of prolonged QT interval in cardiac and noncardiac critically ill patients on antiarryhthmic drugs, differences in measurement of QT interval to identify patients with prolongation in cardiac cycle; use of autotransfusion in hip and knee surgery patients; use of pulse oximetry in pre and pst operative patients; side effects of patient-controlled analgesia; conf. medication histories in hospitalized patients; correlation of patient medication histories to nurses and physicians. Died Feb. 22, 1999.

HELMS, RICHARD MCGARRAH, international consultant, former ambassador; b. St. Davids, Pa., Mar. 30, 1913; s. Herman H. and Marion (McGarrah) H.; m. Julia Bretzman Shields, Sept. 8, 1939 (div. 1968); 1 son, Dennis J.; m. Cynthia McKelvie, 1968. BA, Williams Coll., 1935. Staff corr. UP, Europe, 1935-37; mem. staff Indpls. Times Pub. Co., 1937-42; with CIA, 1947-73, dep. dir., plans, 1962—65, dep. dir., 1965—66, dir., 1966—73; ambassador to Iran, 1973-76; internat. cons., 1977-97. Pres. Safeer Co., Washington, 1977-97. Served with OSS USNR, 1942-46, ETO. Recipient Career Service award Nat. Civil Service League, 1965, Disting. Intelligence medal, 1973, Nat. Security medal, 1983. Mem. Phi Beta Kappa. Died Oct. 22, 2002.

HELPS, ROBERT EUGENE, composer, pianist, educator; b. Passaic, N.J., Sept. 23, 1928; Student, Juilliard Preparatory Dept. and Inst. Musical Arts, 1936-43; student with Felix Salzer, Mannes Coll. Music, 1943-44; pvt. study with Abby Whiteside, Roger Sessions, 1943-60; student, Columbia U., 1947-49, U. Calif., Berkeley, 1949-51; DHL, U. St. Thomas, 1996. Prof. of piano New England Conservatory, San Francisco Conservatory, Princeton Univ., Stanford Univ., Univ. Calif., Berkeley, Manhattan Sch. of Music, Univ. S. Fla., Tampa, presently. Artist-in-residence (pianist) Univ. of Calif., Davis, 1973. Composer and performer in field, also recordings; works pub. by C.F. Peters, Associated Music Pubs., Am. Composers Alliance. Recipient awards in composition NEA, Guggenheim Found., Ford Found., Koussevitzky Music Found. and others. Home: Tampa, Fla. Died Nov. 24, 2001.

HELWIG, ELSON BOWMAN, pathologist; b. Pierceton, Ind., Mar. 5, 1907; s. Llewellyn and Grace (Bowman) H.; m. Mildred Stoelting, Apr. 20, 1933; children— Alan S., Warren B., Ann (Mrs. Thomas Gordon). BS, Ind. U., 1930, MD, 1932, DSc (hon.), 1989. Diplomate: Am. Bd. Pathology. Rotating intern Indpls. City Hosp., 1932-33, resident pathology, 1933- 34; asst. resident pathology Inst. Pathology, Western Res. U., 1934-35; resident pathology Cleve. City Hosp., 1935-36; asst. pathologist New Eng. Deaconess Hosp., Boston, 1936-39; mem. faculty Washington U. Sch. Medicine, St. Louis, 1939-46, asst. prof. pathology, 1946; sr. pathologist, chief skin and gastro-intestinal pathology br.

Armed Forces Inst. Pathology, 1946-80, chief dept. pathology, 1955-74, 1955-74, asso. dir. for consultation, 1967-77, chmn. Ctr. Advanced Pathology, 1974-78; profl. lectr. George Washington U. Sch. Medicine, 1947-64, clin. prof., 1964—; clin. prof. pathology Sch. Medicine, Uniformed Services U. Health Scis., 1976—, chmn. gastrointestinal pathology, from 1980. Vis. profl. dermatol. pathology Temple U. Sch. Medicine, 1958-74, cons. skin and cancer hosp. of univ., 1959-74; cons. Walter Reed Army Hosp., 1953—, WHO, 1965—; Mem. Armed Forces Epidemiol. Bd., 1968-78; Carl V. Weller Meml. lectr. Mich. Soc. Pathologists, 1968, Shields Warren lectr. N.Eng. Soc. Pathologists, 1978. Co-author: International Histopathological Classification of Tumors, 1975; Editor: The Skin, 1971; author: (with others) Dermal Pathology, 1972, Pathology of the Colon, Small Intestine and Anus, 1983; editorial bd.: (with others) Jour. Cancer; Author (with others) numerous articles in field. Mem. dean's coun. Ind. U. Sch. medicine, 1988; charter mem. Sr. Exec. Svc. U.S.A., 1979. Served to col., M.C. AUS, 1942-45, PTO. Recipient Meritorious Civilian Svc. award Dept. Army, Exceptional Civilian Svc. award, 1964, Disting. Civilian Svc. award Dept. Def., 1965; President's award for Disting. Fed. Civilian Svc., 1966, Heath Meml. award, 1975, John Shaw Billings Lifetime Achievement award, Armed Forces Inst. Pathology and Am. Registry of Pathology, 1990. Mem. Coll. Am. Pathologists, Am. Soc. Clin. Pathologists (Arthur Purdy Stout lectr. 1972, H.P. Smith Meml. award 1983), Internat. Assn. Pathologists, Am. Assn. Pathologists and Bacteriologists, AMA, Mass. Med. Soc., Washington Pathology Soc., Washington Dermatol. Soc., Am. Acad. Dermatology, Washington Acad. Medicine, Assn. Mil. Dermatologists, Am. Soc. Dermatopathology (pres. 1964-65, Founders award 1985), Assn. Mil. Surgeons, Histochem. Soc., Stout-Pathology Soc., Am. Dermatol. Assn., Pacific Dermatol. Assn., Soc. Columbiana de Patologica, French Soc. Dermatology and Syphiology (fgn. corr.) Identified and classified adnexal tumors of skin; established relationship between Bowen's disease and internal cancer; identified cloacagenic carcinoma of anus, anatomic and histochem. changes in skin after laser irradiation. Home: Alexandria, Va. Died Nov. 3, 1999.

HEMING, CHARLES E. lawyer; b. N.Y.C., Mar. 1, 1926; s. Charles E. and Lucile (Wolf) H.; m. Olga Landeck, Sept. 21, 1949 (div.); children— Michael, Lucy, Amanda; m Barbara Krueger Meisel, Jan. 1, 1990. Grad., Phillips Acad., Andover, 1944; AB, Princeton U., 1948; LL.B., Columbia U., 1950. Bar; N.Y. 1950, U.S. Dist. Ct. (so. dist.) N.Y. 1951, U.S. Supreme Ct. 1954, U.S. Tax Ct. 1968, U.S. Ct. Appeals (2d cir.) 1962. Ptnr. Wormser, Kiely, Galef & Jacobs, LLP, N.Y.C., 1982-2000, of counsel, from 2000. Trustee Village of Scarsdale, N.Y., 1972-76. Served with USNR, 1944-46 Fellow Am. Bar Found., Am. Coll. Trust and Estate Counsel, N.Y. State Bar Found. (pres.); mem. ABA (ho; of dels.), N.Y. State Bar Assn. (pres. 1986-87), Assn. of Bar of City of N.Y. (past chmn. com. lectures and continuing edn., com. trusts estates surrogate's cts.), Amateur Ski Club of N.Y. (past pres.). Died June 6, 2003.

HEMMETER, CHRISTOPHER BAGWELL, service executive; b. Washington, Oct. 8, 1939; s. George T.and Anne (Bagwell) H.; m. Patricia Kelley, June 21, 1978; children: Mark Maynard, Christopher Rurode, Katherine Kiele, Kelley Patricia, Shane Downey, Brendan Griffin, Holly Maureen. BS, Cornell U., 1962. Chmn., chief exec. officer Hemmeter Corp. (hotel resort developer), Honolulu. Bd. advisors Carter Ctr., Atlanta; bd. dirs. Am. Acad. Achievement, Malibu, Calif. Trustee Cornell U., Ithaca, N.Y. Named Islander of Yr. Honolulu mag., 1988, Entrepreneur of Yr. Johnson Grad. Sch. Cornell U., 1985, Marketer of Yr. Am. Mktg. Assn. (Hawaii chpt.), 1981, Businessman of Yr. Hawaii Bus. mag., 1968, 77; named one of 400 Wealthiest in Am. Forbes mag., 1988. Mem. Young Pres.'s Orgn., Japan-Hawaii Econ. Coun., Waialae Country Club, Oahu Country Club, Outrigger Canoe Club. Republican. Methodist. Home: Honolulu, Hawaii. Died Nov. 27, 2003.

HEMMINGS, DAVID LESLIE EDWARD, actor; b. Nov. 18, 1941; m. Genista Ouvry, 1960; 1 dau.; m. Gayle Hunnicutt, 1969 (dissolved 1975); 1 son; m. Prudence J. de Casembroot, 1976; 2 children. Attended, Glyn Coll., Epsom. In entertainment industry, 1949-2003; appeared in plays including: The Turn of the Screw, English Opera Group, 1954, Jeeves, London, 1975; films include: Five Clues to Fortune, 1957, Saint Joan, 1957, The Heart Within, 1957, Men of Tomorrow, 1958, In The Wake of a Stranger, 1958, No Trees in the Street, 1959, Some People, 1962, Play it Cool, 1962, Live it Up, 1963, Two Left Feet, 1963, The System, 1964, Be My Guest, 1965, Eye of the Devil, 1966, Blow Up, 1966, Camelot, 1967, Barbarella, 1967, Only When I Larf, 1968, The Charge of the Light Brigade, 1968, The Long Day's Dying, 1968, The Best House in London, 1968, Alfred the Great, 1969, Fragment of Fear, 1970, The Walking Stick, 1970, Unman, Wittering & Zigo, 1971, The Love Machine, 1971, Voices, 1973, Don't Worry Momma, 1973, Juggernaut, 1974, Quilp, 1974, Profundo Rosso, 1975, Islands in the Stream, 1975, The Squeeze, 1976, Power Play, 1978, Harlequin, 1980, prisoners, 1981, Beyond Reasonable Doubt, 1982, The Rainbow, 1989, Gladiator, 2000, Last Orders, 2001, Spy Game, 2001, Mean Machine, 2001, Slap Shot 2: Braking the Ice, 2002, Equilibrium, 2002, Gangs of New York, 2002, The Night We Called It a Day, 2003, The League of Extraordinary Gentlemen, 2003; TV movies: Scott Fitzgerald, BBC TV, 1975, The Rime of the Ancient Mariner, ITV, 1978, Charlie Muffin, ITV, 1979, Dr. Jekyll and Mr. Hyde, 1981, Calamity Jane, 1984, Beverly Hills Cowgirl Blues, 1985, The Key to Rebecca, 1985, Harry's Hong Kong, 1987, Three on a Match, 1987, Davy Crockett: Rainbow in the Thunder, 1988, Nightmare Classics, 1989, The Turn of the Screw, 1990, Passport to Murder, 1993, A Mind to Murder, 1995; TV appearances: Out of this World, 1962, Out of the Unknown, 1965, Masquerade, 1983, Airwolf, 1984, Magnum, P.I., 1987, Tales from the Crypt, 1991, L.A. Law, 1991, Northern Exposure, 1992, Kung Fu: The Legend Continues, 1995, Murder in Mind, 2002, Waking the Dead, 2002; dir. feature films: Running Scared, 1972; the 14 (Silver Bear award Berlin Film Festival, 1973), 1973; Disappearance, 1977, Power Play, 1977, David Bowie Stage, 1979, Murder by Decree, 1979, Survivor, 1979, Race to Yankee Zephyr, 1980, Just a Gigolo, 1978, Dark Horse, 1992, Passport to Murder, 1993, Christmas Reunion, 1993, Marker (TV series), 1995; prodr. TV shows Strange Behavior, 1981, Turkey Shoot, 1981; TV miniseries The Key to Rebecca, 1985. Died Dec. 3, 2003.

HENLEY, PRESTON VANFLEET, former banker, financial consultant; b. Fort Madison, Iowa, July 7, 1913; s. Jesse vanFleet and Ruth (Roberts) H.; m. Elizabeth Artis Watts, Mar. 31, 1940 (div. June 1956); children: Preston Edward vanFleet, Stephen Watts, John vanFleet; m. 2d, Helena Margaret Greenslade Nov. 29, 1964; 1 adopted son, Lawrence D. Attended, Tulane U., 1931-34, Loyola U., New Orleans, 1935-36; AB, Calif. State Coll., Santa Barbara, 1939; postgrad., U. Wash., 1939-40, NYU, 1943, 46. Tchg. fellow U. Wash., 1939-40; sr. credit analyst, head credit dept. Chase Nat. Bank, 45th St. br., N.Y.C., 1942-49; Western sales rep. Devoe & Raynolds, Inc., N.Y.C., 1949-51; v.p., comml. loan officer, mgr. credit dept. U.S. Nat. Bank, Portland, Oreg., 1951-72; loan adminstr. Voyageur Bank Group, Eau Claire, Wis.; v.p. Kanabec State Bank, Mora, Minn., Montgomery State Bank, Minn., Park Falls State Bank, Wis., Montello State Bank, Wis., 1972; v.p., mgr. main office, sr. credit officer So. Nev. region Nev. Nat. Bank, Las Vegas, 1973-75; bus. and fin. cons., from 1975. Loan cons. Continental Nat. Bank, Las Vegas, 1983-89; instr. Am. Inst. Banking, Portland, 1952-65, Multomah Coll., Portland, 1956-62, Portland State U., 1961-72, Mt. Hood C.C., 1971-72, Clark county C.C., 1979-83; adv. dir. Vita Plus, Inc., 1979-83; exec. dir. Nev. Minority Purchasing Coun., 1979-80; dir., treas. Consumer Credit Counselling Svc. of Oreg., 1965-72. Contbr. articles to profl. jours. Treas., Oreg. chpt. Leukemia Soc., 1965-66; mem. Menninger Found., 1965-67; trustee, exec. com. St. Rose delima Hosp. Found., 1982-87; dir. So. Nev. chpt. Assn. Part-Time Profls., 1985-87. Served with USNR, 1943-45. Mem. Oreg. Bankers Assn., Robert Morris Assocs. (pres. Oreg. chpt. 1959-60, nat. dir. 1961-64), Nat., Oreg. assns. credit mgmt., Credit Rsch. Found., Inst. Internal Auditors, SAR, Beta Mu, Leaf and Scarab, Alpha Phi Omega, Portland C. of C., Oreg. Reatil Coun. Republican. Episcopalian. Home: Las Vegas, Nev. Died Apr. 12, 2004; Veterans Cemetary Boulder City Nevada.

HENRY, CARL FERDINAND HOWARD, theologian, educator; b. N.Y.C., Jan. 22, 1913; s. Karl F. and Johanna (Vaethroeder) H.; m. Helga Bender, Aug. 17, 1940; children: Paul Brentwood (dec. 1993), Carol Jennifer. BA, Wheaton (Ill.) Coll., 1938, MA, 1940; B.D., No. Baptist Theol. Sem., Chgo., 1941, Th.D., 1942; PhD, Boston U., 1949; Litt.D. (hon.), Seattle-Pacific Coll., 1963, Wheaton Coll., 1968; L.H.D. (hon.), Houghton Coll., 1973; D.D. (hon.), Northwestern Coll., 1979, Gordon-Conwell Theol. Sem., 1984; LL.D (hon.), Hillsdale Coll., 1989. Ordained to ministry Bapt. Ch., 1941; asst. prof., then prof. theology No. Bapt. Theol. Sem., 1942-47; acting dean Fuller Theol. Sem., Pasadena, Calif., 1947, prof., 1947-56, Peyton lectr., 1963, vis. prof., 1980. Vis. prof. theology Wheaton Coll., Gordon Div. Sch., Columbia Bible Coll., 1977, 80, Japan Sch. Theology, 1974, systematic theology and Biblical studies Trinity Evang. Div. Sch., 1974, 87-91, 92-96, Bethel Theol. Sem., W. San Diego, 1988, Denver Conservative Bapt. Sem., 1981, 83, So. Bapt. Theol. Sem., 1988; vis. prof. Eastern Bapt. Theol. Sem., 1969-70, prof.-at-large, 1970-74; lectr.-at-large World Vision, 1974-87; Disting. vis. prof. Christian studies Hillsdale Coll., 1983-84; Disting. vis. prof. systematic theology Calvin Theol. Sem., 1986; faculty mem. flying seminar to Europe and Nr. East, Winona Lake (Ind.) Sch. Theology, 1952; daily radio commentator Sta. KPOL Let the Chips Fall, L.A., 1952-53; chmn. World Congress Evangelism, Berlin, 1966, Consultation Scholars, Washington, 1967; program chmn. Jerusalem Conf. Bibl. Prophecy, Israel, 1971; Latin Am. Theol. Frat. lectr., 1973; lectr. Evangelism Internat., Singapore, 1976, 78, 86, All-India Evang. Conf. on Social Action, Madras, 1979, Liberia Bapt. Theol. Sem., Monrovia, 1982, Cameroun Bapt. Theol. Coll., Ndu, 1982, Japan Christian Inst., Tokyo, 1989; vis. lectr. Asian Ctr. Theol. Studies and Mission, Seoul, Korea, 1974, 74, 76, 78, 80, Teoloski Facultet, Matija Vlacic Illrik, Zagreb, Yugoslavia, 1977, Asian Theol. Sem., Manila, 1980, Soong Sil Univ. Inst. Christian Culture Research, Seoul, 1987, C.S. Lewis Summer Inst., Oxford, 1988, Second Bapt. Ch., Oradea, Romania, 1988, 90, Rutherford Lectures, Edinburgh, Scotland, 1989, Chavanne Scholars' Colloquium on Bibl. Principles and Pub. Policy, Baylor U., 1989, Tyndale Sem., Amsterdam, The Netherlands, 1990, Washington Bapt. Coll. and Sem., 1990-95, Beeson Div. Sch. Samford U., 1994, Acton Soc., 1995, Korea Bapt. Coll. & Sem., Seoul, 1995, So. Baptist Theol. Sem., 1998—; bd. dirs. Inst. Advanced Christian Studies, 1976-79, 81-85, dir. emeritus, 1988—, pres., 1971-74; bd. dirs. Ethics and Pub. Policy Ctr., 1979-96, Inst. Religion and Democracy, 1981-95, v.p., 1985—, Prison Fellowship, 1981—, lectr.-at-large, 1990-94; M.E. Found., 1989—; trustee Gordon Conwell Theol. Sem., 1965-68, Christian Life Commn. Southern Baptist Conv., 1991-93, Elmer Bisbee Found., 1986-91; bd. dirs. Ministers Life and Casualty Union, 1968-77, Riverside Found., 1997, Carl F. H.Henry Inst. for Evangel. Engagement, Sothern Baptist Theological Seminary; co-chmn. Rose Bowl Easter Sunrise Service, 1950-56; main street com. Rockford Inst., 1990—; mem. Christian Life Commn., So. Bapt. Conv., 1991-93; addressed symposium Ctr. Human Values, Moscow, 1993. Author: A Doorway to Heaven, 1941, Successful Church Publicity, 1942, Remaking the Modern Mind, 1948, The Uneasy Conscience of Modern Fundamentalism, 1947, Giving a Reason for Our Hope, 1949, The Protestant Dilemma, 1949, Notes on the Doctrine of God, 1949, Fifty Years of Protestant Theology, 1950, The Drift of Western Thought, 1951, Personal Idealism and Strong's Theology, 1951, Glimpses of a Sacred Land, 1953, Christian Personal Ethics, 1957, Evangelical Responsibility in Contemporary Theology, 1957, Aspects of Christian Social Ethics, 1964, Frontiers in Modern Theology, 1966, The God Who Shows Himself, 1966, Evangelicals at the Brink of Crisis, 1967, Faith at the Frontiers, 1969, A Plea for Evangelical Demonstration, 1971, New Strides of Faith, 1972, Evangelicals in Search of Identity, 1976, God, Revelation and Authority, vols. 1 and 2, 1976, vols. 3 and 4, 1979, vol. 5, 1982, vol. 6,, 1983, The Christian Mindset in a Secular Society, 1984, Christian Countermoves in a Decadent Culture, 1986, Confessions of a Theologian, 1986, Conversations with Carl Henry: Christianity for Today, 1986; Twilight of a Great Civilization, 1988, A Lifetime of Quotable Thoughts: Carl Henry at His Best, 1990, Toward a Recovery of Christian Belief, 1990, The Identity of Jesus of Nazareth, 1992, gods of this age or God of The Ages?, 1994, Has Democracy Had Its Day?, 1996; editor: Contemporary Evangelical Thought, 1957, Revelation and the Bible, 1959, The Biblical Expositor, 1960, Basic Christian Doctrines, 1962, Christian Faith and Modern Theology, 1964, Jesus of Nazareth: Saviour and Lord, 1966, Fundamentals of the Faith, 1969, Horizons of Science, 1978; editor in chief: Baker's Dictionary of Christian Ethics, 1973; co-editor: (with Kenneth Kantzer) Evangelical Affirmations, 1990; cons. editor: Baker's Dictionary of Theology, 1964; editor: Christianity Today, 1956-68, editor-at-large, 1968-77; contbg. editor: World Vision Mag., 1976-87; religion corr. World mag., 1995—. Mem. Capitol Hill Met. Bapt. Ch., Washington, 1956—. Recipient Freedoms Found. award, 1954, 66, Sem. Alumnus of Yr., No. Bapt. Theol. Sem., 1971, Religious Heritage Am. award, 1975, Disting. Social Svc. award Wheaton Coll. Alumni Assn., 1961, J. Elwin Wright award Nat. Assn. of Evangelicals, 1990, Disting. Svc. award Christian Life Commn., So. Bapt. Conv., 1992, 50 Yr. Svc. award Religious Heritage of Am., 1993, Mark O. Hatfield leadership award Cou. Colls. and Univs., 2000; honored with Carl F.H. Henry manuscript collection Syracuse U., 1975—, The Carl F.H. Henry Study and Resource Ctr., Trinity Evang. Divinity Sch., Deerfield, Ill., 1987; fellow Christianity Today Inst., 1987-94; Soc. Sci. Study of Religion fellow, 1992—. Mem. AAAS, Am. Soc. Christian Ethics, Am. Acad. Religion, Am. Theol. Soc. (v.p. 1974-75, pres. 1979-80), Nat. Assn. Envangelicals (bd. adminstrn. 1956-70), Am. Philos. Assn., Am. Soc. Ch. History,Soc. Oriental Rsch. Evang. Theol. Soc. (pres. 1969-70), Conf. Faith and History, Soc. Christian Philosophers, Nat. Assn. Bapt. Profs. of Religion, Evang. Press Assn. (hon. life), Soc. Bible Lit. Achievements include being subject of festschift God and Culture, 1993. Died Dec. 7, 2003.

HENSCHEL, MILTON G. church administrator; b. Pomona, NJ; Mem. governing body Jehovah's Witnesses, Bklyn., 1971—2003; pres. Watch Tower Bible and Tract Society Inc of Pa., 1992—2003. Jehovah'S Witness. Died Mar. 22, 2003.

HENSON, LOUISE ADRIEANNE, political activist; b. Monroeville, Pa., Nov. 21, 1929; m. Phillip C. Henson, Aug. 14, 1947; children: Gail Henson Dahlquist, Helen Henson-Hale, Van Emden. Student, Colo. State U., 1947-48. Activities in Utah Dem. politics include Utah Dem. nat. committeewoman, 1988-96, mem. Utah Clinton/Gore '96 steering com., super del. nat. convs., 1992, 96, del. nat. convs., 1988, 1980, exec. com. Utah Dem. party, 1988-96, campaign mgr. legis. dist. 13, 1990, 92, Davis county coord. Ted Wilson for Gov., 1984, Ted Wilson for Senate, 1982, Matheson for Gov., 1976, 1980; other activities include office vol. Nature Conservancy, 1996, 97, mem. Institutional Coun., Utah Tech. Coll., 1978-82, area capt. Am. Heart Assn., 1986-90, mem. Citizens Adv. Com. Davis Sch. Dist., 1980-82, leader Girl Scouts U.S., Brownies, Cub Scouts, Little League scorekeeper, Sunday Sch. tchr., vol. Am. Cancer Soc., Am. Diabetes Soc., Am. Heart Assn. Recipient Disting. Svc. award Dem. party, 1996, Eleanor Roosevelt award, 1996, Davis County Candidates Appreciation award, 1980. Mem. Nature Conservancy, Nat. Wildlife Assn., Sierra Club, Utahns for Choice, Planned Parenthood, Habitat for Humanity. Home: Oregon City, Oreg. Died Sept. 22, 1999.

HEPBURN, KATHARINE HOUGHTON, actress; d. Thomas N. and Katharine (Houghton) H.; m. Ludlow Ogden Smith (div.) AB, Bryn Mawr Coll., 1928; LHD (hon.), Columbia U., 1992. Actress: (films) A Bill of Divorcement, 1932, Christopher Strong, 1933, Morning Glory, 1933 (Acad. award for best performance by actress 1934), Little Women, 1933, Spitfire, 1934, The Little Minister, 1934, Alice Adams, 1935, Break of Hearts, 1935, Sylvia Scarlett, 1936, Mary of Scotland, 1936, A Woman Rebels, 1936, Quality Street, 1937, Stage Door, 1937, Bringing up Baby, 1938, Holiday, 1938, The Philadelphia Story, 1940 (N.Y. Critic's award 1940), Woman of the Year, 1941, Keeper of the Flame, 1942, Stage Door Canteen, 1943, Dragon Seed, 1944, Without Love, 1945, Undercurrent, 1946, Sea of Grass, 1946, Song of Love, 1947, State of the Union, 1948, Adam's Rib, 1949, The African Queen, 1951, Pat and Mike,

1952, Summertime, 1955, The Rainmaker, 1956, The Iron Petticoat, 1956, The Desk Set, 1957, Suddenly Last Summer, 1959, Long Day's Journey into Night, 1962 (Best Actress, Cannes Internat. Film Festival), Guess Who's Coming to Dinner, 1967, (Acad. award for best actress 1968),The Lion in Winter, 1968 (Acad. award for best actress 1969), Madwoman of Chaillot, 1969, Trojan Women, 1971, A Delicate Balance, 1973, Rooster Cogburn, 1975, Olly, Olly, Oxen Free, 1978, On Golden Pond, 1981 (Acad. award for best actress 1981), George Stevens: A Filmmaker's Journey, 1984, The Ultimate Solution of Grace Quigley, 1985, Love Affair, 1994; (plays) The Czarina, 1928, The Big Pond, 1928, Night Hostess, 1928, These Days, 1928, Death Takes a Holiday, 1929, A Month in the Country, 1930, Art and Mrs. Bottle, 1930, The Warrior's Husband, 1932, Lysistrata, 1932, The Lake, 1933, Jane Eyre, 1937, The Philadelphia Story, 1939, Without Love, 1942, As You Like It, 1950, The Millionairess, Eng. and U.S.A., 1952, The Taming of the Shrew, The Merchant of Venice, Measure for Measure,, Eng. and Australia, 1955, Merchant of Venice, Much Ado about Nothing, Am. Shakespeare Festival, 1957, toured later, 1958, Twelfth Night, Antony and Cleopatra, Am. Shakespeare Festival, 1960, Coco, 1969-70, toured, 1971, The Taming of the Shrew, 1970, A Matter of Gravity, 1976-78, West Side Waltz, 1981, (TV movies) The Glass Menagerie, 1973, Love among the Ruins, 1975, The Corn Is Green, 1979, Mrs. Delafield Wants to Marry, 1986; Laura Lansing Slept Here, 1988, The Man Upstairs, 1992, This Can't Be Love, 1994, One Christmas, 1994; narrator, co-writer documentary Katharine Hepburn: All About Me, 1993; author: The Making of the African Queen, 1987, (autobiography) Me, 1991. Recipient gold medal as world's best motion picture actress Internat. Motion Picture Expn., Venice, Italy, 1934, ann. award Shakespeare Club, N.Y.C., 1950, award Whistler Soc., 1957, Woman of Yr. award Hasty Pudding Club, 1958, outstanding achievement award for fostering finest ideals of acting profession, 1980, lifetime achievement award Coun. Fashion Designers Am., 1986, award Kennedy Ctr. Awards, 1990. Home: New York, NY. Died June 29, 2003.

HERBERT, VICTOR DANIEL, medical educator, educator; b. N.Y.C., Feb. 22, 1927; s. Allan Charles and Rosaline (Margolis) H.; children from previous marriages: Robert, Steven, Kathy, Alissa, Laura. BS in Chemistry, Columbia U., 1948, MD, 1952, JD, 1974. Intern Walter Reed Army Med. Ctr., Washington, 1952-53; resident Montefiore Hosp., Bronx, N.Y., 1954-55; asst. instr., rsch. fellow Albert Einstein Coll. of Medicine, Bronx, 1955-57; rsch. asst. in hematology Mt. Sinai Hosp., N.Y.C., 1958-59; from instr. to asst. prof. Harvard U. Thorndike Lab., Boston, 1959-64; assoc. prof., prof. pathology and medicine Columbia U., N.Y.C., 1964-72; prof. medicine Mt. Sinai Sch. Medicine, N.Y.C., from 1964; prof., asst. chair of medicine SUNY Downstate Med. Ctr., Bklyn., 1976-84; chief hematology & nutrition rsch. lab. Bronx Vets. Affairs Med. Ctr., from 1970. Chmn. medicine Hahnemann U. Sch. Medicine and Med. Ctr., Phila., 1984-85; prof. medicine, chair com. to strenghthen nutrition Mt. Sinai Sch. Medicine, N.Y.C., 1985—; mem. sci. group on nutrition anemias and com. on recommendable dietary nutrient intakes WHO, Geneva, 1964—; mem. com. on dietary requirements for iron, vitamin A, vitamin B12, folic acid, WHO/FAO, 1968—; mem. interdepartmental com. on human nutrition rsch. Exec. Office of the Pres. of the U.S., 1979—. Author: Nutrition Cultism: Facts & Fictions, 1981; co-author: Vitamins & Health Food: The Great American Hustle, 1981, Genetic Nutrition: Designing a Diet Based on Your Family Medical History, 1993 (republished, retitled The Healing Diet 1995), The Vitamin Pushers: How the Health Food Industry is Selling America A Bill of Goods, 1994; editor, author: The Mount Sinai School of Medicine Complete Book of Nutrition, 1990, Total Nutrition: The Only Guide You'll Ever Need: From the Mount Sinai Sch. Medicine, 1995; contbr. more than 800 articles to profl. jours. Lt. col. U.S. Army, ETO, 1944-46, Korea, 1952-54, Vietnam, 1965, 66, 73, Mid. East. 1990-91. Recipient Middleton award U.S. Dept. Vets. Affairs, 1978, Commr.'s Citation, FDA, 1984. Fellow ACP (master), Royal Soc. of Medicine (London); mem. Am. Soc. Hematology (Parliamentarian 1975—), Am. Fedn. Clin. Research, Am. Soc. Clin. Investigation, Assn. Am. Physicians, Am. Inst. Nutrition (Fellow award 1993), Am. Soc. Clin. Nutrition (pres. 1980-81, Herman award 1986, McCollum award 1972, Van Slyke award 1990). Avocations: theatre, Judo. Home: New York, NY. Died Nov. 19, 2002.

HERIN, DAVID V. lawyer; b. Bemidji, Minn., Aug. 17, 1944; s. Robert and Betty (Smithkey) H.; m. Cynthia Ann Duran, Apr. 12, 1969; children: David, Monica Ann. BA, Baylor U., Waco, Tex., 1966; JD, Baylor U., 1969. Bar: Tex. 1969, U.S. Dist. Ct. (so. dist.) Tex. 1973, U.S. Ct. Appeals (5th cir.) 1973, U.S. Tax Ct. 1973, U.S. Supreme Ct. 1973, U.S. Ct. Appeals (11th cir.) 1980. Assoc. Fischer & Fischer, Corpus Christi, Tex., 1973-80, Barnhart & Luther, Corpus Christi, 1980-81; judge 148th Jud. Dist. Tex., Corpus Christi, 1981-83; of counsel Coover & Coover, Corpus Christi, 1983-85; ptnr. Herin & Johnson, Corpus Christi, 1985-87, Herin & Miller, Corpus Christi, 1987-90; pvt. practice law David V. Herin, P.C., Corpus Christi, from 1990. Capt. USAF, 1969-73. Mem. Tex. Bar Assn., Nueces County Bar Assn. (pres. 1980-81, Outstanding Young Lawyer 1981), Tex. Assn. Bank Counsel. Republican. Home: Corpus Christi, Tex. Died Aug. 3, 2000.

HERRING, JACK WILLIAM, retired English language educator; b. Waco, Tex., Aug. 28, 1925; s. Benjamin Oscar and Bertha (Shiplet) H.; m. Daphne L. Norred, June 10, 1944; children— Penny Elizabeth, Paul William. BA, Baylor U., 1947, MA, 1948; PhD, U. Pa., 1958. English instr. Howard Coll., Birmingham, Ala., 1948-50; assoc. prof., acting chmn. dept. English Grand Canyon Coll., Phoenix, 1951-55; asst. prof. English Ariz. State U., Tempe, 1955-59; dir. Armstrong Browning Library, Baylor U., 1959-85, asso. prof. English, 1959-62, prof. English, 1962-73, Margaret Root Brown prof. Robert Browning studies, 1973-97; ret. English prof. Beijing Second Fgn. Lang. Inst., 1984-85, Shaghai Inst. Mech. Engring., 1989-90, People's Republic China. Author: Browning's Old School Fellow, 1972; editor: Complete Poetry of Robert Browning. Mem.: Kiwanis (pres. Waco club 1976-77, lt. gov. div. 23 1983-84). Avocations: travel to united kingdom, europe, china and soviet union. Home: Waco, Tex. Deceased.

HERRMAN, GEORGE ROSS, real estate executive; b. Kokomo, Ind., Dec. 22, 1914; s. George and Ruth (Ross) H.; m. Helen Jeanne Ousley; children: Nancy Jeanne, George R. II, John O. BS, Ind. U., 1938. Enlisted Air Corps U.S. Army, 1940, ret., 1964; airline capt. Pan-Am. Airways-Africa, Ltd., Accra and Khartoum, 1941-42; chief test pilot San Antonio Air Depot, 1942-43; founding. dir. Cen. Test Pilot Sch. U.S. Air Corps, San Antonio, 1943-44, comdr. Cen. India Air Depot Agra, 1944-45; dir. personnel instrn. Air Univ., Maxwell AFB, Ala., 1948-51; chief logistics operation U.S. Army, Washington, 1961-64; sales mgr. Better Homes Realty, Arlington, Va., 1965-66; pres. Rand Real Estate Co., Alexandria, Va., from 1966. Air attache to Buenos Aires and Ascension, Paraguay Dept. State, Washington, 1954-56 Mem. Nat. Assn. Realtors, Va. Assn. Realtors, Northern Va. Bd. Realtors (Pioneer award 1984). Republican. Episcopalian. Avocation: sailing. Home: Alexandria, Va. Deceased.

HERSEY, DAVID FLOYD, information resources management consultant, retired government official; b. Balboa, C.Z., Jan. 7, 1928; s. Ralph George and Marie M. (Ortiz) H.; m. Phyllis May Peterson, Aug. 26, 1961; children: David Floyd, Ruth Ellen, Thomas Owen. BS, Trinity U., 1948; MS, U. Ill., 1949; PhD, Washington U., St. Louis, 1952. Diplomate: Am. Acad. Microbiology. Assoc. dir. Sci. Info. Exch., Smithsonian Instn., Washington, 1961-63, dep. dir., 1964-71, pres., 1972-82; health sci. adminstr. FDA, 1984-90. Mem. virus and rickettsial study sect. USPHS, 1957-61; cons. Microbiol. Assos., Inc., 1960-70, Cooke Engring. Co., Arlington, Va., 1969-72 Contbr. articles on microbiology and info. sci. to profl. jours. Commd. 1st lt. U.S. Air Force, 1952; advanced through grades to col. Res. 1973; chief clin. lab. 3700th USAF Hosp., 1952-54, Lackland AFB, Tex.; established 1st USAF Epidemiol. Lab., 1957-58; asst. chief virology br. Armed Forces Inst. Pathology, 1960-61, Washington; resigned 1961. Decorated Air Force Commendation medal Mem. Acad. Medicine. Home: Silver Spring, Md. Died Aug. 24, 2002.

HERSHCOPF, BERTA RUTH, psychotherapist, writer; b. N.Y.C., Oct. 1, 1924; d. Samuel and Marian (Gzinterman) Feinman; m. Jack Hershcopf, June 11, 1947; children: Shelley, Amy, David. AA, Morris Jr. Coll., Morristown, N.J., 1942; BA, Douglass Coll., 1944; cert., Postgrad. Ctr. for Mental Health, N.Y.C., 1973, N.Y. Med. Coll., 1977. Dir. U.S.O., Nebr., Wyo., N.Y., 1944-46; psychiatric clin. counselor Long Island Jewish Hillside Med. Ctr., New Hyde Park, N.Y., 1974-75; counseling therapist Mt. Sinai Hosp., N.Y.C., 1977-78; asst. dir. Psychoanalytic Ctr., N.Y.C., 1980-82; pvt. practice N.Y.C., from 1973; dir. Am. Counseling and Psychotherapy Svcs., N.Y.C., from 1981. Cons., workshop leader Women's Rsch. Project CUNY, N.Y.C., 1975-76; cons. Nat. Urban League, 1979; workshop leader Ctr. for Interpersonal Growth at Fordham U., N.Y.C., 1979-80. Articles in jour. and nat. newpapers. Environ. activist, N.Y.C., 1993—. Mem. N.Y. State Assn. Practicing Psychotherapists (cert.), Am. Asn. for Counseling and Devel., Am. Mental Health Counselors Assn. Avocations: classical music, ballroom dancing, table tennis, nature, theatre. Died Aug. 25, 2002.

HERSHEY, LINDA ANN, neurology and pharmacology educator; b. Marion, Ind., Jan. 15, 1947; d. Matthew John and Janice Elaine Kwolek; m. Charles Owen Hershey, May 1, 1976; children: Edward, William, Erin. BS, Purdue U., 1968; PhD, Washington U., St. Louis, 1973, MD, 1975. Diplomate Am. Bd. Psychiatry and Neurology. Resident in neurology Barnes Hosp., St. Louis, 1976-78; fellow in clin. pharmacology Strong Meml. Hosp., Rochester, N.Y., 1978-80; asst. prof. neurology Case Western Res. U., Cleve., 1980-86; assoc. prof.neurology and pharmacology SUNY, Buffalo, 1986-94, prof. neurology and pharmacology, from 1994. Chief neurology svc. VA WNY Healthcare Sys., from 1986; sr. examiner Am. Bd. Psychiatry and Neurology, from 1997. Co-author: Handbook of Dementing Illnesses, 1994, Essentials of Pharmacology, 1995, Practice of Geriatrics, 1998, Hypertension Primer, 1999, Management of Ischemic Stroke, 2000, Hypertension Primer, 2002; mem. editl. bd.: Clin. Pharmacology and Therapeutics, from 1993, Stroke, from 1995; co-author: Conn's Curr Ther, 2003. Co-dir. Alzheimers Diseases Assistance Ctr., Buffalo, 1994—99; elder Univ. Presbyn. Ch., Buffalo, 1995—99, from 2002. Grantee, Sterling-Winthrop Co., 1992—96, Lorex Pharms., 1995—96, Parke-Davis, 1990—92, 1996—98, Nat. Inst. Neurol. and Communicative Disorders and Stroke, 1994—98, Bayer Pharms., 1998—99, Ortho-McNeil Pharms., 1999—2002, Novartis Pharms., 2000—02, Schwarz Bioscis., 2001—03, Pharmacia, from 2002, Janssen Pharms., 2002—03, Kyowa Pharms., 2002—03. Fellow Am. Acad. Neurology, Am. Neurol. Assn.; mem. Am. Soc. Clin. Pharmacology and Therapeutics, Am. Heart Assn. (mem. exec. com. stroke coun. 1993-97, chmn. program com. stroke coun. 1993-97). Achievements include evaluating use of MRI in patients with vascular dementia, describing natural history of vascular and mixed dementia, validating cognitive and functional screening instruments in patients with vascular dementia, reviewing stroke types and prevention strategies in women, comparing various presenile dementias, assessing the role of hypertension in the development of dementia and developing VA practice guidelines for treatment of Alzheimer's disease. Home: Amherst, NY. Deceased.

HERSKOWITZ, IRA, molecular geneticist; b. Bklyn., July 14, 1946; BS in Biology, Calif. Inst. Tech., 1967; PhD in Microbiology, MIT, 1971; PhD (hon.), St. Louis U., 1997. From asst. to full prof. biology U. Oreg., Eugene, 1972-81; assoc. Inst. Molecular Biology, U. Oreg., Eugene, 1972-81; prof. dept. biochemistry and biophysics U. Calif., San Francisco, from 1981, chmn. dept., 1990-95, head divsn. genetics, 1981—2000, co-dir. program in human genetics, 1997—2003, prof. dept. biopharm. scis., 2000—03. Mem. genetics study sect. NIH, Bethesda, Md., 1986—90; mem. sci. rev. bd. in genetics Howard Hughes Med. Inst., Bethesda, 1986—94, mem. med. adv. bd., 1995—97; vis. prof. Coll. de France, Paris, 1992; sci. adv. bd. Tularik, Inc., 1992—96; mem. awards jury Albert Lasker Med. Rsch., 1994—2002; mem. sci. adv. com. Inst. Cancer Rsch. Fox Chase Cancer Ctr., 1995—99; bd. sci. counsellors Nat. Cancer Inst., 1996—2000; advisor Merck Genome Rsch. Inst., 1996—2000; mem. sci. adv. bd. Fred Hutchison Cancer Rsch. Ctr., 2000—03, DOE Joint Genome Inst., 2001—03; mem. adv. coun. Nat. Inst. Gen. Med. Scis., NIH, 2002—03. Assoc. editor Virology, 1976-81, Genetics, 1982-87, Ann. Rev. Genetics, 1984-89; editor Jour. Molecular Biology, 1982-86, assoc. editor 1986-87; mem. editl. bd. Molecular Biology of the Cell, 1997-2000, 1986-2003, Trends in Genetics, 1990-2003; mem. bd. reviewing editors Sci., 1991-96. Mem. vis. com. for dept. biology MIT, 1982-2000; mem. vis. com. divsn. biology Calif. Inst. Tech., 1999-2003; mem. coun. Am. Soc. Cell Biology, 1996-99; sci. adv. bd. Sandler Program in Asthma Rsch., 1999-2003. Recipient Howard Taylor Ricketts award, U. Chgo., 1992, Disting. Alumni award Calif. Inst. Tech., 1994, Rosentiel award Brandeis U.; named Streisinger lectr. U. Oreg., 1984, Harvey Soc. lectr., 1986, Mendel lectr. Genetical Soc. Gt. Britain, 1991, Bateson lectr. John Innes Inst., Norwich, UK, Yanofsky lectr., Stanford U., 2001, Hopwood lectr., John Innes Inst., 2001, Lewis S. Rosenthal award, 2003. Fellow: AAAS, Am. Soc. Microbiology (Eli Lilly award 1983), Am. Acad. Arts and Scis., MacArthur Found.; mem.: NAS (sci. reviewing award 1985), Genetics Soc. Am. (pres. 1985, Thomas Hunt Morgan award, medal 1988). Achievements include rsch. in control of gene expression in yeast, cell signalling and growth control, cell morphogenesis, pharmacogenetics and drug resistance. Home: San Francisco, Calif. Died Apr. 28, 2003.

HERTZ, ROY, physician, educator, researcher; b. Cleve., June 19, 1909; s. Aaron Daniel and Bertha (Lichtman) H.; m. Pearl Fennell, June 24, 1934 (dec. 1962); children: Margaret, Jeremy; m. Dorothy Anne Wright Oberdorfer, Nov. 9, 1965. AB, U. Wis., 1930, PhD, 1934, MD, 1939, DSc (hon.), 1986; MPH, Johns Hopkins U., 1940. Rsch. assoc. U. Wis., Madison, 1930-34; instr. pharmacology Howard U., Washington, 1934-35; rsch. fellow Brown U., Providence, 1935-36, U. Wis., 1936-39; chief endocrinology br. Nat. Cancer Inst., Bethesda, Md., 1941-66; sci. dir. Nat. Inst. Child Health, Bethesda, 1966-67; prof. ob-gyn George Washington U., Washington, 1967-68, chief reprodn. rsch., 1968-69; assoc. dir. The Population Council, N.Y.C., 1969-73; rsch. prof. pharmacology, ob-gyn. George Washington U., Washington, 1973-83, prof. emeritus, from 1983. Scientist emeritus NIH, Bethesda, Md., 1987—. Recipient Lasker Med. Research award, N.Y.C., 1972, Cancer Research award Internat. Coll. Surgeons, 1969. Fellow ACP, Am. Coll. Ob-gyn, Am. Assn. Ob-gyn (hon.); mem. AAAS, Nat. Acad. Scis., The Endocrine Soc. (v.p. 1960, Fred Conrad Koch award 1996), Chilean Med. Soc. (hon.), Argentine Med. Soc. (hon.). Avocations: gardening, travel. Home: Hollywood, Md. Died Oct. 28, 2002.

HERWALD, SEYMOUR WILLIS, retired engineering consultant; b. Cleve., Jan. 17, 1917; s. Robert and Sarah (Gidansky) H.; m. Geraldine Greenberger; children: Melvyn, Michelle, Bruce, Steven. BSME, Case Western Res. U., 1938; MSME, U. Pitts., 1940, PhD in Math., 1944. Registered profl. engr., Pa. Mgr. engring. Air Arm div. Westinghouse Electric Co., Balt., 1951-59, v.p. research Pitts., 1959-62, group v.p. electronic components and specialty products, 1962-68, v.p. engring., 1968-75, v.p. strategic resources, 1975-77, v.p. corp. services, 1977-79; pvt. practice cons. Pitts., 1979-82. Mem. adv. com. sci. edn. NSF, Washington, 1975-76, adv. com. Processing Research Inst. Carnegie Mellon U., Pitts., 1972-76, com. sch. engring. U. Pitts., 1968-70; chmn. tech. vis. com. Case Inst. Tech., Cleve., 1972-75, mem. bd. overseers, 1972-75. Patentee in field. Mem. exec. com. bd. trustees Montefiore Hosp., Pitts., 1971-76, chmn., 1977-79; mem. trustees planning com. Univ. Health Ctr. U. Pitts., 1974-76, sci. adv. bd. USAF, 1956-70. Fellow IEEE (pres. 1968, treas. 1965-66, bd. dirs. 1964-72, fin. com. 1966), Inst. Research Engrs.; mem. ASME. Clubs: Duquesne (Pitts.). Avocations: tennis, golfing. Home: Mashpee, Mass. Died Aug. 1998.

HERZOG, RICHARD F. retired science educator; b. Vienna, Mar. 13, 1911; PhD, U. Vienna, 1933, hon. degree, 1983. Prof. physics U. Vienna, 1950-53, Air Force Cambridge Rsch. Ctr., Bedford, Mass., 1953-58; dir. space sci. lab. GCA Corp., Bedford, 1958-73; prof. physics and astronomy U. So. Miss., Hattiesburg. Hon. chmn. Sims-V

Conf., 1985. Issue of Jour. Mass Spectrometry and Ion Physics in his honor, 1971. Mem. Am. Soc. for Mass Spectrometry, Am. Inst. Physics, Sigma Pi Sigma. Home: Pembroke Pines, Fla. Deceased.

HESS, H. OBER, lawyer, director; b. Royersford, Pa., Nov. 8, 1912; s. Samuel Harley and Annamae (Wenger) H.; m. Dolores Groke, May 18, 1940; children: Antonine (Mrs. Joseph J. Gal), Roberta (Mrs. Edward S. Trippe), Liesa (Mrs. Arleigh P. Helfer, Jr.), Kristina (Mrs. Charles H. Bonner). AB, Ursinus Coll., 1933, LL.D. (hon.), 1979; LL.B., Harvard U., 1936; LL.D. (hon.), Muhlenberg Coll., 1964; D.F.A. (hon.), Phila. Coll. Art, 1981. Of counsel to Ballard, Spahr, Andrews & Ingersoll, Phila. Editor: Fiduciary Rev., 1941-2004, The Nature of a Humane Society, 1976. Former mem. exec. coun. Luth. Ch. in Am.; trustee Lankenau Hosp., Phila. U. of the Arts; former chmn. Mary J. Drexel Home, Lankenau Med. Rsch. Ctr.; former bd. dirs., sec. Phila. Orch. Assn., Acad. Music Phila.; former mem. Harvard Overseers Com. to Visit Law Sch.; former nat. chmn. Harvard Law Sch. Fund. Mem. ABA, Pa., Phila., Montgomery County bar assns., Harvard Law Sch. Assn. Clubs: Philadelphia, Union League, Philadelphia Country (Phila.). Home: Gladwyne, Pa. Died Feb. 18, 2004.

HESSELTINE, CLIFFORD WILLIAM, retired microbiologist; b. Brighton, Iowa, Apr. 4, 1917; s. Merlin Jerome and Charlotte Jane (Owen) H.; m. Harriet Elsie Herm, Aug. 8, 1941; children: Christopher, Nancy, Anna, Rise. BS, U. Iowa, 1940; PhD, U. Wis., 1950. Rsch. asst. U. Wis., Madison, 1940-42, instr., 1946-47; researcher Lederle Lab., Pearl River, N.Y., 1947-53; mgr. rsch. USDA, Peoria, Ill., 1953-87; cons. in field, 1987-99. Speaker profl confs. and meetings. Author: (with others) Underexploited Microbial Processes with Potential Economic Value, 1979, Mycotoxins in Human and Animal Health, 1977, Food, Fuel and Fertilizer from Organic Waste, 1981, Indigenous Fermented Food of Non-Western Origin, 1986, Control of the Microbial Contamination of Foods andFeeds in International Trade: Microbial Standards and Specifications, 1982, Mycotoxins: Economic and Health Risks, 1989. With U.S. Army, 1942-46. Recipient numerous awards in field; recipient 3rd Order of Rising Sun award Emperor of Japan, 1983. Fellow Am. Acad. Microbiology; mem. Am. chem. Soc., Bot. Soc. Am., Mycological Soc. Am. (pres. 1963-64), Soc. Ill. Bacteriologists, Soc. Indsl. Microbiology (pres. 1958), Torrey Bot. Club, AAAS, Am. Phytopathology Soc., Brit. Mycological Soc., Japan Mycological Soc., Brit. Soc. Applied Bacteriology, Japanese Assn. Mycotoxicology, Indian Phytopathological Soc. Lutheran. Home: Peoria, Ill. Died Apr. 15, 1999.

HETZEL, FREDERICK ARMSTRONG, publisher, editor; b. Pitts., Sept. 6, 1930; s. Louis and Jean Bowman (Armstrong) H.; m. Nancy Miller, Dec. 14, 1957; children: Jean Armstrong, Jennifer Elizabeth, Frederick Armstrong, Emily Miller. BA, Washington and Jefferson Coll., 1952; MA, U. Va., 1957. Assoc. editor Inst. Early Am. History and Culture, Williamsburg, Va., 1957-61; asso. editor U. Pitts. Press, 1961-64, dir., 1964—94. Sec., dir. United Pocahontas Coal Co., 1960-68; dir. Second Nat. Bank, Connellsville, Pa., 1972-75; commentator WQED-FM, 1976-79 Mem. editorial bd.: Western Pa. Hist. Mag., 1981—1994. Bd. dirs., sec. U. Pitts. Book Center, 1969-72, chmn., 1970-72; bd. dirs. Loaves and Fishes Coffee House, 1969-70; trustee Winchester-Thurston Sch., 1969-77, 79-83, mem. exec. com., 1970-77, 79-83, chmn., 1971-74; bd. dirs. Mendelssohn Choir Pitts., 1977-79; bd. dirs. Pitts. Dance Council, 1977-83, vice pres., 1978-79. Served to 1st lt. AUS, 1952-54, Korea. Decorated Bronze Star. Mem. Assn. Am. Univ. Presses (dir. 1972-74), Am. Hist. Assn., Pitts. History and Landmarks Found., Hist. Soc. Western Pa., Pitts. Bibliophiles (vice chmn. 1970-72, chmn. 1972-73), Phi Beta Kappa, Phi Kappa Sigma, Pi Delta Epsilon. Clubs: University (Pitts.). Presbyterian. Home: Pittsburgh, Pa. Died Sept. 13, 2003.

HEWITT, FRANKIE LEA, theater producer; b. Roger Mills Cty, Okla., June 17, 1931; d. Frank David and Mary Lou (Wood) Teague; m. Alonzo Robert Childers, Dec. 10, 1951 (div. 1955); m. Don S. Hewitt, June 8, 1963 (div. 1974); children: Jilian, Lisa. Grad., Napa (Calif.) High Sch., 1949. Women's editor Napa Daily Register, 1949-51; asst. advt. dir. Rose Marie Reid Swim Suits, L.A., 1951-52; writer Calif. Inst. Social Welfare, L.A., 1954-55; writer, legis. aide Nat. Inst. Social Welfare, Washington, 1956-58; staff dir. U.S. Senate Subcom. to Investigate Juvenile Deliquency, Washington, 1959-61; pub. affairs advisor U.S. Mission to UN, N.Y.C., 1961-63; founder, producing dir. Ford's Theatre Soc., Washington, from 1967. Recipient Congl. Arts Caucus award, 1993; named Washingtonian of Yr., Washingtonian Mag., 1978, Woman of Yr., Women's Equity Action League, 1981, YWCA, 1986. Avocations: needlepoint, hiking. Home: Ardsley, NY. Died Feb. 28, 2003.

HEYMAN, GEORGE HARRISON, JR., securities company executive; b. N.Y.C., June 29, 1916; s. George H. and Anne Heyman; m. Edythe Forman, Mar. 17, 1946; children: William H., John A. BBA, CCNY, 1936; MBA, NYU, 1938. Assoc. Abraham & Co., N.Y.C., 1936-49, gen. partner, 1949-72; pres., dir. Abraham & Co. Inc., 1972-75; chmn. investment com., mng. dir. Lehman Bros. Kuhn Loeb Inc., 1975-83; adv. dir. Lehman Bros. Inc., 1983-97. Pres. Fedn. Jewish Philanthropies N.Y., 1969-71, chmn. bd. trustees, 1977-80; fellow pres.'s coun. Tulane U.; trustee NYU. Capt. AUS, 1941-46. Recipient Louis Marshall medal Jewish Theol. Sem. Am., 1976, Townsend Harris medal Alumni Assn. CCNY, 1976, Gallatin medal NYU. Mem. Harmonie Club, Sunningdale Country Club, Beta Gamma Sigma. Home: New York, NY. Died June 1, 2003.

HEYMAN, THERESE THAU, curator, art historian; b. N.Y.C., Sept. 22, 1930; d. Morris and Mathilda H.; m. Ira Michael Heyman; 1 child, James N. heyman. BA, Smith Coll., Northampton, Mass., 1951; MA, Yale U., 1958. Cert. Mus. Mgmt. Inst., 1981. Curatorial asst. Yale U., New Haven, 1963; sr. curator Oakland (Calif.) Mus., 1963-93; former guest curator Nat. Mus. Am. Art, Washington. Former guest curator Santa Barbara (Calif.) Mus. Art. Exhibited in group shows Oakland Mus., 1972, Oakland Mus., 1973, 74, 78, 82, 85, Calif. Prints, 1975. Bd. dirs. Alameda County Art Commn., Oakland, 1970-79. Mem. Print Coun. Am., Oracle-Photography Group. Home: Berkeley, Calif. Died Jan. 16, 2004.

HICKCOX, CURTISS BRONSON, retired anesthesiologist; b. Watertown, Conn., July 14, 1913; s. Frank Bronson and Elizabeth May (Atwood) H.; m. Helen Theresa Burke, June 7, 1941; children: Maryann Elizabeth, Patricia Katherine, Curtiss Bronson, Edward Frank. S.B., Middlebury (Vt.) Coll., 1934; MD, Tufts Coll., Boston, 1938. Diplomate: Am. Bd. Anesthesiology (dir.; sec.-treas. 1948-58, pres. 1959). Intern Waterbury (Conn.) Hosp., 1938-39, cons. staff, 1955-80; resident in anesthesiology Hartford (Conn.) Hosp., 1939-41, clin. asst., 1942-43, acting chief, 1942-45, asst., 1943-44, asso., 1944-45, acting dir., 1963-64, dir. dept., 1964-73, sr. anesthesiologist, 1959-79, hon. anesthesiologist, 1979—; prof., head dept. anesthesiology Temple U. Med. Sch. and Hosp., 1946-49; med. dir. Hartford Surg. Center, 1976-83. Mem. Adv. Bd. Med. Specialists, 1948-59, exec. com., 1958-59 Mem. Am. Soc. Anesthesiologists (bd. dirs. 1943-49, sec. 1946-49), A.M.A., Conn., Hartford County, Hartford med. socs., New Eng., Conn. socs. anesthesiologists, Kappa Delta Rho. Roman Catholic. Home: Williston, Vt. Deceased.

HIGGINS, DICK (RICHARD CARTER HIGGINS), writer, publisher, composer, artist; b. Cambridge, Eng., Mar. 15, 1938; came to U.S., 1939; s. Carter Chapin and Katharine (Bigelow) H.; m. Alison Knowles, May 31, 1960 (div. 1970); children: Hannah and Jessica (twins); m. Alison Knowles, 1984. Student, Yale U., 1957; BS in English, Columbia U., 1960; postgrad., Manhattan Sch. Printing, 1960-61; MA in English, NYU, 1977; studied with John Cage and Henry Cowell, 1958-59. Co-founder Happenings (Theater) movement, N.Y.C., 1958, Fluxus movement, N.Y.C., 1961; founder Something Else Press, N.Y.C., 1963-73; originator concept, developer (visual, mus. and lit. publs.) Intermedia, 1965; founder, operator Unpublished Edits., West Glover, Vt., 1972-85 (renamed Printed Editions, 1978, in operation until 1986). Operator Something Else Gallery, 1966-69; tchr. Calif. Inst. Arts, 1970-71; mem. lit. panel N.Y. State Coun. on Arts, 1979-81; rsch. assoc. in visual arts, SUNY-Purchase, 1983-89; vis. Clark prof. in art Williams Coll., fall 1987, rsch. assoc. in history of art, 1989—; tchr. Salzburg (Austria) Sommerakademic, 1973, Lund (Sweden) U., 1997. Author: What are legends, 1960, Jefferson's birthday/Postface, 1964, foew & ombwhnw, 1968, Die fabelhafte Geträume von Taifun-Willi, 1969, Computers for the arts, 1970, amigo, 1972, A book about love and war and death, 1972, The Ladder to the moon, 1973, For Eugene in Germany, 1973, Spring Game, 1973, City with all the angles, 1974, Modular Poems, 1975, classic plays, 1976, Legends and Fishnets, 1986, Cat alley, 1977, The Epitaphs/Gli epitaphi, 1977, George Herbert's pattern poems: in their tradition, 1977, Everyone has sher Favorite (his or hers), 1977, The epickall quest of the brothers Dichtung and other outrages, 1977, A dialectic of centuries: notes towards a theory of the new arts, 1978, some recent snowflakes (and other things), 1979, of celebration of morning, 1980, Ten ways of looking at a bird, 1981, Selected early works, 1982, 1959/60, 1982, Art contemporain 10-20, 1983, Horizons: the poetics and theory of the intermedia, 1982 (Japanese edit. 1985), Intermedia, 1985, 2d edit., 1991, Poems, Plain and Fancy, 1986, Visible Language, 1986, Pattern Poetry: A Guide to an Unknown Literature, 1987, The Journey, 1991, The Autobiography of the Moon, 1992, Happytime the Medicine Man, 1992, Buster Keaton Enters Into Paradise, 1994, Octette, 1994, Life Flowers, 1997, Modernism Since Postmodernism, 1997; translator Novalis' Hymne an die Nacht, 1978, 2d edit., 1984, 3d edit., 1988, Czternascie tlumaczen telefonicznych dla Steve'a McCaffery, Poland, 1987, The Journey, 1991, The Autobiography of the Moon, 1992, Happytime the Medicine Man, 1992, Octette, 1994, Buster Keaton Enters Into Paradise, 1994, (with others) The Book, Spiritual Instrument, 1996; editor, annotator On the composition of images, sign and ideas by Giordano Bruno, 1991; musical works include first electronic opera Stacked Deck (with Richard Maxfield), 1958-59, Piano Album: short pieces, 1962-84, 1980, Sonata for prepared piano, 1981, 26 Mountains for Viewing the Sunset From, 1981, Variation on a natural theme, for orch., 1981, 1959/60, 1982, Song for any voice(s) and instrument(s), 1983, Sonata No. 2 for piano, 1983; author numerous plays, movies; editor: (with Wolf Vostell) Pop Architektur, 1969, Fantastic Architecture, 1971; 150 book inclusions; contbr. to numerous periodicals, 1962-95; author mimeo books, acting scripts, small multiples, buttons, postcards, pamphlets, booklets; films include A tiny movie, 1959, The flight of the Florence bird, 1960, The flaming city, 1961-62, The End, 1962, Invocation of canyons and boulders for Stan Brakhage, 1962, Plunk, 1962, For the dead, 1965, Scenario, 1968, Hank and Mary without apologies, 1969, Mysteries, 1969, Men & women and bells, 1970; videotapes include Gentle talk, 1977, A lecture on The Something Else Press and since, 1981, The flaming city, 1961-62, 81, Fluxus at Williams, 1987; radio performance pieces include Die fabelhafte Getraume von Taifun-Willi, 1970, City with all the angles, 1973, Scenes forgotten and otherwise remembered, 1985, Girlande für John, 1987, Five professionals whom you can trust, 1989, Three double helixes that aren't for sale, 1989; mus. publs. include Graphis 144, Wipeout for orchestra, Graphis 143, Softly for orchestra, 1967, Suggested by small swallows, 1973, Emmett Wiliams' ear/L'orecchio di Emmett Williams, 1978; recordings include Telephone music, 1979, Eine zweite heutliche deutliche Sprache, 1972, Danger music 17, 1977, Plug: an acid novel, 1977, "glaslass" in Baobab, 1978, Poems and metapoems, 1983, Session with Bern Porter, 1983, Telephone translation #9, 1983, Bodies electric: arches and requiem for Wagner the criminal mayor, 1985, Glasslass, 1985, Constellations, 1986, Music by Dick Higgins, 1989; one or two-artist shows include Galerie Rene Block, Berlin, 1973, Centro de Arte y Communicacion, Buenos Aires, 1974, Galerie St. Petri, Lund, Sweden, 1974, Galerie Vehicule, Montreal, 1974, Museu de ArtContemporanea, Sao Paulo., Brazil, 1976, Galerie Ecart, Geneva, 1977, La Mamelle, San Francisco, 1977, Studio Morra, Naples, 1977, Galerie Inge Baecker, Bochum, 1978,82, C Space, N.Y.C., 1978, Galleri Sudurgata, Reykjavik, Iceland, Galerie Ars Viva, Berlin, 1982, Galerie A, Amsterdam, 1982, Emily Harvey Artworks, N.Y.C., 1986, 89, Art Gallery, San Diego State U., Calexico, Calif., 1987, Mid-Hudson Arts and Sci. Ctr., Poughkeepsie, N.Y., 1988, Emily Harvey artworks, N.Y, 1989, Galeria Potocka, Krakow, Poland, 1989, Emily Harvey Gallery, N.Y.C., 1990, 93, Gallery Office Art Berry Coll., Rome, Ga., 1991, Schüppenhauer Gallery, Cologne, Germany, 1991, Galérie J.-et-J. Paris, 1993, Emily Harvey Gallery, N.Y.C., 1993, Henie Onstad Art Ctr., Oslo, 1995, Mpls. Mus., 1995, Mcpl. Gallery, Pori, Finland, 1995, Archivio di Nuova Scrittura, Milan, Italy, 1995, Ctr. for Contemporary Art, Warsaw, 1996, Gallery 479, N.Y.C., 1996, Caterina Gualco, Genova, 1997; group exhbns. include Judson Gallery, N.Y.C., 1960, Fine Arts Gallery, U. B.C., 1969, Copenhagen Mus. Modern Art, 1972, Los Angeles Inst. of Contemporary Arts, 1978, Detroit Art Inst., 1979, Neuberger Mus., SUNY, Purchase, N.Y., 1981, Galerie Ars Viva, Berlin, 1982, Hayward Gallery, London, 1983, Staatsgalerie Stuttgart, 1984, Nexus Gallery, Phila., 1985, Mappin Art Gallery, Sheffield, Eng., 1986, Harlekin Art, Wiesbaden, 1987, Galleria Vivita I, Florence, 1988, Stux Gallery, N.Y.C., 1990, others; represented in permanent collections and archives including Berlinische Galerie, Berlin, Gallery of Modern Art, Vienna, Austria, Sonja Henie-Niels Onstad Found., Oslo, Norway, Museu de Arte Contemporanea, Sao Paulo, Brazil, Museum of Modern Art, Copenhagen, Neue Staatsgalerie Stuttgart, Museo Vostell, Caceres, Spain, Jean Brown Archive, John Paul Getty Art Ctr., Los Angeles, Ruth and Marvin Sackner Archive of Visual Poetry, Miami Beach, Fla., Archiv Hanns Sohm, Neue Staatsgalerie Stuttgart; included in pvt. collections of Marcel Fleiss, Paris, Dr. Kenneth Friedman, N.Y.C., Emily Harvey, N.Y.C., Gil Williams, Binghamton, N.Y., Rene Block, Berlin, others; fluxus performances numerous locations U.S.A. and Europe including Moderna Galerija Ljubljana, Solvenia, 1997; numerous creative works including music, art and ephemeral publications since 1958. Ctr. for 20th Century Studies fellow U. Wis., Milw., 1977, DAAD fellow, Berlin, 1981-82, Banff (Alta., Can.) Centre fellow, 1990; N.Y. State Coun. on Arts grantee, 1968—, Collaborations grantee visual arts program N.Y. State Coun. on Arts, 1989—, Purchase Coll. grantee for pattern poetry projects, 1984-86, 88—, Pollock-Krasner Found. grantee, 1993; recipient Bill C. Davis Drama award for The Journey (1986-87), 1988—; residency Banff (Alberta) Centre, 1990. Home: Barrytown, NY. Died Oct., 1998.

HIGGINS, FRANCES STEWART, glass designer; b. Haddock, Ga., Dec. 24, 1912; s. William Jefferson and Elizabeth Frances (Farrar) Stewart; m. Michael H. Higgins. BS, Ga. State Coll. for Women, Milledgeville, 1934; Student, Columbia U., 1936, Ohio State U., 1944; MA, Inst. of Design, Chgo., 1949. Art tchr. Atlanta Pub. Schs., 1935-44; asst. prof. U. Ga., Athens, 1944-48; former designer, craftsman Higgins Glass Studio, Chgo., Riverside, Ill. Two man shows include Art Inst. Chgo., 1959, Glass Gallery, Bethesda, Md., 1984, 88; represented in permanent collections Victoria & Albert Mus., London, Renwick Smithsonian Mus., Metro. Mus., Corning Mus., Milw. Mus. Mem. Nat. Glass Art Soc. (hon. life), Frederick Law Olmsted Soc., Riverside Garden Club. Died Feb. 12, 2004.

HIGGINS, PAMELA WRENN, lawyer; b. Corsicana, Tex., May 5, 1944; d. James M. and Betty Jo (Long) Wrenn; m. Michael L. Higgins, Sept. 26, 1964; (div.); B.A., Rutgers U., 1968; J.D., Temple U., 1972. Bar: Pa. 1972, U.S. Dist. Ct. (ea. dist.) Pa. 1976, U.S. Ct. Appeals (3d cir.) 1979, U.S. Ct. Appeals (2d cir.) 1980, U.S. Supreme Ct. 1981. Asst. dist. atty. Office of Dist. Atty., Phila., 1972-75; assoc. firm David Berger, P.A., Phila., 1975-78, firm Sprague & Rubenstone, Phila., 1980-81; spl. atty. U.S. Dept. Justice, Phila., 1978-80; ptnr. firm Higgins & Madden, Phila., 1981—. Mem. Pa. Bar Assn., Phila. Bar Assn., Brehon Soc. Democrat. Home: Paris, Tex. Died Sept. 14, 2000.

HIGHAM, JOHN, history educator; b. N.Y.C., Oct. 26, 1920; s. LLoyd Stuart and Margaret (Windred) H.; m. Eileen Moss, Aug. 26, 1948; children: Margaret, Jay, Daniel, Constance Vidor. BA, Johns Hopkins U., 1941; PhD, U. Wis., 1949. Instr. history UCLA, 1948-50, asst. prof., 1950-54; asso. prof. Rutgers U., 1954-58, prof., 1958-60; prof. history U. Mich., Ann Arbor, 1961-67, Moses Coit Tyler Univ. prof., 1968-71, 72-73. Vis. assoc. prof. Columbia U., 1958-59; John Martin Vincent prof. Johns Hopkins U.,

1971-89, prof. emeritus, 1989-2003; directeur d'études associé Ecole des Hautes Etudes en Sciences Sociales, Paris, 1981-82; Newman vis. prof. Am. civilization Cornell U., Ithaca, N.Y., 1991-92. Author: Strangers in the Land, 1955, 2nd edit., 1988, History: Humanistic Scholarship in America, 1965, rev. edit., 1989, Writing American History, 1970, Send These to Me, 1975, rev. edit., 1984, Hanging Together: Unity and Diversity in American Culture, 2001; editor: The Reconstruction of American History, 1962, Ethnic Leadership in America, 1978, New Directions in American Intellectual History, 1979, Civil Rights and Social Wrongs: Black-White Relations Since World War II, 1997; co-author: (Peter Kivisto, Dag Blanck, editors) American Immigrants and Their Generations, 1990, Conceptions of National History, 1994. Served with USAAF, 1943-45. Princeton U. Coun. Humanities fellow, 1960-61; Commonwealth Fund lectr. Univ. Coll., London, 1968; Ctr. Advanced Study Behavioral Scis. fellow, 1965-66; Phi Beta Kappa vis. scholar, 1972-73; mem. Inst. Advanced Study, 1973-74; Fulbright-Hays lectr. Kyoto Am. Studies Seminar, 1974; fellow Woodrow Wilson Internat. Ctr. for Scholars, 1976-77, Guggenheim Found. fellow, 1984-85, Fulbright 40th Anniversary Disting. fellow, Argentina, 1986, Mellon Sr. fellow Nat. Humanities Ctr., 1988-89. Mem. Am. Acad. Arts and Scis., Am. Hist. Assn. (coun. and exec. com. 1971-74, rep. to Am. Coun. Learned Socs. 1977-80, founding editor AHA Guide to Hist. Lit., 3d edit. 1987-90, award for disting. scholarship 2002), Orgn. Am. Historians (pres. 1973-74), Mich. Soc. Fellows (sr. fellow 1971-73), New Soc. Letters Lund (Sweden), Am. Antiquarian Soc., Soc. Am. Historians, Immigration and Ethnic History Soc. (pres. 1979-82, 2 Lifetime Achievement awards 2002), Century Club (N.Y.C.). Home: Baltimore, Md. Died July 26, 2003.

HILDEBRAND, DAVID KENT, statistics educator; b. Mpls., June 24, 1940; s. Frank Childs and Joyce (Wadmond) H.; m. Patricia Jane Gach, Mar. 30, 1964; children: Martin Victor, Jeffrey David. BA, Carleton Coll., 1962; MS, Carnegie Inst. Tech., 1965, PhD, 1967; MA (hon.), U. Pa., 1972. Asst. prof. stats. U. Pa., Phila., 1965-71, assoc. prof., 1971-76, prof., from 1976, chair dept. stats., 1985-90. Vis. asst. prof. Carnegie-Mellon U., 1970-71; chair Faculty Senate, U. Pa., 1992-93. Author: Statistical Thinking for Behavioral Scientists, 1986; co-author: Prediction Analysis of Cross-Classification, 1977, Statistical Thinking for Managers, 4th edit., 1998, Basic Statistical Ideas for Managers, 1995. Mem. Am. Statis. Assn. Home: Wynnewood, Pa. Deceased.

HILDEBRAND, DON CECIL, helicopter company executive; b. Camp Cooke, Calif., Dec. 1, 1943; s. Cecil and Gladys Helen (Buschmeier) H.; m. Rita Ann Wojdyla, July 25, 1964 (div. 1991); children: Jeffrey James, Denise Lynn; m. Kathy Glaspie, June 13, 1992. BA, U. Ariz., 1978. Chief pilot Tucson Police Dept., 1981-94; pres. S.W. Helicopters, Inc., Tucson, from 1981. Dir. Airborne Law Enforcement Assn., L.A.a, 1976-78; pilot examiner FAA, Phoenix, 1979-94, counselor accident prevention, 1988. Pres. Vietnam Helicopter Pilot Assn., Phoenix, 1982. With U.S. Army, 1966-69, Vietnam. Mem. SAG, Am. Helicopter Soc., Vietnam Veterans Assn., Veterans of Fgn. Wars, Aircraft Owners & Pilots Assn., The Planetary Soc. Republican. Roman Catholic. Home: Tucson, Ariz. Deceased.

HILGERT, RAYMOND LEWIS, management and industrial relations educator, consultant, arbitrator; b. St. Louis, July 28, 1930; s. Lewis Francis and Frieda Christine (Keune) H.; m. Bernice Alice Nerl, Apr. 28, 1951; children— Brenda, Diane, Jeffrey. BA, Westminster Coll., Fulton, Mo., 1952; MBA, Washington U., St. Louis, 1961; DBA, Washington U., 1963. Mgmt. positions with Southwestern Bell Telephone Co., 1956-60; mem. faculty Olin Sch. Bus. Washington U., St. Louis, 1963—2001, dir. summer workshop Olin Sch. Bus., 1964-68; dir. mgmt. devel. programs Olin Sch. Bus. Washington U., St. Louis, 1967-84; asst. dean, dir. undergrad. program Olin Sch. Bus. Washington U., St. Louis, 1968-69. Cons.; lectr.; labor arbitrator Author: (with C. Ling and Ed Leonard Jr.) Cases, Incidents and Experiential Exercises in Human Resource Management, 1990, 3d edit., 2000; (with David Dilts) Cases in Collective Bargaining and Industrial Relations: A Decisional Approach, 1969, 10th edit., 2002, Labor Agreement Negotiations, 1983, 6th edit., 2001; (with Ed Leonard Jr.) Supervision: Concepts and Practices of Management, 1972, 8th edit., 2001; (with Philip Lochhaas and James Truesdell) Christian Ethics in the Workplace, 2001; contbr. articles to profl. jours. Mem. adv. coun. St. Louis region SBA, 1983-91. Served to 1st lt. USAF, 1952-56 Named Tchr. of Yr., Washington U. Sch. Bus., 1968, 81, 85, 89. Mem. Acad. Mgmt., Indsl. Rels. Rsch. Assn., Soc. for Human Resource Mgmt. (sr. profl. in human resource mgmt.), Am. Mgmt. Assn. Lutheran. Avocations: sports, movies. Home: Kirkwood, Mo. Died Aug. 24, 2003.

HILL, ANITA CARRAWAY, retired state legislator; b. Chatfield, Tex., Aug. 13, 1928; d. Archie Clark and Martha (Butler) Carraway; BA in Journalism, Tex. Woman's U., 1950; m. Harris Hill, Sept. 20, 1952; children: Stephen Victor, Virginia Evelyn. Reporter Garland (Tex.) Daily News, 1950-51; ednl. dir. First Meth. Ch., Garland, 1951-53; chemist Kraft Foods Co., Garland, 1953-56; legis. aide, Tex. Legislature, 1975-77; mem. Tex. Ho. of Reps., 1977-92, mem. mcpl. bond and revenue sharing coms., 1971-74; ret., 1992. Awards chmn. City of Garland Environ. Council; mem. City of Garland Park and Recreation Bd., 1971-77, chmn., 1976-77; life mem. PTA; mem. Dallas County Mental Health Mental Retardation bd. trustees. Named Disting. Alumna, Tex. Woman's U., 1981. Mem. Garland C. of C., Rowlett C. of C., Bus. and Profl. Women's Club (Garland Woman of Year, 1980), AAUW, Tex. Assn. Elected Women. Republican. Methodist. Home: Garland, Tex. Died Oct. 7, 2003.

HILL, ANNA MARIE, manufacturing executive; b. Great Falls, Mont., Nov. 6, 1938; d. Paul Joseph and Alexina Rose (Doyon) Ghekiere. AA, Oakland Jr. Coll., 1959; student, U. Calif., Berkeley, 1960-62. Mgr. ops. OSM, Soquel, Calif., 1963-81; purchasing agt. Arrow Huss, Scotts Valley, Calif., 1981-82; sr. buyer Fairchild Test Systems, San Jose, Calif., 1982-83; materials mgr. Basic Test Systems, San Jose, 1983-86; purchasing mgr. Beta Tech., Santa Cruz, Calif., 1986-87; mgr. purchasing ICON Rev., Carmel, Calif., 1987-88; materials mgr. Integrated Components Test System, Sunnyvale, Calif., 1988-89; mfg. mgr. Forte Comm., Sunnyvale, 1989-94; new products mgr. Cisco Sys., San Jose, from 1994. Cons., No. Calif., 1976—. Counselor Teens Against Drugs, San Jose, 1970, 1/2 Orgn., Santa Cruz, 1975-76. Mem. Am. Prodn. Invention Control, Nat. Assn. Female Execs., Nat. Assn. Purchasing Mgmt., Am. Radio Relay League. Democrat. Avocations: amateur radio operator, music, gardening. Home: Capitola, Calif. Died July 7, 2004.

HILL, (JOHN EDWARD) CHRISTOPHER, history educator, author; b. Feb. 6, 1912; m. Inez Waugh, 1944; 1 dau. (dec.); m. 2d, Bridget Irene Sutton, 1956; 1 son, 2 daus. (1 dec.). BA, Oxford U., 1934, DLitt, 1965; DLitt (hon.), U. Hull, 1966, U. East Anglia, 1968, U. Exeter, 1979, U. Wales, 1979, U. Southampton, 1996, U. Leicester, 1996; LittD (hon.), U. Sheffield, 1967; LLD (hon.), U. Bristol, 1976; DUniv (Hon.), York U., 1978; hon. doctorate Sorbonne, Paris, 1979. Asst. lectr. Univ. Coll., Cardiff, Wales, 1936; fellow and tutor in modern history Balliol Coll., Oxford U., 1938; pvt. field Security Police, commd. Oxford and Buckinghamshire Light Inf., 1940; seconded to Fgn. Office, 1943; lectr. history oxford U., 1959, Ford's lectr., 1962, master of Balliol Coll., 1965-78; vis. prof. Open U., 1978-80, Preston Poly., 1982-84. Recipient Hanford award Milton Soc. Am., 1978. Fellow Brit. Acad.; mem. Am. Acad. Scis. German Democratic Republic (hon. fgn. mem.). Author: The English Revolution 1640, 1940, (under name K. E. Holme) Two Commonwealths, 1945, Lenin and the Russian Revolution, 1947, Economic Problems of the Church, 1956, Puritanism and Revolution, 1958, Oliver Cromwell, 1958, The Century of Revolution, 1961, Society and Puritanism in Pre-Revolutionary England, 1964, Intellectual Origins of the English Revolution, 1965, Reformation to Industrial Revolution, 1967, God's Englishman, 1970, Antichrist in 17th Century England, 1971, The World Turned Upside Down, 1972, Change and Continuity in 17th Century England, 1974, Milton and the English Revolution (Heinemann award), 1978, Some Intellectual Consequences of the English Revolution, 1980, The Experience of Defeat: Milton and Some Contemporaries, 1984, Writing and Revolution in 17th Century England, 1985, Religion and Politics in 17th Century England, 1986, People and Ideas in 17th Century England, 1986), A Turbulent Seditious and Factious People: John Bunyan and his Church (W.H. Smith Lit. award 1989), A Nation of Change and Novelty: Radical Politics, Religion and Literature in 17th Century England, 1990, The English Bible and the 17th Century Revolution, 1993, Liberty Against the Law: Some 17th Century Traditions, 1996; also articles. Editor: (with E. Dell) The Good Old Cause, 1949, The Law of Freedom and Other Writings of Gerrard Winstanley, 1973, (with B. Reay and W. Lamont) The World of the Muggletonians, 1983. Home: Banbury, England. Died Feb. 24, 2003.

HILL, ERROL GASTON, drama educator, director, author; b. Port-of-Spain, Trinidad, Aug. 5, 1921; s. Thomas David and Lydia (Gibson) H.; m. Grace L. E. Hope, Aug. 11, 1956; children: Da'aga, Claudia, Melina, Aaron Grad. diploma, Royal Acad. Dramatic Art, London, 1951; diploma in dramatic art, U. London, 1951; BA summa cum laude, MFA in Playwriting, Yale U., 1962, DFA in Theatre History, 1966. Drama and radio tutor U. W.I., Mona, Jamaica, 1953-58, creative arts tutor, 1962-65, external examiner drama and creative writing, 1982-85; teaching fellow U. Ibadan, Nigeria, 1965-67, external examiner dept. theatre arts, 1977, 78; assoc. prof. drama Richmond Coll., CUNY, S.I., 1967-68, Dartmouth Coll., Hanover, N.H., 1968-69, prof., 1969-89, John D. Willard prof. drama and oratory, 1976-89, John D. Willard prof. emeritus, 1989—2003, dir. summer repertory theatre program, 1979-82, 84, 87. Vis. scholar Bellagio Study and Conf. Ctr., Italy, 1978; vis. prof. U. Calif., San Diego, 1982; Chancellor's disting. prof. U. Calif., Berkeley, 1983; vis. Mellon prof. Tulane U., New Orleans, spring, 1994; evaluator Nat. Assn. Schs. Theatre. Author: (books) The Trinidad Carnival: Mandate for a National Theatre, 1972, Shakespeare in Sable: A History of Black Shakespearean Actors, 1984 (Bertram Joseph award Queens Coll. CUNY 1985, Barnard Hewitt award Am. Theatre Assn. 1985), The Jamaican Stage 1655-1900, 1992, (plays) The Ping Pong, 1953, Wey-Wey, 1957, Strictly Matrimony, 1959, Man Better Man, 1960, Whistling Charlie and the Monster, 1964, Dance Bongo, 1965; co-author: Why Pretend? A Conversation About the Performing Arts, 1973, The Cambridge Guide to African and Caribbean Theatre, 1994; editor: Caribean Plays, vol. 1, 1958, vol. 2, 1965, A Time and a Season: 8 Caribbean Plays, 1976, The Theater of Black Americans, 2 vols., 1980, reprinted single edit. 1987, Plays on Black Heroes, 1989; contbg. editor: Three Caribbean Plays for Secondary Schools, 1979, Plays of Today, 1985; editor Bull. of Black Theatre, 1971-75; contbr. numerous articles to profl. jours.; prodr., dir. over 120 plays and pageants worldwide. Mem. vis. com. Loeb Drama Ctr., Harvard U. Recipient Gold medal for drama Govt. of Trinidad and Tobago, 1973, Regional Citation for teaching and scholarship New Eng. Theatre Conf., 1980; Rockefeller Found. fellow, 1958-60, 65, Theatre Guild of Am. fellow, 1961-62, Guggenheim fellow, 1985-86, Fulbright fellow, 1988. Fellow Coll. Am. Theatre; mem. Am. Soc. Theatre Rsch. (exec. com.), Internat. Fedn. Theatre Rsch., Am. Theatre and Drama Soc., Nat. Conf. Afro-Am. Theatre, Assn. Commonwealth Lang. and Lit. Studies, Caribbean Studies Assn., Phi Beta Kappa (pres. N.H. Alpha chpt. 1982-85). Home: Hanover, NH. Died Sept. 15, 2003.

HILL, FREDRIC WILLIAM, nutritionist, poultry scientist; b. Erie, Pa., Sept. 2, 1918; s. Vaino Alexander and Mary Elvira (Holmstrom) H.; m. Charlotte Henrietta Gummoe, Apr. 1, 1944; children: Linda Charlotte, James Fredric, Dana Edwin. BS, Pa. State U., 1939, MS, 1940; PhD, Cornell U., 1944. Rsch. asst. Pa. State U., 1939-40, Cornell U., 1940-44; head nutrition div. rsch. labs. Western Condensing Co., Appleton, Wis., 1944-48; assoc. prof., then prof. animal nutrition and poultry husbandry Cornell U., 1948-59; prof. poultry husbandry, chmn. dept. U. Calif., Davis, 1959-65, prof. nutrition, from 1965, chmn. dept. nutrition, 1965-73, assoc. dean Coll. Agr., 1965-66, assoc. dean rsch. and internat. programs, 1976-80, coordinator internat. programs, 1976-80, prof. nutrition emeritus, from 1989. Mem. subcom. hormonal relationships and applications com. on Animal Nutrition, NRC, 1953, subcom. poultry nutrition, 1953-74; mem. Food and Nutrition Bd., 1975-78; commr. Calif. Poultry Improvement Commn., 1959-65; participant 8th Easter Sch. Agrl. Scis., U. Nottingham, Eng., 1961, World Conf. Animal Prodn., Rome, Italy, 1963, U.S. AID-Nat. Acad. Sci. Seminar on Protein Foods, Bangkok, 1970, USIA Asia Seminars on Food, Population and Energy, 1974-75; Japan Soc. Promotion Sci. vis. prof. Nagoya U., 1974-75; vis. scientist FDA, 1975, 88, Nutrition Inst., USDA, 1975; cons. Institut National de Recherche Agronomique, France, 1982; plenary speaker 3d Asian-Australian Animal Sci. Congress, Seoul, Republic of Korea, 1985. Contbr. articles profl. jours.; Editorial bd.: Poultry Sci. Jour, 1960-64; editorial bd.: Jour. of Nutrition, 1964-68; editor, 1969-79. Fellow Danforth Found., 1938; recipient Nutrition Rsch. award Am. Feed Mfrs. Assn., 1958, Newman Internat. Rsch. award Brit. Poultry Assn., 1959; Guggenheim Found. fellow Nat. Inst. Med. Rsch., Mill Hill, Eng., Hebrew U., Jerusalem, 1966-67; Alumni fellow Pa. State U., 1983. Fellow AAAS, Poultry Sci. Assn. (Rsch. prize 1957, Borden award 1961), Am. Inst. Nutrition (councillor 1982-85); mem. Soc. Exptl. Biology and Medicine, Nutrition Soc. (Gt. Britain), Coun. Biology Editors, World's Poultry Sci. Assn., Am. Inst. Biol. Scis., Am. Soc. Animal Sci., Am. Chem. Soc., Fedn. Am. Socs. for Exptl. Biology (publs. com. 1987-93, chmn. 1991-93), Sigma Xi, Phi Eta Sigma, Gamma Sigma Delta, Phi Kappa Phi, Delta Theta Sigma, Gamma Alpha. Clubs: Cosmos (Washington); El Macero (Calif.). Home: Davis, Calif. Died Nov. 29, 2003.

HILL, GEORGE ROY, film director; b. Mpls., Dec. 20; s. George Roy and Helen Frances (Owens) H.; m. Louisa Horton, Apr. 7, 1951. BA, Yale U.; B of Lit., Trinity Coll., Dublin, Ireland. Acting debut: (play) The Devil's Disciple, Dublin, 1948; other stage appearances include The Creditors, 1950; toured with Margaret Webster's Shakespeare Repertory Co.; writer, actor: (teleplay) My Brother's Keeper, 1953; writer, producer, dir.: (teleplay) Judgement at Nuremberg, 1957; dir.: (Broadway plays) Look Homeward, Angel, 1957, The Gang's All Here, Period of Adjustment, Greenwillow, 1960, Henry, Sweet Henry, 1967, (off-Broadway show) Moon on a Rainbow Shawl, 1962, (films) Period of Adjustment, 1962, Toys in the Attic, 1963, The World of Henry Orient, 1964, Hawaii, 1966, Thoroughly Modern Millie, 1967, Butch Cassidy and the Sundance Kid, 1969, Slaughterhouse-Five, 1972, The Sting, 1973, The Great Waldo Pepper, 1975, Slap Shot, 1977, A Little Romance, 1979, The World According to Garp, 1982, The Little Drummer Girl, 1984, Funny Farm, 1988. Served as pilot USMC, World War II and Korean War. Recipient Acad. award for best dir. of The Sting, 1973; Emmy award nominations for A Night to Remember, The Helen Morgan Story, Child of Our Time; Acad. award nomination for Butch Cassidy and the Sundance Kid, 1969; Cannes Internat. Film Festival Jury Prize for Slaughterhouse Five, 1972. Died Dec. 27, 2002.

HILL, HAMLIN LEWIS, JR., English language educator; b. Houston, Nov. 7, 1931; s. Hamlin Lewis and Marguerite (Courtin) H.; m. Arlette Crawford, Dec. 27, 1952; children: Cynthia, Joe Scott, Sondra June, William Christian. Student, U. Tex., 1949-51, 1953-54, MA, 1954; BA, U. Houston, 1953; PhD, U. Chgo., 1959. Instr. English U. N.Mex., Albuquerque, 1959-61, asst. prof., 1963-65, asso. prof., 1965-68, prof., 1975-86, chmn. dept., 1979-86; asst. prof. English U. Wyo., 1961-63; prof. English U. Chgo., 1968-75; Ralph R. Thomas prof. liberal arts, head dept. English Tex. A&M U., College Station, 1986-89, Disting. prof. English, from 1988; Salgo prof. Am. studies U. Budapest, Hungary, 1989-91. Vis. prof. U. Nebr., 1960, U. Calif. at Berkeley, 1965, Stanford, 1972-73; dir. Summer Seminar for Coll. Tchrs., Nat. Endowment for Humanities, 1977, 81, Seminar in Residence for Coll. Tchrs., 1978-79, Summer Seminar for Secondary Sch. Tchrs., 1985, 86, 88, 89; mem. Am. lit. selection com. Council Internat. Exchange of Scholars, 1981-84; Fulbright fellow U. Copenhagen, 1966-67; Fulbright prof. U. Würzburg, 1980; acad. specialist, India, 1983; resident scholar in Am. studies USIA, 1984-85; acad. specialist on various countries, 1984-85 Author: Mark Twain and Elisha Bliss, 1964, Mark Twain: God's Fool, 1973; author: (with Walter Blair) Forty Years of Traveling with Mark Twain, 2000, America's Humor, 1978; editor: The Art of Huckleberry Finn, 1962; editor: A Connecticut Yankee in King Arthur's Court, 1963, Mark Twain's Letters to His Publishers, 1967, Wapping Alice by Mark Twain, 1981, Essays on American Humor, 1993, Christian Science, 1996; editor: (with Robert G. Bruce) A Tramp Abroac, 1997; mem. editl. bd.: The Lovingood Papers, 1965—67, Am. Lit. Realism, from 1972, Studies in Am. Humor, from 1974, The Old Northwest, from 1974, Am. Lit., 1982—85; contbr. articles and revs. to scholasioc jours. Am. Council Learned Socs. grantee-in-aid, 1963, 65, 67; Guggenheim fellow, 1971-72; Fulbright 40th Anniversary Disting. fellow, 1986. Mem. MLA, Am. Studies Assn., Am. Humor Studies Assn., Theta Xi. Democrat. Episcopalian. Home: College Station, Tex. Died July 16, 2002.

HILL, SAMUEL RICHARDSON, JR., retired medical educator; b. Greensboro, N.C., May 19, 1923; s. Samuel Richardson and Nona (Sink) Hill; m. Janet Redman, Oct. 28, 1950; children: Susan Hill Lindley, Samuel Richardson III, Elizabeth Hill Humphreys, Margaret Hill Cohn. BA, Duke U., 1943; MD, Wake Forest U., 1946; DSc (hon.), U. Ala., 1975, Wake Forest U., 1979. Intern medicine Peter Bent Brigham Hosp., Boston, 1947—48, asst. resident medicine, 1948—49, asst. medicine, 1949—50; teaching fellow medicine Harvard Sch. Medicine, 1948—49, research fellow medicine, Dazian Med. Found. research fellow, 1949—50; chief resident medicine N.C. Bapt. Hosp., instr. medicine Bowman Gray Sch. Medicine, 1950—51; asst. medicine Harvard Sch. Medicine, also Peter Bent Brigham Hosp., 1953—54; asst. prof. medicine, dir. metabolic and endocrine div. Med. Coll. Ala., also chief metabolic div. VA Hosp., Birmingham, 1954—57; assoc. prof. medicine, dir. metabolic and endocrine div. U. Ala. Med. Ctr. and VA Hosp., Birmingham, 1957—62; prof. medicine, dean U. Ala. Sch. Medicine, Birmingham, 1962—68; prof. medicine U. Ala. Med. Coll., Birmingham, 1968—94; v.p. for health affairs, dir. Med. Ctr., 1968—77; pres. U. Ala., Birmingham, 1977—87, Disting. prof., 1987—93, Disting. prof. emeritus and cons., 1994—98; dir. med. edn. program U. Ala. System, 1972—79. Bd. dirs. Birmingham br. Fed. Res. Bank, Atlanta1981, 1981—83, chmn., 1983. Contbr. articles to med. jours. Bd. regents Nat. Libr. Medicine, 1978—80, chmn. bd. regents, 1979—80. Served to maj. M.C. USAF, 1951—53. Fellow: Royal Soc. Medicine, AAAS, ACP; mem.: Alpha Omega Alpha, Sigma Xi, Assn. Acad. Health Ctrs., Assn. Am. Med. Colls., Med. Assn. State Ala., So. Soc. Clin. Investigation, Inst. Medicine, AMA, Am. Thyroid Soc., Jefferson County Med. Soc., Ala. Diabetes Soc., Endocrine Soc., Am. Fedn. Clin. Rsch., Soc. Exptl. Biology and Medicine. Episcopalian. Home: Birmingham, Ala. Died July 4, 2003.

HILLER, DALE MURRAY, chemistry consultant; b. Chgo., Oct. 13, 1924; s. Cletus Murray and Anna (Keener) H.; m. Mary Aileen Garrett, June 29, 1952; children: Karen Ann, Margaret Ellen, Steven Richard, Eric David. BSEE, U. Nebr., 1947; AB in Chemistry, Miami U., Oxford, Ohio, 1948; PhD in Phys. Chemistry, Iowa State U., 1952. Rsch. assoc. E. I. duPont de Nemours & Co., Inc., Wilmington, Del., 1952-90; pvt. practice cons. Wilmington, from 1990. Contbr. articles to profl. publs.; patentee in field. Chmn. Del. Authority on Radiation Protection, Dover; mem. Rep. State Com., Wilmington, chmn. dist. com.; chmn. bd. dirs. World Federalist Asn., Washington. Master sgt. U.S. Army, 1943-46. Mem. Am. Chem. Soc., Phi Beta Kappa, Sigma Xi, Theta Chi, Omicron Delta Kappa. Episcopalian. Died Nov. 21, 2000.

HILLER, WENDY, actress; b. Stockport, Eng., Aug. 15, 1912; d. Frank and Marie (Stone) H.; m. Ronald Gow, Feb. 25, 1937; children: Ann, Anthony. Ed., Winceby Sch.; LLD (hon.), Manchester U., 1984. Broadway debut in Love on the Dole, 1936; stage appearances in N.Y. include The Heiress, 1947, Moon for the Misbegotten, 1957, Flowering Cherry, 1959, Aspern Papers, 1961-62; London appearances include: Tess of the d'Urbervilles, 1947, Ann Veronica, 1949, The Heiress, 1950, Shakespeare at the Old Vic, 1955-56, John Gabriel Borkman at the National, 1975; appeared in: play Waters of the Moon, Haymarket Theatre, London, 1951, revival 1979, Wings of the Dove, Haymarket Theatre, London, 1963, Crown Matrimonial, Haymarket Theatre, London, 1973, Aspern Papers, Haymarket Theatre, London, 1984, The Importance of Being Earnest, Royalty Theatre, London, 1987, Driving Miss Daisy, Apollo Theatre, London, 1988; motion pictures include Pygmalion, 1939, Major Barbara, 1941, I Know Where I'm Going, 1945, Separate Tables, 1958 (Acad. award for Best Supporting Actress 1958), Sons and Lovers, 1960, Toys in the Attic, 1963, A Man for All Seasons, 1966, David Copperfield, 1969, Murder on the Orient Express, 1973, Voyage of the Damned, 1976, Elephant Man, 1980, Making Love, 1982, Attracta, 1983; TV films include: When We Dead Awaken, 1970, Peer Gynt, 1972, King Richard the Second, 1978, The Curse of King Tut's Tomb, 1980, Country, 1981, The Importance of Being Earnest, 1981, Witness for the Prosecution, 1982, The Kingfisher, 1983, The Comedy of Errors, 1983, The Death of a Heart, 1985, All Passion Spent, 1986, Lord Montbatten: The Last Viceroy (mini-series), 1986, The Lonely Passion of Judith Hearn, 1987, Anne of Green Gables: The Sequel, 1987, Ending Up, 1989, A Taste for Death (mini-series), 1989, The Best of Friends, 1991, The Countess Alice, 1992. Decorated Order Brit. Empire, 1971, Dame Brit. Empire, 1975 Died May 14, 2003.

HINDHEDE, UFFE, mechanical engineering educator, retired; b. Ravning, Jutland, Denmark, Jan. 30, 1922; came to U.S., 1952, naturalized, 1960; s. Mads Hindhede and Kathrine Tang-Jensen; m. Lois Ann Jarnagin, Jan. 28, 1967; children: Karen Marie, Neil Erik. BA, Vejle Gymnasium, Denmark, 1941; MME, Tech. U. Denmark, 1950; MSME, U. Ill., 1964. Engr. Royal Army Arsenal, Copenhagen, 1950-52, Manitowoc (Wis.) Engring. Corp., 1952-54, Barber-Colman Co., Rockford, Ill., 1954-56, F.L. Smidth & Co., N.Y.C., 1956-59, Worthington Corp., Newark, N.J., 1959-61; instr. U Ill., Urbana, 1961-69; mech. engring. prof. Black Hawk Coll., Moline, Ill., 1969-90, ret., 1990. Author: Machine Design Fundamentals, 1983, (with others) Encyclopedia of Physical Science and Technology, 15 vols., 1987. Mem. ASME, Am. Soc. Engring. Edn., Am. Gear Mfg. Assn., Moline Viking Club. Avocations: writing tech. material, swimming, walking, golfing. Home: Moline, Ill. Deceased.

HINDS, GLESTER SAMUEL, financial consultant; b. N.Y.C., July 4, 1951; s. Glester Samuel and Kathryne Elizabeth (Ellison) H. BBA, Bernard M. Baruch Coll., 1973; MBA in Fin., Columbia U., 1975. Cert. Stock broker, ins. broker, financier, notary pub. Staff acct. Peat Marwick Mitchell, N.Y.C., 1975-77; fin. analyst Citicorp, N.Y.C., 1977-79; sr. fin. analyst Am. Express, N.Y.C., 1979-80; owner, cons. Hinds Fin. Svcs., Long Island, N.Y., 1980-87; owner, founder, pres. Emerald Advt. Co., from 1985; program specialist Calif. FTB, Manhasset, N.Y., 1987-2000; founder, dir., pres. New Alliance Inc., from 1999; founder, dir. Worldstar Enterprises, Inc., from 1999. Dir., ptnr. D.H. Holdings, Inc.; cons. Am. Entrepreneur's Assn., L.A., 1980-89, Mildred Burke Prodns., 1982-84, Worldwide Diamonds Assn., 1983-85, Acad. Fin. Aid Matching Svcs., 1983-87; licensee Creative Capital Pubs., Inc., 1983; with Mail Order Assocs., Inc., 1984—; holder minority interest Carlton Blues Football Team, Australia. Editor: Financial Newsletter the H-Club, 1978-82; actor: On Camera TV Acting, 1986; contbr. articles to profl. jours., to Passport For Travel newsletter. Funder U.S. Olympic Com. Team Ptnr. Program, 1999; mem. Presdl. Nat. Steering Com., Rep. Presdl. Task Force; founder Heritage Found., Washington, 1981, Ronald Reagan Rep. Ctr., 1989; founding mem. FDR Meml. Constrn. Project, 1996; mem. chmn.'s com. U.S. Senatorial Bus. Adv. Bd., 1981, 82; mem. Nassau-Suffolk Neighborhood Network; mem. Jim Valvano Found. for Cancer Rsch., Am. Heart Assn., The Children's Charity Fund, N.Y. Sportscene Children's Found. Recipient Edward M. Paster Meml. award, Sigma Alpha award, Beta Gamma Sigma award, Beta Alpha Psi award, Bernard M. Baruch Coll., 1973, Distinction award Am. Express, 1993, 97, Humanitarian Gold Record of Achievement ABI, 1994, Leader in sci. award, 1995, Presdl. Seal of Honor, 1996, Internat. Man of the Yr. award in Sci., 1993, Internat. Cultural Diploma of Honor Am. Biog. Inst., 1994, name permanently enshrined on Nat. Rep. Victory Monument, Ronald Reagan Rep. Ctr., Rep. medal of merit, 1995, task force cert. of merit; named Toronto Sports Club Athlete of Yr., 1987, Nat. Wrestling Hall of Fame, 1991. Mem. Am. Mgmt. Assn., USA Amateur Athletes, Interval Internat., Am. Mus. Natural History (assoc.), Am. Soc. Notaries (life), U.S. Olympic Soc. (life), N.Y. Pub. Interest Rsch. Group, 24K Club, USA Wrestling, Franklin Mint Collectors Soc., Pro-Wrestling Hall of Fame (chmn. until 1994), U.S. Tennis Assn., Nat. Amateur Wrestling Hall of Fame (ptnr., fundraiser), Insiders Money Club, Internat. Platform Assn., Am. Cancer Soc., Am. Inst. Cancer Rsch., Troy Aikman Found., Carter Ctr., Environ. Def. Fund, Internat. Soc. Financiers (cert. 1985), Coram Civic Assn. (acting pres.), Oxford Club (life), Carlton Blues Football Team (Australia). Methodist. Died 2003.

HINES, GREGORY OLIVER, actor, dancer; b. N.Y.C., Feb. 14, 1946; s. Maurice Robert and Alma Iola (Lawless) H.; m. Pamela Koslow (div.), Apr. 12, 1981; children: Daria Hines, Jessica Koslow, Zachary Evan. Appeared with Hines Kids, 1949-55, Hines Bros., 1955-63, Hines, Hines and Dad, 1963-73, An Evening of Tap at Carnegie Hall, 1989; appeared in plays: The Girl in Pink Tights (Broadway debut) 1954, Severance, 1974-77, Eubie!, 1978 (Theater World awazrd), Comin' Uptown, 1980 (Tony award nomination), Sophisticated Ladies, 1981, (Tony award nomination), Parade of Stars Playing the Palace, 1983, I Love Liberty, 1981-82, Twelfth Night, 1989, Jelly's Last Jam, 1992-93 (Tony award, best actor in a musical, 1992); appeared in films: Wolfen, 1981, History of the World Part I, 1981, The Deal of the Century, 1983, The Muppets Take Manhattan, 1984, The Cotton Club, (also choreographer) 1984, White Nights, 1985, Running Scared, 1986, Off Limits, 1988, Tap (also choreographer) 1989, Eve Of Destruction, 1991, A Rage in Harlem, 1991, Renaissance Man, 1994, Waiting to Exhale, 1995, Mad Dog Time, 1996, The Preacher's Wife, 1996, Good Luck, 1997, The Tic Code, 1998, Things You Can Tell Just by Looking at Her, 2000, Once in the Life, 2000; TV appearances: Tap Dance in America (PBS) 1989, Motown Returns to the Apollo, Saturday Night Live (host); TV Series: The Gregory Hines Show, 1997, Stories from my Childhood, 1998, Little Bill, 1999, Will and Grace, 1999-2000, Lost at Home, 2003, (TV movies) White Lie, 1991, T-Bone and Weasel, 1992, Dead Air, 1994, A Stranger in Town, 1995, The Cherokee Kid, 1996, Subway Stories: Tales from the Underground, 1997, Who Killed Atlanta's Children, 2000, Bojangles, 2001, Santa Baby, 2001, The Red Sneakers, 2002. Recipient 3 Tony nominations, 1979, 80, 81, Theater World award, Tor award, Dance Educators Am. award Mem. Actors Equity, Screen Actors Guild, AFTRA. Died Aug. 9, 2003.

HINES, JEROME, opera singer; b. Hollywood, Calif., Nov. 8, 1921; s. Russell Ray and Florence Mildred (Link) Heinz; m. Lucia Evangelista, July 23, 1952; children: David Jerome, Andrew, John, Russell. BA in Chemistry and Math., UCLA; PhD (hon.), Whitworth Coll., Bloomfield Coll., Taylor U., Stevens Inst. Tech., Drew U., Fla. So. Coll., Kean Coll. N.J. Chemist Union Oil Co. of Los Angeles, 1944-45. Began as singer with the Civic Light Opera Co. of Los Angeles, 1940, San Francisco Opera Co., 1941; Hollywood Bowl soloist, 1942, 47, Opera Assn. of Golden West, 1943, with New Orleans Opera Co., 1942, 46, 67, 83, leading basso Met. Opera Co., 1946—, La Scala, Milan, Bolshoi, Moscow, Teatro Colón, Buenos Aires, performed in Glyndebourne, Edinburgh festivals, 1953, Munich Opera Festival, 1953, 54, Wagner Opera Festival, Bayreuth, Germany, 1958, 59, 60, 61, 63, toured, Soviet Union 4 times. Recording artist, London, EMI, Columbia, Victor, Zondervan, Word recording cos.; founder Opera Music Theater Internat., N.J. Author: This is My Story, This is My Song, 1968, Tim Whosoever, 1970, Great Singers on Great Singing; also articles on math. rsch.; composer: opera I Am the Way; 30 songs. Recipient Caruso Scholarship, Cornelia Bliss Scholarhip. Died Feb. 4, 2003.

HINTON, WILLIAM HARWOOD, academic administrator; b. Estelline, Tex., June 18, 1921; m. Bobbie Ruth Duke; children: Julie Ann Hinton Parton, Linda Sue Hinton Frakes. MA, Hardin Simmons U., 1951; EdD, U. Tex., 1955; LittD (hon.), U. St. Thomas, 1987; LLD (hon.), Houston Bapt. U., 1987. Exec. v.p. Howard Payne Coll., Brownwood, Tex.; pres. Texarkana (Tex.) Jr. Coll., Houston Bapt. U., 1962-87, chancellor, 1987—91. Deacon, sunday sch. tchr. 2d Bapt. Ch., Houston. Mem. Tex. State Tchrs. Assn., Baptist Brotherhood, So. Baptist Conv., Shriners, Rotary, Masons. Avocation: golf. Home: Colorado Springs, Colo. Died Apr. 10, 2004.

HIRSCHFELD, ALBERT, artist; b. St. Louis, June 21, 1903; s. Isaac and Rebecca (Rothberg) H.; m. Florence Ruth Hobby, July 13, 1927 (div. Mar. 1941); m. Dorothy Dolly Haas, May 8, 1943 (dec. Sept. 1994); 1 child, Nina; m. Louise Kerz, Oct. 23, 1996. Student, Nat. Acad., Art Students Leaque, County Council, London, Julienne's, Paris; DFA (hon.), U. Hartford, 1982; LHD (hon.), Acad. of Art, 1984; DFA (hon.), NYU, 1985; LHD (hon.), CUNY, 1985, Brandeis U., 1989; DFA (hon.), Pratt Inst., 1994. Caricaturist N.Y. Times, from 1926. Theatre corr. in Moscow for N.Y. Herald Tribune, 1927 Sculptor one-man exhbns. include Newhouse Gallery, 1928, Waldorf Astoria, 1932, Morgan Gallery, 1936, Guy Mayer Gallery, 1942, John Heller Gallery, 1959, Hammer Gallery, 1967, Mus. City N.Y., 1973, Margo Feiden Gallery, 1973, Wako Galleries, Tokyo, 1975, Katonah Art Mus., 1998, Harvard Theater Collection, 1998, Mus. City N.Y., 2002, Motion Picture Acad. Arts and Scis., 2002; theater caricaturist, N.Y. Times, 1925—; represented in permanent collections St. Louis Art Mus., Butler Inst. Am. Art, Whitney Mus. Am. Art, N.Y.C., Cleve. Art Mus., N.Y.C. Mus., N.Y. Pub. Library, Fogg Mus., Bklyn. Mus., Met. Mus. Art, Mus. Modern Art, Davenport Municipal Art Gallery, Mus. U. Wis., Lincoln Center Mus. Performing Arts, N.Y.C., murals in Fifth Ave. Playhouse, Am. Pavilion, World's Fair, Brussels, 1958; author: Manhattan Oases, 1932, Harlem, 1942; musical comedy Sweet Bye and Bye, 1946; The American Theatre, 1961, (with S.J. Perelman) Westward Ha, 1949, Show Business is No Business, 1951, Hirschfeld Folio, 1964, The World of Hirschfeld, 1970, (with Brooks Atkinson) The Lively Years, 1973, Rhythm folio 10 lithographs, Hirschfeld by Hirschfeld, 1979; The Entertainers, 1977, Art and Recollections from 8 Decades, 1991, Hirschfeld on Line, Applause, 1998; U.S. postage stamps of comedians, 1991, of Silent Screen, 1994; (documentary film) The Line King, 1997. Recipient Am. Specialist grant U.S. State Dept., 1960, Spl. Tony award for theatre caricature, 1974, Creative award Art Inst. Boston, 1976, City of N.Y. Arts and Culture award, 1979, Brooks Atkinson Tony award, 1984, Weissberger award Theatre Hall of Fame, 1985, New Eng. Theatre award, 1984, award of honor City of N.Y., 1979, League of N.Y. Theatres and Producers Theatre award, 1975, Life Achievement award Houston Film Festival, 1989, Edwin Booth award CUNY Grad. Sch., ASCAP, 1991, Lotus Club award, 1990, National Arts Club, 1992, Stage Dirs. and Choreographers award, 1992, Living Legend award Libr. of Congress, 2000, 24 Dollar award Mus. of City of N.Y., 2000; honored by mayor of N.Y.C. with Al Hirschfeld Day, May 1, 2000. Mem. Illustrators Club (Hall of Fame 1986, Theater Hall of Fame 1990, N.Y. Living Landmark 1996). Home: New York, NY. Died Jan. 20, 2003.

HIRSCHKLAU, MORTON, lawyer; b. N.Y.C., Mar. 9, 1932; s. Joseph I. and Sylvia (Kleiner) H.; m. Martha R. Silverstein, June 21, 1953; children: Mitchell L., Deborah E. Hirschklau Loeber, Susan I. AB, Syracuse U., 1953, JD, 1959. Bar: N.Y. 1959, N.J. 1960, U.S. Supreme Ct. 1963, U.S. Ct. Appeals (3d cir.) 1982. Law sec. Superior Ct. N.J., Paterson, 1959-60; assoc. Theodore D. Rosenberg, Esquire, Paterson, 1960-63; ptnr. Hirschklau, Wasserman & Welch, Oakland, N.J., 1963-73; pvt. practice Fair Lawn, N.J., 1973-76; ptnr. Hirschklau, Feitlin & Trawinski, Fair Lawn, 1976-84, Muscarella, Hirschklau, Bochet, Feitlin, Trawinski & Edwards, Fair Lawn, 1984-90, Karas, Kilstein, Hirschklau, Feitlin & Youngman, Fair Lawn, 1990-99, Morton Hirschklau, Esq. and Assocs., from 1999. Planning bd. atty. Borough of Fair Lawn, 1961-65, Borough atty., 1965, 81-83; planning bd. atty., Borough of Emerson, 1967-71, zoning bd. atty., 1971-83; zoning bd. atty. Village of Ridgewood, 1977—, Borough of Saddle River, 1996—; spl. counsel Bergen County Park Commn., Paramus, N.J., 1987-88; chmn. N.J. Supreme Ct. Com. on Ethics, 1987-88. Bd. dirs., atty. Fair Lawn Mental Health Ctr., 1965—; bd. dirs., past pres. Opportunity Ctr., Inc., Fair Lawn; pres. Fair Lawn Clean Govt. Assn., 1968-70. Lt. USNR, 1953-56. Mem. N.J.

Bar Assn., Bergen County Bar Assn. (chmn. real estate com.), Fair Lawn Rotary Club (past pres.). Avocations: golf, tennis, collecting porcelains. Home: Fair Lawn, NJ. Died Mar. 15, 2000.

HITTMAIR, OTTO HEINRICH, physics educator; b. Innsbruck, Austria, Mar. 16, 1924; s. Rudolf and Margarete (Schumacher) H.; m. Anni Rauch, Dec. 3, 1956; children: Christine, Elisabeth, Georg, Margarete. PhD, U. Innsbruck, 1949, dozent, 1953; DTech (hon.), Tech. U. Budapest, 1982. Vis. scientist Inst. Advanced Studies, Dublin, 1951, MIT, Cambridge, Mass., 1951-52; attache CNRS, Paris, 1952-54; sr. fellow U. Sydney (Australia), 1954—56; vis. scientist Comision Nacional de Energia Atomica, Buenos Aires, 1957; scientist Atomic Inst. Austrian Us, 1958-60; prof. physics Tech. U. Vienna, 1960—92, prof. emeritus, from 1992, dean Faculty Scis., 1968—69, rector, 1977—79. Author: (with S.T. Butler) Nuclear Stripping Reactions, 1957, Quantum Theory, 1972, (with G. Adam) Theory of Heat, 1971, 4th edit., (with H. Weber) Superconductivity, 1979, (with H. Hunger) Academy of Sciences—Development of an Austrian Research Institution, 1997. Recipient Jubilee medal U. Innsbruck, 1970, prize for sci. and tech. City of Vienna, 1982, Wilhelm Exner medal Austrian Trade Assn., 1980, Prechtl medal Tech. U. Vienna, 1996; Planetoid 10782 named "Hittmair", IAU, 2001. Mem. Austrian Acad. Scis. (sec. 1983-87, pres. 1987-91, v.p. 1991-97, Erwin Schrödinger prize 1974), Internat. Soc. Engring. Edn. (v.p. 1973-97, Ring of Honor 1997), Royal Soc. Scis. Uppsala, Austrian Phys. Soc., European Sci. Found. (exec. coun. 1983-89). Roman Catholic. Home: Innsbruck, Austria. Died May 9, 2003.

HLATKE, MARIE ELENA, elementary school educator; b. Yonkers, N.Y., June 26, 1941; d. Carlos and Amelia (Bernardo) Oliveira; m. Michael J. Hlatke III, Apr. 25, 1964; 1 child, Michael J. IV. BA, Newark State Coll., 1963. Cert. tchr., N.J. Kindergarten tchr. Elizabeth (N.J.) Bd. Edn. Active local PTA. Recipient Chaplains Legion of Honor award, N.J. Gov.'s Tchr. Recognition award, 1989; Elizabeth Project teaching grantee. Mem. NEA, N.J. Edn. Assn., AAUW, Union County Edn. Assn., Elizabeth Edn. Assn., Kdg. Tchrs. Assn. Home: Middlesex, NJ. Died Apr. 23, 2000.

HNATYSHYN, RAMON JOHN, former governor general, commander in chief, lawyer; b. Saskatoon, Sask., Can., Mar. 16, 1934; s. John and Helen Constance (Pitts) H.; m. Karen Gerda Nygaard Andreasen, Jan. 9, 1960; children: John, Carl. BA, U. Sask., Can., 1954; LLB, U. Sask., 1956, LLD (hon.), 1990, Open U. B.C., 1991, Royal Military Coll., 1991, Queen's Univ., 1991, U. Manitoba, 1992, McGill U., 1992, State U. Chernivsti, Ukraine, 1992, Carleton U., 1992, Royal Rds. Mil. Coll., 1994, U. No. B.C., 1994, U. Alta., 1994; D of Civil Law honoris causa, U. Emmanuel Coll., Saskatoon, 1993; D of Canon Law honoris causa, Bishop U., Lennoxville, 1993; doctorate of the univ. (hon.), U. Ottawa, 1991; diploma (hon.), Loyalist Coll., 1992; PhD honoris causa, others, Yonsei U., Republic of Korea, 1994. Called to the bar, Sask., 1957, Ont., 1986; apptd. Queen's Counsel, Sask., 1973, Can., 1988. Pvt. practice, 1957-90; sr. ptnr. Gowling, Strathy & Henderson, Ottawa, Ont., Can., 1988-90; of counsel Hnatyshyn & Co., Saskatoon, 1974-90; mem. Parliament, Can., 1974-88; minister of state for sci. and tech. Govt. Can., 1979, minister energy, mines, resources, 1979-80, minister regulatory affairs, 1986, minister justice, atty.-gen., 1986-88, opposition house leader, 1984, govt. house leader, 1984-86; mem. Queen's Privy Coun. for Can., from 1979, pres., 1985-86; gov. gen. Govt. Can., 1990-95. Pres. Saskatoon Gallery and Conservatory Corp., 1974; campaign chmn. United Way, 1972; dir. United Community Funds, 1968-74. Named Chancellor and Prin. Companion of the Order of Can., Chancellor and Comdr. Order Mil. Merit, 1990; recipient St. Volodymyr medal award World Congress of Ukrainians, 1989; hon. fellow Royal Coll. Physicians and Surgeons, Can., 1990. Mem. Saskatoon Bar Assn., Can. Bar Assn.; hon. life mem., Law Soc. Sask. Died Dec. 15, 2002.

HOADLEY, WALTER EVANS, economist, financial executive, lay worker; b. San Francisco, Aug. 16, 1916; s. Walter Evans Sr. and Marie Howland (Preece) H.; m. Virginia Alm, May 20, 1939; children: Richard Alm, Jean Elizabeth (Mrs. Donald A. Peterson). AB, U. Calif., 1938, MA, 1940, PhD, 1946; D in Comml. Sci., Franklin and Marshall Coll., 1963; LLD (hon.), Golden Gate U., 1968, U. Pacific, 1979; hon. degree, El Instituto Technologico Autonomo de Mexico, 1974. Collaborator U.S. Bur. Agrl. Econs., 1938-39; rsch. economist Calif. Gov.'s Reemployment Commn., 1939, Calif. Gov.'s State Planning Bd., 1941; rsch. economist, teaching fellow U. Calif., 1938-41, supr. indsl. mgmt. war tng. office, 1941-42; econ. adviser U. Chgo. Civil Affairs Tng. Sch., 1945; sr. economist Fed. Res. Bank Chgo., 1942-49; economist Armstrong World Industries, Lancaster, Pa., 1949-54, treas., 1954-60, v.p., treas., 1960-66, dir., 1962-87; sr. v.p., chief economist, mem. mng. com. Bank of Am. NT & SA, San Francisco, 1966-68, exec. v.p., chief economist, mem. mng. com., mem. mgmt. adv. council, chmn. subs., 1968-81; ret., 1981; sr. research fellow Hoover Inst., Stanford U., from 1981. Dep. chmn. Fed. Res. Bank, Phila., 1960-61, chmn., 1962-66; chmn. Conf. Fed. Res. Chmn., 1966; faculty Sch. Banking U. Wis., 1945-49, 55, 58-66; adviser various U.S. Govt. Agys.; Wright Internat. Bd. Econ. and Investment Advisors, 1987—; spl. adviser U.S. Congl. Budget Office, 1975-87; mem. pub. adv. bd. U.S. Dept. Commerce, 1970-74; mem. White House Rev. Com. for Balance Payment Stats., 1963-65, Presdl. Task Force on Growth, 1969-70, Presdl. Task Force on Land Utilization, Presdl. Conf. on Inflation, 1974; gov. Com. on Developing Am. Capitalism, 1977—, chmn., 1987-88; dir. PLM Internat., 1989-97, Transisco Industries, Inc., 1981-95, Davis/Selected/Venture Advisors, 1981-96. Mem. Meth. Ch. Commn. on World Svc. and Fin. Phila. conf., 1957-64, chmn. investment com., 1964-66; bd. dirs., exec. com. Internat. Mgmt. and Devel. Inst., 1976-97; trustee Pacific Sch. Religion, 1968-89; adviser Nat. Commn. to Study Nursing and Nursing Edn., 1968-73; trustee Duke U., 1968-73, pres.'s assoc., 1973-80; trustee Golden Gate U., 1974-94, chmn. investment com., 1977-93; trustee World Wildlife U.S. Fund The Conservation Found., 1987-90; mem. periodic chmn. adminstrv. bd. Trinity United Meth. Ch., Berkeley, Calif., 1966-84; mem. adminstrv. bd., advisor Lafayette (Calif.) United Meth. Ch., 1984—; mem. bd. overseers vis. com. Harvard Coll. Econs., 1969-74; chmn. investment com. Calif.-Nev. Meth. Found., 1968-75, mem., 1976-91; mem. Calif. Gov.'s Coun. Econ. and Bus. Devel., 1978-82, chmn., 1980-82; co-chmn. San Francisco Mcpl. Adv. Com., 1996—, mem. 1981-96; trustee Hudson Inst., 1979-84; chmn. Bay Area Econ. Advisers, 1982—; spl. adviser Presdl. Cabinet Com. Innovation, 1978-79; mem. Calif. State Internat. Adv. Com., 1986-94; regent U. Calif., 1990-91; mem. adv. coun. Calif. Environ. Tech. Ptnrship., 1993-94; mem. econ. adv. coun. Calif. Inst. Fed. Policy Rsch., 1994—; trustee Internat. Ho. U. Calif., 1991—, Devel. Com., 1994—, chmn., 1995-97. Fellow Am. Statis. Assn. (v.p., bd. dirs. 1952-54, pres. 1958), Nat. Assn. Bus. Economists (San Francisco chpt. exec. com. 1989—), Am. Fin. Assn. (bd. dirs. 1955-56, pres. 1969); mem. Conf. Bus. Economists (chmn. 1962), Atlantic Coun. of U.S. (bd. dirs. 1985—), Internat. Acad. Mgmt., 1980—; U.S. Coun. for Internat. Bus. (sr. trustee 1992—), Commonwealth Club of Calif. (pres. 1987, chmn. pub. affairs-comm. com. 1995—), Am. Econ. Assn., Am. Mktg. Assn., Am. Bankers Assn. (chmn. urban and cmty. affairs com. 1972-73, mem. econ. adv. coun. 1976-78), Nat. Bur. Econ. Rsch. (bd. dirs. 1965-81), Western Econ. Assn. (bd. dirs., mem. steering com. 1966-94, 97—), U. Calif. Alumni Assn. (pres. 1989-91, pres. class of 1938 1988—, chmn. investment com. 1983-89, 94-96, Alumnus of Yr. 1993, Chancellor's Highest award 1999), U.S. Nat. Com. on Pacific Econ. Coop. (vice chmn. 1984-89, mem. exec. com. 1989-94), Caux Internat. Roundtable (chmn. steering com. 1993-97), St. Francis Yacht Club, Commonwealth Club, Pacific Union Club, Bankers Club, Silverado Country Club, Phi Beta Kappa Assocs. (bd. dirs. 1986-95), Kappa Alpha. Home: Reno, Nev. Died Feb. 19, 2003.

HOBAN, LILLIAN, writer, illustrator; b. Phila., May 18; d. Jules and Fanny (Godwin) Aberman; children: Phoebe, Abrom, Esmé, Julia. Student, Phila. Mus. Sch., Hanya Holm Sch. Dance, N.Y.C., Martha Graham Sch. Dance. Author, illustrator: (children's books) I Can Read, Arthur Series, 1972—; illustrator: (children's books) Frances Series, 1964— (Notable Book award), First Grade Series, 1967—, Jim Books, Charlie the Tramp (Christopher award). Mem. PEN, Authors Guild, Soc. Children's Book Writers. Democrat. Home: Wilton, Conn. Died Aug., 1998.

HODES, RICHARD S. physician; b. N.Y.C., Apr. 24, 1924; s. Stanley and Rosabel (Palley) H.; m. Marilyn Ann Hodes; m. Marjorie Cohen, May 19, 1946. BS, Tulane U., 1944, postgrad., 1946; MD, U. Minn., 1951. Diplomate Am. Bd. Anesthesiology. Intern U.S. Marine Hosp. Stapleton, Staten Island, N.Y., 1946-47; resident in anesthesiology U. Minn. Hosps., Mpls., 1949-51; dir. dept. anesthesiology Tampa Gen. Hosp., Fla., 1960-66; dir. anesthesiology Meml. Hosp., Tampa, 1992-96; prof., chmn. dept. anesthesiology U. South Fla. Coll. Medicine, Tampa, 1981-85, dep. dean, 1985-87; mem., speaker pro tem, majority leader Fla. Ho. of Reps., Tallahassee, 1966-82. Mem. AMA (del.), Fla. Med. Assn. (prs. 1979-81), Hillsborough County Med. Assn. (pres. 1977-78), Am. Soc. Anesthesiology, Nat. Coun. State Legislatures (pres. 1981-82). Democrat. Jewish. Died Jan. 18, 2002.

HODGES, ROSE MARIE, secondary education educator; b. Ft. Plain, N.Y., Mar. 10, 1927; d. Leo John Cosman Smith and Marion Louise Smith (Dingman) Powers; m. Edward Joseph Doyle, Sept. 4, 1948 (div. Oct. 1963); children: Stephen E. Doyle, Michael W. Doyle, Sharon M. Doyle; m. John H. Hodges, Aug. 25, 1979. BS, Ithaca Coll., 1949. Tchr. drama and English Bainbridge (N.Y.) H.S., 1956-58, Cortland (N.Y.) H.S., 1958-60, Vista (Calif.) Unified Sch. Dist., 1961-87, asst. to psychologist, 1987-88. Author: Rosie's Treasures, Books 1-4, 1993, My Diary Books, 1994. Mem. DAR. Avocations: poetry, oil painting, painting plaster crafts, crochet, embroidery. Home: Murrieta, Calif. Deceased.

HOEFT, DOUGLAS L. state legislator; BA, Denison U., 1964; MAT, Northwestern U., 1965; EdD, No. Ill. U., 1975. Tchr. Am. history Flower H.S., Chgo., 1964-65; tchr. social sci. Elgin (Ill.) H.S., 1965-75; instr. Grad. Sch. Nat. Lewis U., Lombard, Ill., 1985-87; asst. regional supt. schs. Kane County, Ill., 1975-87, supt., 1987-93; Mem. Ill. Ho. of Reps., from 1993. Contbr. articles to profl. jours. Mem. Gov.'s Task Force on Drugs and Alcohol, 1984; mem. adv. bd. Ill. Dept. Children and Family Svc., 1987-90. Deceased.

HOENIGSWALD, HENRY MAX, linguist, educator; b. Breslau, Germany, Apr. 17, 1915; s. Richard and Gertrud (Grunwald) H.; m. Gabriele Schoepflich, Dec. 26, 1944, (dec. 2001); children: Frances Gertrude, Susan Ann. Student, U. Munich, 1932-33, U. Zurich, 1933-34, U. Padua, 1934-36; DLitt, U. Florence, 1936, Perfezionamento, 1937; LHD (hon.), Swarthmore Coll., 1981, U. Pa., 1988, MA (hon.), 1971. Staff mem. Istituto Studi Etruschi, Florence, 1936-38; lectr., rsch. asst., instr. Yale U., 1939-42, 44-45. Lectr., instr. Hartford Sem. Found., 1942-43, 45-46; lectr. Hunter Coll., 1942-43, 46; lectr. charge Army specialized tng. U. Pa., Phila., 1943-44, assoc. prof., 1948-59, prof. linguistics, 1959-85, prof. emeritus, 1985—, chmn. dept. linguistics, 1963-70, co-chmn., 1978-79, cn. Caldwell Prize com., 1989-91; P-4 Fgn. Service Inst., Dept. State, 1946-47; assoc. prof. U. Tex., 1947-48; sr. linguist Deccan Coll., India, 1955; Fulbright lectr., Kiel, 1968, Oxford U., 1976-77; corp. vis. com. fgn. lits. and linguistics MIT, 1968-74; chmn. overseers com. to visit dept. linguistics Harvard U., 1978-84; vis. assoc. prof. U. Mich., 1946, 52, Princeton U., 1959-60; vis. assoc. prof. Georgetown U., 1952-53, 54, Collitz prof., 1955; vis. prof. Yale U., 1961-62, U. Mich., 1968; mem. Seminar, Columbia U., 1965—; vis. staff mem., Leuven, 1986; fellow St. John's Coll., Oxford U., 1976-77; del. Comparative Linguistics Internat. Rsch. and Exchs. Bd., 1986; cons. Etymological Dictionary of Old High German, 1980—; Poultney lectr. Johns Hopkins U., 1991; co-promotor, Leuven, 1992; mem. acad. com. Yarmouk U., 1997. Author: Spoken Hindustani, 1946-47, Language Change and Linguistic Reconstruction, 1960, Studies in Formal Historical Linguistics, 1973; editor: Am. Oriental Series, 1954-58, The European Background of American Linguistics, 1979, (with L. Wiener) Biological Metaphor and Cladistic Classification, 1987, (with M.R. Key) General and American Ethnolinguistics, 1989; assoc. editor Indian Jour. Linguistics, 1977—; cons. editor Jour. History of Ideas, 1978—; adv. bd. Lang. and Style, 1968—, Jour. Indo-European Studies, 1973—, Diachronica, 1984-94, Lynx, 1988—; csr. internat. adviser, cons. editor Internat. Ency. Linguistics, 1986-91, 2d edit., 2000—; editl. cons. Biographical Dictionary of Western Linguistics, 1994—. Am. Council Learned Socs. fellow, 1942-43, 44, Guggenheim fellow, 1950-51, Newberry Library fellow, 1956, NSF and Center Advanced Study Behavioral Scis. fellow, 1962-63, Faculty fellow Modern Langs. Coll. House, 1990-91; Festschrift in his honor, 1987. Fellow British Acad. (corr.), Am. Acad. Arts and Scis.; mem. NAS, Am. Philos. Soc. (rsch. com. 1978-84, libr. com. 1984-94, chmn. 1988-94, membership com. class IV 1984-90, chmn. 1987-90, exec. com. 1988-94, publs. com. 1994—, Henry Allen Moe prize 1991), N.Y. Acad. Scis., Linguistic Soc. Am. (pres. 1958), Am. Oriental Soc. (editor 1954-58, pres. 1966-67), Philol. Soc. (London), Linguistic Soc. India, Linguistics Assn. Gt. Britain, Internat. Soc. Hist. Linguistics, Indogermanische Gesellschaft, Am. Philol. Assn., Classical Assn. Atlantic States, Henry Sweet Soc., Studienkreis Geschichte der Sprachwissenschaft, Deutsch-polnische Gesellschaft der U. Wroclaw/Breslau, N.Am. Assn. History of Lang. Scis., Fulbright Assn., Internat. Soc. Friends of Wroclaw U., Fedn. Am. Scientists. Home: Washington, DC. Died June 16, 2003.

HOFF, SYD(NEY), cartoonist, author; b. N.Y.C., Sept. 4, 1912; s. Ben and Mary H.; m. Dora Berman, May 31, 1937; children: Susan Gross, Bonnie Stillman. Student, NAD. Cartoonist Laugh It Off Comic Strip, King Features Syndicate, 1957-71; cartoonist appearing in Playboy Mag.; author: The Man Who Loved Animals, 1982, The Young Cartoonist, 1983, Happy Birthday, Henrietta!, 1983; illustrator children's books including Oliver, 1960; author juvenile fiction Danny and the Dinosaur, 1958, Sammy the Seal, 1959, Julius, 1959, Where's Prancer, 1960, Who Will Be My Friends?, 1960, Little Chief, 1961, Albert The Albatross, 1961, Chester, 1961, Stanley, 1962, Grizzwold, 1963, I Should Have Stayed In Bed, 1965, Irving and Me, 1967, Horse in Harry's Room, 1970, Thunderhoof, 1971, When Will It Snow, 1971, (also illustrator) My Aunt Rosie, 1972, Katy's Kitten, 1975, Barkley, 1975, Walpole, 1977, Santa's Moose, 1979, Scarface Al and His Uncle Sam, 1980, The Young Cartoonist, 1983, (also illustrator) The Horse in Harry's Room, 1985, (also illustrator) Syd Hoff's Animal Jokes, 1986, (also illustrator) Barney's Horse, 1987, (also illustrator) Mrs. Brice's Mice, 1988, (also illustrator) Bernard on His Own, 1993, (also illustrator) Captain Cat, 1993, Duncan, the Dancing Duck, 1994, Drawing with Letters and Numbers, 1994, The Lighthouse Children, 1994, (also illustrator) Arturo's Stick, 1995, numerous others; illustrator: Rooftop Mystery, 1968, Donald & the Fish That Walked, 1974, The Homework Caper, 1985, Don't Be My Valentine, 1985, I Saw You In the Bathtub & Other Folk Rhymes, 1989, others; also short stories. Mem. Authors Guild. Home: Miami, Fla. Died May 12, 2004.

HOFSTATTER, LEOPOLD, psychiatrist, researcher; b. Vienna, Mar. 11, 1902; came to U.S., 1938, naturalized, 1944; s. Leopold H. and Josefine (Eibuschuetz) H.; m. Lilli Schwarz, Apr. 16, 1930; m. Theresa Adams Mayer, Sept. 4, 1971. MD, U. Vienna, 1926. Demonstrator 1st Anat. Inst., U. Vienna, 1925-27; Intern Allgemeines Krankenhaus Wien, Vienna, 1927-28; resident, demonstrator 1st Surg. Clinic, Vienna, 1928-30; resident Maria Theresien Schloessel, 1930-33; rsch. fellow, fellow in neurosurgery Washington U., St. Louis, 1938-40; resident St. Louis State Hosp., 1941-42, asst. supt., 1942-62, chief gen. med., surg. divsn., 1960-62; mem. staff St. Vincent's Hosp., 1948-62, Deaconess Hosp., 1948-62; supt. St. Louis State Sch. and Hosp., 1962-67. Sr. cons. resident tng. program Mo. Inst. Psychiatry, 1967-69, med. dir., 1972-74; supt. St. Louis State Hosp. Complex, 1970; clin. prof. psychiatry U. Mo. Sigma Xi fellow. Fellow AAAS, Am. Psychiat. Assn. (life); mem. Mo. Hosp. Physicians Assn. (past pres.), Sci. Rsch. Assn. Am., Ea. Mo. Psychiat. Soc., Goldenes Ehrenzeichen fuer Verdienste um das Land Wien (Austria), Sigma Xi. Home: Saint Louis, Mo. Died Dec. 3, 1999.

HOGAN, JOSEPH L. retired Roman Catholic bishop; Ordained Roman Cath. priest, 1942, ordained bishop, 1969. Priest Roman Cath. Ch., Rochester, 1942-69, bishop, 1969-78, ret., 1978. Deceased.

HOLLADAY, WILLIAM EDWARD, internist, cardiologist; b. White Plains, N.Y., Sept. 5, 1926; s. William Edward and Nancy Leigh (Eggleston) H.; m. Betsy Lee McNair, June 21, 1952; children: Elizabeth M., William Edward III, Lynn G., Carol M., John S. BS in Chemistry, U. Richmond, 1948; MD, Med. Coll. Va., 1952. Diplomate Am. Bd. Internal Medicine. Intern Univ. Hosp. of Med. Coll. Ga., Augusta, 1952-53, resident in internal medicine, 1953-56; fellow in cardiology Talmadge Meml. Hosp., Augusta, 1956-57; pvt. practice, Marietta, Ga., from 1957. Chief internal medicine, chmn. coronary care, dir. cardiac rehab. Kennestone Hosp., Marietta, pres. med. staff, 1973-74. With USN, 1944-46. Fellow ACP, Am. Coll. Cardiology, Am. Coll. Chest Physicians; mem. AMA, So. Med. Assn., Cobb County Med. Soc. (pres.), Rotary (pres. Marietta). Presbyterian. Home: Marietta, Ga. Died May 17, 2001.

HOLLAND, HAROLD HERBERT, banker; b. Clifton Forge, Va., Feb. 11, 1932; s. Tristum Shandy and Ida Blanche (Paxton) H.; m. Nellie Mae Thomas, Jan. 15, 1955; children: Richard Long, Michael Wayne Student, Coll. of William and Mary, 1953-54; BA, George Washington U., 1957, MBA, 1958. Tech. asst. Fed. Res. Bd., Washington, 1959-61; v.p. Falls Church (Va.) Bank, 1961-67; exec. v.p. Bank of New River, Radford, Va., 1967-70; pres., CEO Farmers Nat. Bank, Salem, Va., 1970-75; chmn., pres., CEO, dir. Am. Nat. Holding Co., Kalamazoo, 1975-86, Am. Nat. Bank & Trust, Kalamazoo, 1975-86; chmn. bd., dir. Kalamazoo Econ. Devel. Corp., 1977-84; dir. Wynfield Prodns.; chmn. Old Kent Bank of Kalamazoo, 1986-87. Cons. IMCOR, N.Y., 1989—; probate adv. Kalamazoo County Probate Ct. Exec. coun., v.p. S.W. Mich. coun. Boy Scouts Am., Kalamazoo, 1976-86, re-elected exec. coun., 1989—, pres., 1991-95; bd. dirs. Kalamazoo Conv. and Visitors Bur., 1981-82, Jobs for Mich. Grads., 1985-87, Downtown Tomorrow, Inc., 1985, West Mich. Telecom. Found., Blue Ridge Mountains coun. Boy Scouts Am., 1987-90, Jr. Achievement, 1994—; pres. Va. Mental Health Found., 1974-75; chmn. Kalamazoo 2000 Econ. Devel. Com., 1982; chmn., bd. dirs. Western Mich. U. Found., 1985-86; v.p., trustee I.S. Gilmore Found., Kalamazoo, 1976—, Arts Found. Mich.; trustee Borgess Hosp., 1986; chmn. Borgess Capital Campaign, 1986-87; county co-chmn. Gilmore for Congress, 1981; mem. City of Kalamazoo Pension Divestiture Study Com.; mem. campaign cabinet Goodwill Industries; probate adv. Kalamazoo County Probate Ct.; chmn., bd. trustees First United Meth. Ch., Kalamazoo, 1995-97. Recipient Disting. Service award U.S. Jaycees, 1965, Silver Beaver award Boy Scouts Am., 1985. Mem. Mich. Bankers Assn. (strategic planning com.), Mich. Coun. on Founds. (trustee 1994), Assn. of Bank Holding Cos. (dir. 1978-81), Kalamazoo County C. of C. (life, pres. 1981-83, chmn. strategic planning com. 1984), Mad Hatters (pres. Kaalamazoo), Rotary (Paul Harris fellow 1992). Republican. Methodist. Home: Kalamazoo, Mich. Died in July 1, 1999.

HOLLAND, HUBERT BRIAN, lawyer; b. London, Eng., Mar. 28, 1904; came to U.S., 1915, naturalized, 1929; s. Charles Hubert and Lois Amy (Barber) H.; m. Gertrude Bancroft, Aug. 4, 1931 (dec. Dec. 1975); children: Alice Katharine, Charles Howard; m. Helen Buxton, Aug. 21, 1976 (dec. Feb. 1997). Student, Taft Sch., 1918-21; Ph.B., Yale, 1925; LL.B., Harvard U., 1928. Bar: Pa. 1929, Mass. 1935. Assoc. Williams, Brittain & Sinclair, Phila., 1928-30; atty. Dept. Justice, Washington, 1930-35, asst. atty. gen., 1953-56; asso. firm Ropes & Gray., Boston, 1935-42, partner, 1942-53, 56-76, of counsel, 1976—. Lectr. Fed. Tax Inst. N.E., Inst. Fed. Taxation N.Y. U., 1950-51 Hon. trustee Kodaly Mus. Tng. Inst.; bd. dirs. Sharon (N.H.) Art Center, 1978-88. Fellow Am. Bar Found.; mem. Am. Law Inst., Am., Mass., Boston bar assns. Episcopalian. Home: Lexington, Mass. Deceased.

HOLLEMAN, BOYCE, lawyer; b. Wiggins, Miss., Feb. 26, 1924; m. Annie Louise Mounger; 6 children. BA, U. Miss., 1947, JD, 1950. Bar: Miss. 1950, U.S. Supreme Ct. 1973. Mem. Miss. Ho. of Reps., 1947-53; dist. atty. 2d Jud. Dist. Miss., 1953-72; atty. Bd. Suprs. Harrison County, Miss., 1972-89; pvt. practice law Gulfport, Miss. Lectr. in field. Lt. comdr. USN, 1942-46, ret. Fellow Am. Bar Found., Miss. Bar Found. Inc.; mem. ABA, Miss. State Bar (sr. v.p. 1951-52, pres. 1969-70), Assn. Trial Lawyers Am., Miss. Trial Lawyers Assn., Nat. Assn. Criminal Def. Lawyers, SAG (numerous acting roles on stage, TV, movies), Omicron Delta Kappa, Tau Kappa Alpha, Phi Delta Phi. Died Nov. 21, 2003.

HOLLER, JOSEPH, psychologist, consultant; b. Witt, Ill., Dec. 15, 1932; s. Joseph Henry and Jane (Summers) H.; m. Martha Carolyn Delashmit, Apr. 17, 1954 (div. Feb. 1971); 1 child, Joseph. BS magna cum laude, Ball State U., 1972, MA in Clin. Psychology, 1973, MA in Counseling Psychology, 1974; PhD in Counseling Psychology, Purdue U., 1977. Lic. psychologist, clin. marriage and family therapist, arborist; registered landscape architect. Landscape designer Gaar's, Inc., Chesterfield, Ind., 1960-65; pres. Landscape Assocs., Paris, from 1965; sr. ptnr., cons. psychologist Joseph Holler & Assocs., Paris, from 1972. Artist-in-residence Purdue U., 1984-85, vis. scholar, 1979—, mem. pres. coun., 1989—; cons. psychologist Indian Affairs, Pine Ridge, S.D., 1980, Eastern Mont., Glendive, 1982-83. Contbr. numerous articles in field aired on nat. pub. radio. Mem. Chesterfield Boosters Club, 1961-65, City Beautification Com., Anderson, Ind., 1965-69. Served with USAF, 1952-56. Mem. Am. Psychol. Assn., Am. Assn. Marriage and Family Therapy, Am. Orthopsychiat. Assn., Am. Personnel Assn. Lodges: Kiwanis (pres. Chesterfield chpt. 1961-66), Masons. Methodist. Avocations: hiking, gardening, crossword puzzles, writing, lang. study. Died July 10, 2001.

HOLLEY, EDWARD LEE, health care executive; b. Danville, Va., Sept. 27, 1938; s. John William and Nan Maude (Overton) H.; m. Patricia Squire Scheidemantel, Sept. 11, 1965; children: Mary Helen, Kathryn, Annalee. BS, Va. Commonwealth U., 1975. Cert. health care adminstr. Trooper Va. State Police, Richmond, 1963-67; asst. adminstr. Greenville Meml. Hosp., Emporia, Va., 1967-71; reimbursement supr. Blue Cross of Va., Richmond, 1971-78; cons. health care mgmt. Louisville, 1978-82; corp. sec. The King's Daus. & Sons, Louisville, from 1984, treas., from 1986, exec. v.p., from 1982. With U.S. Army, 1956-62. Mem. Lions, Rotary, Kiwanis. Episcopalian. Avocations: body building, reading, writing. Home: Louisville, Ky. Died Feb. 6, 2002.

HOLLEY, LAWRENCE ALVIN, retired labor union official; b. Elkhart, Ind., Nov. 7, 1924; s. Olin Coet and Carrie (Erwin) H.; m. Joyce Reed, Mar. 5, 1946 (dec. Jan. 1997); 1 child, Claudia Joyce. Student public schs., Elkhart. Bus. rep. Vancouver (Wash.) Aluminum Trades Council, 1951-57; pres. Wash. State Card and Label Council, 1952-57; internat. rep. Aluminum Workers Internat. Union, St. Louis, 1957-65, wage engr., 1965, research and ednl. dir., 1967-75, dir. Region 5 Vancouver, Wash., 1975-77; pres. Aluminum Workers Internat. Union (now Aluminum, Brick and Glass Workers Internat. Union), St. Louis, 1977-85; farmer La Center, Wash., 1985-99. V.p. Union Label and Service Trades Dept., AFL-CIO, 1980-85, exec. bd. Maritime Trades Dept., 1981-85, Garde de la Porte, 1986-87, elected chief, 1989-90, Box Car, 1987-88, state chmn. 1987-89, dir., Washington, 1988-89.; chief De Train Voiture, Clark County, Wash., 1989-99, Grand chief de Train, 1991-92, elected Grand chef De Gare Du Washington, 1992-93. Served with U.S. Army, 1943-46, PTO. Decorated Bronze Star with oak leaf cluster. Mem. DAV (life), China Burma India (life), Elks, Voyageur 40/8 Club, Eagles Lodge (life). Democrat. Home: La Center, Wash. Died Dec. 2, 1999.

HOLLISTER, BERNARD CLAIBORNE, secondary school educator; b. Chgo., Mar. 17, 1938; s. Joseph C. and Mildred (Pillinger) H.; m. Victoria Goben, May 28, 1994; 1 child, Suzanne. BA, Roosevelt U., Chgo., 1962; MA, No. Ill. U., 1967; MST, Ill. Inst. tech., 1971. Social worker Cook County Dept. Pub. Aid, Chgo., 1962-63; tchr. Sch. Dist. #88, Villa Park, Ill., 1963-86, 89-90, Ill. Math. and Sci. Acad., Aurora, Ill., 1986-89 and from 90. Tchr. Ctr. for Talent Devel., Northwestern U., summer, 1993, 94, 95, Coll. of Dupage and Nat. Coll.; cons. in field; coach Future Problem Solving Bowl, 1986—, Metro History Fair, 1986—. Author: Grokking the Future, 1973, Mass Media Workbook, 1991; editor: You and Science Fiction, 1990; contbr. articles to profl. jours. Trustee Aurora Hist. Soc., 1990—; mem. bd. Chgo. Metro History Fair, 1991—. NEH fellow, 1984-89, 92, Woodrow Wilson Found. fellow, 1991, James Madison Found. fellow, 1987; recipient Olive Foster award in History, 1993. Mem. Ill. Hist. Soc., Art Inst. Chgo., Chgo. Hist. Soc., Metro. Mus. Art, Nat. Coun. for Social Studies, Ill. Coun. for Social Studies. Democrat. Avocations: collecting political buttons, old time radios. Home: Geneva, Ill. Died Nov. 25, 2000.

HOLMES, FREDERIC LAWRENCE, science historian; b. Cin., Feb. 6, 1932; m. Harriet Holmes, 1959; (dec. 2000), 3 children. BS, MIT, 1954; MA, Harvard U., 1958, PhD, 1962. Asst. prof. history of sci. MIT, 1962-64; asst. prof. to assoc. prof. Yale U., New Haven, 1964-72, prof., chmn. sect. history of medicine, 1979—2003, master Jonathan Edwards Coll., 1982-87; prof. history of sci., chmn. dept. history of medicine and sci. U. Western Ont., 1972-79; Dept. of Hist. of Med. Yale U Schl Med, New Haven, 1979—2003. Author: Claude Bernard and Animal Chemistry, 1974, Lavoisier and the Chemistry of Life, 1985, Eighteenth Century Chemistry as an Investigative Enterprise, 1989, Hans Krebs: The Formation of a Scientific Life, 1991, Hans Krebs: Architect of Intermediary Metabolism, 1993, Antoine Lavoisier-The Next Crucial Year: or the Souras of His Quantitative Method in Chemistry, 1998, Meselson, Stahl, and the Replication of DNA: A History of the Most Beautiful Experience in Biology, 2001; contbr. articles to profl. jours. Rsch. grantee NIH, 1963-67, NSF, 1968-70, 1988-2003, Can. Coun., 1973-74 Mem. History of Sci. Soc. (pres. 1981-83), Am. Assn. History Medicine, Can. Soc. Hist. and Philos. Sci. Died Mar. 27, 2003.

HOLMES, MARJORIE ROSE, writer; b. Storm Lake, Iowa; d. Samuel Arthur and Rosa (Griffith) H.; m. Lynn Mighell, Apr. 9, 1932; children— Marjorie Mighell Croner, Mark, Mallory, Melanie Mighell Dimopoulos; m. George P. Schmieler, July 4, 1981. Student, Buena Vista Coll., 1927-29, DLitt (hon.), 1976; BA, Cornell Coll., 1931, LHD (hon.), 1998. Tchr. writing Cath. U., 1964-65, U. Md., 1967-68. Mem. staff Georgetown Writers Conf., 1959-81 Free-lance writer short stories, articles, verse for mags. including McCall's, Redbook, Reader's Digest; bi-weekly columnist: Love and Laughter, Washington Evening Star, 1959-75; monthly columnist: Woman's Day, 1971-77; author: World By the Tail, 1943, Ten O'Clock Scholar, 1946, Saturday Night, 1959, Cherry Blossom Princess, 1960, Follow Your Dream, 1961, Love is a Hopscotch Thing, 1963, Senior Trip, 1962, Love and Laughter, 1967, I've Got to Talk to Somebody, God, 1969, Writing the Creative Article, 1969, Who Am I, God?, 1971, To Treasure Our Days, 1971, Two from Galilee, 1972, Nobody Else Will Listen, 1973, You and I and Yesterday, 1973, As Tall as My Heart, 1974, How Can I Find You God?, 1975, Beauty in Your Own Back Yard, 1976, Hold Me Up a Little Longer, Lord, 1977, Lord, Let Me Love, 1978, God and Vitamins, 1980, To Help You Through the Hurting, 1983, Three from Galilee—The Young Man from Nazareth, 1985, Writing the Creative Article Today, 1986, Marjorie Holmes' Secrets of Health, Energy and Staying Young, 1987, The Messiah, 1987, At Christmas the Heart Goes Home, 1991, The Inspirational Writings of Marjorie Holmes, 1991, Gifts Freely Given, 1992, Writing Articles From the Heart, 1993, Second Wife, Second Life!, 1993, Still by Your Side-How I Know a Great Love Never Dies, 1996; contbg. editor Guideposts, 1977—; bd. dirs. The Writer, 1975—. Bd. dirs. Found. Christian Living, 1975—. Recipient Honor Iowans award Buena Vista Coll., 1966, Alumni Achievement award Cornell Coll., 1963, Woman of Achievement award Nat. Fedn. Press Women, 1972; Celebrity of Yr. award Women in Communications, 1975; Woman of Yr. award McLean Bus. and Profl. Women, 1976; award Freedom Found. at Valley Forge, 1977; gold medal Marymount Coll. Va., 1978 Mem. Am. Newspaper Women's Club, Nat. Fedn. Press Women, Author's Guild, Washington Nat. Press Club. Home: Manassas, Va. Deceased.

HOLMES, PETER FENWICK, SR., petroleum company executive; b. Athens, Greece, Aug. 27, 1932; s. Gerald Holmes and Caroline Morris Holmes; m. Judith M. Walker, 1955; 3 children. Ed. Malvern Coll., Trinity Coll., Cambridge, Eng. With Shell Group of Cos., 1965—, chief exec. officer Shell Markets, Middle East, Ltd., 1965-68, Shell Cos. in Libya, 1970-73, mng. dir. and chief exec. officer Shell Petroleum Devel. Co. of Nigeria, Ltd., 1977-81, pres. Shell Internat. Trading Co., 1981-83, mng. dir. Shell Transport and Trading, 1982—, chmn. bd., 1985—1993; mng. dir. Royal Dutch/Shell Group, 1982—, vice chmn. com. Author: Mountains and a Monastery, 1958, Nigeria, Giant of Africa, 1985. Avocations: mountaineering; travel; 19th century travel literature. Died Mar. 8, 2002.

HOLMGREN, LATON EARLE, clergyman; b. Mpls., Feb. 20, 1915; s. Frank Albert and Freda Ida (Lindahl) H. Student, U. Minn., 1934-35; AB cum laude, Asbury Coll., 1936; M. Div. summa cum laude, Drew U., 1941; postgrad., Edinburgh (Scotland) U., 1947; D.D., Ill. Wesleyan U., 1956, Asbury Theol. Sem., 1972. Ordained to ministry United Methodist Ch., 1942; assoc. minister Calvary Meth. Ch., East Orange, N.J., 1940-42, Christ Ch. Meth., N.Y.C., 1943-48; minister Tokyo (Japan) Union Ch., 1949-52; lectr. internat. dept. Tokyo U. Commerce, 1950-52; adviser Japanese Fgn. Office, Tokyo, 1951; sec. for Asia Am. Bible Soc., N.Y.C., 1952-54, exec. sec., 1954-62, gen. sec., rec. sec., 1963-78, cons., 1978-91, ret., 1991. Mem. exec. com. United Bible Socs., Stuttgart, Germany, 1957-78, chmn., 1963-72, spl. cons., 1978-88. Recipient Gutenberg award, 1975, Disting. Alumni award Asbury Coll., 1981, Baron von Canstein award, 1982, Disting. Svc. award United Bible Socs., 1990. Home: Rancho Mirage, Calif. Died Jan. 18, 2004.

HOLTER, DON WENDELL, retired bishop; b. Lincoln, Kans., Mar. 24, 1905; s. Henry O. and Lenna (Mater) H.; m. Isabelle Elliott, June 20, 1931; children: Phyllis Holter Dunn, Martha Holter Hudson (dec.), Heather Holter Ellis. BA, Baker U., 1927, DD, 1948; postgrad., Harvard U., 1928; BD, Garrett Theol. Sem., 1930; PhD, U. Chgo., 1934; LLD, Dakota Wesleyan U., 1969; DD, St. Paul Sch. Theology, 1973, Westmar Coll., 1976. Ordained to ministry Meth. Ch. as elder, 1934. Asst. minister Euclid Meth. Ch., Oak Park, Ill., 1930-34; missionary in Philippines, 1935-45; minister Central Ch., Manila, 1935-40; interned with family by the Japanese, Santo Tomas Internment Camp, Manila, 1942-45; prof. Union Theol. Sem., Manila, 1935-40, pres., 1940-45; minister Hamline Meth. Ch., St. Paul, 1946-49; prof. Garrett Theol. Sem., 1949-58; founding pres. St. Paul Sch. Theology, 1958-72; bishop Nebr. area United Meth. Ch., 1972-76. Del. Internat. Missionary Conf., India, 1938; spl. study mission, Africa, 1958; rep., mem. pers. com. Meth. Bd. of Global Ministries, 1964-72; chmn. commn. ministry Gen. Conf., 1968-70, mem. gen. bd. higher edn. and ministry, 1972-76, chmn. div. ordained ministry, 1972-76, del. gen. and jurisdictional confs., 1964, 66, 68, 70, 72 Author: Fire on the Prairie, Methodism in the History of Kansas, 1969, Flames on the Plains, A History of United Methodism in Nebraska, 1983, The Lure of Kansas, The Story of the Evangelicals and United Brethren, 1853-1968, 1990. Trustee St. Paul Sch. Theology. Home: Lees Summit, Mo. Died Sept. 12, 1999.

HOLTER, JOHN WILLIAM, medical instrument manufacturing company executive; b. Chgo., Apr. 1, 1916; s. Charles Robert and Favian (Erskine) H. Grad., Spring Garden (Pa.) Inst., 1938; D.Sc., U. Sheffield (Eng.), 1976. Rsch. technician Socony-Vacuum Oil co., 1946-50; Yale & Towne, 1950-56; founder Holter Co., Bridgeport, Pa., 1956; owner, 1956-67; tech. cons., dir. Extracorporeal Med. Spltys., Inc., King of Prussia, Pa., 1967-77; co-founder Holter-Hausner Internat. V.p. Montgomery County chpt. for Retarded Children, 1960-66; pub. rels. chmn. Metric assn. U.S., 1969. Served with AUS, 1941-45. Recipient A.C.S. award, 1957; named Man of Yr., Norristown, Bridgeport (Pa.) V.F.W., 1958. Mem. Soc. for Rsch. into Hydrocephalus and Spina bifida (hon.), Internat. Soc. Pediat. Neurosurgeons (hon.), European Soc. Pediatric Neurosurgery (assoc.).

Achievements include invention of valve for controlling hydrocephalus; research on artificial heart; patentee med., mech. and yacht devices. Home: Saint Petersburg, Fla. Died Dec. 22, 2003.

HOLTON, JAMES R. atmospheric science educator; BA, Harvard U., 1960; PhD in Meteorology, MIT, 1964. Acting dir. Joint Inst. for Study of Atmosphere and Ocean U. Wash., Seattle, 1981-82, sr. fellow. Mem. numerous adv. coms. and NASA sci. teams; prin. investigator sci. team Upper Atmosphere Rsch. Satellite. Author: An Introduction to Dynamic Meterology; co-author: Middle Atmosphere Dynamics; contbr. numerous articles to profl. jours. Fellow Am. Meteorol. Soc., Am. Geophys. Union (Roger Revelle medal, 2000); mem. NAS (award for sci. reviewing 1998). Achievements includes research on large-scale dynamics, with emphasis on the dynamics of the stratosphere including stratospheric effects of gravity waves generated by convective storms, transport on grace constituents in the stratosphere, and stratosphere-troposphere exchange of mass and constituents. Home: Seattle, Wash. Died Mar. 3, 2004.

HOLTZ, EDGAR WOLFE, lawyer; b. Clarksburg, W.Va., Jan. 18, 1922; s. Dennis Drummond and Oleta (Wolfe) H.; m. Alberta Lee Brinkley, May 6, 1944; children: Diana Hilary, Heidi Johanna. BA, Denison U., 1943; JD, U. Cin., 1949. Bar: Ohio 1949, U.S. Supreme Ct. 1957, D.C. 1961. Assoc. firm Matthews & Matthews, Cin., 1949-53; asst. dean Chase Law Sch., Cin., 1952-55; asst. solicitor City of Cin., 1950-55; asst. chief office of opinions and rev. FCC, Washington, 1955-56, dep. gen. counsel, 1956-60; mem. firm Hogan & Hartson, Washington, 1960—. Trustee Denison U., Granville, Ohio, 1974—: chmn. bd. Ctr. for the Arts, Vero Beach, Fla., 1995-97; bd. dirs. Cultural Coun. Indian River County, 1998—, chmn. 2000-01; bd. dirs. McKee Bot. Garden, 2001. Served to 1st lt. USAAF, 1943-45. Decorated D.F.C., Air medal with 2 clusters, 8 Battle Stars; recipient Alumni citation Denison U., 1993. Fellow Am. Bar Found.; mem. ABA (standing com. on gavel awards), Ohio Bar Assn., D.C. Bar Assn., Fed. Comms. Bar (pres. 1977-78), Am. Juicature Soc., Newcomen Soc. N.Am., Moorings Club (Vero Beach, Fla.), Met. Club (Washington, George Town Club (Washington). Republican. Methodist. Home: New Market, Md. Died Dec. 1, 2003.

HOLTZMEIER, DAWN KAREN, anatomy and physiology educator; b. Marietta, Ohio, Oct. 3, 1941; d. Donald Edwin and Mary Ellen (Covert) Perry; m. Lindell R. Holtzmeier, July 10, 1965; children: Brant, Meri Ann. BS with highest honors and spl. honors, Ohio U., 1963; MS, Purdue U., 1965. Grad. teaching assoc. Purdue U., West Lafayette, Ind., 1964-65, instr. biology, acad. advisor dept. biol. scis., 1965-67; asst. editor South Life Newspaper, Brecksville, Ohio, 1967-68; biology lab. instr., rsch. asst. botany dept. Ohio U., Athens, 1968-69; instr. anatomy & physiology, lab. coord. allied health dept. Hocking Coll., Nelsonville, from 1976. Co-founder, videotape prodr. Tele-Lab, Athens, 1986-87; mem. faculty devel. coun. Hocking Coll., 1990-95, co-chair coun., 1984-86, mem. pres.'s task force, 1983, occupational task analyst, 1983-85, mistress of ceremonies graduation, 1993; participant Pew Higher Edn. Roundtable, 1995. Author: Applied Anatomy and Physiology: A Laboratory Manual and Workbook for Health Careers, 1993; co-author, prodr.: (videotape) Basic Heart Dissection; writer series of computer programs for self-study of anatomy and physiology. Mem., chaplain PEO Sisterhood, Athens, 1972—, pres. chpt. G, 1980-82, treas., 1984-86; deacon United Presbyn. Ch. Recipient Nat. Inst. for Staff and Orgnl. Devel. Tchg. Excellence award U. Tex., 1991, 93. Mem. Ohio Acad. of Sci., Kappa Delta Pi, Phi Beta Kappa. Republican. Achievements include development of science course for all non-science majors, internal human machine course. Home: Athens, Ohio. Died Dec. 16, 1999.

HOLZMAN, PHILIP SEIDMAN, psychologist, educator; b. NYC, May 2, 1922; s. Barnet and Natalie (Seidman) H.; m. Hannah Abarbanell, Sept. 18, 1946; children: Natalie Kay, Carl David, Paul Benjamin. BA, CCNY, 1943; PhD, U. Kans., 1952. Diplomate: Am. Bd. Examiners Profl. Psychology. Psychology intern Topeka VA Hosp., 1946-49; psychologist Topeka State Hosp., 1949-51, cons., 1951-58; psychologist Menninger Found., Topeka, 1949-68, dir. research tng., 1963-68; prof. psychiatry and psychology U. Chgo., 1968-77; prof. psychology dept. psychology Harvard U., 1977-92; prof. dept. psychiatry Med. Sch., 1977-92; Esther and Sidney R. Rabb prof. psychology Harvard U., 1984-92, prof. emeritus, 1992; chief Lab. of Psychology McLean Hosp., Belmont, Mass., 1977—; tng. and supervising psychoanalyst Boston Psychoanalytic Soc. and Inst., 1977—. Vis. prof. U. Minn., 1965, U. Kans., 1966, Boston U., 1973, Jefferson Med. Coll., 1981, U. Pa., 1987; Thomas William Salmon lectr. N.Y. Acad. Medicine, 1994; small grants com. NIMH, 1960-64, clin. projects research rev. com., 1964-68, clin. program projects research rev. com., 1970-74, treatment devel. and assessment rev. com., 1982-86; cons. Ill. State Psychiat. Inst., 1970-77; adv. coms. classification of mental disorders WHO. Author: (with others) Cognitive Control, 1959, Psychoanalysis and Psychopathology, 1970, (with Karl Menninger) The Theory of Psychoanalytic Technique, rev. edit, 1973; editor: (with Merton M. Gill) Psychology Versus Metapsychology, 1975; (with Mary Hollis Johnston) Assessing Schizophrenic Thinking, 1979; bd. editors: Psychol. Issues, 1968-2004, Contemporary Psychology, 1969-76, Bull. of Menninger Clinic, 1961-2004, Psychoanalysis and Contemporary Thought, Jour. Psychiat. Rsch., 1980-92; assoc. editor Schizophrenia Bulletin, Schizophrenia Rsch., Harvard Review of Psychiatry, Harvard Mental Health Letter; contbr. articles to profl. jours. Mem. Topeka Mayor's Com. on Human Rels., 1963-68; chmn. bd. dirs. Founds.' Fund for Rsch. in Psychiatry; mem. program adv. com. MacArthur Found., sci. adv. bd. NIMH, 1986-92; bd. trustees Menninger Found., 1978-2004; mem. sci. coun. Nat. Alliance Rsch. Schizophrenia and Depression, 1989-2004. With AUS, 1943-46. Recipient Career Scientist award NIMH, 1974-77, 92-2002, Stanley Dean award Am. Coll. Psychiatrists, 1984, Lieber prize Nat. Alliance for Rsch. in Schizophrenia and Depression, 1988, Joseph Zubin award Soc. Rsch. in Psychopathology, 1994, Thomas William Salmon medal N.Y. Acad. Medicine, 1994, Townsend Harris medal CCNY, Gold medal for lifetime achievement APA, 1997, William K. Warren award Internat. Congress on Schizophrenia Rsch., 1997, Alexander Gralnick award Am. Psychol. Found., 2002. Fellow APA, AAAS, Am. Acad. Arts and Scis., Am. Coll. Neuropsychopharmacology, Soc. Neurosci.; mem. Am. Psychoanalytic Assn., Boston Psychoanalytic Soc., Am. Psychopath. Assn., Inst. Medicine NAS, Soc. for Rsch. in Psychopathology (pres. 1997-98). Home: Cambridge, Mass. Died June 1, 2004.

HOMAN, RICHARD WARREN, neurologist, academic administrator, medical educator; b. N.Y.C., July 28, 1940; s. H. Frank and Irmgard Homan; m. Katherine Poulos, June 16, 1963; children: Gregory William, Christopher Allen. BA, Colgate U., 1962; MD, SUNY, 1966; MA, U. Tex. Med. Br., 1999-2001. Diplomate Am. Bd. Psychiatry and Neurology, Am. Bd. Clin. Neurophysiology; cert. Nat. Bd. Med. Examiners. Resident in neurology UCLA, 1970; fellow in neurophysiology Albert Einstein Coll. Medicine, Bronx, NY, 1972—74; asst. prof. neurology U. Tex., Southwestern Med. Sch. and Dallas VA Med. Ctr., 1974—82, assoc. prof. neurology, chief neurology svc., 1982—89; prof., chmn. neurology Med. Coll. Ohio, Toledo, 1989—94; chmn. neurology Tex. Tech. U. Health Sci. Ctr., Lubbock, 1994—97, prof. neuropsychiatry and behavioral medicine, pharm. practice, pharm. scis., dir. Ctr. Neuropsychiat. Studies, 1997—99; bioethics cons., 2001—04; mem. bioethics faculty Southwestern Med. Sch., Dallas, 2002—04. Examiner Am. Bd. Clin. Neurophysiology, 1981-94; cons. Tex. State Bd. Med. Examiners, Austin, 1995-2000. Editor (collected sci. manuscripts) Rational Polypharmacy, 1996; contbr. chpts. to books. Mem. profl. adv. bd. Dallas Epilepsy Found., 1985-87, Epilepsy Found. N.W. Ohio, Toledo, 1989-94; mediator South Plains Ctr. for Dispute Resolution, Lubbock, 1998. Fellow Am. Electroencepalographic Soc., Am. Acad. Neurology; mem. Am. Epilepsy Soc., Phi Beta Kappa. Avocations: scuba diving, playing harp. Died Mar. 8, 2003.

HONIG, ELEANOR D. artist; b. N.Y.C., June 20, 1930; d. Israel and Betty (Goldfarb) Wolin; m. Erwin Honig, May 28, 1950; children: Sharon Citrin, Leslie A. BA, Queens Coll., 1967; MA, C.W. Post U., 1972. Cert. secondary supr. in art., N.Y. Fashion designer Betty Lou Jrs., N.Y.C., 1949-52; secondary supr. in art Oyster Bay (N.Y.)-East Norwich Sch. Dist., 1967-79; artist-in-residence BOCES Cultural Arts, Syosset, N.Y., 1979-81; adj. prof. art Nassau C.C., Garden City, N.Y., from 1980. Mem. exec. bd. Discovery Gallery Hempstead Harbor Artists, Glen Cove, N.Y. Exhibited in group show at Heckscher Mus., Huntington, N.Y., 1991; represented in permanent collections Jane Voorhies Zimmerli Art Mus. Rutgers U., N.J., Islip (N.Y.) Art Mus. Recipient 1st prize Wunsch Arts Ctr., 1991, award Parrish Art Mus., Southampton, N.Y., 1992. Mem. Nat. Assn. Women Artists (exec. bd. 1994—, Bronze medal 1988-91, 88), Nat. Drawing Assn., Pastel Soc. Am. Avocations: swimming, hiking, dance. Died Dec. 14, 2001.

HOOD, MORRIS, state legislator; b. June 5, 1934;, Wayne State U. State rep. Dist. 6 Mich. Ho. of Reps., 1970-94, state rep Dist. 11, from 1995. Chmn. Higher Edn. & Regulatory Subcoms., mem. Appropriations Com. Mich. Ho. of Reps. Del. Dem. Nat. Conv., 1980; chmn. Mich. State Black Caucus. Mem. NAACP, Mich. Dem. Black Caucus, Econ. Club, Trade Union Leadership Coun., Urban Alliance, Detroit Urban League. Home: Detroit, Mich. Died 1998.

HOOLE, ALAN NORMAN, British government official; b. Apr. 25, 1942; s. Walter Norman and Elsie Hoole; m. Pauline Claire Bettison, 1962 (diss.); 1 son, 1 dau.; m. Delia Rose Clingham, 1982. Educated, Sheffield U., Coll. of Law, London. Admitted as solicitor, 1964; ptnr. Blakesley & Rooth, Solicitors, Chesterfield, 1965-78; atty. gen. St. Helena, 1978-83, 1983-85, 89-90; chief sec., 1986-88; dep. gov., 1990-91; gov., comdr.-in-chief, 1991-95; gov., 1995-97. Deceased.

HOPE, BOB, actor, comedian, producer, writer; b. Eltham, Eng., May 29, 1903; arrived in US, 1907, naturalized, 1920; s. William Henry Hope, Avis Townes Hope; m. Dolores Reade, Feb. 19, 1934; children: Linda, Anthony, Kelly, Nora. Ed. pub. schs., Cleve.; DFA (hon.), Brown U., Jacksonville (Fla.) U.; LHD (hon.), Quincy (Ill.) Coll., Georgetown U., So. Meth. U., Dallas, Ohio State U., Ind. U., John Carroll U., U. Nev., Monmouth Coll., Whittier Coll., Pa. Mil. Coll., Miami U., Oxford, Ohio, U. Cin., Calif. State Colls., Mercy Coll., N.J., Coll. of Desert, Baldwin-Wallace Coll., St. Louis U., Oral Roberts U., U. Charleston; LLD (hon.), U. Wyo., Northwestern U., Evanston, Ill., St. Bonaventure U., Pace Coll., Pepperdine U., U. Scranton, Western State U., Calif.; HHD (hon.), Ohio Dominican Coll., Bowling Green U., Santa Clara U., Fla. So. Coll., Wilberforce U., Northwood Inst., Mich., Norwich U., Bethel Coll., Tenn., Utah State U., St. Anselm's Coll., N.H., Washington U., St. Louis; D of Internat. Relations (hon.), Salem Coll.; D of Pub. Service (hon.), St. Ambrose Coll.; D of Humane Service (hon.), Drury Coll.; D of Humane Humor (hon.), Benedictine Coll., Kans.; D of Performing Arts (hon.), Dakota Wesleyan U.; LittD (hon.), Gonzaga U. Performer with the USO for U.S. and other Allied troops, 1941-90, Entertainment Coord., USO, 1941-2001. Vaudeville debut in dancing act with partner Mildred Rosequist, 1921; later appeared on stage and in motion pictures, TV, radio; actor: (Broadway) Ballyhoo, 1932, Roberta, 1933, Say When, 1934, Ziegfeld Follies, 1935, Red Hot and Blue, 1936, Smiles, 1938, (films) Going Spanish, 1934, Paree, Paree, 1934, Watch the Birdie, 1935, The Old Grey Mayor, 1935, Double Exposure, 1935, Shop Talk, 1936, Calling all Tars, 1936, The Big Broadcast of 1938, 1938, Thanks for the Memory, 1938, College Swing, 1938, Give Me a Sailor, 1938, Never Say Die, 1939, Some Like It Hot, 1939, The Cat and the Canary, 1939, The Road to Singapore, 1940, The Ghost Breakers, 1940, Caught in the Draft, 1941, Nothing But the Truth, 1941, Road to Zanzibar, 1941, Louisiana Purchase, 1941, Road to Morocco, 1942, My Favorite Blonde, 1942, Star Spangled Rhythm, 1942, They Got Me Covered, 1943, Let's Face It, 1943, The Princess and the Pirate, 1944, The Road to Utopia, 1946, Monsieur Beaucaire, 1946, My Favorite Brunette, 1947, Where There's Life, 1947, Road to Rio, 1947, Paleface, 1948, Sorrowful Jones, 1949, The Great Lover, 1949, Fancy Pants, 1950, The Lemon Drop Kid, 1951, My Favorite Spy, 1951, Greatest Show on Earth, 1952, Son of Paleface, 1952, Road to Bali, 1952, Off Limits, 1953, Here Come the Girls, 1953, Casanova's Big Night, 1954, Seven Little Foys, 1955, That Certain Feeling, 1956, Iron Petticoat, 1956, Beau James, 1957, The Heart of Show Business, 1957, Paris Holiday, 1958, Alias Jesse James, 1959, The Facts of Life, 1960, Bachelor in Paradise, 1961, Road to Hong Kong, 1962, Critic's Choice, 1963, Call Me Bwana, 1963, A Global Affair, 1964, I'll Take Sweden, 1965, Boy, Did I Get a Wrong Number!, 1966, Eight on the Lam, 1967, The Private Navy of Sargeant O'Farrell, 1968, How to Commit Marriage, 1969, Cancel My Reservation, 1972, The Muppet Movie, 1979; appeared on numerous TV variety shows and specials including Star Spangled Rhythm, 1942, Show Business at War, 1943, The All-Star Bond Rally, 1945, The Bob Hope Show, 1952, The Jack Benny Program, 1954-68, The Colgate Comedy Hour, 1955, The Frank Sinatra Show, 1957, This Is Your Life, 1960, The Bob Hope Thanksgiving Special, 1964, The Bob Hope Christmas Show, 1965-94, The Tonight Show Starring Johnny Carson, 1969-92, Bob Hope Presents the Chrysler Theatre, 1963-65, The Dean Martin Show, 1966, Rowan & Martin's Laugh-In, 1968-71, The Bob Hope Christmas Special, 1987, The Bob Hope Birthday Special, 1988, Bob Hope's Yellow Ribbon Party, 1991, Bob Hope: A 90th Birthday Celebration, 1993, Bob Hope: Laughing with the Presidents, 1996; hosted Academy awards ceremony 16 times from 1940-78. TV movies include Where Have All the Children Gone, 1980, A Masterpiece of Murder, 1986; author: They Got Me Covered, 1941, I Never Left Home, 1944, So This is Peace, 1946, Have Tux, Will Travel, 1954, I Owe Russia, 1963, Five Women I Love, 1966, The Last Christmas Show, 1974, Road to Hollywood, 1977, (with Melville Shavelson) Confessions of a Hooker-Lifelong Love Affair with Golf, 1985, Don't Shoot It's Only Me, 1990, Dear Prez, I Wanna Tell Ya!, 1996. Recipient numerous awards and honors including Special Silver Plaque, Acad. of Motion Picture Arts and Sci., 1940, Golden Apple awards, 1941, 43, honorary Acad. awards, 1941, 45, 53, 66, Golden Globe award ambassador of good, 1958, Murray-Green-Meany award for community service, AFL/CIO, 1958, Jean Hersholt Humanitarian award, Acad. of Motion Picture Arts and Sci., 1959, Silver Buffalo award, Boy Scouts of America, 1959, Congressional Gold Medal, 1962, Cecil B. DeMille award, 1963, Golden Globe awards, 1963, Gold Medal, Nat. Inst. of Soc. Sci., 1964, Gold Medal, Acad. of Motion Picture Arts and Sci., 1965, Emmy award, 1966, Life Achievement award, SAG, 1966, Humanitarian award, Variety Clubs Internat., 1967, named first honorary man of the yr., Hasty Pudding Theatricals, Harvard U., 1967, Pres. Medal of Freedom, 1969, Louella Parsons award, Hollywood Women's Press Assn., 1975, Freedom Medal, City of Phila., 1975, inducted into Entertainment Hall of Fame, 1975, Patriot award, Congressional Medal of Honor Soc., 1976, Commander, Order of the British Empire, 1976, inducted into Broadcasting Hall of Fame, Nat. Assn. of Broadcasters, 1977, Bob Jones award, USGA, 1978, Charles Evans Hughes Gold Medal, Nat. Conference of Christians and Jews, 1979, Defense Ind. award for Defense Preparedness, Am. Defense Preparedness Assn., 1980, Jefferson award, greatest public service performed by a private citizen, Am. Inst. for Pub. Service, 1982, inducted into PGA/World Golf Hall of Fame, Professional Golfers' Assn., 1983, Kennedy Center Honors, 1985; Medal of Liberty, Statue of Liberty-Ellis Island Found., 1986, inducted into Hall of Fame, Acad. of Television Arts and Sci., 1987, Christopher award, 1990, honorary knighthood, 1998; named honorary veteran of the U.S. Armed Forces. Achievements include world's most honored entertainer with over 1,500 awards. Died July 27, 2003.

HOPKINS, THOMAS MATTHEWS, former naval officer; b. Balt., Feb. 3, 1927; s. John Howard and Grace Marie (Martin) H.; m. Marjorie Kendall Leonard, Apr. 8, 1950; children: Margaret, Karen, Annette. BS in Mech. Engring, Cornell U., 1948; naval engr. degree, M.I.T., 1955. Commd. ensign U.S. Navy, 1948, advanced through grades to rear adm., 1977; project officer, submarines Bur. Ships and subsequently Naval Ship Systems Command, 1964-68; force maintenance officer U.S. Submarine Force, U.S. Atlantic Fleet, 1968-71; project mgr. Naval Sea Systems Command, Attack Submarine (SSN) Acquisition Project, 1972-76; fleet maintenance officer U.S. Atlantic Fleet, 1977-80; dep. comdr. for ship systems Naval Sea Systems Command, Washington, 1980-82, ret., 1982; exec. cons. Harbridge

House, Inc., Washington, 1982-84, U.S. Maritime Adminstrn., Washington, 1982-84; ind. cons. in naval architecture and marine engring. with emphasis on submarines and ship survivability, 1984—. Adj. rsch. staff mem. Inst. for Def. Analyses,. 1995—. Decorated Meritorious Service medal (2), Legion of Merit. Mem. ASTM (bd. dirs. 1988-90, F-25 com. on ships and marine tech.), Am. Soc. Naval Engrs., Soc. Naval Archs. and Marine Engrs., Internat. Orgn. for Standardization (tech. com. on ships and marine tech., secretariat for piping and machinery subcom. 1995-2000, chmn. 2000-02). Episcopalian. Home: Mc Lean, Va. Died May 18, 2003.

HOPKINS, WILLARD GEORGE, health care administrator; b. Balt., Mar. 30, 1940; s. George Conrad and Laura Elizabeth (Elwell) H.; m. Valerie Jewell Hopkins, June 22, 1963; children— Michelle Marie, Tiffany Lynn. BSCE, U. Md., 1963; MBA, Cornell U., 1969. Cons. Arthur Young & Co. San Francisco, 1969-74, health cons., practice dir., 1974-76, dir. health care, cons. practice dir., Washington, 1976-78; health cons., practice dir. Booz Allen & Hamilton, Washington 1977-79; exec. v.p. Scottsdale Meml. Hosp., Ariz., Scottsdale Meml. Health Service Co., 1979-83; exec. dir. Mednet/Euclid Clinic Found., Ohio, 1983-87; pres. Health Futures, Ariz., 1987-88; pres. Samaritan Physicians Ctr., Phoenix, 1988—. Served with USPHS, 1963-69. Fellow Am. Coll. Hosp. Execs., Soc. Advanced Med. Systems; mem. N.Am. Soc. Corp. Planning, Am. Health Planning Assn., NAM, Assn. Univ. Programs in Health Adminstrn., Comprehensive Health Planning Assn. Contra Costa County (bd. dirs. 1973-77). Mem. editorial adv. bd. Am. Jour. Health Planning, 1976-79; contbr. articles to profl. jours. Presbyterian. Lodge: Rotary. Home: Scottsdale, Ariz.

HORMAN, RICHARD ELIOT, psychologist, hospital management company executive; b. Phila., Oct. 25, 1945; s. Max Bernard and Cecile (Erlichman) H.; m. Karen Loeb; children: Arielle, Shane. AB, Temple U., 1967, EdM, 1968; PhD in Psychology, Ill. Inst. Tech., 1970. Exec. dir. Gov.'s Coun. on Drug and Alcohol Abuse Commonwealth of Pa., Harrisburg, 1972-76; exec. v.p. Psychiat. Insts. of Am., Washington, 1976-79; pres. Fair Oaks Hosp., Summit, N.J., 1976-79; pres., chief exec. officer Nat. Psychiat. Insts., Washington, 1979-82, Internat. Healthcare Corp., Washington, 1983-86; chief exec. officer Addiction Recovery Corp., from 1988. Author: Drug Awareness, 1970; contbr. articles to profl. publs. Trustee Pa. Pub. Health Trust, Harrisburg, 1974-76; commr. Pa. Human Experimentation Commn., Harrisburg, 1972-76; pres. Coun. of Territorial Alcoholism Authorities, Washington, 1974-76. Fellow Pa. Psychol. Assn. (pres.' svc. award 1976); mem. Am. Psychol. Assn., Am. Coll. Mental Health Adminstrs., Nat. Assn. Mental Health Adminstrs., Pisces Club, Desiree Club. Jewish. Home: Las Vegas, Nev. Deceased.

HORTON, KENNETH, investor; b. Newport, Nebr., May 11, 1921; s. Fred and Clara E. (Cottrel) H.; m. Evelyn H. Shafer, Dec. 29, 1939 (div. 1961); children: Kenneth Eugene, Helen Clara Catherine; m. Arlene J. Mitchell, July 23, 1962. AA, Valley Coll., San Bernardino, Calif., 1951; grad., Law Enforcement Officers Tng. Sch., San Bernardino, Calif., 1957. Crew leader 1st suppression fire crew Civilian Conservation Corp, Glendora, Calif., 1937-39; journeyman R.R. Car Shop/Santa Fe R.R., San Bernardino, 1940-44; boy's counselor San Bernardino County Juvenile Hall, 1948-53; supr. state champion drill team Calif. Youth Authority, Whittier, 1954; layout carpenter Bectal Constrn. Co., Oro grande, Calif., 1954-55; patrolman, vice officer Police Dept., San Bernardino, 1956-66; ind. investor Thousand Oaks, Calif., from 1950. Sustaining mem. Rep. Nat. Com., Washington, 1978—. With U.S. Army, 1944-45. Decorated Combat Infantryman medal, Bronze Star medal; recipient Letter of Appreciation for apprehending holdup man Security Pacific Bank, 1974. Lutheran. Avocations: maker of fine furniture, 1st edition book collection, antique automobiles. Died Jan. 1, 2003.

HORTON, PAUL BRADFIELD, lawyer; b. Dallas, Oct. 19, 1920; s. Frank Barrett and Hazel Lillian (Bradfield) H.; m. Susan Jeanne Diggle, May 19, 1949; children: Bradfield Ragland, Bruce Ragsdale. BA, U. Tex., Austin, 1943, student Law Sch., 1941-43; LL.B., So. Methodist U., 1947. Bar: Tex. 1946. Ptnr. McCall, Parkhurst & Horton, Dallas, 1951—. Lectr. mcpl. bond law and pub. finance S.W. Legal Found.; drafter Tex. mcpl. bonds legislation, 1963—. Mem. Gov.'s Com. Tex. Edn. Code, 1967-69. Served to lt. USNR, 1943-46. Mem. ABA, Dallas Bar Assn., Southwestern Legal Found., Nat. Water Resources Assn., Tex. Water Conservation Assn., Govt. Fin. Officers Assn., The Barristers, Dallas Country Club, Crescent Club, Delta Theta Phi, Beta Theta Pi. Home: Dallas, Tex. Died Aug. 19, 2002.

HORTON, THOMAS ROSCOE, business advisor; b. Fort Pierce, Fla, Nov. 17, 1926; s. Charles Montraville Horton and Ruby Mae (Swain) Warren; m. Marilou Deeming, Dec. 19, 1947; children— Susan, Jean, Marilyn. BS, Stetson U., 1949, LHD (hon.), 1982; MS, U. Fla., 1950, PhD, 1954; LLD (hon.), Pace U., 1976; DLitt (hon.), U. Charleston, 1980. Instr., asst. headmaster Bolles Sch., Jacksonville, Fla., 1950-52; with IBM Corp., Armonk, NY, 1954-82; pres., CEO Am. Mgmt. Assn., NYC, 1982-89, chmn., CEO, 1989-91, chmn., 1991-92; advisor Stetson U., DeLand, Fla., 1992-96; pres. emeritus Am. Mgmt. Assn., NYC, 2003. Chmn. The Comml. Bank, 2001-, Techna Health, LLC, 2001-; mem. adv. bd. Who's Who in Fin. and Industry, 1988—, Who's Who in Am., 1999—; panelist White House Conf. on Productivity, 1981; co-chair White House Conf. on Critical Infrastructure Assurance, 2000. Author: What Works for Me, 1986, Beyond the Trust Gap, 1990, The CEO Paradox, 1992, Information Security Governance: What Directors Need to Know, 2001, Information Security Oversight: Essential Board Practices, 2002; editor: Traffic Control--Theory and Implementation, 1965; columnist Mgmt. Rev., 1982-92, Dir. & Bd., 1998—; assoc. prodr. SHO Entertainment, Inc., 1997-2000. Life mem. Salvation Army, Am. Mgmt. Assn., 1990—; trustee Bethune-Cookman Coll., Daytona Beach, Fla., 1971-82, hon., 1982—; trustee Pace U., NYC, 1975-92, emeritus trustee, 1992—; dir. Assn. Governing Bds. Univ. and Coll., 1976-85, chmn., 1982-84, hon. dir., 1987-90; trustee Am. Grad. Sch. Internat. Mgmt., Glendale, Ariz., 1982-92, Stetson U. Bus. Sch. Found., 1992—; mem. econ. devel. com. City of DeLand (Fla.), 1992-98; trustee emeritus Stetson U., 1996—; bd. dir. Kids Voting USA, 1991-2000, chair, 1992-98; adv. bd. Am. C. of C. of Cuba in US, 1996—; bd. dir. Ctr. for Bd. Leadership. Washington, 1999—; bd. visitors The Bolles Sch., Jacksonville, Fla., 1998-2000. Fellow: Internat. Acad. Mgmt. (vice chancellor), Acad. Mgmt.; mem.: Svc. Corps Retired Execs., Mgmt. Exec. Soc., Assn. Internat. des Etudiants en Sci. Econ. et Comml. (hon. dir. from 1990), Am. Coun. Edn. (bd. dirs. 1982—84), Internat. Exec. Svc. Corps, Nat. Coun. on Philanthropy (trustee, vice chmn. 1973—80), Korean Mgmt. Assn. (hon.), Conf. Bd. (sr.), Am. Mgmt. Assn. (life), ASME (hon.), Japan Mgmt. Assn. (hon.), Russian Econ. Soc. (hon.), Internat. Coun. for Innovation in Higher Edn., Corp. Women Dir. Internat. Colloquium (co-chair 2002—03), Inst. Internal Auditors (mem. internatl auditing stds. bd. from 2001), Nat. Assn. Corp. Dir. (mem. Blue Ribbon Commn. on Dir. Professionalism 1996, faculty mem., bd. dirs. from 1996, audit com. 1999, chair 1999—2001, bd. corp. strategy 2000, bd. effectiveness 2001, bd. risk oversight 2002), Pres. Assn. NYC (chmn. 1982—91), European Found. for Mgmt. Devel., Lake Beresford Yacht Club, DeLand Country Club, Sigma Phi Epsilon (co-founder Fla. Beta chpt. from 1949). Baptist. Home: Deland, Fla. Died Aug. 8, 2003.

HOSLER, RUSSELL JOHN, retired education educator; b. DuPont, Ohio, Apr. 2, 1906; s. John Henry and Etta (Spitznaugle) H.; m. Hilda Elizabeth Weible, Dec. 25, 1927 (div. Oct. 1966); children: Philip Eugene, Helen Hosler Daggett, Russell John Jr.; m. Mary Margaret O'Connell, Aug. 23, 1968. AB, Defiance Coll., 1932; MA, Toledo U., 1941; EdD, Ind. U., 1946. Tchr. high sch., Montpelier, Ohio, 1927-34, Fostoria, Ohio, 1934-38, Libbey High Sch., Toledo, 1938-42; asst. prof. commerce Ind. U., 1942-46; faculty U. Wis., Madison, from 1946, prof., 1953-76, emeritus, from 1976, chmn. dept. edn., 1955-59. Co-author: Gregg Shorthand for Colleges, rev. edit, 1958, 65, 73, Gregg Transcription for Colleges, 1959, rev. edit., 1966, 75, Programmed Gregg Shorthand, 1969, Personal Typing, 1979; co-author: (with M. Hosler) The History of the National Business Education Association, 1993; contbr. articles to profl. mags. Recipient John Robert Gregg award, 1966 Mem. Nat. Bus. Edn. Assn. (pres. 1968-69), Nat. Bus. Tchrs. Assn. (pres. 1955), Nat. Assn. Bus. Tchr. Edn. (pres. 1959-61) Home: Milton, Wis. Died Dec. 8, 1999.

HOUGH, LAWRENCE EDWIN, political science educator; b. Flint, Mich., Apr. 19, 1935; s. Jay Edwin and Catherine M. (Lawrence) H.; m. Sandra J. Wurth, Sept. 29, 1967. AB, U. Mich., 1960; MA, Cen. Mich. U., 1965; PhD, U. Okla., 1973. Jr. high tchr. Flint and Flushing Pub. Schs., Mich., 1963-65; instr. U. Okla., Norman, 1968-70; asst. prof. Gustavus Adolphus Coll., St. Peter, Minn., 1968-69; asst./assoc. prof. East Carolina U., Greenville, N.C., from 1970. Asst. dean East Carolina U., Greenville, 1975-81. Elected mem. U. N.C. Faculty Assembly, Chapel Hill, 1982-88, 91—, head ECU Del. Sgt. USMC, 1953-59. Recipient NDEA award, U. Okla., Norman, 1968, NEH award U. Minn., Mpls., 1982, U. Va., Charlottesville, 1989, NSF/AAAS award U. Md., U. Dayton (Ohio), 1979, 80, 81. Mem. AAUP (chpt. pres. 1984-88), Am. Polit. Sci. Assn., Soc. for Utopian Studies (sec.-treas. 1986-90, chair 1990-94), N.C. Polit. Sci. Assn. (v.p., sec.-treas. 1976-81, pres. 1981-82), Assn. Internat. per gli studi sulle Utopie. Democrat. Methodist. Avocations: lapidary, hiking, camping. Home: Greenville, NC. Died Mar. 13, 2000.

HOUSEWRIGHT, RILEY DEE, microbiologist/former scientific society executive; b. Wylie, Tex., Oct. 17, 1913; s. Jick and Lillie (Townsend) H.; m. Marjory Bryant, June 10, 1939 (dec. July 1962); 1 son, Kim Bryant; m. Artemis Skevakis Jegart, Aug. 30, 1969. BS, U. North Tex., 1934; MA, U. Tex., 1938; PhD, U. Chgo., 1944; postgrad., Cambridge (Eng.) U., 1950. Diplomate: Am. Bd. Microbiology, 1961. Pub. sch. tchr., Tex., 1934-36; instr. S.W. Tex. State Coll., San Marcos, 1937-41; chief microbial physiology and chemotherapy br. Ft. Detrick, Md., 1946-50; dep. chief, chief med. bacteriology div., 1950-56; sci. dir. U.S. Army Biol. Labs., 1956-70, U.S. Army Command Mgmt. Sch., 1957; Brookings Instn. Fed. Execs. Programs U.S. Army Biol. Labs., 1960, 64, 69, Aspen Inst. for Adv. Studies, 1968; v.p., sci. dir. Microbiol. Assos. Inc., Bethesda, Md., 1970-75; prin. staff officer Nat. Acad. Sci.-NRC, Washington, 1975-81; exec. dir. Am. Soc. for Microbiology, Washington, 1981-84. Mem. adv. com. to sci. dir. Inst. Microbiology, Rutgers U., 1959-67; pres. 4th Internat. Congress Chemotherapy, 1965; mem. panel on regulatory biology NSF, 1967-70; cons. Office Edn., Dept. Health, Edn. and Welfare, 1973-75; sr. cons. Leonard Wood Found., 1975-82; cons. pharm. and food industry, 1970-81, Ctrs. for Disease Control, Nat. Inst. for Allergy and Infecious Diseases, NASA, Oak Ridge Nat. Lab., Nat. Acad. of Sci.; chmn. Instl. Rev. Bd., Nat. Acad. Scis., 1980-81; mem. Instl. Rev. Bd. Frederick Cancer Research Inst., Nat. Cancer Inst., 1983-93. Author books, articles; editor: Bacteriol. Proc, 1957-59; editor-in-chief, ASM News, 1981-84. Capt. US Naval Reserve, 1944-66, pres. Am. Soc. Microbiology Found., 1973-74; bd. assocs. Hood Coll., Frederick, Md., 1969-80; trustee Am. Type Culture Collection, 1973-81, 87-93, Frederick Meml. Hosp., 1977-83. Served to lt. USNR, 1944-46, capt. Res. ret., 1946-66 U. Chgo. fellow, 1941-42; John and Mary E. Markle fellow, 1942-43; scholarship Am. Mgmt. Assn., 1957; recipient U.S. Patent awards, 1959; Meritorious Civilian Service award Dept. Army, 1962, 64; Distinguished Alumni citation N. Tex. State U., 1965, NAS and U.S. Rep. to Internat. Assn. of Microbiological Socs., Moscow, USSR, 1967; Exceptional Civilian Service award Dept. of Army, 1968 Fellow Am. Acad. Microbiology, AAAS, N.Y. Acad. Scis.; mem. Am. Soc. Microbiology (hon. mem. 1981, pres. 1965-66, Barnett E. Cohen award Md. br. 1967), Soc. Gen. Microbiology (Eng.), Soc. Exptl. Biology and Medicine, Research Soc. Am., Sigma Xi, Phi Delta Kappa, Gamma Alpha Clubs: Cosmos (Washington). Home: Frederick, Md. Died Jan. 11, 2003.

HOWARD, FRANCES ESTELLA HUMPHREY, government official; b. Wallace, S.D., Feb. 18, 1914; d. Hubert Horatio and Christine (Sannes) H.; m. Ray Howard, Dec. 7, 1942 (div. June 1956); children: William, Anne. BA in Sociology, George Washington U., 1937, MA, 1941; HHD (hon.), Lane Coll., 1967; LHD, Seton Hill Coll., 1993, U. Md., Balt., 1993. With U.S. Office Civilian Def., Washington, 1941-43; liaison officer various vol. agys. for fgn. relief, Washington, 1942-60; commd. fgn. service officer Dept. State, Washington, 1960; chief liaison officer vol. agys. AID, Washington, 1960-67; chief spl. project div. Office War Hunger, Washington, 1968; liaison officer vol. health orgns., spl. asst. to assoc. dir. Office Asst. Sec. Health and Sci. Affairs HEW, Washington, 1969-70; spl. asst. to assoc. dir. for extramural programs Nat. Library Medicine, NIH, USPHS, Health and Human Services, Bethesda, Md., from 1970. Lectr. to various orgns. Contbr. articles to nat. periodicals. V.p. U.S. Com. for Refugees, 1975-82; bd. dirs. Universalist-Unitarian Service Com., 1975-80, Mus. African Art, Smithsonian Instn., 1962—, Washington Opera, 1977—, Nat. Theatre Corp., 1980—, Capitol area Chpt. CARE, 1980—, Washington Ctr., 1982-, Capitol Children's Mus., 1982—, Hubert H. Humphrey Inst. Pub. Affairs, U. Minn., 1983—, U.S. Capital Hist. Soc., 1984—, Environics Found. Internat., 1972—, U.N.A. (Capitol Area divsn.), 1984-96, Woodrow Wilson Coun., 1994—. Recipient Disting. Service award Grand Chpt. Delta Sigma Theta, 1966; Women's Honor award Howard U., 1967; No. Va. service award Altrusa Club, 1967; Emblem of Honor award 6th Ann. Pan Am. Congress Conf. on Social Services, 1968. Mem. AAUW, Am. Polit. Sci. Assn., UN Assn., AAAS, The Royal Soc. Arts (London), Cosmos Club. Home: Washington, DC. Died Sept. 23, 2002.

HOWARD, HARLAN PERRY, composer; b. Detroit, Sept. 8, 1927; s. Ralph Hobson and Evelyn (Steed) H.; children: Jennifer Carmella, Harlan Perry Howard Jr., Clementyne Howard; m. Melanie Smith, Aug. 30, 1989. Student pub. schs., Mich. Co-owner Harland Howard Songs and Melanie Howard Music. Composer approximately 4,000 country songs including Pick Me Up on Your Way Down, Heartaches by the Number, I Fall to Pieces, I've Got a Tiger by the Tail, I Won't Forget You, Busted, Your Heart Turned Left, You Comb Her Hair, You Took Her Off My Hands, Second Hand Rose (Second Hand Heart), Above and Beyond (The Call of Love) Foolin' Around, Mommy for a Day, Heartbreak U.S.A., Three Steps to the Phone, Odds and Ends (Bits and Pieces), The Blizzard, No Charge, Life Turned Her That Way, Yours Love. Recipient Song of the Yr. award Acad. Country Music, 1984, Tree Pub., 1989. Mem. Country Music Assn. (mem. bd. 1984-85, awards 1984-89), Broadcast Music Inc. (awards. 1959-89), Nashville Songwriters Assn. (mem. bd. 1982-84, named to Songwriter Hall of Fame 1973), Nashville Entertainment Assn., Nat. Acad. Recording Arts and Scis. Avocations: fishing, reading. Died Mar. 3, 2002.

HOWARD, JOHN, former state legislator; m. Beverly; two children. Past mem. Carrington City Coun.; N.D. State rep. Dist. 29, 1989-96; svc. rep. Otter Tail Power Co. Mem. jud., polit. subdivsn. and ops. divsn. coms.; vice-chmn. appropriations-govt. Mem. Kiwanis, Am. Legion. Home: Carrington, ND. Died Feb. 5, 2002.

HOWE, HAROLD, II, academic administrator, former foundation executive, educator; b. Hartford, Conn., Aug. 17, 1918; s. Arthur and Margaret Marshall (Armstrong) H.; m. Priscilla Foster Lamb, Sept. 4, 1940; children: Catherine Howe Short, Merrill Howe Leavitt, Gordon Armstrong. BA, Yale U., 1940; MA in History, Columbia U., 1947; postgrad., Harvard Grad. Sch. Edn., 1958-59, U. Cin., 1953-55; LLD (hon.), Adelphi U., 1966, U. St. Louis, 1967, U. Notre Dame, 1967, Princeton U., 1968, CUNY-Hunter Coll., 1981, U. Hartford, 1982; LL.D. (hon.), Tulane U., 1991. Tchr. history Darrow Sch., New Lebanon, N.Y., 1940-41, Phillips Acad., Andover, Mass., 1947-50; prin. jr. and sr. high schs. Andover, Mass., 1950-53; prin. Walnut Hills H.S., Cin., 1953-57, Newton (Mass.) H.S., 1957-60; supt. schs. Scarsdale, N.Y., 1960-64; dir. Learning Inst. N.C., 1964-65; U.S. Commr. of Edn., Washington, 1966-68; program advisor on edn. in India Ford Found., 1969-70, v.p. for edn., 1971-81; sr. lectr. Harvard U. Grad. Sch. Edn., 1982-95. Author: Picking Up the Options, 1968, Thinking About Our Kids, 1993. Trustee Yale U., 1962-68, Vassar Coll., Taft Sch., Coll. Entrance Exam. Bd., John Hay Whitney Found., 1973-81; bd. dirs. Kennedy Ctr., Washington, 1967-68; mem. Commn. on Humanities, Am. Coun. Learned Socs., 1962-63; mem. Nat. Coun. on Edn. Rsch., 1978-82, chmn., 1980-82; chmn.

bd. dir. Inst. Ednl. Leadership, 1982, 88; trustee Ednl. Testing Svcs., 1986-95, chairperson, 1990-92. With USNR, 1942-45. Recipient Gold medal for public service NYU, 1968, James Bryant Conant award Edn. Commn. of States, 1986, Harold W. McGraw, Jr. prize in Edn., 1994; Harold Howe II Professorship founded at Harvard U., 2000. Mem. Am. Acad. Art and Scis. Home: Hanover, NH. Died Nov. 30, 2002.

HOWE, JOHN ESTLE, lawyer; b. Washington, Feb. 16, 1947; s. Robert F. and Bettie F. (House) H.; m. Kathleen J. Loftus, June 14, 1969; children: Jennifer E., John E. Jr., Julie E. AB, U. Mo., 1969, JD, 1972. Bar: Mo. 1972, U.S. Ct. Mil. Appeals 1973, U.S. Dist. Ct. (ea. dist.) Mo. 1977, Nev. 1987, U.S. Dist. Ct. Nev. 1988, U.S. Supreme Ct. 1990. Assoc. Mittendorf & Mittendorf, Union, Mo., 1976-79; staff counsel adv. com. Mo. Supreme Ct., Sedalia, 1979-87; bar counsel State Bar of Nev., Las Vegas, 1987-91; chief disciplinary counsel Mo. Supreme Ct., Jefferson City, from 1991. Contbr. articles to profl. jours. Capt. USAF, 1972-76. Mem. Nat. Orgn. Bar Counsel. Avocations: fishing, reading, golf, bridge, hiking. Died Oct. 29, 2001.

HOWIE, JOHN ROBERT, lawyer; b. June 29, 1946; s. Robert H. and Sarah Francis (Caldwell) H.; children: John Robert, Ashley Elizabeth, Lindsey Leigh. BBA, North Tex. State U., 1968; JD, So. Meth. U., 1976. Bar: Tex. 1976, U.S. Dist. Ct. (no. dist.) Tex. 1977, U.S. Ct. Appeals (5th, 9th, 10th and 11th cirs.), U.S. Supreme Ct. 1985, U.S. Dist. Ct. (so., ea. and we. dists.) Tex. 1987; cert. in personal injury trial law Tex. Bd. Legal Specialization, 1982. With Law Offices of Windle Turley, Dallas, 1976-88, Misko & Howie, 1988-95; ptnr. Howie & Sweeney, LLP, from 1995. Adj. prof. trial advocacy So. Meth. U. Sch. Law, 1988-89, 92—, So. Meth. Sch. Law exec. bd. Lt. USN, 1968-73. Named Disting. Alumnus U. of North Tex., 2000, Disting. Alumnus Pvt. Practice, So. Meth. Sch. Law, 2001, Trial Lawyer of Yr., Dallas Bar Assn., 2002. Fellow Am. Coll. Trial Lawyers, Civil Trial Adv.-Nat. Bd. Trial Adv. (cert. civil trial law), Internat. Acad. Trial Lawyers; mem. ABA (vice chmn. aviation law sect. 1986-91, chair 1992), Tex. Trial Lawyers Assn. (bd. dirs. 1983—), Dallas Trial Lawyers Assn. (sec.-treas. 1984, v.p. 1985, pres. 1986), Assn. Trial Lawyers Am. (vice chmn. aviation sect. 1984-85, chmn. 1986), Am. Bd. Trial Advocates (sec. Dallas chpt. 1988, pres. 1989), State Bar Tex. (aviation law sect. coun. 1994—, personal injury trial specialist), Lawyer/Pilots Bar Assn., Ark. Trial Lawyers Assn., Ga. Trial Lawyers Assn., N.Mex. Trial Lawyers Assn., Ind. Trial Lawyers Assn., So. Meth. U. Jour. Air Law and Commerce, Pres.'s Coun. U. North Tex., Internat. Soc. of Barristers. Home: Dallas, Tex. Died Dec. 31, 2002.

HUBER, BILL (CHARLES WILLARD HUBER), communications educator; b. Lewistown, Mont., May 27, 1935; s. Joseph W. and Cecilia F. (Biglen) H.; m. Patricia A. Powers, Aug. 17, 1957; children: Kirk, Matthew, Mark, William, Stacy. BA, Carroll Coll., 1957; MA, U. Mont., 1959. Instr. Sch. Dist. 12, Lima, Mont., 1957-58, Carrol Coll., Helena, Mont., 1959-67, prof. communications, from 1968; prof. comms. Carroll Coll., Washington, 1967-68, chmn., dept. comms. studies Helena, Mont., 1960-72. Coordinator Mont. Pvt. Coll. consortium, Helena, 1970-82. Editor Workbook Basic Communications, 1962. Mem. govt. title I adv. com. Higher Edn. Act, Helena, 1962-85; chmn. Regional Selective Svc. Bd., Helena, 1985—; mem. Helena Citizens Adv. Coun., 1989-91; pres. pastoral coun. St. Helena's Cathedral, 1990-91. Mem. SCAA, WSA. Clubs: Exchange (Helena) (pres. 1979-80). Lodges: KC. Democrat. Roman Catholic. Avocations: sailing, reading, communication theory research. Home: Killeen, Tex. Deceased.

HUDEC, ROBERT EMIL, lawyer, educator; b. Cleve., Dec. 23, 1934; s. Emil and Mary (Tomcho) H.; m. Marianne Miller, Sept. 8, 1956; children: Michael Robert, Katharine Wright. BA, Kenyon Coll., 1956, LL.D. (hon.), 1979; MA, Cambridge U., 1958; LL.B., Yale U., 1961. Bar: D.C. 1963, Minn. 1974. Law clk. to Mr. Justice Potter Stewart, U.S. Supreme Ct., 1961-63; asst. gen. counsel Office Spl. Rep. for Trade Negotiations, Exec. Offices, 1963-65; Rockefeller Found. research fellow, 1965-66; asso. prof. law Yale U. Law Sch., 1966-72; prof. law U. Minn. Law Sch., Mpls., 1972—2000, Melvin C. Steen prof. law, 1986—2000; prof. law Tufts U., Medford, Mass., 2000—03. Author: The Gatt Legal System and World Trade Diplomacy, 1975, 2d edit., 1990, Developing Countries in the Gatt Legal System, 1987, Enforcing International Trade Law: The Evolution of the Modern GATT Legal System, 1993, Essays on the Nature of International Trade Law, 1999; contbr. articles to profl. jours. Mem. Am. Law Inst., Minn. Bar Assn. Home: Newton Highlands, Mass. Died Mar. 12, 2003.

HUDGINS, CATHERINE HARDING, business executive; b. June 25, 1913; d. William Thomas and Mary Alice (Timberlake) Harding; m. Robert Scott Hudgins IV, Aug. 20, 1938; children: Catherine Harding Adams, Deborah Ghiselin, Robert Scott V. BS, N.C. State U., 1933; postgrad., N.C. Sch. for Deaf, 1933-34. Tchr. N.C. Sch. for Deaf, Morganton, 1934-36, N.J. Sch. for Deaf, Trenton, 1937-39; sec. Dr. A.S. Oliver, Raleigh, 1937, Robert S. Hudgins Co., Charlotte, N.C., from 1949, v.p., treas., from 1960; also bd.dirs.; ret. Mem. Jr. Svc. League, Easton, Pa., 1939; project chmn. ladies aux. Profl. Engrs. N.C., 1954-55, pres., 1956-57; pres. Christian H.S. PTA, 1963; program chmn. Charlotte Opera Assn., 1959-61, sec., 1961-63; sec. bd. Hezekiah Alexander House Aux., 1949-52, treas., 1983-84, v.p., 1984-85, pres., 1985-89; sec. Hezekiah Alexander Found., 1986—; past chmn. home missions, annuities and relief Women of Presbyn. Ch., past pres. Sunday Sch. class. Named Woman of Yr. Am. Biog. Soc., 1993. Mem. N.C. Hist. Assn., English Speaking Union, Internat. Platform Assn., Mint Mus. Drama Guild (pres. 1967-69), Internat. Biog. Ctr. Eng. (dep. dir. gen.), Heritage Found. (pres. 1994), Empower Am. (leadership coun. 1995), Daus. Am. Colonists (state chmn. nat. def. 1973-74, corr. sec. Virginia Dare chpt. 1978-79, 84-85, state insignia chmn. 1979-80), DAR (nat. chmn.'s assn., rec. sec. nat. officers club 1990—, chpt. regent 1957-59, chpt. chaplain 1955-57, N.C. program chmn. 1961-63, state chmn. nat. def. 1973-76, state rec. sec. 1977-79, hon. state regent for life, chmn. N.C. Geneal. Register 1982, nat. vice chmn. S.E. region Am. Indians 1989—, rec. sec. Nat. Officers Club 1990-92, v.p. N.C. State Officer's Club 1991-92, pres. 1992-94), Children Am. Revolution (N.C. sr. pres. 1963-66, sr. nat. corr. sec. 1966-68, sr. nat. 1st v.p. 1968-70, sr. nat. pres. 1970-72, hon. sr. nat. pres. life 1972—, 2d v.p. Nat. Officers Club, 1st v.p. 1977-79, pres. 1979-81), Huguenot Soc. N.C., Carmel Country Club (Charlotte), Viewpoint 24 Club (v.p. 1986, pres. 1987). Home: Charlotte, NC. Died Nov. 5, 2003.

HUDLICKY, MILOS, former chemistry educator; b. Prelouc, Czechoslovakia, May 12, 1919; came to U.S., 1968; s. Jaroslav and Marie H.; m. Alena Vyskocilova, July 2, 1946; children: Tomas, Eva. PhD, Tech. U., Prague, 1946. Rsch. chemist Rsch. Inst. of Rubber Tech., Zlin, Czechoslovakia, 1940-45; asst. prof. Inst. of Chemistry and Tech., Prague, 1945-48; postdoctoral fellow Ohio State U., Columbus, 1948; assoc. prof. Inst. Chem. Tech., Prague, 1949-58; rsch. chemist Rsch. Inst. Pharm. Biochemistry, Prague, 1958-68; assoc. to full prof. Va. Polytech. Inst., Blacksburg, Va., 1968-89, prof. emeritus, 1989. Contbr. articles to profl. jours., author books in field. Recipient Alan Clifford award Va. Polytech. Inst., 1989, Votocek medal Czech. Chem. Soc., 1992. Avocations: tennis, hiking, skiing. Home: Blacksburg, Va. Died Aug. 31, 2001.

HUDNUT, DAVID BEECHER, retired leasing company executive, lawyer; b. Cin., Feb. 21, 1935; s. William Herbert and Elizabeth Allen (Kilborne) H.; m. Robin Fraser, Apr. 12, 1958; children: David Beecher, Marjorie Elizabeth, Joshua Fraser, John Marshall, Benjamin Parker. AB, Princeton U., 1957; JD, Cornell U., 1962. Bar: N.Y. 1962, U.S. Supreme Ct. 1967. Assoc. Hughes, Hubbard & Reed, N.Y.C., 1962-67; with Ind. and chem. products div. Ford Motor Co., 1967-69; v.p. U.S. Leasing Internat., Inc., San Francisco, 1969-76, sr. v.p., 1976-90. Bd. dirs. Gary. D. Nelson Assocs., Inc., 1995—, Bread and Roses, 1995-2001, chmn., 1999-2001, Cameron House Found., 1979-98, pres., 1980-92; bd. dirs. Svcs. for Srs., 1970-96, pres. 1990-92, No. Calif. Presbyn. Homes, 1971-77, chmn., 1973-76, 79-86; bd. dirs. Edgewood Children's Ctr., 1979-86, Ind. Colls. No. Calif., 1981-84; mem. adv. bd. Alumnae resources, 1982-94; mem. Calif. Hist. Soc., 1986-92, pres. 1989-91; mem. Calif. Hist. Found., 1997—, chmn., 1999—. Home: Belvedere Tiburon, Calif. Died June 27, 2003.

HUFFMAN, ESTELLE FLETCHER, educator, nurse; b. Yakima, Wash., Sept. 28, 1945; d. John Dee and Edith Marie (Iverson) Fletcher; m. William Walter Huffman, June 22, l975. BS in Nursing, Loma Linda U., l968, MPH with honors, 1972. Standard secondary teaching, health and devel., adminstrv. credentials, Calif.; cert. tchr. gifted and talented, Calif. Sch. nurse Rialto (Calif.) Unified Sch. Dist., l968-69, Hemet (Calif.) Unified Sch. Dist., l969-7l, Sweetwater Union High Sch. Dist., San Diego, l972-83, tchr. sci. and family life edn., from l983; chmn. sci. dept. Montgomery Jr. High Sch., San Diego, l983-84, 86-88. Guest lectr. San Diego State U., 1974-83, master tchr. life sci., 1986, 88; coord. continuing edn. sessions sch. nurses San Diego County, l974-80. Active in support ednl. and sch. health bills in Calif., l968—; mem. heart edn. for young com. Am. Heart Assn., San Diego, l980-85. Recipient cert. of appreciation Am. Heart Assn., l982. Mem. Nat. Sci. Tchrs. Assn., NEA, Calif. Tchrs. Assn., DAV Aux., Yosemite Assn., San Diego Zool. Soc., So. Calif. Convertable Club, Delta Omega. Democrat. Avocations: oils and watercolors, gardening, bird watching, hiking, automobile racing. Home: San Diego, Calif. Deceased.

HUGHES, DWAIN HAROLD, electronics executive; CFO, sr. v.p. Tandy Corp., Ft. Worth. Deceased.

HUGHES, HERSCHEL AUSTIN, retired pastor; b. Grant County, Ind., July 13, 1921; s. Cleftie Aaron and Rachel Ioma (Todd) H.; m. Lorene Lester Whited, June 6, 1942 (div. 1967); m. Carmen Lou Gray, June 27, 1971; children: Charles Evans, Dianne Kaye Hendricks. BS, Owosso (Mich.) Coll., 1942; MS, Fresno (Calif.) State U., 1956; ThM, Chgo. Theol. Sem., 1964. Pastor Wesleyan Ch., Rising Sun, Ind., 1942-44, Terre Haute, Ind., 1944-48; chaplain VA Hosp., Fresno, 1954-57; exec. dir. Community ACtion P., Columbia, Mo., 1968-72; pastor Peace United Ch. of Christ, Hartsburg, Mo., 1968-93; ret., 1993. Bd. dirs. Evang. Children's Home, St. Louis. Mem. Gateway Com. Boone County, Mo., 1990—; pres. South Boone County Schs., Boone County, 1980-86. Mem. Western Assn. Mo. Conf. United Ch. of Christ (pres. 1986-88), Lions (bd. dirs. Hartsburg chpt. 1980-90). Home: Hartsburg, Mo. Died Jan. 18, 2001.

HUGHES, MONICA, writer; b. Liverpool, Eng., Nov. 3, 1925; arrived in Can., 1952; d. Edward Lindsay and Phyllis Ince; m. Glendon Earl Hughes, Apr. 22, 1957; children: Liz, Adrienne, Russell, Tom. With NRC, Ottawa, Canada, 1952-57. Author: (novels) The Keeper of the Isis Light, 1980, Hunter in the Dark, 1982, Space Trap, 1983, My Name is Puala Popowich!, 1983, Devil on my Back, 1984, Sandwriter, 1985, The Dream Catcher, 1986, Blaine's Way, 1988, Log Jam, 1987, The Promise, 1989, The Refuge, 1989, Little Fingering, 1989, Invitation to the Game, 1990, The Crystal Drop, 1992, A Handful of Seeds, 1993, The Gold Aquarians, 1994, Castle Tourmandyne, 1995, Where Have You Been Billy Boy?, 1995, The Seven Magpies, 1996, The Faces of Fear, 1997, The Story Box, 1998, What if...?, 1998, The Other Place, 1999, Storm Warning, 2000, The Maze, 2002, 2 picture books; contbr. short stories to anthologies and collections. With Women's Royal Naval Svc., WWII. Recipient Beaver award, 1980, Vicky Metcalkf award, 1981, 1983, Alta. Culture Juvenile Novel award, 1981, Can. Coun. prize Children's Lit., 1981, 1982, cert. of Honor, IBBY, 1982, Young Adult Novel award, Libr. Assn., 1983, Silver Feather award, Germany, 1986, Alt. Achievement award, 1988, Boeken Leeuw, Book Lion, Belgium, 1987, Cultural Creative Arts award, City of Edmonton, 1988, Phoenix award, 2000; grantee Sr. Writing, Alta. Found. Lit. Arts, 1989. Mem.: Writers' Guild Alta. (sec. 1988—89, R. Ross Annett award 1983, 1984, 1987, 1992), Internat. Bd. Book Young People, SF Can., PEN Can., Illustrators and Performers, Can. Soc. Authors, Writers' Guild Alta., Writers' Union Can., Order of Can. Home: Edmonton, Canada. Died Mar. 7, 2003.

HUGHES, VERNON WILLARD, physics educator, researcher; b. Kankakee, Ill., May 28, 1921; AB, Columbia U., 1941, PhD in Physics, 1950; MS, Calif. Inst. Tech., 1942; PhD (hon.), U. Heidelberg, Germany, 1977. Rsch. assoc. radiation lab. MIT, Cambridge, Mass., 1942-46; instr., lectr. in physics Columbia U., N.Y.C., 1949-52, assoc. prof. physics, 1958-59; asst. prof. U. Pa., Phila., 1952-54; from asst. prof. to prof. Yale U., New Haven, 1954-69, assoc. chmn. dept., 1960-67, chmn. dept., 1961-66, Donner prof., 1969-78, Sterling prof., 1978-91, Sterling prof. physics emeritus, 1991—2003. Vis. I I Rabi prof. Columbia U., 1984, adj. prof., 1984—; trustee Assn. Univs. Inc., 1962-92, hon. trustee, 1992-2003; mem. Naval Rsch. Adv. Com., 1968-74; vis. prof. Japan Soc. Promotion Soc. Sci., 1974, 96; vis. prof. Slac Stanford (Calif.), 1978-79, Col France, 1981, Scuola Normale Superiore, Pisa, Italy, 1982; cons. Los Alamos Sci. Lab., Oak Ridge Nat. Lab., NSF, NRC, Dept. Energy, many others. Recipient Disting. Alumni award Calif. Tech. Inst., 1999. Fellow AAAS, Am. Acad. Arts and Scis., Am. Phys. Soc.; mem. NAS. Died Mar. 25, 2003.

HUGHES, WILLIAM F., JR., internist, allergist and immunologist; b. Marietta, Ohio, Sept. 8, 1922; MD, Case Western Res. U., 1947. Diplomate Am. Bd. Internal Medicine, Am. Bd. Allergy and Immunology. Intern St Lukes Hosp., Cleve., 1947-48, resident in internal medicine, 1948-50; fellow in allergy Buffalo Gen. HOsp., 1965-67; mem. staff Riverside Meth. Hosp., Columbus, Ohio; asst. clin. prof. medicine Ohio State U. Coll. Medicine, Columbus. Mem. AMA, Am. Acad. Allergy, Ohio State Med. Assn. Died Dec. 1, 2000.

HUGUS, Z ZIMMERMAN, JR., chemistry educator; b. Washington, Aug. 14, 1923; s. Z Zimmerman Sr. and Marguerite (Weaver) H.; m. Nancy Anne Regin, June 25, 1947 (dec. Mar. 1998); children: Carily, Z Zimmerman III, Richard Regin, Patricia Helen Hugus Dale. BA, Williams Coll., 1943; PhD, U. Calif. at Berkeley, 1949. Research fellow, instr. U. Calif. at Berkeley, 1949-52; mem. faculty U. Minn., 1952-67; prof., chief inorganic chemistry, 1963-67; prof. N.C. State U., Raleigh, 1967-92, head dept. chemistry, 1967-73, prof. emeritus, from 1993. Served with USNR, 1944-46. Fellow AAAS; mem. Am. Chem. Soc., N.C. Acad. Sci., Phi Beta Kappa, Sigma Xi, Phi Lambda Upsilon, Phi Kappa Phi, Alpha Chi Sigma, Phi Delta Theta. Home: Boone, NC. Deceased.

HULTGREN, HERBERT NILS, cardiologist, educator; b. Santa Rosa, Calif., Aug. 29, 1917; s. Adolf W. and Hilda (Hakanson) H.; m. Barbara Brooke, Aug. 7, 1948; children— Peter B., Bruce H., John B. Jr. certificate, Santa Rosa Jr. Coll., 1937; AB, Stanford, 1939, MD, 1942. Intern San Francisco Gen. Hosp., 1942-43; resident medicine Stanford Hosp., 1943-44, resident pathology, 1946-47; fellow cardiology Thorndike Meml. Lab., Boston, 1947-48; instr. medicine Stanford Med. Sch., 1948-51, asst. prof., 1951-55, asso. prof., 1955-67, prof., 1967—; chief cardiology Service Palo Alto VA Hosp., 1969-88. Chmn. Subspeciality Bd. Cardiovascular Disease, 1972-75; co-chmn. VA Coop. Study Surgery in Coronary Artery Disease, 1972— Contbr. articles to profl. jours. Served from 1st lt. to capt., M.C. AUS, 1944-46, ETO. Markle scholar in med. sci., 1951-56 Mem. Western Soc. Clin. Research (pres.), Western Assn. Physicians (pres.), Assn. U. Cardiologists (pres.), Phi Beta Kappa. Home: Palo Alto, Calif. Deceased.

HUMBER, MARCEL BERTHIER, former naval officer, investment consultant; b. Paris, Nov. 21, 1930; s. Robert Lee and Lucie (Berthier) H. (parents Am. citizens); m. Ann Kimrey, June 20, 1953; children: Robert Lee II, Eileen Genevieve, Stephen Andrew, Carolyn Alexandra. BS, Wake Forest U., 1951; MBA in Fin., George Washington U., 1978, Ph.D. in Fin., 1988; student, French Naval War Coll., Paris, 1965-67. Enlisted USN, 1952, commd. ensign, 1953, advanced through grades to capt., 1972, served as airborne intercept officer, 1953-56, aide to Fleet Adm. C.W. Nimitz, 1961-63, sr. naval advisor Vietnamese Nat. Def. Coll., 1968-69, comdg. officer U.S.S. R.E. Kraus, 1969-70, comdg. officer U.S.S. Columbus, 1972-73, chief spl. ops. div. Joint Chiefs of Staff, 1973-75, ret., 1975; former investment cons. Falls Ch., Va. Lectr. bus. adminstrn. George Washington U.,

1983-1999. Decorated Legion of Merit, Bronze Star with oak leaf cluster. Mem. Sigma Phi Epsilon. Clubs: Army-Navy. Republican. Home: Falls Church, Va. Died Dec. 30, 2003.

HUME, HORACE DELBERT, manufacturing company executive; b. Endeavor, Wis., Aug. 15, 1898; s. James Samuel and Lydia Alberta (Sawyer) H.; student pub. schs.; m. Minnie L. Harlan, June 2, 1926 (dec. May 1972); 1 child, James; m. Sarah D. Lyles Rood, Apr. 6, 1973 (dec. Jan. 1988); m. Dorothy L. Bohan Greenwood, Nov. 15, 1989 (dec. May 1994). Stockman and farmer, 1917-19; with automobile retail business, Garfield, Wash., 1920-21, ptnr. and asst. mgr., 1921-27; automobile and farm machine retailer, Garfield, ptnr., mgr., 1928-35, gen. mgr. Hume-Love Co., Garfield, 1931-35, pres., 1935-57; ptnr., gen. mgr. H.D. Hume Co., Mendota, Ill., 1944-52; pres. H.D. Hume Co., Inc., 1952—; ptnr. Hume and Hume, 1952-72; pres. Hume Products Corp., 1953-95; pres., dir. Hume-Fry Co., Garden City, Kans., 1955-73; dir. Granberry Products, Inc., Eagle River, Wis. Mayor, Garfield, Wash., 1938-40, Hart Carter Co., Mpls., 1965-71. Named to Sr. Illinoisians Hall of Fame, 1995. Bd. dirs. Mendota Hosp. Found., 1949-73, pres., 1949-54; bd. dirs. Mendota Swimming Pool Assn.; mem. City Planning Commn., 1953-72, chmn., 1953-69; mem. Regional Planning Commn., LaSalle County, Ill., 1965-73, chmn., 1965-71; active Schs. Central Com., 1953—, LaSalle County Zoning Commn., 1966—, LaSalle County Care and Treatment Bd., 1970-73; chmn. Mendota Watershed Com., 1967-73; pres. Hume Found., 1993, Mendota Mus. & Hist. Soc., 1993, 95. Recipient Key to City City of Mendota, 1988, Cert. of Appreciation City of Mendota, 1988, Wisdon of Honor award The Wisdom Soc., 1970, Friends of the Graves-Hume Libr. Philanthropic and Humanitarian Svcs. award, Am. Patriot award The Founders Soc., 1994, Cmty. Bldrs. award Mendota Lodge No176AF8AM, 1994; named Grand Marshall Sweet Corn Fesitval Parade by Mendota Ill. C. of C., 1993; recognized part of 100 Most Significant Contbr. to Mechanization of Agr. 1893-1993, by Equipment Mfrs. Inst.; Am. Soc. Agrl. Engring. Hist. Landmark named in honor, 1993. Mem. Am. Soc. Agrl. Engrs., Eagle River (Wis.) C. of C. (pres., dir. 1962-63), Mendota C. of C. (pres. 1948-49, dir. 1946-49, Cmty. Svc. award 1972, H.D. Hume Award named in his honor 1993, Ill. 1st Libr. Ptnrs. Carnegie award 1994). Republican. Presbyterian (elder). Clubs: Kiwanis (pres. 1953, dir. 1954, Paul Harris fellow, George F. Hixson award 1994, Legion of Honor-50Yrs.), Masons (named Master Mason), Shriners, Order Eastern Star, Elks. Patentee in various fields. Home: Mendota, Ill. Deceased.

HUME, WALTER I., JR., surgeon, educator; b. Louisville, Aug. 10, 1925; s. Walter I. and Beulah (Thompson) H.; m. Florence Harding Jenney, June 3, 1950; children: Bradley Royal, Craig Powers, Sarah Hume Kooser. BS, Williams Coll., 1946; MD, Harvard U., 1949. Diplomate Am. Bd. Surgery. Intern Peter B. Brigham Hosp., Boston, 1949-50, resident surgery, 1950, 53-56; pvt. practice gen. surgery Louisville, 1956-90; med. dir. Ky. Med. Ins. Co., 1990—2000. Chief med. advisor Humana, Inc., 1973-86; former clin. prof. surgery U. Louisville Sch. Medicine; emeritus staff Bapt. Hosp. East, Suburban Med. Ctr., U. Louisville Hosp., Norton Hosp., Jewish Hosp., Audubon Regional Med. Ctr. Elder 2nd Presbyn. Ch.; mem. bd. govs. J. Graham Brown Cancer Ctr., 1979-87, v.p., 1983-87; bd. dirs. Louisville Free Pub. Libr. Found., 1987-95, JCMS Outreach Program, Cmty. Found. Louisville, Ky. Cmty. Health Alliance; mem. steering com. on practice parameters Ky. Health Policy Bd., 1995-96; mem., past pres. Transylvania Med., Innominate, and Medico-Chirurgical Socs. Lt. USNR, 1943-56. Fellow ACS; mem. AMA, Internat. Soc. Surgery, So. Surg. Assn., Ky. Surg. Soc., Louisville Surg. Soc. (pres. 1966), Ky. Med. Assn. (assoc. editor jour. 1966-70, editor jour. 1970-76), Jefferson County Med. Soc. (bulletin editor 1963, pres. 1969-70, chmn. bd. govs. 1972-73, mem. jud. coun. 1985-91, chmn. jud. coun. 1987-88, 90-91, mem. found. 1990-97, pres., chmn. bd. dirs. found. 1994-96). Home: Louisville, Ky. Died Dec. 28, 2003.

HUMER, PHILIP WILSON, information systems specialist, patent agent; b. Carlisle, Pa., Nov. 8, 1932; s. Christian Philip and Corinne Barnett (Ramsay) H.; m. Margaret Dysart Barbour, Aug. 15, 1953 (div. Aug. 1978); children: Jean C. Reardon, Kathleen A. Ries, Richard C. Humer; m. Felicia Forsythe Foulkes, June 20, 1981; stepchildren: Alice E. Foulkes-Garcia, Anne M. Foulkes. BS, Dickinson Coll., 1954; postgrad., Dickinson Sch. Law, Carlisle, Pa., 1954-55, U. Pitts., 1957-59; PhD, Pa. State U., 1964. Traffic engr. Pa. Dept. Hwys., Harrisburg, Pa., 1955-59; rsch. chemist Phillips Petroleum Co., Bartlesville, Okla., 1964-69; sr. rsch. chemist Pa. Indsl. Chem. Corp., Clairton, Pa., 1969-73, Hercules, Inc., Clairton, 1973-74; patent liaison FMC Corp., Middleport, N.Y., 1974-78, Princeton, N.J., 1978-94, cons., from 1994. Mem. budget panel United Way, Princeton, 1990-95, campaign area chmn., 1985. Mem. Am. Chem. Soc., Phila. Intellectual Property Law Assn. Republican. Presbyterian. Avocations: gardening, model railroads, handyman repairs. Home: Morrisville, Pa. Died Mar. 5, 2000.

HUMPHREY, ROBERT REGESTER, retired biology educator; b. Palo Alto, Calif., June 14, 1904; s. Harry Baker and Olive Agatha (Mealey) H.; m. Roberta January, Sept. 12, 1929; children: Shirley, Lois, Alan, Beth. BA, U. Minn., 1928, MA, 1929, PhD, 1933. Jr. range examiner U.S. Forest Svc., Tucson, 1933-35; asst. range examiner U.S. Soil Conservation Svc., Albuquerque, 1935-39, assoc. range conservationist Spokane, Wash., 1939-48; assoc. prof. U. Ariz., Tucson, 1948-55, prof., 1955-67, prof. emeritus, from 1967. Prof. range mgmt. AID, Fortaleza, Brazil, 1964-66. Author: Range Ecology, 1962, Desert Grassland History, Botanical Review, 1958, Southwest Grasses, 1958, Ecology of Idria, A Desert Tree, 1974, Vegetational Change on U.S.-Mexican Border, 1987; contbr. more than 100 sci. articles to profl. jours. Recipient Monetary awards NSF, 1968-74, U. Ariz., 1967-80, Nat. Geog. Soc., 1984, Cert. of Merit, AAAS, 1978, Outstanding Achievement award Soc. for Range Mgmt., 1978, Disting. Svc. award Ariz. Water Resources Commn., 1966. Fellow Ariz.-Nev. Acad. Sci., Cactus & Succulent Soc. Am.; mem. Ecol. Soc. Am., Soc. for Range Mgmt. Achievements include development of forage potential technique of rangeland condition analysis. Home: Tucson, Ariz. Died Mar. 13, 2002.

HUMPHREYS, LLOYD GIRTON, research psychologist, educator; b. Lorane, Oreg., Dec. 12, 1913; s. John Pryor H. and Gertrude (Stephenson) H.; m. Dorothy Jane Windes, Dec. 27, 1937 (dec. July 12, 1995); children: John Daniel, Michael Stephenson, Margaret Anne, Susan Jeanne. BS, U. Oreg., 1935; MA, Ind. U., 1936; PhD, Stanford U., 1938. Instr. Northwestern U., 1939-42, asst. prof., 1945-46; assoc. prof. U. Wash., 1946-48, Stanford U., Calif., 1948-51; rsch. psychologist U.S. Air Force, San Antonio, 1951-57, mem., Sci. Adv. Bd. Office of Chief of Staff, 1959—62; prof. psychology U. Ill., Champaign-Urbana, 1957—, chmn. dept. psychology, 1959-69, acting dean Coll. Liberal Arts and Scis., 1979-80. Asst. dir. sci. edn. NSF, 1970-71; mem. bd. human resource data and analyses NRC, 1974-77, Commn. on Human Resources, 1978-82; mem. Ill. Gov.'s Blue Ribbon Commn. on Occupational Licensing, 1977-78; bd. dirs. Am. Insts. for Rsch., 1978-94; mem. expert com. on pediatric neurobehavioral evaluations EPA, 1983, cons. clean air sci. adv. com., mem. sci. adv. bd., 1983. Editor Psychol. Bull., 1964-68, Am. Jour. Psychology, 1968-80. Mem. com. on techniques for the enhancement of human performance NRC, 1985-88; mem. sci. adv. group for Project A and Bldg. the Career Force of Army Rsch. Inst., 1982-93; cons. RGI, Inc. Served from 2d lt. to capt. USAAF, 1942-45. Recipient Rsch. award Am. Ednl. Rsch. Assn., 1995, Ednl. Testing Svc. in Psychometrics award, 1995, Career Rsch. award APA Divsn. 5, 1997, Career Rsch. award Soc. Exptl. Multivariate Rsch., 2000. Mem. AAAS (chmn. sect. I 1962-63, v.p. 1963, council 1974-77, chmn. sect. J 1979-80), Psychometric Soc. (pres. 1959-60), Psychonomic Soc. (chmn. governing bd. 1962-63), Soc. Exptl. Psychologists, Am. Psychol. Soc., Chmns. Grad. Tng. Depts. Psychology (chmn. 1962-66), Phi Beta Kappa, Sigma Xi, Beta Gamma Sigma, Phi Delta Kappa, Delta Upsilon Home: Oakland, Ill. Died Sept. 7, 2003.

HUNT, PETER ROGER, film director, writer, editor; b. London, Mar. 11, 1925; came to U.S., 1975; s. Arthur George and Elizabeth H.; widowed; 1 child, Nicholas Constantine. Student, London Sch. Music. Actor English Repertory Theater, London. Camera asst., asst. editor various documentaries; asst. editor various feature films. London Film Co.; scriptor various films Hill in Korea, Admirable Crichton, Next to No Time, Paradise Lagoon, Cry From the Streets, Greengage Summer (Am. title: Loss of Innocence), Ferry to Hong Kong, H.M.S. Defiant (Am. title: Damn the Defiant), Sink the Bismarck, Operation Snaffu; supervising editor, 2d unit dir.: Dr. No, Call Me Bwana, From Russia with Love, Goldfinger, Ibcress File, Thunderball, You Only Live Twice, Jigsaw Man, Desperate Hours; assoc. producer: Chitty Chitty Bang Bang; dir.: On Her Majesty's Secret Service, Gullivers Travels (film and animated), Gold, Shout at the Devil, Death Hunt, Wild Geese II, Assassination, Hyper Sapien, Marlowe, Shirley's World, Persuaders, (NBC-TV movie) Beasts in the Streets, (ABC-TV mini-series) Last Days of Pompeii, (CBS-TV spl.) Eyes of a Witness. Mem. Assn. Cinematic Technicians Great Britain, Broadcasting Entertainment Cinematograph Theatre Union, Dirs. Guild of Am., Motion Picture Acad. Arts, Acad. TV, Broadcasting, Entertainment, Cinematograph, Theatre Union. Home: Santa Monica, Calif. Died Aug. 14, 2002.

HUNTER, ELMO BOLTON, federal judge; b. St. Louis, Oct. 23, 1915; s. David Riley and Della (Bolton) H.; m. Shirley Arnold, Apr. 5, 1952; 1 child, Nancy Ann (Mrs. Ray Lee Hunt). AB, U. Mo., 1936, LLB, 1938; Cook Grad. fellow, U. Mich., 1941; PhD (hon.), Coll. of Ozarks, 1988. Bar: Mo. 1938. Pvt. practice, Kansas City, 1938-45; sr. asst. city counselor, 1939-40; ptnr. Sebree, Shook, Hardy and Hunter, 1945-51; state circuit judge Mo., 1951-57; Mo. appellate judge, 1957-65; judge U.S. Dist. Ct., Kansas City, Mo., 1965—97, now sr. judge. Instr. law U. Mo., 1952-62; mem. jud. selection Elmo B. Hunter Citizens Ctr., Am. Judicature Soc. Contbr. articles to profl. jours. Mem. Bd. Police Commrs., 1949-51; Trustee Kansas City U., Coll. of Ozarks; fellow William Rockhill Nelson Gallery Art. 1st lt. M.I., AUS, 1943-46. Recipient 1st Ann. Law Day award U. Mo., 1964, Charles E. Whittaker award, 1994, SAR Law Enforcement Commendation medal, 1994, citation of Merit Mo. Law Sch., 1996. Fellow ABA; mem. Fed., Mo. bar assns., Jud. Conf. U.S. (mem. long range planning com., chmn. ct. adminstrn. com.), Am. Judicature Soc. (bd. govs., mem. exec. com., pres., chmn. bd., Devitt Disting. Svc. to Justice award 1987), Acad. Mo. Squires, Order of Coif, Phi Beta Kappa, Phi Delta Phi. Presbyterian (elder). Home: Kansas City, Mo. Died Dec. 27, 2003.

HUNTER, KATHY SUSAN, therapist; b. Joplin, Mo., May 20, 1966; d. James Adam and Geraldine (Bradshaw) H. BES, U. Mo., 1988, MSW, 1992. Substance abuse counselor Ozark Ctr.-New Directions, Joplin, 1989; summer youth counselor Econ. Security Corp., Joplin, 1990; outpatient therapist Clear Pointe, Columbia, Mo., 1991; social work intern Heart of Am., Kansas City, Mo., 1992; team leader Crittenton, Kansas City, Mo., from 1992. Social work intern Fulton (Mo.) State Hosp., 1991. Mem. Hist. Soc. of Kansas City, Young Friends of Art, Play Therapy Network. Lutheran. Avocations: reading, dance, cultural events, tennis. Home: Kansas City, Mo. Deceased.

HUNTER, KIM (JANET COLE), actress; b. Detroit, Nov. 12, 1922; d. Donald and Grace Mabel (Lind) Cole; m. William A. Baldwin, Feb. 11, 1944 (div. Jan. 1946); 1 child, Kathryn Emmett; m. Robert Emmett, Dec. 20, 1951; 1 child, Sean Emmett. Ed. pub. schs., student acting with Charmine Lantaff Camine, 1938-40. Mem. Actors Studio, from 1948. Actor: first stage appearance, 1939, played in stock, 1940—42, (Broadway debut): A Streetcar Named Desire, 1947 (Donaldson award for best supporting actress, 1948), (appeared in tour): Two Blind Mice, 1950, Darkness at Noon, 1951, The Chase, 1952, They Knew What They Wanted, 1952, The Children's Hour, 1952, The Tender Trap, 1954, Write Me a Murder, 1961, Weekend, 1968, The Penny Wars, 1969, And Miss Reardon Drinks a Little, 1971—72, The Glass Menagerie, 1973, The Women, 1973, In Praise of Love, 1975, The Lion in Winter, 1975, The Cherry Orchard, 1976, The Chalk Garden, 1976, Elizabeth the Queen, 1977, Semmelweiss, 1977, The Belle of Amherst, 1978, 1986, The Little Foxes, 1980, To Grandmother's House We Go, 1980, Another Part of the Forest, 1981, Ghosts, 1982, Territorial Rites, 1983, Death of a Salesman, 1983, Cat on a Hot Tin Roof, 1984 (Fla. Carbonell award, 1984), Life With Father, 1984, Sabrina Fair, 1984, Faulkner's Bicycle, 1985, Antique Pink, 1985, A Delicate Balance, 1986, Painting Churches, 1986, Jokers, 1986, Remembrance, 1987, Man and Superman, 1987—88, The Gin Game, 1988, A Murder of Crows, 1988, Watch on the Rhine, 1989, Suddenly Last Summer, 1991, A Smaller Place, 1991, Open Window, 1992, The Cocktail Hour, 1992; actor, actor, actor: The Belle of Amherst, 1992, 1993, The Eye of the Beholder, 1993; actor, actor: Love Letters, 1993, 1994, Do Not Go Gentle, 1994, The Gin Game, 1994—95, All the Way Home, 1995, The Children's Hour, 1995, Middlesex Canal, 1996, In Troubled Waters, 1996, The Visit, 1996, Driving Miss Daisy, 1996, An Ideal Husband, 1996—97, Greytop in Love, 1998, Love Letters, 1999, Love From Shakespeare to Coward, 1999, On Golden Pond, 1999, : (films, debut) The Seventh Victim, 1943; (films) Tender Comrade, 1943, When Strangers Marry (re-released as Betrayed), 1944, You Came Along, 1945, A Canterbury Tale, 1949, Stairway to Heaven, 1946, A Matter of Life and Death, 1995, A Streetcar Named Desire (Oscar award for best supporting actress), Anything Can Happen, 1952, Deadline U.S.A., 1952, Storm Center, 1956, Bermuda Affair, 1957, The Young Stranger, 1957, Money, Women, and Guns, 1958, Lilith, 1964, Planet of the Apes, 1968, The Swimmer, 1968, Beneath the Planet of the Apes, 1970, Escape from the Planet of the Apes, 1971, Dark August, 1975, The Kindred, 1987, Two Evil Eyes, 1991, A Price Above Rubies, 1997, The Hiding Place, 2000, Abilene, 2000, The Virtuoso (Out of the Cold), 1999; (TV films) Requiem for a Heavyweight, 1956, The Comedian, 1957, Give Us Barabbas, 1961, Love, American Style, Colombo, Cannon, Night Gallery, Mission Impossible, The Magician, 1972—73, Marcus Welby, Hec Ramsey, Griff, Police Story, Ironside, Medical Center, Bad Ronald, Born Innocent, 1974, Ellery Queen, 1975, Lucas Tanner, This Side of Innocence, Once an Eagle, Baretta, Gibbsville, Hunter, 1976, The Oregon Trail, 1977, Project UFO, Stubby Pringle's Christmas, 1978, Backstairs at the White House, 1979, Specter on the Bridge, 1979, Edge of Night, 1979—80 (Emmy nomination, 1980), FDR's Last Year, 1980, Skokie, 1981, Scene of the Crime, 1984, Three Sovereigns for Sarah, 1985, Hot Pursuit, 1985, Private Sessions, 1985, Martin Luther King, Jr., The Dream and the Drum, 1986, Drop Out Mother, 1987; (TV films, mini series) Cross of Fire, 1989; (TV films) Murder, She Wrote, 1990, Vivien Leigh: Scarlett and Beyond, 1990, Bloodlines: Murder in the Family, 1993, Class of '96, 1993; (TV series) All My Children, 1993; (TV films) Hurricane Andrew, 1993; (TV series) L.A. Law, 1994, Mad About You, 1994, As The World Turns, 1997, Blue Moon, 1999; performer: (albums) From Morning 'Til Night (and a Bag Full of Poems), 1961, Come, Woo Me, 1964, The Velveteen Rabbit, 1989; author: Kim Hunter: Loose in the Kitchen, 1975. Recipient AMPAS's Oscar, Look award, Hollywood Fgn. Corrs. Golden Globe award, Edwin Forrest award, Walnut St. Theater, 1999. Mem.: AFTRA, ANTA, Screen Actors Guild, Actors Equity Assn. (coun. 1953—59), Acad. Motion Picture Arts and Scis. (Oscar). Home: New York, NY. Died Sept. 11, 2002.

HUNTER, MARVIN THOMAS, plastic surgeon; b. Chattanooga, May 3, 1942; s. Marvin Thomas and Mildred Marie (Hackney) H.; m. Libby Leff, June 16, 1963 (div. 1976); children: Steven, Edward; m. Nancy Jean Zanzinger, Sept. 24, 1976; children: Adam, Mark. AB in Physics, Temple U., 1964; MD, Hahnemann U., 1968. Diplomate Am. Bd. Plastic Surgery. Intern in surgery Hahnemann Hosp., Phila., 1968-69; resident in surgery Abington (Pa.) Hosp., 1969-70, 72-73; resident in plastic surgery Georgetown U., Washington, 1973-75; pvt. practice Plastic Surgery Assocs. Ltd., Doylestown, Pa., from 1975. Chief plastic surgery, chmn. dept. surgery Doylestown Hosp., 1976—, Med. Coll. Hosp. Bucks County Campus, Warmininster, Pa., 1988—. Maj., flight surgeon USAF, 1970-72. Mem. AMA (OHMS rep. 1991—, alt. del. 1995), ACS, Pa. Med. Soc., Am. Soc. Plastic and Reconstructive Surgeons, Am. Soc. Aesthetic Plastic Surgery, Internat. Microsurgery Assn., N.E. Plastic Surgery Soc., Robert Ivy Soc., So. Med. Assn., Phila. Soc. Plastic Surgery, Bucks County (Pa.) Med. Soc. (v.p. 1994, pres.-elect 1995, pres. 1996), Pa. Physician Healthcare Plan, Inc. Avocations: tennis, painting, computers, reading, travel. Home: Doylestown, Pa. Died Aug. 3, 1999.

HUNTER, WILLIAM LOUIS, consultant; b. Ft. Collins, Colo., Apr. 19, 1942; s. Louis E. and Marjorie A. (Hill) H.; m. Katherine G. Jamison, May 31, 1964; children: Kelly, Grant. BA, Coll. Wooster, 1964; MA, U. Oreg., 1965. Adminstrv. aide County of Arlington, Va., 1965-67; mcpl. mgr. Town and Village of Woodstock, Vt., 1967-69; cons. Dept. Community Affairs, Harrisburg, Pa., 1969-70; dir. bur. mgmt. svc. City of Reading, Pa., 1970-75; dir. community devel. Twp. of Cherry Hill, N.J., 1975-77; pres., prin. cons. Hunter Assocs., Cherry Hill, from 1977, Mgmt. Productivity Group, Cherry Hill, from 1986. Bd. dirs. Camden County (N.J.) ARC, 1989-90. Mem. C. of C. So. N.J. (small bus. devel. com.). Avocations: skiing, tennis, golf. Home: Cherry Hill, NJ. Died Aug. 19, 2001.

HUNTLEY, ROBERT ROSS, physician, educator; b. Wadesboro, N.C., Sept. 6, 1926; s. George W. and Louise (Ross) H.; m. Joan Cornoni, Apr. 10, 1976; children: Katherine, Robert, Julia, Elizabeth, Jeffress. BS in Chemistry, Davidson Coll., 1947; MD, Bowman-Gray Sch. Medicine, 1951. Diplomate: Am. Bd. Preventive Medicine (trustee 1974-78), Am. Bd. Family Practice. Intern U. Mich. Hosp., Ann Arbor, 1951-53; resident, fellow N.C. Meml. Hosp., Chapel Hill, 1959-62; pvt. practice medicine Warrenton, N.C., 1953-58; from instr. to assoc. prof. medicine and preventive medicine U. N.C., Chapel Hill, 1959-68; asso. dir. Nat. Center for Health Services Research, HEW, 1968-70; prof., chmn. dept. community and family medicine Georgetown U., 1970-89, prof. emeritus, from 1989; pres. Georgetown U. Community Health Plan, Inc., 1972-80. Chmn. health care tech. study sect. HEW, 1978—82; adj. prof. dept. family medicine U. N.C. Sch. Medicine, 1994—99. Editor various profl. books; contbr. articles to profl. jours. Served with USN, 1945—46. Mem.: Acad. Medicine Washington (emeritus), N.C. Med. Soc., D.C. Med. Soc., Assn. Tchrs. Preventive Medicine (pres. 1974—75). Democrat. Methodist. Died Dec. 8, 2002.

HUPP, HARRY L. federal judge; b. L.A., Apr. 5, 1929; s. Earl L. and Dorothy (Goodspeed) H.; m. Patricia Hupp, Sept. 13, 1953; children: Virginia, Karen, Keith, Brian. AB, Stanford U., 1953, LLB, 1955. Bar: Calif. 1956, U.S. Dist. Ct. (cen. dist.) Calif. 1956, U.S. Supreme Ct. Pvt. practice law Beardsley, Hufstedler and Kemble, L.A., 1955-72; judge Superior Ct. of Los Angeles, 1972-84; appointed fed. dist. judge U.S. Dist. Ct. (cen. dist.) Calif., L.A., 1984-97, sr. judge, 1997—2004. Served with U.S. Army, 1950-52. Mem. Calif. State Bar, Los Angeles County Bar Assn. (Trial Judge of Yr. 1983), Order of Coif, Phi Alpha Delta. Died Jan. 27, 2004.

HUPP, ROBERT PAUL, social services executive, clergyman; b. Wheeler County, Nebr., July 3, 1915; s. Ferdinand Martin and Anna Barbara (Funk) H. Student, St. Louis Prep. Sem.; MA, Kenrick Sem., St. Louis, 1940; L.H.D. (hon.), U. Nebr., Omaha, 1977, Mt. St. Mary's Coll., 1980; LL.D. (hon.), Cath. U. Am., 1980. Ordained priest Roman Cath. Ch., 1940; asst. pastor St. Bridget's Ch., Omaha, 1940-42; dir. Cath. Young Orgn., Archdiocese Omaha, 1946-50; chaplain Home of Good Shepherd, Omaha, 1946-50; pastor St. Mary's Ch., Wayne, Nebr., 1950-53; founding pastor Christ The King Parish, Omaha, 1953-73; vicar gen. Archdiocese Omaha, 1969-72; exec. dir. Father Flanagan's Boys' Home, Boys Town, Nebr., 1973-85, cons., exec. dir. emeritus. U.S. del. 31st Gen. Assembly UN, 1976; chaplain Home of Good Shepherd (Girls Town), Omaha, Newman Club at Wayne (Nebr.) State Coll.; dept. chaplain Am. Legion; dir. Cath. Youth Orgn. Archdiocese Omaha. Served as chaplain USNR, 1943-46. Named hon. alumnus Creighton U., 1973, Man of Year U. Notre Dame, 1976, clergy knight Equestrian Order Holy Sepulchre Jerusalem, 1977; recipient Master Footprinter award, 1976 Life mem. Alpha Sigma Nu. Clubs: K.C. (life), Eagles (life), Elks. Pioneer in devel. youth ednl. programs on drugs. Died Aug. 29, 2003.

HURD, JOHN GAVIN, oil executive, lawyer; BA, Harvard U., 1934, LLB, 1937. Ind. oil prodr., cattle rancher, investor, 1946-70, 75-82; mng. gen. ptnr. Hurd Enterprises, Ltd., Hurd Investments, Ltd.; ptnr. Killam & Hurd; U.S. ambassador to Republic of South Africa U.S. Dept. of State, 1970-75. Mem. Nat. Petroleum Coun., Tex. Ind. Prodrs. and Royalty Owners (past pres.), Tex. Midcontinent Oil and Gas Assn. (bd. dirs.), Ind. Petroleum Assn. Am., Am. Petroleum Inst., Tex. and Southwestern Cattle Raisers Assn., All Am. Wildcatters, Te. Bar Assn., Calif. Bar Assn., Coun. Am. Ambassadors (charter mem., bd. dirs.), Argyle Club, Club Giraud, San Antonio Country Club, Met. Club, Bohemian Club. Deceased.

HURDIS, EVERETT CUSHING, chemistry educator; b. Providence, R.I., Feb. 5, 1918; s. Charles Everett and Elsie Wild (Cushing) H.; m. Marion Elsie Smith, Mar. 16, 1946; children: Helen, Cindy, Holly, Sara. BS in Chemistry, Brown U., 1939; MA, Princeton (N.J.) U., 1941, PhD, 1943. Rsch. chemist U.S. Rubber Co., Passaic, N.J., 1943-58; group mgr. Koppers Co., Verona, Pa., 1958-62; chemistry tchr. Tex. Woman's U., Denton, 1962-94; retired, 1994. Republican. Episcopalian. Home: Denton, Tex. Died Nov. 26, 2000.

HURLEY, JAMES G. lawyer; b. Buffalo, Jan. 3, 1922; s. Jeremiah Joseph and Miriam Ulysses (Casey) H.; m. Joan Alice Cauley, Jan. 24, 1953; children— Mary Hurley Begley, Kathleen A., James G., Alice L. B.A., Princeton U., 1944; LL.B., Harvard U., 1948. Bar: N.Y. 1949, U.S. Supreme Ct. 1958. Assoc. Albrecht, Maguire, Heffern & Gregg, P.C., 1948-53, ptnr., 1954-76, v.p. and sec., 1971-83, pres., 1984-86; counsel, 1987—; dir. Arcade and Attica R.R. Corp., 1961-89, resigned, 1989; trustee, chmn. bd. Messer Found., 1964—; trustee, sec. Vincent and Harriet Palisano Found., 1967—. Trustee Canisius Coll., 1977-83; mem. council D'Youville Coll., 1975-81; trustee Nichols Sch. of Buffalo, 1972-81; mem. adminstrv. bd. Bishop's Lay Council, 1975—. With USAAF, 1944-46. Named Knight of Holy Sepulchre, Roman Cath. Ch., 1982. Mem. N.Y. State Bar Assn., Erie County Bar Assn., Harvard U. Law Sch. Assn. of Western N.Y. Republican. Clubs: Buffalo (bd. dir., sec. 1982-83); Cherry Hill Country, Delray Beach; Mid-Day; Princeton of Western N.Y.; Harvard of Buffalo. Home: Buffalo, NY.

HUSBAND, RICK DOUGLAS, air force officer, test pilot; b. Amarillo, Tex., July 12, 1957; s. Douglas Earl and Jane Virginia (Barbagallo) H.; m. Evelyn June Neely, Feb. 27, 1982; 1 child, Laura Marie. BSME cum laude, Tex. Tech U., 1980; MSME with distinction, Calif. State U., Fresno, 1990. Cons. engr. Abrahamson and Assocs., Amarillo, Tex., 1980; commd. 2d lt. USAF, 1980, advanced through grades to maj., 1993; F-4 aircraft comdr. 69 Tactical Fighter Squadron, Moody AFB, Ga., 1982-85; F-4 instr. pilot 35 Tactical Tng. Squadron, George AFB, Calif., 1985-87; exptl. test pilot 6512 Test Squadron, Edwards AFB, Calif., 1988-89, 6515 Test Squadron, Edwards AFB, 1989-92; fixed wing test squadron RAF Boscombe Down, from 1992. Bd. dirs. First United Meth. Ch., Valdosta, Ga., 1984-85, choir mem., 1983-85; choir mem. Ch. of the Valley, Apple Valley, Calif., 1985-87, Antelope Valley Master Chorale, Lancaster, Calif., 1991-92. Mem. Soc. Exptl. Test Pilots, Air Force Assn., Daedalians, Toastmasters, Tau Beta Pi (engring. hon., V.P. 1978-79), Pi Tau Sigma (engring. hon., sec. 1978). Avocations: golf, travel, skiing, flying, singing. Died Feb. 1, 2003.

HUSTON, JOHN LEWIS, chemistry educator; b. Lancaster, Ohio, Aug. 19, 1919; s. John Allen and Olive Blanche (Wilson) H.; m. Mary Margaret Lally, Sept. 12, 1964. AB, Oberlin Coll., 1942; PhD, U. Calif. at Berkeley, 1946. Instr. chemistry Oreg. State U., Corvallis, 1946-49, asst. prof., 1949-52; mem. faculty Loyola U. at Chgo., 1952—, assoc. prof., 1954-68, prof., 1968-84, prof. emeritus, 1984—. Cons. Argonne (Ill.) Nat. Lab., 1964— Contbr. articles to profl. jours. AEC grantee, 1947-52, NSF grantee, 1953-58 Mem.: Am. Chem. Soc., Sigma Xi, Phi Beta Kappa. Home: Skokie, Ill. Died Jan. 31, 2003.

HYATT, DOROTHY ANN, volunteer; b. N.Y.C., July 14, 1931; d. Gustav Henry and Irene Virginia (Bernad) Stiehl; m. James William Hyatt, Nov. 25, 1950 (div. 1980); children: James W., Kenneth Henry, Catherine Ann Hyatt Costanzo. Grad. H.S., Bronx, N.Y. Author of poetry. Nat. bd. sec. Resources Unltd., New Canaan, Conn., 1984-94, pres. RU Clay Calss, Norwalk, Conn., 1985-95, sec. RU Creative Writing, Stamford, Conn., 1985-92; corp. sect. WCKORP Human Svc. Wickett Inc., Norwalk, 1986—; adminstrv. asst. Abram Heisler, Esq. Atty. at Law, Norwalk, 1992—. Recipient Silver Poet award World of Poetry, Sacramento, 1989. Republican. Roman Catholic. Avocation: creative writing. Home: Norwalk, Conn. Died Mar. 18, 2000.

HYSON, CHARLES DAVID, economist, consultant; b. Hampstead, Md., Dec. 29, 1915; s. Harry Perry and Rose (Miller) H.; m. Winifred Chandler Prince, Sept. 7, 1946; children— David Prince, Pamela Chandler Hyson Martin, Christopher Perry. AB, St. John's Coll., Annapolis, 1937; MS, U. Md., 1939; MA, Harvard, 1942, PhD, 1943. Agrl. economist FCA, 1939—40; staff Surplus Mktg. Adminstrn., Washington, 1940—41; resident tutor, then sr. tutor Harvard U., 1942—49, rsch. assoc., 1943—44, resident cons. Grad. Sch. Pub. Adminstrn., 1943—49, instr. econs., 1946—48, assoc. dir. mktg. rsch. program, 1948—49; regional economist, then chief prices and cost of living br. U.S. Bur. Labor Stats., 1944—46; indsl. economist Fed. Res. Bank Boston, 1946—48; asst. econ. commr. ECA Mission to Norway, Oslo, 1949—50; trade specialist, staff spl. rep. in Europe Paris, 1950; spl. asst. to chief of mission ECA, Mut. Security Agy., Lisbon, Portugal, 1950—52; dep. dir. U.S. Ops. Mission to Portugal, Mut. Security Agy., FOA, ICA, 1952—55; spl. rep. to Portugal ICA, 1955—57, chief Western Europe div., 1957—59, chief European Div., 1959—60; assigned to Nat. War Coll., 1960—61; counsellor of embassy for econ. affairs Am. embassy, Lisbon, 1955—57; dep. dir. for exec. staffing AID, Washington, 1961—62; adviser for econ. affairs Office Material Resources, AID, 1962—63; spl. asst. for econ. and trade affairs AID, 1963—74; cons. economist, from 1975. Dep. nat. coordinator, dep. exec. dir. Cabinet Com. Export Expansion, 1964; mem. White House Conf. on Internat. Coop., 1965; mem. Internat. Secretariat; econ. advisor on human skills in decade of devel., San Juan, PR, 1962. Contbr. numerous articles to econ. jours., books, also monographs. Decorated comdr. Order of Merit, Portugal Fellow Royal Econ. Soc.; mem. Am. Fgn. Service Assn., Am. Acad. Polit. and Social Sci., Am. Econ. Assn., Am. Agrl. Econ. Assn., N.Y. Acad. Scis., AAAS Clubs: Harvard (Washington); Keene Valley (N.Y.) Country; Ausable (St. Huberts, N.Y.); Adirondack Mountain. Died Mar. 8, 2004.

IANNONE, ANTHONY M. physician, neurologist; b. N.Y.C., July 11, 1925; s. Donato and Antoinette (Iannone) I.; m. Mary Iannone, Jan. 11, 1955 (dec. Jan. 1996); children: Antoinette, Mary Ann, Susan, Michael, James, Anthony, Peter (dec.). AB, Columbia U., 1945, MD, 1948. Diplomate in neurology Am. Bd. Psychiatry and Neurology. Instr. neurology U. Buffalo, 1957, U. Minn., Mpls., 1957-60; asst. prof. neurology Stanford U., Palo Alto, Calif., 1960-63, assoc. prof., 1963-68; prof., chmn. dept. neurology Med. Coll. Ohio, Toledo, 1968-70, prof., co-chmn., 1970-85, prof., from 1985. Guest rschr. NIH, Bethesda, Md., 1986. Contbr. articles to profl. jours.; presenter in field. Capt. USAF, 1951-53. Mem. AMA, AAAS, Am. Acad. Neurology, Am. Physiol. Soc., Ohio State Med. Assn., Soc. for Neurosci. Avocations: boating, windsurfing. Home: Toledo, Ohio. Died Oct. 12, 2000.

IGLEHART, T. D. bishop; Bishop Ch. of God in Christ, San Antonio, Tex.; pastor Childress Meml. Ch. of God in Christ, San Antonio. Mem. Ch. Of God In Christ. Deceased.

ILLICH, IVAN, philosophy educator, researcher; b. Vienna, Sept. 4, 1926; s. Peter and Ellen (Regenstreif) I. Lic.U. Philos., Gregorian U., Rome, 1945, Lic.U. Theology, 1950; PhD, U. Salzburg, 1951. Ordained priest Roman Cath. Ch., 1951. Priest in Puerto Rican cmty., N.Y.C., 1951-56; v.p. U. Santa Maria, Ponce, P.R., 1956-60; staff lectr. dept. polit. sci. Fordham U., N.Y.C., 1960-76; rschr. Ctr. Intercultural Documentation, Cuernavaca, Mexico, 1961-76, pres. bd., 1963-68, mem., 1968-76. Mem. Coun. Higher Edn., Commonwealth of P.R., 1959-61; guest prof. U. Kassel, W.Ger., 1979-81; mem. Berlin Inst. Advanced Study, 1981-82; Disting. guest prof. U. Calif., Berkeley, 1982; guest prof. U. Marburg, West Germany, 1983-84; prof. humanities and scis. grad. dept. philosophy Pa. State U., 1986-97; Karl Jaspers prof. U. Oldenburg, West Germany, 1990-91; guest prof. U. Bremen, West Germany, 1991-2002; guest prof. doctoral program in architecture U. Pa., 1990-95. Author: Celebration of Awareness, Deschooling Society, Tools for Conviviality, Energy and Equity, Medical Nemesis, Towards a History of Needs, The Right to Useful Unemployment, Shadow Work, Gender, H2O and the Waters of Forgetfulness, ABC: The Alphabetization of the Popular Mind, In the Mirror of the Past: Lectures and Addresses 1978-90, In the Vineyard of the Text: A Commentary to Hugh's Didascalicon. Mem. Authors Guild. Died Dec. 2, 2002.

IMBERT, JEAN, professor; b. Calais, France, June 23, 1919; s. Leon and Maria (Decobert) I.; m. Thérése Chombart, June 5, 1945; children: Jean-Marie, Cécile, Francois, Bruno. Licence, Faculte de Droit de Toulouse, 1943; Doctorat, Faculte de Droit de Paris, 1945. Prof. Faculte de Droit de Nancy, France, 1947-58, Faculte de Droit de Paris, 1958-88. Detaché comme Doyen Faculte Droit Phnom-Penh, Cambodia, 1959-61, Recteur Universite Yaoundé, Cameron, 1970-73; dir. des enseignements superieurs Nat. Ministry of Edn., Paris, 1976-79. Author: Le procès de Jèsus, 1981, Histoire des Institutions, 1985; contbr. articles to profl. jours. Mem. de L'Institut de France. Home: Paris, France. Died Nov. 13, 1999.

INGERSOLL, JOHN JOSEPH, retired foreign service officer; b. Phila., Jan. 11, 1920; s. Charles Eugene and Winifred Mary (O'Hara) I.; m. Betty Louise Dobson, Oct. 8, 1949; children: Laura Anne, John Dobson. BA, Temple U., 1940; MA, U. Mich., 1957. Vice consul Am. Consultate, Aden, Arabia, 1946-48, legation Jidda, Saudi Arabia, 1947, Am. Consulate Gen., Marseille, France, 1948-50; vice consul Am. Consultate Gen., Tubabao, Philippines, 1950, Amsterdam, The Netherlands, 1950-53, consul Madrid, 1953-56, Am. Embassy, London, 1957-59; asst. officer in charge of Brazilian affairs Dept. State, Washington, 1960, officer in charge of Venezuelan affairs, 1959-60; first sec. Am. Embassy, Buenos Aires, 1961-63; chief tropical products divsn. Bur. Bus. and Econ. Affairs Dept. State, Washington, 1964-71; dir. Office Internat. Commodities, Bureau Bus. and Econ. Affairs Dept. of State, Washington, 1971-76; ret., 1976. Resident U.S. rep. to several internat. commodity orgns., London, 1964-71. Page Dem. Nat. Conv., Phila., 1936. With U.S. Army, 1943-46, ETO. Mem. Am. Fgn. Svc. Assn., Diplomatic and Consular Officers Ret., Soc. of Descendants of the Signers of the U.S. Constn., Cosmos Club. Republican. Roman Catholic. Avocation: handicrafts. Home: Washington, DC. Died May 7, 1999.

INLOW, EDGAR BURKE, political science educator; b. Forest Grove, Oreg., Dec. 14, 1915; s. Harvey Edgar and Eva Lou (Skaggs) I.; m. Louise Maurer, Oct. 21, 1971; children by previous marriage: Rush, Morgan (Mrs. George Douglas), Gerd, Brand, Shane. AB, Wash. State U., 1937; MA, U. Calif., 1939; PhD, Johns Hopkins U., 1949; postgrad., Gen. Theol. Sem., N.Y.C., 1950. Instr. Princeton U., 1947-49; ordained to ministry Episcopal Ch., 1950; parish priest, 1950-57; non-stipendiary priest, 1957-81; ret., 1981; U.S. Dept. of Defense Mil. Asst Inst., Washington, 1957-61; prof. polit. sci. U. Calgary, Alta., Can., 1961-81, chmn. dept., 1961-71, prof. emeritus, 1981—. Project dir. Royal Commn. Health Svcs. Can., 1963—64; cons. Civil Svc. Commn. Can., 1963; vis. prof. Vanderbilt U., Nashville, 1964—65; lectr. St. Paul's U., Japan, 1954, McMaster U., Hamilton, Ont., 1968, U. Tehran, Iran, 1970, U. Pahlavi, Iran, 1970. Author: The Patent Grant, 1949, Studies in Canon Law, 1957, The Health Grant Program in Canada, 1963, The Divine Right of Persian Kings, 1967, Shahan-Shah, The Monarchy of Iran, 1979; contbr. articles to profl. jours. Served with U.S. Army, 1941—45. Recipient Appreciation cert. Def. Dept., 1961, citation His Imperial Majesty Iran, 1967; Social Sci. Rsch. Coun. fellow; Can. Coun. fellow. Mem. Brit. Inst. Persian Studies, SAR (nat. committeeman, pres. Seattle chpt.), Royal Soc. for Asian Affairs (hon. sec. for Can. 1971-81, Phi Beta Kappa. Died Oct. 8, 2003.

INUI, TSUNEO, banker; b. Jan. 28, 1910; m. Atsuko Inui. Grad., Keio U., 1933. Pres., chmn. Sanwa Bank Ltd., 1980; chmn. bd. Orix Corp., Tokyo. Decorated T.C.O. of the Sacred Treasure. Avocations: travel, music appreciation. Home: Hyogo, Japan. Died Oct. 21, 1998.

IRISH, MICHAEL WILLIAM, lawyer; b. Jackson, Mich., July 12, 1942; s. Forrest V. and Sadie B. (Blake) I.; m. Ann Lee Moore, Aug. 15, 1970; children: Jonathan Michael, Elizabeth Ann. BA with high honor, Mich. State U., 1970; JD cum laude, Wayne State U., 1973; MS in Taxation with distinction, F.E. Seidman Coll., 1984. Bar: Mich. 1973. From assoc. to ptnr. Landman, Latimer, Clink & Robb, Muskegon, Mich., 1973-86; ptnr. Culver, Lague & McNally, Muskegon, from 1986. Adj. prof. in estate planning F.E. Seidman Coll., Allendale, Mich., 1984-85. Co-author Michigan Will Drafting, 1988. Bd. dirs. Goodwill Industries, Muskegon County, 1976—, United Way, Muskegon County, 1983—. Served to Sgt. USMC, 1964-67, Vietnam. Fellow Am. Coll. Probate Counsel; mem. ABA, Mich. Bar Assn. (probate council). Clubs: Spring Lake Country, Muskegon Country. Avocations: golf, skiing. Home: Whitehall, Mich. Deceased.

ISBELL, BIRDDIE JEAN, missionary; b. Tampa, Fla., Mar. 5, 1932; d. Atys Severe and Agatha (Nelson) Dickey; children: Robert D. Isbell, Cheryl Del Castillo, Barbara Calkins. Student, Tampa Revival Ctr., 1948. Pres., founder The World is the Field, Inc., Tampa, Fla., from 1964. Coord. The Gospel Crusade in Honduras. Contbr. articles to profl. jours. Mem. Internat. Bd. of the Gospel Crusade, Inc. Home: Tampa, Fla. Deceased.

ISENBERG, JON IRWIN, gastroenterologist, educator; b. Chgo., Mar. 21, 1937; s. Lucien and Roselle (Moss) I.; children: Nancy Beth, Noah William, Rebecca Moss. BS with honors, U. Ill., 1959; MD, U. Ill., Chgo., 1963. Diplomate Am. Bd. Internal Medicine, Am. Bd. Gastroenterology. Assoc. prof. in residence UCLA, 1973-78, prof. medicine in residence, 1978-79; key investigator Ctr. for Ulcer Rsch. and Edn./UCLA, 1979—2003; prof. medicine U. Calif., San Diego, 1979—2003, divsn. head, 1979-92. Vis. scientist Karolinska Hosp. and Inst., Stockholm, 1982-83, U. Uppsala Biomed. Inst., Sweden, 1991-92, 99-2000; sci. com. mem. 5th Internat. Conf. on Peptic Ulcer, Boston, 1985; mem. study sect. GMA-2, NIH, 1988-92. Author: Physicians Guide to Computers and Computing, 1985; editor: Peptic Ulcer Disease: Clinics in Gastroenterology, 1984. Served to maj. U.S. Army, 1968-70. NIH grantee, 1984-2003. Fellow ACP; mem. Western Assn. Physicians (counselor 1981-85, pres. 1989-90), So. Calif. Soc. Gastroenterology (pres. 1978-79), Am. Gastroenterology Assn. (councilor 1993-96, v.p. 1999-2000, pres.-elect 2000-2001, pres. 2001-02), Assn. Am. Physicians, Am. Soc. Clin. Investigation. Democrat. Jewish. Avocation: photography. Home: La Jolla, Calif. Died Oct. 10, 2003.

ISHIHARA, TAKASHI, automotive company executive; b. Tokyo, Mar. 3, 1912; s. Ichiji and Shigeyo (Wakisaka) I.; grad. dept. law Tohoku U., 1937; m. Shizuko; 1 son, Tadashi. With Nissan Motor Co., Ltd., Tokyo, 1937—, gen. mgr. planning, 1948, gen. mgr. fin. and acctg., 1949-54, dir. fin. and acctg., 1954-57, dir. export and overseas ops., 1957-63, mng. dir. export and overseas ops., 1963-65, mng. dir. domestic sales, 1965-69, exec. mng. dir. domestic sales and adminstrv. depts., 1969-73, exec. v.p., 1973-77, pres., 1977-85, chmn., 1985-92, counselor, 1992-95, pres. Nissan Motor Corp. in U.S.A., 1960-65, chmn. Nissan Motor Mfg. Corp. U.S.A., 1980-87. Recipient Blue Ribbon medal Emperor of Japan, 1974, decorated 1st Order of Sacred Treasure (Japan). Home: Tokyo, Japan. Died Dec. 28, 2003.

ISRAEL, STANLEY C. chemistry educator; b. Bklyn., Dec. 30, 1942; s. Henry I. and Lillian I.; m. Sonja F., 1966; 1 child, Aaron M. BS, Parsons Coll., 1965; PhD, Lowell Tech. Inst., 1970. Instr. chemistry Lowell (Mass.) Tech. Inst., 1968-72; asst. prof. chemistry U. Lowell, 1972-77; dir. chem. rsch. Flammability Rsch. Ctr., U. Utah, Salt Lake City, 1975-77; assoc. prof. chemistry U. Lowell, 1977-80, prof. chemistry, 1980—97, head polymer sci. program, 1980-82, former head dept. chemistry, prof. emeritus, 1997—2003; dean, coll. of science Texas St. U., 1997—2003. Cons. in field. Mem. editorial bd. Polymers for Advanced Technologies, N.Y.C. Recipient Div. Officer award Am. Chem. Soc., 1989, 85, 83, Phoenix award, 1989, A.L. Lipschitz award, 1987, Kyoto U. medal, 1986, Student Affiliate Advisor award Am. Chem. Soc., 1978. Mem. AAAS, AAUP, Am. Chem. Soc., Am. Soc. for Mass Spectrometry, N.Y. Acad. Sci., Sigma Xi. Jewish. Achievements include patents in chemistry and polymer science; pioneering research on Direct Pyrolysis-Chemical Ionization Mass Spectrometry for the study of the reactions and mechanisms of thermal decomposition of polymeric materials. Home: Austin, Tex. Died Nov. 2, 2003.

ISRAELS, LYONEL GARRY, hematologist, educator; b. Regina, Sask., Can., July 31, 1926; s. Simon and Sarah (Girtle) I.; m. Esther Hornstein, June 3, 1950; children: Sara, Jared. BA, U. Sask., 1946; MD, U. Man., 1949, MScawd, 1950, DSc (hon.), 1999. Intern Winnipeg Gen. Hosp., 1948-49; resident internal medicine and hematology Salt Lake County Hosp., 1950-52; fellow in hematology Kantonsspital, Zurich, 1952-53; dept. biochemistry U. Man., 1953-55, asst. prof. biochemistry, 1955-59, asst. prof. medicine, 1959-62, assoc. prof. medicine, 1962-66, prof. medicine, 1966—, Disting. prof., 1983—, acting head dept. medicine, 1977-79. Dir. Manitoba Inst. Cell Biology, 1970-73, sr. scientist, 1992—; exec. dir. Manitoba Cancer Treatment and Rsch. Found., 1973-92, 93—; attending physician Health Sci. Centre; mem. Med. Rsch. Coun. Can., 1973-75; chmn. Manitoba Health Rsch. Coun., 1980-87; mem. sci. coun. Internat. Agy. Cancer Rsch., 1989-93, chmn., 1992-93. Contbr. articles on biochem. and immunol. aspects of blood, blood forming organs and cancer to sci. jours. Recipient Humanitarian award, St. Boniface Hosp., Chancellor's award, U. of Manitoba, 2003. Fellow RCPC; mem. Am. Soc. Clin. Investigation, Can. Soc. Clin. Investigation (pres. 1968), Royal Coll. Physicians and Surgeons Can., Can. Hematol. Soc. (pres. 1972-74), Nat. Cancer Inst. Can. (pres. 1976-78), Manitoba Order of Buffalo Hunt. Decorated Order of Can.; L.G. Israels chair in hematology at Ben Gurion U. in his honor, 1996. Home: Winnipeg, Canada. Died Sept. 26, 2003.

ISTOMIN, EUGENE GEORGE, concert pianist; b. N.Y.C., Nov. 26, 1925; s. George T. and Assia (Chavin) I. Grad., Profl. Children's Sch.; pupil, Kyriena Siloti, Rudolf Serkin; student, Mannes Sch., 1935-38, Curtis Inst. Music, 1939-43. Appeared maj. orchs., U.S. and abroad, including six-continent world tour; appeared annually with Pablo Casals at Casals Festivals, mem., Istomin, Stern, Rose trio, recordings for Columbia Masterworks. Winner Phila. Youth Contest and Leventritt award, 1943 Died Oct. 10, 2003.

IVANS, WILLIAM STANLEY, electronics company executive; b. New Rochelle, N.Y., June 17, 1920; s. William S. and Marion (Schultz) I.; m. Rebecca Peck Llewellyn, May 18, 1962; children: Dennis Llewellyn, Denise Ivans Laurent; stepchildren: Virginia Liebner Yates, Joan Renee Liebner de Savigliano. BS in Elec. Engring, Pa. State U., 1942. With Convair div. Gen. Dynamics Corp., San Diego, 1946-57; chief electronics engr., 1954-57; v.p. engring. Cohu Electronics, Inc. (name changed to Cohu, Inc. 1972), San Diego, 1957-65, pres., 1965-83, chief exec. officer, 1968-83, dir., chmn. bd. Bd. dirs. T-Systems Internat.; U.S. rep. gliding com. Fedn. Aero Internat., 1960-65, 66—, v.p., 1974-76, pres., 1976—. Chmn. San Diego Dist. Export Council, 1985, 86, San Diego Internat. Trade Commn., 1987—; bd. dirs. San Diego Opera, 1995—. Served as officer USAAF, 1942-46, ETO. Recipient Lilienthal medal, 1950 Mem. Soaring Soc. Am. (pres. 1963-64), Nat. Aero. Assn. (bd. dirs. 1963-64, 90—, Elder Statesman of Aviation 1994). Home: La Jolla, Calif. Died July 16 1999.

IVERSON, FRANCIS KENNETH, metals company executive; b. Downers Grove, Ill., Sept. 18, 1925; s. Norris Byron and Pearl Irene (Kelsey) Iverson; m. Martha Virginia Miller, Oct. 24, 1945; children: Claudia, Marc Miller. Student, Northwestern U., 1943—44; BS, Cornell U., 1946; MS, Purdue U., 1947, Dr. (hon.), 1988, U. Nebr. Research physicist Internat. Harvester, Chgo., 1947—52; tech. dir. Illium Corp., Freeport, Ill., 1952—54; dir. mktg. Cannon-Muskegon Corp., Mich., 1954—61; exec. v.p. Coast Metals, Little Ferry, NJ, 1961—62; v.p. Nucor Corp. (formerly Nuclear Corp. Am.), Charlotte, NC, 1962—65, pres., chief exec. officer, dir., 1965—85, chmn., chief exec. officer, 1985—96, also bd. dirs., chmn., 1998; ret. Bd. dirs. Wachovia Corp., Wal-Mart Stores Inc., Wikoff Color Corp. Author: Plain; contbr. articles to profl. jours. J.g. USNR, 1943—46. Named Best Chief Exec. Officer in Steel Industry, Wall St. Transcript, 1995; recipient Nat. medal of Tech., 1991. Mem.: Am. Soc. Metals, NAM, AIME, Quail Hollow Country Club. Home: Charlotte, NC. Died 2003.

IVES, DAVID OTIS, television executive; b. Salem, Mass., Apr. 21, 1919; s. Oscar Jackson and Elinor (Goodhue) I.; m. Cecilia Coale van Hollen, Dec. 12, 1953 (div.); children: David van Hollen, Stephen Goodhue; m. Patricia Exton Howard, June 28, 1980; stepchildren: Daggett H. Howard, Jeffrey E. Howard, David M. Howard, Patricia G. Howard. AB, Harvard U., 1941, MBA, 1943; D.H.L. (hon.), Northeastern U., 1975; H.H.D. (hon.), Suffolk U., 1977. Reporter, Salem Evening News, 1947; reporter, desk editor Wall St. Jour., N.Y.C., Detroit and Washington, bur. chief Boston, 1947-58; editorial writer Sta. WBZ-TV-AM, Boston, 1958-60; asst. gen. mgr., dir. devel., pres., vice-chmn. WGBH Ednl. Found., Boston, 1960—2000; vice chmn. bd. mgrs. Public Broadcasting Service, 1974-77; trustee, pres., chmn. exec. com. Eastern Ednl. TV Network, 1976-92; dir. Provident Instn. for Savs. Pres., bd. dirs. Harvard mag., 1986-2000. Pres., Fair Housing, Inc., Boston, 1967-71; v.p. Boston Community-Media Council, 1977-81; bd. dirs. Assoc. Harvard Alumni, 1974-77; trustee Wellesley Coll., 1973-91; mem. overseers com. to vis. dept. visual and environ. studies Harvard U., 1974-80; bd. dirs. New Eng. chpt. Deafness Research Found., 1979—2000; bd. overseers Boston Symphony Orch., 1971-77, chmn., trustee, 1975-77; trustee, chmn. bd. Nat. Assn. Public TV Stas. Recipient Ralph Lowell award for outstanding contbns. to Pub. TV, 1985, Govs. award New Eng. chpt. NATAS, 1988. Mem. Nat. Assn. Pub. TV Stas. (trustee, chmn. 1980-86), Phi Beta Kappa (hon.). Home: Cambridge, Mass. Died May 16, 2003.

IZETBEGOVIC, ALIJA, former government official; b. Bos Šamac, Bosnia-Herzegovinia, Aug. 8, 1925; s. Mustafa and Hiba (Dzabija) I.; m. Halida Repovac, May 26, 1949; children: Lejla, Sabina, Bakir. BS in Law, U. Sarajevo, Bosnia-Herzegovina, 1956. Bar: Boznia-Herzegovina, 1960. Dir. Niskogradnja, Sarajevo, 1950-56; legal advisor PUT, Sarajevo, 1956-64, I.P.S.A., Sarajevo, 1964-81, Sarajevo, 1981-83; chmn. presidency Nat. Govt. Bosnia and Herzegovina, 1990-98; pres. Govt. of Bosnia, 1998—2000. Legal advisor Sarajevo U., 1970-81. Author: Islamic Declaration, 1970, Problems of Islamic Awakening, 1977, Islam Between East and West, 1986. Chmn. Party of Dem. Action, Sarajevo, 1989. Recipient King Faisal Internat. prize for serving Islam, The Selection Com., Riyadh, Saudi Arabia, 1993. Moslem. Home: Sarajevo, Bosnia-Herzegovina. Died Oct. 19, 2003.

JABLONSKI, EDWARD, author; b. Bay City, Mich., Mar. 1, 1922; s. Boleslau and Isabel (Skrypczak) J.; m. Edith Garson, Sept. 2, 1951; children: David, Carla, Emily. AA, Bay City Jr. Coll., 1948; BA, New Sch., N.Y.C., 1950; postgrad., Columbia U., 1950-51. Dir., March of Dimes, N.Y.C., 1951-59; freelance writer, 1959—. Cons. Pub. Broadcasting System TV prodn., 1987. Author: The Gershwin Years, 1958, 73; (with L.D. Stewart) Harold Arlen: Happy With the Blues, 1961, George Gershwin, 1962, The Knighted Skies, 1964, Flying Fortress, 1965, Warriors With Wings, 1966, Ladybirds, 1968, Airwar, 4 vols., 1971-72, Atlantic Fever, 1972, Seawings, 1972, Double Strike, 1974, (with Lowell Thomas) Doolittle, 1976; contbr. to: Music in American Soc, 1976, A Pictorial History of the World War II Years, 1978, A Pictorial History of the World War I Years, 1979, Man with Wings, 1980, Encyclopedia of American Music, 1981, America in the Air War, 1982, A Pictorial History of the Middle East, 1983, Gershwin, 1987, Gershwin Remembered, 1992, Alan Jay Lerner, 1996, Harold Arlen: Rhythm, Rainbows and Blues, 1996, Irving Berlin: American Toubadour, 1999; cons., commentator on PBS TV prodn. Purely Gershwin, 1986; scriptwriter: Gershwin (Alain Resnais), 1991, The Making of Porgy and Bess (with Cyma Rubib), 1995. Served with AUS, 1942-46, PTO. Decorated Bronze Battle Star; recipient Deems Taylor award ASCAP, 1985, ASCAP award, 1989. Home: New York, NY. Died Feb. 10, 2004.

JACKSON, BETTY RUTH, nursing educator; b. Maypearl, Tex., Oct. 12, 1930; d. William Roy and Mary Anne (Underwood) Hutchins; m. James Robert Jackson, Jan. 27, 1952; children: Jamie Clifton, Julie Underriner, George. Diploma, Harris Coll. Nursing, 1951; BSN, West Tex. U., 1975; MSN, U. Tex., 1977. Indsl. nurse Shell Oil, Midland, Tex.; charge nurse Deaconess Hosp., Oklahoma City; head nurse Midland Meml. Hosp.; assoc. prof. Odessa (Tex.) Coll. Bd. dirs. Community Sr. Svcs. Mem. ANA, Tex. Nurse's Assn., Phi Kappa Phi, Sigma Theta Tau. Home: Midland, Tex. Deceased.

JACKSON, CHARLES RAY, surgeon; b. Harper, Kans., June 5, 1927; s. Charles Sutherland and Artie Fern (Comer) J.; m. Charlotte Ann Johnston, Feb. 28, 1953 (div. 1986); children: Thomas Miles, Amy Abigail, Alexander Johnston, Molly Sue; m. Claudia Dianne Arnett, Aug. 13, 1986. BS, Northwestern U., 1949, MD, 1953. Diplomate Am. Bd. Surgery. Surgeon Wichita (Kans.) Clinic, 1959-68; pvt. practice Wichita, 1968-92; ret., 1993. Fellow Am.Coll. Surgeons (pres. Kans. chpt. 1975); mem. Med. Soc. Sedgewick County (pres. 1977). Avocation: computer programming. Home: Wichita, Kans. Died Sept. 16, 1999.

JACKSON, MAYNARD, securities executive; b. Dallas, Mar. 28, 1938; s. Maynard Holbrook and Irene (Dobbs) J.; m. Valerie Richardson; 5 children. BA in Polit. Sci., Morehouse Coll., 1956; JD cum laude, N.C. Cen. U. Atty. NLRB, Atlanta; vice mayor City of Atlanta, 1970—73, mayor, 1973-82, 1990-94; mng. ptnr. Chapman and Cutler, Atlanta, 1982—94; chmn. Jackson Securities Inc., Atlanta, 1994—2002. Mem. exec. com. Dem. Nat. Com., Dem. Party, Ga.; pres. Nat. Conf. Dem. Mayors, Nat. Black Caucus of Local Elected Ofcls.; chmn. U.S. Local Govt. Energy Policy Adv. Com., Urban Residential Fin. Authority, Atlanta, Downtown Devel. Authority, Atlanta, transp. com. Atlanta Regional Commn., Rebuild Am. Coalition U.S. Conf. Mayors; founding chmn. Com. of Arts, U.S. Conf. of Mayors, Atlanta Econ. Devel. Corp.; trustee Atlanta Coun. Internat. Corps.; founder Nat. Assn. Securities Profls. Mem. Phi Beta Kappa. Died June 23, 2003.

JACKSON, R. GRAHAM, architect; b. Sherman, Tex., July 1, 1913; s. Watt J. and Lilly Thompson (Graham) J.; m. Reba Martin, Jan. 6, 1940 (dec. Oct. 1967); m. Violet Stephen Lawrence, May 1, 1971. BS in Architecture, Rice U., 1935. With R. Graham Jackson, Architect, 1936-45; ptnr. Jackson & Dill, Architects, Houston, 1946-53, Wirtz, Calhoun, Tungate & Jackson, Architects, Houston, 1953-65, Calhoun, Tungate & Jackson, Architects, Houston, 1965-75, Calhoun, Tungate, Jackson & Dill, 1975-82, CTJ&D, 1983—. Asst. prof. architecture U. Houston, part time 1947-51; vis. lectr., critic Rice U., 1963-67. Archtl. works include design Lyndon B. Johnson Spacecraft Center, NASA, Houston, Willford Hall Hosp, Lackland AFB, Tex., Ryon Engring. Bldg., Rice U, Houston, Hankammer Sch. Bus., Baylor U, communications bldg. Tex. Tech. U, Darnall Army Hosp, Ft. Hood, Tex., Burleson acad. quadrangle Baylor U, Waco, Tex., Bergstrom AFB Hosp, Austin, Tex., library and performing arts bldgs. Sam Houston State U, Huntsville, Tex., 2d Bapt. Ch, Houston, Vets. Hosp, Temple, Tex., Coll. Tech., U. Houston, master plan Buckner Children's Village, Beaumont, Tex., Westbury Bapt. Ch, Houston, Chem. and Petroleum Engring. Bldg. U. Tex., Austin, 2d Bapt. Ch., Houston. Mem. founding com. Houston Baptist U.; mem. Rice U. Fund Council, Houston Mus. Fine Arts, Friends of Bayou Bend, Houston Symphony Soc. Fellow Constrn. Specifications Inst. (pres. Houston chpt. 1958-59, region dir. 1961-64, chmn. conv. program com. 1965), AIA (treas. Houston chpt. 1950, pres. 1959, mem. nat. adminstrv. office practice com. 1951-53, 67-73, 78-81); mem. Am. Mgmt. Assn., Am. Arbitration Assn. (panel of arbiters), Rice U. Alumni, Rice U. Assos., Houston Baptist U. Alumni Assn. (hon.), Houston C. of C. (edn. com. 1950-53) Baptist (deacon). Clubs: Houston, Rice U. Faculty. Achievements include being one of only 12 persons honored by Fellowship in both AIA & CSI. Home: Lubbock, Tex. Died Oct. 16, 1999.

JACKSON, WARD, artist; b. Petersburg, Va., Sept. 10, 1928; s. Julian Bradley and Evie Allen (Jones) J. BFA, Richmond Profl. Inst. of Coll. of William and Mary, 1951, MFA, 1952; postgrad., Hans Hofmann Sch. Fine Arts, 1952. Co-editor Folio mag., 1949-50; instr. art history, dir. Morse Gallery Art Rollins Coll., 1954-55; head of viewing program, archivist Solomon R. Guggenheim Mus., 1955-94; co-editor Art Now: N.Y., 1969-72; adv. editor Art Now Gallery Guide, from 1969; sec. Am. Abstract Artists, 1990—2004. One-man shows include Fleischman Gallery, N.Y.C, 1958-60, Outer Banks Gallery, Kill Devil Hills, N.C., 1958-73, Va. Mus. Fine Arts, Richmond, 1971, 73, Dept. Art, U. Wis., 1967, Atrium Gallery, Seattle, 1965, Graham Gallery, N.Y.C., 1972, Wilhelm Lehmbruck Mus. der Stadt Duisberg, Germany, 1973, Fine Arts Ctr. Gallery, Ocean County Coll., Toms River, N.J., 1973, Stowe Galleries, Cunningham Arts Ctr., Davidson (N.C.) Coll., 1975, Kendall Galllery, N.Y.C., 1985, J.N. Herlin, N.Y.C., 1986, Galerie Adlung & Kaiser, Berlin, 1988, Museum Morsbroich, Stadtisches Museum Leverkusen, 1991, Kunsthalle Bremen, 1992; exhibited in group shows Am. Abstract Artists, N.Y.C., 1949—, New Art Circle J.B. Neumann Gallery, N.Y.C., 1950-52, Contemporary Arts Gallery, N.Y.C., 1953-56, Art USA, 1958, John Daniels Gallery, N.Y.C., 1964-65, The Contemporaries, N.Y.C., 1965, Phoenix Gallery, N.Y.C., 1966, Coll. of William and Mary, 1967, White House, Washington, 1968, Riverside Mus., N.Y.C., 1968-70, French & Co., N.Y.C., 1971, A.M. Sachs Gallery, N.Y.C., 1971, Hall Galleries, Miami, Fla., 1972, Buecker & Harpsichords, N.Y.C., 1973-82, Terrain Gallery, N.Y.C., 1975-79, Arte Fiere, Bologna, Italy, 1978, Galerie Circulus, Bonn, Fed. Republic Germany, 1978, Inst. Contemporary Art, Richmond, 1980, Summit (N.J.) Art Ctr., 1981, City Gallery, N.Y.C., 1982, Anderson Gallery, Richmond, 1982, Moody Art Gallery, Tuscaloosa, ala., 1983, Westherspoon Gallery, Chapel Hill, 1983, A.I.R. Invitational, N.Y.C., 1984-88, Bronx Mus. of the Arts, N.Y.C., 1985, 86, Columbia (S.C.) Mus. Art, 1987-88, Konkret Sieben, Nürnberg, Kunsthaus, Nürnberg, 1987, Todd Capp Gallery, N.Y.C., 1987, participated in Selections from the Am. Abstract Artists, 1988-92, (exhibition travelled throughout Can. and Europe), Centro Cultural de la Villa, Madrid, 1989, Marilyn Pearl Gallery, N.Y.C., 1988-90, Neuberger Mus., Purchase, N.Y., 1989, Solomon R. Guggenheim Mus., N.Y.C., 1987-90, Marymount Manhattan Coll. Gallery, N.Y.C., 1990, Kyusendo Gallery, Kobe, Japan, 1989-90, Edwin A. Ulrich Mus. Art Wichita State U., Kans., 1992, Noyes Art Mus., Oceanville, N.J., 1994, N.J. State Mus., Trenton, 1995, James Howe Gallery, Kean Coll., Union, N.J., 1996, Westbeth Gallery, N.Y., 1996, Castle Gallery, Coll. New Rochelle (N.Y.), 1996, Sidney Mishkin Gallery, Baruch Coll., N.Y.C., 1996, Mary Washington Coll. Gallery, Frederickberg, Va., 1996, Gibbes Mus. Art, Charleston, S.C., 1997, Sunrise Mus., Charleston, W.Va., 1997, Condeso-Lawler Gallery, N.Y., 1997, Polk Mus. Art, Lakeland, Fla., 1998, Woodward Gallery, N.Y., 1998-2000, Claudra Carr Gallery, N.Y., 2000, Mondrian House Amersfoort, Holland, 2000-01, Kunsthalle Bremen, Germany, 2000, Hill Wood Art Mus., Brookville, N.Y., 2000; represented in permanent collections Nat. Mus. Am. Art, Smithsonian Instn., Elvehjem Art Mus., U. Wis., Bibliotheque Nationale, Paris, Riverside Mus. Collection, Rose Art Mus., Brandeis U., NYU Art Collection, Va. Mus. Fine Arts, Wilhelm Lehmbruck Mus. der Stadt Duisberg, Stowe Galleries, Cunningham Arts Ctr., Davidson Coll., Brit. Mus., London, Solomon R. Guggenheim Mus., Kunsthalle Bremen Met. Mus. Art, Bklyn. Mus., Anderson Gallery, Va. Commonwealth U., N.J. State Mus., Walker Art Ctr., Neuberger Mus., San Francisco Mus. Modern Art, Mus. Fine Arts, Houston, Columbia Mus., S.C., Museum Morsbroich, Stadtisches Museum Leverkusen, Stiftung für Konstructive und Konkrete Kunst, Zurich, Biblioteca di Galleria Nazionale d'Arte Moderna, Rome, Archive '90 Collection, Mondrian House, Amersfoort, Holland. Recipient 1st prize for painting N.Y.C. Ctr.Gallery, 1956, cert. of distinction Va. Mus. Fine Arts, 1963, 66, 71, Materials award Com. for Visual Arts, 1985; Nat. Endowment for Arts Artists fellow, 1975-76, Yaddo Guest fellow, 1997, Va. Ctr. for the Creative Arts fellow, 1998; Richard A. Florsheim Art Fund grantee, 1991-92. Mem. Coll. Art Assn. Am., Am. Abstract Artists (sec. 1990-2004). Home: New York, NY. Died Feb. 3, 2004.

JACKSON, WILLIAM TURRENTINE, history educator; b. Ruston, La., Apr. 5, 1915; s. Brice H. and Luther (Turrentine) J.; m. Barbara Kone, Nov. 28, 1942. AB, Tex. Western Coll., 1935; A.M., U. Tex., 1936, PhD, 1940. Instr. history UCLA, 1940-41, Iowa State U., Ames, 1941-42, asst. prof., 1944-46, assoc. prof., 1946-48; asst. prof. Am. history U. Chgo., 1948-51. Dir. Am. civilization program, asst. prof. Am. history U. Calif. at Davis, 1951-53, assoc. prof. history, 1953-56, prof., 1956-85, chmn. dept., 1959-60; vis. prof. Mont. State U., 1941, univs. Mich., 1944, Wyo., 1945, 63, Minn., 1946, Tex., 1947, So. Calif., 1953, 56, Colo., 1961, San Francisco State Coll., 1962, Yale and R.I., 1964, NDEA History Inst., Chadron (Nebr.) State Coll., 1965, La. State U., 1967, U. Ariz., 1968, U. Alta., 1969, U. Nev., 1970, U. Hawaii, 1970, Colo. State U., 1973, Utah State U., 1975; Walter Prescott Webb lectr. U. Tex., 1976; U.S. Dept. State Disting. Am. Specialist lectr. in Western Europe, 1978; USIA seminar dir. Falkenstein Seminar in Am. Studies, Germany, 1978; cons. hist. sect. Calif. Div. Parks and Recreation, Nat. Park Svc., Wells Fargo Bank, U.S. Army Engrs.; cons. hist. sect. Tetra Tech, Inc., Teknekron, Inc., Sci. Applications, Inc.; cons. legal sect. Calif. Atty. Gen., N.Mex. State Engrs. Office; mem. Calif. Gov.'s History Commn.; dir. Nat. Endowment for Humanities Summer Seminar for Coll. Tchrs., 1976-77, 80, 81; hist. Seminar for Secondary Sch. Tchrs., 1983, 84, 86, 87, 88; adv. com. Sacramento Landmarks Commn.; mem. coordinating bd. Calif. Water Resources Ctr., 1972-81; bd. dirs. Calif. Heritage Coun., Calif. Coun. Humanities; prin. investigator Jackson Rsch. Projects, hist. cons., 1982-91; David E. Miller lectr. U. Utah. Author: Wagon Roads West, 1953, 65 (awards Pacific Coast br. Am. Hist. Assn., Nat. Inst. Graphic Arts, N.Y.C.), When Grass Was King (Merit award Am. Assn. State and Local History 1956), Treasure Hill, 1963 (Merit award Am. Assn. State and Local History), Twenty Years on the Pacific Slope, 1965, The Enterprising Scot, 1968, Gold Rush Diary of a German Sailor, 1970, Lake Tahoe Water, 1972, Water Policy in Sacramento-San Joaquin Delta, 1977, also numerous hist. monographs and articles; bd. editors: Pacific Hist. Rev, 1961-64, 67-70, So. Calif. Quar, 1962—, Arizona and the West, 1968-73, Jour. San Diego History, 1975-90, Red River Valley Hist. Rev. Ensign USNR, 1942-44. Fulbright rsch. fellow Scotland, 1949-50; Rockefeller Found. fellow Huntington Libr., 1953; grantee Am. Philos. Soc., 1955; grantee Social Sci. Rsch. Coun., 1956; grantee Am. Hist. Rsch. Ctr., 1955-56; grantee NSF, 1968-73; grantee Nat. Endowment for Humanities, 1969-70; grantee Humanities Inst., U. Calif., 1971; Guggenheim fellow, 1957-58, 65; Huntington Libr. fellow, 1972; grantee Am. Coun. Learned Socs., 1972; recipient Disting. Teaching award Acad. Senate U. Calif., Davis, 1973-74, Assoc. Students Disting. Teaching award, 1981, Disting. Alumnus award U. Tex., El Paso, award of Merit for disting. contbn. to Western History, 1989, Western Mining Assn. award, 1991, Western History Assn. prize for lifetime of disting. published writing, 1991. Fellow Calif. Hist. Soc. (trustee 1988-89); mem. AAUP, Western History Assn. (pres. 1976-77), Am. Hist. Assn. (adv. com. nat. archives 1983-86), Orgn. Am. Historians (mem. com preservation hist. sites 1960-68, mem. Pelzer award com. 1968-73, Billington Book Prize com. 1982-85), Commonwealth Club, Phi Alpha Theta, Pi Sigma Alpha, Theta Xi. Democrat. Methodist. Home: Davis, Calif. Deceased.

JACOBS, JOHN ARTHUR, earth sciences educator; b. Apr. 13, 1916; m. Daisy Sarah Ann Montgomerie (div. 1974); 2 children; m. Margaret Jones (dissolved 1981); m. Ann Grace Wintle, 1982. BA, U. London, 1937, MA, 1939, PhD, 1949, DSc, 1961; DSc (hon.), U. B.C., 1987. Prof. U. Cambridge; lectr. Royal Holloway Coll. U. London, 1946-51; assoc. prof. U. Toronto, Can., 1951-57; prof. U. B.C., Can., 1957-67; Killam Meml. prof. sci. U. Alta., Can., 1967-74, dir. Inst. Earth and Planetary Physics, 1970-74; prof. geophysics U. Cambridge, 1974-83; hon. prof. Inst. Earth Studies U. Wales, Aberystwyth, from 1989. Author: (with R.D. Russell and J.T. Wilson) Physics and Geology, 1959, 2d edit., 1974, The Earth's Core and Geomagnetism, 1963, Geomagnetic Micropulsations, 1970, A Textbook on Geonomy, 1974, The Earth's Core, 1975, 2d edit., 1987, Reversals of the Earth's Magnetic Field, 1984, 2d edit., 1994, Deep Interior of the Earth, 1992. Recipient Centennial Medal Can., 1967, Can. Assn. Physicists, 1975, J. Tuzo Wilson medal Can. Geophys. Union, 1982, John Adam Fleming medal Am. Geophys. Union, 1994, Price medal RAS, 1994, RAS medal, 2002. Avocations: walking, music. Died Dec. 13, 2003.

JACOBS, SIDNEY J. rabbi, journalist; b. Chgo., May 25, 1917; s. Emanuel and Sarah (Barnett) J.; m. Helen Rosenzweig, Mar. 4, 1951 (div. 1969); children: Nehama Aviva, Michael Ethan, Jonathan Gabriel.; m. Betty J. Lazaroff, July 1, 1971. BSc in Journalism, Northwestern U., 1938; Rabbi, Jewish Inst. Religion, N.Y.C., 1946; MA in Hebrew Letters, Hebrew Union Coll., 1969. Registrar and mem. history faculty Coll. Jewish Studies, Chgo., 1946-49; exec. dir. Chgo. Coun. Am. Jewish Congress, 1949-52; founding rabbi Niles Twp. Jewish Congregation, Skokie, Ill., 1952-70; v.p. Chgo. Bd. Rabbis, 1970-71; mng. editor B'nai B'rith Messenger, L.A., 1971; pres., CEO Jacobs Ladder Pubs., Culver City, Calif., 1985. Vis. rabbi Temple Israel, Duluth, Minn., Congregation Beth Israel, Barstow, Calif., Temple Sinai, Cathedral City, Calif., Temple Ner Tamid, Downey, Calif.; lectr. Univ. Inst., Univ. Judaism, L.A., Earl Warren Inst. Ethics and Human Rels. Author: Jewish Word Book, 1982; co-author Clues About Jews for People Who Aren't, 1985, 122 Clues for Jews Whose Children Intermarry, 1988, Jewish Clues to Your Health and Happiness, 1990; editor: High Holiday Services, 1976; contbr. to numerous mags., newspapers including L.A. Mag., Jewish Spectator, The Lutheran, Westways, L.A. Times, Jewish Encyclopedia and others. Incorporator interfaith com. to aid farm workers of Nat. Migrant Ministry; chmn. Niles Twp. Interfaith Clergy Fellowship, Tikvah Inst. for Childhood Learning Disabilities; mem. Amalgamated Clothing and Textile Workers AFL-CIO, clergy adv. com. L.A. Unified Sch. Dist. Supt.; polit. advocate Fund for Animals, Zero Pet Population Growth; founder-mem. World Theol. Assn. for Animal Rights and many other social orgns. Recipient Thomas J. Crowe award for interracial justice, from Cath. Interracial Coun. Chgo, Solomon Schechter award for social action United Synagogue Am.; citations from numerous charitable orgns. and Ill. State Gen Assembly; Emmy award finalist Mem. Ctrl. Conf. Am. Rabbis, Chgo. Bd. Rabbis (media cons.), Soc. Profl. Journalists, Sigma Delta Chi. Died July 19, 2001.

JACOBS, THEODORE ALAN, scientist, consultant; b. Atlanta, Oct. 19, 1927; s. Samuel Morris and Fay (Williams) J.; m. Joan Granit, Apr. 30, 1961; 1 child, Steven Douglas. BA, Emory U., 1950; MSME, U. So. Calif., 1954; PhD in Chem. Physics, Calif. Inst. Tech., 1960. Designer Douglas Aircraft Co., Santa Monica, Calif., 1951-52; rsch. engr. G. O. Noville and Assocs., Beverly Hills, Calif., 1953-55; rsch. assoc., lectr. mech. engring. U. So. Calif., L.A., 1955-57; sr. rsch. engr. Rocketdyne div. N.Am. Aviation, Inc., Canoga Park, Calif., 1957-58; sr. rsch. fellow Calif. Inst. Tech., Pasadena, 1960-61; head aerophysics dept. Aerospace Corp., El Segundo, Calif., 1961-71; dir. high energy laser tech. TRW Def. & Space Systems Group, Redondo Beach, Calif., 1971-76; supt. optical scis. div. Naval Rsch. Lab., Washington, 1976-78; dep. asst. sec. of the navy Pentagon, Washington, 1978-85; cons. Annandale, Va., 1985—2004. Contbr. articles to numerous sci. publs. Recipient Plasmadynamics and Lasers award AIAA, 1997. Fellow Am. Phys. Soc., Optical Soc. Am.; mem. Am. Chem. Soc., Am. Def. Preparedness Assn., Sigma Xi. Achievements include research in high temperature chemical kinetics, chemical lasers, high energy lasers. Home: Annandale, Va. Died Feb. 23, 2004.

JACOBSEN, JOSEPHINE, author; b. Coburg, Ont., Can., Aug. 19, 1908; d. Joseph Edward and Octavis (Winder) Boylan; m. Eric Jacobsen, Mar. 17, 1932; 1 son, Erlend Ericsen. Grad., Roland Park Country Sch., 1926; LHD (hon.), Coll. Notre Dame Md., 1974, Goucher Coll., 1974; MDiv. (hon.), St. Mary's Seminary & Coll., 1988; hon. degree, Johns Hopkins U., 1993. Critic; short story writer; lectr.; poetry cons. Library of Congress, 1971-73, hon. cons. in Am. letters, 1973-79; v.p. PSA, 1979-80. Author: Let Each Man Remember, 1940, The Human Climate: New Poems, 1953, For the Unlost, 1948, The Animal Inside, 1966, (with William Mueller) The Testament of Samuel Beckett, 1968, Genet and Ionesco Playwrights of Silence, 1968, The Shade-Seller: New and Collected Poems, 1974, A Walk With Raschid and Other Stories, 1978 (Notable Books of 1978), The Chinese Insomniacs, New Poems, 1981, Adios Mr. Moxley, 1986, The Sisters: New and Selected Poems, 1987, On the Island: New and Selected Stories, 1989 Distances, 1992, In the Crevice of Time: New and Collected Poems, 1995, Instant of Knowing: Lectures, Criticism and Occasional Prose, 2000, What Goes Without Saying: Collected Stories of Josephine Jacobsen, 2000; writing also included O. Henry Awards Prize Stories, 1967, 71, 73, 76, 85, 93, Fifty Years of the American Short Story, 1970, On the Island: Stories, 1989, Best Poems, 1991, Pushcart Prizes, 1991. Mem. lit. panel Nat. Endowment for Arts, 1980-84. Recipient MacDowell Colony fellow; Yaddo fellow; Am. Acad. Poets fellow, 1987; recipient Shelly Meml. award for life work PSA, 1993. Mem, Am. Acad. Arts and Letters (Svc. to Lit. award 1982, Lenore Marshall award for best book of poetry pub. in U.S. in 1987, 1988), PEN (nominee Faulkner award for fiction 1990). Democrat. Roman Catholic. Home: Cockeysville, Md. Died July 9, 2003.

JACOBSON, ALBERT HERMAN, JR., industrial and systems engineer, educator; b. St. Paul, Minn., Oct. 27, 1917; s. Albert Herman and Gertrude Jacobson; m. Elaine Swanson, June 1960; children: Keith, Paul. BS Indsl. Engring./Adminstrn. cum laude, Yale U., 1939; SM Bus. and Engring. Mgmt., MIT, 1952; MS in Applied Physics, U. Rochester, 1954; PhD in Indsl. and Mgmt. Engring., Stanford U., 1976. Registered profl. engr., Calif. Pers. asst. Yale U., New Haven, Conn., 1939-40; indsl. engr. in electronics Radio Corp. of Am., Camden, N.J., 1940-43; prodn. officer USN BuORD, 1943-44; RINSMAT USN Colonial Radio Corp. (Sylvania), Buffalo, 1944-45; INSORD USN Eastman Kodak Co., Rochester, N.Y., 1945-46; chief engr., dir. quality control Naval Ordnance Office, Rochester, N.Y., 1946-57; staff engr. Space Satellite Program Eastman Kodak Co., Rochester, 1957-59; assoc. dean Coll. Engring. and Architecture Pa. State U., University Park, Pa., 1959-61; v.p., gen. mgr. to pres. Knapic Electro-Physics Inc., Palo Alto, Calif., 1961-62; prof. of indsl. and systems engring. Coll. of Engring. San Jose State U., from 1962, co-founder, coord. Cybernetic Systems grad. program, 1968-88. Cons. in field, Lockheed, Motorola, Santa Fe R.R., 20th Century Fox, Alcan-Aluminium Corp., Banner Container, Sci. Mgmt. Corp., No. Telecom, Siliconix, others. Author: Military and Civilian Personnel in Naval Administration, 1952, Railroad Consolidations and Transportation Policy, 1975; editor: Design and Engineering of Production Systems, 1984; contbr. articles to profl. jours. Mem., chmn. Pers. Commn. City of Mountain View, Calif., 1968-78; troop chmn., scoutmaster, mem. Stanford Area Coun. Boy Scouts of Am., Palo Alto, 1970-83; chmn. Campus Luth. Coun. San Jose State U., 1981-86; mem. Santa Clara Valley Luth. Parish Coun., 1991—; pres. N.Y. State Young Adults Coun. YMCA, 1954-55. Lt. comdr. USNR. Recipient commendation USN, 1946; Alfred P. Sloan fellow Program Exec. Devel. MIT, 1951-52, NSF fellow, Stanford U., 1965-66; recipient Scouters Key and Award of Merit Stanford Coun. Boy Scouts Am., 1976. Mem. Am. Soc. Engring. Edn., Inst. Indsl. Engrs., Am. Prodn. and Inventory Control Soc. (bd. dirs. 1975—), Masons, Sigma Xi, Tau Beta Pi. Lutheran. Avocations: orchestra and choir, swimming, tennis, skiing, photography. Home: Mountain View, Calif. Died Jan. 15, 2004.

JACOBSON, NATHAN, mathematics educator; b. Warsaw, Sept. 8, 1910; came to U.S., 1917; s. Charles and Pauline (Rosenberg) J.; married Aug. 25, 1942; children— Michael Sidney, Pauline Ida AB, U. Ala., 1930; PhD, Princeton U., 1934; D.Sc. (hon.), U. Chgo., 1972. Asst. Inst. for Advanced Study, 1934-35; lectr. Bryn Mawr Coll., 1935-36; NRC fellow U. Chgo., 1936-37; instr. U. N.C., 1937-38, asst. prof., 1938-40, assoc. prof., 1941-42, Johns Hopkins U., 1943-47; assoc. prof. math. Yale U., New Haven, 1947-49, prof., 1949-81, prof. emeritus, 1981—. Vis. assoc. prof. Johns Hopkins U., 1940-41; vis. prof. U. Chgo., summer 1947, 65; vis. prof. Tata Inst. Fundamental Research, 1969;

vis. prof. Eidgenossiches Technischehochschule, Zurich, 1981; vis. lectr. Japan, Italy, Israel, Peoples Republic China, Taiwan; Sesquicentennial hon. prof. U. Ala., 1981 Author over 10 math. books; contbr. research articles to profl. jours. Served with USN, 1942-43 Fulbright scholar U. Paris, 1951-52; Guggenheim fellow, 1951-52 Mem. Nat. Acad. Scis., Am. Acad. Arts and Scis., Am. Math. Soc. (pres. 1971-73), Internat. Math. Union (v.p. 1972-74), London Math. Soc. (hon.) Avocations: travel; gardening; cinema photography. Home: Norwalk, Conn. Died Oct., 1999.

JACOBY, ALBERTA PETRIE, television producer; b. Worthington, Minn., Sept. 1, 1911; d. Stelle S. and Blanche (Petrie) Smith; m. Kenneth Haycraft (div. 1937); m. Thomas Fair Neblett (div. 1941); m. Oscar Altman (div. 1949); m. Irving Jacoby (dec. 1985); children: Clair, Sara, Peter, Leslie, Tamar, Oren. BS summa cum laude, U. Minn., 1936; M, Yale U., 1967. Reporter Mpls. Star, 1935-36; prof. golfer Women's Tour, 1937-39; writer U.S. Dept. Justice, Washington, 1940-41, U.S. Office War Info., Washington, 1942-44; assoc. dir. communications USPHS, Washington, 1945-48; dir. communications NIMH, Washington, 1949-51; esec. dir. communications Mental Health Film Bd., N.Y.C., from 1952; asst. prof. communications Yale U., New Haven, from 1967; ind. tv producer New Haven, from 1975. Cons. Nat. Conf. Social Workers, Am. Psychiat. Assn., Pres. Com. on Handicapped, Group for Advancement of Psychiatry. Producer 25 films on mental health, 1954— (Golden Eagle, cert. excellence). Mem. Yale Club, Mid Ocean Club, Phi Beta Kappa. Avocations: golf, skiing. Home: Havertown, Pa. Deceased.

JAFFE, LEONARD SIGMUND, financial executive; b. Balt., Oct. 31, 1916; s. Benjamin I. and Anna J. (Berkow) J.; m. Marjorie Dorf, Apr. 24, 1941; children: Carol (Mrs. Fred Levinger), Ellen (Mrs. Robert Davis), Susan A. Jaffe (Mrs. Lisardo Augustin). BA, Johns Hopkins U., 1937; MBA, Harvard U., 1939. Asst. plant mgr. Joseph E. Seagram, N.Y.C., 1942-45, divsn. contr., 1945-56, corp. contr., 1956-58; v.p. fin. Capehart Corp., N.Y.C., 1958-62; v.p. fin., sec.-treas. Rheingold Corp., N.Y.C., 1962-68; v.p. fin. Work Wear Corp., Cleve., 1970-73; exec. v.p. fin. Cook United, Inc., Cleve., 1974-77; pres. Marlen Corp. of Miami, 1978-85, Corp. Fin. Group, Boca Raton, Fla., 1983—. Instr. acctg. U. Louisville, 1946-47. Mem. nat. student alumni coun. Johns Hopkins U. Mem. Fin. Execs. Inst., Inst. of Mgmt. Acctg., Harvard Club (N.Y.C.), Oakwood Club (Cleve.), Harvard Bus. Sch. Club, Clevelander Club, Birchwood Country Club (Westport, Conn.), Rotary. Home: Delray Beach, Fla. Died Sept. 1999.

JAMES, DANIEL J. management consultant; b. Nokomis, Ill., Mar. 21, 1920; s. Daniel and Katie (Lauer) J.; m. Ann Wilder, June 12, 1954; children— Karen Ann, Debra Kay. B.E., Eastern Ill. State U., 1942; MS, U. Ill., 1946, PhD, 1952; Dr. Pedagogy (hon.), Eastern Ill. U., 1958. Chief prodn. scheduling Taylor Instrument Co., Rochester, N.Y., 1946-47; instr. Flint (Mich.) Jr. Coll., 1947-48; asst. prof. Central Mich. Coll., Mt. Pleasant, 1948-50; asst. prof. Atlanta div. U. Ga., 1952-54; prof. marketing U. Ark., Fayetteville, 1954-57; adviser to Govt. of Chile, FAO, UN, 1957-58; program officer AID (formerly ICA), Seoul, Korea, 1959-62; internat. economist Bur. Econ. Affairs, State Dept., 1963; officer in charge politico-econ. affairs Office Near East-South Asian Regional Affairs, 1963-64; econ.-sci. officer Am. Embassy, Taipei, Tawian, 1964-69, polit.-econ., econ.-comml. officer New Delhi, India, 1969-72; dep. dir., spl. projects officer Office of Security Assistance and Sales, Bur. Politico-Mil. Affairs, Dept. of State, 1972-78; fgn. policy adviser to comdr.-in-chief U.S. Army Europe and 7th Army, Heidelberg, Germany, 1978-79; internat. economist Office Internat. Security Ops., Bur. Politico-Mil. Affairs, Dept. State, Washington, 1979-80; v.p. Mgmt. Logistics Internat., Ltd., Arlington, Va., 1980-85, sr. assoc., 1986-88; pvt. mgmt. cons. McLean, Va., from 1988. Served to 1st lt. AUS, 1942-45. Died Sept. 16, 2002.

JAMES, FRANKLIN JOSEPH, JR., public policy educator; b. Tampa, Fla., Nov. 11, 1946; s. Franklin Joseph Sr. and Eve (Keene) J.; m. Melanie Anne Lee, Sept. 9, 1967 (dec. Dec. 1987); children: Charles, Philip. BA in Econs. with honors, U. Ga., 1967; MPhil in Econs., PhD in Econs., Columbia U., 1976. Rsch. asst. Nat. Bur. Econ. Rsch., N.Y.C., 1969-71; sr. rsch. economist Rutgers U., Ctr. for Urban Policy, New Brunswick, N.J., 1971-74; rsch. assoc. The Urban Inst., Washington, 1974-77; dir. urban policy staff U.S. Dept. Housing and Urban Devel., Washington, 1977-81; prof. pub. policy U. Colo., Denver, from 1981; dir. doctoral studies U. Colo. Grad. Sch. Pub. Affairs, Denver, 1992-96. Mem. rsch. adv. com. Fed. Nat. Mortgage Assn., Washington; mem. adv. com. Ctr. Cmty. Devel., N.Y.C. Co-author: President's National Urban Policy Report, 1980, Minorities in the Sunbelt, 1984; co-editor: Future of National Urban Policy, 1990. Staff dir. Colo. Pub. Pvt. Housing State Task Force, Denver; rsch. Gov.'s Task Force on the Homeless, Denver; mem. Mayor's Disbursement Com. for Ryan White Fund, Denver. Mem. Phi Beta Kappa. Democrat. Episcopalian. Avocations: mountain climbing, skiing, hiking, running. Home: Parker, Colo. Died July 4, 2001.

JAMES, SIDNEY LORRAINE, television executive; b. St. Louis, Aug. 6, 1906; s. William Henry and Katherine (Wiese) J.; m. Agnes McCarthy, Oct. 21, 1932 (dec. 1991); children: Christopher, Timothy, Mary, Sidney; m. Donna Petterson, Jan. 14, 1994. Student, Washington U., St. Louis. Mem. editorial staff St. Louis Post-Dispatch, 1928-36; nat. affairs writer Time mag., 1936-38; chief Time, Inc., Chgo., 1938-41, chief Western editorial ops., 1941-46, v.p. corp. mgmt., 1965-67, v.p. Washington, 1967-70; asst. mng. editor Life mag., 1946-54; founding mng. editor Sports Illus. mag., N.Y.C., 1954-60, pub., 1960-65; chmn. bd. Greater Washington Ednl. TV Assn. (WETA), Inc., 1970—2004. 1st vice chmn. bd. Pub. Broadcasting Svc. Author: Paper Trail - A Memoir, Press Pass - The Journalist's Tale, 1994; editor: The Wonderful World of Sport, 1967; author forewords Ben Hogan's The Modern Fundamentals of Golf, 1957, Charles Goren's The Book of Bridge, 1961; contbr. articles to Time and Life mags.; co-developer: (radio program) Quiz Kids; dir. first TV broadcast of polit. conv., Life mag. and NBC, 1948; anchor: (TV spl.) We The People, 1953. Mem. Pres.'s Adv. Com. on Youth Fitness; mem. Peabody Awards Bd.; lay trustee Trinity Coll. Recipient George Foster Peabody award for meritorious svc. in broadcasting, 1979. Mem. Def. Orientation Assn., Nat. Inst. Social Scis., U.S. Srs. Golf Assn., Am. Yacht Club, Apawamis Club (Rye, N.Y.), N.Y. Racquet and Tennis Club, Burning Tree Club, 1925 F St. Club, Nat. Press Club, Internat. (Washington). Home: Oakland, Calif. Died Mar. 11, 2004.

JAMIESON, JOHN ANTHONY, engineering consulting company executive; b. London, Mar. 16, 1929; came to U.S., 1952; s. John Percival and Jean (Kerr) J.; m. Barbara Armstrong, July 6, 1956; children: John Gordon, Sara Felicity, John Douglas. BS summa cum laude, U. London, 1952; PhD, Stanford U., 1957. Scientist, then mgr. electrooptics div. Aerojet-Gen. Corp., Azusa, Calif., 1957-69; asst. dir. U.S. Army Advanced Ballistic Missile Defense Agy., Washington, 1970-73; pres. Jamieson Sci. & Engring., Inc., Washington, 1973-97; chief scientist Vanguard Rsch., Inc., Fairfax, Va., from 1997. Chmn. Sci. & Engring. Support Group to SDIO, Washington, 1985—; mem. sci. adv. bd. USAF, 1990-94; chief scientist Vanguard Rsch., Inc.; bd. dirs. Optelecom, Inc., Gaithersburg, Md., Space Computer Corp., L.A. Author: Infrared Physics & Engineering, 1963; contbr. chpt. in book and articles to profl. jours. Served with RAF, 1947-50. Recipient Space Sys. award AIAA, 1992, award for meritorious civilian svc. U.S. Dept. Air Force, 1990, 94, Thomas B. Dowd Meml. award, 1995, Space-based Infrared Pioneer award USAF, 1999. Republican. Episcopalian. Home: Tucson, Ariz. Died Oct., 1999.

JAMISON, GEORGE MARSHALL SHIPMAN, retired television director and producer; b. Boston, June 16, 1918; s. Walter Washington and Margaret (Shipman) J.; m. Priscilla Langenbach, June 21, 1939 (div. 1948); 1 child, Patricia Ann; m. Janet Rosa, May 14, 1950; children: Janeen, Joshua, Theresa, Marshall, Janet. Student, New Eng. Conservatory of Music, 1936-37, Yale U., 1938-39. Casting dir., asst. Joshua Logan, Leland Hayward, N.Y.C., 1951-56; exec. producer U.S. Steel Hour Theatre Guild Inc., N.Y.C., 1956-58; co-producer Leland Hayward, N.Y.C., 1959-69; dir. ABC-TV, N.Y.C, 1970-71; producer CBS-TV, N.Y.C., 1971-72; exec. producer U. Mid-Am., Lincoln, Nebr., 1974-76; sr. producer U. Nebr. TV, Lincoln, 1976—90. Writer, producer, dir. TNT Communications, Inc., N.Y.C., 1960-74. Dir.: (Broadway plays) By the Beautiful Sea, The Young and Beautiful, On Borrowed Time, Time Limit, 1953-56; dir., producer That Was the Week That Was, 1963-64; Broadway actor, 1948-51. Cons. Rep. Presdl. Conv., Chgo., 1960, coach of speakers, Miami, Fla., 1968, Kansas City, Mo., 1976; coach of speakers Dem. Presdl. Conv., N.Y.C., 1976. Recipient Christopher award Christopher Soc., 1958; numerous Peabody awards, U. Ga. Sch. Journalism, 1953-83, Emmy award TV Acad., 1960, Limelight award, 1960; Ohio State award Ohio State U., 1973. Mem. The Players. Avocations: golf, bridge, swimming, gardening. Home: Altamonte Spg, Fla. Died Sept. 2, 2003.

JAMPLIS, ROBERT WARREN, surgeon, medical foundation executive; b. Chgo., Apr. 1, 1920; s. Mark and Janet (McKenna) J.; m. Roberta Cecelia Prior, Sept. 5, 1947 (dec. 1995); children: Mark Prior, Elizabeth Ann Jamplis Bluestone; m. Cynthia S. Philbin, Dec. 1, 1996. BS, U. Chgo., 1941, MD, 1944; MS, U. Minn., 1951. Diplomate Am. Bd. Surgery, Am. Bd. Thoracic Surgery. Asst. resident in surgery U. Chgo., 1946; fellow in thoracic surgery Mayo Clinic, Rochester, Minn., 1947—52; chief thoracic surgery Palo Alto (Calif.) Med. Clinic, 1958—81, exec. dir., 1965—81; clin. prof. surgery Stanford U. Sch. Medicine, from 1958. Mem. coun. SRI Internat.; chmn. bd. TakeCare Corp.; charter mem., bd. regents Am. Coll. Physician Execs.; mem. staff Stanford Univ. Hosp., Santa Clara Valley Med. Ctr., San Jose, VA Hosp., Palo Alto, Sequoia Hosp., Redwood City, Calif., El Camino Hosp., Mountain View, Calif., Harold D. Chope Cmty. Hosp., San Mateo, Calif.; pres., CEO Palo Alto Med. Found., 1980—2000; past chmn. Fedn. Am. Clinics; dir. Blue Cross Calif.; varsity football team physician Stanford U. Author (with G.A. Lillington)): A Diagnostic Approach to Chest Diseases, 1965, A Diagnostic Approach to Chest Diseases, 2d edit., 1979; contbr. numerous articles to profl. jours. Trustee Santa Barbara Med. Found. Clinic; past pres. Calif. div. Am. Cancer Soc.; past chmn. bd. Group Practice Polit. Action Com.; past mem. athletic bd. Stanford U.; past mem. cabinet U. Chgo.; past trustee No. Calif. Cancer Program; past bd. dirs. Core Communications in Health, Community Blood Res., others; bd. dirs. Herbert Hoover Boys' Club. Lt. USNR, 1944—46, Lt. USNR, 1952—54. Recipient Alumni citation, U. Chgo., 1968, Nat. Divsn. award, Am. Cancer Soc., 1979, Med. Exec. award, Am. Coll. Med. Group Adminstrs., 1981, Russel V. Lee award lectr., Am. Group Practice Assn., 1982, Mayo Disting. Alumnus award, 1991. Mem.: AMA, ACS, Santa Clara County Med. Assn., Calif. Med. Assn., Am. Group Practice Assn. (past pres.), Am. Fedn. Clin. Research, Calif. Acad. Medicine, Am. Coll. Chest Physicians (bd. govs.), Doctors Mayo Soc., San Francisco Surg. Soc. (past pres.), Pacific Coast Surg. Assn., Western Surg. Assn., Western Thoracic Surg. Assn. (past pres.), Soc. Thoracic Surgeons (past pres.), Am. Surg. Assn., Am. Assn. Thoracic Surgery, Inst. Medicine of Nat. Acad. Scis., Portland Surg. Soc. (hon.), Rancheros Visitadores (Santa Barbara, Calif.), Menlo Circus (Atherton, Calif.), Menlo Country Club, Commonwealth Club of California (San Francisco), Bohemian Club, Pacific Union Club, Stanford Club, Golf Club, Sigma Xi. Republican. Roman Catholic. Home: Woodside, Calif. Died Feb. 3, 2003.

JANDL, HENRY ANTHONY, architect, educator; b. Spokane, July 17, 1910; s. Paul and Marie (Zitterbart) J.; m. Gertrude Ward, June 4, 1940 (dec. 1976); children: Margaret M., H. Ward (dec.); m. Nancy Crater, Oct. 2, 1976. Student, Fontainebleau (France) Sch. Fine Arts, 1933; B.Arch., M.Arch., Carnegie Inst. Tech., 1935; M.F.A. in Architecture, Princeton U., 1937; postgrad., Ecole des Beaux Arts, Paris, 1937-39. Faculty Princeton, 1940-43, 45—, prof. architecture, 1957-75, prof. emeritus, 1975—; acting dir. Princeton (Sch. Architecture), 1964; exec. officer Princeton (Sch. Architecture and Urban Planning), 1968-74; plant engr. Corning Glass Works, N.Y., 1943-45; pvt. practice architecture, 1943—. Vis. critic U. Va., 1957; cons. architect; cons. on phys. facilities to comdg. gen., Fort Monmouth, N.J., 1966-67; archtl. cons. art and architecture com. Diocese of Trenton. Mem., vice chmn. bd. Environ. Design Rev. for Princeton Twp.; bd. trustee CB Wellness Found., 2000—. John Stewardson fellow, 1933; Whitney Warren fellow, 1937; Recipient Princeton prize, 1935; honor award for design of Princeton Borough Hall N.J. chpt. AIA, 1966 Fellow AIA (pres. Capitol chpt. N.J. 1961-62, James River chpt. 1978—, Coll. of Fellows 1971—, AIA Sch. medal 1937); mem. Assn. Collegiate Sch. Architecture, Assn. Princeton Grad. Alumni, Nat. Inst. Archtl. Edn., Alpha Rho Chi (medal for excellence 1935), Phi Kappa Phi, Tau Sigma Delta. Clubs: Kennebunk River. Republican. Home: Richmond, Va. Died Jan. 3, 2004.

JANEWAY, CHARLES ALDERSON, JR., immunologist, educator; b. Boston, 1943; BA, Harvard U., 1963, MD, 1969. With Nat. Inst. Med. Rsch., London, NIH, Biomedical Ctr., Uppsala, Sweden; prof. Yale U. Sch. Medicine, New Haven, 1973—2003. Investigator Howard Hughes Med. Inst. Author: Immunobiology: The Immune System in Health and Disease; contbr. articles to profl. jours. Mem.: Nat. Acad. Sci. Died Apr. 12, 2003.

JANSSEN, PAUL ADRIAAN JAN, pharmaceutical company executive; b. Turnhout, Belgium, Sept. 12, 1926; s. Jan Constant and Margriet (Fleerackers) J.; m. Dora Arts, July 1, 1957; children: Graziëlla, Herwig, Yasmine, Pablo, Maroussia. BSc, Fac. Notre Dame de la Paix, 1945; student, U. Louvain, Belgium, 1945-49; MD magna cum laude, State U. Ghent, Belgium, 1951; teaching cert. in chem. pharm., State U. Ghent, 1956. Asst. Inst. Pharmacology and Therapeutics, State U. Ghent, 1950-56, Inst. Pharmacology, U. Cologne, Fed. Republic Germany, 1951-52; pres., dir. rsch. Janssen Pharmaceutica NV, Beerse, Belgium, 1958-91, hon. chmn. bd. dirs., 1991—2003; former chmn. Janssen Rsch. Found. Worldwide. Vice chmn. Johnson & Johnson Internat., 1979-91; lectr. psychiatry U. Liége, Belgium, 1966; prof. medicinal chemistry Liège Notre Dame de la Paix, Namur, Belgium, 1973; pres. Collegium Internat. Neuro-Psychopharm., 1980-82; vis. prof. med. sci. King's Coll., U. London, 1982-83; councillor Belgian Nat. Coun. Mgmt. Scis., 1984-87, Flemish Coun. Mgmt. Scis., 1987—; lectr., Francqui chair Cath. U. Louvain, 1985-86, vis. prof. Sch. Pharm. Scis., 1987-88, prof. extraordinary Inst. Pharm. Scics. Louvain, 1988-91; lectr. in field. Recipient hon. doctorate, Johann Wolfgang Goethe U., Frankfurt, Fed. Republic Germany, 1978, U. Lund, Sweden, 1981, Cath. U. Louvain, 1982, Szeged (Hungary) U. Med. Sch., 1984, State U. Ghent, 1984, U. Dublin, Ireland, 1985, U. Düsseldorf, Fed. Republic Germany, Ben Gurion U. of Negev, Israel, 1986, State U. Liége, Belgium, 1988, U. Granada, Spain, 1989, U. Montreal, 1989, U. Antwerp, 1992. U. Pavia, 1992, U. Istanbul, 1992, U. Rome, 1992, China Pharm. U., 1993, State U. Limburg, Netherlands, 1996, U. Alta., Can., 1996, Charles U., Czech Republic, 1998; recipient numerous awards from profl. orgns. throughout Europe and U.S. Fellow Royal Acad. Medicine Ireland (hon.), Coll. Medicine South Africa (hon.); mem. Royal Soc. Medicine (London), Am. Chem. Soc., N.Y. Acad. Scis., Excerpta Medica Found., European Soc. Study of Drug Toxicity, AAAS, Collegium Internat. Medicinae Psychosomaticae, Am. Coll. Neuropsychopharmacology, Belgian Coll. Neuropsychopharmacology and Biol. Psychiatry, Belgian Soc. Fundamental and Clin. Physiology and Pharmacology, Royal Soc. Sci. Liége, Colombian Soc. Dermatology, numerous others. Home: Vosselaar, Belgium. Died Nov. 11, 2003.

JANTZE, R. DALE, retired educator; b. Milford, Nebr., Apr. 5, 1926; s. Ralph and Esther (Reil) J.; m. Margaret Lorraine Pederson, June 5, 1962. BA, Goshen Coll., 1951; MEd, U. Nebr., 1953, EdD, 1961. Cert. tchr., adminstr., Nebr. Supt. Staplehurst (Nebr.) pub. schs., 1951-54; instr. biology and physics Exeter (Nebr.) pub. schs., 1954-56; supt. Diller (Nebr.) pub. schs., 1956-60; prof., chmn. tchr. edn. Friends U., Wichita, Kans., 1961-78; adminstr. N.W. Wichita Child Devel. Ctr., 1978-94. Cons. Mid-Continent Regional Edn. Lab., Kans. City, Mo., 1966-70, in interaction analysis Emporia State U.; pres. Kans. Assn. Edn. Comm. and Tech., 1968-69, Kans. Assn. Colls. Tchr. Edn., 1972-74; chmn. Kans. Profl. Tchg. Standards Bd., Topeka, 1972-78. Active Mennonite Econ. Devel. Assocs., 1988-98. Mem.

Optimist Internat. (life), Kans. Optimist Dist. (lt. gov. 1975-76), Wichita-W. Optimist Club (pres. 1974-75), Phi Delta Kappa (25 year pin). Home: Wichita, Kans. Died Aug. 9, 2001.

JAQUES, ELLIOTT, organizational consultant, social researcher; b. Toronto, Ont., Can., Jan. 18, 1917; s. John Louis and Pauline (Hirsh) J.; m. Cathryn Cason, Jan. 18, 1989; 1 child, Gemma. BA, U. Toronto, 1937; MD, Johns Hopkins U., 1941; PhD, Harvard U., 1950. Pvt. practice psychoanalysis, indsl. cons., London, 1952-65; head of Sch. of Social Sci. Brunel U., London, 1965-79. Cons. U.S. Army, Washington, 1979-86, CRA Mining Corp., Melbourne, Australia, 1979—; vis. rsch. prof. mgmt. sci. George Washington U., Washington, 1991 Author: Equitable Payment, 1965, General Theory of Bureaucracy, 1976, Requisite Organization, 1989, others. Maj., 1942-46. Mem. Brit. Psychoanalytical Soc. Died Mar. 8, 2003.

JARRELL, DENNIS WALTON, hospital comptroller; b. Clarksville, Tenn., Oct. 7, 1949; s. Julian Walton Jr. and Mavis Rebecca (Fiedler) J.; m. Lisa Katherine Koehn, June 18, 1973; children: Melanie Elaine, Mark Walton. BS in Econs., Austin Peay State U., Clarksville, Tenn., 1971, BS in Acctg., 1972. Acct. Clarksville Meml. Hosp., 1971-73, mgr. acctg., data processing, 1973-82, comptroller, from 1982. V.p., bd. dirs. Clarksville Meml. Hosp. Credit Union, 1974-77, chmn. supervisory com., 1977-78; mem. exec. com. Blue Cross and Blue Shield of Tenn. Hosp. Computer Ctr., Chattanooga, 1982-83. Mem. Tenn. Uniform Billing Com., Nashville, 1979; mem. adminstrv. bd. Hilldale United Meth. Ch., Clarksville, 1983-85, pastor-parish relations com., 1984—. Named one of Outstanding Young Men of Am., 1974, 1979. Mem. Tenn. Hosp. Assn. (mem. com. Tenn. Reimbursement Appeals Program 1982—), Healthcare Fin. Mgmt. Assn. (Follmer merit award Tenn. chpt. 1986), Tenn. Shared Med. Systems Computer Systems Users Group. Lodges: Kiwanis. Republican. Avocations: golf, basketball, softball, auto maintenance and repair. Home: Clarksville, Tenn. Deceased.

JARVIS, JAMES REES, artist; b. Highland Park, Mich., June 19, 1926; s. Emory Harold J. and Ruth Florence (Knouff) Jordan; m. Esther Mary Hendy, Jan. 10, 1948 (div. Sept. 1984); children: Diana Lynn Curry, Patricia Ann Parker, Jean Marie Bentley; m. Cheryl Eileen Randall, Nov. 13, 1984; 1 child, Linda Ray Cooley. BSME, USAF Program, 1964; MS, U. So. Calif., 1989. Comml. pilot Macomb Flyers, Fraser, Mich., 1948-52; design engr. Northrup Aircraft, Hawthorne, Calif., 1966-89. Scoutmaster Boy Scouts Am., 1953-57. Sr. master sgt. USAF, 1944-66, WWII, Korea, Vietnam. Mem. VFW, Am. Legion, L.A. Mountainability Assn. Republican. Lutheran. Avocations: flying, racing cars, writing. Home: Riverside, Calif. Died Jan. 23, 2001.

JAYE, ROBERT DONALD, architect; b. Chgo., Sept. 10, 1927; s. John Leopold and Helene (Statkiewicz) Jasinski; m. Evelyne Marie Campbell, May 20, 1958; children: Robert Donald, Scott M., Kurt W., Eric C.; m. Teruyo Kaneko, Oct. 10, 1975. BS, MS, Pacific Western U., 1984; BS, SUNY, 1985. Registered architect, Calif. Pvt. practice architecture and planning, Chgo., 1957-61, Los Angeles, 1962-85; with Western div., USN Facilities Engring. Command Archtl. Dept., San Bruno, Calif., from 1985. Author plan for Internat. Ctr. Transp. and Trade with off-shore SST airport in Santa Monica Bay, Calif., 1968; co-author plan for deep water internat. port for Chgo. and Gary, Ind., 1958; prin. works include Playboy Mag. Office Bldg., Chgo., 1957, Playboy Townhouse, 1962, Hugh M. Hefner's Brownstone Mansion swimming pool, grotto, recreation area, underwater lounge, 1961, Richard Young Residence, Malibu Colony, Calif., 1963, Tree Houses, West Mag., 1969, Curtis Sch., Los Angeles, 1983. Mem. N.G. and Citizen Soldiers Mus., Old Sacramento, Calif., 1988. Served with USNR, 1944-46, served to lt. col. res. Mem. Soc. Mil. Engrs., Aircraft Owners and Pilots Assn. Deceased.

JAYSON, LESTER SAMUEL, lawyer, educator; b. N.Y.C., Oct. 25, 1915; s. Morris and Mary (Gardner) J.; m. Evelyn Sylvia Lederer, Feb. 6, 1943; children: Diane Frankie, Jill Karen Jayson Ladd. BSS with spl. honors in History and Govt., CCNY, 1936; JD (bd. student advisers), Harvard U., 1939. Bar: N.Y. 1940, U.S. Supreme Ct. 1952, D.C. 1976. With firm Oseas and Pepper, N.Y.C., 1939-40, Marshall, Bratter & Seligson, N.Y.C., 1940-42; spl. asst. to atty. gen. U.S., 1942-50; trial atty. Dept. Justice, 1951-56, chief torts sect. civil div., 1957-60; sr. specialist Am. pub. law, chief Am. law div. Congl. Research Service, Library of Congress, 1960-62, dep. dir. service, 1962-66, dir., 1966-75; prof. law Potomac Sch. Law, 1975-81. Vice chmn. Interdeptl. Fed. Tort Claims Com., 1958-60; rep. Justice Dept. to legal div., air coordinating com. Internat. Civil Aviation Orgn., 1959-60; mem. com. exec. privilege Justice Dept., 1956-60; adv. statutory studies group Commn. Govt. Procurement, 1970-72; mem. adv. council Office Tech. Assessment, 1973-75; cons. govt. relations com. Nat. Assn. Theatre Owners, 1978-79 Author: Handling Federal Tort Claims: Judicial and Administrative Remedies, 1964-95; also articles; supervising editor: The Constitution of the United States of America-Analysis and Interpretation, 1964, 72. Mem. ABA, Fed. Bar Assn. (chmn., then vice chmn. fed. tort claims com. 1963-66, 70-74, chmn. 1967-68, mem. nat. council 1967-73), Am. Friends of Wilton Park, Assn. Trial Lawyers Am., Pi Sigma Alpha (hon.) Clubs: Cosmos (Washington), Harvard (Washington). Home: Bethesda, Md. Died Dec. 30, 1999.

JEFFERS, DONALD E. retired insurance executive, consultant; b. Louisville, Ill., Aug. 21, 1925; s. Byron V. and Alice B. (Burgess) J.; m. Marion D. Benna, Aug. 14, 1948 (dec.); 1 son, Derek; m. Janice C. Smith, Apr. 21, 1979 (dec.). BS in Accountancy, U. Ill., 1948. C.P.A., Ill., D.C. Sr. acct. Coopers & Lybrand, CPAs, N.Y.C. and Chgo., 1948-56; asst. v.p. Continental Casualty Co., Chgo., 1956-64; dep. comptr. First Nat. Bank Boston, 1965-67; exec. v.p., treas. Interstate Nat. Corp., Chgo., 1967-74, pres., chief exec. officer, 1974-85, also dir.; chmn., dir. Interstate Ins. Group and Geo. F. Brown & Sons Inc.; chmn. Jeffers & Assocs., Inc., San Diego, 1985—86; ret., 1986. Former sec., dir. Ill. Ins. Info. Service; underwriting mem. Lloyd's London, 1977-99. Served with inf. AUS, 1943-45. Decorated Purple Heart. Mem. AICPA. Home: San Diego, Calif. Died Aug. 31, 2004.

JEFFREY, MILDRED MARY, secondary school educator; b. Dec. 29, 1911; d. Bert David and Bertha (Merritt) McWilliams; m. Homer Newman Jeffrey (div. 1966); children: Sharon Rose, Daniel Balfour. BA, U. Minn., 1932; MA, Bryn Mawr (Pa.) Coll., 1934. Investigator NIRA, Pa., 1935; ednl. dir. Pa. Joint Bd. Shirt Workers, 1936; gen. organizer Amalgamated Clothing and Textile Workers Union, 1938-39; mem. communications staff War Prodn. Bd., Washington, 1940-43; dir. women's dept. internat. union UAW, Detroit, 1943-50, dir. radio dept., 1950-55, asst. to pres., 1955-70, dir. consumer affairs, 1970-77; freelance cons. Detroit, 1980—2004. Cons. Coalition Labor Union Women, Detroit, 1977-79. Active Detroit Pub. Libr. Commn., 1950-78, Detroit Pks. and Recreation Commn., 1962-69, Mich. Consumer Coun.; apptd. gov.'s commn. on higher edn., 1968-71; mem. exec. com. Dem. Nat. Com.; apptd. Nat. Commn. on Youth Employment, 1961-63, IWY Commn., 1977-78; del. IWY Conv., Houston, 1977; elected chmn. Wayne State U. bd. govs., 1980, 90; bd. dirs. NARAL, Voters for Choice, Women's Campaign Fund; pres. Mich. Women's Found., 1989-2004. pub. mem. bd. dirs. BCBSM, 1987-2004; exec. bd. dirs. Women Meaningful Summit, 1987-2004, Del Soviet Am. Women;s Summit, 1990. Recipient PEACE award WAND, 1989; named Outstanding trustee, 1988, Feminsit of Yr., Mich. NOW, 1982, Mich. Man of Yr., Detroit News, 1992. Mem. NAACP, Ams. for Dem. Action (v.p., Leadership award 1978), Mich. Assn. Trustees Pub. U. (chmn.). Avocation: photography. Home: Detroit, Mich. Died Mar. 17, 2004.

JENKINS, ROY HARRIS (LORD JENKINS OF HILLHEAD), writer, politician; b. Nov. 11, 1920; s. Arthur and Hattie J.; m. Jennifer Morris, 1945; 3 children. Ed., Oxford (Eng.) U.; numerous hon. degrees. Mem. staff Indsl. and Comml. Fin. Corp., 1946-48; Labour Party mem. Ho. of Commons, 1948-77; Social Dem. mem. Ho. of Lords, 1982-87, leader Liberal Dems., 1988-98; pres. Royal Soc. Lit., from 1988. Chmn. Fabian Soc., 1957—58; mem. coun. Britain in Europe; dep. chmn. Common Market campaign, 1961—63; dir. fin. ops. John Lewis Partnership Ltd., 1963—64; min. aviation, 1964—65; chancellor of exchequer, 1967—70; dep. leader Labour Party, 1970—72; home sec., 1974—77; pres. Commn. European Cmtys., 1977—81; privy Councillor, 1964; a founder, first leader Social Dem. Party, 1981—83. Author: Mr. Attlee: An Interim Biography, 1948, Pursuit of Progress, 1953, Mr. Balfour's Poodle, 1954, Sir Charles Dilke: A Victorian Tragedy, 1958, The Labour Case, 1959, Asquith, 1964, Essays and Speeches, 1967, Afternoon on the Potomac, 1972, What Matters Now, 1972, Nine Men of Power, 1974, Partnership of Principle, 1985, Truman, 1986, Baldwin, 1987, Twentieth Century Portraits, 1988, European Diary, 1989, (autogiobraphy) A Life at the Centre, 1991, Portraits and Miniatures, 1993, Gladstone, 1995, The Chancellors, 1998, Churchill, 2001, Twelve Cities, 2002; contbr. New Fabain Essays, 1952. With Royal Arty., 1942-46. Decorated Order of Merit (Luxembourg and Italy), grand cross Order of Charles III (Spain), Comandeur Légion d'Honneur (France), mem. Brit. Order of Merit; recipient Charlemagne prize, 1972, Robert Schuman prize, 1972, Prix Bentinck, 1978. Fellow British Acad.; mem. Am. Acad. Arts and Scis. (hon. fgn.). Home: Oxfordshire, England. Died Jan. 5, 2003.

JENKINSON, MARION ANNE, museum curator; b. Lancaster, Ohio, Apr. 10, 1937; d. Bryan Williamson and Thelma (Cox) J.; m. Robert Morrow Mengel, Dec. 21, 1963; 1 child, Tracy Lynn. BA, BS, Otterbein Coll., 1958; MA, U. Kans., 1964. Tchr. biology Mifflin (Ohio) High Sch., 1958-60; teaching asst. dept. zoology U. Kans., Lawrence, 1960-64, adj. curator ornithology Mus. Nat. History, from 1968. Assoc. editor (sci. jour.) The Auk, 1966-67; contbr., co-contbr. articles to sci. publs. Fellow Am. Ornithologists Union (treas. 1985—, elective councillor 1983-85, bd. dirs. joint venture with Acad. Natural Sci., Birds of N.Am. 1992—, coord. project on Latin Am. libr. enhancement with Coun. Biology Editors 1986—), Cooper Ornithol. Soc., Coun. Biology Editors, Wilson Ornithol. Soc., Kans. Ornithol. Soc. Home: Lawrence, Kans. Deceased.

JENNER, WILLIAM ALEXANDER, meteorologist, educator; b. Indianola, Iowa, Nov. 10, 1915; s. Edwin Alexander; m. Jean Norden, Sept. 1, 1946; children: Carol Beth, Paul William, Susan Lynn. BA, Ctrl. Meth. Coll., Mo., 1938; cert. meteorology, U. Chgo., 1943; MEd, U. Mo., 1947; postgrad., Am. U., 1951-58. Instr. U. Mo., 1946-47; rsch. meteorologist U.S. Weather Bur., Chgo., 1947-49; staff Hdqrs. Air Weather Svc., Andrews AFB, Md., 1949-58, Scott AFB, Ill., 1958-84, dir. tng., 1960-84. Mem. O'Fallon (Ill.) Twp. H.S. Bd. Edn., 1962-99, sec., 1964-71, pres., 1971-83, 85-87, 93-99, v.p., 1990-93; mem. gov. bd. Belleville Area Spl. Svcs. Coop., 1996-99; pres. St. Clair County Regional Vocat. Sys. Bd., 1986-89, active, 1986-99; vice chmn. southwestern divsn. Ill. Assn. Sch. Bds., 1987-89, chmn., 1989-95, dir., 1994-99; comdr. 507th Fighter Group Assn. Inc., 1987-89; mem. O'Fallon Planning Commn., 1973-84, sec., 1979-81, sub-divsn. chmn., 1978-84; alderman City of O'Fallon, 1984-93. With AUS, 1942-46. Recipient Disting. Svc. award O'Fallon PTA, 1968, Exceptional Civilian Svc. award Dept. Air Force, 1984, Disting. Svc. award City of O'Fallon, 1985, Merit cert. St. Clair County, 1987, 99, Cmty. Svc. award O'Fallon Toastmasters Club, 1991, Master Bd. Mem. award Ill. Assn. Sch. Bds., 1991, award of excellence O'Fallon C. of C., 1991, Spl. Recognition award Ill. State Bd. of Edn., 1995, Lifetime Disting. Svc. award, 1998, Disting. Alumni award Ctrl. Meth. Coll., 1999, Those Who Excel award of excellence, 1999, Ill. State Bd. Edn., wisdom award of honor, Wisdom Soc. Advancement Knowledge, 2001; named hall of fame, Renowned Wisdom; Jenmer award established by Air Weather Svc., 1984. Fellow Am. Meteorol. Soc.; mem. AAAS, APA, Am. Psychol. Soc., Wilson Ornithol. Soc., Am. Philatelic Soc., Am. Philatelic Congress, Nat. Soc. Study Edn., Nat. Audubon Soc., Nat. Arbor Day Found., Tree City USA, Nat. Parks and Conservation Assn., Nat. Wildlife Fedn., Nat. Resources Def. Coun., Nature Conservancy, Vt. Inst. Natural Sci., Focus St. Louis, The World Wildlife Fund, N.Y. Acad. Scis., VFW, Am. Legion, The Wilderness Soc., The Wildlife Conservation Soc., Rails to Trails Conservancy, Masons, Shriners, Sierra, Phi Delta Kappa, Psi Chi. Home: O'Fallon, Ill. Died 2003.

JENNINGS, RICHARD WORMINGTON, law educator; b. Bois D'Arc, Mo., Oct. 19, 1907; s. William Thomas and Hattie (Wormington) J.; m. Elizabeth Robison, Aug. 10, 1935; children: Susan Elizabeth, Margaret Anne, William Thomas. AB, Park Coll., Parkville, Mo., 1927, LL.D., 1975; MA, U. Pa., 1934; JD, U. Calif. at Berkeley, 1939. Bar: Calif. 1939. Tchr. high sch., Pinckneyville, Ill., 1927-30, Camden, N.J., 1930-33; asso. firm Jesse H. Steinhart, San Francisco, 1939-45, mem. firm, 1945-47; atty. OPA, 1942; lectr. law U. Calif. at Berkeley, 1940-42, prof., 1947—, James W. and Isabel Coffroth prof., 1955-75, emeritus, 1975—. Fulbright lectr. U. Tokyo, Japan, 1961; vis. prof. Cologne U., summer 1972; lectr. Salzburg Seminar Am. Studies, 1972; Cons. SEC, 1962 Author: (with Harold Marsh, Jr.) Securities Regulation-Cases and Materials, 1963, 6th edit., 1987, (with Richard M. Buxbaum) Corporations-Cases and Materials, 5th edit, 1979. Pres. Internat. Inst. San Francisco, 1949-51. Mem. Am., Calif. bar assns., Am. Law Inst., Am. Bar Found., Order Coif, Phi Beta Kappa. Presbyterian. Home: Oakland, Calif. Deceased.

JENSEN, CARL PETER, lawyer; b. Seattle, Nov. 14, 1925; s. Soren Peter and Ane Catherine (Lehmann) J.; m. Catherine Louise Jensen, Feb. 20, 1946; children— Paul Douglas, Linda Louise. S.B., MIT, 1946; J.D., U. Wash., 1950. Bar: Wash. 1958 U.S. Supreme Ct. 1967. Assoc. Lenihan & Ivers, Seattle, 1950-59, ptnr., 1959-74; pres. Lenihan, Ivers, Jensen & McAteer, Seattle, 1974-75, officer, 1975-76; pres. Carl P. Jensen, P.S., Seattle, 1977-84, Jensen & Black, P.S., Seattle, 1984—. Served to capt. USNR, 1946-76. Mem Wash. Bar Assn., Wash. Trial Lawyers Assn., Naval Architects and Marine Engrs., U.S. Naval Inst. Republican. Lutheran. Home: Seattle, Wash. Deceased.

JENSEN, GERALD RANDOLPH, editor, graphics designer; b. Kalispell, Mont., Aug. 12, 1924; s. Hans Clemen and Mabel (Everson) J.; m. Helen Jeanne Levine, Dec. 11, 1943; 1 child, Marjorie Jeanne. MA, Union U., 1976, PhD, 1978; LittD, Internat. Acad. World Frat. of Scholars, London. Regional and nat. dir. Youth & Christian Edn. Internat., Four Square Los Angeles, 1946-54; dir. San Francisco Youth for Christ, San Francisco, 1955-60; v.p. Sacred Records, Whittier, Calif., 1960-63; dir. pub. Full Gospel Bus. Men's Fellowship, Los Angeles, 1962-69; pres. Triangle Prodns., Burbank, Calif., 1970-79, Claiborne-Jensen Advt., Arcadia, Calif., 1980-82, Jerry Jensen & Assoc., Santa Fe Springs, Calif., 1982-85, editor Full Gospel Bus. Men's Fellowship, Costa Mesa, Calif., from 1985. Bd. dirs. High Adventure Ministries, Van Nuys, Calif., 1970-94, Found. for Airborne Relief, Long Beach, Calif., 1986-89, Ambassadors of Aid, Vancouver, British Columbia, 1978-94, Friends in the West, Seattle, 1969-94, Internat. Bible Inst., Santa Fe Springs, Calif., 1982-94. Bd. regens Golden State U., Los Angeles, 1979-89; advt. & pub. relations Orange County Jesus Rally, Anaheim, Calif., 1980-81. Recipient Award of Merit Golden State U., 1986. Mem. Evang. Press Assn., Am. Mgmt. Assn. Republican. Avocations: golf, stamp collecting. Home: Mission Viejo, Calif. Died Feb. 23, 2002.

JENSEN, HELEN, musical artists management company executive; b. June 30, 1919; d. Frank and Sophia (Kantosky) Leponis; m. Ernest Jensen, Dec. 2, 1939; children: Ernest, Ronald Lee. Student pub. schs., Seattle. Co-chmn. Seattle Cmty. Concert Assn., 1957-62; sec. family concerts Seattle Symphony Orch., 1959-61; hostess radio program Timely Topics, 1959-60; gen. mgr. Western Opera Co., Seattle, 1962-64; v.p., dir., mgr. pub. rels. Seattle Opera Assn., 1964-83, preview artists coord., 1981-84; bus. mgr. Portland (Oreg.) Opera Co., 1968, cons., 1967-69; owner, mgr. Helen Jensen Artists Mgmt., Seattle, 1970-92. Author: An Angel Holds My Hand, 1999. 1st v.p. Music and Art Found., 1981-84, pres., 1984-85. Recipient Cert. Women in Bus. in the Field of Art, 1973, award Seattle Opera Assn., 1974, Outstanding Svc. award Music and Art Found., 1984, Women of Achievement award Women in Comms., 1992, Gold medal in 100 meter sprint USA Track and Field Nat. Masters Championships, 1994, 400 meter sprint, 1999, Gold medal in 100 meter sprint N.W. Regional Championship,

1999, Gold medal in 400 meter sprint N.W. Regional Championship, 1999. Mem.: North Shore Performing Arts Assn. (pres. 1981), Lyric Preview Group (chmn. 1988—92, program chmn. 1998—99, chmn. holiday arts events 1999—2000, 2001, 2002), Aria Preview, Seattle Civic Opera Assn. (pres. from 1981), Portland Opera Guild, Portland Opera Assn., Ballard Symphony League (sec.), Am. Guild Mus. Artists, Seattle Opera Guild (life; bd. dirs. 1988—92, pres., parliamentarian 1987—89, award of distinction 1983), Music and Art Found. (life), Women of Achievement (past pres.'s assembly, chmn.), Pres.'s Forum (1st v.p. 1990—91, program vice-chmn. 1987—88, pres. 1991—92), 200 Plus One, Past Pres. Assembly (pres. 1977—79, parliamentarian 1987—89), Helen Jensen Hiking Club, Women's Century Club (chmn. art, drama, music dept. 1992—93, 1992—97, 1997—98, 1st v.p. 1999—2000, pres. 2000—02). Home: Kenmore, Wash. Died Dec. 28, 2002.

JERVEY, HAROLD EDWARD, JR., medical education consultant, retired; b. Charleston, S.C., Dec. 3, 1920; s. Harold Edward and Stella (White) J.; m. Lillian Pearce Hair, July 13, 1946; children: Harold Edward, III, Nancy Middleton, Margaret Pearce, Harriett Beachum, Helen White, Charles Stewart, Lillian Hair. BS, U. S.C., 1941; MD, Med. U. S.C., 1949. Diplomate Am. Bd. Med. Examiners (mem.). Intern Greenville (S.C.) Gen. Hosp., 1949-50; house officer Bapt. Hosp., Columbia, S.C., 1951-54; gen. practice medicine Columbia, 1951-74; acting head health facilities U. S.C., 1968-70; asst. prof. Med. U. S.C., 1970-77; pres. Fedn. State Med. Bd. U.S., Ft. Worth, 1960-61, exec. v.p., sec., 1978-84; sec., treas. Edit. Bull., 1961-78. Med. cons. S.C. Law Enforcement Agy., 1958-61, S.C. Vocat. Rehab. Dept., 1961-63, S.C. Indsl. Commn., 1963-68, S.C. Dept. Family Practice, 1971-74; med. adv. S.C. Gov. Health and Social Devel., 1973-75; mem. S.C. Bd. Med. Examiners, 1952-72, sec., 1954-56, vice chmn., 1962-64, bd. dirs. Fedn. Assn. Health Regulatory Bds., 1977-80; mem. adv. bd. Am. Bd. Med. Specialties, 1959-70; pres., chmn. bd. Ednl. Commn. Fgn. Med. Grads., 1978-80; past pres. Gen. Practitioners Club Central S.C., pres.Columbia Med. Club; del. Congress Dels. Am. Acad. Gen. Practitioners, 1958-62. Author: (book) Tin Can Sailor, 2000; contbg. editor: Med. Economics; contbr. articles to profl. jours. Episc. lay reader, past vestryman; active Richland County Bd. Health, 1992-93, mem. Bishop's Commn. on Aging, 1997-2001. Lt. comdr. USNR, WWII, 1941-45, capt. M.C., USNR. Decorated Bronze Star, 16 battle stars, Presdl. unit citation. Fellow Am. Acad. Family Practice; mem. AMA (coms.), S.C. Med. Assn., S.C. Med. Soc., S.C. Acad. Family Practice, Columbia Med. Soc., Soc. of Cincinnati, S.C. Hist. Soc., S.C. Writers Workshop, Sertoma, Rotary (v.p. U. S.C. Centurion club 1998?, pres. Centurion club 1999, ex-officio mem. alumni coun. 1999). Episcopalian. Achievements include being 2d in command in boarding party which seized the only Japanese ship captured in WWII, July/Aug. 1945. Died Nov. 28, 2002.

JESTER, JACK D. lawyer; b. Columbus, Ohio, Jan. 31, 1946; BS, Ohio State U., 1968, JD, 1971; LLM, U. Mo., 1972. Bar: Ohio 1971, Ill. 1978. Gen. counsel, atty. inspector Ohio Divsn. Securities, 1973-74; mem. Coffield, Ungaretti & Harris (now named Ungaretti & Harris), Chgo. Spl. counsel City Counselors Office, Kansas City, Mo., 1971-72; counsel Mayor's Environ. Control Task Force, Kansas City, 1971-72. Contbr. articles to profl. jours. Mem. ABA, Urban Land Inst., Mortgage Bankers Assn., Nat. Assn. Bond Lawyers, Ill. State Bar Assn., Ohio State Bar Assn., Internat. Coun. Shopping Ctrs. Deceased.

JETER, MICHAEL, actor; b. Lawrenceberg, Tenn., Sept. 20, 1952; Performances include: (stage) Grand Hotel (Tony award 1990), Only Kidding, The Boy Next Door, Greater Tuna, Cloud Nine, G.R. Point (Theatre World award), Alice, Accidental Death of an Anarchist, Once in a Lifetime, Zoo Story; (films) Hair, 1979, Soup For One, 1982, Zelig, 1983, The Money Pit, 1986, Dead-Bang, 1989, Tango and Cash, 1989, Just Like in the Movies, 1990, Miller's Crossing, 1990, The Fisher King, 1991, Sister Act 2: Back in the Habit, 1993, Bank Robber, 1993, Drop Zone, 1994, Waterworld, 1995, Air Bud, 1997, Mouse Hunt, 1997, Patch Adams, 1998, True Crime, 1999, Jakob the Liar, 1999, The Green Mile, 1999; (TV series) Hothouse, 1988, Evening Shade, 1990-94 (Emmy award Best Supporting Actor, 1992); (TV episodes) Designing Women, Lou Grant, One Life to Live, Sesame Street and others; (TV films) From Here to Eternity, 1979, My Old Man, 1979, Sentimental Journey, 1984, When Love Kills: The Seduction of John Hearn, 1993, Gypsy, 1993, Armistead Maupin's Tales of the City, 1994. Died Mar. 30, 2003.

JETER, ROBERT MCLEAN, JR., lawyer; b. Shreveport, La., Aug. 18, 1918; s. Robert McLean and Marion (Hearne) J.; m. Katherine Brash, May 11, 1946. BS, Washington and Lee U., 1941; LLB, Tulane U., 1944. Bar: La. 1944. Ptnr. Tucker, Jeter, Jackson & Hickman and predecessors, Shreveport, 1946-99. Editor-in-chief Tulane Law Rev., 1943-44; contbr. articles to legal jours. Pres. Goodwill Industries, Shreveport, 1954, Shreveport Little Theatre, 1960; bd. dirs. Shreveport-Bossier Found., 1961-79, chmn., 1969-75. Mem. ABA, La. Bar Assn., Shreveport Bar Assn. (pres. 1969), Am. Coll. Probate Counsel, Shreveport Club (pres. 1979), Order of Coif, Omicron Delta Kappa. Democrat. Baptist. Home: Shreveport, La. Died June 28, 1999.

JOBSON, BETTY SMITH, librarian; b. College Park, Ga., Nov. 22, 1928; d. Horace Lynwood and Mildred Harper (Holt) Smith; m. Robert Bruce Jobson, Jan. 27, 1952; children: Bruce Harris, Brian Adams, Maribeth Elaine. AB in History, Ga. State Woman's Coll., 1949; MA in English, West Ga. Coll., 1970; MLS, Atlanta U., 1983. Sales clk., book buyer, asst. mgr. Miller's Bookstore, Atlanta, 1944-50; placement records supr., sec. to the treas. Agnes Scott Coll., Decatur, Ga., 1950-51; adminstrv. asst. Univ. System Bldg. Authority/State Sch. Bldg. Authority, Atlanta, 1951-52; sec. to editor The Ga. Rev. U. Ga., 1952-53; adminstrv. asst. to the dean U. Ga. Grad. Sch., 1953-56; asst. libr. West Ga. Coll., Carrollton, 1964-68, acting acquisitions libr., 1969-70, asst. prof., acquisitions libr., 1971-76, head tech. svcs. div., 1971-76, assoc. prof., assoc. dir., head tech. svcs., 1983-89, prof., from 1990. Mem. Bus. and Profl. Women's Club, 1984-85, mem. young careerist com., 1985; mem. Carroll County Hist. Soc., 1986—, sec., 1989—; mem. uniform com., Burger-day com. Carrollton Band Boosters Assn., 1969-74; troop leader Brownies, Girl Scouts U.S., 1965-66; den mother Cub Scouts, 1964-65; mem. St. Margaret's Episcopal Ch., 1958—, vestry mem., altar guild chmn., churchwomen's group chmn., children's choir mother, Sunday sch. tchr., 1958-75. Mem. AAUP, Assn. Coll. and Rsch. Libraries, ALA, Southeastern Libr. Assn., Phi Kappa Phi (treas. 1978-80, chmn. awards com. 1980-82, 86-88). Democrat. Home: Marietta, Ga. Died Mar. 9, 2001.

JOE, THOMAS, think-tank; Founder and dir. Ctr. for the Study of Social Policy, Washington, D.C., 1979-1999. Died Oct. 2,1999.

JOHN, RALPH CANDLER, retired college president, educator; b. Prince Frederick, Md., Feb. 18, 1919; s. Byron Wilson and Gladys Bennett (Thomas) J.; m. Dorothy Corinne Prince, Aug. 17, 1943; children: Douglass Prince, Byron Wilson II, Alan Randall. BA, Berea Coll., 1941; student, Duke U., 1941-43; S.T.B., Boston U., 1943, S.T.M., 1944; PhD, Am. U., 1950; L.H.D., Iowa Wesleyan U., 1968; Litt.D., Simpson Coll., 1972; DHL, Western Md. Coll., 1997. Ordained to ministry United Methodist Ch., 1941; asso. minister Foundry Meth. Ch., Washington, 1945-49; chmn. dept. philosophy and religion Am. U., 1949-51, dean students, 1955-58, dean Coll. Arts and Scis., 1958-63, hon. lifetime prof. philosophy, 1963—; pres. Simpson Coll., Indianola, Iowa, 1963-72, Western Md. Coll., Westminster, 1972-84, pres. emeritus, 1984—. Dir. Princor Mut. Funds, Fair Lanes, Inc., Jiffy Lube Internat., Inc., Shore Stop of Berlin, Inc.; chmn. adv. com. Washington Internat. Ctr., 1959-63; mem. commn. on instrl. affairs Assn. Am. Colls. Del., World Meth. Conf., London, 1966; dir. Student Aid Internat., Inc., 1975-86. Trustee Randolph-Macon Acad., 1959-81. Served to capt. AUS, 1951-53; maj. Res. Recipient Alumni Recognition award Am. U., 1968, Disting. Alumnus award Boston U., 1969, Disting. Alumnus award Berea Coll., 1976, Disting. Civilian Service medal Dept. Army, Citation for Disting. Service, Gov. of Md., Disting. Svc. to Higher Edn. award, Berea Coll.; Paul Harris fellow Rotary Internat. Mem. Am. Council on Edn. (commn. on edn. and internat. affairs 1959-63), Am. Philos. Assn., Am. Acad. Religion, Am. Acad. Polit. and Social Sci., Md. Ind. Coll. and Univ. Assn. (chmn. bd., exec. com.), Iowa Assn. Pvt. Colls. and Univs. (chmn. bd., exec. com.), Newcomen Soc. N.Am., Phi Beta Kappa, Phi Kappa Phi, Omicron Delta Kappa, Pi Gamma Mu, Pi Sigma Alpha. Clubs: Prairie (Des Moines); Center (Balt.); Cosmos (Washington); Ocean Pines. Home: Berlin, Md. Died Nov. 25, 1999.

JOHNS, MARGARET BUSH, neuroendocrinologist, painter, researcher, educator; b. Boston, July 31, 1928; d. Ernest William Bush and Ellinor (Brennan) Gazik; m. D. Craig Johns, Jan. 15, 1953 (div. 1982); children: Katherine Adrian, Sara Elizabeth; m. H. Peter Stern, May 30, 1985. Student, George Washington U., 1945-47, NYU, 1951-53; BA, Hunter Coll., N.Y.C., 1971; PhD, Rutgers U., 1979. Postdoctoral NIH rsch. fellow Mt. Sinai Med. Sch., NYC, 1978-81; instr. dept. biol. sci. Hunter Coll., NYC, 1982-83; rsch. scientist NYU, NYC, 1985; ind. rschr. in neuroendocrinology Mountainville, NY, 1985—2003. Cons. Lederle Labs., 1984; reviewer NIH, NSF, 1982-2003. Contbr. articles to Nature, Endocrinology, Annals of N.Y. Acad. Sci. Vol. tutor non-English-speaking children N.Y. Pub. Sch. Sys., N.Y.C., 1964; vol. landscape coord. Neighbors United for Justice in Housing, Newburgh, N.Y., 1988-2003, vol. edn. cons. Harlem Valley Secure Ctr., Wingdale, N.Y., 1998-2003. Fellow: The Endocrine Soc. Democrat. Achievements include first to discover a function of the vomeronasal organ in mammalian physiology; discovered specific and saturable in vitro uptake of serotonin in gonadotrophs in the anterior pituitary of rats and humans and that Prozak blocks it completely; discovered reflex ovulation can be triggered by smell. Avocations: writing, gardening, travel. Home: New York, NY. Died Oct. 25, 2003.

JOHNS, VARNER JAY, JR., medical educator; b. Denver, Jan. 27, 1921; s. Varner Jay and Ruby Charlene (Morrison) J.; m. Dorothy Mae Hippach, Dec. 7, 1944; children: Marcia Johns Hinshaw, Donna Johns Bennett, Varner Jay III. BS, La Sierra Coll., 1944; MD, Coll. Med. Evangelists, 1945. Diplomate Nat. Bd. Med. Examiners, Am. Bd. Internal Medicine, Am. Bd. Cardiovasc. Disease. Intern White Meml. Hosp., Los Angeles, 1944-45, resident, 1945-47; resident pathology Loma Linda (Calif.) U., 1947-48; head physician Los Angeles County Hosp., 1951; assoc. dean Sch. Medicine Loma Linda U., 1951-54, chmn. dept. medicine, 1956-69, 80-86, prof. medicine, 1957-86, prof. emeritus, from 1986; assoc. dean continuing edn. Sch. Medicine Loma Linda U. (Sch. Medicine), 1975-86. Chief med. svc. White Meml. Hosp., Los Angeles, 1956-62, 78-80, hon. vis. physician, 1986—; chief med. svc. Loma Linda U. Hosp., 1964-69, 80-86, hon. vis. physician, 1986—; co-physician in chief Los Angeles County Hosp., 1958-64; cons. Office Surgeon Gen., Dept. Army, 1956-67; vis. colleague Inst. Cardiology, London, 1962-63; hon. vis. physician Nat. Heart Hosp., London, 1962-63; cons. Jerry L. Pettis Meml. VA Hosp., Loma Linda, 1978-86; bd. dirs. Am. Sound and Video Corp., 1986-91. Mem. editl. bd.: Calif. Medicine, 1964—74; contbr. articles to profl. jours. Pres. bd. govs. Alumni Fedn. Loma Linda U., 1970-71; trustee Loma Linda U., 1952-54, Loma Linda Med. Ctr., 1984-86; bd. dirs. Audio/Digest Found., 1975-86, pres. 1986-91. Served to maj. M.C. AUS, 1954-56. Fellow A.C.P. (gov. So. Calif. region II 1972-76), Am. Coll. Cardiology; mem. Los Angeles Acad., Medicine (governing bd. 1965-68, 74-79, treas. 1977-78, v.p. 1978-79, pres. 1979-80), San Bernardino County Heart Assn. (dir. 1966-72), Am. Heart Assn. (fellow council clin. cardiology), Western Assn. Physicians, Royal Soc. Medicine, AMA (del. 1987-91), Calif. Med. Assn. (del. 1974-91), Los Angeles Soc. Internal Medicine (pres. 1961-62), Inland Soc. Internal Medicine (pres. 1988-89), Alpha Omega Alpha, San Bernardino County Med. Soc. (v.p. 1972-73, pres. 1974-75), Redlands Country Club (Calif. bd. dirs. 1995-98). Home: Loma Linda, Calif. Died Apr. 25, 2003; Loma Linda, Calif..

JOHNSON, ANNA GAYLE, artist, educator; b. Camden, N.J., Oct. 17, 1953; d. Roy Irvan and Leonora Anne (Glick) Van Alstine; m. Kenton Laird Johnson, June 12, 1976; children: Claire Hart, Noah Van Alstine. BA in Art, Brown U., 1976; MA in Painting, SUNY, Albany, 1977. Adj. instr. Jr. Coll. of Albany, 1980-84; asst. prof. art Russell Sage Coll., Troy, N.Y., from 1984. Paintings in exhbn. N.Y. State Mus., Nat. Mus. Women in the Arts, 1989-90, U. Gallery, SUNY, Albany, 1986, others; one-woman exhbn. Russell Sage Coll. Gallery. Bd. dirs. Rensselaer County Coun. of the Arts, Troy, 1990—. SUNY Albany grad. assistantship, 1978-79. Home: Troy, NY. Deceased.

JOHNSON, BYRON LINDBERG, economist, educator; b. Chgo., Oct. 12, 1917; s. Theodore and Ruth Emille (Lindberg) J.; m. Catherine Elizabeth (Kay) Teter, Oct. 22, 1938; children: Steven Howard, Christine Ruth, Eric Alan. BA, U. Wis., Madison, 1938, MA, 1940, PhD, 1947. Economist, statistician State of Wis., Madison, 1938-42; fiscal economist Exec. Office Pres., Washington, 1942-44, Social Security Adminstrn., Washington, 1944-47; prof. econs. U. Denver, 1947-56; adm. asst. to gov. State of Colo., Denver, 1957-58; mem. U.S. Congress, Washington, 1959-60; cons. Agy. Internat. Devel. State Dept., Washington, 1961-64; prof. econs. U. Colo., Denver, 1965—, prof. econs. emeritus, from 1985. Cons. economist Commn. R.R. Retirement, Washington, 1971-72, U. Colo Regent, 1970-82. Author: Need is Our Neighbor, 1966; (with Robert Ewegen) B.S.: The Bureaucratic Syndrome, 1982; contbr. articles to profl. jours. Vice-chmn. Denver Regional Transp. Dist., 1983, chmn. 1984, bd. dirs., 1983-84; cons. Colo. Dept. Transp., 1992-93. Recipient Whitehead Meml. award Colo. A.C.L.U., 1960. Mem. Advanced Transit Assn. (chmn. bd. 1986-87, prs. 1992-93). Democrat. Mem. United Ch. of Christ. Club: City (Denver). Avocation: mountaineering. Home: Denver, Colo. Died Jan. 6, 2000.

JOHNSON, CHARLES ARTHUR, technical manufacturing company executive; b. Jacksonville, Fla., Oct. 1, 1925; s. Richard Monroe and Ruby (Chamberlain) J.; m. Lois Rae Patterson, July 29, 1946 (div. Feb. 1964); children: James Arthur, Kristen Ann; m. Sharon Bartz, Feb. 22, 1964 (div. Sept. 1979); children: Paul, Jeffrey; m. Olive Elliott Tudge, Oct. 24, 1980. AA Bus. Adminstrn., Kings River Community Coll.; BS in Aero. Engring., Calif. Poly. State U.; postgrad., UCLA. Mgr. western region corp. mktg. The Marquardt Corp., Van Nuys, Calif., 1951-69; v.p., ptnr. Perrin-Johnson, Inc., Encino, Calif., 1969-73; dir. sales and mktg. Codevintec Pacific, Inc., Woodland Hills, Calif., 1973-80; v.p. sales and mktg. Electronic Frontiers, Inc., Woodland Hills, 1980-81; mgr. advanced programs Litton Data Command Systems, Agoura, Calif., 1984-85; pres. Johnson Transworld, Inc., Reseda, Calif., from 1982. Cons. various electronic and tech. firms. Contbr. articles to profl. jours. Served with USN, 1943-46, PTO. Mem. AIAA (founder west coast conf.), Am. Def. Preparedness Assn., Armed Forces Communications and Electronics Assn., U.S. Naval Inst. Republican. Avocations: hunting, fishing. Home: Canoga Park, Calif. Deceased.

JOHNSON, DAVID GALE, economist, educator; b. Vinton, Iowa, July 10, 1916; s. Albert D. and Myra Jane (Reed) J.; m. Helen Wallace (dec. 1990), Aug. 10, 1938; children: David Wallace, Kay Ann. BS, Iowa State Coll., 1938, PhD, 1945; MS, U. Wis., 1939; student, U. Chgo., 1939-41; LHD (hon.), Iowa State U., 1995. Research assoc. Iowa State Coll., 1941-42, asst. prof. econs., 1942-44; with dept. econs. U. Chgo., 1944—2003, rsch. assoc. to assoc. prof., 1944-54, prof., 1954—86, emeritus prof., 1986—2003, assoc. dean div. social scis., 1957-60, dean, 1960-70, chmn. dept. econs., 1971-75, 80-84, acting dir. library, 1971-72, dir. Office Econ. Analysis, 1975-80, v.p., dean of faculties, 1975, provost, 1976-80; acting dir. William Benton Fellowship in Broadcast Journalism, 1991-92; dir. Ctr. East Asian Studies, 1994-98. Economist OPA, 1942, Dept. State, 1946, Dept. Army, 1948; mem. food adv. com. Office of Tech. Assessment, U.S. Congress, 1974-76; cons. TVA and Rand Corp., AID, 1962-68; pres. Nat. Opinion Rsch. Ctr., 1962-75, 79-85; agrl. adviser Office of Pres.'s Spl. Rep. for Trade Negotiations, 1963-64; mem. Pres.'s Nat. Adv. Commn. on Food and Fiber, 1965-67; adv. bd. Policy Planning Coun. State Dept., 1967-69, Nat. Commn. on Population Growth and the Am. Future, 1970-72; mem. steering com. Pres.'s Food and Nutrition Study, NAS, 1975-77; chmn. bd. dirs. Univ. Savs. and Loan Assn., 1986-88, chmn. exec. com., 1988-92; mem. com. Econ. Edn. and Rsch. in China, 1984-94; co-chmn. working group on population growth and econ. devel. NAS, 1984-86, chmn. delegation to Bulgaria, 1991; team leader World Bank Food Sector Reform Mission to USSR and Republics, 1991-92; cons. European Bank for Reconstrn. and Devel., 1993; mem. internat. adv. com. China Ctr. for Econ. Rsch. Peking U., 1995—; hon. prof. Beijing U., 1999. Author: Forward Prices for Agriculture, 1947, Agriculture and Trade: A Study of Inconsistent Policies, 1950, (with Robert Gustafson) Grain Yields and the American Food Supply, 1962, The Struggle Against World Hunger, 1967, World Agriculture in Disarray, 1973, 2d edit., 1991, World Food Problems and Prospects, 1975, (with Karen Brooks) Prospects for Soviet Agriculture in the 1980's, 1983, The People's Republic of China: 1978-90, 1990, Long-Term Agricultural Policies for Central Europe, 1996; editor Economic Development and Cultural Change, 1986—. Bd. dirs. Wm. Benton Found., 1980-92; pres. S.E. Chgo. Commn., 1980-2002. Recipient Loyola-Mellon Social Sci. award Loyola U. Chgo., 1992. Fellow Am. Acad. Arts and Scis., Am. Agrl. Econs. Assn.; mem. NAS, Social Sci. Rsch. Coun. (dir. 1953-56), Am. Econ. Assn. (pres.-elect 1998, pres. 1999), Am. Farm Econ. Assn. (pres. 1964-65), Phi Kappa Phi, Alpha Zeta. Home: Chicago, Ill. Died Apr. 13, 2003.

JOHNSON, ELLEN S. language arts educator, musician; b. Dearborn, Mich., June 26, 1941; d. George Henry Louis and Emma Lillian Staeheli; m. Michael K. Johnson, June 16, 1963 (div. 1965); 1 child, Laura Ellen. BA, U. Calif., Berkeley, 1964; MS, Calif. State U., Hayward, 1973. Tchr. Livermore (Calif.) High Sch., from 1964; prof. lang. arts Ohlone Coll., Fremont, Calif., from 1990. Vocal soloist Ch. of Christ, Livermore, 1980—, organist, 1990—. Author: The Quality of Life, 1973 (M.S. award 1973). Mem. music selection com. Ch. of Christ, Livermore, 1985—; mem. mentor selection com. Livermore Sch. Dist., 1989—. Ford Found. scholar, 1959. Mem. NEA. Democrat. Avocations: sewing, needlework, walking, gardening. Home: Bellevue, Wash. Died July 10, 2001.

JOHNSON, ERNESTINE HEDGECOCK, educational administrator; b. Roane County, Tenn., June 19, 1938; d. W.E. and Nettie Bailes Hedgecock; m. J.W. Johnson, Jan. 13, 1956; children: Steven L., Jill K., Douglas W., Jeanne E. BS, Jacksonville State U., 1972, MS, 1973; postgrad., Samford U., 1974-75; EdD, U. Ala., 1979. Tchr. Etowah County Sch. System, Gadsden, Ala., 1972-74, Cherokee County Bd. Edn., Centre, Ala., 1975-78, dir. curriculum and instrn., from 1978. Instr. edn. Gadsden State Coll., 1972-74. Mem. NEA, Assn. Supervision and Curriculum Devel., Ala. Edn. Assn., Ala. Council Sch. Adminstrn. and Supervision, Phi Delta Kappa. Home: Gadsden, Ala. Died Apr. 15, 2001.

JOHNSON, HEWITT BONCHAUD, lawyer; b. Harrisonburg, La., Oct. 6, 1919; s. Walter L. and Mary Catherine J.; m. Hazel Mae Pate, Sept. 14, 1944; children— Don H., Neal G. A.B., La. State U., 1940; LL.B., Tulane U., 1948. Bar: La. 1948, U.S. Dist. Ct. (we. dist.) La. 1950, U.S. Dist. Ct. (mid. dist.) La. 1977, U.S. Dist. Ct. (ea. dist.) La. 1981, U.S. Ct. Appeals (5th cir.) 1973, U.S. Supreme Ct. 1978. Sole practice, Monroe, La., 1948-70; ptnr. Johnson & Johnson, Monroe, La., 1970—. Served to lt. (s.g.) USN, 1941-46; PTO. Democrat. Methodist. Home: Monroe, La. Died 1985.

JOHNSON, PAUL OWEN, lawyer; b. Ft. Wayne, Ind., Jan. 26, 1919; s. Paul Ephriam and Pauline May (Ebersole) J.; m. Arlyn Marie Munson, Aug. 3, 1945; m. Louise Marie Skoglund, Feb. 11, 1972; children: Roxanne Marie, Dianne Marie. BSL, U. Minn., 1941, LLB, 1943, JD, 1967. Bar: Minn. 1943, U.S. Dist. Ct. Minn. 1948. V.p., counsel United Capital Life Ins., Mpls., 1965-70; assoc. editor Am. Trial Lawyers Jour., 1970-75; ptnr. Johnson & Ildstad, Edina, Minn., from 1975. Bd. dirs. Interchange Investors, Mpls.; corp. counsel Thunderbird Hotel and Conv. Ctr. Corp.; mem. alt. dispute resolution com. Minn. Supreme Ct. Contbr. articles to Minn. Trial Lawyer Jour. Mem. Mayo Found. Lt. comdr. USN, 1941-46, PTO. Mem. ABA, Am. Arbitration Assn. (lectr.), Am. Judicature Soc., Minn. Bar Assn., Am. Trial Lawyers Assn., Minn. Trial Lawyers Assn. (pres. 1957, bd. dirs.), U.S. Naval Inst., Am. Legion (comdr., judge adv. 1980—), Minn. Alumni Assn. (life), U.S. Navy League (nat. dir. 1995), Submarine Vets. U.S. (life, submarine chaser), VFW, Fireside Investors Club, Masons, Shriners, Gamma Eta Gamma. Episcopalian. Avocations: tennis, boating, travel. Home: Minneapolis, Minn. Died Dec. 2002.

JOHNSON, PHYLLIS JEAN, tour company owner, tour guide; b. Denver, Aug. 28, 1937; d. Paul Houtchens and Helen Mason Gilman (Dow) Parker; m. Lavern O. Johnson, June 21, 1959 (div. 1973); children: Beverly Ann, Brian Paul, Christina Lynn, David Keith. MusB, U. Denver, 1959; cert., Internat. Guide Acad., 1989. Music tchr., performer, Denver, from 1954; sec., office mgr. Johns Manville Corp., Williams Fin. Co., Denver, 1973-85; hostess, driver, guide Historic Denver, Inc., 1984-91; driver, guide Rocky Mountain Park Tours, Estes Park, Colo., 1985-90; step-on guide, tour escort various cos., Denver, from 1984; tchr. Colo. history Internat. Guide Acad., Denver, 1990; owner, driver, guide Colo. Bug Tours, Denver, from 1991. Concert artist Mu Phi Epsilon ann. concert, 1990; host, coord., tchr. youth flute camp, 1989; vol. Alry Flute Choir, Denver, 1992. Mem. Profl. Guide Assn. Am. (conv. booth coord. 1991), Denver Musicians Assn. Avocations: history research, reading, music, nature walks, dance. Home: Denver, Colo. Died Feb. 15, 2002.

JOHNSON, ROBERT EUGENE, physiologist; b. Conrad, Mont., Apr. 8, 1911; s. Arthur D. and Florence May (Disbrow) J.; m. Margaret Hunter, Jan. 11, 1935; children: Thomas Arthur, Charles William, Katherine Helen (dec.). BS in Chemistry, U. Wash., 1931; BA in Physiology (Rhodes scholar), U. Oxford, Eng., 1934, D.Phil. in Biochemistry, 1935; MD, Harvard U., 1941. Research asst. advancing to asst. prof. indsl. physiology Harvard Fatigue Lab., 1935-46; expert cons. QMC 3, AUS, 1941-46; dir. U.S. Army Med. Nutrition Lab., Chgo., 1946-49; prof. physiology U. Ill. at Urbana, 1949-73, head dept., 1949-60, dir. univ. honors program, 1959-67, acting dean Grad. Coll., 1952-53; prof. biology Knox Coll., Galesburg, Ill., 1973-79; coordinator Knox Coll.-Rush U. Med. Program, 1973-79; sci. cons. Presbyn.-St. Luke's Hosp., Chgo., 1973-83; pres. Horn of the Moon Enterprises, Montpelier, Vt., 1980—. Vis. prof. physiology U. Vt., 1983—. Co-author: Metabolic Methods, 1951, Physiological Measurements of Metabolic Functions in Man, 1963; author: Sir John Richardson, 1976; also articles in profl. jours. NSF Sr. Postdoctoral Research fellow, 1957-58; Guggenheim Meml. Found. fellow, 1964-65 Mem. Am. Soc. Clin. Investigation, Am. Physiol. Soc., Nutrition Today, History of Sci. Soc., Phi Beta Kappa, Sigma Xi. Died Sept. 5, 2002.

JOHNSON, ROBERT ROSS, minister; b. Spokane, Wash., June 26, 1920; s. John J. and Metta (Nickleberry) J.; m. Ernestine Norwood, June 3, 1943; children: Michelle Johnson Tompkins, Stephen, John E. BA, Whitworth Coll., 1943; BDiv, MDiv, Colgate-Rochester Divinity Sch., 1946. Ordained to ministry United Ch. Christ, 1945. Pastor 2d Bapt. Ch., LeRoy, N.Y., 1947-48, South Congl. Ch., Chgo., 1948-52, Bklyn. Nazarene Congl. Ch., 1952-56; pastor, founder St. Albans (N.Y.) Congl. Ch., from 1953. Moderator State Conf. United Ch. Christ, 1968-69, conf. chaplain, chmn. ch. extension; bd. dirs. Queens Fedn. Chs.; bd. cooperators, founder, past bd. dirs. Queens Interfaith Clergy Coun.; guest speaker Rotary, Kiwanis, other orgns. Bd. dirs. YMCA (svc. award 1988); chmn. Arthur Ashe Vols. com. United Negro Coll. Fund; mem. N.Y.C. Bd. Higher Edn., 1968-77 (citation mayor of N.Y.C. 1973); bd. dirs. NAACP; mem. Jamaica Queens Dist. 15 Sch. Bd.; bd. dirs. Neighbors Houses; founder Amistad Child Day Care and Family Ctr. (award 1982); supporter Queens Assn. for Edn. Exceptionally Gifted Children Inc., 1973, Self Help Program, Queens. Recipient Scroll of Honor Omega Psi Phi, 1959, Outstanding Contbns. award Nat. Coun. Negro Women Inc., Bklyn., 1963, cert. for outstanding svc. Jamaica C. of C., 1975, Outstanding Svc. award Epsilon Pi Omega chpt. Alpha Kappa Alpha Sorority, 1975, Disting. and Exceptional award Friends of Sr. Citizens, Disting. Svc. award Nu Omicron chpt. Omega Phi Psi, 1979, Disting. Merit citation NCCJ, 1980, Resolution honoring 35th anniversary of ordination as min., Coun. of City of N.Y., 1980, N.Y. Urban League award 1980, Disting. Svc. citation United Negro Coll. Fund, 1980, Religion award NAACP, 1981, Outstanding Leadership to ch. and community award, Jamaica Seventh-day Adventist Ch., 1983, Martin Luther King Jr. Meml. award Congl. Ch. of South Hempstead, 1986, Congratulatory Letter Mayor of N.Y.C. on St. Albans ribbon cutting ceremony, 1987, Roy Wilkins award Rickey Prodn. Caribbean Cultural Assn., 1988, Community Svc. award Jewish War Vets. U.S., 1989, Liberty Bell award Queens County Bar Assn., 1989, Community award Black Tennis and Sports Found., 1989, Outstanding Svc. award Congressman F.H. Flake, 1990, award Black Am. Heritage Found. Inc., 1990, citation of honor Borough of Queens, 1990, Retirement award St. Albans C. of C., 1990; named Clergyman of Yr., NACCJ, Queens Region, 1973, Outstanding Churchman of Yr., Queens Fedn. Chs., 1981. Mem. The Fellas (pres. 1975-80, citation 1980), 100% Right Club, Rotary (award 1982, 88-89), Alpha Phi Alpha. Died Mar. 29, 2000.

JOHNSON, SAM D. federal judge; b. Hubbard, Tex., Nov. 17, 1920; s. Sam D. and Flora (Brown) J.; m. June Page, June 1, 1946; children: Page Johnson Harris, Janet Johnson Clements, Sam J. BBA, Baylor U., 1946; LL.B., U. Tex., 1949. Bar: Tex. 1949. Pvt. practice law, Hillsboro, Tex., 1949—53; county atty. Hill County, Tex., 1953—55; dist. atty. and dist. judge 66th Jud. Dist. of Hill County, Tex., 1955—65; judge 14th Ct. Civil Appeals, Houston, 1967—72; assoc. justice Supreme Ct. Tex., Austin, 1973—79; sr. judge U.S. Ct. Appeals (5th cir.) from 1979. Bd. dirs. Houston Legal Found., 1965—67. With AUS, 1942—45. Recipient Disting. Alumnus award, Baylor U., 1978—79. Mem.: ABA (chmn. appellate judges conf. 1976—77, bd. govs. 1979—82), Baylor Ex-Students Assn. (pres. 1972—73), Houston Bar Assn., Tex. Bar Assn., Am. Judicature Soc., Am. Bar Found. Home: Austin, Tex. Died July 27, 2002.

JOHNSON, SAMUEL CURTIS, chemical company executive; b. Racine, Wis., Mar. 2, 1928; s. Herbert Fisk and Gertrude (Brauner) J.; m. Imogene Powers, May 8, 1954; children: Samuel Curtis III, Helen Johnson-Leipold, Herbert Fisk III, Winifred Johnson Marquart. BA, Cornell U., 1950; MBA, Harvard U., 1952; LLD (hon.), Carthage Coll., 1974, Northland Coll., 1974, Ripon Coll., 1980, Carroll Coll., 1981, U. Surrey, 1985, Marquette U., 1986, Nijenrode U., 1992. With S.C. Johnson & Son, Inc., Racine, from 1954, internat. v.p., 1962-63, exec. v.p., 1963-66, pres., 1966-67, chmn., pres., chief exec. officer, 1967-72, chmn., chief exec. officer, 1972-88, chmn., 1988—2000; CEO S.C. Johnson Commercial Markets, 1996—2000. Bd. dirs. Deere & Co., Moline, Ill., H.J. Heinz Co., Phila., Mobil Corp., N.Y.C.; chmn. bd. dirs. Johnson Worldwide Assocs., Inc., Johnson Internat. Inc. Trustee Am. Mus. Natural History, N.Y.C.; trustee emeritus The Mayo Found., Cornell U., presdl. councillor; chm Johnson's Wax Fund, Inc., Johnson Found., Inc.; founding chmn. emeritus Prairie Sch., Racine; chmn. adv. coun. Cornell U. Grad. Sch. Mgmt.; regent emeritus Smithsonian Instn.; hon. mem. Bus. Coun.; mem. nat. bd. govs. The Nature Conservancy. Mem. Chi Psi. Clubs: Cornell (N.Y.C., Milw.); Univ. (Milw.); Racine Country. Home: Racine, Wis. Died May 22, 2004.

JOHNSON, SUSAN MARIE, communications disorders specialist; b. Mpls., Aug. 25, 1948; d. Joe Al and Ellen Joanne (Syltie) Traen; m. Dean Robert Johnson, July 22, 1978; 1 child, Isaiah. Grad., St. Cloud State U., 1986; MS, S.D. State U., 1993. Cert. counselor. Comm. disorders specialist Remer (Minn.) Pub. Schs., 1971-73, Waconia (Minn.) Pub. Schs., 1973-79; comm. disorders specialist, spl. edn. tchr. Russel, Tyler, Ruthton Schs., Minn., 1979-92; counselor Prineville Schs., Terrebonne, Oreg., 1993-95, 509-S Schs., Madras, Oreg., 1995-99. Ch. tchr. Dayspring Christian Ctr., Terrebonne, 1993-99, recreational tchr. Crooked River Ranch, 1996-99. St. Cloud U. tchg. fellow, 1970; recipient ednl. stipend St. Cloud State U., 1985. Avocations: reading, tennis, swimming, traveling. Home: Terrebonne, Oreg. Died June 17, 1999.

JOHNSON, TERRY CHARLES, biologist, educator; b. St. Paul, Aug. 8, 1936; s. Roy August and Catherine (McKigen) J.; m. Mary Ann Wilhelmy, Nov. 23, 1957; children: James, Gary, Jean. BS, Hamline U., 1958; MS, U. Minn., 1961, PhD, 1964. Postdoctoral fellow U. Calif., Irvine, 1964-66; asst. prof. Med. Sch., Northwestern U., Chgo., 1966-69, assoc. prof., 1969-73, prof., 1973-77; prof. div. biology Kans. State U., Manhattan, from 1977, dir. div. biology, 1977-92, Univ. Disting. prof., 1989. Dir. Konza Prairie Rsch. Area, Manhattan, 1977-92, Ctr. for Basic Cancer Rsch., Manhattan, 1980—, Ctr. for Space Life Scis., Manhattan, 1990-92; co-dir. Bioserve Space Techs., Manhattan, 1989—. Recipient Outstanding Tchr. of Yr. award Med. Sch., Northwestern U., 1975, Outstanding Tchr. award Ill. Coll. Pediatric Medicine, 1976, Disting. Grad. Faculty award Kans. State U., 1987, Outstanding Sci. award Sigma Xi Kans. State U. chpt., 1993, Outstanding Faculty Mem. award Panhellenic and Intrafraternity Couns., Kans., 1998. Mem. AAAS, Am. Soc. for Gravitational and Space Biology, Am. Soc. for Microbiology, Am. Soc. for Neurochemistry, Am. Soc. for Cell Biology, N.Y. Acad. Sci. Avocation: reading. Home: Manhattan, Kans. Died Oct. 27, 2002.

JOHNSON, THOMAS WEBBER, JR., lawyer; b. Indpls., Oct. 18, 1941; s. Thomas W. and Mary Lucinda (Webber) J.; m. Sandra Kay McMahon, Aug. 15, 1964 (div. 1986); m. Deborah Joan Collins, May 17, 1987 (div. 1990); m. Barbara Joyce Walter, Mar. 13, 1992. BS in Edn., Ind. U., 1963, JD summa cum laude, 1969. Bar: Ind. 1969, Calif. 1970. Law clk. Ind. Supreme Ct., Indpls., 1968-69; assoc. Irell & Manella, L.A., 1969-76, ptnr., 1976-84, Irell & Manella, Newport Beach, Calif., 1984—99; atty. Irell & Manella, of counsel, from 2000. Chair Com. on Group Ins. Programs for State Bar of Calif., San Francisco, 1978-79; adj. prof. law UCLA, 1996-2001; lectr. for Practicing Law Inst., Calif. Continuing Edn. of the Bar, Calif. Judges Assn., seminars on ins. and bus. litigation. Editor-in-chief: Ind. Law Review, 1968-69; contbr. articles to profl. jours. With USNR, 1959-65. Named Outstanding Grad. Province XII, Phi Delta Phi legal fraternity, 1969. Mem. ABA (lectr. chair ins. coverage litigation com., tort and ins. practice sec. 1995-96), Calif. Bar Assn., Orange County Bar Assn., Masons, Newport Beach Country Club. Republican. Mem. Christian Ch. Home: Newport Coast, Calif. Died Apr. 19, 2004.

JOHNSON, WINSTON ALVIN, cirriculum administrator, sociology educator; b. Truro, N.S., Can., Mar. 20, 1953; came to U.S., 1970; s. Percy Alvin and Margaret Josephine (Breckenridge) J.; m. Rebecca Ruth Thompson, June 28, 1975; 1 child, Daniel Christopher. BA, Houghton Coll., 1975; MA, Gordon Conwell Sem., 1977; PhD, SUNY, Buffalo, 1991. Asst. v.p. Wold Relief Corp., Wheaton, Ill., 1980-82; asst. prof. The King's Coll., Briarcliff Manor, N.Y., 1982-86; assoc. exec. dir. The Emergency Shelter, N.Y.C., 1986-87, exec. dir., 1987-88; dir. acad. svcs. Nyack (N.Y.) Coll., 1988-89; curriculum coord. Ind. Wesleyan U., Marion, from 1989. Pvt. curriculum cons., 1989—. Author (with others): Christian Perspectives in Sociology, 1982, Gender Matters, 1989. Home: Victor, NY. Died.

JOHNSTON, DAVID CHARLES, judge, lawyer; b. Santa Rosa, Calif., Apr. 24, 1947; s. Donald Clyde and Clara Louise (Swain) J.; m. Rita Ann Murphy, Oct. 26, 1968 (div. Nov. 1995); children: Donald, Katie, Christopher, Thomas. AA, Santa Rosa Jr. Coll., 1966; BA, Stanford U., 1968; JD, Harvard U., 1974. Bar: Colo. 1976, U.S. Dist. Ct. Colo. 1977, U.S. Supreme Ct. 1995. Staff atty. Zuni (N.Mex.) Legal Svcs., 1974-76; ptnr. McCamant and Johnston, Paonia, Colo., 1976-78; pvt. practice Paonia, from 1978; county judge Delta County, Delta, Colo., from 1989. Bd. dirs. Paonia Babe Ruth League. Mem. Tri County League (pres.), Rotary. Avocations: tennis, cross-country skiing, reading. Died Apr. 11, 2001.

JOHNSTON, WALDO CORY MELROSE, museum director; b. Cooperstown, N.Y., Sept. 21, 1913; s. Waldo Cory and Marie (Jones) J.; m. Elinor Doolittle, July 1, 1939; children: Waldo Cory Melrose, Elinor (Mrs. Gilbert Vincent), Carol (Mrs. Amos Galpin), James Andrews Melrose. AB, Yale U., 1937; postgrad., Harvard U., 1938. Tchr. Pomfret (Conn.) Sch., 1939-41, asst. headmaster, 1946-51; exec. sec. Yale Alumni Bd., New Haven, 1951-59, dir. com. on enrollment and scholarships, 1960-65, assoc. dir. alumni rels., 1960-65; dir. Mystic (Conn.) Seaport Mus., 1965-78, dir. emeritus, from 1978, trustee, 1978; headmaster Berkshire Sch., 1978-79, headmaster emeritus, from 1979. Contbr. articles to profl.jours. Mem. adv. com. South St.

Seaport Mus., N.Y.C., 1969-93; trustee Sail Edn. Assn., Woods Hole, Mass., 1971—, Conn. River Found, 1982-88; bd. govs. Chesapeake Bay Maritime Mus., St. Michaels, Md., 1971-82; mem. adv. com. Eleutherian Mills-Hagley Found., Wilmington, Del., 1974-77, adv. coun. Soc. for Preservation New Eng. Antiquities, Boston, 1976-93; bd. dirs. Am. alumni Coun., 1953-60, sec. treas., 1953-58, pres., 1960-61; mem. bd. admissions Yale U., 1955-65; dir. Dwight Hall, 1952-65; bd. dirs. New Haven Coun. Social Agys., 1952-65, Cooperstown Art Assn.; pres. Cooperstown Art Assn., 1955-56, hon., 1961—; trustee Berkshire Sch., Sheffield, Mass., 1956-78, 79-89, headmaster 1978-79, trustee emeritus, 1989—, exec. com. 1963-78; bd. incorporators Lawrence and Meml. Hosps., New London, Conn., 1965-79, Conn. Blue Cross, 1973-74; bd. dirs. Conn. Blue Cross, 1974-79; trustee Nat. Trust for Hist. Preservation, Washington, 1974-80, mem. exec. com., 1975-80, chmn. maritime preservation com., 1976-82; mem. Maritime Task Force, 1982-88; mem. adv. bd. Hartford Nat. Bank, 1965-78. Served from 2d lt. to lt. col. USAAF, 1941-45. Fellow Davenport Coll., Yale U. Mem. Am. Assn. Museums, Coun. Am. Maritime Museums (pres. 1973-78, hon. fellow 1978—), Am. Assn. State and Local History, Newcomen Soc. (hon.), Internat. Congress Maritime Museums (exec. com. 1974-81, hon. founding fellow 1981—), N.Y. State Hist. Assn., Conn. Antiquarian Soc., Am. Sail Tng. Assn., Am. Catboat Assn. (hon.), Scroll and Key, Yeamans Hall Club, Charleston, S.C., N.Am. Sta. Royal Scandinavian Yacht Club (gov. 1973-78), N.Y. Yacht Club, The Century Assn. (N.Y.C.), Mory's Assn. (New Haven), Essex Club (Conn.), Yacht Club, Off Soundings Club (Conn.), Cruising Club Am. Home: Essex, Conn. Died July 21, 2003.

JOHNSTONE, KENNETH ERNEST, electronics and business consultant; b. L.A., Sept. 13, 1929; s. John Ernest and Lorena Hayes (Patterson) J.; m. Edna Mae Iverson, Aug. 20, 1950; children: Bruce, Kent, Anita, Christian, Daniel, Carol, Karen. BSEE, U. Wash., 1966. Registered profl. engr., Wash. Electronics technician The Boeing Co., Seattle, 1955-66, engr., 1966-75; engring. mgr. Boeing Aerosystems Internat., Seattle, 1975-85; ptnr. North Creek Engring., Lynnwood, Wash., 1985-87; pres. SensorLink Corp., Lynnwood, 1987-90; electronics and bus. cons. Bellingham, Wash., from 1991. Internat. cons., lectr. in field. Mem. IEEE (sr.), Tau Beta Pi. Avocations: sailing, amateur radio, languages. Died July 11, 1999.

JONES, ANNE MACFARLANE, pianist, educator; b. Seattle, Dec. 7, 1926; d. Robert Stetson and Vivian Irene (Clemans) Macfarlane; m. Raymond William Jones Jr., Jan. 1, 1949; children: Eudocia M., Andrew M. BA, Smith Coll., 1949, postgrad., 1950-51, Cornish Sch. for Arts; pvt. studies with, Robert & Gaby Casadesus, Paris, 1956, Alfred Cortot. Concert pianist, soloist, U.S. and Europe, 1949-80; pvt. tchr. piano, from 1949; concert accompanist Met. Opera, N.Y.C., 1960-63. Trustee, music councillor Smith Coll., 1962-65; liason rep. Peabody Conservatory and Univ. Catolica, Ponce, P.R., 1967; choral dir., organist Presbyn. Ch. of San Juan, P.R., 1965-69. Mem. Ladies Mus. Club (bd. dirs., 1985, treas. 1985, mem. scholarship com. 1984), Women's Univ. Club, Music Tchrs. Nat. Assn., Wash. State Music Tchrs. Assn., Seattle Music Tchrs. Assn. Died Dec. 26, 2002.

JONES, BRADFORD CLAY, nonprofit organization executive; b. Russellville, Ky., Aug. 4, 1959; s. Bradford Eugene and Sarah Frances (Kennedy) J. BA in Edn., U. Ky., 1981; MPA in Nonprofit Mgmt., U. Mo., Kansas City, 1986. Exec. dir. Kansas div. Am. Cancer Soc., Mission, from 1989. Cons. Civic Coun. Greater Kansas City, 1986, Greater Kansas City Coun. Campfire, 1987; bd. mem. Kansas City AIDS Rsch. Consortium, 1993—. Part-time sports copywriter The Kansas City Star, 1986-90. Adv. Svc. Employees Internat. Union, Kansas City, 1990. 1st lt. USAF, 1981-84. Recipient Exec. Dir. of Yr. award Am. Cancer Soc., 1990, 91. Mem. Am. Soc. for Pub. Adminstrn., Ky. 4-H Alumni Orgn., Phi Delta Theta, Pi Alpha Alpha. Democrat. Avocations: sports, theatre, writing. Home: Kansas City, Mo. Deceased.

JONES, ELVIN RAY, jazz drummer, bandleader; b. Pontiac, Mich., Sept. 9, 1927; m. Keiko Jones; 2 children. Drummer with Teddy Charles, Bud Powell Trio, Tyree Glenn, Harry "Sweets" Edison, J.J. Johnson, 1956—57, Donald Byrd, 1958; mem. John Coltrane Quartet, 1960—65; recorded with Miles Davis, Sonny Rollins; toured with Duke Ellington Orchestra; formed Elvin Jones' Jazz Machine. Musician: (albums) Together!, 1961, Elvin Jones and Company, 1961, Elvin!, 1961, Illumination!, 1963, Dear John C., 1965, And Then Again, 1965, Midnight Walk, 1966, Live at the Village Vanguard, 1968, Puttin' it Together, 1968, The Ultimate Elvin Jones, 1968, Heavy Sounds, 1968, The Prime Element, 1969, Mr. Jones, 1969, Poly-Currents, 1969, Coalition, 1970, Merry-Go-Round, 1971, Genesis, 1971, Live at the Lighthouse Vol. 1, 2, 1972, New Agenda, 1975, Elvin Jones is on the Mountain, 1975, Elvin Jones Live at Town Hall: John Coltrane Memorial Concert, 1976, Summit Meeting, 1976, The Main Force, 1976, Time Capsule, 1977, Remembrance, 1978, Very R.A.R.E., 1978, Love & Peace, 1978, Heart to Heart, 1980, Earth Jones, 1982, For John, 1982, Brother John, 1982, Reunited, 1982, Love Me with All Your Heart, 1983, Live at Pit Inn, 1985, The Elvin Jones Jazz Machine in Europe, 1991, In Europe, 1991, Youngblood, 1992, It Don't Mean a Thing, 1993, When I Was At Aso Mountain, 1993, Going Home, 1993, Live in Japan, 1995, Jazz Machine, 1997, Familiar, 1997, At This Point In Time, 1998; appearance : (films) Zachariah, 1971. Served U.S. Army, 1946—49. Achievements include winning Downbeat Critics' Poll, 1966-77, Downbeat Readers' Poll, 1966, 68, 69, 77, 78. Home: Dinuba, Calif. Died May 18, 2004.

JONES, GEORGE WILLIAMS, medicial educator; b. July 13, 1931; s. Joseph Whitfield and Bernice (Williams) J.; m. Mary T. Jones, June 1963 (div. Aug. 1970); children: Randall, Carleton, Janet; m. Edna Robinson, Oct. 1971; children: George B., Adria Theresa. Degree, N.C. Coll., 1960, Howard U., 1964. Chief urology Howard U. Hosp., Washington, 1967-80; prof. urology Howard U. Med. Sch., Washington, from 1977. Contbr. articles to profl. jours. Recipient Howard O. Gray award Urology sect. Nat. Med. Assn., 1985, Cert. of Appreciation Advancement of Health Care in the U.S. V.I., 1978, Blue Cross and Blue Shield of Nat. Capital Area, 1987, Washington Hosp. Ctr. Cmty. Edn. Svc. award in Appreciation, 1990, Med. Edn. award Dr.'s Coun. of D.C., 1994. Fellow Cosmos Club; mem. Nat. Kidney Found. (bd. dirs. 1989—, chmn. bd. dirs. 1990-91), Am. Cancer Soc. of D.C. (chmn. bd. 1991-92, bd. dirs. 1992—, nat. bd. dirs. 1992—, Nat. Divsnl. award 1995, Physicians award 1991, Plaque 1973). Democrat. Episcopalian. Died Aug. 15, 2001.

JONES, JAMES ARTHUR, retired utilities executive; b. Anderson, S.C., Sept. 18, 1917; s. James Rol and Maude Magdalene (Pendleton) J.; m. Clara Melba Sharpe, May 7, 1942; children: Carolyn J. Summerlin, James Roland, Michael Arthur, Robert Franklin, William Lawrence. BS, N.C. State U., 1951. With Carolina Power & Light Co., Wilmington and Raleigh, N.C., from 1951; v.p. Raleigh, 1969-70; sr. v.p., 1970-73; exec. v.p., from 1973; chief oper. officer, 1976; vice chmn., 1981; also bd. dirs. Past pres. N.C. State U. Engring. Found. Named Disting. Engring. Alumnus, N.C. State U., 1974, Watauga medal, 1993, Outstanding Engr., Raleigh Engrs., 1976 Fellow ASME; mem. NSPE, Am. Soc. Nuclear Engrs., Am. Inst. Indsl. Engr., N.C. Soc. Engrs. (Outstanding Engr. award 1974), N.C. Health Physics Soc., Masons, Pi Tau Sigma, Phi Kappa Phi. Home: Cary, NC. Died Dec. 15, 1999.

JONES, JAMES OGDEN, geologist, educator; b. Punkin Center/Electra, Tex., July 25, 1935; s. Charles Armond and Onis Velva (Carter) J.; m. Marilyn Felty, Aug. 13, 1961; children: James II, Alan. BS, Midwestern State U., Wichita Falls, Tex., 1962; MS, Baylor U., 1966; PhD, U. Iowa, 1971. Welder Nat. Tank Co., Electra, Tex., 1953-57; geologist Shell Oil Co., Wichita Falls, Tex., 1958-60; grad. teaching asst. Baylor U., Waco, Tex., 1962-64, U. Iowa, Iowa City, 1964-68, geologist Texaco, Inc., Wichita Falls, 1966; geology prof. U. So. Miss., Hattiesburg, 1971; dept. head So. Ark. U., Magnolia, 1971-77; geology program chmn. U. Tex., San Antonio, 1978-82, geology prof., from 1977. Commr. Ark. Oil and Gas Commn., 1975-76; researcher in field; lectr. in field. Author: (book) Field Book for the Lower Cretaceous Rocks of South Central Texas 1996, Classic Outcrops of the Trinity Group Lower Cretaceous of South-Central Texas: Sequence Stratigraphic Units of Marine and Non-Marine Stratigraphic Packages; contbr. articles to profl. jours. and field guides in sedimentology, stratigraphy and paleontology. With U.S. Army, 1968-70, lt. col. USAR. Nat. Teaching fellow, 1971-73. Fellow Geol. Soc. Am. (gen. chmn. ann. meeting. 1986, membership com. 1988-90, nominating com. 1995, mgmt. bd. so. ctrl. sect.), North Am. Commn. on Stratigraphic Nomenclature (vice chmn. 1995-96, chmn. 1996-97), Tex. Acad. Sci. (chmn. geology sect. 1986-87, 94-95, 99—, vice chmn. 1985-86, 98-99); mem. South Tex. Geol. Soc. (v.p. 1992-93, pres. 1994-95), Soc. Ind. Profl. Earth Sci. (cert., sec., treas. San Antonio chpt. 1994, v.p. 1995), Soc. Sedimentary Geology (chmn. field trip com. ann. meeting 1989), Gulf Coast Sect. SEPM (v.p. 1995-96, pres. 1997-98), Am. Assn. Petroleum Geologists (ho. of dels. 1995-99, acad. liaison com. 1997—, field trip chmn. ann. meeting 1984, 99), Nat. Assn. Geology Tchrs. (sec., treas. Tex. sect. 1992-94, v.p. 1994-96, pres. 1996-98), Internat. Assn. Sedimentologists, Am. Inst. Profl. Geologists (cert., sec.-treas. Tex. sect. 1997-99), Am. Geol. Inst. (GEO-REF com. 1995-97, 98-2000), Gulf Coast Assn. Geol. Socs. (chmn. awards com. 1996-99), Res. Officers Assn., Am. Legion, Sigma Xi, Phi Sigma Kappa, Sigma Gamma Epsilon. Methodist. Avocations: mineral collecting, travel, skiing. Home: San Antonio, Tex. Deceased.

JONES, JAMES REES, retired oil company executive; b. Britton, S.D., Nov. 26, 1916; s. Buell Fay and Florence (Bockler) J.; m. Betty Jane Preston, May 28, 1943; children— Quentin Buell, Newton James, Preston Lee. BS in Accountancy, U. Ill., 1938. From accountant to sr. accountant Ernst & Ernst (C.P.A.'s), Detroit and Kalamazoo, 1938-41, 46-48; auditor, then div. auditor, chem. plant office mgr. Pan Am. Petroleum Corp., 1948-56; comptroller Amoco Chems. Corp., Chgo., 1956-62; mgr. auditing Standard Oil Co., Ind., 1962-63; controller Murphy Oil Corp., El Dorado, Ark., 1963-74, v.p., 1974-75; also dir.; chmn., mng. dir. Canam Offshore Ltd., Hamilton, Bermuda, 1975—; pres., dir. Mentor Ins. Ltd., Hamilton, 1975—. Controller Ocean Drilling & Exploration Co., El Dorado, 1963-66, also; dir.; controller, dir. Deltic Farm & Timber Co., Inc., El Dorado, 1963-72, v.p., 1963-75 Past mem. El Dorado Water Utilities Commn.; past pres., bd. dirs. United Campaign El Dorado. Served to capt. AUS, 1941-46. Mem. Fin. Execs. Inst., Am. Petroleum Inst., Mid-Continent Oil and Gas Assn., Phi Kappa Psi. Home: Russellville, Ark. Died Dec. 9, 2002.

JONES, JENKIN LLOYD, retired newspaper publisher; b. Madison, Wis., Nov. 1, 1911; s. Richard Lloyd and Georgia (Hayden) J.; m. Ana Maria de Andrada Rocha, July 30, 1976; children: Jenkin Lloyd, David, Georgia; step-children: Maria Alice Glaser, Paulo Rocha. PhB, U. Wis., 1933; various hon. degrees. Reporter Tulsa Tribune, 1933, mng. editor, 1938, editor, 1941-88, pub., 1963-1991; ret., 1992. Author: The Changing World, 1966. Served to lt. comdr. USNR, 1944-46, PTO. Recipient William Allen White award Okla. Hall of Fame, 1957; Fourth Estate award Am. Legion, 1970; Freedom Leadership award Freedoms Found., 1969; Disting. Service award U. Wis., 1970; Disting. Service award U. Okla., 1971; Disting. Service award Okla. State U., 1972. Mem. Am. Soc. Newspaper Editors (pres. 1957), Inter Am. Press Assn., U.S. C. of C. (pres. 1969), Internat. Press Inst. Clubs: So. Hills Country (Tulsa). Republican. Unitarian Universalist. Home: Tulsa, Okla. Died Feb. 24, 2004.

JONES, MARSHALL EDWARD, JR., retired environmentalist, educator; b. St. Cloud, Minn., Nov. 13, 1919; m. Stella Jones; children: Susanne, Michael, Marshall III. Student, Pillsbury Mil. Acad., Owatonna, Minn., 1936-38, Breck Sch., 1938, Smiths Welding Sch., St. Paul, 1940. Instr. horsemanship Breck Sch., 1938; owner milk bus., 1939; welder USN Def., 1940-42; welding foreman Ship Yards, San Francisco, 1942; bus driver San Francisco, also Minn., 1942-44, 1943; driver milk truck, 1944-45; stone carver, foreman, prodn. mgr. Jones Granite Co., 1945-52; rehab. adminstr., founder Green Acres Rehab. Ctr., 1952-59; founder wild life farm Hibbing, Minn., 1959-72; founder Bear Country USA, Black Hills, S.D., 1973; mgr. ranch H. B. P. A., Temecula, Calif., 1974-87; ret., 1987. Founder rehab. ctr. for young men convicted of a felony crime for the first time; tchr. edn. of animals to young children; trainer of horses. Author: Caribou Lake: Reflections of My Father, 2000. Avocations: writing, training dogs for the handicapped. Home: San Jacinto, Calif. Deceased.

JONES, MARY C. CALLAHAN, medical technologist; b. Port Arthur, Tex., Nov. 24, 1941; d. Michael James and Mary Alice (Ingram) Callahan; children: James Patrick Jones, John Stephen Jones. Student, Stephen F. Austin U., McNeese State U. Cert. med. technologist. Phelbotomist W.O. Moss Regional Med. Ctr., Lake Charles, La., technologist. Social chmn. Lab. W.O. Moss Regional Ctr., Lake Charles. Mem. First United Meth. Ch., Lake Charles. Mem. Mardi Gras of Imperial Calcasieu, Soc. Med. Technologists. Avocations: painting, stained glass, cooking, watercolor painting, handwork. Home: Lake Charles, La. Died Mar. 24, 2002.

JONES, PAUL, councilman; City councilman City of Indpls., from 1998. Died July, 1999.

JONES, ROBERT THOMAS, aerospace scientist; b. Macon, Mo., May 28, 1910; s. Edward Seward and Harriet Ellen (Johnson) J.; m. Megan Lillian More, Nov. 23, 1964; children: Edward, Patricia, Harriet, David, Gregory, John. Student, U. Mo., 1928; Sc.D. (hon.), U. Colo., 1971. Aero. research scientist NACA, Langley Field, Va., 1934-46; research scientist Ames Research Center NACA-NASA, Moffet Field, Calif., 1946-62; sr. staff scientist Ames Research Center, NASA, 1970-81, research assoc., 1981—. Scientist Avco-Everett Research Lab., Everett, Mass., 1962-70; cons. prof. Stanford U., 1981 Author: (with Doris Cohen) High Speed Wing Theory, 1960, Collected Works of Robert T. Jones, 1976, Wing Theory, 1987; contbr. (with Doris Cohen) articles to profl. jours. Recipient Reed award Inst. Aero. Scis., 1946, Inventions and Contbns. award NASA, 1975, Prandtl Ring award Deutsche Gesellschaft für Luft and Raumfahrt, 1978, Pres.'s medal for disting. fed. service, 1980, Langley medal Smithsonian Instn., 1981, Excalibur award U.S. Congress, 1981, Aeronautical Engring. award NAS, 1990. Fellow AIAA (hon.); mem. NAS (award in aero. engring. 1989), NAE, Am. Acad. Arts and Scis. Home: Half Moon Bay, Calif. Deceased.

JONES, SHELLEY PRYCE, chemical company executive, writer; b. Cleve., Aug. 19, 1927; s. Shelley Brynt and Ethel (Price) J.; m. Virginia Marie Setlock, Aug. 30, 1967; children: Robert Bruce, Mark Stuart. ME, We. Reserve; LLB, La Salle U.; MBA, Ohio Christian Coll., 1973; PhD, Ohio Christian U., 1974. Petroleum engr. Nat. Refining Co., Finley, Ohio; gen. mgr. A.E.O. Corp., Ft. Wayne, Ind.; div. mgr. Gen. Tire and Rubber Co., Chgo.; v.p. Tech. Maintence Corp., Technidyne Lasers; exec. v.p. tech. maintenance CEO-Internat. Sci. Mgmt. Svcs., Wilmington, Del., 1967-76; pres., CEO Setter Chem. Corp., Indiana, Pa., 1976-99; CEO Setter Chem. Corp. Cons. Firm, Indiana, Pa., 1997-99. Ind. bus., mktg., engring. cons., lectr.; presenter, creator tng. and devel. programs mgmt. seminars; author bus. mgmt. seminars. Mem. Internat. Platform Assn., N.Y. Acad. Scis., Masons, Shriners, Scottish Rite. Episcopalian. Achievements include design of first scallop shucking machine, emergency and new type low cost housing, pump for pressure washers; developed many new formulations for chemical products. Home: Indiana, Pa. Died Aug. 19, 1999.

JONES, THOMAS JOHN, civil and structural engineer; b. Cin., Mar. 17, 1916; s. Harry Parry and Mary Grace (Jones) J.; m. Pollye Richards Diehl, Jun. 17, 1950; children: Mary Jane Borden. ComE in Engring., U. Cin. Registered profl. engr. Ohio, W.Va. Asst. chief engr. Wheeling-Pittsburgh Steel Corp., 1954, chief engr., 1958, staff asst. to v.p. sales, 1962, gen. mgr. mktg. tech. svcs., 1965-78; cons. Mem. product bd., overview rsch. reporter Glaros Products Co. Fellow ASCE, ASTM (chmn. of sub. com. on bldg. serviceability, com. mem. various coms., Merit award 1986); mem. NSPE (life), Am. Concrete Inst. (life), Am. Iron and Steel Inst. (emeritus). Home: Columbus, Ohio. Died Feb. 15, 2002.

JORDAN, JAMES J., JR., advertising agency executive; b. Germantown, PA, Aug. 3, 1930; m. Mary Helen Cronin, 1958. Chmn. Jordan, Case & McGrath Inc., N.Y.C. (now Jordan, McGrath, Case & Taylor Inc.), 1981—95. Died Feb. 4, 2004.

JORDAN, JOHN EMORY, language professional, educator; b. Richmond, Va., Apr. 8, 1919; s. Emory DeShazo and Magdalene (Yarbrough) J.; m. Marie Estelle Keyser, June 14, 1943 (dec. Sept. 1986); children: John Craig, Leigh Keyser, Hugh DeShazo; m. Katherine Lee Lyle, Dec. 4, 1987. BA, U. Richmond, 1940; MA, Johns Hopkins U., 1942, PhD, 1947. Jr. instr. English Johns Hopkins U., 1946-47; mem. faculty U. Calif. at Berkeley, 1947—, prof. English, 1959-85, prof. emeritus, from 1986, vice chmn. dept., 1960-69, chmn. dept., 1969-73, acad. asst. to chancellor, 1962-65, acad. asst. v.p. acad. affairs and personnel, 1974-75. Mem. Calif. Adv. Com. English Framework, 1964-67 Author: Thomas de Quincey, Literary Critic, 1952, reprinted 1972, Stevenson's Silverado Journal, 1954, De Quincey to Wordsworth, 1962, Using Rhetoric, 1965, Why The Lyrical Ballads?, 1976; co-author: English Romantic Poets and Essayists, 2d edit, 1966, English Language Framework, 1968; editor: (Thomas de Quincey) Confessions of an English Opium Eater, 1960, English Mail Coach, 1960, Reminiscences of the English Lake Poets, 1961, (Shelley and Peacock) Defence of Poetry and the Four Ages of Poetry, 1965, Questions of Rhetoric, 1971, Sackville West, A Flame in Sunlight, 1974, Peter Bell (Cornell Wordsworth), 1985; co-editor: Some British Romantics, 1966. Served with USNR, 1942-46. Recipient Honors citation U. Calif.-Berkeley, 1986; Ford fellow, 1954-55, Guggenheim fellow, 1958-59, Humanities rsch. fellow, 1967-68, 73-74; Gayley lectr., 1964 Mem. MLA (chmn. sect. 9 1963-64, contbr. Romantic Bibliography 1965—), Nat. Council Tchrs. English (dir. 1965-68), Phi Beta Kappa, Phi Gamma Delta, Tau Kappa Alpha, Pi Delta Epsilon, Omicron Delta Kappa. Home: Richmond, Va. Died Mar. 14, 2003.

JORDAN, RICHARD CHARLES, engineering executive; b. Mpls., Apr. 16, 1909; s. A.C. and Estelle R. (Martin) J.; m. Freda M. Laudon, Aug. 10, 1935; children: Mary Ann, Carol Lynn, Linda Lee. B. Aero. Engring., U. Minn., 1931, MS, 1933, PhD, 1940. In charge air conditioning div. Mpls. br. Am. Radiator & Standard San. Corp., 1933-36; instr. petroleum engring. U. Tulsa, 1936-37; instr. engring. expt. sta. U. Minn., Mpls., 1937-41, asst. dir., 1941-44, assoc. prof., 1944-45, prof., asst. head mech. engring. dept., 1946-49, prof., head dept. mech. engring., 1950-77, prof., head Sch. Mech. and Aero. Engring., 1966-77, acting assoc. dean Inst. Tech., 1977-78, assoc. dean, 1978-85; pres. Jordan Assocs., from 1985. Dir. Onan Corp. of McGraw-Edison; cons. various refrigeration and air conditioning cos., 1937—; cons. NSF, U.S. Dept. State, Control Data Corp., others.; Mem. engring. sci. adv. panel NSF, 1954-57, chmn., 1957; mem. div. engring. and indsl. research NRC, mem. exec. com., 1957-69, chmn., 1962-65; del. OAS Conf. on Strategy for Tech. Devel. Latin Am., Chile, 1969; chmn. U.S.-Brazil Sci. Coop. Program Com. on Indsl. Research, Rio de Janeiro, 1967, Washington, 1967, Belo Horizonte, 1968, Houston, 1968; del. World Power Conf., Melbourne, 1962; v.p. sci. council Internat. Institut du Froid, 1967-71; cons. to World Bank on alternative energy for Northeastern Brazil, 1976 Author: (with Priester) Refrigeration and Air Conditioning, 1948, rev. edit., 1956, also more than 300 publs. on mech. engring., environ. control, solar energy, energy resources, engring. edn., tech. transfer.; Contbr. Mech. Engring. Recipient F. Paul Anderson medal ASHRAE, 1966, E.K. Campbell award, 1966, Outstanding Publs. Golden Key award, 1994, Outstanding Achievement award U. Minn., 1979; elected to Solar Energy Hall of Fame, 1980; Richard C. Jordan disting. prof. in mech. engring. established in his honor, 1994. Fellow ASME, AAAS, ASHRAE (presdl. mem.); mem. Nat. Acad. Engring., Assn. Applied Solar Energy (adv. council 1958-61), Am. Soc. Refrigerating Engrs. (1st v.p. 1952, pres. 1953, dir., council mem. 1946-53), Am. Soc. Engring. Edn., AAAS, Nat., Minn. (Engr. of Yr. award 1972), socs. profl. engrs., Internat. Inst. Refrigeration (hon. mem., del. NRC to exec. com. 1957-76, v.p. exec. com. 1959-63, v.p. sci. council 1963-71), Engr. Council Profl. Devel. (chmn. regional edn. and accreditation com.), Sigma Xi, Tau Beta Pi, Pi Tau Sigma, Sigma Chi. Clubs: Campus. Died Apr. 12, 2002.

JOYCE, EDMUND PATRICK, clergyman, retired university administrator; b. Tela, Honduras, Jan. 26, 1917; s. Edmund Patrick and Genevieve (Block) J. (parents U.S. citizens). BSC., U. Notre Dame, 1937; postgrad., Holy Cross Coll., 1945-49, Oxford U., 1950-51; LLD, St. Thomas Coll., St. Paul, 1958; LHD, Belmont Abbey Coll., 1967; LHD (hon.), U. S.C., 1984; LLD (hon.), U. Notre Dame, 1986. C.P.A., Spartanburg, S.C., 1939. Entered Congregation of Holy Cross, 1943; ordained priest Roman Cath. Ch., 1949; tchr. religion U. Notre Dame, 1949-51, v.p. bus. affairs, 1951-52, exec. v.p., 1952-87. U.S. del. Atlantic Congress, London, 1959 Trustee Jr. Achievement; bd. visitors U.S. Naval Acad. Recipient Disting. Am. award Nat. Football Found. and Hall of Fame, 1977 Mem. S.C. Assn. C.P.A.s, Oxford Soc. K.C. Home: Notre Dame, Ind. Died May 2, 2004.

JUDGE, ROSEMARY ANN, oil company executive; b. Jersey City; d. Frank T. and Frances M. (O'Brien) J. AB, Seton Hall U. Exec. sec. Socony Vacuum, N.Y.C., 1944-56; sec., confidential asst. to v.p. and dir. Socony Mobil, N.Y.C., 1956-59; sec., confidential asst. to pres. Mobil Oil Co. Div., N.Y.C., 1959-61; sec., adminstrv. asst. to pres. Mobil Oil Corp., N.Y.C., 1961-69, adminstrv. asst. to chmn., 1969-71, asst. to chmn., sec. exec com., 1971-84, corp. sec., 1975-76; asst. to chmn., sec. bd. and exec. com. Mobil Corp., 1976-84; pres. Mobil Found., N.Y.C., 1973-85. Mem. bd. regents Seton Hall U., 1982-88. Mem. Women's Econ. Round Table, Spring Lake (N.J.) Golf Club, Pelican Yacht Club (Fla.). Died June 6, 2003.

JULESZ, BELA, experimental psychologist, educator, electrical engineer; b. Budapest, Hungary, Feb. 19, 1928; came to U.S., 1956; s. Jeno and Klementin (Fleiner) J.; m. Margit Fasy, Aug. 7, 1953 Dipl. Elec. Engring., Tech. U., Budapest, 1950; Dr. Ing., Hungarian Acad. Sci., Budapest, 1956. Asst. prof. dept. communication Tech U. Budapest, Hungary, 1950-51; mem. tech. staff Telecommunication Research Inst., Budapest, 1951-56, Bell Labs., Murray Hill, N.J., 1956-64, head sensory and perceptual processes, 1964-83; rsch. head visual perception rsch. AT&T Bell Labs., Murray Hill, N.J., 1984-89; State of N.J. prof. psychology, dir. lab. of vision rsch. Rutgers U., Piscataway, N.J., 1989-99, prof. emeritus, 1999—2003. Continuing vis. prof. biology dept. Calif. Inst. Tech., Pasadena, 1985-94. Author: Foundations of Cyclopean Perception, 1971, Dialogues on Perception, 1995; author over 200 sci. papers on visual perception; discover computer generated random-dot stereogram technique. Fairchild disting. scholar Calif. Inst. Tech., 1977-79, 87, assoc. Neurosci. Research Progam, 1982; MacArthur Found. fellow, 1983-87; Dr. H.P. Heineken prize Royal Netherlands Acad. Arts and Scis., 1985; Karl Spencer Lashley award Am. Philos. Soc., 1989. Fellow AAAS, Am. Acad. Arts and Scis., Optical Soc. Am.; mem. NAS, Goettingen Acad. Scis. (corr.), Hungarian Acad. Scis. (hon.), Am. Philos. Soc. Home: Warren, NJ. Died Dec. 31, 2003.

JULIAN, PETER JOHN, obstetrician, gynecologist, educator; b. Buffalo, 1924; MD, SUNY, Buffalo, 1947. Diplomate Am. Bd. Ob-Gyn. Intern Jersey City Med. Ctr., 1947-48; resident in ob-gyn. Deaconess Hosp., Buffalo, 1948-51; pvt. practice, Dellas, from 1951. Mem. staff Presbyn. Hosp., Dallas; assoc. clin. prof. U. Tex. Southwestern Med. Sch., Dallas. Fellow ACS, Internat. Coll. Surgeons; mem. ACOG, AMA. Died June 17, 1999.

JUMA, OMAR ALI, government executive; b. Chake Chake, Zanzibar, Tanzania, June 26, 1941; s. Ali and Fatma (Bakari) J.; m. Salma Mwalimu Ali, Oct. 10, 1967; children: Issa, Fatma, Mwalimu, Khalid, Zuhura, Ali, Hafsa, Khairat, Zakia. B Veterinary Medicine and Surgery, Moscow Veterinary Acad., 1967; postgrad. cert. Animal Prodn. & Health, Cairo U., 1970; postgrad. diploma Tropical Vet. Medicine, Edinburgh U., 1977; short course on diseases, U. Fla., 1977; course in Livestock Econs., Reading U., U.K., 1982. Veterinary officer Ministry of Agr., Zanzibar, 1967, asst. veterinary officer, field svcs., 1967-69, veterinary officer, Pemba Region, 1969-70; sr. veterinary officer Minstry of Agr. and Livestock Devel., Zanzibar, 1970-71, livestock officer, Govt. Farms, 1971-72, chief veterinary officer, 1972-78, dir. dept. of livestock devel., 1978-84, prin. sec., 1984-87; chief min. Zanzibar Revolutionary Govt., Zanzibar, 1988-95; v.p. United Republic of Tanzania, 1995—2001. Author: Zanzibar in Perspective, 1990; editor: Agricultural Policy in Zanzibar, 1984. Mem. nat. exec. com. NEC (CCM), 1987-2001, ctrl. com., Tanzania, 1988-2001; mem. Afro-Shirz Party (ASP), Zanzibar, 1958-77; mem. Chama Cha Mapinduzi, Tanzania, 1977-2001. Mem. Tanzania Veterinary Assn., Tanzania Animal Prodn. Soc. Sunni Muslim. Avocations: watching football, movies. Home: Zanzibar, Tanzania. Died July 4, 2001.

JUMP, GORDON, actor; b. Dayton, Ohio, Apr. 1, 1932; m. Anna; children— Cindy, Kiva, Maggi-Jo. Grad., Kans. State U. Prodn. dir. Sta. WIBW-TV, Topeka; later managed spl. broadcast services dept. Sta. WLWD, Dayton and also. Wrote and produced several shows, including High Times; worked as actor in little theaters and showcases, Calif., beginning 1963; regular on TV series McDuff, the Talking Dog, 1976, Soap, 1977, WKRP In Cincinnati, 1978-1982, Growing Pains, 1986-1991, The New WKRP in Cincinnati, 1991; TV appearances include Daniel Boone, Get Smart, T.H.E. Cat, Green Acres, Here Comes the Brides, The Outsider, The Brady Bunch, Mannix, The New Dick Van Dyke Show, Cade's County, Love, American Style,The Partridge Family, The Mary Tyler Moore Show, Thats My Mama, Harry O, Kojak, Apple's Way, The Streets of San Francisco, The Rockford Files, Switch, The Bionic Woman, McMillan and Wife, City of Angels, Alice, The Hardy Boys/Nancy Drew Mysteries, Baa Baa Black Sheep, Lou Grant, Good Times, The Incredible Hulk, THe Love Boat, Diff'rent Strokes, Night Court, Amazing Stories, Simon & Simon, THe Golden Girls, Murder, She Wrote, Who's the Boss, Baywatch, Empty Nest, Caroline in the City, Married-...with Children, Seinfeld, Mike Hammer Private Eye; films include Marriage: What Kind for You, 1967, Conquest of the Planet of the Apes, 1972, Trouble Man, 1972, Skateboard, 1978, The Fury, 1978, House Calls, 1978, Evidence of Power, 1979, Making the Grade, 1984, Moving, 1988, Honeymoon Academy, 1990, Bad Lie, 1998, A Dog's Tale, 1999, The Singles Ward, 2002; TV films include Rolling Man, 1972, A Cry for Help, 1975, Cop on the Beat, 1975, Sybil, 1976, Ruby and Oswald, 1978, Goldie and the Boxer, 1979, The Big Stuffed Dog, 1981, Midnight Offerings, 1981, For Lovers Only, 1981, Just A Little More Love, 1983, Dirkham Detective Agency, 1983, Gus Brown and Midnight Brewster, 1985, On Fire, 1987, Perry Mason: The Case of the Last Love, 1987, Justin Case, 1988, Bitter Vengeance, 1994. Died Sept. 22, 2003.

JUNGWIRTH, RAYMOND VICTOR, physician; b. St. Louis, 1932; s. Raymond Valenine and Evelyn (Verater) J.; wodowed, Jan. 1994; children: Ray. Cheryl, Greg, Bryan, Mary, Theresa, Erich. MD, St. Louis U., 1957. Intern Mt. Carmel Mercy Hosp., Detroit, 1957-58, resident, 1958-62; with Grace Hosp., Detroit, Providence Hosp., Southfield, Mich. Mem. AMA, Am. Coll. Surgeons, Mich. State Med. Soc., Wayne County Med. Soc. Home: Birmingham, Mich. Died Aug. 21, 1999.

JUNKIN, ZELLA EDITH, houseware company executive; b. Enid, Okla., Dec. 5, 1934; d. Vaine V. and Rachel Marie (Woolsey) Crowe; m. John Plank Junkin, Feb. 20, 1963 (dec. Apr. 1981); children: Julie Marie, John Plank. BS in Edn., U. Mo., 1956. Home economist Laciede Gas Co., St. Louis, 1957-60; recreation leader U.S. Civil Svc., Fed. Republic Germany, 1960-63; dir. consumer affairs West Bend (Wis.) Co., 1964-67; cons. Chgo., 1967-76; mgr. consumer affairs and pub. rels. Wilton Enterprises, Woodridge, Ill., 1976-99; dir. Sch. Cake Decorating Wilton Enterprise, Woodridge, Ill., 1980-99. Author: (videos) Cake Decorating, 1987, How to Make Flower, 1987, How to Make Wedding Cakes, 1987, Cake Decorating Made Easy, 1988. Mem. Am. Home Econs. Assn., Am. Inst. Food and Wine, Internat. Assn. Microwave Profls., Home Economist in Bus. (chmn. 1985-86), Les' Dames d' Escoffier (bd. dirs. 1991-99). Avocations: tennis, bridge, skiing, cooking. Home: Chicago, Ill. Died Feb. 23, 1999.

KAGAN, SIOMA, economics educator; b. Riga, Russia, Sept. 29, 1907; came to U.S., 1941, naturalized, 1950; s. Jacques and Berta (Kaplan) K.; m. Jean Batt, Apr. 5, 1947 (div. 1969). Diplom Ingenieur, Technische Hochschule, Berlin, 1931; MA, Am. U., 1949; PhD in Econs, Columbia U., 1954. Sci. asst. Heinrich Hertz Inst., Berlin, 1931-33; partner Laboratoire Electro-Acoustique, Neuilly-sur-Seine, France, 1933-48; chief French Mission Telecom. French Supply Council in N.Am., Washington, 1943-45; mem. telecom. bd. UN, 1946-47, econ. affairs officer, 1947-48; econs. cons. to govt. and industry; asso. prof. econs. Washington U., St. Louis, 1956-59; staff economist Joint Council Econ. Edn., N.Y.C., 1959-60; prof. internat. bus. U. Oreg., Eugene, 1960- 67, U. Mo., St. Louis, 1967-87, prof. emeritus, from 1987. Faculty leader exec. devel. programs Columbia, Northwestern U., NATO Def. Coll., Rome, others. Contbr. numerous articles profl. publs. Served with Free French Army, 1941-43. Decorated Legion of Honor (France). Recipient Thomas Jefferson award U. Mo., 1984 Fellow Latin Am. Studies Assn.; mem. Am. Econ. Assn., Acad. Polit. Sci., Assn. Asian Studies. Clubs: University (St. Louis); Conanicut Yacht (Jamestown, R.I.). Died Dec. 6, 2002.

KAHAN, ROCHELLE LIEBLING, lawyer, concert pianist; b. Chgo., Sept. 5, 1939; d. Arnold Leo and Helly (Ichilson) Liebling; m. Barry D. Kahan, Sept. 22, 1962; 1 child, Kara. BA, Northwestern U., 1959, JD, 1963. Bar: Ill. 1963, Tex. 1977. Atty. Treasury Dept., Chgo., 1964-65, Boston, 1965-66, 68-72, Washington, 1966-67, pvt. practice, Chgo. and Houston, 1972—2002. Mem. ABA, Tex. Bar Assn., Houston Bar Assn., Houston Tuesday Musical Club (pres.), Treble Clef Club (past pres.), Kappa Beta Pi (past pres.), Mu Phi Epsilon. Avocation: early music. Died June 4, 2002.

KAHN, ALBERT MICHAEL, artist, designer; b. Gorky, Russia, July 4, 1917; s. Samson and Bertha (Kashket) K.; came to U.S., 1929, naturalized, 1942; grad. Pratt Inst., 1937, Art Students League, 1938; student U. Mexico, 1946, U. Lima Bellas Artes, 1949; m. Rose Menacer, Dec. 21, 1947 (div. 1970); children: Sharon Beth, Brenda Jo. Art dir. McCann Erickson Advt., 1947; mural painter, Mexico, 1948-50; graphic designer, Washington, 1950, San Francisco, 1951-54, 60-65; instr. San Francisco Art Sch., 1961-65; painter in Central and S.Am., 1955-59, in Europe and Israel, 1966-68; graphic cons. Matson Navigation Co., San Francisco, 1969-70; world painting tour, 1971; painter in Spain, 1972-73; painter, graphic artist Miami, Fla., 1974—; one-man shows include Fine Art Gallery Barry U., Miami, Pomeroy Gallery, San Francisco; represented in permanent collections in museums in U.S., pvt. collections in U.S., Europe, S.Am., Cen. Am. With C.E., U.S. Army, 1940-45. Decorated C.E. Commendation medal, U.S. Army C.E. Surg. Gen. commendation in graphics; recipient Art Dir.'s medal Washington, 1950, Art Dir.'s awards San Francisco, 1962, 63. Mem. Artists Equity Assn., Internat. Soc. Artists, Art Dir.'s Club of San Francisco, Nat. Soc. Pub. Poets, Nat. Writers Club, Am. Assn. Travel Editors, Nat. Geog. Soc. Jewish. Author: Requiem, 1970; travel editor Beach and Town mag. contbr. articles to profl. jours. Home: Miami Beach, Fla.

KAIN, JOHN FORREST, economics educator, academic administrator; b. Ft. Wayne, Ind., Nov. 9, 1935; s. Forrest Morgan and Bessie (Wilder) K.; m. Mary Fan Kiracofe; children: Mary Jo Kain Earle, Joanna Kain Gentsch. AB in Econs. and Polit. Sci., Bowling Green (Ohio) U., 1957; MA, PhD, U. Calif., Berkeley, 1961; AM, Harvard U., 1968. Rsch. economist Rand Corp., Santa Monica, Calif., 1961-62; assoc. prof. econs. U.S. Air Force Acad., 1962-64; visiting rsch. assoc. London Sch. Econs., 1964; dir. program regional and urban econs. Harvard U., Cambridge, Mass., 1967-78, chair dept. city planning, 1975-81, asst. prof. econs., 1964-68, Henry Lee prof. econs., prof. Afro-Am. studies, 1991—97, prof. econs., 1969-90; sr. staff mem. Nat. Bur. Econ. Rsch., Cambridge, 1967-72; acting editor Rev. Econs. and Stats., Cambridge, 1970-71; Cecil and Ida Green chair for study of sci. and soc., prof. econs. U. Tex., Dallas, from

1997. Cons. Govt. of Singapore, 1980-81, Govt. of Thailand, 1982, Govt. of Indonesia, 1987, Govt. of Bulgaria, 1992, Ministry of Fin. Govt. of Guatemala, 1988, U.S. Commn. on Civil Rights, Washington, 1968, U.S. Dept. Housing & Urban Planning, Washington, 1966-68, U.S. EPA, Washington, 1961; vis. prof. U. Tex., Dallas, 1991-92; dir. Cecil & Ida Green Ctr., U. Tex., Dallas, 1998—. Author: Housing Markets and Racial Discrimination, 1975, Essays on Urban Spatial Structures, 1975, Housing and Neighborhood Dynamics, 1985, Increasing the Productivity of the Nation's Urban Transportation Infrastructure, 1992; editor: Race and Poverty, 1969; assoc. editor: Rev. Econs. and Stats., 1965—, Social Sci. Rsch.,a 1972—; contbr. numerous articles to profl. jours. Bowling Green State U. scholar, 1954-57; U. Calif. fellow, 1969-61. Mem. Am. Econ. Assn. Home: Plano, Tex. Died Aug. 4, 2003.

KAISER, BYDUS FRANCIS, minister; b. Vincennes, Ind., Jan. 10, 1931; s. Gay Field and Hattie Ann (Boley) K.; m. Beverly Fay Bramblett, Aug. 10, 1952; children: Gail, Nancy, David. BS, U. Ill., 1952; STB, Boston U., 1957, ThD, 1962. Ordained to ministry United Meth. Ch. as deacon, 1957, as elder, 1959. Pastor Helen L. Lawrence Meml. Meth. Ch., East Pepperell, Mass., 1957-68, Community United Meth. Ch., Wayland, Mass., 1968-72, 1st United Meth. ch., Westborough, Mass., 1972-82; supt. Conn.-Western Mass. Dist., So. New Eng. United Meth. Conf., 1982-88; pastor Rockville (Conn.) United Meth. Ch., from 1988. Chairperson Bd. of Ordained Ministry, So. New Eng. Conf., 1974-80; res. del. Gen. Conf., United Meth. Ch., 1984-88, del., 1988—. 1st lt. U.S. Army, 1952-54, Fed. Republic Germany. Democrat. Died Dec. 1, 2000.

KAISER, PAULA R. anesthesiologist, retired; b. Passaic, N.J., Oct. 6, 1912; MD, U. St. Andrews, Scotland, 1936. Diplomate Am. Bd. Anesthesiology. Intern Bolton Royal Infirmary, England, 1936-37; resident in anesthesiology D.C. Gen. Hosp., Washington, 1940-42; fellow in anesthesiology George Washington U. Hosp., Washington, 1950-56, assoc. prof emeritus anesthesiology, to 1978. Fellow Am. Coll. Anesthesiology; mem. AMA, Am. Soc. Anesthesiology, Am. Coll. Legal Medicine, British Med. Assn. Home: Minneapolis, Minn. Died Mar. 4, 2001.

KAISER BACCUS, LUCY, nurse; b. St. Louis, Apr. 17, 1956; d. Wayne andEdward and Gloria F. (Petry) B.; m. Richard J. Kaiser Jr., Aug. 12, 1978, children: James Preston, Cassandra Leigh, Sabrina Lynn. BSN, Cen. Mo. State U., 1979; M of Nursing, Wichita State U., 1984. Nurse pool Easton (Pa.) Hosp.; supr., relief W.M. Newton Meml. Hosp., Winfield, Kans.; staff nurse, oncology St. Francis REgional Med. Ctr., Wichita; staff nurse, med. ICU Truman Med. Ctr., Kansas City, Mo. Mem. Am. Cancer Soc., ANA, Pa. Nurses Assn., Kansas City Nurses Assn. Home: Bethlehem, Pa. Deceased.

KALBER, FLOYD, TV journalist; b. Omaha, Dec. 23, 1924; Student, Creighton U. Announcer Sta. KGF, Kearney, Nebr., 1946—48; sports dir. Sta. WIRL, Peoria, Ill., 1948—49; news dir. Sta. KMTV, Omaha, 1949—60; anchorman evening news WMAQ-TV, Chgo., 1960—76; newscaster The Today Show, NBC-TV, N.Y.C., 1976—79; reporter NBC News, 1979—84; newscaster WLS-TV, Chgo., 1984—98. Reporter nat. polit. convs., 1960, 64, 68, 72; anchorman covering Apollo 11 and 12 space flights NBC Sunday News. With U.S. Army, WW II. Died May 13, 2004.

KALLAND, LLOYD AUSTIN, retired minister; b. Superior, Wis., Aug. 8, 1914; m. Jean Williams, July 20, 1945; children— Doris Jean Kalland McDowell. AB, Gordon Coll., 1942; B.D., Phila. Theol. Sem., 1945; MA, U. Pa., 1945; M.Th., Westminster Theol. Sem., 1946; Th.D., No. Bapt. Theol. Sem., 1955. Ordained to ministry Am. Bapt. Chs. in U.S.A., 1947. Pastor 1st Bapt. Ch., Slatington, Pa., 1946-49, Calvary Bapt. Ch., Chgo., 1949-55; lectr. N.T., No. Bapt. Theol. Sem., Chgo., 1949-51; exec. v.p. Gordon-Conwell Theol. Sem., South Hamilton, Mass., 1973-81, prof. contemporary theology, 1955-70, prof. Christian ethics, 1971-86; ret., 1986; interim min. in chs., from 1955. Cons. editor The Bible Newsletter; book rev. editor Christian Life mag., 1949-61; contbr. articles to religious jours. Mem. Evang. Theol. Soc., Dietrich Bonhoeffer Soc. (Eng.). Home: South Hamilton, Mass. Died Feb. 9, 2003.

KALTENBACH, JOHN PAUL, retired biochemist; b. Rockford, Ill., Feb. 28, 1920; m. Merle H. Hornor, Sept. 26, 1953; 1 child, John C. BS, Beloit Coll., 1944; MS, U. Iowa, 1947, PhD, 1950. Chief cell metabolism VA Rsch. Hosp., Chgo., 1954-56, sr. biochemist, 1956-57; prof. pathology Northwestern U. Med. Sch., Chgo., 1957-82; acting dir. admissions Northwestern U. Dental Sch., Chgo., 1978-79. Affiliated profl. staff Northwestern U. Meml. Hosp., Chgo., 1973-82. Contbr. articles to profl. jours. Pres. Washburn County unit Am. Cancer Soc., Spooner, Wis., 1986—. Brittingham fellow U. Wis. Med. Sch., Madison, 1950-52, fellow USPHS, 1953-54. Mem. AAAS, Kiwanis. Home: Spooner, Wis. Died Feb. 18, 2001.

KAMEN, MARTIN DAVID, physical biochemist; b. Toronto, Aug. 27, 1913; BS with honors, U. Chgo., 1933, PhD, 1936, ScD (hon.), 1969; PhD (hon.), U. Paris, 1969; ScD (hon.), Washington U., St. Louis, 1977, U. Ill., Chgo., 1978, U. Freiburg, Germany, 1979, Weizmann Inst., Rehovot, Israel, 1987, Brandeis U., 1988. Fellow nuc. chemistry Radiation Lab. U. Calif., 1937-39, rsch. assoc., 1939-41; marine test engr. Kaiser Cargo., Calif., 1944-45; assoc. prof. biochemistry Wash. U., 1945-46; assoc. prof. chemistry and chemist Mallinckrodt Inst., 1945-57; prof. biochemistry Brandeis U., 1957-61; prof. chemistry U. Calif., San Diego, 1961-74, chmn. dept., 1971-73, prof. biol. scis., 1974-78, prof. emeritus biol. scis., from 1978; prof. emeritus chem. scis. U. So. Calif., Los Angeles, from 1978. NSF sr. fellow, 1956, Guggenheim fellow, 1956, 72; recipient C.F. Kettering Award Am. Soc. Plant Physiologists, 1969. Fellow Am. Inst. Chemists, Am. Philos. Soc.; mem. Nat. Acad. Sci., Am. Chem. Soc. (award 1963), Am. Soc. Biol. Chemists (Merck award 1982), Am. Acad. Arts and Scis. (John Scott award Phila., 1989, Einstein award, Fermi award 1996). Home: Santa Barbara, Calif. Died Aug. 31, 2002.

KAMEN, MICHAEL, composer, musician, conductor; b. N.Y.C., Apr. 15, 1948; Scores include (films) The Next Man, 1976, Between the Lines, 1977, Stunts, 1977, (with Chris Stein) Polyester, 1981, Venom, 1982, Pink Floyd-The Wall, 1982, Angelo, My Love, 1983, The Dead Zone, 1983, Brazil, 1985, Lifeforce, 1985, Highlander, 1986, Mona Lisa, 1986, (with George Harrison) Shanghai Surprise, 1986, Rita, Sue and Bob, Too, 1987, (with Eric Clapton and David Sanborn) Lethal Weapon, 1987, Adventures in Babysitting, 1987, Someone to Watch Over Me, 1987, Suspect, 1987, Action Jackson, 1988, Die Hard, 1988, The Raggedy Rawney, 1988, Crusoe, 1988, For Queen and Country, 1988, (with Clapton) Homeboy, 1988, The Adventures of Baron Munchausen, 1989, (with Dave Stewart) Rooftops, 1989, Roadhouse, 1989, Renegades, 1989, License to Kill, 1989, (with Clapton and Sanborn) Lethal Weapon 2, 1989, The Krays, 1990, Die Hard II, 1990, Nothing But Trouble, 1991, (with Robert Kraft) Hudson Hawk, 1991, Robin Hood: Prince of Thieves, 1991, Company Business, 1991, (with Edward Shearmur) Let Him Have It, 1991, The Last Boy Scout, 1991, (with Clapton and Sanborn) Lethal Weapon 3, 1992, Shining Through, 1992, Splitting Heirs, 1993, The Last Action Hero, 1993, Wilder Napalm, 1993, The Three Musketeers, 1993, Die Hard with a Vengeance, 1995, Stonewall, 1995, Mr Holland's Opus, 1995, Jack, 1996, 101 Dalmatians, 1996, Inventing the Abbots, 1997, The Heart Surgeon (TV), 1997, Remember Me?, 1997, Event Horizon, 1997, The Winter Guest, 1997, From the Earth to the Moon (miniseries), 1998, Fear and Loathing in Las Vegas, 1998, Lethal Weapon 4, 1998, What Dreams May Come, 1998, The Iron Giant, 1999, Frequency, 2000, X-Men, 2000, Band of Brothers (miniseries), 2001, Mr. Dreyfuss Goes to Washington (TV), 2001, Open Range, 2003, Against the Ropes, 2004, First Daughter, 2004; songs composed include: (with Bryan Adams and Robert John Lange, from film Don Juan DeMarco) Have Your Ever Really Loved a Woman, 1995 (Acad. award nominee for best original song 1996); (TV movies) Liza's Pioneer Diary, 1976, S*H*E, 1980, (with Clapton) Edge of Darkness, 1986, (with Ray Cooper) Shoot for the Sun, 1986, Blue Ice, 1992. Recipient Ivor Novello award, 1991, 1995, Grammy award, 1992, 1996, 2001. Died Nov. 18, 2003.

KAMENSKE, BERNARD HAROLD, journalist, communications specialist; b. Nashua, N.H., Oct. 11, 1927; s. Nathan and Golda Baila (Glassman) K.; m. Gloria Lee Cheek, Dec. 19, 1960. Grad. pvt. sch., Boston. Writer, editor AP, Boston, 1944-45; news writer, editor Sta. WCOP, Cowles Communications Corp., Boston, 1946-50; news dir. Sta. WORL, Boston, 1950-51; free-lance news writer, 1954; news writer, Latin-Am. news editor Voice of Am., USIA, Washington, 1955-81, chief current affairs div., 1972-73, chief news div., 1973-81; sr. news editor Cable News Network, 1981-83; pres. NewsViews, Inc., Bethesda, Md., from 1983. News ops. cons., lectr. With U.S. Army, 1951-52. Recipient Superior Svc. award USIA/Voice of Am., 1963, Superior Honor award, 1966. Mem. Nat. Assn. Radio and TV News Dirs., Am. Fgn. Svc. Assn., Nat. Press Club (hon.). Died Sept. 25, 2003.

KAMERMAN, KENNETH M. business and management consultant; b. N.Y.C., June 21, 1931; m. Merilee J. Dannemann, Apr. 28, 1991. BS in Textile Engring., U. Lowell, 1953; MBA, U. N.Mex., 1970. Mgr. customer rels. Lytle Corp., Albuquerque, 1956-61; bus. mgr. Teaching Machines Inc., Albuquerque, 1961-65; adminstrv. mgr. Westinghouse Learning Corp., Albuquerque, 1965-71; mgr. pers. and adminstrv. svcs. Bellamah Corp., Albuquerque, 1972-78; v.p. Honor Corp., Albuquerque, 1979-81; firm adminstr. Rogoff, Diamond & Walker, Albuquerque, 1981-82; v.p. Battery Power Specialists, Albuquerque, 1982-87; assoc. broker Lee A. Welsh Real Estate Inc., Albuquerque, 1987-91. Bd. dirs. Design Products Inc., Learning Mgmt. Corp. Vice chmn. Rep. Cen. Com., Bernalillo County, N.Mex., 1978-81, mem. 1976—; N.Mex. Rep. State Cen. Com. mem., 1990—; state senator, 1986-93; chmn. Police Adv. Bd., Albuquerque, 1978-80; sec. bd. trustees Bernalillo County Mental Health/Mental Retardation Ctr., 1981-86, v.p. 1984, pres. 1985; treas. N.Mex. Rep. Legis. Campaign Com., 1987-90. USN, 1953-56. Home: Albuquerque, N.Mex. Deceased.

KAMKIN, ELENA ANDREEVENA, small business owner; b. Lake Baikal, Siberia, U.S.S.R., Sept. 21, 1913; came to U.S., 1949; d. Andrei Afanasievich and Zinaida (Fedorovna) Davidov; m. Victor Petrovich Kamkin, Jan. 21, 1938 (dec. Sept. 1974). D of Dentistry, Dentistry Sch., Harbin, China, 1933. Owner Victor Kamkin Bookstore, Inc., Rockville, Md., from 1974. Active St. Nicholas Cathedral, Washington. Russian Orthodox. Home: Rockville, Md. Died Oct. 27, 2000.

KAMM, HERBERT, journalist; b. Long Branch, NJ, Apr. 1, 1917; s. Louis and Rose (Cohen) K.; m. Phyllis I. Silberblatt, Dec. 6, 1936; children: Laurence R., Lewis R., Robert H. Reporter, sports editor Asbury Park (N.J.) Press, 1935-42; with AP, 1942-43, N.Y. World-Telegram and Sun, 1943-66, successively rewrite man, picture editor, asst. city editor, feature editor, mag. editor, 1943-63, asst. mng. editor, 1963, mng. editor, 1963-66; exec. editor N.Y. World Jour. Tribune, 1966-67; editorial cons. Scripps Howard Newspapers, 1967-69; assoc. editor Cleve. Press, 1969-80, editor, 1980-82, editor emeritus, 1982; edit. dir. Sta. WJW-TV, Cleve., 1982-85. Instr. journalism Case Western Res. U., 1972-75; instr. journalism Calif. Poly., San Luis Obispo, 1991—, spl. asst. to v.p. for univ. advancement, 1998—. Radio and TV news commentator and panelist, 1950-85, TV talk show host, 1974-85; freelance writer, 1985—; author: A Candle for Popsy, 1953; editor: Junior Illustrated Encyclopedia of Sports, 1960. Bd. overseers Case Western Res. U., 1974-78. Two Herb Kamm scholarships in journalism established Kent State U., 1983, Calif. Poly., 1995; inducted Cleve. Journalism Hall of Fame, 1986. Mem. AFTRA, Soc. Profl. Journalists (pres. Calif. Missions chpt. 1986-87), Calif. Ambassadors for Higher Edn. Clubs: City of Cleve. (pres. 1982), Silurians. Died Sept. 25, 2002.

KAMM, LAURENCE RICHARD, television producer, director; b. Long Branch, NJ, Oct. 10, 1939; s. Herbert and Phyllis Irene (Silberblatt) K.; m. Claire Louise Cadieux, Oct. 5, 1977; children: Lauren Michelle, Kristin Marie. BS in Speech, Northwestern U., 1961. Prodn. asst. ABC-TV, NYC, 1962-64; assoc. dir. ABC Sports, NYC, 1964-70, dir., prodr., 1970-95; coord. dir. Turner Sports, Atlanta, 1995—2000, YES Network, 2000—04; Coll. Football Dir. ABC Sports, 2000—04. Dir. numerous major sports events including: Super Bowl XXII, Super Bowl XXV Pre-Game, Half-Time and Post Game Shows, Super Bowl XXXVII Pre-game Show, Super Bowl TV spls., Coll. Football Scoreboard Show, Monday Night Football Half-Time Show, Summer Olympic Games, 1972, 76, 84 (Emmy award 1984), world dir. gymnastics Summer Olympic Game4s, 1996, Winter Olympic Games, 1976-88 (Emmy award 1976), Nagano Olympic Winter Games, 1998, Goodwill Games, 1998, Great Am. Bike Race, 1983 (2 Emmy awards), Indianapolis 500, 1980-87 (Emmy award 1982), Western States 100 Mile Endurance Race, 1985, 86, 20th anniversary spl. for Wide World of Sports (Emmy award 1981), New York Marathon, 1985, 86, Monday Night Football, 1987 (Emmy award), CFA Big 10 and Pac 10 Coll. Football, Major League Baseball, Tour de France Bicycle Race, Profl. Bowler Tours, Grand Prix of Monaco, Indy and NASCAR Racing, Coll. and NBA Basketball, Amateur and Profl. Figure Skating Championships; mem. directing team 25th Anniversary Spl. for Wide World of Sports (Emmy award 1986); scenic design Yes Network Studio (N.Y. local Emmy award); directing team ABC News Coverage Election Night, 1972, 76, 80, 84, 88, 92, 2000, Reagan, Bush and Clinton Inaugurations, numerous ABC News Specials including Millennium 2000; dir. team 1994 World Cup Soccer Championships; coord. dir. Goodwill Games, 1994. Recipient Emmy award for Wide World of Sports, 1986, 88, 90, Individual Achievement Emmy award for Winter Olympics spl. camera mount project, 1988, NY Emmy Award-Scenic Design, YES Network, Lifetime Achievement award in sports Dirs. Guild Am., 1997, Emmy award for tech. achievement TNT Virtual Studio, 1997. Mem.: NATAS, Dir.'s Guild Am. (Lifetime Achievement in Sports award 1996). Home: New York, NY. Died Feb. 13, 2004.

KAMROWSKI, GEROME, artist, educator; b. Warren, Minn., Jan. 29, 1914; s. Felix and Mary (Rizke) K.; m. Mary Jane Dodman, Sept. 12, 1965; children: Felix, Kirby Jay. Student, St. Paul Sch. Art, 1933-36, Art Students League, N.Y.C., 1933-34, New Bau Haus, Chgo., 1937, Hans Hofmann Sch., N.Y.C., 1938. Prof. U. Mich., Ann Arbor, 1946—84, prof. emeritus, 1984—2004. One-man shows Washburn Gallery, 1987; group shows Mus. Modern Art, N.Y.C., 1978, Hayward Gallery, London, 1981, Met. Mus. Art, N.Y.C., 1993. Solomon R. Guggenheim fellow, 1938; Horace H. Rachkam fellow, 1982 Home: Ann Arbor, Mich. Died Mar. 27, 2004.

KANE, CHARLES A. academic administrator; BS, Pepperdine U.; MS, EdD, U. So. Calif. Instr., dean, v.p. Long Beach (Calif.) City Coll., 1964-78; pres., supt. Riverside (Calif.) Community Coll. Dist., 1978-92; chancellor Seattle C.C. Dist., 1992—99; interim superintendent Rio Hondo Coll., Whittier, Calif., 2001—02. Tchr., counselor, basketball coach, dir. student activities Dominguez H.S., Compton, Calif., 1957-64. Mem. Seattle-King County Econ. Devel. Coun., World Affairs Coun. With U.S. Army, 1954-56. Presented with Key to City, Long Beach, Calif.; recipient Pratt cmty. svc. award Urban League of Metro. Seattle; named to Calif. C.C. Hall of Fame. Mem. Wash. Assn. Cmty. and Tech. Colls. Pres., Rotary. Avocations: sports, music, the arts. Home: Seattle, Wash. Died Feb. 9, 2004.

KANT, KRISHNAN, Indian vice president; b. Kot Mohammed Khan, Punjab, Amritsar Dist., India, Feb. 28, 1927; married. MSc in Tech., Banaras Hindu U. Past scientist Coun. Sci. and Indsl. Rsch.; mem. Congress Party Govt. of India, until 1975, mem. Rajya Sabha, 1966-71, elected to Lok Sabha, 1971, nat. exec. mem. Janata Party, 1977-88, v.p., from 1997. Journalist; writer. Mem. Janata Party. Avocation: urdu poetry. Died July 27, 2002.

KANTOR, THEODORE JOSEPH, retired otolaryngologist; b. New York Mills, N.Y., Feb. 22, 1919; s. Stanley John and Karolina (Drozd) K.; m. Doris Cahill, Sept. 25, 1944; children: Leslie Ann Holmberg, Michele Jean Shields. AB, Hamilton Coll., 1941; MD, Albany (N.Y.) Med. Coll., 1944. Diplomate Am. Bd. Otolaryngology. Intern Albany Hosp., 1944-45, resident otolaryngologist, 1945-46, Manhattan Eye, Ear, Nose & Throat Hosp., N.Y.C., 1948-50; pvt.

practice Utica, N.Y., from 1950. Tchr. St. Elizabeth Med. Ctr., 1987—; acad. faculty Utica. Bd. dirs. Mohawk Valley State Bank, Utica, 1968-72, local brs. Bankers Trust N.Y. Corp., Utica, 1972-75. Committeeman Conservative Party of N.Y. State, Oneida County, 1975-95 Mem. AMA, Am. Acad. Otolaryngology-Head & Neck Surgery. Conservative. Roman Catholic. Home: Utica, NY. Died 2004.

KAPLAN, MAX, ophthalmologist; b. Winslow, Ind., Mar. 31, 1911; s. David Louis and Kate (Wolf) K.; m. Ethel Fishman, Jan. 28, 1940 (dec. Apr. 1997); children: David William, Catherine Ellen Levinson. AB, U. Rochester, 1933; MD, U. Ill., Chgo., 1937; postgrad., U. Ill., 1950. Diplomate Am. Bd. Pediatrics. Intern St. Anthony De Padua Hosp., Chgo., 1937, Michael Reese Hosp., Chgo., 1938-39, asst. resident in pediatrics, 1939-40; resident in pediatrics Children's div. Cook County Hosp., Chgo., 1940; resident Ill. Eye-Ear Infirmary, Chgo., 1950-52; asst. med. supt. children's div. Cook County Hosp., Chgo., 1941-42; pvt. practice medicine specializing in pediatrics Denver, 1946-50; pvt. practice medicine specializing in ophthalmology. Former clin. prof. dept. pediatrics U. Colo., clin. prof. dept. ophthalmology; acting med. dir. Children's Hosp., Denver, 1978-79. Contbr. articles to profl. jours.; contbr. chpts. to books. Served to lt. col. Med. Corps, U.S. Army, 1942-46. Fellow Am. Acd. Pediatrics; mem. AMA, Am. Acad. Ophthalmology, Colo. Ophthal. Soc., Physicians for Social Responsibility. Jewish. Avocations: tennis, photography. Home: Denver, Colo. Died Feb. 10, 2004.

KAPLAN, ROBERT BARNETT, musician, educator; b. Brookline, Mass., July 26, 1924; s. Leo Charles and Anna Rachel (Ullian) K. Student, Boston U., 1965-67, NYU, 1973-80. Dir. music Salon Allied Arts, Boston, 1950-54; concert pianist on various radio programs Boston, 1954-77; recitalist, soloist with chamber groups; featured performer Duxbury Art Complex, Peabody Playhouse, Boston; prof. Class Pianoforte Marshfield (Mass.) Schs., 1986-91. Guest lectr. Duxbury Free Library, 1977. Composer numerous orchestral works 1939-57, 70-87; author textbook on orchestration, 1987,; contbr. mus. recs. of masters to archives of New Ventress Library, Marshfield. Founder, dir. music South Shore Philharm. Orch., 1979—; founder Robert Barnett Kaplan Trust. Mem. New Eng. Piano Tchrs. Assn., Am. Composers Soc. (pres., pub. 1979—), Am. Composers Soc. for Propagation and Pub. of 20th Century Masterpieces (pres., founder 1979). Libertarian. Avocation: astronomy. Deceased.

KAPLAN, SAMUEL, pediatric cardiologist; b. Johannesburg, Mar. 28, 1922; came to U.S., 1950, naturalized, 1958; s. Aron Leib and Tema K.; m. Molly Eileen McKenzie, Oct. 17, 1952. MB, BcH., U. Witwatersrand, Johannesburg, 1944, MD, 1949. Diplomate: Am. Bd. Pediatrics. Intern, Johannesburg, 1945; registrar in medicine, 1946; lectr. physiology and medicine U. Witwatersrand, 1946-49; registrar in medicine U. London, 1949-50; fellow in cardiology, rsch. assoc. U. Cin., 1950-54, asst. prof. pediat., 1954-61, assoc. prof. pediat., 1961-66, prof. pediat., 1967-87, asst. prof. medicine, 1954-67, assoc. prof. medicine, 1967-82, prof. medicine, 1982-87; prof. pediat. UCLA, 1987-98, emeritus prof. pediat., 1997—2004. Cons. NIH; hon. prof. U. Santa Tomas, Manila. Mem. editl. bd. Circulation, 1974-80, Am. Jour. Cardiology, 1976-81, Am. Heart Jour., 1981-96, Jour. Electrocardiology, 1977-94, Clin. Cardiology, 1979—, Jour. Am. Coll. Cardiology, 1983-87, Progress Pediat. Cardiology, 1990—. Cecil John Adams fellow, 1949-50; grantee Heart, Lung and Blood Inst. of NIH, 1960-2000. Mem. Am. Pediatric Soc., Am. Soc. Pediatric Rsch., Am. Heart Assn. (med. adv. bd. sect. circulation), Am. Fedn. Clin. Rsch., Am. Coll. Cardiology, Internat. Carviovascular Soc., Am. Acad. Pediatrics, Midwest Soc. Pediatric Rsch. (past pres.), Sigma Xi, Alpha Omega Alpha; hon. mem. Peruvian Soc. Cardiology, Peruvian Soc. Angiology, Chilean Soc. Cardiology, Burma MEd. Assn. Achievements include research and publications on cardiovascular physiology, diagnostic methods, cardiovascular complications of pediatric AIDS and heart disease in infants, children and adolescents. Home: Pacific Palisades, Calif. Died Jan. 21, 2004.

KAPNICK, HARVEY EDWARD, JR., retired corporate executive; b. Palmyra, Mich., June 16, 1925; s. Harvey E. and Beatrice (Bancroft) K.; m. Jean Bradshaw, Apr. 5, 1947 (dec. 1962); m. Mary Redus Johnson, Aug. 5, 1963; children— David Johnson, Richard Bradshaw, Scott Bancroft. Student, James Miliken U., 1942-44; BS, Cleary Coll., 1947, D.Sc. in Bus. Adminstrn. (hon.), 1971; MBA, U. Mich., 1948; D.H.L. (hon.), DePauw U., 1979. C.P.A., Ill. Mem. staff, mgr. Arthur Andersen & Co. (CPAs), Chgo., 1948-56, partner, 1956-62, mng. ptnr. Cleve., 1962-70, chmn., chief exec., 1970-79; dep. chmn. 1st Chgo. Corp., 1st Nat. Bank Chgo., 1979-80; pres. Kapnick Investment Co., 1980-84 and from 89; chmn., pres., CEO Chgo. Pacific Corp., 1984-89; vice chmn. Gen. Dynamics, 1991-94, retired, 1994. Past mem. Adv. Com. on Internat. Investment, TEch. and Devel., Adv. Com. for Trade Negotiations. Mem. Pres.'s Commn. on Pension Policy, Ill. Fiscal Commn., 1977; mem. Adv. Com. Fed. Consol. Fin. Statements, 1976-78; life trustee Mus. Sci. and Industry, Northwestern U., Meninger Found., Orchestral Assn., Lyric Opera Chgo.; trustee Cmty. Found. of Collier County, Fla. 2d lt. USAAF, 1943-46. Mem.: Met. (Washington); Mid-America (gov. 1971-76, treas. 1974-76), Chgo., Univ., Indian Hill, Comml. (Chgo.), Naples Yacht, Hole-in-Wall, Port Royal. Home: Wilmette, Ill. Died Aug. 16, 2002.

KAPPESSER, ROBERT ROY, mechanical engineer; b. St. Louis, Aug. 5, 1943; s. Roy Michael and Adele Josephine (Rhomberg) K.; m. Marlene Helen von Ubin, Sept. 16, 1967; 1 child, Ronald. BS, U. Calif., Berkeley, 1965, MS, 1967, D in Engring., 1970. Staff mem. MIT Lincoln Lab., Boston, 1972-77, Riverside Rsch. Inst., Arlington, Va., 1977-82; group leader W.J. Schafer Assocs., Livermore, from 1982. Mem. ASME. Home: Wallace, Calif. Deceased.

KARLIN, FRED, film composer; b. Chgo., June 16, 1936; BA, Amherst Coll., 1956. Creator, instr. ASCAP/Fred Karlin Film Scoring Workshop, 1988. Composer, arranger for Benny Goodman; composer numerous films, including: Up The Down Staircase, 1967, Yours, Mine and Ours, 1968, The Sterile Cuckoo, 1969, Lovers and Other Strangers, 1970 (Acad. award for Best Song, for For All We Know), Westworld, 1973, The Autobiography of Miss Jane Pittman, 1974 (Emmy award for Original Music), Futureworld, 1976, Leadbelly, 1976, Minstrel Man, 1977 (Image award for Score), The Awakening Land, 1978, The Marva Collins Story, 1981, Inside the Third Reich, 1982, Robert Kennedy and His Times, 1985, Dream West, 1986, A Place to Call Home, 1987, Dadah is Dead, 1988, Bridge to Silence, 1989, Survive the Savage Sea, 1992, The Secret, 1992, Desperate Rescue: The Cathy Mahone Story, 1993, Labor of Love: The Arlette Schweitzer Story, 1993, Lost Treasure of Dos Santos, 1997; author: (with Rayburn Wright) On the Track: A Guide to Contemporary Film Scoring, 1990, Listening to Movies, 1994; producer, dir. Film Music Masters: Jerry Goldsmith, 1995. Died Mar. 26, 2004.

KAROL, ZACHARY R. judge; b. NYC, July 31, 1946; m. Joy S. Kaufman, Aug. 25, 1968; 2 children. BA, Amherst (Mass.) Coll., 1968; JD, Harvard U., 1973. Bar: Mass. 1973, U.S. Dist. Ct. Mass., U.S. Ct. Appeals (1st cir.), U.S. Supreme Ct. Assoc. Bingham, Dana & Gould, Boston, 1973-80, ptnr., 1980-93; U.S. magistrate judge U.S. Dist. Ct., Boston, from 1993. Died 1999.

KASSEL, TICHI WILKERSON, publisher; b. Los Angeles, May 10, 1927; d. Albert Clarence and Beatrice (Velderrain) Noble; m. Arthur M. Kassel, Aug. 23, 1983; children: William Wilkerson Jr., Cynthia Wilkerson. Ed., Sacred Heart Convent, Mex., U. Mex.; HHD, Columbia Coll., 1976. Pub. emeritus Hollywood Reporter. Author: (with Marcia Borie) The Hollywood Reporter: The Golden Years, 1984. Former mem. exec. com. Los Angeles Mayor's Com. Internat. Visitors and Sister Cities; founder Internat. Festival Adv. Council; named ofcl. hostess, Los Angeles, 1974; former mem. adv. com. Hollywood Festival of the Arts; bd. dirs. Friends of U. So. Calif. Libraries, Inst. Advance Planning, Bd. Edn. for Sr. Adults, Los Angeles Music Ctr.; exec. bd. dirs. Bilingual Children's TV; sponsor Make It on Your Own, 1976, Hollywood Reporter Key Art awards, 1971; founder, sponsor Mktg. Concept awards, 1981; active Motion Picture Country Home, Motion Picture and TV Relief Fund, Los Angeles Orphanage; former chair Beverly Hills/Cannes Sister Com.; former mem. adv. com. Hollywood Festival of the Arts. Recipient Treasury Dept. award, 1966, Nat. Theatre Owners award, 1967, cert. Am. Women in Radio and TV, 1968, Disting. Philanthropic Service award Nat. Jewish Hosp., Denver, citation Will Rogers Hosp., citation O'Donnell Meml. Research Labs., citation Montague Library and Study Ctr., letter Program Youth Opportunity Hubert H. Humphrey, 1968, Golden Flame award Calif. Press Women, 1970, Women of Year award Girl Fridays of Show Bus., 1972, Personal Mgrs. Industry award, 1976, Bronze plaque Mayor Los Angeles, 1972, citation Los Angeles City Council, Award of Excellence Imperial Bank, Shofar award United Jewish Appeal, 1976, ShoWest commendation, 1977-86, Angel award Women in Show Bus., 1988, Founder award Women in Film 1988; Officier de l'Ordre des Arts et des Lettres Govt. of France, 1988. Mem. Printing. Industry Am., Cinema Circulus (bd. dirs.), Women of Motion Picture Industry (chair), Am. Women in Radio and TV (bd. dirs.), Calif. Press Women, Nat. Acad. TV Arts and Scis., UN Assn., Internat. Newspaper Promotion Assn., Western Publs. Assn., Dames des Champagne, Calif. Thoroughbreeders Assn., Hollywood C. of C. (bd. dirs., Star on Walk honor 1989), Women in Film (founder, pres. emeritus, Norma Zacky Humanitarian award 1998), L.A. Film Industry Coun. (dir.), Delta Kappa Alpha. Home: Beverly Hills, Calif. Died Mar. 8, 2004.

KATAYAMA, ARTHUR SHOJI, lawyer; b. Los Angeles, June 10, 1927; s. Asaji and Teru (Mori) K.; m. Mie Nakamura, Dec. 23, 1976. AB, Morningside Coll., 1951; LL.B., Pacific Coast U., 1956. Cert: U.S. Dist. Ct. (cen. dist.) Calif. 1959, U.S. Ct. Appeals (9th cir.) 1959, U.S. Tax Ct. 1971, U.S. Supreme Ct. 1971. With intelligence div. U.S. Treasury Dept., Los Angeles, 1953-58; with N. Am. Aviation, Los Angeles, 1958-59; practiced in Los Angeles, 1959-60; mem. firm Mori & Katayama, Los Angeles, 1960-77; prin. Nagata, Masuda & Katayama, 1980-83, Katayama & Nagata, 1983-84; pvt. practice Arthur S. Katayama, P.C., Newport Beach, Calif., from 1984. Mem. adv. bd. Sumitomo Bank of Calif., Los Angeles.; Mem. Calif. Democratic State Ctrl. Com., 1958-60 Served with AUS, 1945-47. Mem. ABA, Los Angeles County, Orange County bar assns. Clubs: Mesa Verde/Costa Mesa Country; Big Canyon Country (Newport Beach). Died Mar. 20, 2003.

KATZ, SIR BERNARD, physiologist; b. Leipzig, Germany, Mar. 26, 1911; s. Max and Eugenie (Rabinowitz) K.; m. Marguerite Penly(dec. 1999), Oct. 27, 1945; children: David, Jonathan. MD, U. Leipzig, Germany, 1934; MD (hon.), U. Leipzig, German Dem. Republic, 1990; PhD, U. London, 1938, DSc, 1943; DSc (hon.), U. Southampton, 1971, U. Melbourne, 1971, Cambridge U., 1980; PhD (hon.), Weizmann Inst. Sci., 1979. Beit Meml. Research fellow, 1938-39; Carnegie Research fellow, 1939-42; asst. dir. biophys. research U. Coll., London, 1946-50, reader, 1950, prof., head biophysics dept., 1952-78, prof. emeritus, 1978—2003. Lectr. univs., socs. Author: Electric Excitation of Nerve, 1939; Nerve, Muscle and Synapse, 1966; The Release of Neural Transmitter Substances, 1969; also articles. Mem. Agrl. Research Council, 1967-77. Recipient Feldberg award, 1965, Copley medal Royal Soc., 1967, Nobel prize in medicine-physiology, 1970, Cothenius medal Deutsche Akademie der Naturforscher Leopoldina, 1989; created knight, 1969. Fellow Royal Soc. (council 1964-65, v.p. 1965, biol. sec. 1968-76), Royal Coll. Physicians (Baly medal 1967); fgn. mem. Royal Danish Acad. Scis. and Letters, Acad. Nat. Lincei, Am. Acad. Arts and Sci., Nat. Acad. Scis. U.S. (fgn. assoc.), Order Pour le Mérite für Wissenschaften und Künste (fgn.) Achievements include research on nerve and muscle function especially transmission of impulses from nerve to muscle fibers. Died Apr. 20, 2003.

KATZ, ISRAEL, retired engineering educator; b. N.Y.C., Nov. 30, 1917; s. Morris and Sarah (Schwarts) K.; m. Betty Steigman, Mar. 29, 1942; children: Susan Raisner, Judith Kessar, Ruth Babai. Journeyman machinist, Boston Trade Sch., 1935; BSME, Northeastern U., 1941; grad. in naval architecture, MIT, 1942; MME, Cornell U., 1944. Registered profl. engr., N.Y., Mass. Test engr. GE Co., Lynn, Mass., Schenectady, N.Y., 1938-42; sr. engr. USN diesel engring. lab. Cornell U., 1942-46, asst. prof. grad. sch. aero. engring., 1946-48; assoc. prof. Sibley Sch. Mech. Engring., Cornell U., 1948-56; consulting engine designer Pratt & Whitney Aircraft Co., 1946-56; mgr. cons. engring. GE Advanced Elec. Ctr., 1956-63; prof., dir. advanced engring. programs Northeastern U., Boston, 1963-88, dean continuing edn., 1967-74, ret., 1988. Examinter Engrs. for Appts. and Promotions Com. Mass., 1964-88; engring. cons. NAS, Washington, 1971-88; cons., lectr. MIT Ctr. Advanced Engring. Study, 1974-82; chmn. seminars Nat. Engrs. Week, 1975-91, dir. New Eng. observance, 1991-93; ednl. advisor NSF, Washington, 1980-88; chmn. Mass. Engring. Coun., Boston, 1981-83; chmn. bd. examiners Dept. Bldg. Constrn., Town of Brookline, Mass., 1994—. Author: (textbook) Principles of Aircraft Propulsion Machinery, 1949; editor various publs. Benwill Publ. Corp., Boston, 1950-88; contbr. articles to profl. jours. Pres. of congregation Temple Beth El, Ithaca, N.Y., 1958-60. Recipient Outstanding Alumnus award Northeastern U., 1992; New Eng. award Engring. Socs. New Eng., 1993; various citations. Mem. Mayflower Lodge (pres. 1990-94), Shriners, B'nai B'rith, Senate Soc., Sigma Xi, Tau Beta Pi. Democrat. Jewish. Achievements include patents for endodontic pressure syringe, low pressure injection oil engine, turbo-compound radial engine, submarine-launched missile system, AN/TPQ-10 close support attack system, bomber fleet automatic traffic control system, CAMAL strategic alert system, others. Home: Brookline, Mass. Died 2003.

KATZELL, RAYMOND A. psychologist, educator; b. Bklyn., Mar. 16, 1919; s. Abraham and Fannie (Skoblow) K.; m. Florence Joyce Goldstein, Sept. 7, 1941; m. Mildred Engberg, May 11, 1953. BS, NYU, 1939, AM, 1941, PhD, 1943; postgrad., Columbia U., 1939. Diplomate: Am. Bd. Examiners in Psychology. Research asst. psychology NRC grant for research on selection and tng.pilots NYU, 1939-42, instr. psychology, 1942-43, adj. assoc. prof. psychology, 1951-53, prof. mgmt. engring. and psychology and dir. research center indsl. behavior, 1957-63, prof. psychology, 1963-84, prof. emeritus, from 1984, head dept., 1963-72; instr. evenings Sch. Bus. Adminstrn. CCNY, 1942-43; asst. prof. psychology U. Tenn., 1945-46, assoc. prof., 1946-48; assoc. prof. personnel psychology, dir. psychol. service center Syracuse (N.Y.) U., 1948-51; lectr. psychology Columbia U., 1955-57; cons. personnel psychology in indsl. orgns., 1945-97; v.p. Richardson, Bellows, Henry & Co., Inc., 1951-57, dir., 1947-68; cons. N.Y.C. Dept. Personnel, 1967-72, U.S. Dept. Labor, 1968-80, HEW, 1968-70, U.S. Dept. Justice, 1969-79, EEOC, 1973. Chmn. Adv. Council Psychologists, N.Y. State, 1963-68; expert cons. USAF, 1950-51; personnel psychologist personnel research sect. Adj. Gen.'s office, U.S. War Dept., 1943-45 Co-author: Testing and Fair Employment, 1968, Work, Productivity and Job Satisfaction, 1975, Guide to Worker Productivity Experiments in the U.S., 1971-77; editor: The Splendid Stutz, 1996; series editor: Frontiers of Industrial and Organizational Psychology, 1984-88; contbr. articles to profl. jours. Recipient Disting. Sci. Contbns. award Soc. for Indsl. and Organizational Psychology, 1988. Fellow APA (pres. divsn. indsl. psychology 1960-61), Am. Psychol. Soc., Met. N.Y. Assn. Applied Psychology (pres. 1955-57); mem. Soc. Advancement Mgmt. (former mem., pres. Cen. N.Y. chpt. 1949-51), N.Y. State Psychol. Assn. (pres. 1958-59), Antique Automobile Assn. Am. (v.p. 1992, pres. 1993, Ankokas region), Soc. Automotive Historians, Classic Car Club Am. (dir. Delaware Valley region 1996), The Stutz Club (v.p. 1992—). Home: Medford, NJ. Died Feb. 5, 2003.

KATZER, JEFFREY, information science educator; Prof. Syracuse (N.Y.) U., 1969—2000, former dean. Recipient Outstanding Sci. Tchr. award, 1992. Died Mar. 4, 2000.

KAUFMAN, HELEN WHEATLEY, mental health nurse, educator; b. Towson, Md., Nov. 26, 1931; Diploma, U. Md., Balt., 1952, BS, 1958, MS, 1965; MEd, John Hopkins U., 1971; EdD, Nova U., 1976. Staff nurse Univ. Hosp., Balt., 1952-53; insvc. instr. Univ. Md. Hosp. and Sch. Nursing, Balt., 1953-55; med.and surg. clin. instr. Univ. Md. Sch.

Nursing, Balt., 1955-56; med. and surg. instr. Ch. Home and Hosp., Balt., 1956-57, head nursing arts dept., 1957-58; adminstrv. supr. Sheppard & Pratt Hosp., Towson, 1959-63; asst. prof. of nursing C.C. of Balt., 1965-66, Catonsville (Md.) C.C., 1966-70; assoc. prof. of nursing Catonsville C.C., 1971-75, prof. of nursing, 1976-94. Treas. Md. State Nurses Assn., Balt., 1956-58. Mem. Sigma Theta Tau, Pi Lamda Theta. Home: Stevensville, Md. Died Nov. 9, 2001.

KAUFMAN, ROBERT, writer, producer; b. N.Y.C., Mar. 22, 1931; s. Leo and Estelle (Mandel)K.; m. Judith Pokempner (div. May, 1976); children: Richard, Melissa, Robin, Christopher; m. Robin Christine Krause. BA, Columbia U., 1952. Freelance publicist, 1952-56; comedy writer working for Dick Shawn, Red Buttons, Groucho Marx, Mort Sahl, N.Y.C., 1956-59; novelist N.Y.C., 1958-62; writer, producer for studios including Warner Bros., Columbia, Filmways, Universal, Metro Goldwyn Mayer, 20th Century Fox, ABC, CBS, NBC, L.A., 1960-88; pres./chief exec. officer Bobka Prodns. Inc., Hollywood, Calif., 1962-88. Screenwriter: Divorce American Style (Acad. award nominee 1967), Getting Straight (Acad. award nominee 1970), (also producer) Love at First Bite, 1979, Freebie and the Bean, 1974; head writer (TV) The Bob Newhart Show (Emmy nomination, 1962); novelist: Isolation Booth, The Right People, Don't Talk to Me, I'm in Training; exec. producer Daddy's Little Girl, 1989; screen wrtier, producer Love at Second Bite, 1989. Writer Robert Kennedy campaign for Pres., L.A., 1968, Gary Hart campaign for Pres., L.A., 1984. Mem. Motion Picture Acad. Fine Arts and Scis., Writers Guild of Am. West, The 918th Club (co-chmn.), 10 Times Negative Cost Club (v.p.), Bijan V.I.P. Club. Democrat. Jewish. Avocations: movie trivia, appearing on johnny carson show (12 times), tennis. Home: Beverly Hills, Calif. Deceased.

KAUFMAN, RONALD PAUL, physician, school official; b. Hartford, Conn., Nov. 30, 1929; s. Louis Elliot and Sarah K.; m. Beth Winkler, Dec. 28, 1968; children: Ronald Paul, Michael, Karyn, Leesa, Jennifer. BS, Trinity Coll., 1951; MD, U. Pa., 1955. Intern Hartford Hosp., 1955-56, resident in internal medicine, 1956-58, chief resident, 1960-61, Asst. dir. dept. medicine, 1966-70, dir. med. edn. dept., 1967-70; med. dir. George Washington U. Hosp., Washington, 1970-75; asso. dean clin. affairs. Univ. Med. Ctr., 1972-73, dean, 1973-77, acting v.p. for med. affairs, 1975-76, v.p. for med. affairs, 1976-87; v.p. for health scis. Health Scis. Ctr. U. So. Fla., 1987-94, prof. medicine, dir. divsn. med. practice mgmt., from 1994; exec. dir. USF Physicians Group, from 1996. Chmn. bd. dirs. Dow Sherwood Corp. Contbr. articles to profl. publs. Mem. D.C. Med. Community com. Mayor's Panel on Human Resources Orgn. and Mgmt. of D.C., 1977. Served to capt. M.C. USAF, 1958-60. Mem. Am. Acad. Med. Dirs., Am. Bd. Med. Mgmt. (treas. 1990, sec. 1991-93, pres. elect 1993, pres. 1994-95, immediate past pres. 1995-96), ACP, AMA, Am. Soc. Internal Medicine, Assn. Acad. Health Ctrs. (chmn. 1986-87), Assn. Am. Med. Colls., Assn. for Hosp. Med. Edn., D.C. Med. Soc., Nat. Bd. Med. Examiners, Am. Coll. Physician Execs. (pres. 1986), Nat. Acad. Med. Examiners (editl. adv. bd. 1991—), World Access Inc., D.C. Consortium Univ. Health Sci. Ctrs., Soc. Med. Adminstrs. (treas. 1992-97), Soc. Med. Assn., D.C. Hosp. Assn., Nat. Assn. Biomed. Rsch. Home: Lutz, Fla. Died June 10, 2003.

KAUPS, MATTI ENN, geography educator; b. Estonia, Sept. 23, 1932; came to U.S., 1949. s. Richard and Salme (Tahe) K.; m. Vaike Kaasik, Mar. 28, 1959; children: Michael Brandon, Kristi Louise. BA, UCLA, 1959; MS, U. Wis., 1960; PhD, U. Minn., 1965. Asst. prof. Macalester Coll., St. Paul, 1965-68; instr. U. Minn., Duluth, 1963-65, assoc. prof., 1968-73, prof., from 1973. Study leader, lectr. fgn. tours Smithsonian Instn., Washington, 1980—. Co-author: American Backwoods Frontier, 1989 (Theodore Saloutos Meml. award 1990, Am. Pioneer Soc. award 1991); contbr. over 30 articles to profl. jours. Cpl. U.S. Army, 1952-54. Decorated Knight 1st Class of the Order of the White Rose of Finland, 1991; recipient Personal Medal of King Carl XVI of Sweden, 1976. Mem. Assn. Am. Geographers, Pioneer Am. Soc., Minn. Hist. Soc., Suomi-Seura (Helsinki, Finland). Home: Duluth, Minn. Deceased.

KAWAI, SABURO, retired insurance company executive; b. Feb. 5, 1908; m. Tamae Kawai. Grad., Tohoku U., 1931. Chief actuary, dir. Kyoei Life Re, Tokyo, Japan, 1935-45; founder Kyoei Life Ins. Co. Ltd., Tokyo, 1947, pres., chmn., 1948-71, hon. chmn. bd., from 1980. Decorated Ordem Nascional do Cruzeiro do Sul (Brazil), Dark Blue Ribbon medal (Japan); recipient Letter of Citation, Minister of Finance of Republic of Korea, 1984, John Bickley Founders award Gold medal for excellence Internat. Ins. Soc., 1995, Appreciation Plaque, Min. Fin. of Republic of Indonesia, 1995, others; named to Ins. Hall of Fame, 1997. Mem. Life Ins. Assn. Japan (bd. dirs., standing mng. dir.), Inst. Actuaries of Japan (chmn. 1959-63), Internat. Congress Actuaries in Tokyo, Inst. of Actuaries (London), Assn. Swiss Actuaries, Assn. Ministry Health and Welfare, Deutche Gesellschaft fur Versicherungsmathemati (hon. overseas mem.). Avocations: golf, photography. Home: Tokyo, Japan. Died Oct. 3, 1998.

KAWAMURA, KENTARO, manufacturing executive; CEO Nippon Yusen, Tokyo, from 1996. Died Aug. 8, 1999.

KAY, SAUL, retired pathologist; b. N.Y.C., Feb. 13, 1914; s. Wolfe and Rose (Savitzky) Kossovsky; m. Grace Calef, Aug. 15, 1940; 1 dau., Deborah. BA, N.Y. U., 1936; MD, N.Y. Med. Coll., 1939. Intern Harlem Hosp., N.Y.C., 1939-41; resident Fordham Hosp., 1941-42, N.Y. Postgrad. Med. Sch. and Hosp., 1946-48, Columbia Presbyn. Med. Ctr., 1948-50; practice medicine specializing in pathology Richmond, Va., 1950-96; ret., 1996. Prof. dept. surg. pathology Med. Coll. Va., 1952-78, emeritus prof., 1978—. Served to maj. AUS, 1942-45. Decorated Bronze Star. Mem. AMA, Coll. Am. Pathology, Va. Med. Soc., Richmond Acad. Medicine, Am. Soc. Clin. Pathology, Internat. Acad. Pathology, Va. Path. Soc. Died Jan. 7, 2004.

KAZAN, ELIA, theatrical, motion picture director and producer, author; b. Constantinople, Turkey, Sept. 7, 1909; s. George and Athena (Sismanoglou) K.; m. Molly Day Thacher, Dec. 2, 1932 (dec.); children: Judy, Chris, Nick, Katharine; m. Barbara Loden, June 5, 1967 (dec.); 1 child, Leo; m. Frances Rudge, June 28, 1982. AB, Williams Coll., 1930; postgrad., Yale U., 1930-32; M.F.A., Wesleyan U., Middletown, Conn., 1955. Co-founder Actors Studio. Actor with Group Theatre, 1932-39; dir. stage plays, 1940-55, including Skin of Our Teeth, Harriet, Jacobowsky and the Colonel, All My Sons, Deep Are the Roots, A Streetcar Named Desire, Death of a Salesman, Camino Real, Tea and Sympathy, Cat on a Hot Tin Roof, The Dark at the Top of the Stairs, J.B (Antoinette Perry award for direction 1958), Sweet Bird of Youth, After the Fall, But for Whom Charlie, The Changeling; numerous motion pictures, 1944—, including A Tree Grows in Brooklyn, Boomerang, Gentlemen's Agreement (Acad. award for best direction 1947), Pinky, Panic in the Streets, A Streetcar Named Desire, Zapata, Man on a Tight Rope, On the Waterfront, (1954 Acad. Award for best direction), East of Eden, Baby Doll, A Face in the Crowd, Wild River, Splendor in the Grass, America, America, The Arrangement, The Visitors, The Last Tycoon; author: America, America, 1962, The Arrangement, 1967, The Assassins, 1972, The Understudy, 1974, Acts of Love, 1978, The Anatolian, 1982, Elia Kazan-A Life, 1988, Beyond the Aegean, 1994. Recipient D.W. Griffith award Dirs. Guild Am., 1987, hon. Oscar (for Long, Disting. and Unparalleled Career), 1999. Died Sept. 28, 2003.

KEACH, STACY, SR., producer, director; b. Chgo., May 29, 1914; s. Walter Edmund and Dora (Stacy) K.; m. Mary Cain Peckham, June 18, 1937; children— Stacy, James. BS, Northwestern U., 1935; MA, 1936; LHD (hon.), Columbia Coll., 1987. Prof. theatrical prodns. Northwestern U., Evanston, Ill., 1935-36, Armstrong Coll., Savannah, Ga., 1936-41, Pasadena (Calif.) Playhouse, 1941-42; pres. Stacy Keach Prodns., Sherman Oaks, Calif., from 1948, Kaydan Record Corp., North Hollywood, 1957-70, Verdict Film Corp., Hollywood, 1972-73. Producer, dir. Universal Studios, Universal City, Calif., 1941-46, RKO Studios, Hollywood, Calif., 1946-48, producer, 1948-50, NBC, Hollywood, 1950-53, Columbia Pictures, Hollywood, 1952-54, appeared as Clarence Birds Eye on Birds Eye Frozen Food commls., 1981-86; spokesman for Nat. Liberty Ins. TV commls., 1988-91. Recipient Rockefeller Found. award, 1941, Freedom Found. award (2), L.A. City Coun. award, 1973; named Man of Yr. Pasadena Playhouse Alumni Assn., 1995. Mem. Assn. Visual Communicators, Pacific Pioneer Broadcasters (bd. dirs. Twice, Diamond Circle award 1995), Rotary (past pres.), Sigma Alpha Epsilon. Died Feb. 13, 2003.

KEARLEY, F. FURMAN, minister, religious educator, magazine editor; b. Montgomery, Ala., Nov. 7, 1932; s. John Ausban and Zelma Olene (Suggs) K.; m. Helen Joy Bowman, July 18, 1951; children: Janice Gail Kearley Mink, Amelia Lynn Kearley Johnson. BA, Ala. Christian Coll., (now Faulkner U.), 1954; MA, Harding U., 1956; MEd, Auburn U., 1960; MRE, ThM, Harding U., 1965; PhD, Hebrew Union Coll.-Jewish Inst. Religion, 1971; LLD (hon.), Lubbock Christian U., 1985. Min. of the Gospel. Evangelist Chs. of Christ, various cities, from 1951; chmn. Bible dept. Faulkner U., Montgomery, 1956-64; chmn., humanities div. Lubbock (Tex.) Christian Univ., 1970-75; dir., grad. studies in religion Abilene (Tex.) Christian Univ., 1975-85; dean Magnolia Bible Coll., 1993-99; prof. Bible, So. Christian U., Montgomery, Ala., 1999-2000; ret. Sec., treas. S.W. Region Evang. Theol. Soc., 1982-85; adv. bd. Gospel Svcs., Houston, 1985-98; pres.'s coun. Lubbock (Tex.) Christian Univ., 1986-98. Author: (book) God's Indwelling Spirit, 1974; editor: (book) Biblical Interpretation, 1986, (religious periodical) Gospel Advocate, 1985—; contbr. over 500 articles to jours. Recipient Alumnus of Yr. award Harding U., Searcy, Ark., 1985, Harding Grad. Sch. Religion, Memphis, 1986, Outstanding Christian Journalism award Freed-Hardeman U., 1994, Christian Journalism award Harding U., 1996, Christian Leadership award Lads to Leaders, 1996. Mem. Soc. Bib. Lit., Evang. Theol. Soc., Nat. Assn. Tchrs. and Profs. of Hebrew. Home: Corsicana, Tex. Deceased.

KEE, WALTER ANDREW, former government official; b. Phila., July 12, 1914; s. Walter Leslie and Regina Veronica (Corcoran) K.; m. Genevieve O'Hair, Dec. 2, 1943; children: Kathleen, Sheila. BS, Purdue U., 1949; M.L.S., Columbia U., 1950. Engring. and phys. sci. librarian N.Y. U., N.Y.C., 1950-51; librarian E.I. DuPont de Nemours, Savannah River Lab., Aiken, S.C., 1951-55; head library and documents sect. Martin Co., Balt., 1955-59; chief library br. AEC, Washington, 1959-74; librarian ERDA, Washington, 1975-76, asst. to dir. div. adminstrv. services, 1976-77, also Freedom of Info. and Privacy Act officer, 1975-77; dir. div. publs. mgmt. Dept. Energy, 1977-78; ret., 1978. Chmn. AEC-Dept. of Def. Joint Atomic Weapon Tech. Info. Group, 1962-72. Contbr.: chpt. to Special Librarianship: A New Reader (Eugene Jackson), 1980. Asst. to chief So. Shores Fire Dept.; sec. Dare County Firemen's Assn., 1980—83; historian So. Shores Civic Assn.; legis. officer Alamance County, N.C. fedn. Nat. Assn. Ret. Fed. Employees, 1994—2002; bd. dirs. Friends Alamance County Librs. Mem. Fed. Library Com., Com. on Sci. and Tech. Info., Spl. Libraries Assn. (cons., pres. nuclear sci. divsn. and info. tech. divsn., pres. Balt. chpt.), Am. Soc. Info. Sci. Home: Burlington, NC. Died Sept. 24, 2003.

KEEN, NOEL THOMAS, plant pathology educator; b. Marshalltown, Iowa, Aug. 13, 1940; s. Walter Thomas and Evelyn Mae (Mayo) K.; m. Diane I. Keen, Nov. 15, 1986. BS, Iowa State U., 1963, MS, 1965; PhD, U. Wis., 1968. Asst. prof. plant pathology U. Calif., Riverside, 1968-72, assoc. prof., 1972-78, prof., from 1978, chmn. dept. plant pathology, 1983-89, chmn. dept. genetics, 1994-97. Faculty rsch. lectr. U. Calif., Riverside, 1995-96. Recipient Ruth Allen award, Am. Phytopathological Soc., 1995, Superior Svc. award USDA, 1996. Fellow: AAAS, Am. Acad. Microbiology, Am. Phytopathol. Soc. (v.p. 1999—2000, pres.-elect 2000—01, pres. from 2001); mem.: NAS, Am. Soc. Plant Biology, Am. Soc. Microbiology, Internat. Soc. Plant Molecular Biology. Home: Riverside, Calif. Died Apr. 18, 2002.

KEENEY, EDMUND LUDLOW, physician; b. Shelbyville, Ind., Aug. 11, 1908; s. Bayard G. and Ethel (Adams) K.; m. Esther Cox Loney Wight, Mar. 14, 1950; children: Edmund Ludlow, Eleanor Seymour (Mrs. Cameron Leroy Smith). AB, Ind. U., 1930; MD, Johns Hopkins U., 1934. Diplomate Am. Bd. Internal Medicine. Intern Johns Hopkins Hosp., 1934-37, vis. physician, instr. internal medicine, 1940-48; practice medicine, specializing internal medicine San Diego, 1948- 55; dir. Scripps Clinic and Research Found., La Jolla, 1955-67, pres., 1967-77, pres. emeritus, 1977—. Dir. rsch. on fungus infections OSRD, 1942-46. Author: Practical Medical Mycology, 1955, Medical Advice for International Travel; contbr. articles on allergy, immunology and mycology to med. jours. Bd. dirs. U. San Diego, Allergy Found. Am. Fellow A.C.P.; mem. A.M.A., Am. Soc. Clin. Investigation, Am. Acad. Allergy (pres. 1964), Western Assn. Physicians, Calif. Med. Assn., Western Soc. Clin. Research, Phi Beta Kappa, Alpha Omega Alpha, Beta Theta Pi. Republican. Presbyterian. Home: La Jolla, Calif. Deceased.

KEESHAN, BOB, television producer, actor; b. N.Y.C., June 27, 1927; s. Joseph and Margaret (Conroy) K.; m. Anne Jeanne Laurie, Dec. 30, 1950; children: Michael Derek, Laurie Margaret, Maeve Jeanne. Student, Fordham U., 1946-49, DFA, 1975; D of Pedagogy, R.I. Coll., 1969; DHL, Alfred U., 1969, L.I. U., 1977, Coll. of New Rochelle, 1980, LeMoyne Coll., 1983, Mt. St. Mary Coll., Newburgh, N.Y., 1984; HHD, Dartmouth Coll., 1975, Bucknell U., 1981; LittD (hon.), Ind. State U., 1978; LLD, Elmira (N.Y.) U., 1980; DL, Marquette U., 1983; DPS, Cen. Mich. U., 1984; DHL, St. Joseph Coll., 1987, Adrian Coll., 1988, SUNY, 1995, Western Med. Coll., 1996. Pres. Robert Keeshan Assocs., 1955—; dir. Marvin Josephson Assocs. Inc., N.Y.C., 1969-77, Bank of Babylon, N.Y., 1973-79, Anchor Savs. Bank, 1976-91. Appeared as Clarabell on Howdy Doody Show, NBC-TV, 1947-52; as Corny the Clown on Time for Fun, ABC-TV, 1953-55, as Tinker the Toymaker on Tinker's Workshop, ABC-TV, 1954-55 (also producer); as Captain Kangaroo on Captain Kangaroo, CBS-TV, 1955-85 (also producer), as Mr. Mayor and the Town Clown on Mr. Mayor, CBS-TV, 1964-65 (also producer); commentator: Subject is Young People, CBS Radio, 1980-82, Up to the Minute, CBS News, 1981-82, CBS Morning News, 1982; author: She Loves Me...She Loves Me Not, 1963, Growing Up Happy, 1989, Family Fun Activity, 1994, Holiday Fun Activity, 1995, Books to Grow By, 1996, Hurry, Murray, Hurry, 1996, Alligator in the Basement, 1996, Good Morning Captain, 1996, Little Bitty Kitty, 1997. Mem. bd. edn. West Islip, N.Y., 1953-58; pres. Suffolk County Hearing and Speech Center, 1966-71, Suffolk County Police Athletic League, 1973-77; mem. Suffolk County council Boy Scouts Am.; bd. dirs. Nat. Assn. Hearing and Speech Agys., 1969-71, United Fund L.I., 1967-68; bd. dirs. Good Samaritan Hosp., West Islip, N.Y., 1969-78, pres., 1978-79, chmn. exec. com., 1979-80; chmn. bd. trustees Coll. New Rochelle, N.Y., 1974-80; chmn. Council of Governing Bds., 1979-80. Served with USMCR, 1945-46. Recipient Sylvania award, 1956, Peabody award, 1958, 72, 79, Jr. Membership award Calif. Fedn. Women's Clubs, 1961, 62, Freedom Found. award, 1962, 72, Page One award, 1965, Ursula Laurus award Coll. New Rochelle, 1958, Ohio State award, 1973, DeWitt Carter Reddick award U. Tex., 1978, Sadie award U. Ala., 1978, Am. Edn. award Edn. Industries Assn., 1978, Disting. Achievement award Ga. Radio and TV Inst.-Pi Gamma Kappa, 1978, Emmy award for outstanding children's entertainment series NATAS, 1978, 81, 82, Emmy award as outstanding performer in children's programming NATAS, 1982, 83, 84, Gabriel award cert. of merit, 1978, 82, James E. Allen Meml. award for disting. service to edn. Albany, N.Y., 1981, Disting. Svc. to Children award Parents Without Partners, 1981, named TV Father of Yr., 1980, recipient Nat. Edn. award, 1982, award Mass. Soc. for Prevention Cruelty to Children, 1982, award Suffolk Early Childhood Edn. Coun., 1983, Abe Lincoln awards So. Bapt. Radio and TV Commn., 1983, Phi Alpha Tau award Emerson Coll., 1983, award N.Y. Elem. Sch. Prins. Assn., 1983, Disting. Svc. award Suffolk Mental Health Assn., 1985, Nat. Pub. Affairs Recognition award Am. Heart Assn., 1987, Friends of Children award Assn. Childhood Edn. Internat., 1987, Frances Holleman Breathitt Award for Excellence Kennedy Ctr. for the Performing Arts, 1987, Disting. Svc. award AMA, 1991; inducted into Clown Hall of Fame, 1990. Fellow Am. Acad. Pediatrics (hon). Clubs: L.I. Yacht (Babylon) (commodore 1964-65); Friars (N.Y.C.); Southward Ho Country (Bay Shore N.Y.). Home: Norwich, Vt. Died Jan. 23, 2004.

KEETON, KATHY MERLE, publisher; b. Republic of South Africa, Feb. 17, 1939; d. Keith and Queenie K.; m. Jan. 17, 1988. Student, Royal Ballet Sch., London. Vice chmn., COO Gen. Media Internat., N.Y.C., from 1969; Pres. Omni mag., N.Y.C., from 1978; pres. Longevity Mag., Compute Mag. Author: (with Yvonne Baskin) Woman of Tomorrow, 1985, Longevity: The Science of Staying Young, 1992; exec. producer TV program Omni: Visions of Tomorrow, The New Frontier. Active Fund for the Aging (City Meals on Wheels), Corp. Blood Drive, Nat. Coalition Against Censorship. Recipient Publisher of Yr. citation, Outstanding Woman in Publishing award March of Dimes, Unity of the City of N.Y. award Mayor Dinkins. Mem. AIAA, Amateur Astronomers Assn., Am. Space Found., Robotics Internat. SME, Space Generation Found., L-5 Soc. Died 1997.

KEIM, ROBERT PHILLIP, retired advertising executive, consultant; b. Ridgewood, N.Y., Jan. 28, 1920; s. William John and Josephine (Becht) K.; m. Gloria Kathleen Smith, Jan. 24, 1943; children: William Gary, Barbara Kathleen. BA magna cum laude, Queens Coll.; student, Grad. Sch. Internat. Relations, U. Md., 1950-51. Trainee Compton Advt., N.Y.C., 1942; campaigns mgr. Advt. Council, Inc., N.Y.C., 1954-61, pres., 1966-88; also dir.; 2d v.p. marketing service Chase Manhattan Bank, N.Y.C., 1962-66; cons. in field, from 1988. Cons. supt. USAF Acad., 1958; Mem. Air Force Res. Policy Com., 1961-63; del. White House Conf. Edn., 1956, White House Conf. Inflation, 1974; mem. Pres.'s Com. Traffic Safety, 1957-62, Nat. Adv. Council on Minority Bus. Enterprise; mem. exec. com. Air Force Acad. Found. for Falcon Stadium Fund, 1960-61; mem. White House Conf. for a Drug Free Am., 1987-88. Author: Air Force Academy Cadet Procurement Study, 1958, Reserve Forces Utilization Study, 1962, A Time in Advertising's Camelot-The Memoirs of a Do-Gooder, 2002; writer, prod.: Air Force Hour, 1946-49, Armed Forces Hour, 1949-50; adv. bd.: Public Relations News, 1977-81. Bd. visitors Ithaca Coll. Sch. Communications, 1974; bd. dirs. Bus. Council for Internat. Understanding; mem. exec. com. James Webb Young Meml. Fund, U. Ill., 1976-81; mem. Pres.'s Council on Energy Efficiency, 1980, Pres.'s Child Safety Partnership Commn., 1986; mem. bd. Queens Coll. Found. Served to col. USAF, 1942-54. Decorated Legion of Merit, Commendation ribbon; elected fellow R.I. Sch. Design, 1982; scholar Queens Coll., 1941; recipient Dept. English 1st in class award, 1942, Ann. award Internat. Advt. Assn., 1982, Douglas A. Fraser award UAW Internat. Union, 1987, Disting. Alumnus award Queens Coll., 1988. Mem. Madison Winter Club, Clinton Country Club, Phi Beta Kappa. Congregationalist. Deceased.

KELALIS, PANAYOTIS, pediatric urologist; b. Nicosia, Cyprus, Jan. 17, 1932; came to U.S., 1960, naturalized, 1969; s. Peter and Julia (Petrides) K.; m. Barbara Wilson, Apr. 8, 1970. Student, U. Edinburgh, 1950-51; MB, BChir, U. Dublin, 1957; MS in Urology, Mayo Grad. Sch. Medicine, 1964. Resident in urology Mayo Grad. Sch. Medicine, Rochester, Minn., 1960-64; asst. to staff Mayo Clinic, 1964, cons. urology, 1965—, head sect. pediatric urology, 1975-91, chmn. dept. urology, 1982-91, 1991-2000, chair internat. activities, from 1991; prof. urology Mayo Med. Sch., from 1975, Anson L. Clark prof. pediatric urology, from 1985. Assoc. dir. surgery and subspecialities Mayo Grad. Sch. Medicine, 1994-2001. Editor: Clinical Pediatric Urology, 2 vols., 1976, 3rd edit., 1992; contbr. numerous sci. articles to profl. jours., chpts. in books. Hon. consul Republic of Cyprus. Recipient Edward J. Noble Found. award, 1964, Pediatric Urology medal, 1996; decorated knight Order of St. Andrew. Fellow ACS; mem. Am. Assn. Genito-Urinary Surgeons, Internat. Soc. Urology, Am. Urol. Assn., Soc. Pediatric Urology (pres.), Am. Acad. Pediatrics (pres., chmn. urology sect., Urology medal 1996), Sociedad Latino Americana de Urologia Infantile (hon.), Assn. Francaise d'Urologie (hon.), Hellenic Urol. Soc. (hon.), Sociedad Argentine de Urologia (corr.), Venezuelan Urol. Soc. (corr.). Deceased.

KELLAWAY, PETER, neurophysiologist, researcher; b. Johannesburg, Republic of South Africa, Oct. 20, 1920; s. Cecil John Rhodes and Doreen Elizabeth (Joubert) K.; m. Josephine Anne Barbieri, Apr. 1957; children: David, Judianne, Kevin, Christina, Jaime. BA, Occidental Coll., 1942, MA, 1943; PhD, McGill U., 1947; MD (hon.), U. Gothenberg, Sweden, 1977. Diplomate Am. Bd. Clin. Neurophysiology, 1953. Lectr. physiology McGill U., Montreal, Que., Can., 1946-47, asst. prof. physiology, 1947-48; assoc. prof. Baylor U. Coll. Medicine, Houston, 1948-61, prof., 1961-78, prof. neurology, 1978—2003, prof. div. neurosci., 1990—2003, dir. lab. clin. electrophysiology, 1948-65; dir. dept. clin. neurophysiology The Meth. Hosp., Houston, 1948-71, mem. attending staff, 1948—2003, chief, 1971-1999, sr. attending Neurophysiology, 1971—2003; cons., neurophysiologist Hermann Hosp., Houston, 1949-73, dir. dept. electroencephalography, 1955-73; dir. electroencephalography lab. Ben Taub Gen. Hosp., Houston, 1965-79; mem. cons. staff, chief neurophysiology svc. Dept. Medicine Tex. Children's Hosp., Houston, 1972—2002; mem. cons. staff neurology St. Luke's Episc. Hosp., Houston, 1971-73, mem. cons. staff neurophysiology, chief neurophysiology svc., 1973—2003. Dir. Blue Bird Circle Children's Clinic Neurol. Disorders The Meth. Hosp., 1949-60, dir. Blue Bird Circle Rsch. Labs., 1960-79, chmn. Instnl. Rev. Bd. Human Rsch., 1974-90, dir. Epilepsy Rsch. Ctr., 1975-99; chmn. appointment and promotions com. Baylor U. Coll. Medicine, 1968-71, chief sect. neurophysiology Dept. Neurology, 1977-98; cons., electrophysiologist VA Hosp., Houston, 1949—; cons. electroencephalography So. Pacific Hosp. Assn., Houston, 1949-57; cons., neurophysiologist M.D. Anderson Hosp. and Tumor Inst., Houston, 1953-62; mem. coun. adminstrs. Tex. Med. Ctr., Houston, 1954-60; cons. electroencephalography sect. NIH, 1961-62; hon. pres. Internat. Congress Clin. Neurophysiology, 1993. Author numerous books; editor Electroencephalography and Clin. Neurophysiology, 1968-71, cons. editor, 1972-75, hon. cons. editor, 1989; mem. editl. bd. Jour. Clin. Neurophysiology, 1995; contbr. over 180 articles to profl. jours. Recipient Sir William Osler medal Am. Assn. History of Medicine, 1946; grantee NIH, NASA; named Grass lectr. Am. Soc. EEG Technologists, 1989; Berger lectr., 1982, 92. Fellow Am. Acad. Pediat. (hon.), Am. Electroencephalographic Soc. (hon., coun. 1954, 64-66, treas. 1956-58, pres.-elect 1962-63, pres. 1963-64, Jasper award 1990)); mem. APA, Am. Epilepsy Soc. (sec.-treas. 1955-58, pres.-elect 1959, pres. 1960, Lennox lectr. 1981, Disting. Clin. Investigator award 1989, Lennox award 1996), Am. Physiol. Soc., Am. Acad. Neurology, Am. Neurol. Assn., Can. Physiol. Soc., Internat. Fedn. Clin. Neurophysiology (hon. pres. internat. congress), Internat. League Against Epilepsy (Am. br.), So. Electroencephalographic Soc. (coun. 1953, v.p. 1954, pres. 1955), Ea. Assn. Electroencephalographic Soc., Ctrl. Encephalographic Soc., Houston Neurol. Soc. (v.p. 1957, pres. 1967, chmn. bd. trustees 1970-73), Soc. Neurosci., Child Neurology Soc., Epilepsy Assn. Houston/Gulf Coast (profl. adv. bd. 1985-92). Avocations: scuba diving, photography. Home: Houston, Tex. Died June 25, 2003.

KELLEN, STEPHEN MAX, investment banker; b. Berlin, Apr. 21, 1914; came to U.S., 1936, naturalized, 1944; s. Max and Leonie (Marcuse) Katzenellenbogen; m. Anna-Maria Arnhold, Mar. 7, 1940; children: Marina Kellen French, Michael. Grad., Royal French Coll., Berlin, 1932. With Berliner Handels-Gesellschaft, Berlin, 1932-35; With Lazard Bros. Ltd., London, Eng., 1936, Loeb, Rhoades & Co., N.Y.C., 1937-40; with Arnhold and S. Bleichroeder, Inc., N.Y.C., 1940—94, pres., 1955-94, co-chmn., from 1994. Trustee Sta. WNET/13, Carnegie Hall Soc., Aldrich Mus. Contemporary Art; mem. trustees coun. Nat. Gallery Art, Washington; bd. dirs. Am. Coun. on Germany. Mem. Investment Bankers Assn. Am. (bd. govs. 1969-71, chmn. fgn. investment com. 1967-72), Securities Industry Assn. (bd. govs. 1972-73, chmn. internat. finance com. 1972-73), Bond Club, City Midday Club, Met. Club. Home: New York, NY. Died Feb. 11, 2004.

KELLEY, ESTEL WOOD, business executive; b. Sharpsville, Ind., Mar. 24, 1917; s. Floyd and Maude (Wood) K.; m. Wilma E. Lippert, June 17, 1939; children: E. Wood, Wayne L., Karen. BA, Ind. U., 1939, LLD, 1971; postgrad., Northwestern U., 1939-41; LLD (hon.), Ind. U., 1973. CPA, Ind. Controller, treas., dir., mem. exec. com. R.H. Macy & Co., Kansas City, Mo., 1951-56; successively gen. mgr. distbn.-sales, treas., pres., gen. mgr. Birds Eye div., corp. v.p. Gen. Foods Corp., White Plains, N.Y., 1956-64; exec. v.p., dir., mem. exec. com. Heublein, Inc., Hartford, 1964-68; corp. v.p. Gulf and Western Industries, Inc., 1968-74; pres. Consumer Products group; pres., chief exec. officer, dir. Fairmont Foods Co., N.Y.C., 1974-82; founder, mng. gen. ptnr. Kelley & Partners, Ltd.; chmn., pres. Kelley, Inc. Chmn., bd. dirs. Consol. Products Inc., King Cola, Inc.; bd. dirs. Steak n' Shake, Inc.; chmn., CEO, bd. dirs. Fairmont Products, Inc.; chmn. Consol. Splty. Restaurants, Inc.; instr. mktg., mfg. cost Columbia U.; co-founder Prickett Chair, Ind. U., founder E.W. Kelley Mktg. Chair. Mem. Fin. and Accounting Fund, Ind. U.; Mayor, Leawood, Kans., 1955-56; bd. dirs. Ind. U. Found.; dean's adv. council Ind. U. Sch. Bus., mem. pres.'s priorities coordinating com.; chmn. YMCA Internat. Div. Com; bd. dirs. Indpls. Symphony Orch., Howard Community Hosp. Found., Kokomo, Ind. Recipient Silver Beaver award Boy Scouts Am.; Disting. Alumni Service award Ind. U., 1985 Mem. Nat. Assn. Accountants, Fin. Execs. Inst. (dir.), Acad. Alumni Fellows, Beta Gamma Sigma (dirs. table) Clubs: Metropolitan (N.Y.C.); Lake Region Yacht and Country (Winter Haven), Fla. Citrus (Winter Haven); Kokomo (Ind.) Country. Lodges: Masons (32 deg.). Mem. Soc. Of Friends. Home: Indianapolis, Ind. Died July 4, 2003.

KELLOGG, GEORGE WILLIAM, psychiatrist; m. Betty L. BS in Chemistry, La. State U., 1963, MD, 1967; JD, U. Chgo., 1975; MBA, Golden Gate U., 1982. Intern Letterman Hosp., San Francisco, 1967-68; resident Walter Redd Hosp., Washington, 1968-71; psychiatrist pvt. practice, Salinas, Calif., from 1974. Maj. U.S. Army, 1966-74, Vietnam. Died Nov. 14, 1999.

KELLOGG, ROBERT LELAND, English language educator; b. Ionia County, Mich., Sept. 2, 1928; s. Charles Edwin and Lucille Jeanette (Reasoner) K.; m. Joan Alice Montgomery, Apr. 4, 1951; children: Elizabeth Joan, Jonathan Montgomery, Stephen Robert. BA, U. Md., 1950; MA, Harvard U., 1952, PhD, 1958. Mem. faculty U. Va., 1957-99, prof. English, 1967-99, chmn. dept., 1974-78, dean Coll. Arts and Scis., 1978-85, prof. emeritus, from 1999; prin. Monroe Hill Coll., 1985-88. Vis. prof. U. Iceland, 1999—2001. Author: (with Robert Scholes) The Nature of Narrative, 1966, A Concordance to Eddic Poetry, 1988; translator of works from Icelandic; contbr. to profl. jours. Served with USAR, 1954-56. Am.-Scandinavian Found. fellow, 1956-57; Guggenheim fellow, 1968-69 Mem. Medieval Acad. Am., Modern Lang. Assn., South Atlantic Modern Lang. Assn. (pres. 1974-75), Raven Soc., Phi Beta Kappa (pres. local chpt. 1981) Clubs: Colonnade. Democrat. Home: Charlottesville, Va. Died Jan. 3, 2004.

KELLY, ABBY NEESE, writer; b. Sedgwick, Maine, Mar. 22, 1911; d. Fred J. and Nellie (Clapp) Sargent; m. Paul Neese, 1948 (dec.); stepchildren: John J. IV, Ann Kelly Porawski, James H. Neese, Joan N. Downing, Richard M. Neese. AB in Latin, U. Maine, 1932, AM in Edn. and Latin (hon.), 1939. With U. Maine, Orono, 1932-33; tchr. area high schs., Maine; tchr. Latin, Spanish, and English high sch., Ardmore, Pa. Pvt. tutor, Pa., 1948—. Author six books. Republican. Methodist. Home: Philadelphia, Pa. Deceased.

KELLY, JAMES, artist; b. Phila., Dec. 19, 1913; s. James Alphonsus and Mabel (Witzel) K.; m. Sonia Gechtoff, June 23, 1953; children— Susannah, Miles. Student, Pa. Acad. Fine Arts, 1938, Barnes Found., 1941; diploma in painting, Calif. Sch. Fine Arts, 1954. Lectr. painting and drawing U. Calif., Berkeley, 1957 One-man shows include San Francisco Art Assn., 1956, Stryke Gallery, N.Y.C., 1963, East Hampton (N.Y.) Gallery, 1965, 69, Albright Coll., Reading, Pa., 1966, L.I. (N.Y.) U., 1968, Westbeth Galleries, N.Y.C., 1971-72, Weigand Gallery, Coll. Notre Dame, Belmont, Calif., 1990; groups shows include Pa. Acad. Fine Arts, Phila., 1951, San Francisco Mus. Art, 1955, 56, 57, 58, 65, Los Angeles County Mus., 1968, Phoenix Art Mus., 1975, Smithsonian Instn., Washington, 1977, Oakland Mus. Art, Calif., 1985, Santa Cruz (Calif.) Art Mus., 1993, Laguna (Calif.) Art Mus., 1996, San Francisco Mus. Modern Art, 1996, Worcester Art Mus., 2001, NAD, 2003; represented in permanent collections San Francisco Mus. Modern Art, Los Agneles County Mus., U. Mass., Oakland Mus. Art, Mus. Modern Art, N.Y.C., Westinghouse Corp.; invitational show Gruenebaum Gallery, N.Y.C., 1988; additional collections Richmond (Calif.) Art Ctr., Crocker Art Mus., Sacramento, NYU, Worcester (Mass.) Art Mus. Served with USAF, 1941-45. Recipient painting awards San Francisco Mus. Art, Phoenix Art Mus., Peter and Madeleine Martin Found. for Creative Arts, San Francisco, 1990; Found. grantee Tamarind Lithography Workshop, Los Angeles, 1963; Nat. Endowment for Arts fellow, 1977 Mem. NAD. Home: New York, NY. Died June 29, 2003.

KELLY, THOMAS FRANKLIN, management educator, academic administrator; b. Kingston, Pa., May 7, 1947; s. Thomas John and Naomi (Flowers) K.; m. Nancy Kay Ritz, May 6, 1947; children: Christopher, Cynthia. BA in Econs. summa cum laude, Wilkes U., 1965-69; MA in Econs., Lehigh U., 1972; PhD in Higher Edn., Cornell U., 1977. Dir. evening and summer coll. Wilkes Coll., Wilkes-Barre, Pa., 1969-71, instr. econs. (part-time), 1969-74, asst to chancellor, 1971-72, dir. devel., 1972-74, dean external affairs, 1977-84; grad. teaching asst. Cornell U., Ithaca, N.Y., 1974-77; assoc. dean sch. of mgmt. SUNY, Binghamton, 1984-85, dean sch. mgmt., 1985-91, prof. mgmt., from 1989, v.p. external affairs, from 1991. Dir. Binghamton Savs. Bank, 1987—; trustee Guthrie Healthcare System, Inc., Sayre, Pa., 1987—; dir. Resources Recycling Techs., Inc., Vestal, N.Y., 1988-92; dir., chmn. of bd. Guthrie Enterprises, Inc., Sayre, 1988—. Mem. editl. bd. Jour. Bus. and Mgmt., 1991—; cons. editor ASHE-ERIC Publs., Inc., 1994. Dir. Broome County C. of C., Binghamton, 1988-94, Binghamton Summer Music Festival, 1991—; mem. WICZ-TV Adv. Bd., Vestal, 1990—; chmn. of bd. First United Meth. Ch., Endicott, N.Y., 1990-94. Mem. Binghamton Club, Harpur Forum. Avocations: golf, cross country skiing. Home: Endicott, NY. Died Jan. 23, 2002.

KELLY, THOMAS JOSEPH, aerospace engineer, consultant; b. Bklyn., June 14, 1929; s. Wilfrid T. and Irene H. Kelly; m. Joan Tantum, Sept. 1, 1951; children: David, Thomas, Edward, Christopher, Jennifer, Peter. BSME, Cornell U., 1951; MSME, Columbia U., 1956; MS in Indsl. Mgmt., MIT, 1970; DSc (hon.), SUNY, Farmingdale, 1983. Registered profl. engr., N.Y. Propulsion engr. Grumman Aerospace Co., Bethpage, N.Y., lunar module engring. mgr., 1962-70, v.p. space sys., 1976, v.p. engring., 1980, v.p. info. resources mgmt., 1986, pres. Space Sta. Integration Divsn., 1991. Cons., Cutchogue, N.Y., 1993—. Contbr. 10 articles to profl. jours 1st lt. USAF, 1956-58. Recipient Disting. Pub. Svc. medal NASA, 1973, Spacecraft Design award AIAA, 1972. Fellow ASME, Am. Soc. Aero. and Astron.; mem. Nat. Acad. Engring., N.Y. State Sci. and Tech. Found. (dir. 1979-99). Roman Catholic. Achievements include chief engineer on Apollo lunar module at Grumman; responsible for designing, building, and testing the spacecraft that took men to the moon and back six times and rescued stranded crew of Apollo 13. Home: Cutchogue, NY. Died Mar. 23, 2002.

KELMAN, CHARLES D. ophthalmologist, educator; b. Bklyn., May 23, 1930; s. David and Eva Kelman; m. Ann Gur-Arie; children: Evan Ari, Jason, Seth; children from previous marriage: David, Lesley, Jennifer. BS, Tufts U., 1950; BMS, U. Geneva, Switzerland, 1952, MD, 1956; LittD (hon.), Jefferson U., 2000. Diplomate Am. Bd. Ophthalmology. Intern Kings County Hosp., N.Y.C., 1956—57; resident Wills Eye Hosp., Pa., 1956—60; with Manhattan Eye, Ear, Nose and Throat Hosp., N.Y.C., N.Y. Eye and Ear Infirmary, N.Y.C. Clin. prof. N.Y. Med. Coll., Valhalla, from 1980; Arthur J. Bedell Meml. lectr., 1991; hon. pres.-elect 1994 World Congress on Lens Implant Surgery. Author: Cataracts--What You Must Know About Them, 1982, Atlas of Cryosurgical Techniques in Ophthalmology, 1966, Phacoemulsification Aspiration-The Kelman Technique of Cataract Extraction, 1975, Through My Eyes, 1985; contbr. numerous articles to profl. jours. Named one of Ten Greatest Living Ophthalmologists, 2000; recipient Gold Plate award, Am. Acad. Achievement, 1969, Congl. Salute, U.S. Senate 97th Congress, 1983, 1st Ann. Innovators award, Am. Internat. Intraocular Lens Congress, 1985, Ridley medal,

Internat. Congress Ophthalmology, 1990, Nat. Medal Tech., 1992, Inventor of Yr. award, Pres. of U.S., 1992, Disting. Svc. award, Tufts U., 1992, Best Ophthalmologist in Am. award, Ophthalmology Times, 1996. Fellow: Am. Acad. Ophthalmology (1st prize for sci. exhibit 1970, Sr. Honor award 1986, Spl. Recognition award); mem.: AMA (Physicians Recognition award), Internat. Retinal Rsch. Fedn. Inc. (v.p.), Soc. for Phacoemulsification and Related Techniques (hon. life pres.), European Phaco-Cataract Soc. (hon. life pres.), N.Y. Acad. Medicine (sec. sect. on ophthalmology), N.Y. State Soc. Ophthalmology, Am. Soc. for Cataracts and Refractive Surgery (former pres., Binkhorst medal 1989, One of Most Influential Ophthalmologists of 20th Century award 1999), Am. Soc. for Contemporary Ophthalmology (1st Outstanding Achievement award 1981), N.Y. Implant Soc., Can. Implant Assn. (award 1982, Ophthalmologist of the Century 1994), Internat. Assn. Ocular Surgeons. Jewish. Avocations: golf, saxophone, composing, flying, writing. Home: New York, NY. Died June 1, 2004.

KELSO, HAROLD GLEN, family practice physician; b. Newport, Ky., Apr. 1, 1929; s. Harold Glen and Alvina Marie (Hehl) K.; m. Janet Rae Cooper, Aug. 12, 1950; children: Harold Glen III, Susan Annette (Mrs. David Thomas Johnson). BS, U. Dayton, 1951; MD, St. Louis U., 1955. Diplomate Am. Bd. Family Practice. Intern St. Elizabeth Hosp., Dayton, Ohio, 1955-56; pvt. practice Centerville, Ohio, 1956-94; mem. teaching staff St. Elizabeth Hosp., Dayton. Mem. staff Kettering (Ohio) Meml. Hosp., chief staff, 1975-76, chief dept. family practice; chief staff Sycamore Med. Ctr., 1978-79; clin. prof. family practice, Wright State U., clin. prof. emeritus, 1994—; mem. faculty Kettering Coll. Med. Arts; med. dir. Kettering Convalescent Ctr. Pres., vice mayor Centerville, 1960-62; pres. Bd. Edn. Centerville City Schs., 1969-72; trustee Western Ohio Found. Med. Care, Kettering Med. Ctr., Sycamore Med. Ctr., Engring. and Sci. Hall of Fame. Named Ohio Family Physician of Yr. Ohio Acad. Family Physicians, 1990. Fellow Am. Acad. Family Practice; mem. AMA, Ohio Med. Assn., Montgomery County Med. Assn. (sec. 1970, pres. 1984), Order Ky. Cols., Dayton Racquet Club, Sugar Valley Country Club, Rotary (local pres. 1974-75, Paul Harris fellow 1979), Masons, Shriners. Republican. Methodist. Avocations: golf, fishing, rose gardening. Home: Centerville, Ohio. Died Dec. 25, 1999.

KEMP, ROBERT FRANCIS, lawyer, educator; b. Chgo., Mar. 11, 1960; s. William Joseph Sr. and Virginia Anne (McHugh) K.; m. Susan Elizabeth Zinner, Aug. 31, 1996. AB, Columbia U., 1982; JD, U. Calif., Berkeley, 1986; MS in Journalism, Northwestern U., 1987; MBA, U. Chgo., 1990; LLM, John Marshall Law Sch., 1990. Bar: Ill. 1987, Minn. 1987, D.C. 1989, U.S. Dist. Ct. (no. dist.) Ill. 1987, U.S. Ct. Appeals (7th cir.) 1988, U.S. Ct. Appeals (fed. cir.) 1990, Supreme Ct. 1990. Extern to Hon. Spencer M. Williams U.S. Dist. Ct. No. Dist. Calif., San Francisco, 1986; law clk. U.S. Ct. Appeals 7th Cir., Chgo., 1987-89; assoc. Willian, Brinks, Olds, Hofer, Gilson & Lione, Chgo., 1990-93, Kegan & Kegan, Ltd., Chgo., 1993-94; ptnr. Kemp & Edelson, Attys. at Law, Chgo., 1994-96; prin. Kemp Law Offices, Chgo., from 1996. Adj. prof. Columbia College, Chgo., 1992, John Marshall Law Sch., Chgo., 1994—, Northwestern Univ. Medill Sch. Journalism, Evanston, 1994—, Northwestern Univ. J.L. Kellogg Grad. Sch. Mgmt., 1992—, Univ. Chgo, 1997—. Co-author: Guide to Education and Career Development in International Law, 1991; contbr. articles to profl. jours. Scholar Rotary Found., 1982-83, English-Speaking Union, 1984-85, H.V. Kaltenborn Found., 1986-87. Mem. Ill. State Bar Assn., Chgo. Bar Assn. (co-chair intellectual property law com., chair intellectual property law com., young lawyers sect. 1990-92), Intellectual Property Law Assn. Chgo. (chair legal edn. com. 1993-95), Internat. Trademark Assn. (internat. com. 1990-93). Republican. Roman Catholic. Avocations: travel, computing, reading, writing, french. Home: La Grange, Ill. Died Mar. 24, 2002.

KEMP, SUSAN GAYLE, language arts coordinator; b. Houston, Nov. 27, 1948; d. Claude Horace McGinnis and B. Maurine (McVoy) Brown; m. James Allen Kemp, Dec. 20, 1970; 1 child, Allison Kirston. BA in Teaching, Sam Houston State U., 1970; MA, U. Tex., San Antonio, 1976; PhD, Tex. A&M U., 1988. Tchr. MacArthur High Sch., San Antonio, 1970-75, 76-86, 1987-89; grad. asst. U. Tex., San Antonio, 1975-76, Tex. A&M U., College Station, 1986-87; coord. Austin (Tex.) Ind. Sch. Dist., from 1989. Bd. dirs. Friends of RIF, Austin, 1993—; presenter in field. Contbr. articles to profl. jours. Mem. San Antonio 100, 1986-90; bd. mem. youth com. Northwest Hills United Meth. Ch., Austin, 1991—, adv. bd., 1993—. Recipient Outstanding Tchr. award San Antonio Greater C. of C., 1986. Mem. ASCD, Am. Ednl. Rsch. Assn., Nat. Coun. Tchrs. English, Internat. Reading Assn. (com. mem. 1987-91, peer reviewer 1990—), Tex. State Reading Assn. (bd. dirs. 1981-89, pres. 1988-89), Phi Delta Kappa. Home: Austin, Tex. Died Feb. 3, 2002.

KENDIG, EDWIN LAWRENCE, JR., pediatrician, educator; b. Victoria, Va., Nov. 12, 1911; s. Edwin Lawrence and Mary McGuire (Yates) K.; m. Emily Virginia Parker, Mar. 22, 1941; children: Anne Randolph (Mrs. R.F. Young), Mary Emily Corbin (Mrs. T.T. Rankin). BA magna cum laude, Hampden-Sydney Coll., 1932, BS magna cum laude, 1933, DSc (hon.), 1971; LHD (hon.), Hampden Sydney Coll., 2001; MD, U. Va., 1936. Diplomate Am. Bd. Pediatrics. House officer Med. Coll. Va. Hosp., Richmond, Bellevue Hosp., N.Y.C., Babies Hosp., Wilmington, N.C., Johns Hopkins Hosp., Balt., 1936-40; instr. pediatrics Johns Hopkins U., 1944; pvt. practice Richmond, 1940-94; dir. child chest clinic Med. Coll. Va., 1944-94, prof. pediatrics, 1958-99; chief of staff St. Mary's Hosp., Richmond, 1966-67. Cons. on diseases of chest in children, 1944-94, William P. Buffum orator Brown U., 1978; Abraham Finkelstein Meml. lectr. U. Md., 1983; Derwin Cooper lectr. Duke U., 1984; Renato Ma Guerrero lectr. U. Santo Tomas, Manila, 1984; Bakwin Meml. lectr. NYU-Bellevue Hosp., 1986. Editor: Disorders of Respiratory Tract in Children, 1967, 1972, 1977; co-editor (with V. Chernick): Disorders of Respiratory Tract in Children, 4th edit., 1983; cons. editor to : V. Chernick, 5th edit, 1990, to V. Chernick and T. Boat, 5th, 6th edit., pub. as Kendig's Disorders of the Respiratory Tract in Children, 1997; co-editor (with C.F. Ferguson): Pediatric Otolaryngology, 1972; contbg. editor: Gellis and Kagan Current Pediatric Therapy, 12 edits., 1993, Burg, Ingelfinger, Wald Current Pediatric Therapy, 14th edit., Antimicrobial Therapy, Kagan, 3 edits., Practice of Pediatrics, Kelley, Practice of Pediatrics, Maurer, Allergic Diseases of Infancy, Childhood and Adolescence, Bierman and Pearlman, Sarcoidosis and Other Granulomatous Diseases, James, 1994, former mem. editl. bd. : Pediat. Pulmonology, Pediat. Annals, Pediat., Alumnews U. Va., 1988. Chmn. Richmond Bd. Health, 1961-63; bd. visitors U. Va., 1961-72; former mem. bd. dirs. Va. Hosp. Svc. Assn.; former ofcl. examiner Am. Bd. Pediatrics; mem. White House Conf. on Children and Youth, 1960; pres. alumni adv. com. U. Va. Sch. Medicine, Charlottesville, 1974-75; past bd. dirs. Maymont Found., Richmond; bd. dirs. Children's Hosp., 1985-97, Children's Hosp. Found., 1997—, Sheltering Arms Hosp.; former mem. adv. bd. Ctr. for Study of Mind and Human Interaction, U. Va. Sch. Medicine, 1988; mem. steering com. One Hundred Twenty Fifth Anniversary, Med. Coll. of VA Hosps., 1986; bd. dirs. St. Mary's Health Care Found., 1990. Recipient resolution of recognition Va. Health Commr., 1978, Obici award Louise Obici Hosp., 1979, Bon Secours award St. Mary's Hosp., 1986, Keating award Hampden-Sydney Coll., 1989, Disting. Citizen award Boy Scouts Am., R.E. Lee chpt., 1996, Disting. Svc. to Cmty. award Richmond Acad. Medicine, 1999, Patrick Henry award, Commonwealth of Va.; named an Outstanding Alumnus Sch. Medicine U. Va., 1986, Oustanding Alumnus, Med. Coll. Va., Va. Commonwealth U., 2001; The Edwin Lawrence Kendig Jr. Disting Professorship in Pediatric Pulmonary medicine named in honor Med. Coll. Va. Commonwealth U., also Edwin Lawrence Kendig Jr. Med. Edn. Rm. at St. Mary's Hosp., 1999. Mem.: AMA (pediat. residency rev. com., Disting. Svc. award 2000), Commonwealth, Raven, Soc. Cin., Med. Soc. Va. (editor Va. Med. Quarterly 1982—98, resolution of recognition), Internat. Pediat. Assn. (cons., standing com., medal 1986), So. Soc. Pediat. Rsch., So. Med. Assn., Am. Pediat. Soc., Va. Pediat. Soc. (past pres.), Richmond Acad. Medicine (pres. 1962, chmn. bd. trustees 1963), Va. Bd. Medicine (former pres.), Am. Acad. Pediat. for Latin Am. (ofcl. adv. to exec. bd. 1988), Am. Acad. Pediat. (mem. exec. bd. 1971—78, nat. pres. 1978—79, past pres. Va. sect., chmn. sect. on diseases of chest, cons. com. on internat. child health, Abraham Jacobi Meml. award with AMA 1987, Lifetime Achievement award Va. chpt. 1999, Edwin L. Kendig Jr. award pulmonary section named in his honor 2001), Farmington Club, Country Club of Va., Omicron Delta Kappa, Kappa Sigma, Tau Kappa Alpha, Alpha Omega Alpha, Phi Beta Kappa. Episcopalian. Home: Richmond, Va. Died Feb. 17, 2003.

KENDLER, TRACY SEEDMAN, psychology educator; b. N.Y.C., Aug. 4, 1918; d. Harry and Elizabeth (Goldfinger) Seedman; m. Howard Harvard Kendler, Sept. 20, 1941; children: Joel Harlan, Kenneth Seedman. BA, Bklyn. Coll., 1940; MA, U. Iowa, 1942, PhD, 1943. Statistician USAF, Washington, 1944-45; instr. U. Colo., Boulder, 1946-48; rsch. assoc. NYU, 1951-54; assoc. prof. Barnard Coll., Columbia U., N.Y.C., 1959-64; prof. U. Calif., Santa Barbara, 1965-89, prof. emeritus, from 1990. Vis. prof. Hebrew U., Jerusalem, Israel, 1974-75, Tel Aviv (Israel) U., 1990. Co-author: Basic Psychology, 1971; contbr. chpts. to books and articles to profl. jours. Rsch. grantee NSF, 1953-76, Pub. Health Svc., 1965-69; Guggenheim fellow, Jerusalem, 1974; Fulbright scholar, Tel Aviv, 1990. Democrat. Jewish. Home: Santa Barbara, Calif. Died July 28, 2001.

KENNA, BERNARD THOMAS, chemistry educator, environmentalist; b. Hays, Kans., Jan. 4, 1935; s. LeRoy Austin and Sara Elisabeth (Shoup) K.; m. Laura-Donna Ashley, June 4, 1960; children: Woodrow Austin, Randall Roy. BS, No. Ariz. U., 1956; MS, U. Miss., 1958; PhD, U. Ark., 1961. Mem. tech. staff Sandia Nat. Lab., Albuquerque, from 1961; lectr. Albuquerque Pub. Schs., 1965-84; prof. chemistry U. N.Mex., Albuquerque, 1966-70. Contbr. articles to profl. jours. Mem. Am. Chem. Soc., FAA (tech. cons.). Republican. Home: Albuquerque, N.Mex. Deceased.

KENNAMER, LORRIN GARFIELD, JR., retired university dean; b. Abilene, Tex., Dec. 20, 1924; s. Lorrin Garfield and Ruie Lee (Hart) K.; m. Laura Helen Durham, Dec. 22, 1948. AB, Eastern Ky. State Coll., 1947; MS, U. Tenn., 1949; PhD, Vanderbilt U./George Peabody Coll., 1952. Tchr. Oak Ridge High Sch., 1947-49; from instr. to asso. prof., chmn. dept. geography and geology East Tex. State Coll., Commerce, 1952-56; mem. faculty U. Tex., 1956-67, prof. geography, 1961-67, chmn. dept., 1961-67, assoc. dean arts and scis., 1961-67; dean arts and scis. Tex. Tech. U., 1967-70; dean U. Tex. Coll. Edn., Austin, 1970-87; prof. emeritus geography U. Tex., from 1998. Vis. summer prof. U. Vt., 1959, Mich. State U., 1961, U. Wash., 1967; Bd. examiners Tex. Edn. Agy., 1964-71; mem. com. exams. Coll. Entrance Exam. Bd., 1965-71, trustee, 1970—, vice-chmn., 1972-74, chmn., 1974-76; pres. Tex. Council Deans Edn., 1973 Author: (with Bowden, Hoffman) Geography Worktext Series, 4th edit., 1979, (with S. Arbingast) Atlas of Texas, rev. edit., 1976, (with W. Chambers) Texans and Their Land, 1964, (with James Reese) Texas-Land of Contrast, 1972, rev., 1978, (with James Reese) We Texans-Our History and Geography, 1987, (with Reese and Crawford) Texas Lone Star Land, 1993, Classroom Atlas of Texas, 1995; mem. editl. bd. Coll. Bd. Guide to 150 Popular Coll. Majors, 1992. Served to lt. (j.g.) USNR, World War II. Recipient Disting. Service award Nat. Council Geog. Edn., 1972, Ruth Knight Millikan Centennial Professorship, U. Tex., Austin, 1987. Hon. life fellow Tex. Acad. Sci.; mem. Nat. Council Geog. Edn. (exec. bd. 1958-65, sec. 1958-64, pres. 1967), Assn. Am. Geographers (exec. council 1962-64, 68-71), Am. Geog. Soc., Southwestern Social Sci. Assn. (pres. 1972-73), Sigma Xi, Omicron Delta Kappa, Pi Gamma Mu, Phi Delta Kappa, Phi Kappa Phi. Unitarian Universalist. Home: Austin, Tex. Died Dec. 23, 1999.

KENNEDY, HARRIET FORTE, museum administrator; b. Cambridge, Mass., 1939; d. Dalton H. and Ruby M. (Scott) Forte; divorced; children: Dana, Judith. Cert. in arts adminstrn., Harvard U., 1974; BA in Art History cum laude, Northeastern U., 1977. Asst. registrar Mus. Fine Arts, Boston, 1968-73; asst. dir., registrar Mus. Nat. Ctr. Afro-Am. Artists, Boston, from 1973, curator, from 1980. Prof. art history Mass. Coll. of Art, Boston, 1980-83, Northeastern U., Boston, 1979-80, Simmons Coll., Boston, 1989-90. Compiler art book: Bessie Smith, 1988, also various catalogues. Mem. Medford (Mass.) Fair Housing Commn., 1985—; mem. Medford Arts Coun., 1970's. Mem. Am. Assn. Mus./Internat. Coun. Mus. (mus. partnership 1983), Afro-Am. Mus. Assn. (past sec., past parliamentarian), Nat. Conf. Artists, Cambridge Art Assn. (past bd. dirs.). Avocation: reading. Home: Medford, Mass. Deceased.

KENNEDY, JAY RICHARD, screenwriter, author, consultant-educator; b. N.Y.C., July 22, 1911; s. Isidore and Erna (Eltes) Solomonick; m. Janet Alterman, May 22, 1943 (div. Nov. 1983); 1 child, Susan A. Kennedy Hile. BA, Antioch U. West, Los Angeles, 1973, MA in Clin. Psychology, 1975; LittD (hon.), Ithaca U., 1958. Mgr. Ritz Theater, N.Y.C., 1929; pres. J.R. Kennedy Mgmt. Corp., N.Y.C., 1943-46, Unique Specialities, N.Y.C., 1940-46; writer, dir. Kennedy Buchman Pictures, Inc., Los Angeles, 1945-48; pres. Kennedy Prodns., Inc., Los Angeles, 1945-54; freelance artistic and fin. cons. to various entertainers N.Y.C., 1948-75; pres. J.R. Kennedy Co., Inc., N.Y.C., 1950-61, Kennedy-Belafonte Prodns., Inc., N.Y.C., 1955-57, Shari Music Pubs., Inc., N.Y.C., 1955-57; cons., collaborator psychosomatic program Montefiore Hosp., N.Y.C., 1956-66; cons., collaborator Career Ladders Progam Gov. State N.Y., N.Y.C., 1964-68; sr. v.p. Sinatra Enterprises, Los Angeles, 1966-70; chmn. bd. Ctr. Human Problems, Inc., Tarzana, Calif., from 1970, exec. dir., sr. cons., clin. educator, from 1976, pres., from 1981. Author: Prince Bart, 1953, Short Term, 1959, Favor The Runner, 1965, The Chairman, 1969; (manuscripts) Jay Richard Kennedy Collection, Boston U. libraries; screenwriter of various movies including, To The Ends of The Earth, 1948, I'll Cry Tomorrow, 1955 (Acad. Award nomination for Best Screenplay 1956), The Chairman, 1972, musical drama, Sing Man Sing, 1956; writer radio shows Dime A Dance, 1943, Rubber Trumpet, 1943; producer, writer radio series The Man Called "X", 1945-54; exec. producer TV series Jean Arthur Show, 1967; creator, producer March on Washington TV spl., 1963. Pres. Ind. Printing Employees Union, N.Y.C., 1931-35; organizer, exec. dir., nat. bd. mem. Am. League Against War & Fascism, N.Y.C., 1932-38; organizer, exec. sec. Com. for Ethiopian Independence, N.Y.C., 1937-38; mem. resolution com. Nat. Assn. Mfrs., 1940-45; mem. Com. on Inter-Am. Affairs, N.Y.C., 1939-44; mem. mgmt. and labor com. Bretton Woods Conf.; mediator between White House and ten leaders of March On Washington, 1963; chmn. 1st Nat. Conf. Human Survival, Hershey, Pa., 1970; trustee Ithaca U., N.Y., 1954-61; advisor to various Pres. and Vice Pres. of the U.S. on Am. Blacks, Africans, Latin and South Am. countries, 1937-68. Recipient Disting. Svc. award Cath. Interracial Coun., Chgo., 1956, Disting. Svc. award Chgo. Conf. Brotherhood, 1956, co-recipient Calif. Civil Rights award United Civil Rights Coun. of L.A., 1966. Mem. ASCAP, Writers Guild of Am., Authors League, N.Y. Stock Exch. Democrat. Home: Newbury Park, Calif. Deceased.

KENNEDY, RAYMOND F. manufacturing executive; m. Mary Kennedy; 3 children. B in Bus. Mgmt., St. John's U.; postgrad., NYU. Pres. Delta and Peerless Faucet Cos., 1978-83; group pres. Masco Corp., 1983-88, pres. bldg. products, 1989-96, pres., COO, 1996—2003. Died Feb. 4, 2003.

KENNEDY, VANN M. broadcast executive; b. 1905; Grad., Southwest Tex. State U.; attended, U. Tex. Bur. chief Austin Internat. News Svc. and Universal Svc.; capital corr. San Antonio Light, Houston Chronicle, Beaumont Enterprise, Dallas Times Herald, others; founder, pres., gen. mgr. Sta. KZTV, Corpus Christi, Tex., Sta. KVTV, Laredo, Tex., Sta. KSIX-Radio, Corpus Christi. Atty.; mem. radio and TV affiliate bds. CBS; mem. com. Lyndon Baines Johnson Disting. Lectr. Series Southwest Tex. State U. Founder, pub. State Observer, South Austin Advocate, Tex. State House Reporter. Decorated Breat Order Yun Hui Republic of China, Battle Star; recipient Disting. Alumnus award Southwest Tex. State U.; Vann M. Kennedy Day proclaimed by Corpus Christi, 1976. Mem. Tex. Assnn. Broadcasters (past dir., named Pioneer Broadcaster 1973), Corpus Christi Rotary Club (past pres.), Corpus Christi C. of C. (past dir.); mem. Corpus Christi Area Devel. Com.; past mem. Nat. Fair Campaign Practices Com., Nat. Coun. USO, pub. rels. com.;

apptd. ad hoc coms.; served six state bds., commns.; Nueces County alternate Coastal Bend Coun. Govts.; Tex. presdl. elector-at-large, 1964; sec. 4 Dem. State Exec. Coms., atty.; sec. 10 Dem. State Convs.; del. 5 Dem. Nat. Convs.; rep. Tex. platform com. Dem. Nat. Conv., 1956, rules com., 1960. With U.S. Army, WWII, CBI, col. USAR. Died Apr. 18, 2004.

KENT, THEODORE CHARLES, psychologist; b. Oct. 13, 1912; m. Shirley Kent, June 7, 1948; children: Donald, Susan, Steven. BA, Yale U., 1935; MA, Columbia U., 1940, Mills Coll., 1953; PhD, U. So. Calif., 1951; DSc, Johannes Gutenberg U., Mainz, Germany, 1960. Diplomate in clin. psychology. Clin. psychologist, behavioral scientist USAF, 1951-65, chief psychologist, 1956-60; head dept. behavioral sci. U. So. Colo., Pueblo, 1965-78, emeritus, from 1978; staff psychologist Yuma Behavioral Health, Ariz., 1978-82, chief profl. svcs., 1982-83; dir. psychol. svcs. Rio Colorado Health Systems, Yuma, 1983-85; clin. psychologist, dir. mental health Ft. Yuma (Calif.) Indian Health Svc., USPHS, 1985-88; exec. dir. Human Sci. Ctr., San Diego, 1987-97. Author: Skills in Living Together, 1983, Conflict Resolution, 1986, A Psychologist Answers Your Questions, 1987, Behind the Therapists's Notes, 1993, Mapping the Human Genome--Reality, Morality and Deity, 1995, Poems for Living, 1995, Genetic Engineering, Yes, No or Maybe--A Look At What's Ahead, 2000, How to Rise Abovre Oneself Transend, 2002; author tests, including symbol arrangement test, 1952, internat. culture free non-verbal intelligence, 1957, self-other location chart, 1970, test of suffering, 1982; author plays and video Three Warriors Against Substance Abuse. Named Outstanding Prof., U. So. Colo., 1977. Fellow APA (disting. visitor undergrad. edn. program); mem. AAAS, Deutsche Gesellschaft für Antropologie, Internat. Assn. Study of Symbols (founder, 1st pres. 1957-61), Japanese Soc. Study KTSA (hon. pres.). Died Jan. 10, 2003.

KERLIN, GILBERT, lawyer; b. Camden, NJ, Oct. 10, 1909; s. Ward Dix Sr. and Jenny (Gilbert) K.; m. Sarah Morrison (dec. 2001), Aug. 23, 1941; children: Sarah Gund, Gilbert Nye, Jonathan Otis. BA, Harvard U., 1933, LLB, 1936. Bar: U.S. Ct. Appeals (2d cir.) 1937, U.S. Supreme Ct. 1945. Of counsel Shearman & Sterling, NYC, 1936—2004. Chmn. bd. dirs. Wave Hill Inc. Served to lt. col. USAF, 1942-46. Democrat. Unitarian. Home: Bronx, NY. Died Apr. 9, 2004.

KERMAN, SHEPPARD, writer, producer; b. Bklyn., Aug. 26, 1928; s. Louis and Leila (Benowitz) K.; m. Ilona Murai, Jan. 19, 1957; 1 child, Christina. BSS, CCNY, 1950. Actor in plays including Boss Tweed, indsl. and army tng. films; appeared in Broadway plays including All for Love, 1950-51, The Prescott Proposals, 1953, Tonight in Samarkand, 1954, The Great Sebastians, 1956, The Sound of Music, 1959-63; producer, dir. Mr. Simian, 1963-64; narrator television comms.; creator multi-media works for industry including speeches, motivational pieces, and musicals such as Seesaw, 1973, Beatlemania, 1977, Platinum, 1978; writer, producer Kenyon & Eckhardt Advt., N.Y.C., 1964-69; writer, producer Charisma Orgn., N.Y.C., 1969-71; creative dir. Stage Right, multi-media producers, N.Y.C., 1971-72; pres., creative dir. In-Perspective Communications, Inc., N.Y.C., 1973—, Affman-Sheral Internat., Inc., N.Y.C., 1988—; mem. faculty Parsons Sch. Design, 1982—, C.W. Post L.I. U., 1984—; author plays including: The Dark and the Day, 1952, Bilby's Doll, 1953, Cut of the Axe, 1960, Players on a Beach, 1961, Mr. Simian, 1963, The Tune of the Times, 1969, Nine Rebels, 1962, The Husband-in-Law, 1968, Distant Relations, 1978; author 1-act musicals including: Orgy on Park Avenue, Roast, Mamma, The Mood Synthesizer, Lady Collona, Funny Business, 1982; author scripts for television shows including: Danger, Matinee Theater, Studio One, Camera 3; lyricist for songwriters, Marvin Hamlisch, Lee Pockriss, John Strauss, Ralph Affoumado; mus. adaptor Picture of Dorian Gray, 1990. Recipient Best radio play for Jacob Rils WNYC student awards, 1946, best actor award as Everyman in Everyman, 1950, best actor award as Marc Antony in All for Love Show Bus., 1951, Obie award for Mr. Simian, 1964, Los Angeles Drama Critics Circle award for overall visual design concept in Beatlemania, 1978; Grand award as writer, creative dir. for Opportunity Unlimited, Internat. Film and TV Festival of N.Y., 1982. Mem. AFTRA, ASCAP, SAG, Dramatists Guild, Actors Equity Assn., Players Club. Died Apr. 15, 1991.

KERR, CLARK, academic administrator emeritus; b. Stony Creek, Pa., May 17, 1911; s. Samuel William and Caroline (Clark) K.; m. Catherine Spaulding, Dec. 25, 1934; children: Clark E., Alexander W., Caroline M. BA, Swarthmore Coll., 1932, LLD, 1952; MA, Stanford U., 1933; postgrad., London Sch. Econs., 1936, 39; PhD, U. Calif., 1939; LLD, Harvard U., 1958, Princeton U., 1959, others. Traveling fellow Am. Friends Svc. Com., 1935-36; instr. econs. Antioch Coll., 1936-37; tchg. fellow U. Calif., 1937-38; Newton Booth fellow, 1938-39; acting asst. prof. labor econs. Stanford, 1939-40; asst., later assoc. prof. U. Wash., 1940-45; assoc. prof., prof., prof. emeritus, dir. Inst. Indsl. Rels., U. Calif., Berkeley, 1945-52, chancellor, 1952-58, pres., 1958-67, pres. emeritus, 1974—2003. Chmn. Carnegie Commn. on Higher Edn., 1967-73, Carnegie Coun. Policy Studies in Higher Edn., 1974-79; vice chmn. divsns. War Labor Bd., 1943-45; nat. arbitrator Armour Co. and United Packing House Workers, 1945-52; impartial chmn. Waterfront Employers, Pacific Coast and Internat. Longshoremen's and Warehousemen's Union, 1946-47; pub. mem. Nat. WSB, 1950-51; various arbitrations in pub. utilities, newspaper, aircraft, canning, oil, local transport and other industries, 1942—; mem. adv. panel Soc. Sci. Rsch., NSF, 1953-57; chmn. Armour Automation Com., 1959-79; chmn. bd. arbitrators U.S. Postal Svc. and Nat. Assn. Letter Carriers (AFL-CIO) and Am. Postal Workers Union (AFL-CIO), 1984 Author: (with E. Wight Bakke) Unions, Management and the Public, rev. edit., 1960, 67, (with Dunlop, Harbison, Myers) Industrialism and Industrial Man, rev. edit., 1964, 73, The Uses of the University, rev. edit., 1972, 82, 95, 2001, Labor and Management in Industrial Society, 1964, Marshall, Marx and Modern Times, 1969, Labor Markets and Wage Determination: The Balkanization of Labor Markets and Other Essays, 1977, Education and National Development: Reflections from an American Perspective during a Period of Global Reassessment, 1979, The Future of Industrial Societies, 1983, (with Marian L. Gade) The Many Lives of Academic Presidents, 1986; editor: (with Paul D. Staudohar) Industrial Relations in a New Age, 1986, Economics of Labor in Industrial Society, 1986, (with Dunlop, Lester, Reynolds; editor Bruce E. Kaufman) How Labor Markets Work: Reflections on Theory and Practice, 1988, (with Marian L. Gade) The Guardians: Boards of Trustees of American Colleges and Universities, 1989, The Great Transformation in Higher Education, 1960-80, 1991, Troubled Times for American Higher Education: The 1990s and Beyond, 1994, Higher Education Cannot Escape History: Issues for the Twenty-First Century, 1994, (with Paul D. Staudohar) Labor Economics and Industrial Relations: Markets and Institutions, 1994, The Gold and the Blue, Vol. 1: Academic Triumphs, 2001. Vol. II Pol. Turmoil, 2003. Trustee Rockefeller Found., 1960-76; mem. bd. mgrs. Swarthmore Coll., 1969-80, life mem., 1981. Recipient Harold W. McGraw Jr. prize in Edn., 1990; named Hon. fellow London Sch. Econs. Mem. Am. Econ. Assn., Royal Econ. Assn., Am. Acad. Arts and Scis., Indsl. Rels. Rsch. Assn., Nat. Acad. Arbitrators, Phi Beta Kappa, Kappa Sigma. Mem. Soc. Of Friends. Home: El Cerrito, Calif. Died Dec. 1, 2003.

KERR, JAMES LEE, III, radiology adminstrator; b. Corpus Christi, Tex., May 27, 1946; s. James Lee and Lois Ann (Wilkinson) K.; m. Bobbie Sue Trentham, Aug. 14, 1971; children: James Robert, Joshua, Jennifer, Nicole, Jana, Jamie, Jesse, John, Joy. BS, American U., 1971. Enlisted USN, 1966, advanced through grades to lt., 1978; retired, 1983; dir. radiology Parkland Meml. Hosp., Dallas, from 1985. Editor mag. Over The Front, 1986; contbr. hist. articles to mags. Cubmaster Boy Scouts Am., Portsmouth, Va., 1981-82. Mem. Am. Hosp. Radiology Adminstrs., League of World War I Aviation Historians (sec.-treas. Dallas 1985—). Avocations: piano, computers, historical research. Home: Mc Kinney, Tex. Deceased.

KESSEL, BARNEY, guitarist; b. Muskogee, Okla., 1923; Ind. jazz guitarist, rec. artist, from 1945. Performed, recorded with Charlie Parker, Lester Young, also played with Ray Brown, Shelly Manne, Oscar Peterson; albums include (with Charlie Parker) Charlie Parker on Dial, Vol. Three, (with Lester Young) Jammin' With Lester, (solo albums) The Pollwinners, Pollwinners Three, Summertime in Montreux, Swinging Easy, Slow Burn, (with Oscar Peterson) Oscar Peterson in Concert. Died May 6, 2004.

KESSLER, WILLIAM HENRY, architect; b. Reading, Pa., Dec. 15, 1924; s. Frederick H. and Lucia W. (Kline) K.; m. Margot Walbrecker, May 11, 1946; children: Tamara Kessler Checkley, Chevonne Kessler Patten. BA in Architecture, Inst. Design, Chgo., 1948; MArch, Harvard U., 1951. Chief designer Yamasaki, Leinweber & Hellmuth, Detroit, 1951-55; prin. Kessler, Francis & Cardoza (formerly William Kessler and Assocs., Inc.), Detroit, 1955—. Adj. prof. U. Mich Coll. Architecture. Prin. works include Ctr. Creative Studies, Detroit, Harvard U. Sch. Pub. Health, Boston, Indsl. Tech. Inst., Ann Arbor, Mich., State of Mich. Libr. Mus. and Archives, Detroit Sci. Ctr., New Detroit Gen. Hosp.-Wayne State U. Health Care Inst., Detroit. Councilman, Grosse Pointe Park, Mich., 1966-67. Served with USAAF, 1943-46. Recipient over 130 archtl. design awards Fellow AIA (Gold medal Detroit chpt. 1974), Mich. Soc. Archs. (Gold medal 1976). Home: Grosse Pointe, Mich. Died Nov. 16, 2002.

KESTIN, NINA REBECCA, law educator; b. N.Y.C., Nov. 24, 1947; d. Krass and Estelle (Greenberg) Kestin; m. Eugene Paul Murphy, Sept. 3, 1967 (div. June 1978); children: Sarabeth Kestin, Sean Joseph. Student, U. Mass., 1965-67; BA, Hunter Coll., 1969; JD, NYU, 1972, LLM, 1976. Bar: N.Y. 1973, U.S. Ct. Appeals (2d cir.) 1977, Va. 1981. Assoc. Mead & Callan, Bay Shore, N.Y., 1972-74; sole practice Levittown, N.Y., 1974-76; prof. law U. of Richmond, Va., from 1976. Mem. Richmond (Va.) First Club, 1986—; bd. dirs. Congregation Beth Ahabeth, Richmond, 1986—. Mem. ABA (tax sect., Outstanding Woman Atty. 1986), Va. Bar Assn. (tax sect., Outstanding Woman Atty. 1986). Clubs: Warsaw Women (Richmond, Va.). B'nai B'rith (adv. bd. Anti-Defamation League 1985—). Democrat. Home: Richmond, Va. Deceased.

KETCHUM, MILO SMITH, civil engineer; b. Denver, Mar. 8, 1910; s. Milo Smith and Esther (Beatty) K.; m. Gretchen Allenbach, Feb. 28, 1944 (dec. Dec. 21, 1990); children: David Milo, Marcia Anne, Matthew Phillip, Mark Allen. BS, U. Ill., 1931, MS, 1932; D.Sc. (hon.), U. Colo., 1976. Asst. prof. Case Sch. Applied Sci., Cleve., 1937-44; engr. F.G. Browne, Marion, Ohio, 1944-45; owner, operator Milo S. Ketchum, Cons. Engrs., Denver, 1945-52; partner, prin. Ketchum, Konkel, Barrett, Nickel & Austin, Cons. Engrs. and predecessor firm, Denver, 1952—; prof. civil engring. U. Conn., Storrs, 1967-78, emeritus, 1978—. Mem. Progressive Architecture Design Awards Jury, 1958, Am. Inst. Steel Constrn. Design Awards Jury, 1975, James F. Lincoln Arc Welding Found. Design Awards Jury, 1977; Stanton Walker lectr. U. Md., 1966 Author: Handbook of Standard Structural Details for Buildings, 1956; editor-in-chief Structural Engineering Practice, 1981-84; contbr. engring. articles to tech. mags. and jours. Recipient Disting. Alumnus award U. Ill., 1979 Mem. Am. Concrete Inst. (hon., bd. dirs., Turner medal 1966), ASCE (hon., pres. Colo. sect.), Am. Cons. Engrs. Coun., Nat. Acad. Engring., Am. Engring. Edn., Structural Engrs. Assn. Colo. (pres.), Cons. Engrs. Coun. Colo. (pres.), Sigma Xi, Tau Beta Ph, Chi Epsilon, Phi Kappa Phi, Alpha Delta Phi. Home: Denver, Colo. Died Dec. 8, 1999.

KEY, MARY RITCHIE (MRS. AUDLEY E. PATTON), linguist, writer, educator; b. San Diego, Mar. 19, 1924; d. George Lawrence and Iris (Lyons) Ritchie; children: Mary Helen Key Ellis, Harold Hayden Key (dec.), Thomas George Key. Student, U. Chgo., summer 1954, U. Mich., 1959; MA, U. Tex., 1960, PhD, 1963; postgrad., UCLA, 1966. Asst. prof. linguistics Chapman Coll., Orange, Calif., 1963-66; asst. prof. linguistics U. Calif., Irvine, 1966-71, assoc. prof., 1971-78, prof., 1978—, chmn. program linguistics, 1969-71, 75-77 and from 87. Cons. Am. Indian langs., Spanish, in Mexico, 1946-55, S.Am., 1955-62, English dialects, 1968-74, Easter Island, 1975, Calif. Dept. Edn., 1966, 70-75, Center Applied Linguistics, Washington, 1967, 69; lectr. in field. Author: Comparative Tacanan Phonology, 1968, Male/Female Language, 1975, 2d edit., 1996, Paralanguage and Kinesics, 1975, Nonverbal Communication, 1977, The Grouping of South American Indian Languages, 1979, The Relationship of Verbal and Nonverbal Communication, 1980, Catherine the Great's Linguistic Contribution, 1980, Polynesian and American Linguistic Connections, 1984, Comparative Linguistics of South American Indian Languages, 1987, General and Amerindian Ethnolinguistics, 1989, Language Change in South American Indian Languages, 1991; founder, editor: newsletter Nonverbal Components of Communication, 1972-76; mem. editoral bd. Forum Linguisticum, 1976—, Lang. Scis., 1978—, La Linguistique, 1979—, Multilingua, 1987—; contbr. articles to profl. jours. Recipient Friends of Libr. Book award, 1976, hon. mention, Rolex awards for Enterprise, project Computerizing the Languages of the World, 1990; U. Calif. Regent's grantee, 1974, Fulbright-Hays grantee, 1975; faculty rsch. fellow, 1984-85. Mem. Linguistic Soc. Am., Am. Dialect Soc. (exec. council; regional sec. 1974-83), Internat. Reading Assn. (dir. 1968-72), Delta Kappa Gamma (local pres. 1974-76). Died Sept. 5, 2003.

KHALDIEH, SALIM A. foreign language educator, consultant, researcher; b. Al-Marj, Bekaa, Lebanon, May 20, 1956; came to U.S., 1985; s. Ahmad A. and Fatima S. (Shaaban) K. MA, Ohio State U., 1987, PhD, 1990. ESL instr. Columbus (Ohio) C.C., 1989-91; lectr. Ohio State U., Columbus, 1990-91; asst. prof. U. Mich., Ann Arbor, from 1991. Lang. and culture cons., 1990—. Home: Ann Arbor, Mich. Died Apr. 10, 2001.

KIBRICK, SIDNEY, retired pediatrics and microbiology educator, virology educator, consultant; b. Boston; s. Joseph and Bessie (Eisenberg) K.; m. Anne Karlon, June 16, 1949; children: Joan Kibrick Amsler, John. AB, Harvard U., 1938; PhD, MIT, 1943; MD, Boston U., 1946. Diplomate Am. Bd. Pediatrics. Intern medicine U. Hosp., Boston, 1946-47; jr. asst. resident in medicine The Children's Hosp. Med. Ctr., Boston, 1950-52; assoc. physician dept. infectious diseases Children's Hosp. Med. Ctr., Boston, 1952-61; tchg. fellow, instr. bacteriology MIT, Cambridge, 1940-42; prof. pediatrics and microbiology Boston U. Sch. Medicine, 1961-81, prof. emeritus, from 1981. Asst. clin. prof. pediatrics Harvard Med. Sch., Boston, 1952-61; chief sect. virology Univ. Hosp.-Boston U. Med. Ctr., 1961-72; cons. polio vaccine field trials Nat. Found. for Infantile Paralysis, 1953-55; cons. on viral and infectious diseases Mass. Health Dept., VA hosps., Chelsea Naval Hosp., also others, 1961-77; mem. rsch. com. Med. Found., Boston, 1972-77; med. cons. disability program Social Security Adminstrn., HHS, 1981-2000; lectr. microbiology Boston U. Sch. Medicine, 1981-2000. Contbr. over 150 articles on viruses and viral diseases to med. jours., chpts. to books. Capt. M.C., U.S. Army, 1947-49. Recipient Disting. Alumni award Alumni Assn. Boston U. Sch. Medicine, 1991. Mem. Soc. for Pediatric Rsch., Infectious Diseases Soc. Am., Am. Soc. Microbiology, Am. Pediatric Soc., Am. Soc. for Virology, Nat. Found. for Infectious Diseases. Home: Auburndale, Mass. Deceased.

KIDDOO, RICHARD CLYDE, retired oil company executive; b. Wilmington, Del., Aug. 31, 1927; s. William Richard and Nellie Louise (Bounds) K.; m. Catherine Schumann, June 25, 1950; children: Jean L., William R., Scott F., David B. BSChemE, U. Del., 1948. With Esso Standard Oil and Esso Internat. Inc., Md., N.J., N.Y., 1948-66; internat. sales mgr. Esso Europe Inc., London, 1966-67; mng. dir., chief exec. officer Esso Pappas Indsl. Co., Athens, Greece, 1967-71; pres. Esso Africa Inc., London, 1971-72; v.p. Esso Europe Inc., London, 1973-81; v.p. mktg. Exxon Co., U.S.A., Houston, 1981-83; pres. Exxon Coal Internat., Coral Gables, Fla., 1983-86, ret. Vice chmn. mktg. com. Am. Petroleum, Washington, 1983. With USMC, 1945-46. Decorated Cross of King George I of Greece; recipient medal of distinction U. Del. Mem. AICE, Am. Petroleum Inst., Gibson Island Club, Circumnavigators Club. Home: Naples, Fla. Died Dec. 10, 1999.

KILEY, DANIEL URBAN, landscape architect, planner; b. Boston, Sept. 2, 1912; s. Louis James and Louise (Baxter) Kiley; m. Anne Lothrop Sturges, June 11, 1942; children:

Kathleen, Kor, Christopher, Antonia, Timothy, Christina, Aaron Alcott, Caleb. Student, Harvard Grad. Sch. Design, 1936—38; LHD (hon.), Green Mountain Coll., 1993. From apprentice to assoc. Warren Manning (landscape design and regional planning), Cambridge, Mass., 1932—38; planning technician Concord (N.H.) City Plan Bd., 1938; arch. Nat. Pk. Svc., 1939, U.S. Housing Authority, 1940; assoc. Town Planning, Washington, 1940; pvt. practice as landscape architect, site planner, architect, 1940—2004. Lectr., critic Balt. Mus., 1949, Worcester (Mass.) Mus., 1950, La. State U., 1950, Cornell U., 1957, Met. Mus., 1959, N.C. State Coll., 1958, Rensselaer Poly. Inst., 1960, Harvard U., 1962—63, Clemson Coll., 1963, also univs. Ill., Minn., Pa. Syracuse, Va., Wash., Tokyo, Kyoto, Hiroshima, Fukuoka, Yale U., U. Calif. Berkeley, U. Utah, Salt Lake City, Harvard U., Archtl. Assn. London, Dallas Inst. Forum, Beijing, China, Nanking (Shanghai, Hangchow, also Osaka U. Japan), Lawrence Tech. U., Detroit, Royal Inst. Architects, London; landscape arch. in residence Am. Acad. in Rome, 1975—76, mem. jury, 1990; Graham Found. lectr., Chgo., 76; mem. design rev. panel Redevel. Land Agy., Washington; participant Symposium on Dan Kiley, 1980; keynote spkr. Am. Soc. Landscape Archs. Fla. chpt.; lectr. U. Va., 1985, NAD, 1990, U. Fla., 1991, symposium N.Y. Botanical Garden, 1991. Author: The Early Gardens, 1999, articles; prin. works include Collier Residence, Falls Ch.urch, Va., 1940, Nuremburg Courtroom, Nuremburg, Germany, 1945, Jefferson Meml. Arch, St. Louis, 1947, Kitimat, B.C., Can. new city, 1951, USAF Acad., Colorado Springs, Colo., 1955, The Miller House, Columbus, Ind., 1955, Rockefeller Inst., N.Y., 1956, Irwin Miller residence, Columbus, Ind., 1956, Union Carbide and Carbon, Westchester, N.Y., 1957, Reynolds Metals Co., Richmond, Va., 1958, Independence Mall, 3d block, Phila, 1959—60, U. Minn., Mpls., 1960, Lincoln Ctr., N.Y.C., 1960, Yale U., 1961, Dulles Internat Airport, Washington, 1961—63, Nat. Acad. Sci., 1961, Cummins Engine Plant, Columbus, Ind., 1962, Chrysler-Cummins Plant, Darlington, Eng., Burr-McManus Plz., Hartford, Conn., 1962, Rochester Inst. Tech., 1962, Oakland (Calif.) Mus., 1962, The Chgo. Filtration Plant, 1962, Nat. Ctr. Atmospheric Rsch., Boulder, Colo., 1963, Fredonia (N.Y.) State Coll., 1963, Potsdam (N.Y.) State Coll., U. Lagos, Nigeria, Ctrl. Filtration Plant, Chgo., Chgo. Art Inst., 1963, Independence Mall, 3d block, Phila., 1963, Dulles Internat. Airport, Chantilly, Va., 1963, Ford Found. Bldg., N.Y.C., 1964, The North Christian Ch., 1964, Irwin Union Bank and Trust Co., 1968, Washington Mall and Tidal Basin, 1968, The Oakland Mus., 1969, Ford Found. Office Bldg., N.Y.C., 1969, 10th St. Overlook, Washington, 1970, Ft. Lawton Pk., Seattle, 1972, La. Defense, Paris, 1972, Victorian Garden, Smithsonian Instn., 1976, N.Y. Bot. Garden master plan, 1973, Ind. Bell Tel., 1974, East Wing Nat. Gallery Art, Washington, 1976, interior ct., Yale Ctr. Brit. Art, 1977, Coca Cola World Hdqs. master plan, Atlanta, 1977, Woodruff Pk., 1977, Cary Arbotetum, Millbrook, N.Y., 1977, N.Y. Bot. Gardens, Bronx, 1978, campus plan, Gallaudet Coll. for Deaf, Washington, J.F. Kennedy Libr., Boston, 1978, Cummins Brussels, Belgium, 1978, Belle Isle Pk., Detroit, 1978, Detroit Art Inst., 1979, Dallas Art Mus., 1980, London Std. Chartered Bank, 1980, San Antonio Art Mus., 1981, Brit. Rys., London, 1981, Bank of Korea, Seoul, 1981, Silicon Valley Fin. Ctr., 1984, N.C. Nat. Bank, Tampa, Fla., 1987, Joslyn Art Mus., Omaha, 1985, U.S. Embassy, Amman, Jordan, 1985, Vanderbilt U. Campus, 1985, Lake Shore Pk., Chgo., 1985—86, St. John's Coll., 1986, Fountain Pl., Dallas, 1986—87, Carnegie Ctr. Charlotte, N.C., 1987, Nelson-Atkins Mus., 1987, Henry Moore Sculpture Pk., 1988, Nat. Sculpture Garden on the Mall, Washington, 1989, A G Group Hdqs., Brussels, 1989, Buck Ctr. for Rsch. on Aging, Novato, Calif., 1989, UMB-Warner, LA, 1989, Washington Internat. U., Va., 1989, Getty Mus., LA, 1989, St. Louis Art Mus., from 1989, Guam Legis. Bldgs., Agana, from 1990, Norman Lear, Brentwood, Calif., 1990, Bailey Plz., Cornell U., 1990, Riverside Pk., Corning, N.Y., 1990, Superblock Master Plan, LA, 1990, Westmount Pub. Libr., Montreal, 1991, Navy Pier, Chgo., from 1991, Twin Farms Inn, Barnard, Vt., from 1991, Pierpont Morgan Libr., N.Y.C., from 1992, U. Ottawa, Can., from 1992, Ct. of Human Rights, Strasbourg, France, 1992, Lehr Res., Miami, 1993, Mashantucket Pequot Mus., Conn., 1993, Kimmel Res., Salisbury, Conn., 1993, Buck Ctr., Novato, Calif., 1993, Lloyd's Register of Shipping Hdqs., Sussex, Eng., from 1993, West Palm Beach Pks., Fla., from 1993, London Archtl. Edn. Econ. Galleries, 1994, Kusko Res., Williamstown, Mass., 1995, numerous others, joint exhbn., USA/USSR, 1990. Mem. BiState Planning Commn. Lake Champlain Basin Region, 1959—63; mem. Pres.'s Adv. Coun. Planning Pennsylvania Ave., Washington, 1962—65, Vt. Bd. Archs. Registration, 1963; jury S.W. Redevel. Area, Washington, Boston Redevel. Authority, 1963, Nat. Honor Awards, Urban Redevel. Authoirity, also FHA, Washington, 1964; design adv. group Cambridge (Mass.) Redevel. Bd., 1978; mem. tech. rev. com. on state use plan State of Vt., 1975. Capt. U.S. Army, World War II. Decorated Legion of Merit; co-recipient 1st prize Jefferson Nat. Expansion Meml. Competition, 1947; named Thomas Jefferson prof. landscape architecture, U. Va., 1988, Daniel Urban Kiley lectr., Harvard U. Grad. Sch. Design, 1983; recipient 1st prize, U. N.H. Student Union Bldg. Competition, 1951, AIA honor award, Concordia State Coll., Ft. Wayne, Ind., 1960, Stiles and Morse Colls., Yale U., 1963, Dulles Airport, Washington, 1963, Ind. Bell Tel. Co., Columbus, hon. mention, Chgo. Tribune Better Homes for Family Living, 1947, award of merit, House and Home mag., 1957, 1st prize, Progressive Architecture mag., 1961, award of merit, Am. Soc. Landscape Archs., 1962, Gold medal, Phila. chpt. AIA, Gov.'s Design award, State of Calif., 1966, Bard award, N.Y.C. Lincoln Ctr. North Ct., 1967, N.Y.C. Ford Found. Ct., 1968, Allied Profession medal, AIA, 1971, Archs. Collaborative award, 1972, Thomas Jefferson medal, 1988, Creative Arts Citation, Brandeis U., 1990, Urban Design award, Dallas, 1989, Dallas Urban Design award, Fountain Pl., 1990, Chgo Archtl. award, Ill. AIA, 1991, Gov.'s award for Excellence in the Arts, Vt. Coun. on the Arts, 1991, Kansas City Urban Design award Excellence, Nelson-Atkins Mus. Art., Henry Moore Sculpture Garden, 1991, Merit award, ASLA, 1991, Excellence on the Waterfront award, NCNB Plz., 1992, Outstanding Lifetime Achievement award, Alumni Coun. Harvard Grad. Sch. Design, 1992, 25 Yr. award Ford Found. Bldg., Am. Inst. Archs., 1995, Arnold W. Brunner prize in Architecture, Am. Acad. Arts and Letters, 1995, Nat. Medal of Arts, President Bill Clinton, 1997, Celebration of Yr. of the Landscape, Am. Acad. Rome, 1990; fellow Disting. Designer, NEA, 1988. Mem.: NAD. Died Feb. 21, 2004.

KILGORE, EUGENE STERLING, JR., former surgeon; b. San Francisco, Feb. 3, 1920; s. Eugene Sterling and Mary (Kirkpatrick) K.; m. Marilynn Wines; children: Eugene Sterling, Marilynn Ann. BS, U. Calif., Berkeley, 1941; MD, U. Calif., San Francisco, 1949. Intern in medicine Harvard service Boston City Hosp., 1949-50; intern in surgery Roosevelt Hosp., N.Y.C., 1950-51, resident gen. surgery, reconstructive hand surgery, 1951-55; practice medicine specializing in reconstructive hand surgery San Francisco, 1955—; asso. clin. prof. surgery U. Calif.-San Francisco, 1955-75, clin. prof., 1975-91, prof. emeritus, from 1991; chief hand surgery dept. surgery U. Calif. Hosp., also San Francisco Gen. Hosp., 1965-91; chief hand service Ft. Miley Vets. Hosp., San Francisco, 1965-91, Martinez (Calif.) Vets. Hosp., 1970-91, Livermore (Calif.) Vets. Hosp., 1965-70; chief hand service plastic surgery tng. service St. Francis Meml. Hosp., 1965-91, chief of surgery, 1979—, chief surgery emeritus, 1984-99; ret., 1999. Cons. hand surgery numerous pvt. hosps., San Francisco, 1955— Author numerous publs. in field. Served to lt. col., inf. AUS, 1941-45. Decorated Bronze Star; recipient Gold Headed Cane, AOA medal; Kaiser award for excellence in teaching U. Calif.-San Francisco Sch. Medicine, 1976, Charlotte Baer Meml. Clin. Faculty award U. Calif., 1993, Alumnus of Yr. award U. Calif. Med. Sch., 1998. Mem. AMA, ACS, Am. Assn. Surgery of Trauma, Am. Trauma Soc., Am. Soc. Surgery of Hand, Carribean Hand Soc., San Francisco Surg. Soc. (pres. 1979-80), Pacific Coast Surg. Assn., City Club. Clubs: Rotary; Bohemian (San Francisco). Home: Belvedere Tiburon, Calif. Died Apr. 6, 2003.

KILLEFFER, ROBERT AYRES, advertising executive; b. N.Y., May 11, 1926; s. David Herbert Quintard and Dorothy Mary (Savage) K.; m. Josephine Biglow MacMillan, June 25, 1949 (div. 1977); children: Robert Ayres Jr., Louis MacMillan, Josephine Ahara; m. Eloise Haines Prescott, Jan. 28, 1978. BS in Chemistry, U. N.C., 1949. Cert. bus. communicator. Chemist R&D Am. Cyanamid Co., Stamford, Conn., 1949-53, advt. mgr. N.Y.C., 1953-55, McKesson & Robbins, Inc., N.Y.C., 1955-56; gen. promotion mgr. Union Carbide Corp., Danbury, Conn., N.Y.C., 1956-83; gen. mgr. pub. rels., advt. Trans-Lux Corp., Norwalk, Conn., 1983-84; gen. mgr. Mktg. Communications, New Canaan, Conn., from 1984. Contbr. Careers and Opportunities in Advt., 1964. With U.S. Army, 1944-46. Mem. Am. Chem. Soc., Bus. Profl. Advt. Assn., The Chemists' Club. Republican. Avocations: model railroading, coin collecting/numismatics, sailing, firearms. Died Oct. 11, 2000.

KIMERER, NEIL BANARD, SR., retired psychiatrist, educator; b. Wauseon, Ohio, Jan. 13, 1918; s. William and Ruby (Upp) K.; m. Ellen Jane Scott, May 22, 1943; children: Susan Leigh, Neil Banard, Brian Scott, Sandra Lynn. BS, U. Toledo, 1941; MD, U. Chgo., 1944; postgrad. (fellow), Menninger Sch., 1947-50. Diplomate Am. Bd. Psychiatry and Neurology. Intern Emanuel Hosp., Portland, Oreg., 1944; resident psychiatry Winter VA Hosp., Topeka, 1947-50; asst. physician Central State Hosp., Norman, Okla., 1950, cons., 1955-98; chief out-patient psychiat. clinic U. Okla. Sch. Medicine, Oklahoma City, 1951-53, instr. dept. psychiatry, neurology and behavioral scis., 1953-61, assoc. prof., 1961-69, clin. prof., 1969-85, clin. prof. emeritus, 1985-98; practice medicine specializing in psychiatry Oklahoma City, 1953-98; med. dir. Oklahoma City Mental Health Clinic, 1953-68; chmn. dept. psychiatry Bapt. Med. Ctr. Okla., 1979-83; ret., 1998. Author: To Get and Beget, 1971, revised, 1996, Independence Means Swim or Sink, 1995; contbr. articles in field to profl. jours. Mem. exec. com. Okla. Family Life Assn., 1958-60; bd. dirs. Oklahoma City Jr. Symphony Soc., 1959. Served as pfc ASTP, 1943-44; to capt. M.C. AUS, 1945-47. Fellow Am. Psychiat. Assn. (life); mem. AMA (life), Okla. Med. Assn., Oklahoma County Med. Soc., Oklahoma City Clin. Soc., AAAS, Alpha Kappa Kappa (pres. Nu chpt. 1943) Lodges: Rotary. Home: Oklahoma City, Okla. Died Mar. 21, 2003.

KINDLE, CECIL HALDANE, geologist, educator, b. Elmira, N.Y., Oct. 16, 1904; s. Edward Marten and Margaret Frances (Ferris) K.; m. Mary Ethel Smyers, Jan. 26, 1941; children: Mary Ann, Elizabeth, Cecil, Millicent. BA, Queen's U., Kingston, Ont., 1926; PhD, Princeton U., 1931. Biology instr. Queen's U., 1926-27; with geol. mapping Geol. Survey of Can., Gaspé, Que., 1928-30 summers; instr. CCNY, N.Y.C., 1931-71, prof., 1971-75, ret. With geol. mapping Nfld. Geol. Survey, West Coast, 1938-39, 45 summers, John Fox Oil Enterprise, West Coast, 1952 summer. Author publs. on Cow Head Groups Western Nfld. Rsch. grantee Geol. Soc. Am., 1955, NSF, 1958. Fellow Geol. Soc. Am., Geol. Assn. Can.; mem. Paleontol. Soc., Empire State Soc. SAR (treas. 1979-83). Republican. Home: Nyack, NY. Died Mar. 10, 2001.

KINDLEBERGER, CHARLES P., II, economist, educator; b. N.Y.C., Oct. 12, 1910; s. E. Crosby and Elizabeth Randall (McIlvaine) K.; m. Sarah Bache Miles(dec. 1997), May 1, 1937; children: Charles P., Richard S., Sarah, E. Randall. AB, U. Pa., 1932, DS (hon.), 1984; AM, Columbia U., 1934, PhD, 1937; Dr. h.c., U. Paris, 1966, U. Ghent, 1975, U. Pa., 1984; Dr. rer.pol. h.c., U. Basle, 1997. Research in internat. trade and fin. Fed. Res. Bank N.Y., 1936-39, Bank Internat. Settlements, 1939-40, Bd. Govs. FRS, 1940-42; Am. sec. Joint Econ. Com. U.S. and Can., 1941-42; served with OSS, Washington, U.K., 1942-44, 45; G-2 12th Army Group, France, 1943-45; chief divsn. German and Austrian Econ. Affairs, Dept. State, Washington, 1945-48; assoc. prof. econs. MIT, 1948-51, prof., 1951-76, prof. emeritus, 1976—2003, chmn. faculty, 1965-67; vis. prof. econs. Brandeis U., 1983-87. Cons. fellow Brit. Acad. Author: International Short-Term Capital Movements, 1937, The Dollar Shortage, 1950, International Economics, 1953, rev. edits., 1973, 78, The Terms of Trade, 1956, Economics Development, 1958, rev. edits., 1965, 77, Foreign Trade and the National Economy, 1962, Economic Growth of France and Britain, 1851-1950, 1964, Europe and the Dollar, 1966, Postwar European Growth, 1967, American Business Abroad, 1969, Power and Money, 1970; editor: The International Corporation, 1970, The World in Depression, 1929-39, 1973, rev. edit., 1986, Economic Response, 1978, Manias, Panics and Crashes, 1978, 4th edit., 2000, International Money, 1981, A Financial History of Western Europe, 1984, rev. edit., 1993, Multinational Excursions, 1984, Keynesianism vs Monetarism, 1985, Marshall Plan Days, 1987, International Capital Movements, 1987, International Economic Order, 1988, The German Economy, 1945-47: Charles P. Kindleberger's Letters from the Field, 1989, Economic Laws and Economy History, 1989, Historical Economics, Art or Science?, 1990, The Life of an Economist: An Autobiography, 1991, Mariners and Markets, 1992, The World Economy and National Finance in Historical Perspective, 1995, World Economic Primacy, 1500-1990, 1996, Centralization vs. Pluralism, 1996, Essays in History, Financial, Economic, Personal, 1999, Comparative Political Economy: A Retrospective, 2000. Intelligence officer 12th Army Group, 1944-45; disch. rank of maj., Gen. Staff Corps. Decorated Legion of Merit, Bronze Star; recipient Harms prize Institut für Weltwirtschaft, Kiel, 1978 Fellow Am. Econ. Assn. (disting., v.p. 1966, pres. 1985), Brit. Acad. (corr.); mem. Am. Acad. Arts and Scis., Am. Philos. Soc., Phi Beta Kappa, Delta Psi. Episcopalian. Home: Cambridge, Mass. Died July 7, 2003.

KINDNESS, THOMAS NORMAN, former congressman, lawyer, consultant; b. Knoxville, Tenn., Aug. 26, 1929; s. Norman Garden and Christine (Gunn) K.; m. Averil J. Stoneback, Jan. 7, 1984; children by previous marriage: Sharon L., David T., Glen J., Adam B. AB, U. Md., 1951; LLB, George Washington U., 1953. Bar: D.C. 1954. Ret.; practiced in Washington, 1954-57; asst. counsel legal dept. Champion Internat. Corp., Hamilton, Ohio, 1957-73; mayor Hamilton, 1964-67; mem. city council, 1968-69; mem. Ohio Ho. of Reps. from 58th Dist., 1971-74, 94th-99th Congresses from 8th Ohio Dist., 1975—87; pvt. practice law, govtl. affairs cons. Washington. Died Jan. 8, 2004.

KINDRICK, ROBERT LEROY, academic administrator, dean, English educator; b. Kansas City, Mo., Aug. 17, 1942; s. Robert William and Waneta LeVeta (Lobdell) K.; m. Carolyn Jean Reed, Aug. 20 1965. BA, Park Coll., 1964; MA, U. Mo., Kansas City, 1967; PhD, U. Tex., 1971. Instr. Ctrl. Mo. State U., Warrenburg, 1967-69, asst. prof. to assoc. prof., 1969-78, prof., 1978-80, head dept. English, 1975-80; dean Coll. Arts and Scis.; prof. English Western Ill. U., Macomb, 1980-84; v.p. acad. affairs, prof. English Emporia State U., Kans., 1984-87; provost, v.p. acad. affairs, prof. English Eastern Ill. U., Charleston, 1987-91; provost, v.p. acad. affairs, dean grad. studies, dean grad. sch., prof. English, U. Mont., 1991-2000; v.p. for acad. affairs and rsch. Wichita State U., 2000—04. Author: Robert Henryson, 1979, A New Classical Rhetoric, 1980, Henryson and the Medieval Arts of Rhetoric, 1993, William Matthews on Caxton and Malory, 1997, The Poems of Robert Henryson, 1997; editor: Teaching the Middle Ages, 1981-2004 (jour.) Studies in Medieval and Renaissance Teaching, 1975-80; co-editor: The Malory Debate, 2000; contbr. articles to profl. jours. Chmn. bd. dirs. Mo. Com. for Humanities, 1979-80, Ill. Humanities Coun., 1991; pres. Park Coll. Young Dems., 1963; v.p. Mo. Young Dems., Jefferson City, 1964; campus coord. United Way, Macomb, Ill., 1983; mem. study com. Emporia Arts Coun., 1985-88; mem. NFL Edn. Adv. Ed., 1995-2004. Recipient CARA Outstanding Svc. award, 2004; U. Tex. fellow, 1965-66; Am. Coun. Learned Socs. travel grantee, 1975; Nat. Endowment for Humanities summer fellow, 1977; Medieval Acad. Am. grantee, 1976; Mo. Com. Humanities grantee, 1975-84; Assn. Scottish Lit. Studies grantee, 1979. Mem. Mo. Assn. Depts. English (pres. 1978 80), Mo. Philol. Assn. (founding pres. 1975-77), Medieval Assn. Midwest (councillor 1977-2004, ex officio bd. 1980-2004, v.p. 1987-88, exec. sec. 1988-2004), Ill. Medieval Assn. (founding exec. sec. 1983-93), Mid-Am. Medieval Assn., Rocky Mtn. MLA, Assn. Scottish Lt. Studies, Early English Text. Soc., Societe Rencesvals, Medieval Acad. N.Am. (exec. sec. com. on ctrs. and regional assns., Outstanding Profl. Svc. award), Internat. Arthurian Soc., Sigma Tau Delta, Phi Kappa Phi, Rotary (editor Warrensburg club). Home: Wichita, Kans. Died May 13, 2004.

KING, ALAN, television entertainer, film producer; b. Bklyn., Dec. 26, 1927; s. Bernard and Minnie (Solomon) K.; m. Jeannette Sprung, Feb. 1, 1947; children: Bobby, Andrew. Ed. pub. schs., Bklyn. Performer Catskill Mountains and burlesque, U.S. Army camps, cafes and vaudeville, U.S. and Eng., Dominion Theatre, London, 1957, Palace Theatre, London, 1959, (with Judy Garland), Palace Theatre, N.Y.C., 1958, Met. Opera House, 1960, Waldorf Astoria Hotel; TV appearances include: Garry Moore Show, Ed Sullivan Show, Perry Como Show, also panel shows; TV producer: Return to Earth, 1976, Pleasure Palace, 1980; numerous appearances in TV spls. and series; appeared in TV mini-series Seventh Avenue; royal command performance for Queen Elizabeth II, Glasgow, Scotland, 1958; produced play The Lion in Winter, 1966; stage appearances include The Impossible Years, 1965, The Investigation, 1966, Dinner at Eight, 1966, Something Different, 1967; appeared in movies Hit the Deck, 1955, Miracle in the Rain, 1956, The Girl He Left Behind, 1956, The Helen Morgan Story, 1957, On the Fiddle, 1961, Bye Bye Braverman, 1968, Anderson Tapes, 1971, Just Tell Me What You Want, 1979, I, the Jury, 1982 Author Author, 1982, Lovesick, 1983, Cat's Eye, 1985, Memories of Me, 1988, Enemies, A Love Story, 1989, Bonfire of the Vanities, 1990 Night and the City, 1992, Under the Gun, 1995, The Infiltrator, 1995, Casino, 1995, Under the Gun, 1995, Brave Little Toaster Goes to Mars (voice only), 1998, Saltwater, 2000, Rush Hour 2, 2001, Sunshine State, 2002, Mind the Gap, 2004; (TV movie) How to Pick Up Girls, 1978, Pinocchio's Christmas (voice only), 1980, Dad, the Angel & Me, 1995, (TV mini-series) Baseball, 1994; producer movies Cat's Eye, Lipstick, Happy Birthday Gemini, Cattle Amie and Little Britches, Wolfen; co-author of: Anybody Who Owns His Own Home Deserves It, 1962; Help. I'm a Prisoner in a Chinese Bakery, 1964; also mag. articles. Mem.: The Friars (N.Y.C.) (monitor). Died May 9, 2004.

KING, LELAND W. architect; b. Battle Creek, Mich., Dec. 17, 1907; s. Leland Wiggins and Elizabeth Gale (Arnold) K.; m. Hametia Fielder, Nov. 29, 1934; children: Sheryl Letia, Louisa Sands. Student, Ga. Sch. Tech., 1927, Armour Inst. Tech. (Chgo. Art Inst., Beaux Arts Design), 1928-29. Registered architect, Colo., Ariz., N.Y., Calif., Nat. Council Archtl. Registration Bds. Archtl. draftsman, designer indsl., sch., hosp. and residential projects, Ga., Ill., Mich., Wis., 1925-32; supr. architect's office U.S. Treasury, 1935-37; field insp. diplomatic and consular bldgs. Dept. State, 1937-40, asso. chief Fgn. Bldg. Ops., 1941-51; dir. and supervising architect, 1952-54; in charge U.S. diplomatic and consular bldg. design and constrn., worldwide; cons. Bd. Edn. White Fish Bay, Milw., 1931-32; tech. adviser to U.S. del. UNESCO Hdqrs. Bldg., Paris, 1952-53; exec. sec. Fgn. Service Bldgs. Com., U.S. Congress, 1952-54; gen. archtl. and indsl. design as asso. Norman Bel Geddes, 1954-55; asso. with James Gordon Carr (Architect), 1956; v.p., dir. architecture Pereira and Luckman, 1956-59; supervising archt. Ampex Corp., 1959-62; pvt. archtl. practice as Leland King, FAIA, 1961—; sr. partner King/Reif & Assos. (architecture and planning), Menlo Park, Calif. Chmn. archtl. and constrn. engring. panel research, adv. council to postmaster gen., 1967, 68; dir., supervising architect U.S. Embassy projects, 1937-54, honor awards Stockholm, Paris, 1953, Memorex project, Santa Clara, Calif., 1972, Mission Control Air Force, 1982; chmn. Bodega Harbour Design Rev. Com. Works exhibited U.S. State Dept., Mus. Modern Art, N.Y.C., 1953, Octagon, 1954, San Jose Mus., 1980. Recipient McGraw-Hill Top Ten Plants award, 1971 Fellow AIA (honor award 1955, chpt. award 1974), Cosmos Club (Washington). Home: Bodega Bay, Calif. Died Apr. 20, 2004.

KING, RUFUS, lawyer; b. Seattle, Mar. 25, 1917; s. Rufus Gunn and Marian (Towle) K.; m. Janice L. Chase, June 15, 1941 (div. June 1951); children: Rufus III, Agnes S.; m. Elvine R. Rankine, Nov. 23, 1973 AB, Princeton U., 1938; postgrad., Stanford U., 1940-41; JD, Yale U., 1943. Bar: N.Y. 1944, D.C. 1948, Md. 1953. Instr. Princeton U., 1938-39; partner Rice & King, Washington, 1953-64; pvt. practice Washington, 1964-75; partner King & Newmyer, Washington, 1977-83; of counsel Berliner & Maloney, Washington, from 1983, Berliner, Corcoran & Rowe, from 1989. Counsel Senate Crime Com., 1951, also other congl. coms.; cons. Nat. Commn. Law Enforcement and Adminstrn. Justice.; Chmn. joint com. on narcotic drugs Am. Bar Assn. and AMA, 1956—; dir. Drug Policy Found., 1988-89, Nat. Orgn. for Reform of Marijuana Laws. Author: You and I, 1940, Manifesto, 1947, Gambling and Organized Crime, 1968, The Drug Hangup, 1971, Stop the Drug War Now, 1991; Contbr. articles to profl. and popular jours. Pres. Montgomery County Community Psychiat. Clinic. Recipient award Drug Policy Found., 1989, Lifetime Achievement award, Assn. Drug Reform Orgns., 1998, svc. award Nat. Orgn. for Reform Marijuana Laws, 1999. Mem. ABA (chmn. criminal law sect. 1957-60, sec. 1954-57, mem. ho. of dels. 1960-66, chmn. spl. com. atomic attack 1962—, del. sect. individual rights, mem. spl. com. on standards for adminstrn. criminal justice), N.Y. State Bar Assn., Md. Bar Assn., Bar Assn. D.C., Am. Law Inst. (life) Clubs: Princeton (N.Y.C.); Metropolitan (Washington). Home: Washington, DC. Died Dec. 28, 1999.

KINGERY, WILLIAM DAVID, ceramics and anthropology educator; b. N.Y.C., July 7, 1926; s. Lisle Byron and Margaret (Reynolds) K.; children: William, Rebekah, Andrew. SB, MIT, 1948, ScD, 1950; PhD (hon.), Tokyo Inst. Tech.; ScD (hon.), Ecole Poly. Federale de Lausanne. From instr. to assoc. prof. MIT, Cambridge, Mass., 1951-62, prof., from 1962, Kyocera prof. ceramics, 1984-88; prof. materials sci. and anthropology U. Ariz., Tucson, from 1988, Regents prof., from 1992. Vis. prof. Imperial Coll. Sci. and Tech., London, 1995—. Author: (text) Introduction to Ceramics, 1960, 2d edit., 1976 (translated into 3 langs.), Ceramic Masterpieces, 1986 (Hon. Mention, Pub. Inst.), others; editor: Ceramic Fabrication Processes, Property Measurements at High Temperatures, Kinetics of High Temperature Processes, Ceramics and Civilization I: Ancient Technology to Modern Science, 1985, Ceramics and Civilization II: Technology and Style, 1986, Ceramics and Civilization III: High Tech Ceramics-Past, Present and Future, 1987, Ceramics and Civilization, 1990, Technolo-gical Innovation, 1991, (with S. Lubar) History from Things, 1993, Learning from Things, 1995; editor-in-chief Ceramics Internat. Chmn. bd. trustees Acad. Ceramics, 1989—. Named Wagener lectr. Tokyo Inst. Tech., 1976, Kurtz lectr. Technion, Haifa, Israel, 1978, Nelson W. Taylor lectr. Pa. State U., 1982; recipient Albert V. Bleininger award, 1977, F.H. Norton award, 1977 recipient of the Pomerance award, Am. Inst. of Archaeology, 1996; Regents fellow Smithsonian Instn., Washington, 1988, Van Horn lectr. Case Western Reserve U., 1995. Fellow Am. Acad. Arts and Scis.; mem. NAE, Am. Ceramic Soc. (life, disting., Ross coffin Purdy award, John Jeppson award 1958, Robert Sosman Meml. Lecture award 1973, Hobart M. Kraner award 1985 outstanding Edn. award, 1992), Cosmos Club, Blue Water Sailing Club, Royal Hamilton Amateur Dinghy Club, Naval Club. Home: Tucson, Ariz. Deceased.

KINNARD, WILLIAM NOBLE, JR., property valuation consultant; b. Phila., Sept. 12, 1926; s. William Noble and Alice C. (Dalton) K.; m. Iris Costikyan, June 11. 1949; children: Susan Jones, Jeffrey B. BA, Swarthmore Coll., 1947; MBA, U. Pa., 1949, PhD, 1956. Cert. real property valuation specialist. Instr. econs. Wesleyan U., Middletown, Conn., 1950-54; dir., urban redevel. City of Middletown, 1954-55; prof. fin. and real estate Univ. Conn., Storrs, 1955-81, dir., Ctr. for Real Estate/Sch. of Bus., 1965-69, 76-80, assoc., acting dean Sch. of Bus., 1969-72, 73-74, prof. emeritus, from 1981; edn. cons. Soc. of Real Estate Appraisers, Chgo., 1965-85; prin. Real Estate Counseling Group Am., St. Petersburg, Fla., from 1977; pres. Real Estate Counseling Group of Conn., Storrs, from 1978. Chmn. Dickey & Kinnard, Inc., Corona del Mar, Calif., 1993—. Author: Income Property Valuation, 1971, Industrial Real Estate, 1967 (AA May award 1969), Appraising Real Property, 1984; cons. editor: Ency. Am., 1955-66, American Heritage Dictionary, 1966. Recipient Alfred E. Reinman award Soc. of Real Estate Appraisers, George Bloom award Am. Real Estate and Urban Econs. Assn., James Graaskamp award, Am. Real Estate Soc.; Disting. Scholar, Beta Gamma Sigma. Avocation: crossword puzzles. Home: Storrs Mansfield, Conn. Died Apr. 6, 2001.

KIRBY, ELIZA JOHNSON, nurse anesthetist; b. Millen, Ga., Aug. 5, 1933; d. Ellis and Daisy (Williams) Johnson; m. Daniel Kirby, July 1960 (dec.); children: Lisa, Toni, Daniel. Diploma, Grady Meml. Hosp., Atlanta, 1954, United Hosp. Sch. Anesthesia, Newark, 1971; BA, Ottawa (Kans.) Univ., 1973. Staff nurse, obstetrics Grady Meml. Hosp.; supr. oper. rm. Babies Hosp., Newark; clin. instr. Sch. Anesthesia United Hosp., Newark; staff nurse-anesthetist Anesthesiology of Cen. Fla., Orlando. Vol. Meals on Wheels; Sunday sch. tchr. Shiloh Bapt. Ch., deaconess bd. Recipient Wayne Densch Svc. award, 1986. Mem. Am. Assn. Nurse Anesthetists, Cen. Fla. Black Nurses Assn. (pres.), Nat. Grady Nurses Alumnae (pres.). Home: Orlando, Fla. Died Mar. 3, 2002.

KIRKLIN, JOHN WEBSTER, surgeon; b. Muncie, Ind., Aug. 5, 1917; m. Margaret Katherine Kirklin; 3 children. BA summa cum laude, U. Minn., 1938; MD magna cum laude, Harvard U., 1942; MD (hon.), U. Munich, 1961; DSc (hon.) (hon.), Hamline U., 1966, U. Ala., Birmingham, 1978, Ind. U., Bloomington, 1983; hon. degree (hon.), U. Bordeaux, France, 1982, Universidad de la República, Uruguay, 1982. Diplomate Am. Bd. Surgery. Intern Hosp. U. Pa., 1942-43; resident in surgery Mayo Clinic and Mayo Grad. Sch. Medicine, Rochester, Minn., 1943-44, 46-48, first asst. in surgery, 1949-50, chmn. dept. surgery, 1964-66; asst. resident in surgery Children's Hosp., Boston, 1948-49; surgeon Mayo Clinic, 1950-66, instr. surgery, 1951-53, asst. prof., 1953-57, asso. prof., 1957-60, prof., 1960-66, bd. govs., 1965-66; surgeon-in-chief U. Ala., Birmingham, 1966-82; Fay Fletcher Kerner prof. surgery U. Ala.-Birmingham Sch. Medicine and Med. Ctr., 1966—82; assoc. chief staffy U. Ala.-Birmingham Hosps., 1966; chmn. dept. surgery U. Ala.-Birmingham Sch. Medicine and Med. Ctr., 1966-82, dir. div. cardiothoracic surgery, dir. Congenital Heart Disease Research and Tng. Ctr., 1982-84, prof. surgery, 1990-98, prof. emeritus, 1998—2004. Mem. task force on prevention and treatment of cardiovascular disease in the young Nat. Heart, Lung and Blood Inst., 1977—78; mem. policy adv. bd. for coronary artery surgery, mem. adv. com. crippled children services regional program NIH. Author (with R.B. Karp)): The Tetralogy of Fallot from a Surgical Viewpoint, 1970; author: (with others)) Cardiac Surgery and the Conduction System, 1983; contbr. articles to profl. jours.; mem. editl. bd.: Am. Heart Jour., 1974—76, Am. Jour. Cardiology, 1974—80, Circulation, 1967—78, Jour. Thoracic and Cardiovascular Surgery, 1971—83, Year Book Cardiovascular Medicine and Surgery, corr. mem. editl bd.: European Jour. Intensive Care Medicine, from 1974, former editl. bd.: Jour. French Soc. Thoracic Surgery. Capt. U.S. Army, 1944—46. Fellow: Assn. Surgeons Gt. Britain and Ireland (hon.), Royal Coll. Surgeons Eng. (hon.), Royal Coll. Surgeons Edinburgh (hon.), Royal Coll. Surgeons Ireland (hon.), Royal Australasian Coll. Surgeons (hon.); mem.: NAS, AAUP, AMA, ACS, So. Surg. Assn., So. Soc. Clin. Investigation, Soc. Vascular Surgery, Soc. Univ. Surgeons, Soc. Thoracic Surgeons, Soc. Surg. Chairmen, Soc. Critical Care Medicine, Soc. Clin. Surgery, Royal Soc. Medicine (affiliate), N.Y. Acad. Scis., Mayo Found. Alumni Assn., Jefferson County Med. Soc., Internat. Surg. Group, Harvard Med. Alumni Assn., Deutsche Gesellschaft Fur Chirurgie, Cardiac Soc. Australia and N.Z. (corr.), Birmingham Surg. Soc., Am. Surg. Assn. (recorder 1967—71), Am. Soc. Critical Care Medicine, Am. Soc. Artificial Internal Organs, Am. Heart Assn., Am. Coll. Cardiology (v.p. bd. govs. 1973—74), Am. Assn. Thoracic Surgery (pres. 1978—79), Am. Acad. Pediatrics, Ala. Heart Assn., Ala. Acad. Sci., Am. Bd. Thoracic Surgery (mem. exam. and tng. programs coms., diplomate), N.Y. Soc. Thoracic Surgery (hon.), Mexican Soc. Cardiology (hon.), European Soc. Cardiovascular Surgery (hon.), Surg. Biology Club. Died Apr. 21, 2004.

KIRKPATRICK, CLAYTON, former newspaper executive; b. Waterman, Ill., Jan. 8, 1915; s. Clayton Matteson and Mable Rose (Swift) K.; m. Thelma Marie De Mott, Feb. 13, 1943 (dec. Dec. 1998); children: Pamela Marie Kirkpatrick Foy, Bruce, Eileen Bea Kirkpatrick Vaughan, James Walter. AB, U. Ill., 1937. Reporter City News Bur., Chgo., 1938; mem. staff Chgo. Tribune, 1938—, day city editor, 1958-61, city editor, 1961-63, asst. mng. editor, 1963-65, mng. editor, 1965-67, exec. editor, 1967-69, editor, 1969-79; v.p. Chgo. Tribune Co., 1967-77, exec. v.p., 1977-79, pres., 1979-81, chmn., 1981; ret., 1981. U.S. del. 19th Gen. Conf., UNESCO, Nairobi, 1976; life trustee Rush-Presbyn.-St. Luke's Med. Ctr.; trustee Robert R. McCormick Trusts, 1976-90. With USAAF, 1942-45. Decorated Bronze Star medal; recipient Elijah Parish Lovejoy award Colby Coll., 1978; William Allen White award U. Kans., 1977; Fourth Estate award Nat. Press Club, 1979 Mem. Chgo. Club, Tavern Club, Comml. Club, Glen Oak Country Club, Phi Beta Kappa, Sigma Delta Chi. Republican. Methodist. Home: Glen Ellyn, Ill. Died June 19, 2004.

KISH, ZAVEN AVEDIS, oriental rug company executive; b. Hadjin, Turkey, July 17, 1911; came to U.S., 1929, naturalized, 1939; s. Avedis H. and Marie (Tufunkjian) K.; student Columbia U., 1929-30; m. Susan Griffin, Aug. 16, 1936; 1 child, Ruth Marie. With Lowenstein's Dept. Store, Memphis, 1930-36; owner oriental rug dept. Goldsmith's Dept. Store, Memphis, 1937-74; pres. Zaven A. Kish Oriental Rug Co., Memphis, 1980-91, ret. 1991; appraiser, lectr. in field. Mem. Oriental Rug Retailers of Am. (a founder). Republican. Episcopalian. Clubs: Civitan, Masons (Shriner). Home: Memphis, Tenn.

KISMARIC, CAROLE LEE, editor, writer, book packaging company executive; b. Orange, N.J., Apr. 28, 1942; d. John Joseph and Alice Felicia (Gruskos) K.; m. Charles Vincent Mikolaycak, Oct. 1, 1970 BA in Psychology, Pa. State U., 1964. Reporter, writer Parkersburg News, W. Va., summers 1960, 61; reporter, writer UPI, Columbus, Ohio, summer 1962; writer Conde Nast Publs., N.Y.C., 1964; picture editor, assoc. editor Time Life Book Div., N.Y.C., 1965-75; editorial dir. Aperture, Inc., N.Y.C., 1976-85; freelance pub. cons., editor, writer N.Y.C., from 1985; co-founder, co-owner book packaging co. Lookout Books, N.Y.C., from 1990; founder Lookout with Marvin Heiferman, comms. co. Mem. visual arts and policy panels NEA, Washington, 1977-81, 93; tchr. grad. sch. photography program Sch. Visual Arts, N.Y.C., 1990—. Author: Duel of the Ironclads, 1969, The Boy Who Tried to Cheat Death, 1971, The Rumor of Pavel and Paali, 1988, A Gift From Saint Nicholas, 1988, Forced Out: The Agony of the Refugee in Our Time, 1989, I'm So Happy, 1990, My Day, 1993, Talking Pictures, 1994, Growing Up With Dick and Jane: Living and Learning and American Dream, 1996, Love is Blind, 1996, Dick Clark's American Bandstand, 1997, Flaming Creature: The Life and Times of Jack Smith, 1997, Self-Portrait: John Coplans, 1997, The Mysterious Case of Nancy Drew and the Hardy Boys, 1998, The Art of the X-Files, 1998, Big Dogs, Little Dogs, 1998, To the Rescue: Eight Artists in an Archive, 1999; author, editor: The Photography Catalogue, 1976; contbr. numerous articles to profl. jours.; assoc. curator From the Picture Press, Mus. Modern Art, 1973; co-curator traveling exhbns. L.A. Mcpl. Art Gallery: Forced Out in Time, 1989-93, Internat. Ctr. of Photography, Talking Pictures, 1994-97, Mus. Modern Art: Fame After Photography, 1999; co-curator: Paradise Now: Picturing the Genetic Revolution, 2000, traveling, 2001-2003. Recipient award Comm. Graphics Assn., 1971-72; Book of Yr. award Am. Inst. Graphic Arts, 1974-75, 91. Avocation: travel. Home: New York, NY. Died Nov. 19, 2002.

KISNER, JACOB, poet, editor, publisher; b. Chelsea, Mass., Apr. 30, 1926; s. Louis and Sarah (Kotel) K.; m. Gladys Selma Feinstein, May 29, 1947; 1 daughter, Lesley Kisner Cafarelli. Student, Calvin Coolidge Coll., 1945-46, Burdett Coll., 1943-45, Harvard Univ. Extension, 1944-48, Mass. State Univ. Extension, 1944-50, Cambridge Ctr. for Adult Edn., 1946-51. With Boston American advt. dept., 1943; Sunday dept. writer Boston Globe, 1943-45; local news editor Jewish Advocate, Boston, 1945-46; founder, editor, pub. Dorchester (Mass.) Herald, 1946-47; copywriter Harold Cabot & Co. Advt. Agy., Boston, 1948; trade reporter Fairchild News Svc., Boston, 1948-49; with Boston Pub. Libr. Cataloguing Dept., 1949; sr. proof-reader Rec. and Statis. Corp., Boston, 1950-54; participant NBC Comedy Writers Devel. Project, 1956; editor Crossroads, Toronto, Ont., Can., 1964-67; Am. editor View, Can., from 1967; rsch. dir. N.Y. bur. Moneytree Publs., N.Y.C., from 1972; stamp and autograph dealer, 1973-82; owner, operator Penthouse F Stamps, from 1982. Discoverer Lord and Taylor find of Finnish postal hist.; free-lance writer, 1943—. Author: (plays) First Came Paula, 1954, Speak of the Devil, 1955, The Monkey's Tail, 1956; (TV plays): The Late Mr. Honeywell, 1957, A World Apart, 1957; (poetry) I Am Hephaestus, 1966; numerous pub. articles, revs., rsch. on stamps and postal hist.; contbr. poetry to various lit. jours. and anthologies; included in Anthology of American Poetry, Vol. X, 1970, Vol. XI, 1971. Saxophonist, leader big band Jack Kenton, 1943-46; philatelic journalist; discussion moderator Great Books Found., Boston, 1948-51; judge of poetry contests, Rochester, N.Y., also N.Y. Poetry Forum, 1969—; sec. Am.-European Friendship Assn., 1948-51; chmn. Nat. Poetry Day Com., 1970; N.Y. State dir. and N.Y.C. chmn. World Poetry Day Com., 1971—; v.p., bd. dirs., incorporator N.Y. Poetry Forum, 1973-75; founder postmaster Park Ave Local Post, 1978—. Recipient Spl. Commendation for poem on death of Martin Luther King, Jr., So. Christian Leadership Conf., 1968, Internat. Who's Who in Poetry award, London, 1969, World Peace award Ky. State Poetry Soc., 1970, Gold Medal award Internat. Poets' Shrine, Hollywood, 1971, Radio award for Poetry of Superior Broadcast Quality, Sta. WEFG-FM, Winchester, Va., 1970, Spl. Citation award Poetry Pageant, 1970, Writer's Digest award, 1971. Mem. Am. Newspaper Guild, Acad. Am. Poets (founder), Wilson MacDonald Poetry Soc. Can. (exec. com. 1967-77, v.p. 1977—), Am. Philatelic Soc., Trans-Miss. Philatelic Soc., Soc. Philatelic Ams., Soc. Israel Philatelists, Am. Revenue Assn., Confederate Stamp Alliance, United Postal Stationery Soc., Scandinavian Collectors Club, Perfins Club, Am. Philatelic Rsch. Libr., Scandinavian Philatelic Libr. So. Calif., N.Mex. Philatelic Assn., Finnish Study Group, Scandinavian Philatelic Found. Died Nov. 17, 2003.

KITCHIN, KATE PARKS, retired guidance counselor and secondary English language educator; b. Scotland Neck, N.C., Apr. 16, 1911; d. John Arrington and Norma (Cloman) K. Grad., St. Mary's Jr. Coll., 1929; AB, U. N.C., Chapel Hill, 1931; MA, Columbia U., N.Y., 1943. Tchr. Woodland (N.C.)-Olney High School, 1931-36; tchr. English, counselor Rocky Mt. High School, 1936-79; guidance asst. summer sch. Appalachian State Tchrs. Coll., Boone, N.C., 1955, co-guidance dir., 1956, guidance dir., 1960. Co-chmn. Report of So. States Work Conf. on Guidance in Pub. Schs., Daytona, S.C., 1956, N.C. Dept. Pub. Instruction. Author: Guidance-Services, 1960; contbr. articles to profl. jours. Pres. N.C. Dean's Assn., 1942-44; exec. sec. N.C. Student Coun. Congress, 1952-56; clk. Vestry Ch. of the Good Shepherd, Rocky Mt., 1979-93. Recipient DAR medal of honor, 1988; named Rocky Mt. Tchr. of the Yr., 1978, Rocky Mt. Woman of Yr., 1950, 65. Mem. Am. Assn. Ret. Persons (NRTA div.), N.C. Assn. Educators, Nash-Edgecombe Ret. Sch. Pers., Rocky Mt. Jr. Guild, Delta Kappa Gamma (pres. N.C. 1950-53). Democrat. Episcopalian. Avocations: reading, bridge, cooking, music, walking. Home: Scotland Neck, NC. Died Mar. 25, 2002.

KITTELLE, POLLY WAYNE, artist; b. Shamokin, Pa., Aug. 31, 1916; d. William Wayne and Elizabeth (Ryon) Wirgman; m. John Kittelle, Jan. 31, 1942 (div. 1947). Grad. diploma, Holton Arms, Washington; student, various art schs., Nat. U., 1936. Paintings exhibited Corcoran Gallery Art, D.C., 1950-53, Nat. Soc. Arts and Letters, D.C., 1949, 50, Arts Club, D.C., 1952, 55, 57, Craft Ctr. of Blue Ridge, 1951-52, The Plains, Va., 1951, 52, Art Gallery, Silver Springs, Md., 1950, 51; represented in pvt. collections; author: Voyage to the Unknown, 1958. Bd. dirs., trustee House of Mercy, D.C., ARC, Salvation Army Aux. Mem.: Westchester (Washington). Republican. Episcopalian. Home: Littleton, Colo. Died Sept. 25, 2000.

KIZER, KELLY THOMPSON, secondary school educator; b. Augusta, Ga., Mar. 25, 1961; d. Theron Theodore and Opal Lexy (Treadway) Thompson; m. Clifton Henry Kizer, June 8, 1985; 1 child, Alexandra Kate. BS, U. S.C., 1983, MSPH, 1986; CNCP, Winthrop Coll., 1988. Cert. critical needs specialist. Tchr. of earth/gen. scis. Orangeburg Dist. 1, Norway, S.C. Mem. NEA, S.C. Edn. Assn., Earth Sci. Assn. Home: Warrenville, SC. Died Oct. 1, 2000.

KJERULFF, GEORGIANA LUDLOW GREENE, journalist, historian, county official; b. N.Y.C., Oct. 26, 1917; d. Thomas Travers and Edith Frances Ludlow (LeComte) Greene; m. Lauritz Toft Kjerulff; children: Clarice, Kristen, Karen, Lauritz, Thomas. Student, N.J. Coll. for Women; BA in Journalism, La. State U., 1939; postgrad., U. Calif., Berkeley, 1946-47. Fashion copywriter Meyer-Both, N.Y.C., 1940-45; feature writer Melbourne (Fla.) Daily Times, 1959-68; mem. Brevard County Hist. Commn., Melbourne, 1983-84 and from 88; feature writer Brevard Mag., 1984-86. Author: Tales of Old Brevard, 1972, Troubled Paradise, Melbourne Village, 1986; editor: Trees of Palo Alto, 1977, Streets of Palo Alto, 1978. Commr. Town of Melbourne Village (Fla.), 1970-72, 85-89, vice mayor, 1985-89. With USNR, 1942-45. Recipient cert. of recognition VA Hosp. Pub. Rels., 1979, spl. awards Mus. of Man, San Diego, 1983, Writers award State of Calif. for The way it Was, 1979. Mem. South Brevard Hist. Soc. (pres. 1986-87), Nat. League Am. Penwomen (bd. dirs. Palo Alto chpt. 1987), LWV (bd. dirs.), AAUW (bd. dirs. Melbourne br. 1960-70), NOW (bd. dirs. Palo Alto 1976-77), Unitarian Fellowship (pres. 1986-87, Leadership award 1988). Democrat. Avocation: photography. Home: Melbourne, Fla. Died July 12, 2000.

KLARMAN, HERBERT ELIAS, economist, educator; b. Chmielnik, Poland, Dec. 21, 1916; arrived in U.S., 1929, naturalized, 1929; s. Joseph Louis and Helen (Klarman) Klarman; m. Mary A. Monk, 1967; children: Seth Andrew, Michael Joseph. AB, Columbia U., 1939; MA, U. Wis., 1941, PhD, 1946. Economist nat. income divsn. Dept. Commerce, 1946—47; asst. prof. econs. Bklyn. Coll., 1947—48; asst., then assoc. dir. Hosp. Coun. Greater N.Y., 1949—51, 1952—62; asst. dir. N.Y. State Hosp. Study, Columbia U., 1948—49; med. economist Nat. Security Resources Bd., 1951—52; mem. faculty Johns Hopkins U., 1962—69, prof. public health adminstrn. and polit. economy, 1965—69; prof. environ. medicine and community health Downstate Med. Center, SUNY, 1969—70; prof. econs. NYU Grad. Sch. Public Adminstrn., N.Y.C., 1970—82; sr. assoc. Johns Hopkins U. Sch. Hygiene and Pub. Health, from 1982. Mem. health svcs. rsch. study sect. NIH, 1962—66; chmn. planning com. 2d Conf. on Econs. Health, 1967—69; mem. U.S. Nat. Com. on Vital and Health Stats., 1967—71, N.Y. State Health Adv. Coun., 1976—83; mem. spl. med. adv. group VA, 1977—81; mem. Inst. Medicine NAS, 1971. Author: Hospital Care in New York City, 1963, Economics of Health, 1965; editor: Empirical Studies in Health Economics, 1970; contbr. chapters to books, articles to profl. jours. Capt. U.S. Army, 1942—46. Recipient 1st Norman A. Welch Meml. award, 1965, Disting. Career award in health svcs. rsch., Assn. for Health Svcs. Rsch., 1989; fellow, Guggenheim, 1976—77. Fellow: APHA, AAAS; mem.: Royal Econ. Soc., Am. Statis. Assn., Am. Econ. Assn., Phi Beta Kappa. Home: Baltimore, Md. Died 1999.

KLASEK, CHARLES BERNARD, university administrator; b. Wilber, Nebr., Dec. 28, 1931; s. Bernard J. and Sylvia F. Klasek; m. Lila Lee Wanek, Aug. 9, 1953; children: Mark, Steve, Terese. BS in English/Polit. Sci., U. Nebr., 1954, MA in History/Prin. of Edn., 1956, PhD in Ednl. Adminstrn., 1971. Asst. prof. instructional matls. So. Ill. U., Carbondale, 1971-76, assoc prof. curriculum, instrn. and media, 1976-81, prof. curriculum and instrn., from 1981, assoc. v.p. acad. affairs/rsch., 1984-90, exec. asst. to pres. internat. and econ. devel., from 1990. Founder, pres. Assn. of Am. Colls. and Univs. in Japan, 1992—; cons. in field; external reviewer U. N.Mex. Author: Instructional Media in the Modern School, 1972, Use of Radio Broadcast for Formal and Nonformal Education in Developing Nations, 1978; editor: Bridges to the Future: Strategies for Internationalizing Higher Education, 1992. Bd. dirs. Children's Survival Fund, St. Louis, 1982—; chmn. Carbondale Cable TV Commn., 1983—; pres. Luth. Ch. Coun., Carbondale, 1986-88. 1st lt. U.S. Army, 1956-58. Recipient Acad. Excellence award, So. Ill. U., Carbondale, 1976; named Tchr. of the Yr., Coll. Edn., So. Ill. U., 1977, King Charles award, Nebr. Czechs of Wilber, 1985. Mem. Assn. U.S. Univ. Dirs. of Internat. Agr. Progs., Nat. Assn. State U. and Land Grant Colls. (bd. dirs. 1987-90), Assn. Internat. Edn. Adminstrs. (chmn. task force 1989—), Golden Key, Kiwanis (lt. gov. 1985-86), Phi Delta Kappa. Lutheran. Avocations: stamp collecting, gardening. Home: Carbondale, Ill. Deceased.

KLAW, BARBARA VAN DOREN, writer, editor; b. N.Y.C., Sept. 17, 1920; d. Carl and Irita (Bradford) Van Doren; m. Spencer Klaw, July 5, 1941; children: Joanna Klaw Schultz, Susan Klaw (Del Tredici), Rebecca Klaw (Feldman), Margaret Klaw (Metcalfe). BA, Vassar Coll., 1941. Writer-researcher OWI, Washington, 1942-43; reporter N.Y. Post, 1943-45; free-lance editor, writer, 1945-63; editor Am. Heritage mag., N.Y.C., 1963-88. Author: One Summer, 1936, One Winter, 1938, A Pony Named Nubbin, 1939, Joan and Michael, 1941, all under pseudonym Martin Gale; under pseudonym Eleanor Benton: The Complete Book of Etiquette, 1956; Camp Follower, 1944; editor folklore anthology, 1960. Home: West Cornwall, Conn. Died Dec. 14, 2002.

KLAW, SPENCER, writer, editor, educator; b. N.Y.C., Jan. 13, 1920; s. Alonzo and Alma (Ash) K.; m. Barbara Van Doren, July 5, 1941; children: Joanna Klaw Schultz, Susan Klaw (Del Tredici), Rebecca Klaw (Feldman), Margaret Klaw (Metcalfe). AB, Harvard U., 1941. Reporter San Francisco Chronicle, 1941; Washington corr. Raleigh (N.C.) News and Observer, and United Press, 1941-43; reporter United Press, N.Y.C., 1946, The New Yorker, 1947-52; asst. to Sunday editor New York Herald Tribune, 1952-54; asso. editor Fortune, 1954-60; free-lance writer, 1960—2004; lectr. in journalism U. Calif., Berkeley, 1968-69, Grad. Sch. Journalism, Columbia U., N.Y.C., 1970-87; editor Columbia Journalism Rev., 1980-89. Author: The New Brahmins: Scientific Life in America, 1968, The Great American Medicine Show, 1975, Without Sin: The Life and Death of the Oneida Community, 1993; contbr. to publs. including American Heritage, Esquire, Fortune, Saturday Evening Post, Natural History, Playboy, Harper's, The Reporter. With U.S. Army, 1943-45. Died June 3, 2004.

KLEIN, DORIS ELAINE, retired primary school educator; b. Crawford County, Iowa, May 13, 1929; d. Arthur Leo Ahrenholtz and Myrtle Fay (Cox) Meyer; m. Clifford John Klein, Aug. 25, 1949; children: Curtiss, Lucinda, Nicolette, Timothy, Mary Beth, Jodine. Normal tng. cert., U. No. Iowa, 1947; student, Drake U., 1955-66; BS, Dana Coll., 1975. Elem. tchr. Crawford County Schs., Denison, Iowa, 1947-49, St. Peter Cath. Sch., Defiance, Iowa, 1965-66; kindergarten tchr. Shelby County Schs., Harlan, Iowa, 1955-65, Harlan (Iowa) Community Schs., 1966-91. Recipient Tchr. Appreciation award Harlan C. of C., 1988, Outstanding Svc. to Students and Profession award Coll. of St. Mary's-Omaha, 1989. Mem. NEA, Iowa Edn. Assn., Harlan Edn. Assn., AAUW, Am. Legion Aux. Democrat. Roman Catholic. Avocations: arts and crafts, sewing, crocheting, walking. Home: Defiance, Iowa. Deceased.

KLEIN, HENRY MORTON, financial company executive; b. N.Y.C., Nov. 27, 1927; s. Joseph and Lena K.; B.BA, CUNY, 1951; m. Eleanore Tand, Dec. 23, 1950; children: Brian Stuart, Karen. Govt. auditor U.S. Army Audit Agy., N.Y.C., 1953-55; auditor, internal Chrysler Corp., Detroit, 1955-58, auditor missile div., 1958-62, mgr. cost, pricing missile div., 1962-64, plant contr., Huntsville (Ala.) space ops., 1964-69, contr. Airtemp Ky. Plant, Bowling Green, 1969-71, contr. Huntsville electronics div., 1971-80; contr. computer products div. Gen. Instrument Corp., El Paso, 1980-85; mgr. fin. and procurement Detroit Ops., Gen. Dynamics Svcs. Co., Sterling Heights, Mich., 1985-89, mgr. acctg., St. Louis, 1989—. mem. part-time faculty U. Ala., Huntsville, 1978-80. Precinct del., city chmn. Oak Park (Mich.) Rep. Party, 1960-63; county and state del. Rep. Conv., Mich., 1961-63; mem. Oakland County Rep. County Com., 1961-63; treas. Tenn. Valley Coun. Boy Scouts Am., 1966-68; treas. Temple B'nai Shalom, Huntsville, 1965-68; bd. dirs., chmn. admissions and budget com. United Way Madison County (Ala.), 1966-67; bd. dirs. Madison County chpt. ARC, 1966-68, 77-80, El Paso chpt., 1981-85. Served with Fin. Corps, U.S. Army, 1951-53. Recipient Meritorious Service award Temple B'nai Sholom, 1969, Man of Yr. award, 1966; Hon. Citizen award City of Huntsville, 1969. Mem. Nat. Assn. Accts. (bd. dirs. Nrth Ala. chpt. 1966-68, v.p. 1968-69, pres. North Ala. chpt. 1977-78, nat. rsch. com. 1978-82, bd. dirs. Dixie coun. 1977-80, sec. 1979-80, nat. dir. 1982-84, v.p. communications and community affairs Oakland chpt. 1986—, v.p. edn. 1987—). Home: Huntsville, Ala.

KLEINMAN, R. E. mathematician, educator; b. N.Y.C., July 27, 1929; married; 2 children. BA, NYU, 1950; MA, U. Mich., 1951; PhD in Applied Math., Delft U. Tech., 1961. Rsch. asst. in math. U. Mich., Ann Arbor, 1951-53, rsch. assoc., 1955-58, from assoc. rsch. mathematician to rsch. mathematician, 1959-68; assoc. prof. U. Del., Newark, 1968-72, prof. math., 1972-95, Unidel prof., from 1995. Vis. prof. math. U. Strathclyde, 1972, 82, Delft U. Tech., 1987, 96, U. Paris, 1993, CNRS, 1993, U. Nice-Sophia Antipolis, France, 1994; vis. scientist David Taylor Naval Ship R&D Ctr., 1982, Naval Rsch. Lab., 1986. Recipient fellowships and grants. Fellow IEEE; mem. Am. Math. Soc., Edinburgh Math. Soc., Gesellschaft Angewandte Math. and Mech., Soc. Indsl. and applied Math., Internat. Sci. Radio Union. Deceased.

KLESTIL, THOMAS, president of Austria; b. Vienna, Nov. 4, 1932; children— Ursula, Thomas, Stefan; m. Margot Klestil-Loffler. MA, U. Econs., Vienna, 1956, PhD, 1957. Staff Office for Econ. Coordination in Fed. Chancellory, Vienna, 1957-59; mem. Austrian del. to OECD, Paris, 1959-62; with Fed. Ministry Fgn. Affairs, 1962-92; staff Austrian Embassy, Washington, 1962—66; consul gen. of Austria Fed. Ministry Fgn. Affairs, L.A., 1969—74, dir. office internat. orgns. Vienna, 1974-78, permanent rep. of Austria to UN N.Y.C., 1978-82, ambassador to U.S. Washington, 1982-87, sec. gen., 1987-92; pres. Austria, 1992—2004. Died July 6, 2004.

KLINGER, SIEGFRIED, retired obstetrician-gynecologist; b. Austria, 1913; came to U.S., 1947; MD, U. Vienna. Diplomate Am. Bd. Ob-Gyn. Intern Albany (N.Y.) Hosp., 1947-49, resident in gynecology, 1947-50; pvt. practice ob-gyn. Albany, N.Y., 1950-95. Home: Albany, NY. Died June 26, 1999.

KLUCK, RUTH MARGARET, cell biologist; b. Toowoomba, Australia; came to U.S., 1995; d. Joseph and Chlorine (Scanlan) K. BS, U. Queensland, 1984, PhD, 1996. Sr. rsch. asst. Dept. of Medicine, U. Queensland, Brisbane, Australia, 1984-87; rsch. asst. Queensland Inst. for Med. Rsch., Brisbane, 1989-95; postdoctoral fellow La Jolla Inst. for Allergy and Immunology, San Diego, from 1995. Home: San Diego, Calif. Deceased.

KNAPHUS, GEORGE, botany educator; b. McCallsburg, Iowa, Aug. 31, 1924; s. Sakarias L. and Inger (Alendal) K.; m. Marie Anna Gjenvick, Aug. 3, 1948; children: Kristopher, Deborah Raines, Dawn Bovenmyer, Daniel. BA in Sci., U. No. Iowa, 1949; MS in Plant Pathology, Iowa State U., 1951, PhD in Plant Pathology, 1964. Sci. tchr., prin. McCallsburg (Iowa) High Sch., 1958-62; instr. dept. botany Iowa State U., Ames, 1962-64, asst. prof. dept. botany, 1964-68, assoc. prof. dept. botany, 1968-72, prof. dept. botany, from 1972-. Chmn. Borlaug Internat. Heritage Project, Cresco, Iowa, 1985--. Co-author: Mushrooms of Midcontinental United States, 1989; contbr. articles to profl. jours. Pres. local sch. bd., McCallsburg, 1952-58; pres. regional sch. bd., Mc-CAllsburg, 1959-66. Sgt. inf. U.S. Army, 1943-45, ETO. Recipient Disting. Svc. award Iowa Acad. Sci., 1980, Gov.'s Sci. medal, Iowa, 1986. Fellow AAAS, Am. Inst. Biol. Sci., Am. Phytopath. Soc., Iowa Acad. Sci. Avocations: softball, shooting. Home: Mc Callsburg, Iowa. Died May 20, 2000.

KNAPP, DENNIS RAYMOND, federal judge; b. Buffalo, W.Va., May 13, 1912; s. Amon Lee and Ora Alice (Forbes) K.; m. Helen Ewers Jordan, June 1, 1935; children: Mary F., Margaret Ann, Dennis Raymond. AB, W.Va. Inst. Tech., 1932, LLD, 1972; AM, W.Va. U., 1934, LLB, 1940. Bar: W.Va. 1940. High sch. tchr., Putnam County, W.Va., 1932-35; supt. schs., 1935-37; practiced in, 1940-56; judge Ct. of Common Pleas, Kanawha County, W.Va., 1957-70; U.S. dist. judge for So. Dist. W.Va., Charleston, 1970-93, sr. judge, from 1993. Vice pres., dir. Bank of Nitro, 1949-70; v.p. Hygeia, Inc., 1968-70 Bd. dirs. Goodwill Industries, Inc., 1968-70; adv. bd. Marshall U., Huntington, W.Va. With AUS, 1944-46. Named Alumnus of Year W.Va. Inst. Tech., 1967 Mem. Am., W.Va. bar assns., W.Va. Jud. Assn., W.Va. Tech. Coll. Alumni Assn. (pres. 1968) Republican. Methodist. Home: Longwood, Fla. Deceased.

KNAPP, WHITMAN, federal judge; b. N.Y.C., Feb. 24, 1909; s. Wallace Percy and Caroline Morgan (Miller) K.; m.

Ann Fallert, May 17, 1962; 1 son, Gregory Wallace; children by previous marriage— Whitman Everett, Caroline Miller (Mrs. Edward M. W. Hines), Marion Elizabeth. Grad., Choate Sch., 1927; BA, Yale, 1931; LLB, Harvard U., 1934; LLD (hon.), CUNY City Coll., 1992. Bar: N.Y. 1935. With firm Cadwalader, Wickersham & Taft, N.Y.C., 1935-37; dep. asst. dist. atty. N.Y.C., 1937-41; with firm Donovan, Leisure, Newton & Lumbard, N.Y.C., 1941; mem. staff dist. atty. N.Y.C., 1942-50; chief indictment bd., 1942-44; chief, appeal bur., 1944-50; partner firm Barrett Knapp Smith Schapiro & Simon (and predecessors), 1950-72; U.S. dist. judge So. Dist. N.Y., 1972-87, sr. dist. judge, 1987—2004. Spl. counsel N.Y. State Youth Commn., 1950-53; Waterfront Commn. N.Y. Harbor, 1953-54; mem. temp. commn. revision N.Y. State penal law and criminal code, 1964-69; chmn. Knapp Commn. to Investigate Allegations of Police Corruption in N.Y.C., 1969-72; gen. counsel Urban League Greater N.Y., 1970-72. Editor: Harvard Law Rev, 1933-34. Sec. Community Council Greater N.Y., 1952-58; pres. Dalton Schs., N.Y.C., 1950-53, Youth House, 1967-68; Trustee Univ. Settlement, 1945-64, Moblzn. for Youth, 1965-70. Mem. ABA, Am. Law Inst., Am. Bar Found., Am. Coll. Trial Lawyers, Assn. Bar City N.Y. (sec. 1946-49, chmn. exec. com. 1971-72). Home: New York, NY. Died June 14, 2004.

KNAPSTEIN, JOHN WILLIAM, psychologist; b. New London, Wis., June 20, 1937; s. John Joseph and Irene Frances (Poepke) K.; m. Betty Ann Wilhelm, Nov. 25, 1966; John Karl, Susan Elise, Eric Steven. BA, St. John's U., Collegeville, Minn., 1959; MA, Marquette U., 1961; PhD, Tex. Tech U., 1970. Lic. psychologist; cert. rehab. counselor, cert. counselor, cert. career counselor. Tchr. Hortonville (Wis.) High Sch., 1959-60; counselor Vocat. and Adult Sch., Racine, Wis., 1961-62; psychologist VA Hosp., St. Louis, 1970-72, Hines, Ill., from 1972. Deacon Diocese of Joliet, Ill., 1982—; bd. dirs., officer Community Service Council of No. Will County, Romeoville, Ill., 1979-96. Served to capt. USAF, 1962-66. Marquette U. scholar, 1960. Mem. APA, Nat. Rehab. Assn., Am. Counseling Assn., Am. Rehab. Counseling Assn., Nat. Career Devel. Assn., Nat. Rehab. Counseling Assn. Lodges: KC. Roman Catholic. Avocations: gardening, reading, computers. Home: Bolingbrook, Ill. Died Oct. 29, 2001.

KNIFFING-LEE, MARY J. medical/surgical and oncology nurse; b. San Diego, June 28, 1944; d. John S. and Margaret C. (Opdycke) Kniffing; m. Barton R. Lee, Feb. 7, 1957; children: Dawn, Paul. Lic. vocat. nurse, Grossmont Vocat. Sch., La Mesa, Calif., 1969; student, Moody Bible Inst., Chgo., 66-67; grad., Grossmont Coll., 1998; student, Bethel Coll., 2000, BA in Orgnl. Studies. Med.-surg. staff nurse Profl. Nurses Bur., San Diego; med. surg. nurse Mercy Hosp., San Diego; staff nurse Valley Med. Ctr., El Cajon, Calif.; staff hospice nurse Grossmont-Sharp Hosp., LaMesa, Calif., 1998-99. Tchr. nursing Maric Coll., S.D., 1996-98. Mem. Nurses Christian Fellowship. Home: Lakeside, Calif. Died May 2, 2001.

KNIGHT, V. C. manufacturing executive; b. Landess, Ind., Aug. 12, 1904; s. Charles and Daisie (Farr) K.; m. Velma Cain, June 30, 1926; children: James, Marilyn. Student, Ind. State U., 1921-24; PhD in Bus. Adminstrn., Adrian Coll., 1977, Hillsdale Coll., 1983. With McCray Refrigerator Co., 1926-47; v.p. ops.; exec. v.p. Betz Corp., Hammond, Ind., 1947-51; with Addison Products Co., 1951—, now chmn. bd. Past trustee Adrian Coll., present trustee emeritus. Deceased.

KNIGHT, WILLARD, manufacturing executive; b. Shadyside, Ohio, Apr. 3, 1915; BA, Linsley Coll., 1942. Pres. Knight Mfg., Inc., Shadyside, Ohio, from 1951. Avocation: fishing. Died Apr. 25, 2000.

KNIGHT, WILLIAM J. (PETE KNIGHT), state legislator, retired air force officer; b. Noblesville, Ind., Nov. 18, 1929; s. William T. and Mary Emma (Illyes) K.; m. Helena A Stone, June 7, 1958; children: William Peter, David, Stephen; m. Gail A. Johnson, Sept. 3, 1983. BS, Air Force Inst. Tech., 1958; student, Indsl. Coll. Armed Forces, 1973-74. Commd. 2d lt. USAF, 1953, advanced through grades to col., 1971; fighter pilot Kinross AFB, Mich., 1953-56; exptl. test pilot Edwards AFB, Calif., 1958-69; exptl. test pilot, 1969-70; dir. test and deployment F-15 program, 1976; dir. Flight Attack System Program Office, 1977-79; vice comdr. Air Force Flight Test Ctr. Edwards AFB, 1979-82; ret. USAF, 1982; mayor City of Palmdale, Calif., 1988-92; mem. Calif. Assembly, Sacramento, 1992-96, Calif. Senate, Sacramento, 1996—2004. V.p. Eidetics Internat., Torrance, Calif., 1988-92. Decorated D.F.C. with 2 oak leaf clusters, Legion of Merit with 2 oak leaf clusters, Air medal with 11 oak leaf clusters, Astronauts Wings; recipient Octave Chanute award, 1968, Harmon Internat. trophy, 1968, citation of honor Air Force Assn., 1969 winner Allison Jet Trophy Race, 1954; named to Nat. Aviation Hall of Fame, 1988, Lancaster Aerospace Walk of Honor, 1990, Internat. Space Hall of Fame, 1998. Fellow AIAA (assoc.), Soc. Exptl. Test Pilots (past pres.); mem. Air Force Assn., Internat. Order of Characters, Aerospace Primus Club, Daedalians, Elks, Shriners. Holder world's speed record for winged aircraft, 4520 m.p.h., 1967. Home: Palmdale, Calif. Died May 7, 2004.

KNOLL, MILENA SEBOROVA, author, travel agency representative; b. Prague, Czechoslovakia, Oct. 18, 1916; came to U.S., 1958; d. Vojtech and Marie Katerina (Koprivova) Sebor. State cert. in langs., Charles U., Prague, 1939. Exec. sec. Czech Nat. Coun., Prague, 1939-41; travel rep. Am. Express Co., N.Y.C., 1960-75, Trans Globe Travel Agy., Denver, from 1975. Author: A Czech Trilogy, 1990; contbr. articles and essays on polit. and social Cen. and Eastern Europe to Am. mags. Cypher clk. Anti-Nazi Czech Resistance, Prague, 1939-41; sec. Anti-Communist Nat. Resistance, Prague, 1945-48. Decorated Anti-Nazi Czeh Resistance medal for bravery Democratic govt. Czechoslovakia, Prague, 1946. Mem. Nat. Mil. Intelligence Assn., Association Nationale des Anciennes Deportees et Internees Resistance (proposition Cross of Legion d'Honneur 1948). Roman Catholic. Avocations: jogging, swimming, analysing foreign press, travel, tennis. Home: Denver, Colo. Died Dec. 11, 2000.

KNOTTS, GLENN R(ICHARD), foundation administrator; b. East Chicago, Ind., May 16, 1934; s. V. Raymond and Opal Ione (Alexander) K. BS, Purdue U., 1956, MS, 1960, PhD, 1968; MS, Ind. U., 1964; Dr. Med. Sci. (hon.), Union Coll., 1975; Sc.D. (hon.), Ricker Coll., 1975. Mem. profl. staff Bapt. Meml. Hosp., San Antonio, 1957-60; instr. chemistry San Antonio Coll., 1958-60; adminstrv. asst. AMA, Chgo., 1960-61, research assoc., 1961-62, dir. advt. eval., div. sci. activities, 1963-69; exec. dir. Am. Sch. Health Assn., Kent, Ohio, 1969-72; vis. disting. prof. health sci. Kent State U., 1969-72, prof., mem. grad. faculty dept. allied health scis., 1972-75, coordinator grad. studies and research, 1975; editor-in-chief, prof. med. journalism U. Tex. M.D. Anderson Cancer Ctr., Houston, 1975-85, head dept. med. info. and publs., 1975-79, dir. div. ednl. resources, 1979-85; dir. devel. U. Tex. Health Sci. Ctr. at Houston, 1985-88; prof. U. Tex. Grad. Sch. Biomed. Scis., 1983—; adj. prof. dept. journalism Coll. Communications U. Tex.-Austin, from 1984; exec. dir. Hermann Eye Fund, Houston, from 1989. Vis. prof. health edn. Madison Coll., Va., summer 1965, Union Coll., Ky., summers 1965, 66, 69; vis. prof. health edn. Utah State U., summer 1965; vis. lectr. Ind. U., 1965-66; vis. lectr. pharmacology Purdue U., 1968-69; vis. prof. Pahlavi U. Med. Sch., Iran, summer 1970; adj. prof. allied health scis. Kent State U., 1975—; prof. dept. biomed. communications U. Tex. Sch. Allied Health Scis., Houston, 1976—; prof. dept. behavioral scis. U. Tex. Sch. Pub. Health, 1977—; cons. health scis. communications, 1969—; pres. Health Scis. Inst., 1973—; mem. exec. com. Internat. Union Sch. and Univ. Health and Medicine, Paris, 1969-72 Co-author various texts and filmstrips on health sci.; contbr. numerous articles to profl. jours.; cons. editor: Clin. Pediatrics, 1971—; contbg. editor: Annals of Allergy, 1972—; exec. editor: Cancer Bull., 1976-85; mem. numerous editorial bds. Bd. dirs. Med. Arts Pub. Found., Houston, 1977-80, Art League of Houston, 1986-88, Delia Stewart Dance Co., Houston, 1988-90; mem. adv. bd. World Meetings Inc., 1971-80, bd. trustees Mus. Art Am. West, 1987-89; trustee Houston Mus. Natural Sci., 1987-89. Served with U.S. Army, 1956-58. Recipient Gold medal French-Am. Allergy Soc., 1973; named Disting. Alumnus Purdue U., 1999. Fellow APHA, Am. Sch. Health Assn. (mem. exec. com. 1968-72, editor Jour. Sch. Health 1975-76, Disting. Service award 1973), Am. Inst. Chemists, Royal Soc. Health; mem. AAUP, AAHPER, AAAS, AMA, Internat. Union Health Edn., Am. Acad. Pharm. Scis., Am. Med. Writers Assn., Am. Pharm. Assn., Am. Chem. Soc., Purdue U. Alumni Assn., Ind. U. Alumni Assn., Union Coll. Alumni Assn., Ricker Coll. Alumni Assn., Rotary, Marines Meml. Club (San Francisco), Univ. Faculty Club, Doctors Club (Houston), Pelican Club (Galveston, Tex.), Petroleum Club (Houston), Argyle Club (San Antonio), Headliners Club (Austin), Internat. Club (Chgo.), Sigma Xi, Rho Chi, Sigma Delta Chi, Eta Sigma Gamma, Phi Delta Kappa, Kappa Psi. Republican. Presbyterian. Home: Houston, Tex. Deceased.

KOCH, CHARLES JOSEPH, banker; b. Cleve., Oct. 29, 1919; s. Charles Frank and Mary (Cunat) K.; m. Elizabeth Rusch, May 7, 1945; children: Charles John, John David. BS, Case Inst. Tech., 1941. Dir. space div. Martin Marietta Corp., Balt., 1941-67; mgr. advanced program McDonnell Douglas Corp., St. Louis, 1967-68; chmn. bd., chief exec. officer Charter One Bank, Fed. Savs. Bank, Cleve., 1980-87; chmn. bd. dirs. Charter One Bank, FSB, Cleve., 1988-95, chmn. emeritus, from 1995. Instr. Johns Hopkins U., U. Md., 1943-47; Mem. adv. com. NASA, 1956-67 Adv. bd. St. Alexis Hosp.; bd. dirs. Am. Cancer Soc. Mem. Northeastern Ohio Savs. and Loan League (Treas., past pres.); Mem. Nat. Council Savs. Instns., Ohio Savs. and Loan League (past chmn., bd. dirs.), Am. Mgmt. Assn., Greater Cleve. Growth Assn., Sigma Xi, Phi Kappa Theta, Tau Beta Pi. Clubs: Rotarian. (Cleve.), Union (Cleve.), Clevelander (Cleve.), Cleve. Athletic (Cleve.), Shaker Heights Country (Cleve.). Deceased.

KOCHER, PAUL HAROLD, humanities educator; b. Trinidad, W.I., Apr. 23, 1907; s. Paul William and Freida (Schwabe) K.; m. Annis Cox, Aug. 31, 1936; children: Paul Dana, Carl Alvin. AB, Columbia U., 1926; JD, Stanford U., 1929, MA, 1932, PhD, 1936. Instr. Stanford U., 1936-38; instr., then asst. prof. U. Wash., 1938-46; prof. U. Nebr., 1948-49, Claremont Grad. Sch., 1949-58; prof. English and humanities Stanford U., 1960-70, prof. emeritus English and humanities, 1971—. Author: Christopher Marlowe, 1946, Science and Religion in Elizabethan England, 1953, Mission San Luis Obispo de Tolosa, 1772-1972, a Historical Sketch, 1972, Master of Middle-Earth: The Fiction of J.R.R. Tolkien, Dutch transl. 1973, French 1981, Swedish 1989, California's Old Missions, 1976, Alabado, Historical Novel of Spanish California, 1978, My Daily Visitor, 1979, A Reader's Guide to The Silmarillion, 1980; Editor: (Marlowe): Doctor Faustus, 1950, Huntington Library Quar, 1952-53; editorial bd.: Jour. History of Ideas, 1951-59, Huntington Library Quar., 1952-53; contbg. editor: Mythlore, 1976—; Contbr. articles to profl. jours. Fellow Folger Shakespeare Library, 1939-40; Guggenheim fellow, 1946-47, 55-56; Huntington Library fellow, 1952-53 Mem. Modern Lang. Assn., Renaissance Soc., Order of Coif. Home: San Luis Obispo, Calif. Died July 19, 1998.

KOEHLER, HENRY M. editor; b. Frankfurt, Germany, Oct. 13, 1931; came to U.S., 1938; s. Otto and Elsa (Kamberg) K.; m. Harriet Blustein, Feb. 3, 1957. MS, Roosevelt U., 1957, MBA, 1960. Chemist ADA, Chgo., 1952-67, editor, 1967-80; cons. Acad. Gen. Dentistry, Chgo., from 1980. Cons. Temket, Inc., Chgo., 1981—. Editor Oral Rsch. Abstracts, ADA, 1967-80; translator: History of Dentistry, 1980. Fellow N.Y. Acad. Scis., AAAS, Am. Chem. Soc., Coun. Biology Editors, Fedn. Dentaire Internat. (communication com.) Home: Chicago, Ill. Died Mar. 19, 2002.

KOESTER, MARY FLATLEY, nurse, educator; b. Glens Falls, N.Y., June 4, 1920; d. Frederick J. and Anna Theresa (Rogers) Flatley; m. Ralph E. Koester, Mar. 14, 1945; 1 child, Frederick E. (dec.). BSN, Coll. St. Rose, 1941; student of drs., Bklyn. Jewish Hosp., from 1953. Tchr. Home Health Aides, Washington County, N.Y.; prof. nursing Speers Meml. Hosp., Dayton, Ky., Glens Falls Hosp.; pvt. counsel in allergy/immunology Greenwich, N.Y. Mem. N.Y. State Nurses Assn. Home: Greenwich, NY. Died Feb. 15, 2002.

KOGER, FRANK WILLIAMS, federal judge; b. Kansas City, Mo., Mar. 20, 1930; s. C.H. and Lelia D. (Williams) K.; m. Jeanine E. Strawhacker, Mar. 19, 1954; children: Lelia Jane, Mary Courtney. AB, Kansas City U., 1951, LLB, 1953; LLM, U. Mo., Kansas City, 1966. Staff judge adv. USAF, Rapid City, S.D., 1953-56; ptnr. Reid, Koger & Reid, Kansas City, 1956-61, Shockley, Reid & Koger, Kansas City, 1961-86; U.S. bankruptcy judge U.S. Dept. Judiciary, Kansas City, from 1986; chief judge 8th Cir. Bankruptcy Appellate Panel, from 1997. Adj. prof. law sch. U. Mo., Columbia, 1990—, U. Mo.-Kansas City, 1992—. Author: (manual) Foreclosure Law in Missouri, 1982, Missouri Collection Law, 1983; author, co-editor: Bankruptcy Handbook, 1992; editor: Bankruptcy Law, 1990. Bd. dirs. Jackson County Pub. Hosp., Kansas City, 1974-79, St. Lukes Hosp., Kansas City, 1970—; chair subcom. Jackson County Charter Transition Com., Kansas City, 1978-79. Capt. USAF, 1953-56. Recipient Shelley Peters Meml. award Am. Inst. Banking, Kansas City, 1986. Fellow Am. Coll. Bankruptcy Judges; mem. Nat. Conf. Bankruptcy Judges (dir. 1990-93, sec. 1994-95, pres.-elect 1995-96, pres. 1996-97), Comml. Law League Am. (pres. 1983-84). Avocations: contract bridge, gardening. Home: Kansas City, Mo. Died Jan. 3, 2003.

KOHL, MATHIAS FRANZ FREDERICK, retired obstetrician/gynecologist; b. Detroit, Aug. 16, 1911; MD, Washington U., St, Louis, 1941. Cert. ob/gyn, 1951. Intern Strong Meml. Hosp., Rochester, 1941-42, resident ob/gyn, 1942-44, fellow pathologist, 1943; MD emeritus Swedish Am., Rockford, Ill., from 1948; ret. Mem. ACS, AMA, Am. Coll. Obstetricians/Gynecologists. Home: Rockford, Ill. Died May 25, 2001.

KOHN, JAMES PAUL, engineering educator; b. Dubuque, Iowa, Oct. 31, 1924; s. Harry Theodore and Kathryn (Piepel) K.; m. Mary Louise McGovern, Aug. 30, 1958; children: Kathleen, Kevin, Mary Louise. BS in Chem. Engring, U. Notre Dame, 1951; MS, U. Mich., 1952; PhD, U. Kans., 1956. Chem. engr. Reilly Tar & Chem. Corp., Indpls., 1946-51; mem. faculty U. Notre Dame, 1955—, prof., 1964-95, prof. emeritus, from 1995; dir. Solar Lab. for Thermal Applications, 1973—. Cons. Am. Oil Co., summer 1958, Imagineering Interprises, 1957-65, Hills-Morrow, 1966-70, Frito Lay Corp., 1982—, South Bend Energy Conservation Commn., 1983—, sec. 1986—. Patentee removal acidic gaseous components from natural gas. Served with U.S. Army, 1943-46. Decorated Bronze star, Purple Heart; recipient Faculty award U. Notre Dame, 1983, Outstanding Tchr. of Yr. award, 1987, Outstanding Faculty mem. minority engring. program, 1995, Spl. Presdl. award Notre Dame, 1995; Donald L. Katz award Gas Processors Assn., 1988. Fellow AIChE; mem. AAAS, Am. Chem. Soc., Sigma Xi. Republican. Roman Catholic. Home: South Bend, Ind. Died May 26, 2003.

KOHRS, LLOYD FREDERICK, electrical engineer; b. St. Charles, Mo., Sept. 6, 1927; s. William August and Lolita Kathrine (Nolle) K.; m. Diana Joyce Button, Mar. 14, 1960; 1 stepchild, Randall Grant Pemberton; 1 child, Charmaine Lynette Kohrs Seavy. BSEE, Washington U., 1950. Test conductor McDonnell Aircraft, St. Louis, 1950-55; mgr. space propulsion Aerojet Gen. Corp., Sacramento, Calif., 1955-67; mgr. propulsion Hughes Aircraft, El Segundo, Calif., 1967-69; chief propulsion engr. McDonnell Douglas Astronautics, St. Louis, Mo., 1969-73, mgr. space shuttle program, 1973-83, mgr. DSP Laser Crosslink program, 1983-89. With U.S. Army, 1945-46. Recipient Disting. Pub. Service medal NASA, 1982. Mem. Am. Inst. Aeronautics and Astronautics (Wyld Propulsion award 1982). Democrat. Avocations: travel, fine arts, theater, photography. Home: Saint Louis, Mo. Deceased.

KOHS, ELLIS BONOFF, composer, educator; b. Chgo., May 12, 1916; s. Samuel Calmin and Paula (Bonoff) K. MA, U. Chgo., 1938; postgrad., Juilliard Sch. Music, 1938-39, Harvard U., 1939-41. Lectr. U. Wis., Madison, 1939; instr. music Kansas City (Mo.) Conservatory of Music, 1946-47; asst. prof. Wesleyan U., Middletown, Conn., 1946-48; assoc. prof. Coll. of the Pacific, Stockton, Calif., 1948-50; lectr. Stanford U., Calif., 1950; from asst. prof. to prof. U. So. Calif., Los Angeles, 1950-85, prof. emeritus, from 1985. Composer (opera) Amerika, 1969, (mus. choreodrama) Lohiau and Hiiaka, 1987, 2 symphonies, 1950, 56, numerous mus. compositions for orch., chorus, keyboard; author: Music Theory (2 vols.), 1961, Musical Form, 1976, Musical Composition, 1980. Served with USAF, 1941-46. Mem. Music Library Assn., Am. Composers Alliance, Am. Music Ctr., Broadcast Music, Inc. Home: Los Angeles, Calif. Died May 17, 2000.

KOLBE, JOHN WILLIAM, newspaper columnist; b. Evanston, Ill., Sept. 21, 1940; s. Walter William and Helen (Reed) K.; m. Mary Bauman, Feb. 24, 1990; stepchildren: Erin Simmons, James Simmons; children by previous marriage: Karen, David. BS in Journalism, Northwestern U., 1961; MA in Polit. Sci., U. Notre Dame, 1962. Feature writer, polit. reporter Rockford (Ill.) Register-Republic, 1964-68; press aide Ogilvie for Gov. campaign, Chgo., 1968; asst. press sec. Office Gov., Springfield, Ill., 1969-73; polit. reporter, columnist Phoenix Gazette, 1973-97; polit. columnist Arizona Republic, from 1997. Elder Valley Presbyn. Ch., Scottsdale, Ariz., 1978-81; bd. dirs. Morrison Inst., Ariz. State U., Tempe, 1982-97. Lt. (j.g.) USNR, 1962-64. Recipient Best Column of Yr. award Ariz. Press Club, 1976, 80, 84. Home: Phoenix, Ariz. Deceased.

KOLLINS, MICHAEL JEROME, automotive engineer, historian, writer; b. Mar. 20, 1912; s. Michael Arthur and Mary Ann (Peck) K.; m. Julia Dolores Advent, Jan. 16, 1934; children: Michael Lewis, Richard, Laura. Student, Coll. City Detroit, 1928—32. Chief sect. svc. engring. and tech. data Studebaker-Packard Corp., Detroit, 1945—55; mgr. tech. svcs. Chrysler Corp., Detroit, 1955—64, mgr. warranty adminstrn., 1964—68, mgr. Highland Park Svc. Ctr., 1968—75; pres. Kollins Design & Engring., Detroit, from 1975. Designer racing cars, 1932—39; designer sports cars, spl. luxury vehicles, from 1951; designer automotive performance and safety devices, from 1946. Author: Motor Torpedo Boat Engr.'s Manual, 1945; co-author: The Technology Century, 1995; author: Pioneers of the U.S. Automobile Industry, 2002; contbr. articles to profl. publs. Trustee Nat. Automotive Hist. Collection, from 1982; active Birmingham (Mich.) Chorale, Meadowbrook (Mich.) Festival Chorus; bd. dirs. Capuchin Charity Guild, from 1983; nat. advisor Motorsports Hall of Fame, from 1988. With USN, 1942—45. Mem.: Am. Automobile Assn. (contest bd.), Engring. Soc. Detroit (industry amb. from 1972), Soc. Automotive Historians, Soc. Automotive Engrs., U.S. Auto Club (vice-chmn. tech. com. 1971—82, dir. cert. com. from 1983). Died Dec. 3, 2003.

KONIG, FRANZ CARDINAL, cardinal, archbishop emeritus of Vienna; b. Rabenstein, Austria, Aug. 3, 1905; D.D.; Ph.D.; hon. degrees univs. Vienna, Innsbruck, Salzburg, Zagreb, Am. univs. Ordained priest Roman Catholic Ch., 1933; prof. high sch.; lectr. U. Vienna, 1946-48, extraordinary prof., from 1948; titular bishop, Livias, 1952, bishop coadjutor, St. Poelten, 1952; archbishop of Vienna, 1956-85; cardinal, 1958; titular ch. St. Eusebius; pres. Secretariat for Non-Believers, 1965-80, Pax Christi Internat., 1985-90; archbishop emeritus of Vienna. Mem. Am. Acad. Arts and Scis. Author: Christus und die Religionen der Erde, 1951, Religionswissenschaftliches Woerterbuch, 1956, Zarathustras Jenseitsvorstellungen und das Alte Testament, 1964, Die Stunde der Welt 1971, Der Aufbruch zum Geist, 1972, Das Zeichen Gottes, 1973, Der Mensch ist fuer die Zukunft angelegt, 1975, Kirche und Welt, 1978, Glaube ist Freiheit, 1981, Der Glaube der Menschen, 1985, Der Weg der Kirche, 1986, Lexikon der Religionen, 1987, König/Ehrlich, Juden und Christen haben eine Zukunft, 1988, Jetzt die Wahrheit leben, 1991, in slowenischer Sprache, 1992. Died Mar. 13, 2004.

KONOPKA, GISELA PEIPER (MRS. ERHARDT PAUL KONOPKA), social worker, author, lecturer, educator; b. Berlin, Fed. Republic Germany, Feb. 11, 1910; came to U.S., 1941, naturalized, 1944; d. Mendel and Bronia (Buttermann) Peiper; m. Erhardt Paul Konopka, June 23, 1941 (dec. Nov. 1976). Student, U. Hamburg, Germany, 1929-33; MS, U. Pitts., 1943; Ph.D Social Welfare, Columbia, 1957; DHL (hon.), Macalester Coll., 1994. Lic. social worker emerita. Psychiat. group worker Child Guidence Clinic, Pitts., 1943-47; lectr. Sch. Social Work, U. Pitts., also Welfare; mem. Gov. Minn. Adv. Com. on Youth; mem. faculty U. Minn., 1947-56, prof., 1956-77, prof. emeritus, 1977—, spl. asst. to v.p. for student affairs, 1969-71; dir. Center for Youth Devel. and Research, 1970-77; adj. U. Minn., 1989. Child welfare expert, group work U.S. High Commr. Med. Affairs, Germany, summers 1950, 51; tchr. social work in Germany Dept. State., summer 1956; tchr. U. Iowa, 1980, Netherlands, 1981; lectr. U. Calif. at Berkeley, 1961-62, in Near and Far East, 1970; lectr. Inst. for Social Services, Montrouge, France, 1971, U. West Indies, Jamaica, 1972, 77; Fulbright lectr., Brazil, 1972, lectr., Israel, Jamaica, 1977, Australia, 1979, Netherlands, 1960-61, 1981; Konopka lectr. U. Minn., 1985; dir. adolescent girl in conflict research project NIMH grant, 1962-65; dir. Project Girl, Lilly Endowment grant, 1973-77, Nat. Youth Worker Edn. Project, 1977-79; cons. VA Hosp., Mpls.; standards for group homes Minn. Research and Evaluation Div., Office Child Devel., Dept. Health, Edn. and Welfare; mem. Gov. Minn. Adv. Com. on Youth, Minn. Supreme Ct. Juvenile Justice Study Commn.; nat. adv. com. Girl Scouts of Am.; also exec. com. group work recreation div.; exec. com. Family and Children's Service, Hennepin County Welfare Council; former cons. Children's Treatment Center, Minn. Welfare Dept.; internat. cons. in social group work by Internat. Conf. Schs. Social Work; mem. Council Internat. Programs Social Workers and Youth Workers, Joint Commn. on Juvenile Justice Standards, Inst. Jud. Adminstrn.-Am. Bar Assn., 1972-76; keynote speaker Internat. Conf. on Youth, Hong Kong, 1989. Author: Therapeutic Group Work with Children, 1940, Group Work in the Institution, 1954, Eduard C. Lindeman and Social Work Philosophy, 1958, Social Group Work: A Helping Process, 1963, 3d edit., 1982, Adolescent Girls in Conflict, 1966, Young Girls: A Portrait of Adolescence, 1976, A Renewed Look at Human Development, Human Needs, Human Services, 1985, Human Dignity: Our Youth and Ourselves, 1986, Courage and Love, 1988, Mit Mut und Liebe, 1996; co-author: Concepts and Methods of Social Work, edited Walter Friedlander, 1958; mem. editorial bd. Social Work With Groups, 1977—; Contbr. numerous articles to profl. jours. Bd. dirs. Mpls. Urban League, 1968, Mpls. Youth Service, 1987 Named outstanding alumnus social work U. Pitts., 1968; recipient award for outstanding svc. Assn. for Blind, 1966; citation U.S. Children's Bur., 1966; citation also Vols. Am.; Highest merit award for rebldg. German social svcs. after World War II Fed. Republic Germany, 1975; 1st Ann. award for excellence in teaching and magnanimous contbn. to cmty. Minn. Conf. Social Work Edn., 1976; Cecil E. Newman humanitarian award Mpls. Urban League, 1977; AAUW Achievement award, 1977; Gisela Konopka lectureship and ann. award established, 1978; award Nat. Conf. Social Welfare, 1979; award Nat. Conf. Children's Homes, 1979; award Big Bros./Big Sisters, 1985, Dr. Martin Luther King, Jr. Humanitarian award Mpls. Cmty. Coll., 1992; Lilly Endowment grantee for treatment of delinquents, 1982-87; A.A. Heckman Cmty. Svc. Lecture award, 1987; Gisela Konopka Day proclaimed by Gov. of Minn., 1990, 95; Konopka Inst. for Best Practices in Adolescent Health established in her name U. Minn., 1998. Fellow Am. Orthopsychiat. Assn. (pres. 1993-94, dir.); mem. AAUP, NASW (chmn. group work sect., Nat. Lifetime Achievement award 1994), Nat. Conf. Social Welfare (v.p., nat. chmn. history of social welfare group 1960, past dir.), Urban League, Nat. Acads. Practice (Disting. practitioner 1983), Consumers League, United World Federalists, Soc. for Adolescent Medicine (hon.). Home: Minneapolis, Minn. Died Dec. 9, 2003.

KONRAD, ADOLF FERDINAND, artist; b. Bremen, Germany, Feb. 21, 1915; came to U.S., 1925, naturalized, 1931; s. Roman and Katherine Heidientje (Engelken) K.; m. Adair Watts, Apr. 26, 1980. Student, Newark Sch. Fine and Indsl. Art, 1930-34, Cummington (Mass.) Sch., 1936-37; DFA, Kean U., 1971. Tchr., advisor N.J. State Council on Arts, 1971-74; artist-in-residence Everhart Mus., Scranton, Pa., 1973, Somerset County Coll. (now Raritan Valley Coll.), Somerville, N.J., 1977-80. Lectr., panelist. One-man shows include Newark Mus., 1966, Everhart Mus., Scranton, Pa., 1973, Mus. Fine Arts, Springfield, Mass., 1973, Montclair Art Mus. and N.J. State Mus., Trenton, 1980, The Newark Mus., 1997; represented in permanent collections Newark Mus., Montclair Art Mus., Mus. Fine Arts, Everhart Mus., N.J. State Mus., NAD, N.Y.C., Newark Public Library, The Forbes Collection, N.Y.C, Ct. Gen. Sessions Painting Collection, Washington, CIBA Geigy, Basle, Switzerland, AT&T, Bedminster, N.J., Crum & Forster Ins. Co., Morristown, N.J., Bell Labs. Murray Hill, N.J., N.J. Public Service, Newark, Schering-Plough Corp., Liberty Corner, N.J., Geraldine R. Dodge Found., Morristown, N.J., Somerset Art Assn., Bedminster, N.J., 2000; mural executed N.J. Vets. Meml. Home, Paramus, 1986; retrospective exhbn. The Morris Mus., Morristown, N.J., 1992, Hunterdon Art Mus., Clinton, N.J., 1996. Louis Comfort Tiffany fellow, 1937; Tiffany Found. fellow, 1961; resident fellow Yaddo, Saratoga Springs, 1956; winner grand prize Atlantic City Fine Arts Festival, 1961, 63; first prize Montclair Art Mus. Ann. Exhbn., 1963; Andrew Carnegie prize NAD Ann., 1967; Audience Choice award Marietta (Ohio) Coll., 1969; Gov.'s citation; N.J. Symphony Ann. Arts award, 1969; David Humphreys Meml. prize Allied Artist of Am., 1971; Artist of Year award Art Educators N.J., 1973; Fellowship award in Painting N.J. State Council on Arts, 1982. Mem. Associated Artists N.J. (pres. 1960-65), Artists Equity Assn. N.J. (pres. 1952-60, NAD (academician; Thomas B. Clark prize 1956). Home: Annandale, NJ. Died Jan. 14, 2004.

KONVITZ, MILTON RIDBAZ, law educator; b. Safad, Israel, Mar. 12, 1908; came to U.S., 1915, naturalized, 1926; s. Rabbi Joseph and Welia (Ridbaz-Willowski) K.; m. Mary Traub, June 18, 1942; 1 son, Josef. BS, NYU, 1928, AM, JD, NYU, 1930; PhD (Sage fellow in philosophy 1932-33), Cornell U., 1933; LittD, Rutgers U., 1954, Dropsie U., 1975; DCL, U. Liberia, 1962; LHD, Hebrew Union Coll-Jewish Inst. Religion, 1966, Yeshiva U., 1972; LLD, Syracuse U., 1971, Jewish Theol. Sem., 1972. Bar: N.J. 1932. Practice law, Jersey City and Newark, 1933-46; lectr. on law and pub. adminstrn. NYU, 1938-46; asst. gen. counsel NAACP Legal Def. and Edn. Fund, 1943-46; mem. faculty New Sch. for Social Rsch., 1944-46; prof. indsl. and labor rels. N.Y. State Sch. Indsl. and Labor Rels., Cornell U., 1946-73; prof. Law Sch. Cornell U., 1956-73, prof. emeritus, 1973—2003. Vis. prof., assoc. dir. Truman Ctr. for Peace Rsch., Hebrew U., 1970; dir. Liberian Codification of Laws project, 1952-80; gen. counsel Newark Housing Authority, 1938-43, N.J. State Housing Authority, 1943-45; Pub. rep. Nat. War Labor Bd. region 2, 1943-46; mem. enforcement commn. and hearing commn. Wage Stablzn. Bd., 1952-53; chmn. nat. com. study of Jewish Edn. in U.S., 1958-59; faculty Salzburg (Austria) Seminar Am. Studies, 1952; panel Fed. Mediation and Conciliation Svc., N.Y. Mediation Bd., Am. Arbitration Assn., N.Y. State Pub. Employment Rels. Author: On the Nature of Value: Philosophy of Samuel Alexander, 1946, The Alien and the Asiatic in American Law, 1946, Constitution and Civil Rights, 1946, Civil Rights in Immigration, 1953, Bill of Rights Reader, 1954, Fundamental Liberties of a Free People, 1957, A Century of Civil Rights, 1961, Expanding Liberties: Freedom's Gains in Postwar America, 1966, Religious Liberty and Conscience, 1968, Judaism and Human Rights, 1972, Judaism and the American Idea, 1978, Torah and Constitution, 1998, Nine American Jewish Thinkers, 2000, Fundamental Rights: History of a Constitutional Doctrine, 2001; founding editor: Industrial and Labor Relations Rev. (vols. 1-5), 1947-52, Liberian Code of Laws (5 vols.), 1958 60, Liberian Code of Laws Revised, 1973—, Liberian Law Reports (27 vols.); co-founder and chmn. editl. bd. Midstream Mag.; co-chmn. emeritus adv. editl. bd. Jour. Law and Religion; co-editor: Jewish Social Studies, 1975-93; co-founder: Judaism Mag.; mem. editl. bd. Ency. Judaica. Chmn. Hebrew Culture Found., 1956-95; mem. commn. for reorgn. World Zionist Orgn. Decorated comdr. Order Star of Africa, grand band (Liberia); recipient NYU Washington Sq. Coll. Disting. Alumni award, 1964, Mordecai ben David Disting. award Yeshiva U., 1965, Morris J. Kaplun internat. prize for scholarship Hebrew U., 1969, Tercentenary medal Jewish Community of Essex County, N.J., 1954; Ford Found. Faculty fellow, 1952-53, Guggenheim fellow, 1953-54, Fund for the Republic fellow, 1955, Inst. Advanced Study fellow, 1959-60, Ctr. Advanced Study Behavioral Scis. fellow, 1964-65, NEH fellow, 1975-76. Fellow Am. Acad. Arts and Scis.; mem. AAUP (mem. coun. 1961-64), ACLU (mem. nat. com.), Am. Philos. Assn., Am. Acad. Jewish Rsch., Law and Soc. Assn., Indsl. Rels. Rsch. Assn., Workers Def. League (mem. adv. bd.), Am. Jewish League for Israel (mem. adv. bd.), Internat. Assn. Jewish Law, Internat. Assn. Jewish Lawyers and Jurists, Order of Coif, Phi Beta Kappa. Home: Oakhurst, NJ. Died Sept. 5, 2003.

KOOPMAN, KARL FRIEDRICH, curator; b. Honolulu, Apr. 1, 1920; s. Karl Henry and Martha Johnston (Brown) K. BA, Columbia U., 1943, MA, 1945, PhD, 1950. Instr. Middletown (N.Y.) Collegiate Ctr., 1949-50, Queens Coll., Flushing, N.Y., 1952-58; asst. curator Acad. Natural Scis. Phila., 1958-59, Field Mus. Natural History, Chgo., 1959-61, Am. Mus. Natural History, N.Y.C., 1961-65, assoc. curator, 1966-78, curator, 1978-86, curator emeritus, from 1986. Mem. Am. Soc. Mammalogists (hon.). Home: New York, NY. Deceased.

KOPPETT, LEONARD, columnist, journalist, author; b. Moscow, Sept. 15, 1923; s. David and Marie (Dvoretskya) Kopeliovitch; m. Suzanne Silberstein, Apr. 24, 1964; children: Katherine, David. BA, Columbia U., 1946. Sportswriter, columnist N.Y. Herald Tribune, 1948-54, N.Y. Post, 1954-63, N.Y. Times, 1963-78, 88-91, Sporting News, 1967-82; exec. sports editor Peninsula Times Tribune, 1980-81, editor, 1982-84, editor emeritus, 1984-93; free-lance columnist, 1978—2003. Tchr. journalism and law Stanford (Calif.) U., 1977—81, 1987—2003, San Jose State U., 1988—89. Books include A Thinking Man's Guide to Baseball, 1967, 24 Seconds to Shoot, 1969, The N.Y. Times Guide to Spectator Sports, 1970, The New York Mets, 1970, The Essence of the Game is Deception, 1974, Sports Illusion, Sports Reality, 1981, The New Thinking Fan's Guide to Baseball, 1991, 2d edit., 2000, The Man in the Dugout, 1993, 2d edit., 1999, Koppett's Concise History of Major League Baseball, 1998. Served with U.S. Army, 1943-45. Named to writer's wing Baseball Hall of Fame, 1992, Basketball Hall of Fame, 1994. Mem. Baseball Writers Assn. Am., Profl. Football Writers, Authors Guild. Democrat. Jewish. Home: Palo Alto, Calif. Died June 22, 2003.

KORFHAGE, ROBERT ROY, information sciences educator, consultant; b. Syracuse, N.Y., Dec. 2, 1930; s. Roy Fred and Loretta Margaret (Krohn) K.; m. Ann Hobart Willard, June 14, 1955; children: Willard, Margaret, Lisa, David. BSE in Math., U. Mich., 1952, MS, 1955, PhD, 1962. Asst. prof. N.C. State U., Raleigh, 1960-62, Purdue U., West Lafayette, Ind., 1962-67, assoc. prof., 1967-70; prof. So. Meth. U., Dallas, 1970-86, U. Pitts., from 1986. Pres. DOM, Inc., Pitts., 1983—. Author: Discrete Computational Structures, 1984, Logic and Algorithms, 1967; co-author: Calculus, 1970, Principles of Data Structure and Algos, 1988; co-editor: Visual Languages and Applications, 1990; contbr. articles to profl. jours. Fulbright-Hayes fellow U.S. Govt., 1973-75. Mem. IEEE Computing Soc., Assn. Computing Machinery (coun. 1975-81), Am. Inst. Info. Sci., Sigma Xi. Avocations: music, reading, antiques, fossils. Home: Pittsburgh, Pa. Deceased.

KORWEK, ALEXANDER DONALD, management consultant; b. Madison, Ill., Feb. 20, 1932; s. Alexander and Constance (Gulewicz) K.; m. Katherine Moore, Oct. 24, 1954 (div. Nov. 1974; dec.); children: Alexander D., Brian P., Lizabeth E.; M. Judith Joy, Jan. 11, 1975; 1 child, Theodore Sofianos. BSBA, Washington U., St. Louis, 1962; MBA, U. Utah, 1967. Cert. in data processing, 1962. Asst. sec., asst. treas. Hoechst (Hystron) Fiber, N.Y.C., 1966-72; v.p. fin. Reeves/Teletape, N.Y.C., 1972-76; prin. A.D. Korwek Cons., North Babylon, N.Y., 1975-77; bus. mgr., CFO Queens Coll., CUNY, Flushing, N.Y., 1977-79; mng. dir. ASCE, N.Y.C., 1979-81; sec., gen. mgr., CEO United Engring. Trustees, N.Y.C., 1981-90; prin. A.D. Korwek Mgmt. Cons., 1990—2003. Exec. sec. Engring. Found., N.Y.C., 1981-90, Engring. Socs. Library, N.Y.C., 1981-90; sec. Daniel Guggenheim Medal Bd., N.Y.C., 1981-90, John Fritz Medal Bd., N.Y.C., 1981-90, Frank F. Aplan Award Bd., N.Y.C., 1989-90; bd. dirs. Daytona Beach C.C. Author: Cost Estimating Relationships, 1967, A Dissertation on Management, 1978; author manuals in field. Commr. Norwalk-Wilton Conv. and Visitors Bur., Conn., 1985; vol. bd. bank mem., bd. instr. Volusia/Flagler United Way, Fla.,

1992-95; bd. dirs. Marineland Found., Inc., 1988-2000; trustee Daytona Beach C.C., 1999-2003 Recipient award of Appreciation Queen's Coll. Student Body, 1979. Mem. ASCE, IAJBBSC (bd. dirs. dist. 10 1989-90), Coun. of Engr. and Sci. Soc. Execs., N.Y. Soc. Assn. Execs., N.Y. Acad. Sci., Assn. for a Better N.Y., N.Y.C. C. of C., Conn. Specialty Club (pres. Norwalk 1985-90), Elks (treas. lodge 2709 1992-94). Avocations: decanter collecting, golf, stamp collecting/philately, coin collecting/numismatics. Died July 24, 2003.

KORZENIOWSKI, OKSANA M. infectious disease physician; b. Jaroslaw, Ukraine, Apr. 11, 1945; BA in Biology, U. Pa., Phila., 1967; MD, U. Rochester, N.Y., 1971. Diplomate Am. Bd. Internal Medicine, subspecialty bd. infectious diseases. Intern mixed medicine/surgery, resident medicine U. Va. Sch. Medicine, Charlottesville, Va., 1971-74; ptnr. emergency rm. medicine Lynchburg (Va.) Gen. Hosp., 1974-75; fellow infectious diseases U. Bahia, Salvador U. Va. Sch. Medicine, Charlottesville, 1975-76, fellow infectious diseases, 1976-78, chief resident dept. internal medicine, 1978-79; asst. prof. medicine Med. Coll. Pa., Phila., 1979-85, assoc. prof., 1985-95; prof. Med. Coll. Pa./Hahnemann U., Phila., from 1995. Med. dir. inpatient med. svcs. Eastern Pa. Psychiat. Inst., 1985-93; asst. med. dir. Med. Coll. Hosps., Main Clin. Campus, 1993—, med. dir. quality assessment, 1993—, hosp. epidemiologist, 1993—, pres. med./dental staff, 1995-97, 99—. Contbr. articles to profl. jours., chpts. to books. Fellow ACP; mem. Am. Coll. Microbiology, Am. Fedn. Clin. Rsch., Infectious Diseases Soc. Am., Soc. Healthcare Epidemiology Am., Alpha Omega Alpha. Died Mar. 29, 2002.

KOSTENBADER, KENNETH DAVID, virologist; b. Allentown, Pa., May 6, 1941; s. Kenneth David and Margaret Blanche (Shinton) K.; m. Jean Louise Jensen, June 16, 1977. BS, Albright Coll., 1964. Microbiologist I Pa. Dept. Health Labs., Phila., 1965-66; rsch. specialist Food Rsch. Inst., U. Wis., Madison, 1966-85, researcher, from 1985. Collaborator WHO Collaborating Ctr. on Food Virology, U. Wis., Madison, 1975—. Contbr. articles to Appl. Microbiol., Appl. Env. Microbiol., Jour. Food Protection, Internat. Jour. Food Microbiology. Vol. campaigner state legis. races, Madison, Middleton, Wis. and surrounding areas, 1982—. Nat. Merit scholar. Mem. AAAS, Am. Soc. for Microbiology. Achievements include methods for virus recovery from food and water that are still in use worldwide. Home: Madison, Wis. Deceased.

KOSTER, DONALD NELSON, English language educator; b. N.Y.C., Aug. 4, 1910; s. Albert Clarence and Anna Adele (Nelson) K.; m. Rosemary Therese Lawson, Feb. 24, 1930; children: Donald Nelson Jr., Harold Albert. AB, U. Pa., Phila., 1931, BS in Edn., 1932, PhD, 1942. Asst. instr. in English U. Pa., Phila., 1933-35, instr. in English, 1935-46; asst. prof. English Adelphi U., Garden City, N.Y., 1946-53, assoc. prof. English, 1953-59, prof. English, 1959-78, prof. emeritus English, from 1978. Cons. in field, 1965—; chair N.Y. State AAUP Conf. Com. on Acad. Freedom and Tenure, 1976-78; mem. seminar on higher edn. Columbia U. Author: The Theme of Divorce in American Drama, 1942, Transcendentalism in America, 1975, American Literature and Language, 1982; co-author: Modern Journalism, 1962; editor 14 books in Gale's American Studies Information Guide series. Mem. MLA, AAUP (pres. assembly of state confs. 1962-63), Am. Studies Assn. (bibliographer 1965-75). Democrat. Avocations: travel, reading, hiking, golf. Home: Whitney Point, NY. Died Sept. 21, 2000.

KOVACH, BARBARA ELLEN, management and psychology educator; b. Ann Arbor, Mich, Dec. 28, 1941; d. Harry Arnold and Margaret Mayne (Buell) Lusk; m. Craig Randall Duncan, Dec. 28, 1963 (div. 1973); children: Deborah Louise, Mark Randall; m. Randall Louis Kovach, May 2, 1981; 1 child, Jennifer Elizabeth. BA magna cum laude, Stanford U., 1963, MA, 1964; PhD, U. Md., 1973. Asst. prof. psychology U. Mich., Dearborn, 1973-77, assoc. prof., 1977-82, prof., 1982-84, chair dept. behavioral scis., 1980-83; dean Univ. Coll. Rutgers U., New Brunswick, NJ, 1984-88, prof. mgmt. and psychology, from 1984, dir. leadership devel. program, from 1988. Pres. Leadership Devel. Inst., Princeton, NJ, 1990—; cons. Rochester (NY) Products-GM, Grand Rapids, Mich., 1982-87, Ford Motor Co., Dearborn, 1981-82, Mich. Bell Telephone, 1980-81, Rockwell Internat., Troy, Mich, 1993-97, Meritor Automotive, Troy, 1997-98, Johnson & Johnson, 1995-97, 2000, Std. Product Co., 1998-99. Author: Sex Roles and Personal Awareness, 1978, 90, Power and Love, 1982, Organizational Synch, 1983, Adolescent Experience, 1983, The Flexible Organization, 1984, Survival on the Fast Track, 1988, 93, Organization Gameboard, 1989, Leaders in Place, 1994, More About Survival on the Fast Track, 1996; producer (videotape series) Keys to Leadership I, 1991-93, II, 1993-94, III, 1995-97; contbr. articles to profl. jours. Daniel E. Prescott fellow U. Md., 1972; recipient Susan B. Anthony and Faculty Recognition awards U. Mich., 1980. Mem. Am. Psychol. Assn., Acad. Mgmt., Organizational Devel. Network, Phi Beta Kappa. Republican. Episcopalian. Home: Skillman, NJ. Died July 28, 2003.

KOVAK, ELLEN B. public relations firm executive; b. N.Y.C., Nov. 28, 1948; m. Stanley Kovak, Apr. 20, 1971; 1 child, Janet (J.J.) BA, Skidmore Coll.; postgrad., Brown U. Sr. acct. supr. Creamer Dickson Basford, Inc., N.Y.C., 1977-80; exec. v.p. Lobsenz-Stevens Inc., N.Y.C., 1980-85; pres. Kovak-Thomas Pub. Relations, Inc., N.Y.C., 1985-96, Kovak Likiy, from 1997. Mem. Pub. Relations Soc. Am., Am. Horse Show Assn. Avocation: horseback riding (show and own hunter horses). Home: Wilton, Conn. Deceased.

KOVARIK, JOSEPH LEWIS, surgeon; b. Omaha, Sept. 16, 1927; m. Delores Marie Casey, June 20, 1953; children: Jane Ann, Joseph Edward, Patricia Marie, James John, Karen Rose, Kenneth Michael. Student, Creighton U., 1944, Ctrl. Mo. State U., Warrensburg, 1945, Brown U., 1945-46; MD, U. Nebr., 1950. Diplomate Am. Bd. Surgery, Am. Bd. Thoracic Surgery; lic. physician Nebr., Ill., Colo. Intern U. Ill. Rsch. and Ednl. Hosps., Chgo., 1950-51; resident in gen. surgery St. Francis Hosp., Peoria, Ill., 1951-53, Presbyn. Hosp., Chgo., 1953-55; resident in thoracic surgery Chgo. State Tuberculosis Sanitarium, 1955, VA Hosp., Hines, Ill., 1956; fellow in thoracic and cardiovascular surgery Rush-Presbyn.-St. Luke's Med. Ctr., Chgo., 1957; pvt. practice surgery Englewood, Colo. Active staff Presbyn.-St. Luke's Med. Ctr., Denver; staff St. Joseph Hosp., Denver; cons. in thoracic surgery VA Hosp., Albuquerque, 1961-66; cons. in surgery Colo. State Hosp., Pueblo, Colo., 1960-80; attending in thoracic surgery VA Hosp., Denver, 1959-85; asst. clin. prof. surgery U. Colo. Health Scis. Ctr., Denver, 1965-76, assoc. clin. prof., 1976-87, clin. prof. surgery, 1987—; staff surgeon Gates Med. Clinic, Denver, 1973-93. Contbr. numerous articles to profl. jours.; mem. physician's adv. panel Med. World News, 1980. Pres. Colo. divsn. Am. Cancer Soc., 1981-83, adv. com., 1986—, exec. com., 1965-86); bd. dirs., chmn. profl. adv. com. Cmty. Homemaker Svc., Denver, 1964-68; v.p., chmn. med. adv. com. Colo. Cystic Fibrosis Assn., 1964-69; surg. rev. com. Blue Cross/Blue Shield of Colo., 1981-88, cons., 1988—; bd. govs. QuaLife Wellness Cmty., Denver, 1988-91; bd. dirs. Denver Boys, Inc., 1992-93; health care adminstrv. adv. bd. Denver Tech. Coll., 1993—; physician advisor Colo. Found. Med. Care, 1988—. With U.S. Naval Air Corps, 1945-46. Mem. ACS (bd. govs. 1979-85, Colo. chpt. pres. 1976-77), AMA, Southwestern Surg. Congress (pres. 1986-87), Denver Med. Soc. (pres. 1969-70, chmn. bd. trustees 1970-71), Colo. Med. Soc. (del. 1982-85), Rush Surg. Soc. (pres. 1989-90), Western Thoracic Surg. Assn., Am. Assn. for Thoracic Surgery, Western Surg. Assn., Am. Coll. Chest Physicians, Colo. Trudeau Soc., Am. Thoracic Soc., Denver Acad. Surgery (bd. dirs. 1985-86), Rotary. Died Jan. 31, 2002.

KOZMETSKY, GEORGE, computer science educator; b. Seattle, Oct. 5, 1917; s. George and Nadya (Omelan) Kozmetsky; m. Ronya Keosiff, Nov. 5, 1943. BA, U. Wash., 1938; MBA, Harvard U., 1947, DCCS, 1957. Instr. Harvard U., 1947—50; asst. prof. Carnegie-Mellon U., Pitts., 1950—52; mem. tech. staff Hughes Aircraft Co., Los Angeles, 1952—54; dir. computer, controls lab. Litton Co., Los Angeles, 1954—59, v.p., asst. gen. mgr. electronic equipment div., 1959—60; exec. v.p. Teledyne Corp., Beverly Hills, Calif., 1960—66; prof. mgmt. and computer sci., dean Coll. Bus. Adminstrn. and Grad. Sch. Bus., U. Tex. at Austin, 1966—82, exec. assoc. for econ. affairs univ. system, 1966—82. Leatherbee lectr. Harvard U., 1967; vis. scholar U. Wash., 1968, Walker-Ames prof., 70. Author: Financial Reports of Labor Unions, 1950; author: (with Simon and Guetzkow) Centralization Versus Decentralization in Organizing the Controller's Department, 1954; author: (with Paul Kircher) Electronic Computers and Management Control, 1956; author: (with Ronya Kozmetsky) Making It Together, 1981, Transformational Management, 1985; author: (with Gill and Smilor) Financing and Managing Fast-Growth Companies, 1985, Creating the Technopolis, 1988; author: (with Matsumoto and Smilor) Pacific Cooperation and Development, 1988; author: (with Peterson and Albaum) Modern American Capitalism, 1990; author: (with Yue) Global Economic Competition, 1997. With AUS, 1942-45. Decorated Silver Star, Bronze Star with oak leaf cluster, Purple Heart; recipient Nat. Medal of Tech., NSF, 1993. Fellow: AAAS; mem.: Am. Soc. Oceanography, Brit. Interplanetary Soc., Assn. Advancement of Med. Instrumentation, Inst. Mgmt. Sci. (chmn. bd., pres.). Home: Austin, Tex. Died Apr. 30, 2003.

KRAMER, FERDINAND, mortgage banker; b. Chgo., Aug. 10, 1901; s. Adolph F. and Ray (Friedberg) K.; m. Stephanie Shambaugh, Dec. 22, 1932 (dec. Feb. 1973); children: Barbara Shambaugh Kramer Bailey, Douglas, Anthony; m. Julia Wood McDermott, Aug. 19, 1975. PhB, U. Chgo., 1922. Engaged in real estate bus. and mortgage banker, Chgo., from 1922; with Draper & Kramer, Inc., Chgo., from 1922, chmn. bd., 1944-95, chmn. emeritus, from 1995. Dir., mem. exec. com. Chgo. 21 Corp.; Program supr. Div. Def. Housing Coordination (and successor Nat. Housing Agy.), Washington, 1941-42; past pres. Met. Housing and Planning Council, Chgo., Actions, Inc.; past mem. Pres.'s Com. Equal Opportunity in Housing. Past chmn. steering com. United Negro Fund; mem. vis. com. dept. design and visual arts Harvard, 1963-64; life trustee U. Chgo. Recipient citation of merit U. Chgo. Alumni Assn., 1947, Individual Disting. Housing and Redevel. Svc. award Nat. Assn. Housing Ofcls., 1952, Disting. Alumnus award, 1982, Alumni Svc. medal, 1997, Disting. Pub. Svc. award Union League Club, Chgo., 1994. Mem. Chgo. Mortgage Bankers Assn. (past pres.), Mortgage Bankers Assn. Am., Nat. Assn. Housing Ofcls., Chgo. Assn. Commerce and Industry. Clubs: Chicago, Quadrangle, Standard, Tavern, Mid-Town Tennis, Commercial (Chgo.). Died July 16, 2002.

KRAMER, JONATHAN DONALD, composer, music theorist, educator; b. Hartford, Conn., Dec. 7, 1942; s. Maxwell and Pauline (Klein) K.; m. Norma Berson, Aug. 28, 1966; children: Zachary, Stephanie. A.B. magna cum laude, Harvard U., 1965; M.A., U. Calif.-Berkeley, 1967, Ph.D., 1969; postgrad. U. Calif.-Irvine, 1976. Lectr. music theory and composition U. Calif., Berkeley, 1969-70; prof. conservatory music Oberlin (Ohio) Coll., 1970-71; prof. dept. music Yale U., New Haven, 1971-78, dir. undergrad. composition, 1972-78; prof., dir. electronic music Coll. Conservatory Music, U. Cin., 1978-90; prof. Columbia U., 1988-2004; hon. research assoc. U. London, 1985-86; program annotator San Francisco Symphony, 1967-70; former program annotator Cin. Symphony, new music advisor, composer in residence, 1984-92; weekly radio program host Sta. WGUC, Cin., 1982-88; lectr. in field. Nat. Endowment Arts grantee, 1976, 85, 87; NEH grantee, 1976, 85; Martha Baird Rockefeller Fund grantee, 1978; Morse fellow, 1975; Ohio Arts Council grantee, 1982, 84, 87; recipient Ohio Gov.'s award, 1984, Alienor Harpsichord Conposition award, 1990. Mem. Cin. Composers Guild (chmn. adv. bd.), Nat. Assn. Composers (nat. council), Soc. Music Theory (publs. com.), Am. Soc. Univ. Composers (dir. nat. festival), AAUP, Coll. Music Soc., Internat. Soc. for Study of Time (v.p.), Am. Music Ctr. Compositions performed at Lincoln Ctr., Aspen Music Festival, Carnegie Hall, World Music Days, Composers' Forum, Peru, Brazil, Korea, Japan, Eng., Denmark, Israel, Argentina, Norway, France, Can., Germany, Belgium, Austria, Holland, Spain, Australia, Poland; composer: music for orch., chorus, piano, clarinet, band, dance, theater, electronics, chamber ensembles, percussion.; compositions rec. by Grenadilla, Opus One, Leonarda, Orion Records, pub. by G. Schirmer and MMB; performances by London Philharm. Orch., Cin., Symphony Orch., Am. Composers Orch., Seattle Symphony, Nat. Orch. of El Salvador, Seoul Philharm., Warsaw Philharm.; author: Listen to the Music, 1988, The Time of Music, 1988; contbr. articles to profl. jours. and books. Home: New York, NY. Died June 3, 2004.

KRAUSE, ROY CHARLES, retired religious studies educator, writer; b. Rogers City, Mich., Feb. 3, 1917; s. Louis Frederick and Lenora (Pagels) K.; m. Leona Ann Dieckhoff, Mar. 24, 1940; children: David Leroy, Dianne Lavonne, Donna Lorraine, Daniel Lewis. Diploma, Concordia Tchrs.' Coll., River Forest, Ill., 1938; BS in Edn., S.E. Mo. State Coll., Cape Girardeau, 1942; MS in Edn., Wayne State U., Detroit, 1950; PhD in Edn., U. Nebr., 1974. Cert. secondary tchr., Mich. Prin., tchr. Immanuel Luth. Sch., Rosebud, Mo., 1938-40, Carrollton, Mo., 1940-42, Christ Luth. Sch., St. Louis, 1942-43, Redmption Luth. Sch., Detroit, 1943-46; prin., tchr., coach Holy Ghost Luth. Sch., Monroe, Mich., 1946-53, East Bethlehem Luth. Sch., Detroit, 1953-62; asst. supt. Luth. sch. Mich. Dist. Luth. Ch., Ann Arbor, 1962-67; prof. edn. Concordia Tchrs.' Coll., Seward, Nebr., 1967-82, prof. emeritus, from 1982. Author: The Role of the Lutheran Teacher, 1978, Decisions, 1994, Destination: Silver Valley, 1995, And God Also Created Teachers and Children, 1995. Mem. bd. ch. missions Luth. Ch. of Mich., Ann Arbor, 1955-62; mem. bd. edn. Luth. Ch. Mich. Dist., Ann Arbor, 1962-67; chmn. Beautiful Savior Luth. Ch., Lehigh Acres, Fla. Mem. AARP (pres. local chpt. Lehigh Acres 1983-85, chaplain 1985-97). Republican. Avocations: sports, bridge, reading, travel. Home: Lehigh Acres, Fla. Deceased.

KRAUSE, WALTER, retired economics educator, consultant; b. Portland, Oreg., Jan. 12, 1919; PhD, Harvard U., 1945. John F. Murray prof. internat. bus. and econs. emeritus U. Iowa, Iowa City, from 1987. Mem. Phi Beta Kappa Home: Iowa City, Iowa. Deceased.

KRAY, ANTOINETTE, actress; b. Chgo., June 13, 1911; d. Meyer and Lizaveta Markovna (Taranova) Krawitz. Student, Art Inst., Chgo., 1928-30. Children's illustrator Jr. Life, Chgo., 1930-31, Hygeia, Chgo., 1930-31. Actress (off broadway plays) The Chief Thing, Marouf, The Glass Menagerie, Slow Night in Elk City, Widower's Houses, The Blue Bird, Don Perlimplin; (TV shows) The Doctors, Search for Tomorrow, World Apart, East Side, West Side, The Reporter, The Defenders, For the People, Trials of O'Brien, Consumer Survival Kit, Lucky Pup (commls.) Bell Telephone, Sylvania, WXYZ-TV (News Promo), Balt. Fed. Loan (cable TV) Well Hello Fanny; author: Isn't it a Lovely Day, 1978, Mother Bickerdyke & Me, 1988. Mem. Actors Equity Assn., Screen Actors Guild, Am. Fedn. of TV and Radio Actors, Dramatists Guild, Inc. Home: Cliffside Park, NJ. Died Aug. 31, 2001.

KREN, GEORGE MICHAEL, history educator; b. Linz, Austria, June 3, 1926; s. Frank and Gertrude (Bloch) K.; m. Claudia Wilson (div. 1967); 1 child, Stefan; m. Margo Hemphill, June 1, 1969. BA in History, Colby Coll., 1948; MA in History, U. Wis., 1949, PhD, 1960. Instr. Oberlin (Ohio) Coll., 1958-59; asst. prof. Elmira (N.Y.) Coll., 1959-60, Lake Forest (Ill.) Coll., 1960-65; assoc. prof. Kans. State U., Manhattan, 1965-76, prof. history, from 1976. Co-author: (with Leon Rappoport) The Holocaust and the Crisis of Human Behavior, 1980, (with George Christakes) Scholars and Personal Computers: Microcomputing in the Humanities and Social Sciences, 1988; co-editor: (with Leon Rappoport) Varieties of Psychohistory, 1976; bd. editors Psychohistory Rev.; contbr. chpts. to books and articles to profl. jours. With Inf., 1944-46, ETO. Avocation: photography. Home: Manhattan, Kans. Died July 24, 2000.

KREPPS, ETHEL CONSTANCE, lawyer; b. Mountain View, Okla., Oct. 31, 1937; d. Howard Haswell and Pearl (Moore) Goomda. R.N., St. John's Med. Center, 1971; B.S., U. Tulsa, 1974, J.D., 1979; m. George Randolph Krepps, Apr. 10, 1954; children: George Randolph, Edward Howard Moore. Nurse St. John's Med. Ctr., Tulsa, 1971-75. Bar: Okla., 1979. pvt. practice law, Tulsa, 1979-96; mem. Indian law alumni com. U. Tulsa Coll. Law; atty., dir. Indian Child Welfare Program, 1981-96; nat. v.p. A.I.L.S.A.; sec. bd. dirs.

Okla. Indian Legal Svcs, 1986-96; administrative law judge, Dept. Health Enforcement Unit, Okla; bd. dirs. North Am. Coun. on Adoption of Children; mem. Okla. adv. commn. civil rights; atty. Native Am. Coalition, Inc., Kiowa Tribe Okla., Tulsa Indian Youth Council, Legal Rsch. Okla. Indian Affairs Commn. Chmn., Okla. Indian Child Welfare Orgn., 1981-96; tribal sec. Kiowa Tribe Okla., 1979-81; atty. nurse aide registry Okla. Dept. Health, 1994-96. Mem. ABA, Fed. Bar Assn., Tulsa Women Lawyers Assn., Am. Indian Bar Assn., Okla. Indian Bar Assn., Okla. Bar Assn., Tulsa County Bar Assn., Oklahoma County Bar Assn., Am. Indian Nurses Assn. (v.p.), Okla. Women Lawyers Assn., Nat. Indian Social Workers Assn. (pres. 1984-96), Assn. Trial Lawyers Am., Phi Alpha Delta, Nat. Native Am. C. of C. (sec. 1980-96), Internat. Indian Child Conf. (founder, chair). Democrat. Baptist. Author: A Strong Medicine Wind, 1979; Oklahoma Memories, 1981. Died July 15, 1996. Home: Oklahoma City, Okla.

KRESS, ROY ALFRED, psychology educator; b. Elmira, N.Y., Oct. 4, 1916; s. Roy Alfred and Alice Elmira (Whitaker) K.; m. Doris Ethel Parker, Mar. 29, 1940 (dec. July 1969); children: Keith Denton, Lance Whitaker, Gene Gordon; m. Eleanor Murphy Ladd, Dec. 4, 1969. BS in Edn., Lock Haven State Coll., 1938; Ed.M., Temple U., 1949, PhD, 1956. Tchr. Woods Schs., Langhorne, Pa., 1938-43; tng. supr. VA, Phila., 1946-49; lectr. Temple U., Phila., 1949-55, prof. psychology, 1963-68, chmn. psychology of reading dept., 1968-70; assoc. dean Temple U. (Grad. Sch.), 1970-73, prof. psychology of reading, 1973-79, prof. emeritus, 1979—2004; acting dean Temple U. (Coll. Edn.), 1974-75. Ednl. dir. Shady Brook Schs., Richardson, Tex., 1955-58; asso. prof. Syracuse (N.Y.) U., 1958-63; vis. lectr. Tex. Women's U., 1956, So. State Coll. Ark., 1957, U. Ark., 1958, State U. N.Y., 1960, U. Colo., 1961, Appalachian State U., 1970-79, U. S.C., 1980, Furman U., 1980; cons. edn. and psychology, U.S., Can., Australia. Author: A Place to Start, 1963, (with Marjorie S. Johnson) Informal Reading Inventories, 1965, (with J. Pikulskie), rev. edit., 1987, (with M.S. Johnson and J. McNeil) The Read System, rev. edit, 1971, American Book Company Reading Program, 1977. Editor: That All May Learn to Read, 1959, (with M.S. Johnson) Corrective Reading in the Elementary Classroom, 1967 (Outstanding Education Book of 1967, Pi Lambda Theta), Proc. Ann. Reading Insts. Temple U., 1963-70; proc. The Reading Teacher, 1967-71; editorial adv. bd.: Reading Research Quar, 1965-70, Jour. Learning Disability, 1968—, The Reading Tchr, 1971-72; adv. bd.: ERIC/CRIER, 1968-71, 73-75. Instl. rep., scoutmaster Circle Ten council, Onondaga Valley council Boy Scouts Am., 1955-63; faculty sponsor Alpha Phi Omega, Syracuse U., 1958-63. Served with USMCR, 1943-46. Recipient Disting. Service award Lock Haven State Coll. Alumni Assn., 1973; Disting. Service award Internat. Reading Assn., 1976; named to Reading Hall of Fame, 1986; Research grantee Phila. Bd. Edn., 1965-68 Mem. Am. Psychol. Assn., Internat. Reading Assn. (mem. bd. 1964-67), Nat. Council Research in English (bd. 1966-69, sec.-treas. 1972-75), Coll. Reading Assn. (bd. dirs. 1971-74, A.B. Herr award for disting. service in reading 1983), Nat. Soc. Study Edn., Am. Edn. Research Assn., Nat. Council Grad. Sch. Deans, Sigma Pi, Phi Delta Kappa, Alpha Phi Omega. Clubs: Masons. Home: Kutztown, Pa. Died Jan. 9, 2004.

KREVSKY, SEYMOUR, electronics engineer, consultant; b. Elizabeth, N.J., July 2, 1920; s. Louis J. and Rose (Zipkin) K.; m. Gladys Welt Krevsky, Jan. 9, 1944; children: Ell Miocene, Joan Cambria Whelan. BSEE, Newark Coll. Engring., 1942, MSEE, 1950. Registered profl. engr., N.J. Sr. mem. tech. staff RCA, Princeton, N.J., 1958-68; dep. dir. engring. U.S. Army Communications Systems Agy., Fort Monmouth, N.J., 1968-80; sr. engr. PRC Inc., Eatontown, N.J., 1980-84; mem. tech. staff Mitre Corp., Eatontown, 1984-85; prin. engr. Analytics, Inc., Tinton Falls, N.J., 1985-89, C3I Systems Group Inc., Eatontown, 1989-90; prin. staff mem. BDM Internat., Inc., Eatontown, 1990-91. Editor: IEEE N.J. Coast sect. Centennial Jour., 1984. Emergency mgmt. coord. Borough of Little Silver, N.J., 1989-95; apptd. FEMA, NAt. Def. Exec. Res. Fellow AAAS, Radio Club Am.; mem. IEEE (life sr., pres. Engring. Mgmt. Soc. 1992-93), Internat. Test and Evaluation Assn. (pres. Ft. Monmouth chpt. 1986—), Am. Acad. Environ. Engrs. (diplomate, specialist in radiation), Jewish War Vets U.S. (nat. emergency mgmt. officer 1980-90, dept. N.J. vice comdr. 4th dist. 1981-88, comdr. Post 515, Red Banks, N.J. 1972-73, 97—). Avocation: radio amature. Died June 3, 2001.

KRIEG, DOROTHY LINDEN, soprano, performing artist, educator; b. Moline, Ill. d. Carl Victor Lundin and Maybelle Eugenia (Bohman) Linden; m. Eugene D. Krieg, Nov. 24, 1949; m. John C. Ludke, Feb. 1, 1996. Studied piano, voice, pvt. instrs., from 1932; student, Am. Conservatory, 1938-44; studied, opera and oratorio with numerous Maestri. Tchr. Midwestern Conservatory, Chgo., 1947-49; pvt. practice teaching singing Chgo., 1952-94, L.A., from 1994. Past treas. Nat. Assn. Tchrs. Singing Chgo. Began singing career in vaudeville at age 4, later appeared with Midwest Opera Co.; artist Moments of Opera show, Colosimo's and on TV; appearances in Chgo. area include supper clubs Singer's Rendevous, Caruso's, Singing Sorinis, Pucci's, Black Forest in Three Lakes, Wis., Northernaire Showboat in Three Lakes, Wis., ballrooms Drake Hotel, Conrad Hilton Hotel, Blackstone Hotel, others, polit. convs., USO shows; concert artist Chgo. Symphony Orch., from 1950's appearing at Orch. Hall, on tour and on TV with condrs. Fritz Reiner, Rafael Kubelic, George Schick, others; soprano soloist ann. performances Messiah, Marshall Field Choral Soc., 27 yrs., Bryn Mawr Community Ch., Chgo., 17 yrs., Chgo. Temple, 10 yrs., other chs. and temples throughout Chgo.; soloist major oratorio socs. including Swedish Choral Club, Apollo Club, Rockefeller Chapel Choir, Collegium Musicum, St. Louis Bach Soc., Cornell Coll., Calvin Coll., Testor Chorus, Rockford, Ill.; soloist U.S. premieres Vivaldi's Gloria and Handel's Psalm 112, Orch. Hall with Chgo. Symphony; female soloist Chgo. Swedish Glee Club, Chgo. Swedish Male Chorus, Schwaebisher Saengerbund, Chgo. Master Bakers Chorus, Combined German Male Choruses at Civic Opera Ho., others; tchr. voice prodn., phrasing, stage deportment, coach opera, oratorio, English, French and Italian lit., German lieder. 1st pl. winner West Side div. Chicagoland Music Festival Contest, 1939; named Western Springs Music Club scholar. Mem. Seal Watch (Can., Magdalen Islands), Greenpeace, Internat. Fund Animal Welfare, Internat. Soc. Animal Rights, People for Ethical Treatment of Animals, Whale Adoption Project. Avocations: cats, gemology, stereo and video recording, swedish culture. Died Dec. 30, 2002.

KRIENKE, CAROL BELLE MANIKOWSKE (MRS. OLIVER KENNETH KRIENKE), realtor; b. Oakland, Calif., June 19, 1917; d. George and Ethel (Purdon) Manikowske; m. Oliver Kenneth Krienke, June 4, 1941 (dec. Dec. 1988); children: Diane Krienke Denny, Judith Krienke Giss, Debra Louise Krienke Davalos. Student, U. Mo., 1937; BS, U. Minn., 1940; postgrad., UCLA, 1949. Demonstrator Gen. Foods Corp., Mpls., 1940; youth leadership State Minn. Congl. Conf., U. Minn., Mpls., 1940-41; war prodn. worker Airesearch Mfg. Co., L.A., 1944; tchr. L.A. City Schs., 1945-49; realtor DBA Ethel Purdon, Manhattan Beach, Calif., 1949; buyer Purdon Furniture & Appliances, Manhattan Beach, 1950-58; realtor O.K. Krienke Realty, Manhattan Beach, from 1958. Manhattan Beach bd. rep. Cmty. Chest for Girl Scouts U.S., 1957; bd. dirs. South Bay coun. Girl Scouts U.S.A., 1957-62; mem. Manhattan Beach Coord. Coun., 1956-68, South Coast Botanic Garden Found., 1989—; v.p. Long Beach Area Childrens Home Soc., 1967-68, pres., 1979; charter mem. Beach Pixies, 1957-93, pres., 1967; chmn. United Way, 1967; sponsor Beach Cities Symphony, 1953—, Little League Umpires, 1981-91; active Cmty. ch., pres. women's fellowship, 1970-71. Recipient Longstanding Local Bus. award City of Manhattan Beach, 1993. Mem. DAR (life, citizenship chmn. 1972-73, v.p. 1979, 83—), Calif. Retired Tchrs. Assn. (life), Colonial Dames XVII Century (charter mem. Jared Eliot chpt. 1977, v.p., pres. 1979-81, 83-84), Friends of Libr., South Bay Assn. Realtors, Nat. Soc. New Eng. Women (life, Calif. Poppy Colony), Internat. Platform Assn., Soc. Descs. of Founders of Hartford (life), Friends of Banning Mus., Hist. Soc. Centinela Valley, Manhattan Beach Hist. Soc., Manhattan Beach C. of C. (Rose and Scroll award 1985), U. Minn. Alumni (life). Republican. Home: Manhattan Beach, Calif. Died Dec. 8, 1999.

KRINSLY, STUART Z. lawyer, manufacturing company executive; b. N.Y.C., May 19, 1917; m. Charlotte Wolf, Aug. 18, 1944; children: EllinJane, Joan Susan. BA, Princeton U., 1938; LLB, Harvard U., 1941. Bar: N.Y. 1941. Asst. U.S. atty. So. Dist. N.Y., 1942-45; mem. firm Schlesinger & Krinsly, 1945-57; sec. Sun Chem. Corp., N.Y.C., 1957-65, v.p., gen. counsel, 1965-76, sr. v.p., gen. counsel, 1976-78, exec. v.p., gen. counsel, 1978-82, also bd. dirs.; sr. exec. v.p., gen. counsel Sequa Corp., N.Y.C., 1982—2002, also bd. dirs. Mem. Beach Point Club, Princeton Club N.Y. Home: Mamaroneck, NY. Died Nov. 16, 2002.

KRIT, ROBERT LEE, development executive; b. Chgo., Apr. 6, 1920; s. Jacob and Tania (Etzkowitz) K.; BS in Commerce, DePaul U., 1946; ABA, N. Park Coll., 1939; children: Melissa, Margaret, Justin. Dir. Chgo. Herald Am. Mercy Fleet charity drives, 1940-41; asst. exec. dir. cancer rsch. found. U. Chgo., 1947-48; state campaign dir. Am. Cancer Soc., Inc., Chgo., 1948-63; dir. med. devel. U. Chgo., 1963-67; v.p. devel. Finch U. Health Scis./Chgo. Med. Sch, 1967—. Moderator, NBC-TV series Tension in Modern Living, Drug Abuse, Aging and Retirement, Health and Devel. Children, Cancer, Bridge For Tomorrow, Healthy Life Style, NBC Ednl. Exchange; host producer TV series Med. Looking Glass, Relevant Issues in Health and Medicine, Coping, Su Salud, Spanish TV series, Chgo. Med. Sch. Reports, radio series; Author: The Fund Raising Handbook, 1991, Scott Foresman Professional Books. chmn. Ill. Comm. for Nat. Health Agys. Fed. Svc. Campaigns; mem. adv. bd. Cen. States Inst. for Addiction Svcs.; v.p. Drug Abuse Coun. of Ill.; bd. dirs. Lawson YMCA, United Way Lake County, Ill. Found. Dentistry for the Handicapped; vice chmn. North Chgo. Citizens Against Drug & Alcohol Abuse. Served to 1st lt. USAAF, 1942-46. Fellow Inst. Medicine Chgo. (co-chmn. com. on public info., editorial bd. Procs.; Disting. Service award); mem. NATAS, Chgo. Soc. Fund Raising Execs. (pres. 1964-65), Chgo. Assn. Commerce and Industry (health-in-industry com.). Home: Clinton, Ill.

KRUGER, WILLIAM ARNOLD, consulting civil engineer, b. St. Louis, June 13, 1937; s. Reynold and Olinda (Siefker) K.; m. Carole Ann Hofer, Oct. 17, 1959. BCE, U. Mo.-Rolla, 1959; MS, U. Ill., 1968. Lic. profl. engr., Ill., Mo., Fla., Miss., N.Y., Iowa, Del., Ohio, Ind.; lic. profl. land surveyor, Ill. Civil engr. City of St. Louis, 1959; with Clark, Dietz & Assocs., and predecessors, Urbana, Ill., 1961-79, sr. design engr., 1963-67, dir. transp. div., 1968-79; civil engr. div. hwys. Ill. Dept. Transp., Paris, 1979-83; part-owner ESCA Cons., Inc., Urbana, 1983-88; civil engr. Zurheide-Herrmann, Inc., Champaign, 1988-95, v.p., from 1995. Instr. Parkland Coll., Champaign, 1972; mem. Ill. Prof. Engrs. Examining Com., 1982-89; mem. Ill. State Bd. Profl. Engrs., 1990—, vice chmn., 1993-94, chmn., 1995—. With C.E., AUS, 1959-61. Mem. ASTM, ASCE (br. pres. 1982-83, sect. pres. 1988-89, chmn. dist. coun. 1989), NSPE, Ill. Soc. Profl. Engrs. (chpt. pres. 1974, state chmn. registration laws com. 1973, 78), Ill. Assn. Hwy. Engrs., Am. Pub. Works Assn. (sect. dir. 1974-77, 80), Inst. Transp. Engrs., Ill. Profl. Land Surveyors Assn., Soc. Am. Mil. Engrs., Nat. Coun. Examiners for Engring. and Surveying (Disting. Svc. award 1992), U. Mo.-Rolla Acad. Civil Engrs., Ill. Engring. Coun. (dir. 1996-2000), Ill. Architect-Engr. Coun., U. Mo.-Rolla Alumni Assn., Champaign Ski Club, Theta Tau, Tau Beta Pi, Chi Epsilon, Pi Kappa Alpha. Home: Saint Louis, Mo. Deceased.

KRUMHANSL, JAMES ARTHUR, physicist, educator, industrial consultant; b. Cleve., Aug. 2, 1919; s. James and Marcella (Kelly) K.; m. Barbara Dean Schminck, Dec. 26, 1944 (div. 1983); children: James Lee, Carol Lynne, Peter Allen; m. Marilyn Cupp Dahl, Feb. 19, 1983. BS in Elec. Engring, U. Dayton, 1939; MS, Case Inst. Tech., 1940, D.Sc. (hon.), 1980; PhD in Physics, Cornell U., 1943. Instr. Cornell U., 1943-44; physicist Stromberg-Carlson Co., 1944-46; mem. faculty Brown U., 1946-48, assoc. prof., 1947-48; asst. prof., then asso. prof. Cornell U., 1948-55; asst. dir. research Nat. Carbon Co., 1955-57, asso. dir. research, 1957-58; prof. physics Cornell U., 1959—90, prof. emeritus, 1990—2004, Horace White prof., 1980. Dir. Lab. Atomic and Solid State Physics, 1960-64; adj. prof. U. Pa., 1979; fellow Los Alamos Lab., 1980; asst. dir. for math., phys. sci. and engring. NSF, 1977-79; cons. to industry, 1946; adv. com for AEC, Dept. Def., Nat. Acad. Sci.; vis. fellow All Souls Coll., Oxford U., 1977, Gonville and Caius Coll., Cambridge U., 1983, Royal Soc. London, 1983; Fulbright lectr., Yugoslavia, 1975. Editor Jour. Applied Physics, 1957-60; assoc. editor Solid State Communications, 1963-85, Rev. Modern Physics, 1968-73; editor Phys. Rev. Letters, 1974-78, physics Oxford U. Press, 1980-87; Contbr. articles to profl. jours. Guggenheim fellow, 1959-60; NSF sr. postdoctoral fellow Oxford U., 1966-67 Fellow Am. Phys. Soc. (chmn. div. solid state physics 1968, councillor 1970-74, pres. 1989), AAAS, Am. Inst. Physics (governing bd. 1987); mem. AAUP, Sigma Xi, Phi Kappa Phi. Clubs: Ithaca Yacht. Republican. Presbyterian. Home: Hanover, NH. Died May 6, 2004.

KRYSIAK, JOSEPH FRANCIS, manufacturing executive; b. Southbridge, Mass., Oct. 17, 1915; s. Paul Teophile and Amelia Barbara (Serdinski) K.; m. Julian Annette Kennedy, May 30, 1942; children: Carole Ann, Grant Joseph, Veda Gaye. Student, Cole Trade, 1931-34, Northeastern U., 1936-39, 39-43, Mass. State Coll., 1942-45. Machinist, toolmaker Am. Optical Co., Southbridge, 1934-36; toolmaker Westinghouse Electric Co., Springfield, Mass., from 1936; instr., asst. supr., supr. Matthews Mfg. Co., Worcester, Mass., 1936-39; specialist toolmaker Leland & Gifford, Worcester, 1939-40; toolmaker, designer, methods engr. Boston Navy Yard, 1940-46; pres., treas., gen. mgr. Atlantic Optical Moulding Co., Dudley, Mass., from 1946, also bd. dirs. Active Webster coun. Boys Scouts Am., Webster-Dudley Boys Club, Rotary Club, 1958-75. Avocations: swimming, fishing, dance. Home: Webster, Mass. Died Apr. 14, 2002.

KUBO, WATARU, Japanese government official; b. Jan. 15, 1929; Sec.-gen. Social Democratic Party of Japan; dep. prime min., min. of fin. Govt. of Japan, from 1996; mem. Ho. of Councillors. Died June 3, 2003; Japan.

KUISK, HANS, retired radiologist; b. Tallinn, Estonia, Oct. 16, 1913; came to U.S., 1949, citizen, 1955; MD, U. Tartu, Estonia, 1939, DSc. in Microbiology, 1941. Diplomate Am. Bd. Radiology. Chief asst. Inst. Microbiology U. Tartu, Estonia, 1941-44; intern St. Lukes Hosp., Fargo, N.D., 1950-51; pvt. practice Rutland, N.D., 1951-56; physician VAMC, Fargo, N.D., 1956-60; resident in radiology U. Minn., 1960-64, instr., 1964-67, asst. prof., 1967-73, assoc. prof. therapeutic radiology, 1973-76; chief Therapeutic Radiation Svc. VA Med. Ctr., Mpls., 1967-76; asst., acting chief Radiation Therapy Svc. VA W. L.A. Med. Ctr., 1976-90. Cons. VA West L.A. Med. Ctr.; clin. prof. UCLA. Sr. med. officer UN Relief and Rehab. Adminstrn., 1945-48. Fellow Am. Coll. Radiologists, Am. Soc. Therapeutic Radiology and Oncology; mem. Radiol. Soc. N.Am. Home: Los Angeles, Calif. Died Apr. 22, 2002.

KULLBERG, JOHN FRANCIS, not-for-profit administrator; b. Cranston, R.I., Apr. 16, 1939; s. Paul Frederick and Katherine Frances (Smith) K.; m. Karol Marie Runing, Sept. 15, 1979; children: Kathryn Marie, Kristen Frances, Evan Andrew. BA, Cath. U. Am., 1962; MA, U. R.I., 1967; postgrad., U. Ill., 1967-69; EdD, Columbia U., 1976. Chmn. dept. English, St. Raphael Acad., Pawtucket, R.I., 1962-64, Parkland Coll., Champaign, Ill., 1967-69; coordinator instrn. The Baldridge Reading Services, Greenwich, Conn., 1964-66; counselor Columbia Coll., Columbia U., N.Y.C., 1969-71; cons. The Dictaphone Corp., Rye, N.Y., 1969-71; dir. admissions, asst. dean Columbia U. Sch. Law, N.Y.C., 1971-77; postdoctoral fellow Office of Sec., Dept. HEW, Washington, 1977-78; pres. Am. Soc. Prevention Cruelty to Animals, N.Y.C., 1978-91, Guiding Eyes for the Blind, Yorktown Hgts., N.Y., 1991-93, cons., 1993-94; exec. dir. The Humane Soc. U.S. Wildlife Land Trust, 1994—2003. Advisor to N.Y. State Atty. Gen. on animal welfare legislation, 1974-77; pres. Soc. Animal Protective Legislation; lectr. in field. Author: The Communication Laboratory, 1971, also numerous essays; appearances in various TV and radio programs. Bd. dirs. Am. Soc. Prevention Cruelty to Animals, N.Y.C., 1976-78, N.Y. State Humane Assn., 1979-81, Am. Humane Assn., 1984-86, Wildlife Land Trust,

1998—, Farm Animal Reform Movement, 1999—; chmn. bd. Nat. Coalition to Protect Our Pets, 1986-89. Kellogg fellow Columbia U., 1971-73; recipient Man of Yr. award East Manhattan C. of C., 1986; Disting. Alumnus award Teachers Coll., Columbia U., 1992, Leadership in Habitat Preservation award Pegasus Found., 2000. Home: Germantown, Md. Died Apr. 20, 2003.

KUMLER, ROSE MARIE, career counselor, educator; b. Detroit, Dec. 22, 1935; d. Charles and Aida (Oliveri) Fiorini; m. Frank Wozniak, May 17, 1958 (div. 1975); children: Corrine, Paul. BBA, Western Internat. U., 1982; MA, U. Phoenix, 1985. Lic. career counselor, Ariz. Sales rep. Vestal Labs., Phoenix, 1978-79; personnel cons. Ford Personnel Cons. Inc., Phoenix, 1979-81; owner, career counselor Specialized Employment Evaluation Devel., Phoenix, from 1980; dist. supr. Grand Canyon Color Lab., Phoenix, 1981-83. Acad. dean Lamson Colls., Glendale, Ariz., 1983-86, instr. Phoenix Coll., Ottawa U., Phoenix, 1986—; speaker in field, 1987—. Chair subcom. of task force Ariz. Gov.'s Offices Women's Svcs.; active Ariz. Affirmative Action Assn., 1990—. Mem. Fellow Impact (strategic planning com. 1988, edn. com. 1988), The Network, Ariz. Career Devel. Assn. (pres. 1994-95), Am. Bus. Women's Assn. (sec. 1975), Soroptimists (judge 1988). Roman Catholic. Avocations: reading, swimming, dance, golf, cycling. Died Dec. 3, 2000.

KUPCINET, IRV, columnist; b. Chgo., July 31, 1912; s. Max and Anna (Paswell) K.; m. Essee Joan Solomon, Feb. 12, 1939; children: Karyn (dec.), Jerry Solomon. AB, Northwestern U., 1930-32, U. N.D., 1935. Columnist Chgo. Daily Times, 1935-43, Kup's Column, Chgo. Sun Times, 1943—; host TV program Kup's Show, Chgo., from 1959; commentator WBBM-TV, Chgo.; former commentator Chgo. Bears football broadcasts. Spl. cons. in charge of columnists for War Fin. Divsn., drives U.S. Treasury Dept. V.p. Dr. Jerome D. Solomon Meml. Found.; originator, host Purple Heart Cruise. Recipient 14 Emmy awards, numerous civic and profl. awards; Wabash Ave. Bridge, Chgo. renamed Irv Kupcinet Bridge, 1986. Mem. Newspaper Guild, Nat. Press Club (Washington), Chgo. Press Club, Tau Delta Phi. Home: Chicago, Ill. Died Nov. 10, 2003.

KUPFER, SHERMAN, physician, educator, researcher; b. Jersey City, Apr. 28, 1926; s. Max C. and Mildred Kupfer; m. Adele Glassman, Nov. 21, 1951; children: Marcia Ann, Joel Michael, Kenneth Charles. Student, Cornell U., 1942-44, MD, 1948. Intern Mt. Sinai Hosp., N.Y.C., 1948-49, chief resident medicine, 1951-53; instr. physiology Case-Western Res. U., Cleve., 1949-50, Cornell U. Med. Coll., N.Y.C., 1950-51, asst. prof. physiology, 1955-66; assoc. prof. to prof. physiology, biophysics and medicine Mt. Sinai Sch. Medicine, N.Y.C., from 1968, prin. investigator, dir. Clin. Research Ctr., 1962-86, asst. dean, assoc. dean, sr. assoc. dean, dep. dean, sr. v.p. research and edn., 1966-85. Assoc. editor, editor-in-chief The Mount Sinai Jour. of Medicine, 1986—. Trustee Free Synagogue, 1974-77, chmn. Jewish Chautauqua Soc., Westchester, 1976-77; sec., treas., trustee Med. Library Ctr., N.Y.C., 1974-85. Served to capt. USAF, 1953-55 Recipient research awards NIH, 1956, 62, U.S. Army, 1957 Fellow ACP; mem. Am. Physiol. Soc., Am. Soc. Artificial Internal Organs, Am. Heart Assn., Harvey Soc., N.Y. Acad. Medicine, N.Y. Acad. Sci., N.Y. Heart Assn., Assn. Med. Schs. (sec., treas. 1974-85) Home: New York, NY. Died Dec. 1, 2003.

KUPFERMAN, MEYER, composer; b. N.Y.C., July 3, 1926; s. Elias and Fanny (Hoffman) K.; m. Sylvia Kasten, June 16, 1946 (div.); 1 dau., Lisa; m. Pei-fen Chin, July 24, 1973. Student, Queens Coll., 1944-46. Co-dir. New Chamber Music Soc., 1946-48, Bolton Music Festival, Bolton Landing, N.Y., 1947-48; mem. forum group bd. N.Y. chpt. Internat. Soc. Contemporary Music, 1949-50; tchr. composition, chamber music, music for theatre Sarah Lawrence Coll., 1951-93, prof. emeritus, 1955—2003, chmn. music dept., 1979; dir., founder Sarah Lawrence Improvisational Ensemble, from 1967; composer-in-residence Calif. Music Ctr., 1977-80; former pres. Soundspells Prodns.; composer-in-residence N.Y. Virtuosi, 1997; condr. Monte Carlo Orch., 1999. Concert lectr. Colgate U., 1996, SUNY-New Paltz, 1996. Composer: debut, Steinway Hall, N.Y.C., 1946, film scores Hallelujah the Hills, 1962, A X'mas Memory, 1966, Blast of Silence, 1960, Faces of America, 1965, Goldstein, 1964, Black Like Me, 1964, Cool Wind, 1961, Among the Paths to Eden, 1968; (operas) In a Garden, 1948, The Curious Fern, 1957, Voices for a Mirror, 1957, Draagenfut Girl, 1958, Doctor Faustus Lights the Lights, 1963, The Judgement, 1966-67, Prometheus, 1976, The Proscenium, 1991; symphony Symphony No. 10: FDR, 1982, Clarinet Concerto, 1984, Ode to Shreveport, 1985, Sound Phantoms, #8, 1983, Challenger (for large orch.), 1983, A Little Ivory Concerto, 1986, Jazz Symphony, 1988, Savage Landscape, 1989, Double Concerto for 2 clarinets and orch. commd. by Nassau Symphony for soloists Stanley and Naomi Druker, 4 Piano Retrospective on March 8, at Katheryn Bache Miller Theatre featuring premieres of Symphonic Odyssey, Vilnius, Lithuania, 1990, Red Sonata, Snow and In Quiet Measure, with pianists Morton Estrin, Kuzuko Hayami, Christopher Vassiliades and Svetlana Gorokhovich, 1992, Ice Cream Concerto, 1992, The Moor's Concerto, 1993, Fantasy Concerto for Violin and Orchestra, 1997, Strata for Solo Flute, N.Y.C., 1997, Percussion Symphony, Ithaea Percussion Ensemble, 1997, Quasar Symphony, Vilnius, 1997, Sound Phantoms # 8, Sinfonia Brevis II, Vilnius, 1997; chamber music Cycle of Infinities, 1962-67, Images of Chagall, 1988, (recs.) Images of Chagall, Jazz Symphony and Challenger with Lithuauian Nat. Philharm., Clarinet Concerto with Pro Arte Chamber Orch. of Boston; (choreographed by Martha Graham) ballet score O Thou Desire, 1977, Concerto for Guitar and Orch. premiered by Orquesta de Baja Calif., Chaccone Sonata premiered by Laurel Ann Mauer, Hexagon Skies for guitar and orch., Infinites Projection for small orch., winter symphony for orch., 1999; author: Atonal Jazz; Third Piano Concerto, commd. by Christopher Vassiliades, 1999, Speculum Symphony '99 and Music for Guitar and Orchestra commd. by Robert Limon and the Orquestra de Baja Calif., 1998; commd. Concerto Brevis for Flute and Orch., Nat. Flute Assn., 1999: Concerto Brevis, A Faust Concerto, Lunar Symphony, 1999, Speculum Symphony, 1999, Tinker Hill, 1999, Fly by Night (for two solo clarients and orch.), 2000, Icon Symphony, 2000, Quantum Symphony, 2000, Structures for Orchestra, 2001, Elegy for the Vanished, 2001, Violin Concerto: The Voyager, 2001, Concerto for Guitar and Strings, Tuba and Orchestra, 2002. First recipient La Guardia Meml. award outstanding achievement field music, 1958, Music award Am. Acad. and Inst. Arts and Letters, 1981, Dutchess County Individual Artist's award, 1991; Nat. Endowment Arts grantee, 1974; Guggenheim fellow, 1974-75; Ford Found. grantee, 1975-76 Mem. ASCAP (mem. Deems Taylor Award com. of judges). Died Dec. 3, 2003.

KUPFERMAN, THEODORE R. former state justice, lawyer; b. N.Y.C., May 12, 1920; s. Samuel H. and Gertrude Kupferman; m. Dorothee Hering, Dec. 21, 1957 (dec. June 1969); children: Theodore R. Jr., Stephanie Elisabeth; m. Fran Liner, Sept. 12, 1975. BS, City Coll. N.Y.; LLB (Kent scholar, editor Law Rev.), Columbia U. Bar: N.Y., U.S. Supreme Ct. Law sec. presiding Judge D.W. Peck, appellate divsn. N.Y. State Supreme Ct., 1948-49; mem. legal dept. Warner Bros. Pictures, Inc., 1949-51, NBC, 1951-53; sec., v.p., gen. counsel Cinerama Prodns. Corp., 1953-59; ptnr. Kupferman & Price, 1959-66; counsel firm Battle, Fowler, Stokes & Kheel, N.Y.C., 1966-69; justice Supreme Ct., State of N.Y., 1969-70; assoc. justice Appellate Divsn., 1st Dept., 1971-96; formerly counsel Tunick, Kupferman & Creadore; former ptnr. Kupferman & Kupferman. Mem. State Indsl. Bd. Appeals, 2000-01; asst., then adj. prof. law N.Y. Law Sch., 1959-64; counsel, legis. asst. minority leader S.M. Isaacs, N.Y. City Coun., 1958-62 Former Editor-in-chief Comm. and the Law Quar. Mem. N.Y. City Coun., 1962-66; mem. 89-90th Congress 17th Dist. N.Y.; past chmn. youth svcs. com., former bd. dirs. YMCA, N.Y.C.; pres. Layman's Nat. Bible Com., 1975-80, chmn. bd., 1980-86; former bd. dirs. Practising Law Inst. Col. J.A.G. N.Y. State Guard, 1979-88. Recipient Finley award for mcpl. svc. Mem. ABA (past editor bull. sect. internat. and comparative law, Congl. affairs editor Internat. Lawyer), N.Y. State Bar Assn. (former chmn. judges speakers bur., spl. com. on cts. and community), Fed. Bar Coun. (pres. 1954-56, chmn. bd. dirs. 1956-60), Consular Law Soc. (past pres., trustee), Am. Arbitration Assn. (former mem. panel arbitrators), Theodore Roosevelt Assn. (pres. 1986-90), Acad. Polit. Sci., Internat. Radio and TV Soc., Med. Jurisprudence Soc. (chmn. bd., past pres.), City Club (past pres. N.Y.C. chpt.) Phi Beta Kappa (past pres. Gamma chpt., bd. dirs. Phi Beta Kappa Assocs.). Republican. Home: New York, NY. Died Sept. 20, 2003.

KUPFERMANN, IRVING, neurobiology educator, researcher; b. Jan. 26, 1938; s. Paul and Anna Kupfermann; m. Aug. 19, 1965; children: David, Celina. BS, U. Fla., 1959; PhD, U. Chgo., 1964. Asst. prof. NYU, N.Y.C., 1969-73, assoc. prof., 1973-74; assoc. rsch. scientist N.Y. State Psychiat. Inst., N.Y.C., from 1973; Columbia U., N.Y.C., from 1979, prof., from 1979. Assoc. rsch. scientist N.Y. State Psychiat. Inst., N.Y.C., 1974—. Contbr. over 100 articles to profl. jours. Grantee NIMH; recipient Merit award NIMH, Career Devel. award. Home: Port Washington, NY. Died Feb. 19, 2002.

KUPSCH, WALTER OSCAR, geologist; b. Amsterdam, Netherlands, Mar. 2, 1919; emigrated to Can., 1950, naturalized, 1956; s. Richard Leopold and Elizabeth (Heuser) K.; m. Emmy Helene de Jong, Oct. 2, 1945; children— Helen Elizabeth, Yvonne Irene, Richard Christopher. M. Cand, U. Amsterdam, 1943; M.Sc., U. Mich., 1948, PhD, 1950, LLD (hon.), 1997. Asst. prof. geology U. Sask., Saskatoon, Can., 1950-56, assoc. prof., 1956-64, prof., 1964-86, emeritus prof., from 1986. Dir. Inst. North Studies, 1965-73, Churchill River Study, 1973-76, Sask. Heritage Assocs. Ltd., 1973-76; bd. govs. Arctic Inst. N.Am., 1969-74, chmn., 1973-74; mem. Sci. Coun. Can., 1976-82; vice chmn. sci. adv. bd. N.W. Terrs., 1976-85; exec. dir. adv. com. Devel. of Govt. in N.W. Terrs., 1965-66; petroleum advisor to Govt. N.W. Terrs., 1980-85; mem. North Devel. adv. coun. to Govt. Sask., 1985-88; mem. BHP Diamond Mine Environ. Rev. Panel, N.W. Terrs., 1994-96. Contbr. articles to profl. jours. Served with Netherlands Army, 1939-40. Recipient Pub. Svc. award Commr. N.W.T., 1992, Queen's Golden Jubilee medal, 2002; named mem. Order of Can., 1996. Fellow Royal Soc. Can., Geol. Soc. Am., Royal Can. Geographic Soc., Geol. Assn. Can., Arctic Inst. N.Am.; mem. Am. Assn. Petroleum Geologists, Sask. Geol. Soc. Home: Saskatoon, Canada. Died July 6, 2003.

KURSUNOGLU, BEHRAM N. physicist, researcher; b. Caykara, Turkey, Mar. 14, 1922; came to U.S., 1958; s. Ismail and Hanife (Esenulku) K.; m. Sevda Arif, Sept. 25, 1952; children— Sevil, Ayda, Ismet. B.Sc., Edinburgh (Scotland) U., 1949; PhD, Cambridge (Eng.) U., 1952; D.Sci. (hon.), Fla. Inst. Tech., 1982. Mem. faculty Cornell U., 1952-54, Yale, 1955; with Turkish Gen. Staff on Atomic Matters, 1956-58, Turkish Atomic Energy Commn., 1956-58; dean faculty nuclear scis. and tech. Middle East Tech. U., Ankara, Turkey, 1956-58; vis. prof. physics U.Miami, Coral Gables, Fla., 1954-55; prof. physics U. Miami, 1958-92; mem. NATO Scis. Com., 1958; dir. Center for Theoretical Studies, 1965-92. Chmn. ann. Internat. Sci. Forum on Energy, 1977-92; cons. Oak Ridge Nat. Lab., 1962-64, Brit. Atomic Energy Establishment, 1961, Max Planck-Institut fur Physik and Astrophysik, 1961 Author: Modern Quantum Theory, 1962; editor: (with Eugene Wigner) Reminiscences of a Great Physicist, Paul Adrien Maurice Dirac, 1987; contbr. articles to profl.jours. Former Pres. Global Found. Recipient Sci. prize of Turkey, 1972 Fellow Am. Phys. Soc.; mem. Sigma Xi. Research on elementary particles, gen. relativity, statis. mechanics, nuclear energy and environment and arms control issues. Home: Miami, Fla. Died Oct. 25, 2003.

KURTICH, JOHN WILLIAM, architect, film-maker, educator; b. Salinas, Calif., Oct. 18, 1935; s. John Joseph and Elizabeth (Lyons) K. BA in Theatre and Cinematography, UCLA, 1957; BArch, U. Calif., Berkeley, 1966; MS in Architecture and Urban Design, Columbia U., 1968. Filmmaker SMP Architects, San Francisco, 1960-61; film-maker, archtl. draftsman McCue & Assocs., San Francisco, 1962-66; freelance film-maker, designer Friedberg, N.Y., 1968; instr. Sch. of Art Inst., Chgo., 1968-70, asst. prof., 1970-74, assoc. prof., 1974-82, prof., 1982—2004, chmn. dept. design and communication, 1981-85, area head interior arch., 1987-94, chmn. undergrad. divsn. Staff arch. Am. Excavations, Samothrace, Greece, 1970-2004; archtl. cons. Fed. Res. Bank Chgo., 1978; William Bronson Mitchell and Grayce Slovet Mitchell endowed chair in Interior Architecture, 1995-2004. Multi-media prodns. include: Hellas, Columbia U., N.Y.C., 1968, Art Inst. Chgo., 1971, 79, Muncie: Microsm of America (NEA grante), Muncie, Ind., 1972, Legend of the Minotaur, Art Inst. Chgo., 1973, The Seasons, Shapes, Contrasts, Art Inst. Chgo., 1977, 83, 84, Canal du Midi, Art Inst. Chgo., 1987, Light: A History of Architecture from Stonehenge to the Fall Of Western Civilization, Graham Found., 1988, The Desert of Rets, Graham Found., 1989, The Mysteries of Samothrace, Art Inst. Chgo., 1989, Echoes of Eternity, Art Inst. Chgo., 1989, Porno Versailles, Graham Found., 1990, Monuments and Memorials, State Ill. Art Gallery, 1990, The Art Institute of Chicago: The Corporation, Art Inst. Chgo., 1990, The Seven Wonders of the World, Mus. Contemporary Art, 1991, Design in the Fourth Dimension Space-Time, Neo Con/Chgo. Architecture Found., 1993, The Ancient World, Art Inst. Chgo., 1994, Ilumine: The Architecture of Light, Graham Found., 1995, Recent Excavations at Samothrace, Graham Found., 1996. Served with USNR, 1957-60. Recipient Architecture medal Alpha Rho Chi, 1966; William Kinne fellow Columbia U., Fgn. Travelling fellow; grantee NEA, 1972, Woman's Bd. Art Inst. Chgo., 1973, Union Ind. Colls. Art, 1974, Fulbright-Hays (Eng.), 1976, Fulbright-Hays (Jordan), 1981, Ford Foun./Art Inst Chgo. Faculty Enrichment, 1982, 87, 91, 93, 2000, Graham Found. for Advanced Studies in Fine Arts, 1988. Fellow Royal Soc. Arts (London); mem. AIA (corp. mem.), Soc. Archtl. Historians, Nat. Com. for Interiors, Chgo. Archtl. Club. Home: Chicago, Ill. Died Mar. 29, 2004.

KYL, JOHN HENRY, former business executive; b. Wisner, Nebr., May 9, 1919; s. John George and Johanna (Boonstra) K.; m. Arlene Pearl Griffith, May 16, 1941; children— Jon, Jannene Kyl Martin, Jayne. AB, Nebr. State Tchrs. Coll., 1940; MA in Sch. Adminstrn, U. Nebr., 1947; postgrad., Drake U., U. Nebr. Mem. 86th-88th, 90th-92d Congresses from 4th Iowa Dist.; asst. sec. congl. legis. affairs U.S. Dept. Interior, Washington, 1973-77; exec. v.p. Occidental Internat. Corp., Washington, 1977-85. Trustee Herbert Hoover Presdl. Library, 1973—, Iowa Natural Heritage Found.; mem. Public Land Law Rev. Commn., Outdoor Recreational Resources Commn., Lewis and Clark Trail Commn. Republican. Presbyterian. Home: Phoenix, Ariz. Died Dec. 23, 2002.

LABALME, PATRICIA HOCHSCHILD, foundation administrator; b. N.Y.C., Feb. 26, 1927; d. Walter and Kathrin (Samstag) Hochschild; m. George Labalme, Jr., June 6, 1958; children: Jennifer R., Henry G., Lisa G., Victoria A. BA magna cum laude, Bryn Mawr Coll., 1948; MA, Harvard U., 1950, PhD, 1958. Instr. history Wellesley Coll., Mass., 1952-57; tchr. history Brearley Sch., N.Y.C., 1957-59; lectr. Barnard Coll., N.Y.C., 1961-77; adj. assoc. prof. history Hunter Coll., N.Y.C., 1979; lectr. NYU, N.Y.C., 1980-82, adj. prof. history, 1986-87; assoc. dir. Inst. for Advanced Study, Princeton, N.J., 1982-88, sec. corp., 1982-92, asst. to dir., 1992-97, visitor Sch. Hist. Studies, 1997-98; mem. adv. bd. Gladys Krieble Delmas Found., N.Y.C., 1976—79, trustee, from 1979. Trustee Am. Acad. in Rome, N.Y.C., 1979—99; exec. dir. Renaissance Soc. Am., N.Y.C., 1982—85, trustee, 1982—89, N.Y.C., from 1998. Author: Bernardo Giustiniani: A Venetian of the Quattrocento, 1969; contbg. editor: Beyond Their Sex: Learned Women of the European Past, 1980, A Century Recalled: Essays in Honor of Bryn Mawr College, 1987; contbr. articles to profl. jours. and publs. Trustee Brearley Sch., 1975-83, pres., 1978-82, hon. trustee, 1983—; trustee Lawrenceville Sch., 1985-96, trustee emerita, 1996—. Recipient Caroline A. Wilby prize Radcliffe Coll., 1958 Mem. Am. Hist. Assn., Soc. for Renaissance Studies, Renaissance Soc. Am., Ateneo Veneto, Cosmopolitan Club, Harvard Club (N.Y.C.), Cream Hill Lake Assn. (West Cornwall, Conn.), Phi Beta Kappa. Home: New York, NY. Died Oct. 11, 2002.

LACOMBE, MICHAEL, information technology executive; Grad., Ecole Supérieure Libre des Sciences Commerciales Appliquées, 1977. Sales engr. Sharp Electronics Corp.; retail sales mgr. Microsoft, Redmond, Wash., 1983, dep. gen. mgr. sales and mktg. ops., 1984, regional dir. So. Europe, 1991; v.p. Microsoft Europe; sr. v.p., chmn. Microsoft Europe, Middle East and Africa. Died Jan. 2003.

LACY, MARGARET ROSE, retired educator; b. Wellston, Ohio, July 13, 1922; d. Harry and Ruth Russell (Rockwell) L. BS in Bus. Edn. cum laude, Miami U., 1964; MA in Bus. Edn., Ohio State U., 1967. Sec., co-mgr. Fowler's Camera Shop, Portsmouth, Ohio, 1940-58; sec., loan dept. Security Cen. Nat. Bank, Portsmouth, 1958-62; tchr., bus. edn. Cleveland Heights (Ohio) Sch. Dist., 1964-66; tchr., vocat. bus. edn. Minford (Ohio) Local Sch. Dist., 1966-71, Scioto County Joint Vocat. Sch., Lucasville, Ohio, 1971-84; med. transcriptionist Kendall L. Stewart, MD, Portsmouth, 1990-91. Real estate photographer Portsmouth Daily Times, 1994—. Mem. Ret. Sr. Vol. Program, 1985—; vol. Bur. Svcs. for Visually Impaired, 1986—. Mem. Nat. Bus. Edn. Assn., Am. Vocat. Assn., Ohio Vocat. Assn., Ohio Bus. Edn. Assn., North-Cen. Bus. Edn. Assn. Republican. Presbyterian. Avocations: photography travel, walking, reading, family. Home: Portsmouth, Ohio. Died May 3, 2002.

LACY, STEVE, jazz musician; b. N.Y.C., 1934; Played soprano sax at Schillinger House, Boston; performed with Pee Wee Russell, Rex Stewart, Buck Clayton, Jimmy Rushing, Dicky Wells, Walter Page, N.Y.C., 1953-54; played with Cecil Taylor; then with Gil Evans' orch., 1957; formed quartet with Roswell Rudd, experimenting with chord-free improvisation and unusual song forms, early 1960s; formed sextet, 1970; played regular duets with Mal Waldron. Recordings include Soprano Sax (debut), 1957, Reflections: Steve Lacy Plays Thelonius Monk, 1958, Evidence (with Don Cherry), 1961, Paris Blues (with Gil Evans), Raps, 1977, Steve Lacy Three: New York Capers, 1979, The Way, 1979, Ballets, 1980, Herbe de L'Oubli & Snake Out (with Mal Waldron), 1981, Songs (with Brion Gysin), 1985, 86, Let's Call This (with Mal Waldron), Prospectus, 1986, Steve Lacy Two, Five & Six: Blinks, 1986, Steve Lacy Nine: Futurities, 1986, The Straight Horn of Steve Lacy, The Door (duos, trios, etc.), 1989, Anthem, 1990, Hot House (with Mal Waldron), 1991, Live at Sweet Basil, 1992, Steve Lacy Solo, 1993, Vespers, 1993, Spirit of Mingus (with Eric Watson), 1996; composed/played musical score Landing live for D. Dunn, 1992. Frequent winner Down Beat Mag. poll, best soprano saxist, 1992. Died June 5, 2004.

LADYZHENSKAYA, OLGA ALEXANDROVNA, physics educator; Grad., Moscow State U., 1947; PhD, Leningrad State U., 1949; DS, Moscow State U., 1953. Prof. physics Acad. Scis. Russia, Dkeklov Math. Inst., St. Petersburg. Mem. Soc. Indsl. & Appled Math. Died Jan. 12, 2004.

LAGARDÈRE, JEAN-LUC, engineering executive; b. Aubiet, France, Feb. 10, 1928; s. André Lagardère and Marthe Fourcade; 1 child, Arnaud. BS in Engring., École Supérieure d'Électricité. Engr., dept. head gen. aero. Marcel Dassault, 1951-62; exec. dir.-gen. Sociéte Matra, 1963-76; pres., dir.-gen. Société Matra and divsns., 1977-92, Société Hachette, 1981-92; exec. dir. Europe 1 Images et Son, 1972, v.p., 1973, pres., 1979-81, Matra Hachette et Gérant, from 1992; co-chmn. European Aeronautic Def. and Space Co., Paris, from 2000. Bd. dirs. Renault; pres. Found. Hachette, 1989—; adv. com. Chase Manhattan Bank, N.Y., 1990. Internat. adv. bd. Chase Manhattan Bank, N.Y.C. Decorated officier Légion d'Honneur (France), comdr. l'Ordre Nat. du Merité; named Mgr. of Yr., Nouvel Economiste, 1979. Avocations: soccer, tennis, skiing. Died Mar. 14, 2003.

LAIDLAW, HARRY HYDE, JR., entomology educator; b. Apr. 12, 1907; s. Harry Hyde and Elizabeth Louisa (Quinn) L.; m. Ruth Grant Collins, Oct. 26, 1946; 1 child, Barbara Scott Laidlaw Murphy. BS, La. State U., 1933, MS, 1934; PhD, U. Wis., 1939. Tchg. asst. La. State U., 1933—34, rsch. asst., 1934—35; prof. biol. sci. Oakland City (Ind.) Coll., 1934—91; state apiarist Ala. Dept. Agr. and Industries, Montgomery, 1941—42; entomologist First Army, N.Y.C., 1946—47; asst. prof. entomology, asst. apiculturist U. Calif., Davis, 1947—53, assoc. prof. entomology, assoc. apiculturist, 1953—59, prof. entomology, apiculturist, 1959—74, prof. entomology emeritus, apicultureist emeritus, 1974; assoc. dean Coll. Agr., 1960—64, chair agr. faculty, staff, 1965—66. Coord. U. Calif.-Egypt Agrl. Devel. Program AID, 1979—83. Author (with J.E. Eckert): Queen Rearing, 1950; author: Instrumental Insemination of Honey Bee Queens, 1977, Contemporary Queen Rearing, 1979, (slide set) Instrumental Insemination of Queen Honey Bees, 1976; author: (with R.E. Page Jr.) Queen Rearing and Bee Breeding, 1998. Trustee Yolo County (Calif.) Med. Soc. Scholarship Com., 1965—83. Capt. AUS, 1942—46, capt. AUSR, 1952, maj. AUSR, 1952, LTC AUSR, 1956. Named honored guest, Tamagawa U., Tokyo, 1980; recipient Cert. of Merit, Am. Bee Jour., 1957, Merit award, Calif. Ctrl. Valley Bee Club, 1974, Apicultural Soc., 1980, Gold Merit award, Internat. Fedn. Beekeepers' Assns., 1986, Disting. Svc. award, Ariz. Beekeepers Assn., 1987, Cert. of Appreciation, Calif. State Beekeepers's Assn., 1987, award, Alan Clemson Meml. Found., 1989, Award of Distinction, Coll. Agrl. and Environ. Scis. U. Calif. Davis, 1997; fellow Genetics fellow, Alumni Rsch. Found.; grantee, Rockefeller Found., Brazil, 1954—55, NIH, 1963—66, NSF, 1966—74. Fellow: Soc. Am., Entomol. Soc. Am. (honoree spl. symposium 1990, C.W. Woodworth award Pacific br. 1981), AAAS; mem.: Ret. Officers Assn. (2nd v.p. Sacramento chpt. 1984—86), Nat. Assn. Uniformed Svcs., Am. Soc. Integrative Biology, Am. Inst. Biol. Scis., Scabbard and Blade, Sigma Xi (treas. Davis chpt. 1959—60, v.p. chpt. 1966—67), Alpha Gamma Rho (pres. La. chpt. 1933—34, counsellor We. Province 1960—66). Democrat. Presbyterian. Achievements include determination of cause of failure of attempts to artificially inseminate queen honey bees; invention of instruments and procedures to consistently accomplish same; elucidation of genetic relationships of individuals of polyandrous honey bee colonies; design of genetic procedures for behavioral study and breeding of honey bees for general and specific uses. Home: Davis, Calif. Died Sept. 2003.

LAING, EDWARD ARTHUR, government official, judge; b. Belize City, Belize, Feb. 27, 1942; s. Edward Arthur and Marjorie Eunice (Dunn) L.; m. Margery Victoria Fairweather, Apr. 5, 1969; children: Nyasha, Obi. BA, Cambridge U., 1964, LLM, 1966, Columbia U., 1968. Bar: Eng. 1966, Ill. 1969, Belize 1970, Barbados 1972, D.C. 1985. Assoc. Baker & McKenzie, Chgo. and N.Y.C., 1968-69; sr. lectr. U. West Indies, Barbados and Jamaica, 1970-75; asst. prof. Notre Dame U., Ind., 1974-76; assoc. prof. U. Md., Balt., 1976-81; prof. Howard U., Washington, 1980-85; amb. to U.S. and Can. Govt. of Belize, Washington, 1985-90; prof. N.Y. Law Sch., 1990-93; elected judge Internat. Tribunal for the Law of the Sea, Hamburg, from 1996; permanent rep. of Belize to UN, 1993-97; magistrate, crown counsel Belize Govt., 1966-67. Faculty adviser Internat. Trade Law Jour., Balt., 1976-81; participant numerous Summit Confs. and exec. bd. UN Devel. Program; internat. adjudicator trade and bus. law, law of the sea; cons. to UN agys. on internat. devel. and governance, consolidation of democracy and human rights, legal edn. Author: Introduction to Caribean Law, 1973; contbr. articles to profl. jours. Ind. advisor Belize C. of C., 1981; founder, 1st pres. N.Y. Belizean Com., N.Y.C., 1999, Consortium for Belizean Devel., Washington, 1985. Govt. of Belize scholar, 1961-66; Fulbright travel grantee, 1967; Ford Found. rsch. grantee, 1972; World Intellectual Property Orgn. Acad. grantee, 1997. Mem. Am. Soc. Internat. Law. Avocations: outdoors, camping, canoeing. Home: New Rochelle, NY. Died Sept. 2001.

LAITONE, EDMUND VICTOR, mechanical engineer; b. San Francisco, Sept. 6, 1915; s. Victor S. L.; m. Dorothy Bishop, Sept. 1, 1951; children: Victoria, Jonathan A. BSME, U. Calif., Berkeley, 1938; PhD in Applied Mechanics, Stanford U., 1960. Aero. engr. Nat. Adv. Com. for Aeros., Langley Field, Va., 1938-45; sect. head, flight engr. Cornell Aero. Lab., Buffalo, 1945-47; prof. U. Calif., Berkeley, from 1947. Cons. aero. engr. Hughes Aircraft & Douglas Aircraft, 1948-78; U.S. acad. rep. to flight mechanics AGARD/NATO, 1984-88; chmn. engring. dept. U. Calif. Extension, Berkeley, 1979-96. Author: Surface Waves, 1960; author, editor: Integrated Design of Advanced Fighter Aircraft, 1987; contbr. articles to Jour. Aero. Scis., Aircraft and Math. Jour. Named Miller Rsch. prof., 1960, U.S. Exch. prof., Moscow, 1964; vis. fellow Balliol Coll., 1968; vis. prof. Northwestern Poly. Inst., Xian, China, 1980. Fellow AIAA (San Francisco region chmn. 1960-61, assoc. fellow 1964-88); mem. Am. Math Soc., Am. Soc. for Engring. Edn. Achievements include discovery of effect of acceleration on longitudinal dynamic stability of a missile; nonlinear dynamic stability of space vehicles entering or leaving atmosphere; higher approximations to nonlinear water waves. Home: Moraga, Calif. Died Dec. 18, 2000.

LAKE, ANN WINSLOW, lawyer; b. Lowell, Mass., May 14, 1919; d. Frank and Helen Jablonski; BS, Lowell State Coll., 1940; JD, U. Detroit, 1946; MA, Boston State Coll., 1964, Boston U., 1967; m. Thomas E. Lake, Sept. 5, 1942; children: Beverly Wilkes, Douglas, Warren. Tchr. schs. in Maine, Ga. and Detroit, 1940-43; admitted to Mass. bar, 1946; ind. practice, Dedham, Mass., 1946—; prof. law Salem (Mass.) State Coll., 1970-90, prof. emerita, 1990; mem. Mass. Commn. Study Labor Laws, 1972-74, Mass. Mental Health Legal Advisers Com., 1974-79; mem. mktg. bd. ABA-GPS, 1993—; mem. ABA commn. coll. and univ. legal studies, 1994—. Mem. Mass. Adv. Commn. Acad. Talented Pupils, 1960-64, Mass. State Coll. Bldg. Authority, 1964-67, Mass. Com. to Recruit and Screen Candidates for Office Atty. Gen., 1974-78, U. Lowell Found., 1977-82; chmn. Dedham (Mass.) Coun. on Aging, 1993—. Recipient award Mass. State Coll. Alumni Assn., 1963, 64, 72, Mass. Assn. Mental Health, 1969, 72. Fellow Am. Bar Found. (life), Mass. Bar Found. (life); mem. Nat. Assn. Women Lawyers (pres. 1980-81), Polish Bus. and Profl. Women's Club Greater Boston (pres. 1977-79), Norfolk Mental Health Assn. (pres. 1972-73), Mass. Assn. Women Lawyers (pres. 1971-72), Assn. Mass. State Colls. Alumni (pres. 1961-64), Riverdale Improvement Assn. (pres. 1959). Republican. Died Feb. 28, 2003.

LAKSHMINARAYANA, BUDUGUR, aerospace engineering educator; b. Shimoga, India, Feb. 15, 1935; came to U.S., 1963, naturalized, 1971; m. Saroja Lakshminarayana; children: Anita, Arvind. BME, Mysore U., India, 1958; PhD, U. Liverpool, Eng., 1963, DEng, 1981. Asst. mech. engr. Kolar (India) Gold Mining Undertakings, 1958-60; rschr. in mech. engring. U. Liverpool, 1960-63, Leverhulme fellow, 1962-63; asst. prof. aerospace engring. Pa. State U., University Park, 1963-69, assoc. prof., 1969-74, prof., 1974-85, dir. computational fluid dynamics studies, 1980-87, disting. alumni prof., 1985-86, Evan Pugh prof., from 1986, dir. Ctr. for Gas Turbines and Power, from 1994. Vis. fellow scientist Cambridge U., St. John's Coll., Eng., 1971-72; vis. assoc. prof. aeros. and astronautics MIT, 1972; vis. prof. dept. mech. engring. Indian Inst. Sci., 1979; aerospace engr. computational fluid mechanics group NASA Ames Rsch. Ctr., Moffett Field, Calif., 1979; CNRS vis. prof. Laboratoire de Mecanique des Fluides at d'Acoustique, Ecole Centrale de Lyon, France, 1987-88; vis. prof. Tech. U. of Aachen, Germany, 1988; adv. prof. Inst. Thermophysics Chinese Acad. Scis., 1993, Shanghai Jiao Tong U., China, 1993; cons. Pratt & Whitney Aircraft, GE Aircraft Engine Div., Allied Signal, Allison Engine Co., Teledyne CAE, Inc.; UN, NATO/AGARD lectr.; Gen. Motors, Rolls Royce, European Space Agy.; mem. NASA adv. group on computational fluid dynamics, 1980; lectr. in field. Author: Fluid Dynamics and Heat Transfer of Turbomachinery, 1995; editor 2 books; contbr. numerous articles on fluid dynamics, turbomachinery, computational fluid dynamics, turbulence modelling and acoustics to profl. publs. Recipient Henry R. Worthington N.Am. tech. award, 1977, sr. prof. Fulbright award, 1988, Arch. T. Colwell merit award Soc. Automotive Engrs., 1992, Worcester Reed Warner medal, 2001; merit scholar Mysore U., 1953-57; grantee NSF, numerous others. Fellow AIAA (chmn. Ctrl. Pa. chpt. 1970, Pendrey Lit. award 1989, Airbreathing Propulsion award 1994), ASME (Freeman Scholar award 1990, Fluids Engring. award 1996, IGTI aircraft engine tech. award 1997, Worcester Reed Warner medal). Home: State College, Pa. Died 2002.

LALLY, RICHARD FRANCIS, aviation security consultant, former association executive, former government official; b. Newark, Nov. 23, 1925; s. Francis J. and Helen (Fennesy) L.; m. Doris P. Yasko, Sept. 10, 1949; children: Barbara J. Lally-Dittler, Joan E. BS, Upsala Coll., 1950. Spl. agt. FBI, Atlanta, Cin. and Washington, 1951-60; area dir., chief gen. investigations Dept. Labor, Newark and Washington, 1960-63; dep. dir. compliance and security FAA, Washington, 1963-65, dir. compliance and security, 1965-67; dir. investigations and security Dept. Transp., Washington, 1967-70, dir. equal opportunity, 1967-70, dir. civil rights, 1970-72, dir. transp. security, 1972-74; dir. civil aviation security FAA, 1974-82; v.p. security Air Transport Assn. Am., 1982-91; aviation security consultant, from 1991. Served with AC U.S. Army, 1944-46. Recipient Exceptional Svc. citation Dept. Trans., 1969, Meritorious Achievement award, 1970, Sec.'s award, 1973, Superior Achievement award, 1970, Sec.'s award, 1973, Superior Achievement award, 1973, 76, Superior Achievement in Equal Opportunity award, 1977, Disting. Alumnus award Upsala Coll., 1979, Presdl. Rank Sr. Exec. award, 1980, Extraordinary Svc. award FAA, 1991, Internat. Security Mgmt. Assn. J. Paul Breslin Recognition award, 1993. Died Jan. 3, 2004.

LAMBERT, ELEANOR (MRS. SEYMOUR BERKSON), public relations executive, fashion authority, journalist; b. Crawfordsville, Ind., Aug. 10, 1903; d. Henry Clay and Helen Houghton (Craig) L.; m. Seymour Berkson, 1936 (dec. 1959); 1 son, William Craig Berkson. Student, John Herron Art Inst., Chgo. Art Inst.; DFA (hon.), Parsons Sch. Design, 1993. Pioneer publicist for Am. art and artists and later for creative talents in Am. fashion; originator, coordinator Coty Am. Fashion Critics Award and Cotton Fashion Awards; originator, founder, coord. Nat. Fashion Press weeks and ann. Internat. Best Dressed polls; pres. Eleanor Lambert Ltd., N.Y.C. Original dir. ILGWU's consumer svc. program; prodr. large fashion shows; spl. cons. on uniforms WAC and U.S. Army Nurse Corps, 1943-45; mem. NRC adv. com. to q.m. on women's mil. clothing; mem. adv. com. Costume Inst., Met. Mus. Art; apptd. by Pres. Johnson as mem. Nat. Coun. on Arts, 1965-66; founder, charter mem. Coun. Fashion Designers of Am., 1963; mem. N.Y. Mayor's Com. World Fashion Ctr.; mem. Mayor's Hospitality Com., N.Y.; bd. dirs. N.Y. World's Fair, 1964; founder, organizer Fashion Inst. Tech. Sch. Author: World of Fashion, 1973, syndicated column on women's interests. Recipient N.Y. Bd. of Trade gold medal award for outstanding contbns. to Am. fashion industries, 1960; Honor award Girls Clubs Am.; Matrix award in pub. rels. N.Y. Women in Communications, 1985; Lifetime Achievement awards Coun. Fashion Designers of Am., 1988, 94. Mem. N.Y. Fashion Group (v.p. 1961-63). Presbyterian. Home: New York, NY. Died Oct. 7, 2003.

LAMBOS, CONSTANTINE PETER, lawyer; b. Aug. 4, 1926; s. Peter Constantine and Elizabeth (Malaspinas) L.; m. Theodora Kaganis, June 15, 1952; children: Peter, William, Andrew. LLB, NYU, 1948. Bar: N.Y. 1948, U.S. Dist. Ct. (so. and ea. dists.) N.Y., U.S. Ct. Appeals (2d, 3d, 4th, 5th & 11th cirs.), U.S. Supreme Ct. Atty. AT&T, 1948-51; assoc. McLanahan, Merritt & Ingraham, 1951-54, Lorenz, Finn & Giardino, 1955-58; ptnr. Lorenz, Finn. Giardino & Lambos, N.Y.C., 1958-81; sr. ptnr. Lambos, Flynn, Nyland & Giardino, N.Y.C., 1981-96, Lambos & Junge, from 1996. Adj. prof. law N.Y. Law Sch. Pres., Taxpayes Assn. N.E. Yonkers, 1963-65; pres. bd. trustees Holy Trinity Greek Orthodox Ch., 1961-64. Editor-in-chief NYU Law Quar. Rev. Served with AUS, 1944-46. Mem. ABA, N.Y. State Bar Assn., N.Y. County Lawyers Bar Assn. Democrat. Home: Odessa, Fla. Died Feb. 8, 2003.

LAMONTAGNE, NORMAND EDWARD, safety consultant; b. New Bedford, Mass., Apr. 14, 1925; s. Herman G. and Cora Alma (Messier) LaM.; m. Mary Curtin, June 9, 1951; children: Paula, Anne, Lisa, Anthony, Gregg. BS in Indsl. Engring., Northeastern U., Boston, 1951. Cert. safety profl., Ill., 1972; registered profl. engr., Calif., 1975. Engr. supr. Am. Ins. Group, various locations, 1951-59; asst. v.p. loss control Johnson & Higgins, N.Y.C., Boston, 1959-90; ret., 1990; safety cons., from 1990. Commr. Pond Meadow Park, Weymouth, Mass., 1973—. Lt. USAF, 1943-45, ETO. Mem. Am. Soc. Safety Engrs. (dir. 1983-87; safety profl. of the yr., region XI, 1980, U.S.A., 1989; adminstr. Healthcare div., 1987-89). Roman Catholic. Avocations: golf, sailing, woodworking. Died Mar. 20, 2002.

LAMPELL, MILLARD, writer; b. Paterson, N.J., Jan. 10, 1919; s. Charles and Bertha (Unger) L.; m. Ramona Love Estep; children: Guruka Singh Khalsa, Jane Peebles, Stephanie Davis, Richard Key. BA, W.Va. U., 1940. Author: The Long Way Home, 1946, The Hero, 1949, Journey to the Cape, 1959, California to the New York Island, 1960, The Inheritance, 1964, The Pig with One Nostril, 1975, O, Appalachia, 1989, (feature films) Saturday's Hero, 1951, Chance Meeting, 1959, Escape from East Berlin, 1962, The Idol, 1966, Eagle in a Cage, 1970, (documentaries) The Journey, 1951, American Frontier, 1956, The Wilderness of Zin, 1958, Sometime Before Morning, (Peabody award 1959), The Inheritance, 1964, Do Not Fold, Staple, Spindle or Mutilate (Montreal Festival award, 1967), (TV) Eastside/Westside, 1964, Eternal Light, 1964, Eagle in a Cage (Emmy award 1964), The Visitor, 1965, The Adams Chronicles, 1976, Rich Man, Poor Man, 1977, Wheels, 1978, Orphan Train (Writers Guild award, 1979), The Wall (Christopher award 1982, Peabody award 1982); lyricist: The Lonesome Train, 1945, Morning Star, 1946, (stage plays) The Wall, 1960, Hard Travelin', 1963, A Public Nuisance, 1965; author poetry, novels screenplays for a variety of films. Served with USAF, 1942-45. Mem. Writers Guild Am. Deceased.

LAMSON, GEORGE HERBERT, economics educator; b. Hartford, Conn., Feb. 21, 1940; s. Arroll Liscomb and Marguerite (Brechbuhler) L.; m. Susan Kathryn Lippert, Sept. 7, 1968; children: Scott, Brandon. AB, Princeton U., 1963; MA, Northwestern U., 1966, PhD, 1971. Research asst. Northwestern U. Econ. Survery of Liberia, Monrovia, 1962-63; instr. dept. econs. Loyola U., Chgo., 1967-68, U. Conn., Storrs, 1968-69; asst. prof. then assoc. prof. dept. econs. Carleton Coll., Northfield, Minn., 1969-80, Williams prof., 1981—, chmn. dept., 1978-84, 99-00. Cons. Minn. Higher Edn. Coordinating Com., St. Paul, 1971-72; textbook reviewer John Wiley & Sons, N.Y.C., 1979-82; reviewer NSF grad. fellowship program, 1988-90; vis. prof. U. Internat. Bus. and Econs., Beijing, China, 1994, 98; dir. Carleton Oversees seminar in econs. Cambridge, U.K., 1986, 91, 97, 2002; vis. scholar Chinese Acad. Social Scis., Beijing, 2001. Intersocietal studies fellow Northwestern U., 1966-67; recipient Faculty Devel. awards 1979, 90-91. Mem. Am. Econ. Assn., Midwest Econ. Assn., Minn. Econ. Assn. (bd. dirs. 1981-83, pres. 1984) Home: Dundas, Minn. Died Oct. 14, 2002.

LANCASTER, KELVIN JOHN, economics educator; b. Sydney, Australia, Dec. 10, 1924; s. John Kelvin and Margaret Louise (Gray) L.; m. Deborah Grunfeld, June 10, 1963; children— Clifton John, Gilead. BSc, Sydney U., 1948, BA, 1949, MA, 1953; BSc in Econs., London U., 1953, PhD, 1958. Asst. lectr., lectr. London Sch. Economics, 1954-59; reader economics U. London, 1959-62; prof. polit. economy Johns Hopkins U., 1962-66; prof. econs., 1966-78; John Bates Clark prof. econs., 1978—, Columbia U., N.Y.C.; Ford faculty fellow, 1968-69; chmn. dept. econs., 1970-73, 89-90; Wesley Clair Mitchell research prof., 1973-74. Vis. prof. U. Birmingham, Brown U., 1961-62, CUNY, 1965-66, NYU, Australian Nat. U., 1969-77, Ottawa U., 1972; fellow Inst. Advanced Studies Hebrew U., Jerusalem, 1976-77; dir. Nat. Bur. Econ. Rsch., 1971-73; trustee BT Investment Funds, 1986—. Author: Mathematical Economics, 1968, Introduction to Modern Microeconomics, 1969, Consumer Demand: A New Approach, 1971, Modern Economics: Principles and Policy, 1973, Variety, Equity and Efficiency, 1979, Modern Consumer Theory, 1991, Trade, Markets and Welfare, 1996; contbr. articles in econs. to profl. jours. Served with Royal Australian Air Force, 1943-45. Fellow Econometric Soc., Am. Acad. Arts and Scis., Am. Econ. Assn. (disting.); mem. N.Y. State Econ. Assn. (pres. 1974-75). Home: New York, NY. Deceased.

LANCE, BONNIE JEAN, retired financial director, clerk; b. Ohio, Oct. 7, 1926; d. Mehl and Frances Maria (Schuck) Garmong; (div. 1978); children: Linda Ann, Barbara Kay, Bobbi Jean, Stephen R. Student, U. Ashland. Billing clk. Simmons Mfg., Ashland, Ohio, 1944-46; IBM key punch operator Hess & Clark, Ashland, 1946-47; clk., sec. Ashland County Meml. Park, 1958-60; computer operator, office mgr., asst. dir. Office of Dir. of Fin., Ashland, 1966-88; nite clk. Heyl Funeral, Ashland, from 1987. Lutheran. Home: Ashland, Ohio. Died Mar. 10, 2002.

LANDAHL, HERBERT DANIEL, biophysicist, mathematical biologist, researcher, consultant; b. Fancheng, China, Apr. 23, 1913; (parents Am. citizens); s. Carl W. and Alice (Holmberg) L.; m. Evelyn Christine Blomberg, Aug. 23, 1940; children: Carl David, Carol Ann Landahl Kubai, Linda C. Landahl Shidner. Student, U. Minn., 1931-32; AB, St. Olaf Coll., Northfield, Minn., 1934; SM, U. Chgo., 1936, PhD, 1941. Rsch. asst. psychometric lab. U. Chgo., 1937-39, rsch. asst. math. biophysics, 1938-41, instr., 1942-45, asst. prof. com. on math. biology, 1945-48, assoc. prof., 1949-56, prof., 1956-68, acting. chmn., 1965-67; prof. biophysics and math. U. Calif., San Francisco, 1968-80, prof. emeritus, from 1980. Cons. Respiratory Project, U. Chgo., 1944-46, toxicity lab. U. Chgo., 1947-51, USAF radiation lab., U. Chgo., 1951-67, dept. biomath. U. Tex., Houston, 1968-89; mem. NIH com. on epidemiology and biometry, Bethesda, Md., 1960-64. Co-author: Mathematical Biophysics of Central Nervous System, 1945; contbr. approximately 190 sci. papers to various jours.; chief editor Bull. Math. Biology, 1973-80; mem. editl. Computers in Biology and Medicine, 1971-90. Recipient Career Devel. award NIH, 1962-67, Career Achievement award Soc. Toxicology, 1987; grantee NIH, 1963-67. Fellow AAAS; mem. Biophys. Soc., Biometric Soc. (charter), Bioengring. Soc. (charter), Latin Am. Biomath. Soc. (charter), Soc. for Math. Biology (founding, pres. 1981-83). Home: San Francisco, Calif. Died May 23, 2003.

LANG, EDWARD GEORGE, chemical engineer; b. Galveston, Tex., Aug. 19, 1925; s. Edward George and Amelia (Muzar) L.; m. Flora Kowis, June 7, 1947; children: Lucia Gates, Michelene Lopez, Eileen Baker, Helen Lang, Mary Lang, Cathy Frettas. BS in Chem. Engring., Rice U., 1949. Rsch. engr. Texaco, Port Arthur, Tex., 1949-51; chem. engr. Stauffer Chem., Houston, Tex., 1952-58, plant mgr. Bay Town, Tex., 1958-60, plant manager Hammond, Ind., 1960-63, Houston, 1963-71, dir. technology group, 1971-85; dir. tech. group Rhone Poulemc, Houston, 1985-91. Author: (Encyclopedia) Sulfuric Acid REGN, 1992. Past pres. Rotary Club, Harrisburg, Tex., Civic Club, Crown Point, Ind.; dir. lakes Sandalwood Civic Assn., Houton, 1997-98. Mem. AIChE. Roman Catholic. Achievements include the conception and preliminary design of world's largest sulfur burning sulfuric acid plant, 1965; and the conception, preliminary design of the world's largest REGN sulfuric acid plant, 1989-90. Died Jan. 22, 2001.

LANGE, CRYSTAL MARIE, university official, nursing educator; b. Snover, Mich., Aug. 22, 1927; d. Bazil H. and Crystal S. (Hilborn) Morse; m. Elmer William Lange, June 10, 1961; children: Gregory, Frederick, Helen, Charles, G. Benson, Robert, Larry. BSN, U. Mich., 1949; MSN, Wayne State U., 1961; PhD, Mich. State U., 1972. Pvt. duty nurse, Richmond, Ind., 1949-50; asst. DON, nursing supr., instr. St. Mary's Hosp., Tucson, 1950-58; night supr. Pima County Hosp., Tucson, 1958-59; asst. dir. Sch. Nursing, Saginaw (Mich.) Gen. Hosp., 1959-60; from instr. to prof., chmn. divsn. Delta Coll., University Center, Mich., 1962-76; dean Sch. Nursing and Allied Health Scis., prof. nursing Saginaw Valley State U., University Center, 1976-96, asst. to v.p. acad. affairs, 1976-96, assoc. v.p. acad. affairs, 1996—99. Mem. vis. com. U. Mich. Med. Ctr., Ann Arbor, 1978-81. Author: Leadership for Quality, 1966, Instructor's Guide—Nursing Skills and Techniques, 1969, The Use of the Auto-Tutorial Laboratory and the Mobile Tutorial Unit in Teaching, 1969, Instructor's Guide—Nursing Skills and Techniques—Films 76-126, 1972, Films 127-151, 1971, Auto-Tutorial Techniques in Nursing Education, 1971, Future Education: Diagnosis Prescriptions Evaluation, 1971; contbr. articles to profl. jours. Bd. dirs. Saginaw chpt. ARC, Saginaw Vis. Nurse Assn. Recipient award Mich. Acad. Sci., Arts and Letters, 1970, Monsour Found. lecturership award Health Edn. Media Assn., 1977; named Woman of Distinction Bay Area coun. Girl Scouts U.S.A., 1997; fellow NEH, 1983. Fellow Am. Acad. Nursing (governing coun., sec. 1978-80); mem. ANA, Am. Acad. Arts and Scis., AAUP (chpt. v.p. 1975, award citation 1970), Am. Ednl. Scis., Mich. Nurses Assn., Saginaw Dist. Nurses Assn. (bd. dirs.), U. Mich. Alumnae Assn., Wayne State U. Alumnae Assn., Phi Kappa Phi, Sigma Theta Tau. Home: Saginaw, Mich. Died Nov. 1, 1999.

LANGE, HOPE, actress; b. Redding Ridge, Conn., Nov. 28, 1938; d. John and Minnette (Buddecke) L.; m. Don Murray; m. Alan S. Pakula, 1963 (div. 1971); m. Charles Hollerith, Jr., 1986 Ed., Barmore Jr. Coll., Reed Coll., Oreg. Appeared as dancer Jackie Gleason TV program; also Kraft TV plays; TV films include: That Certain Summer, 1973, I Love You...Goodbye, 1974, Crowhaven Farm, 1970, A Family Tree, The Henry Ford Story, Fer de Lance, 1974, The Secret Night Caller, 1975, The Love Boat II, 1977, Like Normal People, 1979, The Day Christ Died, 1980, Pleasure Palace, 1980, Private Lessons, 1985, Dead Before Dawn, 1993, Message from Nam, 1993, Cooperstown, 1993, also miniseries Beulah Land, 1980, Man and the Machine; motion pictures include: Bus Stop, The True Story of Jesse James, Peyton Place, The Young Lions, A Pocketful of Miracles, Love Is a Ball, Jigsaw, Death Wish, Best of Everything, I Am the Cheese, 1983, The Prodigal, 1984, A Nightmare on Elm Street: Part 2, 1985, Blue Velvet, 1986, Tune In Tomorrow, Clear and Present Danger, 1994, Just Cause, 1995, others; leading actress in TV series The Ghost and Mrs. Muir, 1968-70, New Dick Van Dyke Show, 1971-74 Recipient Emmy award 1968, 69. Died Dec. 19, 2003.

LANGHORNE, KATHRYN PAYNE, secondary school educator; b. Norfolk, Va., Aug. 24, 1905; d. Charles Anton and Alma Gennette (Burton) Smith; m. Maurice Bilisoly Langhorne, Apr. 8, 1944 (dec. 1986). BS, Radford U., 1928; MA, Columbia U., 1941. Tchr. Sch. Bd. Norfolk City, Va., 1930-72, Substitute Mathews County Sch., 1973-78. Mem. choir Kingston Parish Christ Ch., 1974—. Republican. Episcopolian. Home: Mathews, Va. Deceased.

LANGLINAIS, JOSEPH WILLIS, educator, chaplain; b. San Antonio, Aug. 12, 1922; s. Joseph Willis and Marie Nellie (St. Julien) L. BS in Edn, U. Dayton, 1943; STD, U. Fribourg, Switzerland, 1954. Joined Soc. Mary of St. Louis, 1940; ordained priest Roman Cath. Ch., 1952. Joined Soc. Mary, 1940; tchr. high schs. in Mo., Ill. and Man., Can., 1943-48; dir. admissions Chaminade Coll. Prep. Sch., St. Louis, 1957-59; dir. Archdiocesan High Sch. Sodality Union St. Louis, 1958-59, Marianist Novitiate, Galesville, Wis., 1959-63; mem. faculty St. Mary's U., San Antonio, from 1963, dean Sch. Arts and Scis., 1964-75, acad. v.p., 1975-81, dir. instnl. self-study, 1970-72, 82-84, chmn. theology dept., 1981-83, dean Sch. Humanities and Social Scis., 1986, chaplain Sch. of Bus., 1988—2002, Univ. Prof., 1993—2002; pres. Cen. Cath. Marianist High Sch., San Antonio, 1987-91. Dir. semester in Puebla, Mex. St. Mary's U., 1994; pres. Holy Rosary Sch. Bd., 1995-99; archdiocesan ecumenical rep., 1996—, counselor, 1997—; bd. dirs. Mariological Soc. Am., 1997—. Contbr.: Catholic Encyclopedia America, Encyclopedic Dictionary of Religion, 1979. Pres. United Svcs. Orgn. South Tex., 1985-87, Holy Rosary Elem. Sch., San Antonio, 1997-99; mem. bd. Tex. Bach Choir; pres. sch. bd. Ctrl. Cath. H.S., 1987-91; chaplain Marianist Residence at St. Mary's U., 1999—. Named Champion of Compassion, B'nai B'rith, San Antonio, 1990, Nat. Commn. Comty. and Justice, 2001. Mem. AAUP, Cath. Theol. Soc. Am., Mariological Soc. Am., Archaeol. Soc. Am., Torch Internat., Nat. Soc. Arts and Letters, Rotary. Roman Catholic. Avocations: horticulture, classical music. Died Aug. 3, 2002.

LANGTON, BASIL CEDRIC, actor, stage director; b. Bristol, Eng., Jan. 9, 1912; s. Samuel Calvert and Esther (Shandel) L.; m. Louise Soelberg (div. 1959); 1 dau., Jessica L. Andrews (Mrs. Timothy Toothman); m. Nancy Wickwire (div. 1969). Privately ed. Mem. faculty Mahattan Sch. Music, 1958-81, UCLA, 1987. Mem. Council Participating Dirs., Boston U.; co-founder, stage dir. Empire State Music Festival; v.p. Music Now Inc. With Vancouver Little Theatre, Can., Theatre of Dance-Mime and Jooss Leder Sch. Dance, Dartington, Eng.; played: Hamlet at Shakespeare Meml. Theatre, 1940; with maj., Brit. Repertory Theatres, including Birmingham Repertory and Old Vic; founder Travelling Repertory Theatre during World War II at Kings Theatre, London Theatre Royal, Bristol on tour of France, Belgium, Holland, Germany; has appeared in leading roles on Broadway and London's West End in The Affair, Soldiers, Camelot, on nat. tour of Hostile Witness appeared stock cos., Westport, Olney, Bucks County, and in The Birthday Party and Tartuffe at Los Angeles Theatre Ctr., 1986; has appeared on TV shows for BBC, Playhouse 90, Robert Montgomery Presents, Omnibus, Philco TV Playhouse, Kraft Theatre, Alcoa Theatre, Hallmark, 1952-65, The Secret Storm, Love of Life, General Hospital, Love of Life, 1983-84 and PBS, 1986, Highway to Heaven, 1987, Murphy Brown, 1990, Star Trek Voyager, 1994, Mrs Warren's Profession, 1996; moderator Lucien Clergue, CBS-TV Spl., 1967; stage dir. plays and operas including Romeo and Juliet, In Time to Come, The Moon Is Down, Pygmalion (London); dir. operas Carmen, La Boheme, premieres of Medee, Volo di Notte, Goyesoas, Ariadne Auf Naxos and The Would-Be Gentleman, L'Arlesienne; exec. producer, v.p. TV shows Music Now Inc., 1970—; stage dir. world premiere Yerma, opera by Villa-Lobos, Santa Fe, 1971, Arlesienne, N.Y.C., 1971; N.Y. premiere Boulevard Solitude, 1972, Don Pasquale, Manhattan Sch. Music, N.Y.C., 1974, 13 Rue de l'Amour, Chgo., 1974; dir.: N.Y. premiere Hay Fever, Chgo., 1975, Major Barbara, Juilliard, N.Y.C., 1976, 13 Rue de l'Amour, N.Y.C. and tour, 1978, for Elizabethan Theatre Trust, Melbourne and Sydney, Australia, 1980; stage dir., librettist: N.Y. premiere The Free Lance (Sousa) at, Iowa State Center and Acad. Music, Phila. for, Opera Co. Phila., 1979; dir.: N.Y. premiere Wolf Trap, 1980; chmn. drama com. N.Y. premiere, Fulbright-Hays-Inst. Internat. Edn., faculty, Sarah Lawrence Coll., Western Res. U., Cath. univs., Manhattan Sch. Music, N.Y.C., (Julliard), RADA, London Theatre Studio, St. Denis, 1958—, lectr., Yale U., Antioch Coll., Hunter Coll., Carnegie Inst. Tech., Am. Theatre Wing.; narrator: T.S. Eliot's The Wasteland, with Cin. Symphony Orch.; one man shows include McGrath Gallery, L.A., 1988-89, L.A. County Mus. and Met. Mus., N.Y., 1988-90, Tobey C. Moss Gallery, L.A., 1988-90; contbr.: photographs and articles to Opera News, Life, N.Y. Times, Horizon, others. John Hay Whitney Found. grantee, 1949-50, MacDowell Colony grantee, 1960, 69; Nat. Endowment Arts grantee, 1974, 75; Guggenheim fellow, 1957. Mem. Dramatists Guild, Actors Equity, AFTRA, AGMA, ASCAP, Soc. Stage Dirs. and Choreographers. Home: Santa Monica, Calif. Died May 29, 2003.

LANS, ASHER BOB, lawyer; b. N.Y.C., Dec. 4, 1918; s. Arthur Louis and Sophie (Bob) L.; m. Barbara Eisner, Dec. 5, 1946 (div.); children: Deborah, Stephen, Alan; m. Mary Themo, Nov. 1, 1966 (div.); 1 child, Tracy (dec.); m. Shirley Johnson, June 26, 1967 (div.); 1 child, Andrea Elisabeth; m. Margaret Catherine Clancy, June 12, 1993. AB, Dartmouth Coll., 1938; MA, Columbia U., 1939; LLB, Yale U., 1944. Bar: N.Y. 1945, U.S. Dist. Ct. (so. and ea. dists.) N.Y., U.S. Tax Ct., U.S. Ct. Appeals (2d cir.), U.S. Supreme Ct. Law clk. Trustees of Assoc. G&E Corp., 1942-44; rsch. asst. Yale U., New Haven, 1944; assoc. Coudert Bros., 1945-47; ptnr. Lans, Goldstein, Golenbock & Abrams, N.Y.C., 1948-50; pvt. practice N.Y.C., 1951-57, 69; ptnr. Kramer & Lans, N.Y.C., 1958-65, Lans & Fink, N.Y.C., 1966-68, Lans, Feinberg & Cohen, N.Y.C., 1970-84, Summit, Rovins & Feldesman, N.Y.C., 1984-91; of counsel Jackson & Nash, N.Y.C., from 1991. Dir., sec. Charbert, Inc. and related cos., N.Y.C., 1964—, J.K. Gallery, Inc., 1994—. Co-author: Studies in World Public Order, 1960; contbr. articles to profl. jours. Mem. Alumni Coun., Dartmouth Coll., Hanover, N.H., 1988-92; elector Spanish Portuguese Synagogue, N.Y.C., 1971—; v.p., bd. dirs. Gramercy Neighborhood Assn., 1993-97, pres., 1997—. Mem. ABA, Yale Club, Nat. Arts Club. Democrat. Jewish. Home: New York, NY. Died Feb. 27, 2002.

LAPIDUS, NORMAN ISRAEL, food broker; b. N.Y.C., July 20, 1930; s. Rueben and Laurette (Goldsmith) L.;m. Myrna Sue Cohen, Nov. 20, 1960; children: Robin Anne, Jody Beth BBA, CCNY, 1952; postgrad. internat. Relations, CCNY, NYU, 1957-60. Salesman Rueben Lapidus Co., N.Y.C., 1954-56, pres., from 1960; sales trainee Cohn-Hall-Marx, N.Y.C., 1955; salesman to v.p. Julius Levy Co., Millburn, N.J., 1964-66, pres., from 1966; salesman Harry

W. Freedman Co., Millburn, N.J., 1975-76, v.p., treas., 1976-84, pres., from 1984, Julius Levy/Rueben Lapidus and Harry W. Freedman Cos. div. Pezrow Corp., Millburn, N.J., 1985-86, L&H Food Brokers, Millburn, N.J., 1986-87; v.p. M&H Sales and Mktg., Tarrytown, N.Y., from 1998, Reichenbach and Assocs., Glen Head, N.Y., from 1998. Mem. Maplewood (N.J.) Bd. Adjustment, 1975-82, Bedminster (N.J.) Bd. Adjustment, 1996—; gen. chmn. Maplewood Citizens Budget Adv. Com., 1977-79; chmn. Maplewood United Jewish Appeal Drive, 1975-76, 83-84; vice-chmn. Maplewood 1st Aid Squad Bldg. Fund Dr., 1978-79; co-founder Citizens for Charter Change in Essex County, N.J., 1974, mem. exec. bd., 1974—, treas., 1983-84; founder, chmn. Music Theatre of Maplewood; pres. Maplewood Civic Assn., 1983-85; mem. bd. mgrs. Essex County unit Am. Cancer Soc., v.p., 1984-87, chmn. 1991—; mem. adv. bd. Essex County Coll., West Essex, N.J., chairperson bd., 1991—; mem., sec., bd. dirs. Knollcrest Neighborhood Assn., 1994—, pres., 1991-96, 96—; committeeman Bedminster Twp. Com., 1997—; commr. Suburban Mcpl. Joint Ins. Fund, 1997—; mem. Bedminster Hills Housing Corp., 1997—. Recipient Leadership Medallion United Jewish Appeal, 1970, 84 Mem. Nat. Food Brokers Assn. (regional dir., Cert. Exceptionally Meritorious Svc.), Nat. Food Svc. Sales Com., Met. Food Brokers Assn. (chmn. 1982-90), Assn. Food Industries (bd. dirs.), Nat. Food Processors Assn., Young Guard Soc., Old Guard Soc., CCNY Alumni Assn., U.S. Navy Inst., Acad. Polit. Sci., Archaeol. Inst. Am., Nat. Trust for Historic Preservation, Assn. Food Distbrs., Knollcrest Homeowners Assn. (bd. trustees), LWV, Am. Legion, Lions (bd. dirs.), B'nai Brith. Clubs: Maplewood Glee. Republican. Jewish. Home: Bedminster, NJ. Died: July 5, 1999.

LA PLANTE, SUSAN KATHERINE, nursing administrator, geriatrics nurse; b. Helena, Mont., Nov. 24, 1944; d. William and Katherine (Harrison) Bates; m. Michael La Plante, Sept. 18, 1971; children: Sarah, Rachel. Student, U. Calif., Davis, 1966; RN, St. Luke's Sch. of Nursing, 1967. Charge nurse Benewah Comunity Hosp., St. Maries, Idaho; dir. nursing svcs. Valley Vista Convalescent Ctr., St. Maries; home health nurse Panhandle dist. State of Idaho, St. Maries; dir. client svcs. Valley Vista Care Ctr., St. Maries. Charter mem. ANA, Idaho Nurse's Assn. Home: Saint Maries, Idaho. Deceased.

LAPOE, WAYNE GILPIN, retired business executive; b. Waynesburg, Pa., July 13, 1924; s. James Lindsay and Mary (Gilpin) LaP.; m. Margaret Louise Clark, Feb. 21, 1953; children: Deborah Jean, Marqui Lynne. BA, Pa. State U., 1947. With personnel and sales depts. Armstrong Cork Co., Lancaster, Pa., 1947-53, Chgo., 1947-53, San Francisco, 1947-53; personnel dir. Safeco Ins. Group., 1953-63, v.p., 1963-86, Safeco Corp., Seattle, 1976-80, sr. v.p., 1980-86; v.p. Gen. Ins. Co. Am., 1963-86, Safeco Ins. Co. Am., 1963-86, Safeco Life Ins. Co., 1963-86, First Nat. Ins. Co. Am., Seattle, 1963-86, Safeco Nat. Ins. Co., St. Louis, 1972-86. Mem. White House Conf. Children and Youth, 1960; bd. dirs. Ind. Colls. Washington. Capt. USAAF, 1943-46, USAF, 1951-52. Decorated D.F.C.; decorated Air medal with three oak leaf clusters Mem. Mus. Flight Seattle, Ocean Liner Mus. N.Y., Am. Polit. Items Collectors (past pres.), Am. Aviation Hist. Soc., SS Hist. Soc. Am., Assn. Des Amis Des Paquebots, Nat. Trust Hist. Preservation, Phi Kappa Tau. Republican. Home: Lake Forest Park, Wash. Died Mar. 15, 2004.

LARGUIER, EVERETT HENRY, mathematician, educator; b. New Orleans, Jan. 26, 1910; s. Henry Joseph and Ella Nora (Foley) L. BA, St. Louis U., 1934, MS, 1936, PhL, 1937, STL, 1942; PhD, U. Mich., 1947. Instr. math. and physics Spring Hill Coll., Mobile, Ala., 1937-38; math asst. St. Louis U., 1939-41; instr. Loyola U., New Orleans, 1942; prof. math, dept. chmn. Spring Hill Coll., 1947-72, prof., 1973-75, prof. emeritus, from 1975. Carl Jacobs vis. prof. U. Wis., Stevens Point, 1972-73; trustee Spring Hill Coll., 1952-59. Author: Algebraic Structures, 1989; editor, author 2 vols. Gautrelet Publications, 1980—; contbr. articles to Duke Math. Jour., Pacific Jour. Math., Scripta Mathematica, others. Mem. Am. Math. Soc., Math. Assn. Am., Sigma Xi. Home: New Orleans, La. Died Sept. 20, 2000.

LARKIN, FRANCES HESSE, community health professional; b. Boston, Mar. 11, 1946; BA in English, Salem State Coll., 1968, BSN magna cum laude, 1979; MS, U. Lowell, 1989. RN, Mass. Coord. community health Addison Gilbert Hosp., Gloucester, Mass., from 1985. Active Internat. Bluegrass Music Assn., North Shore Assn. for Retarded Citizens, Mus. Fine Arts, Boston; founding pres. Salem State Coll. Nursing Honor Soc., 1980-82; co-founder, first chair Nursing Honor Socs. Alliance, 1982-85; bd. dirs. local chpt. Am. Cancer Soc., ARC. Mem. ANA (dist. IV chair nurse practice com. 1980-82, 83-85, chair nominating com. 1987-88), Diabetes Educators Ea. Mass., Am. Diabetes Assn. (local bd. dirs.), Mass. Nurse's Assn. (cabinet on nursing practice 1985, spkr.'s bur. on proposed nurse practice act 1986, awards com. 1988-91), Sigma Theta Tau (del. to biennial conv. 1981, 83, 85, 89, charter mem. Eta Tau chpt.). Home: Beverly, Mass. Died July 18, 2001.

LARRABEE, MARTIN GLOVER, biophysics educator; b. Boston, Jan. 25, 1910; s. Ralph Clinton and Ada Perkins Miller L.; m. Sylvia Kimball, Sept. 10, 1932 (div. 1944); 1 son, Benjamin Larrabee Scherer; m. Barbara Belcher, Mar. 25, 1944 (dec. 1996); 1 son, David Belcher Larrabee; m. Sarah B. Galloway, July 11, 1998. BA, Harvard U., 1932; PhD, U. Pa., 1937; MD (hon.), U. Lausanne, Switzerland, 1974. Research asst., fellow U. Pa., Phila., 1934-40, assoc. to assoc. prof., 1941-49; asst. prof. physiology Cornell U. Med. Coll., N.Y.C., 1940-41; assoc. prof. Johns Hopkins U., Balt., 1949-63, prof. biophysics, 1963-99, prof. emeritus biophys., from 1999. Contbr. articles to scientific jours. Mem.: Soc. for Neurosci. (treas. 1970—75), Nat. Acad. Scis., Internat. Neurochem. Soc., Am. Soc. Neurochemistry, Biophys. Soc., Am. Physiol. Soc., English Physiol. Soc. (assoc.), Mountain of Md., Sierra, Appalachian Mountain, Phi Beta Kappa. Achievements include research in circulatory, respiratory and nervous systems of animals, especially on synaptic and metabolic mechanisms in sympathetic ganglia, 1934-99; wartime research on oxygen lack, decompression sickness, nerve injury, infrared viewing devices, 1941-45. Home: Glen Arm, Md. Died June 16, 2003.

LARSEN, MICHAEL JOHN, research mycologist; b. London, Apr. 27, 1938; came to U.S., 1949; s. J. Futter and Nancy (Stevens) L.; m. Audrey Helen Sutherland, Jan. 4, 1970 (dec. 1977); children: Emily, Caitlin; m. Nancy Jo Onsager, Jan. 14, 1982; children: Scott, John, Anne, Christopher, Steven, Jaime. BS, Syracuse U., 1960; MS, N.Y. State Coll. Forestry, 1963, PhD, 1967. Rsch. scientist Canadian Forestry Svc. So. Rsch. Sta., Maple, Ontario, Canada, 1966-67, Great Lakes Forest Rsch. Ctr. Canadian Forestry Svc., Sault St. Marie, Ontario, Canada, 1967-70; rsch. mycologist U.S. Forest Svc., Ctr. for Forest Mycology Rsch., Madison, Wis., 1971-92, Forestry Scis. Lab., Moscow, Idaho, from 1993. Adj. prof. Plant Pathology Dept., U. Wis., 1974-92, Dept. Forestry, Mich. Tech. U., Houghton, 1976—; adj. assoc. prof. Dept. Forest Scis., U. Idaho. Author: Tomentelloid Fungi of NA, 1968, A Contribution to the Taxonomy of the Genus Tomentella, 1974, The Genus Phellinus - A World Survey, 1990; contbr. numberous articles to profl. jours. Mem. Lodi (Wis.) Plan Commn., 1989-93, Lodi Land Use Planning Commn., 1989-93. Recipient Grad. Student honorarium N.Y. State Mus. Sci. Svc., 1964; NSF fellow, 1963-66. Mem. Mycol. Soc. Am. (counselor 1978-80, chmn. nomenclature com. 1988-90), Am. Inst. Biol. Sci. Internat. Mycol. Assocs. Home: Chaska, Minn. Died June 7, 2000.

LASAGNA, LOUIS CESARE, medical educator; b. N.Y.C., Feb. 22, 1923; s. Joseph and Carmen (Boccignone) Lasagna; m. Helen Chester Gersten; children: Nina, David, Maria, Kristin, Lisa, Lisa, Peter, Christopher. BS, Rutgers U., 1943; MD, Columbia U., 1947; DSc (hon.), Hahnemann U., 1980; DSc (hon.), Rutgers U., 1983. Asst. prof. medicine Johns Hopkins U., Balt., 1954—57, asst. prof. pharmacology, 1954—59, assoc. prof. medicine, 1957—70, assoc. prof. pharmacology, 1959—70; prof. pharmacology and toxicology U. Rochester, 1970—86, prof. medicine, 1970—94; dean Sackler Sch. Med., Tufts U., 1984—2002, prof. pharmacology and psychiatry, from 1984. Author: The Doctors' Dilemmas, 1962, Life, Death and the Doctor, 1968, Phenylpropanolamine, A Review, 1988; editor: Controversies in Therapeutics, 1980. Sr. asst. surgeon USPHS, 1952—54. Named Disting prof., Tufts U., 1994; recipient Oscar B. Hunter award, Am. Soc. Clin. Pharmacology, 1975, ASPET award, Am. Soc. Pharmacology and Exptl. Therapeutics, 1976, Lilly prize, Brit. Pharm. Soc., 1985, Rutgers U., 1993, Allyn Taylor Internat. prize in Medicine, 1996. Mem.: Am. Coll. Neuropsychopharmacology (pres. 1979—80), Inst. Medicine. Republican. Roman Catholic. Home: Auburndale, Mass. Died Aug. 7, 2003.

LASHER, STEVEN HOWE, electric power industry executive, lawyer; b. Chgo., May 23, 1944; s. Stuart Blodgett and Bette (Howe) L.; m. Bernadine Perry, Oct. 25, 1968; children: Anthoney P., Angela J. BS, Wayne State U., 1972; JD, Detroit U., 1977. Tax analyst GM, Detroit, 1971-78; dir. taxes Am. Natural Resources, Detroit, 1978-85; treas., tax counsel Continental Mortgage Investors, Livonia, Mich., 1985-87; v.p., gen. counsel Midland (Mich.) Cogeneration Venture, from 1987. Pres. Walled Lake (Mich.) Sch. Bd., 1975-81. Sgt. U.S. Army, 1966-69, ETO. Mem. ABA, Mich. Bar Assn., Midland C. of C. (vice chmn. 1988—). Avocations: softball, racquetball, tennis, golf. Home: Midland, Mich. Deceased.

LASIC, DANILO DUSAN, physicist; b. Ljubljana, Slovenia, Aug. 7, 1952; came to U.S., 1988; s. Dusan H. and Vida (Tom) L.; m. Alenka Dvorzak, Jan. 7, 1988; 1 child, Eva. BS in Chemistry, U. Ljubljana, 1975, MS in Chemistry, 1977, PhD in Physics, 1979. Rsch. assoc. Inst. J. Stefan, Ljubljana, 1977-81; postdoctoral fellow Duke U., Durham, N.C., 1981-82; vis. scientist Eidgenossische Technische Hochschule, Zurich, Switzerland, 1982-84; prof. Biophysics U. Ljubljana, 1984-86; vis. prof. U. Waterloo (Ont., Can.), 1986-88; sr. scientist Liposome Tech. Inc., Menlo Park, Calif., 1988-94, Mega Bios Corp., San Carlos, Calif., 1994-96; ind. cons. liposomes, drug and gene delivery, from 1996. Dir. Nuclear Magnetic Resonance Inst. U. Waterloo, Ont., 1986-88; cons. Immunotherapeutics, Fargo, N.D., 1987-88, Liposome Tech. Inc., Menlo Park, 1994—. Author: Liposomes: From Physics to Applications, 1993, Liposomes in Gene Delivery, 1997; co-editor: Nuclear Magnetic Resonance in Physics, Chemistry and Biology, 1989, Stealth Liposomes, 1995, Nonmedical Applications of Liposomes, Vols. I, II, III, and IV, 1996, Medical Applications of Liposomes, 1998; contbr. numerous articles to profl. jours. Avocations: music, painting, nature, tennis, skiing. Home: San Leandro, Calif. Died Oct. 14, 2000.

LASKER, GABRIEL WARD, anthropologist, educator; b. York, Eng., Apr. 29, 1912; s. Bruno and Margaret Naomi (Ward) L.; m. Bernice Kaplan, July 31, 1949; children: Robert Alexander, Edward Meyer, Ann Titania. Student, U. Wis., 1928-30; AB, U. Mich., 1934; A.M., Harvard U., 1940, PhD, 1945; DSC (hon.), U. Turin, Italy, 2000. Instr. English Chiao T'ung U., Peking, China, 1936-37; teaching fellow in anatomy Harvard Med. Sch., 1941-42; mem. faculty dept. anatomy Wayne State U. Sch. Medicine, Detroit, from 1946, asst. prof., 1947-55, assoc. prof., 1955-64, prof., 1964-82, prof. emeritus, from 1982; fellow commoner Churchill Coll., Cambridge U., 1983-84. Conducted Wayne U.-Viking Fund field trip to Mexico to study effects of migration on phys. characteristics of Mexicans, 1948 Author: Physical Anthropology, The Evolution of Man, Surnames and Genetic Structure, Happenings and Hearsay: Experiences of a Biological Anthropologist, 1999; editor: Yearbook of Phys. Anthropology, 1945-51, Human Biology, 1953-87, Research Strategies in Human Biology: Field and Survey Studies, 1993; contbr. articles to profl. jours. Fellow Am. Anthrop. Assn., AAAS (v.p. 1968); mem. Am. Assn. Phys. Anthropologists (sec.-treas. 1947-51, v.p. 1960-62, pres. 1963-65, Charles Darwin award 1993), Am. Assn. Anatomists, Human Biology Assn., (pres. 1982-84, First Franz Boas Prize, 1996), Soc. Study Human Biology (U.K.), Asociación Mexicana de Antropología Biológica, Sigma Xi. Home: Beverly Hills, Mich. Died Aug. 27, 2002.

LASKOWSKI, JOANNE FRANCES, nurse; b. Phila., Feb. 24, 1954; d. Stanley Joseph Laskowski. Lic. in practical nursing, Ea. Montgomery County Vo-Tech, 1975; student, Mercer Med. Ctr. Sch. Nursing, 1975-78. Staff nurse medicine and cardiology units Palm Beach-Martin County Med. Ctr., Jupiter, Fla., 1980-82; pvt. duty, hosp. and in-home nurse Med. Pers. Pool, Tulsa, 1982-85; staff nurse med. unit Shands Hosp., U. Fla., Gainesville, 1990-92; nurse Upjohn Healthcare Svcs., Fla. Cons. Internat. Acad. Oral Medicine and Toxicology, 1990—. Mem. Nat. Ctr. Homeopathy, Gainesville Homeopathic Study Group, Fla. Nurses Assn., Dental Amalgam Mercury Syndrome of North Ctrl. Fla., Inc. (founder, pres.). Avocations: sewing, physical fitness, reading, knitting, needlepoint. Deceased.

LASON, SANDRA WOOLMAN, linguistics, ESL, and gifted educator; b. Chgo., July 30, 1934; d. Irwin Robert and Annette (Hassman) Woolman; m. Marvin Mitchell Lason, Feb. 8, 1959 (dec. 1972); children: Caryn Anne, Joel Steven, Scott David. BS with highest distinction, Northwestern U., 1956; MA, Northeastern Ill. U., 1976; postgrad., U. Okla., from 1982. Cert. K-12 tchr. Tchr. Sch. Dist. 69, Skokie, Ill., tchr., dir. gifted students, 1972-76; tchr., adminstr. MONA-CEP, Morton Grove, Ill.; freelance writer-editor; curriculum writer-editor The Economy Co., Oklahoma City; instr., assoc. dir. freshman English dept. U. Okla., Norman; prof., ESL coord. Oklahoma City Community Coll., 1983-95, ret. Ptnr. Communication Consultants; adj. prof. ESL Austin Coll., Sherman, Tex.; judge Okla. Olympics Mind, Mensokie Essay Contest; chmn. com. for ESL Okla. State Regents; mem. state legis. com. for internat. devel.; speaker presentations on writing, ESL and educating the gifted. Author: (with others) Gifted Galaxy: Oklahoma State Gifted Guide; writer, editor: K-8 Language Arts Series: Expressways; editor books and articles; contbr. articles to profl. jours. Officer Karen Brown chpt. Bobs Roberts Hosp., Chgo., Children's Meml. Hosp., Chgo.; bd. dirs. Okla. Hillel Found., Women's Resource Ctr., Norman; officer Kenton PTA. Mem. Tchrs. English as Second Lang., Okla. Tchrs. English as Second Lang., Mensa (gifted child coord. Ill. chpt.), Pi Lambda Theta, Alpha Epsilon Phi (officer alumnae chpt.). Avocations: raising children, dance, reading, travel, art. Home: Flower Mound, Tex. Died Nov. 11, 2000.

LASSAW, IBRAM, sculptor, painter; b. Alexandria, Egypt, May 4, 1913; s. Philip and Bertha (Zaleski) L.; m. Ernestine Blumberg, Dec. 15, 1944; 1 dau., Denise. Student, Clay Club, 1927-32, Beaux Arts Inst. Design, N.Y.C., 1930-31, CCNY, 1931-32; student art, Amedée Ozenfant; ArtsD (hon.), DFA (hon.), L.I. U., 1990. Benjamin N. Duke prof. Duke U., 1962-63; tchr. U. Calif. at Berkeley, 1965-66, Am. U., 1950, Colo. Coll., Colorado Springs, 1965; former adj. faculty Southampton (L.I.) Coll. Vis. prof. Brandeis U., 1975, Mt. Holyoke Coll., 1978 One-man shows Kootz Gallery, N.Y.C., 1951, 52, 54, 58, 60, 63, 64, MIT, 1958, Duke U., 1963, Benson Gallery, 1966, Gertrude Kasle Gallery, Detroit, 1968, Zabriskie Gallery, N.Y.C., 1977, Mus. Art, Carnegie Inst., Pitts., 1983, Whitney Mus., N.Y., 1984, Sid Deutsch Gallery, N.Y.C., 1986, The Third Dimension, Whitney Mus. Am. Art, 1984, Sid Deutsh Gallery, N.Y.C., Sculpture Am., Internat. Biennial of Contemporary Sculpture, Matera, Italy, 1990, Harmon-Meek Gallery, Naples, Fla., 1991, others; exhibited at museums, univs., art insts. in U.S., Japan, France, Italy, Holland, Denmark, Switzerland, Eng., S. Am., USSR; also Internat. Exhbn. Sculpture, Musée Rodin, Paris, 1956, retrospective, Heckscher Mus., Huntington, N.Y., 1973, Smithsonian Instn., 1975, Whitney Mus. Am. Art, 1976, 78, U. N.Mex., Albuquerque, 1977, Guild Hall Mus., East Hampton, N.Y., 1978, 88, Nat. Mus. Am. Art, Washington, 1989, Baruch Coll., N.Y.C., 1994; group shows Hirschhorn Mus., Washington, 1982, Ten Sculptors of N.Y. Sch., 1992, M. Silverman Gallery, L.A., 1992; represented in permanent collections Nat. Gallery, Washington, Mus. Modern Art, N.Y.C., Whitney Mus. Am. Art, N.Y.C., Museu de Arte Moderna, Rio de Janeiro, Brazil, Gallery Contemporary Art, Carnegie-Mellon U., Pitts., Balt. Mus. Art, Washington U., St. Louis, Albright Knox Art Gallery, Buffalo, Wadsworth Atheneum, Hartford, Conn., Fogg Mus. of Harvard U., Newark Mus., Worcester (Mass.) Art Mus., U. Calif. Mus., Berkeley, U. N.C., Greensboro, Birla Mus., Calcutta, India, Israel Mus., Jerusalem, Wichita (Kans.) Art Mus., Bklyn. Mus., Corcoran Gallery, Washington, Guggenheim Mus., N.Y.C., Nat. Gallery, Washington, McNay Art Mus., San Antonio, Rhode Island Sch. Design, Met. Mus., Sheldon Art Gallery, Nat.

Gallery, Washington, Anital Saposky Gallery, N.Y., Chgo. Internat. Art Expo., McNay Art Mus., San Antonio, RISD; works in pvt. collections including, Nelson Rockefeller, William A. M. Burden, Nat. Gallery, Washington; one of five U.S. reps. to, Venice Biennale, 1954; prin. commns. include: large sculpture Pillar of Fire, Temple Beth-El, Springfield, Mass., 1953; sculptures, Temple Beth-El, Providence, 1954, Sculpture Pantheon, Celanese Bldg., N.Y.C., also residential archtl. sculpture, Work reproduced in numerous books. Served as pvt. AUS, World War II. Mem. Am. Abstract Artists (pres. 1946-48), Am. Acad. Arts and Letters, Century Assn. Pioneer welding techniques in sculpting. Home: East Hampton, NY. Died Dec. 30, 2003.

LATHAM, ALLEN, JR., manufacturing company consultant; b. Norwich, Conn., May 23, 1908; s. Allen and Caroline (Walker) L.; m. Ruth Nichols, Nov. 11, 1933 (dec. 1992); children: W. Nichols, Harriet Latham Robinson, David W., Thomas W.; m. Charlotte T. Goldsmith, July 4, 1992. BS in Mech. Engring, MIT, 1930, Sloan fellow, 1936. Devel. engr. E.I. duPont, Belle, W.Va., 1930-35; engr., treas. Polaroid Corp., Cambridge, Mass., 1936-41; engr., v.p. Arthur D. Little, Cambridge, 1941-66; pres. Cryogenic Tech., Waltham, Mass., 1966-71; founder Haemonetics, Braintree, Mass., 1971—2003. Patentee in blood processing equipment and processes. Recipient New Eng. Inventor award, 1987, Morton Grove-Rasmussen award Am. Assn. Blood Banks, 1989; named Engr. of Yr. Socs. New Eng. Engring., 1970. Mem. AAAS, ASME (hon.), AIChE, Instrument Soc. Am., Nat. Acad. Engring. Clubs: Country (Brookline, Mass.). Home: Jamaica Plain, Mass. Died Aug. 5, 2003.

LATHAM, WILLIAM PETERS, composer, former educator; b. Shreveport, La., Jan. 4, 1917; s. Lawrence L. and Eugenia (Peters) L.; m. Joan Seyler, Apr. 18, 1946; children: Leslie Virginia, William Peters, Carol Jean. Student, Asbury Coll., Wilmore, Ky., 1933-35, Cin. Conservatory Music, 1936-38; BSc in Music Edn, U. Cin., 1938; BMus, Coll. Music Cin., 1940, MusM, 1941; PhD, Eastman Sch. Music, 1951; pupil composition with, Eugene Goossens, Howard Hanson, Herbert Elwell. Mem. faculty N. Tex. State Tchrs. Coll., 1938-39, Eastern Ill. State Tchrs. Coll., 1946, State Coll. Iowa, 1946-65, prof. music, 1959-65; prof. composition Sch. Music, U. N. Tex., Denton, 1965-84, dir. grad. studies, 1969-84, disting. prof., 1978-84, prof. emeritus, 1984—2004. Composer numerous works, 1938-2004, including works for orch., band, chorus, chamber groups, soloists, one opera and one ballet; compositions since 1980 include (chorus) Gaudeamus Academe, 1981, Bitter Land, 1985, My Heart Sings, 1988, Missa Novella, 1989, Only in Texas!, 1994; (chamber music) Ion, The Rhapsode for clarinet and piano, 1985, Metaphors, three songs for soprano, 1988, A Green Voice, cantata for soprano and tenor, 1989, (three songs for high voice) Requiem for My Love, 1994, (orch.) The Sacred Flame, Cantata for Baritone and Orch., 1990, Excelsior K-2 for Orch., 1994, (band) Suite Summertime, three movements for band, 1995,, Y2K, The New Millennium March for Concert Band, 1999 (scenic cantata for orch., chorus, soloists and ballet) Orpheus out West, 1997. Served to 2d lt. AUS, 1942-46. Scholar in composition Cin. Coll. Music, 1939-41; recipient numerous awards and commns. Mem. ASCAP (ann. awards 1962—2004), Coll. Mus. Soc., Phi Mu Alpha, Pi Kappa Lambda. Home: Denton, Tex. Died Feb. 24, 2004.

LATIMER, JOHN THOMAS, law educator; b. Hamilton, Ohio, May 25, 1922; s. Homer H. and Mayme (Hazeltine) L.; m. Eleanor Grace Millikin, Oct. 18, 1948; children: Carolyn E., Bruce M., John H. BS, U. Pa., 1944; JD, U. Cin., 1947. Bar: Ohio 1947. Assoc. Millikin & Fitton, Hamilton, Ohio, 1947-52, ptnr., 1952-73; lectr. law, Miami U., Oxford, Ohio, 1970-73, prof. dept. fin., sch. bus., 1973—, prof. emeritus, 1989—. Mem. Am. Bus. Law Assn. Democrat. Unitarian. Avocation: history. Home: Fairfield, Ohio. Died Feb. 28, 2002.

LAUDER, ESTEE, cosmetics company executive; b. Corona, Queens, NY, 1908; m. Joseph Lauter (later changed to Lauder), 1930 (dec.); children: Leonard, Ronald. LLD (hon.), U. Pa., 1986. Founding chmn. & CEO Estee Lauder, Inc., 1946—82; chmn Estee Lauder, Inc, 1982—95. Author: Estee: A Success Story, 1985. Decorated chevalier Legion of Honor France; named one of 100 Women of Achievement, Harpers Bazaar, 1967, Top Ten Outstanding Women in Business, 1970; named to Laureate Nat. Bus. Hall of Fame., 1988; recipient Neiman-Marcus Fashion award, 1962, Spirit of Achievement award, Albert Einstein Coll. Medicine, 1968, Kaufmann's Fashion Fortnight award, 1969, Bamberger's Designer's award, 1969, Gimbel's Fashion Forum award, 1969, Internat. Achievement award, Frost Bros., 1975, Pogue's Ann. Fashion award, 1975, medaille de Vermeil, de la Ville de Paris, 1979, 4th Ann. award for Humanitarian Svc., Girls' Club N.Y., 1979, 25th Anniversary award Greater N.Y. council, Boy Scouts Am., 1979, L.S. Ayres award, 1981, Achievement award, Girl Scouts U.S.A., 1983, Outstanding Mother award, 1984, Athena award, 1985, Golda Meir 90th Anniversary Tribute award, 1988, Pres. award, Cosmetic Exec. Women, 1989, Neiman-Marcus Fashion award, 1992, honored Lincoln Ctr., World of Style, 1986. Died Apr. 24, 2004.

LAW, WARREN AUBREY, business educator, consultant; b. Dallas, Apr. 16, 1924; s. Aubrey Clarence and Inez Lucille (Talley) L.; m. Betty Lewis, Jan. 26, 1950; children—Elizabeth, Amy BBA, So. Methodist U., 1943; MBA, Harvard U., 1948, A.M., 1952, PhD, 1953. Assoc. prof. So. Methodist, Dallas, 1953-58; prof. Harvard U., Cambridge, Mass., 1958—90, prof. emeritus, 1990—2003. Dir. Security Capital Corp., N.Y., Charter Power Systems, PA, Crompton & Knowles, N.Y., Dynatech Corp., Burlington, Mass; former chmn. Mezzanine Capital Corp., Grand Cayman Contbr. articles to profl. jours. Served to lt. (j.g.) USNR, 1943-46 Mem. Fin. Mgmt. Assn. Home: Belmont, Mass. Died Dec. 11, 2003.

LAWRENCE, FRANCES ELIZABETH, secondary school educator; b. Glendale, Calif., Feb. 26, 1925; d. Felix William and Bessie Marie Powers; m. Vester Blount Lawrence, Apr. 2, 1955 (div.); children: Elizabeth Gail, Mark William, Cynthia Sue Cherry. AA, Pasadena Jr. Coll., 1945; BA, Whittier Coll., 1949. Tchr. Victor Sch. Dist., Victorville, Calif., 1949-56, Adelanto (Calif.) Sch. Dist., 1965-93. Mem. planning bd. San Bernardino County Spelling Connection Com., 1985, Adelanto Dist. Curriculum Com., 1985-86; spl. edn. tchr., 2 yrs. Served with USNR, 1945-49. Mem. Nat. Assn. for Edn. Young Children, Calif. Assn. for Edn. Young Children, Early Childhood Caucus Calif. Tchrs. Assn., Adelanto Dist. Tchrs. Assn. (rep.). Lodges: Job's Daus. (majority mem.), Order Eastern Star. Democrat. Avocations: travel, grandchildren. Home: Maryville, Tenn. Died Nov. 22, 2001.

LAWRENCE, HENRY SHERWOOD, retired physician; b. N.Y.C., Sept. 22, 1916; s. Victor John and Agnes (Whalen) Lawrence; m. Dorothea Wetherbee, Nov. 13, 1943; children: Dorothea, Victor, Geoffrey. AB, NYU, 1938, MD, 1943. Diplomate Am. Bd. Internal Medicine. Mem. faculty NYU, N.Y.C., 1949—2001, John Wyckoff fellow in medicine, 1948—49, dir. student health, 1950—57, head infectious disease & immunology div., 1959—2000, prof. medicine, 1961—79, Jeffrey Bergstein prof. medicine, 1979—2000, co-dir. med. svcs., 1964—2000; dir. Cancer Ctr., 1974—79, Ctr. for AIDS Rsch., 1989—94. Vis. physician Tisch Hosp., Bellevue Hosp., 1964—2000; cons. medicine Manhattan VA Hosp., 1964—2000; infectious disease program com. VA Rsch. Svc., 1960—63; cons. allergy and immunology study sect. USPHS, 1960—63, chmn., 1963—65; assoc. mem. commn. on streptococcal and staphylococcal diseases Armed Forces Epidemiol. Bd., Dept. Def., 1956—74; mem. coms. NAS-NRC, 1957—65, chmn. com. transplantation, 1963—65; mem. NRC, 1970—72; mem. allergy and infectious disease panel Health Rsch. Coun., N.Y.C., 1962—75, co-chmn., 1968—75; mem. sci. adv. coun. Am. Cancer Soc., 1973—75. Editor: Medical Clinics of North America, 1957, Cellular and Humoral Aspects of Hypersensitive States, 1959; editor: (with M. Landy) Mediators of Cellular Immunity, 1969; editor: (with Kirkpatrick and Burger) Immunobiology of Transfer Factor, 1983; mem. editl. bd.: Transplantation, Ann. of Internal Medicine, 1965—71, mem. editl. adv. bd.: Transplantation Procs., from 1960, founder, editor in chief: Cellular Immunology, 1970—96. Lt. M.C. USNR, World War II. Recipient Rsch. Career Devel. award, USPHS, 1960—65, prize, Alpha Omega Alpha, 1943, Meritorious Sci. Achievement award, NYU Alumni Assn., 1970, von Pirquet Gold medal, Ann. Forum on Allergy, 1972, award for disting. achievement in sci. of medicine, ACP, 1973, Sci. Achievement award, Am. Coll. Allergists, 1974, Sci. medal, N.Y. Acad. Medicine, 1974, Bristol Sci. award, Infectious Diseases Soc. Am., 1974, Charles V. Chapin medal, 1975, Lila Gruber honor award for cancer rsch., Am. Acad. Dermatology, 1975, Alumni Achievement award, NYU Washington Sq. Coll., 1979; fellow Commonwealth Fund fellow, U. Coll., London, 1959. Fellow: ACP (Bronze medal 1973), Royal Coll. Physicians and Surgeons Glasgow (hon.), Am. Acad. Allergy (hon.); mem.: NAS, Internat. Transplantation Soc. (chmn. constnr. com., councillor), Royal Soc. Medicine (affiliate, Eng.), Infectious Diseases Soc. Am. (charter, councillor 1970—72, Bristol Sci. award 1974), Peripatetic Clin. Soc., Harvey Soc. (sec. 1957—60, lectr. from 1973, councillor 1974—77), Interurban Clin. Club, Soc. for Exptl. Biology and Medicine (editl. bd. procs.), Am. Soc. for Clin. Investigation, Assn. Am. Physicians, Soc. Francaise d'Allergie (corr.), Alpha Omega Alpha. Achievements include discovery of Transfer Factor - a product of lymphocytes (T-cells) which confers and/or augments immunity to mycobacterial, viral and fungal infections when administered to non-immune individuals; research in mechanisms tissue damage and homograft rejection in man. Home: New York, NY. Died Apr. 5, 2004.

LAWRENCE, JEROME, playwright, director, educator; b. Cleve., July 14, 1915; s. Samuel and Sarah (Rogen) L. BA, Ohio State U., 1937, LHD (hon.), 1963; DLitt, Fairleigh Dickinson U., 1968; DFA (hon.), Villanova U., 1969; LittD, Coll. Wooster, 1983. Dir. various summer theaters, Pa. and Mass., 1934-37; reporter, telegraph editor Wilmington (Ohio) News Jour., 1937; editor Lexington Daily News, Ohio, 1937; continuity editor radio Sta. KMPC, Beverly Hills, Calif., 1938-39; sr. staff writer CBS, Hollywood, Calif. and N.Y.C., 1939-42; former pres., writer, dir. Lawrence & Lee, Hollywood, N.Y.C. and London. Vis. prof. Ohio State Univ., 1969, Salzburg Seminar in Am. Studies, 1972, Baylor Univ., 1978; former prof. playwriting Univ. So. Calif. Grad. Sch.; co-founder, judge Margo Jones award, N.Y.C.; co-founder, pres. Am. Playwrights Theatre, Columbus, Ohio, 1970-85; bd. dirs. Am. Conservatory Theatre, San Francisco, 1970-80, Stella Adler Theatre, L.A., Plumstead Playhouse, 1986; keynote speaker Bicentennial of Bill of Rights, Congress Hall, Phila., 1991; hon. mem. Nat. Theatre Conf., 1993; former adv. bd. Am. Theatre in Lit. Contemporary Arts Ednl. Project; playwright. Scenario writer Paramount Studios, 1941; master playwright NYU Inst. Performing Arts, 1967-69; author-dir. for: radio and television UN Broadcasts; Army-Navy programs D-Day, VE-Day, VJ-Day; author: Railroad Hour, Hallmark Playhouse, Columbia Workshop; author: Off Mike, 1944, (biography, later made into PBS-TV spl.) Actor: Life and Times of Paul Muni, 1978 (libretto and lyrics by Lawrence and Lee, music by Billy Goldenberg); co-author, dir.: (album) One God; playwright: Live Spelled Backwards, 1969, Off Mike, (mus. with Robert E. Lee) Look, Ma, I'm Dancin', 1948 (music by Hugh Martin), Shangri-La, 1956 (music by Harry Warren, lyrics by James Hilton, Lawrence and Lee), Mame, 1966 (score by Jerry Herman), Dear World, 1969 (score by Jerry Herman), (non-mus.) Inherit the Wind (translated and performed in 34 langs., named best fgn. play of year London Critics Poll 1960), Auntie Mame, 1956, The Gang's All Here, 1959, Only in America, 1959, A Call on Kuprin, 1961, Diamond Orchid (revised as Sparks Fly Upward, 1966), 1965, The Incomparable Max, 1969, The Crocodile Smile, 1970, The Night Thoreau Spent in Jail, 1970, (play and screenplay) First Monday in October, 1978, (written for opening of Thurber Theatre, Columbus) Jabberwock: Improbablilities Lived and Imagined by James Thurber in the Fictional City of Columbus, Ohio, 1974, (with Robert E. Lee) Whisper in the Mind, 1994, The Angels Weep, 1992, (novel) A Golden Circle: A Tale of the Stage and the Screen and Music of Yesterday and Now and Tomorrow and Maybe the Day After Tomorrow, 1993; Decca Dramatic Albums, Musi-Plays., Selected Plays of Lawrence and Lee, 1996; contbg. editor Dramatics mag., mem. adv. bd., contbr. Writer's Digest; Lawrence and Lee collections at Libr. and Mus. of the Performing Arts, Lincoln Ctr., N.Y., Harvard's Widener Libr., Cambridge, Mass., Jerome Lawrence & Robert E. Lee Theatre Rsch. Inst. at Ohio State U., Columbus, est. 1986. A founder, overseas corr. Armed Forces Radio Service; mem. Am. Theatre Planning Bd.; bd. dirs. Nat. Repertory Theatre, Plumstead Playhouse; mem. adv. bd. USDAN Center for Creative and Performing Arts, East-West Players, Performing Arts Theatre of Handicapped., Inst. Outdoor Drama; mem. State Dept. Cultural Exchange Drama Panel, 1961-69; del. Chinese-Am. Writers Conf., 1982, 86, Soviet-Am. Writers Conf., 1984, 85; Am. Writers rep. to Hiroshima 40th Anniversary Commemorative, Japan, 1985; mem. U.S. Cultural Exchange visit to theatre communities of Beijing and Shanghai, 1985; former adv. coun. Calif. Ednl. Theatre Assn., Calif. State U., Calif. Repertory Co., Long Beach. Recipient N.Y. Press Club award, 1942, CCNY award, 1948, Radio-TV Life award, 1948, Mirror awards, 1952, 53, Peabody award, 1949, 52, Variety Showmanship award 1954, Variety Critics poll 1955, Outer-Circle Critics award 1955, Donaldson award, 1955, Ohioana award, 1955, Ohio Press Club award, 1959, Brit. Drama Critics award, 1960, Moss Hart Meml. award, 1967, State Dept. medal, 1968, Pegasus award, 1970, Lifetime Achievement award Am. Theatre Assn., 1979, Nat. Thespian Soc. award, 1980, Pioneer Broadcasters award, 1981, 95, Diamond Circle award Pacific Pioneer Broadcasters, 1995, Ohioana Library career medal, Master of Arts award Rocky Mountain Writers Guild, 1982, Centennial Award medal Ohio State U., 1970, William Inge award and lectureship Independence Community Coll., 1983, 86-2004, Disting. Contbr. award Psychologists for Social Responsibility, 1985, ann. awards San Francisco State U., Pepperdine U., Career award Southeastern Theatre Conf., 1990; named Playwright of Yr. Baldwin-Wallace Coll., 1960; named to Honorable Order of Ky. Colonels, 1965, Tenn. Colonels, 1988; named to Theater Hall of Fame, 1990. Fellow Coll. Am. Theatre, Kennedy Ctr.; mem. Nat. Theatre Conf. (hon.), Acad. Motion Picture Arts and Scis. (nominating com. best fgn. films 1997), Acad. TV Arts and Scis. (2 Emmy award 1988), Authors League (coun.), ANTA (dir., v.p.), Ohio State U. Assn. (dir.), Radio Writers' Guild (founder, pres.), Writers Guild Am. (dir., founding mem. Valentine Davies award), Dramatists Guild (coun.), ASCAP, Calif. Ednl. Theatre Assn. (Profl. Artist award 1992), Century Club N.Y., Phi Beta Kappa, Sigma Delta Chi. Avocations: traveling, photography, swimming. Home: Malibu, Calif. Died Feb. 29, 2004.

LAWRENCE, RAYMOND EUGENE, minister, academic administrator; b. Elliston, Ky., Nov. 14, 1921; s. Ray and Mary (Sams) L.; m. Eula Whiteker, Sept. 8, 1948; children: Deborah, Dora. BA, Georgetown Coll., 1949; MDiv, So. Bapt. Sem., 1973. Ordained to ministry, 1947. Pastor 1st Bapt. Ch., Mt. Vernon, Ky., 1953-57, Shelbyville, Ky., 1957-62, Cen. Bapt. Ch., Corbin, Ky., 1962-72; asst. to pres. Cumberland Coll., Williamsburg, Ky., 1972-80; pres. Mid-Continent Bapt. Coll., Mayfield, Ky., 1981-87; dir. Kelley Univ. Coll. S.W. Bapt. U., Joplin, Mo., from 1987. Author: History of Ten Mile Association, 1948, Don't Give Up the Ship, 1972, Whiteker Dunn, 1976. Trustee Southeastern Bapt. Hosp., 1962-82, Cumberland Coll., 1970-72; bd. dirs. Western Recorder, 1965-70. With AUS, 1943-45. Home: Joplin, Mo. Died Apr. 26, 2001.

LAWSON, A(BRAM) VENABLE, retired librarian; b. South Boston, Va., Jan. 9, 1922; s. Abram Venable and Vivien Strudwick (Moseley) L.; children: Janet Lee, Abram Venable, Mary Vivian. BA, U. Ala., 1946; M.Ln., Emory U., 1950; D Libr. Sci., Columbia U., 1969. Auditor Socony Mobil Oil Co., 1947-48; teller 1st Nat. Bank, Altavista, Va., 1948-49; library asst. Harvard Coll. Library, 1951-54; head reference dept. Atlanta Pub. Libr., 1954-56, coord. pub. svcs., 1956-60; asst. prof. Fla. State U., 1960-65; dir. div. librarianship Emory U., Atlanta, 1965-89. Vis. prof. Clark Atlanta U., 1989-90. Advisor Friends of Librs. U.S.A., 1990-93; bd. dirs. Episcopal Charities Found. With USAF, 1942-46. Recipient George Virgil Fuller award Columbia U., 1964, Nick Davies award Friends of Atlanta Fulton Pub. Libr., 1993, Emory medal, 2002. Mem. ALA, AAUP, Assn. Libr. and Info. Sci. Edn., Southeastern Libr. Assn., Ga. Libr. Assn. (Nix-Jones award for disting. svc. to Ga. librarianship 1989). Home: Atlanta, Ga. Died May 14, 2004.

LAWSON, GREGORY ALLEN, medical physicist, radiation consultant; b. Cleve., Jan. 13, 1958; s. William Allen and Virginia Jo (Hannah) Maynor; m. Katherine Lee (Ruberti) Reese, Aug. 14, 1982 (div. Dec. 1994); 1 child, Katherine Jalaine Lawson. AS in Radiologic Tech., Chattanooga State C.C., 1980; BS in Physics, U. Tenn., Chattanooga, 1983; MS in Health Physics, Ga. Inst. Tech., 1985. Diplomate Am. Bd. Radiology. Radiologic technologist Bradley Meml. Hosp., Cleveland, Tenn., 1980-84; clin. instr. radiology Chattanooga State Tech. Coll., 1984-85; jr. med. physicist Mission Meml. Hosp., Asheville, N.C., 1985-86; med. physicist Gadsden (Ala.) Cancer Ctr., 1986-87, Southeastern Cancer Ctr., Chattanooga, 1987-91; consulting med. physicist Hamilton Med. Ctr., Dalton, Ga., 1990-95, Cleveland Regional Cancer Ctr., from 1989. Executor Radiation Physics & Engring., Cleveland, 1996-97. Mem. Am. Assn. of Physicists in Medicine, Am. Coll. Radiology, Health Physics Soc. Home: Cleveland, Tenn. Died Oct. 31, 2000.

LAWSON, JAMES RAYMOND, carillonneur; b. Cody, Wyo., May 25, 1919; s. Leslie and Celeste (Sellers) L. BA, U. Chgo., 1941; postgrad., Stanford, 1942; laureate, Ecole de Carillon Malines, Belgium, 1949. Lectr. dept. music Lehman Coll., U. City N.Y., 1969-89. Carillonneur, Hoover War Library, Stanford, 1941-48, guest carillonneur, Scottish Rite Cathedral, Indpls., 1946-47, carillonneur, Rockefeller Chapel, U. Chgo., 1953-60, Riverside Ch., N.Y.C., 1960-89, Crystal Cathedral, Garden Grove, Calif., 1991; editor: quart. jour. Am. Guild English Handbell Ringers Overtones, 1960-64. Mem. Guild Carillonneurs N.A., Coll. of Campanology (Eng.), Sussex County Assn. Change Ringers (Eng.). Died Oct. 14, 2003.

LAZARUS, BARBARA BETH, academic administrator; b. Chgo., Apr. 17, 1946; d. David and Betty (Ross) L.; m. Marvin Alan Sirbu, Jan. 6, 1979; children: Margaret Ann, Benjamin James. AB cum laude, Brown U., 1967; MA in Anthropology, U. Conn., 1969; EdD in Ednl. Anthropology, U. Mass., 1973. Instr. dept. anthropology U. Conn., Storrs, 1967-72; info. unit dir. Ednl. Devel. Ctr., Newton, Mass., 1972-75; dir. Ctr. for Women's Careers Wellesley (Mass.) Coll., 1975-85; assoc. dean, sch. pub. affairs Carnegie-Mellon U., Pitts., 1985-87, assoc. provost for acad. affairs, adj. assoc. prof., 1988—2003. Co-dir. Commn. on Women and Work, Asian Women's Inst., 1978-88; vis. staff mem. Oxford U., St. Hilda's Coll., Fall, 1980; steering com. Women for Asian Devel., 1990—. Author: A Call for Action, 1985; co-editor: Aspirations: Women and Work in Asia, 1985, Women's Studies, Women's Lives, The Equity Equation, 1995. Bd. mem. Cancer Guidance Inst., Pitts., B'nai B'rith Hillel, Pitts., Criminal Justice Tng. Task Force, Pa. Commn. on Crime and Delinquency, Va. Gildersleeve Internat. Fund for U. Women; adv. bd. Women's Desk of New Voices Radio Pub. Internat Video Network; women's concerns com. United Bd. for Christian Higher Edn. in Asia; rev. com. United Way of Allegheny County. Grantee Doris Duke Found., 1968. Mem. Assn. N.Am. Cooperating Agys. of Overseas Women's Christian Coll. (cons.), Coun. on Anthropology and Edn., Assn. for Women in Devel., Am. Assn. Higher Edn., Corss Univ. Rsch. in Engring. & Sci. (founder, mem. steering com.), Phi Kappa Phi. Democrat. Jewish. Home: Pittsburgh, Pa. Died July 15, 2003.

LAZARUS, MAURICE, retired retail executive; b. Columbus, Ohio, June 27, 1915; s. Fred, Jr. and Meta (Marx) L.; m. Nancy Stix, June 7, 1942 (dec. 1985); children: Carol, Jill; m. Nell P. Eurich, Nov. 25, 1988. Student, Ohio State U.; BA, Harvard, 1937; LL.D., Am. Internat. Coll., 1969. Div. mdse. mgr. John Shillito Co., Columbus, 1937-41; head service and control Foley's, Houston, 1945-48, exec. v.p., 1948-58; pres., treas. Filene's, Boston, 1958-64, chmn. bd., 1964-65; vice chmn. Federated Dept. Stores, Inc., Boston, 1965-70, chmn. finance com., 1971-82, also dir. Mem. adv. com. on nat. health ins. issues HEW, 1977-78; bd. dirs. Cambridge Ctr. Adult Edn., 1974-75; mem. adv. Council Pres.'s Commn. on Status of Women, 1963-68; chmn. exec. com. Public Agenda Found., 1987-99; mem. div. health scis. and tech. Harvard U.-M.I.T., 1978-87, Harvard Cmty. Health Plan Found. Bd., 1984—2002, chmn., 1996-99; mem. adv. bd. Schlesinger Library Women's Archives, Radcliffe Coll., 1972-76; mem. bd. overseers Harvard Coll., 1977-83; mem. ethics adv. bd. HEW, 1978-80; vis. com., chmn. central services, Med. Sch. and Dental Medicine, Sch. Public Health Harvard U., 1978-85, mem. governance com., 1968-71, mem. working group div. health policy research and edn.; chmn. adv. com. Joint Center Urban Studies., 1977-82; trustee Mass. Gen. Hosp., Old Sturbridge Village, 1965-78, Marine Biol. Lab., 1977-84, McLean Hosp., 1980-2004, Tufts U. Civic Edn. Found. of Lincoln Filene Center for Citizenship and Public Affairs, 1972-80, New Eng. Med. Center Hosp., 1960-78, Beth Israel Hosp., 1958-65, Bennington Coll., 1965-72, Combined Jewish Philanthropy Greater Boston, 1962-65; chmn. exec. com. Pub. Agenda Found., 1977-99; bd. dirs. Boston chpt. ARC, 1962-64; dir. Med. Found., 1987—2002; chmn. Harvard Cmty. Health Plan, 1984-93; bd. overseers Boston Symphony Orch., 1971-74; bd. dirs. Salzburg Seminars in Am. Studies, Assoc. Harvard Alumni, 1966-73; pres. Assoc. Harvard Alumni, 1972-73; mem. Mass. Higher Edn. Facilities Commn., 1970-74; mem. corp. Northeastern U., Peter Bent Brigham Hosp.; bd. overseers Boston Symphony Orch., 1971-74; mem. M.I.T. Council Arts, 1972-77, Harvard Med. Center, 1977-79; mem. adv. com. hosp. initiatives in long-term care Am. Hosp. Assn.; chmn. bd. dirs. Harvard Cmty. Health Plan, dir. emeritus, 1994-2004; mem. adv. bd. Brandeis U. Ctr. Social Policy in Middle East, 1978-88. Fellow Am. Acad. Arts and Scis. Clubs: Bay (Boston), Harvard (N.Y.C.); Univ. (N.Y.C.); St. Botolph (Boston), Comml.-Mchts. (Boston). Died May 4, 2004.

LAZARUS, RICHARD STANLEY, psychology educator; b. N.Y.C., Mar. 3, 1922; s. Abe and Matilda (Marks) L.; m. Bernice H. Newman, Sept. 2, 1945; children: David Alan, Nancy Eve. AB, CCNY, 1942; MS, U. Pitts., 1947, PhD, 1948; Dr. honoris causa, Johannes Gutenberg U., Mainz, Germany, 1988, U. Haifa, Israel, 1995. Diplomate in clin. psychology Am. Bd. Examiners in Profl. Psychology. Asst. prof. Johns Hopkins, 1948-53; psychol. cons. VA, from 1952; assoc. prof. psychology, dir. clin. tng. program Clark U., Worcester, Mass., 1953-57; assoc. prof. psychology U. Calif., Berkeley, 1957-59, prof., 1959-91, prof. emeritus, from 1991. Prin. investigator Air Force contracts dealing with psychol. stress, 1951-53, USPHS grant on personality psychol. stress, 1953-70; NIA, NIDA, and NCI grantee on stress, coping and health, 1977-81, MacArthur Found. research grantee, 1981-84; USPHS spl. fellow Waseda U., Japan, 1963-64 Author 23 books, including (autobiography) The Life and Work of an Eminent Psychologist, 1998; also numerous publs. in sci. jours. 1st lt. AUS, 1943-46. Recipient Disting. Sci. Achievement award Calif. State Psychol. Assn., 1984, Div. 38 Health Psychology, 1989; Guggenheim fellow, 1969-70; Army Rsch. Inst. rsch. grantee, 1973-75 Fellow AAAS, APA (Disting. Sci. Contbn. award 1989); mem. Western Psychol. Assn., Argentina Med. Assn. (hon.). Home: Walnut Creek, Calif. Died Nov. 24, 2002.

LAZERUS, GILBERT, lawyer; b. New York City; s. Jacob and Bessie Lazerus; m. Judith Lazerus, Dec. 25, 1940 (dec.); children: Bruce and June. PhB, Yale U., 1931; JD, Columbia U., 1934. Bar: N.Y., 1934, U.S. Dist. Ct. (so. dist.) N.Y., 1940, U.S. Dist. Ct. (ea. dist.) N.Y., 1940, U.S. Supreme Ct., 1940. Assoc. Joseph V. McKee, 1938—45; ptnr. Strook, Strook, and Lavan, N.Y.C., 1945—83, of counsel, 1983—2004. Master arbitrator Dept. Ins., State of N.Y.; adminstrv. law judge Transit Dept., City of N.Y.; mem. panel of arbitrators Civil Ct. City N.Y., Am. Arbitration Assn., N.Y. Stock Exch., Am. Stock Exch., Nat. Assn. Security Dealers. Mem. Yale Club, Columbia Club N.Y.C. Home: New York, NY. Died May 25, 2004.

LEACH, RUSSELL, judge; b. Columbus, Ohio, Aug. 1, 1922; s. Charles Albert and Hazel Kirk (Thatcher) L.; m. Helen M. Sharpe, Feb. 17, 1945; children: Susan Sharpe Snyder, Terry Donnell, Ann Dunham Samuelson. BA, Ohio State U., 1946, JD, 1949. Bar: Ohio 1949. Clk. U.S. Geol. Survey, Columbus, 1948-49; reference and teaching asst. Coll. Law, Ohio State U., 1949-51; asst. city atty. City of Columbus, 1951, 53-57, city atty., 1957-63, presiding judge mcpl. ct., 1964-66; ptnr. Bricker & Eckler, 1966-88, chmn. exec. com., 1982-87; judge Ohio Ct. Claims, 1988—2002. Commr., Columbus Met. Housing Authority, 1968-74; chmn. Franklin County Republican Com., 1974-78. Served with AUS, 1942-46, 51-53 Named One of 10 Outstanding Young Men of Columbus, Columbus Jaycees, 1956, 57 Mem. ABA, FBA, Ohio Bar Assn. (coun. of dels. 1970-75), Columbus Bar Assn. (pres. 1973-74, Svc. medal 1993), Am. Judicature Soc., Pres.' Club Ohio State U., Am. Legion, Delta Theta Phi, Chi Phi. Presbyterian. Died June 15, 2002.

LEACH-CLARK, MARY A. educator, counselor of handicapped; b. Wichita, Kans., Aug. 5, 1931; d. Frank and May Jean (Hollow) Leach; m. Courtney Clark, June 12, 1954 (div.); children: David Courtney, Bruce Colin, Anne Clark Nelson, Jeffrey Charles. BS in Edn., U. Kans., 1954; MEd in Counseling, Wichita State U., 1978. Lic. counselor, Kans.; cert. nat. counselor, 1983. Tchr. gifted and emotionally disturbed Dist. 110, Overland Park, Kans., 1954-56; activity dir. Booth Meml. Hosp., Wichita, 1978; tchr. personal and social adjustment classes, Wichita, 1979-81; therapist Aidance Devel. Programs, 1980—; elem. sch. counselor Dist. 259, Wichita, 1986-93; dist. resource cons. Kans. Resource Tng. Systems, 1986-87; instr. interior design AIM's Community Coll., Greeley, Colo., 1983; art curriculum coordinator Creative Arts Ctr., Greeley, 1983; instr. interior design and piano improvisation Wichita State Free U., 1983-85; interior design instr. Marcus Ctr., Wichita State U., 1984-87, also workshop dir. interior design Small Bus. Devel. Ctr., 1985-92; home bound spl. edn. tchr. Wichita Pub. Schs. Dist. 259, 1983-93; developmental program tchr. in classrooms Adolescent Psychiat. Unit, St. Francis Hosp., Wichita, 1984. Prin. works include personal art display in State Capitol Rotunda; gallery black and white photography display China Surfaces, 1985, displayed Topeka, 1986; personal photography display Botanica Galleries, Wichita, 1990; producer musical video STOP. Vol., dir. Off-Broadway Lewis St. Troupers, Downtown Sr. Ctr., 1984-86. Interior design cons. Kaleidiscope Segment KAKE TV; counselor registry Behavorial Sci. Bd. State of Kans., 1989-93, apprentice master gardner Kans. State Ext., Wichita, 1990-91. Grantee Kans. Arts for Mus. Prodns., Wichita Pub. Schs. grantee, 1990. Mem. ACA, Am. Mental Health Counselor's Assn., Family Counselor's Assn., Kans. Counseling Assn., Kans. Mental Health Counselor's Assn., Women in the Arts, Kans. Author's Club, Alpha Chi Omega, Delta Rho Sigma. Home: Wichita, Kans.

LEAMAN, PAUL CALVIN, minister; b. New Lexington, Ohio, Feb. 10, 1929; s. Glen and Anna C. (Rickets) L.; m. Alice Marie Anderson, Sept. 25, 1948; children: Linda, Keith, Bruce, Neil, Kevin. Student, Apostolic Bible Inst., 1946-48. Pastor The Apostolic Ch., New Straitsville, Ohio, 1948-53; state youth pres. Ohio dist. United Pentecostal Ch., 1950-54; founder, pastor The Apostolic Ch., Jackson, Ohio, 1953-60, pastor Detroit, 1960-75, 1st United Pentecostal Ch., Saginaw, Mich., from 1984. Mich. dist. presbyter United Pentecostal Ch. Internat., 1961-75, 85-87, mem. fgn. missionary bd., United Pentecostal Ch. Internat., Hazelwood, Mo., 1970-75, regional field supr. fgn. missions, Latin Am./Caribbbean Region, 1975-84, Mich. dist. supt., 1987—. Home: Bridgeport, Mich. Deceased.

LEAVITT, MYRON E. state supreme court justice; b. Las Vegas, Oct. 27, 1930; m. Shirley Leavitt; 11 children. BA journalism, U. Nev., Reno; JD, U. Utah Coll. Law. Lt. gov State of Nev., Carson City, Nev., 1979—83; dist. judge Carson City, Nev., 1984—98; justice Nev. Supreme Court, Carson City, Nev., 1999—2004. Died Jan. 9, 2004.

LEAYCRAFT, EDGAR CRAWFORD, retired engineer; b. N.Y.C., July 2, 1918; s. Edgar Crawford and Julia Searing Leaycraft; m. Nancy McMahan, Aug. 1, 1945 (div. Nov. 1953); children: Cathy, Bruce Cleveland; m. Winifred Riley, Nov. 28, 1953; children: Matthew Thomas, Timothy, William. BA, Harvard U., 1941; M of Econs., New Sch. for Social Rsch., 1950. Office mgr. J. E. Leaycraft & Co., N.Y.C., 1946-50; tchr. East Woods Sch., Oyster Bay, N.Y., 1950-53; engr. Ferroxcube Corp., Saugerties, N.Y., 1953-55, Collins Radio, Burbank, Calif., 1956, Westinghouse Electric Co., Balt., 1956; staff engr. IBM, Poughkeepsie and Hopewell Junction, N.J., 1956-85; ret., 1985. Contbr. articles to profl. jours.; patentee in field. Model builder of mills Woodstock (N.Y.) Hist. Soc., 1975-85; town historian, Woodstock, 1965—, town justice, 1969. Sgt. U.S. Army Air Force, 1942-46. Mem. Ofcl. Historians of N.Y. State, Ulster County Geneal. Soc., Hist. Soc. Woodstock (pres. 1960-75), Saugerties Hist. Soc. Avocations: model boats and planes, carpentry. Home: Woodstock, NY. Died Apr. 16, 2002.

LECOURS, MICHEL, electrical engineering educator; b. Montreal, Que., Can., Aug. 1, 1940; s. Henri and Germaine (L'Archeveque) L.; m. Almut Lange, July 14, 1966; children: Christiane, Mireille, Jean-Yves. BScA, Ecole Poly., Montreal, 1963; PhD, Imperial Coll., London, 1966. Registered profl. engr., Que. Mem. sci. staff Bell-No. Rsch., Ottawa, Ont., Can., 1971-72; head dept. U. Laval, Quebec City, Que., 1975-77, vice dean, 1977-85, prof. elec. engring., 1967—2001. Cons. Lab-Volt (Que.) Ltd., Quebec City, 1981—; vis. researcher Nippon Tel. & Tel., Yokosuka, Japan, 1986. Contbr. numerous articles on electronics and communications to sci. jours.; patentee for short range high resolution radar. Recipient ann. merit award Ecole Poly., 1986, Larry K. Wilson award IEEE, 1997. Fellow IEEE, Engring. Inst. Can. (John B. Stirling medal 1997) Home: Sainte-Foy Quebec, Canada. Died Oct. 21, 2002.

LEDERBERG, VICTORIA, judge, former state legislator, lawyer; b. Providence, July 7, 1937; d. Frank and Victoria Santopietro; m. Seymour Lederberg, 1959; children: Tobias, Sarah. AB, Pembroke Coll., 1959; AM, Brown U., 1961, PhD, 1966; JD, Suffolk U., 1976, LLD, 1995, Roger Williams U., 2001. Mem. R.I. Ho. of Reps., 1975-82, chmn. subcom. on edn., fin. com., 1975-82; chmn. nat. adv. panel on financing elem. and secondary edn. Washington, 1979-82; mem. R.I. State Senate, 1985-91, chmn. fin. com. subcom. on social svcs., 1985-89, dep. majority leader, 1989-91; prof. psychology R.I. Coll., 1968-93; pvt. practice Providence, 1977-93; justice R.I. Supreme Ct., Providence, from 1993, chmn. com. on judicial performance evaluation, from 1993, mem. com. jud. edn., from 1993, chmn. com. on user-friendly cts., 1994-97, chmn. lawday com., 1996-2001; trustee Suffolk U., from 2001. Trustee Brown U., 1983—89, com. on biomed. affairs, 1990—2002; trustee Roger Williams U., from 1980, vice chmn. corp., dir. Sch. Law, Butler Hosp., 1985—93, also sec. of corp., from 2000. USPHS fellow physiol. psychology, 1964-66. Mem. ABA, New Eng. Psychol. Assn., R.I. Bar Assn., Am. Judicature Soc., Nat. Assn. Women Judges, Sigma Xi. Died Dec. 29, 2002.

LEDERER, JEROME, aerospace safety consultant, engineer; b. N.Y.C., Sept. 26, 1902; m. Sarah Bojarsky, Nov. 1, 1935; children: Nancy, Susan. BSc in Mech. Engring., NYU, 1924, MEngring., 1925. Registred profl. engr., N.Y. Aero. engr. USAir mail svc., 1926-27; chief engr. Aero Ins. Underwriters, N.Y.C., 1929-40; dir. safety bur. CAB, Washington, 1940-42; mgr. Airlines War Tng. Inst., 1942-44, U.S. Strategic Bombing Survey, 1945; pres. Flight Safety Found., 1947-67, pres. emeritus, from 1967; dir. Cornell-Guggenheim Aviation Safety Rsch. Ctr., N.Y.C., 1950-67, Office Manned Space Flight Safety, NASA, Washington, 1967-70, dir. safety, 1970-72; ret., 1972. Adj. prof. Inst. Safety and System Mgmt., U. So. Calif., ret.; past mem. adv. council Inst. Nuclear Power Ops., Atlanta, 1980-85; former cons., Laguna Hills, Calif. Author books and articles on aviation and space safety. Recipient NASA Exceptional Svc. medal, Daniel Guggenheim medal, Wright Bros. trophy, Amelia Earhart medal, Ziolkowski and Yuri Gagarin medals, Soviet Fedn. Cosmonauts, Von Baumhauer medal Royal Dutch Aero. Soc., Laura Taber Barbour award, U.S. Congress Ho. of Reps. award for exemplary svc. for aviation safety, many others; named to Safety and Health Hall of Fame Internat., OX5 Club Hall of Fame, Internat. Space Hall of Fame. Fellow AIAA (hon., Life Achievement award 1997), Am. Astronautics Assn., Soc. Automotive Engrs., Royal Aero. Soc., Human Factors Soc.; mem. NAE, Airline Pilots Assn. (hon.), Mil. Order Daedalions (hon.), Wings Club (N.Y.). Home: Laguna Hills, Calif. Died Feb. 8, 2004.

LEE, ALLAN WREN, clergyman; b. Yakima, Wash., June 3, 1924; s. Percy Anson and Agnes May (Wren) L.; m. Mildred Elaine Ferguson, June 16, 1946; 1 dau., Cynthia Ann. BA, Phillips U., Enid, Okla., 1949; MA, Peabody Coll.

Tchrs., 1953; B.D., Tex. Christian U., 1955, D.D. (hon.), 1968. Ordained minister Christian Ch. (Disciples of Christ), 1949; pastor chs. in Tex. and Wash., 1955—60, 1970—2004; gen. sec. World Conv. Chs. of Christ, Dallas, 1971-92; mem. gen. bd. Christian Ch., 1971-73; pres. Seattle Christian Ch. Missionary Union, 1964-66, Wash.-No. Idaho Conv. Christian Chs., 1966; pastor Park Ave Christian Ch., N.Y.C., 1999. TV panel mem. Am. Religious Town Hall, 1988-97. Author: Bridges of Benevolence, 1962, Wit and Wisdom, 1963, The Burro and the Bibles, 1968, Under the Shadow of the Nine Dragons, 1969, Reflections Along the Reef, 1970, Disciple Down Under, 1971, Meet My Mexican Amigos, 1972, One Great Fellowship, 1974, Fifty Years of Faith and Fellowship, 1980, Recollections of a Dandy Little Up-to-Date Town, 1985, also articles. Bd. trustees N.W. Christian Coll., Eugene, Oreg., 1985-93; bd. dirs. Melissa Pub. Libr., 1992-94, I.H.S. Hosp., 1998-2004; mem. Thai Christian Found., 1996-2004. With USNR, 1943-46. Recipient Disting. Service citation Children's Home Soc. Wash., 1967, Disting. Service award Bremerton Jaycees, 1959; Jamaica Tourist Bd. citation, 1984 Mem. Disciples of Christ Hist. Soc. (founder, life mem. 1992), Religious Conv. Mgrs. Assn. (v.p. 1972-92), Am. Bible Soc. (nat. adv. coun. 1985-94). Mem. Christian Ch. Died Mar. 8, 2004.

LEE, EDITH W. retired nursing administrator, educator; b. Enfield, N.C., Feb. 1, 1926; d. Luther and Celia (Robinson) Wade; m. John Linzie Lee, May 25, 1962. Diploma, Lincoln Hosp. Sch. Nursing, Durham, N.C., 1947; BS in Nursing Edn., U. Md., 1958, MS in Adminstrn., 1988. Instr., program coord. Crownsville (Md.) Hosp. Ctr.; supr., head nurse, asst. DON Provident Hosp., Balt.; night supr. St. Agnes Hosp., Raleigh, N.C.; dir. nursing edn. Crownsville (Md.) Hosp. Ctr.; ret., 1986. Mem. NLN, ANA, Md. League for Nursing, Md. Nurses Assn. Home: Baltimore, Md. Died Jan. 16, 2002.

LEE, IVY, JR., public relations consultant; b. N.Y.C., July 31, 1909; s. Ivy and Cornelia (Bigelow) L.; m. Marie F. Devin, Oct. 14, 1988; children: Peter Ivy III (dec.), Jean Downey. BA, Princeton U., 1931; MBA, Harvard U. Bus. Sch., 1933. Ptnr. Ivy Lee & T.J. Ross, N.Y.C., 1933-45; with Pan Am. World Airways, Miami, Fla. and San Francisco, 1942-45; adminstrv. asst. S.D. Bechtel, Bechtel Cos., San Francisco, 1950-54; pres. Ivy Lee Jr. & Assocs., San Francisco, 1945-85; pres., cons. Ivy Lee Jr. & Assocs., Inc., San Francisco, from 1985. Trustee Princeton (N.J.) U., 1965-69; bd. dirs. San Francisco TB Assn., Bay Area Red Cross, San Francisco, Edgewood Childrens Ctr. Mem. Pub. Relations Soc. Am., Internat. Pub. Relations Assn. (pres. 1976-77). Clubs: Bohemian, Pacific Union. Republican. Presbyterian. Home: San Francisco, Calif. Died Oct. 21, 2003.

LEE, ROBERT ANDREW, librarian; b. Washington, Dec. 7, 1923; s. Frederic Edward and Edna (Stewart) L. BA in English, Oberlin Coll., 1947; MLS, U. So. Calif., 1966. Jr. cataloger Columbia U. Law Library, 1950-51; reference librarian N.Y. Daily Mirror, 1952-54; researcher for Dore Schary MGM, Culver City, Calif., 1955; with Universal City Studios, Calif., from 1955, research librarian, 1960-69, head research dept., 1969-89. Contbr. articles to profl. jours. Served with AUS, 1943-46. Decorated Bronze Star with oak leaf cluster. Mem. Acad. Motion Picture Arts and Scis. (gov. 1973-75), Acad. TV Arts and Scis., Am. Film Inst., Am. Cinematheque. Home: Harrisburg, Pa. Died May 15, 2002.

LEE, ROSA ZUNG ZA, obstetrician/gynecologist; b. Seoul, Korea, 1932; MD, Korea U., 1958. Diplomate Am. Bd. Ob-Gyn. Intern, resident ob-gyn Ill. Masonic Hosp., Chgo., 1959-61, 62-64; resident ob-gyn Grant Hosp., Chgo., 1961-62; ob-gyn Walter Reed Army Med. Ctr., Washington, from 1962. Home: Bethesda, Md. Deceased.

LEEDY, DANIEL LONEY, retired ecologist; b. Butler, Ohio, Feb. 17, 1912; s. Charles Monroe and Bernice Camilla (Loney) L.; m. Barbara E. Sturges, Nov. 25, 1945 (dec. Mar. 12, 1988); children: Robert Raymond, Kathleen Eleanor; m. Virginia Lee Bittenbender, Sept. 22, 1989. AB with honors, Miami U., Oxford, Ohio, 1934, B.Sc., 1935; M.Sc., Ohio State U., 1938, PhD, 1940. Asst. geology and zoology depts. Miami U., 1933-35; instr. wildlife mgmt. Ohio State U., 1940-42; leader Ohio Coop. Wildlife Research Unit, 1945-48; biologist charge coop. wildlife research units U.S. Fish and Wildlife Service, Washington, 1949-57; mem. biol. sci. com. Dept. Agr. Grad. Sch., 1950-75; pres. Wildlife Soc., 1952, exec. sec., 1953-57; chief br. wildlife research U.S. Fish and Wildlife Service, 1957-63; chief div. research Bur. Outdoor Recreation, Dept. Interior, 1963-65; water resources research scientist Office Water Resources Research, 1965-74; ret., 1974; sr. scientist Nat. Inst. Urban Wildlife, Columbia, Md., 1975-95. Contbr. over 100 articles to profl. publs. Served to capt. USAAF, 1942-45. Decorated Bronze medal; recipient cert. of merit Nash Conservation awards program, 1953, Am. Motors Conservation award, 1958, U.S. Dept. Interior Disting. Svc. award, 1972, Disting. Alumni award Ohio State U., 1975, Daniel L. Leedy Urban Wildlife Conservation award established in his honor Nat. Inst. Urban Wildlife, 1985. Fellow AAAS; mem. Wildlife Soc. (hon., Aldo Leopold award for disting. service to wildlife conservation 1983), Am. Ornithologists Union (elective mem.), Wilson Ornithol. Soc., Am. Fisheries Soc., Sigma Xi. Clubs: Field Biologists, Cosmos (Washington). Home: Silver Spring, Md. Died Jan. 20, 2003.

LEFEBVRE, ARTHUR HENRY, mechanical engineer, educator; b. Long Eaton, Eng., Mar. 14, 1923; came to U.S., 1976; s. Henri and May (Brown) L.; m. Elizabeth Marcella Betts, Dec. 20, 1952; children: David Ivan, Paul Henry, Anne Marie. B.Sc., Nottingham U., 1946; PhD, Imperial Coll., London, 1952, D.Sc., 1975, Cranfield Inst. Tech., 1989. Combustion engr. Rolls Royce, Derby, Eng., 1952-61; prof. aircraft propulsion Cranfield Inst. Tech., Eng., 1961-71, prof., head Sch. Mech. Engring., 1971-76; prof., head Sch. Mech. Engring., Purdue U., West Lafayette, Ind., 1976-80, Reilly prof. combustion engring., 1980-93, emeritus Reilly prof. combustion engring., from 1993; emeritus prof. Cranfield U., from 1997. Cons. on combustion to various cos., Britain, Europe and U.S.A.; mem. propulsion and energetics panel Adv. Group Aero. Research and Devel., 1972-76 Author: Gas Turbine Combustion, 1983, Atomization and Sprays, 1989; contbr. tech. articles to profl. jours.; patentee combustion equipment. Fellow Royal Aero. Soc., Instn. Mech. Engrs., Royal Soc. Arts, ASME and Royal Acad. Engring.(Gas Turbine award 1984, R. Tom Sawyer award 1984, Internat. Gas Turbine Inst. scholar award 1995, Aircraft Engine Tech. award, 1996, George Westinghouse Gold medal 2002); mem. AIAA (Propellants and Combustion award 1990). Home: Stratford-upon-Avon, England. Died Nov. 24, 2003.

LEFOR, MICHAEL WILLIAM, botanist; b. Yonkers, N.Y., Apr. 1, 1943; s. Nicholas Stephen and Bertha (Buteux) L. BA in Biology, Hobart Coll., 1965; MS in Plant Systematics, U. Conn., 1968, PhD in Plant Systematics, 1972. Lab. tech. New Eng. Inst. for Med. Rsch., Ridgefield, Conn., 1966; rsch. assoc., cons. biologist State Conn. Wetland Programs U. Conn., Storrs, 1972-90, asst. prof.-in-residence depts. geography and civil engring., from 1988; prin. Factum Erit Environ. & Engring. Consultants, from 1992. Bd. dirs. Aton Forest Inc. Ecosystem Rsch. Sta., 1992—; cons. biologist to clients of Robinson & Cole, Hartford, Conn., DeLeuw-Cather Engrs., Inc., other cos. Editor Conn. Bot. Soc., 1980-93; assoc. editor Rhodora (New Eng. Bot. Club), 1984—; co-editor Inst. Water Resources Conf. Procs. 1-4, 1973-86; contbr. articles to profl. jours. Presented testimony on behalf of State of Conn.'s Wetland programs in many hearings and ct. appearances. Grantee of many orgns. including Conn. Dept. of Transp. Mem. New Eng. Bot. Club, Conn. Bot. Soc., Assn. Am. Geographers, Am. Assn. Univ. Profs., Soc. of Wetland Scientists, Am. Assn. Photogrammetry & Remote Sensing (cert. photogrammetrist 1978). Democrat. Episcopalian. Avocations: music, musical instruments. Home: Storrs Mansfield, Conn. Died Sept. 3, 2000.

LEFRAK, SAMUEL JAYSON, housing and building corporation executive; b. N.Y.C., Feb. 12, 1918; s. Harry and Sarah (Schwarz) LeF.; m. Ethel Stone, May 14, 1941; children: Denise, Richard, Francine, Jacqueline. Grad., U. Md., 1940; postgrad., Columbia U., Harvard U.; LLD (hon.), U. of Studies, Rome, 1971, N.Y. Law Sch., 1974, Colgate U., 1979; HHD (hon.), Pratt Inst., 1988, U. Md., 1990, Queens Coll., 1994, Mich. State U., 1995, St. John's U., 1996. Pres. Lefrak Orgn., from 1948, chmn. bd., from 1975; creator, sponsor, builder LeFrak City, Battery Park City, Gateway Pla., Newport Complex. Mem. adv. bd. Sta. WHLI, 1955; commr. Landmarks Preservation Commn., N.Y.C., 1966; commr. pub. works Borough Manhattan, 1956-58; commr. Interstate Sanitation Commn., 1958; Saratoga Springs Commn., 1962—; mem. adv. bd. Chem Bank.; guest lectr. Harvard Grad. Sch. Bus. Adminstrn., 1971, Yale, 1975, NYU, 1977; guest speaker Fin. Women's Assn., N.Y., 1975; guest lectr. Princeton U., U. Haifa, 1983, Oxford U., 1984, Pratt Inst., 1987, Harvard U., 1987, Columbia Sch. Bus., 1988, Wharton Sch. Bus., 1989, Sch. Bus. NYU, 1989; speaker UN, 1988; featured speaker Instl. Investment Real Estate Conf., 1975, Fed. Home Loan Bank Conf., 1990; guest lectr. Japanese Govt., Finnish Govt., Switzerland, 1967; U.S. del. Internat. Conf. Housing and Urban Devel., Switzerland, 1967; dir. N.Y. World's Fair Corp., 1964-65, N.Y. Indsl. Devel. Corp., 1975—, chmn. bd. L.I. Post; pres. N.Y.C. Comml. Devel. Corp., 1967-71, chmn., 1971—; founding mem. World Business Coun., Inc., 1970; mem. Pres.'s Com. Employment Handicapped; spl. cons. urban affairs State Dept., 1969; mem. adv. coun. Real Estate Inst., N.Y. U., 1970—; mem. gov. fin. Pres.'s Club U. Md., 1971, com. N.Y. State Traffic Safety Council, 1966; bd. visitors Sch. Law, Columbia U., 1983; commr. Saratoga-Capital dist. N.Y. State Park and Recreation Commn., 1973; mem. real estate coun. exec. com. Met. Mus. Art, 1982; mem. N.Y.C. Pub. Devel. Corp., Nat. Energy Coun., U.S. Dept. Commerce, Mayor's Com. on Housing Devel., N.Y.C., 1974—; mem. exec. com. Citizen's Budget Com. for N.Y.C., Inc., 1975—; mem. Gov. Cuomo's Adv. Coun., 1983, N.Y. State Gov.'s Task Force on Housing, 1974; establish Lefrak Lecture Series, U. Md., 1982; creator, developer residential and business property. Vice chmn.-at-large ARC, N.Y.; mem. U.S. com. UN Orgn., 1957; chmn. nat. bd. Histadrut, 1967—; mem. Israel Bonds Prime Minister Com., 1980; dir. Ronald McDonald House, 1986; chmn. bldg. com. Saratoga Performing Arts Ctr.; mem. Fifth Ave. Assn.; dir., chmn. real estate div. Greater N.Y. Fund; hon. com. AAU; Queens chmn. United Greek Orthodox Charities, 1973; chmn. Celebrity Sports Night-Human Resources Ctr., 1973-74, Sports Assn. Hebrew U. of Jerusalem, 1979; patron Met. Mus. Art; sponsor Israel Philharm. Orch., Jan Groth Exhibit, Guggenheim Mus.; trustee, dir. Beth-El Hosp.; bd. dirs. USO, Citizens Housing and Planning Council, N.Y., 1957—, Interfaith Movement, Diabetics Found., Queens Cultural Assn., Consumer Credit Counseling Svc. Greater N.Y., Astoria Motion Picture and TV Ctr. Found.; trustee N.Y. Law Sch., Queens Art and Cultural Ctr., Jewish Hosp. at Denver, N.Y Civic Budget Com.; trustee, med. adv. bd. Brookdale Hosp. Med. Ctr., Pace U.; mem. exec. bd. Greater N.Y. couns. Boy Scouts Am.; founder Albert Einstein Sch. Medicine; mem. Bretton Woods Com.; bd. govs. Invest-in-Am. Nat. Coun.; mem. task force on energy conservation Div. Community Housing, 1981—; mem. com. N.Y. State Traffic Safety Coun., 1966; chmn. Scandinavia Today, 1981—; bd. visitors Sch. Law Columbia U., 1983; mem. adv. bd. The Explorer's Club, 1984; mem. Nat. Com. on U.S.-China Rels. Inc.; bd. dirs. Inst. Nautical Archaeology; trustee Queens Coll., 1989; adv. dir. Met. Opera, 1990; conf. bd. Keynote Address-Annual Fin. Seminar, 1987; mem. Lambda Alpha Internat. bd. trustees Guggenheim Mus., 1993; mem. bd. trustees Dana Farber Cancer Inst. Harvard Med. Sch., 1992. Decorated officer Order of Lion of Finland, 1980, Medal of Parliament, 1988; officer Order St. John of Jerusalem Knights of Malta, 1982; Order of the North Star of Sweden, 1982; comdr. Royal Norwegian Order of Merit, 1987; Chevalier des Artes et des Lettres medal, France, 1996, Commendatore Order of Merit, Italy, 1997; recipient Mayor N.Y.C. award outstanding citizenship, 1960; Nat. Boys Club award, 1960; Citizen of Year award B'nai Brith, 1963; Am. Achievement award, 1984; Disting. Achievement award Pratt Inst., 1967; Man of Year award VFW, 1963; Brotherhood award NCCJ, 1964; Chief Rabbi Herzog gold medal; Torah Fellowship citation Religious Zionist Am., 1966; John F. Kennedy Peace award, 1966; Man of Year award Bklyn. Community Hosp., 1967; Builder of Excellence award Brandeis U., 1968; Master Builder award N.Y. Cardiac Ctr., 1968; Disting. Citizen award M Club Found. U. Md., 1970; Disting. Alumnus award U. Md. Alumni Assn., 1970; Disting. Citizen and Outstanding Community Svc. award United Way, 1986; Am. Achievement award Ency. Britannica, 1984; Am. Eagle award nat. coun. Invest-in Am., 1972; Exec. Sportsman award Human Resources Ctr., 1973; Archtl. award Fifth Av. Assn., 1974; Excellence in Design award Queens C. of C., 1974; Flame Truth award Fund Higher Edn., 1986; LeFrak Forum Mich. State U., 1997; elected hon. citizen Md., 1970; Citizen of Yr. award Bklyn. Philharm. Orch., 1983; dedication of Samuel J. LeFrak Hall U. Md., 1982, LeFrak Gymnasium, Amherst Coll., 1986, LeFrak Terrace Explorers Club, 1996, LeFrak Moot Ct., N.Y. Law Sch., 1990, LeFrak Meadow, N.Y.C., 1991, LeFrak Concert Hall, Queens Coll., LeFrak Gallery and Sculpture Terrace, Guggenheim Mus.; LeFrak Lecture Series at U. Md. established, 1982, LeFrak Learning Ctr. Temple Emanuel, 1995; LeFrak Gymnasium and Scholarship Barnard Coll., 1997; LeFrak IMAX Theatre in Am. Mus. Natural History; Comdr. of the Royal Norwegian Order of Merit, presented by King Olav V, 1987; Rough Riders award Boy Scouts Am., 1987; Torch of Progress Assoc. Builders and Owners Greater N.Y.; award Soc. Fgn. Consuls, 1988, Gold medal and Man of Yr. award Israel Bonds Found., 1990, Developer of the Yr. Associated Builders and Owners of Greater N.Y., 1990; award Assn. Graphics Arts, 1990, Disting. Citizen of World award UN, 1994, Alumni Hall of Fame award U. Md., 1995, award N.J. Hist. Soc., 1999, hon. N.Y. Ear and Ear Infirmary, 1999; named to Nat. Sales Club Hall of Fame, 1990, Songwriter's Hall of Fame, 1997, Samuel J. LeFrak Day named in hon. gov. N.Y., N.Y. State license plate deicated in hon., 1998, Man of Yr. gov. Philippines, 1999, 100 most important New Yorkers during past 400 yrs. whose work contributed to city's cultural and econ. success Crain Mag., 1999. Mem. Sales Execs. Club N.Y. (dir.), United Hunts Racing Assn., Philharm. Symphony Soc. N.Y., Explorers Club (dir.), Newcomen Soc. U.S., Phi Kappa Phi, Tau Epsilon Phi (established Samuel J. LeFrak scholarship award 1975). Clubs: U. Md. Pres.'s (mem. Gov. N.Y. fin.), Lotos (bd. dirs. 1975—, Merit award 1973), Grand Street Boys, Friars (dir. Found.), Advertising, Economic, Downtown Athletic (N.Y.C.); Town, Turf and Field; Cat Cay (Nassau, Bahamas); Xanadu Yacht (Freeport, Grand Bahamas); Palm Bay (Miami Beach, Fla.); Seawane; Ocean Reef (Key Largo); Sag Harbor Yacht (L.I.). Lodges: Masons (32d degree), Shriners. Died Apr. 16, 2003.

LEGGETT, GLENN, former English language educator, academic administrator; b. Ashtabula, Ohio, Mar. 29, 1918; s. Glenn H. and Celinda (Sheldon) L.; m. Doris Ruth James, June 14, 1941 (dec.); children: Leslie Ann Leggett Leonard, Susan Cady Leggett Jones, Celinda Sheldon Leggett Conrad, Joanna Ruth Leggett Sinnwell; m. Russelle Seeberger Jones, Mar. 11, 1973; children: Brian Edward Jones, Sarah Lorene Jones Krumm. AB, Middlebury (Vt.) Coll., 1940, LL.D., 1971; MA, Ohio State U., 1941, PhD, 1949; L.H.D., Rockford Coll., 1967, Ripon Coll., 1968, Coll. Idaho, 1974, Grinnell Coll., 1975; LL.D., Morningside Coll., 1975; Litt.D., Lawrence U., 1968. Instr. in English Mass. Inst. Tech., 1942-44; instr., then asst. prof. English Ohio State U., 1946-52; asso. prof. English U. Wash., 1952-58, asst. to pres., 1958-61, vice provost, 1961-63, provost, 1963-65; prof. English, pres. Grinnell Coll., 1965-75, pres. emeritus, 1979—; v.p. corporate communications Deere & Co., 1975-79. Mem. commn. English Coll. Entrance Exam. Bd., 1957-65, trustee, 1965-76, vice chmn., 1970-72, chmn., 1972-74; pres. Mayflower Retirement Homes, Inc., 1986-88. Author: (with Mead and Kramer) Handbook for Writers, 12th edit., 1995, A Conservative View, The New Professors, 1960; editor: Twelve Poets, 1959, (with Daniel and Beardsley) Theme and Form: An Introduction to Literature, 4th edit., 1975, (with Daniel) The Written Word, 1960, (with Steiner) Twelve Poets, alt. edit., 1967, Years of Turmoil: Years of Change, 1978, Teacher to Teacher: Selected Papers on Teaching, Writing, and Higher Education, 1979. Chmn. Ill.-Iowa Assn. Children with Learning Disabilities, 1976-79; bd. dirs. Quad-Cities Grad. Study Center, 1975-79, chmn., 1977-79; chmn. Conf. Coll. Composition, 1959, Iowa Coll. Found., pres., 1974-75; trustee Marycrest Coll., 1975-80; curator Stephens Coll., 1976-83; mem. exec. com. Iowa Natural Heritage Found., 1979-93; mem. Iowa Natural Resources Commn., 1982-83; bd. dirs. Stewart Library, pres., 1987-88. Served with USNR, 1944-46. Danforth grantee, 1971; recipient Edward S. Noyes award Coll. Bd.,

1979 Mem. MLA, Nat. Council Tchrs. English (chmn. coll. sect. 1963-65, chmn. survey undergrad. curriculum in English 1964-67, task force career edn. 1978-79), Iowa Assn. Pvt. Colls. (pres. 1969-71), Assoc. Colls. Midwest (chmn. 1971-73), Chi Psi. Congregationalist. Home: Grinnell, Iowa. Died June 2, 2003.

LEHR, ELLEN, pediatric psychologist; b. St. Louis, Apr. 3, 1946; d. Clarence Henry and Augusta (Stahmer) Kremmel; m. William Lehr, Jan. 29, 1967; children: Aaron Sung, Adam Manop. AB, Boston U., 1971, EdM, 1972; PhD, Boston Coll., 1978. Lic. psychologist, Wash.; cert. sch. psychologist, Wash.; Diplomate Am. Bd. Med. Psychotherapists. Asst. prof. U. Wis., Milw., 1977-79; postdoctoral fellow Georgetown Univ. Hosp., Washington, 1979-81; sr. pediatric psychologist Rehab. Inst. of Chgo., 1981-88; clin. assoc. prof. Univ. of Medicine and Dentistry of N.J., New Brunswick, 1988-89; assoc. program dir. New Medico Community Re-entry Svcs. of Wash., Seattle, 1989-90; psychologist pvt. practice Seattle, from 1990. Disability examiner Social Security Adminstrn., Seattle, 1993—; participant U.S. Dept. of Edn. and the Nat. Inst. of Disability and Rehab. Rsch. Author: Psychological Management of Traumatic Brain Inuries in Children and Adolescents, 1990. Mem. APA, Internat. Neuropsychol. Soc., Nat. Acad. of Neuropsychology, Nat. Head Injury Found. Home: Seattle, Wash. Died Apr. 20, 2002.

LEININGER, STEVEN J. advertising executive; b. Frankfort, Ind., Mar. 17, 1948; s. Earel G. and Madge (Reagan) L.; m. Donna Kay Reeder, June 8, 1969; children: Amy Marie, Thomas J. Student, Ind. State U., 1967-69; BA in Speech, Ball State U., 1971. Classified mgr. Elwood (Ind.) Call Leader, 1976-79; adv. mgr. Alexandria (Ind.) Times-Tribune, 1979-81, Apple Press, Frankfort, 1981-83; adv. account rep. Frankfort Times, 1983-86; adv. dir. Peru (Ind.) Daily Tribune, from 1986. Author: (8 books) Official Joke Books, 1980-84; writer for cartoonists, 1976-84, actor with Red Barn Summer Theatre, Frankfort, 1983-86. Cocah Bunker Hill (Ind.) Little League, 1987-90, Maconaquah Babe Turh, Bunker Hill, 1990-92. Mem. Internat. Circus Hall of Fame (bd. dirs. 1992-94, art dir. 1990—), Hoosier State Press Assn. (20 awards for advt. layout and design). Republican. Baptist. Avocations: sports card collecting, drawing, painting, macintosh computers. Home: Peru, Ind. Died Mar. 21, 1994.

LEIS, HENRY PATRICK, JR., surgeon, educator; b. Saranac Lake, N.Y., Aug. 12, 1914; s. Henry P. and Mary A. (Disco) L.; m. Winogene Barnette, Jan. 8, 1944; children: Henry Patrick III, Thomas Frederick BS cum laude, Fordham U., 1936; MD, N.Y. Med. Coll., 1941. Diplomate Am. Bd. Surgery. Intern Flower and Fifth Ave Hosps., N.Y.C., 1941-42, resident, 1943-44, 46-49, attending surgeon, chief breast service, 1960-81; resident in surgery Kanawa Valley Hosp., Charleston, W.Va., 1942-43; attending surgeon, chief breast svc. Met. Hosp., N.Y.C., 1960-81, emeritus chief breast svc., 1982—; attending surgeon Coler Meml. Hosp., N.Y.C., 1960-76; chief breast surgery Cabrini Hosp. Med. Ctr., 1978-85, cons. breast surgery, from 1985; emeritus surgeon Lenox Hill Hosp., N.Y.C., 1980-83; hon. mem. surg. staff Lenox Hill Hosp., N.Y.C., 1984—, Drs. Hosp., N.Y.C.; hon. mem. surg. staff, cons. breast surgery Breast Ctr. Grand Strand Regional Med. Ctr., Myrtle Beach, S.C., 1985—; attending surgeon Westchester County Med. Ctr., 1977-81, emeritus surgeon, 1982—; clin. prof. surgery U. S.C. Sch. Medicine, Breast Surg. Oncology, Columbia, 1985-2000, prof. emeritus, from 2000; hon. dir. breast cancer ctr., cons. in breast surgery Winthrop Univ. Hosp., Mineola, from 1971; cons. in breast surgery VA Hosp., Columbia, S.C., 1985—; breast surg. oncologist Carolina Cancer Ctr., from 1997. Cons. in breast surgery St. Claires Hosp., N.Y.C., 1979; attending surg. staff Richland Meml. Hosp., Columbia, 1986-90; clin. prof. surgery, 1960-81, prof. emeritus, 1982—, co-dir. Inst. Breast Diseases, 1978-82, emeritus, 1982—, chief breast svc. N.Y. Med. Coll., 1960-81, emeritus, 1982—; cons. in breast surgery SUNY Div. Rehab., 1965—, Med. and Surg. Specialists Plan N.Y.; mem. Am. Joint Com. on Breast Cancer Staging and End Results; v.p. N.Y. Met. Breast Cancer Group, 1975-76, pres., 1977-79; cons. Med. Advs. Selective Svc. System, N.Y.C. Alumni trustee N.Y. Med. Coll., 1971-76; adv. coun. Fordham Coll. Pharmacy, 1968; bd. dirs. Hall Fame and Mus. Surg. History and Related Scis. Author: Diagnosis and Treatment of Breast Lesions: The Breast, 1970, Management of Breast Lesions, 1978, Breast Cancer: Conservative and Reconstructive Surgery, 1989, Breast Lesions: Diagnosis and Treatment, 1988; co-editor: Breast; hon. editor Internat. Surgery Jour.; mem. editorial bd. jour. Senolgia, 1982—, Breast: An Internat. Jour.; contbr. articles to profl. jours. Mem. Women's Cancer Task Force of S.C. Capt. M.C., AUS, 1944-46, PTO. Decorated knight Grand Cross Equestrian Order Holy Sepulchre Jerusalem, knight Mil., Order of Malta, Knight Noble Co. of the Rose; recipient award of Merit Am. Cancer Soc., 1969, 87, cert. and award for outstanding and devoted services to indigent sick City N.Y., 1965, Dr. George Hohman Meml. medal, 1936, N.Y. Apothecaries medal, 1936, Internat. cert. merit for disting. service to surgery, 1970, award of merit N.Y. Met. Breast Cancer Group, 1976, medal of Ambrogino (Italy), 1977, Service award of Honor N.Y. Med. Coll., 1969, medaille d'Honneur (France), medal of City of Paris, 1979, Silver Palm Jerusalem award 1996, citation for svcs. to indigent sick in S.C.; Henry P. Leis, Jr. Breast and Women's Ctr. named in his honor, Grand Strand Reg. Med. Ctr., Myrtle Beach, S.C., 1999. Fellow ACS (cancer liaison physician Surgeons commn. on Cancer 1988-98, emeritus cancer liaison physician commn. on Cancer 1999—, Cancer Liaison Physician Merit award Grand Strand Regional Med. Ctr., 1988-98), Peruvian Acad. Surgery (hon.), Am. Acad. Compensation Medicine, Am. Soc. Clin. Oncology, Am. Assn. Cancer Rsch., Am. Geriats. Soc., Indsl. Med. Assn., Internat. Coll. Surgeons (1st v.p. 1973-74, pres. 1977-78, v.p., chmn. coun. examiners U.S. sect. 1962-68, pres. 1971, Svc. award of honor 1971), Internat. Paleopathology Assn. (founder), N.Y. Acad. Medicine, N.Y. Coun. Surgeons, Royal Soc. Health (Eng.); mem. AMA, AAAS, AAUP, Am. Cancer Soc. (com. breast cancer), Am. Med. Writers Assn., Am. Soc. Breast Diseases and Breast Surgeons, S. Carolina Women's Cancer Coalition, Breast Surgical Cons. of Carolina Cancer Ctrs. (mem. profl. edn. and risk factors coms.), Am. Profl. Practice Assn., Assn. Am. Med. Colls., Am. Coll. Radiology (com. mammography and breast cancer), Assn. Mil. Surgeons U.S., Am. Soc. Breast Diseases, Am. Soc. Breast Surgeons, Cath. Physicians Guild (pres. N.Y. 1970-78), Gerontol. Soc., Internat. Platform Assn., N.Y. Cancer Soc., N.Y. County Med. Soc., N.Y. Surg. Soc., Pan Am Med. Assn. (v.p. N.Am. sect. on cancer 1967—), Pan Pacific Surg. Assn. (v.p. 1980, Res. Officers Assn. U.S., Soc. Acad. Achievement (mem. editl. bd. 1969—), Nat. Consortium Breast Ctrs. (bd. dirs. 1991-96), Soc. Med. Jurisprudence, Soc. Nuc. Medicine Surg. Soc. N.Y. Med. Coll., WHO, World Med. Assn., Alumni Assn. N.Y. Med. Coll. (gov. 1960—, pres. 1971), Assn. Mil. Surgeons U.S., Catholic War Vets. Assn., VFW, Hollywood Acad. Medicine (hon.), Alpha Omega Alpha, Phi Chi; hon. mem. Argentine Soc. Mammary Pathology, Argentina Cardiac and Thoracic Surg. Soc., Ecuador Med. Assn., Mo. Surg. Soc., Venezuela Surg. Soc., Italian Surg. Soc., S.C. Oncology Soc., So. Med. Assn. Clubs: Surf, Rotary. Lodges: K.C. (4th deg.). Died Mar. 7, 2002.

LEISER, ERNEST STERN, journalist; b. Phila., Feb. 26, 1921; s. Monroe Felsenthal and Gertrude (Stern) L.; m. Caroline Thomas Camp, Oct. 26, 1946; children: Nancy, Shelley, Nicholas. AB, U. Chgo., 1941. Reporter City News Bur. Chgo., 1941; asst. picture editor Chgo. Herald-Am., 1941-42, 46; corr. Overseas News Agy., 1947-52; successively corr., producer, dir. TV news, exec. producer CBS News, N.Y.C., 1953-72, sr. producer, producer bicentennial coverage, spl. reports, 1975-79, v.p. spl. events and polit. coverage, 1979-81, v.p., dep. dir. news, 1981-85; exec. producer ABC News, N.Y.C., 1972-75; sr. fellow Gannett Ctr. for Media Studies, 1987-88. Author: This is Germany, 1950; contbr. articles to mags. Served with AUS, 1942-46. Decorated Bronze Star, Croix de Guerre; recipient Sigma Delta Chi award for TV reporting, 1956, Peabody awards for TV reporting and producing, 1956, 77, Ohio State awards, 1969, 77, Nat. Acad. TV Arts and Scis. award, 1968-71. Home: South Nyack, NY. Died Nov. 26, 2002.

LEISURE, GEORGE STANLEY, JR., retired lawyer; b. N.Y.C., Sept. 16, 1924; s. George S. and Lucille E. (Pelouze) L.; m. Joan Casey, June 22, 1949; children: Constance, Timothy, Matthew, George III. BA, Yale U., 1948; LLB, Harvard U., 1951. Bar: N.Y. 1953, U.S. Supreme Ct. 1966. Asst. U.S. atty. So. Dist. N.Y., 1954-56; trial atty. antitrust divsn. Dept. Justice, N.Y.C., 1956-57; ptnr. Donovan Leisure Newton & Irvine, N.Y.C., 1957-93. Spl. counsel to Gen. William Westmoreland in Westmoreland vs. CBS, 1984-85. With USN, 1943-46, lt. USNR, 1951-53. Fellow Am. Coll. Trial Lawyers (chmn. N.Y. downstate com. 1975-77); mem. Fed. Bar Council (pres. 1976-78), Assn. Bar City N.Y. (exec. com. 1962-66), Fed. Bar Assn., ABA, N.Y. State Bar Assn., N.Y. County Lawyers Assn. Home: Sea Island, Ga. Died Aug. 25, 2003.

LEITH, JOHN HADDON, clergyman, theology educator; b. Due West, S.C., Sept. 10, 1919; s. William H. and Lucy Ann (Haddon) L.; m. Ann Caroline White, Sept. 2, 1943; children— Henry White, Caroline Haddon. AB, Erskine Coll., 1940, DD (hon.), 1972; BD, Columbia Theol. Sem., 1943; MA, Vanderbilt U., 1946; PhD, Yale U., 1949; DD (hon.), Davidson Coll., 1978; DLitt (hon.), Presbyn. Coll., 1990. Ordained to ministry Presbyn. Ch. 1943. Pastor chs. in Nashville and Auburn, Ala., 1944-59; Pemberton prof. theology Union Theol. Sem., Richmond, Va., 1959-90. Vis. prof. Columbia Theol. Sem., Eckerd Coll., New Coll. at U. Edinburgh; adj. prof. Va. Commonwealth U.; mem. ad interim com. to revise book of ch. order Presbyn. Ch. U.S., 1955-61, mem. com. to write brief statement of faith, 1960-62, mem. com. to prepare brief statement of reformed faith, 1984-91; chmn. com. revision of chpt. 3 of Confession of Faith, 1959-60, mem. permanent nominating com. gen. assembly, 1972-75; chmn. bd. Presbyn. Survey, 1961-70; bd. dirs. Presbyn. Outlook Mag., 1962-99; moderator Presbyn. Synod N.C., 1977-78; mem. Gov.'s Commn. on Seasonal and Migrant Farm Workers, 1982-94; mem. adv. coun. Ctr. of Theol. Inquiry, Princeton, N.J., 1989-94. Author: Creeds of the Churches, 1963, 3d. rev. edit., 1982, The Church, A Believing Fellowship, 1965, rev., 1980, Assembly at Westminster, 1973, Greenville Church, The Story of a People, 1973, rev. edit. 1997, The Reformed Tradition, A Way of Being the Christian Community, 2d edit., 1981, John Calvin, the Christian Life, 1984, The Reformed Imperative, 1988, John Calvin's Doctrine of the Christian Life, 1989; editor: Guides to Reformed Theology, The Reformed Imperative, 1988, From Generation to Generation, 1990, Basic Christian Doctrine, 1993; editor (with Stacy Johnson) A Reformed Reader, A Source Book for Christian Theology, 1993, Crisis in the Church, the Plight of Theological Education, 1997, The Pilgrimage of a Presbyterian, 2000. Trustee Erskine Coll.; bd. dirs. Inst. Religion and Democracy, 1985-93; mem. Richmond City com. Dem. Party, 1973-93. Kent fellow, 1946-48; Folger Library fellow, 1964; grantee Advanced Religious Studies Found., 1974 Mem. Calvin Studies Soc. (pres. 1980-83) Home: Easley, SC. Died Aug. 12, 2002.

LEIZEAR, CHARLES WILLIAM, retired information services executive; b. Balt., Dec. 15, 1922; s. Charles R. and Nellie Beyer L.; m. Jean Smith, Nov. 26, 1947; children: Robin DeBarry, Kathy King. Charles R. II BS cum laude, Loyola Coll., Balt., 1949. With Burroughs Co., 1949-71; v.p. mktg. data systems Singer Co., NYC, 1972-76; group v.p. cash mgmt. services Nat. Data Corp., Atlanta, 1976-81, exec. v.p. fin. service and systems, 1981-83, exec. v.p. ops., 1983-85, exec. v.p. retail systems, 1984, sr. v.p., 1985-88; mktg. and quality process cons. Charles Assoc., Atlanta, 1989-98; ret., 1998. Bd. dirs. Lupus Specialists, Inc., Atlanta; pres. Fairhaven Residents Assn., Inc., 2003-04. With US Army, 1942-45. Recipient Susan Anthony award for highest acad. achievement Loyola U., 1947 Mem.: Fairhaven Residents Assoc., Inc. (pres. 2003). Home: Sykesville, Md. Died Jan. 20, 2004.

LEMONICK, AARON, physicist, researcher; b. Phila., Feb. 2, 1923; s. Samuel and Mary (Ferman) L.; m. Eleanor Leah Drutt, Feb. 12, 1950; children— Michael Drutt, David Morris. BA, U. Pa., 1950; MA, Princeton U., 1952, PhD, 1954. Asst. prof. physics Haverford Coll., Pa., 1954-57, assoc. prof., 1957-61, Princeton U., N.J., 1961-64, prof., 1964-94, assoc. chmn. dept. physics, 1967-69, dean grad. sch., 1969-73, dean faculty, 1973-89, dean of faculty emeritus, from 1989; assoc. dir. Princeton-Pa. Accelerator, 1961-67; prof. physics emeritus Princeton U., N.J., from 1994; v.p. Princeton U. Press, 1973—; dep. dir. Princeton Plasma Physics Lab., 1989-90. Trustee Bryn Mawr Coll., 1988—, Princeton Day Sch., Princeton Adult Sch. Fellow AAAS, Am. Phys. Soc.; mem. AAUP, Am. Assn. Physics Tchrs., Phi Beta Kappa, Sigma Xi. Home: Hightstown, NJ. Deceased.

LENGA, J. THOMAS, lawyer; b. Toledo, Dec. 16, 1942; s. Casimir M. and Rose C. (Sturniolo) L.; children by previous marriage: Christina M., John Thomas Jr., Peter M. BA, U. Toledo, 1965, JD, 1968. Bar: Mich. 1968, Ohio 1968. Capt. JAGC U.S. Army, 1968—72; mem. Dykema Gossett PLLC, Detroit, 1972-96, Clark Hill P.L.C., Detroit, from 1996, CEO, from 2001. Mem. com. on std. jury instrns. Mich. Supreme Ct.; advocate Am. Bd. of Trial Advocates. Named Disting. Alumnus, Coll. Law, U. Toledo, 1987. Fellow: Am. Coll. Trial Lawyers, Internat. Acad. Trial Lawyers; mem.: Internat. Assn. Def, Counsel, State Bar Mich. (bd. commrs. from 1992, treas. 1995—96, v.p. 1996—97, pres. elect 1997—98, pres. 1998—99), Detroit Bar Assn. (pres. 1989—90). Died 2002.

LENKEY, SUSAN VILMA, art historian, educator; b. Budapest, Hungary, Nov. 8, 1910; came to U.S., 1958; m. Andrew Lenkey, 1931 (dec. 1967); 1 child, Maryll Telegdy. B, Gisella U., Budapest, 1928; tchrs. diploma, Pazmany U., Budapest, 1934, PhD in Art History summa cum laude, 1946. Asst. prof. art history U. Budapest, 1946-54; catalog-ing asst. Yale U. Libr., New Haven, 1958-60; rare book libr. Stanford (Calif.) U., 1960-76, lectr. humanities, 1961-80; lectr. art history Extension of U. Calif., 1961-76; lectr. ecclesiastical art St. Patrick's Sem., Menlo Park, Calif., from 1981. Vis. prof. art history World Campus Afloat, 1969, 71, 74, 75, 77, 79, 80, mem. faculty coun., 1972. Author: An Unknown Leonardo Self-Portrait, 1963, Portraits, 1972, Stanford Incunabula, 1976, Census of Aldines in California, 1974, others; contbr. articles on art history, museology and bibliography to profl. jours. Mem. Archaeol. Inst. (hon. v.p. Stanford chpt. 1965), Royal Commonwealth Soc. Roman Catholic. Avocations: travel, photography, music. Home: Mountain View, Calif. Deceased.

LEONARD, EASON HARRIS, architect; b. El Reno, Okla., June 5, 1920; s. Carl Van Every and Zadeth Amy (Dutcher) L.; m. Jeanne A. Mason, Nov. 1945 (dec. Sept. 1965); children— Bruce, Craig; m. Jeanne A. Burton, June 21, 1970; adopted Polly Burton B.Arch., Okla. State U., 1943. Asso. William Lescaze Architect, N.Y.C., 1947-49, Chauncey W. Riley Architect, N.Y.C., 1949, 1953; assoc. I.M. Pei & Ptnrs., N.Y.C., 1953-55; mng. ptnr. Pei Cobb Freed & Ptnrs. (formerly I.M. Pei & Ptnrs.), N.Y.C., 1955—90. Major works include Bank of China, Hong Kong, Meyerson Symphony Ctr., Dallas, Mile High Ctr., Denver, Dallas City Hall, Raffles City, Singapore. Served with C.E. U.S. Army, 1943-46. Fellow AIA; mem. Archtl. Registration Council U.K., Royal Inst. Brit. Architects (corp. mem.), Archtl. League, N.Y. Bldg. Congress, Nat. Council Archtl. Registration Bds., Singapore Register of Architects, Metropolitan Club. Republican. Methodist. Home: Carmel, Calif. Died Nov. 13, 2003.

LEPPER, ROBERT LEWIS, artist, educator; b. Aspinwall, Pa., Sept. 10, 1906; s. Charles William and Elizabeth Lloyd (Hutchinson) L.; widowed; 1 child, Susan J. BA, Carnegie Inst. Tech., 1927; postgrad., Harvard U., 1943. Prof. painting and design Carnegie Inst. Tech., Carnegie-Mellon U., Pitts., 1930-75; disting. lectr. Carnegie Mellon U., 1989, Executed murals W.Va. U., 1941, Carnegie-Mellon U., 1952; represented in pub. collections Mus. Modern Art, N.Y., Carnegie Mus. Art, Stedelijk, Amsterdam, Ind. U., Sheldon, Nebr.; contbr. articles to prof. jours. Recipient Purchase/Sculpture award Carnegie Mus. Art, 1963, Educator award Indsl. Design Soc. Am., 1989, Pa. Soc. Architects medal AIA, 1963; named Honored Artist, Carnegie Mus. Art., 1970. Home: Washington, DC. Deceased.

LERNER, ALFRED, professional sports team executive, real estate and financial executive; b. Brooklyn, New York, May 8, 1933; s. Abraham and Clara (Abrahmson) Lerner; m. Norma Wokloff, Aug. 7, 1955; children: Nancy Faith, Randolph David. BA, Columbia U., 1955. Chmn. bd., chief exec. officer Multi-Amp Corp., Dallas, 1970—80, Realty

Refund Trust, Cleve., 1971—90; pres., chief exec. officer Refund Advisers, Inc., from 1971, Town & Country Mgmt. Corp., 1979—93; chmn., dir. Equitable Bancorp., Balt., 1981—90; chmn., bd. dirs. Prog. Corp., Cleve., 1988—93; chmn., CEO, pres. MBNA Corp., Newark, from 1991; chmn., CEO Town & Country Trust, from 1993; co-owner, chair Cleveland Browns, from 1998. Chmn., bd. dirs. MNC Corp., Balt., 1991—93. Trustee Columbia U., Case Western Res. U.; pres. Cleve. Clin. 1st lt. Res. USMC, 1955—57. Mem.: Young Pres. Orgn., Harmonie Club (N.Y.C.), Beechmont Club (Cleve.). Jewish. Home: Cleveland, Ohio. Died Oct. 23, 2002.

LEROY, EDWARD CARWILE, rheumatologist; b. Elizabeth City, N.C., Jan. 19, 1933; s. J. Henry and Grace Brown (Carwile) LeR.; m. Garnette DeFord Hughes, June 11, 1960; children: Garnette DeFord, Edward Carwile. BS summa cum laude, Wake Forest Coll., 1955; MS in Pathology, U. N.C., 1958, MD with honors, 1960. Med. intern Presbyn. Hosp., N.Y.C., 1960-61, resident, 1961-62; clin. asso. Nat. Heart Inst., Bethesda, Md., 1962-65; fellow in rheumatology Columbia U., 1965-67; dir. Edward Daniels Faulkner Arthritis Clinic; asso. attending physician Presbyn. Hosp., N.Y.C., 1970-75; asso. prof. Columbia U. Coll. Phys. and Surg., 1970-75; prof. medicine, dir. div. rheumatology and immunology Med. U. S.C., Charleston, 1975-95, prof., chmn. dept. microbiology and immunology, 1995-2000, disting. univ. prof. Bd. dirs. Arthritis Found. Contbr. articles med. jours. Recipient Alexander von Humboldt prize U. Cologne (Germany), 1995-96. Master: ACR, ACP; fellow: Am. Coll. Rheumatology, Am. Coll. Physicians; mem.: AAAS, Usher First Scots Presbyn., Orthopedic Rsch. Soc., Assn. Am.Physicians, So. Soc. Clin. Investigation, N.Y. Acad. Scis., Microvascular Soc., Am. Soc. Clin. Investigation, Soc. Exptl. Biology and Medicine, Am. Assn. Immunologists, Harvey Soc., Am. Fedn. Clin. Rsch., Carolina Yacht, Yeamans Hall. First Scots Presbyterian. Clubs: Yeamans Hall, Carolina Yacht. Home: Charleston, SC. Deceased.

LESTER, TERRY LEROY, actor; b. Indpls., Apr. 13, 1950; s. Ernest LeRoy and Carol Ann (Gipson) L. BA, DePauw U., 1975. Actor, "The Young and the Restless" Sta. CBS-TV, 1980—89. With U.S. Army, 1971-74. Mem. Acad. TV Arts and Scis. (daytime Emmy awards com. 1988, nominated for Best Actor Emmy awards 1983-86). Avocations: music, computers, golf, tennis, skiing. Home: Los Angeles, Calif. Died Nov. 28, 2003.

LETULLE, JOAN ANN, parochial school educator; b. Port Arthur, Tex., Mar. 17, 1933; d. Ernest Paul and Pearl Valerie (Pepper) L. BA magna cum laude, Lamar U., 1976. Sec. Texaco, Inc., Port Arthur, Tex., 1951-53; tutor Port Arthur, Tex., 1955-64; dictaphone typist Bone & Joint Clinic, Port Arthur, Tex., 1964-70; tchr. St. James Elem. Sch., Port Arthur, Tex., 1977-79; English tchr. Bishop Byrne High Sch., Port Arthur, Tex., 1979-83; tchr. Cen. Cath. Sch., Port Arthur, Tex., from 1983. Vol. tutor Port Arthur, 1977—; vol. drama coach Bishop Byrne High Sch., 1964-68; vol. tchr. Adult Religious Edn., Port Arthur, 1986—. Author short stories: Substitute Player, 1967, Safe Son, 1964, Moment of Decision, 1962. Vol. Juvenile Probation Office, Jefferson County, Tex., 1979—, Hospitality Ctr. for the Poor, Port Arthur, 1989—; apptd. Mayor's Handicapped Com.; liaison for the handicapped with coll. pres., Lamar U., 1970-76. Named Handicapped Texan of the Yr., Gov.'s Handicapped Com., Austin, 1969-70, Port Arthur's Woman of Yr., Quota Internat., 1986, Profl. Women of Yr. in Port Arthur, Pilot Club, 1979, One of Outstanding Young Women in Am., 1970; inductee S.E. Tex. Women's Hall of Fame, 1990, Nat. Hall of Fame for Persons with Disablities, 1992; recipient Youth Svc. award La Sertoma Club, 1977, Guarnere Meml. award Diocese of Beaumont, 1991. Mem. AAUW (sec. 1988-91), Lamar U. Beaumont Alumni Assn. (Disting. Alumna award 1992-94), Lamar U. Port Arthur Alumni Assn., Nat. Cath. United for Spiritual Action, Phi Kappa Phi. Democrat. Roman Catholic. Avocations: theatre, reading, movies, sports, "trivial pursuit". Home: Port Arthur, Tex. Died Feb. 22, 2002.

LEVENSON, ALAN BRADLEY, lawyer; b. Long Beach, N.Y., Dec. 13, 1935; s. Cyrus O. and Jean (Kotler) L.; m. Joan Marlene Levenson, Aug. 19, 1956; children: Scott Keith, Julie Jo. AB, Dartmouth Coll., 1956; BA, Oxford U., Eng., 1958, MA, 1962; LLB, Yale U., 1961. Bar: N.Y. 1962, U.S. Dist. Ct. D.C. 1964, U.S. Ct. Appeals (D.C. cir.) 1965, U.S. Supreme Ct. 1965. Law clk., trainee div. corp. fin. SEC, Washington, 1961-62, gen. atty., 1962, trial atty., 1963, br. chief, 1963-65, asst. dir., 1965-68, exec. asst. dir., 1968, dir., 1970-76; v.p. Shareholders Mgmt. Co., L.A., 1969, sr. v.p., 1969-70, exec. v.p., 1970; ptnr. Fulbright & Jaworski, Washington, from 1976. Lectr. Cath. U. Am., 1964-68, Columbia U., 1973; adj. prof. Georgetown U., 1964, 77, 79-81, U.S. rep. working party OECD, Paris, 1974-75; adv. com. SEC, 1976-77; mem. adv. bd. Securities Regulation Inst., U. Calif., San Diego, 1973—, vice chmn. exec. com., 1979-83, chmn., 1983-87, emeritus chmn., 1988—; mem. adv. coun. SEC Inst., U. So. Calif., L.A., Sch. Acctg., 1981-85; mem. adv. com. Nat. Ctr. Fin. Svcs,. U. Calif.-Berkeley, 1985-89; mem. planning com. Ray Garrett Ann. Securities Regulation Inst. Northwestern U. Law Sch.; mem. adv. panel to U.S. compt.-gen. on stock market decline, 1987, panel of cons., 1989-98; mem. audit adv. com. GAO, 1992—. Mem. bd. editl. advisors U. Iowa Jour. Corp. Law, 1978—; Bur. Nat. Affairs adv. bd. Securities Regulation and Law Report, 1976—; bd. editors N.Y. Law Jour., 1976—; bd. advisors, corp. and securities law advisor Prentice Hall Law & Bus., 1991-95; contbr. articles to profl. jours.; mem. adv. bd. Banking Policy Report. Trustee, chair audit com., chair oral history com. SEC Hist. Soc. Recipient Disting. Service award SEC, 1972; James B. Richardson fellow Oxford U., 1956 Mem. ABA (adv. com., fed. regulation securities com., task force rev. fed. securities laws, former chair subcom. on securities activities banks), Fed. Bar Assn. (emeritus mem. exec. com. securities law com.), Am. Law Inst., Practicing Law Inst. (nat. adv. com. 1974, adv. com. ann. securities reg. inst.), AICPA (pub. dir., bd. dirs. 1984-91, fin. com. 1984-91, chmn. adv. coun. auditing standards bd. 1979-80, future issues com. 1982-85), Nat. Assn. Securities Dealers (corp. fin. com. 1981-87, nat. arbitration com. 1983-87, gov.-at-large, bd. govs. 1984-87, exec. com. 1986-87, long range planning com. 1987-90, chmn. legal adv. bd. 1988-93, spl. com. governance and structure 1989-90, numerous adv. coms.), Transparency Internat. USA (bd. dirs.). Home: Potomac, Md. Died May 11, 2003.

LEVERENZ, HUMBOLDT WALTER, retired chemical research engineer; b. Chgo., July 11, 1909; s. Paul Frederick and Lydia (Humboldt) L.; m. Edith Ruggles Langmuir, Nov. 30, 1940; children: David, Edith, Julia, Ellen. BA in Chemistry, Stanford U., 1930; postgrad., U. Muenster, 1930-31. Rsch. engr. RCA Mfg. Co., Camden, Harrison, N.J., 1931-42, RCA Labs., Princeton, N.J., 1942-54, dir. physics and chem. rsch. lab., 1954-57, asst. dir. rsch., 1957-59, dir. rsch., 1959-61, assoc. dir., 1961-68; staff v.p. RCA Corp., Princeton, 1968-74. Mem. Materials Adv. Bd., Washington, 1964-68. Author: Luminescence of Solids, 1950, 70; contbr. articles to profl. publs. Named Modern Pioneer Nat. Assn. Manufacturers, 1940; recipient Frank P. Brown medal Franklin Inst., 1954. Fellow Am. Phys. Soc., Optical Soc. Am., IEEE; mem. Nat. Acad. Engring., Am. Chem. Soc., Sigma Xi. Achievements include 67 patents; devel. of phosphors and luminescent screens used in fluorescent lamps and picture tubes, ferrites for TV receivers. Home: Williamsburg, Va. Died May 20, 2004.

LEVERMANN, THOMAS WERNER, environmental educator; b. Omaha, May 27, 1943; s. Werner Friedrick and Lela Beryl (Melvin) L.; m. Sandra June Levermann, Jan. 1965 (div.); children: Eric Thomas, Elizabeth Cathleen; m. Barbara Joan Wake, Mar. 18, 1989. BCS, U. Nebr., 1973; postgrad., U. Va., 1984. Producer/dir. KETV, Omaha, 1963-67; engr. WOW-TV, Omaha, 1967-68; Omaha Women's Job Corp. Burroughs Corp., Omaha, 1968-69; prog. coordinator Joslyn Art Mus., Omaha, 1969; urban conservationist Douglas SWCD, 1969-72; dir. info. and edn. Papio Natural Res. Dist., Omaha, 1972-76; pub. info. officer Soil Conservation Svcs./U.S. Dept. Agr., Lexington, Ky., 1976-77, head. ednl. rels. Washington, 1979-90, with, from 1976. Co-founder B3J, Inc., internat. environ. edn. orgn., 1989. Contbr. articles to profl. jours. Com. mem. Boy Scouts Am., Fairfax, Va.; mem. Boy Scouts Nat. Conservation Com., Touch Am. Project, Keep Am. Beautiful, Alliance for Environ. Edn. (past pres.), KAB Nat. Pub. Lands, others. Mem. Soil and Water Conservation Soc., N. Am. Assn. Environ. Edn., Keep Am. Beautiful (mem. nat. adv. com.). Lutheran. Avocations: soccer, photography, travel. Home: Fairfax, Va. Died Apr. 18, 2002.

LE VIEN, JOHN DOUGLAS (JACK LE VIEN), motion picture and television producer, director; b. N.Y.C., July 18, 1918; s. Christopher Luke and Rose Jeanette Le V. Chmn. bd. TCA Travel Corp. Am., 1979—. Chmn. bd. Electronic Pub. Co., London. Div. News editor: Pathé News, 1946-57; ind. motion picture and TV dir. and producer, 1958—; producer: (TV series) Valiant Years, 1959-60; exec. producer: (film) Black Fox, 1962 (Acad. award); producer and dir.: (films) Finest Hours, 1963-64, A King's Story, 1965, Churchill Centenary, 1974; (TV shows) Other World of Winston Churchill, 1964, The Gathering Storm, 1973, The Amazing Voyage of Daffodil and Daisy, 1974, Cicero, 1975, Where the Lotus Fell, 1976, Flames Over the Sahara, 1977, Children of the Lotus, 1978, Churchill and The Generals, 1980; pres., exec. producer TV movies, Le Vien Internat. Prodns. Ltd., N.Y.C., 1958—; chmn. bd., exec. producer TV shows, Le Vien Films Ltd., London, Eng., 1963—; author: The Valiant Years, 1961, The Finest Hours, 1964, (with Lady Mosley) The Duchess of Windsor, 1979, (with Barrie Pitt) Churchill and The Generals. Served to col. AUS, World War II, ETO; col. Res. Decorated Legion of Merit, Bronze Star; Legion of Honor; Croix de Guerre France). Mem. Brit. Acad. Film & Television Arts. Clubs: Overseas Press (N.Y.C.). Home: London, England. Died Nov. 9, 1999.

LEVIN, CARL, public and government relations consultant, inventor; b. Ringgold, La. m. Doris Wechsler; m. Sonia Atlas, Oct. 13, 1958; children: Judith Friedman, Richard (dec.), Virginia Levin Vinik, Alan Schwartzbach. Student, CCNY, 1930-33. Corr. CCNY N.Y. Herald Tribune, 1930-34, staff reporter, 1934-43, Washington corr., 1943-45, 46-50, war and fgn. corr., 1945-46; free lance mag. writer, 1942-50; Washington mgr. William H. Weintraub & Co. (advt. and pub. rels.), 1950-52; charge Washington activities Schenley Industries, Inc., 1952-62, v.p. Washington activities, 1952-62; dir. pub. support Trade Expansion Act, White House, 1962; pres. Carl Levin Assos., Inc., 1962-68; v.p., gen. mgr. Burson-Marsteller, Washington, 1968-72, v.p., sr. cons., 1972-83, sr. v.p., 1983-87; pub. affairs cons., writer, from 1987. Mem. Nat. Small Bus. Adv. Coun., 1964-68. Collaborator books on journalism, postwar security investigations; contbr. to nat. mags. Active in founding Am.-Israel Pub. Affairs Soc.; bd. dirs. Interracial Coun. Bus. Opportunity, 1972-75; mem. bd. Com. Accuracy on Middle East Reporting in Am., 1985-91, Am. Gas Index Fund, 1990-2000; trustee Opera Soc. Washington, 1963-70, Ford's Theater, Washington, 1975-81; co-chmn. Citizens Com. Opera, 1963. Mem. Soc. Profl. Journalists, Lotos Club (N.Y.C.). Home: Bethesda, Md. Died Apr. 18, 2002.

LEVIN, LEONARD, writer, producer, director; b. Spring Hole, N.C., Sept. 13, 1928; s. Maurice Israel and Sadye Hannah (Samburg) L.; m. Shirley Weiner. Student, Balt. Polytech. Producer, dir. WBAL-TV, Balt., 1955-66; broadcast producer WB Doner & Co., Balt., 1966-69; exec. producer WFIL-TV, Phila., 1969-70; owner, pres. Levin Prodns., Balt., from 1970. Dir. TV documentaries, 1963 (Emmy award 1963), govt. tng. films, 1983, comml. 1985; producer, dir. TV comml., 1985. Sgt. U.S. Army, 1952-54. Democrat. Jewish. Avocation: golf. Died Aug. 14, 2001.

LEVIN, MARSHALL ABBOTT, judge, educator; b. Balt., Nov. 22, 1920; s. Harry Oscar and Rose (DeLaviez) L.; m. Beverly Edelman, Aug. 6, 1948; children: Robert B., Susan R. Lieman, Burton H. BA, U. Va., 1941; JD, Harvard Law Sch., 1947. Bar: Md. 1947, U.S. Dist. Ct. Md. 1947, U.S. Ct. Appeals (4th cir.) 1950, U.S. Supreme Ct. 1953. Bill drafter, legis. asst. Dept. Legis. Reference, Annapolis, Md., 1948-49; rsch. asst. Workers Compensation Commn., 1951, police magistrate, 1951-55, magistrate housing ct., 1955-58; ptnr. Levin & Levin, Balt., 1947-66; pvt. practice Balt., 1966-68; ptnr. Edelman, Levin, Levy & Rubenstein, Balt., 1968-71; judge cir. ct. City of Balt., 1971-87, judge for asbestos litigation, 1987-97. Lectr. nationally on toxic torts, complex litigation, asbestos; lectr. Nat. Conf. on Child Abuse, 1976; dir. Legal Aid Soc., Balt., 1979-81; chmn. jud. bd. sentencing State of Md., 1979-83, chmn. sentencing guidelines bd., 1983-87; instituted One Trial/One Day jury system, Balt., 1983; adj. prof. mass torts, legal & ethical studies grad. sch. U. Balt., 1979-90; charter mem. faculty coun., coord. and faculty general jurisdiction, current issues in civil litigation Nat. Jud. Coll.; mem. vis. faculty trial advocacy workshop Harvard Law Sch. Contbr. articles to law revs. Mem. Jud. Disability Commn., 1980-87; chmn. Mass Tort Litigation Com., 1991-95. NEH fellow, 1976. Mem. ABA (vice chmn. mass tort and litigation com.), Md. State Bar Assn. (Leadership award 1984), Balt. City Bar Assn. (commendation 1982). Home: Baltimore, Md. Died Feb. 1, 2004.

LEVIN, MYRON JAME, physician, educator, consultant; b. Los Angeles, Mar. 6, 1912; s. Ben S. and Elsie (Jame) L.; m. Anita Dresner, July 7, 1940; children— Harold D., Marilyn Jean. B.S., U. Ill., 1935, M.S. in Bacteriology, 1937, M.D., 1937. Diplomate Am. Bd. Anesthesiology. Intern, Woodlawn Hosp., Chgo., 1937-38; resident in anesthesiology Hines VA Hosp. (Ill.), 1949-51, asst. chief anesthesiology, 1951-72, cons., 1951—; dir. anesthesiology Am. Hosp., Chgo., 1956-70; chmn. anesthesiology Gottlieb Meml. Hosp., Melrose Park, Ill., 1961-78, cons., 1978—; sr. attending anesthesiology, chmn. dept. Pain Mgmt. Clinic, Cook County Hosp., Chgo., 1981—; clin. assoc. prof. anesthesiology U. Ill. Coll. Medicine, Chgo., 1951-75; clin. prof. anesthesiology Chgo. Med. Sch., 1975—, acting chmn. anesthesiology, 1980-81; cons. VA Hosp., North Chicago, Ill., 1979—; field rep. Joint Commn. on Accreditation of Hosps., 1976-78. Contbr. articles to profl. jours., chpts. to books. Served to capt. M.C., AUS, 1942-46. Fellow Am. Coll. Anesthesiologists, Internat. Coll. Surgeons; mem. AMA, Chgo. Med. Soc., Ill. State Med. Soc., Am. Soc. Anesthesiologists, Ill. Soc. Anesthesiologists, Chgo. Soc. Anesthesiologists (pres. 1956-57). Lodges: Masons, Shriners. Died June 8, 1999. Home: Northbrook, Ill.

LEVINE, ISRAEL E. writer, public relations company executive; b. N.Y.C., Aug. 30, 1923; s. Albert Ely and Sonia (Silver) L.; m. Joy Elaine Michael, June 23, 1946; children: David, Carol. BS, CCNY, 1946. Asst. dir. pub. rels. CCNY, 1946-54, dir., 1954-77, editor Alumnus Mag., 1952-74, 87-89; editor Health Care Week, 1977-79, William H. White Publs., 1979-81; dir. comm. Am. Jewish Congress, 1981-87; COO, Richard Cohen Assocs., N.Y.C., 1987-99; pres. I.E. Levine Pub. Rels., N.Y.C., 2000—03. Author: (with A. Lateiner) The Techniques of Supervision, 1954; The Discoverer of Insulin: Dr. Frederick G. Banting, 1959, Conqueror of Smallpox: Dr. Edward Jenner, 1960, Behind the Silken Curtain: The Story of Townsend Harris, 1961, Inventive Wizard: George Westinghouse, 1962, Champion of World Peace: Dag Hammarskjold, 1962, Miracle Man of Printing: Ottmar Mergenthaler, 1963, Electronics Pioneer: Lee DeForest, 1964, Young Man in the White House: John Fitzgerald Kennedy, 1964, 91, Oliver Cromwell, 1966, Spokesman for the Free World: Adlai Stevenson, 1967, Lenin: The Man Who Made a Revolution, 1969, The Many Faces of Slavery, 1975; contbr. over 200 articles to mags. Mem. exec. com. Com. for Pub. Higher Edn., N.Y.C., 1987-2003. 2d lt., navigator USAAF, 1943-45, ETO. Decorated Air medal with 3 oak leaf clusters, 3 battle stars USAAF; recipient 125th Anniversary medal; CCNY, 1972, Svc. medal CCNY Alumni Assn., 1974. Mem. The Authors Guild, Authors' League Am., Soc. of Silurians, 2d Air Divsn. Assn. Jewish. Avocation: gardening. Died May 10, 2003.

LEVINE, RICHARD LAWRENCE, physician; b. N.Y.C., Oct. 13, 1949; s. Murray and Ethel (Schildt) L.; m. Diane Marie Kellner, Nov. 11, 1979; children: Maren Leah, Sydne Anne. BS in Biology cum laude, Bucknell U., 1971; MD summa cum laude, SUNY Downstate, Bklyn., 1975. Diplomate Nat. Bd. Med. Examiners. Internship gen. surgery NYU, Bellevue, N.Y.C., 1975-76, residency gen. surgery, 1976-77, SUNY Downstate, Bklyn, 1977-79; staff emergency physician Helene Fuld Med. Ctr., Trenton, N.J., 1979, asst. dir. emergency dept., 1979-80, dir. emergency dept., 1980-82; fin. dir., bd. dirs., ptnr. Emergency Med. Assoc., Mountainside, N.J., 1980-81; med. dir.,physician, pres.

Profl. Emergency Svcs. of Lawrenceville (N.J.), 1982-87, Profl. Med. Svcs. of Lawrenceville, from 1988; pres. Primed, Inc., Lawrenceville, N.J., 1984-85. Med. advisor Emergency Med. Svcs. City of Trenton, N.J., 1979-81; bd. dirs. Mercer County Disaster Com., Trenton, 1979-81; trauma advisor Mercer County Mobile Intensive Care, Trenton, 1979-82; v.p. Am. Heart Assn., Princeton, N.J., 1988-89. Recipient Bklyn. Soc. Internal Medicine Award of Excellence, 1975, Physician's Recognition award AMA, 1980, 83, 85, 89, Continuing Edn. award Am. Coll. Emergency Medicine, 1985, 88; named N.J. Sml. Bus. Person of the Yr., 1991. Fellow Am. Coll. Urgent Care Physicians; mem. Am. Coll. Emergency Physicians, N.J. Med. Soc., Mercer County Med. Soc., Mercer County C. of C., Princeton C. of C., Chaine des Rotisseurs (Princeton), Phi Beta Kappa, Alpha Omega Alpha. Jewish. Avocations: swimming, racquetball, skiing. Home: Cliffside Park, NJ. Died.

LEVINE, RUTH ROTHENBERG, biomedical science educator; b. N.Y.C. d. Jacob and Jeannette (Bandel) Rothenberg; m. Martin J. Levine, June 21, 1953. BA magna cum laude, Hunter Coll., 1938; MA, Columbia U., 1939; PhD, Tufts U., 1955. Asst. prof. sch. medicine Tufts U., 1955-58; asst. prof. pharmacology sch. medicine Boston U., 1958-61, assoc. prof. sch. medicine, 1961-65, prof. sch. medicine, 1965—, univ. prof., 1972—; chmn. grad. div. med. and dental scis. Boston U. Sch. Medicine, 1964-89, assoc. dean grad. biomed. scis., 1981-89, assoc. dean emeritus, from 1989. Mem. sci. adv. bd. U.S. EPA, 1976-82, Internat. Joint Commn., State Dept., 1983-89. Author: Pharmacology, Drug Actions and Reactions, 1973, 6th edit., 2000; coord. internat. symposia of subtypes of muscarinic receptors. Named to Hall of Fame, Hunter Coll. of City of N.Y. Fellow AAAS; mem. Am. Soc. Pharmacology and Exptl. Therapeutics (sec.-treas. 1975-76), Biophys. Soc., Am. Chem. Soc., Am. Pharm. Assn., Acad. Scis., Phi Beta Kappa, Sigma Xi. Died Feb. 23, 2003.

LEVINSKY, NORMAN GEORGE, physician, educator; b. Boston, Apr. 27, 1929; s. Harry and Gertrude (Kipperman) Levinsky; m. Elena Sartori, June 17, 1956; children: Harold, Andrew, Nancy. AB summa cum laude, Harvard U., 1950, MD cum laude, 1954. Diplomate Am. Bd. Internal Medicine. Intern Beth Israel Hosp., Boston, 1954—55, resident, 1955—56; commd. med. officer USPHS., 1956; clin. assoc. Nat. Heart Inst., Bethesda, Md., 1956—58; NIH fellow Boston U. Med. Center, 1958—60; practice medicine, specializing in internal medicine and nephrology Boston, 1960—2004; chief of medicine Boston City Hosp., 1968—72, 1993—97; physician-in-chief, dir. Boston U. Med. Ctr. Hosp., Boston, 1972—97; asst. prof., then assoc. prof. medicine Boston U., 1960—68, Wesselhoeft prof., 1968—72, Wade prof. medicine, 1972—97, chmn. medicine, 1972—97, prof. medicine, assoc. provost, 1997—2004. Mem. drug efficacy panelNRC; mem. nephrology test com. AM. Bd. Internal Medicine, 1971—76; mem. gen. medicine B rev. group NIH; mem. comprehensive test com. Nat. Bd. Med. Examiners, 1986—89; chmn. com. to study end-stage renal disease program NAS/Inst. Medicine, 1988—90, chmn. com. on Xenografts, 1995. Editor (with R.W. Wilkins): Medicine: Essentials of Clinical Practice, 3d edit., 1983; editor: (with R. Rettig) Kidney Disease and the Federal Government, 1991; editor: Ethics and the Kidney, 2001; contbr. chapters to books, sci. articles to med. jours. Master: ACP (Disting. Tchr. award 1992); mem.: AAAS, Interurban Clin. Club (pres. 1985—86), Inst. Medicine NAS, Am. Soc. Nephrology, Assn. Profs. Medicine (sec., treas. 1984—87, pres.-elect 1987—88, pres. 1988—89), Am. Physiol. Soc., Assn. Am. Physicians, Am. Heart Assn., Am. Soc. Clin. Investigation, Am. Fedn. Clin. Rsch., Alpha Omega Alpha, Phi Beta Kappa. Home: Newton, Mass. Died Mar. 8, 2004.

LEVITT, ELEANOR SOSNOW, counseling psychologist, volunteer; b. Hackensack, N.J., Mar. 13, 1936; d. Louis U. and Anna Lillian (Miller) Sosnow; m. Harry Levitt, June 15, 1969; 1 child, David Avrum. BA, Cornell U., 1958; MA, NYU, 1965, PhD, 1970. Employment interviewer, counselor N.Y. State Employment Svc. Profl. Placement Ctr., N.Y.C., 1960-65; counseling coord. Hofstra U., Hempstead, N.Y., 1969-71; asst. prof. County Coll. Morris, Dover, N.J., 1975-76; counselor Project Eve Kean Coll., Union, N.J., 1977; asst. dir. Career Counseling and Placement Office William Paterson Coll., Wayne, N.J., 1978-79; vol. advocate for institutionalized elderly Ombudsman Office State of N.J., Trenton, from 1993. Adj. instr. psychology Kean Coll., Union, 1976-77. Treas. LWV, Livingston, N.J., 1975-77; vol. Am. Coun. Jewish Women, Livingston, 1992—. NDEA fellow, 1965-67. Mem. Phi Beta Kappa, Psi Chi. Avocations: creative writing, gardening. Home: Bodega Bay, Calif. Died Sept. 11, 2000.

LEVSTIK, FRANK RICHARD, archivist; b. Chgo., Mar. 3, 1943; s. Frank Richard and Anna Katherine (Dickman) L.; m. Linda Suzanne Thoms, June 15, 1968; children: Jeremy, Jennifer. BA in History, Pikeville Coll., 1966; MA in History, Va. Polytech. Inst., 1968; PhD in History, Ohio State U., 1981. Archives specialist Ohio Hist. Soc., Columbus, 1969-72, asst. state archivist, 1972-76, state archivist, 1976-82; prin. archivist Ky. Dept. Librs./ Archives, Frankfort, 1982-83, 85-87, archives & records adminstr., from 1987; libr. U. Ky., Lexington, 1983-85. Treas. Soc. Ohio Archivists, Columbus, 1980-82; state hist. records adv. bd. Ohio State Hist. Soc., Columbus, 1976-82; chmn., sec. State Records Commn., Columbus, 1972-82. Author: Kentucky Historical Records Needs Assessment Report, 1983; coauthor: Union Bibliography of Ohio Printed State Documents, 1974. 2d v.p. Bluegrass Assn. Retarded, Lexington, 1992—; bd. dirs. Southside Settlement House, Columbus, 1980-82. Mem. Hist. Confedn. Ky. (treas., bd. dirs. 1985—), Ky. Coun. Archives (bd. dirs.). Presbyterian. Home: Lexington, Ky. Died June 4, 2000.

LEVY, JAY ROBERT, construction executive, property manager; b. Denver, Aug. 23, 1936; s. Mandell Nathan and Gertrude Sylvia (Mastrosky) L.; m. Harriet Bernice Shaiman, Sept. 5, 1939; children: Mindy Sue, Laurie Ann. BS-BA Bldg. Industry, Real Estate, U. Denver, 1958. Pres. Hallmark Industries, Denver, 1963-69, Cellular Corp. Colo., Denver, 1969-75, Concrete Placers, Denver, 1969-75, J&B Bldg. Co., Denver, from 1972. Bd. dirs. recovery unit Alcohol Unit and Drug Addictions, Rocky Mountain Hosp., Denver, 1983-88; bd. dirs. Yeshiva Toras Chaim, Denver, 1984-86, honor award, 1987; bd. dirs. Jewish Community Ctr., Denver, 1989-91. Recipient honor award Women's Am. ORT, 1989. Avocations: skiing, fishing, classical music, classic sports cars. Home: Denver, Colo. Died Mar. 2, 2001.

LEVY, JERROLD EDGAR, anthropology educator; b. N.Y.C., Mar. 9, 1930; s. Julien Samson Levy and Joella Synara (Haweis) Bayer; m. Patricia Blake (div. Dec. 1963); 1 child, Kimrey; m. Marie Dolores Charley, Mar. 1964; children: Modesta, Jonathan. Student, Black Mountain Coll., 1947-50; MA, U. Chgo., 1956, PhD, 1959. Lectr. in pub. health U. Calif., Berkeley, 1959-62; rsch. ethnologist USPHS Indian Health Svc., Navajo Reservation, 1962-64; prof. anthropology Portland (Oreg.) State U., 1964-72, U. Ariz., Tucson, from 1972; prof. emeritys, from 1995. Mem. profl. adv. bd. Epilepsy Found. Am., Landover, Md., 1979-87; mem. suicide task force USPHS Indian Health Svc., Washington, 1986—; mem. bd. advisors Nat. Ctr. for Am. Indian and Alaska Native Mental Health Rsch., Denver, 1981. Author: (with others) Indian Drinking, 1974, Hand Trembling, Frenzy Witchcraft and North Mdness, 1987, Navajo Aging, 1991, Orayvi Revisited, 1992. Recipient Career Devel. award NIMH, 1966-71; Resident scholar NEH, Sch. Am. Rsch., Santa Fe, 1988-89. Fellow AAAS, Am. Anthropol. Assn.; mem. Soc. for Med. Anthropology, Soc. Psychol. Anthropology, Am. Ethnol. Soc., Soc. for Cross-Cultural Rsch. Avocation: photography. Home: Tucson, Ariz. Died Feb. 7, 2002.

LEVY, LEON, investment company executive, b. N.Y.C., Sept. 13, 1925; s. Jerome and Sadie (Samuelson) L.; m. Roxanne Wruble, Dec. 13, 1959 (div.); m. Shelby White, Aug. 12, 1983. BSS, City Coll., 1948. Security analyst Hirsch & Co., N.Y.C., 1948-51; gen. ptnr. Odyssey Ptnrs. (formerly Oppenheimer & Co.), N.Y.C., 1951—2003; chmn. bd. dirs. Oppenheimer Mutual Funds (now Odyssey Ptnrs.). Chmn. bd. dirs. Avatar Holdings, Inc.; bd. dirs. United Kingdom Fund; lectr. CCNY, 1952-59. Trustee Bard Coll., Inst. Fine Arts, NYU; pres. Inst. Advanced Studies, Rockefeller U., Jerome Levy Inst. for Econ. Rsch., N.Y.C.; bd. dirs. Internat. Found. Art Rsch., John Simon Guggenheim Found. Home: New York, NY. Died Apr. 6, 2003.

LEVY, NORMAN J. state legislator; b. Rockville Centre, N.Y., Jan. 24, 1931; s. Emanuel and Rose (Ferraro) L.; m. Joy Saslow, 1968. BA, Bucknell U., 1952; postgrad., U. Pa.; JD, Bklyn. Law Sch., 1958. Individual practice law, N.Y.C., 1958-98; asst. dist. atty. Nassau County, N.Y., 1959-70; chief Nassau County Rackets Bur., 1962-70; mem. N.Y. State Senate, 1971-98, chmn. standing com. on transp., 1982-98, mem. legis. commn. on critical transp. choices, mem. task force on drunk driving. Del., Rep. Nat. Conv. 2d lt. USAR, 1957-60. Recipient Humanities award Anti-Defamation League, Christopher Columbus award Nat. Columbus Day Soc., Man of Yr. award Merrick C. of C., 1978, Naassau County Aux. Police award. Mem. Masons, B'nai B'rith, Elks, Jewish War Vets. (Law Enforcement award, Pub. Svc. award), Sons of Italy, Hist. Soc. the Merricks, Phi Alpha Theta, Sigma Alpha Mu. Deceased.

LEWERT, ROBERT MURDOCH, microbiologist, educator; b. Scranton, Pa., Sept. 30, 1919; s. Philip John and Nell (Bertholf) L.; m. Evelyn P. Allen, Feb. 19, 1948; children—Philip Allen, Barbara Joan. BS, U. Mich., 1941; MS, Lehigh U., 1943; Sc.D., Johns Hopkins, 1948. Diplomate: in parasitology Am. Bd. Microbiologists. Instr. biology Lehigh U., 1941-43, Hobart and William Smith Colls., Geneva, N.Y., 1943-44; instr. dept. bacteriology and parasitology U. Chgo., 1948-52, asst. prof., 1952-56, assoc. prof. microbiology, 1957-61, prof., 1961-85, prof. emeritus dept. molecular genetics and cell biology, 1985—. Vis. prof. parasitology U. Philippines Inst. Hygiene, 1961, 63-66; mem. com. on parasitic diseases Armed Forces Epidemiological Bd., 1955-73; cons. to surgeon gen. Dept. Army, 1956-75; cons. on parasitic diseases Hines (Ill.) VA Hosp., 1975-82; mem. tropical medicine and parasitology study sect. USPHS, 1965-69, allergy and infectious diseases tng. grant com., 1969-73 Mem. editorial bd.: Jour. Parasitology, 1958-64, Abstracts of Bioanalytic Tech, 1959-63, Jour. Infectious Disease, Am. Jour. Epidemiology, Am. Jour. Tropical Medicine and Hygiene. Served with USNR, 1944-46. Fulbright fellow, 1961; Guggenheim fellow, 1961; recipient U. Chgo. Med. Alumni Gold Key award, 1997. Fellow Am. Acad. Microbiology; mem. Am. Soc. Tropical Medicine and Hygiene, Nippon Bijitsu Token Hozon Kyokai (life), Japanese Sword Soc. of U.S. (chmn. 1977-83), Nihontoken Hozon Kai, Kunzan-Sensei Ni Manabu-Kai, Token Soc. Gt. Britian, Sigma Xi. Achievements include research on immunity to schistosomiasis, histochem. and cytochem. studies on invasiveness of parasites, biochemistry of host-parasite relationships. Died Sept. 27, 2003.

LEWIS, ARTHUR BEVERLY, physicist, educator; b. Forest, Miss., Nov. 21, 1901; s. Benjamin Franklin and Mary Frances (Otkin) L.; m. Alma Gochenour, June 20, 1930; children: Arthur Beverly, Mary Frances Lewis Poole, Roger Clay, George Leighton. BA with distinction, U. Miss., 1923, MA, 1925; PhD, Johns Hopkins U., 1930. Asst. prof. U. Miss., Oxford, 1925; jr. physicist Nat. Bur. Standards, Washington, 1926-30, asst. physicist, 1930-36; assoc. prof. math. and physics U. Miss., Oxford, 1936-41, prof. math. and physics, 1941-47, chmn., dept. physics, 1952-57, dean Coll. Liberal Arts, 1957-71, prof. emeritus of physics, from 1971. Contbr. articles to profl. jours. Fellow AAAS; mem. Am. Physical Soc., Am. Soc. Physics Tchrs., Masons. Methodist. Home: Oxford, Miss. Died May 22, 2000.

LEWIS, EVELYN HODGES, social worker; b. Logan, Utah, Feb. 1, 1907; d. William N. Hodges and Clara (Nelson) Hodges; m. Theodore R. E. Lewis, June 23, 1945; 1 child, Theodore William. BS, Utah State U., 1929; MS, U. Chgo., 1939. Nat. Assn. Social Workers, cert. social worker, Utah. Social worker Nat. Woman's Relief Soc., Salt Lake City, 1929-33; supr. Dept. Pub. Welfare Salt Lake County, Salt Lake City, 1935-38; prof. social work Utah State U., Logan, 1938-70, prof. emeritus, from 1970. Social worker War Relocation Authority, Topaz, Utah, 1943, Dept. Youth Brigham City, Utah, 1944; adj. prof. U. Utah, Salt Lake City, 1942; dir. No. Utah Mental Health Clinic, Logan, 1950-63. Editor (jour.) Rural Social Workers, 1938. V.p., pres. Utah Woman's Legis. Coun., Salt Lake City, 1938, v.p. Utah Mental Health Assn., 1962-64; bd. dirs. Com. Juvenile Detention State Utah, 1960-61, Com. for Aged, 1955-60; vol. YMCA, 1970-89. Avocations: photography, hiking. Home: San Bernardino, Calif. Deceased.

LEWIS, JAMES ROSS, SR., retired pharmacist; b. Charlottesville, Va., Sept. 12, 1919; s. Eugene Buckingham Lewis and Alma (Galletin) Yowell; m. Ann Louise Guthrie, Sept. 22, 1943 (dec. Sept. 1993); children: Dorothy Ann, James Ross, Cynthia Lee. BS, M.C.V. Sch. Pharmacy, 1943. Cert. pharmacist, real estate appraiser. Asst. mgr. Peoples Drug Co., Richmond, Va., 1946-48; mgr. Hughes Drug, Ashland, Va., 1948-53; field rep. Hoffman-La Roche Labs., 1953-58; owner Hudgins Durg-Surg. Supply, Mathews, Va., 1958-85. Bd. dirs. Chesapeake Fin. Shares, Chesapeake Mortgage Co., Chesapeake Title Ins. Co. Appointee by Gov. of Va. Vol. Formulary Bd.; deacon Ashland Presbyn. Ch., 1945-58; mem. Presbyn. Ch., Gloucester, Va. Lt. USNR, 1943-57, PTO. Decorated 11 battle stars and various unit citations. Fellow Am. Coll. Apothecaries; mem. Nat. Assn. Real Estate Appraisers (cert. 1988), Am. Pharm Assn., Res. Officers Assn., U.S. Navy League, Va. Pharm. Assn., Chesapeake Pharmacist Assn. (pres. 1963), Mathews (Va.) C. of C., Mathews Yacht Club (bd. dirs. 1980-84), Mathews Ruritan Club (pres. 1979-80). Conservative. Avocations: writing, travel, fishing. Home: Mathews, Va. Deceased.

LEWIS, JEROME XAVIER, II, lawyer, retired army officer; b. Chgo., June 12, 1938; s. Michael John and Eva (Lisewski) Brown; m. Mary Caroline Kickham, Sept. 17, 1960; children: Michael John, Thaddeus Thomas, John William, Mary Caroline. BS, U.S. Mil. Acad., 1960; JD, Georgetown U., 1965. Bar: D.C. 1966, U.S. Supreme Ct. 1980. Commd. 2d lt. U.S. Army, 1960, advanced through grades to col., 1981; sr. advisor to judge adv. gen. Republic of Vietnam, 1970-71; assoc. prof., dep. judge adv. law dept. U.S. Mil. Acad., West Point, N.Y., 1970-71, assoc. prof., acting prof., head dept. law, 1983-87; staff judge adv. 2d Armored Div., Ft. Hood, Tex., 1975-78, U.S. Army Cen. Command/3d Army, Ft. McPherson, Ga., 1987-90; appellate judge U.S. Army Ct. Mil. Rev., Washington, 1978-83; ret., 1990; dir. adminstrn., mng. atty. law dept. Digital Equipment Corp., Maynard, Mass., 1990-93; adminstr. Deutsch Williams et al., Boston, from 1993. Mem. various governing bds. U.S. Mil. Acad., 1983-87 Contbr. book revs. to legal jour. Decorated Bronze Star, Legion of Merit with 2 oak leaf clusters. Mem. Assn. Legal Adminstrs., D.C. Bar Assn. Republican. Roman Catholic. Avocations: music, reading, computing. Home: Concord, Mass. Died July 6, 2001.

LEWIS, SHERMAN RICHARD, JR., investment banker; b. Ottawa, Ill., Dec. 11, 1936; s. Sherman Richard and Julia Audrey (Rusteen) L.; m. Dorothy Marie Downie, Sept. 9, 1967; children: Thomas, Catherine, Elizabeth, Michael. AB, Northwestern U., 1958; MBA, U. Chgo., 1964. With investment dept. Am. Nat. Bank & Trust Co., Chgo., 1961-64; v.p. Halsey, Stuart & Co., N.Y.C., 1964-70, v.p. in charge corp. fin. dept., 1970-73; v.p. C.J. Lawrence & Sons, N.Y.C., 1970; ptnr. Loeb, Rhoades & Co., N.Y.C., 1973-76, ptnr. in charge corp. fin. dept., 1975-76, exec. v.p., bd. dirs., 1976-77, pres., co-chief exec. officer, 1977-78; vice chmn., co-chief exec. officer Loeb Rhoades, Hornblower & Co., N.Y.C., 1978-79; pres. Shearson/Am. Express Inc., N.Y.C., 1979-82, vice chmn., 1983-84, Shearson Lehman/Am. Express Inc., 1984-85, Shearson Lehman Bros. Inc., 1985-87, Shearson Lehman Hutton Inc., 1988-89; co-chief exec. officer, vice chmn., chmn. exec. com. Lehman Bros., 1990; vice chmn. Shearson Lehman Bros. Holdings, Inc., N.Y.C., 1990-93, Lehman Bros. Holdings, Inc., 1990—93, Lehman Bros. Inc., 1993—2004. Bd. dirs. Infraworks Corp., Resolution Capital Mgmt., EuroAmer. Mem. Pres.'s Commn. on Housing, 1981—82, Pres.'s Coun. on Internat. Youth Exch., 1982—88, Marine Corps Heritage Ctr. Founders' Group, 2000—04; bd. dirs. The Korea Soc.; trustee Northwestern U., 1992—2004, regent, 1990—97, mem. bd. visitors Weinberg Coll. Arts and Scis., 1981—2004, chmn. bd. visitors Weinberg Coll. Arts and Scis., 1990—96; mem. coun. Grad. Sch. of Bus. U. Chgo., 1991—2004; bd. dirs. U.S.-Greece Bus. Coun., N.Y. Eye and Ear Infirmary. Commd. officer

USMC, 1958—61. Mem. Coun. on Fgn. Rels., The Pilgrims, Bond Club, Univ. Club, Quogue Field Club, Shinnecock Yacht Club, Quantuck Beach Club. Home: New York, NY. Died Mar. 11, 2004.

LEWTER, ALICE JENKINS, history and political science educator; b. Roanoke Rapids, N.C., Aug. 16, 1946; d. Thomas George and Parthenia (Jones) Jenkins; m. Dennis Lacon Lewter, Oct. 3, 1980; 1 child, Sonya Desett Jenkins. BA, N.C. Ctrl. U., 1969, MA, 1975; EdD, N.C. State U., 1995. Cert. tchr. adult and c.c. adminstrn. Instr. Halifax County (N.C.) Schs., 1969-70, Durham (N.C.) City Schs., 1970-72; adminstrv. asst. Found. for Rsch. and Edn. in Sickle Cell Disease, N.Y.C., 1972-73; instr. history/polit. sci. Halifax C.C., Weldon, N.C., from 1973, divsn. chair, 1986-90; program dir. MSIP U.S. Dept. Edn., Washington, 1986-89; adj. prof. Chowan Coll., Murfreesboro, N.C., from 1994. Advisor African-Am. Soc., Weldon, 1990-93. Co-author: American History: An Introduction, 1996. Judge Precinct #11, Bd. of Elections, Halifax County, 1978-87; coord. 5-A-Day program Black Chs. United for Better Health, Raleigh, 1992—. Named Educator of the Yr., Halifax-Northampton Opportunities Indsl. Corp., 1994; U.S. Dept. Edn. Minority Sci. Improvement grantee, 1986-89. Mem. Am. Coll. and Univ. Women, Am. Assn. Polit. Scientists, Am. Assn. Women in C.C.'s, The Smithsonian Club, Order Ea. Star, Alpha Kappa Alpha. Democrat. Baptist. Avocations: dance, bowling, reading, travel, walking. Home: Roanoke Rapids, NC. Died Sept. 7, 2000.

LIBENSKY, STANISLAV, art educator; b. Sezemice, Czech Republic, Mar. 27, 1921; s. Emil and Hedvika (Mizlerova) L.; m. Jaroslava Brychtova, Apr. 1963; children: Jaroslav, Milos, Alena. MFA, Acad. Applied Art, Praha, Czech Republic, 1963-87; D (hon.), Royal Coll. Art, London, 1994, U. Suntherland, Eng., 1999, R.I. Sch. Design, 2000, Royal Coll. Art; DA (hon.), U. Suntherland G. Britanien; DFA (hon.), RISD. Prof., chair dept. glass Acad. Applied Art, Praha, 1963-87. Chair Czech Glass Artists Union, Prague, 1989-92, Czech Artist Union, Prague, 1968-69, lectr., Ohio State, Berkeley, Pilchuck Glass Sch. (established Libensky award); exhbns. include IUC Hall, Paris, 1962-64, Prague Castle, 1964-69, River of Life Expo, Osaka, 1967-70, Cornin Mus., N.Y., 1978-80, Chapel Horsvskytyn, 1990-91, Corning Inc. Bldg., N.Y.C., 1991-93, Kioi Hall, Tokyo, 1994-95, Kameoka, Kyoto, Japan, 1998, Sao Paulo, 1965, Rio de Janeiro, 1966, Finland, 1984, Zurich, 1990, Yokohama, 1995, Nat. Gallery, Prague, 1989, Am. Craft Mus., N.Y., 1996, Brno, Czech Republic, 1996, Venezia Palazzo Ducale, 1996, Lausane Museé des Art, 1997, Bergamo Piazza Vecchia, 1998, Prague Carolinum, 2000. Decorated chevalier Order Arts and Letters (France); recipient Grand Prix Expo 58 Brussels; Gold medal VIII Biennale Sao Paulo, Brasil, 1966, Herder prize Vienna, Austria, 1975; Libensky award est. in his name at Pilchuck Glass Sch. Home: Brod, Czech Republic. Died Feb. 2, 2002; Zelezny Brod, Czech..

LIEBHERR, HANS, construction executive; b. Kaufbeuren, Germany, Apr. 1, 1915; children: Hans, Willy, Hubert, Marcus, Isolde. Student in civil engring., Baumeisterschule Ulm; DEng (hon.), Tech. U. Aachen, 1964. With family bldg. constrn. firm family bldg. constrn. firm (now Liebherr Internat. Ag), from 1945, established main office, 1954, established several subs. cos., 1955-59; chmn. bd. dirs. Liebherr Internat. Ag, Bulle, Switzerland. Named hon. senator U. Karlsruhe, Germany, 1974, Eberhard-Karls U., Tübingen, Germany, 1974; hon. citizen Kirchdorf/Iller, Biberach/Riss, Germany, and Bischofshofen. Died 1993.

LIEDTKE, JOHN HUGH, petroleum company executive; b. Tulsa, Feb. 10, 1922; m. Betty Lyn; children: Karen, Kristin, John Hugh, Blake, Kathryn. BA, Amherst Coll., 1942; postgrad., Harvard Grad. Sch., Bus. Adminstrn., 1943; LL.B., U. Tex., 1947. Pres. Zapata Petroleum Corp., 1953-62; pres., chief exec. officer Pennzoil Co., Houston, 1962-68, chmn., 1968—94, chief exec. officer, dir., 1953—88, also bd. dirs. Trustee Kinkaid Sch., Houston, Baylor Coll. Medicine, U.S. Naval Acad. Found.; council overseers Jesse H. Jones Grad. Sch. Adminstrn. Rice U. Served to lt. USN, 1942-45. Mem. Tex. Mid-Continent Oil and Gas Assn. (dir.), Am. Petroleum Inst. (dir.), Nat. Petroleum Council (dir.), Nat. Petroleum Refiners Assn. (bd. dirs.), Ind. Petroleum Assn. Am. (bd. dirs.), Penn Grade Assn. (bd. dirs.), Houston C. of C. (dir.), Beta Theta Pi, Phi Alpha Delta. Clubs: Houston Country, Ramada, Petroleum; Rolling Rock (Ligonier, Pa.); Racquet (Midland, Tex.); Calgary (Alta., Can.). Died Mar. 28, 2003.

LIGHT, KENNETH FREEMAN, college administrator; b. Detroit, Jan. 22, 1922; s. Delbert Bertram and Hilma (Stolt) L.; m. Shirley Claire Bower, Jan. 7, 1944 (dec. 1984); children— Karen Christine, Kevin Harold, Brian Curtis; m. Betty Jensen Pritchett, Nov. 23, 1985 BS, U. Ill., 1949; MA, Mich. State U., 1952, PhD, 1967. Instr. mech. engring. dept. Mich. Tech. U., 1956-60, assoc. prof., coord. for tech. edn., 1960-65; vice chancellor for acad. affairs, v.p. for acad. affairs Lake Superior State Coll., Sault Ste. Marie, Mich., 1965-76, pres., 1982-86, Oreg. Inst. Tech., Klamath Falls, 1976-82. Pres. Upper Peninsula Health Edn. Corp., 1975-76; mem. Mich. Manpower Commn., 1973-74, Vocat. Edn. Adv. Council, 1973-76, Oreg. Career and Vocat. Adv. Council, 1977-82, Oreg. Manpower Commn., 1978-80; mem. Econ. Devel. Corp. Chippewa County, 1982-86. Served with USAF, 1942-45, to maj., USAFR, 1945-62. Mem. AAUP, Am. Soc. Engring. Edn., Am. Soc. Mil. Engrs., Air Force Assn., Phi Delta Kappa. Home: Gresham, Oreg. Died Aug. 16, 2003.

LILLEVANG, OMAR JOHANSEN, civil engineer; b. Los Angeles, Sept. 8, 1914; s. Gunnar Johansen and Nina (Christiansen) L.; m. D. Miriam Guest, Sept. 10, 1939 (dec. Sept. 1990); children— Ralph Glen, Carol Ellen. AA, Los Angeles Jr. Coll., 1935; BS, U. Calif., Berkeley, 1937, postgrad., 1950-51. Registered profl. engr., Alaska, Calif., Hawaii, N.J., Oreg., Utah, Wash., Wis. Topographic surveyor Calif. Hwy. Commn., 1937; asst. engr. Coachella Valley County (Calif.) Water and Stormwater Dist., 1938; harbor constrn. engr., 1939-40; cantonment design and constrn. engr., 1941; constrn. engr. dams, aqueduct, tunnel, pump plants, 1942; water resources analyst, 1943; with Leeds, Hill, Barnard and Jewett (Cons. Engrs., and successors), Los Angeles, 1938-43, 46-61, supervising engr., 1950-61; v.p., dir. Leeds, Hill & Jewett Inc. (Cons. Engrs.), Los Angeles, 1961-64; cons. civil engring., especially for harbors, rivers, lakes, seas, coastal processes L.A., Whittier, 1964—. Mem. advisory panel for shore erosion protection U.S. Army Chief Engrs. Contbr.: articles to profl. jours. including Shore & Beach mag. Trustee, chmn. bldg. com. Plymouth Congregational Ch. of Whittier, Calif. Served with USN, 1943-46. Fellow ASCE (mem. task groups, John G. Moffatt-Frank E. Nichol Meml. award 1981); mem. Am. Shore Beach Preservation Assn., Permanent Internat. Assn. Navigation Congresses, U.S. Power Squadrons. Clubs: Rotary Internat. Deceased.

LIMBAUGH, RUSH HUDSON, lawyer; b. nr. Sedgewickville, Mo., Sept. 27, 1891; s. Joseph Headley and Susan Frances (Presnell) L.; m. Bee Seabaugh, Aug. 29, 1914 (dec.); children: Rush Hudson, Manley O., Stephen Nathaniel. Student, Cape Girardeau (Mo.) Normal Sch., 1907-08, 09-12; AB, U. Mo., 1916. Bar: Mo., 1916. Tchr. rural sch., Mo., 1908-09; since practiced in; sr. mem. firm Limbaugh, Russell & Syler (and predecessor firm), 1946—96. City counselor, Cape Girardeau, 1924-30; commr. St. Louis Ct. Appeals, 1935, Supreme Ct. Mo., 1950-51; Nelson Meml. lectr. U. Mo., 1955; Dept. State lectr., India, 1958 Author: Missouri Practice; Contbr. articles to profl. jours. in, U.S. and India. Served as rep. 56th Gen. Assembly, Mo., 1931-33; mem. Mo. Commn. Human Rights, 1965-73; adv. bd. Salvation Army; trustee Old McKendree Chapel (nat. Meth. Shrine); trystee S.E. Mo. Univ. Found. Recipient S.E. Mo. State U. Alumni award, 1961; U. Mo. at Columbia award for distinguished service in law, 1964 Fellow Am. Bar. Found., Am. Coll. Trial Lawyers, Am. Coll. Probate Counsel; mem. Am. Soc. Internat. Law, Am. Judicature Soc., Am. Law Inst., Am. Bar Assn. (mem. council, sect. real property, probate and trust law 1950-54, chmn. sect. 1954-55, mem. ho. dels. 1955-59, standing com. bill of rights 1959-66, chmn. com. 1960-61, 63-65), Inst. Jud. Adminstrn., Am. Soc. Legal History, Inter-Am. Bar Assn., Mo. Bar Found., Selden Soc., Mo. Bar (pres. 1955-56, Spurgeon Smithson award 1984), State Hist. Soc. Mo. (trustee, past pres.), Cape Girardeau County Bar Assn. (pres. 1929-31), Order Coif (hon.), All India Law Tchrs. Assn. (hon. life), Scribes, Phi Delta Phi, Delta Sigma Rho. Clubs: Mason, Missouri Athletic, Cape Girardeau Country, Rotary (pres. 1948-49, Paul Harris Fellow). Republican. Methodist. Home: Cape Girardeau, Mo. Died Apr. 8, 1996.

LIMMER, RUTH, writer, editor; b. N.Y.C., Nov. 23, 1927; d. Kurt Alfred Limmer and Jennie Levinson. BA, Bklyn. Coll., 1948; MA, Mills Coll., 1950. Prof. English Western Coll. for Women, Oxford, Ohio, 1954-74, Goucher Coll., Towson, Md., 1974-78; writer, editor Dept. Housing and Urban Devel., Washington, 1978-80, Nat. Endowment for Arts, Washington, 1980-81; dir. publs. Hunter Coll., N.Y.C., 1981-84, asst. to pres., 1984-88; adj. prof. Sch. Continuing Edn. NYU, N.Y.C., 1989-90. Author: Six Heritage Tours of the Lower East Side, 1997; editor: What the Woman Lived, 1973, Journey Around My Room, 1980; editor The Hunter mag., 1981-84; co-editor: A Poet's Alphabet, 1970; writer, editor (periodical) Tenement Times, 1989—, bio. essay, Letters of Rolfe Humphries, 1992; intro. Streets, 1995; contbr. articles to newspapers and mags. Pres., bd. dirs. Roosevelt Island Community Libr., N.Y.C., 1990-91. Democrat. Jewish. Died Oct. 31, 2001.

LIN, TUNG YEN, civil engineer, educator; b. Foochow, China, Nov. 14, 1911; arrived in U.S., 1946, naturalized, 1951; s. Ting Chang and Feng Yi (Kuo) Lin; m. Margaret Kao, July 20, 1941; children: Paul, Verna. BSCE, Chiaotung U., Tangshan, Republic of China, 1931; MS, U. Calif., Berkeley, 1933; LLD, Chinese U. Hong Kong, 1972, Golden Gate U., San Francisco, 1982, Tongji U., Shanghai, 1987, Chiaotung U., Taiwan, 1987. Chief bridge engr., chief design engr. Chinese Govt. Rys., 1933—46; from asst. to assoc. prof. U. Calif., 1946—55, prof., 1955—76, chmn. div. structural engring., 1960—63, dir. structural lab., 1960—63; chmn. bd. T.Y. Lin Internat., 1953—87, hon. chmn. bd., 1987—92; pres. Inter-Continental Peace Bridge, Inc., 1968—2003. Chmn. World Conf. Prestressed Concrete, 1957, Western Conf. Prestressed Concrete Bldgs., 1960; chmn. bd. Lin Tung Yen, China, from 1993; cons. in field. Author: Design of Prestressed Concrete Structures, 1955, rev. edition, 1963; author: (with N.H. Burns) 3rd edit., 1981; author: (with B. Bresler, Jack Scalzi) Design of Steel Structures, 1968; author: (with S.D. Statesbury) Structural Concepts and Systems, 1981, 2d edit., 1988; contbr. articles to profl. jours. Named Alumnus of Yr., U. Calif. Alumni Assn., 1994; recipient Berkeley citation, 1976, Quarter Century award, NRC, 1977, Honor award, AIA, 1984, Pres.'s Nat. Med. of Sci., 1986, Merit award, Am. Cons. Engrs. Coun., 1987, John A. Roebling medal, Bridge Engring., 1990, Leadership award, Am. Segmental Bridge Inst., 1992, Outstanding Paper of Yr. award, Internat. Assn. Bridge and Structural Engring., 1993, Lifetime Achievement award, Asian Am. Archs. and Engring. Assn., 1993, Outstanding Achievement award of So. Calif., Prix Albert Caquot award, Assn. Française pour Constrn., 1995; fellow, U. Calif., Berkeley. Mem.: ASCE (hon. Wellington award, Howard medal, OPAL award), Chinese Acad. Sci., Prestressed Concrete Inst. (medal of honor), Internat. Fedn. Prestressing (Freyssinet medal), Academia Sinica, Chinese Acad. Sci., Nat. Acad. Engring., Am. Concrete Inst. (hon.), Chi Epsilon (hon.). Home: El Cerrito, Calif. Died Nov. 15, 2003.

LINCOLN, CARL CLIFFORD, JR., auditor; b. Connellsville, Pa., Sept. 23, 1928; s. Carl Clifford and Mary Elizabeth (Pierce) L.; m. Clara May Collins, May 1, 1950; children: Patricia J., William E., Carl Clifford III (dec.), Ralph C., Charles D., James B., John D., Richard D. Student, LaSalle Extension U., 1962; comml. flight tng., 1948-49. Flight crew All Am. Airways (now US Airway), Pitts., 1951-52; prodn. control expeditor Bryant Heaters, Inc., Cleve., 1952-53; asst. to plant engr. Osborne Mfg. Co., Cleve., 1953-54; driver salesman Nat. Biscuit Co., Cleve., 1954-55; prodn. control expeditor Rockwell Mfg. Co., Uniontown, Pa., 1955-56; clk., salesman various cos., Connellsville, Pa., 1956-65; investigator tax Dept. Revenue Pa., Harrisburg, 1965-68; revenue adminstr. indsl. collections Pa. State Gen. Hosp., Harrisburg, 1968-70; field office mgr., field insp., field auditor, constrn. Pa. Turnpike Commn., Harrisburg, from 1970; ret., 1991. County chmn. Young Reps., Uniontown, 1965-69; chmn. Western Pa. chpt. Am. heart Assn., Connellsville, 1968; mem. Rep. Coun. Cmty. Leaders, State Ho. of Reps., Harrisburg, 1987-98. With USN, 1944, 46-48, ETO. Mem. SAR (pres., v.p., publicity chmn. dep. dir. dist. 5 Pa. Somerset Cambria chpt. 1991), USS Wyo. BB-32 Assn. (treas., reunion chmn., membership chmn. 1995-99), Am. Battleship Assn., USS Franklin CV-13 Assn., Am. Legion, Berlin Hist. Soc., Pa. Assn. Ret. Employees, VFW (life), Toastmasters, Last Man's Club WWII Vets., Masons, Ancient Accepted Scottish Rite (32 degree, pres., v.p.). Mem. Ch. of Christ. Home: Berlin, Pa. Died June 14, 1999.

LINDH, ANNA, Swedish government official; b. Enskede, Stockholm, June 19, 1957; BA in Law, U. Uppsala, 1982. Mem. parliament Swedish Govt., Stockholm, 1982-85, chmn. Govt. Coun. on Alcohol and Drug Policy, 1986-90; vice-mayor, mem. Stockholm City Coun., 1991-94; min. environment Swedish Govt., Stockholm, 1994-98, min of foreign affairs, 1998—2003. Mem. Mcpl. Coun., Enköping, 1977-79; ct. clk. Stockholm Dist. Ct., 1982-83. Chmn. Social Dem. Youth League, Uppsala, 1977-80, pres. 1984-90; mem. exec. com. Social Dem. Party, 1991—; chmn. Stockholm City Culture com., Leisure Svcs. Com, Stockholm City Theater, 1991-94. Died Sept. 11, 2003.

LINDSAY, GEORGE EDMUND, museum director; b. Pomona, Calif., Aug. 17, 1916; s. Charles Wesley and Alice (Foster) L.; m. Geraldine Kendrick Morris, 1972. Student, San Diego State Coll., 1936-39; BA, Stanford U., 1951, PhD, 1956. Dir. Desert Bot. Gardes, Phoenix, 1939-40, San Diego Natural History Mus., 1956-63, Calif. Acad. Scis., San Francisco, 1963-82, dir. emeritus, 1982—. Served to capt. USAAF, 1943-46. Decorated Air medal with 3 clusters, Bronze Star. Fellow San Diego Soc. Natural History, Zool. Soc. San Diego, Calif. Acad. Scis., A.A.A.S., Cactus and Succulent Soc. Achievements include spl. rsch. taxonomy desert plants, Cactaceae of Baja Calif., Mex. Home: Belvedere Tiburon, Calif. Died July 16, 2002.

LINDSAY, KATHERINE ANN, principal; b. Decatur, Ill., Apr. 18, 1946; d. Frank Merrill and Margery (Crawford) L. BS, Millikin U., Decatur, 1968; MEd, U. Ill., 1969. Cert. ednl. adminstr., guidance counselor, Ill. Tchr. Decatur Pub. Sch. Dist., 1969-75, adminstrv. intern, 1975-76, prin. Pershing Sch., 1976-82, prin. South Shores Elem. Sch., from 1982. Ednl. adv. com. Millikin U., Decatur, 1976—. Co-author, illustrator: (book) Decatur, Today and Yesterday, 1979. Pres. Mental Health Assn. of Macon County, Decatur, 1972; bd. dirs. ARC, Macon County chpt., Decatur, 1981-84, 85-88, YWCA, Decatur, 1986-88, Am. Cancer Soc., Macon County chpt., Decatur, 1988—; deacon, elder Cen. Christian Ch., Decatur, 1986—. Named Outstanding Young Educator award Decatur Jaycees, 1972, Young Alumnus of Yr. Millikin U., 1973, Outstanding Educator Alpha Delta Kappa, 1982, Adminstr. of Yr. Decatur Assn. Ednl. Office Personnel, 1983; recipient Those Who Excel award Ill. Bd. Edn., 1985. Mem. Assn. Supervision and Curriculum Devel., Decatur Assn. Bldg. Adminstrs. (past pres.), Delta Kappa Gamma, Phi Delta Kappa. Lodges: Zonta. Avocations: photography, collecting carousel horses, gardening. Home: Decatur, Ill. Deceased.

LING, TIMOTHY H. oil company executive; b. Phila. BS, Cornell U., 1982; MBA, Stanford U., 1989. Resource geologist U.S. Geol. Survey, Woods Hole, Mass.; with McKinsey & Co., 1989-97, ptnr., 1994-97; CFO Unocal Corp., El Segundo Corp., 1997—2000, exec. v.p., North American ops. El Segundo, Calif., 1997—2000, pres., COO, 2000—04. Co-author: Real Change Leaders. Bd. dirs., officer L.A. Philharm. Died Jan. 28, 2004.

LINMAN, JAMES WILLIAM, retired physician, educator; b. Monmouth, Ill., July 20, 1924; s. Chester E. and Ruth L. (Pearson) L.; m. Frances Firth, Aug. 31, 1946; children— John, Jean, James, Jeffrey. BS, U. Ill., 1945, MD, 1947. Intern, resident internal medicine Med. Sch., U. Mich., Ann Arbor, 1947-51, fellow in hematology, 1951-52, 54-56, asst. prof. internal medicine, 1955-56; chief hematology sect. VA Research Hosp. Chgo.; assoc. prof. medicine Med. Sch., Northwestern U., Evanston, Ill., 1956-65; prof. internal medicine Mayo Grad. Sch. Medicine, U. Minn., Mpls.; cons.

hematology and head spl. hematology sect. Mayo Clinic-Found., Rochester, Minn., 1965-72; prof. medicine, dir. Osgood Leukemia Ctr., Health Sci. Ctr., U. Oreg., Portland, 1972-79, head hematology div., 1974-78; prof. medicine John A. Burns Sch. Medicine, U. Hawaii, Honolulu, 1979-92; emeritus prof., from 1992; chmn. admissions com. John A. Burns Sch. Medicine, U. Hawaii, Honolulu, 1983-92, asst. dean for admissions, 1988-92. Chmn. State of Hawaii Adv. Commn. on Drug Abuse and Controlled Substances, 1986-88; dir. med. edn. The Queen's Med. Ctr., Honolulu, 1987-88. Author: Principles of Hematology, 1966, Factors Controlling Erythropoiesis, 1960, The Leukemias, 1971, Hematology, 1975; Contbr. articles to profl. jours. Served with USAF, 1952-54. Recipient Tchr. of Year award Mayo Fellows Assn., 1970, Tchr. of Year award U. Hawaii, 1980, 81 Mem. Am. Soc. Clin. Investigation, Central Soc. Clin. Research, Am., Internat. socs. hematology, A.C.P., Western Assn. Physicians, Western Soc. Clin. Research, Pacific Interurban Clin. Club, Alpha Omega Alpha, Phi Kappa Phi. Clubs: Oahu Country. Home: Honolulu, Hawaii. Died Sept. 13, 2003.

LINSTEDT, WALTER GRIFFITHS, lawyer, banker; b. Turlock, Calif., Mar. 16, 1933; s. Daniel Henry and Wanda Mae (Griffiths) L.; m. Kathleen Dawson, Apr. 1956 (div. 1977); children: Adam, Laurel, Pamela; m. MaryLou Campbell, Apr. 29, 1978. BA, Stanford U., 1955; JD, U. Calif., San Francisco, 1960. Bar: Calif. 1961, Ill. 1976. Counsel Calif. Pub. Utilities Commn., San Francisco, 1960-63; assoc. Erskine & Tulley, San Francisco, 1963-66; v.p., assoc. gen. counsel Crocker Bank, San Francisco, 1966-74; ptnr. Macdonald, Halsted & Laybourne, L.A., 1974-76; v.p., assoc. gen. counsel Continental Ill. Nat. Bank and Trust Co. Chgo., 1976-88; asst. gen. counsel Bank of Am., L.A., 1988-99. Trustee Calif. Indian Legal Svcs., San Francisco, 1968-75, 860 Lake Shore Dr. Trust, Chgo., 1985-88. Avocations: tennis, photography. Home: Pasadena, Calif. Died Aug. 22, 1999.

LINTZ, PAUL RODGERS, physicist, engineer, patent examiner; b. Dallas, Feb. 8, 1941; s. Norman Edmund and Sarah Kathleen (Powers) L.; m. Mary Grace Caggiano, Nov. 27, 1965; children: Matthew Thomas, Eileen Sarita, Jerome Peter, Elizabeth Irene. BA cum laude, U. Dallas, 1963; MS, Cath. U. Am., 1965, PhD, 1977. Mem. tech. staff Tex. Instruments, Dallas, 1965-67; rsch. physicist Teledyne Geotech. Co., Alexandria, Va., 1967-74; scientist Planning Systems Inc., McLean, Va., 1974-76; prin. investigator Sci. Applications Internat. Corp., McLean, 1976-84; systems engr. Mitre Corp., McLean, 1984-87; ind. cons. Vienna, Va., 1987-92; patent examiner U.S. Patent and Trademark Office, Washington, from 1992. Mem. Providence Dist. Dem. Com., Vienna, 1985; com. mem. Vienna area Boy Scouts Am., 1986-90; pres. Tysons Woods Civic Assn., Vienna, 1991. Mem. IEEE, D.C. Bar Assn. (social mem.), Internat. Platform Assn., Sigma Xi. Roman Catholic. Achievements include development of digital signal processing techniques for defense purposes in seismic detection of underground nuclear blasts, submarine sonar signal processing, passive bistatic radar signal processing, detection, tracking. Home: Vienna, Va. Died Jan. 13, 2002.

LIPMAN, WYNONA M. state legislator; b. Ga.; children: Karyne Anne, William (dec.). BA, Talladega Coll.; MA, Atlanta U.; Ph.D., Columbia U.; LL.D. (hon.), Kean Coll., Bloomfield Coll. Former high sch. tchr., lectr. Seton Hall U., Assoc. prof. Essex County Coll.; mem. N.J. State Senate, 1971-99, Human Svcs. com., budget and appropriation com., Women, Children Family Svcs com. chmn., Commn. on Sex Discrimination in the Statutes. Mem. NAACP, Nat. Coun. Negro Women, Women's Polit. Caucus, Essex County Urban League. Recipient Outstanding Woman award Assn. Women Bus Owners, 1983. Democrat.Died May 1999.

LIPPER, JEROME, lawyer; b. N.Y.C., July 19, 1936; s. George and Sally (Hollander) L.; m. Binnette Blatt, Dec. 23, 1961; children: David, Allen. BA magna cum laude, Long Island U., 1957; LLM cum laude, NYU, 1960, LLB in Internat. Law, 1963. Bar: N.Y. 1960, U.S. Dist. Ct. (so. dist.) N.Y. 1961, U.S. Ct. Appeals (2nd cir.) 1961, D.C. 1969, U.S. Supreme Ct. 1975, U.S. Ct. Appeals (5th cir.) 1984. Law clk. to judge U.S. Dist. Ct., N.Y.C., 1960-61; assoc. Feldman, Kramer, Bam & Nessen, N.Y.C., 1962-66, ptnr., 1966, Fly, Shuebruk, Blume & Gaguine, 1967-70, Leon, Weill & Mahony, 1970-84, Tenzer, Greenblatt, Fallon & Kaplan, from 1984. Chmn., bd. dirs. Ansbacher Bank, Dublin, Ireland; lectr. Cambridge (End.) U., 1988. Author: (with others) The Law of International Drainage Basins, 1969; exec. editor NYU Law Rev., 1959-60; asst. editor Internat. Rivers Rsch. Project NYU, 1961-62; contbr. articles N.Y. Law Jour., 1959-69. Trustee Law Ctr. Found. NYU, N.C.C., 1982—, Fairleigh S. Dickinson, Jr. Found., 1980—, Ansley Family Found., The Bahamas, 1981—; bd. govs. Weizmann Inst. Sci., Israel, 1987—; treas., exec. com. Am. Com. for Weizmann Inst., N.Y.C., 1979—; mem. commn. Office of Protocol City of N.Y., 1983-88; vice chmn. Nat. Com. on Am. Fgn. Policy, 1979-82. Fellow Aspen Inst. Humanistic Studies, 1983; recipient law teaching fellowship Ford Found. for NYU, 1962. Mem. ABA, Assn. of Bar of City of N.Y. (chmn. com. on profession 1988—), Internat. Law Assn. (exec. com.), NYU Law Alumni Assn. (pres. 1979-81), Aspen Inst. Alumni Assn. (pres. N.Y.C. chpt. 1982-86), Order of Coif. Avocations: hiking, travel. Home: White Plains, NY. Deceased.

LIPPINCOTT, JOSEPH WHARTON, JR., publisher; b. Bethayres, Pa., Oct. 2, 1914; s. Joseph Wharton and Elizabeth Schuyler (Mills) L.; m. Josephine Drexel Henry, 1937 (div.); 1 child, Elizabeth Seton; m. Marie Louise Beck, Dec. 8, 1950; 1 child, Joseph Wharton III. Student, St. Paul's Sch., 1928-33, Princeton, 1933-37. With J.B. Lippincott Co., Phila., 1937-78, dir., 1940-78, sec., 1942-46, exec. v.p., 1953-58, pres., 1958-78, chmn. bd., 1974-78; sec. Med. Sci., Inc., 1956-68; v.p., dir. A.J. Holman Co., 1962-73, chmn. bd., 1973-78. Dir. Harper & Row Pubs., Inc. Trustee Ludington Pub. Library, Free Library Phila.; bd. dirs. Am. Ednl. Pubs. Inst., 1967-70, U. Pa. Press, 1971-76, Urban Libraries Council, 1978-87. Served with Am. Field Service, 1943-45. Mem. Am. Book Pubs. Council (dir. 1962-65), Booksellers Assn. Phila. (dir. 1960-66, pres. 1964-65), ALA (council 1968-72), Hist. Soc. Pa. (dir. 1966-78), Pa. Soc. Sons of Revolution. Clubs: Franklin Inn, Wilderness (Phila.); Merion Cricket (Haverford); Field (Sarasota, Fla.); Princeton (N.Y.C.). Home: Bryn Mawr, Pa. Died Jan. 25, 2003.

LIPPMAN, MURIEL MARIANNE, biomedical scientist; b. N.Y.C., Oct. 16, 1930; d. Louis George and Erna (Hirsch) L. BA, Syracuse U., 1951; MS, U. Pa., 1955; postgrad., Tufts U., 1965-66, Yale U., 1966-67; PhD, U. Chgo., 1970. Chmn. sci. dept. St. Agnes H.S., Rochester, N.Y., 1957-59, Nazareth Acad., Rochester, 1959-63; asst. prof. biology, rsch. dir. Nazareth Coll., Rochester, 1963-65; scientist Retina Found., Boston, 1965-66; vis. scientist Karolinska Inst., Stockholm, 1967; assoc. prof. biology Seton Hall U., South Orange, N.J., 1970-71; sr. staff fellow Nat. Cancer Inst., Bethesda, Md., 1971-76; sr. scientist Food and Drug Adminstrn. Bur. Med. Devices, Silver Spring, Md., 1976-77; sr. staff scientist Nat. Acad. Scis., Washington, 1977-78; dir. scientific planning and review Clement Assocs., Washington, 1978-79; pres. ERNACO, Inc., Silver Spring, from 1979, MMLI Biomed. Comm., Silver Spring, from 1998. Adj. prof. biology Am. U., Washington, 1981-83; vis. prof. Cook Coll., Rutgers State U., N.J., 1985-86; adj. prof. anatomy Frederick (Md.) C.C., 1991, No. Va. C.C., Sterling, 1992-96; vis. prof. biology U. Md., 1996, 97. Contbr. articles to profl. jours. Mem. Human Relations Commn. Montgomery County, Md., 1982-83. Recipient numerous grants and fellowships including Cancer Rsch. grantee Damon Runyon Found., 1964, Am. Cancer Soc. grantee, 1969-70, Biomedical rsch. grantee Evans Found., 1984-91, Nat. Heart, Lung and Blood Inst. NIH, 1986-87; U.S. Pub. Health fellow, 1965-66, KC Rsch. fellow, 1967, Danforth Teaching fellow U. Chgo., 1970; Teaching Excellence award Rochester Acad. Scis., 1963. Mem. Am. Med. Writers Assn., Drug Info. Assn., Sigma Xi. Home: Silver Spring, Md. Deceased.

LIPPOLD, RICHARD, sculptor; b. Milw., May 3, 1915; s. Adolph and Elsa (Schmidt) L.; m. Louise Greuel, Aug. 24, 1940; children— Lisa, Tiana, Ero. Student, U. Chgo., 1934-37; B.F.A., Art Inst. Chgo., 1937; D.F.A. (hon.), Ripon Coll., 1968. Tchr. Layton Sch. Art, Milw., 1940-41, U. Mich., 1941-44, Goddard Coll., 1945-47; head art sect. Trenton (N.J.) Jr. Coll., 1948-52; prof. Hunter Coll., N.Y.C., 1952-67. Works exhibited Inst. Arts, Detroit, 1946-47, St. Louis City Mus., 1946, Toronto (Ont.) Mus., 1947, Whitney Mus., N.Y.C., 1947, 49, 51-53, 76, Calif. Palace Legion of Honor, San Francisco, 1948, Fundacao de Arte Moderne, Sao Paulo, Brazil, 1948, Mus. Modern Art, N.Y.C., 1951-53, 63, Tate Gallery, London, 1953, Musée d'Art Moderne, Paris, 1955, Nat. Collection Fine Arts, Washington, 1976, Nat. Air and Space Mus., Washington, 1976, Biennale, Venice, 1988; one-man show Willard Gallery, N.Y.C., 1947-48, 50, 53, 62, 68, 73, Arts Club, Chgo., Layton Art Gallery, Milw., 1953, Haggerty Mus., Milw., 1990, 20th Century Sculpture, Nssau County Mus. of Art, NY, 1999, The Amer. Century, Whitney Mus. of Art, NY, 1999; represented in collections Addison Gallery Am. Art, Andover, Mass., Fogg Mus., Harvard U., Wadsworth Atheneum, Hartford, Mus. Modern Art, Whitney Mus., N.Y.C., Newark Mus., Met. Mus. Art, N.Y.C., Detroit Art Inst., Des Moines Art Inst., Brooks Gallery, Memphis, Mobile (Ala.) Art Mus., Musée de Vin, Pavillac, France, Munson-Williams-Proctor Inst., Utica, N.Y., Va. Mus. Fine Arts, Milw. Art Center, Yale U. Art Gallery, others, also pvt. collections, U.S. and Europe; commns. include Harvard U., 1950, Inland Steel Bldg, Chgo., 1958, Four Seasons Restaurant, Seagram Bldg., N.Y.C., 1959, Stage Set, Spoleto, Italy, 1959; Portsmouth (R.I.) Priory Ch, 1960, Pan Am Bldg., N.Y.C., 1961, Avery Fisher Hall, Lincoln Center, N.Y.C., 1961, Jesse Jones Hall, Houston, 1965, St. Mary's Cathedral, San Francisco, 1967, Christian Sci. Center, Boston, 1974, Hyatt Regency Atlanta, 1975, Fairlane Plaza, Dearborn, Mich., 1975; 115 foot stainless steel sculpture on mall in front, Air and Space Mus., Washington, 1976; King's Retiring Room, Riyadh, Saudi Arabia, 1977, Columbia (S.C.) Mall, 1977, Kish Island, Iran, 1978, Hyatt Regency, Milw., 1980, Shiga Sacred Garden, Kyoto, Japan, 1981; 250 foot sculpture Park Ave Atrium Bldg., N.Y.C., 1981, One Fin. Ctr., Boston, 1984, Deutsche Bank, Frankfurt, W. Ger., 1985, First Interstate Bank, Seattle, 1985, Sohio Hdqrs., Cleve., 1986, 200 foot high outdoor sculpture, Seoul, South Korea, 1986, Atrium Sculpture for Crystal City, Va., 1986, Marina Square, Singapore, 1986, Orange County Ctr. for Performing Arts, Costa Mesa, Calif., 1987, Atrium Sculpture and Tapestry, Alexandria, Va., 1988, Atrium Sculpture, San Diego, 1990, 95, Haggerty Mus. Retrospective, Marquette U., Milw., 1991, Montrone Residence, La Jolla, 1992, Conv. Ctr., Charlotte, N.C., 1995. Recipient 3d prize Internat. Sculpture Competition, Inst. Contemporary Arts, London, 1953, Creative Arts award Brandeis U., 1958, Silver medal Archtl. League N.Y., 1960, Honor award Mcpl. Art Soc. N.Y., 1963, Fine Arts medal AIA, 1970 Mem. Nat. Inst. Arts and Letters (v.p. 1966) Died Aug. 22, 2002.

LIPSON, RICHARD LEWIS, rheumatologist, physician, researcher; b. Phila., July 21, 1931; s. Samuel Arthur and Norma Leah (Bershtein) L.; m. Mavis Lipson; children: Jonathan, Amy Sue. AB in Biology cum laude, Lafayette Coll., Easton, Pa., 1952; MD, Jefferson Med. Coll., Phila., 1956; MSc in Medicine, U. Minn., 1960. Intern Jefferson Med. Coll. Hosp., Phila., 1956-57; fellow in internal medicine and rheumatology Mayo Clinic and Found., Rochester, Minn., 1957-60, research asst. biophysics sect., 1962-63; asst. prof. medicine U. Vt., Burlington, 1963-68, clin. asst. prof., 1968-85, clin. assoc. prof., from 1985. Med. attendant Med. Ctr. Hosp. Vt., Burlington, 1963—; cons. in rheumatology Fanny Allen Hosp., Winooski, Vt., 1968—. Contbr. numerous articles to profl. jours. Served with USAF, 1960-62. Fellow ACP, Am. Rheumatism Assn. (founding); mem. Am. Coll. Rheumatology (founding), Biophys. Soc., Am. Fedn. Clin. Rsch., Royal Soc. Medicine, Sigma Xi. Home: Grand Isle, Vt. Deceased.

LIPTAK, DOROTHY ANNE, controller, freelance writer; b. Passaic, N.J., Dec. 16, 1938; d. George J. and Anna J. (Strelec) L. BA, Rutgers U., 1966; MBA, Fairleigh Dickinson U., 1973. Pers. reviewer Prudential Ins. Co., Newark, 1956-65, pers. cons., 1965-75, tng. specialist, 1975-83, head rsch. assoc., 1983-84, controller adminstrv. prodn., from 1984. Adminstrv. asst. Gov.'s Commn. to Evaluate Capital Needs of N.J., 1966, 75. Mem. AAUW (editor 1971-73), Rutgers U. Alumni Assn., Rutgers U. Coll. Women's Club (pres. 1964-65), Prudential Ins. Co. Athletic Assn. (sec., treas., v.p. 1959-89), Rutherford Garden Club (v.p. 1985-87), Phi Chi Theta chpt. Alpha Omega (1964-74). Republican. Roman Catholic. Avocations: travel, indoor gardening. Home: Rutherford, NJ. Deceased.

LISKIN, BARBARA ANN, psychiatrist; b. Englewood, NJ, Nov. 24, 1952; d. Louis and Anita (Merker) L.; m. Vincent Robert Bonagura, June 3, 1982; children: Elizabeth, Rebecca. AB, Smith Coll., Northampton, 1974; MS, Columbia U., N.Y.C., 1974, MD, 1979. Boarded in Pediatrics and Psychiatry. Research asst. Columbia U., N.Y.C., 1974-75, asst. psychiat. instr., 1985-87, asst. clin. prof. pediatrics and psychiatry, from 1987, dir. young adult psychiatry, from 1987; clin. dir. Barnard Coll. Mental Health Svcs., from 1988; pvt. practice psychiatry, from 1985. Recipient NIMH Jr. Faculty award 1985; Resident Research award 1985. Mem. Am. Psychiatry Assn. Home: Ridgefield, NJ. Deceased.

LITCHFORD, GEORGE B. aeronautical engineer; b. Long Beach, Calif., Aug. 12, 1918; BA, Reed Coll., 1941. Fellow IEEE (past chmn. awards com. K.I. sect., Pioneer award AES-S 1974, Lamme medal 1981, AIAA (Wright Bros. medal/lectureship 1978); mem. Aerospace and Electronic Sys. Soc. Deceased.

LIU, WEN DAVID, civil, structural engineer; b. Taipei, Taiwan, Dec. 7, 1952; came to U.S., 1978; s. Ching-Tang and Chu-Chin (Yao) L.; m. Nan Wang, Feb. 14, 1992. BS, Nat. Cheng-Kung U., Taiwan, 1974; MS, Nat. Taiwan U., Taiwan, 1976; PhD, U. Calif., Berkeley, 1983. Registered profl. engr., Calif. Rsch. engr. Earthquake Engring. Rsch. Ctr., U. Calif., Berkeley, 1982-84, Engring. Computer Corp., Sacramento, 1984-86; dir. Imbsen & Assocs., Inc., Sacramento, from 1986, assoc., 1986-90, prin., tech. dir., 1990-96, prin., bridge engr., from 1996. Author papers in field. Mem. Am. Concrete Inst., Seiosmol. Soc. Am., Earthquake Engring. Rsch. Inst. Home: Folsom, Calif. Died June 27, 2001.

LIVE, ANNA HARRIS, linguist, educator; b. Balta, Russia, Mar. 5, 1908; arrived in U.S., 1913, naturalized; d. Hyman Hirsch and Rachel (Selinger) Harris; m. Israel Live, Nov. 25, 1936; children: Theodore, David. BS, U. Pa., 1929, MA, 1931, PhD, 1959; postgrad., Sorbonne U., 1961. Tchr. English Phila. Sr. H.S., 1930—63; instr. English for fgn. students U. Pa., Phila., 1959—64, dir. English Program for Fgn. Students, 1964—78, lectr. Linguistics, 1964—68. Vis. prof., lectr. Seton Hall U., 1962, St. Joseph's U., Phila., 1964—65, Swarthmore Coll., 1966—68. Author: Yesterday and Today in the U.S.A., 1977, 1988; co-author (with S. Sankowsky): American Mosaic, 1980; author: From Sea to Shining Sea, 1985; contbr. articles to profl. jours. Mayor's scholar, 1925—29. Mem.: Tchrs. English to Spkrs. Other Langs., Nat. Coun. Tchrs. English, Linguistic Soc. Am. Home: Philadelphia, Pa. Died Jan. 14, 2002.

LOCALIO, S. ARTHUR, retired surgeon, educator; b. N.Y.C., Oct. 4, 1911; s. Joseph and Carmella (Franco) L.; m. Ruth Virginia Adkins, July 14, 1945; children: William Hale, Susan Emily, Arthur Russell, David Charles. AB, Cornell U., 1932; MD, U. Rochester, 1936; D.Sc., Columbia, 1942. Diplomate Am. Bd. Surgery. Intern pathology N.Y. U. Hosp., 1936-37, intern medicine, 1937-38, asst. resident in surgery, 1938-40, sr. resident, 1940-42, asst. surgeon, 1945-47, asst. attending surgeon, 1947-49, asso. attending surgeon, 1949-52, attending surgeon, 1952—; clin. asst. vis. surgeon 4th surg. div. Bellevue Hosp., N.Y.C., 1945-46, asst. vis. surgeon, 1946-48, asso. vis. surgeon, 1948-52, vis. surgeon, 1952—; practice medicine specializing in surgery N.Y.C., 1945—; instr. surgery Columbia Postgrad. Med. Sch., N.Y.C., 1945-48, asst. prof., 1948-49; asst. prof. surgery N.Y. U. Schs. Medicine, N.Y.C., 1949-50, asso. prof., 1950-53, prof., 1953—; Johnson and Johnson Disting. prof. surgery N.Y.U. Schs. Medicine, 1972-92, Johnson and Johnson Disting. prof. surgery emeritus, from 1992. Cons. in surgery Riverview Hosp., Red Bank, N.J., 1952—, Monmouth Meml. Hosp., Long Branch, N.J., 1952—, St. Barnabas Hosp., N.Y.C., 1958—, VA Hosp., N.Y.C., Wyckoff Heights Hosp., Bklyn., N.Y. Infirmary, N.Y.C., Booth Meml.

Hosp., Flushing, N.Y., Brookhaven Meml. Hosp., Patchogue, N.Y. Contbr. articles to med. jours. Trustee Deerfield (Mass.) Acad., 1984-94. Served from capt. to lt. col. M.C. AUS, 1942-45, PTO. Mem. Am. Gastroent. Assn., N.Y. Gastroent. Assn., ACS, AMA, Am. Assn. for Surgery of Trauma, Soc. for Surgery Alimentary Tract, N.Y. Acad. Medicine (trustee 1971-75), N.Y. Acad. Scis., N.Y. Cancer Soc., N.Y. Soc. Colon and Rectal Surgeons, Pan Am. Med. Soc. (N.Am. chmn. sect. gen. surgery 1972—), N.Y. County Med. Soc., N.Y. State Med. Soc., Sociedad Colombiana de Cirujanos, Société Internationale de Chirurgie, Collegium Internationale Chirurgie Digestivae, Royal Soc. Medicine, N.Y. Surg. Soc., B.C. Surg. Soc., Transplantation Soc., Am. Surg. Assn., Sigma Xi. Home: Deerfield, Mass. Deceased.

LOCKHART, AILEENE SIMPSON, retired dance, kinesiology, physical education educator and editor; b. Atlanta, Mar. 18, 1911; d. Thomas Ellis and Aileene Reeves (Simpson) Lockhart. BS, Tex. Woman's U., 1932; MS, U. Wis., 1937, PhD, 1942; DSc (hon.), U. Nebr., 1967. Mem. faculty Mary Hardin Baylor Coll., Belton, Tex., 1937-42, U. Wis., 1941-42; asst. prof., then assoc. prof. phys. edn. and pharmacology U. Nebr., 1942-49; assoc. prof., then prof. U. So. Calif., 1949-73; dean, prof. Coll. Health, Phys. Edn., Recreation and Dance Tex. Woman's U., 1973-78, Cornaro prof., 1973-78, prof. dance and phys. edn., chmn. dept. dance, 1978-83, adj. prof., 1983-88, Rachel Bryant Meml. lectr., 1997. Clare Small lectr. U. Colo., 1975; Ethel Martus Lawther lectr. U. N.C., 1978; Army Morris Homans lectr., Milw., 76; Donna Mae Miller Humanities scholar/lectr. U. Ariz., Tucson, 1989; vis. prof./lectr. Iowa State U., univs., Wash., Oreg., Wiss., Mass., N.C., Colo., N.H., Calif., State U., Long Beach, Springfield Coll., Mass., Smith Coll., Wellesely Coll., U. Maine-Presque Isle, Dunfermline Coll., Edinburgh, Scotland, U. Brazil, Brasilia; cons. editor William C. Brown Pub. Co., Dubuque, Iowa, 1954—95. Author or co-author: 12 books; contbr. articles to profl. jours.; cons. editor or editor: over 300 books. Recipient Alumnae award, Tex. Woman's U., 1971, Disting. Alumnae award, U. Wis.-Madison, 1981, Cornaro award, 1980, Honor award, Ministry Edn., Taiwan, 1981, Heritage award, Nat. Dance Assn., 1985, honra ao Merito, Ministerio de Educator and Cultura Brazilla, Brazil, 1977; fellow Amy Morris Homans, 1961—62; scholar Minnie Stevens Piper Found., State of Tex., 1983, Nat. Dance Assn., 1986—87, Tex. Assn. Health, Phys. Edn., Recreation and Dance, 1986. Fellow: Am. Acad. Phys. Edn. (pres. 1980—81, Hetherington award 1992), Am. Alliance Health, Phys. Edn., Recreation and Dance (Honor award 1963, Luther Halsey Gulick medal 1980), Am. Coll. Sports Medicine; mem.: Nat. Assn. Phys. Edn. in Higher Edn., So. Assn. Phys. Edn. Coll. Women, Nat. Dance Assn., Nat. Assn. Girls and Women in Sports (Honor award 1991, Rachel Bryant Meml. lectr. 1997), Phi Kappa Phi. Presbyterian. Home: Denton, Tex. Died Feb. 16, 2004.

LOEPFE, OTTP, mechanical engineer, air transportation executive; b. Switzerland, Mar. 23, 1936; m.; 3 children. Degree in mech. engring., Swiss Fed. Inst. Tech. With engring. and maintenance dept. Swissair, 1969, head power plant overhaul, 1970-73, head planning and quality supervision, 1974-78, v.p. engring. and maintenance, 1979-83, v.p. info. sys., 1984-86, dep. pres., 1987, pres., CEO, from 1988. Bd. dirs. Credit Suisse, Zurich, Winterthur. Mem. Assn. European Airlines (mem. pres. assembly). Died March 1998.

LOEVINGER, LEE, lawyer, science writer; b. St. Paul, Apr. 24, 1913; s. Gustavus and Millie (Strouse) L.; m. Ruth Howe (dec. 2003), Mar. 4, 1950; children: Barbara L., Eric H., Peter H. BA summa cum laude, U. Minn., 1933, JD, 1936. Bar: Minn. 1936, Mo. 1937, DC 1966, US Supreme Ct., 1941. Assoc. Watson, Ess, Groner, Barnett & Whittaker, Kans. City, Mo., 1936-37; atty., regional atty. NLRB, 1937-41; with antitrust div. Dept. Justice, 1941-46; ptnr. Larson, Loevinger, Lindquist & Fraser, Mpls., 1946-60; assoc. justice Minn. Supreme Ct., 1960-61; asst. U.S. atty. gen. charge antitrust div. Dept. Justice, 1961-63; commr. FCC, 1963-68; ptnr. Hogan & Hartson, Washington, 1968-85, of counsel, 1986—; v.p., dir. Craig-Hallum Corp., Mpls., 1968-73. Dir. Petrolite Corp., St. Louis, 1978-83; US rep. com. on restrictive bus. practices Orgn. for Econ. Coop. and Devel., 1961-64; spl. asst. to US atty. gen., 1963-64; spl. counsel com. small bus. US Senate, 1951-52; lectr. U. Minn., 1953-60; vis. prof. jurisprudence U. Minn. (Law Sch.), 1961; professorial lectr. Am. U., 1968-70; chmn. Minn. Atomic Devel. Problems Com., 1957-59; mem. Adminstrv. Conf. US, 1972-74; del. White House Conf. on Inflation, 1974; US del. UNESCO Conf. on Mass Media, 1975, Internat. Telecomms. Conf. on Radio Frequencies, 1964, 66. Author: The Law of Free Enterprise, 1949, An Introduction to Legal Logic, 1952, Defending Antitrust Lawsuits, 1977, Science As Evidence, 1995; author first article to use term: jurimetrics, 1949; contbr. articles to profl. and sci. jours.; editor, contbr.: Basic Data on Atomic Devel. Problems in Minnesota, 1958; adv. bd. Antitrust Bull., Jurimetrics Jour. Served to lt. comdr. USNR, 1942-45. Recipient Outstanding Achievement award U. Minn., 1968; Freedoms Found. award, 1977, 84. Fellow Am. Acad. Appellate Lawyers; mem. ABA (del. of sci. and tech. sect. to Ho. of Dels. 1974-80, del. to joint conf. with AAAS 1974-76, co-chair 1990-93, liaison 1984-90, 93-98, chmn. sci. and tech. sect. 1982-83, coun. 1986-89, standing com. on nat. conf. groups 1984-90), AAAS, Minn. Bar Assn., Hennepin County Bar Assn., NY Acad. Sci., DC Bar Assn., FCC Bar Assn., Broadcast Pioneers, US C. of C. (antitrust coun. 1980-94), Am. Arbitration Assn. (comml. panel), Atlantic Legal Found. (adv. coun.), Cosmos Club (pres. 1990), City Club (Washington), Phi Beta Kappa, Sigma Xi, Delta Sigma Rho, Sigma Delta Chi, Phi Delta Gamma, Tau Kappa Alpha, Alpha Epsilon Rho. Home: Chevy Chase, Md. Died Apr. 26, 2004.

LOEW, ROBERT MARCUS, broadcast executive; b. Santa Monica, Calif., Oct. 15, 1946; s. Marcus II and Ethel Loew; children: Adam, Stephen, Rebecca. BS, U. Calif., Berkeley, 1968, M of Engring., 1969; MBA, Stanford U., 1971. V.p. KHVH, Inc., Honolulu, 1976-84; pres., gen. mgr. Loew Broadcasting Corp. doing bus. as Stas. KDEO-FM-KORL-FM, Waipahu, Hawaii, from 1984. Mem. Hawaii Assn. Broadcasters (treas. 1986-96), Waipahu Bus. Assn., Oahu Country Club, Rotary (past pres. West Pearl Harbor). Avocations: golf, softball, swimming. Home: Honolulu, Hawaii. Died Nov. 22, 2000.

LO GERFO, PAUL, surgeon; b. Middletown, N.Y., 1939; MD, SUNY, Syracuse, 1967. Cert. in surgery. Intern Columbia-Presbyn. Med. Ctr., 1967-68, resident, 1968-73; former surgeon Presbyn. Hosp., N.Y.C. Prof. surgery Columbia Coll. Physicians and Surgeons. Died Sept. 16, 2003.

LOLLEY, RICHARD N. health science adiministrator, educator; b. Blaine, Kans., May 25, 1933; s. Loran Newton and Catherine Agnes (Caffrey) L.; m. Hazel Ruth Bauerrichter, June 4, 1959; children: Emily Ruth, Melissa Anne, Cybil Marie. BS in Pharmacy, U. Kans., 1955, PhD in Physiology, 1961. Registered pharmacist. Postdoctoral research fellow Maudsley Hosp., U. London, 1961-62; postdoctoral fellow in neuropathology McLean Hosp., Harvard U., Boston, 1962-64; rsch. pharmacologist VA Med. Ctr., Sepulveda, Calif., 1965-71, assoc. chief staff rsch. and devel., 1978-80, chief devel. neurology lab., from 1971; asst. prof. anatomy Sch. Medicine, UCLA, 1966-70, assoc. prof. anatomy, 1970-76, prof. anatomy, from 1976, cons. Jules Stein Eye Inst., 1972-78, mem. staff Jules Stein Eye Inst., from 1981, mem. med. scientist tng. program and med. sch. admissions, 1982-87. Chmn. rsch. and devel. com. VA Med. Ctr., 1985-88; chmn. adv. com. geriatric rsch. Edn. and Clin. Ctr., Sepulveda; mem. Nat. Adv. Eye Coun., Nat. Eye Inst., 1979-84; mem. rsch. scientist evaluation com. VA Cen. Office, Washington, 1981-84. Editor: Neurochemistry of the Retina, 1980; mem. editorial bd. Investigative Ophthamology and Visual Sci., 1982-87. Named Rsch. Career Scientist, VA, 1979; rsch. grantee, NSF, VA, Nat. Eye Inst., Nat, Retinitis Pigmentosa Found. Mem. AAAS, Assn. Rsch. in Vision and Ophthamology (trustee), Soc. Neurosci., Am. Soc. Neurochemistry, Internat. Soc. Neurochemistry, Am. Soc. Anatomists, Internation Soc. Eye Rsch. Home: Santa Barbara, Calif. Died Apr. 3, 2000.

LOMAX, ALAN, anthropologist; Student, Harvard Coll., 1932—33; BA in Philosophy, U. Tex., 1936; postgrad., Columbia U., 1939. Dir. Cantometrics and Choreometrics Rsch. Project Columbia U.-Ctr. for Social Scis., 1962—89, rsch. assoc. dept. anthropology, 1962—89; dir. Assn. for Cultural Equity, rsch. assoc. anthropology Hunter Coll., from 1989. Asst. dir. Archive of Am. Folk Song, Libr. Congress; dir.-prodr. CBS Radio, BBC Radio, London. Author: Milster Jelly Roll, 1950, Mister Jelly Roll, reissued, 1993, Harriet and Her Harmonium, 1955, The Rainbow Sign, 1959, The Folk Songs of North America, 1960, (audio-cassettes and handbook) Cantometrics: A Method of Musical Anthropology, 1977, Land Wehere the Blues Began, 1993 (Nat. Book Critics award for non-fiction, 1993); co-author (with John A. Lomax): American Ballads and Folk Songs, 1934; co-author: Negro Folk Songs as Sung by Leadbelly, 1936, Cowboy Sings, 1937, Our Singing Country, 1938, Folk Songs: USA, 1946; co-author: (with W. Guthrie and P. Seeger) Hard-Hitting Songs for Hard-Hit People, 1967; co-author: (with Cantometrics staff) Folk Song Style and Culture, 1968; co-author: (with R. Abdul) 3000 Years of Black Poetry, 1969; contbr. numerous articles to profl. jours.; scriptwriter : To Hear My Banjo Play, 1945; scriptwriter, dir. with P. Kennedy and G. Pickow : Oss, Oss Wee Oss, 1951; scriptwriter, dir., prodr. with F. Paulay : Dance and Human History, 1976; scriptwriter, dir., prodr. : Step Style, 1979; Palm Play, 1979; The Longest Trail, 1979; The Land Where the Blues Began, 1985 (blue ribbon Am. Film Festival, 1985). Fellow, Guggenheim, 1946, ACLS fellow dept. anthropology, Columbia U., 1960—61; grantee, ACLS, 1939, Rockefeller Found., 1962, 1975, 1977—78, NIMH, 1963—76. Mem.: Phi Beta Kappa. Died July 19, 2002.

LONG, GERALD DEAN, electrical engineer; b. Lehigh, Iowa, Mar. 8, 1934; s. Ronald Earl and Anna Geneva (Dosland) L.; married Aug. 17, 1953 (div. Feb. 1976); children: Ronald E., Debra A., Steven M.; m. Jexix Elizabeth Gibson, Dec. 28, 1977. Student, Iowa State U., 1951-53; BA in Physics, U. No. Iowa, 1957; MS in Tng. and Organic Devel., Eastern Wash. U., 1986. Project mgr. Bendix Aviation, Towson, Md., 1959-60; dir. cust. tng. Reliance Electric Co., Cleve., 1960-64; maint. supr. Kaiser Aluminum and Chemical Co., Trentwood, Wash., 1964-75, 78-85, mgr. tng., 1975-78, sr. elec. engr., 1985-99. Contbr. articles to profl. jours. Served with U.S. Army, 1957-59. Mem. Am. Soc. Tng. and Devel. (treas. 1983). Democrat. Avocations: electronic repair, metalworking. Home: Spokane, Wash. Died Apr. 6, 1999.

LONG, ROBERT BYRON, engineering consultant; b. Annville, Pa., Feb. 18, 1923; s. Morris Miller and Elizabeth Catherine (Fencil) L.; m. Marie Parker, June 24, 1944 (dec. May 1991); children: Gretchen, Gilbert, Robin, Kate, James, Bonnie. BSChemE, Pa. State U., 1944, MSChemE, 1947, PhD in Chem. Engring., 1951. Registered profl. engr., Vt. Rsch. engr. Exxon Rsch. and Engring. Co., Linden, N.J., 1950-53, project leader, 1953-57, rsch. assoc., 1957-64, sr. rsch. assoc., 1964-69, sci. advisor, 1969-84; pres. Long Cons., Inc., Atlantic Highlands, N.J., 1984-88, Stowe, Vt., 1988-93, Austin, Tex., 1993-95, College Station, Tex., from 1995. Mem. adv. bd. Petroleum Rsch. Fund, Washington, 1983-88; mem. profl. adv. coun. Pa. State Coll. Engring., State College, 1985-87; chmn. conf. Gordon Rsch. Confs., 1969. Author: Separation Processes in Waste Minimization, 1995; 66 patents in field; contbr. numerous articles to profl. jours.; internat. editor Fuel, 1976-78. Named Outstanding Engring. Alumnus, Pa. State U., 1987. Mem. AIChE, Am. Soc. Profl. Engrs., Masons (chaplain 1994). Republican. Avocation: barbershop singing. Deceased.

LONGLEY, LAWRENCE DOUGLAS, political science educator; b. Bronxville, N.Y., Nov. 12, 1939; s. Henry Nathaniel and Effie (Devers) L.; m. Judith Hostetter, June 23, 1979; children: Rebecca, Susan Richards. BA, Oberlin Coll., 1962; MA, Vanderbilt U., 1964, PhD, 1969. From instr. to assoc. prof. govt. Lawrence U., Appleton, Wis., 1965-89, prof., from 1989. Vis. assoc. prof. govt. Am. U., Washington, 1978; guest lectr. politics Imperial Coll. U. London, 1985; Fulbright chair polit. sci. Budapest (Hungary) U. Econs., 1994-95. Co-author: Politics of Electoral College Reform, 1975, The People's President, 1981, Politics of Broadcast Regulation, 1982, Bicameral Politics, 1989, Two Into One, 1991, Democrats Must Lead, 1992, Working Papers on Comparative Legislative Studies, 1994, 97, 98, 2000, The New Roles of Parliamentary Committees, 1998, The Electoral College Primer 2000, 1999, The Uneasy Relationship Between Parliamentary Members and Leaders, 2000. Mem. Dem. Nat. Com., Washington, 1989—, exec. com. 1996; mem. adminstrv. com. Wis. State Dem. Party, 1971—, exec. com., 1989—; mem. task force structure & participation Dem. Nat. Com., 1993, credentials com., 1993—; mem. Presdl. Electoral Coll., 1988, 92; coord. Wis. campaign Anderson Presdl. Campaign, 1980; John Marshall chair in Hungary Fulbright Commn., 1994-95. Mem. Internat. Polit. Sci. Assn. (co-chair electoral systems rsch. com. 1985-94, co-chair com. legis. specialists 1991—, mem. exec. coun. 1991-94), Am. Polit. Sci. Assn., Midwest Polit. Sci. Assn. (exec. coun. 1988-91), Wis. Polit. Sci. Assn. (pres. 1969-70). Democrat. Home: Appleton, Wis. Died Mar. 20, 2002.

LONGMIRE, WILLIAM POLK, JR., physician, surgeon; b. Sapulpa, Okla., Sept. 14, 1913; s. William Polk and Grace May (Weeks) L.; m. Jane Jarvis Cornelius, Oct. 28, 1939; children— William Polk III (dec.), Gill, Sarah Jane. AB, U. Okla., 1934; MD, Johns Hopkins, 1938; MD hon. degrees, U. Athens, Greece, 1972, Northwestern U., 1976, U. Lund, Sweden, 1976; MD (h.c.), U. Heidelberg, Germany, 1974. Diplomate Am. Bd. Surgery (chmn. 1961-62). Intern surgery Johns Hopkins Hosp., Balt., 1938-39, resident surgery, 1944, surgeon in charge plastic out-patient clinic, 1946-48, surgeon, 1947-48; Harvey Cushing fellow exptl. surgery Johns Hopkins, 1939-40, Halsted fellow surg. pathology, 1940, successively instr., asst. prof. assoc. prof. surgery, 1943-48; prof. surgery UCLA, 1948-81, prof. emeritus, 1981—2003, chmn. dept., 1948-76. Cons. surgery Wadsworth VA Hosp., Los Angeles County Harbor Hosp., 1945-76, VA disting. physician, 1982-87; guest prof. spl. surgery Free U. Berlin, Fed. Republic Germany, 1952-54; vis. prof. surgery Mayo Grad. Sch. Medicine, 1968, Royal Coll. Physicians and Surgeons of Can., 1968; chmn. surgery study sect. NIH, USPHS, 1961-64; mem. Conf. Com. on Grad. Edn. in Surgery, 1959-66, chmn., 1964-66; mem. spl. med. adv. group to med. dir. VA, 1963-68, vice chmn., 1967-68; chmn. surgery tng. com. NIH, 1969-70; mem. pres.' cancer panel Nat. Cancer Inst., 1982-91; Wade vis. prof. Royal Coll. Surgeons Edinburgh, 1972; nat. civilian cons. surgery Air Surgeon USAF; surg. cons. Surgeon Gen. U.S. Army, 1961-88; commr. Joint Commn. on Accreditation of Hosps., 1975-80. Editor: Advances in Surgery, 1975-76; editorial bd.: Annals of Surgery, 1965—2000. Served as maj. USAF, 1952-54; spl. cons. Air Surgeon Gen.'s Office. Recipient hon. certificate for advancement cardiovascular surgery Free U. of Berlin, 1954, certificate for high profl. achievement USAF, 1954, Gold medal UCLA, 1980, prize Societe Internationale De Chirurgie, 1987, Disting. Med. Alumni award Johns Hopkins Univ. Sch. Medicine, 1999; inducted into Okla. Hall of Fame, 1980. Fellow ACS (chmn. forum com. fundamental surg. problems 1961-62, regent 1962-71, chmn. bd. regents 1969-71, pres. 1971-73, Sheen award N.J. chpt. 1987); hon. fellow Assn. Surgeons Great Britain and Ireland, Royal Coll. Surgeons Ireland, Royal Coll. Surgeons Edinburgh, Royal Coll. Surgeons Eng., Italian Surg. Soc., Association Française de Chirurgie, Japan Surg. Soc.; mem. AMA (mem. council on med. edn. 1964-69), Soc. Scholars of Johns Hopkins U., Soc. Clin. Surgeons, Am. Surg. Assn. (pres. 1967-68), Pacific Coast Surg. Assn., Western Surg. Assn., So. Surg. Assn., Soc. U. Surgeons, Internat. Soc. Surgery, Internat. Fedn. Surg. Colls. (pres. 1984-87), Internat. Surgical Group, (pres. 1993), Am. Assn. Thoracic Surgery, Pan-Pacific Surg. Assn., Los Angeles Surg. Soc. (pres. 1956), Bay Dist. Surg. Soc., Soc. Surgery Alimentary Tract (pres. 1975-76), Calif. Med. Assn. (sec. surg. sect. 1950-51, chmn. sci. bd. 1966-67, Golden Apple award 1990), James IV Assn. Surgeons (pres. 1981), Soc. Surg. Chairmen (pres. 1970-72), Sociédad Argentina di Cirugia Digestiva (hon.), So. Surg. Assn. (hon.), Italian Surg. Soc. (hon.), Phi Beta Kappa, Alpha Omega Alpha; corr. mem. Deutsche Gesellschaft fur Chirugie. Home: Los Angeles, Calif. Died May 9, 2003.

LONGSTRETH, W. THACHER, city official; b. Haverford, Pa., Nov. 4, 1920; s. Williams Collins and Nella (Thacher) L. Grad., Princeton U., 1941. Merchandising specialist, space salesman, 1946-53; v.p. svcs. and new bus. Geare-Marston Advt., 1953-55; v.p. new bus., acct. supr. Aitkin-Kynett Advt., 1956-64; pres., CEO Greater Phila. C. of C., 1964-83; bd. dirs. Deleware Funds, 1977-98; ptnr. MLW Assocs.; councilman City of Phila., 1984—2003. City coun.-at-large, Phila., 1968-71, 84—; founder, pres., CEO Penjerdel Coun., 1972-88; ptnr. MLW Assocs., 1983—; vice chair Packquisition Corp., 1988—; chair Microleague Interactive Software. Co-author: The Main Line Wasp. Bd. dirs. Chestnut Hill Acad., Friends Select; bd. dirs. Phila. Convention & Vis. Bur., 1964—; founder Greater Delaware Valley chpt. Nat. Multiple Sclerosis Soc., 1951, chair, 1951—, emeritus bd. dirs.; mem. Southeastern Pa.chpt. ARC; bd. dirs. Pa.-Jersey Regional Blood Svc. Served in USN, 1942-46. Named outstanding grad. Haverford Sch., 1990. Mem. AFTRA, Coll. Physicians P hila., Pa. Hist. Soc. Mem. Soc. Friends. Died Apr. 11, 2003.

LOOMIE, ALBERT JOSEPH, historian; b. N.Y.C., July 29, 1922; s. Leo Stephen and Loretta Felicity (Murphy) L.; B.A., Loyola Coll., Chgo., 1944; Ph.L., West Baden U., 1946; M.A., Fordham U., 1949; S.T.L., Woodstock U., 1953; Ph.D., London U., 1957. Joined Jesuit order, 1939; ordained priest Roman Catholic Ch., 1952; mem. dept. history Fordham U., Bronx, N.Y., 1958—93, prof. history, 1969—93, prof. emeritus, 1993-2002, chmn. dept., 1978-81. Recipient Award of Merit, Am. Assn. State and Local History, 1954; Folger Library fellow, 1960, 61, 62, 70; Guggenheim fellow, 1965-66; Huntington Library fellow, 1967. Fellow Real Academia de Historia (corr.), Royal Hist. Soc. (Eng.); mem. Hispanic Soc. Am. (corr.), Am. Hist. Assn., Cath. Hist. Assn., Renaissance Soc. Am., Conf. Brit. Studies. Democrat. Roman Catholic. Author: Spanish Elizabethans, 1963, Toleration and Diplomacy, 1963, Spain and the Jacobean Catholics, 2 vols., 1973, 78, Guy Fawkes in Spain, 1971, Ceremonies of Charles I, 1987; contbr. articles in field to profl. jours. Home: New York, NY. Died Nov. 11, 2002.

LOOMIS, MARY ELLEN, psychologist; b. Detroit, Feb. 28, 1929; d. John Cochran and Margaret (McGregor) Stewart; m. Robert Gordon Loomis, Mar. 8, 1951; children: Carrie, Pamela, Margaret, Barbara, Robert, Elizabeth. BA, Mich. State U., 1950; MA in English, Wayne State U., 1974, MA in Psychology, 1978, PhD, 1980. Diplomate in analytical psychology, 1982. Writer The Detroit News, 1950-52; substitute tchr. Detroit and Grosse Pointe (Mich.) Pub. Schs., 1973-75; instr., grad. asst. Wayne State U., Detroit, 1975-80; mem. faculty C.G. Jung Inst., Chgo., from 1983, C.G. Jung Ctr., Grosse Pointe, from 1983; pvt. practice Jungian analysis Grosse Pointe, from 1982. Author: Dancing the Wheel, 1991, Her Father's Daughter, 1994; co-author personality test S.L.I.P., 1983. Trustee C.G. Jung Inst., Chgo., 1984-87, C.G. Jung Ctr., Detroit, 1981—. Mich. State U. Alumni scholarship, 1946. Mem. Internat. Assn. Analytical Psychologists, Chgo. Soc. Jungian Analysts, Am. Psychol. Assn., Mich. Psychol. Assn., Ctr. for Jung Studies of Detroit (various offices), Phi Kappa Phi. Home: Grosse Pointe, Mich. Died Sept. 23, 2000.

LOOMIS, WESLEY HORACE, III, former publishing company executive; b. Kansas City, Mo., July 29, 1913; s. Wesley Horace, Jr. and Mary (Gary) L.; m. Mary Bradford Paine, Apr. 17, 1937 (dec. Feb. 1998); children: Mary Elizabeth (Mrs. R.M. Norton), Jonathan Lee (dec.), Frederick Pierson. Grad., Hackley Sch., Tarrytown, N.Y., 1931; BS in Engring. and Bus. Adminstrn, MIT, 1935. Indsl. engr. Automatic Elec. Co., Chgo., 1935-42; pres. Loomis Advt. Co., 1946-55, Gen. Telephone Directory Co., Des Plaines, Ill., 1956-78; v.p. Dominion Directory Co., Vancouver, B.C., 1956-64, pres., 1964-78, Courtnay Pty., Ltd., Adelaide, Courtnay Pty., Ltd. S.A. Australia, Directories (Australia) Pty., Ltd., Melbourne, Australia, Gen. Telephone Directory Co. C por A, Santo Domingo, 1971-78, Directorio Telefonico Centroamericano, S.A., 1972-78; dir. Directorio Telefonico de El Salvador (SA). Pres. Episc. Charities 1969-70, dir., 1962-83, now life trustee; trustee emeritus U.S. Naval Acad. Found., Annapolis, Md.; bd. dirs. Traveler Aid Soc. Met. Chgo./Immigrants' Service League, 1957-80, pres., 1960-61; chmn. Travelers Aid Internat., Social Service Am., 1973-77; bd. dirs. Travelers Aid Assn. Am., 1977-82, pres., 1978-80; pres. Ind. Telephone Hist. Found., 1967-81, trustee, 1981-98; trustee emeritus Colby-Sawyer Coll., New London, N.H., sec., 1976-81; mem. corp. devel. com. M.I.T., 1979-81; trustee Ill. Bus. Hall of Fame, 1981-83; bd. dirs., trustee, chmn. planning com. Mote Marine Lab., Sarasota, Fla., 1983—. Served to lt. col., Ordnance AUS, 1942-46. Decorated hon. mil. mem. Order Brit. Empire; laureate Am. Nat. Bus. Hall of Fame, 1980; recipient APPY award of excellence Yellow Pages Pubs. Assn., 1998; elected to Ind. Telephone Hall of Fame, 1981, Calif. chpt., 1990. Mem. Ind. Telephone Pioneers Assn. (pres. 1964-66), Racquet Club (Chgo.), Field and Bird Key Yacht (Sarasota), Masons (32 deg.), Phi Gamma Delta. Republican. Episcopalian (warden). Home: Sarasota, Fla. Deceased.

LOPER, GEORGE WILSON, JR., physical education educator; b. Phila., Sept. 1, 1927; s. George Wilson Sr. and Emma Margaretta (Davis) L.; m. Eleanor Ruth Shell, mar. 10, 1951 (div. Aug. 1967); children: George Wilson III, Carol Ann Loper Cloud; m. Jeanne Ann Lodeski, Aug. 12, 1967; children: Lynn Jeanne Loper Sakers, Anne Marie Loper Todd, John Vincent. BS, W. Chester State U., 1954; MEd, Temple U., 1957. Cert. tchr. Fla. Tchr., coach Media (Pa.) Pub. Schs., 1954-63, Duval County Sch. System, Jacksonville, Fla., 1963-67; tchr., dept. chmn., coach Bradford County Sch. System, Starke, Fla., from 1967. Dir. March Dimes Walkathon, Starke, 1970; coord. Spl. Olympics, Starke, 1970-89; chmn. Adminstrv. Bd. First Meth. Ch., Starke, 1970; co-chmn. Toys for Tots USMC, Starke, 1976, 78. With USMC Res., 1945-87. Named Coach of Yr. Fla. Times Union, 1966, 67, Coach of Yr. Cross Country Gainesville Sun, 1985, 86; recipient Lifetime Achievement award Govs. Coun. on Phys. Fitness and Sports, 1997, Award Hartwell Conklin Golden South Classic, 1997. Mem. AAHPERD (life), NEA, Nat. Health Assn. (life), Nat. High Sch. Coaches Assn., Fla. Athletic Coaches Assn. (state vice chmn. 1972—, Meritorious Svc. awrd 1988, Nat. Boys Track Coach of Yr. 1991, Life Membership award 1992), The Athletic Congress (lead instr. 1987—, internat. level track ofcl. 1983—, Track Hall of Fame 1987), Fla. Ofcls. Assn. (high sch. games com. 1964—, state vice chmn. track 1972—), Bradford Edn. Assn. (v.p. 1977-79) Democrat. Methodist. Avocations: reading, music, art, swimming and track officiating. Home: Starke, Fla. Died Sept. 18, 2000.

LOPEZ, EUGENIO, holding company executive; b. Manila, Nov. 4, 1928; married; 7 children. Owner Manila Chronicle; pres., CEO Benpres Holdings Corp., Manila, ABS-CBN Broadcasting Corp., Manila Elec. Corp.; co-owner Philippine Comml. Internat. Bank. Polit. prisioner, The Philippines, 1972-77. Died 1999.

LOPEZ LARA, JOSE, bishop; b. Moroleon, Mex., Mar. 19, 1927; Ordained priest Roman Cath. Ch., 1953. Bishop of, Huajuapan de Leon, Mex., 1968-82, San Juan de los Lagos, Mex., from 1982. Died Apr. 27, 1987.

LORANTAS, RAYMOND MARTIN, historian, educator; b. Elizabeth, Pa., Feb. 1, 1928; s. Justin and Agnes (Supanis) L.; m. Barbara Anne Bradshaw, Aug. 2, 1969; 1 child, Glenn Seng. PhD, U. Pa., 1963. Asst. to assoc. prof. Drexel U., Phila.; sr. lectr. The Chinese U. of Hong Kong; prof. Tianjin Fgn. Langs. Inst., China. Co-host Conf. of the Chinese Soc. of Ancient and Medieval World Historians, Tianjin, 1993. Recipient fellowships NEH, 1976, 80, Mary and Christian Lindback Teaching award, 1968, Educator of Yr. award Interfraternity Coun., Drexel U., 1976. Mem. World History Assn. (pres. 1992-94), Am. Hist. Assn. (Africa travel/study grant 1982), Modern European Historians of Phila. (pres. 1965-66, 75-76), Assn. Asian Studies, N.Am. Assn. for Cameroonian Studies, ACLU, AAUP, Nat. History Teaching Alliance. Home: Flourtown, Pa. Died Apr. 14, 2000.

LORAS, JAMES, small business owner; b. El Paso, Apr. 12, 1928; s. James E. and Kyriake (Tollias) L.; m. Doris Jean Loras; children: Dorothy Jean, Steve, Scott; m. Wanda Lee. BS, U. Tex., El Paso, 1951; MS, So. Meth. U., 1960. Dir. engring. E-Systems, Dallas, 1951-71; chmn. bd. Rsch. Tech., Inc., Dallas, 1971-76; pres. Loras Industries Inc., Dallas, from 1977. Cons. F&M Systems, Dallas, 1976-78. With USN, 1946-47, Japan, China. Republican. Avocations: swimming, tennis, fishing, boating, golf. Home: Dallas, Tex. Deceased.

LORD, ARTHUR ABRAM, television producer; b. N.Y.C., Mar. 3, 1942; s. Benjamin and Kathryn (Zucker) L.; m. Susan E. Tallman, Aug. 28, 1965; children: Michael, Sharon. Student, Ohio Wesleyan U., 1961; BS in Journalism, U. Fla., 1963. Newswriter NBC, N.Y.C., 1967-71, war corr. Saigon, Vietnam, 1971-73, S.W. bur. dir. Houston, 1973-79, network news dir. Burbank, Calif., 1979-82, producer, from 1982. Cons. (TV movie) Special Bulletin, 1983. Producer news feature Heart Transplant, 1980 (Emmy award 1981): Writer news spl. Apollo to the Moon, 1970 (Emmy award 1970); contbr. articles to TV Guide. Served to capt. USAF, 1963-67. Recipient Nat. Merit award Houston Urban League, 1975, Peabody award, 1985. Mem. TV News Dirs. Assn. Clubs: Mid Valley Athletic. Jewish. Avocations: pvt. pilot, tennis, freelance writing. Home: Tarzana, Calif. Died Sept. 25, 2002.

LORD JENKINS OF HILLHEAD, See JENKINS, ROY HARRIS

LORSCH, HAROLD GOETZ, research engineering educator; b. Frankfurt, Germany, Aug. 25, 1919; came to U.S., 1941; s. William B. and Erna E. (Landau) L.; m. Edith Ilse Feistman, Nov. 16, 1947; children: Tim, Rita, Jeffrey. MS, MIT, 1942; PhD, Columbia U., 1953. Registered profl. engr., N.Y. Draftsman Stone & Webster, Boston, 1941-42; designer, draftsman Irington Form & Tank, N.Y.C., 1946-47; structural designer D.B. Steinman, N.Y.C., 1947-48; instr. NYU, N.Y.C., 1948-50; asst. prof. CCNY, N.Y.C., 1950-57; civil engr. Lublin McGaughey, Paris, 1955; head of stress analysis Curtiss-Wright Corp., Wood-Ridge, N.J., 1957-60; mgr. in space divsn. GE, Valley Forge, Pa., 1960-70; rschr. in energy U. Pa., Phila., 1970-73; mgr. Franklin Inst., Phila., 1973-83; prof. Drexel U., Phila., from 1983. Mem. Tech. Adv. Com., State of Pa., Harrisburg, 1988—. Translator: Influence Lines, 1952, Rigid Frame Formulas, 1953; editor: Air Conditioning System Design, 1993; contbr. numerous papers and reports on energy topics to profl. publs.; patentee in field. Mem. Citizens Coalition for Energy Efficiency, Phila., 1988—, PennJerDel, Phila., 1992—. With U.S. Army, 1943-46, PTO. Fellow ASHRAE (com. mem. 1973—), ASCE (life). Avocations: skiing, hiking, tennis, piano. Died Nov. 28, 2001.

LOTZ, WALTER EDWARD, JR., retired army officer, government scientist, engineer; b. Johnsonburg, Pa., Aug. 21, 1916; s. Walter Edward and Maude (Colvin) L.; m. Shirley Carter Colton, Dec. 23, 1939; children: Shirley Virginia, Roger Colton, Anne Colvin. BS, U.S. Mil. Acad., 1938; MS in Elec. Engring, U. Ill., 1947; PhD in Physics, U. Va., 1953; D.Sc. (hon.), Fla. Inst. Tech., 1971. Commd. 2d lt. U.S. Army, 1938, advanced through grades to lt. gen., 1971; dep. comdg. gen. Ft. Monmouth, 1962-63; dir. army research Washington, 1963-65; asst. chief staff, communications-electronics U.S. Mil. Assistance Command, Vietnam, 1965-66; chief communications-electronics Dept. Army, 1966-68; comdg. gen. U.S. Army Strategic Communications Command, 1968-69, U.S. Army Electronics Command, 1969-71; dep. dir. gen. NATO Integrated Communications System Mgmt. Agy., 1971-74; ret., 1974; dir. test and evaluation Dept. Def., Washington, 1975-77; cons. TRW, Inc., 1980—; dir. Genisco Tech. Corp., 1980—. Decorated D.S.M. (2), Legion of Merit (4), Army Commendation medal (2), Bronze Star; named Distinguished Alumnus Electronics Engring. U. Ill., 1972 Fellow IEEE, Radio Club Am.; mem. Tau Beta Pi. Home: Alexandria, Va. Deceased.

LOUBE, IRVING, lawyer, corporation executive; b. Winnepeg, Can., Dec. 19, 1918; s. Samuel and Alice (Chasin) L.; m. Shirley P. Lombardero, Feb. 22, 1922; children: Garrett David, Suzanne Adrienne. AB, U. Calif., Berkeley, 1941, JD, 1951. Bar: Calif. 1951, U.S. Dist. Ct. (no. dist.) Calif., U.S. Ct. Apls. (9th cir.). Assoc., Harold Strom, 1952-53; ptnr. Loube & Rounseville, 1954-60, Loube & Lewis, 1961-66, Loube, Lewis & Blum, 1967-72, Loube, Lewis, Lowen & Albers, 1973-80, Loube, Lewis, Lowen, Albers & Klein, 1981-82; sr. ptnr. Loube, Lewis, Lowen, Klein & Lando, 1983—; bd. dirs. Convalescent Hosp. Honolulu, Park Marino Health Ctr., Loube & Loube, Calif., Found. for Cardiac Rsch., Diversified Health Svcs., Van Nuys Psychiat. Hosp. Mem. Calif. Bar Assn., County Alameda Bar Assn. Republican. Jewish. Clubs: St. Francis Yacht, Waikiki Yacht, The Family, Richmond Yacht. Died 2003.

LOUDON, DOROTHY, actress; b. Boston, Sept. 17, 1933; d. James E. and Dorothy Helen (Shaw) L.; m. Norman Paris, Dec. 18, 1971 (dec.) Student, Syracuse U., 1950-51, Emerson Coll., summers 1950, 51, Alviene Sch. Dramatic Art, 1952, 53, The Am. Acad. Dramatic Art. Appeared in nat. repertory cos. of The Effect of Gamma Rays on Man in the Moon Marigolds, 1970, Plaza Suite, 1971, Luv, 1965, Anything Goes, 1967; appeared in Broadway prodns. Nowhere to Go But Up, 1962 (Theatre World award), Sweet Potato, 1968, Fig Leaves Are Falling, 1969 (Tony nominee), Three Men on a Horse, 1969 (Drama Desk award), The Women, 1973, Annie (Tony award, Drama Desk award, Outer Critics Circle award), 1976 (Dance Educators Am. award), Ballroom, 1979 (Tony nominee), Sweeney Todd, 1980, West Side Waltz, 1981 (Sarah Siddons award), Noises Off, 1983 (Tony nomination), Jerry's Girls, 1985 (Tony nomination), Driving Miss Daisy, 1988, Annie 2, 1990, Comedy Tonight, 1994, Love Letters, 1995, Showboat, 1996, N.Y. Encore series, 1997; appeared in film Garbo Talks, 1984, Midnight in the Garden of Good and Evil, 1997; numerous appearances on TV variety and talk shows; latest TV appearances In Performance at the White House, A Salute to Stephen Sondheim at Carnegie Hall, 1992; star TV show Dorothy, 1979; appeared in supper clubs The Blue Angel, Le Ruban Bleu, Persian Room; rec.: (CDs) Saloon, Broadway Baby. Mem. SAG, AFTRA, Actors Equity. Died Nov. 15, 2003.

LOUGHRIN, HARRY JOSEPH, physician; b. Cadillac, Mich., Oct. 30, 1926; MD, Univ. Mich., 1953. Intern Indiana Gen. Hosp., Indpls., 1953-54; resident ob-gyn Univ. Hosp., Cleveland, Ohio, 1957-60; ob-gyn E W Sparrow Hosp., Lansing, Mich., from 1992; clinical prof. ob-gyn Mich. State Univ., East Lansing, from 1990, ret. Mem. Am. Coll. Obstetricians & Gynecologists. Home: Holland, Mich. Died Aug. 14, 2000.

LOURIE, DANIEL NORMAN, retired educator, librarian; b. Johannesburg, Dec. 14, 1928; came to U.S., 1940; s. Arthur and Clara Ruth (Chase) L. BA, Brandeis U., 1957. Mem. staff Brandeis U., Waltham, Mass., 1959-60, asst. reference librarian, 1966-76; asst. librarian London U., 1961-62; tchr. ESL to fgn. grad. students and vis. scholars, 1983-86. Vol. Cultural Survival, Cambridge, Mass., 1973—, Am. Friends Svc. Com., 1980, Medford Pub. Libr., 1981-82, transitional yr. program Brandeis U., 1982, Boston Ctr. for Internat. Visitors, 1978-79. Mem. Soc. for Preservation New Eng. Activities (life). Democrat. Jewish. Avocations: stamp collecting/philately, travel. Home: Cambridge, Mass. Deceased.

LOVE, DOROTHY MCGUIRE, nursing educator; b. Pitts., Nov. 12, 1931; d. Audrey and Alene McGuire; m. May 1, 1953; children: Kimberly, Michael. Diploma, West Penn Hosp. Sch. Nursing, Pitts., 1953; BSN, U. Pitts., 1973. Cert. orthopaedic nurse. Staff nurse, head nurse labor and delivery room West Penn Hosp., 1953-58; prof. nursing C.C. Allegheny County, Pitts., 1973-91. Mem. Nat. Assn. Orthopaedic Nurses, Sigma Theta Tau. Home: Pittsburgh, Pa. Died Nov. 11, 2000.

LOVE, EDWARD A. art educator; Archtl. design student, U. So. Calif., 1960-61; BFA in Sculpture, UCLA, 1965-66, MFA in Design, 1966-67; student, U. Uppsala, Sweden, 1967-68. Sr. engring. draftsman Norht Am. Aviation Corp., Downey, Calif., 1961-65; prof. art, dir. sculpture program Howard U., Washington, 1968-87; founding dean visual arts div. New World Sch. Arts, Miami, Fla., 1987-90; prof. art, dir. undergrad studies Fla. State U., Tallahassee, 1990-99. Archtl. designer interim asst. project. Outdoor Recreational Ctrs., Washington, 1969; artist-in-residence Workshops for

Careers in Arts, Washington, 1973-74; bd. advisors Washington Project for Arts, 1981-82; bd. advisors Nat. Found. Advancement of Arts, Miami, 1988-90. One-man exhibits: the Corcoran Gallery of Ary, Washington, 1975, Washington Project for Arts, 1981, Howard U., Washington, 1986, Montpelier Arts Ctr., Laurel, Md., 1987, Miami-Dade Community Coll., Fla., 1988, Brickell Square, Miami, 1989, U. Gallery, Tallahassee, 1990, The Forum, St. Louis, 1991; traveling exhibitions: Southeastern Ctr. for Contemporaty Art, 1992-99, Dallas Museum of Art, 1989-91, U.S. Info. Agy., 1990-91; speaker and writer in field. Active Habitat for Humanity, 1991-99, The Project Box, 1988-99. With USAF, 1954-58. Recipient Individual Arts award D.C. Commn. on Arts, 1986, Mayor's award D.C., 1987, Art Educator Recognition award The Pratt Inst., 1990, Disting. Alumni award Calif. State U.; Guggenheim fellow 1987. Mem. Am. Assn. U. Profs., Nat. Conf. of Artists. Home: Amherst, Mass. Died Mar. 22, 1999.

LOVELAND, LAURIE JEAN, lawyer; b. Minot, N.D., Sept. 5, 1958; d. George Newell Loveland and Caroline Ruth (Borgen) Weninger. BA, N.D. State U., 1979; JD, Yale U., 1983. Bar: Ill. 1983, N.D. 1985, U.S. Dist. Ct. (no. dist.) Ill. 1983, U.S. Dist. Ct. N.D. 1985, U.S. Ct. Appeals (8th cir.) 1985, U.S. Supreme Ct. 1987. Assoc. Sonnenschein, Carlin, Nath & Rosenthal, Chgo., 1983-84; law clk. to Hon. Albert J. Engel U.S. Ct. Appeals, 6th cir., Grand Rapids, Mich., 1984-85; asst. atty. gen. N.D. Atty. Gen.'s Office, Bismarck, 1985-89, dir. state and local govt., 1989, solicitor gen., from 1989. Reading tutor Bismarck Adult Learning Ctr., 1988-91. Mem. Nat. Assn. Attys. Gen. (fellow). Home: Bismarck, ND. Died Apr. 18, 2002.

LOVER, MYRON JORDAN, pharmaceutical chemist; b. N.Y.C., July 26, 1924; s. Earle J. and Sally (Swade) L.; m. Vera Martha Markus, Sept. 15, 1953; children: Melanie, Melissa. BA, N.Y. U., 1944, MS, 1947, PhD, 1950. Post doctoral fellow U. Va., 1950-51; dir. rsch. Am. Home Products, Cranford, N.J., 1951-64; staff asst. Revlon Rsch. Ctr., Bronx, N.Y., 1964-65; dir. devel. rsch. Merck & Co., Inc., Rahway, N.J., 1965-72; dir. devel. Alcon Labs, Owen Labs. Div., Ft. Worth, 1972-73; dir. rsch. Reed & Carnrick, Piscataway, N.J., 1973-90; pres. Mountainside (N.J.) Assoc., Inc., from 1990. Treas. NYU Chemistry Alumni, N.Y.C., 1968-72; sec. Aerosol com. Am. Assn. Pharm. Scis., Washington, 1985-90; dir. Medenta Corp., Ft. Lauderdale, Fla., 1991-92. Contbr. articles to scholarly jours. With U.S. Army, 1944-46. Mem. Am. Chemical Soc., Am. Assn. Pharm. Scientists, Sigma Xi, Phi Lamba Upsilon. Achievements include over 200 U.S. and foreign patents. Home: Westwood, NJ. Deceased.

LOWE, FLORENCE SEGAL, retired public relations executive; b. N.Y.C.; d. Samuel I. and Rose (Cantor) Segal; BS in Edn., U. Pa., 1930; postgrad. Sch. Social Svc., 1935-36; m. Herman Albert Lowe, June 27, 1935; children: Lesley Ellen Lowe Israel, Roger Bernard. Guidance counsellor Phila. Pub. Schs., 1935-41; Washington corr. Variety and Daily Variety, Phila. Daily News, Manchester Union Leader, TV Guide, 1942-58; spl. pub. rels. Radio Sta. WIP, Phila. and Metromedia, 1958-60; coord. spl. projects Metromedia, 1960-70; spl. asst. to chmn. pub. affairs NEA, Washington, 1970-86; sr. cons. arts and cultural comm. Kamber Group, 1986-93, ret., 1994. Mem. pub. rels. and advt. com. Nat. Symphony, 1952-56; mem. Sec. State's Commn. on Travel, 1970-71; mem. Coordinating Com. for Ellis Island, 1982-87; bd. dirs. Women of the Year award banquet, 1994-95; mem. Com. for Nancy Hanks Endowment for Arts, Duke U. Recipient All-Army Entertainment Contest award, 1958; spl. achievement award Nat. Endowment for Arts Chmn., 1983; Spl. Merit award Fed. Govt., 1981, Spl. Achievement award, 1983, Disting. Svc. award, 1985. Mem. Am. Women in Radio and TV (founder, pres. 1954-55), Am. News Women's Club (Woman of Yr. com.), Coun. Jewish Women, Women in Communications (citation for meritorious reporting 1962), Nat. Press Club, Women's Nat. Press Club (treas. 1954, v.p. 1956), Washington Press Club (bd. dirs. 1968-71, 83-84), Am. News Women's Club (v.p. 1969-70), Washington Press Club Found. Home: Washington, DC. Died Nov. 14, 2002.

LOWE, RONALD, SR., chief of police; b. Dayton, Ohio; Student, U. Dayton, Wright State U., Ohio State U., Sinclair C.C.; grad., FBI Acad., 1988; grad. Sr. Exec. Inst., U. Va. Police officer Dayton Police Dept., 1974-83, sgt., 1983-87, police maj., supt. profl. stds., 1987-90, police maj., supt. ops., 1990-83; chief of police Chatham, Ga., 1993-95; dir., chief of police Dayton Police Dept., from 1995. Recipient Police medal of honor, Masonic Comty. Svc. award, Soc. Bank Officer of Yr. award, Legis. awards for outstanding svc. U.S. Congress, Ohio House and Senate, Ga. House and Senate, numerous comty. svc. awards and honors; named Police Officer of Yr. Mem. Internat. Assn. Chiefs of Police, Pub. Mgmt. Assn., Profl. Exec. Leadership Coll. Assn., Nat. Orgn. Black Law Enforcement Execs., Am. Colls. Criminal Justice Scis., FBI Nat. Acad., FBI Law Enforcement Exec. Devel. Assn., U.S. Secret Svc. Dignitary Protection Affiliate, Ohio Assn. Chiefs of Police, Montgomery County Chiefs of Police Assn. Avocations: computers, music, reading, weight lifting. Died Nov. 2002.

LOWENSTINE, MAURICE RICHARD, JR., retired steel executive; b. Valparaiso, Ind., Feb. 28, 1910; s. Maurice Richard and Etta (Hamburger) L.; m. Miriam Jean Richards, Nov. 9, 1940; children: Martha Jean, Linda Jane, Mark Richards. Student, U. Mich., 1928-29, U. Ariz., 1929-30. With Central Steel & Wire Co., Chgo., 1932-71, exec. v.p., treas., dir., 1942-71. Chmn. exec. com. Steel Service Center Inst., 1962-64 Chmn. bd. Greater Hinsdale Cmty. Chest, 1960; bd. dirs. Chgo. area coun. Boy Scouts Am., 1957-2001, Hinsdale Cmty. House, 1961-64; vice commodore Chgo. Sea Explorer Scouts, 1973-2001. Mem.: Chgo. Yacht; Ruth Lake Country. Episcopalian. Deceased.

LOWERY, BILL, music publisher, consultant; b. Leesville, La., Oct. 21, 1924; s. William J. and Elizabeth (McCracken).; m. Billie Green, Sept. 29, 1924; children: Cheryl Gene, Terri Lynn, Bill Jr. Grad., Leesville High Sch. Radio announcer Sta. KWKH, Shreveport, La., 1942-43, Sta. KTHS, Hot Springs, Ark., 1943-44, Sta. KTOK, Oklahoma City, 1944, Sta. KWFT, Wichita Falls, Tex., 1944-45; mgr. Sta. WBEJ, Elizabethtown, Tenn., 1945-46; DJ program dir. Sta. WQXI, Atlanta, 1946-48; radio personality Sta. WGST, Atlanta, 1948-54; TV personality Sta. WLW-A, Atlanta, 1954-56; music pub. The Lowery Group Mus. Pub. Cos. (music pubs. over 39 yrs.), Atlanta, 1953-88. More than 5,000 records including million performance songs: all-time-classic Be-Bop-A-Lula, I Love the Nightlife, Champagne Jam, So In To You, Games People Play (two Grammy awards 1969), Rose Garden (Robert Burton award 1971), Walk On By, Down In The Boondocks, Young Love, Key Largo, What Kind of Fool Do You Think I Am., Spooky, Traces, Stormy, Imaginary Lover. Pres. Country Music Found., Friends Ga. Music Festival, 1978-88; mem. elections com. Ga. Music Hall of Fame. Inducted into Ga. Music Hall of Fame, 1978, named by Gov. to Ga. Mus. Hall of Fave Authority to build Hall of Fame; Bill Lowery Scholarship Fund was established at Ga. State U. Sch. Comml. Music., 1977. Mem. NARAS (past nat. pres.), Nat. Music Pubs. Assn. (bd. dirs.), Nat. Acad. Popular Music, Country Music Assn. (bd. dirs.), Variety Club, Omicron Delta Kappa. At age 21 the youngest sta. mgr. in Am. radio. Home: Atlanta, Ga. Died June 8, 2004.

LOWMAN, GEORGE FREDERICK, lawyer; b. N.Y.C., Oct. 29, 1916; s. William H. and Mary (Canty) L.; m. Mary Farrell, Oct. 4, 1947; children— John F., Peter H., Patricia A. AB, Harvard U., 1938, JD, 1942. Bar: Conn. 1946. Since practiced in, Stamford; assoc. Cummings & Lockwood, 1946-52, ptnr., 1952-86, of counsel, from 1986. Chmn. bd. dirs., chmn. exec. com. Farrell Lines, Inc.; bd. dirs. S.S. Owners Mutual Protection and Indemnity Assn., Inc.; bd. govs. Nat. Maritime Coun.; bd. mgrs. Am. Bur. Shipping, 1980-86. Chmn. Darien YMCA-YWCA fund campaign, 1956; chmn. fund campaign Darien ARC, 1953-54, bd. dirs., 1953-59; mem. exec. com. Alfred W. Dater council Boy Scouts Am., 1956; chmn. Darien Cancer Fund, 1959-60; pres., bd. dirs. Silvermine Guild Artists, 1967-77; bd. dirs., trustee King Sch., Stamford; trustee Low-Heywood Sch.; advisory com. U. Bridgeport Law Sch.; pres. B/G India House, N.Y.C., 1980—; trustee Am. Merchant Marine Mus., 1997—. Lt. col. AUS, 1942-46. Decorated Legion of Merit, Bronze Star; recipient Admiral of the Sea Aotos award United Seamen's Svc., 1998; named to Internat. Hall of Fame Maritime Assn. of N.Y., N.J., 1996. Fellow Am. Coll. Trial Lawyers, Internat. Acad. Trial Lawyers, Am. Bar Found.; mem. ABA, Conn. Bar Assn. (past pres.), Stamford Bar Assn. (past pres., Conn. state trial referee 1983-96), Harvard U. Alumni Assn. (v.p.), Marine Soc. N.Y.C. (hon.), St. Andrew's Soc., Conn. Srs. Golf Assn., Delta Upsilon. Home: Darien, Conn. Died Oct. 2, 1999.

LOWREY, RICHARD WILLIAM, architect; b. Phila., June 11, 1938; s. Charles William and Ethel May (Straley) L.; m. Eileen Joanne Wallace, Jan. 28, 1989; children: Jodi, Erika, Melanie, Ian. BArch, Pa. State U., 1962. Registered architect, Mass., Pa.; registered real estate salesman, Mass. Project mgr. Nolen, Swinburne & Assocs., Phila., 1962-64, project architect, 1968-69; project architect Harold E. Wagoner FAIA, Phila., 1964-68; constrn. mgr. Cape Lands Realty & Bldg. Corp., Brewster, Mass., 1969-70; v.p. David M. Crawley Assocs., Inc., Plymouth, Mass., 1970-75; owner Lowrey Assocs., Architects, Plymouth, 1975-84; pres. Architects Lowrey & Blanchard, Inc., Plymouth, 1984-88; pvt. practice Plymouth, from 1988. South Shore editor Mugs Away, 1989-90. Mem. Plymouth Hist. Dist. Commn., 1979-95; trustee Old Colony Natural History Soc., 1979-95; corp. mem. Plymouth Pub. Libr., 1984—, Old Colony Club, 1986—; chmn. design com. Plymouth Downtown/Harbor Project. Recipient Plymouth County Renaissance award, 1980, 87, 88. Mem. Minute Man Dart League (award 1989, area rep. 1989-90, capt. Parrotheads dart team 1992—), Am. Darts Orgn. (area coord. 1989-90), Nat. Coun. Archtl. Registration Bds. (cert.), Masons, Kiwanis (disting. past pres. Plymouth chpt. 1980-81). Congregationalist. Avocations: music, photography, reading, darts. Died Jan. 2, 1999.

LOWRY, BATES, art historian, museum director; b. Cin., June 21, 1923; s. Bates and Eleanor (Meyer) L.; m. Isabel Barrett (dec. 2003), Dec. 7, 1946; children: Anne, Patricia. PhB, U. Chgo., 1944, MA, 1952, PhD, 1955. Asst. prof. U. Calif., Riverside, 1954-57, Inst. Fin. Arts NYU, 1957-59; prof., chmn. dept. art Pomona Coll., Claremont, 1959-63, Brown U., Providence, 1963-68; dir. Mus. Modern Art, N.Y.C., 1968-69; prof., chmn. dept. art U. Mass., Boston, 1971-80; dir. Nat. Bldg. Mus., Washington, 1980-87. Cons. dept. photography Getty Mus., 1992; disting. vis. prof. U. Del. Newark, 1988-89; founder, pres. Com. to Rescue Italian Art, 1966-76; mem. arts coun. MIT, 1974-80. Author: Visual Experience, 1961, Renaissance Architecture, 1962, Muse or Ego, 1963, Building a National Image, 1985, Looking for Leonardo, 1993, The Silver Canvas, 1998; editor: College Art Association Monograph Series, 1957-59, 65-68, Architecture of Washington, D.C., 1977-79, Art Bull., 1965-68; mem. editorial bd. Smithsonian Instn. Press, 1981-87. Mem. bd. cons. NEH, 1975-81. With U.S. Army, 1942-45. Decorated Grand Officer of Order of Star of Solidarity, Italy, 1967; recipient Gov.'s award for contbn. to art, R.I., 1967; fellow Guggenheim Found., 1972, Inst. for Advanced Study, 1971. Mem. Coll. Art Assn. (bd. dirs. 1962-65), Soc. Archtl. Historians (bd. dirs. 1959-61, 63-65), Dunlap Soc. (pres. 1974-92), Academia del Disegno (hon. mem. Italy). Home: Boston, Mass. Died Mar. 12, 2004.

LUBKIN, YALE JAY, electrical engineer, consultant; b. Bklyn., June 30, 1931; s. Samuel and Frances (Rosen) L.; m. Gloria Becker, June 18, 1953 (div. Apr. 1968); children: David, Sharon; m. Veronica Mary Pole, May 13, 1968; children: Sara, Adam, Judith, Samantha, Jeremy, Barbara, Jennifer, Avram, Emily, Rachel, Arik. BSEE, U. Penna., 1953; MSEE, MIT, 1954; MS in Math., NYU, 1963; PhD in Applied Math., Sussex (Eng.) Coll. Tech., 1970. Registered profl. engr., N.Y., Pa. Sr. engr. W.L. Maxson Corp, 1956-57; engr. Airborne Instrument Labs., 1957-59; mgr. advanced devel. Consol. Avionics Corp., 1959-60; prin. sys. engr. Loral Electronics, 1960-62; pres. Lubkin Assocs., Inc., cons., 1962-70; dept. head intelligence and acoustics Eljim, Israel, 1970-72; dir. advanced tech. Litton Amecom, 1985-86; pres. Ben Franklin Industries, Owings, Md., 1972-85 and from 87. Assoc. prof., dept. head N.Y. Inst. Tech., Bklyn. Poly. Grad. Sch. Author 4 books; contbr. over 100 articles to sci. jours. Lt. Ordnance Corps, U.S. Army, 1954-56; col. USAR, 1953-86. Fellow NSF, N.Y. Bd. Regents. Fellow ISPE; mem. Triple Nine Soc., Old Crows (charter). Republican. Jewish. Achievements include invention of permissive action link as used by U.S. and Russian allies to prevent unauthorized arming of nuclear weapons. Died Aug. 12, 2001.

LUCKING, PETER STEPHEN, marketing consultant, industrial engineer; b. Kalamazoo, Oct. 11, 1945; s. Henry William, Sr., and Mary (Lynn) L.; m. Marilyn Barbara Jensen, Dec. 18, 1971. BA, Western Mich. U., 1968; BS in Indsl. Engring., 1973. Indsl. engr. Motorola, Phoenix, 1974, Revlon, Inc., Phoenix, 1974-75; indsl. engr. Hooker Chem. and Plastics Co., Niagara Falls, N.Y., 1975-76, sr. corp. indsl. engr., 1976-77; indsl. engr. Carborundum Co., Niagara Falls, 1977-78; cons. H.B. Maynard and Co., Pitts., 1978-85; mgr. indsl. engring. Carrier, Tyler, Tex., 1985-88; cons. H.B. Maynard and Co., Pitts., 1988-92; pres., mktg. cons. MARPET Systems, Inc., 1992—; sr. specialist mfg. engring. Boeing Co., 1997—; lectr. in field, 1989; co-chmn. Florissant Post Office Adv. Coun. Advisor, Jr. Achievement, Niagara Falls, 1977. Author chpts. to books. Sec. Lewis Clark chpt. Vietnam Vets. Am.; served with U.S. Army, 1969-70, Vietnam. Mem. Inst. Indsl. Engrs. (sr. mem., region v.p. 1983-85), Inst. Indsl. Engrs. (pres. Niagara Frontier chpt. 1977-78, paper presented fall conf.), St. Louis Fencer's Club (v.p.). Democrat. Roman Catholic.

LUDGIN, CHESTER HALL, baritone, actor; b. N.Y.C., May 20, 1925; s. Michael and Dora Josephine L. Student, Lafayette Coll., 1943, Am. Theatre Wing Profl. Tng. Program, 1948-50. Premiere leading baritone roles in: The Crucible, 1961, The Golem, 1962, Angle of Repose, 1976, A Quiet Place, 1983; appeared in major opera houses throughout the world, including San Francisco Opera Co., N.Y.C. Opera Co., Netherlands Opera, La Scala Opera, Vienna State Opera; singing actor in: musical comedies including Kismet, summer 1972, Most Happy Fella, summer 1977, Shenandoah, summer, 1978, Student Prince, summer 1980, South Pacific, summer 1981, Fanny, summer 1986. Co-chmn. exec. com. Norman Treigle Meml. Fund, 1975—2003. Served with inf. U.S. Army, 1943-46. Mem. Am. Guild Musical Artists, Actors Equity, AGVA, AFTRA. Home: New York, NY. Died Aug. 9, 2003.

LUDWIG, RICHARD MILTON, English literature educator, librarian; b. Reading, Pa., Nov. 24, 1920; s. Ralph O. and Millie (Smeltzer) L. AB, U. Mich., 1942; A.M., Harvard U., 1943, PhD, 1950. Mem. faculty Princeton U., 1950-86, prof. English, 1968-86, prof. emeritus, 1986—2003, dir. spl. program humanities, 1956-64; dir. Am. civilization program, 1969-71, assoc. univ. librarian for rare books and spl. collections, 1974-85. Teaching fellow Harvard, 1946-50, mem. faculty summer sch., 1951, 52 Editor Princeton U. Library Chronicle, 1977-85; editor: Aspects of American Poetry, 1963, Letters of Ford Madox Ford, 1965, Dr. Panofsky & Mr. Tarkington, 1974; co-editor: Major American Writers, 1952, Nine Short Novels, 1952, Guide to American Literature and Its Backgrounds, Since 1890, 1972, Literary History of the United States, 1974, Advanced Composition, 1977, Annals of American Literature, 1986, 89. Served with AUS, 1944-46. Dexter traveling fellow Harvard, 1950; Jonathan Edwards preceptor Princeton, 1954-57; McCosh Faculty fellow, 1967-68 Mem. MLA, Am. Studies Assn. Home: Princeton, NJ. Died Apr. 28, 2003.

LUNA, GREGORY, lawyer, state legislator; BA, Trinity U.; JD, St. Mary's U., 1965. Mem. Tex. Ho. of Reps., 1985-92, vice-chair pub. edn. com., mem. select joint com. on edn., others; mem. Tex. Senate, from 1993, vice chair edn. com., vice chmn. vets. affairs and mil. installations com., mem. jurisprudence com., mem. state affairs com., others. Founder, past bd. chair Mexican Am. Legal Def. and Ednl. Fund; chair bd. dirs. Inman Christian Ctr.; nat. bd. dirs. Project SER; bd. dirs. Big Bros./Big Sisters, United Way; mem. State and Bexar County Dem. Exec. Com. Recipient Nat. and State Premier award for extraordinary svc. Mexican Am. Legal Def. and Ednl. Fund, 1991, award Tex. State Tchrs. Assn. Alamo Dist., 1991, Recognition award Assn. Tex. Profl. Educators, 1991, Friend of Edn. award Tex. State Tchrs. Assn., 1992. Democrat. Home: San Antonio, Tex. Deceased.

LUNDBERG, LARRY THOMAS, business executive; b. Pleasanton, Kans., Mar. 19, 1938; s. William Rex and Lucille Maxine (Rosebrook) L.; m. Sharon Colleen Kirksey, Jan. 26, 1957; children: Julie, John, William. BA, U. Wash., 1965; postgrad., Wash. State U., 1974-80. Cert. secondary tchr. Clerk G.N.Ry., Wenatchee/Seattle, 1957-65; tchr. Grandview (Wash.) Sch. Dist., 1965-66, South Kitsap Sch. Dist., Port Orchard, Wash., 1966-67; acctg. supr. Weyerheauser Co., Tacoma, 1967-69; pres., chief exec. officer Commander Bd. Wash., Seattle, 1969-70; asst. exec. dir. Wash. State Sch. Dirs., Olympia, 1970-80; gen. mgr., CEO Trout, Inc., Chelan, Wash., from 1980. Author: Negotiations, 1978. Bd. dirs. Traffic Assn., Wenatchee, Wash., 1987—; commr. Wash. State Apple, 1995. With U.S. Army, 1957-60. Mem. Internat. Apple Inst. (bd. dirs. 1988—), Chelan, Wash. C. of C. (bd. dirs. 1989—). Deceased.

LUNDIN, ANDREW PETER, III, physician; b. Kansas City, Mo., Jan. 4, 1944; s. Andrew Peter and Virginia Ann Lundin; m. Maureen Fitzgerald, Sept. 14, 1974 (dec. 2000). BA in Biology, Stanford U., 1968; MD summa cum laude, SUNY, Bklyn., 1972. Resident medicine Kings County SUNY Downstate, Bklyn., 1972-74; fellow in nephrology rsch. Peter Bent Brigham, Boston, 1974-76; fellow in clin. nephrology Kings County Hosp. Ctr. SUNY Downstate, Bklyn., 1976-77; chief nephrology VA Med. Ctr., Bklyn., 1977-80; dir. ambulatory hemodialysis SUNY Downstate, Bklyn., 1980-89, Kings County Hosp., Bklyn., 1989-2001. Cons. in field. Mem. Am. Assn. Kidney Patients (pres. 1990-94), Alpha Omega Alpha. Avocations: reading, traveling. Home: Brooklyn, NY. Deceased.

LURVEY, IRA HAROLD, lawyer; b. Chgo., Apr. 6, 1935; s. Louis and Faye (Grey) L.; m. Barbara Ann Sirvint, June 24, 1962; children: Nathana, Lawrence, Jennifer, Jonathan, David, Robert. BS, U. Ill., 1956; MS, Northwestern U., 1961; JD, U. Calif., Berkeley, 1965. Bar: Calif. 1965, Nev. 1966, U.S. Dist. Ct. (cen. dist.) Calif. 1966, U.S. Tax Ct. 1966, U.S. Ct. Appeals (9th cir.) 1966, U.S. Supreme Ct. 1975. Law clk. to hon. justices Nev. Supreme Ct., Carson City, 1965-66; from assoc. to ptnr. Pacht, Ross, Warne, Bernhard & Sears, Inc., 1966-84; predecessor firm Shea & Gould, L.A.; founding ptnr. Lurvey & Shapiro, L.A., from 1984. Lectr. legal edn. programs; mem. Chief Justice's Commns. on Ct. Reform, Weighted Caseloads; mediator family law L.A. Superior Ct. Editor Community Property Jour., 1979-80, Primary Consultant CFL 2d, 1994; columnist Calif. Family Law Monthly; contbr. articles to profl. jours. Former chmn. L.A. Jr. Arts Ctr.; past pres. Cheviot Hills Homeowners Assn.; exec. v.p., counsel Hillel Acad. Sch., Beverly Hills, Calif., 1977—. With U.S. Army, 1957-58. Fellow Am. Acad. Matrimonial Lawyers (pres. So. Calif. chpt. 1991-92, mem. nat. bd. govs. 1992-94), Internat. Acad. Matrimonial Lawyers; mem. ABA (chair family law sect. 1996-97, liaison family law to sr. lawyers' divsn. 1998—, exec. com. 1991-97, governing coun. 1986—, fin. officer 1991-92, chmn. support com., chmn. CLE, chmn. policy and issues com., vice chmn. com. arbitration and mediation, bd. of editors Family Adv. mag., chmn. issues com. sr. lawyer divsn. 2001—), Calif. Bar Assn. (editor jour. 1982-85, chmn. family law sect. 1986-87, exec. com. family law sect. 1982-88, specialization adv. bd. family law 1979-82), L.A. County Bar Assn. (chmn. family law sect. 1981-82, exec. com. family law 1989-92), Beverly Hills Bar Assn. (chmn. family law sect. 1976-77,). Home: Los Angeles, Calif. Died Jan. 26, 2003.

LUSGARTEN, MARC A. communications executive; Vice chmn. Cablevision Sys. Corp., Woodbury, N.Y. Died in August of 1999.

LUTERS, AINA, librarian; b. Freudenstadt, Schwartz., Fed. Republic Germany, Dec. 9, 1944; came to U.S., 1962; d. Vladimirs and Vera (Lielbiksis) L. BA in Anthropology, U. of the Ams., Mexico, 1969; MA equivalent/Anthropology, U. Calif., Riverside, 1972; MLS, U. Ariz., 1976. Photo archivist, libr. EQE, San Francisco; libr. Riverside (Calif.) Pub. Libr.; indexer Office of Arid Land Studies, Tucson; photo editor Follett Pub. Co., Chgo.; researcher Capital Times, Madison, Wis.; rsch. asst. PIMA Alcoholism Consortium; field rsch. supr. Elrick & Lavidge, Inc., San Francisco; social sci. researcher U. Ariz.; researcher R & D dept. EQE Engring., San Francisco; prin. Luters Rsch. Cons. in field. Mem. Am. Assn. Ind. Info. Profls., Spl. Librs. Assn., ALA, Am. Anthropol. Assn., Soc. for Med. Anthropology, Soc. for Psychol. Anthropology, Soc. for Visual Anthropology. Home: San Francisco, Calif. Died Mar. 8, 2000.

LUTZE, FREDERICK HENRY, JR., aerospace and ocean engineering educator; b. Bklyn., Nov. 27, 1937; s. Frederick Henry and Beatrice (Nodine) L.; m. Jeanne Soults, Aug. 14, 1965. BSME, Worcester Poly. Inst., 1959; MS in Aero. Engring., U. Ariz., 1964, PhD in Aero. Engring., 1967. Project engr. Bendix Corp., Teterboro, N.J., 1959-60, 61, Boeing Co., Seattle, 1963, N.Am. Co., Downey, Calif., 1964; instr. U. Ariz., Tucson, 1965-66; asst. prof. Va. Poly. Inst. and State U., Blacksburg, 1966-69, assoc. prof., 1969-82, prof. aero. and ocean engring., 1982—2003. Cons. in field. Former assoc. editor, Jour. Spacecraft and Rockets; patentee slow angular rates measuring device; contbr. articles to sci. publs. Cons. Va. Gov.'s Sch. Sci. and Tech., Roanoke, 1986-93. Fellow AIAA (assoc.); mem. Am. Astron. Soc., Sigma Gamma Tau (former nat. v.p.). Presbyterian. Avocations: flying, basketball, bowling. Home: Blacksburg, Va. Died Dec. 2, 2003.

LYALL, SANTOKH S. internist, emergency physician, educator; b. Delhi, India, 1943; MD, Delhi U., 1965. Diplomate Am. Bd. Internal Medicine, Am. Bd. Emergency Medicine. Rotating intern Hosp. St. Raphael, New Haven, 1968-69, resident in internal medicine, 1969-71, fellow in endocrinology and metabolism, 1971-73, attending physician, 1976-95; pvt. practice. Asst. clin. prof. Yale U. Sch. Medicine, New Haven, 1988—. Fellow ACP, Am. Coll. Emergency Physicians. Died Aug. 3, 2000.

LYDECKER, ANN MARIE, college administrator; BA, Oberlin (Ohio) Coll., 1966, MAT, 1972; PhD, U. Mich., 1982. Prof., chair curriculum and instrn. dept. Mankato (Minn.) State U., 1987-92; dean Sch. Edn. and Allied Studies Bridgewater (Mass.) State Coll., 1992-95, acting v.p. acad. affairs, 1995-96, provost, v.p. acad. affairs, 1995-2000; chancellor U. Wisc., River Falls, 2000—04. Died Mar. 25, 2004.

LYLE, JOHN TILLMAN, architect, landscape architecture educator; b. Houston, Aug. 10, 1934; s. Leo Tillman and Martha Ellen (Rawlins) L.; m. Harriett Laverna Fancher, Dec. 28, 1967; children: Alexander Tillman, Cybele Katsura. BArch, Tulane U., 1957; postgrad., Royal Acad. of Fine Arts, Copenhagen, 1965-67; M of Landscape Architecture, U. Calif., Berkeley, 1966. Registered architect, Calif. Architect Stanford (Calif.) U., 1959-62; urban designer John Carl Warnecke & Assocs., San Francisco, 1963-65; prof. emeritus Calif. State Poly. U., Pomona, from 1968. Vis. prof. Liubliana (Yugoslavia) U., 1982, Instituto Universitario Di Architectura, Venice, Italy, 1988, U. Sao Paulo, Brazil, 1989, Kyushu Inst. Design, Fukuoka, Japan, 1990; dir. design bldg. and landscape Ctr. for Regenerative Studies, 1984—. Author: Design for Human Ecosystems, 1985 (award Assn. Am. Pubs. 1985, Am. Soc. Landscape Architects 1986), Regenerative Design for Sustainable Development, 1994; contbr. articles to profl. jours. Mem. bd. govs. Desert Studies Consortium, Mojave Desert, 1984-88. Recipient Honor award Calif. Coun. Landscape Architects, 1988, Disting. Educator award Coun. Educators in Landscape Architecture, 1989; named Fulbright Disting. prof. U.S. Dept. State, 1982. Fellow Am. Soc. Landscape Archs. (ASLA medal 1996). Democrat. Avocations: hiking, skiing. Died 1999.

LYLE, MARGUERITE RICHARD, communications consultant; b. Lafayette, La., Sept. 13, 1929; d. Clarence Phillip and Jacqueline Mathilde (Weil) Richard; m. Michael G. Lyle, Aug. 3, 1952 (dec. May 1986); children: Melinda, Jacqueline, Michael, Elizabeth. BA, U. Southwestern La., 1950, MA, 1971. Tchr. Lake Charles (La.) City Sch. System, 1950-51, Allen Parish Sch. System, Oberlin, La., 1951-64; assoc. prof. U. Southwestern La., Lafayette, 1964-84; bd. mem., chair instructional com. Lafayette Parish Sch. System, from 1981; communications cons., from 1978. Author: Effective Oral Communications, 1971, Design for Speaking, 1971; editor: (booklets) Supervision for the 70's, 1972, Building Together, 1972; contbr. articles to profl. jours. Founder Lafayette Natural History Mus. and Planetarium, 1968; bd. dirs., sec. Downtown Lafayette Unltd., 1987—; past curriculum chair Leadership Lafayette, 1986-88. Named Hon. Mem. Future Farmers of Am., 1963; recipient Achievement award La. Women in Politics, 1987, Outstanding Pub. Servant award Ind. Arts Coun., 1989-90, Outstanding Vol. Activist from Vol. Ctr., 1990-91. Mem. Internat. Listening Assn. (pres. 1983-84, Pres. award 1982), Lafayette Natural History Mus. Assn. (com. chair 1972-73, 77-88), La. Wildflower Assn., RSVP. Democrat. Roman Catholic. Avocations: travel, needlework, gardening. Deceased.

LYNCH, PETER GEORGE, artist; b. Aug. 5, 1932; BFA, Pratt Inst., Bklyn., 1954; postgrad., CCNY. Pub.: Limited Editions Prints (11 eds.), CONTACT News-'n'-ViewsLetter, 1992—, Concerns Artists, Art, Crafts and Marketing, Peter G. Lynch's Catalog of Art and Fine Craft, 1996—; advisor Tri-State (Pa., N.J., Del.) Art Mktg. Task Force for Living ARtists, 1998—. Exhibitions include: (internat. and nat.) The Art Gallery of La Merced, Maracaibo, Venezuela, Nepenthe Mundi Internat. Competition, Allied Artist Am., Nat. Arts Club, Chautauqua Instn., Acad. Artist Assn. Nat. Exhibition, Internat. Festival of The Arts, Mexico-Douglas, Ariz., Wiesner Gallery Intertnat., Global Visions, Fed. Pla., Gallery Cozumel, Yergeau Mus. Internat. d'Art, Montreal, Que. (Named One of Best Am. Painters, One of Best Am. Printmakers, 1991, Deuxieme prix Ann. Ctr. P.R.D. Montreal Exhbn., 1992), and numerous others; (regional and local) Arsenal Gallery, Coler Meml., Vega Fine Arts, Casino Gallery, Fulton Gallery, Artifax Galleries, Cabrini Gallery, Ten Talents Gallery, Inroads Multimedia Ctr. among others; author: (dossiers), Collaborative Photolithographic Prints: Publishing Your Own, 1990, Direct Marketing: Survival Factors and the Artist, 1990, Succeeding as a Fine Artist: Professionalism in a Difficult Environment, 1991, Artist's Eye vs. Photographers Eye: Shooting Your Art Right, 1991, Overused and Underexplored: The Paradox of Print Media: Effective Advertising for Creative People, 1991, Direct-Contact Marketing: Art Fairs and Festivals, 1991, The Video Portfolio: A New User-Friendly Marketing Tool, 1991, Survival Factors and The Artist; Keeping Up or Dropping Out, 1994, Creativity-What On Earth Is It? Where Can We Get Some?, 1994; featured writer ArtScope newsletter, 2000. With U.S. Army, 1956-58. Recipient Citation for Superior Competence, U.S. Army Air Def. Command, 1958, Hon. Mention Nat. Exhibition at Bakersfield, 1985, Second Place Assn. Artist Nat. Exhibition, 1985, Cert. of Merit, Academic Artist Assn. Annual Nat. Exhibition, 1986, First Place Nepenthe Mundi Internat. Art Competition, 1987, Watson-Guptill award Lake Worth Silver Anniversary Exhbn., 1991. Home: Brooklyn, NY. Died Jan. 28, 2002.

LYNG, RICHARD EDMUND, former secretary of agriculture; b. San Francisco, June 29, 1918; s. Edmund John and Sarah Cecilia (McGrath) L.; m. Bethyl Ball, June 25, 1944; children: Jeanette (Mrs. Gary Robinson), Marilyn (Mrs. Daniel O'Connell). Ph.B. cum laude, U. Notre Dame, 1940; PhD (hon.), Carroll Coll., 1988. With Ed J. Lyng Co., Modesto, Calif., 1945-66, pres., 1949-66; dir. Calif. Dept. Agr., 1967-69; asst. sec. Dept. Agr., Washington, 1969-73, dep. sec., 1981-85; vice chmn. Commodity Credit Corp., 1981-85; pres. Lyng & Lesher, Inc., Washington, 1985-86; Sec. of Agr. Dept. Agr., Washington, 1986-89. Pres. Am. Meat Inst., Washington, 1973-79; pvt. cons., 1980; dir. Commodity Credit Corp., 1969-73, Nat. Livestock and Meat Bd., 1973-76, Tri-Valley Growers, 1975-81; bd. govs. Refrigeration Rsch. Found., 1974-77, Chgo. Merc. Exch.; chmn. food industry trade adv. com. Commerce Dept.; chmn. U.S. Child Nutrition Adv. Com., 1971-73; mem. animal health com. NAS; sr. rsch. fellow Harvard U. Sch. Bus. Adminstrn., 1989-91; chmn. export adv. com. Nat. Dairy Bd., 1989—; bd. dirs. Ecosci., Corp, 1991—; trustee Internat. Life Sci. Inst., 1990— Chmn. Stanislaus County (Calif.) Republican Central Com., 1961-62; dir. agr. div. Pres. Ford Com., 1976; co-dir. farm and food div. Reagan-Bush Campaign, 1980. Served with AUS, 1941-45. Mem. Washington Golf and Country Club, Del Rio Country Club (hon.). Roman Catholic. Died Feb. 1, 2003.

LYNN, EUGENE MATTHEW, insurance company executive; b. Kansas City, Mo., Nov. 6, 1918; s. Eugene M. and Marthield (Ellis) L.; m. Mary E. Spoors, Mar. 12, 1947 (dec.); 1 dau., Diane E.; m. Christine E. Koppl, Jan. 19, 1980. Student John B. Stetson U., 1937-39. Pilot Trans World Airlines, 1944-47; v.p. U.S. Epperson Underwriting Co., Boca Raton, Fla., 1949-55, pres., 1955—; pres. LIG Ins. Agy., Inc., Boca Raton, 1978—; v.p. Universal Underwriters Ins. Co., Kansas City, 1949-55, pres., 1955-82. Hon. chmn. bd., trustee Boca Raton Community Hosp.; trustee Lynn U. Boca Raton. Clubs: Boca Raton Hotel and Club, Royal Palm Yacht and Country (Boca Raton, Fla.), Delray Beach (Fla.), Ocean Reef (Key Largo, Fla.), Indian Creek Country, (Miami Beach), Fisher Island Surf (Miami Beach). Home: Boca Raton, Fla.

LYNN, MARGARET E. b. Dallas, Apr. 28; BA in Speech and Drama, Northwestern U., So. Meth. U.; MA in Theatre Arts, Cath. U. Am. Dancer/actress Prof. Theatre, N.Y.C.; dancer/actress Nat. Touring Cos. of Broadway Prodns.; dancer-mgr. Tarnower Concert Dancers, N.Y.C., Martha Graham Co.; dir., actress, choreographer Straight Wharf Theatre, Nantucket Island, Mass.; civilian actress technician U.S. Army ETO; entertainment cons., dir. Dept. Army, Washington, staff entertainment dir. Hdqr. Third U.S. Army, Hdqrs. 8th U.S. Army, Hdqrs. Army Forces Far East, Hdqrs. Second U.S. Army; dir. army music program Dept. Army, Washington, dir. Army entertainment program, dir. performing arts, dir. arts mgmt. and career devel. of personnel. Instr. dance, choreography U. Heidelberg, Ger., Sofia U., Tokyo; instr. theatre history U. Va.; condr. workshops in field; cons., dir. spl. events Walt Disney Prodns., Inc.; exec. dir. Am. Theatre Assn., Washington; exec. com., dir. New Nat. Theatre Corp.; developer prodns. for performance in various theatres France, Germany, Austria, Korea, Okinawa Islands. Author: Production Guide I— A Technical Guide to Thematic Production; Show Band Book I, Tech. Music Companion to Production Guide I; Production Guide II— A Technical Guide to Adaptations, Dramatic Themes, and Incidental Music for Show Bands; Show Band Book II, Musical Adaptations for Dramatic Themes and Incidental Music; Design Guide for Music and Theatre Facilities. Disting. Woman of Am. Theater Assn.; Decoration for meritorious Civilian Service, Sec. of Army; Internat. Theater award, Arts Council of Rome, Italy, others. Mem. (hon.) Acad. Olympians, Internat. Theatre of Berlin. Home: Reston, Va. Died June 11, 2002.

LYNN, PAULINE JUDITH WARDLOW, lawyer; b. Columbus, Ohio, Nov. 14, 1920; d. Charles and Helen P. (Christman) Wardlow; student Wellesley Coll., 1938-40; B.A., Ohio State U., 1942, J.D., 1948; m. Arthur D. Lynn, Jr., Dec. 29, 1943; children— Pamela Wardlow, Constance Karen, Deborah Joanne, Patricia Diane. Admitted to Ohio bar, 1948; practiced in Columbus, 1948-49. Troop leader Girl Scouts U.S.A., 1969-71. Mem. ABA, Columbus Bar Assn., Phi Beta Kappa, Kappa Kappa Gamma (mem. research com. Heritage mus. 1981-87), Pi Sigma Alpha. Republican. Episcopalian. Died May 8, 1995. Home: Columbus, Ohio.

LYONS, DANIEL CARSON, sales executive; b. Torrington, Conn., Dec. 30, 1930; s. William H. and Mary (Carson) L.; m. Suzanne N. Steers, Oct. 5, 1957; children: Daniel C. Jr., Lisa, Michael, Leslie, Cahterine, Thomas. Student, Gen. Motors Inst., 1957. Pres. Lyons Pont-Cad Inc., Montpelier, Vt., from 1959. Bd. dirs. Vt. Fin. Services Holding Co., Brattleboro, 1972—. Chmn. Heart Fund, Montpelier, 1972-75; trustee Wood Art Gallery; chmn. Vt. State Environ. Bd., 1961-80. Served with Nat. Def. Exec. Res., 1962-75. Mem. Vt. Auto Dealers Assn. (treas. 1972-78). Clubs: Saronnet Golf (Little Compton, R.I.), Coral Beach (Bermuda). Lodges: Elks. Avocations: walking, boating, reading. Home: Montpelier, Vt. Deceased.

LYSYK, KENNETH MARTIN, judge; b. Weyburn, Sask., Can., July 1, 1934; s. Michael and Anna (Maradyn) L.; m. Patricia Kinnon, Oct. 2, 1959; children: Joanne, Karen (dec.), Stephanie. BA, McGill U., 1954; LL.B., U. Sask., 1957; B.C.L., Oxford U., 1960. Bar: Sask., B.C., Yukon, apptd. Queen's counsel 1973. Lectr. U. B.C., 1960-62, asst.

prof., 1962-65, assoc. prof., 1965-68, prof., 1968-69; adviser Constl. Rev. sect. Privy Council Office, Govt. of Can., Ottawa, 1969-70; prof. Faculty of Law U. Toronto, 1970-72; dep. atty. gen. Govt. of Sask., Regina, 1972-76; dean Law Sch., U. B.C., Vancouver, 1976-82; judge Supreme Ct. of B.C., Vancouver, from 1983. Dep. judge Supreme Ct. Yukon, 1991—, N.W. Territories, 1991—; judge Ct. Martial Appeal Ct. Can., 1995—; assoc. dir. Nat. Jud. Inst., 1996-98; chmn. Alaska Hwy. Pipeline Inquiry, 1977; sole commr. Yukon Electoral Boundaries Commn., 1991. Mem. Can. Bar Assn., Internat. Commn. Jurists (Can. sect.; v.p. for B.C. 1992-2002), Can. Inst. for Adminstrn. of Justice (pres. 1989-91). Home: Vancouver, Canada. Died July 28, 2003.

MACAULAY, COLIN ALEXANDER, mining engineer; b. Montreal, Que., Can., Dec. 26, 1931; s. Kenneth Douglas and Eunice S. (Guild) M.; m. Elizabeth Ann Rowsell, Aug. 27, 1955; children: Douglas C., James. R., Robert C. B.Engring. in Mining, McGill U., Montreal, 1954, M.Engring., 1955. Registered profl. engr., Ont. Gen. mgr., dir. Palabora Mining Co., Transvaal, Republic South Africa, 1972-82; dep. chmn., mng. dir., chief exec. Rössing Uranium Ltd., Namibia, 1982-88; pres., chief operating officer Rio Algom Ltd., Toronto, Ont., Can., 1988-91, pres., ceo, from 1991. Chmn. bd. dirs. Highland Valley Copper, B.C. Mem. Ont. Mining Assn. (bd. dirs. 1990-91), Mining Assn. Can. (dir.), Can. Inst. Mining and Metallurgy, Assn. Profl. Engrs. Ont. Home: Toronto, Canada. Deceased.

MACAULAY, ROBERT ERWIN, education educator; b. Duluth, Minn., Mar. 2, 1930; s. George Mackenzie and Francis (Erwin) M.; m. Dona Ylinen, Mar. 4, 1956; children: Robert, Catherine, James, George, Carolyn. Grad., MacAlester Coll., 1955; student, Winona State U., 1979-80, U. Minn., 1980. Mgmt. trainee Glass Block, Duluth, Minn., 1955-56; supt. Roots, Terre Haute, Ind., 1956-61; owner Macaulay's, Moose Lake, Minn., 1961-80; mgr. ops. and pers. Justers, Mpls., 1971-73; instr. Red Wing (Minn.) Tech. Inst., 1979-81; dir. Dakota County Tech. Coll., Minn., from 1981. Pres. Devel. Corp., Moose Lake, 1968-70; city councilman, 1968-70; vice-chmn. County Airport Commn., Cloquet, 1968-72. With USAF, 1950-56. Mem. South St. Paul C. of C. (cons. 1984-91), Moose Lake C. of C. (pres. 1967), Kiwanis, Flying Club (pres. 1975-77). Republican. Lutheran. Avocations: fishing, hunting, gardening. Home: Red Wing, Minn. Deceased.

MACDONALD, DONALD ARTHUR, publishing executive; b. Union City, N.J., Nov. 30, 1919; s. Richard A. and Marie (McDonald) M.; m. Ruth Moran, Dec. 21, 1942; children: Ronald A., Martha J., Marie C., Donald A., Charles A. BS cum laude, NYU, 1948, MBA, 1950. Advt. sales rep. Wall St. Jour., Dow Jones & Co., Inc., N.Y.C., 1953-55, mgr. New Eng. and Can. ter., 1955-58, ea. advt. mgr., 1958-61, exec. advt. mgr., 1961-63, advt. dir. sales promotion and prodn. depts., 1963-67, v.p. advt. sales, 1970-74, sr. v.p., retired dir.; vice chmn. Dow Jones & Co. Inc., N.Y.C., 1979—86; dir. Far Ea. Econ. Rev., Hong Kong. Chmn. coun. judges Advt. Hall of Fame, 1972-78. Author: An Arrow for Your Quiver, 1994. Capt. AUS, 1942-46, World War II. Named to Advt. Hall of Fame, 1985. Mem. Am. Advt. Fedn. (dir. 1962—, past chmn., Barton A. Cummings Gold Medal award, 1995), Advt. Fedn. Am. (past gov. 2d dist., past chmn. joint commn., past chmn.), Advt. Council (dir.), N.Y. Advt. Club (past dir., Silver medal award 1965), Beta Gamma Sigma. Clubs: Downtown Athletic (N.Y.C.), Yale (N.Y.C.); Rumson Country (N.J.). Home: Rumson, NJ. Died June 13, 2003.

MACDONALD, JEAN MARIE, social worker; b. Mpls., Dec. 20, 1960; d. Gene Laverne and Marie Yvonne (Olin) Blomquist; m. Stuart David Macdonald, June 11, 1988. BA cum laude in Psych., Hamline U., 1983; MSW, Washington U., 1985. Housing coordinator Independence Ctr., St. Louis, 1985-87; therapist Community Counseling Ctr., Alton, Ill., 1987; clin. social worker community placement program St. Louis State Hosp., 1987-89; clin. coord. Community Counseling Ctr., Alton, 1989-99. Presenter seminar in field. Vol. Ramsey County Community Human Svcs., St. Paul, 1980-81; mem. World Wildlife Fund, 1987-99. Mem. Pi Gamma Mu. Unitarian Universalist. Avocations: camping, sewing, furniture refinishing. Home: Eden Prairie, Minn. Died Apr. 14, 1999.

MACFARLAND, NANCY FOLEY, dietitian; b. Denver, Jan. 22, 1952; d. Thomas Henry and Kathryn Marie (Kelley) Foley; m. Robert Scott MacFarland, June 27, 1974; children: Kelley Patrick, Natalie Anne. BS in Nutrition, Ariz. State U., 1974. Registered dietitian. Dietitian Okla. Children's Hosp., Oklahoma City, 1976-77, Hayden (Colo.) Sch. Dist., 1978-80; consulting dietitian The Meml. Hosp., Craig, Colo., 1984-99, Routt Meml. Hosp., Steamboat Springs, Colo., 1985-99; instr. Colo. Mountain Coll., Steamboat Springs, 1985-87, Colo. Northwest Community Coll., Craig, 1985-86. Cons. dietitian Grand Junction (Colo.) Care Ctr., 1992-99. Pres. Lit Toots Ski Club, Steamboat Springs, 1982, Sch. Improvement Com., Steamboat, 1989-99; pres. Steamboat Springs Swim Team, 1992-99. Mem. Am. Dietetic Assn., Sport and Cardiovascular Dietitians, Cons. Dietitians, Am. Diabetes Assn., Beta Sigma Phi. Republican. Roman Catholic. Avocations: skiing, reading, ski diving. Home: Steamboat Springs, Colo. Died Feb. 13, 1999.

MACGREGOR, CLARK, museum executive, retired manufacturing executive; b. Mpls., July 12, 1922; s. William Edwin and Edith (Clark) MacG.; m. Barbara Porter Spicer, June 16, 1948; children: Susan Clark, Laurie Miller, Eleanor Martin. Grad. cum laude, Dartmouth, 1946; JD, U. Minn., 1948. Bar: Minn. 1948. Practiced in, Mpls., until 1961; partner firm King & MacGregor, 1952-61; mem. 87th-91st Congress, 3d Dist. Minn., mem. jud. com., com. on banking and currency; counsel to Pres. for congl. affairs, 1971-72; Nixon campaign dir., 1972; sr. v.p. United Technologies Corp., 1972-87; pres. Nat. Hist. Intelligence Mus. Served to 2d lt. AUS, 1942-45, CBI. Decorated Bronze Star, Legion of Merit. Mem.: Burning Tree, Metropolitan, Chevy Chase. Republican. Presbyterian. Home: Washington, DC. Died Feb. 10, 2003.

MACHENBERG, JEAN P. foundation director; b. Syracuse, N.Y., June 15, 1942; d. Loren Brandt and Eleanor Ruth (Hess) Plopper; m. Alan Paul Machenberg, June 13, 1970; children: Eleanor Lynn, Christopher Charles. BS, Syracuse U., 1964; MBA, U. Richmond (Va.), 1990. Exec. dir. Adult Devel. Ctr., Richmond, 1980-84, Cen. Va. Foodbank, Inc., Richmond, 1984-89, Nat. Kidney Found. of Va., Richmond, from 1990. Bd. dirs. Standing Room Only Housing, Richmond, LifeNet, Richmond. Home: Chesterfield, Va. Deceased.

MACIAG, THOMAS, biochemist, cell and molecular biologist; b. Bayonne, N.J., Nov. 19, 1946; s. Edward and Agnes (Wernock) M.; m. Lorraine Ann Rogers, Aug. 17, 1974; 1 child, Andrei Rogers. BA in Biology, Rutgers U., 1968; PhD in Molecular Biology, U. Pa., 1975. Postdoctoral fellow U. Pa., Phila., 1975-76; scientist Collaborative Rsch. Inc., Waltham, Mass., 1976-79; asst. prof. Harvard Med. Sch., Boston, 1979-83; dir. cell biology Revlon Biotechnology Rsch. Ctr., Rockville, Md., 1983-86; head molecular biology dept. Jerome H. Holland Lab. for Biomedical Scis. ARC, Rockville, 1986—97; scientific dir., Ctr. for Molecular Medicine Maine Med. Ctr. Rsch. Inst., Freeport, 1997—2004. Former adj. prof. biochemistry George Washington U., Washington; adv. bd. Upstate Biotechnology Inc., Lake Placid, N.Y., Molecular Biology Resources, Milw.; cons. ICOS Corp., Bothell, Wash., 1991-92, Geron, Inc., Palo Alto, Calif., Berlex Bioscis., Inc., Richmond, Calif. Contbr. articles to Procs. Nat. Acad. Sci., Jour. Cell Biology, Nature Sci., Jour. Biol. Chemistry, Ann. Rev. Biochemistry. With U.S. Army, 1969-71. Grantee NIH. Mem. Am. Soc. Biochemistry and Molecular Biology, Am. Soc. Cell Biology, Molecular Cytology Study Sect. div. rsch. grants of NIH. Home: Freeport, Maine. Died Mar. 8, 2004.

MACIVER, JOHN KENNETH, lawyer; b. Milw., Mar. 22, 1931; s. Wallace and Elizabeth (MacRae) MacI.; m. Margaret J. Vail, Sept. 4, 1954; children: Douglas B., Carolyn V., Kenneth D., Laura E. BS, U. Wisc., 1953, LLB, 1955; D Laws & Econ. Devel. (hon.), Milw. Sch. Engring., 1997. Bar: Wisc. 1955. Sr. ptnr. Michael Best & Friedrich LLP, Milw., from 1955. Mem. various bds. dirs. Chmn. Thompson for Gov. steering coms., 1986, 90, 94, 98; state chmn. Wisc. Bush for Pres. coms., 1980, 88, 92; chmn. Wis. Nixon for Pres. com., 1968, 72, Olson for Gov. com., 1970; co-chmn. Wis. George W. Bush for Pres., state co-chair, 2000; vice chmn. Knowles for Gov. com., 1964, 66; bd. dirs. Milw. Symphony Orch., 1968-96, pres. 1981-82; trustee Milw. Symphony Endowment Trust, 1988—; chmn. exec. com., bd. govs. East-West Ctr., 1970-76 (Disting. svc. award Honolulu 1976); pres., chmn. bd. dirs. Nat. Coun. Alcoholism, 1974-77, bd. dirs. 1968-78 (Silver Key award N.Y. 1975); pres., campaign co-chmn. United Performing Arts Fund Greater Milw., 1974-76 (Stiemke award Arts 1988); bd. dirs., exec. com. Greater Milw. Edn. Trust, 1988-97, Project New Hope, 1991—; sec., gen. counsel Wisc. Mfrs. and Commerce, 1980—; regent, sec., gen. counsel Milw. Sch. Engring., 1987—; bd. dirs., sec. Pettit Nat. Ice Tng. Ctr., 1992—; bd. dirs. Milw. Nat. Heart Project; bd. dirs., exec. com., founding mem., sec. Competitive Wisc. Inc., 1982—; bd. dirs., vice-chair Met. Milw. Assn. Commerce, 1987—; mem. Greater Milw. Com. 1985—; trustee Milw. County Pub. Mus., 1989-92. Recipient Wisc. Gov's. awards in Support of Arts, 1989, cmty. svc. award Assoc. Gen. Contractors of Greater Milw. Mem. Wis. Bar Assn. (chmn. commn. litigation costs and delay, past chmn. labor law sect., commn. on jud. elections and ethics), Milw. Bar Assn. (chmn. jud. selection and qualifications com.), Milw. Club, Town Club. Republican. Avocations: Am. history, tennis, charities, politics. Home: Milwaukee, Wis. Died Sept. 2003.

MACK, MAYNARD, English language educator, writer; b. Hillsdale, Mich., Oct. 27, 1909; s. Jesse Floyd and Pearl (Vore) M.; m. Florence Brocklebank, Aug. 5, 1933; children: Prudence Allen, Sara Bennett, Maynard Jr. BA, Yale U., 1932, PhD, 1936; LittD, Duke U., Lawrence U., No. Mich. U., Oberlin Coll., Kalamazoo Coll.; DHL, Towson (Md.) State U. From instr. to prof. English Yale U., New Haven, Conn., 1936-48, Sterling prof., from 1965. Chmn. dept. English Yale U., 1965-68, dir. divsn. humanities Faculty of Arts and Scis., 1962-64, assoc. dir. Shakespeare Inst., 1953-62; dir. Nat. Humanities Inst., 1974-77; Walker-Ames vis. prof. U. Wash., Seattle, 1956; W.J. Alexander lectr. U. Toronto, Ont., Can., 1963; Elizabeth M. Beckman vis. prof. U. Calif., Berkeley, 1964; Lord Northcliff lectr. U. London, 1972; Elizabeth Drew vis. prof. Smith Coll., 1973; Charles Homer Haskins lectr. Am. Coun. Learned Socs., 1983. Author: King Lear in Our Time, 1965, The Garden and the City, 1969, Collected in Himself, 1982, The Last and Greatest Art, 1984, Alexander Pope: A Life, 1986 (Best Biography of Yr., L.A. Times, Christian Gauss award Phi Beta Kappa), Prose and Cons: Monologues on Several Occasions, 1989, Everybody's Shakespeare: Reflections Chiefly on the Tragedies, 1993; editor: The Twickenham Edition of the Poems of Alexander Pope, Vol. 3:1 and vols. 7-11, 1951-69, Twentieth Century Views, Collections of Critical Essays on Individual Authors, 143 vols., 1960-81, Twentieth Century Interpretations, Collections of Critical Essays on Individual Works, 97 vols., 1965-81, New Century Views, Collections of Critical Essays on Individual Authors, 17 vols., 1991—. V.p. New Haven Bd. Edn., 1954-59; trustee Am. Shakespeare Theatre, Ctr. for Theatre in Edn., Pub. Broadcasting Assocs. Recipient cert. of honor for disting. svc. to humanities Nat. Coun. Tchrs. of English, 1970, Wilbur Lucius Cross award Friends of the Conn. Humanities Coun., 1986; Faculty fellow Ford Found., 1952-53, fellow Guggenheim Found., 1942-43, 64-65, 81-82, Sr. Rsch. fellow NEH, 1968-69, 77-78, Vis. fellow Ctr. for Advanced Study in the Behavioral Scis., 1971-72, Sr. fellow William Andrews Clark Libr., L.A., 1974, Sr. fellow Huntington Libr., 1979-80, Sr. fellow Nat. Humanities Ctr., 1984, 86; Sr. Rsch. scholar Fulbright Found., U. London, 1959-60; endowed performance lectr. on Shakespeare established in his honor, 1990, endowed professorship established in his honor, 1994. Fellow Am. Acad. Arts and Scis., Brit. Acad. (corr.); mem. MLA (pres. 1970, Lifetime Scholarly Achievement award 1996), Am. Coun. on Edn. (commn. on faculty affairs 1971-73), Shakespeare Assn. Am. (trustee 1972-77, pres. 1975-76), Internat. Shakespeare Assn. (v.p. 1976-86), Modern Humanities Rsch. Assn. (pres. 1984), Internat. Assn. Univ. Profs. of English, Soc. Scholars and Critics. Home: New Haven, Conn. Deceased.

MACKE, HARRY JERRY, mechanical engineer, consultant; b. Newport, Ky., Aug. 26, 1922; s. Harry Jerome and Mildred Ruth (Rauch) M.; m. Virginia Heinlein, Apr. 1, 1948; children: Janice Macke Zwolshen, Jennifer. BS, U. Ky., 1947; MS, Harvard U., 1948, DSc, 1951. Registered profl. engr., Ohio. Mech. engr. aircraft engine group GE, Boston, 1951-52, Cin., 1952-71, cons. engring. mechanics, 1971-77, mgr. applied exptl. stress, 1977-87; cons. GE Aircraft Engines, Cin., from 1988. Adj. assoc. prof. aerospace engring. U. Cin., 1961-66, 83. 1st lt. U.S. Army, 1943-46. Mem. ASME, Soc. Exptl. Mechanics, Engrs. Scientists Cin., Sigma Xi, Tau Beta Pi. Home: Cincinnati, Ohio. Deceased.

MACLEAN, DAVID BAILEY, chemistry educator, researcher; b. Summerside, P.E.I., Can., July 15, 1923; s. William and Lulu Adelaide (Stewart) McL.; m. Helen Shirley Canning, Dec. 28, 1945 (dec. 1950); 1 child, Susan; m. Regina Lane, Sept. 21, 1951; children— David, Richard, Robert, Gillian, stepchildren— Gary Hutton, Dariel Hutton B.Sc., Acadia U., 1942; PhD, McGill U., 1946. Research chemist Dominion Rubber Co., Guelph, Ont., Can., 1946-49; assoc. prof. chemistry N.S. Tech. Coll., Halifax, Can., 1949-54, McMaster U., Hamilton, Ont., 1954-60, prof., 1960-89, prof. emeritus, from 1989. Mem. Council of Ont. Univs., Toronto, 1982-84 Fellow Royal Soc. Can., Chem. Inst. Can.; mem. Am. Chem. Soc., Am. Soc. Mass Spectroscopy Home: Hamilton, Canada. Deceased.

MACLEISH, ANDREW, English and linguistics educator; b. Phila., Aug. 30, 1923; s. Norman Hillard and Lenore (McCall) MacL.; m. Ann Pullen, June 1950 (dec. May 1971); children: Andrew, Eve, Spencer; m. Barbara K. Christensen, June 1985. AB, Roosevelt U., 1950; MA, U. Chgo., 1951; PhD, U. Wis., 1961. Instr. English Valparaiso (Ind.) U., 1951-53, Rockford (Ill.) Coll., 1956-58; asst. prof. No. Ill. U., DeKalb, 1958-67; prof. U. Minn., Mpls., from 1967. Author: The Middle-English Subject-Verb Cluster, 1969; editor: The American Revolution Through British Eyes, 1962, Oedipus: Myth and Drama, 1967, The Medieval Monastery, 1988. With USNR, ret. Grantee U.S. Office of Edn., 1961, Minn. Humanities Commn., 1985. Mem. Am. Dialect Soc., Celtic Assn. N.Am., Medieval Acad. Am. Home: Minneapolis, Minn. Died Jan. 12, 2001.

MACLEOD, ROBERT FREDRIC, editor, publisher; b. Chgo., Oct. 15, 1917; s. Ernest F. and Martha W. (Ruzicka) MacL.; children— Merrill, Robert Fredric, E. Jay, Ian. BA, Dartmouth Coll., 1939. Advt. mgr. Town & Country mag., N.Y.C., 1949; v.p., pub. Harper's Bazaar, N.Y.C., 1950-55, 55-60; v.p., advt. dir. Hearst Mags., N.Y.C., 1960-62; pub. Seventeen mag., N.Y.C., 1962-63; v.p., dir. mktg. Subscription TV Inc., Santa Monica, Calif., 1963-64; editor, pub. 'Teen Mag., Los Angeles, 1965—, now editorial dir., exec. pub.; sr. v.p. Petersen Pub. Co., L.A., 1976-95; ret., 1995; pub. cons., from 1995. Served to maj. USMC, 1941-46. Named to Football Hall of Fame, 1977 Mem.: Bel Air Country. Home: Malibu, Calif. Died Jan. 13, 2003.

MACNICHOL, EDWARD FORD, JR., biophysicist, educator, consultant; b. Toledo, Oct. 24, 1918; s. Edward Ford and Adelaide (Foster) MacN.; m. Anne Proctor Ayer, Sept. 7, 1940; (dec. Nov. 1996); children: Edward Ford III, Anne (Mrs. David A. Brownell); m. Dorothy B. Thorne, Apr. 5, 1998. AB, Princeton, 1941; student, U. Pa., 1946-48; PhD, Johns Hopkins, 1952. Staff mem. radiation lab. Mass. Inst. Tech., 1941-46; from instr. to prof. biophysics Johns Hopkins, 1952-68; research biophysicist, asst. dir. Marine Biol. Lab., Woods Hole, Mass., 1972-76; dir. Lab. Sensory Physiology, 1973-84. Prof. physiology Boston U. Med. Sch., 1973-2001, prof. emeritus, 2001—; dir. Nat. Inst. Neurol. Diseases and Stroke, 1968-72; acting dir. Nat. Eye Inst., NIH, 1968-69; Mem. visual scis. study sect. NIH, 1963-66; mem. bd. sci. counsellors Nat. Inst. Neurol. Disease, and Blindness, 1965-68, chmn., 1968—; mem. U.S. Nat. Com. Photobiology, 1966-68, U.S. Nat. Com. Pure and Applied Biophysics, 1966 Co-editor: Sensory Processes, 1978-82. Bd. dirs. Deafness Research Found., 1973-83, sec., 1976-78. Recipient certificate of appreciation War Dept.-Navy Dept., 1947 Fellow IEEE (life, Engring. in Biology and Medicine prize award 1965, Centennial medal 1984, editor trans. biomed. engring. 1963-65); mem. AAAS (life), Am. Phys.

Soc., Am. Physiol. Soc., Biophys. Soc., Soc. for Neurosci., Assn. Rsch. Vision and Ophthalmology (hon. life), Corp. Bermuda Biol. Sta. Rsch. (life trustee 2001). Achievements include research in neurophysiology of vision; design instrumentation biol. research. Home: Concord, Mass. Died Mar. 14, 2003.

MACOMBER, WILLIAM BUTTS, museum executive; b. Rochester, N.Y., Mar. 28, 1921; s. William Butts and Elizabeth Currie (Ranlet) M.; grad. Phillips Andover Acad., 1940; A.B., Yale U., 1943, M.A., 1947; LL.B., Harvard U., 1949; M.A., U. Chgo., 1951; m. Phyllis D. Bernau, Dec. 28, 1963. Lectr. govt. Boston U., 1947-49; with CIA, Washington, 1951-53; spl. asst. to spl. asst. to sec. for intelligence Dept. State, Washington, 1953-54; adminstrv. asst. to Sen. John Sherman Cooper, 1954-55; spl. asst. to under sec. of state Herbert Hoover, Jr., 1955, to sec. of state John Foster Dulles, 1955-57; asst. sec of state for congl. relations, 1957-61; A.E. and P. to Jordan, 1961-64; asst. adminstr. in Near East and South Asia, AID, Washington, 1964-67; asst. sec. for congl. relations Dept. State, 1967-69, dep. under sec. of state for mgmt., 1969-73; U.S. ambassador to Turkey, 1973-77; pres. Met. Mus. Art. N.Y.C., 1978-86; tchr. social sci. Nantucket (Mass.) High Sch., 1986-91; Author: The Angels' Game: A Handbook of Modern Diplomacy, 1975; former mem. Nantucket Sch. Com.; bd. dirs. Becton Dickinson and Co., 1985-94; trustee AARP-Scudder, Stevens and Clark. Trustee emerites, Carnegie Endowment for Internat. Peace, Hayes Hist. Soc., 1983-90; bd. overseers Hoover Inst. on War, Revolution and Peace; Am. Acad. Diplomacy. Served as lt. USMC, 1943-46. Club; Genesee (Rochester, N.Y.); Century (N.Y.C.). Home: Nantucket, Mass. Died Nov. 19, 2003.

MAC VITTIE, ROBERT WILLIAM, retired college administrator; b. Middletown, N.Y., Dec. 29, 1920; s. Mortimer, Jr. and Mary (Thompson) MacV.; m. Margaret L. Cooper, July 15, 1944; children— Robert William II, Beth Ann, Geralyn Amy. B.Ed., State U. N.Y., Oneonta, 1944; MA, N.Y. U., 1946; Ed.D., 1954. Elementary tchr. Pine Plains (N.Y.) Central Sch., 1944; social sci. tchr. Meml. Jr. High Sch., Middletown, N.Y., 1944-48; supervising prin. Montowese Sch., North Haven, Conn., 1948-52, Ridge Rd. Sch., North Haven, 1952-53; prof. sch. adminstrn., prin. lab. sch. N.Y. State Coll. Tchrs., Buffalo, 1954-56; dir. div. elementary and secondary edn. State U. N.Y. Coll., Buffalo, 1956-58, dean coll., 1958-63; pres. State U. Coll., Geneseo, 1963-79, emeritus, 1979—; interim pres. SUNY-Fredonia, N.Y., 1985, SUNY-Geneseo, 1988-89. Mem. regional adv. bd. Key Bank, N.A., Oneonta, N.Y., 1978-86; mem. SUNY Commn. Univ. Purposes and Priorities; exec. com. Rochester Area Colls., Inc., 1972-79, SUNY Council Pres.'s, 1970-72, 76-78; bd. dirs. Adams Art Gallery. Author: Handbook for Substitute Teachers, 3d edit, 1959, also numerous articles. Mem. citizens salary adv. com. Kenmore, N.Y., 1957; cons. sch. program evaluation team Tchrs. Coll., Temple U., 1956-57; mem. Livingston County Planning Bd., 1967-73, chmn., 1972-73; bd. dirs. Chautauqua Co. Automobile Club, Inc., Am. Automobile Assn., 1986-93, No. Chautauqua Community Foundation, 1985—, Chautauqua Adult Day Care Ctrs., 1991-92, D.R. Barker Libr., 1992—; mem. adv. bd. Auto Club Western N.Y., 1993—. Paul Harris fellow Rotary Internat.; Robert W. MacVittie Coll. Union named in his honor SUNY-Geneseo, 1989. Mem. Am. Assn. Higher Edn., Am. Assn. Sch. Adminstrs., Am. Assn. Univ. Adminstrs. (pres. 1971-73, dir. 1977-79, gen. sec. 1979-81, Disting. Svc. award 1994), Am. Assn. State Colls. and Univs. (bd. dirs. 1977-79), Am. Acad. Polit. and Social Scis., Livingston C. of C. (dir. 1970-79), Phi Delta Kappa, Kappa Delta Pi, Rotary Internat., SUNY of N.Y. and Conferations of SUNY Alumni Assns. (spl. citation Disting. Alumni Svc. award 1994). Lodges: Rotary Internat. Died Apr. 1997.

MADANSKY, LEON, particle physicist, educator; b. Bklyn., Jan. 11, 1923; BS, U. Mich., 1942, MS, 1944, PhD in Physics, 1948. From asst. prof. to assoc. prof. Johns Hopkins U., Balt., 1948-58, chmn. dept., 1965-68, prof. physics, 1958-77, Decker prof., 1978-98, Decker prof. emeritus, 1998; research physicist Brookhaven Nat. Lab., 1952-53. Fellow NSF, 1961, 69, John S. Guggenheim Meml. Found., 1974-75. Fellow Am. Phys. Soc. Home: Baltimore, Md. Deceased.

MADDEN, BARTLEY JOSEPH, economist; b. N.Y.C., Nov. 3, 1943; s. Bartley Joseph and Genevieve Helen (Ghegan) Madden; m. Maricela Elizondo, 1995; children: Lucinda, Miranda, Jeffrey, Gregory. BS in Mech. Engring., U. So. Calif., Los Angeles, 1965; MBA, U. Calif., Berkeley, 1970. V.p. Callard, Madden & Assocs., Chgo., 1970—83; sr. v.p. Harbor Capital Advisors, Chgo., 1983—92; ptnr. Holt Value Assocs., Chgo., 1993—2001; mng. dir. CSFB Holt, Chgo., from 2002. Author: CFROI Valuation: A Total System Approach to Valuing the Firm, 1999. With U.S. Army, 1966-68. Mem. Tau Beta Pi, Beta Gamma Sigma. Deceased.

MADDOUX, MARLIN, broadcast executive, journalist, author; Founder, former pres., CEO USA Radio Networks, Dallas. Former host (radio talk show) Point of View. Died Mar. 4, 2004.

MADSEN, SVEN DYRLOEV, retired corporate executive; b. Nakskov, Denmark, Mar. 12, 1935; s. Harry Christian Dyrloev and Sigrid Marie (Fjelde) M.; m. Anna Lone Mathiesen, Nov. 9, 1963; children: Mads Christian, Lars Peter. Grad., Royal Vet. Coll., Copenhagen, 1959; M in Commerce, Coll. Econs. and Bus. Adminst., Copenhagen, 1962. Submgr. DAT-Schaub, Copenhagen, 1959-62; from dep. mgr. to pres., mng. dir. ESS Food, Copenhagen, 1962-85; pres., mng. dir. J. Lauritzen Holding Ltd., Copenhagen, 1985-95; ret., 1995. Chmn., non-exec. bd. mem. several founds. and indsl. cos., Denmark, from 1995. Decorated 1st Degree knight of Dannebrog. Home: Holte, Denmark. Died Nov. 25, 2003.

MAEHR, JOAN, interior designer; b. Cedar Rapids, Iowa, Mar. 14, 1928; d. Bedford Paul and Alta (Booton) Lattner; m. Edwin Maehr, Apr. 1, 1950 (dec. Oct. 1986); children: Deborah Maehr Aldridge, Judith Maehr Evans, Stephanie Ann. BS in Applied Art, Iowa State U., 1950. Sr. designer Gabbert's Design Studio, Dallas, 1973-84; pres. Joan Maehr, Inc., Addison, Tex., from 1984. Mem. Lyon Furniture Merc. Agy., Allied Bd. Trade. Prin. works include: Theta Showhouse, Degolyer Estate Library; contbr. articles to local publs. Mem. Nat. Trust for Historic Preservation, Tex. Hist. Found., Smithsonian Assocs., Allied Bd. Trade. Mem. Am. Soc. Interior Designers (profl.), Am. Craft Guild, Internat. Arabian Horse Assn., Tex. Horse Racing Assn., Metrocrest C. of C. Home: The Colony, Tex. Died Oct. 29, 2000.

MAFFETT, ANDREW LEWIS, mathematician, consultant; b. Port Royat, Pa., Oct. 23, 1921; s. Harvey Lewis and Mary Hamer (Crozier) M.; m. Pauline Catherine Lupp Maffett, May 1, 1943. AB, Gettysburg Coll., Pa., 1943; MA, U. Mich., 1948. Instr. Gettysburg (Pa.) Coll., 1946-47; rsch. assoc. Willow Run (Mich.) Lab., 1951-52; asst. prof. Gettysburg (Pa.) Coll., 1952-54; rsch. engr. Engring. Rsch. Inst., Ann Arbor, Mich., 1954-60; rsch. mathematician Conduction Corp., Ann Arbor, Mich., 1961-67; rsch. mathmetician KMS Industries, Ann Arbor, Mich., 1967-69; prof. math. U. Mich., Dearborn, Mich., 1969-85; cons., Signature Theory various orgns., Dexter, Mich., 1969-94; retired, from 1994. Cons. Johns Hopkins U. Applied Physics Lab., Laurel, Md., 1972-85, Environ. Rsch. Inst. Mich., Ann Arbor, 1972—; mem. adv. bd. Radar Target Scatter Facilitiy, Holloman AFB, N.Mex., 1984-89. Author: Topics for a Statistical Description of Radar Cross Section, 1989; guest editor Electromagnetics, 1984. Treas. Soil Conservation Dist. Bd. Washtenaw County, Ann Arbor, Mich., 1972-78. 1st lt. U.S. Army, 1943-46, 51. Mem. La Confrerie des Chevaliers du Tastevin, Nuits St. Georges, France, Sigma Xi. Home: Dexter, Mich. Died July 2, 1999.

MAGGIO, MICHAEL JOHN, artistic director; b. Chgo., July 3, 1951; s. Carlo and Genevieve (Sparacino) M.; m. Janice St. John, Sept. 7, 1974 (div. June 1977); m. Julie Carol Jackson, Mar. 29, 1980 (div. Dec. 1994); 1 child, Ben. BA, U. Ariz., 1973, MA, 1974. Artistic dir. Woodstock (Ill.) Music Theatre Festival, 1980-82, Northlight Theatre, Evanston, Ill., 1983-87; assoc. artistic dir. Goodman Theatre, Chgo., from 1987; dean Theatre Sch. De Paul U., from 1999. Artistic advisor Columbia Coll., Chgo., 1987-97; assoc. prof. acting and directing, Theatre Sch. DePaul U., 1997—. Directed As You Like It, All the Rage, Arcadia, Another Midsummer Night, Brutality of Fact, Black Snow, Wings, Shakespeare's A Midsummer Night's Dream, Romeo and Juliet, Uncle Vanya, 1989-90, A Flea In Her Ear, A Christmas Carol, Sunday In The Park With George, Cyrano De Bergerac, The Front Page, The Dining Room; artistic dir. Northlight Theatre premieres of Dealing, City On The Make, Heart of A Dog, (Am. premiere) Ballerina, (world premiere) Sondheim Suite; dir. The Real Thing, West Memphis Mojo, Highest Standard of Living, Endgame, The Winter's Tale, Travesties, Tartuffe, Spokesong, Ladies In Waiting; dir. prodn. of Titus Andronicus for N.Y. Shakespeare Festival; prodns. include McCarter Theatre, Guthrie Theater in Mpls., The Cleve. Playhouse, Ariz. Theatre Co., Actors Theatre of Louisville, Seattle Repertory Co. Chmn. Michael Merritt Award and Endowment Fund, Colubmia Coll, Chgo. Recipient Joseph Jefferson "Jeff" Citation 1975-76. 78, 93-94, Father of Yr. award, Chgo. Father's Day Com., 1986, Excellence in Arts award De Paul U. Theatre Sch., 1993, Obie award, 1993, Home: Chicago, Ill. Deceased.

MAGLIOCHETTI, JOSEPH M. automotive executive; BA, U. Ill. With Victor Mfg. Co. subs. Dana Corp., Chgo., 1967-78; gen. mgr. spicer clutch divsn. Dana Corp., Toledo, 1978-80, pres. London, 1980-85, group v.p. N.Am. ops. Toledo, 1985-90, pres. automotive N.Am. ops., 1990-92, pres. N.Am. ops., 1992-96, pres., 1996-97, pres., COO, 1997-99, pres., CEO & chmn., 1999—2003. Died Sept. 22, 2003.

MAGOON, JOHN HENRY, JR., airlines executive; b. Honolulu, Dec. 2, 1915; s. John H. and Juliet (Carroll) M.; m. Adele Whitlock, Oct. 28, 1939 (dec. Jan. 29, 1975); 1 dau., Sara.; m. Cynthia Jeanette Baker, Mar. 19, 1976. Student, U. Calif.-Berkeley, 1933-35. Pres. Hawaiian Linen Supply, Ltd., 1941-60; pres., dir. Hawaiian Securities & Realty, Ltd., Honolulu, from 1955; former chmn. Hawaiian Airlines, Inc., Honolulu, former CEO, former pres., bd. dirs. Dir. Hawaiian Trust Co., Ltd., Castle & Cooke, Inc., Magoon Bros., Ltd., Magoon Estate, Ltd., First Ins. Co. Hawaii, Ltd., Cox Broadcasting Corp., Atlanta Mem. C. of C. Hawaii (dir.), Phi Kappa Psi. Clubs: Outrigger Canoe, Pacific, Oahu Country, Waialae Country, Diamond Head Tennis; Met. (Washington). Home: Honolulu, Hawaii. Died Nov. 24, 2003.

MAJOR, JOHN KEENE, radio broadcasting executive; b. Kansas City, Missouri, Aug. 3, 1924; s. Ralph Hermon and Margaret Norman (Jackson) M.; m. Gracemary Somers (Westing), Apr. 9, 1950 (div.); children: John Westing, Ann Somers, Richard Jackson; m. Lee Adair (Jordan), June 25, 1970. Attended, U. Kansas City, 1940—41; BS, Yale U., 1943; MS, 1947; DSc, U. Paris, 1951. Lab. asst. physics Yale U., 1943—44; sci. staff spl. studies group, div. war rsch. Columbia U., SC, 1944; sci. cons. Sonar Analysis Group, 1946—47; instr. physics and chemistry Am. Cmty. Sch., Paris, 1948—49; research fellow Ctr. Nat. Rsch. Sci. Lab. de Chimie Nuclear, Coll. France, Paris, 1951; Carnegie Found. fellow Laboratoire Curie, Inst. Radium, Paris, 1951; instr., research asst. physics Yale U., 1952—55; assoc. prof. physics Western Res. U., 1955—57, chmn. dept., 1955—60, Perkins prof. physics, 1957—66, chmn. dept., 1960—64; staff assoc. U. sci. devel. sect. div. instl. programs NSF, 1964—68, cons., 1968—69; prof. physics, dean Grad. Sch. Arts and Sci., U. Cin., 1968—71; prof. physics N.Y. Univ., 1971—74, dean Grad. Sch. Arts and Sci., 1971—73; vis. scholar Alfred P. Sloan Sch. Mgmt., Mass. Inst. Tech., 1973—74; prof. physics Northeastern Ill. U., Chgo., 1974—77, v.p. acad. affairs, 1974—75; gen. mgr. Sta. WONO, Syracuse, NY, 1977; dir. rsch. and mktg. Sta. WFMT, Chgo., 1978—81; chmn. bd., pres. KCMA, Inc., from 1980; gen. mgr. Sta. KCMA, 1981—88. Mem. exec. com. radio project Ctr. for Pub. Resources, 1980-81; vis. prof. U. Mysore, 1967, Sardar Patel U., 1968; sci. equation specialist U. Tunis, 1968. Contbr. articles to profl. journals. Bd. dir. Concertime, 1985—, pres. 1993-95; bd. dir. Tulsa Opera, 1984-95, Tulsa Philharm. Soc., 1988-95; vol. exec. Internat. Exec. Svc. Corps, Bulgaria, 1993, Armenia 1995, Ga. 1996. Fellow Lab. für Technische Physik, Technische Hochschule Munich, 1960-61; Fulbright Fellow U. Paris, 1949-50. Mem. Classical Music Broadcasters Assn. (exec. v.p., 1979-80, bd. dir. 1979-82, 85-87, 89-93, pres. 1980-81, 90-91, Walter Neiman Award 1998), Cosmos Club, Washington, Sigma Xi. Home: Lakeside, Ariz. Died Mar. 13, 2003.

MAKELA, BENJAMIN R. editor, research director; b. Hancock, Mich., Mar. 23, 1922; s. Charles Robert and Engel (Kruka) M.; m. Betty Virginia Shade, June 26, 1954; 1 son, Gregory Strickler. BA, George Washington U., 1943; MA, Stanford, 1954. Statistician Dept. Commerce, 1946; statistician Nat. Fertilizer Assn., 1947-48; research economist U.S. C. of C., 1948-53; asso. dir. Financial Execs. Inst., N.Y.C., 1953-63; editor Financial Exec., 1963-72; research dir. Financial Execs. Research Found., 1966-83. Cons., 1983— Editor: (with Richard F. Vancil) The CFO's Handbook, 1970, How to Use and Invest in Letter Stock, 1970, (with William Chatlos) Strategy of Corporate Tender Offers, 1971, (with D.R. Carmichael) Corporate Financial Reporting: The Benefits and Problems of Disclosure, 1986, (with Mark E. Haskins) The CFO Handbook, 1997: mem. editorial adv. bd. also author chpt. Financial Exec.'s Handbook. Served with AUS, 1943-46, 51-53. Mem. Am. Acctg. Assn., Stanford Alumni Club, Squadron A Club, Halifax Club, Smyrna Yacht Club, Men's Garden Club of New Smyrna Beach, Phi Beta Kappa, Pi Gamma Mu, Omicron Delta Gamma, Sigma Nu. Republican. Baptist. Home: Holly Hill, Fla. Died Nov. 5, 2002.

MALAMED, SASHA, anatomy and embryology educator, cell biologist; b. Bklyn., May 6, 1928; s. Harry and Fannie (Felman) M.; m. Lyanne Schneider, Aug. 12, 1956; 1 child, David. BA, U. Pa., 1948, MS, 1950; PhD, Columbia U., 1955. Rsch. assoc. U. Iowa, Iowa City, 1954-55; instr. CUNY, N.Y.C., 1955; rsch. assoc. Columbia U., N.Y.C., 1955-56; instr. Albert Einstein Coll. of Medicine, Bronx, N.Y., 1958-59, asst. prof., 1959-67; assoc. prof. Robert Wood Johnson Med. Sch. U. Medicine & Dentistry of N.J., Piscataway, 1967-74, prof. Robert Wood Johnson Med. Sch., from 1974. Vis. prof. St. Bartholomews Hosp. Med. Sch., London, 1986-87. Contbr. articles to Jour. Biol. Chemistry, Endocrinology, Jour. Cell Biology, Cell Tissue Research. USPHS fellow Columbia U., 1952-54, Case Western Res. U., 1956-58. Achievements include research in osmotic behavior of mitochondria, steroid self-suppression of adrenocortical cells, ACTH stimulation of changes in actin in adrenocortical cells, neurotrophic and neural control of ovarian follicle formation. Home: Bridgewater, NJ. Died Sept. 19, 2001.

MALMSTADT, HOWARD VINCENT, university chancellor; b. Marinette, Wis., Feb. 17, 1922; s. Guy August and Nellie (RUsch) M.; m. Carolyn Gay Hart, Aug. 3, 1947; children: Cynthia Sue, Alice Ann, Jonathan Howard. BS, U. Wis., 1943, MS, 1948, PhD, 1950. Postdoctoral rsch. assoc. U. Wis., Madison, 1950-51; mem. faculty U. Ill., Urbana, from 1951, prof. chemistry, 1961-78, emeritus, from 1978, dir. electronic insts., 1960-74; dean sci. and tech., provost, internat. v.p. acad. affairs U. of the Nations, 1978—2001, internat. chancellor, from 2001. Fulbright-Hays disting. prof., Romania, 1978; cons. to govt. and industry. Author textbooks and articles in field; mem. adv. bds. profl. jours.; patentee sci. instruments. Served as officer USNR, 1943-46. Recipient award in edn. Instrument Soc. Am., 1970, Outstanding Analytical Chemist award Pitts. Conf. Analytical Chemistry and Applied Spectroscopy, 1978, ISCO award for contbns. biochem instrumentation, 1980, award for Outstanding Contbns. in Chemistry, ANACHEM, 1987; Guggenheim fellow, 1960; grantee NSF, 1965-78, NIH, 1975-80. Mem. Am. Chem. Soc. (award instrumentation 1963, award analytical chemistry 1976, award for excellence in tchg. 1984), Soc. Applied Spectroscopy (M.F. Hasler award 1995), Am. Assn. Clin. Chemists. Died July 7, 2003.

MALONE, MICHAEL PETER, academic administrator, historian; b. Pomeroy, Wash., Apr. 18, 1940; s. John Albert and Dolores Frances (Cheyne) M.; m. Kathleen Malone, Apr. 17, 1983; children: John Thomas, Molly Christine. BA in History, Gonzaga U., 1962; PhD in Am. Studies, Wash. State U., Pullman, 1966. Asst. prof. history Tex. A&M U., College Station, 1966-67; asst. prof., prof. history Mont.

State U., Bozeman, from 1967, dean grad. studies, 1979-88, v.p. acad. affairs, 1988-90, pres., from 1991. Bd. dirs. Buttrey Food and Drug, Commn. on Colls. of N.W. Assn. of Schs. and Colls. Author: The Battle for Butte, 1981 (Sick award 1981), Historians and The American West, 1983, (with others) Montana: A History of Two Centuries, 1976, 2d edit., 1991, The American West: A 20th Century History, 1989, James J. Hill, Empire Builder of the Northwest, 1995. Mem. Western History Assn., Nat. Assn. State Univs. and Land-Grant Colls. (exec. bd. dirs.). Home: Bozeman, Mont. Died Dec. 1999.

MALOOF, WALEED GABRIEL, urologist; b. N.Y.C., Feb. 28, 1924; s. Joseph and Afdokiah (Gabriel) M.; m. Ardyce Brown, June 10, 1972. BA, Columbia U., 1946; MD, N.Y. Med. Coll., 1948. Diplomate Am. Bd. Urologists. Intern Fordham Hosp., Bronx, N.Y., 1948-49, resident, 1949-50, urology resident, 1950-51, Queens (N.Y.) Gen. Hosp., 1951-52, St. Luke's Hosp., N.Y.C., 1954-55, Manhattan VA Hosp., N.Y.C., 1955-56; urology fellow Meml. Hosp., N.Y.C., 1956-59; pub. health physician N.Y. State Dept. Health, N.Y.C., 1976-97. Instr. urology Coll. Physicians and Surgeons, N.Y.C., 1975-85; med. dir. Luteran Community Svcs. Capt. USAF, 1952-54. Fellow Am. Coll. Surgeons, Internat. Coll. Surgeons, Fertility Soc., N.Y. Acad. Sci. Republican. Roman Catholic. Deceased.

MANCHESTER, WILLIAM, writer; b. Attleboro, Mass., Apr. 1, 1922; s. William Raymond and Sallie Elizabeth (Thompson) M.; m. Julia Brown Marshall, Mar. 27, 1948 (dec. May 1998); children: John Kennerly, Julie Thompson, Laurie. BA, U. Mass., 1946; AM, U. Mo., 1947; LHD (hon.), U. Mass., 1965, U. New Haven, 1979, Russell Sage Coll., 1990; LittD (hon.), Skidmore Coll., 1987, U. Richmond, 1988; LittD (hon.), Wesleyan U., 2002. Reporter Daily Oklahoman, 1945-46; reporter, fgn. corr., war corr. Balt. Sun, 1947-55; mng. editor Wesleyan U. Publs., 1955-64; fellow Ctr. for Advanced Studies Wesleyan U., Middletown, Conn., 1959-60, writer-in-residence, 1975—2004, adj. prof. history, 1979-92; fellow Pierson Coll. Yale U., from 1991; prof. of history emeritus Wesleyan U., 1992—2004. Author: Disturber of the Peace, 1951, The City of Anger, 1953, Shadow of the Monsoon, 1956, Beard the Lion, 1958, A Rockefeller Family Portrait, 1959, The Long Gainer, 1961, Portrait of a President, 1962, The Death of a President, 1967 (Book-of-the-Month Club selection), The Arms of Krupp, 1968 (Lit. Guild selection), The Glory and the Dream, 1974 (Lit. Guild selection), Controversy and Other Essays in Journalism, 1976, American Caesar: Douglas MacArthur, 1880-1964, 1978 (Book-of-Month Club selection), Goodbye, Darkness, 1980 (Book-of-the-Month Club selection), The Last Lion: Winston Spencer Churchill Visions of Glory 1874-1932, 1983 (Book-of-the-Month Club selection), One Brief Shining Moment: Remembering Kennedy, 1983 (Book-of-the-Month Club selection), The Last Lion: Winston Spencer Churchill Alone 1932-1940, 1988 (Book-of-the-Month Club selection), In Our Time, 1989, A World Lit Only by Fire: The Medieval Mind and the Renaissance, Portrait of an Age, 1992; contbr. to Ency. Brit., various publs. Pres. bd. trustees Friends of U. Mass. Libr., 1970-71, trustee, 1970-74; bd. dirs. Winston Churchill Travelling Fellowships, 1990-99. Sgt. USMC, 1942-45, PTO. Decorated Purple Heart; recipient Dag Hammarskjöld prize Assn. Internationale Correspondents Diplomatiques, Rome, 1967, citation for best book on fgn. affairs Overseas Press Club, 1968, U. Mo. Honor award for disting. svc. in journalism, 1969, Conn. Book award, 1975, Pres.'s Cabinet award U. Detroit, 1981, Frederick S. Troy medal U. Mass., 1981, McConnaughy award Wesleyan U., 1981, N.Y. Pub. Libr. Lit. Lion award, 1983, Disting. Pub. Svc. award Conn. Bar Assn., 1985, Lincoln Lit. award Union League Club N.Y., 1983, Blenheim award Internat. Churchill Soc., 1986, Washington Irving award, 1988, Sarah Josepha Hale award, 1993, Helmerich Disting. Author award, 2000, Nat. Humanities medal, 2002; Guggenheim fellow, 1959-60. Mem. PEN, Soc. Am. Historians, Am. Hist. Assn., Authors Guild, Century Club. Democrat. Avocation: photography. Home: Middletown, Conn. Died June 1, 2004.

MANDEL, CAROLA PANERAI (MRS. LEON MANDEL), foundation trustee; b. Havana, Cuba, 1920; d. Camilo and Elvira (Bertini) Panerai; m. Leon Mandel, Apr. 9, 1938. Mem. women's bd. Northwestern Meml. Hosp., Chgo.; trustee Carola and Leon Mandel Fund Loyola U. Foundation trustee; b. Havana, Cuba; d. Camilo and Elvira (Bertini) Panerai; ed. pvt. schs., Havana and Europe; m. Leon Mandel, Apr. 9, 1938. Mem. women's bd. Northwestern Meml. Hosp., Chgo. Trustee Carola and Leon Mandel Fund Loyola U., Chgo. Life mem. Chgo. Hist. Soc., Guild of Chgo. Hist. Soc., Smithsonian Assos., Nat. Skeet Shooting Assn. Frequently named among Ten Best Dressed Women in U.S.; chevalier Confrerie des Chevaliers du Tastevin. Capt. All-Am. Women's Skeet Team, 1952, 53, 54, 55, 56; only woman to win a men's nat. championship, 20 gauge, 1954, also high average in world over men, 1956, in 12 gauge with 99.4 per cent; European women's live bird shooting championship, Venice, Italy, 1957, Porto, Portugal, 1961; European woman's target championship, Torino, Italy, 1958; woman's world champion live-bird shooting, Sevilla, Spain, 1959, Am. Contract Bridge League Life Master, 1987. Named to Nat. Skeet Shooting Assn. Hall of Fame, 1970; inducted in U.S. Pigeon shooting Fedn. Hall of Fame, 1992. Mem. Soc. Four Arts. Club: Everglades (Palm Beach, Fla.), The Beach. Capt. All-Am. Women's Skeet Team, 1952, 53, 54, 55, 56. Frequently named among Ten Best Dressed Women in U.S.; chevalier Confrerie des Chevaliers du Tastevein; only woman to win a men's nat. championship, 20 gauge, 1954; high average in world over men, 1956, in 12 gauge with 99.4 per cent; European woman's world champion live-bird shooting, Sevilla, Spain, 1595, Am. Contract Bridge League Life Master, 1987; inducted to U.S. Pigeon Shooting Fedn. Hall of Fame, 1992. Mem. Chgo. Hist. Soc., Guild Chgo. Hist. Soc., Smithsonian Assn., Nat. Skeet Shooting Assn. (named to Hall of Fame 1970), Soc. Four Arts, Everglades Club, Beach Club. Home: Palm Beach, Fla. Died June 23, 2002.

MANDEVILLE, GILBERT HARRISON, consulting engineering executive; b. Bklyn., July 6, 1910; s. Gilbert Spier and Minnie (Ross) M.; m. Mildred Schwagerman, June 20, 1936; 1 child, Terry Melinda BS, Seattle U., 1953. Registered profl. engr., Wash. Exec. dir., v.p. Leo O. Daly Co., Seattle, 1952-57; ptnr., cons. engr. Mandeville & Berge, Architects and Engrs., Seattle, 1957-83. Dir., sec.-treas. Riverfront Assocs.; dir. U.S. Devel. Co. Chmn. Seattle City Planning Commn., 1960-62, Puget Sound Regional Planning Coun., 1960-62. Lt. comdr. USNR, 1947-52. Fellow ASCE (life); mem. IEEE (life), Am. Arbitration Assn. Clubs: Seattle Engring. Presbyterian. Home: Woodinville, Wash. Deceased.

MANGIONE, JERRE GERLANDO, author, educator; b. Rochester, N.Y., Mar. 20, 1909; s. Gaspare and Giuseppina (Polizzi) M.; m. Patricia Anthony, Feb. 18, 1957. BA, Syracuse U., 1931; MA (hon.), U. Pa., 1971, LittD (hon.), 1980; LHD (hon.), SUNY, Brockport, 1987. Writer, Time mag., 1931; book editor Robert M. McBride & Co., N.Y.C., 1934-37; nat. coordinating editor Fed. Writers' Project, 1937-39; spl. asst. to U.S. commr. immigration and naturalization, 1942-48; advt. writer, pub. relations dir., 1948-61; mem. faculty U. Pa., 1961-98, dir. writing program, 1965-77, prof. English, 1968-77, emeritus, 1977—, founding dir. Italian Studies Center, 1978-80, coord. cultural events, 1980-82. Vis. lectr. Bryn Mawr Coll., 1966-67; vis. prof. Trinity Coll., Rome, summer 1973, Queens Coll., 1980; chmn. Leon lectr. com. U. Pa., 1964-85; acting dir. Yaddo, 1977-78; editor WFLM Phila. Guide, 1960-61; book reviewer, 1931—; adv. editor Italian Americana, 1974-84, 90—; mem. lit. panel NEA, 1980-81; spkr. main address Symposium on Italian and Italian-Am. Women in '90s, SUNY, Stony Brook, 1993. Author: Mount Allegro: A Memoir of Italian Life, 1943, 7th edit., 1998 (hist. marker commemorating area erected in Rochester, 1986, stage adaptation premiere, Rochester), 1992, Spanish edit., 1944, Italian edit., 1947, rev., 1983, (novel) Ship and the Flame, 1948, Swedish edit., 1949, Reunion in Sicily, 1950, 2d edit., 1984, Italian edit., 1992, Night Search, 1965, To Walk the Night, Brit. edit., 1966, Italian edit., 1987, Life Sentences for Everybody, 1966, (fables) A Passion for Sicilians: The World Around Danilo Dolci, 1968, 3d edit., 1985, America is Also Italian, 1969, The Dream and the Deal: Federal Writers Project (1935-43), 1972, 3d edit., 1983 (nominated for Nat. Book award 1972), Mussolini's March on Rome, 1975, An Ethnic At Large: A Memoir of America in the Thirties and Forties, 1978, 2d edit., 1983, (with Ben Morreale) La Storia: Five Centuries of the Italian American Experience, 1992; (pamphlet on Phila. lit. history) By Reason of Birth or Residence, 1988; contbr. to newspapers and mags. Chmn. lit. arts com. Phila. Art Alliance, 1958-61; mem. adv. bd. U. Pa. Press, 1983-84; founding mem. exec. bd. Am.-Italy Soc., 1959-94, Inst. Contemporary Art U. Pa., 1964-77, Am. Italian Hist. Assn., 1969—, Am. Inst. Italian Studies, 1975-82, Amici, 1981—; pres. Friends Danilo Dolci, Inc., 1969-71. Guggenhiem fellow,1945; Fulbright Rsch. fellow, 1965; MacDowell Colony fellow, Yaddo fellow; Va. Ctr. Arts fellow; Rockefeller grantee, 1968; Am. Philos. Soc. grantee, 1971; Earhart Found. grantee, 1975; NEH grantee, 1980-83; decorated Knight Comdr. Order Star Solidarity, Italy, 1971; recipient Key to City Rochester, 1963, 10th Ann. Lit. award Friends Rochester Pub. Libr., 1966, Justinian Soc. award, 1966, Phila. Athenaeum Lit. award, 1973, Presdl. award Am. Inst. for Italian Culture, 1979, Outstanding Achievement award Am.-Italian Hist. Assn., 1985, Key to City New Orleans, 1988, Pa. Gov.'s award for Excellence in Humanities, 1989, Leonardo da Vinci award Italian Heritage and Culture Month Com., 1989; named Person of Yr. Italian Ams. Delaware County, 197, 86, Premio Nazionale Empedocie, 1984, Legion of Honor medal Chapel Four Chaplains, 1984; Mangione papers housed at U. Rochester Libr. Dept. of Rare Books and Spl. Collections; recipient Internat. Arts award Columbus Countdown, 1990, 92; honored by Libr. of Congress for lit. career with an exhibit titled: Jerre Mangione, An Ethnic at Large, 1992, Fed. Writer's Project, Christopher Columbus Qunicentenary award, 1992, Mariano DiVito Human Achievement award Amici Friends of Italian Studies U. Pa., 1993, Distinction in Lit. Achievement award Columbus Citizens Found., 1993. Fellow Soc. Am. Historians; mem. Author's Guild, Franklin Inn, Assn. Writers of Agrigento in Sicily (nominated hon. pres. 1994), Sons of Italy. Home: Haverford, Pa. Died Aug. 17, 1998.

MANISCHEWITZ, BERNARD, food products company executive; b. Cin., Dec. 24, 1913; s. Jacob U. and Pearl (Quitman) M.; m. Esther Manischewitz, July 19, 1932 (div.); children: Elaine (Mrs. Yehiel Sorki), Ruby (Mrs. Yitzchok Gass), Edith E. (Mrs. Howard Best); m. Beatrice Hoffman, Apr. 11, 1976. Certificate in factory mgmt, U. Cin., 1940; B.C.S., N.Y.U., 1944. Asst. supt. B. Manischewitz Co., 1934-42, dir., sec., 1942-49, pres., 1949-76, chmn. bd., 1976-78, chmn. exec. com. and chief exec. officer, 1978-80, chmn. bd., chmn. exec. com., cons., 1980—90. Ofcl. del. 7th-11th Internat. Mgmt. Congresses. Chmn. Manhattan div. State of Israel Bonds, 1960-61. Mem. Chief Execs. Forum, Inc. Home: Boynton Beach, Fla. Died Sept. 20, 2003.

MANN, HERBIE, flutist; b. N.Y.C., Apr. 16, 1930; s. Harry C. and Ruth (Brecher) Solomon; m. Ruth Shore, Sept. 8, 1956 (div. 1971); children: Paul J., Claudia; m. Jan Clonts, July 11, 1971 (div. 1990); 2 children: Laura, Geoffrey; m. Susan Janeal Arison, 1991. Student, Manhattan Sch. Music, 1952-54. Founder, pres. Herbie Mann Music Corp., N.Y.C., from 1959; founder Kokopelli Music, Santa Fe, from 1992. Toured Africa for Dept. State, 1960, Brazil, 1961-62, Japan, 1964, Scandanavia, Cyprus and Turkey, 1971; pres. Herbie Mann Orch., Inc., 5 Face of Music Prodns., Inc., Rupadia Music, Inc. Recorded over 100 albums under own name, 1954-2003; African Suite, 1959, At the Village Gate, 1962, Brasil, Bossa Nova & Blues, 1962, Latin Mann, 1965, Memphis Underground, 1969, Memphis Two step, 1971 Push, Push, 1971, Missippi Gambler, 1974, Bird in a Silver Cage, 1977, Caminho De Casa, 1990. Deep Pocket, 1992, The Evolution of Mann: The Herbie Mann Anthology, 1994, Eastern European Roots, 2000. Served with AUS, 1948-52. Recipient Downbeat award for flute, 1958-70 Mem. ASCAP, Nat. Acad. Rec. Arts and Scis. Died July 1, 2003.

MANSHIP, DOUGLAS, broadcast and newspaper executive; b. Baton Rouge, Nov. 3, 1918; s. Charles P. and Leora (Douthit) M.; m. Jane French, Jan. 31, 1942 (div. 1981); children: Douglas Lewis, Richard French, David Charles, Dina. Student, La. State U., 1936-41, U. Heidelberg, 1937, U. Colo., 1938-39. Reporter State Times and Morning Advocate, 1945-47, pub., from 1970; with Baton Rouge Broadcasting Co., from 1947, pres., from 1948; pres., chmn. bd. La IV Broadcasting Corp., from 1953; vice chmn. bd. Radio Free Europe/Radio Liberty, from 1978. Chmn. Mobile Video Tapes, Inc., 1960; pres. emeritus Capital City Press; bd. dirs. City Nat. Bank, TV Stas. Inc. Campaign chmn. Community Chest, 1950, bd. dirs., 1950-52, pres., 1951. With USAAF, World War II. Mem. Baton Rouge C. of C. (pres. 1963), La. C. of C. (v.p.), Assn. for Profl. Broadcasting Edn., Council for A Better La., Assn. La. Chambers Commerce, So. Newspaper Pubs. Assn. (pres. 1977-78), Kappa Alpha, Sigma Delta Chi. Episcopalian. Home: Baton Rouge, La. Deceased.

MANSON, GORDON, pediatrician; b. Burlington, Vt., June 5, 1922; s. David and Anna (Cross) M.; m. Mary Elizabeth Eckelman, Aug. 6, 1943; children: David, Andrew. Student, U. Vt., 1941; BA, U. Kans., 1948; MD, U. Vt., 1952. Intern Iowa Meth. Hosp., Des Moines, 1952-53; resident pediatrics Blank Children's Hosp., Des Moines, 1953-55; staff pediatrician Henry Ford Hosp., Detroit, 1955-91; clin. assoc. prof. pediatrics U. Mich., Ann Arbor, 1974-91; retired, 1991. Pediatrician Franklin Settlement House Pediatric Clinic, Detroit, 1962-65, Community Health and Social Svcs. Clinic, Detroit, 1972-87. Contbr. rsch. papers and articles to profl. jours. Adult leader Boy Scouts Am., Detroit, 1959-71. 1st lt. U.S. Army, 1942-46. Decorated Bronze star, Purple Heart. Fellow Am. Acad. Pediatrics; mem. AMA, AM. Bd. Pediatrics, Prismatic Club Detroit (pres. 1991), Detroit Pediatric Soc. (pres. 1971). Avocations: hist. lit., smallarms, target shooting. Home: Holly, Mich. Died Mar. 7, 2001.

MANSOOR, MENAHEM, emeritus Semitic languages educator, author; b. Port Said, Egypt, Aug. 4, 1911; came to U.S., 1954, naturalized, 1963; s. Asher S. and Yonah H. (Shalom) M.; m. Claire Dora Kramer, Nov. 29, 1951; children: Yardena Miriam, Daniel Jonathan. Student in oriental studies, U. London, 1934-39; BA with honors, Trinity Coll., Dublin, Ireland, 1941, MA, 1942, PhD, 1944; PhD (hon.), Edgewood Coll., 1986. Sr. edn. officer, Jerusalem, 1946-49; asst. press attache Brit. Fgn. Service, Tel Aviv, 1949-54; research fellow, lectr. Johns Hopkins Oriental Sem., 1954-55; mem. faculty U. Wis., 1955-82, prof. Semitic langs., 1955-77, chmn. dept. Semitic langs. and lits., 1955-77, Joseph L. Baron prof., 1973-82, emeritus prof., 1982—2001. Mem. accreditation team North Central Assn. Colls. and Univs.; Chmn. Hebrew com. Coll. Entrance Exam. Bd., 1964-69; chmn., founder Madison Bibl. Archaeol. Soc., 1967; mem. bd. Wis. Writers' Council, 1964— Author: Thanksgiving Hymns, 1960, English Arabic Dictionary of Political, Diplomatic and Conference Terms, 1960, The Dead Sea Scrolls, 1966, Legal and Documentary Arabic Readers, 1966, Political and Diplomatic History of the Arab World, Chronological Study, 7 vols, 1977, Advanced Modern Hebrew Literature Readers, 1971, Duties of the Heart, 1973, Biographical Dictionary of the Arab World, 1975, Political and Diplomatic History of the Arab World, Documentary Study, 8 vols, 1977, Contemporary Hebrew, 1976, Biblical Hebrew Step by Step, 1978, vol. 2, 1982, Modern Hebrew Conversation Course, Linguaphone, 1973, (with Fuad Megally) Modern Standard Arabic Course, linguaphone, 1978, Jewish History and Thought: An Introduction, 1992; also textbooks, articles; editor: Hebrew Studies, Iggeret, 1978-81. Fulbright fellow, 1954-55; grantee Am. Philos. Soc., 1958; grantee Wis. Soc. Jewish Learning, 1965, 75; recipient Kohut award Yale, 1955; research fellow Harvard, 1962-63, 64-65; Am. Council Learned Socs. award, 1958-59; Lang. research award NDEA, 1959, 1965, 68-71, 72-73 Mem. Soc. Bibl. Lit. (Midwest pres. 1969-70), Am. Oriental Soc. (Midwest pres. 1970-71), MLA, Wis. Acad. Arts, Scis. and Letters (v.p. 1986-87), Middle East Studies Assn., Assn. Jewish Studies, Nat. Assn. Hebrew Profs. Home: Madison, Wis. Died Oct. 20, 2001.

MANUEL, FRANK EDWARD, writer, educator; b. Boston, Sept. 12, 1910; s. Morris and Jessica (Fredson) M.; m. Fritzie Wilhelmina Prigohzy, Oct. 6, 1936. AB, Harvard U., 1930, AM, 1931, PhD, 1933; diploma, Ecole des Hautes Etudes Politiques et Sociales, Paris, 1933; LittD (hon.), Jewish Theol. Seminary Am., N.Y., 1979; LHD (hon.),

Brandeis U., 1986. Various govt. positions, Washington, 1938-43, 45-47; prof. history Brandeis U., Waltham, Mass., 1949-65, 77-86; prof. emeritus, 1986—2003; prof. history NYU, N.Y.C., 1965-76, prof. emeritus, 1976—2003. Vis. prof. Harvard U., 1960, Hebrew U., Jerusalem, 1972, Oxford (Eng.) U., 1972-73, U. Chgo., 1975, U. Calif., 1976, 85, Boston U., 1986, 87-88; editl. cons. Pegasus Publs., N.Y.C., 1966-67; vis. rsch. fellow Australian Nat. U., Canberra, 1974; vis. scholar Phi Beta Kappa, 1978. Author: The Politics of Modern Spain, 1938, American-Palestine Relations, 1949, The Age of Reason, 1951, The Eighteenth Century Confronts the Gods, 1959, The Prophets of Paris, 1962, Isaac Newton, Historian, 1963, The New World of Henri Saint-Simon, 1956, Shapes of Philosophical History, 1965, A Portrait of Isaac Newton, 1968, Freedom from History and Other Untimely Essays, 1971, The Religion of Isaac Newton, 1974, The Changing of the Gods, 1983, The Broken Staff, 1992, A Requiem for Karl Marx, 1995; co-author: Utopian Thought in the Western World, 1979 (Melcher prize, Emerson award Phi Beta Kappa, Am. Book award); editor: The Enlightenment, 1965, Utopias and Utopian Thought, 1966, Herder's Reflections on the Philosophy of the History of Mankind, 1968; co-editor: French Utopias: An Anthology of Ideal Societies, 1966; mem. editl. bd. Dictionary of the History of Ideas, 1969-70; cons. editor Psychoanalysis and Contemporary Science, 1970; mem. adv. bd. Clio, 1971—. Lt. U.S. Army, 1943-45. Decorated Bronze Star; Guggenheim fellow, 1957-58, fellow Ctr. for Advanced Study in the Behavioral Scis., 1962-63, Inst. for Advanced Study, Princeton, 1976-77. Fellow Am. Acad. Arts and Scis., Phi Beta Kappa. Home: Boston, Mass. Died Apr. 23, 2003.

MARCH, MARION D. writer, astrologer, consultant; b. Nürnberg, Germany, Feb. 10, 1923; came to the U.S., 1941; d. Franz and Grete Dispeker; m. Nico D. March, Sept. 1, 1948; children: Michele, Nico F. Diploma, Ecole de Commerce, Lausanne; attended, Columbia U. Cons. astrologer, L.A., from 1970; founder, pres., tchr. Aquarius Workshops, L.A., from 1975. Internat. lectr. in field, 1976—; chmn. bd. dirs., convention dir. United Astrology Congress, 1986, 89, 92; co-founder, mem. bd. dirs. Assn. for Astrological Networking; cons. in astrology to psychology profls. Author: (books) (with Joan McEvers) The Only Way To... Learn Astrology, 1981-94 (6 vol. series; bestseller), Astrology: Old Theme, New Thoughts, 1984; editor (mag.) ASPECTS, 1976-93; contbr. numerous articles to jours. in field. Recipient Regulus award for edn. United Astrology Congress, 1989, for community svc., 1992, lifetime achievement award 1998, PAI Annual award Profl. Astrologers, Inc., 1990, Syotisha Ratna award Syotish Samsthan of Bombay, India, 1986, Robert Carl Jansky Astrology Leadership award, 1994, Life Achievement award, 1998. Mem. Nat. Coun. for Geocosmic Rsch. (mem. adv. bd.), Internat. Soc. Astrological Rsch., Profl. Astrologers Inc., Astrological Assn. Great Britain, United Astrology Congress. Avocations: reading, gardening, music, skiing, travelling. Home: Encino, Calif. Died May 28, 2001.

MARCUS, MARIE ELEANOR, pianist; b. Roxbury, Mass., May 25, 1914; d. Frank John and Mary Veronica (McDonough) Doherty; (widowed 1965); children: Jack Brown, Mary Liles, Billy Marcus, Barbara Marcus. Grad. high sch., Roxbury. Freelance jazz pianist various clubs including Venetian Palace, 52d Swing Club, from 1933; freelance jazz pianist for depression era entrepreneurs Dutch Schultz, Frank Costello, from 1933. Performer piano jazz series with Mario McPartland, 1982 (George Foster Peabody medal 1982); features in book: Alec Wilder and His Friends (Whitney Balliet), 1972, also features in video about her life, family and career, 1989. Pres. emeritus Cape Cod Jazz Soc., Dennisport, Mass., From 1983. Recipient 50th Anniversary in Show Bus. tribute Am. Heart Assn., 1982; honored Cape Cod Jazz Soc., 1997; recipient Living Treasure award Cape Cod Profl. Women's Assn., 1998. Democrat. Roman Catholic. Avocation: swimming. Died Oct. 10, 2003.

MARGRAVE, JOHN LEE, chemist, educator, university administrator; b. Kansas City, Kans., Apr. 13, 1924; s. Orville Frank and Bernice J. (Hamilton) M.; m. Mary Lou Davis, June 11, 1950; children: David Russell, Karen Sue. BS in Engring. Physics, U. Kans., 1948, PhD in Chemistry, 1950. AEC postdoctoral fellow U. Calif. at Berkeley, 1951-52; from instr. to prof. chemistry U. Wis., Madison, 1952-63; prof. chemistry Rice U., 1963—2004, E.D. Butcher chair, 1986—2004, chmn. dept., 1967-72, dean advanced studies and rsch., 1972-80, v.p., 1980-86. V.p. rsch. Houston Advanced Rsch. Ctr., chief sci. officer, 1989—2004; vis. prof. chemistry Tex. So. U., 1993; vis. disting. prof. U. Wis., 1968, U. Iowa, 1969, Ga. Inst. Tech., 1970, U. Colo., 1975; dir. HARC Materials Sci. Ctr., 1986—93, Coun. Chem. Rsch., 1985—88, Woodlands Sci. and Art Ctr., 1999—2004; various nat. and internat. confs. on chem. vapor deposition of thin diamond films, 1989—98; advisor NROTC Assn., 1984—2004; mem. Wilhelm und Else Heraeus Stiffung Found. Symposium on Alkali Metal Reactions, Germany, 1988; mem. com. on stockpile of chem. weapons NRC, 2001—04; Reilly lectr. Notre Dame, 1968; Patrick lectr. Kans. State U., 2002; Dupont lectr. U. S.C., 1971; Abbott lectr. U. N.D., 1972; Cyanamid lectr. U. Conn., 1973; Sandia lectr. U. N.Mex., 1981; Phi Lambda Upsilon lectr. Kans. State U., 1995; Seydel-Wooley lectr. Ga. Inst. Tech., 1970; lectr. NSF-Japan Joint Thermophys. Properties Symposium, 1983, Ohio Aerospace Inst., 1999; orgnl. com. NATO Conf. on Supercooled Metals, Il Ciocio, Italy, 1993, Internat. Symposia Fluorine Chemistry, Santa Cruz, 1988, Vancouver, B.C., 96, Durham, England, 2000, First, Second, Third and Fourth World Superconductivity Congresses, 1989, 90, 92, 94; chmn. com. chem. processes in severe nuc. accidents NRC, 1987—88, mem. com. on armor and armaments, from 1994, chmn. molten salt reactor panel, 1996—99, mem. com. alt. techs. demilitarization assembled chem. weapons, 1997—2000; cons. to govt. and industry, from 1954; dir. Rice Design Ctr., Houston Area Rsch. Ctr., U. Kans. Rsch. Found., Gulf Univs. Rsch. Consortium, Energy Rsch. and Edn. Found., Spectroscopic Assocs., World Congress on Superconductivity; mem. adv. coms. chem., materials sci., rsch. U. Tenn., Knoxville, Ohio State U., Tex. So. U., La. Bd. Regents; sci. adv. bd. SI Diamond Tech., 1992—96, BioNumerik, 1993—2004, Intrepid Tech., 1994—96; pres. Mar Chem., Inc., 1970—2004, High Temperature Sci., Inc., 1976—99. Editor: Modern High Temperature Sci., 1984; contbg. editor Characterization of High Temperature Vapors, 1967, Mass. Spectrometry in Inorganic Chemistry, 1968; editor High Temperature Sci., 1969-99, Procs. XXIII and XXIV Confs. on Mass Spectrometry, 1975, 76; author: (with others) Bibliography of Matrix Isolation Spectroscopy, 1950-85, 87; contbr. articles to profl. jours.; patentee in field. Served with AUS, 1943-46; capt. Res. ret. Sloan rsch. fellow, 1957-58; Guggenheim fellow, 1960; recipient Kiekhofer Teaching award U. Wis., 1957; IR-100 award for CFX lubricant powder, 1970, IR-100 award for Cryolink, 1986; Tex. Honor Scroll award, 1978; Disting. Alumni citation U. Kans., 1981, Sci. and Tech. award North Harris Montgomery Cmty. Coll., 1994. Fellow AAAS, Am. Inst. Chemists (Chem. Pioneer award 2002), Am. Phys. Soc., Tex. Acad. Sci.; mem. AAUP, NAS, Am. Chem. Soc. (Inorganic Chemistry award 1967, S.W. Regional award 1978, Fluorine Chemistry award 1980, S.E. Tex. Sect. award 1993, chem. edn. com. 1968-70, publs. com. 1973-74, patents and related matters com. 1994-96), Am. Ceramic Soc., Am. Soc. Mass Spectrometry (dir.), Am. Soc. Metals, Electrochem. Soc., Chem. Soc. London, Tex. Philos. Soc., Materials Rsch. Soc., Sigma Xi (Disting. Svc. award 1994), Omicron Delta Kappa, Sigma Tau, Tau Beta Pi, Alpha Chi Sigma. Methodist. Home: Bellaire, Tex. Died Dec. 18, 2003.

MARIER, RAYMOND CONRAD, lawyer; b. Ottawa, Ont., Can., Jan. 4, 1945; s. Conrad Lucien and Mildred Ann (Patton) M.; m. Cheryl Lynn Rutherford, July 18, 1970; children: Megan Leigh, Leslie Lucienne, Elizabeth Ann. BChE, Manhattan Coll., Riverdale, N.Y., 1966; JD, Cornell U., 1969. Bar: N.Y. 1969. Law clk. N.Y. Superior Ct., Appellate divsn. 3d Dept., Albany, 1969-70; assoc. Fish & Neave, N.Y.C., 1970-73; assoc. counsel Corning Inc., Corning, N.Y., 1973-90; sr. v.p., gen. counsel Corning Life Scis., Inc., N.Y.C., 1990-96, Metpath, Inc., Tetersboro, N.J., 1992-96; v.p., gen. counsel Quest Diagnostics Inc., Tetersboro, from 1997. Instr. Cornell Law Sch., Ithaca, 1976-78; pres., dir. South Tier Legal Svcs., Bath, N.Y., 1976-88. Mng. editor Cornell Law Rev., 1968-69. Vice pres., dir. Chemung County Hist. Soc., Elmira, N.Y., 1990-92; dir. Monroe County Legal Assist Corp., Rochester, N.Y., 1976-80. Republican. Roman Catholic. Home: Mountain Lakes, NJ. Died Nov. 3, 2000.

MARIETTA, MARY BLACKFORD, clinical social worker; b. Gallup, N.Mex., Mar. 17, 1929; d. Clyde Walter and Edna (Elder) Blackford; m. Wallace Cameron Sweat, Aug. 31, 1951 (div. Mar. 1958); children: Eric Kevin (dec.), Cynthia Eileen Moriarty; m. George Albert Marietta, June 18, 1967. BS, Ariz. State U., 1951; MSW, UCLA, 1967. Lic. clin. social worker, Calif. Social worker Los Angeles County Dept. Welfare, 1953-57; probation officer Los Angeles Dept. Probation, 1957-70, clin. social worker, 1967-70; social services dir. Epworth Village, York, Nebr., 1970-71; clin. social worker Mental Health Ctr., Lincoln, Nebr., 1971-77; child protective services social worker San Diego County Dept. Social Services, Oceanside, Calif., 1977-87, supr., from 1988; pvt. practice clin. social worker Oceanside, from 1977. Cons. Group Home for Girls, Lincoln, 1972-77; field instr. U. Nebr., Lincoln, 1970-77. Mem. Nat. Assn. Social Workers, Nat. Assn. Social Workers Clin. Registry, N. County Child Abuse Coalition (treas. 1986), Sierra Club. Baha'I. Avocations: dance, reading, gardening, sewing, music. Home: Johnstown, Colo. Deceased.

MARINACCIO, ALEXANDER TERESIO, club administrator; b. Thompsonville, Conn., Dec. 21, 1912; s. Teresio and Alessandrina (Tancredi) M.; m. Gertrude Agnes Bombard, Nov. 4, 1941 (dec. Aug. 1984); children: Alan, Ann Marie, Alice Jean, David, Barbara, Mark; m. Nelle K. Branch, May 2, 1987. Grad. in bus. adminstrn. Baypath Inst., Springfield, Mass., 1935. Editor, Enfield Advertiser 1935; founder Inventors Club Am. Enfield, Conn., 1935—, pres. chmn. bd. 1968—; lectr. on invention process Ga. Inst. Tech., Western New Eng. Coll., other leading univs.; guest appearances on (radio shows) Larry King Radio Show, Voice of Am., (TV shows) 60 Minutes Lifestyles of Rich and Famous; ptnr. Home Appliance Outlet, Enfield, Conn., 1938-42, 45-50; chief research Trinity Research Found., Hartford, Conn., 1950-55; founder, owner Nat. Cons., Enfield, 1955-69. Author: Mistakes Inventors Make, 1960; How to Shape an Idea into an Invention, 1969; How to Protect Your Patent, 1969; Adventures of Mr. Happy Birthday, 1980. Interviewed on TV and radio shows. Adv. bd. U. Conn. Served with USN, 1941-45. Recipient Humanitarian award Inventors Club Am., 1981. Mem. World Invention Orgn., Am. Vets., Sons of Italy, St. Joseph Soc. Roman Catholic. Club: Top Pond (Ware, Mass.). Home: Atlanta, Ga. Died July 31, 2000.

MARKE, JULIUS JAY, law librarian, educator; b. N.Y.C., Jan. 12, 1913; s. Isidore and Anna (Taylor) M.; m. Sylvia Bolotin, Dec. 15, 1946; 1 child, Elisa Hope. BS, CCNY, 1934; LLB, NYU, 1937; BS in Libr. Sci., Columbia U., 1942. Bar: N.Y. 1938. Ref. asst. N.Y. Pub. Libr., 1937—42; pvt. practice law N.Y.C., 1939—41; prof. law, law libr. NYU, 1949—83, prof. law emeritus, from 1983, interim dean of librs., 1975—77; Disting. Prof., dir. Law Libr. St. John's U. Sch. Law, 1983—95, disting. rsch. prof. law, from 1995. Lectr. Columbia Sch. Library Service, 1962-78, adj. prof., 1978-85; cons. Orientation Program Am. Law, 1965-68, Found. Overseas Law Libraries Am. Law, 1968-79, copyright Ford Found., law libraries, Coun. Fgn. Rels., 1990—, Shubert Archives, 1991, others. Author: Vignettes of Legal History, 1965, 2d series, 1977, rev. edit., 2000, Copyright and Intellectual Property, 1967 (with R. Sloane) Legal Research and Law Library Management, rev. edit., 1990, 2003; editor: Modern Legal Forms, 1953, The Holmes Reader, 1955, The Docket Series, 1955—, Bender's Legal Business Forms, 4 vols., 1962; compiler, editor: A Catalogue of the Law Collection at NYU with Selected Annotations, 1953, Dean's List of Recommended Reading for Pre-Law and Law Students, 1958, 84, and others; chmn. editl. bd. Oceana Group, 1977—, Index to Legal Periodicals and Books, 1978—; columnist N.Y. Law Jour., 1970—; contbr. articles to profl. jours. Mem. publs. coun. N.Y.U., 1964-80. Sgt. AUS, 1943-45. Decorated Bronze Star. Mem. ABA, Am. Assn. Law Librs. (pres. 1962-63, Disting. Svc. award 1986, Presdl. cert. of merit 2002), Assn. Am. Law Schs., Coun. of Nat. Libr. Assns. (exec. bd., v.p. 1959, 60), Law Libr. Assn. Greater N.Y. (pres. 1949, 50, chmn. joint com. on libr. edn. 1950-52, 60-61), NYU Law Alumni Assn. (Judge Edward Weinfeld award 1987, mem. exec. bd. 1988—), Columbia Sch. Libr. Svc. Alumni Assn. (pres. 1973-75), Order of Coif (pres. NYU Law Sch. br. 1970-83), NYU Faculty Club (pres. 1966-68), Field Inn, Phi Delta Phi. Home: New York, NY. Died May 30, 2003.

MARKLE, GEORGE BUSHAR, IV, surgeon; b. Hazleton, Pa., Oct. 29, 1921; s. Alvan and Gladys (Jones) M.; m. Mildred Donna Umstead, July 3, 1944; children: Donna Markle Partee, Melanie Jones Markle, George Bushar, Christian; m. Teresa Damm, Mar. 31, 1996. BS, Yale U., 1943; MD, U. Pa., 1946. Diplomate Am. Bd. Surgery. Intern Geisinger Med. Ctr., Danville, Pa., 1946-47, resident, 1947-49; surg. fellow Mayo Clinic, Rochester, Minn., 1949-52; chief surgery U.S. Army Hosp., Ft. Monroe, Va., 1952-54; practice gen. surgery Carlsbad, N.Mex., 1954-94; surg. staff Carlsbad Regional Med. Ctr., 1954-77, Guadalupe Med. Ctr., 1977-94; ret., 1994. Panelist Voice of Am. Author: Ill Health and Other Foolishness, 1966, How to Stay Healthy All Your Life, 1968, The Teka Stone, 1983, How to Be Healthy, Wealthy and Wise, 1991, Donna's Story, 1991, Beyond Ophir, 1998; contbr. articles to profl. jours., radio health series. Mem. Eddy County Ctrl. Rep. Com.; candidate N.Mex. Ho. of Reps., 1996. With M.C., U.S. Army, 1952-54. Recipient Distinguished Service award Jr. C. of C., 1956 Fellow Internat. Coll. Surgeons (regent, Regent of Yr. 1991), Southwestern Surg. Congress, Priestley surg. Soc., Western Surg. Assn.; mem. Eddy County Med. Soc., Kiwanis. Presbyterian. Home: Carlsbad, N.Mex. Died Oct. 1, 1999.

MARKS, EDWIN S. investment company executive; b. N.Y.C., June 3, 1926; s. Carl and Edith R. (Smith) M.; m. Nancy Lucille Abeles, June 21, 1949; children: Carolyn Gail, Linda Beth, Constance Ann. Student, Princeton U., 1944-45; BS, U.S. Mil. Acad., 1949. V.p. Carl Marks & Co., Inc., N.Y.C., 1958-61, pres., 1961-2000, also bd. dirs., chmn., 2000; dir., exec. v.p. CMNY Capital Co. Inc., from 1962. Chmn. emeritus North Shore Hosp.'s Rsch. Inst. Author: What I Know about Foreign Securities, 1958. Trustee Lincoln Ctr. Fund, 1966-77, Hofstra U., 1974-79, Sarah Lawrence Coll., 1979-81, North Shore Univ. Hosp., Manhasset, N.Y.; chmn. bd. overseers Rsch. Lab., North Shore Univ. Hosp.; bd. dirs. Chief Execs. Orgn. Cold Spring Harbor Labs., 1992, vice chmn.; bd. dirs. Smith New Court PLC, London, 1988-94; bd. dirs., exec. com. Lincoln Ctr. for the Performing Arts, vice chmn., 1998—. Mem. West Point Soc., N.Y. Bd. Trade, Harmonie Club. Died Apr. 24, 2003.

MARKS, JEROME, lawyer; b. N.Y.C., June 24, 1931; m. Margarita A. Marks; children: Susan Marks Schmetterer, David J., Ilyse Marks Kelly, Laurence K. BA, Northwestern U., 1952, JD summa cum laude, 1955. Bar: Ill. 1955. Assoc. Friedman & Koven, Chgo., 1956-63, ptnr., 1963-86, Rudnick & Wolfe, Chgo., from 1986. Asst. editor-in-chief Northwestern U. Law Rev., 1954-55. Co-chmn. No. Suburbs div. Operation Breadbasket, Chgo. and Highland Park (Ill.), 1968-72. Mem. Chgo. Bar Assn., Order of Coif. Democrat. Avocations: walking, swimming, horse racing. Home: Northbrook, Ill. Died 1999.

MARKS, STANLEY JACOB, lawyer, historian, educator, writer; b. Chgo., Apr. 26, 1914; s. Samuel and Sarah Marks; m. Ethel Milgrom, Aug. 1, 1936; 1 child, Roberta E. AB, U. Ill., 1934; LLB, JD, John Marshall Law Sch., Chgo., 1937. Bar: Ill. 1939. Pres., chmn. bd. Beauti-Dor, Inc., Chgo., from 1939, Glamour Glass Door, Inc., Chgo., from 1939; pvt. practice Calif., from 1964; internat. and nat. legal and bus. labor cons., from 1964. Lectr. on polit. and social/econ. events worldwide. Author: (with Ethel Marks) The Bear That Walks Like a Man, 1943, Murder Most Foul, 1967, Two Days of Infamy, 1969, Coup d'Etat!, 1970, Through Distorted Mirrors, 1974, Judaism Looks at Christianity, 1986, A Year in the Lives of the Damned, Reagn, Reaganism, 1986, The 1991 U.S. Consumer Market, 1991, Yes, Americans, A Conspiracy Murdered JFK!, 1992, Jews, Judaism and the U.S., 1992, Justice For Whom?, 1996, If this Be Treason, 1996others; playwright: Judgement Day, 1998, Judaism - Civilization's Las Hope, 1998; pub. weekly polit. newsletter Diogenes, 1984, 88, 90. Writer Dem. Nat. Com., 1936, 40, 48, 52, 60, 91, 96. With AUS, 1946-47. Recipient various Army decorations. Mem. Am. Acad. Polit.

and Social Scis., Soc. Am. Mil. Engrs., Authors League Am., Libr. of Congress Assn., Anti-Defamation League, Dramatists Guild (life), Masons, Shriners, Anti Discrimination League, World Jewish Congress, Dramatist Guild. Home: Los Angeles, Calif. Deceased.

MARLEY, MARY LOUISE, psychologist; b. Columbia, Pa., Apr. 18, 1923; d. William Edward and Carrie Cook (Lockard) M. BS in Edn., Millersville (Pa.) State U., 1944; MEd in Psychology and Audiology, Franklin and Marshall Coll., 1952. Lic. psychologist, speech pathologist, audiologist, Pa. Cons. remedial reading Dearborn (Mich.) Elem. Schs., 1944-49; tchr. spl. edn. Hershey (Pa.) Elem. Sch., 1949-52; speech pathologist York (Pa.) County Schs. Office, 1952-55, asst. psychologist, 1955-68; clin. psychologist stroke unit York Hosp., 1968-74; pvt. practice clin. psychology York, from 1974. Cons. to police depts. of Gettysburg, Glen Rock Boro, Hanover Boro, Hazleton, Jackson Twp., Manheim Twp., Eastern Adams Regional, North Codorus Twp., Northeastern, No. Regional, Penn Twp., Red. Lion, Spring Garden Twp., Springettsbury Twp., West Manchester Twp., West Manheim Twp., West York, Windsor Twp., Wrightsville, York City, York Twp.; cons. to fire depts. of Spring Garden, Emigsville, Hanover; cons. York County Parks and Recreation. Author: Organic Brain Pathology and the Bender Gestalt Test, 1982. Mem. Pa. Psychol. Assn., Nat. Assn. Neuropsychology, Nat. Register Clin. Psychology, York County Psychol. Assn. Republican. Methodist. Avocations: fishing, gourmet cooking. Home: York, Pa. Died Apr. 21, 2002.

MARLIER, JOHN THOMAS, communication educator; b. Pitts., Nov. 25, 1948; s. Raymond Murray Jr. and Gladys Marie (Johnson) M.; m. Ada Jane Focer, July 31, 1971; children: Ian, Grace. BA, Bucknell U., 1970; MA, W.Va. U., 1973; PhD, Mich. State U., 1976. News writer Sta. WKOK, Sunbury, Pa., 1970; salesman Sta. WUDO, Lewisburg, Pa., 1970-71, sales mgr., 1971; grad. asst. W.Va. U., Morgantown, 1971-73, Mich. State U., East Lansing, 1973-76; asst. prof. Northeastern U., Boston, 1976-83; assoc. prof. Curry Coll., Milton, Mass., 1983-84; prin. cons. Marlier & Assocs., Boston, from 1983; assoc. prof. communication Emerson Coll., Boston, from 1984, grad. prog. coord., from 1990, faculty assembly chmn., 1989-91. Author: (with others) Multidimensional Scaling Software Galileo, 1977; assoc. editor: Communication Jour. of Mass., 1989—; contbr. articles to profl. jours. Disposition panelist and trainer Urban Ct. Program Dorchester Dist. Ct., 1979-81; founder, charter mem. bd. dirs. Codman Sq. Community Devel. Corp., Boston, 1979; vol. cons. The Boston Com., 1980-83, City of Boston Neighborhood Devel. Agy., 1980-81; bd. dirs. New England Hemophilia Assn., Dedham, Mass., 1982-84, Dorchester YMCA, Boston, 1981-84; trustee The Advent Sch., Boston, 1989—. Mem. Am. Arbitration Assn., Internat. Communication Assn. (top paper award 1983), Speech Communication Assn. (top paper award 1974), Communication Assn. of Mass. (v.p. 1988—), Mass. Faculty Devel. Consortium (adv. coun. 1989—), Indsl. Rels. Rsch. Assn., Boston Athletic Club. Mem. Trinity Ch. Avocations: photography, camping. Home: Dorchester, Mass. Deceased.

MARMOR, JUDD, psychiatrist, educator; b. London, May 1, 1910; came to U.S., 1911, naturalized, 1916; s. Clement K. and Sarah (Levene) M.; m. Katherine Stern (dec. 1999), May 1, 1938; 1 son, Michael Franklin. AB, Columbia U., 1930, MD, 1933; DHL, Hebrew Union Coll., 1972. Diplomate: Am. Bd. Psychiatry and Neurology, Nat. Bd. Med. Examiners. Intern St. Elizabeth Hosp., Washington, 1933-35; resident neurologist Montefiore Hosp., N.Y.C., 1935-37; psychiatrist Bklyn. State Hosp., 1937; psychoanalytic tng. N.Y. Psychoanalytic Inst., N.Y.C., 1937-41; pvt. practice psychiatry, psychoanalysis and neurology N.Y.C., 1937-46, L.A., 1946—2003; adj. neurologist, neurologist-in-charge clinic Mt. Sinai Hosp., N.Y.C., 1939-46; lectr. New Sch. Social Rsch., N.Y.C., 1942-43; vis. prof. social welfare UCLA, 1949-64, clin. prof. psychiatry sch. medicine, 1953-80, adj. prof. psychiatry, 1980-85, emeritus prof., 1985—2003. Tng. analyst, also pres. So. Calif. Psychoanalytic Inst., 1955-57; sr. attending psychiatrist L.A. County Gen. Hosp., 1954-80; dir. divs. psychiatry Cedars-Sinai Med. Ctr., L.A., 1965-72; Franz Alexander prof. psychiatry U. So. Calif. Sch. Medicine, 1972-80, emeritus, 1980—; sr. cons. regional office social svc. VA, L.A., 1946-50; cons. psychiatry Brentwood VA Hosp., Calif., 1955-65; mem. Coun. Mental Health of Western Interstate Commn. Higher Edn., 1966-72. Editor: Sexual Inversion-The Multiple Roots of Homosexuality, Modern Psychoanalysis: New Directions and Perspectives, Psychiatry in Transition: Selected Papers of Judd Marmor, Homosexual Behavior: A Modern Reappraisal; (with S. Woods) The Interface Between the Psychodynamic and Behavioral Therapies, Psychiatrists & Their Patients: A National Study of Private Office Practice; (with S. Elsenstein and N.A. Levy) The Dyadic Transaction: An Investigation into the Nature of the Psychotherapeutic Process; (with P. Nardi and D. Sanders) Growing Up Before Stonewall; mem. editl. bd. Am. Jour. Psychoanalysis, Contemporary Psychoanalysis, Archives Sexual Behavior; contbr. articles in field to profl. jours. Served as sr. attending surgeon USPHS USNR, 1944-45. Fellow Am. Psychiat. Assn. (life mem., pres. 1975-76), N.Y. Acad. Medicine (life mem.), Am. Acad. Psychoanalysis (pres. 1965-66), Am. Orthopsychiat. Assn. (dir. 1968-71), AAAS, Am. Coll. Psychiatrists; mem. AMA, Calif. Med. Assn., Group for Advancement Psychiatry (dir. 1968-70, pres. 1973-75), Am. Fund for Psychiatry (dir. 1955-57), So. Calif. Psychiat. Soc., So. Calif. Psychoanalytic Soc. (pres. 1960-61), Am. Psychoanalytic Assn., Los Angeles County Med. Soc., Phi Beta Kappa, Alpha Omega Alpha. Died Dec. 16, 2003.

MARQUEZ, AWILDA ROSE, federal official; b. San Juan, P.R., Jan. 23, 1949; BS in Fgn. Svc., Georgetown U., 1980; JD with honors, U. Md., 1988. Bar: Md. 1988. Assoc. litigation divsn. Piper & Marbury, 1988-93; commd. officer U.S. Fgn. Svc., 1984-97; chief counsel Econ. Devel. Adminstrn., U.S. Dept. Commerce, Washington, from 1998, asst. sec. and dir. gen., 1997-98. White House liaison Dept. of State; asst. sec. U.S. & Fgn. Comml. Svc. Internat. Trade Adminstrn. U.S. Dept. Commerce, 1988—. Home: Arlington, Va. Deceased.

MARS, FORREST E., SR., candy company executive; s. Frank and Ethel Mars; children: Forrest Jr., John, Jacqueline Chmn. Mars Inc., McLean, Va. Died July 2, 1999.

MARSEE, STUART (EARL), educational consultant, retired; b. Gardener, Oreg., Sept. 30, 1917; s. William and Clare (Grimes) M.; m. Audrey Belfield, June 1, 1940; children: Frederic, Jeffrey, Wayne. BS, U. Oreg., 1939, MS, 1942; EdD, U. So. Calif., 1947; LLD, Pepperdine U., 1977. Asst. supt. for bus. Pasadena City Schs., Calif., 1949-57, acting supt., 1957-58, asst. supt., 1949-58; pres. El Camino Coll., 1958-82, cons., from 1982. Lectr. UCLA, 1965, U. So. Calif., 1956-57; adj. prof. Pepperdine U., 1978-79 Author: History of the Rotary Club of Torrance, 1962-74, 1974; contbr. articles to profl. jours. Recipient Disting. Service award Los Angeles County Bd. Suprs., 1958, Disting. Service Leadership award Kiwanis Internat., 1970; named Citizen of Yr., Torrance, Calif., 1981, Redondo Beach, Calif., 1986. Mem. Am. Assn. Cmty. and Jr. Colls. (pres. 1968), Nat. Commn. Accrediting (dir. 1970-74), Coun. Postsecondary Accreditation (dir. 1974-78), Western Coll. Assn. (mem. exec. com. 1978-81). Died Aug. 17, 2002.

MARSH, JEREMIAH, lawyer; b. Freeborn County, Minn., 1933; AB magna cum laude, Harvard U., 1955, JD, 1958. Bar: Ill. 1958. Mem. faculty John Marshall Law Sch., Chgo., 1959—68, former mem. faculty; former chmn., ptnr. Hopkins & Sutter, Chgo.; legis asst. to U.S. Senator Edward M. Kennedy, 1963—64; spl. counsel to Gov. Richard B. Ogilvie, Ill., 1969—72. Ill. commr. Uniform State Laws, 1969—73, former Ill. commr.; former chmn. Ill. Del., 1979, Ill. Adminstrv. Rules Commn., 1977; former trustee Ill. Ins. Exch., 1979. Mem. Harvard Med. Sch. Com. on Resources, from 1979, Mayor's Airport Study Commn., 1980—83, Ill. Atty. Gen.'s Profl. Adv. Commn.; chmn. Ill. Gov.'s Task Force Fin. Svcs., 1985—86. Mem.: Phi Beta Kappa. Died Jan. 19, 2004.

MARSHALL, BURKE, law educator; b. Plainfield, N.J., Oct. 1, 1922; AB, Yale U., 1944, LL.B., 1951, MA, 1970. Bar: D.C. bar 1952. Assoc., then partner firm Covington and Burling, Washington, 1951-61; asst. atty. gen. U.S., 1961-65; gen. counsel IBM Corp., Armonk, N.Y., 1965-69, sr. v.p., 1969-70; prof. law Yale U. Law Sch., 1970—2003, Nicholas deB. Katzenbach prof. emeritus. Chmn. Nat. Adv. Commn. SSS, 1967. Author: Federalism and Civil Rights, 1965; co-author: The Mylai Massacre and Its Cover-up, 1975; editor: The Supreme Court and Human Rights, 1982, A Workable Government?, 1989; contbr. articles, revs. to legal publs. Bd. dirs. Ctr. Community Change, Washington, 1968-98, Robert F. Kennedy Meml., 1969-98, Vera Inst. Justice, N.Y.C., 1965-1985. Recipient Eleanor Roosevelt award for human rights, 1999. Home: Newtown, Conn. Died June 2, 2003.

MARSHALL, CHARLES BURTON, political science consultant; b. Catskill, N.Y., Mar. 25, 1908; s. Caleb Carey and Alice (Beeman) M.; m. Betty Louise O'Brien, Aug. 1, 1958 (dec. July, 1991); children (by previous marriage) Charles Richard, Jean Marshall Vickery. BA, U. Tex., 1931, MA, 1932; PhD, Harvard U., 1939; LHD, Johns Hopkins U., 1987. With newspapers in, El Paso and Austin, Tex., 1925-31; With newspapers in Detroit, 1934-38; instr., tutor govt. Harvard U. and Radcliffe Coll., 1938-42; vis. lectr. Harvard U., summer 1963; cons. Intergovtl. Com. Refugees, 1946-47; staff cons. com. fgn. affairs U.S. Ho. of Reps., 1947-50; mem. policy planning staff State Dept., 1950-53; adviser to prime minister Pakistan, 1955-57; research assoc. Washington Center Fgn. Policy Research, 1957-74, acting dir., 1969-70; vis. prof. Sch. Advanced Internat. Studies, Johns Hopkins, 1965-66, prof., 1966-67, Paul H. Nitze prof. internat. politics, 1967-75; Alumni prof. internat. studies U. N.C., 1960-61; Centennial vis. prof. Tex. A&M U., 1976; cons. in field, from 1961. U.S. govt. rep. XIV Conf. Internat. Red Cross, Toronto, Can., 1952; mem. Gen. Adv. Com. Arms Control and Disarmament, 1982-92. Author: The Limits of Foreign Policy, 1954, The Exercise of Sovereignty, 1965, The Cold War: A Concise History, 1965, Crisis Over Rhodesia: A Skeptical View, 1967; Cons. editor: New Republic, 1959-64; contbg. editor: Nat. Rev, 1979-83. Served to lt. col. AUS, 1942-46. Fellow Carnegie Endowment Internat. Peace, 1934-35; vis. scholar, 1958-59 Mem. Washington Inst. Fgn. Affairs, Cosmos Club. Home: Beaverton, Oreg. Died Dec. 22, 1999.

MARSHALL, GEOFFREY, retired university official; b. Lancaster, Pa., Feb. 6, 1938; s. Ray Ardell and Mary (Elsen) M.; m. Mary Gale Beckwith, June 17, 1961; children: Eden Elizabeth, Erin Elizabeth. BA, Franklin and Marshall Coll., 1959; MA, Rice U., 1961, PhD, 1965; LHD (hon.), Mansfield State Coll., 1980, Ursinus Coll., 1990. Assoc. prof. English U. Okla., Norman, 1964-74; asst. provost U.Okla., Norman, 1973-74; dir. div. state programs Nat. Endowment for Humanities, Washington, 1974-78, dir. div. edn. programs, 1978-80, dep. chmn., 1981-85; assoc. provost and dean for acad. affairs Grad. Sch. CUNY, 1985-92, acting provost and v.p. for acad. affairs, 1992-94, provost, sr. v.p., 1994-98, ret., 1998. Bd. dirs. Ursinus Coll., 1986—. Author: Restoration Serious Drama, 1975; contbr. articles to profl. jours. Trustee Norman Pub. Library, 1970-74; chmn. Okla. Humanities Com., 1971-74; mem. Norman Human Rights Commn., 1972-73. Assoc. Danforth Found., 1968-74; recipient Couch Scholars award for excellence in undergrad. edn. U. Okla., 1967 Mem. MLA, Nat. Council Tchrs. English, Am. Soc. 18th Century Studies, Nat. Collegiate Honors Council (exec. com. 1972-74) Home: Monroe Township, NJ. Deceased.

MARSHALL, PRENTICE HENRY, federal judge; b. 1926; BS, 1949; JD, U. Ill., 1951. Bar: Ill. bar 1951. Judge U.S. Dist. Ct. (no. dist.) Ill., 1973—; assoc. firm Johnston Thompson Raymond & Mayer, Chgo., 1953-60; ptnr. Raymond Mayer Jenner & Block, Chgo., 1961-67; spl. asst. atty. gen. State of Ill., 1964-67; hearing officer Ill. Fair Employment Practices Commn., 1967-72. Faculty Am. Law Inst.; adj. prof. law Ill. Inst. Tech., Chgo.-Kent Coll. Law, 1975—; prof. law U. Ill., 1967-73 Served with USN, 1944-46. Mem. ABA, Am. Coll. Trial Lawyers, Am. Law Inst., Am. Judicature Soc., Chgo. Bar Assn., Bar Assn. of 7th Cir., Order of the Coif, Phi Kappa Phi. Died May 24, 2004.

MARSTON, ROBERT QUARLES, retired university president; b. Toano, Va., Feb. 12, 1923; s. Warren and Helen (Smith) M.; m. Ann Carter Garnett, Dec. 21, 1946; children: Ann, Robert, Wesley. BS, Va. Mil. Inst., 1943; MD, Med. Coll. Va., 1947; B.Sc. (Rhodes scholar 1947-49), Oxford (Eng.) U., 1949; B.Sc. 6 hon. degrees. Intern Johns Hopkins Hosp., 1949—50; resident Vanderbilt U. Hosp., 1950—51, Med. Coll. Va., 1953—54, asst. prof. medicine, 1954; asst. prof. bacteriology and immunology U. Minn., 1958—59; asso. prof. medicine, asst. dean charge student affairs Med. Coll. Va., 1959—61; dean U. Miss. Sch. Medicine, 1961—66; dir. U. Miss. Sch. Medicine (Med. Center), 1961—65, vice chancellor, 1965—66; asso. dir. div. regional med. programs NIH, 1966—68; adminstr. Fed. Health Services and Mental Health Adminstrn., 1968; dir. NIH, Bethesda, Md., 1968—73; scholar in residence U. Va., Charlottesville, 1973—74; Disting. fellow Inst. of Medicine, Nat. Acad. Scis., 1973—74; pres. U. Fla., 1974—84, pres. emeritus, emeritus prof. medicine, emeritus prof. fish and aquaculture. Bd. dirs. Johnson and Johnson, Nat. Bank Alachua, Wackenhut Corp.; chmn. bd. dirs. Cordis Corp.; chmn., mem. Fla. Marine Fisheries Commn. Author articles in field. Chmn. Commn. on Med. Edn. for Robert Wood Found.; chmn. Safety Adv. Bd. Three Mile Island; chmn. adv. com. med. implications of nuclear war NAS; exec. coun. Assn. Am. Med. Coll., 1964-67; past chmn. exec. com. Nat. Assn. State Univs. and Land Grant Colls., chmn., 1982. 1st lt. AUS, 1951-53. 1st lt. AUS, 1951—53. Decorated Knight of North Star (Sweden); Markle scholar, 1954-59; hon. fellow Lincoln Coll. Oxford U. Fellow Am. Pub. Health Assn.; mem. Inst. Medicine of NAS, AAAS, Am. Hosp. Assn. (hon.), Nat. Med. Assn. (hon.), Assn. Am. Rhodes Scholars, Assn. Am. Physicians, Assn. Am. Med. Colls. (disting. mem.), Am. Clin. and Climatol. Assn., Soc. Scholars Johns Hopkins, Alpha Omega Alpha. Episcopalian. Home: Alachua, Fla. Died Mar. 14, 1999.

MARTE, ANNABELLE LEE, nursing educator; b. Kellersburg, Pa., July 17, 1940; d. Lester E. and Flossie (Young) Sanford; m. Jay G. Marte, Aug. 24, 1967; children: Timothy J., Jennifer A. Diploma, Shadyside Hosp. Sch. Nursing, 1961; BSN, Slippery Rock U., 1976; MS in Nursing, Duquesne U., 1977; postgrad. in adult edn., Pa. State U. Cert. nursing adminstrn., gerontology nurse, nursing continuing edn./staff devel. ANA. Undergrad. nursing faculty Duquesne U., Pitts.; head nurse psychogeriatrics Dept. Vets. Affairs Med. Ctr., Pitts., assoc. chief, nursing svc. for edn., edn. coord. Med. Ctr. Butler, Pa. Contbr. articles to profl. jours. Capt. U.S. Army Nurse Corps, 1962-68. Mem. Geriatric Edn. Ctr. Pa. (Excellence award 1989, faculty fellow), Sigma Theta Tau, several other nursing edn. spl. interest groups. Home: Butler, Pa. Died June 4, 2001.

MARTENS, S.K. legal administrator, retired; Pres. Supreme Ct. of The Netherlands, The Hague, ret., 2000. Died Jan. 2001.

MARTIN, ARCHER JOHN PORTER, retired chemistry educator; b. London, Mar. 1, 1910; s. William Archer Porter and Lilian Kate (Brown) M.; m. Judith Bagenal, Jan. 9, 1943; 5 children. Student, Peterhouse, Cambridge, Eng., 1929-32, MA, 1936; PhD, DSc, Leeds U., 1968; LLD (hon.), U. Glasgow, Scotland, 1973; laurea honoris causa, U. Urbino, Italy, 1985. Chemist Nutritional Lab., Cambridge, 1933-38, Wool Industries Rsch. Assn., Leeds, 1938-46; mem. rsch. dept. Boots Pure Drug Co., Nottingham, Eng., 1946-48; mem. staff Med. Rsch. Coun., 1948-52; head phys. chemistry div. Nat. Inst. Med. Rsch., Mill Hill, 1952-56; chem. cons., 1956-59; dir. Abbotsbury (Eng.) Labs. Ltd., 1959-73; profl. fellow U. Sussex, Eng., 1973-77; Robert A. Welch prof. chemistry U. Houston, 1974-78. Guest prof. Ecole Polytechnique Fed. de Lausanne, Switzerland, 1980-85; cons. Wellcome Rsch. Labs., Beckenham, Eng., 1970-73; Extraordinary prof. Tech. U., Eindhoven, The Netherlands, 1965-74. Decorated comdr. Brit. Empire; Order of Rising Sun Japan; recipient Berzelius Gold medal Swedish Med. Soc., 1951, Nobel prize chemistry (with R.L.M. Synge) for invention of partition chromatography, 1952, John Scott award, 1958, John Price Wetherill medal, 1959, Franklin Inst. medal, 1959, Koltoff medal Acad. Pharm. Sci., 1969, Callendar medal Inst. Measurement & Control, 1971,

Fritz-Pregl medal Austrian Chemical Soc., 1985. Fellow Royal Soc. (Leverhulme medal 1964). Clubs: Chemist's (N.Y.C.) (hon.). Home: Leominster, England. Died July 28, 2002.

MARTIN, JAMES GILBERT, university provost emeritus; b. Paris, Ill., Dec. 10, 1926; s. James and Ruth Ann (Gilbert) M.; m. Doris E. Edmonson, Aug. 23, 1969; children— Bradley Keith, Philip Roger. BA, Ind. State Coll., 1952, MA, 1953; PhD, Ind. U., 1957. Instr. Ind. State Coll., Terre Haute, 1952-53; lectr. Ind. U., Bloomington, 1953-56; instr. sociology Okla. U., Norman, 1956-57; asst. prof. sociology No. Ill. U., DeKalb, 1957-65, asso. prof., 1959-64; asst. dean Coll. Arts and Scis., Ohio State U., Columbus, 1965-68; asso. dean Coll. Arts and Scis., Ohio State U. (Coll. Social and Behavioral Scis.), 1968-70, acting dean, 1970-71; v.p., provost U. No. Iowa, Cedar Falls, 1971-89, provost emeritus, 1989-99. Intern academic adminstrn. E.L. Phillips Found., 1963-64 Author: The Tolerant Personality, 1964, Minority Group Relations, 1973. Mem. Iowa Peace Inst. Bd., 1989-92. With AUS, 1945-48. Home: Dayton, Ohio. Died Dec. 14, 1999.

MARTIN, JOHN RUPERT, art and archaeology educator; b. Hamilton, Ont., Can., Sept. 27, 1916; came to U.S., 1941, naturalized, 1959; s. John Smith and Elizabeth (Hutchinson) M.; m. Barbara Janet Malcolm, Aug. 23, 1941; 1 dau., Hilary Jane. BA, McMaster U., 1938, D.Litt., 1976; M.F.A., Princeton, 1941, PhD, 1947. Instr. art U. Iowa, 1941-42; mem. faculty Princeton U., 1947-87, prof. art and archaeology, 1961-87, Marquand prof. art and archaeology, 1970-87, chmn. dept. art and archaeology, 1973-79. Mem. Comité Internat. d'Histoire de l'Art. Author: The Illustration of the Heavenly Ladder of John Climacus, 1954, The Portrait of John Milton at Princeton and Its Place in Milton Iconography, 1961, The Farnese Gallery, 1965, The Ceiling Paintings by Rubens for the Jesuit Church in Antwerp, 1968, Rubens: the Antwerp Altarpieces, 1969, The Decorations for the Pompa Introitus Ferdinandi, 1972, Baroque, Style and Civilization, 1977, (with G. Feigenbaum) Van Dyck as Religious Artist, 1979; also articles; Editor: Rubens before 1620, 1972; editor in chief Art Bull., 1971-74. Served to maj. Canadian Army, 1942-46. Recipient Charles Rufus Morey book award Coll. Art Assn., 1974. Fellow Royal Soc. Arts; mem. Coll. Art Assn. Am. (pres. 1984-86), Am. Philos. Soc., Renaissance Soc. Am. Home: Princeton, NJ. Died July 26, 2000.

MARTIN, ROBERT L. state legislator, insurance company executive, farmer; b. Nov. 8, 1912; m. Sue Martin. Grad. high sch., Bethel, N.C. Farmer, Bethel; pres. Pitt Farmers Ins., Bethel; mem. N.C. Senate, Raleigh, from 1984. Chmn. appropriations on natural and econ. resources com., mem. appropriations/base budget com., info. tech. com., rules and ops. of senate com., select com. on tobacco settlement issues, transp. com., ways and means com., vice chmn. commerce com., ins. com. Mem. Farmers Mut. Life Ins. Assn. (pres.). Democrat. Died May 22, 2003.

MARTIN, ROY BUTLER, JR., museum director, retired broker; b. Norfolk, Va., May 13, 1921; s. Roy Butler and Anne (Holman) M.; m. Louise Eggleston, Apr. 17, 1948; children: Roy Butler III, Anne Beverly Martin Sessoms. Student, William and Mary Coll., Norfolk, 1939-40; BS in Commerce, U. Va., 1943. Chmn. bd. Commonwealth Brokers Inc., 1955-88; mayor City of Norfolk, 1962-74; pres. Chrysler Mus., Norfolk, from 1989-961989. Pres. U.S. Conf. Mayors, Washington, 1973-74; trustee Sentara Health System, 1985-96. Chmn. Douglas MacArthur Found., 1963-2000, Civic Facilities Commn., Norfolk, 1986—; bd. dirs. Norfolk Forum; exec. com., pres. Va. Mcpl. League, 1968-69; past mem. Va. State Water Control Bd.; past mem. exec. com., adv. bd. Nat. League of Cities, com. on community devel., U.S. Conf. Mayors, Southeastern Va. Planning Dist. Commn; chmn. Southeastern Tidewater Area Manpower Planning System, Mayor's Youth Commn.; Gov.'s Com. on Youth; past bd. dirs. Norfolk Urban Coalition; past mem. VALC Zoning Procedures Com.; past bd. dirs. Norfolk Symphony Orch., Boys Club Norfolk, Old Dominion U. Edns. Found.; past mem. Norfolk Cerebral Palsy Tng. Ctr., vestry Ch. of Good Shepherd, Norfolk. Lt. USNR, 1943-46, USNR, 1948-52. Decorated officer in Order of the Crown (Belgium); recipient Outstanding Alumni award Old Dominion U., 1964, Sales of Yr. award Sales and Mktg. Club Tidewater, 1971, Meritorious Pub. Svc. Citation Dept. Navy, 1974, Cmty. Svc. award Jewish Cmty. Ctr., 1974, Cert. Appreciation Va. Food Dealers Assn., 1974, Fall Guy award Saints and Sinners, 1974, Brotherhood award NCCJ, 1976, First Citizen award City of Norfolk, 1974. Mem. Norfolk Yacht and Country Club (pres. 1990-92), Va. Club (bd. dirs. 1991-93), Chi Phi, Alpha Kappa Psi. Episcopalian. Home: Virginia Beach, Va. Died May 20, 2002.

MARTIN, WILLIAM CHARLES, retired lawyer, law educator; b. Shenandoah, Iowa, May 25, 1923; s. J. Stuart and Chloe Irene (Anderson) M.; m. Marilyn Forbes, Oct. 18, 1947 (div. 1979); children: Ann, James; m. Kathryn Ann Fehr, Sept. 17, 1979. BA, U. Iowa, 1946, JD, 1947. Bar: Iowa 1947, Oreg. 1948. Sr. ptnr. Martin, Bischoff, Templeton, Biggs & Ericsson, Portland, Oreg., 1951-86. Mem. Oreg. Bd. Bar Examiners, 1966-69; instr. Lewis and Clark Coll. Law, 1973-75, U. Hawaii-Hilo, West Hawaii, 1989-97. Bd. dirs. Eastmoreland Gen. Hosp., Portland, 1960-84, chmn., 1978-81; mem. Lawyers Com. for Civil Rights Under Law, Jackson, Miss., 1965; bd. dirs. Lake Oswego (Oreg.) Pub. Libr., 1981-84, chmn., 1982-84; mem. Kona bd. Am. Cancer Soc. 1st lt. USAAF, WWII. Mem. ABA, Oreg. State Bar, Kona Heavens Assn. (pres. 1994-95), Univ. Club, Kona Outdoor Cir. (Kailua Kona), Keauhou Yacht Club (bd. dirs. 1996—), Phi Delta Phi, Sigma Nu. Democrat. Roman Catholic. Home: Kailua Kona, Hawaii. Died Nov. 15, 2001.

MARTIN, WILLIAM T. nurse administrator; b. Marmaduke, Ark., Sept. 4, 1929; s. Jamie Paul and Hattie (Wallace) M.; m. Jenny C. Martin, Apr. 30, 1949; 1 child, Andrew. Diploma, St. Luke's Hosp. Sch. Nursing, New Bedford, Mass., 1962; BS (magna cum laude), Roger Williams Coll., 1976; MS, Salve Regina Coll., 1983. Cert. personnel mgr. Asst. dir. nursing St. Luke's Hosp., New Bedford, Mass., dir. personnel; v.p. Employee and Community Svc., Newport (R.I.) Hosp.; dir., mgr. ambulatory surgery Charlton Meml. Hosp., Fall River, Mass. Recipient Nat. Pfizer award for Planning of Emergency Care. Mem. AORN, Mass. and R.I. Gov.'s Coms., R.I. and Mass. Personnel Dirs. Assn. (pres.), Region 1 ASHPA (bd. dir. 1978-80), Am. Soc. Hosp. Personnel Adminstrs., Am. soc. Personnel Adminstrs. Home: Naples, Fla. Died Apr. 27, 1999.

MARTINEZ, VIRGINIA MARCELINA, dietitian; b. Denver, June 2, 1942; d. Maxcimo and Maria R. (Salas) M.; m. Jimmy Allen Tanhoff, Nov. 15, 1967 (div. Dec. 1989). MS, Mont. State U., 1990, BS, 1987. Lic. nutritionist Mont. Bd. Med. Examiners; registered dietitian. Sr. acctg. clk. 1st Bank Bozeman, Mont., 1974-80; rsch. asst. Mont. State U., Bozeman, 1984-90; nutritionist County of Big Horn, Hardin, 1992-95, Indian Health Svc./Crow Agy., 1995-97; dietitian Yellowstone, Billings, Mont., from 1996. Part-time instr. Little Big Horn Coll., Crow Agency, Mont., 1991—; part-time women, infants and children program dir. No. Cheyenne Bd. of Health, Lame Deer, Mont., 1992-96; with Deering Cmty. Health Ctr., Billings. With USN, 1960-63. Recipient Outstanding Presentation award U. Minn., 1986; scholar Mont. Pub. health Assn., Am. Dietetic Assn., Mont. State U. Coll. Edn., Mex.-Am. Nat. Women's Assn. Mem. Am. Dietetic Assn., Pub. Health Nutrition Practice Group (MDA nominating com. 1997-98). Roman Catholic. Avocations: skiing, weight lifting, dance, singing, handicrafts. Home: Hardin, Mont. Died Dec. 8, 2001.

MARVIN, JOHN GEORGE, clergyman, church organization executive; b. Summit, N.J., May 8, 1912; s. George and Caroline (Whitman) M.; m. Elizabeth Anne Wheater, June 30, 1944; children: Caroline Wheater Dorney, Elizabeth Anne West, Martha Jane Hobbs, Frances Alice Heidel. BS, Davidson Coll., 1933; ThB, Princeton Theol. Sem., 1936; DD, Coll. of Emporia, 1964; LLD, Tarkio Coll., 1964. Ordained to ministry Presbyn. Ch., 1936. Pastor, Windsor, N.Y., 1936-37, Montrose, Pa., 1937-44, Lewistown, Pa., 1944-52, Denton, Tex., 1952-61; presbytery exec. Greater Kansas City, Mo., 1961-65; pastor 1st Presbyn. Ch., Bartlesville, Okla., 1965-69; sr. min. Chevy Chase Presbyn. Ch., Washington, 1969-77, pastor emeritus, from 1978. Interim sr. min. Catonsville Ch., Balt., 1978, 3d Ch., Rochester, N.Y., 1978-79, 1st Ch., Ft. Worth, 1979-80, Gaithersburg, Md., 1980-81, Westfield, N.J., 1981-82, Ch. of Palms, Sarasota, Fla., 1982-83, Bethel Ch., Balt., 1983-84, Pine Shores Ch., Sarasota, Fla., 1984, Interfaith Chapel, Silver Spring, Md., 1984-87; mem. exec. com. Pa. Coun. Chs., 1949-52, Tex. Coun. Chs., 1953-61; mem. exec. com., long range chmn. Greater Kansas City Coun. Chs., 1962-65; chmn. campus Christian Life Tex. Synod, 1958-61; chmn. nat. mission Pa. Synod, 1949-52; sec. nominations com. Gen. Assemly U.P. Ch., 1955-58, chmn. com. on baptized children, 1969-70, mem. com. of nine on synods bounderies, 1970-72. Contbr. articles to religious publs. Bd. dirs. Midwest Christian Counseling Ctr., Kansas City, Mo., 1963-69, Presbyn. Homes of Okla., Inc., 1966-69; mem. jud. commn. Synod of Okla.-Ark., 1966-69; mem. strategy com. Bd. Nat. Missions, 1968-70, British-Am. Preaching Exch., preaching missions to Alaska and Mex.; leader and lectr. on religious heritage tours in Europe, Middle East, Egypt, Caribbean and Orient, 1972-84; bd. dirs. Tarkio Coll., 1961-67, Westminster Found., Pa. State U., 1945-52, North Tex. State U., 1952-61; mem. ministerial rels. com. Nat. Capital Union Presbytery, 1973-78; bd. visitors Warren Wilson Coll. Mem. Rotary, Beta Theta Pi. Republican. Home: Silver Spring, Md. Died Jan. 4, 2004.

MARX, GERTIE FLORENTINE, anesthesiologist; b. Frankfurt am Main, Germany, Feb. 13, 1912; came to U.S., 1937, naturalized, 1943; d. Joseph and Elsa (Scheuer) M.; m. Eric P. Reiss, Sept. 26, 1940 (dec. 1968). Student, U. Frankfurt, Germany, 1931-36; MD, U. Bern, Switzerland, 1937. Diplomate: Nat. Bd. Med. Examiners, Am. Bd. Anesthesiology. Intern, resident in anesthesiology Beth Israel Hosp., N.Y.C., 1939-43, adj. anesthesiologist, 1943-50, assoc. anesthesiologist, 1950-55; attending anesthesiologist Bronx Municipal Hosp. Center, 1955-95, Bronx VA Hosp., 1966-72, cons., 1972-84. Asst. prof. anesthesiology Albert Einstein Coll. Medicine, 1955-60, assoc. prof., 1960-70, prof., 1970-95, prof. emeritus, 1995-2004. Author: (with Orkin) Physiology of Obstetric Anesthesia, 1969; assoc. editor: Survey Anesthesiology, 1957-83; editor: Parturition and Perinatology, 1973, Clinical Management of Mother and Newborn, 1979, (with G. M. Bassell) Obstetric Analgesia and Anesthesia, 1980, Obstetric Anesthesia Digest, 1981; former cons. editor Internat. Jour. Obstetric Anesthesia; contbr. articles to profl. jours. Recipient Nils Lofgren award, 1990, Coll. medal Royal Coll. Anaesthetists, 1993. Fellow Am. Coll. Anesthesiology, N.Y. Acad. Medicine, Am. Coll. Obstetricians and Gynecologists; mem. AMA, Am. Soc. Anesthesiologists (Disting. Svc. award 1988), N.Y. State Soc. Anesthesiologists, Am. Soc. Regional Anesthesia (Disting. Svc. award 1990), Bronx County Med. Soc., N.Y. Acad. Scis. Home: Southbury, Conn. Died Jan. 25, 2004.

MASAMUNE, SATORU, chemistry educator, consultant; b. Fukuoka, Japan, July 24, 1928; came to U.S., 1953; s. Hajime and Chikako (Kondo) M.; m. Takako Nozoe, July 25, 1956; children: Hiroko, Tohoru. BS, Tohoko U., Sendai, Japan, 1953; PhD, U. Calif. at Berkeley, 1957. Postdoctoral fellow U. Wis., Madison, 1957-59, lectr., 1959-61; rsch. fellow Mellon Inst., Pitts., 1961-64; assoc. prof. U. Alta., Edmonton, Can., 1964-67; prof. U. Alta, Edmonton, Can., 1967-79, MIT, Cambridge, 1978-91, A.C. Cope prof., 1991—2000. Cons. Abbott Labs., North Chicago, Ill., 1982-88, Kao Corp., Tokyo, Toyo Akuzo, Tokyo. Editor: Reaction Intermediate, 1976, Organic Synthesis, 1970-78; contbr. 220 sci. articles to profl. jours. Recipient Hamilton award U. Nebr., 1984. Fellow Am. Acad. Arts and Scis., Royal Soc. Can.; mem. Am. Chem. Soc. (Organic Synthesis award 1978, A.C. Cope scholar 1987), Chem. Soc. of London (Centenary lectr. 1980). Home: Newton, Mass. Died Nov. 9, 2003.

MASLAND, RICHARD LAMBERT, neurologist, educator; b. Phila., Mar. 24, 1910; s. Charles William and Mary Jane (Gillinder) M.; m. Mary Wootton, Nov. 2, 1940; children: Richard H., Frances W., Sarah E., Thomas W. BA, Haverford (Pa.) Coll., 1931, LLD, 1975; MD, U. Pa., Phila., 1935. Diplomate Am. Bd. Neurology-Psychiatry. Intern Pa. Hosp., Phila., 1936-37; fellow U. Pa., 1940-46; asst. prof. to prof. Bowman Gray Sch. Medicine, Winston-Salem, N.C., 1947-57; asst. dir., dir. Nat. Inst. Neurol. Disease, Washington, 1957-68; chmn. dept. neurology Columbia U., N.Y.C., 1968-73, H.H. Merritt prof. emeritus, 1973—2003. Chmn. Commn. for Control of Epilepsy, 1976. Author: Mental Subnormality, 1958. Former bd. mem. Epilepsy Found. Am., Washington. Capt.-maj. U.S. Army, 1942-45. Fellow Am. Neurol. Soc. (v.p. 1964), Royal Soc. Medicine, Am. Acad. Neurology (councillor 1956-59); mem. Can. Neurol. Soc., World Fedn. Neurology (pres. 1981-89), Epilepsy Internat. (sec. 1981-89). Died Dec. 19, 2003.

MASON, BARBARA MENTZER, environmental specialist; b. Atlanta, Jan. 2, 1937; d. Maxwell Richardson and Martha Jean (Osborne) Mentzer; m. John Augustus Lee (div. 1978); children: George A., Martha J.A., Sara Lee Fernandez, Maxwell R.M., Rebecca D.C.; m. Edward Augustus Mason, Sept. 22, 1979. BS, Fla. State U., 1959. Tchr. sci. Atlanta Pub. Sch. System, 1959-60, tchr. home econs., 1960-62, 1967-70; specialist mktg. Ga. Egg Commn., Atlanta, 1976-77, coordinator consumer program, 1977-78; state dir. Ga. Clean and Beautiful Dept. Community Affairs State of Ga., Atlanta, 1978-89; exec. dir. Clean Fla. Commn., Tallahassee, from 1989. Tchr. Sunday sch., vacation Bible sch. St. Philips Episc. Cathedral, 1962-67; chmn. com. orgn. Atlanta Clean City Commn, 1976; pres. Peachtree Battle Alliance Civic Assn., 1974-76, v.p., 1975, chmn. beautification, 1977; mem. Council Vol. Adminstrs., Ga. Assn. Vol. Adminstrn., 1986—, Ga. Conservency, 1980—, Ga. Environ. Council, 1986—. Named Outstanding Citizen, Fultop County Bd. Commrs., 1986, Outstanding Citizen State Cobb County Clean Commn., Ga., 1987; recipient Profl. leadership award Keep Am. Beautiful Inc., 1983, leadership award State of Ga., 1989 Mem. NEA (Ga. chpt.), Am. Home Econs. Assn. (Ga. chpt.), Nat. Assn. Female Execs., Atlanta Womens' Network, DAR Jr. Com. (pres. 1963), Delta Gamma Alumnae (pres. 1963, chmn. recommendations 1959). Home: Waleska, Ga. Died Dec. 29, 2000.

MASON, JOHN MILTON (JACK MASON), judge; b. Mankato, Minn., Oct. 31, 1938; s. Milton Donald and Marion (Dailey) M.; m. Vivian McFerran, Aug. 25, 1962; children: Kathleen, Peter, Michael. BA cum laude, Macalester Coll., 1960; JD, Harvard U., 1963. Bar: Minn. 1963, U.S. Supreme Ct. 1970. Assoc. Dorsey & Whitney, Mpls., 1963-68, ptnr., 1969-71, 73-95; solicitor gen. State of Minn., St. Paul, 1971, chief dep. atty. gen., 1972-73; U.S. magistrate judge Dist. of Minn., St. Paul, 1995—2002. Bd. dirs. Macalester Coll., St. Paul, 1971-77, St. Paul Chamber Orch., 1979-88, U. Minn. Hosps. and Clinics, St. Paul, 1979-83, Mpls. Bd. Edn., 1973-80, Minn. Chorale, 1990-95, MacPhail Ctr. for Arts, 1990-96, Ordway Music Theatre, 1990-99, 2000-02; mem. nat. adv. bd. Concordia Lang. Villages, 1996-2002, Theatre de la Jeune Lune, 1998-2001. With USAF, 1957, with Res., 1957-65. Jack Mason Endowed scholar Macalester Coll. St. Paul, Concordia Coll., Moorhead, Minn. Mem. Harvard Law Sch. Assn. (pres. Minn. sect. 1980-81), Minn. Assn. Black Lawyers (Profile Courage award 2002), Fed. Bar Assn. (Jack Mason Meml. lectr., Minn. chpt. 2003). Avocations: classical piano, bicycling, accordion, foreign languages. Home: Minneapolis, Minn. Died June 8, 2002.

MASON, ROBERT THEODORE, federal agency administrator; b. Floral Park, N.Y., Jan. 29, 1937; s. Theodore and Millicent Virginia (Carpenter) M.; m. Joan Marie Baumgartner; children: Leigh Ann, Cynthia Marie, Paul Robert. AS, Orange County C.C., 1959; BS, Adelphi Coll., 1962; sr. exec. fellows, Harvard U., 1991. Ops. analysis exec. Grumman Aircraft Engring. Corp., Bethpage, N.Y., 1955-69; systems analyst Ctr. for Naval Analyses, 1969-72; sr. mgmt. Ops. Rsch., Inc., Va. Rsch. Inc., 1972-75; sr. ops. rsch. analyst Manpower Analysis and Rsch. Ctr., Washington, 1975-78; systems analyst Maintenance Policy Office, Washington, 1978-88; former asst. dep. under sec. for maintenance policy Office of Sec. of Def., Washington. Avocations: exercise, gardening. Home: Potomac, Md. Died Apr. 24, 2004.

MASSEY, DONALD WAYNE, clergyman, small business owner; b. Durham, N.C., Mar. 7, 1938; s. Gordon Davis and Lucille Alma (Gregory) M.; m. Violet Sue McIlvain, Nov. 2, 1958; children: Kimberly Shan (dec.), Leon Dale, Donn Krichele, Anthony Donn Prestarri. Student, U. Hawaii, 1959, U. Ky., 1965, 66, U. Va., 1970, Piedmont C.C., 1982. Ordained Hookerton Christian Ch., 1999. Head microfilm sect. Ky. Hist. Soc., Frankfort, 1961; dir. microfilm ctr. U. Ky., Lexington, 1962—67; dir. photog. svcs. and graphics U. Va., Charlottesville, 1967—73; pres. Micrographics II, Charlottesville, Charleston, SC, from 1973; min. Hookerton (N.C.) Christian Ch., 1999—2001, Bethel Christian Ch., Grifton, 1999—2001, Park St. Christian Ch., Charlottesville, from 2002; supply min. Louisa Christian Ch., from 2001, Rochelle Christian Ch., from 2001. Instr. U. Va. Sch. Continuing Edn., 1971—72, Ctrl. Va. Piedmont C.C., 1976; cons. Microform Systems and Copying Ctrs.; owner Massland Farm, Shadwell, Va.; basketball coach Rock Hill Acad., 1975—77; chaplain Cedars Nursing Home, Charlottesville, 1992—94, Colonnades Charlottesville, from 1992, Our Lady Peace Charlottesville, from 1996, Manor House, from 1999, Britthaven, Snow Hill, NC, 1999—2000, Winterhaven, Charlottesville, from 2002; vol. chaplaincy program Martha Jefferson Hosp., Charlottesville, from 2002. Pub.: Micropublishing Series, 18th Century Sources for Study of English Lit. and Culture, Women Authors 18th and 19th Centuries, 1993, Va. Colonial History, 1994—, Theology in the 18th and 19th Centuries, 1995; author: Episcopal Churches in the Diocese of Virginia, 1989, A Catechism for Children, 1995, A Guide to Colonial Churches in Virginia, 1996, The Christian Philosphy of Patrick Henry, In Memoriam to the Rt. Rev. William Meade, Third Bishop of Virginia, 1996, Jamestown, the Beginning of the Church in Virginia, 1996, Christ Epsicopal Church, Monticello Parish, Charlottesville, Va.. The First 100 Years, 1924-1924, 1996, Ministry in Nursing Homes and Health Care Centers, 1997, St. John's-Waldrop a Church History, 1845-1997, 1998, Jamestown and the Colonial Churches in Virginia, 1999, 2002, Twelve Gates to the Kingdom of God, Apostles of Christ, 1999; contbg. editor Va. Libr., 1970-71; contbr. articles to profl. jours. Introduced and Leader of Fest. of Carols and Liturgy in Retirement and Nursing Homes, 1995—98; with USMCR, 1957—73; rep. Senatorial Inner Cir., 1990, George Bush Rep. Task Force, 1990; chmn. bd. Park St. Christian Ch., 1969—76; mem. Emmanuel Epsic. Ch., Greenwood, Va., Grace Episc. Ch., Cismont, Va.; pres. region XV Episc. Diocese Va.; chalice bearer St. Luke's Chapel, Simeon, Va., Christ Ch., Charlottesville, 1992, lay eucharistic min., from 1993; lay reader eucharistic min. Christ Episcopal Ch., Charlottesville; chaplain Cedars Nursing Home, Charlottesville, from 1991; eucharistic min. Grace Episc. Ch., Cismont, from 1996; chaplain Comyn Hall, Charlottesville, from 2001; pres. Rock Hill Acad. Aux., 1975—76; pres. bd. Workshop V for handicapped, Charlottesville, 1972—73. Named Ky. Col.; recipient Key award Workshop V. Mem. ALA, Va. Libr. Assn., Soc. Reprodn. Engrs., Nat. Microfilm Assn. (libr. rels. com. 1973), Va. microfilm Assn. (pres. 1971-72, v.p. 1973-74, program chmn. ann. conf. 1974, Pioneer award 1973, fellow 1976), Ky. Microfilm Assn. (Oustanding award 1967, pres. 1964-67), Assn. Info. and Image Mgmt., Va. Gamebird Assn., Thoroughbred Owners and Breeders Assn., Am. Rose Soc., Thomas Jefferson Rose Soc. (charter), NRA, Nat. Trust Hist. Preservation, Va. Microfilm Assn. (contbg. editor Micro-News 1983-85). Home: Keswick, Va. Died Feb. 24, 2003.

MASSEY, LEON R. (R.L. MASSEY), professional association administrator; b. Grand Island, Nebr., Jan. 16, 1930; s. James Moore and Iva Pearl (Richardson) M.; m. Jean M. Nielsen, June 17, 1951; children: Dean R., Maureen L. Student, U. Colo., 1948-49; BA, U. Nebr., 1955; postgrad., N.Y. Inst. Fin., 1963. Salesman consumer products Union Carbide Corp., Memphis, 1956-57, Greenville, Miss., 1957-58, Albuquerque, 1958-61, Dallas, 1962-63; regional sales mgr. GC Electric div. Textron Corp., Dayton, Ohio, 1963-64; account exec. Merrill Turben Co., Dayton, 1964-66; with Nat. Electric Contractors Assn., Dayton, 1967-72, Denver, 1972-83, exec. sec., 1967-83, also bd. dirs. Rocky Mountain chpt.; pres. RLM's Assocs., Englewood, Colo., 1983—2002. Instr. adult edn. Wayne State U., Dayton, 1964-66. City councilman City of Greenwood Village, Colo., 1986-90; pres. Cherry Creek Civic Assn., 1979-80, bd. dirs. 1973-74; bd. dirs. Assn. Operating Rm. Nurses, Cherry Creek Village Water Dist., 1992-95; bd. dirs. Goldsmith Gulch Sanitation Dist., 1990—, pres., 1992—; bd. dirs. The Retreat Assn., 1996-99, Highlands Ranch Met. Dist., 1999; active Dem. Party, 1960. With USAF, 1950-54, Korea. Mem. Am. Soc. Assn. Execs. (cert., bd. dirs.), Colo. Soc. Assn. Execs. (life, pres. 1979), Civitan Club, Masons, Phi Kappa Psi. Died May 21, 2002.

MATHAI, JOSEPH, information scientist; b. Trivandrum, Kerala, India, Mar. 27, 1952; s. Chacko and Aleyamma (John) M.; m. Teresa Louzado, Feb. 12, 1989; children: Michelle, Robert. BS, Kerala U., 1973; MBA, Columbia U., 1976. Mgmt. cons. Am. Mgmt. Systems, Arlington, Va., 1976-77; asst. v.p. Paine Weber, N.Y.C., 1977-82; systems mgr. Merrill Lynch Capital Markets, N.Y.C., 1982-85; mng. dir. N.Y. Stock Exch., N.Y.C., 1985-91; chief strategist Instinet Corp., N.Y.C., 1991-94; v.p. technologies Fidelity Investments, Boston, from 1994. Named to All Star Data Processing/Mgmt. Info. Systems Team, Wall St. Computer Rev., 1989. Died Sept. 11, 2001.

MATHER, JOHN RUSSELL, climatologist, educator; b. Boston, Oct. 9, 1923; s. John and Mabelle (Russell) M.; m. Amy L. Nelson, 1946 (dec. 1994); children: Susan, Thomas, Ellen; m. Sandra F. Pritchard, 1997. BA, Williams Coll., 1945; BS in Meteorology, MIT, 1947, MS, 1948; PhD in Geography-Climatology, Johns Hopkins U., 1951. Rsch. assoc., climatologist Lab. Climatology, Seabrook, N.J., 1948-54, prin. rsch. scientist Centerton, N.J., 1954-63; pres. Lab. Climatology, C.W. Thornthwaite Assoc., Centerton, 1963-72; asst. prof. Johns Hopkins U., 1951-53; assoc. prof. climatology Drexel Inst. Tech., Phila., 1957-60; prof. geography U. Del., Newark, 1963-99, prof. emeritus, from 1999, chmn. dept. geography, 1966-89; state climatologist Del., 1978-92. Vis. lectr. geography U. Chgo., 1957-61; vis. prof. U.S. Mil. Acad., 1989. Author 2 books on applied climatology, 1 book on water resources; co-author biography of C.W. Thornthwaite; U.S. editor joint U.S.-USSR book on global change; contbr. numerous articles to tech. jours. Recipient Lifetime Achievement award in climatology, 1999. Fellow AAAS; mem. Am. Meteorol. Soc., Assn. Am. Geographers (v.p. 1990-91, pres. 1991-92, Lifetime Achievement award 1998), Am. Geog. Soc. (councilor 1981-99, sec. 1982-99, Charles P. Daly medal), Am. Water Resources Assn., Tau Beta Pi, Phi Kappa Phi. Achievements include contributing to concept of potential evapotranspiration, its measurement, use in climatic water balance; moisture factor in climate; application of climatic water balance to studies in agr., hydrology, applied climatology. Home: Avondale, Pa. Died Jan. 3, 2003.

MATHEW, MARTHA SUE CRYDER, retired education educator; b. Hallsville, Ohio, Feb. 21, 1928; d. Earl and Minnie Ada (Hough) Cryder; m. Guy Wilbur Mathew, Mar. 25, 1949; children: John G., Jeffrey Bruce. BS, Ohio No. U., 1966. Cert. tchr., Ohio. Tchr. Immaculate Conception Sch., Celina, Ohio, 1961-64, Zane Trace Local Sch., Chillicothe, Ohio, 1964-93; ret., 1993. Mem. Juvenile Ct. Rev. Bd., Ross County, Chillicothe. Vol. ARC; band mem. Cicleville Pumpkin Show. Named Educator of Yr., Zane Trace Local, Ross County, 1993. Mem. Order Ea. Star (Worthy Matron 1976, 88, Evergreen chpt. 169, Adelphi), Ladies Oriental Shrine (treas., sec., v.p., pres.), Delta Kappa Gamma (com.). Republican. Methodist. Home: Kingston, Ohio. Died July 22, 2000.

MATHEWS, KENNETH PINE, internist, educator; b. Schenectady, N.Y., Apr. 1, 1921; s. Raymond and Marguerite Elizabeth (Pine) Mathews; m. Alice Jean Elliot, Jan. 26, 1952 (dec.); children: Susan Kay, Ronald Elliott, Robert Pine; m. Winona Beatrice Rosenburg, Nov. 8, 1975. AB, U. Mich., 1941, MD, 1943. Diplomate Am. Bd. Allergy and Immunology (past sec.). Intern, asst. resident, resident in medicine Univ. Hosp., Ann Arbor, Mich., 1943-45, 48-50; mem. faculty dept. medicine Med. Sch. U. Mich., 1950—, assoc. prof. internal medicine, 1956-61, prof., 1961-86, prof. emeritus, from 1986, head divsn. allergy, 1967-83. Adj. mem. Scripps Clinic and Rsch. Found., La Jolla, Calif., from 1986; past chmn. residency rev. com. allergy and immunology, past chmn. allergy and immunology rsch. com. NIH. Co-author: (book) A Manual of Clinical Allergy, 2d edit., 1967; editor: Jour. Allergy and Clin. Immunology, 1968—72; contbr. articles to profl. jours. Served to capt. M.C. U.S. Army, 1946—48. Recipient Disting. Svc. award, Am. Acad. Allergy, 1976. Fellow: ACP (emeritus), Am. Acad. Allergy (past pres.); mem.: Am. Fedn. Clin. Rsch., Ctrl. Soc. Clin. Rsch. (emeritus), Am. Assn. Immunologists (emeritus), Phi Beta Kappa, Alpha Omega Alpha. Died Dec. 28, 2002.

MATHIS, WILLIAM LOWREY, lawyer; b. Jackson, Tenn., Dec. 19, 1926; s. Harry Fletcher and Syrene (Lowrey) M.; m. Marilyn Jayne Cason, Sept. 10, 1949; children: Amanda Mathis Miller, Amy Mathis Webb, Peter Andrew, Perry Alexander, Anne Mathis Mandigo. B.M.E., Duke U., 1947; JD with honors, George Washington U., 1951. Bar: D.C. bar 1951, Fla. bar 1972, Va. bar 1977. Examiner U.S. Patent Office, 1947-52; mem. Swecker & Mathis, Washington, 1952-61; of counsel Burns, Doane, Swecker & Mathis, Alexandria, Va., from 1961. Adj. prof. law Georgetown U. Law Center, 1974— Co-author: Trademark Litigation in the Trademark Office and Federal Courts, 1977; also chpt. in Handbook of Modern Marketing, 2d edit., 1986. Mem. Am., D.C. Bar Assns., Am. Intellectual Property Law Assn., IN Trademark Assn., Order of Coif. Roman Catholic. Home: Annandale, Va. Died Dec. 25, 2002.

MATHUR, KAILASH, nutritionist, educator; b. Jodhpur, India, Feb. 21, 1934; came to the U.S., 1962; s. Vijey Mal and Mohan Kaur Mathur; m. Savita Mathur, July 29, 1964; children: Shikha, Sameer. BS, Jaswant Coll., Jodhpur, 1955; DVM, Vet. Coll., Bikaner, India, 1960; MS, N.C. State U., 1964; PhD, U. Ill., 1975. Mgr. coll. clinics Vet. Coll., Bikaner, 1960-62; assoc. prof. dairy sci. S.C. State U., Orangeburg, 1965-71, project dir. human nutrition rsch., 1971-80, prof., advisor to nutritional scis. grad. program, from 1982; tech. Southeastern Consortium for Internat. Devel., Kenya, 1980-82. Specialist, cons. for nutrition edn. project, vis. prof. food sci. Clemson (S.C.) U., 1979-80; field dir. health measurements program sch. pub. health U. S.C., Columbia, 1976-77; local project officer Head Start Orangeburg Com. for Econ. Progress, 1968; adj. prof. nutrition Med. U. S.C., Charleston. Contbr. articles to profl. jours. Bd. dirs. Orangeburg divsn. Am. Heart Assn.; mem. adv. bd. assoc. degree in nursing divsn. Orangeburg Calhoun Tech. Coll. Recipient Gov.'s Disting. Prof. award, 1991; apptd. by Pres. Clinton to Nat. Nutrition Monitoring Adv. Coun.; honored for disting. cmty. svc. by concurrent resolution passed by N.C. Ho. of Reps. and Senate, 1997. Mem. Am. Dietetic Assn., S.C. Dietetic Assn. (bd. dirs. 1986-87, 90—, chmn. licensure and legis. network coord.), Edisto Dietetic Assn. (pres. 1986-87), Am. Soc. Microbiology, Nutrition Today Soc., Soc. for Nutrition Edn., S.C. Acad. Scis., S.C. Soc. Microbiology (pres. awards com.), S.C. State Nutrition Coun. (mem. exec. bd., chmn. nominating com.), S.C. Pub. Health Assn., S.C. Soc. Allied Health Professions (sec.-treas. 1976-77), Greater Orangeburg C. of C. (chmn. health care nutrition com.). Avocations: reading, community work, gardening. Home: Orangeburg, SC. Died Jan. 28, 2001.

MATSUI, JIRO, importer, wholesaler, small business owner; b. Honolulu, Hawaii, Apr. 5, 1919; s. Juro and Tsuta (Murai) M.; m. Barbara Toshiko Tanji; children: Kenneth Jiro, Alan Kiyoshi, Carol Ritsu. BA, U. Hawaii, 1949. Owner Honolulu Aquarium and Pet Supply, Honolulu, 1946-77, Bird House, Honolulu, 1957-61; owner, pres., chmn. Petland, Inc., Honolulu, 1961-99, Pets Pacifica, Inc., Honolulu, 1977-99, Global Pet Industries, Honolulu, 1975-99. Organizer, coord. first Pet Consumer Show in U.S., 1979, pres. 1979-82; first Internat. Pet Show; cons. Japan Pet Product Mfr. Assn. Fair, Japan, 1981-99. Pres. Waikiki Vets. Club, Kapahulu, Oahu, Hawaii, 1948-66, Waiawa (Oahu) Farmers, 1948-88; sr. adv. com. plants and animals State of Hawaii, 1974-99. Sgt. U.S. Army, 1941-46. Decorated Bronze Star; named retailer of yr. Retail Merchants of Hawaii, 1993. Mem. Am. Pet Soc. (pres. 1979-82, chmn. 1989-92), World Wide Pet Supply Assn. (bd. dirs. 1974-93, pres. 1989-90, Edward B. Price award 1982), Honolulu C. of C. (bd. dirs. 1974-99), Merchants of Hawaii. Avocations: fishing, gardening,. Home: Pearl City, Hawaii. Died Mar. 6, 1999.

MATTHES, HOWARD KURT, computer consultant and researcher; b. Chgo., June 18, 1929; s. Otto Kurt and Dora Ella (Fleischer) M.; m. Theressa Burton, Aug. 31, 1952; children: Patrice, Marcia, Linda, David Kurt, Ruth. BS, U. Utah, 1954; MS, Utah State U., 1967; PhD, Rutgers U., 1973. Communs. staff cons. Sperry Univac, Salt Lake City, 1972-74, mgr. network systems tech. support Americas div. Blue Bell, Pa., 1974-77, mgr. communs. design and devel. Devel. and Mfg. div., 1977-78; dir. network systems Billings Computer Corp., Provo, Utah, 1978-79; mgr. data communs. devel. Gould/Modicon, Andover, Mass., 1980-82; mgr. software devel. ITT Courier Terminal Systems, Tempe, Ariz., 1982-85; founder, pres. Computer Rsch. Inc., Tempe, 1985-89; dir. tng./computer Tempe Tech. Inst., Phoenix, 1989-90; pres. Computer Rsch. Inc., Salt Lake City, from 1991. Adj. prof. computer sci. Salt Lake C.C., 1991-92. Author: Introduction to DOS, 1991, Introduction to Word Processing, 1991, Increasing Your Productivity with Lotus1-2-3 Release 2.2, 1992. Chair dist. Rep. Party, Salt Lake City, 1958. With U.S. Army, 1954-56, Germany. Mem. Lds Ch. Died Apr. 25, 2001.

MATTHEWS, DANIEL GEORGE, editorial consultant; b. Lawrenceville, Va., Dec. 18, 1932; s. George Daniel and Evelyn (Goodrich) M.; student George Washington U., 1956-64, U.S. Fgn. Service Inst., 1960-64; m. Linda L. Fink, Oct. 25, 1975; children: Strelka Jamila, Francesca Alina. Analyst, VA, Washington, 1953-54; libr. asst. cataloging U.S. Dept. State, Washington, 1954-63, intelligence and rsch. specialist, 1964-66; editor-in-chief African Bibliog. Ctr., Washington, 1963-83, exec. dir., 1966-83; v.p. Afritec cons. firm, 1983-85; ptnr. The Matthews Assocs., former editor Africa Insider, biweekly newsletter on U.S.-African rels.; former editor African Fgn. Affairs; editorial cons. Greenwood Press, N.Y.C., 1967—; pres. Washington Task Force on African Affairs, 1969-79, African Communications Liaison Svc., 1979-84; mem. exec. com. coordinating coun. Internat. Ednl. Exch., 1969-87; program dir. So. African Devel. Documentation and Info. Exch., 1979-83; acting Am. dir. U.S./S. Africa Leader Exch. program, 1987-88; dir. Congl. African program Internat. Ctr. for Dynamics of Devel., 1989-90; lectr., cons. to acad. instns. on Africana collections and U.S. fgn. policy toward Africa; N.Am. liaison Orgn. African Unity/UN; mem. Econ. Commn. on Africa's Pan African Devel. Info. System, 1979-82. Bd. dirs. U.S.-South Africa Leader Exch. Program, 1980-90, chmn. exec. com., 1985-87; bd. dirs. Internat. Ctr. for Dynamics Devel., 1985-90; dir. ICDD Congressional Africa Program, 1989-90; pres. Internat. Ctr. for Devel. Initiatives, 1991-93; exec. dir. Operation Hunger, 1992-93. With AUS, 1950-53. Mem. ALA, African Studies Assn. (publs. com. 1974), African Heritage Studies Assn. (assoc.; award for outstanding contbn. to Africa 1975), Internat. Inst. Edn. (South African program bd.). Author: Soviet View of Africa, 1957; A Current Bibliography on Ethiopian Affairs, 1967, 72; editor-in-chief A Current Bibliography on African Affairs, 1963-84, editor emeritus, 1984—; editor: African affairs for General Reader, 1967; Current Themes in African Historical Studies, 1970; editorial bd. African Books in Print, Ife, Nigeria. Home: Rockville, Md. Died Dec. 28, 2003.

MATUSOW, HARVEY JOB, peace center administrator, consultant; b. Bronx, N.Y., Oct. 3, 1926; s. Herman Jay and Sylvia (Stolpen) M.; widowed, July 1989; children: Ann, Chuck. Student, Bairritz Am. U., 1945, CCNY, 1947-48, Taos Valley Art Sch., 1950, Am. U., 1953. Dir. Hooker Haven, N.Y.C., 1973-74, Ammal's Garden, Orange, Mass., 1974-77, Magic Mouse Theater, Tucson, 1977-82, Natural Balance Cafe, Tucson, 1981-82, A-OK Survival Ctr., Orange, 1982-83, Gandhi Peace Ctr., Warwick, Mass. and Tucson, from 1983. Part-time worker Bit Info. Svcs., London, 1966-72; chmnm. bd. dirs. People Serving People, Tucson. Author: False Witness, 1955, Art Almanac, 1965, Beast of Baseness, 1968, Magic Mouse, 1981. Mem. cemetary commn. Town of Wendell, Mass., 1976-77; chmn. bd. dirs. Specialized Home Care, Hadley, Mass., 1985-86; bd.

dirs. People Helping People, Boston, 1986-88. Staff sgt. U.S. Army, 1943-46, ETO, UASF, 1950-51. Recipient Humanitarian award Interfaith Coun., Boston, 1987. Mem. Lds Ch. Died Jan. 17, 2002.

MATZ, PETER S. composer, conductor, arranger; b. Pitts., Nov. 6, 1928; s. Louis N. and Alice (Krieger) M.; m. Janet Perry, Jan. 20, 1960 (div. 1978); children: P. Zachary, Jonas C.; m. Marilynn Lovell, June 21, 1987. BS, UCLA, 1950. Music dir. (TV shows) My Name Is Barbra, 1964 (Emmy award), Kraft Music Hall, 1968-71 (Emmy award), Carol Burnett Show, 1971-78 (Emmy award); composer (TV scores) Emergency!, 1972, I Heard the Owl Call My Name, 1973, Larry, 1974, In This House of Brede, 1975, The Dark Side of Innocence, 1976, Just an Old Sweet Song, 1976, The Call of the Wild, 1976, The Great Houdinis, 1976, Terraces, 1977, The Last Hurrah, 1977, Special Olympics, 1978, One in a Million, 1978, Happily Ever After, 1978, The Grass is Always Greener Over the Septic Tank, 1978, First You Cry, 1978 (Emmy award nominee), Love for Rent, 1979, Can You Hear the Laughter?, 1979, I Know Why the Caged Bird Sings, 1979, The Tenth Month, 1979, The Man in the Santa Claus Suit, 1979, Valentine Magic on Love Island, 19, White Mama, 1980, Fun and Games, 1980, Father Damien, 1980 (Emmy award nominee), Crazy Times, 1981, The Killing of Randy Webster, 1981, Take Your Best Shot, 1982, Drop-Out Father, 1982 (Emmy award nominee), Mrs. Delafield Wants to Marry, 1986, Stone Fox, 1987, Mercy or Murder?, 1987, Laura Lansing Slept Here, 1988, When We Were Young, 1989; orchestrator (Broadway mus.) Grand Hotel, 1989; arranger, condr. (rec.) People, 1964 (Gramy award), (comml.) Lena Horne Schaefer, 1965 (Clio award); producer, arranger, condr. (albums) The Broadway Album, 1986, Tab Tribute Album, 1988; arranger, condr., composer (movie score) Bye Bye Braverman, 1968, Marlowe, 1969, Rivals, 1972, Funny Lady, 1975 (Acad. award nominee), The Prize Fighter, 1979, The Private Eyes, 1980, Lust in the Dust, 1985, Torch Song Trilogy, 1988, The Gum Shoe Kid, 1989; composer, condr. TV scores for numerous shows, 1971—. Recipient Spl. L.A. award L.A. City Hall, 1990. Democrat. Jewish. Avocations: sports, musical events, politics. Home: Los Angeles, Calif. Died Aug. 9, 2002.

MATZNER, EGON, economics educator; b. Klagenfurt, Austria, Mar. 2, 1938; s. Heinrich and Josefine (Posautz) M.; m. Monica Siegel, Mar. 2, 1959 (div. 1983); children: Joerg, Robert; m. Gabriele Holzer, Oct. 14, 1984; 1 child, Sissela. M in Econs., U. Econs., Vienna, PhD, 1961; Docent, U. Linz, 1970. Asst. dir. Bank for Labor and Industry, Vienna, Austria, 1962-65; rsch. fellow Internat. Inst., Stockholm (Sweden) U., 1965-67; dean of faculty U. Tech., Vienna, Austria, 1992-95; dir. Sci. Ctr., Berlin, Germany, 1984-89; dir. rsch. unit for socio-econs. Austrian Acad. Sci., Vienna, Austria, 1992-98; fellow Max Weber Coll., 1998—2002. Cons. Fed. Min. Fin., Vienna, 1970-79, OECD, Paris, 1975; coord. Fed. Ministry Tech., Bonn, Germany, 1986-88; vis. prof. U. B.C., Vancouver, 2001—. Author: Monopolar World Order, 2000, The Wasted Republic, 2001; co-editor: Barriers to Full Employment, 1988, Beyond Keynesianism: The Socio-Economics of Production and Full Employment, 1991, The Market Shock, 1992. Mem. German Econ. Assn., SASE, European Assn. Polit. Economy. Avocation: mountaineering. Home: Vienna, Austria. Died Sept. 2003.

MAULDIN, WILLIAM HENRY (BILL MAULDIN), cartoonist; b. Mountain Park, N.Mex., Oct. 29, 1921; s. Sidney Albert and Edith Katrina (Bemis) M.; m. Norma Jean Humphries, Feb. 28, 1942 (div. 1946); children— Bruce Patrick, Timothy; m. Natalie Sarah Evans, June 27, 1947 (dec. Aug. 1971); children— Andrew, David, John, Nathaniel; m. Christine Ruth Lund, July 29, 1972; children: Kaja Lisa, Samuel Lund. Ed. pub. schs. and high schs., N.Mex. and Ariz.; studied art, Chicago Acad. of Fine Arts; MA (hon.), Conn. Wesleyan U., 1946; Litt.D. (hon.), Albion Coll., 1970, N.Mex. State U., Las Cruces, 1972; L.H.D. (hon.), Lincoln Coll., 1970, Wash. U., St. Louis, 1984, Coll. of Santa Fe, 1986. Cartoonist St. Louis Post-Dispatch, until 1962, Chgo. Sun-Times, 1962-91. Tech. adviser, actor film Teresa, 1950; actor film The Red Badge of Courage, 1950; author or cartoonist: Star Spangle Banter, 1941, Sicily Sketch Book, 1943, Mud, Mules and Mountains, 1943, This Damn Tree Leaks, 1945, Up Front (Book of the Month selection), 1945, Back Home (Book of the Month seleaction), 1947, A Sort of a Saga, 1949, Bill Mauldin's Army, 1951, Bill Mauldin in Korea, 1952, What's Got Your Back Up?, 1961, I've Decided I Want My Seat Back, 1965, The Brass Ring, 1971 (Book of Month Club selection), Mud and Guts, 1978: Let's Declare Ourselves Winners and Get the Hell Out, 1985; illustrator: Bradley: A Soldier's Story, 1978; author, illustrator numerous articles Sports Illus., Life, Collier's. Served with U.S. Army, 1940-45, 45th Inf. Div. and Stars and Stripes; campaigns Sicily, Italy, France, Germany. Decorated Purple Heart, Legion of Merit; recipient Pulitzer prize for cartoons 1944, 59, Sigma Delta Chi award for cartoons 1963, 69, 72; Prix Charles Huard de dessin de presse Fondation pour l'Art et la Recherche Paris, 1974, Walter Cronkite award for journalistic excellence Ariz. State U., 1985. Fellow Sigma Delta Chi. Died Jan. 22, 2003.

MAURICE, DAVID MYER, physiology researcher; b. London, Apr. 3, 1922; came to U.S., 1968; BSc in Physics, Reading U., Eng., 1942; PhD, London U., 1950. Jr. sci. officer Telecommunications Rsch. Establishment, Eng., 1942-45; reader U. London, 1963-68; sr. scientist Stanford (Calif.) U., 1968-85, prof. rsch., 1985-95; prof. ocular physiology Columbia U., N.Y.C., from 1995. Mem. NIH study sect., 1972-76; lectr. Harvard U., Boston, 1974-90. Author: (with others) The Cornea and Sclera, 1986, Pharmacokinetics of the Eye, 1986, Fluorophotometry of Anterior Segment, 1990; contbr. over 200 articles to profl. publs. Recipient Borsa di Studio, Govt. of Italy, Rome, 1951, Friedenwald award Assn. Rsch. in Ophthalmology, 1967, Castroviejo medal Castroviejo Soc., 1986, Prentice medal Am. Acad. Optometry, 1989; Fulbright fellow U.S. Govt., San Francisco, 1954, Guggenheim Found. fellow, Paris, 1979, others. Mem. Physiol. Soc., Assn. Rsch. in Opththalmology, Internat. Soc. Ocular Fluorophotometry (pres. 1988-90), Redwood City Eton Fives Club (hon. chaplain 1990). Home: New York, NY. Died July 20, 2002.

MAXWELL, ROBERT HAWORTH, agricultural consultant; b. Earlham, Iowa, Oct. 8, 1927; s. Charles Erich and Mildred Grace M.; m. Betty Ruth Michener, Dec. 24, 1950; children: Robert Steven, Daniel Guy, Timothy Charles, Kristen Kimuli. Student, Earlham Coll., 1946-48; BS in Farm Ops., Iowa State U., 1950, MS in Agrl. Edn., 1964; PhD in Agrl. Edn., Cornell U., 1970. Cert. tchr., Iowa. Farm operator, Iowa, 1952-60; instr. Earlham Coll., Richmond, Ind., 1960-62; tchr. vocat. agr. Earlham (Iowa) Community Sch., 1963-64; asst. prof. agrl. edn. W.Va. U., Morgantown, 1964-68, assoc. prof. agrl. edn., 1970-75, prof. agrl. edn., 1975-79, asst. dean coll. agr. & forestry, acting chmn. divsn. animal & vet. scis., 1980, assoc. dean coll. agr. & forestry, chmn. divsn. internat. agr. & forestry, 1980-84, interim dean coll. agr. & forestry, interim dir. W.Va. agrl. & forestry experiment sta., 1984-85, dean coll. agr. & forestry, dir. W.Va. agrl. & forestry experiment sta., 1985-93; prof. agr., coord. internat. agr. U. W.Va., Morgantown, 1994-95, assoc. provost for ext. and pub. svc., dir. coop. ext. svc., 1995-97. Vocat. agr. tchr. Dexfield Community Schs., Redfield, Iowa, 1958-60; grad. asst. dept. edn. Cornell U., 1969-70; contract AID agrl. edn. advisor Kenya Ministry Edn., 1960-62, 64-68, spl. asst. dir. manpower devel. divsn. Tanzania Ministry Agr., 1975-79; dir. Allegheny Highlands Project, 1970-75; bd. dirs. Northeast Regional Ctr. Rural Devel., W.Va. U. Rsch. Corp.; lectr. in field. Author: (with others) Agriculture for Primary School series, 1979, 82, 85; editor Empire State Vo-Ag Teacher Jour., 1969-70; pub. papers and reports; contbr. articles to profl. jours. Unit leader United Way, Elkins, W.Va., 1970-75, Morgantown, 1979-93. With U.S. Army, 1950-52. Named Disting. West Virginian Gov. W.Va., 1993; recipient Commemorative medal U. Agr., Nitra, Slovakia, 1993; named to W.Va. Agriculture and Forestry Hall of Fame, 1995. Mem. AAAS, Am. Assn. Agrl. Edn., Am. Farmland Trust (life), Am. Soc. Agrl. Conss. (Meritorious Svc. award 1994), Am. Soc. Agrl. Conss. Internat. (cert., bd. dirs.), Nat. Assn. Colls. and Tchrs. Agr., Nat. Peace Inst., World Future Soc., Assn. Internat. Agrl. and Extension Educators (pres.-elect, pres. 1994, Outstanding Svc. 1991), Assn. Internat. Agr. and Rural Devel. (Outstanding Svc. 1992), Coun. Agrl. Sci. and Tech., Northeast Regional Assn. Agrl. Experiment Sta. Dirs. (Svc. Commendation 1993), UN Assn. of the USA, Soil and Water Conservation Soc. (life), Kenya Assn. Tchrs. Agr. (life), Tanzanian Soc. Agr. Edn. and Extension (life), W.Va. Shepherd's Fedn., W.Va. Poultry Assn., W.Va. Cattlemen's Assn., W.Va. Farm Bur., Iowa Farm Bur., W.Va. Horticultural Soc., Agriculture and Forestry Hall of Fame Found. W.Va. (past pres.), Upshur Livestock Assn. (life), Morgantown Rotary Club, Iowa State U. Alumni Assn. (life), Cornell U. Alumni Assn. (life), W.Va. U. Alumni Assn. (life), FFA Alumni Assn. (life), Phi Delta Kappa, Gamma Sigma Delta (Disting. Svc. W. Va. Agrl. award 1999), Alpha Zeta (Centennial Honor Roll 1997), Phi Mu Alpha (life). Mem. Soc. Of Friends. Died Oct. 1999.

MAY, ERNEST MAX, charitable organization official; b. Newark, July 24, 1913; s. Otto Bernard and Eugenie (Morgenstern) M.; m. Harriet Elizabeth Dewey, Oct. 12, 1940; children: Ernest Dewey, James Northrup, Susan Elizabeth. BA, Princeton, 1934, MA, 1935; PhD in Organic Chemistry, U. Chgo., 1938; LittD (hon.), Montclair State Coll., 1989. With Otto B. May, Inc., Newark, 1938-73, successively chemist, gen. mgr., 1938-52, pres., 1952-73; trustee Youth Consultation Service Diocese of Newark, 1952-59, 61-66, 68-75, pres., 1971-75, hon. trustee, from 1975; dir. Cone Mills Corp., 1961-73, mem. exec. com., 1968-71. Tech. adviser to spl. rep. trade negotiations, 1964-67. Councilman, Summit, N.J., 1963-70; mem. Summit Environ. Com., 1971-75, chmn., 1974-75; pres. Family Svc. Assn. Summit, 1959-61, Mental Health Assn. Summit, 1954, Summit Coun. Chs. Christ, 1962-63; mem. exec. com. Christ Hosp., Jersey City, 1971—, v.p., chmn., 1974-93; chmn. Summit Hwy. Adv. Com., 1976-94; trustee, organizer Summer Organic Chemistry Inst., Choate Sch., Wallingford, Conn.; mem. Union County Mental Health Bd., 1973-76; bd. dirs. N.J. Mental Health Assn., 1974-81; trustee Montclair (N.J.) State Univ., 1975-85, vice-chmn., 1976-80, chmn., 1980-83; adviser applied prof. psychology Rutgers U., 1976—; mem. Nat. commn. on Nursing, 1980-83; adviser dept. music Princeton U.; trustee Assn. for Children in N.J., 1975—, Citizen's Com. on Biomed. Ethics in N.J., 1984-95, N.J. Health Decisions, 1995-97; advisor Nat. Exec. Svcs. Corps Health Care Consulting Group, 1994—; mem. N.J. Early Early Care and Edn. Coalition, 1999—, N.J. Child Care Adv. Coun., 1999—. Fellow Am. Inst. Chemists; mem. Am. Chem. Soc., Synthetic Organic Chem. Mfrs. Assn. (bd. govs. 1952-54, 63-70, v.p. 1966-68, chmn. internat. comml. rels. com. 1968-73, hon. mem.), Vol. Trustees Not-for-Profit Hosps. (trustee 1986-88, 94-98), Chemists Club (N.Y.), Beacon Hill Club (Summit, N.J.), Nassau Club (Princeton), N.J. Hosp. Assn. (coun. on edn. 1990-91), Sigma Xi. Republican. Episcopalian (vestry 1950-60). Home: Summit, NJ. Died Dec. 6, 2002.

MAY, GEORGES (CLAUDE), French language and literature educator, university official; b. Paris, Oct. 7, 1920; came to U.S., 1942, naturalized, 1943; s. Lucien and Germaine (Samuel) M.; m. Martha Corkery, Feb. 19, 1949 (dec. Dec. 1997); children: Anne May Berwind, Catherine May Dias. BA, U. Paris, 1937; Licence es Lettres, U. Montpellier, France, 1941; Diplome, d'Etudes Superieures, 1941; PhD, U. Ill., 1947; LHD, U. New Haven, 1990, Quinnipiac Coll., 1996, Wesleyan U., 1997, Albertus Magnus Coll., 2000. Asst. U. Ill., 1942-43, 46-47; faculty Yale, 1947—, successively instr., asst. prof., assoc. prof., 1947-56, prof. French, 1956-71; dean Yale Coll., 1963-71, Sterling prof. French, 1971-91, prof. emeritus, from 1991. Chmn. dept. French, 1978-79, provost, 1979-81; prof. summers U. Ill., 1946, Middlebury Coll., 1951, 54, U. Minn., 1948, U. Mich., 1952, U. Calif. at Berkeley, 1959; sec. Fourth Internat. Congress Enlightenment, 1975 Author: Tragedie cornélienne, tragedie racinienne, 1948, D'Ovide a Racine, 1949, Quatre Visages de Denis Diderot, 1951, Diderot et La Religieuse, 1954, Rousseau par lui-meme, 1961, Le Dilemme du roman au XVIIIe siecle, 1963, L'Autobiographie, 1979, Les Mille et une nuits d'Antoine Galland, ou le Chef-d'oeuvre invisible, 1986, La Perruque de Dom Juan, ou Du bon usage des énigmes dans la littérature de l'âge classique, 1995; editor: Corneille's Polyeucte and Le Menteur, 1964, Diderot's Commentary on Hemsterhuis' Lettre sur l'homme, 1964, Diderot's La Religieuse, 1975, Diderot's Sur Terence, 1980, Jean-Jacques Rousseau et Madame de LaTour/Correspondance, 1998, Antoine Hamilton's Les Quatre Facardins, 2001; contbr. articles on French lit. to profl. pubs. Trustee Hopkins Grammar Day Prospect Hill Sch., 1970-78; bd. dirs. Am. Council Learned Socs., 1979-89, chmn. bd., 1982-89, chmn. emeritus, 1989-95. Served with French Army, 1939-40; Served with AUS, 1943-45. Decorated chevalier French Legion of Honor; Guggenheim Found. fellow, 1950-51, 84-85 Mem. Am. Acad. Arts and Scis., Am. Philos. Soc., Am. Soc. 18th Century Studies (pres. 1974-75), Internat. Coun. Philosophy and Humanistic Studies (v.p. 1982-84), Am. Assn. Tchrs. French, Union Academique Internationale (bd. dirs. 1983-86, v.p. 1986-89, pres. 1989-92), MLA, Assn. des Etudes Francaises, Soc. d'Etude du XVIIIe Siecle, Phi Beta Kappa. Home: New Haven, Conn. Died Feb. 28, 2003.

MAYBERRY, HERBERT SYLVESTER, lawyer; b. Enid, Okla., Jan. 20, 1927; s. Herbert Sylvester and Pearl Wilma (Bridal) M.; m. Gladys Anne Cody, Nov. 21, 1951 (div. Feb. 1974); children: Martha Rebecca, Molly Nanette; m. Joan Wilma Burnette, Dec. 28, 1974. BS in Geology, U. Okla., 1949; JD, U. Denver, 1959. Bar: Colo. 1959, Tex. 1979. Geologist Shell Oil Co., Denver, 1949-58; mgr. Ball Assocs. Ltd., Denver, 1958-65; exec. asst. Western Geophys. Co., Shreveport, La., 1965-66; v.p., gen. counsel, sec. McAlester (Okla.) Fuel Co., 1966-81; assoc. gen. counsel Enstar Corp., Houston, 1977-84; v.p., gen. counsel, sec. Ultramar Oil and Gas Co., Houston, 1985-89; pvt. practice Grand Junction, Colo., from 1989. With USNR, 1945-46. Mem.: ABA, Am. Assn. Petroleum Geologists. Home: Grand Junction, Colo. Died June 7, 2003.

MAYER, EGON, sociology educator; b. Caux Sur Montreaux, Switzerland, Dec. 23, 1944; came to U.S., 1956; s. Eugene and Hedy Mayer; m. Susan Feldman Sept. 4, 1967 (div. Dec. 1986); 1 child, Daphne; m. Marcia J. Kramer-Friedman, June 26, 1988. BA in Sociology, Bklyn. Coll., 1967; MA in Sociology, New Sch. for Social Rsch., 1969; PhD in Sociology, Rutgers U., 1975. Asst. prof. Bklyn. Coll., 1970-75, assoc. prof., 1976-83, prof., 1984—2004. Sr. rsch. fellow Ctr. for Jewish Studies, CUNY Grad. Sch.; dir. instnl. grants program Wexner Found., 1987-88; rsch. cons. Am. Jewish Com., Coun. Jewish Fedns., Union of Am. Hebrew Congregations, United Jewish Appeal, others; organizer, co-sponsor confs. 94th Ann. Conf. Jewish Communal Svcs. Assn., 1992, Ctr. for Jewish Studies/CUNY Grad. Sch. and Jewish Outreach Inst., 1989, 90; presenter in field nat. and internat. confs. Author: From Suburb to Shtetl: The Jews of Boro Park, 1979, Love & Tradition: Marriage Between Jews & Christians, 1985, (monographs) Children of Intermarriage, 1983, The Boro Park Community Survey, 1982-83, 1984, Intermarriage and Rabbinic Officiation, 1989; editor: Jewish Intermarriage, Conversion and Outreach, 1990, The Imperatives of Jewish Outreach, 1991, Jewish Connections for Interfaith Families: A National Directory of Outreach Programs, 1992; contbr. articles to profl. jours. Home: Laurel Hollow, NY. Died Jan. 30, 2004.

MAYES, CHARLOTTE, city councilwoman; b. Dallas, Aug. 27, 1947; m. Johnnie Mayes; children: Maury, Tory, Sir, Jonyelle. AS, Eastfield C.C., 1979; BS, East Tex. State U., 1982. City councilwoman Dist. 7, Dallas, 1991—99, mem. pub. safety, fin., arts, edn., privatization coms., chmn. legis. com.; dep. mayor pro tem Dallas City Coun.; owner Charlotte Mayes & Assoc. Cons. pub. rels. dept. AT&T. Died Feb. 24, 2004.

MAYHALL, MICHAEL WAYNE, secondary school educator; b. Haleyville, Ala., Dec. 11, 1953; s. Benjamin Franklin and Gladys (Whitman) M. AS, N.W. Ala. State Jr. Coll., 1974; BS, Auburn (Ala.) U., 1976. Cert. secondary math. tchr., Ga. Tchr., dept. head East Coweta High Sch., Sharpsburg, Ga., from 1976. Invitation chmn. GCTM State Math. Tournament, Atlanta, 1989—. Author: History of Eastern Coweta County Schools and Indian Heritage, 1988. Named Tchr. of the Yr., 1979, 89. Mem. Nat. Coun. Tchrs. Math., Math. Assn. Am., Assn. Computing Machinery, Assn. for Supervision and Curriculum Devel., Am. Math. Soc., Atlanta Auburn Club. Democrat. Baptist. Avocations: traveling, puzzle solving. Home: Palmetto, Ga. Deceased.

MAYO, ROBERT PORTER, banker; b. Seattle, Mar. 15, 1916; s. Carl Asa and Edna Alberta (Nelson) M.; m. Marian Aldridge Nicholson, Aug. 28, 1942; children: Margaret Alice, Richard Carl, Carolyn Ruth (Mrs. Gregory Brown), Robert Nelson. AB magna cum laude, U. Wash., 1937, MBA, 1938. Research asst., auditor Wash. State Tax Commn., 1938-41; economist U.S. Treasury, 1941-47, asst. dir. office of tech. staff, 1948-53, chief debt div. analysis staff, 1953-59; asst. to sec. Treasury Dept., 1959-60; v.p. Continental Ill. Nat. Bank & Trust Co. of Chgo., 1960-69; chmn. Boye Needle Co., 1963-67; staff dir. Pres. Commn. on Budget Concepts, 1967; dir. U.S. Bur. of Budget, 1969-70; counsellor to Pres. U.S., 1970; pres. Fed. Res. Bank of Chgo., 1970-81, 81-95, ret. Trustee No. Trust Benchmark Funds, Goldman Sachs Funds, CNA Income Shares; Duff and Phelps Utilities Income Fund. Trustee YMCA, Chgo.; bd. dirs. Exec. Svc. Corps, Chgo. Mem. Comml. Club Chgo., Econ. Club Chgo., Bartlett-on-the-Greens Homeowner's Assn., Phi Beta Kappa. Presbyterian. Home: Bartlett, Ill. Died Jan. 25, 2003.

MAZZAWY, MARY, oncology nurse; Diploma, St. Peter's Sch. Nursing, 1965; BSN, U. Va., 1973; MSN, Tex. Woman's U., 1976. Cert. oncology nurse. Teaching asst. Tex. Woman's U., 1974-76; instr. U. Tex. Sch. Nursing, 1976-77; clin. dir. oncology and med. nursing Hermann Hosp., 1977-79; instr. Tex. Woman's U., 1979-84; clin. asst. prof. U. Tex. Sch. Nursing, from 1985; oncology clin. nurse specialist, nurse thanatologist Meth. Hosp., Houston, from 1979. Contbr. articles to profl. jours. Active Am. Cancer Soc.; lay pastor, lay eucharistic minister, mem. choir St. Stephen's Episc. Ch. Mem. Am. Assn. Suicidology, Am. Nurses Assn., Assn. Death Educators and Counselors, Oncology Nursing Soc., Lupus Found. Am., Found. of Thanatology. Home: Houston, Tex. Deceased.

MAZZOCCHI, ANTHONY, labor union executive; b. Bklyn., June 13, 1926; s. Joseph and Angelina M.; m. Susan Kleinwaks, Mar. 18, 1970; children: Geraldine, Carol, Linda, Anthony, Kristina and Elizabeth (twins). Student public schs. Assembly line worker Ford Motor Co., 1946-50; pres. Oil, Chem. and Atomic Workers Local 8-149, 1952-65; mem. internat. exec. bd. Oil, Chem. and Atomic Workers Internat. Union, Denver, legis. dir., 1965-77, v.p., 1977-79, health and safety dir., 1979-81, dir. workers policy project, 1981—. Mem. vis. faculty Harvard U. Sch. Public Health, Albert Einstein Coll. Medicine. Mem. Nassau County (L.I.) Planning Commn., 1964-72. Served with U.S. Army, 1943-46, ETO. Recipient Presdl. citation Am. Pub. Health Assn., 1983 Home: New York, NY. Died Oct. 5, 2002.

MCATEER, JOYCELEE, consultant, human services administrator; b. Denver, June 13, 1933; d. Roy Raymond and Merry Charlotte (Palmer) Lee; (div.); children: Gary Lee, Larry Allen, Henry Arthur. BA in Polit. Sci., Human Svcs., New Hampshire Coll., 1976, MS in Adminstrn., Gerontology, 1978. Chief exec. officer Champlain Valley OEO, St. Albans, Vt., Haverhill (Mass.) Communication, Peoples Alliance, Columbia, Ind.; field rep. State Office Elder Affairs, Boston, Mass.; chmn. grad. gerontology program New Hampshire Coll., Manchester; chief exec. officer Columbia Club of Seattle. Columnist; contbr. articles to profl. jours. Bd. dirs. Nat. Rural Housing Alliance, Community Econ. Devel. Recipient Excellence award, Cites of Bourne, Palmer, Malden, Lawrence, Lowell, Weymouth, Springfield, Mass. Mem. Nat. Assn. Couns. on Aging, Nat. Assn. Sr. Ctrs., Wash. Assn. of Execs. Downtown Seattle Assn. of Execs. Avocations: flying, horseback riding, travel, orchids. Home: Seattle, Wash. Died Apr. 26, 1999.

MCBAY, ARTHUR JOHN, toxicologist, consultant; b. Medford, Mass., Jan. 6, 1919; s. Arthur and Virginia (Davito) McB.; m. Avis Louise Botsford, Aug. 24, 1946; children: John, Robert. BS, Mass. Coll. Pharmacy, 1940, MS, 1942; PhD, Purdue U., 1948. Diplomate Am. Bd. Forensic Toxicology, cert. toxicol. chemist Am. Bd. Clin. Chemistry; registered pharmacist, Mass. Asst. prof. chemistry Mass. Coll. Pharmacy, Boston, 1948—53, 63asst. in legal medicine, dept. legal medicine, 1953; lectr. legal medicine Harvard U.; toxicologist, criminalist, cons. Mass. State Police Chemistry Lab., 1955—63; instr. Northeastern U., 1962—63; assoc. prof. toxicology Law-Medicine Inst. Boston U., 1963—69, assoc. prof. pharmacology Med. Sch., 1963-69; supr. lab. Mass. Dept. Pub. Safety, Boston, 1963—69; assoc. prof. pathology and toxicology U. N.C., Chapel Hill, 1969—73, prof., 1973—89, prof. emeritus pharmacy and pathology, from 1989; chief toxicologist Office Chief Med. Examiner, Chapel Hill, 1969—89. Mem. task force on alcohol, other drugs and transp. NRC; cons. toxicology resource com. Coll. Am. Pathologists, 1975-95, Bur. Med. Devices and Diagnostic Products, FDA, 1975-91, N.C. Drug Authority, 1971-75; dir. Mass. Alcohol Project, 1968-69. Mem. editl. bd. Jour. Forensic Scis., 1981-95; bd. editors Yearbook of Pathology, 1981-91; contbr. numerous articles on toxicology to profl. jours. Served to capt. USAAF, 1943-45. Fellow Am. Acad. Forensic Scis.; mem. Internat. Assn. Forensic Toxicologists, Nat. Safety Coun. (exec. bd. com. on alcohol and drugs 1981-91), Am. Pharm. Assn. (sec., treas. sci. sect. 1954-57), Soc. Forensic Toxicologists (dir. 1978), Am. Chem. Soc., Sigma Xi, Rho Chi, Phi Lambda Upsilon. Democrat. Roman Catholic. Home: Chapel Hill, NC. Deceased.

MCBEATH, ANDREW ALAN, orthopedic surgery educator; b. Milw., Mar. 4, 1936; s. Ivor Charles and Lida McBeath; m. Margaret McBeath; children: Craig Matthew, Drew Alan. BS, U. Wis., 1958, MD, 1961. Diplomate Am. Bd. Orthopaedic Surgery (oral examiner). Intern, resident Hartford (Conn.) Hosp., 1961-63; resident in orthopedic surgery U. Iowa, Iowa City, 1963-66; asst. prof. div. orthopedic surgery div. surgery U. Wis., Madison, 1968-72, assoc. prof., 1972-79, prof., from 1979, Frederick J. Gaenslen prof., 1980, acting chmn. div., 1972-75, chmn. div., 1975-2000. Contbr. over 75 articles, chpt. to books. Capt. M.C., USAF, 1966-68. Mem. AMA, Am. Acad. Orthopaedic Surgeons, Orthopaedic Rsch. Soc., Am. Orthopaedic Assn., Hip Soc., Wis. Orthopaedic Soc., Rotary, Alpha Omega Alpha. Avocations: bicycling, skiing, reading. Home: Madison, Wis. Died June 2, 2002.

MC BRIDE, THOMAS FREDERICK, lawyer, former university dean, government official; b. Elgin, Ill., Feb. 8, 1929; m. Catherine Higgs Milton, Aug. 23, 1975; children: Matthew (dec.), Elizabeth, John, Raphael, Luke. BA, NYU, 1952; LLB, Columbia U., 1956. Bar: N.Y. 1956, D.C. 1966, Calif. 1989, Conn. 2000, U.S. Supreme Ct. 1963. Asst. dist. atty., N.Y. County, 1956-59; trial atty. organized crime sect. Dept. Justice, 1961-65; ofcl. Peace Corps, 1965-68; assoc. spl. prosecutor Watergate, 1973-75; insp. gen. U.S. Dept. Agr., Washington, 1977-81, U.S. Dept. Labor, Washington, 1981-82; assoc. dean Stanford Law Sch., Calif., 1982-89; mem. Pres.'s Commn. Organized Crime, 1983-86, Calif. Council on Mental Health, 1986-90; dir. environ. health and safety Stanford U., 1990-92; counselor U.S. Dept. Energy, Washington, 1993-95. Spl. asst. to pres. Save the Children, 1997-99. With AUS, 1946-47. Died Oct. 31, 2003.

MCBRYDE, THOMAS HENRY, lawyer; b. New Albany, Miss., Oct. 26, 1925; s. Henry Thornton and Mary Catherine (Davis) McB.; m. Barbara White, Dec. 28, 1946; children: Elise, William Henry, John Thomas. BS, U.S. Mil. Acad., 1946; LLB, U. Va., 1952. Bar: Va. 1952, N.Y. 1959. Commd. 2d lt. U.S. Army, 1946, advanced through grades to capt., 1950; assigned to Japan, ETO and U.S.; instr. law U.S. Mil. Acad., 1956-57; resigned, 1957; asst. counsel N.Y. State Banking Dept., 1960-61; assoc. Rogers & Wells and predecessors, N.Y.C., 1957-60, 61-65, ptnr., 1965-93, sr. counsel, from 1993; chief counsel N.Y. State Joint Legis. Com. to Revise Banking Law, 1962-65, minority counsel, 1965-66. Mem. comml. panel Am. Arbitration Assn., 1976—; mem. adv. com. supervision mut. instns. Office N.Y. Banking Supt., 1966-67 Mem. Assn. Grads. U.S. Mil. Acad., Order of Coif, Am. Yacht Club, Heritage Club. Republican. Episcopalian. Home: Gainesville, Fla. Died Aug. 31, 2002.

MCCAIN, H. HARRISON, frozen food products company executive; b. Florenceville, N.B., Can., Nov. 3, 1927; s. A. D. and Laura B. (Perley) McC.; m. Marion M. McNair, Oct. 4, 1952; children: Mark, Peter, Laura, Ann, Gillian. BA, Acadia U.; LLD (hon.), U. N.B., Can., 1986. Chmn. McCain Foods Ltd., Florenceville, N.B., Can., former chmn. Scarborough. Chmn. bd. McCain Alimentaire S.A.R.L., Harnes, France, McCain Europa bv, Hoofddorp, Netherlands, Day & Ross Inc., Hartland, N.B.; bd. dirs. McCain Espana S.A., Burgos, Spain, McCain Foods Inc. Pty. Ltd., Wendouree, Australia, McCain Foods Inc., U.S.A., McCain Refrigerated Foods Inc., Oakville, Ont., Bilopage Inc., Que., Thomas Equipment Ltd., Centreville, N.B., Britfish Ltd., Hull, Eng., Valley Farms Ltd., McCain Citrus Inc., Chgo., Beau Marais S.A.R.L., Bethune, France, McCain Foods Western, Inc., Othello, Wash., McCain Sunnyland B.V., Turnhout, Belgium, McCain Processing, Inc., Presque Isle, Maine, McCain Foods Ltd., Tokyo, Right-O-Way, Inc., Tustin, Calif.; assoc. McCain Group Cos., Bank of N.S., Petro-Can. Decorated officer Order of Canada; recipient Canadian Bus. Statesman award Harvard Bus. Sch., 1988. Presbyterian. Avocation: skiing. Died Mar. 18, 2004.

MCCALL, DAVID WARREN, retired chemistry research director, consultant; b. Omaha, Dec. 1, 1928; s. H. Bryron and Grace (Cox) McC.; m. Charlotte Marion Dunham, July 30, 1955; children: William Christopher, John Dunham BS, U. Wichita, 1950; MS, U. Ill., 1951, PhD, 1953. Mem. tech. staff AT&T Bell Labs, Murray Hill, N.J., 1953-62, head dept. phys. chemistry, 1962-69, asst. chem. dir., 1969-73, dir. chem. rsch. lab., 1973-91, dir. environ. chemistry rsch., 1991-92. Chmn. bd. trustees Gordon Rsch. Confs.; mem. adv. bd. Chem. Abstract Svcs.; chmn. Nat. Commn. on Super-conductivity; chmn. panels on advanced composites, electronic packaging, fire suppression for USN, and shipboard pollution control NRC; mem. Naval Studies Bd. Fellow: AAAS, Royal Soc. Chemistry London, Am. Phys. Soc.; mem.: AICE, NAE (chmn. materials engrng. sect., chmn. membership com.), Am. Chem. Soc. (com. on chemistry and pub. affairs, Barnes award 1992). Home: Far Hills, NJ. Died June 5, 2002.

MCCALL, HOWARD WEAVER, JR., retired banker; b. Chattanooga, Aug. 11, 1907; s. Howard W. and Juliet (Hotzclaw) McC.; m. Jane Ewart, Oct. 21, 1938; children: Nancy E. McCall Watson, Howard W. III, Jane E. McCall Politi. BA, U. Va., 1928; postgrad., Rutgers U., 1939. With Chem. Bank, N.Y.C., 1928-72, pres., 1966-72, ret., 1972. Advisor Chem. Bank, N.Y.C.; pres., bd. dirs. Chem. N.Y. Corp.; bd. dirs. Inmont Corp. and predecessors, LTV Corp. and predecessors, MassMut. Income Investors, Texaco, Inc.; trustee MONY. Life trustee NYU Med. Ctr.; trustee Internat. Inst. Rural Reconstrn.; dir. Salvation Army; mem. alumni bd. dirs. U. Va. Endowment Fund; mem. coun. Miller Ctr. Pub. Affairs U. Va., also trustee Grad. Sch. Bus. Adminstrn., bd. visitors. Mem. Am. Bankers Assn. (exec. coun.), Assn. Res. City Bankers (dir.), Augusta Nat. Golf Club, Blind Brook Club, Clove Valley Rod and Gun Club, Pilgrims of U.S. Club, The Links Club, Univ. Club (N.Y.C.), Wee Burn Country Club. Republican. Avocations: golf, fishing, wing shooting. Home: Darien, Conn. Deceased.

MC CAMBRIDGE, MERCEDES, actress; b. Joliet, Ill., Mar. 17, 1918; d. John Patrick and Marie (Mahaffry) McC. AB, Mundelein Coll., 1937; 9 hon. doctorates. Appearances on stage include Glass Menagerie, Cat on A Hot Tin Roof, The Little Foxes, The Miracle Worker, The Medea, Cabaret, Macbeth, Madwoman of Chailott, Woman Bites Dog, The Young and Fair, Who's Afraid of Virginia Woolf, Agnes of God, Night, Mother, Lost in Yonkers; films include All the King's Men (Acad. award Best Supporting Actress 1950), 1949, Inside Straight, 1951, The Scarf, 1951, Lightning Strikes Twice, 1951, Johnny Guitar, 1954, Giant, (Acad. award nomination 1956), 1956, A Farewell to Arms, 1957, A Touch of Evil, 1958, Suddenly Last Summer, 1959, Cimarron, 1961, Angel Baby, 1961, Run Home Slow, 1965, 99 Women, 1969, Marquis de Sade: Justine, 1969, Last Generation, 1971, The Other Side of the World, 1972, Sixteen, 1973, The Exorcist (voice only), 1973, Thieves, 1977, The Concorde-Airport '79, 1979, Echoes, 1983; TV films: The Counterfeit Killer, 1968, Killer by Night, 1972, Two for the Money, 1972, The Girls of Huntington House, 1973, The President's Plane Is Missing, 1973, Who Is the Black Dahlia?, 1975, The Sacketts, 1979; artist-in-residence, Cath. U., Washington, 1972-73; Author: The Two of Us, 1960, The Quality of Mercy, 1981. Recipient Drama award Mundelein Coll., 1937; AP Poll, Look award, 1950; Fgn. Corr. award for Best Newcomer 1950 Fgn. Corr. award for Best Supporting Actress, 1950; nominated for Tony award, 1972. Died Mar. 2, 2004.

MCCARTER, LOWELL HAROLD, lawyer; b. Alma, Mich., Aug. 4, 1934; s. Donal Liston and Ruby Anna (Porter) McC.; m. Mary Ann Dalton, Nov. 30, 1963; children: Martin Devroe, Michael Lowell. BS in Chem. Engring., Purdue U., 1957; JD, John Marshall Law Sch., 1962; MBA, Northeastern U., 1987. Bar: Ind. 1962, Ill. 1962, U.S. Patent Office 1963, Mich. 1965, Mass. 1968. Assoc. patent counsel BASF Wyandotte (Mich.) Chem. Co., 1964-67; patent counsel Kennecott Corp., Lexington, Mass., 1967-77, W.R. Grace & Co., Cambridge, Mass., 1977-80, Instrumentation Lab., Lexington, 1980-87; mgr. legal affairs Genzyme Corp., Boston, from 1987. Instr. bus. law Middlesex Community Coll., Bedford, Mass., 1976. Chmn. Town Bldg. Com., Carlisle, Mass., 1972-74; coach Town Recreation Program, Carlisle, 1974-79; umpire Town Recreation Baseball Program, Carlisle, 1980-82. Served with U.S. Army, 1959. Mem. Am. Intellectual Property Law Assn., Boston Patent Law Assn. (bd. govs., chmn. inventors, recognition com. 1982-87), Inventors Assn. New Eng., Phi Alpha Delta. Home: Windham, NH. Died June 4, 2000.

MCCASKEY, EDWARD W. professional football team executive; b. Phila., Apr. 27, 1919; m. Virginia Halas; 11 children. Student, U. Pa., 1940. Mgr. merchandising Nat. Retail Tea and Coffee Assn., Chgo.; exec. v.p. Mdse. Services, Inc., Chgo.; account exec. E.F. McDonald Co., Chgo.; v.p., treas. Chgo. Bears, 1967-83, chmn. bd. dirs., 1983-99, chmn. emeritus, 1999—2003. Served to capt., AUS. Died Apr. 8, 2003.

MCCLANAHAN, JAMES FREDERICK, insurance executive; b. Dallas, Aug. 31, 1933; s. James Orion and Isabelle (Kitchens) McC.; m. June Beverly Fisher, Jan., 1966 (div. 1981); children: Lorrie McClanahan Street, William Frederick; m. Claire Adele Meyers, Aug. 8, 1985. BBA, N. Tex. State Coll., 1955. With Associated Aviation Underwriters, Dallas, from 1963, asst. mgr., acting v.p. L.A., 1971-75, mgr., v.p San Francisco, from 1975. Capt. USAF, 1955-63. Mem. Olympic Club. Republican. Presbyterian. Avocation: golf. Home: Walnut Creek, Calif. Deceased.

MCCLATCHEY, KENNETH D. pathology educator; degree, DDS, MD, degree in medicine, U. Mich. Dir. clin. microbiology and virology lab. U. Mich. Med. Ctr., 1978-96, assoc. chmn., dir. labs., 1981-91; Helen M. & Raymond M. Galvin prof., Loyola U. Chgo. Stritch Sch. Medicine, Maywood, Ill., 1991—2002; chmn., dept. pathology, 1996—2002. Mem. Nat. Com. for Clin. Lab. Stds. Author: Clinical Laboratory Medicine; editor Archives of Pathology and Lab. Medicine; mem. editl. bd. jour. AMA; contbr. over 150 articles to profl. jours., chpts. to books. Mem. Coll. Am. Pathologists, Am. Soc. Clin. Pathologists, World Assn. Socs. Pathology. Died Dec. 21, 2003.

MCCLAUGHERTY, JOHN LEWIS, lawyer; b. Bluefield, W.Va., Feb. 13, 1931; s. William N. and N. Louisa (Shelton) McC.; m. Sallie M. Fredeking, June 27, 1953; children: Martha M. Nepa, John W. BS, Northwestern U., 1953; LLB, W.Va. U., 1956. Bar: W.Va. 1956, U.S. Dist. Ct. (so. dist.) W.Va. 1956, U.S. Ct. Appeals (4th cir.) 1956, U.S. Supreme Ct. 1975, U.S. Ct. Mil. Appeals 1957. Assoc. Jackson & Kelly, Charleston, W.Va., 1959-65, ptnr., 1965-86; mng. mem., CEO Jackson & Kelly Pllc, Charleston, 1986—2002. Mem. com. Nat. Conf. Commrs. on Uniform State Laws, Chgo., 1977—, pres. 1999-01; pres. Ea. Mineral Law Found., Lexington, Ky., 1983-84. Contbr. articles to profl. jours., chpts. to books. Pres. W.Va. Symphony Orch., Charleston, 1982—; vice-chmn. Am. Symphony Orch. League, Washington, 1991-00, W.Va. Wesleyan Coll., Buckhannon, 1989-94; bd. dirs. Charleston Renaissance Corp., Fund for Arts; past mem. exec. com. Arts Advocacy Com. of W.Va., Inc.; former trustee United Meth. Charities of W.Va., Inc.; vice chmn. Clay Ctr. for Arts and Scis. of W.Va. 1st lt. USAF, 1956-59. Recipient Mayor's award for Arts Vol., 1990, Individual Art Patron of Yr. award Coll. of Creative Arts of W.Va. U., 1998, YMCA's Spirit of Valley award, 1998, Professionalism award U.S. Ct. Appeals (4th cir.), 1999, James R. Thomas II Outstanding Vol. award Charleston Renaissance Corp., 1999, Sam Walton Bus. Leader award Sam's Club and Wal-mart, 1999, Disting. Reader award Read Aloud W.Va., 1999, Outstanding Vol. Fund Raiser award W.Va. chpt. Nat. Soc. Fund Raising Execs., 2000, Disting. W.Va. award Gov. W.Va. Fellow Am. Bar Found. (life); mem. ABA, W.Va. Bar Found. (pres. 1994-98, Lawyer Citizen of Yr. award 1998), Am. Judicature Soc., W.Va. Bar Assn. (pres. 1995-96, award of merit 2002), Kanawha County Bar Assn. (pres. 1980-82, Outstanding Achievement award for meritorious svc. to the legal profession and the cmty. 1995), 2nd Cent. Leadership award, W.V. State Coll. Found., W.Va. State C. of C. (chmn. workers compensation and unemployment compensation com., past chmn., bd. dirs., exec. com.), Kiwanis, Masons, Shriners, Order of Coif. Democrat. Methodist. Home: Charleston, W.Va. Died Mar. 4, 2003.

MCCLELLAN, DAVID LAWRENCE, physician; b. Burlington, Iowa, Feb. 13, 1930; s. Harold L. and LaVon H. McC.; children: David, Steven, Mark, Jeffrey. BA, U. Iowa, 1952, MD, 1955. Intern U.S. Naval Hosp., San Diego, 1955-56; med. officer USS Nereus, 1956-58; pvt. practice Garland Med. Office, Spokane, Wash., 1958-64; pres. DeRe Medica Med. Clinic, Spokane, 1964-93; pvt. practice in family medicine Spokane, from 1993; CFO, mgmt. cons. A.C. LaRocco Co., from 1996. Pres., chmn. bd. North Spokane Profl. Bldg., Inc., 1966-86; pres. Inland Health Assocs., Inc., Spokane, 1984-92; pres., bd. dirs. Bio-Chem Environ. Svcs., Seattle, 1984-90; v.p. Forest Resources, 1978-86; pres. Omnex, 1980-86; chief exec. officer Double N Orchards, 1980-87; gen. ptnr. Double N Investments, 1987—; ptnr. Recovre, Inc.; mem. staff Holy Family Hosp.; fin. cons. Asia-Pacific Timber Co., 1991—. Contbr. articles and papers to med. jours. Lt. USN, 1955-58. Fellow Am. Acad. Family Practice; mem. AMA, Am. Profl. Practice Assn., Wash. State Med. Soc., Spokane County Med. Soc., Inland Empire Acad. Family Practice, Internat. Platform Assn. Republican. Roman Catholic. Avocations: art collecting, antique collecting, boating, miniature sculpting, landscaping. Home: Spokane, Wash. Died June 6, 2001.

MCCLENDON, SARAH NEWCOMB, news service executive, writer; b. Tyler, Tex., July 8, 1910; d. Sidney Smith and Annie Rebecca (Bonner) McClendon; 1 child, Sally Newcomb Mac Donald. Grad., Tyler Jr. Coll., U. Mo. Mem. staff Tyler Courier-Times and Tyler Morning Telegraph, 1931-39; reporter Beaumont (Tex.) Enterprise; Washington corr. Phila. Daily News, 1944; founder McClendon News Svc., Washington, from 1946. Talk show host Ind. Broadcasters Network; lectr. Faneuil Hall, Boston, Poor Richard's Club, Phila., Cobo Hall, Detroit, Chautauqua Instn., N.Y., Comstock Club, Sacramento, others; adv. to Senior Beacon; v.p. Nat. Press Club, hostess Study Group, 1991—. Author: My Eight Presidents, 1978 (1st prize), Mr. President, Mr. President! My Fifty Years of Covering the White House, 1996; contbr. articles to mags. including Esquire, Penthouse, Diplomat; TV appearances include Merv Griffin Show, Tomorrow, Inside the White House, PBS, NBC Meet the Press, KUP Show, NBC Today Show, C-Span, CNN, Fox Morning News, Late Night with David Letterman, Michael Jackson Show (L.A. radio). Mem. VA Adv. Bd. on Women Vets, def. adv. com. Women in the Svcs.; army advisor, mem. task force Women in the Army Policy Rev.; bd. dir. Sam Rayburn Libr., In Our Own Way, So. Poverty Relief Orgn. Served with WAC. Recipient Woman of Achievement award Tex. Press Women, 1978, 2d prize Nat. Fedn. Press Women, 1979, Headliner award Women in Comm., 1st Pres. award for Journalism in Washington, Nat. Fedn. Press Women, Pub. Rels. award Am. Legion, Bob Considine award, 1990, Am. Woman award Women's Rsch. Edn. Inst., 1991. Mem. DAR (Nat. Constn. award 1990), U. Mo. Alumni Assn. (chpt. pres.), Women in Comm. (Margaret Caskey award), Am. Legion (post comdr.), Nat. Woman's Party (v.p.), Nat. Coun., Soc. Profl. Journalists (Hall of Fame Washington chpt.), Nat. Press Club (v.p.), Am. Newspaper Women's Club (pres.), Capitol Hill First Friday Club (pres.). Clubs: Capitol Hill First Friday (pres.). Died Jan. 9, 2003.

MCCLOSKEY, FRANK, congressman; b. Phila., June 12, 1939; s. Frank and Helen (Warner) McC.; m. Roberta Ann Barker, Dec. 23, 1962; children: Helen Marie, Mark. AB in Govt., Ind. U., 1968, JD, 1971. Bar: Ind. 1971. Newspaper reporter Bloomington Herald-Telephone, Indpls. Star, Ind., 1963-69, City News Bur., Chgo., 1963-69; mayor City of Bloomington, Ind., 1972-83; mem. 98th-103rd Congresses from 8th Ind. dist., 1983—94. Mem. armed svcs. com., chmn. civil svc. subcom. on post office, mem. fgn. affairs com. Former pres. Ind. Assn. Cities and Towns. With USAF, 1957-61. Democrat. Roman Catholic. Home: Bloomington, Ind. Died Nov. 2, 2003.

MCCLURE, WILLIAM KYLE, journalist; b. Knoxville, Tenn., Sept. 8, 1922; s. Wallace Mitchell and Helen (Mellen) McC.; m. V. Jane Catherine Gittins, June 25, 1946; children: Cathy, Robert, Anne, David. Student, U. Tenn., Knoxville, 1939-41; postgrad., Cath. U., 1942. Corr. UPI, Washington, 1941-42; editor in chief Georgetown News, Washington, 1941-42; reporter UP, 1946; dir. pub. rels. RKO Pathe, N.Y.C., 1946-47, Berlin corr., 1948-51; European corr. CBS News "See It Now" Program, Paris, London, 1951-58; documentary producer, dir. CBS News "CBS Reports" Program, London, 1958-68; former European producer CBS News "60 Minutes" Program, London. European dir. ops. CBS News "Small World" Program. Dir., cameraman for feature motion picture African Conflict; dir., cameraman documentary All the World's Children, 1950. With Signal Corps U.S. Army, 1943-46, ETO, PTO. Recipient (4) Emmy awards, others. Mem. Overseas Press Club, Internat. Documentary Assn., British Acad. Film Arts. Avocations: film festivals, travel. Home: London, England. Died July 2, 2004.

MCCONNELL, DAVID MOFFATT, lawyer; b. Chester, S.C., June 12, 1912; s. Harvey Elzaphon and Elizabeth (Simpson) McC.; m. Ona Altman, Dec. 31, 1952; children: David Moffatt, Lynn Torbit, Joseph Moore. BS summa cum laude, Davidson Coll., 1933; student, Harvard. Grad. Bus. Sch., 1933-34, Law Sch., 1934-35; JD, Georgetown U., 1939, LLM, 1940; LLD, Mex. Acad. Internat. Law, 1987. Bar: S.C. 1936, D.C. 1945, N.C. 1946, U.S. Supreme Ct 1946. With firm Henry & Henry, Chester, 1936; counsel com. govt. reorgn. U.S. Senate, 1937-38; spl. atty. to chief counsel Internal Revenue Service, 1938-41; practice in Charlotte, N.C., 1946—. V.p., gen. counsel Belk Stores, Charlotte, 1946-76; gen. counsel Leggett Stores, 1946-76; dir. So. Nat. Bank, Lumberton, N.C., also chmn. Charlotte bd., 1970-76; U.S. ambassador to UN, 1968-69; Spl. adviser UN Econ. and Social Council; mem. U.S. delegation Fed. Republic Germany Marshall Plan, 1967 Chmn., sec. N.C. Bd. Elections, 1952-62; chmn. exec. com. Mecklenburg County (N.C.) Democratic Party, 1952-57; mem. nat. platform com. Dem. Party, 1964-72; elector U.S. Electoral Coll., 1948, 52; Donor McConnell Collection Tibetan Art to Baton Rouge Arts Mus., 1965; bd. dirs. emeritus Billy Graham Evangelistic Assn.; bd. visitors Davidson Coll., 1972-76; trustee Erskine Coll., Due West, S.C., 1954-58, bd. advisers, 1968-72; trustee Robert Lee Stowe, Jr. Found. Served to col. U.S. Army, 1940-46, CBI; brig. gen. N.C. State Militia. Decorated Legion of Merit with oak leaf cluster; Order Cloud with banner (Republic China); knight comdr. Order of the Knights of Malta Fellow Mexican Acad. Internat. Law; mem. Am., N.C., 26th Jud. Dist. bar assns., St. Andrews Soc., Newcomen Soc., Phi Beta Kappa, Kappa Alpha. Clubs: Mason (Charlotte) (Shriner), Charlotte Country (Charlotte), City (Charlotte), University (Washington). Presbyterian. Home: Charlotte, NC. Deceased.

MCCOOL, WILLIAM C. astronaut, military officer; b. San Diego, Calif., Sept. 23, 1961; married. BS in Applied Sci., USN Acad., Annapolis, 1983; MS in Computer Sci., U. Md., 1985; MS in Aero. Engring., USN Postgrad. Sch., 1992. Student pilot USN Flight Tng. Sch., 1983—86; trainee Squadron 129, Whidby Island, Wash., 1986; pilot Tactical Electronic Warfare Squadron 122, USS Coral Sea in Mediterranean, 1986—89; student Test Pilot Sch., Calif., 1989—92; test pilot USN Flight Systems Dept., Patuxent River, Md., 1992—94; adminstrv. and ops. officer Tactical Electronic Warfare Squadron 132 aboard USS Enterprise, 1992—96; astronaut NASA Johnson Space Ctr., Houston, from 1996. Mem.: US Naval Acad. Alumni Assn. Died Feb. 1, 2003.

MCCORMACK, MARK HUME, advertising executive, lawyer; b. Chgo., Nov. 6, 1930; s. Ned and Grace (Wolfe) McC.; m. Nancy Ann Breckenridge, Oct. 9, 1954 (div.); children: Breck, Todd, Leslie; m. Betsy Nagelsen, 1986; 1 child, Maggie. BA, William and Mary Coll., 1951; LLB, Yale U., 1954; PhD (hon.), St. Lawrence U., 1991; LHD, Coll. William and Mary, 1997. Assoc. Arter and Hadden, Cleve., 1957-63, ptnr., from 1963; pres., CEO IMG, The Mark McCormack Group of Cos., Cleve., 1964—2003. Editor: The World of Professional Golf, 1967-2000, 2002; author: Arnie, The Evolution of a Legend, 1967, Arnie, The Man and the Legend, 1967 (British edit.), Arnie, What They Don't Teach You at Harvard Business School, 1984, The Terrible Truth About Lawyers, 1987, What They Still Don't Teach You at Harvard Business School, 1989, The 110% Solution, 1991, Hit the Ground Running, 1993, Getting Results for Dummies, 2000, Staying Street Smart in the Internet Age, 2000, Never Wrestle with a Pig, 2002. With U.S. Army, 1955-56. Decorated Order of the Polar Star (Sweden). Mem. Cleve. Bar Assn., Author's Guild, Royal and Ancient Club (St. Andrews, Scotland), Union Club, Pepper Pike Club, The Club (Cleve.), Isleworth Club, Deepdale Club, All England Club, Theta Delta Chi. Home: Windermere, Fla. Died May 16, 2003.

MCCORMICK, EDWARD JAMES, JR., lawyer; b. Toledo, May 11, 1921; s. Edward James and Josephine (Beck) McC.; m. Mary Jane Blank, Jan. 27, 1951; children: Mary McCormick Krueger, Edward James III, Patrick William, Michael J. B.S., John Carroll U., 1943; J.D., Western Res. U., 1948. Bar: Ohio 1948, U.S. Supreme Ct. 1980. Mem. teaching staff St. Vincent Hosp. Sch. Nursing, 1951-67. Pvt. practice 1948—; Trustee Toledo Small Bus. Assn., 1950-75, pres., 1954-55, 56-58, 67-68; trustee Goodwill Industries Toledo, 1961-74, chmn. meml. gifts com., mem. exec. com., 1965-70; trustee Lucas County unit Am. Cancer Soc., 1950-61, sec., 1953, v.p., 1954-56, pres., 1957-58; founder, incorporator, sec., trustee Cancer Cytology Research Fund Toledo, Inc., 1956-79; trustee Ohio Cerebral Palsy Assn., 1963-70; incorporator, sec., trustee N.W. Ohio Clin. Engring. Ctr., 1972-74; trustee Friendly Ctr., 1973-83, Ohio Blind Assn., 1970-79; founder-incorporator, trustee, sec. Western Lake Erie Hist. Soc., 1978-85; mem. Toledo Deanery Diocesan Coun. Cath. Men; asst. gen. counsel U.S. Power and Sail Squadrons; life mem. China, Burma and India Vets. Assn., Inc. 1st lt. U.S. Army, 1942-46, USAR, 1946-52. Named Outstanding Young Man of Yr., Toledo Jr. C. of C., 1951; Man of Nation, Woodmen of World, Omaha, 1952. Fellow Ohio State Assn.; mem. ABA, Ohio Bar Assn. (chmn. Am. citizenship com. 1958-67, mem. pub. rels. com. 1967-72, estate planning, probate and trust law com.), Toledo Bar Assn. (chmn. pub. rels. com. 1979, mem. grievance com. 1974-92, chmn. probate, estate planning and trust law com. 1986-90, Disting. Svc. award in memory Robert A. Kelb, Esq. 1993), Lucas County Bar Assn. (chmn. Am. citizenship com.), Assn. Trial Lawyers Am., Am. Judicature Soc., Am. Arbitration Assn., Conf. Pvt. Orgns. (sec.-treas.), Toledo C. of C., Toledo Yacht Club (mem. com. 1970-71), Toledo Torch Club, Blue Gavel, Elks (grand esteemed leading knight 1964-65, mem. grand forum 1965-70), Lions (trustee, legal advisor Ohio Eye Research Found. 1956-70; pres. 1957-58, chmn. permanent membership com. 1961-85, hon. mem. 1984, pres. 1957, A.B. Snyder award 1979), Ky. Col. Deceased. Home: Toledo, Ohio.

MCCOWN, JUDITH PORTER, volunteer; b. Dallas, Sept. 19, 1904; d. Frederic Howard and Pauline Phillips (Gambrell) Porter; m. Henry Young McCown, Nov. 6, 1928 (Dec. 6, 1983); children: Frederic, Henry, Fairfax (dec.). BA, U. Tex., 1924. With advt. dept. A. Harris & Co., Dallas, 1926-28. Asst. editor The Daily Texas, 1923-24. Vol. Adult Day Care Ctr., Austin, 1986-88; tutor Travis County Adult Lit. Coun., Austin, 1985-89; del. Austin Met. Ministeries, 1988—; bd. mem. West Austin Care Givers, 1987—; pres. Episcopal Women, Good Shepherd, 1962. Recipient Teaching Excellence award Travis County Adult Lit., Austin, 1988. Mem. Pan Am. Round Table (dir. 1982), Austin Art League (pres. 1965-66), Phi Mu, Theta Sigma Phi. Republican. Episcopalian. Avocations: travel, reading, volunteering, politics, music. Home: Austin, Tex. Died June 2, 2000.

MCCRONE, WALTER COX, research institute executive; b. Wilmington, Del., June 9, 1916; s. Walter Cox and Bessie Lillian (Cook) McC.; m. Lucy Morris Beman, July 13, 1957. B Chemistry, Cornell U., 1938, PhD, 1942. Microscopist, sr. scientist Armour Research Found., Ill. Inst. Tech., Chgo., 1944-56; chmn. bd. Walter C. McCrone Assos. Inc., Chgo., 1956-81, sr. research advisor, 1956-78; pres. McCrone Research Inst., Inc., 1961-94, chmn. bd., from 1961. Vis. prof. chem. microscopy Cornell U., 1984—; adj. prof. IIT, 1950-94, 2000—, NYU, 1974—, U. Ill., 1989-95. Author: Fusion Methods in Chemical Microscopy, 1957, The Particle Atlas, 1967, Particle Atlas Two 6 vols., 1973-78, Particle Atlas Three Electronic CD-ROM edit., 1992, Polarized Light Microscopy, 1978, Asbestos Particle Atlas, 1980, Asbestos Identification, 1987, Judgment Day for the Turin Shroud, 1997, Judgment Day Pres. bd. dirs. Ada S. McKinley Cmty. Svcs., 1962-95, emeritus pres., 1995—; chmn. bd. trustees Vandercook Coll. Music, 1986-95, emeritus chair, 1995—; trustee Campbell Ctr., 1990—. Recipient Benedetti-Pichler award Am. Microchem. Soc., 1970, Anachem award Assn. Analytical Chemists, 1981, cert. of merit Franklin Inst., 1982, Forensic Sci. Found., 1983, Madden Disting. Svc. award Vandercook Coll. Music, 1988, Fortissimo award, 1991, Irving Selikoff award Nat. Asbestos Coun., 1990, Founder's Day award Calif. Assn. Criminalists, 1990, Roger Green award, 1991, Pub. Affairs award Chgo. Pub. Schs., 1993, Chamot award Ill. Micros. Soc., 1998, Disting. Svc. award USAF AFTAC program, Analytical Chemistry award Am. Chem. Soc., 2000. Mem. Am. Chem. Soc. (Pub. Affairs award 1993, Disting. Svc. award USAF AFTAC Program 1994), Am. Phys. Soc., Am. Acad. Forensic Sci. (Criminalist of Yr. award 1984), Am. Inst. Conservators Art (hon.), Internat. Inst. Conservators, Australian Micros. Soc., N.Y. Micros. Soc. (hon., Ernst Abbe award 1977), Ga. Micros. Soc., Can. Micros. Soc., Midwest Forensic Soc., Royal Micros. Soc. Internat. Inst. for Conservation of Art, Quekett Micros. Club, Sigma Xi, Phi Kappa Phi, Alpha Chi Sigma. Achievements include discovery of highly sensitive polymorphs of HMX and development of a safe prodn. method, improved prodn. method for casting of artillery rounds with TNT; proved the Vinland map to be a modern forgery, 1974, the Turin Shroud to be a medieval painting, 1980; developed the EPA analytical methods for detection and identification of asbestos; first city zoning ordinance based on performance stds. instituted in Chgo. Home: Chicago, Ill. Died July 10, 2002.

MCCULLY, BRUCE CALVIN, videographer, director; b. Evanston, Ill., July 8, 1952; Student, Coll. Lake County, 1973. Cert. in TV prodn. 2nd shift computer ops. supr., 1st shift lead operator Americana Interstate, Mundelein, Ill.; computer problem solver, schedular AllState Ins., Northbrook, Ill.; sound engr. Cheyenne Winter (Country Rock Band), Vancouver, Can., 1979-85; videographer Cabac Prodns. Inc., Waukegan, Ill., 1986-97; dir. Reid Prodns., Evanston, 1988-92; videographer MainStream Prodns. Inc., Lindenhurst, Ill., 1988-2000; freelance videographer Chgo., from 2000. Avocations: travel, music, art, hiking. Home: Round Lk Bch, Ill. Deceased.

MCDANIEL, MICHAEL CONWAY DIXON, bishop, retired theology educator; b. Mt. Pleasant, N.C., Apr. 8, 1929; s. John Henry and Mildred Juanita (Barrier) McD.; m. Marjorie Ruth Schneiter, Nov. 26, 1953; 1 son, John Robert Michael. BA, U. N.C., 1951; B.D., Wittenberg U., 1954; MA, U. Chgo., 1969, PhD, 1978; D.D. (hon.), Lenoir-Rhyne Coll., 1983; LL.D., Belmont Abbey Coll., 1984. Ordained to ministry United Lutheran Ch. in America, 1954. Pastor Faith (N.C.) Luth. Ch., 1954-58, Ch. of the Ascension, Savannah, Ga., 1958-60; assoc. dir. evangelism United Luth. Ch. in Am., N.Y.C., 1960-62; sr. pastor Edgebrook Luth. Ch., Chgo., 1962-67; pastor, guest lectr. Wittenberg U., Springfield, Ohio, 1970-71; prof. Lenoir-Rhyne Coll., Hickory, N.C., 1971-82, Raymond Morris Bost disting. prof., 1982, founding dir. Ctr. for Theology, 1991-99, emeritus, from 1999; bishop N.C. Luth. Ch. in Am., Salisbury, 1982-87, Evang. Luth. Ch. Am., Salisbury, 1988-91. Chmn. humanities div. Lenoir-Rhyne Coll., 1973-82; cons., grant coord. NEH, 1977-79; master tchr. Hickory Humanities Forum, 1981—; chmn. task force on ecumenical and interfaith relationships Commn. Forming a New Luth. Ch., 1983-87;

rep. Luth. Orthodox Dialogue In U.S.A., 1983-89;; chmn., cons. bishops governing coun. Evang. Luth. Ch. Am., 1987-89. Author: Welcome to the Lord's Table, 1972. Mem. Englewood Human Rels. Coun., N.J., 1959-60; pres., trustee Edgebrook Symphony, Chgo., 1965-67; sec. Chgo. Astron. Soc., 1966-67; pres. Cmty. Concerts Assn., Hickory, N.C., 1977-80, Western Piedmont Symphony Soc., 1993-94. Served to sgt. U.S. Army, 1946-48, Korea. Luth. World Fedn. fellow, 1967-69, Mansfield Coll. fellow U. Oxford, 1989; recipient Disting. Alumnus award Trinity Luth. Sem., 1990. Home: Hickory, NC. Died Dec. 18, 2003.

MC DERMOTT, DENNIS, trade union executive; b. Portsmouth, Eng., Nov. 3, 1922; s. John and Beatrice (Sutton) McD.; m. Mary Claire Elizabeth Caza, Oct. 22, 1976; children: Michael, Mark, Patrick, William, Maureen. Student public schs. Assembler and welder Massey-Ferguson, Toronto, Ont., Can., 1948-54; internat. rep. United Automobile Workers Am., 1954-68, Can. dir., 1968-78; pres. Can. Labour Congress, Ottawa, Ont., 1978-86; ambassador to Ireland Dublin, 1986—89. Lectr. on arbitration and labor law at univs. and Labour Coll. Can.; mem. Ont. Labour Relations Bd. Mem. Ont. provincial exec. and fed. exec. New Democratic Party; bd. dirs. Can. Inst. for Internat. Peace and Security. Served with Royal Navy, 1939-46. Decorated Centennial medal. Died Feb. 13, 2003.

MCDONALD, PATRICK HILL, JR., engineering educator; b. Carthage, N.C., Dec. 25, 1924; s. Patrick Hill and Mary (Bruton) McD.; m. Virginia Mabel Ackerman, June 14, 1951; children: Virginia Janet, Patrick Donald, Clyde Malcolm, Charles Thomas (dec.). BS, N.C. State U., 1947; MS, Northwestern U., 1951, PhD (Cabell fellow), 1953. Instr. mech. engring. N.C. State U. at Raleigh, 1947-48, former mem. faculty, former prof., head dept. engring. mech., 1960-76, former Harrelson prof., prof. emeritus. Instr. mechanics and hydraulics Clemson (S.C.) U., 1948-50 Author: Unified Mechanics, 1964; Contbr. articles to profl. jours. Served with AUS, 1943-45. Recipient Research award Am. Soc. Engring. Edn., 1959 Mem. Am. Soc. Engring. Edn., ASME, Am. Acad. Mechanics, Soc. Exptl. Stress Analysis, N.C. Soc. Engrs., Sigma Xi, Tau Beta Pi, Pi Tau Sigma. (Gold medal 1957) Presbyn. (elder). Home: Raleigh, NC. Died Oct. 16, 2003.

MCDOUGAL, MYRES SMITH, law educator, lawyer; b. Burtons, Miss., Nov. 23, 1906; s. Luther Love and Lulu Bell (Smith) McD.; m. Frances McDannold Lee, Dec. 27, 1933; 1 son, John Lee. A.B., U. Miss., 1926, A.M., 1927, LL.B., 1935; B.A., Oxford (Eng.) U., 1929, B.C.L., 1930; J.S.D., Yale U., 1931; L.H.D. (hon.), Columbia U., 1954, Temple U., 1975; LL.D. (hon.), Northwestern U., 1966, York U. (Can.), 1970, U. New Haven, 1975. Bar: Miss. 1935, U.S. Supreme Ct. 1963. Asst. prof. law U. Ill., 1931-34; assoc. prof. Yale U., 1934-39, prof., 1939—, William K. Townsend prof. law, 1944-58, Sterling prof. law, 1958-75; lectr. Fulbright Conf. Am. Studies, Cambridge (Eng.) U., 1952; vis. prof. Cairo U., 1959-60; Cardozo Meml. lectr. Assn. Bar City N.Y., 1978; atty. to asst. gen. counsel Lend-Lease Administrn., 1942; gen. counsel Office Fgn. Relief and Rehab. Ops., Dept. State, 1943; mem. U.S. panel Permanent Ct. Arbitration, 1963-69; mem. U.S. del. UN Conf. on Law of Treaties, Vienna, Austria, 1969; of counsel Govt. Saudi Arabia in Aramco Arbitration, 1955-56. Mem. ABA, Am. Soc. Internat. Law (pres. 1958, hon. pres. 1973-76, Hudson medal 1976), Am. Acad. Arts and Scis., Institut de Droit International, Assn. Am. Law Schs. (pres. 1966), Kappa Sigma. Clubs: Masons; Grads., Lawn (New Haven); Yale (N.Y.C.); Cosmos (Washington). Author law books including: (with others) Studies in World Public Order, 1960; (with Feliciano) Law and Minimum World Public Order: The Legal Regulation of International Coercion, 1961; (with Burke) The Public Order of the Oceans: A Contemporary International Law of the Sea, 1962; (with Lasswell and Vlasic) Law and Public Order in Space, 1963; (with Lasswell and Miller) The Interpretation of Agreements and World Public Order: Principles of Content and Procedures, 1967; (with Lasswell and Chen) Human Rights and World Public Order, 1980; (with Reisman) International Law in Contemporary Perspective, 1981; International Law Essays, 1981; contbr. numerous articles to legal jours. Died: May 7, 1998. Home: New Haven, Conn.

MCELROY, BERNARD PATRICK, English language educator; b. Newark, Sept. 25, 1938; s. Bernard P. and Agnes Marie (Donnelly) McE. BA, U. Notre Dame, 1960; MA, Cornell U., 1969, PhD, 1971. Asst. prof. English Loyola U., Chgo., 1971-75, assoc. prof., 1975-87, prof., from 1988. Vis. prof. English Rice U., Houston, 1978, 82. Author: Shakespeare's Mature Tragedies, 1973, Fiction of the Modern Grotesque, 1988; contbr. articles to profl. jours. 1st lt. USA, 1960-64, Germany. Guggenheim Found. fellow, 1979-80; recipient Younger Humanist award Nat. Endowment for Humanities, 1974. Mem. MLA, U. Chgo. Renaissance Seminar. Avocations: drama, opera, music. Home: Chicago, Ill. Deceased.

MCELWAIN, JOSEPH M. state legislator, contractor; b. Tippah County, Miss., Mar. 14, 1941; Student, U. Miss. State legislator Miss. Ho. of Reps., Jackson, 1988-91, 93-97. Vice chmn. transp. com. Miss. Ho. of Reps., mem. conservation, judiciary B, public utilities, ways and means coms. Forestry commr. Tenn-Tom Water Way Commn. Mem. Rotary Club, Am. Legion, Tippah Devel. Democrat. Methodist. Home: Falkner, Miss. Died 1998.

MCERLEAN, KEITH ALAN, psychotherapist, social worker; b. Southampton, N.Y., June 3, 1954; s. Harold J. and Viola (Tomasheski) Mc. AAS, Rockland Community Coll., 1976; BA, Fairleigh Dickinson U., Teaneck, N.Y., 1978; MSW, NYU, 1979. Social worker State Edn. Dept., Albany, N.Y., from 1980. Mem. NASW, N.Y. Milton Erickson Soc. for Psychotherapy & Hypnosis (bd. dirs.). Episcopalian. Home: New York, NY. Died Mar. 5, 2002.

MCGARRY, ROBERT GEORGE, safety engineer; b. Mpls., Jan. 4, 1917; s. Emmett Frank and Ethel Florence (Bryant) McG.; m. Janalee Judy, Sept. 22, 1986; children from previous marriage: Mary Kathleen, Nancy Margaret, Susan Elaine, Kevin Robert. BS in Engring., U. Minn., 1939; MS in Safety Engring., Ga. Inst. Tech., 1947. Registered profl. engr., Calif.; cert. safety profl. Sr. safety engr. U.S. Fidelity & Guaranty Co., Atlanta, Mpls., 1950-63; sr. safety engr. Bechtel Corp., San Francisco, 1963-77; corp. safety engr. Burns & McDonnell Engrs., Cons., Kansas City, Mo., 1977-82; cons. in safety engring., forensic engring. (heavy constrn.) Kansas City, Mo., from 1982. With USN, 1942-45. Recipient Minn. Gov.'s Outstanding Achievement award, 1969; scholar Advanced Inst. Nuclear Studies; decorated 3 Silver Stars, USN. Mem. NSPE, Am. Soc. Safety Engrs. (chmn. engring. com.), Vets. of Safety Internat. (dir.-at-large), Mo. Soc. Profl. Engrs., Profl. Engrs. in Pvt. Practice, Am. Arbitration Assn. (arbitrator), Masons, Shriners. Died May 11, 2000.

MCGEE, DOROTHY HORTON, writer, historian; b. West Point, N.Y., Nov. 30, 1913; d. Hugh Henry and Dorothy (Brown) M. Ed., Sch. of St. Mary, 1920-21, Gren Vale Sch., 1921-28, Brearley Sch., 1928-29, Fermata Sch., 1929-31. Asst. Historian Inc. Village of Roslyn, N.Y., 1950-58; historian Inc. Village of Matinecock, from 1966. Author: Skipper Sandra, 1950, Sally Townsend, Patriot, 1952, The Boarding School Mystery, 1953, Famous Signers of the Declaration, 1955, Alexander Hamilton-New Yorker, 1957, Herbert Hoover: Engineer, Humanitarian, Statesman, 1959, rev. edit., 1965, The Pearl Pendant Mystery, 1960, Framers of the Constitution, 1968; author booklets, articles hist. and sailing subjects. Chmn. Oyster Bay Bicentennial Revolution Commn., 1971—, historian Town of Oyster Bay, 1982—, mem. Nassau County Am. Revolution Bicentennial Commn., hon. dir. The Friends of Raynham Hall, Inc., treas. Family Welfare Assn. Nassau County, Inc., 1956-58, dir. Family Svc. Assn. Nassau County, 1958-69. Recipient Cert. of award for outstanding contbn. children's lit. N.Y. State Assn. Elem. Sch. Prins., 1959, award Nat. Soc. Children of Am. Revolution, 1960, award N.Y. Assn. Supervision and Curriculum Devel., 1961, hist. award Town of Oyster Bay, 1963, Cert. Theodore Roosevelt Assn., 1976, Franklin D. Roosevelt award, Local Govt. Historian's Prof. Achievement award Office of State Historian and Assn. Pub. Historians N.Y. State, 1999. Fellow Soc. Am. Historians, mem. Soc. Preservation L.I. Antiquities (hon. dir.), Nat. Trust Hist. Preservation, N.Y. Geneal. and Biol. Soc. (dir., trustee), Oyster Bay Hist. Soc. (hon. pres. 1971-75, chmn. 1975-79, trustee), Theodore Roosevelt Assn. (trustee), Townsend Soc. Am. (trustee). Republican. Died Oct. 12, 2003.

MCGEE, PATRICIA SABYNA, small business owner; b. Beacon Falls, Conn., June 24, 1921; d. John and Sabyna (O'Flynn) Malone; m. B. J. Bolander, Jr.,l May 7, 1977 (dec. 1988). Student, Boston U., 1971, Columbia U., 1972, U. Conn., 1973-74. Broadcaster radio and TV, Hartford, Conn., 1960-64; dir. Nat. Multiple Sclerosis Soc., Hartford, 1964-73, Nat. Kidney Found., Miami, Fla., 1973-76; dir. adminstrv. svcs. Children's Psychiatric Clinics, Miami, 1976-77, Shelnut & Assocs., Augusta, Ga., 1977-81; dir. pub. rels. Telfair Inns, Augusta, 1981-83; ptnr. Bolender Holley Surveying Co., Augusta, from 1984. Bd. dirs. Women in Ga. Power, Augusta, 1982; v.p. Aux. to Augusta Shrine Club, 1983; mem. Dem. State Com. Conn., 1972-73; sec.-treas. Classic South, 1981. Mem. Pub. Rls. Soc. Am. (pres. 1974-75), Nat. Soc. Fund Raisers (pores. 1975-76), Bus. and Profl. Women's Club (pres. 1974 76), Am. Women in Radio and TV (pres. 1973, 75), Ga. Hospitality and Travel Assn. (treas. 1982-83), Women in Constrn. (dir. 198-90), SBA, Civitan Club (v.p. 1983-84). Democrat. Roman Catholic. Avocations: swimming, reading. Home: Augusta, Ga. Deceased.

MCGEHEE, THOMAS RIVES, paper company executive, director; b. Jacksonville, Fla., July 12, 1924; s. Clifford Graham and Ray (Sutton) McG.; m. Delia Houser, Nov. 3, 1950; children: Delia McGehee II, Thomas R. Jr. Student, Davidson Coll., 1942-43; BS in Chemistry, U. Ala., 1948. V.p. Jacksonville Paper Co., 1948-56, pres., 1956-64, Mac Papers, Inc., Jacksonville, 1964-79, co-founder, chief exec. officer, chmn. bd., from 1979. Co-chmn., chief exec. officer Mac Papers Converters, Inc., 1965—, pres., North Fla. TV-47, Inc., 1979-90; pres. Higley Pub. Co., 1968-90; bd. dirs. Barnett Bank of Jacksonville,, 1961-89; chmn. exec. com. Sta. WTLV-TV 12, 1972-78; numerous real estate interests. Chmn. and founder Greater Jacksonville Community Found., 1964-84, trustee, 1984-89; trustee Jacksonville U., 1959—, vice chmn., 1962-65, chmn., 1991-92; trustee Regent U., 1996—; mem. U. Fla. Pres.' Coun., U. Fla. Health & Sci. Ctr.; mem. post secondary edn. planning commn. State of Fla., 1987-90; bd. dirs. Dreams Come True, pres. and founder 1984-90, chmn. emeritus, 1990—; bd. dirs. Bapt. Hosp. Found., 1986-90; vice chmn. Every Home For Christ, 1987—; past mem., officer numerous other community orgs. Served with U.S. Army, 1943-46, ETO. Decorated 3 Battle Stars; recipient Fla. Gov.'s award as Outstanding Industrialist, 1962, Top Mgmt. award Sales and Mktg. Execs. of Jacksonville, 1981, Outstanding Vol. Leadership award, Patriot of Yr. award Duval County Rep. Party, 1991, Disting. Bus. Man award, Prime F. Osborne Disting. Citizen award U. North Fla., 1998, Disting. Citizen award Boy Scouts Am., 1999, others; named Philanthropist of Yr. Nat. Soc. Fundraising Execs., 1999. Mem. NAM (dir. 1964-66), Asso. Industries Fla. (dir. 1961-63), Nat. Paper Trade Assn., So. Paper Trade Assn., Nat. Assn. Broadcasters, Fla. State C. of C., Phi Gamma Delta (pres. 1948). Republican. Episcopalian. Clubs: River (dir. 1980-83), Fla. Yacht, Timuquana Country, Ponte Vedra, Blowing Rock Country (bd. dirs. 1991-94), Lodge Country Clubs. Home: Jacksonville, Fla. Died Aug. 9, 2002.

MC GILLEM, CLARE DUANE, electrical engineering educator; b. Clinton, Mich., Oct. 9, 1923; s. Virgil and Starlie (Weaver) McG.; m. Frances Ann Wilson, Nov. 29, 1947; 1 child, Mary Ann. BSEE, U. Mich., 1947; MSE, Purdue U., 1949, PhD, 1955. Rsch. engr. Diamond Chain Co. Inc., Indpls., 1947-51; head functional design U.S. Naval Avionics Ctr., Indpls., 1951-56; head mil. and elec. engring. AC Spark Plug, GM, Flint, Mich., 1956-58, dir. elec. and applied rsch. Milw., 1958-59; program mgr. def. rsch. div. GM, Santa Barbara, Calif., 1959-62; prof. elec. engring. Purdue U., West Lafayette, Ind., 1963-92, assoc. dean engring., 1968-72, prof. emeritus of elec. engring., from 1992, dir. engring. expt. sta. Bd. dirs. VETRONICS Inc., West Lafayette, 1984-97, pres., 1984-87; pres. Tech. Assocs. Inc., West Lafayette, 1977-96. Co-author: Modern Communications and Spread Spectrum, 1986, Continuous and Discrete Signal and System Analysis, 3d edit., 1991, Modern Communications and Spread Spectrum, 1986, Probabilistic Methods of Signal and System Analysis, 3d edit., 1998. Lt. (j.g.) USN, 1943-46, PTO. Recipient Meritorious Civilian Svc. award USN, 1955. Fellow IEEE (Centennial award 1984, J. Fred Peoples award 1988). Avocations: duplicate bridge, amateur radio. Home: West Lafayette, Ind. Died Mar. 6, 1999.

MCGILLEY, SISTER MARY JANET, nun, educator, writer, academic administrator; b. Kansas City, Mo., Dec. 4, 1924; d. James P. and Peg (Ryan) McG. BA, St. Mary Coll., 1945; MA, Boston Coll., 1951; PhD, Fordham U., 1956; postgrad., U. Notre Dame, 1960, Columbia U., 1964. Joined Sisters of Charity, Roman Catholic Ch., 1946. Social worker, Kansas City, 1945-46; tchr. English Hayden H.S., Topeka, 1948-50, Billings (Mont.) Central H.S., 1951-53; faculty dept. English St. Mary Coll., Leavenworth, Kans., 1956-64, pres., 1964-89, disting. prof. English and Liberal Studies, 1990-96, pres. emeritus, 1989—2003. Contbr. articles, fiction and poetry to various jours. Bd. dirs. United Way of Leavenworth, 1966-85; mem. Mayor's Adv. Coun., 1967-72; bd. dirs. Kans. Ind. Coll. Fund, 1964-89, exec. com., 1985-86, vice chmn., 1984-85, chmn., 1985-86. Recipient Alumnae award St. Mary Coll., 1969; Disting. Service award Baker U., 1981, Leavenworth Bus. Woman of Yr. Athena award, 1986. Mem. Nat. Coun. Tchrs. of English, Nat. Assn. Ind. Colls. and Univs. (bd. dirs. 1982-85), Kans. Ind. Coll. Assn. (bd. dirs. 1964-89, treas. 1982-84, v.p. 1984-85, chmn. exec. com. 1985-86), Am. Coun. Edn. (com. on women in higher edn. 1980-85), Am. Assn. Higher Edn., Kansas City Regional Coun. for Higher Edn. (bd. dirs. 1965-89, treas. 1984-85, v.p. 1986-88), Ind. Coll. Funds Am. (exec. com. 1974-77, trustee-at-large 1975-76), North Cen. Assn. Colls. and Schs. (exec. commr. Com. on Insts. Higher Edn. 1980-88, vice chair 1985-86, chair 1987-88), Leavenworth C. of C. (bd. dirs. 1964-89), Assn. Am. Colls. (commn. liberal learning 1970-73, com. on curriculum and faculty devel. 1979-82) St. Mary Alumni Assn. (hon. pres. 1964-89), Delta Epsilon Sigma. Democrat. Died Sept. 13, 2003.

MCGIVERN, BRIAN, physician; b. L.A., 1940; BA, UCLA, Ireland, 1963; MD, Nat. U., Ireland, 1968. Intern Maricopa County Hosp., 1968-69; resident Santa Barbara Gen. Hosp., 1969-72; with Kaweah Delta Dist. Hosp., Visalia, Calif. Assoc. prof. U. Calif., San Francisco. Mem. Am. Coll. Radiology, Calif. Med. Assn. Died Apr. 1, 1999.

MCGLYNN, JOSEPH LEO, JR., federal judge; b. Phila., Feb. 13, 1925; s. Joseph Leo and Margaret Loretta (Ryan) McG.; m. Jocelyn M. Gates, Aug. 26, 1950; children: Jocelyn, Leo, Timothy, Suzanne, Alisa, Deirdre, Caroline, Elizabeth, Meghan, Brendan. BS, Mt. St. Mary's Coll., 1948; LL.B., U. Pa., 1951. Bar: Pa. 1952. Asst. U.S. atty., Phila., 1953-60; 1st asst., 1957-60; assoc., then ptnr. Blank Rudenko Klaus & Rome, Phila., 1960-65; judge County Ct. of Phila., 1965-68, Ct. of Common Pleas, 1st Jud. Dist. of Pa., 1968-74, U.S. Dist. Ct. (ea. dist.) Pa., Phila., 1974-90, sr. judge, from 1990. Mem. County Bd. Law Examiners, 1961-65, adv. com. bankruptcy rules U.S. Judicial Conf., 1987-93. Mem. bd. mgrs. Phila. Youth Study Ctr., 1961-65. Served with USN, 1943-46, PTO. Mem. Phila. Bar Assn. Home: Washington Crossing, Pa. Deceased.

MCGOVERN, JOHN HUGH, urologist, educator; b. Bayonne, N.J., Dec. 18, 1924; s. Patrick and Mary (McGovern) McG.; m. Mary Alice Cavazos, Aug. 2, 1980; children by previous marriage: John Hugh, Robert, Ward, Raymond. BS, Columbia U., 1947; MD, SUNY, Bklyn., 1952. Diplomate Am. Bd. Urology. Rotating intern Bklyn. Hosp., 1952-53; asst. resident in surgery Bklyn. VA Hosp., 1953-54; with urology N.Y. Hosp., 1954-56; exchange surg. registrar West London Hosp., Eng., 1956-57; resident in urol. surgery N.Y. Hosp., 1957-58, rsch. asst. pediatric urology, 1958-59, asst. attending surgeon James Buchanan Brady Found., 1959-61, assoc. attending surgeon, 1961-66, attending surgeon, from 1966; asst. in surgery Med. Coll. Cornell U., 1957-59, asst. prof. clin. surgery, 1959-64, assoc. prof., 1964-72, prof., from 1972; attending staff in urology Lenox Hill Hosp., from 1969, in-charge urology, 1969-83. Cons. urology Rockefeller Inst., St. Vincent's Hosp., Mercy Hosp., Phelps Meml. Hosp.; chmn. coun. on urology Nat. Kidney Found., 1982. Contbr. articles to profl. jours., chpts. to books. Lt. M.C., U.S. Army, 1942-45. Recipient Conatvoy mos medal Chile, 1975, Tree of Life award Nat. Kidney Found., 1990; named Huesped de Honor, Mimunicipalidad de Guayaquil (Ecuador), 1976; award in urology Kidney Found. N.Y., 1977, Sir Peter Freyer medal, Galway, Ireland, 1980. Fellow N.Y. Acad. Medicine (exec. com. urol. sect. 1968-72, chmn. 1972), ACS (credentials com. 1991—), Am. Acad. Pediatrics (urological); mem. AMA (diagnostic and therapeutic tech. assessment bd. 1991—, diagnostic and therepautic tech. assessment program panel 1991, DATTA panel 1991—), Am. Assn. G.U. Surgeons, N.Y. State Med. Soc. (chmn. urol. sect. 1975), Med. Soc. County N.Y., Am. Urol. Assn. (hon. mem. 1994—, pres.-elect 1988-89, pres. 1989-90, pres. N.Y. sect. 1979-80, N.Y. rep. exec. com. 1982-87, socioecons. com. 1987, chmn. fiscal affairs rev. com. 1987, chmn. awards com. 1990, time and place com. 1989-90), N.Y. State Urol. Soc. (exec. com. 1982—), Pan Pacific Surg. Assn., Am. Assn. Clin. Urologists (pres.-elect 1987-88, pres. 1988-89, bd. dirs. 1984—, mem. interpersonal rels. com. 1975—, govt. rels. com. 1989-90, program com. 1989-90, nominating com. 1989-90), Assn. Am. Physicians and Surgeons, Pan Am. Med. Assn. (diplomate 1981—), Urol. Investigators Forum, Soc. Pediatric Urology (pres.-elect 1979-80, pres. 1980-81), Am. Trauma Soc., Kidney Found. (med. adv. bd. N.Y. sect., trustee, 1979) Société Internationale d'Urologie (exec. com. U.S. sect.); hon. mem. Sociedad Peruana de Urología, Sociedad Guatemale de Urología, Sociedad Ecuadorians de Urología, Royal Coll. Surgeons (London). Deceased.

MCGRATH, J. NICHOLAS, lawyer; b. Hollywood, Calif., Feb. 12, 1940; children: Nicholas Gerald, Molly Inez. BA with honors, Lehigh U., 1962; LLB magna cum laude, Columbia U., 1965. Bar: D.C. 1966, Calif. 1969, U.S. Supreme Ct. 1970, Colo. 1971. Law clk. U.S. Ct. Appeals (D.C. cir.), 1965-66; law clk. to assoc. justice Thurgood Marshall U.S. Supreme Ct., Washington, 1967-68; pvt. practice Aspen, from 1971. Chmn. grievance com. Colo. Supreme Ct., 1989, mem. 1984-89. Mem. bd. editors Columbia Law Review, 1964-65. Mem. planning commn. Town of Basalt, Colo., 1992—93, town trustee, 1993—94; lectr. nat. and state CLE programs on ethics, litigations, and land use subjects; pres. Basalt Children's Recreation Fund, Inc., from 1994, Basalt Soccer Club, 1997—99. Mem. Colo. Bar Assn. (v.p. 1991-92), Pitkin County Bar Assn. (pres. 1977). Democrat. Home: Basalt, Colo. Died 2002.

MC GRORY, MARY, columnist; b. Boston, Aug. 22, 1918; d. Edward Patrick and Mary (Jacobs) McGrory. AB, Emmanuel Coll. Reporter Boston Herald Traveler, 1942-47; book reviewer Washington Star, 1947 54, feature writer for nat. staff, 1954-81; syndicated columnist The Washington Post, Universal Press Syndicate, 1981—2003. Recipient George Polk Meml. award; Pulitzer prize for commentary, 1975 Died Apr. 21, 2004.

MCGUIRE, ANTHONY BARTHOLOMEW, engineering executive; b. Bklyn., Jan. 19, 1945; s. Edward Sylvester and Frances Mary (Wojciechowicz) M.; m. Lynn Marie Andersen, Mar. 16, 1968; children: Christopher, Hillary, Kathryn, Susan. BE, Manhattan Coll., 1966. Registered profl. engr., Ill., Ind., N.Y., Ohio, Mich., Wis., Mass., N.J., Mo., Conn., Md., Ky., Minn., Va., Pa., Nebr., Nev., Iowa, others. Project mgr., engr. various firms, 1966-80; v.p. Perkins and Will, Chgo., 1980-83, Environ. Systems Design, Chgo., 1983-86; pres. McGuire Engrs., Chgo., from 1986. Contbr. articles to profl. jours. Mem. Ill. regional insulation adv. com. City of Chgo. code rev. com. Named Outstanding Engring. Grad., Manhattan Coll., 1992. Mem. ASHRAE (award of Merit 1975, chpt. pres. 1988-90), NSPE (Young Engr. of Yr. award 1975), Am. Soc.Plumbing Engrs., Chgo. Architecture Found., Stewart Club, Chgo. Hist. Soc., Western Trade Assn., Chgo. Bldg. Congress. Home: Chicago, Ill. Deceased.

MCHUGH, JOSEPHINE FLAHERTY, association administrator; b. Pontiac, Mich., May 13, 1947; d. Joseph Francis and Mary Burns Flaherty; m. Richard Alan McHugh, Aug. 31, 1974; children: Sean Joseph, Bridget Kathleen. Grad. summa cum laude, Romana Sch., Rome, 1967; grad., Chandler Secretarial Sch., 1969. Sr. sec. Mass. Eye and Ear Infirmary, Boston, 1969-73; exec. sec. Dean's Office Preventative Medicine U. Colo. Health Scis. Ctr., Denver, 1973-80; clin. coordinator U. Hosp., Denver, 1980-90; exec. dir. Parker C. of C., from 1990. Mem. long-range planning commn. Douglas County (Colo.) Sch. Dist., 1988-90; adv. bd. Arapahoe C.C., 1991-92; del. Dist. 40, rep. State Senate Race at County Assemblies, Douglas County Women's Crisis Ctr., 1990-91. Mem. NAFE, Am. Soc. Profl. and Exec. Women, Parker Club, Breakfast Club (pres. 1987, 88, sec. 1989-90), Optimist Club (bd. dirs. Parker club 1992), Jaycees (Parker), Rotary. Republican. Roman Catholic. Avocations: draft horses, golf, camping. Home: Franktown, Colo. Died Dec. 13, 2000.

MCKESSON, JOHN ALEXANDER, III, international relations educator; b. N.Y.C., Mar. 29, 1922; s. John Alexander and Mildred Fleming (Warner) McK.; m. Erna Jensson, Jan. 4, 1950 (dec. May 1971); 1 child, John A. IV. AB, Columbia U., 1941, MA in Internat. Rels., 1942, MA in Art History, 1982; LLD (hon.), Ea. Mich. U., 1972. Fgn. svc. officer Dept. of State, Washington and abroad, 1947-75; Am. amb. Libreville, Gabon, 1971-75; v.p. Etudes Travaux et Gestion, Paris, 1975-78; editor-in-chief UN Plaza Mag., N.Y.C., 1980-81; prof. NYU, N.Y.C., from 1983. Contbr. articles to profl. jours. Lt. USN, 1942-46. Decorated Commdr. Order of Equatorial Star of Gabon, 1975, Nat. Order of Senegal, 1967. Mem. Fgn. Svc. Assn., Regency Club. Episcopalian. Avocation: bridge. Home: New York, NY. Died May 21, 2002.

MCKINLEY, LARAINE J. primary care nurse; b. Balt., Apr. 3, 1942; d. Herbert and Helen (Brown) McK. Diploma, Md. Gen. Hosp. Sch., Balt., 1962; AA, Community Coll. of Balt., 1962; BSN, Coll. of Notre Dame Md., 1990. Head nurse med.-surg. Md. Gen. Hosp., Balt., staff nurse intensive care unit; GSN, H.N. clin. mgr. RACU GBMC, Towson, Md., staff nurse intervention radiology. Mem. Md. Assn. Radiology Nurses, ASPAN, Md. Assn. Post Anesthesia Nurses, Sigma Theta Tau (charter mem. Mu Eta chpt.). Home: Baltimore, Md. Died Aug. 15, 2000.

MCKINLEY, LOREN DHUE, museum director; b. Tillamook, Oreg., Feb. 1, 1920; s. Henry Raymond and Flora (Phillips) McK.; m. Mary Eileen Sessions, May 22, 1942; children: Candace Eileen, Scott Dhu, Kevin Loren, Laurie Lee, Maris Colleen. Student, Oreg. State U., U. Oreg.; D.Sc., U. Portland, 1973. Advt. mgr. Headlight Herald, Tillamook, 1946; partner Kenwood Press, Tillamook, 1949; dir. Oreg. Mus. Sci. and Industry, Portland, 1960-78, chief exec. officer, 1978—. Bd. dirs. Fred Hutchinson Cancer Rsch. Ctr. Found., Oreg. Mus. Sci. and Industry; sr. devel. officer Office of Devel. Oreg. State U. Mayor of Tillamook, 1954-60; pres. Leukemia Assn. Oreg. Inc., 1983—; bd. dirs. St. Mary's Acad., 1993—; bd. trustees Oreg. Mus. Sci. and Industry; mem. Oreg. State U Found. Served with AUS, World War II, ETO, MTO. Decorated Bronze Star with oak leaf cluster; named 1st Citizen of Oreg., 1951; recipient award Oreg. Mus. Sci. and Industry, 1965, Elsie M.B. Naumberg award as outstanding sci. mus. dir., 1968, citation for outstanding svc. Oreg. Acad. Sci., 1971, Aubrey Watzek award Lewis and Clark Coll., 1973, Barbara Stallcup Miller Profl. Achievement award Willamette Valley Devel. Officers, 1999; named alumni of yr. Oreg. State U., 1999, recipient heart of gold award, 1999. Mem. Assn. Sci. and Tech. Ctrs. Am. (pres. 1973—), League Oreg. Cities (past pres.), Kappa Sigma. Republican. Died Aug. 28, 2003.

MC KINNEY, ALEXIS, public relations consultant; b. Cin., Mar. 13, 1907; s. John Austin and Gertrude (Kofler) McK.; m. Esther Ryker Simmons, Aug. 27, 1930 (dec. 1985); 1 dau., Eunice Christine; m. Margaret Jane Miles, Sept. 14, 1986 (dec. 1990); m. Irene Voigt Stevenson, Apr. 6, 1991. Ed. pub. schs., Colo., and Tex. Enlisted in U.S. Navy, 1923, served aboard U.S.S. New Mexico, 1923 27; circulation mgt. Pueblo (Colo.) Star-Jour., 1928; reporter Pueblo Chieftain, 1929, state editor, 1930, city editor, 1931-32; co-pub. and editor Rocky Ford Tribune, 1933-34; news editor Alamosa (Colo.) Daily Courier, 1934-42; statehouse reporter Denver Post, 1942-45; information officer U.S. Bur. Reclamation, Denver, 1945-46; asst. city editor Denver Post, 1946, city editor, 1946-47, mng. editor, 1947-49, asst. pub., 1949-63; project dir. Rio Grande-land, Durango, Colo., 1963-65; dir. pub. relations Denver & Rio Grande Western R.R. Co., 1965-73; pub. relations cons. Rio Grande Industries, Inc., 1973—. Trustee Colo. R.R. Hist. Found. and Mus. Mem. all-Navy championship rifle team, 1927. Mem. Pub. Relations Soc. Am., R.R. Pub. Relations Assn., Soc. Profl. Journalists. Congregationalist. Died Mar. 26, 2003.

MCKINNEY, CHARLES MICHAEL, artist, educator; b. Clinton, Okla., Dec. 1, 1951; s. Charles Bert and Catherine Georgene McKinney; m. Denise Ann Wardell Kirkes, Apr. 15, 1972 (div. Sept. 1983); children: Gary Michael, Charles Justin; m. Rose Caterina Vartuli, Aug. 15, 1992; children: Sean Patrick, Catherine Maedb, Paul Devon Ross. BA in Journalism, U. Okla., Norman, 1987; MFA in Creative Writing, McNeese State U., 1990. Freelance journalist The Daily Oklahoman, Oklahoma City Times, Oklahoma City, 1972-75; editor Wyo. Outdoor Reporter, Buffalo, 1979-82; profl. photographer Paseo Photo Works, Oklahoma City, 1982-86; grad. tchg. asst. McNeese State U., Lake Charles, La., 1987-90, U. Southwestern La., Lafayette, 1990-91; instr. IV Southwestern Okla. State U., Sayre, Okla., from 1991. Copy editor Westview: A Jour. of Western Okla., Southwestern Okla. State, Weatherford; cons. Arts in Prisons program Instn. Programs Inc., Oklahoma City. Author: (poetry) Whispers on the Wind, 1997; contbr. to jours., mags. Mem. citizen's adv. commn. Okla. State Reformatory, Granite, 1994—; pres.-elect faculty senate Southwestern Okla. State U., 1998—. With U.S. Army, 1976-79. Recipient Addy award for photography Oklahoma City Advt. Club, 1985. Mem. Phi Theta Kappa Internat. (faculty advisor Beta Iota Gamma chpt. 2000—). Democrat. Avocations: flyfishing, wildflower taxonomy and collecting, collecting antiques, gardening. Home: Leedey, Okla. Died Nov. 11, 2002.

MCLAIN, JOHN HOWARD, retired military officer; b. Pitts., Jan. 21, 1919; s. Theodore Raybert and Marion Cora (Kidd) McLain; m. Patricia Ann O'Connor, Nov. 28, 1953; children: Wendy Ray, John Howard, Jr., Sarah Annabelle, Marion Kathleen. AB with honors, U. Pitts., 1947, MA, 1954; postgrad., Fla. State U., 1950; grad. with honors Inst. for Orgn. Mgmt., Mich. State U., 1958. Commd. 2d lt. US Army, 1940, advanced thru grades to brigadier gen., 1972; served Panama CZ, 3d Army, Battle of the Bulge and Relief of Bastogne, World War II, 1st Cav. Divsn., Japan; sr. advisor Korean Mil. Adv. Group, 99th ROK Arty. Bn.; comdg. gen. 99th U.S. Arrmy Res. Command; active duty Dept. Def. Guard and Res., Total Force study com., 1974; ret., 1977. Lectr. history U. Pitts., 1947; asst. prof. English Presbyn. Jr. Coll., Maxton, NC, 1948; head English dept. Adm. Farragut Acad., St. Petersburg, Fla., 1949—50; grad. asst. English Fla. State U., 1950; instr. English St. Petersburg Sr. H.S., 1951—52; lectr. English U. Pitts., 1954—57; instr. English Edgewood H.S., 1954—55; nat. adv. coun. employer support for guard and res. US Dept. Def.; bd. dirs. Bus. and Job Devel. Corp. Mgr., govtl. and ednl. affairs Greater Pitts. C. of C., 1956—58, staff dir., 1959, exec. dir., 1960—65, exec. v.p., 1965—72, mgmt. cons., 1972—77; co-sec. Greater Pitts. Labor-Mgmt. Adv. Coun.; regional export expansion coun. US Dept. Commerce; trustee Cmty. Svcs. Pa.; exec. com. Allegheny Children and Youth Svcs. Coun.; chmn. City of Hope Greater Pitts. Citizens Coun., 1970—74; bd. dirs. Am. Wind Symphony Orch.; past pres. Allegheny County Easter Seal Soc.; bd. dirs., v.p. United Mental Health Svcs. Allegheny County. Decorated Bronze Star, Legion of Merit; named Man of Yr., Jaycees, 1962; named to Field Artillery Sch. Officer Candidate Sch. Hall of Fame, 1976; recipient Cert. Appreciation, Govt. France, Govt. Korea, Cert., Goodwill Industries, 1971, Brace for an Ace award, Pa. Easter Seal Soc., 1971. Mem.: VFW (life), Am. Arbitration Assn. (regional adv. coun.), Ret. Officers Club (pres. Sarasota chpt. 1990), Military Order of the World Wars, Res. Officers Assn. (life; dir. membership affairs 1978—84), Mil. Officer Assn. Am. (life), Army War College Alumni Assn. (life), Military Order Cooties, Shriners, Am. Legion, Sahib Shrine Legion Honor, Rotary (past pres. Pitts. chpt.), Masons (32 degree), Sons of Am. Revolution, Pi Kappa Alpha, Kappa Phi Kappa. Home: Sarasota, Fla. Died Sept. 23, 2003; Arlington Nat. Cemetary.

MCLAMB, CHARLES HAROLD, real estate executive, lawyer; b. Fayetteville, N.C., July 24, 1951; s. Charles Henry Jr. and Edith (Buck) McL.; m. Janet Elizabeth Hudson, May 20, 1973; children: Charles Brandon, Nathan Buck. BSBA, U. N.C., 1973, JD, 1977. Bar: N.C. 1977, U.S. Dist. Ct. (mid. dist.) N.C. 1977, U.S. Tax Ct. 1978. Acct. Arthur Andersen and Co., Charlotte, N.C., 1973-74, Greensboro, N.C., 1974-75; ptnr. Tuggle Duggins Mescham & Elrod, Greensboro, 1977-85; v.p., gen. counsel, prin. Adaron Group, Inc., Durham, N.C., from 1985. Mem. N.C. Bar Assn., N.C. Assn. CPA's, Phi Beta Kappa, Phi Eta Sigma. Democrat. Methodist. Avocations: travel, tennis, golf. Home: Chapel Hill, NC. Deceased.

MCLANE, JOHN ROY, lawyer; b. Manchester, N.H., Feb. 19, 1916; s. John R. and Elisabeth (Bancroft) Mc L.; m. Blanche Marshall, Feb. 15, 1935; children: John Roy III, Andrew M. (dec.), Lyn, Blanche M., Angus; m. 2d, Elisabeth Deane, Dec. 30, 1960 (dec. 1999); children: Towner D., Virginia W., Kathryn E., Duncan C. Bar: N.H. 1941. Practiced in, Manchester, since 1941; dir. firm McLane, Graf, Raulerson & Middleton, P.A., 1941-42, 45-93, of counsel, 1997-98, retired, from 1998. Alderman, Manchester, 1952-53; trustee Spaulding-Potter Charitable Trusts, 1958-72, N.H. State Hosp., 1949-62, Hurricane Island Outward Bound Sch., 1972-79; chmn. N.H. Adv. Commn. on Health and Welfare, 1965-68; trustee, sec. Norwin S. and Elizabeth N. Bean Found., 1967-94; trustee, clk. St. Paul's Sch., 1952-83; distbg. dir. N.H. Charitable Fund, 1962-69; bd. dirs. Coun. on Founds, 1968-74, chmn., 1970-72; bd. dirs. Child and Family Svcs. N.H., 1946-71, pres., 1963-71; bd. dirs. Palace Theatre Trust, 1974-2000. Lt. USNR, 1942-45. Mem. ABA, N.H. Bar Assn., Manchester Bar Assn. Republican. Episcopalian (vestry 1963, 68). Home: Shelburne, Vt. Deceased.

MCLANE, ROBERT JOEL, playwright; b. Macon, Ga., Aug. 4, 1944; s. Henry Joel and Sylvia (Lamb) McL. BA, Furman U., 1968; MA, Goddard Coll., 1983. Lic. marriage, family and child counselor, Calif. Case mgr. AIDS Project L.A., 1982-84; counseling coord. Inland AIDS Project, Riverside, Calif., 1987-91. Author: (play) Triptch-Ducks, Rattlesnakes & Roses, 1984, Emma, 1987, Freedom, 1989-90; adaptor: (play) Journeyman, 1988. Fellow Sundance Playwright Lab., Provo, Utah, 1986, Ucross Found., Sheridan, Wyo., 1986. Democrat. Avocations: camping, paper making, hiking. Home: Riverside, Calif. Deceased.

MCLARNAN, DONALD EDWARD, banker, corporation executive; b. Nashua, Iowa, Dec. 19, 1906; s. Samuel and Grace (Prudhon) McL.; m. Virginia Rickard, May 5, 1939; children: Marilyn, Marcia, Roxane. AB, U. So. Calif., 1930; grad., Southwestern U. Law Sch., 1933; postgrad., Cambridge U. Trust appraiser, property mgr. Security-Pacific Nat. Bank, Los Angeles, 1935-54; regional dir. SBA for, So. Calif., Ariz., Nev., 1954-61, area adminstr., 1969-73; pres. Am. MARC, Inc. (offshore oil drillers and mfr. diesel engines), 1961-63, Terminal Drilling & Prodn. Co., Haney & Williams Drilling Co., Western Offshore, 1961-63; v.p., dir. Edgemar Dairy, Santa Monica Dairy Co., 1954-70; founder, pres., chmn. bd. Mission Nat. Bank, 1963-67; pres. Demco Trading Co., Mut. Trading Co. Dir. Coast Fed. Savs. & Loan; cons. numerous corps.; guest lectr. various univs. Contbr. articles on mgmt. and fin. to profl. jours. Chmn. fed. agys. div. Community Chest, 1956; nat. pres. Teachers Day, 1956; bd. councillors U. So. Calif.; founder, chmn., pres. Soc. Care and Protection Injured Innocent; adv. bd. Los Angeles City Coll.; bd. dirs. Calif. Easter Seal Soc.; nat. chmn. U. So. Calif. Drug Abuse Program. Recipient Los Angeles City and County Civic Leadership award, 1959 Mem. Nat. Assn. People with Disabilities (pres.); Mem. Skull and Dagger, Delta Chi. Clubs: Mason (Los Angeles) (K.T., Shriner), Los Angeles (Los Angeles), Jonathan (Los Angeles). Home: Los Angeles, Calif. Died Dec. 27, 1985.

MCLAURIN, KAREN GREER, mathematics educator; b. Manchester, N.H., July 10, 1939; d. Lloyd Elsworth and Theresa Evelyn (Cabasino) Greer; m. Leroy Evans; children: Brent, Lloyd, Scot. BS, MS in Math., U. S.C. Tchr. Poyner Jr. H.S., Florence, S.C., Orangeburg-Calhoun Tech., Orangeburg, S.C., Willington Acad., Orangeburg, Wade Hampton Acad., Orangeburg; instr. Ctrl. Carolina Tech. Coll., Sumter, S.C. Dir. honor soc. Ctrl. Carolina Tech. Coll., Sumter. Recipient Tchg. Excellence award NISOD, 1996-97. Mem. S.C. Tech. Edn. Assn., S.C. Coun. Tchrs. of Math. Avocations: art, music, bridge, travel. Home: Sumter, SC. Died 1998.

MC LUCAS, JOHN LUTHER, aerospace company executive; b. Fayetteville, N.C., Aug. 22, 1920; s. John Luther and Viola (Conley) McL.; m. Patricia Knapp, July 27, 1946 (div. 1981); children: Pamela McLucas Byers, Susan, John C., Roderick K.; m. Harriet D. Black, Sept. 25, 1981. BS, Davidson Coll., 1941; MS, Tulane U., 1943; PhD, Pa. State U., 1950, D.Sc., 1974. V.p., tech. dir. Haller, Raymond & Brown, Inc., State College, Pa., 1950-57; pres. HRB-Singer, Inc., State College, 1958-62; dep. dir. rsch. and engring. Dept. Def., 1962-64; pres., chief exec. officer Mitre Corp., Bedford, Mass., 1966-69; undersec. of Air Force, 1969-73; sec. of Air Force, 1973-75; adminstr. FAA, 1975-77; pres. Comsat Gen. Corp., Washington, 1977-79; exec. v.p. COMSAT, 1979-80, pres. world systems div., 1980-83, exec. v.p., chief strategic officer, 1983-85. Bd. dirs. Orbital Scis. Corp.; mem. USAF Sci. Adv. Bd., 1967-69, 77-84, Def. Sci. Bd., 1968-69; chmn. USAF SDAG, 1979-83; chmn. bd. dirs. Internat. Space U., 1987-93, active, 1987—. Author: Space Commerce, 1991; contbr. articles to tech. lit.; patentee and author in field. Chmn. bd. Wolf Trap Found., 1986-88; chmn. bd. Arthur C. Clarke Found. of U.S.; chmn. bd. dirs. ISY Internat. Space Yr. Assn. U.S., 1987-93; chmn. NASA adv. council, 1988-91. Served with USNR, 1943-46. Recipient Disting. Service award Dept. Def., 1964, 1st bronze palm, 1973, silver palm, 1975 Fellow IEEE, AAAS, AIAA (hon., pres.); mem. NAE (coun. 1988-93), Nat. Rsch. Coun. (chmn. Air Force studies bd. 1987-91), Belle Haven Club, Sigma Xi, Sigma Pi Sigma. Died Dec. 1, 2002.

MCMAHON, ELEANOR MARIE, education educator; b. Pawtucket, R.I., Oct. 25, 1929; d. William Frank and Anne Angela (Cunningham) Hess; m. Richard P. McMahon, Feb. 14, 1927. BS summa cum laude, Coll. St. Elizabeth, Convent Station, N.J., 1950; HHD (hon.), Coll. St. Elizabeth, 1975; MA, Brown U., 1954; EdD, Harvard U., 1967; D in Pedagogy (hon.), Mt. St. Joseph Coll., Wakefield, R.I., 1974, Sem. Our Lady Providence, 1975; Hum.D (hon.), Providence Coll., 1976; LLD, Regis Coll., 1985; EdD (hon.), Roger Williams Coll., 1986; D in Pub. Svc. (hon.), R.I. Coll., 1988. Dir. lab. experiences R.I. Coll., Providence, 1968-70, assoc. dean ednl. studies, 1970-71, dean ednl. studies, 1971-77, acting exec. dir. coll. advancement and support, 1977-78, provost, v.p. acad. affairs, 1978-82; commr. higher edn. State of R.I., Providence, 1982-89; regent Seton Hall U., South Orange, N.J., from 1992. Disting. vis. prof. Alfred Taubman Ctr., Brown U., 1989—; vis. prof. dept. govt. Georgetown U., 1990-94; mem. Edn. Commn. of States, Denver, 1983-89, New Eng. Bd. Higher Edn., Boston, 1984—, chair-elect, 1996-97, chair, 1997-98; chair Cath. Sch. Bd. Diocese Providence, 1999—. Contbr. articles to profl. jours. Trustee Coll. St. Elizabeth, 1967-72, Providence Country Day Sch., East Providence, R.I., 1975-81, 90-92; mem. corp., mem. exec. com. Providence Coll., 1974-82, pres. coun., 1982—; mem. R.I. Strategic Devel. Commn., 1982-84; mem. gov. vis. com. U. Maine, 1984-86; alumnae trustee Brown U., 1985-88, bd. of fellows, 1988-99; mem. R.I. Commn. EC 1992, 1989-92, Gov. Econ. Strategy Task Force, 1991-92; mem. Rockefeller Brothers Fund Minority Fellowship Program, 1990-94; mem. steering com. R.I. Project Rethinking Govt., 1992-96; mem. Providence Blueprint Edn. Commn., 1991-93. Recipient Outstanding Cmty. Svc. award Blackstone Valley Jr. Women's Club, 1976, Outstanding Woman award R.I. chpt. Internat. Fedn. Cath. Alumnae, 1977, Disting. Svc. award R.I. Bd. Govs., 1989, Disting. Pub. Svc. award R.I. ASPA, 1989, Disting. Svc. award, R.I. Pub. Expenditure Coun., 1987, Brotherhood award NCCJ, 1992; Brown U. fellow, 1988-99; Named to R.I. Hall of Fame, 1986. Mem. Nat. Com. Higher Edn. Governance. Roman Catholic. Avocations: traveling, reading. Home: Pawtucket, RI. Died June 1, 2002.

MCMAHON, MARIA O'NEIL, social work educator; b. Hartford, Conn., Jan. 2, 1937; d. John Joseph and Margaret (Galvin) O'Neil; m. Dennis Richard McMahon, June 10, 1988; stepchildren: Lezlie, Nora, Kelly, Stacie, Michael. BA, St. Joseph Coll., West Hartford, Conn., 1958; MSW, Cath. U. Am., 1964, D. Social Work, 1978. Supr., child and family therapist Highland Heights Residential Treatment Ctr., New Haven, 1964-71; chair dept. sociolgy and social work St. Joseph Coll., 1971-84; prof. E. Carolina U., Greenville, N.C., from 1985, dean Sch. Social Work, 1985-91. Cons. to various univs., 1970—; trainer Conn. Dept. Social Svcs., 1982-84, N.C. Dept. Social Svcs., 1987-89. Author: The General Method of Social Work Practice, 1984, 2d edit., 1990, 3d edit., 1996, Advanced Generalist Practice, With An International Perspective, 1994; editor report in field; contbr. articles, book revs. to profl. publs. Commr. Nat. Coun. Social Work Edn., Alexandria, Va., 1983-85; chair bd. dirs. Ea. N.C. Poverty Com., 1987—, Cath. Social Ministries of Archdiocese of Raleigh (N.C.), 1989-92. Recipient Outstanding Educator award AAUW, 1981, Disting. Alumnae award, Cath. U. of Am., 1994. Mem. Nat. Assn. Social Workers (Outstanding Social Worker of Yr., Conn. chpt. 1981), Acad. Cert. Social Workers, Am. Correctional Assn., Nat. Assn. Women Deans, Nat. Coun. Social Work Edn. Democrat. Roman Catholic. Avocations: dance, reading, walking. Home: Pompano Beach, Fla. Deceased.

MCMAHON, THOMAS ARTHUR, biology and applied mechanics educator; b. Dayton, Ohio, Apr. 21, 1943; s. Howard Oldford and Lucille (Nelson) McM.; m. Carol Ehlers, June 20, 1965; children: James Robert, Elizabeth Kirsten. BS, Cornell U., 1965; S.M., MIT, 1967, PhD, 1970. Postdoctoral fellow Harvard U., Cambridge, Mass., 1969-70, lectr. bioengring., 1970-71, asst. prof., 1971-74, assoc. prof., 1974-77, prof. applied mechanics and biology, 1977—. Cons. numerous industries, legal firms Author: (novels), Principles of American Nuclear Chemistry, 1970, McKay's Bees, 1979, Loving Little Egypt, 1987; (non-Fiction) Muscles, Reflexes and Locomotion, 1984; (with others) On Size and Life, 1983. Grantee NIH; System Devel. Found., Sloan Found.; recipient Richard and Hinde Rosenthal award Am. Acad. and Inst. Arts and Letters, 1988. Mem. Biomed. Engring. Soc., Am. Physiol. Soc., N.Y. Acad. Scis., PEN Home: Wellesley, Mass. Died Feb. 21, 1999.

MCMAKEN, LYNDA HAMILTON, lawyer, consultant; b. Chgo. m. James A. Lagdon, Nov. 12, 1988. BS, Ind. U.; JD, Ind. U., Indpls., 1987. Bar: Wash. 1988, U.S. Dist. Ct. Wash. 1991. Project specialist City of Indpls., 1980-81; chief adminstr. officer sch. plan Saturday Evening Post, Indpls., 1981-82; brokerage mgr. Golden Rule Ins. Co., Indpls., 1982; pres. The Mgmt. Co., Indpls., 1983-87. Lectr. Ind. U., Bloomington, 1984, Mich. Arts Sci. Coun. Inc., South Bend, Ind., 1987, Ind. Assn. Women Bus. Owners, Indpls., 1987 Vol. Big Sisters Greater Indpls., 1982-87; organizing chair, bd. dirs. Big Bros. Big Sisters Kitsap County, 1990-91, pres. bd. dirs., 1992—; chair corp. sponsorships Bainbridge Classic, 1990-91; bd. dirs. United Way, 1993—; chair Needs Assessment Com., 1994. Recipient cert. appreciation United Way, 1984, recognition for support svc., Big Sister. 1984. Mem. ABA, Network Women in Bus., Women Leader Round Table. Deceased.

MCMILLAN, ANN ENDICOTT, composer; b. N.Y.C., Mar. 23, 1923; d. Andrew and Dorothy York (Wadhams) McM. BA, Bennington Coll., 1945. Music editor RCA, 1949-55; with non-comml. radio Radio Diffusion TV Francaise (France), Can. Broadcasting Corp. (Can.), Pacifica Radio, Voice of Am. USA, 1957-72; freelance composer, from 1972. Concerts commissioned by Hollander, Moses Asch, Manuel Enriquez, Max Lifchitz, 1986-90, Quintet of the Americas, 1990; guest editor Contemporary Music Rev., 1990—. Recipient Guggenheim fellow, 1972, Rockefeller Found. fellow, 1979. Mem. Broadcast Music Inc., Am. Composers Alliance, Am. Music Ctr. Home: Ann Arbor, Mich. Deceased.

MCMILLAN, COLIN RILEY, federal agency administrator; b. Houston, July 27, 1935; s. Hugh Dix and Edna (Self) McM.; m. Kay Anderson Ruth, July 26, 1958; children: Lynda Kay McMillan Ballard, Colin Riley III, Susan Ann, Michael Allen. BS in Geology, U. N.C., 1957. Jr. geophysicist Texaco, Inc., Roswell, N.Mex. and Midland, Tex., 1960-64; founder, pres., chief exec. officer Permian Exploration Corp., Roswell, 1964-90; asst. sec. def. for prodn. and logistics Dept. Def., Washington, 1990—92. Founder, ptnr. Three River Cattle Co., Roswell, 1984-90; founder, owner Roswell Vegetable Farms, Inc., 1988-90; mem. N.Mex. State Legislature, Santa Fe, 1971-82, minority whip, chmn. taxation and revenue com., 1979-82; sec. bd. fin. State of N.Mex., Santa Fe, 1986-89; chmn. Gov.'s Task Force on Oil and Gas Econ. Devel., 1986-89; cons. geophysicist, 1964-90. Chmn. Chaves County Rep. Party, N.Mex., 1966, Ford presdl. campaign, N.Mex., 1976; fin. and campaign co-chmn. Bush presdl. campaign, N.Mex., 1988. Maj. USMC, 1957-60; res., 1960-72. Mem. N.Mex. Oil and Gas Assn. (pres. 1975), Ind. Petroleum Assn. N.Mex., N.Mex. Cattle Growers Assn., Soc. Exploration Geophysicists, Phi Beta Kappa. Methodist. Avocations: airline transport pilot, golf, swimming. Home: Roswell, N.Mex. Died July 24, 2003.

MC MULLEN, EDWIN WALLACE, JR., English language educator; b. Quincy, Fla., Dec. 8, 1915; s. Edwin Wallace and Sara Della (Moore) McM.; m. Marian Elizabeth Hoper, June 9, 1946; children: William Wallace, Charles Edwin. BA, U. Fla., 1936; MA, Columbia U., 1939, PhD, 1950. Instr. English Pa. State U., 1946-48, State U. Iowa, 1950-52; spl. instr. in report writing U.S. Dept. Def., Washington, 1953, sr. reporter, 1952-57; asst. editor Merriam Webster Dictionary Co., 1957; asst. prof. English Lehigh U., 1957-61, Fairleigh Dickinson U., Madison, N.J., 1961-62, assoc. prof., 1962-72, prof., 1973-82, chmn. dept. lang. and lit., 1962-65, emeritus, 1982; founder, dir. Names Inst., 1962-86. Chmn. publs. subcom. Morris County Tercentenary Com., N.J., 1962-63 Author: English Topographic Terms in Florida, 1563-1874, 1953; contbr. articles to profl. publs.; editor: Names, 1962-65; editor, contbr.: Pubs, Place-Names and Patronymics: Selected Papers of the Names Institute, 1980; editor, contbr. Names New and Old: Papers of the Names Inst., 1993, 2d edit., 2002. Served with Signal Corps, U.S. Army, 1942-46. Mem. MLA, Am. Name Soc. (pres. 1976), Internat. Congress on Onomastic Scis., Internat. Linguistic Assn., Am. Dialect Soc., English Place-Name Soc., Morris County Hist. Soc., Old Guard of Summit (N.J.), Nat. Coun. Tchrs. English, Meth. Friendship Club (past co-pres.). Democrat. Methodist. Home: Madison, NJ. Died July 27, 2002.

MCNABB, TALMADGE FORD, religious organization administrator, retired military chaplain; b. Johnson City, Tenn., Mar. 22, 1924; s. Robert Pierce and Dora Isabelle (Bailey) McN.; m. Nesbia Orlene Boswell, Dec. 3, 1950 (dec.); children: Darlene Roberta, Marla Dawn; m. Pirkko Marjotta Pelttari, Nov. 11, 1962; children: Valerie Anne, Lisa Rhea, Marcus Duane. Student, East Tenn. State U., 1941-43, 46; BA, Southwestern U. Assemblies of God, Waxahachie, Tex., 1947, BTh, 1949; BS, Birmingham Southern Coll., 1952; MA, U. Ala., 1957; HHD (hon.), S.E. Univ., Greenville, S.C., 1978. Ordained to ministry Assemblies of God, 1950. Evangelist Assemblies of God, 1948-49; pastor 1st Assembly of God, Warrior, Ala., 1949-53, Tuscaloosa, Ala., 1955-56; commd. 1st lt. U.S. Army, 1955, advanced through grades to lt. col., 1966, chaplain, 1953-54, 1954-55, 1957-59, 1959-61, 1961-66, Ft. Dix, N.J., 1967-69, chaplain William Beaumont Hosp. El Paso, Tex., 1971-72, ret., 1972; writer, evangelist, speaker, from 1973; founder, pres. Worldwide Christian Ministries, Browns Mills, N.J., from 1981. Ministered in Ecuador, India, Russia, China, France, Belgium, The Netherlands. Contbr. articles on religious and ethnic topics to newspapers and mags. Mem. DAV (life), Mil. Ret. Officers Assn. (life), Mil. Chaplains Assn. (life, del.). Republican. Deceased.

MCNALLY, JAMES RAND, JR., fusion energy consultant; b. Boston, Nov. 10, 1917; s. James Rand and Margaret (Turley) McN.; m. Margaret Anne McKenna, Nov. 26, 1942; children: Randy, Peter, Mary Ellen, Francis, Therese, Michael, Peggy. BS in Physics, Boston Coll., Chestnut Hill, Mass., 1939; MS in Physics, MIT, 1941, PhD in Physics, 1943. Rsch. asst. MIT, Cambridge, Mass., 1939-44, instr., 1944-48; sr. physicist stable isotopes divsn. Union Carbide, Oak Ridge, Tenn., 1948-56, assoc. dir. stable isotopes divsn., 1956-58, sr. physicist fusion divsn., 1958-82; fusion energy cons. Oak Ridge, from 1982. Contbr. articles to profl. jours. Trustee Dedham (Mass.) Pub. Libr., 1946-48; mem. parish bd. St. Mary's Parish, Oak Ridge, 1970-73, eucharistic minister, lector, midnight mass commentator. Recipient Manhattan Dist. award U.S. Govt., Cambridge, 1946; named Alumnus of Yr. Dedham H.S., 1980. Fellow AAAS, Optical Soc. Am.; mem. Am. Physics Soc. Republican. Roman Catholic. Achievements include discovery of properties of a nuclear tornado, zeeman effects of several atoms, consultant on film A State of Emergency. Deceased.

MCWHIRTER, NORRIS DEWAR, publisher, author, broadcaster; b. London, Aug. 12, 1925; s. William Allan and Margaret Moffat (Williamson) McW.; m. Carole Eckert, Dec. 28, 1957 (dec. 1987); children: Jane Margaret, Alasdair William; m. Tessa Mary Pocock, Mar. 26, 1991. Student Marlborough Coll., 1939-43; BA in Econs., Trinity Coll., Oxford, 1947, MA in Contract Law, 1950. Founder and dir. McWhirter Twins Ltd., London, 1951-2004; athletics corr. The Star, 1951-64, The Observer, 1951-67; editor and pub. Athletics World, 1952-57; dir. Guinness Superlatives Ltd. (now Guinness Publs. Ltd.), London, 1954-96; mng. dir., 1954-76; commentator Olympic Games BBC radio, 1952-56, TV, 1960-72; presenter BBC TV Record Breakers, London, 1972-92; founding editor Guinness Book of Records, London, 1954-86; founder, chmn. Redwood Press, Trowbridge, Wiltshire, England, 1966-72; dir. Gieves Group plc, 1972-95; chmn. William McWhirter & Sons, Glasgow, 1955-87, Ross Films Ltd., 1998-2004. Publications include: Get To Your Marks, 1951; Guinness Book of World Records (founder, editor and compiler in 37 langs. 1955-86); Dunlop Books of Facts, 1964, 1966; Guinness Book of Answers, 1976-93; Ross, Story of a Shared Life, 1976, Treason at Maastricht, 1994, Time and Space, 1998. Parliamentary candidate Conservative Party, Orpington, Kent, 1962-66; mem. Sports Coun. for England, 1970-74; co-founder, chmn. The Freedom Assn., London, 1975. Served sub.-lt. R.N.V.R., 1943-46. Named Comdr. Order Brit. Empire, 1980; recipient Free Enterprise Spl. award Aims of Industry, London, 1983. Anglican. Clubs: Vincent's (Oxford); Carlton (London). Died Apr. 19, 2004.

MECHEM, EDWIN LEARD, judge; b. Alamogordo, N.Mex., July 2, 1912; s. Edwin and Eunice (Leard) M.; Dorothy Heller, Dec. 30, 1932 (dec. 1972); children: Martha M. Vigil, John H., Jesse (dec. 1968), Walter M.; m. Josephine Donavan, May 28, 1976 L.L.B., U. Ark., 1939; L.L.D. (hon.), N.Mex. State U., 1975. Bar: N.Mex. 1939, U.S. Dist. Ct. N.Mex. 1939. Lawyer, Las Cruces and Albuquerque, 1939-70; judge U.S. Dist. Ct. N.Mex., Albuquerque, 1970-82, sr. judge, from 1982; spl. agt. FBI Dept. Justice, various locations, 1942-45; mem. legislature State of N.Mex., 1947-48, gov., 1951-54, 57-58, 61-62; senator U.S. Govt., Washington, 1963-64. Mem. ABA, N.Mex. Bar Assn., Am. Law Inst. Republican. Methodist. Avocation: travel. Died Nov. 27, 2002.

MECHIGIAN, NANCY LEE, word processing company executive; b. Highland Park, Mich., Feb. 8, 1941; d. John Peniamin and Arpie (Abajian) M. Student secretarial sci., Highland Park Jr. Coll., 1959-61; legal sec. studies, Florence Rose Study Course, Southfield, Mich., 1969. Sec. Mich. Employment Security Commn., Detroit, 1961-68; legal sec. Law Offices Stephen A. Crane, Southfield, Mich., 1969-71, Sheldon M. Lutz, Southfield, 1971-73, Clarence G. Carlson, Bloomfield Hills, Mich., 1975-76, Rubenstein, Allen & Isaacs, Southfield, 1976; owner, mgr. Typing By Nan, Southfield, 1977-85; account exec. 55Plus/Golden Yrs. newspaper, Southfield, 1985; sr. mcht. cons. Mich. Credit Card Svcs., Southfield, 1985; adminstrv. asst. Cliff Adams, CLU, ChFC, Troy, Mich., 1987; owner, mgr. Efficient Word Processing Svcs., Southfield, from 1987; owner Scholarships for Students, Southfield, 1989-92. Data entry cons. St. John's Armenian Ch., Southfield, 1988-90, computer operator Armenia Earthquake Fund, 1988-90; nominated sec. of the day St. John's Armenian Ch. Parish Coun. Meeting, 1985. Avocations: dance, gardening, movies, photography. Died Oct. 14, 2001.

MECHLIN, GEORGE FRANCIS, electrical manufacturing company executive; b. Pitts., July 23, 1923; s. George Francis and Ruth (Butler) Mechlin; m. Mary Louise Megaffin, June 25, 1949; children: David Whitehead, Thomas, Elizabeth Thompson, Ann Louise. BS in Physics, U. Pitts., 1944, MS in Physics, 1949, PhD in Physics, 1951. With Westinghouse Electric Corp., 1949-87, gen. mgr. astronuclear/oceanic div., 1971-72, v.p. astronuclear lab., oceanic and marine divs., 1972-73, v.p. R & D Pitts., 1973-87; pub. svc. cons., from 1990. Past bd. dirs. Buhl Planatarium. Recipient Meritorious Public Service award U.S. Navy, 1961, John J. Montgomery award Nat. Soc. Aerospace Profls. and San Diego Aerospace Mus., 1961; Order of Merit award Westinghouse Electric Corp., 1961 Mem.: AIAA, Nat. Acad. Engring., Am. Phys. Soc., Sigma Xi. Home: Aptos, Calif. Died Dec. 12, 2003.

MEDINA, STANDISH FORDE, JR., lawyer; b. Orange, N.J., June 16, 1940; s. Standish F. and Hope Tyler (Kiesewetter) M.; m. Kathryn L. Bach, Apr. 20, 1968; 1 child, Nathaniel Forde. AB cum laude, Princeton U., 1962; LL.B. magna cum laude, Columbia U., 1965, LL.M., 1966. Bar: N.Y. 1965, U.S. Supreme Ct. 1970, U.S. Dist. Ct. (so. dist., ea. dist.) N.Y., U.S. Ct. Appeals (2d, 3d, 4th, 5th, 7th, 11th, D.C. cirs.). Assoc. in law Columbia Law Sch., 1965-66, lectr., 1992; instr. law orientation program in Am. law Princeton U., summer 1966; assoc. Debevoise & Plimpton, N.Y.C., 1966-72, ptnr., 1973—. Author: Settlement Practices in the Second Circuit, 1988, Reflections Below, 1991, Things Magic, 1998. Trustee The Hill Sch., Pottstown, Pa., 1976-91, St. Bernard's Sch., N.Y.C., 1992—, Episc. Sch., N.Y.C., 1988-93. Fellow Am. Coll. of Trial Lawyers; mem. ABA (vice-chmn. com. on fed. cts., litigation sect. 1981-82, co-chmn. com. pleadings motions and pretrial 1986-87), Fed. Bar Coun., N.Y. State Bar Assn., Assn. of Bar of City of N.Y. (mem. exec. com. 1982-86, chmn. membership com. 1986-90, chmn. com. fed. cts. 1978-81, mem. judiciary com. 1978-81, 96—, mem. nominating com. 1986-87, mem. com. on ct. requirements 1978-81, mem. fed. legis. com. 1971-75), Am. Law Inst., 2d Cir. Com. on Improvement Civil Litigation (chmn. 1986-90), Legal Aid Soc. (chmn. assoc. and young lawyers com. 1972). Home: New York, NY. Died June 1999.

MEECHAM, WILLIAM CORYELL, engineering educator; b. Detroit; s. William Edward and Mabel Catherine (Wilcox) M.; m. Barbara Jane Brown, Sept. 4, 1948 (dec.); children: Janice Lynn, William James; m. Della Fern Carson BS, MS, U. Mich., 1948; PhD in Physics, U. Mich. and Brown U., 1954. Head acoustics lab. Willow Run Labs., Ann Arbor, Mich., 1959-60; asst. prof. U. Mich., Ann Arbor, 1958-60; prof. U. Minn., Mpls., 1960-67; prof. fluid mechanics and acoustics UCLA, 1967—, chmn. dept. mechanics and structures, 1972-73. Cons. Aerospace Corp., El Segundo, Calif., 1975-80, Rand Corp., Santa Monica, Calif., 1964-74, Bolt, Beranek and Newman, Cambridge, Mass., 1968-73, Arete Assocs., Encino, Calif., 1976—, CRT Corp., Chatsworth, Calif., 1985—; expert witness numerous cmty. noise ct. cases, L.A., Las Vegas, 1986—. Author: (with R. Lutomirski) Lasar Systems, 1973; author 140 papers on fluid mechanics and acoustics. Treas. Unitarian Ch., Ann Arbor, Mich., 1958-60; advisor U.S. Congress Com. on Pub. Works, Congl. Record Report N.J., 1972; mem. Calif. Space and Def. Council, U.S. Congress, 1982—. Served with U.S. Army, 1944-46. Mich. Alumni scholar 1942-44, Donovan scholar U. Mich., 1944-45; UCLA senate rsch. grantee, 1968—, NASA rsch. grantee, 1971—, Office Naval Rsch. grantee, 1977-85; recipient Disting. Svc. award U.S. Army. Fellow Acoustical Soc. Am. (gen. chmn. meeting 1973), AIAA (assoc. fellow); mem. Internat. Inst. Acoustics and Vibration, Am. Phys. Soc. (fluid dynamics div.), Inst. Noise Control Engring., Sigma Xi, Tau Beta Pi Home: Pacific Palisades, Calif. Died Oct. 2002.

MEEHL, PAUL EVERETT, psychologist, educator; b. Mpls., Minn., Jan. 3, 1920; s. Otto John and Blanche Edna (Duncan) Swedal; m. Alyce M. Roworth, Sept. 6, 1941 (dec. 1972); children: Karen, Erik; m. Leslie Jane Yonce, Nov. 17, 1973. AB, U. Minn., 1941, PhD, 1945; ScD, Adelphi U., 1984, U. Minn., 2001. Diplomate Am. Bd. Profl. Psychology (clin. psychology, bd. dirs.1957-62, Disting. Svc. and Outstanding Contbns. award 1989). Instr., asst., assoc. prof., chmn. dept. psychology U. Minn., 1951-57, prof., 1952—, prof. dept. psychiatry Med. Sch., 1952-90, regents' prof. psychology, 1968-89, Hathaway-Meehl prof. psychology, 1990-93, regent's prof. psychology emeritus, from 1993; prof. Minn. Ctr. for Philosophy of Sci., 1953-56 and from 69, prof. philosophy, 1971—; acting chief clin. psychology VA Hosp., Mpls., 1947-49; participant Dartmouth Conf. on Behavior Theory, 1950; mem. panel on criminal deterrence Nat. Acad. Sci., 1975-77; practice psychotherapy, 1951-94; staff Nicollet Clinic, 1970-80. Author: (with S.R. Hathaway) Atlas for Clinical Use of MMPI, 1951, (with others) Modern Learning Theory, 1954, Clinical Versus Statistical Prediction, 1954, What, Then, Is Man?, 1958, Psychodiagnosis, 1973, Selected Philosophical and Methodological Papers, 1991, (with N. Waller) Multivariate Taxometric Procedures, 1998; contbr. articles to profl., legal and philos. jours. Recipient Ednl. Testing Svc. award for contbns. to measurement, 1994, Clin. Psychology Centennial prize for lifetime achievement APA, Bruno Klopfer disting. contbn. award, 1979, Gold medal for life achievement application of psychology Am. Psychol. Found., 1989, Disting. Svc. award Am. Bd. Profl. Psychologists, 1989, Joseph Zubin prize lifetime contbns. to psychopathology, 1993; William James fellow Am. Psychol. Soc., 1989. Fellow Am. Psychol. Soc. (James McKeen Cattell fellow 1998), Inst. for Advanced Study in Rational Psychotherapy; mem. APA (pres. 1961-62, Disting. Contbr. award clin. divsn. 1967, Disting. Sci. Contr. award 1958, Disting. Scientist award 1976, Disting. Contbn. to Knowledge award 1993, award for Outstanding Lifetime Contbn. to Psychology 1996), Am. Acad. Arts and Scis., Nat. Acad. Sci., Philosophy of Sci. Assn., Phi Beta Kappa, Sigma Xi, Psi Chi. Home: Minneapolis, Minn. Died Feb. 14, 2003.

MEIER, AUGUST, historian, educator; b. N.Y.C., Apr. 30, 1923; s. Frank A. and Clara (Cohen) M. AB, Oberlin Coll., 1945; AM, Columbia U., 1949, PhD, 1957; LittD, Rutgers U., 1994. Asst. prof. history Tougaloo (Miss.) Coll., 1945-49; rsch. asst. to Charles S. Johnson, 1953; asst. prof. history Fisk U., 1953-56; asst., assoc. prof. history Morgan State Coll., Balt., 1957-64; prof. history Roosevelt U., Chgo., 1964-67, Kent (Ohio) State U., 1967-69, univ. prof., 1969-93; univ. prof. emeritus, 1993—2003. Author: Negro Thought in America, 1880-1915, 1963, (with Elliott Rudwick) From Plantation to Ghetto, 1966, 3d edit., 1976, (with Elliott Rudwick) Black Detroit and the Rise of the UAW, 1979, (with Elliott Rudwick) CORE: A Study In The Civil Rights Movement, 1942-68, 1973, (with Elliott Rudwick) Along the Color Line: Explorations in the Black Experience, 1976, (with Elliott Rudwick) Black History and the Historical Profession, 1986, A White Scholar and the Black Community, 1945-1965, 1993; editor: (with Francis Broderick) Negro Protest Thought in the Twentieth Century, 1966, (with Francis Broderick and Elliott Rudwick) rev. edit. renamed Black Protest Thought in The Twentieth Century, 1971, (with Elliott Rudwick and John H. Bracey, Jr.), Black Nationalism in America, 1970, (with John Hope Franklin) Black Leaders of the Twentieth Century, 1982, (with Leon Litwack) Black Leaders of the Nineteenth Century, 1988; gen. editor: Atheneum Negro in Am. Life Series, 1966-74, University of Illinois Press Blacks in the New World Series, 1972-89, (with John H. Bracey), 1994-97, (with Elliott Rudwick and John Bracey) University Publications of America Black Studies Research Sources on Microfilm, 1980-2003; mem. editorial adv. bd.: Booker T. Washington Papers, 1967-85, Civil War History, 1970-2003, Jour. Am. History, 1974-77. Sec. Newark br. NAACP, 1951-52, 56-57; chmn. Balt. chpt. Ams. for Democratic Action, 1960-61, mem. nat. bd., exec. com., 1960-61; active Newark chpt. CORE, 1963-64, Balt. chpt. SNCC, 1960-63. Advanced grad. fellow Am. Council Learned Socs., 1952; Guggenheim fellow, 1971-72; Nat. Endowment for Humanities fellow, 1975-77; Center for Advanced Study in Behavioral Scis. fellow, 1976-77; recipient Am. Hist. Assn. award Scholarly Distinction, 1998. Mem. Am. Hist. Assn., So. Hist. Assn. (pres. 1992), Assn. Study Negro Life and History, Orgn. Am. Historians (del. to Am. Coun. Learned Socs. 1979-83, chmn. program com. 1990). Unitarian Universalist. Home: Edgewater, NJ. Died Mar. 19, 2003.

MEIJER, HENDRIK, retail company executive; b. 1952; With Meijer Inc., Grand Rapids, Mich., from 1963, co-chmn., from 1990. Deceased.

MEINDRE, ROGER LUCIEN, archbishop; b. Ruynes-en-Margeride, Cantal, France, Aug. 31, 1931; Ordained priest, 1956. Prof. philosophy Grand Séminaire, Saint-Flour, head Clermont-Ferrano, 1968-82; curate Riom, 1982-83; vicar gen. Saint-Flour, 1983; bishop Mende, 1983-89; archbishop Albi, from 1989. Died Oct. 8, 1999.

MEISEL, GEORGE IRA, lawyer; b. Cleve., May 5, 1920; s. Herman George and Ethel Lynn (Wright) M.; m. Gladys Ulch, 1946; children: Scott, Craig, David, Keith. AB, Case Western Res. U., 1942; LL.B., Harvard U., 1948. Bar: Ohio 1948. Assoc. Williams, Eversman & Morgan, Toledo, 1948-51, Squire, Sanders & Dempsey, Cleve., 1951-58, ptnr., from 1958, vice chmn. mgmt. com., 1980-81, chmn. mgmt. com., 1981-86, sr. ptnr., 1986-87, ret., 1987. Bd. dirs. Harris Corp., Melbourne, Fla., 1983-92. Pres. Cleve. Hearing & Speech Center, 1960-61; sec.-treas. Greater Cleve. Growth Assn., 1980-81, chmn. 1984-86. Served with USAAF, 1942-46. Mem. ABA (chmn. litigation sect. 1973-74), Ohio Bar Assn., Bar Assn. Greater Cleve. (pres. 1975-76), Am. Coll. Trial Lawyers, Internat. Assn. Def. Counsel (exec. com. 1977-80, sec.-treas. 1987-90) 6th Circuit Jud. Conf. Home: Palm City, Fla. Deceased.

MEISSLER, GEORGE R. psychologist; b. Phila., May 25, 1930; s. George Aloysious and Lillian Rose (McCann) M. BA, LaSalle U., Phila., 1959; MED, Temple U., Phila., 1961; PhD, Catholic U. Am., Washington D.C., 1970. School psychologist Bd. Edn. Anne Arundel Co., Annapolis, Md., 1961-71; psychologist dir. Ea. State Sch. & Hosp., Trevose, Pa., 1971-82; clin. psychotherapist Police & Fire Med. Assocs., Phila., from 1984, Ct. of Common Pleas, Phila., 1986-89; chief clin. psychologist Juvenile Forensic Unit Pa., Trevose, 1989-94; clin. counseling psychologist Pvt. Practice, Phila., from 1974; lectr. Bucks County C.C., Newtown, Pa., 1975-82; ind. contractor Phila., from 1994. Expert witness Ct. Common Pleas, Phila., 1990—. With USN, 1951-55. Mem. Am. Psychol. Assn., Nat. Register Health Svc. Providers in Psychology, Pa. Psychol. Assn., Knights of Columbus. Republican. Roman Catholic. Avocations: reading, puzzles, physical fitness. Home: Philadelphia, Pa. Died May 21, 1999.

MELARAGNO, MICHELE, architecture educator; b. Rome, Oct. 25, 1928; came to U.S., 1959; s. Attilio and Amelia (Castaldi) M.; m. Helen P. Melaragno, May 1958 (div. 1984); children: Patricia, Elizabeth, Mark; m. Deborah Frazier, Dec. 1987. Diploma, Coll. Nazareno, Rome, 1948; D in Civil Engring., U. Bari, 1959. Registered engr. R.I., Mass., N.C., Va., Kans. Asst. prof. architecture and bldg. scis. Kans. State U., Manhattan, 1966-69; assoc. prof. Clemson (S.C.) U., 1969-74; prof. architecture and bldg. scis. U. N.C., Charlotte, from 1974; dir. Grad. Studies Ctr. Clemson U., Genova, Italy, 1973-74. Structural cons., worker in engring. field various firms. Author: Simplified Truss Design, Wind in Architectural and Environmental Design, An Introduction to Shell Structures: The Art and Science of Vaulting, Severe Storm Engineering for Structural Design, Unita de Misura, Quantification in Science: The VNR Dictionary of Engineering Units and Measures, Preliminary Design of Bridges for Architects and Engineers; contbr. articles to profl. jours., chpts. to books. Rsch. grantee Kans. State U., Clemson U., U. N.C., Charlotte; recipient awards Internat. Inst. for Advanced Studies in Systems Rsch. and Cybernetics, 1993, 96. Home: Charlotte, NC. Died Feb. 10, 2001.

MELIKOVA, GENIA, dance educator; b. Marseille, France; Studies with Sedova, Egorova, Gzovsky, Perretti, Vilzak, Schollar, Fedorova, Craske, Schwetzoff, France and U.S. Dance faculty Bennett Coll., 1970-71, Igor Youskevitch Sch. of Ballet, 1970-77; ballet tchr. Alvin Ailey Am. Dance Ctr., 1972-79; artistic dir., choreographer Greater Bridgeport Ballet Co. of Conn., 1974-75, Bernhard Ballet, Westport, Conn., 1976-80; faculty The Juilliard Sch., N.Y.C., 1969—95. Guest tchr. dance dept. Reed Coll., Portland, Oreg., summer 1982-83, U. Hawaii, Manoa. Performed with Ballet de Monte Carlo, Am. Ballet Theater; ballerina (with Rudolf Nureyev, Andre Prokovsky and Henning Kronstam) Internat. Ballet de Marquis de Cuevas, Paris, 1954-62; TV performances in England, France, Spain, Belgium, Switzerland; also worked with Balanchine, Cranko, Lichine, Nijinska, Tara, Tudor; ballet mistress Andre Eglevsky Co., 1969. Died Mar. 5, 2004.

MELNER, SINCLAIR LEWIS, retired military officer; b. Reno, Apr. 6, 1928; s. Abraham H. and Carol Rachel (Myers) M.; m. Roma F. Garner, Dec. 26, 1949; children: Catherine, Michael, Joan. BS, U. Nev., 1949; MS in Internat. Affairs, George Washington U., 1969. Commd. 2d lt. U.S. Army, 1949, advanced through grades to lt. gen., formerly comdg. gen.; later dep. chmn. NATO Mil. Command, Brussels; ret., 1984; v.p., corp. sec. Hudson Inst., 1984-88; sr. advisor Am. Amicable Life Ins. Co. Tex., 1989-95; ret., 1995. Decorated Silver Star with oak leaf cluster, Def. Superior Service medal, Def. D.S.M., Army D.S.M., Legion of Merit with oak leaf cluster. Home: Fort Belvoir, Va. Died June 8, 2002.

MELOAN, TAYLOR WELLS, marketing educator; b. St. Louis, July 31, 1919; s. Taylor Wells and Edith (Graham) M.; m. Anna Geraldine Leukering, Dec. 17, 1944 (div. 1974); children: Michael David, Steven Lee; m. Jane Innes Bierlich, Jan. 30, 1975. BS cum laude, St. Louis U., 1949; MBA, Washington U., St. Louis, 1950; D of Bus. Admin., Ind. U., 1953. Advt. mgr. Herz Corp., St. Louis, 1941—42; sales promotion supr. Liggett & Myers Tobacco Co., St. Louis, 1942—43; asst. prof. mktg. U. Okla., Norman, 1953; asst., then assoc. prof. mktg. Ind. U., Bloomington, 1953—59; prof., chmn. dept. mktg. U. So. Calif., L.A., 1959—69, prof. mktg., 1969—92, Robert E. Brooker prof. mktg., 1970—79, disting. prof. mktg. emeritus, from 1997, dean Sch. Bus. Adminstrn., 1969—71, assoc. v.p. acad. adminstrn. and research, 1971—81. Prof. bus. adminstrn. U. Karachi, Pakistan, 1962; vis. prof. mktg. Istituto Post U. Per Lo Studio Dell Organizzazione Aziendale, Turin, Italy, 1964, U. Hawaii, 1993, Madrid Bus. Sch., 1993; disting. vis. prof. U. Witwatersrand, Johannesburg, 1978, U. Hawaii, 1993; editl. advisor bus. adminstrn. Houghton Mifflin Co., Boston, 1959-73; cons. to industry and govt., 1953; bd. dirs Inst. Shipboard Edn. Author: New Career Opportunities, 1978, Innovation Strategy and Management, 1979, Direct Marketing: Vehicle for Department Store Expansion, 1984, Preparing the Exporting Entrepreneur, 1986, The New Competition: Dilemma of Department Stores in the 1980's, 1987, Franchise Marketing: A Retrospective and Prospective View of a Contractual Vertical Marketing System, 1988; co-author: Managerial Marketing, 1970, Internationalizing the Business Curriculum, 1968, Handbook of Modern Marketing, contbg. author, 1986; co-author, co-editor: International and Global Marketing: Concepts and Cases, 1994, International and Global Marketing Concepts and Cases, Vol. 2, 1997; bd. editors Jour. Mktg., 1965-72. Trustee World Affairs Coun. Orange County, 1994—. Lt. (j.g.) U.S. Maritime Svc., 1943-46. Mem. Am. Mktg. Assn. (pres. L.A. chpt. 1963-64), Order of Artus, Beta Gamma Sigma, Delta Pi Epsilon, Calif. Yacht Club, Univ. Club, Rotary. Died Nov. 4, 2002.

MELZER, JOHN DENNIES, engineer; b. Green Bay, Milw., Jan. 28, 1910; s. Eva Marie Pratt; m. Adelle Marie Cumber; children: John A., LeRoy F., Valerie M., Keith C. Diploma, Mich. Coll. Mines, Houltan, 1930. Owner Melzer Sheet Metal, Appleton, Wis., 1928-33; rsch. engr. Kimberly Clark, Badger Globe, Appleton, 1933-72. Mem. St. Vincent DePaul Soc. (pres. 1960-85). Republican. Roman Catholic. Avocations: lapidary, gold and silver working, stamp and coin collecting. Home: Appleton, Wis. Deceased.

MENOCAL, PEDRO GARCIA, portrait painter; b. Havana, Cuba, July 3, 1928; came to U.S., 1961; s. Mario Garcia and Hortensia (de Almagro) M.; m. Magda del Valle, Oct. 2, 1954 (div. 1979); children: Magdalena, Mario, Pedro; m. Magali Rubiera, Jan. 3, 1987. Student, U. Havana,

1947—51. Owner rice plantation, Camaguey Province, Cuba, 1951-61; interpreter U.S. State Dept., 1961; portrait painter, from 1964. Republican. Roman Catholic. Avocations: reading, golf, bridge. Died July 13, 2001.

MERCHANT, DONALD JOSEPH, retired microbiologist and educator; b. Biltmore, N.C., Sept. 7, 1921; s. Oscar Lowell and Bess Lee (Clark) M.; m. Marian Adelaide Yeager, May 31, 1943; children— Nancy Adele, Barry Scott, Karen Ruth. AB, Berea Coll., 1942; MS, U. Mich., 1947, PhD, 1950; Diploma of Merit, Gen. Assembly/Presbyn. Ch. of, Kinshasa, Rep. of the Congo, 2000. Instr. U. Mich., 1948-51, asst. prof., 1951-58, asso. prof., 1958-64, prof., 1964-69; dir., scientist W. Alton Jones Cell Sci. Center, Tissue Culture Assn., Lake Placid, N.Y., 1969-72; prof. U. Vt., 1969-72; prof., chmn. dept. microbiology and immunology Eastern Va. Med. Sch., Norfolk, 1973-86, prof. emeritus, from 1986. Dir. Tidewater Regional Cancer Network, 1974-88; cons. U.S. Army Biol. Lab., 1966-68; mem. sci. adv. bd. Found. for Research on the Nervous System, Boston, 1965-69, Masonic Med. Research Lab., Utica, N.Y., 1970-75; mem. Nat. Prostatic Cancer Task Force, Nat. Cancer Inst., 1972-79, 83-86. Author: (with others) Handbook of Cell and Organ Culture, 1960, 2d edit., 1964; Editor: (with J.V. Neel) Approaches to the Genetic Analysis of Mammalian Cells, 1962, Cell Cultures for Virus Vaccine Production, 1968, (with others) Biology of Connective Tissue Cells, 1962; contbr. articles to profl. jours., chpts. to books. Served with U.S. Army, 1944-46. Mem. Am. Acad. Microbiology, Am. Soc. Microbiology (past pres. Mich. br.), Soc. Exptl. Biology and Medicine, Am. Soc. Cell Biology, Tissue Culture Assn. (pres. 1964-68), Va. Acad. Sci., N.Y. Acad. Sci., Assn. Community Cancer Centers, Brit. Soc. Cell Biology, Royal Soc. Medicine. Presbyterian. Home: Virginia Beach, Va. Died Aug. 9, 2002.

MEREDITH, HOWARD LYNN, American Indian studies educator; b. Galveston, Tex., May 25, 1938; s. Howard and Lillian (Pitts) M.; m. Mary Ellen Meredith; m. Lynn, Lee. BS, U. Tex., 1961; MA, Stephen F. Austin State U., 1963; PhD, U. Okla., 1970. Asst. prof. history Ky. Wesleyan Coll., Owensboro, 1967-71; exec. Indian work Exec. Coun. Episcopal Ch., N.Y.C., 1971-75; dir., hist. pres. Okla. Hist. Soc., Oklahoma City, 1975-79; adminstr., editor Eco. Co., Ginn, C. Merrill & Bacone, Oklahoma City, 1979-85; regents prof. interdisciplinary studies U. Sci. and Arts of Okla., Chickasha, from 1985. Author: Bartley Milam: Principal Chief, 1985, Hasinai, 1988 (award 1989), Modern American Indian Tribal Government, 1993-94, Dancing on Common Ground, 1995, Elohi, 1997 (award 1998), Short History of Native Americans in the United States, 2001. Bd. mem., sec. Red Earth, Oklahoma City, 1988-94; bd. mem. Nat. Indian Hall of Fame, Anadarko, 1990—; bd. dirs., chmn. Pan-Am. Indian Humanities Ctr., Chickasha. Recipient Muriel Wright award Okla. Hist. Soc., Oklahoma City, 1980, Co-Founders Book award Westerners Internat., Tucson, 1989, McCasland award Okla. Heritage Assn., Oklahoma City, 1994, Coke Wood award for Best Monograph, 1998. Episcopalian. Avocation: water colors. Home: Oklahoma City, Okla. Died May 2003.

MERKLE, HANS L. manufacturing executive; b. Pforzheim, Germany, Jan. 1, 1913; s. Emil M. and Zeline (Kilgus) M.; m. Annemarie Schlerff. Student law and econs. Mem. exec. bd. Ullrich Gminder AG, Reutlingen, Fed. Republic Germany, 1949-58; mng. dir. Robert Bosch GmbH, 1958-83, chmn. exec. bd., 1984-88, now hon. chmn.; former ptnr. Robert Bosch Industrietreuhand KG, Stuttgart, now hon. chmn. Chmn. supervisory bd. BASF AG, Continental Gummiwerke, Deutsche Bank AG; mem. supervisory bd. Allianz Vers./AG, AKZO N.V., Arnheim, Otto Wolff AG, Royal Dutch Petroleum Co., Volkswagenwerk AG, Allianz AG Holding, Munich, Klöckner-Humboldt-Deutz AG, Cologne. Author: Inflation und öffentliche Finanzen, 1975. Chmn. curatorium Fritz Thyssen Found., Cologne, 1986—. Mem. Max-Planck-Gesellschaft (mem. sci. coun.). Avocation: collecting german 1st editions. Home: Stuttgart, Germany. Deceased.

MERKLE, ROBERT W., JR., law educator; b. WA; US atty. mid. Fla., Tampa, Fla., 1982—88. Died May 5, 2003.

MERRITT, SHARON LOUISE, nurse, educator; b. Chgo., June 24, 1940; d. George R. and Lorraine E. (Neybert) Gibson; m. Frank J. Merritt, Oct. 17, 1964; children: Michelle, Melissa. BSN, St. Louis U., 1962; MSN, U. Calif., San Fracisco, 1964; EdD, U. Mo., St. Louis, 1982; postgrad, U. Ill., Chgo., 1981-82. RN; Lic. nurse Calif., Ill., Mo. Staff nurse Firmin Desloge Hosp., St. Louis, 1962; staff and charge nurse St. Lukes Hosp., Chgo., 1962-63; assoc. in nursing U. Calif Sch. Nursing San Francisco Med. Ctr., 1965-66, instr. nursing, 1970-71; cons. nursing service VA Hosp., Calif., 1968-69, 1968-69; asst. prof. Coll. Nursing, U. Ill., Chgo., 1973-77, project dir., 1977-80; acting coord., assoc. prof., project dir. 1981-82, 1981-87; asst. prof. U. Ill., Chgo., 1987—2004, dir., rsch. ctr. for narcolepsy, 1994—2004. Clin. nurse reviewer C. V. Mosby; nurse clinician, researcher Barnes Hosp.1983-87, Am. Edn. Research Assn. 1986, Nat. Inst. of Health Research 1986, N. Am. Nursing Diagnoses Assn. 1987, Computers in Nursing, Soc. Research Nursing Edn. 1985-2004, Midwest Nursing Reseach Soc. 1987; Manuscript reviewer Mosby Pub. Co., Western Jour. of Nursing Research, Applied Nursing Research and Nursing Research. Mem. soc. Behavioral Medicine. Avocations: tennis, walking, skiing. Home: Hinsdale, Ill. Died July 10, 2004.

MERTON, ROBERT K. sociologist, educator; b. Phila., July 4, 1910; s. Harry David and Ida (Rosoff) Schkolnick; m. Suzanne Carhart, 1934 (sep. 1968, dec. 1992); children: Stephanie, Robert C., Vanessa; companion Harriet Zuckerman, 1968-92, m. June, 1993. AB, Temple U., 1931, LLD (hon.), 1956; MA, Harvard U., 1932, PhD, 1936, LLD (hon.), 1980; LHD (hon.), Emory U., 1965, Loyola U., Chgo., 1970, Kalamazoo Coll., 1970, Cleve. State U., 1977, U. Pa., 1979, Brandeis U., 1983, SUNY-Albany, 1986, New Sch. Social Rsch., 1995, Long Island U., 1996; Dr. honoris causa, U. Leyden, 1965, Jagiellonian U., Cracow, Poland, 1989; LLD (hon.), Western Res. U., 1966, U. Chgo., 1968, Tulane U., 1971, U. Md., 1982; LittD (hon.), Colgate U., 1967, SUNY, 1984, Columbia U., 1985, SUNY, Albany, 1986, Oxford U., 1986; Dr. Social Sci. (hon.), Yale U., 1968; DSC in Econ. (hon.), U. Wales, 1968; PhD (hon.), Hebrew U. of Jerusalem, 1980, U. Oslo, Norway, 1991; D of Polit. Sci. (hon.), U. Bologna, 1996; D honoris causa, U. Madrid, 1999, U. Athens, 1999, U. Rome, 2001. Tutor, instr. sociology Harvard U., 1936-39; prof., chmn. dept. Tulane U., 1939-41; from asst. prof. to prof. Columbia U., 1941-63, Giddings prof., 1963-74, univ. prof., 1974-79, spl. svc. prof., 1979-84, Univ. prof. emeritus, 1979—2003. Assoc. dir. Bur. Applied Social Rsch., 1942-71; adj. faculty Rockefeller U., 1979-2003; George Sarton prof. hist. sci. U. Ghent, Belgium, 1986-88; adv. editor sociology Harcourt Brace 1947-98; ednl. adv. bd. Guggenheim Found., 1963-79, chmn., 1971-79. Author: Science Technology and Society in 17th Century England, 3rd edit., 2001, Mass Persuasion, 3d edit., 2002, Social Theory and Social Structure, rev. edit., 1968, On the Shoulders of Giants, 1965, bicennial edit., 1985, post-Italianate edit., 1993, On Theoretical Sociology, 1967, The Sociology of Science, 1973, Sociological Ambivalence, 1976, Sociology of Science: An Episodic Memoir, 1979, Social Research and the Practicing Professions, 1982, Opportunity Structure, 1995, On Social Structure and Science, 1996; co-author: the Focused Interview, rev. edit., 1956, 3d edit., 1990, Freedom to Read, 1957, I Viaggi e le Avventura della "Serendipity", 2002, The Travels and Adventures of Serendipity: A Study in Sociolajica Semantics and the Sociology of Science, 2003; co-editor, co-author: Continuities in Social Research, 1951, Social Policy and Social Research in Housing, 1951, Reader in Bureaucracy, 1952, The Student-Physician, 1957, Sociology Today, 1959, Contemporary Social Problems, 4th edit., 1976, The Sociology of Science in Europe, 1977, Toward a Metric of Science, 1978, Qualitative and Quantitative Social Research: Papers in Honor of Paul F. Lazarsfeld, 1979, Sociological Traditions from Generation to Generation, 1980, Continuities in Structural Inquiry, 1981; co-editor Social Sci. Quotations, 2000. Trustee Ctr. Advanced Study Behavioral Scis., 1952-75, Temple U., 1964-68, Inst. Sci. Info., 1968-2003; mem. bd. guarantors Italian Acad. for Advanced Studies in Am., 1992-2000. Recipient MacArthur Prize fellow, 1983-88, Nat. Medal of Sci., 1994, Common Wealth award for Disting. Svc. to Sociology, 1979, award Meml. Sloan-Kettering Cancer Ctr., 1981, Derek Price award Scientometrics, 1995, Sutherland award Am. Soc. Criminology, 1996, Dinerman prize World Assn. Pub. Opinion Rsch., 2000; Disting. scholar in humanities Am. Coun. Learned Socs., 1962, Russell Sage Found. scholar, 1979-99, emeritus, 1999-2003, Haskins lectr., 1994; NIH lectr. in recognition of outstanding sci. achievement, 1964; Guggenheim fellow, 1962. Fellow Am. Acad. Arts and Scis. (Talcott Parsons prize 1979), Brit. Acad. (fgn.); mem. NAS, Am. Philos. Soc., Sociol. Rsch. Assn. (pres. 1968), Nat. Acad. Edn., Nat. Inst. Medicine, Am. Sociol. Assn. (pres. 1957, Disting. Scholarship award 1980, Cooley-Mead Award in social psychology 1997), Ea. Sociol. Soc. (pres. 1969), History of Sci. Soc., World Acad. Arts and Scis., Soc. Social Studies of Sci. (pres. 1975, Bernal prize), Royal Swedish Acad. Scis. (fgn.), Academia Europaea (fgn.), Polish Acad. Scis. (fgn.), N.Y. Acad. Scis. (hon. life mem.). Home: East Hampton, NY. Died Feb. 23, 2003.

MESSING, HAROLD, lawyer, theatrical producer, educator, writer; b. N.Y.C., May 4, 1935; s. Paul and Mary (Bromberg) M.; m. Marcia Yoffe, Feb. 18, 1984. B.A., NYU, 1956, J.D., 1966; M.A., Stanford U., 1958. Bar: N.Y. 1966, U.S. Supreme Ct. 1970, U.S. Ct. Appeals (2d cir.) 1972, U.S. Dist. Ct. (so. and ea. dists.) N.Y. 1974, Calif. 1977,Fla. 1977. Atty., asst. gen. counsel Embassy Pictures, N.Y.C., 1967-68; assoc. law firm Katz, Moselle & Schier, N.Y.C., 1968-69, Greenbaum, Wolff & Ernst, N.Y.C., 1969-70; ptnr. law firm Bomser & Messing, N.Y.C., 1970-72; sole practice, N.Y.C., 1972-74; ptnr. law firm Kosmas & Messing, N.Y.C., 1974-76; sole practice, N.Y.C., 1976—; mem. faculty New Sch., 1974—; lectr. Am. Film Inst., Washington, 1979—; producer: Herringbone, 1982. Contbg. author: Your Legal Rights, 1970; contbr. articles to mags. Recipient TV Programming award Nat. Acad. TV Artsand Scis., 1960. Mem. ABA, N.Y. State Bar Assn. Calif. Bar Assn., League of Off Broadway Theatres and Producers, Dirs. Guild Am. Club: Friars. Home: Santa Monica, Calif.

MEYER, HELEN (MRS. ABRAHAM J. MEYER), retired editorial consultant; b. Bklyn., Dec. 4, 1907; d. Bertolen and Esther (Greenfield) Honig; m. Abraham J. Meyer(dec. 1993), Sept. 1, 1929; children— Adele Meyer Brodkin, Robert L. Grad. pub. schs. With Popular Sci., McCall's mag., 1921-22; pres., dir. Dell Pub. Co., Inc., N.Y.C., 1923-57, Dell Distbg., Inc., from 1957, Dell Internat., Inc., from 1957; pres. Dell Pub. Co., Inc., Montville Warehousing Co., Inc.; chmn. bd. Noble & Noble Pubs., Inc.; v.p. Dellprint, Inc., Dunellen, N.J.; pres. Dial Press.; later editorial cons. Doubleday & Co., N.Y.C.; cons. Fgn. Rights, N.Y.C. Bd. dirs. United Cerebral Palsy. Named to Pub.'s Hall of Fame, 1986. Mem. Assn. Am. Pubs. (dir.) Home: Verona, NJ. Died Apr. 21, 2003.

MEYER, HOWARD LEE, clergyman; b. Jefferson City, Mo., Dec. 21, 1937; s. Arnold J. and Clara Mae (Barger) M.; m. Shirley J. Frank, Aug. 24, 1957 (div. 1985); children: Stephen Rex, Thomas Nelson. AB, Okla. Bapt. U., 1959; MDiv, Midwest Bapt. Theol. Sem., 1963. Minister So. Bapt. Ch., Linn, Mo., 1960-65, minister Palmyra, Mo., 1965-68; denominational exec. Mo. Bapt. conv., Jefferson City, 1968-74; adminstr. Mo. Bapt. Children's Home, Bridgeton, Mo., 1975-78; pres. Bluffmont Corp., Jefferson City, from 1979. Pres. Ministerial Assn., Palmyra, 1966, Bethel Bapt. Minister's Conf., Hannibal, Mo., 1967; chmn. bd. Christian Counseling Svcs., Inc., Jefferson City, 1973-75; v.p. So. Bapt. Child Care Execs., St. Louis, 1978. Contbr. articles to profl. jours. Bd. dirs. Osage County Libr., Linn, Mo., 1963-65, Gov.'s Coun. on Comprehensive Health Planning, Jefferson City, 1973-74; v.p. Kiwanis Club, Palmyra, 1967; mem. Mo. Health Assn., Jefferson City, 1973-74. Republican. Avocations: flying, architecture, psychology, theater, woodworking. Home: Abilene, Tex. Deceased.

MEYERS, MARVIN, retired history educator; b. Norfolk, Va., Apr. 5, 1921; s. Peter and Jeanette (Greenberg) M.; m. Edith Cooper, Aug. 31, 1932; 1 child, Daniel. BA, Rutgers U., 1942; MA, Columbia U., 1947, PhD, 1957. Instr., asst. prof., assoc. prof. history U. Chgo., 1948-63; Truman prof. history Brandeis U., Waltham, Mass., 1963-85, Truman prof. emeritus, from 1985. Vis. lectr. U. P.R., Rio Piedras, 1952-53; vis. scholar Claremont (Calif.) Grad. Sch., 1959-60; cons. NEH, Washington, 1972—; bd. dirs. Univ. Ctrs. for Rational Alternatives, N.Y.C., 1968—; resident fellow Ctr. for Advanced Study in Behavioral Scis., Stanford, Calif., 1955-56, Nat. Humanities Ctr., Research Triangle Park, N.C., 1981-82; humanities fellow-in-residence Am. Enterprise Inst., Washington, 1978; seminar mem. program on constl. govt. Harvard U., 1985—. Author: The Jacksonian Persuasion, 1957 (Dunning prize Am. Hist. Assn. 1958); contbg. author: Liberty and Equality under the Constitution, 1983; editor: The Mind of the Founder, 1973, 2d edit. 1981; co-editor: Sources of the American Republic, 2 vols., 1960, 69-92. Sgt. USAAF, 1942-46. Fellow NEH, 1976-77. Mem. Am. Hist. Assn., Mass. Assn. Scholars. Republican. Jewish. Avocations: listening to music, japanese prints, bonsai. Home: Denver, Colo. Died Apr. 8, 2000.

MICHAEL, PHYLLIS CALLENDER, composer; b. near Berwick, Pa., Dec. 24, 1908; d. Bruce Miles and Emma (Harvey) C.; m. Arthur L. Michael, Aug. 21, 1933; children: Robert Bruce, Keith Winton. Grad., Bloomsburg Coll., 1928; MusB, U. Extension Conservatory, Chgo., 1953. Tchr. Berwick (Pa.) Elem. Schs., 1928-33; substitute tchr. Shickshinny and N.W. Area, Pa., 1954-66; tchr. N.W. Area H.S., 1966-71; tchr. piano, organ, theory and voice pvt. practice, Shickshinny, Pa., 1943-89; hymn writer, poet, author, composer, from 1943. Author: Poems for Mothers, 1963, Poems from My Heart, 1964, Beside Still Waters, 1970, Fun To Do Showers, 1971, Bridal Shower Ideas, 1972, Is My Head on Straight, 1976, This is Christmas, 1985, Quotes, 1986, Hi, Lord!, 1987, Bright Tomorrows, 1989, Home Sweet Home, 1991, Reach for the Rose, 1992, God Promised, 1992, Why Me, Lord, 1993, Golden Gems, 1993, Oops, 1994, Mountains, Molehills and Mustard Seed, 1995, Surely Goodness and Mercy, 1995, Some Golden Daybreak, 1995, When Petals Fall, 1996, Peace in the Valley, 1996, Snippets from Mother's Diary, 1997, God Cares, 1998; contbr. songs, gospel songs, anthems, articles, poems to books, hymnbooks, booklets, mags. and other nat. and internat. publs. Adv. mem. MBLS. Recipient first place in Nat. Favorite Hymns contest for Take Thou My Hand, 1953, cert. of merit for disting. svc. to composition of outstanding hymns, 1967. Mem. Nat. Ret. Tchrs. Assn., Internat. Platform Assn., Nat. Soc. Lit. and the Arts, Hymn Soc. Am. Deceased.

MICHAELS, LEONARD, English educator; b. N.Y.C., Jan. 2, 1933; s. Leon and Anna (Czeskies) M.; m. Priscilla Drake Older, June 9, 1966 (div.); children: Ethan, Jesse; m. Brenda Lynn Hillman, Aug. 8, 1976 (div.); 1 child, Louisa Alice. BA, NYU, 1953; MA, U. Mich., 1956, PhD, 1967. Prof. English Paterson (N.J.) State Coll., 1961-62, U. Calif., Davis, 1966-68, Berkeley, from 1969. Author: Going Places, 1969, I Would Have Saved Them If I Could, 1975, The Men's Club, 1981 (also wrote screenplay); editor various lit. mags.; co-editor: (with Christopher Ricks) The State of the Language, 1979, 89, (with David Reid and Raquel Scherr) West of the West, 1989, Shuffle, 1990, Sylvia, 1993, (essays) To Feel These Things, 1993; contbr. short stories, book revs., critical essays to Best Am. Essays, Best Am. Stories, other publs. Recipient award Nat. Found. on Arts and Humanities, 1967, award Am. Nat. Acad. Arts and Letters, 1972; Guggenheim fellow, 1970 Died May 10, 2003.

MIDDLETON, JOHN ALBERT, retired communications executive; b. Bradford, Yorkshire, Eng., Mar. 20, 1915; came to U.S., 1922; s. Albert Henry and Priscilla (Lambert) Ml; m. Marjorie Frances Crossett, May 29, 1942; children: John Gary, Pamela Mary, Gregory Chester, Susan Jeanne. Grad. H.S., Manchester Ctrl. H.S., Manchester, 1934. Repair supr. New Eng. Telephone, Claremont, N.H., 1946-77; ret., 1977. City councilor, Claremont, 1986-94, asst. mayor, 1987-88, 90, 93-94, mayor, 1991; state rep., Concord, N.H., 1989-92; Justice of the Peace, N.H., 1990—; vice-chair fin. Sullivan County Delegation, N.H., 1989-92; mem. Sullivan County Econ. Devel. Coun., 1986-95; mem. Claremont Indsl. Devel. Authority, 1994, chmn. traffic com., 1987-90; chmn. health com., Claremont, 1993-94; mem. strategic planning com.

Claremont Sch. Dist., 1994-95; sr. warden Union Ch., Claremont; grand marshall Independence Day Parade, July 4, 1997. With U.S. Army, 1942-46, PTO. Mem. VFW (life), Am. Legion (life), Am. Vets. (life), Shrine Legion of Honor (life), Hist. Soc. (writer historical document Civil War Tablets at City Hall 1987), Telephone Pioneers Am. (pres. 1985-86, 95), Anniversary Lodge (charter), William Pitt Tavern Lodge (charter), Sullivan Hugh-De Payens (treas. 1979-89), Hiram Lodge (Master Hiram # 9, 1963,83, 84, 85, 86, sec. 1987-89), Masons (Maj. Gen. John Sulivan medal, Disting. Svc. award 1986, Cheshire/Webb chpt. # 4 High Priest 1987-88, Columbian/St. Johns chpt. # 2 master 1983-90). Republican. Episcopalian. Avocation: woodworking. Home: Claremont, NH. Died Dec. 2, 2002.

MIDDLETON, S. GUY, state legislator; m. Anita; children: Dana Atkins, Lisa Davis, Sally Edwards. Grad., Ga. Tech. Farmer; mem. Ga. Senate, Atlanta, from 1992, chmn. health and human svcs. com., vice chmn. agr., reapportionment coms., sec. banking and fin. instns. com., mem. appropriations, edn., ethics coms. Chmn. Lumpkin County Water and Sewer Authority, 1985-92, Lumpkin County Econ. Growth and Steering Com., 1991-92; bd. dirs Chestatee-Chattahoochee Resource Conservation and Devel. Coun.; active Upper Chattahoochee Soil and Conservation Dist. With U.S. Marine Corps. Mem. C. of C. Democrat. Deceased.

MIES, THOMAS GERALD, lawyer; b. Detroit, Sept. 23, 1953; s. James E. and Mary P. (McBride) M.; m. Paula A. Diamond, Jan. 21, 1984; children: Jeffrey T., Lauren A. BSBA, Wayne State U., 1975, JD cum laude, 1981. Bar: Mich. 1981; CPA, Mich. Acct. Perrin Fordrec & Co., Troy, Mich., 1976-78, Thomas G. Mies, P.C., Livonia, Mich., 1978-82; ptnr., prin. Fried & Mies. P.C., Livonia, Mich., 1982-92; prin. Mies & Assocs., P.C., Livonia, Mich., from 1992. Treas. Mich. Tng. and Resource Ctr., Inc., 1988-91, v.p., 1991-92, also bd. dirs.; mem. adv. bd. Wayne County Office Nutrition Svcs., 1989-92. Mem. Detroit Wayne County Cmty. Mental Health Bd., 1993—, treas. 1995-97, vice chairperson, 1997. Mem. AICPA, Am. Assn. Attys. and CPAs, State Bar Mich. (chair practice and procedure com. 1991-93, mem. tax coun. 1993-96), Mich. Assn. CPAs, Optimists (treas. 1984-86). Died May 16, 2001.

MIKO, ANDRAS, opera producer, educator; b. Budapest, Hungary, June 30, 1922; s. Strelinger Karoly and Maria (Kriser) M.; m. Eva Rehak. Producer State Opera, Budapest, from 1946; prof. Acad. Music, Budapest, from 1950. Producer of operas at Covent Garden, London, Teato Colon, Buenos Aires, Copenhage, Helsinki, Savonlinna, Finland, Moscow, East Berlin, Teatro Regio, Torino, Genva, Cologne, Warsaw, others. Home: Budapest, Hungary. Deceased.

MILES, VERONICA LEVOLA, academic coordinator; b. Crisfield, Md., Jan. 13, 1949; d. Charles and Madgline (Merrill) Matn; m. William T. Miles, Aug. 17, 1974; 1 child, Jennifer Y. BA in Social Sci., U. Md., 1972, MEd in Guidance and Counseling, 1997. Cert. test adminstr. Employment security splst. trainee Md. Dept. Employemnt and Econ. Devel., Crisfield, 1980-85; coord. T.A.T.A.S. U. Md., Princess Anne, 1981, implementation developer, 1985-92, career developer, 1992-98, student advising coord., from 1998. Med. records clk., outreach worker Delmarva Rural Ministries, Princess Anne, 1982-92; test ctr. mgr., proctor Assessment Sys. Inc., Bala Cynwyd, Pa., 1985—; proctor, supr. Ednl. Testing Svcs., Princeton, 1985-98. Mem. United Meth. Ch., Princess Anne, 1995. Mem. Coll. Placement Coun. Mid-Atlantic Assn., U. Med. Ea. Shore Tri-County Alumni Assn., Kappa Delta Pi (pres. 1997-99). Home: Princess Anne, Md. Died Jan. 3, 2002.

MILEY, HUGH HOWARD, retired physician; b. Wauseon, Ohio, Apr. 24, 1902; s. Howard Harland Miley and Edith (Martin) Esterline; m. Anna Horwitz, June 26, 1935; children: Ruth Eliza Jane, Howard Charles. BA, Ohio State U., 1924, MS, 1925, PhD, 1927; MD, Wayne State U., 1935. Intern Grace Hosp., Detroit, 1934-35; extern Delray Gen. Hosp., 1933-35; instr. physiology Detroit Coll. Medicine and Surgery, 1927-33; practice indsl. medicine Dodge Main Hosp., Chrysler Motor Co., Hamtramick, Mich., 1935-37; gen. practice indsl. medicine Marygrove Indsl. Clinics, Detroit, 1937-67; long-term care physician Wayne County Gen. Hosp., Eloise, Mich., 1967-72; gen. practice clinics Highland Park, Mich., 1972-82; gen. practice medicine Herman Kiefer Hosp. Bldg., Detroit, 1982-83. Participant charity welfare programs North End Clinic, Grace Hosp., Detroit. Contbr. articles to profl. jours. Physician vaccination and examination programs Detroit Pub. Schs., 1935-40, Neighborhood Health Svc. Ctr., Inc., 1972. Res. officer Tng. Corps., ROTC, 1924-25. Mem. AMA, Wayne County Med. Soc., Mich. State Med. Soc., Hon. Pathology Soc., Sigma Xi. Avocations: reading books, fishing, traveling, geriatrics. Home: Scotts Valley, Calif. Died Mar. 10, 1999.

MILLARD, CHARLES F. F. soft drink executive; b. Paterson, N.J., Sept. 4, 1932; s. James C.B. and Mary (Orr) M.; m. Marylou Slattery, Sept. 25, 1954; children: Marylou, Charles, Christopher, Maureen, Margaret, Suzanne, Kathleen, Gregory. AB, Coll. Holy Cross, 1954. Vice pres., account supr. Benton & Bowles, Inc., 1958-64, William Esty Co., Inc., 1964-66; sr. v.p., dir. client services Gilbert Advt. Agy., Inc., 1966-67; v.p., mgmt. supr. Benton & Bowles, Inc., 1967; pres. Coca-Cola Bottling Co., N.Y., Inc., 1967-68, chief exec. officer, chmn. bd., 1968-86; chmn. Coca-Cola Bottling Co. of No. New Eng., Inc., 1986-87; chmn., chief exec. officer Premium Beverages, Inc., Fairfield, Conn., 1984-90; chmn. Lance Inc., 1989—95. Bd. dirs. BF Enterprises; mng. ptnr. Millard/O'Reilly Enterprises, Fairfield. Past chmn. bd. dirs. N.Y. Urban League; past trustee Nat. Urban League; past chmn. exec. com. Newark Archbishop's Com. of Laity; trustee, exec. com., past. chmn. Coll. Holy Cross.; bd. dirs. Am. Irish Found.; bd. dirs. Canterbury Sch., New Milford, Ct. Mem. River Club (N.Y.C.), Links (N.Y.C.), Pine Valley Club, Jupiter Island Club. Home: Hobe Sound, Fla. Died Oct. 20, 2003.

MILLARD, MALCOLM STUART, retired lawyer; b. Highland Park, Ill., Mar. 22, 1914; s. Everett L. and Elizabeth (Boynton) M.; m. Joanne T. Blakeman; 1 child, Anne W. Benjamin. BA, Harvard U., 1936; JD, Northwestern U., 1939. Bar: Ill. 1939, Calif. 1951. Ptnr. Farr & Millard, Carmel, Calif., 1951-55, Millard, Tourangeau, Morris & Staples, P.C., Carmel, 1955-91, Millard, Morris & Staples, Carmel, 1991-94, ret., 1994. Dir. Leslie Salt Co., 1975-81. Trustee Community Hosp. of Monterey Peninsula, 1982-88, Monterey Inst. Fgn. Studies, 1955-76, Community Found. Monterey County, 1988-99; pres. Community Chest of Monterey Peninsula, 1958. Served to lt. USN, 1943-46. Mem. Monterey Inst. Internat. Relations (hon. lifetime trustee 1982-99, hon. DHL 1991), Ill. State Bar, Calif. State Bar, Monterey County Bar Assn. (pres.), Old Capital Club, Harvard Club. Avocations: environmental interests, travel, ranching. Home: Carmel Valley, Calif. Died Feb. 8, 1999.

MILLER, ANN (LUCILLE ANN COLLIER), actress, dancer, singer; b. Houston, Apr. 12, 1923; d. John Alfred and Clara Emma (Birdwell) Collier. Student, Lawlors Profl. Sch., Los Angeles, 1937. Appeared in numerous motion pictures, including: You Can't Take It With You, 1939, Room Service, 1939, Easter Parade, 1949, Kiss Me Kate, 1956, On the Town, 1950, Hit the Deck, 1955, Opposite Sex, 1956, Great American Pastime, 1956, That's Entertainment, Part 1, 1976, Part 2, 1977, Won Ton Ton, 1976, That's Entertainment!III, 1994, Mulholland Drive, 2001; star: stage show Mame on Broadway, 1969-70, also in, Los Angeles, Fla., Ohio, Ga., 1970-71; Broadway show Sugar Babies, 1979-82 (Tony nomination 1980), (on tour), 1982-84; appeared: TV shows including Perry Como, 1961, Magic of Christmas, 1968, Bob Hope Show, 1961, Jonathan Winters Show, 1969, Ed Sullivan Show, 1958, 59, 4 Palace Shows, 1966-68, also, Heinz Soup Comml, 1971; appeared in: TV shows including Hello Dolly in, Ohio and Indpls., 1971; tour with Cactus Flower, 1978-79; TV spl. Dames at Sea, 1971, Can Can, 1972; appearances on all talk shows; semi-regular on: Merv Griffin Show; Author: Miller's High Life, 1972, Tops in Taps, 1981. Created dame Knights of Malta; recipient Israeli Cultural award, 1980; Woman of Yr. award Anti-Defamation League, 1980 Home: Beverly Hills, Calif. Died Jan. 22, 2004.

MILLER, ANNE HARMON, lawyer, labor arbitrator; b. Kansas City, Mo., Apr. 28, 1926; d. Harmon and Josephine Anne (Coppinger) Chase; m. Edward Boone Miller, Feb. 14,1969; children: Thomas Christopher Phillips, Sarah Harmon Phillips. AB, St. Louis U., 1947; JD, Loyola U., Chgo., 1968. Bar: Ill. 1968. Editor (with Barreca & Zimny) Labor Arbitrator Development, 1983. Mem. ABA (coun. mem. 1985-91, labor & employment law sect.), Nat. Acad. Arbitrators. Home: Glenview, Ill. Died Dec. 4, 2001.

MILLER, CHARLES GARY, lawyer; b. Bklyn., June 21, 1957; s. Paul and Sandra Cora (Peps) M. BA, Tulane U., 1979; JD, Touro Coll., 1983. Bar: N.Y. 1987. Pvt. practice, N.Y.C., from 1987. Republican. Jewish. Deceased.

MILLER, CHARLES LESLIE, civil engineer, planner, consultant; b. Tampa, Fla., June 5, 1929; s. Charles H. and Myrle Iona (Walstrom) M.; m. Roberta Jean Pye, Sept. 9, 1949; children— Charles Henry, Stephen, Jonathan, Matthew. BCE, MIT, 1951, MCE, 1958. Registered profl. engr., Mass., Fla., Tenn., N.H., R.I., P.R. Successively field engr., project engr., exec. engr. Michael Baker, Jr., Inc. (cons. engrs.), Rochester, Pa., 1951-55; asst. prof. surveying, dir. photogrammetry lab. Mass. Inst. Tech., 1955-59, asso. prof. civil engring., head data engring. div., 1959-61, prof. civil engring., 1961-77, head dept., 1961-70, dir. urban systems lab., 1968-75, dir. civil engring. systems lab., 1961-65, dir. inter-Am. program civil engring., 1961-65, asso. dean engring., 1970-71; cons. engr., 1955—; chmn. bd., sr. cons., pres. CLM Systems, Inc., C.L. Miller Co., Inc. Adviser Commonwealth of P.R; dir. Geo-Transport Found.; Chmn. Pres.-elect's Task Force on Transp., 1968-69 Author: The COGO Book, 1990; contbr. articles to tech. jours. Recipient Outstanding Young Man of Greater Boston award, Computing in Civil Engring. award, 1998. Fellow ASCE (Computing in Civil Engring. award 1998), Am. Acad. Arts and Scis.; mem. Am. Inst. Cons. Engrs., Am. Soc. Engring. Edn. (George Westinghouse award), Am. Soc. Photogrammetry, Am. Congress Surveying and Mapping, Am. Rd. Builders Assn., Transp. Rsch. Bd., Assn. Computing Machinery, Sigma Xi, Chi Epsilon, Tau Beta Pi. Achievements include originating DTM, COGO, ICES, CEAL computer systems. Deceased.

MILLER, DANIEL MARTIN, surgeon, oncologist; b. Edmonton, Alberta, Can., Dec. 16, 1917; came to U.S., 1922; s. David and Lena (Horwich) M.; m. Harriet R. Rosen, Mar. 7, 1943; children: Neil R., Craig R., Alexander R. BS in Medicine, Creighton U., 1938, MD, 1942. Attending surgeon Meth. Hosp., Omaha, 1952-95, Bishop Clarkson Hosp., Omaha, 1952-95; asst. prof. surgery U. Nebr. Med. Sch., Omaha, 1952-55, assoc. prof. surgery, 1955-95. Med. dir. Bishop Clarkson Hosp., 1985-94. Maj. USAF, 1942-46. Mem. AMA, Am. Coll. Surgeons, Am. Assn. Cancer Rsch., Nebr. Med. Assn., Omaha Douglas County Med. Soc., Assn. Clin. Oncology, Ewing Soc. Independent. Jewish. Avocation: fishing. Home: Omaha, Nebr. Died Apr. 10, 1999.

MILLER, DAVID, lawyer, advertising executive; b. Fort Worth, Dec. 12, 1906; s. Max and Tillie (Hoffman) M.; m. Rosalie Agress, Jan 31, 1929; children— Allan David, Martha Sally. AB cum laude, U. Tex., 1926; LL.B. cum laude, Harvard, 1929. Bar: N.Y. State bar 1931. With law firm of Jones, Clark & Higson, N.Y. City, 1929-33; pvt. practice with Harold W. Newman, Jr., 1937-44; mem. law firm of Engel, Judge & Miller, 1944-74; counsel RFC, Washington, 1933-34; asst. gen. counsel Md. Casualty Co., Balt., 1934-36; with Office of Gen. Counsel, Securities & Exchange Commn., 1936-37; v.p. and gen. counsel Young & Rubicam, Inc. (Advt. agy.), 1951-71, sec., dir., sr. v.p., 1971; counsel Squadron, Ellenoff & Plesent, 1974—. V.p., sec., gen. counsel The Music Project for TV, Inc., 1973—; Trustee Motion Picture Players Welfare Fund, Am. Fedn. TV & Radio Artists Pension and Welfare Fund.; Cons. joint policy com. Am. Assn. Advt. Agys.-Assn. Nat. Advertisers. Lecturer on radio and TV law for professional groups.; Editor: Harvard Law Review, 1927-29. Mem. Am. Bar Assn., Assn. Bar City N.Y., N.Y. County Lawyers' Assn., Am. Assn. Advt. Agencies (cons. broadcast business affairs com.), Phi Beta Kappa. Clubs: Harvard (N.Y.). Home: Great Neck, NY. Deceased.

MILLER, JOHN E. retired cardiovascular surgeon; b. Cochranville, Pa., Apr. 25, 1918; s. John Wilbur and Esther Elizabeth (Cunningham) M.; m. Cleta Young, Nov. 25, 1945; children: Bradford, Toy, Kim, Garth. BA, Pa. State, 1938; MD, Jefferson Med. Coll., 1942. Diplomate Am. Bd. General Surgery, Am. Bd. Thoracic Surgery. Fellow thoracic surgery U. Mich., Ann Arbor, 1948-50; chief thoracic and vascular surgery Md. Gen. Hosp., Balt., 1950-86, St. Joseph's Hosp., Towson, Md., 1974-86; ret., 1986. Instr. surgery John Hopkins U., 1971—86; assoc. prof. surgery U. Md., 1973—86. Trustee Bon Secours Hosp., Balt., 1988-96. Capt. USAR, 1943-46. Fellow Am. Coll. Surgeons (Md. chpt. pres. 1966-67), Am. Coll. Chest Physicians; mem. AMA, Am. Thoracic Soc., Am. Heart Assn., Am. Lung Assn. (pres.), So. Assn. Thoracic Surgery, Md. Thoracic Soc. (pres. 1965-67), Md. Lung Assn. (pres. 1977-78), Balt. City Med. Soc., Soc. Thoracic Surgeons, Am. Trauma Soc. (founding mem.). Home: Lutherville Timonium, Md. Died May 30, 2004.

MILLER, JOHN FRANCIS, association executive, social scientist; b. Canton, Ill., Aug. 3, 1908; s. Frank Lewis and Minnie Grace (Fyerly) M.; m. Ruth Roby, May 29, 1937; children: Joan, Kent R., Dana R. AB, U. Ill., 1929, AM, 1930; postgrad., Columbia U., 1930-31, 34-35; German-Am. student exch. fellow, U. Frankfurt on Main, 1931-33. Staff Commn. Inquiry on Pub. Svc. Pers., 1934-35, Regent's Inquiry Character and Cost Pub. Edn., 1936; cons. Pres.'s Com. on Adminstrv. Mgmt., 1936-37, Com. Civil Svc. Improvement, 1939, Inst. Pub. Adminstrn., 1937-38, Pub. Adminstrn. Clearing House, 1938; chief field svc. Nat. Resources Planning Bd., 1938-43; asst. dir. Nat. Planning Assn., 1943-50, asst. chmn., 1951-77, exec. sec., 1951-71, pres., 1971-79, vice chmn., 1977-89, trustee, from 1977. Sec. Canadian-Am. Com., 1957-76, N.Am. sec. Brit.-N.Am. Com., 1969-85 Author: Veteran Preference in the Public Service, 1935. Trustee, mem. adv. com. Nat. Conf. on Family, 1946-49; mem. adv. council social security Senate Com. on Finance, 1947-48. Mem. The Planning Forum, Am. Econ. Assn., Am. Polit. Sci. Assn., Am. Hist. Assn., Cosmos Club (Washington), Univ. Club (N.Y.), Phi Beta Kappa. Home: Chocorua, NH. Died Dec. 28, 1999.

MILLER, LOIS KATHRYN, virology educator; b. Lebanon, Pa., Oct. 8, 1945; d. Clarence Elmer and Naomi Alice (Gibson) M.; m. Karl Edward Espelie, June 13, 1974; 1 child, Erin Marie. BS, Upsala Coll., 1967; PhD, U. Wis., 1972. Postdoctoral fellow Calif. Inst. Tech., Pasadena, 1972-74, Imperial Cancer Rsch. Fund, London, 1974-76; prof. U. Idaho, Moscow, 1976-86, U. Ga., Athens, from 1986. Co-author: Baculovirus Expression Vectors; editor: The Baculoviruses; co-editor: The Insect Viruses; contbr. numerous articles to profl. jours. Recipient Merit award NIH, 1986, Chiron Corp. Biotechnology Rsch. award Am. Soc. Microbiology, 1996. Fellow AAAS (coun. 1987-89), NAS, Am. Soc. Virology (coun. 1989-91), Am. Acad. Microbiology. Achievements include invention of several technologies relating to baculovirus expression vectors and biopesticides. Home: Athens, Ga. Died Nov. 9, 1999.

MILLER, MICHAEL CARL, chemist, researcher; b. Chgo., July 8, 1955; s. Arthur Martin and Mary K. (Brunkala) M.; m. Debra Marie Jakimauskas, Aug. 30, 1981; children: Stephanie Anne, Brenda Michelle. BS in Forensic Chemistry, U. Ill., 1979; postgrad., Roosevelt U., from 1983. Quality assurance chemistry technician William Wrigley Jr. Co., Chgo., 1979-81; R & D analytical chemist Velsicol Chem. Corp., Chgo., 1981-85; R & D sr. chemist materials characterization Helene Curtis Industry, Inc., Chgo., 1985-87; chemistry mgr. Silliker Labs., Chicago Heights, Ill., 1987-88; cons. JEMS Assocs., Glenview, Ill., 1988; rsch. dir. Regenex Rsch. Corp./CJR Processing Inc., Des Plaines, Ill., 1988-93; mgr. product support Bohdan Automation, Mundelein, Ill., 1994-96. Mem. AIChE, ASTM (engine coolant subcom. 1990—, oil and insulation subcoms.), Am. Chem. Soc., Assn. Official Analytical Chemists, U. Ill. Alumni Assn. (life), Trout Unltd. Roman Catholic. Avocations: fly fishing, racquetball, tennis, ping pong/table tennis. Home: Downers Grove, Ill. Died Oct. 21, 2001.

MILLER, RENE HARCOURT, aerospace engineer, educator; b. Tenafly, N.J., May 19, 1916; s. Arthur C. and Elizabeth M. (Tobin) M.; m. Marcelle Hansotte, July 16, 1948 (div. 1968); children: Christal L., John M.; m. Maureen Michael, Nov. 20, 1973. BA, Cambridge U., 1937, MA, 1954. Registered profl. engr., Mass. Aero. engr. G.L. Martin Co., Balt., 1937-39; chief aero. and devel. McDonnell Aircraft Corp., St. Louis, 1939-44; mem. faculty aero. engring. MIT, Cambridge, 1944—, prof., 1957-86, Slater prof. flight transp., 1962-86, head dept. aeros. and astronautics, 1968-78, prof. emeritus, from 1986; v.p. engring. Kaman Aircraft Corp., Bloomfield, Conn., 1952-54. Mem. tech. adv. bd. FAA, 1964-66; mem. Aircraft panel Pres.'s Sci. Adv. Com., 1960-72, Army Sci. Adv. Panel, 1966-73; chmn. Army Aviation Sci. Adv. Group, 1963-73; mem. Air Force Sci. Adv. Bd., 1959-70; com. on aircraft aerodynamics NASA, 1960-70 Contbr. articles to profl. jours. Recipient U.S. Army Decoration for Meritorious Civilian Service, 1967, 70; recipient L.B. Laskowitz award N.Y. Acad. Scis., 1976 Fellow Am. Helicopter Soc. (hon. tech. dir. 1957-59, editor jour. 1957-59, Klemin award, Hon. Nikolski lectr. 1983), AIAA (hon., pres. 1977-78, Sylvanus Albert Reed award), Royal Aero. Soc. (Great Britain); mem. Nat. Acad. Engring., Internat. Acad. Astronautics, Academie National de L'Air et de L'Espace France. Died Jan. 28, 2003.

MILLER, RONALD RU, advertising executive, writer; b. Phila., June 27, 1933; s. Rudolph Wilhelm and Jessie Herbster (Cloward) M.; m. Winona Kate Graf, Dec. 18, 1954; children: Marjorie, Curtis, Christopher, Matthew. Grad. high sch., Phila. Pres. Barbetta-Miller Advt., Upper Montclair, N.J., 1965-76, Gen. Constrn. Equipment Corp., S.I., N.Y., 1970-73; v.p., div. mgr. Hagen Communications Inc., Upper Montclair, N.J., 1976-78; pres. Curtis/Matthews Assocs., Shipbottom, N.J., 1978-89; pres., v.p. mktg. Scurrier Boat Co., Miami, Fla., from 1978; dir. U.S. ops. C M Christopher Assocs., Beach Haven Terrace, N.J., N.Y.C. and Beijing, from 1973. Pres., cons. Ronald R. Miller & Co., Beach Haven Terrace, 1971—. Author: (children's book) Littledog and Souffle, 1985; author: Marketing Construction Products in the United States, 1972, The Long Beach Island Coloring Book, 1981, The European Connection: Marketing Overseas Products in the United States; author annual Complete Guide to Fishing on Long Beach Island. Pres. N.J. chpt. Nat. Leukemia Assn., East Orange, 1975; active Island Civic Players, Surf City, N.J.; mem. Alliance for a Living Ocean, 1988—. With USAF, 1953-57. Named N.J. Advt. Man of Yr. Bus. and Profl. Advt. Assn., Clifton, N.J., 1974. Mem. Long Beach Island Hist. Assn. (exec. com. 1982-87). Clubs: Beach Haven Yacht. Republican. Presbyterian. Avocations: writing, theater, boating, fishing, sports car racing. Home: Beach Haven, NJ. Deceased.

MILLER, SANDRA JEAN, retired special education educator; b. Tonawanda, N.Y., July 15, 1937; d. Glenn W. Sisson and Ruth Ellen Baker; m. David Timothy Miller, Feb. 7, 1970 (dec. Oct. 1988). BS in Edn., SUNY, Buffalo, 1960; postgrad., SUNY, 1960-65, Syracuse U., 1961-65. Tchr. partially sighted Niagara Falls (N.Y.) Bd. Edn., 1960-65, tchr. educable mentally retarded, 1967-69; tchr. spl. edn. Buffalo Bd. Edn., 1965-67; tchr. of learning disabled Niagara Orleans Bd. Coop. Ednl. Svcs., Medina, N.Y., 1969-72; tchr. 5th grade Diocese of Buffalo, Niagara Falls, 1978-79; tchr. visually impaired Erie Bd. Coop. Ednl. Svcs., Lancaster, N.Y., 1979-92. Pres. Niagara Falls Philharmonic Guild, 1978-79. Mem. Coun. Exceptional Children, Assn. Edn. and Rehab. of Blind, Pub. Broadcasting of Western N.Y. (founder's club mem), Art Park and Co., Women of Moose (chmn. libr. com. 1989-91). Avocations: reading, music, piano, needlework, travel. Home: N Tonawanda, NY. Died June 15, 2000.

MILLER, WARREN CANFIELD, secondary school educator; b. Geauga County, Ohio, Nov. 2, 1893; s. William Hale and Millicent Rhoda (Canfield) M.; m. Nelle Elizabeth Dallas, June 5, 1920 (dec. May 1978); children: Donald, Marilyn. BA, Hiram Coll., 1917; MS in Entomology, Ohio State U., 1927. Cert. tchr., Ohio. Prin. pub. sch., Macedonia, Ohio, 1919-23; tchr. music, biology high sch., Bedford, Ohio, 1923-26; prin. Bedford, 1927-53; dir. curriculum, 1953-62. Lectr. entomology. Ensign USN, 1918-19. Mem. NEA, Am. Legion, Ohio Acad. Sci., Ohio Retired Tchrs. Assn., Rotary (life, pres. 1930-31), Sigma Xi. Disciple of Christ. Avocations: studying and lecturing to various organizations, solving insect problems. Home: Silver Lake, Ohio. Deceased.

MILLER, WILLIAM LESLIE, pathologist, laboratory administrator; b. Louisville, May 10, 1934; s. Leslie and Lillie Mae (Parson) M.; m. Hilda Fae Cook, Sept. 3, 1956; children: William Marcus, Leslie Scott, Jennifer Carson, Leslyn Fae. BS, U. Louisville, 1956, MD cum laude, 1959. Diplomate Am. Bd. Pathology; lic. physician, Ky., Ind., Ariz., Tenn., Ill., Mo. Intern Mallory Inst. Pathology, Boston, 1960; resident Mass. Gen. Hosp., Boston, 1961, Louisville Gen. Hosp., 1962-63, staff pathologist, 1963-66, Ft. Walton Beach, Fla., 1968-70; staff pathologist, chief hematopathology Ariz. Med. Ctr., Tucson, 1970-72; staff pathologist, acting chief pathology svc. VA Hosp., Tucson, 1971; vice chmn. and chief clin. pathology U. Tenn. Med. Units, Memphis, 1972-73; dir. hematopathology, dep. dir. clin. lab. City of Memphis Hosps., 1972-73; chief pathologist, dir. labs. Muhlenberg Cmty. Hosp., Greenville, Ky., from 1973. Chmn. tumor bd. Muhlenberg Cmty. Hosp., Greenville, 1989—. Contbr. articles to profl. jours. Capt. M.C. U.S. Army, lt. col. USAR, 1966—. Recipient Mosby Book Co. awards, 1957, 59; NIH Cancer Rsch. fellow, 1961-63; U. Louisville Flexner scholar, 1952-55. Fellow Am. Soc. Clin. Pathologists, Coll. Am. Pathologists, Internat. Assn. Pathologists; mem. AMA, Am. Soc. Hematology, Ky. Soc. Pathology, (pres.), Ky. Med. Assn. (trustee 1989-92), Greenville-Muhlenberg C. of C. (pres.), Kiwanis (chpt. pres.), Alpha Omega Alpha, Phi Kappa Kappa. Republican. Baptist. Avocations: flying, fishing, handy-man projects. Home: Morgantown, Ky. Died Sept. 1, 2001.

MILLS, GARY BERNARD, history educator; b. Marshall, Tex., Sept. 10, 1944; s. Harold Garland and Hazel Cecilia (Rachal) M.; m. Elizabeth Shown; children: Clayton Bernard, Donna Rachal, Daniel Garland. BA in History and Bus. Adminstrn., Delta State U., 1967; MA in History, Miss. State U., 1969, PhD in History, 1974. Instr. history McNeese State U., Lake Charles, La., 1969-72, U. Ctr., Jackson, Miss., 1972-75; asst. prof. U. Ala., Gadsden, 1976-79, assoc. prof., 1979-82, Tuscaloosa, 1982-83, prof. history, 1984[0089]. Cons. in field. Author numerous books; co-editor Nat. Geneal. Soc. Quar., 1987+; contbr. numerous articles to profl. jours. Del. Am.-Russian Archival Adv., Washington, Moscow, Minsk, 1989-91; mem. adv. bd. Archive Am. Minority Cultures, U. Ala., 1983-90. Fellow Huntington Libr., San Marino, Calif., 1988. Fellow Grady McWhiney Hist. Rsch. Found. (sr.); mem. Nat. Geneal. Soc., Am. Hist. Assn., Ala. Hist. Assn., La. Hist. Assn. (bd. dirs. 1972-94), Orgn. Ala. Historians, So. Hist. Assn. (various coms. 1981-86), St. George Tucker Soc. (fellow 1992+). Independent. Roman Catholic. Avocations: music, genealogy. Home: Tuscaloosa, Ala. Died Jan. 26, 2002.

MILLS, HARLAN DUNCAN, software engineer, mathematician, educator; b. Liberty Center, Iowa, Mar. 14, 1919; s. Oral Harlan and Joy Gladys (Duncan) M.; m. Luella Christine Sprecher, June 21, 1940. BSc, Iowa State U., 1948, MS, 1950, PhD, 1952. Pres. Mathematica, Princeton, N.J., 1959-63; fellow Johns Hopkins U., Balt., 1965-73; prof. U. Md., College Park, 1973-87, U. Fla., Gainesville, 1987-88, Fla. Inst. Tech., Melbourne, from 1988; pres. Software Engring. Tech., Vero Beach, Fla., from 1987. Author: Baseball Statistics, 1973, Structured Programming, 1979, Software Productivity, 1983, Information Systems, 1986. Lt. gen. U.S. Army, 1986-90. Hon. fellow Wesleyan U., 1968, IBM fellow IBM Corp., 1964-87. Fellow IEEE; mem. Am. Math. Soc., Am. Statis. Soc., Am. Computing Machinery, Data Processing Mgmt. Assn. (Man of Yr. award 1986). Home: Vero Beach, Fla. Deceased.

MILNER, MAX, food and nutrition consultant; b. Edmonton, Alta., Can., Jan. 24, 1914; came to U.S., 1939, naturalized, 1944; s. Morris Abram and Rose (Lertzman) M.; m. Elizabeth Banen, Aug. 9, 1942; children— Ruth Sharon, Marcia Ann. B.Sc., U. Sask., 1938; LL.D. (hon.), 1979; MS, U. Minn., 1941, PhD, 1945. Research chemist Pillsbury Mills Inc., Mpls., 1939-40; prof. grain sci. and industry Kans. State U., Manhattan, 1947-59; sr. food technologist UNICEF, N.Y.C., 1959-71; chief nutrition br. AID, 1966-67; dir. secretariat protein calorie adv. group UN, 1971-75; assoc. dir. internat. nutrition program M.I.T., 1975-78; exec. officer Am. Inst. Nutrition, Bethesda, Md., 1978-84; mem. U.S. Wheat Industry Council, 1980-83; mem. expert evaluation panel Bd. Internat. Food and Agrl. Devel., 1983—. Chmn. Gordon Research Conf. Food and Nutrition, 1968; Gen. Food Co. (Can.) disting. internat. lectr., 1975 Co-author: Protein Resources and Technology, 1978, Postharvest Biology and Biotechnology, 1978; Editor: Protein-enriched Cereal Foods for World Needs, 1969, Nutrition Improvement of Food Legumes by Breeding, 1975; Contbr. articles to profl. jours., chpts. to monographs. Bd. dirs., exec. com. Meals for Million/Freedom From Hunger Found., 1975-83, cons. in field. Fellow AAAS, Inst. Food Technologists (Internat. award 1968, lectr. sci. series 1971-72, Disting. Food Service award N.Y. sect. 1975), Am. Soc. Nutritional Scis.; mem. Am. Chem. Soc., Am. Assn. Cereal Chemists Home: Chevy Chase, Md. Died Dec. 7, 2002.

MILSTEIN, HENRIETTA, retail executive; Sec., exec. v.p. Burlington (N.J.) Coat Factory. Died Aug. 17, 2001.

MINDEL, ADRIENNE RAUCHWERGER, historian, educator; b. Bayonne, N.J.; d. Joseph and Blanche (Vitriol) Rauchwerger; m. Robert G. Spivack, 1940 (dec. 1970); children— Lorna Ellen Spivack, Miranda Sheila Spivack; m. 2d, Joseph Mindel, 1975. B.A., NYU, 1941; M.A., Am. U., 1966, Ph.D., 1976. Editorial assoc. Roscoe Drummond, newspaper columnist, Washington, 1960-63; teaching asst. Am. U., Washington, 1966-68, Massey fellow, 1968-69, univ. fellow, 1969-70; asst. prof. history Hood Coll., Frederick, Md., 1970-76, assoc. prof., 1976-84, prof., 1984—; commentator Duquesne U. History Forum, 1985; mem. Wye faculty seminar Aspen Inst., 1983; cons. town planning Town of Reston (Va.), 1963-64; humanities scholar and panelist Md. Com. for Humanities, 1977, 78, com. mem., 1979-86; panelist Western Soc. for French Hist. Annual Conf., 1986. Assoc. editor Contemporary Affairs, 1963-64; contbg. editor: China and U.S. Far East Policy, 1967; contbr. articles to profl. jours. Mem. Va. Gildersleeve Internat. Fund for Univ. Women, 1981—; mem. Md. br. Nat. Coordinating Com. for Promotion of History, 1982—, AAUW Coll. Faculty Program scholar, 1964. Mem. Am. Hist. Assn., French Hist. Studies Assn., AAUP, AAUW, So. Assn. Women Historians, Phi Alpha Theta. Deceased.

MINER, JAN, actress; b. Boston, Oct. 15, 1917; d. Walter Curtis and Ethel Lindsey (Chase) M.; Richard Merrell, May 5, 1963. Student, Vesper George Sch. Design, Boston, 1937; studies with Don Richardson, Ira Cirker, Lee Strasberg, N.Y.C. Mem. Am. Shakespeare Co., Stratford, Conn. Broadway appearances: Heartbreak House (with Rex Harrison and Amy Irving), Watch on the Rhine (directed by Arrim Brown), Romeo and Juliet, Circle in the Square for Ted Mann, The Heiress, Saturday Sunday Monday (directed by Franco Zepperelli), The Women, Othello, Lady of the Camelias; TV appearances: Cagney and Lacey, Friends and Lovers, Picasso/Net, Robert Montgomery Presents, Great Performances Out of Our Father's House, PBS Great Performanaces, CBS Studio One, NYPD, The Jackie Gleason Show, Cire T.V., Gertrude Stein and a Companion (ACE award nomination for Best Actress, stage and film directed by Ira Cerker), Stood Up (ABC Afterschool Spl.), others; films: Lenny, Willie and Phil, Endless Love, For the Women (directed by Monton DaCosta, Internat. Film award) Mermaids, 1990; regional and off-Broadway stage appearances include Peg O' My Heart, Glass Menagerie, Astopova, Creve Couer, Danndy Dick, Gertrude Stein and a Companion, Philadelphia Story, The Showoff, Major Barbara, The Music Keeper, Night Must Fall, Eve, Ladies in Retirement; portrayed Madge in TV comml. for Palmolive Liquid. Recipient Radio Favorite Dramatic Actress award 1950, 51, 52, 53, 54, 55, 56, 57, Outer Circle Critics award, Internat. Film award, Chgo. Film award, Emmé award for Best Film, ACE award nomination for Best Actress, Blue Ribbon award Chgo. Internat. Film Festival, Silve Hugo award Am. Film Inst., 1987, Nat. Ednl. Film and Video Bronze Apple award, ACE award Theatrical Spl. Best Actress award, 1987. Home: Southbury, Conn. Died Feb. 15, 2004.

MINER, JOHN RONALD, bioengineer; b. Scottsburg, Ind., July 4, 1938; s. Gerald Lamont and Alice Mae (Murphy) M.; m. Betty Katheron Emery, Aug. 4, 1963; children: Saralena Marie, Katherine Alice, Frederick Gerald. BSChemE, U. Kans., 1959; MS in San. Engring., U. Mich., 1960; PhD in Chem. Engring. and Microbiology, Kans. State U., 1967. Lic. profl. engr., Kans., Oreg. San. engr. Kans. Dept. Health, Topeka, 1959-64; grad. rsch. asst. Kans. State U., Manhattan, 1964-67; asst. prof. agrl. engring. Iowa State U., 1967-71, assoc. prof., 1971-72; assoc. prof. agrl. engring. Oreg. State U., 1972-76, prof., from 1976, head dept., 1976-86, acting assoc. dean Coll. Agrl. Sci., 1983-84, assoc. dir. Office Internat. R & D, 1986-90, ext. water quality specialist, 1991—2003; environ. engr. FAO of UN, Singapore, 1980-81. Fulbright scholar U. Malawi, 1997-98; internat. cons.; cons. to livestock feeding ops., agrl. devel. firms. Co-author 2 books on livestock waste mgmt.; author 3 books of children's sermons; contbr. numerous articles on livestock prodn., pollution control, control of odors associated with livestock prodn. to profl. publs. Fellow Am. Soc. Agrl. Engrs. (bd. dirs. 1985-87); mem. Water Pollution Control Fedn., Sigma Xi, Gamma Sigma Delta, Alpha Epsilon, Tau Beta Pi. Presbyterian. Home: Corvallis, Oreg. Died Feb. 10, 2004.

MINES, HERBERT THOMAS, executive recruiter; b. Fall River, Mass., Jan. 30, 1929; s. Abraham and Fanny (Lepes) M.; m. Barbara Goldberg, Oct. 23, 1960; 1 child, Susan. BS in Econs., Babson Coll., 1949; MS in Indsl. and Labor Rels., Cornell U., 1954. Supr., asst. buyer, employment supr. G. Fox & Co., Hartford, Conn., 1949-52; adminstr. divsn. tng.-exec. devel. and orgn. planning R.H. Macy & Co., N.Y.C., 1954-66; v.p. pers. Neiman Marcus Co., Dallas, 1966-68, sr. v.p. pers., 1968-70; v.p. pers. Revlon, Inc., N.Y.C., 1970-73; pres. Bus. Careers, Inc., 1973-78, chmn., 1978-81; pres. Exec. Search and Cons. divsn. Wells Mgmt. Corp., 1978-81, Herbert Mines Assocs., Inc., 1981-93, chmn., CEO, 1993-99, chmn., 1999—2004. Mem. editl. bd. Commentary Mag., bd. dirs.; contbr. articles to trade publs. Bd. dirs. Fashion Inst. Tech., Am. Jewish Com., Assn. of Exec. Search Cons. Died Mar. 2004.

MINICUCCI, ANERICO JOSEPH, construction executive, engineer; b. New Rochelle, N.Y., Apr. 2, 1925; m. Mary Louise Wenk, May 7, 1959; children: Mary Alice, Laura Jean, Americo Jr., Sean Martin. BS in Civil Engring., Columbia U., 1949. Registered profl. engr. Constrn. supt. Pettinicichi Corp., White Plains, N.Y., 1949-52; chief field engr. Madrid, 1954-56; chief constrn. dept. U.S. Army, Columbia, Md., 1956 84; pres. Maric Corp., Atlanta, from 1984; chief exec. officer Replacement Plus, Atlanta, from 1986. Bd. dirs. GO-Internat., Atlanta; bd. dirs., engr., supt. pub. works Peach Tree City, Ga., 1985; cons. Calif. Sparkman-Photo, 1989—, Lawn Care Specialist, Peachtree City, 1988—. Author: Abstract Photo, 1989. Chmn. Am. Heart Fund, Fayette, Ga.; mem. Nat. Rep. Congl. Com., 1981—. Sgt. U.S. Army, 1943-45, PTO. Decorated Purple Heart (with oak leaf cluster); recipient Cert. of Appreciation, HQ Forscom, 1986. Mem. Kiwanis (publicity chmn. Peachtree City chpt. 1989—, Disting. Svc. award 1988, Outstanding Kiwanian award 1989). Avocations: boating, fishing, photography, bicycle riding, writing. Home: Peachtree City, Ga. Deceased.

MINK, PATSY TAKEMOTO, congresswoman; b. Paia, Maui, Hawaii, Dec. 6, 1927; d. Suematsu and Mitama (Tateyama) Takemoto; m. John Francis Mink, Jan. 27, 1951; 1 child, Gwendolyn. Student, Wilson Coll., 1946, U. Nebr., 1947; BA, U. Hawaii, 1948; LLD, U. Chgo., 1951; DHL (hon.), Chaminade Coll., 1975, Syracuse U., 1976, Whitman Coll., 1981. Bar: Hawaii. Pvt. practice, Honolulu, 1953-65; lectr. U. Hawaii, 1952-56, 59-62, 79-80; atty. Territorial Ho. of Reps., 1955; mem. Hawaii Ho. of Reps., 1956-58, Ter. Hawaii Senate, 1958-59, Hawaii State Senate, 1962-64, Congresses from 2nd Hawaii dist., 1965—77, 1991—2002; mem. edn. and workforce com., mem. budget com.; mem. com. on govt. reform 106th Congresses from 2d dist. Hawaii. Mem. govt. reform com., mem. U.S. del. to UN Law of Sea, 1975-76, Internat. Woman's Yr., 1975, UN Environ. Program, 1977, Internat. Whaling Commn., 1977; asst. sec.

of state U.S. Dept. State, 1977-78. Charter pres. Young Dem. Club Oahu, 1954-56, Ter. Hawaii Young Dems., 1956-58; del. Dem. Nat. Conv., 1960, 72, 80; nat. v.p. Young Dem. Clubs Am., 1957-59; v.p. Ams. for Dem. Action, 1974-76, nat. pres., 1978-81; mem. nat. adv. com. White House Conf. on Families, 1979-80; mem. nat. adv. coun. Federally Employed Women. Recipient Leadership for Freedom award Roosevelt Coll., Chgo., 1968, Alii award 4-H Clubs Hawaii, 1969, Nisei of Biennium award, Freedom award Honolulu chpt. NAACP, 1971, Disting. Humanitarian award YWCA, St. Louis, 1972, Creative Leadership in Women's Rights award NEA, 1977, Human Rights award Am. Fedn. Tchrs., 1975, Feminist of Yr. award Feminist Majority Found., 1991, Margaret Brent award ABA, 1992, Outstanding Woman of Yr. award Nat. Assn. Profl. Am. Women, 1992, Environ. Leadership award Nat. League Conservation Voters, 1993, Jessie Bernard Wise Women award Ctr. for Women Policy Studies, 1993, Hawaii's Health Mother award, 1994, Hispanic Health Leadership award, 1995, Women Work! Nat. Network for Women's Employment, 1995, Women at Work Pub. Policy award, 1995, Justice in Action award Asian Am. Legal Def. and Edn. Fund, 1996, Daniel K. Inouye award Hawaii Psychol. Assn., 1996, Indsl. Union Dept. Lewis-Murray-Reuther Social Justice award AFL-CIO, 1996, Top Rating for Global Internat. Trade Watch, Pub. Citizens/Nat. Farmers Union/Friends of the Earth, 1996, award Inferfaith IMPACT for Justice and Peace, 1996, Hawaii Coun. on Lang. Planning and Policy cert. for opposition to English-only legislation, 1996, Hawai'i Women Lawyers Lifetime Achievement award 1997, Legis. Leadership award Nat. Assn. of WIC Dirs., 1997, Judges of the US Dist. Ct., Dist. of Hawaii and Hawaii Chpt. of the Fed. Bar Assn.Lifetime Membership Award, 2002. Democrat. Died Sept. 28, 2002.

MINKOFF, HARVEY ALLEN, English educator; b. N.Y.C., Apr. 9, 1944; s. Michael and Mildred (Falk) M. BA in English, CCNY, 1965, MA in Am. studies, 1966; PhD in Linguistics, CUNY, 1970. Adj. lectr. CCNY, 1966; tchg. fellow CUNY, 1967-68; asst. prof. Iona Coll., New Rochelle, N.Y., 1968-71, Hunter Coll., N.Y.C., 1971-76, assoc. prof., 1976-91, prof. English and linquistics, from 1991. Author: Mysteries of The Dead Sea Scrolls, 1998, The Book of Heaven, 1996, Exploring America, 1995; editor: Approaches to the Bible, 2 vols., 1994-95; editor Peer Tutoring newsletter, 1975-76; mng. editor Empire State Investigator, 1979-89; contbr. articles to profl. jours. Youth leader Temple Beth Shalom, Mahopec, N.Y., 1983-95; adult edn. vol. Congregaton Agudath Israel, Caldwell, N.J., 1996—. Mem. Am. Fedn. tchrs., Linguistic Soc. Am., Am. Jewish History Soc. Home: N Caldwell, NJ. Died May 4, 2002.

MINOT, OTIS NORTHROP, writer, researcher; b. Cambridge, Mass., Nov. 2, 1916; s. Henry Davis and Harriet (Northrop) M.; m. Edna Louise Gross; children: Edward Otis, Alfred Henry, David Thomas. AB in Physics, Harvard U., 1939, EdD, 1954. Asst. dean Coll. Harvard U., Cambridge, 1946-48, asst. dean Bus. Sch., 1950-52; researcher NSC, Washington, 1949-50, Minot Informatic Devices, Lexington, Mass., 1953-56, Lexington Rsch., 1960-67, 71-81; electronic scientist USN Electronics Lab., San Diego, 1957-60; lectr. U. Mass., Boston, 1968-71, acting dir. admissions, 1968; rsch., writer Brunswick, Maine, from 1981. Pres. Inventors Coop. Svc., Lexington, 1957-60; sec., treas. first Internat. Joint Conf. on Artificial Intelligence, Washington, sect. chmn. second conf., London. Author children's books, 1960—; inventor 2 U.S. patents on electrical devices; achievements include research in Fechner Benham effect and mixed cathode ray tube phosphors.; contbr. articles on artificial intelligence to profl. jours. Sustaining membership chmn. Boy Scouts Am., La Jolla, Calif., 1959-60; contbg. corr. Simulation in Svc. Society, La Jolla, 1965—; trustee Browne and Nichols Sch., Cambridge, 1968-72. Lt. comdr. USN, 1941-45, ret. Mem. IEEE, Soc. for Computer Simulation, Assn. Ind. Researchers and Cons. (coord. 1965-91), Third Friday Munch Soc. (Lexington, co-founder), Mere Point Yacht Club (sec. 1986-92), Phi Delta Kappa. Unitarian Universalist. Avocations: tennis, woodworking, writing stories. Deceased.

MINTON, SHERMAN ANTHONY, medical zoologist; b. New Albany, Ind., Feb. 24, 1919; s. Sherman and Gertrude (Gurtz) M.; m. Madge Shortridge Rutherford, Oct. 10, 1943; children: Brooks, April, Holly. AB, Ind. U., 1939, MD, 1942. Asst. prof. Ind. U. Sch. Medicine, Indpls., 1947-58; vis. prof. Jinnah Postgrad. Med. Ctr., Karachi, Pakistan, 1958-62; assoc. prof. Ind. U. Sch. Medicine, Indpls., 1963-71, prof., 1971-84, prof. emeritus, from 1984. Rsch. assoc. Am. Mus. Natural History, N.Y.C., 1957—; tropical med. fellow La. State U., Baton Rouge, 1957; vis. prof. U. New Eng., Armidale, Australia, 1980. Co-author: Venomous Reptiles, 1969, Giant Reptiles, 1973; author: Venom Diseases, 1974. Lt. USN, 1943-46, PTO. Fellow Ind. Acad. Sci.; mem. Internat. Soc. Toxinology (pres. 1966-68, Redi award 1985), Am. Soc. Ichthyologists and Herpetologists, Am. Soc. Tropical Medicine and Hygiene, Soc. for Study of Amphibians and Reptiles (pres. 1986), Herpetologists League, N.Y. Acad. Sci. Avocations: photography, swimming. Home: Indianapolis, Ind. Died Jun. 1, 1999.

MIRACLE, ROBERT WARREN, retired banker; b. Casper, Wyo. m. Maggie Zanoni; children: Mark, John BS in Law, U. Wyo., 1951; grad. with honors, Pacific Coast Banking Sch., 1960. With Wyo. Nat. Bank (now Norwest Bank Casper N.A.), 1954-91; exec. v.p. Wyo. Nat. Bank of Casper, 1967; pres., chief exec. officer Wyo. Nat. Bank of Casper (now Norwest Bank Casper N.A.)_, 1968-87; chmn. Wyo. Nat. Bank of Casper (formerly Norwest Bank Casper N.A.), 1983-91, also bd. dirs.; pres., chief exec. officer, dir. Wyo. Nat. Bancorp. (formerly Affiliated Bank Corp Wyo.), Casper, 1970-91; mgr. Kemmerer LaBarge Royalties LLC, from 1999. Instr. bank mgmt. U. Colo., 1971-75. Bd. dirs. United Fund of Natrona County, Wyo., 1963-85, campaign co-chmn., 1973-78; trustee The Myra Fox Skelton Found., 1963—, Goodstein Found., 1992—; bd. dirs., pres. Investment in Casper, 1967-70; Wyo. treas. Radio Free Europe, 1967-72; trustee Casper Coll. Foun., 1967-91, pres., 1973-75, 85-91; trustee U. Wyo. Found., 1972-87; chmn. Casper Downtown Improvement Assn., 1974-75; bd. dirs. Cen. Wyo. Fair Bd., 1974-79, pres., 1977-78; dir. Mountain States Employers Coun., 1979-91; bd. dirs. Wyo. Natural Gas Pipeline Authority, 1991-97; trustee Meml. Hosp. Natrona County, 1993-96, pres. 1995-96; bd. dirs. Wyo. Med. Ctr., 1996-99. Capt. USMC, 1951-53. Recipient James C. Scarboro Meml. award Colo. Sch. Banking., 1977; Disting. Service in Bus. award U. Wyo. Coll. Commerce and Industry, 1980 Mem. Wyo. Bankers Assn. (chmn. legis. com. 1969-80, pres. 1974-75), Am. Bankers Assn. (mem. governing coun. 1974-75, 81-83), Am. Mgmt. Assn., Rocky Mountain Oil and Gas Assn., Newcomer Soc. in N.Am., Casper C. of C. (pres. 1965-66, Disting. Svc. award 1981), VFW, Casper Petroleum Club, Casper Country Club (pres. 1993-94), Casper Rotary Club (hon. Rotarian award 1996-97), Masons, Lions. Home: Casper, Wyo. Died Sept. 11, 2002.

MIRISCH, MARVIN ELLIOT, motion picture producer; b. N.Y.C., Mar. 19, 1918; s. Max and Josephine (Urbach) M.; m. Florene Smuckler, Dec. 28, 1941; children— Donald, Carol, Lynn. BA, Coll. City N.Y., 1940. With contract and print depts., then office mgr. Grand Nat. Films, Inc., N.Y.C., 1936-40; organized theatre concession bus. Theatres Candy Co., Inc., Milw., 1940; exec., corporate officer Allied Artists Pictures Corp., Hollywood, Calif., 1953-57; co-organizer Mirisch Co., Inc. (motion picture producers), Hollywood, Calif., 1957, v.p., dir., 1957—; chmn., chief exec. officer Mirisch Prodns., Inc., 1968—. Chmn. permanent charities com. Motion Picture and TV Industries. (Recipient Best Picture of Year award Acad. Motion Picture Arts and Scis. for The Apartment, 1961, West Side Story, 1962, In the Heat of the Night 1968, Producer of Year award Nat. Assn. Theatre Owners 1972). Bd. govs. Cedars-Sinai Med. Ctr. Mem. Assn. Motion Picture and TV Producers Am. (dir., vice-chmn.), Los Angeles Art Inst., Acad. Motion Picture Arts and Scis. (bd. govs., 1st v.p.) Clubs: Motion Picture Pioneers, Hillcrest Country. Jewish. Home: Los Angeles, Calif. Died Nov. 17, 2002.

MIRRIELEES, JAMES FAY, III, publishing executive; b. Cin., Nov. 2, 1939; s. James Fay and Alicia Lucille (Beatty) M.; m. Gillian C. Hanlon, July, 1986; 1 child, Hillary Evan, from previous marriage. BA, U. Cin. Editorial dir. McGraw-Hill Coll. Pub. Co., N.Y.C., 1975-77; v.p. Holt-Rinehart & Winston, N.Y.C., 1977-79; pres. CBS Coll. Pub., N.Y.C., 1979-81, 83-85, CBS Internat. Pub., 1981-83; mng. dir. European ops. Ashton-Tate, London, 1985-86; pres. Somerset House Edn. and Profl. Pubs., 1986-87; chief exec. officer Raintree Pub. Inc., 1987-88; chmn., pres. Raintree I Ltd. Partnership, 1988-91; pres. Coronet/MTI Film & Video, Deerfield, Ill., 1991-93; v.p. mktg. Edunetics Corp., Arlington, Va., 1993-95; v.p. bus. devel. Jennings & Keefe Media, 1995; pres. Blue Aegean Media, Arlington, Va., from 1996; mng. ptnr. Waterside E-Ventures, Arlington, Va., 2000—01; exec. v.p. Digital Learning Interactive, 2001—02. Democrat. Died Jan. 25, 2004.

MIRRO, ROBERT, pediatrician, educator; b. Pitts., Mar. 15, 1951; s. Joseph and Romilda (Sacchet) M.; children: Benjamin, Andrea. BS, Pa. State U., 1973; MD, Temple U., 1977. Intern Children''s Hosp., Pitts., resident, fellow; asst. prof. pediatrics U. Toronto (Can.), 1982-85; assoc. prof. pediatrics U. Tenn., Memphis, from 1985. Contbr. articles to scholarly and profl. jours. Clin. Investigator award NIH, 1986. Mem. Am. Acad. Pediatrics, Soc. Pediatric Rsch., Am. Physiol. Soc. Deceased.

MIRSKY, SONYA WOHL, librarian, curator; b. N.Y.C., Nov. 12, 1925; d. Louis and Anna (Steiger) Wohl; m. Alfred Ezra Mirsky, Aug. 24, 1967 (dec. June 1974). BS in Edn., CCNY, 1948; MSL.S., Columbia U., 1950. Asst. libr. Rockefeller U., N.Y.C., 1949-60, assoc. libr., 1960-77, univ. libr., 1977-91, univ. libr. emeritus, from 1991. Trustee Med. Libr. Ctr. N.Y., 1965-91, v.p., 1980-88; cons. libr. mgmt. Mem. Bibliog. Soc. Am., Bibliog. Soc. Can., Bibliog. Soc. Gt. Britain, Soc. Bibliography of Natural History Home: New York, NY. Died Apr. 18, 2003.

MISHLER, JACOB, federal judge; b. N.Y.C., Apr. 20, 1911; s. Abraham and Rebecca M.; m. Lola Mishler, Sept. 1, 1936; m. Helen Mishler, Aug. 26, 1970; children: Alan, Susan Lubitz; stepchildren: Bruce Shillet, Gail Shillet Unger. Degree, NYU, 1931, JD, 1933. Pvt. practice, L.I. City, N.Y., 1934-50; ptnr. Mishler & Wohl, 1950-59, 60; judge N.Y. State Supreme Ct., 1959; sr. judge U.S. Dist. Ct. (ea. dist.), Uniondale, NY, 1960—2004; chief judge U.S. Dist. Ct., 1969-80. Mem. U.S. Jud. Conf., Dist. Judge Rep., 2nd cir., 1974-77. Died Jan. 26, 2004.

MITBY, NORMAN PETER, college president; b. Cashton, Wis., May 21, 1916; s. Chester M. and Margaret (Murray) M.; m. Luvern J. Jensen, June 15, 1941; children: John C., Margaret N. BS, Whitewater (Wis.) State Coll., 1938; postgrad., U. Wis., 1947-48; MS, Stout State U., 1949. Tchr. high sch., vocat. sch., Cornell, Wis., 1938-41, Antigo, Wis., 1941-46; asst. dir. LaCrosse (Wis.) Vocat. and Adult Schs., 1946-54; dir. vocat. and adult sch. Oshkosh, Wis., 1954-55, Green Bay, Wis., 1955-60, Madison, Wis., 1960-67; dist. dir. tech. and adult edn. dist. Madison Area Tech. Coll., 1967, pres., 1967-88; prof. Stout State U. Grad. Sch., Menomonie, Wis. Mem. adv. council U. Wis. Schs. Edn., Madison and Milw., 1961-64; cons., examiner North Central Assn. Colls. and Secondary Schs., 1970-88; mem. pres.'s adv. com. Assn. Community Coll. Trustees, 1978-79; mem. joint adminstrv. com. on acad. programs U. Wis. Vocat., Tech. and Adult Edn. System, 1985-88. Mem. Community Welfare Council Madison, 1960-63, mem. needs and priorities com., 1964; sponsor Wis. Heart Assn.; chmn. pub. employees div. Cancer Fund drive, 1963; mem. Mayor's Com. for Employment Handicapped, 1964-68, Nat. Adv. Com. on Health Occupations Tng., 1964-68; chmn. gov.'s adv. com. Title I, Higher Edn. Act, 1965-74; mem. adv. council Midwest Community Coll., Leadership Council, 1968-73; mem. Wis. Gov.'s Adv. Council on Vocat. Edn., 1969-74, Wis. Gov.'s Health Planning and Policy Task Force, 1971-73; adv. com. Wis. State Bd. Nursing, 1972-74; mem. Wis. Council Safety, 1960-73; bd. dirs. Madison Civic Music Assn., 1960-88, Oakwood Found. Inc., 1990-97. Recipient Disting. Svc. Alumni award U. Wis.-Whitewater, Spl. award NAACP, 1987, cert. recognition Phi Delta Kappa-U. Wis. chpt., 1987, Rotary Sr. Svc. award, 1992, award for advocating equal opportunity initiative at Madison Area Tech. Coll., 1998; named to Madison Area Tech. Coll. Athletic Hall of Fame, 1989; Paul Harris fellow, 1998. Mem. Am. Assn. Community and Jr. Colls. (dir. 1975-78, Leadership award 1988), Am. Vocat. Assn. Merit award Region 3 1988), Wis. Assn. for Vocat. and Adult Edn. (Disting. Svc. award 1988), Wis. Assn. Dirs. Vocat. and Adult Edn. (pres. 1960-61), Sigma Tau Gamma, Epsilon Pi Tau, Delta Pi Epsilon. Clubs: Rotarian, Elk, Nakoma Golf. Home: Madison, Wis. DIED 1999.

MITCHELL, ARTHUR HARRIS, newspaper columnist; b. St. John, N.B., Can., Nov. 8, 1916; s. Stuart Campbell and Marjorie (Harris) M.; m. Mary Moliawko, Nov. 6, 1944; children: John Stuart, Marjorie Starr. Student, Columbia Sch. Journalism, 1945-46. Travelling freelance writer various U.S., Can. mags., 1946-48; syndicated newspaper columnist, from 1971; editor Mitchell Press Ltd., Vancouver, B.C.; founding editor Can. Pulp and Paper Industry mag., Western Homes & Living mag., 1948-66; editor Can. Homes mag., Southstar Publs. Ltd., Toronto, Ont., 1967-80; Can. cons. Time-Life Books, N.Y.C., 1976-82. Author: You Wanted to Know, 1971, Easy Furniture Finishing, 1974, The Basement Book, 1977. Served with Brit. and U.S. Mcht. Marine, 1940-45. Home: Scarborough, Canada. Died Oct. 17, 2003.

MITCHELL, HERBERT HALL, former university dean, educational consultant; b. New Market, Ala., Dec. 10, 1916; s. Walter Hall and Vera Pearl (Johnston) M.; m. Audrey Elizabeth Taylor, Oct. 30, 1942; children: William Hall, Robert Michael, Richard Lee, Mary Ann. BS, U. Ala., 1939, MS, 1950; PhD, U. N.C., 1954. Asst. to dean of men U. Ala., 1939-42, asst. dean of men, 1942-43, asst. to dean of students, 1946-48; instr. U. N.C., 1948-51; asst. prof. Ala. Poly. Inst., 1951-55, assoc. prof., 1955-56; prof., head dept. bus. adminstrn. Miss State U., 1956-60; prof., chmn. dept. bus. adminstrn. Va. Poly. Inst., 1960-61, dean Sch. Bus., 1961-81, dean emeritus, 1981—2003; dean Coll. Commerce and Bus. Adminstrn. U. Ala., 1981-86, dean emeritus, 1986—2003; ednl. cons. and lectr., 1986—2003. Vis. prof. finance grad. program in England and Germany U. Ark., 1972; mem. adv. bd. Intercollegiate Case Clearing House, Harvard U., 1973-76, 77-78 Contbr. articles to jours. Bd. dirs. Ala. Council Econ. Edn., 1982—; trustee Joint Council on Econ. Edn., 1982-86. Capt. Transp. Corps, AUS, 1943-46, col. Res., ret. Edn. fellow Joseph T. Ryerson & Son, Inc., Chgo., summer 1956 Mem. So Bus. Adminstrn. Assn. (pres. 1968-69), Am. Assembly Collegiate Schs. Bus. (dir. 1973-80, v.p. 1977, pres. 1978), Anderson Soc., Ret. Officers Assn., West Ala. Ret. Officers Club (pres. 1989), Indian Hills Country Club, Rotary, Phi Eta Sigma, Delta Sigma Pi, Beta Alpha Psi, Omicron Delta Epsilon, Beta Gamma Sigma (nat. bd. govs. 1980-84), Omicron Delta Kappa (G. Burke Johnston award 1981), Mu Kappa Tau, Gamma Iota Sigma. Methodist. Home: Tuscaloosa, Ala. Died Oct. 30, 2003.

MITCHELL, JACOB NEAFIE, lawyer; b. Hartford, Conn., Nov. 15, 1919; s. Jacob Neafie and Madelin L. (Gray) M.; m. Jane Spotts, Sept. 26, 1942; children— Edward S., Patricia Mitchell Fegley, Christine Mitchell Fox, Susan Mitchell Nagy. Ph.B., Dickinson Coll. 1941; LL.B., Dickinson Sch. Law, 1943. Bar: Pa. 1946, U.S. Dist. Ct. (mid. dist.) Pa. 1949, U.S. Ct. Appeals (3d cir.) 1980. Assoc. Candor, Youngman & Gibson, Williamsport, Pa., 1946-51, ptnr. 1951-64; ptnr. Greevy, Knittle & Mitchell, Williamsport, 1964-75; sr. ptnr. Mitchell & Mitchell, Williamsport, 1976-80; pres. Mitchell, Mitchell & Gray, P.C., Williamsport, 1980—. Served with USN 1943-46. Mem. ABA, Lycoming Law Assn. (pres. 1959, chmn. med.-legal com. 1974-81, chmn. pub. relations com. 1964-75, bench-bar com. 1983—), Pa. Bar Assn. (bd. govs. 1959-60, ethics com. 1969-70), Pa. Trial Lawyers Assn., Pa. Def. Inst., Def. Research Inst., Am. Judicature Soc. Republican. Episcopalian. Clubs: Williamsport Wheel, Ross (Williamsport), Antlers Country (Williamsport); Grays Run Hunting (Trout Run, Pa.). Home: Williamsport, Pa. Died June 8, 1996.

MITCHELL, JAMES (WILLIAM) (JAMES MUNRO), writer; b. 1926; Lectr. in English South Shields Tech. Coll., 1950-59; TV writer London, 1959-63; lectr. in Liberal Studies Sunderland Coll. of Art, 1963-64. Author: The Lady is Waiting, 1958, The Way Back, 1960, Steady Boys Steady, 1960, Among Arabian Sands, 1962, Magnum for Schneider, 1969, A Red File for Callan, 1971, Ilion Like a Mist, 1969,

The Winners, 1970, Russian Roulette, 1973, Death and Bright Water, 1974, Smear Job, 1975, The Evil Ones, 1982, Sometimes You Could Die, 1985, Dead Ernest, 1986, Dying Day, 1988, A Woman to be Loved, 1990, An Impossible Woman, 1992, Leading Lady, 1993; (as James Munro) The Man Who Sold Death, 1964, Die Rich, Die Happy, 1965, The Money That Money Can't Buy, 1967, The Innocent Bystanders, 1969. Died Sept. 15, 2002.

MITCHELL, LUCIUS QUINN, financial management consultant, real estate consultant; b. Atlanta, Dec. 12, 1959; s. Lucius R. and Dorothy (Nash) M. Student, Cornell Coll., 1977-78; BA cum laude, Morehouse Coll., 1981. Acct. and fin. Equitable Real Estate, Atlanta, 1980-85; intern Equitable Life Ins., N.Y., 1980, appraisal trainee, intern Atlanta, 1981-82; v.p. Cen. Atlantic Realty Co., Inc., Atlanta, 1985-87; pres. So. Am., Atlanta, 1984-86; v.p. Atlantic Assn., Inc., Atlanta, from 1985; vice chmn. Rogers & Logan, Inc., Atlanta, 1986-87; v.p. The Hines Bus Network, Inc., Atlanta, 1987-88; pres. Global Real Estate and Investment Co., Atlanta, from 1988. Co-founder Socius Strata, Inc., Atlanta, 1982—; mem. Hist. Oakland Cemetery, Inc., Atlanta, 1984—, Metro Fair Housing, Inc., Decatur, Ga., 1979—; pres. Westside Bus. and Community Assn., 1990—; acting chmn. Olympic Games Community Coalition, 1990-91; chmn. Community Countdown Coalition, Inc., 1991—. Mem. Jr. Entrepreneurial Traders Assn. (charter), Jaycees (Outstanding Young Man Am. 1983), Westside Bus. and Community Assn. (pres. 1990—). Congregationalist. Avocations: photography, travel, tennis, writing. Home: Atlanta, Ga. Deceased.

MITCHELL, MAURICE MCCLELLAN, JR., chemist, researcher; b. Lansdowne, Pa., Nov. 27, 1929; s. Maurice McClellan and Agnes Stewart (Kerr) M.; m. Marilyn M. Badger, June 14, 1952. BS in Chemistry, Carnegie-Mellon U., 1951, MS in Chemistry, 1957, PhD in Phys. Chemistry, 1960. Group leader rsch. and devel. U.S. Steel Corp., Pitts., 1951-61; br. head phys. chemistry rsch. and devel. Melpar Inc., Falls Church, Va., 1961-64; group leader rsch. and devel. Atlantic Richfield Co., Phila., 1964-73; dir. rsch. and devel. Houdry div. Air Products and Chems., Inc., 1973-81, Ashland (Ky.) Oil Inc., 1981-86, v.p. rsch. and devel., 1986-93; vis. lectr. dept. chem. Coll. Arts and Scis. Ohio U. Southern Campus, Ironton, 1993-96. Cons. in field, 1993. Contbr. articles to profl. jours.; patentee in field. Fellow Am. Inst. Chemists; mem. Am. Chem. Soc., Am. Inst. Chem. Engrs., Catalysis Soc. N.Am. (pres. 1985-89), AAAS, Sigma Xi. Died Apr. 18, 2003.

MITCHELL, ROY DEVOY, industrial engineer; b. Hot Springs, Ark., Sept. 11, 1922; s. Watson W. and Marie (Stewart) M.; m. Jane Caroline Gibson, Feb. 14, 1958; children: Michael, Marilyn, Martha, Stewart, Nancy. BS, Okla. State U., 1948, MS, 1950; B of Indsl. Mgmt., Auburn U., 1960. Registered profl. engr., Ala., Miss. Instr. Odessa (Tex.) Coll., 1953-56; prof. engring. graphics Auburn (Ala.) U., 1956-63; field engr. HHFA, Cmty. Facilities Adminstrn., Atlanta and Jackson, Miss., 1963-71; area engr. Met. Devel. Office, HUD, 1971-72, chief architecture and engring., 1972-75, chief program planning and support br., 1975, dir. archtl. br., Jackson, 1975-77, chief archtl. br. and engring. br., 1977-84, cmty. planning and devel. rep., 1984-88; prin. Mitchell Mgmt. and Engring., 1988—; cons. Army Balistic Missile Agy., Huntsville, Ala., 1957-58, Auburn Rsch. Found., NASA, 1963; mem. state tech. action panel Coop. Area Manpower Planning System; elected pub. ofcl., chmn. Bd. of Election Commrs., Rankin County, Miss. Mem. Cen. Miss. Fed. Personnel Adv. Council; mem. House and Home mag. adv. panel, 1977; trustee, bd. dirs. Meth. Ch., 1959-60; docent Miss. Mus. Art, 1993—; bd. dirs. Am. Heart Assn., Rankin County, 1994. Served with USNR, 1943-46. Recipient Outstanding Achievement award HUD, Commendation by Sec. HUD. Mem. NSPE, Am. Soc. for Engring. Edn., Miss. Soc. Profl. Engrs., Nat. Assn. Govt. Engrs. (charter mem.), Jackson Fed. Execs. Assn., Ctrl. Miss. Safety Coun., Am. Water Works Assn., Iota Lambda Sigma. Club: River Hills (Jackson). Deceased.

MOCKRIDGE, NORTON, writer, editor; b. N.Y.C., Sept. 29, 1915; s. Frank Walter and Fredricka (Apfel) M.; m. Margaret Gleason, 1946 (div. 1961); m. Valborg Palmer, 1963; children: Phillip, Nancy Mockridge Miner, John Student, pub. schs., Mt. Kisco, N.Y. Journalist Mt. Kisco Recorder, N.Y., 1933-36; journalist White Plains Daily Reporter, N.Y., 1936-40; with World-Telegram & Sun, N.Y.C., 1940-66, city editor, 1956-63, humor columnist, 1963-66; with World Jour. Tribune, 1967; syndicated humor columnist Scripps-Howard newspapers and United Feature Syndicate, 1963-80; editor Customized Communications div. Med. Econs. Co., Litton Publs., Oradell, N.J., 1971-81; fgn. corr. Ind. News Alliance div. United Feature Syndicate, 1980; pres. Valnor Prodns., Inc., 1981. Author: 17 books including This is Costello, 1951, The Big Fix, 1954, Costello on the Spot, 1957, Fractured English, 1965, A Funny Thing Happened, 1966, Mockridge, You're Slipping, 1967, The Scrawl of the Wild, 1968, Eye on the Odds, 1976, Types of Medical Practice: Making Your Choice, 1982; contbr. Medical Economics Encyclopedia of Practice and Financial Management, 1986; contbr. articles to mags.; author numerous film story outlines; tech. adviser film Teacher's Pet, 1957; lectr. Keedick Lecture Bur.; host daily radio show Sta.-WCBS, 1963-64, CBS radio network, 1964-70 Served to 1st lt. AUS, 1942-45 Recipient Christopher award the Christophers, 1949; Pulitzer prize for best local news reporting in U.S. (with World-Telegram city news staff), 1963; Jesse H. Neal cert of merit, 1974. Mem. 7th Regt. Vets. Assn. (life), Silurian Soc., N.Y. Vet. Police Assn., Sigma Delta Chi Clubs: Players, Dutch Treat, River, Coffee House, Regency, Casino (Chgo.); Cuernavaca Croquet (Mex.), Balboa Beach. Episcopalian. Home: Tucson, Ariz. Died Apr. 18, 2004.

MODIGLIANI, FRANCO, economist, educator, finance educator; b. Rome, June 18, 1918; arrived in U.S., 1939, naturalized, 1946; s. Enrico and Olga (Flaschel) Modigliani; m. Serena Calabi, May 22, 1939; children: Andre, Sergio. D. Jurisprudence, U. Rome, 1939; D. Social Sci., New Sch. Social Rsch., 1944; LLD (hon.), U. Chgo., 1967; D. honoris causa (hon.), U. Louvain, Belgium, 1974, Istituto Universitario di Bergamo, 1979, Hartford U.; LHD (hon.), Bard Coll., 1985, Brandeis U., 1986, New Sch. Social Research, 1989; LLD, Mich. State U., 1989; D (hon.), U. Ill., 1990, U. Valencia, Spain, 1992; D in Managerial Engring. (hon.), U. Naples, 1998. Instr. econs. and statistics N.J. Coll. Women, New Brunswick, 1942; instr., then asso. econs. and statistics Bard Coll., Columbia, 1942—44; lectr., asst. prof. math. econs. and econometrics New Sch. Social Rsch., 1943—44, 1946—48; rsch. asso., chief statistician Inst. World Affairs, N.Y.C., 1945—48; rsch. cons. Cowles Commn. Rsch. in Econs. U. Chgo., 1949—54; asso. prof., then prof. econs. U. Ill., 1949—52; prof. econs. and indsl. adminstrn. Carnegie Inst. Tech., 1952—60; vis. prof. econs. Harvard U., 1957—58; prof. econs. Northwestern U., 1960—62; vis. prof. econs. MIT, 1960—61, prof. econs. and finance, from 1962, Inst. prof., 1970—88, Inst. prof. emeritus, 1988—2003. Fellow polit. economy U. Chgo., 1948; Fulbright lectr. U. Rome, also, Palermo, Italy, 1955. Author: The Debate Over Stabilization Policy, 1986, Il Caso Italia, 1986, The Collected Papers of Franco Modigliani, 3 vols., 1980, The Collected Papers of Franco Modigliani, 4th and 5th vols., 1989; co-author: National Incomes and International Trade, 1953, Planning Production Inventories and Work Forces, 1960, The Role of Anticipations and Plans in Economic Behavior and Their Use in Economic Analysis and Forecasting, 1961, New Mortgage Designs for Stable Housing in an Inflationary Environment, 1975; co-author: (with Frank J. Fabozzi) Capital Markets: Institutions and Instruments, 1991, Mortgage and Mortgage-Backed Security Markets, 1992; co-author: (with Frank J. Fabozzi, Michael G. Ferri) Foundations of Financial Markets and Institutions, 1994; co-author: Le Avventure di un Economista: Mia Vita, Le Mie Idee, La Nostra Epoca, 1999, (English edit.) Adventures of an Economist, 2001. Named hon. citizen, Town of Modigliana, Italy, 1993, Town of Chiavari, Italy, 1996, Jan Timbergen Meml. lectr., Rotterdam, 1994; recipient Bank of Sweden Alfred Nobel Memorial award in econ. sci., The Royal Swedish Academy of Sciences, 1985, Cavaliere Di Gran Croce Repubblica Italiana, 1985, Premio Coltura for Econs., Repubblica Italiana, 1988, Premio APE award, 1988, Graham and Dodd award, 1975, 1980, James R. Killian Jr. Faculty Achievement award, 1985, Lord Found. prize, 1989, Italy Premio Columbus, 1989, Italy Premio Guido Dorso, 1989, Italy Premio Stivale D'oro, 1991, Italy Premio Campione D'Italia, 1992, Premio Scanno, 1997. Fellow: NAS, Internat. Econ. Assn. (v.p. 1977—83, hon. pres. 1983—2003), Am. Acad. Arts and Scis., Am. Econ. Assn. (v.p. 1971, pres. 1976), Econometric Soc. (coun. 1960, v.p. 1961, pres. 1962); mem.: Shadow Fin. Regulatory Com., Accademia Nazionale dei Lincei (Rome), Boston Security Analysts Soc. (hon.), Am. Fin. Assn. (pres. 1981). Home: Cambridge, Mass. Died Sept. 25, 2003.

MOESCH, JANNETTE IVY, compensation consultant; b. Ludlow, Mass., Sept. 7, 1944; d. William Rennie and Ivy Pearl (maylott) Hill; m. Michael J. Haskell (div. Feb. 1978; children: Michael J., Derek J.; m. Richard F. Moesch, Oct. 6, 1990. Grad. high sch., Ludlow, Mass. Asst. dir. compensation Mass Mutual, Springfield, Mass., 1972-81; asst. v.p. compensation and tech. tng. svcs. CIGNA, Phila., 1981-95; mng. prin. Ctr. for Compensation Solutions, Orwell, Vt., from 1995. Spkr. Internat. Quality and Productivity Ctr., Little Falls, N.J., 1993—. Mem. Open Pantry, Springfield, 1979-80. Mem. Am. Compensation Assn., Soc. for Human Resource Mgmt., Phila. Human Resources Planning Group, Vt. Cons.'s Network. Avocations: travel, reading, model trains. Home: Orwell, Vt. Died Nov. 4, 2001.

MOHOLY, NOEL FRANCIS, clergyman; b. San Francisco, May 26, 1916; s. John Joseph and Eva Gertrude (Cippa) Moholy. Grad., St. Anthony's Sem., Santa Barbara; STB, Faculte de Theologie, Universite Laval, Quebec, Que., Can., 1944, STL, 1945, STD, 1948. Joined Franciscan Friars, 1935; ordained priest Roman Cath. Ch., 1941; tchr. fundamental theology Old Mission Santa Barbara, 1942—43, sacred theology, 1947—58; tchr. langs. St. Anthony's Sem., 1943—44; Am. adminstr. (handling affairs of the cause in U.S.) Cause of Padre Junipero Serra, 1950—55, vice postulator, from 1958; retreat master San Damiano Retreat, Danville, Calif., 1964—67. Mem. Ann. Assay Commn. U.S. Mint, 1964; Occupied numerous pulpits, assisted in several Franciscan Retreat Houses; condr. series illustrated lectrs. on cause of canonization of Padre Junipero Serra to students of all Franciscan study houses in U.S., summer 1952; also spkr. in field at various clubs of Serra Internat. in U.S., Europe and Far East; on NBC in documentary with Edwin Newman, Padre Serra, Founding Father, 85; PBS on Firing Line with William F. Buckley: Junipero Serra-Saint or Sinner, 89; CBS, ABC broadcasts and conducted own local TV series; nat. and internat. authority on Saint Irenaeus, mariology, Calif. history (particularly history of Father Serra). Author: (books) Our Last Chance, 1931, Saint Irenaeus; the Father of Mariology, 1952, The Calif. Mission Story, 1975, The First Californian, 1976; co-author (with Don DeNevi): (book) Junipero Serra, 1985; prodr.: (phonograph records) Songs of the Calif. Missions, 1951, Christmas at Mission Santa Barbara, 1953, St. Francis Peace Record, 1957, VCR The Founding Father of the West, 1976. Pres. Calif. Bicentennial Celebration Commn., 1967—70; mem. Bldg. Com. for Restoration Hist. Towers and Facade of Old Mission Santa Barbara, 1950—53; exec. dir., treas. Old Mission Restoration Project, 1954—58; mem. Calif. Hist. Landmarks Adv. Com., 1967—70; pres. Serra Bicentennial commn., 1983—86; dir. Old Spanish Days in Santa Barbara, Inc., 1950—58; pres. Father Junipero Serra 250th Anniversary Assn., Inc., from 1964. Decorated Knight comdr. Order of Isabella la Catolica; named hon. citizen Petra de Mallorca, 1969; recipient Palma de Mallorca, 1976, Cross of Merit, Sovereign Mil. Order of Knights Malta, 1989, Knight in the Equestrian order of the Holy Sepulchre of Jerusalem, 1997. Mem.: Calif. Missions Study Assn., Associacion de los Amigos de Padre Serra, Native Sons Golden West, Mariol. Soc. Am., K.C. Deceased.

MOLL, CLARENCE RUSSEL, retired university president, consultant; b. Chalfont, Pa., Oct. 31, 1913; s. George A. and Anna A. (Schmidt) M.; m. Ruth E. Henderson, Nov. 19, 1941; children: Robert Henderson, Jonathan George. BS, Temple U., 1934, EdM, 1937; LHD, Pa. Mil. Coll., 1949; PhD, NYU, 1955; LLD, Temple U., 1963; ScD, Chungang U., Seoul, Korea, 1969; LLD, Swarthmore Coll., 1970, Gannon U., 1981; LittD, Delaware Valley Coll., 1976; Ped D, Widener U., 1981. Instr. physics and chemistry Conshohocken (Pa.) H.S., 1935-37; instr. sci. Freehold (N.J.) H.S., 1937-38; instr. physics, chemistry Meml. H.S., Haddonfield, N.J., 1938-42; instr. electronics and radar USN, Phila., 1942-43; assoc. prof. physics and elec. engring. Pa. Mil. Coll., Chester, Pa., 1943-45, registrar, coord. engring. program, 1945-47, dean admissions, student pers., prof. edn., 1947-56, v.p., dean pers. svcs., 1956-59, pres. coll., 1959-72; pres. Widener U. (formerly PMC Colls.), 1972-81, chancellor, 1981-88, pres. emeritus, from 1988; pres. RC Assocs., Inc., from 1981. Instr. electronics Temple U., 1944-46; headmaster Pa. Mil. Prep. Sch., 1945-47; trustee Ironworkers Bank., Project Mgrs. Edn. Found.; trustee emeritus Crozer Keystone Health Sys.; commr. Project Mgmt. Inst./Global Accreditation Commn. Author: History of PA Military College, 1955; contbr. numerous mag. articles. Chmn. Pa. Commn. Ind. Colls., 1969, Found. for Ind. Colls. Pa., 1970; chmn. Com. for Financing Higher Edn. in Pa., 1975; trustee Pa. Inst. Tech., 1985—; commr. Am. Assn. Homes for Aging Cont. Care Accrediting Commn., 1985-95. Recipient Horatio Alger award, 1962, Disting. Alumnus award Temple U., 1964, Cert. of Honor Temple U., 1997, B'nai B'rith Citizen Service award, 1966, Distinguished Citizen award, 1971, Themis award Del. County Bar, 1976, Good Citizenship award Phila. Bar, 1976, Exec. of Yr. award Soc. Advancement Mgmt., 1978, Gallery of Success award, Temple U., 1999. Mem. Assn. Mil. Colls. and Schs. (pres. 1969), Pa. Assn. Colls. and Univs. (chmn. 1970, Sheepskin award 1982), Am. Soc. Engring. Edn., Springhaven Club (Wallingford, Pa.), Tau Beta Pi, Phi Delta Kappa, Alpha Sigma Lambda, Phi Kappa Phi. Lutheran. Home: Media, Pa. Died Dec. 29, 2002.

MONAHAN, RITA SHORT, nursing educator; b. Waterloo, Iowa, Sept. 16, 1954; d. Andrew T. and Lillian R. (Weber) Short; m. W. Gregory Monahan, Jr., June 2, 1976; children: Andrew G., Catherine R. BSN, U. Iowa, 1976; MS in Nursing, Duke U., 1980; EdD, W.Va. U., 1986. Cert. gerontology clin. nurse specialist. From instr. to asst. prof. sch. nursing W.Va. U., Morgantown, 1981-86; assoc. prof. sch. nursing Oreg. Health Scis. U., LaGrande, 1986-99. Contbr. articles to profl. jours. Mem. ANA, AAUW, Am. Diabetes Assn., Oreg. Nurses Assn., Sigma Theta Tau. Avocations: biking, gardening. Home: La Grande, Oreg. Died July 14, 1999.

MONDOK, PASTOR DACIO, retired engineer; b. Philippines, July 26, 1913; came to U.S., 1947; s. EMilio G. and Caliyta (Sadio) Mondok; married, Jan. 6, 1951; children: D. Raymondo, Emilio Pastor, Nestor, Arlen, Fidelis. BSCE, Mapua U., 1942. Registered profl. engr., Guam Chief clk. Municipality of Natividad, 1938-47; acct., auditor Gen. Auditing Office, Philippine Govt., Manila, 1938-47; civil engr. Guan Engr. Dist., 19477-64; owner, appraiser Mondok Adjustment Co., Guam, 1962-64; constrn. negr. San Francisco, 1964-67, Edwards AFB, Calif., 1967-88; pres., chmn. bd. dirs. Mondok's Enterprises, Palmdale, Calif., from 1990. Cons. engr. Corld Cultural City Mktd. Corp., Palmdale, 1990. Mem. Mapua Alumni Assn. (Outstanding Sr. Civil Engr. 1991), Filipin Assn. Antelope Valley (pres. 1970-72), Fil-Am. Assn. Antelope Valley. Democrat. Roman Catholic. Avocations: home repair, gardening, reading, lotto and sweepstakes. Home: Palmdale, Calif. Deceased.

MONGE, JOSEPH PAUL, business executive; b. N.Y.C., Feb. 29, 1912; s. Frank R. and Johanna (Bott) M.; m. Dorothy Oschmann, July 4, 1940; 1 son, Jay Parry. AB, Wagner Coll., 1934, D.H.L., 1981; LL.B., Harvard, 1937. Various positions Internat. Paper Co., N.Y.C., 1937-40, budget dir., 1940-44, treas., 1954-70, v.p., 1961-70, sr. v.p. adminstrn. and finance, 1970-71, exec. v.p., 1971-72, chmn. finance com., chief financial, planning and adminstrv. officer, 1972-74, vice chmn. bd., 1974-77, also dir.; chmn., chief exec. officer Calif. Life Corp. and subs., 1979-83. Dir. Canadian Internat. Paper Co., pres., chief exec. officer, 1971-72, chmn. bd., 1972-77; chmn. bd., chief exec. officer, dir. Calif. Life; dir. Royal Bank Can., Bradford Nat. Corp., S.A.S. Bd. dirs. Nat. Multiple Sclerosis Soc. Nat. Office Mgmt. Assn. fellow, 1954 Mem. Canadian Soc. N.Y., Am., N.Y. bar assns. Clubs: Sky,; Mount Royal (Can.). Home: Rancho Santa Fe, Calif. Deceased.

MONROE, BROOKS, investment banker; b. Greenville, S.C., July 24, 1925; s. Clarence Jenningsand Edith Cabot (Johnson) M.; m. Hilda Marie Meredith, June 30, 1956. BS in Commerce, U. Va., 1948, JD, 1951; grad., Inst. Investment Banking, U. Pa., 1959. Dir. pub. relations Scott, Horner & Co., Lynchburg, Va., 1951-53, with Richmond, Va., 1953-56, v.p., gen. sales mgr. Lynchburg, 1956-59; sales mgr. nat. and underwriting Francis I. duPont & Co., N.Y.C., 1959-61, gen. ptnr., ptnr. in charge West Coast, L.A., 1961-66; gen. ptnr., ptnr. in charge adminstrn. br. offices sys. Paine, Webber, Jackson & Curtis, N.Y.C., 1966-69; pres., chief exec. officer Brooks Monroe & Co., Inc., N.Y.C., 1969—. Chmn. HHM Corp., Wilmington and Beverly Hills, Calif., 1969—, Bargeland Corp., Phila., 1970—, IGAS Corp., Pitts., 1975—; founder, chmn. Execs. Guardian Co., N.Y.C., 1971—; Tchr. U. Va., 1949-51; asso. mem. Am., N.Y. stock exchanges, 1961-72; mem. Pacific Stock Exchange, 1962-66, Chgo. Bd. Trade, 1962-66 Bd. dirs. McIntire Sch. Commerce U. Va., 1979-94. Served with USAAF, 1943-46, PTO. Mem. U. Va. Alumni Assn. (N.Y. pres. 1978-81), Colonnade Club Pavillion VII (Charlottesville), Sigma Chi, Delta Sigma Rho, Pi Delta Epsilon, Omicron Delta Kappa, Delta Theta Pi. Republican. Presbyterian. (trustee). Clubs: Boar's Head Sport, (Charlottesville, Va.), Farmington Country (Charlottesville); Bond, City Midday, Union League (N.Y.C.); Quogue (N.Y.) Field, Quogue Beach; Clan Munro (Scotland and U.S.). Home: Charlottesville, Va. Deceased.

MONROE, MURRAY SHIPLEY, lawyer; b. Cin., Sept. 25, 1925; s. James and Martha (Shipley) M.; m. Sally Longstreth, May 11, 1963; children: Tracy, Murray, Courtney, David. BE, Yale U., 1946, BS, 1947; LLB, U. Pa., 1950. Bar: Ohio 1950, U.S. Dist. Ct. (so. dist.) Ohio 1954, U.S. Dist. Ct. (mid. dist.) Tenn. 1981, US. Dist. Ct. (mid. dist.) N.C. 1974, U.S. Dist. Ct. (mid. dist.) Pa. 1986, U.S. Dist. (ea. dist.) Pa. 1960, U.S. Dist. Ct. (we. dist.) Mo. 1974, U.S. Dist. Ct. Mass. 1978, U.S. Dist. Ct. (ea. dist.) La. 1979, U.S. Dist. Ct. (no. dist.) Ill. 1980, U.S. Ct. Appeals (4th cir.) 1984, U.S. Ct. Appeals (6th cir.) 1969, U.S. Supreme Ct. 1977, U.S. Ct. Appeals (3d cir.) 1990. Assoc. Taft, Stettinus & Hollister, Cin., 1950-58, ptnr., 1958-96; of counsel, from 1997. Mem. lawyers com. Nat. Ctr. for State Cts., 1985-96; faculty Ohio Legal Ctr. Inst., 1970-93. Contbr. articles to profl. jours. Trustee, treas. The Coll. Prep. Sch., 1972-76; trustee The Seven Hills Schs., 1982-88, chmn. bd., 1982-85. 2d lt. USNR, 1943-46. Recipient award Seven Hills Schs., 1985. Fellow Ohio Bar Found.; mem. ABA (speaker symposiums), Ohio Bar Assn. (coun. dels. 1977-82, bd. govs. antitrust sect. 1960-95, dir. emeritus 1995—, chmn. bd. govs. 1973-75, Merit award 1976, speaker symposiums), Bankers Club (Cin.), Cin. Country Club, Met. Club, Tau Beta Pi. Republican. Episcopalian. Avocations: sailing, tennis. Home: Cincinnati, Ohio. Died Sept. 2003.

MONTGOMERY, ROGER, dean; b. N.Y.C., May 28, 1925; s. Graham Livingston and Ann Katharine (Cook) M.; m. Mary Elizabeth Hoyt, Apr. 23, 1949 (dec. Feb. 1980); children: Richard W., Thomas V., John L., Peter G. Student, Oberlin Coll., 1942-44, 47, N.C. State U., 1953-55; MArch, Harvard U., 1957. Architect Zeller & Hunter, Springfield, Ohio, 1948-53; assoc. prof. architecture Washington U., St. Louis, 1957-64, prof. architecture, 1964-67; architect, planner Anselevicius & Montgomery, St. Louis, 1957-70; prof. U. Calif., Berkeley, 1967—95, assoc. dean environ. design, 1976-79, 81-84, acting dean, 1988-89, dean, 1989—96; emeritus prof., 1995—2003; emeritus dean, 1996—2003. Pres. Calif. Council on Archtl. Edn., 1986, bd. dirs., 1983-87. Co-author: Architecture in State of Washington, 1980; co-editor: Housing in America, 1979, Housing Policy for the 1980's; contbr. articles to profl. jours. Mem. Redevel. Commn., Berkeley, 1978-80, pres. 1980. Served with U.S. Army, 1945-47. Mem. AIA, Am. Planning Assn. Home: Berkeley, Calif. Died Oct. 25, 2003.

MONTGOMERY, WILLIAM WAYNE, surgeon; b. Proctor, Vt., Aug. 20, 1923; s. Charles Lynn and Ann (Jones) M. AB, Middlebury (Vt.) Coll., 1944; MD, U. Vt., 1947. Diplomate: Am. Bd. Otolaryngology. Intern Mary Fletcher Hosp., Burlington, Vt., 1947-48; gen. practice medicine W. Rutland, Vt., 1948-50; resident otolaryngology Mass. Eye and Ear Infirmary, 1952-55, mem. staff, 1956—, sr. surgeon in otolaryngology, 1966—; mem. staff Mass. Gen. Hosp., 1956—, surgeon otolaryngology, 1966-86. Prof. Harvard Med. Sch., 1986-94, John W. Merriam prof. otology and laryngology, 1994—, med. dir. voice lab., 1993. Author: Surgery of the Upper Respiratory System, vol. I, II, The Mustache that Walks Like a Man, 1995; contbr. articles to med. jours. Served as batallion surgeon USMCR, 1950-52, Korea. Decorated Purple Heart, Bronze Star, Commendation medal; recipient Disting. Alumni award U. Vt. Med. Sch., 1968, Alumni Achievement award Middlebury Coll., 1985. Fellow ACS; mem. AMA, Am. Acad. Ophthalmology and Otolaryngology (instr. 1963-67), Am. Broncho-Esophagological Assn., Am. Laryngol. Assn. (James E. Newcomb award 1990), Am. Otologic Soc., Am. Laryngol., Rhinol. and Otol. Soc. (Cert. of merit 1990), Pan Am. Med. Assn., Mass. Med. Soc. (program chmn. 1966—), Suffolk Med. Soc., Am. Triological Soc. (Mosher award 1963, v.p. 1987), New Eng. Otolaryngol. Soc. (pres. 1977-78), Am. Soc. Head and Neck Surgery, Am. Acad. Facial Plastic and Reconstructive Surgery. Achievements include spl. research paranasal sinuses and laryngeal surgery. Home: Chestnut Hill, Mass. Died Nov. 7, 2003.

MOODY, GRAHAM BLAIR, lawyer; b. Roswell, N. Mex., July 20, 1925; s. Graham Blair and Vinnie Charlotte (Burton) M.; m. Linda Alden Swanson, Apr. 11, 1970 (div.); children: Graham Blair III, Stuart, Katherine, Charlotte, Douglas, Margaret. BA, Yale U., 1947; MBA, Harvard U., 1947; LLB, U. Calif., Berkeley, 1955. Bar: Calif. 1956, U.S. Dist. Ct. (no. dist.) Calif. 1956, U.S. Ct. Appeals (9th cir.) 1956, U.S. Supreme Ct. 1963. Asst. to dist. mgr. producing dept. Standard Oil of Calif., L.A., 1948-52; head law clk. to chief justice U.S. Supreme Ct., Washington, 1955-56; assoc. McCutchen, Doyle, Brown & Enersen, San Francisco, 1956-64, ptnr., 1964-85, of counsel, 1985-86; ptnr. Moody & Moody, 1987-94. Vestryman St. Clement's Episc. Ch., then All Souls Episc. Ch., 1960-68, Ch. of Our Savior, 1988-90; bd. dirs., 1st pres. Eugene O'Neill Found., Tao House, Danville, Calif., 1975-76; bd. dirs. League to Save Lake Tahoe, 1978-98, pres., 1980-82, 88-90, mem. exec. com., 1980-93; bd. dirs. Trauma Found., 1988—, Point Reyes Bird Obs., Stinson Beach, Calif., 1991—, mem. exec. com. vice chair, 1996—, chair, 1997-98; bd. dirs. Calif. Kidney Cancer Found., 1994—, sec., 1997—; bd. dirs. Henry Ohloff House, San Francisco, 1994—, Friends of Redwoods, Mill Valley, Calif., 1991-92. Supply officer USN. Mem. ABA, Am. Law Inst. (life), Yale Club (past pres. local club). Home: Mill Valley, Calif. Died Oct. 6, 1999.

MOORADIAN, LEO, corporate executive; b. Brantford, Ontario, Canada, Aug. 21, 1909; came to U.S., 1940; s. George and Sadie (Berberian) M.; m. Lucy Achdjian, Jan. 28, 1967; 1 child, Nancy. B in Communications, McMaster U., Hamilton, Canada, 1932. Auditor, tax cons. Ernest & Ernest, Atlanta, 1941-44; organizer Morradian Pulpwood & Timber Co., Atlanta, from 1945. Mem. So. Pulpwood Dealers Assn. (pres. 1946-47). Republican. Episcopalian. Home: Atlanta, Ga. Deceased.

MOORE, CONSTANCE SMITH, retired medical/surgical nurse; b. New Britain, Conn., Jan. 18, 1914; d. Patrick and Mary (Hart) Smith; m. Martin Moore, Oct. 16, 1943 (dec. May 1947). RN, New Britain Gen. Hosp., 1935; BS, New Britain Tchrs. Coll., 1956. Sr. nurse Berlin Pub. Health, 1956; med./surg. supr./instr. New Britain Gen. Hosp.; indsl. nurse U.S. Civil Svc., Aberdeen Proving Ground, Md.; head nurse med. dept. New Britain Gen. Hosp.; sch. nurse New Britain Consol. Sch. Dist.; ret., 1979. Vol., info. desk New Britain Gen. Hosp., 1979-98. Mem. Berlin Grad. Nurses Assn., New Britain Gen. Hosp. Alumni Assn., Cath. Nurses Assn., Coun. Cath. Women, Women's Club New Britain. Home: New Britain, Conn. Died May 22, 2001.

MOORE, DAVID LEWIS, trade association executive; b. Arvin, Calif., Aug. 22, 1931; s. John Chessher and Bonnie (Carter) M.; m. Priscella Jane Martin, Aug. 1, 1953; children: John, Leslie, David, Elizabeth, Andrew. BS, U. So. Calif., 1954. Owner, operator White Wolf Potato Co., 1956-87; chmn. Western Growers Assn., Irvine, Calif., 1984-87, pres., chief exec. officer, from 1987. Apptd. Fed. Res. Bd., 1992—; mem. Coun. on Calif. Competitiveness, 1992, Eximbank Adv. Com., 1990—, Agrl. Policy Adv. Com. for Trade, 1987—, Calif. Econ. Devel. Corp., 1987—, Calif. Fgn. Market Devel. Export Incentive Com., 1986-87, Kern County Water Resources Bd., 1978-87; pres. Arvin Co-op Gin, 1968-75, Arvin-Edison Water Storage Dist., 1971-87; vice chmn. Cal-Cot, 1971-76. Former vestryman St. Paul's Episc. Ch., Bakersfield, Calif.; trustee Bakersfield Coll. Found., 1986-87; founder presdl. assocs. U. So. Calif., L.A. Capt. USAF, 1954-56. Republican. Avocations: golf, tennis, travel. Home: Corona Del Mar, Calif. Died June 6, 2001.

MOORE, EDWARD FORREST, computer scientist, mathematician, former educator; b. Balt., Nov. 23, 1925; s. James Bernard and Edith (Thorn) M.; m. Elinor Constance Martin, July 30, 1950; children— Nancy, Shirley, Martha. BS in Chemistry, Va. Poly. Inst., 1947; MS in Math., Brown U., 1949, PhD in Math., 1950. Asst. prof. math. U. Ill., 1950-51; mem. tech. staff Bell Tel. Labs., Murray Hill, N.J., 1951-61, 62-66. Vis. prof. elec. engring. MIT, 1961-62; vis. lectr. applied math. Harvard U., 1961-62; prof. computer scis., math. U. Wis., Madison, 1966-85; now ret. Author: Sequential Machines, 1964. Membership chmn. Fair Housing Com. of Chathams, N.J., 1964; treas. Francis Wayland Found., 1970-73; bd. dirs. Madison Campus Ministry, 1970-75. Served with USNR, 1944-46. Mem. AAAS, Nat. Speleological Soc., Wis. Speleological Soc., Am. Math. Soc., Math. Assn. Am., Bat Conservation Internat., State Hist. Soc. Wis., Sigma Xi, Phi Kappa Phi, Phi Lambda Upsilon. Baptist. Home: Madison, Wis. Died June 14, 2003.

MOORE, JOHN GEORGE, JR., medical educator; b. Berkeley, Calif., Sept. 17, 1917; s. John George and Mercedes (Sullivan) M.; m. Mary Louise Laffer, Feb. 8, 1946; children: Barbara Ann, Douglas Terence, Bruce MacDonald, Martha Christine. BA, U. Calif., Berkeley, 1939; MD, U. Calif., San Francisco, 1942. Diplomate: Am. Bd. Ob-Gyn (pres. 1974-78, chmn. 1978-82). Asst. prof. U. Iowa, 1950-51; assoc. prof. UCLA, 1951-65, prof., chmn. dept. ob-gyn, 1968-88, Columbia U. Coll. Physicians and Surgeons, N.Y.C., 1965-68; chief gynecology VA Hosp., Sepulveda, Calif., 1988-94. Contbr. articles to profl. jours. Served to maj. M.C. U.S. Army, 1942-46. Decorated Silver Star, Bronze Star, Purple Heart.; NIH grantee U. Copenhagen; Royal Postgrad. Sch. Medicine, London Mem. ACS, ACOG, Soc. Gynecol. Investigation (pres. 1967), Assn. Profs. Gynecology and Obstetrics (pres. 1975), Western Assn. Gynecol. Oncologists (pres. 1976), Am. Gynecol. Soc., Pacific Coast Ob-Gyn. Soc., L.A. Ob-Gyn. Soc., Pepperdine U. Assocs. Home: Malibu, Calif. Died Oct. 30, 2003.

MOORE, PAUL, JR., bishop; b. Morristown, N.J., Nov. 15, 1919; s. Paul and Fanny Weber (Hanna) M.; m. Jenny McKean, Nov. 26, 1944 (dec.); children: Honor, Paul III, Adelia, Rosemary, George Mead, Marian Shaw, Daniel Sargent, Susanna McKean, Patience; m. Brenda Hughes Eagle, May 16, 1975 (dec.). Grad., St. Paul's Sch., Concord, N.H., 1937; BA, Yale U., 1941; S.T.B., Gen. Theol. Sem., N.Y.C., 1949, S.T.D. (hon.), 1960; D.D. (hon.), Va. Theol. Sem., 1964, Berkeley Divinity Sch., 1971; PhD (hon.), City Coll. N.Y. Ordained to ministry Episcopal Ch., 1949. Mem. team ministry Grace Ch., Jersey City, 1949-57; dean Christ Ch. Cathedral, Indpls., 1957-64; suffragan bishop Washington, 1964-70; bishop coadjutor Diocese, N.Y., 1970-72, bishop, 1972-89. Lectr. St. Augustine's Coll., Canterbury, Eng., 1960; chmn. commn. Delta ministry Nat. Coun. Chgs., 1964-67; mem. urban divsn., nat. exec. coun. Episcopal Ch., 1952-68; dep. to Gen. Conv., 1961, Anglican Congress, 1963; chmn. com. 100; legal def. fund NAACP. Author: The Church Reclaims the City, 2d edit, 1970, Take A Bishop Like Me, 1979, Presences, 1997. Trustee Bard Coll.; former trustee Gen. Theol. Sem., Trinity Sch., Berkeley Div. Sch. at Yale U., N.Y.C.; mem. Human Rights Watch; mem. adv. coun. Gov.'s Com. on AIDS, 1983-87; chmn. The Timor Project, Project on Religion and Human Rights; adv. coun. Anglican Office, UN. Capt. USMCR, 1941-45, PTO. Decorated Navy Cross, Silver Star, Purple Heart; recipient Margaret Sanger award Planned Parenthood, 1984, Frederick Douglas award North Star Fund, 1989, Freedom of Worship medal Franklin and Eleanor Roosevelt Inst., 1991, Gen. John Russell Leadership award USMC Found., Patrick Moynihan medal Citizens Com. of N.Y.C., St. Paul's Sch. Alumni Assn. award, Lifetime Achievement award Cathedral Heritage, Louisville; Yale Corp. sr. fellow, 1964-90. Mem.: Anglers Club (N.Y.C.), Century Club (N.Y.C.). Episcopalian. Died May 1, 2003.

MOORE, PHILIP LAWTON, judge; b. Santurce, Puerto Rico, Dec. 12, 1944; s. Thomas Howard Moore and Jane Lawton (Lunt) Moore Payson; m. Susanna Elizabeth Long, June 1, 1968 (div. Aug. 1984); children: Jane, Nathaniel; m. Patricia Jean Henry, Aug. 27, 1984. BSBA, Bucknell U., 1967; JD, George Washington U., 1970. Bar: D.C. 1970, U.S. Dist. Ct. D.C. 1970, U.S. Ct. Appeals (D.C. cir.) 1971, Maine 1972, U.S. Dist. Ct. Maine 1973. Atty. office of proceedings interstate Commerce Commn., Washington, 1970-73, 78-81; gen. atty. Maine Ctrl. R.R. Co., Portland, 1973-78; fed. adminstrv. law judge Social Security Adminstrn., Pitts., from 1981. Home: Pittsburgh, Pa. Deceased.

MOORE, THOMAS CARROL, botanist, retired educator; b. Sanger, Tex., Sept. 22, 1936; s. Thomas M. and Willie Mae M.; m. Arvida Inmon DePriest, Sept. 1, 1956; children— Cynthia, Linda, Alan. BA in Biology, U. N. Tex., Denton, 1956; MA in Botany, U. Colo., 1958, PhD (Outstanding Grad. Student in Biology award 1960, USPHS predoctoral fellow 1960-61), 1961. Instr. biology, then part-time instr. U. Colo., 1958-60; asst. prof. Ariz. State Coll., Flagstaff, 1961-63; mem. faculty Oreg. State U., Corvallis, 1963-93, prof. botany, 1971-93, prof. emeritus, from 1993, chmn. dept. botany and plant pathology, 1973-86, asst. to v.p. for rsch. and grad. studies, 1972-73. Vis. prof. Colo. State Coll., 1963. Mem. editorial bd. Plant Physiology, 1981-86; editor in chief Jour. Plant Growth Regulation, 1982-99; contbr. articles to profl. jours. Recipient Mosser award outstanding undergrad. teaching Oreg. State U., 1966 Mem.: Internat. Plant Growth Substances Assn., Am. Soc. Plant Physiologists. Democrat. Home: Corvallis, Oreg. Died Aug. 30, 2002.

MOORE, WALTER JOHN, physical chemistry educator; b. N.Y.C., Mar. 25, 1918; s. Walter John and Ruth Edith (Hart) M.; m. Patricia Bacon, Dec. 4, 1943; children: Anthony, Julia, Catherine. BS, NYU, 1937; PhD, Princeton U., 1940. Rsch. fellow Calif. Inst. Tech., Pasadena, 1941-42; asst. prof., then assoc. prof. Cath. U. Am., Washington, 1946-52; prof. Ind. U., Bloomington, 1952-73, adj. prof., from 1990; prof. of chemistry U. Sydney, Australia, 1973-83, prof. emeritus, from 1984. Author: Seven Solid States, 1967, Physical Chemistry, 1972, Basic Physical Chemistry, 1983, Schrödinger, Life and Thought, 1989. Fellow Royal Australian Inst. Chemistry; mem. Am. Chem. Soc. (Norris Teaching award 1960). Democrat. Roman Catholic. Achievements include co-discovery of origin of color of amethysts. Home: Bloomington, Ind. Died Dec. 20, 2001.

MOORER, THOMAS HINMAN, retired naval officer; b. Mt. Willing, Ala., Feb. 9, 1912; s. Richard Randolph and Hulda (Hill) M.; m. Carrie Ellen Foy, Nov. 28, 1935; children: Thomas Randolph, Mary Ellen, Richard Foy, Robert Hill. BS, U.S. Naval Acad., 1933; grad., Naval War Coll., 1953; LL.D. (hon.), Sanford U., Auburn U., Troy U., The Citadel. Commd. ensign U.S. Navy, 1933, advanced through grades to adm., 1957; held several fleet commands at sea; chief naval ops., 1967-70; chmn. joint chiefs of staff, 1970-74; ret., 1974; dir. Blount Inc., Montgomery, Ala., 1974—. Dir. U.S. Life Ins. Corp., Arlington, Va., CACI, Arlington; adviser Center Strategic and Internat. Studies, The Citadel. Co-author: U.S. Overseas Bases: Problems of Projecting American Military Power Abroad, 1977, Sea Power and Strategy in the Indian Ocean, 1981. Chmn. Naval Aviation Mus. Found., Inc. Decorated Def. Dept. D.S.M. with oak leaf cluster, Navy D.S.M. with 4 stars, Army D.S.M., Air Force D.S.M., Silver Star, Legion of Merit, D.F.C., Purple Heart, others; recipient Forrestal award, 1975; named to Nat. Aviation Hall of Fame, 1987, Naval Aviation Hall of Honor, 1988 Mem. U.S. Naval Acad.

Alumni Assn., U.S. Naval Inst., Ret. Officers Assn., Assn. Naval Aviation, Chevy Chase Club, Army-Navy Club. Republican. Baptist. Home: Bethesda, Md. Died Feb. 5, 2004.

MORBEY, GRAHAM KENNETH, management educator; b. Birmingham, Eng., Apr. 5, 1935; came to U.S., 1956; m. Gillian M. Grist, Feb. 13, 1960; children: Alison J., Karen J. BScChemE with honors, U. Birmingham, 1956; MASc in Applied Chemistry, U. Toronto, 1957; MA, PhD, Princeton U., 1961. Rsch. scientist Dunlop Tire, Toronto, 1960-63; dir. product devel. Celanese, Charlotte, N.C., 1963-69; tech. dir. Hoechst Fibers Inc., Spartanburg, S.C., 1969-72; dir. R&D Johnson & Johnson Personal Products, Milltown, N.J., 1972-79; v.p. R&D Texon-Emhart, South Hadley, Mass., 1979-85; v.p. Lydall Inc., Manchester, Conn., 1989-92; assoc. prof. U. Mass., Amherst, from 1985. Cons. Aminco, Amherst, 1985—. Contbr. articles to profl. jours. Hon. rsch. fellow Textile Rsch. Inst., Princeton. Mem. TAPPI, Product Devel. Mgmt. Assn., Princeton Club N.Y., Sigma Xi. Achievements include patents for absorbtive and thermal barrier products. Home: Northampton, Mass. Deceased.

MOREN, LESLIE ARTHUR, physician; b. Webster, Wis., Jan. 28, 1914; s. John Arthur and Jennie (Anderson) M.; m. Laurena Ann McBride, Sept. 9, 1939 (dec. Aug. 1987); children: Ann Nisbet, Allen, Kristin Madden, James A. BA, U. Minn., 1934, MD, 1938. Diplomate Am. Bd. Family Practice. Pvt. practice physician, Eklo, Nev., 1938-40, St. Paul, 1940-42, Elko Regional Med. Ctr., from 1946. Maj. AUS, 1943-45, ETO. Mem. Nev. State Bd. Med. Examiners (pres. Reno chpt. 1950-77), Nev. State Med. Assn. (pres. Reno chpt. 1938-40, 46—), Rotary. Republican. Episcopalian. Avocation: reading. Home: Elko, Nev. Deceased.

MORGAN, FREDERICK, poet, editor; b. N.Y.C., Apr. 25, 1922; s. John Williams and Marion Haviland (Burt) M.; m. Constance Canfield, Dec. 20, 1942 (div. Aug. 1957); children: Gaylen, Veronica, George F.; m. Rose Fillmore, Aug. 14, 1957 (div. Aug. 1969); m. Paula Deitz, Nov. 30, 1969. AB magna cum laude, Princeton U., 1943. Founder, editor The Hudson Rev., N.Y.C., 1947, editor, pres., 1947—98; chmn. adv. council dept. Romance langs. and lits. Princeton U., NJ, 1973-91. Author: A Book of Change, 1972, Poems of the Two Worlds, 1977, The Tarot of Cornelius Agrippa, 1978, Death Mother and Other Poems, 1979, The River, 1980, Refractions, 1981, Northbook, 1982, Eleven Poems, 1983, The Fountain and Other Fables, 1985, Poems: New and Selected, 1987, Poems for Paula, 1995, The Night Sky, 2002, The One Abiding, 2003. Served with U.S. Army, 1943-45. Decorated chevalier de l'Ordre des Arts et des Lettres (France); recipient Aiken Taylor award for poetry, 2001. Mem.: Univ. Club, Knickerbocker Club (gov. 1981—89). Home: New York, NY. Died Feb. 20, 2004.

MORGAN, MARK ALLEN, obstetrician, gynecologist; b. Enid, Okla., June 17, 1957; s. Wayne Thomas and Della Mae (Goodhue) M.; m. Sharyl Jaleen Scharn, June 7, 1980; children: Robert Wayne, Jamie Lynn. BS, So. Nazarene U., 1979; MD, Okla. U., 1983. Diplomate Am. Bd. Obstetrics and Gynecology. Intern, then resident obstetrics & gynecology, chief adminstrv. resident Okla. U. Health Scis. Ctr., Oklahoma City, 1983-87, fellow maternal fetal medicine, 1987-89, asst. prof., dir. primate colony, 1989-91; asst. prof. obstetrics-gynecology Irvine Med. Ctr. U. Calif., Orange, 1991-94; prof., dir. obstetrics and maternal-fetal medicine U. Pa. Sch. Medicine, Phila., from 1994. Med. cons. Emerson Teen Parent Program, Oklahoma City, 1987-91, adv. bd., 1988-91. Reviewer Am. Jour. Obstetrics and Gynecology, 1991—. Fellow Am. Coll. Obstetricians and Gynecologists; mem. So. Med. Assn., Soc. Perinatal Obstetricians, Phi Delta Lambda. Republican. Nazarene. Avocations: golf, reading. Home: Gwynedd, Pa. Died Apr. 4, 1999.

MORITZ, EDWARD, historian, educator; b. Columbia, S.C., Jan. 24, 1920; s. Edward and Edith (Jumper) M.; m. Betty Gene Reid, Apr. 8, 1946; children— Stephen Edward, John Reid, Richard Douglas, Sarah Anne. BA, Miami U., Oxford, Ohio, 1949; MA (Taft scholar), U. Cin., 1950; PhD (Knapp scholar), U. Wis., 1953. Instr. U. Wis., Madison, 1953-55; mem. faculty Kalamazoo (Mich.) Coll., 1955—, prof. history, 1963—, chmn. dept., 1965-88, prof. emeritus, from 1988. Vis. prof. Oxford, Eng., 1971-72 Author: Winston Churchill, Parliamentary Career, 1908-12. Served with USAAF, 1942-46. Kellog fellow, 1971 Mem. Am. Hist. Assn., Conf. Brit. Studies, AAUP, Phi Beta Kappa, Phi Eta Sigma. Home: Kalamazoo, Mich. Died Dec. 3, 1999.

MORRIS, NORVAL, criminologist, educator; b. Auckland, New Zealand, Oct. 1, 1923; s. Louis and Vera (Burke) M.; m. Elaine Richardson, Mar. 18, 1947; children: Gareth, Malcolm, Christoper. LLB, U. Melbourne, Australia, 1946, LLM, 1947; PhD in Criminology (Hutchinson Silver medal 1950), London Sch. Econs., 1949. Bar: called to Australian bar 1953. Asst. lectr. London Sch. Econs., 1949-50; sr. lectr. law U. Melbourne, 1950-58, prof. criminology, 1955-58; Ezra Ripley Thayer teaching fellow Harvard Law Sch., 1955-56, vis. prof., 1961-62; Boynthon prof., dean faculty law U. Adelaide, Australia, 1958-62; dir. UN Inst. Prevention Crime and Treatment of Offenders, Tokyo, 1962-64; Julius Kreeger prof. law and criminology U. Chgo., 1964—2004, dean Law Sch., 1975-79. Chmn. Commn. Inquiry Capital Punishment in Ceylon, 1958-59; mem. Social Sci. Rsch. Coun. Australia, 1958-59; Australian del. confs. div. human rights and sect. social def. UN, 1955-66; mem. standing adv. com. experts prevention crime and treatment offenders. Author: The Habitual Criminal, 1951, Report of the Commission of Inquiry on Capital Punishment, 1959, (with W. Morison and R. Sharwood) Cases in Torts, 1962, (with Colon Howard) Studies in Criminal Law, 1964, (with G. Hawkins) The Honest Politicians Guide to Crime Control, 1970, The Future of Imprisonment, 1974, Letter to the President on Crime Control, 1977, Madness and the Criminal Law, 1983, Between Prison and Probation, 1990, The Brothel Boy and Other Parables of the Law, 1992, The Oxford History of the Prison, 1995, Maconochie's Gentlemen, 2001. Served with Australian Army, World War II, PTO. Decorated Japanese Order Sacred Treasure 3d Class. Fellow Am. Acad. Arts and Scis. Home: Chicago, Ill. Died Feb. 21, 2004.

MORRIS, RALPH ODELL, physician; b. Gray, Okla., Dec. 20, 1917; s. Jay Thomas and Tessa (Clark) M.; m. Manuela Frasquella, Aug. 28, 1990; children: Aurora Morris Coppola, Jean Morris Roberts, Marrian Morris De Leon, Magale, Wanda Morris Lent, Thomas, Linda Morris Hargrove, Fred, Ketty Morris Arrazote (dec.). BA, Whittier Coll.; DO, Coll. Osteopathic Medicine; MD, Calif. Coll. Medicine. Pvt. practice med. hypnosis, from 1966. Home: Torrance, Calif. Deceased.

MORRISON, GEORGE, artist; b. Grand Marais, Minn., Sept. 30, 1919; s. James and Barbara (Mesaba) M.; m. Hazel Belvo, Dec. 13, 1960; 1 child, Briand Mesaba. Student, Art Students League, N.Y.C., 1946, U. Aix-Marseille, France, 1952; M.F.A. (hon.), Mpls. Coll. Art Design, 1969. Asst. prof. R.I. Sch. Design, Providence, 1963-68, asso. prof., 1968-70; prof. art U. Minn., Mpls., 1973-87. Vis. artist Cornell U., 1962, Pa. State U., 1963 One-man shows include, Walker Art Center, Mpls., 1973, Mpls. Inst. Art, 1976, U. Calif., Davis, group shows include, Heard Mus., Phoenix, 1977, Landmark Center, St. Paul, 1979; represented in permanent collections, Whitney Mus., N.Y.C., Phila. Mus., Minn. Mus., St. Paul, Chgo. Art Inst., Dayton (Ohio) Art Inst. Vanderlip scholar, 1943; Fulbright grantee, 1952; John Hay Whitney fellow, 1953 Mem. Audubon Artists, Fedn. Modern Painters and Sculptors. Home: Grand Portage, Minn. Deceased.

MORTOLA, EDWARD JOSEPH, academic administrator emeritus; b. N.Y.C., Feb. 5, 1917; s. John and Letitia (Pellarano) M.; m. Doris Slater, May 3, 1941; children: Doreen Mortola LeMoult, Elaine Mortola Clark. BA, Fordham U., 1938, MA, 1941, PhD, 1946, L.H.D. (hon.), 1964; postgrad., Columbia U., 1946; L.H.D. (hon.), Medaille Coll., 1980; LL.D. (hon.), Bryant Coll., 1965, Syracuse U., 1967, N.Y. Law Sch., 1968; Litt.D. (hon.), Manhattan Coll., 1967, Coll. St. Rose, 1971; LL.D. (hon.), Western State U., 1985; L.H.D. (hon.), Pace U., 1987. Grad. fellow, sch. edn. Fordham U., 1938-39, asst. registrar, 1939-41, asst. registrar, city hall div., lectr. grad. faculty, sch. edn., 1946-47; instr. math. Cooper Union and Townsend Harris High Sch., N.Y.C., 1941-42; mem. faculty St. Peter's Coll., Jersey City, part time 1946-47; with Pace U., N.Y.C., 1947—, asst. dean, 1947-49, dean, 1949-50, provost, 1950-54, v.p., 1954-60, pres., 1960-84, chancellor, 1984-90, chancellor emeritus, from 1990. Mem. Community Planning Bd. 1, Borough Manhattan, 1954-66, chmn., 1956-58; mem., chmn. legis. com. Assn. Colls. and Univs. State N.Y., v.p., 1965-66, pres., 1967-68; mem. adv. council on higher edn. State Edn. Dept.; trustee, past pres. Com. on Ind. Colls. and Univs.; mem. Middle States Assn. Colls. and Schs., N.Y. Gov.'s Commn. on Quality, Cost and Finance of N.Y. State Elementary and Secondary Edn., 1969-71, Westchester Planning Commn., 1966-73, Westchester County Assn., N.Y.C. Council on Econ. Edn., Commn. on Ind. Colls. and Univs. State N.Y., chmn., 1961-63; mem. council Fordham U.; mem. Mayor's Com. on Long-Term Fin. of N.Y.C.; former mem. adv. bd. Elizabeth Seton Coll.; past dir. and sec. Greater N.Y. Council Fgn. Students; chmn. bd. govs. Fordham U. Alumni Fedn., 1958-60; formerly trustee Rosemont Coll., St. Joseph's Sem., Yonkers, N.Y.; co-chmn. N.Y. State Edn. Dept. Task Force on Teaching Profession, 1987-88; chmn. Lincoln Ctr. Inst., 1987; bd. dirs. Lincoln Ctr., 1987 ; hon. dir. N.Y.C. Partnership, 1987—; bd. dirs. N.Y. Telephone Co., Bank of N.Y., J.C. Penney Co., Nat. Reins. Co., Continental Ins. Co. Bd. govs. New Rochelle Hosp.; hon. bd. govs. White Plains Hosp.; Downtown-Lower Manhattan Assn., Econ. Devel. Council; former trustee Instructional TV. Served with USNR, 1942-46; lt. comdr. Res. Decorated Knight of Malta, Knight Comdr. Order of Merit of Republic of Italy; recipient Ann. Achievement award in edn. Fordham Coll., 1960, William O'Brien award Cardinal Newman Found., 1964, Ednl. award Westchester chpt. Am. Com. Italian-Immigration, 1969, James E. Allen Jr. Meml. award Disting. Svc. to Edn. Bd. Regents N.Y. State, 1977, Leadership in Edn. award Assn. Colls. and Univs. State of N.Y., 1986, Outstanding Achievement award 100 Yr. Assn. of N.Y., 1983, Big Bros. of N.Y. Achievement award, 1987, Distinguished Alumni award Fordham U. Sch. Edn. Alumni Assn., 1970, Outstanding Achievement award One Hundred Yr. Assn., 1983, Achievement award in edn. Big Bros. N.Y., 1987, Starr award Good Counsel Acad., 1991, Family of Yr. award Family Svc. of Westchester, 1990; named Man of Yr. B'nai B'rith Youth Services, 1975 Mem. N.Y. Acad. Pub. Edn. (pres. 1962-64, dir.), N.Y. C. of C. (chmn. edn. com. 1966-68, mem. exec. com.), Nat. Office Mgmt. Assn., NEA, N.Y. Adult Edn. Coun., Knights of Malta. Clubs: Metropolitan (N.Y.C.), Univ. (N.Y.C.); Larchmont Yacht Club. Died Oct. 21, 2002.

MOSBY, RALPH JOSEPH, minister, educator; b. Kansas City, Mo., Feb. 11, 1931; s. Ralph Mosby Sr. and Ruth (Robinson) Collier; m. Kathleen Theresa Johnson, May 29, 1971; children: Audwin Joaquin, Gregory Johnson. BA, Redlands U., 1962; MDiv, Am. Bapt. Sem., 1968; PhD, Calif. Grad. Sch. Theology, 1973. Ordained to ministry Bapt. Ch.; cert. adult edn. tchr. (life). Assoc. min. Trinity Bapt. Ch., L.A., 1965-71; sr. pastor Immanuel Bapt. Ch., L.A., 1971-73, St. John Bapt. Ch., Long Beach, Calif., 1974-99. Instr. Am. Bapt. Sem. of West, Covina, Calif., 1968-69, Angeles Bible Coll., Hawthorne, Calif., 1974-75, L.A. Trade Tech. Coll., 1974-80, Long Beach City Coll., 1974-90. Bd. dirs. Long Beach Area Citizenship Involved, 1975-99, Cable Com. Adv. Commn., Long Beach, 1983-99, African Am. Coordinating Coun., Long Beach, 1989-99; pres. Long Beach Housing Action Assn., 1976-78. Recipient Commendation of Svc. award County of L.A., City of Long Beach, 1983-86. Mem. South Coast Ecumenical Coun. (pres. 1988-89 Pastor of Yr. 1984), Christian Fellowship Union of Chs. (pres. 1985-88), Black Am. Bapt. of Pacific S.W. (pres. 1985-88, Svc. award 1988), Theta Alpha Phi. Home: Long Beach, Calif. Died Apr. 30, 1999.

MOSES, JEFFREY MICHAEL, customer services executive; b. Nov. 16, 1945; s. George John and Mildred (Kronz) M.; m. Barbrae Danowsky, Apr. 24, 1976; children: Apryl Richelle, Heather Lorien. AA, Eckel's Coll., Phila. Sales supr. Internat. Tariff Svcs., Inc., Washington, 1970-71; transp. analyst to mgr. of tariff pub. Charles Donley & Assocs., Pitts., 1973-81; transp. mgr. Texas Aromatics, Houston, 1981-83; dir. customer svcs. ChemCoast, Inc., LaPorte, Tex., 1983-91, v.p., 1991-96; dir. svcs. United Surveyors of Chems., Baytown, Tex., from 1997; pres. Compliance Packaging & Svcs., from 1996; dir. of svcs. United Surveyors of Chems., Inc., 1997. Mem. adv. bd. Tex. Workers' Compensation Ins. Fund. Mem. Internat. Hazardous Materials Inst. (chmn. bd. 1993, 94, cert. master transp. specialist), Am. Assn. Inspection and Lab. Cos. (chmn.). Home: Galveston, Tex. Died Oct. 25, 1999.

MOSS, HENRY TULLY, art expert; b. Kansas City, Mo., July 6, 1924; s. Henry Tully Sr. and Bonnie (Rafferyt) M.; m. Ruth Brunkhorst, May 31, 1952; children: Henry Tully III, Melinda Ann, Elaine Moss Smoot. BA cum laude, Syracuse (N.Y.) U., 1948. CLU. Cons. Mass. Mut. Life, Kansas City, Mo., 1950-68; v.p. Lincoln Consol., 1968-75; founder, owner Henry Ruth Fine Arts, from 1975. Bd. dis. Kansas City Philharm., 1981-82; pres. Homes Assn., Mission Hills, Kans., 1982. Fellow Appraisers Assn. of Am.; mem. The Carriage, Rotary. Republican. Episcopalian. Avocations: music, hiking, art history. Home: Prairie Vlg, Kans. Deceased.

MOST, JOHN ANTHONY, nursing educator, consultant, physician; b. Dubuque, Iowa, Aug. 12, 1928; s. George Henry and Mary Caroline (Fay) M.; children: John George, Wiliam Andrew, Sara Ann, Gregory Patrick Joseph, Ann Caroline. Student, Loras Coll., Dubuque, 1946-49; MD, St. Louis U., 1953. Diplomate Nat. Bd. Med. Examiners, Am. Bd. Family Practice. Surg. intern Univ. Hosp., Little Rock, 1953-54; resident surgery U.S. Naval Hosp., Chelsea, Mass., 1960-61; pvt. practice Carlsbad, N.Mex., 1961-99. Mem. staff Guadalupe Med. Ctr., Carlsbad; mem. assoc. faculty N.Mex. State U., Carlsbad. Bd. dirs. N.Mex. Lung Assn., Albuquerque; past pres. Boys' Club, Carlsbad; past chmn. bd. trustees Guadalupe Med. Ctr., Carlsbad. Lt. comdr. USNR, 1954-61. Fellow AMA, Am. Acad. Family Physicians (past state pres.); mem. Am. Soc. Law and Medicine, Hasting Ctr. (assoc.), Thoracic Soc. (past v.p.). Republican. Roman Catholic. Avocations: writing, woodworking. Home: Carlsbad, N.Mex. Died May 7, 1999.

MOSTILER, JOHNNY BAXTER, lawyer; b. Spartanburg, S.C., Feb. 23, 1947; s. John L. and Nora Elizabeth (Morgan) M.; m. Diane Turnell Park, Aug. 14, 1971; children: John Clifton, Stephanie Diane. BA, Furman U., Greenville, S.C., 1969; JD, U. Ga., 1972. Bar: Ga. 1972, U.S. Dist. Ct. Ga. 1977, U.S. Tax Ct. 1973. Student asst. Office of Chief Counsel, IRS, Atlanta, 1971, tax atty. Houston, 1973-77; sole practitioner Griffin, Ga., from 1977; pub. defender Spalding County, Ga., from 1990. Pub. defender Spalding County, Ga., 1990—. Bd. dirs. Ga. affiliate Am. Heart Assn., 1978—, state sec., 1983-84, state v.p., 1984-85, chmn. bd. dirs., 1985-86, pro bono gen. counsel, 1989—; mem. state bd. dirs. Assn. for Retarded Citizens; bd. dirs. Griffin Assn. for Retarded Citizens, 1980—, v.p., 1985-86, pres., 1984, 87; mem. Spalding County Dem. Com.; mem. Griffin Footlight Players. Recipient various recognitions Am. Heart Assn. Mem. ABA, State Bar Ga., Spalding County Bar Assn., Assn. Trial Lawyers Am., Ga. Trial Lawyers Assn., Kiwanis Internat. (chmn. laws and regulations com. 1990-91). Baptist. Home: Griffin, Ga. Died Apr. 1, 2000.

MOURANT, WALTER BYRON, composer; b. Chgo., Aug. 29, 1910; s. Arthur John and Addie May (Morris) M.; children: Susannah Abitz, Peter. BM, Eastman U., 1934, MM, 1935. Arranger, composer Mark Warnow Hit Parade, N.Y.C., 1937-42; arranger Raymond Scott Orchestra, N.Y.C., 1942-55, A. Kostelanetz N.Y. Philharmonic, N.Y.C., 1969, 70. Composer (TV film) Prisoner of Zenda, 1965; various symphonic compositions rec. by London Symphony, N.Y. Philharmonic and Hamburg Symphony. Mem. Broadcast Music, Inc., Am. Composers Alliance. Democrat. Avocations: golf, Scrabble. Home: Los Osos, Calif. Deceased.

MOYLE, BENNETT ISAAC, computer software company executive, consultant; b. Columbus, Ohio, Mar. 24, 1946; s. Bennett Oliver and Mary Alice (Lawler) M. BA, U. Minn., 1968. Sys. programmer Fed. Res. Bank, Mpls., 1968-78; owner, mgr. B.I. Moyle Assocs., Inc., Mpls., from 1978. Gen. ptnr. Reno Air. Contbr. articles to profl. jours. Mem.

Minn. DOS Users Group (pres. 1970-72), Ind. Computer Cons. Assn. (dir. 1981-84, 87-88), Am. Arbitration Assn. (arbitrator 1987-92). Died July 26, 2001.

MOYNIHAN, DANIEL PATRICK, former senator, educator; b. Tulsa, Mar. 16, 1927; s. John Henry and Margaret Ann (Phipps) M.; m. Elizabeth Therese Brennan, May 29, 1955; children: Timothy Patrick, Maura Russell, John McCloskey. Student, CCNY, 1943; BA cum laude, Tufts U., 1948; MA, Fletcher Sch. Law and Diplomacy, 1949, PhD, 1961, LLD (hon.), 1968; Fulbright fellow, London (Eng.) Sch. Econs. and Polit. Sci., 1950-51; LLD (hon.), Cath. U. Am., 1968, New Sch. Social Rsch., 1968, U. Notre Dame, 1969, Fordham U., 1970, St. Bonaventure U., 1972, Boston Coll., 1976, Yeshiva U., 1978, Rensselaer Polytech. Inst., 1983, Syracuse U. Sch. Law, 1984, Columbia U., 1987, U. Rochester, 1994; LLD (hon.), Yale U., 2000, Harvard U., 2002; D in Pub. Adminstrn. (hon.), Hamilton Coll., 1968; DSI (hon.), Defense Intelligence Coll., 1984; numerous other hon. degrees. With Internat. Rescue Com., 1954; successively asst. to sec., asst. sec., acting sec. to gov. State of N.Y., 1955-58, dir. Syracuse U. govt. rsch. project, 1959-61, spl. asst. to sec. labor, 1961-62, exec. asst. to sec., 1962-63, asst. sec. labor, 1963-65; dir. Joint Ctr. for Urban Studies MIT and Harvard U., 1966-69; prof. edn. and urban politics Kennedy Sch. Govt., Harvard U., 1966-73, sr. mem., 1966-77, prof. govt., 1973-77; asst. for urban affairs to Pres. U.S., 1969-70; counsellor to Pres. U.S., mem. Cabinet, 1969-70, cons. to Pres. U.S., 1971-73; mem. U.S. del. 26th Gen. Assembly, UN, 1971, Pres.'s Sci. Adv. Com., 1971-73; ambassador to India New Delhi, 1973-75; U.S. permanent rep. to UN, N.Y.C., 1975-76; U.S. senator from N.Y., 1977-2001; chmn. senate fin. com., 1993-94; ranking mem., senate fin. com., 1995-2001; prof. Syracuse U. Maxwell Sch. Citizenship/Pub. Affairs, from 2001. Chmn. commn. on Reducing and Protecting Govt. Secrecy, 1994-97,vice chmn. Pres.'s Temp. Commn. on Pennsylvania Avenue, 1964-73; chmn. adv. com. traffic safety dept. HEW; fellow Ctr. Advanced Studies, Wesleyan U., 1965-66; hon. fellow London Sch. Econs. and Polit. Sci., 1970—; sec. pub. affairs com. N.Y. State Dem. Com., 1958-60; alt. del. Dem. Nat. Conv., 1960, 76; sr. pub. policy scholar Woodrow Wilson Policy Ctr., 2001. Author: Maximum Feasible Misunderstanding, 1969, The Politics of a Guaranteed Income, 1973, Coping: On the Practice of Government, 1974, A Dangerous Place, 1978, Counting Our Blessings, 1980, Loyalties, 1984, Family and Nation, 1986, Came the Revolution: Argument in the Reagan Era, 1988, On the Law of Nations, 1990, Pandaemonium: Ethnicity in International Politics, 1993, Miles To Go: A Personal History Of Social Policy, 1996, Secrecy: The American Experience, 1998; co-author: Beyond the Melting Pot, 1963; editor: The Defenses of Freedom, 1966, On Understanding Poverty, 1969, Ethnicity: Theory and Experience, 1975, others; editorial bd. Pub. Interest; contbr. articles to profl. jours. Vice chmn. Woodrow Wilson Internat. Ctr. for Scholars, 1971-76; chmn. bd. trustees Joseph H. Hirshhorn Mus. and Sculpture Garden, 1971-85; mem. bd. regents Smithsonian Instn., 1987—. With USN, 1944-47. Recipient Meritorious Svc. award U.S. Dept. Labor, 1965, Centennial medal Syracuse U., 1969, Internat. League for Human Rights award, 1975, John LaFarge award for Interracial Justice, 1980, Medallion SUNY Albany, 1984, Henry medal Smithsonian Instn., 1985, SEAL Medallion, CIA, 1986, Meml. Sloan-Kettering Cancer Ctr. medal, 1986, Britannica award, 1986, Notre Dame U. Laetare medal, 1992, Thomas Jefferson award AIA, 1993. Mem. AAAS (vice chmn. 1971, dir. 1972-73), Am. Philos. Soc. (Hubert Humphrey award 1983, Thomas Jefferson medal 1993), Nat. Acad. Pub. Adminstrn., Am. Acad. Arts and Scis. (chmn. seminar on poverty), Century Club, Harvard Club. Democrat. Home: Washington, DC. Died Mar. 26, 2003.

MUKI, ROKURO, engineering educator; b. Morioka, Japan, Apr. 27, 1928; s. Tetsuo and Tomi (Oyama) M.; m. Kiyo Muki, Oct. 12, 1958; children— Yoshio, Mari BS, Keio U., Tokyo, Japan, 1951; PhD, Keio U., 1959. Vis. research assoc. Brown U., Providence, 1958-60; assoc. prof. Keio U., Tokyo, 1960-65; vis. assoc. prof. Calif. Inst. Tech., Pasadena, 1965-66, sr. research fellow, 1966-67; assoc. prof. UCLA, 1967-69, prof. dept. mechanics and structures, 1969—93. Fellow Am. Acad. Mechanics; mem. ASME Home: Los Angeles, Calif. Died Feb. 10, 2004.

MULLIGAN, JAMES FRANCIS, retired business executive, lawyer; b. Attleboro, Mass., Aug. 27, 1925; s. Henry D. and Eleanor R. (Carey) M.; m. Mary Alice Mangels, Aug. 28, 1948; 1 child, Christopher. AB, Tufts U., 1947; JD, Columbia U., 1950. Bar: N.Y. 1950, Pa. 1968, U.S. Supreme Ct. 1986. Gen. atty. Erie-Lackawanna R.R., Cleve. and N.Y.C., 1950-61; gen. counsel Monroe Internat. div. Litton Industries, Orange, N.J., 1961-67; v.p., sec., gen. counsel Lukens Steel Co., Coatesville, Pa., 1967-83; v.p. law and corp. affairs, sec. Lukens, Inc., Coatesville, Pa., 1983-88, ret., 1988. Pres. United Way Chester County, West Chester, Pa., 1980-81. Lt. (j.g.) USNR, 1943-46. Mem. Springhaven Country Club. Avocation: computers. Home: Media, Pa. Died Nov. 12, 2002.

MULLIKIN, HARRY COPELAND, mathematics educator; b. Flintville, Tenn., July 10, 1940; s. Houston Yost and Daisy (Copeland) M.; m. Gary W. Parker. Student, U. Paris, France, 1960-61; BA, U. the South, Sewanee, Tenn., 1963; MA, U. Wis., Madison, 1964, PhD, 1968. Asst. prof. math. Pomona Coll., Claremont, Calif., 1968-74, assoc. prof. math., 1974-82, prof. math., 1982—, chmn. dept. math., 1979-85, William Polk Russell prof. math., 1984—, acting assoc. dean of students, 1982. Bd. dirs. Calif. br. Humane Soc. U.S., Long Beach, 1974-78; bd. dirs. Golden State Humane Soc., Garden Grove, Calif., 1974-82, sec., 1978-82. Woodrow Wilson fellow, 1963-64; recipient Disting. Prof. award Pomona Coll., 1972, 76, 80, 90, 96. Mem. Am. Math. Soc., Math. Soc. Am., Assn. Computing Machinery, So. Calif. Phi Beta Kappa Alumni Assn. (treas. 1990-94), Phi Beta Kappa (chpt. pres. 1973-74, sec.-treas. 1979-80, 82-83). Democrat. Home: Los Angeles, Calif. DIED JUNE 30, 1998.

MULVEY, JUDITH ANNE, secondary school educator; b. Sharon, Conn., Sept. 25, 1950; d. Edward Joseph and Winifred Judith (Morrison) M. BA, Marist Coll., 1972. Tchr., math. Prince George Coll., Canada, 1972-74, John Jay Sr. High Sch., Fishkill, N.Y., 1974-75, Franciscan Acad., Syracuse, N.Y., 1978-79, Marist Bros. High Sch., Pago Pago, A.S., 1975-78, 79-81, Spaulding High Sch., Rochester, N.H., from 1981. Vol. Riverside Rest Home, Dover, N.H., 1982—. Recipient Presdl. award for Excellence in Math. Teaching NSF, 1987. Mem. Nat. Coun. Tchrs. Math., Math. Assn. Am., Assn. Tchrs. Math. New England, Assn. Supervision Curriculum Devel., Coun. Presdl. Awardees Math., Delta Kappa Gamma. Democrat. Roman Catholic. Avocations: reading, swimming, cross-country skiing, calligraphy. Home: Danvers, Mass. Died Apr. 8, 2000.

MUMFORD, MANLY WHITMAN, lawyer; b. Evanston, Ill., Feb. 25, 1925; s. Manly Stearns and Helen (Whitman) M.; m. Luigi Thorne Horne, July 1, 1961; children— Shaw, Dodge. AB, Harvard U., 1947; JD, Northwestern U, Chgo., 1950. Bar: Ill. 1950, U.S. Supreme Ct. 1969. Assoc. Chapman and Cutler, Chgo., 1950-62, ptnr., 1963-90. Author: The Old Family Fire, 1997; contbr. articles to profl. jours. Served with USNR, 1942-46. Fellow Am. Coll. Bond Counsel (hon.); mem. Nat. Assn. Bond Lawyers (Bernard P. Friel medal 1987). Clubs: Cliff Dwellers, University, Chgo. Literary. Democrat. Avocation: computers. Home: Chicago, Ill. Died Dec. 31, 2003.

MUNRO, JAMES See MITCHELL, JAMES (WILLIAM)

MUNSON, PAUL LEWIS, pharmacologist; b. Washta, Iowa, Aug. 21, 1910; s. Lewis Sylvester and Alice E. (Orser) M.; m. Aileen Geisinger, Mar. 7, 1931 (div. 1948); 1 dau., Abigail (Mrs. Mark Krumel); m. Mary Ellen Jones, Aug. 15, 1948 (div. 1971); children: Ethan Vincent, Catherine Laura; m. Yu Chen, Feb. 27, 1987; 1 stepchild, Ming An Chen. BA, Antioch Coll., 1933; MA, U. Wis., 1937; PhD, U. Chgo., 1942; MA (hon.), Harvard, 1955. Fellow, asst. biochemistry U. Chgo., 1939-42; research biochemist William S. Merrell Co., Cin., 1942-43; research biochemist, head endocrinology research Armour Labs., Chgo., 1943-48; research asst., then research asso. Yale Sch. Medicine, 1948-50; asst. prof., asso. prof. pharmacology, then prof. Harvard Sch. Dental Medicine, 1950-65; prof. pharmacology, chmn. dept. U. N.C. Sch. Medicine, 1965-77, Sarah Graham Kenan prof., 1970—. Mem. U.S. Pharmacopeia Panel on Corticotropin, 1951-55; mem. pharmacology test com. Nat. Bd. Med. Examiners, 1966-71; mem. gen. medicine B study section NIH, 1966-70, chmn., 1969-70, mem. pharmacology-toxicology rev. com., 1972-76 Author numerous articles on hormones; co-editor: Vitamins and Hormones, 1968-82; editl. bd. Endocrinology, 1957-63, Jour. Pharmacology and Exptl. Therapeutics, 1959-65, Jour. Dental Rsch., 1962-64, Biochem. Medicine, 1967-84, Am. Jour. Chinese Medicine, 1973-79, 99—, Pharmacol. Revs., 1967-70, editor-in-chief, 1977-81; editor-in-chief: Principles of Pharmacology, 1981-94. Fellow AAAS, Am. Acad. Arts and Scis.; mem. Am. Soc. Pharmacology and Exptl. Therapeutics (council 1970-73, sec.-treas. 1971-72), Am. Soc. Biol. Chemists, Endocrine Soc. (council 1963-65, Fred Conrad Koch award 1976), Am. Soc. Bone and Mineral Research (William F. Neuman award 1982), Am. Chem. Soc., Biometrics Soc., Internat. Assn. Dental Research (councillor 1957-59), AAUP, ACLU (mem. internat. confs. on calcium regulating hormones, Elsevier Sci. Pubs. award 1989), Assn. Med. Sch. Pharmacology (council 1971-73, sec. 1972-73, pres. 1974-76), Am. Thyroid Assn. (nominating com. 1973), Sigma Xi. Dem. Socialist. Unitarian. Died May 15, 2003.

MURANY, ERNEST ELMER, exploration geologist, consultant; b. Avella, Pa., Mar. 28, 1923; s. Joseph and Rose Botz (Botz) M.; m. Judith Vivian Taylor; children: Peter Taylor, Paul Alexander BS, Kent State U., 1950; PhD, U. Utah, 1963. Cert. petroleum geologist. Exploration advisor Belco Petroleum Inc., Maracaibo, Venezuela, 1973-77; sr. exploration advisor Ministry of Petroleum, Muscat, Oman, 1977-80; dist. mgr. Tetratech Inc., Columbus, Ohio, 1980-82; exploration advisor Superior Oil Co., Houston, 1982-84; pres. Murex Internat. Inc., Houston, 1984-94, Jemco Internat. Inc., Houston, from 1994. Cons. geologist Tenneco Oil Co., Houston, 1984-86, Cambrian Oil Co., Houston, 1986-89. Contbr. articles to Bull. Am. Assn. Petroleum Geologists, Intermountain Assn. Petroleum Geologists. Cpl. USMC, 1941-45. Mem. Am. Assn. Petroleum Geologists, Am. Geophys. Union, Houston Geol. Soc. Home: Houston, Tex. Died Aug. 27, 2000.

MURNANE, WILLIAM J., JR., Egyptologist, educator; b. White Plains, N.Y., Mar. 22, 1945; s. William Joseph and Marie Eleanor (Cardone) M. BA, St. Anselm's Coll., 1966; MA, U. Chgo., 1968, PhD, 1973. Staff Egyptologist Oriental Inst. epigraphic survey U. Chgo., 1972-86, assoc. prof., 1982-87; vis. assoc. prof. U. Calif., Berkeley, 1986-87; assoc. prof. Memphis State U. (now U. Memphis), 1989-94, prof., from 1994. Field dir. Amarna Boundary Stelae project U. Chgo. and U. Memphis, 1984-89, field dir. Karnak Hypostyle Hall project, 1979—; mem. editl. bd. jour. KMT, 1990—; mem. editl. bd. translation series Soc. Biblical Lit., 1993—. Author: Ancient Egyptian Coregencies, 1977, Penguin Guide to Ancient Eqypt, 1983, 96, The Road to Kadesh, 1985, 90, (with C.C. Van Siclen) The Boundary Stelae of Akhenaten, 1993, Texts from the Amarna Period in Egypt, 1995, 98. Mem. AAUP (campus pres. 1996—), Am. Rsch. Ctr. in Egypt, Archeol. Inst. Am. Avocation: opera. Home: Memphis, Tenn. Died Nov. 17, 2000.

MUROFF, ELENA MARIE, lawyer; b. Waterbury, Conn., Mar. 14, 1957; d. John Andrew Muroff. AS in Bus. Adminstrn. summa cum laude, Teikyo Post Coll., Waterbury, 1979, BS in Mktg. in summa cum laude, 1981; JD, U. Bridgeport, 1986; postgrad., U. Conn. Bar: Conn., U.S. Dist. Ct. Conn. Legal intern Fl. Woodward Lewis, Yalesville, Conn., 1986-87; clk. New Haven Superior Ct., 1987-88; asst. appellate clk. Supreme and Appellate Ct., Hartford, Conn., 1988-89; asst. atty. gen. Office Atty. Gen., Hartford, 1990-91; pvt. practice, pro bono Waterbury, 1989-90 and from 91. Legal instr. Nat. Acad. Paralegal Studies, West Hartford, Conn., 1991; instr. living skills Greenshire Sch., Cheshire, Conn., 1988; care provider to mentally challenged Respite Resources, Wallingford, Conn., 1994—; co-facilitator group therapy Mental Health Assn., Wethersfield, Conn., 1995—; spkr. Rose Traurig scholars program Teikyo Post U., 1992, also for legal asst. program. Mem. Dem. Nat. Com.; U.S. del. Moscow Conf. Law and Bilateral Econ. Rels., 1990. Recipient letter of commendation Conn. Valley Hosp., 1990; scholar Teikyo Post Coll., 1980-81, Max Traurig scholar, 1981; Bank of Boston Marguerite McGraw scholar U. Bridgeport, 1983, Conn. grad. scholar, 1983, Sch. Law scholar, 1983-86. Mem. ATLA, ACLU, NOW, Conn. Bar Assn., Conn. Edn. and Legal Fund, Conn. Mental Health Assn., Conn. Assn. for Human Svcs., Campaign for Children, So. Poverty Law Ctr. Roman Catholic. Avocations: writing poetry, music and arts, avidly following politics. Died Apr. 13, 2001.

MURPHY, BRIANNE, cinematographer; b. London, Eng., Apr. 1, 1937; d. Gerald Leslie and Mary Kathleen (Nobel) Murphy; m. Ralph Brook, Apr. 1, 1958 (dec.). MA, Brown U., 1952; student, Neighborhood Playhouse, 1952—54. Cinematographer: (TV series) Little House on the Prairie, Mulligan's Stew, Kaz, Married: The First Yr., Trapper John, M.D., Breaking Away (Emmy nomination for Cinematography, 1981), Stone, Father Murphy, Square Pegs, For Love and Honor, Highway to Heaven, In the Heat of the Night, Shades of LA, Love & War; (TV films) Like Mom, Like Me, 1977, Merlene of the Movies, 1981, Little House: Look Back to Yesterday, 1983, Kung Fu: The Next Generation, 1987, Destined to Live, 1988, My Dad Can't Be Crazy, Can He?, 1989, In the Best Interest of the Child, 1990; (films) Panchito y el gringo, 1962, The Magic Tide, 1962, Fatso, 1980, Cheech & Chong's Nice Dreams, 1981, There Were Times, Dear, 1985, Blackbird Fly, 1991, To Die, To Sleep (also dir.), 1992, (NBC Spl.) Five Finger Discount (Emmy award for Cinematography, 1978). Recipient Acad. Award for design, concept and manufacture of Misi Safety Car and Trailer, 1982. Mem.: Am. Film Inst., Acad. TV Arts and Scis., Acad. Motion Picture Arts and Scis., Soc. Motion Picture Technicians and Engrs., Internat. Alliance Theatrical and Stage Employees, Am. Soc. Cinematographers. Died Aug. 20, 2003.

MURPHY, FRANCIS SEWARD, retired journalist; b. Portland, Oreg., Sept. 9, 1914; s. Francis H. and Blanche (Livesay) M.; m. Clare Eastham Cooke, Sept. 20, 1974 (dec. Apr. 1990). BA, Reed Coll., 1936. With The Oregonian, Portland, 1936-79, TV editor, Behind the Mike columnist, 1952-79. Archeol. explorer Mayan ruins, Yucatan, Mex., 1950-87, mem. Am. Quintana Roo Expdn., 1965, 66, 68. Author: Dragon Mask Temples in Central Yucatan, 1988. With U.S. Army, 1942-46. Mem. Am. Philat. Soc. (life), Royal Asiatic Soc., City Club, Am. Club of Hong Kong, Explorer's Club, Oreg. Hist. Soc., Soc. Am. Archaeology, Hong Kong Philat Soc., World Wide Fund Nature, Hong Kong Jockey Club. Democrat. Congregationalist. Home: Portland, Oreg. Died Mar. 24, 2003.

MURPHY, JOHN CULLEN, illustrator; b. N.Y.C., May 3, 1919; s. Robert Francis and Jane (Finn) M.; m. Katherine Joan Byrne, July 14, 1951; children: John Cullen, Mary Cullene, Katherine Siobhan, Joan Byrne, Robert Finn, Brendan Woods, Cait Naughton, Mairead Walsh. Student, Phoenix Art Inst., Chgo. Art Inst., Art Students League, N.Y.C. Illustrator: numerous mags. including Colliers, 1946-51; illustrator: comic strip King Features Syndicate, 1950-69, Prince Valiant, King Features Syndicate, 1970—2004; Illustrator numerous books. Co-founder of The Wild Geese (an Irish-Am. Cultural Assn.). Maj. U.S. Army, 1941-46. Decorated Bronze star. Recipient 6 Best Story Strip Artist awards Nat. Cartoonists Soc., 1988. Mem. Nat. Cartoonists Soc. (pres., Best Story Strip Cartoonist award (6), Segar award 1983), Soc. Illustrators, Artists and Writers Assn. Roman Catholic. Died July 2, 2004.

MURPHY, JOHN J. retired university administrator, economist; b. Holyoke, Mass., 1927; BA, Catholic U. Am., 1952; MA, Yale U., 1953, PhD, 1961. Instr. Yale U., 1954-57; from asst. prof. to prof. economics Catholic U. Am., 1957—92, dean Grad. Sch., 1968-73, provost, exec. v.p., 1979—86. Contbr. articles to profl. jours. Mem. Am. Econ. Assn. Died Oct. 2, 2003.

MURPHY, TERRENCE JOHN, priest, college president; b. Watkins, Minn., Dec. 21, 1920; s. Frank and Mary (Lee) M. BA, St. Paul Sem., 1946; MA, U. Minn., 1956; PhD,

Georgetown U., 1959. Ordained priest, Roman Catholic church, 1946, became monsignor, 1966. Asst. pastor various parishes, 1946-49; chaplain USAF, 1949-54; mem. faculty Coll. St. Thomas, St. Paul, 1954-61, dean of students, 1961-62, exec. v.p., 1962-66, pres., 1966—91. Del. Congress Cath. Edn., Rome, 1972; mem. Minn. Pvt. Coll. Council., Minn. Pvt. Coll. Fund.; bd. dirs. Am. Nat. Bank, St. Paul, Waldorf Corp., St. Paul. Author: Censorship: Government and Obscenity, 1963. Bd. dirs. Mt. St. Mary's Coll. of Md., Associated Colls. Twin Cities, Minn. Wellspring. Mem. Nat. Cath. Ednl. Assn., Assn. Post-Secondary Ednl. Instns. Minn., Assn. Am. Colls., Internat. Fedn. Cath. Univs. (dir.). Died Feb. 25, 2004.

MURPHY, WILLIAM HOST, sales executive, retired; b. South Bend, Ind., June 7, 1926; s. Joseph Patrick and Edna Emma (Host) M.; m. Dorothy A. Dubala, Jan. 29, 1949 (div. 1968); m. Barbara Joan Mellinger, Sept. 11, 1987; children: Kent Alan, Thomas Aquinas, Catherine Ann, Molly Teresa. BS in Commerce, U. Notre Dame. Lic. English and Math tchr. Salesman Lyon Metal Products, Inc., Aurora, Ill., 1954; sales tng. dir. Lyon Metal Products, Aurora, 1987-99, ret., now part time, from 1999. With US Navy, 1944-46. Mem. Mensa, South Bend Press Club. Christian. Avocation: science. Died May 20, 2001.

MURRAY, BARBARA ANN, lay minister; b. Ft. Knox, Ky., June 29, 1948; d. Leonard Orrie and Karen Lydia (Grabis) M. AA, Elizabethtown (Ky.) Community Coll., 1968; BA magna cum laude, Cardinal Stritch Coll., Milw., 1988. Min. youth Holy Family Ch., Ashland, Ky., 1988-90; coord. youth ministries Roman Cath. Diocese of Lexington, Ky., 1991. Corr. The Messenger jour., 1989, Cross Roads, 1990-91. Mem. Nat. Assn. Religious Women, Pax Christi U.S.A., Kappa Gamma Pi. Democrat. Home: Lexington, Ky. Died Dec. 7, 2001.

MURRAY, FLORENCE KERINS, retired state supreme court justice; b. Newport, R.I., Oct. 21, 1916; d. John X. and Florence (MacDonald) Kerins; m. Paul F. Murray, Oct. 21, 1943 (dec. June 2, 1995); 1 child, Paul F. AB, Syracuse U., 1938; LLB, Boston U., 1942; EdD, R.I. Coll. Edn., 1956; grad., Nat. Coll. State Trial Judges, 1966; LLD (hon.), Bryant Coll., 1956, U. R.I., 1963, Mt. St. Joseph Coll., 1972, Providence Coll., 1974, Roger Williams Coll., 1976, Salve Regina Coll., 1977, Johnson and Wales Coll., 1977, Suffolk U., 1981, So. New Eng. Law Sch., 1995; D (hon.), New England Inst. Tech., 1998. Bar: Mass. 1942, R.I. 1947, U.S. Dist. Ct. 1948, U.S. Tax Ct. 1948, U.S. Supreme Ct. 1948. Sole practice, Newport, 1947-52; mem. firm Murray & Murray, Newport, 1952-56; assoc. judge R.I. Superior Ct., 1956-78; presiding justice Superior Ct. R.I., 1978-79; assoc. justice (ret.-active) R.I. Supreme Ct., 1979—96. Staff, faculty adv. Nat. Jud. Coll., Reno, Nev., 1971-72, dir., 1975-77, chmn., 1979-87, chair emeritus, 1990-2004; mem. com. Legal Edn. and Practice and Economy of New Eng., 1975-2004; former instr. Prudence Island Sch.; legal adv. R.I. Girl Scouts; sec. Commn. Jud. Tenure and Discipline, 1975-79; apptd. by Pres. Clinton to bd. dirs. State Justice Inst., 1994-99; participant, leader various legal seminars; presdl. appointment R.I. State Justice Inst. Mem. R.I. Senate, 1948-56; chmn. spl. legis. com.; mem. Newport Sch. Com., 1948-57, chmn., 1951-57; mem. Gov.'s Jud. Coun., 1950-60, White House Conf. Youth and Children, 1950, Ann. Essay Commn., 1952, Nat. Def. Adv. Com. on Women in Service, 1952-58, Gov.'s Adv. Com. Mental Health, 1954, R.I. Alcoholic Adv. Com., 1955-58, R.I. Com. Youth and Children, Gov.'s Adv. Com. on Revision Election Laws, Gov.'s Adv. Com. Social Welfare, Army Adv. Com. for 1st Army Area; mem. civil and polit. rights com. Pres.'s Commn. on Status of Women, 1960-63; mem. R.I. Com. Humanities, 1972-2004, chmn., 1972-77; mem. Family Ct. Study Com., R.I. com. Nat. Endowment Humanities; bd. dirs. Newport YMCA; sec. Bd. Physicians Service; bd. visitors Law Sch., Boston U.; bd. dirs. NCCJ; mem. edn. policy and devel. com. Roger Williams Jr. Coll.; trustee Syracuse U.; pres. Newport Girls Club, 1974-75, R.I. Supreme Ct. Hist. Soc., 1988-2004; chair Supreme Ct. Mandatory Continuing Legal Edn. Com., 1993-2004; apptd. bd. dirs. Touro Synague; apptd. R.I. Found. Served to lt. col. WAC, World War II. Decorated Legion of Merit; named named Judge of Yr., Nat. Assn. Women Judges, 1984, Outstanding Woman, Bus. and Profl. Women, 1972, Citizen of Yr., R.I. Trial Lawyers Assn., Newport courthouse renamed in her honor, 1990; recipient Arents Alumni award, Syracuse U., 1956, Carroll award, R.I. Inst. Instn., 1956, Brotherhood award, NCCJ, 1983, Herbert Harley award, Am. Judicature Soc., 1988, Silver Citizenship award, DAR, R.I., 1980s, Gold Citizenship award, DAR, 1990s, Merit award, R.I. Bar Assn., 1994, John Manson/Carl Robinson award, Nat. Probation Officers Assn., 1996, Longfellow Humanitarian award, ARC, 1997. Mem. ABA (chmn. credentials com. nat. conf. state trial judges 1971-73, chair judges adv. com. on standing com. on ethics and profl. responsibility 1991—, joint com. on jud. discipline of standing com. on profl. discipline 1991-94), R.I. Found. (bd. dirs. 1998—), AAUW (chmn. state edn. com. 1954-56), Am. Arbitration Assn., Nat. Trial Judges Conf. (state chmn. membership com., sec. exec. com.), New Eng. Trial Judges Conf. (com. chmn. 1967), Boston U. Alumni Coun., Am. Legion (judge adv. post 7, mem. nat. exec. com.), Bus. and Profl. Women's Club (past state v.p., past pres. Newport chpt., past pres. Nat. legis. com.), Auota Club (past gov. internat., past pres. Newport chpt.), Alpha Omega, Kappa Beta Pi. Died Mar. 28, 2003.

MURRAY, WILLIAM JAMES, anesthesiology educator, clinical pharmacologist; b. Janesville, Wis., July 20, 1933; s. James Arthur and Mary Helen (De Porter) M.; m. Therese Rose Dooley, June 25, 1955; children: Michael, James, Anne. BS, U. Wis., 1955, PhD, 1959; MD, U. N.C., 1962. Diplomate Am. Bd. Anesthesiology. Rsch. asst. U. Wis., Madison, 1955-59; instr. pharmacology U. N.C., Chapel Hill, 1959-62, resident and fellow in surgery (anesthesiology), 1962-64, instr., 1964-65, asst. prof., 1965-68; asst. to dir. for drug availability FDA, Washington, 1968-69; assoc. prof. pharmacology, clin. pharmacology and anesthesiology U. Mich., Ann Arbor, 1969-72; assoc. prof. anesthesiology Duke U., Durham, N.C., 1972-81, prof., from 1981. Assoc. dir. Upjohn Ctr. for Clin. Pharmacology, Ann Arbor, 1969-72. Mem. AMA, Am. Soc. Anesthesiologists, Internat. Anesthesia Rsch. Soc., Soc. for Ambulatory Anesthesia, Am. Pharm. Assn., N.Y. Acad. Scis., N.C. Soc. Anesthesiologists, Am. Soc. Hosp. Pharmacists, U.S. Pharmacopeial Conv., Am. Coll. Clin. Pharmacology, Am. Soc. for Clin. and Therapeutic Pharmacology, Am. Soc. Pharmacology and Exptl. Therapeutics, N.C. Soc. Hosp. Pharmacists, So. Med. Assn., Annals Pharmacotherapy, Am. Med. Writers Assn. Republican. Roman Catholic. Home: Durham, NC. Deceased.

MURTAGH, JOHN EDWARD, alcohol production consultant; b. Wallington, Surrey, Eng., Sept. 12, 1936; arrived in U.S., 1982; s. Thomas Henry and Elsie (Kershaw Paterson) M.; m. Eithne Anne Fawsitt, July 18, 1959; children: Catherine, Rhoda, Sean, Aidan, Doreen. BSc, U. Wales, 1959, MSc, 1970, PhD, 1972. Rsch. coord. House of Seagram, Long Pond, Jamaica, 1959-63, whisky distillery mgr. Beaupre, Que., Can., 1963-65, rum distillery mgr. Richibucto, N.B., Can., 1965-68, rsch. mgr. Montreal, Que., 1968-70; alcohol prodn. cons. Murtagh & Assocs., Buttevant, Ireland, 1972-77, 79-82, Winchester, Va., from 1982; vodka distillery mgr. Iran Beverages, Tehran, 1977-79. Ethanol tech. cons., adv. bd. Info. Resources, Inc., Washington, 1988-98; lectr. Alltech Ann. Alcohol Sch., Lexington, Ky., 1982-97; chmn. Ann. World Ethanol Conf., London, 1998-2001; cons. in field. Author: Glossary of Fuel-Ethanol Terms, 1990; co-author, editor: The Alcohol Textbook, 1995; editor: Worldwide Directory of Distilleries, 1996; contbr. articles to profl. jours. Adv. bd. Byrd Sch. Bus., Shenandoah U., Winchester, Va., 1989-95. Recipient Millers Mut. prize, U. Wales, 1959. Fellow Am. Inst. Chemists, Inst. Chemistry of Ireland, Inst. Food Sci. and Tech. of Ireland; mem. Royal Soc. Chemistry (chartered), Am. Arbitration Assn. (arbitrator nat. comml. panel 1990-2000). Achievements include development of processes for the prodn. of high-quality neutral alcohol from a wide range of feedstocks. Died Jan. 25, 2003.

MUZENDA, SIMON VENGAI, vice president of Zimbabwe; b. Gutu, Masvingo Province, Zimbabwe, Oct. 28, 1922; m. Maude Muzenda; 8 children. Diploma in carpentry, Marianhill Coll., South Africa, 1948. Instr. Mazenod Sch., Mayville, South Africa, 1948-50. Carpenter, Bulawayo twp. of Barbourfields, from 1953, also Umvuma; co-founder Barbourfields Tenants Assn.; co-founder Nat. Democratic Party; chmn. Umvuma br., organizing sec. for Masvingo province, 1960-61, party banned, 1962; adminstrv. sec. Masvingo, Zimbabwe African People's Union, 1962, dep. organizing sec. 1st Congress Zimbabwe African Nat. Union; dep. adminstrv. sec. Zambia, 1975-76, minister fgn. affairs, 1980-81; with Zimbabwe African Nat. Liberation Army, 1977-80; dep. prime minister Republic of Zimbabwe, 1980-88, v.p., 1988-2003. Died Sept. 20, 2003.

MYERS, MINOR, JR., academic administrator, political science educator; b. Akron, Ohio, Aug. 13, 1942; s. Minor and Ruth (Libby) M.; m. Ellen Achin, Mar. 21, 1970; children: Minor III, Joffre V.A. BA, Carleton Coll., Northfield, Minn., 1964; MA, Princeton U., 1967, PhD, 1972. From instr. to assoc. prof. Conn. Coll., New London, 1968-81, prof. govt., 1981-84; provost, dean of faculty, prof. polit. sci. Hobart and William Smith Colls., Geneva, N.Y., 1984-89; pres., prof. polit. sci. Ill. Wesleyan U., Bloomington, 1989—2003. Adv. Numismatic Collection Yale U., 1975-84; chmn. adv. coun. Lyman Allyn Mus., 1976-81, 82-84, pres., 1982-84. Author: Liberty Without Anarchy: A History of the Society of the Cincinnati, 1983, The Insignia of the Society of the Cincinnati, 1998; ((with others) Illinois Wesleyan University: Continuity and Change 1850-2001, 2001, with others) Arnold O. Beckman, One Hundred Years of Excellence, 2000, (with others) New London County Furniture, 1974, (with others) The Princeton Graduate School: A History, 1978, 2nd edit., 1997, (with others) American Interiors: A Documentary History from the Colonial Era to 1915, 1980. Asst. sec. gen. Soc. of the Cin., 1983-86, sec.-gen., 1986-89; trustee Inst. for Internat. Edn. Students, 1992-98, Found. for Ind. Higher Edn., 1999-2001, Nat. Merit Scholarship Corp., 1999-2002; pres. Associated Colls. Ill., 1999-2001. Mem. Grolier Club (N.Y.C.), Princeton Club (N.Y.C.), University Club (Chgo.), Caxton Club (Chgo.), Phi Beta Kappa, Sigma Xi. Home: Bloomington, Ill. Died July 22, 2003.

MYERS, ORIE EUGENE, JR., university official; b. Hagan, Ga., Oct. 14, 1920; s. Orie Eugene and Betty (Shuman) M.; m. Margaret Elizabeth Nesbit, June 7, 1941; children: Orie Eugene III, Curtis Alan, Adrian Marvyn. Student, Ga. Inst. Tech., 1937-38; AB, Emory U., 1941, MA, 1957. Personnel asst. Atlanta Personnel Bd., 1940-41; personnel officer Nat. Youth Adminstrn., 1941-43, Office Emergency Mgmt., 1943-44, VA, 1946-48; dir. personnel Emory U., 1948-61, bus. mgr., 1961, dean adminstrn., dir. health services, 1961-64, v.p. bus., 1973-89, sr. bus. analyst, 1989-91; v.p. bus., dir. Woodruff Med. Center, 1964-73. Past chmn. bd. Prime Bancshares, Inc., Prime Bank FSB. Trustee, chmn. med. com. Wesley Homes; bd. dirs., past chmn. DeKalb County unit Am. Cancer Soc. Served to 1st lt. USAAF, 1944-46. Mem. Coll. and Univ. Personnel Assn. (past pres.), Nat. Assn. Coll. and Univ. Bus. Officers (past pres.), So. Assn. Coll. and Univ. Bus. Officers (past pres.), DeKalb C. of C. (past pres.), Sigma Nu. Democrat. Baptist. Home: Decatur, Ga. Died Dec. 24, 1999.

MYERSON, ALBERT LEON, physical chemist; b. N.Y.C., Nov. 14, 1919; s. Myer and Dora (Weiner) M.; m. Arline Harriet Rosenfield, May 10, 1953; children: Aimee Lenore, Lorraine Patrice, Paul Andrew. BS, Pa. State U., 1941; postgrad., Columbia U., 1942-45; PhD, U. Wis., 1948. Rsch. asst. Manhattan Project Columbia U., N.Y.C., 1941-45; sr. rsch. chemist Franklin Inst. Labs., Phila., 1948-56; mgr. phys. chemistry Gen. Electric Co., Phila., 1956-60; prin. phys. chemist Aero. Lab. Cornell U., Buffalo, 1960-68; rsch. assoc. Exxon Rsch. and Engring. Co., Linden, N.J., 1969-79; head phys. chemistry sect. Mote Marine Lab., Sarasota, Fla., 1979-85. Cons. in field. Co-editor: Physical Chemistry in Aerodynamics and Space Flight, 1961; contbr. articles in field to profl. jours.; patentee in field. Mem. Am. Phys. Soc., Am. Chem. Soc., Combustion Inst., Pa. State U. Alumni Assn., Sigma Xi, Phi Lambda Upsilon. Avocations: violin, fine antique china and porcelain. Died Mar. 31, 2004.

MYRON, ROBERT ELIAS, art history educator, appraiser; b. N.Y.C., Mar. 15, 1926; s. Joseph and Sophie (Cantor) M.; m. Marie-Rose Gantois, 1954; children: Daniel, Jacques. BA, NYU, l949; MA, Inst. Fine Arts, N.Y.C., l950; PhD, Ohio State U., l953. Prof. art history Hofstra U., Hempstead, N.Y., from l954. Vis. prof. St. John's U., l955-59, Mich. State U., East Lansing, l956, Adelphi U., l965. Author: Two Faces of Asia: India and China, 1967, Prehistoric Art, 1975, American Art, 2 vols., 1975, Shadow of the Hawk, 1978, Mounds, Towns and Totems, 1979, Italian Renaissance, 1976. With AUS, l944-45. Ohio State U. fellow, l950-53, Belgium-Am. Found. fellow, l955. Mem. Appraisers Assn. Am. (bd. dirs. 1985—), Am. Soc. Appraisers (sr. mem.). Home: Garden City South, NY. Died Mar. 10, 2000.

NABORS, JOHN C. lawyer; b. Gatesville, Tex., Sept. 9, 1944; BBA, U. Tex., 1965, LLB with honors, 1967. Bar: Tex. 1967. Mem. Gardere & Wynne, Dallas. Assoc. editor: Tex. Law Rev., 1966-67. Mem. ABA, State Bar Tex., Dallas Bar Assn., Houston Bar Assn., Order of Coif, Chancellors, Phi Delta Phi. Died June 14, 2004.

NABRIT, SAMUEL MILTON, retired embryologist; b. Macon, Ga., Feb. 21, 1905; BS, Morehouse Coll., 1925; MS, Brown U., 1928, PhD in Biology, 1932; 13 hon. degrees, various U.S. univs. Instr. zoology Morehouse Coll., 1925—27, prof., 1928—31, Atlanta U., 1932—55; pres. Tex. So. U., 1955—66; commr. U.S. AEC, 1966—67; exec. dir. So. Fellows Fund, 1967—81. Exch. prof. Atlanta U., 1930, dean Grad. Sch.; gen. edn. bd. fellow Columbia U., 1943; rsch. fellow U. Brussels, 1950; coord. Carnegie Expn. Grant-in-Aid Rsch. Program; mem. sci. bd. NSF, 1956—60; mem. corp. Marine Biol. Lab., Woods Hole; mem. Marine Biol. Labs., AEC, 1966—67; exec. dir. Nat. Fellows Fund, 1967—81; interim dir. Atlanta U. Ctr., 1989—91. Named to Hall of Fame, NSF, Sayles Hall of Fame Brown U. Fellow: AAAS; mem.: Inst. Medicine-NAS, Societ+248 d'honneur Francaise, Am. Soc. Zoology, Nat. Inst. Sci. (pres. 1945), Nat. Assn. Rsch. Sci. Tchg., Soc. Devel. Biology, Sigma Xi, Pi Delta Phi, Phi Beta Kappa. Died Dec. 30, 2003.

NACHMAN, NORMAN HARRY, lawyer; b. Chgo.; s. Harry and Mary (Leibowitz) N.; m. Anne Lev, June 19, 1932; children: Nancy Nachman Laskow, James Lev, Susan Lev. PhB, U. Chgo., 1930, JD, 1932. Bar: Ill. 1932, U.S. Dist. Ct. (no. dist.) Ill. 1932, U.S. Dist. Ct. (we. dist.) Tex. 1978, U.S. Ct. Appeals (7th cir.) 1942, U.S. Ct. Appeals (4th cir.) 1978, U.S. Ct. Appeals (8th cir.) 1994, U.S. Supreme Ct. 1942. Assoc. Michael Gesas, Chgo., 1932-35; assoc. Schwartz & Cooper, Chgo., 1936-40, ptnr., 1940-46; pvt. practice, Chgo., 1947-67; founder, sr. ptnr. Nachman, Munitz & Sweig, Ltd., Chgo., 1967-87; ptnr. Winston & Strawn, 1987-94; counsel McDermott, Will & Emery, 1994—; mem. adv. com. bankruptcy rules Jud. Conf. U.S., 1960-76, 78-88; mem. Nat. Bankruptcy Conf., 1952—, mem. com. bankruptcy reorganization plans and securities problems, 1977-85; mem. faculty numerous bankruptcy seminars throughout U.S. Contbg. editor: Collier on Bankruptcy, 1981, 84. Chmn. appeals bd. Chgo. Dept. Environ. Control, 1960-80. Served to lt. USN, 1943-46. Mem. ABA (past chmn. comml. bankruptcy com.), Chgo. Bar Assn. (pres. 1963-64), Ill. Bar Assn., Standard Club, Law Club. Jewish. Deceased.

NADLER, HARRY, artist, art educator; b. L.A., Feb. 17, 1930; s. Jacob and Etta (Greenberg) N.; m. Helen Sturges, Mar. 24, 1971. BA, UCLA, 1956, MA, 1958. Instr. Bklyn. Mus. Art Sch., 1960-65; asst. prof. art Wesleyan U., Middletown, Conn., 1965-71; assoc. prof. art U. N.Mex., Albuquerque, 1971-80, prof. art, from 1980. Instr. Liberal Arts NYU, 1960-65. One-man shows include Dwan Gallery, L.A., 1959, 62, Santa Barbara Mus. of Art, Calif., 1960, Nebli Gallery, Madrid, 1961, Drawing Shop Gallery, N.Y., 1963, Wesleyan U., Middletown, Conn., 1971, Bertha Schaefer Gallery, N.Y., 1969, 72, 1974, London Arts Gallery, Detroit, 1973, Janus Gallery, Santa Fe, 1973, Cantor/Lemberg Gallery, Birmingham, Mich., 1981, Fine Art Mus.-U. of N.Mex., 1983, Peter Eller Gallery, Albuquerque, 1987, Sena Gallery East, Santa Fe, 1989; group shows include L.A. County Mus. Anns., San Francisco Mus. Ann., Denver Mus. Ann., Butler Inst. Art, Libr. Congress, N.W. Printmakers Ann.,

Guggenheim Mus., N.Y., 1980, Bologna-Lani Gallery, East Hampton, 1984, Shippee Gallery, N.Y., 1988; pub. and pvt. collections include The Alan I. Kay Co., Albuquerque Mus., U. Calif., Cin. Art Mus., Container Corp. of Am., Detroit Inst. Art, Guild Hall Mus., Hyatt Corp., Landmark Systems Corp., U. Mass., Milton Co., Nikko Corp., Pa. Acad. of the Fine Arts, Storm King Art Ctr., Tyson's Dulles Pla. Fulbright grantee Fulbright Commn., 1959; recipient Childe Hassam Purchase award Nat. Inst. of Arts and Letters, 1971. Mem. Coll. Art Assn., Chelsea Arts Club (London chpt.). Avocation: study of tia-chi-chuan. Home: Albuquerque, N.Mex. Deceased.

NAFEY, WILLIAM BROOKS, audio-visual services supervisor; b. North Bergen, N.J., Sept. 5, 1926; s. Raymond and Olga Sophia (Stroem) N.; m. Marguerite Mary Bahr, Mar. 21, 1948; children: Stuart Brian, Carol Ann Nafey Kutz. Photographer U.S. Army Electronics Command, Eatontown, N.J., 1955-76; visual info. specialist Naval Research Laboratory, Washington, D.C., 1976-84; audio-visual supr. North Va. Community Coll., Loudoun, Sterling, Va., 1984-87. Ind. cons. Visual Impressions, Reston, Va., 1982-87; sr. photography instr. Reston Community Ctr., 1980-87. Photographer received 12 awards, 1982-87. President Laurel Park Civic Assn., Parlin, N.J., 1970-73, Council and Congregation Lutheran ch., Parlin, 1973-75; pres., chmn. Citizens Action Com., Parlin, 1970-72; chmn. Citizens for Moral Decency, Sayreville, N.J., 1971. Served with USNR 1943-83, PTO. Mem.: F and AM. Avocations: needlepoint, rock hound, salt water fishing. Home: Reston, Va. Deceased.

NAGLEE, ELFRIEDE KURZ, retired medical nurse; b. Phila., Mar. 13, 1932; d. Emil and Frida (Keppler) Kurz; m. David I. Naglee, Sept. 6, 1952 (dec. Jan. 20, 1998); children: Joy, Miriam, Deborah, Joanna, David. Grad., Phila. Gen. Hosp., 1952. RN, Ga. Dir. nursing City County Hosp., LaGrange, Ga.; house supr. West Ga. Med. Ctr., LaGrange, from 1967, staff nurse med. fl. LaGange, to 1995; ret., 1995. Vol. West Ga. Med. Ctr., 1995—. Mem. Ga. Nursing Assn. Home: Lagrange, Ga. Died Oct. 31, 2001.

NAKAMURA, KAZUO, artist; b. Vancouver, Can., Oct. 13, 1926; s. Toichi and Yoshiyo (Uyemoto) N.; m. Lillian Yuriko Kobayakawa, Sept. 15, 1967; children: Elaine Yukae, Bryan Kazuto. Student, Central Tech. Sch., Toronto, 1948-51. Exhibited in one man shows at, Picture Loan Soc., 1952, Hart House, U. Toronto, 1953, Gallery of Contemporary Art, Toronto, 1956, 58, Jerrold Morris Gallery, Toronto, 1962, 65, 67-70, R. McLaughlin Gallery, Oshawa and Can. Tour, 1974-75, Christopher Cutts Gallery, Toronto, 1991, 96; exhibited in group shows at, Fifth Internat. Hallmark Art Award Exhbn., N.Y.C., 1960, Canadian Prints, Drawings and Watercolor, Am. Fedn. Arts Tour, 1960, Seconde Biennale, Musee d'Art Moderne, Paris, France, 1961, Canadian Painting, Polish Tour, 1962, Canadian Painting, Central Africa, 1962, Nineteen Canadian Painters, Louisville, 1962, Commonwealth Painting, London, Eng., 1962, Recent Acquisitions, Mus. Modern Art, N.Y.C., 1963, Canadian Painting, London, 1963, Member's Loan Gallery Acquisitions, Albright-Knox Gallery, Buffalo, 1963, World Show, Washington Sq. Gallery, N.Y.C., 1964, Cardiff Commonwealth Exhbn. of Drawings, Wales, 1965, Centennial Exhbn. of Canadian Prints and Drawings, Australian Tour, 1967, Painters Eleven in Retrospect, Can. tour, 1979-81, Ont. Heritage Found. Firestone Collection, European tour, 1983-84, Nat. Gallery Can., Ottawa, 1989, Nat. Gallery Can., Ottawa, Can. tour, 1993, Mead Mus., Amherst Coll., 1994, Art Forum, Berlin, 1998, others; represented in permanent collections at Nat. Gallery Can., Mus. Modern Art, N.Y.C., Art Gallery of Ont., Toronto, Musée d'Art contemporain, Montreal, R. McLaughlin Gallery, Oshawa, Hirshhorn Mus., Washington, British Mus., London, Art Gallery of Hamilton, Winnipeg Art Gallery, MacKenzie Art Gallery, Regina Edmonton Art Gallery, Vancouver Art Gallery, Beaverbrook Art Gallery, Fredericton, N.B., Windsor (Ont.) Art Gallery, Lugano Collection, Hart House, U. Toronto, Victoria Coll., U. Toronto, U. Western Ont., U. Guelph, Concordia U., Univ. Club Montreal, commd. 2 sculptures, Toronto Internat. Airport. (Recipient prize 4th Internat. Exhbn. Drawings and Engravings, Lugano, Switzerland 1956, Purchase award 5th Internat. Hallmark Art Award Exhbn., N.Y.C. 1960). Home: Toronto, Canada. Died 2003.

NAPARSTEK, ARTHUR J. social work educator; b. N.Y.C., June 1, 1938; s. Abe and Clara (Meltzer) N.; m. Belleruth Krepon, Sept. 5, 1965; children: Aaron, Keila, Abram. BS, Ill. Wesleyan U., Bloomington, 1960; MSW, NYU, 1962; PhD, Brandeis U., 1972. Sr. health educator USPHS, Chgo., 1962-65; dir. Urban Devel. Inst. Purdue U., Hammond, Ind., 1965-69; dir. rsch. Cath. U., Nat. Ctr. Ethnic Affairs, Washington, 1972-76; dir., prof. Washington Pub. Affairs Ctr. U. So. Calif., Washington, 1976-83; dean, prof. Mandel Sch. Applied Social Sci., Case Western Res. U., Cleve., 1983-88, prof. social work, 1988—2004; Grace Longwell Coyle prof. Case Western Res. U., Cleve., 1989—2004. Pres. Premier Indsl. Found., Cleve., 1987-89, cons. 1989-2004. Author: Neighborhood Networks, 1982, Community Support, 1982; author legislation for city govt., 1976-78. Mem. White House Commn. on Neighborhoods, Washington, 1979-80; trustee Corp. for Nat. Svc. Cleve. Found. sr. fellow, 1993-95; sr. assoc. Urban Inst., 1995-2004. Democrat. Jewish. Home: Cleveland, Ohio. Died Apr. 24, 2004.

NARDONI, ENRIQUE, priest, theology educator; b. Rosario, Argentina, Nov. 15, 1924; came to U.S., 1974; s. Francisco and Enriqueta (Piermarini) N. MA in Theology, Cath. U., Buenos Aires, 1948; MA in Bibl. Studies, Pontifical Biblicas Inst., Rome, 1953, PhD in Bibl. Studies, 1975. Ordained priest Roman Cath. Ch., 1948. Tchr. theology Major Sem., Rosario, 1954-70, dean studies, 1958-70; tchr. anthropology State U., Rosario, 1960-70; tchr. Bibl. interpretation St. Thomas Sem., Seattle, 1974-77, St. Mary's Sem., Balt., 1977-78, U. Dallas, Irving, Tex., from 1978, prof., from 1980, chmn. theology, 1985-90, chmn. emeritus, from 2001. Author: El Hijo del Hombre, 1961, La Transfiguracion, 1977, Those Who Seek Justice, 1998; (art) Catholic Biblical Quarterly, 1993, New Testament Studies, 1991, Theologicas Studies, 1992, Revista Biblica, 1994-98; contbr. Internat. Bible Commentary, 1998. Recipient Scholarships Argentinian Govt., Rome, 1949-52, Adveniat, German Inst., Rome, 1971-74; resident fellow Ctr. for Study Religion in Greek-Roman World, 1983-94; invested Knight of Equestrian Order of Holy Sepulchre of Jerusalem, 1994. Mem. Cath. Bibl. Assn., Soc. Bibl. Lit. Roman Catholic. Avocation: photography. Home: Dallas, Tex. Died Mar. 28, 2002.

NARUM, WILLIAM HOWARD KENNETH, philosophy and religion educator; b. Fargo, N.D., Aug. 22, 1921; s. William and Helen Clara (Fossum) N.; m. Jeanne Lois Kunau, Sept. 1, 1957; children: Paul, Peter, David. BA, St. Olaf Coll., 1943; BTh, Luther Theol. Sem., 1945; ThM, Princeton Theol. Sem., 1946, ThD, 1951. Instr. St. Olaf Coll., Northfield, Minn., 1947-49, asst. prof., 1949-53, assoc. prof., 1953-57, prof., 1957-91, prof. emeritus, from 1991. Vis. prof. U. Iowa, 1957-58, U. Philippines, 1964-65. Co-editor, contbg. author: Quest for a Viable Saga, 1977; contbg. author: Christian Faith and the Liberal Arts, 1960; contbr. articles to profl. jours. Fulbright grantee, 1954-55, Rockefeller grantee, U. Philippines, 1964-65; fellow E.-W. Ctr., 1972, NEH, 1978-79; recipient Harbison award Danforth Found., 1963-64. Mem. Am. Acad. Religion, Am. Philos. Assn., Assn. for Asian Studies, Soc. Christian Philosophers, Metaphys. Soc. Am. Democrat. Home: Northfield, Minn. Died May 23, 2000.

NASH, GERALD DAVID, historian; b. Berlin, July 16, 1928; came to U.S., 1938, naturalized, 1944; s. Alfred and Alice (Kantorowicz) N.; m. Marie L. Norris, Aug. 19, 1967; 1 dau., Stephanie Ann. BA, NYU, 1950; MA, Columbia U., 1952; PhD, U. Calif., Berkeley, 1957. Instr. history Stanford U., 1957-58, vis. asst. prof., 1959-60; asst. prof. No. Ill. U., DeKalb, 1958-59; postdoctoral fellow Harvard U., 1960-61, mem. faculty U. N.Mex., Albuquerque, 1961—, prof. history, 1968—, chmn. dept., 1974-80, Presdl. prof., 1985-90, Disting. prof., from 1990. Faculty rsch. lectr., 1970; vis. assoc. prof. NYU, 1965-66; George Bancroft prof. Am. History U. Goettingen, Fed. Republic Germany, 1990-91. Author: State Government and Economic Development, 1964, U.S. Oil Policy, 1968, Perspectives on Adminstration, 1969, The Great Transition, 1971, American West in 20th Century, 1973, Great Depression and World War II, 1979, The American West Transformed: The Impact of World War II, 1985, World War II and the West: Reshaping the Economy, 1990; editor: Issues in American Economic History, 3d edit., 1980, F.D. Roosevelt, 1967, Urban West, 1979 (with Noel Pugach and Richard Tomasson) Social Security in the U.S.-The First Half Century, 1988, (with Richard Etulain) Perspectives on the 20th Century West, 1989, Creating the West: Historical Interpretations, 1991, A.P. Giannini and the Bank of America, 1992, The Crucial Era, 1992 editor: (with Richard Etulain) Research Opportunities in 20th Century Western History, 1996, Federal Landscape: An Economic History of the Twentieth Century West, 1999, A Brief History of the American West since 1945, 2000; editor The Historian, 1974-84. Fellow Newberry Library, 1959, Huntington Library, 1979; sr. fellow NEH, 1981; Project 87 fellow, 1982-83 Mem. Am. Hist. Assn., Orgn. Am. Historians, Bus. History Soc., Agrl. History Soc., Western History Assn., Phi Beta Kappa. Clubs: Commonwealth. Home: Albuquerque, N.Mex. Deceased.

NATANSON, ALVIN S. surgeon; b. Boston, Feb. 15, 1920; MD, Tufts U., 1949. Intern Boston City Hosp., 1949-50, resident in surgery, 1950-54; staff Peninsula Hosp., Burlingame, Calif. Fellow Am. Coll. Surgeons; mem. AMA. Home: San Mateo, Calif. Died Apr. 28, 1999.

NEAL, STEVEN GEORGE, journalist; b. Coos Bay, Oreg., July 3, 1949; s. Ernest L. and Ellen Louise (Williams) N.; m. Susan Christine Simmons, May 8, 1971; children: Erin, Shannon. BS in Journalism, U. Oreg., 1971; MS in Journalism, Columbia U., 1972. Reporter Oreg. Jour., Portland, 1971, Phila. Inquirer, 1972-78; gen. assignment reporter, White House corr., polit. writer Chgo. Tribune, 1979-87; polit. editor Chgo. Sun-Times, 1987-92, polit. columnist, 1987—2004. Bd. govs. White House Corrs. Assn., Washington, 1981-83. Co-author: Tom McCall: Maverick, 1977; author: The Eisenhowers, 1978, Dark Horse: A Biography of Wendell Willkie, 1984, McNary of Oregon, 1985, Rolling on the River: The Best of Steve Neal, 1999, Harry and Ike: The Partnership that Remade The Postwar World, 2002; editor: They Never Go Back to Pocatello: The Essays of Richard Neuberger, 1988, HST: Memories of the Truman Years, 2003; contbr. to Am. Heritage, The Nation, The N.Y. Times Books Rev., Dictionary of Am. Biography. Recipient William H. Jones award Chgo. Tribune, 1984; Robert W. Ruhl lectr. U. Oreg., Eugene, 1984; Col. Robert R. McCormick fellow, McCormick Found., Chgo., 1989; Hoover Libr. Assn. scholar, West Branch, Iowa, 1989. Roman Catholic. Home: Hinsdale, Ill. Died Feb. 18, 2004.

NEELY, CHARLES LEA, JR., retired physician; b. Memphis, Aug. 3, 1927; s. Charles Lea and Ruby Perry (Mayes) N.; m. Mary Louise Buckingham, Mar. 30, 1957; children: Louise Mayes, Charles Buckingham. AB, Princeton U., 1950; MD, Washington U., St. Louis, 1954. Diplomate: Am. Bd. Internal Medicine. Intern Cornell Service, Bellevue Hosp., N.Y.C., 1954-55; resident Barnes Hosp., St. Louis, 1955-57, fellow in hematology, 1957-58; dir. U. Tenn. Cancer Clinic, 1979-87. Mem. staffs Bapt. Meml. Hosp., Regional Med. Ctr. at Memphis, U. Tenn. Med. Center; prof. medicine and pathology U. Tenn., 1971-87. Served with USNR, 1945-47. Fellow A.C.P.; mem. AMA, Am. Soc. Clin. Oncology, Am. Soc. Hematology, Am. Fedn. Clin. Research, Sigma Xi, Alpha Omega Alpha. Home: Memphis, Tenn. Died Aug. 22, 2000.

NEGSTAD, RICHARD B. former state legislator; m. Mary Negstad; 2 children. Student, S.D. State U. Mem. S.D. Ho. of Reps., mem. agr. and natural resources coms., mem. taxation and health and human resource coms.; mem S.D. Senate; elec. engr.; farmer. Home: Volga, SD. Died Jan. 11, 1997.

NEILSON, ELIZABETH ANASTASIA, health sciences educator, association executive, author, editor; b. Medford, Mass., Oct. 13, 1913; d. William H. and Anastasia (Mahony) N. Diploma, Tufts U., 1933; BS in Edn, Boston U., 1934, MEd, 1945, EdD, 1957. Tchr. pub. schs., Medford, 1934-43; instr. health and phys. edn. Boston Coll., 1954-55; mem. faculty State Coll., Lowell, Mass., 1944-72, prof. edn., chmn. dept. health and phys. edn., 1966-72; dir. continuing edn. Am. Sch. Health Assn., Kent, Ohio, 1972—2001; adj. prof. Kent State U., 1971-77; adj. prof. health edn. Boston-Bouvé Coll. Human Devel. Professions, Northeastern U., 1974—2001; lectr. extension div. Harvard U., 1975—2001. Vis. prof. Boston U., 1960-62, Ind. U., summers 1966-72, Utah State U., summer 1968; del. Internat. Conf. Health and Edn., Madrid, 1965, Pa., 1962, Dusseldorf, Germany, 1959; health edn. cons. to govt. agys., industry, ednl. instns.; del. White House Conf. Children and Youth, 1970; mem. membership com. Am. Nat. Council for Health, 1967-73; chmn. resources council Mass. Sch. Health Council, 1964-69; mem. Nat. Adv. Council on Smoking and Health Edn., 1966-74, Gov.'s Council for Health and Fitness, 1964-69, Gov.'s Council for Nutrition Edn., 1971-74; mem. program evaluation team N.H. State Bd. Edn. Author: Health Living Program, 1977, also school health textbooks; contbg. author: coll. text Personal and Community Health; editor in chief coll. text Journal-Health Values: Achieving High Level Wellness, 1976—; contbr. articles to profl. jours. V.p. bd. dirs. March Against Dental Disease Found.; bd. dirs. Middlesex TB and Health Assn., Mass. Cancer Soc., Lowell MEntal Health Assn., Lowell Heart Assn., Lowell Diabetes Assn., New Hampshire Lung Assn.; mem. Jackson Sch. Bd.; trustee Jackson Libr.; pres., bd. dirs. Flintlock Village Assn.Inc., Wells, Maine, 1988—; founder Elizabeth A. Neilson-George H. Neilson Advanced Grad. Endowed Scholarship Fund for the Promotion of Health Edn., dept. physiology and health scis., Ball State U., 1992. Recipient William A. Howe award Am. Sch. Health Assn., 1969, Disting. Svc. award 1965, Disting. Svc. award ea. dist. AAHPER, 1967, Profl. Svc. award Mass. chpt. 1965, Svc. award Nat. ARC, 1960, Disting. Alumni award Northeastern U., Boston, 1983, Profl. Svc. award Am. Alliance for Health Edn., 1987; inducted into Mass. Hall of Fame, Medford High, 1990; hon. fellow Ball State U., Muncie, Ind., 1993, named to Fellows Soc. and Pres.'s Cir., 1996. Fellow Am. Sch. Health Assn. (life, pres. 1964-66, chmn. study coms. 1969-72, mem. governing assn. 1960-65, Howe award), Royal Soc. Health; mem. Am. Assn. Higher Edn., Am. Soc. Assn. Execs., Nat. Bus. and Profl. Women's Club, Assn. Supervision and Curriculum Devel., UN Assn. U.S.A., Internat. Union for Health, Smithsonian Assos., Nat. Parks and Conservation Assn., New Eng. Health Assn., Am. Coll. Health Assn. (research council 1954-57), Am. (editorial bd. 1958-60, chmn. coll. health com. Eastern dist. 1948-51, chmn. resolutions com. sch. health div. 1951-53), Mass. assns. health, phys. edn. and recreation, Am. Pub. Health Assn., Soc. Pub. Health Educators, Fellows Soc. Ball State U., Pres. Cir. Ball State U., Phi Lambda Theta. Died Oct. 4, 2001.

NEILSON, ROGER, professional hockey coach; b. Toronto, June 16, 1934; BS, McMaster U., Ontario. Head coach Peterborough Petes, 1966—76, Toronto (Can.) Maple Leafs, 1977—79; asst. coach Buffalo Sabres, 1980—81; head coach Vancouver (Can.) Canucks, 1981—83, L.A. Kings, 1983—84; asst. coach Chgo. Blackhawks, 1984—85, 1986—87; head coach New York Rangers, 1989—93, Florida Panthers, Ft. Lauderdale, 1993—95; asst. coach St. Louis Blues, 1995—96, 1997—98; head coach Philadelphia Flyers, 1997—2000; asst. coach Ottawa Senators, 2000—03. Died June 21, 2003.

NELKIN, DOROTHY, sociology and science policy educator; b. Boston, July 30, 1933; d. Henry and Helen (Fine) Wolfers; m. Mark Nelkin, Aug. 31, 1952; children: Lisa, Laurie. BA, Cornell U., 1954. Research assoc. Cornell U., Ithaca, 1963-69, sr. research assoc., 1970-72, assoc. prof., 1972-76, prof. sci. tech. sociology program, 1976-90, prof. sociology, 1977-90; univ. prof., prof. sociology, affiliate prof. law NYU, 1990—2003, Clare Boothe Luce vis. prof., 1988-90. Cons. OECD, Paris, 1975-76, Inst. Environ., Berlin, 1978-79; maitre de conference U. Paris, 1975-76; maitre de recherche Ecole Polytechnique, Paris, 1980-81. Author: The Atom Besieged, 1981, The Creation Controversy, 1982, Science as Intellectual Property, 1983, Workers at Risk, 1984, Selling Science: How the Press Covers Science and Technology, 1987, 2d edit., 1995, Dangerous Diagnostics: The Social Power of Biological Information, 1989, 2d edit., 1994, A Disease of Society: Cultural Impact ofAIDS, 1991,

The Animal Rights Crusade, 1991, Controversy: Politics of Technical Decision, 3d edit., 1992, The DNA Mystique: The Gene as Cultural Icon, 1995, Body Bazaar: The Market for Body Tissue in the Biotechnology Age, 2001. Adviser Office Tech. Assessment, 1977-79, 82-83; expert witness ACLU, Ark., 1982; mem. Nat. Adv. Coun. to NIH Human Genome Project, 1991-95; mem. exec. com. NIH Ethical, Legal and Social Issues Working Group, Commn. on Embryo Rsch., 1998-99; mem. Working Group for Nat. Commn. on Future of DNA Evidence, 1998-2000. Vis. scholar Resources for the Futures, 1980-81; vis. scholar Russell Sage Found., N.Y.C., 1983; Guggenheim fellow, 1983-84. Fellow AAAS (bd. dirs.), Hastings Inst. Soc. Ethics and Life Scis.; mem. NAS Inst. of Medicine, Soc. for Social Studies Sci. (pres. 1978-79). Home: New York, NY. Died May 28, 2003.

NELSON, EDWIN L. federal judge; b. 1940; Student, U. Ala., 1962-63, Samford U., 1965-66, LLB, 1969. Mem. firm French & Nelson, Ft. Payne, Ala., 1969-73; pvt. practice Ft. Payne, Ala., from 1974; magistrate U.S. Dist. Ct. (no. dist.) Ala., Birmingham, 1974-90, judge, from 1990. With USN, 1958-62. Mem. Ala. Bar Assn., Birmingham Bar Assn., 11th Cir. Assn. U.S. Magistrates, Nat. Coun. Magistrates, Phi Alpha Delta. Died May 17, 2003.

NELSON, MARK BRUCE, interior designer; b. Los Angeles, Dec. 8, 1921; s. Mark Bruce and Rubie (Henrionnet) N. BA in Art, U. Calif., Los Angeles, 1943, postgrad., 1949-50, Art Center Sch., 1946-49. Tchr. Pasadena (Calif.) City Coll., 1950-54; propr. Mark Nelson Interiors, Los Angeles, 1954—; designer DuPont Corp. exhibit N.Y. World's Fair, 1964; co-chmn. Los Angeles show com. Am. Inst. Interior Designers, 1960-67, Living with Famous Paintings, 1964-65. Mem. Los Angeles adv. council Am. Arbitration Assn., 1971-72; chmn. Los Angeles N.C.I.D.Q., 1973-80, Design House West, 1978 Mem. Los Angeles Beautiful Com., 1966. Served as officer USNR, 1942-46, 52-53, ETO, Korea. Fellow Am. Soc. Interior Designers (life mem., exam. chmn. 1972—, chmn. nat. by-laws com. 1973, pres. Los Angeles 1969-71, Calif. regional v.p. 1970-73, pres. Los Angeles found. 1980, Presdl. citation 1973); mem. Phi Kappa Sigma. Died Oct. 16, 2003.

NELSON, RICHARD HENRY, manufacturing executive; b. Norfolk, Va., May 24, 1939; s. Irvin Joseph and Ethel Blair (Levy) N.; m. Carole Ellen Rosen, Mar. 12, 1966; children: Christopher, Karin. BA, Princeton U., 1961; postgrad., Georgetown U., 1962-63. Spl. asst. to dir. Peace Corps, Washington, 1961-62; mil. aide to U.S. v.p. Office of the V.P., Washington, 1962-63; asst. to U.S. Pres. Office of the Pres., Washington, 1963-66; spl. asst. to sec. HUD, Washington, 1966-68; v.p. Am. Internat. Bank, N.Y.C., 1968-70, Studebaker-Worthington, N.Y.C., 1970-73; pres. Sartex Corp., N.Y.C., 1973-80; pres., CEO Cogenic Energy Systems, Inc., N.Y.C., 1981-91; CEO U.S. Energy Systems, Inc., West Palm Beach, Fla., from 1992. Bd. dirs. Nelco Corp., Laurel, Md.; chmn. bd. Powersave, Inc., N.Y.C., 1984-92. Bd. dirs. Nat. Hypertension Assn., N.Y.C., 1982-90; exec. com. Southampton Assn., N.Y., 1983—. 1st lt. U.S. Army, 1962-64. Recipient Presdl. Medal Office of Pres. of U.S., 1965. Mem. Nev. Geothermal Industry Coun., Nat. Sporting Clays Assn., Amateur Trap Assn., U.S. Polo Assn., Princeton Club, Southampton Hunt and Polo Club, Palm Beach Polo and Country Club, Meadow Club, Palm Beach Yacht Club. Democrat. Avocations: horseback riding, trap and skeet shooting. Home: West Palm Beach, Fla. Deceased.

NÉMETHY, GEORGE, chemistry educator; b. Budapest, Hungary, Oct. 11, 1934; came to U.S., 1954; s. Imre and Mária (Mikó) N.; m. Judith Kesserü, Apr. 26, 1975; children: Kinga, Mária. BA, Lincoln U., 1956; PhD, Cornell U., 1962. Rsch. chemist GE Rsch. Lab., Schenectady, N.Y., 1962-63; asst. prof. of phys. chemistry Rockefeller U., N.Y.C., 1963-72; vis. prof. of biochemistry U. Paris XI, Orsay, France, 1972-74; vis. assoc. prof. of chemistry SUNY, Binghamton, 1974-75; sr. rsch. assoc. of chemistry Cornell U., Ithaca, N.Y., 1975-89; prof. of biomath. sci. Mt. Sinai Sch. Medicine, N.Y.C., from 1989. Vis. prof. chemistry U. Federico II, Naples, Italy, 1984, 86; vis. lectr. Inst. Superiore di Sanità, Rome, 1970; lectr. NYU Med. Ctr., N.Y.C., 1971-72. Contbr. over 150 sci. articles to profl. publs. Recipient Pius XI Gold medal Pontifical Acad. Sci., 1972; European Molecular Biology Orgn. sr. fellow, 1973-74. Mem. Am. Chem. Soc., N.Y. Acad. Scis., Am. Soc. Biochemistry, Molecular Biology, Hungarian Scouts Assn. in Exteris (pres. 1973—). Mem. Reformed Ch. Achievements include research in structure of proteins, theory of macromolecular conformation, enzyme activity, structure of aqueous solutions, thermodynamics, statistical mechanics. Deceased.

NESBITT, LENORE CARRERO, federal judge; b. 1932; m. Joseph Nesbitt; children: Sarah, Thomas. AA, Stephens Coll., 1952; BS, Northwestern U, 1954; student, U. Fla. Law Sch., 1954—55; LLB, U. Miami, 1957. Rsch. asst. Dist. Ct. Appeal, 1957—59; assoc. Dade County Cir. Ct., 1963—65; pvt. practice Nesbitt & Nesbitt, 1960—63; spl. asst. atty. gen., 1961—63; with Law Offices of John Robert Terry, 1969—73; counsel Fla. State Bd. Med. Examiners, Fla., 1970—71; with Petersen McGowan & Feder, 1973—75; judge Fla. Cir. Ct., 1975—82, US Dist. Ct. (so. dist.), Miami, Fla., from 1983. Mem.: Women's Forum, FBA, Internat., Miami Children's Hosp. (bd. dir.), Fla. Bd. trustees, US Dist. Ct. (so. dist.). Died Oct. 5, 2001.

NESS, ALBERT KENNETH, artist; b. St. Ignace, Mich., June 21, 1903; s. Albert Klingberg and Violet Matilda (Sutherland); m. Lenore Consuelo Chrisman, Aug. 4, 1926; children: Peter, James Kenneth, Jane Lenore. Student U. Detroit, 1923-24, Detroit Sch. of Applied Art, 1924-26, Wicker Sch. of Fine Art, 1926-28; Diploma, Sch. of Art Inst., 1932. Show-card writer, window display man S.S. Kresge Co., Detroit, 1923-24; artist poster and advt. Cunningham Drugs, Detroit, 1924-26; artist layout lettering and design W.L. Flemming Studios, Detroit, 1926-28, McAleer Displays, Chgo., 1929-32; artist, design asst. Layman-Whitney Assocs., 1933 World's Fair, Chgo.; layout artist, poster designer Elevated Advt. Co., Chgo., 1934-37; instr., art dir. Sch. of Applied Art, Chgo., 1938-40; Carnegie resident artist U. N.C., Chapel Hill, 1941-43, dir. War Art Ctr., 1942-43, resident artist, assoc. prof. art, 1943-49, acting head, dept. art, acting dir. Person Hall Art Gallery, 1944-45, resident artist, prof. art, 1949-73, acting head dept. of art, acting dir. Person Hall Art Gallery, 1955, 57-58, resident artist, prof. emeritus, 1973—. One man shows include: Chester Johnson Galleries, Chgo., 1932, Evanston Art Ctr., Ill., 1940, Person Hall Art Gallery, 1941, N.C. Art Soc. Gallery, Raleigh, 1942, Duke U. Art Gallery, Durham, N.C., 1955, Louisburg Coll. Gallery, N.C., 1964, Ackland Art Mus., U.N.C. Chapel Hill, 1973; Internat. Water Color Exhbn. Chgo. Art Inst., 1934-39; Golden Gate Internat. Exposition, San Francisco, 1939, exhibited in group shows: Whitney Mus., N.Y.C., 1933, U. Chattanooga, Tenn., 1946, Centennial Exhbn. U. Fla., Gainesville, 1953, Jacksonville Art Mus, Fla., 1960; exhibited nationally Am. Artists' Anns., Chgo. Art Inst., 1935-37, Butler Art Inst., Youngstown, Ohio, 1951, Pa. Acad. Am. Annuals, Phila., 1953-54, Optique Gallery, Lambertville, N.J., 1991—, Ross-Constantine Gallery, N.Y.C., 1991—, others; works in pub. collections include: N.C. Mus., Raleigh, Ackland Art Mus., Reynolds Found., Winston Salem, Duke U. Art Mus., Durham. Contbr. to local and state newspapers. Editor, designer, photographer: A brochure on art study, 1964. Recipient Jenkins Meml. prize 38th Ann. Chgo. Artists' Exhbn., 1934, Purchase award N.C. Artists' Ann., Raleigh, 1953; 2-Star award Movie Maker Competition, London, 1970, N.C. award in Fine Arts, 1973, Purchase award Reynolds Competition, Winston Salem, 1977. Deceased. Home: Chapel Hill, NC.

NEUMAN, ROBERT HENRY, lawyer; b. N.Y.C., Oct. 14, 1936; s. Sydney A. and Ethel (Pekelner) N.; m. Emily Mann, Dec. 30, 1960 (div. 1975); children: David Marshall, Anthony Howard, Amanda Sarah; m. Joyce Thompson, May 5, 1975; 1 child, Nicole Sydney. AB magna cum laude, Harvard U., 1958, JD, 1961. Bar: N.Y. 1962, D.C. 1962. Ford Found. fellow, West Africa, 1961-62; assoc. Meyers & Batzell, Washington, 1962-64; asst. legal advisor U.S. Dept. of State, Washington, 1964-70; ptnr. Arent, Fox, Kintner, Plotkin & Kahn, Washington, 1970-93, Baker & Hostetler, Washington, 1993-98. Adj. prof. The George Washington U., 1998, Elliott Sch. Internat. Affairs, 2001-02. U.S. rep. to UN Conf. on Marine Pollution, 1969. Recipient Superior Honor award Dept. State, 1965. Mem. ABA, FBA, Am. Soc. Internat. Law, Internat. Bar Assn., Phi Beta Kappa. Avocation: sailing. Home: Kiawah Island, SC. Died Feb. 15, 2004.

NEUMANN, EDNA LEE, nursing educator; b. Tenn., Jan. 7, 1937; d. Parmon Lee and E. Sue Kincaid (Bishop) Dutton; m. Pierre Joel Janda, Dec. 23, 1983; children: Jamie Heather Neumann, David Lawrence Neumann. Diploma, Deaconess Hosp. Sch. Nursing, 1957; BSN, U. Utah, 1959, MS in Nursing, 1962, PhD, 1972. Chmn. nursing dept. Wichita State U., Kans., 1971-76; chmn. West Minster Coll. Nursing, Salt Lake City, 1972-74; dean Coll. Health Scis. Lamar U., Beaumont, Tex., 1976-82; prof. Corpus Christi (Tex.) State U., 1982-84; dean, prof. CCNY, from 1984; asst. dir. nursing Bergen Pines County Hosp., from 1991. Cons. hosp. nursing adminstrn. Mem. editorial bd. dirs. Advances in Nursing Science. Mem. N.Y. State Nurses Assn. (human rights coun.). Home: Fort Lee, NJ. Deceased.

NEUSCHEL, ROBERT PERCY, management consultant, educator; b. Hamburg, N.Y., Mar. 13, 1919; s. Percy J. and Anna (Becker) N.; m. Dorothy Virginia Maxwell, Oct. 20, 1944; children: Kerr Anne Ziprick, Carla Becker Neuschel Wyckoff, Robert Friedrich (Fritz). BA, Denison U., 1941; MBA, Harvard U., 1947. Indsl. engr. Sylvania Elec. Products Co., Inc., 1947-49; with McKinsey & Co., Inc., 1950-79, sr. partner, dir., 1967-79; prof. corp. governance, assoc. dean J. L. Kellogg Grad. Sch. Mgmt., 1977—2004. Mem. exec. bd. Internat. Air Cargo Forum, 1988-2004; mem. com. study air passenger svc. and safety NRC, 1989-2004; bd. dirs. Butler Mfg. Co., Combined Ins. Co. Am., Templeton, Kenley & Co., U.S. Freightways Co.; lectr. in field; mem. McKinsey Found. Mgmt. Rsch., Inc.; transp. task force Reagan transition team; chmn. bd. dirs. Internat. Intermodal Expn. Atlanta. Author: The Servant Leader: Unleashing the Power of Your People, 1998; co-author: Emerging Issues in Corporate Governance, 1983; contbr. over 125 articles to profl. jours. Pres. Bd. Edn., Lake Forest, Ill., 1965-70; rep. Nat. council Boy Scouts Am., 1970-2004, mem. N.E. exec. coun., 1969-2004; chmn. bd. Lake Forest Symphony, 1973; bd. dirs. Loyola U., Chgo., Chgo. Boys' Club, Nat. Ctr. Voluntary Action, Inst. Mgmt. Consultants; trustee N. Suburban Mass Transit, 1972-73, Loyola Med. Ctr.; mem. adv. coun. Kellogg Grad. Sch. Mgmt., Northwestern U., White House conferee Drug Free Am.; mem. Nat. Petroleum Coun. Transp. and Supply Com. Served to capt. USAAF, World War II. Named Transporation Man of Yr. Chitransp. Assoc., 1994; recipient Salzberg medallion Syracuse U., 1999. Fellow Acad. Advancement Corp. Governance; mem. Transp. Assn. Am., Nat. Def. Transp. Assn. (subcom. transp. tech. agenda 1990—), Intermodal Assn. N.Am. (chmn. bd. dirs.), Harvard Bus. Sch. Club (pres. 1964-65), Economic Club (named Internat. Educator of Yr., 2000), Exec. Club, Chgo. (Ill.) Club, Mid-Am. Club, Mid-Day Club. Presbyn. Home: Lake Forest, Ill. Died Feb. 9, 2004.

NEUSTADT, RICHARD ELLIOTT, political scientist, educator; b. Phila., June 26, 1919; s. Richard Mitchells and Elizabeth (Neufeld) N.; m. Bertha Frances Cummings, Dec. 21, 1945 (Dec. 1984); children: Richard Mitchells (Dec. 1995), Elizabeth Ann; m. Shirley Williams, Dec. 19, 1987. AB, U. Calif., Berkeley, 1939; MA, Harvard U., 1941, PhD, 1951. Economist OPA, 1942; mem. staff Bur. Budget, 1946-50, White House, 1950-53; prof. pub. adminstrn. Cornell U., 1953-54; prof. govt. Columbia U., 1954-64, Harvard U., 1965-78, Lucius N. Littauer prof. pub. adminstrn., 1978-87, Douglas Dillon prof., 1987-89, assoc. dean John F. Kennedy Sch. Govt., 1965-75, dir. Inst. Politics, 1966-71, Douglas Dillon prof. emeritus, 1989—2003. Spl. cons. subcom. on nat. policy machinery U.S. Senate, 1959-61; mem. adv. bd. Commn. Money and Credit, 1960-61; spl. cons. to Pres. elect Kennedy, 1960-61; to subcom. on nat. security staffing and ops. U.S. Senate, 1962-68; cons. to Pres. Kennedy, 1961-63, Pres. Johnson, 1964-66, Dept. State, 1962-69, Bur. Budget, 1961-70, AEC, 1962-68, Rand Corp., 1964-79, Pres.'s Reorgn. Project, Office Mgmt. and Budget, 1977-79; chmn. adv. com. candidate selection Commn. Presdl. Debates, 1988, 92, 96; vis. lectr. Nuffield Coll., Oxford, Eng., 1961-62, assoc. mem., 1965-67, 90-92; vis. prof., Princeton U., 1957, U. Calif., Berkeley, 1986, Cornell U., 1992, U. Essex, UK, 1994-96. Author: Presidential Power, 1960, rev., 1990, Alliance Politics, 1970; (with Harvey V. Fineberg) The Swine Flu Affair, 1978, reissued as The Epidemic That Never Was, 1983; (with Ernest R. May) Thinking in Time, 1986; Presidents, Politics, and Analysis, 1986; Report to JFK, 1999, Preparing to be President, 2000; contbr. articles to mags., revs. Mem. staff Dem. Platform Com., 1952, 56, chmn., 1972; trustee Radcliffe Coll., 1976-80; mem. exec. bd. Coll. Letters & Scis., U. Calif., Berkeley, 1994-97. With USNR, 1942-46. Fellow Ctr. Advanced Study in the Behavioral Scis., 1978-79; recipient Grawemeyer award U. Louisville, 1988, Paul Peck prize Smithsonian Instn., 2002. Fellow Am. Acad. Arts Scis; mem. Am. Polit. Sci. Assn. (Woodrow Wilson award 1961, Hubert H. Humphrey award 1993, Charles Merriam award 1986), Nat. Acad. Pub. Adminstrn., Council Fgn. Rels., Inst. Strategic Studies, Am. Philos. Soc., Cosmos Club. Home: Herts, England. Died Oct. 31, 2003.

NEVES, LUCAS MOREIRA CARDINAL, archbishop; b. Sao Joao del Rei, Brazil, Sept. 16, 1925; ordained priest Roman Cath. Ch., 1950, as titular bishop, 1967. V.p. Pontifical Commn. for Laity, 1974-79; archbishop, 1979; sec. Congregation for Bishops, 1979-87; titular see Vescovia, 1987; archbishop Sao Salvador da Bahia, 1987-98; cardinal, from 1988; prefect Congregation of Bishops, Vatican City, 1998-2000, prefect emeritus, from 2000. Titular ch. Sts. Boniface and Alexius; curial mem. Secretariat of State (2nd sect.), Doctrine of the Faith, Bishops (congregations), Family, Culture (couns.) Latin Am. (commn.). Home: Rome, Italy. Died Sept. 8, 2002.

NEVILLE, RICHARD FRANCIS, university administrator; b. Bklyn., Sept. 6, 1931; s. Richard Stephen and Mary (Kyne) N.; m. Roselyn Rae Bryson (dec. 1990), Aug. 14, 1956; children— Richard, Shannon, Elizabeth, John, Mary, Heather, Barbara. B.S., Central Conn. State Coll.; M.A., Columbia U.; Ph.D., U. Conn. Assoc. prof. edn., asst. to dean U. Md., College Park, 1964-69; prof., chmn. dept. edn. U. Md.-Balt. County, Balt., 1969-77, acting dean of faculty, 1978-79, dean of faculty, 1979-80, dean arts and scis., 1980-89; sr. advisor to pres. and provost, 1989-91, acting provost, U. Md. Biotechnology Inst. 1991-94, ret. 1995; rsch. assoc. Nat. Coun. for Accreditation Tchr. Edn., Washington, 1977-78; dir. Tchr. Corps., Balt. Author: (with others) Foundations of Elementary School Teaching, 1963; (with Alfonso, Firth) Instructional Supervision: A Behavior System, 1975, 2d edit., 1980-81. Mem. Assn. for Supervision and Curriculum Devel., Md., Assn. for Supervision and Curriculum Devel., Phi Delta Kappa, Kappa Delta Pi. Democrat. Roman Catholic. Home: Silver Spring, Md. Died Mar. 1, 2004.

NEWCOMB, ROBERT WHITNEY, biotechnologist, neuroscience researcher; b. Redwood City, Calif., Apr. 19, 1956; s. Robert Wayne and Sarah Elenor N.; m. Marcelle Nguyen, Oct. 12, 1985. BA in Chemistry, Molecular Biology, U. Colo., 1977; PhD in Biochemistry, Biophysics, U. Hawaii, 1983. Teaching asst. dept. chemistry U. Hawaii, Honolulu, 1977-78, rsch. asst. dept. biochemistry, 1978-83, postdoctoral researcher Bekesy Lab. Neurobiology, 1983-85, asst. prof. Pacific Biomed. Rsch. Ctr., 1987-89; postdoctoral researcher in biol. scis. Stanford (Calif.) U., 1985-87; INSERM fellow Ctr. Neurochemistry, U. Louis Pasteur, Strasbourg, France, 1987; scientist, project coord. analytical biochemistry Neurex Corp., Menlo Park, Calif., from 1989. Contbr. articles to Jour. Neurosci., Jour. Neurochemistry, other profl. publs. Grantee NIH, 1985, 86. Mem. Phi Beta Kappa. Died Nov. 24, 2000.

NEWHOUSE, Mrs. EDWARD See DELAY, DOROTHY

NEWMAN, DAVID, freelance/self-employed writer; b. N.Y.C., Feb. 4, 1937; s. Herman and Rose (Spatz) N.; m. Leslie Harris England, June 22, 1958; children: Nathan, Catherine. BA, U. Mich., 1958; MA, U. Mich., 1959. Editor Esquire mag., 1960-64, contbg. editor, 1964—; free-lance writer, 1964—; columnist Mademoiselle mag., 1964-74. Co-author: Bonnie and Clyde, 1967, There Was A Crooked Man, 1970, Floreana, What's Up, Doc?, 1971, (with Robert Benton) Money's Tight, Bad Company, 1972, (with Leslie Newman) The Crazy American Girl, 1975, (with Leslie Newman and Robert Benton) Superman: The Movie, 1978, (with Leslie Newman) Superman II, 1981,(with Burt Blessing) Jinxed, 1982, (with Robert Benton) Still of the Night, 1982, Superman III, 1983,The Santa Claus: The Movie, 1985, Le Trampa de Fu Manchu, 2002. Writings:O, Calcutta, 1969, Extremism, 1966, Esquire World of Humor, 1964, Esquire Book of Gambling, 1963; (with Leslie Newman-).Screenplays: Superman, 1978, Sheena, 1984, Moonwalker, 1988, Takedown, 2000. Produced: He Who Rides A Tiger, 1966, R.O.T.O.R.(assoc. prod.), 1989, The Secret Lives of Dentists(exec. prod.), 2002, Off the Map(exec. prod.), 2003. Plays: It's a Bird, It's a Plane, It's Superman, 1966 Recipient Avery Hopwood Fiction award, 1957; Hopwood Drama award, 1958; N.Y. Film Critics Best Screenplay award, 1967; Nat. Film Critics Best Screeplay award, 1967; award best drama and best original for Bonnie and Clyde Writers Guild Am., 1967 Died June 27, 2003.

NEWMAN, FRANCES LAMBERT RUSSELL MOODY, foundation executive; b. Parsons, Kan, Nov. 4, 1906; m. Shearn Moody, Aug. 26, 1931 (dec. 1936); children: Shearn Moody Jr(dec.), Robert Lewis Lee Moody; m. August James Newman, 1953 (dec. 1977). With The Moody Found., Galveston, Tex., from 1942, chairperson. Died Aug. 10, 2003; buried Galveston Memorial Park Cemetery, Hitchcock, TX.

NEWMAN, JAMES WILSON, business executive; b. Clemson, S.C., Nov. 3, 1909; s. Charles Carter and Grace (Strode) N.; m. Clara Collier, July 1934; children: Clare Adelaide, Mildred Bledsoe, James Wilson, Charles Carter II. BS, Clemson U., 1931, also LL.D. (hon.); student, Am. Inst. Banking, 1931-32; JD, N.Y. U., 1937. Bar: N.Y. bar 1937. Reporter R.G. Dun & Co., 1931-46; v.p. Dun & Bradstreet, Inc., 1946-52, pres., chief exec. officer, 1952-60, chmn., chief exec. officer, 1960-68, chmn. finance com., 1968-80, dir., 1968—80. Adv. bd. Chem. Bank, Gen. Foods Corp., 1963-81, Internat. Paper Co., until 1982; trustee Atlantic Mut. Ins. Co., Mut. Life Ins. Co. Am., until 1982; chmn. spl. rev. com. Lockheed Corp., 1976-78 Chmn. Pres.'s Task Force on Small Bus., 1969; mem. Commn. on Bankruptcy Laws U.S., 1970-73; chmn. Nat. Bur. Econ. Rsch., 1974-78; trustee Com. Econ. Devel., Va. Mus. Fine Arts, 1978-94; mem. coun. Miller Ctr. Pub. Affairs, U. Va., 1983-94; mem. Price Commn., 1971-72; chmn. Sweet Briar Coll., 1963-69. Mem. ABA, Farmington Country Club (Va.), Phi Delta Phi. Home: Charlottesville, Va. Died July 8, 2003.

NEWMAN, RICHARD ALAN, publisher, editor and consultant; b. Watertown, N.Y., Mar. 30, 1930; s. Gordon Leon and Belle (Burton) N.; m. Ann Cowan Meredith, 1955 (div. 1960); m. Peggy J. Hoyt, 1964 (div. 1978); m. Belynda Blair Bady, 1996. BA, Maryville Coll., 1952; M.Div., Union Theol. Sem., 1955, postgrad., Syracuse U., 1959-61, Harvard U., 1966. Ordained to ministry Presbyn. Ch., 1955, demitted, 1977; minister Westminster Presbyn. Ch., Syracuse, N.Y., 1955-59; instr. religion Vassar Coll., Poughkeepsie, N.Y., 1962-63; prof., chmn. dept. social scis. Boston U., 1964-73; sr. editor G.K. Hall Co., Boston, 1973-79; exec. editor Garland Pub. Co., N.Y.C., 1978-81; mgr. publs. N.Y. Pub. Libr., 1981-92. Cons. Columbia U., N.Y.C., 1992-93; publs. officer, mng. editor The Harvard Guide to African-Am. History, W.E.B. DuBois Inst., Harvard U., 1993-95, fellows officer, 1995-2003, rsch. officer, 1997-2003. Author: Black Index, 1981, Bless All Thy Creatures, Lord, 1982, Lemuel Haynes, 1984, Afro-American Education, 1984, Black Access: A Bibliography, 1984, Black Power and Black Religion, 1987, Words Like Freedom, 1989, Black Preacher to White America, 1990; editor: Treasures From the New York Public Library, 1985, This Far By Faith, 1996, Everybody Say Freedom, 1996, Go Down, Moses, 1997, African-American Quotations, 1998; contbr. articles to profl. jours. Dem. candidate for N.Y. State Assembly from Onondaga County, 1960. Mem. New Eng. Hist. Genealogical Soc., Friends of Union Sem. Libr., Boston Athenaeum, Studio Mus. in Harlem, Friends of Amistad Rsch. Ctr., Schomburg Commn. for Preservation of Black Culture. Home: Boston, Mass. Died July 7, 2003.

NEWPORT, JOHN PAUL, philosophy of religion educator, former academic administrator; b. Buffalo, Mo., June 16, 1917; s. Marvin Jackson and Mildred (Morrow) N.; m. Eddie Belle Leavell, Nov. 14, 1941; children: Martha Ellen, Frank M., John P. Jr. BA, William Jewell Coll., Liberty, Mo., 1938; ThM, So. Bapt. Theol. Sem., Louisville, 1941, ThD, 1946; PhD, U. Edinburgh, Scotland, 1953; MA, Tex. Christian U., 1968; LittD, William Jewell Coll., 1967. Assoc. prof. Baylor U., 1949-51, New Orleans Bapt. Theol. Sem, 1951-52; prof. Southwestern Bapt. Theol. Sem, Ft. Worth, 1952-76, Rice U., 1976-79; v.p. acad. affairs, provost Southwestern Bapt. Theol. Sem., 1979-90, v.p. emeritus, spl. asst. to pres., from 1990, disting. prof. philosophy of religion, from 1990. Vis. prof. Princeton Theol. Sem., 1982. Author: Theology and Contemporary Art Forms, 1971, Demons, Demons, Demons, 1972, Why Christians Fight over the Bible, 1974, Christ and the New Consciousness, 1978, Christianity and Contemporary Art Forms, 1979, Nineteenth Century Devotional Thought, 1981, Paul Tillich, 1984, What Is Christian Doctrine? 1984, The Lion and the Lamb, 1986, Life's Ultimate Questions, 1989, The New Age Movement and the Biblical Worldview: Conflict and Dialogue, 1998; contbr. numerous articles to jours. and mags. Seatlantic fellowship Rockefeller Found., Harvard U., 1958-59. Mem. Am. Acad. Religion (pres. S.W. div. 1967-68), Soc. Bibl. Lit. and Exegesis, Southwestern Philos. Assn., N.Am. Paul Tillich Soc. (dir. 1984-86), Southside C. of C. (Ft. Worth), Downtown Rotary Cub (Ft. Worth), Ft. Worth Club. Democrat. Avocations: golf, swimming, tennis. Home: Fort Worth, Tex. Deceased.

NEWTON, JAMES QUIGG, JR., lawyer; b. Denver, 1911; s. James Quigg and Nelle (Singleton) N.; m. Virginia Shafroth, June 6, 1942; children: Nancy Grusin, Nelle Grainger, Abby Hornung, Virginia Rice. AB, Yale U., 1933, LLB, 1936, MA (hon.), 1951; DPS (hon.), U. Denver, 1952; LLD, Adams State Coll., 1960, Colo. Coll., 1962, U. Colo., 1975. Bar: Colo. 1938. Legal sec. to W.O. Douglas SEC, 1936-37; practiced in Denver, 1938-42, 46-47; lectr. U. Denver, 1938-41; with Ford Found., N.Y.C., 1955-56, v.p., 1956; pres. U. Colo., 1956-63, Commonwealth Fund, N.Y.C., 1963-75, vice chmn., 1975-76, dir., 1951-55, 57-78; sr. cons. Henry J. Kaiser Family Found., Menlo Park, Calif., 1978-80; of counsel firm Davis, Graham & Stubbs, 1981—2003. Dir. N.Y. Life Fund, 1972-95, Kaiser Found. Hosps./Health Plan, 1972-80; trustee Dry Dock Savs. Bank; mem. Yale Corp., 1951-55, Western Interstate Com. Higher Edn., 1957-63; mem. nat. adv. mental health coun. NIH, 1964-68; mem. Inst. Medicine, Nat. Acad. Scis., 1972-2003, VA Spl. Med. Adv. Group, 1968-74; fellow Ctr. for Advanced Study in Behavioral Scis., 1977-78. Mayor, City and County of Denver, 1947-55; Sec. bd. trustees U. Denver, 1938-42, pres., 1946-47; pub. trustee Nutrition Found.; chmn. bd. YMCA Greater N.Y., 1976-77. Served with USNR, 1942-46. Fellow Am. Acad. Arts and Scis.; mem. Am. Municipal Assn. (pres. 1950), Am. Council Edn. (dir. 1959-62), Am. Arbitration Assn. (dir., exec. com.), Fgn. Bondholders Protective Council (bd. dirs. 1975—2003), Phi Delta Phi, Alpha Delta Phi. Home: Denver, Colo. Died Apr. 4, 2003.

NEWTSON, RICHARD EVAN, stockbroker; b. Decatur, Ill., Aug. 17, 1950; s. Raymond Earl and Evelyn Lucille (Johnson) N.; m. Robyn Elaine Bock, Dec. 21, 1974; children: Rachel Elizabeth, Randall Eric. BS, Culver-Stockton Coll., 1973. Registered rep. Investors Diversified Svcs., Springfield, Ill., 1972-74; securities broker Reinholdt & Gardner, Springfield, 1975-78, A.G. Edwards & Sons, Inc., Springfield, from 1978, v.p. investments, from 1981. Fin. industry appointee Ill. Coal Devel. Bd., 1990—. With USAR, 1971-77. Melvin Jones fellow, 1994. Mem. Lions (pres. Springfield Noon club 1980, zone chmn. dist. 1-L 1981-82). Republican. Presbyterian. Avocations: woodworking, cooking, sports. Home: Springfield, Ill. Died May 27, 2001.

NGAI, SHIH HSUN, physician; b. Wuchang, China, Sept. 15, 1920; came to U.S., 1946, naturalized, 1953; s. Chih F. and Shen (Shih) N.; m. Hsueh-hwa Wang, Nov. 6, 1948; children: Mae, Janet, John. M.B., Nat. Central U. Sch. Medicine, China, 1944. Mem. staff Presbyn. Hosp., N.Y.C., 1949-88, attending anesthesiologist, 1965-88; faculty Columbia Coll. Phys. and Surg., 1949—, prof. anesthesiology, 1965-88, prof. pharmacology, 1974-88, prof. emeritus and from 1988, chmn. dept. anesthesiology, 1970-73; mem. com. on anesthesia NRC-Nat. Acad. Scis., 1961-70. Cons. NIH, 1963-67, 78-82 Author: Manual of Anesthesiology, 1959, 62, Metabolic Effects of Anesthesia, 1962, Highlights of Clinical Anesthesiology, 1971; contbr. to: Physiol. Pharmacology, 1963, Handbook of Physiology, 1964, Modern Trends in Anesthesia, 1966, Advances in Anesthesiology-Muscle Relaxants, 1967, Handbook of Experimental Pharmacology XXX, Modern Inhalation Anesthetics, 1972, Muscle Relaxants, 1975, Enzymes in Anesthesiology, 1978; editor: Anesthesiology, 1967-77. Mem. Am. Physiol. Soc., Am. Soc. Pharmacology and Exptl. Therapeutics, Assn. Univ. Anesthetists, Am. Soc. Anesthesiologists, Academia Sinica. Home: Teaneck, NJ. Died July 8, 1999.

NIBLOCK, WALTER RAYMOND, lawyer; b. Little Rock, Nov. 19, 1927; s. Freeman John and Nellie (Wolfe) N.; m. Marjorie Lee Hammond, Oct. 17, 1953; children: Fred William, George Hammond, Walter Lester, Raymond Lee. Student, Tex. A&M Coll., 1945, Little Rock Jr. Coll., 1947; BS, U. Ark., 1951, JD, 1953. Bar: Ark. 1953. Field dir. ARC, 1953-59; asst. gen. mgr., dir. Industria de Pollos (S.A.), Cali, Colombia, 1959-61; practice in Fayetteville, 1961—; now sr. ptnr. Niblock Law Firm. Exec. sec. Ark. Judiciary Commn., 1963-65; U.S. commr. Fayetteville div. U.S. Dist. Ct., Western Dist. Ark.; part-time mem. U.S. Magistrate, 1965-79; mem. Jud. Ethics Com. State Ark., 1978-83, Supreme Ct. Com. on Prof. Conduct, 1979-86, chmn., 1981; mem. com. U.S.-Soviet Rels., 1992—. Bd. dirs. Washington County chpt. ARC.; mem. Pub. Employees Retirement Study Commn., 1983-85; trustee Iolta Found., 1989—. Served with AUS, 1945-47. Recipient Meritorious Service award ARC, 1963 Fellow Ark. Bar Found. (sec.-treas. 1973-74, chmn. 1976-77), Roscoe Pound Found.; mem. ABA, ATLA (bd. govs. 1978-90, home office and budget com. 1987-88, chair, key person com. 1987-88, chair ATLA PAC taskforce com. 1988-89, co-chair membership com. 1989-90, co-chair state fund devel. com. 1989-90, mem. exec. com. 1989-90, bd. dirs. ATLA assurance 1991—, PAC trustee 1993—, chair Group Ins. Trust 1994—), Am. Bd. Trial Advocates, So. Trial Lawyers Assn. (gov. 1988—, War Horse award 1992, parliamentarian 1995-96, sec. 1996-97, treas. 1997-98), Ark. Trial Lawyers Assn. (pres. 1974-76), Ark. Bar Assn. (pres. 1977-78), Washington County Bar Assn. (v.p. 1973-74, pres. 1974-75), N.Y. Trial Lawyers Assn., Am. Inns. Ct. (master 1989), William B. Putnam Inn, Delta Theta Phi. Democrat. Home: Fayetteville, Ark. Died 1999.

NICHOLAS, LAURIE STEVENS, marketing consultant; b. Urbana, Ill., Oct. 2, 1959; d. Richard Charles and Rosemary (Vose) Stevens; m. Robert Arthur Nicholas, Aug. 6, 1983; children: Kali, Connor, Quentin. BS with honors, U. Wyo., 1981, postgrad., 1981-82, MBA, 1983. Asst. product mgr. Unicover Corp., Cheyenne, Wyo., 1983-85, 87-89; mktg. cons. Noble Internat. Travel Agy., Lander, Wyo., 1986, Wyo. State Jour., Lander, 1986; cons. joint legis. and exec. study State of Wyo., Cheyenne, 1987; market researcher Unicover Corp., Cheyenne, 1989-91; instr. Ctrl. Wyo. Coll., Riverton, 1991. Active Econ. Devel. Commn., Lander, 1986, Friends of the Symphony, Cheyenne, 1987. Mem. Fremont County Rep. Women's Club, Local Book Club, Riverton Country Club. Republican. Roman Catholic. Avocations: reading, horses, cooking, golfing, gardening. Home: Riverton, Wyo. Died July 7, 2000.

NICHOLAS, PETER, medical educator; b. Little Falls, N.Y., June 5, 1942; s. Peter Sr. and Helen K. N.; m. Joan Marie Popadak, 1970. BS magna cum laude, Union Coll., 1964; MD, Yale U., 1968. Intern Mt. Sinai Hosp., N.Y.C., 1968-69, resident, 1969-70, 70-71, chief resident, 1971-72; instr. assoc., asst. prof. medicine, assoc. prof. CCNY, Mt. Sinai Sch. Medicine, from 1971; attending physician City Hosp. Ctr. Mt. Sinai Svcs., from 1987; assoc. dean. Lic. physician N.Y., 1969. Contbr. articles to profl. jours. Fellow Am. Coll. Physicians, N.Y. Acad. Medicine; mem. Am. Soc. Microbiology, AMA, Assn. Asm. Med. Colls., Soc. Hosp. Epidemiologists Am., N.Y. Heart Assn., N.Y. Sco. Tropical Medicine, Soc. Health and Human Values, Assn. Practitioners in Infection Control. Home: New York, NY. Died in November of 1999.

NICHOLS, WILLIAM H. physicist, educator, priest; b. Cleve., Mar. 15, 1928; s. Rexford A. and Helen Marie (Gavigan) N. AB, Loyola U., Chgo., 1950; LicPhil, West Baden Coll., West Baden Springs, Ind., 1952; SB, MIT, 1955, PhD, 1958. Joined S.J., 1945, ordained priest Roman Cath. Ch., 1960. Instr. French, algebra and physics Loyola Acad., Chgo., 1952-53; postdoctoral student in physics U. Vienna, 1962-63; asst. prof. physics U. Detroit, 1963-67; from assoc. prof. to prof. physics John Carroll U., University Heights, Ohio, from 1967. Contbr. articles to profl. jours. Trustee Walsh Jesuit High Sch., Stow, Ohio, 1987—. Mem. Am. Phys. Soc., Am. Assn. Physics Tchrs. (treas. Ohio sect.), Inst. for Theol. Encounter with Sci. and Tech., Sigma Xi. Home: Cleveland, Ohio. Died May 2, 2001.

NIEBEL, BENJAMIN WILLARD, industrial engineer, educator; b. Liling, Hunan, China, May 7, 1918; came to U.S., 1927; s. Benjamin Earl and Alice Eva (Haney) N.; m. Doris Mae Middleton, Oct. 22, 1942; children: Benjamin E., Douglas A., Joseph A., Mary Alice. BS in Indsl. Engring., Pa. State U., 1939, MS in Indsl. Engring., 1947, I.E. in Indsl. Engring., 1952. Registered profl. engr., Pa. Chief indsl. engr. Lord Mfg. Co., Eric, Pa., 1939-47; from asst. prof. to prof. Pa. State U., University Park, 1947-55, head dept. indsl. engring., 1955-79; prin. B.W. Niebel & Assocs., State College, from 1979. Author 23 books in areas of methods, process planning, standards, designing for production, 1955—. Pres. College Twp. Indsl. Devel. Authority, State College, 1985—; bd. dirs. Centre County C. of Bus. and Industry, State College, 1990—. Recipient Frank and Lillian Gilbreth award Am. Inst. Indsl. Engrs., 1976, fellow, 1965, Outstanding Engring. Alumni award Pa. State U., 1992. Fellow Inst. Indsl. Engrs. (past chpt. pres., Phil Carroll award 1984); mem. Soc. Mfg. Engrs. (life, past chpt. pres.), Am. Soc. for Engring. Edn. (life, past chpt. pres.). Methodist. Achievements include patents for calculus disintegrator; for animated intestinal tube; for perfect circle hemmorrhoidal excisor; for surgical strip stitch; for mole remover. Home: State College, Pa. Died May 10, 1999.

NIEHAUS, CHLOE MAE, elementary school educator; b. Tompkinsville, Ky., Dec. 7, 1929; d. Herbert J. and Hallie (Wheat) Turner; m. Charles L. Niehaus, June 29, 1957 (dec. 1973). Student, Western U., Bowling Green, Ky., 1948-49, Lindsey Wilson Coll., Columbia, Ky., 1950, 51; BS, Butler U., 1960; MS, Ind. U., 1971. Cert. elem. tchr., Ky., Ind. Elem. tchr. Monroe County Schs., Tompkinsville, 1949-52, Hancock County Schs., Mt. Comfort, Ind., 1953-55, Marion County Sch. Ctr. Twp., Margaret McFarland Sch., Indpls., 1955-62, Indpls. Pub. Schs., Margaret McFarland Sch., 1962-89, ret., 1989. Named to Outstanding Elem. Tchrs. Am., 1972. Mem. Ind. Ret. Tchrs. Orgn., Marion County Ret. Tchrs. Assn., Butler U. Alumni Assn., Ind. U. Alumni Assn., Sigma Delta Pi. Democrat. Roman Catholic. Avocations: reading, travel, walking, gardening, shopping. Home: Indianapolis, Ind. Deceased.

NIEHAUS, ROBERT JAMES, investment banking executive; b. Ann Arbor, Mich., Jan. 6, 1930; s. Julius Herman and Mary Johanna (Koch) N.; m. Jacqueline C. Mallier, Aug. 5, 1982. BBA, U. Mich., 1951; MBA, U. Detroit, 1958. Asst. sr. buyer Ford Motor Co., Dearborn, Mich., 1954-58; gen. purchasing agt. Hercules Motors Co., Canton, Ohio, 1959-60; v.p. procurement Schwitzer Corp., Indpls., 1960-66; sr. v.p. Wallace Murray Corp., N.Y.C., 1966-82; v.p. spl. projects Fischbach Corp., N.Y.C., 1983-84, sr. v.p., 1985-87; pres., chief exec. officer, vice chmn. Fischbach & Moore, Inc., Dallas, 1987-90; pres. Fischbach Corp., 1989-90, 1st Phila. Corp., Radnor, Pa., 1991-92, Computone corp., Atlanta, 1993; dir. Computone Corp., Atlanta, Ga., 1993-95; pres. Mile Marker, Inc., Pompano Beach, Fla., 1994-95. Bd. dirs. Software Group, Barrie, Ont., Can. Bd. dirs., found. chmn. South Fla. Blood Bank, West Palm Beach; bd dirs. Broward Sheriffs' Adv. Coun., sec. Served to lt. USN, 1951-54. Mem. Am. Mgmt. Assn. (gen. mgmt. council 1982—), Lighthouse Point (Fla.) Yacht and Racket Club, Tower Club (dir.), U.S. Navy League, Union League Club (N.Y.C.) Avocations: boating, music, tennis, golf. Home: Fort Lauderdale, Fla. Died Nov. 17, 2003.

NIITAMO, OLAVI ENSIO, Finnish government official; b. Kotka, Finland, Nov. 23, 1926; s. Tenho Armas and Alja Elisabeth (Valiaho) N.; m. Helka Helena Narinen, June 21, 1953; children— Satu, Petteri, Veli-Pekka, Olli-Mikko. M.A., U. Helsinki, 1949, Licenciate of Econs., 1953, Dr.Econs., 1958. Chief econ. stats. div. Central Statis. Office of Finland, Helsinki, 1959-63, chief nat. income stats. div., 1963-71, chief planning dept., 1971-78, dir., 1979-82, dir. gen., 1982—; docent of econs. U. Helsinki, 1962—, acting prof. econs., 1964-65, acting prof., 1971-72; vis. prof. Harvard U., 1966-67, U. Calif.-Berkeley; mem. Central Research Bd., Acad. Finland, 1971-73, Bd. Nordic Statis. Secretariat, 1979—, Statis. Commn., UN, 1981—. Contbr. articles to profl. jours. Served with Finnish Army, 1944. Decorated knight 1st class, White Rose of Finland. Mem. Econ. Soc. Finland, Inst. Mgmt. Sci., Internat. Assn. Research in Income and Wealth, Internat. Statis. Inst., Future Soc. Finland. Home: Helsinki, Finland. Deceased.

NILLES, ANDREW J. lawyer; b. Racine, Wis., Nov. 22, 1960; s. James E. and Ruth A. (Ross) N.; m. Carrie D. Nilles, Apr. 11, 1987. BSEE, U. Wis., 1982; JD, Hamline U., 1985. Bar: Wis. 1985, U.S. Dist. Ct. (ea. and we. dists.) Wis. 1985, Calif. 1988, U.S. Dist. Ct. (cen. dist.) Calif. 1988, U.S. Ct. Appeals (fed. dist.) 1988; registered U.S. patent atty. Intern to judge U.S. Dist. Ct. Minn., 1983-84; law clk. to judge U.S. Ct. Appeals (Fed. Cir.), Washington, 1985-87; ptnr. Nilles & Nilles, S.C., Milw., from 1990. Contbr. chpt. to textbook. Mem. ABA, Wis. Bar Assn., Fed. Cir. Bar Assn., Am. Intellectual Property Law Assn., Wis. Intellectual Property Law Assn., Racine County Bar Assn. Republican. Roman Catholic. Avocations: commercial pilot, flight instructor. Home: Racine, Wis. Died Aug. 17, 2001.

NIMMONS, RALPH WILSON, JR., federal judge; BA, U. Fla., 1960, JD, 1963. Deceased.

NIMS, JOHN FREDERICK, writer, educator; b. Muskegon, Mich., Nov. 20, 1913; s. Frank McReynolds and Anne (McDonald) N.; m. Bonnie Larkin, Sept. 11, 1947; children— John (dec.), Frank, George (dec.), Sarah Hoyt, Emily Anne. AB, U. Notre Dame, 1937, MA, 1939; PhD, U. Chgo., 1945. Mem. faculty U. Notre Dame, 1939-45, 46-52, 54-58, U. Toronto, 1945-46, Bocconi U., Milan, Italy, 1952-53, U. Florence, Italy, 1953-54, U. Madrid, 1958-60, Harvard U., 1964, 68-69, summer 1974, U. Ill.-Urbana, 1961-65, U. Ill., at Chgo., 1965-85, Bread Loaf Writers Conf., 1958-71, Bread Loaf Sch. English, 1965-69, U. Fla., fall 1972, 73-77. Margaret Scott Bundy prof. lit. Williams Coll., fall 1975; prof. lit. Coll. of Charleston, spring 1981; mem. editorial bd. Poetry mag., 1945-48, vis. editor, 1960-61, editor, 1978-84; Phi Beta Kappa poet Harvard U., 1978; Cockefair chair U. Mo., Kansas City, spring 1986; Kilby cons. in poetry Wheaton (Ill.) Coll., fall 1988; editl. advisor Princeton U. Press, 1975-82. Author: The Iron Pastoral, 1947, A Fountain in Kentucky, 1950, The Poems of St. John of the Cross, 1959, rev., 1979, Knowledge of the Evening, 1960, Of Flesh and Bone, 1967, Sappho to Valéry: Poems in Translation, 1971, rev. edit., 1990, Western Wind, 1974, rev. edit., 1992, The Kiss: A Jambalaya, 1982, Selected Poems, 1982, A Local Habitation; Essays on Poetry, 1985, The Six Cornered Snowflake, 1990, Zany in Denim, 1990, Complete Poems of Michelangelo, 1998; contbr.: Five Young American Poets, 1944, The Complete Greek Tragedies, 1959, Euripides, 2, 1998; also anthologies, mags.; editor: Ovid's Metamorphoses, 1965, (James Shirley) Love's Cruelty, 1980, Harper Anthology of Poetry, 1981; assoc. editor: The Poem Itself, 1960. Recipient Harriet Monroe Meml. award Poetry mag., 1942, Guarantors prize, 1943, Levinson prize, 1944, Disting. fellowship Acad. Am. Poets, 1982; Fulbright grantee, 1952, 53; Smith Mundt grantee, 1958, 59; Nat. Found. Arts and Humanities grantee, 1967-68; award for creative writing Am. Acad. Arts and Letters, 1968, Aiken Taylor award, 1991, Melville Cane award 1992, Hardison Poetry prize, 1993; Creative Arts citation in Poetry Brandeis U., 1974; fellow Inst. Humanities U. Ill., 1983-84; Guggenheim fellow, 1986-87. Democrat. Roman Catholic. Died January 19, 1999.

NISSENBAUM, GERALD, physician, educator, inventor; b. Jersey City, Feb. 5, 1932; m. Sylvia Sinakin, Sept. 4, 1957; children: Gary David, Eliot Mark, Robert Samuel. BA, Yeshiva U., 1954; MD, SUNY, 1958. Intern Brookdale Hosp., Bklyn., 1958-59, resident, 1959-60; sr. resident Jersey City Med. Ctr., 1960-61; NIH research fellow in gastroenterology Nat. Cancer Inst., 1962-63; asst. med. dir. Hebrew Hosp., Jersey City, 1962-73; clin. instr. medicine U. Medicine and Dentistry N.J., 1963-72; asst. attending dept. medicine Jersey City Med. Ctr., 1963-68, assoc. attending, 1968-69, attending, from 1970, dir. gastroenterology, 1973-76; clin. asst. prof. medicine U. Medicine and Dentistry N.J., from 1972; pvt. practice internal medicine and gastroenterology Jersey City; adminstrv. dir. gastroenterology Jersey City Med. Ctr., from 1996. Contbr. articles to profl. jours.; developed classic cytol. reagt. used worldwide in medicine and microbiology, "Nissenbaum's Fixative", 1953; patentee device for localizing gastrointestinal bleeding; inventor various med. devices. Capt. M.C., U.S. Army. Recipient Bernard Revel Meml. award Yeshiva U., 1972. Mem. AMA, Soc. Protozoologists, N.J. Med. Soc., NRA, Phi Lambda Kappa. Died Aug. 29, 2002.

NIWANO, NIKKYO, religion and peace foundation administrator; b. Tokamachi-City, Japan, Nov. 15, 1906; m. Sai Abé (dec. 1994); 6 children. LLD, Meadville Lombard Theol. Sch., 1975. Founder Rissho Kosei-Kai, from 1938, pres., 1938-91, Asian Conf. on Religion and Peace, 1977-96, hon. pres., from 1996, World Conf. on Religion and Peace, from 1979, Internat. Assn. for Religious Freedom, from 1987; chmn. Shinshuren: Union of Fedn. New Religious Orgns. of Japan, 1965-92, hon. chmn., from 1992. Trustee Japan Religious League; pres. Japanese Com. for World Conf. on Religion and Peace, 1972-96, hon. pres., 1996—. Decorated knight comdr. with silver star Order St. Gregory the Great; recipient Imperial Household Agy. medal of honor with dark navy blue ribbon, 1958; Templeton Found. prize for progress in religion, 1979; UN plaque, 1983; Internat. Humanitarian award Boys' Town Italy, 1984; Interfaith medallion Internat. Coun. Christians and Jews, 1993. Buddhist. Died 1999.

NIX, ROBERT N(ELSON) C(ORNELIUS), JR., retired state supreme court chief justice; b. Phila., July 13, 1928; s. Robert Nelson Cornelius and Ethel (Lanier) N.; m. Renate Bryant; children from previous marriage: Dorothy Lewis (dec.), Robert Nelson Cornelius III, Michael, Anthony, S. Jude. AB, LLD (hon.), Villanova U.; JD, U. Pa.; postgrad. bus. adminstrn. and econs., Temple U.; LLD (hon.), St. Charles Sem., Dickinson U. Sch. Law, Scranton U., Delaware Law Sch., Lafayette Coll. Bar: Pa. 1956, U.S. Dist. Ct. (ea. dist.) Pa., U.S. Ct. Appeals (3d cir.). Dep. atty. gen. Commonwealth of Pa., 1956-58; ptnr. Nix, Rhodes & Nix, Phila., 1958-68; judge Common Pleas Ct., Phila., 1968-71; justice Supreme Ct. Pa., Phila., 1972-84, chief justice, 1984-96. Chmn. bd. dirs. Nat. Ctr. for State Cts., 1990-91. Bd. dirs. Nat. Ctr. for State Cts., 1985—, Scranton U., Duquesne U., Lincoln U.; life mem. bd. consultors Villanova U., trustee, 1986—; bd. overseers U. Pa. Sch. Law, 1987—; bd. mgrs. Archdiocese of Phila. Served with AUS, 1953-55. Recipient First Pa. award, Benjamin Franklin award Poor Richard Club Pa., James Madison award Soc. Profl. Journalists; named Knight Comdr. Order of St. Gregory the Great. Fellow Am. Bar Found.; mem. ABA, Pa. Bar Assn., Phila. Bar Assn., Nat. Bar Assn. (past chmn. jud. coun.), Barristers Club, Am. Law Inst., Conf. of Chief Justices (bd. dirs., pres. 1990-91), The Legal Club, Omega Psi Phi. Lodges: KC. Home: Philadelphia, Pa. Died Aug. 22, 2003.

NIXON, JOAN LOWERY, writer; b. L.A., Feb. 3, 1927; d. Joseph Michael and Margaret Mary (Meyer) Lowery; m. Hershell Howard Nixon, Aug. 6, 1949; children: Kathleen Nixon Brush, Maureen Nixon Quinlan, Joseph Michael, Eileen Nixon McGowan. BA in Journalism, U. So. Calif., L.A., 1947; Elem. Edn. Credentials, Calif. State Coll., L.A., 1949. Tchr. L.A. Elem. Schs., 1947-50; free-lance writer Houston, 1944—2003; creative writing tchr. Midland (Tex.) Jr. Coll., 1971-73, U. Houston Continuing Edn., 1974-77; columnist The Houston Post, 1969-76. Author: The Mystery of Hurricane Castle, 1964, The Mystery of the Grinning Idol, 1965, The Mystery of the Hidden Cockatoo, 1966, The Mystery of the Haunted Woods, 1967, The Mystery of the Secret Stowaway, 1968, Delbert, The Plainclothes Detective, 1971, The Alligator under the Bed, 1974 (Tex. Inst. Letters award, 1975), The Secret Box Mystery, 1974 (Jr. Lit. Guild), The Mysterious Red Tape Gang, 1974 (Edgar scroll Mystery Writers of Am. 1975), The Mysterious Prowler, 1976, Who Is My Neighbor?, 1976, Five Loaves and Two Fishes, 1976, The Son Who Came Home Again, 1977, Writing Mysteries for Young People, 1977, The Boy Who Could Find Anything, 1978 (reprinted Scott Foresman text), Danger in Dinosaur Valley, 1978, (Jr. Lit. Guild), Muffie Mouse and the Busy Birthday, 1978, (Jr. Lit. Guild), When God Speaks, 1978, When God Listens, 1978, The Kidnapping of Christina Lattimore, 1979 (Edgar Allan Poe award Mystery Writers Am., 1980), The Grandmothers's Book, 1979, The New Year's Day Mystery, 1978, The Halloween Mystery, 1979, The Butterfly Tree, 1979, Bigfoot Makes a Movie, 1979, The Valentine's Day Mystery, 1979, The Happy Birthday Mystery, 1979, The Seance, 1980 (Edgar Allan Poe award best juvenile mystery 1981), Gloria Chipmunk, Star! 1980, If You Say So, Claude, 1980 (Book of Month Club), Before You Were Born, 1980, Casey and the Great Idea, 1980, The Thanksgiving Day Mystery, 1980, The April Fools Day Mystery, 1980, Kleep, The Space Detective Series: Kidnapped on Astarr, The Mysterious Queen of Magic, The Mystery Dolls of Planet Ur, 1981, The Christmas Eve Mystery, 1981, The Easter Mystery, 1981, The Spotlight Gang and the Backstage Ghost, 1981, The Specter, 1982, The Gift, 1983, Days of Fear, 1983, Magnolia's Mixed-Up Magic, 1983 (Crabbery childrens choice award Prince George County, Md.), A Deadly Game of Magic, 1983 (Ind. Young Adult Hoosier award 1989), The Ghosts of Now, 1984 (Edgar Allan Poe award nomination), The House on Hackman's Hill (Mich. Children's Choice award 1987), The Stalker, 1985 (Calif. Young Readers medal 1989), Maggie, Too, 1987, Beats Me, Claude, 1986 (Lit. Guild), The Other Side of Dark, 1987 (Edgar award Mystery Writers Am., other awards, Calif. Young Readers medal 1990), And Maggie Makes Three, 1986, Haunted Island, 1987, Maggie Forevermore, 1987, Fat Chance, Claude, 1987, The Dark and Deadly Pool, 1987, Orphan Train Quartet: (vol. 1) A Family Apart, 1987 (Best Juvenile Western Book award Western Writers Am.), (vol. 2) Caught in the Act, 1988, (vol.3) In The Face Of Danger, 1988 (Best Juvenile Western Book award We. Writers of Am. 1989), (vol. 4) A Place to Belong, 1989, If You Were a Writer, 1988 (Jr. Lit. Guild), Secret, Silent Screams, 1988, The Island of Dangerous Dreams, 1989, You Bet Your Britches, Claude, 1989, Whispers From the Dead, 1989, Hollywood Daughters: A Family Triology: (vol. 1) Star Baby, 1989, (vol. 2) Overnight Sensation, 1990, (vol. 3) Encore, 1990, A Candidate for Murder, 1991, The Nic-Nacs and the Nic-Nac News Series (The Mystery Box, Watch Out for Dinosaurs, The Honeycutt Street Celebrities, and The Haunted House on Honeycutt Street), 1991, High Trail to Danger, 1991, The Deadly Promise, 1992, The Weekend Was Murder!, 1992, Ellis Island: Land of Hope, 1992, That's the Spirit, Claude, 1992, The Name of the Game Was Murder, 1993 (Edgar award Mystery Writers Am. 1994), Land of Promise, 1993, Land of Dreams, 1994, When I Am Eight, 1994, Will You Give Me A Dream?, 1994, A Dangerous Promise, 1994, Shadowmaker, 1994, Keeping Secrets, 1995, Spirit Seeker, 1995, The Statue Walks at Night, 1995, The Legend of Deadman's Mine, 1995, Backstage with a Ghost, 1995, Check in to Danger, 1995, The House Has Eyes, 1996, Secret of the Time Capsule, 1996, Beware the Pirate Ghost, 1996, Don't Scream, 1996, Search for the Shadowman, 1996; co-author textbooks: This I Can Be, 1975, People and Me, 1975; co-author: (with Hershell Nixon) Oil and Gas, from Fossils to Fuels, 1977, Volcanoes: Nature's Fireworks, 1978 (Outstanding Sci. Books for Children cert. Nat. Sci. Tchrs. Assn. and Children's Book Coun.), Glaciers: Nature's Frozen Rivers, 1980 (Outstanding Sci. Books for Children cert. Nat. Sci. Tchrs. Assn. and Children's Book Coun.), Earthquakes: Nature in Motion, 1981 (Outstanding Sci. Books for Children cert. Nat. Sci. Tchrs. Assn. and Children's Book Coun.), Land Under the Seas, 1985; author under pseudonym Jaye Ellen: The Trouble With Charlie, 1982; numerous of these books pub. in fgn. langs., paperbacks, reprints. Recipient Children's Choice awards in over 7 states, 1984-89, Best Children's Book award Tex. Inst. Letters, Austin, 1975, Outstanding Contbn. to Children's Lit. award Bishop Byrne Chpt. Cath. Librs. Am., 1980, Cen. Mo. State U., 1982. Mem. Mystery Writers of Am., Inc. (regional v.p. southwest chpt. 1984-86, gen. awards chmn. N.Y. 1988-89, nat. bd. dirs.), Tex. Inst. Letters, Soc. Children's Book Writers (bd. dirs. 1974-78), Am. Crime Writers League, Western Writers Am., The Authors Guild, Sisters in Crime, Kappa Delta. Republican. Roman Catholic. Avocations: reading, travel. Home: Houston, Tex. Died July 5, 2003.

NOBLE, BEN, JR., gemological consultant; b. Galveston, Tex., Dec. 23, 1919; s. Ben Z. and Wsther (Littman) N.; m. Carmen B., Feb. 1950 (div. 1960); children: Brian P., Melissa E. Student, U. Fla., 1942, U. Houston, 1938-40, 49-52, Gemological Inst. Am., 1954-59 and from 75. Pres. Houston Advt. Agy., 1946-53, Eureka Gem Instrument Co., from 1956; sales, cons. Ben Noble-Gemological Cons., 1946-53, owner, from 1953. Writer, producer, dir. (radio program) Gems and Music, 1950-53. Staff sgt. USAF, 1940-42, 42-45. Recipient John B. Van Ness award, 1965, 75, Big Mouth award, Speaker com., 1984, 85, 86, 87. Mem. Houston Livestock Show and Rodeo Assn. (life), Houston Farm and Ranch Assn. (life), Houston Gem and Mineral Soc. (life), Jewish War Vets. (life), U. Houston Alumni Assn. (life). Jewish. Avocations: lapidary, hunting, fishing, ranching, politics, rsch. in gemology. Deceased.

NOBLE, RICHARD LLOYD, lawyer; b. Oklahoma City, Oct. 11, 1939; s. Samuel Lloyd and Eloise Joyce (Millard) N. AB with distinction, Stanford, 1961, LLB, 1964. Bar: Calif. 1964. Assoc. firm Cooper, White & Cooper, San Francisco, 1965-67; assoc., ptnr. firm Voegelin, Barton, Harris & Callister, Los Angeles, 1967-70; ptnr. Noble & Campbell, Los Angeles, San Francisco, from 1970. Dir. Langdale Corp., L.A., Gt. Pacific Fin. Co., Sacramento; lectr. Tax Inst. U. So. Calif., 1970; mem. bd. law and bus. program Stanford Law Sch. Contbr. articles to legal jours. Bd. govs. St. Thomas Aquinas Coll. Recipient Hilmer Dehlman Jr. award Stanford Law Sch., 1962; Benjamin Harrison fellow Stanford U., 1967. Mem. ABA, State Bar Calif., L.A. Bar Assn., San Francisco Bar Assn., Commercial Club (San Francisco), Petroleum Club (L.A.), Capitol Hill Club (Washington), Pi Sigma Alpha. Republican. Home: Los Angeles, Calif. Deceased.

NOBLE, WALTER MORRIS HART, physician, educator; b. San Francisco, Mar. 24, 1933; s. Charles A. Jr. and Agnes (Von Adelung) N.; m. Winifred Brady, Sept. 21, 1962; children: Christopher (dec.), Morris, William. BA cum laude, Harvard U., 1954, MD, 1958. Diplomate Am. Bd. of Internal Med. Intern and resident U. N.C., 1958-60; resident San Francisco Gen. Hosp., 1962-63, H.C. Moffitt Hosp., San Francisco, 1963-64, instr. to clin. prof., 1964-83; acting chmn. dept. of medicine Children's Hosp., San Francisco, 1981-82, bd. dirs., from 1984. Sec., treas. Pacific Interurban Clin. Club, 1978-82, chmn. 1988-89; trustee Town Sch. San Francisco, 1966-84, Thacher Sch., Ojai, Calif., 1967-73; bd. govs. San Francisco Heart Assn. 1967-72. Capt. U.S. Army Med. Corps, 1960-62, Korea. Mem. AMA, San Francisco Med. Soc., ACP, Am. Soc. of Internal Med., Pacific Union (San Francisco, bd. dirs. 1994—), Calif. Tennis Club (bd. dirs. 1994-97). Avocations: tennis, riding. Home: San Francisco, Calif. Died July 28, 2000.

NOIROT, MARY RUTH WHITSON (MRS. LEO NOIROT), retired adult and secondary education educator; b. Westfield, Ill., Nov. 27, 1905; d. Perry Edward and Estrella (Porterfield) Whitson; m. George Leo Noirot, Aug. 24, 1929 (dec. Jan. 1991); children: Jacqueline, Dona, George Leo III, Nannette. Student, Mich. State U., Lansing, Mich. U., Ann Arbor; EdD, Ea. Ill. U., 1925. Cert. master flower show judge, NCGC, Ind., Ohio, Fla., landscape design critic. Substitute tchr. DeKalb County Bd. Edn., Auburn, Ind.; prof. horticulture and floral design Tri State U., Angola, Ind., Purdue U., Ft. Wayne, Ind., Ind. Univ., Ft. Wayne; ret. Contbr. articles to profl. jours. Mem. Nat. Coun. Garden Clubs (master flower show judges), N.E. Garden Clubs (dist. 6 dir.). Home: Waterloo, Ind. Deceased.

NORBY, WILLIAM CHARLES, financial consultant; b. Chgo., Aug. 10, 1915; s. Oscar Maurice and Louise (Godejohann) N.; m. Camilla Edbrooke, June 12, 1943; children: Martha Norby Fraundorf, Richard James. AB, U. Chgo.,

1935. With Harris Trust & Savs. Bank, Chgo., 1935-70, v.p., 1953-64, sr. v.p., 1964-70; exec. dir. Fin. Analysts Fedn., N.Y.C., 1970-72; sr. v.p., bd. dirs. Duff & Phelps, Inc., Chgo., 1973-81. Mem. Fin. Acctg. Standards Adv. Coun., 1975-79. Mem. Fin. Acctg. Stds. Adv. Coun., 1975-79. Mem. AICPA (com. on auditors responsibilities 1975-78), Fin. Analysts Fedn. (bd. dirs. 1962-68, pres. 1963-64, Disting. Svc. award 1973, Nicholas Molodovsky award 1979), Investment Analysts Soc. Chgo. (pres. 1955-56), U. Chgo. Alumni Assn. (citation 1961), Phi Beta Kappa. Congregationalist (trustee 1950-56, chmn. 1955-56). Home: La Grange Park, Ill. Deceased.

NORMAN, JAMES WILLIAM, JR., retired lawyer; b. Gainesville, Fla., Jan. 17, 1921; s. James William and Lucile (Pullen) N.; m. Nancy Rossetter, Mar. 3, 1945; children: Nancy, James III, Lucile, Martin. BA, U. Fla., 1941, JD, 1947; LLM, Harvard U., 1947. Bar: Fla., 1947. Asst. prof. Stetson Coll. of Law, De Land, Fla., 1947-49; mem. faculty Coll. of Law U. Fla., Gainesville, 1948; pvt. practice West Palm Beach, Fla., 1949; ptnr. Buck and Norman, Jacksonville, Fla., 1950; adminstrv. asst. to Charles E. Bennett, mem. U.S. Ho. of Reps., Washington, 1951-60; legis. asst. to U.S. Senator Spessard L. Holland, Washington, 1960-63; staff dir. spl. com. on aging. U.S. Senate, Washington, 1963-67, atty., 1967-69; legis. analyst U.S. Adminstrn. on Aging, Washington, 1969-86; tax law specialist Fla. Dept. Revenue, Tallahassee, 1986-96. Lt. (s.g.) USNR, 1943-46. Named one of Five Outstanding Young Men of Fla., Fla. State Jaycees, 1954. Mem. Fla. Bar Assn. Democrat. Baptist. Home: Tallahassee, Fla. Deceased.

NORTH, ROBERT CARVER, political science educator; b. Walton, N.Y., Nov. 17, 1914; s. Arthur W. and Irene (Davenport) N.; m. Dorothy Anderson, Mar. 12, 1977; children by previous marriage: Woesha Kristina, Mary Davenport, Elizabeth Katrynka, Robert Cloud, Renya Catarina. AB, Union Coll., 1936; MA, Stanford U., 1948, PhD, 1957. Tchr. English, History Milford (Conn.) Sch., 1939-42; research asst. Hoover Instn., Stanford, Calif., 1948-50, research assoc., 1950-57; assoc. prof. polit. sci. Stanford (Calif.) U., 1957-62, prof., 1962-85, prof. emeritus, from 1985. Author: Revolt in San Marcos, 1941 (Commonwealth Gold medal), Moscow and Chinese Communists, 1952, The World That Could Be, 1976, (with Nazli Choucri) Nations in Conflict, 1975, War, Peace, Survival, 1990, (with Nazli Choucri and Susumu Yamakage) The Challenge of Japan: Before World War II and After, 1992. Served to capt. USAAF, 1942-46. Recipient Prix Mondial, U. Geneva, Hautes Etudes Internats., 1998. Mem. Am. Polit. Sci. Assn. (Conflicts Processes Sect. Lifetime Achievement award 1993), Internat. Studies Assn. (Disting. scholar award in fgn. policy analysis, pres. 1970-71), Internat. Peace-Sci. Assn., Explorers Club Democrat. Unitarian Universalist. Home: Woodside, Calif. Died July 15, 2002.

NORTON, CLIFFORD CHARLES, actor, director; b. Chgo., Mar. 21, 1918; s. Benjamin Wolf and Sophia (Sholdar) N.; m. Florence Robinson, Feb. 23, 1974; children from previous marriage— Clifford Charles, Susan; 1 stepdau., Stacey Robinson Ulyate. Student public schs., Chgo. Appearances include: (radio) FBI; TV Garroway at Large; films Funny Lady; night clubs, Empire Rm., Chgo., Elmwood Casino, Windsor, Ont.; currently appearing on various TV comms. Served with U.S. Army Air Corps, WW II. Mem. Actors Equity Assn., Screen Actors Guild, Actors Fund of Am., AFTRA, Acad. Motion Picture Arts and Scis., Am. Film Inst. Died Jan. 25, 2003.

NORTON, (WILLIAM) ELLIOT, retired drama critic; b. Boston, May 17, 1903; s. William L. and Mary E. (Fitzgerald) N.; m. Florence E. Stelmach (dec.); AB, Harvard, 1926; MA (hon.) Emerson Coll. 1955, LittD, 1963; D of Journalism (hon.), Suffolk U., 1956; LHD, Fairfield (Conn.) U., 1964, Boston Coll., 1970, St. Francis Coll., 1970, St. Joseph's Coll., 1976, Assumption Coll., 1979; D.Litt., Northeastern U., 1966, Merrimack Coll., 1977, Boston U., 1980; m. Florence E. Stelmach, Sept. 9, 1934; children— Elizabeth Noel, Jane Florence, David Andrew. Reporter, 1926-34; drama critic Boston Post, 1934-56, Boston Daily Record and Boston Sunday Advertiser, 1956-62, Boston Record Am. and Sunday Advertiser, 1962-73, Boston Herald Am., 1973-82; part time mem. faculty Emerson Coll., 1935-62, Boston Coll., 1948-62; lectr. dramatic lit. Boston U. Sch. Fine and Applied Arts, 1954-67, adj. prof. dramatic lit., 1967-81, prof. emeritus, 1981—; Phi Beta Kappa orator Tufts U., 1967; lectr. Drama Workshop Fgn. Studies League London, Nottingham, 1967, Reading (Eng.), 1968; star TV program Elliot Norton Revs., 1958-82. Pres. New Eng. Theatre Conf., 1951-53; vice chmn. Mass. Council Arts and Humanities, 1966-71; mem. pres.'s council Fairfield U. 1967-69; exec. com. Am. Theatre Critics Assn., 1974-79; mem. Pulitzer Prize Play Jury, 1964-68, 72-73; delivered Bi-Centennial Lectr. Forum Third Lantern Old North Church, Boston, 1976. Recipient First Ann. Citation Merit, Boston Coll., 1947; Connor Meml. award Emerson Coll., 1956; Rodgers and Hammerstein Coll. President's award, 1962; Peabody award for Elliot Norton Revs., 1962; George Jean Nathan award, 1963-64; Spl. Antoinette Perry award, 1971; citation Nat. Council Tchrs. English, 1971; gold medal Am. Coll. Theater Festival, 1973; Nat. award New Eng. Theatre Conf., 1974; Yankee Quill award Acad. NE Journalists, 1976; award for outstanding achievement in arts Mass. chpt. Nat. Multiple Sclerosis Soc., 1977; named Grand Bostonian, City of Boston, 1977; theater park named in his honor, Boston, 1977; O'Reilly-Conway medal The Pilot, 1980; annual Elliot Norton Awards for Excellence instituted in his honor, 1983; inducted to Am. Theatre Hall of Fame, 1988; honored for Dist. Contbns. to the Theatre City of Boston, 1993. Fellow Am. Acad. Arts and Scis.; mem. Nat. Theatre Conf. (hon.) Clubs: Boston Press (pres. 1950-52), Harvard; Players (N.Y.C.). Author: Broadway Down East, 1978; contbr. Theatre Arts, Shakespeare Quarterly, N.Y. Times, N.Y. Herald Tribune, Boston Globe. Home: Newton, Mass. Died July 20, 2003.

NORTON, MARY, retired researcher; b. Oak Park, Ill., July 25, 1932; d. John Joseph and Laura Ellen (Canning) Bledsoe; m. James Joseph Norton, Oct. 19, 1963; children: Susan Elizabeth, Amy Patricia. BS in Humanities, Loyola U., Chgo., 1954; cert. in French lang., U. Paris, 1957. Head edn. rsch. World Book, Inc., Chgo., 1958-64, dir. rsch. and libr. svcs., 1979-96, ret., 1996. Mem. Chgo. Book Clinic, 1989-96; donor, mem. Nat. Dem. Com., Washington, 1992—. Recipient scholarship Alliance Française de N.Y., 1956-57. Mem. ALA, Alliance Française. Roman Catholic. Avocations: antiquing, travel, reading, decorating. Home: Chicago, Ill. Died Nov. 23, 2001.

NOSAKA, KOKEN, Japanese government official; Elected mem. Lower House, Tottori; mem. Prefectural Assembly; Minister of Constrn. Govt. of Japan, 1994-96. Chmn. diet affairs com. Social Dem. Party of Japan. Mem. Social Dem. Party of Japan. Died Apr. 18, 2004.

NOTARO, MICHAEL R. data processing and computer service executive; b. Chgo., Nov. 1, 1914; s. Anthony and Felicia (Franzese) N.; m. Irene Hapsude, May 5, 1936 (dec.); children: Michael R., Phyllis Ann; m. Ruth Bostrom, Mar. 10, 1984 Student, Northwestern U. Sch. Commerce, 1930-36, Chgo. Law Sch., 1930-32; LL.D., DePaul U. Dir. St. Paul Fed. Savs. Bank Bd. dirs. Cath. Charities of Archdiocese of Chgo., Boys Clubs Chgo., Loyola U.; trustee De Paul U. Decorated knight Malta, knight St. Gregory, Knight comdr. Order Merit Italy). Roman Catholic (lay trustee). Clubs: Union League, Mid-Am., Tavern, Chgo. Athletic Assn. (Chgo.); Butterfield Country (Hinsdale, Ill.). Died July 4, 1998.

NOVICH, MIJA, voice educator; b. Chgo., May 11, 1928; d. Božidar and Zorka (Miljkovich) Mijanovich; 1 child, Elena. BEd, Northwestern U., 1949; MusM, Duquesne U., 1976. Operatic soprano, 1956-70; former prof. voice Duquesne U., Pitts., former dir. opera workshop. Performed operatic prodns. in N.Y.C., New Orleans, Houston, Pitts., Montreal, Can., Teatro Colon Buenos Aries, Teatro Mcpl., Santiago, Chile, Colo., Stadt Theater, Aachen, Germany; operalogue lectr. Pitts. Opera. Scholar Mannes Coll. Music, 1954, Aspen Inst. Music, 1953; recipient Martha Baird Rockefeller award Rockefeller Found., 1956; Hunkele grantee Duquesne U., 1980. Mem. Nat. Assn. Tchrs. Singing. Avocations: photography, collecting books and music, travel, theater. Home: Pittsburgh, Pa. Died Oct. 13, 2003.

NYALALI, FRANCIS LUCAS, former chief justice; b. Mwanza, Tanzania, Feb. 3, 1935; s. Lucas Makali and Salome (Sato) Madiya; m. Loyce Phares, Dec. 28, 1968; children— Emmanueli, Karoli, Victor, Lulu. B.A. with honors (London), Univ. Coll. of East Africa, Makerere, 1961. Mem. Lincoln's Inn, London, 1965. Bar: Tanzania. Resident magistrate Judiciary Dept., Tanzania, 1966-71, judge High Ct., 1974-77, chief justice, 1977-2000; chmn. labor tribunal, Labor Dept., Tanzania, 1971-74. Author: Aspect of Industrial Conflicts in Tanzania, 1978. Chmn. presdl. commns. on polit. pluralsim in Tanzania, 1991-92; patron Tanzania Youth Assn., 1993—; appointer Tanzania Social Action Trust Fund, 1994—. Decorated Order of United Republic (Tanzania). Mem. Tanzania Judges and Magistrates Assn. (patron), Soc. For Reform in Internat. Criminal Law, Indian Soc. Internat. Law (hon.) Lincolns Inn Ct. (hon. bencher). Avocations: reading; nature watching. E-mail: flnyalali@raha.com; vmb@raha.com. Died 2003.

NYGAARD, JENS, conductor, music educator; b. Longview, Tex., Oct. 26, 1931; s. Marius Jensen Nygaard and Lois McClurkin. BS, Juilliard Sch. Music, 1957, MS, 1958. Founder, condr. Westchester Chamber Chorus and Orch., White Plains, N.Y., 1967-79, Jupiter Symphony, N.Y.C., from 1979; condr. Naumburg Orch., N.Y.C., 1979-93, Rutgers U. Orch., New Brunswick, N.J., 1983-93; tchr. conducting Columbia U., N.Y.C., 1981-83. Organist, harpsichordist Mostly Mozart, N.Y.C. Composer Stephen Foster Medley, cadenzas for various Mozart concertos, various marches and waltzes. Organizer musical activities Washington Heights YMHA, N.Y.C., 1970-93, Jewish Guild for the Blind, N.Y.C., 1985-88; presenter numerous concerts for underprivileged and handicapped, 1960's—. Avocation: reading. Died Sept. 24, 2001.

NYSTRAND, RAPHAEL OWENS, university dean, educator; b. Maryville, Mo., Nov. 6, 1937; s. Phillip Owens and Emily (Martin) M.; m. Suzanne Rose Duval, Apr. 1, 1961; children: Kathryn Lee, Kristin Sue. BA, Cornell Coll., 1959; MAT., Johns Hopkins U., 1960; PhD, Northwestern U., 1966. Tchr. Lyons Twp. High Sch., La Grange, Ill., 1960-64; research assoc. Research Council of Great Cities Program for Sch. Improvement, Chgo., 1965-66; asst. prof. Coll. Edn., Ohio State U., Columbus, 1967-69, assoc. prof., 1969-71, prof., chmn. dept., 1972-78; dean Sch. Edn., U. Louisville, 1978—, prof., 1978—; sec. edn. and humanities cabinet Commonwealth of Ky., 1984 (on leave). Postdoctoral fellow U. Chgo., 1966-67, vis. lectr., 1967; vis. prof. U. Victoria, B.C., Can., 1977; cons. various sch. dists., state agys.; v.p. Holmes Group, 1990—; mem. Nat. Policy Bd. for Ednl. Adminstrn., 1991-93, Nat. Coun. Accreditation Tchr. Edn. State Partnership Bd., 1994—, Ky. Edn. Profl. Stds. bd., 1993—. Co-author: The Organization and Control of American Schools, 6th edit., 1990, Introduction to Educational Administration, 6th edit., 1983; co-editor: Educational Administration: The Developing Decades, 1977, Strategies for Educational Change, 1981. Trustee Columbus Met. Sch., 1974-78, Fairmount Fund, 1980—, Louisville Youth Choir, 1983-85, Louisville Art Gallery, 1985-87, Wesley Comty. House, 1986-90, Stage One, 1989-91, Ky. Derby Festival, 1990-92, Jewish Hosp. Health Care Svcs., 1998—; adv. bd. Inst. Creative Learning, Inc., Louisville, 1980-90, Jr. League Louisville, 1984-87, Gov.'s Sch. for Arts, 1986-87; mem. Ky. Edn. Profl. Stds. Bd., 1993—. Mem. Am. Ednl. Rsch. Assn., Nat. Soc. Study Edn., Phi Delta Kappa. Methodist. Home: Louisville, Ky. Deceased.

NZO, ALFRED BAPHETHUXOLO, South African government official; b. Benoni, South Africa, June 19, 1925; BSc, U. Ft. Hare. Joined African Nat. Congress, 1950; health insp. Alexander Health Commn., 1951-58; organizer Transvaal and Natal Exec. Com., 1958; repeated banned and arrested, 1959-61; served in prison 6 months, 1961; placed under 24 hour house arrest, 1962-65; detained under 90-day detention Act, 1963; released, 1964; joined external mission African Nat. Congress, 1964, dep. rep., 1964-67, chief rep. New Delhi, India, 1967-69, sec.-gen., 1969-91, mem. nat. exec. com., from 1991; min. fgn. affairs Govt. of South Africa, Pretoria, from 1994. Contbr. articles to profl. jours. Died Jan. 13, 2000.

O'BANNON, FRANK LEWIS, governor, lawyer; b. Louisville, Jan. 30, 1930; s. Robert Pressley and Rosella Faith (Dropsey) O'B.; m. Judith Mae Asmus, Aug. 18, 1957; children: Polly, Jennifer, Jonathan. AB, Ind. U., 1952, JD, 1957. Pvt. practice, Corydon; ptnr. Hays, O'Bannon & Funk, Corydon, 1966-80, O'Bannon, Funk & Simpson, Corydon, 1980-88; mem. Ind. Senate, Corydon, 1970-89, minority floor leader, 1979-89, asst. minority floor leader, 1972-76; lt. gov. State of Ind., 1989-97, gov., 1997—2003. Chmn., dir. O'Bannon Pub. Co., Inc.; chair Dem. Govs.' Assn., 1999; chair human resources com. Nat. Govs.' Assn., 2002-03. Served with USAF, 1952-54. Mem. Ind. Dem. Editorial Assn. (pres. 1961), Am. Judicature Soc., Am. Bar Assn., Ind. Bar Assn. Democrat. Methodist. Died Sept. 13, 2003.

OBERREIT, WALTER WILLIAM, lawyer; b. Paterson, N.J., Oct. 7, 1928; s. William and Gertrud (Limpert) O.; m. Anne-Marie Gohier, July 6, 1955; children: Stephan, Alexis, Jerome BA, U. Mich., 1951; diploma, U. Paris Inst. Polit. Studies, 1955; JD, Yale U., 1958. Bar: N.Y. Assoc. Cleary, Gottlieb, Steen & Hamilton, N.Y.C., 1958-62, Paris, 1962-66, Brussels, 1966-67, ptnr., 1968-98, of counsel, from 1999. Contbr. articles to profl. jours., chpts. to books. Lt. (j.g.) USN, 1953-55. Mem. ABA, Assn. of Bar of City of N.Y. (co-chmn. com. on rels. with European Bars 1981—), Am. Arbitration Assn., Ctr. European Policy Studies, Inst. Royal Rels. Internat., Union Internat. Des Avocats. Clubs: Cercle Royal Gaulois. Avocations: sailing, tennis, skiing. Home: Brussels, Belgium. Deceased.

OBI, ROBERT TOSHIO, anesthesiologist; b. L.A., Sept. 25, 1918; MD, Wayne State U., 1948. Diplomate Am. Bd. Anesthesiology. Intern L.A. County - U. So. Calif. Med. Ctr., 1948-49, resident in anesthesiology, 1949-51; asst. clin. prof. anesthesiology U. So. Calif. Sch. Medicine, from 1970, assoc. clin. prof. anesthesiology, from 1974, emeritus prof. Fellow Am. Coll. Anesthesiology; mem. AMA, Am. Soc. Anesthesiology, Calif. Med. Assn. Home: South Pasadena, Calif. Died Dec. 3, 1999.

O'BRIEN, DONALD JOSEPH, retired lawyer; b. Chgo., Oct. 4, 1913; s. Donald and Julia (Steger) O'B.; m. Helen C. McGinnis, Feb. 26, 1938; children: Donald J. Jr., Nancy S. Brown, Terrence M., Dennis F., Richard M. JD, De Paul U., 1936. Bar: Ill. 1936, U.S. Dist. Ct. (no. dist.) Ill. 1936, U.S. Ct. Appeals (7th cir.) 1936. State senator Ill. Legislature, Chgo., 1950-64; ward committeeman Cook County Dem. Orgn., Chgo., 1953-63, mem. exec. com., 1953-64; judge Cir. Ct., 1964-80; presiding judge Chancery Div. Cook County, Chgo., 1968-80. Senate minority leader Ill. Legislature, 1956-64. Contbr. articles to profl. jours. Disting. service award Nordic Law Club, Chgo., 1972, Celtic Legal Soc., Chgo., 1970, Catholic Lawyers Guild, Chgo., 1978, Chgo. Bar Assn., Young Lawyers 1978. Mem. ABA, Ill. State Bar Assn., Chgo. Bar Assn., Am. Coll. Trial Lawyers, Internat. Acad. Trial Lawyers, Soc. Trial Lawyers Ill., Butterfield Country Club, K.C. Democrat. Roman Catholic. Avocations: fishing, hunting, golf. Home: Indianhead Park, Ill. Died Dec. 15, 2001.

O'BRIEN, DONOUGH, pediatrician, educator; b. Edinburgh, Scotland, May 9, 1923; came to U.S., 1957, naturalized, 1963. s. Arthur John Rushton and Catherine Henderson (Aikman) O'B.; children— Turlough, Rushton, Quentin MA, Cambridge U., 1944, M.B., 1947, MD, 1950. Diplomate Am. Bd. of Pediatrics. Intern St. Thomas Hosp., London, 1946; resident Guy's Hosp. and Hosp. Sick Children, London, 1948; former prof. pediatrics U. Colo. Med. Ctr., Denver, dir. Barbara Davis Ctr. Childhood Diabetes, 1982-89. Contbr. articles to profl. jours. Served to maj. RAMC, 1946-57 Markle Found. scholar, 1958, U. Colo. medal, 2000. Democrat. Episcopalian. Home: Denver, Colo. Died Mar. 16, 2004.

O'BRIEN, MARGARET JOSEPHINE, retired community health nurse; b. N.Y.C., Dec. 5, 1918; d. John J. and Nellie (Coyle) O'B. BS, St.John's U., 1954, MS, 1962; MPH, Columbia U., 1964. With Health Dept., City of New York, 1943-81, assoc. dir. Bur. Pub. Health Nursing, dir.

Pub. Health Nursing Svc., asst. commr. pub. health nursing; professional respite provider for caregivers of frail ederly Westchester Jewish Comty. Svcs., from 1997. Contbr. articles to profl. jours. Recipient Outstanding Alumnus of Columbia U. Sch. of Pub. Health award, 1994. Mem. ANA, APHA, NLN, N.Y. State Nurses Assn., N.Y.C. Pub. Health Assn. Died June 23, 1999.

O'BRIEN, RICHARD, health facility executive; b. Brighton, Mass., Apr. 2, 1943; s. Francis Charles and Dorothy Marie (Keefe) O'B.; m. Mary Kathleen Rogers, July 25, 1964; children: Michelle Lynn, Kevin Richard, Stephanie Patricia. BA, Fla. Atlantic U., 1968, MPA, 1981. Cert. health care exec. V.p. materials mgmt. St. Mary's Hosp., West Palm Beach, Fla., 1979-81; exec. v.p., COO Palm Beach Blood Bank, Inc., West Palm Beach, Fla., 1981-89; pres., chief exec. officer Assn. Ind. Blood Ctrs., Inc., West Palm Beach, Fla., from 1990; pres. Auxiliary Power Systems, Inc., West Palm Beach, Fla., from 1989, Negotiation Agts., Internat., West Palm Beach, Fla., 1988—0. Cons. Baxter Health Care, Deerfield, Ill., 1988—, Abbott Labs., diagnostic div., Chgo., 1988—. Pres. Palm Beach County Kidney Assn., West Palm Beach, 1982, 84; bd. dirs. State of Fla. Kidney Assn., Tallahassee, Fla., 1981; del. End Stage Renal Disease Network 19, Tallahassee, 1980. Recipient Disting. Svc. award Palm Beach County Kidney Assn., 1983. Mem. Am. Assn. Blood Banks, Fla. Assn. Blood Banks, Inc. (chmn. 1991), Am. Coll. Health Care Execs. Republican. Roman Catholic. Avocations: horse raising, tennis, golf. Home: Jupiter, Fla. Deceased.

O'BRIEN, SUE, journalist; b. Waukon, Iowa, Mar. 6, 1939; d. John Gordon and Jean (Schadel) O'B.; m. John Seifert, Sept. 14, 1991; children from previous marriage: Peter, Sarah, Andrew. BA, Grinnell Coll., 1959; MPA, Harvard U., 1985. Reporter KTLN/KTLK Radio, Denver, 1968-70; anchor, reporter KBTR-AM, Denver, 1970-73; anchor, reporter, commentator KOA-AM/TV, Denver, 1973-75; corr. NBC Radio, N.Y.C., 1975-76; news. dir., exec. editor KOA AM/FM/TV, Denver, 1976-80; press sec. Gov. Colo., Denver, 1980-85; campaign mgr. Roy Romer, 1985-86; asst. city editor The Denver Post, 1987-88; assoc. prof. journalism, dir. masters program Sch. Journalism & Mass Comm., U. Colo., Boulder, 1988-95; editl. page dir. The Denver Post, 1995—2003. Adj. assoc. prof. U. Colo. Grad. Sch. Pub. Adminstrn., 1986-95. Chmn. Christian Social REls. divsn. Episc. Diocese Colo., 1964-68; bd. dirs. Colo. Journalism Rev., 1974-75; press sec. Coloradans for Lamm/Dick, 1982. Recipient Headliner award Women in Comm. Colo., 1972, Women of Achievement award, 1992, Big Hat award U. Colo. Soc. Profl. Journalists, 1973, Alumni award Grinnell Coll., 1974. Mem. Soc. Profl. Journalists (v.p. 1977-78), Assn. for Edn. in Journalism & Mass Comm. (head newspaper divsn. 1992—), Radio and TV News Dirs. Assn., Denver Press Club, Martar Bd., Phi Beta Kappa. Democrat. Episcopalian. Died Aug. 6, 2003.

O'BRIEN, WILLIAM VINCENT, government educator; b. Washington, July 9, 1923; s. William Colombo and Theresa (Matthews) O'B.; m. Madge Laura Roberts (dec.1996), Sept. 19, 1951. BS in Fgn. Svc., Georgetown U., 1946, MS in Fgn. Svc., 1948, PhD Internat. Relations, 1953. Instr. dept. govt. Georgetown U., Washington, 1950-51; Fulbright fellow Faculte de droit, Sorbonne, Paris, 1951-52; asst. prof. dept. govt. Georgetown U., Washington, 1952-57, assoc. prof. dept govt., 1957-66, prof. dept. govt., 1966-89, chmn. dept. govt., 1974-77, 84-85. Co-dir. summer institutes NEH, U. Mass., Amherst, 1979. Editor, co-author: World Polity, Vols. I-III, 1957, 60, 65, The Nuclear Dilemma and the Just War Tradition, 1986; author: War and/or Survival, 1969, The Conduct of Just and Limited War, 1981. Sgt. U.S. Army, 1943-46, PTO, lt. col. USAR, 1951-75. Research grantee U.S. Institutes of Peace, 1989. Mem. Am. soc. Internat. Law, Internat. Studies Assn. Roman Catholic. Avocations: collecting art, walking. Home: Washington, DC. Died July 8, 2003.

O'CONNELL, BRIAN JAMES, priest, former university president; b. Hartford, Conn., Aug. 21, 1940; s. Jerry and Mary (Moloney) O'C. AB, Mary Immaculate Sem., 1964, MDiv, 1968; MA, St. John's U., Jamaica, N.Y., 1970; PhD, Ohio State U., 1974. Ordained priest Roman Cath. Ch., 1968. Social studies tchr. St. John's Prep. Sch., Bklyn., 1968-70; lectr. sociology St. John's U., Jamaica, 1970-71, asst. prof. sociology, 1974-79, assoc. prof., 1979-87, assoc. dean arts and scis., 1987-88, also bd. dirs., 1989-99; exec. v.p. Niagara U., N.Y., 1988-89, pres., 1989-95; chaplain Providence Hosp., Washington, 1996-99; dean arts and scis. St. John's U., Jamaica, 1999. Author: Blacks in White Collar Jobs, 1979; also articles. Cons. Bklyn. Ecumenical Coops., 1981-88. Mem. Niagara Falls C. of C. (bd. dirs. 1989-95). Home: Jamaica, NY. Died Feb. 28, 2000.

O'CONNELL, JOHN F. lawyer, retired law educator; b. Mahanoy City, Pa., Jan. 4, 1919; s. Thomas Vincent O'Connell and Mary Elizabeth Cunningham; m. Rosemary Teresa O'Connell, Jan. 9, 1943 (dec. June 1990); children: Paul, Rosemarie, Dennis, Michael, Patricia, Kevin; m. Yvonne Louise O'Connell, Dec. 2, 1993. BA, La Salle Coll., 1940; JD, Western Reserve U., 1950; MA, U. Md., 1960; PhD, So. Calif. U., 1995. Commd. 2d lt. USAF, 1943, advanced through grades to col., ret., 1968; dean, law prof. Western State U. Coll. Law, Fullerton, Calif., 1975-87; law prof. Am. Coll. Law, Brea, Calif., 1987-89; dean So. Calif. Coll. Law, Brea, 1989-91, ret., 1991. Author: Remedies in a Nutshell, 1985. Decorated Legion of Merit, Bronze Star, Army Commendation medal, Air Force Commendation medal. Mem. Air Force Office Spl. Agts., Delta Theta Phi. Republican. Roman Catholic. Home: Las Vegas, Nev. Died Feb. 27, 2002.

O'CONNOR, ROBERT B. retired federal judge; b. 1919; Student, San Antonio Jr. Coll., 1937-39, U. Tex. Sch. Law, 1942. Pvt. practice, 1946-79; apptd. magistrate judge we. dist. U.S. Dist. Ct. Tex., 1979; ret. With U.S. Army Air Corps, 1942-45. Mem. Fed. Bar Assn., State Bar Tex., San Antonio Bar Assn. Deceased.

ODDI, SILVIO CARDINAL, archbishop; b. Morfasso, Piacenza, Italy, Nov. 14, 1910; s. Agostino and Esther (Oddi) O.; Doctorate in Canon Law, Rome, 1936; Dr. honoris causa, U. Buenos Aires, 1944, St. John's U., N.Y.C., 1981, St. Charles Sem., Phila. Ordained priest Roman Cath. Ch., 1933; named archbishop titular of Mesembria, 1953, cardinal, 1969. Mem. Vatican Diplomatic Service, Iran, Lebanon, Syria, Palestine, Egypt, France, Yugoslavia, Belgium and Luxembourg, 1936-69; spl. missions to Central Africa, Latin Am., Philippines, Cuba and Dominican Rep., 1961-74; mem. Congregations for Causes of Saints, Bishops, Oriental Chs. of Pub. Affairs of the Ch., Supreme Tribunal of Apostolic Segnatura, Amministrazionedel Patrimonio della Sede Apostolica, Congregation per l'Evangelizzazione dei Popoli, Sanctuaries of Loreto and Pompei; pontifical legate to Basilica and Convent of St. Francis (Assisi). Home: Rome, Italy. Died June 29, 2001.

ODEGAARD, CHARLES EDWIN, history educator; b. Chicago Heights, Ill., Jan. 10, 1911; s. Charles Alfred and Mary (Cord) O.; m. Elizabeth Jane Ketchum, Apr. 12, 1941 (dec. 1980); 1 child, Mary Ann Quarton AB, Dartmouth Coll., 1932; MA, Harvard U., 1933, PhD, 1937; L.H.D., Lawrence Coll., 1951; LL.D., Miami U., Oxford, Ohio, 1955, U. B.C., Can., 1959, Gonzaga U., 1962, UCLA, 1962, Seattle U., 1965, U. Mich., 1969; Litt.D., U. Puget Sound, 1963. Asst. in history Radcliffe Coll., 1935-37; from instr. to prof. U. Ill., 1937-48; exec. dir. Am. Council Learned Soc., Washington, 1948-52; prof. history, dean Coll. Lit. Sci. and Arts U. Mich., Ann Arbor, 1952-58; pres. U. Wash., Seattle, 1958-73, pres. emeritus, prof. higher edn., 1974—, prof. biomed. history, 1975—. Mem. U.S. Nat. Commn. UNESCO, 1949-55, advisor U.S. del. 5th Gen. Conf., Florence, Italy, 1950; chmn. Commn. Human Resources and Advanced Tng., 1949-53, pres. Internat. Council of Philosophy and Humanistic Studies, 1959-65; mem. adv. com. cultural info. USIA, 1955-62, Western Interstate Com. on Higher Edn., 1959-70, Citizens Com. on Grad. Med. Edn., 1963-66, Nat. Adv. Health Counci USPHS, 1964-68, Nat. Adv. Health Manpower, 1965-67, NEH, 1966-72, Study Commn. Pharmacy, 1973-75; mem. Macy Study Commn. on Acad. Psychiatry, 1978-79 Author: Fideles and Vassi in the Carolingian Empire, 1945; Minorities in Medicine, 1977, Area Health Education Centers, 1979, Dear Doctor: A Personal Letter to a Physician, 1986; contbr. articles on mediaeval history and higher edn. to profl. jours. Bd. regents Uniformed U. Health Scis., 1973-80; chmn. Wash. State Bd. Continuing Legal Edn., 1976-79. Served from lt. (j.g.) to lt. comdr. USNR, 1942-46 Recipient Medal of Merit State of Wash., 1989. Mem. Am. Coun. on Edn. (dir., chmn. 1962-63), Am. Hist. Assn., NAS, Medieval Acad. Am., Tchrs. Ins. and Annuity Assn. (dir. 1963-69, trustee 1970-86, coll. retirement equity fund 1970-86), Inst. Medicine, Phi Beta Kappa, Phi Eta Sigma, Beta Theta Pi, Seattle Yacht Club, Univ. Club (Seattle), Cosmos Club (Washington), Bohemian Club (San Francisco), Rotary. Deceased.

ODEN, HOWARD WAYNE, management educator; b. Altamont, Ill., Dec. 26, 1929; s. Chester Raleigh and Lola Iva (Krohn) O.; m. Carmela Maria Perrone, Nov. 24, 1956; children: Wayne Anthony, Madeline Marlo. BS, U.S. Naval Acad., 1952; BSEE, USN Postgrad. Sch., Monterey, Calif., 1960; M in Engring. Adminstrn., George Washington U., 1971; MPA, U. North Colo., 1977; MBA, Boston U., 1982, DBA, 1986. Cert. profl. engr. indsl. engring., mfg. engr. Commd. ensign USN, 1952, advanced through grades to capt., 1972; exec. officer USS Salmon, San Diego, 1962-64; comdg. officer USS Bluegill, San Diego, 1965-67; project mgr. submarine sys. Naval Ship Engring. Ctr., Washington, 1967-70; project mgr. sonar systems Naval Sea Systems Command, Washington, 1970-74; chief staff officer USN Underwater Ctr., Newport, R.I., 1974-77; ret. USN, 1977; asst. prof. bus. adminstrn. Nichols Coll., Dudley, Mass., 1977-82, assoc. prof. mgmt., from 1990; asst. prof. mgmt. Worcester (Mass.) Poly. Inst., 1982-89; assoc. prof. mgmt. U. Bridgeport, Conn., 1989-90. Project rschr., cons. Mgmt. of Advanced Automation Tech. Program Worcester Poly. Inst., 1982-89. Author: Handbook of Material and Capacity Requirements Planning, 1993; contbr. articles to profl. jours. Mem. Am. Prodn. & Inventory Control Soc., Am. Soc. for Quality Control, Inst. Indsl. Engrs., Computer & Advanced Systems Assn., Soc. Mfg. Engrs., Inst. Mgmt. Sci., Prodn. & Ops. Mgmt. Soc., Beta Gamma Sigma. Episcopalian. Home: Thompson, Conn. Died May 30, 2000.

ODHIAMBO, THOMAS RISLEY, entomologist, educator; Ph.D. hon., U. Oslo, 1986. Chmn., prof. Kenya Nat. Acad. Scis., Nairobi, 1982-85; founder, pres. African Acad. Scis., 1985—2003; founder, dir. Internat. Ctr. of Insect Physiology and Ecology, Kenya, 1967—92. Mem. internat. adv. council Inst. Internat. Studies. Albert Einstein Medal, 1979, Co-recipient Africa Prize for Leadership for the Sustainable End of Hunger, 1987. Home: Nairobi, Kenya. Died May 26, 2003.

O'DOAN, DOROTHY O'CONNOR, elementary school educator; b. Evanston, Wyo., May 25, 1930; d. Harry T. and Dorothy (Snow) O'Connor; m. William L O'Doan, June 14, 1952; children: Susan Maloney, Elizabeth Riches, Margaret Devish, Fred, Tom, Patricia Bue. Student, Loretto Heights Coll., Denver, 1950; BA, San Jose State U., 1952; MEd, Lesley Coll., Cambridge, Mass., 1988. Tchr. Fremont Sch. Dist. 25, Riverton, Wyo. Mem. NEA, ASCD, Wyo. Edn. Assn., Riverton Edn. Assn. Home: Riverton, Wyo. Deceased.

O'DONOHUE, WALTER JOHN, JR., medical educator; b. Washington, Sept. 23, 1934; s. Walter John and Mavis Leota (Terry) O'D.; m. Cynthia Ann Halmintoller, Aug. 10, 1957 (div. 1978); 1 child, Diane Louise; m. Maria Theresa Sauer, Nov. 27, 1978; children: Walter John III, Mary Theresa. BA, Va. Mil. Inst., 1957; MD, Med. Coll. Va., 1961. Diplomate Am. Bd. Internal Medicine, Am. Bd. Pulmonary Medicine. Resident internal medicine Med. Coll. Va., Richmond, 1961-63, 65-66, chief med. resident, 1966-67, cardiopulmonary fellow, 1967-69, asst. prof. medicine, 1968-73, assoc. prof., 1973-77; prof. Creighton U., Omaha, Nebr., from 1977, chief pulmonary medicine div., from 1977, chmn. dept. medicine, 1985-96, assoc. chair for edn., from 1996, dir. internal medicine residency program, 1985-98, assoc. dean grad. med. edn., from 1998. Editor: Current Advances in Respiratory Care, 1984, Long-term Oxygen Therapy: Scientific Basis and Clinical Application, 1995, Accurate Coding for Critical Care Services and Pulmonary Medicine, 1996-2002; contbr. more than 100 articles to med. jours., 30 chpts. to books. Served to capt. M.C., U.S. Army, 1963-65. Fellow ACP, Am. Coll. Chest PHysicians (regent 1986-88, gov. for Nebr. 1982-88); mem. AMA (CPT adv. com. 1992—, mem. ho. of dels., alt. del. for Am. Coll. Chest Physicians 1998—), Am. Lung Assn. (bd. dirs. 1981-87), Nebr. Lung Assn. (bd. dirs., pres. 1979-81), Am. Assn. Respiratory Care (chmn. bd. med. advisors 1986-87), Nat. Assn. Med. Dirs. for Respiratory Care (pres. 1995-97). Republican. Roman Catholic. Avocations: hunting, fishing. Home: Omaha, Nebr. Died 2002.

ODUM, EUGENE PLEASANTS, ecologist, educator; b. Lake Sunapee, N.H., Sept. 17, 1913; s. Howard Washington and Anna Louise (Kranz) O.; m. Martha Ann Huff, Nov. 18, 1940; 1 child, William Eugene. AB, U. N.C., 1934, A.M., 1936; PhD, U. Ill., 1939; hon. degree, Hofstra U., 1980, Ferum Coll., 1986, U. N.C., Ashville, 1990. Instr. Western Res. U., Cleve., 1936-37; resident biologist Edmund Niles Huyck Preserve, Rensselaerville, N.Y., 1939-40; instr., asst. prof., assoc. prof., prof. U. Ga., Athens, 1940-58, Alumni Found. disting. prof. zoology, 1957-85, prof. emeritus, 1985—, Callaway prof. ecology, 1973-85, prof. emeritus, 1985—, dir. Inst. Ecology, 1960-65, dir. emeritus Inst. Ecology, 1985—. Instr. in charge marine ecology tng. program Marine Biol. Lab., Woods Hole, Mass., 1957-61; cons. and lectr. in field Author: Fundamentals of Ecology, 3d edit., 1971, Ecology, 1963, 3d edit., 1989; co-author: Birds of Georgia, 1945, (with H.H. Brimley) A North Carolina Naturalist, 1949, Basic Ecology, 1983; contbr. articles to profl. jours. Recipient Michael award U. Ga., 1945, Internat. award L'Institut de la Vie, Paris, 1975, Tyler Ecology award, Educator of Yr. award Nat. Wildlife Fedn., 1977, Crafoord prize Royal Swedish Acad., 1987, Disting. Alumni Svc. award U. N.C., U. Ill., Theodore Roosevelt Disting. Svc. award, 1991; named Scientist of Yr., State of Ga., 1968, Conservationist of Yr., 1976, NSF sr. postdoctoral fellow, 1958-59 Fellow AAAS, Am. Acad. Arts and Scis., Am. Ornithologists Union; mem. Nat. Acad. Sci., Ecol. Soc. Am. (pres. 1964-65, Mercer award 1956, Eminent Ecologist's award 1975), Am. Inst. Biol. Scis. (Disting. Service award 1978), Estuarine Rsch. Fedn., Internat. Soc. Ecol. Econs., Am. Naturalist Soc., Sigma Xi (exec. com. 1965-67), Phi Sigma, Phi Kappa Phi. Died Aug. 10, 2002.

OESCHGER, HANS A. physicist, educator, deceased; Prof. physics Inst. Applied Physics U. Bern, Switzerland. Recipient Roger Revelle medal Am. Geophysical Union, 1997. Died, 1999.

OGG, GEORGE WESLEY, retired foreign service officer; b. Washington, June 13, 1932; s. William Raymond and Carrie (Blair) O.; m. Frances Zabilsky, Sept. 17, 1954; children: David Stuart, Carolyn Ogg Tripp. AB, Colgate U., N.Y., 1954; MA, George Washington U., Washington, 1970; postgrad., U. Md., College Park, 1968-69, Nat. Def. Coll., Can., 1977-78. Chief econ. sect. U.S. Embassy, San Jose, Costa Rica, 1974-77; chief commodities and developing countries div. Dept. of State, 1978-80; dep. dir. Office Canadian Affairs, Dept. of State, 1980-82; consul gen. U.S. Consulate Gen., Vancouver, B.C., Can., 1982-86; prof. internat. rels. Nat. Defense U., Washington, 1986-91. Served to 1st lt. USAF, 1954-57 Recipient Superior Honor award U.S. Dept. State, 1974, Meritorious Honor award, 1980 Avocations: tennis, photography. Home: Rockville, Md. Died Jan. 29, 2003.

OGILVIE, JOHN BLACK, retired surgeon; b. N.Y.C., Mar. 3, 1910; MD, Yale U., 1934. Intern N.Y. Hosp., 1934-35, resident in surgery, 1935-41; retired. Home: Riverside, Conn. Died May 1, 1999.

O'HARE, MARILYNN RYAN, artist; b. Berkeley, Calif., Aug. 6, 1926; d. Lawrence and Linnie Marie (Ryan) Atkins; m. Lawrence Bernard O'Hare, Sept. 20, 1947; children: Timothy Lawrence, Kevin Roy, Shannon John, Kacey Sophia, Kelly Katherine. Student, Jean Turner Art Sch., San Francisco, 1944, 45, 46. Artist Cherubs children's dept. store, San Francisco, 1946, 47, Emporium Art Dept., San

Francisco, 1947-54; freelance artist Capwells-Emporium, Liberty House, San Francisco, Oakland, 1955-64. Artist-in-residence, coord. art program Childrens Fairyland USA, Oakland, 1962—; commissioned painting for Moffit Hosp., San Francisco, 1970, Havens Sch. Libr., Piedmont, Calif., 1975. Painter children's portraits; designer greeting cards; executed murals Children's Fairyland, Oakland, 1965, 66, 73, Kaiser Hosp., Martinez, Calif., 1974. Vol. art tchr. Oakland Pub. Schs., 1958-62; vol. Oak Mus., 1965—, Convelescant Hosp., Berkeley, Calif., 1975-97. Named Mother of Yr., City of Oakland, 1993. Mem. Oakland Art Assn. Democrat. Avocations: reading, craft design, garage sales. Home: Oakland, Calif. Died Jan. 29, 2000.

OKE, JOHN BEVERLEY, astronomy educator; b. Sault Ste. Marie, Ont., Can., Mar. 23, 1928; s. Charles Clare and Lyla Jane (Partushek) O.; m. Nancy Sparling, Aug. 20, 1955; children— Christopher, Kevin, Jennifer, Valerie. BA, U. Toronto, 1949, MA, 1950; PhD, Princeton U., 1953. Lectr. U. Toronto, 1953-55, asst. prof., 1955-58, Calif. Inst. Tech., Pasadena, 1958-61, assoc. prof., 1961-64, prof., 1964-92, prof. emeritus, 1992—2004; assoc. dir. Hale Observatories, 1970-78. Vis. Dominion Astrophysical Observatory, 1992-2004 Mem. Astron. Soc. of the Pacific, Am. Astronomical Soc. (councillor 1969-72), Internat. Astronomical Union. Died Mar. 2, 2004.

OLDE, ERNEST J. investment company executive; Chmn. bd. dirs. Olde Fin. Corp., Detroit, until 1999. Died 2003.

O'LEARY, WILLIAM MICHAEL, microbiology educator; b. Columbus, Ohio, Oct. 9, 1928; s. Francis Michael and Bernadine Carolyn (Murdick) O'L.; m. Anna Mae Vandale, Sept. 1, 1951. BS, U. Pitts., 1951, MS, 1952, PhD, 1957. Rsch. fellow div. biol. and med. rsch. Argonne Labs., Lemont, Ill., 1957-59; from asst. prof. to full prof. Cornell U., N.Y.C., from 1959. Editor: Critical Revs. in Microbiology; contbr. over 100 articles to profl. jours. With U.S. Army, 1946-53, Korea and CBI. Sinshiemer Found. fellow Cornell U. Med. Ctr., 1961. Mem. Am. Acad. Microbiology, N.Y. Acad. Medicine, Harvey Soc., Sigma Xi, Phi Beta Kappa. Achievements include discovery of human idiopathic infertility can be due to otherwise harmless infections of ureaplasmas which can be alleviated by appropriate antibiotic therapy thus leading to successful pregnancy and birth of well-borns. Died Apr. 21, 2002.

OLENICK, ARNOLD JEROME, accountant, financial management consultant; b. N.Y.C., Sept. 2, 1918; s. Jesse and Eleanor (Rothenberg) O.; m. Bernice Rosenblum, Nov. 4, 1945; children: Philip R., Steven E. BS in Acctg., NYU, 1940, MBA in Mktg., 1947. CPA. Sr. acct. I.A. Rosenblum, CPA, N.Y.C., 1948-54; ptnr. Olenick & Needleman, CPAs, N.Y.C., 1955-60; pvt. practice N.Y.C., 1960-66; assoc. prof. acctg. N.Y. Inst. Tech., Westbury, 1966-71; assoc. prof. acctg./fin. CUNY, Staten Island, 1971-76; prof. acctg./fin. U. Mass., Boston, 1976-83; pres. Fin. Mgmt. Solutions, Inc., Boston, from 1985. Cons. Mass. Dept. Atty. Gen., Boston, 1984, Mass. Office Refugees and Immigrants, Boston, 1988-91. Author: Managing the Company Tax Function, 1976, Managing to Have Profits, 1989, (talking book) Expanding Your Nonprofit Organization Skills, 1995; co-author: Nonprofit Operating Manual, 1991. Chair, bd. mem. Great Neck (N.Y.) Commn. for Human Rights, 1962-65; treas. Americans for Dem. Action, Boston, 1985-88, Waltham (Mass.) Alliance to Create Housing, 1988-92. Capt. USAAF, 1940-45. Mem. ASCAP, N.Y. Accts. for Pub. Interest (chpt. pres., bd. mem. 1972-76), Mass. Accts. for Pub. Interest (pres., bd. mem. 1976-80), Mass. Soc. CPAs. Avocations: writing, politics. Died June 4, 2001.

OLIANSKY, JOEL, author, director; b. N.Y.C., Oct. 11, 1935; s. Albert and Florence (Shaw) O.; children: Ingrid, Adam. M.F.A., Yale, 1962; BA, Hofstra U., Hempstead, N.Y., 1959. Playwright-in-residence Yale, 1962-64; co-founder Hartford Stage Co., 1963; writer Universal Studios, 1974—. Author: Shame, Shame on the Johnson Boys!, 1966; writer, dir.: The Competition, 1980, The Silence at Bethany, 1987, Bird, 1988. Recipient Emmy award, 1971, Humanitas prize, 1975, Writers Guild award 1975. Died July 26, 2002.

OLIPHANT, BETTY, retired ballet school director; b. London, Eng., Aug. 5, 1918; Studied classical ballet under Tamara Karsavina and Laurent Novikoff; student, Queen's and St. Mary's Colls.; LLD (hon.), Queen's U., 1978, Brock U., 1978, U. Toronto., 1980; DLitt, York U., 1992. Prin. dancer and arranger Prince & Emile Littler Prodns., London, 1936-46; dance arranger Howard & Wyndham, London, 1936-46; tchr. ballet London, 1936-40; dancer, dance arranger and ballet mistress Blue Pencils Concert Party, Eng., 1944-46; tchr. ballet Oliphant Sch., Toronto, Can., 1948-59; ballet mistress Nat. Ballet of Can., Toronto, 1951-62; prin. and dir. Nat. Ballet Sch., 1959; asso. artistic dir. Nat. Ballet of Can., 1969-75, artistic dir., 1975-89; founder Nat. Ballet Sch., 1959, dir., prin., ret., 1989, tchr., artistic advisor, 1989-91. Reorganized Ballet Sch. of Royal Swedish Opera, 1967, Royal Danish Theatre, 1978; mem. jury Internat. Ballet Competition, Moscow, 1977-81, III Internat. Ballet Competition, Jackson, MIss., 1986. Author: Miss O: My Life in Dance, 1996; contbr. articles on dance and teaching to profl. publs. Decorated officer Order of Can., 1972, Companion Order of Can., 1985; recipient Centennial medal, 1967, Molson prize, 1978, Diplome d'Honneur Can. Conf. Arts, 1982, Lifetime Achievement award, Toronto Arts Awards Found., 1989, Order of Napoleon, France, 1990, Commemorative medal 125th Anniversary Can., 1992, Gov. Gen.'s Performing Arts award, 1997, Order of Ontario, 2000; named Disting. Educator, Ont. Inst. for Studies in Edn., 1985. Fellow Imperial Soc. Tchrs. of Dancing (examiner); mem. Can. Dance Tchrs. Assn. (founder, past pres.), Internat. Soc. Tchrs. Dancing, Can. Assn. Profl. Dance Orgns. (founding mem.). Died July 12, 2004.

OLMSTEAD, CLARENCE WALTER, geography educator, retired; b. Ludington, Mich., Nov. 4, 1912; s. Verne Lloyd and Anna Mary (Rinebolt) O.; m. Rhea Nancy Donnelly, Aug. 18, 1939; children: Clarence W., Jr., Nancy, John V. BA, Cen. Mich. U., 1937; MS, U. Mich., 1938, PhD, 1951. Tchr. Lincoln Valley Sch., Mason County, Mich., 1931-34; instr. Cen. Mich. Coll., Mt. Pleasant, Mich., 1938-40; grad. tchrs. asst. U. Calif., Berkeley, 1940-42; goegrapher, analyst Office Strategic Svc./Dept. State, Washington, 1942-46; asst. prof. geography and edn. U. Wis., Madison, 1946-50, asst. prof. to prof. geography, 1950-81, emeritus prof. geography, from 1981. Vis. prof. geography, George Peabody Coll. Tchrs., Nashville, 1951, UCLA, 1959, Syracuse U., Greeley, Colo., 1964, U. Auckland, New Zealand, 1968; active various coms. including Commn. on Agrl. Typology, Internat. Geograph. Union, 1968-76, others. Collaborator: North America, A Regional Geography, 7th edit., 1984; contbr. articles and book chpts. to publs. in field. Lt. USN Res., 1943-46, ETO. Mem. Assn. Am. Geographers (various coms.), Nat. Coun. Geographic Edn., AAUP. Unitarian Universalist. Avocations: study, travel, photography, environmental preservation. Home: New York, NY. Died Dec. 12, 2000.

OLSEN, ARTHUR MARTIN, physician, educator; b. Chgo., Aug. 29, 1909; s. Martin I. and Aagot (Rovelstad) O.; m. Yelena Pavlinova, Sept. 16, 1936; children: Margaret Ann (Mrs. Frank A. Jost), David Martin, Karen Yelena (Mrs. Dori Kanellos), Mary Elizabeth. AB, Dartmouth Coll., 1930; MD, U. Chgo., 1935; MS, U. Minn., 1938. Diplomate Am. Bd. Internal Medicine. Intern Cook County Hosp., Chgo., 1935-36; fellow in medicine, resident Mayo Found., U. Minn., 1936-40, from instr. to prof. medicine, 1950-57, prof., 1957—. Cons. medicine Mayo Clinic, Rochester, Minn., 1940-76, chmn. divsn. thoracic diseases, 1968-71. Author numerous publs. on diseases of the lungs and esophagus. Mem. nat. heart and lung adv. coun. NIH, 1970-71; trustee Mayo Found., 1961-68, mem. subsplty. bd. pulmonary diseases, 1958—, chmn., 1961-63. Recipient Alexander B. Vishnevski medal Inst. Surgery, Moscow, 1966, Andres Bello medal Govt. of Venezuela, 1987, Disting. Alumnus award Rush Med. Coll., U. Chgo., 1989. Fellow ACP, Am. Coll. Chest Physicians (master, regent 1955—, chmn. 1959-66, pres. 1970, Disting. Fellow award 1978, dir. internat. activities 1976-83, cons. internat. activities 1983-85); mem. AMA (Billings gold meadl for exhibit on esophagitis 1955), Am. Soc. Gastrointestinal Endoscopy (pres. 1962-63), Minn. Respiratory Health Assn. (pres. 1964-68), Minn. Med. Assn., Am. Assn. Thoracic Surgery, Am. Thoracic Soc., Minn. Thoracic Soc. (pres. 1952), Am. Bronchoesophagol. Assn. (pres. 1969-70, Chevalier Jackson award 1973), Internat. Bronchoesophagol. Soc. (pres. 1979-81), Minn. Soc. Internal Medicine, Brit. Thoracic Soc. (hon.), Nat. Acad. Medicine of Buenos Aires (hon.), Portuguese Soc. Respiratory Pathology (corr.), Sigma Xi., Alpha Omega Alpha. Episcopalian. Home: Rochester, Minn. Died Aug. 7, 2002; Oakwood Cemetery.

OLSHAKER, BENNETT, physician, writer; b. Balt., Oct. 5, 1921; s. Samuel M. and Fannie L. (Klavan) O.; m. Thelma Abramson; children: Mark B., Robert A., Jonathan S. BA, George Washington U., 1943, MD, 1945. Diplomate Am. Bd. Pediatrics, Am. Bd. Psychiatry and Neurology. Med. officer U.S. Army, KYUSHU, Japan, 1946-48; pediatrician pvt. practice, Washington, 1950-55, child psychiatrist, 1955-74; med. officer St. Elizabeth's Hosp., Washington, 1974-78; former psychiatrist pvt. practice, Washington; clin. prof. pediatrics George Washington U. Sch. Medicine, 1979—2002, clin. prof. psychiatry and behav. scis., 1979—2002. Author: What Shall We Tell the Kids, 1971, The Child As A Work of Art, 1975. Capt. U.S. Army, 1946-48. Fellow: Am. Psychiat. Assn., Am. Acad. Pediatrics, Am. Acad. Child & Adolescent Psychiatry, Am. Orthopsyciatric Assn. Jewish. Died Mar. 8, 2004.

OLSON, FREDERICK IRVING, retired history educator; b. Milw., May 30, 1916; s. Frank and Clara (Hansen) O.; m. Jane Marian Correll, June 8, 1946; children: David Frederick, Donald Frank, Roger Alan. BA magna cum laude, Harvard U., 1938, MA (George W. Dillaway fellow 1938-39), 1939, PhD in History, 1952. Mem. faculty U. Wis., Milw., 1946-85, prof. history, 1956-85, chmn. com. on univ. future, 1959-60, chmn. dept. history, 1960-62, 67-70, assoc. dean Coll. Letters and Sci., 1971-76, acting dean Sch. Library Sci., 1977-79; exec. dir. Milw. Humanities Program, 1979-84. Vis. prof. history U. Wis.-Madison, summer 1957; assoc. dean U. Wis. extension, Mil., 1960-68. Author: (with Harry H. Anderson) Milwaukee: At the Gathering of the Waters, 1981, 2d edit., 1984, (with Frank Cassell and J. Martin Klotsche) The University of Wisconsin-Milwaukee: A Historical Profile, 1885-1992, 1992, (with Jane Correll Olson) Dear Jane: A Soldier's Letters from Africa and the Middle East, 1942-45, 1994; contbr. articles and book revs. to profl. jours. Trustee Milw. Pub. Mus., 1951-52; bd. dirs. Milw. County Hist. Soc., 1947-85, 95—, pres., 1953-57, 72-75; bd. curators State Hist. Soc. Wis., 1961-91; mem. Milw. Landmarks Commn., 1964-71, Milw. County Landmarks Commn., 1976—, chmn., 1976-82; mem. rev. bd. Wis. Hist. Preservation, 1978-89; bd. dirs. Wis. Heritages, Inc., 1983-93, pres., 1989-90; bd. dirs. Wauwatosa Hist. Soc., 1984-96; mem. City of Wauwatosa Hist. Preservation Commn., 2001-. With AUS, 1942-45. Named Wauwatosa's Disting. Citizen of Yr., 2000. Mem. Orgn. Am. Historians, Wis. Acad. Scis., Arts and Letters, Lincoln Group (Boston), North Hills Country Club (Waukesha, Wis.), Phi Beta Kappa, Phi Alpha Theta, Phi Kappa Phi. Lutheran. Home: Milwaukee, Wis. Died Oct. 5, 2004.

OLSON, JAMES ALLEN, biochemist, educator; b. Mpls., Oct. 10, 1924; s. Ralph William and Minnie Azalea (Holtin) O.; m. Giovanna F. Del Nero, Dec. 10, 1953; children: Daniel, Lisa, Eric. BS, Gustavus Adolphus Coll., 1946; PhD, Harvard U., 1952; Doctor Honoris Causa, U. Ghent, Belgium, 1988. Postdoctoral fellow NIH, Rome, 1952-54; rsch. assoc. Harvard U., Cambridge, Mass., 1954-56; from asst. prof. to prof. U. Fla. Coll. Medicine, Gainesville, 1956-66; prof., chmn. dept. biochemistry Mahidol U., Bangkok, 1966-74; prof. biomed. sci. dept. biochemistry U. Bahia, Salvador, Brazil, 1974-75; prof., chmn. dept. biochemistry Iowa State U., Ames, 1975-85, disting. prof. dept. biochemistry, from 1984. Cons. NIH, Bethesda, Md., NSF, Washington, other agys. and industries; plenary lectr. FAOBMB, 1994, European Retinoid lectr., 1993. Editor: Modern Nutrition in Health and Disease, 1989—; contbr. over 400 articles and revs. to profl. jours. Lt. USN, 1942-44. Named Atwater Meml. Lectr., 1992, Wellcome Lectr. Burroughs-Wellcome Co., 1991, Kullavanijaya Lectr., U. Leeds, 1990; recipient Disting. Alumni Citation Gustavus Adolphus Coll., 1973, Disting. Svc. award Mahidol U., 1975. Fellow Am. Inst. Nutrition (pres. 1986-87, Borden award 1989); mem. Soc. Exptl. Biology (councilor 1989-92). Achievements include patents on therapeutically active vitamin A derivatives; research on vitamin A and carotenoids. Home: Ames, Iowa. Died Sept. 22, 2000.

OLSON, PATRICIA JOANNE, artist, educator; b. Chgo., Aug. 22, 1927; d. Fred William and Fern Leslie (Shaffer) Kohler; m. Paul J. Olson, Jan. 21, 1950 (dec. July 1968); adopted children: Paulette, Dominic; stepchildren: Cindy, Katie, Larry, Daniel. BA, Northeastern Ill. U., 1976; MA, Loyola U., 1981. Advt. art dir. Chas. A. Stevens Dept. Store, Chgo., 1950-55; art dir. McCann, Erickson Advt. Agy., Chgo., 1955-57; pres. Olson Studio, Chgo., 1957-75; dept. chair, mem. faculty Chgo. Acad. Fine Art, 1974-78; exhibiting artist Chicago and Santa Barbara, Calif., from 1981. Instr. Old Town Triangle Art Ctr., Chgo., 1978—, Bernard Horwich Ctr., Chgo., 1982-86, Art Inst. Chgo., 1987; prof. Columbia Coll., Chgo., 1978—; panelist Chgo. Cultural Ctr.; spkr., demonstrator Skokie Cultural Ctr., 1992, Joliet Art Ctr., 1992; guest spkr. AAUW, Evanston, Ill., 1991, Columbia Coll. Humanities, Chgo., 1992. Author: Women of Different Sizes, 1981; contbr. poetry to mags.; one woman shows include Artemesia Gallery, 1985, Highland Park H.S., 1987, One Ill. Ctr., 1987, Gallery 6000, 1988, Countryside Gallery of New Work, 1991, Old Town Triangle Gallery, 1991, Loyola U. Gallery, 1991; exhibited in group shows New Horizons, Art Inst. Gallery, 1975, 90, Beverly Art Ctr., 1978, 79, 82, 87, 89, 90, Beacon St. Gallery, 1984, 89, Art Inst. Chgo., 1984, Galex 19 Internat., Galesburg, Ill., 1985, Suburban Art League, 1986, Natalini Gallery, 1987, Societe des Pastellistes de France, 1987, Campanile Gallery, 1987, Artemsia Gallery, 1987, Delora Cultural Ctr., 1988, Alexandrian Mus., 1988, Gallery Genesis, 1988, 89, Adler Cultural Ctr., 1989, Post Rd. Gallery, 1989, Evanston Co-op Gallery, 1990, Pilsen Gallery, 1991, Old Town Triangle Gallery, 1991, Loyola U. Gallery, 1991, Chgo. Soc. Artists, 1992, R.H. Love Gallery, 1992, Chgo. Cultural Ctr., 1992, Wood St. Gallery, 1994, North Lakeside Cultural Ctr., 1994, State of Ill. Bldg. Chgo. Sr. Citizen Art Network (award), others. Hostess Rogers Park (Ill.) Hist. Soc., 1993. Named to Sr. Hall of Fame, Mayor Daley, Chgo., 1991, Womens Mus., Washington. Mem. Chgo. Soc. Artists, Chgo. Womens Caucus for Art (curator 1989-90), North Lakeside Cultural Ctr. (mem. art adv. bd. 1990—), Am. Jewish Art Club (juror, curator, speaker 1991), Wizo (juror 1989), Sr. Citizens Art Network. Democrat. Avocations: writing poetry, theatre, photography, hiking, reading. Home: Chicago, Ill. Died Apr. 22, 2001.

OLSON, ROBERT LEONARD, retired insurance company executive; b. Auburn, Mass, Aug. 11, 1930; s. Henry Leroy and Marie Albertina (Holquist) O.; m. Muriel E. Storms, Mar. 22, 1958; children: Cynthia L., Mark W., Keith E. AAS, Becker Jr. Coll., 1956; BBA, Clark U., 1958; grad. exec. program, Dartmouth Coll., 1986. Supr. payroll and expense acctg. Allmerica Financial Life, Worcester, 1958-66, asst. mgr. budget fiscal planning, 1966-68, mgr. cost acctg., 1968-72, asst. contr., 1972-75, asst. v.p., 1975-82, 2d v.p. fin. planning and reporting, 1982-85, v.p. fin. planning and reporting, 1985-87, v.p., contr., 1987-90, also bd. dirs. Asst. treas. Mass. affiliate Am. Heart Assn., 1982-90, mem. budget, fin. and audit com., 1983-90; treas. Auburn Dist. Nursing Assn., 1972—. Mem. Inst. Mgmt. Accts., Fin. Execs. Inst., Bus. Planning Bd., Am. Mgmt. Assn. (cert. mgmt. course 1982). Avocations: antique and classic cars, boating. Home: Auburn, Mass. Died Mar. 3, 2003.

OMAN, JULIA TREVELYAN, theatrical designer; b. London, July 11, 1930; d. Charles Chichele and Joan (Trevelyan) O.; m. Roy Strong, 1971. Ed., Royal Coll. Art; DLitt (hon.), Bristol U., 1987. Designer BBC-TV, 1955-67; designer for theater, opera and ballet, London, N.Y.C., Boston, Toronto, Vienna, Stockholm and, West Germany, Japan, The Netherlands and Italy, from 1967. Designer Mme. Tussand's Hall of Historical Tableaux, 1979; art dir. various films including The Charge of the Light Brigade, 1967, Laughter in the Dark, 1968; prodn. designer film Julius Caesar, 1969; design cons. film Straw Dogs, 1971; dir. Oman Prodns. Ltd.; author: (with B.S. Johnson) Street Children, 1964; (with R. Strong) Elizabeth R., 1971, Mary Queen of Scots, 1972, The English Year, 1982, A Celebration of Gardens, 1991, (with R.

Strong) A Country Life, 1994, Vanitas Designs, Gianni Versace, 1994, (with R. Strong) Happiness, 1997, (with R. Strong) Garden Party, 2000. Mem. vis. com. dept. edn. and sci. Royal Coll. of Art, 1980. Decorated Comdr. of the Order of the Brit. Empire; recipient Silver medal Royal Coll. of Art, Designer of Yr. award, 1967, ACE award for best art direction NCTA, 1983; named Royal scholar; elected Royal Designer for Industry, 1977. Died Oct. 10, 2003.

O'MORCHOE, PATRICIA JEAN, pathologist, educator; b. Halifax, Eng., Sept. 15, 1930; came to U.S., 1968; d. Alfred Eric and Florence Patricia (Pearson) Richardson; m. Charles Christopher Creagh O'Morchoe, Sept. 15, 1955; children: Charles E.C., David J.C. BA, Dublin U., Ireland, 1953, MB, Bch., BAO, 1955, MA, 1966, MD. Intern Halifax (Yorkshire) Gen. Hosp., Eng., 1955-57; instr., lectr. physiology Dublin U., 1957-61, 63-68; instr. pathology Johns Hopkins U., Balt., 1961-62, 68-72, asst. prof. pathology, 1972-74; rsch. assoc. surgery, pathology Harvard U., Boston, 1962-63; asst. prof. anatomy U. Md., 1970-74; assoc.prof., prof. pathology, anatomy Loyola U. Chgo., 1974-84; prof. pathology, cell and structural biology U. Ill., Urbana, from 1984, assoc. head dept. pathology, 1991-94, head dept. pathology coll. medicine, 1994-98; staff pathologist VA Hosp., Danville, Ill., 1989-98. Courtesy staff pathologist Covenant Hosp., Urbana, 1984-98, Carle Clinic, Urbana, 1990-98. Contbr. numerous articles to profl. jours. Recipient Excellence in Teaching award U. Ill., 1996, Spl. Recognition award U. Ill. Coll. Medicine at Urbana-Champaign, 1998. Mem. Internat. Acad. Cytology, Internat. Soc. Lymphology (auditor 1989-91, exec. com. 1991-93), N.Am. Soc. Lymphology (sec. 1988-90, treas. 1990-92, v.p. 1992-94, pres. 1994-98), Am. Soc. Cytology, Am. Assn. Anatomists, Ill. Soc. Cytology. Avocations: boating, needlework. Home: Poulsbo, Wash. Deceased.

O'NEILL, HUGH A. retired radiologist; b. Pitts., Aug. 23, 1914; MD, St. Louis U., 1938. Intern Mercy Hosp., Pitts., resident; res. in radiology Thomas Jefferson U. Hosp.; resident in radiology Meml. Hosp. Cancer, N.Y.C.; adj. pvt. practice St. Petersburg, Fla.; retired, 1980. Died Apr. 16, 2000.

O'NEILL, LEO C. finance company executive; BA in Econs. & Polit. Sci., Hobart Coll. Analyst in equities svcs. divsn., then exec. mng. dir. Standard & Poor's, N.Y.C., 1968-89, pres., chief rating officer, rating services ops., 1989—99, pres., 1999—2004. Bd. dirs. Credit Rating Investor Svcs. India; mem. sr. ops. com., pension and investment com. McGraw-Hill Cos.; mem. Fin. Leaders Group. Active leadership coun. W. Paul Stillman Sch. Bus., Seton Hall U. Recipient medal of excellence Hobart Coll. Alumni Assn., 1995. Died Apr. 20, 2004.

O'NEILL, MICHAEL WAYNE, civil engineer, educator; b. San Antonio, Feb. 17, 1940; s. Wayne Jackson and Delores Hazel (Shaw) O'N.; m. Jerilyne Arleen Busse, Jan. 22, 1972; 1 child, Ronald Christopher. PhD, U. Tex., 1970. Registered profl. engr., Tex. Rsch. assoc. U. Tex., Austin, 1970-71; divsn. mgr. Southwestern Labs., Inc., Houston, 1971-74; prof. U. Houston, from 1974, chmn. engring. dept., 1989-93. Author: Design of Structures and Foundations for Machines, 1979, (with others) Construction and Design of Drilled Shafts, 1988, 1999 (2nd edition); contbr. articles to profl. jours. Capt. U.S. Army, 1965—67. Recipient Geo-Hero award, ADSC and The Geo-Inst. of ASCE, 2004. Fellow ASCE (chmn. deep founds. com. 1982-86, John B. Hawley award 1975, 81, 90, Walter L. Huber Rsch. prize, 1986, Karl Terzaghi lecturship 1998, Martin S. Kapp award 2003); mem. NSPE, Transp. Rsch. Bd., Internat. Soc. for Soil, Mechanics and Geotech. Engring. (chmn. exec. com. 1994-95), Internat. Assn. Found. Drilling (Outstanding Svc. award 1990), Deep Founds. Inst. (Disting. Svc. award 2002). Lutheran. Achievements include research in reliability of load transfer on drilled shafts, interaction among piles in a group. Home: Houston, Tex. Died Aug. 2, 2003.

ONG, WALTER JACKSON, English educator, historian; b. Kansas City, Mo., Nov. 30, 1912; s. Walter Jackson Ong Sr. and Blanche Eugenia Mense. BA, Rockhurst Coll.; MA in English, St. Louis U., 1948, DHL (hon.), 1984; PhD in English, Harvard U., 1955; D (hon.), U. Glasgow, Scotland. Joined S.J., 1935, ordained priest, 1956. William E. Haren prof. English St. Louis U., prof. humanities Sch. Medicine, prof. emeritus, 1984—2003. Vis. prof. NYU, U. Chgo., Ind. U., Washington U., St. Louis; vis. scholar Phi Beta Kappa, 1969-70; Licoln lectr. U.S. Bd. Fgn. Scholars, Central and West Africa, 1974. Author: Rhetoric, Romance, and Technology, 1971, The Presence of Word, 1976, Fighting for Life: Contest, Sexuality, and Consciousness, 1981, Hopkins, the Self, and God, 1982, Orality and Literacy: The Technologizing of the Word, 1982, The Written Word: Literacy in Transition, 1985; contbr. articles to profl. jours. Mem. Fulbright Nat. Selection Com., France, 1957-58, Rockefeller Found. Commn. Humanities, 1978-80; mem. Nat. Coun. Humanities, 1968-74, vice chair, 1971-74; co-chair Adv. Com. Sci., Tech. and Human Values, 1974-78; trustee Nat. Humanities Faculty, 1974-89, pres., chmn. bd. trustees, 1974-75; priest St. Francis Xavier Ch., St. Louis. Decorated Chevalier l'Ordre Palmes Académiques (France); Guggenheim fellow, 1950-53, Weleyan U. fellow, 1961-62. Mem. Am. Acad. Arts and Scis. Died Aug. 12, 2003.

OPPENHEIMER, JAMES RICHARD, lawyer; b. St. Paul, July 27, 1921; s. William Henry and Marion Louise (Joslin) O.; m. Mary Ensign Dunning, Jan. 14, 1944 (div. 1957); m. Christine Kurth White, Oct. 14, 1960 (dec. 1979); 1 child, Susan. BA, Dartmouth Coll., 1942; JD, Yale U., 1948. Bar: Minn. 1948, U.S. Dist. Ct. Minn., 1950, U.S. Ct. Appeals (8th cir.) 1963. Assoc. Oppenheimer Wolff & Donnelly and predecessor firm, St. Paul, 1948-54, ptnr., 1954-91, of counsel, from 1992. Trustee Charles K. Blandin Found., Grand Rapids, Minn., 1958—, pres. and chair, 1972-89; trustee Charles K. Blandin Residuary Trust, Mpls., 1968—, Tozer Found., St. Paul, 1978—. Lt. (j.g.) USN, 1943-46, PTO and Atlantic. Mem. ABA, Minn. Bar Assn., Ramsey County Bar Assn., St. Paul C. of C. (bd. dirs. 1978-81), Rotary (St. Paul club pres. 1957-58), White Bear Yacht Club (commodore 1988-89). Unitarian Universalist. Home: Minneapolis, Minn. Deceased.

ORBAN, EDMOND HENRY, political science educator; b. Heron, Liege, Belgium, Apr. 25, 1925; emigrated to Can., 1961; s. Edmond and Maria (Jamar) O.; m. Anne Marie Anciaux, May 10, 1955; children: Margaret, Christine, Yvon, Francois, Benoit. PhD in Polit. Sci., U. Louvain, Belgium, 1967. Asst. adminstr. Province of Kasaï Govt. of Belgium, 1951-59, adminstr. Province of Kasaï, 1961; prof. polit. sci. U. Montreal, Que., Can., 1961—. Vis. prof. Peoples Republic China, 1996-2000. Author: La Presidence moderne, 1974, Le Conseil legislatif, 1967, Le Conseil nordique, 1978; author-editor: Mecanismes constitutionnels, 1982, Dynamique de la Centralisation dans l'Etat Fédéral, 1984, Le Systeme politique des Etats-Unis, 1987, Federalism and Supreme Courts, 1991, Federalism, 1992, Systéme Politique Américain, 2001. Served as info.-commando Belgium Army, 1950-51. Decorated Medal of the Resistance, 1945, chevalier de l'Ordre de la Couronne (Belgium), 3 other decorations. Roman Catholic. Home: Saint-Sauveur, Canada. Died Aug. 17, 2002.

O'REILLY, DON, reporter, writer, photographer; b. Attleboro, Mass., May 1, 1913; s. Dennis Charles and Helen Louise (Barden) O'R.; m. Edith Lillian Macomber, July 9, 1938; 1 child, Howard (dec.). Owner, operator Eagle Press, 1930-37; reporter, photographer Attleboro (Mass.) Sun, 1937-39, N. Attleboro Chronicle, 1939-40, New London (Conn.) Day, 1940-42, Washington Post, 1945-47; editor, pub. Speed Age Mag., Washington, 1947-53; mgr. NASCAR News Bur., Daytona Beach, Fla., 1953-56; sports broadcaster NBC Radio Monitor, various locations, 1956-59, Stas. WESH-TV, WROD, Daytona Beach, 1956-59; dir. pub. rels. Atlanta Internat. Raceway, 1959-64; mgr. automotive divsn., writer, prodn. asst., unit mgr. sports documentaries Dynamic Films, Inc., 1964-68; pub. rels. Am. Motor Corp., 1971-75; broadcaster Mutual, ABC, NBC, 1968-80; writer Popular Mechanics, Sat. Evening Post, Stock Car Racing, Argosy, Small Cars, Illustrated Speedway News, others, 1968-80; bur. chief, reporter, photographer News-Jour., Daytona Beach, 1976-80; feature writer Circle Track Mag., Speed Age, Stock Car Racing, Racing Pictorial, others, 1980-90; columnist various newspapers, 1980-90; feature writer newspapers, mags., books, from 1991. Stringer Boston Post, Globe, Herald-Traveler, 1937-39; dir. press rels. U.S. Grand Prix; self-syndicated columnist Inside Auto Racing, Motorcade USA, 1956-85. Author: Mr. Hockey: The World of Gordie Howe, The Complete Book of Motor Camping, Sports Review-Motorspeed, Auto Racing Guide, (with Curtis Crider) The Road to Daytona. Chief photographers mate U.S. Coast Guard, 1942-45. Elected to Nat. Auto Racing Hall of Fame by Nat. Old Timers Auto Racing Club, Flemington, N.J., 1988; named Living Legend of Auto Racing by Living Legends, Port Orange, Fla., 1993, Hon. Order of Ky. Cols., Louisville, 1990. Mem. Nat. Motorsports Press Assn., Ea. Motorsports Press Assn. (1st pl. award in feature writing 1990), Nat. Press Club, Am. Assn. Auto Racing Writers (v.p.), Nat. Press Photographers Assn. (charter, life), Am. Auto Racing Writers and Broadcasters Assn. (Best Column of Yr. 1989), Nat. Sportswriters and Sportscasters Assn., Soc. Profl. Journalists, Nikon Profl. Svcs., Fla. Freelance Writers Assn., Halifax Hist. Soc., Bay State Old Timers Racing Assn., Williams Grove Old Timers, Indpls. 500 Old Timers Club (charter, life). Deceased.

OREM, HENRY PHILIP, retired chemist, chemical engineer, consultant; b. Campbellsburg, Ky., Feb. 28, 1910; s. Mal Lee and Alice (Green) O.; m. Lydia C. Orem (dec. Feb. 1988). BS in Indsl. Chemistry, U. Ky., 1932, MS, 1934; postgrad., Pa. State U., 1934-36. Grad. asst. phys. chemistry U. Ky., 1933; grad. rsch. scholar Pa. State Coll., 1934-37; with rsch. dept. Calco Chem. Co. subs. Am. Cyanamid Co., Bound Brook, N.J., 1937-39; plant rschr./process developer Am. Cyanamid Co., Bound Brook, 1939-42; asst. chief chemist Azo Dye and Intermediate divsn. Am. Cyanamid Co., Bound Brook, N.J., 1942-46, departmental chemist, 1947, tech. supt., 1947-50; rsch. chemist Sloss Sheffield Steel and Iron Co. (now U.S. Pipe and Foundry Co. subs. Jim Walter Co.), Birmingham, Ala., 1950-52, rsch. ehcm. engr., 1952-65, group leader, 1965-75, ret., 1975. Cons. Jim Walter Resources, Inc., Arichem, Inc. (now subs. Jim Walter Resources, Inc.). Contbr. articles to on black powder and ballistics to publs. Fellow Am. Inst. Chemists (profl. accredited chemist); mem. AIChE (life, 1st sec. N.J. sect. 1949-50, chmn. 1963, treas. Ala. sect. 1971, 72), Am. Chem. Soc. (emeritus life, sec.-treas. Raritan Valley group N.J. sect. 1948, chmn. 1950, sec. Ala. sect. 1956-57), NRA (life), Nat. Muzzle Loading Rifle Assn. (life, contbr. and reviewer articles Muzzle Blasts, technical advisor muzzle blasts, powder and ballistics), U.S. Revolver Assn. (life), Ala. Gun Collectors Assn. (life), Magic City Gun Club (life), Va. Gun Collectors Assn. (life), Kate Carpenter Muzzleloaders Inc., Stonewall Rifle and Pistol Club (Churchville, Va.), Shenandale Gun Club (Buffalo Gap, Va.), Homestead Shooting Club (Hot Springs, Va.), Va. Muzzle Loading Rifle Assn., Va. State Rifle and Revolver Assn., Ft. Lewis Hunting Club (life), Am. Def. Preparedness Assn., Sigma Xi. Achievements include 22 patents in field (U.S. and Can.), numerous publs. in chemistry and ballistics. Home: Hot Springs, Va. Deceased.

ORMAN, HELEN BELTON, humanities educator, artist; b. Houston, Sept. 1, 1938; d. John Dickerson and Clarice Evelyn (Maercky) B.; m. Benjamin Franklin Orman, Sept. 3, 1959 (div. 1982); children: Mark McDonald, Benjamin Neil. Student, Rice U., 1956-59; BA in Comparative Lit., U. N.C., 1961, MA in Comparative Lit., 1967; postgrad., Glassell Sch. Art, 1979-82. Tchg. fellow in English composition U. Houston, 1962-63; English instr. GED program U.S. Army, Mannheim, Germany, 1965-66; art instr. older adults program Glassell Sch. Art, Houston, 1981-84; ptnr. Cosgrove/Orman Photo Images, Houston, 1982-90; English instr. Houston C.C., Stafford, 1986-92, head dept. lit. and philosophy, 1992-97, chair lit. and lang., 1997—2003, chair lit., lang. philosphy and edn., 2003—04. Resident, fellow Vt. Studio Ctr., 2001; lectr., presenter in field. One-woman shows include McMurtrey Gallery, Houston, 1984, Anne Dean Turk Fine Arts Ctr., Kilgore, Tex., 1995, C.G. Jung Ednl. Ctr., Houston, 1996, Gallery 3, Houston, 2002; exhibited in group shows at U. Houston, Clear Lake, 1980, 84, Boulevard Gallery, Houston, 1981-82, McMurtrey Gallery, Houston, 1983, 85-86, Little Egypt Enterprises, Houston, 1983, Houston Womens Caucus for Art, 1984, Midtown Art Ctr., Houston, 1985, Art League Houston, 1985, 2001, 03, Houston Ctr. for Photography, 1986, Lawndale Art Ctr., Houston, 1987, Mus. Fine Arts, Houston, 1991, Blaffer Gallery, Houston, 1996, Women and Their Work, Austin, Tex., 1997, 98, Mus. East Tex., Lufkin, 1998, C.G. Jung Ctr., Houston, 1999, O'Kane Gallery, Houston, 1999, Longview Mus. Fine Arts, 1999, 2002, Art Ctr. of Waco, 2001, Lawndale Art Ctr., Houston, 2001; Wayfinding Project artist Cultural Arts Coun. Houston, 2000, Coll. of the Mainland Gallery, Texas City, 2001, Art Mus. of S.E. Tex., Beaumont, 2002, Tex. Nat., 2003, Nagadoches, Tex., 2003, 37th Ann. Drawing and Small Sculture Show, Del Mar Coll. Corpus Christi, 2003, Visual Arts Alliance 20th Ann. Open-Juried Exhbn., Houston, 2003; represented in permanent collections Transco, Mus. of Fine Arts, Houston; contbr. articles to profl. jours. Deacon St. Philip Presbyn. Ch., Houston, 1992-94, AIDS care team vol., 1993-95. Recipient HCC Bedichek Disting. Svc. award, 2000. Mem. Two-Yr. Coll. English Tchrs. Assn., Nat. Coun. Tchrs. English, South Ctrl. MLA, Art League Houston (artistic dir. 1985-87, chair 1985-86), Houston Ctr. for Photography, Diverse Works, Houston C.C. Faculty Senate (sec. 1993-94, pres. 1999-2000). Democrat. Presbyterian. Avocations: travel, film, theater, walking. Home: Houston, Tex. Died Mar. 20, 2004.

ORR, ROBERT DUNKERSON, diplomat, former governor; b. Ann Arbor, Mich., Nov. 17, 1917; s. Samuel Lowry and Louise (Dunkerson) O.; m. Joanne Wallace, Dec. 16, 1944; children: Robert Dunkerson, Susan Orr Jones, Marjorie R. Orr Hail. AB, Yale U., 1940; postgrad., Harvard Bus. Sch., 1940-42; hon. degrees, Ind. State U., 1973, Hanover Coll., 1974, Butler U., 1977, U. Evansville, 1985, U. So. Ind., 1986, Ind. U., 1986; hon., Tri-State U., 1986, Purdue U., 1987. Officer, dir. Orr Iron Co., 1946-60, Sign Crafters, Inc., 1957-74, Hahn, Inc., 1957-69, Indian Industries, Inc., 1962-73; mem. Ind. Senate, 1968-72; lt. gov. Ind., 1973-81; gov., 1980-89; U.S. amb. to Singapore U.S. Dept. State, 1989—92. Former dir. Nat. Passenger Rail Co. (Amtrak). Leader Fgn. Ops. Adminstrn. evaluation team to, Vietnam, 1954; Pres. Buffalo Trace council Boy Scouts Am., 1957-58; v.p. Evansville's Future, Inc., 1958-62; Chmn. Vanderburgh County Republican Com., 1965-71; alternate del. Rep. Nat. Conv., 1956, 76, del. 1984, 88; Trustee Hanover Coll., Willard Library, Evansville YMCA, 1950-70; trustee, elder, deacon Presbyn. Ch. Served to maj. AUS, 1942-46. Decorated Legion of Merit. Mem. Scroll and Key Soc., Meridian Hills Club, Columbia Club, Rotary, Delta Kappa Epsilon. Presbyn. (elder, trustee, deacon). Home: Evansville, Ind. Died Mar. 10, 2004.

ORRICK, WILLIAM HORSLEY, JR., federal judge; b. San Francisco, Oct. 10, 1915; s. William Horsley and Mary (Downey) O.; m. Marion Naffziger, Dec. 5, 1947 (dec. Feb. 1995); children: Mary-Louise, Marion, William Horsley III; m. Suzanne Rogers, Jan. 19, 1996. Grad., Hotchkiss Sch., 1933; BA, Yale, 1937; LL.B., U. Calif.-Berkeley, 1941. Bar: Calif. 1941. Partner Orrick, Dahlquist, Herrington & Sutcliffe, San Francisco, 1941-61; asst. atty. gen. civil div. Dept Justice, 1961-62, antitrust div., 1963-65; dep. under sec. state for adminstrn. Dept. State, 1962-63; practice law San Francisco, 1965-74; former partner firm Orrick, Herrington, Rowley & Sutcliffe; U.S. dist. judge No. Dist. Calif., 1974-85, sr. judge, 1985—2003. Past pres. San Francisco Opera Assn., Trustee, World Affairs Council; former trustee San Francisco Law Library, San Francisco Found., Children's Hosp. San Francisco, Grace Cathedral Corp. Served to capt. M.I. AUS, 1942-46. Recipient Alumnus of Yr. award Boalt Hall Alumni Assn., U. Calif., 1980. Fellow Am. Bar Found.; mem. Bar Assn. San Francisco (past trustee, treas.) Home: San Francisco, Calif. Died Aug. 15, 2003.

ORSZULAK, RICHARD STEWART, accountant, educator; b. Girard, Kans., Oct. 4, 1957; s. John Andrew and Cleo Nadine (Shaffer) O. BS in Bus. Adminstrn., Pittsburg (Kans.) State U. 1979, MS in C.C. Teaching, 1989, EdS in C.C. and Higher Edn., 1991. Acct., Biron, Inc., Chanute, Kans., 1981-82, DFW Petroleum, Inc., Iola, Kans., 1982-83; chief acct., asst. to pres. Hagman Corp., Pittsburg, Kans., 1983-84; contr. Helio Aircraft, Inc., Pittsburg, 1984, contr., 1984-85, Extrusions, Inc., Ft. Scott, Kans., 1985-87; instr. Labette C.C., Parsons, Kans., 1988—, Ft. Scott C.C.,

1988—, Vatterott Coll., St. Ann, Mo., 1992-93. Missions treas. Girard (Kans.) Bible Ch., 1979, 84, ch. treas., 1980-83. Mem. Am. Acctg. Assn., Nat. Bus. Edn. Assn., Kans. Bus. Edn. Assn., Pittsburg State U. Alumni Assn. Republican. Baptist. Died July 23, 1997. Home: Girard, Kans.

ORTLIP, MARY KRUEGER, artist; b. Scranton, Pa. d. John A. and Ida Mae (Phillips) Smale; m. Emmanuel Krueger, June, 1940 (dec. Nov. 1979); children: Diane, Keith; m. Paul D. Ortlip, June 26, 1981. Student, New Sch. Social Rsch., N.Y.C., 1957-59, Margarita Madrigal Langs., Montclair (N.J.) Art Mus. Sch., 1978-79; Nomina Accademico Conferita, Accademia Italia, Italy, 1986; DFA (hon.), Houghton Coll., 1988. Dancer, dance instr. Fleischer Dance Studio, Scranton, Pa., 1934-38. One-woman shows include Curzon Gallery of Boca Raton, Fla. and London, 1986-93, Galerie Les Amis des Arts, Aix-en-Provence, France, 1987; group exhbns.: Salmagundi Club, N.Y.C., 1980, James Hunt Barker Galleries, Nantucket, Mass. and N.Y.C., 1983, Salon Internationale Musée Parc Rochteau à Revin, France, 1985, 90, Accademia Italia, Milan, 1986, many others in Europe and Am.; permanent collections Musée de parc Rocheteau, Revin, France, Pinacothèque Arduinna, Charleville-Meziéres, France. Named Invité d'Honneur, Le Salon des Nations a Retenu L'oeuvre, Paris, 1983, Artist of the Year, La Cote des Arts, France, 1986; recipient La Medaille d'Or, Du 13ème Salon Internationale al du Parc Rocheau au Revin, France, 1985, Medaille d' Honneur Ville de Marseille, France, 1987, Targo D'Oro, Accademia Italia Premio D'Italia, 1986; Trophy Arts Internationale Exposition de Peinture Marseille, Plaquette d' Honneur, Palais des Arts, 1987, Grand Prix Salon de Automne Club Internationale, 1987, Connaissance de Notre Europa Ardennes Eifel, Revin, France, 1990. Mem. Nat. Mus. Women in Arts, Accademia Italia (charter), Instituo D'Art Contemporanea Di Milano, Nat. Soc. Arts and Letters, Gov.'s Club, Salmagundi Club. Home: Highland Beach, Fla. Deceased.

OSBORNE, ADAM, computer company executive; b. Thailand, Mar. 6, 1939; BS, U. Birmingham, Eng., 1961; MS, U. Del., PhD, 1968. With M.W. Kellogg Co., 1961-64, Shell Devel. Corp., Emeryville, Calif., 1967-70; established Osborne & Assocs., Berkeley, Calif., 1970, pub., writer, programming cons., 1970-79; established Osborne Computer Corp., Hayward, Calif., 1981, pres., chief exec. officer, chmn.; founder Paperback Software Internat., Berkeley, 1984, former pres., chief exec. officer. Author: Running Wild: The Next Industrial Revolution, 1979, Introduction to Microcomputers, 1980; (with John Dvorak) Hypergrowth: The Rise and Fall of Osborne Computer Corporation, 1984; contbr. articles to computer mags. Achievements include invention of portable computer. Died Mar. 18, 2003.

OSBORNE, STANLEY DE JONGH, investment banker; b. San Jose, Costa Rica, Mar. 27, 1905; m. Elizabeth Ide, Oct. 28, 1929 (dec. Sept. 1984); children: Mary Ide (Mrs. John Witherbee), Richard de Jongh, Cynthia Adams (Mrs. Richard M. Hoskin). Student, Phillips Acad., Andover, Mass., 1918-22; AB cum laude, Harvard U., 1926, postgrad. bus. sch., 1926-27. Dir. publicity Harvard Athletic Assn., 1927-28; with Old Colony Corp., Boston, 1928-29; asst. to pres. Atlantic Coast Fisheries Co., 1929-30, treas., 1930-36, 39-43, sec., 1932-42, v.p., 1936-43; spl. asst. to rubber dir. Washington, 1942-43; v.p. Eastern Airlines, Inc., 1944-50; fin. v.p. Mathieson Chem. Corp., Balt., 1950-54; exec. v.p. Olin Mathieson Chem. Corp., 1954-57, pres., chmn. dir., 1957-64; gen. ptnr. Lazard Freres & Co., N.Y.C., 1963-69, ltd. ptnr., 1970—2004. Chmn. Pvt. Investment Corp. for Asia, Singapore, 1980-85. Spl. asst. to Pres., Am. Olympic Team, Gen. Douglas McArthur, Amsterdam, 1928; spl. adviser to Pres. John F. Kennedy, 1963-64; mem. Pres.'s Adv. Com. Supersonic Transport, 1964-67; spl. cons. to adminstr. NASA, 1966-68; bd. govs. Soc. N.Y. Hosp.-Cornell Med. Ctr., N.Y.C., 1957-2004, pres., 1975-80, chmn., 1980-85, hon. chmn., 1986-2004. Mem. Harvard Club, Brook Club, River Club. Episcopalian. Home: New York, NY. Died Apr. 9, 2004.

OSKOLKOFF, GRASSIM, Native American Indian tribal chief; b. Ninilchik, Alaska, Oct. 14, 1926; s. Michael and Zoya (Darien) O.; m. Marion Emma Encelewski, Oct. 30, 1952; children: Debra, Marla, Bruce, Gary, Becky. Student, Ninilchik Sch., Alaska. With Alaska R.R., Anchorage; comml. fisherman Ninilchik, Alaska; pres., dir. Ninilchik Native Assn., Inc., Alaska, 1971-82; chief, pres. Ninilchik Traditional Coun., Alaska, from 1982. Former rep. Alaska Fedn. Natives, Anchorage; rep. Alaska Inter-Tribal Coun., Anchorage, Cook Inlet Treaty Tribes, Alaska; commr. Alaska Sea Otter Commn., Fairbanks. Bd. dirs. Russian Orthodox Ch., Ninilchik; environ. adv. Promotion of Peace Among People and Nations. With inf. AUS, WWII, PTO. Avocations: fishing, hunting. Home: Ninilchik, Alaska. Deceased.

OSTER, DEAN HOWARD, psychologist; b. Ferguson, Mo., Oct. 25, 1929; s. George Gibson and Florence (Christy) O.; m. La Vern Velma Schmidt, July 8, 1951; children: Jolinda Sue, Kurt Eugene. Student, Washington U., 1961; BS, St. Louis U., 1963; M. Psychology, U. Md., 1965; PhD in Behavioral Sci., U. N.Y., 1969. Owner, mgr. Presto Food Products Co., Inc., St. Louis, 1959-64, Der Wagon Putzerie, Inc., St. Louis, 1964-80; fgn. missionary Tower Grove Bapt. Ch., St. Louis, 1978-81; fgn. missionary in Japan and Taiwan Christian Counselors Internat., Inc., St. Louis, from 1969. Editor: Biblical Tools and Thoughts for the Noodle; designer in field. Active candidate Rep. Com., St. Louis, 1968; escort, housing St. Louis Counsel World Affairs, 1970; exchange, housing Servas, St. Louis, 1970, People to People, St. Louis, 1970. 2d sgt. AUS, 1947-54. Decorated 2 Good Conduct medals; recipient Trophy for designing car V.W. Factory & Club, 1965, Gold Trophy and Ribbons, Toastmaster Am., 1966. Baptist. Deceased.

OSTERMAN, LESTER, theatrical producer; b. Bklyn., Dec. 31, 1914; s. Lester and Adrienne (Pinover) O.; m. Marjorie Ruth Korn, June 3, 1937; children: Patricia Ann, Lester Thomas. Student, U. Va. Former owner, operator theatres including: The Eugene O'Neill, The Alvin, The 46th St., The Helen Hayes, The Mocosco; Assoc. producer: Leonard Bernstein/Lillian Hellman Candide on Broadway; producer: Butley (Tony award), The Rothschilds, (Tony award), (directed by Noel Coward) High Spirits, Hadrian VII, (Tony award), Sizwe Banzi Is Dead, The Island, (Tony award), A Moon for the Misbegotten, (Tony award), The Shadow Box, (Tony award, Pulitzer prize), Da, (Tony award, Drama Critics award); Off-Broadway play Getting Out; Execution of Justice Mem. League of N.Y. Theatres and Producers (bd. govs.) Died Jan. 28, 2003.

OSTERWALD, BIBI (MARGARET VIRGINIA OSTERWALD), actress; b. New Brunswick, N.J., Feb. 3, 1920; d. Rudolf Engelhard and Dagmar (Kvastad) O.; m. Edward Justin Arndt, Jan. 14, 1951; 1 son, Christopher Justin. Ed., Washington Sch. Secs., George Washington U., Cath. U. Actress appearing in theatre, motion pictures and television; theater credits include Sing Out Sweet Land, 1944; Three to Make Ready, 1946, Bus Stop, 1955, Golden Apple, 1955, Look Homeward Angel, 1957, New Girl in Town, 1957; standby (also performed N.Y.C.): Gentlemen Prefer Blondes, 1949-51, Hello Dolly, 1964, Gallows Humor at Acad. Playhouse, summer 1973; motion picture credits include Parish, 1961; The World of Henry Orient, 1964, Fine Madness, 1967, The Tiger Makes Out, 1968, The Bank Shot, 1973, The Great Smokey Roadblock, 1978, Moving, 1988, Caddyshack II, 1988, Angie, I Says, 1991, Paper Brigade, 1995, Glimmer Man, 1996, As Good As It Gets, 1997; has appeared on: numerous television shows including feature role on Where the Heart Is series, 1970-71; as Sophie Steinberg on: Bridget Loves Bernie, 1972; numerous TV commls.; comedienne, LeRuban Bleau Bon Soir and 1 Fifth Av., N.Y.C., 1951-58; guest star numerous TV shows: Remington Steele, Too Close for Comfort, Quincy, Beulah-Land, Home Improvement, Simon, Donato & Daughter, Tales for the Crypt, Star, Still Watch, voice-overs for cartoons including Rugrats, Cow and Chicken; appearing in nat. co.: 42d Street, U.S. and Can., 1983-86; appeared in General Hospital, daytime TV series, 1980—; narrator (film) Whispers, 1997. Recipient Outer Critics award for best supporting player in Golden Apple, 1955-56 Mem. Nat. Acad. TV Arts and Scis. (past gov.), Actors Equity (past council) Died Jan. 2, 2002.

OSTREM, DONALD L. lawyer; b. Great Falls, Mont., Dec. 17, 1940; s. Ernest and Anita (Mannering) O.; m. Suzanne Walker, Mar. 5, 1966; children: Scott E., David W., Peter L. BS in Commerce, Mont. State U., 1962; JD, U. Mont., 1965. Bar: Mont. 1965, U.S. Dist. Ct. Mont. 1965, U.S. Ct. Appeals (9th cir.) 1969, U.S. Tax Ct. 1992. Ptnr. Graybill, Ostrem, & Crotty, Great Falls, Mont., from 1965. Mayor Great Falls 1975-77; city atty. Great Falls 1968-71; city commnr. Great Falls 1973-77; Great Falls Libr. Bd. 1977-78; Great Falls Airport Authority 1978-84. Mem. ABA, Assn. Trial Lawyers Am., Mont. Bar Assn., Cascade County Bar Assn. (pres. 1989). Democrat. Avocations: boating, skiing, fishing, travel. Home: Bigfork, Mont. Died May 21, 2000.

OTUNGA, MAURICE MICHAEL CARDINAL, archbishop; b. Chebukwa, Kenya, Jan. 1923; Ordained priest Roman Catholic Ch., 1950; Formerly tchr. Kisumu Maj. Sem.; attaché apostolic del. Mombasa, 1953-56; titular bishop of Tacape; also aux., 1957; bishop of Kisii, 1961; titular archbishop of Bomarzo, 1969; coadjutor of Nairobi, 1969-71; archbishop of Baitobi, 1971-98; archbishop emeritus of Nairobi, 1998—2003. Elevated to Sacred Coll. of Cardinals, 1973; titular ch. St. Gregory Barbarigo; mil. vicar of Kenya, 1981; primate of Kenya, 1983; dir. Castrense for Kenya. Mem. Congregation of Sacraments and Divine Worship, Congregation of Religious and Secular Insts., Commn. Revision Code of Canon Law. Died Sept. 6, 2003.

OUTLAND, ORLAND T, civic leader, retired army officer; b. Dennison, Ohio, Apr. 27, 1923; s. Orland and Mary Alice (Chambers) O.; m. Anna Mae Greer, May 29, 1961; 1 child, Orland V. Joined U.S. Army, 1940, advanced through grades to maj., intelligence officer, 1962; ret., 1962; ins. cons. Met. Life Ins. Co., Fresno, Calif., 1962-63; ins. broker, Fresno, 1963-64; sr. adminstrn. analyst Pacific Fidelity Life Ins. Co., L.A., 1964-66, agy. mgr. Downey, Calif., 1966-67; office mgr. H & R Block, San Bernardino, Calif., 1969, owner, mgr., cons. Outland's Tax and Bus. Svc., Reno, 1969-75. Pres. Consumer Action No. Nev., Reno, 1975; chmn. Common Cause Nev., 1976, 81-83, Washoe County Bd. Equalization, Reno, 1981-82; lobbyist on campaign financing, ethics in govt., health care, and taxation, 1974—; chmn. platform com. Washoe County Rep. Com., 1977-78; chmn. John Anderson Nev. Presdl. Campaign, Nev., 1980; trustee Washoe County Sr. Citizens Svc. Ctr., 1991—; vice chmn. citizens adv. com. Regional Transp. Commn., Reno, 1991—; mem. cen. com. Washoe County Dem. Com., 1992, quality of life task force Truckee Meadows Regional Planning Agy, 1992—; others. Decorated Bronze Star Medal. Mem. Nat. Coun. Sr. Citizens (v.p. Nev. coun. chpt. 4539, 1991—), Am. Assn. Ret. Persons (chmn. Nev. legis. com. 1989-90, trustee chpt. 416, 1991—, activist Nev. health care and long term care campaign 1988—), Ret. Officers Assn., 37th Div. Assn. Avocations: political activism, writing. Home: Reno, Nev. Died July 12, 2000.

OVERMAN, GLENN DELBERT, college dean emeritus; b. Camden, Ark., Apr. 23, 1916; s. George D. and Mattie D. (Scott) O.; m. Roberta Marie Thomas, May 20, 1939; children— Priscilla Ann, George Dan. BS, Central State U., Edmond, Okla., 1937; MS, Okla. State U., 1946; D.BA, Ind. U., 1954. Cert. for labor arbitration Fed. Mediation and Conciliation Service, also Am. Arbitration Assn. Tchr. bus. high sch., Fairfax, Okla., 1937-39; Okla. rep. South-Western Publishing Co., 1939-42; dir. Sch. Intensive Bus. Tng., Okla. State U. Coll. Bus., 1946-50; dean Oklahoma City U. Sch. Bus., 1952-56, Ariz. State U. Coll. Bus. Adminstrn., 1956-85, dean emeritus, 1985—; hon. prof. Autonomous U. Guadalajara, Mex., from 1990. Mem. Dept. Navy, Naval Audit Svc. U.S.A., 1972-75. Author: Economics Concepts Everyone Should Know, 1956. Mem. law adv. bd. S.W. Found. Med. Rsch. and Edn.; mem. U.S. Office Edn. Appeal Bd., 1985-88. Served to lt. (s.g.), Supply Corps USNR, 1942-46. Mem. Soc. Advancement Mgmt., Financial Execs. Inst., Systems and Procedures Assn. Am., Am. Marketing Assn., Newcomen Soc. Am., Red Red Rose, Am. Right of Way Assn., Beta Gamma Sigma, Delta Sigma Pi, Pi Sigma Epsilon, Lambda Chi Alpha, Phi Kappa Phi, Delta Pi Epsilon, Phi Delta Kappa, Alpha Phi Sigma, Kappa Delta Pi, Delta Nu Alpha. Methodist. Home: Tempe, Ariz. Deceased.

OWEN, WILFRED, consulting transportation economist; b. Birmingham, Eng., Dec. 19, 1912; came to U.S., 1915; s. Wilfred and Miriam (Hanlon) O.; m. Ellie Bowen, Apr. 10, 1941; children: Wilfred, Kristen, Jane. AB, Harvard U., 1934. Researcher NRC, Washington, 1935-39; economist Nat. Resources Planning Bd., Exec. Office of Pres., Washington, 1939-43; sr. fellow Brookings Instn., Washington, 1946--78; cons. transp. economist, from 1978. Cons. Harvard Adv. Svc., Pakistan, 1958, Port of N.Y. Authority, N.Y.C., 1949-51, govts. of Japan, 1956, Brazil, Colombia, Taiwan, World Bank, India, 1966, Asian Devel. Bank, Manila, 1970 72; lectr. U. Calif., Berkeley, 1976; condr. seminars on transp. U. Va., Charlottesville, 1984-92, Ariz. State U., Tempe, 1984-90. Co-author: National Transportation Policy, 1949; author: Metropolitan Transportation, 1956, Cities in the Motor Age, 1959, Distance and Development, 1966, The Accessible City, 1972, Transportation for Cities, 1976, Transportation and World Development, 1987. Mem. Arlington County Econ. Devel. Commn., Arlington, Va., 1980—, Com. of 100, Arlington, 1980—. Recipient ann. transp. award Am. Econ. Assn., 1978; travel grantee Ford Found., 1967-68. Mem. Cosmos Club, Phi Beta Kappa. Died Nov. 28, 2001.

OWENS, A(RNOLD) DEAN, lawyer; b. Visalia, Calif., June 14, 1943; s. Clarence Cecil and Eula Mae (Boaz) O.; m. Marilyn Joyce Hatfield, Sept. 16, 1967; children: Eric, Rachel. BS, U. Calif., Berkeley, 1966; JD, U. Oreg., 1969. Bar: Oreg. 1969. Assoc. O'Reilly, Anderson, Richmonds & Adkins, Eugene, Oreg., 1969-71; ptnr. Anderson, Richmond & Owens, Eugene, 1971-74, Owens & Loomis, Eugene, 1975-79, Owens & Platt, Eugene, 1982-85; pvt. practice, Eugene, 1979-82 and from 85. Atty. City of Coburg, Oreg., 1971-79, City of Lowell, Oreg., 1973-79; hearings officer Lane County, Eugene, 1972—. Author: Advising Oregon Business Chpter 13, 1979; editor Lane County Bar News, 1980-87; also articles. Pres. Lane County Muscular Dystrophy Assn., Eugene, 1969-71; chmn. Eugene Human Rights Commn., 1969-71; bd. dirs. Asian Counseling Ctr., Eugene, 1991—; mem. exec. com. Lane County Rep. Party, Eugene, 1993—; mem. Eugene econ. devel. City of Eugene, 1989—; bd. dirs. Eugene-Springfield Met. Partnership, Inc., 1989-90; mem. exec. com. Eugene/Springfield Community Partnership, 1991—. Recipient cert. of appreciation Lane County Law Libr. Adv. Com., 1976-78, Bd. Lane County Legal Aid and Sr. Law Svcs., 1987, 90, spl. award and recognition of vol. svc. Eugene Sports Program, 1982. Mem. Eugene Area C. of C. (bd. dirs. 1986-90, pres. 1989, Disting. Svc. award 1986, 88), Emerald Exec. Assn. (pres. 1984), Eugene Swim and Tennis Club (pres. 1982), Eugene Country Club (chmn. tennis com. 1975-79), Downtown Athletic Club, Tri-Pass Water Ski Club, Eugene Active 20-30 Club (hon. life, editor newsletter 1969-72). Republican. Avocations: tennis, basketball, running, reading, water and snow skiing. Home: Eugene, Oreg. Deceased.

OWENS, GARLAND CHESTER, accounting educator; b. Wilson, N.C., Dec. 12, 1922; s. James F. and Leona (Owens) O.; m. Mary Elizabeth Wade, June 19, 1948; 1 dau., Lynn Carol. BS, U. Richmond, 1947; MS, Columbia U., 1948, PhD, 1956. C.P.A., N.Y. State. Acct. Arthur Young & Co. (C.P.A.s), N.Y.C., 1950-53; mem. faculty Columbia Grad. Sch. Bus., N.Y.C., 1956-86, prof., 1964-86; prof. emeritus Columbia U., 1986; assoc. dean Columbia Grad. Sch. Bus., 1962-70; prof. Mercer U. Sch. Bus., 1986-93; prof. emeritus Mercer U., 1993; program dir. Mgmt. Devel. Center, Belo Horizonte Minas Gerais, Brazil, 1973-75. Controller Arctic Inst. N.Am., 1957-77 Author: Cost Basis in Business Combinations, 1956, (with James A. Cashin) Auditing, 1963; former reading editor: Jour. Accountancy. Mem. bd. edn. Union Free Sch. Dist. 5, Greenburgh, N.Y., 1964-69, v.p., 1965-68, pres., 1968-69; mem. N.E. Regional Postmaster Selection Bd., U.S. Postal Service, 1969-75. Served to capt. USAAF, 1942-45. Decorated D.F.C., Air medal Mem. Am. Inst. C.P.A.s, N.Y. State Soc. C.P.A.s, Ga. State Soc. C.P.A.'s, Am. Acctg. Assn., Beta Gamma Sigma. Methodist. Home: Palm Coast, Fla. Died Sept. 4, 2003.

OWENS, (DOUGLAS) WAYNE, former congressman; b. Panguitch, Utah, May 2, 1937; m. Marlene Wessel; 5 children. Grad., U. Utah, JD, 1964. Mem. Congress, 1972-74; pvt. practice Salt Lake City and Washington, 1974, 78-80; pres. Montreal Mission for Ch. of Jesus Christ of Latter-Day Saints, Que., Can., 1974-78; mem. 100th-102nd Congresses from 2d Utah dist., 1987-92, mem. interior and insular affairs com., fgn. affairs com., Dem. steering and policy com., house intelligence com., house aging com. Adminstrv. asst. Sen. Edward Kennedy, 1969. Coordinator western states Roberty Kennedy for Pres., 1968, Edward Kennedy for Pres., 1980; candidate for U.S. Senate, 1974, 1992; for gov. of Utah, 1984. Named one of 200 Leaders for the Future, Time Mag., 1974. Died Dec. 18, 2002.

PACHMAN, DANIEL J. physician, educator; b. N.Y.C., Dec. 20, 1911; s. Louis and Ann (Kleinman) P.; m. Vivian Allison Futter, Nov. 8, 1935; children— Lauren Merle, Grace Allison. AB, U. N.C., 1931; MD, Duke U., 1934. Diplomate Nat. Bd. Med. Examiners, Am. Bd. Pediatrics. Intern pediatrics U. Chgo., 1934-35, instr. pediatrics, 1937-40; intern pediatrics N.Y. Hosp., 1935-36; resident pediatrics, attending pediatrician Duke Hosp., Durham, N.C., 1936-37; instr. Duke U., 1936-37, Northwestern U., 1940-42; practice medicine specializing in pediatrics Chgo., 1940-96; ret., 1996; clin. asst. prof. pediatrics U. Ill., 1950-59, clin. assoc. prof., 1960-67, clin. prof., 1967-81, emeritus prof., 1981—. Attending pediatrician Ill. Research and Edn. Hosp., 1950-81; cons. Presbyn.-St. Luke's Hosp., Chgo., 1971-81, South Shore Hosp., 1955-60, Ill. Central Hosp., 1970-72, chmn. dept. pediatrics, 1962-70; attending pediatrician Trinity Hosp., 1971—; prof. pediatrics Rush Med. Coll., 1971-81, emeritus prof., 1981—; staff Children's Meml. Hosp.; courtesy staff Chgo. Lying-in Hosp; Med. cons. Bd. Edn., S. Shore High Sch., 1954-56; mem. advisory com. on sch. health Chgo. Bd. Health, 1962—, Chgo. Bd. Edn., 1962-66; pediatric cons. Ill. Council for Mentally Retarded Children, 1960-66; chmn. subcom. on sch. health Chgo. Med. Sch., 1961-67; chmn. Ill. Pediatric Coordinating Council, 1969-76 Contbr. numerous articles to profl. jours. Mem. com. on rights of minors Ill. Commn. on Children, 1975-77; mem. Mayor's Com. on Sch. Bd. Nominations, 1965-68; mem., co-chmn. Ill. Bd. for Opinions on Profl. Nursing, 1980—. Served to lt. col. M.C. U.S. Army, 1942-46. Recipient Archibald L. Hoyne award Chgo. Pediatric Soc., 1977 Fellow Am. Acad. Pediatrics (mem. exec. com. Ill. 1961-69, rep. to adv. council on child health Nat. Congress Parents and Tchrs., chmn. sci. exhibits com. 1964-72), Am. Cancer Soc. (pub. edn. com. 1967-69), Chgo. Inst. Medicine (mem.-at-large jt. com. on sch. services 1961-64), Chgo. Med. Soc. (past chmn. child health com.), Chgo. Pediatric Soc., AMA (med./edn. com. on sch. and coll. health), Phi Beta Kappa, Sigma Xi. Clubs: Quadrangle (bd. dirs. 1969-72), Carlton. Home: Chicago, Ill. Deceased.

PADDOCK, AUSTIN JOSEPH, retired engineering executive; b. Washington Court House, Ohio, July 18, 1908; s. Leon A. and Nellie (Hare) P.; m. Janet Nevin, Aug. 3, 1934 (dec. Aug. 1964); children: Larry C. and Linda M. (twins), Jane M.; m. JoAnn Rourke, May 1966; 1 child, Jennifer Jo. BSCE, U. Mich., 1929. With Am. Bridge divsn. U.S. Steel Corp., 1929-61; from timekeeper constrn. dept., through ops. and sales to pres.; corp. adminstrv. v.p. fabrication and mfg. U.S. Steel Corp., 1961-69; chmn. bd., pres., CEO Blount, Inc., 1969-75; exec. v.p., COO Pa. Engring. Corp., Pitts., 1975-78, vice-chmn. bd., dir., 1978-87. Dir., exec. com. Pitts.-Des Moines Corp.; past dir. bldg. research adv. bd. Nat. Acad. Sci.; past dir. Am. Standards Inst., Steel Structures Paint Council; past dir. constrn. affairs com. U.S. C. of C.; past chmn. research tech. com. Am. Iron and Steel Inst. Past bd. dirs. Allegheny council Boy Scouts Am. Mem. NAM (past dir.), Duquesne Club (Pitts.), Montgomery Country Club. Home: Montgomery, Ala. Died Oct. 24, 2002.

PADDOCK, STUART R., JR., publishing executive; Bd. chmn. Daily Herald/Sunday Herald, Arlington Heights, Ill.; pub. emeritus Daily Herald, Arlington Heights, Ill. Deceased.

PAINTER, MAX WESLEY, surgeon; b. Glasgow, Ky., Nov. 11, 1939; Grad., U. Tenn., 1960, grad., 1963. Bd. cert. Am. Bd. Thoracic Surgery, Am. Bd. Surgery; lic. physician, Tenn., Ark., Miss., Ala. Intern U. Tenn., Memphis, 1964-65, resident, 1965-69, thoracic resident, 1971-72, 74-75; fellow Thoracic & Cardiovasc. Surgery Assn., Memphis, 1974; courtesy staff Sumner County Meml. Hosp., Tenn., 1972-74; with St. Joseph Hosp., 1980-98; courtesy staff Senatobia Cmty. Hosp., Miss., 1988-90, Humana Hosp., Shoals, Ala., 1987-90, Florence, Ala., 1988-90, Jackson-Madison County Gen. Hosp., Tenn., 1982-98, Eliza Coffee Meml. Hosp., Florence, 1987-90, Bapt. Hosp. Desoto, Southaven, Miss., 1989-98, Bapt. Meml. Hosp., Booneville, Miss., from 1993. Cons. St. Francis Hosp., 1975—, Tippah County Hosp., Ripley, Miss., 1997—; courtesy staff Meth. Hosp., 1975—, Eastwood Hosp., 1977—, St. Bernard's Regional Med. Ctr., 1982—; active staff Bapt. Meml. Hosp., 1980—, Bapt. Hosp. East, 1980—; clin. asst. prof. dept. surgery Coll. Medicine, U. Tenn., 1979-96; presenter in field. Maj. USAF, 1969-71, Vietnam. Decorated Bronze Star. Fellow ACS; mem. AMA, Am. Coll. Chest Physicians, Southeastern Surg. Congress Assn., So. Assn. Vascular Surgery, So. Thoracic Surg. Assn., Tenn. Med. Assn., Memphis-Shelby City Med. Soc. Home: Memphis, Tenn. Died Feb. 10, 2002.

PAKE, GEORGE EDWARD, research executive, physicist; b. Jeffersonville, Ohio, Apr. 1, 1924; s. Edward Howe and Mary Mabel (Fry) P.; m. Marjorie Elizabeth Semon, May 31, 1947; children— Warren E., Catherine E., Stephen G., Bruce E. BS, MS, Carnegie Inst. Tech., 1945; PhD, Harvard U., 1948. Physicist Westinghouse Research Labs., 1945-46; mem. faculty Washington U., St. Louis, 1948-56, 62-70, prof. physics, provost, 1962-69, exec. vice chancellor, 1965-69, Edward Mallinckrodt prof. physics, 1969-70; v.p. Xerox Corp.; mgr. Xerox Palo Alto (Calif.) Research Center, 1970-78, v.p. corp. research, 1978-83, group v.p., 1983-86; dir. Inst. for Research on Learning, Palo Alto, Calif., 1987-91, dir. emeritus, 1991—2004. Prof. physics Stanford U., 1956-62 Author: (with E. Feenberg) Quantum Theory of Angular Momentum, 1953, Paramagnetic Resonance, 1962, (with T. Estle) The Physical Principles of Electron Paramagnetic Resonance, 1973. Mem. gov. bd. Am. Inst. Physics, 1957-59; bd. dirs. St. Louis Research Council, 1964-70; mem. physics adv. panel NSF, 1958-60, 63, 66; chmn. physics survey com. Nat. Acad. Sci.-NRC, 1964-66; Mem. St. Louis County Bus. and Indl. Devel. Commn., 1963-66; chmn. bd. Regional Indsl. Devel. Corp., St. Louis, 1966-67, St. Louis Research Council, 1967-70; mem. President's Sci. Adv. Com., 1965-69; Bd. dirs. St. Louis Country Day Sch., 1964-70, Central Inst. for Deaf, 1965-70; trustee Washington U., 1970—, Danforth Found., 1971-99, U. Rochester; trustee Ctr. for Advanced Study in Behavioral Scis., Palo Alto, 1986-92, The Exploratorium, San Francisco, 1987-98; bd. overseers Superconducting Super Collider, Univs. Rsch. Assn., 1984-89. Recipient Nat. Medal Science, 1987. Fellow Am. Phys. Soc. (pres. 1977); mem. Am. Assn. Physics Tchrs., AAUP, AAAS, Am. Acad. Arts and Scis., Nat. Acad. Sci., Sigma Xi, Tau Beta Pi. Home: Tucson, Ariz. Died Mar. 4, 2004.

PALAY, SANFORD LOUIS, retired scientist, educator; b. Cleve., Sept. 23, 1918; s. Harry and Lena (Sugarman) P.; m. Victoria Chan Curtis, 1970 (div. Nov. 1990); children: Victoria Li-Mei, Rebecca Li-Ming. AB, Oberlin Coll., 1940; MD (Hoover prize scholar 1943), Western Res. U., 1943. Teaching fellow medicine, rsch. assoc. anatomy Western Res. U., Cleve., 1945-46; NRC fellow med. scis. Rockefeller Inst., 1948, vis. investigator, 1953; from instr. anatomy to assoc. prof. anatomy Yale U., 1949-56; chief sect. neurocytology, lab. neuroanatomical scis. Nat. Inst. Neurol. Diseases and Blindness, NIH, Washington, 1956-61, chief lab. neuroanatomical scis., 1960-61; Bullard prof. neuroanatomy Harvard, Boston, 1961-89, prof. emeritus, from 1989. Linnean Soc. lectr., London, 1959; vis. investigator Middlesex Hosp. (Bland-Sutton Inst.), London, Eng., 1961; Phillips lectr. Haverford Coll., 1959; Ramsay Henderson Trust lectr. U. Edinburgh, Scotland, 1962; George H. Bishop lectr.. Washington U., St. Louis, 1990; Disting. Scientist lectr. Tulane U. Sch. Medicine, 1969, 75; vis. prof. U. Wash., 1969; Rogowski Meml. lectr. Yale, 1973; Disting. lectr. biol. structure U. Miami, 1974; Disting. Scientist lectr. U. Ark., 1977; Disting. scholar-in-residence dept. biology Boston Coll., Chestnut Hill, Mass., 1994—; other Disting. lectureships; vis. prof. U. Osaka, Japan, 1978, Nat. U. Singapore, 1983; spl. vis. prof. U. Osaka, 1988; chmn. study sect. on behavioral and neural scis. NIH, 1984-86; mem. fellowship bd. NIH, 1958-61, cell biology study sect., 1959-65, adv. com. high voltage electron microscope resources, 1973-80, mem. rev. com. behavioral and neurol. scis. fellowships, 1979-86; chmn. Gordon Research Conf. Cell Structure and Metabolism, 1960; asso. Neuroscis. Research Program, 1962-67, cons. assoc., 1975—; mem. anat. scis. tng. com. Nat. Inst. Gen. Med. Scis., 1968-72; mem. sci. adv. com. Oreg. Regional Primate Research Center, 1971-76 Author: The Fine Structure of the Nervous System, 1970, 3d edit., 1991, Cerebellar Cortex, Cytology and Organization, 1974; editor: Frontiers of Cytology, 1958, The Cerebellum, New Vistas, 1982; mem. sci. coun. Progress in Neuropharmacology and Jour. Neuropharmacology, 1961-66; mem. editorial bd. Exptl. Neurology, 1959-76, Jour. Cell Biology, 1962-67, Brain Research, 1965-71, Jour. Comparative Neurology, 1966—, Jour. Ultrastructure Research, 1966-86, Jour. of Neurocytology, 1972-87, Exptl. Brain Research, 1965-76, Neurosci, 1975-95, Anatomy and Embryology, 1968; co-mng. editor, 1978-88, editor in chief Jour. Comparative Neurology, 1981-93, editor emeritus, 1994—; mem. adv. bd. editors Jour. Neuropathology and Exptl. Neurology, 1963-82, Internat. Jour. Neurosci, 1969-74, Tissue and Cell, 1969-86; contbr. articles to profl. jours. Served to capt. M.C. AUS, 1946-47. Recipient 50 Best Books of 1974 award Internat. Book Fair, Frankfurt, Fed. Republic Germany, Best Book in Profl. Readership award Am. Med. Writers Assn., 1975, Biomed. Rsch. award Assn. Am. Med. Colls., 1989, Lashley award Am. Philos. Soc., 1991, Camillo Golgi award Fidia Rsch. Found., 1992; Guggenheim fellow, 1971-72; Fogarty scholar-in-residence NIH, Bethesda, 1980-81. Fellow Am. Acad. Arts and Scis.; mem. NAS, Am. Assn. Anatomists (chmn. nominating com. 1964, mem. exec. com. 1970-74, anat. nomenclature com. 1975-78, pres. 1980-81, Henry Gray award 1990), Histochem. Soc., Electron Microscope Soc. Am., AAAS, Am. Soc. Cell Biology (program com. 1975), Internat. Soc. Cell Biology, Soc. for Neurosci. (Gerard award 1990), Washington Soc. Electron Microscopy (organizing com., sec.-treas. 1956-58), Soc. Francaise de Microscopie Electronique (hon.), Royal Microscopical Soc. (hon.), Golgi Soc. (hon.), Anat. Soc. Gr. Britain and Ireland (hon.), Cajal Club (pres. 1973-74), Am. Philos. Soc., Phi Beta Kappa, Sigma Xi, Alpha Omega Alpha. Home: Concord, Mass. Died Aug. 5, 2002.

PALLADINO, NUNZIO JOSEPH, retired nuclear engineer; b. Allentown, Pa., Nov. 10, 1916; s. Joseph and Angelina (Trentalange) P.; m. Virginia Marchetto, June 16, 1945; children: Linda Susan, Lisa Anne, Cynthia Madaline. BS, Lehigh U., 1938, MS, 1939, D.Eng. (hon.), 1964. Registered profl. engr., Pa. Engr. Westinghouse Electric Co., Phila., 1939-42; nuclear reactor designer Oak Ridge Nat. Lab., 1946-48; staff asst. to div. mgr. Argonne Nat. Lab., Lemont, Ill., 1948-50; mgr. PWR reactor design subdiv. Westinghouse Electric Corp., Pitts., 1950-59; head nuclear engring. dept. Pa. State U., University Park, 1959-66, dean Coll. Engring., 1966-81; chmn. Nuclear Regulatory Commn., Washington, 1981-86. Past mem. Pa. Gov.'s Sci. Adv. Com., Gov.'s Energy Coun., Pa.'s Commn. To Investigate Three Mile Island; mem. Nat. Nuclear Accrediting Bd., 1989-92. Contbr. tech. articles to profl. jours. Served to capt. AUS, 1942-45. Recipient Order of Merit Westinghouse Electric Corp. Fellow ASME (Prime Movers award), Am. Nuclear Soc. (past pres., A.H. Compton award, W. Zinn award), Am. Soc. Engring. Edn.; mem. NAE, NSPE, Argonne Univs. Assn. (past interim pres., past bd. dirs.). Clubs: Rotary. Roman Catholic. Home: State College, Pa. Died Dec. 12, 1999.

PALMER, ERWIN GEORGE, language professional, educator; b. Sodus, N.Y., May 11, 1908; s. George W. and May F. (Pierson) P.; m. Catherine Mary Whitney, Nov. 21, 1940; children— Suzanne M. (Mrs. Philip Forbes), Gerard Erwin. AB, Syracuse U., 1934, PhD, 1952; MA, Middlebury Coll., 1946. Tchr. Ontario Dist. 4, 1927-30, Churchville (N.Y.) High Sch., 1934-41, Catskill (N.Y.) HIgh Sch., 1941-46; faculty State U. N.Y. at Oswego, 1946—, chmn. dept. English, 1961-69. Contbr. to publs. Served with AUS, 1943-45. Recipient N.Y. State research grants, 1964, 66; N.Y. State Summer fellow, 1968 Fellow N.Y. State English Assn. (pres. 1963-64); mem. Mensa, Sigma Phi Epsilon. Home: Oswego, NY. Deceased.

PALMER, FRED ALDEN, broadcast executive; b. Van Wert, Ohio, July 22, 1904; s. Joseph Watson and Emma (Bowers) P.; m. Miriam Frances Painter, June 18, 1934; children: Carol Angene, David William. Student, Ohio No. U., 1924-26, Wooster Coll., 1926-28. Mgr. Sta. WAIU, Columbus, Ohio, 1929-32; pres., mgr. Sta. WBNS, Columbus, 1932-36; v.p., mgr. Sta. KOY, Phoenix, 1936-40; mgr. Sta. WCKY, Cin., 1940-44; owner Fred A. Palmer Co., Columbus, 1944-77, Stas. WATH and WXTQ, Athens, Ohio, from 1973, Sta. WRAP, Norfolk, Va., from 1987. Lectr. various clubs and assns., 1948-73; mem. broadcasting and film com. Nat. Council of Chs. Trustee Ohio No. U., Ada, 1954. Mem. Nat. Assn. Broadcasters (Hall of Fame 1985), Ohio Assn. Broadcasters (founder, pres. 1937, Disting. Service award 1982), Broadcast Pioneers Club, Athens C. of C. (pres. 1974, Disting. Service award 1980). Lodges: Rotary. Presbyterian. Home: Athens, Ohio. Deceased.

PALMER, LESLIE HOWARD, literature educator; b. Memphis, Jan. 25, 1941; s. Milton Howard and Janie Lee (Weaver) P.; m. Joyce Arline Cornette, Aug. 27, 1965; children: David Leslie, Rachel Joyce. BA, Memphis State U., 1962; MA, U. Tenn., 1963, PhD, 1966. Instr. U. Tenn., Knoxville, 1966-67; prof. English U. North Tex., Denton, 1967—2003. Mem. athletic coun. U. North Tex., 1975-82, scholarship com., 1988-94; presenter poetry readings and guest lectrs. in field. Author: (poetry books) A Red Sox Flag, 1983, Ode to a Frozen Dog: and Other Poems, 1992, Artemis' Bow, 1993, The Devil Sells Ice Cream, 1994, The Bryn Mawr Poems, 1998, Swollen Foot, 1999, Disgraceland, 2000, Last Bite, 2001; asst. editor: Studies in the Novel, 1973-86; contbr. articles to profl. jours. Faculty sponsor Amnesty Internat., U. North Tex., 1984-86, North Tex. Chess Club, Denton, 1978-90; sch. vol. Denton Ind. Sch. Dist., 1977-2003; bd. dirs. Friends Abilene Christian U. Libr. Recipient Beaudoin Gemstone award, Memphis, 1963, 64, Mid-South Free Verse award, Memphis, 1965, Outstanding Poet mention Pushcart Press, 1981. Mem. MLA, Modern Humanities Rsch. Assn., PEN, Denton C. of C. (cons.), Mensa, Phi Kappa Phi. Home: Denton, Tex. Died July 16, 2003.

PALMER, ROBERT, vocalist, composer, musician; b. Batley, Yorkshire, Eng., Jan. 19, 1949; Solo career, from 1974; vocalist Power Station band, 1985. Albums include Sneakin' Sally thru the Alley, 1974, Pressure Drop, 1975, Some People Can Do What They Like, 1976, Double Fun, 1978, Secrets, 1979, Clues, 1980, Maybe It's Alive, 1982, Pride, 1983, Riptide, 1985, Heavy Nova, 1988, Addictions Vol. 1, 1989, Ridin High, 1992, Very Best of Robert Palmer, 1997, Best of Robert Palmer, 1999, Don't Explain, 1999, Rhythm & Blues, 1999; singles include Every Kinda People, 1978, Bad Case of Lovin' You (Doctor, Doctor), 1979, Some Guys Have All the Luck, 1982, (with Power Station) Some Like It Hot, (with Power Station) Get It On, 1985, Addicted to Love, Simply Irresistible, 1988. Home: London, England. Died Sept. 26, 2003.

PALMER, ROBERT ROSWELL, historian, educator; b. Chgo., Jan. 11, 1909; s. Roswell Roy and Blanche (Steere) P.; m. Esther Howard, Dec. 19, 1942; children: Stanley, Richard, Emily. Ph.B., U. Chgo., 1931, LL.D., 1963; PhD, Cornell U., 1934; Litt.D., Washington U., St. Louis, 1962; L.H.D., Kenyon Coll., 1963, U. New Haven, 1980; Dr. honoris causa, U. Toulouse, France, 1965, U. Uppsala, Sweden, 1977. Mem. faculty Princeton U., 1936-63, 66-69, prof. history, 1946-63, Dodge prof. history, 1952-63; dean faculty arts and sci., prof. history Washington U., St. Louis, 1963-66; prof. history Yale U., 1969-77, emeritus, 1977. Adj. prof. U. Mich., 1977-80; vis. prof. U. Chgo., summer 1947, U. Colo., summer 1951, U. Calif. at Berkeley, summer 1962, U. Mich., 1969, 75 Author: Catholics and Unbelievers in 18th Century France, 1939, Twelve Who Ruled, 1941, A History of the Modern World, 1950, (with Joel Colton) A History of the Modern World, 2d edit., 1955, 8th edit. 1994, also in Swedish, Italian, Finnish, Spanish and Chinese, The Age of the Democratic Revolution, 1959, vol. II, 1964, also

German, Italian edits., World of the French Revolution, 1971, also in French, School of the French Revolution, 1975, The Improvement of Humanity: Education and the French Revolution, 1985, From Jacobin to Liberal, Marc-Antoine Jullien 1775-1848, 1993, J.b. Say Economist in Troubled Times, 1997; editor, translator: The Two Tocquevilles, Father and Son on the Coming of the French Revolution, 1987; co-author: Organization of Ground Combat Troops, 1947, Procurement and Training of Ground Combat Troops, 1948; editor: Rand McNally Atlas of World History, 1957. Served hist. div. U.S. Army, 1943-45. Recipient of ACLS Spl. prize, 1960, Bancroft prize, 1960, Antonio Feltrinelli Internat. prize, Rome, 1990. Mem. Am. Acad. Arts and Scis., Mass. Hist. Soc., Am. Philos. Soc., Am. Hist. Assn. (pres. 1970), Soc. French Hist. Studies (pres. 1961), Acad. Naz. dei Lincei. Home: Newtown, Pa. Died June 11, 2002.

PANAJOTOVIC, ILIJA SVETISLAV, producer, director, writer; b. Belgrade, Yugoslavia, Apr. 25, 1932; came to U.S. 1962; s. Svetislav and Stanka P.; m. Elena Maria Panajotovic; children: Eric, Sonja. Diploma in piano, Mokranjac Music Sch., Belgrade, 1954; Law degree, Belgrade U., 1957; BA in Polit. Sci., UCLA, 1963. Sole practice, Belgrade, 1957-62; prin. Noble Prodns., Inc., Los Angeles, from 1966. Assoc. producer: (films) Brown Eye Evil Eye, 1966, Curse of the Faithful Wife, 1968, Togetherness, 1970; producer, writer Operation Cross Eagles, 1969, Last Train to Berlin, 1973, Dirty Rebel, 1984, Wildwind, U.S., Yugoslavia, USSR co-prodn., 1986; producer Bomb at 10:10, 1967, Hell River, 1977, Cruise Missile, 1978, Day of the Assassin, 1981; U.S. and Yugoslavia coordinator Skalawag, 1972; producer, dir., author original story (film) Last Nazi at Large, 1994; co-writer, producer Massacre At Noon, 1989, Derwishes, 1995. Named Tennis Nat. Jr. Singles Champion, 1948, 49, All-Nat. Singles Champion, 1959. Mem. Acad. Motion Picture Arts and Scis., Am. Film Mktg. Assn. (worldwide film distbr. 1984), Arbitration Assn. Am. Clubs: Hollywood (Calif.) Fgn. Press. Serbian Orthodox. Avocation: tennis. Participated in Jr. Wimbledon semi-finals, 1948; mem. Nat. Davis-Cup Team for 11 years, Wimbledon 1/4 finals in doubles, 1958; Nat. Yugoslav champion in singles, 1959. Died July 18, 2001.

PANG, HERBERT GEORGE, ophthalmologist; b. Honolulu, Dec. 23, 1922; s. See Hung and Hong Jim (Chuu) P.; m. Dorothea Lopez, Dec. 27, 1953. Student, St. Louis Coll., 1941; BS, Northwestern U., 1944. Diplomate Am. Bd. Ophthalmology. Intern Queen's Hosp., Honolulu, 1947-48; postgrad. course ophthalmology N.Y.U. Med. Sch., 1948-49; resident ophthalmology Jersey City Med. Ctr., 1949-50, Manhattan Eye, Ear, & Throat Hosp., N.Y.C., 1950-52; practice medicine specializing in ophthalmology Honolulu, 1952-54 and from 56. Mem. staffs Kuakini Hosp., Children's Hosp., Castle Meml. Hosp., Queen's Hosp., St. Francis Hosp.; asst. clin. prof. ophthalmology U. Hawaii Sch. Medicine, 1966-73, now asso. clin. prof. Cons. Bur. Crippled Children, 1952-73, Kapiolani Maternity Hosp., 1952-73, Leahi Tb. Hosp., 1952-62. Mem. AMA, Am. Acad. Ophthalmology and Otolaryngology, Assn. for Rsch. Ophthalmology, ACS, Hawaii Med. Soc. (gov. med. practice com. 1958-62, chmn. med. spkrs. com. 1957-58), Hawaii Eye, Ear, Nose and Throat Soc. (pres. 1960), Pacific Coast Oto-Ophthalmological Soc., Pan Am. Assn. Ophthalmology, Mason, Shriner, Eye Study Club (pres. 1972—). Home: Honolulu, Hawaii. Deceased.

PANKOW, CHARLES J. civil engineer; Chmn. New Century Ptnrs.; owner, operator Charles Pankow Builders, LTD. Contbr. articles in field. Mem. Nat. Acad. Engring., Civil Engring. Rsch. Found. Died Jan. 12, 2004.

PANTON, VERNER, architect; b. Gamtofte, Fyn, Denmark, Feb. 13, 1926; arrived in Switzerland, 1963; s. Henry and Ellen (Koch-Hansen) P.; m. Marianne Pherson, July 17, 1964; 1 child, Carin. Degree in bldg. constrn., Odense (Denmark) Tech. Sch., 1947; MArch, Royal Acad. Arts, Copenhagen, 1951. Owner, architect, designer Verner Panton AG, Basel, Switzerland, from 1964. Vis. prof. indsl. design Hochschule für Gestaltung, Offenbach, Fed. Republic of Germany, 1984. Fellow Royal Soc. Arts; mem. Acad. Arkitektforening, Danske Arkitekters Landsforbund, Indsl. Designers Denmark, Schweizerischer Werkbund. Died Sept. 5, 1998.

PANUSH, IRENE E(STHER), social worker; b. Detroit, Jan. 31, 1921; d. Martin and Regina (Eichner) Siegel; m. Irving Panush, Aug. 30, 1942; 1 child, Deborah Aviva. BS, Wayne State U., 1943; postgrad., U. Mich., 1947-48; MS with honors, Columbia U., 1960; MSW, Wayne State U., 1980. Clin. social worker, Mich.; diplomate Nat. Bd. Examiners in Clin. Social Work. Libr. Wayne State U. Gen. Libr., Detroit, 1960-62; asst. prof. anatomy and physiology Oakland Community Coll. Highland Lakes, Auburn HillS, Mich., 1971-78; therapist Community Mental Health Ctr., Highland Park, Mich., 1978-79, Cath. Social Svcs. Oakland County, Royal Oak, Southfield, Mich., 1979-88; pvt. practice, Birmingham, Mich., 1988-99; retired. Cons. Ostomy Assn. Oakland County, Mich., 1988—. Editor: (booklet) Facts About Bloomfield Hills Schools, 1970. V.p., community chmn. LWV, Detroit, 1957-58, bd. dirs., community chmn., Birmingham, Bloomfield, Mich., 1968-75. Med. Coll. scholar Student Aid Found., 1942-44, grad. scholar Wayne State U., 1978-80; Libr. Sch. fellow Columbia U., 1959-60. Fellow Am. Orthopsychiat. Assn.; mem. Friends of Mich. Psychoanalytic Assn., Mich. Soc. Clin. Social Workers, Nat. Assn. Social Workers, Alliance Mental Health Svcs., Planned Parenthood, NOW, Women of Religions for Abortion, Beta Phi Mu. Jewish. Deceased.

PAPPAS, ROBERTA LYNN, computer educational consultant; b. Rockville Ctr., N.Y., Apr. 28, 1951; d. Jerome and Frances (Mayer) North; m. John S. Pappas, Apr. 21, 1985; 1 child, Louis Samuel. BA in Internat. Law, Goucher Coll., Balt., 1973; MBA in Fin., Golden Gate U., 1984. Tech. rep., database specialist Nat. CSS, San Francisco, 1974-81; mgr. fin. products worldwide Bank of Am. Hdqrs., San Francisco, 1981-85; mgr. ad hoc reporting Wells Fargo, San Francisco, 1985-87; computer ednl. cons. Fed. Home Loan Bank, San Francisco, from 1988. Rep. World Book, San Francisco. Author: User Friendly Systems, 1986; pub. newsletter Clipper Cove, 1988; contbr. articles to profl. jours. Mem. Raoul Wallenberg Dems. Mem. Assn. Women in Computing, U.S. Tennis Assn. Home: Alameda, Calif. Deceased.

PAPPER, EMANUEL MARTIN, anesthesiologist; b. N.Y.C., July 12, 1915; s. Max and Lillian (Weitzner) P.; m. Patricia Meyer, Nov. 30, 1975; children: Richard Nelson Papper, Patrick Goldstein, Amy Goldstein. AB, Columbia U., 1935; MD, NYU, 1938; MD (hon.), Univ. Uppsala, Sweden, 1964, U. Turin, Italy, 1969, U. Vienna, Austria, 1977; DSc (hon.), Columbia U., 1988; PhD, U. Miami, 1990. Diplomate Am. Bd. Anesthesiology (dir. 1956-65, pres. 1964-65). Fellow medicine NYU, 1938-39, fellow physiology, 1940, asst. prof., 1946-49, assoc. prof., 1949; intern Bellevue Hosp., 1939-40, resident in anesthesiology, 1940-42; prof. anesthesiology, chmn. dept. Columbia U.; also dir. anesthesiology service Presbyn. Hosp., 1949- 69; dir. anesthesiology, vis. anesthesiologst Francis Delafield Hosp., 1951-69; v.p. med affairs, dean, prof. anesthesiology U. Miami, 1969-81, prof. pharmacology, 1972-81. Dir. Abbott Labs., No. Trust Bank of Fla., Miami; cons. div. med. scis. NRC, 1954-69, Huntington (N.Y.) Hosp., 1949-69; nat. cons. surgeon gen. USAF, 1963-70; mem. surgery study sect. NIH, 1958-62; civilian cons. First Army, USN; prin. cons. Nat. Inst. Gen. Med. Scis., 1965-66, chmn. project com. gen. med. research program, 1966-70; mem. nat. heart council NIH, 1962-66; hon. cons. Royal Prince Alfred Hosp., Sydney, Australia Author 350 sci. papers pub. in various med. jours., 3 textbooks, 2 non-fiction books. Bd. dirs. PBS-Channel 2, Miami, 1984—. Served from 1st lt. to maj. M.C. U.S. Army, 1942-46; chief anesthesiology sect. Torney, Dibble and Walter Reed hosps. Recipient Silver medal City of Paris, 1972, 1st prize History of Medicine, Am. Med. Writers Assn., 1996, Davdi M. Little prize Am. Anesthesia Assn., 1998; established E.M. Papper chair in anesthesiology Columbia U. Coll. Physicians and Surgeons, 1984, E.M. Papper lectures in anesthesiology Columbia U. and UCLA, 1978 Hon. fellow Royal Coll. Anaesthetists (England), Royal Coll. Surgeons (Ireland, faculty anaesthetists), Royal Soc. Medicine (England), Australian and New Zealand Coll. Anesthesiologists; mem. N.Y. Acad. Medicine (1st pres. sect. anesthesiology), Am. Surg. Assn., Am. Soc. Anesthesiologists (pres. 1967-68), N.Y. State Soc. Anesthesiologists (past pres.), NRC (chmn. com. anesthesia 1962-67), Am. Coll. Anesthesiologists, World Fedn. Soc. Anesthesiologists (v.p.), Am. Soc. Pharmacology and Exptl. Therapeutics, AMA, N.Y. Acad. Scis., N.Y. Co. Med. Soc., Am., N.Y. socs. anesthesiologists, AAAS, Am. Assn. Thoracic Surgery, Harvey Soc, Am. Soc. Clin. Investigation, Am. Thoracic Soc., Assn. Univ. Anesthetists (co-founder, 1st pres.), Pan Am. Med. Assn., Assn. Anaesthestists Gt. Britain and Ireland (hon.), Swedish Soc. Anesthesiologists (hon. mem.), Finnish Soc. Anesthesiologists (hon. mem.), Israeli Soc. Anesthesiologists (hon. mem.), Australian Soc. Anaesthesiologists (hon. mem.), N.Y. State Soc. Anesthesiologists (hon. mem.), D.C. Soc. Anesthesiologists (hon. mem.), Calif. Soc. Anesthesiologists (hon. mem.), German Soc. Anesthesiologists (hon. mem.), Halsted Soc., Japan Soc. Anesthesiologists (hon.), Am. Soc. Anesthesiologists (pres. 1969), European Acad. Anesthesiology (hon., Gold medal), Grolier Club (N.Y.C.), Phi Beta Kappa, Sigma Xi, Alpha Omega Alpha. Clubs: Cosmos (Washington); Century Assn. (N.Y.C.). Died Dec. 3, 2002.

PARIS, DEMETRIUS THEODORE, electrical engineering educator; b. Stavroupolis, Thrace, Greece, Sept. 27, 1928; came to U.S., 1947, naturalized, 1954; s. Theodore P. and Aspasia (Yannakis) Paraskevopoulos; m. Elsie Edwards, Jan. 5, 1952. BS, Miss. State U., 1951; MS, Ga. Inst. Tech., 1958, PhD, 1962. With Westinghouse Electric Corp., 1952-58, Lockheed-Ga. Co., 1958-59; asst. prof. elec. engring. Ga. Inst. Tech., 1959-63, assoc. prof., 1963-66, prof., 1966—, asst. dir. elec. engring., 1966-69, dir., 1969-89, v.p for rsch. and grad. programs, 1989-95. Cons.Sci.-Atlanta, Inc., Lockheed-Ga. Co., U.S. Army Ltd. War Lab., Aberdeen, Md.; chair internat. activities com. Accreditation Bd. for Engring. and Tech., 1991—. Author: Basic Electromagnetic Theory, 1969. Recipient Sigma Xi award for best research paper by a mem. Ga. Inst. Tech. faculty, 1965 Fellow IEEE (editor trans. on edn. 1976-79, Centennial medal 1984, ednl. activities bd. meritorious svc. citation 1989, IEEE rep. to Accreditation Bd. for Engring. and Tech. bd. dirs. 1990-95), Accreditation Bd. for Engring. and Tech.; mem. IEEE Edn. Soc. (Achievement award 1980, pres. 1986), Am. Soc. Engring. Edn., Sigma Xi, Kappa Mu Epsilon, Tau Beta Pi, Eta Kappa Nu, Phi Kappa Phi. Home: Atlanta, Ga. Deceased.

PARK, JOHN FAIRCLOTH, cantor; b. Greenville, S.C., Apr. 15, 1930; s. John Andrew and M. Inez (Faircloth) P. Student, Furman U., 1947-50; BA, U. N.C., 1951, MA, 1954; student, Cin. Conservatory of Music, 1954-55; EdD, Columbia U., 1962. Cantor Temple Emanuel, Kingston, N.Y., from 1967. Chmn. div. humanities and social scis. Ulster County Community Coll., Stone Ridge, N.Y., 1963-85. Composer various works for cantor and cantor and choir. Mem. Am. Conf. Cantors. Home: Poughkeepsie, NY. Died Jan. 14, 2001.

PARKER, BOBBY EUGENE, SR., college president; b. Wortham, Tex., May 28, 1925; s. Thomas W. and Stacy (Beasley) P.; m. Marietta Vickrey, Sept. 1, 1946; children: Bobby Eugene Jr., Mark. AA, Westminster Jr. Coll., 1948; BS, Sam Houston State Coll., 1951; MS, Baylor U., 1954, EdD, 1964; LLD (hon.), Houston Bapt. U., 1990; HHD (hon.), U. Mary Hardin-Baylor, 1996. Prin., counselor pub. schs., Richland and Mexia, Tex., 1948-57; dean students Howard Payne Coll., Brownwood, Tex., 1957-59; mem. faculty Baylor U., Waco, Tex., 1960-69; v.p. Mary Hardin-Baylor Coll., Belton, Tex., 1969-71; pres. U. Mary Hardin-Baylor, 1971-91, chancellor, 1991-99, pres. emeritus, 1996-99; hon. chancellor Ebino (Japan) Kohgen Internat. Coll., 1994. Hon. pres. Allen Jr. Coll., Kuji Iwate Japan, 1992. Mem. King's Daus. Hosp. Assn., Heart O' Tex. coun. nat. Boy Scouts Am., pres. 1995; trustee Bell County Mus. History and Art; bd. dirs. Greater Waco Safety Coun., 1963-67, Waco Girl's Club, 1967-69, Tex. Safety Assn., 1963; pres. coun. Heart of Tex. Athletic Conf. With USNR, 1943-46. Recipient Spl. Safety award Tex. Safety Assn., 1965, Exemplary medal San Marcos Bapt. Acad., 1991, Good Shepherd award Boy Scouts Am., 1996; named Man of Yr. Belton Area C. of C., 1978, Outstanding Christian Educator Mexican Bapt. Conv.; fellow Paul Harris. Mem. Internat. Platform Assn., Tex. Baptist Sch. Adminstrs. Assn., Tex. Found. Vol. Supported Colls. and Univs. (former chmn. bd.), Assn. Am. Colls., Am. Council Edn., Ind. Colls. and Univs. of Tex. (former mem. exec. bd.), Nat. Assn. Intercollegiate Athletics (former pres. adv. com.), Belton C. of C. (past bd. dirs.), East Tex. C. of C., Killeen C. of C., Temple C. of C., Friends of Scott and White. Lodges: Rotary Internat. (Gov. 1984, Dist. Gov.'s Role of Fame; Gov. Dist. 587. 1986-87). Home: Belton, Tex. Died Dec. 16, 1999.

PARKER, DANIEL LOUIS, lawyer; b. Smithfield, N.C., Sept. 2, 1924; s. James Daniel and Agnes Augusta (Toussaint) P.; m. Mae Comer Osborne, Aug. 2, 1958. AB, U. N.C., 1947, LLB, 1950. Bar: N.C. 1950. With escrow sect. mortgage loan dept. Pilot Life Ins. Co., Greensboro, N.C., 1950-53, with trust dept. N.C. Nat. Bank, Greensboro, 1953-62; investment counsel Pilot Life Ins. Co., 1962-71, counsel 71-77, 2d v.p., 1977-84; 2nd v.p., asst. gen. counsel Jefferson Standard Life Ins. Co. (now Jefferson-Pilot Life Ins. Co.), Greensboro, 1984-90; with Ivey, Ivey, McClellan & Gatton, Greensboro, 1990-94. Bd. dirs., treas. Ctr. for Creative Arts, Greenboro, 1984-93. With U.S. Army, 1944-46. Mem. N.C. Bar Assn., Assn. Life Ins. Counsel, Greensboro Bar Assn., Greensboro Jr. C. of C., Phi Beta Kappa. Republican. Roman Catholic. Died Apr. 30, 1994. Home: Greensboro, NC.

PARKER, FRED I. federal judge; b. Boston, 1938; BA, U. Mass., 1962; LLB, Georgetown U., 1965. With Lyne, Woodworth & Everts, Boston, 1965—66; dep. atty. gen. Office Atty. Gen., Montpelier, Vt., 1969—72; with Langrock and Sperry, Middlebury, Vt., 1972—75; ptnr. Langrock, Sperry, Parker & Stahl, Middlebury, 1975—82, Langrock, Sperry, Parker & Wool, Middlebury, 1982—90; fed. judge U.S. Dist. Ct. (Vt. dist.), 1990—91, chief judge, 1991—94; fed. judge U.S. Ct. Appeals (2d cir.), 1994—2003. Mem. conduct bd. Vt. Supreme Ct., 1975—79, jud. conduct bd., 1982—88. Active Vt. Lawyers Project. With USMC, 1955—62. Mem.: Chittenden County Bar Assn., Vt. Bar Assn. (chair spl. com. reform of judiciary 1988—89). Died Aug. 12, 2003.

PARKIN, EVELYN HOPE, retired medical social worker; b. Owatonna, Minn., Aug. 2, 1910; d. Wilbur L. and Verta (Cowles) Parkin. BA, Carleton Coll., 1931; postgrad., U. Minn. Sch. Social Work, 1939-41. Desk attendant Mayo Clinic, Rochester, Minn., 1931-39; pediatric social worker U. Minn. Hosp., Mpls., 1941-45; supr. social svc. dept. Mayo Clinic, Rochester, Minn., 1953-75, dir. social svc. dept., 1952-75, staff mem., 1973-75, emeritus staff mem., 1975-99. Sec. Mayo Clinic Credit Union, 1958-65. Treas., Young Rep.League, Rochester, 1952; sec. Olmsted County Rep. Com., 1953-55; bd. dirs. YWCA, Rochester, 1953-54, Minn. Heart Assn., 1959-64, Am. Heart Assn., N.Y.C., 1958-62; sec. Minn. Welfare Conf., 1954-99. Honored for social work with open heart surgery patients, Germany, 1975. Mem. NASW. Republican. Presbyterian. Home: Rochester, Minn. Died Jan. 22, 1999.

PARKINSON, BENJAMIN HENRY, JR., lawyer; b. Portland, Oreg., Mar. 2, 1922; s. Benjamin Henry and Fayette Wunifred (Harbaugh) P.; m. Virginia Ellen Kaley, June 10, 1943; children: Kaley Roger, Linda Jean Hamadani, Benjamin H. III. BA, Stanford U., 1943, JD, 1949. Bar: Calif. 1949, U.S. Dist. Ct. (no. dist.) Calif. 1949, U.S. Supreme Ct. 1980. Assoc. Orrick Dahlquist Neff & Herrington, San Francisco, 1949-51, 53, Johnston & Johnston, San Francisco, 1953-57; ptnr. Ackermann Johnston Campbell & Parkinson & Predecessor Firms, San Francisco, 1957-87; of counsel Steinhart & Falconer, San Francisco, 1987-95. City atty. Town of Atherton, Calif., 1968-76. Bd. dirs. Bar Assn. San Francisco, 1966-67. 1st lt. F.A., 1943-46, JAGC, 1951-53. Fellow Am. Bar Found.; mem. Order of Coif. Democrat. Home: Palo Alto, Calif. Died June 1, 2001.

PARKS, MADELYN N. nurse, retired army officer, university official; b. Jordan, Okla. Diploma, Corpus Christi (Tex.) Sch. Nursing, 1943; BSN., Incarnate Word Coll., San Antonio, 1961; M.H.A. in Health Care Adminstrn, Baylor

U., 1965. Commd. 2d lt. Army Nurse Corps, 1943, advanced through grades to brig. gen., 1975; basic tng. Fort Meade, Md., 1944; staff nurse eye ward Valley Forge (Pa.) Gen. Hosp., 1944; served in India, Iran, Italy, 1944-45; gen. duty staff nurse, 1951; nurse eye clinic Tripler Army Med. Center, Hawaii, 1951-54; staff nurse eye, ear, nose and throat ward Brooke Army Med. Center, San Antonio, 1954-57; ednl. coordinator Fort Dix, N.J., 1957-58; instr., supr. enlisted med. tng. U.S. Army Med. Tng. Center, Fort Sam Houston, Tex., 1959-61; chief nurse surg. field hosp. 62d Med. Group, Germany, 1961-62, sr. nurse coordinator, 1962-63; adminstrn. resident Letterman Gen. Hosp., San Francisco, 1964-65, dir. clin. specialist course, 1965-67; chief nurse 85th Evacuation Hosp., Qui Nhon, Vietnam, 1967-68; asst. chief nursing sci. div., asst. prof. Med. Field Service Sch., U.S. Army-Baylor U. Program in Health Care Adminstrn., 1968-72; chief nurse surgeons office Hdqrs. Continental Army Command, Fort Monroe, Va., 1972-73; chief dept. nursing Walter Reed Army Med. Center, Washington, 1973-75; chief Army Nurse Corps, Office of Surgeon Gen., Dept. Army, Washington, 1975-79, ret., 1979; faculty assoc. adminstr. U. Md., 1974-78. Decorated D.S.M., Army Commendation medal with 2 oak leaf clusters, Legion of Merit, Meritorious Service medal; recipient Alumna of Distinction award Incarnate Word Coll., 1981 Mem. Ret. Officers Assn., AMEDD Mus. Found. Died Nov. 24, 2002.

PARKS, ROBERT EMMETT, JR., medical science educator; b. Glendale, N.Y., July 29, 1921; s. Robert Emmett and Carolyn M. (Heinemann) P.; m. Margaret Ellen Ward, June 15, 1945; children: Robert Emmett III, Walter Ward, Christopher Carr. AB, Brown U., 1944; MD, Harvard U., 1945; PhD, U. Wis., 1954. Intern Boston's Children's Hosp., 1945-46; rsch. assoc. Amherst (Mass.) Coll., 1948-51; post-doctoral fellow Enzyme Inst., Madison, Wis., 1951-54; mem. faculty U. Wis. Med. Sch., 1954-63, prof. pharmacology, 1961-63; prof. med. sci. Brown U., Providence, 1963-91, prof. emeritus, from 1991, dir. grad. program in pharmacology and exptl. pathology, 1978-81, chmn. sect. biochem. pharmacology, 1963-78, 83-91. Cons. in field. Contbr. articles to profl. jours. With AUS, 1943-45, 46-48. Acad. medicine scholar John and Mary Markle Found., 1956-61. Mem. Am. Soc. Pharmacology and Exptl. Therapeutics, Am. Soc. Biol. Chemists, Am. Assn. Cancer Rsch. (bd. dirs. 1982-86), Sigma Xi. Home: Providence, RI. Deceased.

PARKS, VINCENT JOSEPH, civil engineering educator; b. Chgo., May 5, 1928; s. Joseph and Nora (Carr) P.; m. Julia Catherine Pyles, Feb. 12, 1955; children: Sean, Michael, David, Nora, Joseph, Gregory, Laurence. AS, Lewis Coll. Sci., 1948; BSME, Ill. Inst. Tech., 1953; MCE, Cath. U. Am., 1963, PhD, 1968. Engr. Andrew Corp., Orland Park, Ill., 1953-55; rsch. engr. Armour Rsch. Found., Chgo., 1955-61; rsch. assoc. Cath. Univ. Am., Washington, 1961-65, asst. prof., 1965-68, assoc. prof., 1968-73, prof., 1973-95; ret., 1995. Rsch. cons. U.S. Naval Rsch. Lab., Washington, 1973-90, Sandia Nat. Lab., Albuquerque, 1980-94. Co-author: Moire Analysis of Strain, 1970; editor: Progress in Experimental Mechanics, 1975. Recipient Resident Rsch. Associateship, Nat. Rsch. Coun., Washington, 1971-72, Faculty Rsch. grant Am. Soc. for Engring. Edn., Washington, 1983-89. Fellow ASME, Soc. Experimental Mechanics (Hetenyi 1974, Frocht 1981); mem. Am. Acad. Mechanics, Sigma Xi. Democrat. Roman Catholic. Home: Washington, DC. Died Apr. 16, 2001.

PARKS, WILLIAM ROBERT, former university president; b. Lincoln County, Tenn., Oct. 13, 1915; s. Benjamin N. and Minnie A. (Taylor) P.; m. Ellen R. Sorge, July 1, 1940; children: Andrea, Cynthia. BA, Berea Coll., 1937, LL.D. (hon.), 1966; MA, U. Ky., 1938, D.Sc. (hon.), 1973; PhD, U. Wis., 1948; LL.D., Drake U., 1968; L.H.D., Westmar Coll., 1968. Economist bur. agrl. econs. Dept. Agr., 1940-48; prof. govt. Iowa State Coll., 1948-56; prof. agrl. econs. U. Wis., 1956-58; dean of instrn. Iowa State U., 1958-61; v.p. academic affairs, 1961-65; pres., 1965-86; pres. emeritus, 1986—2003. Cons. TVA, part-time 1956-57, also Dept. Interior; dir. Northwestern Bell Telephone Co., Central Life Assurance Co., 1972-86. Contbr. articles to profl. jours. Trustee Coll. Retirement Equity Fund, 1971-83. Served to lt. (j.g.) USNR, 1943-46. Mem. Assn. Am. Univs. (pres. 1977, chmn. 1978), Mid-Am. State Univs. Assn. (pres. 1965), Nat. Assn. State Univs. and Land Grant Colls. (pres. 1973) Home: Ames, Iowa. Died July 13, 2003.

PARR, THURMOND CHARLES, JR., accountant; b. Winchester, Tex., Nov. 1, 1925; s. Thurmond Charles and Jewel (Hubbard) P.; m. Dorothea Ann Pfanstiel, Sept. 15, 1951; children: Thurmond Charles Parr III, Richard Marshall Parr. BBA in Acctg. cum laude, St. Mary's U., 1958. CPA, Tex. Salesman Straus-Frank Co., San Antonio, 1953-55; teller Highland Park State Bank, San Antonio, 1955-56; acct. Gasoline Prodn. Corp., San Antonio, 1956-60; tchr. St. Mary's U., San Antonio, 1959-63; pvt. practice San Antonio, from 1960. 1st lt. U.S. Army, 1950-53. Mem. AICPA, SAR, Tex. Soc. CPAs (San Antonio chpt.), Sons of Confederate Vets., Masonic Order Knight Templar. Republican. Presbyterian. Avocations: golf, hunting, leather tooling. Home: San Antonio, Tex. Died June 3, 2001.

PARSONS, GEORGE RAYMOND, JR., lawyer; b. N.Y.C., May 5, 1938; s. George Raymond and Gertrude (Blackburn) P.; m. Katharine P. Sook, Oct. 16, 1982; children: Timothy, Geoffrey, Amy, Julia, Elizabeth. BA with distinction, Wesleyan U., 1959; LLB with honors, Cornell U., 1962. Bar: N.Y. 1962, U.S. Dist. Ct. (we. and no. dists.) N.Y. 1962, Fla. 1974. Assoc. Nixon, Hargrave, Davans & Doyle LLP, Rochester, N.Y., 1962-69, ptnr., 1970—. Lectr. continuing legal edn. programs Editor-in-chief, contbr. articles to Cornell Law Rev., 1961-62, New Republic; contbr. John Updike Newsletter. Officer, bd. dirs. Rochester Philharm. Orch., 1976-83; pres. Friends of Rochester Pub. Libr., 1972-75; trustee Monroe County Libr. Sys., 1986-87, 94-96, Reynolds Libr., 1987— (pres. 1996—), Rochester Regional Libr. Coun., 1988-98, pres. 1994-97; bd. dirs. Rundel Libr. Found., Inc., 1989—; pres. Friends of U. Rochester Librs., 1989-91; trustee Rochester Pub. Libr., 1978-81, 83-99, pres. 1986-87, 94-96; bd. dirs. Writers and Books, 1991-97; del. N.Y. State Gov.'s Conf. on Librs. and Info. Svcs., 1990; mem. adv. com. librs. U. Rochester, 1991-95, 97—; trustee Halycon Hill Found., 1992—; trustee Rochester Grantmakers Forum, 1997-98. Mem. N.Y. Bar Assn., Monroe County Bar Assn., Am. Coll. of Trust and Estate Counsel, Estate Planning Council Rochester Democrat. Home: Rochester, NY. Deceased.

PARSONS, HOWARD LEE, philosophy educator; b. Jacksonville, Fla., July 9, 1918; s. Howard Lee and Edna Alice (Powell) P. BA, U. Chgo., 1942, PhD, 1946. Asst. prof. U. So. Calif., 1946-47; instr. U. Ill., 1947-49; prof. U. Tenn., 1949-57, Coe Coll., Cedar Rapids, Iowa, 1957-65, chmn. dept., 1959-65, U. Bridgeport, Conn., 1965-88, prof. emeritus, from 1988. Prof. Columbia U., 1952, Idaho State Coll., Pocatello, 1959, Victoria (B.C., Can.) Coll., 1961, Moscow State U., 1980, 90, 93, Moscow State Inst. Internat. Rels., 1991; lectr. in field, Tokyo, 1971, 73, Dem. People's Republic of Korea, 1971, India, 1973, 75-76; mem. sci. coun. Internat. Inst. for Peace; rep. World Peace Conf., UN, N.Y.C.; past mem. adv. com. World Peace Conf., Praxis, Yugoslavia; presenter in field at internat. and nat. confs. Author: Humanism and Marx's Thought, 1971, Man Today-Problems, Values and Fulfillment, 1973, Man East and West, 1975, Self, Global Issues, and Ethics, 1977, Marx and Engels on Ecology, 1977, The Soviet People and the Soviet Union: Perspectives of an American Philosopher, 1980, Buddhism as Humanism, 1982, Marxism, Christianity, and Human Values: Essays Toward Dialogue and Common Action, 1981, Man in the Contemporary World, 1985, Christianity Today in the USSR, 1987; co-editor: (with John Somerville) Dialogues on the Philosophy of Marxism, 1974, Marxism, Revolution and Peace, 1976; contbr. 200 articles and 7 monographs to philos., religious and ednl. jours. Past bd. dirs. World Fellowship of Faiths; past sponsor Am. com. for Protection of Fgn.-Born. William Rainey Harper fellow U. Chgo., 1945-46, Mellon rsch. fellow, 1985, 88; rsch. grantee Wenner-Gren Found. for Anthrop. Rsch., 1956, Kavir Inst., 1963-64, travel grantee Am. Coun. Learned Socs., 1975-76, Internat. Rsch. and Exchs. Bd., 1977, 78, 80. Mem. AAUP (pres. Coe Coll. chpt. 1961-61, U. Bridgeport chpt. 1970-71), Am. Philos. Assn., So. Soc. for Philosophy in Religion (pres. 1959-60), Soc. for Values in Higher Edn., Soc. for Philos. Study Marxism (pres. 1962-63, 87-93, v.p. 1963-87), Found. for Philosophy of Creativity (bd. dirs.), Am. Inst. for Marxist Studies (founding sponsor, bd. dirs.), Soc. Européene de Culture, Soc. for Asian and Comparative Philosophy, World Fedn. Sci. Workers, Hegel Soc. Am. Home: Milford, Conn. Died Dec. 28, 2000.

PASCHEN, HENRY DANIEL, contracting company executive; b. Chgo., Feb. 1, 1927; s. Henry Daniel and Lillian Margaret (Field) P.; 1 child, Margaret Moore Paschen Wright; m. Maria Tallchief, June 3, 1956; 1 child, Elise Maria BA, DePaul U., 1951. Corp. purchasing officer Paschen Contractors, Inc., Chgo., 1953-59, dir., v.p., 1959-75, exec. v.p., treas., 1975-77, pres., 1977-83, former chief exec. officer, chmn., treas.; mem. Lloyds of London. Former trustee, regent Lincoln Acad., Ill.; mem. Felix Neck Wildlife Sanctuary. Served with U.S. Army, 1945-47. Recipient Variety Club Ball King award 18th Ann. Variety Club Celebrity Ball, Chgo., 1985 Mem. Friends of Long Point Wildlife Refuge (trustee of reservations), Beavers. Clubs: Chgo., Chgo. Yacht, Racquet, Tavern (Chgo.); Bob-O-Link (Highland Park, Ill.); Edgartown Yacht, Casino, Arts. Avocations: tennis; opera; ballet; golf; skiing. Home: Chicago, Ill. Died June 2, 2004.

PASK, JOSEPH ADAM, ceramic engineering educator; b. Chgo., Feb. 14, 1913; s. Adam Poskoczem and Catherine (Ramanauskas) P.; m. Margaret J. Gault, June 11, 1938; children: Thomas Joseph, Kathryn Edyth. BS, U. Ill., 1934, PhD, 1941; MS, U. Wash., 1935. Ceramic engr. Willamina Clay Products Co., Oreg., 1935-36; teaching asst. ceramic engring. U. Ill., 1938, instr., 1938-41; asst. ceramic engr. electrotech. lab. U.S. Bur. Mines, 1941; assoc. ceramic engr. N.W. Exptl. Sta., 1942-43; asst. prof. ceramic engring., head dept. Coll. of Mines, U. Wash., Seattle, 1941-43; research ceramist, lamp div. Westinghouse Electric Corp., N.J., 1943-46, research engr. ceramic sect., 1946-48; assoc. prof. ceramic engring., head ceramic group div. materials sci. and engring. U. Calif. at Berkeley, 1948-53, founder program ceramic engring. and sci., 1948, prof., 1953-80, prof. emeritus, 1980—, vice chmn. div., 1956-57, chmn. dept., 1957-61; asso. dean grad. student affairs U. Calif. at Berkeley (Coll. Engring.), 1969-80; sr. faculty scientist Lawrence Berkeley Lab. John Dorn Meml. lectr. Northwestern U., 1977; mem. clay mineral com. NRC; mem. materials adv. bd., chmn. ad hoc com. ceramic processing, adv. commn. metallurgy div. U.S. Bur. Standards; chmn. NSF study objective criteria in ceramic engring. edn., U.S.-China Seminar on Basic Sci. of Ceramics, Shanghai, 1983 Recipient John F. Bergeron Meml. Svc. award Ceramic Engring. div. U. Wash., Seattle, 1969, gold medal for research and devel. French Soc. for Research and Devel., 1979, Berkeley citation U. Calif., 1980, Alumni honor award for disting. service in engring. U. Ill. Coll. Engring., 1982, Outstanding Achievement in Edn. award Com. of Confucius, 1982, Internat. Prize Japan Fine Ceramics Assn., 1988, Engring. Alumni Achievement award U. Wash. Coll. Engring., 1991. Fellow AAAS, Am. Ceramic Soc. (disting. life mem., v.p. 1953-54, pres. ednl. coun. 1954-55, trustee 1959-62, chmn. electronics div. 1959-60, John Jeppson award 1967, Ross Coffin Purdy award 1979), Mineral Soc., Acad. Dental Materials; mem. NAE, Nat. Inst. Ceramics Engrs., N.Y. Acad. Scis., Am. Soc. Matls, Brit. Ceramic Soc., Internat. Acad. Ceramics,, Am. Soc. Engring. Edn. (chmn. materials com. 1961-63, Centennial Cert. 1993), Clay Minerals Soc., Ceramics Soc. Japan (hon., Centennial medal 1991), Materials Rsch. Soc. Japan (hon.), Keramos, Sigma XI, Tau Bet Pi, Alpha Sigma Mu. Home: Berkeley, Calif. Died June 14, 2003.

PASSIN, HERBERT, sociologist; b. Chgo., Dec. 16, 1916; s. Hyman and Edith (Block) P.; m. Helen Wood Latham, Dec. 18, 1964; 1 son, Thomas. Student, U. Ill., 1935-36; MA, U. Chgo., 1941; Dr.h.c., Kwansei Gakuin U., 1984. Instr. Northwestern U., 1941-42; chief pub. opinion and sociol. research div., civil info. and edn. G.H.Q., SCAP, Tokyo, 1946-51; prof. Far Eastern studies U. Wash., Seattle, 1959-62; prof. sociology Columbia U., 1962-87, chmn. dept., 1973-78, 80-81, prof. emeritus sociology, from 1987; chmn. bd. editorial advisers TBS-Britannica, Tokyo, 1969-73, now cons. Dir. Assn. Asian studies, 1965-68. Author: (with others) The Japanese Village in Transition, 1951, (with J.W. Bennett) In Search of Identity, 1958, China's Cultural Diplomacy, 1962, Society and Education in Japan, 1965, The United States and Japan, 1975, Language and Cultural Change, 1979; editor: Encounter at Shimoda, 1979, A Season of Voting, 1979, Japanese and The Japanese, 1980, Encounter with Japan, 1983. Served to 1st lt. AUS, 1944-47. Decorated Imperial Order of the Sacred Treas. Mem. Am. Anthrop. Assn., Soc. Applied Anthropology, Assn. Asian Studies, Internat. House Japan, Am. Sociol. Assn. Home: New York, NY. Died Feb. 26, 2003.

PASTORELLI, ROBERT, actor; b. New Brunswick, N.J., June 21, 1954; Student, N.Y. Acad. Theatrical Arts, Actors Studio. Appeared in: (plays) Rebel Without a Cause, N.Y. Theatre Ensemble, End as a Man, Death of a Salesman, Bus Stop, The Rainmaker, One Flew Over the Cuckoo's Nest, Lovers and Other Strangers, Grey Spades, Ensemble Studio Theatre, Cosmo's in Love, Mere Mortals, Dice and Cards, (with actor Bill Murray) Down the Tubes, (TV series) Hill Street Blues, 1983, 85, Miami Vice, 1987, Cagney and Lacey, 1983, Beauty and the Beast, 1988, Murphy Brown, 1988-94, Double Rush, 1995, Cracker, 1997, Touched by an Angel, 2002; (TV movies) I Married a Centerfold, 1984, California Girls, 1985, Braker, 1985, hands of a Stranger, 1987, The Spirit, 1987, Lady Mobster, 1988, Sex, Shock & Censorship, 1993, Harmful Intent, 1993, The Yarn Princess, 1994, The West Side Waltz, 1995, The Ballad of Lucy Whipple, 2001, South Pacific, 2001, Women vs. Men, 2002, Murphy Brown: TV Tales, 2002; (films) Outrageous Fortune, 1987, Beverly Hills Cop II, 1987, Memories of Me, 1988, Dances with Wolves, 1990, FernGully: The Last Rainforest, 1992, Folks, 1992, The Paint Job, 1992, Striking Distance, 1993, Sister Act II: Back in the Habit, 1993, Folks, Eraser, 1996, Michael, 1996, A Simple Wish, 1997, Scotch and Milk, 1998, Modern Vampires, 1998, Bait, 2000. Died Mar. 9, 2004.

PATTEN, BEBE HARRISON, minister, academic administrator; b. Waverly, Tenn., Sept. 3, 1913; d. Newton Felix and Mattie Priscilla (Whitson) Harrison; m. Carl Thomas Patten, Oct. 23, 1935; children: Priscilla Carla and Bebe Rebecca (twins), Carl Thomas. D.D., McKinley-Roosevelt Coll., 1941; D.Litt., Temple Hall Coll. and Sem., 1943. Ordained to ministry Ministerial Assn. of Evangelism, 1935; evangelist in various cities of U.S., 1933-50; founder, pres. Christian Evang. Chs. Am., Inc., Oakland, Calif., 1944—2004, Patten Acad. Christian Edn., Oakland, 1944—, Patten Bible Coll., Oakland, 1944-83; chancellor Patten Coll., Oakland, 1983—2004; founder, pastor Christian Cathedral of Oakland, 1950—2004. Held pvt. interviews with David Ben-Gurion, 1972, Menachim Begin, 1977, Yitzhak Shamir, 1991; condr. Sta. KUSW world-wide radio ministry, 70 countries around the world, 1989-90, Stas. WHRI and WWCR world coverage short wave, 1990-2004 Founder, condr.: radio program The Shepherd Hour, 1934—2004; daily TV, 1976—2004, nationwide telecast, 1979—2004; Author: Give Me Back My Soul, 1973; Editor: Trumpet Call, 1953—2004; composer 20 gospel and religious songs, 1945—2004. Mem. exec. bd. Bar-Ilan U. Assn., Israel, 1983; mem. global bd. trustees Bar-Ilan U., 1991. Recipient numerous awards including medallion Ministry of Religious Affairs, Israel, 1969; medal Govt. Press Office, Jerusalem, 1971; Christian honoree of yr. Jewish Nat. Fund of No. Calif., 1975; Hidden Heroine award San Francisco Bay coun. Girl Scouts U.S.A., 1976, Golden State award Who's Who Hist. Soc., 1988; Ben-Gurion medallion Ben-Gurion Rsch. Inst., 1977; Resolutions of Commendation, Calif. Senate Rules Com., 1978, 94, Disting. Leadership award Ch. of God Sch. of Theology, 1996; hon. fellow Bar-Ilan U., Israel, 1981; Dr. Bebe Patten Social Action chair established Bar-Ilan U., 1982. Mem. Am. Assn. for Higher Edn., Religious Edn. Assn., Am. Acad. Religion and Soc. Bibl. Lit., Zionist Orgn. Am., Am. Assn. Pres. of Ind. Colls. and Univs., Am. Jewish Hist. Soc., Am.-Isreal Pub. Affairs Com. Died Jan. 25, 2004.

PATTERSON, MARY MARVIN BRECKINRIDGE (MRS. JEFFERSON PATTERSON), photographer, writer, broadcaster; b. N.Y.C., Oct. 2, 1905; d. John Cabell and Isabella (Goodrich) Breckinridge; m. Jefferson Patterson, June 20, 1940; children: Patricia Marvin, Mark Julian (dec.).

Ed. schs. in Cannes, France, N.Y.C. and Milton, Mass.; AB, Vassar Coll., 1927; student photography, Clarence White Sch., N.Y.C., 1936; L.H.D. (hon.), Bowdoin Coll., 1975, Georgetown U., 1984; L.D. (hon.), U. Ky., 1988. European broadcaster World News Roundup Program, CBS, 1939-40. Mem. women's com. Corcoran Gallery Art, 1953—, Smithsonian Instn. Assocs., 1971—; nat. council Soc. Woman Geographers, 1972-78; mem. internat. council Folger Shakespeare Library, 1978-86. Photographer, film maker: She Goes To Vassar, Forgotten Frontier, others; contbr. articles to Town and Country; contbr. photographs in Life, others; also in: Olivia's African Diary-Cape Town to Cairo, 1932, 1980. Trustee Frontier Nursing Service, 1934, gov., 1955, nat. chmn., 1960-75, hon. chmn., 1975—; mem. founders bd. Transylvania U., Lexington, Ky., 1978-80; mem. Patterson Homestead Adv. Commn., Dayton, Ohio, 1978—; trustee Meridian House Internat., 1979-85, counselor, 1985—; mem. Dacor/Bacon House adv. com., 1985-87; bd. dirs. Internat. Student House, 1981-85; dir.-at-large Am. Assn. Mus. Vols., 1983-85, mem. adv. bd., 1985-88; mem. adv. coun. Murrow Ctr., Fletcher Sch. Law and Diplomacy, Tufts U., 1981—; mem. adv. com. J. Patterson Pk. and Mus., Md., 1983—, Dacon/Bacon House Found., 1985-88; mem. US/ICOMOS Nat. Adv. Com., 1986-89, Coun. of Friends of Waterford, Va., 1986-90; hon. chmn. cultural edn. com. Smithsonian Instn., 1987-91. Recipient award for achievements in preservation in Ky., Ohio and Maine Historic House Assn. Am., 1980, Calvert prize State of Md., 1984, Conservation award Piscataqua Garden Club of Maine, 1987, Folger award Folger Shakespeare Libr., 1989; named Outstanding Citizen State of Md., 1983, Iona House, 1990. Mem. Nat. Soc. Arts and Letters. Clubs: Colony, Cosmopolitan (N.Y.C.); Sulgrave, Am. News Women's (Washington). Died Dec. 4, 2002.

PATTON, GEORGE SMITH, retired military officer; b. Boston, Dec. 24, 1923; s. George Smith, Jr. and Beatrice Banning (Ayer) P.; m. Joanne Holbrook, June 14, 1952; children: Margaret, George, Robert, Helen, Benjamin. BS, U.S. Mil. Acad., 1946; M in Internat. Affairs, George Washington U., 1965. Commd. 2d lt. U.S. Army, 1946, advanced through grades to maj. gen., 1973; parachutist Germany, 1947-51; assigned Armor Br., 1949; instr. tank offense sect. Armored Sch., 1952-53; comdr. Co. A, 140th Tank Bn., 1953; exec. officer I, Corps Reconnaissance Bn., 1953-54; co. tactical officer dept. tactics U.S. Mil. Acad., 1954-56; officer exec. dept. U.S. Naval Acad., 1956-57; assigned Command and Gen. Staff Coll., Fort Leavenworth, Kans., 1957-58; a.d.c. comdg. gen. 7th Army and comdr. in chief U.S. Army, Europe, 1958-60; exec. officer 1st squadron 11th Armored Cav. Regt. Straubing, Germany, 1960-61; assigned Armed Forces Staff Coll. Norfolk, Va., 1961-62; assigned U.S. Army War Coll. Carlisle Barracks, Pa., 1964-65; spl. forces ops. officer Mil. Assistance Command, 1962-63; comdr. 2/81 Armor, 1st Armored Div., 1963-64; chief Mainland S.E. Asia br. Far East-Pacific div. Office Dep. Chief Staff for Mil. Ops., Dept. Army, 1965-67; chief force devel. div. U.S. Army, Vietnam, 1967-68; comdg. officer 11th Armored Cav. Regt. Vietnam, 1968-69; assigned U.S. Army Primary Helicopter Ctr., Ft. Wolters, Tex., 1969-70, Ft. Rucker, Ala., 1969-70; asst. div. comdr. for support 4th Armored div. Hdqrs. U.S. Army, Europe, 1970-71; comdt. U.S. Army Armor Sch. Fort Knox, 1971-73; dir. security assistance Hdqrs. U.S. European Command, 1973-74; comdr. Army Readiness Region, 1974-75; comdr. 2d Armored Div., 1975-77; dep. comdg. gen. U.S. VII Corps, 1977-79; dir. readiness Hdqrs. Dept. Army Materiel Devel. and Readiness Command, 1979-80; ret., 1980; owner Green Meadows Farm, Hamilton, from 1980. Owner Green Meadows Farm, Hamilton, Mass. 1980-2004; instr. history U. Md., 1960-61. Mem. West Point Fund, Alexandria, Va.; trustee Essex Agrl. and Tech. Inst., Hathorne, Mass. Decorated D.S.C. with oak leaf cluster, Silver Star with oak leaf cluster, Legion of Merit with two oak leaf clusters, D.F.C., Bronze Star with oak leaf cluster, Purple Heart; Cross of Gallantry with gold, silver and bronze stars Vietnam; Army Forces Honor medal 1st class. Mem. Assn. U.S. Army, Armor Assn., Blackhorse Assn., Ducks Unltd., N.E. Farm Bur., Legion of Valor, Am. Legion. Home: South Hamilton, Mass. Died June 27, 2004.

PAUL, COURTLAND PRICE, landscape architect, planner; b. Pasadena, Calif., Mar. 11, 1927; s. Charles Price and Ethyle Louisa (Stanyer) P.; m. Kathryn Nadine Knauss, July 5, 1947; children: Pamela Kathryn, Courtland Scott, Kimberly Carol, Robyn Annette, Sanford Elliott. AA, John Muir Coll., 1948; student, Calif. Poly. U., 1948-49. Lic. landscape architect Ariz., Nebr., Nev., Calif. Founder, sr. prin., landscape architect Peridian Group, P.C., Pasadena, 1951-96; ret., 1996. Apptd. Calif. State Bd. Landscape Architects, 1960, 1964, pres., 1964; lectr. Calif. Poly. U., Pomona, Tex. A&M U., UCLA, Orange Coast Coll. Bd. dirs. Landscape Architecture Found., 1981-85 (pres. 1983). Served with USN, 1944-46. Recipient Achievement award Calif. Landscape Contractors Assn., 1963, citation award Pasadena Beautiful Found., 1969, Landscape Architecture award of merit Calif. Garden Clubs, 1970, commendation resolution Calif. State Senate Rules Com.,1 986, Profl. of Yr. Life Mem. award, 1986, 1st outstanding svc. to industry and environ. award Long Beach/O.C., Meridian award Landscape Contractors Assn., Max Tipton Meml. award, 1993; named Man of Yr. Landscape and Irrigation mag., 1987. Fellow Am. Soc. Landscape Archs. (at-large coun. fellows); mem. Calif. Coun. Landscape Archs. (pres. 1958, Outstanding Svc. citation 1984). Home: San Juan Capistrano, Calif. Died Jan. 28, 2003.

PAUL, GABRIEL (GABE PAUL), former professional baseball club executive; b. Rochester, N.Y., Jan. 4, 1910; s. Morris and Celia (Snyder) P.; m. Mary Frances Copps, Apr. 17, 1939; children: Gabriel, Warren, Michael, Jennie Lou, Henry. Ed. pub. schs., Rochester. Reporter Rochester Democrat and Chronicle, 1926-28; publicity mgr., ticket mgr. Rochester Baseball Club, 1928-34, traveling sec., dir., 1934-36; publicity dir. Cin. Reds Baseball Club, 1937, traveling sec., 1938-50, asst. to pres., 1948-49, v.p., 1949-60, gen. mgr., 1951-60, v.p., 1949-60; v.p., gen. mgr. Houston Astros Baseball Club, 1960-61; gen. mgr. Cleve. Indians Baseball Club, 1961-63, pres., treas., 1963-72, pres., 1978-84, N.Y. Yankees, 1973-77, ret., 1984. Dir. or trustee various charitable instns. Served with inf. AUS, 1943-45. Named Major League Exec. of Yr. Sporting News, 1956, 74, Sports Exec. of Yr. Gen. Sports Time, 1956, Exec. of Yr., Braves 400 Club, 1974, Baseball Exec. Yr., Milw. Baseball Writers, 1976, Major League Exec. of Yr. UPI, 1976; recipient J. Lewis Comiskey Meml. award Chgo. chpt. Baseball Writers Assn. Am., 1961, Judge Emil Fuchs Meml. award Boston chpt., 1967, Bill Slocum award N.Y. chpt., 1975, Sports Torch of Learning award, 1976; named to Ohio Baseball Hall of Fame, 1980 Mem.: Palma Ceia Country (Tampa, Fla.), Centre Club (Tampa). Home: Tampa, Fla. Died April 26, 1998.

PAUL, JAMES MACKAY, retired otolaryngologist; b. Salt Lake City, 1918; BS, Harvard Coll., 1940; MD, Johns Hopkins U., 1943. Diplomate Am. Bd. Otolaryngology. Intern York Hosp., 1944; resident in otolaryngology Washington U. Sch. Medicine, St. Louis, 1947-48, Geisinger Meml. Hosp., Danville, Pa., 1948-50; pvt. practice Redwood City, Calif., 1950-55, Denver, 1956-58, 60-74, York, Pa., 1959-60; group practice San Gabriel Valley ENT Med. Group, Inc., Glendora, Calif., 1974-79. Home: Denver, Colo. Died Dec. 1, 1999.

PAVLOV, VALENTIN, government official; Former amb. of USSR to Benin; prime minister, 1991. Died Mar. 30, 2003.

PAYNE, VIRGINIA C. nurse educator; b. Greenville, N.C., July 23, 1949; d. Richard L. and Dora (Gurganus) Craft; m. Jim Payne, Nov. 27, 1969; 1 child, Joey. BS in Nursing, East Carolina U., Greenville, N.C., 1971, MSHE in Child Devel. and Family Rels., 1976, MS in Nursing, 1979. Mental health nurse II Wake County Mental Health Clinic, Raleigh, N.C., 1974; instr., asst. prof. East Carolina U., Greenville, 1974-79; asst. prof. Atlantic Christian Coll., Wilson, N.C., 1979-82; asst. prof., level II coord. U. N.C. at Wilmington Sch. Nursing, 1982-88; ednl. nurse specialist, coord. nursing edn. Pitt County Meml. Hosp., Greenville, from 1988. Presenter seminars and workshops on mental health topics for nurses and other profls. in N.C., Va., Washington. Contbr. articles to profl. jours. Mem. Nat. League Nursing, Am. Nurses Assn., N.C. League Nursing (pres., pres.-elect, program chair), N.C. Nurses Assn. (psychiat.-mental health div. chair, commn. on practice, ad hoc task force on credentialing, vice-chair psychiat.-mental health div., dist. pres., nominating com. baccalaureate and higher degree forum), Sigma Theta Tau (chpt. sec.) Home: Springfield, Va. Died Apr. 6, 2001.

PEACOCK, THOMAS H., JR., surgeon; b. Birmingham, Ala., Feb. 17, 1937; MD, U. Ala., 1963. Diplomate Am. Bd. Surgery. Intern U. Hosp.-Hillman Clinic, Birmingham, 1963-64, resident in gen. surgery, 1964-68; pvt. practice Birmingham, from 1968. Died Aug. 31, 1999.

PEARCE, MORTON LEE, physician, educator; b. Chgo., Aug. 22, 1920; s. James William and Lydia (Lee) P.; m. Ruth Elizabeth Schwartz, Mar. 11, 1944 (div. 1977); children—Katherine, Michael, David; m. Inger Christensen, Dec. 28, 1977. BS, U. Chgo., 1941, MD, 1944. Intern Los Angeles County Hosp., 1945, resident in medicine, 1945-48; research asso. U. Calif. at Los Angeles, 1948-51; fellow in medicine Johns Hopkins, 1951-52; instr. Vanderbilt U., 1952-53, asst. prof., 1953-56; asso. prof. U. Calif. at Los Angeles, 1956-63, prof. medicine/cardiology, 1963—86, chief of cardiology, ctr. for health sciences, 1969—75, prof. emeritus, 1986—2004; chief of cardiology Vets. Adminstrn. Hosp., Westwood, 1965—69. Cons. Rand Corp., VA Hosp., Los Angeles. Mem. Los Angeles Soc. Internal Medicine (past pres.), Am. Heart Assn. (past pres. Los Angeles affiliate), Am. Fedn. Clin. Research, Western Soc. for Clin. Research, Assn. U. Cardiologists, Western Assn. Physicians, Am. Physiol. Soc., AAAS. Research in cardiology. Died Mar. 1, 2004.

PEARINCOTT, JOSEPH VERGHESE, educator, physiologist; b. Travancore, India, May 26, 1929; s. George F. and Elizabeth (Kottakaram) P.; B.Sc., Travancore U., 1949; M.Sc., Aligarh U., 1951; Ph.D., Fordham U., 1959; m. Michaeleen Ferrara, May 1, 1958; 1 son, George Joseph. Came to U.S., 1952, naturalized, 1959. Instr. biology Fordham U., N.Y.C., 1952-56; postdoctoral fellow Columbia Coll. Physicians and Surgeons, N.Y.C., 1959-61; research asso., dept. physiology and pharmacology N.Y. Med. Coll., N.Y.C., 1961-62; asst. prof. biology Northeastern U., Boston, 1962-68, asso. prof. biology, 1968—. Mem. N.Y. Acad. Scis., AAAS, Am. Soc. Zoologists, Entomol. Soc. Am., AAUP, Sigma Xi. Home: Lexington, Mass. Deceased.

PEARSON, NATHAN WILLIAMS, investment management executive; b. N.Y.C., Nov. 26, 1911; s. James A. and Elizabeth (Williams) P.; m. Kathleen P. McMurtry, Apr. 9, 1947; children: James S. (dec.), Nathan Williams. AB, Dartmouth Coll., 1932; MBA, Harvard U., 1934; LLD, Thiel Coll., 1972. With U.S. Steel Corp., 1939-42; mgr. research Matson Navigation Co., 1946-47; controller Carborundum Co., 1947-48; with T. Mellon and Sons, Pitts., 1948-70, v.p., gov., 1957-70; chmn., chief exec. officer, chmn. emeritus Mellon Bank N.A. & Mellon Bank Corp., Pitts., from 1987. Fin. exec. for Paul Mellon, 1948-99. Chmn. Pitts. Theol. Sem., 1987. Served from lt. (j.g.) to comdr. USNR, 1942-46. Mem. Allegheny Country Club, Harvard-Yale Princeton Club, Duquesne Club, Edgeworth Club, Rolling Rock Club (Ligonier, Pa.). Republican. Presbyterian. Home: Sewickley, Pa. Died June 11, 2002.

PEARSON, RUDOLPH W. otolaryngology; b. Newport, R.I., July 27, 1906; MD, Tufts Univ., 1931. Intern Jersey City Medical Ctr., 1931, resident ob-gyn, 1931-32. Fellow Am. Acad. Otolaryngology Head & Neck Surgery. Home: Sarasota, Fla. Died Oct. 14, 1999.

PEASE, DONALD JAMES, former congressman, political educator; b. Toledo, Sept. 26, 1931; s. Russell Everett and Helen Mary (Mullen) P.; m. Jeanne Camille Wendt, Aug. 29, 1953; 1 child, Jennifer. BS in Journalism, Ohio U., Athens, 1953, MA in Govt., 1955; Fulbright scholar, Kings Coll., U. Durham, Eng., 1954-55. Mem. Ohio Senate, 1965-66, 75-76, Ohio Ho. of Reps., 1969-74, 95th to 102nd Congresses from 13th Ohio Dist., 1977-92; vis. Disting. prof. politics Oberlin Coll., from 1993. Chmn. Oberlin (Ohio) Pub. Utilities Commn., 1960-61; mem. Oberlin City Council, 1961-63. Served with AUS, 1955-57. Home: Oberlin, Ohio. Died July 28, 2002.

PEASE, SARA GOODING, lay worker; b. Berlin, N.H., Nov. 12, 1918; d. Willard Merrill and Dorothy Quincy (Gay) Gooding; m. Donald Frederick Pease; children: Nancy Gay (dec.), Janet Meserve Pease Moore, Marcia Merrill Pease Lebhar. B in Religious Communications, George Mason U., 1987. Pres. Ch. Women United Frederick (Md.) County, 1981-82; ctr. assoc. Lancaster (Pa.) Theol. Sem., 1985-91. Mem. task force Frederick Sch. Religion, 1984-90; sec. fellowship of faiths Mt. Holyoke Coll., South Hadley, Mass., 1937-38; mem. ministerial com. Hospice of Frederick County, 1983-84. Contbg. author: Advent Devotionals, 1981; editor newsletter Covenant Call, 1975-77, Ch. Women United in Frederick County, 1982, Ch. Woman in Md., 1988-90; contbr. articles, litany in field. Sherman scholar Mt. Holyoke Coll., 1936-39, Charles Merrill Smith scholar Ill. Wesleyan U. Writer's Conf., 1986. Mem. Nat. Assn. Parliamentarians (profl. registered parliamentarian 1968-91), LWV (dir. Frederick County chpt. 1980-81). Presbyterian. Home: Newville, Pa. Died Feb. 21, 2002.

PECK, GREGORY (ELDRED GREGORY PECK), actor; b. La Jolla, Calif., Apr. 5, 1916; m. Greta Rice, 1942 (div. 1949); m. Veronique Passani, 1955; 5 children. Student, U. Calif. Founder, prodr. La Jolla Playhouse, 1947-52. Actor: (plays) various productions at Neighborhood Playhouse, N.Y.C., broadway debut, 1942; (films) Days of Glory, 1944, The Keys of the Kingdom, 1944, The Valley of Decision, 1945, Spellbound, 1945, The Yearling, 1946 (Golden Globe award best actor, 1947), Duel in the Sun, 1946, The Macomber Affair, 1947, Gentlemen's Agreement, 1947, The Paradine Case, 1947, Yellow Sky, 1949, The Great Sinner, 1949, Twelve O'Clock High, 1949 (NY Film Critics Circle award best actor, 1950), The Gunfighter, 1950, Captain Horatio Hornblower, 1951, Only the Valiant, 1951, David and Bathsheba, 1951, The Snows of Kilamanjaro, 1952, The World in His Arms, 1952, Roman Holiday, 1953, The Million Pound Note, 1953, Boum sur Paris, 1954, Night People, 1954, The Purple Plain, 1954, The Man in the Gray Flannel Suit, 1956, Moby Dick, 1956, Designing Woman, 1957, The Bravados, 1958, Pork Chop Hill, 1959, Beloved Infidel, 1959, On The Beach, 1959, The Guns of Navarone, 1961, To Kill a Mockingbird, 1962 (Acad. award best actor, 1963, Golden Globe best actor, 1963), Cape Fear, 1962, How the West Was Won, 1962, Captain Newman, M.D, 1963, Behold a Pale Horse, 1964, Mirage, 1965, Arabesque, 1966, Mackenna's Gold, 1969, The Chairman, 1969, The Stalking Moon, 1969, Marooned, 1969, I Walk the Line, 1970, Shoot Out, 1971, Billy Two Hats, 1974, The Omen, 1976, MacArthur, 1977, The Boys From Brazil, 1978, Sea Wolves: The Last Charge of the Calcutta Light Horse, 1980, Amazing Grace and Chuck, 1987, Old Gringo, 1989, Cape Fear, 1991, Other People's Money, 1991, (voice) The Art of Norton Simon, 1999, The Story of Joseph Smith, 2000; actor, prodr.: The Big Country, 1958; prodr.: The Trial of the Catonsville Nine, 1972, The Dove, 1974; actor: (TV films) The Blue and the Gray, 1982, The Scarlet and the Black, 1983, Moby Dick, 1998 (Golden Globe award best sup. actor, 1999); actor, exec. prodr.: The Portrait, 1993; voice: (TV miniseries) Baseball, 1994; rec.: (audio cassette) The New Testament, 1985-86. Chmn. Am. Cancer Soc., 1966, chmn. Motion Picture & TV Relief Fund, 1971, hon. chair. LA Library Foundation, 1995. Recipient Jean Hersholt Humanitarian award, 1967, Golden Laurel award, 1967, Cecil B. Demille award Hollywood Fgn. Press, 1969, Presdl. Medal of Freedom, 1969, Life Achievement award SAG, 1971, Life Achievement award Am. Film Inst., 1989, Career award Cannes Film Festival, 1989, Bd. of Govs. award Am. Soc. of Cinematographers, 1990, Kennedy Ctr. Honors, 1991, Lifetime Achievement award Lincoln Ctr., N.Y.C., 1992, Legion d'Honneur, France, 1993. Mem. Acad. Motion Picture Arts and Scis. (pres., 1967-70), Am. Film Inst. (founding chmn. bd. trustees, 1967-69), Nat. Council on the Arts, 1964-66, 68-74. Died June 12, 2003.

PEDEN, ROBERT F., JR., retired lawyer; b. Ft. Worth, July 26, 1911; s. Robert F. and Laura (Phillips) P.; LLB, Cumberland U., 1933; m. Virginia LeTulle, May 25, 1939.

Bar: Tex. 1934; practice law, Bay City, 1934-91; ret. 1991; city atty., Bay City, 1935-38, 65-79; county atty. Matagorda County, Tex., 1939-46, 50-54. Bd. dirs. Bay City Library Assn., 1969-88; pres. men. of ch. South Tex. Presbytery, 1959. Mem. ABA, Am. Judicature Soc., State Bar Tex., Matagorda County Bar Assn. (pres. 1961-62, v.p. 1967-69), Lambda Chi Alpha. Presbyterian (clk. session 1969-71, elder 1969—). Rotarian (v.p. 1968-69, pres. 1969-70). Club: Knife and Fork (dir. 1968-69, pres. 1970-71). Home: Bay City, Tex. Died 2003.

PEKER, LEON KAUFMAN, nuclear physicist, consultant; b. Winniza, Ukraine, Apr. 3, 1929; came to U.S., 1976; s. Kaufman-Aron Leiser and Polin Aron (Derbaremdiker) P.; m. Nina Moses Rabinovich, Apr. 25, 1958; 1 child, Mark Leon. MA in Physics, Leningrad U., 1952; PhD in Physics-Math., Physiko-Tech. Inst., Leningrad, 1956; DSc in Physics-Math., Kharkov (Russia) U., 1966. Tchr. physics, Leningrad, 1952-54; nuc. scientist Libr. of Acad. of Sci., Leningrad, 1954-56; sr. scientist Leningrad U., 1956-66; chmn. dept. nuc. physics Metrological Inst., Leningrad, 1966-76; prof. Amsterdam (The Netherlands) Free U., 1976-78; sr. physicist Brookhaven Nat. Lab., Upton, N.Y., 1978-94. Adj. prof. Vanderbilt U., Nashville, 1981—. Contbr. over 270 articles to profl. jours. Mem. Am. Phys. Soc. Home: Monsey, NY. Died Aug. 1, 2000.

PELLETIER, S. WILLIAM, chemistry educator; b. Kankakee, Ill., July 3, 1924; s. Anthony Amos and Estella Edith (Hays) P.; m. Leona Jane Bledsoe, June 18, 1949; children: William Timothy, Jonathan Daniel, Rebecca Jane, Lucy Ruth, David Mark, Sarah Lynn. BS in Chem. Engring. with highest honors, U. Ill., 1947; PhD in Organic Chemistry, Cornell U., 1950. Instr. chemistry U. Ill., 1950-51; mem. staff Rockefeller Inst., 1951-62, assoc. prof. organic chemistry, 1961-62; prof. chemistry, head dept. U. Ga., 1962-69, Alumni Found. disting. prof., 1969—, provost, 1969-76, Univ. prof., 1976—; dir. Inst. for Natural Products Research, 1976—. Gordon lectr., New Hampton, N.H., 1955, 59, 69; lectr. German Acad. Agrl. Scis., 1959; Am. Swiss Found. lectr., Zurich, Basel, Bern, Geneva, Switzerland, 1960; Commemorative dedication lectr. Shionogi Rsch. Lab., Osaka, Japan, 1961; Victor Coulter lectr. U. Miss., 1965; Nason-Piston lectr. Boston Pub. Libr., 1982; Plenary lectr. 32d Internat. Congress on Medicinal Plant Rsch., Antwerp, Belgium, 1984; lectr. for internat. symposia in Berlin, Melbourne, Hong Kong, Latvia, Prague, Stockholm, London, Riga, Latvia, Varna, Bulgaria, Istanbul, Turkey, Cairo also other lectures in Eng., Italy, India, Israel, Taiwan, Japan; mem. health medicinal chemistry study panel NIH, 1968-72. Author: Chemistry of the Alkaloids, 1970, 7 monograms on am. etcher John Taylor Arms, 1975—93, Alkaloids: Chemical and Biological Perspectives vols. 1-15, 1983—2001, catalog of etchings of Charles Meryon and Jean-Francois Millet, 1994, Adriaen van Ostade, Etchings of Peasant Life in Holland's Golden Age, 1994, From Rembrandt and his Studio: Two Paintings from the Bader Collection, 1998, Everyday Life in Holland's Golden Age: The Complete Etchings of Adriaen van Ostade, 1998, Sir Muirhead Bone: His Etched and Drypointed Portraits and Figure Studies, 1999; mem. editl. bd.: Jour. Organic Chemistry, 1966—70, Heterocycles, from 1979, Jour. Natural Products, 1980—2001, Phytochem. Analysis, 1989—99, Trends in Heterocyclic Chemistry, 1994, Recent Rsch. Devel. in Heterocyclic Chemistry, 1994, Turkish Jour. Chemistry, from 1996; contbr. articles to profl. jours. Pres. bd. Flushing Christian Day Sch., 1956-60; bd. advisers Ga. Mus. Art, 1968—; bd. dirs. Center for Research Libraries, Chgo., 1975-81. With USNR, 1944-46. Fellow AAAS, Royal Soc. Arts (London), Royal Soc. Chemistry (London); mem. Am. Chem. Soc. (chmn. N.E. Ga. sect. 1968, Charles Herty medal 1971, So. Chemists award 1972), Am. Soc. Pharmacognosy (hon. life, Rsch. Achievement award 1991, v.p. 2000, pres. 2001), Worldwide Discipleship Assn. (bd. dirs. 1980-88), Sigma Xi, Phi Eta Sigma, Tau Beta Pi, Sigma Tau. Presbyn. (elder). Achievements include research in structure and stereochemistry diterpenoid alkaloids, applications of carbon-13 nuclear magnetic resonance to structure determination, synthesis of terpenes, X-ray crystallographic structures of natural products. Home: Athens, Ga. Died Feb. 21, 2004.

PENCE, LELAND HADLEY, organic chemist; b. Kearney, Mo., Oct. 1, 1911; s. Samuel Anderson and Rosa Louise (Reid) P.; m. Mary Ellen Elliott, Aug. 6, 1938; children: Jean, Daniel, Elizabeth. BS, U. Fla., 1932; MS, U. Mich., 1933, PhD, 1937. Teaching fellow U. Mich. Dept. Chemistry, Ann Arbor, 1933-37; organic rsch. chemist Biochem. Rsch. Found. of Franklin Inst., Phila., 1937-39; instr. Reed Coll., Portland, Oreg., 1939-42, asst. prof., 1942-45; sr. scientist Difco Labs., Inc., Detroit, 1945-83. Organic rsch. chemist Mayo Clinic, Rochester, Minn., summer 1940; rsch. fellow Calif. Inst. Tech., Pasadena, 1943. Author: Phytohemagglutinin Preparations, 1962; co-contbr. articles to jour. Am. Chem. Soc. Active Tax Rev. Bd., Ferndale, Mich., 1990—; trustee Presbyn. Ch., 1969-75, 1978-81. Fellow AAAS; mem. Am. Chem. Soc. (emeritus, Detroit exec. bd. 1950-52, cert.), Tissue Culture Assn., Audubon Soc., Sierra Club, Nature Conservancy, Wilderness Soc., World Wildlife Fund, Nat. Wildlife Fedn., Circumnavigators Club, Detroit Econs. Club, Sigma Xi, Kappa Kappa Psi. Achievements include research on the preparation of pure carcinogenic hydrocarbons and their derivatives, estrogens, bile acids, steroids, sulfanilamide reagents, cardiolipin, lecithin, cholesterol, serological reagents, fluorescent antibodies, phytohemagglutinin, mitogens, chromosome reagents, lectins, immunochemistry, tissue culture, monoclonal antibodies. Home: Ferndale, Mich. Died Oct. 30, 2002.

PENNING, JOHN RUSSELL, JR., research engineer; b. Spokane, Wash., Dec. 13, 1922; s. John Russell Sr. and Mildred Evelyn (Clark) P.; m. Dorothy June Benn, Dec. 20, 1960 (dec. Jan. 1975); m. Hak Sun Kim, June 7, 1975; 1 child, Flora Meehwa. BS, U. Wash., 1948, PhD, 1956. Research scientist Space Tech. Labs., Los Angeles, 1956-59; research engr. Northrop Corp., Newbury Park, Calif., 1963-65; research scientist Boeing Co., Seattle, 1959-63, 65-91; retired, 1991. Contbr. articles to profl. jours. Served as sgt. USAF, 1942-45, ETO. Mem. Am. Phys. Soc., Phi Beta Kappa, Sigma Xi. Home: Federal Way, Wash. Died Feb. 27, 2002.

PEO, ROGER EDWIN, therapist, educator, engineer; b. Rochester, N.Y., Feb. 23, 1936; s. Horace Edwin and Florence May (Webb) P.; m. Judith Ann Briskie, Apr. 4, 1959 (div. June 1979); children: Melissa Ann, Christine Beth; m. Victoria King Powell, Aug. 31, 1985. BS, Clarkson U., 1957; PhD, Inst. Advanced Study of Human Sexuality, 1984. Cert. sex counselor, cert. sexologist. Electronics engr. Stromberg-Carlson, 1957-58; physicist Bausch & Lomb, 1959-60; physicist, engr. Hamilton Standard, 1961; mgr. IBM, 1969-81, sr. engr., from 1961; pvt. practice therapist/educator Poughkeepsie, from 1983. Profl. advisor Metamorphosis Med. Rsch. Found., 1984-88; profl. cons. human sexuality spl. interest group CompuServ Network, 1985—; profl. cons. Tri Ess, 1985—; mem. adv. com. Renaissance Edn. Assn., Inc., 1989—; mem. Transgender World Bull. Bd., Delphi Computer Network, Am. Sexology Spl. Interest Group, 1985-86; mem. Dutchess County Youth Bur., Adolescent Health and Sexualty Consortium, 1986—; presentations various orgns., media, workshops and seminars. Profl. advisor, columnist TV-TS Tapestry mag., 1984—; contbr. articles to profl. jours. Mem. task force for edn. in human sexuality N.Y. Ann. Conf. United Meth. Ch., 1975-84; founding mem., fin. chmn., pres. bd. dirs. Meals on Wheels of Great Poughkeepsie, 1970-81; choir mem., fin. chmn., youth leader Trinity United Meth. Ch.; bd. dris. Internat. Found. Gender Edn., 1987—, chmn. publs. com., 1987—. 2d lt. Signal Corps U.S. Army, 1958. Mem. IEEE, Am. Bd. Sexology, Am. Coll. Sexologists, Assn. Sexologists, Sex Info. and Edn. Coun. U.S., Soc. Sci. Study Sex, Harry Benjamin Internat. Gender Dysphoria Assn. Died Feb. 2, 1995.

PEOPLES, JAMES BLAIR, surgeon, educator; b. Altoona, Pa., Feb. 13, 1945; s. Don Miguel and Beverly Jane (Yingling) P.; m. Charlotte Virginia Fretz, May 27, 1967 (div. 1977); 1 child, Jessica Lynn; m. Kathleen Terry, Aug. 30, 1977. AB, Franklin and Marshall Coll., 1967; MD, NYU, 1971. Diplomate Am. Bd. Surgery. Intern U. Pitts., 1971-72, resident in surgery, 1972-77; asst. prof. surgery Wright State U., Dayton, Ohio, 1979-85, assoc. prof., 1985-89, prof., chair, from 1990, dir. surg. techs. lab., 1980-90. Surg. cons. USAF Hosp., Dayton, 1980—; coord. surg. edn. Good Samaritan Hosp., Dayton, 1983-89. Contbr. articles to profl. jours. Recipient Resident's award Pitts. Surg. Soc., 1976. Fellow ACS (Resident's award S.W. Pa. chpt. 1976); mem. Soc. Surgery of Alimentary Tract, Midwest Surg. Assn., Ctrl. Surg. Assn., Phi Beta Kappa, Alpha Omega Alpha. Republican. Lutheran. Avocations: model railroading, gardening, cooking, wine. Home: Dayton, Ohio. Died July 19, 2002.

PEPITONE, BYRON VINCENT, former government official; b. New Brunswick, N.J., June 9, 1918; s. Joseph James and Sarah Frances (Byron) P.; m. Marolynn Mary Mills, June 9, 1940; children: Byron II, James S. Student, U.S. Army Command and Gen. Staff Coll., 1944, Air. U. Air Command and Staff Coll., 1950, NATO Def. Coll., 1955. Commd. 2d lt. USAAF, 1942; advanced through grades to col. USAF, 1953; ret., 1970; dep. dir. SSS, Washington, 1970-72, acting dir., 1972-73, dir., 1973-77; ret., 1977. Decorated D.S.M., Legion of Merit with 2 oak leaf clusters, USAF Commendation medal, U.S. Army Commendation medal with oak leaf cluster; recipient Distinguished Service medal SSS, 1972 Mem. USAF Assn. Home: Palm City, Fla. Died Sept. 11, 2003.

PEPLOW, RICHARD CHARLES, librarian; b. Chgo., Mar. 10, 1950; s. Raymond Albert and Ruth Elizabeth (Hegstrom) P. BS, Ill. State U., 1974; MLS, Rosary Coll., 1988. Cataloger, libr. binding asst. Newberry Libr., Chgo., 1975-85; asst. libr. Schiff, Hardin & Waite, Chgo., 1985-87; tech. svcs. libr. Boston Cons. Group, Chgo., 1987-89; cataloger C. Berger & Co., Carol Stream, Ill., 1989; tech. svcs. libr. Ameritech Information Systems, Chgo., from 1989. Tenor 1 Chgo. Symphony Chorus, 1968-69, 80-83, Grant Park Symphony Chorus, Chgo., 1979-82, William Ferris Chorale, Chgo., 1978-79. Recipient Grammy awards for recordings by Chgo. Symphony Chorus, 1981, 82, 83, Margaret Hillis Fellowship, Margaret Hillis Fellowship Fund for Study of Voice, Chgo., 1981, 82, 83. Mem. ALA, Special Librs. Assn., Chgo. Assn. Law Librs., Nat. Assn. Recording Arts (voting mem.), Nat. Wildlife Fedn., Assn. Rsch. and Enlightenment. Lutheran. Home: Sherrard, Ill. Deceased.

PERHAM, ROY GATES, artist; b. Paterson, N.J., Apr. 18, 1916; s. Roy Gates and Alice Jeannette (Parsons) P.; m. Titania Joan Robbitts, Mar. 10, 1956; 1 child, Roy Gates 3d. Student, Grand Central Art Sch., N.Y.C., 1936-37. Instr. portrait painting Englewood Adult Sch.; lectr. in field. Work represented Diocesan Coll., McGill U., Montreal, Can., South Jersey Coll., Rutgers U., The Conf. Bd., N.Y.C., Peninsula Gen. Hosp. Salisbury, Md., Plimoth Plantation, Plymouth, Mass., Centreal Coll., Pella, Iowa, Felician Coll., Lodi, N.J., Americana Collection, U. S.C.; portrait of former U.S. Sec. of State Edmund S. Muskie, 1986, protrait for Franlkin Delano Roosevelt Jr., 1989, portrait of Senator William S. Cohen, 1993. Sec., chmn. Hasbrouck Heights (N.J.) Juvenile Conf. Com., 1967-85; mem. Rent Leveling Bd., Hasbrouck Heights, 1980—. Mem.: Lions (pres. 1966-67, zone chmn. 1974-75, Hasbrouck Heights club). Deceased.

PERKES, DANIEL, news agency executive; b. Bklyn., Feb. 17, 1931; s. A. and Edith (Sherman) P.; m. Norma Jean O'Mary, Dec. 6, 1952; children: Kimberly, Daniel. BA in Journalism, Tex. Tech U., 1957. Part-time reporter Amarillo (Tex.) Globe-News, 1952-54; reporter Lubbock (Tex.) Avalanche, 1954-57; with AP, 1957, chief bur., 1964-67, Iowa-Nebr., 1967-69; gen. exec. AP Newsfeatures, N.Y.C., 1969-78; asst. gen. mgr. AP, 1978. Author: Eyewitness to Disaster, 1976, Shipwreck, 1983; Editor-in-chief: AP Sports Almanac, 1974-77, AP News Annual, 1969-77, Century of Sports, 1971, Century of Champions, 1976. Served with USAF, 1950-54. Mem. Assn. Sunday and Feature Editors, Sigma Delta Chi. Clubs: N.Y. Athletic, Masons. Died Apr. 27, 2004.

PERKINS, JAMES WINSLOW, international business consultant, builder, contractor; b. Southington, Conn., Sept. 15, 1955; s. Robert Winslow and Florence Corinne (Angelone) P. Student, Tunxis C.C., Farmington, Conn., 1973-75. Owner Town & Country Club, Smithfield, R.I., 1975-80, Ad Mark of Mass, Inc., Ludlow, Mass., 1980-84, Car Stereo Distbrs., Inc., West Palm Beach, Fla., 1983-85, Internat. Imports, Lauderdale Lakes, Fla., 1985-88, Modern Sectional Homes, Inc., Southington, Conn., 1989-93. Mem. Nat. Assn. Realtors, Cen. Conn. Bd. Realtors, Mayflower Soc., 100 Club Conn. Republican. Avocations: sailing, water skiing. Home: Marion, Conn. Died 2002.

PETERKIN, ALBERT GORDON, retired education educator; b. Phila., May 25, 1915; s. Albert Gordon and Eleanor Frances (Fricke) P.; m. Helen Webster, June 14, 1947; children: Eleanor Fricke, Scott Boddington, Mark Webster. BA, U. Pa., 1936; MAT, Harvard U., 1946; EdD, Columbia U., 1954. Cert. sch. adminstr., N.J., Conn., Ill. Tchr. Arms Acad., Shelburne Falls, Mass., 1938-39, Park Sch. of Buffalo, Snyder, N.Y., 1939-41; asst. prof. Lehigh U., Bethlehem, Pa., 1948-55; founding supt. Watchung Hills Regional H.S., Warren, N.J., 1955-60; supt. Westport (Conn.) Pub. Schs., 1960-70, Winnetka (Ill.) Sch. Dist. 36, 1971-77; prof. edn. Vanderbilt U., Nashville, 1977-81; ret., 1981. Cons. Nat. Assn. Sch. Bus. Officers, Washington, 1968-70, Tenn. State U., Nashville, 1980-81; advisor Coun. Basic Edn., Washington, 1975; trustee Country Sch., Madison, Conn., 1985-91; chmn. master's program Iranian Sch. Devel., 1978-80, assessment instrument student devel., 1974; initiator Cooperative Individualized Reading Project, U.S. Office Edn., 1970-73. Initiator Urban Coalition Sch. Study, Bridgeport, Conn., 1969-70; pres. Friends of Libr., Madison, 1984-85; prodr. cmty. TV, Madison, 1984-90; mem. Madison Inland Wetlands Commn., 1985—, chmn., 1990-92. Lt. comdr. USNR, 1941-45. John Hay fellow Greenwood Found., 1965; Kettering Found. fellow, 1966, 69; Whitehead fellow Harvard Sch. Edn., 1970-71; named to Supt.'s Hall of Fame Sch. Mgmt. Study Group, 1973. Mem. Am. Assn. Sch. Adminstrs., Suburban Sch. Supts., Madison Beach Club, Phi Delta Kappa. Mem. Religious Soc. of Friends. Avocations: garden design, travel, home video, golf, music. Home: North Branford, Conn. Died Oct. 27, 2002.

PETERS, ALTON EMIL, lawyer; b. Albany, N.Y., Mar. 21, 1935; s. Emil and Winifred (Rosch) P.; m. Elizabeth Irving Berlin, Feb. 27, 1970; children: Rachel Canfield, Emily Anstice Fletcher. AB cum laude, Harvard U., 1955, Ll.B., 1958. Bar: N.Y. 1958, U.S. Dist. Ct. (so. dist.) N.Y. 1963. Assoc. Bleakley, Platt, Schmidt & Fritz, 1959-65, mem., 1956-81; ptnr. Miller, Montgomery, Sogi & Brady, 1981-83, Kelley Drye & Warren, N.Y.C., 1983—. Bd. dirs. Am. Friends of Covent Garden and the Royal Ballet, N.Y.C., 1971—, v.p., 1971—; mem. coun. Am. Mus. in Britain, Bath, Eng., 1970—, chmn. U.S.A., 1975-92; bd. dirs. Brit. Am. Arts Assn., N.Y.C., 1983—, chmn., 1984—; bd. dirs. N.Y. br. English-Speaking Union U.S., 1963-97, chmn., 1972-88; bd. dirs. Goodwill Industries of Greater N.Y., 1965—, pres., 1970-82, chmn., 1982—; mng. dir. Met. Opera Assn., N.Y.C., 1966—, sec., 1974-86, v.p., 1986-93, chmn. Exec. Com., 1993—; bd. dirs. Met. Opera Guild, Inc., N.Y.C., 1965—, chmn. exec. com., 1968-70, 74-79, 1st v.p., 1979-86, pres., 1986—; bd. dirs. Lincoln Ctr. for Performing Arts, N.Y.C., 1986—; trustee Signet Assocs., Cambridge, Mass., 1957-73, treas., 1957-73, hon. trustee, 1973—; Coun. Fellows Pierpont Morgan Libr., 1995—, vice chmn., 1996—, fellow Frick Collection; trustee Acad. Am. Poets, N.Y.C., 1988—, treas., 1993—; trustee Cathedral of St. John the Divine, 1991-95. Decorated Knight Order of St. John of Jerusalem, Officer Order of Brit. Empire. Mem. ABA, N.Y. State Bar Assn., Assn. of Bar of City of N.Y., Am. Judicature Soc., Am. Coll. Probate Counsel, Century Assn., Church Club, Grolier Club (coun. 1994—), Harvard Club N.Y.C., Knickerbocker Club (bd. govs. 1986-92, 94-98), Pilgrims Club of Odd Volumes. Home: New York, NY. Died 30 May, 1999.

PETERS, THOMAS ROBERT, English language educator, writer; b. Detroit, Nov. 14, 1929; s. Norman Addison and Eleanor H. (Schneider) P.; m. Lillian J. Tremonti, Aug. 21, 1954; children: Jennifer Leigh Hartman, Thomas R. Jr., Sarah Jeanne. BA, Hillsdale Coll., 1954; MA, Wayne State U., 1963. Screen writer Jam Handy Film Prodns., Detroit, 1956-59; secondary tchr. English, Detroit Pub. Schs., 1960-69; edn. coord. Detroit Free Press, 1969-72; mgr. pub. rels. Blue Cross, Blue Shield Mich., Detroit, 1972-86; prof.

English Macomb C.C, Warren, Mich., 1986-95, Ctr. for Creative Studies, Detroit, from 1998. Guest speaker Mich. Schs. and Colls., 1970—. Author: (novels) Education of Tom Webber, 1977, Two Weeks in the Forties, 1988 (Opus Magnum award 1996), Selected Works, 1995, (with others) The Third Coast: Contemporary Michigan Fiction, 1982, (play) Mensa Meeting, 1987; contbr. numerous stories, articles and poems to nat. mags., anthologies; writer several published speeches. Bd. dirs. Friends of Grosse Pointe Librs., 1978-84. With U.S. Army, 1948-49; U.S. Army Res. 1950-55. Recipient Alumni Achievement award in Literature Hillsdale Coll., 1993; grantee: Grosse Pointe Found., 1978, Utica Community Schs., 1989. Mem. Fine Arts Soc. Detroit (pres. 1978-79). Roman Catholic. Avocations: pianist, actor, tennis player. Home: Grosse Pointe, Mich. Died July 21, 2000.

PETERSON, JOHN EDWARD, minister; b. Seattle, Aug. 12, 1953; s. Wilbur Glen and Donna Jean (Nielsen) P.; m. Judith Arlene Coleman, Dec. 19, 1975; children: Bjorn Karl, Christine Anna, Joel Thomas. BA in Polit. Sci., Bethel Coll., 1976; MDiv. in Ch. History, Bethel Theol. Sem., 1980, D of Ministry, 1993. Ordained min. Bapt. Ch., 1982. Pastor Bethel Bapt. Ch., Hartford, Conn., 1980-83, Ord, Nebr., 1983-98, 1st Bapt. Ch., La Crescento, Calif., from 1998. Chmn. bd. trustees Great Plains Bapt. Conf., Omaha, 1990-92; trustee S.W. Bapt. Conf., 1999—; bd. regents Bethel Coll. and Sem., St. Paul, 1990-95. Unit commr. Boy Scouts Am., Ord, 1988-95; pres. Ord Twp. Libr. Found., 1995-97; moderator, Great Plains Bapt. Conf., Omaha, 1995-96; bd. overseers Heartland Bapt. Dist., 1996-98. Mem. Am. Soc. Ch. History. Republican. Home: Glendale, Calif. Died Feb. 12, 2001.

PETERSON, LESLIE ERNEST, bishop; b. Noranda, Que., Can., Nov. 4, 1928; s. Ernest Victor and Blanche (Marsh) P.; m. Yvonne Hazel Lawton, July 16, 1953; children— Shauna Peterson Van Hoof, Tom, Jennifer Peterson Glage, Kathryn Peterson Scott, Jonathan BA, U. Western Ont., London, Ont., Can., 1952; L.T.H., Huron Coll., London, Ont., Can., 1954, D.D. (hon.), 1984; tchr.'s cert., North Bay Tchrs. Coll., Ont., 1970. Ordained to ministry Anglican Ch., 1954. Priest Diocese of Algoma, Coniston, Ont., 1954-58, priest Elliot Lake, Ont., 1959-63, rural dean, 1961-63, priest North Bay, 1963-78, Parry Sound, Ont., 1978-83, archdeacon, 1980-83, bishop Sault Ste. Marie, Ont., 1983-94; tchr. North Bay Elem. Sch., 1970-78; ret., 1994. Anglican. Avocations: canoeing, woodworking, gardening. Died July 25, 2002.

PETERSON, PAUL QUAYLE, retired university dean, physician; b. Marissa, Ill., June 30, 1912; s. Charles Logan and Phoebe (Lewis) P.; m. Kathryn Lentz, Aug. 1936; children— Philip Lewis, Frances Anne; m. Mildred Cook Allison, Dec. 7, 1957; foster children— Patricia Elaine Allison, Susan Claire Allison. BS, U. Ill., 1933, MD, 1937; MPH, U. Mich., 1946. Diplomte Am. Bd. Preventive Medicine (service mem., vice chmn. 1976—). Intern Bethesda Hosp., Cin., 1936-37; gen. resident Meml. Hosp., Lima, Ohio, 1937-38; gen. practice medicine McLeansboro, Ill., 1939-40; practice medicine specializing in preventive medicine, 1940-46; health officer, 1940-41, Warren, Simpson and Allen counties, 1942-45; regional cons., div. local health Ky. Health Dept., 1946-47; chief bur. direct services, asst. to dir. Ohio Dept. Health, 1948-51; asst. prof. preventive medicine Ohio State U., 1948-51; chief health div. Mut. Security Mission to China, Taipei, Taiwan, 1952-53; chief health and sanitation div. USOM (asso. states Cambodia, Laos and Vietnam), 1954; chief program services, div. internat. health USPHS, Washington, 1955, chronic disease program, 1957; asst. dir. Nat. Inst. Allergy and Infectious Diseases, NIH, 1958-61; dep. chief div. pub. health methods Office Surgeon Gen., 1961-62, chief div., 1962-64; asst. surgeon gen. USPHS, 1964, asso. chief bur. state services (community health), 1964-67; dep. dir. Bur. Health Services, 1967-68; asso. adminstr. Health Services and Mental Health Adminstrn., 1968-70; dep. surgeon gen., 1970; dean Grad. Sch. Pub. Health, U. Ill., Chgo., 1971-82, dean emeritus, from 1982; dir. office rsch. Ctr. Study Patient Care, U. Ill. Med. Ctr., 1979-86. Dir. Ill. Dept. Pub. Health, 1977-79, Am. Bur. Med. Aid to China; mem. residency rev. com. Liaison Com. Grad. Med. Edn., 1976—; cons. Ctr. for Health Services Research, 1982— Mem. editorial bd. Pub. Health Service World, Mil. Medicine. Commr. USPHS, 1941. Recipient Disting. Service award U. Ill. Alumni Assn., 1984 Fellow Am. Pub. Health Assn. (chmn. program area com. pub. health adminstrn.); mem. Am. Assn. Pub. Health Physicians (pres. 1975-76), AMA (interspity. adv. bd. 1975-77), Assn. Schs. Pub. Health (exec. com. 1975—), Pub. Health Service Commd. Officers Assn. (sec. D.C. 1959), AAAS, Assn. Mil Surgeons, Am. Coll. Preventive Medicine (regent 1975—), Ill. Hosp. Assn. (exec. bd. 1974-77, cert. correctional health com. of profl. cert. bd. 1990), Nat. Inst. of Health Alumni Assn. (bd. dirs., 1993—, Alumni award 1999), U. Ill. Pres. Club, U. Ill. Pres. Coun., Phi Beta Pi (pres. 1935), Delta Omega. Methodist. Home: Arlington, Va. Deceased.

PETERSON, RUDOLPH A. banker; b. Svenljunga, Sweden, Dec. 6, 1904; s. Aaron and Anna (Johannson) P.; m. Patricia Price, 1927 (dec. 1960); children: Linnea Peterson Bennett, R. Price; m. Barbara Welser Lindsay, Dec. 25, 1962; stepchildren: Robert I. Lindsay, Lorna Lindsay, Anne Lindsay, Margaret Lindsay. BS in Commerce, U. Calif., 1925, LLD, 1968; LHD, U. Redlands, 1967. With Comml. Credit Co., 1925-36, successively asst. mgr., v.p., gen. mgr. Mexico City, div. operations mgr. Chgo.; dist. mgr. Bank Am. Nat. Trust & Savs. Assn., Fresno, Calif., 1936-41, v.p. San Francisco, 1941-46; pres., chief exec. officer Allied Bldg. Credits, 1946-52; v.p. Transam. Corp., San Francisco, 1952-55; pres., chief exec. officer Bank of Hawaii, Honolulu, 1956-61; pres., CEO BankAm. Corp., San Francisco, 1961-70, chmn. exec. com., 1970-76, also dir., 1968-98; adminstr. UN Devel. Programme, 1971-76. Bd. dirs. Alza Corp., Asia Found.; chmn. Euro Can. Bank, 1982-94; adminstr. UN Devel. Programme, 1972-76. Mem. adv. coun. Calif. Acad. Scis. Decorated Grand Cross of Civil Merit Spain; Order of Merit Italy; named Swedish-Am. of Year Vasa Order, 1965; U. Calif. Alumnus of Year, 1968; recipient Capt. Robert Dollar Meml. award for contbn. to advancement Am. fgn. trade, 1970, Chancellor's award U. Calif., 1992, Great Swedish Heritage award, 1996. Mem.: Bohemian (San Francisco), Pacific-Union (San Francisco). Home: Piedmont, Calif. Died Dec. 2, 2003.

PETERSON, WILLIAM FRANK, retired physician, administrator; b. Newark, Sept. 28, 1922; s. Edgar Charles and Margaret Benedict (Heyn) P.; m. Margaret Henderson Lee, June 28, 1946 (div. 1978); children: Margaret Lee, Edward Charles; m. 2d, Mary Ann Estelle McGrath, Nov. 29, 1980. Student, Cornell U., 1940-43; MD, N.Y. Med. Coll., 1946. Commd. lt. U.S. Air Force, 1946, advanced through grades to col., 1963; med. officer U.S. Air Force, 1946-70; chmn. dept. ob-gyn Washington Hosp. Ctr. 1970-92; dir. Women's Clinic. Washington, 1971-96, Ob-Gyn Ultrasound Lab., Washington, 1974-92; ret. 1996. Contbr. articles to profl. jours. Chmn., Maternal Mortality Com., 1981-96. Decorated Legion of Merit, 1960, 70; Cert. Achievement, Office Surgeon Gen., USAF, 1967. Fellow Am. Coll. Ob-Gyn, ACS, Nat. Bd. Med. Examiners (diplomate), Washington Gynecol. Soc. (exec. council 1980-85). Republican. Episcopalian. Home: Colesville, Md. Died Jan. 14, 2003.

PETTIJOHN, FRANCIS JOHN, geology educator; b. Waterford, Wis., June 20, 1904; m. Dorothy Bracken, 1930 (dec.); children: Norma Pettijohn Friedemann, Clare Pettijohn Maher, Loren; m. Virginia Romberger, 1990 (dec.). AB, U. Minn., 1924, A.M., 1925, PhD, 1930; D.H.L. (hon.), Johns Hopkins U., 1978; Sc.D. (hon.), U. Minn., 1986. Instr. Macalester Coll., 1924-25, Oberlin Coll., 1925-29, U. Minn., 1928-29; instr. U. Chgo., 1929-31, asst. prof., 1931-39, asso. prof., 1939-46, prof., 1946-52, Johns Hopkins U., Balt., 1952-73, prof. emeritus, 1973—, chmn. dept. geology, 1963-68, acting chmn. dept. earth and planetary scis., 1970; geologist U.S. Geol. Survey, 1943-53. Cons. Shell Oil Co., 1953-63; mem. adv. panel for earth scis. NSF, 1959-62; mem. adv. bd. Petroleum Research Fund., 1963-65 Author: numerous books in field including Sedimentary Rocks, 1949, 3d edit., 1973, (with P.E. Potter) Paleocurrents and Basin Analysis, 1963, 2d edit., 1977, (with P.E. Potter, R. Siever) Sand and Sandstone, 1987, 2d edit.; contbr. articles to profl. jours.; editor: Jour. Geology, 1947-52. Recipient Sorby medal Internat. Assn. Sedimentologists, 1982. Fellow AAAS, Geol. Soc. London (Wollaston medal 1974), Geol. Soc. Am. (Penrose medal 1975); mem. Soc. Econ. Paleontologists and Mineralogists (hon., pres. 1955-56, Twenhofel medal 1974), Geol. Soc. India (hon.), Geol. Soc. Finland (corr.), Soc. for Sedimentary Geology (established Francis J. Pettijohn medal 1992), Am. Assn. Petroleum Geologists, Am. Acad. Arts and Scis., Nat. Acad. Scis., Explorers Club (life), Phi Beta Kappa, Sigma Xi. Home: Glen Arm, Md. Died Apr. 23, 1999.

PÉWÉ, TROY LEWIS, geologist, educator; b. Rock Island, Ill., June 28, 1918; s. Richard E. and Olga (Pomrank) P.; m. Mary Jean Hill, Dec. 21, 1944; children: David Lee, Richard Hill, Elizabeth Anne. AB in Geology, Augustana Coll., 1940; MS, State U. Iowa, 1942; PhD, Stanford U., 1952; DSc (hon.), U. Alaska, 1991. Head dept. geology Augustana Coll., 1942-46; civilian instr. USAAC, 1943-44; instr. geomorphology Stanford, 1946; geologist Alaskan br. U.S. Geol. Survey, 1946-93; chief glacial geologist U.S. Nat. Com. Internat. Geophys. Year, Antarctica, 1958; prof. geology, head dept. U. Alaska, 1958-65; prof. geology Ariz. State U., 1965-88, prof. emeritus, from 1988, chmn. dept., 1965-76; dir. Mus. Geology, 1976-97, dir. emeritus, from 1997. Lectr. in field, 1942—; mem. organizing com. 1st Internat. Permafrost Conf. Nat. Acad. Sci., 1962-63, chmn. U.S. planning com. 2d Internat. Permafrost Conf., 1972-74, chmn. U.S. del. 3d Internat. Permafrost Conf., 1978, chmn. U.S. organizing com. 4th Internat. Permafrost Conf., 1979-83; com. to study Good Friday Alaska Earthquake Nat. Acad. Scis., 1964-70, mem. glaciological com. polar research bd., 1971-73, founding chmn. permafrost com., mem. polar research bd., 1975-81; organizing chmn. Internat. Assn. Quarternary Research Symposium and Internat. Field Trip Alaska, 1965; mem. Internat. Commn. Periglacial Morophology, 1964-71, 80-88; mem. polar research bd. NRC, 1975-78, late Cenozoic study group, sci. com. Antarctic research, 1977-80 Contbr. numerous papers to profl. lit. Recipient U.S. Antarctic Svc. medal, 1966, Outstanding Achievement award Augustana Coll., 1969, Disting. Alumnus award U. Iowa, 1994, Internat. Geophysics medal USSR Nat. Acad. Sci., 1985, Disting. Career award The Geol. Soc. Am., 1999; named 2d hon. internat. fellow Chinese Soc. Glaciology and Geocryology, 1985; Troy L. Péwé Climate Change Permafrost Res., Fairbanks, Alaska, named in his honor, 1999. Fellow AAAS (pres. Alaska div. 1956, com. on arid lands 1972-79), Geol. Soc. Am. (editorial bd. 1975-82, chmn. cordilleran sect. 1979-80, chmn. geomorphology div. 1981-82, Disting. Career award 1999), Arctic Inst. N.Am. (bd. govs. 1969-74, exec. bd. 1972-73), Iowa Acad. Sci., Ariz. Acad. Sci. (pres. 1982-83); mem. Internat. Permafrost Assn. (founding v.p. 1983, pres. 1988-93), Am. Quaternary Assn. (pres. 1984-86), Internat. Geog. Union. Clubs: Cosmos. Home: Tempe, Ariz. Died Oct. 21, 1999.

PEYSER, MINNA POST, psychiatrist, educator; b. N.Y., May 17, 1922; d. Philip Mansfield and Ann (Nadler) Urdon; m. Seymour M. Peyser, Feb. 27, 1949 (div. Sept. 1968); children: Andrea Peyser Abbott, Jull Peyser Curtis, Michael N. BA, UCLA, 1943; grad. pub. law, Columbia Univ., 1954; computer sci. political psychiatry, CUNY, 1975. Deputy probation officer L.A. Probation Dept., L.A., 1944-45; exec. dir. Nat. Citizens Political Action Com., L.A., 1945-48, Civil Liberties Edn. Found., N.Y., 1954-62; nat. assembly exec. dir. Teaching the Principles of the Bill of Rights, N.Y., 1962-65; found., co-dir. Ctr. for Rsch. & Edn. in Am. Liberities, from 1965; edn. and telecom. cons. M.P. Peyser & Assocs., N.Y., 1969-76; found., pres. The Ecodemocracy Found., Inc., N.Y., from 1984. Project dir. Williamstown Workshop for Inservice Tchr. Training, 1963-64; tchr. training & media cons. U.S. Office of Edn., 1964-65; cons. The Network Project, Pub. Interest Satellite Assn., 1967-72. Author: A Metasystem Perspective on the First Amendment, 1967; co-author: The Legal Rights of the Married Working Women, 1965; editor: A Bibliography of Civil Rights & Civil Liberties for Secondary Sch. Tchrs., 1962, A Program to Improve Bill of Rights Teaching in the U.S., 1963; TV producer, host Our Constituional Future, 1989-91. Chmn. Official Constitutional Bicentennial Observance, Key West and Monroe County, Fla., 1986-92; coord., founder Key West 2000, 1992-97; cons. Pres. Colum,bia Univ., 1967—, Pres. Carter's Commn. A Nat. Agenda for the Eighties, 1980. Recipient MEritoriuos Ednl. Program award U.S. Bicentennial Commn., 1991, COnstitutional Observance Drama of Schs. award Fla. Endowment for the Arts, 1989-91, Disting. Svc. award Monroe County Commn., 1991. Mem. Am. Political Sci. Assn., Union of Concerned Scientists, Inter. Soc. of Political Psychology, World Future Soc., Nat. Coun. for the Social Studies, Am. Assn. for Advancement of Sci. Home: Key West, Fla. Died Nov. 5, 2001.

PFEIL, DON CURTIS, retired real estate executive; b. Wausa, Nebr., Dec. 4, 1923; s. Leonard W. and Katherine A. (Peterson) P.; m. Jane Cole Magee, Sept. 14, 1946; children: Bruce, Mark, Joan. Grad. high sch., Wausa. Farmer, Wausa, 1946-64; pres. Don C. Pfeil & Assoc., Inc., Wausa, 1964-90; ret., 1990. Bd. dirs., sec. Cedar-Knox Pub. Power Dist., Hartington, Nebr., 1962-99; chmn. governing bd. N.E. C.C., Norfolk, Nebr., 1972-88; mem. Nebr. Coun. on Vocat. Edn., Lincoln, chmn., 1983-92; bd. dirs. Osmond (Nebr.) Gen. Hosp., 1970-77; mem. Nebr. Jud. Nominating Commn., 1991-95. Sgt. AC, U.S. Army, 1943-45. Mem. Realtors Land Inst., Am. Soc. Farm Mgrs. and Rural Appraisers, Lewis and Clark Bd. Realtors (pres. 1970), Grad Realtors Inst. (dean 1978-83). Democrat. Lutheran. Avocations: fishing, gardening, photography. Home: Wausa, Nebr. Died June 13, 1999.

PHELPS, GALE MCDONOUGH, lawyer; b. Fondulac, Wis., Aug. 19, 1947; d. Charles A. and Irene S. McDonough; m. Thomas O. Phelps, Aug. 23, 1969; children: Elizabeth, Kathleen. BA, Butler U., 1969; JD, Ind. U., 1976. Bar: Ind. 1976, U.S. Dist. Ct. (so. dist.) Ind. 1976, U.S. Supreme Ct. 1981. Pvt. practice, Indpls., 1976—88; part-time atty. Marion County Prosecutor's Office, Indpls., 1980—81; ptnr. Phelps & Fara, Indpls., from 1988. Treas. Ind. Bar Found., Indpls., 1999—2001, v.p., from 2001, pres. elect., 2001—02; bd. mgrs., treas. Ind. State Bar Assn.; co-chair Family Law Ind. Cert. Bd., Indpls., from 1999. Contbr. articles to profl. jours. Mem.: Am. Acad. Matrimonial Lawyers. Home: Fishers, Ind. Died May 10, 2003.

PHIBBS, HARRY ALBERT, interior designer, professional speaker, lecturer; b. Denver, Jan. 9, 1933; s. Harry Andrew and Mary May (Perriam) P.; m. Alice Conners Glynn, Oct. 23, 1957 (div. Jan. 1988); children: Kathleen Ann Phibbs Pierz, Paul Robert, Mary Alice Phibbs Hettle, Michael John, Peter James, Daniel Edward; m. Nevelle Haley Jones, Feb. 1988. BA, U. Colo., 1954, B.F.A., 1957. Interior designer Howard Lorton, Inc., Denver, 1957-68; interior designer, v.p. Ronald Ansay Inc., Wheatridge, Colo., 1969-71; interior designer, pres. Phibbs Design Assos., Inc., Denver, 1972-78; interior designer, mgr. Howard Lorton, Inc., Colorado Springs, Colo., 1979-93; prin. Phibbs Design, Colorado Springs, 1993—2003. Pres. Interior Designers Housing Devel. Corp., 1969-72; chmn. adv. com. interior design program Pikes Peak C.C., 1998—; adj. faculty, Pike's Peak C.C., 2000-2003. V.p. Arvada (Colo.) Hist. Soc., 1973; bd. dirs. Colo. Opera Festival, also pres., 1984, 86; bd. dirs. Downtown Colorado Springs, Inc., also pres., 1984; chmn. bd. trustees Interior Design Internship Denver, 1991-94. With U.S. Army, 1954-56. Fellow Am. Soc. Interior Designers (nat. pres. 1977); mem. Am. Arbitration Assn., Theta Xi (pres. Denver Area alumni club 1958-64) Democrat. Roman Catholic. Died Jan. 23, 2003.

PHILLIPS, JERRY JUAN, law educator; b. Charlotte, N.C., June 16, 1935; s. Vergil Ernest and Mary Blanche (Wade) P.; m. Anne Butler Colville, June 6, 1959; children: Sherman Wade, Dorothy Colville. BA, Yale U., 1956, JD, 1961; BA, Cambridge (Eng.) U., 1958, MA (hon.), 1964. Bar: Tenn. bar 1961. Assoc. firm Miller & Martin, Chattanooga, 1961-67; asst. prof. law U. Tenn., 1967-72, assoc. prof., 1972-73, prof., 1973—, W.P. Toms prof., 1980—. Advisor Tenn. Law Revision Commn., 1968-70; mem. Tenn. Jud. Council, 1970-74; adv. Fed. Interagy. Task Force on Products Liability, 1976-77; lectr. in field. Author: Products Liability in a Nutshell, 5th edit., 1998, Products Liability Cases and Materials on Torts and Related Law, 1980, Products Liability Treatise, 3 vols., 1986, Cases and Materials on Tort Law, 1992, 2d edit., 1997, Products Liability-Cases, Materials, Problems, 1994; advisor Tenn. U. Law Rev., 1977—. U. Tenn. grantee, 1978 Mem. ABA, Am. Law

Inst., Knoxville Bar Assn., Am. Assn. Law Schs., Order of Coif, Phi Beta Kappa. Clubs: Knoxville Racquet. Democrat. Episcopalian. Home: Knoxville, Tenn. Deceased.

PHILLIPS, PATRICK EDWARD, fire protection engineer; b. Birmingham, Ala., May 5, 1931; s. John Bunyon and Frances (Fede) P.; m. Fern L. Schalund, Nov. 24, 1954 (div. May 1979); children: Matthew, Craig, Tracey, Karla; m. Paula Lynn Jacobson, Nov., 1990. B.S. in Fire Protection and Safety Engrng., Ill. Inst. Tech. Registered profl. engr., Calif., Mass. with Mich. Inspection Bur., Detroit, 1950-65, AEC, Richland, Wash., 1965-68, U.S. Dept. Energy, Las Vegas, 1968-91, ret., 1991; cons., Las Vegas, 1975—; cons. consulting svc. in fire protection. Co-author: Fire Protection for the Design Professional, 1975. Served with U.S. Army, 1953-55. Named Man of Yr. Automatic Fire Alarm Assn., 1975. Fellow Soc. Fire Protection Engrs.; mem. Am. Soc. Safety Engrs., System Safety Soc., Cert. Safety Profls., Nat. Fire Protection Assn. (former life, chmn. signalling systems correlating com., 1978-93, former chair com. on initiating devices, 1974-88, halon com., former mem. com. systems concepts for bldg. fire safety, NFPA Standards med 1993), Underwriter's Labs. Fire Council. Lodges: Elks, Masons (master 1979), Shrine Club (pres. 1980, unit capt. 1977, 90), Scottish Rite (ven master, wise master), York Rite (high priest in royal arch), Grotto (past monatch), Order of the Eastern Star (treas., 1991—). Died Mar. 17, 2000.

PICKERING, WILLIAM HAYWARD, physicist, educator, research scientist; b. Wellington, N.Z., Dec. 24, 1910; s. Albert William and Elizabeth (Hayward) Pickering; m. Muriel Bowler, Dec. 30, 1932 (dec. Mar. 1992); children: William B., Anne E.; m. Inez Chapman, July 28, 1994. BS, Calif. Inst. Tech., 1932, MS, 1933, PhD in Physics, 1936; degree (hon.), Clark U., 1966, Occidental Coll., 1966, U. Bologna, 1974; PhD (hon.), Canterbury Univ., New Zealand, 2003. Mem. Cosmic Ray Expdn. to India, 1939, Cosmic Ray Expdn. to Mex., 1941; faculty Calif. Inst. Tech., 1940—2004, prof. elec. engring., 1946—80, prof. emeritus, 1980—2004, dir. jet propulsion lab., 1954—76; mem. sci. adv. bd. USAF, 1945—48; chmn. panel on test range instrumentation (Research and Devel. Bd.), 1948—49; mem. U.S. nat. com. tech. panel Earth Satellite Program, 1955—60; mem. Army Sci. Adv. Panel, 1960—64. Dir. rsch. inst. U. Petroleum and Minerals, Dharan, Saudi Arabia, 1977—79; pres. Pickering Rsch. Corp., 1980—91, Lignetics, Inc., 1983—94, chmn., from 1994. Decorated Order of Merit Italy, knight comdr. Order Brit. Empire, Order of New Zealand; recipient James Wyld Meml. award, Am. Rocket Soc., 1957, Columbus medal, Genoa, 1964, Prix Galabert for Astronautics, Goddard trophy, Nat. Space Club, 1965, Disting. Svc. medal, NASA, 1965, Army Disting. Civilian Svc. award, 1959, Spirit of St. Louis medal, 1965, Crozier medal, Am. Ordnance Assn., 1965, Man of Yr. award, Indsl. Rsch. Inst., 1968, Interprofl. Coop. award, Soc. Mfg. Engrs., 1970, Marconi medal, Marconi Found., 1974, Nat. medal of Sci., 1976, Fahrney medal, Franklin Inst., 1976, award of merit, Am. Cons. Engrs. Coun., 1976, Francoix-Xavier Bagnoud Internat. award, 1993, Japan prize, Sci. and Tech. Found. Japan, 1994, Daniel Guggenheim medal for promotion of aeronautics, Guggenheim Fund, 2000. Fellow: IEEE (Edison medal 1972), NAE, AIAA (pres. 1963, Louis W. Hill Transp. award 1968, Aerospace Pioneer award 1986, AIAA Guggenheim medal 2001), AAAS; mem.: NAS, Internat. Astronautical Fedn. (pres. 1965—66), Am. Geophys. Union. Home: Flintridge, Calif. Died Mar. 15, 2004.

PICKETT, DOYLE C. employment counselor; b. Greencastle, Ind., July 15, 1930; s. Joseph Virgil and Lora Clay (Phillips) P.; m. Judith Ann Marshall, 1956 (div. 1961); children: Brian Doyle, Marsha Ann; m. Dorothy Newgent McGinnis, 1964. AB, Wabash Coll., 1952; MBA, Ind. U., 1953. Exec. trainee, various staff and line exec. positions, asst. store mgr. L.S. Ayres & Co., Lafayette and Indpls., Ind., 1953-64; mgmt. analyst Cummins Engine Co., Columbus, Ind., 1964-67; adminstrv. asst. to pres., other exec. positions Baker & Taylor Co., 1967-80; v.p. mktg. Baker & Taylor Co. subs. W.R. Grace Co., N.Y.C., Somerville, N.J., 1980-82; pres. UNIPUB subs. Xerox Co., N.Y.C., 1982-86; mem. exec. com. R.R. Bowker Co., N.Y.C., 1982-86; pres. D.C. Pickett Assocs., 1986-93; counselor Work Force Devel. Program N.J. Dept. Labor, Somerville, Perth Amboy, 1993-94, counselor Project Reemployment Opportunities Sys. Somerville, 1994-96; counselor, facilitator Career Transition Ctr., Somerville, 1996-98, field office supr., 1998—2001. Mem. adv. bd. Fourth Internat. Conf. on Approval Plans/Collection Devel., 1979. Co-author: Approval Plans and Academic Libraries, 1977; mem. editorial adv. bd. Technicalities, 1980-81; contbr. articles to profl. jours. Chair membership com. Ctrl. Ind. Coun., Boy Scouts Am., 1961-62; mem. Dean's Assocs., Ind. U. Kelly Sch. Bus., Bloomington, 1983-90, 97-99, 2001—; mem. Friends Somerset County/Bridgewater Libr.; mem. alumni admissions coun. Wabash Coll., 1996—. With U.S. Army, 1953-55. Mem. Assn. Coll. and Rsch. Librs. (publs. com. 1983-87), Soc. Logistics Engrs. (adv. bd. 1981-91), Nat. Assn. Wabash Men (bd. dirs. 1983-90), Am. Legion, Kiwanis (charter pres. N.W. Indpls. club 1958-59, dir. 1960-61, Ind. dist. zone chmn. membership and attendance, 1960-61, Ind. and N.J. clubs officer, chair com. 1962-68), Masons, Blue Key, Alpha Phi Omega, Delta Tau Delta (North Jersey coord. N.Y. area alumni chpt. 1986-88). Mem. Christian Ch. Home: Bridgewater, NJ. Died Mar. 3, 2003.

PICKETT, GEORGE BIBB, JR., retired military officer; b. Montgomery, Ala., Mar. 20, 1918; s. George B. and Marie (Dow) P.; BS, U.S. Mil. Acad., 1941; student Nat. War Coll., 1959-60; m. Beryl Arlene Robinson, Dec. 27, 1941; children: Barbara Pickett Harrell, James, Kathleen, Thomas; m. Rachel Copeland Peeples, July 1981. Commd. 2d lt. U.S. Army, 1941, advanced through grades to maj. gen., 1966; instr. Inf. Sch., Fort Benning, Ga., 1947-50, instr. Armed Forces Staff Coll., Norfolk, Va., 1956-59; comdg. officer 2d Armored Cav. Regt., 1961-63; chief of staff Combat Devel. Command, 1963-66; comdg. gen. 2d inf. divsn., Korea, 1966-67; ret., 1973; field rep. Nat. Rifle Assn., 1973-85. Decorated Purple Heart with oak leaf cluster, D.S.M. with two oak leaf clusters, Bronze Star with two oak leaf clusters and V device, Silver Star, Legion of Merit with two oak leaf clusters, Commendation medal with two oak leaf clusters. Mem. SAR (pres. Ala. Soc. 1984), Old South Hist. Assn. Episcopalian. Club: Kiwanis. Author: (with others) Joint and Combined Staff Officers Manual, 1959; contbr. articles on mil. affairs to profl. jours. Home: Montgomery, Ala. Died Jan. 4, 2003.

PIERCE, FRANKLIN HANKINSON, judge; b. Augusta, Ga., Oct. 13, 1916; s. Benjamin E. Sr. and Esse (Hankinson) P.; m. Hilda Evans, Jan. 16, 1941; children: Mariam Pierce Brown, Melissa Pierce Beaver. Student, Jr. Coll. Augusta; LLB, Augusta Law Sch., 1939, LLD (hon.), 1975. Bar: Ga. 1937, U.S. Dist. Ct. Ga., U.S. Ct. Appeals (5th cir.), U.S. Supreme Ct. Atty. Richmond County, Ga., 1947-72; sr. judge Augusta Superior Ct., from 1973. Served to 1st lt. USAAC, 1942-45. Mem.: Augusta Country, Methodist Ch, Masons, Elks, Shriners. Avocations: fishing, hunting, skeet shooting, golf. Home: Augusta, Ga. Died May 14, 2002.

PIERSON, WILLARD JAMES, geophysicist, educator, geophysicist, researcher; b. N.Y.C., July 7, 1922; s. Willard James and Mary Abagail (Hand) Pierson; m. Joy Mary Kell, July 3, 1954 (dec. July 1999); children: Mary Jean, Arthur, Mark. BS, U. Chgo., 1944; PhD, NYU, 1949. From asst. prof. to assoc. prof. NYU, N.Y.C., 1949-61, prof., 1961-73, CUNY, N.Y.C., 1973-92, rsch. prof., from 1992. Co-author: (book) HO Pub 603, 1957, Principles of Physical Oceanography, 1966. Capt. USAF. Recipient Exceptional Sci. Achievement award, NASA, 1980, cert. of Appreciation, Soc. Naval Arch. Marine Engrs., 1973. Fellow: AAAS, IEEE (life), Am. Meterol. Soc., Am. Geophys. Union (Sverdrup Gold medal). Methodist. Achievements include research in on remote sensing and ocean waves; on radar scatterometry; on radar altimetry; on ship motions. Home: West Hempstead, NY. Died June 7, 2003.

PIERSON, WILLIAM ROY, chemist; b. Charleston, W.Va., Oct. 21, 1930; s. Roy H. Pierson and Gay Harris; m. Juliet T. Strong, May 20, 1961; children: Elizabeth T., Anne H. Veis. BSE, Princeton U., 1952; PhD, MIT, 1959. Rsch. assoc. Enrico Fermi Inst. for Nuclear Studies U. Chgo., 1959-62; rsch. scientist Ford Motor Co., Dearborn, Mich., 1962-87; exec dir. Energy and Environ. Engring. Ctr. Desert Rsch. Inst., Reno, 1987-95, rsch. prof., 1996-98, Desert Rsch. Inst., from 1998. Former dir. energy and environ. engring. ctr. Desert Rsch. Inst. Contbr. over 100 articles to profl. jours. Bd. dirs Reno Chamber Orch., 1992-96, 98—. Lt. USN, 1952-55. Fellow Air and Waste Mgmt. Assn. (Chambers award 1995); mem. AAAS, Am. Phys. Soc., Am. Chem. Soc., Am. Assn. for Aerosol Rsch. (bd. dirs. 1982-85). Home: Reno, Nev. Deceased.

PIGMAN, GLADYS HARGREAVES, aeronautical engineer; b. Tifton, Ga., Jan. 21, 1909; d. Leon Abraham and Essie (Blitch) H.; m. Ward Pigman (dec. Sept. 1977). BS, U. Ga., 1935, MS, 1941. Tchr. high schs., Ga., 1935; physicist S.C. Rsch. Labs., Ft. Monmouth, N.J., 1942-43; instr. in physics U. Ga., Athens, 1943-44; physicist Tenn Eastman Corp., 1944-50; rsch. assoc. Sch. of Dental Medicine Tufts U., 1952-56; rsch. assoc. Naval Air Engring. Ctr., Phila., 1956-67; with Naval Air Devel. Ctr., Warminster, Pa., 1967-70, aero. materials engr., 1970-76, ret., 1976; pvt. practice cons. Athens, from 1976. Contbr. numerous articles to profl. jours. Vol., Athens Internat. Orgn., U. Ga. Fellow AAAS, Am. Inst. Chemists; mem. Am. Chem. Soc. (bd.dirs. 1963-66, 71-74), Grad. Women in Sci. (nat. v.p., pres. elect, pres. 1978-80), Am. Phys. Soc., N.Y. Acad. Sci. Home: Athens, Ga. Deceased.

PILCHIK, ELY EMANUEL, rabbi, writer; b. Russia, June 12, 1913; came to U.S., 1920, naturalized, 1920; s. Abraham and Rebecca (Lipovitch) P.; m. Ruth Schuchat, Nov. 20, 1941 (dec. 1977); children: Susan Pilchik Rosenbaum, Judith Pilchik Zucker; m. Harriet Krichman Perlmutter, June, 1981. AB, U. Cin., 1935; M.Hebrew Lit., Hebrew Union Coll., 1936, D.D., 1964. Ordained rabbi, 1939; founder, dir. Hillel Found. at U. Md., 1939-40; asst. rabbi Har Sinai Temple, Balt., 1940-41; rabbi Temple Israel, Tulsa, 1942-47, Temple B'nai Jeshurun, Short Hills, N.J., 1947-81; prof. Jewish Thought Upsala Coll., 1969—. Pres. Jewish Book Council Am., 1957-58 Author: books, including Hillel, 1951, From the Beginning, 1956, Judaism Outside the Holy Land, 1964, Jeshurun Essays, 1967, A Psalm of David, 1967, Talmud Thought, 1983, Midrash Memoir, 1984, Touches of Einstein, 1987, Luzzatto on Loving Kindness, 1987, Prayer in History, 1989; author: play Toby, 1968; lyricist 6 cantatas; contbr. articles to profl. and gen. jours. Bd. dirs. Newark Mus.; mem. ethics com. N.J. Bar Assn. Served as chaplain USNR, 1944-46. Mem. N.J. Bd. Rabbis (pres. 1955-57), Central Conf. Am. Rabbis (pres. 1977-79) Died Jan. 6, 2003.

PILKINGTON, ROGER WINDLE, author; b. St. Helens, Lancashire, Eng., Jan. 17, 1915; s. Richard Austin and Hope (Cozens-Hardy) P.; m. Miriam Jaboor, July 28, 1937 (div.); children: Cynthia, Hugh; m. Ingrid Geijer(dec. 2002), 1973. Student, Freiburg U., 1933; MA, Magdalene Coll., Cambridge, Eng., 1937, PhD, 1942. Free-lance writer, 1948-2003. Author: Males and Females, 1948, Stringer's Folly, 1949, Sons and Daughters, 1951, Biology, Man and God, 1951, Revelation through Science, 1954, Thames Waters, 1956, The Ways of the Sea, 1957, Robert Boyle, Father of Chemistry, 1959, World Without End, 1960, Who's Who and Why, 1961, The Ways of the Air, 1961, How Ships Are Navigated, 1963, Heavens Alive, 1963, Waterways in Europe, 1972, One Foot in France, 1992; (series) Small Boat, 1957-71; (children's books) The Facts of Life, 1955, Jan's Treasure, 1955, In the Beginning, 1955, The Chesterfield Gold, 1957, The Great South Sea, 1957, The Missing Panel, 1958, The Dahlia's Cargo, 1959, How Boats Go Uphill, 1959, Don John's Ducats, 1960, Nepomuk of the River, 1962, Boats Overland, 1963, The Eisenbart Mystery, 1963, How Ships Are Navigated, 1963, The River, 1964, Glass, 1965, The Boy from Stink Alley, 1965 (published as I Sailed on the Mayflower 1966), The Ormering Tide, 1974, The Face in the River, 1976, Small Boat in the Midi, 1983, Small Boat Down the Years, 1987, One Foot in France, 1992, View from the Shore, 1995. Died May 5, 2003.

PIMIENTA, GILBERT, anesthesiologist; b. L.A., Mar. 14, 1957; s. Ruben G. and Esther (Ojeda) P. AA, El Camino Coll., 1977; BS, U. Calif., Irvine, 1979; MD, U. Calif., San Diego, 1984. Intern in internal medicine Good Samaritan Med. Ctr., Phoenix, 1984-85; resident in anesthesiology U. Ariz., Phoenix, 1985-87; pvt. practice Phoenix, from 1987-. Mem. AMA, Internat. Anesthesia Rsch. Soc., Am. Soc. Anesthesiologists. Home: Phoenix, Ariz. Died Jul. 4, 1999.

PINELLAS, XAVIER CLINTON, counselor, consultant; b. Eustis, Fla., Dec. 26, 1947; s. Louis Cornelius and Dorothy (Anderson) P.; m. Doris Jackson, July 18, 1973; 1 child, Xaundria Kini. BS, Bethune-Cookman Coll., 1969; MS, Ft. Valley State Coll., 1973; EdS, Boston State Coll., 1975; EdD, U. Ariz., 1992. Pub. sch. tchr. State of Fla., 1970-72; pub. sch. counselor State of Mass., 1973-76; founder, pres. Project Reach Inc., World Acad. Excellence, 1976-79; pub. sch. counselor State of Ariz., 1980-84; coord. pub. sch. work edn. Tucson Unified Sch. Dist., 1984-87; pres. Ctr. Devel. Human Potential, Kissimmee, Fla., 1988-90. Cons. Pima County Sports Hall Fame, Tucson, 1990. Pres. Concerned Black Citizens, Kissimmee, 1977-79; bd. dirs. Osceola County Housing Rev. Bd., 1988-90; co-founder Who's Who Among African Am. Students Convocation, Tucson, 1987. Fellow U. Ariz. Minority Affairs Office, Tucson, 1990, Ft. Valley (Ga.) State Coll., 1971. Mem. NEA, Coun. Black Edn., Ariz. Counselors Assn., Mass. Counselors Assn., NAACP (pres. Kissimmee br. 1976-79). Avocations: reading profl. jours., writing, pub. speaking, designing progs. for at-risk students. Died Feb. 20, 2001.

PINKETT, MARY, city councilwoman; b. Bklyn., 1931; d. Junius and Arwelda (Harvey) Glover; m. William Daniel Pinkett; 1 child, William D. (dec.). Student, Bklyn. Coll., 1970-72. With Mcpl. Dept. Hosp., Bklyn., 1961-66, Dept. Social Svc., from 1966; liaison Mayor's Pension Com.; city councilwoman Dist. 28, N.Y.C., 1974-91, Dist. 35, N.Y.C., 1991—2001. Chairwoman aging com. N.Y.C. Coun., mem. fin., consumer affairs, state legis. com. V.p. Social Svc. Employees Union Local 371, 1971-73, pres., 1973-74; mem. Stuyvesant Dem. Club. Mem. NAACP,. Nat. Coun. Negro Women, State Mcpl. Employees Union (v.p. dist. coun. 37), Am. Legion Women's Aus. Kings County. Died Dec. 4, 2003.

PIPER, ANSON CONANT, former language educator; b. Newton, Mass., Aug. 14, 1918; s. Luther Warren and Elizabeth (Smith) P.; m. Miriam Etna Simms, Nov. 12, 1945; children— Jonathan, Victoria, Gregory. BA, Williams Coll., 1940; MA, U. Wis., 1947, PhD, 1953. Grad. asst. Spanish U. Wis., 1941-42, 46-49; mem. staff NDEA Summer Inst., 1961; mem. faculty Williams Coll., 1949-86, prof. Romanic langs., 1961-86; mem. staff Colby Coll. Summer Sch. Langs., 1956-58, 60, 62, 68; Fulbright lectr. Brazil, 1963-64. Co-dir. of study radiophonic teaching in Latin Am. for Internat. Research Assos., 1961-63 Author: Asi es la vida, 1958; also articles.; co-editor: Portuguese: A Fundamental Vocabulary, 1968. Co-dir. Williamstown United Fund. Served with USNR, 1942-46. Williams Found. grantee for study in Argentina, 1951-52; Gulbenkian grant for Portuguese studies, 1967 Mem. Am. Assn. Tchrs. Spanish and Portuguese (pres. Western Mass. chpt. 1966-68), Inst. Internat. Edn. (mem. nat. screening com. 1973-74, 76-77), Phi Beta Kappa. Conglist. (moderator 1959-61, 72-75). Home: Williamstown, Mass. Died Jan. 28, 2004.

PIPER, RICHARD GLENN, human resources specialist; b. Elizabeth, N.J., Sept. 14, 1930; s. Wilbur Glenn and Violet (Geehr) P.; m. Joan Anne Porcher, Apr. 7, 1956; children: Richard G., Kim Suzanne Piper Landis, William G. BSChemE, Lafayette Coll., 1952. Engr., foreman E.I. DuPont, Camden, S.C., 1952-54, supr., 1956-59, supr. and sr. engr. Waynesboro, Va., 1959-62, staff asst., planner Wilmington, Del., 1962-65, area supr., plant designer Camden, S.C., 1965-68, mf. supt., mgr. Wilmington, N.C., 1968-81, human resources career cons., from 1981. Commr. New Hanover County Human Rels. Commn., Wilmington, 1989; bd. dirs. Girls Club, 1982, Waterway Commn., 1986-91. Sgt. U.S. Army, 1954-56. Mem. Friends of Human Relations, Wilmington C. of C. Republican. Roman Catholic. Avocations: tennis, fishing, carpentry, gardening, travel. Home: Wilmington, NC. Deceased.

PITELKA, FRANK ALOIS, zoologist, educator; b. Chgo., Mar. 27, 1916; s. Frank Joseph and Frances (Laga) P.; m. Dorothy Getchell Riggs, Feb. 5, 1943; children: Louis Frank, Wenzel Karl, Vlasta Kazi Helen. BS with highest honors, U. Ill., 1939; summer student, U. Mich., 1938, U. Wash., 1940; PhD, U. Calif. at Berkeley, 1946; PhD (hon.), Masaryk U., Brno, Czech Republic, 1997. Mem. faculty U. Calif. at Berkeley, 1944—85, prof. zoology, 1958-85; prof. emeritus, 1985—2003; chmn. dept. U. Calif. at Berkeley, 1963-66, 69-71, Miller research prof., 1965-66; curator birds Mus. Vertebrate Zoology, 1945-63, assoc. dir., 1982-97; exec. com. Miller Inst. Basic Rsch. in Sci., 1967-71, chmn., 1967-70. Panel environ. biology NSF, 1959-62, panel polar programs, 1978-80; mem. panel biol. and med. scis., com. polar research Nat. Acad. Scis., 1960-65; research assoc. Naval Arctic Research Lab., Barrow, Alaska, 1951-80; ecol. adv. com. AEC, 1956-1958; adv. coms. U.S. Internat. Biol. Program, 1965-69; mem. adv. com. U. Colo. Inst. Arctic and Alpine Research, 1968-73; mem. U.S. Tundra Biome Program, 1968-73, dir., 1968-69; vis. prof. U. Wash. Friday Harbor Labs, summer 1968; mem. U.S. Commn. for UNESCO, 1970-72 Contbr. research papers in field.; Editorial bd.: Ecology, 1949-51, 60-62, editor, 1962-64; mem. editorial bd. U. Calif. Press, 1953-62, chmn., 1959-62; mem. editorial bd. Pacific Coast Avifauna, 1947-60, Ecol. Monographs, 1957-60, Systematic Zoology, 1961-64, The Veliger, 1961-85, Studies in Ecology, 1972-84, Current Ornithology, 1980-85; asst. editor Condor, 1943-45, assoc. editor, 1945-62; mem. editorial bd. Studies in Avian Biology, 1979-84, editor, 1984-87. Guggenheim fellow, 1949-50; NSF sr. postdoctoral fellow Oxford (Eng.) U., 1957-58; Research fellow Ctr. for Advanced Study in Behavioral Scis., Stanford, 1971; recipient Disting. Teaching award U. Calif.-Berkeley, 1984; The Berkeley citation, 1985, Alumnus Achievement award, U. Ill., 1993, Lifetime Achievement award Pt. Reyes Bird Obs., 2000. Fellow Arctic Inst. N.Am., Am. Ornithologists Union (Brewster award 1980), Calif. Acad. Scis. (medal 1997), AAAS, Animal Behavior Soc.; mem. Ecol. Soc. Am. (Mercer award 1953, Eminent Ecologist award 1992), Soc. Study Evolution, Cooper Ornithol. Soc. (hon. mem.; pres. 1948-50), Brit. Ecol. Soc., Am. Soc. Mammalogists, Am. Soc. Naturalists, Am. Inst. Biol. Scis., Western Soc. Naturalists (pres. 1963-64), Nat. Audubon Soc., Sierra Club, Phi Beta Kappa, Sigma Xi. Home: Altadena, Calif. Died Oct. 10, 2003.

PITTMAN, DAVID JOSHUA, sociologist, educator; b. Rocky Mount, N.C., Sept. 18, 1927; BA, U. N.C., 1949, MA, 1950; postgrad., Columbia U., 1953; PhD, U. Chgo., 1956. Asst. prof. sociology Washington U., St. Louis, 1958-60, assoc. prof., 1960-64, prof., 1964-91, prof. sociology in psychology, 1991-92, prof. psychology, 1992-93, prof. emeritus, from 1993, chmn. dept. sociology, 1976-86, dir. Social Sci. Inst., 1963-76. Cons. Jellinek Clinic, Amsterdam, Netherlands, 1965—68, Wine Inst., 1985—94; mem. sci. adv. com. Distilled Spirits Coun., Washington, 1976—86; Dent Meml. lectr. U. London, 1989. Author: (book) The Revolving Door: A Study of Chronic Police Case Inebriates, 1958, The Drug Scene in Great Britain, 1967, Primary Prevention of Alcoholism, 1980; editor: Socity, Culture and Drinking Patterns, 1962, Alcoholism, 1967, Society, Culture and Drinking Patterns Reexamined, 1991; field editor: Jour. Study Alcohol, 1985—92, mem. editl. bd.:, 1992—2000, Internat. Jour. Advt., 1990—97. Chmn. 28th Internat. Congress Alcohol and Alcoholism, Washington, 1968; pres. N.Am. Assn. Alcoholism Programs, 1965—67; chmn. Mo. Adv. Coun. Alcoholism and Drug Abuse, Jefferson City, 1972—75, 1987—91; mem. Mo. Mental Health Commn., Jefferson City, 1975—78; bd. dirs. Nat. Gay and Lesbian Task Force, 1993—97. Recipient Page One Civic award, St. Louis Newspaper Guild, 1967, Bronze key, St. Louis Coun. Alcoholism, 1976, Silver key, Nat. Coun. Alcoholism, 1978, Biennial Rsch. award, Soc. Med. Friends of Wine, 1992; fellow Spl., NIMH, 1966. Fellow: Am. Sociol. Soc.; mem.: Am. Sociol. Assn. (chmn. alcohol and drugs sect. 1992), Internat. Coun. Alcohol and Addictions (exec. com. 1968—84), Soc. Study Social Problems (chmn. alcoholism com. 1957—59, Disting. Sr. Scholar award 1993), Univ. Club, Phi Beta Kappa, Omicron Delta Kappa, Sigma Xi. Episcopalian. Avocations: collecting elephant replicas, collecting political memorabilia. Home: Orlando, Fla. Deceased.

PLATTHY, JENO, cultural association executive; b. Dunapataj, Hungary, Aug. 13, 1920; s. Joseph K. and Maria (Dobor) P.; m. Carol Louise Abell, Sept. 25, 1976 Diploma, Peter Pazmany U., Budapest, Hungary, 1942; PhD, Ferencz J. U., Kolozsvar, Hungary, 1944; MS, Cath. U., 1965; PhD (hon.), Yangminshan U., Taiwan, 1975; DLitt (hon.), U. Libre Asie, Philippines, 1977. Lectr. various univs., 1956-59; sec. Internat. Inst. Boston, 1959-62; adminstrv. asst. Trustees of Harvard U., Washington, 1962-85; exec. dir. Fedn. Internat. Poetry Assns., 1976—. Pub. New Muses Quar., 1976— Author: Winter Tunes, 1974, Ch'u Yuan, His Life and Works, 1975, Springtide, 1976, Opera Bamboo, Collected Poems, 1981, The Poems of Jesus, 1982, Holiness in a Worldly Garment, 1984, Ut Pictures Poeta, 1984, European Odes, 1985, The Mythical Poets of Greece, 1985, Book of Dithyrambs, 1986, Asian Elegies, 1987, Space Ecologues, 1988, Cosmograms, 1988, Nova Comoedia, 1988, vols. II-III, 1992, Bartok: A Critical Biography, 1988, Plato: A Critical Biography, 1990, Near-Death Experiences in Antiquity, 1992, Celebration of Life, 1992, Idylls, 1992, Elegies Asiatiques, 1992, Paeans, 1993, Rhapsodies, 1994, Prosodia, 1994, Visions, 1994, Prophecies, 1994, Epyllia, 1994, Budapesttol Tokyoig, 1994, 2d edit., 1995, Walking Two Feet Above the Earth, 1995, Dictionarium Cumanico Hungaricum, 1996, Emblems, 1996, Epodes, 1996, Aeolian Lilts, 1996, Transformations, 1996, Inexpressions, 1996, Songs of the Soul, 1996, Sacrifices, 1996, Gifts with Poetic Horizons, 1997, Imperceptions, Hermeneutics of Poetry, 1997, From Silence to Silence, New Perspectives in Poetry, 1997, Lincoln the Poet, an Epic Poem, 1997, Looking Away, 1998, Commitments, 1998, The Duino Elegies of Rilke, 1999, Symmetries with Poetic Discoveries, Part I, 1999, Cosmos Flowers with Poetic Discoveries, Part II, 1999, Dreamtide with Principia Spiritualia I (Discoveries III), 2000, Demonstrations with Principia Spiritualia II-III (Discoveries IV-V), 2000, Pictorial Bio-Bibliography, 2000, also numerous others, also translations; editor-in-chief Monumenta Classica Perennia, 1967-84. Named Poet Laureate 2d World Congress of Poets, 1973; recipient Confucius award Chinese Poetry Soc., 1974, Yunus Emre award 12th Internat. Congress of Poets, Istanbul, Turkey, 1991, Jacques Raphael-Leygues prize Société des Poètes Français, 1992, French Ordre des Arts et des Lettres (officer), 1992. Mem. PEN, ASCAP, Internat. Soc. Lit., Die Literarische Union, Internat. Poetry Soc., Acad. Am. Poets, Assn. Lit. Scholars and Critics, 3d Internat. Congress Poets (pres. 1976, poet laureate 1976), Nat. Assn. of Scholars. Home: Santa Claus, Ind. Died Dec. 6, 2002.

PLESICH, THOMAS DAVID, educator; b. Steubenville, Ohio, Apr. 27, 1939; s. Joseph Michael and Margaret Ann (Pishok) P.; m. George-Anna Hartley, Nov. 16, 1963; children: William, Jansen, David. BS, U. Steubenville, 1962; postgrad., Am. U., Washington, 1964-65; MAT, Duquesne U., 1971. Staff announcer Radio Sta. WEIR, Weirton, W.Va., 1961-62; tchr. Weir High Sch., Weirton, W.Va., 1962-63; programmer Tech. Ops., Inc., Washington, 1963-65; expediter Nat. Steel Corp., Weirton, 1966-69; owner, assoc. publisher TV Facts Mag., Weirton, Steubenville, 1982-83; assoc. prof. Jefferson Tech. Coll., Steubenville, from 1969, Belmont Tech. Coll., from 1991. Instr. W.Va. No. Community Coll., Weirton, 1973—, Am. Inst. Banking, Steubenville, 1973, Wheeling Coll., W.Va., 1980, Community Coll. Allegheny County, Pitts., 1987—; cons. Brooke, Hancock, Jefferson Planning Commn., Steubenville, 1975; reviewer Prentice Hall Pub., Old Tappan, N.J., 1984. Mem. NEA, Ohio Edn. Assn., Nat. Eagle Scout Assn., Moose, Elks. Democrat. Roman Catholic. Home: Steubenville, Ohio. Died Oct. 24, 2000.

PLIMPTON, GEORGE AMES, writer, editor, television host; b. NYC, Mar. 18, 1927; s. Francis T.P. and Pauline (Ames) P.; m. Freddy Medora Espy, 1968 (div. 1988); children: Medora Ames, Taylor Ames; m. Sarah Whitehead Dudley, 1991; children: Olivia Hartley, Laura Dudley. Student, Phillips Exeter Acad., 1944; AB, Harvard U., 1948; MA, Cambridge (Eng.) U., 1952; L.H.D. (hon.), Franklin Pierce Coll., 1968; Litt.D. (hon.), Hobart Smith Coll., 1978, Stonehill Coll., 1982, L.I.U., 1984, U. S.C., 1986, Pine Manor Coll., 1988. Editor in chief Paris Rev., 1953—2003, Paris Rev. Edits. (subs. Doubleday and Co.), 1965-72; editor-in-chief Paris Rev. Edits. (subs. Brit. Am. Publ.), 1987—2003; instr. Barnard Coll., 1956-58; assoc. editor Horizon mag., 1959-61; dir. Am. Lit. Anthology program, 1967-71; assoc. editor Harper's mag., 1972-81; contbg. editor Food and Wine Mag., 1978; editorial adv. bd. Realities, 1978; TV host Dupont Plimpton Spl., 1967-69, Greatest Sports Legends, 1979-81, The Ultimate High, 1980, Survival Anglia, 1980—2003, Writers' Workshop, 1982, Mousterpiece Theater, 1983—2003, Challenge, 1987. Spl. contbr. Sports Illustrated, 1968—2003; bd. dir. Int. Film Investors, 1979-82, Leisure Dynamics, 1983-85; curator Tennis Week, 1990-2003. Author: Rabbit's Umbrella, 1956, Out of My League, 1961, Paper Lion, 1966, The Bogey Man, 1968, Mad Ducks and Bears, 1973, One for the Record, 1974, Shadow-Box, 1976, One More July, 1976, (with Neil Leifer) Sports!, 1978, (with Arnold Roth) A Sports Bestiary, 1982, Fireworks, 1984, Open Net, 1985, The Curious Case of Sidd Finch, 1987, The X-Factor, 1990, The Best of Plimpton, 1990, Truman Capote, In Which Various Friends, Enemies, Acquantances and Detractors Recall His Turbulent Career, Pet Peeves, 2000, Shackleton, 2003; also numerous articles.; editor; Writers at Work, Vol. 1, 1957, Vol. 11, 1963, Vol. 111, 1967, Vol. IV, 1976, Vol. V, 1981, Vol. VI, 1984, Vol. VII, 1987, Vol. VIII, 1989, Vol. IX, 1992, (with Jean Stein) American Journey: The Times of Robert Kennedy, 1970, Pierre's Book, 1971, The Fancy, 1973, (with Jean Stein) Edie, An American Biography, 1982, (with Christopher Hemphill) D.V., 1984; The Paris Review Anthology, 1989, The Writer's Chapbook, 1989, Women Writers at Work, 1989, Poets at Work, 1989, The Norton Book of Sports, 1992, (with Jean Kennedy Smith) Chronicles of Courage, 1992, Home Run, 2001; contbg. editor Gentlemen's Quar., 1983-85, Smart mag., 1988-90, Esquire mag., 1990; actor films including Lawrence of Arabia, 1962, The Detective, 1968, Reds, 1981, The Bonfire of the Vanities, 1990, Little Man Tate, 1991, Nixon, 1995, When We Were Kings, 1996, Good Will Hunting, 1997; actor TV mini-series The Civil War, 1990, Baseball, 1994, Nero Wolfe, 2000-2002. Commr. fireworks, NYC, 1973—2003; trustee WNET, 1973-81, Nat. Art Mus. Sport, 1967—2003, Police Athletic League, 1976-90, African Wildlife Leadership Found., 1980—2003, Guild Hall, East Hampton, 1980—2003, NY Zool. Soc., 1985-2003; bd. dir. Dynamite Mus., Nat. Tennis Found., 1979—2003, Squaw Valley Center for Written and Dramatic Arts, 1979—2003, Authors Trust Am., 1979, Friends of the Masai Mara, 1986, Friends of Conservation, 1988-2002, Roger Tory Peterson Inst., The Carnegie Cook Ctr. for the Arts; chmn. Books Across the Sea, English Speaking Union, 1988-2003; bd. dir., pres. NY Philomusica, Pen/Faulkner, 1995; mem. adv. bd. Coordinating Council Lit. Mags., 1979, Yoknapatawpha Press, Am. Chess Found., East Harlem Tutorial, Boy's Harbor. Served to 2d lt. AUS, 1945-48. Assoc. fellow Trumbull Coll., Yale, 1967; recipient Disting. Achievement award U. So. Calif., 1967, Blue Pencil award Columbia Spectator, 1981, Mark Twain award Internat. Platform Assn., 1982, Chancellor's award L.I. U., 1986, l'Ordre des Arts et des Lettres, France, 1994, Guild Hall Lifetime Achievement award, 2002, Chevalier Legio d'honeur, 2002, small Press Ben Franklin Award, 2003. Mem. NFL Alumni Assn., Am. Pyrotechnics Assn., Acad. Arts Letters, Pyrotechnics Guild Internat., Explorers Club., Linnean Soc., PEN, Mayflower Descendants Soc. Clubs: Century Assn, Racquet and Tennis, Brook, Piping Rock, Dutch Treat, River, Coffee House, Devon Yacht; Travellers (Paris). Died Sept. 25, 2003.

PLOGER, ROBERT RIIS, retired military officer, engineer; b. Mackay, Idaho, Aug. 12, 1915; s. Robert and Elfrieda (Riis) P.; m. Marguerite Anne Fiehrer, June 13, 1939 (dec. Feb. 1982); children: Wayne David, Robert Riis III, Daniel Bruce, Marguerite Anne, Marianne Ploger Hill, Gregory Fiehrer; m. Jeanne Allys Pray, Nov. 20, 1982 (dec. Aug., 1998). BS, U.S. Mil. Acad., 1939; MS in Engring., Cornell U., 1947; MBA, George Washington U., 1963. Registered civil engr., D.C. Commd. 2d lt. U.S. Army, 1939, served in corps of engrs., 1939-65, advanced through grades to maj. gen., 1966, div. engr. New England div., 1965, comdg. gen. 18th engr. brigade, 1965-66, comdg. gen. engr. command, Vietnam, 1966-67, dir. topography and mil. engring., Office Chief Engrs., 1967-70; comdg. gen. Ft. Belvoir and commandant U.S. Army Engr. Sch. Va., 1970-73; ret. U.S. Army, 1973; engr. specialist Bechtel Power Corp., Ann Arbor, 1974-80, mgr. adminstrv. services, 1980-81; counselor SCORE, Ann Arbor, Mich., from 1984, ret., from 2002. Lectr. Indsl. Coll. Armed Forces, 1962-65. Author: Vietnam Studies, U.S. Army Engineers 1965-70; contbr. numerous articles on war and mil. engring. to profl. jours. Chmn. gift com. Class of 1939 50th Reunion of U.S. Mil. Acad., 1985-89; pres.-elect residents assn. Glacier Hills Retirement Ctr., Ann Arbor, Mich., 2001—, pres., 2002—. Decorated DSM with oak leaf cluster, Legion of Merit, Silver Star with oak leaf cluster, Bronze Star with oak leaf cluster, Air medal, Purple Heart, Korean Order Mil. Merit Chung Mu, Nat. Order 5th Class Republic of Vietnam; recipient George Washington medal ICAF, 1965, Wheeler medal Soc. Am. Mil. Engrs., 1966, Silver Beaver award Boy Scouts Am., 1973, Médaille du Jubilé, Vire, France, 1994. Fellow Soc. Am. Mil. Engrs.; mem. NSPE (priviliged; chpt. pres. 1979-80), 29th Inf. Divsn. Assn. (Phila. award 1985), West Point Soc. Mich. (pres. 1981-84), SCORE (at-large exec. com. 1991, counselor chpt. 18, chpt. 655 2000—, membership com. chmn. chpt. 655 2000—), Ann Arbor C. of C. (counselor svc. corps ret. execs.), Army Engr. Assn. (life, Silver Order de Fleury medal 1995), SHAPE Officers Assn. (life). Baptist. Avocations: tennis, skiing, sailboarding. Home: Ann Arbor, Mich. Deceased.

PLUMMER, ROGER SHERMAN, JR., oil company executive, consultant; b. Portland, Oreg., Aug. 4, 1922; s. Roger Sherman and Ruth (Barlow) P.; m. Lois Virginia Ross, Aug. 15, 1960; 1 dau., Pamela Ruth Martin. B.A., U. Tex., 1948, M.A. in Geology, 1949. Geologist, Socony Mobil Oil Co., Caracas, Venezuela, 1949-53; chief subsurface geologist Internat. Petroleum Colombia, Bogota, 1952-56; exploration mgr. Libyan Am. Oil Co., Benghazi, Libya, 1956-58, gen. mgr., 1958-60, v.p., gen. mgr., Benghazi, 1961-64; v.p., dir. Grace Petroleum Corp., Benghazi, 1965-66, exec. v.p., dir. Grace Petroleum Corp., Grace Oil Corp. (Italy). Rome, 1966-68; pres., chief exec. officer, dir. Champlin Petroleum Co., Fort Worth, 1968-75, cons., 1975-77; internat. petroleum cons., 1978-96; teaching fellow U. Tex., 1948-49, mem. Geology Found.; instr. Southwestern U., 1948-49; dir. Continental Nat. Bank of Fort Worth. Served to 1st lt. USAAF, 1942-46. Mem. Am. Assn. Petroleum Geologists, AIME Tex. Mid-Continent Oil and Gas Assn., Am. Petroleum Inst. (dir.), Am. Inst. Profl. Geologists, Fort Worth C. of C. (dir.), Explorers Club, Sulphur Springs Country Club, Ft. Worth Petroleum Club, Phi Beta Kappa, Sigma Xi, Sigma Gamma Epsilon. Republican. Methodist. Died Oct. 13, 1996. Home: Sulphur Springs, Tex.

POFFENBERGER, PAUL ROUTZAHN, economics educator; b. Hagerstown, Md., Jan. 28, 1913; s. George F. and Elizabeth (Routzahn) P.; m. Gladys Maud Leonard, Apr. 5, 1947; children: Linda Lee, Gail Patrice. BS, U. Md., 1935, MS, 1937; PhD, Am. U., 1953. Asst. prof. dept. agrl. econs. U. Md., College Park, 1940-43, asso. prof., 1946-54, prof., head dept., 1954-61, asst. dean instrn. Coll. Agr., 1956-69, prof. agrl. econs., asso. dean, 1969-81, prof. emeritus, asso. dean emeritus, 1981—. Contbr. articles profl. jours. Pres. Columbia Rd. Citizens Assn., 1963; bd. dirs. Nations Capital council Girl Scouts U.S., 1982-88. Served with USNR, 1943-46. Recipient hon. Am. Farmer degree Nat. Future Farmers Am. Fellow AAAS; mem. Am. Agrl. Econs. Assn., Alpha Gamma Rho, Alpha Zeta, Omicron Delta Kappa, Pi Delta Epsilon, Phi Kappa Phi. Clubs: Toastmasters (Silver Spring) (ednl. v.p. 1965, pres. 1966). Lutheran. Home: Arnold, Md. Deceased.

POGUE, L(LOYD) WELCH, lawyer; b. Grant, Iowa, Oct. 21, 1899; s. Leander Welch and Myrtle Viola (Casey) P.; m. Mary Ellen Edgerton(dec. 2001), Sept. 8, 1926; children: Richard Welch, William Lloyd, John Marshall. AB, U. Nebr., 1924; JD, U. Mich., 1926; SJD, Harvard U., 1927. Bar: Mass., N.Y., D.C., Ohio, U.S. Supreme Ct. Assoc. Ropes, Gray, Boyden and Perkins, 1927-33; ptnr. affiliated firm Searle, James and Crawford, N.Y.C., 1933-38; asst. gen. counsel CAB, 1938-39, gen. counsel, through 1941, chmn. bd., 1942-46; mem., mng. ptnr. Pogue & Neal, Washington, 1946-67; Washington mng. ptnr. Jones, Day, Reavis &

Pogue, Washington, 1967-79, ret., 1981. Lindbergh Meml. lectr. Nat. Air and Space Mus., Smithsonian Inst., 1991; presenter essay 50th Ann. Internat. Civil Aviation Orgn., Montreal, 1994; Wright Bros. Meml. lectr., 1999; spkr. and lectr. in field. Author: International Civil Air Transport—Transition Following WW II, 1979, Pogue/Pollock/Polk Genealogy as Mirrored in History, 1990 (1st pl. in Anna Ford Family history book contest 1991, Nat. Geneal. Soc. award for excellence genealogy and family history 1992, William H. and Benjamin Harrison Book award Coun. Ohio Genealogists 1992, Outstanding Achievement award County and Regional History category Ohio Assn. Hist. Socs. and Mus. 1992, 1st pl. award Iowa Washington County Geneal. Soc. 1994, cert. commendation Am. Assn. State and Local History 1994, 1st place award Lake Havasu Geneal. Soc. 1996), Airline Deregulation, Before and After: What Next? (Lindbergh Meml. lectr. 1991), The International Civil Aviation Conference, 1944, and Its Sequel, The Anglo-American Bermuda Air Transport Agreement, 1946, 1994; The Wright Brothers Memorial Lecture (Annually given) NASA Langley Research Center, 1999; contbr. articles to profl. publs. Mem. U.S. dels.: Chgo. Internat. Civil Aviation Conf., 1944; vice chmn. Bermuda United Kingdom-U.S. Conf., 1946; vice chmn. Provisional Internat. Civil Aviation Orgn. Assembly, 1946; active Internat. Civil Aviation Orgn. Assembly, 1947. With AUS, 1918. Recipient Elder Statesman of Aviation award Nat. Aeronautic Assn., 1993, Golden Eagle award Soc. Sr. Aerospace Execs., 1988, 1st annual recipient of L. Welch Pogue award for Aviation Achievement, McGraw-Hill Orgn.'s Aviation Week Group, 1994, Aviation Week's Laurel Legend award and named to its Laureates Hall of Fame, 2002; (hon.)fellow Am. Helicopter Soc. Internat., Benjamin Franklin fellow Royal Soc. Arts. Fellow Royal Aero. Soc.; mem. AIAA (hon., Certificate of 60 yrs. continuous membership), Soc. of Sr. Aerospace Execs. (hon.), Helicopter Assn. Internat. (hon. mem.), Am. Air Mus. in Britain (founding mem.), Can. Aeronautics and Space Inst., Nat. Aeronautic Assn. (pres. 1947), Nat. Air and Space Soc. (founder), Soc. of Sr. Aerospace Execs., Nat. Geneal. Soc., New Eng. Hist. Geneal. Soc. (life, former trustee), Ohio Geneal. Soc. (life), Md. Geneal. Soc. (life), Md. Hist. Soc. (life), Provincial Families of Md., First Families of Ohio, Met. Club (50-yr. mem.), Univ. Club, Wings Club (hon., N.Y.C.), Bohemian Club (San Francisco, 40-yr. mem.), Cosmos Club, Masons, Order of the First World War (charter), Nat. Aviation Club, Aero Club of Washington (hon. mem., Donald D. Engen trophy for aviation excellence, 2001), Am. Legion (cert. of 80 years continuous membership, Life Membership, 2002). Home: Chevy Chase, Md. Died May 10, 2003; Quantico Nat. Cemetary.

POGUE, MARY ELLEN E. (MRS. L(LOYD) WELCH POGUE), youth and community worker; b. Fremont, Nebr., Oct. 27, 1904; d. Frank Eugene and Mary Nettie (Coe) Edgerton; m. L. Welch Pogue, Sept. 8, 1926; children: Richard Welch, William Lloyd, John Marshall. BFA in Edn. Music, U. Nebr., 1926; studied violin with Harrison Keller, Boston Conservatory of Music, 1926-28; studied violin with Kemp Stillings, Violin Master Class, 1935-37. Mem. Potomac String Ensemble, Washington, 1939-80. Compiler, editor: Favorite Menus and Recipes of Mary Edgerton of Aurora, Nebraska, 1963, Family History of Frank Eugene Edgerton and Mary Coe Edgerton of Aurora, Nebraska, 1965. Historian, Gov. William Bradford Compact, 1966—; vice chmn. Montgomery County (Md.) Victory Garden Ctr., 1946-47; pres. Bethesda Cmty. Garden Club, 1946-47; founder Montgomery County YWCA, bd. dirs., 1946-50, 52-55; founder Welcome to Washington Internat. Club Music Group, 1967—; co-founder Group Piano in Montgomery County, Md. schs., 1954. Recipient Gov. William Bradford Compact Cert. of Merit award, 1970, Outstanding Svc. award Bethesda United Meth. Ch., 1984, Bethesda Cmty. Garden Club award, 1985, 93, Devoted Svc. award Mayflower Descendants in D.C., 1985, 89, Welcome to Washington Internat. Club award, 1986, Mortar Board award, 1986. Mem. Gen. Soc. Mayflower Descs., Soc. Mayflower Descs. D.C. (dir. D.C. 1954—, elder 1974-92, elder emeritus 1992—), Nat. Soc. Daus. Founders and Patriots Am., PEO Sisterhood (pres. 1957-59, charter mem. chpt. R, 75 Year Mem. Tribute), Mortar Bd. Alumnae Club (pres. 1965-67, award 1986, 75 Year Member Honor.), Nat. Capitol Area Fedn. Garden Clubs, Nat. Coun. State Garden Clubs, Bethesda United Meth. Women, Nat. Geneal. Soc., New Eng. Historic Geneal. Soc. (life), Ohio Geneal. Soc. (life), Md. Geneal. Soc., Md. Hist. Soc., Conn. Soc. Genealogists, Pilgrim Soc. (life), Plimoth Plantation, Hereditary Order Descs. Colonial Govs., Nat. Soc. Magna Charta Dames, Colonial Order of Crown, Sovereign Colonial Soc. Ams. Royal Descent, Order of Descs. Colonial Physicians and Chirurgiens, Hereditary Soc. Blue Book (perpetual mem.), Nat. Soc. Women Descs. Ancient and Hon. Arty. Co., First Families Ohio, First Families Nebr., Century Families Nebr., Oreg. Trail Pioneers, Sons and Daus. Colonial and Antebellum Bench and Bar 1565-1861 (charter), Welcome to Washington Internat. Club, Ind. Agy. Women (assoc.), Capital Spkrs. Club (Washington), The Plantagenet Soc., Soc. Descs. Knights of Most Noble Order of Garter, DAR, Order Ams. Armorial Ancestry, Saybrook Colony Founders Assn., Soc. Founders Norwich Conn. (cert. desc. Richard Edgerton), Kenwood Country Club, Alpha Phi (75 yr. mem. cert.), Alpha Rho Tau, Delta Omicron Music (life). Methodist. Avocations: genealogy, gardening, music. Home: Chevy Chase, Md. Died Sept. 19, 2001; Quantico Nat. Cemetery.

POIS, ROBERT AUGUST, historian; b. Washington, Apr. 24, 1940; s. Joseph and Rose (Tomarkin) P.; m. Anne Marie Messerschmitt, July 2, 1972; children— Haia Rebecca, Erica Leah, Emily Tamara. AB, Grinnell (Iowa) Coll., 1961; MA, U. Wis., 1962, PhD, 1965. Mem. faculty U. Colo., Boulder, 1965—2004, prof. history, 1975—2004. Del. Citizens Amb. Exch. Program, Russia, 1991. Author: Friedrich Meinecke and German Politics in the 20th Century, 1972, The Bourgeois Democrats of Weimar Germany, 1976, Emil Nolde, 1982, National Socialism and the Religion of Nature, 1986, The Great War, 1994. Del. Boulder County Dem. Conv., 1970. Woodrow Wilson fellow, 1961; recipient Student Orgn. Alumni Relations teaching award, 1987, 93, Boulder Faculty Assembly teaching award, 1987; Pres.' Tchg. scholar, 1990. Mem. Am. Hist. Assn., Am. Fedn. Tchrs., Phi Beta Kappa. Jewish. Home: Boulder, Colo. Died Jan. 18, 2004.

POJMAN, PAUL J. lawyer; b. Cleve., Aug. 22, 1917; s. Joseph F. and Cecilia Pojman; widower; children: Paul E., Marianne, Jeanne, Raymond, Richard, Elizabeth. BS in Tchg., Baldwin Wallace U., 1943; MA, Case Western Res. U., 1948, LD, 1942; PhB, John Carroll U., 1939. Pvt. practice, Parma Heights, Ohio, from 1942. Mem. coun. Walton Hills Village, 1950-51. Mem. Cleve. Bar Assn., Parma Bar Assn. Home: Walton Hills, Ohio. Died Aug. 7, 2001.

POLICOFF, LEONARD DAVID, physician, educator; b. Wilmington, Del., Apr. 22, 1918; s. David and Rosalie (Rochkind) P.; m. Naomi Lewis, June 25, 1942; children: Susan, Stephen. BS, U. Richmond, 1938; MD, Med. Coll. Va., 1942. Diplomate Am. Bd. Internal Medicine, Am. Bd. Phys. Medicine and Rehab. (mem. 1968-80). Asst. prof. Med. Coll. Va., 1948-55; prof., chmn. dept. phys. medicine and rehab. Albany Med. Coll., Union U., 1955-67, Temple U., Phila., 1967-70; prof., chmn. Hahnemann Med. Coll., Phila., 1970-71; prof. clin. phys. medicine U. Pa.; chmn. dept. rehab. medicine Princeton (N.J.) Hosp., 1971-75, cons., 1975-78; dir. rehab. medicine Somerset Hosp., Somerville, N.J., 1975-78; acting chmn., prof. clin. phys. medicine Rutgers Med. Sch., 1976-78; clin. prof. phys. medicine and rehab. U. Calif.-Davis Sch. Medicine, 1980-86; chmn. dept. rehab. medicine Pacific Med. Center, San Francisco, 1978-81. Med. cons. Dept. Health Svcs., State of Calif., 1987-91; chief rehab. medicine svc. VA Med. Ctr., Martinez, Calif., 1983-85; med. dir. Rehab. Ctr., John Muir Meml. Hosp., Walnut Creek, Calif., 1985-87; mem. Bd. Med. Examiners, N.Y. State, 1962-67; chief of staff VA Hosp., Livermore, Calif., 1987-88. Contbr. articles to profl. jours., textbooks. Bd. dirs. Commn. on Edn. in Phys. Medicine and Rehab., 1968-80, com. for Handicapped People-to-People Program, 1967-75. Served to maj. M.C., AUS, 1943-46. Nat. Inst. Neurologic Diseases fellow, 1953-55 Fellow ACP, Am. Acad. Phys. Medicine and Rehab., Am. Acad. Cerebral Palsy; mem. Am. Congress Rehab. Medicine (pres. 1971), Assn. Acad. Physiatrists, AMA (chmn. phys. medicine sect. 1965-66), Phi Beta Kappa, Alpha Omega Alpha, Sigma Zeta. Home: Berkeley, Calif. Died Jan. 3, 2004.

POLIN, RAYMOND, political scientist, educator; b. Westport, Mass., Aug. 9, 1918; s. Israel and Ida (Posnick) P.; m. Constance Fay Caplan, Nov. 9, 1957; children: Jane, Lawrence, Kenneth, Ellen, Theodore. BA, NYU, 1940, MA, 1941, PhD, 1959. N.Y. permanent social studies cert. From clk. to chief clk. U.S. War Dept., 1941-43; from instr. to asst. prof. L.I. U., Bklyn., 1946-59; asst. prof., dept. chmn. Yeshiva U., N.Y.C., 1959-62; assoc. prof. St. John's U., Jamaica, N.Y., 1962-67, prof., 1967-90, prof. emeritus, 1990. Vis. asst. prof. NYU, N.Y.C., 1961-62, vis. assoc. prof., 1962-67; mem. supts. curriculum adv. com. N.Y.C. Pub. Schs., 1960-62; cons. Internat. Fair Cons., N.Y.C., 1961-64; dir. Multi-Ethnic Curriculum Task Force, Pub. Schs., Mt. Vernon, N.Y., 1969-70; on-camera lectr., participant CBS and NBC tv, N.Y.C., 1975-80. Author: Marxian Foundations of Communism, 1966 (Harry J. Carman Meml. medal 1965), Modern Government and Constitutionalism, 1979, Plato and Aristotle on Constitutionalism, 1998. Recipient Dwight D. Eisenhower award U.S. Dept. of the Army, ROTC, 1971; Penfield fellow Grad. Sch. Arts and Scis., NYU, 1948-49. Mem. AAUP, Am. Hist. Soc., Am. Polit. Sci. Assn., Middle States Coun. for the Social Studies (pres. 1968-70, Disting. Svc. medal 1979), N.-Y. Hist. Soc., Scarsdale Town and Village Club, Soc. for Greek Polit. Thought. Democrat. Jewish. Avocations: gardening, photography, musical record collecting. Home: Scarsdale, NY. Died Apr. 25, 2002.

POLITZ, HENRY ANTHONY, federal judge; b. Napoleonville, La., May 9, 1932; s. Anthony and Virginia (Russo) P.; m. Jane Marie Simoneaux, Apr. 29, 1952; children: Nyle, Bennett, Mark, Angela, Scott, Jane, Michael, Henry, Alisa, John, Nina. BA, La. State U., 1958, JD, 1959. Bar: La. 1959. Assoc., then ptnr. firm Booth, Lockard, Jack, Pleasant & LeSage, Shreveport, 1959-79; circuit judge U.S. Ct. Appeals (5th cir.), Shreveport, 1979—92, chief judge, 1992-99, sr. judge, 1999—2002. Vis. prof. La. State U. Law Center; bd. dirs. Am. Prepaid Legal Services Inst., 1975—; mem. La. Judiciary Commn., 1978-79; mem. U.S. Jud. Conf., 1992-99, exec. com., 1996-99. Mem. editl. bd. La. State U. Law Rev., 1958-59. Mem. Shreveport Airport Authority, 1973-79, chmn., 1977; bd. dirs. Rutherford House, Shreveport, 1975—, pres., 1978; pres. Caddo Parish Bd. Election Suprs., 1975-79; mem. Electoral Coll., 1976. Served with USAF, 1951-55. Named Outstanding Young Lawyer in La., 1971, Outstanding Alumnus La. State U. Law Sch., 1991; inducted in La. State U. Hall of Distinction, 1992. Mem. Am. Bar Assn., Am. Judicature Soc., Internat. Soc. Barristers, La. Bar Assn., La. Trial Lawyers Assn., Shreveport Bar Assn., Justinian Soc., K.C., Omicron Delta Kappa. Democrat. Roman Catholic. Died May 25, 2002.

POLLICOVE, HARVEY MYLES, manufacturing executive; b. Utica, NY, May 28, 1944; s. Maxwell Hymen and Carolyn (Vogel) P.; m. Catherine Mary Keady, Aug. 3, 1968; children: Carolyn, Sarah. AAS, Monroe Community Coll., 1968; BS, U. Rochester, 1973. Sr. engr. supr. optics Eastman Kodak Co., Rochester, 1978-82, engring. mgr. optics, 1982-84, mfg. mgr., 1984-86, mgr. tech. mkts. (internat.), 1986-89; dir. Ctr. for Optics Mfg. U. Rochester, from 1989. U.S. del. (optics) to Internat. Stds. Orgn., 1995—; bd. mem. Optics and Electro-Optics Standards Coun., 1999—, chmn. ASC OP Nat. Optics Standards, 2001-; hon. advisor Hong Kong Photographic and Optics Mfrs. Assn., 2000—; lectr. in field. Editorial adv. bd. (optics mag. for mfg.) Laser Focus World, 1990-2000; contbr. articles to profl. jours. Advisor High Tech. of Rochester, 1988-89; advisor tech. applications rev. bd. Strategic Def. Initiative Orgn., 1990-92, Ballistic Missile Def. Orgn., 1993-96, mem. lasers and optics working group Inst. Def. Analysis, 2002; industry advisor Monroe C.C., 1986-97. Recipient Dept. of Def. Mfg. Tech. Achievement award, 1992, 2000, R&D 100 award, 2001. Mem. ASME/Optics Stds. (chmn.), Am. Precision Optics Mfrs. Assn. (exec. com. 1987—), Internat. Soc. for Optical Engring., Optical Soc. Am. (hon. mem. Rochester sect. 1996). Home: Rochester, NY. Died Jan. 25, 2004.

POMERANTZ, JERALD MICHAEL, lawyer; b. Springfield, Mass., July 9, 1954; s. Lawrence Louis Pomerantz and Dolores (Barez) Chaudoir. BA in Econs. cum laude, Brandeis U., 1976; JD, Vanderbilt U., 1979; student, Am. Inst. Banking, 1983-99. Atty., McAllen, Tex., 1979-80, Weslaco, Tex., 1980-85; gen. counsel, sec. Tex. Valley Bancshares, Inc., Weslaco, 1985-87; atty. for Hidalgo County Rural Fire Prevention Dist., Tex., 1982-88; atty. SBA, Harlingen, Tex., 1987; pvt. practice Weslaco, Tex., 1987-89; adv. dir. South Tex. Fed. Credit Union, 1995-98. Atty. Elsa (Tex.) Housing Authority, from 1993, Weslaco (Tex.) Housing Authority, from 1995, Econ. Devel. Corp. Weslaco, 2001—02. Mem. Weslaco Charter Review Com., 1981-82,; drafted S.B. 139 (amending Tex. bus. and commerce code sect. 9.402(g)) regular session Tex. Legislature), 1989, S.B. 140, 1989, enacted as H.B. 2005 (amending Tex. Credit Code sect. 1.06) regular session Tex. Legislature, 1993; commr. Weslaco Planning and Zoning Com., 2002—. Recipient continuing edn. award Banking Law Inst., 1992. Mem.: Rio Grande Valley Bankruptcy Bar Assn. (v.p. 2000—01), Hidalgo County Bar Assn. (law libr. com. from 1999), Coll. State Bar Tex. (bd.dirs. 1990—95), Conf. on Consumer Fin. Law, State Bar Tex., Tex. Assn. Bank Counsel (bd. dirs. 1990—95, 1997—2000, v.p. 2001—02, pres.-elect 2002—03, pres. from 2003). Died Nov. 27, 2003.

POMEROY, HARLAN, lawyer; b. Cleve., May 7, 1923; s. Lawrence Alson and Frances (Macdonald) P.; m. Barbara Lesser, Aug. 24, 1962; children: Robert Charles, Caroline Macdonald, Harlan III BS, Yale U., 1945; JD, Harvard U., 1948. Bar: Conn. 1949, U.S. Supreme Ct. 1954, U.S. Ct. Appeals (fed. cir.) 1954, Ohio 1958, U.S. Dist. Ct. (no. dist.) Ohio 1958, U.S. Claims Ct. 1958, U.S. Ct. Appeals (6th cir.) 1958, U.S. Tax Ct. 1958, D.C. 1975, Md. 1981, U.S. Dist. Ct. (D.C. dist.) 1984, U.S. Ct. Internat. Trade 1984, U.S. Ct. Appeals (D.C. cir.) 1986; cert. county ct. mediator, Fla. Atty. trial sect. tax div. Dept. Justice, Washington, 1952-58; assoc. Baker & Hostetler, Cleve., 1958-62, ptnr., 1962-75, Washington, 1975-92. Gen. chmn. Cleve. Tax Inst., 1971; fgn. legal advisor to Romanian Securities Mkts., 1997, Macedonia, 1998, UN Interim Adminstrn. Mission in Kosovo, 2000-2001; arbitrator Nat. Assn. Securities Dealers, 1992—, N.Y. Stock Exch., 1995—, Sarasota Better Bus. Coun., 1997—; arbitrator Multistate Tax Commn., 1996—, mem. neutral roster IRS mediation program; lectr. on tax and comml. law. Author: (monographs) The Privatization Process in Bulgaria; Bulgarian Government Structure and Operation-An Overview; contbr. articles to profl. jours. Treas. Shaker Heights (Ohio) Dem. Club, 1960-62; trustee, mem. exec. com. 1st Unitarian Ch. Cleve., 1965-68; trustee River Road Unitarian Ch., Bethesda, Md., 1988-90; gen. counsel, former asst. treas. John Glenn Presdl. Com., 1983-87; participant Vol. Lawyers Project, Legal Counsel for Elderly, Washington, 1983-92; vol. Guardian Ad Litem Program, Sarasota, Fla., 1990-92, GED-H.S. Equivalency Program, Sarasota, 1990-92; participant Guardianship Monitoring program 12th Jud. Cir., Fla., 1996-97; vol. exec. fgn. legal advisor Internat. Exec. Svc. Corps. with Privatization Ministry, Prague, Czech Republic, 1994-95; mem. spl. mission to Bulgarian Ministry of Fin., U.S. Dept. Treasury, 1995. Ensign USN, 1943—46. Mem. ABA (resident liaison Bulgaria for Ctrl. and East European Law Initiative 1992-93), Am. Arbitration Assn. (arbitrator 1992-2000), D.C. Bar Assn., The Field Club (Sarasota, Fla.), Yale Club of the Suncoast (pres. 1999-2000), Ivy League Club. Home: Sarasota, Fla. Died Feb. 28, 2003.

PONZER, JOHN LEWIS, engineering executive; b. Brinkley, Ark., Feb. 20, 1913; s. Karl Lewis and Grace (Short) P.; m. Willetta Woody, Nov. 26, 1945; children: Grace Stratton, Janet Lee. BSEE, N.C. State U., 1935. Supt. REA, Wilson, N.C., 1935-37; jr. indsl. engr. Carolina Power & Light Co., Asheville, N.C., 1937-41, sr. indsl. engr. Southern Pines, N.C., 1946-66, lighting specialist Raleigh, N.C., 1966-78; pres., chief exec. Energy Assocs., Southern Pines, from 1978. Tech. cons. N.C. Dept. Labor, Raleigh, 1963-70; lighting chmn. N.Y.C. Edison Electric Inst. Electrification Council, 1968-70; keynote speaker All-Industry Conv., Myrtle Beach, S.C., 1968; conceived, co-developed Research Triangle Park, Durham, N.C., 1953; created Total Environ. Program Nat. Elec. Contractors Assn., 1967; lectr., speaker numerous colls., assns. Contbr. numerous articles to profl. jours. Chmn. Southern Pines Indsl. Com., 1958; exec.

bd. N.C. Cong. PTA's, 1964-65; dir. engring. sect. Civil Def.; chmn. fund drive ARC, 1960; lay reader Emmanuel Episc. Ch., Southern Pines, 1959-66. Served to col. U.S. Army, 1941-46, ETO, grad. Command and Gen. Staff Sch. Decorated four battle stars; recipient Outstanding Scouter award Boy Scouts Am., Southern Pines, 1954, Elec. Man of Yr. award Nat. Elec. Contractors Assn., 1970; named Eagle Scout, Boy Scouts Am. Mem. IEEE (chmn. nat. textile com., 1957, chmn. indsl. com. 1962, Outstanding Service award 1961), Illuminating Engring. Soc. (dir. 1958-60, section pres. 1968-69, Disting. Service award 1969), N.C. Engring. Soc., Nat. Assn. Lighting Maintenance, N.C. State U. Alumni Assn. (pres. 1953), Phi Eta Sigma, Sigma Phi Epsilon. Clubs: Mens' Garden (Southern Pines) (pres.); Cotillion (Asheville); City (Raleigh); Southern Pines Country; North Ridge Country; Biltmore Forest Country. Lodges: Royal Brigade Guards, Kiwanis (pres. Southern Pines club 1955-56, Lt. gov. Carolinas dist. 1957, Disting. Service award 1962), Elks, Masons, Brotherhood St. Andrews (pres. 1958). Avocations: civic work, fishing, gardening, golf. Home: Raleigh, NC. Deceased.

POOL, JAMES LAWRENCE, neurosurgeon, emeritus educator; b. N.Y.C., Aug. 23, 1906; s. Eugene H. and Esther (Hoppin) P.; m. Angeline K. James, June 14, 1940; children: James Lawrence, Eugene H. II, Daniel S. AB, Harvard U., 1928; MD, Columbia U., 1932, D.MS, 1941. Diplomate: Am. Bd. Neurol. Surgery. Intern N.Y.-Cornell, 1932-33, Presbyn. Hosp., N.Y.C., 1934-36; Neurol. Inst., 1936-38, chief resident neurol. surgery, 1938-39; neurosurgeon Bellevue Hosp., 1939-47, Neurol. Inst., 1947; prof. neurol. surgery and dir. dept. Presbyn. Hosp. and Columbia Coll. Physicians and Surgeons, 1949-72, emeritus, 1972—2004. Cons. Englewood (N.J.) Hosp.; Trustee St. Pauls Sch., Concord, N.H., 1954-64; Am. Mus. Natural History, 1956-60; bd. overseers Harvard Coll., 1948-54 Author: Neurosurgical Treatment of Paraplegia, 1951, (with Arthur Pava) Acoustic Nerve Tumors, 1957, 2d edit., 1971, (with Gordon Potts) Aneurysms and AVM of the Brain, 1965, Your Brain and Nerves, 1973, paperback edit., 1978, Izaak Walton, Life and Times, 1975, The Neurological Institute of N.Y.: 1909-1972, 1974, America's Valley Forges and Valley Furnaces, 1982, Nature's Masterpiece: The Brain and How It Works, 1987, Adventures and Ventures of a New York Neurosurgeon, 1988. Served to lt. col. M.C. AUS, World War II. Recipient Disting. Service award Soc. Neurol. Surgeons, 1983; Medal of Honour 8th Internat. Congress Neurol. Surgery, 1985. Fellow A.C.S. (gov. 1959-62); mem. AMA, Am. Neurology Assn., Am. Acad. Neurol. Surgery (pres. 1952-53), Harvey Cushing Soc., Neurosurg. Soc., World Fedn. Neurol. Surgeons (treas. 1965-73), Harvard Alumni Assn. (pres. 1958-59) Clubs: Anglers (N.Y.C.), Century (N.Y.C.), Harvard (N.Y.C.); British Royal Ocean Racing. Home: West Cornwall, Conn. Died May 4, 2004.

POORE, JAMES ALBERT, III, lawyer; b. Butte, Mont., June 28, 1943; s. James A. Jr. and Jesse (Wild) P.; m. Shelley A. Borgstede, Feb. 12, 1989; children: James IV, Jeffrey. AB, Stanford U., 1965; JD with honors, U. Mont., 1968. Bar: Mont. 1968, U.S. Dist. Ct. Mont. 1968, U.S. Ct. Appeals (9th cir.) 1972, U.S. Supreme Ct. 1973. Assoc. Poore, Poore, McKenzie & Roth, Butte, 1968-74; prin., v.p. Poore, Roth & Robinson, P.C., Butte, 1974-96; ptnr. Knight, Masar & Poore, LLP, Missoula, Mont., 1996-98, Poore & Hopkins PLLP, Missoula, Mont., 1998-99. Speaker in field. Assoc. editor U. Mont. Law Rev., 1967-68; contbg. editor Product Liability Desk Reference, 1999; contbr. articles to profl. publs. Dist. dir. Boy Scouts Am., S.W. Mont., 1969; dir. YMCA, Butte, 1981-83; founding bd. dirs. Hospice of Butte, 1982-85, Butte Community Theater, 1977-80; pres. Butte Uptown Assn., 1974; dir. Butte Silverbow Am. Cancer Soc. Bd., 1992-95. Fellow Am. Bar Found.; mem. ABA, State Bar Mont., Am. Judicature Soc., Silver Bow Bar Assn., Western Mont. Bar Assn., Phi Delta Phi. Home: Missoula, Mont. Died Aug. 11, 1999.

POPLE, SIR JOHN ANTHONY, chemistry educator; b. Burnham, Somerset, Eng., Oct. 31, 1925; arrived in U.S., 1964; s. Herbert Keith and Frances (Jones) Pople; m. Joy Cynthia Pople, Sept. 22, 1952 (dec. 2002); children: Hilary Jane, Adrian John, Mark Stephen, Andrew Keith. BA in Math., Cambridge U., Eng., 1946, MA in Math., 1950, PhD in Math., 1951. Rsch. fellow Trinity Coll., Cambridge (Eng.) U., 1951—54, lectr. in math., 1954—58; Ford vis. prof. chemistry Carnegie Inst. Tech., Pitts., 1961—62; Carnegie prof. chem. physics Carnegie-Mellon U., Pitts., 1964—74, J.C. Warner prof., 1974—91; prof. Northwestern U., Evanston, Ill., 1986—2004. Named Knight Comdr., British Empire, 2003; recipient Chemistry prize, Wolf Found., 1992, Kirkwood medal, Am. Chem. Soc., 1994, J.O. Hirschfelder prize in theoretical chemistry, U. Wis., Theoretical Chemistry Inst., 1994, Nobel prize in chemistry, 1998. Fellow: AAAS, Royal Soc. London, mem.: NAS. Home: Chicago, Ill. Died Mar. 15, 2004.

PORDY, LEON, coffee company executive, cardiologist; b. N.Y.C., July 5, 1919; s. William and Sadie (Fogel) P.; m. Ruth Gansberg, Feb. 11, 1951; children: William Todd, Robert Craig, Melissa Jane. BS, NYU, 1938; MD, La. State U., 1943. Intern Morrisania City Hosp., N.Y.C., 1943-44; resident in cardiology Mt. Sinai Hosp., N.Y.C., 1946-48; assoc. clin. prof. cardiology Mount Sinai Sch. Medicine, N.Y.C., 1966-87, assoc. attending cardiologist, 1966-87; exec. v.p. corp. affairs Chock Full O'Nuts Corp., N.Y.C., 1979-81, pres., 1981-84, chmn. bd., CEO, 1983-92, dir., 1976-92. Exec. v.p. Cro-Med. Bionics, Chromalloy-Am. Corp., St. Louis, 1968-76; bd. dirs. Cardionics, Union Miniere, Brussels, 1968-76; former sec. Nat. H.H.C. Corp., bd. dirs.; bd. dirs. Family Med. Ctrs. Am., N.Y.C. Author: Computer Electrocardiography: Present Status and Criteria, 1977; contbr. articles to profl. jours. Served to capt. M.C. U.S. Army, 1944-46. Recipient Nat. Kidney Found. Humanitarian award in medicine, 1977 Mem. AMA, N.Y. State Med. Assn., N.Y.C. Med. Assn., Am. Heart Assn., Am. Geriatrics Soc., Am. Acad. Compensation Medicine, Soc. Computer Medicine, Nat. Coffee Assn. (scientific adv. group). Lodges: Masons. Republican. Jewish. Died Nov. 14, 2003.

PORGES, WALTER RUDOLF, television news executive; b. Vienna, Nov. 26, 1931; s. Paul and Charlotte (Posamentier) P.; m. Jean Belle Mlotok, Dec. 22, 1953; children: Donald F., Marian E., Lawrence M. BA, CCNY, 1953. News writer radio sta. WOR, N.Y.C., 1955-56, WCBS Radio and TV, N.Y.C., 1956-57; news writer ABC Radio Network, N.Y.C., 1958-60, news editor, 1960-63, asst. dir. radio news, 1963-65; asst. assignment mgr. ABC-TV, 1965-68; asso. producer ABC-TV Evening News, 1968-70, sr. producer, 1973-75; European producer ABC News, London, 1970-73; producer ABC-TV spl. events, N.Y.C., 1975-76; coordinating producer ABC News (Republican Nat. Conv.), 1976; editorial producer, chief writer ABC Evening News, 1976-77, sr. producer, 1977-80, ABC World News Tonight, 1978-83; fgn. news dir. ABC News, N.Y.C., 1983-89, v.p. news practices, 1989-93. Assoc. Exec. TV, 1993. Served with U.S. Army, 1953-55. Home: Hastings Hdsn, NY. Died Sept., 1999.

PORPHY, WILLIAM GERALD, advertising executive; b. Dover, N.J., Apr. 24, 1938; s. Albert R. and Agnes E. (Bedner) P.; m. Carol Ann Krepela, Nov. 30, 1960; children: William, Dawn, Jeffrey. Student, Fairleigh Dickinson U., 1963. Tech. writer Hercules, Inc., Kenvil, N.J., 1956-64; supr. tech. info. Thiokol Chem. Co., Denville, N.J., 1965-69; mng. editor Star-Journal, Ledgewood, N.J., 1969-70; sr. accounts supr. Elastimold, Hackettstown, N.J., 1971-79; mktg. communication mgr. Thomas & Betts, Raritan, N.J., 1979-80; pres. WGP & Assocs., Budd Lake, N.J., 1980-82; mktg. communication mgr. Automatic Switch Co., Florham Park, N.J., from 1982. Avocations: sports, country music. Home: Budd Lake, NJ. Deceased.

PORTER, DARRELL RAY, professional baseball player; b. Joplin, Mo., Jan. 17, 1952; With Milw. Brewers, 1971-76, Kansas City (Mo.) Royals, 1976-80, St. Louis Cardinals, 1981-85, Tex. Rangers, from 1986. Mem. Am. League All-Star Team, 1974, 78, 79, 80; played with St. Louis Cardinals in World Series, 1982, 85 Died Aug. 5, 2002.

PORTER, DON CECIL, SR., actor, theatre director; b. Miami, Okla., Sept. 24, 1912; s. Jesse Bradley and Hazel Margaret (Wills) P.; m. Peggy Randall Converse, Apr. 30, 1943; 1 child, Don Cecil Jr. Freelance actor and dir., from 1936. Actor: (play) The Best Man, 1962, Any Wednesday, 1964-65, Plaza Suite, 1970-71, Generation, 1974-75, (film) Eagle Squadron, 1941, 711 Ocean Drive, 1949, The Savage, 1950 The Racket, 1950, The Candidate, 1972, Mame, 1980, (TV series) Private Secretary, 1952-61, Gidget, 1965-66. Master sgt. U.S. Army, 1943-45. Avocations: golf, tennis. Home: Beverly Hills, Calif. Deceased.

PORTER, LORD GEORGE, chemist, educator; b. Stainforth, Yorkshire, Eng., Dec. 6, 1920; s. John Smith and Alice Ann (Roebuck) Porter; m. Stella Jean Brooke, Aug. 12, 1949; children: John B., Andrew C.G. B.Sc., U. Leeds, Eng., 1941; MA, PhD, Cambridge (Eng.) U., 1949, Sc.D., 1959; D.Sc. (hon.), U. Utah, 1968, Sheffield U., 1968, U. East Anglia, U. Surrey, U. Durham, 1970, U. Leicester, U. Leeds, U. Heriot-Watt, City U., 1971, U. Manchester, U. St. Andrews, London U., 1972, Kent U., 1973, Oxford U., 1974, U. Hull, 1980, U. Rio de Janiero, 1980, Inst. Quimico de Sarria, Barcelona, 1984, U. Coimbra, Portugal, 1984, Open U., U. Pa., 1984, U. Philippines, 1985, U. Notre Dame, U. Bristol, U. Reading, 1986, U. Loughborough, 1984, U. Brunel, U. Bologna. Asst. research dir. phys. chemistry Cambridge U., 1952—54; asst. dir. Brit. Rayon Research, 1954—55; prof. phys. chemistry U. Sheffield, England, 1955—63, Firth prof., head dept. chemistry, 1963—66; dir., Fullerian prof. chemistry Royal Instn., 1966—85; pres. The Royal Soc., from 1985; chmn. Ctr. for Photomolecular Scis. Imperial Coll., London, from 1990. Prof. photochemistry Imperial Coll.; vis. prof. chemistry Univ. Coll. London; hon. fellow Emmanuel Coll., Cambridge; hon. prof. phys. chemistry U. Kent; Richard Dimbleby lectr., 1988; John P. McGovern lectr., 88. Author: Chemistry for the Modern World, 1962, (BBC TV series) Laws of Disorder, 1965, Time Machines, 1969—70, Natural History of a Sunbeam, 1976; editor: Progress in Reaction Kinetics; contbr. articles to profl. jours. Pres. London Internat. Youth Sci. Fortnight, 1987, 1988, trustee Bristol Exploratory, from 1986. Served with Royal Navy, 1941—45. Decorated knight, mem. Order of Merit; co-recipient (with M. Eigen and R.G. W. Norrish, Nobel Prize in chemistry, 1967; recipient Kalinga prize, 1977. Fellow: Royal Soc. of Edinburgh, Royal Scottish Soc. of Arts, Royal Soc. (pres. 1985—90, Davy medal 1971, Rumford medal 1978, Copley medal 1992, Michael Faraday award 1992); mem.: Nat. Assn. Gifted Children (pres. 1975—80), Acad. Lincei (Rome), Indian Acad. Sci., Hungarian Acad. Scis., La Real Academia de Ciencias (Madrid) (corr.), Am. Acad. Arts and Scis. (fgn.) (hon.), N.Y. Acad. Scis. (hon.), Göttingen Acad. Sci. (corr.), Soviet Acad. Scis., Pontifical Acad. Sci., Comite Internat. de Photobiologie (pres. 1968—72), Sci. Rsch. Coun. Brit. (coun. sci. bd. 1976—80), Chem. Soc. (pres. 1970—72, pres. Faraday divsn. 1973—74, Faraday medal 1979, 1980, Longstaff medal 1981), NAS (fgn. assoc. Washington). Achievements include research in on fast chemical reactions, photochemistry, photosynthesis. Died Aug. 31, 2002.

PORTMAN, NANCY ANN, artist, art educator; b. Bath, N.Y., Dec. 10, 1936; d. Lewis Menzo Peck and Neva Irene (Keeler) Wheeler; m. Warren Conrad Portman, Apr. 1, 1961; children: Lorraine Jean Portman, Errol Lawrence. BA with honors, SUNY, New Paltz, 1958; MA with honors, NYU, 1965; postgrad., Coll. New Rochelle, 1982-86, SUNY, Purchase, 1985-90, Pace U., 1990. Permanent tchg. cert., N.Y. Art tchr. Yorktown Ctrl. Schs., Yorktown Heights, N.Y., 1958-60, 61-65, 1971-91, Pearl River (N.Y.) Schs., 1960-61. Group shows include Jacksonville Watercolor Soc., St. Augustine Art Assn., Crescdnt Beach Art Gallery. Campaigner for Steve Alexander, State Dist. Atty. Fla., St. Augustine, 1992. Mem. Fla. Watercolor Soc., Jacksonville Watercolor Soc. (chair fall show 1994, co-chair fall show 1995, 1st v.p. and show chmn. 1996-97), St. Augustine Art Assn., Jacksonville Mus., Cummen Mus. Republican. Methodist. Avocations: drawing, photography, reading, sewing, gardening. Home: Saint Augustine, Fla. Died Oct. 29, 2001.

POSNER, IRWIN, publishing company executive; b. Bklyn., Oct. 9, 1924; s. Melvin and Helen (Kaufman) P.; m. Lois Ackerman, June 20, 1948; children: Mitchell, Jonathan. Publs. mgr. Fairchild Pub., N.Y.C., 1946-48; prodn. mgr. Erland Advt. Agy., N.Y.C., 1948-52; account exec. N. Fein Advt. Agy., N.Y.C., 1952-54; ea. sales mgr. Frosted Food Field, N.Y.C., 1954-57; regional sales mgr. Whitney Pub., N.Y.C., 1958-68; ea. sales mgr. InfoSystems mag., N.Y.C., 1968-92; co-pub., owner M-I Pub., N.Y.C., from 1994. V.p. Jewish Coun. of Yonkers, N.Y., 1984—, Westchester Jewish Conf., White Plains, N.Y., 1986—; pres., chmn. bd. dirs. Congregation Sons of Israel, Yonkers, 1990—; mem. cabinet Westchester region UJA/Fedn., White Plains, 1990—. with Signal Corps, 1942-45. Decorated Victory medal, Philippines Liberation medal, Asiatic Pacific Svc. medal, others. Mem. Odd Fellows. Democrat. Avocations: sports, stamp collecting, reading, photography, cmty. activities. Home: Yonkers, NY. Died Mar. 22, 2000.

POST, ROBERT WILEY, lawyer; b. Cuero, Tex., Mar. 4, 1942; s. Nathan Wilber and Hattie (Kleiber) P.; m. Sara Ann Armstrong, Sept. 2, 1967; children— Kelly Christine, Nathan Matthew. A.A., Victoria Coll., Tex., 1962; B.A., U. Tex., 1964, LL.B., 1967. Bar: Tex. 1967. Sole practice, Cuero, Tex., 1967-70; DeWitt County Atty., Cuero, 1970—. City councilman City of Cuero, 1969-70. Recipient Outstanding Young Man award Cuero Jaycees, 1970, Top Hand award U. Tex. Student Assn., Austin, 1984, Outstanding Bus. and Profl. Person DeWitt Soil and Water Conservation Dist., 1984. Mem. DeWitt County Bar Assn., Cuero C. of C. (pres. 1970-71). Democrat. Roman Catholic. Lodge: Lions. Died Feb. 2, 1994. Home: Cuero, Tex.

POSTAL, MAXINE, county official; b. Bklyn. d. Jacob Levy and Pauline Lang; m. Jeffrey L. Postal June 30, 1963 (div. June 1988); children: Gregory J., Eric S. BA, Bklyn. Coll. CUNY, 1962; MA, 1965. Cert. art tchr. nursery-12. Tchr. Jr. H.S., Bklyn., 1962-63, James Madison H.S., Bklyn., 1963-64, Midwood H.S., Bklyn., 1964-65, Sheepshead Bay H.S., Bklyn., 1965-68; owner, dir. Busy Bee Nursery Sch. and Kindergarten, Bklyn., 1968-76, Amityville, NY, 1976-90; legislator Suffolk County, Hauppage, NY, 1988—2002; presiding officer Suffolk County Legislature, Hauppage, 2003. Mem. student adv. bd. L.A. Wilson Tech. Child Care, Dix Hills, N.Y., 1976-80. Mem. adv. com. Long Is. Progressive Coalition, Massapequa, N.Y., 1998-2004, Literacy Vols. Am., Bellport, N.Y., 1999; v.p. Amityville Bd. Edn., 1984-88; treas. Friends of Amityville Libr., 1980-84; pres. Hauppage Libr. Bd., 1976-77. Recipient Unsung Heroine award NOW, 1989, Major Braxton award NAACP, 1990; named Hon. Guardian of Yr. Suffolk County Guardians, 1999. Democrat. Jewish. Avocations: jogging, reading, travel. Died Jan. 1, 2004.

POSTEN, HARRY OWEN, statistics educator; b. Middletown, N.Y., Feb. 6, 1928; s. Harry O. and Keziah M. (Wells) P.; m. Gail Marcia Keller, Aug. 24, 1957; children: Catherine, Thomas, June. BS, Central Conn. State U., 1956; MS, Kans. State U., 1958; PhD, Va. Polytechnic Inst., 1960. Research staff IBM Research Ctr., Yorktown Hgts., N.Y., 1960-62; asst. prof. U. R.I., Kingston, 1962-63; prof. U. Conn., Storrs, from 1963. Contbr. 41 articles to profl. jours. With USN, 1948-52. Recipient Kaiser Disting. Alumnus Service award, Central Conn. State U., 1985. Fellow Am. Statis. Assn. Home: Storrs Mansfield, Conn. Died Feb. 23, 2002.

POSTMAN, LEO JOSEPH, psychologist; b. St. Petersburg, Russia, June 7, 1918; came to U.S., naturalized, 1944; s. Joseph and Elizabeth (Leites) P.; m. Dorothy Lerman, June 27, 1945. BSS., Coll. City N.Y., 1943; MA, Harvard U., 1944, PhD, 1946. Instr. Harvard U., 1946-47, asst. prof., 1948-50, Ind. U., 1947-48; mem. faculty U. Calif., Berkeley, 1950—87, prof. psychology, 1957-87, prof. emeritus, 1987—2004. Co-author: Experimental Psychology, 1949; editor: Psychology in the Making, 1962; co-editor: Verbal Learning and Memory, 1969; editor: Jour. Verbal Learning and Verbal Behavior, 1961-68, Am. Jour. Psychology, 1976-86; asso. editor: Jour. Exptl. Psychology, 1968-74; contbr. articles to profl. jours., chpts. to books. Mem. Nat. Acad. Scis., Soc. Exptl. Psychologists (Warren medal 1974), Am. Psychol. Assn. (past pres. div. exptl. psychology, gen. psychology), Psychyonomic Soc., AAAS (past v.p.). Home: Berkeley, Calif. Died Apr. 22, 2004.

POTTER, KENNETH ROY, retired minister; b. Pittsfield, Mass., Dec. 29, 1919; s. Roy Wilder and Lillian Bertha (Clark) P.; m. Julia Helen Morris, June 12, 1943; children: Susan Elaine Potter Goslin, Terry LaVerne Potter Rowe, Ronald Duane. Student, Anderson (Ind.) U., 1946-48; BTh, Warner Pacific Coll., 1950. Ordained to ministry Ch. of God (Anderson, Ind.), 1956. Min. music Church of God, Couer d'Alene, Idaho, 1950-51; pastor Ch. of God, Salt Lake City, 1951-52, West Side Ch. of God, Mt. Carmel, Ill., 1952-54, First Ch. of God, Springfield, Oreg., 1954-56, Ch. of God, Laton, Calif., 1957-59, Missoula, Mont., 1959-62, Gary, Ind., 1962-74, Southlake Ch. of God, Merrillville, Ind., 1974-77, Ch. of God, California City, Calif., 1977-78, Eastgate Ch. of God, Fresno, Calif., 1978-79, Ch. of God, Mt. Ayr, Ind., 1979-81, Southlake First Ch. of God, Merrillville, Ind., 1981-82, Oakview Community Ch. of God, Scio, Oreg., 1984-86, First Ch. of God, Coquille, Oreg., 1986-98; ret., 1998. Pres. Laton (Calif.) Ministerial Assn., 1958-59; treas. Missoula (Mont.) Evang. Ministerial Alliance, 1961-62; counselor Gary Contact-Help, Gary-Merrillville, 1973-75; pres. Scio Ministerial Assn., 1985-86, Coquille Ministerial Assn., 1990-98; former mem. Napa, Calif. Art Assn. Crafted model automobile, Fisher Body Craftsman's Guild competition (2nd prize state award, Va.), 1937. Staff sgt. USAF, 1941-45, PTO. Mem. Coquille Valley Art Assn. Home: Coquille, Oreg. Died Feb. 18, 2002.

POTTER, MARIANNE BRYANT, women's health nurse educator; b. Buffalo, Feb. 15, 1952; BSN, Russell Sage Coll., 1974; MSN, SUNY, Buffalo, 1977. RN, N.Y.; cert. adult nurse practitioner. Pvt. practive childbirth educator; dir. edn. Western N.Y. Poison Control Ctr., Buffalo; asst. prof. Daemen Coll., Amherst, N.Y. Founder, dir. Women's Cancer Network. Editor: Positive Images newsletter. Bd. dirs. Am. Cancer Soc., Erie County div., chair of chemo coach adv. bd. Mem. NAACOG, ASPO (cert. Lamaze childbirth educator, Profl. Recognition award, chair profl. coalition, pres. chpt., bd. dirs.). Home: Grand Island, NY. Deceased.

POUJADE, PIERRE, newspaper executive; b. St. Cere, Lot, France, Dec. 1, 1920; m. Yvette Seva, Feb. 19, 1943; children: Yves, Patric, Magg-Noele, Alain, Marie-Paule. Grad., Coll. St. Eugene, Aurillac, France, 1936. Founder, pres. Union Defense Commercants et Artisans, from 1953; founder Union et Fraternit4 Francaise, 1955-58; founder, dir. Union et Defene daily, Fraternite Francaise weekly. Newspaper executive; b. St.-Cere, Lot, Quercy, France, Dec. 1, 1920; s. Gabriel and Louise (Roux) P.; m. Yvette Seva, Feb. 19, 1943; children— Yves, Patrick, Magg-Noele, Alain, Marie-Paule. Grad. College St.-Eugene, Aurillac, France, 1936. Founder, pres. Union de Defense de Commercants et Artisans, 1953—2003; founder Union et Fraternite Francaise, 1955-58; founder, dir. Union et Defense daily, Fraternite Francaise weekly. Author: J'ai Choisi le combat, 1954; A l'heure de la colere, 1974. Conseiller Economique Social de la Republique Francaise. Mem. Mcpl. Council St.-Cere; pres. Confederation National des Travailleurs Independents, 1970—2003, Caisse National d'Assurance Maladie Independants, 1971—2003, National Association l'Utilisation des Resources Energetiques Francais, 1980—2003; dir. Caisse Regionale, Midi-Pyrenees, 1972—2003; founder Union pour la Defense des Libertes, 1978; mem. Commission Nationale de Carburants de Substitution, Ministry Energy, Paris, 1984; founder, pres. Poujadist Movement; promoter agro-motor fuel. Decorated Cross of Voluntary Combat, medaille des Evades. Mem. C. of C. and Industry Lot, Occitanie Caraïbes (pres. 1986). Author: J'ai Choisi le Combat, 1954, A l'heure de la colere, 1974, Histoire Sans Masque, 2003. Conseiller Economique Social de la Republique Francaise; mem. Mcpl. Coun. St. Cere; pres. Confedn. Nat. Travailleurs Independents, 1970-2003, Caisse Nat. d'Assurance Mailadie Independents, 1971-2003, Nat. Assn. Utilisation des Resources Energetiques Francais, 1980-2003; dir. Caisse Regionale, Midi-Pyrenees, 1972-2003; founder Union pour la Defense des Libertes, 1978; mem. Commn. Nat. Carburants de Substitution, Ministry Energy, Paris, 1984; founder, pres. Poujadist Movement; prmoter agro-motor fuel. Decorated Cross of Vol. Combat, medaille des Evades. Mem. C. of C. and Industry Lot, Occitanie Caraibes (pres. 1986). Died Aug. 27, 2003.

POVISH, KENNETH JOSEPH, retired bishop; b. Alpena, Mich., Apr. 19, 1924; s. Joseph Francis and Elizabeth (Jachcik) P.. AB, Sacred Heart Sem., Detroit, 1946; MA, Cath. U. Am., 1950; postgrad., No. Mich. U., 1961, postgrad., 1963. Ordained priest Roman Cath. Ch., 1950. Asst. pastorships, 1950—56; pastor in Port Sanilac, 1956—57, 1957—60, Bay City, Mich., 1966—70; dean St. Paul Sem., Saginaw, Mich., 1960—66, vice rector, 1962—66; bishop of Crookston Minn., 1970—75; bishop of Lansing, 1975—95. Bd. consulators Diocese of Saginaw, 1966—70; instr. Latin and U.S. history St. Paul Sem., 1960—66. Weekly columnist: Saginaw and Lansing diocesan newspapers. Bd. dirs. Cath. Charities Diocese Saginaw, 1969—70. Mem.: Bay County Hist. Soc., Mich. Hist. Soc., Kiwanis, KC (pres. Mich. Cath. Conf. 1985—95), Lions Club. Roman Catholic. Died Sept. 5, 2003.

POWELL, SIR PHILIP, architect; b. Bedford, Eng., Mar. 15, 1921; s. Arnold and Winnifred (Walker) P.; m. Philippa Powell, Jan. 17, 1953; children: Dido, Ben. AA Diploma Sch. Architecture, Epsom Coll. Ptnr. Powell and Moya, London, 1946-91. Prin. works include Churchill Gardens flats, Westminster, 1948-62, Skylon for Festival of Britain, 1951, Chichester Theater, 1962, Brit. Pavilion Expo70, Osaka, Japan, 1970, Mayfield Sch., Putney, 1955, Picture Gallery Christ Ch., Oxford, 1967, Mus. of London, 1977, London and Manchester Assurance HQ, 1978, Queen Elizabeth II Conf. Ctr., 1986, Queen's Bldg., Royal Holloway Coll., Egham and labs., 1986-90; extensions Brasenose Coll., Oxford, 1961, Christ Ch., 1967, Corpus Christi Coll., Oxford, 1969, St. John's Coll. Cambridge, 1967, Wolfson Coll., Oxford, 1974, Queens' Coll., Cambridge, 1976, Hosps. at Swindon, Slough, High Wycombe, Wythenshawe, Woolwich, Maidstone, Hastings, Ashington, Great Ormond Street (London), 1960-92. Mem. Royal Fin. Art Commn., London, 1969-94; trustee Soane Mus., London, 1978-2001. Decorated officer Order Brit. Empire, 1957, Knight, 1975, Companion of Honour, 1984; recipient Royal Gold medal Royal Inst. Brit. Architects, 1974. Mem. Royal Acad. Arts (trustee and treas. 1985-95). Home: London, England. Died May 5, 2003.

POWELL, RICHARD PITTS, writer; b. Phila., Nov. 28, 1908; s. Richard Percival and Lida Catherine (Pitts) P.; m. Marian Carleton Roberts, Sept. 6, 1932 (dec. Nov. 1979); children: Stephen Barnes, Dorothy Louise; m. Margaret M. Cooper, 1980. Grad., Episcopal Acad., 1926; AB, Princeton, 1930. Reporter Phila. Evening Ledger, 1930-40; with N.W. Ayer & Son, Phila., 1940-58, mem. pub. relations dept., 1940-42, charge info. services, 1949-58, v.p., 1951-58. Author: mystery books Don't Catch Me, 1943, All Over but the Shooting, 1944, Lay That Pistol Down, 1945, Shoot If You Must, 1946, And Hope to Die, 1947, Shark River, 1950, Shell Game, 1950, A Shot in the Dark, 1952, Say It with Bullets, 1953, False Colors, 1955; novels The Philadelphian, 1957, Pioneer, Go Home, 1959, The Soldier, 1960, I Take This Land, 1963, Daily and Sunday, 1965, Don Quixote, U.S.A, 1966, Tickets to the Devil, 1968, Whom the Gods Would Destroy, 1970, Florida: A Picture Tour, 1972; novel under pen name Jeremy Kirk The Build-Up Boys, 1951; Contbr. short stories, articles, serials to mags. Served as lt. col. AUS, 1942-46; chief news censor 1945, S.W. Pacific Theatre. Home: Fort Myers, Fla. Deceased.

POWERS, DENNIS ALPHA, biology educator; b. Detroit, May 4, 1938; S. Virginia (Ward) P.; m. 1963 (div. 1993); children: Kathy M., Wendy R., Julie A. BA, Ottawa U., 1963; PhD, U. Kans., 1970. AEC postdoctoral fellow Argonne (Ill.) Nat. Lab.; NSF postdoctoral fellow Marine Biol. Lab., Woods Hole, Mass., 1971-72, SUNY, Stony Brook, 1971-72; asst. prof. biology Johns Hopkins U., Balt., 1973-79, assoc. prof., 1979-82, prof. biology, McCollum-Pratt prof., 1982-89, dir. McCollum-Pratt Inst., chmn. dept. biology, 1983-88; acting dir. Chesapeake Bay Inst., Shady Side, Md., 1984-87; Harold A. Miller prof. biol. sci., dir. Hopkins Marine Sta. Stanford (Calif.) U., 1988—2000. Prin. rsch. scientist Ctr. Marine Biotech., U. Md., Balt., 1986-89; bd. advisors Nat. Aqaurium, Balt. Mem. editorial bd. Sci., Molecular Biology and Evolution, Molecular Phylogenetics and Evolution, Physiol. Zoology, Zool. Studies, Molecular Marine Biology and Biotech.; mem. editorial adv. bd. Advances in Marine Biotech.; contbr. more than 200 articles to profl. jours. Trustee Monterey Bay Aquarium; bd. dirs. Monterey Bay Aquarium Rsch. Inst. With USMC, 1957-59, USMCR, 1959-63. Grantee NSF, NIH, NOAA, others; numerous honors and awards. Fellow AAAS, Calif. Acad. Sci., Japanese Soc. Promotion of Sci. Fellowship; mem. Am. Soc. Biochem. and Molecular Biologists, Am. Soc. of Limnology and Oceanography, Am. Chem. Soc., Am. Soc. Molecular Marine Biology and Biotechnology (pres. editor-in-chief jour.), Soc. Study Evolution, Genetics Soc., Am. Soc. Zoologists, Biophys. Soc., N.Y. Acad. Sci., The Protein Soc., Am. Soc. Biol. Chemists, Sigma Xi. Died Dec. 8, 2003.

POWERS, KATHLEEN JAY, management consultant, educator; b. N.J., Aug. 1, 1946; d. George Paul and Eileen May (Dennison) Swanick; m. James Michael Powers, Sept. 13, 1969 (div. Dec. 1982); children: Roslyn Ann Hart, Samantha Rae. BBA, Fla. Internat. U., 1974, MBA, 1975; PhD, U. Fla., 1986. Prodn. coord. Studio Masters, Inc., North Miami, Fla., 1969-72, Advercolor, Inc., Hialeah, Fla., 1972; mfrs. rep. assoc. Bassett (Va.) Furniture Industries, 1965-77; instr. dept. bus. Miami (Fla.) Dade Community Coll.-South, 1978-80; acad. admissions advisor Miami Edn. Consortium, Barry Coll. & Emery-Riddle Aero. U., Miami Shores, Fla., 1980; rsch. assoc. Univ. Fla., Gainesville, 1980-85, teaching asst., 1981-85; asst. prof. mgmt. Tex. Tech. Univ., Lubbock, 1986-89; asst. prof. health orgn. mgmt. Tex. Tech. Univ. Health Scis. Ctr., Lubbock, 1987-89; asst. prof. human resources mgmt. George H. Atkinson Grad. Sch. Mgmt.-Willamette Univ., Salem, Oreg., 1989-93, assoc. prof., from 1994. Cons. Asten Dryer Fabrics, Salem, Compton, English & Hunsaker, Salem, exec. dept. The State of Oreg., Salem, Furr's Inc., Lubbock, Moore Bus. Forms and Systems Div., Salem, United Coupon Clearing House, Lubbock; mem. Oreg. State mgmt. curriculum adv. com., 1990; presenter in field. Contbr. articles to profl. jours. Recipient numerous grants. Mem. APA, Acad. Mgmt., Soc. for Human Resource Mgmt., Indsl. Rels. Rsch. Assn., Internat. Acad. Mgmt. and Mktg., Sigma Iota Epsilon. Avocations: reading, opera, classical music, gardening, pets. Home: Portland, Oreg. Died Jan. 7, 2002.

POYNTZ, WALTER JOHN, musician, actor, artistic director, retired music educator; b. Pitts., Aug. 17, 1898; s. Thomas and Mary Mathias (Barclay) P.; m. Margaret Jane Vivian, Dec. 25, 1934 (dec. Aug. 1973). BA, Carnegie Tech., 1928; MA, Columbia U., 1934; postgrad., U. Colo., 1945, U. Mex., Mexico City, 1947, U. Guatamala, Guatamala City, 1948. Pianist, organist various orchs., chs., vaudeville shows, Pitts., 1920-28; tchr. music Pub. Sch. System, New Rochelle, N.Y., 1928-60; founder, actor, producer Pohai Nani Players, Kaneohe, Hawaii, 1966-89, prodn. cons., from 1989; actor Honolulu Theatre for Youth, 1960-66, treas., acct., 1964-80, v.p., controller, 1983-89, v.p. emeritus, 19896. Organist, pianist Pohai Nani Vesper Services, Kaneohe, 1980—. Served with USNRF, 1918-19. Mem. Hawaii State Theatre Council (Po'okela award 1985, Po'kela Pierre Bowman award 1987), Arts Council of Hawaii, Phi Mu Alpha. Lodges: Masons. Republican. Presbyterian. Deceased.

PRASAD, B.H. utility company executive; b. Rudrur, India, Aug. 1, 1955; came to U.S. 1978; s. Krishna Murthy and Sudha (Murthy) Rao; m. Sheela Prasad, May 30, 1985; children: Neil B., Megan B. BSME, Osmania U., Hyderabad, India, 1977; MSIE, Okla. State U., 1980. Methods engr. in tng. Okla. Gas & Elec., Oklahoma City, 1980-82, methods engr., 1982-84, sr. engr. HVAC, 1984-87, mgr. mkt. svcs., 1987-89, mgr. load mgmt., 1989-92; mgr. Demand Side Mgmt., from 1993. Mem. ASHRAE (Profl. Award of Excellence 1988, Vol. of the Yr. 1991, pres. 1992-93, Golden Gavel award), Assn. of Demand Side Mgmt. Profls. (bd. dirs. 1989—, exec. v.p. 1991-92, pres., 1993—), Toastmasters. Home: Edmond, Okla. Died May 15, 1999.

PRATT, ALBERT, financial consultant, trustee; b. Newton, Mass., May 23, 1911; s. Frederick Sanford and Ella Winifred (Nickerson) P.; m. Alice Mathea Lee, May 24, 1940 (dec. 1976); children: Alice Mathea, Cornelia S., Nina L., Frederick H., Kate Nickerson Pratt Lapping; m. Fanny Gray Little Morgan, Jan. 2, 1977. Grad., Country Day Sch., Newton, 1929; AB, Harvard, 1933, JD, 1936. Bar: Mass. bar 1936. With firm Goodwin, Procter & Hoar, Boston, 1936-40; with Paine, Webber, Jackson & Curtis, Inc., Boston, 1946-80, vice chmn., 1970-76, cons., 1976-80, gen. partner, 1950-54, 57-70, ltd. partner, 1954-57; adv. dir. Blyth, Eastman Paine Webber Inc., Boston, 1980-83. Dir., chmn. investment com. Paine Webber Properties, Inc., 1980-84, pres., 1984, cons., 1985-2003; ptnr. F.S. Pratt & Son, 1946-87; asst. sec. navy, 1954-57; bd. govs. N.Y. Stock Exchange, 1963-66 Pres. United Fund Boston, 1962-64. Served to comdr. USNR, 1940-45. Mem. Investment Bankers Assn. (chmn. N.E. group 1952-53, gov. 1957-60, 64-67, chmn. securities act com. 1959-63, pres. 1965-66), Assn. Harvard Alumni (dir. 1964-70), Boston C. of C. (dir. 1958-61), Assn. Harvard Clubs (pres. 1962-63), Harvard Alumni Assn. (dir. 1958-63), Cruising Club Am., N.Y. Yacht Club, Wianno Club (Osterville, Mass.). Home: Key Largo, Fla. Died May 16, 2003.

PRATT, EDMUND TAYLOR, JR., pharmaceutical company executive; b. Savannah, Ga., Feb. 22, 1927; s. Edmund T. and Rose (Miller) P.; m. Jeanette Louise Carneale, Feb. 10, 1951; children: Randolf Ryland, Keith Taylor. BSEE magna cum laude, Duke U., 1947; MBA, U. Pa., 1949; hon. degrees, L.I. U., Marymount Manhattan Coll., Poly. U. of N.Y., St. Francis Coll. With IBM Corp., 1949-52, 54-57, asst. to exec. v.p., 1956-57; with IBM World Trade Corp., 1958-62, contr., 1958-62; asst. sec. fin. mgmt. Dept. Army, 1962-64; contr. Pfizer, Inc., N.Y.C., 1964-67, v.p. ops. internat. subs., 1967-69, chmn. bd., pres. internat. subs., 1969-71, exec. v.p., 1970-71, pres., 1971-72, chmn., chief exec. officer, 1972-91, chmn., 1972-92, chmn. emeritus, from 1992, also bd. dirs. Bd. dirs. Chase Manhattan Corp., Internat. Paper Co., GM, Minerals Techs., Inc., Hughes Electronics; trustee Logistics Mgmt. Inst. Lt. (j.g.) USNR, 1952-54. Mem. Bus. Coun., Bus. Roundtable (past chmn., mem. policy com.), Phi Beta Kappa. Home: Port Washington, NY. Died Sept. 5, 2002.

PREISKEL, BARBARA SCOTT, lawyer, association executive; b. Washington, July 6, 1924; d. James and B. Beatrix Scott; m. Robert H. Preiskel, Oct. 28, 1950; children: John S., Richard A. BA, Wellesley Coll., 1945; LLB, Yale U., 1947. Bar: D.C. 1948, N.Y. 1948, U.S. Supreme Ct. 1960. Law clk. U.S. Dist. Ct., Boston, 1948-49; assoc. Poletti, Diamond, Roosevelt, Freidin & Mackay, N.Y.C., 1949-50, Dwight, Royall, Harris, Hoegel & Caskey, N.Y.C., 1950-54, legal cons., 1954-59; cons. Ford Found. Fund for the Republic, N.Y.C., 1954; dep. atty. Motion Picture Assn. Am., Inc., N.Y.C., 1959-71, v.p., legis. counsel, 1971-77, sr. v.p., gen. atty., 1977-83; pvt. practice N.Y.C., from 1983. Bd. dirs. Am. Stores Co., Salt Lake City, The Washington (D.C.) Post Co., brd. dirs., Textron Inc., 1975-98, brd. dirs., General Electric Co., 1982-98. Mem. Pres.'s Commn. on Obscenity and Pornography, 1968-70, Am. Arbitration Assn., 1971-87, N.Y.C. Bd. Ethics, 1976-89, Inst. Civil Justice, 1984-86, Citizens Com. for Children, N.Y.C., 1966-72, 85-91, Child Adoptive Svc. of State Charities Aid Assn., N.Y.C., 1961-68, Hillcrest Ctr. for Children, N.Y.C., 1958-61, Fedn. Protestant Welfare Agys., N.Y.C., 1959-61, 64-92, N.Y. Philharm. Soc., 1971-94, Am. Women's Econ. Devel. Corp., 1981-93, Med. Edn. for South African Blacks, Inc., Washington, 1985-89; bd. dirs. Wiltwyck Sch., N.Y.C., 1968-78, chmn. bd. dirs., 1950, Mass. Mutual Life Ins. Co., Springfield, 1983-97; successor trustee Yale Corp., New Haven, 1977-89; trustee Ford Found., N.Y.C., 1982-94, Am. Mus. of Moving Image, 1986-96, Wellesley Coll., 1988—; mem. distbn. com. N.Y. Cmty. Trust, Inc., N.Y.C. 1978-95, chmn. dist. com. N.Y. Cmty. Trust, 1990-95; chmn. coun. Advisors Hunter Coll. Sch. Social Work, 1985-89; mem. Dumpson chair com., Fordham U., N.Y.C., 1981-89; bd. dirs. Tougaloo Coll. Econ. Devel. Corp., 1991—, The Bold Initiative, 1998—. Recipient Meritorious award Nat. Assn. Theatre Owners, 1970, 72, Alumni Achievement award Wellesley Coll., 1975, Tribute to Women in Internat. Industry award YWCA, 1984, Elizabeth Cutter Morrow award, 1985, Outstanding Contbrs. award Am. Women's Econ. Devel., 1985, Dirs. Choice award Nat. Women's Econ. Alliance Found., 1989, Keystone award Fedn. Protestant Welfare Agys., 1991, Civic award

Citizen's Union of City of N.Y., 1995, Nat. Equal Justice award NAACP, 1996, Dir. of Yr. award Nat. Assn. Corp. Dirs., 1996. Mem. ABA, Assn. of Bar of City of N.Y. (mem. exec. com. 1972-76), Century Assn., Cosmopolitan Club, Wellesley Club. Episcopalian. Home: New York, NY. Died June 6, 2002.

PRESCOTT, PETER SHERWIN, writer; b. N.Y.C., July 15, 1935; s. Orville and Lilias (Ward-Smith) P.; m. Anne Courthope Kirsopp Lake, June 22, 1957; children: David Sherwin, Antonia Courthope. AB magna cum laude, Harvard, 1957. Editor E.P. Dutton Co., N.Y.C., 1958-67; lit. editor, syndicated columnist Women's Wear Daily, N.Y.C., 1964-68; mem. faculty Pubs. Sch. for Writers, N.Y.C., 1965-66; lit. editor, columnist Look mag., 1968-71; book critic Newsweek mag., N.Y.C., 1971-91, sr. writer, 1978-91; lectr. U.S. State Dept., 1978; adj. prof. Grad. Sch. Journalism, Columbia U., 1979-86. Vis. prof. Barnard Coll., 2001, 02. Author: A World of Our Own: Notes on Life and Learning in a Boys' Preparatory School, 1970, Soundings: Encounters with Contemporary Books, 1972, A Darkening Green: Notes from the Silent Generation, 1974, The Child Savers: Juvenile Justice Observed, 1981, Never in Doubt: Critical Essays on American Books, 1972-85, 1986, The Norton Book of American Short Stories, 1988. Mem. Dem. town Com., New Canaan, 1969-72, 1999-2001; constable Town of New Canaan, 1969-73; bd. dirs. Authors Guild Found., 1970-95, pres., 1971-93; exec. bd. Authors League Fund, 1987—, 1st v.p., 1994-97, pres., 1997—; trustee New Canaan Libr., 1998-01. With USAR, 1958-64. Recipient George Polk award criticism, 1978, 1st prize Robert F. Kennedy Book Awards, 1981; fellow Guggenheim Found., 1977, NEH, 1993. Mem. PEN Am. Center (exec. bd. 1974-76), Authors League Am. (exec. bd. 1974-76), Assn. Literary Scholars and Critics, Authors Guild (exec. bd. 1971-91), Nat. Book Critics Circle (exec. bd. 1973-75, 92-93), Century Assn., Harvard Club (N.Y.C.), Phi Beta Kappa. Died Apr. 23, 2004.

PRESEMENT, IAN JEFFREY, psychotherapist; b. Toronto, Ont., Can., July 29, 1958; came to U.S., 1981; s. Harvey I. and Ruth Presement. BSc, U. Toronto, 1980; MA, John F. Kennedy U., 1984; PhD, Summit U., 1991. Cert. marriage, family, child counselor, Calif. Mental health counselor Pacific Presbyn. Hosp., N.E.L., San Francisco, 1984-85; psychiat. counselor Jail Psychiat. Svcs., San Francisco, 1985-88; part-time dual diagnosis coord. Walden House, Inc., San Francisco, 1987-88, mgr. clin. svcs., from 1988. Pvt. practice psychotherapy, San Francisco, 1989—; cons. Calif. Youth Authority, San Francisco, 1989—; moderator dual diagnosis conf. Double Trouble, 1988; mem. San Francisco Dual Diagnosis Task Force, 1987, 88, 89, San Francisco AIDS and Substance Abuse Task Force, 1989-90. Avocations: computers, downhill skiing, hiking, camping, mountain biking. Deceased.

PREVOZNIK, STEPHEN JOSEPH, retired anesthesiologist; b. McAdoo, Pa., June 21, 1929; s. John George and Mary Margaret (Ficek) P.; m. Rita Agnes Kellett, Aug. 20, 1955; children— Mary Therese, Stephen Joseph, John Cyril, Michael Edward, Margaret Anne, Rita Marie, Thomas William, Jean Marie. R.N., St. Joseph Hosp. Sch. Nursing, Phila., 1951; BS, U. Notre Dame, 1955; MD, U. Pa., 1959. Intern Fitzgerald Mercy Hosp., Darby, Pa., 1959-60; resident in anesthesia U. Pa., Phila., 1960-62; practice medicine specializing in anesthesiology Phila., 1962-94; mem. staff U. Pa. Hosp.; prof. anesthesia U. Pa., 1977-94, dir. clin. activities, 1971-89; ret., 1994. Chmn. Residency Rev. Com. for Anesthesiology, 1991-93. Contbr. to textbooks on anesthesiology. Mem. AMA, Am. Soc. Anesthesiologists, Pa. Soc. Anesthesiologists, Phila. Soc. Anesthesiologists (pres. 1975-77), Internat. Anesthesia Rsch. Soc., Assn. Univ. Anesthesiologists (exec. coun. 1977-79, sec. 1981-84, dir. anesthesiology pain mgmt. program 1992-94). Home: Havertown, Pa. Died Nov. 12, 2002.

PRIBBLE, EASTON, artist; b. Falmouth, Ky., July 31, 1917; s. Thaddeus Sewell and Louise Ella (Parker) P. Student, U. Cin., 1941. Ind. tchr., N.Y.C., 1950-57; instr. painting and history of art Munson-Williams-Proctor Inst., Utica, N.Y., 1957—. Instr. history of art Utica Coll., Syracuse U., 1960-74 One-man exhbns. include Pinacotheca Gallery, N.Y.C., 1947, 48, Alan Gallery, N.Y.C., 1953, 55, 59, Hamilton Coll., Clinton, N.Y., 1975, Munson-Williams-Proctor Inst. Mus. Art, 1957, 76, 82, Kirkland Art Ctr., Clinton, N.Y., 1988, Rome (N.Y.) Art Ctr., 1990, Utica Coll. of Syracuse U., 1997; represented in permanent collections Sheldon Swope Art Mus., Savannah Coll. of Art and Design Mus. of Art, Whitney Mus. Am. Art, Hirschorn Mus. and Sulpture Garden, Smithsonian Instn., Parrish Mus., Southampton, N.Y., Munson-Williams-Proctor Inst. Mus. Art., Fallingwater (Frank Lloyd Wright House), Mill Run, Pa., Hudson River Mus., Yonkers, N.Y., Everson Mus., Syracuse, N.Y., Emerson Gallery, Hamilton Coll., The Farnsworth Mus. Art, Rockland, Maine, Colgate U. Art Gallery, Hamilton, Savannah Coll. of Art and Design. Fellow Yaddo, Saratoga Springs, N.Y., 1954, 55, 68 Mem. Artists Equity. Home: Utica, NY. Deceased.

PRICE, CHARLES E. petroleum engineer, consultant; b. Smackover, Ark., Nov. 27, 1924; s. Charles E. and Wilhemina B. (Bookter) P.; m. Ouida D. Driggers, Dec. 1, 1950; children: Kathy, Connie, Kelly. BS, U. Tuscaloosa (Ala.), 1949. Registered petroleum engr., La. Engr. P.G. Lake, Inc., Tyler, Tex., 1949-51; divsn. engr. Murphy Oil Co., Eldorado, Ark., 1951-59; v.p. Crystal Oil Co., Shreveport, La., 1959-77; dir., 1970-75; v.p. Callon Petroleum, Natchez, Miss., 1977-83; dir., 1980-82; pres. Price-Sayers, Inc., Shreveport, La., from 1985. Served with U.S. Army Air Force, 1944-45. Republican. Mem. So. Bapt. Ch. Home: Shreveport, La. Deceased.

PRICE, LUCILE BRICKNER BROWN, retired civic worker; b. Decorah, Iowa, May 31, 1902; d. Sidney Eugene and Cora (Drake) Brickner; B.S., Iowa State U., 1925; M.A., Northwestern U., 1940; m. Maynard Wilson Brown, July 2, 1928 (dec. Apr. 1937); m. 2d, Charles Edward Price, Jan. 14, 1961 (dec. Dec. 1983). Asst. dean women Kans. State U., Manhattan, 1925-28; mem. bd. student personnel adminstrn. Northwestern U., 1937-41; personnel research Sears Roebuck & Co., Chgo., 1941-42, overseas club dir. ARC, Eng., Africa, Italy, 1942-45; dir. Child Edn. Found., N.Y.C., 1946-56. Participant 1st and 2d Iowa Humanists Summer Symposiums, 1974, 75. Del. Mid Century White House Conf. on Children and Youth, 1950; mem. com. on program and research of Children's Internat. summer villages, 1952-53; mem. bd. N.E. Iowa Mental Health Ctr., 1959-62, pres. bd., 1960-61; mem. Iowa State Extension Adv. Com., 1973-75; project chmn. Decorah Hist. Dist. (listed Nat. Register Historic Places); trustee Porter House Mus., Decorah, 1966-78, emerita bd. dirs., 1982—; participant N. Cen. Regional Workshop Am. Assn. State and Local History, Mpls., 1975, Midwest Workshop Hist. Preservation and Conservation, Iowa State U., 1976, 77; mem. Winneshiek County (Iowa) Civil Service Commn., 1978-87; rep. Class of 1940 Northwestern U. Sch. Edn. and Social Policy, 1986-88. Recipient Alumni Merit award Iowa State U., 1975, Cert. of Appreciation Iowa State U. Extension, 1988. Mem. Am. Coll. Personnel Assn., (life), ARC Overseas Assn. (life, nat. bd.), AAUW (life, mem. bd. Decorah, Named Gift award 1977), Nat. Assn. Mental Health (del. nat. conf. 1958), Norwegian-Am. Mus. (life, Vesterheim fellow), Internat. Platform Assn., Winneshiek County Hist. Soc. (life, cert. of appreciation 1984), DAR, Luther Coll. Heritage Club (life, pres.'s coun. 1993), Pi Lambda Theta, Chi Omega. Designer, builder house for retirement living. Avocation: remembering WWII. Home: Decorah, Iowa. Died July 20, 2002.

PRICE, ROBERT ALFRED, mechanical engineer; b. Chgo., July 12, 1924; s. Alfred F. and Marie G. (Coleman) P.; m. Jananne Sivill, Sept. 12, 1947; children: Denise, Todd, Alan. BSME, Northwestern U., 1948; MBA, Mich. State U., 1964. Registered profl. engr., Mich., Ind. Plant engr. U.S. Rubber Co., Mishawaka, Ind., 1948-50; design engr. Bendix Automotive, South Bend, Ind., 1950-51; engring. specialist Douglas Aircraft Co., Santa Monica, Calif., 1951-59; engring. supr. Bendix Aerospace, South Bend, 1959-62; engring. and sales specialist Bendix Energy Controls, South Bend, 1963-70; project engr. Sullair Corp., Michigan City, Ind., 1970-74; v.p. ops. Pure Aire Corp. subs. Sullair Corp., Charlotte, N.C., 1974-76; sr. engr. Sullair Corp., Michigan City, 1976-89; cons., designer compressed air sys. Lakeside, Mich., from 1990. Co. rep. CAGI Pneurop, Michigan City, 1987-90. Mem. Sch. Bd., River Valley, Mich., 1968; pres. Birchwood Assn. (Home Owner's Assn.), Harbert, Mich., 1964-88; zoning adminstr. Chikaming Twp., Berrien County, Mich. Mem. Elks, Beta Gamma Sigma, Phi Kappa Psi. Achievements include patents for helicopter rotor brake, for mono-rail brake; design of DC-8 landing Gear-Ford T-Bird separate unit power steering system many rotary screw compressor packages and compressed air dryer systems. Home: Lakeside, Mich. Died Dec. 1, 2001.

PRIGOGINE, ILYA, physics educator; b. Moscow, Jan. 25, 1917; s. Roman and Julie (Wichmann) Prigogine; m. Marina Prokopowicz, Feb. 25, 1961; children: Yves, Pascal. Licencié en sciences chimiques, licencié en sciences physiques, Free U. Brussels, 1939, PhD, 1941, agrégé de l'Enseignement Supérieur en Chimie Physique, 1945; DHC (hon.), U. Newcastle, Eng., 1966, U. Poitiers, France, 1966, U. Chgo., 1969, U. Bordeaux, France, 1972, U. de Liège, Belgium, 1977, U. Uppsala, Sweden, 1977, U de Droit, D'Economie et des Scis., d'Aix-Marseille, France, 1979, U. Georgetown, 1980, U. Cracovie, Poland, 1981, U. Rio de Janeiro, 1981, Stevens Inst. Tech., Hoboken, 1981, Heriot-Watt U., Scotland, 1985, Universidad Nacional de Educacion a Distancia, Madrid, 1985, U. Francois Rabelais de Tours, 1986, U. Beijing, People's Republic of China, 1986, U. Buenos Aires, 1989, U. Cagliari, Sardinia, Italy, 1990, U. Sienna, Italy, 1990; DSc (hon.), Gustavus Adolphus Coll., 1990; Membre d'Honneur (hon.), l'Academie Nationale d'Argenti, 1989, l'Academie des Sciences Naturelles de Republique Federale de Russie, 1991; Pres. d'Honneur (hon.), l'Acad. Nat. des Scis. de Republique de San Marino, 1991; Membre d'Honneur (hon.), l'Academie Chilienne des Scis., 1991, de l'Université de Nice-Sophia-Antipolis, Nice, France, 1991, de l'Univ. Philippines System, Quezon City, 1991, del'Université de Santiago, Chile, del'Université de Tucumán, Argentine, 1991; DHC (hon.), Université Lomonosov de Moscow, Russia, 1993, L'Univ. de A L.I. Cuza IASI, Iasi, Romania, 1994, U. de San Luis, Argentina, 1994, U. de Palermo, 1994, Institut Nat. Polytechnique, Lorraine, France, 1994, SUNY, Binghamton, 1995, Vrije U. Brussel, Brussels, Belgium, 1995, Internat. Assn. U. Pres., Seoul, 1995; Doyen d'honneur Honoris Causa (hon.), l'Institut Royal des Elites du Travail de Belgique Albert I, Brussels, 1995; DHC (hon.), U. Valladolid, Espagne, 1995, l'Universite de Saint-Petersbourg, Saint-Patersbourg, Russia, 1995; Laurea ad honorem in philosophy (hon.), U. degli Studi Inst. Filosofia, Urbino, Italy, 1996; DHC (hon.), U. Salvador, Buenos Aires, 1996, U. Xanthi, Greece, 1996; Degree in Sci. and Applied Sci. (hon.), Aristoteles U. of Thessaloniki, Thessaloniki, Greece, 1998; Degree (hon.), Nat. Inst. Astrophysics, Optics & Electronics, Puebla, Mex., 1998; DHC (hon.), Universidad Nacional Autonomade Mex., Mex., 1998; Degree (hon.), Wesleyan U., Ill., 1998; DHC (hon.), Wroclaw U. Tech., Wroclaw, Poland, 1998; numerous other honorary degrees (hon.), 1998-2000. Prof. Free U. Brussels, 1947—2003; dir. Internat. Insts. Physics and Chemistry, Solvay, Belgium, 1959—2003; prof. physics and chem. engring. U. Tex., Austin, 1967—2003, dir. Ilya Prigogine Ctr. Studies Statis. Mechs./Complex Sys., 1967—2003; hon. dir. Internat. Inst. Rsch. U. del Salvador, Buenos Aires, 1999—2003. Hon. prof. U. Nankin, China, 1986; Ashbel Smith regental prof. U. Tex., Austin, from 1984; Dir.'s Disting. visitor Inst. for Advanced Study, Princeton (N.J.) U., 1993; conseiller spl. Commn. des Communautés Européennes, 1993; internat. advisor de l'Internat. Inst. Advanced Studies, Kyoto, 1994; hon. dir. Inst. Internat. Investigaciones Cientficas U. Salvador, 1996, hon. chmn., Greece, 96; mem. adv. bd. Kothari Ctr. Sci., Ethics and Edn. U. Delhi, 1995; mem. Internat. Info. Acad, Moscow, Moscow, 1996, Académie de Yuste-Fauteuil J.S. Bach, Moscow, 1996; hon. pres. Ctr. FĪ No Linear Sistemas Complejos U. Santiago, Chile, from 1996; with Ctr L.Am. Estudios U. Nacional San Luis, Argentina, 1994; with U. Lomonosov, Moscow, 1995, Haute Ecole Libre Ilya Prigogine, Brussels, 1996, Inst. Documentazione Ricerca Sull, Italy, 1996, Opere di Ilya Prigogine, CISST, Brugine, Padova, Italy, 1996; Ilya Prigogine chair philosophy scis. U. Palermo, Argentina, 1996; pres. seminar Penser la Sci., U. Libre de Bruxelles, 1997; hon. pres. Inst. Philosophy, Naples, Italy, 1997; Prigogine lectr. U. Lombarde, Como, Italy, 1999; hon. prof. Internat. U. Albert Schweitzer, 2001; mem. internat. sci. adv. bd. UNESCO, 1996; numerous others; hon. prof. U. Ninking, China, 1986; Ashbel Smith regimental prof. U. Tex., Austin, from 1984; Dir.'s Disting. visitor Inst. for Advanced Study, Princeton (N.J.) U., 1993; conseiller spl. Commn. des Communautes Europeennes, 1993; internat. advisor Internat. Inst. Advanced Studies, Kyoto, 1994; hon. dir. Inst. Internat. Investigaciones Cientificas U. Salvador, 1996; hon. chmn. Inst. Complex Sys., Thrace, Greece, 1996; mem. adv. bd. Kothari Ctr. Sci., Ethics and Edn., U. Delhi, 1995; mem. internat. Info. Acad., Moscow, 96; mem. Acad. de Yuste-Fauteuil J.S. Bach, Madrid, 1996; hon. pres.Ctr. FĪ No Linear Sistemas Complejos U. Santiago, Chile, from 1996; with Ctr. L.Am. Estudios, U. Nacional San Luis Argentina, 1994, U. Lomonosov, Moscow, 1995, Haute Ecole Libre Ilya Prigogine, Brussels, 1996, Inst. Documentazione Ricerca Sull, Italy, 1996, Opere di Ilya Prigogine, CISST, Brugine, Padova, Italy, 1996; Ilya Prigogine chair philosophy scis. U. Palermo, Argentina, 1996; pres. seminar Penser la Sci., U. Libre de Bruxelles, 1997; Prigogine lectr. U. Lombarde, Como, Italy, 1999; hon. prof. Internat. U. Albert Schweitzer, 2001; mem. internat. sci. adv. bd. UNESCO, 1996; numerous others. Author (with R. Defay): Traite de Thermodynamique, conformement aux methodes de Gibbs et de Donder, 1944, 1950; author: Etude Thermodynamique des Phenomenes Irreversibles, 1947, Introduction to Thermodynamics of Irreversible Processes, 1954, 1962, 1967; author: (translation) Russian, Serbo-Croatian, French, Italian and Spanish; author: (with A. Bellemans, V. Mathot) The Molecular Theory of Solutions, 1957; author: Nonequilibrium Statistical Mechanics, 1962; author: (with R. Herman) Kinetic Theory of Vehicular Traffic, 1971; author: (with R. Glansdorff) Thermodynamic Theory of Structure, Stability and Fluctuations, 1971; author: (with G. Nicolis) Self-Organization in Nonequilibrium Systems, 1977; author: From Being to Becoming--Time and Complexity in Physical Sciences, 1980; author: (translation) French, German, Japanese, Russian, Chinese, Italian, Romanian and Portuguese edits.; author: (with I. Stengers) Order Out of Chaos, 1983; author: La Nouvelle Alliance, Les Metamorphoses de la Science, 1979; author: (translations) German, English, Italian, Spanish, Serbo-Croatian, Romanian, Swedish, Dutch, Russian, Japanese, Chinese, Portuguese, Bulgarian, Greek, Korean, Polish, Danish, Turkish & Hungarian edits. Mem. sci. adv. bd. Internat. Acad. for Biomed. Drug Rsch., 1990; mem. adv. com. Internat. Coun. Human Duties, U. degli Studi di Trieste, Italy, 1996. Decorated comdr. Legion d'Honneur France, comdr. de L'Ordre de Leopold; named Viscount, King of Belgium, 1989; recipient Medaille de la Resistance, comdr. de l'ordre Leopold II, 1961, Grande Croix de l'Ordre de Leopold II, 1977, Medaille Civique de Premiere Classe, 1972, comdr. de l'Ordre Natoinale du Merite, France, 1977, comdr. de l'Ordre des Arts et des Lettres, 1984, Titulaire de l' Ordre du Soleil Levant, avec Médaille d' Or et d' Argent, Japan, 1990, prix Franqui, 1955, Nobel prize in Chemistry, 1977, prix Solvay, 1965, Honda prize, 1983, Rumford Gold medal, Royal Soc. London, 1976, Karcher medal, Am. Crystallographic Assn., 1978, Descartes medal, U. Paris, 1979, award, Gravity Rsch. Found., 1988, prix Umberto Biancamano, 1987, Artificial Intelligence Sci. Achievement award, Internat. Found. for Artificial Intelligence, 1990, prix Summa de l'Universite Laval, Can., 1993, Medaille de l'Ecole Normale Superieure, Paris, 1995, Medaille Piotr Kapitza decernee par l'Academie des Scis. Naturelles de Russie, from 1996, Medaille d'Honneur de l'Inst. Phys. Chemistry, Polish Acad. Scis., from 1996, others; fellow RKG Found. Centennial, U. Tex., 1989—90. Fellow: Nat. Acad. Sci. India (hon.); mem.: Internat. Acad. Russia, Consejo Academico, Belorussian Acad. Sci., Conseil Consultatif Sci. Internat. de l'UNESCO, Internat. Soc. Theoretical Chem. Physics (hon. bd. mem.), Etranger ACad. Scis., Communautes Europeenne, Assemblee Europeenne Scis. Tech., World Inst. Sci., World Acad. Arts and Scis., Internat. Acad. Philosophy Sci., N.Y. Acad. Sci., Internat. Soc. Gen. Systems Rsch.. (pres.-elect 1988), Deutscher Acad. der Naturforscher Leopoldina (Cothenius medal 1970), Acad. Gottingen Germany, Royal Soc. Scis. Uppsala (Sweden), Korean Soc. Chemistry, NAS (assoc.), Ukrainian Nat. Acad. Sci., Am. Acad. Sci. (medal 1975), Royal Acad. Belgium (pres.), Osterreichische Acad. der

Wissenschaften (corr.), Soc. Royale des Scis Liege Belgium (corr.), Korean Acad. Sci. and Tech. (hon.), Royal Acad. Medicine (hon.), Soc. Coreenne de Chimie (hon.), Royal Soc. Chemistry Belgium (hon.), Chem. Soc. Poland (hon.), Commn. Mondiale de la Culture et du Devel. de l'UNESCO (hon.), Acad. Nationale des Scis., des Lettres et des Arts de Modena (Italy) (hon.). Died May 28, 2003.

PRINCE, MARTHA, botanic illustrator, writer, photographer; b. Birmingham, Ala., Aug. 8, 1925; d. Frank Hartley and Martha (Fort) Anderson; m. Jordan Herbert Prince, June 20, 1946. BA, Piedmont Coll., 1944; student of Reginald Marsh, Art Students League, N.Y.C., 1944-46; postgrad., N.Y. State Coll. Ceramics, 1949; studied with, Trafton and Reginald Marsh. Artist, illustrator U.S. Army, Bklyn., 1945-46; art dir. Mears Advt., N.Y.C., 1946-48; freelance artist, writer, photographer, Locust Valley, N.Y., from 1949. Notecards artist George Caspari, Inc., 1978, Doehla, Inc., 1978, Arboretum Press, 1979; porcelain plate artist Royal Hort. Soc., 1981. One-woman shows include U.S. Nat. Arboretum, Washington, 1978, Am. Hort. Soc. Hdqrs., Va., 1978, Callaway Gardens, Ga., 1974; exhibited in group shows Hunt Inst. Bot. Documentation, 1978; represented in permanent collections Hunt Inst. Bot. Documentation, Carnegie Mellon U., Pitts., Mus. of Garden History, London, Planting Fields Arboretum Libr., Oyster Bay, N.Y., Seaford Libr., N.Y.; writer, designer: (booklet) Native Azaleas, 1975; contbr. illustrations and articles to Gourmet mag., Am. Horticulturist, Wilderness, Horticulture, Rock Garden Quar., Jour. Am. Rhododendron Soc., numerous others. Bd. dirs. Planting Fields Arboretum, Oyster Bay, N.Y., 1991-95. Fellow Royal Hort. Soc.; mem. AAUW, Avocations: travel, gardening, music. Home: Locust Valley, NY. Died June 24, 2000.

PRINGLE, PETER LEE, retired systems engineer; b. Santa Monica, Calif., May 10, 1936; s. Gayland Paul and Helen (Schmidt) P.; m. Evamaria Rother, May 3, 1958; children: Ronald Lee, Karen Diane, Lynn Denise. BSChemE, Seattle U., 1958; MBA, Boise State U., 1973. With prodn. dept. Boise Cascade, Salem, Oreg., 1958-65; ops. research Boise (Idaho) Cascade, 1966-73, Kaiser Aluminum, Oakland, Calif., 1973-78, indsl. engring. Trentwood, Wash., 1978-83, with automated systems, 1983-89, Kaiser Aluminum DTC, 1989-96; info. sys. specialist Kaiser Aluminum, Mead, Wash., 1996-98; ret., 1998. Mem. Inst. Mgmt. Sci., Lake Merritt Sailing Club (commorore 1978), Lake Pend Oreille Tacht Club. Avocations: sailing, skiing, theatre. Home: Oakland, Calif. Died Sept. 29, 2001.

PROBASCO, GENE ARLEN, lawyer; b. Creston, Iowa, May 17, 1931; s. Fred Theodore and LaVada Vesta (Hoffman) P.; m. Patricia Ann Shoemaker, Mar. 8, 1952; children: Sheryl L. Cobb, Debra A. Amick, Cynthia J. Aspeotis, Craig G. BS in Acctg., U. Iowa, 1956, JD, 1957. Bar: U.S. Dist. Ct. (no. dist.) Iowa 1957, U.S. Tax Ct. 1957, Iowa Supreme Ct. 1957. Ptnr. Goldberg, Probasco & Berenstien, later Goldberg, Mayne, Probasco & Berenstien, Sioux City, Iowa, 1957-84, Rawlings, Nieland, Probasco, Killinger, Ellwanger, Jacobs & Monrhauser, Sioux City, Iowa, 1984-99. Mem. Sioux City Bd. Adjustment 1964-66, Sioux City Estate Planning Council exec. com. Served to sgt. USAF, 1951-53, Korea (air medal 3 oak leaf clusters). Mem. Sioux City and Woodbury County Bar Assns. (pres. 1969), Iowa State Bar Assn. Clubs: Sertoma (pres., v.p., bd. dirs. 1969), Sioux City Country (pres., v.p., bd. dirs. 1979-80), Sioux City Lawyers (pres. 1961). Republican. Methodist. Home: Sioux City, Iowa. Died May 26, 1999.

PROFFITT, JUDY KAY, past computer programmer analyst; b. Beech Grove, Ind., Nov. 7, 1958; d. William Logan Sr. and Shirley Mae (Tuttle) Linhart; m. Michael Norman Proffitt, June 15, 1991; children: Amber Kay, Joshua Michael. BS, Butler U., 1981, MBA, 1988. Computer operator Holcomb Research Inst., Indpls., 1980-81; programmer analyst Alverno Adminstrv. Services Inc., Beech Grove, 1981-85, AFNB, Indpls., 1985-86, Polygram Records, Inc., Indpls., 1987-94. Mem. Eastlawn Wesleyan Ch., mem. ch. choir. Mem. Kappa Mu Epsilon, Delta Delta Delta (corresponding sec. Indpls. alumni chpt. 1986-88, rec. sec. 1990-92, v.p. 1994-96). Democrat. Mem. Wesleyan Ch. Avocations: skiing, needlecrafts. Home: New Palestine, Ind. Died Apr. 9, 2001.

PROUDFOOT, SISTER BERNADETTE AGNES, biology educator; b. Jersey, N.J., June 22, 1921; d. George Francis and Lillian Agnes (Fay) P. BA, Caldwell Coll., 1952; MS, St. Thomas Inst., 1959, PhD, 1972. Joined Order of Preachers, Roman Cath. Ch., 1939. Researcher Spring Hill Coll., Mobile, Ala., 1954-55; instr. biology Caldwell (N.J.) Coll., 1955-60, asst. prof. biology, 1961-64, assoc. prof. biology, 1964-72, tenured prof. biology, chair nat. sci., 1972-83, tenured prof. biology, 1983-92. Master fellow St. Thomas Inst., Palm Beach, Fla., 1958-59, doctoral fellow, Cinn., 1971-72; grantee Nat. Sci. for Genetics, U. N.C., Raleigh, 1963. Mem. N.Y. Acad. Sci. Home: Caldwell, NJ. Deceased.

PUDNEY, BETTY ANN, state official; b. Oneonta, N.Y., May 6, 1931; d. Cecil Loren and Mary Harriet (Lawless) P. BS in Journalism, Northwestern U., Evanston, Ill., 1953; postgrad., Cornell U., 1955-56. Asst. publicity dir. Harper & Bros. (now Harper & Row), N.Y.C., 1959-62; edn. editor Nat. Instructional TV Libr., N.Y.C., 1962-64; special researcher for pub. rels. Cunningham & Walsh, N.Y.C., 1964; reporter Nat. Lutheran Ch. in Am., N.Y.C., 1965; pub. information dir. Div. Employment Opportunities, Mobilization for Youth, N.Y.C., 1965-73; asst. rsch. scientist Narcotic and Drug Rsch., Inc., N.Y.C., 1974-76; dir., Concerns of Children Campaign Odyssey Inst., N.Y.C., 1977; tax compliance agt. N.Y. State Dept. Labor, Unemployment Div., Bronx, 1977-79; staff analyst, Office Appraisal Rsch. N.Y.C. Dept. Fin., 1979-80; investigator N.Y. State Liquour Authority, N.Y.C., from 1980. Co-author: (monograph) The Utilization of Industrial Advisory Committees to Increase Employment Opportunities, 1973 and others. Mem. Coalition Labor Union Women, 1980—, Pub. Employees Fedn., AFL-CIO. Mem. Assn. State Liquor Enforcement Agys. (sec. 1988—). Liberal. Lutheran. Avocations: horseback riding, sailing, collecting antiques, swimming. Home: New York, NY. Deceased.

PUFFER, MERLE E. opera company executive; b. Rochester, N.Y., Oct. 16, 1915; m. Deena P. Founder, former artistic dir. Nev. Opera Assn., Reno; former chmn. U. Nevada, Reno; prof. Manhattan Sch. of Music, 1994—2003. Died Oct. 22, 2003.

PUNDT, JOAN SCHRADER, elementary and middle school educator; b. Colorado Springs, Colo., June 21, 1936; d. Walter Herman and Melba Lorene (Weisdorfer) Schrader; m. George Harold Pundt, Aug. 7, 1955; children: George Harold Jr., Joseph Steven, Raymond Addison. BS in Elem. Edn., Winthrop Coll., 1959, MA in Teaching, 1964; PhD in Edn., U. S.C., 1990. Cert. elem. tchr., prin., supr., S.C. Math. and phys. edn. tchr. Lancaster (S.C.) Jr. High Sch., 1958-60; 5th and 6th grade tchr. Ebinport Elem. Sch., 1960-69; 7th and 8th grade sci. tchr. Sullivan Jr. High Sch., 1969-72; 7th, 8th and 9th grade math. tchr. Rawlinson Rd. Jr. High Sch., 1972-76; 5th and 6th grade math. and sci. tchr. Belleview Elem. Sch., 1976-84, remedial and compensatory coord. tchr., 1984-89, 6th grade tchr., 1989-90; 8th grade earth sci. tchr. Sullivan Middle Sch., from 1990. Adv. Bd.: Science Scope jour., 1991-93. Mem. NEA, S.C. Edn. Assn., Rock Hill Edn. Assn., Nat. Coun. Tchrs. of Math., S.C. Coun. Tchrs. of Math., Nat. Sci. Tchrs. Assn., Catawba Regional Math. Coun. (pres. 1989—), Phi Delta Kappa (co-chmn. rsch. 1989—). Presbyterian. Avocations: watercolors, gardening, environmental and conservation activities. Died Apr. 7, 2000.

PURCELL, KENNETH, psychology educator, university dean; b. N.Y.C., Oct. 21, 1928; s. Herman and Ann (Bulkin) P.; m. Claire Dickson Kepler, Dec. 17, 1949 (div. Dec. 1986); children: Kathleen Ann, Andrew Kepler; m. Marjorie Bayes, Jan. 17, 1987. BA, PhD, U. Nebr. Asst. prof. U. Ky., 1956-58; dir. behavior sci. div. Children's Asthma Research Inst.; asst. prof. U. Colo. Med. Center, 1958-68; prof., dir. clin. tng. psychology U. Mass., 1968-69, chmn. dept. psychology, 1969-70; prof., chmn. psychology U. Denver, 1970—76, dean Coll. Arts and Scis., 1976-84, prof. psychology, 1984—94, prof. emeritus, 1994. Author papers in field. Served to 1st lt. AUS, 1953—56. Fellow Am. Psychol. Assn., Soc. Research Child Devel., AAAS, Colo. Psychol. Assn. (dir. 1962-64) Home: Aurora, Colo. Died Dec. 11, 2003.

PURDY, JOHN EDGAR, retired manufacturing executive; b. Detroit, June 17, 1919; s. William Everett and May Adeline (Fountain) P.; m. Elizabeth Anne Van Dyne; 1 child, Vannessa Anne. Grad. h.s., Mich. Founder, chmn. Dayton (Ohio) Showcase Co., 1947-87; pres. P-38 Nat. Assn., ret., from 1987. Capt. USAF, 1942-46. Decorated DFC with 2 oak leaf clusters, Purple Heart, Air medal with 6 oak leaf clusters. Mem. Am. Fighter Aces Assn. (pres. 1983-84), Am. Fighter Aces Mus. Found. (chmn. 1984-91), Nat. Aviation Hall of Fame (trustee 1978-86), Nat. Aviation Hall of Fame (bd. dirs. bd. of nominations), P-38 Nat. Assn. (pres. 1999-2001), Internat. Fighter Pilots Mus. Found. (trustee 1999—). Avocations: golf, aviation historian. Home: Dayton, Ohio. Died Sept. 8, 2003.

PUTNEY, PAUL WILLIAM, lawyer; b. Phila., Feb. 6, 1940; s. R. Emerson and Dorothea (Schulz) P.; m. Joan E. High, June 9, 1961; children: Joanna E., Andrew E. AB, Princeton U., 1962; JD, Harvard U., 1965. Bar: Pa. 1965, U.S. Dist. Ct. (ea. dist.) Pa. 1966, U.S. Supreme Ct. 1977, N.Y. 1988. Assoc. Dechert Price & Rhoads, Phila., 1965-73, ptnr., 1973—74, Dechert Price & Rhoads LLP, 1977—2004, mng. ptnr. N.Y.C., 1987—94, chmn. trust and estates dept., 1994—2001; dep. chief broadcast bur. FCC, Washington, 1974-77. Chmn. Phila. Presbytery Homes, Inc., 1987-93. Mem.: ABA. Home: Huntingdon Valley, Pa. Died June 5, 2004.

QUADRACCI, HARRY V. printing company executive, lawyer; b. 1936; BA, Regis Coll; JD, Columbia U, 1959. Assoc., N.Y.C., Milw., 1961—71; corp. counsel W.A. Krueger Co., Brookfield, Wis., 1961—71; pres. Quad Graphics, Inc., Pewaukee, Wis., 1971—2002. Died July 29, 2002.

QUALTERE, THOMAS JOHN, clinical psychologist; b. Kingston, N.Y., Feb. 9, 1923; s. Anthony Qualtere and Angelina Sisco; m. Maria Conchita DiRenzo; children: Mary, Theresa, Thomas, Jennie, Frank, Louise, Agnes. PhD, Syracuse U., 1957. Lic. psychologist, N.Y. Clin. psychologist Ellis Hosp., Schenectady, N.Y., 1953-60; asst. prof. Russell Sage Coll., Troy, N.Y., 1961-66, assoc. prof., 1966-71, prof., 1971-90; cons. psychologist St. Colman's Home, Watervliet, N.Y., from 1953, Van Der Hyden Hall, Troy, N.Y., 1954-89. Cons. psychologist The Charlton Sch., Burnt Hills, N.Y., 1955-56, Albany Mental Health Clinic, 1955-59, Schenectady Sch. System, 1955-65. Pres. St. Anthonys Sch., Schenectady, 1965. Sgt. U.S. Army, 1944-46. Mem. Sons of Italy, Psi Chi, Phi Delta Kappa, Sigma Psi. Roman Catholic. Avocations: fishing, baseball, playing cards, hiking. Home: Schenectady, NY. Died Mar. 1, 2001.

QUILLEN, JAMES HENRY (JIMMY QUILLEN), former congressman; b. Wayland, Va., Jan. 11, 1916; s. John A. and Hannah (Chapman) Q.; m. Cecile Cox (dec. 2002), Aug. 9, 1952. Ed. high sch.; LL.D. (hon.), Milligan Coll., Tenn., 1978. With Kingsport Press, 1934-35; with Kingsport Times, 1935-36; founder newspaper Kingsport Mirror (semi-weekly), 1936, pub., 1936-39; founder Johnson City (Tenn.) Times, 1939, pub., 1939-44, Johnson City (Tenn.) Times (converted to daily), 1940; mem. Tenn. Ho. of Reps., 1954-62, minority leader, 1959-60, mem. legislative council, 1957, 59, 61, mem. rules com., subcom. legis. process, Rep. chmn. emeritus; mem. U.S. Congress from Tenn., 1963-97. Served to lt. USNR, 1942-46. Mem. Am. Legion, VFW, C. of C. Clubs: Lions, Ridgefields Country (Kingsport); Capitol Hill (Washington). Republican. Methodist. Home: Kingsport, Tenn. Died Nov. 2, 2003.

QUINN, JANE, journalist; b. San Antonio, Tex., Oct. 5, 1916; d. James Edward and Willie Stell (Mitchell) Q. BA, Fla. State U., 1938; MS in Social Work, Cath. U. of Am., 1945. Reporter St. Augustine (Fla.) Record, 1938-41; journalist, editl. staff The Fla. Cath. for Diocese of St. Augustine, 1940-68, The Fla. Cath., St. Augustine, 1940—68, The Fla. Cath. for Diocese of Orlando, Fla., 1968—88; archivist Diocese of Orlando, 1988—2001. Author: Minorcans in Florida, 1975, Story of a Nun: Jeanie Gordon Brown, 1979, others; contbr. articles to profl. jours. Recipient Papal award Pro Ecclesia et Pontifice, 1979, citation Cath. Press Assn. of U.S. and Can., 1994. Fellow: Orlando Interfaith Sponsoring Com.; mem.: DAR, St. Joseph Alumni Assn., Orlando Diocesan Coun. Cath. Women (life) (hon.), Assocs. of Josephite Nuns, Alpha Xi Delta. Roman Catholic. Avocations: reading biographies, Florida history books, collecting US commemoratives. Home: Orlando, Fla. Died Dec. 1, 2003.

QUINN, LINDA CATHERINE, lawyer; b. Rockville Centre, N.Y., 1948; BA, Mt. Holyoke Coll., 1969; JD, Georgetown U., 1972. Bar: N.Y. 1973. Law clk. Hon. J. Joseph Smith U.S. Ct. Appeals (2d cir.), 1972-73; assoc. Sullivan & Cromwell, 1973-80; atty. fellow SEC, 1980-82, assoc. dir. divsn. corp. fin., 1982-84, exec. asst. to chmn., 1984-86, dir. corp. fin. divsn., 1986-96; ptnr. Shearman & Sterling, N.Y.C., 1996—2003. Named one of 50 Top Women Lawyers Nat. Law Jour., 1998. Mem.: ABA. Home: New York, NY. Died Nov. 11, 2003.

QUITTMEYER, CHARLES LOREAUX, business educator; b. Peekskill, N.Y., Dec. 23, 1917; s. Ernest Martin and Edith Grace (Loreaux) Q.; m. Maureen J. Rankin, June 2, 1956; children: Peter Charles, David Rankin, Andrew Robert, Jane Loreaux. AB, Coll. William and Mary, 1940; MBA, Harvard U., 1947; PhD (fellow), Columbia U., 1955. Bus. and govt. positions, 1941-42, 47-48; asst. prof. bus. adminstrn. Coll. William and Mary, Williamsburg, Va., 1948-54, prof., head dept., 1962-68, founding dean Sch. Bus. Adminstrn., 1968-83, Floyd Dewey Gottwald prof. bus. adminstrn., 1982-88, Floyd Dewey Gottwald prof. bus. adminstrn. emeritus, from 1988. Lectr., asst. prof. mktg. U. Buffalo, 1954-57; rsch. assoc., assoc. prof. commerce U. Va., 1957-61; sr. scientist Tech. Ops., Inc., 1961-62; dir., adv. bd. First & Mchts. Nat. Bank, Peninsula, 1972-83; dir., treas., exec. com. Williamsburg Landing, Inc., 1983-89. Contbr. to Ency. Brit., also papers in field. Mem. bd. suprs. James City County, 1969-71, chmn., 1971; mem. Peninsula Airport Commn., 1971-81, sec., 1973-81; lifetime mem. Sch. Bus. Adminstrn. Bd. Sponsors, Inc. Coll. of William and Mary. Served to capt., F.A. and M.I. AUS, 1942-46. Recipient William and Mary Alumni medallion, 1976 Mem. Acad. Mgmt., Am. Econ. Assn., So. Bus. Adminstrn. Assn. (pres. 1976-77), Soc. of Alumni Coll. William and Mary (dir. 1984-90), Phi Beta Kappa, Beta Gamma Sigma. Clubs: Harvard of Virginia. Episcopalian. Home: Mobile, Ala. Died Apr. 22, 2004.

RABB, MAXWELL MILTON, lawyer, former ambassador; b. Boston, Sept. 28, 1910; s. Solomon and Rose (Kostick) R.; m. Ruth Creidenberg, Nov. 2, 1939; children: Bruce, Sheila Rabb Weidenfeld, Emily Rabb Livingston, Priscilla Rabb Ayres. AB, Harvard U., 1932, LLB, 1935; LLD (hon.), Wilberforce U., 1957; DHL (hon.), Mt. St. Mary's Coll., 1983; LLB (hon.), Pepperdine U., 1985, St. Thomas U., 1986; DHL (hon.), Hebrew Union Coll., 1990. Bar: Mass. 1935, N.Y. 1958. Mem. firm Rabb & Rabb, Boston, 1935-37; adminstrv. asst. to U.S. Senator H.C. Lodge Jr., Mass., 1937-43; adminstrv. asst. U.S. Senator Sinclair Weeks, Mass., 1944; legal and legis. cons. Sec. Navy Forrestal, 1946; practice law Boston, 1946-51; cons. U.S. Senate Rules Com., 1952; presdl. asst. to Pres. Eisenhower; sec. to Cabinet, 1953-59; partner Stroock & Stroock & Lavan, N.Y.C., 1959-81, of counsel, 1989-91, Kramer, Levin, Naftalis & Frankel LLP, N.Y.C., 1991—2002; amb. to Italy, 1981-89. Bd. dirs. Sterling Nat. Bank, Sister City Program City of N.Y., MIC Industries, Data Software Sys. Inc., Dwight Eisenhower Nat. adv. bd., Oak Tree Med. Sys., Inc. Exec. asst. campaign mgr. Eisenhower presdl. campaign, 1951-52; del. Republican Nat. Conv., 1952, 56, 76, 80; mem. exec. com. U.S. Commn. for UNESCO, 1959-60; chmn. U.S. del. UNESCO conf., Paris, 1958; mem. Coun. on Fgn. Rels., 1978-2002; pres. Congregation Emanu-El, N.Y.C., 1973-81; former mem. bd. advisors John F. Kennedy Sch. Govt., Harvard U. Sch. Pub. Health; trustee Cardinals Cooke and O'Connor Inner City Scholarship Fund, The Lighthouse, 1995—, Eisenhower Libr., George Marshall

Internat. Ctr.; mem. bd. mgrs. Seamen's Ch. Inst.; mem. presdl. adv. panel on South Asian Relief assistance, 1971; mem. panel conciliators World Bank Internat. Ctr. for Settlement of Investment Disputes, 1967-73, U.S. rep., 1974-77; mem. Presdl. Commn. on Income Maintenance Programs, 1968-69; hon. chmn. bd. Am. Friends of Alliance Israelite Universelle; vice chmn. United Cerebral Palsy, Inc., Nat. Com. on Am. Fgn. Policy; mem. adv. bd. Auburn U. Served as lt. amphibious corps USNR, 1944-46. Decorated Commendatore Order of Merit, 1958, Grand Cross of Order of Merit (Italy), 1982, Commendation ribbon USN; Grand Cross of Order of Malta, 1989; Brandeis U. fellow. Mem. ABA, Am. Law Inst., Amb.'s Club of Reps. Abroad (hon. chmn.), Harvard Club (N.Y.C.), Harmonie Club (N.Y.C.), Army and Navy Club (Washington), Met. Club (Washington). Home: New York, NY. Died June 9, 2002.

RABENSTEIN, MANFRED, rabbi; b. Tann, Hesse, Germany, July 13, 1911; came to U.S., 1938; s. Hugo and Lina (Fichtelberger) R.; m. Flora Plaut, Mar. 31, 1936; children: Aaron A., Bernard H., Naomi D. Rabenstein Miller, Jacob S. BEd, Jewish Cantorial & Tchrs. Sem., Cologne, Germany, 1932. Chaver, Rabbinical Coll. Kol Torah, Jerusalem, 1971. Pub. sch. and Hebrew tchr., Darmstadt, Germany, 1932-38; rabbi Congregation New Hope, Cin., from 1939. Mem. Orthodox Union N.Y.C. Home: Cincinnati, Ohio. Died June 21, 2001.

RABIN, RHODA, music educator, writer, musician; b. N.Y.C., Jan. 20, 1927; d. Irving and Sylvia L. Shapiro; m. Marvin Rabin, Jan. 31, 1948; children: Ralph, David, Martha. Student, Music and Art High Sch. Columbia U., N.Y.C., 1946; MusB, Eastman Sch. Music, Rochester, 1948; student, Julliard Sch. Music, N.Y.C., 1949. Prof. music, piano and double bass U. La., Louisville, 1948—50; lectr. U. Ky., Lexington, 1951—58; tchr., presch. piano and double bass Boston U., 1959—61; tchr. presch. piano and pedagogy New Eng. Conservatory of Music, Boston, 1961—66; lectr. U. Wis., Madison, 1968—88; pvt. piano tchr., 1948—95. Author: At the Beginning: Teaching Piano to the Very Young Child, 1996; contbr. articles to profl. jours. Home: Madison, Wis. Died Apr. 11, 2003.

RABINOW, JACOB, electrical engineer, consultant; b. Kharkov, Russia, Jan. 8, 1910; came to U.S., 1921, naturalized, 1930; s. Aaron and Helen (Fleisher) Rabinovich; m. Gladys Lieder, Sept. 26, 1943; children: Jean Ellen, Clare Lynn. BS in Elec. Engring, Coll. City N.Y., 1933, E.E., 1934; D.H.L. (hon.), Towson State U., 1983. Radio serviceman, N.Y.C., 1934-38; mech. engr. Nat. Bur. Standards, Washington, 1938-54; pres. Rabinow Engring. Co., Washington, 1954-64; v.p. Control Data Corp., Washington, 1964-72; research engr. Nat. Bur. Standards, 1972-89; cons. Inst. Standards and Tech., Gaithersburg, Md., from 1989. Regent's lectr. U. Calif.-Berkeley, 1972; lectr., cons. in field. Author; patentee in field. Recipient Pres.'s Certificate of Merit, 1948; certificate appreciation War Dept., 1949; Exceptional Service award Dept. Commerce, 1949; Edward Longstreth medal Franklin Inst., 1959; Jefferson medal N.J. Patent Law Assn., 1973; Lamelson-MIT Lifetime Achievment award, 1998; Cosmos Club award, 1999; named Scientist of Yr. Indsl. R&D mag., 1980. Fellow IEEE (Harry Diamond award 1977), AAAS; mem. Nat. Acad. Engring., Philos. Soc. Washington, Audio Engring. Soc., Sigma Xi. Clubs: Cosmos (Washington). Home: Bethesda, Md. Died Sept. 11, 1999.

RABINOWITZ, JESSE CHARLES, biochemist, educator; b. N.Y.C., Apr. 28, 1925; s. Julius and Frances (Pincus) R. BS, Poly. Inst. Bklyn., 1945; PhD, U. Wis., Madison, 1949. Chemist NIH, Bethesda, Md., 1953-57; assoc. prof. biochemistry U. Calif., Berkeley, 1957-63, prof., 1963—91, chmn. dept. biochemistry, 1978-83, prof. emeritus, 1991—2003. Guggenheim fellow, 1977-78 Mem. Am. Soc. Biol. Chemistry and Molecular Biology, Am. Soc. Microbiology, Am. Chem. Soc., Nat. Acad. Scis. Home: Kensington, Calif. Died Sept. 9, 2003.

RABY, TEDDY LEE, clergyman; b. Kingston, Tenn., May 26, 1928; s. Sanie David and Jessie (Gordon) R.; m. Mable Zora Nelson, Feb. 4, 1947 (dec.); children: Betty Jean, Evelyn L. (dec.), Edward, Samuel, Denise, Robin, Teddy Lee II, Lisa, Donna; m. Margie Juanita Stephens, Apr. 3, 1992. Grad. Theology, Pioneer Theol. Sem., 1952, DTh, 1958; MTh, Colonial Acad., 1954, D Bible Philosophy, 1960; DD (hon.), Bapt. Christian Coll., Shreveport, La., 1988; D Ministry (hon.), Theol. Sem. Bowling Green, Ky., 1989, ThD (hon.), 1991. Ordained to ministry Bapt. Ch., 1951. Pastor Swan Pond Bapt. Ch., Kingston, Tenn., 1951-52, Little Valley Bapt. Ch., Blaine, Tenn., 1952-53, Union Valley Bapt. Ch., Oliver Springs, Tenn., 1953-55, Victory Bapt. Ch., Maryville, Tenn., 1959-79, New Fairview Bapt. Ch., Oliver Springs, 1955-79, 83-92, Faith Bapt. Ch., Oak Ridge, Tenn., 1993-95. Chair bd. Bapt. Internat. Bible Inst., Harriman, Tenn., 1983—; trustee World Bapt. Coll., Ft. Worth, 1950-52, Colonial Theol. Sem., Rockford, Ill., 1950-54. Author: Christ is Conqueror, 1958, He is Coming Again, 1959, The Blood of Jesus Christ, God's Son Cleanseth Us From All Sin, 1993; author sermon: Jerusalem, A Burdensome Stone, 1991—. Sgt. U.S. Army, 1946-49. Deceased.

RADCLIFF, WILLIAM FRANKLIN, lawyer, director; b. Fredericksburg, Ind., May 21, 1922; s. Samuel Pearl and Hester Susan (Sherwood) R.; m. Elizabeth Louise Doeller Haines, May 15, 1982; children— Forrest Lee, Stephanie Anne; foster children— Cheryl Lynn, Sandra Lee, Richard Alan, Lezlie Laverne; stepchildren— Mark David, Laura Louise, Pamela Lynn, Veronica Leigh. BA, Yale U., 1948; JD, Ind. U., 1951. Bar: Ind. 1951. With DeFur, Voran, Hanley, Radcliff & Reed and predecessors, Muncie, Ind., 1951—, ptnr., 1954—. Dir., mem. exec. com. Am. Nat. Bank and Trust Co., Muncie. Author: Sherman Minton: Indiana's Supreme Court Justice, 1996, Sagamore of the Wabash. Pres. Delaware County Mental Health Assn., 1962-63; founding mem. Ind. Mental Health Meml. Found., 1962, sec., 1962-84; bd. dirs. Delaware County Cancer Soc.; trustee Acad. Community Leadership. Served with AUS, 1940-46, PTO Mem. ABA, Ind. Bar Assn., Muncie Bar Assn., Muncie-Delaware County C. of C. (pres. 1972-73) Clubs: Muncie Tennis and Country (bd. dirs., sec.), Muncie, Delaware Country (pres. 1972-73), Exchange (pres. 1962) (Muncie). Lodges: Masons. Home: Muncie, Ind. Died July 16, 2002.

RADCLIFFE, S. VICTOR, international executive; b. Cheshire, Eng., July 28, 1927; came to U.S., 1956; s. Andrew Hunter and Ellen (Waring) R.; m. Wanda (Reid) Koskinen, June 4, 1977. B Engring., U. Liverpool, Eng., 1948, PhD, 1956. Chartered engr. Rsch. metallurgist Rylands Bros. Ltd., also Lancashire Steel Corp., 1958-53; rsch. assoc. MIT, Cambridge, Mass., 1956-62; rsch. mgr. Man Labs. Inc., Cambridge, Mass., 1961-63; mem. faculty Case Western Res. U., Cleve., 1963-75, prof. metallurgy, 1966-75, head dept. metallurgy and materials sci., 1969-75; sr. policy analyst Office Sci. Adviser to Pres., Washington, 1974-75; sr. fellow Resources for the Future, Washington, 1976-79; v.p. corp. devel. Nat. Forge Co., N.Y.C., 1979-89; former pres. RAN Internat. Inc., Washington, London, Paris. Cons. to industry, U.S. govt., internal orgns.; bd. dirs. IMT Inc., Boston. Mem. study group sci. and engring. edn. in Mex., Ford Found., 1966; dir. survey of meterial sci. and engring. NAS, 1971-74; mem. Apollo Lunar Sci. Program. Univ. fellow Liverpool U., Eng., 1953-56. Fellow Instn. Metallurgists; mem. Am. Chem. Soc., Am. Phys. Soc., AIME, Nat. Assn. Bus. Economists, ASM Internat., Internat. Soc. for Planning and Strategic Mgmt., Nat. Economists Club, Cosmos Club. Home: Washington, DC. Died Nov. 16, 2003.

RADKE, VENITA, community health nurse; b. Slaton, Tex., Feb. 26, 1950; d. BB and Rita (James) Miles; m. Lonnie W. Radke, Apr. 16, 1974. Diploma, Hilcrest Bapt. Hosp. Sch. Nursing, 1971; BSN, U. Tex., Arlington, 1982, postgrad. Cert. CPR instr. and trainer, blood pressure instr. and trainer. Head nurse Hillcrest Bapt. Med. Ctr., Waco, Tex., educator nursing, mgr. Home Health Hospice. Cons. in field. Mem. ANA, Tex. Nurses Assn. (scholarship chair person), Tex. Assn. Home Health Adminstrs., NAHC, Sigma Theta Tau. Home: Hewitt, Tex. Deceased.

RADWAY, LAURENCE INGRAM, political science educator; b. Staten Island, N.Y., Feb. 2, 1919; s. Frederick and Dorothy (Segall) R.; m. Patricia Ann Headland, Aug. 20, 1949; children: Robert Russell, Carol Sinclair, Michael Porter, Deborah Brooke. BS, Harvard U., 1940, MA, 1948, PhD, 1950; M.P.A., U. Minn., 1943; MA (hon.), Dartmouth, 1959. Jr. economist OPA, 1941; intern U.S. Bur. Budget, 1941-42, Nat. Inst. Pub. Affairs, 1941-42; teaching fellow govt. dept. Harvard U., 1946-50; instr. govt. dept. Dartmouth U., 1950-52, asst. prof., 1952-57, assoc. prof., 1957-58, prof., 1958—89, chmn. dept., 1959-62, 70-72, 77-80, dir. Comparative Studies Ctr., 1963-68. Cons. ODM, 1952; prof. Nat. War Coll., 1962-63; civilian aide to sec. army, 1962-70; mem. N.H. Ho. Reps., 1968-72 Author: (with John W. Masland) Soldiers and Scholars, 1957, Military Behavior in International Organizations, 1962, Foreign Policy and National Defense, 1969. Chmn. Hanover Democratic Com., 1954-56; mem. N.H. Dem. Com., 1958-60, chmn. Platform Conf., 1959, 60, chmn., 1975-77; chmn. Grafton County Dem. Com., 1956-58; mem. Dem. Nat. Com., 1975-77; Bd. dirs. N.H. World Affairs Council, 1955-81; bd. advisers Indsl. Coll. Armed Forces, 1958-62. Served from pvt. to capt., Transp. Corps AUS, 1943-46. Pub. Adminstrn. fellow U. Minn., 1940-42; Social Sci. Research Council fellow, 1957 Mem. Council Fgn. Relations, Internat. Inst. Strategic Studies, Am. Polit. Sci. Assn. (nat. council 1965-67), Royal Inst. Internat. Affairs, New Eng. Polit. Sci. Assn. (mem. com. 1959-60, pres. 1964-65), Phi Beta Kappa. Presbyterian. Home: West Lebanon, NH. Died May 7, 2003.

RAIDER, LOUIS, retired physician, radiologist; b. Chattanooga, Sept. 7, 1913; s. Leaha Reevin; m. Emma Silberstein, Oct. 19, 1940; children: Lynne Dianne, David Bernard, Paula Raider Olichney. BS, Bklyn. Coll., 1935; MD, Dalhousie U., 1941. Diplomate, cert. Am. Bd. Radiology. Intern Met. Hosp., N.Y.C., 1940-41, resident in radiology, 1941-42; resident in radiation therapy Bellevue Hosp., N.Y.C., 1942-43; fellow in cancer therapy NIH, N.Y.C., 1943-44; chief of radiology Vets. Hosp., New Orleans, 1947-50; radiologist, chief radiology Providence Hosp., Mobile, Ala., 1950-76; clin. prof. Med. Sch. U. South Ala., Mobile, 1987-97; ret., 1997. Contbr. articles to profl. jours. Maj. AUS, 1944-47. Fellow Am. Coll. Radiology, Am. Coll. Chest Physicians; mem. Radiol. Soc. N.Am., Am. Roentgen Ray Soc., AMA, Ala. Acad. Radiology (pres. 1970-71, Silver medal 1989), So. Med. Assn. (chmn. sect. radiology 1973-74), Soc. Thoracic Radiology, So. Radiol. Conf., Am. Soc. Emergency Radiology. Democrat. Jewish. Home: Mobile, Ala. Deceased.

RAINBOLT, RANDY JOE, oncological nurse; b. Batesville, Ark., Feb. 3, 1961; s. Joe T. and Norma (Tuggle) R. Student, Ark. Coll., Batesville, 1979-81; EMT, East Ark. Community Coll., Forrest City, 1982; ADN, U. Ark., 1989; student, SUNY. RN, Ark. Cert. ACLS. Charge nurse Rebsamen Regional Med. Ctr., Jacksonville, Ark.; charge nurse, staff nurse cardiac stepdown unit; staff nurse cardiac stepdown unit, ICU supr., house supr. Advocate Death and Dying Ednl. Coun. N.Y.; dir. nursing svc. Van Buren County Meml. Hosp., Clinton, Ark.; health and safety inspector USDA. Leader com. quality improvement, chmn. pub. edn. Jacksonville unit Am. Cancer Soc.; vol. lectr. cancer prevention, chem. dependency. Recipient Quorum Excellence in Nursing award. Mem. ANA, Internat. Union Nurses Against Cancer, Nat. Coun. Nursing Adminstrn., Ark. State Nurses Assn., Am. Oncology Nurses Assn. Home: Pleasant Plains, Ark. Died Sept. 18, 2000.

RALL, DAVID PLATT, pharmacologist, environmentalist; b. Aurora, Ill., Aug. 3, 1926; s. Edward Everett and Nell (Platt) Rall; m. Mary Gloria Monteiro, Apr. 22, 1989; children from previous marriage: Jonathan D., Catharyn E. BS, North Ctrl. Coll., Naperville, Ill., 1946; MS, Northwestern U., 1948, MD, PhD, 1951. Intern Bellevue Hosp., N.Y.C., 1952—53; officer USPHS, 1953—90, asst. surgeon gen., 1971—90. Sr. investigator Lab. Chem. Pharmacology Nat. Cancer Inst., NIH, Bethesda, Md., 1953—55, Clin. Pharmacology and Exptl. Therapeutics Svc., 1956—58, head svc., 1958—63; chief Clin. Pharmacology and Exptl. Therapeutics Svc. (Lab. Chem. Pharmacology), 1963—69; assoc. sci. dir. for exptl. therapeutics Nat. Cancer Inst., 1966—71; dir. Nat. Inst. Environ. Health Scis., 1971—90, Nat. Toxicology Program, 1978—90; adj. prof. pharmacology U. N.C., Chapel Hill, 1972—90; Fgn. Sec. NAS Inst. Medicine, 1994—98. Trustee Environ. Def. Fund, 1991—99; treas. Collegium Ramazzini, 1992—99. Fellow: AAAS; mem.: Soc. Toxicology, Am. Soc. Pharmacology and Exptl. Therapeutics, Am. Soc. Clin. Investigation, Am. Assn. Cancer Rsch. Died Sept. 28, 1999.

RAMIREZ, CARLOS DAVID, publisher; b. San Juan, P.R., Aug. 19, 1946; s. Carlos David and Maria (Melendez) R.; children: Christine, David. AAS, CCNY, 1969, BBA, 1972; PhD, Pace U., 1995. Asst. controller TRW, London Am. Mktg. Corp. (Midland Bank), Meridien Mktg. Corp.; dep. dir. fin. svcs. ITM Group, N.Y.C., 1980; controller El Diario-La Prensa, N.Y.C., from 1981, pres., pubr., 1984-98, pub., from 1998. Exec. v.p. Latin Comm. Group Inc.; mem. bd. dirs. and sec. Latin Comm. Arcup, Inc. Mem. El Museo del Barrio; trustee Pace U., Partnership for a Drug-Free Am. Mem. N.Y. Press Club., Am. Newspapers Pubs. Assn.,, Nat. Assn. Hispanic Journalists, Nat. Assn. Hispanic Pubs., N.Y. C. of C. (bd. dirs.), Nat. Advt. Bur., Nat. Hispanic Coalition. Roman Catholic. Home: Bronx, NY. Died in July of 1999.

RAMON, ILAN, astronaut; b. Tel Aviv, June 20, 1954; m. Rona Ramon; 4 children. Grad., Israel Air Force Flight Sch., 1974; student, A-4 Basic Tng. and Ops., 1974—76, Mirage III-C Tng. and Ops., 1976—80, F-16 Tng. Course, Hill AFB, Utah, 1980; BS in Electronics and Computer Engring., U. Tel Aviv, 1987. Mem. establishment team F-16 squadron Israel Air Force, 1980, dep. comdr. B, F-16 squadron, 1981—83, dep. comdr. A, F-4 Phantom squadron, 1988—90, comdr. F-16 squadron, 1990—92, head aircraft br. dept. ops. requirement, 1992—94, head dept. operational requirement for weapon devel. and acquisition, 1994—98; payload specialist astronaut NASA, 1997—98. Col. Israeli Air Force, Yom Kippur War, Operation Peace for Galilee. Achievements include logging over 1,500 flight hours in an F-16, 3,000 flight hours total. Avocations: snow skiing, hiking. Died Feb. 1, 2003.

RAMSAY, LOUIS LAFAYETTE, JR., lawyer, banker; b. Fordyce, Ark., Oct. 11, 1918; s. Louis Lafayette and Carmile (Jones) R.; m. Joy Bond, Oct. 3, 1945; children: Joy Blankenship, Richard Louis. JD, U. Ark., 1947; LLD (hon.), U. Ark., Fayetteville, 1988, U. Ark., Pine Bluff, 1992. Bar: Ark. 1947, U.S. Dist. Ct. Ark. 1947, U.S. Ct. Appeals (8th cir.) 1948, U.S. Supreme Ct. 1952. Of counsel Ramsay, Bridgforth, Harrelson & Starling and predecessor firm Ramsay, Cox, Lile, Bridgforth, Gilbert, Harrelson & Starling, Pine Bluff, Ark., 1948—; pres. Simmons First Nat. Bank, Pine Bluff, Ark., 1970-78, CEO, chmn. bd. dirs., 1978-83. Chmn. exec. com., bd. dirs. Blue Cross-Blue Shield of Ark., Usable Life Ins. Co.; chmn. exec. com. Simmons First Nat. Corp. With USAF, 1942-45, maj. Res., 1945-49. Recipient Disting. Alumnus award U. Ark., 1982, Outstanding Lawyer award Ark. Bar Assn./Ark. Bar Found., 1966, 87; named to Ark. Bus. Hall of Fame, 2003. Mem. ABA (mem. spl. com. on presdl. inability and vice presdl. vacancy 1966), Ark. Bar Assn. (pres. 1963-64), Ark. Bar Found. (pres. 1960-61, Joint Bar Assn.,-Bar Found. Outstanding Lawyer award 1966, Lawyer Citizen award 1987), Ark. Bankers Assn. (pres. 1980-81), Pine Bluff C. of C. (pres. 1968), Rotary (pres. Pine Bluff 1954-55). Methodist. Home: Pine Bluff, Ark. Died Jan. 4, 2004.

RAMSEY, ROBERT RUSSELL, JR., higher education consultant; b. Stewart County, Tenn., Apr. 22, 1929; s. Robert Russell and Bonnie Kate (Goforth) R.; m. Susan Charlotte Randolph, June 30, 1962. BA, Yale U., 1950; EdM, Harvard U., 1954, EdD, 1959; LLD (hon.), Alderson-Broaddus Coll., 1981. Asst. to dir. admissions Harvard U. Law Sch., 1954-57; asst. in financial aid office, head proctor, mem. bd. freshman advisers Harvard Coll., 1957-59; asst. dean freshman year, asst. dir. Office Ednl. Research, 1959-61, asst. master Branford Coll., 1960-63, dir. admissions and freshman scholarships, Yale U., 1961-66; asst. dir. program devel. Va. Council Higher Edn., 1966-68, assoc. dir., 1968-69; dir. evaluation Commn. Instns. Higher Edn., New Eng. Assn. Schs. and Colls., 1969-76; sec. edn. Gov.'s Cabinet, Commonwealth of Va., 1976-78; Va. commr. Edn. Commn. States, 1976-78; ednl. cons., 1978-80; chancellor W.Va. Bd. Regents, 1980-83; W.Va. mem. So. Regional Edn. Bd., 1981-83; W.Va. mem. Edn. Commn. States, 1982-83; dep. commr. coordinating bd. Tex. Coll. and Univ. System,

Austin, 1983-85; higher edn. cons., 1985-87; interim v.p. fin. and adminstrv. svcs. Murray State U., 1987-88; former higher edn. cons.; mem. Accrediting Commn. of the Nat. Home Study Coun., Washington. With AUS, 1950-53. Mem. Am. Psychol. Assn., Am. Sociol. Assn. (assoc.). Died Sept. 12, 2003.

RAMSEY, WALLACE ZANE, English educator; b. Bertrand, Mo., Mar. 22, 1923; s. Robert Hurley and Mina Dillard (Vick) R.; m. Betty Ann Day, May 20, 1951; children: Robert Winston, Malissa Anne. BS in Edn., S.E. Mo. State U., 1947; MEd, U. Mo., 1952, EdD, 1956. Tchr. grades 4-8 Rural Sch., Bell City, Mo., 1942-44; tchr. of English Mo. Mil. Acad., Mexico, 1947-50, DeSoto (Mo.) H.S., 1950-51; supr. elem. edn. Bolivar (Mo.) Schs., 1952-53; instr. in edn. Ill. State U., Normal, 1953-55; asst. prof. edn. Purdue U., West Lafayette, Ind., 1956-61; prof. edn. U. Ky., Lexington, 1961-67, dir. NDEA Insts., 1965-66; prof. edn. U. Mo., St. Louis, 1967-90. Cons. in reading, various sch. systems, Ind., Mo., 1953-89; cons., workshops in Reading and Lang. Arts, Colo. State Coll., summers, 1956, 61; mem. Edn. DoctoralFaculty Coun., 1974, U. Wide Doctoral Faculty, 1974, 80; mem. Thomas Jefferson Award Com. 1977-78; scholarship com., 1978—, adminstrv. structure rev. com. 1978-79, acad. rev. com. 1976—, Speakers Bur., 1970—; chmn. grad. grievance com., 1977-78; Edn. dept. chmn. 1971-74, mem. promotion and tenure com., 1975-79, many other coms. in Sch. of Edn., Campus and Univ. wide. Editor: (book) Organizing for Individual Differences, 1967; contbr. over 50 articles to profl. jours., 1955-80. Mem. Bd. trustees Presbyn. Sch. of Christian Edn., 1973-79; elder Bonhomme Presbyterian Ch., Ballwin, Mo. 1972-75, mem. Christian Edn. Commn., 1973-75, 77-79, choir mem. 1977—; mem. Gov.'s Reading Coun., 1975-76, Ad Hoc Com. on Elem. Tchr. Certification, 1977-78; pres. Mo. Orgn. of Tchr. Educators in Reading, 1977-79. Recipient Disting. Svc. award So. Coun. of Optometrists, Atlanta, 1965; named Hon. Lectr. Mid Am. State Univs., 1978-79. Mem. AAUP, Internat. Reading Assn. (bd. dirs. Mo. chpt., v.p. elect, 1979-80, pres. elect 1980-81, pres. 1981-82., pres. St. Louis suburban coun., 1975, treas. 1978-80, Reading Tchr. of Yr. St. Louis Suburban Coun., 1972-73), Nat. Coun. Tchrs. of English, Am. Ednl. Rsch. Assn., Nat. Conf. on Rsch. in English, Phi Beta Kappa. Avocations: photography, woodworking. Home: Hermitage, Tenn. Died May 16, 2001.

RANA, JAI PRATAP, ambassador; b. Tansen, Palpa Dist., Nepal, June 6, 1937; married; 3 children. Postgrad. degree in polit. sci.; student internat. affairs, U. London, Fletcher Sch.Law and Diplomacy. Various pos., to additional fgn. sec. Ministry Fgn. Affairs, Nepal, 1961—92; 2d sec. Royal Nepalese Embassy, London; 1st sec. Royal Nepalese Mission, Washington, Permanent Mission of Nepal to the UN, N.Y.C.; counselor, dep. chief of mission Royal Nepalese Embassy, New Delhi, 1975—80; amb., permanent resident rep. of Nepal to UN N.Y.C., 1985—91; also amb. to Argentina, Brazil, Chile, Cuba, Peru and Venezuela, 1985—91; Nepal's chief rep. to UN Security Coun., 1988—89; various pos., including v.p. General Assembly UN, N.Y.C., 1988—90; apptd. mem. sec., CEO King Mahendra Trust for Nature Conservation, Nepal, 1994—2001; Royal Nepalese amb. to the U.S. Washington, 2002—04. Co-editor: book on Nepal and non-alignment. Recipient Order of Suprashiddha Prabal Gorhadakshin Bahu, 1st, Govt. Nepal, Subikhyat Trishaktipatta, 2d. Died Mar. 16, 2004.

RAND, SIDNEY ANDERS, retired college administrator; b. Eldred, Minn., May 9, 1916; s. Charles William and Ida Alice (Pedersen) R.; m. Dorothy Alice Holm, Sept. 1, 1942 (dec. Jan. 1974); children: Peter Anders, Mary Alice; m. Lois Schiager Ekeren, Nov. 23, 1974. BA, Concordia Coll., Moorhead, Minn., 1938, DD (hon.), 1956; degree in theology, Luther Sem., St. Paul, 1943; LHD (hon.), Colo. Coll., 1976; LLD (hon.), Carleton Coll., 1980, St. Olaf Coll., 1980, Coll. of St. Scholastica, 1985; DTh (hon.), St. John's U., 1980; LHD (hon.), Augustana Coll., 1988; DD (hon.), Luther Coll., 1997. Faculty Concordia Coll., Moorhead, Minn., 1945-51; pres. Waldorf Coll., Forest City, Iowa, 1951-56; exec. dir. coll. edn. Am. Luth. Ch., Mpls., 1956-63; pres. St. Olaf Coll., Northfield, Minn., 1963-80; U.S. ambassador to Norway, Oslo, 1980-81; pres. Augustana Coll., Sioux Falls, S.D., 1986-87, 92-93, Suomi Coll., Hancock, Mich., 1990-91. Sr. cons. Minn. Pvt. Coll. Council, St. Paul, 1981-87. Pastor Nashwauk (Minn.) Luth. Ch., 1943-45; chmn. Fund for Theol. Edn., Princeton, N.J., 1984-87; mem. Gov.'s Tax Commn., Minn., 1984-86; chmn. Minn. Citizens for Ct. Reform, 1984-87. Decorated comdr. Norwegian Order of Merit, comdr. Norwegian Order of Merit with star, Knight 1st Class Order of St. Olaf, Kingdom of Norway; recipient Wittenberg award, 1996. Mem. AIA (hon.), Phi Beta Kappa. Home: Northfield, Minn. Died Dec. 16, 2003.

RANDALL, TONY (LEONARD ROSENBERG), actor; b. Tulsa, Feb. 26, 1920; m. Florence Gibbs (dec.), m. Heather Harlan; 2 children, Julia Laurette and Jefferson Salvini. Student, Northwestern U., Columbia; studies, Neighborhood Playhouse Sch. of Theater, N.Y.C. Founder, artistic dir. Nat. Actors' Theatre, N.Y.C. Appearances include: (theatre) Circle of Chalk, 1941, Candida, 1941, The Corn is Green, 1942, The Barretts of Wimpole St., 1947, Antony and Cleopatra, 1948, Caesar and Cleopatra, 1950, Oh Men, Oh Women, 1954, Inherit the Wind, 1955-56, Oh Captain, 1958, UTBU, 1966, Two Into One, 1988, M. Butterfly, 1989, A Little Hotel on the Side, 1992, Three Men on a Horse, 1993, Fatal Instinct, 1993, The Government Inspector, 1994, tour with Jack Klugman The Odd Couple, 1994; (tv) Mr. Peepers, 1952-55, Max Liebman Spectaculars, Tonight Show, 1956, The Odd Couple, 1970-75, also The Tony Randall Show, 1976-77, Love Sydney, 1981-83; (motion pictures) Oh Men, Oh Women, 1957, Will Success Spoil Rock Hunter, 1957, The Mating Game, 1959, Pillow Talk, 1959, Let's Make Love 1960, Lover Come Back, 1962, Bang, Bang, You're Dead, 1966, Huckleberry Finn, 1974, Scavenger Hunt, 1979, Foolin' Around, 1980, The King of Comedy, 1983, My Little Pony, 1986, That's Adequate, It Had to Be You; appeared in TV movies: Kate Bliss and the Ticker Tape Kid, 1978, Sidney Shorr: A Girl's Best Friend, 1981, Off Sides, 1984, The Man in the Brown Suit, 1989, The Odd Couple Returns, 1993, Fatal Instinct, 1993, Down with Love, 2003; author: (with Michael Mindlin) Which Reminds Me, 1989. Served from pvt. to 1st lt. Signal Corps, AUS, 1942-46. Recipient Emmy award for The Odd Couple 1975. Died May 17, 2004.

RANDALL, WILLIAM B. manufacturing executive, director; b. Phila., Jan. 8, 1921; s. Albert and Ann (Fine) R.; m. Geraldine Kempson, Aug. 10, 1943; children: Robert, Erica Lynn, Lisa. Student, Rider Coll., Trenton, N.J., 1940-41. Gen. Sales mgr. Lowres Optical Mfg. Co., Newark, 1946-49; pres., founder Rand Sales Co., N.Y.C., 1949-58; gen. mgr. Sea & Ski Co. div. Botany Industries, Inc., Millbrae, Calif., 1958-61, pres., dir., 1961-66, v.p., 1961-65; pres. Renauld of France, Reno, 1967-68; chmn. bd. Renauld Internat., Reading, Pa., 1963-65; pres., chief operating officer Renauld Internat., Ltd., Burlingame and Reno, 1966-67; pres., chmn. bd. Randall Internat., Ltd., 1967-68; sr. exec. v.p. Forty-two Prods. Ltd., 1969-71; pres. Exec. Products Internat. Ltd., 1969-71, New Product Devel. Ctr., Carlsbad, Calif., 1971—2001; pres. Internat. Concept Ctr. Exec. Products Internat. Ltd., Irvine, 1971—2001, pres. Sun Research Ctr., 1974—2001; pres. La Costa Products Internat., 1975-86; mng. dir. merchandising La Costa Hotel and Spa, 1986-88; pres., chief exec. officer Randall Internat., Carlsbad, 1989—2001. Bd. dirs. Bank of La Costa, Garden Botanika. Served to 1st lt., navigator USAAF, 1942-45. Mem. Am. Mgmt. Assn., Nat. Wholesale Druggists Assn., Nat. Assn. Chain Drug Stores, Hon. Order Ky. Cols., Baja Beach and Tennis Club (bd. dirs.). Home: Carlsbad, Calif. Died Nov. 2, 2001.

RANDOLPH, JOHN, actor; b. Bronx, June 1, 1915; s. Louis and Dorothy (Shore) Cohen; Jan. 3, 1942; m. Sarah Cunningham Randolph; children— Martha Eoline, Harrison Henry. Student, CCNY, 1932-35, Columbia U., summer 1934. Artistic cons. Phila. Drama Guild Appeared in Broadway plays Broadway Bound, 1986-87 (Tony award 1986-87), The Visit; films Serpico, Heaven Can Wait, Prizzi's Honor; numerous TV appearances including Lucas Tanner, Blind Ambition, M*A*S*H, Bob Newhart Show, Roseanne, Grand, A Foreign Field; adaptations include Portrait of an Artist (J. Joyce), 1961-62, Magic Mountain (T. Mann), 1963; TV drama Jew in Old Country, 1965, The Unknown Chekhov, 1965. V.p. U.S. Com. for Friendship with German Dem. Republic, 1978-90; chmn. Nat. Council for U.S. Soviet Friendship, 1987-90; bd. dirs. Theatricum Botanicum, Topanga, Calif., Access Theater of Santa Barbara; bd. dirs. Nat. Com. Against Racist and Polit. Repression; mem. adv. com. TransAfrica. With USAAF, 1942-46. Recipient Paul Robeson medal German Democratic Republic Soc., Berlin, 1980, Drama Desk award, 1986-87, Plaque award Abraham Lincoln Brigade. Mem. Actors Equity Assn. (council 1958-63, dir.), Acad. Motion Picture Arts and Scis., Nat. TV Acad., Screen Actors Guild (dir. 1972-97), AFTRA (bd. dirs. 1986-97), Actors Fund Am. (life). Home: Los Angeles, Calif. Died Feb. 24, 2004.

RANKIN, ALICK MICHAEL, brewery executive; b. Jan. 23, 1935; s. Arthur Niall Talbot and Jean R.; m. Susan Margaret Dewhurst, 1958 (dissolved 1976; 4 children; m. Suzetta Barber. Student, Ludgrove, Eton Coll.; DL (hon.), U. Edinburgh, 1996. With Wood Gundy & Co. Investment Dealers, Toronto, 1956-59; joined Scottish & Newcastle Breweries, 1960; dir. retail Scottish Brewers, 1965-69, chmn., 1982-83; dep. chmn., 1987-89; chmn., mng. dir. Waverley Vintners, 1969-76, dir., 1974, mktg. dir., 1977-82; ceo Scottish & Newcastle plc, 1983-91, chmn., 1989-97. Non-exec. dir. Bank of Scotland plc, 1987—, Sears plc, 1991—, Securities Trust of Scotland, 1991—, James Finlay, 1994—. Chmn. Holyroof Brewers Found., 1990—. With Scots Guards, 1954-56. Decorated knight, 1992 Fellow Royal Soc. Arts; mem. Royal Co. Archers, Edinburgh Festival Soc. (dir. 1996—), The Brewers' Soc. (chmn. 1989-90), Hon. Co. Edinburgh Golfers, Royal and Ancient Golf, I Zingari, Eton Ramblers Cricket, Vanderbilt Tennis, Boodle's. Avocations: fishing, shooting, golf, tennis, ornithology. Died Aug. 5, 1999.

RANKIN, HELEN CROSS, cattle rancher, guest ranch executive; b. Mojave, Calif; d. John Whisman and Cleo Rebecca (Tilley) Cross; m. Leroy Rankin, Jan. 4, 1936 (dec. 1954); children— Julia Jane, Patricia Helen Denvir, William John. A.B., Calif. State U.-Fresno, 1935. Owner, operator Rankin Cattle Ranch, Caliente, Calif., 1954—; founder, pres. Rankin Ranch, Inc., Guest Ranch, 1965—; mem. sect. 15, U.S. Bur. Land Mgmt.; mem. U.S. Food and Agrl. Leaders Tour China, 1983, Australia and N.Z., 1985; dir. U.S. Bur. Land Mgmt. sect. 15. Pres., Children's Home Soc. Calif., 1945; mem. adv. bd. Camp Ronald McDonald. Recipient award Calif. Hist. Soc., 1983, Kern River Valley Hist. Soc., 1983. Mem. Am. Nat. Cattlemen's Assn., Calif. Cattlemen's Assn., Kern County Cattlemen's Assn., Kern County Cowbelles (pres. 1949, Cattlewoman of Yr. 1988), Calif. Cowbelles, Nat. Cowbelles, Bakersfield Country Club, Bakersfield Raquet Club. Republican. Baptist. Died Feb. 17, 2003.

RANSOM, DAVID MICHAEL, retired ambassador; b. St. Louis, Nov. 23, 1938; s. Clifford Fredic and Inez Natalie (Green) R.; m. Marjorie Ann (Marilley) Ransom; children: Elizabeth Inez, Katherine Hope, Sarah Grace. AB, Princeton U., 1960; MA, Johns Hopkins Sch. of Advanced Internat. Studies, 1962; student, The Nat. War Coll., 1982-83. With U.S. Dept. State, Yemen, Iran, Lebanon, Saudi Arabia, 1965-71, nat. security coun. staff White House Washington, 1971-73; dep. chief mission Am. Embassy, Sana'a, Yemen Arab Rep., 1975-78; dir., dept. dir. near east divsn. internat. security affairs Office of Sec. of Def., U.S. Dept. of Def., Washington, 1978-82; dep. chief mission Am. Embassy, Abu Dhabi, United Arab Emirates, 1983-85, dep. chief of mission Damascus, Syria, 1985-88; country dir. Arabian Peninsula-Near East Bur., U.S. Dept. State, 1988-90, country dir. Greece, Turkey, Cyprus-European Bur., 1990-93; amb. to Bahrain, Am. Embassy, Manama, 1994-97; ret., 1997; prin. DM Ransom Assocs., Washington, from 1997. 1st lt. inf. USMC, 1962-65. Mem. Met. Club (Washington). Episcopalian. Avocations: scuba diving, canoeing, skiing. Died Dec. 4, 2003.

RAO, SATHYANARAYAN S. electrical and computer engineering educator, administrator; BSEE, Osmania U., India, 1961; MSEE, U. Kans., 1963, PhD, 1966. Mem. faculty Villanova (Pa.) U., 1968—2004, prof., chair dept. electrical engring., 1983—2004. Vis. assoc. prof. Stanford (Calif.) U., 1979; dir. undergrad. cirriculum project CAUSE/CAD, NSF, 1982-83. Contbr. articles to sci. journals; author papers in field. Grantee Naval Air Devel., GE, Sonic Scis., Bio-Automation. Mem. IEEE (sr., transactions reviewer, mem. circuits and systems soc., signal processing computers soc., comm. soc., control systems soc., edn. soc., chair ASSP chpt. Phila. sect. 1977-78), Nat. Elec. Engring. Dept. Heads Assn. (Pa. coun.), Eta Kappa Nu (mem. Jury of Award com. 1991), Phi Kappa Phi, Sigma Xi, Tau Beta Phi, ASEE, FIE. Died Apr. 22, 2004.

RAPPAPORT, BARRY NEIL, computer engineer, researcher; b. Bklyn., Aug. 3, 1960; s. Walter and Jean (Sapol) R. BS in Astronomy, Case Western Res. U., 1982; MS in Astronomy, N.Mex. State U., Las Cruces, 1988, MSEE, 1989. Mem. tech. staff Jet Propulsion Lab., Pasadena, Calif., 1983-90; staff scientist III Sci. & Tech. Corp., Las Cruces, from 1987; grad. rsch. asst., coll. instr. Los Alamos (Calif.) Nat. Lab., from 1991. Author: Cape Photographic Durchamsterung, 1984, Uranometria 2000, vol. I, 1987, vol. II, 1988, Field Guide to Uranometria 2000, 1993. Mem. Am. Astron. Soc., Assn. Computing Machinery. Research in field. Deceased.

RASCO, KAY FRANCES, antique dealer; b. Rienzi, Miss., Nov. 13, 1925; d. Robert Franklin and Sophia Agnes (Kinningham) Dilworth; m. H. Manfred Ray, July 9, 1943 (div. 1950); 1 child, Manfred Ray; m. Lavon Rasco, Mar. 22, 1951; children: Francine, Karen. BA, U. Miss., 1948, MA, 1953; PhD, Northwestern U., 1966. Instr. English Western Ill. U., 1953-54, 56-60, Northwestern U., 1960-61; lectr. De Paul U., Chgo., 1969, 71-74; master tchr. English Yale U., New Haven, Conn., summers 1963,64, 66,67; tchr. English New Trier High Sch., Winnetka, Ill., 1961-69, 71-73; assoc. prof. English Am. U., Cairo, 1969-71; prof. drama Al Azhar U., Cairo, 1976-77; sales assoc. Merrill Lynch Realty, Evanston, Ill., 1973-76, 78-83, mgr. area sales, 1983-89; owner Sarah Bustle Antiques, Evanston, Ill., from 1989. Mem. Rotary Internat. (pres. Evanston Lighthouse Rotary 1999-2000). Home: Evanston, Ill. Died Feb. 27, 2004.

RASMUSSEN, NORMAN CARL, nuclear engineer, educator; b. Harrisburg, Pa., Nov. 12, 1927; s. Frederick and Faith (Elliott) R.; m. Thalia Tichenor, Aug. 23, 1952; children: Neil, Arlene. BA, Gettysburg (Pa.) Coll., 1950, ScD (hon.), 1968; PhD, MIT, 1956; Dr honoris causa, Cath. U. Leuven, Belgium, 1980. Mem. faculty MIT, 1958—94, prof. nuclear engring., 1965—94, McAfee prof. engring., 1983—94, head dept., 1975-81; dir. reactor safety study AEC, 1972-75; mem. Def. Sci. Bd., 1974-78, sr. cons., 1978-84; mem. nat. sci bd. NSF, 1982-88; prof. emeritus MIT, 1993—2003. Mem. Presdl. Adv. Group on Contbns. Tech. to Econs. Strength, 1975; dir. Bedford Engring. Corp.; adv. com. components tech. div. Argonne Univs. Assn., 1977-80; chmn. sci. rev. com. Idaho Nat. Engring. Lab., 1977-86; mem. adv. council Princeton Plasma Physics Lab., 1983-91; mem. safety adv. bd. Three Mile Island Unit-2 Program, 1980-90; trustee N.E. Utilities, 1977— Co-author: Modern Physics for Engineers, 1966; contbr. articles to profl. jours. Chmn. Lincoln-Sudbury Sch. Com., 1971-72; bd. dirs. Atomic Indsl. Forum, 1980-84; mem. Utility Sci. Review Council for Nuclear Safety Analysis Center. Served with USNR, 1945-46. Recipient Disting. Achievement award Health Physics Soc., 1976; Disting. Service award NRC, 1976; Disting. Alumni award Gettysburg Coll., 1983; Enrico Fermi award Dept. Energy, 1985 Fellow Am. Nuclear Soc. (spl. award nuclear power reactor safety 1976, Theos J. Thompson award nuclear reactor safety div. 1981, bd. dirs. 1976-80, Ahlstrom prize 1990); mem. Am. Acad. Arts and Scis., Nat. Acad. Engring., Nat. Acad. Sci., Soc. Risk Analysis, Health Physics Soc. Home: Concord, Mass. Died July 18, 2003.

RASTIELLO, MICHAEL KENNETH, aeronautical engineer, consultant; b. Newark, Feb. 19, 1921; s. Salvatore Paul and Louisa (Nappi) R.; m. Helen Carlotta Lord, July 13, 1952; 1 child, Margaret Anne. Student, N.Y. State U., Syracuse, 1946-47; BS in Aero. Engring., Aeronautical U., Chgo., 1950; postgrad., U. Buffalo, 1966-67, Pa. State U., 1967-82. Aero-flight mechanics engr. Thiokol Corp. Wasatch Div., Brigham City, Utah, 1976-77; systems analysis engr. Info. Spectrum, Inc., Warminster, Pa., 1977-79; logistics systems engr. G.D. Electric Boat Div., Groton, Conn., 1979-80; prin. engr. Computer Scis. Corp., Huntington Valley, Pa., 1979-80; aero. design specialist Gen. Dynamics Corp., Ft. Worth, 1980-81; aerodynamics design specialist Bendix Guidance Systems Div., Mishawaka, Ind., 1981-82, Gulfstream Aerospace Corp., Bethany, Okla., 1983-85; aerodynamicist, missile systems div. Rockwell Internat., Duluth, Ga., 1985-86; aerodynamics cons. Hatboro, Pa., from 1986. With USN, 1943-46, PTO. Mem. AIAA, Am. Astronautical Soc., IPMS U.S.A. Episcopalian. Avocations: model aircraft, camping, fishing. Deceased.

RAULSTON, ROBERT OWEN, urologist, educator; b. Oct. 13, 1943; AB, U. Chattanooga, 1964; MD, Med. Coll. Ga., 1968. Intern Walter Reed Gen. Hosp., Washington, 1968-69; resident Washington Hosp. Ctr., 1971-72; resident in urology U. Okla. Health Scis. Ctr., Oklahoma City, 1972-75, assoc. clin. prof. dept. urology, from 1985; pvt. practice, Oklahoma City, from 1975. Fellow ACS, Societe Internationale d'Urologie, diplomate, Amer. Bd. Urology, Rotary. Home: Oklahoma City, Okla. Died Oct. 4, 2001.

RAWLS, EUGENIA, actress; b. Macon, Ga. d. Hubert Fields and Louise (Roberts) R.; m. Donald Ray Seawell, Apr. 5, 1941; children: Brook Ashley, Donald Brockman. Grad., Wesleyan Conservatory, Macon, 1932; student, U. N.C., 1933; L.H.D., U. No. Colo., Greeley, 1978; D.F.A., Wesleyan Coll., Macon, Ga., 1982. Participant 25th Anniversary of Lillian Smith Book Awards, Atlanta, 1993. Author: Tallulah— A Memory, 1979; Broadway appearances include The Children's Hour, 1934, Pride and Prejudice, 1936, The Little Foxes, 1939, 41, Guest in the House, 1942, Rebecca, 1945, The Second Mrs. Tanqueray, 1940, The Shrike, 1952, Private Lives, 1949, The Great Sebastians, 1956, First Love, 1961, The Glass Menagerie, 1964, 67, Our Town, 1967, Tallulah: A Memory; appeared at Lincoln Ctr., 1971, London, 1974, U.S. tour, 1979, Denver Ctr. Performing Arts, 1980, Theatre of Mus., N.Y.C., 1980, Four Arts Soc., Palm Beach, Fla., 1981, Herbst Theater, San Francisco, 1981, Kennedy Ctr. (cable TV), 1981, Nat. Theatre Great Britain, 1984, Queen Elizabeth II, 1984-86; one-woman show Affectionately Yours Fanny Kemble, London, 1974, U.S. tour, 1979, Nat. Portrait Gallery, Washington, 1983, Grolier Club Exhbn., N.Y.C., 1988; appeared in The Enchanted, 1973, Sweet Bird of Youth, 1975, 76, Daughter of the Regiment, 1978, Just the Immediate Family, 1978, Women of the West, U.S. tour, 1979, Am. Mus. in Britain, Bath, Eng., 1981, Kennedy Ctr. and Denver Ctr. Performing Arts, 1980; one-woman show Fanny Kemble, Arts Theatre, London, 1969, Queen's Hall, Edinburgh, 1980, St. Peter's Ch., N.Y.C., 1980, Internat. Theater Festival, Denver, 1982, also Kennedy Center; appeared as Emily, Denver, 1976; with Abbey Theatre, Dublin, Ireland, 1972; one-woman show tour of Europe, 1972; appeared as: Fanny Kemble, Shakespeare World Congress, Washington, 1976; TV appearances, U.S. Steel Hour, Love of Life, Women of the West; (for ednl. TV) Tallulah: A Memory (performed for presdl. inauguration), 1977; Memory of a Large Christmas, Folger Shakespeare Library, 1977, Memory of a Large Christmas, 1996; mem., Sarah Caldwell Opera Co., Boston, 1978; rec. talking books for blind; mem. com.: Plays for Living, 1964-67; Rockefeller Found. artist-in-residence, Denver U., 1967, 68, U. Tampa, Fla., 1970, artist-in-residence, U. No. Colo., 1971, 72, 73; artist Annenberg Theatre, Desert Art Mus., Palm Springs, Calif., 1988, 89, "Our Town" Pitts. Pub. Theatre, 1990; author: (poems) A Moment Ago, 1984; participant Edwin Forrest Day Celebrating Shakespeare's 427th Birthday The Actors' Fund of Am.'s Nursing and Retirement Home Lucille Lortel Theatre, 1991; appeared in Our Town, Pitts. Pub. Theater, 1990-91, Three Sisters, 1991—. Mem. Internat. Women's Forum, Vail, Colo., 1989. Recipient Alumna award U. N.C., 1969; Disting. Achievement award Wesleyan Coll., 1969; Gold Chair award Central City (Colo.) Opera House Assn., 1973; (with husband) Frederick H. Koch Drama award U. N.C., 1974; citation Smithsonian Instn., 1977 DIED 11/08/00.

RAWLS, JOHN, philosopher, educator; b. Balt., Feb. 21, 1921; s. William Lee and Anna Abel (Stump) R.; m. Margaret Warfield Fox, June 28, 1949; children: Anne Warfield, Robert Lee, Alexander Emory, Elizabeth Fox. Grad., Kent Sch., 1939; AB, Princeton, 1943, PhD, 1950; postgrad., Cornell U., 1947-48. Instr. Princeton, 1950-52; asst., then asso. prof. Cornell U., 1953-59; prof. MIT, 1960-62; vis. prof. Harvard U., 1959-60, prof., from 1962, James Bryant Conant Univ. prof. emeritus, from 1979. Author: A Theory of Justice, 1971, Political Liberalism, 1993; co-editor Philos. Rev., 1956-59; contbr. articles to profl. jours. Served with AUS, 1943-46, PTO Fulbright fellow Oxford (Eng.) U., 1952-53; recipient Nat. Humanities medal White House, 1999. Mem. Am. Philos. Assn. (exec. com. Eastern div. 1959-62, v.p. 1973, pres. 1974), Am. Acad. Arts and Scis., Am. Assn. Polit. and Legal Philosophy (pres. 1970-72), Am. Philos. Soc. Died Nov. 24, 2002.

RAY, JOSEPH T. communication arts educator; b. Charleston, W.Va., Feb. 2, 1952; s. Paul A. and Virginia Ann (Miller) R.; m. DeLora Lee Caudill, Aug. 6, 1983; children: Paul, Hilary, David. BA, Marshall U., 1974, MA, 1976; EdD, U. Tenn., Knoxville, 1993. Assoc. prof. comm. arts Tenn. Temple U., Chattoonaga, from 1977, dir. instnl. rsch., from 1991, dir. grad. studies, from 1993. Adj. faculty Chattanooga State Tech. C.C., 1987—; cons. WDYN-FM, Chattanooga, 1985-88. Mem. Assn. for Instnl. Rsch., Tenn. Coun. for Grad. Schs., Broadcast Edn. Assn. Home: Harrison, Tenn. Died Apr. 5, 2000.

RAY, MARY VIRGINIA, retired federal government worker; b. Essex, Va., June 13, 1924; d. William Ernest and Mary Ida (Johnson) W.; m. Robert Edward Bates, Feb. 14, 1942 (div. 1947); children: Robert E., James A.; m. Frederick Lacey Ray, Oct. 23, 1947; children: Fredericka A., Natalia F. Mgmt. Devel. Program for Women, Nat. Sch. of Home Study, N.Y.C., 1984; Paralegal Study in Civil Litigation, The Sch. of Paralegal Studies, Atlanta, 1991. Display mgr. Lerner Shops, Arlington, Va., 1948-55; card punch operator USCG, Washington, 1955-56, Interstate Commerce Commn., Washington, 1956-60, accident report reviewer, analyst, 1960-67; hwy. safety mgmt. specialist Fed. Hwy. Adminstrn., Washington, 1967-76, 76-78, 1978-80, 1978-80, 1980-85; ret., 1985; paralegal Banks & Assocs. Law Firm, Woodbridge, Va., 1990-92; spl. police crossing guard Prince William County Police Dept., Manassas, Va., 1990-92. Mem. Sr. Choir, 1947—, Gospel choir, 1952—; music coord. Starlighter Gospel Singers, 1982—; pastor's wife Mount Olive Bapt. Ch., Woodbridge, 1972—, pres. Mount Olive Bapt. Ch. Deaconess & Women's Aux., Woodbridge, 1978—; religious affairs chairwoman NAACP, Prince William County, Va., 1986—; committee chairwoman Woodbridge Dem. Magisterial Dist., 1992-95; sch. crossing guard Prince William Police Dept., 1989-91. Recipient Superior Achievement on the Job Performance award Dept. Transp., 1976, Superior Achievement award Freedom of Information, 1979, Afro-Am. Achievement award program Disting. Achievement in the field of pub. svc., 1994. Democrat. Baptist. Avocations: singing in the choir, travel, bible study, counseling, relaxing on the beach with a good book. Home: Woodbridge, Va. Died Sept. 15, 2001.

RAY, WILLIAM LEE, real estate executive; b. Coos Bay, Oreg., Mar. 29, 1922; s. Maurice Wade and Jessie Elanor (Norton) R.; m. Stella Ann Holub (dec.); children: William Lee II, Kenneth Wade; m. Rita Jo Carlile. Student, U. Oreg., 1941-42, Cen. Wash. Coll., 1954. Commd. USAF, 1942, advanced through grades to maj., retired, 1963, pilot in tng., 1943-44, flight engr., 1945, pilot, 1946-47, with tactical dept., 1947-48; prof. air sci. and tactics ROTC U. Wash., Seattle, 1949-51, Cen. Wash. Coll., Ellensburg, 1951-53, comdr. airbase squadron Thule AFB, Greenland, 1954-55, base adjutant Geiger Field Spokane, Wash., 1955-59; pres. ERA Jordan Assocs., Inc., Arlington, Tex., from 1980. Cons. mktg. Burroughs Corp., Radnor, Pa., 1963-65, LTV Aerospace Corp., Dallas, 1965-72; pres. North Tex. Exercycle, Inc., Arlington, 1972-78. Mem. Nat. Assn. Realtors, Am. Ordnance Assn. (life), Airforce Assn. (life). Clubs: Toastmasters (Spokane) (pres. 1957). Republican. Methodist. Home: Arlington, Tex. Deceased.

READ, ALLAN ALEXANDER, minister; b. Toronto, Ont., Can., Sept. 19, 1923; s. Alec P. and Lillice (Matthews) R.; m. Mary Beverly Roberts, Sept. 28, 1949; children: John Allan, Elizabeth Anne, Peter Michael, Martha Ruth. BA, U. Toronto, Can., 1946; Licentiate in Theology, Trinity Coll., Toronto, 1947, D.D., 1972, Wycliffe Coll., 1972; D.S.T. (hon.), Thornloe Coll., Sudbury, Ont., 1982. Ordained diaconate, 1948, priest, 1949, Anglican Ch. of Can.; lic. Diocese of Albany, N.Y., 1996—. Rector 7 chs. Diocese Toronto-Anglican Ch., Parish of East and West Mono, Ont., Can., 1947-54; rector Diocese of Toronto-Trinity Anglican Ch., Christ Ch. Vespra, Barrie, Ont., Can., 1954-72; founder Barrie East End Mission, Parish of St. Giles, 1954; chaplain Simcoe County Gaol, 1954-72; Suffragan bishop Diocese of Toronto-Anglican Ch., Toronto, Ont., Can., 1972-81; bishop Diocese of Ont., Kingston, Ont., Can., 1981-92. Canon St. James Cathedral, Toronto, 1957-61; mem., chmn. provincial synod rural chmn. com., 1953-63, Diocese of Toronto Exec. Com., 1959-71, Diocesan Com. Prayer and Evang., 1950-70, Ont. Guelph Agr. Coll. Planning Com. on Courses for Clergy in Rural Areas, 1950-54, Anglican Gen. Synod Com. on Ministry in Rural Areas, 1952-65; Diocesan Com. Corrections, 1950-72, Gen. Synod Com. Music and Hymn Book, 1965-71, chmn. and chaplin, Boy Scout Com., Barrie #1, 1954-71, Govt. of Ont. Dept. Lands and Forests adv. com. on reforestation, 1950-54, provincial synod, 1955-91, rural ch. unit gen. synod Anglican Ch. Can., 1959-89; archdeacon of Simcoe, 1961-72, Can. churchmn. bd. trustees; participant World Anglican Congress, Toronto, 1963; mem. Anglican World Wide Lambeth Conf., 1978, 88; dir. Anglican Found., Toronto; priest-in-charge St. Patrick's Cathedral, Trim, Ireland, 1992, Parish of Dunster Diocese of Bath and Wells, Eng., 1993, Parish of St. Ippolyts, Diocese St. Alban's, Eng., 1994, Parish of St. Mary the Virgin Westerham, Dioscese of Rochester Eng., 1995, Cathedral of St. John and St. Patrick, Ch. of Ireland, Eire, 1956; hon. asst. St. George's Cath., Kingston, Ont., 1992—. Author: Unto The Hills, 1951; Shepherds in Green Pastures, 1953. Patron Grenville Christian Coll., Brockville, Ont., 1981—; mem., hon. pres. Can. Coll. Organists, Simcoe Br., 1954-71; hon. Reeve, Black Creek Pioneer Village, 1981-82; mem. Barrie and Dist. High Sch. Bd., 1961-70; exec. com. Alcohol and Drug Concerns, 1971-83; asst. organist Grace Ch.-on-the-Hill, Toronto, 1941-47; hon. asst. St. George's Cathedral, Kingston, 1991-2003. Named Citizen of Yr., City of Barrie, 1967; recipient Rural Workers Fellowship award, Episcopal Ch. U.S., 1952, Citizenship awards, Gov. Ont., 1980, 1985, 1990, Queen Elizabeth II Golden Jubilee medal, adopted by Mohawks, given name Tehahswahthe-than-the one who lights the way, Bay of Quinte, Deseronto. Mem. Rural Workers Fellowship (hon. pres. 1967-2003), Barrie Ministerial Assn. (sec. 1954-81). Home: Kingston, Canada. Died Nov. 15, 2003.

READ, CHARLES ARTHUR, lawyer; b. Washington, Dec. 14, 1919; s. Ernest James and Florence Albertine (Gude) R.; m. Marian Berky, May 23, 1953; children: Susan, Charles, Andrew. BS in Commerce, U. Va., 1941, JD, 1947. Bar: Va. 1947, N.Y. 1948, U.S. Supreme Ct. 1962, D.C. 1965. Biology instr. U. Va., 1938-40; instr. naval scis. Notre Dame U., 1942-43; asst. prof. naval scis. Ga. Inst. Tech., 1946; assoc. Reid & Priest, N.Y.C., 1947-55, ptnr., 1956-86, mng. ptnr., 1981-86, sr. counsel, 1987—; gen. counsel Pub. Power Corp., Athens, Greece, 1950-52. Chmn. Rep. Party, Upper Montclair, N.J., 1960-72; chmn. bd. Perkiomen Sch., 1971-79. Lt. USNR, 1942-46. Recipient Raven award U. Va., 1941. Mem. ABA, N.Y. State Bar Assn., Va. Bar Assn., D.C. Bar Assn., U. Va. Alumni Assn. (trustee 1976-82, pres. 1980-81), U. Va. Law Sch. Alumni Assn. (trustee 1982—, pres. 1987-89), U. Va. Law Sch. Found. (bd. dirs. 1988—), Beta Gamma Sigma, Omicron Delta Kappa. Episcopalian. Clubs: Union League, Down Town Assn., Club at World Trade Center, Wall St., Montclair Golf, Farmington Country. Home: Montclair, NJ.

READ, DONALD WILLIAM, conductor, music educator, tenor; b. Saugus, Mass., Sept. 19, 1914; s. William Martin and Helen Cleveland (Parker) R.; m. Saimi Lucina Keto, Apr. 21, 1943; 1 child, Elaine Gwyneth Read Cook. BA, Boston U., 1938, MA, 1939; diploma, Juilliard Sch. Music, 1950, postgrad. diploma, 1951. French tchr. Juilliard Sch. Music, 1946-49, diction tchr., 1949-69; voice tchr. Manhattan Sch. Music, N.Y.C., from 1969. Condr. UN Singers concerts worldwide, 1955-72; tchr. French, fgn. dictions Mannes Coll. Music, 1972-79. Editor, choral arranger UN Singers Folk Series, 1959—; condr. various recs., 1959, 61; contbr. articles to profl. jours.; tenor soloist. Served as sgt. USAAF, 1942-45. Recipient Medal of Merit, mayor of Ystad, Sweden, 1965. Mem. Am. Acad. Tchrs. of Singing (treas. 1975-90, chmn. 1991—), N.Y. Singing Tchrs. Assn. (pres. 1972-74), Nat. Assn. Tchrs. of Singing (pres. N.Y. chpt. 1969-71). Avocations: traveling, carpentry, stamp collecting. Home: East Elmhurst, NY. Deceased.

READ, ROBERT EMMS, organic chemist; b. Stoke on Trent, Eng., Jan. 30, 1933; came to U.S., 1939; s. Bernard E. and Katherine L. (Henderson) R.; m. Marjory Fair, Sept. 9, 1955; children: Katherine R., Howard C. BS, Haverford Coll., 1955; MS, U. Del., 1957, PhD, 1960. Chemist, supr., rsch. dir. head, rsch. mgr. DuPont, Wilmington, Del., 1960-91; mgr. bus. and devel. Terumo Med., Elkton, Md., 1991-94; cons. Newark, Del., from 1994. Mem. Am. Chem. Soc. (prs. cell divsn. 1980), Am. Assn. Textile Chemists and Technologists, Sigma Xi. Achievements include U.S. patents in field. Home: Wilmington, Del. Died May 16, 2000.

REAGAN, BARBARA BENTON, economics educator; BS with honors, U. Tex., 1941; MA in Stats., Am. U., 1947; MA in Econs., Harvard U., 1949, PhD in Econs., 1952. Econ. researcher Dept. Agr., 1942-47; sr. project leader Agrl. Research Service, Washington, 1949-55; prof. econs. Tex. Woman's U., Denton, 1959-67, So. Meth. U., Dallas, 1967-90, prof. emeritus, from 1990, chmn. dept., 1984-90, dir. interdisciplinary research project, 1969-70, dir. undergrad. studics econs. dept., 1972-75, assoc. dean Univ. Coll., 1975, asst. to pres. for student acad. services, 1975-76, pres. faculty senate, 1981-82, mem. exec. com., 1981-84; dir. Region IX Fed. Home Loan Bank, 1981-85; mem. Dallas Morning News Bd. Economists, 1982-88. Dir. Agrl. Rsch. Svc. Project, Dallas, 1970-71; mem. adv. bd. econs. USA Wharton Econometric Forecasting Assocs., 1983-85; mem. adv. bd. Nat. Women's Mus., Dallas, 1998—; reviewer NSF; disting. vis. prof. econs. Kenyon Coll., spring, 1979; bd. dirs. 1st Am. Savs. Bank, 1990-95, North Tex. Mesbic, 1991-93, Tex. Guaranteed Student Loan Corp., 1991-97, sec., exec. com., chmn. policy com., 1992-93, chmn. bd., 1993-95. Author: Economic Foundations of Labor Supply of Women, 1981; co-editor, contbg. author: Women in the Workplace: Implications of Occupational Segregation, 1976; editor, contbg. author: Issues in Federal Statistical Needs Relating to Women, 1979; bd. editors: Jour. Econ. Lit., 1977-79, Jour. Econ. Edn., 1984-92; referee profl. jours. contbr. articles to profl. publs. Mem. Nat. Adv. Food and Drug Coun., 1968-71; mem. adv. com. Nat. Rsch. Inst. on Family, 1973-76; nat. coord. on issues in fed. statis. needs for women Census Bur. Conf., 1978; mem. Tex. adv. bd. Tex Coastal Mgmt. Program, 1977-78; mem. adv. com. White House Conf. on Balance Nat. Growth and Econ. Devel., 1977-78; bd. dirs. League for Ednl. Advancement in Dallas, 1972-75; trustee, mem. instrnl. TV com. Pub. Comm. Found. North Tex., 1973-76; mem. North Tex. Coun. Govts.' Manpower Coun., 1972-74; mem. adv. bd. Women's Ctr. Dallas, 1975-79, 82-85, 95—, pres. 1981, bd. dirs. 1990-92; bd. dirs. Dallas Urban League, 1975-79, co-chmn. com. on skills bank, 1977-79; Leadership Am., 1989-90. Ferguson fellow Harvard U., 1947-49; named Outstanding Tchr., So. Meth. U. 1972; recipient Women's Ctr. Dallas award as one of Dallas Outstanding Women, 1980,So. Meth. U. M award 1972, Willis M. Tate award as outstanding faculty mem., 1982, Laurel award AAUW, 1983, Headliner award Dallas Press Club, 1985, 86, Disting. Alumna award Mary Baldwin Coll., 1986. Mem. Am. Econ. Assn. (chmn. sessions 1977, 80, chmn. com. on status of women in econs. profession 1974-78), Southwestern Social Sci. Assn. (exec. com. 1977-80, pres. 1978-79), Assn. Am. Colls. (faculty rep. 1984), Dallas Economists Club, Dallas C. of C. (com. on urban affairs 1975), Phi Beta Kappa (pres. So. Meth. U. chpt. 1975-76), Town and Gown Club (pres. 1986-87), The Dallas Summit (exec. com. 1990-92). Home: Dallas, Tex. Died Dec. 9, 2002.

REAGAN, RONALD WILSON, 40th President of the United States; b. Tampico, Ill., Feb. 6, 1911; s. John Edward and Nelle (Wilson) R.; m. Jane Wyman, Jan. 25, 1940 (div. 1948); children: Maureen E. (dec. 2001), Michael E.; m. Nancy Davis, Mar. 4, 1952; children: Patricia, Ronald. AB,

Eureka Coll., 1932, MA (hon.), 1957. Actor GE Theatre, 1954-62; host TV series Death Valley Days, 1962-66; gov. State of Calif., 1967-74; businessman, rancher, commentator on public policy, 1975-80; Pres. of U.S., 1981-89. Sports announcer, motion picture and TV actor, 1932—66; author: Where's the Rest of Me?, Speaking My Mind: Selected Speeches, 1989, An American Life: The Autobiography, 1990; actor: (films) Love is on the Air, 1937, Sergeant Murphy, 1937, Swing Your Lady, 1938, Accidents Will Happen, 1938, Cowboy from Brooklyn, 1938, Boy Meets Girl, 1938, Girls on Probation, 1938, Brother Rat, 1938, Going Places, 1938, Secret Service of the Air, 1939, Dark Victory, 1939, Naughty But Nice, 1939, Hell's Kitchen, 1939, The Angels Wash Their Faces, 1939, Smashing the Money Ring, 1939, Code of the Secret Service, 1939, Brother Rat and a Baby, 1940, An Angel from Texas, 1940, Knute Rockne All American, 1940, Tugboat Annie Sails Again, 1940, Santa Fe Trail, 1940, The Bad Man, 1941, Million Dollar Baby, 1941, International Squadron, 1941, Nine Lives Are Not Enough, 1941, Kings Row, 1942, Juke Girl, 1942, This is the Army, 1943, For God and Country, 1943, Cadet Classification, 1943, Stallion Road, 1947, The Hagen Girl, 1947, The Voice of the Turtle, 1947, John Loves Mary, 1949, Murder in the Air, 1949, Night Unto Night, 1949, The Girl from Jones Beach, 1949, The Hasty Heart, 1949, Louisa, 1950, Storm Warning, 1951, The Last Outpost, 1951, Bedtime for Bonzo, 1951, The Big Truth, 1951, Hong Kong, 1952, The Winning Team, 1952, She's Working Her Way Through College, 1952, Law and Order, 1953, Tropic Zone, 1953, Prisoner of War, 1954, The Jungle Trap, 1954, Cattle Queen of Montana, 1955, Tennessee's Partner, 1955, Hellcats of the Navy, 1957, The Killers, 1964, (voice): The Young Doctors, 1961, : (TV series) The Orchid Award, 1953—54. Mem. Calif. State Rep. Ctrl. Com., 1964-66; del. Rep. Nat. Conv., 1968, 72; chmn. Rep. Gov. Assn., 1968-73; mem. presdl. Commn. CIA Activities Within U.S., 1975; bd. dirs. Com. Present Danger, Washington, 1977; cand. for Rep. nomination for Pres., 1976. Served as capt. USAAF, 1942-45. Recipient Great Am. Decade award, Va. Young Am. Freedom, Man Yr. Free Enterprise award, San Fernando Valley Bus. & Profl. award, 1964, Am. Legion award, 1965, Horation Alger award, 1969, George Washington Honor medal, Freedoms Found. Valley Forge award, 1971, Disting. Am. award; inducted into Nat. Football Found. Hall Fame, Am. Patriots Hall Fame. Mem. SAG (pres. 1947-52, 59), Am. Fedn. Radio & TV Artists, Lions, Friars, Tau Kappa Epsilon. Republican. Died June 5, 2004.

RECHTIEN, JOHN GERHARDT, English language educator; b. New London, Wis., Jan. 17, 1937; BA, St. Mary's U., 1959; MA, St. Louis U., 1964, PhD, 1975; STL, U. Fribourg, 1970. Ordained priest Roman Cath. Ch., 1970. Tchr. McBridge High Sch., St. Louis, 1959-64, Vianney High Sch., St. Louis, 1964-65, Villa St. Jean, Fribourg, Switzerland, 1965-69; prof. St. Mary's U., San Antonio, from 1974. Contbr. essays to profl. jours. Bd. dirs. Habitat for HUmanity, San Antonio, 1982-90, sec., 1983-84, 86-90, pres., 1985. Recipient Piper professorship Minnie Stevens Piper Found., 1988. Mem. MLA, Erasmus of Rotterdam Soc. (charter), Phi Beta Kappa (pres. San Antonio chpt. 1977). Home: San Antonio, Tex. Died Sept. 7, 2001.

REDLICH, FREDRICK CARL (FRITZ), psychiatrist, educator; b. Vienna, June 2, 1910; married; 2 children. MD, U. Vienna, 1935. Intern Allgemeines Krankenhaus, Vienna, 1935-36; resident Univ. Psychiat. Clin., U. Vienna, 1936-38; asst. physician State Hosp. Iowa, 1938-40; resident neurol. unit Boston City Hosp., 1940-42; from instr. to assoc. prof. psychiat. Yale U., New Haven, 1942-50, prof. psychiat., chmn. dept., 1950-67, dean Sch. Medicine, assoc. provost med. affairs, 1967-72, prof. psychiatry, 1972-77; assoc. chief of staff edn. VA Med. Ctr., Brentwood, 1977-82; prof. psychiatry UCLA, 1977-82; prof. emeritus UCLA and Yale U., 1982—2004. Fellow AAAS, Am. Psychiat. Assn., Am. Orthopsychiat. Assn.; mem. Inst. Medicine of NAS, Am. Psychoanalytic Assn. Home: Hamden, Conn. Died Jan. 1, 2004.

REDMOND, WALTER T. food products company executive; b. 1923; Student, Mich. State U. With Kellogg Co., Battle Creek, Mich., 1948—, controller, 1961-67, v.p., controller, 1967-75, exec. v.p., 1975-81, pres., chief adminstrv. officer, 1981—85, also dir. Died Dec. 2, 2003.

REED, JOHN FRANKLIN, instrument manufacturing company executive; b. Winfield, Mo., Aug. 10, 1917; s. Claude F. and Inez (Crenshaw) R.; m. Ann M. Walter, Aug. 31, 1940; children: John Franklin, James D., Thomas W., William C., Robert D. BS in Mining Engring, Mo. Sch. Mines and Metallurgy, 1940. Indsl. engr. Tenn. Coal Iron R.R. Co., 1940-42; time study methods engr. McDonnell Aircraft Corp., 1943; prodn. planner, chief estimator Fairchild Aircraft Co., 1944; joined Manning, Maxwell & Moore, Inc., Stratford, Conn., 1944, works mgr. Tulsa, Shaw Box, Crane and Hoist div., Muskegon, Mich., 1951-57; gen. mgr. Instrument and Gauge div., 1957-59, v.p., gen. mgr., 1959, exec. v.p., 1959-62, pres., chief exec. officer, dir., 1962-65; pres., dir. Manning, Maxwell and Moore of Can., Ltd., Galt, Ont., 1962-65; pres., chief oper. officer Hupp Corp., Cleve., 1965-67, pres., dir., 1967-68; pres., chief exec. officer, dir. Hercules Galion Products, Inc., Ohio, 1968-69; pres., chief exec., dir. Canrad Inc., Newark, 1969—, chmn., 1976-86; mem. exec. com. Canrad-Hanovia Inc., 1984-89, also bd. dirs., 1984-89. Bd. dirs. Rhein Med., Tampa, Fla., Am. Health Capital, Naples, Fla. Mem. Royal Poinciana Golf. Presbyterian. Home: Naples, Fla. Deceased.

REELING, GLENN EUGENE, psychology educator, researcher; b. Dover, Pa., Aug. 21, 1930; s. Irvin Roy and Dora lMay (Swartz) R.; m. Patricia ann Glueck, Aug. 18, 1962; children: Craig, Aimée. BS, Pa. State U., 1952; MS, U. N.Mex., 1958; postgrad., U. Cin., 1958-59; EdD, Ind. U., 1962. Tchr. math. and sci. Kennard-Dale Jr. and Sr. High Sch., Fawn Grove, Pa., 1954-55; tchr. 5th grade Newberrytown (Pa.) Elem. Sch., 1955-56; tchr. gen. math. grade 9 Albuquerque Pub. Schs., 1956-59; tchr. math. and sci. jr. and sr. high schs. Cin. Pub. Schs., 1959-60; teaching assoc. Ind. U., Bloomington, 1960-62; test editor Houghton Mifflin Co., Boston, 1962-63; dir. testing and rsch. Montclair (N.J.) Pub. Schs., 1963-66; prof. psychology and edn. Jersey City State Coll., from 1966. Cpl. U.S. Army, 1952-54, Korea. Mem. AACD, Am. Edn. Rsch. Assn., Am. Psychol. Assn., Am. Assn. Higher Edn., New Jersey Edn. Assn. Higher Edn. (bd. dirs. 1978—), Phi Delta Kappa. Lutheran. Home: Waretown, NJ. Died Mar. 15, 2000.

REES, THOMAS MANKELL, former congressman; b. Los Angeles, Mar. 26, 1925; s. Caradoc and Mildred (Melgaard) R.; m. Leanne Boccardo, Apr. 16, 1960; children— Evan Boccardo, James Caradoc. BA, Occidental Coll., 1950. Bar: Calif. bar, D.C. bar. Pres. Compania del Pacifico, Inc., Los Angeles, 1951-70; mem. Calif. Assembly, 1955-62, Calif. Senate from Los Angeles County, 1962-65, 89th-94th Congresses from 23d Calif. Dist., 1965—77; mem. banking, currency and housing com., chmn. internat. trade investment and monetary policy subcom., mem. com. on D.C.; U.S. adv. to U.S. del. ann. World Bank and Inter-Am. Bank, 1967-76; adv. to U.S. del. UN Trade and Devel. Meeting, Nairobi, Kenya, 1976; retired atty. private practice, Washington. Mem. Nat. Commn. Supplies and Shortages on Nat. and Internat. Levels; mem. adv. com. on internat. investment, tech. and devel. Dept. State; chmn. small bus. and internat. trade task force Pres. Carter's White House Conf. on Small Bus. Bd. dirs., chmn. bd. Am. Near East Refugee Aid.; Del. Democratic Nat. Convs., 1956, 60, 64, 68. Served with inf. AUS, ETO, World War II. Decorated Bronze star medal. Mem. Former Mems. Congress, Calif. State Soc., Am. Women Composers (bd. dirs.), Los Angeles County Mus. Art Assos. Home: Santa Cruz, Calif. Died Dec. 9, 2003.

REGAN, DONALD THOMAS, financier, artist, lecturer; b. Cambridge, Mass., Dec. 21, 1918; m. Ann G. Buchanan, July 11, 1942. BA, Harvard U., 1940; LLD, Hahnemann Med. Coll. Hosp., 1968, U. Pa., 1972, Pace U., 1973, Middlebury Coll., 1999; DHL (hon.), Colgate U. With Merrill Lynch, Pierce, Fenner & Smith Inc. (and predecessor), 1946-81, exec. v.p., 1964-68, pres., 1968-70, chmn., chief exec. officer, 1971-80; chmn. bd., chief exec. officer Merrill Lynch & Co. Inc., 1973-81; sec. Dept. of Treasury, Washington, 1981-85; White House chief of staff Washington, 1985-87. Vice chmn., dir. N.Y. Stock Exchange, 1972-75. Author: A View from the Street, 1972, For the Record, 1988. Chmn. bd. trustees U. Pa., 1974-78, life trustee, 1971-80. Lt. col. USMCR, World War II. Laureat Bus. Hall of Fame, 1981; Commdr. Legion of Honor. Mem. Army-Navy Club (Washington). Died June 10, 2003.

REHM, LEO FRANK, civil engineer; b. Milw., Jan. 8, 1916; s. Joseph V. and Theresa (Binder) R.; m. Irene R. Kegel, Aug. 24, 1940; children: Judith Ann LeDoux, Cecelia C. Nelson. B.C.E., Marquette U., 1938. Civil engr. Consoer Townsend & Quinlan, Chgo., 1938-43; asso. Consoer Townsend & Assocs. (Cons. Engrs.), Chgo., 1946-53, gen. partner, 1953-74, mng. partner, 1974-76; pres. PRC Consoer Townsend, Chgo., 1976-83, pres. emeritus, 1983-85; v.p. PRC Engring., Inc., Chgo., 1976-85. Chmn. bd. Environ. Engring., Inc., 1976-83, Consoer Townsend Harris Internat., Inc., 1976-83; dir., v.p. Planning Research Corp., 1976-80; Mem. planning and adv. bd. Village of River Forest (Ill.), 1964-76; mem. exec. senate Marquette U., Milw., 1978—; mem., chmn. adv. council Marquette U. (Coll. Engring.), 1976-89. Mem. bldg. bd. appeals Village of River Forest, Ill., 1977-87, pres.'s adv. council Rosary Coll., River Forest, 1986-91, Exec. Svc. Corps Chgo. With U.S. Army, 1943-46. Recipient Disting. Engring. Alumnus award Marquette U. Coll. Engring., 1975; Alumnus of Yr. award Marquette U., 1983 Mem. Am. Public Works Assn., Am. Water Resources Assn., Am. Water Works Assn., Water Environ. Fedn., Inter-Am. Assn. San. Engring., NSPE, Western Soc. Engrs., Ill. State C. of C. (bd. dirs. 1981-85), VFW, KC, Country Club of Naples. Roman Catholic. Home: Lombard, Ill. Deceased.

REICHERT, JACK FRANK, manufacturing executive; b. West Allis, Wis., Sept. 27, 1930; s. Arthur Andrew and Emily Bertha (Wallinger) R.; m. Corrine Violet Helf, Apr. 5, 1952; children: Susan Marie, John Arthur. Cert. mktg., U. Wis., Milw., 1957; AMP, Harvard U., 1970; LLD (hon.), Marian Coll., 1994. Various mktg. positions GE, 1948-57; with Brunswick Corp., Lake Forest, Ill., 1957-95, pres. Mercury Marine div., 1972-77, corp. v.p., 1974-77, group v.p. Marine Power Group, 1974-77, pres., COO, 1977-93, CEO, 1982-95, chmn. bd. dirs., 1983-95, dir., 1977-82, chmn. emeritus, 1995—2004. Bd. dirs. Viad Corp., Phoenix, Strike Ten Entertainment, Inc. Trustee Carroll Coll., Waukesha, Wis., 1972; indsl. chmn. Fond du Lac United Fund, 1977; chmn. Internat. Bowling Mus. and Hall of Fame. With C.E. U.S. Army, 1951-53. Named Disting. Alumnus of the Yr., U. Wis., Milw. 1979, Top Chief Exec. Officer in Multi-Industry Group, Fin. World Mag., 1984; recipient Gold award in leisure industry Wall St. Transcript, 1983, 86, Bronze award in multi-industry category Wall St. Transcript, 1985, Leisure Industry Silver award, 1988. Mem. Am. Mgmt. Assn., U. Wis.-Milw. Alumni Assn., Knollwood Club, Harvard Club, Mid-Am. Club, Beta Gamma Sigma (hon.). Presbyterian. Avocations: golf, reading. Home: Lake Forest, Ill. Died May 9, 2004.

REID, BONNIE LEE, junior high school principal; b. St. Louis, Jan. 30, 1937; d. William Charles Lovrenic and Fern Lee (Swingler) Reiman; m. Thomas James Fitzsimmons, Aug. 16, 1958 (div. Aug. 1966); children: Susan Lee, Scott James; m. Donald Francis Reid, Nov. 18, 1966; stepchildren: Christopher Kearns, Donald Francis Jr., Connie Ann, Britton Anthony, Douglas Nye. BE, U. Mo., 1958; MA in Adminstrn., Washington U., St. Louis, 1977, postgrad., 1978-80. Cert. tchr., Mo.; cert. secondary adminstr., Mo. Tchr. Webster Groves (Mo.) High Sch., 1958-60; tchr., dept. chmn. Parkway Sch. Dist., Chesterfield, Mo., 1971-81, asst. prin., 1982-83, assoc. prin., 1984, interim prin., 1985; prin. Parkway E. Jr. High Sch., Chesterfield, from 1986. Mem. governance com. Gov.'s Conf. Edn., 1978; prin. Nat. Secondary Sch. Recognition Sch., 1986-87. Team leader Danforth Found. Marginal Students Responsive Schs. Consortium, 1989—; mem. mid. sch. task force Boy Scouts Am. Recipient award of excellence U.S. Dept. Edn., 1987. Fellow Prin.'s Acad.; mem. Nat. Assn. Secondary Sch. Prins., Assn. Supervision and Curriculum Devel. (consortium sch. team leader 1986-89), Nat. Middle Sch. Assn. (conf. edn.), Mortar Bd., Mo. State Future Tchrs. Am., Parkway Ind. Community Tchrs. Assn. (pres. 1976-78), Greater St. Louis Tchrs. Assn. (pres. 1977-78), Delta Kappa Gamma, Kappa Alpha Theta, Pi Lambda Theta, Phi Sigma Iota, Kappa Epsilon Alpha, Sigma Rho Sigma. Republican. Presbyterian. Avocations: travel, needlepoint. Home: Ballwin, Mo. Deceased.

REID, PAT, sports association executive; Mem. exec com. Can. Olympic Assn.; instr. & coach curling. V.p. organizing com. World Culring Championships, 1984—86; Can. rep. World Curling Fedn.; team leader Olympic Winter Games, Nagano, Japan, 1998; chair curling qualification com. Can. Winter Games, 1991. Recipient Byrce Taylor Meml. award for Vol. Leadership, 2000, Ontario Women's Curling Championship, 1979, Ontario Sr. Curling Champion, 1999. Mem.: Can. Olympic Assn. (bd. dirs. from 1992, 2010 site rev. com., parlismentary outreach com., governance com., nominating com., winter sport com., chair women in sports com.), Can. Curling Assn. (bd. dirs. 1992—97, chair tech. develop. com., chair rules com., chair high performance com., chair athlete liason com., chair olympic com., Ray Kingsmith award 1999, Named to Can. Curling Hall of Fame Exec. Honour Roll 1999), Ontario Ladies' Curling Assn. (pres. 1990), So. Ontario Ladies' Curling Assn. (former pres.), Toronto Curling Assn. (del., mixed championships com., women's 25th anniversary championships com., Oustanding Contbn. award 1989), Toronto Women's Major League (chair 1980—85, former chair), Blvd. Club (Mrs. Blvd. Club Svc. award 1984), Dixie Club (chair bonspiel com., chair mixed competition com., chair games com., chair jr. com.). Died Mar. 27, 2002.

REID, WILLIAM JAMES, social work educator; b. Detroit, Nov. 14, 1928; s. James Macknight and Sophie Amelia (Schneider) R.; m. Anne E. Fortune, May 22, 1988; children by previous marriage: Valerie, Steven. BA, U. Mich., 1950, MSW, 1952; DSW, Columbia U., 1963. Caseworker-in-charge Family Service of Westchester, Mt. Kisco, N.Y., 1956-59; asst. prof. social work U. Chgo., 1962-65, prof., 1968-75, George Herbert Jones prof., 1975-80; prof. Sch. Social Welfare, SUNY, Albany, 1980-98, disting. prof., 1998—2003. Dir. Center for Social Casework Rsch., Cmty. Svc. Soc., N.Y.C., 1965-68. Author: Brief and Extended Casework, 1969, Task-Centered Casework, 1972, Task-Centered Practice, 1977, The Task-Centered System, 1978, Models of Family Treatment, 1981, Research in Social Work, 1981, 3d edit., 1999, Family Problem Solving, 1985, The Role-Sharing Marriage, 1986, Advances in Clinical Social Work Research, 1990, Task Strategies, 1992, Qualitative Research in Social Work, 1994, Generalist Practice: A Task-Centered Approach, 1994, 2d edit., 2003, The Task Planner, 2000, Science and Social Work, 2001, Educational Supervision in Social Work, 2002. With U.S. Army, 1952-56. Recipient excellence in rsch. award Nat. Assn. Social Workers, 1990, Disting. Svc. award Soc. for Social Work and Rsch. Mem. Phi Beta Kappa. Home: Rensselaer, NY. Died Nov. 17, 2003.

REILLY, JAMES OWEN, interior design executive; b. Des Moines, Apr. 26, 1925; s. Walter Eugene and Minne Mae (Owen) R.; m. Joan Bond, June 18, 1948; children: John, Ann, Thomas. BA, Drake U., 1948; M in Fgn. Trade, Am. Inst. Fgn. Trade, Phoenix, 1949. V.p. Cowles Co., Des Moines, 1950-60; pres. Prairie Lee Co., Inc., Des Plaines, Ill., 1961-99; assoc. pub. Popular Communications, Hicksville, N.Y., 1980-84. Bd. mem. Sch. Dist. #62, Des Plaines, 1968-74; pres. Des Plaines Merchants Assn., 1980-86. With USN, 1942-46. Mem. Elks. Republican. Home: Arlington Heights, Ill. Died May 1, 1999.

REINA IDIAQUEZ, CARLOS ROBERTO, former president of Honduras; b. Mar. 13, 1926; m. Bessie Watson; childre: Karla Marina, Lolita, Florencia. Student, Nat. Autonomous U. Honduras, U. London, U. Cambridge, U. Paris, London Inst. Internat. Affairs. Ct. judge, Tegucigalpa, 1953; with Embassy Honduras, Paris, 1960-65; dep. Nat. Constituent Assembly, 1965; dir. El Pueblo, 1966; Francisco Morazán dep. Nat. Congress, 1971-77; judge Inter-Am. Ct. Human Rights, 1979; pres. of Honduras, 1994—98. Lectr. law Nat. Autonomous U. Honduras; reg. lectr. fgn. univs.

Author: El Reto Democrático en Centro America, Honduras: Realidad Nacional y Crisis, El Agora y el Aula, Una Senda hacia el Nuevo Siglo, La Patria Vacilante. Died Aug. 19, 2003.

REINHARDT, MAX, publisher; b. Istanbul, Nov. 30, 1915; s. Ernest and Frieda (Darr) R.; m. Joan MacDonald, 1957; 2 daus. Student, English H.S. for Boys, Istanbul, Ecole des Hautes Etudes Commerciales, Paris, London Sch. Econs. Chmn. HFL (Pulishers) Ltd. (now Reinhardt Books Ltd.), London, 1948, Max Reinhardt Ltd., London, 1948-87, Nonesuch Press, Ltd., from 1985. Bd. dirs. The Bodley Head, chmn. 1982-87. Mem. coun. Royal Acad. Dramatic Art, 1965-96, Pilgrim, 1965. Mem. Publishers Assn. (mem. coun. 1963-69), Royal Soc. Arts. Died Nov. 19, 2002.

REINKE, JOHN HENRY, academic administrator, priest; b. Covington, Ky., Sept. 14, 1915; s. Henry Tilden and Helena (Ungeheuer) R. BA, Loyola U., 1937, MA, 1942, postgrad., 1947-54, UCLA, 1948-49. Ordained priest Roman Cath. Ch., 1945; instr. psychology Loyola U., Chgo., 1947-54, vice chancellor, 1975-76, chancellor, 1976—86; instr. psychology Xavier U., Cin., 1954-56, asst. prof., 1956-59; dir. guidance Loyola Acad., Wilmette, Ill., 1959-60, headmaster, 1960-65, pres., 1965-75; instr. music therapy Ind. U., Bloomington, summers 1958-60; trustee Regis Coll., Denver, Xavier U., Hadley Sch. for Blind, Winnetka; chancellor emeritus Loyola U. of Chgo., Chgo., 1993—2003. Mem. Nat. Cath. Ednl. Assn., Nat. Sch. Public Relations Assn., Conf. Religious Dirs. Edn., Chgo. Art Inst., Field Mus., Nat. Assn. Ind. Schs., Jesuit Adminstrs. Assn., Nat. Cath. Guidance Conf. Clubs: Mid-Am, Internat, Plaza. Lodges: K.C. Achievements include 1st U.S. priest to appear as soloist with maj. symphony orch., Cin., 1956, 57, 60. Home: Chicago, Ill. Died Feb. 25, 2003.

REIS, DONALD JEFFERY, neurologist, neurobiologist, educator; b. N.Y.C., Sept. 9, 1931; s. Samuel H. and Alice (Kiesler) R.; m. Cornelia Langer Noland, Apr. 13, 1985 AB, Cornell U., 1953, MD, 1956. Intern N.Y. Hosp., N.Y.C., 1956; resident in neurology Boston City Hosp.-Harvard Med. Sch., 1957-59; Fulbright fellow, United Cerebral Palsy Found. fellow London and Stockholm, 1959-60; rsch. assoc. NIMH, Bethesda, Md., 1960-62; spl. fellow NIH, Nobel Neurophysiology Inst., Stockholm, 1962-63; asst. prof. neurology Cornell U. Med. Sch., N.Y.C., 1963-67, assoc. prof. neurology and psychiatry, 1967-71, prof., 1971—, First George C. Cotzias Disting. prof. neurology, neurosci., 1982—. Mem. U.S.-Soviet Exch. Program; mem. adv. coun. NIH; bd. sci. advisers Merck, Sharpe & Dohm, Sterling Rsch. Group; cons. Eli Lilly, Servier Pharms.; bd. dirs. China Seas, Inc., Charles masterson Burke Rsch. Found. Contbr. articles to profl. jours.; mem. editorial bd. various profl. jours. Recipient CIBA Prize award Am. Heart Assn. Fellow AAAS, ACP; mem. Am. Physiol. Soc., Am. Neurol. Assn., Am. Pharmacol. Soc., Am. Assn. Physicians, Telluride Assn., Am. Soc. Clin. Investigation, Century Assn., Ellis Island Yacht Club (commadore), Phi Beta Kappa, Sigma Xi, Alpha Omega Alpha. Home: New York, NY. Deceased.

REISZ, KAREL, film director; b. Ostrava, Czechoslovakia, July 21, 1926; arrived in Eng., 1939; s. Josef and Frederika Reisz; m. Julia Coppard (dissolved); m. Betsy Blair, 1963; 3 children. Student, Emmanuel Coll., Cambridge. Freelance journalist, lectr. and tchr.; films officer Ford Motor Co.; now film dir. and prodr. Co-dir. (with Tony Richardson): Mamma Don't Allow, 1954; dir. We Are the Lambeth Boys, 1958, Saturday Night and Sunday Morning, 1959, Night Must Fall, 1963, Morgan—A Suitable Case for Treatment, 1965, Isadora, 1969, The Gambler, 1974, Dog Soldiers, 1977, The French Lieutenant's Woman, 1981, Sweet Dreams, 1985, Everybody Wins, 1989, The Gigli Concert, 1991, The Deep Blue Sea, 1993, The Doll's House, 1994, A Kind of Alaska, 1996; (theater) The Gigli Concert, 1991, The Deep Blue Sea, 1992, The Dolls House, 1993, Moonlight, 1994, Happy Days, 1996; prodr.: Every Day Except Christmas, 1958, This Sporting Life, 1962; author: The Technique of Film Editing, 1953. With RAF, 1944-46. Avocation: gardening. Died Nov. 25, 2002.

REMENICK, SEYMOUR, artist, educator; b. Detroit, Apr. 3, 1923; s. Oscar and Luba (Shackman) R.; m. Diane Kathryn Thommen, Aug. 30, 1950; children: Richard Vincent, Catherine Ann. Student, Tyles Sch. Fine Arts, Phila., 1940-42, 46, Hans Hofmann Sch., N.Y.C., 1946-48, Pa. Acad. Fine Arts, 1948. Instr. Pa. Acad. Fine Arts, Phila., 1977—;, 1977-96. Exhibited one-man shows: Davis Gallery, N.Y.C., annually, 1954-62, Peridot Gallery, N.Y.C., annually, 1967-71, Pearl Fox Gallery, Pa., 1969, 73, 76, Gross McCleaf Gallery, Phila., 1981, Gallery K, Washington, 1983, Mangel Gallery, Phila., 1997, (retrospective) Rosemont Coll., Pa., 1983; group shows: 3d Biennial Exhbn., Italy, 1955, Am. Painting, Rome, 1955, Paris exhbn., 1956, 57, Pa. Acad. Fine Arts, 1957, 59, 64, 68, Festival of Arts, Spoleto, 1959, Nat. Acad., 1960, 63, 66, Phila. Mus. Art. Served with U.S. Army, 1942-45, ETO. Recipient Tiffany Found. award NAD, N.Y.C., 1955; recipient Altman Landscape Prize, 1960, Hallmark Purchase award Hallmark Co., 1960 Mem. NAD (academician 1983) Home: Philadelphia, Pa. Died Sept. 2, 1999.

RENNING, ELISE LORRAINE, physician; b. Kasson, Minn., Jan. 6, 1910; d. Frank and Lydia (Vetsch) R. BA, Macalester Coll., 1931; MD, U. Minn. Diplomate Am. Bd. Ob-Gyn. Intern Jersey City Med. Ctr., 1939-41, New England Hosp. for Women and Children, Boston, 1941-42, Doctors Hosp., N.Y.C., 1943-44; resident Womens Hosp., N.Y.C., 1944-46, chief resident, 1946-47; pvt. practice N.Y.C., 1946-98, Bronxville, N.Y., 1950-85. Fellow ACS, World Med. Assn.; mem. AMA, N.Y. Gynecology Soc., N.Y. County Med. Soc., Westchester County Med. Soc., Westchester Ob-Gyn. Soc., Am. Med. Women's Assn. Avocations: ballroom dancing, gardening. Home: Becket, Mass. Died Dec. 13, 2001.

RENTSCHLER, CARL THOMAS, real estate executive, consultant; s. Franklin K. Rentschler and Della Diana Bucks; m. Madelynne Layden, Aug. 31, 1946; children: Patricia, Laron, Deborah. BS in Indsl. Edn., Pa. State U., 1942. Mem. Alaska Territorial Legis., Juneau, 1952; active in organization of First Fed. Savings and Loan, Anchorage, 1955, Anchorage Real Estate Multiple Listing Svc., 1955, Alaska Mutual Savings Bank, Anchorage, 1960. Capt. Army Air Corps, 1944-47. Republican. Baptist. Avocations: golfing, traveling, hunting, fishing. Home: Anchorage, Alaska. Died Apr. 15, 2004.

REPLOGLE, ARTHUR SEEDS, community development executive; b. Altoona, Pa., May 30, 1922; s. Arthur M. and Mary E. (Seeds) R.; m. Ruth E. Heiges, Sept. 7, 1946; children: Scott, Mark, Susan. BA, Washington & Jefferson Coll., 1943. Lic. real estate sales assoc., Ill. With Replogle Globes, Inc., Chgo., 1946-73; pres. Oak Park (Ill.) Devel. Corp., from 1974. V.p., dir. Downtown Oak Park Corp., 1985—; dir. Civic Arts Coun., Oak Park, 1987-92; life trustee Frank Lloyd Wright Home & Studio Found., Oak Park; sec., dir. West Suburban Coll. of Nursing, Oak Park, 1982—; mem., sec., pres. Bd. Edn. Oak Park/River Forest H.S., 1973-79; dir., past chmn. West Suburban Hosp. Med. Ctr., Oak Park, 1971-93; pres. Thatcher Woods Area Coun. Boy Scouts Am., Oak Park, 1970-72; mem. pres.'s coun. Rosary Coll., River Forest. Lt. USNR, 1944-46. Recipient Silver Antelope, Silver Beaver Boy Scouts Am., 1975, 76, Disting. Citizen award, 1976, Pres.'s award Concordia U., 1991; named to Rib Hall of Fame, 1997. Mem. Geog. Soc. Chgo. (dir., past pres.), River Forest Tennis Club (pres. 1976), Econ. Club of Chgo., Oak Park Country Club, Rotary (pres. 1966, Community Merit award 1991). Republican. Avocations: tennis, public speaking. Home: Moraga, Calif. Died Jul. 12, 1999.

RERES, MARY EPIPHANY, health care and administration consultant; b. Kansas City, Mo., Jan. 31, 1941; d. Mathew and Mary Ellen (Connelly) R. BS in Nursing, Creighton U., Omaha, 1963; M.Psychiat. Nursing, U. Nebr., 1965; Ed.D in Adminstrn., Columbia U., 1970. Staff nurse Nebr. Psychiat. Inst., 1963-65; clin. specialist Norfolk (Nebr.) State Hosp., 1965-66; instr. Creighton U. Sch. Nursing, 1966-68; prof. nursing, medicine and edn. U. Va., 1970-77; prof., dean Sch. Nursing, UCLA, 1977-85, prof.-at-large Med. Sch., 1977-85. Pres. Human Services Tng. and Research Corp., 1974-85; co-chmn. Gov.'s Mental Health and Mental Retardation Adv. Bd., 1973-76; rsch. review com. VA; cons. in field. Co-author: Your Future in Nursing Careers, 1972; editor Am. Psychiat. Nurses Assn. Newsletter, 1989; former mem. editorial bd. JAPNA; book rev. editor: Jour. Psychosocial Nursing, 1980-94. Former mem. bd. dirs. Kaiser Permanente Health Plan and Hosps., Med. Media Group; former mem. adv. bd. hosp. adminstrn. program Charles A. Drew Med. Ctr. Recipient Outstanding Alumni award Creighton U. Sch. Nursing, 1972; named Disting. Vis. Scholar U. Tex., Arlington, 1986. Mem. Am. Acad. Nursing (pres. 1974), Am. Nurses Assn., Am. Assn. Colls. Nursing, Western Interstat Am. Hosp Higher Edn., Am. Psychosocial Nursing Assn. (bd. dirs., sec. 1986-90), Am. Hosp. Assn. (alt. Calif. del. 1992, former trustee rep. regional policy bd., regional policy bd.), Calif. Assn. Hosps. and Health Systems (Gov.'s Forum, nominating com. 1992. pub. affairs com., vice chmn. program com. 1992), Governance Forum (former chmn., CAHHS trustee, trustee 1993-94), Am. Psychiat. Nurses Assn. (Disting. Leadership and Meritorious Svc. award 1989, vice chmn. progs. 1991-93, mem. pub. policy com.), Delta Sigma Rho, Alpha Sigma Nu, Sigma Theta Tau. Democrat. Roman Catholic. Died Dec. 17, 2003.

RESNICK, MILTON, artist; b. Bratslav, Russia, Jan. 7, 1917; Student, Pratt Inst., 1932, Am. Artists Sch., 1933-37. Tchr. Pratt Inst., NYU, U. Wis., R.I. Sch. Design, N.Y. Studio Sch., Barnard Coll., Va. Commonwealth U., U. Calif., Berkeley, 1954—2004. One man shows include M.H. de Young Mus., San Francisco, 1955, Poindexter Gallery, N.Y., 1955, 57, 59, 75, Ellison Gallery, Fort Worth, 1959, Holland-Goldowsky Gallery, Chgo., 1959, Howard Wise Gallery, Cleve., N.Y., 1960, 61, 64, Feiner Gallery, N.Y., 1962, 63, 64, Zabriskie Gallery, Provincetown, Mass., 1963, Madison Art Ctr., Wis., 1967, Reed Coll., Portland, Oreg., 1968, Arden Anderson Gallery, Edgartown, Mass., 1969, Roswell Mus. and Art Ctr., N. Mex., 1971, Fort Worth Art Ctr., 1971, Max Hutchinson Gallery, N.Y., 1972, 77, 79, 80, 82, Kent State U., Ohio, 1973, Robert Miller Gallery, N.Y., 1979, 85, 86, 88, 91, 92, Gruenebaum Gallery, N.Y., 1983, San Jose State U., Calif., 1983, Mus. Contemporary Art, Houston, 1985, Hand in Hand Galleries, N.Y., 1985, Galerie Biedermann, Munich, 1986, Galerie Urban, Nagoya, 1986, Galerie Montenay, Delsol, Paris, 1987, Meredith Long Gallery, Houston, 1985, 87, Compassrose Gallery, Chgo., 1987, Daniel Weinberg Gallery, 1988, d.p. Fong and Spratt Galleries, San Jose, Calif., 1992; exhibited in numerous group shows, N.Y.C., Tex., Pa., Ill., Ohio, Minn., N.C., Mich., Conn., Washington, Calif.; represented in permanent collections Met. Mus. Art, N.Y., Guggenheim Mus., N.Y., Milw. Art Mus., Nat. Mus. Am. Art at the Smithsonian, Akron Art Inst., Australian Nat. Gallery, Mus. Modern Art N.Y., Nat. Gallery Art, Washington, Nat. Collection Fine Arts, Washington, Calif. Mus. Fine Arts, Mil. Art Ctr., Bundy Art Gallery, N.Y.U., Whitney Mus. Am. Arts, N.Y., U. Calif. Art Gallery, Reed Coll., Oreg., Weatherspoon Gallery, Cleve. Mus. Art, Roswell Mus. and Art Ctr., N. Mex., Honolulu Acad. Arts, Nat. Gallery Can., Fort Worth Art Mus. Died Mar. 12, 2004.

REYCRAFT, GEORGE DEWEY, lawyer; b. New Haven, May 2, 1924; s. George Dewey and Katherine Vivien R.; children: George C., Thomas C., Thaddeus J., Ann K., Nancy J., Pamela C., Sheilah M. BA with honors and distinction, Wesleyan U., 1947; LL.B., Harvard U., 1950; postgrad., Georgetown U., 1952, Wayne U., 1953. Bar: D.C. 1951, N.Y. 1964. Ptnr. Cadwalader, Wickersham & Taft, N.Y.C., 1963-93; vis. prof. George Washington Law Sch., Washington, 1967; atty. Office Gen. Counsel, Dept. Navy, Washington, 1952; trial atty. U.S. Dept. Justice, Washington, 1952-57, asst. chief gen. litigation sect., 1957-58, chief spl. trial sect., 1958-60, chief sect. ops., 1960-63; vice chmn. M.A. Schapiro & Co. Inc., 1993-95, former chmn. Served to maj. USAF, 1943-45, 50-52. Mem. Am. Bar Assn., Fed. Bar Assn., Fed. Bar Council, Am. Bar Found., Am. Coll. Trial Lawyers, N.Y. State Bar Assn. (past chmn. antitrust sect.), Assn. Bar City N.Y. (past chmn. com. on trade regulation) Clubs: Harvard (N.Y.C.); Univ. (Washington); Ocean Reef, Shelter Island Yacht, Key Largo Anglers Club. Died Mar. 1, 2004.

REYES, DAVID CENTENO, cardiovascular surgeon; b. Tegucigalpa, Honduras, July 3, 1934; came to U.S., 1964; s. Manuel and Rosa (Centeno) R.; m. Anna Marie West, June 21, 1969. MD, U. Nat. Autonoma de Honduras, Tegucigalpa, 1964. Diplomate Am. Bd. Surgery, Am. Bd. Thoracic Surgery, spl. qualification in vascular surgery, Am. Bd. Med. Mgmt. Intern Presbyn. Hosp., Phila., 1964-65; resident in gen. surgery Rochester (N.Y.) Gen. Hosp., 1965-66, Harlem Hosp., N.Y.C., 1966-68; chief resident in gen. surgery Ohio Valley Med. Ctr., Wheeling, W.Va., 1968-69; resident in thoracic surgery St. Vincent Hosp., Cleve., 1969-70; chief resident in thoracic surgery U. S.C., Charleston, 1970-71; surgery officer Weirton (W.Va.) Gen. Hosp., 1971-73; emergency room physician Mercy Hosp., Columbus, Ohio, 1973-75; fellow in cardiovascular surgery Tex. Heart Inst., Houston, 1975-76, mem. med. staff Bay Med. Ctr., Bay City, Mich., from 1976. Fellow ACS; mem. Internat. Soc. Cardiovascular Surgeons (N.Am. chpt.), Soc. Thoracic Surgeons, Bay County Med. Soc. (pres. 1995). Roman Catholic. Avocation: golf. Home: Bay City, Mich. Died Feb. 24, 2001.

REYNOLDS, HARRY LINCOLN, physicist, researcher; b. Port Chester, N.Y., Mar. 31, 1925; s. Harry Benson and Lydia (Wilde) R.; m. Katherine Haile, 1950; children: Patricia Reynolds Cabral, Margaret Benson Neufeld. BS, Rensselaer Poly. Inst., 1947; PhD, U. Rochester, 1951. Sr. scientist Oak Ridge Nat. Lab., 1951-55; physicist Lawrence Livermore Nat. Lab., 1955-65; asst. program mgr. NASA Manned Spacecraft Center, Houston, 1965; asso. dir. nuclear test, nuclear design and nuclear explosives programs Lawrence Livermore Nat. Lab., Calif., 1965-80, spl. asst. to dir., 1980-81; dep. asso. dir. advanced concepts Los Alamos Nat. Lab., 1981-85; dir. advanced concepts Rockwell Internat. Corp., Seal Beach, Calif., 1985-94. Cons. in field. Contbr. articles to profl. jours. Trustee Valley Meml. Hosp., Livermore, 1980-81; mem. Army Sci. Bd., 1982-88. Served with U.S. Navy, 1944-46. AEC fellow, 1947-49 Fellow Am. Phys. Soc. Home: Lafayette, Calif. Died May 26, 2002.

REYNOLDS, RALPH DUANE, oncologist, educator; b. Powhatan Point, Ohio, Feb. 22, 1934; s. Ray Campbell and Edna Louise (Corbett) R.; m. Gertrude Elaine Manifold, June 15, 1957 (div. 1982); children: Daniel Ralph, Barry Duane, Ronald Arthur; m. Norita Rose Sholly, Nov. 6, 1982; children: Nancy Lee, Susan. BS, Muskingum Coll., 1956; MD, Ohio State U., 1960. Diplomate Am. Bd. Internal Medicine. Commd. 2d lt. USAF, 1959, advanced through grades to col., 1972, served in various locations including Vietnam, 1959-82, ret., 1982; intern Madigan Gen. Hosp., Tacoma, Wash., 1960-61; resident, then chief med. resident Wilford Hall Med. Ctr., San Antonio, 1961-64, fellow in hematology, oncology, 1964-65; chief hematology-oncology svc. David Grant Med. Ctr., Fairfield, Calif., 1965-82; med. dir. Ellis Fischel Cancer Ctr., Columbia, Mo., 1982-87; assoc. dir. oncology Adria Labs., Columbus, Ohio, from 1987. Clin. prof. medicine U. Calif.-Davis, Sacramento, 1967-82, U. Mo. Sch. Medicine, Columbia, 1982-87; prin. investigator Nat. Cancer Inst., Bethesda, Md., 1967-87; dir. med. edn. David Grant Med. Ctr., 1969-81; sr. scientist, dir. clin. rsch. Cancer Rsch. Ctr., Columbia, 1982-87; sr. dir. cancer R&D U.S. Bioscience, 1993—. Patentee high-dose cancer therapy; author, editor: Cancer and the Heart, 1986; contbr. articles on cancer therapy and diagnosis to profl. publs. Treas. Meth. Ch., San Antonio, 1964-65; pres. Little League and Babe Ruth Baseball, Vacaville, Calif., 1970-73; commr. Babe Ruth Baseball, Trenton, 1977-87. Decorated Legion of Merit, Bronze Star medal; recipient Med. Rsch. in Cancer award Surgeon Gen., 1982; named Man of Yr. Babe Ruth Baseball, Trenton, 1982; grantee NIH, 1986. Fellow ACP (region pres. 1981-82, Physician of Yr. Air Force region 1981); mem. AMA, Soc. Air Force Physicians (bd. govs. 1977-79), Am. Soc. Clin. Oncology, Am. Soc. Hematology. Presbyterian. Avocations: baseball, history. Home: Kirksville, Mo. Died Oct. 19, 2001.

REYNOLDS, RONALD DAVISON, family physician; b. Boston, July 31, 1958; s. Orland Bruce and Moira (Davison) R.; m. Diana May Prieur; children: Brittany, Andrew, Avery, Isabelle. BS in Biochemistry, No. Mich. U., 1980; MD, U. Mich., 1984. Bd. cert. family practice. Resident family practice Flower Meml. Hosp., Sylvania, Ohio, 1984-87;

family physician New Richmond (Ohio) Family Practice, from 1987; instr. family medicine U. Cin. Coll. Medicine, 1988-98, asst. prof., 1996-98, assoc. prof., from 1999; ctr. dir. New Richmond Family Practice, from 1993. Mem. quality assurance com. So. Ohio Health Svcs. Network, Cin., 1993—; mem. Tri Health steering com. for computerized med. records, 1996-97; faculty Nat. Procedures Inst., Midland, Mich., 1996-98; beta tester Logician Internet, Med. Logic Corp., 1999-2000; mem. logician internet clin. adv. team Bur. of Primary Healthcare, 2000; presenter in field. Reviewer Am. Family Physician, Jour. Family Practice, Mosby-Year Book Publishers; contbr. chpts. to books and articles to profl. jours. Fellow Am. Acad. Family Physicians; mem. Ohio Acad. Family Physicians, Southwestern Ohio Soc. Family Physicians, Assn. for Voluntary Surg. Contraception. Achievements include: development of Modified U. technique of Norplant removal; trainer in No-scalpel vasectomy; coined Limbic Dysfunction to describe depressive illness; discovered way to reverse antidepressant-induced sexual dysfunction; authority on Mogen technique of circumcision; discovered danger in using common saline solution for breathing treatments. Home: Cincinnati, Ohio. Deceased.

REYNOLDS, TELFER B. physician, educator, researcher; b. Regina, Sask., Can., July 30, 1921; s. Telfer Barkley and Agnes (Dougans) R.; m. Elsie B. Chambers, Apr. 2, 1955; children— John, Ann AB, UCLA, 1941, MD, 1944. Diplomate Am. Bd. Internal Medicine. Intern Los Angeles County-U. So. Calif. Med. Ctr., Los Angeles, 1945-46, resident, 1948-51; practice medicine specializing in internal medicine; former chief of hepatology Los Angeles County-U. So. Calif. Med. Ctr., Los Angeles; Clayton G. Loosli prof. of medicine U. So. Calif., Los Angeles. Contbr. over 30 chpts. on liver diease to books, more than 150 articles to profl. jours. Served to maj. U.S. Army, 1946-48. Giannini Found. research fellow, London, 1952; recipient Hoffman award for Teaching U. So. Calif., 1971, 72, Kaiser Teaching award, 1977, 79, 84. Mem. Assn. Am Physicians, Am. Soc. Clin. Investigation, Western Assn. Physicians. Clubs: Lakeside Golf (North Hollywood, Calif.). Avocations: golf; snow skiing. Home: North Hollywood, Calif. Died June 5, 2004.

REYNOLDS, WILLIAM CRAIG, mechanical engineer, educator; b. Berkeley, Calif., Mar. 16, 1933; s. Merrill and Patricia Pope (Galt) R.; m. Janice Erma Reynolds, Sept. 18, 1953; children: Russell, Peter, Margery. BS in Mech. Engring., Stanford U., 1954, MS in Mech. Engring., 1955, PhD in Mech. Engring., 1957; D in Engring. (hon.), UMIST, U.K., 2000. Faculty mech. engring. Stanford U., 1957—2004, chmn. dept. mech. engring., 1972-82, 89-93, Donald Whittier prof. mech. engring., 1986—2004, chmn. Inst. for Energy Studies, 1974-81; staff scientist NASA/Ames Rsch. Ctr., 1998—2004; dir. Ctr. for Integrated Turbulence Simulations, 1997—2003. Author: books, including Engineering Thermodynamics, 2d edit, 1976; contbr. numerous articles to profl. jours. NSF sr. scientist fellow Eng., 1964, Otto Laporte awd., Am. Physical Soc., 1992. Fellow: ASME (Fluids Engring. award 1989), Am. Phys. Soc.; mem.: AIAA (Fluid Dynamic award), Am. Acad. Arts & Scis., Nat. Acad. Engrs., Stanford Integrated Mfg. Assn. (co-chmn. 1990—94, dir. Stanford Ctr. Integrated Turbulence Simulation), Tau Beta Pi. Achievements include research in fluid mechanics and applied thermodynamics. Died Jan. 3, 2004.

RHINE, LARRY, television screenwriter, consultant; b. San Francisco, May 26, 1912; s. Elias and Esther (Lesser) R.; m. Hazel Shermet, May 5, 1950; children: Vicki, Robert. BA, U. Calif., Berkeley, 1933. Writer, announcer Sta. KGB, San Diego, 1934-35; screenwriter Universal/20th Century-Fox, Hollywood, Calif., 1936-40; head writer Duffy's Tavern Radio, 1949-51; staff writer TV shows Mr. Ed Show, 1963-66, Red Skelton Show, 1963-66, Bob Hope Show, 1968-69, Lucille Ball Show, 1969-70, The Brady Bunch, 1972-74, The Odd Couple, 1974, All in the Family, 1975-78; editor Tandem TV Prodns., Hollywood, 1970-80; creative cons. Harps TV Prodns., Hollywood, 1987. Trustee to Producer-Writers Pension Plan, Los Angeles, 1960-70 (chmn. 1968); lectr. various colls., Calif. Contbr. travel articles to newspapers. Chief Philippines div. Office of War Info., San Francisco, 1941-45. Recipient Humanitas Award Human Family Inst., 1978. Mem. Acad. TV Arts and Scis. (Emmy award nominations 1966-78), Writers Guild (award 1977, Producer-Writers Pension Plan (Founders plaque 1980), Pioneer Broadcasters. Avocation: traveling. Home: Los Angeles, Calif. Deceased.

RHODES, JOHN JACOB, retired lawyer, former congressman; b. Council Grove, Kans., Sept. 18, 1916; s. John Jacob and Gladys Anne (Thomas) R.; m. Mary Elizabeth Harvey, May 24, 1942; children: John Jacob 3d, Thomas H., Elizabeth C. Rhodes Reich, James Scott. BS, Kans. State U., 1938; LLB, Harvard U., 1942. Bar: Kans. 1942, Ariz. 1945, D.C. 1965. Mem. 83d-97th congresses from 1st Dist. Ariz., 1952—81; House minority leader, 1973—80; of counsel Hunton & Williams, Washington, 1985-97; mem. bd. overseers Hoover Instn., 1984-92. Chmn. platform com. Nat. Rep. Conv., 1972, permanent chmn., 1976, 80 Mem. Ariz. Bd. Pub. Welfare, 1951-52. Served with AUS, World War II; Col., ret. Recipient 1st Congl. Disting. Svc. award, 2003. Mem. Mesa C. of C. (pres. 1950), SAR, Am. Legion, Ariz. Club, Mesa Golf and Country Club, Capitol Hill Club, Met. Club, Burning Tree Club (Bethesda, Md.), Pinetop Country Club, Masons (33 deg., Grand Cross), KP, Elks, Moose, Rotary, Beta Theta Pi (internat. pres. 1984-87). Republican. Methodist. Home: Mesa, Ariz. Died Aug. 24, 2003.

RHYNE, CHARLES SYLVANUS, lawyer; b. Charlotte, N.C., June 23, 1912; s. Sydneyham S. and Mary (Wilson) R.; m. Sue Cotton, Sept. 16, 1932 (dec. Mar. 1974); children: Mary Margaret, William Sylvanus; m. Sarah P. Hendon, Oct. 2, 1976; children: Sarah Wilson, Elizabeth Parkhill. BA, Duke U., 1934, LLD, 1958; JD, George Washington U., 1937, DCL, 1958; LLD, Loyola U., Calif., 1958, Dickinson Law Sch., 1959, Ohio No. U., 1966, De Paul U., 1968, Centre, 1969, U. Richmond, 1970, Howard U., 1975, Belmont Abbey, 1982. Bar: D.C. 1937. Pvt. practice, Washington; sr. ptnr. Rhyne & Rhyne. Gen. counsel Nat. Inst. Mcpl. Law Officers, 1937-88, of counsel; prof. govt. and aviation law George Washington U., 1948-53; prof. govt. Am. U., 1939-44; gen. counsel Fed. Commn. Jud. and Congl. Salaries, 1953-54; spl. cons. Pres. Eisenhower, 1957-60; Dir. Nat. Savs. & Trust Co., 1941-76, ACCIA Life Ins. Co., 1966-84; Mem. Internat Commn. Rules Judicial Procedures, 1959-61, Pres.'s Commn. on UN, 1969-71; spl. ambassador, personal rep. of Pres. U.S. to UN High Commr. for Refugees, 1971-73 Author: Civil Aeronautics Act, Annotated, 1939, Airports and the Courts, 1944, Aviation Accident Law, 1947, Airport Lease and Concession Agreements, 1948, Cases on Aviation Law, 1950, The Law of Municipal Contracts, 1952, Municipal Law, 1957, International Law, 1971, Renowned Law Givers and Great Law Documents of Humankind, 1975, International Refugee Law, 1976, Law and Judicial Systems of Nations, 1978, Law of Local Government Operations, 1980, (autobiography) Working for Justice in America and Justice in the World, 1996; editor Mcpl. Atty., 1937-88; contbr. articles to profl. jours. Trustee George Washington U., 1957-67, Duke U., 1961-85, now trustee emeritus. Recipient Freedoms Found. award for creation Law Day-U.S.A., 1959; Alumni Achievement award George Washington U., 1960; Nat. Bar Assn. Stradford award, 1962; 1st Whitney M. Young award, 1972; Harris award Rotary, 1974; U.S. Dept. State appreciation award, 1976; Nansen Ring for refugee work, 1976, 1st Peacemaker award Rotary Internat., 1988. Mem. ABA (life mem. ho. dels., pres. 1957-58, chmn. ho. dels. 1956-58, chmn. commn. world peace through law 1958-66, chmn. com. aero. law 1946-48, 51-54, chmn. internat. and comparative law sect. 1948-49, chmn. UN com., chmn. commn. on nat. inst. justice 1972-76, nat. chmn. Jr. Bar Conf. 1944-45, ABA Gold Medal 1966, Advocacy award state and local govt. sect. 1999), D.C. Bar Assn. (pres. 1955-56, Grotius Peace award 1958, Disting. Svc. award, 1975, Heroes in Law award 1999), Inter-Am. Bar Assn. (v.p. 1957-59), Am. Bar Found. (pres. 1957-58, chmn. fellows 1958-59), Internat. Bar (founder patron 1947, v.p. 1957-58), Am. Judicature Soc. (dir. life), Am. Law Inst. (life), Am. Soc. Internat. Law (life), World Peace Through Law Ctr. (pres. 1963-89), World Jurist Assn. (pres. 1989-91, hon. life pres.), Nat. Aero. Assn. (bd. dirs. 1945-47), Washington Bd. Trade, Duke U. Alumni Assn. (chmn. nat. coun. 1955-56, pres. 1959-60), Barristers, Met. Club Washington (life), Nat. Press Club, Congl. Country Club (life), Nat. Lawyers Club (life), Univ. Club, Order of Coif (life), Scribes, Delta Theta Phi (life), Omicron Delta Kappa. Died July 27, 2003.

RIACH, DOUGLAS ALEXANDER, retired marketing executive, retired military officer; b. Victoria, B.C., Can., Oct. 8, 1919; came to U.S., 1925, naturalized, 1942; s. Alex and Gladys (Provis) R.; m. Eleanor Montague, Mar. 28, 1942; 1 child, Sandra Jean. BA, UCLA, 1948; postgrad., Fenn Coll., 1959; student, Grad. Sch. Sales Mgmt., 1959-60, Armed Forces Staff Coll., 1968, Indsl. Coll. Armed Forces, 1970-71; DMS, Am. Cornerstone U., 1999. With Gen. Foods Corp., 1948-80; terr. sales mgr. San Francisco, 1962-80; with Food Brokers, San Francisco, 1980-90; exec. v.p. Visual Market Plans Inc., Novato, Calif., 1984-87; terr. mgr. Ibbotson, Berri, DeNola Brokerage, Inc., Emeryville, Calif., 1990-96; acct. exec. Sales Max Inc., Richmond, Calif., 1996-97; terr. mgr. Kelly Clarke, Inc., Pleasanton, Calif., 1997-98, Acosta Sales & Mktg., Pleasanton, Calif., 1997-2000; ret., 2000. Capt. inf. AUS, 1941-46, ETO; col. inf. USAR, 1946-79; from comdr. 2nd inf. brigade Calif. State mil. res., 1984-87 to brigadier gen. (ret.) 1990. Decorated Legion of Merit, Medal of Merit, Commendation medal, Bronze Star with V device and oak leaf cluster, Purple Heart, Combat Infantry Badge, Croix de Guerre avec palme (France and Belgium), Combattant Cross-Vol. (France), Combattant Cross-Soldier (France), Medaille Commemorative de la Liberee (France), Medaille Commemorative Francais, Medaille-War Wounded (France), Medaille Commemorative Belgique, Medaille Reconnoisance (Belgium), Medaille du Vol. (Belgium), Cross of Freedom (Poland), Virtuti Militari- Silver Cross (Poland), Royal Commemorative War Cross (Yugoslavia), knight Order of the Compassionate Heart (internat.), knight Magnus Officialis (GOTJ), Sovereign Mil. Order, Temple of Jerusalem (Knights Templar), CDR Commandery of Calif. (Knights Templar), knight comdr. of grace Sovereign Order of St. John of Jerusalem (knights hospitaller), comdr. Commandery of St. Francis (mil.) San Francisco, Knights Hospitaller), Knight Comdr. Cross with Star (class II), Polonia Restituta (Poland), knight Grand Cross Order St. Stanislaus, comdr. Commandery of San Francisco, Order of St. Stanislas, 1996-97, dep. prior Priory of Calif. Order of St. Stanislas, 1997, prior, 1998-2000, Cross of Justice, Silver Cross of Merit Order of St. Stanislas, 1997, Sword of Honor Order of St. Stanislas 1999; named to U.S. Army Inf. Hall of Fame, 1982. Mem. Long Beach Food Sales Assn. (pres. 1950), Assn. Grocers Mfrs. Reps. (dir. 1955), Am. Security Coun. (nat. adv. bd. 1975—), Res. Officers Assn. (pres. San Francisco Presidio 1974-76, v.p. 1977-82, v.p. dept. Calif. 1979, exec. v.p. 1980, pres. 1981, nat. councilman 1981-82), Nat. Assn. Uniformed Svcs., Exchange Club (v.p. Long Beach 1955), St. Andrews Soc. Queens Club San Francisco, Combat Infantry Assn., Assn. U.S. Army, Am. Legion, Vets. Battle of the Bulge Asn., Assn. Former Intelligence Officers, Presidio Soc., Navy League, Ret. Officers Assn., Mil. Order Purple Heart, DAV, Psychol. Ops. Assn., Nat. Guard Assn. Calif., State Def. Force Assn. Calif., State Guard Assn. of U.S., Internat. Diplomacy Coun. San Francisco, Merchandising Execs. San Francisco (dir. 1970-75, sec. 1976-77, v.p. 1978-79, pres. 1980, bd. dirs. 1981-89), Commonwealth of Club Calif. (nat. def. sect. vice chmn. 1964-66, chmn. 1967-72), Elks, Masons (master, lodge 400, Shrine, Islam temple, 32nd degree Scottish Rite, sojourner chpt. # 277). Republican. Episcopalian. Home: Omaha, Nebr. Died Mar. 1, 2003.

RICE, ARGYLL PRYOR, Hispanic studies and Spanish language educator; b. Va.; d. Theodorick Pryor and Argyll (Campbell) R. BA, Smith Coll., 1952; MA, Yale U., 1956, PhD, 1961. Inst. Spanish, Yale U., New Haven, 1959-60, 61-63; asst. prof. Spanish, Conn. Coll., New London, 1964-67, assoc. prof., 1967-72, prof., 1972—, chair dept. Hispanic Studies, 1971-74, 77-84. Author: Emilio Ballagas: poeta o poesia, 1967, Emilio Ballagas, Latin American Writers III; editor in chief Carlos A. Sole, Charles Scribner's Sons, 1989. Mem. MLA, Am. Assn. Tchrs. Spanish and Portuguese, New Eng. Coun. L.Am. Studies, U.S. Tennis Assn. (New Eng. Hall of Fame), Phi Beta Kappa. Avocations: music, tennis. Home: New London, Conn. Deceased.

RICE, EMILY MARIE, administrative judge, lawyer; b. St. Louis, June 24, 1922; d. Herman and Freda S. (Cohn) Cronheim; m. Bernard Rice, July 3, 1954; children: Ellen Sue Rice Wiley, Nancy Rice Watkins, Andrew, Henry, Rosemary. BA, Washington U., St. Louis, 1942, JD, 1944. Deputy dir. Mayors Coun. on Youth, St. Louis, 1969-74; exec. dir. Mo. State Arts Coun., St. Louis, 1974-76; appeals officer U.S. Civil Svc. Commn., St. Louis, 1977-79; adminstrn. judge EEOC, St. Louis, from 1979. Sec. Delcrest Sr. Apts., St. Louis, 1991; bd. dirs. Grace Hill Neighborhood Svcs., St. Louis, 1991, St. Louis Parkinsons Assn., 1991; mem. allocation panel United Way, St. Louis, 1991-93; vice chmn. Jewish Fedn. Campaign, St. Louis, 1991, 92. Mem. Phi Beta Kappa, Order of Coif. Home: Richardson, Tex. Deceased.

RICE, JAMES I. former state legislator; b. Oct. 1925; m. Jill Rice; 8 children. SLA, U. Minn. Mem. Minn. Ho. of Reps., St. Paul, 1971-97. Mem. labor mgmt. rels. com., ways and means com., econ. devel. com., chmn. econ. devel. com., infrastructure com., regulation fin. com., mem. other coms.; fin. writer. Democrat. Died 1997.

RICE, JONATHAN C. retired educational television executive; b. St. Louis, Feb. 19, 1916; s. Charles M. and May R. (Goldman) R.; m. Kathleen Feiblman, Aug. 6, 1946 (dec. June 1964); children: Jefferson Charles, Kit (dec.), May Nanette. AB, Stanford U., 1938. War photographer, reporter Acme Newspix/NEA Svc., PTO of WWII, 1941-43; picture book editor Look Mag., N.Y.C., 1947-48; news/spl. events dir. Sta. KTLA-TV, L.A., 1948-53; program mgr. Sta. KQED-TV, San Francisco, 1953-67, dir. program ops., 1967-78, asst. to pres., 1978-90, bd. dirs., 1990-96, spl. advisor to the bd., from 1997, bd. dirs., 1990-96. Cons. NET, PBS, Corp. for Pub. Broadcasting, Ford Found., TV Lima Peru, Sta. WGBH-TV, Boston, Sta. WNET-TV, N.Y.C., French TV, Europe Eastern Edn. TV, Dept. Justice, 1955-90; lectr. Stanford U., 1958-77. Editor: Look at America, The South, Official Picture Story of the FBI, 1947. Bd. dirs. NATAS, San Francisco, Planned Parenthood, San Francisco and Marin County, Calif. Maj. USMC, 1943-47, PTO. Recipient George Foster Peabody award, 1956, Thomas Alva Edison award for best station, N.Y.C., 1960, Gov.'s award NATAS, 1972-73, Ralph Lowell award Corp. for Pub. Broadcasting, 1972; Jonathan Rice Studio named in his honor, 1986. Avocations: rowing, cooking, photography, travel. Home: San Francisco, Calif. Died July 22, 2001.

RICE, ROSS R(ICHARD), political science educator; b. Shenandoah, Iowa, Jan. 13, 1922; s. Bird O. and Della (Goodner) R.; m. Marie Puzach, Mar. 20, 1948; children: Marilyn, Roxanne, Valerie, Laurie. Student, Creighton U., 1939-41, U. No. Iowa, 1941-42; MA, U. Chgo., 1949, PhD, 1956. Elem. sch. tchr., 1941-42; Instr. Ariz. State U., Tempe, 1950-53, asst. prof., 1953-57, assoc. prof., 1957-60, prof. polit. sci., 1960-89, prof. emeritus, from 1989. Vis. prof. U. Calif., Santa Barbara, 1962-63. Author: Extremist Politics, 1964, An Annotated Bibliography of Arizona Politics and Government, 1976, Carl Hayden: Builder of the American West, 1994; contbr. numerous articles to scholarly publs. Mem. council, mayor City of Tempe, 1958-62. With Air Corps U.S. Army, 1942-45. NEH grantee, 1972. Mem. Tempe Hist. Soc. (pres. 1971-73), Am. Polit. Sci. Assn., Western Polit. Sci. Assn. Democrat. Home: Tempe, Ariz. Died Oct. 2002.

RICE, STAN, JR., poet, painter, English language educator; b. Dallas, Nov. 7, 1942; s. Stanley Travis and Margaret Nolia (Cruse) R.; m. Anne O'Brien, Oct. 14, 1961; children: Michele (dec.), Christopher. BA, San Francisco State U., 1963, MA, 1965. Asst. prof. San Francisco State U., 1965-71, assoc. prof., 1971-76, prof. English and creative writing, 1977-88, asst. dir. Poetry Ctr., 1964-72, chmn. dept. creative writing, 1980-88, ret. Author: Some Lamb, 1975, Whiteboy, 1976 (Edgar Allen Poe award Acad. Am. Poets 1977), Body of Work, 1983, Singing Yet: New and Selected Poems, 1992, Fear Itself, 1995, Paintings—Stan Rice, 1997, The Radiance of Pigs, 1999, Red to the Rind, 2002; one-man show of paintings Gallerie Simone Stern, New Orleans, La., 1992. Nat. Endowment Arts grantee, 1966, writing fellow, 1972; recipient Joseph Henry Jackson award San Francisco Found., 1968 Home: New Orleans, La. Died Dec. 9, 2002.

RICHARDSON, DOUGLAS FIELDING, lawyer; b. Glendale, Calif., Mar. 17, 1929; s. James D. and Dorothy (Huskins) R.; m. Leni Tempelaar-Lietz, June 26, 1959; children— Arthur Wilhelm, John Douglas AB, UCLA, 1950; JD, Harvard U., 1953. Bar: Calif. 1953. Assoc. O'Melveny & Myers, Los Angeles, 1953-68, ptnr., 1968-86, of counsel, from 1986. Author: (with others) Drafting Agreements for the Sale of Businesses, 1971, Term Loan Handbook, 1983. Bd. govs. Town Hall of Calif., L.A., 1974-87, sec., 1977, v.p., 1978-79, pres., 1984, mem. adv. coun., 1987—, chmn. sect. on legis. and adminstrn. of justice, 1968-70, pres. Town Hall West, 1975, mem. exec. bd., 1973-93; bd. dirs. Hist. Soc. Calif., 1976-82, pres., 1980-81; bd. dirs. Alliance Francaise de Pasadena, 1993-98, treas., 1993-95. Mem. ABA (com. on devels. in bus. financing, com. state regulation of securities, com. corp. law and acctg., com. employee benefits and exec. compensation of sect corp. banking and bus. law.), Calif. Bar Assn., Los Angeles County Bar Assn. (chmn. com. Law Day 1968, exec. com. comml. law sect. 1974-78, exec. com. corp. law sect. 1975-86), Kiwanis, Phi Beta Kappa Republican. Presbyterian (elder). Clubs: California, Harvard So. Calif. Home: Glendale, Calif. Died Dec. 17, 1999.

RICHARDSON, FRANK KELLOGG, lawyer, former state justice; b. St. Helena, Calif., Feb. 13, 1914; s. Channing Alonzo and Jessie May (Kellogg) R.; m. Elizabeth Kingdon, Jan. 23. 1943; children: Stuart Channing, Paul Kellogg, Eric Kingdon, David Huntington. Student, U. Pa., 1931-32; AB with distinction, Stanford U., 1935, LL.B., 1938; LL.D. (hon.), Western State U., San Diego, 1976, Mid-Valley Coll. Law, Los Angeles, 1977, Pepperdine U., 1981. Bar: Calif. 1938. Sole practice, Oroville, Calif., 1939-42, Sacramento, Calif., 1946-71; presiding justice Calif. Ct. of Appeal (3d Dist.), 1971-74; assoc. justice Calif. Supreme Ct., Sacramento, 1974-83; solicitor U.S. Dept. Interior, 1984-85. Prof. law U. Pacific., 1946-51; disting. vis. prof. law Pepperdine U., Los Angeles, 1984; dir. Fedco, Inc. Pres. Methodist Hosp., Sacramento, 1965-71, Sacramento Community Welfare Council, 1956-57, Sacramento YMCA, World Affairs Council Sacramento, 1970-71; bd. visitors, mem. exec. com. law sch. Stanford (Calif.) U., 1966-69; bd. dirs. Meth. Hosp. of Sacramento Valley Health Care Found. Served with USAAF, 1942-43; Served with U.S. Army, 1943-45. Fellow Am. Coll. Probate Counsel, Am. Bar Found., Am. Coll. Trust and Estate Counsel Found.; mem. Calif. Judges Assn., State Bar Calif. (mem. exec. com. 1965-69), Presiding Justice Cts. Appeal, Sacramento County Bar Assn. (pres. 1962-63), Order of Coif (hon.), Phi Beta Kappa, Delta Theta Phi, Pi Sigma Alpha, Phi Delta Phi (hon.). Clubs: Sutter (hon.). Methodist. Home: Sacramento, Calif. Deceased.

RICHLAND, W. BERNARD, lawyer; b. Liverpool, Eng., 1909; came to U.S., 1925; m. Pauline Diamond (dec. 1993), 1933; 2 children: Robin, Lisa. Grad., NYU, 1936. Bar: N.Y. 1937, U.S. Dist. Ct. (so. and ea. dists.) N.Y., U.S. Ct. Appeals (2d cir.), U.S. Supreme Ct. Counsel O'Dwyer & Bernstein, 1964-73; corp. counsel City of N.Y., 1975-77; counsel Botein Hays & Sklar, 1978-88; adj. prof. local govt. law N.Y. Law Sch., 1978-89; spl. master for appeals Agt. Orange Adminstrn., N.Y., from 1988. Spl. counsel N.Y. World's Fair, 1964-65; counsel Nassau County Commn. on Govtl. Revision, 1964-66; mem. adv. bd. Kings County Hosp., 1958-75; gen. counsel State Charter Revision Commn. for N.Y.C., 1973-75; lectr. in field. Author: You Can Beat City Hall, 1980; author book revs.; mem. editorial bd. N.Y. Law Jour.; contbr. articles to profl. jours. Mem. Gov. Harriman's Commn. on Home Rule, 1958; gen. coun. Mayor Wagner's Spl. Study of Housing and Urban Renewal, 1960; chmn. N.Y. State Commn. on Govtl. Ops., N.Y.C., 1961; mem. tech. adv. com. N.Y.-N.J.-Conn. Met. Regional Coun., 1960-65; mem. Commn. on Home Rule of the N.Y. State Office for Local Govt., 1960-64, N.Y.C. Mayoralty Transition Team, 1973-74, Mayor's Com. on the Judiciary, 1974-75; commr. N.Y.C. Charter Revision Commn., 1986-88. Mem. Am. Acad. Polit. Sci., Assn. Bar of City of N.Y. (state legis. com., mcpl. affairs com., adminstrv. law com., others), Nat. Mcpl. League. Home: Brooklyn, NY. Died Aug. 14, 2003.

RICHMAN, JOAN F. retired television consultant; b. St. Louis, Apr. 10, 1939; d. Stanley M. and Barbara (Friedman) R. BA, Wellesley (Mass.) Coll., 1961. Asst. producer Sta. WNDT, N.Y.C., 1964-65; researcher CBS News, N.Y.C., 1961-64, researcher spl. events unit, 1965-67; mgr. rsch. CBS News (Rep. and Dem. nat. convs.), N.Y.C., 1968; assoc. producer CBS News, N.Y.C., 1968, producer spl. events, 1969-72; sr. producer The Reasoner Report, ABC News, N.Y.C., 1972-75; exec. producer Sports Spectacular CBS, N.Y.C., 1975-76; exec. producer CBS Evening News weekend broadcasts CBS News, N.Y.C., 1976-81, v.p., dir. spl. events, 1982-87, v.p. news coverage, 1987-89. Fellow Inst. Politics, John F. Kennedy Sch. Govt., Harvard U., 1990. Chair nat. patrons com. Opera Theatre St. Louis. Recipient Emmy award for CBS News space coverage Nat. TV Acad. Arts and Scis., 1970-71; Alumnae Achievement award Wellesley Coll., 1973 Mem. Coun. on Fgn. Rels., Wellesley Coll. Alumnae Assn. (pres. class of 1961, 1966-70). Home: Erwinna, Pa. Died Apr. 2, 2004.

RICKER, WILLIAM EDWIN, retired biologist; b. Waterdown, Ont., Can., Aug. 11, 1908; s. Harry Edwin and Rebecca Helena (Rouse) R.; m. Marion Torrance Cardwell, Mar. 30, 1935 (dec.); children: Karl Edwin, John Fraser, Eric William, Angus Clemens BA, U. Toronto, 1930, MA, 1931, PhD, 1936; D.Sc. (hon.), U. Man., 1970; LL.D., Dalhousie U., 1972; DSc (hon.), U. Guelph, 1996. Sci. asst. Fisheries Research Bd. Can., Nanaimo, B.C., 1931-38, editor publs., 1950-62, biol. cons. to chmn. and staff, 1962-63, acting chmn. Ottawa, 1963-64, chief scientist Nanaimo, 1964-73; jr. scientist Internat. Pacific Salmon Fisheries Commn., New Westminster, B.C., 1938-39; asst. prof., assoc. prof., prof. zoology Ind. U., 1939-50; dir. Ind. Lake and Stream Survey Ind. Dept. Conservation, 1939-50; vol., contract investigator Pacific Biol. Sta., Nanaimo, 1973-96. Contbr. articles to profl. jours. Decorated officer Order of Can., 1986; named Eminent Ecologist Ecol. Soc. Am., 1990; recipient Murray Newman award Vancouver Aquarium, 1995. Fellow Royal Soc. Can. (Flavelle medal 1970), AAAS; mem. Wildlife Soc. (awards 1956, 59), Profl. Inst. Pub. Service Can. (gold medal 1966), Am. Fisheries Soc. (award of excellence 1969), Can. Soc. Zoologists (F.E.J. Fry medal 1983), Am. Soc. Limnology and Oceanography (pres. 1959), Arctic Inst. N.Am., Can. Soc. Wildlife and Fishery Biologists, Entomol. Soc. B.C., Internat. Assn. Limnology, Ottawa Field-Naturalists Club, Sigma Xi Home: Nanaimo, Canada. Died Sept. 8, 2001.

RICKEY, GEORGE WARREN, artist, sculptor, educator; b. South Bend, Ind., June 6, 1907; s. Walter J. and Grace (Landon) R.; m. Edith Leighton, May 24, 1947 (wid. June 1995); children: Stuart Ross, Philip J.L. Ed., Trinity Coll., Glenalmond, Scotland, 1921-26; BA, Balliol Coll., Oxford U., 1929, MA, 1940; postgrad., Acad. Lhote, Paris, 1929-30, Inst. Fine Arts, NYU, 1945-46, State U. Iowa, 1947, Inst. Design, Chgo., 1948-49; PhD (hon.), Union Coll., Schenectady, 1973, Ind. U., 1974, Kalamazoo Coll., 1977; hon. doctorates, York U., Can., 1978; PhD (hon.), Tulane U., 1983, Rensselaer Polytechnic Inst., Troy, N.Y., 1990, U. Notre Dame, 2000. Tchr. Groton Sch., 1930-33; artist-in-residence Olivet Coll., 1937-39, Kalamazoo Coll., 1939-40, Knox Coll., 1940-41; head dept. art Muhlenberg Coll., 1941-42, 46-48; assoc. prof. design Ind. U., Bloomington, 1949-55; prof. Tulane U., New Orleans, 1955-61, head dept., 1955-59; prof. art Sch. Architecture Rensselaer Poly. Inst., Troy, N.Y., 1962-65. Sculptor, DAAD Art Program, Berlin, Germany, 1968-69, 71-72. Exhibited Denver Mus., 1945, 48, Met. Mus. Art, 1951, Pa. Acad. Ann., 1952-54, Whitney Mus., 1952-53, 64, Mus. Modern Art, 1959, Albright-Knox Gallery, 1965, Mus. Modern Art Internat. Council, 1965, Stedelijk Mus., Amsterdam, Holland, 1965, Mus. Tel Aviv, 1965, St. Louis Bicentennial Sculpture Exhbn., 1965, Dag Hammerskjold Plaza, N.Y.C., 1977, Pier and Ocean, Hayward Gallery, London, 1980, Whitney Mus., 1983, Neuer Berliner Kunstverein, 1987, Am. Fedn. Arts, 1991, Found. Maeght, France, 1992, Lumiere et Mouvement, Paris, 1996, Indpls. Mus., 2000, New Orleans Mus. Art, 2001, other U.S. and fgn. galleries; one man shows: Maxwell Davidson Gallery, N.Y.C., John Herron Art Mus., Indpls., 1953, Delgado Mus., New Orleans, 1955, Kraushaar Gallery, 1955, 1959, Amerika Haus, Hamburg, Germany, 1957, Santa Barbara Mus., 1960, Kunstverein, Düsseldorf, Fed. Republic Germany, 1962, Kunsthalle, Hamburg, 1962, Inst. Contemporary Arts, Boston, 1964, Corcoran Gallery, Washington, 1966, UCLA, 1971, Kestner Gesellschaft, Hannover, 1973, Nationalgalerie, Berlin, 1973-74, Amerika Haus, Berlin, 1979, Guggenheim Mus., 1979, Montreal Musée d'Art Contemporain, 1981, Nat. Sculpture Trust, Glasgow, Scotland, 1982, Sculpture Park, Yorkshire, Eng., 1982, Fairweather Hardin Gallery, 1982, Tulane U. Art Gallery, New Orleans, 1983, Bauhaus Archiv., Berlin, Fed. Republic Germany, 1984, Josef Albers Mus., Bottrop, Fed. Republic Germany, 1984, George Rickey in South Bend, 1985, Neuer Berliner Kunstverein, Berlin, 1986, Neuberger Mus., Purchase, N.Y., 1987, Veranneman Found., Holland, 1988, Mus. Boymans-van Beuningen, Rotterdam, Holland, 1989, Gallery Kasahara, Osaka, Japan, 1989, Artcurial, Paris, 1990, Katonah Mus. Art, 1991, Berlinische Galerie, Berlin, 1992, Foundation Maeght, Vence, France, 1992, UCLA Wright Art Gallery, L.A., 1993, Harenberg Verlag, Dortmund, Germany, 1994, Staatliches Mus., Schwerin, Germany, 1995, The Snite Mus. Art, Notre Dame, Ind., 1997, Veraqnneman Found., Kruishoutem, Belgium, 1998, Gallery Kasahara, Tokyo, 2000, Maxwell Davidson Gallery, N.Y.C., 2001, numerous others; represented in permanent collections: Dallas Mus., Kunsthalle, Hamburg, Whitney Mus., Mus. Modern Art, Albright-Knox Gallery, Tate Gallery, London, U. Glasgow, U. Heidelberg, Nationalgalerie, Berlin, Corcoran Gallery of Arts, Washington, Louisiana Mus., Humlebaek, Denmark, Auckland City Art Gallery, New Zealand, Tokyo City Hall, Japan, City of Nurnberg, Germany, Nat. Mus. Fine Art, Osaka, Japan, New Theatre, Rotterdam, Parliament Bldg., Dusseldorf, Fed. Republic Germany, Hara Mus., Tokyo, Berlinische Galerie, Berlin, U. Art Mus., Santa Barbara, Calif., others, also pvt. collections; executed commns. Ft. Worth City Hall, 1974, Fed. Courthouse, Honolulu, 1976, Tech. U., Ulm, Germany, 1977, Ruhr U., Bochum, Ger., 1978, K.B. Plaza, New Orleans, 1978, Central Trust Center, Cin., 1979, Nat. City Ctr., Cleve., 1980, Pitts. Nat. Steel Ctr., 1982, Gerald Ford Library, Ann Arbor, Mich., 1982, Musée de Grenoble, France, 1991, Nat. Gallery, Washington, 1992, Martin Gropius Bau, Berlin, 1992, Nat. Mus. of Fine Arts, Osaka, 1993, Met. Mus. of Art, N.Y.C., 1994; author: Constructivism: Origins and Evolution, 1967, 95; contbr. to publs. in field. Decorated Order of Merit 1st Class, Germany, 1993; recipient Fine Arts medal AIA, 1972, Skowhegan medal for sculpture Skowhegan Sch. Painting and Sculpture, 1973, Ind. Arts. Commn. award for sculpture, 1975, Creative Arts Award medal Brandeis U., 1979; Guggenheim fellow, 1960-62. Mem. Am. Acad. Arts and Letters (Gold medal for sculpture 1995), Coll. Art Assn., Akademie der Kunste (Berlin). Clubs: Century Assn. (N.Y.C.). Episcopalian. Home: East Chatham, NY. Died July 17, 2002.

RIDDER, BERNARD HERMAN, JR., retired newspaper publisher; b. N.Y.C., Dec. 8, 1916; s. Bernard Herman and Nell (Hickey) R.; m. Jane Delano, Feb. 24, 1939; children: Laura, Paul A., Peter, Robin, Jill. BA, Princeton U., 1938. Advt. dir. Duluth News-Tribune, 1941-42, gen. mgr., 1947-52, pub., 1952-72, St. Paul Dispatch-Pioneer Press, 1959-73; pres. Ridder Publs., Inc., 1969-98; chmn. bd. Knight-Ridder Newspapers, 1979-83. Dir. AP, 1954-64, Seattle Times Served from ensign to lt. USNR, 1942-45. Recipient Journalism award U. Minn., also Regents award. Mem. U.S. Golf Assn. (mem. exec. com. 1958-64), Inland Daily Press Assn. (pres. 1954). Clubs: Royal and Ancient Golf (St. Andrews, Scotland); Somerset Country (St. Paul); Augusta Nat. Golf (Ga.), Gulf Stream Golf (Delray Beach, Fla.). Died Oct. 10, 2002.

RIDDLE, STURGIS LEE, minister; b. Stephenville, Tex., May 26, 1909; s. Lee and Linda (McKinney) R.; m. Elisabeth Pope Sloan, Oct. 14, 1939. BA magna cum laude, Stanford U., 1931; student, Gen. Theol. Sem., N.Y.C., 1931-32; B.D. cum laude, Episcopal Theol. Sch., Cambridge, Mass., 1934; D.D., Seabury Western Theol. Sem., Evanston, Ill., 1957. Ordained deacon P.E. Ch., 1934, priest, 1935; Episcopal chaplain U. Calif., 1934-37; instr. church Div. Sch. of Pacific, 1934-37; rector Caroline Ch., Setauket, L.I., 1937-40; asst. minister St. Thomas Ch., N.Y.C., 1940-46; rector St. James Ch., Florence, Italy, 1947-49; dean Am. Cathedral of Holy Trinity, Paris, 1949-74, dean emeritus, 1974—2003. Exchange preacher Trinity Ch., N.Y.C., 1956-57, 62, St. Bartholomew's Ch., N.Y.C., 1958, 63, 73, St. John's Cathedral, Denver, 1959, Grace Cathedral, San Francisco, 1960, Nat. Cathedral, Washington, 1961, Trinity Ch. Boston, 1964, St. Andrew's Cathedral, Honolulu, 1965, St. John's Ch., Washington, 1966, 67, 68, 70, 73, St. Thomas' Ch., N.Y., 1968, 73, St. Paul's Cathedral, Boston, 1969; clerical dep. Europe to Gen. Conv. P.E. Ch., 1949-60, 64, 70 Author: One Hundred Years, 1950; contbg. Author: We Believe in Prayer, 1958, That Day with God, 1965. Hon. gov. Am. Hosp. in Paris; fellow Morgan Library, N.Y.C., trustee bd. fgn. parishes; chmn. Friends of the Am. Cathedral in Paris. Decorated Legion of Honor France; grand cross and grand prelate Sovereign Order St. John of Jerusalem Knights of Malta, grand cross Ordre du Milice de Jesus Christ; Patriarchal Order Mt. Athos. Mem. Nat. Inst. Social Sci., Am. Soc. French Legion of Honor, Phi Beta Kappa. Clubs: Union, University, Pilgrims, Spouting Rock Beach Assn. Home: New York, NY. Died Dec. 9, 2003.

RIEDER, ROLAND CONRAD, foundation administrator; b. L.A., July 25, 1931; s. Cecil Clyde and Cecilia Rosemond (LeMon) R. BA, UCLA, 1953, MA, 1955; PhD, Harvard U., 1958. Cert. coll. tchr., Mich. Instr. Mich. State U., East Lansing, 1955-58; jr. govt. aide China Lake (Calif.) Naval Base, 1958-60; archivist Nat. Archives, Washington, 1960-63; prof. history/math. Brandon Hall Found., Dunwoody, Ga., 1963-77, dean of faculty, 1977-84, dir., 1984-96, dir. emeritus, from 1996. Author: Provisional Government of Cuba, 1963; contbr. articles to profl. jours. Mich. State U. Grad. Coun.. fellow, 1956, Harvard Grad. fellow, 1958. Mem. Assn. Am. Archivists (nat. del. 1963—), Am. Ordnance Assn., Southern Assn., Ga. Assn., Phi Beta Kappa. Avocations: travel, mathematical topology. Died Dec. 16, 2000.

RIEFENSTAHL, LENI, author, photographer, film director; b. Berlin, Aug. 22, 1902; d. Alfred and Berta (Scherlach) R.; m. Peter Jacob, Mar. 21, 1944 (div. 1946). Student, Russian Ballet, Mary Wigmann Sch. for Dance, Dresden, Jutta Klamt Sch. for Dance, Berlin. Modern dancer, Germany and abroad, 1923-24; actress various prodns. including Der Heilige Berg, 1926, Der Grosse Sprung, 1927, Das Schicksaal derer von Habsburg, 1928, Die Weisse Holle von Piz Palu, 1929, Sturm uber dem Montblanc, 1930, Der Weisse Rausch, 1931, SOS Eisberg, 1932; founder L.R. Film Prodn., Berlin, 1931; producer, dir., actress Das Blaue Licht, 1931, Tiefland, 1954; dir. Sieg des Glaubens, 1933; producer, dir. Triumpf des Willens, 1934, Tag der Freiheit, 1935, Olympia, part 1, part 2, 1936-38; author: Kampf in Schnee und Eis, 1933, Schonheit in Olympische Kampf, 1938, The Last of the Nuba, 1974, The People of Kau, 1976, Coral Gardens, 1978, Mein Afrika, 1982, Memoiren, 1987, Wonders Under Water, 1991, The Sieve of Time, 1992; one person photography show, Tokyo, 1980. Recipient Silver medal (Das Blaue Licht) Biennale Venice, 1932, Gold medal (Triumpf des Willens), 1935, Gold medal (Olympia films), 1938, Gold medals World Exposition (Triumpf des Willens, Das Blaue Licht), 1937, 1st prize and Olympic Gold medals (Olympia films), 1948, Best Photography of Yr., Art Dirs. Club, 1977. Died Sept. 8, 2003.

RIEGERT, ROBERT ADOLF, law educator, consultant; b. Cin., Apr. 21, 1923; s. Adolf and Hulda (Basler) R.; m. Roswitha Victoria Bigalke, Oct. 28, 1966; children: Christine Rose, Douglas Louis. BS, U. Cin., 1948; LLB cum laude, Harvard U., 1953; Doctoris Juris Utriusque magna cum laude, U. Heidelberg, Germany, 1966; postgrad., U. Mich., Harvard U., Yale U., MIT. Bar: D.C. 1953, Cts. Allied High Commn. Germany 1954. Mem. Harvard Legal Aid Bur., 1952-53; sole practice Heidelberg, 1954-63; vis. assoc. prof. So. Meth. U. Law Sch., Dallas, 1967-71; prof. law Cumberland Law Sch., Samford U., Birmingham, Ala., 1971-97, prof. emeritus, from 1997; dir. Cumberland Summer Law Program, Heidelberg, 1981-94. Disting. vis. prof. Salmon P. Chase Coll. Law, 1983-84. Author: (With Robert Braucher) Introduction to Commercial Transactions, 1977, Documents of Title, 1978; contbr. articles to profl. jours. Served to 1st lt. USAAF, 1943-46 Grantee Dana Fund for Internat. and Comparative Law, 1979; grantee Am. Bar

Found., 1966-67; German Acad. Exchange, 1953-55, mem. Harvard Legal Aid Bur., Salmon P. Chase Coll. law scholar, 1950; Pres.'s scholar U. Cin., 1941 Mem. ABA (com. on new payment systems), Internat. Acad. Comml. and Consumer Law, Am. Law Inst., Ala. Law Inst. (coun.), Assn. Am. Law Schs. (sect. internat. legal exchs., subcom. on com. laws), German Comparative Law Assn., Acad. Soc. German Supreme Cts., Army-Navy Club (Washington). Home: Birmingham, Ala. Deceased.

RIGGS, MEADE DAVID, clinical psychologist, priest, bishop; b. Cortland, N.Y., Sept. 6, 1923; s. Charles Morrell and Sadie (Bersson); m. Jane Elizabeth Nass Pabst, Jan. 8, 1994; 1 child, Michelle. BA, Ohio Wesleyan U., 1944; MDiv, Yale U., 1947; MEd, U. Kans., 1951; MA, Hartford Sem. Found., 1952; PhD, U. So. Calif., 1959; LHD, Newport U., 1984; DD, St. Andrews Sem., 1993; PhD (hon.), So. Pacific U., 1999. Lic. psychologist, Calif.; cert. child, marriage and family counselor, Calif. Exec. dir., chief of staff Riggs & Assoc. Psychol. Svcs. Ctr., Anaheim, Calif., 1964-80; prin. assoc., cons. Closson, Riggs & Assoc., Anaheim, Calif., 1980-94; assoc. Stanley F. Hansen, M.D., Costa Mesa, Calif., 1980-91; mem. staff Successful Living Counseling Ctr., Garden Grove, Calif., from 1986, dir., 1986-91; assoc. dir., chaplain Halfway Homes Inc., Huntington Beach, Calif., 1990-94; clin. dir. Cope Ctr., Costa Mesa, from 1991; mental health staff Universal Care Med. Group, Bellflower and Garden Grove, Calif., from 1995. Cons. Rigg & Assocs., Anaheim, 1976—. Mem. Citizen's Traffic Adv. Com., Cypress, Calif., 1968, Citizen's Capital Improvement Com., Anaheim, 1977; del. mem. Orange County Health Planning Coun., 1985; consecrated bishop Philippine Ind. Cath. Ch., Los Alamitos, Calif., 1993—. Recipient 1st ann. Most Spirit award Orange County Grad. chpt. Phi Gamma Delta, 1984. Mem. Am. Assn. Clin. Counselors (diplomate), Am. Bd. Adminstrs. Psychology (diplomate), Am. B. Med. Psychotherapists and Psychodiagnosticians (diplomate), Masons. Democrat. Avocations: pipe collecting, american stamps, basketball, bridge, reading. Home: Stanton, Calif. Died May 18, 2000.

RIKER, WALTER F., JR., pharmacologist, physician; b. N.Y.C., Mar. 8, 1916; s. Walter F. and Eleanore Louise (Scafard) R.; m. Virginia Helene Jaeger, Nov. 28, 1941; children: Donald K., Walter F., Wayne S. BS, Columbia U., 1939; MD, Cornell U., 1943; D.Sc. (hon.), Med. Coll. Ohio, 1980. Instr. pharmacology Cornell U. Med. Coll., N.Y.C., 1944-47, instr. medicine, 1945-46, asst. prof. pharmacology, 1947-50, assoc. prof., 1950-56, prof., chmn. dept. pharmacology, 1956-83, Revlon chair pharmacology and toxicology, 1980-83, prof. emeritus, 1983—2004. Mem. study sect. NIH, 1956-63, 65-68; mem. Nat. Inst. Gen. Med. Scis. Council., 1963-64, Nat. Inst. Environ. Health Scis. Council, 1971-75, Pres.'s Sci. Adv. Com. on Toxicology, 1964-65; vis. prof. pharmacology U. Kans. Med. Coll., 1953; mem. Unitarian Service Med. Exchange Program, Japan, 1956; mem. sci. adv. com. Pharm. Mfrs.'s Assn. Found., 1966-87; adj. mem. Roche Inst. Molecular Biology, 1972-80; med. advisor on drugs Nat. Football League, 1973-84; adv. com. Irma T. Hirschl Found., N.Y.C., 1973—; bd. sci. advisors Sterling Drug, 1973-76; dir. Richardson-Vicks Inc., 1979-85. Recipient Teaching award Cornell U. Med. Coll., 1968, 78, citation Pharm. Mfrs.'s Assn. Found., 1972, 87, Award of Distinction Cornell U. Med. Coll. Alumni Assn., 1981, Maurice R. Greenberg Svc. award N.Y. Hosp./Cornell U. Med. Ctr., 1990; Sterling Drug vis. professorship established in honor at Cornell U. Med. Coll., 1979; named Hon. Fellow, Am. Coll. Clin. Pharmacology, 1987. Fellow AAAS, N.Y. Acad. Medicine, Harvey Soc.; mem. Am. Soc. Pharmacology and Exptl. Therapeutics (chmn. membership com. 1956-59, councillor 1959-62, bd. publs. trustees 1962-64, chmn. bd. publs. trustees 1964-70, chmn. com. ednl. and profl. affairs 1972-74, John Jacob Abel award 1951, Publs. citation 1970, Torald Sollman award 1986, Oscar B. Hunter award 1990), Japanese Pharmacology Soc., Am. Soc. Clin. Pharmacology and Therapeutics, N.Y. Acad. Scis., Sigma Xi, Alpha Omega Alpha. Home: Fort Lee, NJ. Died Feb. 20, 2004.

RILEY, ANTHONY WILLIAM, German language and literature educator; b. Radcliffe-on-Trent, Eng., July 23, 1929; s. Cyril Frederick and Winifred Mary (White) R.; m. Maria Theresia Walter, July 16, 1955; children: Christopher, Katherine, Angela. BA with honors, U. Manchester, Eng., 1952; DrPhil, U. Tübingen, Germany, 1958. Lectr. U. Tübingen, 1957-59, 60-62; asst. lectr. Queen Mary Coll., U. London, Eng., 1959-60; asst. prof. German lang. and lit. Queen's U., Kingston, Ont., Can., 1962-65, asso. prof., 1965-68, prof., 1968-92, emeritus prof., from 1993, head dept. German lang. and lit., 1967-76, acting head dept., 1979-80, 86-87. Vis. prof. U. Munich, 1996. Author: Elisabeth Langgässer Bibliographie mit Nachlassbericht, 1970; also articles on Elisabeth Langgässer, Alfred Döblin, Thomas Mann, Herman Hesse, Frederick Philip Grove, Joseph Wittig, Cordelia Edvardson; co-editor: The Master Mason's House (F.P. Grove), 1976, Echoes and Influences of German Romanticism, 1987, Muse and Reason, The Relation of Arts and Sciences 1650-1850, 1994; co-translator, co-editor: Fanny Essler, 2 vols. (Grove), 1984; editor: Der Oberst und der Dichter/Die Pilgerin Aetheria (Alfred Döblin), 1978, Der unsterbliche Mensch/Der Kampf mit dem Engel (Alfred Döblin), 1980, Jagende Rosse/Der schwarze Vorhang (Alfred Döblin), 1981, Wadzeks Kampf mit der Dampfturbine (Alfred Döblin), Kleine Schriften I (1902-1921) (Döblin), 1985, Kleine Schriften II (1922-24) (Döblin), 1990, Schicksalsreise (Döblin), 1993, Kleine Schriften III (1925-33), 1999. Served with Brit. Army, 1947-49. Summer fellow Weil Inst. for Studies in Religion and the Humanities, Cin., 1965; Can. Council Leave fellow, 1969-70, 76-77, 83-84 Fellow Royal Soc. Can. (sec. acad. humanities and social scis. 1992-95, editor 1995-98); mem. Can. Assn. Univ. Tchrs. German (v.p. 1973-75, pres. 1975-76, Hermann Boeschenstein medal 1987, prize for Excellence in Rsch. 1983, Konrad Adenauer rsch. award Alexander von Humboldt Found. 1989, Humboldt rsch. grant 1999), Deutsche Schillergesellschaft, Internat. Alfred Döblin-Gesellschaft (cofounder, v.p. 1984-95), Internat. Assn. for German Studies, Elisabeth Langgässer-Gesellschaft (Darmstadt). Home: Kingston, Canada. Died 2003.

RILEY, ROBERT COONS, business educator; b. Waynesboro, Pa., Apr. 14, 1921; s. Earl Harold and Anna (Coons) R.; m. Ruth Eleanor Ruppersberger, Nov. 20, 1971. BS in Edn., Shippensburg U., 1941; MS, Columbia U., 1947; PhD, NYU, 1962. Cert. purchasing mgr. Asst. prof. Gettysburg (Pa.) Coll., 1947-51; assoc. prof. econs. and bus. adminstrn., prof., div. chmn. Lebanon Valley Coll., Annville, Pa., 1951-67, v.p., contr., 1967-86. Cons. Pa. Dept. Edn., Harrisburg, Pa. Dept. Revenue. Co-author: Money & Banking, 1957, Public Finance, 1968, Texts in Accounting, 1959; editor: Proceedings of Pa. Conf. of Econs., 1965-67. Recipient scholarship award, Shippensburg (Pa.) U., 1941, Hawkin & Sells faculty award, NYU, 1958, Founders Day award, NYU, 1963. Avocations: reading, travel, gardening. Home: Venice, Fla. Deceased.

RILEY, WILLIAM FRANKLIN, mechanical engineering educator; b. Allenport, Pa., Mar. 1, 1925; s. William Andrew and Margaret (James) R.; m. Helen Elizabeth Chilzer, Nov. 5, 1945; children— Carol Ann, William Franklin BS in Mech. Engring., Carnegie Inst. Tech., 1951; MS in Mechanics, Ill. Inst. Tech., 1958. Mech. engr. Mesta Machine Co., West Homestead, Pa., 1951-54; research engr. Armour Research Found., Chgo., 1954-61; sect. mgr. IIT Research Inst., Chgo., 1961-64, sci. adviser, 1964-66; prof. Iowa State U., Ames, 1966-78, Disting. prof. engring., 1978-88, prof. emeritus, from 1989. Ednl. cons. Bihar Inst. Tech., Sindri, India, 1966, Indian Inst. Tech., Kanpur, summer 1970 Author: (with A.J. Durelli) Introduction to Photmechanics, 1965; (with J. W. Dally) Experimental Stress Analysis, 1991; (with D. Young, K. McConnell and T. Rogge) Essentials of Mechanics, 1974; (with L.D. Sturges and D.H. Morris) mechanics of Materials, Fifth edit., 1999; (with J. Dally and K. McConnell) Instrumentation for Engineering Measurements, 1993; (with L.W. Zachary) Introduction to Mechanics of Materials, 1989, (with L.D. Sturges) Engineering Mechanics-Statics and Dynamics, 1993, 2d edit., 1996, (with L.D. Sturges and D.H. Morris) Statics and Mechanics of Materials, 1996, Mechanics of Materials, 1999; also numerous articles and tech. papers. Served to lt. col. USAAF, 1943-46 Fellow Soc. for Exptl. Mechanics (hon. mem.); mem. Soc. for Exptl. Stress Analysis (hon., M.M. Frocht award 1977) Home: Ames, Iowa. Died Jan. 6, 2000.

RIMILLER, RONALD WAYNE, podiatrist; b. Rome, N.Y., July 21, 1949; s. Harold Henry and Ida (Scherz) R.; m. Janice Ann Bombara, June 30, 1973; children: Joseph Harold, Lori Ann. BA, Colgate U., 1971; D Podiatric Medicine, Pa. Coll. Podiatric Medicine, 1979. Diplomate Am. Bd. Podiatric Orthopedics. Pvt. practice, Elmwood, Conn., from 1979. Cons. Hartford (Conn.) Hosp., 1982—. Lt., EMT, Tunxis Hose Co. No. 1, Unionville, Conn., 1990—. Recipient achievement award Tunxis Hose Co. No. 1, 1989. Fellow Am. Coll. Foot Orthopedists; mem. APHA, Internat. Coll. Podiatric Laser Surgery (assoc.), Acad. Ambulatory Foot Surgery (assoc.), Am. Acad. Podiatric Sports Medicine (assoc.), Am. Acad. Sports Medicine, Am. Podiatric Med. Assn. Roman Catholic. Avocations: gardening, sports, reading. Home: Unionville, Conn. Died May 22, 2002.

RIMROTT, FRIEDRICH PAUL JOHANNES, engineer, educator; b. Halle, Germany, Aug. 4, 1927; emigrated to Can., 1952; s. Hans and Margarete (Hofmeister) R.; m. Doreen McConnell, Apr. 7, 1955; children: Karla, Robert, Kira, Elizabeth-Ann. Dipl. Ing., U. Karlsruhe, Germany, 1951; MASc, U. Toronto, Ont., Can., 1955; PhD, Pa. State U., 1958; Dr Ing., Tech. U., Darmstadt, Germany, 1961; P.Eng., Ontario Prov., 1954; C.Eng., U.K., 1987; D.Eng. (hon.), U. Victoria, 1992; DSc (hon.), St. Petersburg State U., 1996; Dr.Ing. (hon.), Otto-von-Guericke-U., Magdeburg, 1997. Asst. prof. engring. mechanics Pa. State U., 1958-60; mem. faculty dept. mech. engring. U. Toronto, from 1960, assoc. prof., 1962-67, prof., 1967-93, prof. emeritus, from 1993. Vis. prof. Tech. U. Vienna, 1969—70, 1986, Tech. U. Hanover (Germany), 1970, U. Bochum (Germany), 1971, U. Havana (Cuba), 1972, U. Wuppertal, Germany, 1987, 89, U. Lanzhou, China, 1989, Otto-von-Guericke-U., Magdeburg, 1992, 93, 94, 95, 96, 97; mng. dir. German Lang. Sch. (Metro Toronto) Inc., 1967—91; pres. 15th Internat. Congress Theoret. and Applied Mechs., 1980, CSME Mech. Engring. Forum, 1990. Author: Introductory Attitude Dynamics, 1988, Introductory Orbit Dynamics, 1989, (with K.Y. Yeh) Orbital Mechanics Introduction, Chinese edit., 1993, (with B. Tabarrok) Variational Methods and Complementary Formulations in Dynamics, 1994, (with Yongxi Yu) Satellite Gyrodynamics, Chinese edit., 1996; editor: (with J. Schwaighofer) Mechanics of the Solid State, 1968, (with L.E. Jones) Proceedings CANCAM 67, 1968, (with J.T. Pindera, H.H.E. Leipholz, D.E. Grierson) Experimental Mechanics in Research and Development, 1973, (with W. Eichenlaub) Was Du ererbt, 1978, (with B. Tabarrok) Theoretical and Applied Mechanics, 1980. Mem. Can. Council on Multiculturalism, 1972-79. NRC postdoctoral fellow, 1959, Alexander von Humboldt sr. fellow, 1962, NRC sr. rsch. fellow, 1969-70; recipient Can. Congress Applied Mechanics award, 1989, Alexander von Humboldt Rsch. prize, 1993. Fellow ASME, Instn. Mech. Engrs., Engring. Inst. Can., Can. Soc. Mech. Engring. (pres. 1974-75), Can. Aero. and Space Inst.; mem. Can. Congress Applied Mechanics (ctrl. com., chmn. congress com. 1967, 69, 71, 77), Can. Metric Assn. (pres. 1971-72), Soc. German Engrs. (Germany), Soc. for Applied Math. and Mechanics (Germany) (dir. 1971-79). Home: Minden, Canada. Died June 25, 2003.

RINGWALD, RICHARD COCHRANE, construction engineering educator; b. Chillicothe, Ohio, Sept. 28, 1925; s. William Eli and Georgia (Cochrane) R.; m. Marjorie Jane Reinhart, Sept. 10, 1949; children: Rebecca Jane, Richard Scott. BSCE, Bucknell U., 1949; MSCE, U. Mich., 1950. Registered profl. engr., Ohio, Iowa. Ptnr. W. E. Ringwald & Sons, Chillicothe, 1950-69; area mgr. Denton Constrn. Co., Grosse Pointe Woods, Mich., 1969-71, Armco Steel Corp., South Bend, Ind., 1971-77; project mgr. Stannard Constrn. Co., Wichita, 1977-79; assoc. prof. constrn. engring. Iowa State U., Ames, Iowa, 1979-93, ret. emeritus, 1993. Expert witness Iowa Dept. Transp., Ames; arbitrator Am. Arbritation Assn., 1985—. Author: Means Heavy Construction Handbook, 1993; contbr. articles to profl. jours. V.p., pres. Ross County Council Chs., Chillicothe. With U.S. Army, 1944-46. Recipient Outstanding Contbn. Educator award Assoc. Gen. Contractors Am., 1993. Mem. NSPE, Am. Inst. Constructors (bd. dirs. 1987—), Iowa Engrs. Soc., New Benders Club (founding co-pres.), Jaycees (local sec., v.p., pres., nat. dir., internat. senator), Sigma Lambda Xi. Republican. Episcopalian. Home: Ames, Iowa. Died Apr. 8, 2000.

RIPLEY, ALEXANDRA BRAID, author; b. Charleston, S.C., Jan. 8, 1934; m. Leonard Ripley, 1958 (div. 1963); m. John Graham, 1981 (div. 2002); children Elizabeth, Merrill. BA in Russian, Vassar Coll., 1955. Former tour guide, travel agent, underwear buyer; former manuscript reader, publicity director. Author: Who's That Lady in the President's Bed?, 1972, Charleston, 1981, On Leaving Charleston, 1984, The Time Returns: A Novel of Friends and Mortal Enemies in Fifteenth Century Florence, 1985, New Orleans Legacy, 1987, Scarlett: The Sequel to Margaret Mitchell's Gone With the Wind, 1991, From Fields of Gold, 1994, A Love Divine, 1996. Home: Richmond, Va. Died Jan. 10, 2004.

RIPPEL, HARRY CONRAD, mechanical engineer, consultant; b. Phila., Feb. 19, 1926; s. Philip and Emma (Metzger) R.; m. Dorothy Ann Tartala, Nov. 20, 1948; children— Linda Jean, Richard Peter. B.M.E., Drexel U., Phila., 1952, MS, 1957. Registered profl. engr., Pa. With Franklin Research Center, div. Franklin Inst., Phila., 1952-87, Inst. fellow, 1978—2004; cons. in tribology, 1987—2004; resident consultant Rotor Bearing Tech. & Software Inc., 1987—2004. Mem. Com. on Sci. and the Arts, Franklin Inst., Phila. Author manuals and articles in field. Chalice bearer, layreader St. James Episcopal Ch., Phila.; bd. dirs. Turbo Rsch. Found. With AUS, WWII, ETO. Decorated Bronze Star. Fellow ASME, Soc. Tribologists and Lubrication Engrs.; mem. Sigma Xi, Pi Tau Sigma. Home: Sharon Hill, Pa. Died Mar. 27, 2004.

RIPPEL, JOHN CHARLES, insurance executive; b. Balt., Feb. 12, 1926; s. Henry Charles Conrad and Bertha (Becker) R.; m. Elaine Kirkpatrick, June 10, 1955; children: Henry Charles II, Noel Elaine. Cert. underwriting, Am. Coll., 1983. CLU. With MONY Fin. Svcs., Balt., from 1969. Mem. coun. 1st English Luth. Ch., Balt., 1977-80, 85-87, 88—; pres. N. Balt. County Rep. Club, Parkton, Md., 1968-72. Mem. Balt. Assn. Life Underwriters, Md. Life Underwriters Assn., Nat. Assn. Life Underwriters. Home: Baltimore, Md. Deceased.

RIPPY, FRANCES MARGUERITE MAYHEW, English language educator; b. Ft. Worth, Sept. 16, 1929; d. Henry Grady and Marguerite Christine (O'Neill) Mayhew; m. Noble Merrill Rippy, Aug. 29, 1955 (dec. Sept. 1980); children: Felix O'Neill, Conrad Mayhew, Marguerite Hailey. BA, Tex. Christian U., 1949; MA, Vanderbilt U., 1951, PhD, 1957; postgrad., U. London, 1952-53. Instr. Tex. Christian U., 1953-55; instr. to asst. prof. Lamar State U., 1955-59; asst. prof. English Ball State U., Muncie, Ind., 1959-64; assoc. prof. English, Ball State U., 1964-68, prof., 1968—2001, dir. grad. studies in English, 1966-87; editor Ball State U. Forum, 1960-89. Vis. asst. prof. Sam Houston State U., 1957; vis. lectr., prof. U. P.R., summers 1959, 60, 61; exch. prof. Westminster Coll., Oxford, Eng., 1988; former cons.-evaluator North Cen. Assn. Colls. and Schs., commn.-at-large, 1987-91; cons.-evaluator New Eng. Assn. Schs. and Colls., 1983. Author: Matthew Prior, 1986; contbr. articles to profl. jours., encys., ref. guides, chpts. to anthology; contbr. to Dictionary of Literary Biography. Recipient McClintock award, 1966; Danforth grantee, 1964, Ball State U. Rsch. grantee, 1960, 62, 70, 73, 76, 87, 88, 89, 90, 92, 93, 95, 96, 98, Lilly Libr. Rsch., 1978; Fulbright scholar U. London, 1952-53; recipient Outstanding Faculty award Ball State U., 1992, Ind. Coll. Tchr./Scholar of 1994, Ind. Coll. English Assn., 1994. Mem. MLA, AAUP, Coll. English Assn, Nat. Coun. Tchrs. English, Am. Soc. 18th Century Studies, Am. Fedn. Tchrs., Ind. Coll. English Assn. (pres. 1984-85) Johnson Soc. Midwest (sec. 1961-62). Home: Georgetown, Tex. Died Dec. 20, 2003.

RISHER, JOHN ROBERT, JR., lawyer; b. Washington, Sept. 23, 1938; s. John Robert and Yvonne Gwendolyn (Jones) R.; m. Carol Adrienne Seeger, June 9, 1974; children— John David, Michael Temple, Mark Eliot, Conrad Zachary. BA, Morgan Coll., 1960; LL.B., U. So. Calif., 1963; postgrad., John F. Kennedy Sch., Harvard U., 1977. Bar: Calif. 1963, D.C. 1967, U.S. Supreme Ct. 1975. Mem. staff Pres.'s Com. on EEO, Washington, 1965; atty. criminal fraud sect. Dept. Justice, Washington, 1965-68; assoc. Arent, Fox, Kintner, Plotkin & Kahn, Washington, 1968-75, ptnr., 1975-76; corp. counsel D.C., 1976-78; ptnr. Arent, Fox, Kintner, Plotkin & Kahn, Washington, 1978—. Chmn. D.C. Criminal Justice Coord. Bd., 1976-78, D.C. Bar spl. com. on federal judiciary, 1985-87; trustee, exec. com. Supreme Ct. Hist. Soc., 1990—; fellow Am. Bar Found., 1994—; trustee Frederick B. Abramson Meml. Found., 1996—; exec. com. The Smithsonian Instn. Washington Coun., 1997—. Chmn. budget com. Jewish Social Svc. Agy., 1980-85; chmn. D.C. Commn. on Licensure to Practice Healing Arts, 1976-78; chmn. nominating com. D.C. Bd. Elections and Ethics, 1974-76; bd. dirs. D.C. Pub. Defender Svc., 1974-76; chmn. Montgomery County Civil Liberties Union, 1970-71; mem. exec. com. Nat. Capital Area Civil Liberties Union, 1969-71; pres. D.C. Jewish Cmty. Ctr., 1985-87, bd. dirs., 1985—; trustee, bd. dirs. capital camps United Jewish Appeal Fedn., 1987-93; bd. dirs. Washington Symphony Orch., 1990—. Mem. ABA, Bar Assn. D.C., Calif. Bar Assn., Fed. Bar Assn., Washington Bar Assn.. DePriest 15. Democrat. Jewish. Home: Washington, DC. Deceased.

RISLEY, HENRY BRAINARD, protective service official; b. Torrington, Conn., Feb. 12, 1946; s. Henry Brainard and Margery (Utz) R.; m. Suzanne K. Stanton, May 10, 1967, (div. May 1979); m. Peggy M. Madore, July 3, 1981; children: Henry, Matthew, Amy. BS, Mich. State U., 1968, MS, 1970. Vocational counselor RGC, State Prison So. Mich., Jackson, 1970-72, asst. dep. warden, 1974-77; supr. program planning Dept. of Corrections, Lansing, Mich., 1972-74; dep. warden Mich. Tng. Unit, Ionia, 1977-78; reception ctr. administrator Riverside Correction Facility, Ionia, 1978-81; dep. warden Ypsilanti (Mich.) Mens Correction Facility, 1981; warden Montanta State Prison, Deer Lodge, 1981-88; adult bur. chief Del. Dept. of Corrections, Smyrna, 1988-93; sr. project mgr. CRSS Constructors, Houston, 1994-95; dep. sec. Kans. Dept. Corrections, 1995-98; commr. Dept. Corrections, State of N.H., from 1998. Mem. Del. Criminal Justice Coun., 1988-93. Bd. dirs. Highlands Coop. (low income housing), Lansing, 1973-74; v.p. Powell County Med. Found., Deer Lodge, 1987. Mem. Am. Corrections Assn. (mem. tech. com. 1993—), N.Am. Assn. Wardens and Supts., Nat. Law Enforcement and Corrections Tech. (adv. coun. 1995—), Mont. Corrections Assn. (bd. dirs. 1984-88), Wc. Corrections Assn. (bd. dirs. 1984-88), Mich. Corrections Assn. (program chmn. 1973-74), Mid. Atlantic States Correctional Assn., Del. Corrections Assn., Mich. State U. Sch. Criminal Justice Alumni Assn. (bd. dirs. 1992-98), Deer Lodge C. of C. (pres. 1987), Deer Lodge Rotary (pres. 1987), Dover Capital City Rotary, Topeka Rotary, Bow Rotary. Avocations: hunting, fishing, camping, skiing, hiking, photography. Home: Scott Depot, W.Va. Died Sept. 26, 1999.

RISLEY, JOHN HOLLISTER, sculptor, educator; b. Brookline, Mass., Sept. 20, 1919; s. Edward Hammond and Ada (Simpson) R.; m. Mary Kring, June 2, 1949; children: Kathryn Hanford, John Hollister Jr. BA, Amherst Coll., 1942; BFA, RISD, 1949; MFA, Cranbrook Acad., Bloomfield, Mich., 1951. Cons. Mut. Security Agy., The Philippines, 1951-52; prof. art Wesleyan U., Middletown, Conn., from 1954. Cons. U.S. govt., Taipai, Taiwan, 1960, Peace Corps, P.R., 1964. One-man show Full House Gallery, N.Y.C., 1989; represented in permanent collections Henry Hunting Art Gallery, Calif., Fred Olsen Found., Conn., Rose Art Gallery, Brandeis U., Waltham, Mass., Cleve. Garden Ctr., South Kent Sch., Conn., Ea. Conn. State Coll., Hartford (Conn.) Jewish Community Ctr., Gaylord Hosp., Conn., Ford Found., Colby Coll., Maine, Wesleyan U., U. Conn., U. Maine, Taft Sch., Slater Meml. Mus., Conn., Mus. Contemporary Crafts, also others. Mem. examining bd. Charter Oak Coll., Farmington, Conn., 1987—; mem. Commn. on Arts and Culture, Middletown, 1987—. 1st lt. AUS, 1942-46, PTO. Recipient sculpture award Maine Arts Festival, 1961, sculpture prize Silvermine Guild Art, 1964, 1st prize Festival Human and Satire, Bulgaria, 1981, purchase prize Beth El Temple, West Hartford, Conn., 1982. Mem. Soc. Conn. Craftsmen (master craftsman award 1991). Home: Brooklyn, NY. Died Feb. 19, 2002.

RITCHIE, MICHAEL BRUNSWICK, film director and producer; b. Waukesha, Wis., Nov. 28, 1938; s. Benbow Ferguson and Patricia (Graney) R.; m. Jimmie Bly, Oct. 1982; children from previous marriage: Lauren, Steven, Jessica; stepchildren: Lillian, Miriam, Nelly, Billy. AB, Harvard U., 1960. Television dir., 1963-68; now dir. films. Dir.: Downhill Racer, 1969, Prime Cut, 1972, The Candidate, 1972, Smile, 1975, Bad News Bears, 1976, Semi Tough, 1977, The Island, 1980, Bette Midler's Divine Madness, 1980, The Survivors, 1983, Fletch, 1985, Wildcats, 1986, The Golden Child, 1986, The Couch Trip, 1987, Fletch Lives, 1989, Diggstown, 1989, Cops and Robbersons, 1994, The Scout, 1994; dir., writer: The Bad News Bears Go to Japan, 1978, An Almost Perfect Affair, 1979; (TV series) Profiles in Courage (also prod.), Man from U.N.C.L.E., Run for Your Life, Dr. Kildare, The Big Valley, others; TV films include The Positively True Adventures of the Alleged Texas Cheerleader-Murdering Mom, 1993; films invited to Venice Film Festival and U.S. Film Festival. Mem. Dirs. Guild Am. Died Apr. 16, 2001.

RITER, ROBERT CARL, lawyer; b. Carroll, Iowa, Jan. 9, 1912; s. Charles L. and Lillian (Furchner) R.; children—Charles, Paula Kay, Robert. LL.B., U. S.D., 1935. Bar: S.D. 1935, U.S. Dist. Ct. S.D. 1936, U.S. Ct. Appeals (8th cir.) 1964. Assoc. Waggoner & Stordahl, Sioux Falls, S.D., 1935-39, O'Keefee & Stephens, Pierre, S.D., 1941-44; ptnr. Stephens & Riter, Pierre, 1944-47; sr. ptnr. Riter, Mayer, Hofer & Riter, Pierre, 1965—; asst. atty. gen., Pierre, 1939-41; states atty. Hughes County (S.D.), 1944-48. Del. S.D. State Republican Conv., 1944. Recipient McKusick award State Bar S.D. and S.D. U. Law Sch., 1981. Mem. State Bar S.D. (pres. 1968-69, ABA, S.D. Trial Lawyers Assn., Am. Bar Found., S.D. Law Sch. Found., Am. Coll. Probate Counsel, Am. Coll. Trial Lawyers, Internat. Soc. Barristers, Am. Judicature Soc., Law Sci. Acad., Phi Delta Phi, Pi Kappa Delta. Mem. United Ch. of Christ. Club: Elks. Home: Pierre, SD. Deceased.

RITTER, JOHN(ATHAN) (SOUTHWORTH), actor; b. Burbank, Calif., Sept. 17, 1948; s. Tex and Dorothy Fay (Southworth) R. BFA, U. So. Calif., 1971. Actor: (films) The Barefoot Executive, 1970, The Other, 1972, Nickelodeon, 1976, Americathon, 1979, Wholly Moses, 1980, Hero at Large, 1980, They All Laughed, 1981, Real Men, 1987, Skin Deep, 1989, Problem Child, 1990, Noises Off, 1992, Stay Tuned, 1992, North, 1994, Sling Blade, 1996, Nowhere, 1997, Shadow of Doubt, 1998, Montana, 1998, A Gun, a Car, a Blonde, 1998, Bride of Chucky, 1998, TripFall, 1999, Panic, 2000, Tadpole, 2002, Man of the Year, 2002, Manhood, 2003, Bad Santa, 2003; (plays) Feiffer's People, Butterflies Are Free, The Glass Menagerie, The Tempest, As You Like It, The Unvarnished Truth, Love Letters, (TV shows) Who's Happy Now, Theatre in America, The Lie, Playhouse 90, (TV spl.) John Ritter: Being of Sound Mind and Body, 1980; (TV movies) Leave Yesterday Behind, The Comeback Kid, In Love With An Older Woman, Pray TV, Sunset Limousine, Love Thy Neighbor, Letting Go, Unnatural Causes, The Last Fling, A Prison for Children, My Brother's Wife, The Dreamer of Oz: The L. Frank Baum Story, 1990, The Summer My Father Grew Up, 1991, It, 1991, Danielle Steele's Heartbeat, 1993, The Only Way Out, 1993, Gramps, 1995, The Colony, 1995, Unforgivable, 1996, Hacks, 1997, Nowhere, 1997, It Came From the Sky, 1998, I Woke Up Early the Day I Died, 1998, Gun, a Car, a Blonde, 1998, Shadow of Doubt, 1998, Lethal Vows, 1999; star (TV series) Three's Company, 1977-84 (Emmy award for best actor, Golden Globe award for best actor), Three's A Crowd, 1984-85, Hooperman, 1987-89 (Emmy nomination Best Actor, People's Choice award), Hearts Afire, 1992-95, Clifford the Big Red Dog (voice), 2000, Felicity, 2000-2002, 8 Simple Rules for Dating My Teenage Daughter, 2002-2003; prodr.: (series) Have Faith, 1989, Anything But Love, 1989-92. Host United Cerebral Palsy Assn. telethons. Mem. Screen Actors Guild, AFTRA, Actor's Equity. Died Sept. 11, 2003.

RITTER, LAWRENCE (STANLEY), finance educator; b. N.Y.C., May 23, 1922; s. Irving Ritter and Bella Gerwitz; m. Claire Ritter, 1942 (div. 1951); 1 child, Stephen; m. Elisabeth R.G. Ritter, Oct. 27, 1979. BA, Ind. U., 1942; MA, U. Wis., 1948, PhD, 1951. Asst. prof. econs. Mich. State U., 1950-55; economist Fed. Res. Bank N.Y., 1955-60; prof. fin. NYU, from 1960. Author: The Glory of Their Times, 1966, The Story of Baseball, 1983, (with William Silber) Money, 1970, Principles of Money, Banking and Financial Markets, 1974, (with Donald Honig) The Image of Their Greatness, 1979, The 100 Greatest Baseball Players of All Time, 1981, (with Mark Rucker) Babe: A Life in Pictures, 1988. Served to lt. (j.g.) USN, 1942-46, PTO. Mem. Am. Econ. Assn., Am. Fin. Assn. (pres. 1969), Royal Econ. Soc. Home: New York, NY. Died Feb. 15, 2004.

RIVERS, LARRY, artist; b. N.Y.C., Aug. 17, 1923; m. Augusta Berger, 1945 (div.); 2 sons; m. Clarice Price, 1961; 2 children. Grad., N.Y. U.; student painting with, Hans Hofmann. Exhibited one-man shows including: N.Y.C. galleries, 1949—, Kestner Gesellschaf, 1980-81, Staatliche Kunsthalle, Berlin, 1981, 82, Galerie Biederman, Munich, 1981, Hirshhorn Mus. and Sculpture Garden, Washington, 1981, Marlborough Gallery, N.Y.C., 1982, Gloria Loria Gallery, Bay Harbor, Islands, Fla., 1982, Lowe Art Mus., U. Miami, 1983, Guild Hall Mus., East Hampton, N.Y., 1983, Jewish Mus., N.Y.C., 1984, Hooks-Epstein Galleries, Houston, 1984, Mus. Guggenheim, Bilbao, Spain, 1998, Susquehanna Art Mus., Pa., 1998; exhibited group shows: Vanguard Gallery, Paris, France, 1953, Am. Fedn. Arts traveling exhbn., 1954-55, Mus. Modern Art, N.Y.C., 1956, Museum de Arte Moderne, São Paulo, Brazil, 1957, Art Inst. Chgo., Mpls. Inst. Arts, La Jolla Mus. Art, 1980, Bklyn. Mus., 1980, 81, N.Y.U., 1981, Allen Mus., Berlin, 1981, Marquette U., Milw., 1981, Whitney Mus. Am. Art, 1981, 82, Los Angeles County Mus. Art, 1982, Nat. Gallery of Victoria, B.C., 1982, spl. exhbn. sponsored, Mus. Modern Art, Japan, Mus. Mexico City, Hirshhorn Gallery, Washington, Los Angeles County Mus., Mus. Caracas, Venezuela, 1979-80, Hanover (Ger.) Mus., 1980, permanent works in collections, William Rockhill Nelson Gallery Art, Kansas City, Mpls. Inst. Arts, State U. Coll. Edn., New Paltz, N.Y., Bklyn. Mus. Art, Met. Mus. Art, Mus. Modern Art, Whitney Mus. Am. Art, N.Y.C., R.I. Sch. Design, Providence, N.C. Mus. Art, Raleigh, Corcoran Gallery Art, Washington, also pvt. collections; stage designer: play The Toilet; appearance: film Pull My Daisy; executed mural History of the Russian Revolution.; Author: Drawings and Digressions, 1979, (with Arnold Weinstein) What Did I Do?, 1993. Recipient spl. awards Corcoran Gallery Art, 1954, spl. awards Arts Festival, Spoleto, Italy, also; Newport, R.I., 1958 Mem. NAD (assoc.) Home: New York, NY. Died Aug. 14, 2002.

RIVLIN, HARRY NATHANIEL, dean; b. N.Y.C., Dec. 30, 1904; s. Samuel and Jennie (Feldman) R.; m. Eugenie Graciany, Aug. 23, 1924; children: Richard Saul, Paula Glickman. BS, CCNY, 1924; MA, Columbia U., 1926, PhD, 1930. Lic. psychologist, N.Y. Tchr. Bd. Edn., N.Y.C., 1924-30; assoc. prof. CCNY, 1930-39; prof., dept. chmn. Queens Coll., N.Y.C., 1939-57, dir. army specialized tng. div. test construction ctr., 1943-44; dean, tchr. edn. div. CUNY, N.Y.C., 1957-66, dean emeritus, from 1966; acting pres. CCNY, N.y.C., 1961-62; dean grad. sch. edn. Fordham U., N.Y.C., 1966-73, dean emeritus, from 1973. Tech. advisor to dir. examinations Mcp. Civil Svc. Commn., N.Y.C., 1939-54; chmn. testa and measurements com. Ednl. Testing Svc., Princeton, N.J., 1970-72. Author: Educating for Adjustment, 1936, Teaching Adolescents in Secondary schools, 1948l editor: Encyclpedia of Modern Education, 1943, The First years in College, 1965; author and editor 4 books. Dir. Leadership Tng. Inst., U.S. Office of Edn., Washington, 1968-73; trustee Bank St. Coll., N.Y.C., 1973—. Recipient George Johnson award Catholic U. Am., 1973; Outstanding Svc. medal Am. Jewish Com., N.Y.C., 1982, Disting. Svc. medal Columbia U., 1982. Fellow APA (pres. ednl. psychology div. 1956-57), Am. Orthopsychiatric Assn. (pres. N.Y. div. 1949-50), N.Y. Acad. Sci., Nat. Commn. Tchr. Edn. Pracitce and Standards. Home: New York, NY. Deceased.

ROACH, JOHN ROBERT, retired archbishop; b. Prior Lake, Minn., July 31, 1921; s. Simon J. and Mary (Regan) Roach. BA, St. Paul Sem., 1946; MA, U. Minn., 1957; LHD (hon.), Gustavus Adolphus Coll., St. Mary's Coll., St. Xavier U., Villanova U., U. St. Thomas, Coll. St. Catherine. Ordained priest Roman Catholic Ch., 1946. From instr. to headmaster St. Thomas Acad., 1946—68; named domestic prelate, 1966; rector St. John Vianney Sem., 1968—71; aux. bishop St. Paul and Mpls., 1971; consecrated bishop, 1971; pastor St. Charles Borromeo Ch., Mpls., 1971—73, St. Cecilia Ch., St. Paul, 1973—75; archbishop of St. Paul, 1975—95. Appointed vicar for parishes, 1971; vicar for clergy, from 1972; Episc. moderator Nat. Apostolate for Mentally Retarded, 1974; v.p. Nat. Conf. Cath. Bishops, 1977—80, pres., 1980—83, chmn. ad hoc com. on call to action, 1977; chmn. internat. policy com. U.S. Catholic Conf., 1990—93; mem. Priests Senate, 1968—72; pres. Priests Senate and Presbytery, 1970; chmn. Com. on Accreditation Pvt. Schs. in Minn., 1952—57; adv. com. Coll. Entrance Exam. Bd., 1964; Episc. mem. Bishops and Pres.'s Com.; chmn. Bishops Com. to Oversee Implementation of the Call to Action Program, 1979—80, chmn. priestly formation com.; mem. Cath. Charity Bd.; chmn. task force on food and agr. Nat. Cath. Rural Life Conf., 1987—89; adminstrv. com., priestly formation com., chmn. vocations com., priorities and plans com., com. on sexual abuse Nat. Conf. Cath. Bishops; com. on social devel. and world peace U.S. Cath. Conf., 1990—93, priorities and plans com. Trustee St. Paul Sem. Sch. Divinity, 1971—75, chmn., 1975—95; trustee Cath. U. Am, 1978—81, Coll. St. Catherine, 1975—95; chmn. bd. trustees St. Thomas Acad., U. St. Thomas, St. John Vianney Sem. Mem.: Nat. Cath. Edn. Assn. (chmn. bd. dirs.), North Cen. Assn. Colls. and Secondary Schs., Assn. Mil. Colls. and Schs. U.S. (past pres.), Minn. Cath. Edn. Assn. (past pres.), Am. Coun. Edn. (del. 1963—65). Roman Catholic. Died July 11, 2003.

ROACH, WILLIAM RUSSELL, training and education executive; b. Bedford, Ind., 1940; s. George H. and Beatrice M. (Schoenlaub) R.; m. Margaret R. Balogh, 1961 (div. 1994); children: Kathleen L., Keith W. BS in Fin. and Acctg., UCLA, 1961. CPA, Calif. Internal auditor Hughes Aircraft Corp., L.A., 1962; sr. acct. Haskins & Sells, L.A., 1962-66; asst. to group v.p., asst. corp. contr. Lear Siegler, Inc., Santa Monica, Calif., 1966-71; exec. v.p., corp. sec., dir. Optimum Sys. Inc., Santa Clara, Calif., 1972-79; pres., dir. Banking Sys. Inc. subs. Optimum Sys. Inc., Dallas, 1976-79, BancSystems, Inc., Santa Clara, 1976-79, DMA/Optimum Honolulu, 1978-79; v.p. URS Corp., San Mateo, Calif., 1979-81; pres. URS Internat., Inc., 1980-81; pres., CEO, dir. Advanced Sys., Inc., 1981-88. Pres., CEO, dir. Applied Learning Internat., Inc. (formed from merger of Advanced Systems, Inc and Deltak Training Corp.), Naperville, Ill., 1981-88; sr. v.p., bd. dirs. Nat. Edn. Corp. (parent co. Applied Learning Internat.), Irvine, Calif., 1988-89; chmn. bd., CEO Plato Learning Inc. (former known as TRO Learning Inc. (acquisition and edn. group Control Data Corp.), Hoffman Estates, Ill., 1989-2000; guest speaker numerous industry related funtions including Rep. Platform Com., 1988. Mem. AICPA, Calif. Soc. CPAs, Biltmore Country Club, Marco Island Yacht and Sailing Club, Theta Delta Chi. Home: Barrington, Ill. Died Feb. 12, 2003.

ROBB, ALEXANDER FORBES, aeronautical engineer; b. Bklyn., Nov. 27, 1919; s. Alexander Riddle and Helen (Forbes) R. B in Aero. Engring., Polytech. Inst. of N.Y., 1942; MS, Adelphi U., 1956; postgrad., MIT, 1958-63. Aerodynamicist Grumman Aircraft, Bethpage, N.Y., 1942-47; sr. test engr. Wright Aero., Patterson, N.J., 1947-49; project engr. Curtiss-Wright, Caldwell, N.J., 1948-50; sr. aerodynamicist Republic Aviation, Farmingdale, N.Y., 1950-56; sr. staff scientist AVCO, Wilmington, Mass., 1956-68; design engr. Atkins & Merrill, Maynard, Mass., 1968-70; sr. analyst Kentron Internat., Cambridge, Mass., 1970-79; project engr. H.H. Aerospace, Bedford, Mass., 1980-83; sr. analyst, ADP Support services Unisys, Cambridge, from 1983. Mem. Boston Computer Soc. Clubs: Palmer Cove Yacht. Lodges: Masons. Democrat. Methodist. Avocations: flying, sailing, skiing. Home: Danvers, Mass. Deceased.

ROBBINS, FREDERICK CHAPMAN, retired physician, medical school dean emeritus; b. Auburn, Ala., Aug. 25, 1916; s. William J. and Christine (Chapman) Robbins; m. Alice Havemeyer Northrop, June 19, 1948; children: Alice, Louise. AB, U. Mo., 1936, BS, 1938; MD, Harvard U., 1940; DSc (hon.), John Carroll U., 1955, U. Mo., 1958, U. N.C., 1979, Tufts U., 1983, Med. Coll. Ohio, 1983; LLD (hon.), U. N.Mex., 1968. Diplomate Am. Bd. Pediatrics.

Intern Children's Hosp., Boston, 1941—42, resident, 1940—41, resident in pediat., 1946—48; sr. fellow virus disease Nat. Rsch. Coun., 1948—50; staff rsch. divsn. infectious diseases Children's Hosp., Boston, 1948—50, assoc. physician, assoc. dir. isolation svc., assoc. rsch. divsn. infectious diseases, 1950—52; instr., assoc. in pediat. Harvard Med. Sch., 1950—52; dir. dept. pediatrics and contagious diseases Cleve. Met. Gen. Hosp., 1952—66; prof. pediatrics Case Western Res. U., 1950—80; dean Case Western Res. U. Sch. Medicine, 1966—80, dean emeritus, from 1980; prof. emeritus Case Western Res. U., from 1987, dir. Ctr. Adolescent Health Sch. Medicine; pres. Inst. Medicine, NAS, 1980—85. Vis. scientist Donner Lab. U. Calif., 1963—64. Pres. Soc. Pediatric Rsch., 1961—62. Maj. U.S. Army, 1942—46. Decorated Bronze Star; co-recipient Nobel prize in physiology and medicine, 1954; recipient 1st Mead Johnson prize application tissue culture methods to study of viral infections, 1953, Med. Mut. Honor award, 1969, Ohio Gov.'s award, 1971, NASA Public Service Award, 1989, Frank and Dorothy Humel Hovorka Prize, Case Western Res. U., 1992, Benjamin Franklin Medal, Amer. Philosophical Soc., 1999. Mem.: Am. Philos. Soc., Am. Pediatric Soc., Am. Acad. Pediatrics, Am. Acad. Arts and Scis., Nat. Acad. Scis., Assn. Am. Med. Colls. (Abraham Flexner award 1987), Phi Gamma Delta, Sigma Xi, Phi Beta Kappa. Home: Cleveland, Ohio. Died Aug. 4, 2003.

ROBBINS, STANLEY LEONARD, pathologist, educator; b. Portland, Maine, Feb. 27, 1915; BS, MIT, 1936; MD, Tufts U., 1940. Diplomate Am. Bd. Pathology. Intern Mallory Inst. Pathology, Boston, 1940-41, resident, 1941-44, asst. pathologist, 1945-53, assoc. dir., 1953-66, dir., 1966-72; asst. prof. Sch. Medicine, Boston U., 1947-50, assoc. prof., 1950-57, prof. pathology, 1957-80, chmn. dept. pathology, 1964-80; asst. prof. Med. Sch., Tufts U., Boston, 1947-50, prof. emeritus, 1990; vis. prof. Med. Sch., Harvard U., Boston, 1980—2003; pathologist Brigham and Women's Hosp., Boston, 1980—2002; ret., 2002. Vis. prof. U. Glasgow, Scotland, 1959-60, Hebrew U., Jerusalem, 1976-77; cons. VA Hosp., Boston, 1965-80, Univ. Hosp., Boston, 1970-80. Author: Robbins Pathologic Basis of Disease, 7th edit., 1997, Basic Pathology, 7th edit., 2002, Companion Handbook to Robbins Pathologic Basis of Disease, 4th edit., 2002 Trustee Boston Med. Libr., Combined Jewish Philanthropies; bd. dirs. Jewish Family Children's Svc.; past chmn. rsch. allocation com. Mass. Heart Assn. Fellow Am. Soc. Clin. Pathologists (hon.); mem. AAAS, U.S. and Can. Acad. Pathology (designated Disting. Pathologist 1990), Mass. Med. Soc. (Disting. Leader in Am. Medicine 1980), New Eng. Soc. Pathologists (pres. 1955), Am. Assn. Pathologists (Gold-Headed Cane award 1992), Am. Assn. Med. Mus., Am. Soc. Clin. Investigation, Alpha Omega Alpha. Home: Cambridge, Mass. Died Oct. 7, 2003.

ROBERGE, A. ROLAND, commissioner, state; Commr. N.H. State Banking Dept., Concord, 1977—2001. Died July 28, 2001.

ROBERTS, LUCILLE, owner fitness agency, operator; b. Leninabad, USSR, Dec. 7, 1943; came to U.S., 1943; d. Henry and Celia (Raifinoff) Spindel; m. Bob Roberts, Apr. 20, 1967; children: Kevin Van, Kirk Van. BA, U. Pa., 1964; cert. O.P.M., Harvard U., 1985. Tchr. N.Y.C. Bd. Edn., 1964-65; buyer Mays Dept. Store, N.Y.C., 1965-67; mgr. accessory mdse. Kitty Kelly Inc., N.Y.C., 1967-69; chief exec. officer Lucille Roberts Fitness Pl., N.Y.C., 1969—2003. Cons. AWED, 1984-2003, N.Y. Women Bus. Owners, N.Y.C., 1983-2003. Author: Computercise, 1984. Mem. Nat. Multiple Sclerosis Soc., 1987-2003; vol. Meals on Wheels, 1986-2003. Named Woman Yr. Cosmopolitan mag., 1985. Mem. Young Pres. Orgn. Republican. Avocations: tennis, aerobics, reading, traveling. Home: New York, NY. Died July 17, 2003.

ROBINER, DONALD MAXWELL, lawyer, former federal official; b. Detroit, Feb. 4, 1935; s. Max and Lucia (Chassman) Robiner; m. Phyllis F Goodman; children: Brian Roberts, Marc Roberts, Steven Ralph, Lawrence Alan. BA, U. Mich., 1957; postgrad., Wayne State U., 1957-58; JD, Case Western Res. U., 1961. Bar: Ohio 1961, US Supreme Ct 1964, US Ct Appeals (6th cir) 1965. Assoc. Metzenbaum, Gaines, Schwartz, Krupansky, Finley & Stern, Cleve., 1961-67; ptnr. Metzenbaum, Gaines, Krupansky, Finley & Stern, Cleve., 1967-72; v.p. Metzenbaum, Gaines, Finley & Stern Co., L.P.A., Cleve., 1972-77, Gaines, Stern, Schwarzwald & Robiner Co., Cleve., 1977-81; exec. v.p., sec. Schwarzwald, Robiner & Rock Co. LPA, Cleve., 1981-90; prin. Buckingham, Doolittle & Burroughs Co, LPA, Cleve., 1991-94; U.S. Trustee Ohio and Mich. region 9 U.S. Dept. of Justice, 1994—2001; of counsel Belkin, Billick & Harrold Co., LPA, Cleve., from 2002. V.p., sec. Richard L. Bowen & Assocs. Inc., Cleve., 1969—94; acting judge Shaker Heights Mcpl. Ct., 1973; mem. bd. bar examiners State of Ohio, Columbus, 1974—79; life mem. 6th Cir. Jud. Conf.; mediator alternate dispute resolution panel U.S. Dist. Ct. (no. dist.) Ohio, 1993—94. Sec. Friends of Beachwood Libr. Inc, Ohio, 1981—88; trustee Friends of Beachwood Libr. Inc., Ohio, 1981—96. Recipient Cert Appreciation, Ohio Supreme Ct, 1974—79, Appreciation Award, Am Soc Appraisers, 1975. Mem.: Fed. Bar Assn., Ohio State Bar Assn., Ohio Coun. Sch. Bd. Attys. (mem. exec. com. 1990—94), Am. Arbitration Assn. (Serv Award 1975), Jud. Conf. 8th Appellate Dist. Ohio (life; charter mem.), KP. Home: Beachwood, Ohio. Died Jan. 12, 2004.

ROBINSON, BERT GILBERT, consulting company executive; b. N.Y.C., May 12, 1942; s. William and Sadie (Sheines) R.; m. Ilene Early, May 18, 1968 (div. 1978); m. Maureen Ryan, Oct. 31, 1981; 1 child, Ryan Gordon. Student, Poly. Inst. N.Y., 1959-60. Corp. dir. fin. planning Kinney Shoe Corp., N.Y.C., 1960-72; dir. corp. budget F.W. Woolworth Co., 1972-76; CFO Vida Shoes Internat., 1976-77; pres. R.R.A. Cons. Svcs., Inc., from 1977; sr. v.p. Ballet Makers, Inc., Totowa, N.J., 1989-92. Fund raiser Sta. WNET-TV, PBS, N.Y.C., 1975. Mem. Planning Forum, Am. Mgmt. Assn. Democrat. Jewish. Avocations: gourmet cooking, wines, electronics, fishing, chess. Home: New York, NY. Deceased.

ROBINSON, CLARENCE GUY, physician; b. Chgo., Sept. 19, 1920; s. Clarence Guy Sr. and Mary Ardella (Taylor) R.; m. Thelma Muriel Lennard, May 28, 1946; children: David, Michael, Mary Robinson Cohen. BS, U. Chgo., 1942; MD, Meharry Med. Coll., 1945. Diplomate Am. Bd. Internal Medicine. Attending physician Coney Island Hosp., Bklyn., from 1963; assoc. attending physician Maimonides Med. Ctr., Bklyn., from 1965, Kings County Hosp. Ctr., Bklyn., from 1971; cons. physician SUNY Health Sci. Ctr., Bklyn., from 1982; emeritus staff Cmty. Hosp., Bklyn., from 1985. Police surgeon N.Y.C. Police Dept., 1970-73; chief surgeon, 1973-80; supervising chief surgeon, 1980-85; clin. instr. medicine SUNY Downstate Med. Ctr., Bklyn., 1962-69, clin. asst. prof. medicine, 1969—. Contbr. articles to profl. jours. Recipient Clarence G. Robinson MD Self-Teaching Rm. award Coney Island Hosp., 1973, Humanitarian award Nursing Dept. Coney Island Hosp., 1978, Spl. award Honor Legion N.Y.C. Police Dept., 1981, commendation Pres.'s Coun. on Phys. Fitness & Sports, 1983, Disting. Physician award of African-Am. Heritage Com. of Coney Island Hosp., 2000. Fellow ACP; mem. N.Y.C. Employees' Ret. Sys. (mem. med. bd. 1988-97, chmn. 1997—). Died July 26, 2001.

ROBINSON, DUDLEY, retired financial executive; b. St. Paul, Nov. 17, 1915; s. Charles Dudley and Edith Helen (McMillan) R.; m. Ruth Emily Vehe, Apr. 28, 1943; children: John Dudley, Daniel Vehe. BA, Harvard U., 1937. Asst. buyer Carson Pirie Scott & Co., Chgo., 1937-40; salesman Coopers, Inc., Kenosha, Ill., 1940-41; estimator, mng. ptnr., then pres. H.R. Barney & Co., Chgo. and Skokie, Ill., 1946-66, dir. govt. affairs, 1966-90; ret., 1990. Cons. on state sales tax. Active Evanston United Fund; bd. dirs. Kendall Coll., 1962—, chmn., 1981-90. Capt. U.S. Army, 1941-46, ETO. Republican. Congregationalist. Avocations: gardening, reading, travel. Home: Evanston, Ill. Deceased.

ROBINSON, PETER CLARK, general management executive; b. Brighton, Mass., Nov. 16, 1938; s. Richard and Mary Elizabeth (Cooper) R.; m. Sylvia Phyllis Petschek, Aug. 26, 1961 (div. 1973); children: Marc Louis, Nicholas Daniel, Andrea Suzanne; m. Sarah Lingham, Jan. 1, 1984. BS in Fgn. Service, Georgetown U., 1961; MBA, Babson Inst., 1963; AMP, Harvard U., 1986. Asst. supt. prodn. Mass. Broken Stone Co., Weston, 1961-62, night shift supt., 1962-65, v.p. ops., 1968, v.p., 1969-75, 85-94, sr. v.p., from 1995, also dir.; gen. supt. Berlin Stone Co., 1965-67, v.p. ops., 1968; v.p. Holden Trap Rock Co., to 1975, also dir., v.p., 1985-94, sr. v.p., from 1995; pres. Blount Materials Inc., Saginaw, Mich., 1975-81; v.p. corp. mktg. Blount, Inc., Montgomery, 1978-79, v.p. corp. planning and mktg., 1979-92, v.p. corp. planning and devel., 1992-94; group exec., pres. Blount Agri/Indsl. Corp., 1984-90; pres. P.C. Robinson & Co., Montgomery, from 1994. Bd. dirs. Mass. Broken Stone Co. Mem. Nat. Stone Assn. (dir., exec. com., chmn. govt. affairs com., chmn. bd.), Am. Mgmt. Assn., Am. Soc. Agrl. Engrs., Newcomen Soc., Engring. Soc. Detroit, Pres. Assn., SME-AIME. Clubs: Montgomery Country, Capital City (Montgomery), Harvard (Boston). Home: Montgomery, Ala. Deceased.

ROBINSON, RAY CHARLES See CHARLES, RAY

ROBISON, BARBARA JANE, tax accountant; b. Bkln., Oct. 17, 1924; d. Matthews and Sara (Birnbaum) Brilliant; m. Morris Moses Robison, Aug. 30, 1945; 1 child, Susan Kay. BS, Ohio State U., 1945; MBA, Xavier U., 1976. CPA. Acct. Antenna Research Lab. Inc., Columbus, Ohio, 1948-51; office mgr. Master Distributors, Inc., Columbus, 1951-57; treas. Antlab Inc., Columbus, 1957-69; tax acct. AcuRay Corp., Columbus, 1969-76, tax mgr., 1976-92; pvt. practice Powell, Ohio, 1992-99. Mem. AICPA, Ohio Soc. CPA's, Am. soc. Women Accts. (pres. 1978-79). Home: Powell, Ohio. Died May 1, 1999.

ROCHLIS, JAMES JOSEPH, manufacturing executive; b. Phila., Apr. 12, 1916; s. Aaron and Gussie (Pearlene) R.; m. Riva Singer, Mar. 21, 1943; children: Jeffrey A., Susan J. Ed. pub. schs. Salesman Mid-City Tire Co., Phila., 1945-46, gen. mgr., 1946-49; pres. Ram Rubber Co., Phila., 1948-49; rep. Blair & Co., Phila., 1949-61, bus. analyst, 1955-61; pres., chief exec. officer Baldwin-Montrose Chem. Co., Inc., N.Y.C., 1961-68; v.p. Chris-Craft Industries, Inc., N.Y.C., 1968-69; pres. Chris-Craft Corp., Pompano Beach, Fla., 1969-71; exec. v.p. Chris-Craft Industries, Inc., N.Y.C., 1969-87, also bd. dirs.; pres. Baldwin-NAFI Industries div. Chris-Craft Industries, 1968—2003, Chris-Craft Internat., 1977-87, Chris-Craft Indsl. Products, Inc., Pompano Beach, 1981-86, chmn., bd. dirs., cons., 1986—2003. Bd. dirs. Montrose Chem. Co. Calif., Torrance and Mex., So. Mass. Cablevision Corp., N.Y.C., Piper Aircraft Corp., Lock Haven, Pa., Chris-Craft Pacific, Inc., Calif. Mem. AIAA, Fin. Analysts Soc. Phila., Soc. Naval Architects and Marine Engrs., Antique and Classic Boat Soc. Clubs: Lotus (N.Y.C.). Died Jan. 14, 2003.

ROCKEFELLER, LAURANCE S. philanthropist; b. N.Y.C., May 26, 1910; s. John Davison, Jr. and Abby Greene (Aldrich) R.; m. Mary French, Aug. 15, 1934; children: Laura Rockefeller Chasin, Marion French Rockefeller Weber, Lucy Rockefeller Waletzky, Laurance. BA, Princeton U., 1932; LLD (hon.), SUNY Sch. Forestry at Syracuse U., 1961, U. Vt., 1968; D.Pub. Svc. (hon.), George Washington U., 1964; LHD (hon.), Tex. Tech. Coll., 1966, Duke U., 1981, Marymount Coll., 1983; HHD (hon.), Princeton U., 1987. Chmn. Rockefeller Center, Inc., 1953-56, 58-66, dir., 1936-78; founding trustee, pres., chmn. Rockefeller Bros. Fund, 1958-80, vice chmn., 1980-82, adv. trustee, 1982-85. Dir. Ea. Airlines, 1938-60, 77-81, adv. dir., 1981-87; chmn. Woodstock Resort Corp.; bd. dirs. Readers Digest Assn., 1973-93. Mem. Nat. Cancer Adv. Bd., 1972-79; hon. chmn. N.Y. Zool. Soc., 1975; life trustee Wildlife Conservation Soc.; Meml. Sloan-Kettering Cancer Ctr., 1947-60, chmn. 1960-82, hon. chmn. 1982—; chmn. Citizens Adv. Coun. on Environ. Quality, 1969-73, Jackson Hole Preserve, Inc., pres., 1940-87, chmn. and trustee, 1987-96, chmn. emeritus and trustee, 1997-2004; commr. Palisades Interstate Pk. Commn., 1939-78, pres., 1970-77, commr. emeritus, 1978-2004; chmn. Outdoor Recreation Resources Rev. Commn., 1958-65, N.Y. State Coun. of Pks., 1963-73, White House Conf. on Natural Beauty, 1965; life mem. corp. MIT; trustee emeritus Princeton U.; hon. trustee Nat. Geog. Soc.; trustee Alfred P. Sloan Found., 1950-82, Greenacre Found., Nat. Pk. Found., 1968-76, Sleepy Hollow Restorations, 1975-87, chmn., 1981-85; trustee Hist. Hudson Valley, 1987-2004, chmn. emeritus, 1997-2004; chmn. Woodstock Found., 1968-97, chmn. emeritus, 1997-2004; hon. dir. Nat. Wildflower Ctr., 1988-2004. Decorated commandeur de Ordre Royal du Lion, Belgium, 1950; comdr. most excellent Order Brit. Empire, 1971; recipient Conservation Service award U.S. Dept. Interior, 1956, 62, Horace Marden Albright Scenic Preservation medal, 1957, Disting. Service medal Theodore Roosevelt Assn., 1963, Audubon medal, 1964, Nat. Inst. Social Scis. award, 1959, 67, Alfred P. Sloan, Jr. Meml. award Am. Cancer Soc., 1969, Medal of Freedom, 1969, Cert. of Award, Am. Assn. for Cancer Research, 1980, James Ewing Layman's award Soc. Surg. Oncology, 1980, Congl. gold medal, 1990, McAneny Hist. Pres. medal, 1993, Chmn.'s award Nat. Geograph. Soc., 1995, Theodore Roosevelt Nat. Park medal of honor, 1995, Lady Bird Johnson Conservation award Lifetime Achievement, 1997, Gov.'s Parks & Preservation award, N.Y., 1997. Mem. Am. Conservation Assn. (pres. 1958-80, chmn. 1980-85, hon. chmn. 1985-2004), Princeton Club, University Club, Brook Club, Capitol Hill Club, Cosmos Club, Boone and Crockett Club, Knickerbocker Club, Lotos Club (N.Y.C.), Sleepy Hollow Club (Tarrytown). Died July 11, 2004.

ROCKELMAN, GEORGIA F(OWLER) BENZ, retail furniture executive; b. Jefferson City, Mo., June 7, 1920; d. Charles Herman and Marinda Julia (Fowler) Benz; m. Elvin John Henry Rockelman, Nov. 9, 1940; 1 child, Barbara Jean. BBA, Lincoln U., 1964, MBA, 1977. Sec./acct. Harry Benz Enterprises, Jefferson City, 1932-52; ptnr. Benz Furniture Co., Jefferson City, 1952-59, Benz-Rockelman Furniture Co., Jefferson City, 1961-82; v.p., sec. Benz-Rockelman Ltd., Jefferson City, 1982-93, pres., sec., 1993-94. Pres. Trinity-Luth. PTA, Jefferson City, 1952-54; pres. Jefferson City Council Nat. Congress PTA, 1954-56; mem. City Water Flouridation com., 1956; candidate Jefferson City Council, 1983; bd. dirs. Southside Bus. League, Jefferson City, 1981-82, v.p., 1983-84; Rep. com. women Cole County, 1984, 86; asst. leader, leader Girl Scouts and Brownies, 1949-52. Mem. AAUW (sec. 1990-94), DAR, Am. Legion, Cole County Hist. Soc., Hist. City of Jefferson City, Cole County Rep. Women's Club. Lutheran. Home: Volant, Pa. Died Apr. 27, 1999.

ROCKWELL, R(ONALD) JAMES, JR., laser and electro-optics consultant; b. Cin., May 7, 1937; s. Ronald James and Mary Cornelius (Thornton) R.; m. Diane Lundin, Feb. 3, 1968; children: James Gregory, Christopher Derrick. BS, U. Cin., 1960, MS, 1964. Directing physicist, assoc. prof. laser scis., laser research labs. Med. Center, U. Cin., 1963-76; dir. continuing edn. services Electro-Optical Systems Design Jour., Cin., 1976-77; v.p. laser/electro-optics Control Dynamics, Inc., Cin., 1977-79; pres. Rockwell Assocs., Inc. (cons. lasers, optics and electro-optics), Cin., 1979-89; pres., chief exec. officer Rockwell Laser Industries (cons. lasers, optics and electro-optics), Cin., from 1989. Exec. com. safe use lasers com. Am. Nat. Standards Inst., 1971-2000, chmn. control measures tech. com., 1971—; exec. sec. Laser Inst. Am., 1976-77, dir., 1972-92, pres., 1974; mem. adv. com. Laser History Project, 1983-89; dir. Laserworks, Inc., Rockwell Devel. Co.; cons. WHO, Internat. Electrotechnical Commn., founder Consortium of Laser and Tech. Cons., 1988; mem. tech. com. Laser Fire Protection of the Nat. Fire Protection Assn., 1991—. Co-author: Lasers in Medicine, 1971; author: Laser Safety Training Manual, 1982, Laser Safety in Surgery and Medicine, 1985, Laser Safety: Concepts, Analysis and Controls, 1992, Laser Safety: Modularized Training Package, 1994, Users Guide for Laser Safety, 1997, Multi-Lingual Laser Safety Training Program, 1998, Laser Accidents, a 30 Year Review, 2000, Medical User's Guide for Laser Safety, 2000; created software program: Laser Hazard Analysis, 1987, LAZAN for Windows, 1995, SKYZAN for Windows, 1996; co-developer: LASERNET page on the World-Wide Web (Internet), 1996; contbr. chpts. to books and articles to profl. jours.; editor jours. in field; mem. editl. bd. Jour. Laser Applications, 1994-99. Co-chmn. Internat. Laser Safety Conf., 1990, 92, mem. planning com., keynote spkr., 1997. Recipient Pres.' award Laser Inst. Am., 1985, Safety and Health award Am. Welding Soc., 2001. Fellow: Laser Inst.

Am.; mem.: IEEE, Internat. Laser Display Assn., Midwest Bio-Laser Inst., Am. Soc. Laser Medicine and Surgery, N.Y. Acad. Scis., Newcomen Soc., Delta Tau Delta (dir. acad. affairs, nat. bd. dirs. 1975—83, D.S.C. award 1985), Sigma Xi (nat. lectr. 1971—75). Methodist. Achievements include designer, builder portable laser entertainment system in laser light artistic shows; patentee in field; co-developer laser safety awareness training program for world-wide web. Home: Cincinnati, Ohio. Died June 2003.

RODERICK, ROBERT LEE, aerospace executive; b. Chgo., Oct. 19, 1925; s. Albert Lee and Betha Manilla (Powers) R.; m. Lisa Wolf, Dec. 28, 1950 (dec. Feb. 1995); children: Diane Gale, Robert Kirk; m. Susan U. Eckert, May 30, 1997. Student, Iowa State U., 1943; BSEE, Ill. Inst. Tech., 1948; PhD, Brown U., 1951. V.p. Litton Industries, Beverly Hills, Calif., 1968-73; group v.p. Hughes Aircraft Co., Canoga Park, Calif., 1973-87, v.p. corp. tech. ctrs. L.A., 1987-90. Patentee instanteous vertical speed indicator. With USN, 1943-46. Recipient Spl. Recognition award Ill. Inst. Tech., 1967, named to Hall of Fame, 1983; recipient Pub. Svc. award NASA, 1967, Am. Machinist's award Am. Machinists Assn., 1970. Mem. Assn. U.S. Army, Am. Def. Preparedness Assn., Sigma Xi, Tau Beta Phi, Eta Kappa Nu. Avocations: tennis, personal computing. Home: West Palm Beach, Fla. Died Aug. 12, 2003.

RODGERS, JOHN, geologist, educator; b. Albany, N.Y., July 11, 1914; s. Henry D. and Louise W. (Allen) R. BA, Cornell U., 1936, MS, 1937; PhD, Yale U., 1944. Geologist, U.S. Geol. Survey, 1938-46, intermittently, 1946-95; sci. cons. U.S. Army Engrs., 1944-46; instr. geology Yale U., New Haven, 1946-47, asst. prof., 1947-52, asso. prof., 1952-59, prof., 1959-62, Silliman prof., 1962-85, Silliman prof. emeritus, 1985—2004. Vis. lectr. Coll. de France, Paris, 1960; sec.-gen. commn. on stratigraphy Internat. Geol. Congress, 1952-60; commr. Conn. Geol. and Natural History Survey, 1960-71. Author: (with C.O. Dunbar) Principles of Stratigraphy, 1957, The Tectonics of the Appalachians, 1970; also articles in field.; editor Symposium on the Cambrian System, 3 vols., 1956, 61; recording artist: (with W. Ruff) The Harmony of the World, 1979; asst. editor Am. Jour. Sci., 1948-54, editor, 1954-95, editor emeritus, 1995-2004. NSF Sr. postdoctoral fellow France, 1959-60; exchange visitor Geol. Inst., Acad. Scis. USSR, 1967; Guggenheim fellow Australia, 1973-74; recipient Medal of Freedom U.S. Army, 1947, James Hall medal N.Y. State Geol. Survey, 1986; exchange scholar Inst. of Geology Academia Sinica (Beijing) 1986; recipient Médaille Paul Fourmarier Académie Royale des Sciences, Lettres et Beaux-Arts de Belgique, 1987, William Clyde DeVane medal Phi Beta Kappa, 1990; named hon. prof. Inst. Geology and Geophysics. Chinese Acad. Scis., Beijing, 2000. Fellow AAAS, Geol. Soc. Am. (councillor 1962-65, pres. 1970, Penrose medal 1981), Am. Geophys. Union; mem. NAS, Am. Acad. Arts and Scis., Am. Assn. Petroleum Geologists, Conn. Acad. Sci. and Engring. (charter), Conn. Acad. Arts and Scis. (pres. 1969), Geol. Soc. London (hon.), Société géologique de France (assoc. mem., v.p. 1960, Prix Gaudry 1987), Am. Philos. Soc., Russian Acad. Scis. (hon. fgn. mem.), Academia Real de Ciencias y Artes Barcelona (fgn. corr. mem.), Phi Kappa Phi, Sigma Xi, Phi Beta Kappa. Clubs: Elizabethan (New Haven). Died Mar. 7, 2004.

ROEMER, EDWARD PIER, neurologist; b. Milw., Feb. 10, 1908; s. John Henry and Caroline Hamilton (Pier) R.; m. Helen Ann Fraser, Mar. 28, 1935 (dec.); children: Kate Pier, Caroline Pier; m. Marion Clare Zimmer, May 24, 1980. BA, U. Wis., 1930; MD, Cornell U., 1934. Diplomate Am. Bd. Neurology. Intern Yale-New Haven Hosp., 1934-36; resident internal medicine N.Y. Hosp., 1936; resident neurology Bellevue Hosp., N.Y.C., 1936-38; instr. Med. Sch. Yale U., New Haven, 1935-36; asst. prof. neurology Cornell U., N.Y.C., 1936-41; prof. neurology U. Wis., Madison, 1946-64; chief of neurology Huntington Meml. Hosp., Pasadena, Calif., 1964-78; pvt. practice Capistrano Beach, Calif., 1978-99. Founder, dir. Wis. Neurol. Found., Madison, 1946-64; dir. Wis. Multiple Sclerosis Clinic, Madison, 1946-64; adv. bd. Inst. Antiquities and Christianity, Claremont Grad. Sch., 1970-99; dir. found. Univ Good Hope, S.Africa. Contbr. rsch. articles on multiple sclerosis, neuropathies to profl. jours. Lt. col. med. corps U.S. Army, 1941-46, ETO. Fellow ACP, Royal Coll. Medicine, L.S.B. Leakey Found.; mem. Rotary Internat., Annandale Golf Club, El Niguel Country Club, Nu Sigma Nu, Phi Delta Theta. Republican. Achievements include significant findings in field of anthropology and archaeology in Egypt and southwest U. S. relative to prehistory and PreColumbian European influences. Home: Capo Beach, Calif. Died May 29, 1999.

ROEMING, ROBERT FREDERICK, foreign language educator; b. Milw., Dec. 12, 1911; s. Ferdinand August and Wanda E. (Radtke) R.; m. Alice Mae Voss, Aug. 30, 1941; 1 child, Pamela Alice. BA in Econs./Acctg., U. Wis., 1934, MA in Italian, 1936, PhD in French, 1941. Mem. faculty U. Wis.-Milw., from 1937, prof. French and Italian, from 1956, assoc. dean Coll. Letters and Sci., asst. to provost for devel. of spl. programs, 1957-62, sole dir. dept. lang. labs., 1964-70, dir. English as 2d lang., 1967-70, founder and dir. Ctr. Twentieth Century Studies, 1970-74, prof. emeritus, from 1980; founder, chief investigator Camus Bibliography Research Collection, Golda Meir Library, from 1985. Rep. D.C. Heath Co., 1943-46; cons., 1946-50; cons. computer systems Harnischfeger Corp., Milw., 1953-57; chmn. tech. sect. Internat. Congress on Fgn. Lang. Tchg., Pädagogisches Zentrum, Berlin, summer 1964; guest InterAm. Congress of Linguists, Montevideo, Uruguay, 1966; ofcl. guest Romanian govt. 10th Internat. Congress Linguists, summer 1967; dir. Insts. in Adult Basic Edn., 1969, U.S. Office Edn.; pres., treas. Electronic Rsch. Instruments Co., Inc., Nashotah, Wis., 1969-93. Author: In the Land of the Immortals, 1934, (with C.E. Young) Introduction to French, 1951, Camus, A Bibliography, 1969, rev. and augmented computer-microfiche, 15th edit., 2000, Little Magazine Catalog, 1976, 77 (NEH grantee); editor: Modern Lang. Jour, 1963-70; contbr. numerous monographs and articles to profl. jours., 72 taped radio programs on French Black lit. Chmn. bldg. commn. Village of Chenequa, Wis., 1972-88; trustee, chmn. Midwest chpt. Jose Greco Found. for Hispanic Dance, Inc., 1970-76; mem. Wis. Bd. Nursing, 1977-79, chmn., 1979; mem. numerous nat. conservation orgns. and local civic groups. Decorated chevalier, officier, commandeur Ordre Palmes Académiques (France); recipient Travel award Italian Govt., summer, 1934. Mem. MLA (life, index com. 1970-79), Nat. Fedn. Modern Lang. Tchrs. Assn. (exec. com. 1963-70), Verband Deutscher Schriftsteller, Wis. News Photographers Assn. (hon. life, Pres.'s award 1972), Soc. des Etudes Camusiennes, Am. Assn. of French Acad. Palms, Wis. Assn. for the Blind and Physically Handicapped, Chenequa Country Club, Lake Country Racquet and Athletic Club, Phi Eta Sigma, Phi Kappa Phi, Tau Kappa Epsilon. Achievements include research in application of the computer to humanities, applied linguistics and contemporary French and Italian Literature. Home: Nashotah, Wis. Died Jan. 11, 2004.

ROESELER, WOLFGANG GUENTHER JOACHIM, city planner; b. Berlin, Mar. 30, 1925; s. Karl Ludwig and Therese (Guenther) R.; m. Eva Maria Jante, Mar. 12, 1947; children: Marion, Joanie, Karl. PhD, Philipps State U. of Hesse, Marburg, Germany, 1949; LLB, Blackstone Sch. Law, Chgo., 1958. Assoc. planner Kansas City (Mo.) Planning Commn., 1950-52; city planning dir. City of Palm Springs, Calif., 1952-54; sr. city planner Kansas City, 1954-56; prin. assoc. Ladislas Segoe & Assocs., Cin., 1956-64; dir. urban and regional planning Howard, Needles, Tammen & Bergendoff, cons., Kansas City and N.Y.C., 1964-68; owner W.G. Roeseler, Cons. City Planner and Transp. Specialist, Bryan, Tex., 1969—90. Head dept. urban and regional planning Tex. A&M U., 1975-81, 85-88, prof., 1975-90, dir. Tex A&M Ctr. Urban Affairs, 1984-88, exec. officer for edn. Coll. of Architecture, 1987-88, prof. emeritus, 1990-2004. Author: Successful American Urban Plans, 1982; author tech. reports; contbr. articles to profl. jours. Fellow Am. Inst. Cert. Planners; mem. Am. Planning Assn., Transport Planners Coun., Urban Land Inst. Died Jan. 7, 2004.

ROESLER, HELMUT, structural engineer; b. Mexico City, Dec. 21, 1930; came to U.S., 1963; s. Georg Maximilian and Erika (Froemberg) R.; m. Ingrid Schlueter, June 1, 1955 (div. July 1962); children: Helmut, Wilhelm, Regina; m. Renate Irmgard Bagdahn, Dec. 18, 1962; children: Christina, Erika. MSCE, U. Mex., 1953; student, Project Mgmt. Inst., Phila., 1985. Registered prof. engr., Pa.; cert. project. mgmt. profl. Engr., project engr. La Latino Americana, Mexico City, 1953-56; owner, pres. Engring. and Gen. Constrn., Mexico City, 1956-60; project engr., project mgr. Wayss & Freytagg/Brown Boverie, Manheim, Germany, 1961-63; asst. constrn. mgr. S. Jevy Co., Camden, N.J., 1963-64; project engr. The Austin Co., Roselle, N.J., 1964-65; mgr. projects Catalytic Inc., Phila., 1965-87; mgr. projects Seacor subs. Day & Zimmerman Inc., Moorestown, N.J., 1987-99. Mgr. engring. and constrn. Catalytic Caribe, Ponce, P.R., 1971; cons. Roesler, Phila., 1987-99. Author articles. Active Main Line Dist. coun. Boy Scouts Am., Lower Merion, Pa., 1972-86. Mem. NSPE, Project Mgmt. Inst. (pres. 1992, chmn. 1993), Soc. Am. Mil. Engrs., Cynwyd Club, The Clinkers (v.p., pres.). Avocations: rowing, tennis, silhouette cutting, home repairs. Home: Narberth, Pa. Died May 13, 1999.

ROETTGER, NORMAN CHARLES, JR., federal judge; b. Lucasville, Ohio, Nov. 3, 1930; s. Norman Charles and Emma Eleanora Roettger; children: Virginia, Peggy. BA, Ohio State U., 1952; LLB magna cum laude, Washington and Lee U., 1958. Bar: Ohio 1958, Fla. 1958. Assoc. Frost & Jacobs, Cin., 1958—59; assoc. Fleming, O'Bryan & Fleming, Ft. Lauderdale, Fla., 1959—63, ptnr., 1963—69, 1971—72; dep. gen. counsel HUD, Washington, 1969—71; judge U.S. Dist. Ct. (so. dist.), Ft. Lauderdale, 1972—97; sr. judge U.S. Dist. Ct. (so. dist.), Ft. Lauderdale, from 1997. Lt. (j.g.) USN, 1952—55, capt. USNR, 1972. Mem.: ABA, Am. Judicature Soc., Broward County Bar Assn., Fla. Bar Assn., Fed. Bar Assn., Ridge Yacht Club, Masons, Order of Coif, Kappa Delta Rho, Omicron Delta Kappa. Presbyterian. Home: Fort Lauderdale, Fla. Died July 26, 2003.

ROGERS, FRED MCFEELY, television producer and host; b. Latrobe, Pa., Mar. 20, 1928; s. James Hillis and Nancy (McFeely) Flagg; m. Sara Joanne Byrd, July 9, 1952; children: James Byrd, John Frederick. MusB, Rollins Coll., 1951; MDiv, Pitts. Theol. Sem., 1962; DHL (hon.), Thiel Coll., 1969; HHD (hon.), Eastern Mich. U., 1973; LittD (hon.), St. Vincent Coll., 1973; DD (hon.), Christian Theol. Sem., 1973, Washington and Jefferson Coll., 1984, Westminster Coll., 1987; LHD (hon.), Yale U., 1974, Lafayette Coll., 1977, Washington and Jefferson Coll., 1984, Linfield Coll., 1982, Duquesne U., 1982, Slippery Rock Coll., 1982, U. S.C., 1985, MacMurray Coll., 1986, Drury Coll., 1986, Bowling Green State U., 1987; DFA (hon.), Carnegie-Mellon U., 1976; MusD (hon.), Waynesburg Coll., 1978, U. Ind., 1988; LLD (hon.), Hobart and William Smith Colls., 1985, U. Conn., 1991, Ind. U., Pa., 1992, Boston U., 1992, Moravian Coll., 1992; hon. degree, Goucher Coll., 1993, U. Pitts., 1993, N.C. State, 1996; DHL (hon.), U. W.Va., 1995; D Pub. Svc. (hon.), Edinboro (Pa.) U., 1998; hon. degree, Westminster Choir Coll., 1999, Marist Coll., 1999, Old Dominion U., 2000; LHD, Marguette U., 2001, Middlebury Coll., 2001. Adj. prof. U. Pitts., 1976; C.E.O., Family Comm., Inc., Pitts.; asst. producer NBC, N.Y.C., 1951-53; exec. producer Sta. WQED, Pitts., 1953-62; producer, host CBC, Toronto, Ont., 1962-64; exec. producer, host Mister Rogers' Neighborhood (PBS), Pitts., from 1965; prodr., host Old Friends, New Friends PBS interview series, 1979-81; host Fred Rogers' Heros PBS, 1994. Author: Mister Rogers Talks with Parents, 1983, Mister Rogers' First Experiences Books, 1985, Mister Rogers' Playbook, 1986, Mr. Rogers Talks About Divorce, 1987, Mister Rogers-How Families Grow, 1988, You are Special, 1994, Let's Talk About It: Divorce, 1995, Let's Talk About It: Adoption, 1996, Dear Mister Rogers, 1996, Let's Talk About Stepfamilies, 1999, Let's Talk About It: Extraordinary Friends, 2000, The Giving Box, 2000; producer five audio cassettes of original songs-Many Ways to Say I Love You, audio cassettes and CD Bedtime, 1992, Growing, 1992, You Are Special, 1995, Coming and Going, 1997; composer: Mr. Rogers' Songbook, Mister Rogers EZ Play Today Songbook, 1998, It's a Beautiful Day with Mister Rogers Songbook, 1998; host, writer, producer five one hour videocassettes home videos CBS, 1987-88, eight 30 minute home videos, 1995-96. Chmn. child devel. and mass media forum White House Conf. on Children; mem. Esther Island Preserve Assn.; bd. dirs. McFeely Rogers Found.; hon. chmn. Nat. PTA, 1992-94. Recipient Children's Trust award Children's Med. Ctr., Chgo., 1997, Pittsburgher of Yr. award Pitts. mag., 1997, Lifetime Achievement TV Critics Assn., 1997, Lifetime Achievement Nat. Acad. TV Arts and Scis., 1997, Lifetime Achievement award Gold Angel Internat. Angel Awards, 1998, Emmy award for performer, children's series, 1999, Spirit of Am. award Nat. Coun. for the Social Studies, 1999, Pa. Founder's award Pa. Hist. and Mus. Commn., 1999, Parents' Choice Classic award, 1999; star on Hollywood Walk of Fame, Hollywood C. of C., 1998; inducted to TV Hall of Fame Nat. Acad. TV Arts and Scis., 1999, Library of Congress LIveing Legend Award, 2000, Lifetime Acievement Award, 2000, National Exceptional Service Award, Salvation Army, 2000, Strong Kids award YMCA, 2001, Mental Health award Psychology Today, 2001, Christophers award, 2001, James Bryant Conant award Edn. Commn. of States, 2001. Mem. Luxor Ministerial Assn., Nat. Assn. TV Program Execs. Presbyterian. Died Feb. 27, 2003.

ROGERS, LLOYD SLOAN, surgeon; b. Waukegan, Ill., Apr. 23, 1914; s. Irvin Lloyd and Maude Elizabeth (Sloan) R. BS, Trinity Coll., Hartford, Conn., 1936; MD, U. Rochester, N.Y., 1941. Decorated Purple Heart. Intern surgery Strong Meml. Hosp., Rochester, N.Y., 1941-42; resident surgery U. Rochester (N.Y.) Hosps., 1946-50; asst. chief surgeon Crile VA Hosp., Celve., 1951-53; chief surgical svc. VA Hosp., Syracuse, N.Y., 1953-81; from asst. prof. to assoc. prof. surgery SUNY Health Sci. Ctr., Syracuse, 1953-67, prof. surgery, 1967-84, acting chmn. surgery, 1967-70, vice chmn. surgery, 1970-84, prof. emeritus, from 1984. Mem. VA Surgical Oncology Group, Washington, 1960-83, NIH Surgical Study sect., Bethesda, Md., 1963-68; cancer coord. SUNY Health Sci. Ctr., Syracuse, 1967-72. Contbr 35 articles to peer reviewed surgical jours., 1957-84. Maj. U.S. Army Med. Corps, 1942-46, ETO. Recipient Pres.'s award for Disting. Svc., Health Sci. Ctr. Syracuse, 1991. Fellow ACS; mem. AMA, Assn. VA Surgeons (pres. 1967, Disting. Svc. award 1973), Ctrl. Surgical Assn., Internat. Surgical Soc., Soc. for Surgery Alimentary Tract. Avocations: boating, fishing. Home: Syracuse, NY. Died May 29, 2001.

ROGERS, PALMER, microbiology educator, researcher; b. N.Y.C., Sept. 7, 1927; s. Palmer David and Ruth Leslie (Clingan) R.; m. Mary Jean Giles, June 9, 1951 (div. Oct. 1974); children: David Bruce, Ethan Waid, Seth Palmer, Meredith; m. Donna Marie Beerninck Gunderson, Apr. 25, 1981. BS, Yale U., 1950; PhD, Johns Hopkins U., 1957. Rsch. asst. Johns Hopkins U., Balt., 1954-57; postdoctoral fellow Oak Ridge (Tenn.) Nat. Lab., 1957-59; asst. prof. biochemistry Ohio State U., Columbus, 1959-62; assoc. prof. microbiology U. Minn., Mpls., 1962-67, prof., from 1968. Spl. fellow Max Planck Inst. Med. Rsch., Heidelberg, Fed. Republic Germany, 1972-73; asst. program mgr. energy bioscis. Dept. Energy, Washington, 1980, cons. div. energy bioscis., 1980-81; program mgr. alcohol fuels program USDA, Washington, 1990. Editor: (symposium) Basic Biology of New Developments in Biotechnology, 1983; mem. editorial bd. Jour. Bacteriology, 1975-82; contbr. articles to Applied Environ. Microbiology, Jour. Bacteriology. Bd. dirs. Univ. Episcopal Ctr., Mpls., 1976-78. Lt. (j.g.) USN, 1947-53. Fellow NIH, 1956, 57, spl. fellow in rsch., 1972-73; fellow Am. Cancer Soc., 1957-59. Fellow AAAS; mem. Am. Soc. for Microbiology, Am. Soc. for Biochemistry and Molecular Biology, Soc. for Indsl. Microbiology, Phi Beta Kappa, Sigma Xi. Democrat. Achievements include research on mechanism of regulation of Argiuine biosynthesis in Eschericlum coli, regulation of solvent fermentation of Clostridium acetobutylicum. Home: Minneapolis, Minn. Died May 6, 2002.

ROGERS, STEPHEN, newspaper publisher; b. Lansing, Mich., Feb. 24, 1912; s. Anthony and Anna (Kruszewska) R.; m. Athenia A. Andros, Oct. 19, 1935; children: Stephen A., Christopher A., Elizabeth A. AB, Mich. State Coll., 1933; LLD (hon.), Syracuse U., 1988. Writer Detroit Times, 1934-35; copy editor N.Y. Herald-Tribune (European edit.), Paris, France, 1936-37; spl. writer Newark Ledger, 1937-38; editorial writer, city editor Long Island Daily Press, 1938-41; editor Long Island Star-Jour., 1941-55; pub. Post Standard, Syracuse, N.Y., 1955-58, Herald-Journal, Herald-Am.,

Syracuse; and pres. The Herald Co., 1958—. Dir. N.Y. Dental Service Corp., N.Y.C., Mchts. Nat. Bank; pres. Met. Devel. Assn., 1980—. Bd. dirs. Crouse-Irving Hosp., Syracuse. Mem. N.Y. State Pubs. Assn. (pres. 1963), Am. Newspaper Pubs. Assn. Roman Catholic. Died Nov. 14, 2002.

ROGERS, WARREN JOSEPH, JR., journalist; b. New Orleans, May 6, 1922; s. Warren Joseph and Rose Agatha (Tennyson) R.; m. Hilda Kenny, Dec. 23, 1943 (dec.); children: Patricia Ann, Sean; m. Alla Bilajiw, Dec. 26, 1973; 1 son, Michael (dec.). Student, Tulane U., 1940-41, La. State U., 1951. Copy boy, cub reporter New Orleans Tribune, 1939-41; copyreader, columnist New Orleans Item, 1945-47; reporter A.P., Baton Rouge, 1947-51, Washington, 1951-53, diplomatic corr., 1953-59; mil., fgn. affairs corr. assignments abroad Wash. Bur. N.Y. Herald Tribune, 1959-63; chief Washington corr. Hearst Newspapers, assignments abroad, 1963-66; Washington editor LOOK mag., 1966-69, chief, 1969-70; mil., fgn. affairs corr. Washington bur. Los Angeles Times, 1970-71; Washington columnist Chgo. Tribune-N.Y. News syndicate, 1971-73; v.p. pub. affairs Nat. Forest Products Assn., Washington, 1973-76; editorial dir. Plus Publs., Washington, 1977-78, v.p., editor-in-chief, 1978-79; free-lance, 1979—. Washington bur. chief The Trib of N.Y., 1977-78; editor White House Weekly, 1981-89; exec. editor Associated Features, Inc., Washington editor, 1992—; editor This Week in the White House, 1989-90, Georgetown Courier, 1991-92; bd. dirs. Nat. Press Found., Internet Guide, Inc.; founder Robert F. Kennedy Journalism awards; lectr. presdl. politics, mil. and fgn. affairs. Author: The Floating Revolution, 1962, Outpost of Freedom, 1965, (with others) An Honorable Profession: A Tribute to Robert F. Kennedy, 1968, (with Paul Watson) Sea Shepherd, 1982, When I think of Bobby: A Personal Memoir of the Kennedy Years, 1993. Served with USMCR, 1941-45. Recipient citation Overseas Press Club N.Y., 1963, Disting. Svc. award Nat. Press Found., 1991. Mem.: Nat. Press (pres. 1972), Federal City Club, Gridiron Club, Washington Ind. Writers. Home: Washington, DC. Died Aug. 31, 2003.

ROGERSON, CONSTANCE JEAN, guidance counselor; b. Staples, Minn., May 17, 1921; d. John Frank and Nina (Hagen) Grace; m. Richard T. Rogerson, May 28, 1944 (div.); children: Thomas, Richard, John. BA in Chemistry, Linfield Coll., McMinnville, Oreg., 1943; postgrad., Fla. State U., 1960-63, Ga. So. Coll., 1968-69. Instr. Everett (Wash.) Jr. Coll., 1944-47, W.Va. U., Morgantown, 1947-49; elem. tchr. Hermiston (Oreg.) Schs., 1950-58; tchr. math. Duval County Schs., Jacksonville, Fla., 1959-60, counselor, from 1961, ret., 1992. Vol. counselor Duval County, 1992—; instr. parenting skills Fla. Jr. Coll., Jacksonville, 1968-82. Grantee Fla. Dept. Edn., 1975-76. Mem. Duval Tchrs. United (exec. bd. 1989-91), Delta Kappa Gamma (pres. 1964-68), Kappa Delta Pi. Republican. Avocations: ceramics, classical music, poetry. Home: Jacksonville, Fla. Died Jan. 29, 1999.

ROHMER, LEONARD, psychotherapist; b. N.Y.C., Apr. 13, 1916; s. Joseph Rohmer and Sonia (Portnoy) Oberstein; m. Mildred Holzer, Aug. 23, 1936; children: Judith, Daniel. B Social Sci. magna cum laude, CCNY, 1941; MSW, U. Pitts., 1943. Cert. social worker, cert. for ins. reimbursement, N.Y. Casework supr. Jewish Social Svc. Bur., Pitts., 1946-48; unit supr. Jewish Family Svc., N.Y.C., 1948-56; exec. dir. Westchester Jewish Community Svcs., White Plains, N.Y., 1957-81; psychotherapist Whitehill Counseling Svc., Yorktown Heights, N.Y., from 1981. Assoc. prof. casework NYU, N.Y.C., 1960-62; mem. adv. com. schs. social work Fordham U., NYU, Columbia U., Yeshiva U.; chmn. com. on children Westchester Dept. Mental Health; presenter profl. confs. Contbr. articles and book revs. to profl. jours. Bd. dirs. Westchester Jewish Community Svcs., Hartsdale, 1983—; mem. allocations com. United Way Putnam, Carmel, N.Y., 1987—; chmn. fin. com., past mem. bd. dirs. Three Arrows Coop. Soc., Putnam Valley, N.Y. With AUS, 1944-46. Recipient Lehman prize Lehman Prize Found., 1968; Leonard Rohmer Day designated by Westchester Legislature, 1981. Fellow Am. Orthopsychiat. Assn., Am. Group Psychotherapy Assn.; mem. NASW (past chmn. com. on inquiry N.Y. State chpt., Disting. Svc. award 1981), Acad. Cert. Social Workers, Phi Beta Kappa. Jewish. Avocations: outdoor activities, hi fi buff, classical music, gardening. Home: Goshen, NY. Died Dec. 30, 2001.

ROLAND, BRENDA, medical/surgical and mental health nurse; b. Gainesville, Tex., Nov. 1, 1950; d. George W. Jr. and Joyce (Moore) R. Diploma, BS, Cameron U., Lawton, Okla., 1978; student, North Tex. State U., Denton. RN. Charge nurse, mental health and med.-surg. Med. Plaza Hosp., Sherman, Tex.; staff nurse in mental health Brookhaven Hosp., Dallas; med.-surg. staff nurse Texoma Med. Ctr., Denison, Tex. Mem. Nat. Profl. Psychiat. Nurses Am. Home: Whitesboro, Tex. Deceased.

ROLFE, MICHAEL N. management consulting firm executive; b. Chgo., Sept. 9, 1937; s. Mark Alexander and Antoinette (Wittgenstein) R.; m. Judith Mary Lewis, June 16, 1959; children— Andrew, Lisa, James AB in Econs., U. Mich., 1959; MBA, U. Chgo., 1996. Sales staff Lewis Co., Northbrook, Ill., 1961-62; systems mgmt. staff Brunswick Corp., Chgo., 1962-68; v.p. Kearney Mgmt. Cons., Chgo., 1968-81; ptnr. KPMG/Peat Marwick, Chgo., 1981-92; dir. Keystone Group, Evanston, Ill., 1992-99. Author: AMA Management Handbook, 1969 Bd. dirs. Common, Chgo., 1972-75, U. Chgo. Cancer Rsch., 1985-88, Am. Cancer Soc., Chgo., 1985—; trustee Michael Reese Med. Ctr., 1986-91; pres. Sch. Bd. Dist. 113, Highland Park, Ill., 1977-83, Sch.Dist. 113 Found., 1993—; mem. Am. Jewish Com., 1996—. Lt. (j.g.) USNR, 1959-61. Mem.: Northmoor Country (Highland Park); Standard (Chgo.). Home: Highland Park, Ill. Died Mar. 31, 1999.

ROLLINS, JOHN W., JR., transportation executive, environmental services administrator; b. 1942; BBA, So. Meth. U., 1942; MBA, Northwestern U., 1965. With Rollins Truck Leasing Corp., Wilmington, Del., from 1965, sr. v.p., 1973, exec. v.p., 1975, pres., COO, 1975; with Rollins Eviron. Svcs. Inc., Wilmington, from 1982, chmn. bd. dirs., 1982, vice chmn., 1983, sr. vice chmn., 1988; with Matlack Systems Inc., Wilmington, from 1988, chmn. bd. dirs.; pres., CEO Rollins Truck Leasing Corp., from 2000. Deceased.

ROMAGOSA, ELMO LAWRENCE, retired clergyman, retired editor; b. Thibodaux, La., Jan. 11, 1924; s. Lawrence Gabriel and Lydie (Achee) R. Ed., St. Joseph Sem., Notre Dame Sem., New Orleans, 1947. Ordained priest Roman Cath. Ch., 1947. Asst. pastor, Cut Off, La., 1947-50, New Orleans, 1950-58; chaplain Ursuline Convent and Nat. Shrine Our Lady of Prompt Succor, 1958-63; pastor St. John's Ch., New Orleans, 1963-70; asst. dir. Soc. for Propagation of Faith, 1950-60, dir., 1962; communications dir. Archdiocese New Orleans, 1962; founding editor Clarion Herald newspaper, 1963-74; priest in residence Sts. Peter and Paul Ch., New Orleans, 1970-72; pastor Holy Trinity Ch., New Orleans, 1972-74, St. Rose of Lima Ch., New Orleans, 1974-76, St. Clement of Rome Ch., Metairie, La., 1976-84; chaplain Port of New Orleans, 1984-88; pastor Ch. of Infant Jesus, Harvey, La., from 1988. Nat. sec. Cath. Broadcasters Assn., 1963-65; mem. U.S. Cath. bishops subcoms. on Cath.-Jewish relations, 1965; named prelate of honor, 1980. Editor Airtime, 1963-64. Dir. Stella Maris Maritime Ctr., 1984-88; chaplain Harbor Police, Port of New Orleans, 1984-88; mem. Nat. Conf. Seafarers, 1984, pres., 1986—, mem. legal adv. com. Ctr. for Seafarers Rights, 1986; mem. Nat. Cath. Conf. for Seafarers, 1984, pres., 1986-88. Recipient First Place award for best editorial and best feature photo Press Club New Orleans, 1965, First Place award for best column Press Club New Orleans, 1972; named Prelate of Honor, Pope John II, 1980. Mem. Cath. Press Assn. (1st Place awards for gen. excellence 1963-65), Sociedad Espanola New Orleans (founding sec.-treas.), Equestrian Order of Holy Sepulchre of Jerusalem (knight 1978, knight comdr. 1983, master of ceremonies 1986, Gold Palms of Jerusalem medallion 1993). Republican. Home: Lafayette, La. Deceased.

ROMANTINI, IRIS C. special and adult education educator; b. Phila., Sept. 11, 1952; d. George H. Sr. and Iris (Barrett) Carter; m. Anthony Romantini, Jan. 14, 1984; children: Heather, Samantha. BS, Cheyney (Pa.) U., 1974; MEd, Antioch U., 1983. Cert. elem. and mentally retarded tchr., Pa. Teaching asst. Temple U., Phila.; tchr. Phila. Sch. Dist. Student and coop. tchr., 1990; mentor tchr. Pa. Tchr. Induction Program, 1990—; chmn. lower sch., 1992—; active Phila. Writing Project; mem. Adopt-A-Sch. Com., 1993. Teacher sponsor Homework Club, 1988—, Student Coun., 1990—. P.A.T.H./P.R.I.S.M. grantee, 1990-91; U. Pa. fellow, 1992-93. Mem. ASCD, Pa. Fedn. Tchrs., Black Women's Ednl. Alliance (South Jersey chpt.), Alpha Kappa Alpha (Svc. awards). Home: Sicklerville, NJ. Died Oct. 30, 2001.

ROMOND, JAMES, principal; Prin. La Salle Inst., Troy, N.Y., from 1981. Recipient Blue Ribbon Sch. award U.S. Dept. Edn., 1990-91. Deceased.

ROOT, MARGARET GOHEEN, public relations executive; b. Quinwood, W.Va., Mar. 27, 1937; d. Martin Richard and Maysel Irene (Brown) Goheen; m. Arthur Ross Sleasman, Jr., Mar. 6, 1959; 1 child, Christopher Squire; m. Stephen Noble Root, Aug. 27, 1970. AA, Towson State U., 1957; BA, U. Md., 1959; MA, Ball State U., 1983. Accredited in pub. rels. Pub. health info. officer Balt. County Dept. Health, Towson, Md., 1969-71; pub. info. officer State Ill., Springfield, 1971-72; dir. pub. rels. Mount Saint Vincent U., Halifax, N.S., Can., 1973-77; mgr. comm. Blue Cross & Blue Shield Iowa, Des Moines, 1977-78; asst. v.p. pub. rels. Ind. Nat. Bank, Indpls., 1978-82; v.p. corp. comm. Conn. Nat. Bank, Hartford, 1982-91; v.p. pub. rels. St. Francis Hosp. & Med. Ctr., Hartford, 1991-93; exec. dir. corp. comm. Tenneco, Inc., Houston, from 1993. Women's exec. com. Greater Hartford C. of C., 1992-93, comm. com., 1990, 93; exec. com. Conn. Jount Coun. Econ. Edn., Storrs, 1986-90; bd. dirs. Alley Theatre, Houston, 1994-95; bd. dirs. Stamford (Conn.) Theatre Works, 1996—, pres. bd., 1997—. Recipient Ohio State award Ohio State U., 1977, Merit award Can. Pub. Rels. Soc., 1977. Mem. Pub. Rels. Soc. Am. (chmn., vice chmn., sec. Northeast dist. 1986-88, pres., v.p., treas. Hoosier chpt. 1979-82). Home: Annapolis, Md. Deceased.

ROPER, BURNS WORTHINGTON, retired opinion research company executive; b. Creston, Iowa, Feb. 26, 1925; s. Elmo Burns and Dorothy Camille (Shaw) R.; m. Elizabeth Kellock, Feb. 7, 1945 (div.); children: Bruce, David, Douglas; m. Helen Gillette Lanagan, Dec. 26, 1958 (dec. Apr. 1990); 1 child, Candace Gillette; m. Helen Grinnell Page, Sept. 19, 1991. Hon. doctorate, Colgate U., 1996. Rsch. asst. Elmo Roper, N.Y.C., 1946-48, project dir., 1948-55; ptnr. Elmo Roper & Assocs., N.Y.C., 1955-66; pres., chmn. bd. Roper Rsch. Assocs., N.Y.C., 1967-70, The Roper Orgn., Inc., N.Y.C., 1970-93; exec. v.p. Roper Starch Worldwide, Mamaroneck, N.Y., 1981-94. Chmn. bd. The Roper Pub. Opinion Rsch. Ctr., Storrs, Conn., 1970-94, trustee 1947—. Contbr. numerous articles on polls to profl. jours., book chpts. Trustee Nat. Urban League, N.Y.C., 1955-64, UN Assn. Am., N.Y.C., 1964-97, Freedom House, N.Y.C., 1970-97. 1st lt. USAAF, 1943-45, ETO. Decorated DFC, Air medal with five oak leaf clusters. Mem. Am. Assn. Pub. Opinion Rsch. (nat. pres. 1982-83, award 1988), Nat. Coun. on Pub. Polls (bd. dirs. 1969—, chmn. bd. trustees 1980-93), Market Rsch. Coun. (pres. 1967-68, inducted into Hall of Fame 1990), Wings Club. Democrat. Home: Bourne, Mass. Died Jan. 20, 2003.

ROSE, BEATRICE BESTOR, retired teacher of English; b. Bakersfield, Calif., Feb. 10, 1915; d. Perry and Edna Altha (Weingart) Bestor; m. Herbert E. Rose, Aug. 31, 1982. BA, Grinnell Coll., 1936; MA in English, Wash. State Coll., 1939. Cert. secondary educator. Tchr. Wash. State Coll., Pullman, 1937-39; tchr. English Winterset (Iowa) Jr. High Sch., 1936-37, Portland, Oreg., 1939-41; hosp. worker ARC, Riverside, Calif., 1941-46; tchr. English Bakersfield (Calif.) High Sch., 1947-59, Arcadia (Calif.) High Sch., 1959-61, East Bakersfield High Sch., 1961-79; retired tchr., from 1979. Pres. Lori Brock Children's Mus., Bakersfield, 1983—; vol. 60+ Club of Calif. State U., Bakersfield. Home: Bakersfield, Calif. Died Jan. 26, 2001.

ROSE, DONALD L. physician, educator; b. St. Charles, Mo., July 20, 1911; s. William Albert and Estelle Mattie (Sherry) R.; m. Martha Jane Koontz, Mar. 6, 1937; children: Nancy Kathryn Rose Harling, William Donald. BA, U. Colo., 1933, MA, MD, 1936. Diplomate Am. Bd. Phys. Medicine and Rehab. Intern Miami Valley Hosp., Dayton, Ohio, 1936-37, resident, 1937-38; rsch. assoc. Kettering Inst. Med. Rsch., Dayton, 1938-41; asst. prof. sch. medicine Univ. Kans., Kansas City, 1947-49, assoc. prof., 1949-51, prof., 1951-74, prof. emeritus, from 1974. Cons. Phys. Med. Surgeon Gen.'s Office, Washington, 1957-65, nat. cons. USAF, 1959-61; bd. govs. Am. Bd. Phys. Medicine and Rehab., Rochester, Minn., 1957-67. Contbr. chpt. An Atlas of Amputations, 1947, Postgraduate Medicine and Surgery, 1951, Therapeutic Heat, 1958. Med. advisor NFIP Wyandotte County, Kansas City, 1947-60, Johnson County chpt., 1950-60, MDA Kansas City, 1965-74. Fellow Baruch Found., Boston, 1946-47. Mem. AMA, Am. Acad. Phys. Medicine and Rehab. (pres. 1953-54, Disting. Clin. award 1983), Am. Congress Rehab. Medicine (pres. 1957-58), Kans. Med. Soc., Wyandotte County Med. Soc. Republican. Methodist. Avocations: golf, boating. Home: Bella Vista, Ark. Died Jan. 10, 2004.

ROSE, JOAN B. former business owner; m. Leonard Rose. BA in English Lit., Radcliffe Coll., 1952; grad., Simmons Coll. Asst. to exec. dir. Nat. Braille Press; founder, pres., CEO Braille Inc., East Falmouth, Mass., 1972-2000; ret., 2000. Classical piano profl. tchr. Vol. braillist, tchr. braille transcribing. Died 2003.

ROSE, JOHN A. former government executive; b. Winchester, Ky., June 1, 1940; s. James Alex and Leona (Coldiron) R.; children: Debbie, Susan, Stephanie. BS in Math., Ea. Ky. U., Richmond, 1963. Senator State of Ky., Frankfort, 1978-84, asst. pres. pro tempore, 1985-86, pres. pro tempore, from 1987. Co-chmn. Legis. Rsch. Com., Frankfort, 1987—. Named Outstanding Young Farmer of Yr. Ky. Young Farmers Assn.; recipient Disting Svc. award Ky. Cir. Judges Assn., 1981, EKU's Disting. Alumni award Ea. Ky. U., 1987. Mem. Clark County Young Farmers Assn., Ky. Walking Horses Assn., Jaycees. Democrat. Methodist. Deceased.

ROSE, ROBERT LEONARD, newspaperman; b. Detroit, Apr. 21, 1924; s. Leonard Cecil and Mildred Ernestine (Brothers) R.; m. Beverly Bain McKee, Aug. 1, 1947 (dec. Sept. 1978); 1 son, Michael; m. LuNeill Divine, Aug. 30, 1980. Student, U. Colo., 1941-42, Drexel Inst. Tech., 1942-43, U. Del., 1943, U. Denver, 1947. Reporter (Daily Plainsman), Huron, S.D., 1947-49; bur. mgr. U.P., St. Paul-Mpls., 1949-53, Des Moines, 1953-56; reporter-rewriteman, asst. city editor Chgo. Daily News, 1956-60, 1st asst. editor, 1961-63, city editor, 1964-66, West Coast bur. chief, 1966-78; polit. editor Spokane Spokesman-Rev., 1979-80, city editor, 1981-83, Washington bur. chief, 1983—87. Served with AUS, 1942-46. Mem. Sigma Chi. Clubs: Press, LaSalle St. Rod and Gun (Chgo.). Lodges: Masons, Shriners, Elks. Episcopalian. Died Aug. 6, 2001.

ROSE, RUTH ORMSBY, retired English educator; b. Chgo. d. John Alexander and Nellie Arnold Rose. BA, Smith Coll., 1926; MA, Harvard U., 1927, PhD, 1929. Instr. English Coker Coll., Hartsville, S.C., So. Ill. Tchrs. Coll., Wheaton Coll., Norton, Mass., Milwaukee Downer, Western Coll., Oxford, Ohio; prof., head dept. English MacMurray Coll., Jacksonville, Ill.; ret., 1973. Home: Newtonville, Mass. Died July 29, 2002.

ROSE, STEPHEN JAY, advertising company executive; b. N.Y.C., Nov. 24, 1925; s. Herman and Harriet (Greenspan) R.; m. Margitta Braun; children by previous marriage: John Stephen, Daniel Jay. AB, Univ. Heights Coll., NYU, 1948. Dir. radio-TV-rec. Sol Hurok, N.Y.C., 1948-57; mktg. dir. Revlon, Inc., N.Y.C., 1957-60; account exec. Ogilvie & Mather, N.Y.C., 1960-61; v.p. mktg. Maradel, N.Y.C., 1961-63, J.B. Williams, N.Y.C., 1963-65; with AC&R Advt., Inc., N.Y.C., 1965-87, exec. v.p., sec., 1965-72, CEO, chmn. bd., 1972—87, chmn. exec. com.; chmn. bd., CEO Saatchi & Saatchi Advt. Affiliates, N.Y.C., 1987. Chmn. AC&R Pub. Relations, Inc., AC&R Hellas, Athens, Greece; pres. Ted Bates Internat. Ops., 1977; dir. Ted Bates Advt., Inc. Served with USNR, 1942-46. Mem.: Orienta Yacht. Home: Ancram, NY. Died Sept. 30, 2003.

ROSE, TED, graphic designer; b. Milw., Aug. 13, 1940; s. Francis John and Ann (Voelkel) R.; m. Polly Towers, July 1, 1967; children: Jesse, Molly. BFA, U. Ill., 1962. Artist, illustrator, book designer Kalmbach Pubs. Co., Milw., 1959-63; cartographer City of Santa Fe, 1967-69, art dir., 1971-76, Eberline Inst Co., Santa Fe, 1969-71; graphic designer Hod Carriers Ink, Santa Fe, from 1971; art dir. Stereophile Mag., Santa Fe, 1985-86. Watercolor artist, 1954-60, 80—; graphic cons. Los Alamos (N.Mex.) Nat. Lab., 1978-80; instr. color graphics Santa Fe Community Coll., 1984-85. Designer, artist (calendar) The Chili Line, 1984; photographer N.Am. Steam Locomotives, 1955-62; photo exhibits, 1973, 76. Graphic designer Santa Fe Rape Crisis Ctr., 1983, Santa Fe Symphony, 1985-87, Santa Fe Dance Found., 1987—. Served with U.S. Army, 1963-65, Vietnam. Mem. No. N.Mex. Advt. Fedn. (pres. 1987, graphic design awards 1982, 83, 84, 86,87, print advt. awards 1982, 83, 84, 86), Am. Advt. Fedn. (print advt. awards 1982, 85), N.Mex. Watercolor Soc., Nat. Assn. R.R. Passengers, Santa Fe C. of C. Democrat. Avocation: photography. Home: Santa Fe, N.Mex. Died July 26, 2002.

ROSEN, CHARLES ABRAHAM, electrical engineer, consultant; b. Toronto, Ont., Can., Dec. 7, 1917; came to U.S., 1950; s. Morris and Ida (Muscet) R.; m. Blanche Jacobson, May 15, 1941; children: Hal, Steven, Naomi, Sema. BEE, Cooper Union, 1940; M in Engring., McGill U., 1950; PhD, Syracuse U., 1957. Founder, CEO Electrolabs Registered, Montreal, Can., 1946-50; semiconductor designer GE, Syracuse, N.Y., 1950-52, mgr. dielectrics group, 1952-57; mgr. applied physics SRI Internat., Menlo Park, Calif., 1957-62, dir. artificial intelligence, 1962-78; founder, chmn. Machine Intelligence Corp., Sunnyvale, Calif., 1980-85; co-founder, dir. Ridge Vineyards, Cupertino, Calif., 1962-87; CEO Cultured Foods Corp., San Francisco, 1988-92, also bd. dirs.; pvt. practice cons. Atherton, Calif., from 1988. Cons. Ricoh Rsch., Menlo Park, 1989-2001, Food Machinery, Sunnyvale, 1989-2001; adv. com. Nat. Rsch. Coun., Washington, 1990-92; dir. Techniquip Corp., Livermore, Calif., 1995—, Electric Mobility Sys., Los Altos, Calif., 1996-2000. Co-author Principles of Transistor Circuits, 1953, Solid State Dielectric Design, 1959; contbr. articles to profl. jours.; patentee in field. P.O. Air Force, Can., 1944-45. Recipient Engelberger award Robot Inst. Am., 1982. Fellow IEEE (Taylor award 1975), Am. Assn. Artificial Intelligence; mem. AAAS, Am. Physical Soc. Avocations: winemaking, horticulture, hydroponics, inventions. Home: Atherton, Calif. Died Dec. 8, 2002.

ROSENBAUM, EDWYNNE C. "POLLY", state legislator; b. Ollie, Iowa, Sept. 4, 1899; m. William G. Rosenbaum BA, U. Colo.; MEd, U. So. Calif. Former tchr., stenographer, gen. office worker copper and asbestos industrys, law, real estate appraisal, savings and loan, dental receptionist; former county clk. and recs. offices; mem. Ariz. Ho. of Reps., 1949—94, mem. appropriations com., edn. com., rules com., human resources and aging com., rules com. Mem. Gila County Tuberc Control Bd. Mem. Globe Bus. and Profl. Women's Club, Zonta Internat., Eastern Star (Winkleman chpt., past matron). Democrat. Died Dec. 28, 2003.

ROSENBERG, LEONARD See RANDALL, TONY

ROSENBERG, WILLIAM, retired food chain executive, horse breeder; b. Boston, 1916; Founder, chmn. emeritus Dunkin' Donuts Inc., Randolph, Mass.; founder N.H. Sire Stakes Program. Past chmn., trustee N.H. Standardbred Breeders and Owners Devel. Agy.; founder, past owner Wilrose Farms, Standardbred breeding facility, East Kingston, Kingston, N.H.; donated William Rosenberg chair of Dana Farber Cancer Inst. to Harvard U., 1988. Named to New Eng. Harness Writer's Hall of Fame Mem. Internat. Franchise Assn. (founder, past pres. Hall of Fame 1980), Am. Standardbred Breeders Assn. (dir.), New Eng. Standardbred Breeders and Owners Assn. (founder, past pres.), Standardbred Breeders and Owners Assn. N.H., N.Am. Harness Racing Mktg. Assn. (founder, chmn. 1983). Wilrose Farms donated to U. N.H. as William Rosenberg Conf. Center for continuing study of franchising and small bus., 1980. Died Sept. 20, 2002.

ROSENBLATT, LESTER, naval architect; b. N.Y.C., Apr. 13, 1920; s. Mandell and Rosa (Wolff) R. BS, CCNY; BS in Naval Architecture and Marine Engring., U. Mich., 1942; DSc (hon.), Webb Inst. Naval Architecture, 1993. Registered profl. engr., N.Y., Mass. Naval architect John H. Wells, Inc., 1942-47; naval acrhitect USN Pearl Harbor Navy Yard, 1944-46; co-founder, chmn., chief exec. officer, naval architect M. Rosenblatt & Son Inc., Naval Architects and Marine Engrs., N.Y.C. and throughout U.S., 1947-2000. Designer maj. ships, U.S. and fgn. Contbr. numerous tech. papers. Trustee (hon.) Webb Inst. Naval Architecture; mem. United Jewish Appeal N.Y., Maritime Friends of Seamen's Ch. Inst. Recipient U. Mich. Sesquicentennial award in ship design, 1967, 1st Rosenblatt-Mich. award, U. Mich., 1992; Admiral's honoree SUNY Maritime Coll., 1992. Fellow Soc. Naval Architects and Engrs. (pres. 1978-80, nat. chmn. membership com. 1964-78, mem. coun. and exec. com., Land medalist, hon. mem., chmn. N.Y. sect. 1961-62); mem. Am. Bur. Shipping, Bur. Veritas, Am. Soc. Naval Engrs. (Harold Saunders award 1987), Marine Soc. N.Y. (hon.), Internat. Maritime Hall of Fame, Soc. Marine Cons., N.Y. Yacht Club, Tau Beta Pi. Home: New York, NY. Deceased.

ROSENBLUTH, MARSHALL NICHOLAS, physicist; b. Albany, N.Y., Feb. 5, 1927; s. Robert and Margaret (Sondhein) Rosenbluth; m. Sara Unger, Feb. 6, 1979; children from previous marriage: Alan Edward, Robin Ann, Mary Louise, Jean Pamela. BA, Harvard U., 1945; MS, U. Chgo., 1947, PhD, 1949. Instr. Stanford U., 1949—50; staff mem. Los Alamos Sci. Lab., 1950—56; sr. research adviser Gen. Atomic Corp., San Diego, 1956—67; prof. U. Calif., San Diego, 1960—67, Inst. for Advanced Study, Princeton (N.J.) U., 1967—80; dir. Inst. for Fusion Studies, U. Tex., 1980-87; prof. U. Calif., San Diego, 1987—92; former chief U.S. scientist Internat. Thermonuclear Engring. Reactor. Lectr. with rank prof. in astrophys. scis. Princeton U., also vis. sr. research physicist, Plasma Physics Lab., 1967—80; Andrew D. White vis. prof. Cornell U., 1976; cons. AEC, NASA, Inst. Def. Analysis. Served with USNR, 1944—46. Recipient E.O. Lawrence award, 1964, Albert Einstein award, 1967, Maxwell prize, 1976, Enrico Fermi award, Dept. Energy, 1985, Nat. medal of Sci., Pres. U.S., 1998, Disting. Assoc. award, U.S. Dept. Energy, 2002, Hannes Alfven prize, European Phys. Soc., 2002. Mem.: NAS, Am. Acad. Arts and Scis., Am. Phys. Soc. (Nicholson medal for humanitarian svc. 2000), Am. Philos. Soc. Home: La Jolla, Calif. Died Sept. 28, 2003.

ROSENKOETTER, GERALD EDWIN, engineering and construction company executive; b. St. Louis, Mar. 16, 1927; s. Herbert Charles and Edna Mary (Englege) R.; m. Ruth June Beekman, Sept. 10, 1949; children: Claudia Ruth, Carole Lee. BSCE, Washington U., St. Louis, 1951; MSCE, Sever Inst. Tech., St. Louis, 1957. Registered profl. engr. Colo., Del., D.C., Fla., Ga., Idaho, Kans., Mass., Mich., Mo., N.C., N.J., Ohio, Pa., Tex., Utah, Wis., Ind. Sr. structural engr. Sverdrup & Parcel, Inc., St. Louis, 1951-56, project engr., 1956-60, engring. mgr. Denver, 1960-62; project mgr. Sverdrup & Parcel & Assocs., St. Louis, 1962-69, chief engr., 1969-74, v.p., 1974-80; pres., CEO SPCM, Inc., St. Louis, 1980-85; exec. v.p. Sverdrup Corp., St. Louis, 1985-88, vice-chmn., 1988-93; pres., CEO Sverdrup Hydro, Inc., 1988-93; engr. and fin. cons. Sarasota, from 1993. Assoc. prof. Washington U., 1955-60; ptnr. 3 Sverdrup Partnerships, 1977-93; expert witness Sverdrup & Parcel & Assocs., 1970-75; cons. engring. and constrn. projects, 1993—; bd. dirs. 17 corps. Councilman City of Berkeley, Mo., 1956-58, councilman-at-large, 1958-60, chmn. city planning and zoning com., 1963-65; dir. Conservatory and Sch. Arts, St. Louis, 1989-92. Sgt. U.S. Army, 1945-46. Engrs. Club of St. Louis scholar, 1950. Mem. ASCE (chmn. continuing edn. 1965-66, named Outstanding Sr. Engring. Student 1951), Bent Tree Country Club (Sarasota, Fla.). Lutheran. Avocations: golfing, travel. Died May 2002.

ROSENTHAL, AARON, management consultant; b. N.Y.C., July 12, 1914; s. Zelig and Sarah (Shapinsky) R.; m. Edna Blanche Finkel, Sept. 3, 1940; children— Stephen Mark, Marjorie Ann. BA, Coll. City N.Y., 1934, MS in Edn, 1935; postgrad., Georgetown U. Law Sch., 1937-39, Am. U., 1950-53. Dir. Internal Audit Service, VA, Washington, 1953-58; controller VA, 1958-60; dir. financial mgmt. NASA, 1960-61; comptroller NSF, 1961-69, Nat. Acad. Scis., 1969-76; exec. cons. Coopers & Lybrand. Fin. cons. to Ctr. for Devel. and Population Activities; fin. and mgmt. cons. to Joint Oceanographic Instns. Inc.; U.S. rep. supr. Radiation Effects Rsch. Found., Hiroshima, Japan; mem. nat. adv. coun. nat. Ctr. for Higher Edn. Mgmt. Systems; bd. dirs. TCOA, Inc., Manchester Center, Vt. Trustee Sci. Service Inc. Served with AUS, 1943-45. Recipient Exceptional Service award VA, 1960; Merit citation Nat. Civil Service League, 1957; Distinguished Service award NSF, 1969 Fellow AAAS; mem. Am. Soc. Pub. Adminstrn., Assn. Govt. Accts. Home: Washington, DC. Died Nov. 2003.

ROSENTHAL, FRANZ, language educator, educator; b. Berlin, Aug. 31, 1914; came to U.S., 1940, naturalized, 1943; s. Kurt W. and Elsa (Kirschstein) R. PhD, U. Berlin, 1935; DHL (hon.), Hebrew Union Coll., 1987; PhD (hon.), Hebrew U., 1987, Tel Aviv U., 1992, U. Tübingen, 1993, Columbia U., 1996. Asst. prof. Semitic langs. Hebrew Union Coll., Cin., 1940-48; prof. Arabic, U. Pa., 1948-56; Louis M. Rabinowitz prof. Yale U., 1956-67, Sterling prof. Near Eastern langs., 1967-85, prof. emeritus, 1985—2003. Author: Aramaistische Forschung, 1939, Technique and Approach of Muslim Scholarship, 1947, Hist. of Muslim Historiography, 1952, Humor in Early Islam, 1956, Ibn Khaldun, The Muqaddimah, 1958, The Muslim Concept of Freedom, 1960, Fortleben der Antike im Islam, 1965, Knowledge Triumphant, 1970, The Herb: Hashish versus Medieval Muslim Society, 1971, Gambling in Islam, 1975, Sweeter than Hope, 1983, History of al-Tabari, vols. 1 and 38, 1985, 89, Muslim Intellectual and Social History: A Collection of Essays, 1990. Served with AUS, OSS, 1943-45. Fellow AAAS, Brit. Acad. (corr.); mem. Am. Philos. Soc., Am. Oriental Soc. (pres. 1964-65), Accademia Nazionale dei Lincei, Société Asiatique (hon.), Deutsche Morgenländische Ges (hon.). Home: Hamden, Conn. Died Apr. 8, 2003.

ROSENTHAL, HAROLD LESLIE, biochemistry educator; b. Elizabeth, N.J., Mar. 26, 1922; s. Isadore and Sophia (Shapiro) R.; m. Rose Schwartz, June 7, 1947; children: Jenifer Ann, Pamela Susan. B.Sc., U. N. Mex., 1944; PhD, Rutgers U., 1951. Rsch. asst. Rutgers U., New Brunswick, N.J., 1948-51; instr. Tulane U., New Orleans, 1951-53; chief biochemist Rochester Gen. Hosp., N.Y., 1953-58; prof. biomed. scis. Washington U., St. Louis, 1958-87, prof. emeritus, from 1987. Vis. scientist Minerva Found., Finland, 1966, Nat. Acad. Sci., Hungary, 1974. Served with USN, 1943-46 Fellow AAAS; mem. Am. Chem. Soc. (emeritus), Am. Inst. Nutrition, Am. Soc. for Biochemistry and Molecular Biology, Sigma Xi. Avocations: gardening; oenology. Home: Saint Louis, Mo. Died Nov. 2002.

ROSENTHAL, LEIGHTON A. aviation company executive; b. Buffalo, Jan. 27, 1915; s. Samuel and Sadie (Dosberg) R.; m. Honey Rousuck, June 30, 1940; children: Cynthia, Jane. Student, Phila. Textile Sch.; grad. Wharton Sch., U. Pa.; hon. doctorate, Cleve. Coll. Jewish Studies, 1973. Pres. Cleve. Overall Co., 1956-61, Work Wear Corp., 1961-86, The Purity Uniform Service Inc., 1986-89, Lars Mgmt. div. Purity Uniform Service Inc., 1986-89, Lars Aviation Inc., from 1990. Chmn. Architecture Commn., City of Palm Beach, 1988-96. Trustee Jewish Cmty. Fedn. Cleve., Leighton A. Rosenthal Family Found.; bd. dirs. Ohio Motorists Assn. Fellow Am. Assn. Jewish Edn., Oakwood Club, Union Club, Poinciana Club, Marks Club, Annabels Club, Doubles Club, Harmonie Club. Deceased.

ROSENZWEIG, CAROL BARBARA, writer, art publisher; b. N.Y.C. d. Sidney and Sadie (Greenberg) Kupersmith; m. Saul Louis Rosenzweig, Feb. 11, 1961; children: Davy, Laurance. BA, Pa. State U., 1951. Acct. exec., v.p. Pub. Relations Research Inc., Pitts., 1951-60; freelance writer St. Louis, Los Angeles, Palm Springs, Calif., 1961-80; pres. Rosebranch, Inc., Los Angeles, 1980-86, Artist Editions Ltd., Beverly Hills, Calif., from 1985. V.p. R.Z. Group, Inc., Los Angeles, 1986—. Author: (TV shows) House Husband, 1983, 21 Days of America, 1985 (Heritage award), Women of the World, 1987. Chmn. emeritus Young Talent award com. Los Angeles County Mus. Art, 1985—; pres. Carol and Saul Rosenzweig Family Found., Los Angeles, 1987. Mem. Women in Film, Royal TV Soc., Modern and Contemp. Art Council (bd. dirs. 1976-85). Clubs: Mountaingate (Los Angeles). Jewish. Avocations: running, travel, poetry. Died May 20, 2002.

ROSENZWEIG, OSCAR JOHN, obstetrician, gynecologist; b. Novisad, Yugoslavia, July 9, 1922; came to U.S., 1949; s. John A. Rosenzweig and Natalia D. Gillich. MD, U. Vienna, Austria, 1947. Diplomate Am. Bd. Ob-Gyn. Resident ob-gyn Landeskrankenhaus, Salzburg, Austria, 1947-49; intern Luth. Deaconess Hosp., Chgo., 1949-50, resident ob-gyn, 1950-52, Chgo. Maternity Ctr., 1952-53, U. Ill., Alton, 1953-54; practice medicine specializing in ob-gyn Chgo., from 1957; clin. assoc. prof. ob/gyn U. Ill. Bd. dirs. Ravenswood Hosp. Med. Ctr., Bank Ravenswood; chmn. bd. dirs. Ravenswood Pvt. Paid Med. Group. Served to maj. USAF, 1955-57. Decorated Cross of Merit (Fed. Republic Germany). Mem. ACS, Ama, Am. Coll. Ob-Gyn, Am. Coll. Abdominal Surgeons, Internat. Coll. Surgeons. Lodges: Order of St. John Jerusalem (knight). Home: Chicago, Ill. Deceased.

ROSICKY, BOHUMIR, parasitologist, educator; b. Brno, Czech Republic, Apr. 18, 1922; Dr.rer.nat., DSc, Charles U., Prague, Czechoslovakia. Mem. staff Rovnost (Brno daily paper), 1945-46; chem. rsch. worker, lab. head, chem. industry, 1947-50; specialist Ctrl. Biol. Inst., Prague, 1950-53; head dept. parasitology Biol. Inst., Czechoslovak Acad. Scis., Prague, 1954-61; dir. Inst. Parasitology, Prague, 1962-80, Inst. Hygiene and Epidemiology, 1980-90; prof. natural scis. Comenius U., Bratislava, from 1965. Dep. Czech Nat. Coun., 1969-91, mem. presidium, from 1969; WHO cons., India, 1964-65; mem. Joint WHO/FAO UN Panel of Zoonoses. Author: Czechoslovak Fauna-Aphaniptera, 1957; co-author: Modern Insecticides, 1951, Parasitologische Arbeitsmethoden, 1965, Med. Entomology and Environ., 1989, Probleme der Stadthygiene-Tierische Umwelt, 1992, Salmonelloses, 1994; author numerous papers on ecology, taxonomy, entomology, med. zoology and parasitology. Decorated Order Cyril and Method, Bulgaria, Krzyz Oficerski, Poland, Order Labor; recipient State prize, 1954, G. Mendel Gold medal, 1970; co-recipient Klement Gottwald State prize, 1956, 72. Mem. Czechoslovak Acad. Scis. (academician 1970-92, v.p. 1970-77, Silver plaque 1972, Gold 1987), Bulgarian Acad. Scis., Polish Acad. Scis. (corr., pres. 3d and 8th Cong. of Acarology). Died Apr. 2, 2002.

ROSOW, JEROME MORRIS, institute executive; b. Chgo., Dec. 2, 1919; s. Morris and Mary (Cornick) R.; m. Rosalyn Levin, Sept. 28, 1941; children: Michael, Joel. BA cum laude, U. Chgo., 1942. Position classification analyst Dept. Army, Washington, 1942-43, orgn. and methods examiner, asst. mgr. wage and salary div., 1948-51; dir. compensation War Assets Adminstrn., Washington, 1946-48; dir. policy, salary stblzn. bd. Econ. Stblzn. Agy., 1952-53; with Creole Petroleum Corp. subs. Standard Oil N.J., Caracas, Venezuela, 1953-55; exec. mem., coord. compensation, indsl. rels. rsch. Standard Oil N.J., N.Y.C., 1955-66; mgr. employee relations dept. ESSO Europe, Inc., London, 1966-69; asst. sec. labor for policy, evaluation and rsch. Dept. Labor, 1969-71; planning mgr. pub. affairs. dept. Exxon Corp., 1971-77; founder, chmn., CEO Work in Am. Inst., 1975—2002. Cons. fed. pay plans U.S. Bur. Budget and U.S. CSC, 1964; mem. bus. adv. rsch com. Bur. Labor Stats., 1958-65; chmn. coun. of compensation Nat. Indsl. Conf. Bd., 1959-66; assoc. seminar on labor, Columbia U., 1961-91; dir. N.Y.C. Vocat. Adv. Svc., 1961-69, chmn. fin. com., 1962-65; mem. White House Working Group on Welfare Reform, 1969-71; chmn. cabinet com. White House Conf. Children and Youth, 1970-71; chmn. subcabinet com. nat. growth policy; U.S. del OECD Ministers Conf., Paris, 1970, 74; vice-chmn. Nat. Productivity Commn., 1971; chmn. tech. experts multinat. indsl. relations OECD, Paris, 1972; chmn. subcom. manpower and social affairs; chmn. Pres.'s Adv. Com. Fed. Pay, 1971-83; adviser Pres. U.S.; chmn. Am. assembly The Changing World at Work. Editor: American Men in Government, 1949, The Worker and the Job: Coping with Change, 1974; (with Clark Kerr) Work in America: The Decade Ahead, 1979, Productivity: Prospects for Growth, 1981, Views from the Top, 1985, Teamwork: Joint Labor-

Management Programs in America, 1986, Global Marketplace, 1988, Training-The Competitive Edge, 1988, Allies in Education Reform, 1988; contbr. articles to profl. jours. Bd. dirs. Young Audiences; trustee Nat. Com. Employment of Youth; former adviser Com. Econ. Devel., Nat. Planning Assn.; mem. Nat. Commn. Productivity and Quality of Work, 1975; former v.p. Population Edn. Inc.; mem. Study Group Work and Edn. in China, 1978; cons. comptroller gen. U.S., 1972-83, Ford Found.; mem. Mayor's Commn. on Gainsharing, N.Y.C., 1993. With AUS, 1943-46. Recipient Comptroller Gen.'s Public Service award, 1980. Mem. Indsl. Relations Rsch. Assn. (life, exec. bd., pres. 1979). Jewish. Home: Scarsdale, NY. Died Oct. 11, 2002.

ROSS, CHARLES ROBERT, lawyer, consultant; b. Middlebury, Vt., Feb. 24, 1920; s. Jacob Johnson and Hannah Elizabeth (Holmes) R.; m. Charlotte Sells Hoyt, Aug 28, 1948; children— Jacqueline Hoyt, Peter Holmes, Charles Robert. AB, U. Mich., 1941, MBA, LL.B., U. Mich., 1948. Bar: Ky. 1949, Vt. 1954, U.S. Supreme Ct. 1968. Instr. Oreg. State Coll., 1948-49; practice law Louisville and Burlington, Vt., 1949-59; chmn. Vt. Pub. Service Commn., 1959-61; commr. FPC, 1961-68; mem. U.S. sect. Internat. Joint Commn., 1962-81; mem. Nat. Consumers Energy Com., 1973-74; pub. mem. Adminstrv. Conf. U.S., 1971-74; adj. prof. econs. U. Vt., 1969-74. Served to capt. USAAF, 1942-46. Home: Shelburne, Vt. Died 2003.

ROSS, HERBERT DAVID, film director; b. Bklyn., May 13, 1927; m. Nora Kaye, Aug. 21, 1959 (dec. 1987); m. Lee Radziwill, Sept., 1988. Dir. motion pictures Goodbye Mr. Chips, 1969, The Owl and The Pussycat, 1970, T. R. Baskin, 1971, Play It Again Sam, 1972, The Last of Sheila, 1973, Funny Lady, 1975, The Sunshine Boys, 1975, The Seven Percent Solution, 1976, The Goodbye Girl, 1977, The Turning Point, 1977, California Suite, 1978, Nijinsky, 1980, Pennies From Heaven, 1981, I Ought To Be in Pictures, 1982, Max Dugan Returns, 1983, Footloose, 1984, Protocol, 1984, The Secret of My Sucess, 1987, Dancers, 1987, Steel Magnolias, 1988, Undercover Blues, 1993; dir., producer: My Blue Heaven, 1989, True Colors, 1990, Boys On The Side, 1995; exec. prodr. Soapdish, 1991, choreographer: Spoleto (Italy) Festival, Berlin (Germany) Festival; active in numerous Broadway prodns., including Anyone Can Whistle; dir.: Broadway Chpt. Two, I Ought to Be in Pictures, 1980; opera dir. La Boheme, L.A. Music Ctr., 1993; recipient Golden Globe award 1978, award of distinction Dance mag. 1980. Home: East Hampton, NY. Died Oct. 9, 2001.

ROSS, JOHN MICHAEL, editor, magazine publisher; b. Bklyn., Oct. 17, 1919; s. Albert Henry and Dorothy Veronica (Murray) R.; m. Kathleen M. Courtney; children: Donna Patricia Ross Easterbrook, Maureen Courtney Ross Fay. Student pub. schs., N.Y.C. Sports writer Bklyn. Eagle, 1937-41, The Newspaper PM, 1946-47; editor Am. Law Tennis mag., 1947-50, Macfadden Publs., 1950-51, 60-61; contbg. editor Am. Weekly, 1952-60; editor-in-chief Golf mag., 1961-67, Golf Bus. mag., 1963-65, Golfdom mag., 1965-67; v.p. Universal Pub. and Distbn. Corp., 1965-67; pres. Golf Promotions, Inc., 1967-70; pub. Golf Bus. Almanac, also Golf TV Guide, 1969; pub. relations dir. Profl. Golfers Assn. Golf Tour, 1970-71; editor-in-chief Golf mag., 1972-79, assoc. pub., 1979-84; publishing dir., v.p. The Golf Link, 1985-87; editorial dir. Am. Golf mag., 1990-94; sr. ptnr. J.M. Ross Assocs., Westport, Conn., from 1994. Bd. dirs. World Golf Hall of Fame, 1974-83, mem. adv. bd. 1993-97; chmn. Women's Golf Scholarship Fund, 1976-82; exec. dir. World Cup Golf Internat. Golf Assn., 1977-84; columnist Paradigm Syndicate, 2000-03. Co-author: Nothing But The Truth, 1960; editor: Encyclopedia of Golf, 1977; author: (feature column) Paradigm Syndicate, 1999-2003; contbr. numerous articles to nat. publs. including Reader's Digest, Life, Sports Illustrated. Justice of peace, Newtown, Conn., 1960-64. Served with AUS, 1942-46. Recipient Christopher award for best mag. story, 1957; recipient Lincoln Werden award for golf journalism, 1991. Mem. U.S. Golf Assn. (nat. com. 1977-99), Lawn Tennis Writers Assn. (sec. 1949-50), Golf Writers Assn. Am. (gov. 1966-67), Met. Golf Writers Assn. (pres. 1975-76), Assn. of Golf Writers (Great Britain), Am. Soc. Mag. Editors, Overseas Press Club (N.Y.C.), Patterson Club (Fairfield, Conn.). Roman Catholic. Home: Weston, Conn. Died Dec. 29, 2003.

ROSSE, JAMES N. newspaper publishing executive; Ph.D, U. Minn. Provost Stanford U., 1984—92; CEO Freedom Comms., Irvine, Calif., 1992—99. Died Feb. 16, 2004.

ROSTOW, EUGENE VICTOR, lawyer, educator, economist; b. Bklyn., Aug. 25, 1913; s. Victor A. and Lillian (Helman) R.; m. Edna Berman Greenberg; children: Victor A. D., Jessica, Charles Nicholas. AB, Yale U., 1933, LLB, 1937, AM, 1944; postgrad., King's Coll., Cambridge (Eng.) U., 1933-34; MA, Cambridge U., 1959, LL.D., 1962, Boston U., 1976, U. New Haven, 1981, N.Y. Law Sch., 1984. Bar: N.Y. 1938, U.S. Supreme Ct. 1962. Practice in N.Y.C., 1937-38; mem. faculty Law Sch. Yale, 1938—, prof. law, 1944-84, prof. emeritus, sr. research scholar, 1984—, dean, 1955-65, Sterling prof. law and pub. affairs, 1964-84; master Trumbull Coll., 1966; dir. ACDA, 1981-83. Disting. vis. research prof. law and diplomacy Nat. Def. U., 1984-90, 92—; under-sec. state for polit. affairs, 1966-69; pres. Atlantic Treaty Assn., 1973-76; vis. prof. U. Chgo., 1941; Pitt prof. Am. history and instns., professorial fellow King's Coll., Cambridge U., 1959-60; William W. Cook lectr. Mich. U., 1958; John R. Coen lectr. U. Colo., 1961; Leary lectr. U. Utah, 1965; Brandeis lectr. Brandeis U., 1965; Rosenthal lectr. Northwestern U., 1965; George Eastman vis. prof., fellow Balliol Coll., Oxford (Eng.) U., 1970-71; Adviser Dept. State, 1942-44; asst. exec. sec. Econ. Commn. for Europe, UN, 1949-50; mem. Jud. Council of Conn., 1955-66, Atty. Gen.'s Nat. Com. Study Antitrust Laws, 1954-55; chmn. exec. com. Com. on the Present Danger, 1976-81, 86-92. Author: Planning for Freedom, 1959, The Sovereign Prerogative, 1962, Law, Power and the Pursuit of Peace, 1968, Peace in the Balance, 1972, The Ideal in Law, 1978, Toward Managed Peace, 1993, A Breakfast for Bonaparte, 1994; editor: Is Law Dead?, 1971. Decorated Chevalier Legion d'Honneur (France), Grand Cross Order of Crown (Belgium); recipient Disting. Civilian Svc. award U.S. Army, 1990; Guggenheim fellow, 1959-60, Randolph fellow U.S. Inst. Peace, 1990-92, hon. fellow Hebrew U. of Jerusalem, 1992—. Fellow Am. Acad. Arts and Scis.; mem. Am. Law Inst., Phi Beta Kappa, Alpha Delta Phi, Elizabethan Yale Club, Century Assn. N.Y.C. Club, Cosmos Club Washington. Democrat. Jewish. Died Nov. 26, 2002.

ROSTOW, WALT WHITMAN, economist, educator; b. N.Y.C., Oct. 7, 1916; s. Victor Aaron and Lillian (Helman) R.; m. Elspeth Vaughan Davies, June 26, 1947; children: Peter Vaughan, Ann Larner. BA, Yale U., 1936, PhD, 1940. Instr. econs. Columbia U., 1940-41; asst. chief German-Austrian econ. div. Dept. State, 1945-46; Harmsworth prof. Am. history Oxford (Eng.) U., 1946-47; asst. to exec. sec. Econ. Commn. for Europe, 1947-49; Pitt. prof. Am. history Cambridge (Eng.) U., 1949-50; prof. econ. history MIT, 1950-60; staff mem. Center Internat. Studies, 1951-60; dep. spl. asst. to Pres. for nat. security affairs, 1961; counselor, chmn. policy planning council Dept. State, 1961-66; spl. asst. to Pres., 1966-69; U.S. rep., ambassador Inter-Am. Com. Alliance for Progress, 1964-66; now Rex G. Baker Jr. prof. polit. economy, depts. econs. and history U. Tex., Austin, prof. emeritus. Mem. Bd. Fgn. Scholarships, 1969-72, Austin Project, 1982—. Author: The American Diplomatic Revolution, 1947, Essays on the British Economy of the Nineteenth Century, 1948, The Process of Economic Growth, 1953, 2d edit., 1960, (with A.D. Gayer, A.J. Schwartz) The Growth and Fluctuation of the British Economy, 1790-1850, 1953, 2d edit., 1975, (with A. Levin, others) The Dynamics of Soviet Society, 1953, (with others) The Prospects for Communist China, 1954, (with R.W. Hatch) An American Policy in Asia, 1955, (with M.F. Millikan) A Proposal: Key to an Effective Foreign Policy, 1957, The United States in the World Arena, 1960, The Stages of Economic Growth, 1960, 2d edit., 1971, 3d edit., 1990, A View from the Seventh Floor, 1964, A Design for Asian Development, 1965, (with William E. Griffith) East-West Relations: Is Detente Possible?, 1969, Politics and the Stages of Growth, 1971, The Diffusion of Power, 1972, How It All Began, 1975, The World Economy: History and Prospect, 1978, Getting From Here to There, 1978, Why the Poor Get Richer and the Rich Slow Down, 1980, Pre-Invasion Bombing Strategy: General Eisenhower's Decision of March 25, 1944, 1981, British Trade Fluctuations, 1868-1896: A Chronicle and a Commentary, 1981, The Division of Europe After World War II: 1946, 1981, Europe After Stalin: Eisenhower's Three Decisions of March 11, 1953, 1982, Open Skies: Eisenhower's Proposal of July 21, 1955, 1982, The Barbaric Counter-Revolution: Cause and Cure, 1983, Eisenhower, Kennedy, and Foreign Aid, 1985, The United States and the Regional Organization of Asia and the Pacific: 1965-1985, 1986, Rich Countries and Poor Countries, 1987, Essays on a Half Century: Ideas, Policies and Action, 1988, History, Policy, and Economic Theory, 1989, Theorists of Economic Growth From David Hume to the Present with a Perspective on the Next Century, 1990, The Great Population Spike, 1998, Concept and Controversy, 2003; editor: The Economics of Take-Off Into Sustained Growth, 1963. Maj. OSS, AUS, 1942-45. Decorated Legion of Merit, Hon. Order Brit. Empire (mil.); recipient Presdl. Medal of Freedom with distinction; Rhodes scholar Balliol Coll., 1936-38, Outstanding Work in Social Scis. award Assn. Am. Pubs., 1990. Mem. Am. Acad. Arts and Scis., Am. Philos. Soc., Mass. Hist. Soc., Tex. Philos. Soc., Cosmos Club, Elizabethan Club. Clubs: Cosmos (Washington); Elizabethan (New Haven). Home: Austin, Tex. Died Feb. 13, 2003.

ROTH, JACK JOSEPH, historian, educator; b. Dec. 17, 1920; s. Max and Dinah (Kraus) R.; m. Sheilagh Goldstone. BA, U. Chgo., 1942, PhD, 1955; postgrad., Inst. d'Études Politiques, Paris, 1949-50. Mem. faculty Roosevelt U., 1951-68, prof. history, chmn. dept., 1960-68; prof. history Case Western Res. U., Cleve., 1968—, chmn. dept., 1968-73; vis. asso. prof. history U. Chgo., 1962, professorial lectr. history, 1968; vis. prof. history U. Wis., 1964-65. Project dir.: The Persistence of Surrealism, Nat. Endowment for Humanities, festival, 1979, film, 1982; Translator: (Georges Sorel): Reflections on Violence, 1951, Sorel und die Totalitären Systeme, 1958, Revolution and Morale in Modern French Thought: Sorel and the Sorelians, 1963, The First World War: A Turning Point in Modern History, 1967, The Roots of Italian Fascism, 1967, Georges Sorel: on Lenin and Mussolini, 1977, The Revolution of the Mind: The Politics of Surrealism Reconsidered, 1977, The Cult of Violence: Sorel and the Sorelians, 1980; Contbr. articles to profl. jours., chpts. to books. Served with AUS, 1942-46. Recipient Penrose Fund award Am. Philos. Soc., 1964 Home: Beachwood, Ohio. Died May 7, 2003.

ROTH, RICHARD HARRISON, petrochemical inspection company executive; b. Washington, July 8, 1955; s. Donald Davis and June Martha (Pleacher) R.; m. Julia Ann Hamel, Dec. 16, 1978 (div. Oct. 1990); 1 child, Martha Marie; m. Holly Lee Hilbrink, May 18, 1991 (div. June 1997); 1 child, Carina Michelle; m. Paula Ann Toepfer, Aug. 22, 1998; 1 step-child, Jenna Michelle Toepfer. BS in Biology, U. N.C., 1977. Cert. grade II wastewater treatment plant operator, N.C. Chemist, supr. SGS Control Svcs. Inc., Wilmington, N.C., 1981-85, br., lab. mgr. Savannah, Ga., from 1990; chemist, wastewater plant operator Republic Refining, Wilmington, 1985-86; chemist Oxford Lab., Wilmington, 1986-88, 89-90; rsch. asst. Hazleton Labs. Am., Inc., Vienna, Va., 1988-89. Author: Manual of Operations for ATC Petroleum Refinery, 1979, Crude Assay Handbook, 1979. Mem. Propeller Club of U.S., Savannah Kennel Club (pres. 1994-98, bd. dirs. 1999-2001). Republican. Lutheran. Achievements include implementation of ISO 9002 quality program laboratory. Died Nov. 2001.

ROTH, WILLIAM V., JR., former senator; b. Great Falls, Mont., July 22, 1921; m. Jane K. Richards; children: William V. III, Katharine Kellond. BA, U. Oreg., 1944; MBA, Harvard U., 1947, LLB, 1949. Bar: Del., U.S. Supreme Ct., Calif. Mem. 90th-91st congresses at large from, Del., 1967-71; senator State of Del., 1971-2001; former chmn. senate fin. com., former chmn govt affairs com.; chmn. U.S.-EU-Slovakia Action Comm., Washington. Chmn. Del. Rep. State Com., 1961-64; mem. Rep. Nat. Com., 1961-64; pres. North Atlantic Assembly, 1996-98. Served to capt. AUS, 1943-46. Decorated Bronze Star medal. Mem. ABA, Del. Bar Assn. Republican. Episcopalian. Died Dec. 13, 2003.

ROTHING, FRANK JOHN, government official; b. Chgo., July 4, 1924; s. Frank Joseph and Eva A. (Buhl) R.; m. Carita Reiss Corbett, June 16, 1951; children: Frank John, Reginald, Peter, James, Richard, Joseph, Thomas, Carita Ann. BS, U. Notre Dame, 1948. C.P.A., U. Ill., 1954. Pub. accountant Arthur Young & Co., Chgo., 1948-55; v.p. Midwest Stock Exchange, 1955-60, v.p., treas., 1960-66, sr. v.p., 1966-71; exec. v.p., sec., dir. Ill. Co., 1971-74; v.p. 1st Nat. Bank Chgo., 1974-75; exec. v.p. Front St. Securities, Inc., 1975-78; mem. Chgo. Office SEC, 1978, ret., 1989; chmn. bd. Chgo. Bd. Options Exchange Clearing Corp. Mem. Chgo. Bd. Trade. Adviser Jr. Achievement Chgo.; bd. dirs. St. Elizabeth's Hosp., Chgo.; mem. citizens bd. U. Chgo.; Bd. dirs., mem. exec. bd. North Shore Area Boy Scouts Am.; chmn. bd. trustees St. Mary of Woods Coll., Terre Haute, Ind. Served to 1st lt. USAAF, 1943-45. Decorated D.F.C., Air medal. Mem. VFW, Am. Legion, Am. Inst. Accountants, Ill. Soc. C.P.A.s, Am. Accounting Assn., Newcomen Soc., Navy League U.S., Ill. Athletic Club. Clubs: Michigan Shores; Bond of Chicago (dir.), Economic, Chgo. Athletic, Notre Dame (dir.), Attic (Chgo.). Home: Wilmette, Ill. Died Jan. 26, 2003.

ROTMAN, MORRIS BERNARD, public relations consultant, author; b. Chgo., June 6, 1918; s. Louis and Etta (Harris) R.; m. Sylvia Sugar, Mar. 1, 1944; children: Betty Ruth, Jesse, Richard. Student, Wright Jr. Coll., 1936-37, Northwestern U., 1937-39. Editor Times Neighborhood publs., Chgo., 1938-40; asst. editor City News Bur., 1940-42; mng. editor Scott Field Broadcaster, USAAF, 1942-43; publicity dir. Community and War Fund of Met. Chgo., 1943-45; v.p. William R. Harshe Assocs., 1945-49, pres., 1949-66; chmn. bd., chief exec. officer Harshe-Rotman & Druck, Inc. (formerly William R. Harshe), 1966-81, pres., 1982, Ruder Finn & Rotman, Inc. (merger of Harshe-Rotman & Druck and Ruder & Finn), 1981—88; founder Morris B. Rotman & Assocs., Chgo., from 1989. Former adj. prof. comm. Coll. of the Desert, Palm Desert, Calif. Author: Opportunities in Public Relations Careers, Dear Betty Chronicles. A Memoir of 40 Years in Public Relations. Chmn. solicitations pub. rels. div. Community Fund Chgo., 1948-49, spl. events chmn., 1953; chmn. comms. div. Jewish Fedn. Chgo., 1965, Combined Jewish Appeal, 1966; life dir. Rehab. Inst. Chgo.; U.S. dir. The Shakespeare Globe Centre (N.Am.) Inc.; trustee emeritus Roosevelt U. Recipient Prime Minister Israel medal, 1969 Mem. Pub. Rels. Soc. Am. (past dir.), Chgo. Presidents' Orgn. (pres. 1970-71), Acad. Motion Picture Arts and Scis. (assoc.), Am. Film Inst., World Chief Execs. Orgn., Standard Club, Tamarisk Country Club, Desert Rats (chair, King Rat Emeritus). Home: Rancho Mirage, Calif. Died June 8, 2003.

ROTZOLL, KIM BREWER, advertising and communications educator; b. Altoona, Pa., Aug. 21, 1935; s. Fredrick Charles and Anna (Brewer) R.; m. Nancy Benson, Aug. 26, 1961; children: Keith, Kristine, Amanda, Jason. BA in Advt., Pa. State U., 1957, MA in Journalism, 1965, PhD in Sociology, 1971. Account exec. Ketchum, Macleod and Grove, Pitts., 1957-61; instr. advt. Pa. State U., University Park, 1961-71; asst. prof. advt. U. Ill, Urbana, 1971-72, assoc. prof., 1972-78, prof., from 1978, rsch. prof., head advt. dept., 1983-92; dean Coll. Comms., from 1992. Lectr. in People's Republic of China, Bahrain, Pamplona, Spain Author, co-author, editor: Is There Any Hope for Advertising, 1986, Advertising in Contemporary Society, 1990, 96, Media Ethics, 1995, 97, 2000, The Book of Gossage, 1995, Last Rights: Revisiting Four Theories of the Press, 1995. Named Disting. Advt. Educator of Yr. by Am. Advt. Fedn., 1992. Fellow Am. Acad. Advt. (pres. 1991, Charles Sandage Tchg. award 2000); mem. Ill. Press Assn. Bd., Alpha Kappa Delta, Phi Kappa Phi. Democrat. Presbyterian. Avocations: reading, films, cycling. Home: Champaign, Ill. Died Nov. 4, 2003.

ROUBAL, GERALD GREGORY, construction executive; b. Barron County, Wis., Sept. 5, 1936; s. Joseph Phillip and Irene Sarah (Zastoupil) R.; m. Eula Grace Kuykendall; children: Deanna Ruth Kuykendall, Craig, Kyle Miles. BS, U. Wis., 1960; M of City Planning, U. Calif., Berkeley, 1966. Lic. gen. contractor, real estate broker, N.Mex. Asst. planner City of Corpus Christi, Tex., 1960-64; assoc. planner

San Diego County, 1966-68; regional planner Mid Rio Grande Council of Govts., Albuquerque, 1968-72; mgr. planning McIntire & Quiros, Albuquerque, 1972-75; owner, operator Roubal & Assocs., Albuquerque, from 1975. Cons. project mgr. Mountain Run Shopping Ctr., Albuquerque, 1983-85; past pres. RIW, Inc., Albuquerque. Past bd. dirs. Christian Profl. Counseling Svc., Mid-Rio Grande Health Planning Coun., Vis. Nursing Svc., Albuquerque. Democrat. Baptist. Avocations: directing Sunday sch., home bible study. Deceased.

ROUDIEZ, LEON SAMUEL, JR., French literature educator; b. Bronxville, N.Y., Nov. 18, 1917; s. Leon Samuel and Lulu Gray (Horan) R.; m. Jacqueline Strich, May 7, 1945; children: Genevieve Strich, Francis Horan. Baccalaureat es Scis., U. Paris, 1936, Baccalaureat en Droit, 1938; MA, Columbia U., 1940, PhD, 1950. Instr. French Columbia U., 1946-50; from instr. to assoc. prof. Romance langs. Pa. State U., 1950-59; mem. faculty Columbia U., 1959-87, prof. emeritus, 1988—2004, prof. French grad. faculties, 1962-87, acting chmn. dept., 1968-69, chmn., 1971-74. Acad. coordinator programs in Paris Columbia-Barnard, 1975-92. Author: Maurras Jusqu'a L'Action Française, 1957, Michel Butor, 1965, French Fiction Today, 1972, French Fiction Revisited, 1991; editor, translator: Desire in Language (Julia Kristeva), 1980; translator: Powers of Horror (Julia Kristeva), 1982, Tales of Love (Julia Kristeva), 1987, Black Sun (Julia Kristeva), 1989, Strangers to Ourselves (Julia Kristeva), 1991, Nations Without Nationalism (Julia Kristeva), 1993; mng. editor, editor French Rev., 1953-65. Served to capt. AUS, 1940-45, Alaska, ETO. Mem. MLA, Am. Assn. Tchrs. French (exec. council 1953-65) Home: Stevensville, Md. Died June 18, 2004.

ROUSE, WILLARD G., III, property trust company executive; b. Balt. m. Susannah Rouse; 5 children. Grad., U. Va., 1966. With U.S. Army. Died May 27, 2003.

ROUTIEN, JOHN BRODERICK, mycologist; b. Mt. Vernon, Ind., Jan. 23, 1913; s. William Evert and Frances Lolita (Broderick) R.; m. Helen Harrison Boyd, Mar. 11, 1944 (dec. 1965); m. Constance C. Connolly, Feb. 22, 1967 (dec. 1996). BA, DePauw U., 1934; MA, Northwestern U., 1936; PhD, Mich. State Coll., 1939. Instr. botany U. Mo., 1939-42; mycologist Pfizer, Inc., N.Y.C., 1946-77, research adviser, 1974-77. Editorial bd.: Applied Microbiology, 1964-71, Antimicrobial Agts. and Chemotherapy, 1974-77. Recipient Comml. Solvents award in antibiotics, 1950 Mem. Mycol. Soc. Am., Bot. Soc. Am., Soc. Am. Bacteriologists, Soc. Indsl. Microbiology. Achievements include research on molds producing new antibiotics, strain improvement of cultures, identification of fungi. Home: Fayetteville, NY. Deceased.

ROWE, JAMES ARNOLD, retired education administrator, real estate agent; b. Washington, Ohio, June 14, 1924; s. David Walter and Ollie (Cook) R.; m. Gloreen Nell, June 25, 1955; children: Shelley Marie Fanning, Jeffrey James, Tuio Alph. BS, Cedarville Coll., 1949; MA, U. Redlands, 1956; EdD, U. So. Calif., 1969. Tchr. Mira Loma (Calif.) Sch. Dist., 1948-55; supt. Pedley (Calif.) Sch. Dist., 1955-64; dir. edn. Riverside (Calif.) County Schs., 1964-67; assoc. supt. Santa Barbara (Calif.) County Sch. Dist., 1962-83; lobbyist Kern County Supt., Bakersfield, Calif., 1984-95; stock broker Robert Thomas Securities, Bakersfield, Calif., 1984-98; real estate agt. Century 21, Santa Barbara, Calif., 1997-98. Vol. YMCA, Riverside (Calif.), 1952-65, ARC, Riverside, 1955-65, PTA Pedley (Calif.) Sch. Dist., 1955-65. Republican. Avocations: basketball, running, hiking, back packing, sports. Home: Santa Barbara, Calif. Died May 19, 2001.

ROWE, JOSEPH EVERETT, electrical engineering educator, administrator; b. Highland Park, Mich., June 4, 1927; s. Joseph and Lillian May (Osbourne) R.; m. Margaret Anne Prine, Sept. 1, 1950; children: Jonathan Dale, Carol Kay. BSEE, BS Engring. in Math., U. Mich., 1951, MSEE, 1952, PhD, 1955. Mem. faculty U. Mich., Ann Arbor, 1953-74, prof. elec. engring., 1960-74, dir. electron physics lab., 1958-68, chmn. dept. elec. and computer engring., 1968-74; vice provost, dean engring. Case Western Res. U., Cleve., 1974-76; provost Case Inst. Tech., 1976-78; v.p. tech. Harris Corp., Melbourne, Fla., 1978-81; v.p., gen. mgr. Controls divsn. Harris Corp., 1981-82; exec. v.p. rsch. and def. Gould Inc., 1982, vice chmn., chief tech. officer, 1983-87; sr. v.p., chief technologist Inst. Rsch., Ill. Inst. Tech., Chgo., 1987; v.p. and chief scientist PPG Industries, Inc., Pitts., 1987-92; v.p., dir. Rsch. Inst., U. Dayton, Ohio, 1992-97. Cons. to industry; mem. adv. group electron devices Dept. Def., 1966-78, 93-97; bd. govs. Rsch. inst. of Ill. Inst. Tech.; chmn. Coalition for Advancement of Indsl. Tech., U. Ill.; mem. indsl. adv. bd. U. Ill. at Chgo.; mem. Army Sci. Bd., 1985-91, 93-2001. Author: Nonlinear Electron-Wave Interaction Phenomena, 1965, also articles. Fellow AAAS, IEEE (chmn. adminstrv. com. group electron devices 1968-69, editor procs. 1971-73, Harrell V. Nobel award 1994, Millenium medal 2000); mem. NAE, Am. Phys. Soc., Am. Soc. Engring. Edn. (Curtis McGraw Rsch. award 1964), Am. Mgmt. Assn. (R&D), Sigma Xi, Phi Kappa Phi, Tau Beta Pi, Eta Kappa Nu. Home: Palm City, Fla. Died Oct. 28, 2002.

ROWE, MAE IRENE, investment company executive; b. Gardner, Mass., Dec. 6, 1927; d. Clifford Wesley and Mertie (Moore) Mann; m. Willard Chase Rowe, June 18, 1951 (div. 1979); children: Gail B. Rowe Simons, Bruce C.; m. Paul Kimball, Sept. 26, 1997. BA with high honor, Am. Internat. Coll., 1949. Cert. real property adminstr. Social worker City of Montague, Turners Falls, Mass., 1949-51; mgr. Park Investment Co., Cleve., 1979-94; ret. 1994. Pres., v.p., bd. dirs. Park Ridge Counseling Svc., Ill., 1972-76; clk. Village of Kildeer, Ill., 1977; bd. dirs. Maine Township Mental Health Svc., Park Ridge, 1975-76; bd. dirs., recording sec. Manatee County Audubon Soc.; trustee Heathermore Condominium Assn., 1987, 93, pres. 1988, 93-94, sec.-treas., 1989. Mem. Cleve. Bldg. Owners Mgrs. Assn. (mem. edn. com. 1983—), Bldg. Owners Mgrs. Assn. Internat., Soc. Real Property Adminstrs. (cert.), LWV (v.p., mem. city adv. com. 1973-76), Am. Mensa Soc., Manatee County Audubon Soc. bd. dirs., rec. sec.), Cleve. Racquet Club, Kiwanis (bd. dirs., pres., trustee, v.p. Kiwanis Found. Cleve.). Republican. Unitarian. Avocation: tennis. Died June 2, 1999. Home: Richmond, Va.

ROWLAND, DOROTHY ESTHER, library science educator retired; b. Waterbury, Conn., Jan. 25, 1914; d. Clifford Frank and Esther Emaranth (Gothberg) Rowland. BS, U. Conn., 1937; MS in Libr. Sci., Syracuse U., 1950. Chief of art, music room, head of films and recordings Hartford (Conn.) Pub. Libr., 1937-50; asst. prof., librarian, head of pub. svcs. Westfield (Mass.) State Coll., 1952-69. Part time lectr. to groups, 1941—. Mem. Women's Fellowship, Prospect Sr. Citizens, Amaranth (historian 1981—), Order of the Eastern Star, Beta Phi Mu. Republican. Congregationalist. Avocations: ecology, horticulture, antiques. While at Hartford Pub. Libr., initiated record library which began a trend to include records and, later, films in library circulating depts. Home: Prospect, Conn. Died Jan. 27, 2002.

RUBENSTONE, ALBERT IRVING, pathologist; b. Elkton, Md., Apr. 21, 1919; s. Jacob and Annie (Diamond) R.; m. Eva Mae Dinnenberg; 1 child, Georgette. BA, U. Pa., 1941; MD, U. Md., Balt., 1944. Prof. pathology, chmn. Chgo. Med. Sch., 1965-75; chmn. pathology Mt. Sinai Hosp., Chgo., from 1965. Author chpt. in book; contbr. articles to pathology jours. Home: Glenview, Ill. Died Aug. 13, 2000.

RUBIN, HARRIS B. psychology educator; b. Jersey City, May 12, 1932; s. Eli L. and Doris R.; m. Angela Battaglia, June 11, 1960; children: Amy L., Chad A., Thea F., Garth A. BA in Psychology, So. Ill. U., 1959; PhD, U. Chgo., 1965. Research scientist behavior research lab. Anna State Hosp., Ill., 1965-72; asst. prof. rehab. inst. So. Ill. U., Carbondale, 1966-71, assoc. prof. behavioral sci. Sch. Medicine and Rehab. Inst., 1972-78, prof., 1978-95, interim asst. dean student affairs, 1994-96, prof. emeritus, from 1996. Cons. Ill. Dept. Corrections, Ill. Dept. Mental Health Bd. editors Jour. Applied Behavior Analysis, 1972-75, Jour. Exptl. Analysis of Behavior, 1973-75, The Behavior Analyst, 1986-90; adv. editor various jours.; contbr. articles to profl. jours. Mem. Carbondale Human Relations Com., 1968-73, chmn., 1969-72. Served with U.S. Army, 1952-54 Fellow APA, Am. Psychol. Soc., Am. Assn. Applied and Preventive Psychology; mem. Assn. Behavior Analysis, Midwest Psychol. Assn., Behavior Analysis Soc. Ill. (pres. 1989-90). Home: Carbondale, Ill. Deceased.

RUBIN, JACOB CARL, mechanical research engineer; b. N.Y.C., Nov. 22, 1926; s. Abraham and Bessie (Tockman) R.; m. Nancy Jean Weinstein, Aug. 2, 1952; children: Sara Lee, Jeffrey Daniel. BSME, CUNY, 1945; MMechE, NYU, 1947; MS of Applied Statistics, Rochester (N.Y.) Inst. Tech., 1969, MSEE, 1971, MS in Imaging Sci., 1975. Registered profl. engr., N.Y., D.C. Design group leader MacDonnell Aircraft Corp., St. Louis, 1955-56; mem. research staff U. Mich., Ann Arbor, 1956-57; staff engr. IBM, Vestal, N.Y., 1957-58; engr. advance design GE, Johnson City, N.Y., 1958-60, program engr. Phila., 1960-62; mgr. standards engring. Martin-Marietta Corp., Balt., 1962-63; mgr. product design dept. Am. Car & Foundry Co., Rockville, Md., 1963-64; cons. reliability NASA, Greenbelt, Md., 1964-65; project engr. Eastman Kodak Co., Rochester, 1965-75, sr. rsch. assoc., 1975-90; staff mech. engr. Med. Lab. Automation, Inc., Pleasantville, N.Y., 1990-91; prin. engr. instrument div. Dresser Industries, Stratford, Conn., 1992; sr. mech. engr. Materials Rsch. Corp., Congers, N.Y., 1993; sr. mech. design engr. Electronics Retailing Sys. Inc., Wilton, Conn., 1993-94; mfg. engr. Contact Sys. Inc., Danbury, Conn., 1995; sr. mech. engr. Barnes engring. divsn. EDO Corp., Shelton, Conn., 1995-96; mech. engr. Screen Tech, Oakville, Conn., 1996-97, Premier Microwave Corp., Port Chester, N.Y., 1997-98; prin. mech. engr. Microphase Corp., Norwalk, Conn., 1998; cons. product engr. Walboro Automotive, Meriden, Conn., 1998; cons. project engr. Ingersoll-Rand Corp., Watertown, Conn., 1999-2000; sr. mech. engr. Electro Energy, Inc., Danbury, Conn., 2000-01; engring. cons. BAE Systems, Cheshire, Conn., from 2002. Course dir. Ctr. Profl. Advancement, East Brunswick, N.J., 1975—; adj. faculty Rochester Inst. Tech., 1965-90; assoc. prof. mech. engring. Bridgeport Engring. Inst., 1991-94, Fairfield U., 1994—. Patentee artificial kidney, piezo-electric generator. Pres. Grove Place Neighborhood Assn., Rochester, 1984. Mem. NSPE (life), N.Y. State Soc. Profl. Engrs. Republican. Jewish. Avocations: teaching Sunday sch., music appreciation, theater, travel. Home: Southbury, Conn. Died Jan. 31, 2004.

RUDDER, CLAUDE BENNETT, brokerage firm executive; b. Atlanta, Jan. 4, 1952; s. James Maclin and Virginia (Bennett) R.; m. Lynn Mount, Dec. 29, 1977; children: Virginia Lynn, Bennett, Allison, Haynes. BBA, BA in Econs., Vanderbilt U., 1974; grad., Gemological Inst. Am., 1975. Mgr. Maier & Berkele, Atlanta, 1975-84; acct. exec. Dean Witter, Atlanta, 1984-88, v.p., sales mgr., asst. br. mgr., 1988-89, v.p., br. office mgr. Louisville, 1989-91, v.p., retirement plan coord. Atlanta, 1991-92, v.p., regional ins. coord., 1992-94; sr. v.p., br. mgr. Atlanta Interstate/Johnson Lane, from 1994. Mem. Investment Mgrs. Consulting Assn., Sr. Living Assn. Ga., Buckhead Bus. Assn. (v.p. econ. devel. 1991), Rotary Club Buckhead (interact adv. 1983, New Rotarian of Yr. 1983). Avocation: jogging. Home: Atlanta, Ga. Died Apr. 29, 2002.

RUDDY, JOHN MICHAEL, consulting engineer; b. Scranton, Pa., Mar. 24, 1909; s. John A. and Anna R. (Gannon) R.; m. Florence E. Buchan, Mar. 2, 1935 (div. 1965); children: Robert, John, Thomas; m. Gertrude G. Schunk, May 16, 1967; 1 child, Jeffry. BS in Engring., Manhattan Coll., 1931, MCE, 1932. Registered profl. engr., land surveyor. Asst. plant engr. Sperry Gyroscope, Lake Success, L.I., N.Y., 1942-47; chief engr. planning Brookhaven (N.Y.) Atomic Research Lab., 1947-62; resident engr., mgr. Skidmore, Owings & Merril, Puako, Hawaii, 1962-65; chief engr. TAPCO, Honolulu, 1965-77; consulting engr., assoc. Syntech, Ltd., Honolulu, from 1977. Fellow ASCE; mem. ASHRAE. Lodges: Lions. Home: Honolulu, Hawaii. Deceased.

RUDOLPH, FREDERICK BYRON, biochemistry educator; b. St. Joseph, Mo., Oct. 17, 1944; s. John Max and Maxine Leah (Wood) R.; m. Glenda M. Myers, June 18, 1971; children: Anna Dorine, William K. BS in Chemistry, U. Mo., Rolla, 1966; PhD in Biochemistry, Iowa State U., 1971. Prof. biochemistry Rice U., Houston, from 1972, chair biochemistry and cell biology, 1995—2003, dir. Lab. for Biochem. and Genetic Engring., from 1986, exec. dir. Inst. Biosci. and Bioengring., 1993—2003; dir. Inst. Biosci. and Bioengring., Houston, from 2003. Cons. World Book, Chgo., 1972—; mem. biochemistry study sect. NIH, Bethesda, Md., 1983-87; bd. dirs. Coun. Biotech. Ctrs., Tex. Healthcare & Bioscis. Inst. Contbr. over 160 articles to profl. jours. including Jour. Biol. Chemistry, Biochemistry, Transplantation, Exptl. Hematology, Jour. Parenteral and Enteral Nutrition, Jour. Molecular Biology, Applied and Environ. Microbiology, Life Scis., Archives Biochem. Biophysics, Critical Care Medicine, Archives Surgery, Sci.; also chpts. in books. Recipient Disting. Alumnus award Iowa State U., 1980, 99, 2000. Fellow AAAS; mem. Am. Chem. Soc., Am. Soc. for Biochemistry and Molecular Biology, Am. Soc. Nutritional Scis. Achievements include research on dietary requirements for immune function, new enteral feeding formulas and infant formulas, new techniques for protein purification, new methods for kinetic analysis of enzymes, structure and function of various enzymes. Home: Houston, Tex. Died Oct. 10, 2003.

RUE, OLAV HR, publishing executive; b. Hovin, Telemark, Norway, Feb. 28, 1930; s. Halvor and Gro R.; m. Torunn Hammer, May 9, 1964; children: Torborg, Hallvard. Cand. Mag., U. Oslo, 1962. Editor Det Norske Samlaget, Oslo, 1964-77, chief editor, 1978-84, sr. sec., from 1985. Sub-editor Syn Og Segn, 1964-83, writer, translator; editor various books. With Norwegian Air Force, 1952-54. Mem. Norwegian Pubs. Assn. Mem. Norwegian State Ch. Avocation: book collector. Home: Oslo, Norway. Died: Feb. 12, 1999.

RUGG, MARJORIE ALICE, retired secondary school educator; b. Charleston, W. Va., Nov. 4, 1916; d. Charles and Helen Pauline (Gurski) Listing; m. Charles Richard Rugg, June 18, 1938 (dec. Sept., 1989); children: Judith Ann Benson, Jennifer Helen Cantine. BS in Journalism, Northwestern U., 1938; MA in Edn., U. Northern Iowa, 1965. Cert. tchr., Iowa. Reporter Cedar Falls Gazette, Cedar Rapids, Iowa, 1940; tchr. Cedar Falls (Iowa) High Sch., 1965-81. Pres. Gladbrook, Iowa Sch. Bd., 1951-60; pres. Iowa Social Studies Coun., 1967-71; organizer, charter pres. Friends of Cedar Falls Pub. Libr., 1982, bd. dirs., 1982-91; bd. dirs., trustee Cedar Falls Pub. Libr., 1984—. Mem. AAUW, Iowa Libr. Assn., Iowa Artists, Waterloo Art Assn. Presbyterian. Home: Cedar Falls, Iowa. Deceased.

RUGGLES, DOROTHY WALKER, county official; b. St. Louis, Feb. 26, 1941; d. Lewis and Agnes (Turner) Bennett; m. James W. Walker; children: James L. Walker, Diane E. Walker Romero; m. John Ruggles. BA in Bus., Eckerd Coll., 1983. Lic. real estate agt.; cert. supr. elections, Fla. Adminstrv. asst. Office Supr. Elections, Clearwater, Fla., 1977-78, dep. adminstr., 1989-88, supr. elections, from 1988; mem. staff Congressman C.W. Bill Young, Washington, 1981. Bd. dirs. Pinellas County United Way, St. Petersburg, Fla., 1991-94, Tiger Bay, St. Petersburg, 1993-94; adv. bd. Pinellas Emergency Med., Pinellas Park. Mem. Internat. Assn. Clks., Recorders, Elected Ofcls. and Treas., Clearwater C. of C. (govt. com.), Alpha Xi Delta. Republican. Avocations: sking, roller blading, scuba, reading. Home: Clearwater, Fla. Died May 16, 2000.

RUMELY, EMMET SCOTT, retired automobile company executive, banker; b. N.Y.C., Feb. 15, 1918; s. Edward A. and Fanny (Scott) R.; grad. Phillips Exeter Acad., 1935; B.S., Yale, 1939; postgrad. U. Mich., 1940-41; m. Elizabeth Hodges, July 5, 1947; children— Virginia H., Elizabeth Scott Visser, Scott Hodges. Mgr., Marenisco Farms, La Porte County, Ind., 1939-73; dir. La Porte Hotel Co., Inc., 1938-70, pres., 1965-70; pres., dir. Rumely Corp., 1970—; product planning mgr. tractor ops. Ford Motor Co., Birmingham, Mich., 1961-70, asst. to v.p., gen. mgr., 1970-75; dir., mem. exec. com. 1st Nat. Bank & Trust Co., La Porte. Mem. Detroit Inst. Arts Founders Soc., Am. Soc. Agrl. Engrs., Soc. Automotive Engrs., Am. Mktg. Assn. Clubs: Orchard Lake (Mich.) Country; Huron Mountain (Big Bay, Mich.); Yale (Detroit). Died Nov. 23, 1987. Home: Birmingham, Mich.

RUNYON, MARVIN TRAVIS, former postmaster general; b. Ft. Worth, Sept. 16, 1924; s. Marvin T. and Lora Lee (Whittington) R.; children: Marvin, Elizabeth Anne, Paul, James. BS in Mgmt. Engring., Tex. A&M U., 1948. Staff mem. mfg. engring. areas assembly plants Ford Motor Co., 1943-60, asst., plant mgr. various assembly plants, 1960-70, mgr. assembly engring. automotive assembly div. gen. office, 1970-72, gen. mgr. automotive assembly div., 1972-73, v.p. body and assembly ops., 1973-77, v.p. powertrain and chassis ops., 1977-78, v.p. body and assembly ops., 1979-80; pres., chief exec. officer Nissan Motor Mfg. Corp. U.S.A., Smyrna, Tenn., 1980—87; chmn. bd. TVA, Knoxville, Tenn., 1988—92; postmaster gen./CEO U.S. Postal Svc., Washington, 1992-98. Mem. at large Nuclear Power Oversight Com., 1991-92. Bd. dirs. United Way Knoxville, 1988-92, mem. campaign adv. com. 1990; bd. dirs. Downtown Orgn., Knoxville, 1988-92, Tenn. Tech. Found., 1982, NCCJ, 1985-88, Nashville-Davidson County unit Am. Cancer Soc., 1986-88, United Way Rutherford County, 1986-89, Cumberland Mus., Nashville, 1986; participant Leadership Nashville Assn., pres., 1986, Leadership Knoxville, 1989, Leadership Memphis, 1990-91; hon. chmn. Clinic Bowl, Nashville, 1986; mem. devel. adv. bd. Ctr. for Internat. Bus. Studies Tex. A&M U., 1987, mem. coll. bus. adminstrv. devel. coun., 1984-87; mem. outreach com. Knoxville Bicentennial '91 Coord. Coun.; former mem. adv. bd. Inroads/Nashville, Inc.; mem. devel. adv. bd. Nashville State Tech. Inst., 1987; chmn. corp. adv. com. Middle Tenn. Regional Minority Purchasing Coun., 1982-83; mem. gov.'s adv. bd. to S.E./U.S. Japan Assn., 1981; gen. campaign chmn. United Way Nashville and Middle Tenn., 1985-86, trustee, 1984-86; former trustee Automotive Hall of Fame; chmn. Tenn. Minority Bus. Opportunity Fair, 1987-89, 1992 Trade Fair, Midsouth Minority Purchasing Coun., 1991-92;, Sr. Ptnrs. Bd. for May 1992 World Congress of Indsl. Devel. Rsch. Coun., 1991-92; bd. dir. Memphis in May Internat. Festival Inc., 1991-92, Met. Nashville Pub. Edn. Found., 1991-92; former mem. U. Tenn. Devel. Coun., Nucleus Fund Com. and Internat. Programs Resource Devel. Com., Tex. A&M U. Named Outstanding Man of Year Soc. Advanced Mgmt., 1968, Pres. slot on 1985 Model Yr. Automotive News All-Star Team, Automotive News; recipient Mgr. of Yr. award Avco Aerostructures chpt. Nat. Mgmt. Assn., 1985, CEO of Yr., Advantage mag., 1985, Disting. Service citation Automotive Hall of Fame, 1986, Salesman of Yr., Nashville chpt. Sales and Mktg. Exec. Club, 1985, award Tenn.-Japan Friends in Commerce, 1989; hon. gen. com. Internat. Fedn. Automotive Engring. Socs. 1988 Congress; recipient Human Rels. award NCCJ Nashville chpt., 1990, Spl. Recognition award Minority Bus. Devel. Agy., 1990, Gold Knight of Mgmt. award Nat. Mgmt. Assn., 1992, Exec. of Yr. award Nat. Mgmt. Assn., 1992, Adv. Mail Mktg. Assns. J. Edward Day award, 1993. Mem. Soc. Automotive Engrs., Engring. Soc. Detroit, Nashville Area C. of C. (bd. govs. 1983-85), Knoxville C. of C. (bd. dirs. 1988-92), Memphis C. of C. (bd. dirs. 1990-92), Tenn. Assn. Bus. (bd. dirs.), Soc. Internat. Bus Fellows, Belle Meade Country Club (Nashville). Episcopalian. Died May 3, 2004.

RUOTOLO, LUCIO PETER, English language educator; b. N.Y.C., Mar. 14, 1927; s. Onorio and Lucia (Sperling) R.; m. Marcia Mauney, June 11, 1960; children: Cristina, Vanessa, Peter. BA, Colgate U., 1951; MA, Columbia U., 1954, PhD, 1960. Part-time lectr. Hofstra Coll., Hempstead, N.Y., 1956-57; lectr. New Sch. for Social Rsch., N.Y.C., 1957; acting instr., prof. English Stanford (Calif.) U., 1957—94, prof. emeritus English, 1994—2003. Cons. panelist NEH, Washington, 1974-75; reader Nat. Humanities Ctr., N.C., 1986; film editor Christianity and Crisis, N.Y.C., 1965-66. Author: Six Existential Heroes, 1973 (Wilson prize 1972), The Interrupted Moment: A View of Virginia Woolf's Novels, 1986; editor: Virginia Woolf's Freshwater, 1976; founding editor Virginia Woolf Miscellany, 1973—. Co-chmn. Stanford/Palo Alto (Calif.) Dem. Club, 1968; co-pres. bd. Palo Alto Chamber Orch., 1980; bd. dirs. Peninsula Drama Guild, Palo Alto, 1964-67. Rsch. grantee NEH, 1973. Mem. MLA, Virginia Woolf Soc. (pres. 1983-87). Presbyterian. Avocations: steelhead and salmon fishing, tennis, baseball, poker. Home: Stanford, Calif. Died July 4, 2003.

RUSH, J. RICHARD, archivist; b. St. Joseph, Mo., Jan. 4, 1918; s. Harry E. and Elizabeth Rose (Smith) R. BA, St. Mary's Coll., Winona, Minn., 1940; MA, DePaul U., Chgo., 1943; MA in Libr. Sci., Rosary Coll., River Forest, Ill., 1975. Lic. spiritual theology Dominican House of Studies, River Forest, Casa Generalizia, Fratres Scholarum Christianorum, Rome. Tchr., counselor, prin. St. Mel. High Sch., Chgo., 1940-41, 52-64; tchr., counselor Boys Town, Nebr., 1942-44, De La Salle Acad., Kansas City, Mo., 1944-45, De La Salle Inst., Chgo., 1945-49, LaSalle Inst., Glencoe, Mo., 1950-52; Plato Consultants, Chgo., from 1994; tchr., counselor La-Salle High Sch., Cin., 1965-66; tchr., counselor, dean studies, rector St. Charles Borromeo Sem., Romeoville, Ill., 1966-80; tchr. Montini Cath. High Sch., Lombard, Ill., 1980-82; archivist publs. Christian Bros. Confs., Romeoville, 1982-89. Dir. summer workshops/tchr. tng.; pres. Joliet Diocesan Sch. Bd. Mem. Nat. Cath. Edn. Assn., Nat. Coun. Tchrs. English, Nat. Cath. Libr. Assn., Beta Phi Mu. Roman Catholic. Avocations: hiking, reading. Deceased.

RUSSELL, FRED MCFERRIN, former journalist, author, lawyer; b. Nashville, Aug. 27, 1906; s. John E. and Mabel Lee (McFerrin) R.; m. Katherine Wyche Early, Nov. 2, 1933; children: Katherine (Mrs. Earl Beasley), Ellen (Mrs. Robert Sadler), Lee (Mrs. John Brown, Carolyn Russell. Student, Vanderbilt U., 1923-27. Bar: Tenn. 1928. Atty. Real Estate Title Co., 1928; reporter Nashville Banner, 1929, sports editor, 1930-69, sports dir., 1969-87, v.p., 1955-99; ret. Chmn. honors ct. Nat. Football Found. and Hall of Fame, 1967-92; So. chmn. Heisman Trophy Com., 1946-92. Author: 50 Years of Vanderbilt Football, 1938, I'll Go Quietly, 1944, I'll Try Anything Twice, 1945, Funny Thing About Sport, 1948, Bury Me in an Old Press Box, 1957, Big Bowl Football, 1963; contbr. to mags. including Saturday Evening Post, 1939-63. A founder Harpeth Hall Sch., 1951, trustee, 1951-55; nat. pres. Vanderbilt Alumni Assn., 1960-61; dir. Children's Regional Med. Center, 1970-72. Recipient Nat. Headliners award, 1936; Grantland Rice award for sports writing, 1955; Jake Wade award, 1966; Coll. Football Centennial award, 1969; writing award Golf Writers Assn. Am., 1972; award for disting. journalism U.S. Olympic Com., 1976; Disting. Am. award Nat. Football Found. and Hall of Fame, 1980; Amos Alonzo Stagg award Am. Football Coaches Assn., 1981; award Nat. Turf Writers Assn., 1983; Red Smith award AP Sports Editors, 1984; named to Tenn. Sports Hall of Fame, 1974, Nat. Sportscasters and Sportswriters Hall of Fame, 1988. Mem. Football Writers Assn. Am. (pres. 1960-61), Sigma Delta Chi, Kappa Sigma (nat. man of yr. 1983), Omicron Delta Kappa. Clubs: Belle Meade Country, Univ. Lodges: Masons (33 degree), Shriners. Methodist. Home: Nashville, Tenn. Died Jan. 26, 2003.

RUSSELL, JOHN ROBERT, neurosurgeon; b. Bloomington, Ind., Mar. 17, 1922; s. John Dale and Elsie Violet Russell; m. Jane Elizabeth Bureau, Aug. 21, 1943; children: Thomas William, John Bureau, Ann Elizabeth, Amy Catherine. BS, U. Chgo., 1941, MS, 1942, MD, 1945. Diplomate Am. Bd. Neurol. Surgery. Intern Chgo. Meml. Hosp., 1945-46, resident, 1948-50, Bapt. Meml. Hosp, Memphis, 1950-51; mem. faculty Ind. U. Sch. Medicine, Indpls., 1951-59; ptnr. pvt. practice neurosurgery Indpls., 1959-71; pres. pvt. practice neurosurgery Indpls. Neurosurg. Group, 1971-84; neurosurg. cons. forensic medicine Chiron/EMC, Madison, Wis., 1991-97. V.p. Neurosurg. Soc. Ind., 1976-77. Fellow ACS; mem. Am. Assn. Neurol. Surgeons (bd. dirs. 1967-70), Congress Neurol. Surgeons (sec. 1962-65, pres. 1967). Avocations: woodworking, swimming. Home: Sewickley, Pa. Died Feb. 14, 2004.

RUSSELL, MARION CARR, secondary education educator, volunteer fundraiser; b. Cherokee, Iowa, Feb. 22, 1913; d. Sigel Warren and Inez M. (Phipps) Carr; m. Ocrel M. Russell, May 14, 1943; children: Nancy Russell, Polly Russell Nelson, Ned H. BS in Child Devel., Iowa State U., Ames, 1938; MS in Child Devel., Ohio State U., 1940. Nursery sch. instr. Pa. State U., University Park, 1940-43; dir. nursery sch. Ohio State U., Columbus, 1943-44; dir. children's sch. Pacific Oaks Coll., Pasadena, Calif., 1957-60; founder, dir. Hillsdale Children's Sch./Hillsdale Meth. Ch., San Mateo, Calif., 1962-64; dir. community presch. program San Francisco Unified Sch. Dist., 1964-66; head tchr. lab. sch. San Francisco State U., 1966-70; vol. coord. Pescadero (Calif.) Play Sch., 1980-91. Pres., treas., fundraiser, cons. South Coast Svcs., Inc., Pescadero, 1978-91. Friends of the libr. Pescadero High Sch., 1987-91. Recipient Dorothy Kraus award Child Care Coordinating Coun. San Mateo County, 1985, Robert Koshland prize Peninsula Community Found., 1986, Celebrate Literacy award San Mateo County Reading Assn., 1990; inducted into Women's Hall of Fame, San Mateo Adv. Coun. on Women, 1988. Mem. Assn. Edn. of Young Children (pres. Pasadena chpt. 1954-55), AAUW, Pi Beta Phi Alumni Assn. Republican. Avocations: gardening, flower arranging, children's books, children's music. Home: Arroyo Grande, Calif. Died Sept. 10, 2001.

RUSSELL, OLGA WESTER, foreign language educator; b. Hartford, Conn., June 20, 1913; d. Thomas Nielsen and Olga S.K. (Iversen) Wester; m. Henry G. Russell, Mar. 8, 1938; 1 child, Lauren Rusk. Diploma, U. Paris, 1933; AB, Conn. Coll., 1934; MA, U. Calif., Berkeley, 1939; AM, PhD, Harvard U., 1944, 57. Asst. in French U. Calif., Berkeley, 1939; instr. Cambridge Jr. Coll., 1943-44, Wheaton Coll., Mass., 1944-46, Tufts U., 1946-48, 51-52; asst prof. Chatham Coll., Pitts., 1956-61; tchr. WQED Ednl. TV, Pitts., 1956-60; asst. prof. U. South Fla., Tampa, 1961-63; prof., chmn. dept. fgn. langs. Longwood Coll., Va., 1963-65; assoc. prof. Ea. Ill. U., 1965-66; prof. emerita U. Maine, Orono, from 1966. Author: Etude historique et critique des Burgraves de Victor Hugo, 1962, Humor in Pascal, 1977. Fellow Radcliffe Coll., 1955. Mem. MLA, Phi Beta Kappa. Home: Palo Alto, Calif. Died June 2, 2000.

RUSSELL, WILLIAM LAWSON, geneticist, consultant; b. Newhaven, Eng., Aug. 19, 1910; came to U.S., 1932; s. Robert Lawson and Ellen Frances (Frost) R.; m. Elizabeth Buckley Shull, Aug. 29, 1936 (div.); children— Richard L. (dec.), John S., James J., Ellen M.; m. Liane Ruth Brauch, Sept. 23, 1947; children— David L., Evelyn R. BA, Oxford U., Eng., 1932; PhD, U. Chgo., 1937. Sherman Pratt fellow Amherst Coll., Mass., 1932-33; fellow, asst. U. Chgo., 1933-36; research assoc. Jackson Lab., Bar Harbor, Maine, 1937-47; prin. geneticist Oak Ridge Nat. Lab., 1947-77, ret., 1977. Del. UN Confs. on Peaceful Uses Atomic Energy, 1955, 58, 71, UN Sci. Com. on Effects Atomic Radiation, 1962; mem. coms. on biol. effects of atomic (ionizing) radiation Nat. Acad. Scis., 1955-80; adviser Fed. Radiation Council, 1964-70 Contbr. numerous articles to profl. jours., chpts. to books Founder Tenn. Citizens for Wilderness Planning, 1971, pres., 1971-73, 81-85 Recipient Roentgen medal, 1973, Enrico Fermi medal, 1976 Fellow Health Physics Soc.; mem. Nat. Acad. Scis., Genetics Soc. Am. (sec. 1959-61, pres. 1965, Disting. Achievement award 1976), Environ. Mutagen Soc. (councilor), Nat. Council on Radiation Protection and Measurements (hon.) Avocation: preservation of wilderness areas. Home: Oak Ridge, Tenn. Died July 23, 2003.

RUSSO, WENONA BERRIE, business educator; b. Columbia, Mo., Feb. 11, 1916; d. Howard William and Mabel Gertrude (Young) Berrie; m. Joseph R. Russo, June 16, 1942; children: Wenona Josephine Russo Fatton, Mary Ann Russo Reiter. BS in Edn., U. Mo., 1939, MEd, 1941. Tchr. bus. edn. Liberty (Mo.) High Sch.; tchr. remedial reading 4th-6th grades Somerville, N.J.; reading tchr. 4th-8th grades, Somerville, N.J.; tchr. bus. Scotch Plains, N.J., St. Claire Shores (Mich.) Schs. Active ednl. and community roles. With USN, 1944-45. Mem. NEA, N.J. Edn. Assn.-Reading. Home: Flemington, NJ. Died May 6, 2000.

RUSSO, WILLIAM, composer, educator; b. Chgo., Ill., June 25, 1928; s. William Joseph and Evelyn Viola (Guarno) R.; m. Shelby Davis, Mar. 13, 1947 (div. 1953); 1 child, Camille; m. Jeremy Warburg, Feb. 6, 1960 (div. 1973); children: Condee Nast, Alexander William; m. Carol Loverde, Aug. 23, 1982 (div. 1992). BA, Roosevelt U., Chgo., 1955. Composer, trombonist Stan Kenton Orch., L.A., 1950-54; composer, dir. The Russo Orch., N.Y.C., 1958-60, The London Jazz Orch., 1962-65; dir. Ctr. for New Music, Chgo., Ill., 1965-75; composer in residence City and County of San Francisco, 1975-76; dir. Contemporary Am. Music program Columbia Coll., Chgo., Ill., 1976—. Guest condr. Minn. Orch., Kansas City Philharm., New Am. Orch., Chgo. Chamber Orch.; condr., dir. Chgo. Jazz Ensemble, 1965—. Composer (operas) John Hooton, 1963, The Island, 1963, Land of Milk and Honey, 1964, Talking to the Sun, 1989, The Sacrifice, 1990, The General Opera, 1976, The Shepherds' Christmas, 1979, Sonata for Violin and Piano, 1986, Dubrovsky, 1988, Women, 1990, The Seasons, 1991; (film score) Everybody Rides the Carousel, 1976; (chamber pieces) The Carousel Suite, 1974, The English Concerto, 1963, Memphis, 1988; (mus. story) The Golden Bird, 1984; (cantata) Touro Cantata, 1988; (symphonic pieces) Street Music, 1975, Three Pieces for Blues Band and Orch., 1968, Urban Trilogy, 1981, numerous pieces for jazz orch. including America, 1966, The New Age Suite, 1984, The World of Alcina, 1954, 62; author: (symphony) Symphony # 2 in C (Koussevitsky award), Jazz Composition and Orchestration, 1968, 74, Composing for the Jazz Orchestra, 1961, 73, Composing Music, A New Approach, 1988, Listen Beneath, 1993, The Golden Bird, 1993, In Memoriam, Hermann Connaway, 1994, The Chicago Suite No. 1, 1995; composed for films: Everybody Rides the Carousel (CBS-TV 1976), Wrapped in Steel, Five Short films by Faith Hubley; record albums with own orch.: The English Concerto, Stonehenge, The Seven Deadly Sins, The School of Rebellion, Jump for Joy, with Cannonball Adderly, An Image, with Lee Konitz, The World of Alcina, An Experiment in Jazz. Recipient 25th Anniversary award Roosevelt Alumni Assn., 1970, Golden Eagle award, 1975-76, Grand Prix du Disc award, 1978, Italia, BBC submission, 1963, ASCAP Spl. award, 1961—, NARAS Lifetime Achievement award, 1990, Collaborative Artists of the Yr., 1991; inducted into 1st Navy Pier Hall of Fame, 1981. Mem. ASCAP, Ctr. for Black Music Rsch. (nat. adv. bd.), Arts Club (Chgo.). Home: Chicago, Ill. Died Jan. 11, 2003.

RUTLEDGE, ERNESTINE, school nurse; b. Nashville, Apr. 26, 1931; d. Ferdie Bethel Sr. and Tommie Irene (Hittson) Cassel; m. John Ellis Rutledge Jr., Dec. 19, 1958 (div. May 1981); children: Ernest B., John E. III. BSN, Northwestern State U., 1955; postgrad., U. Mich., 1957-58. RN, Tex., La. Staff nurse, pub. health nurse Jefferson Parish Health Dept., Harvey, La., 1955-58; supr. surg. svc. Bapt. Hosp., Beaumont, Tex., 1962-63; dir. health svcs. Beaumont Ind. Sch. Dist., from 1963. Bd. dirs. Am. Cancer Soc., Beaumont, 1965—, Am. Heart Assn., Beaumont, 1991—. Mem. Tex. Assn. Sch. Nurses (pres. dist. V 1965-66, various offices), Tex. State Tchrs. Assn., Assn. Tex. Profl. Educators, Sigma Theta Tau (Kappa Kappa chpt.), Delta Kappa Gamma (various offices Eta Mu chpt.). Baptist. Avocations: photography, plants, reading. Home: Vidor, Tex. Died Jan. 26, 2002.

RUZICKA, FRANCIS F., JR., radiologist; b. Balt., June 30, 1917; s. F. Frederick and Anne (Kaspar) R.; m. Margaret M. Kernan, May 31, 1941; children: M. Margaret Anne, Mary Frances, John F., Francis Frederick III, M. Therese, Joseph T. AB, Holy Cross Coll., Worcester, Mass., 1939; MD, Johns Hopkins U., 1943. Diplomate Am. Bd. Radiology. Intern Univ. Hosp. Md., Balt., 1943, resident in roentgenology, 1944-45; fellow in radiology Univ. Hosp. Minn., Mpls., 1948-49; instr. radiology U. Minn., Mpls., 1949-50; assoc. clin. prof. radiology NYU Sch. Medicine, N.Y.C., 1950-54; dir. radiology St. Vincent's Hosp. Med. Ctr., N.Y.C., 1950-73; clin. prof. radiology NYU Sch. Medicine, N.Y.C., 1954-73; chief diagnostic imaging rsch. br. Nat. Cancer Inst.-NIH, Bethesda, Md., 1984-88; prof. radiology U. Wis., Madison, 1973-84, chmn., 1976-81, prof. emeritus, from 1984. Cons., com. mem. VA Hosp., NAS, 1975; acting chmn. radiology, prof. N.J. Coll. Medicine, Newark, 1964-67. Author/editor: Vascular Roentgenology, 1964; editor: Modern Imaging of Liver, 1989. Pres., Conf. of St. Vincent De Paul Soc., Easton, Md., 1990-96. Fellow emeritus Am. Coll. Radiology, Soc. of Cardiovascular and Interventional Radiology; mem. AMA, Radio. Soc. N.Am., Am. Gastroenterol. Assn., Am. Roetgen Ray Soc., N.Y. Roentgen Soc. (pres. 1964-65), K.C. (chancellor 1993-95). Republican. Roman Catholic. Home: Bethesda, Md. Died July 12, 2000.

RYAN, GEORGE EDWARD, journalist; b. Boston, Aug. 6, 1925; s. Edward Patrick and Mildred Marie (Curtis) R.; m. Caroline Menslage, Sept. 24, 1966 (dec. 1993); children: Fredrick (dec. 1980), David, Caroline, Patricia, Colleen, Caitlin. BS in Social Sci., Boston Coll., 1951, MA in English, 1953. Dir. Archdiocesan News Bur., Boston, 1952-80; staff writer The Pilot, Boston, 1952-90, entertainment editor, 1960-90, mng. editor, 1986-88, sr. writer, 1988-90, contbg. columnist, 1993-2000. Freelance writer, 1952-2000; editl. adv. bd. Boston College Alumni Mag., Newton, Mass., 1989-92; cons. Archdiocesan Office Comm., Boston, 1985-86. Author: Botolph of Boston, 1971, Figures in Our Catholic History, 1979, Richard Cardinal Cushing: An Appreciation, 1959, A Life of Band Master Richard Willis: First Teacher of Music at West Point, 2001; contbr. articles to numerous mags. and newspapers. Mem. Scituate (Mass.) Town Libr., 1966-2000, Scituate Maritime and Mossing Mus., 1997-2000, Scituate Hist. Soc., Friends of Scituate Town Libr. Recipient Rasle medallion Boston Coll., 1976. Mem. Eire Soc. Boston (pres. 1965-67, editor 1964-99, bd. dirs. 1957-2000, gold medal award 1981), Bostonian Soc., Scituate Hist. Soc., Boston Athenaeum. Democrat. Roman Catholic. Avocations: stamp collecting/philately, irish history, theater, film, french foreign legion. Died Sept. 19, 2000.

RYAN, MATTHEW J. state legislator; b. Phila., Apr. 27, 1932; s. Thomas F. and Kathleen (Mullin) R.; m. Patricia H. Jenkins. BS, Villanova U., 1954, JD, 1959. Bar: Pa. 1960. Pvt. practice Pa. Ho. of Reps., 1962—2003; rep. Dist. 168 State of Pa., Harrisburg, 1963—2003. Majority chmn. Liquor Control com., 1967-68; chmn. Policy com., 1971-72; majority whip, 1973-74; minority whip, 1975-78; majority leader, 1979-80; spkr. of house 1981-83, 1994-2003. Mem. Rep. State Com., Del. County Rep. Com. 1st lt. USMC, 1954-56. Named Legislator of Yr. Nat. Conf. State Legislators; recipient Humanitarian Svc. award Elwyn Inst., Cert. of Valued Svc. Pa. Cancer Control, Prevention and Rsch. Adv. Bd., Cmty. Svc. award Crozer Chester Med. Ctr., Delaware County Am. Spirit Preservation award, Guardian of Small Bus. award Nat. Fedn. Ind. Bus. Republican. Avocations: boating, fishing. Died Mar. 30, 2003.

RYAN, STEVEN DANIEL, English language educator; b. Hoboken, N.J., Oct. 6, 1948; s. Daniel Patrick and Dorothy Ann (Herbert) R.; m. Leslie Hinckley, June 8, 1974; children: Kathryn, Jessica, Zachary. BA, Fairfield U., 1970; MA, U. R.I., 1972; PhD, Fordham U., 1988. Prof. English, Bergen C.C., Paramus, N.J., from 1973, head dept., from 1996. Author: (novel) O'Leary's Law, 2000. Soccer and baseball coach, Woodcliff Lake, N.J., 1983—. Mem. NEA, Two-Yr. Coll. Assn. Home: Woodcliff Lk, NJ. Died Mar. 12, 2002.

RYAN, TERRY, scriptwriter; b. Cleve., Nov. 26, 1922; s. Reginald and Julia (Terry) R.; m. Maren Wixsom, May 12, 1962; children: Cynthia, Douglas. Student, Western Res. U., 1939-41. Pianist Russ Carlyle band, 1941-43; scriptwriter Fred Allen Show, N.Y.C., 1946-49, Inside U.S.A., N.Y.C., 1950, Phil Silvers Show, N.Y.C., 1954-58, Car 54, Where Are You?, N.Y.C., 1960-62, Love American Style, Los Angeles, 1969-74, Flyin' High, Los Angeles, 1978; freelance writer, N.Y.C., from 1979. Served as staff sgt. U.S. Army, 1943-46. Recipient Emmy award for Phil Silvers Show Acad. TV Arts and Scis, 1955, 57, Emmy nomination for Car 54 Acad. TV Arts and Scis., 1962. Mem. Writers Guild Am. East. Home: New York, NY. Died May 5, 2001.

RYAN, THOMAS PATRICK, JR., mayor; b. Rochester, Dec. 4, 1929; s. Thomas Patrick and Delia (Mulkeen) R.; m. Charlotte Carpenter; 1 dau., Mary. BA, St. Bonaventure U., 1952; LL.B., Syracuse U., 1956. Bar: N.Y. bar 1956. Partner firm Kennedy & Ryan, 1957—2003; mem. Monroe County (N.Y.) Bd. Suprs., 1962-67; city councilman Rochester, 1967-85; mayor, 1974—94. Served in USMC, 1946-48. Mem. Am., N.Y. State, Monroe County bar assns., Phi Alpha Delta. Democrat. Died Mar. 14, 2003.

RYCHECK, JAYNE BOGUS (MRS. ROY RICHARD RYCHECK), retired educational administrator; b. Schenectady; d. Peter and Sylvia (Cywinski) Bogus; M.A., N.Y. U., 1953; B.S., State U. N.Y., Albany, 1941; postgrad. Syracuse U., 1957-66; m. R. Richard Rycheck, July 26, 1942. Tchr. various schs., 1935-43; elementary sch. tchr. Schenectady (N.Y.) City Schs., 1943-51, leadership intern, 1951-52, elementary sch. prin., 1952-61, dir. spl. edn., 1961-72. Instr. Russell Sage Coll., 1955-58, State U. N.Y., Oneonta, 1956; cons. bur. handicapped children N.Y. Edn. Dept., 1966-76, mem. commrs. and hoc coms., 1964-72, State Planning Com. Insts. for In-Service Edn., 1964-67; rep. to Community Welfare Council Schenectady County, 1961-62; adv. council N.Y. State Joint Legislative Com. Mental and Phys. Handicapped, 1970 72; mem. adv. com. Schenectady County Office for Aging, 1976-81, vice chmn., 1977-78, chmn., 1978-81; advisory com. Older Ams. Act program N.Y. State Office of Aging, 1977-80. Trustee, chmn. edn. Schenectady Mus., 1974-77; mem. human services adv. com. Schenectady County Community Coll., 1977-92; rec. sec. Ladies of Charity, 1992-94, Schenectady-Albany diocese Cath. Daus. Ct. 128, 1992, Our Lady of Fatima Ch. Rosary Soc., 1981-97; chair, coord sr. club activities Our Lady of Fatima Ch., 1981-92. Recipient Humanitarian service awards United Cerebral Palsy Schenectady County, 1966, 67, Capital dist. Assn. for Brain-Injured Children, 1967, Today's Woman award Schenectady YWCA, 1987, various citations from N.Y. State Sen. and Assembly, Am. Assn. Ret. People, AAUW, Schenectady County Legis., N.Y. State Legis., 1986, and others; named Sr. Citizen of Yr. Schenectady County, 1986; recipient Meritorious Alumni award State U. N.Y. Coll. at Oneonta, 1972; Capitol Dist. Speech and Hearing award, 1972, Distinguished Service award N.Y. Fedn. chpts. Council for Exceptional Children, 1972, Joseph P. Kennedy, Jr. Found. award for outstanding activity for the mentally retarded, 1972, Achievement award for contbns. to quality of life for sr. citizens N.Y. State Legislature, 1979, Disting. Service award Council Adminstrs. Spl. Edn., 1980, N.Y. State Achievement award by Senate Com. on Aging and Assembly Standing Com. on Aging for outstanding dedication to task improving quality on N.Y. State sr. citizen, 1986, Schenectady YWCA Recognition award for Today's Women, 1987; cert. of appreciation for community service by the City of Schenectady Coun. and Mayor Karen B. Johnson, 1986; cert. of merit for outstanding com. service N.Y. State Senator Hugh T. Farley, 1986, cert. in recognition of valuable pub. service Schenectady County Bd. of Reps., 1986, citation N.Y. State Assembly, 1986. Mem. N.Y. State (sec. 1967-68), Nat. councils adminstrs. spl. edn., Assn. Childhood Edn. (state sec. 1952-55, state exec. bd. 1951-59), Council Exceptional Children (mem. chpt. regional and state bds. 1966-78, state regional dir. 1966-68, state adv. bd. 1966-72, v.p. 1968-69, state pres. 1970), Schenectady County Assn. Childhood Edn. (treas. and v.p. 1952), N.Y. State Assn. Childhood Edn. Internat. (sec., v.p. 1962-65), Am. Assn. Mental Deficiency, N.Y. State Assn. Brain-Injured Children (state adv. bd. 1963-67, dist. adv. bd. 1966-72), Nat. Soc. Autistic Children, Assn. Retarded Children (adv. bd.), Gifted Children Soc. (adv. com.), Schenectady C. of C. (edn. com.), Schenectady County Ret. Tchrs. Assn. (v.p. 1973, pres. 1974-76), AARP (program com. chpt. #490 1973-76, legis. chmn., dir. 1981-84, cert. of appreciation for dedicated service 1986, 87), AAUW (topic chmn. 1977-79, chpt. Name Grant honoree 1981), N.Y. Assn. Elementary Prins. (hon. life), N.Y. State Ret. Tchrs. Assn. (county dir. Eastern zone, del. state conv. 1974-76), Schenectady County Hist. Soc. (rec. sec. 1982-84, 92, dir. exec. bd 1982-84, 97, 1st v.p. 1986-87), Delta Kappa Gamma (chmn. chpt. profl. affairs com. 1972-76, del. state legis. forum 1974-79, mem. state com. profl. affairs 1974-75). Contbr. articles to publs. Home: Saratoga Springs, NY. Died Jan. 19, 1999.

SABANCI, SAKIP, holdings company executive; b. Akçakaya, Kayseri, Turkey, Apr. 7, 1933; s. Haci Ömer and Sadika (Sapan) S.; m. Türkan Civelek, June, 1957; children: Dilek, Metin, Sevil. D of Mgmt., U. Anatolia, Eskisehir, Turkey, 1984; LHD, Hampshire Coll., 1986; Docotrate (hon.), Anatolan U., Eskisehir, 1984, New Hampshire U., U.S.A, 1986, Yildiz U., Istanbul, 1992, Kayseri-Erciyes U., 1993, Mimar Sinan U., Istanbul, 1997, 18 Mart U., Canakkale, 1997, Istanbul U., 1997, Washington Southeastern U., 1998, Çukurova U., 1999. Chmn. bd. Haci Ömer Sabanci Holdings, Istanbul, Turkey, 1967—2004. Chmn. Chamber of Industry, Adana, Turkey, 1964-74, Izmit, Turkey, 1978, 84, mem. Istandbul chamber of Industry, chmn. bd., TUSIAD, founder Haci Ömer Sabanci Found. Author: Iste Hayatim, Gönül Galerimden, Rusya'dan Amerika'ya, Para Basarinin, Mükafatidir, Ücret Pazarligi mi?, Degisen ve Gelisen Türkiye, Basari Simdi Aslanin Agzinda, Daha Fazla İs, Daha Fazala As, Dogu ANadolu Raporu, Hayat Bazen Tatlidir, This Is My Life (English and Japanese), 1985, From the Gallery of My Heart, 1987, Money, 1988, From Russia to America, 1989, Wage Bargaining or Sheep Bargaining?, 1990, Changing and Developing Turkey (English and Japanese), 1991; collections: Ottoman Calligraphy, Sakip Sabanci Museum, Metroploitan Museum of Art, NY, 1999, Arthur M. Sackler Museum, 1999-2000, Deutsche Guggenheim Berlin, 2001, Frankfurt museums für Angewandte Kunst, 2001. Recipient award Gold Mercury Internat. Com., Cairo, 1979, Turkey, 1983, Spl. Friends award Edward M. Kennedy, 1983; Rank of Commodore of Order of King Leopold II, 1982; named Hon. West Virginian, Gov. of Va., 1985, Rank of Commodore of the Order of King Leopold II, Belgium, 1987, Good Will Amb., Mayor of Houston, 1989, Gold and Silver Stars, Japanese Govt., 1992, Crystal Globe Award, European Economic Inst., Turkish State Dist. Service Medal, Pres. Turkish Republic, Hon. Award, Soc. Law Sovereign, 1997, Award for Promoting Turkey, Turkish-American Businessman Assn., 1999, hon. townmanship of Artvin, Erzurum, Kirikkale, New Hampshire, Houston, Beverly Hills. Mem. Turkish Industrialists and Businessmen's Assn. (chmn. 1986-2004, chmn. supreme coun. 1987-89), Turkey Kinya Petrol, lastik ve Plastik San Isverenleri Sendikosi (chmn. supreme coun.). Home: Istanbul, Turkey. Died Apr. 10, 2004.

SABAROFF, ROSE EPSTEIN, retired education educator; b. Cleve., Sept. 4, 1918; d. Hyman Israel and Bertha (Glaser) Epstein; m. Bernard Joseph Sabaroff, Dec. 28, 1940; children: Ronald Asher, Katya Nina. BA, U. Ariz., 1941; MA, San Francisco State U., 1954; EdD, Stanford U., 1957. Tchr. Presidio Hill Elem. Sch., San Francisco, 1951-55; asst. prof. edn. Oreg. State U., Corvallis, 1958-61; asst. dir., then dir. elem. edn. Harvard Grad. Sch. Edn., Cambridge, Mass., 1961-66; prof. edn., head elem. edn., head reading program Va. Poly. Inst. and State U., Blacksburg, 1967-82; dir. Grad. Edn. Ctr. Calif. Luth. Coll., North Hollywood, 1982-84; reading specialist How to Learn, Inc., West Los Angeles, Calif., 1983-88. Author: (with Hanna, Davies, Farrar) Geography in the Teaching of Social Studies, 1966, (with Mary Ann Hanna) The Open Classroom, 1974, Teaching Reading with a Linguistic Approach, 1980, Developing Linguistic Awareness, 1981; contbr. articles to profl. jours. Recipient Disting. Research award Va. Edn. Research Assn., 1977; Phi Delta Kappa grantee, 1980 Mem. AAUP, Internat. Reading Assn., NEA, Va. Edn. Assn., Va. Coll. Reading Educators (pres. 1976-77), Va. Reading Assn., Phi Delta Kappa, Pi Lambda Theta, Gamma Theta Upsilon. Democrat. Jewish. Achievements include conducting 15 month study abroad comparing ednl. sys. in 4 European countries with differing social-econ. sys. Died June 12, 2002.

SABLAN, SUZANNE BARBARA, secondary school educator; b. Plainview, N.Y., Aug. 25, 1962; d. Anthony and Elaine Florence (Frecth) Pellegrino; m. Joseph Andrew Sablan, Aug. 26, 1982. Student, NYU, 1981; AA, Valencia Community Coll., 1985; BA, Rollins Coll., 1987. Night auditor Days Inns Am., Orlando, Fla., 1981-82, Sheraton World Resort, Orlando, 1982-84; dividend processor Sun Banks, Inc., Orlando, 1984, supr., 1984-88; tchr. gifted edn., secondary English Dr. Phillips High Sch., Orlando, from 1988. Sponsor Dr. Phillips High Sch. Nat. Honor Soc. Author: (poem) Slipping Away; contbg. poet On the Threshold of a Dream. Sponsor Nat. Honor Soc.; liaison Dr. Phillips High Sch. Campus News. Mem. Orange County Tchrs. Assn., Tchrs. USA, Nat. Writers Club. Democrat. Episcopalian. Home: Bay Shore, NY. Deceased.

SABOLISH, GEORGE, chemist; b. Cannonsburg, Pa., July 12, 1950; s. Emil and Virginia (Salutric) S.; divorced; children: Leanne, Jordan, David. BS, U. Mich., Flint, 1972. Dairy chemist Mich. Dept. Agr., East Lansing, 1972-80, feed and fertilizers chemist, 1980-90, feed and fertilizer mgr., 1990-95, food, dairy and beverage mgr., from 1995. Mem. Assn. Ofcl. Analytical Chemists (past pres. 1997), Mich. Environ. Health Assn., Inst. Food Tech., Mich. State Employees Assn. (bd. dirs. 1980-82), Mich. Profl. Employees Soc. (bd. dirs. 1982-85). Avocations: bike riding, golf, woodworking. Home: Flint, Mich. Died Apr. 14, 2001.

SACHS, ROBERT GREEN, physicist, educator, laboratory administrator; b. Hagerstown, Md., May 4, 1916; s. Harry Maurice and Anna (Green) S.; m. Selma Solomon, Aug. 28, 1941; m. Jean K. Woolf, Dec. 17, 1950; children: Rebecca, Jennifer, Jeffrey, Judith, Joel; m. Carolyn L. Wolf, Aug. 21, 1968; stepchildren: Thomas Wolf, Jacqueline Wolf, Katherine Wolf. PhD, Johns Hopkins U., 1939; D.Sc. (hon.), Purdue U., 1967, U. Ill., 1977, Elmhurst Coll., 1987. Research fellow George Washington U., 1939-41; instr. physics Purdue U., 1941-43; on leave as lectr., research fellow U. Calif. at Berkeley, 1941; sect. chief Ballistic Rsch. Lab., Aberdeen Proving Ground, Md., 1943-46; dir. theoretical physics divsn. Argonne (Ill.) Nat. Lab., Ill., 1946-47; asso. prof. physics U. Wis., 1947-48, prof., 1948-64; assoc. dir. Argonne Nat. Lab., 1964-68, dir., 1973-79; prof. physics U. Chgo., 1964-86, prof. emeritus, 1986—; dir. Enrico Fermi Inst., 1968-73, 83-86. Higgins vis. prof. Princeton U., 1955 56; vis. prof. U. Paris, 1959-60, Tohoku U., Japan, 1974; cons. Ballistic Research Labs., 1945-59, Argonne Nat. Lab., 1947 50, 60 64; cons. radiation lab. U. Calif. at Berkeley, 1955-59; adv. panel physics NSF, 1958-61; mem. physics survey com., chmn. elem. particle physics panel Nat. Acad. Scis., 1969-72; high energy physics adv. panel div. research AEC, 1966-69; mem. steering com. (Sci. and Tech., A Five Year Outlook), 1979; mem. DOE task force on energy rsch. priorities, 1991-93. Author: Nuclear Theory, 1953, The Physics of Time Reversal, 1987; chief editor: High Energy Nuclear Physics, 1957; editor: National Energy Issues: How Do We Decide, 1980, The Nuclear Chain Reaction--Forty Years Later, 1984. Recipient Disting. Svc. to Engrng. citation U. Wis., 1977; Guggenheim fellow, 1959-60. Fellow Am. Phys. Soc. (coun. 1968-71, regional sec. Cen. States 1964-69), Am. Acad. Arts and Scis. (v.p. Midwest Ctr. 1980-83); mem. NAS (chmn. physics sect. 1977-80, chmn. Class I Math. and Phys. Scis. 1980-83), AAAS (v.p., chmn. physics sect. 1970-71), Am. Inst. Physics (mem. gov. bd. 1969-71), Phi Beta Kappa, Sigma Xi. Achievements include reseach in theoretical particle, nuclear and solid state physics, terminal ballistics, nuclear power reactors. Home: Chicago, Ill. Deceased.

SADKER, MYRA POLLACK, educator, dean; b. Portland, Maine, Mar. 5, 1943; d. Louis and Shirley (Schilling) Pollack; m. David Sadker, July 4, 1965; children: Robin, Jackie. BA, Boston U., 1964; MAT, Harvard U., 1965; EdD, U. Mass., 1971. Asst. prof. U. Wis., Racine, 1971-72; assoc. prof. Am. U., Washington, 1972-77, dean Sch. Edn., 1979-84 and from 88, prof., from 1978. Dir. U.S. Dept. Edn. grants: Project Intersect, 1980-83, Effectiveness and Equity in College Teaching, 1983-85, Principal Effectiveness, Pupil Achievement, 1985-86, Equity of Education Reform, 1986-87. Author: Sexism in School and Society, 1973, Now upon a Time, 1977, Sex Equity Handbook for Schools, 1982, Teachers, School and Society, 1988; contbr. articles to profl. jours. Recipient Women Educators award Am. Ednl. Research Assn., 1980, William Cosby Alumni award U. Mass., 1981, Andrew Mellon Sr. Scholar award Am. U., 1986, Edn. Press award Ednl. Press Assn. Am., 1988. Home: Bethesda, Md. Deceased.

SAFAR, PETER, anesthesiologist, researcher; b. Vienna, Apr. 12, 1924; came to U.S., 1949; s. Karl and Vinca (Landauer) S.; m. Eva Kyzivat, July 6, 1950; children: Elizabeth, Philip, Paul. MD, U. Vienna, 1948; Dr. Hon. Causa, Gutenberg U., Germany, 1972, U. Campinas, Brazil. Resident in surgery U. Vienna and Yale U., 1948-50; resident in anesthesiology U. Pa., Phila., 1950-52; chief anesthesiologist Nat. Cancer Hosp., Lima, Peru, 1953, Balt. City Hosp., 1955-61; anesthesiologist Johns Hopkins Hosp., Balt., 1954; asst. prof. anesthesiology Johns Hopkins U., Balt., 1955-61; prof., chmn. dept. anesthesiology, founder U. Pitts. Med. Ctr., 1961-78; founder, dir. U. Pitts., 1978-94, disting. svc. prof. resuscitation medicine, from 1978. Co-initiator cardiopulmonary-cerebral resuscitation; researcher in field; mem. emergency med. svcs. and resuscitation coms.

NRC/NAS, Washington, 1950-70; mem. Emergency Med. Svcs. Interagy. Com., Washington, 1974-76. Co-author nat. and internat. guidelines for modern resuscitation. Considered Father of Modern Resuscitation. Mem. Soc. Critical Care Medicine (pres., co-initiator 1972, 82), Am. Coll. Emergency Physicians (hon.), Nat. Assn. Emergency Med. Svcs. Physicians (hon.), Soc. Acad. Emergency Medicine (hon.), German Acad. Natural Scis., Leopoldina (hon., corr.), Austrian Acad. Scis. (hon., corr.), Czechoslovak Med. Soc., J.E. Purkinje (Hon., corr.), European Resuscitation Coun. (hon.), Club of Mainz, World Assn. Disaster and Emergency Medicine. Avocations: snow skiing, mountaineering, water sports, music, piano. Home: Pittsburgh, Pa. Died Aug. 3, 2003.

SAFFELS, DALE EMERSON, federal judge; b. Moline, Kans., Aug. 13, 1921; s. Edwin Clayton and Lillian May (Cook) S.; m. Margaret Elaine Nieman, Apr. 2, 1976; children by previous marriage: Suzanne Saffels Gravitt, Deborah Saffels Godowns, James B.; stepchildren: Lynda Cowger Harris, Christopher Cowger. AB, Emporia State U., 1947; JD cum laude, LLB cum laude, Washburn U., 1949. Bar: Kans. 1949. Pvt. practice law, Garden City, Kans., 1949-71, Topeka, 1971-75, Wichita, Kans., 1975-79; U.S. dist. judge Dist. of Kans., Topeka, 1979—2002. County atty. Finney County, Kans., 1951-55; chmn. bd. Fed. Home Loan Bank Topeka, 1978-79; mem. Jud. Conf. Com. on Fin. Disclosure, 1993-99. Mem. bd. govs. Sch. Law Washburn U., 1973-85; pres. Kans. Dem. Club, 1957; Dem. nominee Gov. of Kans., 1962; mem. Kans. Ho. of Reps., 1955-63, minority leader, 1961-63; mem. Kans. Corp. Commn., 1967-75, chmn., 1968-75; mem. Kans. Legis. Coun., 1957-63; Kans. rep. Interstate Oil Compact Commn., 1967-75, 1st vice chmn., 1971-72; pres. Midwest Assn. Regulatory Commn., 1972-73, Midwest Assn. R.R. and Utilities Commrs., 1972-73; trustee Emporia State U. Endowment Assn.; bd. dirs. Nat. Assn. Regulatory Utility Commrs., 1972-75. Maj. Signal Corps U.S. Army, 1942-46. Fellow Am. Bar Found., Kans. Bar Found.; mem. ABA, Kans. Bar Assn., Wichita Bar assn., Am. Judicture Soc., Delta Theta Phi. Lutheran. Home: Topeka, Kans. Died Nov. 14, 2002.

SAFRAN, NADAV, government educator; b. Cairo, Aug. 25, 1925; came to U.S., 1950, naturalized, 1962; s. Joseph and Jeanne (Abadi) S.; m. Anna Balicka, June 9, 1955; children— Janina, Abigail, Elizabeth. BA summa cum laude, Brandeis U., 1954; MA, Harvard, 1956, PhD, 1958. Dir. Ctr. for Middle Eastern studies Harvard U., Cambridge, Mass., 1958—86, prof., 1959—2002. Author: Egypt in Search of Political Community, 1961, The U.S. and Israel, 1963, From War to War, 1969, Israel— The Embattled Ally, 1978, Saudi Arabia— the Ceaseless Quest for Security, 1985, contbr. articles to profl. jours. Adviser State Dept.; spl. counsel Senate coms. Served as 1st lt. Israel Armed Forces, 1948-49. Recipient Politics prize Brandeis U., 1954, Chase prize, 1958; Sheldon fellow, 1956-57; Guggenheim fellow, 1963-64; Ford fellow, 1968-69 Mem. Council on Fgn. Relations, Harvard Acad. Internat. Relations, Phi Beta Kappa. Home: Cambridge, Mass. Died July 5, 2003.

SAGER, RODERICK COOPER, retired life insurance company executive; b. Washington, May 25, 1923; s. Theron Parker and Rebecca (Ward) S.; m. Ruth Regina Ross, Sept. 2, 1947; children: Lawrence Cooper, Jonathan Ward, Timothy Charles. AB, Syracuse U., 1948, JD, 1950. Bar: N.Y. 1951, U.S. Supreme Ct. 1958; C.L.U., 1969; chartered fin. cons. Assoc. Mackenzie, Smith, Lewis, Michell and Hughes, Syracuse, 1950-62; gen. counsel Farmers and Traders Life Ins. Co., Syracuse, 1962-66, v.p., gen. counsel, 1966-69, sr. v.p., gen. counsel, 1969-74, exec. v.p., gen. counsel, 1974-79, pres., chief exec. officer, 1979-89, also bd. dirs., ret., 1989. Chmn. Life Ins. Council, N.Y., 1984 Trustee Jamesville-DeWitt Cen. Sch. Dist., 1956-69, Onondaga Community Coll., 1971-75; bd. dirs. N.Y. State Tchrs. Retirement System, 1977-92, Onondaga Indsl. Devel. Corp., 1984-89, Lit. Vols. of Greater Syracuse, Inc., 1990-91; trustee Rescue Mission Alliance, Syracuse, 1980-96, pres., 1985-86. 1st lt. U.S. Army, 1943-46, 51-52. Mem. Onondaga County Bar Assn., Assn. Life Ins. Counsel. Clubs: Century (Syracuse); Onondaga Golf and Country (Fayetteville, N.Y.). Lodges: Rotary. Home: Fayetteville, NY. Died Nov. 17, 2002.

SAGUNSKY, BYRON THOMAS, surgeon; b. Butte, Mont., June 30, 1944; s. Walter Gustav and Edith Sagunsky; m. Katherine Leone, May 6, 1972; children— David Lee, Anita Marie. B.A., Ripon Coll., 1966; M.D., U. Utah, 1970. Diplomate Am. Bd. Surgery. Intern Good Samaritan Hosp., Phoenix, 1970-71; resident in surgery U. Calif. Med. Ctr., Sacramento, 1974-78; practice medicine specializing in gen. surgery, Klamath Falls, Oreg., 1978—. Served as capt. USAF, 1971-74. Fellow ACS. Home: Klamath Falls, Oreg. Deceased.

SAID, EDWARD W. English language and literature educator; b. Jerusalem, Palestine, Nov. 1, 1935; s. Wadie A. and Hilda (Musa) S.; m. Mariam Cortas, Dec. 15, 1970; children: Wadie, Najla. AB, Princeton U., 1957; A.M., Harvard U., 1960, PhD, 1964; degree (hon.), U. Chicago, Bir Zeit U., Jawaharlal Nehru U., U. Michigan, U. Edinburgh, Nat. U. Ireland. Tutor history and lit. Harvard U., 1961-63; instr. Columbia U., 1963-65, asst. prof. English, 1965-67, assoc. prof., 1968-70, prof., 1970-77, Parr prof. English and comparative lit., 1977-89, Old Dominion Found. prof. humanities, 1989—2003. Vis. prof. Harvard U., 1974, Johns Hopkins, spring 1979, Yale U., fall 1985; fellow Ctr. for Advanced Study in Behavioral Scis., Palo Alto, Calif., 1975-76; Christian Gauss lectr. in criticism Princeton U., spring 1977, T.S. Eliot lectr. U. Kent, Canterbury, U.K., 1985, Messenger lectr. Cornell U., 1986, Little lectr. Princeton U., 1988, Raymond Williams Meml. lectr., London, 1989, Wilson lectr. Wellesley Coll., 1991, Amnesty lectr. Oxford U., 1992, Lord Northcliffe lectr., U. Coll., London, 1993, Reith lectr. BBC, London, 1993, others; Carpenter prof. U. Chgo., 1983; Northrop Frye chair U. Toronto, fall 1986. Author: Joseph Conrad and the Fiction of autobiography, 1966, Beginnings: Intention and Method, 1975, Orientalism, 1978, The Question of Palestine, 1979, Covering Islam, 1980, The World, The Text and the Critic, 1983, After the Last Sky, 1986, Blaming the Victims, 1988, Musical Elaborations, 1991, Culture and Imperialism, 1993, Representations of the Intellectual, 1994, Politics of Dispossession, 1994, Peace and Its Discontents, 1996, Out of Place, 1999, The End of the Peace Process, 2000, Reflections on Exile and Other Essays, 2000; editor: Literature and Society, 1979, Ghazzah-Arihah: Salam Amriki, 1994, Henry James' Completed Stories 1884-1891, 1999. Social Sci. Research fellow, 1975; Guggenheim fellow, 1972-73; Recipient Lionel Trilling award Columbia U., 1976, 94, Sultan Owais Prize, 1998, Spinoza Prize, 1999, New Yorker Book Award for Non-Fiction, 1999, Year 2000 Anisfeld-Wolf Book Award for Non-Fiction, Morton Dauwen Zabel Award in Literature, 2000. Mem. AAAS, MLA, Assn. Arab Am. U. Grads. (past v.p.), N.Y. Coun. Fgn. Rels., Am. Comparative Lit. Assn. (René Wellek award 1985), PEN (exec. bd. 1989—), Am. Acad. Arts and Scis., Royal Soc. Literature, Am. Philosophical Soc., Modern Language Assn. (pres. 1999). Died Sept. 25, 2003.

SAINT-COME, CLAUDE MARC, science educator, consultant; b. Saint Marc, Haiti, May 23, 1949; came to U.S., 1968; s. Ernest and Marie Therese (Viau) Saint-Come; m. Cicely Patricia Leacock, Oct. 19, 1985. BS, Fordham Coll., 1975; MS, L.I. U., 1978; PhD, NYU, 1985. Adj., lectr. Medgar Evers Coll., Bklyn., 1975-78; lab. coord. NYU, N.Y.C., 1980-84; rsch. assoc. U. Mass. Med. Sch., Worcester, 1985-87; asst. prof. Bates Coll., Lewiston, Maine, 1987-88, So. Univ., Baton Rouge, 1988-89, U. S.C., Sumter, 1989-91, DeKalb Coll., Clarkston, Ga., from 1991. Cons. NYU, 1990-91; advisor ednl. programs N.Y. Acad. Scis., N.Y.C., 1983-84. Co-author: Laboratory Manual, 1984, Teacher's Manual, 1983; contbr. articles to profl. jours. Asst. to coord. Community Ednl. Tng. Program, Medgar Evers Coll., Bklyn., 1977. Recipient Rsch. Devel. grant Biomeasure Inc., 1989, Conf. fellowship Multiple Sclerosis Soc., 1987, Postdoctoral fellowship Porter Devel., 1985-87, Dissertation fellowship NYU, 1983. Mem. AAAS, Human Anatomy and Physiology, Sigma Xi (assoc.). Achievements include research in the release of atrial natriuretic peptides from the right atrium of the rat is modulated by pressure in the pulmonary trunk; in administration of modified ACTH peptides during the early phases of nerve regeneration prevents degenerative changes in associated muscles. Deceased.

ST. JOHN, HAROLD BERNARD, Barbados politician, lawyer; b. Christ Church, Barbados, Aug. 16, 1931; LL.B., Univ. Coll., London U.; m. Stella Hope; children— Charmaine Jane, Nicole Alice, Harold Bryte Ian. Bar: Barbados, 1954. Sole practice, Barbados and Eastern Caribbean; created queen's counsel, 1969; mem. Barbados Senate, 1964-66, 71-76, M.P., 1966-71; former minister of Caribbean Affairs, External Trade and Tourism; minister of Trade, Industry and Tourism, 1981-85, prime minister, 1985-86, dep.prime minister, 1991-99. Leader Barbados Labor Party. Died Feb. 29, 2004.

ST. JOHN, RICHARD See HARRIS, RICHARD

SAKER, JOSEPH MICHAEL, JR., lawyer; b. Warren, Ohio, Mar. 30, 1926; s. Joseph Michael Sr. and Victoria (Abraham) S.; m. Jeanette Julia Khoury; children: Joseph, Jean, James, Jeffrey (dec.), John. JD, Youngstown (Ohio) State U., 1955. Bar: Ohio 1955. Ptnr. Saker and Saker, Warren, from 1955. Acting judge Warren Mcpl. Ct., 1980-86; chmn. Warren City Civl Svc. Commn., 1981-87. Trustee Nat. Shrine of Our Lady of Lebanon, N. Jackson, Ohio, 1989—. Mem. Trumbull County Bar Assn. (pres. 1966), K.C., Elks, Moose. Democrat. Roman Catholic. Avocations: stamp collecting, music. Deceased.

SAKITA, BUNJI, physicist, retired educator; b. Inami, Toyama-ken, Japan, June 6, 1930; came to U.S., 1956; s. Eiichi and Fumi (Morimatsu) S.; children— Mariko, Taro. BS, Kanazawa U., 1953; MS, Nagoya U., 1956; PhD, U. Rochester, 1959. Rsch. assoc. U. Wis., Madison, 1959-62, asst. prof., 1962-64, prof., 1966-70; assoc. physicist Argonne (Ill.) Nat. Lab., 1964-66; disting. prof. City Coll. CUNY, N.Y.C., 1970-99, disting. prof. emeritus, from 1999. Vis. prof. IHES, Bures-sur-Yvette, France, 1970-71, Ecole Normale Superieur, Paris, 1979-80, 88, U. Tokyo, 1987; Pandit Jawaharlal Nehru chair U. Hyderabad, India, 2000. Recipient Nishina prize, 1974; Guggenheim fellow, 1970-71, Japan Soc. Promotion Sci. fellow, 1975, 80, 87, 95. Fellow Am. Phys. Soc. Home: Fort Lee, NJ. Died 2002.

SALAZAR, HERNANDO, surgical gynecological pathologist, educator; b. Ibague, Colombia, Nov. 21, 1931; s. Julio Ernesto and Alicia (Navarro) S.; m. Lolita Sanchez, Nov. 17, 1956; children: Fernando, Clara Lucia, Rodrigo, Oscar. BS, Coll. San Simon, Ibague, 1950; MD, Nat. U. Colombia, 1958; MPH, U. Pitts., 1971. Diplomate Am. Bd. Pathology. Instr. of physiology Nat. U. Med. Sch., Bogota, 1952-57, instr. morphology, 1958-60; fellow in cell biology Wash. U. Med. Sch., St. Louis, Mo., 1960-63; asst. prof. morhology Valle U., Cali, Colombia, 1963-66; from instr. to assoc. prof. pathology U. Pitts., 1966-83; med. dir. of labs. Med-Chek Labs., Pitts., 1983-92; chief surg. pathology Fox Chase Cancer Ctr., Phila., 1992-94, The Reading Hosp. Med. Ctr., West Reading, Pa., from 1994. Acad. sec., asst. dean Nat. U. Med. Sch., Bogota, 1959-60, Valle U. Med. Sch., Cali, 1963-66; sr. mem. Fox Chase Cancer Ctr., Phila., 1992-94; clin. prof. patology Jefferson Med. Sch., Phila., 1995—. Postdoctoral fellow Rockefeller Found. Washington U., 1960-63; rsch. fellow Monsour Med. Found. Oxford U., 1973-74. Fellow Coll. Am. Pathologists; mem. L.Am. Soc. Pathology, Internat. Acad. Pathology, Internat. Soc. Gynecol. Pathologists (pres. 1984-86), Latinamerican Pathology Found. (pres. 1981-83). Avocation: Ham radio. Achievements include identification of non-secretory cell type in the human hypophisis, identification of specific cells of endodermal origin in human yolk sac tumors; recognition of a pre-neoplastic phenotype in the ovaries of women at high risk for ovarian cancer. Home: West Reading, Pa. Died July 16, 2000.

SALMERON, FERNANDO, philosopher, researcher; b. Córdoba, Veracruz, Mex., Oct. 30, 1925; s. Fernando Salmerón-Díaz and Ana María Roiz; m. Alicia Castro; children: Fernando, Leonardo, Jorge, Alicia, Gabriel, Ana María. Lic. in law, U. Veracruzana, Veracruz, 1948, DHC (hon.), 1980; M of Philosophy, UNAM, Mex., 1955, PhD, 1965. Dir. faculty philosophy U. Veracruzana, 1956-58, rector, 1961-63; dir. Inst. Philos. Research, UNAM, 1966-78, researcher complete time, from 1981; rector iztapalapa sect. Met. Autonomus U., Mex., 1978-79, gen. rector, 1979-81. Author: Las mocedades de Ortega, 1959, 3d edit., 1983, Cuestiones educativas y Págs sobre Mexico, 1962, 2d edit., 1980, La filosofía y las actitudes morales, 1971, 3d edit., 1986, Ortega y Gasset, 1984, Etica y análisis, 1985, Ensayos filosóficos, 1988, Enseñanza y filosifia, 1991, The Origins of Analytic Moral Philosophy and Other Essays, 1998, Perfiles y recuerdos, 1998, Diversidad cultural y tolerancia, 1998, Etica analitica y derecho, 2000, Ensayos de filosifia moderna y contemporanea, 2000, Escritos sobre José Gaos, 2000. Rockefeller Found. scholar, 1959-60; Sistema Nacional Investigadores fellow, Mex., 1984—, Premio Nacional de Ciencias y Artes, 1993, Premio Universidad Nacional, 1993. Mem. Colegio Nacional, Inst. Internat. Philosophie, Acad. Investigación Cientifica, Acad. Mex. Lengua, Assn. Filosófica Mex. (pres. 1988—). Home: Tlalpan, Mexico. Died May 31, 1997.

SALMON, SYDNEY ELIAS, medical educator, director; b. S.I., N.Y., May 8, 1936; m. Joan; children: Howard, Julia, Laura, Stewart, Russell. BA cum laude, U. Ariz., 1958; MD, Washington U., St. Louis, 1962. Intern, then resident in medicine Strong Meml. Hosp., Rochester, N.Y., 1962-64; rsch. fellow in immunology dept. pediats. Harvard U. Med. Sch., Boston, 1965-66; rsch. fellow dept. medicine Medicine and Cancer Rsch. Inst. U. Calif., San Francisco, 1966-68, asst. prof. medicine dept. medicine, 1968-72; assoc. prof. medicine U. Ariz., Tucson, 1972-74, head sect. hematology and oncology, 1972-81, prof. medicine, 1974-89, founding dir. Ariz. Cancer Ctr., from 1976, regents prof. medicine, from 1989. NIH spl. fellow Cancer Rsch. Inst., U. Calif., San Francisco, 1966-68, rsch. assoc., 1968-72; mem. nat. cancer adv. bd. Nat. Cancer Inst., 1990—; founding sci. Selectide Corp., 1990; mem. sci. adv. bds. Amplimed Corp., SUGEN Corp.; bd. dirs. Synergen Devel. Corp., Repligen Devel. Corp. Editor: Cloning of Human Tumor Cells, Human Tumor Cloning, Adjuvant Therapies of Cancer, 1982, Clinics of Haematology, 1982; mem. adv. bd. Cancer Treatment Reports, 1979-82; mem. editl. bd. Stell Cells, Jour. Clin. Oncology; patentee in field; contbr. articles to profl. jours. Surgeon USPHS, 1964-66. Recipient Lectureship award Gold Headed Cane Soc., 1979, Alumni Achievement award U. Ariz., 1986. Mem. AAAS, Am. Soc. Hematology, Am. Soc. Clin. Investigation, Am. Soc. Clin. Oncology (pres. 1984-85), Am. Cancer Soc. (bd. dirs. Ariz. divsn.), Leukemia Soc. Am., Am. Assn. Cancer Rsch., Assn. Am. Cancer Insts. (pres. 1988-89). Died 1999.

SALUJA, SUNDAR S. international engineering consultant; b. Wasu, Punjab, India, June 23, 1927; came to U.S., 1981; s. Wadhaya Mal and Gur Devi (Bagga) S.; m. Kamla S. Grover Saluja, Oct. 12, 1953; children: Bhupinder, Urvashi, Dipender. AISM, Indian Sch. of Mines, Dhanbad, India, 1950; postgrad. diploma, U. Sheffield, United Kingdom, 1955; MS, U. Ill., 1961; PhD, U. Wis., 1963. Cert. mine surveyor and mine mgr., India. Mine engr., surveyor Mining Industry, 1950-53, mine mgr., 1953-57; prof. of coal mining Banaras Hindu U., Varanasi, India, 1957-66, head dept of mining engring., 1966-71, prin. coll. mining & met., 1966-68, dean faculty of engring. & tech., 1968-71, dir. inst. tech., 1971-81; prof. mining engring. U. N.D., Grand Forks, 1982-96, prof. emeritus, from 1997. Mem. Univ. Grants, Commn. India, 1976-79; pres. assn. engring., sci. sect. Indian Sci. Congress, 1980. Co-author: Handbook on Mechanical Properties of Rocks, vol. 1, 1974, translated in Japanese, 1989. Mem. state adv. com. U.S. Commn. on Civil Rights, 1993-95; founder, pres. Gt. Plains Forum, Grand Forks, N.D., 1985—, ROUSE Found. For Reclamation of Our Spiritual Environ.; advisor N.D. State Pub. Svc. Commn., 1983-84; founder, pres. Global Arouse Alliance for the Reclamation of our Spiritual Environment, 1998—; vol. Kaiser Permanente Health Edn. Dept., No. Claif., 1998. Grad. fellowship, Colombo Plan, 1954-55, fellowship in Engring., Nuffield Found., 1959, Commonwealth U. Tchrs. Exch., Australia, 1960, TCM fellowship, U.S Ag. for Int. Devel., 1961; recipient Dr. Rajendra Pasad Meml. Gold medal Inst. of Engrs., Calcutta, India, 1978. Mem. Mining, Geol. & Met. Inst. of India (coun. mem. 1966-69), Am. Soc. Engring. Edn., Am. Soc. Mining Met. & Exploration, Indian

Sci. Congress Assn. (pres. en gring. 1979-80), Global Alliance for the Reclamation of Our Spiritual Environ. (founder, pres.). Achievements include pioneer rsch. on roof bolting (1954-66), blasting mechanics (1961-71), mining of thick coal seams (1964-71), airlift pumping (1976-78), Nat. Reconstruction Corps. (1972), architect of engr. clinic c prototype dev. centres (1963-78), Indian Energy Policy (1979-81), World Energy Policy (1982—), leadership role in saving the $ 3.8 billion coal gasification plant in N.D. (1984-86), rsch. in environ. of human mind to improve the quality of life and its impact on soc. (1992—). Home: Cupertino, Calif. Died Mar. 15, 2000.

SAMUEL, HOWARD DAVID, union official; b. N.Y.C., Nov. 16, 1924; s. Ralph E. and Florence (Weingarten) S.; m. Ruth H. Zamkin, Apr. 15, 1948; children: Robert H., Donald F., William H. BA, Dartmouth Coll., 1948. Various positions Amalgamated Clothing and Textile Workers (formerly Amalgamated Clothing Workers Am.), N.Y.C., 1949-60, asst. pres., 1960-64, v.p., 1966-77; dep. under sec. Bur. Internat. Labor Affairs Dept. Labor, Washington, 1977-79; pres. Indsl. Union Dept. AFL-CIO, Washington, 1979-92; v.p. New Sch. for Social Rsch., N.Y.C., 1964-65, Econ. Strategy Inst., 1992-98. Vice chmn. N.Y. Urban Coalition, 1968-74; mem. governing bd. Common Cause, 1971-77; sec. Nat. Com. Full Employment, 1975-77, sec.-treas., 1977-89; mem. Pres.'s Commn. on Indsl. Competitiveness, 1983-85; sr. fellow Coun. on Competitiveness, 1993-97, vice chmn., 1986-92; mem. U.S. Dept. Labor Task Force on Econ. Adjustment, and Worker Dislocation, 1985-87; mem. vis. com. advanced tech. Nat. Inst. Stds. and Tech., 1995-2000; mem. adv. com. Export-Import Bank. Author: (with Stephen K. Bailey) Congress at Work, 1952; Government in America, 1957; editor: Toward a Better America, 1968; author numerous mag. articles. Mem. Nat. Manpower Adv. Com., 1969-74; mem. Commn. Population Growth and the Am. Future, 1970-72; mem. Def. Mfg. Bd., 1988-89, Def. Sci. Bd., 1989-92; chmn. White Plains Dem. Com., 1960-64; vice-chmn. Westchester County com., 1957-70, alt. del. nat. conv., 1964; mem. Nat. Dem. Charter Revision Com., 1972-73; exec. dir. Nat. Labor Com. McGovern-Shriver, 1972; del. Dem. Conv. on Party Orgn. and Policy, Kansas City, 1974, Nat. Dem. Conv., 1976; trustee Carnegie Corp., 1971-77, Joint Coun. Econ. Edn., 1971-77; bd. dirs. ACLU, 1966-68; trustee Brookings Instn.; overseer RAND Inst. for Civil Justice, 1987-93. With AUS, 1943-46. Mem. Coun. on Fgn. Rels., Phi Beta Kappa. Home: Chevy Chase, Md. Died June 19, 2003.

SANDBACK, FREDERICK LANE, artist; b. Bronxville, N.Y., Aug. 29, 1943; s. Edward C. and Helen E. (Kowalewski) S.; m. Margaret Alden Bovey, Jan. 25, 1964 (div. 1972); children— Annika M., Peter F.; m. Amy Baker, May 25, 1982. BA, Yale Coll., 1966; B.F.A., M.F.A., Yale Sch. Art and Architecture, 1969. Numerous one-man shows of drawings, prints, and sculpture including, John Weber Gallery, N.Y.C., 1976, Brooke Alexander, Inc., N.Y.C., 1976, Galerie Annemarie Verna, Zurich, Switzerland, 1976, Galerie Heiner Friedrich, Cologne, W. Ger., 1976, 78, Galleria Primo Piano, Rome, 1976, Galerie Heiner Friedrich, Munich, W. Ger., 1977, Lisson Gallery, London, 1977, Hester Van Royen Gallery, London, 1977, Heiner Friedrich, Inc., N.Y.C., 1978, Mus. Modern Art, N.Y.C., Yale U. Sch. of Art and Architecture, New Haven, 1978, Marian Goodman, N.Y.C., 1985, Kunsthaus Zurich, Switzerland, 1985, Kunsthalle Mannheim, Fed. Republic Germany, 1986, Galerie Fred Jahn, Munich, 1986, Kestner Gesellschaft, Hannover, Fed. Republic Germany, 1987, Westfalian Kunstuerein, Münster, Fed. Republic Germany, 1987, David Nolan, N.Y.C., Fred Jahn, Munich, Liliane and Michel Durand-Dessert, Paris, Dia Art Found., N.Y.C., Villa Arson, Nice, Contemporary Arts Mus., Houston, 1989, Yale Art Gallery, New Haven, 1989, Burnett Miller Gallery, L.A., 1989; group shows, 1967-2003, including, Mus. Modern Art, N.Y.C., 1976, Biennale of Sydney, Australia, 1976, Heiner Friedrich, Inc., N.Y.C., 1976, Cannaviello Studio d'Arte, Rome, 1976, Visual Arts Mus., N.Y.C., 1976, Galerie Heiner Friedrich, Cologne, 1977, Chgo. Art Inst., 1979, Lisson Gallery, London, 1980, Hayward Gallery, London, 1980, The New Provincetown Gallery, Provincetown, Mass., 1980, Kunsthaus, Zurich, 1980. Guggenheim fellow; Nat. Endowment for the Arts grantee. Died June 23, 2003.

SANDERS, PAUL HAMPTON, lawyer, retired educator, arbitrator/mediator; b. Sherman, Tex., Feb. 26, 1909; s. Jewell Richard and Louisa Jane (Gaskill) S.; m. Pauline Cameron, Feb. 23, 1935. AB, Austin Coll., 1931, LL.D., 1960; JD, Duke U., 1934. Bar: Tex. 1934, Ga. 1944, N.C. 1946, Tenn. 1951. Practiced with Leo Brewer, San Antonio, 1934; asst. to dir. of nat. bar program Am. Bar Assn., Chgo., 1934-36; asst. prof. law Duke U., 1936-40, assoc. prof. law, 1940-45, prof. law, from 1946; practiced with firm of Wilson and Sanders, Atlanta, 1946-47; vis. prof. law Sch. Jurisprudence, U. Calif. at Berkeley, 1947-48; prof. law Vanderbilt U., 1948-74, prof. emeritus, 1974—, past lectr. Sch. Medicine, adj. prof. mgmt. Grad. Sch. Mgmt.; regional atty. U.S. Dept. of Labor, 1951-53; prin. mediation officer Nat. War Labor Bd., Washington, 1942, regional atty., hdqrs. Atlanta, 1942-44, regional vice chmn., 1944; regional atty. Nat. Wage Stblzn. Bd., Atlanta, 1946. Past lectr. Nashville Sch. Social Work; cons. Fed. Civil Rights Commn., 1958-61; dir. Race Relations Law Reporter, 1955-59; apptd. mem. bd. inquiry, labor disputes in atomic energy installations, Oak Ridge, also Ky.; pub. mem., chmn. Industry Com. on Minimum Wages, Puerto Rico, 1950, 56-58, 60-61, 63, 67, 69, 71, 73, 75, 77; apptd. mem. various Presdl. emergency boards to consider labor disputes. Assoc. editor: Law and Contemporary Problems, 1937-46; editor symposia on Unauthorized Practice of Law, The Wage and Hour Law, Governmental Tort Liability, Alcoholic Beverage Control, Combating the Loan Shark, Labor in Wartime and Labor Dispute Settlement, all in Duke Univ., 1938-46; contbr. articles to profl. jours. Indsl. relations specialist, 12th Naval Dist. 1944-46, San Francisco; lt. USNR, 1945-53. Mem. ABA (council mem., sec. labor relations sect. 1949-52), Am. Law Inst. (life), Nat. Acad. Arbitrators (past mem., past bd. govs., regional chmn. Southeastern states 1968-74), Am. Arbitration Assn. (labor panel), Nat. Conf. Jud. Councils, Soc. Profls. in Dispute Resolution, Scholarship Soc. S., Order of Coif, Pi Gamma Mu, Phi Delta Phi. Democrat. Baptist (vice chmn. Christian Life Commn., So. Bapt. Conv. 1953-59). Club: University (Nashville). Home: Nashville, Tenn. Died Nov. 1999.

SANDESON, WILLIAM SEYMOUR, cartoonist; b. Mound City, Ill., Dec. 16, 1913; s. William Stephen and Jessie Mae (Mertz) S.; m. Ione Wear, June 4, 1938 (dec. 1975); 1 son, William Scott; m. Ruth Cress, Dec. 31, 1978. Student, Chgo. Acad. Fine Arts, 1931-32. Free-lance cartoonist for nat. mags., 1932-37; editorial cartoonist New Orleans Item-Tribune, 1937-41; cartoonist, picture editor and art dir. St. Louis Star-Times, 1941-51; editorial cartoonist Ft. Wayne (Ind.) News-Sentinel, 1951-82; ret., 1982. Drew daily cartoon feature for, Star-Times, Sketching Up With the News. Recipient Honor medal Freedoms Found., 1952, 53, 56, George Washington Honor medal, 1954, 55, 57, 58, 59, 60, Disting. Service award, 1961-72, cartoon award, 1982;, Ind. Sch. Bell award, 1967, Disting. Service awards, 1971-76, prin. cartoon award, 1977, cartoon award, 1978; co-recipient Pulitzer prize for gen. local reporting, 1982 Mem. Nat. Cartoonist Soc., Assn. Am. Editorial Cartoonists. Clubs: Fort Wayne Press (pres. 1965). Congregationalist. Home: Fort Wayne, Ind. Died Dec. 30, 2003.

SANDS, MARVIN, wine company executive; b. Cleve., Jan. 28, 1924; s. Mack E. and Sally (Kipnis) S.; m. Marilyn Alpert, May 30, 1947; children: Laurie, Richard, Robert. BSBA, U. N.C., 1946. Chmn., dir. Canandaigua Wine Co., Inc., N.Y., from 1945; pres., dir. Tenner Bros., Inc., Patrick, N.C., from 1965, Roberts Trading Corp., Canandaigua, from 1959; v.p., dir. Bisceglia Bros. Wine Co., Madera, Calif., from 1975. Pres. F.F. Thompson Health Sys., Inc., 1990—; past pres., dir. F.F. Thompson Hosp., Canandaigua, 1970—, Finger Lakes Area Hosp. Corp., Geneva, N.Y., 1980—; trustee YMCA, Canandaigua. Served with USN, 1943-46. Mem. Nat. Wine Assn. (treas., dir.), N.Y. State Finger Lakes Wine Growers Assn. (past pres., bd. dirs. 1979—), Assn. Am. Vintners (bd. dirs.). Home: Canandaigua, NY. Died 1999.

SANFORD, ISABEL GWENDOLYN, actress; b. N.Y.C., Aug. 29; d. James Edward and Josephine (Perry) S.; m. William Edward Richmond (dec.); children: Pamela (Mrs. Eddie Ruff), William Eric, Sanford Keith. Ed. pub. schs. Stage appearances in off-Broadway prodns., also in L.A.; Broadway appearance in Amen Corner; film appearances include Guess Who's Coming to Dinner, 1968, Pendulum, 1969, Stand Up and Be Counted, 1972, The New Centurions, 1972, Love at First Bite, 1979, Original Gangstas, 1996, Sprung, 1997, Mafia!, 1999, Jackie's Back, 1999, Click Three Times, 1999; appeared in TV film The Great Man's Whiskers, 1973, series All in the Family, numerous guest appearances various series, The Carol Burnett Show; co-star: TV series The Jeffersons, 1974-85, Hearts Are Wild, 1992, South Beach, 1992, Living Single, 1994, Hangin' with Mr. Cooper, 1994, The Fresh Prince of Bel Air, Cybill, Lois & Clark: The New Adventures of Superman, Roseanne, The Parkers, 2000. Mem. Kwanza Found. Died July 9, 2004.

SANTAMARIA, MONGO, percussionist; Mem. Cuban bands Perez Prado, Tito Puente and Cal Tjader; performed with various artists including Willie Bobo, Chick Corea, Dizzy Gillespie; albums include Afro Roots, Skins, Watermelon Man, Greatest Hits, (with Dizzy Gillespie) Summertime; compositions include Afro-Blue. Died Feb. 1, 2003.

SAPP, JAMES WINSTON, neuropsychiatrist, psychotherapist; b. Nov. 20, 1932; s. James W. Sr. and Helen (Bowen) S. MS in Rsch. Psychiatry, Temple U., 1964; MD, Emory U., 1957. Diplomate Am. Bd. Psychiatry and Neurology, Internat. and Am. Bd. Med. Psychotherapy, Internat. Acad. Behavioral Medicine, Counseling and Psychotherapy. Intern, Long Beach, Va., 1957-58; resident in psychiatry U. Pa. Hosp., Phila., 1958-59, Temple U. Hosp., Phila., 1959-61, fellow in rsch. psychiatry, 1961-64; psychotherapist, neuropsychiatrist Camarillo (Calif.) State Hosp. Lt. USN, 1958—. Mem. Am. Psychiat. Assn. Avocations: sports cars, collecting fine art. Home: Port Hueneme, Calif. Deceased.

SARETT, LEWIS HASTINGS, chemist, retired inventor, retired health/medical products executive; b. Champaign, Ill., Dec. 22, 1917; BS, Northwestern U., 1939; PhD, Princeton U., 1942. With Merck Rsch. Labs., Rahway, N.J., 1942, sr. v.p. science and tech.; ret., 1982. Inducted to Nat. Inventors Hall of Fame, 1980. Achievements include development of synthetic cortisone. Died Nov. 29, 1999.

SARNOFF, PAUL, metals consultant, author, editor; b. Bklyn., Apr. 21, 1918; s. Nathan and Rose (Gelfand) S.; m. Lucille Levitt, Oct. 13, 1940; children: Alan Jan, Mitchell Ira, Steven Arthur. BS, MBA, CCNY. Various Wall St. positions, 1937-57; owner Sarnoff Co.-Stockbrokers, N.Y.C., 1955-57; sales mgr. Thomas Haab & Botts, N.Y.C., 1957-67; lectr.-in-fin. Hofstra U., Hempstead, N.Y., 1967-71; v.p. Herzog & Co., N.Y.C., 1972-76; research dir. ContiCommodity Services, N.Y.C., 1976-80, Rudolph Wolff, N.Y.C., 1980-82; corp. v.p. Paine Webber Jackson Curtis, N.Y.C., 1982-86; dir. The Metals Consultancy, Baldwin, N.Y., from 1986. History editor Banker's Mag., Boston, 1965-71; exec. editor Sci. & Tech., N.Y.C., 1968-71; dir. Inst. for Bus. & Urban Rsch., Hempstead, N.Y., 1969-70; curator econ. history U. Wyo., Laramie, 1966—; founding pres. Futures Industry Assn. options div. and rsch. div. Author more than 60 books, including biographies, histories, children's books, fin. volumes; editor spl. projects for Euromoney in London; columnist Japan Econ. Jour., 1981—; contbg. editor fin. newsletters and publs., 1987—. Founding dir. Oceanside (N.Y.) Jewish Ctr., Inst. for Children's Lit., Redding Ridge, Conn. Served to 2d lt. U.S. Army, 1944-46. Mem. Internat. Precious Metals Inst., Soc. Mining Engrs., N.W. Mining Assn., Authors Guild. Democrat. Jewish. Home: Wakefield, RI. Deceased.

SARTORI, GIOVANNI MARIA, archbishop; b. Vicenza, July 11, 1925; Degree, Vicenza Sem.; degree in canon law, Pontifical Lateran U., Rome. Ordained priest, Roman Cath. Ch., 1948. Sec. Cath. Action Diocesan Com., 1948-49, 1948-49, diocesan social asst., 1948-49, episcopal del., 1959-69; editor Voce Dei Berici; rector sem., 1969-77; bishop Adria/Rovigo Roman Cath. Ch., 1977, archbishop Curia Arcivescovile, from 1987. Regional asst. Cath. Action, judge Ecclesiastical Tribunal of Veneto; ecclesiastical advisor Smallholders' Provincial Fedn.; asst. UCSI. Author: Essere Chiesa in Polesine. Named Pvt. Valet of His Holiness and Prelate of Honour. Mem. Accademia dei Concordi, Rovigo. Avocation: classica music. Deceased.

SARTORIS, DAVID JOHN, radiologist; b. Chgo., Nov. 25, 1955; s. Cornelius Ugo and Helen Louise (Lesjak); m. Cyd Clariza Grepo. BS in Biol. Scis., Stanford U., 1976, MD, 1980. Diplomate Am. Bd. Radiology. Intern, diagnostic radiology Stanford (Calif.) Univ. Med. Ctr., 1980-81; resident, diagnostic radiology Stanford U. and Affil. Hosps., 1981-84; fellow, musculoskeletal radiology U. Calif. and Affil. Hosps., San Diego, 1984-85; asst. prof. radiology U. Calif., San Diego, 1985-87, assoc. prof. radiology, 1987-94, prof. radiology, from 1994; chief, musculoskeletal IMG U. Calif. San Diego Med. Ctr., 1985-91, chief, quantitative bone densitometry, 1985-94. Lectr. in field; cons. Rsch. and Edn. Fund/Radiol. Soc. North Am.; vis. prof. numerous univs. including Creighton U. Med. Ctr., Omaha, 1993, U. Pitts., 1990, VA Med. Ctr., Long Beach, Calif., 1990, U. Ottawa/Ottawa Gen. Hosp., Ont., Can., 1987, others; served on numerous coms. in field. Contbr. over 400 articles to profl. jours., numerous chpts. to books in field; editorial adv. bd. Chem. Rubber Co. Pres., Inc., Boca Raton, Fla., Diagnostic Imaging mag., 1987, Thieme Med. Pubs., Inc., N.Y.C., Year Book Med. Pubs., Chgo., Applied Radiology Jour.; asst. editor: AJR/musculoskeletal sect., 1987-88; reviewer jours. Rsch. grantee The Arthritis Soc., Toronto, Ont.; recipient Silver Spoon awards from residents at U. Calif., San Diego, 1986, 93, 94, others. Mem. Am. Coll. Radiology, Am. Roentgen Ray Soc., Assn. U. Radiologists, Radiol. Soc. N. Am., Calif. Radiol. Soc., Physicians for Social Responsibility, Internat. Skeletal Soc. (Youngest-Ever New Mem. award 1987, Pres.'s medal 1989), So. Calif. Bone and Mineral Club, New Bone Densitometry Soc., Bone Dysplasia Soc., Phi Beta Kappa. Avocations: swimming, stamp collecting. Home: La Jolla, Calif. Died June 17, 2000.

SATANOWSKI, ROBERT, conductor, deceased; b. Łódź, Poland, June 20, 1918; s. Jakub and Maria Ida (Kolska) S.; m. Dunuta Balicka, 1960 (div. 1987); children: Jeny, Grzegorz; m. Grazyna Mieszkowicz-Adamowier, Mar. 12, 1988. Student, Tech. U., 1935-39; MA, Musical Acad., Łódź, 1951. Condr. Philharm. State Orch., Lublin, Poland, 1951-54, artistic dir. Bydgoszoz, Poland, 1954-58; gen. music dir. Städtische Bühnen, Chemnitz, East Germany, 1960-62; gen. and artistic. dir. Philharm. State Orch., Poznan, Poland, 1961-63, State Opera House, Poznan, 1963-69; gen. music dir. Vereinigte Städtische Bühnen, Krafeld-Monchengladbach, 1969-76; gen. and artistic dir. City Opera House, Cracow, Poland, 1975-77, State Opera House, Wroclaw, Poland, 1976-82, Nat. Opera House, Warsaw, 1981-91. Author of music critiques; composer of various works for chamber and symphony orch. Mem. Parlament, Warsaw, Poland, 1985-89. Gen. Polish Army, 1941-49. Decorated Labour Banner First Class (Poland), Commdr. Cross with Star (Poland), Das Grosse Verdienstkrwuz award Der Bundespresident (Germany) and various other military awards. Mem. Assn. Polish Musicians (hon., pres. 1965-70, 81-88), Intern. Assn. Opera Houses (bd. dirs. 1991—), Le Circle Lyrique Internat. (v.p. 1987—), Assn. Mil. Veterans. Home: Warsaw, Poland. Died, 1997.

SATOVSKY, ABRAHAM, lawyer; b. Detroit, Oct. 15, 1907; s. Samuel and Stella (Benenson) Satovsky; m. Toby Nayer, Sept. 4, 1938 (dec.); children: Sheldon Baer, James Bennett. BA, U. Mich., 1928, JD, 1930. Bar: Mich. 1930, U.S. Supreme Ct. 1930. Assoc. William Henry Gallagher, Detroit, 1930-65. Bldg. chmn. lawyers com. United Found. and Torch Dr. Active fund raiser Greater Miami United Jewish Appeal; mem. fund dr. com. U. Mich. Law Sch.; trustee Clover Hill Park Cemetery, 1978—81, trustee emeritus, from 1982; co-chmn. profl. divsn. Allied Jewish Campaign; mem. adv. coun. United Synagogue Am.; del. Jewish Cmty. Coun., Detroit; v.p. Mosies Chetim Orgn., Detroit; bd. dirs. Congregation Shaarey Zedek, Southfield, Mich., past pres., 1959—62; bd. dirs. Detroit Svc. Group, past chmn. fgn. mission. Recipient Sem. award, Jewish Theol. Sem. Am., 1952, citation of merit, Jewish Welfare Fedn., Detroit, Jerusalem award, State of Israel Bond Orgn., others. Mem.: ABA, Am. Judicature Soc., Am. Arbitration Assn., Oakland County Bar Assn., Detroit Bar Assn., Mich. Bar Assn., Am.

Jewish Hist. Soc., Jewish Hist. Soc. Mich. (mem. adv. bd.), Std. Club, Men's Club Congregation Shaarey Zedek (past pres., hon. life pres.), Nat. Fedn. Jewish Men's Clubs (founder, past pres., hon. life pres., Gt. Lakes Regional award 1977, Ma'Asim Tovim (Good Deeds) award 1989), B'nai B'rith (past pres. Detroit), Hadassah (life), Phi Beta Delta (merged with Pi Lambda Phi. Died Sept. 20, 2003.

SATTEN, ROBERT ARNOLD, physics educator; b. Chgo., Aug. 4, 1922; s. Frank and Mabel Satten; m. Erica Dorothee Simone, Oct. 19, 1946; children: Corey Douglas, Glen Alan. BS, U. Chgo., 1944; MA, UCLA, 1947, PhD, 1951. Instr. UCLA, 1951-52, asst. prof., 1953-58, assoc. prof. physics, 1958-63, prof. physics, 1963-91, prof. emeritus, from 1991, vice chmn. dept. physics, 1968-69, 70-73, vice chmn. acad. affairs, 1987-91; asst. prof. physics MIT, 1952-53. Resident rsch. assoc. Argonne (Ill.) Nat. Lab., summer 1957; cons. in field. Contbr. articles to profl. jours. Fulbright Rsch. scholar, France, 1961-62, Ger., 1969-70; Erskine fellow, U. Canterbury, N.Z., 1971. Fellow Am. Phys. Soc.; mem. Am. Assn. Physics Tchrs., AAAS, AAUP, Phi Beta Kappa. Avocations: folk dancing, skiing. Home: Los Angeles, Calif. Died Sept. 26, 2001.

SAUBERLICH, HOWERDE EDWIN, biochemistry educator, nutritionist; b. Ellington, Wis., Jan. 23, 1919; s. George Henry and Ann Gertrude (Ray) S.; m. Irene Kathryn Cartwright, Sept. 15, 1945; children: Melissa Kay, Howerde Edwin II. BA, Lawrence U., 1944; MS, U. Wis., 1946, PhD, 1948. Diplomate Am. Bd. Nutrition. Prof. biochemistry Auburn (Ala.) U., 1948-58, U. Indonesia/Ky., Bogor, 1957-59; chief chemistry div. Fitzsimons Hosp., Denver, 1960-73; assoc. prof. Iowa State U., Ames, 1959; chief div. nutrition tech. Letterman Inst., San Francisco, 1974-80; acting dir. Western Human Nutrition Rsch. Ctr. USDA, San Francisco, 1980-82; prof. dept. nutrition sci. U. Ala., Birmingham, from 1982. Rsch. fellow U. Tenn., Knoxville, 1951; vis. prof. Vanderbilt U., Nashville, 1970-71; adj. prof. U. Miami, 1990—. Author, co-author books, chpts. in books; contbr. over 300 articles to sci. jours. Recipient Meritorious Civilian Svc. award Dept. Army, 1964, McLester award, 1965, Rsch. award Sec. of Army, 1970, Disting. Svc. award Lawrence U., 1994. Fellow Am. Inst. Nutrition (Meade-Johnson award 1952, Borden award 1971); mem. Am. Assn. Cancer Rsch., Am. Soc. Biochemistry Molecular Biology, Am. Soc. Clin. Nutrition, numerous others. Achievements include research in nutrition sciences, human and clinical nutrition, antibiotics, trace elements, vitamins, clinical chemistry, cancer research, microbiologgy, animal science, proteins. Home: Birmingham, Ala. Died May 14, 2001.

SAX, HELEN SPIGEL, lawyer; b. Phila., June 2, 1915; d. D. Hays and Erna (Sultan) Solis-Cohen; m. Herbert Spigel (dec. 1951), Aug. 31, 1939; children: Frank, Robert, James; m. James E. Sax, June 15, 1969 BA, Swarthmore Coll., 1937; LL.B., U. Pa., 1940. Bar: Ill. 1941, Pa. 1945. With War Labor Bd., Chgo., 1940-41; mem. Wolf Block Schorr & Solis-Cohen, Phila., 1945—98. Former trustee Rosenbach Mus. and Libr., Nat. Mus. Am. Jewish History; bd. dirs. Big Bros.-Big Sisters Assn. Phila; mem. women's bd. Thomas Jefferson U. Hosp.; mem. adv. bd. Phila. Found.; mem. Juvenile Justice Alliance-Citizens Crime Commn.; former pres., mem. fin. com. Girl Scouts of Greater Phila. Mem. ABA, Pa. Bar Assn., Phila. Bar Assn., Phila. Lawyers Club, Phi Beta Kappa Home: Albuquerque, N.Mex. Died May 2, 2004.

SCACE, WILLIAM BUELL, retired manufacturing executive; b. Chgo., May 27, 1905; s. Stephen Birch and Mae (Emmert) S. PhB, U. Chgo., 1928. Commd. 2d lt. USAR, 1928, advanced through grades to lt. col., 1946, ret., 1965; trainee Sears Roebuck and Co., Chgo., 1928-31, investment adviser, 1932-34; 1st lt. in command civilian Conservation Corp. camp U.S. Army, 1935-37; co-founder, pres. Scrambled Signs Co., Chgo., 1938; prodn. mgr. Speed Way Mfg. Co., Cicero, Ill., 1939-41; co-founder, asst. commanding officer Army Electronic Standards Agy., World War II, 1942-46; v.p. Speed Way Mfg. Co., La Grange Park, Ill., 1947-65, pres., 1951-63, chmn., 1963-65, ret., 1965. Donor U. Wyo. Transp. History, Laramie, 1968, Am. Heritage Ctr., 1990. Decorated Legion of Merit; set Bonneville Nat. B Motosports speed record (219.665 mph), 1968. Mem. Acad. Polit. Scis. (life), Ret. Officers Assn. (life), Res. Officers Assn. (life), Union League Club, Bonneville Zoo MPH Club (life), U.S. Auto Club (life), Masons. Republican. Lutheran. Home: Oak Park, Ill. Deceased.

SCAVULLO, FRANCESCO, photographer; b. Staten Island, N.Y., Jan. 16, 1929; s. Angelo and Margaret (Pavis) S.; m. Carol McCallson, 1952. Student pub. schs., N.Y.C. Asst. photographer Horst at Vogue Studio, N.Y.C., 1946-48; photographer Seventeen mag., N.Y.C., 1948-50, Town and Country mag., 1950, Harper's Bazaar mag., 1960, Cosmopolitan mag., 1965, Vogue mag., 1970. Owner The Scavullo Gallery, 1988. Represented in permanent collection, Met. Mus. Art., Amon Carter Mus., Ft. Worth; author: Scavullo on Beauty, 1976, Scavullo Men, 1977, Scavullo Women, 1982, Scavullo, 1984. Recipient Photograph of Yr. award, 1977, numerous awards advt. art dirs. clubs. Mem. Dirs. Guild Am. Roman Catholic. Died Jan. 6, 2004.

SCHACHTER, OSCAR, lawyer, educator, arbitrator; b. N.Y.C., June 19, 1915; s. Max and Fannie (Javits) S.; m. Mollie Miller, Aug. 9, 1936 (dec. July 1980); children: Judith (Mrs. Albrecht Funk), Ellen (Mrs. John P. Leventhal); m. Muriel L. Sackler, June 14, 1982. BSS, Coll. City N.Y., 1936; JD, Columbia, 1939, LLD (hon.), 2000. Bar: N.Y. 1939. Editor-in-chief Columbia Law Rev., 1938-39; pvt. practice N.Y.C., 1939-40; atty. U.S. Dept. of Labor, Washington, 1940; chief nat. defense sect. in law dept. FCC, 1941; sect. of law com. and adviser on internat. communications Bd. of War Communications, 1941-42; prin., divisional asst., adviser on wartime econ. controls and on European liberated areas U.S. Dept. State, 1942-43; asst. gen. counsel UNRRA, 1944-46; drafting officer UNRRA council sessions, 1944-45; legal adv. UNRRA del. to USSR and Poland, 1945; legal counselor UN, 1946-52, dir. gen. legal div., 1952-66; dep. exec. dir., dir. studies UN Inst. for Tng. and Research, 1966-75; lectr. law Yale U. Law Sch., 1955-71; Carnegie lectr. Hague Acad. Internat. Law, 1963-82; Rosenthal lectr. Northwestern U. Law Sch., 1974; prof. Law Sch. and Faculty Internat. Affairs Columbia U., from 1975, Hamilton Fish prof. internat. law and diplomacy Law Sch. and Faculty Internat. Affairs, 1980-85, prof. emeritus Law Sch. and Faculty Internat. Affairs, from 1985. Vis. prof Harvard Law Sch., 1982; chmn. legal com. UN Maritime Conf., 1948; legal cons. UNESCO, 1948; past dir. Gen. Legal Div. of UN; served as legal adviser various internat. confs. and UN couns. and coms.; sec. legal adv. com. UN Atomic Energy Commn., 1946-47; vice chmn. Internat. Investment Law Conf., 1958; exec. sec. Internat. Arbitration Conf., 1958; mem. panel arbitrators Internat. Ctr. for Settlement of Investment Disputes, 1980-87; judge Ct. Arbitration in Canada-France Maritime Boundary dispute, 1989-92; expert advisor UN com. on transnational corps., 1990-93. Author: Relation of Law, Politics and Action in the U.N, 1964, Sharing the World's Resources, 1977, International Law in Theory and Practice, 1985, rev. edit., 1991; co-author: Across the Space Frontier, 1952, Toward Wider Acceptance of UN Treaties, 1971, International Law Cases and Materials, 1980, 3rd edit., 1993, United Nations Legal Order, 2 vols., 1995; contbr. articles and monographs on internat. law, internat. instns., legal philosophy, human rights, internat. peace and security, internat. resources to legal jours.; editor-in-chief Am. Jour. Internat. Law, 1978-84, hon. editor, 1985—; co-editor: Competition in International Business, 1981; editorial bd. Marine Policy. Bd. dirs. Internat. Peace Acad., 1970-82. Recipient Friedman award Columbia Law Sch., 1983, Carl Fulda award U. Tex. Law Sch., 1990, Columbia Law medal for excellence, 1991. Fellow Am. Acad. Arts and Scis., World Acad. Art and Sci.; mem. ABA, Am. Soc. Internat. Law (pres. 1968-70, hon. v.p., exec. coun., hon. pres. 1994-96, Manley Hudson medal 1981, Cert. of Merit for creative scholarship 1992), Coun. on Fgn. Rels., Inst. de Droit Internat. (v.p. 1991-93), Internat. Law Assn., Internat. Astronautical Acad., Phi Beta Kappa. Home: New York, NY. Died Dec. 13, 2003.

SCHALGE, ROGER DONALD, mechanical engineer; b. Akron, N.Y., Mar. 28, 1932; s. Alvin Carl and Clara (Sardes) S.; m. Patricia Ann, Aug. 10, 1985; children: Linda, Rosemary, Roger Jr., Christopher. BSME, Poly. Inst., Bklyn., 1965. Product mgr. Patent Scaffold, N.Y.C., 1965-75; v.p. SPG Steel Scaffold, Linden, N.J., 1975-79; project mgr. Fenix & Scisson, Tulsa, 1979-90, PB-KBB, Inc., Houston, from 1990. With USN, 1949-53, Korea. Mem. ASME, Soc. Petroleum Engrs. Home: Houston, Tex. Died Sept. 6, 2000.

SCHEIBER, SANDOR, clergyman, educational administrator; b. Budapest, Hungary, July 9, 1913; s. Lajos and Maria (Adler) S.; m. Livia Bernath, 1942; 1 dau. Ed. Budapest U., Nat. Rabbinical Sem., Budapest, and in U.K.; Dr. (hon.), Hebrew Union Coll., Cin., Balt. Hebrew Coll., Jewish Theol. Sem. Am. Chief rabbi, Dunafoldvar, 1940-44; prof. Nat. Rabbinical Sem., 1945-50, dir., 1950—; pvt. docent Szeged U., 1949. Author: Mikszath Kalman es a keleti folklor, 1949; Magyarorszagi zsido feliratok, 1960; Heber kodexmaradvanyok magyarorszagi kotestablakban, 1969; Folklor es targytortenet I-II, 1974, 77; Genizah Studies, 1981; editor: Monumenta Hungariae Judaica, vols. V-XVIII, Kodex Maimonides, 1980. Recipient Gold medal (Freeman), Oppido, Italy, Kaplan prize, Phila. Mem. Jewish Hist. Soc. (Eng.) (corr.), Am. Acad. Jewish Research (corr.), World Union Jewish Studies (council); hon. mem. Mekize Nirdamim, Assn. Jewish Studies. Died 1985.

SCHEINBERG, LABE CHARLES, neurologist, educator; b. Memphis, Dec. 11, 1925; m. Louise Goldman, Jan. 6, 1952 (dec. Jan. 2000): children: Susan, David, Ellen, Amy. AB, U. N.C., 1945; MD, U. Tenn., 1948. Intern Wesley Meml. Hosp., Chgo., 1949; resident psychiatry Elgin (Ill.) State Hosp., 1950; resident, asst. neurology Neurol. Inst., N.Y., 1952-56; mem. faculty Albert Einstein Coll. Medicine, 1956-93, prof. neurology, asst. dean, 1968-69, assoc. dean, 1969-70, prof. rehab. medicine and psychiatry, dean, 1970-72; dir. neurology Hosp., 1966-73; dir. dept. neurology and psychiatry St. Barnabas Hosp., Bronx, N.Y., 1974-79; prof. neurology emeritus Albert Einstein Coll. Medicine, N.Y.C., 1995—2004. Cons. editor: N.Y. Acad. Scis., 1964, 84; founding editor-in-chief Jour. Neurologic Rehab., Rehab. Reports, Multiple Sclerosis Rsch. Reports. Served as capt. M.C. USAF, 1951-52. Fellow Am. Acad. Neurology; mem. Am. Neurol. Assn., Am. Assn. Neuro-pathology, Am. Soc. Exptl. Pathology, Phi Beta Kappa, Alpha Omega Alpha. Died Feb. 22, 2004.

SCHELL, JOZEF STEPHAAN (JEFF SCHELL), molecular biologist, science administrator; b. Antwerp, Belgium, July 20, 1935; s. Franciscus Josephus Joannes and Mathildis Adolphina J. (Springael) S.; m. Elizabeth Warren Frederick, Sept. 14, 1968; children: Peter Frederick Warren, Bart Frank Frederick. Lic. in zoology, State U. Ghent, Belgium, 1957, PhD in Microbiology (hon.), 1960. Extraordinary prof. Free U. Brussels, 1972-78; assoc. prof., dir. State U. Ghent, 1967-70, prof., dept. head, 1970-78, dept. head, 1978-87, extraordinary prof., 1978—2003; dir. Max Planck Inst. Plant Breeding Rsch., Cologne, Germany, 1978-94; prof. Coll. de France, Paris, 1994—2003; hon. prof. U. Cologne, 1980—2003. Mem. John Innes Coun., Norwich, Eng., 1990-2003; chmn. coun. EMBO, Heidelberg, 1991—; mem. peer adv. bd. IRRI, Manila, 1990-2000; chmn. coun. EMBO, Heidelberg, Germany, 1991-2002. Editor-in-chief EMBO Jour., 1991-2002; sr. editor Plant Jour., 1990-2003; mem. editl. bd. Current Opinion in Biotech., 1988-2003, Molecular and Gen. Genetics, 1978-2003. Mem. adv. bd. KOWI, Bonn, Germany, 1994. Recipient Francqui prize Francqui Fonds, Brussels, 1979, Wolf prize in Agriculture, Wolf Found., Israel, 1990, Australia prize Sci. and Tech. Awareness Program, Govt. of Australia, 1990. Mem. NAS (fgn. assoc.), Acad. Arts and Scis. (fgn. hon.), Hungarian Acad. Scis. (hon.), Leopoldina. Achievements include patents, including that for process for introduction of expressable genes into plant cell genomes and Agrobacterium strains carrying hybrid Ti plasmid vectors useful to this process, various others. Died Apr. 17, 2003.

SCHELLPEPER, STAN, state legislator; b. Hoskins, Nebr., Jan. 27, 1934; m. Faye Wiedeman, 1957; children: Jeffrey, Thomas, Nancy (Mrs. Morfeld). Grad., Stanton H.S. Farmer, livestock breeder, Nebr.; mem. from dist. 18 Nebr. State Senate, Lincoln, from 1986, mem. agr. and revenue coms., chmn. gov. affairs com. Past state pres. Nebr. Rural Elec. Assn.; past sec. Sch. Dist. 13, Nebr.; sec., mgr. Stanton County Fair Bd.; mem. Nebr. State Fair Bd. Named Area Farmer of Yr., Norfolk Kiwanis, 1985. Mem. Stanton County Livestock Feeders Assn. (past pres.). Died April 4, 1999.

SCHERICK, EDGAR J. film producer; Producer films The Birthday Party, 1968, For Love of Ivy, 1968, Ring of Bright Water, 1969, Homer, 1970, Jenny, 1970, To Kill a Clown, 1972, The Heartbreak Kid, 1972, Gordon's War, 1973, Law and Disorder, 1974, The Taking of Pelham 1-2-3, 1974, The Stepford Wives, 1975, I Never Promised You a Rose Garden, 1977, Shoot the Moon, 1982, I'm Dancing As Fast As I Can, 1982, Reckless, 1984, Mrs Soffel, 1984, Rambling Rose, 1991, others. Died Dec. 3, 2002.

SCHEUER, PAUL JOSEF, chemistry educator; b. Heilbronn, Germany, May 25, 1915; came to U.S., 1938; s. Albert and Emma (Neu) S.; m. Alice Elizabeth Dash, Sept. 5, 1950; children: Elizabeth E., Deborah A., David A., Jonathan L.L. BS with honors, Northeastern U., Boston, 1943; MA, Harvard U., 1947, PhD, 1950. Asst. prof. chemistry U. Hawaii, Honolulu, 1950-55, assoc. prof. chemistry, 1956-61, prof. chemistry, 1961-85, prof. chemistry emeritus, from 1985. Vis. prof. Orsted Inst., U. Copenhagen, 1977, 89; Toyo Suisan vis. prof. U. Tokyo, 1992. Author: Chemistry of Marine Natural Products, 1973, editor 12 series, 1978-93; contbr. over 290 articles to profl. jours. Spl. agt. U.S. Army, 1944-46, ETO. Recipient Rsch. Achievement award Am. Soc. Pharmacognosy, 1994, Regents award for rsch. excellence U. Hawaii, 1972; named P.J. Scheuer award Marine Chemists, 1992, Disting. Rsch. Scientist, Hawaii Acad. Sci., 2002; NATO fellow, 1975. Fellow AAAS, Royal Soc. Chemistry; mem. Am. Chem. Soc. (sect. chair 1956, 87, Hawaii sect. award 1996, Ernest Guenther award 1994), Northeastern U. Alumni Assn. (Disting. Alumni award 1984). Home: Honolulu, Hawaii. Deceased.

SCHIFF, STEFAN OTTO, zoologist, educator; b. Braunschweig, Germany, July 22, 1930; came to U.S., 1941, naturalized, 1943; s. Walter and Johanne Ilse (Muller) S.; m. Laura Frances Ward, June 6, 1957; children— Sena, Stefanie BS, Roanoke Coll., 1952; PhD, U. Tenn., 1964. USPHS trainee, 1961-63; mem. faculty George Washington U., Washington, 1964—95, prof. zoology, 1976-95, prof. emeritus, 1995—2004, chmn. dept. biol. scis., 1977-87, dir. grad. genetics program, 1971-95. Author: Twenty-One Afternoons of Biology, 3d edit., 1986, Buttons: Art in Miniature, 1980 Lutheran. Home: Fairfax, Va. Died Feb. 6, 2004.

SCHINZINGER, ROLAND, electrical and computer engineering educator; b. Osaka, Japan, Nov. 22, 1926; s. Robert Karl Edmund and Annelise (Hebting) S.; m. Jane Harris, June 19, 1952 (dec.); children: Stefan, Annelise, Barbara; m. Shirley Price, 1994. BSEE, U. Calif., Berkeley, 1953, MSEE, 1954, PhD in Elec. Engring., 1966. Registered profl. engr., Calif. Mem. liaison staff Nippon Steel Tube Co., Tsurumi Shipyard, Japan, 1946-47; asst. mgr. Far Eastern Equip. Co., Ltd., Tokyo, 1947-48; lectr. U. Pitts., 1955-58; elec. engr. Westinghouse Elec. Corp., East Pittsburgh, 1954-58; asst./assoc. prof. Robert Coll., Istanbul, Turkey, 1958-63; mem. faculty dept. elec. and computer engring. and mgmt. U. Calif., Irvine, 1965-92, prof., assoc. dean, 1979-83, 85-86. Author: (with M. Martin) Ethics in Engineering, 1983, 4th edit., 1999, (with P.A. Laura) Conformal Mapping: Modern Applications and Methods, 1991; contbr. articles to profl. jours., chpts. to books. Sci. faculty fellow NSF, 1964. Fellow IEEE (Centennial medal 1983, award for Contbn. to Professionalism 1993), AAAS, Inst. for Advancement Engring.; mem. Ops. Rsch. Soc. Am., Am. Soc. for Engring. Edn., Soc. for Philosophy and Tech., Computer Scientists for Social Responsibility, Sigma Xi, Tau Beta Pi, Eta Kappa Nu. Avocations: photography, travel, peace education. Home: Irvine, Calif. Died Jan. 25, 2004.

SCHLANT, ROBERT CARL, cardiologist, educator; b. El Paso, Tex., Apr. 16, 1929; s. Edward Bernard and Elaine Almstaedt (Acker) S.; m. Maria Honnef Ellingsen, Apr. 4, 1980; 1 child, Ernestine Stephanie. BA, Vanderbilt U., 1948, MD, 1951. Diplomate: Am. Bd. Internal Medicine, Am. Bd. Cardiovascular Disease (bd. dirs. 1977-78). Intern Peter Bent Brigham Hosp., Boston, 1951-53, jr. asst. resident,

1952-53, sr. asst. resident, 1955-66, asst. med., 1956-58; research fellow medicine Harvard U., 1956-58; asst. prof. medicine Sch. Medicine Emory U., Atlanta, 1958-62, asso. prof., 1962-66, prof. medicine (cardiology), 1967-87, dir. div. of cardiology, 1968-88. Co-editor: (textbook) The Heart, 1974, 6th edit., 1994, contbr., 1966, 70, editor, 1994; author, editor, co-editor, contbr. books, sci. and med. articles in field; editorial bds. ten sci. jours. Served with U.S. Army, 1953-55. Fellow ACP, Am. Coll. Cardiology (asst. treas., long-range planning com., norms com., trustee, extramural continuing med. edn. com. 1992—, chmn. 1995—); mem. AMA, Am. Heart Assn. (fellow coun. on clin. cardiology, exec. com., mem. sci. adv. com., James B. Herrick award 1994), Ga. Heart Assn. (bd. dirs. 1970-76), Assn. U. Cardiologists (pres. 1982-83), So. Soc. Clin. Investigation, Am. Fedn. Clin. Rsch., Am. Physiol. Soc., Am. Acad. Sports Physicians (bd. govs. 1984-92), Internat. Atherosclerosis Soc., Internat. Soc. Cardiovascular Pharmacotherapy, Internat. Soc. Fed. Cardiology Coun. (chmn. coun. clin. cardiology 1997—), Phi Beta Kappa, Alpha Omega Alpha, Omicron Delta Kappa, Phi Delta Theta, Phi Chi. Home: Atlanta, Ga. Died Dec. 12, 2002.

SCHLAU, PHILIP, retired lawyer; b. N.Y.C., Sept. 25, 1922; s. Joseph and Bella (Brown) S.; m. Florence Schlau, Jan. 31, 1947; children: Stacey, Bethel. BBA cum laude, CCNY, 1943; JD, Harvard U., 1949. Bar: N.Y. 1949, U.S. Dist. Ct. (so. dist.) N.Y. 1950, U.S. Dist. Ct. (ea. dist.) N.Y. 1950, U.S. Ct. Appeals (2d cir.) 1951, U.S. Supreme Ct. 1959. Sr. trial atty. U.S. Fidelity & Guaranty Co., 1950-57; ptnr. Schlau & Nadelson and predecessors, N.Y.C., 1959-70; sr. ptnr. Newman & Schlau PC, N.Y.C., 1970-84, Newman, Schlau, Fitch & Burns PC, N.Y.C., 1984-96. Capt. AUS, 1943-46. Mem. ABA, N.Y. State Bar Assn., N.Y. County Lawyers Assn., Def. Rsch. Inst. Home: New York, NY. Died Feb. 24, 2001.

SCHLEI, NORBERT ANTHONY, lawyer; b. Dayton, Ohio, June 14, 1929; s. William Frank and Norma (Lindsley) S.; m. Jane Moore, Aug. 26, 1950 (div. 1963); children: Anne C. Buczynski, William K., Andrew M.; m. Barbara Lindemann, Mar. 7, 1965 (div. 1981); children: Bradford L., Graham L. (dec. 1995), Norbert L. (dec. 1996), Blake Lindsley, Elizabeth Eldridge; m. Joan Masson, Dec. 29, 1995. BA, Ohio State U., 1950; LLB magna cum laude, Yale U., 1956. Bar: Ohio 1956, Calif. 1958, D.C. 1963, U.S. Supreme Ct. 1963. Law clk. to Justice Harlan U.S. Supreme Ct., 1956-57; assoc. atty. O'Melveny & Myers, L.A., 1957-59; ptnr. Greenberg, Shafton & Schlei, L.A., 1959-62; asst. atty. gen. U.S. Dept. Justice, Washington, 1962-66; ptnr. Munger, Tolles, Hills & Rickershauser, 1968-70, Kane, Shulman & Schlei, Washington, 1968-70; ptnr.-in-charge Hughes Hubbard & Reed, L.A., 1972-89; pres., CEO Kahala Capital Corp., Santa Monica, Calif., from 1983; pvt. practice Santa Monica, 1989—2003. Author: (with M.S. McDougal and others) Studies in World Public Order, 1961 (Am. Soc. Internat. Law ann. book award); State Regulation of Corporate Financial Practices, 1962; editor-in-chief Yale Law Jour., 1955-56. Dem. nominee for Calif. Assembly, 1962, for sec. of state Calif., 1966. Mem. Riviera Country Club (Pacific Palisades, Calif.). Avocations: tennis, golf, skiing, sailing. Died Apr. 17, 2003.

SCHLESINGER, JOHN RICHARD, film, opera and theater director; b. London, Feb. 16, 1926; s. Bernard Edward and Winifred Henrietta (Regensburg) S. BA, Balliol Coll., Oxford U., 1950. Dir. BBC TV, 1958-60. Dir. feature films including Terminus, 1961 (Golden Lion award Venice Film Festival, Brit. Acad. award), A Kind of Loving, 1962 (Golden Bear award Berlin Film Festival), Billy Liar, 1963, Darling, 1965 (N.Y. Critics award, Acad. nomination), Far From the Madding Crowd, 1967, Midnight Cowboy, 1968 (Acad. award best dir., best film, Brit. Acad. award best dir., best film), Sunday Bloody Sunday, 1970 (David di Donatello award), Day of the Locust, 1974, Marathon Man, 1976, Yanks, 1978 (Nat. Bd. Rev. award, New Std. award), Honky Tonk Freeway, 1980, The Falcon and the Snowman (also prod.), 1983, The Believers(also prod.), 1986, Madame Sousatzka, 1988, Pacific Heights, 1991, The Innocent, 1993, Cold Comfort Farm (BBC/ Thames), 1994, Eye for an Eye, 1995, The Next Best Thing, 2000; TV films including Separate Tables, 1982, An Englishman Abroad (BBC), 1983 (David Wark Griffith award for best TV film, Brit. Acad. award, Best Single Drama, Broadcasting Press Guild award, Best Single Drama, Best Fiction Film, Barcelon Film Festival), A Question of Attribution (PBS), 1992 (Brit. Acad. award best single drama), The Tale of Sweeney Todd, 1998; plays including Days in the Trees, 1966, I and Albert, 1972, Heartbreak House, 1975, Julius Caesar, 1977, True West, 1981, operas including Les Contes d'Hoffmann, 1980-81 (Soc. West End Theatre award), Der Rosenkavalier, 1984-85, Un Ballo in Maschera, 1989 (Salzburg Festival), Peter Grimes La Scala, Milan, L.A. Opera; assoc. dir. Nat. Theatre, London, 1973-80. Served with Royal Engrs., 1943-48. Recipient David di Donatello Spl. Dir. award, 1980, Shakespeare prize, 1981, The Hamptons Internat. Film Festival Disting. Achievement award, 1995; BAFTA fellow, 1995. Died July 25, 2003.

SCHLESINGER, ROBERT WALTER, microbiologist, microbiology educator emeritus; b. Hamburg, Germany, Mar. 27, 1913; came to U.S., 1938, naturalized, 1943; s. Emil and Flora (Strelitz) S.; m. Adeline P. Sacks, Jan. 7, 1942; children: Robert, Ann. Student, U. Hamburg Med. Sch., 1931-34; MD, U. Basel, Switzerland, 1937. Guest investigator Inst. Bacteriology and Hygiene, U. Basel, 1937-38; intern Beekman Hosp., N.Y.C., Stamford (Conn.) Hosp., 1938-40; fellow, asst. pathology and bacteriology Rockefeller Inst., N.Y.C., 1940-46; assoc. research prof. pathology, head virus research lab. U. Pitts. Sch. Medicine, 1946-47; assoc. mem., div. infectious diseases Pub. Health Research Inst., City of N.Y., Inc., 1947-55; prof., chmn. dept. microbiology St. Louis U. Sch. Medicine, 1955-63, U. Medicine and Dentistry N.J.-Robt. Wood Johnson Med. Sch., Piscataway, 1963-83, emeritus disting. prof., 1984—, chmn., 1963-80, also acting dean. Cons. Sec. War, 1946; mem., chmn. virology study sect. NIH; mem., chmn. microbiology and infectious disease adv. com. Nat. Inst. Allergy and Infectious Disease, NIH; mem. adv. com. Nat. Cancer Inst.; mem. cell biology and virology adv. com. Am. Cancer Soc. Editor: Virology; contbr. articles to sci. jours., chpts. to books. Mem. initial sci. adv. com. St. Jude Children's Rsch. Hosp., Memphis, 1962-68, chmn., 1966-68, bd. govs., 1968-70, also mem. search coms. for dirs. and rsch. staff mems. Capt. M.C., AUS, 1944-46. Recipient Danny Thomas award in recognition of outstanding efforts in furthering goals of St. Jude Children's Rsch. Hosp., 1970, Humboldt award Govt. of Germany, 1981; Guggenheim fellow, 1972-73. Mem. Am. Acad. Microbiology, Am. Assn. Immunologists, Am. Soc. Microbiology, Am. Soc. Cancer Rsch., AAAS, Am. Soc. Virology, N.Y. Acad. Scis., Sigma Xi, Alpha Omega Alpha. Died Jan. 11, 2003.

SCHLOEMANN, ERNST FRITZ (RUDOLF AUGUST), physicist, engineer; b. Borgholzhausen, Germany, Dec. 13, 1926; came to U.S., 1954, naturalized, 1965; s. Hermann Wilhelm and Auguste Wilhelmine (Koch) S.; m. Gisela Mattiat, June 19, 1955 (dec. 1990); children: Susan C., Sonia G., Barbara I.; m. Sally (Duren) Heatter, Nov. 5, 1994. BS, U. Göttingen, Fed. Republic of Germany, 1951, MS, 1953, PhD, 1954. With rsch. div. Raytheon Co., Lexington, Mass., 1955-94, electronics sys. divsn., 1994-95; ind. cons. Weston, Mass., 1995—2003. Cons. scientist, 1964-95; vis. assoc. prof. Stanford U., 1961-62; vis. prof. U. Hamburg, Germany, 1966. Assoc. editor: Jour. Applied Physics, 1974-76; contbr. numerous articles to profl. jours. Recipient T.L. Phillips award for Excellence in Tech., 1990. Fellow IEEE, Am. Phys. Soc., Sigma Xi. Democrat. Unitarian Universalist. Achievements include patents in field of magnetic materials and their application to microwave technology. Died Mar. 2, 2003.

SCHMITZ, CHARLES EDISON, evangelist; b. Mendota, Ill., July 18, 1919; s. Charles Francis Schmitz and Lucetta Margaret (Foulk) Schmitz Kaufmann; m. Eunice Magdalene Ewy, June 1, 1942 (dec. Mar. 26, 2000); children: Charles Elwood, Jon Lee; m. Irene I. Cords Walter, Jan. 1, 2001. Student, Wheaton Coll., 1936-37, 38, 39; BA, Wartburg Coll., Waverly, Iowa, 1940; BD, Wartburg Theol. Sem., Dubuque, Iowa, 1942, MDiv, 1977. Ordained to ministry Am. Luth. Ch., 1942. Founding pastor Ascension Luth. Ch., L.A., 1942-48, Am. Evang. Luth. Ch., Phoenix, 1948-65; dir. intermountain missions, founding pastor 14 Evang. Luth. Parishes, Calif., Ariz., N.Mex., Fla., 1942-89; evangelist Am. Luth. Ch., Mpls., 1965-73; sr. pastor Peace Luth. Ch., Palm Bay, Fla., 1973-89; pastor-at-large Am. Evang. Luth. Ch., Phoenix, from 1989. Charter mem. Navajo Luth. Mission, Rock Point, Ariz., 1960—; chmn. Greater Phoenix Evangelical Ministers Assn., 1998-99; pastoral advisor Ariz. Luth. Outdoor Ministry Assn., Prescott, 1958-65, 89—; Kogudus Internat. Retreat master and chaplain, Fla., Berlin and Marbach, Germany, 1990; mem. transition team Fla. Synod, Evang. Luth. Ch. Am., 1985-89. Author: Evangelism for the Seventies, 1970; co-author: ABC's of Life, 1968; assoc. editor Good News mag., 1965-71. Founder, chmn. Ariz. Ch. Conf. on Adult and Youth Problems, 1956-65; vice chmn. synod worship & ch. music com. Am. Luth. Ch., Mpls., 1960-66; chmn. Space Coast Luth. Retirement Ctr., Palm Bay, Fla., 1985-89; chaplain Ariz. chpt. Luth. Brotherhood, 1991-2000. Named Citizen of Yr., Palm Bay C. of C., 1979. Mem. Nat. Assn. Evangelicals, Greater Phoenix Assn. of Evangelicals (pres.), German Am. Nat. Congress (nat. chaplain 1970), Lions (life mem., officer Phoenix and Palm Bay clubs 1952—, Ariz. Dist. 21A chaplain 1994-95, Melvin Jones fellow 1995), Kiwanis (bd. dirs. L.A. chpt. 1942-48). Republican. Home: Granada Hills, Calif. Deceased.

SCHMUTTE, STEPHEN JAMES, economics educator; b. Indpls., May 10, 1944; s. Clarence William and Ann Elizabeth (Williams) S.; m. Judith Ann Warner, Feb. 1, 1964; children: Lori Ann, Pamela Sue. AB, Wabash Coll., 1966; MS, Purdue U., 1968, PhD, 1971. Instr. econ. Wabash Coll., Crawfordsville, Ind., 1968-71, asst. prof., 1971-73, assoc. prof., 1973-89, prof., from 1989. Fellow Woodrow Wilson Nat. Fellowship Found., 1966. Mem. Am. Econ. Assn. Home: Zionsville, Ind. Died Dec. 14, 2000.

SCHNEIDER, EUGENE SAUL, retired microbiologist, laboratory administrator; b. N.Y.C., Apr. 28, 1920; s. Isreal and Gertrude (Mendelsohn) S.; m. Bertha Gollan, Feb. 18, 1945; 1 child, Myles Gordon. BS in Microbiology, Cornell U., 1942. Cert. med. technologist, microbiologist. Microbiologist 50th Gen. Hosp., 1942-45, Morrisania City Hosp., Bronx, N.Y., 1946; rsch. microbiologist Coll. Phys. and Surg., N.Y.C., 1946; microbiologist Tacoma Gen. Hosp., 1946-48; lab. dir. Pierce County Hosp., Tacoma, 1948-52, St. Helens Med. Labs., Tacoma, 1952-68, Nat. Health Labs., Kent, Wash., 1985-92, Meridian Valley Lab., Kent, from 1992. Founding pres. Wash. State Soc. Med. Tch., 1947-48, Wash. Soc. AMTs, 1963-66; mem. Stae Commn. on Alcoholism. Contbr. articles to profl. jours.; presenter in field. Mem. Tacoma Coun. on Alcoholism, 1961-75. 1st lt. U.S. Army, 1949-52. Recipient Disting. Citizen award, Olympia, Wash., 1972, Order of Golden Microscope, AMT, 1963. Mem. Anaerobic Soc. of the Ams. Democrat. Jewish. Avocations: painting, model railroading. Home: Tacoma, Wash. Died Dec. 2, 2003.

SCHNEIDERMAN, BARRY ALAN, lawyer; b. Seattle, June 28, 1933; s. Harry and Margaret S.; m. Judith Arron, July 1, 1968; children: Paul L., Leah. BA, U. Wash., 1955, JD, 1957. Bar: Wash. 1957. Dep. King County Pros. Atty.'s Office, Seattle, 1959-61; ptnr. Burns & Schneiderman, Seattle, 1961-67, pres., 1968-77, Burns Schneiderman & Finkle, Seattle, from 1977. Asst. to gen. counsel U.S. Army (IMA), 1979-84; commdr. 6th JAG Mil. Law Ctr., 1974-78. Trustee Temple DeHirsch Sinai, Seattle, 1976-84; pres. bd. dirs. Caroline Kline Galland Home Aged, Seattle, 1980-83. Served as officer AUS, 1957-59; col. JAGC res., ret. Mem. ABA, Fed. Bar Assn., Wash. Bar Assn., Seattle-King County Bar Assn., B'Nai B'Rith (pres. 1967-68). Clubs: Wash. Athletic, College (Seattle), Rainier (Seattle), Seattle Tennis. Lodges: Shriners, Seattle. Home: Tacoma, Wash. Deceased.

SCHODER, WENDELL LOUIS, lawyer; b. Battle Creek, Mich., July 11, 1926; s. Harold Maurice and Hildred Angeline (Baird) S.; m. Helen Marie Bauman, Feb. 3, 1951; children: Patrice Schoder Emmerson, Robert, Gerald, Martha Schoder Terry, Mary Collins, David. Student, Georgetown U., 1946-47; JD, U. Detroit, 1951. Bar: Mich. 1951, U.S. Dist. Ct. (we. dist.) Mich. 1953. Sole practice, Battle Creek, 1951-64; cir. ct. commr. Calhoun County, Marshall, Mich., 1954-60, asst. pros. atty., 1960-64, probate judge, 1965-84; of counsel Holmes, Mumford, Schubel, Norlander & Macfarlane, Battle Creek, 1984-88. Instr. law Kellogg Community Coll., Battle Creek, 1974-79; lectr. in field. Contbr. articles to profl. jours. Apptd. Mich. Mental Health Adv. Council, Lansing, 1975-77; chmn. Mich. Mental Health Research, Lansing, 1975-77; pres. Goodwill Industries/Family Services, Battle Creek, 1969-70. Served with U.S. Army, 1944-46. Recipient Mental Health Services award VA, 1981, Commendation Chief Atty. VA, 1984; Snyder-Kok award Mental Health Assn. for Mich., 1983. Mem. Mich. Bar (chmn. probate and estate planning council 1987-88), Calhoun County Bar Assn. (pres. 1963-64), Mich. Assn. Probate Judges. Clubs: Exchange (pres. 1973-74) (Battle Creek). Lodges: K.C. (4 degree). Republican. Roman Catholic. Deceased.

SCHOENECK, HENRY W., JR., obstetrician-gynecologist; b. Syracuse, N.Y., June 17, 1923; MD, SUNY, Syracuse, 1947. Intern Syracuse Med. Ctr., 1947-48, resident, 1948-49, N.Y. Womens Hosp., 1950-53, N.Y. Drs. Hosp.; physician pvt. practice, Syracuse, 1955-81; med. dir. Planned Parenthoot Cul. & No. Ariz., 1982-86, Plannes Parenthood Ctr., Syracuse, 1991-93. Assoc. clin. prof. SUNY. Fellow Am. Coll. Ob-gyn.; Mem. AMA, N.Y. Med. Assn., Syracuse Med. Assn., Alpha Omega Alpha. Home: Syracuse, NY. Died Mar. 15, 2002.

SCHONBERG, HAROLD CHARLES, music critic, columnist; b. N.Y.C., Nov. 29, 1915; s. David and Minnie (Kirsch) S.; m. Rosalyn Krokover (dec. 1973), Nov. 28, 1942; m. Helene Cornell (dec. 2003), May 10, 1975. BA cum laude, Bklyn. Coll., 1937; MA, NYU, 1938; LittD, Temple U., 1964; LHD, Grinnell Coll., 1967. Assoc. editor Am. Music Lover, 1939-41; contbr. editor Mus. Digest, 1946-48; music critic N.Y. Sun, 1946-50; contbg. editor, record columnist Mus. Courier, 1948-52; music and record critic N.Y. Times, 1950-60, sr. music critic, 1960-80, cultural corr., 1980-85. Columnist on The Gramophone of London, 1948-60; judge many internat. piano competitions. Author: The Guide to Long-Playing Records, Chamber and Solo Instrumental Music, 1955, The Collector's Chopin and Schumann, 1959, The Great Pianists, 1963, The Great Conductors, 1967, Lives of the Great Composers, 1970, Grandmasters of Chess, 1973, Facing the Music, 1981, The Glorious Ones--Classical Music's Legendary Performers, 1985, Horowitz: His Life and Music, 1992; illustrated own articles with caricatures; contbg. editor Internat. Ency. Music and Musicians, New Grove Dictionary of Music and Musicians; reviewer mystery fiction Sunday N.Y. Times Book Review (under name of Newgate Callendar), 1971-95. Served as 1st lt. Airborne Signal Corps AUS, 1942-46. Recipient Pulitzer prize for criticism, 1971 Mem.: Manhattan Chess, Century Assn., Army and Navy. Home: New York, NY. Died July 26, 2003.

SCHÖNHOFF, ROBERT LEE, marketing and advertising executive; b. Detroit, May 24, 1919; s. John Clement and Olympia Regina (Diebold) S.; m. Kathleen O'Hara, Dec. 24, 1971; children: Rita, Elise, Robert. Student, Wayne State U., 1940-41. Artist J.L. Hudson, 1939-42; v.p. advt. and mktg. Dillard Dept. Stores, Little Rock & San Antonio, 1963-77; owner R.L. Schonhoff Advt. and Mktg., San Antonio, 1977-83, Ad Graphics, AMC Printers Inc. Former ltd. ptnr. New Orleans Saints football team; mem. faculty Bus. Sch., St. Mary's U., 1975-81; bd. dirs. Groos Bank, San Antonio. Permanent deacon Roman Cath. Ch., San Antonio Diocese. 1st lt. USAF, 1942-46. Mem.: Am. Mktg. Assn. (founding dir. San Antonio chpt.). Home: San Antonio, Tex. Died Jan. 4, 2004.

SCHOON, WARREN EUGENE, automotive executive; b. Ash Creek, Minn., Oct. 3, 1921; s. Jacob and Viola (Hansen) S.; m. Elizabeth Johnson, Dec. 25, 1943 (div. 1969); children: Steven, Susan, Peter, Christian, Robert; m. Marjorie Costello, Oct. 10, 1969. BA, U. Minn., 1943. Various jr. exec. positions GM, Mpls. and St. Louis, 1947-50, nat. advt. and N.Y. zone mgr., Pontiac div. N.Y.C., 1957-60; ptnr. McKean and Schoon Ford, Sioux Falls, S.D., 1951-54; pres.

and owner Schoon Motors, Luverne, Minn., from 1960; pres. New Chrysler Inc., Luverne, from 1977, Luverne Oil Co., from 1971. Master adv. bd. dirs. Met. Fin. Corp., Fargo, N.D.; chmn. bd. dirs. Dakota Savs. and Loan, Sioux Falls (merger Met. Fed. Bank, Fargo), 1982-86. Mayor City of Luverne, 1955-57; small bus. adv. com. U.S. Sen. R. Boschwitz, Minn., 1982—, U.S. Sen. Pressler, S.D., 1985—; adv. bd. McKennan Hosp., Sioux Falls, 1985—, pres. 1988—; bd. dirs. S. Dakota Crippled Children's Sch., 1986—; chmn. Rock County (Minn.) Reps., 1954-57, 60-70; mem. Nat. Bd. Ctr. Western Studies Augustana Coll., Sioux Falls. Served to lt. (j.g.) USN, 1943-47, PTO. Mem. Oldsmobile Zone Deal Coun. (chmn. 1984-85), U. Minn. Alumni Assn. (pres. Rochester chpt. 1974-75), Minn./S.D. Cadillac Dealer's Mktg. Assn. (pres. 1986-88), Am. Legion, VFW, Phi Beta Kappa. Republican. Presbyterian. Club: Minnehaha Country (Sioux Falls). Lodges: Rotary (bd. dirs. Sioux Falls Downtown Club 1984-85), Masons, Shriners, Elks. Home: Sioux Falls, SD. Deceased.

SCHOPLER, JOHN HENRY, psychologist, educator; b. Fuerth, Fed. Republic Germany, Nov. 5, 1930; came to U.S., 1938, naturalized, 1943; s. Ernest H. and Erna (Oppenheimer) S.; m. Janice E. Hough, Dec. 12, 1969; children: Kari, Lisa, Andrew, David. BA, U. Rochester, 1952; MA, U. N.Mex., 1953; PhD, U. Colo., 1958. Mem. faculty U. N.C., Chapel Hill, 1957—, asso. prof. psychology, 1964-69, prof., 1969—, chmn. dept., 1976-83. NSF sr. postdoctoral fellow London Sch. Econs. and Polit. Sci., 1966-67, Kenan prof., 1983-84 Author: (with Chester Insko) Experimental Social Psychology, 1972; co-founder, asso. editor: (with John Thibaut) Jour. Exptl. Social Psychology, 1964-69; contbr. (with Chester Insko) articles to profl. jours. Fulbright scholar, 1974-75 Fellow Am. Psychol. Assn., Soc. Psychol. Study Social Issues, N.C. Psychol. Assn.; mem. Soc. Explt. Social Psychology. Home: Chapel Hill, NC. Deceased.

SCHORR, MARTIN MARK, forensic examiner, psychologist, educator, screenwriter; b. Sept. 16, 1923; m. Dolores Gene Tyson, June 14, 1952; 1 child, Jeanne Ann. Student, Oxford (Eng.) U., 1945-46; AB cum laude, Adelphi U., 1949; postgrad., U. Tex., 1949-50; MS, Purdue U., 1953; PhD, U. Denver, 1960; postgrad., U. Tex. Diplomate in psychology, Am. Bd. Profl. Disability Cons., Am. Bd. Forensic Examiners, Am. Bd. Forensic Medicine; lic. clin. psychologist. Chief clin. psychol. svcs. San Diego County Mental Hosp., 1963-67; clin. dir. human services San Diego County, 1963-76; pvt. practice San Diego, from 1962. Forensic examiner superior, fed. and mil. cts., San Diego, 1962—; prof. abnormal psychology San Diego State U., 1965-68; chief dept. psychology Center City (Calif.) Hosp., 1976-79; cons. Dept. Corrections State of Calif., Minnewawa, 1970-73, Disability Evaluation Dept. Health, 1972-75, Calif. State Indsl. Accident Commn., 1972-78, Calif. Criminal Justice Adminstrn., 1975-77, Vista Hill Found., Mercy Hosp. Mental Health, Foodmaker Corp., Convent Sacred Heart, El Cajon, FAA Examiner; lectr. S.D. Police Acad. Author: Death by Prescription, 1988; author short stories. Recipient award for aid in developing Whistle Blower Law Calif. Assembly, 1986, Man of Yr. award, 1995. Fellow Internat. Assn. Social Psychiatry, Am. Coll. Forensic Examiners (life); mem. AAAS, PEN, APA, Am. Acad. Forensic Scis. (qualified med. evaluator), Internat. Platform Assn., World Mental Health Assn., Mystery Writers Am., Nat. Writers Club, Mensa. Home: San Diego, Calif. Died Feb. 2003.

SCHOTT, MARGE, former professional baseball team executive; b. 1928; d. Edward and Charlotte Unnewehr; m. Charles J. Schott, 1952 (dec. 1968). Owner Schottco, Cin.; ltd. ptnr. Cin. Reds, 1981-84, gen. ptnr., 1984—99, owner, pres., 1985—99, former chief exec. officer. Died Mar. 2, 2004.

SCHRAMM, TEXAS E. football league executive; b. San Gabriel, Calif., June 20, 1920; m. Marty Schramm (dec. 2002); children: Mardee, Christi, Kandy. Grad., U. Tex. Publicity dir., then gen. mgr. Los Angeles Rams, 1947-57; asst. dir. sports CBS, 1957-60; gen. mgr. Dallas Cowboys, 1960-89, pres., resigned 1989, World League of Am. Football, 1989-91. Named NFL Exec. of the Yr., The Sporting News, 1978; recipient Bert Bell award, 1978; named Dallas Father of the Yr., 1987. Died July 15, 2003.

SCHROEDER, DAVID HAROLD, healthcare facility executive; b. Chgo., Oct. 22, 1940; s. Harry T. and Clara D. (Dexter) Schroeder; m. Clara Doorn, Dec. 27, 1964; children: Gregory D., Elizabeth M. BBA, Kans. State Coll., 1965; MBA, Wichita State U., 1968; postgrad., U. Ill., 1968-69. CPA Ill. Supt. cost acctg. Boeing Co., Wichita, Kans., 1965-68; sr. v.p., treas. Riverside Med. Ctr., Kankakee, Ill., from 1971; v.p., bd. dirs. Service Med., Inc., from 1999. Treas. Riverside Health Sys., from 1982, Kankakee Valley Health Inc., from 1985, Health Info. Sys. Coop., from 1991; v.p., treas. Oakside Corp., Kankakee, from 1982; bd. dirs. Harmony Home Health Svc., Inc., Naperville, Ill.; treas. Oak Surg. Inst., from 2001; mem. faculty various profl. orgns.; preceptor Gov.'s State U., University Park, Ill., from 1987, adj. prof. econs. divsn. health adminstrn., 1990—95; trustee Riverside Found. Trust, from 1989, RMC Found., from 1989, Sr. Living Ctr., from 1989, Alzehimer's Assn., 1997; pres. Kankakee County Mental Health Ctr., 1982—84. Contbg. author: book Cost Containment in Hospitals, 1980; contbr. articles to profl. jours. Active Make A Wish Found., from 1994; founder Kankakee Trinity Acad., 1980, Riverview Hist. Dist., 1982; dir. Kankakee County Hist. Soc., 1995, pres., 2001; mem. adv. bd. Students in Free Enterprise, Olivet Nazarene U., Kankakee, from 1989; pres. United Way Kankadee County, 1984—85; trustee, treas. Am. Luth. Ch.; pres. Riverside Employees Credit Union, 1976—79; chmn. Ill. Provider Trust, Naperville, 1983—85; dir. IPT Physician's Ins. Co. Ltd., from 2001; chmn. Ill. Provider Trust, Naperville, from 2002. Capt. U.S. Army, 1969—71. Fellow: Fin. Analysts Fedn. (bd. cert. in healthcare mgmt.), Healthcare Fin. Mgmt. Assn. (pres. 1975—76), Am. Coll. Healthcare Execs.; mem.: AICPA, Investment Analysts Soc. Chgo., Inc., Healthcare Fin. Mgmt. Assn. (William G. Follimer award 1977, Robert H. Reeves award 1981, Muncie Gold award 1987, Founders medal of honor 1990), Ill. CPA Soc., Fin. Exec. Inst., Nat. Assn. Accts., Inst. Chartered Fin. Analysts, Ill. Hosp. Assn. (chmn. coun. health fin. 1982—85), Packard Club, Classic Car Club Am., Masons, Kiwanis (pres.), Sigma Chi, Alpha Kappa Psi. Avocations: classical automobile restoration, architectural preservation, computers. Home: Kankakee, Ill. Died July 21, 2002.

SCHROETER, DONALD GARRISON, oil company executive; b. Cin., Nov. 16, 1921; s. Garrison B. and Dorothy Carter (Kendal) S.; m. Phyllis Jean Hannah, July 7, 1945; 1 child, Paul Allen. BS in Chemistry, U. Cin., 1943; MS ChemE, Ohio State U., 1947. Asst. dean of men Ohio State U., Columbus, 1946-48; chem. engr., other positions Amoco Corp., Tex., Ind. and Ill., 1949-69; mgr. employee and pub. relations Amoco Research Ctr., Naperville, Ill., 1970-79; exec. dir., sec. Amoco Found. and Amoco Corp., Chgo., 1980-86; retired, 1986. Bd. dirs. JETS. Bd. dirs. Donors Forum Chgo., 1983-86, Naperville United Way, 1987-89, Exec. Svc. Corps Chgo., 1991—; pres. Naperville YMCA, 1973, trustee; trustee Naperville Edn. Fedn., 1992—. Lt. USN, 1943-46. Mem. AAAS, Am. Chem. Soc., Am. Inst. Chem. Engrs. (chmn. fuels & petrochems. div. 1968), Am. Assn. Engring. Socs. (chmn. engring. manpower commn. 1985-86), Cress Creek Club. Avocation: golf. Home: Naperville, Ill. Died Nov. 3, 2000.

SCHUBERT, ARLINE FLORENCE, lawyer; b. Van Houten, N.Mex., Sept. 19, 1936; d. Jesse Franklen and Esther Helen (McDougall) Short; m. George W. Schubert, May 5, 1956; children: Kathlene Jane Schubert Hall, Cheryl Lynn Schubert Madsen. BS, U. N.D., 1967, MA, 1973, JD, 1982. Bar: N.D. 1983, U.S. Dist. Ct. (fed. dist.) N.D. 1983. Tchr. Pub. Schs., various locations, 1967-76; instr. U. Minn., Crookston, 1976-79, U. N.D., Grand Forks, 1983-87; ptnr. Schubert & Schubert-Madsen, Grand Forks, from 1983. Contbr. articles to profl. jours. Mem. sch. bd. Grand Forks Pub. Schs., 1987. Mem. State Bar Assn. of N.D. (com. chmn.), Am. Trial Lawyers Assn., Grand Forks County Bar Assn., Quota Club (pres. Grand Forks chpt. 1987—), PEO (pres. Grand Forks chpt. 1987—). Republican. Methodist. Avocations: golf, tennis, speaker to groups on preventive legal matters. Home: Edmonds, Wash. Deceased.

SCHULTE, THERESA M. critical care nurse; b. Beardsley, Minn., Aug. 19, 1931; d. Bernard Henry and Marie Rose (Guenther) Leisdon; m. Charles Edward Schulte, May 9, 1953; children: Kathryn, Martin, Carolyn, Marvin, Barbara, Robert. Diploma, St. Gabriels Sch. of Nursing, 1952; cert. in coronary care nursing, Methodist Hosp., 1973. RN, Minn; ACLS, BCLS. Med./ surg. charge nurse Meth. Hosp., Mpls., charge nurse PAR, evening supr.; supr. Douglas County Hosp., Alexandria, Minn., clin. dir. ICU, critical care unit. Mem. INS Home: Miltona, Minn. Died Apr. 19, 2002.

SCHULZE, LEROY JAMES, engineer; b. Stewart, Minn., Mar. 17, 1944; s. William John and Nora Augusta (Kuehn) S.; m. Gloria Vasquez, Sept. 15, 1973 (div. 1990); 1 child, Angela Maria. Student, St. Cloud State Coll., 1964, Air U., 1968, U. Minn. Electric service engr. Westinghouse Electric Corp., Mpls., 1968-69, Des Moines, 1969-72, product engr. Newark, 1972-76; specialist relay systems Marini & Daminelli S.A., Sao Paulo, Brazil, 1976-79; design engr. Gen. Electric Co., Burlington, Iowa, 1979-80; relay application engr. Asea Inc., Arlington Heights, Ill., 1980-83; field application engr. Asea Electric, Arlington Heights, Ill., 1983-88; regional tech. mgr. Asea Brown Boveri, Arlington Heights, 1988-90; sales engr. Electro Midwest, Blackduck, Minn., 1991. Instr. Hands-on-Relay Sch., Wash. State U.; Dakota County AVTI for ASEA Relay Seminar; mem. Minn. Power Systems Planning Com. Contbr. articles to profl. publications; patentee in field. Sgt. USAF, 1965-68. Mem. IEEE (chmn. Working Group, speaker Nebr. sect.). Died Dec. 17, 2001.

SCHUPP, JAMES LOUIS, JR., lawyer; b. New Orleans, Nov. 25, 1936; s. James Louis and May Arthemise (Wright) S.; m. Harriet Agnes Barry, June 25, 1960; children: Walker A., Benjamin O. BA, Tulane U., 1958, LLB, 1960. Bar: La. 1960, U.S. Dist. Ct. (ea. and mid. dists.) La. 1960, U.S. Dist. Ct. (we. dist.) La. 1965, U.S. Ct. Appeals (5th cir.) 1963. Assoc. Terriberry, Carroll & Yancey, New Orleans, 1960-66, ptnr., from 1966. Mem. World Trade Ctr., New Orleans, 1960—, Bd. of Trade, New Orleans, 1987—; bd. dirs. Norwegian-Am. C. of C., New Orleans, 1992. Capt. USAR, 1960-68. Hon. Consul, Finland, 1980—. Mem. ABA, La. State Bar Assn., New Orleans Bar Assn., Maritime Law Assn., Southeastern Admiralty Law Inst. (chmn. 1979), Internat. Bar Assn., Phi Delta Phi, Omicron Delta Kappa. Avocation: farming. Home: New Orleans, La. Died June 15, 2000.

SCHWAB, GLENN ORVILLE, retired agricultural engineering educator, consultant; b. Gridley, Kans., Dec. 30, 1919; s. Edward and Lizzie (Sauder) S.; married Lois Saul (dec. Oct. 16, 1998); children: Richard, Lawrence,Mary Kay. BS, Kans. State. U., 1942; MS, Iowa State U., 1947, PhD, 1951; postdoctoral, Utah State U., 1966. Registered profl. engr., Ohio. Instr. to prof. agrl. engring. Iowa State U., Ames, 1947-56; prof. agrl. engring. Ohio State U., Columbus, 1956-85, ret., 1985, prof. emeritus, from 1985. Co-author: Soil and Water Conservation Engineering, 4th edit., 1993, Agricultural and Forest Hydrology, 1986, Soil and Water Management Systems, 4th edit., 1996; contbr. articles to profl. jours. Served to capt. U.S. Army, 1942-46. Fellow Am. Soc. Agrl. Engrs. (bd. dirs. soil and water div. 1976-78, Hancock Brick and Tile Drainage Engr. 1968, John Deere medal 1987), ASTM, Soil and Water Conservation Soc. Am., Am. Geophys. Union, Internat. Commn. Irrigation and Drainage. Avocations: rock polishing, wood working, photography, traveling. Home: Powell, Ohio. Died Mar. 12, 2003.

SCHWARTZ, ALLEN G. federal judge; b. Bklyn., Aug. 23, 1934; s. Herbert and Florence (Safier) S.; m. Joan Ruth Teitel, Jan. 17, 1965; children: David Aaron, Rachel Ann, Deborah Eve. BBA, CCNY, 1955; LLB, U. Pa., 1958. Bar: N.Y. 1958. Asst. dist. atty. Office of Dist. Atty., N.Y. County, 1959-62; assoc. firm Paskus Gordon & Hyman, N.Y.C., 1962-65; ptnr. firm Koch Lankenau Schwartz & Kovner, N.Y.C., 1965-69, Dornbush Mensch Mandelstam & Schwartz, N.Y.C., 1969-75; mem. Schwartz & Schreiber, P.C., N.Y.C., 1975-77; corp. counsel City of N.Y., 1978-81; mem. Schwartz Klink & Schreiber, P.C., 1982-87; ptnr. Proskauer Rose Goetz & Mendelsohn, N.Y.C., 1987-94; judge U.S. Dist. Ct. (so. dist.) N.Y., N.Y.C., 1994—2003. Mem. ex officio N.Y.C. Bd. Ethics, 1978-81; pro bono sports commr. City of N.Y., 1982-83. Research editor: U. Pa. Law Rev, 1957-58. Recipient Award of Achievement, Sch. Bus. Alumni, Soc. of the City Coll., 1981, Hogan-Morganthau Assocs. award, 1980, Corp. Coun. ann. award, 1995, Frank S. Hogan Assocs. award, 1995, Pres.'s medal Baruch Coll., 2001. Died Mar. 22, 2003.

SCHWARTZ, DORIS RUHBEL, nursing educator, consultant; b. Bklyn., May 30, 1915; d. Henry and Florence Marie (Shuttleworth) Schwartz. BS, NYU, 1953, MS, 1958. RN N.Y. Staff nurse Meth. Hosp., Bklyn., 1942—43; pub. health nurse Vis. Nurse Assn., Bklyn., 1947—51, Cornell U. Med. Coll., Cornell-N.Y. Hosp. Sch. Nursing, N.Y.C., 1951—61, tchr. pub. health nursing, geriatric nursing, 1961—80; ret., 1990. Sr. fellow U. Pa. Sch. Nursing, Phila., 1981—90; mem. bd. dirs. Elders With Adult Dependants. Author: Give Us to Go Blithely, 1990 (Book of Yr. award Am. Jour. Nursing, 1991); author: (sr.) The Elderly Chronically Ill Patient: Nursing and Psychosocial Needs, 1963; co-author: Geriatrics and Geriatric Nursing, 1983 (Book of Yr. award Am. Jour. Nursing, 1984); contbr. articles to profl. jours. Vol. Foulkeways Continuing Care Retirement Cmty., Gwynedd, Pa.; mem. adv. com. nursing WHO, Geneva, 1971—79; adv. com. Robert Wood Johnson Found., Tchg. Nursing Home Project, Princeton, NJ, U. Pa. Wharton Sch. Study of Continuing Care Retirement Communities, 1981—83. Capt. U.S. Army, 1943—47, PTO. Recipient Diamond Jubilee Nursing award, N.Y. County RNs Assn., 1979; fellow Rockefeller fellow, U. Toronto, 1950—51, Mary Roberts fellow, Am. Jour. Nursing, 1955, Fogarty fellow, NIH, 1975—76. Fellow: Am. Acad. Nursing (charter coun. 1973—74, designated A Living Legend 1997), APHA (Disting. Career award nursing sect. 1979), Inst. Medicine of NAS; mem.: ANA (Pearl McIver award 1979), Soroptimist (v.p. N.Y. club 1974—75), Sigma Theta Tau (Founders award 1979, Mentor award Alpha Upsilon chpt. 1992). Democrat. Mem. Soc. Of Friends. Avocations: travel, writing, people. Deceased.

SCHWARTZ, EDWARD J. federal judge; b. 1912; Judge Mcpl. Ct, San Diego, 1959—63, Superior Ct., San Diego, 1963—68, U.S. Dist. Ct. for So. Dist. Calif., 1968—2000, former chief judge, former sr. judge. Died Mar. 22, 2000.

SCHWARTZ, LAURENT, retired mathematician; b. Paris, Mar. 5, 1915; AgrÉgation de Mathématique, Ecole Normale Supérieure, Paris, 1937; DSc, U. Strasbourg, 1943; D (hon.), Humboldt U., 1960, Brussels U., 1962, Lund U., 1981, Tel-Aviv U., 1981, Montreal U., 1985, U. Athens, 1993. Lectr. Faculty Sci., Grenoble, 1944-45, prof. Nancy, France, 1945-53, Ecole Normale Supérieure, Paris, 1953-59, Ecole Polytechnique, Paris, 1959-80; tchr. U. Paris, 1980-83. Founder Ctr. Math., Ecole Polytechnique, 1966. Contbr. articles to profl. jours. Recipient Fields medal Internat. Congress in Harvard, 1950, prizes Paris Acad. Scis., 1955, 64, 72. Mem. Paris Acad. Scis. Achievements include development of theory of distributions and stochastic differential calculus. Died July 4, 2002.

SCHWARTZ, LOUIS BROWN, law educator; b. Phila., Feb. 22, 1913; s. Samuel and Rose (Brown) S.; m. Berta Wilson, Mar. 29, 1937 (div. 1954); children: Johanna, Victoria; m. Miriam Robbins Humboldt, Sept. 16, 1964. BS in Econs, U. Pa., 1932, JD, 1935. Bar: Pa. 1935, U.S. Supreme Ct. 1942. Atty. SEC, Washington, 1935-39; chief gen. crimes and spl. projects sect. Dept. Justice, 1939-43, chief judgment and enforcement sect. antitrust div., 1945-46; also mem. inter-departmental coms. on war crimes and status-of-forces treaties; prof. law U. Pa. Law Sch., 1946-83, Benjamin Franklin prof., 1964-83; prof. law Hastings Coll. Law, U. Calif., 1983-98, emeritus prof., from 1998. Vis. prof. Harvard U., Columbia U., U. Calif. at Berkeley, Cambridge (Eng.) U.; Ford vis. Am. prof. Inst. Advanced Legal Studies, U. London (Eng.), 1974; vis. disting. prof. Ariz. State U., 1980; mem. Atty. Gen.'s Nat. Com. Study Antitrust Laws, 1954-55, Pa. Gov.'s Commn. on Penal and Correctional Affairs, 1956-60; adv. commn. Revision Pa. Penal Code, 1963-68; nat. adv. council Nat. Defender Project, 1964-69; dir. Nat. Commn. on Reform of Fed.

Criminal Laws, 1968-71; co-reporter Model Penal Code Am. Law Inst., 1962; cons. FTC, Dept. Justice, other agencies. Author: Free Enterprise and Economic Organization, 1959, 6th edit. (with John J. Flynn, Harry First) titled Antitrust and Government Regulation, 1983-85 (2 vols.), Le Système Pénal des Etats-Unis, 1964, Law Enforcement Handbook for Police, 1970, 2d edit., 1979, Proposed Federal Criminal Code, (with Comments and Working Papers), 1971; contbr. numerous articles to profl. jours. Served as lt. (j.g.) USNR, 1944-45. Mem. Ams. Democratic Action (nat. bd.), Am. Law Inst. (adv. com. pre-arraignment code), Order of Coif. Home: San Francisco, Calif. Died Jan. 23, 2003.

SCHWARTZ, MILDRED B. interior designer, art consultant; b. Pitts., Apr. 7, 1927; d. David and Jennie (Handelsman) Bernstein; m. Leonard Schwartz, Sept. 8, 1946; children: Debra Lynn Schwartz Bailey, Jodi Sue Schwartz Lindner. Student, U. Pitts., 1968. Pres., interior designer Millie Schwartz Assoc., Inc., Pitts., 1971-94, ret., 1994. Art cons. Reynolds Gallery, Pitts., 1989-94. Home: Pittsburgh, Pa. Died May 16, 2002.

SCHWARTZ, RALPH JEROME, speech pathologist, audiologist; b. Chgo., Mar. 14, 1919; s. Adolf Joseph and Mildred (Cohen) S.; m. Jane King Sherwin, Oct. 29, 1966. BS, Northwestern U., 1941; MA, Marquette U., 1948; PhD, Purdue U., 1958. Cert. speech pathologist and audiologist. Head, speech clinic McPherson (Kans.) County Chpt. Am. Red Cross, 1947-52; speech clinician Inst. Logopedics, Wichita, Kans., 1952-53; speech therapist and acting head, speech and hearing dept. Children's Rehab. Inst., Inc., Baltimore, Md., 1953-55; asst. prof. logopedics U. Wichita, 1957-63; asst. prof. speech U. No. Iowa, Cedar Falls, 1963-68, assoc. prof. speech pathology and audiology, 1968-89, prof. emeritus speech pathology and audiology, from 1989. Vis. asst. prof. speech pathology, Syracuse U., summer 1963. Mem. Am. Speech-Lang.-Hearing Assn. (life), Am. Assn. Phonetic Sci., Acoustical Soc. Am. (emeritus), Internat. Assn. Logopedics and Phoniatrics, Internat. Soc. Phonetic Sci. (emeritus), Iowa Speech and Hearing Assn. (life). Home: Cedar Falls, Iowa. Deceased.

SCHWARTZ, WILLIAM A(LLEN), broadcasting and cable executive; b. Detroit, Nov. 29, 1938; m. Marlene J. Cohen; children: Jonathan, Cynthia, Michael. BA in Mktg. and Broadcasting, Wayne State U., 1961; postgrad., Bernard Baruch Grad. Sch. Bus. Mgr. rsch. products NBC, 1963-66; asst. dir. rsch. Columbia Pictures, 1966; v.p., gen. mgr. Sta. WUAB-TV, Cleve., 1968-73; v.p. ops. Telerep, Inc., N.Y.C., 1973-74; v.p., gen. mgr. Sta. KTVU-TV, Oakland, Calif., 1974-79; pres. Cox Broadcasting, Atlanta, 1979-81, Cox Comm., Inc., Atlanta, 1981-87, CEO, 1983-87; pres., COO Cox Enterprises, Inc., Atlanta, 1985-87; chmn., CEO Capital Cable, 1988-2000. Pres., CEO Cannell Comm., L.P., 1989-95, First Media Television, L.P., 1995-97; pres. FMB Enterprises, Inc., 1987—. Vice chair, CEO Nat. Prostate Cancer Coalition, 1999—. Home: Atlanta, Ga. Died Sept. 9, 2002.

SCHWARTZMAN, GLENDA JOY, artist; b. L.A., Dec. 24, 1939; d. Morton and Thelma Lorrain (Bryer) S.; m. Leonard I. Schwartzman, June 21, 1961 (div. Sept. 1973); children: James Elliot, Eric Bennett. Student, Otis Art Inst., Calif., 1958, Chouinard Art Inst., 1959-60. One-woman shows include: Angeles Press, L.A., 1990, Boringer Gallery, Dallas, 1988, Krieger Gallery, Santa Barbara, Calif., 1987, SOMA Exhbns., Denver, 1986, De Vorsan Gallery, 1987, Inamori, Beverly Hills, Calif., 1982, Lelia Ivy Gallery, Santa Monica, Calif., 1982, others; group shows include TransAmerica Bldg., San Francisco, 1990, Wells Fargo Bank, L.A., 1990, La Jolla (Calif.) Mus., 1990, 1989, Col.-Jems Studios, others; work in pub. and pvt. collections; author: (book) Art in California, 1990. Mem. Dems., Calif., Benedict Canyon. Recipient fine art scholarship Otist Art Inst. Mem. Calif. Yacht Club, So. Calif. Women's Caucas for Art. Jewish. Avocations: chess, bridge, boating. Home: Venice, Calif. Died May 9, 2000.

SCHWARZ, J(AMES) CONRAD, psychology educator; b. Hartford, Conn., Sept. 19, 1936; s. William Merlin and Violet May (List) S.; m. Lois J. Stonebraker, 1956 (div. 1981); m. Carolina A.B. Herfkens, Oct. 12, 1984. BS, Pa. State U., 1958; MA, Ohio State U., 1961, PhD, 1963. Lic. clin. psychologist, Conn.; cert. psychologist, N.Y. Rsch. asst. Pa. State U., 1957-58; psychol. trainee Chillicothe (Ohio) VA N.P. Hosp., 1958-60; psychol. intern Columbus (Ohio) VA Out-Patient Clinic, 1960-61; instr. psychology Bowling Green (Ohio) State U., 1962-64, asst. prof., 1964-65; asst. prof., mem. teaching faculty grad. tng. Syracuse U, 1965-70, assoc. prof., 1970-72; assoc. prof., mem. teaching faculty grad. tng. program U. Conn., Storrs, 1972-75, prof., mem. teaching faculty grad. tng. program, from 1975; pvt. practice clin. psychology Mansfield Ctr., Conn., 1973-94, North Windham, Conn., 1995-96. Asst. field assessment officer Peace Corps Tng. Programs, 1967-68; clin. psychology cons. VA Out-Patient Clinic, Syracuse, 1968-72, Onodaga Co. Mental Health Clinic, Syracuse, 1969-72; with Windham Pub. Schs.-Project Self-Search, 1974-76; cons. Ea. Conn. Mental Health Group, 1974-83, Bermuda Govt., Child Devel. Project, 1979-82, Optimum Resource, Inc., Software for Learning Disabled Children. Author: Deck-a-Dot Manual: An Educational Card Game Program to Develop Arithmetic Readiness, 1970; If This Is Love, Why Do I Feel So Insecure?, 1989, 90, Teacher's Manual for Optimum Resource Reading Program, 1991; cons. editor Devel. Psychology, 1981-84; co-developer The Optimum Resource Reading Program, 1991; contbr. articles to profl. jours. USPHS fellow, 1958-59, 61-62; grantee Nat. Lab. Early Childhood Edn. Ctr. Syracuse U., 1968-71, NIMH, 1978-83, 84-85, Nat. Inst. Alcohol Abuse and Addiction, 1986-89, U. Conn. Rsch. Found., 1985-87. Mem. APA (div. clin., family psychology), Sigma Xi, Phi Beta Kappa, Psi Chi, Phi Eta Sigma, Phi Kappa Phi. Avocations: tennis, landscape gardening. Home: Storrs Mansfield, Conn. Died May 15, 2003.

SCHWARZ, JOSEPHINE LINDEMAN, retired ballet company director, choreographer; b. Dayton, Ohio, Apr. 8, 1908; d. Joseph and Hannah (Lindeman) S. D.F.A. (hon.), U. Dayton, 1974; H.H.D. (hon.), Wright State U., 1983. Founder, dir. Schwarz Sch. Dance, Dayton, 1927-84, Exptl. Group for Young Dancers (now Dayton Ballet), 1937-79; mem. Weidman Theatre Dance Co., 1934-37. Guest tchr., lectr., choreographer Hunter Coll., N.Y.C., YM-YWHA, N.Y.C., also regional dance companies in, Cleve., Phila., Indpls., Houston; pres. N.E. Regional Ballet Assn., 1961; chmn. dance adv. panel Ohio Arts Council, 1967-70; founder, program dir. Nat. Craft Choreography Confs., 1968-70; dance advisory panels Nat. Endowment for Arts, 1975-78; also Ohio Arts Council, 1975-78 Profl. dancer Adolph Bolm's Ballet Intime, Ravinia Opera Ballet, Chgo., 1925-27; European study and performances, 1929-30; author articles. Recipient award Ohio Arts Council, 1977, Spl. Achievement award YWCA, 1982, Brotherhood award Dayton chpt. NCCJ, 1984, Pegasus award Ohioana Library Assn., 1987, Northeast award Regional Dance Am., 1990; inducted into Ohio Women's Hall of Fame, 1991. Mem. Nat. Assn. Regional Ballet (bd. dirs. 1970-75), Am. Dance Guild (award 1985), Friends Dayton Ballet, Dayton Art Inst. Jewish. Home: Boulder, Colo. Died Feb. 27, 2004.

SCHWARZ, ROBERT DEVLIN, art dealer; b. Atlantic City, N.J., July 11, 1942; s. Frank Samuel and Marie (Devlin) S.; m. Pamela Pillion; children: Robert, Jr., Elizabeth, Jonathan. BS, Dickinson Coll., 1964. Curator Stephen Girard Collection, Phila., 1970-80; former pres., curator The Schwarz Gallery, Phila.; pres., owner. Author: Catalogue of the Stephen Girard Collection, 1980, A Gallery Collects Peale, 1987, One hundred Fifty Years of Philadelphia Still-Life Painting, 1997. Mem. bd. dirs. Conservation Ctr., 1995. Mem. Art Dealers Assn. Am., Art and Antiques Deales League Am. Republican. Presbyterian. Home: Gladwyne, Pa. Died Mar. 18, 2004.

SCHWED, PETER, author, retired editor and publisher; b. N.Y.C., Jan. 18, 1911; s. Frederick and Bertie (Stiefel) S.; m. Antonia Sanxay Holding, Mar. 6, 1947; children: Katharine Holding (Mrs. Eric F. Wood), Peter Gregory, Laura Sanxay (Mrs. Michael Sirico), Roger Eaton. Grad., Lawrenceville (N.J.) Sch., 1928; student, Princeton, 1929-32. Asst. v.p. Provident Loan Soc. N.Y., 1932-42; with Simon & Schuster, Inc., N.Y.C., 1946-84, v.p., exec. editor, 1957-62, exec. v.p., 1962-66, pub. trade books, 1966-72, chmn. editorial bd., 1972-82, editorial chmn. emeritus, 1982-84, dir., 1966-72. Author: Sinister Tennis, 1975, God Bless Pawnbrokers, 1975, The Serve and the Overhead Smash, 1976, Hanging in There, 1977; (with Nancy Lopez) The Education of a Woman Golfer, 1979, Test Your Tennis IQ, 1981, Turning the Pages, 1984, Overtime: A 20th Century Sports Odyssey, 1987, How to Talk Tennis, 1988, Quality Tennis after 50...Or 60...Or 70...Or..., 1990, The Common Cold Crusade: A Novel Not to be Sneezed At, 1994, Plum to Peter: Letters of P.G. Wodehouse to his Editor, 1996, Say, Could That Lad Be I?, 1998; compiler: The Cook Charts, 1949; editor: (with H.W. Wind) Great Stories From the World of Sports, 1958; (with Allison Danzig) The Fireside Book of Tennis, 1972; contbr. articles to jours. Trustee Lawrenceville Sch., 1968-72. Capt. F.A. AUS, World War II. Decorated Bronze Star, Purple Heart. Mem. Authors Guild, Century Assn. Democrat. Home: New York, NY. Died July 31, 2003.

SCOFIELD, MILTON N. lawyer; b. N.Y.C., Aug. 11, 1911; s. Elias and Celia (Neinken) S.; m. Nanette Eisler, Sept. 5, 1945; children: Elizabeth M., Anthony L. AB, Columbia U., 1932, JD, 1935. Bar: N.Y. 1935. Asst. N.Y.C. Law Revision Com. 1935; assoc. Stroock & Stroock & Lavan and predecessor Stroock & Stroock N.Y.C., 1942—, 43-45, ptnr., 1945—, sr. ptnr., 1960-88, of counsel, 1989—; chief counsel food rationing div. Office Price Adminstrn., 1942; adv. on rationing to Sec. War, 1943; police magistrate, Scarsdale, N.Y., 1961-62; dir. Vishay Intertech., Inc. Corp. Mem. ABA, N.Y. County Law Assn., Assn. of Bar of City of N.Y. Home: Hollowville, NY. Deceased.

SCOGGIN, JAMES FRANKLIN, JR., electrical engineering educator; b. Laurel, Miss., Aug. 3, 1921; s. James Franklin and Berenice Evans (Phares) S.; m. Madeline Eve Lannelle, Mar. 6, 1948; children: Tracy Catherine, Beryl Evans, James Franklin. BS in Math., Miss. State U., 1941; BS in Mil. Engring., U.S. Mil. Acad., 1944; MA in Physics, Johns Hopkins U., 1951; PhD in Physics, U. Va., 1957. Commd. 2nd lt. U.S. Army, 1944, advanced through grades to col., 1966, editor German WWII mil. history, R&D mgr., ret., 1968; prof. elec. engring. The Citadel, Charleston, S.C., 1968-91, prof. emeritus, from 1991. Fellow Radio Club of Am.; mem. IEEE (Centennial medal), Am. Nuclear Soc., Tau Beta Pi (chief faculty adviser Citadel's chpt. 197992). Presbyterian. Home: Charleston, SC. Died Aug. 7, 2000.

SCONFITTO, GERARD CARL, real estate broker, real estate executive; b. Rochester, N.Y., Feb. 1, 1942; s. Joseph Sconfitto and Mary D'Agata; m. Estella Ann McMindes, Sept. 11, 1971. Grad., Empire State U. Lic. real estate broker, N.Y. Pres. Comml. Design Consultants, Rochester, 1986-87, Sconfitto Group Ltd., Rochester, from 1987, Com-Pro Realty Inc., Rochester, from 1988; with Jay Birnbaum Co. Asset Mgmt., Pittsford, N.Y., from 1993. Chmn. Rep. Leaders Coun., 1993-94; mem. Monroe County Rep. Fin. Com., 1991. Died.

SCOTT, BRENDA M. city official; BA, MA, Wayne State U., Detroit. City councilwoman, Detroit, Mich., from 1993. Past exec., adminstrv. asst. Detroit City Councilmen Mel Ravitz & Herbert McFadden, Jr.; past congl. intern to Congressman John Coyers; mem. bd. govs. Wayne State U., 1990-95, vice chair, 1995—; bd. mem. Detroit Entrepreneurship Inst. and Resnaissance Women's Group. Recipient Exemplary Pub. Svc. award Greenlawn Book Club, cert. of appreciation Devel. Ctr. Inc., Wayne County C.C. and Wayne County Bd. Commrs., Mayoral Recognition award City of Detroit, Outstanding Woman award Detroit Sci. Ctr., Sisterhood award, 1994, Outstanding Young Woman of Am. award, Outstanding Svc. award Michael Lee Searcy Cmty. & Devel. Ctr., 1995, William Patrick Disting. Pub. Servant award Safe Ctr., Inc., 1997. Mem. Wayne State U. Alumni Assn. (mem. exec. bd.), Wayne State U. Orgn. Black Alumni (award), Assn. Gov. Bds. for Colls. and Univs. Roman Catholic. Died Sept. 2, 2002.

SCOTT, JAMES MICHAEL, artist, filmmaker; b. Wells, England, July 9, 1941; came to U.S., 1989; s. William George and Hilda Mary Scott; m. Anna Katherine Partridge, Feb. 19, 1966 (div. 1976); children: Alexander, Rosie; m. Yolanda Orozco, 1995; 1 child, Paloma. Art scholar, Bryanston Sch., Sorbonne, Paris, 1959; student painting and theatre design, Slade Sch. Fine Art, London, 1960-61, Slade Sch. Fine Art, Berlin, 1964. Ind. filmmaker Maya Film Prodns., London, 1964-70; film prodr. and dir. Flamingo Pictures, London, 1980-88; artist Santa Monica, from 1989. Tchr., lectr. cinema Bath Acad. Art, U.K., Maidstone Coll. Art, U.K., Royal Coll. Art, London, Nat. Film Sch., U.K., U. So. Calif. Writer, dir.: (feature films) The Sea, 1962, Adult Fun, 1972, Coilin and Platonida, 1976, Loser Takes All, 1989, (films about artists) Love's Presentation, 1966, R.B. Kitaj, 1967, Richard Hamilton, 1969, The Great Ice Cream Robbery, 1970, Antoni Tapies, 1974, Chance, History, Art..., 1979; dir.: (TV films) Every Picture Tells a Story, 1984, Getting Even, 1985, Inspector Morse - The Last Enemy, 1988, (documentaries) Night Cleaners, 1974, Hajj 75, 1975, '36 to '77, 1978, (shorts) The Rocking Horse, 1962, In Separation, 1965, A Shocking Accident (Acad. award best short film 1983, Brit. Acad. award nominee best live action short film 1983), People Are the Same the Universe Over, 1987, Crime in the City, 1987, (info. films and commls.) Ejectoret, Stamp Exhibition - Olympia, Patrick McGrath; writer: (screenplays) Circle of Fear, Darkroom Window, Dibs, Someone, Somewhere. Recipient Silver Boomerang award Melbourne, Australia, 1979. Mem. Am. Acad. Motion Picture Arts, Dirs. Guild Am., Dirs. Guild Great Britain, Brit. Acad. Film and TV Arts, Assn. Cinematograph and Allied Techs. Avocations: reading, photography, travel. Died Jan. 5, 2002.

SCOTT, JOHN CARLYLE, retired gynecologist, oncologist; b. Mpls., Sept. 24, 1933; s. Horace Golden and Grace (Melges) S.; m. Beth Krause, 1958 (div. 1977); m. Paola Maria Martini, Feb. 8, 1986; children: Jeff, David, Suzanne, Danielle. AB, Princeton U., 1956; BS, MD, U. Minn., 1961. Diplomate Am. Coll. Ob-gyn., Pan Am. Ob-gyn. Soc. Intern Sch. Medicine Marquette U., Milw., 1961-62, resident Sch. Medicine, 1962-66; resident Harvard Med. Sch., Boston, 1965; Am. Cancer fellow Marquette Med. Sch., Milw., 1966-67, instr. ob-gyn., 1966-67; clin. instr. ob-gyn. U. Wash. Med. Sch., Seattle, 1968-75, clin. asst. prof., 1975-85, clin. assoc. prof., from 1985, ret., 1998. Mem. faculty adv. com. dept. ob-gyn. U. Wash., Seattle, 1973-97; adj. prof. dept. ob-gyn. U. S.C., 1995—. Author: First Aid for N.W. Boaters, 1977; author Am. Jour. Ob-Gyn., 1970, 75, 77, 97, Jour. Neurologic and Orthopedic Surgery. Bd. dirs. Renton (Wash.) Handicapped Ctr., 1968-70, March of Dimes, 1974-79; bd. dirs. enabling sys. U. Hawaii, Honolulu, 1977-80. Capt. U.S. Army, 1950-52, Korea. Decorated U.S. Senate Medal of Freedom, Bronze and Silver Stars, Pres. Ronald Reagan's Task Force Medal of Merit and Eternal Flame of Freedom. Fellow Royal Soc. Medicine (gynecology and oncology sects.), Am. Coll. Ob-Gyn, Internat. Coll. Surgeons (v.p. 1997—, pres. 1999-2001, past pres. 2001—); mem. Seattle Gynecol. Soc. (pres. 1978), Baker Channing Soc., Sigma Xi. Avocations: photography, sailing, skiing, construction, ornithology. Home: Seattle, Wash. Deceased.

SCOTT, ROLAND BOYD, pediatrician; b. Houston, Apr. 18, 1909; s. Ernest John and Cordie (Clark) S.; m. Sarah Rosetta Weaver, June 24, 1935 (dec.); children— Roland Boyd, Venice Rosetta, Estelle Irene. BS, Howard U., 1931, MD, 1934, DSc (hon.), 1987. Diplomate Nat. Bd. Med. Examiners, Am. Bd. Pediatrics. Gen. Edn. Bd. fellow U. Chgo., 1936-39; faculty Howard U., Washington, 1939—, prof. pediatrics, 1952-77, disting. prof. pediatrics and child health, 1977—, chmn. dept. pediatrics, 1945-73; dir. Ctr. for Sickle Cell Anemia, 1973—; chief pediatrician Freedmen's Hosp., 1947-73; professorial lectr. in child health and devel. George Washington U. Sch. Medicine, 1971-75. Staff Children's Hosp., Providence Hosp., Columbia Hosp., D.C. Gen. Hosp., Washington Hosp. Center; cons. in pediatrics to NIH, hosps.; Mem. com. Pub. Health Adv. Council, 1964—, U.S. Children's Bur., 1964-70; mem. Nat. Com. for Children and Youth.; mem. sickle cell adv. com. NIH, 1983-88. Author: (with Althea D. Kessler) Sickle Cell Anemia and Your Child, (with C.G. Uy) Guidelines For Care of Patients With Sickle Cell Disease; Editor: Procs. 1st Internat. Conf. on Sickle Cell Disease: A World Health Problem, 1979; Mem. editorial bd.: Advances in the Pathophysiology, Diagnosis and Treatment of Sickle Cell Disease, 1982, Clin. Pediatrics, 1962-80, Jour. Nat. Med. Assn, 1978; cons. editor: Medical Aspects of Human Sexuality; editorial bd.: Annals of Allergy, 1977-82, Pediatrics, 1988. Recipient Sci. and Community award Medico-Chirurgical Med. Soc. D.C., 1971, Community Service award Med. Soc. D.C., 1972, award for contbns. to sickle cell research Delta Sigma Theta, 1973, 34 years Dedicated and Disting. Service award in pediatrics dept. pediatrics Howard U., 1973, Faculty award for excellence in research, 1974, Alumni award for Service and Dedication, 1984, spl. recognition plaque for contbns. to research and edn., 1985, Ronald McDonald Children Charities award, 1987; certificate of appreciation Sickle Cell Anemia Research and Edn., 1977; Mead Johnson award D.C. chpt. Am. Acad. Pediatrics, 1978; Percy L. Julian award We Do Care, Chgo., 1979; Abraham Jacobi Meml. award AMA and Acad. Pediatrics, 1985; also plaques for work in sickle cell disease various orgns. including Columbia U. Sickle Cell Ctr., 1984, Elks, Nat. Assn. Med. Minority Educators, NIH, 1980-82. Fellow Am. Coll. Allergists (Disting. Service award 1977); mem. AMA, Am. Hematology Soc., Am. Pediatric Soc. (John Howland award 1991), Soc. Pediatric Research, Am. Acad. Allergy (v.p. 1966-67), Am. Acad. Pediatrics (mem. com. on children with handicaps, cons. head start program), Am. Fedn. Clin. Research, Nat. Med. Assn. (Disting. Service medal 1966), AAAS, Internat. Corr. Soc. Allergists, Assn. Ambulatory Pediatric Services, AAUP, Internat. Congress Pediatrics, Can. Sickle Cell Soc. (hon. life), Phi Beta Kappa, Sigma Xi (Percy L. Julian award Howard U. chpt. 1977), Kappa Pi, Beta Kappa Chi, Alpha Omega Alpha, others. Achievements include research and publications on sickle cell anemia, growth and devel. of infants and children, allergy in children. Home: Silver Spring, Md. Died Dec. 10, 2002.

SCOTT, STANLEY SOUTHALL, public relations executive; b. Bolivar, Tenn., July 2, 1933; s. Lewis Augustus and Clinora Neely (Hamer) S.; m. Bettye L. Lovejoy, Dec. 23, 1962; children: Kenneth Earl, Susan Lovejoy, Stanley Southall II. Student, U. Kans., Lawrence, 1951-53; BS in Journalism, Lincoln U., Jefferson City, Mo., 1959. Editor, gen. mgr. Memphis World, 1960-61; gen. assignment news reporter, copy editor, editorial writer Atlanta Daily World, 1961-64; gen. assignment news reporter UPI, N.Y.C., 1964-66; asst. dir. public relations NAACP, N.Y.C., 1966-67; radio newsman Westinghouse Broadcasting Corp., N.Y.C., 1967-71; asst. to dir. communications exec. br. White House, Washington, 1971-73, spl. asst. to pres., 1973-75; asst. adminstr. AID, 1975-77; asst. dir. corp. relations Philip Morris, Inc., N.Y.C., 1977, dir. corp. public affairs, 1978-79, v.p. public affairs, 1979-84, dir. corp. affairs, from 1984; pres., sole owner Crescent Distbg. Co., New Orleans, from 1988. V.p. Philip Morris Cos., Inc., 1984—; bd. dirs. Fed. Res. Bank, New Orleans, Am. Bank & Trust Co., New Orleans, New Orleans Bus. Coun. Bd. dirs. New Orleans Audubon Zoo; bd. trustees Xavier U., New Orleans; mem. Pres.' Commn. on White House fellowships; mem. N.Y. State Martin Luther King Jr. Commn.; nat. com. mem. Nat. Mus. African Art, Smithsonian Inst.; adv. bd. John Jay Coll. Criminal Justice. Served with U.S. Army, 1954-56. Recipient Russwurm award for excellence in radio news reporting, 1967, Silurians award, 1965, Pulitzer nomination for Malcolm X coverage, 1965, Wisemens award for series on police-minority community confrontation in Atlanta, 1961 Mem. NAACP, Urban League New Orleans. Republican. Presbyterian. Home: New Orleans, La. Died Apr. 1992.

SCRIBNER, BELDING HIBBARD, retired medical educator, nephrologist; b. Chgo., Jan. 18, 1921; s. Carleton Spear and Mary Elizabeth (Belding) Scribner; m. Elizabeth F. Browne, Dec. 28, 1942 (div. Dec. 1965); children: Peter B., Robert R., B. Thomas, A. Elizabeth; m. Ethel Victoria Hackett, Jan. 28, 1966. AB, U. Calif., Berkeley, 1941; MD, Stanford U., 1945; MA, U. Minn., 1951; D (hon.), U. Goteborg, 1981; postgrad., Med. Sch. London, 1985. Asst. to staff Mayo Clinic, Rochester, Minn., 1950—51; instr. medicine U. Wash., Seattle, 1951—55, asst. prof. medicine, 1955—58, assoc. prof. medicine, 1958—64, prof. medicine, 1964—82, prof. emeritus, 1982—98. With USN, 1941—44. Recipient Gaindner Found. award, Toronto, 1969, David Hume award, Nat. Kidney Found., 1975, Mayo Soley award, Western Soc. Clin. Investigation, 1982, Jean Hamburger award, Internat. Soc. Nephrology, 1987, Gov.'s medal, State of Wash., 1989; scholar, Markle Found., 1954—59. Mem.: Inst. Medicine, Assn. Am. Physicians, Am. Soc. Nephrology (pres. 1978—79, John P. Peters award 1986), Am. Soc. Artificial Organs (pres. 1963—64), Am. Soc. Clin. Investigation. Achievements include patents for medical device. Home: Seattle, Wash. Died June 19, 2003.

SCUDDER, EDWARD WALLACE, JR., newspaper and broadcasting executive; b. Newark, Dec. 8, 1911; s. Edward Wallace and Katherine (Hollifield) Scudder; m. Louise Bagby Fry (dec. 1998), Jan. 19, 1945; children: Katherine Allison Tiballi, Mary Gale Doe, Edward, Robert. AB, Princeton, 1935. Pres. Newark Evening News, 1950-70; former pres. Newark Broadcasting, Newark. Trustee Paper Mill Playhouse, Millburn, N.J., Newark Mus., Lake Placid (N.Y.) Edn. Found. Lt. (j.g.) to lt. comdr. USNR Air Force, 1942-46. Mem. Short Hills Club, Gulfstream Golf Club, Gulfstream Bath and Tennis Club. Home: Lake Placid, NY. Died Nov. 27, 2003.

SCUDDER, JACK HOWARD, newspaper editor; b. Mpls., Nov. 23, 1919; s. Clarence and Ethel Elizabeth (Johnson) S.; m. Josephine Louise Woodward, Feb. 26, 1944; children: Janet Louise, James Howard, David Woodward, John Douglas. BA cum laude, U. Minn., 1942. Editor Idaho Free Press, Nampa, 1955-66; pub. Daily-Record Gazette, Banning and Beaumont, Calif., 1966-68; dir. rsch. Scripps League of Newspapers, Seattle, 1968-75, J.G. Scripps Newspapers, Seattle, 1975-86; pres. Scudder/Western Rsch., Inc., Nampa, Idaho, 1986-89. Pres. Comty. Concert Assn., Little Falls, Minn., 1954, Banning C. of C., 1967; bd. dirs. Nampa Area United Way, 1964-66, Idaho Press Club, Boise, 1964-66, Rotary, Banning, 1968, Arts for Idaho, 1994—; pres. Nampa Civic Ctr. Aux., 1991-93, Nampa Civic Ctr. Commn., 1991—. Mem. Soc. Profl. Journalists. Methodist. Avocations: photography, piano, organ, writing. Home: Nampa, Idaho. Died Apr. 10, 2000.

SCURLOCK, ARCH CHILTON, chemical engineer; b. Beaumont, Tex., Jan. 29, 1920; s. Marvin and Mary (Chilton) S.; m. Maurine Spurbeck, Nov. 27, 1945 (div.); children: Arch, Susan, Marvin Curtis; m. Nancy Morrison Yonick, Nov. 16, 1962; children: Mary, Nancy, Margaret Ann. BS in Chem. Engring, AB in Physics, U. Tex., 1941; MS, Mass. Inst. Tech., 1943, Sc.D., 1948; spl. course meteorology, U. Chgo., 1944. Research asso. chem. engring. dept. Mass. Inst. Tech., 1946-48; asst. dir. chemistry Engring. Research Assocs., 1948-49; pres. Atlantic Research Corp., Alexandria, Va., 1949-62, chmn. bd., 1962-65; pres., dir. Research Industries Inc., Alexandria, 1968—. Chmn. TransTechnology Corp., 1969-92, Halifax Corp. Served to lt. (s.g.) USNR, 1943-46. Mem. AAAS, AIAA, Am. Inst. Chem. Engrs., Am. Chem. Soc., Am. Phys. Soc., Am. Meteorol. Soc., Am. Def. Preparedness Assn., Combustion Inst., Univ. Club (Washington), Belle Haven (Va.) Country Club, Army Navy Country Club (Va.), Mid-Ocean Club (Tuckers Town, Bermuda), Phi Beta Kappa, Sigma Xi, Tau Beta Pi. Home: Arlington, Va. Died Dec. 9, 2002.

SEALTS, MERTON MILLER, JR., English language educator; b. Lima, Ohio, Dec. 8, 1915; s. Merton Miller and Daisy (Hathaway) S.; m. Ruth Mackenzie, Nov. 17, 1942 (dec. 1995). BA, Coll. of Wooster, 1937, DLitt (hon.), 1974; PhD, Yale U., 1942. Instr. in English U. Mo., Columbia, 1941-42, Wellesley Coll., 1946-48; asst. prof. English Lawrence Coll., Appleton, Wis., 1948-51; assoc. prof. English, 1951-58; prof. English Lawrence Coll./U., Appleton, Wis., 1958-65, U. Wis., Madison, 1965-75, Henry A. Pochmann prof. English, 1975-82, Henry A. Pochmann prof. English emeritus, from 1982. Author: Melville as Lecturer, 1957, Melville's Reading, 1966, The Early Lives of Melville: Nineteenth-Century Biographical Sketches and Their Authors, 1974, Pursuing Melville: Chapters and Essays, 1982, Melville's Reading: Revised and Enlarged Edition, 1988, Emerson on the Scholar, 1992, Beyond the Classroom: Essays on American Authors, 1996; editor: The Journals and Miscellaneous Notebooks of Ralph Waldo Emerson, vol. V (1835-1838), 1965, vol. X (1847-1848), 1973; co-editor: Billy Budd, Sailor (by Herman Melville), 1962, Emerson's Nature: Origin, Growth, Meaning, 1969, 79. Pvt.-maj. USAAC, 1942-46. Fellow Ford Found., 1953-54, J. S. Guggenheim Found., 1962-63, NEH, 1975; Am. Coun. Learned Socs. grantee, 1970; recipient Tchg. award E. and R. Uhrig Found., 1965, Disting. Alumni award Coll. of Wooster, 1994. Mem. MLA (Jau B. Hubbell medal Am. Lit. sect. 1992), Am. Lit. Assn., Melville Soc. (pres. 1953), Ralph Ealdo Emerson Soc. (Disting. Achievement award 1995), Thoreau Soc. Avocations: reading, classical music. Died June 4, 2000.

SEALY, WILL CAMP, cardiovascular and thoracic surgeon, educator; b. Roberta, Ga., Nov. 6, 1912; s. Hugh Key and Marjorie Parkie (Camp) S.; m. Marian Blinn Sanford, 1941 (dec. 1959); children: Leigh, Marjorie, Neil, Brian; m. Jacqueline Wamble, Apr. 30, 1965; children: Karen, Jacqueline. BS, Emory U., 1933, MD, 1936. Diplomate Am. Bd. Surgery, Am. Bd. Thoracic and Cardiovascular Surgery (bd. dirs. 1971-77). Intern, resident in surgery Duke U., Durham, N.C., 1936-42, prof. surgery, 1946-83, prof. emeritus, 1983; prof. surgery Mercer U., Macon, Ga., from 1984, chair surgery dept., 1984-91. Vol. fellow thoracic surgery U. Mich., Ann Arbor, 1950-51; mem. surgical study sect B NIH, Washington, 1960-66. Mem. editorial bd. Annals of Thoracic Surgery, St. Louis, 1977-83; contbr. articles to jours. Hypothermia Open Heart Surgery, Paradoxical Hypertension, Surgery for WPW, Post Septal Space & WPW, Artrial Conduction. Lt. col. M.C. U.S. Army, 1942-46, ETO (Decorated Bronze star). Recipient Ray Fish award Tex. Heart Inst., 1979, Disting. Scientist award N.Am. Soc. Pacing and Electrophysiology, Boston, 1987. Mem. Am. Surgical Assn., Soc. Univ. Surgery, South Surgical Assn., Soc. Thoracic Surgery (pres. 1971). Democrat. Methodist. Achievements include first to incorporate moderate and profound hypothermia combined with extracorporeal circulation for open heart surgery; first to correct arrhythmias in WPW; research on causes of hypertension and coarctation of aorta, on characteristics of low atrial pacemakers, on postoperative paradoxical hypertension and coarction repair. Home: Greenville, NC. Died Jan. 27, 2001.

SEARS, WILLIAM REES, engineering educator; b. Mpls., Mar. 1, 1913; s. William Everett and Gertrude (Rees) S.; m. Mabel Jeannette Rhodes, Mar. 20, 1936; children: David William, Susan Carol. BS in Aero. Engring, U. Minn., 1934; PhD, aeronautics, Calif. Inst. Tech., 1938; DSc (hon.), U. Ariz., 1987. Asst. prof. Calif. Inst. Tech., 1939-41; chief aerodynamics Northrop Aircraft, Inc., 1941-46; dir. Grad. Sch. Aero. Engring., Cornell U., Ithaca, N.Y., 1946-63, Center Applied Math., 1963-67, J.L. Given prof. engring., 1962-74; prof. aerospace and mech. engring. U. Ariz., Tucson, 1974-88, prof. emeritus, from 1988. F. W. Lanchester lectr. Royal Aero. Soc., 1973, Gardner lectr. MIT, 1987, Guggenheim lectr. Internat. Congress Aero. Scis., 1988; cons. aerodynamics. Author: The Airplane and its Components, 1941, Stories from a 20th-Century Life, 1994; editor: Jet Propulsion and High-Speed Aerodynamics, vol. VI, 1954, Jour. Aerospace Scis., 1956-63, Ann. Revs. of Fluid Mechanics, Vol. I. Recipient Vincent Bendix award Am. Soc. Engring. Edn., 1965, Prandtl Ring Deutsche Gesellschaft für Luft-und Raumfahrt, 1974, Von Karman medal AGARD (NATO), 1977, ASME medal, 1989, NAS Award in Aeronautical Engrng Nat. Acad of Sciences, 1995; named to Ariz. Aviation Hall of Fame, 1996. Fellow AIAA (hon., G. Edward Pendray award 1975, S.A. Reed Aeros. award 1981, Von Karman lectr. 1968, Daniel Guggenheim medal 1996); mem. NAE, NAS, Am. Acad. Arts and Scis., Nat. Acad. Engring. Mex. (fgn.), Am. Phys. Soc. (Fluid Dynamics prize 1992). Home: Tucson, Ariz. Died Oct. 12, 2002.

SEEBASS, ALFRED RICHARD, III, aerospace engineer, educator, university dean; b. Denver, Mar. 27, 1936; s. Alfred Richard Jr. and Marie Estelle (Wright) S.; m. Nancy Jane Palm, June 20, 1958; children: Erik Peter, Scott Gregory. BS in Engring. magna cum laude, Princeton U., 1958, MS in Engring., 1961; PhD, Cornell U., 1962. Asst. prof., assoc. prof. Cornell U., Ithaca, N.Y., 1962-72, prof. aerospace engring., assoc. dean engring., 1972-75; hdqrs. staff rsch. divsn. NASA, 1966-67; prof. aerospace engring., mech. engring. and math. U. Ariz., Tucson, 1975-81; dean U. Colo. Coll. Engring. and Applied Sci., Boulder, 1981-94; John R. Woodhull prof. and chair aerospace engring. scis. U. Colo., Boulder, 1993-94; faculty assoc. Boeing Sci. Rsch. Labs., 1970. Cons. in field; mem. coms. NAE, NAS, NRC, NASA, Dept. Transp., sci. adv. bd. Air Force, Aero. and Space Engring. Bd., Los Alamos Nat. Lab; grant investigator NASA, Office Naval Rsch., Air Force Office Sci. Rsch., 1966—; mem. U.S.-Israel Bi-nat. Fund; aeronautics and space engring. bd. NRC, 1977-84, vice-chmn., 1979-81, chmn., 1981-83, mem. Commn. on Engring. and Tech. Sys., 1982-83; mem. Numerical Aerodynamics Simulator Adv. Group, 1978-97; chmn. Air Force Office Scientific Rsch. rev. panel Flight Dynamics Lab., Wright-Patterson AFB, 1979; adv. coun. NASA, 1981-83; survey com. on plasma physics and fluids, subcom. on fluids NRC, 1983-84; engring. rsch. bd. Panel on Transp. Sys. Rsch., 1984-85; sci. adv. bd. USAF, 1984-88, chmn. Air Force Operational Test & Evaluation Ctr. Divsn. Adv. Group, 1986-88, mem. Arnold Engring. & Devel. Ctr. Divsn. Adv. Group, 1984-88, aerospace vehicles panel, 1984-88; adv. coun. univ. study planning group NASA, 1988-97; bd. dirs. Aerosonde, Ltd.; mech. and electronic external adv. com. Los Alamos (N.Mex.) Nat. Lab., 1991-93, chair divsn. rev. com. Engring. Scis. & Applications, Los Alamos, 1995-98; mem. NASA Adv. Coun. U. Rels. Task Force, 1991-93; mem. Commn. on Phys. Scis., Math. & Applications NRC, 1992-95; chmn. NRC Com. Air Force Hypersonics Tech., 1997-98. Editor: Sonic Boom Research, 1967, Nonlinear Waves 1974, Russian, 1977; assoc. editor: Physics of Fluids, 1978-80; mem. editl. bd. Ann. Rev. Fluid Mechanics, Phys. Fluids, AIAA Jour.; editor-in-chief (book series) Progress Astronautics and Aeronautics, 1990-95; contbg. author: Handbook of Applied Mathematics, 1974; contbr. articles to profl. jours., chpts. to books; reviewer Jour. Fluid Mechanics, Physics of Fluids, Jour. Acoustical Soc. Am., AIAA Jour., Jour. Aircraft, Jour. Applied Mechanics, NSF. Daniel and Florence Guggenheim fellow Princeton U., 1958-59, Woodrow Wilson fellow Cornell U., 1959-60; recipient Disting. Engring. Alumni award U. Colo., 1983, Meritorious Civilian Svc. award Dept. Air Force, 1988, (with H. Sobieczky) Max Planck Rsch. prize, Germany, 1991, U. Colo. medal 1994, U. Colo. Coll. of Engring. Centennial medal 1994, Frank J. Malina medal Internat. Astronautics Fedn., 1994. Fellow AAAS (mem. engring. sect. nominating com. 1987-90, chair 1990, coun. del. engring. sect. 1991-94, vice chair, chair engring. sect. 1995-97), AIAA (mem. fluid mechanics tech. com. 1977-80, tech. dir. bd. dirs. 1978-81, exec com. 1980-81, assoc. editor jour. 1981-83, Disting. lectr. 1995-98); mem. Nat. Acad. Engring. (aerospace peer com. 1987-90, 99—, chair 1990, mem. com. on membership 1991-93, vice chmn. 1991, chair 1992, acad. adv. bd. 1997-98), Am. Soc. Engring. Edn. (mem. sr. rsch. award com. 1990-93, chair 1993), Sigma Xi, Tau Beta Pi. Home: Denver, Colo. Deceased.

SEEDLOCK, ROBERT FRANCIS, engineering and construction company executive; b. Newark, Feb. 6, 1913; s. Frank Andrew and Mary Elizabeth (Prosner) S.; m. Hortense Orcutt Norton, Sept. 1, 1937 (dec. Aug. 2000); children: Robert Francis, Elizabeth Munsell Seedlock Morrissette, Walter Norton, Mary Marion. Grad., Armed Forces Staff Coll., 1948, Nat. War Coll., 1958. Registered profl. engr., D.C., Pa. Commd. 2d lt. U.S. Army, 1937, advanced through grades to maj. gen., 1963; asst. to dist. engr. Pitts., 1937-39, Tulsa Aircraft Assembly Plant, 1941; regtl. exec. bn. comdr. Engr. Unit Tng. Ctr., Camp Claiborne, La., 1942; asst. theatre engr. CBI; also comdr. Burma Road Engrs.; also chief engr. Shanghai Base Command, 1943-45; mem. Gen. Marshall's Mediation Mission, Peking, 1946-47; mem. gen. staff U.S. Army; mem. Am. del. Far Ea. Commn., 1948-49; aide to chief staff U.S. Army, 1949-54; mem. U.S. del. NATO Ministerial Conf., 1952-53, dep. divsn. engr. Mediterranean divsn., 1954-57, mil. asst. to asst. sec. def. for pub. affairs, 1958-62. Div. engr. Missouri River, Omaha, 1962-63; sr. mem. UN Mil. Armistice Commn., Korea, 1963-64; dir. mil. personnel Office dep. chief of staff for personnel Dept. Army, 1964-66; dir. mil. constrn. Office Chief of Engrs., 1966; commdg. gen. U.S. Army Engr. Ctr. and Ft. Belvoir, Va. and comdt. U.S. Army Engr. Sch., Ft. Belvoir, 1966-68, ret., 1968; pres. Yuba Industries, 1968-69, v.p. Standards Prudential Corp. (merged with Yuba Industries), 1969-70; vice pres., dir. Petro-Chem. Devel. Co., Inc., N.Y.C., 1968-70, Petchem. Constrn. Co., N.Y.C., 1968-70,

Petrochem Isoflow Furnaces, Ltd. (Can.), 1968-70; dir. constrn. and devel. Port Authority of Allegheny County, Pitts., 1970-73; assoc. Parsons, Brinckerhoff-Tudor-Bechtel, Atlanta, 1973-77; prog. dir. Ralph M. Parsons Co., Pasadena, Calif., Phila. and Washington, 1977-83; cons. 1983-97; dir. T.Y. Lin Internat., 1985-89; chief liaison, cons. Chinese Acad. Sci. for Beijing Inst. Mgmt., 1985-89; U.S. rep. to Permanent Tech. Com. Number 1 of Permanent Internat. Assn. of Navigation Congresses, 1984-93; pres. First Am. chapt. Burma Star Assn., 1984-98; chmn. Sino-Am. Ventures Inc., 1987-2004; cons. The Knowledge Co., 1989-92, Dove & Assocs., 1990. Contbr. to mil. and engring. jours. Bd. dirs. Army and Air Force Exch. and Motion Picture Svc., 1964; mem. Miss. River Commn., 1962-63, Bd. Engrs. Rivers and Harbor, 1962-63, Def. Adv. Commn. Edn., 1964; chmn. Mo. Basin Inter-Agy. Com., 1962-63; fed. rep., chmn. Big Blue River Compact Commn., 1962-63; mem. U.S. Com. on Large Dams, 1962-82; exec. bd. Nat. Capital Area coun. Boy Scouts Am., 1967-68, Atlanta area coun., 1975-77. Decorated DSM, Legion of Merit with oak leaf cluster; chevalier Legion of Honor (France); 1st class grade A medal Army, Navy, Air Force, also spl. breast order Yun Hui (China); named Engr. of Yr., Met. Atlanta Engring. Soc., 1976, Ga. Engr. of Yr. in Govt., Ga. Soc. profl. Engrs., 1976; recipient Silver Beaver award Boy Scouts Am., 1977, Case Alumni Assn. Golf medal, 1985. Fellow Soc. Am. Mil. Engrs. (nat. dir., Cathedral Latin Alumni Assn. Man of the Yr. award 1992); mem. ASCE (hon., aerospace divsn. program com. 1980-82, sec. exec. com. 1982-83, chmn. 1984-85, editor Jour. Aerospace Engring. 1986-93), Assn. U.S. Army, West Point Soc. N.Y. (life), West Point Soc. Atlanta (pres. 1976), Burma Star Assn. (pres. 1st Am. chpt. 1982-98), Army-Navy Country Club (sec., chmn. bd. govs. 1952-54, 61-62), Met. Club (N.Y.C.), Oglethorpe Club (Savannah, Ga.), Ansley Golf Club (Atlanta). Roman Catholic. Died May 5, 2004.

SEGAL, GERALDINE ROSENBAUM, sociologist; b. Aug. 26, 1908; d. Harry and Mena (Hamburg) Rosenbaum; m. Bernard Gerard Segal, Oct. 22, 1933; children: Loretta Joan Cohen, Richard Murry. BS in Edn., U. Pa., 1930, MA in Human Rels., 1963, PhD in Sociology, 1978; MS in Libr. Sci., Drexel U., 1968; LittD (hon.), Franklin & Marshall Coll., 1990. Social worker County Relief Bd., Phila., 1931-35; sociologist Phila., from 1935. Cons. and lectr. in field. Author: In Any Fight Some Fall, 1975, Blacks in the Law, 1983. Bd. dirs. NCCJ, 1937-47, 82—, sec., 1983-91; bd. overseers U. Pa. Sch. Social Work, 1983-97; bd. dirs. Juvenile Law Ctr., 1984-98; chair Phila. Tutorial Project, 1966-68; 1st v.p. U. Pa. Alumnae Assn., 1967-70. Co-recipient Nat. Neighbors Disting. Leadership in Civil Rights award, 1988; recipient Drum Major award for Human Rights, Phila. Martin Luther King, Jr. Assn. for Nonviolence, 1990, Brotherhood Sisterhood award NCCJ, 1994. Democrat. Jewish. Died Jan. 14, 2003.

SEGAL, IRVING RANDALL, lawyer; b. Allentown, Pa., Oct. 15, 1914; s. Samuel I. and Rose (Kantor) S.; m. Eleanor F. Smolens, Dec. 26, 1943; children: Betsy A. Segal Carter, Kathy J., Robert J. BA, U. Pa., 1935; LLB, 1938. Bar: Pa. 1938. Instr. polit. sci. U. Pa., 1938-42; law clk. Ct. Common Pleas No. 4, Phila. County, Pa., 1938-39; assoc. Schnader, Harrison, Segal & Lewis, Phila., 1939-49, ptnr., 1949-92, sr. counsel, 1993—2002. Permanent mem. Jud. Conf. 3d Circuit U.S. Ct. Appeals; regional rationing atty. OPA, 1942 Author: May It Please the Court, 1998. V.p. Nat. Kidney Disease Found., 1954-59, hon. life del., 1959-64; pres. Nephrosis Found., Phila., 1953-56; bd. mgrs. Woman's Hosp. Phila., 1957-64, v.p., 1962-63; bd. Jewish Edn., Phila., 1948-72; trustee YMHA, YWHA, 1954-58. Served to capt. Judge Adv. Gen. Dept. AUS, 1942-46. Decorated Mil. Commendation medal. Fellow Am. Coll. Trial Lawyers (regent 1976-79, sec. 1979-80); mem. ABA (corrections com. 1980-87, jud. selection tenure and compensation com. 1988-93, com. on legal problems of the elderly 1997-99), Pa. Bar Assn., Phila. Bar Assn. (chmn. sr. lawyers 1996-99), Am. Law Inst., Am. Bar Found. (50-yr. award 1999), Am. Judicature Soc., World Peace Through Law, Am. Acad. Polit. and Social Sci., Order of Coif, Phi Beta Kappa, Pi Gamma Mu (pres., 1934-35), Delta Sigma Rho. Jewish (dir., v.p. temple). Clubs: Phila. Lawyers, Art Alliance, Locust, Army and Navy of Washington Home: Philadelphia, Pa. Died Nov. 25, 2002.

SEHLMEYER, RICHARD GEORGE, real estate broker, educator; b. Mineola, N.Y., July 4, 1934; s. Ernest Ferdinand and Anna Francis (Wighaus) S.; m. Joanne Elizabeth Hanlon, Nov. 30, 1957; children: Richard George Jr., Deborah Ann, James Joseph, Daniel David, Elizabeth Joanne. Grad., Realtor's Inst., Albany, N.Y., 1976. Cert. real estate appraiser, Ariz.; cert. environ. insp., N.Y.; lic. and cert. gen. real estate appraisals, N.Y. Electrician Local #25, Internat. Brotherhood Elec. Workers, Westbury, N.Y., 1952-63; real estate broker Lake Luzerne Real Estate Co., Lake Luzerene, N.Y., from 1969, Sacandaga Real Estate, Day, N.Y., from 1986, Corinth Real Estate, Corinth, Lake George, from 1986; real estate instr. Adirondack Community Coll., Queensbury, N.Y., from 1974; instr. Nat. Assn. Real Estate Appraisers, Scottsdale, Ariz., from 1991; training dir., pres. Sellmeyer Inc., Hadley, N.Y., from 1987. Hearing officer N.Y. State Supreme Ct., 4th Jud. Dist., 1985—, N.Y. Author: Sure-Sell System, 1989. Br. chmn. ARC, Glen Falls, N.Y., 1982—; planning bd. Town of Hadley, N.Y., 1974; Dem. chmn. Town of Hadley, 1986; mem. Great Sacandaga Lake Assn., Edinburg, N.Y., 1985. Mem. Nat. Assn. Real Estate Appraisers (cert. instr., chmn. Adirondack chpt. 1991—), Lake Luzerne C. of C. (bd. dirs. 1970—, Man of Yr. award). Democrat. Roman Catholic. Home: Hadley, NY. Died Feb. 7, 2001.

SEIB, CHARLES BACH, journalist; b. Kingston, N.Y., Aug. 22, 1919; s. Charles Bach and Elizabeth (Meyer) S.; m. Shirley Jane Mayer, Oct. 1, 1945; children— Philip, Caroline. BA, Lehigh U., 1941. Reporter Allentown (Pa.) Chronicle, 1942-44, A.P., 1944-45; deskman Phila. Record, 1945-46; reporter I.N.S., 1946-52; asst. bur. chief Gannett News Service, Washington, 1952-54; with Washington Star, 1954-74, mng. editor, 1968-74; assoc. editor, ombudsman Washington Post, 1974-79; columnist The News Business, 1974-79. Vis. prof. Newhouse Sch., Syracuse (N.Y.) U., 1981-83; lectr. U. Md., 1985 Author: The Woods, 1971. Fellow Inst. Politics, Harvard U., 1980 Home: Spruce Head, Maine. Died Oct. 23, 2003.

SEILER, WALLACE URBAN, chemical engineer; b. Evansville, Ind., Aug. 31, 1914; s. Samuel Alfred and Anna Beatrice (Grossman) S.; m. Charlotte Woody, Oct. 10, 1942; children: Patricia Anne, Janet Alice. Student, U. Evansville, 1932-34; BS, Purdue U., 1937; postgrad., U. Mich., 1945-46. Engr. Dow Chem. Co., Midland, Mich., 1937-39, cons. rsch. engr. Ann Arbor, Mich., 1939-49, tech. sve. engr. Midland, 1950-55, mgr. solvents field svc., 1955-64, contract R & D specialist, 1964-80. Chemical engineer; b. Evansville, Ind., Aug. 31, 1914; s. Samuel Alfred and Anna Beatrice (Grossman) S.; student U. Evansville, 1932-34; BS, Purdue U., 1937; postgrad. U. Mich., 1945-46; m. Charlotte Woody, Oct. 10, 1942; children: Patricia Anne, Janet Alice. With Dow Chem. Co., 1937-80, engr., Midland, Mich., 1937-39, cons. rsch. engr., Ann Arbor, Mich., 1939-49, tech. svc. engr., Midland, 1950-55, mgr. solvents field svc., 1955-64, contract R & D specialist, 1964-80. Mem. AAAS, Am. Chem. Soc., Am. Inst. Chemists, Sigma Xi, Tau Beta Pi, Phi Lambda Upsilon. Mem. AAAS, Am. Chem. Soc., Am. Inst. Chemists, Sigma Xi, Tau Beta Pi, Phi Lambda Upsilon. Home: North Port, Fla. Died Aug. 2, 2002.

SELBY, HUBERT, JR., writer; b. N.Y.C., July 23, 1928; s. Hubert and Adalin (Layne) S.; m. Inez Taylor, Apr. 23, 1955 (div. 1960); children: Claudia, Kyle; Suzanne Schwartzman, Dec. 26, 1969; children: Rachel, William. Student public schs., Bklyn. Author: Last Exit to Brooklyn, 1964, The Room, 1971, The Demon, 1976, Requiem for a Dream, 1978, Song of the Silent Snow, 1986, The Willow Tree, 1998, Waiting Period, 2002; screenwriter: Day and Night, 1986, Remember the Sabath Day, 1974, Love Your Buddy Week, 1978, Solder of Fortune, 1990, Requiem for a Dream, 1998, Fear the X, 2000. Served with U.S. Mcht. Marine, 1944-46. Mem. Writers Guild Am. (West chpt.), Authors Guild. Died Apr. 26, 2004.

SELECMAN, CHARLES EDWARD, business executive; b. Dallas, Sept. 17, 1928; s. Frank A. and Eloise (Olive) S.; m. Nan Harton Nash, May 11, 1951 (div. 1975); children: Mary Lucinda, Nan Elizabeth, Amy Eloise; m. Judith Wallace Pollard, Feb. 6, 1976 (div. 1984); m. Barbara Ann Calvert, Apr. 18, 1985. BA, So. Meth. U., 1951. Bus. mgmt. clk. Buick Motor div. Gen. Motor Corp., Dallas, 1951-52; pers. dept. Chance Vought Aircraft, Inc., Dallas, 1952-56; div. pers. mgr. U.S. Industries, Inc., Longview, Tex., 1956-64, div. v.p. mktg., 1964-66; div. exec. v.p. Axelson div. U.S. Industries, Inc., 1966-67, div. pres., 1967; corp. v.p. U.S. Industries, Inc., N.Y.C., 1967-68, corp. exec. v.p., dir., 1968-70, pres., 1970-73, vice chmn., CEO, 1973-74, also dir.; pres., CEO E.T. Barwick Industries, Inc., 1975-78; ptnr. Marshalsea Texas Partners, Dallas, 1978-83; chmn., pres., CEO Input/Output Inc., Houston, 1984-93, chmn., from 1993. Dir. Triton Oil & Gas Corp., 1975-93. Mem. Soc. Exploration Geophysicists, Sigma Alpha Epsilon. Home: Palm Coast, Fla. Died Sept. 20, 1999.

SELINGER, CARL M. legal educator, dean; b. 1934. B.A., U. Calif.-Berkeley, 1955; J.D., Harvard U., 1958. Bar: Calif. 1958, Hawaii 1976, Mich. 1980, W.Va. 1983. Pvt. practice, Calif., 1958-59; teaching fellow Harvard U., Cambridge, Mass., 1960-61; prof. law Albany (N.Y.) Coll., 1961-63, U. N.Mex., Albuquerque, 1963-68; acad. dean Bard Coll., Annandale-on-Hudson, N.Y., 1968-75; prof. sch. law, assoc. dean U. Hawaii, Honolulu, 1975-79; dean Sch. Law, U. Detroit, 1979-82; dean Coll. Law, W.Va. U., Morgantown, 1982—; cons. Deceased.

SELLERS, JOHN LEWIS, advertising design educator; b. Alexander City, Ala., Aug. 28, 1934; s. Clyde Chapman and Mary Nell (Slaton) S.; m. Ann Vary Ford, Aug. 20, 1955; children: Mary Elizabeth, Reed Chapman, Serena Slaton, Anna Lucille, Ford Hunter. BA, Auburn U., 1955; MA, Vanderbilt U., 1963. Artist Williams Printing Co., Nashville, 1957-58; art dir., asst. editor Tenn. Mag., Nashville, 1958-60; promotion mgr. Meth. Pub. House, Nashville, 1960-65; assoc. creative dir. McDonald & Saussy Advt., Nashville, 1965-67; art dir. Motive Mag., Nashville, 1967-68; v.p., creative dir. Les Hart Advt., Nashville, 1967-70; assoc. prof. advt. design Syracuse (N.Y.) U., 1970-73, prof. advt. design, from 1973, chmn. dept. visual communication, from 1973. Chmn. MFA program, Syracuse U., 1972—; dir. Sports Learning Corp., N.Y.C.; judge Conn. Art Dirs. Club, 1986; speaker in field. Author: Prize Winning Painting, 1965; art dir. Syracuse Scholar, 1978-86, editor, 1986. Pres. Tenn. chpt. Arthritis Found. Am., 1966-69, bd. dirs. N.Y. chpt., 1970-80 (Disting. Service award 1969). 1st lt. U.S. Army, 1955-57. Recipient over 100 awards in advt., design and painting. Mem. Am. Inst. Graphic Art, N.Y. Art Dirs. Club (chmn. educators conf. 1976, judge 1976-87), Crescent Yacht Club (cmmodore 1991—), Harbor Island Yacht Club. Republican. Avocations: sailing, photography, boat bldg., antiques, travel. Home: Chaumont, NY. Died Apr. 5, 2000.

SEMM, KURT KARL STEPHAN, obstetrics and gynecology researcher; b. Munich, Mar. 23, 1927; MD, U. Munich, 1951; DVM (hon.), U. Hannover, 1980; MD honoris causa, U. Rostock, 1994. Prof. ob-gyn. univ. clinic U. Munich, 1953-70; dir. dept. ob-gyn. Michaelis Midwifery Sch., Christian Albrechts U., Kiel, Germany, 1970-95; ret., 1995. Father Surg. Endoscopy, 1990-95. More than 693 publ. in fields endocrin., perinat., gyn., obst., books include Operative Manual of Operative Endoscopic Abdominal Surgery (German, English, Italian, Japanese, Chinese, French languages, 30,000 eds.), 1984, Pelviscopy-Operative Guidlines (German, Chinese, English, Italian, Japanese, Yugoslavian, 30,000 eds.), Intrafascial Hysterectomy, TUMA, IVH, 1993, Chronic of the Univeristy Womens Clinic and Michaelis-Midwifery School 1805-1995, 1995, Manual of Pelviscopy and Hysteroscopy, 1976 (German, English, Spain, French), 1984, Manual of Laparoscopic Surgery, 1984, (German, English, Japanese, Italian) 1980. Decorated Gt. Order of Merit on band (Germany), 1980; pvt. audience with Pope Pius XII, 1954, with Pope John Paul II, 1997. Fellow Royal Coll. Ob-Gyn., Internat. Coll. Surgery (hon.); mem. German Soc. Fertility, Sterility, (founder, sec. gen. 1957-75, pres. 1975-83, hon. mem. 1983-2003), German Soc. Ob-Gyn. (hon. mem. 1996—), German Soc. Nature Scientists and Physicians, European Sterility Congress Org., (founder, sec. gen. 1966-90, pres. 1981 in Berlin), German Soc. Endoscopy, (pres. 1977-78, Kiel and 1989-90, Munich), European Endoscopy Congress Org. (founder, sec. gen. 1968-72), German Soc. Photography, European Congress Endoscopy-,(pres.), Internat. Fed. Fertility Soc. (sec. gen. 1977-80, v.p. 1983-86, pres. 1986-89, pres. 13th World Congress IFFS Marrakesh, Marocco, 1986-89, chmn. Sci. Program Comm., 1989-92), German Soc. Endoscopy Gyn. (founder, treas. 1975-92), German Soc. Prenatal Med., Soc. Schleswig-Holstein U., Acad. Human Reproduction (pres. 3rd World Congress Human Reproduction 1981, 92, 93), German-French Soc. for Ob-Gyn. (founder, pres. 1976-88), Internat. Fed. of Fertility Socs. (sec.-gen. 1976-84, v.p. 1984-95), European Sterility Congress Orgn. (sec.-gen. 1965-95), Internat. Fedn. of Gynaecologic Endoscopists (v.p. 1984-95), pres. French Soc. Gyn., 1995; hon. mem. 29 gynecol. socs. Home: Gruenwald/Munich, Germany. Died July 16, 2003.

SENECA, JEFFREY DALE, merchandising company executive; b. Orange, N.J., Oct. 3, 1947; s. Joseph C. and Florida T. (Gili) S. Student, RCA Inst. Tech., N.Y.C., 1966, Rutgers U., 1967, Fairleigh Dickinson U., 1970; grad., Computer Learning Ctr., Paramus, N.J., 1988. Tax acct. U.S. Fed. Ct. (4th dist.), N.Y.C., 1970-73; owner, pres. Internat. Merchandising Co., Orange, N.J., 1973-99. Roman Catholic. Home: Willowdale, Canada. Died Aug. 5, 1999.

SERNA, JOE, JR., mayor; b. Stockton, Calif. m. Isabel Serna; children: Phillip, Lisa. BA in Social Sci., Govt., Sacramento State Coll., 1966; postgrad., U. Calif., Davis. Vol. Peace Corps., Guatemala, 1966; edn. advisor Lt.-Gov. Mervyn Dymally, 1975-77; prof. govt. Calif State U., Sacramento, from 1969; mayor City of Sacramento, 1992-99. Bd. dirs. Freddie Mac, McLean, Va. Mem. Sacramento City Coun. 5th Dist., 1981-92, law and legis. com., 1989-92, Housing & Devel. Commn., Sacramento, chmn. budget and fin. com., 1981-89, transp. and cmty. devel. com., 1989-92; dir. United Farmworkers Am.'s Support Com. in Sacramento County, 1970-75; co-trustee Crocker Art Mus. Assn.; founder Thursday Night Market, Mayor's Summer Reading Camp; mem. Sacramento Housing & Devel. Commn.; bd. dirs. Regional Transit. Died Nov. 7, 1999.

SEROW, WILLIAM JOHN, economics educator; b. N.Y.C., Apr. 8, 1946; s. William John and Dorothea (Goyette) S.; m. Elizabeth Goetz, Aug. 24, 1968; 1 child, Erika. BA, Boston Coll., 1967; MA, Duke U., 1970, PhD, 1972. Rsch. dir. Univ. Va., Charlottesville, 1970-81; prof., dir. Fla. State U., Tallahassee, from 1981. Editor: Handbook of International Migration, 1990; author: Population Aging in the United States, 1990. Capt. U.S. Army, 1967-73. Grantee Fla. Health Care Cost Containment Bd., 1988-90, Nat. Instn. Aging, 1983-89, NIMH, 1984-86, Govt. of Indonesia, 1992-98, TVA, 1997-98, 99-00, Fla. Dept. Environ. Protection, 2002-03. Mem. Internat. Union for Scientific Study of Population, Population Assn. Am., Am. and Western Econ. Assns., So. Demographic Assn. (pres. 1986-87), So. Regional Sci. Assn. (pres. 1982-83), Gerontol. Soc. Am. Avocations: railroads, sherlock holmes, baseball rsch. Home: Tallahassee, Fla. Died Nov. 5, 2003.

SETON, FENMORE ROGER, manufacturing company executive, civic worker; b. Bridgeport, Conn., Nov. 27, 1917; m. Phyllis Winifred Zimmerman, Apr. 5, 1942; 1 child, Diana Seton Adams Wakerley. BA in English, Yale U., 1938; EdM, So. Conn. State Coll./Yale U., 1956; LLD (hon.), U. New Haven, 1990; DHL (hon.), Albertus Magnus Coll., 1994. Asst. prof. air sci. and tactics Yale U., New Haven, 1952-56; pres., chief exec. officer Seton Name Plate Corp., New Haven, 1956-81. Pres. Nat. Assn. Metal Etchers, Washington, 1968-69, Internat. Mktg. Device Assn., Chgo., 1973-74, mfrs. div. New Haven C. of C., 1974-79; chmn. Am. Nat. Standards Com. A13, N.Y.C., 1972-82. Apptd. Pres.'s Com. on Employment of People With Disabilities, Washington, 1973; world pres. Rehab. Internat., World Secretariat in N.Y.C., 1988-92; bd. govs. U. New Haven; treas. Save the Children Fedn., Westport, Conn., 1984-88; assoc. fellow Calhoun Coll. Yale U.; bd. dirs. Gaylord Hosp.; trustee Albert B. Sabin Vaccine Found. Recipient

Citation of Honor Sec. HEW, Washington, 1976, Preminger medallion People-To-People program Com. for Handicapped, Washington, 1988, Elm and Ivy award Yale U., 1985, Pub. Svc. award Social Security Adminstrn., 1992, Yale medal Pres. Yale U. on behalf of Bd. Govs. Assn. Yale Alumni, 1992, Disting. Svc. award Pres. of U.S., 1992, Seal of City of New Haven, Conn., 1999; named. Nat. Vol. of Yr., Easter Seal Soc., 1997. Fellow Inst. Dirs. (U.K.); mem. Cercle de l'Union Interallié (Paris), Explorers Club (N.Y.C.), Circumnavigators Club (N.Y.C.), Elizabethan Club (New Haven), Mory's Assn. (New Haven), New Haven Country Club. Republican. Home: Hamden, Conn. Died May 26, 2003.

SETTLE, EDWIN THEODORE, religion educator; b. Covington, Ky., Sept. 27, 1901; s. Edwin Theodore and Mary Ella (McGill) S.; m. Mary Louise Stacy, Aug. 15, 1931; 1 child, Louise Carroll. BA, U. Cin., 1923; ThM, So. Bapt. Theol. Sem., 1926; PhD, Yale U., 1931; postgrad., Oxford (Eng.) U., 1966. Minister First Bapt. Ch., West Haven, Conn., 1931-43; prof. religion and philosophy Doane Coll., Crete, Nebr., 1946-48, Coe Coll., Cedar Rapids, Iowa, 1948-69. Author: Why Doesn't God Do Something?, 1988; contbr. articles to profl. jours. Pres. Civic Forum, West Haven, Conn., 1941, Coun. on World Questions, Cedar Rapids, 1948. Major, chaplain, U.S. Army, 1943-46, ETO, PTO. Fellow NYU, 1959, Danforth Found., 1962. Mem. Am. Acad. Religion (pres. midwest sect. 1964), Am. Philos. Assn. (sec. Iowa sect. 1962-64), Soc. for Sci. Study Religion), UNA (congl. liaison 1986), Rotary (chmn. internat. svc. projects India-Thailand-Japan, North Stockton Calif. chpt. 1975-77). Home: Stockton, Calif. Deceased.

SETZEKORN, WILLIAM DAVID, retired architect, consultant, author; b. Mt. Vernon, Ill., Mar. 12, 1935; s. Merrett Everet and Audrey (Ferguson) S.; m. Georgia Sue Brown, Feb. 4, 1958 (div. 1968); children: Jeffrey Merle, Timothy Michael. BArch, Kans. State U., 1957; cert. in computer graphics, Harvard U., 1968; BA with MA equivalency in Humanities, Western Ill. U., 1982. Registered arch., Calif. Coord. design and constrn. Cal-Expo, Sacramento, 1968; pvt. practice, Los Altos and Redding, Calif., Seattle, 1968-85; cons. Contra Costa County, Martinez, Calif., 1985-89, El Dorado County, Placerville, Calif., 1985-89, Somerset, Calif., from 1989. Cons. Fed. Emergency Mgmt. Agy., The Presidio, San Francisco, 1989-95, Gov. Keating's task force for disaster recovery, Oklahoma City, 1995; apptd. Calif. State Grand Jury, 1996-97. Author: Formerly British Honduras: A Profile of the New Nation of Belize, 1975, 4 other titles; contbr. articles to mags. Recipient Ofcl. Commendation, State of Calif., 1968, U.S. Presdl. Medal of Merit, Ronald Reagan, 1988. Fellow Augustan Soc. (bd. dirs. 1994-96); mem. Noble Co. of the Rose (knight 1979, lt. magister rosae 1995-97), Mil. and Hospitaller Order of St. Lazarus (comdr.), numerous other internat. orders of chivalry, Family Setzekorn Assn. (prin. officer 1979—), San Leandro (Calif.) Yacht Club (founding), Kiwanis. Republican. Unitarian Universalist. Avocations: genealogy, medieval history, heraldry, travel. Deceased.

SEVIER, ERNEST YOULE, lawyer; b. Sacramento, June 20, 1932; s. Ernest and Helen Faye (McDonald) S.; m. Constance McKenna, Apr. 12, 1969; children: Carolyn Stewart, Katherine Danielle. AB, Stanford U., 1954, JD, 1956. Bar: Calif. 1956, U.S. Supreme Ct. 1965. Asso. mem. firm Sedgwick, Detert, Moran & Arnold, San Francisco, 1958-62; mem. firm Severson & Werson, San Francisco, 1962-99. Served with USAF, 1956-57. Fellow Am. Bar Found.; mem. ABA (chmn. tort and ins. practice sect. 1982-83, exec. coun. 1976-84, chmn. standing com. on assoc. comms. 1988-90, chmn. coord. com. on Outreach to Pub. 1989-90, chmn. standing com. on lawyers responsibility for client protection 1991-94, commn. on non-lawyer practice 1992-95), Calif. Bar Assn. Died Nov. 3, 2002.

SEWELL, CHARLES HASLETT, banker; b. Buford, Ga., Jan. 16, 1928; s. Grover C. and Jennie G. (Haslett) S.; m. Margaret Gillespie, Sept. 9, 1985; children: Anna E., William H., John L. BA, Emory U., 1951. Econs., mgmt. cons. Rsch. and Cons. Corp., Atlanta, 1952-72; sr. v.p. Deposit Guaranty Nat. Bank, Jackson, Miss., 1972-74, exec. v.p., from 1974; chmn., CEO Deposit Guaranty Mortgage Co., Jackson, Miss., 1976-91; acting dean Millsaps Coll. Grad. Sch. Mgmt., Jackson, 1994. Cons. in field; chmn. Miss. Econ. Council, 1983—; chmn. Sml. Bus. Devel. Ctr. U. Miss, Oxford, 1979— Contbr. articles to profl. jours. Trustee Miss. State Libr. Commn., 1983—; chmn. Miss. Com. for Humanities, 1983—; pres. Miss. Symphony Orch., 1988-89; chmn. Miss. internat. adv. bd. Emory U. Coll. Arts and Scis., 1992—; exec.-in-residence Else Sch. Mgmt., Millsaps Coll. Mem. University Club (Jackson). Republican. Presbyterian. Deceased.

SHAFFER, HARRY GARD, JR., advertising executive; b. Clearfield, Pa., Apr. 6, 1932; s. Harry Gard and Harriet (McCloskey) S.; m. Janet Evelyn Bayliss, Oct. 15, 1961 (div. Nov. 1971); children: Lynne, Harry Gard III, Karen, Kurt; m. Geraldine Louise Adams, Dec. 12, 1976. BS, U. Hawaii, 1957. Account exec. K.M. and G., Inc., Pitts., 1959-61; account supr. Sykes Advt., Inc., Pitts., 1961-64; v.p., media dir. Carlton Advt. Co., Pitts., 1964-70; account supr. M and F Advt., Inc., Cleve., 1970-72; exec. v.p. Palm and Patterson, Cleve., 1972-78; pres., creative dir. Shaffer Shaffer Shaffer, Inc. Cleve., 1979-96; exec. sec. Florists Assn. of Greater Cleve., 1976—; Creative dir. (TV program) Singing Angels Sing America, 1975 (Best TV Entertainment Spl. award, 2 NATAS Emmy comml. awards). Capt. Hawaii Olympic Ocean Swimming and Surfing Team, Melbourne, Australia, 1956; pub. relations dir. Swimming Hall of Fame, Fort Lauderdale, Fla., 1967-71; Underwater Demolition Team swimming team #2; commdg. officer recruit tng. in swimming USMC. Served with USMC, 1951-54. Recipient Emmy award, 26 Best Radio Comml. awards, 28 Best TV Comml. awards, 7 Nat. Telly awards, 31 Silver Nat. Microphone awards, Bronze medal Australian Surf Life Saving Assn. Mem. Mensa, Singing Angels Found. (bd. dirs.), Cleve. Ad Club, Pitts. Ad Club, Pitts. Athletic Assn., Masons, Shriners, Rotary. Republican. Presbyterian. Avocation: power yachting. Died Jan. 13, 1996; buried Hillcrest Cemetery, Clearfield, Pa. Died Jan 13, 1996. Home: Cleveland, Ohio.

SHALACK, JOAN HELEN, psychiatrist; b. Jersery City, Mar. 6, 1932; d. Edward William and Adele Helen S.; widowed. Student, Farleigh Dickinson U., 1950-51; BA cum laude, NYU, 1954; MD, Women's Med. Coll. Pa., 1958. Intern Akron (Ohio) Gen. Hosp., 1958-59; resident in psychiatry Camarillo (Calif.) State Hosp., 1959-62; resident in physchiatry UCLA Neuropsychiat. Inst., 1962, U. So. Calif., L.A., 1963; pvt. practice Beverly Hills, Calif., 1963-83, Century City L.A., Calif., 1983-86, Pasadena, Calif., from 1986. Pres., chair bd. dirs. Totizo Inc., Beverly Hills, 1969-71; mem. staff Westwood Hosp., 1970-75. Mem. Physicians for Social Responsibility, Union of Concerned Scientists, Phi Beta Kappa, Mu Chi Sigma. Avocations: archaeology, gardening, tennis, bicycling, economics. Died Mar. 6, 2001.

SHALLON, DAVID, conductor, music director; b. Tel Aviv, Oct. 15, 1950; s. Efraim and Pnina Shallon. Condr. diploma, Hochsschule Für Musik, Vienna, 1975; studies with Henri Dutilleux, Leonard Bernstein, Krzysztof Penderecki, Hans Werner Henze, Luigi Nono, Gottfried von Einem and Noam Sheriff. Gen. music dir. Düsseldorf Symphony Orch., Fed. Republic of Germany, 1987-2000, chief condr., 1987-93. Conducted many prominent orchs. worldwide including the London Symphony Orch., Berlin Philarmonic Orch., Santa-Cecilia-Rome, San Francisco Symphony, Vienna Symphony, Cin. Symphony, St. Paul Chamber Orch., L'Orchestre Nat. de France, L'Orchestre dela Suisse Romande, Tonhalle Orch. Zürich, Helsinki Philarmonic, Danish Kopenhaguen, various top orchs. in Japan, among others; opera conductions include Fidelio at the Vienna Staatsoper, Jesu Hochzeit (world premiere) at the Theater an der Wien, (with Alfredo Kraus) Massenet's Werther at the Frankfurt Opera, The Tales of Hoffmann and Aida at the Deutsche Oper am Rhein, The Rosenkavalier and Carmen at the Nederlands Opera. Home: Dusseldorf 30, Germany. Deceased.

SHAMBROOM, WILLIAM DAVID, SR., marketing, communications educator, consultant; b. Bklyn., June 11, 1921; s. Henry and Edna (Epstein) S.; m. Gloria Perryman, Mar. 21, 1947 (div. Dec. 1981); children: William David Jr., Donald Henry, Glenn George, Paul Dennis, Eric James, John Richard. BS, Harvard U., 1943. V.p. mfg. Windsor Mfg. Co., Clifton, N.J., 1946-50; advt. mgr., gen. mgr. Flo-Ball Pen div. Clary Corp., N.Y.C., 1950-54; account supr. Mogul Baker Byrnes Weiss, N.Y.C., 1954-69, Jameson Advt., N.Y.C., 1969-74, A. Eicoff and Co., N.Y.C., Chgo., 1974-82; cons., dir. tech. communications Merrick Corp. subs. Penn Va. Corp., Roseland, N.J., 1981-86; adj. asst. prof. Mktg. and Communications Arts Iona Coll., New Rochelle, N.Y., from 1982; bus. lectr. mktg. and mktg. communications Caldwell (N.J.) Coll., from 1986; lectr. mktg. and mktg. communications Fairleigh Dickinson U., Teaneck, N.J., from 1986. Active athletic coach, Boy Scouts (scoutmaster, commr.), Teaneck, 1958-74; mem. Teaneck Parks Bd., 1974-82; trustee Teaneck Vol. Ambulance Corps, Teaneck, 1985-86; pres. Teaneck City Club, 1986. Served with USN, 1943-46, ETO and PTO. Jewish. Avocations: music, theater, athletics. Deceased.

SHANAHAN, EILEEN, journalist; b. Washington, Feb. 29, 1924; d. Thomas Francis and Vena (Karpeles) S.; m. John Virgil Waits, Jr., Sept. 16, 1944; children: Mary Beth, Kathleen. DHL (hon.), Colby Coll., 1993. Reporter UPI, Washington, 1944-47, Cronkite Radio News Bur., Washington, 1949-50, Rsch. Inst. Am., Washington, 1951-56, Jour. Commerce, Washington, 1956-61, N.Y. Times, Washington, 1962-77; spl. asst. to asst. sec. U.S. Dept. Treasury, Washington, 1961-62; asst. sec. pub. affairs U.S. Dept. Health, Edn. and Welfare, Washington, 1977-79; asst. mng. editor Washington Star, 1979-81, Pitts. Post-Gazette, 1981-84; assoc. prof. Medill Sch. Journalism, Evanston, Ill., 1984-85; reporter Congl. Quar., Washington, 1986; co-founder, exec. editor Governing mag., Washington, 1987-91; Washington corr. St. Petersburg Times, 1991-94. Mem. exec. com. Reporters Com. for Freedom of Press, Washington, 1972-76, Oral History Project, Washington Press Club, 1987—; mem. adv. com. Nieman Found., Cambridge, Mass., 1976-76, 79-82; vis. faculty Inst. for Journalism Edn. U. Calif., Berkeley, 1976-88, U. Ariz., 1988—. Mem. Pub.-Pvt. Partnership Coun., D.C. Pub. Schs. Communications Program, Washington, 1984—. Recipient Bus. Journalism award U. Mo., 1966, Alumni Achievement award George Washington U., 1982, Disting. Lifetime Svc. Journalism award U. Mo., 1991, Elijah Parish Lovejoy award for contbns. to journalism Colby Coll., 1993, Pres.'s 21st Century award Nat. Women's Hall of Fame, 1994; named Newspaper Woman of Yr., N.Y. Women in Comms., 1975. Fellow Nat. Acad. Pub. Adminstrn. Home: Silver Spring, Md. Died Nov. 2, 2001.

SHANNON, JAMES PATRICK, foundation consultant, retired food company executive; b. South St. Paul, Minn., Feb. 16, 1921; s. Patrick Joseph and Mary Alice (McAuliffe) S.; m. Ruth Church Wilkinson, Aug. 2, 1969. BA in Classics, Coll. St. Thomas, St. Paul, 1941; MA in English, U. Minn., 1951; PhD, Yale U., 1955; JD, U. N.Mex., 1973; LL.D., U. Notre Dame, 1964, Macalester Coll., 1964; LLD, Lora Coll., 1964, DePaul U., 1965, St. Mary's Coll., 1965, Carleton Coll., 1965; LL.D., Creighton U., 1966; LLD, Northland Coll., Ashland, Wis., 1979, William Mitchell Coll. Law, 1980; LittD, Seton Hall, 1965, Coe Coll., Cedar Rapids, Iowa, 1966, U. Minn., 1966; JUD, Lawrence U., 1969. Ordained priest Roman Catholic Ch., 1946; asst. prof. history Coll. St. Thomas, 1954-56, pres., 1956-66; aux. bishop Archdiocese of St. Paul, 1965-68; pastor St. Helna Parish, Mpls., 1966-68; tutor Greek St. John's Coll., Santa Fe, 1969-70, v.p., 1969-70; columnist, writer, found. cons., 1970-79, 88-90; mem. firm Sutin, Thayer & Browne, Albuquerque, Santa Fe, 1973-74; exec. dir. Mpls. Found., 1974-78; v.p. Gen. Mills, Inc., 1980-88; sr. cons. Nat. Coun. on Founds., Washington, 1988—2003. Dir. Midwest Importers, Inc., 1988-96. Author: Catholic Colonization on the Western Frontier, 1957, Reluctant Dissenter, 1998. Bd. dirs. James J. Hill Libr., St. Paul, 1985-94, Inst. Ecumenical and Cultural Rsch., Collegeville, Minn., 1985-2003, chmn., 1990-94; bd. dirs. Ind. Sector, Washington, 1988-94, N.Mex. Cmty. Found., 1991-95, Gen. Svc. Found., 1991-94; coun. Conf. Bd., 1982-88; chmn. Rhodes Scholarship Selection Com. for Upper Midwest Selection Com., 1976-86; chmn. coun. founds., Washington, 1984-85; vice chmn. Found. Ctr., N.Y.C.; sr. cons. Coun. on Founds. Mem. D.C. Bar Assn., N.Mex. Bar Assn., Minn. Bar Assn., Mpls. Club (bd. govs. 1989-96, pres. 1994-95). Democrat. Died Aug. 28, 2003.

SHAPIRO, FRED LOUIS, nephrologist, educator; b. Mpls., Aug. 18, 1934; s. Ralph Samuel and Dora (Cullen) S.; m. Merle Sandra Rosenzweig, June 23, 1957; children: Wendy Judith, Richard Scott. BA magna cum laude, U. Minn., 1958, BS, MD, U. Minn., 1961. Intern Hennepin County Med. Ctr., Mpls., 1961-62, resident in internal medicine, 1962-65, instr., 1965-68, chief nephrology, 1965-84; med. dir. Regional Kidney Disease Program, 1966-84; asst. prof. U. Minn., Mpls., 1968-71, assoc. prof., 1971-75, prof., from 1975. Pres. Hennepin Faculty Assocs., 1983-95. Contbr. articles to profl. jours. With USNR, 1953-55. Mem. Phi Beta Kappa, Sigma Xi, Alpha Omega Alpha. Home: Minnetonka, Minn. Died Apr. 13, 2004.

SHAPIRO, GILBERT, physicist, researcher; b. Phila., Mar. 17, 1934; s. Harry M. and Reba S.; m. Harriet Lerman, Oct. 12, 1958; children: James, Dinah, Susan. BA, U. Pa., 1955; MA, Columbia U., 1957, PhD, 1959. Rsch. assoc. Columbia U., N.Y.C., 1959-61; rsch. physicist Lawrence Berkeley (Calif.) Lab., from 1961. From. asst. prof. to prof. U. Calif., Berkeley, 1963—. Author: Physics Without Math, 1978, A Skeleton in the Darkroom, 1986; contbr. articles to Physical Rev., Physical Rev. Letters, others. Home: Moraga, Calif. Died Dec. 5, 2001.

SHARP, HELEN TAYLOR, Spanish language educator; b. El Dorado, Ark., Aug. 2, 1937; d. Proctor Jesse and Reba (Hightower) Taylor; m. John Berlin Sharp Jr., Apr. 1, 1961; children: Laura Hampton Sharp Mills, Alice Taylor. BM, Miss. U. for Women, 1959; MA, Miss. State U., 1985. Stewardess Pan Am, Miami, Fla., 1959-61; tchr. Winston Acad., Louisville, Miss., 1973-86; teaching asst. Miss. State U., Starkville, 1982-85, instr., teaching asst. supr., from 1986. Mem. Jr. Aux., Louisville, Miss., 1973-79, pres., 1978-79. MLA fellow, 1989; State of Miss. and Nat. Coll. Bd. grantee, 1990. Mem. South Cen. MLA, Am. Assn. Tchrs. Spanish and Portuguese (dir. nat. Spanish exam. for Miss. 1986—), Miss. Fgn. Lang. Assn., Sigma Delta Pi. Republican. Presbyterian. Avocations: reading, knitting, golf. Home: Louisville, Miss. Died June 3, 2001.

SHARP, MITCHELL WILLIAM, former advisor to prime minister; b. Winnipeg, Man., Can., May 11, 1911; s. Thomas and Elizabeth (Little) S.; m. Daisy Boyd, Apr. 23, 1938 (dec.); 1 son, Noel; m. Jeannette Dugal, Apr. 14, 1976 (dec.); m. Jeanne d'Arc Labrecque, Sept. 1, 2000. BA, U. Man., 1934, LL.D. (hon.), 1965; postgrad., London Sch. Econs., 1937-38; hon. Dr. Social Sci., U. Ottawa, 1970; LLD (hon.), U. Western Ont., 1977, Carleton U., 1994, McMaster U., 1995. Statistician Sanford Evans Statis. Service, 1926-36; economist James Richardson & Sons, Ltd., 1936-42; officer Canadian Dept. Fin., Ottawa, 1942-51, dir. econ. policy div., 1947-51; assoc. dep. minister Canadian Dept. Trade and Commerce, 1951-57, dep. minister, 1957-58; v.p. Brazilian Traction, Toronto, Can., 1958-62; mem. Can. Ho. of Commons, from 1963; minister trade and commerce, 1963-65; minister fin., 1965-68; sec. state external affairs, 1968-74; pres. Privy Council, house leader, 1974-76; resigned, 1978; pers. advisor to prime min. of Can., 1993—2003. Commr. No. Pipeline Agy., 1978-88. Decorated companion Order of Can. Fellow Royal Conservatory Music (hon.). Died Mar. 19, 2004.

SHARP, ROBERT PHILLIP, geology educator; b. Oxnard, Calif., June 24, 1911; s. Julian Hebner Sharp and Alice Sharp Darling; m. Jean Prescott Todd, Sept. 7, 1938; adopted children: Kristin Todd, Bruce Todd. BS, Calif. Inst. Tech., Pasadena, 1934, MS, 1935; MA, Harvard U., Cambridge, Mass., 1936, PhD, 1938. Asst. prof. U. Ill., Urbana, 1938-43; prof. U. Minn., Mpls., 1946-47, Calif. Inst. Tech., Pasadena, 1947-79, chmn., 1952-67, prof. emeritus, 1979—2004. Robert P. Sharp prof. Calif. Inst. Tech., 1978. Author: Glaciers, 1960, Field Guide-Southern California, 1972, Field Guide-Coastal Southern California, 1978, Living Ice-Understanding Glaciers and Glaciation, 1988; author: (with A.F. Glazner) Geology Under Foot in Southern California, 1993; author: Geology Underfoot in Death Valley and Owens Valley, 1997. Capt. USAF, 1943—46. Recipient

Exceptional Sci. Achievement medal, NASA, 1971, Nat. Medal Sci., 1989, Charles P. Daly medal, Am. Geog. Soc., 1991. Fellow: Am. Geophys. Union, Geol. Soc. Am. (councillor, Kirk Bryan award 1964, Penrose medal 1977, G.K. Gilbert and Disting. Career award 1996), Internat. Glaciological Soc. (hon.); mem.: NAS. Republican. Avocations: fly fishing, snorkeling, camping. Home: Santa Barbara, Calif. Died May 25, 2004.

SHARPE, ROCHELLE PHYLLIS, journalist; b. Gary, Ind., Apr. 27, 1956; d. Norman Nathaniel and Shirley (Kaplan) Sharpe. BA, Yale U., 1978. Reporter Concord (N.H.) Monitor, 1979—81; statehouse rep. Wilmington News Jour., Dover, Del., 1981—85; statehouse corr. Gannett News Svc., Albany, NY, 1985, nat. reporter Washington, 1986—93; staff reporter social issues The Wall St. Jour., Washington, from 1993. Contbr. articles to profl. jours. Recipient Pulitzer Prize for series in child abuse, Columbia U., 1991. Home: Brookline, Mass. Deceased.

SHATTUCK, JOSEPH BOARDMAN, JR., insurance company executive; b. Damariscotta, Maine, Aug. 2, 1925; s. Joseph Boardman and Marcia Vivian (Parker) S.; m. Mildred Louise Delano, June 14, 1949 (div. 1969); children: Henry, June, Pamela, Patricia, William; m. Marie Laraine David, May 18, 1980; stepchildren: Gordon, Anne, Arthur, Matthew. BA, U. Maine, Orono, 1949. Registered profl. engr., Mass. Inspector Liberty Mut. Ins. Co., N.Y.C., 1949-51, engr. Phila., 1951-52, dist. engr. Buffalo, 1953-55, div. engr., 1955-57, sect. engr. Boston, 1957-62, mgr., 1962-69, svc. mgr. fire protection div., 1969-77, tech. dir., 1977-89, ret., 1989. Mem. Finance Bd., Salisbury, Mass., 1964-65, Planning Bd., Salisbury, 1965-71. With USAF, 1943-45. Mem. Am. Mut. Ins. Engrs. (past pres. 1978-79), Am. Soc. Safety Engrs., Soc. Fire Protection Engrs. (past pres. 1966-67), Masons, Shriners. Home: Salisbury, Mass. Deceased.

SHAVER, HAROLD C. mass communications educator, public relations consultant; b. Cuyahoga Falls, Ohio, Oct. 19, 1938; s. Herschel C. and Margaret (Housley) S.; m. Marilyn L. Cole, Mar. 26, 1966; children: Melanie, Wendy. BA in Speech and English, MuskingumColl., New Concord, Ohio, 1960; MS in Broadcasting, Syracuse U., 1963, PhD in Mass Communications, 1976. Tchr. South Euclid (Ohio)-Lyndhurst Schs., 1960-62, Liverpool (N.Y.) Schs., 1963-65; instr. speech SUNY, Oswego, 1965-68; asst. dir. mental health info. program Syracuse U., 1968-70; asst. prof. pub. rels. and advt. Drake U., Des Moines, 1970-72; dir. mental health, mass communications program Kans. State U., Manhattan, 1972-75, assoc. prof. journalism and mass communications, 1972-82; prof. communications, head dept. Bethany (W.Va.) Coll., 1982-90; prof. Journalism, dir. sch. Journalism/Mass Communications Marshall U., Huntington, W.Va., 1990—2004. Account supr. Ketchum Pub. Rels., Pitts., 1988-89; freelance cons. to non-profit orgns., 1970-2004. Contbr. articles to mags. Pres. Riley County Mental Health Assn., Manhattan, 1977-78; tchr. Sunday sch., supt. Grace Bapt. Ch., Manhattan, 1978-82; elder, tchr. Sunday sch., dir. music Ind. Bible Ch., Wellsburg, W.Va., 1982-90. Mem. Pub. Rels. Soc. Am. (accredited), Assn. Edn. in Journalism and Mass Communications. Republican. Home: Huntington, W.Va. Died Mar. 1, 2004.

SHAW, BYNUM GILLETTE, educator; b. Burlington, N.C., July 10, 1923; s. William Carroll and Martha (Saunders) S.; m. Louise N. Brantley, Aug. 30, 1948 (dec. 1980); children: Bonnie L., Susan S.; m. Charlotte E. Reeder, Nov. 26, 1986. BA, Wake Forest Coll., 1951. Reporter Virginian-Pilot, Norfolk, Va., 1948-51; reporter, Washington correspondent The Sun, Balt., 1951-65; prof. journalism Wake Forest U., Winston Salem, N.C., 1965-93. Chmn. N.C. Writers Conf., Raleigh, 1972. Author: Sound of Small Hammers, 1965, The Nazi Hunter, 1969, Days of Power, Nights of Fear, 1982, Oh, Promised Land!, 1992. Purser USCG, 1943-46. Recipient Sir Walter Raleigh award in Fiction N.C. Hist. Book Club, 1969, Disting. Teaching award Wake Forest U., 1986. Democrat. Baptist. Avocations: gardening, stamp collecting/philately, fishing, model shipbuilding. Home: Winston Salem, NC. Died Aug. 27, 2001.

SHAW, GEORGE BERNARD, consulting engineer, educator; b. Dayton, Ohio, Feb. 25, 1940; s. William E. and Edna E. (Hartley) S.; m. Carol M. Crawford, Aug. 6, 1966. A in Mech. Engring., U. Dayton, 1963, BCE, 1967, MSCE, 1971. Diplomate Am. Acad. Environ. Engrs.; registered profl. engr., Ohio, Va., Ind., Ky., Tenn., W.Va., Fla., Kans., Mich., Mo., Okla., Ill., Tex.; lic. profl. surveyor, Ohio. Asst. to chief engr. Northmont Engrs., Vandalia, Ohio, 1960-66; estimator Oberer Constrn., Dayton, 1966-67; sanitary engr. Alden E. Stilson & Assocs., Columbus, 1967-68; staff cons. Miami Conservancy Dist., Dayton, 1969 71; assoc. prof. civil and environ. engring. U. Dayton, from 1967; dir. environ. and engring. program; pres., chmn. Shaw, Weiss & De Naples, Dayton, from 1968. Pres., chmn. GBS Environ., 1989—; chmn. Panterra Corp., 1990—. Contbr. articles to profl. jours. Pres. Engrs. Club Dayton Found.; pres. Dayton chpt. United Cerebral Palsy; chmn. govt. affairs com. on transp. Dayton C. of C. Mem. NSPE, ASCE, Am. Consulting Engrs. Coun., Soc. Am. Mil. Engrs., Water Environment Fedn., Inter-Am. Assn. Sanitary Engring., Am. Water Works Assn. Avocation: travel. Home: Dayton, Ohio. Died in August of 1999.

SHAW, JAMES, information technology specialist; b. Salt Lake City, June 26, 1944; s. James Irvin and Cleo Lea (Bell) S. Student, San Antonio Coll., 1962—64; BA in History, St. Mary's U., San Antonio, 1966. With VA Automation Ctr., Austin, Tex., 1967-99, sr. computer programmer analyst, 1984-87, supervisory computer programmer analyst, 1987-88, computer sys. analyst, 1988-94, sr. computer sys. analyst, 1994-99; sr. computer specialist VA Fin. Svcs. Ctr., Austin, from 1999. Conversion team manual to computerized acctg. VA, 1974-76; team leader conversion computerized acctg. sys. to database, 1984-88; team leader complete replacement of VA computerized acctg. sys., 1989-95, transfer NARA applications to VA Automation Ctr., 1997-98; sr. technician VA Electronic Healthcare Billing Project, 1999—. Active Smithsonian Instn., Planned Parenthood, Met. Mus. Art, Austin Mus. Art. Mem. Am. Assn. Individual Investors. Democrat. Home: Austin, Tex. Died Jan. 23, 2004.

SHAW, JAMES RENFREW, retired music educator; b. Phila., Aug. 27, 1930; s. Alexander Renfrew and Marion Hesther (Richardson) S.; m. Barbara Ann Kindig, June 4, 1955 (div. 1968); children: Debra Lee, Bryan Richard, Gretchen Kristina, Leslie Anne; m. Joanna Gibbs Miller, Nov. 21, 1969. MusB, Pa. State U., 1954; MusM Edn., Temple U., 1959; student, U. Arizona, 1961-62, U. Ind. Tchr. Scott High Sch., Coatesville, Pa., 1954, Pennridge High Sch., Perkasie, Pa., 1956-61, Niagara-Wheatfield High Sch., Sanborn, N.Y., 1962-63; prof. music Glassboro (N.J.) State Coll., 1963-93, ret., 1993. Composer (opera) The Minion and the Three Riddles, 1988, (children's shows) Penny and The Magic Medallion, 1974, Beanstalk, 1975, Legend of the Sun Child, 1976, Showdown at the Sugarcane Saloon, 1979, Once Upon A Shoe, 1981, The Princess, The Poet, and the Little Gray Man, 1977, (adult mus.) Ashes, Ashes, All Fall Down, 1983, Dear Me, The Sky is Falling, 1991, (cantata) The Lovely Shall Be Choosers, 1990. Served as 1st lt. Signal Corp., 1954-56. Mem. Nat. Assn. Tchrs. Singing (N.J. and nat. chpts.), Gloucester County Fine Arts Assn., Gloucester County Art League. Avocations: bridge, watercolor painting, tropical fish, stamp collecting/philately. Home: Pitman, NJ. Died Aug. 25, 2001.

SHEAFFER, JAY MICHAEL, electronics executive; b. Harrisburg, Pa., Oct. 12, 1950; s. Jason P. and Vivian (Nell) S.; 1 child, Jack Brett. BBA, Tex. Tech. U., Lubbock, 1975. Adminstrv. Hi-Line Electric Co., Dallas, 1975-76, salesman, 1976-78, regional sales mgr., 1978-79, purchasing dir., 1979-81, nat. sales dir., 1981-86, pres., chief exec. officer, from 1986. Cons. Jr. Achievement, Dallas, 1985—; corp. dir. Hi-Line Electric Co., 1987—, Roxor, Inc., Dallas, 1987—; dir. Brookhaven Men's Tennis League, Dallas, 1987—. Fellow mem. Dallas Young Republicans, 1986—. Mem. Nat. Assn. Wholesalers. Clubs: Chief Exec. Officers, The Exec. Com., Jr. Achievement, CEO. Republican. Avocations: tennis, flying. Deceased.

SHEARER, HUGH LAWSON, Jamaican governmental official; b. Martha Brae, Trelawny, Jamaica May 18, 1923; ed. St. Simon's Coll.; LL.D. (hon.), Howard U., 1968 Journalist, editorial staff Jamaica Worker, 1941-47; mem. Kingston and St. Andrew Corp. Council, 1947-51; mem. Jamaican Ho. of Reps., 1955-59; mem. Legis. Council (now Senate), 1961-66; minister without portfolio and leader of govt. bus. in Senate, 1962-67; dept. chief mission Jamaican del. to UN, 1962-67; former mem. Jamacian Ho. of Reps., minister of external affairs, 1967-72, prime minister, 1967-72, former mem. privy council, leader of the opposition, 1972-74, dep. prime minister, minister of fgn. affairs and fgn. trade, 1980-89; former mem. Bustamante Indsl. Trade Union, asst. gen. sec., 1947-53, island supr., 1953-60, v.p., 1960-77, former pres.; leader Jamaican Labor Party, 1967-74; Jamaican rep. Non-Aligned Movement, from 1981; Jamaican del. Commonwealth Heads of Govt. Conf., 1969, 71, 83; mem. African, Caribbean and Pacific Council of Ministers, pres., 1984; mem. CARICOM Council of Ministers. Decorated 1st class Order of Francisco de Miranda, Govt. of Republic of Venezuela. Died July 5, 2004.

SHEARER, JONATHAN TURBITT, lawyer; b. West Reading, Pa., Dec. 4, 1945; s. Robert Keiser and Velma Elizabeth (Turbitt) S. BA, Columbia U., 1966; JD, Fordham U., 1971. Bar: N.Y. 1971, U.S. Dist. Ct. (so. and ea. dists.) N.Y. 1973, U.S. Ct. Appeals (2d cir.) 1974, U.S. Supreme Ct. 1975, U.S. Dist. Ct. (no. dist.) N.Y. 1977, U.S. Ct. Appeals (5th cir.) 1983, Tex. 1984, U.S. Dist. Ct. (no. dist.) Tex. 1985, Pa. 1989. Atty. City of N.Y., 1971-72, State of N.Y., N.Y.C., 1972-74; pvt. practice law, N.Y.C., 1974-82; with IRS, Dallas, 1983-84; with Jones, Day, Reavis & Pogue, Dallas, 1984-85; pvt. practice law, Dallas, 1985—. Local counsel Vietnam Vets. Coalition, Dallas, 1984—. With U.S. Army, 1966-68, Vietnam. Mem. Pa. Bar Assn. (com. alcoholism and drug addiction). Died, Sept. 3, 1992.

SHEARER, PAUL VICTOR, lawyer; b. Columbus Junction, Iowa, Jan. 21, 1919; s. Brainard Hayes and Maude Sarah (Hanft) S.; m. Barbara Jean Smith, June 11, 1943; children: Mark S., Jane M. BA, U. Iowa, 1940, JD, 1942. Bar: Iowa 1942, U.S. Dist. Ct. (so. dist.) Iowa 1972. Atty. County of Washington, Iowa, 1949-51; ptnr. Stewart & Shearer, Washington, 1951-78, Stewart, Shearer & Tindal, Washington, 1978-80, Stewart, Shearer, Owen & Tindal, Washington, 1980-85, Shearer & Tindal, Washington, from 1985. Bd. dirs. Washington Fed. Savs. & Loan; pres., pub. The Columbus Gazette, Columbus Junction, Iowa, 1979—; pres. Washington County Abstract Co., 1980—. Columnist The Columbus Gazette, 1979—. Bd. fellows Sch. Religion, U. Iowa, Iowa City, 1973—; trustee Garrett-Evang. Theol. Sem., Evanston, Ill., 1972-78; gen. counsel on ministries United Meth. Ch., Dayton, Ohio, 1976-84. With U.S. Army, 1942-46. Mem. ABA, Iowa Bar Assn. (Cert. Outstanding Svc. 1962), Washington County Bar Assn. (pres. 1961-62), Rotary (Community Svc. award 1986), Masons, Am. Legion, YMCA (pres. 1954-56). Democrat. Home: Washington, Iowa. Deceased.

SHEEHAN, MARY ANDERSON, retired fundraiser; b. Pitts., Jan. 26, 1932; d. Donald C. and Dorothy (Fagan) Anderson; m. Thomas E. Sheehan, Nov. 25, 1961; children: Mark, David. BA, Chatham Coll., Pitts., 1954. Copy writer Sta. WQED, Pitts., 1954-60; trainer Gimbel's, Pitts., 1960-61; spl. events staff United Way, Pitts., 1961; mem. fund raising staff Harmarville Rehab. Ctr., Pitts., 1979-80; dir. devel. and alumnae rels. Chatham Coll., 1980-84, exec. asst. to pres., 1984-92; dir. devel. Goodwill Industries of Pitts., 1993-95; ret. Chmn. Mercy Hosp. Found. Bd., Pitts., 1990-93, 99—; pres. Fedn. Ind. Sch. Alumnae, 1993-01; dir. Canterbury Pl., 1998—; treas. Alpha House, 2000—. Avocations: tennis, reading, bridge. Home: Pittsburgh, Pa. Died Jan. 31, 2002.

SHEELINE, PAUL CUSHING, hotel executive; b. Boston, June 6, 1921; s. Paul Daniel and Mary (Child) S.; m. Harriet White Moffat, May 23, 1948 (dec. 1962); children: Christopher White, William Emerson, Mary Child, Leonora Moffat; m. Sandra Dudley Wahl, July 24, 1965; 1 child, Abby Tucker. BS, Harvard U., 1943, JD, 1948. Bar: N.Y. 1949, D.C. 1986. Assoc. Sullivan & Cromwell, N.Y.C., 1948-54; with Lambert & Co., N.Y.C., 1954-65, gen. ptnr., 1958-65; chief fin. officer Intercontinental Hotels Corp., N.Y.C., 1966-71, pres., 1971-74, chief exec. officer, 1971-85, chmn. bd., 1972-87, cons., 1987-92; of counsel Verner, Liipfert, Bernhard, McPherson & Hand, Washington, 1986-93. Mem. Presdl. Bd. Advisors on Pvt. Sector Initiatives, Washington, 1987-89. Vice chmn. Community Service Soc. of N.Y., 1962-63; dir. Am. Assn. for UN, 1951-58; former mem. Harvard Overseers Com. to visit Center for Internat. Affairs and Dept. Romance Langs.; trustee East Woods Sch., Oyster Bay Cove, N.Y., 1959-68, Camargo Found., 1971—, St. Luke's/Roosevelt Hosp. Ctr., 1982-97; bd. dirs. Bus. Council for Internat. Understanding., 1975-88, Fgn. Policy Assn., 1981-90, Scientists' Inst. Pub. Info., 1984-91, Battle of Normandy Found., 1986-91; mem. bd. zoning appeals Village of Lloyd Harbor, N.Y., 1988—. Served to capt. USAAF, 1942-46. Decorated Silver Star medal, French Legion of Honor, Croix de Guerre with palm, Moroccan Ouissam Alaouite. Mem. Am.-Arab Assn. Commerce and Industry (chmn. bd. 1984-86), Phi Beta Kappa. Clubs: Cold Spring Harbor Beach; Harvard (N.Y.C.); North Haven Casino (Maine). Died Aug. 6, 2003.

SHEFFIELD, LESLIE FLOYD, retired agricultural educator; b. Orafino, Nebr., Apr. 13, 1925; s. Floyd L. and Edith A. (Presler) S.; m. Doris Fay Fenimore, Aug. 20, 1947; children: Larry Wayne, Linda Fay (Mrs. Bernard Eric Hempelman), Susan Elaine (Mrs. Randy Thorman). BS in Agronomy with high distinction, U. Nebr., 1950; MS, 1964, PhD, 1971; postgrad., U. Minn., summer 1965. County ext. agt., Lexington and Schuyler, Nebr., 1951-52; exec. sec. Nebr. Grain Improvement Assn., Lincoln, 1952-56; chief Nebr. Wheat Commn., Lincoln, 1956-59; exec. sec. market devel. Great Plains Wheat, Inc., Garden City, Kans., 1959-61; asst. to dean Coll Agr. U. Nebr., Lincoln, 1961-66; supt. North Platte Expt. sta., 1966-71; asst. to vice chancellor Inst. Agr. and Natural Resources, 1975-84; also extension farm mgmt. splst., assoc. prof. agrl. econs., 1975-94; ret., 1994. Cons. econs. of irrigation N.D., Minn., S.D., Brazil, 1975, 88, 92, Sudan, Kuwait, Iran, 1976, China, 1977, 81, Argentina, 1978, 92, Hong Kong, 1981, Japan, 1981, South Africa, 1985, Paraguay, 1992, Australia, 1994, New Zealand, 1994. Author: Economic Impact of Irrigated Agriculture, 1985; co-author: Flat Water-A History of Nebraska and Its Water, 1993; contbr. chpt. to book; editor: Procs. of Nebr. Water Resources and Irrigation Devel. for 1970;s, 1972; contbg. editor Irrigation Age Mag., St. Paul, 1974-86; contbr. articles to profl. jours. V.p. U. Nebr. Found., 1982-86; sec.-treas. Circle 4S-L Acres, Wallace, Nebr., 1973-87. With U.S. Army, 1944-46, ETO. Rsch. grantee NASA, 1972-77; recipient Hon. State Farmer award Future Farmers Am., 1955, Hon. Chpt. Farmer award, North Platte chpt., 1973, fellowship grad. award Chgo. Bd. Trade, 1964, Agrl. Achievement award Ak-Sar-Ben, 1969, Citizen award U.S. Dept. Interior Bur. Reclamation, 1984, Pub. Svc. award for contbns. to Nebr. agr. Nebr. Agribus Club, 1984, Ditch Rider award Four States Irrigation Coun., 1988, Disting. Svc. award Am. Soc. Farm Mgrs. and Rural Appraisers Nebr. chpt., 1993, alumnus of Yr. award U. Nebr.-Lincoln Coll. Agr. and Natural Resources Alumni Asn., 1993, Headgate award Four States Irrigation Coun., 1995, Pioneer Irrigation award Nebr. Water Conf. Coun. and U. Nebr. Lincoln, 1995; inducated Nebr. Hall of Agrl. Achievement, 1988; named Irrigation Man of Yr. Irrigation Assn., 1988; honoree Disting. Svc. Nebr. Hall Agrl. Achievement, 1996, Silver Eagle award Nebr. Farm Bur. Fedn., 1996, Kremer Groundwater Ach. award Groundwater Found., Lincoln, 1998, Mem. Am. Soc. Farm Mgrs. Rural Appraisers, Am. Agrl. Econs. Assn., Am. Nat. Water Resources assn., Nat. Water Resources Assn., Nebr. Water Resources Assn. (Pres.'s award 1979, award for commitment to irrigated agr. 1993, bd. dirs. 1995—), Nebr. Irrigation Assn., Nebr. Assn. Resource Dists., Orgn. Profl. Employees of U.S. Dept. Agr., Lincoln C. of C. (chmn. agrl. com. 1974-77), Rotary (dir. 1965-66), Gamma Sigma Delta, Alpha Zeta (v.p. Nebr. agrl. rels. coun. 1993-94). Home: Lincoln, Nebr. Deceased.

SHEINKMAN, JACK, union official, lawyer; b. N.Y.C., Dec. 6, 1926; s. Shaia and Bertha (Rosenkrantz) S.; m. Betty Francis Johnson, May 31, 1954; children: Michael, Joshua, Mark. BS, Cornell U., 1948, LL.B., 1952; cert. in econs.,

Oxford U., 1949. Bar: N.Y. 1952. Atty. NLRB, Washington, 1952-53, Amalgamated Clothing Workers Am., N.Y.C., 1953-58, gen. counsel, 1958-72, v.p., 1968-72, sec.-treas., 1972-76, Amalgamated Clothing and Textile Workers Union, N.Y.C., 1976-87, pres., 1987-95, pres. emeritus, 1995—2004. Chmn. bd. Amalgamated Bank of N.Y.; mem. exec. coun., v.p. AFL-CIO, 1987-95; mem. indsl. union dept. Internat. Textile, Garment and Leather Workers Fedn., Brussels, 1972-95. Dir. internat. rescue com. N.Y. Hist. Soc.; bd. dirs. Martin Luther King Jr. Inst., Economists Allied Against Arts; vice chmn. Coun. Competitiveness United Housing Found.; trustee Aspen Inst.; mem. Pres.'s Adv. Com. on Trade Policy Negotiations, 1987-95; trustee emeritus Cornell U. Lt. (j.g.) USNR, 1944-46, PTO. Mem. Workers Def. League (dir.), Am. Arbitration Assn. (dir.) Coun. Fgn. Rels., UN Assn. U.S.A. (bd. govs.), Brit.-N.Am. Com. (exec. com.), Nat. Planning Com. (exec. com.). Democrat. Jewish. Home: New York, NY. Died Jan. 29, 2004.

SHELTON, LEONARD AGEE, lawyer; b. Ardmore, Okla., Feb. 10, 1911; s. Leonard G. and Alice (Agee) S.; m. Frances Dundas, Aug. 19, 1937; children: John, Jane, Thomas, Robert. AB, Pomona Coll., 1932; LLB, U. Calif., Berkeley, 1935; LLD, U. Calif., 1981. Bar: Calif. 1935. Assoc. Fogle, Beman and Jones, Santa Monica, Calif., 1936-41; ptnr. Allard, Shelton & O'Connor, Pomona, from 1946. Trustee Pomona Coll., Claremont, Calif., 1956-80, Internat. Crane Found., Baraboo, Wis., 1983-91; bd. dirs. Nat. Audubon Soc., N.Y.C., 1970-76. Lt. col. USAF, 1941-46. Decorated Legion of Merit. Mem. Calif. Bar Assn. (bd. govs. 1961-63), L.A. County Bar Assn. (trustee 1948). Home: Claremont, Calif. Deceased.

SHENTON, JAMES PATRICK, history educator; b. Passaic, N.J., Mar. 17, 1925; s. Walter Gardiner and Lillian (Spitzel) S. AB, Columbia, 1949, MA, 1950, PhD, 1954. Mem. faculty Columbia U., N.Y.C., 1951—2003, prof. Am. history, 1967—2003, departmental rep. history dept., 1963-69. Author: Robert John Walker, A Politician from Jackson to Lincoln, 1960, Reconstruction, The South After the War, 1963, A Historian's History of the United States, 1966, Melting Pot, 1971, These United States, 1978; lectr. edn. Sta. WNDT-TV, 1963-64. Served with AUS, 1943-46. Mem. Am. Hist. Assn., AAUP, Am. Cath. Hist. Assn. (bd. dirs. 1962-65) Home: Passaic, NJ. Died July 25, 2003.

SHEPS, CECIL GEORGE, physician; b. Winnipeg, Man., Can., July 24, 1913; came to U.S., 1946, naturalized, 1956; s. George and Polly (Lirenman) S.; m. Mindel Cherniack, May 29, 1937 (dec. Jan. 1973); 1 child, Samuel B.; m. Ann Shepherd. MD, U. Man., 1936, DSc (hon.), 1985; MPH, Yale U., 1947; DSc (hon.), Chgo. Med. Sch., 1970; PhD (hon.), Ben Gurion U. of the Negev, 1983. Intern St. Joseph's Hosp. Gen. Hosp., Winnipeg; resident Corbett Gen. Hosp., Stourbridge, Eng., Queen Mary's Hosp. for East End, London, 1938, Camp Shilo Mil. Hosp., Can., Ft. Osborne Mil. Hosp., Can.; asst. dep. min. Dept. Health Sask., Can., 1944-46; gen. dir. Beth Israel hosp., Boston; also clin. prof. preventive medicine Med. Sch. Harvard U., 1953-60; prof. med. and hosp. adminstrn. Grad. Sch. Pub. Health U. Pitts., 1960-65; prof. community medicine Mt. Sinai Sch. Medicine; also gen. dir. Beth Israel Med. Ctr., N.Y.C., 1965-68; prof. social medicine U. N.C., 1969-79, former Taylor Grandy Disting. prof. social medicine, dir. Health Svcs. Rsch. Ctr., 1968-72, vice chancellor health scis., 1971-76, prof. emeritus, 1986. Cons. in field, 1947— Author: Needed Research in Health and Medical Care-A Biosocial Approach, 1954, Community Organization-Action and Inaction, 1956, Medical Schools and Hospitals, 1965, The Sick Citadel: The American Academic Medical Center and the Public Interest, 1983, and five other books. Chmn. health svcs. rsch. study sect. NIH, 1958-62; cons med. affairs Welfare Adminstrn., HEW, 1964-67; mem. spl. commn. social scis. NSF, 1968-69; chmn. Milbank Meml. Fund Commn. on Higher Edn. for Pub. Health, 1972-75. Capt. M.C., Royal Can. Army, 1943-46. Mem. NAS, Inst. Medicine (sr.), Nat. Coun. Aging (v.p., bd. dir.), Am. Nurses Found. (bd. mem., sec.-treas.). Home: Chapel Hill, NC. Died Feb. 8, 2004.

SHER, NORMAN, physician, psychiatrist, consultant; b. Phila., Jan. 21, 1931; s. Max and Emma (Friedman) S.; m. Joanna Hollenberg, Dec. 27, 1955 (dec. July 1992); children: Jonathan, Katherine Sher Baker. BA, Swarthmore Coll., 1952; MD, U. Chgo., 1956. Rotating intern Kings County Hosp./SUNY, Bklyn., 1956-57, resident in psychiatry, 1957-58, Manhattan Psychiat. Ctr., N.Y.C., 1960-62; fellow in child psychiatry Bklyn. Psychiat. Ctr., 1962-64; dir. child psychiatry Maimonides Med. Ctr., Bklyn., 1964-68, dir. child psychiatry tng., 1968-78, dir. gen. residency tng., 1973-82; pvt. practice child and adult psychiatry Bklyn., from 1964. Contbr. articles to profl. jours. Capt. M.C., U.S. Army, 1958-60. Fellow Am. Psychiat. Assn. (life), Bklyn. Psychiat. Soc. (Disting. life, pres. 1975-76), Am. Acad. Child Psychiatry (life); mem. Soc. Adolescent Psychiatry (life). Democrat. Jewish. Avocations: reading, swimming, squash, gardening, theater-going. Home: Abington, Pa. Died 2002.

SHERBOURNE, ARCHIBALD NORBERT, civil engineering educator; b. Bombay, July 8, 1929; s. Manekji and Sarah Agnes (Sherbourne) Bulsara; m. Jean Ducan Nicol, Aug. 15, 1959; children: Mary, Sarah, Jeffrey, Nicolas, Jonathan, Simon. B.Sc., U. London, 1953, D.Sc., 1970; BS, Lehigh U., 1955, MS, 1957; MA, Cambridge U., 1959, PhD, 1960. Registered profl. engr., Ont.; chartered engr. U.K., European Engr. Mem. faculty U. Waterloo, Ont., Can., 1961-96, prof. civil engring., 1963-96; dean U. Waterloo (Faculty Engring.), 1966-74. Dir. Sherbourne Consultants Ltd.; vis. sr. lectr. U. Coll. London, 1963-64; vis. prof. U. W.I., Trinidad, 1969-70, Nat. C.E. Lab., Lisbon, Portugal, 1970, Ecole Polytechnique Federale, Lausanne, Switzerland, 1975-77; DAAD vis. fellow, W. Ger., 1975, NATO sr. scientist fellow, vis. lectr., 1975-76; advisor-cons. Commonwealth Africa study group on tech. edn. in industry Commonwealth Secretariat London, 1978; Gledden vis. sr. fellow U. Western Australia, Perth, 1978; acad. adviser Centre for Sci. and Tech., Fed. U. Paraiba, Campina Grande, Brazil, 1979; prin. cons. acad. planning Faculty Engring., U. Victoria, B.C., Can., 1979-80; advisor Tata Sons Ltd., Bombay, 1980; vis. prof. civil engring. Mich. Technol. U., Houghton, 1980-81, 82-83, U. Melbourne, 1983; spl. cons. technol. edn. for developing countries Can. Internat. Devel. Agy., Internat. Am. Devel. Bank, Orgn. Am. States in West Africa, Cuba, Brazil, West Indies; vis. prof. ocean engring. Fla. Atlantic U., Boca Raton, 1985, archtl. engring. N.C. A & T State U., Greensboro, 1987; vis. prof. aerospace engring. I.I. Sci., Bangalore, India, 1990, vis. prof. civil engring. U. Cape Town, S. Africa, 1995—. Contbr. articles to profl. jours. OECD fellow Switzerland, 1964; recipient Engring. medal Assn. Profl. Engrs., Province Ont., 1975, Leipholz medal Can. Soc. Civil Engring., 1997, Julian C. Smith medal Engring. Inst. of Can. Fellow Instn. Structural Engrs. (London), Royal Soc. Arts, Can. Soc. Civil Engring., Can. Acad. Engring. Home: Waterloo, Canada. Died Dec. 17, 1999.

SHERLOCK, PAUL V. state legislator; b. Pawtucket, R.I., Apr. 5, 1930; m. Ann E. Devine; children: Kathleen A., Timothy P., Patrick J., Martin D., Mary E. BA, Providence Coll., 1951; MA, R.I. Coll., 1960; DEd, Boston U., 1969, postgrad., 1983. Dir., spl. edn. State of R.I., 1959—66; mem. R.I. Ho. of Reps., Providence, 1978—2004, vice chmn. fin. com.; former prof. edn. of handicapped and spl. edn. R.I. Coll. Bd. dirs. Insight, Vis. Nurses Assn. Mem. R.I. and Kent County Assn. Retarded Citizens. Died Jan. 17, 2004.

SHERMAN, WILLIAM EURASTI, lawyer; b. Tampa, Fla., Apr. 28, 1927; s. William Eurasti and Maryetta (Abbott) S.; B.A., U. Fla., 1950, J.D., 1953; m. Frances Rogers, 1950 (div. 1973); children— William Eurasti III, Valerie Ann; m. Vicki Lynn Peterson, June 9, 1974. Bar: Fla. 1953. Spl. asst. to atty. gen. Fla., Tallahassee, 1953; assoc. Francis P. Whitehair, DeLand, Fla., 1954-57; practiced in DeLand, 1958—; mem. firm Hall, Sweeney & Godbee, 1958-59, Hull, Landis, Graham & French, 1960-66, Landis, Graham, French, Husfeld and Sherman, 1966-69, Landis, Graham, French, Husfeld, Sherman & Ford, P.A., 1969—. Mem. Volusia County Charter Study Commn., 1969-71, Volusia County Charter Rev. Commn., 1975; mem. nominating commn. 5th Dist. Ct. Appeals, 1979, 82. Bd. dirs. Internat. Music Festivals, Inc., 1969-71, Montreat (N.C.)-Anderson Coll., 1961-71, Mountain Retreat Assn., 1961-71. Served with Signal Corps, U.S. Army, World War II. Mem. Fla. Bar (gov. 1970-76, chmn. legis. com. 1973-76, exec. com. real property probate and trust sect. 1972—, dir. probate guardianship and trust law div. 1981-83, chmn.-elect 1983, mem. Uniform Probate Code Study Commn.; mem. Marketable Record Title Act Commn. 1984-85), ABA, Volusia County Bar Assn. (pres. 1969-70, MRTA Commn. 1985-86, chmn. estate planning and probate cert. com.), DeLand C. of C. (v.p. 1970-71), Phi Delta Phi, Pi Kappa Alpha, Alpha Delta Sigma. Democrat. Presbyterian (elder). Clubs: Rotary, Halifax. E-mail: wsherman@landispa.com. Died May 27, 2000. Home: De Land, Fla.

SHERWOOD, MARY PASCO, environmentalist; b. Hartford, Conn., May 1, 1906; d. Arthur Joseph and Mary (Lundy) Pasco. BS in Forestry, U. Conn., 1934; MS in Wildlife, Cornell U., 1937. Jr. forester State of Wis., Madison, 1944-45; ecologist State of Conn., Storrs, 1934-35, 38-44; creator, chmn. Walden Forever Wild, Inc., Concord, Mass., from 1980; owner native plant nursery Falls Village, Conn., from 1945. Curator Conn. State Forest Mus., 2 summers; program dir Mass. Audubon Soc., 1961-62; worker herbarium, Nantucket, Mass.; creator A.E. Moss Forest, Wildlife, Wildflower Sanctuary, Storrs, Conn., 1988. Creator, editor The Saunterer, 1967-68, Thoreau Jour. Quar., 1968-78. Creator Thoreau Lyceum, Concord, 1967, Thoreau Fellowship, Old Town Maine, 1968-80. Grantee Colson, Corcord, 1936-37, Women's Farm and Garden, 1961-62; recipient Plaque, EPA, 1987, E-Mag. award, 1992, Medallion, U. Conn., Storrs, 1992. Mem. Thoreau Soc. (nominating com. 1992), New Eng. and Wildflower Soc. (book reviewer 1984-91). Avocations: wildflower and bird chasing, conservation items, writing. Home: Storrs, Conn. Died July 29, 2001.

SHETTLES, LANDRUM BREWER, obstetrician-gynecologist; b. Pontotoc, Miss., Nov. 21, 1909; s. Basil Manly and Sue (Mounce) S.; m. Priscilla Elinor Schmidt, Dec. 18, 1948; children— Susan Flora, Frances Louise, Lana Brewer, Landrum Brewer, David Ernest, Harold Manly and Alice Annmarie (twins). BA, Miss. Coll., 1933, D.Sc. (hon.), 1966; MS (fellow 1933-34), U. N.M., 1934; PhD, Johns Hopkins, 1937, MD, 1943. Diplomate: Am. Bd. Obstretrics and Gynecology, N. Am. sect. obstetrics and gynecology Pan Am. Med. Assn. Instr. biology Miss. Coll., 1932-33; biologist U.S. Bur. Fisheries, 1934; instr. biology Johns Hopkins, 1934-37, research fellow, 1937-38, Nat. Com. Maternal Health, N.Y.C., 1938-43; intern Johns Hopkins Hosp., 1943-44; resident Columbia-Presbyn. Med. Center, N.Y.C., 1947-51, attending obstetrician-gynecologist, 1951-73, Doctors, Polyclinic and Flower-Fifth Av hosps., N.Y.C., 1974-75; chief obstetrician-gynecologist Gifford Meml. Hosp., Randolph, Vt., 1975-81, Star Clinic, Las Vegas, Nev., 1981-82, Oasis Clinic, Las Vegas, Nev., 1982-85; attending gynecologist-obstetrician Women's Hosp., Las Vegas, Nev., 1981-94, Sunrise Hosp. and Med. Ctr., from 1994. Markle Found. scholar Columbia Coll. Phys. and Surg., 1951-56; assoc. prof. clin. obstetrics-gynecology Coll. Phys. and Surg., Columbia, 1951-73; individual practice, N.Y.C., 1951-75; dir. research N.Y. Fertility Research Found., 1974-75; Anglo-Am. lectr. Royal Coll. Obstetricians and Gynecologists, London, Eng., 1959; Research cons. Office Naval Research, Am. embassy, London, 1951-52 Author: Ovum Humanum, 1960, Your Baby's Sex, Now You Can Choose, 1970, From Conception to Birth, 1971, Choose Your Baby's Sex, 1976, The Rites of Life: The Scientific Evidence of Life Before Birth, 1983, How to Choose Your Baby's Sex, 1984, 89, 21st Century Edition: How To Choose the Sex of Your Baby, 1997; also numerous articles. Served to maj., M.C. AUS, 1944-46. Editorial bd. Infertility Recipient Ortho medal and award Am. Soc. Study Fertility, Sterility and Allied Subjects, 1960, Order of the Golden Arrow award Miss. Coll., 1993, Disting. Alumnus award Miss. Coll., 1993. Fellow ACS, AAAS, Am. Coll. Obstetricians and Gynecologists, World Med. Assn., Royal Soc. of Health (London), Royal Soc. Medicine (London); mem. AMA, Am. Soc. Zoologists, Am. Physiol. Soc., Soc. Exptl. Biology and Medicine, Libr. of Congress, Vt. Med. Soc., Soc. U. Gynecologists, N.Y. Obstet. Soc., Harvey Soc., Wisdom Soc., N.Y. State Med. Assn., N.Y. County Nev. Med. Assn., Clarke County Med. Assn., 50 Yr. Club of Miss. Coll., 50 Yr. Club of Johns Hopkins U., 50 Year Club of Vt. State Med. Soc., 50 Yr. Club of AMA, 25 Yr. Club of Columbia-Presbyn. Med. Ctr., Phi Beta Kappa, Sigma Xi, Omicron Delta Kappa, Gamma Alpha. Spl. rsch. fisheries biology, physiology, human reprodn., fertility and sterility, hemorrhagic disease in newborn infants, sperm biology; discovered, identified male and female producing sperms; achieved gamete intrafallopian transfer, 1978; human in vitro fertilization, 1951; method for chorionic villi sampling, 1979. Home: Saint Petersburg, Fla. Died Feb. 6, 2003.

SHEYNES, MARIA, journalist; b. Moscow, July 7, 1935; came to U.S., 1996; d. Alexander Zinovii and Victoria Alexander (Lelchin) Krieger; m. Boris Isaac Sheynes, Apr. 17, 1969; 1 child, Matthew Boris. BA in English Lang., Moscow State Inst. Fgn. Langs., 1960. Cert. English tchr., Moscow. Guide Intourist, Moscow, 1960-64; radio and TV translator Moscow, 1964-65; editor Rovesnik youth mag., Moscow, 1965-74; translator Moscow State U., 1974-83; sec. Orthogenic Sch., U. Chgo., 1988-93; sec. dept. pathology U. Chgo. Med. Ctr., 1993-95; sec. Adminstrn. Office U. Chgo. Libr., 1995-96, serial recorder, from 1996. Russian interpreter Fed. Immigration Ct., Chgo., 1980—; freelance translator various Russian mags., Moscow, 1960-85. Vol. English tchr. Jewish Vocat. Svc., Chgo., 1995. Avocations: history of art, foreign languages. Home: Chicago, Ill. Died July 20, 2000.

SHICKMAN, BARRY LOUIS, physician, obstetrician, gynecologist; b. Phila., May 29, 1939; s. Charles Bernard and Adele (Levy) S.; m. Merle Sandra Rachlin, May 30, 1965 (dec. June 1973); 1 child, Joel Nathan; m. Dora Ann Moore, Mar. 13, 1994. BA, Franklin & Marshall Coll., 1961; MD, U. Pa., 1965. Diplomate Am. Bd. Ob-Gyn. Intern U. Rochester (N.Y.) Strong Meml. Hsop., 1965-66; resident Kaiser FOund. Hosp., Oakland, Calif., 1968-71; ob-gyn. physician Berkeley (Calif.) Health Dept., 1971, Charles R. Drew Med. Ctr., East Palo Alto, Calif., 1971-76, Health Alliance of No. Calif., San Jose, 1976-79, Pacific Med. Clinic, Saratoga, Calif., 1979-83, City of Houston Health Dept., 1983-93, Riverwalk Ob-Gyn. Assocs., San Antonio, 1993-94. Cons. Clinica Sierra Vista, Lamont, Calif., 1972-81. Capt. U.S. Army, 1966-68. Mem. Tex. Med. Assn., Bexar County Med. Assn. Republican. Jewish. Avocations: choral singing, flying, cooking, camping, swimming. Home: Houston, Tex. Died Mar. 6, 2002.

SHIELDS, CAROL ANN, writer, educator; b. Oak Park, Ill., June 2, 1935; came to Can., 1957, naturalized, 1974. d. Robert Elmer and Inez Adelle (Sellgren) Warner; m. Donald Hugh Shields, July 20, 1957; chldren: John, Anne, Catherine, Margaret, Sara. BA, Hanover Coll., 1957; MA, U. Ottawa, Ont., Can., 1975; hon. degree, U. Ottawa, 1995, Hanover Coll., 1996, Queen's U., 1996, U. Winnipeg, 1996, U.B.C., 1996, U. Western Ont., 1997, U. Toronto, 1998, Concordia U., 1998, Carleton U., 2000, Wilfrid Laurier U., 2000, Univ. Victoria, 2001, Lakehead Univ., 2001, U. Calgary, 2001, U. Man., 2003, Malaspina U. and Coll., 2003. Editl. asst. Can. Slavonic Papers, Ottawa, 1972-74; lectr. U. Ottawa, 1976-77, U.B.C., Vancouver, Can., 1978-80; prof. U. Man., Winnipeg, Can., 1980-2000, prof. emerita, 2000—03; chancellor U. Winnipeg, 1996-2000; chancellor emerita, 2000—03. Author: (poems) Others, 1972, Intersect, 1974, Coming to Canada, 1991, (novels) Small Ceremonies, 1976, The Box Garden, 1977, Happenstance, 1980, A Fairly Conventional Women, 1982, Swann: A Mystery, 1987, The Republic of Love, 1992, The Stone Diaries, 1993 (Nat. Book Critics Circle award for fiction, 1995, Pulitzer Prize for fiction, 1995), Larry's Party, 1997 (Orange prize for fiction, 1998), Unless, 2002, (biography) Jane Austen, 2000, (plays) Women Waiting, 1983, Departures and Arrivals, 1984, Thirteen Hands, 1993; author: (with Catherine Shields) Fashion Power Guilt; author: (with David Williamson) Anniversary, 1998; author: (story collections) Various Miracles, 1985, The Orange Fish, 1989, Dressing Up for the Carnival, 2000; co-editor (with Marjorie Anderson): Dropped Threads, 2001, Dropped Threads 2, 2003; author: (novels) Unless, 2000. Named Can. Booksellers Author of Yr., 2001, Order of Can., Companion to the Order of Can., 2002; recipient prize, CBC, 1983, 1984, Nat. Mag. award, 1985, Arthur Ellis award, 1987, Can. Book Sellers' award,

1994, 2003, Manitoba Book of the Yr., 1994, Marian Engel award, 1990, Gov. Gen's award, Can. Coun., 1993, Nat. Book Critics Circle award, 1995, Pulitzer prize, 1995, Chevalier de l'Ordre des Arts et des Lettres, 2000, Order of Manitoba, 2001, Charles Taylor Prize, 2002; fellow Guggenheim, 1999; grantee, Can. Coun., 1973, 1976, 1978, 1986, Man Arts Coun., 1984, 1985. Mem. PEN, Writers Union Can., Writers Guild Man., Jane Austen Soc., Royal Soc. Can. Home: Victoria, Canada. Died July 16, 2003.

SHIHATA, IBRAHIM FAHMY IBRAHIM, retired bank executive, lawyer, writer; b. Damietta, Egypt, Aug. 19, 1937; s. Ibrahim and Neamat (El Ashmawy) S.; m. Samia S. Farid, June 18, 1967; children: Sharif, Yasmine, Nadia. LL.B., U. Cairo, 1957, diploma in pub. law and fin., 1958, diploma in pvt. law, 1959; S.JD, Harvard U., 1964; LLD (hon.), U. Dundee, Scotland, 1995, U. Paris Panthéon, Sorbonne, France, 1996, Am. U., Cairo, 2000. Mem. Conseil d'Etat, UAR, 1957-60, Tech. Bur. of Pres., Egypt, 1959-60; from lectr. to assoc. prof. internat. law Ain-Shams U., Cairo, 1964-66, 70-72; legal adviser Kuwait Fund for Arab Econ. Devel., 1966-70, 72-76; dir. gen. OPEC Fund for Internat. Devel., Vienna, 1976-83; exec. dir. Internat. Fund for Agrl. Devel., Rome, 1977-83; sr. v.p., gen. counsel World Bank, Washington, 1983-98; ret., 1998. Sec. gen. Internat. Ctr. Settlement of Investment Disputes, Washington, 1983—; chmn. bd. Internat. Devel. Law Inst., Rome, 1983—; chmn. Egyptian Ctr. Econ. Studies, Cairo, 1999—; bd. dirs. Internat. Fertilizer Devel. Ctr., Muscle Shoals, Ala., 1979-84, Vienna Devel. Inst.; mem. exec. coun. Am. Soc. Internat. Law, Washington, 1984-87; adv. com. Rsch. Ctr. Internat. Law, Cambridge, Eng., 1985—; founding adv., bd. dirs. Inst. Transnat. Arbitration, Houston, 1986—; hon. fellow Inst. Advance Legal Studies, U. London. Author: The Power of the International Court to Determine Its Own Jurisdiction, 1965, International Air and Space Law, 1966, International Economic Joint Ventures, 1969, International Guarantee for Foreign Investments, 1971, Treatment of Foreign Investments in Egypt, 1972, Secure and Recognized Boundaries, 1974, The Arab Oil Embargo, 1975, The Other Face of OPEC, 1982, The OPEC Fund for International Development-The Formative Years, 1983, A Program for Tomorrow-Challenges and Prospects of the Egyptian Economy in a Changing World, 1987, MIGA and Foreign Investment, 1988, The European Bank for Reconstruction and Development, 1990, The World Bank and the Arab World, 1990, The World Bank and in a Changing World, vol. 1, 1991, Legal Treatment of Foreign Investment: The World Bank Guidelines, 1993, Towards Comprehensive Reforms, 1993, The World Bank Inspection Panel, 1994, 2d edit., rev. 1999, The World Bank in a Changing World, vol. 1, 1991, vol. 2, 1995, vol. 3, 1999, Complementary Reform: Essays on Legal, Judicial and Other Institutional Reform Supported by the World Bank, 1997; editor ICSID Rev.-Fgn. Investment Law Jour. Sr. v.p. IBRD, 1983-99, v.p., 1983-98. Decorated Grosses Silbernes Ehrenzeichen am Bande fuer Verdienste um die Republik Oesterreich (Austria), 1983; recipient Babcock prize, 1964, Kuwait prize for sci. progress in social scis., 1983. Mem. Am. Soc. Internat. Law, Institut de Droit Internat. (Geneva), Social Scis. Acad. (Chile). Home: Washington, DC. Died May 28, 2001.

SHIMEK, JOHN LYLE, copywriter, consultant; b. Weimar, Tex., June 30, 1914; s. John and Isabel (Lyle) S.; m. Louise M. Mansfield, June 8, 1941 (dec. Apr. 1970); 1 child, John Neal; m. Jeanette M. Fox, 1980. BBA, U. Tex., 1947. Editor U. Ill., Urbana, 1949-53; advt. mgr. The Fox Co., San Antonio, 1953-54; promotion writer Sports Illustrated, N.Y.C., 1954-56, Parents mag., N.Y.C., 1956-58, McCall's mag. & Redbook, N.Y.C., 1958-62; creative dir. Mail Advt. Corp. of Am., 1962-73, Metromail, Lincoln, 1973-74; advt. mgr. Thompson Cigar Co., Tampa, Fla., 1974-85; pvt. practice Lutz, Fla., from 1985. Author: Billions of False Impressions, 1969. With USN, 1941-45. Recipient Golden Gavel award Direct Mktg. Assn., 1969, Direct Mktg. Assn. award, 1969. Fla. Direct Mktg. Assn. Democrat. Unitarian Universalist. Avocations: gardening, traveling. Died Nov. 18, 2000.

SHIPLEY, JEAN SCOTT, financial planner; b. Seattle, Jan. 10, 1936; d. Morris Robert Scott and Ruth Marietta Boyer Pack; m. George T. Gruber (dec.); m. Howard V. Shipley (div.); children: Ivan, Brenda (dec.), Theresa, Eric, George, Michael, Sharon, Jennifer. Student, Radcliffe U., 1952-54; BA, George Washington U., 1957; postgrad., Washington State Coll., Cheny, 1965-66. CLU, chartered fin. cons; cert. tchr. Calif. Tchr. Petaluma (Calif.) Ind. Sch. Dist., 1966-68; hostess Welcome Wagon, Inc., 1973; ins. agt. Met. Life, 1974-79, USAA Life, San Antonio, 1980-88, fin. planner, from 1988. Vol. displaced homemakers. 2nd lt. USAF, 1957-58. Republican. Roman Catholic. Avocations: photography, computers. Home: San Antonio, Tex. Deceased.

SHOEMAKER, BILL (WILLIAM LEE SHOEMAKER), retired jockey, horse trainer; b. Fabens, Tex., Aug. 19, 1931; s. B. B. and Ruby (Call) Shoemaker; 1 child, Amanda Elisabeth. Jockey, 1949—90; ret., 1990; horse trainer, 1990—97. Author: Stalking Horse, 1994, Fire Horse, 1995, Dark Horse, 1996. Named winner, Ky. Derby, 1955, 1959, 1965, 1986, Belmont Stakes, 1957, 1959, 1962, 1967, 1975, Preakness Stakes, 1963, 1967. Achievements include Retired with 8,833 wins including over 1000 Stakes wins. Died Oct. 12, 2003.

SHOPE, ROBERT ELLIS, epidemiology educator; b. Princeton, N.J., Feb. 21, 1929; s. Richard Edwin Shope and Helen Madden (Ellis) Flemer; m. Virginia Elizabeth Barbour, Dec. 27, 1958; children: Peter, Steven, Deborah, Bonnie BA, Cornell U., 1951, MD, 1954. Intern then resident Grace-New Haven Hosp., 1954-58; mem. staff Rockefeller Found., Belem, Brazil, 1959-65; dir. Belem Virus Lab., Brazil, 1963-65; from asst. to assoc. prof. epidemiology Yale Sch. Medicine, New Haven, 1965-75, prof., 1975-95; prof. pathology U. Tex. Med. Br., Galveston, 1995—2004. Adv. bd. Gorgas Inst., Panama City, 1972—90; mem. WHO Expert Panel Arboviruses, Geneva, from 1974; U.S. del. U.S.-Japan Coop. Med. Scis. Program, Washington, 1977—2003, Pan Am. Health Orgn. Commn. for Dengue, Washington, 1980. Served to capt. U.S. Army, 1955-57, Southeast Asia Fellow Am. Acad. Microbiology; mem. Am. Soc. Tropical Medicine and Hygiene (pres. 1980, Bailey K. Ashford award 1974, Walter Reed award 1993), Am. Soc. Virology, Am. Soc. Epidemiology, Infectious Diseases Soc. Am. Democrat. Home: Galveston, Tex. Died Jan. 19, 2004.

SHULL, RICHARD BRUCE, actor; b. Evanston, Ill., Feb. 24, 1929; s. Ulysses Homer and Zana Marie (Brown) S.; m. Margaret Ann Haddy, July 14, 1951 (div. 1956); m. Peggy Joan Barringer, June 9, 1957 (div. 1967); m. Marilyn Sandra Swartz, July 6, 1969 (div. 1985); remarried July 7, 1989 (dec. 1997); m. Deborah Lee Thomas, Dec. 12, 1998. BA in Drama, State U. Iowa, 1950; AA in Humanities, Kemper Mil. Sch., 1986. Exec. asst. producer Gordon W. Pollock Prodns., 1953-56; stage mgr. Hyde Park Playhouse, 1954-55; prodn. mgr. Kaufman Auditorium, N.Y.C., 1956; gen. mgr. Music Circle Theatre, Detroit, 1957; prodn. supr. Ford Motor Co. Am. Road Show, 1959; prodn. mgr. (film) Dana Prodns. Inc., 1959-60; dir. Lake Luzerne Playhouse, 1962, 64, Showboat Dinner Theatre, 1968-69; art dir. (film) Tears are for Tomorrow, 1960. Freelance theatrical stage mgr. and dir., N.Y.C., 1950-70; appeared in plays, N.Y.C., including Each in His Own Way, 1950, Wake Up Darling, 1956, Minnie's Boys, 1970, Goodtime Charley (Tony nominee, Drama Desk nomination), 1975, Fools, 1981, Oh, Brother!, 1981, Desire Under the Elms, 1983, Fade the Game, 1984, The Marriage of Bette and Boo (Obie award), 1985, The Front Page, 1986, Opera Comique, 1987, Rough Crossing, 1990, One of the All-Time Greats, 1992, Ain't Broadway Grand, 1993, The Gig, 1994, Victor/Victoria, 1995-97, A Flea In Her Ear, 1998; plays in L.A., including Mr. Ferris and The Model, 1967, The Tempest, 1979; film appearances include The Anderson Tapes and B.S., I Love You, 1970, Hail to the Chief and Such Good Friends, 1971, Slither and Ssssss, 1972, Cockfighter, 1974, The Fortune, The Black Bird and The Big Bus, 1975, The Pack, 1977, Lovesick, 1983, Spring Break, 1983, Unfaithfully Yours, 1984, Splash, 1984, Garbo Talks, 1984, My Blue Heaven, 1990, Tune in Tomorrow, 1990, Housesitter, 1992, For Love or Money, 1993, Trapped in Paradise, 1994, Café Society, 1995, Private Parts, 1996, Two Family House, 1999—; appearances on TV include Your Hit Parade, 1950, Robert Montgomery Presents, 1950, Diana, 1973, Ironsides, 1975, Goodtimes, 1975, Holmes and YoYo, 1976, The Rockford Files, 1978, Ziegfeld, A Man and His Women, 1978, Studs Lonigan, 1979, Hart to Hart, 1979, Lou Grant, 1980, The Ropers, 1980, Alice, 1980, Nurse, 1981, Will There Really Be a Morning?, 1982, The Boy Who Loved Trolls, 1984, Keeping the Faith, 1984, Seize the Day, 1985, The Conan O'Brien Show, 1993, As the World Turns, 1997; dir. Man Without a Shadow, 1958; author: motion picture story and screenplay Aroused, 1964, Pamela, Pamela You Are, 1967; program dir. Armed Forces Radio Sta. GYPSY; created AFKN Network program Concert in Jazz. Served with U.S. Army, 1951-53, Korea. Mem. AFTRA, Actors Equity Assn. (founding editl. bd., constl. rev. com. 1975), Screen Actors Guild, Acad. Motion Picture Arts and Scis., Episcopal Actors Guild (life), Actors Fund (life), SR, Soc. Colonial Wars, St. Nicholas Soc. (steward, bd. mgrs.), N.Y. Vet. Corps. Artillery (councillor), Gen. Soc. War of 1812 (pres. N.Y. State soc.), Colonial Order Acorn, Sons of Union Vets, Civil War (treas. Tilden Camp), First Families Ohio, Soc., Ind. Pioneers, Pioneer Assn. State Wash., Sons. Am. Colonists (gov. N.Y. chpt.), Hon. Order Ky. Cols., Lambs Club (life), Players Club, Friars Club, Dutch Treat Club, Univ. Club (N.Y.C.), Sloane Club (London), India House (N.Y.C.), Ends of the Earth, Pumpkin Papers Irregulars, Baker St. Irregulars. Democrat. Avocation: antique autos and railroading. Home: New York, NY. Died Oct. 14, 1999.

SHULTZ, SHELLEY MARLENE, probation officer; b. Warren, Ohio, Nov. 10, 1952; d. Archie Gilbert and Martha (Petrovich) DeCapite; m. John Franklin, May 5, 1979; children: Christopher John Shultz, Ashley Lisbeth Shultz. BS in Corrections, Youngstown State U., 1974. Probation officer Mahoning County Juvenile Ct., Youngstown, Ohio, 1974-79, restitution investigator, 1979-84, intake officer, 1984-87, chief probation officer, from 1987. Bd. dirs. Diagnostic & Evaluation Clinic, Youngstown, 1989—; mem. meeting mgtm. Fortnightly III, Youngstown, 1987, PTA, Youngstown, 1985. Mem. Jr. League Youngstown (fund raising), Mahoning County Bar Aux. (membership chmn. 1980), Am. Corrections Assn., Nat. Inst. Corrections, Ohio Juvenile Ct. and Detention Workers Assn., Gov.'s Coun., Cath. Collegiate (membership chmn. 1985-86). Democrat. Roman Catholic. Home: Youngstown, Ohio. Died Nov. 3, 2001.

SHUMEJDA, JOHN M. agricultural products executive; BS in Automotive Engring., Western Mich. U., 1969. Mgr. ea. regionsl Uniroyal, inc.; mgr. sales, product devel., truck sales, fleet mktg. Internat. Harvester Co., 1970-83; sr. v.p., sales AGCO Corp, Duluth, Ga., 1983-98, pres., CEO, 1998—2002. Died Jan. 4, 2002.

SICKELS, ROBERT JUDD, political science educator; b. Nyack, N.Y., June 26, 1931; s. Robert and Dorothy (Judd) S.; m. Alice Esterer; children: Stephen Judd, Wendy. BA, U. Chgo., 1950, MA, 1954; PhD, Johns Hopkins U., 1960. Asst. staff dir. Pres.'s Commn. on Registration and Voting Participation, Washington, 1963-64; asso. dir. exec. insts. U.S. CSC, Washington, 1964-65; asso. prof. polit. sci. Purdue U., West Lafayette, Ind., 1965-68; assoc. prof. polit. sci. U. N.Mex., Albuquerque, 1968-73, prof., 1973-95, prof. emeritus, from 1995, chmn. dept., 1976-81. Author: Race, Marriage, and the Law, 1972, Presidential Transactions, 1974, The Presidency, 1980, John Paul Stevens and The Constitution: The Search for Balance, 1988; contbr. articles to profl. jours. Home: Albuquerque, N.Mex. Died June 12, 2003; Vista Verde Crematory.

SICKLES, CARLTON RALPH, employee benefit consultant; b. Hamden, Conn., June 15, 1921; s. Carlton Wilbur and Louise Edith (Torelli) S.; m. Simone Semailovna Shornick, Feb. 16, 1947 (dec. Jan. 1990); 1 child, Simone Louise Rockstroh; m. Jacqueline Bridewell Eig, Mar. 4, 1997. BSS cum laude, Georgetown U., 1943, JD, 1948. Bar: Md. Asst. gen. counsel United Mine Workers of Am. Welfare/Retirement Fund, 1949-51; atty., 1952-89; ptnr. Carday Assocs., Inc., 1952-59, part owner, v.p. and sec., 1960-70, pres., 1970-97, sr. v.p., from 1997; ptnr. Goldberg, Thompson, Pasternak & Sickles, 1979-86. Gen. counsel Internat. Assn. of Heat and Frost Insulators and Asbestos Workers, 1954-63; adj. prof. Georgetown U. Law Sch., 1960-67; mem. U.S. Congress, 1963-67, Md. Congress-at-Large; del. Md. Constnl. Conv., 1967-68, Md. Ho. of Dels., 1955-62, chmn. labor com., 1959-62; profl. neutral trustee United Mine Workers Combined Health Fund, 1993-98; pension reporter, mem. adv. com. Bur. Nat. Affairs, 1976-84. Bd. dirs. Washington Met. Area Transit Authority, 1967-73, chmn. 1971, alt. dir. 1975-78, 81—; commr. Washington Suburban Transit Commn., 1967-73, chmn. 1967, 75-79, chmn. 1977, 81—, chmn. 1992; mem. Internat. Met. R.R.s Com., Internat. Union of Pub. Transit, 1987—; commr. Md. State Planning Commn., 1969-80; mem. Washington Met. Coun. of Govts., chmn. 1962, 63; mem. Joint Commn. to Study Passenger Carrier Facilities in Met. Washington Area, 1955-66; chmn. Coun. of Govts. adv. com. on health info. systems, 1973-76; mem. U.S. Dept. HEW task force, 1974; bd. dirs. Prince George's Gen. Hosp. and Med. Ctr., 1974-76; chmn. Gov.'s Commn. to Study the Md. Pub. Svc. Commn., 1977-80; bd. dirs. Assn. of Pvt. Pension and Welfare Plans, Inc., 1969-79, pres., 1975-77, numerous others; bd. mem. Strathmore Found. Art Ctr., Montgomery County, 1980—, treas., 1989—; bd. dirs. Internat. Found. Employee Benefit Plans, 1965-67, 69-74, pres., chmn. bd., 1974, mem. various coms., 1974—; mem. nat. coordinating com. Multi-Employer Plans, chmn. adminstrs. adv. com., 1976—. Served in U.S. Army, Inf., 1943-46, USAF, 1951-52, Korea. Mem. D.C. Bar assn., Prince George's County Bar Assn., Former Mems. of Congress (bd. dirs. 1965-67, 69-74, bd.d irs. 1965-67, 69-74, pres., chmn. bd. 1974, counselor 1983—), Cosmos Club Washington. Democrat. Roman Catholic. Avocations: music, photography. Home: North Bethesda, Md. Died Jan. 2004.

SIDGMORE, JOHN, telecommunications executive; BA in Econ., SUNY, 1973. V.p., gen. mgr. GE Info. Svc. GEIS N.Am.; pres., CEO CSC Intelicom (formerly Intelicom Solutions), 1989-91, CEO, 1989-94; pres., CEO UUNET Techs. (now WorldCom Inc.), 1994-96; pres. (after merger) UUNET and MFS Comm. Co., 1996; vice chmn., COO WorldCom, Inc., 1996—2002, pres., 2002, consultant, 2002—03. Died Dec. 11, 2003.

SIDGMORE, JOHN W. former telecommunications executive; b. Suffern, NY, Apr. 9, 1951; BA in Econs., SUNY, 1973. With Litton Industries; v.p., gen. mgr. GE Info. Svcs., Rockville, Md.; pres., CEO CSC Intelicom, Bethesda, Md., 1991-94, UUNET Tech., Inc., Falls Church, Va., 1994-2000; chmn. bd. dirs. Strategy.com Personal Intelligence Network, Vienna, Va., 2000—02; pres., CEO WorldCom, Clinton, Miss., 2002. Died Dec. 11, 2003.

SIEGEL, MARTIN, history educator; b. Jan. 27, 1928; BA, Rutgers Coll., 1949; MA, Columbia U., 1950, PhD, 1965. Prof. history Kean U., Union, N.J., from 1960. Nat. corr. U.S.A. Internat. Commn. History and Theory Historiography, 1980—. Home: Swartswood, NJ. Died Oct. 26, 2000.

SIEMANKOWSKI, FRANCIS THEODORE, geology educator; b. Buffalo, Nov. 12, 1914; s. Frank and Rose (Rusinski) S.; m. Stephanie Theresa Zajaczek, May 16, 1942; children: Raymond, Michael. BS, Buffalo State Tchrs. Coll., 1939; MEd, U. Buffalo, 1950; EdD, SUNY, Buffalo, 1970. Cert. secondary tchr., N.Y. Sci., English tchr. Sloan (N.Y.) High Sch., 1939-41; sci. tchr. J.F. Kennedy High Sch., Cheektowaga, N.Y., 1946-63; coord. East European and Slavic studies program State U. Coll., Buffalo, 1974-79, prof. dept. geoscience, physics, interdisciplinary sci., 1964-79, prof. emeritus, from 1979. Cons. U.S. Tchr. Corps, Buffalo, 1971-73, U.S. Peace Corp, Afghanistan Sci. program, Buffalo, 1971-73, Individualized Instrn., Buffalo, 1970-79. Author: College Geology Textbook, 1976, Study Guide to College Geology, 1976, Physical Geology Laboratory Manual, 1971; contbr. articles to profl. jours. Pres. St. Vincent de Paul Soc., 1960-65. Capt. U.S. Army, 1941-45. Recipient L'Ordre Du Merite Culturel, Ministry of Culture, Warsaw, Poland, 1975. Mem. Nat. Assn. Geology Tchrs., N.Y. Acad. Sci, Polish Am. Hist. Assn., Polish Inst. Arts and

Scis. in Am., Kosciuszko Found. Western N.Y. (dir. 1990), Phi Delta Kappa (pres. 1962). Democrat. Roman Catholic. Avocations: reading, music, sports. Home: Tucson, Ariz. Died Jan. 21, 2001.

SIESS, CHESTER PAUL, civil engineering educator; b. Alexandria, La., July 28, 1916; s. Leo C. and Adele (Liebreich) S.; m. Helen Kranson, Oct. 5, 1941; 1 dau., Judith Ann. BS, La. State U., 1936; MS, U. Ill., 1939, PhD, 1948. Party chief La. Hwy. Commn., 1936-37; research asst. U. Ill., 1937-39; soil engr. Chgo. Subway Project, 1939-41; engr., draftsman N.Y.C. R.R. Co., 1941; mem. faculty U. Ill., 1941—, prof. civil engring., 1955-78, emeritus, head dept. civil engring., 1973-78. Mem. adv. com. on reactor safeguards Nuclear Regulatory Commn., 1968-92, chmn., 1972 Recipient award Concrete Reinforcing Steel Inst., 1956, Alumni Honor award for disting. service in engring. U. Ill., 1985, Disting. Service award NRC, 1987; named to Engring. Hall of Distinction, La. State U., 1979. Mem. ASCE (hon. mem., Rsch. prize 1956, Howard medal 1968, Reese award 1970), Nat. Acad. Engring., Am. Concrete Inst. (pres. 1974-75, Wason medal 1949, Turner medal 1964, hon. mem.), Reinforced Concrete Rsch. coun. (chmn. 1968-80, Boase award 1974), Internat. Assn. Bridge and Structural Engring., Sigma Xi, Tau Beta Pi, Phi Kappa Phi, Omicron Delta Kappa, Gamma Alpha, Chi Epsilon (chap. hon., nat. hon.). Achievements include research in reinforced and prestressed concrete structures and hwy. bridges. Home: Savoy, Ill. Died Jan. 14, 2004.

SIEVERTS, FRANK ARNE, association executive; b. Frankfurt, Fed. Republic Germany, June 19, 1933; s. Helmut J. and Cecile M. (Behrendt) S.; m. Jane Woodbridge, Dec. 31, 1957 (div.); children: Lisa, Michael; m. Sue Hubbell, Feb. 13, 1988; 1 stepchild, Brian. BA, Swarthmore Coll., 1955; PhB (Rhodes Scholar), Balliol Coll. Oxford U., 1957; postgrad., Nuffield Coll., 1957-59. News corr. Time mag., London and Washington, 1959-60; legis. asst. U.S. Senator Washington, 1960-62; with Dept. of State, Washington, 1962-86, spl. asst. to ambassador at large Averell Harriman, 1966-68, adviser on prisoners of war to U.S. delegation to Vietnam peace talks, spl. asst. to dep. sec. of state for prisoners of war., 1969-75, dep. asst. sec. for prisoners of war and missing in action, 1976—78, dep. asst. sec. for refugee and migration affairs, 1978—80; minister-counselor for humanitarian affairs U.S. Mission, Geneva, 1980-81; spl. asst. for refugee programs, 1982-86; spokesman for Com. on Fgn. Relations U.S. Senate, 1987-95; asst. to head of delegation for U.S., Can. Internat. Com. Red Cross, Washington, 1995—2004. Mem. advance team for release Am. prisoners of war, Hanoi, 1973. Mem. U.S. delegation to 20th Internat. Conf. Red Cross, Vienna, 1965, 21st Conf., Istanbul, 1969, 22d Conf., Tehran, 1973; chmn. 23d Conf., Bucharest, 1977, 24th Conf., Manila, 1981, 25th Conf., Geneva, 1986; U.S. del. Diplomatic Conf. on Humanitarian Law in Armed Conflicts, Geneva, 1974-77, to exec. com. of UN High Commn. for Refugees, 1978, 79, 80; staff dir. Indochinese Refugee panel, 1986. Mem. Am. Assn. Rhodes Scholars (bd. dirs.). Died Mar. 31, 2004.

SIGWARD, ANGELA MARIA, social services administrator; b. N.Y.C., Dec. 28, 1908; d. Vincent and Maria (Armato) Cosumano; m. Roderick Sigward, Feb. 4, 1942 (dec. 1966); children: Ellen, Eric. BA, Hunter Coll., 1930; MA, Columbia U., 1934, MSW, 1939; postgrad., William Alanson White Inst., 1959. Lic. social worker, N.Y. Social worker, supr. Community Svc. Soc., N.Y.C., 1931-38, Eastchester Neighborhood Assn. and Child Guidance Clinic, Tuckahoe, N.Y., 1939-42; dir. Family Svc. Jersey City, 1944-46; supr. Maimonides Hosp., Bklyn., 1957-59; psychiat. social worker Jewish Bd. Guardians, N.Y.C., 1959-60; asst. dir., dep. dir. N.Y.C. Youth Bd., 1960-73; sr. svc. adminstr., acting dir. dept. social svc. Group Health, Inc.-Homemaking Svc., N.Y.C., 1973-79; pvt. practice, cons. N.Y.C., from 1980. Mem. Messinger's Sr. Adv. Com., N.Y.C., 1990— . Mem. Nat. Assn. Social Workers (chair subcom. ret. social workers 1989—). Home: New York, NY. Died Jan. 7, 2002.

SILVERBLATT, ARTHUR, lawyer; b. Wilkes-Barre, Pa., July 27, 1910; s. Jacob and Henrietta (Menkle) S.; m. Elizabeth Friend, Apr. 27, 1946; children— Anne Silverblatt Greenwald, Arthur F. A.B., Harvard U., 1930, J.D., 1933. Bar: Pa. 1934, U.S. Dist. Ct. (11th dist.) Pa. 1934, U.S. Ct. Appeals (3d cir.). Sole practice, Wilkes-Barre, 1933-50; ptnr. Silverblatt & Townend, Wilkes-Barre, 1950—; 1st asst. dist. atty. Luzerne County, Pa., 1955-59; dir. Pa. Millers Mut. Ins. Co., 1968—, also gen. counsel. Chmn. Luzerne County Mental Health Bd., 1968-71; Luzerene County Bicentennial Commn., 1975-76; pres. Osterhout Free Library, 1978-81; mem. Family Service Assn. bd. Children's Service Ctr.; pres. Wyoming Valley United Fund, 1963-64. Served to capt. AUS, 1942-46. Recipient Award of Merit, Pa. Mental Health, 1966; Citation NCCJ, 1964. Mem. Wilkes-Barre Law and Library Assn., Pa. Bar Assn., ABA, Am. Bar Found., Internat. Assn. Ins. Counsel, Wyoming Valley C. of C. (pres. 1969-70). Republican. Jewish. Club: Westmoreland (Wilkes-Barre). Home: Kingston, Pa. Died May 30, 1994.

SILVERMAN, FRANKLIN HAROLD, speech pathologist, educator; b. Providence, Aug. 16, 1933; s. Meyer and Reba (Sack) Silverman; m. Ellen-Marie Loebel, Feb. 1, 1967 (div. Feb. 1981); 1 child, Catherine; m. Evelyn Ellen Chanda, Nov. 13, 1983. BS in Speech, Emerson Coll., 1960; MA, Northwestern U., 1961; PhD, U. Iowa, 1966. Lic. speech-lang. pathologist Wis. Rsch. assoc. U. Iowa, Iowa City, 1965-67; asst. prof. U. Ill., Champaign, 1968-71; assoc. prof. Marquette U., Milw., 1971-77, prof., from 1978; clin. prof. Med. Coll. Wis., Wauwatosa, from 1978. Mem. adv. bd. Wis. Telecomm. Relay Svcs., Madison, from 1991; cons. USAID Palestinian Speech Pathology Tng. Program, Gaza City, from 1993, Joint Centre for Rsch. Prosthetics and Orthotics and Rehab. Programmes, Riyadh, Saudi Arabia, from 1995, Disabled Children's Assn., Riyadh, Saudi Arabia, from 1998. Author: Speech, Language, and Hearing Disorders, 1995, Communication for the Speechless, 3d edit, 1995, Stuttering and Other Fluency Disorders, 2d edit., 1996, Computer Applications for Augmenting the Management of Speech, Language and Hearing Disorders, 1997, Research Design and Evaluation in Speech-Language Pathology and Audiology, 4th edit., 1998, Authoring Books and Materials for Students, Academics, and Professionals, 1998, Telecommunication Relay Service Handbook, 1999, Professional Issues in Speech-Language Pathology and Audiology, 1999, Fundamentals of Electronics for Speech Language Pathologists and Audiologists, 1999, Publishing for Tenure and Beyond, 1999, Self-Publishing Books and Materials for Students, Academics and Professionals, 1999, Second Thoughts About Stuttering, 2000, Teaching for Tenure and Beyond, 2001, The Impact of a Unique Cooperative American University USAID Funded Speech-Language Pathologist, Audiologist and Deaf Educator BS Degree Program in the Gaza Strip, 2002, Essentials of Speech, Language, and Hearing Disorders, 2002, Essentials of Professional Issues in Speech-Language Pathology and Audiology, 2003; contbr. numerous rsch. papers to profl. jours. Fellow: Text and Acad. Authors Assn. (sec. 1993—94, pres.-elect 1996, pres. 1997), Am. Speech-Lang.-Hearing Assn. Jewish. Avocation: photography. Home: Greendale, Wis. Died Dec. 10, 2003.

SILVERMAN, HERBERT R. corporate financial executive; b. N.Y.C., June 10, 1914; s. Jacob and Minnie (Stein) S.; m. Roslyn Moskowitz, Dec. 17, 1933 (dec. Dec. 1965); children: Karen Silverman Mayers, Henry; m. Nadia Gray, Oct. 17, 1967 (dec. June 1994). BS, NYU, 1932; JD, St. Lawrence U., 1935. Bar: N.Y. bar 1935. Organizer, pres. Centaur Credit Corp. (merged with James Talcott, Inc. of N.Y.), 1945; v.p. James Talcott, Inc., 1944-46, exec. v.p., 1956-58, dir., 1956-75, pres., 1958-64, chmn. bd., chief exec. officer, 1961-73; chmn., chief exec. officer Talcott Nat. Corp., 1968-73, also chmn. exec. com., dir., 1968-75. Pres. Nat. Comml. Fin. Conf., 1948-52, chmn., 1952-58; sr. advisor Bank Julius Baer; adj. prof. fin. NYU Coll. Bus. and Pub. Adminstrn., 1973—; trustee med. ctr., vice chmn. bd. NYU. Named Man of Yr. banking and finance Phi Alpha Kappa; recipient Golden Medallion for humanitarian services B'nai B'rith, Albert Gallatin award NYU, 1978 Mem. ABA, N.Y. Bar Assn., N.Y. Univ. Alumni Fedn. (pres. 1958-60), Phi Alpha Kappa, Iota Theta. Clubs: Harmonie (N.Y.C.); N.Y. Univ. (past pres.). Home: New York, NY. Died Aug. 21, 2003.

SILVERMAN, JOSEPH ROBERT, electrical engineer, educator; b. Lawrence, Mass., July 31, 1936; s. Jacob David and Norma (Illman) S.; m. Hedda Leah Medjuck, Apr. 1, 1967; children: Jeffrey David, Brian Norman. BSEE, Northeastern U., 1959; MS in Engring., George Washington U., 1968, DSc, 1977. Student engr. Tung-Sol Elec., Bloomfield, N.J., 1956-59; elec. engr. U.S. Army/Signal Corps, Ft. Monmouth, N.J., 1960-62, Nat. Aero. and Space Adminstrn., Greenbelt, Md., 1962-72, Nat. Oceanic and Atmospheric Adminstrn., Suitland, Md., 1972-83; supervisory elec. engr. Gen. Svcs. Adminstrn., Washington, 1983-85; ops. data mgr. Hubble space telescope Nat. Aero. and Space Adminstrn./Goddard Space Flight Ctr., Greenbelt, 1985-91; program mgr. Earth Observing Sys. Nat. Aero. and Space Adminstrn./Headquarters, Washington, from 1991. Adj. prof. George Washington U., Washington, 1970—. Patentee programmable telemetry system. 1st Lt. Signal Corps U.S. Army. Recipient Invention awards NASA, 1969, 70, 80, Group Achievement awards. Mem. IEEE (sr.), AAAS. Avocations: photography, woodworking, electronics, aerobics, biking. Home: Silver Spring, Md. Died Dec. 16, 2000.

SILVERMAN, SAMUEL, psychiatrist; b. Boston, Aug. 29, 1912; s. Harry and Fannie (Messing) S.; m. Edith R. Levine, 1942 (div. 1970); children: Harry J., Neil M. BA, Harvard U., 1933, MD, 1938. Diplomate Am. Bd. Psychiatry and Neurology. Med. intern Boston City Hosp., 1939-40; jr. and sr. physician in psychiatry Boston State Hosp., 1940-42; asst. chief neuropsychiat. svc. Cushing VA Hosp., Framingham, Mass., 1946-52; chief psychosomatic sect. VA Hosp., Boston, 1952-59; attending psychiatrist McLean Hosp., Belmont, Mass., 1959-63, dir. clin. psychiatry, 1963-65; pvt. practice Boston and Brookline, Mass., from 1946. Asst. prof. psychiatry Tufts U. and Boston U. Med. Schs., 1952-60; asst. clin. prof. psychiatry Harvard U. Med. Sch., Boston, 1961-73, assoc. clin. prof. psychiatry, 1973-79; hon. psychiatrist Mass. Gen. Hosp., 1980—; tng. analyst Boston Psychoanalytic Soc.-Inst., Psychoanalytic Inst. New England East. Author: Psychological Aspects of Physical Symptoms, 1968, Psychological Cues in Forecasting Physical Symptoms, 1970, How Will You Feel Tomorrow?, 1973; frequentcontbr. articles to profl. jours. Lt. to maj. U.S. Army, 1942-46. Fellow Am. Psychoanalytic Assn. (cert. bd. profl. stds.), Am. Psychiat. Assn., Internat. Psycho-Analytic Assn., Mass. Med. Soc. Avocation: gardening. Home: Canton, Mass. Died Jan. 30, 2002.

SIMBRO, WILLIAM CHARLES, journalist; b. Eldon, Iowa, Mar. 9, 1933; s. Elmer Leroy and Miriam Edna (Sheldon) S.; m. Shirley Jo Taylor Hunt, Jan. 18, 1976 (div. Apr. 1990); children: Robert Paul, David William. BA, William Penn Coll., 1956; MDiv, Garrett-Evang. Theol. Sem., 1961; postgrad., U. Iowa, 1958-59, 65-66. Ordained to ministry Meth. Ch., 1962. Pastor Ainsworth (Iowa) Meth. Ch., 1960-64, Coralville (Iowa) Meth. Ch., 1964-66; reporter Cedar Rapids (Iowa) Gazette, 1966-67; chief Cedar Rapids bur. The Des Moines Register, 1967-76, religion writer, 1976—98. Cons. Rockefeller Found., N.Y.C., 1980. Contbr. articles to profl. jours. Former mem. bd. dirs. Moingona coun. Girl Scouts U.S. Recipient Faith and Freedom award Religious Heritage Am., 1980. Mem. Religion Newswriters Assn. (treas. 1980-82, Supple Meml. award 1978). Avocations: power walking, traveling, radio reading to the blind. Home: West Des Moines, Iowa. Died Mar. 20, 2004.

SIMON, JULIAN LINCOLN, economics educator; b. Newark, Feb. 12, 1932; s. Philip Mordechai and Mae (Goodstein) S.; m. Rita Mintz James, June 25, 1961; children: David Meyer, Judith Debs, Daniel Hillel. BA, Harvard U., 1953; MBA, U. Chgo., 1960, PhD, 1961. Advt. copywriter William Douglas McAdams Inc., N.Y.C., 1956; with sale promotion Ziff-Davis Pub. Co., N.Y.C., 1957-61; owner Julian Simon Assocs., Newark, 1961-63; prof. econs., mktg. and advt. U. Ill., Urbana, from 1963; now prof. mgmt. U. Md., College Park, from 1983. Prof. Hebrew U., Jerusalem, 1968, 70-71, 74-75. Author: How to Start and Operate a Mail-Order Business, 1965, 4th edit., 1986, Basic Research Methods in Social Science, 1969, 3d edit., 1985; (with Herman H. Fussler) Patterns of Use of Books in Large Research Libraries, 1969; Issues in the Economics of Advertising, 1970, The Management of Advertising, 1971, The Effects of Income on Fertility, 1974, Applied Managerial Economics, 1975, The Economics of Population Growth, 1977, The Ultimate Resource, 1981, Theory of Population and Economic Growth, 1986, Effort, Opportunity, and Wealth, 1987, The Economic Consequences of Immigration, 1989, Population Matters: People, Resources, Environment and Immigration, 1990, editor: Research in Population Economics, Vol. I, 1978, Vol. II (with Julie daVanzo), 1978, Vol. III (with Peter Lindert), Vol. IV (with Peter Lindert), 1982, (with Herman Kahn) The Resourceful Earth: A Response to the Global 2000 Report, 1984. Served to lt. (j.g.) USN, 1953-56. Mem. Am. Statis. Assn., Am. Econ. Assn., Pop Assn. Am., Population Assn. Am. Jewish. Home: Chevy Chase, Md. Died Feb. 8, 1998.

SIMON, PAUL, former senator, educator, writer; b. Eugene, Oreg., Nov. 29, 1928; s. Martin Paul and Ruth (Troemel) S.; m. Jeanne Hurley, Apr. 21, 1960 (dec. Feb. 20, 2000); children: Sheila, Martin; m. Patricia Derge, May 20, 2001. Student, U. Oreg., 1945-46, Dana Coll., Blair, Nebr., 1946-48; 55 hon. doctorates. Pub. Troy (Ill.) Tribune and 12 other So. Ill. weeklies., 1948-66; mem. Ill. Ho. of Reps., 1955-63, Ill. Senate, 1963-69; lt. gov. Ill., 1969-73; fellow John F. Kennedy Sch. Govt., Harvard U., 1972-73; founded pub. affairs reporting program Sangamon State U., Springfield, Ill., 1972-73; mem. 94th-98th Congresses from 22d and 24th Dists. 94th-98th Congresses from 24th and 22d Dists. Ill., Ill., 1975-85; U.S. Senator from Ill., 1985-96; dir. Pub. Policy Inst. So. Ill. U., from 1996. U.S. presdl. candidate, 1987-88. Author: Lovejoy: Martyr to Freedom, 1964, Lincoln's Preparation for Greatness, 1965, A Hungry World, 1966, You Want to Change the World, So Change It, 1971, The Tongue-Tied American, 1980, The Once and Future Democrats, 1982, The Glass House: Politics and Morality in The Nation's Capitol, 1984, Beginnings, 1986, Let's Put America Back to Work, 1986, Winners and Losers, 1989, (with Jeanne Hurley Simon) Protestant-Catholic Marriages Can Succeed, 1967, (with Arthur Simon) The Politics of World Hunger, 1973, Advice and Consent, 1992, Freedom's Champion: Elijah Lovejoy, 1994, The Dollar Crisis (with Ross Perot), 1996, Tapped Out: The Coming World Crisis in Water and What We Can Do About It, 1998, Autobiography of Paul Simon, 1999, (with Michael Dukakis) How to Get Into Politics and Why, 2000. With CIC, AUS, 1951-53. Recipient Am. Polit. Sci. Assn. award, 1957, Harry Truman Pub. Svc. award, 2003; named Best Legislator by Ind. Voters of Ill., 7 times. Mem. Luth. Human Rels. Assn., Am. Legion, VFW, NAACP, Urban League. Democrat. Lutheran. Home: Makanda, Ill. Died Dec. 9, 2003.

SIMONE, NINA (EUNICE WAYMON), singer; b. Tyron, N.C., Feb. 21, 1933; Student, Julliard Sch. of Music; HHD (hon.), Malcolm X U.; MusD (hon.), U. Mass. Ind. jazz vocalist, rec. artist, from 1959. Albums include Baltimore, Here Comes the Sun, It's Finished, Pure Gold, The Best of Nina Simone, Nina Simone Sings the Blues, The Most Beautiful Songs of...Nina Simone, Nina's Back; songs include I Loves You, Porgy, I Put a Spell On You, Ain't Got No-I Got Life, Mississippi Goddam, Compensation, The Backlash Blues, To Be Young, Gifted and Black, Four Women. Died Apr. 21, 2003.

SIMONSON, HANA MALKA, coordinator special education program; b. Bklyn., Apr. 10, 1929; d. Charles and Shifra (Kalech) Gutwillig; m. Solomon Simonson, Jan. 27, 1957; children: Charles, Rayze, Alexander. BA, Bklyn. Coll., 1953; MS, CUNY, 1959; PhD, Columbia U., 1972. Cert. impartial hearing officer, tchr., spl. edn. tchr., sch. psychologist, N.Y. Instr. Psychology Rockland C.C., Rockland County, N.Y., 1964-65; rsch. cons. Ctr. for Urban Edn., N.Y.C., 1966; rsch. assoc. Columbia U., N.Y.C., 1970-73; coord., prof. Spl. Edn. CUNY, Jamaica, from 1973. Project assoc. grants HEW, Jamaica, 1975-77, assoc. dir. grants N.Y. Edn. Dept. Bilingual Spl. Edn., 1980-82. Speaker Bur. Child Protective Svcs., Rockland County, 1982-84. Columbia U. fellow, N.Y.C., 1967-70. Mem. APA, Coun. Exceptional Children, Am. Edn. Rsch. Assn. Home: Englewood, NJ. Died Apr. 26, 2001.

SIMPSON, JAMES JAY BEASLEY, priest, journalist; b. Mansfield, Ark., Sept. 13, 1926; s. Earl H. and Elsie Marjorie (Simpson) Beasley. BSc in Journalism, Northwestern U., 1949; postgrad., U. Edinburgh, U.K., 1951; Licentiate in Theology, Nashotah House, 1967. Ordained priest Episcopal Ch., 1967. News editor INS, UPI, AP, NBC, N.Y.C., 1949-54; account exec. Grant Advt., Ellington Co., BBDO, Columbia Gas, N.Y.C., 1954-64; curate Christ Ch., Rye, N.Y., 1967-70, rector Middletown, N.J., 1970-80; dir. Episcopal Book Club, 1980-84; editor Anglican Digest, 1980-84; assoc. St. Michael's Ch., N.Y.C., 1983-86; interim rector St. Alban's Ch., Tokyo, 1991; assoc. Ascension and St. Agnes, Washington, from 1988; chaplain Georgetown Retirement Residence, from 1990; Washington corr. Church Times, London, from 1988, The Living Ch., Milw., from 1995. Author: The Hundredth Archbishop of Canterbury, 1962, Regent of the Sea, 1988, Veil and Cowl, 1988; (with Edward M. Story) The Long Shadows of Lambeth X, 1969, Stars in His Crown: A Chronicle of the Community of St. John Baptist Told in the Context of the History of Religious Orders in the Episcopal Church, 1976, Discerning God's Will: Lambeth 1978, 1979; (with Robert A.K. Runcie) Seasons of the Spirit, 1983; Veil and Cowl, 1994; (with George H. Eatman) A Treasury of Anglican Art, 1998; editor continuing edits. Simpson's Contemporary Quotations, 1957, 64, 88, 97; contbr. articles to profl. jours. Paul Harris fellow Rotary Internat., 1950-51, Rsch. fellow Kaltenborn Found., 1953, Resident fellow MacDowell Colony, 1966. Mem. Cosmos Club (Washington), Sigma Delta Chi. Died Mar. 11, 2002.

SIMPSON, JOHN ALEXANDER, physicist; b. Portland, Oreg., Nov. 3, 1916; s. John A. and Janet (Br) S.; m. Elizabeth Alice Hilts, Nov. 30, 1946 (div. Sept. 1977); children: Mary Ann, John Alexander; m. Elizabeth Scott Johnson, Aug. 23, 1980. AB, Reed Coll., 1940, D.Sc. (hon.), 1981; MS, NYU, 1942, PhD, 1943. Research assoc. OSRD, 1941-42; sci. group leader Manhattan Project, 1943-46; instr. U. Chgo., 1945-47, asst. prof., 1947-49, assoc. prof., 1949-54, chmn. com. on biophysics, 1951; prof. physics, dept. physics and Fermi Inst. Nuclear Studies, 1954- 68, Edward L. Ryerson Disting. Service prof. physics, 1968-74, Arthur H. Compton Disting. Service prof. physics, 1974-87, Arthur H. Compton Disting. prof. emeritus, from 1987; also dir. Enrico Fermi Inst., 1973-78. Mem. Internat. Com. IGY; chmn. bd. Ednl. Found. Nuclear Sci.; mem. tech. panel cosmic rays NRC; chair Internat. Commn. Cosmic Radiation, 1963-67; mem. astronomy missions bd. NASA, 1968; vis. assoc. physics Calif. Inst. Tech.; vis. scholar U. Calif., Berkeley.; founder Lab. Astrophysics and Space Research in Enrico Fermi Inst., 1962, Space Sci. Working Group, Washington, 1982. Bd. overseers, vis. com. astronomy Harvard; mem. Pres. Ford's Sci. Adv. Group on Sci. Problems, 1975-76; life trustee Adler Planetarium, 1977—. Recipient medal for exceptional sci. achievement NASA, Quantrell award for excellence in teaching, Gagarin medal Nat. Soviet Socialists Rep. Acad. of Scis., Cospar award UN Com. on Space Rsch., 1990, Leo Szilard award Am. Phys. Soc., 1999, O'Ceilleague medal Internat. Union of Pure and Applied Physics, 1999, Foster-Schultz Disting. Svc. award Reed Coll., 2000; fellow Ctr. Policy Study, U. Chgo., Guggenheim fellow, 1972, 84-85; Nora and Edward Ryerson lectr., 1986; A. H. Compton Centennial lectr., 1992. Fellow Am. Acad. Arts and Scis., Am. Geophys. Union (Parker lectr. 1992, William Bowie medal 2000), Am. Phys. Soc. (chmn. cosmic physics div. 1970-71); mem. NAS (elected, mem. space sci. bd., Henryk Arctowski medal and premium 1993), Am. Philosophical Soc. (elected 1996, co-winner First Norman MacLean Faculty award for educating young scientists 1997), Internat. Union Pure and Applied Physics (pres. cosmic ray commn. 1963-67), Atomic Scientists Chgo. (chmn. 1945-46, cofounder, bd. bull. 1945—, pres. bull. bd. sponsors 1993—), Am. Astron. Soc. (Bruno Rossi prize 1991), Internat. Acad. Astronautics, Smithsonian Inst. (Martin Marietta chair in history of space sci. 1987-88, Glennan, Webb, Seamans Group 1986—), Phi Beta Kappa, Sigma Xi (Victor Hess Meml. Lectr. 25th Internat. Cosmic Ray Conf. 1997). Achievements include research in nuclear radiation and instrumentation inventions, also origin of cosmic radiation, solar physics, magnetospheric physics, high energy astrophys. problems, and acceleration and isotopic and elemental composition of charged particles in space; prin. investigator for 33 expts. in earth satellites and deep space probes, also 1st probes to Mercury, Mars, Jupiter and Saturn, fly by at Venus, 9 planetary encounters, comet dust expts. on the 2 Vega spacecraft to Halley's comet, 1986; Ulysses space craft experiments over poles of the sun, 1990—, Pioneer 10 space craft outside solar system to 72 astronomical units. Home: Chicago, Ill. Deceased.

SIMS, JOHN LEROY, gastroenterology and internal medicine educator, physician; b. Houston, Sept. 21, 1912; s. Frank Jacob and Jennie Elisabeth (Ramsay) S.; m. Anne M. Schurch, May 30, 1942; children: John Ernest, Elizabeth Anne, Thomas LeRoy. AB, Rice U., 1933; MD, U. Tex., Galveston, 1937. Diplomate Am. Bd. Internal Medicine. Intern Wis. Gen. Hosp., Madison, 1937-38, resident in medicine, 1939-42; resident Midway Hosp, St. Paul, 1938-39; mem. faculty Sch. Medicine U. Wis., Madison, from 1946, prof. Sch. Medicine, 1959-83, prof. emeritus, from 1983; coord. outreach continuing med. edn. U. Wis. Med. Sch. and Hosps., 1983-95; ret., 1995. With AUS, 1942-46, col. ret. USAR, 1966. Fellow ACP (gov. Wis. 1963-69); mem. AAAS, AMA, Am. Fedn. Clin. Rsch., Cen. Soc. Clin. Rsch., Cen. Clin. Rsch. Club, Wis. Soc. Internal Medicine (pres. 1959-60), Phi Beta Kappa, Sigma Xi, Alpha Omega Alpha. Presbyterian. Home: Madison, Wis. Died Sept. 6, 1999.

SIMS, THOMAS AUBURN, retired shipbuilding company executive; b. Little Rock, Miss., Oct. 20, 1925; s. Thomas Alexander and Evie Jane (Riche) S.; m. Ruby Pearl Graham, Oct. 6, 1946; children: Gloria Jean, Judy Ann, Janet Lea. AA, East Central Jr. Coll., 1948; BS, U. Md., 1957; MBA, Babson Coll., 1962. Commd. 2d lt. U.S. Army, 1949, advanced through grades to lt. col., retired, 1967; asst. to purchasing agt. Ingalls Shipbuilding, Inc., Pascagoula, Miss., 1968-69, purchasing mgr., 1970-77, dir. procurement, 1978-93. Mem. Gov. of Miss. Minority Adv. Bd., Jackson, 1972-75; bd. dirs. Miss. Minority Supplier Devel. Coun., Jackson, 1980-93; deacon, Sunday sch. tchr. 1st Bapt. Ch., Ocean Springs, Miss., 1972—. With USN, 1943-46, PTO. Mem. Nat. Contract Mgmt. Assn. (bd. dirs. 1980-82, mem. coun. fellows 1993), Retired Officers Assn. Avocation: public speaking. Home: Ocean Springs, Miss. Died Feb. 2, 2003; VA Cemetery, Biloxi, Miss..

SIMS, WILLIAM JOSEPHUS, retired military officer, retired college dean; b. Phoenix, Dec. 8, 1920; s. John William and Anita (Neri) S.; m. Mary Louise Rickel, May 31, 1943; children: William J. III, Joseph R., John M., Mary Anita, Bobbye Lou. AA, Phoenix Jr. Coll., 1940; student, Ariz. State U., 1940-41; BS, U. Md., 1958, MS in Internat. Rels., 1967. Commd. 2d lt. USMC, 1939, advanced through grades to col., 1962; comdg. officer Marine Corps Air Sta., Yuma, 1967-70, exec. officer, 1963-63; ret., 1970; prof. govt. Ariz. Western Coll., Yuma, 1970-72, acting pres., 1977; dir., owner, mgr. SIMSCO, Yuma, from 1988; dean instnl. svcs. Ariz. Western Coll., Yuma, 1972-88; exec. sec. Western Coll. Found., Yuma, 1972-86. Advisor model UN student group, 1983-88; staff mem. Yuma County Town Hall, 1985-88; chmn. High Sch. Adv. Coun., Yuma, 1985; chmn. Strategic Planning Group, Yuma, 1989-90; mem. Desert Trails coun. Boy Scouts Am., 1972-77, com. chmn. cub pack 58, Yuma, 1963-64; bd. dirs. United Way Fund, Yuma, 1980-83; mem. parish coun. Immaculate Conception Ch., Yuma, 1970-77, chmn. fin. com., 1972-73; mem. Yuma Fine Arts Assn., 1985-87, Yuma Crossing Park Coun. Recipient Svc. award Yuma Jaycees, 1963, Navy Relief Soc., 1970, various awards troop 95 and Desert Trails coun. Boy Scouts Am., 1970-77, plaque Sr. Fgn. Officers Naval Amphibious Sch., 1970, award Williams AFB, Ariz., 1970; Bill Sims Broadcast Studio named in his honor Sta. KAWC, 1988, nominated Citizen of Yr., Yuma County, 1990. Mem. Caballeros de Yuma (hon.), Optimists (President's Svc. award Yuma 1988). Democrat. Avocations: woodworking, computers, golf, travel. Died Jan. 9, 2002.

SINGER, ALMA I. investor; b. Munich, Jan. 7, 1907; came to U.S., 1936; d. Paul and Lina (Bach) Haimann; m. Walter Wasserman, July, 1927 (div. 1939); children: Inga Dujack, Klaus; m. Isaac Bashevis Singer, Feb. 14, 1940 (dec.). Student, U. Lausanne, Switzerland, 1927, U. Munich. Lectr. Hadassah, Miami, Fla., 1987. Lectr. Womens Club Miami U., Hadassa, others. Mem. Women's Club of Miami U. Republican. Jewish. Avocations: antique collector, reading, animal activist, world traveller, investing. Home: New York, NY. Deceased.

SINGER, MARGARET THALER, research psychologist; b. Denver, July 29, 1921; d. Raymond Willard and Margaret Burke Coleman (McDonough) Thaler; m. Jerome Ralph Singer, June 28, 1956; children— Samuel Robert Thaler, Martha Rachel Thaler. BA, U. Denver, 1943, MA, 1945, PhD, 1952. Med. psychologist U. Colo. Med. Sch., 1945-52; sr. psychologist Walter Reed Army Inst. Research, 1952-58; spl. cons. research asso. NIMH, 1958-73; mem. faculty U. Calif. Med. Sch., San Francisco, 1958-85; former mem. faculty U. Rochester (N.Y.) Med. Sch.; adj. prof. psychology U. Calif., Berkeley, 1964—91, prof. emeritus, 1991—2003. Mem. World Mental Health Assn. com. on victims, 1980 Author papers, reports in field; editorial bd. profl. jours. Recipient Hofheimer prize Am. Psychiat. Assn., 1966, Stanley R. Dean award Am. Coll. Psychiatrists, 1976, McAlpin award U.S. Mental Health Assn., 1977, award Am. Family Therapy Assn., 1981 Mem. Am. Psychosomatic Soc. (pres. 1972-73), Internat. Soc. Polit. Psychology, Am. Psychol. Assn. Died Nov. 23, 2003.

SINGER, RAY ELEAZER, writer; b. N.Y.C., Oct. 24, 1916; s. William Zachary and Esther (Sadolsky) S.; m. Monia Abramson, Oct. 13, 1940; children: Laurie Patricia, John Harris. Student, CCNY, 1934-36. Writer Phil Baker, N.Y.C., 1939, Henny Youngman, N.Y.C., 1939; writer, radio Milton Berle show, Hollywood, Calif., 1941-42, Bing Crosby show, Hollywood, 1942-43, Sealtest Village Store, Hollywood, 1942-47; creator, writer, producer TV series It's a Great Life, Hollywood, 1953-56; writer, radio Phil Harris--Alice Faye show, Hollywood, 1947-53; writer, producer NBC, Hollywood, 1953-57; writer Metro Goldwyn Mayer pictures, Hollywood, 1960-62; TV writer for various performers including Frank Sinatra, Danny Thomas, Jack Benny, Hollywood, 1963-67; producer, writer TV series Joey Bishop Show, 1964; producer TV series Donna Reed show, 1965, No Time for Sargeants, 1966; writer, creator Here's Lucy, Hollywood, 1967-71; freelance playwright Hollywood, 1972-88. Assoc. prof. Calif. State U., Northridge, 1976-77; instr. UCLA, Los Angeles, 1975-88. Recipient Emmy award nomination, 1968. Mem. Pacific Broadcast Pioneers, Nat. Acad. TV Arts and Scis. (bd. govs., nat. trustee 1971-73), Writers Guild Am., Dramatists Guild. Democrat. Jewish. Avocations: golf, swimming. Deceased.

SINGER, SAMUEL L(OEWENBERG), retired journalist; b. Phila., May 2, 1911; s. Benjamin and Hattie May (Loewenberg) S.; m. Betty Janet Levi (dec. 2002), June 12, 1939; children: Ruth Babette, Samuel Lawrence, Robert Benjamin. BS in Journalism, Temple U., 1934. Mem. staff Phila. Inquirer, 1934-81, music editor, 1955-81, emeritus, 1981—, public service editor, 1973-81; tchr. undergrad. journalism course Temple U., 1946-92, tchr. music criticism, 1965-70, adj. prof. journalism, 1973-92. Tchr. theatre and music reviewing Main Line Sch. Night, 1994-2004 Condr. radio program This Week's Music, 1961-72; author: Reviewing the Performing Arts, 1973. Organist Congregation Temple Judea, 1933-41, Phila. Ethical Soc., 1942-56, Main Line Reform Temple, 1951-55, Beth Israel, Phila., 1956-65, Coatesville, Pa., 1966-88, Zion Evang. Luth. Ch., 1956-82, St. Matthew's Evang. Luth. Ch., 1972-82, IHS Episcopal Ch., Drexel Hill, Pa, 1984-99, emeritus, 1999—. Served with USNR, 1943-45. Named Outstanding 1934 Journalism Alumnus, Temple U., 1988. Mem. Am. Guild Organists (editor Phila. chpt. publ. Crescendo 1971-76), Newspaper Guild, Phila. Press Assn., Mus. Fund Soc. Phila., Music Critics Assn., Phila. Orch. Assn., Sigma Delta Chi (life) Home: Wynnewood, Pa. Died May 31, 2004.

SINGLETARY, OTIS ARNOLD, JR., university president emeritus; b. Gulfport, Miss., Oct. 31, 1921; s. Otis Arnold and May Charlotte (Walker) S.; m. Gloria Walton, June 6, 1944; children: Bonnie, Scot, Kendall Ann. BA, Millsaps Coll., 1947; MA, La State U., 1949, PhD, 1954. Mem. faculty U. Tex., Austin, 1954-61, prof. history, 1960-61, assoc. dean Sch. Arts and Scis., 1956-59, asst. to pres., 1960-61; chancellor U. N.C., Greensboro, 1961-66; v.p. Am. Council on Edn., Washington, 1966-68; on leave as dir. Job Corps, OEO, Washington, 1964-65; exec. vice chancellor acad. affairs U. Tex. System, 1968-69; pres. U. Ky., Lexington, 1969-87, prof. emeritus, 1987—2003. Bd. dirs. Howell Corp. Author: Negro Militia and the Reconstruction, 1957, The Mexican War, 1960; editor: American Universities and Colleges, 1968. Regional chmn. Woodrow Wilson Nat. Fellowship Found., 1959-61; chmn. N.C. Rhodes Scholarship Com., 1964-66; chmn. Ky. Rhodes Scholarship Com., 1970-71, 73-74, 77, 80-81, 84-86; mem. So. Regional Edn. Bd., 1969—; chmn. dept. Army history adv. com., 1972-80; bd. visitors Air U., Maxwell AFB, 1973-76. Served with USNR, 1943-46, 51-54. Recipient Scarborough Teaching Excellence award U. Tex., 1958, Students Assn. Teaching Excellence award, 1958, 59; Carnegie Corp. grantee, 1961 Mem. Am. Hist. Assn., So. Hist. Assn., Am. Mil. Inst. (Moncado Book Fund award 1954), Am. Assn. Higher Edn. (dir. 1969—), Phi Beta Kappa (senator 1977-94, v.p. 1985-88, pres. 1988-91), Phi Alpha Theta, Omicron Delta Kappa, Pi Kappa Alpha. Democrat. Methodist. Died Sept. 20, 2003.

SINGLETON, HENRY EARL, retired industrialist; b. Haslet, Tex., Nov. 27, 1916; s. John Bartholomew and Victoria (Flores) S.; m. Caroline A. Wood, Nov. 30, 1942; children: Christina, John, William, James, Diana. S.B., S.M., Mass. Inst. Tech., 1940, Sc.D., 1950. V.p. Litton Industries, Inc., Beverly Hills, Calif., 1954-60; CEO Teledyne Inc., Los Angeles, 1960-86, chmn., 1960-91, Singleton Group, Beverly Hills, Calif., 1991-96; chmn. exec. com. Teledyne, Inc., L.A., 1991-96, retired; bd. dirs. Argonaut Group Inc., L.A. Died 1999.

SINGLEY, MARK ELDRIDGE, agricultural engineering educator; b. Delano, Pa., Jan. 25, 1921; s. Maurice and Clara (Rhodes) S.; m. Janet Twichell, Oct. 3, 1942; children: Donald Heath, Frances Marvin, Jeremy Mark, Paul Victor. BS, Pa. State U., 1942; MS, Rutgers U., 1949. Adminstrv. asst. UNRRA, 1946; prof. II biol. and agrl. engring. Rutgers U., New Brunswick, N.J., 1947-87, chmn. dept., 1961-71; v.p. rsch. and devel. Bedminster Bioconversion Corp., Haddonfield, N.J., 1987-95; cons. New Holland N.Am., from 1993. Bd. dirs. Agriplane. Chmn. Hillsborough Twp., Somerset County (N.J.) Planning Bd., 1956-73; pres. Hillsborough Twp. (N.J.) Democratic Club, 1979-80, Agrl. Mus. State of N.J., 1983—, pres. bd. trustee, 1984-89. With USNR, 1942-46. Named Prof. of Yr. Cook Coll., 1985. Fellow AAAS (sect. com. O), Am. Soc. Agrl. Engrs. (chmn. North Atlantic region 1966, bd. dir. 1973-75, Massey-Ferguson medal 1987); mem. Am. Forage and Grassland Council (bd. dir. 1966-69) Died October 18, 1999.

SISSON, ROBERT F. photographer, writer, lecturer, educator; b. Glen Ridge, N.J., May 30, 1923; s. Horace R. and Frances A. S.; m. Patricia Matthews, Oct. 15, 1978; 1 son by previous marriage, Robert F.H.; 1 stepson, James A. Matthews. With Nat. Geographic Soc., Washington, 1942-88, chief nat. sci. photographer, 1981-88; free-lance photographer, from 1988. Lectr. in field; mem. nature staff Sarasota Mag., 1989; owner Macro/Nature Workshops, Englewood, Fla. Photographer one-man shows, Nat. Geog. Soc., Washington, 1974, Washington Press Club, 1976, Berkshire (Mass.) Mus., 1976, Brooks Inst., Santa Barbara, Calif., 1980, U. Miami, 1993, Sea Ctr., Santa Barbara, Calif., 1993, Corcoran Gallery of Art's Spl. World Tour, 1988, permanent collections, Mus. Art, N.Y.C. Recipient 1st prize for color photograph White House News Photographers Assn., 1961; recipient Canadian Natural Sci. award, 1967, Louis Schmidt award, 1991. Fellow Biol. Photographers Assn.; mem. Biol. Photog. Assn. (awards for color prints 1967), Nat. Audubon Soc., Nat. Geog. Soc., Nat. Wildlife Fedn., Soc. Photog. Scientists and Engrs., N.Y. Acad. Scis., N.Am. Nature Photography Assn. (bd. dirs., Lifetime Achievement award 1999), Sigma Delta Chi. Died Dec. 20, 2002.

SKEEN, JOSEPH RICHARD, congressman; b. Roswell, N.Mex., June 30, 1927; s. Thomas Dudley and Ilah (Adamson) S.; m. Mary Helen Jones, Nov. 17, 1945; children: Mary Elisa, Mikell Lee. BS, Tex. A&M U., 1950. Soil and water engr. Ramah Navajo and Zuni Indians, 1951, 1951; rancher Lincoln County, N.Mex., 1952—; mem. N.Mex. Senate,

1960-70, 97th-103rd Congresses from 2nd N.Mex. dist., Washington, D.C., from 1981; mem. appropriations com., subcom. chair Interior, agr., chmn. appropriations com., subcom. def.; mem. subcom. interior. Chmn. N.Mex. Republican Party, 1963-66. Served with USN, 1945-46; Served with USAFR, 1949-52. Mem. Nat. Woolgrowers Assn., Nat. Cattle Growers Assn., N.Mex. Woolgrowers Assn., N.Mex. Cattle Growers Assn., N.Mex. Farm and Livestock Bur. Clubs: Elks. Republican. Home: Picacho, N.Mex. Died Dec. 7, 2003.

SKIBITZKE, HERBERT ERNST, JR., hydrologist; b. Benton Harbor, Mich., Mar. 30, 1921; s. Herbert Ernst and Jennie (Richie) S.; m. Eva Hegel, Mar. 22, 1943; 1 child, Herbert William (dec.). Student, Ariz. State U., 1947; Hon. ScD, U. Ariz., 1988. Registered profl. engr., 11 states; registered profl. land surveyor, Ariz.; registered ground water hydrologist. Mathematician U.S. Geol. Survey, Phoenix, 1948-54, rsch. hydrologist, 1954-76; pres., sr. hydrologist Hydro Data, Inc., Tempe, Ariz., 1976-85; cons. Skibitzke Engrs. & Assocs., Phoenix, 1986-90; co-founder, pres., sr. hydrologist Hydro Analysis, Inc., Tempe, from 1990. Co-founder, instr. Sch. Hydrology, U. Ariz., Tucson, 1960-64; adv. bd. Sch. Hydrology, Tarleton State U., Stephensville, Tex., 1986-90, Am. Inst. Hydrology, Mpls., 1989—; rep. Office Pres. John F. Kennedy in congl. hearings regarding water salinity problems in Pakistan, 1962. Contbr. articles to profl. jours., chpts. to books. Lt. USN, 1943-46. Recipient Lifetime Svc. awards, U. Ariz. Fellow ASCE; mem. Am. Inst. Hydrology (C.V. Theis award 1991), Assn. Ground Water Scientists and Engrs., Geol. Soc. Washington, Nat. Water Well Assn. Achievements include development of first computer (electric analog) applied to GW studies; patent on electronic flowmeter for U.S. Geol. Survey; pioneered development/application of remote sensing techniques to collect information on water resources; methods to analyze contaminant movement in ground water systems; development of state of the art analytical methods for hydrologic occurrences. Died July 24, 2001.

SKILLIN, EDWARD SIMEON, magazine publisher; b. N.Y.C., Jan. 23, 1904; s. Edward Simeon and Geraldine Madeleine (Fearons) S.; m. Jane Anne Edwards, Jan. 27, 1945; children: Edward John, Elizabeth Ann Skillin Flanagan, Arthur Paul, Susan Geraldine Skillin Thuvanuti, Mary Jane Skillin Davis. Grad., Phillips Acad., Andover, Mass., 1921; AB, Williams Coll., 1925; MA, Columbia U., 1933; LHD (hon.), St. Benedict's Coll., Atchison, Kans., 1954, Fordham U., 1974; LLD, St. Vincent's Coll., Latrobe, Pa., 1959, St. Francis Xavier U., Antigonish, N.S., Can., 1966, Stonehill Coll., 1979. With ednl. dept. Henry Holt & Co., N.Y.C., 1925-32; mem. staff Commonweal Found., N.Y.C., 1933-38, editor, 1938-67, pub., from 1967, pub. emeritus. Editor: The Commonweal Reader, 1949. Recipient Centennial citation St. John's U., Collegeville, Minn., 1957, St. Francis de Sales award Cath. Press Assn., 1987, Pax Christi award St. John's U., 1990. Mem. Cath. Commn. on Intellectual and Cultural Affairs, Phi Beta Kappa, Phi Gamma Delta. Home: Montclair, NJ. Deceased.

SKINNER, BARBARA F. elementary school educator; b. N.Y.C., July 16, 1932; d. Walter and Magdalena Elizabeth (Mutzberg) Feddern; m. Albert F. Skinner, Dec. 31, 1959; children: Walter C., Charles B., James E., Teri E., Lori F. BS, Fla. State U., 1954. Tchr. 5th grade J.H. Wilson Elem. Sch., Lake Wales, Fla.; tchr. Highlander Sch., Lake Wales, Spookhill Elem. Sch., Lake Wales, Lake Wales Jr. High Sch., Hillcrest Elem. Sch., Lake Wales. Mem. sch. bd. Lake Wales Evang. Luth. Ch. and Sch. Mem. NEA (life), Polk Edn. Assn. (past rec. sec. past bldg. rep.), FTP, Alpha Delta Kappa. Home: Hartsville, SC. Died Mar. 27, 2002.

SKINNER, DAVID BERNT, surgeon, educator, health facility administrator; b. Joliet, Ill., Apr. 28, 1935; s. James Madden and Bertha Elinor (Tapper) S.; m. May Elinor May Elinor Tischer, Aug. 25, 1956; children: Linda Elinor, Kristin Anne, Carise Berntine, Margaret Leigh. BA with high honors, U. Rochester, N.Y., 1958, ScD (hon.) (hon.), 1980; MD cum laude, Yale U., 1959; MD (hon.) (hon.), U. Lund, 1994, Technishe U. Munich, 1995. Diplomate Am. Bd. Thoracic Surgery. Intern, then resident in surgery Mass. Gen. Hosp., Boston, 1959—65; sr. registrar in thoracic surgery Frenchay Hosp., Bristol, England, 1963—64; teaching fellow Harvard U. Med. Sch., 1965; from asst. prof. surgery to prof. Johns Hopkins U. Med. Sch., also surgeon Johns Hopkins Hosp., 1968—72; Dallas B. Phemister prof. surgery, chmn. dept. U. Chgo. Hosps. and Clinics, 1972—87; prof. orthopedic surgery Cornell U., from 1987. Pres., CEO, N.Y. Hosp., from 1987; vice chair, CEO N.Y. and Presbyn. Hosps., 1996—2000; dir. Omnis Surg. Inc., 1984—85, Churchill Livingston, 1990—93, Lab. Corp. Am.; mem. Pres.' Biomed. Rsch. Panel, 1975—76, pres. emeritus, from 2000. Author: Atlas of Esophageal Surgery, 1991; author: (with others) Gastroesophageal Reflux and Hiatal Hernia, 1972, Management of Esophageal Diseases, 1988; editor: Surgical Practice Illustrated, 1988—95, Current Topics in Surg. Rsch., 1969—71, Jour. Surg. Rsch., 1972—83; co-editor: Surg. Treatment of Digestive Disease, 1985, Esophageal Disorders, 1985, Reconstructive Surgery of the Gastrointestinal Tract, 1985, Primary Motility Disorders of the Esophagus, 1991; mem. editl. bd.: Jour. Thoracic and Cardiovasc. Surgery; contbr. articles to profl. jours., chpts. to books. Bd. visitors Cornell U. Med. Coll., 1980—87; trustee Fifth Ave. Presbyn. Ch., N.Y.C., 1999—2000; Elder Fourth Presbyn. Ch., Chgo., 1976—87, clk. of session, 1978—82, 1984—87. Maj. M.C. USAF, 1966—68. Decorated chevalier Nat. Order of Merit France, Cross of Honor Arts and Scis. 1st class Austria; scholar John and Mary Markle scholar acad. medicine, 1969—74. Mem.: AMA, ACS, Soc. Med. Adminstrs., Greater N.Y. Hosp. Assn. (chair 1996—97), Soc. Clin. Surgery (pres. 1986—88), Halsted Soc., Assn. Acad. Surgery, Internat. Soc. Diseases Esophagus (pres. 1992—95), Ctrl. Surg. Soc., Am. Coll. Chest Physicians, Collegium Internat. de Chirurgie Digestivae, Soc. Internat. de Chirurgie, Soc. Surgery Alimentary Tract, Soc. Pelvic Surgeons, Soc. Thoracic Surgery, Soc. Vascular Surgery, Am. Assn. Thoracic Surgery (pres. 1996—97), Soc. Surg. Chmn. (pres. 1980—82), Am. Soc. Artificial Internal Organs (pres. 1977), Soc. Univ. Surgeons (pres. 1978—79), Western So. Surg. Assn., Am. So. Surg. Assn., Internat. Surg. Group (pres. 1997—98), Am. Bd. Surgery (dir. 1974—80), River Club, Univ. Club, Cosmos Club (Washington), Quadrangle (Chgo.), Alpha Omega Alpha, Phi Beta Kappa. Home: New York, NY. Died Jan. 24, 2003.

SKOOG, FOLKE KARL, botany educator; b. Fjärås, Sweden, July 15, 1908; arrived in U.S., 1925, naturalized, 1935; s. Karl Gustav and Sigrid (Person) Skoog; m. Birgit Anna Lisa Berner, Jan. 31, 1947; 1 child, Karin. BS, Calif. Inst. Tech., 1932, PhD, 1936; PhD (hon.), U. Lund, Sweden, 1956; DSc (hon.), U. Ill., 1980; DAgr. Sci., U. Pisa, Italy, 1991, Swedish U. Agrl. Scis., Uppsala, 1991. Teaching asst., research fellow biology Calif. Inst. Tech., 1934-36; NRC fellow U. Calif., Berkeley, 1936-37, summer 1938; instr., tutor biology Harvard U., 1937-41, research assoc., 1941; assoc., assoc. prof. biology Johns Hopkins U., 1941-44; chemist Q.M.C.; also tech. rep. U.S. Army ETO, 1944-46; asso. prof. botany U. Wis.-Madison, 1947-49, prof., from 1949, C. Leonard Huskins prof. botany, now emeritus. Vis. physiologist Pineapple Rsch. Inst. U. Hawaii, 1938—39; assoc. physiologist NIH, USPHS, 1943; vis. lectr. Wahington U., 1946, Swedish U. Agrl. Scis., Ultuna, 1952; v.p. physiologist sect. Internat. Bot. Congress, Paris, 1954, Edinburgh, Scotland, 64, Leningrad, 75. Editor: (sci. jours.) Plant Growth Substances, 1951, 1980; contbr. articles to profl. jours. Mem Olympic Track and Field Tea, Sweden, 1932. Recipient Cert. of Merit, Bot. Soc. Am., 1956, Nat. Medal of Science, U.S., 1991, Cosimo Ridolfi medal, 1991, John Ericsson medal, 1992. Mem.: NAS, Russian Soc. Plant Physiologists (hon. life mem.), Tissue Culture Assn. (hon. life mem. 1991, Life Achievement award 1992), Swedish Royal Acad. Scis., Deutssche Akad. der Naturforscher Leopoldina, Am. Acad. Arts and Scis., Am. Soc. Biol. Chemists, Internat. Plant Growth Substances Assn. (v.p. 1976—79, pres. 1979—82, hon. life mem.), Am. Soc. Gen. Physiologists (v.p. 1955—57, pres. 1957—58), Soc. Devel. Biology (pres. 1971), Am. Soc. Plant Physiologists (v.p. 1955—57, pres. 1957—58, Stephen Hales award 1954, Reid Barnes life mem. award 1970), Bot. Soc. Am. (chmn. phyiol. sect. 1954—55). Achievements include patents in field. Home: Madison, Wis. Deceased.

SLATER, JOSEPH ELLIOTT, educational institute administrator; b. Salt Lake City, Aug. 17, 1922; m. Annelore Kremser, Dec. 20, 1947; children: Bonnie Karen Hurst, Sandra Marian Slater BA with honors, postgrad., U. Calif., Berkeley, 1943; LLB with honors, Colo. Coll.; PhD (hon.), U. Denver, U. N.H., Kung Hee, Korea. Teaching asst., reader U. Calif.-Berkeley, 1942-43; dep. U.S. sec. Allied Control Council, Berlin, Germany, 1945-48; UN planning staff Dept. State, Washington, 1949; sec.-gen. Allied High Commn. for Germany, Bonn, 1949-52; exec. sec., U.S. spl. rep. in Europe, U.S. sec. to U.S. del. to NATO and OEEC, Paris, France, 1952-53; chief economist Creole Petroleum Corp. (Standard Oil Co. N.J.), Caracas, Venezuela, 1954-57; mem. and dir. internat. affairs program Ford Found., 1957-68, study dir. spl. com. to establish policies and programs, 1961-62; asst. mng. dir. Devel. Loan Fund, Washington, 1960-61; dep. asst. sec. state for edn. and cultural affairs, 1961-62; pres. Salk Inst., LaJolla, Calif., 1967-72, hon. trustee, pres. emeritus; pres., CEO trustee Aspen Inst. for Humanistic Studies, 1969-86, pres. emeritus, trustee, sr. fellow, from 1986; chmn. John J. McCloy Internat. Ctr., from 1986. Pres. Anderson Found., N.Y.C., 1969-72; adv. bd. Volvo Internat.; dir. Volvo N.Am. Sec. Pres.'s Com. on Fgn. Assistance (Draper Com.), 1959; del. Atlantic Conf., 1959; mem. devel. assistance panel Pres.'s Sci. Adv. Com., 1960-61; cons. Dept. State, 1961-68; founder, dir., bd. dirs. Creole Found., 1956-57; trustee Carnegie Hall Corp., 1960-86, Asia Soc., 1971-86, Am. Coun. on Germany, 1971—; mem. vis. com., dept. philosophy MIT, 1971-83; trustee Acad. for Ednl. Devel., Internat. Council Ednl. Devel., John J. McCloy Fund; bd. dirs. Eisenhower Exchange Fellowships, Internat. Inst. Environ. Devel., Ctr. for Pub. Resources. Served to lt. USNR, 1943-46; mil. govt. planning officer London, Paris, Berlin; trustee Lovelace Med. Found., 1993—. Decorated Order of Merit Fed. Republic Germany). Mem. NAS (mem. pres.'s cir.), Century Assn., Coun. Fgn. Rels., Phi Beta Kappa. Clubs: Century Assn. (N.Y.C.), Mid-Atlantic (N.Y.C.). Home: New York, NY. Died Nov. 25, 2002.

SLAUGHTER, ENOS, retired baseball player; b. Roxboro, N.C., Apr. 27, 1916; Baseball player St. Louis Cardinals, 1938-42, 46-53, N.Y. Yankees, 1954, 56-59, Kansas City Athletics, 1955-56, Milw. Braves, 1959. With USAF, 1943-45. Named to Baseball Hall of Fame, 1985; selected All-Star Team, 1941-42, 46-53; mem. World Series Champions, 1942, 46, 56-58. Died Aug. 12, 2002.

SLAVITT, EARL BENTON, lawyer; b. Chgo., Sept. 12, 1939; s. Harold Hal and Rose (Hoffman) S.; m. Amy Lerner, July 12, 1987; 1 child, Gabriel Harrel; children from previous marriage: Andrew Miller, Lesley Deborah. BS in Econs., U. Pa., 1961, JD, 1964. Bar: Ill. 1964, U.S. Dist. Ct. (no. dist.) Ill. 1964, U.S. Supreme Ct. 1971. Assoc. Wisch, Crane & Kravets, Chgo., 1964-67, Ressman & Tishler, Chgo., 1967-69; assoc., then ptnr. Levy & Erens, Chgo., 1969-78; ptnr. Tash & Slavitt, Chgo., 1978-81, Katten Muchin, Zavis Rosenman, Chgo., 1981—2004. Contbr. articles to profl. jours.; author poems and plays. Vol. Hospice of Ill. Masonic Med. Ctr., Chgo., 1987-89, Pro bono Advocates, 1989, Chgo. Ho., 1991 (recipient Outstanding Vol. award), Lawyers for the Creative Arts, Bus. Vols. for the Arts, 1992-2004; bd. dirs. Playwrights Ctr., Chgo., 1987, Jewish Reconstructionist Congregation, Chgo., 1978, 91, 92, Legal Clinic for the Disabled, 1993-96, pres., 1995-96, Sarah's Circle, 1994-96. Mem. Ill. State Bar Assn. (mem. real estate com. 1976, recipient Pro Bono Cert. Accomplishment 1994), Chgo. Bar Assn. (mem. real estate com. 1976, real estate fin. com. 1982), Chgo. Coun. Lawyers (mem. jud. selection com. 1969), Lawyers in Mensa (bd. govs. 1983). Democrat. Jewish. Home: Los Angeles, Calif. Died Nov. 20, 2003.

SLAYTON, WILLIAM LAREW, planning consultant, former government official; b. Topeka, Dec. 2, 1916; s. Clarence Harvey and Mary (Larew) S.; m. Mary Prichard, Aug. 30, 1941; children: Mary Elizabeth Slayton Campbell, Barbara Slayton Shelton. Student, U. Omaha, 1937-39; AB, U. Chgo., 1940, MA, 1942; DHL (hon.), Clarkson Coll. Tech., 1965. Polit. sec. Alderman Paul H. Douglas, Chgo., 1940-42; planning analyst Milw. Planning Commn., 1944-45, 46-47; municipal reference librarian Milw., 1947-48; asso. dir. Urban Redevel. Study, Chgo., 1948-50; field rep. div. slum clearance and urban redevel. HHFA, Washington, 1950; dir. redevel. Nat. Assn. Housing and Redevel. Ofcls., Washington, 1950-55; v.p. planning, redevel. Webb & Knapp, Inc., Washington, 1955-60; planning partner I.M. Pei & Partners, N.Y.C., 1956-61; commr. Urban Renewal Adminstrn., HHFA, HUD, Washington, 1961-66; dir. Urban Policy Center, Urban Am., Inc., Washington, 1966; exec. v.p. Urban Am., Inc., 1966-69, pres., 1969; exec. v.p. AIA, Washington, 1969-77, AIA Found., 1970-77; mem. bd. AIA Corp., 1970-77; vice chmn. AIA Research Corp., 1973-77; chmn. urban devel. advisory com. HUD, 1967-68; mem. U.S. del. Econ. Commn. for Europe, 1970; dep. asst. sec. of state for fgn. bldgs., 1978-83; cons. Nat. Assn. Housing and Redevel. Ofcls., 1983-87, Am. Planning Assn., from 1986. Bd. dirs. Met. Washington Ear, 1995—. With USNR, 1945-46. Recipient gold medal Royal Instn. Chartered Surveyors, Great Britain, 1965, Justin Herman award Nat. Assn. Housing and Redevel. Ofcls., 1994. Mem. Potomac Inst. (dir.), AIA (hon.), Am. Planning Assn., Am. Inst. Cert. Planners. Home: Arlington, Va. Deceased.

SLEPECKY, NORMA B. cell biologist; b. Montgomery, Ala., Jan. 2, 1944; BS, Syracuse U., 1965, MS, 1968; PhD, SUNY, Syracuse, 1985. Rsch. scientist dept. physiology Karolinska Inst., Stockholm, 1985-86, NIH, Nat. Inst. Deafness and Other Communicative Disorders, Bethesda, Md., from 1991; assoc. prof. dept. bioengring. and neurosci. Syracuse U, from 1986. Contbr. over 40 articles to profl. jours. Mem. Am. Soc. Cell Biology, Electron Microscope Am., Assn. Rsch. in Otolaryngology. Achievements include research in cell biology of the sensory cells of the inner ear. Died May 2, 2001.

SLEPIN, MATTHEW MORGAN, lawyer; b. N.Y.C., May 22, 1908; s. Harry Yale and Rose (Goldstein) S.; m. Lynne Judith Davis, May 28, 1935 (dec. Feb. 1991); children: Stephen Marc, Susan Davis. LLB, Rutgers U., 1928, JD, 1960. Bar: N.J. 1931, Fla. 1949, U.S. Dist. Ct. N.J. 1931, U.S. Dist. Ct. (so. dist.) Fla. 1949, U.S. Tax Ct. 1949, U.S. Ct. Appeals (11th cir.) 1949, U.S. Supreme Ct. 1970, Republic of Korea, 1952. Ptnr. Slepin & Slepin, Tallahassee, from 1993. Judge Mcpl. Ct., Miamim, 1954-58; mem. adv. bd. Attys.' Title Svcs., Miami, 1980—. Chmn. West Miami (Fla.) Zoning Bd., 1947-51, 82-85, West Miami Code Enforcement Bd., 1985-87, Dade County Rep. Com., 1954-58; councilman, vice-mayor City of West Miami, 1958-78. With U.S. Army, ETO, 1940-46, 51-52. Mem. N.J. Bar Assn., Fla. Bar Assn., VFW, DAV, Armed Forces League, Mil. Order World Wars, Ret. Officers Assn., Res. Officers Assn., Am. Legion, Country Club Coral Gables, Masons, Shriners, Order Ea. Star and others. Jewish. Avocations: golf, swimming. Home: Miami, Fla. Died Sept. 2, 2000.

SLIWINSKI, ZDZISLAW, music and theater executive; b. Dolina, July 20, 1910; s. Jan and Maria (Steslowicz) S.; grad. Higher Coll. Commerce, Warsaw; m. Alicja Woszczynska, Mar. 25, 1938; 1 dau., Maria Sliwinska Furman. Head of sect., dept. music Ministry Art and Culture, 1945-46; vice dir. Polish Music Publ. Cracow, 1946-47; gen. dir. Philharm. Orch., Poznan, 1948-58; gen. dir. Nat. Philharm. Warsaw, 1958-69; gen. dir. Grand Opera House Teatr Wielki, Warsaw, 1965-66, 70-80; mem. organizing com. Internat. Chopin Competition, 1949—; pres. Internat. Festivals of Autumn in Warsaw Contemporary Music, 1958—; pres. Orgn. Internat. H. Wieniawski Competition, Poznan, 1952, 57. Decorated Gold Cross of Merit, knight and officers Order Polonia Restituta, Order Banner of Labor, Badge of Merit for cultural activity. Mem. Polish Soc. Authors ZAIKS.

SLOAN, MARJORIE HAWKINS, science educator, retired advertising executive; b. Kansas City, Kans., Oct. 22, 1923; d. Ernest Henry Hawkins and Louisa Eola Fouché; m. Raymond Charles Sloan, July 21, 1949 (dec. Mar. 1994); children: Roger Charles, Jeffrey Craig. BS, Kans. State U., 1945; MS, Iowa State U., 1948. Cert. life tchg. license Kans., Calif. Tchr. Fredonia (Kans.) H.S., 1945—47; blend chemist Phillips Petroleum Co., Kansas City, Kans., 1947; asst. prof. Whittier (Calif.) Coll., 1948—50, Sacramento State U., 1950—51; tchr. L.A. Unified Sch. Dist., 1951—52,

Torrance (Calif.) Unified Sch. Dist., 1957—60, L.A. Unified Sch. Dist., 1962—81; advt. account exec. Sloan, Sloan & Charles, Reseda, Canoga Park, Eureka, Calif., 1981—93; ret., 1993. Pinochle facilitator Prescott Adult Ctr., Prescott, Ariz., from 2000; staff Prescott Sr. Olympic Games, 2002, 2003. Mem.: LWV, AAUW (bd. dirs. 1996—97, Eleanor Roosevelt award 2000), Iota Sigma Pi, Omicron Nu, Phi Kappa Phi. Avocations: book clubs, wine tasting, foreign and domestic travel. Home: Cave Creek, Ariz. Died Mar. 21, 2003.

SLOANE, ROBERT MALCOLM, university administrator; b. Boston, Feb. 11, 1933; s. Alvin and Florence (Goldberg) S.; m. Beverly LeBov, Sept. 27, 1959; 1 child, Alison Sloane Gaylin. AB, Brown U., 1954; MS, Columbia U., 1958. Adminstrv. resident Mt. Auburn Hosp., Cambridge, Mass., 1957-58; med. adminstr. AT&T, N.Y.C., 1959-60; asst. dir. Yale New Haven Hosp., 1961-67; assoc. adminstr. Monmouth Med. Center, Long Branch, N.J., 1967-69; adminstr. City of Hope Nat. Med. Center, Duarte, Calif., 1969-80; pres. Los Angeles Orthopedic Hosp., Los Angeles Orthopedic Found., 1980-86; pres., CEO Anaheim (Calif.) Meml. Hosp., 1986-94; pres. Vol. Hosp. Am. West, Inc., L.A., 1995; healthcare cons. Monrovia, Calif., 1996-98; v.p. Rudolph Dew and Assocs., Torrance, Calif., 1997-98; dir. health adminstrn. program U. So. Calif., L.A., 1998—2001. Mem. faculty Columbia U. Sch. Medicine, 1958—59, Yale U. Sch. Medicine, 1963—67, 1963—67, Pasadena City Coll., 1972—73, Calif. Inst. Tech., 1973—85, U. So. Calif., 1976—96, clin. prof., 1987—95, from 1998, UCLA, 1985—87; chmn. bd. Health Data Net, 1971—73; bd. dirs. Intervalley Health Plan, 1995—2001; pres. Anaheim Meml. Devel. Found., 1986—94; pres., CEO InTech Health Sys., Inc., 1996—2001; sr. cons. APM, Inc., 1996—97. Author: (with B. L. Sloane) An Introduction to Health Care Delivery Organization: Functions and Management, 1971, 2d edit., 1977, 3d edit., 1992, (with Richard Harder) 4th edit., 1999; mem. editl. and adv. bd. Health Devices, 1972-90; contbr. articles to hosp. jours. Bd. dirs. Health Systems Agy. Los Angeles County, 1977-78, Vol. Hosps. of Am., 1986-95, chmn., 1993-94, pres., 1995; bd. dirs. Calif. Hosp. Polit. Action Com., 1979-87, vice chmn., 1980-83, chmn., 1983-85. Served to lt. (j.g.) USNR, 1954-56. Fellow Am. Coll. Healthcare Execs. (regent 1989-93, nominations com. 1994-97); mem. Am. Hosp. Assn., Healthcare Assn. So. Calif. (bd. dirs., sec. 1982, treas. 1983, chmn. elect 1984, chmn. 1985, past chmn. 1986, 89), Calif. Healthcare Assn. (bd. dirs. exec. com. 1984-86, 89), Anaheim C. of C. (bd. dirs. 1994). Home: Arcadia, Calif. Died June 16, 2002.

SLOBADIN, STEPHEN, retired foundation executive; b. N.Y.C., July 25, 1918; s. Maxsym and Alexandra (Triuda) S.; m. Elizabeth A. Rogers, Nov. 6, 1976. BA, U. Mich., 1940; MBA, NYU, 1942. Exec. dir. Prescott Neighborhood House, N.Y.C., 1947-58, Christodona Found., N.Y.C. and Bound Brook, N.J., 1958-83; pres., bd. dirs. Prescott Fund for Children and Youth, Inc., N.Y.C., from 1984; bd. dirs. Day Care Coun. N.Y., N.Y.C., from 1947, v.p., treas., 1973-77; bd. dirs. Christodora Found., N.Y.C., from 1983. Trustee Local 1707 Day Care Coun. Welfare Fund, 1974-78; bd. dirs. MFY Day Care Ctr., 1977-80. Mem. Nat. Arts Club. Republican. Episcopalian. Home: Somerset, NJ. Died.

SMALL, MICHAEL, composer; b. NY, May 30, 1939; Composer Marks Mgmt. Scores include (films) Out of It, 1969, Puzzle of a Downfall Child, 1970, Jenny, 1970, The Revoltionary, 1970, The Sporting Club, 1971, Klute, 1971, Child's Play, 1972, Dealing: Or the Berkeley-to-Boston Forty-Brick Lost-Bag Blues, 1972, Love and Pain and the Whole Damned Thing, 1973, The Parallax View, 1974, The Drowning Pool, 1975, The Stepford Wives, 1975, Night Moves, 1975, Marathon Man, 1976, Audrey Rose, 1977, Girlfriends, 1978, The Driver, 1978, Comes a Horseman, 1978, Going in Style, 1979, Those Lips, Those Eyes, 1980, The Postman Always Rings Twice, 1981, Continental Divide, 1981, Rollover, 1981, The Star Chamber, 1983, Kidco, 1984, Firstborn, 1984, Target, 1985, Dream Lover, 1986, Brighton Beach Memoirs, 1986, Black Widow, 1987, Orphans, 1987, Jaws the Revenge, 1987, 1969, 1988, See You in the Morning, 1989, Mountains of the Moon, 1990, Mobsters, 1991, Consenting Adults, 1992, Wagons East!, 1994, Into My Heart, 1998; (documentaries) Pumping Iron, 1977, American Dream, 1989, (TV movies) The Boy Who Drank Too Much, 1980, The Lathe of Heaven, 1980, Chiefs, 1983, Nobody's Child, 1986, Queen, 1993, Poodle Springs, 1998, Golden Spiders: A Nreo Wolfe Mystery, 2000. Died Nov. 24, 2003.

SMITH, ADELINE MERCER, retired librarian; b. Saratoga Springs, N.Y., May 28, 1915; d. Thomas Elwood and Hazel Belle (Farrington) Mercer; m. Jack Monroe Smith, Mar. 3, 1946; 1 child, Jeffrey Monroe. BS in Libr. Sci., N.Y. State Coll. Tchrs., 1937; MS in Libr. Sci., SUNY, Albany, 1968. Designer, sample maker Van Raalte Co., Ladies Lingerie, Saratoga Springs, 1939-63; high sch. libr. Hoosic Valley Ctrl. Sch., Schaghticoke, N.Y., 1964-78; dir. dist. libr. svcs. Hoosic Valley Ctrl. Sch. Dist., Schaghticoke, 1975-78; practicing retired libr., cataloger James L. Hamner Pub. Libr., Amelia, Va., from 1989. Mem. adv. bd. Index to Free Periodicals, Ann Arbor, Mich., 1977—. Author: Free Magazines for Libraries, 1980, 2nd edit., 1985; co-author: Free Magazines for Libraries, 3d edit., 1989, 4th edit., 1994; contbr. articles to libr. jours., mags. Mem. ALA, Nat. Ret. Tchrs. Assn., N.Y. State United Tchrs., Va. Ret. Tchrs. Assn., Beta Phi Mu. Baptist. Avocations: library volunteer, genealogy, gardening, needlework. Home: Amelia Court House, Va. Died Oct. 2002.

SMITH, ALEXANDER GOUDY, physics and astronomy educator; b. Clarksburg, W.Va., Aug. 12, 1919; s. Edgell Ohr and Helen (Reitz) S.; m. Mary Elizabeth Ellsworth, Apr. 19, 1942; children: Alexander G. III, Sally Jean. BS, Mass. Inst. Tech., 1943; PhD, Duke U., 1949. Physicist Mass. Inst. Tech., Radiation Lab., Cambridge, 1943-46; research asst. Duke U., Durham, 1946-48; asst. prof. to prof. physics U. Fla., Gainesville, 1948-61, asst. dean grad. sch., 1961-69, acting dean grad. sch., 1971-73, chmn. dept. astronomy, 1962-71, prof. physics and astronomy, 1956—, Disting. prof., 1981—. Dir. U. Fla. Radio Obs., 1956-85, Rosemary Hill Obs., 1989—. Author: (with others) Microwave Magnetrons, 1958, (with T.D. Carr) Radio Exploration of the Planetary System, 1964 (also Swedish, Spanish and Polish edits), Radio Exploration of the Sun, 1966; also numerous articles in field. Fellow AAAS, Optical Soc. Am., Am. Phys. Soc., Royal Micros. Soc.; mem. Am. Astron. Soc. (editor Photo-Bull. 1975-87), Astron. Soc. Pacific, Internat. Astron. Union, Internat. Sci. Radio Union, Fla. Acad. Scis. (treas. 1957-62, pres. 1963-64, medal 1965), Assn. Univs. for Rsch. in Astronomy (dir., cons.), S.E. Univs. Rsch. Assn. (trustee 1981-91), Soc. Photog. Scientists and Engrs., Athenaeum Club (past pres.), Db Racquet Club, Gainesville Country Club, Sigma Xi (nat. lectr. 1968, past pres. Fla. chpt.), Phi Kappa Phi, Sigma Pi Sigma. Republican. Christian Scientist. Home: Cedar Rapids, Iowa. Died 2001.

SMITH, BARNEY OVEYETTE, JR., lawyer; b. Mobile, Ala., July 29, 1952; s. Barney O. Sr. and Delores (Long) S.; m. Rita Ward, May 31, 1975; children: Barney O. III, Berkley Lauren. BA, Furman U., 1973; JD, U. S.C., 1976. Bar: S.C. 1976, U.S. Dist. Ct. S.C. 1976, U.S. Ct. Appeals (4th cir.) 1981, U.S. Supreme Ct. 1981. Ptnr. Parham & Smith, Greenville, S.C., from 1976. Fellow Nat. Bd. Trial Advocates, So. Trial Lawyers Assn.; mem. ABA, Am. Bd. Trial Advocates, Assn. Trial Lawyers Am. (sustaining), S.C. Trial Lawyers Assn. (bd. dirs. 1984—, pres. elect 1986-87, pres. 1987-88). Democrat. Home: Simpsonville, SC. Died Aug. 16, 1996.

SMITH, BRUCE DAVID, economics educator, consultant; b. St. Paul, Sept. 21, 1954; s. Samuel and Marian Smith; m. Valerie R. Bencivenga, Oct. 27, 1987. BS, U. Minn., 1977; PhD, MIT, 1981. Asst. prof. Boston Coll., 1981-82; economist Fed. Res. Bank, Mpls., 1982-86; asst. prof. Carnegie-Mellon U., Pitts., 1986-87; assoc. prof. U. Western Ont., London, Ont., Can., 1987-90; prof. Cornell U., Ithaca, N.Y., 1990-96, U. Tex., Austin, from 1996. Cons. Fed. Res. Bank, Kansas City, from 1997, Mpls., 1986—96, Cleve., from 1996, Atlanta, from 1994; adv. World Bank. Contbr. articles to profl. jours. Mem. Am. Econs. Assn., Econometric Soc. Home: Austin, Tex. Died July 9, 2002; Acacia Park Cemetary.

SMITH, DAVID HAMILTON, foundation administrator; b. Canton, Ohio; m. Joan Smith. Grad., Ohio Wesleyan U., 1953; MC, U. Rochester Sch. Med., 1958. Chief infectious diseases Boston Children's Hosp.; chmn. pediatrics dept. U. of Rochester, 1978—83; founder Praxis Biologics (bought by Am. Cyanamid), Rochester, NY, 1983—89; chmn, chief scientific officer Lederle-Praxis (formerly Praxis Biologics), 1989—90; pres. David H. Smith Found., N.Y.C. Recipient Albert Lasker Clin. Med. Rsch. award, 1996, Children's Vaccine Initiative Pasteur award WHO, 1996. Died Feb. 23, 1999.

SMITH, SISTER DORIS HELEN, college president; b. Cleve., June 1, 1930; d. Harold Peter and Ellen Mary (Keane) S. B.S., Coll. of Mt. St. Vincent, 1952; M.A., NYU, 1957; postgrad. Fordham U., 1960-65; L.H.D., (hon.), Manhattan Coll., 1979. Joined Sisters of Charity (N.Y.), 1952. Mem. faculty Coll. of Mount St. Vincent, Bronx, N.Y., 1955-71, adminstrv. asst. to pres., 1971-72, exec. v.p., 1972-73, pres., 1973—92; spl. asst. to pres. Chatham Coll., Pitts., 1970-71; dir. Hudson River Trust of Equitable Variable Life Ins., N.Y.C.; trustee Higher Edn. Service Corp., Albany, N.Y., 1980-85, Com. on Independent Colls. and Univs., Albany, 1980-83. Recipient Higher Edn. Leadership award Com. on Independent Colls. and Corning Glass Works, 1983, several interfaith and brotherhood awards; named Riverdalian of Yr. Riverdale Community Council, 1978; Am. Council Edn. fellow, 1970-71. Mem. Assn. Colls. and Univs. of State of N.Y. (trustee), Bronx C. of C. Roman Catholic. Died Jan. 19, 2004.

SMITH, ELVIE LAWRENCE, retired corporate director; b. Eatonia, Sask., Can., Jan. 8, 1926; s. Harry Burton and Laura Mae (Fullerton) S.; m. Jacqueline Moy Colleary, Dec. 15, 1956; children: Ronald, Paul, David, Marguerite. BS with great distinction, U. Sask., 1947; MSME, Purdue U., 1949; LLD (hon.), Concordia U., 1983; D in Engring., Carleton U., 1984, Purdue U., 1987; DS (hon.), U. Saskatchewan, 1997. Exptl. engr. Nat. Research Council, Ottawa, Ont., Can., 1949-56; with Pratt & Whitney Can. Inc., 1957—, exec. v.p. ops., 1978-80, pres., CEO, 1980-84, chmn., 1984-94, dir., 1970-96. Decorated Order of Can., 1992; recipient Sawyer award ASME, 1986, Gold Medal Polish People's Republic, 1985, Aerospace Leadership award SAE, 1994; named to Can. Aviation Hall of Fame, 1993. Fellow Can. Aeronautics and Space Inst. (McCurty award 1976, C.D. Howe award 1983); mem. Aerospace Industries Assn. Can. (life, chmn. 1982-83), Gatineau Gliding Club. Deceased.

SMITH, EVA JOYCE, retired nurse; b. New Eagle, Pa., Mar. 16, 1932; d. Harold Elwood John and Vera Lena (Herd) Schlosser; m. Lyell G. Smith (div. 1980); children: Stephen Mark, Stephanie Anne, Shari Linne. Student, Marshall Coll., 1949-50; diploma, Wheeling Hosp. Sch. Nursing, W.Va., 1953; BS, Coll. St. Francis, Joliet, Ill., 1982, MS, 1986. R.N., Ill. Staff nurse Didsbury (Alta.) Hosp., Can., 1957-60, Annapolis Hosp., Wayne, Mich., 1963-64, Stagg Clinic, Hartford, Mich., 1969-72, Hinsdale (Ill.) Sanitorium and Hosp., 1972-76; staff nurse, instr., then clin. edn. coord. St. Luke's Med. Ctr., Phoenix, Ill., 1977-85; asst. dir. health arts program Coll. St. Francis, Joliet, 1985-87; clinic dir. Memory Assessment Clinics, Inc., Scottsdale, Ariz., 1988-96; clin. rsch. adminstr. Phoenix Ctr. for Clin. Rsch., from 1996. Mem. NAFE, Profl. Assn. Gerontology Educators and Svcs. (sec. 1985), Drug Info. Assn. (assoc. in clin. pharmacology 1995—). Republican. Baptist. Avocations: piano, organ. Home: Phoenix, Ariz. Died July 30, 2000.

SMITH, FREDA L. retired elementary education educator; b. Birds, Ill., Oct. 3, 1923; d. Loney W. and Mattie A. (Perrott) Thomas; m. Lloyd Preston, May 18, 1947 (dec. 1991); 1 child, Thelma. BS, U. Western Ky., 1959. Tchr. Jefferson Sch., Robinson, Ill., 1953-54, Franklin County (Tenn.) Sch., 1954-56, Muhlenberg (Ky.) Pub. Schs., 1956-58, Livingston County Pub. Schs., Salem, Ky., 1958-61, Custer (S.D.) Elem. Sch., 1961-64, Chugwater (Wyo.) Elem. Sch., 1964-87. Vol. Headstart, Wheatland, Wyo., 1991—, Lauback Internat., Kingman, Ariz., 1987-91. With WAVES, 1944-46. Mem. AAUW (pres. 1980-81), NEA, Chugwater Edn. Assn. Episcopalian. Avocations: hiking, reading, knitting. Home: Rapid City, SD. Died July 8, 2001.

SMITH, GEORGE FOSTER, retired aerospace company executive; b. Franklin, Ind., May 9, 1922; s. John Earl and Ruth (Foster) S.; m. Jean Arthur Farnsworth, June 3, 1950; children: David Foster, Craig Farnsworth, Sharon Windsor. BS in Physics, Calif. Inst. Tech., 1944, MS, 1948, PhD magna cum laude, 1952. Founding staff mem. Engring. Rsch. Assocs., St. Paul, 1946-48; tchg. fellow, resident assoc. Calif. Inst. Tech., 1948-52; staff Hughes Rsch. Labs., Malibu, Calif., 1952-87, assoc. dir., 1962-69, dir., 1969-87; v.p. Hughes Aircraft Co., 1965-81, sr. v.p., 1981-87, policy bd., 1966-87. Adj. assoc. prof. elec. engring. U. So. Calif., 1959-62; cons. Army Sci. Adv. Panel, 1975-78. Contbr. numerous articles to profl. jours. Adv. local Explorer post Boy Scouts Am., 1965-70; bd. mgrs. Westchester YMCA, 1974-, chmn., 1979-81; chmn. trustees Pacific Presbyn. Ch., L.A., 1959-62. Served to lt. (j.g.) USNR, 1944-46. Std. Oil fellow, 1949-50; recipient Disting. Alumnus award Calif. Inst. Tech., 1991. Fellow IEEE (pres. Sorenson fellows 1972-73, Frederick Philips award 1988), Am. Phys. Soc.; mem. AAAS, Caltech Assocs. (bd. dirs. 1990—, pres. 1993-94), Sierra Club, Sigma Xi (chpt. pres. 1957-58), Tau Beta Pi. Achievements include 6 patents in field; directed leading industrial research in electronics, lasers, and electro-optics; conducted first laser range finder experiments. Home: Manhattan Beach, Calif. Died Nov. 8, 2003.

SMITH, HELENE SHEILA CARETTNAY, microbiologist; b. Phila., Feb. 13, 1941; d. Joseph Cohen; m. Allan Smith; 1 child, Joshua. BS in Edn. cum laude, U. Pa., 1962, PhD in Microbiology, 1967. Postdoctoral rsch. fellow Princeton U., 1967-69, Nat. Cancer Inst., 1969-71; asst. rsch. virologist cell culture lab. sch. pub. health U. Calif., Berkeley, 1971-75, assoc. rsch. virologist, 1975-77; staff Peralta Cancer Rsch. Inst., Oakland, Calif., 1975-89, asst. dir., 1980-85, assoc. dir., 1985-89; dir. Geraldine Brush Cancer Rsch. Inst., San Francisco, from 1989. Lectr. sch. pub. health U. Calif., Berkeley, 1973-78; staff Donner Lab. Lawrence Berkeley Lab. U. Calif., 1977-82; grad. group in genetics U. Calif., 1979-82, adj. assoc. prof., San Francisco, 1984—; speaker in field; mem. spl. rev. com. Nat. Cancer Inst., 1991, reviewer metabolic pathology study sect., 1991, spl. rev. com. program project, 1988, ad hoc reviewer, 1988, 87; ad. com. oral contraceptives and breast cancer Inst. Medicine, 1989-90; mem. cell biology study sect. NSF, 1980-84. Contbr. numerous articles to profl. jours. Speaker Am. Cancer Soc., 1986. Recipient Award of Distinction Susan G. Komen Found., 1987, 89, 90, 91. Mem. Am. Assn. for Cancer Rsch., Am. Soc. for Cell Biology, Soc. for Analytic Cytology, Tissue Culture Assn. Home: San Francisco, Calif. Deceased.

SMITH, HOKE LAFOLLETTE, former university president; b. Galesburg, Ill., May 7, 1931; s. Claude Hoke and Bernice (LaFollette) Smith; m. Barbara E. Walvoord, June 30, 1979 (div. 2001); children from previous marriage: Kevin, Kerry, Amy, Glen. BA (Harold fellow), Knox Coll., 1953; MA, U. Va., 1954; PhD (fellow 1958), Emory U., 1958; hon. degree, Sung Kyun Kwan U., Korea, 1993, Knox Coll., 1995; prof. (hon.), St. Petersburg Electrotech. U., 2001. Asst. prof. polit. sci. Hiram Coll., Ohio, 1958-64, assoc. prof. polit. sci., 1964-67; asst. to pres., prof. polit. sci. Drake U., Des Moines, 1967-70, chmn. interim governing com., 1971-72, v.p. acad. adminstrn., 1970-79; pres. Towson (Md.) U., 1979—2001, pres. emeritus, 2001—04. Vis. prof. U. Md., College Park, 2001—03; mem. univ. adv. coun. Life Ins. Coun. Am., 1969—71; mem. task force to study the governance, structure and funding U. Sys. Md., 1998—99. Chmn. exec. com. Coun. Econ. Edn., Towson, Md., 1979—2001; bd. dirs. Balt. Coun. on Fgn. Rels.; chmn. Very Spl. Arts of Md.; bd. dirs. Greater Homewood Cmty. Corp.; commr. Md. Higher Edn. Commn., from 2003. With U.S. Army, 1954—56. Recipient Eileen Tosney award, Am. Assn. Univ. Administrs., 1991; Congl. fellow, Am. Polit. Sci. Assn., 1964—65. Mem.: St. Petersburg Intenat. Consortium of Colls. and Univs. (co-chair 1997), Met. and Urban Colls. and Univs. (co-chair 1996—98), Soc. for Coll. and Univ. Planning (bd. dirs. 1986—88), Am. Assn. Higher Edn., Am. Coun. Edn. (exec. com. 1988—94, chmn. elect 1991—92, chmn. 1992—93, past chmn. 1993—94, bd. dirs.), Am.

Assn. State Colls. and Univs. (bd. dirs. 1984—88, chmn. elect 1985—86, Found. bd. dirs. 1985—87, chmn. 1986—87), Renaissance Group (exec. com.), Balt. C. of C. (adv. coun.), Pi Sigma Alpha, Gamma Gamma, Delta Sigma Tho, Omicron Delta Kappa, Phi Kappa Phi, Phi Beta Kappa. Home: Baltimore, Md. Died Mar. 27, 2004.

SMITH, HOWARD EDWARD, chemistry educator; b. San Francisco, Aug. 1, 1925; s. Charles Augustus and Gertrude Bernadette (Higgins) S.; m. Louise Meier, Nov. 18, 1960; children: David Charles, Marie-Louise, Erika Bernadette. BS, U. Calif., Berkeley, 1951; MS, Stanford U., 1954, PhD, 1957. Asst. rsch. chemist Calif. Rsch. Corp., Richmond, 1951-52; rsch. assoc. Stanford U., 1956; USPHS postdoctoral fellow Wayne State U., Detroit, 1956-58, Swiss Fed. Inst. Tech., Zurich, 1958-59; asst. prof. chemistry Vanderbilt U., Nashville, 1959-63, assoc. prof. chemistry, 1963-71, prof. chemistry, 1971-93, prof. chemistry emeritus, from 1993. Contbr. articles to profl. jours. Grantee NSF, NIH. Fellow AAAS; mem. Am. Chem. Soc. (chmn. Nashville sect. 1971), Royal Soc. Chemistry, Tenn. Acad. Sci., Sigma Xi, Phi Lambda Upsilon. Democrat. Roman Catholic. Home: Nashville, Tenn. Died Sept. 23, 2000.

SMITH, JACK PRESCOTT, journalist; b. Paris, Apr. 25, 1945; s. Howard Kingsbury and Benedicte (Traberg) S.; divorced; 1 child, Alexander Kingsbury. BA in History, Carnegie-Mellon U., 1971, Oxford (Eng.) U., 1974. Writer-producer Sta. WIIC-TV News, Pitts., 1969-70; producer-reporter Sta. WLS-TV News, Chgo., 1974-76; fgn. corr. ABC-TV News, Paris, 1976-80, corr. Washington, 1980—2000. Served with inf. U.S. Army, 1964-67. Decorated Purple Heart, Bronze Star, Army commendation medal; recipient citation for best mag. reporting in fgn. affairs Overseas Press Club, 1967, Emmy award, 1997. Died Apr. 7, 2004.

SMITH, JAMES BIGELOW, SR., electrical engineer; b. Hamilton, Ont., Can., Dec. 18, 1908; s. Percy Merrihew and Ethel Burgess (Torrey) S.; m. Elizabeth Perry Dane, Mar. 1936 (div. 1954); children: James Bigelow Jr., Sylvia Perry, David Prentiss; m. Catharine Dean Temple, Jan. 17, 1959. BSEE, MIT, 1932, MSEE, 1933. Registered profl. engr., Mass. Quality control engr. Sylvania Electric Products Co., Salem, Mass., 1933; claims adjuster Liberty Mutual Ins. Soc., N.Y.C. and Lynn, Mass., 1933-35; lab. engr. engr.-in-charge sect. Factory Mutual Rsch. Corp., Norwood, Mass., 1935-74, asst. chief engr. to chief engr., v.p., mgr. applied rsch.; assoc. cons. engr. Lement & Assocs., Waltham, MA, from 1974. Chair black liquor recovery boiler adv. com. for pulp and paper industry, 1960's. Patentee fire protection methods and systems apparatus. Fellow Soc. Fire Protection Engrs. (life, charter mem., pres. New Eng. chpt. 1962-63, historian 1980—, bd. dirs. 1980—, Richard E. Stevens award 1985), Nat. Fire Protection Assn. (life, past chair oven and furnace com.), Fire Detection Inst. (past chair). Died May 17, 2001.

SMITH, JEFFREY L. cooking expert, television personality, author; b. Seattle, Jan. 22, 1939; s. Emely S.; m. Patricia M. Dailey, 1964; children: Jason, Channing. BA, U. Puget Sound, 1962, DHL (hon.), 1987; MDiv, Drew U., 1965, DDiv (hon.), 1993. Ordained to ministry United Meth. Ch., 1965. Served Meth. chs., Hartsdale, N.Y., rural, Wash.; chaplain, asst. prof. religion U. Puget Sound, Tacoma, 1966-72; founder The Chaplain's Pantry, Tacoma, 1972-83; host Seattle Today TV program The Frugal Gourmet (formerly Cooking Fish Creatively), 1973-77; host PBS program The Frugal Gourmet, 1983—97. Author: The Frugal Gourmet, 1984, The Frugal Gourmet Cooks with Wine, 1986, The Frugal Gourmet Cooks American, 1987, The Frugal Gourmet Cooks Three Ancient Cuisines: China, Greece and Rome, 1989, The Frugal Gourmet on Our Immigrant Ancestors: Recipes You Should Have Gotten From Your Grandmother, 1990, The Frugal Gourmet's Culinary Handbook, 1991, The Frugal Gourmet Celebrates Christmas, 1991, The Frugal Gourmet Whole Family Cookbook, 1992, The Frugal Gourmet Cooks Italian: Recipes from the New and Old World Simplified for the American Kitchen, 1993, The Frugal Gourmet Keeps the Feast: Past, Present and Future, 1995. Recipient Daytime Emmy nominations (5), Best of the West Edn. TV award Western Ednl. Network, 1986. Died July 7, 2004.

SMITH, JERRY NEIL, music educator; b. Lefors, Tex., Feb. 20, 1935; s. Jess Lee and Audrey Eileen (Sutton) S.; m. Joan L. Templar, Dec. 26, 1956; children: Julie Eileen, Blaine. B in Music Edn., U. Tex., 1956, MusM, 1957; PhD, Eastman Sch. Music, 1963. Instr. woodwind Tex. City (Tex.) Pub. Schs., 1957-58; dir. jr. high band Henderson (Tex.) Pub. Schs., 1958-59; instr. woodwind U. Southwest La., Lafayette, 1959-60, U. Fla., Gainsville, 1961-64; asst. prof. woodwinds U. Colo., Boulder, 1964-72; head dept. music U. No. Iowa, Cedar Falls, 1972-75; dir. sch. music U. Okla., Norman, 1975-80, prof. music, from 1980. Chmn. dept. music Calif. State U., Long Beach, 1986-87. Contbr. articles to the Instumentalist, Selmer Bandwagon, 1960, 61; arranger Shapiro-Bernstein Co., 1965-75; composer: Epilog, 1967, Fanfare and Celebration, 1976; clarinet/saxophone Okla. Symphony, 1975—; condr. Norman Chamber Orch., 1980—; prin. clarinetist Oklahoma City Philharm., 1989—. Grantee So. Faculty Fellowship Fund, 1960-61, U. Colo., 1966, composition grantee MacDowell Colony, 1981; commn. Okla. Music Tchrs. Assn., 1977. Mem. ASCAP, Music Educators Nat. Conv., Music Tchs. Nat. Assn., Phi Mu Alpha, Pi Kappa Lambda. Home: Norman, Okla. Died Dec. 14, 2001.

SMITH, JUDY LYNN, interior designer; b. Myrtle Beach, S.C., May 8, 1965; d. Jesse Therman and Eula Mae (McFadden) Lancaster; m. Edward Jerome Williams III, Aug. 1, 1987 (div. Aug. 17, 1990); m. Calvin Eugene Smith III, Sept. 15, 1992; children: Jessica Lynn Smith, Caleb Mason Smith. BS in Interior Design, Western Carolina U., 1987. Interior designer The Decorators Inn, Easley, S.C., 1987, Allen Funks Wallpaper, Spartanburg, S.C., 1987-88, Color Tile, Spartanburg, S.C., 1988, Hodge Carpets, Spartanburg, S.C., 1988-89, Hines Lighting, Charlotte, N.C., 1990-91, Henderson Furniture, Greenville, S.C., 1992-93; detention officer Spartanburg County Detention Ctr., 1994-95; owner A-OK Bail Bonding, from 1992. Interior designer, Spartanburg, 1987—. Baptist. Died 2000.

SMITH, LAWRENCE J. lawyer; b. Oct. 10, 1938; s. Lawrence C. and Ora Lee (Beyer) S.; m. Dianne Ermon; children from first marriage: Lawrence J. II, Kathleen Ann. BBA, Loyola U., New Orleans, 1961, JD, 1962. Bar: La., 1962; U.S. Dist. Ct. Appeals (5th cir.); U.S. Dist. Ct. (ea. dist.) La., U.S. Dist. Ct. (we. dist.) Miss.; Diplomate Am. Bd. Profl. Liability Attys., Am. Bd. Trial Advocacy. Pvt. practice, New Orleans, 1964-70; ptnr. Levy, Smith, Gennusa, New Orleans, 1977-85, Levy, Smith, New Orleans, 1973-77, Levy, Smith, Pailet, New Orleans, 1970-73. Editorial adv. bd. Jour. of Med. and Hosp. Malpractice, Nat. Law Reporter; contbr. articles to profl. jours./publs. Fellow Am. Coll. Legal Medicine, Am. Bd. Trial Advocacy; mem. La. State Bar Assn. (various coms.), ATLA (bd. govs. 1968-69, 71-72, numerous coms., Disting. Leadership award 1972, chmn. traumatic brain injury litig. group), La. Trial Lawyers Assn. (bd. govs. 1970-71, numerous coms.), Am. Soc. Law and Medicine, Calif. Trial Lawyers Assn., Am. Judicature Soc., ABA, Fla. Trial Lawyers Assn., Assn. Behavioral Cons., New Orleans Bar Assn., Trial Lawyers for Pub. Justice, Nat. Coll. Advocacy, others. Avocation: magician. Died Dec. 12, 2001.

SMITH, LEONARD BINGLEY, musician; b. Poughkeepsie, N.Y., Sept. 5, 1915; s. Frank Roderick and Ethel (Schubert) S.; m. Helen Gladys Rowe, Apr. 20, 1940 (dec. 1993); 1 dau., Sandra Victoria. Student, N.Y. Mil. Acad., 1930-33, Ernest Williams Sch. Music, 1933-36, NYU, 1936-37, Curtis Inst. Music, 1943-45; H.H.D., Detroit Inst. Tech., 1965. Pres. Accompaniments Unltd., Inc., from 1952. Cornet soloist, Ernest Williams Band, 1933-36, The Goldman Band, summers 1936-42; 1st trumpet, Barrere Little Symphony, 1935-37, Detroit Symphony Orch., 1937-42, Ford Sunday Evening Hour, 1937-42; condr., The Leonard Smith Concert Band, 1945—, Detroit Concert Band, 1945—, U. Detroit Bands, 1949-50, Moslem AAONMS Band, 1945-57, Scandinavian Symphony Orch. of Detroit, 1959-61, guest condr., Indpls. Symphony Orch., 1967; guest condr., soloist, clinician numerous concerts, U.S., Can.; mus. dir. John Philip Sousa documentary for BBC, 1970; Sousa Am. Bicentennial Recorded Collection; record series Gems concert band, Blossom Festival Band; condr. Blossom Festival Concert Band, 1972—; The Indomitable Teddy Roosevelt; producer: Our Am. Heritage in Music, 1970; pres., Bandland, Inc., 1951-61; Author: Treasury of Scales; over 350 pub. compositions; mem. bd. advisors Instrumentalist mag. Chmn. music com. Mich. Civil War Centennial Commn., 1961-64; gov. bd. Mac Award. With USNR, 1942-45. Recipient spl. medal Mich. Polish Legion Am. Vets., Distinguished Service medal Kappa Kappa Psi; Mich. Minuteman Gov.'s award, 1973; Freedom Found. award, 1975; Gen. William Booth award, 1976, Embassy Mich. Tourism award, 1979; named Alumnus of Distinction N.Y. Mil. Acad., 1976 Mem. ASCAP, Philippine Bandsmen's Assn. (hon.), Am. Fedn. Musicians, Internat. Platform Assn., Assn. Concert Bands (pres. 1982-83). Clubs: Masons (33 deg.), Shriners, K.T, Jesters. Home: Scottsdale, Ariz. Died July 2002.

SMITH, LLOYD HILTON, independent oil and gas producer; b. Pitts., July 9, 1905; s. Roland Hilton and Jane (Lloyd) S.; m. Jane Clay Zevely, Sept. 7, 1931; children: Camilla; m. Elizabeth Keith Wiess, May 25, 1940; children: Sandra Keith, Sharon Lloyd, Sydney Carothers. Ph.B., Yale U., 1929. Statistician Biggs, Mohrman & Co., N.Y.C., 1932; mgr. New York office Laird & Co., 1933-34; v.p. Argus Research Corp., 1934-35; chmn., dir. Paraffine Oil Corp., 1949-81. Past dir. 1st City Nat. Bank Houston, Nat. Rev., Curtiss-Wright Corp., Info. Storage Systems, Falcon Seaboard, Inc. Mem. Houston Mus. Sci.; trustee Pine Manor Coll., 1963-74; past dir. DeBakey Med. Found. Lt. comdr. USNR, 1942-45. Mem.: Bayou (Houston); Everglades, Bath and Tennis (Palm Beach); Racquet and Tennis (N.Y.C.), Brook (N.Y.C.), River (N.Y.C.); Nat. Golf Links of America, Southampton, Meadow. Republican. Home: Palm Beach, Fla. Deceased.

SMITH, LOUIS DESPAIN, retired microbiologist, consultant; b. Odessa, Wash., Oct. 12, 1910; s. Charles Mortimer and Martha (Wolfe) S.; m. Norma Longeteig, May 5, 1936; children: Celia, Frances, Ellen. BS, U. Idaho, 1932, ScD (hon.), 1971, MS, 1935; PhD, U. Wash., 1948; ScD, Mont. State U., 1976. Diplomate Am. Bd. Microbiology (emeritus). From assoc. prof. microbiology to prof. and dean dept. Mont. State U., Bozeman, 1950-67; prof. Va. Poly. Inst., Blacksburg, 1967-76, prof. emeritus, from 1976; affiliate prof. U. Wash., Seattle, from 1976. Author: Introduction to the Pathogenic Anaerobes, 1955, The Pathogenic Anaerobes, 2d. edit., 1975, Botulism: The Organism, Its Toxins, The Disease, 1977; co-author: Physiologic Effects of Wounds, 1952, The Pathogenic Anaerobes, 1st. edit., 1968, 3d. edit., 1984, Botulism, 1988; contbr. chpts. to books, articles to profl. jours. Served to capt. U.S. Army, 1943-45. Fellow AAAS; mem. Am. Soc. Microbiology (hon). Avocations: winemaking, fishing. Home: Wenatchee, Wash. Deceased.

SMITH, MARSHALL FRANCIS, diversified company executive; b. Chgo., Apr. 30, 1929; s. Marshall E. and Suzanne (Vernia) S.; m. Catherine A. Kerin, Sept. 9, 1955; children— Thomas, Kathryn, Suzanne, Elizabeth. BS in Accounting, U. Ill., 1951; postgrad., U. Chgo., 1954, Northwestern U., 1955. Div. controller U.S. Steel Corp., N.Y.C., 1966-67; asst. controller Indian Head, Inc., N.Y.C., 1967-68; v.p., asst. gen. mgr. Wayne Corp. div. Indian Head Co., Richmond, Ind., 1969; v.p., controller Indian Head, Inc., N.Y.C., 1969-72, exec. v.p., 1972-74, pres., chief exec. officer, dir., 1974-84; bd. mgmt. T-B Inc., 1977-84; pres., chief exec. officer Commodore Internat. Ltd., 1984-86. Dir. Madera Glass Co., Hapad, Inc.; adv. bd. Mfrs. Hanover Trust Co. Former mem. adv. council Clarkson Coll.; former mem. U. Ill. Found. Mem. Psi Upsilon. Died Feb. 29, 2004.

SMITH, MICHAEL, management consultant; b. Hartford, Conn., Nov. 25, 1953; s. Robert Smith and Evelyn (Levine) Lieberman, m. Judy Beth Ludwig, Oct. 21, 1984. BA in Econs., U. Miami, Coral Gables, Fla., 1974; MBA in Fin., George Washington U., 1980. Rsch. analyst gov. ops. com. Senate, Washington, 1976-77; assoc. A.T. Kearney, Inc., Washington, Chgo., 1977-82; dir. mktg. Kwikasair Express, Inc., Mt. Prospect, Ill., 1982-83; dir. acquisitions/product mgr. new bus. devel. Alberto-Culver Co., Melrose Park, Ill., 1983-85; sr. mgr. Ernst & Whinney, Chgo., 1985-89; sr. cons. Buccino & Assocs., Chgo., from 1989. Pres. young leadership div. Jewish United Fund, Chgo., 1987-88; bd. dirs. Jewish Family and Community Svc., Chgo., 1988. Mem. Standard Club. Democrat. Home: Deerfield, Ill. Deceased.

SMITH, NELSON STUART, electrical engineer; b. Weirton, W.Va., Aug. 9, 1929; s. Nelson Stuart and Sara Kathyrn (Campbell) S.; m. Rhea Pauline Baker, Oct. 26, 1951; children: Nelson Stuart III, Sherri Kay, Vicki Lynn. BSEE, W.Va. U., 1956, MSEE, 1958; PhD, U. Pitts., 1962. From instr. to prof. elec. engring. W.Va. U., Morgantown, from 1956. Rsch. engr. U.S. Dept. Energy, Morgantown, 1965-93; electrical engr. U.S. Bur. Mines, Morgantown, 1957-60. Mem. IEEE, Elks, Moose. Avocations: travel, hiking, history. Patentee in field. Home: Morgantown, W.Va. Died Mar. 29, 2002.

SMITH, OLIVE IRENE PERRY, realty company executive; b. nr. Shelbyville, Ill., Dec. 13; d. Joseph Luther and Pearl (Bushart) Perry; grad. Sparks Coll., 1928; student Milligan U., 1929, Northwestern U., 1934-36, UCLA, 1959-60; m. William Smith, May 11, 1942. Hosp. librarian, registrar Chgo. State Hosp., Cook County, 1929-40; dep. assessor San Diego County, Calif., 1951-52; real estate broker O.I. Smith, Hemet, Calif., 1953—; real estate investment and loan counselor. Local rep. Nat. Inst. Real Estate Bds. Active Southland Water Com., 1960-68. Mem. adv. bd. San Jacinto (Calif.) Jr. Coll., 1967-68. Mem. Nat. Inst. Real Estate Brokers, Nat. Traders, Comml., and Investment Brokers Div. (pres. 1961), Hemet-San Jacinto Bd. Realtors (sec. 1960), Calif. Real Estate Assn. (regional v.p. 1964-65), Riverside Art Assn. Republican. Club: Soroptimist (San Jacinto-Hemet, Calif.). Home: Riverside, Calif.

SMITH, OLIVER ANDERSON, JR., realtor, developer; b. Knox County, Tenn., June 24, 1915; s. Oliver Anderson and Alva Belle (Seaton) S.; m. Evelyn Dooley, Dec. 14, 1939; children: Oliver Anderson III, E. Diana Smith Flaherty, Carol Mae Smith Tombras. BS, U. Tenn., 1939. Supr. USDA, Clinton, Tenn., 1939-41; appraiser Fed. Land Bank, 1941-43; prin. Oliver Smith Realty & Auction Co., Knoxville, Tenn., from 1939. Owner various other businesses including bldg. materials outlets; estate mgr., shopping ctr. developer, Knoxville. Former trustee Covenant Coll., Lookout Mountain, Tenn.; organizer, trustee PCA Presbyn. Ch., Knoxville; founder Oliver A. and Evelyn Smith Irrevocable Trust, Oliver A. and Evelyn Smith Found. Mem. Nat. Realtors Assn., Nat. Appraisers Assn., Nat. Auctioneers Assn., Nat. Platform Assn., Masons (32 degree), Optimists (past pres. Knoxville chpt.). Democrat. Home: Knoxville, Tenn. Deceased.

SMITH, RICHARD BLOTENBERGER, lawyer; b. Lancaster, Pa., July 9, 1928; s. Richard H. and May F. (Blotenberger) S.; m. Patricia Hamilton, July 18, 1987; children from previous marriage: Landis (Mrs. Bruce Bernstein), Leslie (Mrs. Keith McDaniel), Thompson, Eliza. BA, Yale U., 1949; LLB, U. Pa., 1953. Bar: N.Y. 1955, U.S. Supreme Ct. 1972. Assoc. Reavis & McGrath, N.Y.C., 1953-55, 57-63, ptnr., 1963-67; atty. W.R. Grace Co., N.Y.C., 1955-57; commr. SEC, Washington, 1967-71; ptnr. firm Davis Polk & Wardwell, N.Y.C., 1971-90, sr. counsel, 1991—2003. Mem. council Adminstrv. Conf. U.S., 1971-74 Trustee N.Y.C. Citizens Budget Commn., 1976-88, vice chmn. 1976-84. Mem. ABA (vice chmn. commn. on law and economy 1975-79, mem. council sect. on corp., banking and bus. law 1979-84, nat. conf. lawyers and CPAs, 1982-87), N.Y. State Bar Assn., Assn. Bar City N.Y., Am. Law Inst. (adviser Fed. Securities Code 1970-80, corp. governance project 1981-93, N.Y. Uniform Law Commn. 1998-2002). Died Nov. 2, 2003.

SMITH, SAMUEL BOYD, history educator; b. Adams, Tenn., Oct. 23, 1929; s. Carl S. and Annie (Tolleson) S.; m. Martha Sue Fitzsimmons, Dec. 23, 1956; children— David Fitzsimmons, Mark Tolleson, Stephen Boyd. Student, Milligan Coll., 1947-48, U. Tenn., 1948-49, Syracuse U., 1951-52; BS, Peabody Coll., 1956; MA, Vanderbilt U., 1960, PhD, 1962. Asst. prof. history U. South Fla., 1961-64; state librarian and archivist, chmn. Tenn. Hist. Commn., 1964-69; lectr. history Peabody Coll., 1965-66; assoc. prof. history U. Tenn., 1969-72, prof., editor Andrew Jackson Presdl. Papers, 1972-79; prof. Tenn. State U., Nashville, 1979-97. Co-author: This is Tennessee, 1973; Editor and compiler: Tennessee History: A Bibliography, 1974; co-editor: The Papers of Andrew Jackson, vol. I, 1980. Served with USAF, 1951-54. Mem. Tenn. Hist. Soc., Shakespeare Club, Univ. Club. Democrat. Methodist. Died Jan. 17, 2003.

SMITH, THOMAS S. state legislator; b. Bloomfield, Dec. 14, 1917; Student, Howard U. Mayor, Asbury Park, N.J., 1989-93; assemblyman dist. 11 N.J. State Assembly, from 1992. Named police chief of yr. Nat. Assn. Police Commr. Rels., Nat. Orgn. Christians & Jews. Mem. Monmouth-Ocean Christians & Jews. Died Sept. 26, 2002.

SMITH, VINCENT DACOSTA, artist; b. Bklyn., Dec. 12, 1929; s. Beresford Leopold and Louise S.; m. Cynthia I. Linton, July 15, 1972. Student, Art Students League, N.Y.C., 1953, Bklyn. Mus. Sch., 1955-56; B. Profl. Services, Empire State Coll., 1980. Instr. painting and graphics Whitney Mus. Art, N.Y.C., 1967-76; instr. painting Ceda Project, 1978-80. Artist in residence Smithsonian Conf. Center, Elkridge, Md., 1967, Cite des Arts Internat., Paris, 1978, 1999; participant 2d World Black and African Festival Arts and Culture, Lagos, Nigeria, 1977; commns. include Impressions: Our World Portfolio of Prints, 1974, mural at Boys and Girls High Sch., Bklyn., 1976, mural for Tremont/Crotona Social Svc. Ctr. Human Resources Adminstrn. and CETA Project, N.Y.C., 1980, mural for Oberia D. Dempsey Multi-Svc. Ctr. for Cen. Harlem, Dept. Cultural Affairs, N.Y.C., 1988, 2 murals for 116 St. Sta., N.Y.C. Met. Transit Authority, Portrait of Reginald F. Lewis, Harvard U., Cambridge; film tapes and videos include Bernie Casey: Black Dimensions in Contemporary Am. Art, Carnation Co., Los Angeles, 1971, Tee Collins, Barbara Cobb: The First Water, Theatre Eleven, 1977, Robert Fassbinder: The Creative Pulse of Afro-Am. Culture, WTVG, N.J., 1978, Bearden Plays Bearden, Third World Cinema, 1980, Works on Paper, Storefront Mus./Paul Robeson Theatre, Jamaica, N.Y., 1981; host bi-weekly program, discussions with 45 activists WBAI-FM Radio. Illustrator: Folklore Stories from Africa, 1974; exhbns. include Hall of Springs Mus., Saratoga, N.Y., 1970, Contemporary Black Am. Artists, Whitney Mus. Am. Art, N.Y.C., 1971, Two Generations, Newark Mus., 1971, Mus. of Sci. and Industry, Chgo., 1975, Bronx Mus. Art, 1977, Bklyn. Mus., 1979; one-man exhbns. include Lacarda Gallery, N.Y.C., 1967, 68, 70, 73, 75, 77, Paa Ya Paa Gallery, Nairobi, Kenya, 1973, Chemchemi Creative Arts Center, Arusha, Tanzania, 1973, Kibo Art Gallery, Mt. Kilimanjaro, Tanzania, 1973, Portland (Maine) Art Mus., 1974, Reading (Pa.) Public Mus., 1974, Erie (Pa.) Art Center, 1977, Gallery 7, Detroit, 1977; represented in permanent collections, Mus. Modern Art, N.Y.C., Newark Mus., Bklyn. Mus., U. Va. Art Mus.; also subject of TV film; host Vincent Smith Dialogues with Contemporary Artists, Radio Sta. WPAI-FM, 1986-88. Served with U.S. Army, 1948-49. Recipient Thomas B. Clark prize N.A.D., 1974; Winslow and Newton prize Nat. Soc. Painters in Casein and Acrylic, 1978; John Hay Whitney fellow, 1959; Nat. Endowment Arts grantee, 1973; Nat. Inst. Arts and Letters grantee, 1968; Cultural Council Found. grantee, 1971 Mem. Nat. Conf. Artists. Home: New York, NY. Died Dec. 27, 2003.

SMITH, WAYLAND RUFUS, retired county official; b. Sterling, Colo., Dec. 11, 1936; s. Eldon Emerson and Edith Marie Smith; m. Barbara Hartshorne, Dec. 27, 1959; children: Gregory T., Douglas S., Kristen M. BA, U. Denver, 1958. Project mgr. Denver Housing Authority, 1958-60; housing rehab. specialist Redevel. Land Agy., Washington, 1961-62, asst. chief rehab. divsn., 1963-64; asst. exec. dir. Cumberland (Md.) Urban Renewal Agy., 1965-66; exec. dir. Parkersburg (W.Va.) Urban Renewal Authority, 1967-71, Fayette County Redevel. Authority, Uniontown, Pa., 1971-98; ret. Facilities chmn. State Theater Ctr. for the Arts, Uniontown, 1999. Mem. Nat. Assn. of Housing and Redevel. Ofcls. (v.p. profl. devel. 1985-87, pres. Pitts. chpt. 1983-85, pres. Middle Atlantic Regional Coun. 1995-97, bd. govs. 1985-87, 95-99). Democrat. Avocations: cookie baking, woodworking. Home: Uniontown, Pa. Died Feb. 14, 2000.

SMITH, WILLIAM A. philosophy educator; b. Newburgh, N.Y., Dec. 12, 1929; s. William A. Sr. and Marion L. (McIntyre) S.; m. Joyce Eleanor Comeau, Apr. 12, 1958; children: Stephen, Christopher, James, Timothy, Kerry Ann. PhB, Gregorian U., Rome, 1952, PhL, 1953, STB, 1955; PhD, St. John's U., 1967. Instr. in philosophy Coll. of New Rochelle, N.Y., 1956-57; analyst CIA, Washington, 1957-59; instr. to full prof. Seton Hall U., South Orange, N.J., from 1959. Home: Maplewood, NJ. Died Jan. 20, 2002.

SMITH, WILLIAM LANCASTER, lawyer; b. Lebanon, Ky., June 14, 1923; s. William Lancaster and Dorothy (Spalding) S.; m. Jacquelyn Ann Hilbert, June 5, 1948 (dec. Jan. 1993); children: Lancaster Jr., Scott, Terry, Sherry, Michael, Stephen, Patrick, Christopher, Matthew, Shane. JD, U. Notre Dame, 1950. Bar: Ky. 1950, Ind. 1950, Tex. 1950, U.S. Ct. Mil. Appeals 1960, U.S. Supreme Ct. 1960, U.S. Ct. Appeals (5th cir.) 1969, U.S. Dist. Ct. (ea., we., so. and no. dists.) Tex. Asst. dist. atty., Dallas, 1954-57; ptnr. Smith, Smith & Smith, Dallas, from 1957. Coach football team Dallas Jesuit High Sch., 1953; pres. Dallas Citizens for Decent Lit., 1963. Served to sgt. USAF, 1942-46. Recipient Man of Yr. award Notre Dame U., Dallas, 1954. Mem. Nat. Notre Dame Alumni Assn. (pres. 1965-66), Notre Dame Monogram Club (pres. 1987-88), KC (grand knight 1963, coun. 799). Roman Catholic. Home: Dallas, Tex. Died July 12, 2000.

SMITHSON, PETER DENHAM, architect; b. Stockton-on-Tees, Eng., Sept. 18, 1923; s. William Blenkiron and Elizabeth (Denham) S.; m. Alison Margaret Gill, 1949 (dec. Aug. 1993); 3 children. Ed., Stockton-on-Tees Grammar Sch., U. Durham, Royal Acad. Schs., London. Asst. L.C.C., 1949-50; pvt. practice architect with Alison Smithson, 1950-93. Prin. works include Hunstanton Sch., Economist Bldg., London, Robin Hood Gardens, G.L.C. Housing in Tower Hamlets, Garden Bldg. St. Hilda's Coll., Oxford, Amenity Bldg., U. Bath, Second Arts Bldg. 6 East, U. Bath, Arts Barn, U. Bath, 1978—90, Porch at Ansty Plum, Porches at Tecta, Lauenforde, 1992—99, Hexenbesenraum, Karlshafen, 1991—96, Hexenhaus Bridge and Pier, 1997, Hexenhaus Tea-House, Panorama Porch, Tecta, Lauenforde, 1997—98, Hexenhaus Lantern Pavilion, 2001—03, exhibitions include House of the Future, 1956, Milan Triennale, 1968, Venice Biennale, 1976, Tichleindeckdich, Cologne and Berlin, 1993, On the Floor-Off the Floor, Cologne, 1998, The Lattice Idea, 1999, 2000, Madrid, 2000; author: Ordinariness and Light, 1970, Urban Structuring Studies, 1971, Without Rhetoric, 1979, The Heroic Period of Modern Architecture, 1981, The Shift, 1982, Monographs, The 1930's, 1985, Italian Thoughts, 1993, Changing the Art of Inhabitation, 1994, Bath Walks Within Walls: Oxford and Cambridge Walks (all with A. Smithson) Book Work, 1995, Italienische Gedanken, 1996, The Charged Void: Architecture, 2002; co-author (with K. Unglaub): Flying Furniture, 1999. Died Mar. 3, 2003.

SMOCK, WALTER WILSON, communications executive, educator; b. Bandung, Indonesia, July 11, 1923; s. Wilson Walter and Christina Wilhemia (Vanas) S.; m. Jean Vivian O'Levich, Aug. 11, 1946 (div. Mar. 1963); children: Bari Lynne, Gregg, Peter; m. Carolyn Ruth Baker, Jan. 10, 1971. BSEE, U. Scranton, 1948; MS in Math., Villanova U., 1956; MS in Sociology, U. Del., 1980, PhD, 1982. Registered profl. engr., Del. Exec. v.p. Sci-Tek, Inc., Wilmington, Del., 1969-73; pres. Telemarc, Inc., Wilmington, from 1971, Rollins Communications, Atlanta, 1973-74; dir. nat. account Litton Industries, Los Angeles, 1974-78; asst. prof. Rutgers U., Camden, N.J., 1982-88; prof. mgmt. Sch. Bus. and Pub. Policy West Chester U. Pa., 1988-91; pvt. practice psychol. counseling West Chester, 1991; ret., 1991. Cons. Dept. Environ. Protection, Trenton, N.J., 1982-83; tech./bus. cons. Amenex Assocs., West Chester, Pa.; psychol. counselor VA; mem. SCORE. Author: A User's MIS Concepts and Applications, 1986. Cons. Mayor's Adv. Council, Phila., 1972-73; bd. dirs. fin. affairs St. Peter's Roman Cath. Cathedral, Wilmington, 1980. Served to capt. U.S. Army, 1943-46, ETO. Mem. IEEE, DAV, Data Processing Mgrs. Assn., Ret. Officers Assn.. Republican. Roman Catholic. Avocations: sailing, flying, writing, travel. Home: Wilmington, Del. Died May 20, 2002.

SMUCKER, PAUL HIGHNAM, food company executive; b. Orrville, Ohio, Apr. 21, 1917; s. Willard Earl and Letha (Highnam) S.; m. Lorraine Evangeline Smith, June 29, 1940; children— Susan Diane Wagstaff, Timothy Paul, Richard Kim. BS in Bus., Miami U., Oxford, Ohio, 1939. With J. M. Smucker Co., Orrville, 1939—, gen. mgr., 1946-61, pres., 1961-70, chmn., chief exec. officer, 1970-87, chmn. exec. com., chief executive officer, from 1987. Co-trustee Kellogg Trust, Nat. Bank Orrville. Lt. (j.g.) USNR, 1943-46, PTO. Mem. Nat. Preservers Assn. (pres. 1956-57), Grocery Mfrs. Am. (dir.), Am. Mgmt. Assn., Am. Acad. Achievement, Phi Delta Theta. Republican. Home: Orrville, Ohio. Died Dec. 17, 1998.

SMYTHE, SHEILA MARY, academic dean and administrator; b. N.Y.C., Nov. 1, 1932; d. Patrick John and Mary Catherine (Gonley) S. BA, Creighton U., 1952, Manhattanville Coll., 1952; MS, Columbia U., N.Y.C., 1956; LHD (hon.), Manhattanville Coll., 1974. From rsch. assoc. to asst. dir. of rsch. and planning Blue Cross Assn., Chgo., 1957-63; exec. assoc. to pres. Empire Blue Cross & Blue Shield, N.Y.C., 1963-72, v.p., 1972-74, sr. v.p., 1974-78, exec. v.p., 1978-82, pres., chief oper. officer, 1982-85; health fin. and mgmt. cons. N.Y.C. and Washington, 1986-87; chief health policy advisor, cons. GAO, Washington, 1987-95, exec. v.p., 1995—2003; dean Sch. Pub. Health N.Y. Med. Coll., N.Y.C., 1990—2003. Adj. asst. prof. Grad. Sch. Pub. Health, Columbia U., 1980—86; bd. dirs. Mut. of Am., product and mktg. com., 1991—93, nominating com., 1992—94, audit com., 1993—2003, strategic planning com., 1994—97, investment com., from 1997; bd. dirs. Nat. Health Coun., Inc., mem. fin. com., 1987—94; bd. dirs. Hudson Valley Health Sys. Agy., sec., 1993—94, 1st v.p., 1994—95, pres., 1995—2000; mem. N.Y. State Hosp. and Rev. Planning Coun., 1994—2001. Chmn. bd. Manhattanville Coll., Purchase, NY, 1982—86, 1994—97, vice-chair, 1997—2003, trustee affairs, acad. affairs, exec. coms.; bd. dirs. March of Dimes Birth Defects Found., 1989—2001, vice chair, mem. fin. com., chair pub. affairs com., chair trustee affairs com.; bd. dirs. Greater N.Y. March of Dimes, 1985—89; trustee Dominican Acad., N.Y.C., 2000—03, chair, from 2002; bd. dirs. Visiting Nurse Svc. Westchester, 1999—2003, chair nominating com., 2000—03, chmn. bd., 2003; bd. dirs. Cath. Charities-U.S.A., 1989—95, mem. exec. pers. coms. Recipient Elizabeth Cutter Morrow award YWCA, N.Y., 1977, Disting. Alumni award Manhattanville Coll., 1981, 97, Excellence in Leadership award Greater N.Y. March of Dimes, 1989, First Westchester County Pub. Health Leadership award, 2002. Mem. Nat. Arts Club N.Y.C. Roman Catholic. Home: Washington, DC. Died Nov. 4, 2003.

SNAPP, ROY BAKER, lawyer; b. Strang, Okla., May 9, 1916; s. Harry Moore and Verda Mildred (Austin) S.; m. Dorothy Faye Loftis, Jan. 27, 1942; children: Deborah, Bryan Austin, Martha Lynn, Barbara, James. Lawyer. BS in Pub. Adminstrn, U. Mo., 1936; LL.B., Georgetown U., 1941, LL.M., 1942. With U.S. State Dept., 1941; spl. adviser comdg. gen. (Manhattan (Atomic Bomb) Project), 1946; dir. internat. affairs U.S. AEC, 1947, 1st sec., 1948-54, asst. to chmn., 1954-55, sr. staff mem. nat. security coun., 1953-55; v.p. atomic div. (Am. Machine & Foundry), 1957; v.p. Am. Machine & Foundry Co., Washington office, 1961. Bd. dirs. Electro-Nucleonics, Inc.; ptnr. Bechhoefer, Snapp and Trippe, 1966. Commd. ensign USNR 1942; assigned secretariat of U.S. Joint Chiefs of Staff and Combined (U.S.-Brit), Chiefs of Staff; naval mem. 1945; Intelligence Staff of Joint Cheifs Staff and Combined Chiefs Staff promoted to lt. comdr. 1945. Recipient D.S.M. AEC, 1955 Mem. Phi Gamma Mu, Delta Theta Phi. Clubs: Univ. (Washington), Columbia Country (Washington). Baptist. Home: Fredericksburg, Va. Died Dec. 30, 2002.

SNELL, ALAN HAROLD, optometrist; b. Liberty, Nebr., June 22, 1940; s. J. Harold and Elizabeth (Finney) S.; m. Phyllis Lea Moses, Aug. 25, 1963; children: Lennah, Michelle, Dawn. B.A., Tarkio Coll., 1963; O.D., Pacific U., 1966. Optometrist, Dr. Watts-Snell, Leavenworth, Kans., 1966-69; practice optometry, Leavenworth, 1969-72, Lansing, Kans., 1972-96. Mem. sch. bd. Lansing Sch. Dist. #469, Kans., 1981-89, pres., 1985. Mem. Am. Optometric Assn. (sports sect., contact lens sect.), Kans. Optometric Assn., Heart Am. Contact Lens Assn., Leavenworth Area C. of C. (bd. dirs., 2d v.p. 1985). Republican. Died Dec. 13, 1996. Home: Leavenworth, Kans.

SNELL, JOHN RAYMOND, civil engineer; b. Suzhou, China, Dec. 9, 1912; (parents Am. citizens); s. John A. and Grace (Birkett) S.; m. Florence Moffett, Dec. 8, 1939; children: Chica Dorothea, Karen Snell Dailey, Martha E. Snell Rood, John Raymond Jr., David Moffett. BE, Vanderbilt U., 1934; MS, U. Ill, 1936; DSc, Harvard U., 1939. Registered profl. engr., Mass., Mich., Ohio, Ill., Ind., La. Wis., N.Y., Tex. Fla., Idaho, Oreg., Ont., Can.; cert. san. engr.; diplomate Am. Acad. Environ. Engrs. Instr. civil engring. Hangchow U., 1934-35; with Water Supply Fed. Pub. Works Dept., Venezuela, 1939-40; design engr. Metcalf & Eddy, also Fay Spofford and Thorndyke, Stone & Webster, Boston, 1941-42; san. engr., head water and sewage sect. 1st Svc. Command, Boston, 1946; assigned UNRA restoration water, sewage, solid wastes 5 no. provinces China San. Engring. Services Inc., 1945-46; project engr. Burns & Kenerson, Boston, 1947; pres., chief engr. Engring. Svcs. Inc., Boston, 1948-51; lectr. MIT, 1949-51; prof., head dept. civil and san. engring. Mich. State U., 1951-55; owner John R. Snell & Assocs., 1956; sr. prin. Mich. Assocs., cons. engrs., 1956-60; pres. John R. Snell Engrs. Inc., 1960-75, Snell Environ. Group, 1975-80, hon. chmn. bd., spl. cons., 1980-88; joint venturer Snell-Republic Assocs. Ltd., Lahore, West Pakistan, 1961-80; with Assoc. Architects & Engrs., Dacca, Bangladesh, 1965-80; pres. Caribbean Devel. Corp. and subs. Gen. Shrimp Ltd., Belize, 1984-92. Sr. adj. scientist Mich. Biotech. Inst., 1990—; 1994 guest of China-Suzhou Hosp. 110 Aniv.; solid waste cons. Xiaogan Recycling Treatment Utilization of Organics, Peoples Republic of China, 1995—; founder Trans Mich. Waterway Inc., S.W. Waterway (Ont.) Ltd., N.Y.; spl. cons. on ast high rate compost plant to Govt. of Japan, 1955-56; cons. in Orient, WHO, 1956; chmn. bd. Bootstrap Internat. Inc., 1972; chmn. bd. Save Our Spaceship/nc.NFP 2001 (to abate pollution, sustainability and population control); expert witness on over 50 ct. cases. Author: Toward a Better World, 1997, trans. into Chinese, 1999, 12 sects. Environment Engineering Handbook; co-author: Municipal Solid Waste Disposal; contbr. articles to profl. jours.; patentee in composting field. Maj. USPHS, 1945-47. Recipient Prescott Eddy award, 1944. Mem. Nat., Mich. (life) socs. profl. engrs., Am. Water Works Assn., Hwy. Rsch. Bd., ASTM, ASCE, Am. Pub. Works Assn., Water Pollution Control Fedn. (life), Mich. Engring. Soc. (life), Cons. Engrs. Coun. (past dir.), Cons. Engrs. Assn. Mich. (past pres.), Inter-Am. Assn. San. Engrs., World Aquaculture Soc., Composters Inc. (pres. Worldwide Techs. Inc. East Lansing 1980—), Rotary, Tau Beta Pi, Chi Epsilon. Died Apr. 4, 2003.

SNIDER, ROBERT CUSATOR, retired educator; b. Jamestown, N.D., Apr. 17, 1924; s. Argalis and Sybella Catherine (Cusator) S.; m. Dorothy Louise Olson, Aug. 5, 1950; 1 child, Robert Jr. BA, Jamestown Coll., 1947; MS, Ind. U., 1949, EdD, 1956. Tchr. English Marine Corps Inst. Pacific, Honolulu, 1945-46, Breckenridge (Minn.) Pub. Schs., 1947-48; mem. faculty U. Minn., Mankato, 1949-51; asst. to dean Ind. U., Bloomington, 1951-53; asst. dir. edn. communication svc. U. Chgo., 1953-54, mem. faculty, 1953-58; sr. staff mem. NEA, Washington, 1958-86. Adj. faculty Fed. City Coll., Washington, 1969-71; staff mem. Fed. Commn. on Instructional Tech., 1969-70; writer, cons. Words & Pictures, Inc., Chevy Chase, Md. Editor Monitor newsletter, NEA, 1975-78; contbr. to numerous ednl. publs. Lender collection of books on Am. photography, Georgetown U. Rare Book Library, 1980. With USMC, 1943-46. Mem. NEA, Coun. Internat. Nonthetrical Events (bd. dirs. 1982-90), Washington Rare Book Group, St. Andrew's Soc. Washington, Phi Delta Kappa. Republican. Presbyterian. Avocation: rare books on american photography. Home: Bethesda, Md. Deceased.

SNOOK, JOHN MCCLURE, telephone company executive; b. Toledo, May 31, 1917; s. Ward H. and Grace (McClure) S.; m. Marjorie Younce; student Ohio State U., 1936-43. Instr. history, fine arts and scis. Ohio State U., Columbus; exec. v.p. Gulf Telephone Co., Foley, Ala., 1955-71, pres., 1971-90, chmn. bd., chief exec. officer, 1990—. Chmn., Baldwin Sesquicentennial, 1969; mem. Baldwin County Bicentennial Commn.; pageant chmn., dir. Ft. Morgan Bicentennial Program, 1976; mem. hon. staff Gov. Ala., 1967—; past pres. Friends of Library Assn.; asso. sponsor Gulf Shores Mardi Gras Assn. Named Hon. A.D.C. Lt. Col. Ala., Ala. State Trooper; recipient Citizen of Year award Gulf Shores, 1956-57. Mem. NRA (hon.), Ala.-Miss. Ind. Telephone Assn. (past pres.), Am. Ordnance Assn., South Baldwin C. of C., Delaware County, Baldwin County (pres.) hist. assns., Defiance and Williams' Hist. Soc., Am. Mus. Nat. History Assn., Nat. Hist. Soc., Nat. Wildlife Fedn., Clan McLeod Soc., Smithsonian Assn., Am. Heritage Soc., Nat. Fedn. Blind, Ohio State Alumni Assn., Ala. Ind. Telephone Assn., Telephone Pioneers, Ind. Pioneers. Clubs: Lions (past pres.), Kiwanis (past pres.; asst. chmn. ann. Christmas Party and Parade).Died 1995.

SNYDER, JOHN CRAYTON, population and public health consultant; b. Salt Lake City, May 24, 1910; s. Crayton Chambers and Flora (Macdonald) S.; m. Virginia Townsend Ferry, June 14, 1942; children: Virginia Snyder MacNeil, John Macdonald, Gordon Mansfield. AB, Stanford U., 1931; MD, Harvard U., 1935, LLD (hon.), 1964. Diplomate Am. Bd. Preventive Medicine. Rsch. fellow in surgery Harvard/Mass. Gen. Hosp., Boston, 1936-37; jr. fellow Harvard Soc. Fellows/Harvard U., Cambridge, Mass., 1939-40; staff mem. internat. health divsn. Rockefeller Found., N.Y.C., 1940-46; prof. pub. health bacteriology, head dept. Harvard Sch. Pub. Health, Boston, 1946-54, dean faculty, 1954-71; med. dir. Ctr. for Population Studies Harvard U., Boston, 1971-76, prof. emeritus population and pub. health Sch. Pub. Health, from 1976. Cons. on population policy Pathfinder Fund, Chestnut Hill, mass., 1976-79, Univ. Assoc. for Internat. Health, Boston, 1977-83; bd. dirs. Emerson Hosp., Concord, Mass., 1980-85; chmn. expert com. on trachoma WHO, Geneva, 1961; mem. study sect. NIH, Bethesda, Md.; mem. Armed Forces Epidemiol. Bd., 1962-72, rickettsial diseases com., 1951-72; mem. U.S.A. Typhus Com., 1942-46. Contbr. articles to profl. jours. Lt. col. U.S. Army Med. Corps, 1942-45. Recipient medal USA Typhus Commn., 1942-45, Order of the Nile medal Egyptian Govt., 1944. Fellow AAAS, Am. Acad. Arts and Scis.; mem. Am. Assn. Physicians, Am. Epidemiol. Soc., Alpha Omega Alpha, Phi Beta Kappa. Avocations: music, tennis. Home: Harrisville, NH. Died Feb. 19, 2002.

SNYDER, LEWIS SAMUEL, stock brokerage executive; b. Bethlehem, Pa., Apr. 30, 1913; s. Oran Charles and Mary Dixon (Saeger) S.; m. Aleen Julia Ballou, June 12, 1938; children: Julia Ann Scarisbrick, Laura Jane Begler. AA, Riverside (Calif.) City Coll., 1933; BBA, Woodbury Coll., 1935. Clk. Mobil Oil Co., San Diego, 1935-41; agt. FBI, Birmingham, Ala., 1941; dist. auditor Def. Plant Corp., Kansas City, Mo., 1942-46; stockbroker Pacific Co., Riverside, Calif., 1946-52; br. mgr. Lester, Ryons & Co., Riverside, 1952-68; v.p., stockbroker Wagenseller & Durst, Riverside, 1968-78, Wedbush Co., Riverside, 1978-89, Bateman Eichler & Co., Riverside, 1989-91; sr. account exec. A.G. Edwards & Sons, Riverside, from 1991. Mem. Riverside Optimist Club (pres. 1956), Masons (master Riverside lodge # 635 F&AM 1957). Republican. Presbyterian. Avocations: hiking, traveling. Home: Riverside, Calif. Deceased.

SOBIESKI, CAROLINE BUSH O'BRIEN, screenwriter; b. Chgo., Mar. 16, 1939; d. Francis Thomas and Emeline Ruth (Bush) O'Brien; m. James Louis Sobieski, Nov. 21, 1964; children: Emeline, Mona, James. BA, Smith Coll., Northampton, Mass., 1960; M. Litt., Trinity Coll., Dublin, Ireland, 1961. Writer TV shows Mr. Novak, The Mod Squad, Fame is the Name of the Game, 1964-68; staff writer TV series Peyton Place, 1965-67; writer TV pilots Dial Hot Line, Paper Moon, Sunshine, Two Marriages, 1970-83; writer TV movies including Where the Ladies Go, Sunshine Christmas, Amelia Earhart, The Neon Ceiling, from 1971; writer TV mini-series The Women's Room, The Bourne Identity; writer feature films Honeysuckle Rose, Annie, Casey's Shadow, The Toy, Sylvester, Winter People, from 1978. Adj. prof. U. So. Calif. Cinema Sch., Los Angeles, 1987. Recipient Anthology award San Francisco Film Festival, 1971, Emmy nomination, 1976, Women in TV and Film award, 1977, 80. Mem. Acad. Motion Picture Arts and Scis., Writers Guild Found. (bd. dirs.), Writers Guild Am. West (Outreach com., Awards com., awards 1971, 73, 77). Episcopalian. Avocations: horses, flying, theater, children. Home: Pasadena, Calif. Deceased.

SOBIN, SIDNEY S. physiology and biophysics educator, researcher; b. Bayonne, NJ, Jan. 1, 1914; s. Eva (Newman); m. Venus K. Karalis, Nov. 27, 1959; children: Paul B., Dione D. BS, U. Mich., 1935, PhD, 1938, MD, 1941. Diplomate Am. Bd. Internal Medicine. Prof. physiology U. So. Calif., Los Angeles, 1947-56 and from 1966; research prof. medicine Loma Linda U., Los Angeles, 1957-66. Dir. U. So. Calif. Cardiovascular Research Lab., 1957—. Contbr. numerous articles on microcirculation, aging and hypertension to profl. jours. Med. Scis. fellow NRC, 1944-46; Rsch. Career award NIH, 1962. Fellow ACP, AAAS; mem. Am. Physiol. Soc., Microcirculatory Soc. (pres. 1965-67, Landis award 1980), Alpha Omega Alpha. Died Oct. 25, 2001.

SOCHUREK, HOWARD JAMES, graphic arts company executive, author; b. Milw., Nov. 27, 1924; s. Edward Aloys Sochurek and Gertrude Hildegarde Herbst; m. Tatiana Alexandra Akhonin, May 7, 1965; 1 child, Tatiana. Student, Marquette U., 1942, Princeton U., 1942-44, Harvard U., 1960. Mem. staff Milw. Jour., 1946-50; mem. staff Life mag. Time, Inc., N.Y.C., 1950-65; pres., chief exec. officer Howard Sochurek, Inc., N.Y.C., from 1965. Author: The First Siberians, 1969, The New Russia, 1970, Siberia at Work, 1971, Medicine's New Vision, 1988. Capt. U.S. Army, 1943-46. Named Mag. Photographer of Yr. U Mo., 1956; recipient award Nat. Art Dirs. Club N.Y., 1956; Nieman fellow Harvard U., 1960. Mem. Overseas Press Club (Robert Capa award 1955), Bronxville Field Club. Home: Ocean Ridge, Fla. Deceased.

SOKOLOF, PHIL, industrialist, consumer advocate; b. Omaha, Dec. 14, 1922; s. Louis and Rose (Jacobson) S.; m. Ruth Rosinsky, June 1, 1947 (dec. Feb. 1982); children: Steven, Karen Sokolof Javitch. Grad. H.S., Omaha, 1939. Founder, CEO Phillips Mfg. Co., Omaha, 1955-92; founder, pres. Nat. Heart Savers Assn., Omaha, 1985—2004. Author: Bridge Philosophy, 1971, Add Years to Your Life: Maintain or Regain a Healthy Heart, 2002; contbg. editor N.Y. Times, 1991; featured in Time mag., Mar. 1990, in Jour. of Am. Medicine, Dec. 1990 as catalyst of Am. pub.'s cholesterol consciousness; contbg. editor Sunday New York Times, 1991. Designated by Congress hon. co-sponsor 1990 Nutrition Labeling and Edn. Act; conducted Poisoning of Am. nat. media campaigns for high cholesterol, high fat content in foods, 1988-93 (citation FDA 1993); activist in lowering fat content Nat. Sch. Lunch Program; conducted, funded $1 million Nutrition Facts sweepstakes quiz to educate pub. regarding nutrition food labels, 1994; ran nat. advt. campaign promoting skim milk and alerting Ams. that 2% milk is not low fat, 1995; ran nat. advt. campaigns advising pub. of lifesaving cholesterol-lowering drugs, 1996, 98; pioneered citywide cholesterol testing in U.S., 1985-88, testing over 200,000 people in 16 states; created, won congl. approval designating Apr. as Nat. Know Your Cholesterol Month, 1987, Cholesterol Kills pub. svc. announcements featured on over 1000 TV stas., 1987-2004; nat. spokesperson of danger of cholesterol and saturated fats in food products which promote heart disease; ran $2.5 million TV ad on Super Bowl urging Ams. take breakthrough cholesterol-lowering drugs, 2000; successfully lobbied Can. Govt. for nutrition facts labels, 2003. Named Person of Week, ABC News, Mar. 15, 1991; recipient FDA Commr's. Spl. Achievement citation, 1993, C. Everett Koop Health Adv. award Am. Hosp. Assn., 1994, Am. award Norman Vincent Peale Found., 1997, Nat. award Caring Inst., 2001. Mem. Am. Contract Bridge League (life master), King Solomon's Cir. Philanthropy (charter). Died Apr. 15, 2004.

SOKOLOW, MAURICE, physician, educator; b. N.Y.C., May 19, 1911; s. Alexander and Anna (Spiegelman) S.; m. Ethel Schwabacher, June 30, 1941 (dec. 1970); children: Gail Anne, Jane Carol (dec.), Anne May. AB cum laude, U. Calif., Berkeley, 1932; MD, U. Calif., San Francisco, 1936. Intern San Francisco Gen. Hosp., 1935-36; resident U. Calif., San Francisco, 1936-37, rsch. fellow, 1939-40; resident New Eng. Med. Ctr., Boston, 1937-38; rsch. fellow Michael Reese Hosp., Chgo., 1938-39; gen. practice medicine San Francisco, 1946-62; faculty cardiovascular divsn. Sch. Medicine, U. Calif., San Francisco, from 1946, assoc. prof. medicine, 1952-58, prof., 1958-78, prof. emeritus, from 1978, chief electrocardiograph dept., chief hypertension clinic, 1946-78, chief cardiovascular divsn., 1955-73; program and founding dir. cardiology tng. grant USPHS, San Francisco, 1960-73; sr. and founding mem. Cardiovascular Rsch. Inst., from 1957. Cons. in field. Author: Clinical Cardiology, 1977, 6th edit., 1993; contbr. articles to profl. jours.; mem. editorial bd. Jour. Cardiovascular Medicine, 1975—, Western Jour. Medicine, 1946-68. Bd. dirs. Fromm Inst Life Long Learning, U. San Francisco. Lt. comdr. M.C. USN, 1942-46. Rsch. fellow U. Calif., 1939-40; Nat. Heart Inst. grant, 1950-78; named U. Calif. San Francisco Alumnus of Yr., 1986. Fellow Am. Coll. Cardiology (hon.); mem. Am. Fedn. Clin. Research (v.p. 1948-49), Assn. Univ. Cardiologists, Am. Soc. Clin. Investigation, Brit. Cardiac Soc. (corr.), Am. Heart Assn., San Francisco Heart Assn. (pres. 1950-51), Menlo Circus Club. Clubs: Menlo Circus. Deceased.

SOLDO, JOHN J. educator, writer; b. Bklyn., May 16, 1945; s. Victor and Mildred Carmela (Ferrari) S.; m. Martha Schwink, Aug. 24, 1968 (div. Apr. 1971). BA magna cum laude, Fordham U., 1966; MA, Harvard U., 1968, PhD, 1972. Asst. prof. Wells Coll., Aurora, N.Y., Bronx (N.Y.) C.C., Kingsborough C.C., Bklyn., Columbia U., N.Y.C.; chmn. dept. langs. and lit. Ea. N.Mex. U.; prof. Five Towns Coll., Dix Hills, N.Y. Author: The Tempering of T.S. Eliot, 1983; (poetry) Delano in American, 1972, Odes and Cycles, 1983, In An Arid Clime, 1984, In the Indies, 1991, Sonnets for our Risorgimento, 1992. Bd. advisors N.Y. Poetry Forum, N.Y.C.; chancelor N.Mex. State Poetry Soc. Mem. Internat. Spkrs. Platform. Democrat. Home: Brooklyn, NY. Deceased.

SOLECKI, RAY, government agency administrator; b. N.Y.C., Apr. 6, 1945; BA, Manhattan Coll., N.Y.C., 1965; MA, N.C. State U., 1972. In planning Dept. HUD, 1972-84, regional dir. for fair housing, 1984-90, spl. asst. to asst. sec. for fair housing Washington, 1990-92, dir. affirmative employment, 1992-97, dir. EEO, from 1997. Capt. USAF, 1965-70. Deceased.

SOLENDER, SANFORD, social worker, consultant; b. Pleasantville, N.Y., Aug. 23, 1914; s. Samuel Solender and Catharine (Goldsmith); m. Ethel Klonick (dec. 1995), June 19, 1935; children: Stephen, Ellen, Susan(dec.), Peter. BS, NYU, 1935; MS, Columbia U., 1937. Dir. activities Neighborhood House, Bklyn., 1935-36; asst. headworker Bronx House, N.Y., 1936-39; headworker Madison House, N.Y.C., 1939-42; exec. dir. Coun. Ednl. Alliance, Cleve., 1942-48; dir. bur. pers. and tng., also dir. Jewish community ctr. div. Nat. Jewish Welfare Bd., N.Y.C., 1948-60, exec. v.p. bd., 1960-70; exec. v.p. Fedn. Jewish Philanthropies N.Y., 1970-81, exec. cons., 1982-86. Exec. v.p. United Jewish Appeal Fedn. Campaign, 1975-81; past pres. Nat. Conf. Jewish Communal Svc.; past chmn. planning com. Internat. Conf. Jewish Communal Svc.; chmn. Task Force on N.Y.C. Crisis, 1976-81; chmn. temporary inter-assn. coun. to organize NASW, 1957-1959. Contbr. articles to profl. jours., chpts. in books. Chmn. ad hoc. com. to study fed. govt. social welfare programs HEW, 1962, adv. coun. pub. welfare, 1963—65; active Mid East Watch-Human Rights Watch, Jewish Mus., from 1982, bd. dirs.; mem. Gov. Hugh Carey's Task Force on Human Svcs., NY, 1975; bd. dirs. Nat. Jewish Ctr. for Learning and Leadership, from 1984; adv. bd. Brandeis U., Hornstein Program in Jewish Communal Svc.; bd. dirs. Americans for Peace Now, from 1995, Nat. Found. for Jewish Culture, from 1985; mem. Mt. Vernon Bd. Edn., NY, 1953—58, pres., 1957—58; bd. dirs. Herman Muehlstein Found. Named Most Disting. Citizen of Mt. Vernon, 1960; recipient Joseph E. Kappel award Nat. Conf. Jewish Communal Svc., 1968, Florence G. Heller award Nat. Jewish Welfare Bd., 1972. Mem. Nat. Assn. Jewish Ctr. Workers (past pres.), Nat. Conf. Social Welfare (past pres.). Home: Sarasota, Fla. Died Aug. 30, 2003.

SOLLIN, INGMAR ADOLPH, economist; b. Rugby, N.D., May 4, 1918; s. Thorvald and Margaret Caroline (Grebe) s.; m. Raeanna G. Gudgeon, Sept. 5, 1959; stepchildren: Gary E. Shrout, Barbara R. Johnson. BS, N.D. State U., 1948, MS, 1949; PhD, Pa. State U., 1952. Sr. research chemist Internat. Minerals and Chem. Corp., Skokie, Ill., 1952-59, tech. service rep., 1959-61, product mgr., 1961-66, indsl. research economist, 1966-69; indsl. economist Minn. Dept. Econ. Devel., St. Paul, 1969-81, Minn. Office Tourism, St. Paul, 1981-90; ret., 1990. Patentee in field. Decorated Bronze Star. Mem. Travel and Tourism Research Assn., Phi Kappa Phi. Lutheran. Avocations: reading, bridge, auto mechanics, bowling. Home: Saint Paul, Minn. Deceased.

SOLOMON, AMELIA KROLL, artist; b. Zwenigorodka-Kiev, Russia, Nov. 24, 1908; d. Abraham Krugliak Kroll and Nora Pipco; m. Herman Lampert Solomon, July 31, 1931 (dec. 1989); children: Ernest, Suzon, Semyon T., Sheba S. Studied with Ralph Stackpole, 1947; attended, Patri Sch. Fine Art, 1950, Foothill Coll., 1969, San Miguel de Allenda Art Inst., 1970; student, DeAnza Coll.; BA magna cum laude, San Jose State U., 1979, MFA, 1986. Lectr. in field. Solo shows include Stanford (Calif.) U., 1982, 83, Oakland (Calif.) Art Assn., 1985, Open Studio, San Jose, 1989, 90, Rosicrucian Egyptian Mus., San Jose, 1989, Metro Contemporary Art Gallery, Foster City, Calif., 1989, Koret Gallery, Palo Alto, Calif., 1992, Cooper-Molera Adobe, Monterey, Calif., 1998, Los Altos Hills (Calif.) Town Hall, 1999; group shows include Palo Alto Art Club, 1966, 69, San Mateo Floral Fiesta, 1970, Livermore (Calif.) Art Assn., 1979, San Francisco Women Artists, 1980, 81, Ana Gardner Gallery, 1980, Soma Gallery, San Francisco, 1980, Open Studio, 1986, Fenwick's Estate Art Show, Los Altos Hills, Calif., 1987, San Jose Inst. Contemporary Arts, 1987, 94, Gallery III, San Jose, 1990, Olive Hyde Gallery, Fremont, Calif., 1990, Lincoln Ctr., N.Y., 1992, San Jose Art League, 1993, Los Gatos (Calif.) Tait Mus., 1993, 94, Gallery Tanantzin, San Juan Bautista, 1993, Syntex Gallery, Palo Alto, 1993, Synopsis Gallery, Mountain View, Calif., 1993, Solomon Dubnick Gallery, Sacramento, 1994, Seippe Gallery, Palo Alto, 1994, Koret Gallery, 1995, Contract Design Ctr. Juried Show, San Francisco, 1996, Ironstone Gallery Juried Show, Sonora, Calif., 1996, Memory Park Invitational, Monterey, 1996, Merced (Calif.) Coll. Art Gallery, 1996, Anne Frank Exhibit, Mt. View (Calif.) Cultural Ctr., 1996, Works Gallery Mem. Show, San Jose, 1997, Cooper-Molera Adobe Sculpture Show, Monterey, 1997, 98, Cogswell Coll., Sunnyvale, Calif., 1998, San Jose (Calif.) State U., 1998, 99, 2000 Euphrat Mus. Art, Cupertino, Calif., 1998, Los Altos Hills Town Hall, 1999, Hayward City Hall, 1999., Contract Design Center, 2000. Recipient 1st prize for sculpture, San Mateo, Calif., 1969, 75-77. Mem. San Jose State U. Sculptors Guild (treas. 1978-99), League Nat. PEN Women, Womens Caucus for Arts, Internat. Sculpture Ctr. Home: Los Altos, Calif. Died Mar. 23, 2002.

SOLOMON, EZRA, economist, educator; b. Rangoon, Burma, Mar. 20, 1920; came to U.S., 1947, naturalized, 1951; s. Ezra and Emily (Rose) S.; m. Janet Lorraine Cameron, May 7, 1949; children: Catherine Shan, Janet Mingulay, Lorna Cameron. AB (hons.), U. Rangoon, 1940; PhD, U. Chgo., 1950. Instr. U. Chgo., 1948-51, asst. prof. fin., 1951-55, assoc. prof., 1955-57, prof., 1957-61; Dean Witter prof. fin. Stanford U., 1961-71, 73-90; dir. Internat. Ctr. Mgmt. Edn.; mem. Coun. Econ. Advisers, 1971-73. Author: The Theory of Financial Management, 1963, Money and Banking, 5th edit, 1968, The Management of Corporate Capital, 1959, Metropolitan Chicago: An Economic Analysis, 1958, The Anxious Economy, 1975, An Introduction to Financial Management, 2d edit, 1980, Beyond the Turning Point, 1981; editor: International Patterns of Inflation: A Study in Contrasts, 1984, Jour. Bus, 1953-57; bd. editors Jour. of Finance, 1965-66, Jour. Bus. Finance, 1969-73, Jour.

Quantitative and Financial Analysis, 1969-71. Served as lt., Burma div. Royal Naval Vol. Res., 1942-47. Mem. Am. Econ. Assn. Home: Stanford, Calif. Died Dec. 9, 2002.

SOLOMON, SYD, artist; b. Uniontown, Pa., July 12, 1917; s. Jack E. and Edith (Bennett) S.; m. Ann F. Cohen, Dec. 29, 1941; children— Michele R., Michael. Student, Chgo. Art Inst., 1934, Ecole des Beaux Arts, Paris, 1945. Instr. Art Inst. Pitts., 1947; dir. painting classes Ringling Mus. Art, Sarasota, 1948-50; dir. Sarasota (Fla.) Sch. Art, 1950, 55; mem. of guiding faculty Famous Artists Schs., Inc., Westport, Conn., 1954-70; prof. of art New Coll., Sarasota, 1964-65; vis. instr. painting U. Ill., 1968; vis. instr. Robertson Ctr. Arts and Scis., Binghamton, N.Y., 1969, Tampa Bay (Fla.) Art Ctr., 1972, U. Calif., 1976, Boca Raton (Fla.) Ctr. Art, 1977. Exhbns. include Met. Mus., 1952, Delgado Mus., New Orleans, 1951-57, Butler Mus., Youngstown, 1954-56, Carnegie Inst., 1956, Dallas Mus., 1954, Houston Mus., 1955, Balt. Mus., 1952, High Mus., Atlanta, 1956, Free State Israel Mus., Jerusalem, 1956, Williams Proctor Inst., Utica, N.Y., 1956, Nat. Acad. Art, 1951-56, Birmingham Mus., 1952-62, Saidenberg Gallery, N.Y., 1959-70, Ringling Mus. Art, 1975, N.Y. Cultural Ctr., 1975, Tampa (Fla.) Bay Art Ctr., 1975, Benson Gallery, N.Y., 1975, Adley Gallery, 1978-79, Mus. Fine Arts, St. Petersburg, Fla., Genesis Gallery, N.Y.C., 1981, Art and Culture Ctr., Hollywood, Fla., Nardin Gallery, N.Y.C., 1982, Carone Gallery, Ft. Lauderdale, Phoenix Gallery, Washington, 1983, Boca Raton Mus. Arts, John & Mable Ringling Mus. Art, 1990-91, Polk Mus. Art, Lakeland, Fla., 1992, Butler Inst. Am. Art, Youngstown, Ohio, 1992, Philharm. Ctr. Arts, Naples, Fla., 1993; group exhbn. Painting in the South, 1564-1980, 1984-85; represented in permanent collections including Phila. Mus. Art, Rose Mus., Brandeis U., La. State Mus., Baton Rouge, Guggenheim Mus., Whitney Mus. Am. Art, Wadsworth Athenaeum, Ringling Mus., Birmingham Mus., High Mus., Florida So. Coll., Clearwater (Fla.) Art Mus., Miss. Art Assn., Jackson, Fla., Fedn. Art Miami, Mus. Fine Arts, St. Petersburg, Miami Dade Collection, Fla., Balt. Mus., Weatherspoon Gallery, U. N.C., Corcoran Gallery Art, Washington, Herbert F. Johnson Mus. Art, Cornell U., Lowe Gallery Mus., Miami, Fla., Cin. Mus. Art, Walter P. Chrysler, Jr. Collections, Dewitt Mus., Joseph Hirschhorn Collection, Delgado Mus., Adelphi U. Mus., Tel Aviv Mus., Norton Mus., Ft. Lauderdale Mus., Polk Pub. Mus., Guild Hall, E. Hampton, N.Y., Mus. of South, Memphis, Tampa Bay Art Ctr., camouflage designer: Engrs. Bd, Washington, 1942. Recipient Hallmark Internat. award, 1952, Purchases prize Fla. Internat., 1952, Lowe Gallery Ann. award, 1953, Southeaster ann. award, 1953, High Mus. award, 1956, Casein Soc. medal of honor, 1957, Audobon Soc. medal of honor, 1957, 1st Purchase watercolor award Butler Mus. Art, 1957, 58, 1st Purchase prize Sarasota Art Assn., Childe Hassam purchase award Hassam and Speicher Fund, 1979, Fla. prize award N.Y. Times, 1987. Mem. Nat. Soc. Lit. and Arts, Artists Equity, Allied Arts Coun. Died Jan. 28, 2004.

SOMANI, SATU MOTILAL, pharmacologist, toxicologist, educator; b. Hingoli, India, Mar. 14, 1937; came to U.S., 1961; s. Motilal B. and Tulsabal Somani; m. Shipra Somani, Nov. 5, 1966; children: Indira, Sheila. MSc in Biochemistry, Poona (India) U., 1959; MS in Pharmacy, Duquesne U., 1964; PhD in Pharmacology, Liverpool (Eng.) U., 1969. Rsch. fellow U. Pitts., 1969-70, instr., 1970-71; asst. prof. pharmacology Univ. Pitts., 1971-74; assoc. prof. So. Ill. U. Sch. Medicine, Springfield, 1974-82, prof. pharmacology and toxicology, from 1982. Contbr. articles to profl. jours.; editor: Environmental Toxicology: Principles and Policies, 1981, Chemical Warfare Agents, 1992, Pharmacology in Exercise and Sports, 1996, Chemical Warfare Agents: Toxicity at Low Level, 2001. Founder, treas. First Hindu Temple in U.S., Pitts., 1970-74; chair Asian Indian Polit. Action Com. Ctrl. Ill., 1989-92. Ellis T. Davies fellow, 1967-69; NIH fellow, 1969-70; grantee U.S. EPA, U.S. Army, Am. Heart Assn., invitee of U.S. Congress to testify on Gulf War Syndrome, 1997; presentor workshop on Problem Based Learning Curriculum in med. sch., India, 1997, 99. Mem. AAAS, Am. Soc. Pharmacology and Exptl. Therapeutics, Soc. Toxicology, Am. Chem. Soc. (chair Decatur-Springfield chpt. 1981-83), Assn. Scientists of Indian Origin (chair 1987-88). Hindu. Achievements include first to show the metabolic pathway of quaternary ammonium compound (neosigmine) and glucuronide formation; contributions include research in physostigmine as an antidote (pretreatment) for soman-nerve agent pharmacokinetics and pharmacodynamics studies; showed the effectiveness of caffeine and theophylline for treatment of apneic episodes in premature infants; exercise ameliorate antioxidant enzymes in heart, brain and tissues after alcohol. Home: Springfield, Ill. Died Oct. 2.

SOMERVILLE, WILLIAM GLASSELL, JR., lawyer; b. Memphis, July 27, 1933; s. William Glassell and Hilda (Deeth) S.; m. Mary Hateley Quincey, June 13, 1959 (div. Oct., 1985); children: William Glassell, John Quincey, Mary Campbell, Sarah Guerrant. AB, Princeton U., 1955; LLB, U. Va., 1961. Bar: Ala. 1961, U.S. Ct. Appeals (5th cir.) 1963, U.S. Supreme Ct. 1964, U.S. Ct. Appeals (8th cir.) 1968, U.S. Ct. Appeals (11th cir.) 1981. Law clk. to chief judge U.S. Dist. Ct. (no. dist.) Ala., 1961-63; assoc. Lange, Simpson, Robinson & Somerville, Birmingham, Ala., 1963-66, ptnr., 1966—; mem. supreme ct. adv. com. on rules of Ala. appellate procedure, 1972-77; mem. standing com. on Ala. rules of appellate procedure, 1979-86. Served with CIC U.S. Army, 1955-58. Mem. ABA, Ala. Bar Assn., Birmingham Bar Assn., Am. Judicature Soc., Ivy (Princeton), Birmingham Country Club, Rotary. Episcopalian. Deceased.

SOMLYO, ANDREW PAUL, physiology, biophysics and cardiology educator; b. Budapest, Hungary; s. Anton and Clara Maria (Kiss) S.; m. Avril V. Russell, May 25, 1961; 1 child, Andrew Paul. BS, U. Ill., 1954, MS, MD, U. Ill., 1956; MS, Drexel Inst. Tech., Phila., 1963; MA (hon.), U. Pa., Phila., 1981; hon. D, U. Catholique de Louvain, Belgium, 1997. Asst. physician Columbia-Presbyn. Med. Ctr., N.Y.C., 1960-61; rsch. assoc. Presbyn. Hosp., Phila., 1961-67; asst. prof. pathology U. Pa., Phila., 1964-67, assoc. prof., 1967-71, prof., 1971-88, prof. physiology and pathology, 1973-88, dir. Pa. Muscle Inst., 1973-88; Charles Slaughter prof. molecular physiology-biol. physics U. Va., Charlottesville, from 1988, chmn. dept., from 1988, prof. cardiology, from 1988, dir. ctr. structural biology, from 1997. Cons. NIH; Brit. Heart Found. vis. prof. Hammersmith Hosp., London, Shanghai (China) Med. U.. Author: (with others) Vascular Neuroeffector Systems, 1971, The Handbook of Physiology, Vascular Smooth Muscle, 1981, Microprobe Analysis of Biological Systems, 1981, Recent Advances in Light and Optical Imaging in Biology and Medicine, 1986; editor: Jour. Muscle Research and Cell Motility, 1987, FASEB Jour., 1996; contbr. numerous articles to jours. including Biol. Chemistry, Jour. Physiology, Am. Heart Jour., Jour. Pediatrics, Jour. Cell Biology, Cell Calcium, others; mem. editl. bd. Blood Vessels, Am. Jour. Physiology, 1979-83, Magnesium: Experimental and Clinical Rsch., Jour. Structural Biology. Recipient The Louis and Artur Lucian award for rsch. in circulatory diseases, 1996; Biophysical Soc. fellow, 1999. Fellow AAAS; mem. Soc. Gen. Physiologists, Am. Physiol. Soc. Biophys. Soc., Electron Microscopy Soc., Microbeam Analysis Soc. (Presdl. Sci. award 1996), Am. Soc. for Cell Biology, Hungarian Physiol. Soc. (hon.), Microscopy Soc. Am. (Disting. Scientist award for biol. scis. 1994), Alpha Omega Alpha Med. Soc. (CIBA-GEIGY award for Hypertension Rsch. 1991). Home: Charlottesville, Va. Died Jan. 14, 2004.

SOREL, CLAUDETTE MARGUERITE, pianist; b. Paris; d. Michel M. and Elizabeth S. Grad. with top honors, Juilliard Sch. Music, 1947, postgrad., 1948; student of, Sigismund Stojowski, Sari Biro, Olga Samaroff Stokowski, Mieczyslaw Horszowski, Rudolf Serkin; ensemble with, Felix Salmond; musicology with, Dr. Robert Tangeman; music history with, Marian Bauer; grad., Curtis Inst. Music, 1953; BS cum laude in Math., Columbia U., 1954. Music faculty, vis. prof. Kans. U., 1961-62; assoc. prof. music Ohio State U., 1962-64; prof. music, head piano dept. SUNY Fredonia, 1964— , Disting. Univ. prof., 1969—, univ. artist, 1969—, faculty exchange scholar, 1976—; mem. internat. jury Van Cliburn Internat. Piano Competition, Tex., 1966, Que. and Ont. Music Festivals, 1967, 75; chmn. music panel Presdl. Scholars in Arts Program, 1979—; juror numerous nat. and internat. music competitions; cons. Ednl. Testing Service, Princeton; pres. Elizabeth and Michel Sorel C.O. Inc. Author: Compendium of Piano Technique, 1970, 2d edit., 1987, Japanese edit., 1987, Mind Your Musical Manners - Off and On Stage, 1972, 3d revised edit., 1995, The 24 Magic Keys, 3 vols., 1974, The Three Nocturnes of Rachmaninoff, 1974, 2d edit., 1975, 3d edit. with cassette in compact disc, 1988, Fifteen Smorgasbord Studies for the Piano, 1975, 2d edit., 1995, 17 Little Piano Studies, 1995, Arensky Piano Etudes, 1976, To Madam with Love: Letters of Olga Samaroff Stokowski, 1999, From Madam: Selected Writings of her Julliard Years, 1999; spl. editor: Music Insider; painter of oil portraits; contbr. articles to profl. mags.; compiler: The Modern Music of Today, 1974, Serge Prokofieff - His Life and Works, 1947, The Ornamentations in Mozart's Music, 1984; debut at Town Hall, N.Y.C., 1943; since appeared in leading cities of U.S.; performed with N.Y. Philharm., London Philharm., Zurich, Boston, San Antonio, Milw., NBC, Phila., New Orleans and Cin. symphony orchs., Youth Orch. of Am., 200 others; appeared at Aspen, Berkshire, Chautauqua, other festivals, European concert tours, 1956, 57, 58, to Eng., Sweden, Holland, Germany, Switzerland, France; appeared on various radio, TV programs; made recs. for RCA Victor Rec. Co., Monitor Records, Mus. Heritage; compact disc MacDowell Piano Concerto #2 with N.Y. Philharm. Orch., 1993; 2 CD-set Piano Music of Rachmaninoff, 1998, Am. Piano Concertos,1999; 2000 solo appearances, U.S. and Europe. Bd. dirs. Olga Samaroff Found.; Jr. com. aux. bd. N.Y. Philharmonic Symphony Orch., N.Y. State Nat. Fedn. Music Clubs; mem. adv. bd. Univ. Library Soc.; pres. Shelton Apartments, Inc., Elizabeth and Michel Sorel Charitable Orgn., Inc. Fulbright fellow, 1951; Ford Found. Concert grantee, 1962; winner Phila. Orch. Youth Auditions, 1950, to appear with orch. under direction of Eugene Ormandy; U.S. Senatorial Bus. Adv. Com. Fulbright scholar, 1951; recipient Harry Rosenberg Meml., Frank Damrosch prizes, 1947, Nat. Fedn. Music Clubs Young Artist award, 1951; citation svc. to Am. music Nat. Fedn. Music Clubs, 1966, citations Nat. Assn. Composers & Condrs., 1967, Mu Phi Epsilon, 1968, Freedom medal U.S. Senatorial Com., 1994; nominated Kyoto Japan Humanitarian award, 1989, 92; Claudette Sorel Scholarship for Women Ctr. in Music created by NYU. Mem. Nat. Music Coun. (dir. 1973—, chmn. performance com.), Nat. Arts Club, Music Critics Assn., Broadcast Music Incorp., Columbia Univ. Club (N.Y.C.), Nat. Arts Club, Pi Kappa Lambda, Mu Phi Epsilon (dir. Meml. Found., nat. chmn. Sterling Staff Concert Series, citation 1968). Home: New York, NY. Deceased.

SØRENSEN, AAGE BØTTGER, sociology educator; b. Silkeborg, Denmark, May 13, 1941; came to U.S., 1968; s. Harry and Nanna Bøttger (Jensen) S.; m. Annemette Kristensen, Jan. 25, 1964; 1 child, Jesper Bøttger. MSc, U. Copenhagen, 1967; PhD, Johns Hopkins U., 1971. Rsch. assoc. Johns Hopkins U., Balt., 1970-71; asst. prof. U. Wis., Madison, 1971-74, assoc. prof., 1974-77, prof., 1978-84, dept. chmn., 1979-82; prof., dept. chmn. Harvard U., Cambridge, Mass., 1984-92. Asst. dir. Rsch. of Poverty, Univ. Wis., Madison, 1975-78; prof. Univ. Oslo, Norway, 1978-79. Editor: Human Development: Multidisciplinary Perspective, 1986; assoc. editor numerous profl. jours., 1975—; contbr. articles to Am. Jour. Sociology, Am. Sociol. Rev., Annual Rev. of Sociology, Sociology of Edn., others. Bd. dirs. Danish Nat. Rsch. Found. Recipient fellowship Woodrow Wilson Found., 1970, Ctr. for Advanced Study in the Behavioral Sci., Stanford, Calif., 1977-78; grantee NSF, Nat. Inst. Aging, Nat. Inst. Child Health Devel., Nat. Inst. Edn., 1973—. Fellow AAAS; mem. Max Planck Inst. (adv. bd. 1984-93), Sociol. Rsch. Assn. Home: Chestnut Hill, Mass. Died Apr. 1, 2001.

SORREL, WILLIAM EDWIN, psychiatrist, educator, psychoanalyst; b. N.Y.C., May 27, 1913; s. Simon and Lee (Lesenger) S.; m. Rita Marcus, July 1, 1950; children: Ellyn Gail, Joy Shelley, Beth Mara. BS, NYU, 1932; MA, Columbia U., 1934, MD, 1939; PhD, NYU, 1963. Diplomate Am. Bd. Med. Psychotherapists (profl. adv. coun. 1992—); qualified psychiatrist, also cert.examiner N.Y. State Dept. Mental Hygiene. Intern Madison (Tenn.) Sanitarium and Hosp., 1939; resident physician Alexian Bros. Hosp., St. Louis, 1940; officer instrn. St. Louis U. Sch. Medicine, 1940-41; asst. psychiatrist Central State Hosp., Nashville, 1941; assoc. psychiatrist Eastern State Hosp., Knoxville, 1942-44; assoc. attending neuropsychiatrist, chief clin. psychiatry Jewish Meml. Hosp., N.Y.C., 1946-59; assoc. attending neuropsychiatrist, chief clin. child psychiatry Lebanon Hosp., Bronx, N.Y., 1947-65; psychiatrist-in-chief Psychiatry Clinic, Yeshiva U., 1950-66, asst. prof. psychiatry, 1952-54, assoc. prof., 1954-58, prof., 1959-62, psychiatrist-in-chief, assoc. dir. Psychol. Center, 1957-67; prof. emeritus human behavior Touro Coll., from 1974; attending psychiatrist St. Clare's Hosp., N.Y.C., from 1983; asst. prof. clin. psychiatry Albert Einstein Coll. Medicine, from 1986. Psychiat. cons. SSS, 1951, N.Y. State Workmens Compensation Bd., 1951—, Bronx-Lebanon Med. Ctr., 1985—; vis. psychiatrist Fordham Hosp., N.Y.C., 1951; attending neuropsychiatrist, chief mental hygiene svc. Beth-David Hosp., 1950-60; attending neuropsychiatrist Grand Central Hosp., 1958-66, Morrisania Hosp., 1959-72; psychiatrist-in-chief Beth Abraham Hosp., 1954-60; psychiat. cons. L.I. U. Guidance Ctr., 1955-60, Daytop Village, 1970-71; assoc. psychiatrist Seton City Hosp., 1955; guest lectr. U. London, 1947; vis. prof. Jerusalem, Israel Acad. Med., 1960, Hebrew U., 1960; mem. psychiat. staff Gracie Sq. Hosp., 1960—; chief psychiatry Trafalgar Hosp., 1962-72; vis. prof. psychiatry Tokyo U. Sch. Medicine, 1964; adj. prof. N.Y. Inst. Tech., 1968; vis. lectr. in psychiatry N.Y. U., 1971-73; Am. del. Internat. Conf. Mental Health, London, 1948; mem. Am. Psychiat. Commn. to USSR, Poland and Finland, 1963, Empire State Med., Sci. and Ednl. Found. Author: (booklets) Neurosis in a Child, 1949, A Psychiatric Viewpoint on Child Adoption, 1954, Shock Therapy in Psychiatric Practice, 1957, The Genesis of Neurosis, 1958, The Prejudiced Personality, 1962, The Schizophrenic Process, 1962, The Prognosis of Electroshock Therapy Success, 1963, Psychodynamic Effects of Abortion, 1967, Violence Towards Self, 1971, Basic Concepts of Transference in Psychoanalysis, 1973, A Study in Suicide, 1972, Masochism, 1973, Emotional Factors Involved in Skeletal Deformities, 1977, Cults and Cult Suicide, 1979, Further Viewpoints on the Genesis of Neurosis, 1996; assoc. editor Jour. Pan Am. Med. Assn., 1992—; contbr. articles on the psychoses. Vice pres. Golden Years Found.; N.Y.C. chmn. Com. Med. Standards in Psychiatry, 1952-54. Recipient Sir William Osler Internat. Honor Med. Soc. Gold Key; 3d prize oil paintings N.Y. State Med. Art Exhibit, 1954; NYU Founders Day award, 1963; Presdl. Achievement award, 1984, medal for med. excellence Pan Am. Med. Assn., 1997, others. Fellow Am. Psychiat. Assn. (life, pres. Bronx dist. 1960-61, other offices, Gold medal 1974, 94), Am. Assn. Psychoanalytic Physicians (pres. 1971-72, bd. govs. 1972—); mem. AMA, Ea. Psychiat. Assn., N.Y. State Soc. Med. Rsch., Am. Med. Writers Assn., N.Y. Med. Soc., N.Y. County Med. Soc., N.Y. Soc. for Clin. Psychiatry, Pan Am. Med. Assn. (various offices including pres. 1989—, assoc. editor jour. 1992—, Disting. Med. Svc. award 1997), Assn. for Advancement Psychotherapy, Bronx Soc. Neurology and Psychotherapy (pres. 1960-61, Silver medal 1970), Mensa. Home: Scarsdale, NY. Died Nov. 16, 2002.

SORSA, KALEVI, government representative; b. Keuruu, Finland, Dec. 21, 1930; s. Kaarlo O. and Elsa S. (Leinonen) S.; m. Elli Irene Laakari, July 23, 1953. Ed., U. Tampere. Chief editor Vihuri, 1954-56; bd. dirs. Bank of Finland, Helsinki, 1987-96 (ret.). Lit. editor Tammi Pub. House, 1956-59; program asst. specialist UNESCO, 1959-65; sec.-gen. Finnish UNESCO Com., 1965-69; dep. dir. Ministry Edn., Govt. of Finland, 1967-69, mem. Parliament, 1970-91, minister for fgn. affairs, 1972, 75-76, 87-89, prime minister, 1972-75, 77-79, 82-83, 83-87, spkr. Parliament, 1989-91; chmn. fgn. affairs com., 1970-72, 77, 79-82; chmn. bd. adminstrn. Finnair, 1981-94, chmn. bd., 1994-97. Author books; contbr. articles to profl. jours. Sec.-gen. Social Democratic Party Finland, 1969-75, pres., 1975-87; chmn. study group on disarmament Socialist Internat., 1978-80, v.p., 1980-2004; v.p., chmn. adv. com. on disarmament, 1980-96, Socialist Internat., 1980-96. Decorated Grand Decoration of Honor (Austria), Grand Cross Order of Dannebrog (Denmark), Grand Star Order of Star of Friendship Between Peoples of German Dem. Republic; Grand Cross Order Icelandic Falcon; Order of Banner (Hungarian People's Republic); 1st class Grand Cross Order St. Michael and St. George, Eng.; Grand Cross Order Merit (Fed.

Republic Germany); comdr. Grand Cross Order of White Rose Finland; Grand Cross Order of Orange-Nassau (Netherlands), Grand Cross Order of Merit of Polish People's Republic, Grand Cross Order of St. Marinus / San Marino, Grand Cross Order of Merit of Senegal, Grand Cross Royal Order of No. Star (Sweden), Grand Cross Order of So. Cross (Brazil), Grand Cross Order of Star (Jordan), Grand Cross Order of Isabella the Cath. (Spain), Order of Trishakti-Patta (Nepal). Died Jan. 16, 2004.

SOUERWINE, ANDREW HARRY, management consultant; b. Slatington, Pa., Feb. 29, 1924; s. Harry Wilbur and Katie (Anthony) S.; m. Jane Dorell Day, Aug. 27, 1949; children: David Anthony, Andrew Day. BA, Ursinus Coll., Collegeville, Pa., 1947; MA, U. Pa., 1948; PhD, U. Conn., 1954. Lic. psychologist, Conn. Asst. dept. psychology U. Pa., Phila., 1947-49; asst. prof., acting chmn. dept. psychology Trinity Coll., Hartford, Conn., 1949-58; dir. career planning and devel. Travelers Corp., Hartford, 1958-67; dir. MBA prog. U. Conn., Hartford, 1967-77, prof. mgmt. and orgn., 1971-84, prof. emeritus, from 1984; pres., owner Career Planning Svcs., Wethersfield, Conn., from 1980. Adj. faculty U. Hartford, 1959-61, Hartford Coll. for Women, 1960-62, U. Conn., 1963-67; cons. in field. Author: Career Strategies, 1978; contbr. articles to profl. jours.; mem. editorial adv. bd. Staff Care Rev. jour., 1989-90, Am. Soc. for Tng. and Devel. Jour., 1983-91. Bd. dir. Ch. Homes, Inc., 1986-89, chmn. pers. com., 1986-89; mem. adv. bd. Elliott Berv Assocs., 1989-90; bd. dirs. United Way of Hartford, 1975-77, Rsch. Ctr. of New Eng., 1977, Bristol Brass Corp., 1978-83, Community Coun. Greater Hartford, 1977-80. With U.S. Army, 1943-46, ETO. Mem. Am. Psychol. Assn., Am. Soc. Tng. and Devel., Pi Gamma Mu, Alpha Psi Omega, Beta Gamma Sigma, Tau Kappa Alpha. Congregationalist. Avocations: gardening, tennis, reading, writing. Died Mar. 15, 2000.

SOUTELLO-ALVES, LAURO EDUARDO, diplomat; b. Rio de Janeiro, R.J., Brazil, May 10, 1958; s. Lauro and Maria Eugenia (Ribeiro) Soutello-A.; m. Maria de Fatima Faria, Aug. 31, 1994. BA, NYU, 1981; diploma, Fgn. Svc. Inst., Brazil, 1984; Brevet d'Adminstrn. Pub., Nat. Sch. Adminstrn., France, 1999. Chief of staff dept. spl. affairs Brazilian Fgn. Ministry, 1986-89, mem. permanent mission to UN, 1989-92, chief of staff dept. UN and disarmament affairs, 1995-98; head econ. sect. Brazilian Embassy, Mex., 1992-95, head OECD liaison sect., from 1999; dep. dir. for environ. policy and sustainable devel. Brazilian Fgn. Ministry, Brasilia. Lectr. Brazilian Naval Acad., 1988, Brazilian Army Staff Coll., 1998, Brazilian War Coll., 1998. Contbr. articles to profl. jours. Recipient Order of Merit, Brazilian Armed Svcs., 1998. Home: Brasilia, Brazil. Died Mar. 2002.

SOUTHALL, FRANCIS GENEVA, retired education educator music; b. New Orlean, Dec. 5, 1925; d. William Talbot and Darthney Pauline (Pleasant) Handy; 1 child, Patricia Camille Jones. BA, Dillard U., 1945; MusM, Am. Conservatory, 1958; PhD, U. Iowa, 1966. Artist diploma, Nat. Guild of Piano Tchrs., 1953. Instr. piano Paul Quinn Coll., Waco, Tex., 1958-59; chair piano dept. Knoxville (Tenn.) Coll., 1959-61; asst. prof. piano/music history S.C. State, Orangeburg, 1962-64; teaching asst. piano U. Iowa, Iowa City, 1964-66; prof. piano/music history Grambline (La.) State U., 1966-70; prof. Afro-Am. music U. Minn., Mpls., 1970-92; ret. Mem. bd. dirs. Dillard U., New Orleans. Author: (book) Blind Tom, Book I, 1979, Blind Tom, Book II, 1983; pianist (cassette tape) Piano Music of Blind Tom, 1983, Blind Tom, The Black Pianist-Composter: Continually Enslaved, In Celebration of Black Music, 1984-94. Referee Minn. Humanities Commn., St. Paul, 1983-87; editl. bd. Black Music Rsch. Jour., 1984-94; bd. trustees Camphor United Meth. Ch., St. Paul, 1995—. Recipient Prix de Martell Achievement award Minn. Orch., 1992, MLK Cmty. Svc. award Found. for Social Action, 1992; nmaed Hon. Sterling patron Mu Phi Epsilon Music Frat., 1993, Nat. Women of Yr., Iota Phi Lambda Sorority, 1979. Mem. AAUW (long range planning com., program com. 1994-96), NAACP (coord. music events NAACP conv. 1995), Nat. Assn. Negro Musicians (chair scholarship competition 1989). Methodist. Avocations: travel, reading. Home: Minneapolis, Minn. Died Jan. 2, 2004.

SOUTHAM, CHESTER MILTON, physician; b. Salem, Mass., Oct. 4, 1919; s. Walter Aloysius and Elizabeth Effie (Furbish) S.; m. Anna Lenore Skow, Sept. 24, 1939 (div.); children: Lawrence Albert, Lenore Elizabeth, Arthur Milton; m. Gertrude Elizabeth Lundin, June 9, 1973. BS, U. Idaho, 1941, MS, 1943; MD, Columbia U., 1947. Intern Presbyn. Hosp., N.Y.C., 1947-48; rsch. fellow to full mem., chief divsn. virology/immunology Sloan-Kettering Inst. Cancer Rsch., N.Y.C., 1948-71; from clin. fellow to attending physician Meml. Hosp. for Cancer, N.Y.C., 1948-71; from instr. to assoc. prof. medicine Cornell U. Med. Ctr., N.Y.C., 1951-71; head Div. Med. Oncology Thomas Jefferson U. Med. Coll., Phila., 1971-79, prof. medicine, from 1971; attending physician Dept. Medicine Thomas Jefferson U. Hosp., Phila., from 1971. Contbr. articles to profl. jours. Trustee Leopold Shepp Found., N.Y.C., 1961-67, Strang Clinic and Preventive Medicine Inst., N.Y.C., 1963-68; adv. com. on rsch. and therapy cancer Am. Cancer Soc., N.Y.C., 1961-66; sci. adv. com. Damon Runyon Fund, N.Y.C., 1961-68; com. virology and immunology Internat. Union Against Cancer, Geneva, 1966-90; adv. com. tobacco and health rsch. AMA Edn. and Rsch. Found., Chgo., 1965-66; bd. dirs. Am. Assn. Cancer Rsch., 1966-70, pres., 1968-69. Capt. U.S. Army, 1953-55. Mem. Am. Soc. Clin. Oncologists. Avocations: ice skating, swimming, music, ballet, gardening. Died Apr. 5, 2002.

SOUTHERN, EILEEN (MRS. JOSEPH SOUTHERN), writer, music educator, African American educator; b. Mpls., Feb. 19, 1920; d. Walter Wade and Lilla (Gibson) Jackson; m. Joseph Southern, Aug. 22, 1942; children: April, Edward. AB, U. Chgo., 1940, MA, 1941; PhD, NYU, 1961; MA (hon.), Harvard U., 1976; D.A. (hon.), Columbia Coll., Chgo., 1985. Instr. Prairie View U., Hempstead, Tex., 1941-42; asst. prof. So. U., Baton Rouge, 1943-45, 49-51; tchr. N.Y.C. Bd. Edn., 1954-60; instr. Bklyn. Coll., CUNY, 1960-64, asst. prof., 1964-69; assoc. prof. York Coll., CUNY, 1969-71, prof., 1972-75; prof. music Harvard U., Cambridge, Mass., 1976-87, chmn. dept. Afro-Am. studies, 1976-79, prof. emeritus, from 1987. Concert pianist, 1940-55; author: The Buxheim Organ Book, 1963, The Music of Black Americans: A History, 1971, 3d edit., 1997, Readings in Black American Music, 1971, 2d edit., 1983, Anonymous Chansons in MS El Escorial Biblioteca del Monasterio, IV a 24, 1981, Biographical Dictionary of Afro-American and African Musicians, 1982, African-American Traditions in Song, Sermon, Tale, and Dance, 1630-1920; An Annotated Bibliography, 1990 (with Josephine Wright); editor: The Black Perspective in Music (1973-90), Nineteenth Century African-American Musical Theater, 1994; contbr. articles to profl. jours. Active Girl Scouts U.S.A., 1954-63; chmn. mgmt. com. Queens Area YWCA, 1970-73. Recipient Alumni Achievement award U. Chgo., 1970, Deems Taylor award ASCAP, 1973, Peabody medal Johns Hopkins U., 1991, Nat. Humanities medal Pres. of U.S., 2002; NEH grantee, 1979-83. Mem. NAACP, Internat. Musicol. Soc., Am. Musicol. Soc. (hon., bd. dirs. 1974-76), Sonneck Am. Music Soc. (bd. dirs. 1986-88), Renaissance Soc., Phi Beta Kappa (hon. Radcliffe Coll.), Alpha Kappa Alpha. Died Oct. 17, 2002.

SOVIE, MARGARET DOE, nursing administrator, educator, clinician, researcher; b. Ogdensburg, N.Y., July 7, 1934; d. William Gordon and Mary Rose (Bruyere) Doe; m. Alfred L. Sovie, May 8, 1954; 1 child, Scot Marc. Student, U. Rochester, 1950—51; diploma in nursing, St. Lawrence State Hosp. Sch. Nursing, Ogdensburg, 1954; student, St. Lawrence U., 1956—60; BSN summa cum laude, Syracuse U., 1964, MS in Edn., 1968, PhD in Edn., 1972; DSc (hon.), Health Sci. Ctr. SUNY, Syracuse, 1989; MSN, U. Pa., 1995, adult health nurse practitioner, 1996. Cert. post-masters gerontol. nurse practitioner. Staff nurse, clin. instr. St. Lawrence State Hosp., Ogdensburg, 1954—55, instr. nursing, 1955—62; staff nurse Good Shepherd Hosp., Syracuse, 1962; nursing supr. SUNY Upstate Med. Ctr., Syracuse, 1963—65, insvc. instr., 1965—66, edn. dir. and coord. nursing svc., 1966—71, asst. dean Coll. Health Related Professions, 1972—84, assoc. prof. nursing, 1973—76, dir. continuing edn. in nursing, 1974—76, assoc. dean and dir. div. continuing edn. Coll. Health Related Professions, 1974—76; spl. assignment in pres.'s office SUNY Upstate Med. Ctr. and Syracuse U., 1972—73; assoc. dean for nursing U. Rochester, NY, 1976—88, assoc. prof. nursing, 1976—85, prof., 1985—88; assoc. dir. for nursing Strong Meml. Hosp., U. Rochester Med. Ctr., 1976—88; chief nursing officer Hosp. U. Pa., Phila., 1988—96, assoc. exec. dir., 1988—94, assoc. dean for nursing practice Sch. Nursing, 1988—96; prin. investigator hosp. restructuring NINR U. Pa., Phila., 1996—2000, Jane Delano prof. nursing adminstrn. Sch. Nursing, from 1988, sr. fellow Leonard Davis Inst. Health Econs., from 1992; trustee bd. U. Pa. Health Sys., Phila., 1993—96; NP PNN Health Annex, Phila., 1998—2001. Nursing coord. and project dir. Ctrl. N.Y. Regional Med. Program, Syracuse, 1968—71; mem. edn. dept. State Bd. Nursing, Albany, NY, 1974—84, chmn., 1981—83, chmn. practice com., 1975—80, mem. joint practice com., 1975—80, vice chmn., 1980—81; mem. adv. com. to clin. nurse scholars program Robert Wood Johnson Found., Princeton, NJ, 1982—88; adj. assoc. prof. Syracuse U. Sch. Nursing, 1973—76, chmn. vis. com. Coll. Nursing, 1996—99; mem. Gov.'s Health Adv. Panel N.Y. State Health Planning Commn., 1976—82, task force on health manpower policy, 1978, informal support networks sect. steering com., 80; mem. health manpower tng. and utilization task force State N.Y. Commn. on Health Edn. and Illness Prevention, 1979; mem. task force on nursing pers. N.Y. State Health Adv. Coun., 1980; mem. adv. panel on nursing svcs. U.S. Pharm. Conv., Inc., Washington, 1985—90; cons. Nat. Ctr. for Svcs. Rsch. and Health Care Tech. Assessment, Rockville, Md., 1987; mem. nursing stds. task force Joint Commn. Accreditation Health Care Orgns., 1988—90; mem. various other adv. coms.; lectr. in field. Mem. editl. bd. Health Care Supr., 1982—87, Nursing Econs., from 1983, Best Practices and Benchmarking in Health Care, 1995—98, mem. manuscript rev. panel Nursing Outlook, 1987—91, mem. editl. bd. Seminars for Nurse Mgrs., from 1994; contbr. articles to profl. jours., chapters to books. Bd. visitors Sch. Nursing, U. Md., Balt., 1984—89; mem. bd. mgrs. Strong Meml. Hosp., Rochester, 1983—88; bd. dirs. Monroe County Assn. for Hearing, Rochester, 1979—82, Vis. Nurse Svc. of Rochester and Monroe County, 1978, Southeastern Pa. chpt. ARC, 1991—97. Recipient Ann. Margaret D. Sovie lectureship inaugurated, Strong Meml. Hosp., U. Rochester, 1989, Dean's Outstanding Alumni award, Coll. of Nursing, Syracuse U., 1994; fellow spl. nurse rsch. fellow, NIH, 1971—72; grantee various orgns. Fellow: Am. Acad. Nursing (program com. 1980—81, task force on hosp. nursing 1981—83, chair expert panel on quality health care 1994—97, mem. panel from 1994); mem.: Inst. Medicine of NAS (com. design strategy for quality rev. and assurance in Medicare 1988—90), N.Y. State Nurses Assn. (med. surg. nursing group, chmn. edn. com. dist. 4 1974—76, chmn. cmty. planning group for nursing dist. 4 1974—75, coun. on regional planning in nursing 1974—76, del. to conv. 1978, Nursing Svc. Adminstrn. award 1985), Am. Orgn. Nurse Execs. (stds. task force 1987, rsch. com. 1997—98), ANA (nat. rev. com. for expanded role programs 1975—78, site visitor to programs requesting accreditation 1976—78, cabinet on nursing svcs. 1986—90, cert. bd. nursing adminstrn. 1983—86, ad hoc com. on advanced practice 1992—95), Sigma Theta Tau. Republican. Roman Catholic. Avocations: golf, cross-country skiing, swimming, dancing. Home: Media, Pa. Died Aug. 16, 2002.

SPAHN, WARREN, retired baseball player; b. Buffalo, N.Y., Apr. 23, 1921; Pitcher Boston Braves, 1946-52, Milw. Braves, 1953-64, N.Y. Mets, 1965, San Francisco Giants, 1965. Recipient Cy Young award, 1957; named to Baseball Hall of Fame, 1973. Achievements include led or tied for most wins in Nat. League 1949, 50, 53, 57-61, led Nat. League strikeouts 1949, 50, 52, led Nat. League ERA 1947, 53, 61, led Nat. League in complete games, 1949, 51, 57-59, no-hitters against Phila., 1960, San Francisco, 1961, All-star game, 1947, 49-54, 56-63, mem. World Series Champions, 1957, winningest left-hander in game's history with 363 victories. Died Nov. 24, 2003.

SPECHALSKE, PHYLLIS VALAND, media specialist, educator; b. Stonega, Va., Mar. 18, 1931; m. Frank H. Spechalske, June 18, 1954; children: Richard, Janine, Jon, Robert. BA, Baldwin Wallace Coll., 1953; postgrad., Ea. Mont. U., 1969-71; MEd, U. South Ala., 1979. Cert. tchr., Ohio, Pa., Ala. Media specialist Billings (Mont.) Pub. Schs., 1972-77; tchr. Mobile (Ala.) County Pub. Schs., 1979-81, media specialist, from 1982. Mem. South Ala. Botanical Soc., Mobile, 1985-88. Recipient 4-H Club Leaders award, Ala. Coop. Extention Svc., 1985. Mem. Ala. Instrnl. Media Assn. (pres. 1985, 87), Ala. Libr. Assn., Bay Area Libr. Assn. (pres. 1992), Jubilee Story League, Mystic Maskers (treas. Mobile 1986, rec. sec. 1988), Nat. Assn. for Preservation and Perpetuation Storytelling. Republican. Lutheran. Home: Mobile, Ala. Deceased.

SPECK, GERALD BENNETT, financial executive; b. Phila., Jan. 31, 1923; s. James Gavin and Lora (Bennett) S.; B.S., Temple U., 1956; m. Bridget Christina McGuire, Dec. 29, 1956; children: Gerald, Ellen, Lora, Bridget. CPA, Pa. Mid-Atlantic region acct. Liquid Carbonic Corp., Phila., 1957-58; sr. staff acct. Main Hurdman, CPAs, Fernald & Co., Phila., 1958-63; asst. dir. acctg. and fin. Phila. Bd. Edn., 1963-69; controller Gannett Fleming Corddry and Carpenter, Inc., Harrisburg, Pa., 1969-81; v.p., controller Gannett Fleming, Inc., Harrisburg, 1982-87; v.p. fin., 1987-89, also dir., ret., 1989, prin., 1989-90; instr. acctg. Villanova (Pa.) U., 1964-67; adj. prof. Phila. Coll. Textiles and Sci., Phila., 1967-69; instr. acctg. St. Joseph's U., Phila., 1967-70. Recipient Scholarship award Credit Mens Assn. Eastern Pa., 1956. Mem. AICPA, Fin. Execs. Inst. (past dir. Central Pa. chpt.), Assn. Govt. Accts., Profl. Services Mgmt. Assn., Pa. Inst. CPAs (chmn. govt. contracts com.). Republican. Roman Catholic. Clubs: KC, U.S. Navy Commd. Officers Mess. Home: New Cumberland, Pa.

SPECTOR, BARBARA HOLMES, retired communications administrator; b. Manchester, N.H., June 15, 1927; d. Kenneth Morris and Frances A. (Hall) Holmes; m. Saul James Spector, Oct. 27, 1953 (dec. Apr. 1986); children: Pamela Jill, Mark James. Student, Hesser Bus. Sch., Manchester, 1945-46. Operator New England Telephone, Manchester, 1946-51, repair clk., 1951-54, repair observer, 1959-71, cen. office foreman Nashua, N.H., 1972-73, staff instr., svc. ctr. foreman Boston, Concord, N.H., 1973-75, asst. staff mgr. Manchester, 1975-83, ret., 1983. Mem. N.H. Rep. Women's Club, 1987—. Mem. Telephone Pioneers. Episcopalian. Avocations: travel, reading, antiques, gardening, painting. Home: Manchester, NH. Deceased.

SPECTOR, LOUIS, retired federal judge, lawyer, arbitrator, consultant; b. Niagara Falls, N.Y., Apr. 4, 1918; s. Jacob and Gussie (Yochelson) S.; children: Gale Anne Spector Pasternack, Arthur George, James Aland. Student (N.Y. State scholar), Niagara U., 1936-37; LL.B. with honors, U. Buffalo (later State U. N.Y.), 1940. Bar: N.Y. bar 1940, D.C. bar 1972, U.S. Supreme Ct. bar 1971, U.S. Ct. Claims bar 1968. Asso. firm Saperston, McNaughton & Saperston, Buffalo, 1941-42; asst. chief legal div. U.S. Army C.E., Buffalo Dist., 1942-43; chief sect. claims appeals and litigation U.S. Army C.E. (Great Lakes Div.), Chgo., 1946, chief legal br. and real estate div. Buffalo Dist., 1946-53; exec. dir. Buffalo Port Authority, 1953-54; mem. Bd. Contract Appeals, Washington, 1954-59; chmn. Army panel Armed Services Bd. Contract Appeals, Washington, 1959-62, Unified Armed Services Bd. Contract Appeals, 1962-68; trial judge U.S. Ct. Claims, Washington, 1968-82, judge, 1982-85; cons., arbitrator, mediator Falls Church, Va., from 1985. Lectr., speaker, writer public contracts; Congressional appearances, 1953, 66, 69, 77 Contbr. articles to profl. publs. Served with C.E. U.S. Army, 1943-46. Recipient Freshman medal Niagara U., 1936, Sophomore medal, 1937 Fellow Am. Bar Found.; mem. ABA (chmn. sect. pub. contract law 1967-68); Fellow Nat. Contract Mgmt. Assn. (nat. bd. advisers 1967—); mem. ABA (ho. of dels. 1968-70), Fed. Bar Assn. (gen. editor jour. 1960-74, nat. chmn. com. govt. contracts and procurement law 1961-63, Distinguished Service award D.C. chpt. 1974), Lincoln Law Soc. (alumni pres. 1951) Clubs: Cosmos. Home: Falls Church, Va. Died Jan. 4, 2003.

SPENCER, JAMES CALVIN, SR., humanities educator; b. Detroit, Oct. 21, 1941; s. Donald and Beulah S.; m. Linda J. Voloshen, Nov. 21, 1987; children: James, Anne. BA, Calif. State U., 1966; MA, SUNY, 1970, PhD in Philosophy, 1973. NDEA fellow SUNY, Buffalo, 1968-70, SUNY fellow, 1970-71; instr. Cuyahoga C.C., Parma, Ohio, 1971-73, asst.

prof., 1973-77, assoc. prof., 1977-81, prof. philosophy and art, from 1981. Cons. continuing edn. divsn. Kans. State U., 1986, Case Western U., Cleve., 1973, Ford Motor Co., Brookport, Ohio, 1990, Campus Planning Inst., Cleve., 1991-94, PBS Nat. Faculty Referral Network, 1996—; pres. Spencer Enterprises, Brecksville, Ohio, 1991—; reviewer manuscripts for Wadsworth Pub. and McGraw-Hill Pub. Author: The Nightmare Never Ends, 1992; co-author: Instructor's Manual for the Voyage of Discovery: A History of Western Philosophy, 1996; contbr. articles to profl. jours. Ward com. Democratic Party, Ashland, Brecksville, Ohio, Libertarian Party, Buffalo, N.Y.; vice chancelier Argentier, Bailli de la Chaine des Rotisseurs, Chevalier Ordre Mondial, 1996—. NSF grantee, 1979, 87, 97, 99. Mem. Soc. Wine Educators, Am. Wine Soc. Home: Brecksville, Ohio. Died June 15, 2000.

SPENCER, MARILYN J. artist; b. Detroit, July 10; d. John and Dorothy Jensen; m. Andrew R. Spencer, July 24, 1948; children: Gary, Linda, James. BA, Wayne State U., 1947. Tchr. Detroit Pub. Schs., 1947-52; sub. tchr. Troy and Birmingham (Mich.) Schs., 1966-76; art instr. Pontiac (Mich.) Art Ctr., 1980, 81. Exhbns. in group shows include various local, state and nat. shows in Mich. and U.S., 1968—; 12 one-woman shows in Mich. galleries; represented in over 300 pvt. and pub. collections. Docent Cranbrook Inst. Sci., Bloomfield Hills, Mich., 1973-76; contbr. paintings Channel 56 Art Auctions, Detroit, Birmingham-Bloomfield Art Assn.; exhbn. art chmn. Birmingham-Bloomfield Art Assn., Pontiac Art Ctr. Recipient numerous awards. Mem. Birmingham Soc. Women Painters, Ariz. Artists Guild, Traverse Area Arts Coun., Detroit Art Inst. (founder soc. 1963—). Avocations: birding, bridge, reading, writing, travel. Home: Bloomfield Hills, Mich. Died June 28, 2003.

SPENCER, WILLIAM ARTHUR, public relations consultant; b. Huntington, Ind., Jan. 30, 1921; s. Lowell G. and Edith Evangeline (Augustine) S.; m. Jo Ann Whipple, May 26, 1951; children: Nancy, Thomas, Kevin. AB, Ind. U., 1942. Reporter New Enterprise, Corinth, N.Y., 1947; asst. dir. pub. rels. Armour Rsch. Found./Ill. Inst. Tech., Chgo., 1948-52; dir. office info. svcs. NYU, N.Y.C., 1952-66; univ. rels. officer Ind. U. Indpls., 1966-70; asst. to chancellor Ind. U.-Purdue U. at Indpls., 1970-91; pub. rels. cons., from 1991. Lectr. in field. Elder Presbyn. Ch., Indpls. Capt. AUS, 1943-46, ETO. Decorated Bronze Star medal. Mem. Internat. Brotherhood Magicians (ring pres. 1988-90), Pub. Rels. Soc. Am. (pres. Hoosier chpt. 1970, Nat. Coll. Fellows), Coun. for Advancement and Support of Edn. (life mem.), Indpls. Lit. Club. Avocation: collecting old magic books. Home: Indianapolis, Ind. Died May 2, 2002.

SPEZZANO, VINCENT EDWARD, newspaper publisher; b. Retsof, N.Y., Apr. 3, 1926; s. Frank and Lucy S.; m. Marjorie Elliott, Dec. 18, 1948; children: Steve, Judy, Mark, Christine (dec.). BA in Journalism, Syracuse (N.Y.) U., 1950. Reporter Livingston Republican, Geneseo, N.Y., 1950-51, Lynchburg (Va.) News, 1951-54, St. Louis Globe-Democrat, 1954-55; polit. writer, then dir. public service and research Rochester (N.Y.) Times Union, 1955-68; dir. public service, then dir. promotion and public service Gannett Co., Inc., 1968-75; pres., publisher Cape Publs., Inc., Cocoa, Fla., 1975-84, chmn., 1984-91; asst., then v.p. Gannett/South, Gannett Co., Inc., 1977-79; pres. Gannett Southeast Newspaper Group, Gannett Co., Inc., 1979-82; exec. v.p. USA Today, 1982-83, pres., 1983; sr. v.p. communications Gannett Co., 1983-84, bd. dirs.; pres., pub. Gannett Rochester Newspapers, 1984-90, chmn., 1990-91; pres. Gannett N.E. Div., 1984-86. Past mem. journalism endowment adv. com. U. Fla.; bd. dirs. Marine Midland Bank. Editor handbook. Past trustee St. John Fisher Coll., Rochester; trustee Brevard Art Ctr. and Mus., Melbourne, Fla.; bd. dirs. Cape Canaveral Hosp., 1991—, Fla. Inst. Tech., 1991—, Astronauts Meml. Found., 1991—, vice-chmn., space camp adv. bd.; bd. vice-chmn. Rochester Conv. Bur., 1986-91; mem. Founder's Com. The Rochesterians, 1986—; mem. adv. bd. Space Pioneers, Inc. With A.C., USNR, 1944-46. Recipient News Ariting award Va. Press Assn., 1953, Citizen of Yr. award Citizens Club Rochester, 1960, Disting. Svc. award for non-members Kiwanis Club, 1960, Pub. Svc. Reporting award Am. Polit. Sci. Assn., 1963; named NE Kiwanis Citizen of Yr., 1987, Boss of Yr. Coca Beach chpt. Nat. Secretaries Assn., 1977, Rochester Communicator of Yr., 1987, Rochester Citizen of Yr., 1987, Cavaliere (Knight) in Order of Merit Republic of Italy, 1994. Mem. Internat. Newspaper Promotion Assn. (pres. 1970-71, Silver Shovel award 1975), Am. Newspapers Pubs. Assn., So. Newspaper Pubs. Assn. Found (chmn.), Fla. Press Assn. (bd. dir., pres. 1984), N.Y. Newspaper Pubs. Assn. (bd. dirs.), Cocoa Beach Area C. of C., Rochester Area C. of C. (bd. dir. 1985—, chmn. bd. 1989-90). Roman Catholic. Home: Cocoa Beach, Fla. Died 1999.

SPIEGEL, ABRAHAM, savings and loan association executive; b. 1906; m. Edita Spiegel. Chmn. Columbia Savs. and Loan Assn., Beverly Hills, Calif., 1974—90, also bd. dirs. Achievements include the Spiegel Family Building at the Museum of the Jewish Diaspora in Tel Aviv; the Children's Memorial at the Yad Vashem Holocaust memorial in Jerusalem; the Spiegel Family Park in Tel Aviv. Died Apr. 10, 2004.

SPINRAD, BERNARD ISRAEL, physicist, researcher; b. N.Y.C., Apr. 16, 1924; s. Abraham and Rose (Sorrin) S.; m. Marion Eisen, June 29, 1951; children: Alexander Abraham, Mark David, Jeremy Paul, Diana Esther; m. Lois Ringstrom Helton, Jan. 28, 1983. BS with honors, Yale, 1942, MS, 1944, PhD in Phys. Chemistry, 1945, Sterling fellow postdoctoral research, 1945-46. Physicist Oak Ridge Nat. Lab., 1946-48; mem. staff Argonne Nat. Lab., 1949-67, 70-72, dir. reactor engring. div., 1957-63, sr. physicist applied physics div., 1963-67, 70-72; dir. div. nuclear power and reactors IAEA, Vienna, Austria, 1967-70; prof. nuclear engring. Oreg. State U., Corvallis, 1972-82, prof. emeritus, from 1983; prof., chmn. dept. nuclear engring. Iowa State U., Ames, 1983-90, prof. emeritus, from 1990. Adviser and participant U.S. delegation Internat. Conf. Peaceful Uses Atomic Energy, Geneva, 1955, 58; cons. IAEA, 1961, 63, 72, 74; chmn. European-Am. Com. Reactor Physics, 1962-64; mem. com. nuclear and alternative energy systems NRC, 1974-79, com. innovative concepts and approaches to energy conservation, 1984-85, com. univ. research reactors, 1986-88; vis. researcher Internat. Inst. Applied Systems Analysis, Vienna, 1978-79, chmn. nuclear engring. dept. head orgn., 1986-87. Author books, papers and reports in field; mem. editorial bd. Annals of Nuclear Energy. Named Man of Year Chgo., 1956, Man of Year Hinsdale, Ill., 1958 Fellow Am. Phys. Soc., Am. Nuclear Soc. (past dir.); mem. AAAS, Am. Chem. Soc., UN Assn. Am., Sigma Xi. Died Mar. 1999.

SPITZ, LEWIS WILLIAM, historian, educator; b. Bertrand, Nebr., Dec. 14, 1922; s. Lewis William and Pauline Marie (Griebel) S.; m. Edna Marie Huttenmaier, Aug. 14, 1948; children: Stephen Andrew, Philip Mathew. AB, Concordia Coll., 1944; MDiv, Concordia Sem., 1946; MA, U. Mo., 1947; PhD, Harvard U., 1954; DD (hon.), Concordia Theol. Sem., 1977; LLD (hon.), Valparaiso (Ind.) U., 1978; LittD (hon.), Wittenberg U., 1983; DLitt (hon.), Concordia Coll., 1988. With U. Mo., Columbia, 1953-60, assoc. prof. history, 1958-60; Fulbright prof. U. Mainz, Germany, 1960-61; prof. history Stanford (Calif.) U., 1960—, William R. Kenan Jr. prof., from 1974, assoc. dean humanities and scis., 1973-77. Vis. prof. Harvard U., Cambridge, Mass., 1964-65; dir. rsch. Ctr. for Reformation Rsch., Clayton, Mo., summer 1964, mem. bd. control, 1973—; sr. fellow South Eastern Medieval and Renaissance Inst., Duke U., summer 1968; vis. prof. Barnard Coll., 1980-81; sr. fellow Inst. Advanced Study Princeton U., 1979-80; vis. prof. Institut für Europäische Geschichte, Mainz, 1992. Author: Conrad Celtis: The German Arch-Humanist, 1957, The Religious Renaissance of the German Humanists, 1963, Life in Two Worlds: A Biography of William Sihler, 1968, The Renaissance and Reformation Movements, 2 vols., 1987, Humanismus und Reformation in der Deutschen Geschichte, 1980, The Protestant Reformation, 1517-1559, 1985; contbr. The Harvest of Humanism in Central Europe: Essays in Honor of Lewis W. Spitz, 1992; co-author (with Barbara Sher Tinsley): Johann Sturm on Education, 1995, Luther and German Humanism, 1996, The Reformation: Education and History, 1997; editor: The Protestant Reformation: Major Documents, 1997; mem. editl. bd. Soundings, 1973-79; mng. editor: Archive for Reformation History, 1968-76. Recipient Harbison award for tchg. Danforth Found., 1964; Guggenheim fellow, 1956; Nat. Endowment for Humanities sr. fellow, 1965; Am. Coun. Learned Socs. fellow, 1971; Huntington Libr. fellow, 1959; Inst. Advanced Study Princeton fellow, 1979-80; Pew Found. fellow, 1983 Fellow Am. Acad. Arts and Scis.; mem. Am. Soc. Reformation Rsch. (pres. 1963-64), Am. Hist. Assn., No. Calif. Renaissance Soc. (pres. 1964-65), Am. Soc. Ch. History (pres. 1976-77). Home: Stanford, Calif. Died Dec. 22, 1999.

SPRAGUE, IRVINE HENRY, government official; b. San Francisco, July 4, 1921; s. Irvine Henry and Claire Dolores (Kelly) S.; m. Margery Eleanor Craw, Nov. 3, 1940; children: Michael Irvine, Terry Earl, Kristine Ann. BA, U. Pacific, 1947; student, Stockton Coll., 1940-41, U. Ind., 1943; postgrad., George Washington Law Sch., 1957; grad., Advanced Mgmt. Program, Harvard, 1972. Reporter Stockton (Calif.) Record, 1938-56; adminstrv. asst. to congressman, 1957-62; dep. dir. finance, 1963-66; asst. to Pres. Lyndon B. Johnson, White House, Washington, 1967-68; dir. FDIC, Washington, 1969-72; adminstrv. asst. U.S. Ho. of Reps. Majority Whip, 1973-76; exec. dir. Ho. of Reps. Steering and Policy Com., 1977-78; chmn. FDIC, 1979-81, dir., 1982-86. Del. Nat. Dem. Conv., 1964 Served to 1st lt. AUS, 1943-46; Res. 1946-70; lt. col., ret. Decorated Bronze Star with cluster, Purple Heart, Combat Inf. Badge; recipient Calif. medal of merit. Mem. DAV. Home: Great Falls, Va. Died Feb. 17, 2004.

SPRAGUE, JAMES MATHER, medical scientist, educator; b. Kansas City, Mo., Aug. 31, 1916; s. James P. and Lelia (Mather) S.; m. Dolores Marie Eberhart, Nov. 25, 1959; 1 son, James B. BS, U. Kans., 1938, MA, 1940; PhD, Harvard U., 1942; AM (hon.), U. Pa., 1971. From asst. to asst. prof. anatomy Hopkins Med. Sch., 1942-50; asst. prof. to prof. anatomy U. Pa. Med. Sch., Phila., 1950-83, chmn. dept., 1967-76, Joseph Leidy prof. anatomy, 1973-83, emeritus Joseph Leidy prof., from 1983, dir. Inst. Neurol. Sci., 1973-80, chmn. univ. faculty senate, 1963. Vis. prof. Northwestern U., 1948, U. Oxford, 1949, Rockefeller U., 1955, Cambridge U., 1956, U. Pisa, 1966, 74-75, U. Leuven, 1984-95, Kyushu U., 1988; sci. cons. NIH, 1957-60. Co-editor: Progress in Psychobiology and Physiological Psychology, 1966-84; asso. editor: Acta Neurobiol. Exper., 1976; contbr. articles to profl. jours. Recipient Macy faculty award, 1974-75, Disting. Tchg. award Lindbach Found., 1965; Guggenheim fellow, 1948-49 Mem. NAS, Am. Assn. Anatomists (v.p. 1976-78), Japanese Assn. Anatomists (hon.), Soc. Neurosci. (founding coun.). Democrat. Home: Berwyn, Pa. Died Dec. 22, 2002.

SPROUL, LORETTA ANN SCHROEDER, elementary school educator, reading specialist; b. Milw., Oct. 25, 1938; d. Paul Frederick and M. Faye (Brown) Schroeder; m. Hugh Bell Sproul III, July 30, 1966; children: Mary-Faye AnnTeresa, Hugh Bell IV. BS, Mount Mary Coll., 1960; MS, U. Wis., 1966, James Madison U., 1978. Cert. elem. tchr., reading specialist. Tchr. Milw. Pub. Schs., 1960-62, 63-64, 1965-66, 67-68, Dept. Def. Overseas Sch., Fed. Republic Germany, 1962-63, 1964-65, Muscogee County Schs., Columbus, Ga., 1966-67, Ft. Bragg (N.C.) Schs., 1974-76; reading and math. specialist Staunton (Va.) Pub. Schs., from 1976. Facilitator Summer Ednl. Experiences for Knowledge program Bessie Weller Sch., Staunton, Va., 1989—. Bd. dirs. Community Child Care, Staunton, 1984-87; den mother Cub Scouts Am., Staunton, 1978-79; troop leader Girl Scouts U.S., Staunton, 1977-78; founder Children's Libr. Program, Martin, Tenn., 1970-73; vol. Meals on Wheels, Staunton, 1983-88, ARC Hosp., 1973-74. Recipient Outstanding Young Woman of Am. award, 1970, Excellence in Edn. award Va. Polytechnic Inst., 1989. Mem. MADD, Nat. Edn. Assn., AAUW (named Outstanding Young Woman of Am. 1970), Va. Reading Assn., Nat. Coun. Tchrs. of Math., Alpha Delta Kappa (treas.). Roman Catholic. Avocations: reading, camping, traveling, knitting, swimming. Home: Staunton, Va. Died July 20, 2000.

SPROUSE, JAMES MARSHALL, retired judge; b. Williamson, W.Va., Dec. 3, 1923; s. James and Garnet (Lawson) S.; m. June Dolores Burt, Sept. 25, 1952; children: Tracy Sprouse Ferguson, Jeffrey Marshall, Andrew Michael, Sherry Lee Sprouse Shinholser, Shelly Lynn Sprouse Schneider. AB, St. Bonaventure (N.Y.) U., 1947; LLB, Columbia U., 1949; postgrad. in internat. law, U. Bordeaux, France, 1950. Bar: W.Va. 1949. Asst. atty. gen. State of W.Va., 1949; with CIA, 1952-57; pvt. practice W.Va., 1957-72, 75-79; justice W.Va. Supreme Ct. Appeals, 1972-75; judge U.S. Ct. Appeals (4th cir.), Richmond, Va., 1979-92, sr. cir. judge, 1992-95; ret., 1995; pvt. practice, 1995—2001. With AUS, 1942—45. Fulbright scholar. Mem. ABA, W.Va. State Bar, W.Va. Bar Assn., W.Va. Trial Lawyers Assn., Kanawha County Bar Assn., VFW, Am. Legion, Shriners, Aheppa. Democrat. Presbyterian. Died July 3, 2004.

SQUIRES, PATRICIA EILEEN COLEMAN, freelance journalist, writer; b. Beaver Falls, Pa., Jan. 28, 1927; d. John Wiley and Helen Marie (Barstow) Purtell; m. Mark B. Squires Sr., June 30, 1951; children: Sally Regan, Mark B., Susan Barstow. BA in Journalism, Ind. U., 1949. Staff reporter LaPorte (Ind.) Herald-Argus, 1949-51, sect. editor, 1949-51, daily columnist, 1950-51; women's news and feature writer Muskegon (Mich.) bur. Grand Rapids Herald, 1956-57; editor suburban sect. North Shore Line, Chicago-land Mag., Chgo., 1967-69; staff writer Fairpress, Westport, Conn., 1972-73; regular contbr. New Canaan (Conn.) Advertiser, 1975-78, Bridgeport (Conn.) Sunday Post, 1976-78, Soundings, Essex, Conn., 1977-78, N.Y. Times, N.Y.C., 1976-94. Tchr. English, journalism, social studies, jr. and sr. pub. high schs., Jackson, Mich., 1966-67, Niles Twp., Skokie, Ill., 1967-68; editor: The Island Sun, Isla de Sol, St. Petersburg, Fla.; mem. Acad. Sr. Profls. Eckerd Coll. Vol. tutor Social Cultural Ednl. Enrichment Program, Protestant Cmty. Ctr., 1979-86; pub. rels., promotion dir. Ella Sharp Mus., Jackson, 1964-66; publicity chmn. New Canaan Soc. for Arts, 1977-78; bd. dirs. Centennial Celebration Com., Winnetka, Ill., 1968-69; Cmty. Coun. New Canaan, 1972-75; New Canaan Bicentennial Com., 1975-76; publicity chmn. parent-tchr. coun. Frost Jr. H.S., Jackson, 1963-64; active Girl Scouts Am. Mem. AAUW, Soc. Profl. Journalists, Ind. U. Alumni Assn. (assoc. acad. sr. profl. at Eckerd Coll. Fla.), Cedar Point Yacht Club (Westport, Conn.), Lake Mohawk Golf Club (Sparta, N.J.), Isla Del Sol Yacht and Country Club. Episcopalian. Home: Washington, DC. Died Oct. 2, 1999.

SQUIRES, RICHARD C. marketing executive; b. N.Y.C., Sept. 27, 1931; s. William Haywood and Fay H. (Hochstetler) S.; m. Ruth Black, Sept. 23, 1955 (div. 1975); children: Gary, Cathleen, Pamela; m. Joan A. Finn, Sept. 20, 1986. BA in Liberal Arts, Williams Coll., Williamstown, Pa., 1953. Salesman ALCOA, Pitts., 1953-61, ARCATA Nat., N.Y.C., 1961-70; founder, pres. Sports Mktg. Assocs. Corp., Norwalk, Conn., 1971-77; dir. Downtown Racquet Club, New Haven, 1978-82; mgr. nat. equipment Tennis mag., Trumbull, Conn., from 1983; pub. Tennis Buyer's Guide, Trumbull, from 1983. Author: How To Play Platform Tennis, 1968, The Complete Book of Platform Tennis, 1973, The Other Racquet Sports, 1978; contbg. editor (monthly column) Tennis mag., 1971-78. Republican. Episcopalian. Avocations: tennis, writing. Home: Norwalk, Conn. Died Nov. 12, 2003.

SRIVASTAVA, UMA SHANKAR, zoologist, educator; b. Allahabad, India, Mar. 24, 1924; m. Prem Srivastava; children: Rashmi, Ravi. PhD, U. Allahabad, 1947. Asst. prof. U. Allahabad, 1947-63, prof., head zoology, 1969-84, dean sci., 1978-81; prof., head zoology Bihar U., Muzaffarpur, India, 1963-69, dean sci., 1964-66; pres. NAS, India, coord. sci. communication programme. Vis. sci. Imperial Coll., London, 1957-58; vis. prof. N.W. Univ., Evanston, Ill., 1967-68; nat. lectr. Univ. Grants Commn., India, 1979; emeritus sci. Coun. Sci. and Indsl. Rsch., New Delhi. Editor: Glimpses of Science in India, (with others) Utilization of Living Resources of the Indian Seas, Space in Pursuit of New Horizons, Inputs of Science and Technology for Development of Wastelands; authored over 100 papers. Recipient Sir J.C. Bose award. Fellow NAS (India), Indian Nat. Sci. Acad., Etomology Soc. India (past v.p.), Zoological Soc. India (past sec. gen.); mem. Indian Soc. Devel. Biologists (past pres.). Deceased.

STACK, ROBERT LANGFORD, actor; b. Los Angeles, Jan. 13, 1919; s. James Langford and Elizabeth (Wood) S.; m. Rosemarie Bowe, Jan. 23, 1956; children: Elizabeth Langford, Charles Robert. Student, U. So. Calif., 1937-38. Pres. St. Pierre Prodns., Los Angeles, from 1959. Actor, co-producer: (TV series) The Untouchables, 1959-63 (2 nominations, 1 Emmy award); actor: The Name of the Game, 1968-71, Most Wanted, 1976-77, Strike Force, 1982-83, Unsolved Mysteries, 1986-1999; actor: (TV movies) The Strange and Deadly Occurence, 1974, The Adventure of the Queen, 1975, Murder on Flight 502, 1975, Undercover with the KKK, 1979 (narrator), Perry Mason: The Curse of the Sinister Spirit, 1987, The Return of Elliot Ness, 1991, Sealed with a Kiss, 1999, H.U.D.,2000; (TV miniseries) George Washington, 1984, Hollywood Wives; (films) including First Love, 1940, When the Daltons Rode, 1940, Mortal Storm, 1940, Nice Girl, 1941, Badlands of Dakota, 1941, To Be or Not To Be, 1942, Eagle Squadron, 1942, Men of Texas Fighter Squadron, 1948, Date with Judy, 1948, Miss Tatlock's Millions, 1948, Mr. Music, 1950, The Bullfighter and the Lady, 1950, My Outlaw Brother, 1951, Bwana Devil, 1952, War Paint, 1953, The High and the Mighty, 1953, Iron Glove, 1954, Written on the Wind, 1956 (Acad. Award nomination for best supporting actor), The Last Voyage, 1959, John Paul Jones, 1959, The Caretakers, 1963, The Corrupt Ones, 1967, Story of a Woman, 1970, '1941', 1979, Airplane!, 1980, Uncommon Valor, 1983, Big Trouble, 1984, Glory Days, 1987, Caddyshack II, 1988, Plain Clothes, 1988, Dangerous Curves,1988, Joe Verses the Volcano, 1990, Wild Bill: A Hollywood Maverick, 1995, Beavis and Butt-head Do America, 1996, My Kingdom For, 1997, BASEketball, 1998, Hercules (TV series) 1998, Waylon & Buzz, 1999, Killer Bud, 2001. Served with USN, WWII. Recipient Emmy award Acad. TV Arts and Scis. Home: Los Angeles, Calif. Died May 14, 2003.

STADNICKI, STANLEY WALTER, JR., health science association administrator; b. Norwich, Conn., Sept. 30, 1943; s. Stanley Walter Sr. and Beatrice Catherine (Dumais) S.; m. Jeanne Marie Couture, Sept. 6, 1965; children: Sandra, Scott, Steven, Robert. BA, Assumption Coll., Worcester, Mass., 1965; MA, Clark U., Worcester, 1970; PhD, Worcester Poly. Inst., 1976. Neurophysiologist Dept. Toxicology and Pharmacology, E.G. & G. Mason Research Inst., Worcester, 1967-70, sect. head, 1970-75, research scientist, 1975-76; toxicologist Drug Safety Evaluation, Pfizer, Inc., Groton, Conn., 1976-79, sr. toxicologist, 1979-81, project leader, 1981-85, mgr., 1985-86, asst. dir., from 1986. Contbr. articles to profl. jours. Leader Cub Scouts, East Lyme, Conn., 1978; mgr. East Lyme Little League Baseball, 1978-83; coach Babe Ruth Baseball, East Lyme, 1984-86; mem. Athletic Booster Club, East Lyme, 1984—. Clark U. grad. fellow, 1965-66. Mem. IEEE, Am. Soc. Pharmacology and Exptl. Therapeutics, Am. Coll. Toxicology, Soc. Toxicology (pres. N.E. chpt. 1990-92), Can. Soc. Toxicology. Roman Catholic. Avocations: racquetball, golf, volleyball. Home: East Lyme, Conn. Died June 30, 2000.

STAFF, CHARLES BANCROFT, JR., music and theater critic; b. Franklin, Ind., July 2, 1929; s. Charles Bancroft and Clara Margaret (Jennings) S. AB, Franklin Coll., 1951; BM, Ind. U., 1955. Copy editor Indpls. News, 1955-58, movie, TV critic, 1958-65, music, drama critic, from 1965. Pianist dance band, Franklin, 1943-46. Composer numerous musical pieces string quartet, 1954, wind quintet, 1954, violin sonata, 1955, Deat Under A Tree, Wicked Tales for Evil Children, 1980. Organist Presbyn. Ch., Franklin, 1945-48, Bapt. Ch. Franklin, 1948-51. Recipient Best Critical Writing award Indpls. Press Club, 1977, 78. Democrat. Home: Indianapolis, Ind. Died Jan. 1999.

STAHL, BARBARA JAFFE, biologist, educator; b. Bklyn., Apr. 17, 1930; d. Samuel and Sophie (Kalison) Jaffe; m. David G. Stahl, July 7, 1951; children: Susan E. Hardy, Nancy R. Wilsker, Sarah A., John S. BA, Wellesley Coll., 1952; AM, Radcliffe Coll., 1953; PhD, Harvard U., 1965; DSc (hon.), St. Anselm Coll., 1993. Prof. biology St. Anselm Coll., Manchester, NH, 1954—2004. Instl. rev. bd. mem. Cath. Med. Ctr., Manchester, 1987-2004. Author: Vertebrate History: Problems in Evolution, 1974, 1985, Chondrichthyes III: Holocephali (Handbook of Paleoichthyology, Vol. 4), 1999; contbr. articles to profl. jours. Trustee The Derryfield Sch., Manchester, 1965-2004. Disting. alumna award Albany Acad. for Girls, Albany, N.Y., 1993. Mem. AAAS, AAUP, Am. Soc. Ichthyology and Herpetology, Nat. Assn. Advisors for Health Professions, Soc. Vertebrate Paleontology, N.E. Assn. Advisors for Health Professions (treas. 1981-97), Sigma Xi. Home: Manchester, NH. Died Jan. 16, 2004.

STAMPER, JOE ALLEN, lawyer; b. Okemah, Okla., Jan. 30, 1914; s. Horace Allen and Ann (Stephens) S.; m. Johnnie Lee Bell, June 4, 1936; 1 child, Jane Allen (Mrs. Ernest F. Godlove). BA, U. Okla., 1933, LL.B., 1935, JD, 1970. Bar: Okla. bar 1935. Practice in, Antlers, 1935-36, 46—; mem. firm Stamper, Hadley & Reasor, 1974—; atty. Pushmataha County, 1936-39; spl. justice Okla. Supreme Ct., 1948. Mem. Okla. Indsl. Commn., 1939-40; pres. Antlers Sch. Bd., 1956-67, Pushmataha Found., 1957—; mem. Okla. Bicentennial Com., 1971—; vice chmn. bd. U. Okla. Law Center, 1975-78; mgr. Okla. Democratic party, 1946, dist. chmn., 1946-50; alt. del. Dem. Nat. Conv., 1952. Served to col. AUS, 1935-46, E O. Decorated Bronze Star. Fellow Am. Bar Found., Am. Coll. Trial Lawyers, Am. Bd. Trial Advocates (advocate); mem. ABA (del. 1974-91, state del. 1975-86, mem. com. on law book pub. practices 1974-76, bd. govs. 1986-89, standing com. on fed. jud. improvement 1989-92), SAR, Okla. Bar Assn. (bd. govs. 1969-73, Pres.'s award 1977, 80, 93, 2001), Okla. Bar Found. (pres. 1977), Mil. Order World Wars, Pi Kappa Alpha. Baptist (deacon). Clubs: Petroleum (Oklahoma City). Lodges: Masons, Shriners, Lions. Home: Antlers, Okla. Died Feb. 5, 2004.

STANDISH, SAMUEL MILES, oral pathologist, college dean; b. Campbellsburg, Ind., July 6, 1923; s. Irvin Arthur and Etta May (Smedley) S.; m. Gertrude Elizabeth Eberle, Aug. 6, 1949; children— Nancy Jo, Linda Sue. D.D.S., Ind. U., 1945, MS, 1956. Diplomate: Am. Bd. Oral Pathology (dir. 1973-80), Am. Bd. Forensic Odontology. Practice dentistry, specializing in oral pathology, Indpls., 1948-58; mem. faculty Sch. Dentistry Ind. U., 1958-88, emeritus prof. oral pathology, 1967-88, chmn. div. clin. oral pathology, 1967-77, asst. dean sch., 1969-74, asso. dean, 1974-88. Cons. Nat. Cancer Inst., 1969-73, Nat. Bd. Dental Examiners, 1966-74, ADA, 1971-77. Author: (with others) Oral Diagnosis/Oral Medicine, 1978, Maxillofacial Prosthetics: Multidisciplinary Practice, 1972, Outline of Forensic Dentistry, 1982. Served with USNR, 1945-47. With USN, 1945—47, with USNR, 1948—83. Fellow Am. Acad. Oral Pathology (pres. 1972-73); mem. ADA, Internat. Assn. Dental Research, Am. Acad. Forensic Sci., Sigma Xi, Omicron Kappa Upsilon, Xi Psi Phi. Home: Indianapolis, Ind. Died Sept. 21, 2003.

STANFIELD, ROBERT LORNE, Canadian legislator; b. Truro, N.S., Can., Apr. 11, 1914; s. Frank and Sarah E. (Thomas) S.; m. N. Joyce Frazee, June 5, 1940 (dec. July 1954); children: Sarah, Robert M., Judith, Miriam; m. Mary M. Hall, May 10, 1957 (dec. Oct. 1977); m. Anne M. Austin, Aug. 10, 1978. BA, Dalhousie U., 1936; LL.B. cum laude, Harvard U., 1939; LL.D., U. N.B., 1958, St. Dunstan's U., 1964, McGill U., 1967. Bar: Called to N.S. bar 1940, Queen's counsel 1950. Privy council, 1967; asst. sec. Acadia Trust Co., Truro, 1940-41; regional rentals officer Wartime Prices and Trades Bd., Halifax, N.S., 1942-45; mem. firm McInnes & Stanfield, Halifax, 1945-57; pres. N.S. Progressive-Conservative Assn., 1947; leader Progressive-Conservative party in N.S., 1948-67; mem. House of Assembly for Colchester, 1949-67; chmn. N.S. Power Commn., 1956-60; minister edn., 1960-67; premier N.S., 1956-67; mem. House of Commons, Can., 1967-76; leader opposition; leader Progressive Conservative Party Can.; mem. Parliament, 1976-79. Spl. rep. of Govt. Can. to Middle East, 1979-80; former chmn. Inst. for Rsch. on Pub. Policy; former dir., Can. Life Assurance Co. Chmn. Commonwealth Found., 1987-91. Mem. Anglican Ch. Clubs: Halifax, Saraguay. Home: Rockcliffe, Canada. Died Dec. 16, 2003.

STANGLAND, EIDER CLIFFORD, broadcast executive; b. Hetland, S.D., Feb. 7, 1922; s. Ole Hanson and Gurine Olsdtr. (Dahl) S.; m. Norma A. Andersen, Nov. 16, 1949; children: Susan Andrea, Jeffrey James. BA, U. S.D., 1949. Announcer Sta. KSOO, Sioux Falls, S.D., 1941-56; gen. mgr., ptnr. Sta. KBRK, Brookings, S.D., 1956-60; owner, pres. Sta. KCHF, Sioux Falls, 1969-77, Sta. KIWA, Sheldon, Iowa, from 1961, Norse Press, Sioux Falls, from 1973. Author: How to Become Your Own Boss, 1983, Norwegian Jokes, 1978, O LUTEFISK, 1985, Ole & Lena Jokes, 1986, Norwegian Home Companion, 1990, Roast Somebody, 1991. V.p. Keystone Drug and Alcohol Found., Sioux Falls, 1977-83; co-founder, chmn. Concerned Citizens Orgn., Sioux Falls, 1985. Served with USN, 1942-45. Mem. Nat. Assn. Broadcasters, Iowa Broadcasters Assn., S.D. Broadcasters Assn. (pres. 1975). Lodges: Elks, Moose, Masons, El Riad Shrine, El Riad Clowns (pres. 1970), Sons of Norway (pres. Sioux Falls chpt. 1979). Republican. Lutheran. Avocations: boating, travel, writing poetry, photography. Home: Sioux Falls, SD. Deceased.

STANLEY, CHARLES MALCOLM, JR., management professional; b. Honolulu, May 10, 1933; s. Charles Malcolm and Eva (Perry) S.; m. Joyce Eernisse, Dec. 27, 1951; children: Gordon, Jacqueline, Herbert, Cynthia, Becky. B in Gen. Studies, U. Nebr., Omaha, 1970; MPA, U. Mo., Kansas City, 1973. Commd. USAF, 1951, advanced through grades to capt.; commd. U.S. Army, 1967, advanced through grades to col., 1980, ret., 1987; chief of plans U.S. Support Activities Group, Thailand, 1973-74; various positions to dep. chief of staff ops. info. systems command U.S. Army Info. System, Ft. Huachuca, Ariz., 1984-87; group mgr. Automation Rsch. Systems, Alexandria, Va., 1987-90, Sierra Vista, Ariz., from 1990. Ops. officer various BNS, Okinawa, Vietnam. Decorated Disting. Svc. medal Legion of Merit. Mem. Armed Forces Communications Electronics Assn., 1600 Communication Assn., Nat. Contract Mgmt. Assn., Am. Radio Relay League. Republican. Avocations: amateur radio, golf, computers. Home: Oxford, Ala. Died Dec. 9, 2001.

STANNETT, VIVIAN THOMAS, chemical engineering educator; b. Langley, Eng., Sept. 1, 1917; came to U.S., 1947, naturalized, 1957; s. Ernest and Dorothy Grace (Rustell) S.; m. Flora Susanne Sulzbacher, May 30, 1946; 1 dau., Rosemary Anthia. BS, London Poly., 1939; PhD, Poly. Inst. Bklyn., 1950. Chemist, govt. and industry, Eng., 1939-47; research assoc. Mellon Inst., Pitts., 1950-51; research chemist Koppers Co., Pitts., 1951-52; prof. polymer chemistry State U. Coll. Forestry, Syracuse, N.Y., 1952-61; asso. dir. Camille Dreyfus Labs., Research Triangle Inst., Durham, N.C., 1961-67; Camille Dreyfus prof. chem. engring. N.C. State U., Raleigh, from 1967, vice provost, dean Grad. Sch., 1975-82. Author: Cellulose Acetate Plastics, 1950, Handbook of Chemical Technology, 1953; contbr. articles to profl. jours. Recipient Borden award Am. Chem. Soc., 1974, Anselm Payen award, 1974, O. Max Gardner award U. N.C., 1984, Polymer Chemistry award Am. Chem. Soc., 1987. Olney medal Am. Assn. Textile Chemists and Colorists, 1995. Fellow Royal Soc. Chemistry, TAPPI (Silver medal synthetic divsn. 1967), N.Y. Acad. Scis., Soc. Plastics Engrs. (Internat. award and gold medal 1978, N.C. Sci. medal 1981); mem. NAE. Home: Raleigh, NC. Died Oct. 1, 2002.

STANTON, CHARLES P. corporate executive; b. Zurich, Dec. 27, 1935; came to U.S., 1936; s. Fred J. and Hella (Kaufmann) S.; m. Julia Henning, May 31, 1969; children: Julia D., Charlotte Y. AB, Cornell U.; MBA, NYU; JD, Columbia Univ. Bar: N.Y. V.p. J.P. Morgan, N.Y.C., 1963-84; exec. v.p. Hypobank, N.Y.C., 1984-87; pres., CEO Charles Pratt & Co. L.L.C., N.Y.C., from 1988. Treas. Grace Ch., Brooklyn Heights, 1991-95, clk., 1996—. 1st lt. U.S. Army, 1958-59. Home: Brooklyn, NY. Died Feb. 27, 2001.

STARK, NATHAN J. medical administrator, health policy consultant, lawyer; b. Mpls., Nov. 9, 1920; s. Harold and Anna (Berlow) Stark; m. Lucile D. Seidler, Nov. 28, 1943; children: Paul S., David H., Robert, Margaret J. AA, Woodrow Wilson Jr. Coll., Chgo., 1940; BS, U.S. Mcht. Marine Acad., 1943; JD, Ill. Inst. Tech., 1948; LLD (hon.) (hon.), Park Coll., 1969, U. Mo., 1980; DHL, Scholl Coll., Hahnemann U., 1987. Bar: Ill. 1947, Mo. 1952. Plant mgr. Englander Co., Inc., Chgo., 1948—51; partner law firm Downey, Abrams, Stark & Sullivan, Kansas City, Mo., 1952—53; v.p. Rival Mfg. Co., Kansas City, 1954—59; sr. v.p. ops. Hallmark Cards, Inc., Kansas City, 1959—74, dir., 1960—74; pres., chmn. Crown Center Redevel. Corp., 1971—74; sr. vice chancellor health scis. Schs. Health Professions, U. Pitts., 1974—84, sr. vice chancellor emeritus, from 1984, also pres. Univ. Health Center, 1974—79, also prof. Grad. Sch. Public Health; undersec. HEW, Washington, 1979—81; of counsel Fort & Schlefor, Washington; lawyer, treas., pres., CEO Nat. Acad. of Social Ins., 1992—95, also pres. Univ. Health Center, from 1981. Dir. ERC Corp., 1970—79, Hallmark Continental Ltd., Ireland, 1971—73; mem. exec. bd. Nat. Bd. Med.; mem. sci. adv. bd. NE Regional Ctr., from 2000. Contbr. articles to profl. and bus. jours. Legal counsel Lyric Opera Theatre, Kansas City, Mo., 1958—72; mem. com. undergrad. med. edn. AMA, 1966—73; chmn. cmty. hosp.-med. staff group practice program Robert Wood Johnson Found., 1974—79; vice chmn. health ins. benefits adv. com. HEW, 1965—70; sec. Task Force on Medicaid, 1960—70, chmn. adv. commn. incentive reimbursement experimentation, 1968—70; chmn. capital investment conf. HEW-HRA, 1976; mem. liaison com. Am. Assn. Med. Colls.-AMA, 1970—74; chmn. task force life-long learning opportunities Kellogg Found., 1975—77; mem.-a-large Nat. Bd. Med. Examiners; mem. bd. Blue Cross Western Pa., 1975—79, Am. Nurses Found., 1975—77, Health Sys. Agy. SW Pa., from 1976; v.p. Kansas City Philharm. Assn., 1954; sec. Eddie Jacobson Meml. Found., from 1960; mem. tech. bd. Milbank Meml. Fund, 1976—78; pres., chmn. Kansas City Gen. Hosp. and Med. Ctr., 1962—74; trustee Allegheny Found., from 1975, Pitts. Ballet Theater, 1977—79, Pitts. Chamber Opera Theater, from 1978; mem. VA Scholars Bd. Governance, from 1979; hon. fellow, trustee Hastings Ctr., 1981; v.p. Pitts. Opera; adv. bd. trustees St. Joseph Coll., trustee, 1994. Recipient Chancellor's medal, U. Mo. at Kansas City, 1969, Pro-Meritus award, Rockhurst Coll., 1967, Layman award, AMA, 1974. Fellow: Am. Acad. Pediatrics (hon.); mem.: Nat. Acad. Social Ins. (bd. trustees, pres. 1992—94, treas. from 1994), Am. Coll. Hosp Adminstrs., Inst. Medicine of NAS (coun. 1973—76), Am. Hosp. Assn. (hon. Trustee award 1968). Home: Washington, DC. Died Nov. 11, 2002.

STARK, RAY, motion picture producer; b. Chgo., Oct. 3, 1914; Student, Rutgers U. Publicity agt.; lit. agt.; talent agt. Famous Artist Agy., to 1957; co-founder Seven Arts Prodn. Co., 1957; ind. film producer, 1966—. Producer : (films) The World of Suzie Wong, 1960, The Night of the Iguana, 1964, Reflections in a Golden Eye, 1967, Funny Girl, 1968, The Owl and the Pussycat, 1970, Fat City, 1972, The Way We Were, 1973, Funny Lady, 1975, The Sunshine Boys, 1975, Murder By Death, 1976, Smokey and the Bandit, 1977, The Goodbye Girl, 1977, The Cheap Detective, 1978, California Suite, 1978, Chapter Two, 1979, The Electric Horseman, 1979, Seems Like Old Times, 1980, Annie, 1982, Blue Thunder, 1983, Nothing in Common, 1986, Peggy Sue Got Married, 1986, The Secret of My Success, 1987, Biloxi Blues, 1988. Steel Magnolias, 1989, Revenge, 1990, Lost in Yonkers, 1993, Barbarians at the Gate, 1993 (Emmy award Outstanding Made to Television Movie 1993), Mr. Jones, 1993, Dr. Jekyll and Ms. Hyde, 1995, Mariette in Ecstacy, 1996, To Gillian on Her 37th Birthday, 1996, Harriet the Spy, 1996, Random Hearts, 1999, Night of the Iguana, 2001. Recipient Thalberg award Acad. Motion Picture Arts and Scis., 1980 Died Jan. 17, 2004.

STARR, JUNE O. law educator; b. Cin., Apr. 1, 1934; d. M. Herbert and Jane (Rauh) Oettinger; m. George A. Starr, Mar. 23, 1958 (div. 1968); 1 child, Stephen Z. BA, Smith Coll., 1956; MA, Columbia U., 1961; PhD, U. Calif., Berkeley, 1970; MSL, Yale U., 1990; JD, Stanford U., 1992. From asst. prof. to prof. anthropology SUNY, Stony Brook, 1970-93, dir. sociol. legal studies, 1983-87, 93-94; assoc. prof. law Ind. U., Indpls., from 1994; Fulbright prof. Indian Law Inst., New Delhi, 1979, Ankara (Turkey) Law Sch., 1989. Vis. scholar Stanford Law Sch., Palo Alto, Calif., 1992-93, Socio-Legal Ctr., Oxford U., 1981-82. Mem. Assn.

Law Schs., Am. Anthropol. Assn., Turkish Studies Assn., Law and Soc. Assn. (trustee 1976-79, 89-92), Assoc. Polit. and Legal Anthropologists. Avocations: hiking, sailing, reading. Home: Palo Alto, Calif. Died Apr. 28, 2001.

STASIAK, DAVID B. nursing administrator and educator; b. Detroit, Sept. 11, 1956; s. Thomas Donald and Bernice (Zuk) S. Diploma, Grace Hosp., Detroit, 1977; BS with distinction, Wayne State U., 1979, MEd, 1982, MS in Nursing, 1990. Cert. nurse anesthetist. Clin. and didactic instr. Henry Ford Hosp., Detroit, clin. edn. coord.; adminstrv. dir. Horizon Health Systems, Warren, Mich., Mercy Hosps., Detroit. Mem. task force on continued competency in nursing Mich. State Bd. Nursing, 1985-87; assoc. prof., dir. grad. program of nurse anesthesiology Mercy Coll. Detroit. Contbr. articles to profl. jours. Mem. Am. Nurses Assn., Am. Assn. Nurse Anesthetists (bd. dirs. 1990-92, chmn. pub. rels. com. 1989), Mich. Nurses Assn., Mich. Assn. Nurse Anesthetists (chmn. govt. rels. com. 1984-87, bd. dirs. Dist. I 1983-86, polit. action com., chmn. scholarship com., pres. 1987-88), Transcultural Nursing Soc., Inst. for Human Caring, Sigma Theta Tau, Eta Sigma Gamma. Home: Southfield, Mich. Deceased.

STAUFFER, EDWARD SHANNON, orthopedic surgeon, educator; b. Lancaster, Pa., June 30, 1931; s. Carry Emmett and Ruby Rebecca (Driver) S.; m. Dawn Marie Moser, Aug. 28, 1954; children: Pamela, Randall, Lisa, Amy, Beth, Scott. BS, Franklin & Marshall Coll., 1955; MD, Temple U., 1959. Diplomate Am. Bd. Orthopedic Surgery. Resident in orthops. U. Pitts., 1960-64; fellow U. So. Calif.-Rancho Los Amigos Hosp., Downey, 1964-65; chief Spinal Injury Ctr. L.A. County Hosp., Downey, 1965-75; prof. orthop. surgery So. Ill. U., Springfield, from 1975. Editor: The American Academy of Orthopaedic Surgeons Instructional Course Lectures, 1985, Am. Acad. of Orthopedics, 1995; contbr. numerous articles to profl. jours., chpts. to books. Recipient Rsch. award Nat. Parapleig Assn., 1973. Mem. Cervical Spine Rsch. Soc. (pres. 1987-88), Assn. Bone and Joint Surgeons (pres. 1988-89), Acad. Orthp. Soc. (pres. 1989-90). Home: Chatham, Ill. Died May 16, 2002.

STEARNS, FORST W. ecologist, consultant; b. Milw., Sept. 10, 1918; s. Perry J. and Maebelle (Brook) S.; m. Hope Hartley, Apr. 23, 1943 (dec. Sept. 1953); children: Carlin, Andrea, Jay; m. Ruth Heitz, Aug. 3, 1956; 1 child, Timothy (dec.). AB, Harvard U., 1939; MPH, U. Wis., 1940, PhD, 1947. Cert. sr. ecologist. Asst. prof. Purdue U., Lafayette, Ind., 1947-57; ecologist, project leader So. Forest Experiment Sta., U.S. Forest Svc., Vicksburg, Miss., 1957-61; project leader, wildlife habitat Lek States Forest Experiment Sta., St. Paul, 1961-64, N.C. Forest Experiment Sta., Rhinelander, Wis., 1964-68; prof. U. Wis., Milw., 1968-87, prof. emeritus, 1987-99. Chair Wis. Sci. Areas Preservation Coun., Madison, 1975-89; cons. Conservation Found., Washington, 1986-88. Co-editor: The Urban Ecosystem--A Holistic Approach, 1974. Mem. tech. com. S.E. Wis. Coalition for Clean Air, Milw., 1976-82. 1st lt. USAF, 1943-46. Recipient Wis. Idea award Ctrs. for Resource Policy Studies, U. Wis., 1990; named Outstanding Environmentalist, Coll. Natural Resources/U. Wis., Stevens Point, 1991. Fellow AAAS, Ecol. Soc. Am. (pres. 1975-76, editor), The Wildlife Soc., Wis. Acad. Sci., Arts and Letters (coun. 1976-79, editor Transactions 1978-81, Citation 1986). Home: Humbird, Wis. Died Sept. 8, 1999.

STEELE, EARL LARSEN, electrical engineering educator; b. Denver, Sept. 24, 1923; s. Earl Harold and Jennie (Larsen) S.; m. Martha C. Hennessey, June 27, 1953; children: Karl Thomas, Earl Robert, Karen Lynn, Kevin Douglas, Lisa Louise, Colleen Carol. BS with honors, U. Utah, 1945; PhD, Cornell U., 1952. Research physicist Gen. Electric Co., 1952-56; chief device devel. Motorola, Inc., 1956-58; mgr. devel. lab. Hughes Aircraft Co., 1958-64; research scientist N.Am. Rockwell Corp., 1964-69; prof. elec. engring. U. Ky., Lexington, 1969-90, prof. emeritus, from 1991, chmn. dept., 1971-80, 1988-89. Affiliate prof. Ariz. State U., 1956-58, U. Calif.-Irvine, 1966-69; adviser So. Calif. Coll., Costa Mesa, 1963-64; charter mem. Orange County Academic Decathlon (Calif.); bd. dirs. Southeastern Center for Elec. Engring. Edn., 1975—, treas., 1980-81, v.p., 1981-82, resident dir., 1981-82, 89-90, pres., 1982-83, mem. coun. of pres.', 1983—. Author: Optical Lasers in Electronics; contbr. articles to profl. jours. Fellow IEEE; mem. Am. Soc. Engring. Edn. (U. Ky. Coll. Engring. rep. to ASEE, 1988-90), Am. Phys. Soc., Internat. Soc. Hybrid Microelectronics, Sigma Xi, Tau Beta Pi, Eta Kappa Nu (dir. 1974-76, v.p. 1983-84, pres. 1984-85). Mem. Lds Ch. Home: Lexington, Ky. Died July 27, 2003.

STEER, HELEN VANE, theatre director, educator, stage dialect coach; b. Manchester, Eng., May 20, 1926; d. Charles Burrell Llewellyn and Dorothy Alice (Rice) S. BA, La. State U., 1954, MA, 1958, PhD, 1967. Instr., theatre dir. Howard Coll. (name changed to Samford U.), Birmingham, Ala., 1956-59; teaching asst. La. State U., Baton Rouge, 1960-63; assoc. prof. East Carolina U., Greenvillle, N.C., 1963-88, ret., 1988. Dialect coach The Lost Colony, Manteo, N.C., 1985; dir. Actors Theatre S.E., Greenville, 1988. Editor: Your Speech, 1975, 3d edit. revised, 1996; drama editor So. Speech Jour., 1966-69; contbr. articles and book revs. to profl. jours. Mem. So. Speech Comm. Assn. (hon. life), Speech Comm. Assn., Southeastern Theatre Conf., N.C. Speech and drama Assn. (pres. 1971), Greenville Singles Club (parliamentarian 1987-97), Skinner Inst. (cert.), Phi Kappa Phi (v.p. LSU chpt. 1954). Avocation: music. Home: Durham, NC. Died Aug. 14, 2001.

STEFFENS, DOROTHY RUTH, political economist; b. N.Y.C., May 5, 1921; d. Saul M. and Pearl Y. (Reiter) Cantor; m. Jerome Steffens, Nov. 19, 1940; children: Heidi Sue, Nina Ellen. BBA, CCNY, 1941; MEd, Temple U., 1961; PhD, Anthony U., 1981. Economist Nat. War Labor Bd., Washington, 1941-44, United Elec. Radio Machine Workers, Phila., 1944-46; instr. group dynamics Temple U., Phila., 1955-57; seminar program dir. Soc. Friends, Washington, 1958-61; tng. dir. Nat. Coun. Negro Women, Washington, 1967-68; edn. cons. Peace Corps, Nigeria, 1969-70; exec. dir. Women's Internat. League for Peace and Freedom, Phila., 1971-77, Fund for Open Info. and Accountability, Inc., 1978-80; conf. dir. Haverford Coll., 1980-84; exec. sec. Nigerian Women's Com., 1968-69; del. African Women's Seminar UN, Accra, Ghana, 1969; mem. Africa panel Am. Friends Svc. Com., 1976-88, mem. internat. divsn. exec. com., 1977-84. Resource lectr. Internat. Women's Seminar, Lillehammer, Norway, 1991. Author: The Day after Summer, 1966; editorial bd. The Churchman, 1977—; mem. nat. bd. Gray Panthers, 1989-91; contbr. articles to profl. jours., newspapers, mags. N.Y. C. of C. scholar, N.Y. State Regents scholar CCNY, 1941. Mem. Soc. Of Friends. Home: Silver Spring, Md. Died July 17, 1999.

STEIG, WILLIAM, author, artist; b. N.Y.C., Nov. 14, 1907; s. Joseph and Laura (Ebel) S.; m. Elizabeth Mead, Jan. 2, 1936 (div.); children: Lucy, Jeremy; m. Kari Homestead, 1950 (div. 1963); 1 child, Margit Laura; m. Stephanie Healey, Dec. 12, 1964 (div. Dec. 1966); m. Jeanne Doron, 1969. Ed., Coll. City N.Y., 1923-25, NAD, 1925-29. Cartoonist New Yorker, N.Y.C., from 1930; author, illustrator for children's books, from 1968. Artist drawings in mags., water color collections, Bklyn. Mus.; one-man show wood sculpture Downtown Gallery, N.Y.C., 1939; exhibited drawsing and sculpture Smith Coll., 1940; author: Man About Town, 1932, About People: A Book of Symbolic Drawings, 1939, The Lonely Ones, a book of drawings, 1942, All Embarrassed, 1944, Small Fry, 1944, Persistent Faces, 1945, Till Death Do Us Part, 1947, The Agony in the Kindergarten, 1950, The Rejected Lovers, 1951, The Steig Album. Seven Complete Books, 1953, Dreams of Glory, 1953, Roland, the Minstrel Pig, 1968, CDB, 1968, Sylvester and the Magic Pebble, 1969 (Caldecott medal 1970), The Bad Island, 1969, An Eye for Elephants, 1970, The Bad Speller, 1970, Amos and Boris, 1971, Male/Female, 1971, Dominic, 1972 (Christopher award 1973, Priz de la Fondation de France 1983), The Real Thief, 1973 (Best Children's Book prize, Italy 1990), Farmer Palmer's Wagon Ride, 1974, Abel's Island, 1976 (Newbery Honor book), The Amazing Bone, 1976 (Caldecott Honor book), Caleb and Kate, 1977, Tiffky Doofky, 1978, Drawings, 1979, Gorky Rises, 1980, Doctor de Soto, 1982 (Am. Book award 1983), Yellow & Pink, 1984, Ruminations, 1984, Solomon and the Rusty Nail, 1984, Brave Irene, 1986, CDC?, 1986, Zabajaba Jungle, 1987, Spinky Sulks, 1988, Shrek!, 1990, Our Miserable Life, 1990, Doctor De Soto Goes to Africa, 1992, (book of drawings) Strutters and Fretters, 1992, Zeke Pippin, 1994, Grown-ups Get to Do All the Driving, 1995, The Toy Brother, 1996, Toby, Where Are You?, 1997, Pete's a Pizza, 1998, Made for Each Other, 2000, Wizzil, 2000, Potch & Polly, 2002; executed Wood sculpture R.I. Mus., Providence, Smith Coll. Mus., Northampton, Mass. Recipient William Allen White award, 1975; Irma Simonton Black award, 1981 Home: Boston, Mass. Died Oct. 3, 2003.

STEIGER, JANET DEMPSEY, government official; b. Oshkosh, Wis., June 10, 1939; 1 child, William Raymond. BA, Lawrence Coll., 1961; postgrad., U. Reading, Eng., 1961-62, U. Wis., 1962-63; LLD (hon.), Lawrence U., 1992. Legis. aide Office of Gov., Wis., 1965; v.p. The Work Place, Inc., 1975-80; commr. Postal Rate Commn., Washington, 1980-89, acting chmn., 1981-82, chmn., 1982-89; commr. FTC, Washington, 1989—95. Former U.S. del. OECD, Paris. Author: Law Enforcement and Juvenile Justice in Wisconsin, 1965; co-author: To Light One Candle, a Handbook on Organizing, Funding and Maintaining Public Service Projects, 1978, 2d edit., 1980. Chmn. Commn. on Vets. Edn. Policy, 1987-90. Woodrow Wilson scholar; Fulbright scholar, 1961. Mem. Phi Beta Kappa. Died Apr. 3, 2004.

STEINER, KURT, educator, lawyer, political scientist; b. Vienna, June 10, 1912; came to U.S., 1938, naturalized, 1944; s. Jacob and Olga (Weil) S.; m. Josepha (dec. 2003), Aug, 26, 1939. D.Jurisprudence, U. Vienna, 1935; PhD in Polit. Sci, Stanford U., 1955; honorary doctorate, U. Vienna, 1990. Jud. asst., later atty., Vienna, 1935-38; instr., asst. dir., then dir. Berlitz Schs. Langs., Cleve., Pitts., 1939-43; prosecutor, spl. asst. to chief counsel, prosecution sect. Internat. Mil. Tribunal Far East, Tokyo, 1948; pros. atty., legal sect. SCAP, Tokyo, 1948-49, legis. atty., later chief civil affairs and civil liberties br., legislation and justice div., legal sect., 1949-51; vis. research scholar Center Internat. Studies, Princeton, 1954-55; faculty Stanford U., 1955—77, prof. polit. sci., 1962—77; prof. emeritus Stanford U, 1977—2003; asso. exec. head dept. Stanford U., 1959-63; chmn. com. East Asian Studies, 1964-65; dir. Stanford in, Germany, summer 1961, Stanford Center Japanese Studies, Tokyo, 1962. Ofcl. escort Japanese Legal Edn. Mission to U.S., 1950-51 Author: Local Government in Japan, 1965, Politics in Austria, 1972; co-author, co-editor: Political Opposition and Local Politics in Japan, 1981; editor: Modern Austria, 1981, Tradition and Innovation in Contemporary Austria, 1982; Contbr. articles to publs., chpts. to books. Served with AUS, 1944-48, PTO. Ford Found. fellow, 1953-54; recipient Austrian Cross of Honor for Sci. and the Arts, 1981, Austrian Golden Order of Merit, 1989. Mem. Am. Polit. Sci. Assn., Assn. Asian Studies, AAUP, Japanese Am. Soc. Legal Studies (councillor 1965—) Home: Palo Alto, Calif. Died Oct. 20, 2003.

STEINKAMP, DOROTHY DEMAURO, nursing educator, educator; b. Middletown, Conn., Aug. 29, 1936; d. Harry S. and Marian (Carta) DiMauro; m. Erwin A. Steinkamp, Dec. 6, 1969; children: Mark LaBella, Robin LaBella, Suzanne Steinkamp, Steven Steinkamp, Cynthia Steinkamp. RN, Middlesex Meml. Hosp., 1957. Dir. nursing Forestville (Conn.) Nursing Home, 1986; cons. Dogwood Acres, Durham, Conn., 1986-89; tech. supr., tchr. Greater Hartford (Conn.) Community Coll., 1988-89; infection control nurse Middletown (Conn.) Health Care, 1988-89; staff nurse Golf Coast Home Health Svcs., Spring Hill, Fla., 1990-91, DNS Royal Oak Nursing Ctr., Dade City, Fla., 1991-93; DON Cypress Cove Care Ctr., 1993-95; quality assurance nurse Cmty. Home Health Care, Spring Hill, Fla., 1995-98, Mederi Home Care, Brooksville, Fla., 1995-98; ret., 1998. Mem. Infection Control Nurses of Conn. (treas. Hartford group). Home: Middletown, Conn. Died Apr. 10, 2000.

STEINPFAD, RUSSELL ALEXANDER GUSTAVE, engineer; b. Los Angeles, Jan. 5, 1933; s. Russell Stunz and Alexanderina (Bethune) S.; m. Lois Jean Paul, Oct. 23, 1953 (div. June 1961); children: Craig Alexander, Karen Annette, Christie Lee; m. Margaret Anne Coulson, June 23, 1962 BA, Antioch Coll., 1977; MA, U. Redlands, 1983. Registered profl. engr. Service engr. Harvey Aluminum, Inc., Torrance, Calif., 1958-60; sales engr. Connor Spring Co., Los Angeles, 1960-62, div. mgr. Phoenix, 1962-67; sales rep. Assoc. Spring Corp., Gardenia, Calif., 1967-69, territory sales mgr., 1969-75, mgr., engring., from 1975. Active Los Angeles County Mus. Art, 1978—, So. Calif. Cultural Heritage Founders, Los Angeles, 1983—, Mus. Natural History, Los Angeles, 1985—, Mus. Contemporary Art, Los Angeles, 1986—. Served with USN, 1951-55, Korea. Decorated Air medal. Mem. Soc. Mfg. Engrs. (chmn. 1974-75), Nat. Soc. Profl. ENgrs., soc. Automotive Engrs., Am. Soc. For Quality Control, ASTM, YMCA. Republican. Episcopalian. Avocations: swimming, reading, gardening,. Home: La Crescenta, Calif. Deceased.

STEMBRIDGE, VERNIE A(LBERT), pathologist, educator; b. El Paso, Tex., June 7, 1924; s. Vernie Albert and Anna Marie (Lawless) S.; m. Aileen Cofer Marston, June 14, 1944; children— Shirley (Mrs. J.P. Watkins), Ann (Mrs. Donald M. Connell), Vivian (Mrs. Lance E. Porter). BA, U. Tex. at El Paso (formerly Tex. Coll. Mines), 1943; MD, U. Tex., Galveston, 1948. Diplomate: Am. Bd. Pathology (trustee 1969-80, sec. 1976-79, pres. 1980). Intern U.S. Marine Hosp., Norfolk, Va., 1948-49; resident in pathology Med. Br., U. Tex., Galveston, 1949-52, asst. prof. pathology, 1952-54, asso. prof., 1954-56, Southwestern Med. Sch., Dallas, 1959-61, prof., 1961—2000, Ashbel Smith prof., 1991—2000, chmn. dept. pathology, 1966-88, chmn. emeritus, 1992—2000, interim dean Sch. Allied Health Scis. U. Tex., 1988-91; assoc. dir. clin. labs. U. Tex. Med. Br. Hosps., 1952-56; sr. pathologist, chief aviation pathology sect. Armed Forces Inst. Pathology, Washington, 1956-59; dir. pathology labs. Parkland Hosp., Dallas, 1966-85. Cons. VA Hosp., Dallas; cons. to surgeon gen. USAF; civil air surgeon FAA; chmn. sci. adv. bd. Armed Forces Inst. Pathology; mem. State of Tex. Radiation Adv. Bd., 1987-94. Contbr. articles to med. jours. Served with USAF, 1956-59. Decorated Legion of Merit; named Outstanding Alumnus U. Tex. at El Paso, 1978, Hon. Alumnus, U. Tex. Southwestern Med. Sch., 1964, Ashbel Smith outstanding alumnus U. Tex. Med. Br., 1982; recipient Joint Disting. Service award Am. Soc. Clin. Pathologists/Coll. Am. Pathologists, 1987. Mem. Internat. Acad. Pathology (counselor 1970-73), Am. Soc. Clin. Pathologists (bd. dirs. 1973-79, pres. 1977-78, bd. registry, gov. 1983-90, Ward Burdick award for outstanding contbns. 1981, Bd. Registry Disting. Svc. award 1995), AMA (residency rev. com. of pathology 1972-78, chmn. 1977-78, residency rev. com. nuclear medicine 1972-78), Intersoc. Pathology Coun. (sec. 1979-84), Coll. Am. Pathologists, Am. Assn. Pathologists, Assn. Pathology Chairmen (mem. coun., pres. 1979, Disting. Svc. award 1996), Am. Assn. Blood Banks, Tex. Soc. Pathologists (pres. 1966, Caldwell award 1967, annual lectureship established in honor), Tex. Med. Assn. (ho. of dels. 1966-86), Dallas County Med. Soc. (pres. 1985, Max Cole Leadership award 1991), Am. Registry Pathology (bd. dirs. 1986-91, chmn. 1989-90, Disting. Svc. award 1995), Sigma Xi, Phi Rho Sigma, Mu Delta, Alpha Omega Alpha. Home: Dallas, Tex. Died Dec. 1, 2000; Dallas, Tex..

STEPHENS, PAULA CHRISTINE (POLLY), arbitrator, consultant; b. St. Louis, July 17, 1932; d. Herbert and Irene Lovey (Caldwell) Kuenzel; m. John James Stephens, Aug. 27, 1957 (div. Feb. 1971); children: David A., Nancy S. BA in Sociology, U. Mich., 1955. Registered rep. NASD; lic. real estate salesperson, Ohio, Fla., in uniform securities NYSE, ASE. Fin. cons. trainer, fin. cons. Merrill Lynch, various locations, 1978-87, field strategy mgr., tng. mgr. Princeton, N.J., 1987-89, Venice, Fla., 1989-91; litigation cons. Sarasota, Fla., 1991-95; arbitrator Fla. State's Atty. Gen., Tallahassee, 1996-99; litigation cons. Stephens Reven & Assocs., Sarasota, 1995-99. Arbitrator Am. Arbitrator Assn., Miami and N.Y.C., 1992-99, Nat. Assn. Securities Dealers, 1992-99; cons. Women's Resource Ctr. Displaced Homemaker Program, 1989-91; water safety coor. ARC, Tuscaloosa, Ala., 1954; supplemental recreation activities overseas employee ARC, Korea, 1956-57. Bd. dirs. Women's Resource Ctr., 1978-79, 94-95. Mem. U.S. Coast Guard Aux. Republican. Avocations: bridge, travel, swimming, tennis, reading. Home: Sarasota, Fla. Died July 23, 1999.

STEPHENS, RICHARD DALE, banker, real estate and insurance agency executive; b. Del Norte, Colo., Aug. 20, 1932; s. Charles William and Evelyn Aileen (Mount) S.; m. Virginia Lee Brown, June 29, 1951; children: Charles J., Candace S., Julia A. Cert. in real estate law, Parriot Del Monte Sch., Jackson, Wyo., 1978. Lic. real estate broker, ins. agt., Wyo. Owner, mgr. service sta. Standard Oil Co., Pine Bluffs, Wyo., 1953-56; owner, mgr. Stephens Ins., Pine Bluffs, 1958-99, Stephens Realty, Pine Bluffs, 1970-99; pres. Farmers State Bank, Pine Bluffs, 1978-99, also. bd. dirs. Councilman, Town of Pine Bluffs, 1969-75, mayor, 1975-79. With USAF, 1950-54, Korea. Mem. Wyo. Bankers Assn., Wyo. Jaycees (treas., v.p. 1960-64), Masons, Order Eastern Star, Lions (pres. Pine Bluffs lodge 1978-79). Republican. Methodist. Avocation: golf. Home: Pine Bluffs, Wyo. Died July 6, 1999.

STEPKA, WILLIAM, pharmacologist, educator; b. Veseli, Minn., Apr. 13, 1917; s. John J. and Mary (Jasan) S.; m. Bonnie Gene Thomas, July 15, 1948; 1 child, Donald Thomas. BA, U. Rochester, 1946; PhD, U. Calif., Berkeley, 1951. Grad. teaching asst. U. Rochester, 1946-47; grad. rsch. asst. U. Calif., Berkeley, 1948-49; rsch. assoc. U. Pa., Phila., 1951-54, ass.t prof. botany, 1954-55; sr. scientist The Am. Tobacco Co., Richmond, Va., 1955-68; asst. prof. rsch. physiology Med. Coll. Va., Richmond, Va., 1955-60, assoc. prof. rsch. physiology, 1960-67, assoc. prof. rsch. pharmacology, 1967-68; prof. pharmacognosy Va. Commonwealth U., Richmond, 1968-82, prof. emeritus, from 1982. Cons. Va. Commonwealth U., 1982—, chmn. Sch. Pharmacy Reaccreditation Com., 1977, 82, 88, radiation safety com., 1955-82. Contbr. articles to profl. jours., chpts. to books. Magisterial rep. Henrico County Dem. Com., 1988-94; lobbyist Faculty Interests and Higher Edn. in Va., 1979—. 1st lt. USAAF, 1943-46. AEC predoctoral fellow, 1949-51. Mem. AAUP (chair com. on pub. affairs 1978, pres. Va. conf. 1991), Sigma Xi, Rho Chi. Democrat. Avocations: gardening, music, travel. Died Feb. 6, 2001.

STERMER, RAYMOND ANDREW, agricultural engineer; b. Barclay, Tex., July 22, 1924; s. Henry Jacob and Roseline (Voltin) S.; m. Gladys Freida Hoelscher, June 15, 1948; children: Linda Gayle, Nancy Louise. BS, Tex. A&M U., 1950, MS, 1958, PhD, 1971. Registered profl. engr., Tex. Agrl. engr. Soil Conservation Svc. USDA, various cities, Tex., 1950-55, agrl. engr. Agrl. Mktg. Svc. College Station, Tex., 1955-62, agrl. engr. Agrl. Rsch. Svc., 1962-89; agrl. engr. Tex. Agrl. Exptl. Sta.-Tex. A&M U., College Station, from 1989. Contbr. to profl. publs. Mem. Am. Soc. Agrl. Engrs., Sigma Xi. Home: Bryan, Tex. Died Dec. 5, 2000.

STERN, ARNOLD JAY, lawyer; b. Omaha, Nov. 10, 1931; s. Samuel H. and Bess (Haykin) S.; m. Carolyn R. Cohn, Nov. 23, 1958; children: John, Richard, Jeffrey. BS in Law, U. Nebr., 1954; JD, Creighton U., 1957. Bar: Nebr. 1957, U.S. Dist. Ct. Nebr. 1957., U.S. Ct. Appeals (8th cir.) 1960. Assoc. Stern, Harris & Feldman, Omaha, 1961-65; ptnr. Fellman & Stern, Omaha, 1965-74, Eisenstatt, Higgins et al, Omaha, 1974-79; ptnr., pres. Arnold J. Stern & Assocs., Omaha, 1979-86, Stern, Swanson & Stickman, Omaha, 1986-99. Pres. Variety Club Nebr., Omaha, 1970-74, Beth El Synagogue, Omaha, 1975-76, Meyer Inst. Bd., Omaha, 1978-80. Served to 1st lt. U.S. Army, 1954-56. Recipient award Meyer Children's Rehab. Inst. Mem. ABA, Nebr. Bar Assn., Omaha Bar Assn., Omaha Estate Planning Council, Omaha Tennis Assn. (pres. 1977-79). Democrat. Jewish. Home: Omaha, Nebr. Died Mar. 13, 1999.

STERN, FREDERICK C. English language and literature educator; b. Vienna, Apr. 28, 1929; came to U.S., 1939; s. George G. and Tony (Holzer) S.; m. Naomi Landy, Jan. 1, 1950; children: Carrie, David, Paul, Jeremy. MA, U. Chgo., 1963; PhD, Purdue U., 1970. Lectr. in English Ind. U. N.W., Gary, 1964; instr. English Purdue U. Calumet, Hammond, Ind., 1964-65, U. Ill. at Chgo., 1966-70, asst. prof., 1970-81, assoc. prof., 1981-91, prof., from 1991. Author: E.O. Matthiessen, Christian Socialist as Critic, 1981; editor: The Revolutionary Poet in the United States: The Poetry of Thomas McGrath, 1989; contbr. articles to profl. jours. Bd. dirs., officer Ind. Civil Liberties Union; bd. dirs. Midwest Com. for Mil. Counseling, Chgo., New Jewish Agenda, Gary. Mem. MLA, Midwest MLA, Soc. for Studyof Midwestern Lit. (bd. dirs. 1986-92, v.p. 1992—, MidAm. award 1992), others. Jewish. Home: Gary, Ind. Deceased.

STERN, MARVIN, psychiatrist, educator; b. N.Y.C., Jan. 6, 1916; s. Jacob and Mary (Kappel) S.; m. Libby Rifkin, Jan. 18, 1942; children: Carol S., Robert M., Theodore A. BS, CCNY, 1935; MD, NYU, 1939. Diplomate Am. Bd. Psychiatry and Neurology. Intern in medicine and surgery Bellevue Hosp., N.Y.C., 1939-40, resident in medicine and psychiatry, 1940-42, fellow in psychiatry, 1946-47; practice medicine specializing in psychiatry N.Y.C., 1947—; asst. prof. psychiatry NYU Med. Ctr., N.Y.C., 1948-55, assoc. prof., 1955-62, prof., 1962-79, Menas S. Gregory prof. psychiatry, 1979-86, prof., 1986-95; prof. emeritus, from 1995, NYU Med. Ctr., N.Y.C., from 1995, exec. chmn. dept. psychiatry, 1976-86. Mem. staff NYU Hosp., Bellevue Hosp.; cons. psychiatrist VA Hosp.; cons. psychiatrist emeritus Brookdale Hosp. Served to maj. AUS, 1942-46. Fellow Am. Psychiat. Assn. (sec. dist. br. 1956-63, pres. dist. br. 1964, area chmn. 1962-63); mem. Am. Psychosomatic Assn., N.Y.C. Acad. Medicine, Harvey Soc., NYU Med. Alumni Assn. (pres. 1979-80), Phi Beta Kappa, Sigma Xi, Alpha Omega Alpha Home: New York, NY. Died May 13, 2003.

STERNBERG, PAUL, retired ophthalmologist; b. Chgo., Dec. 18, 1917; s. David M. and Sarah (Kopeka) S.; m. Dorie Betty Feitler, Dec. 24, 1949; children— Daniel P., Patricia F., Paul, Susan P., David. BS, Northwestern U., 1938, MD, 1940. Intern Michael Reese Hosp., Chgo., 1940-41, resident ophthalmology, Ill. Eye & Ear Infirmary U. Ill.; spl. fellow ophthalmology Cornell U. Med. Center, N.Y. Hosp., Wilmer Inst. Johns Hopkins, 1941-44; practice medicine, specializing in ophthalmology Chgo., 1945—89. Attending ophthalmologist Cook County Hosp., Michael Reese Hosp., Highland Park (Ill.) Hosp., Louis Weiss Meml. Hosp.; prof. ophthalmology Chgo. Med. Sch., U. Ill. Med. Sch. Contbr. sci. articles to med. and ophthal. jours. Trustee Art Inst. Chgo. Fellow A.C.S.; mem. Assn. for Research in Ophthalmology, Am. Assn. Ophthalmology, Am. Acad. Ophthalmology, Chgo. Ophthal. Soc., Pan-Am. Congress Ophthalmology, Merit Country Club, Standard Club, Lake Shore Country Club. Home: Glencoe, Ill. Died Mar. 2, 2004.

STERNGLASS, MARILYN SEINER, english composition studies educator; b. Pitts., Aug. 21, 1932; d. Harry and Eva (Price) Seiner; m. Ernest J. Sternglass, Sept. 21, 1957; children: Daniel, Susan. BS, Carnegie-Mellon U., 1954, MA, 1967; PhD in Linguistics, U. Pitts., 1973. Instr. Carnegie-Mellon U., Pitts., 1967-72, asst. prof. English, 1973-75; assoc. prof. English Indiana U. Pa., 1975-79, Ind. U., Bloomington, 1979-85, City Coll. of CUNY, 1985-87, prof., 1987-96, prof. emerita, 1996—2004. Author: The Presence of Thought, 1988, Reading, Writing and Reasoning, 1991, 92, 93; Time to Know Them: A Longitudinal Study of Writing and Learning at the college Level, 1997; contbr. articles to profl. jours. Profl. Staff Congress/CUNY rsch. grantee, 1991, 93, 94, Nat. Coun. Tchrs. English grantee, 1992, 93. Jewish. Home: Pittsburgh, Pa. Died Jan. 6, 2004.

STEVENS, HAROLD, retired neurology educator; b. Salem, N.J., Oct. 18, 1911; s. Bernard and Bessie (Klein) S.; m. Dorothy C. Stevens (dec. 1998), children: David, Roger. BS, Pa. State U., 1933; MA, U. Pa., 1934, PhD, 1937, MD, 1941. Cert. Am. Bd. Psychiatry and Neurology. Internship U. of Mich. Hosp., 1941-42; resident St. Eliz Hosp., 1942-46; prof. neurology George Washington U., Washington, 1955—78; disting. prof. dept. neurology Uniformed Svcs. Health Scis., Bethesda, Md., 1983. Neurology cons. D.C. Health Dept., Washington, 1946, VA Hosp., Washington, 1946, Walter Reed Hosp., Washington, 1958, FDA, 1974; lectr. Joseph Gitt Meml., Wash. U. Sch. Medicine, 1976. Pres. Jacobi Med. Soc., Washington, 1960, D.C. Doctors Orch., Washington, 1968, Washington chpt. Soc. for Hist. Medicine, 1972. Univ. scholar in psychology, 1934-35, Harrison scholar U. Pa., 1934-36; recipient spl. citation FDA, 1979, award D.C. Assn. for Retarded Citizens, 1977. Fellow Am. Coll. Physicians, Am. Acad. Neurology; mem. Am. Psychiat. Assn., D.C. Med. Soc., Am. Neurological Assn., COSMOS Club. Home: Bethesda, Md. Died Aug. 26, 2003.

STEVENS, PAUL LAWRENCE, lawyer; b. Glen Ridge, N.J., Aug. 18, 1947; s. Mead Ferrin and Mary Nealtha (Cherry) S.; m. Cathy Lee Danskin, Sept. 13, 1969; children: Todd Benjamin, Laura Catherine. BA, U. N.H., 1969; JD cum laude, Dickinson Sch. of Law, 1975. Bar: Pa. 1975, U.S. Dist. Ct. (ea. and mid. dists.) Pa. 1975, U.S. Ct. Appeals (3d cir.) 1979, U.S. Supreme Ct. 1980. Law clk. to pres. judge Pa. Superior Ct., Carlisle, 1975-76; ptnr. Sweet, Stevens, Tucker & Katz, Doylestown, Pa., from 1985. Editor Dickinson Law Rev., 1975. Bd. govs. Dickinson Sch. Law, 2001—. Served to 1st lt. U.S. Army, 1969-82. Mem. ABA (Spl. Achievement award 1983), Pa. Bar Assn. (bd. govs. 1981-84, chmn. ho. of dels. 1987-89, pres. 1994-95), Bucks County Bar Assn. (bd. dirs. 1978-80), Pa. Sch Bd. Solicitors' Assn. (v.p. 1985-87, pres. 1987-88). Republican. Avocations: photography, skiing. Home: Doylestown, Pa. Died Sept. 12, 2001.

STEVENSON, ROBERT EDWARD, corporate executive, business owner; b. East Orange, N.J., May 19, 1932; s. William Chipman and Hilda (Moss) S.; m. Cynthia Dunbar, Aug. 25, 1957; children: Mark Dunbar, Laurie Lynn, Lisa Anne. Grad. high sch., Baldwinsville, N.Y. Owner Stevenson Studios, Baldwinsville, 1952-90, Photography as an Art, St. Thomas, U.S. V.I., from 1969; pres. Concepts Unltd., Marcellus, from 1985. Lectr. in field; cons. Coppinger & Affiliates, Cleveland, Tenn., 1982—. Mem. Am. Soc. Photographers (assoc.), Profl. Photographers of Am. (Nat. award 1985), Profl. Photography Soc. of N.Y. (bd. govs. 1968). Avocations: racquetball, skiing, music, canoeing, travel. Home: Marcellus, NY. Died Aug. 26, 2000.

STEVOFF, AUDREY LAZNICKA, investment analyst, telecommunications specialist; b. Chgo., Dec. 13, 1934; d. Frank and Bessie (Srp) Laznicka; m. Nick Spiro Stevoff, Dec. 26, 1970; children— Nadine, Sheryl. B.S. in Acctg., U. Ill., 1956; M.B.A., Northwestern U., 1965. Acct. Arthur Andersen & Co., Chgo., 1956; statistical analyst Standard Oil (Ind.), Chgo., 1956-66; public utility analyst Harris Trust & Savs. Bank, Chgo., 1966-71; telecommunications analyst Duff & Phelps, Inc., Chgo., 1982—, asst. v.p., 1984-86, v.p., 1986—. Mem. Investment Analysts Soc. Chgo. (chmn. membership com. 1985-87, arrangments com. 1987-88, program com. 1989-90), Inst. Chartered Fin. Analysts (cert.), Fin. Analysts Fedn., Pub. Utility Securities Club Chgo. (treas. 1968-69, sec. 1969-70). Club: Women's Assn. 1st Presbyterian Ch. Deerfield (treas. 1978-79, v.p. 1980-81, pres. 1981-82), Townley Golf (treas. 1979-80) (Deerfield). Avocations: golf, travel, arts and crafts, attending concerts and theater. Home: Wilmette, Ill.

STEYERT, WILLIAM ALBERT, physicist; b. Allentown, Pa., Sept. 20, 1932; s. William Albert Sr. and Anna (Jones) S.; m. Lila J. Oderkirk, June 10, 1961; children: David William, Ann Eileen. BS in Physics, MIT, 1954; MS in Physics, Calif. Inst. Tech., 1956, PhD in Physics and Math., 1960. Postdoctoral research assoc. U. Ill., Urbana, 1960-61; staff mem. Los Alamos (N.Mex.) Nat. Lab., 1961-82; sr. research assoc. Air Products and Chems., Inc., Allentown, Pa., 1982-87, APD Cryogenics, Inc. subs. Intermagnetics Gen. Corp., Allentown, from 1987. Cons. Jet Propulsion Lab., Pasadena, Calif., 1980-81. Contbr. articles to profl. jours.; patentee in field. Mem. troop com. Explorer Post Boy Scouts of Am., Los Alamos, 1970-78. Sr. fellow NSF U. Tokyo, 1969. Fellow Am. Phys. Soc. Home: Center Valley, Pa. Deceased.

STILES, NED BERRY, lawyer; b. Mays Lick, Ky., Aug. 7, 1932; s. Andrew Jackson and Frances (Berry) S.; m. Patricia Pollard, Nov. 23, 1953 (div. 1959); 1 son, Michael P.; m. Lynn Shattuck, Apr. 16, 1966 (div. 1976); children: Andrew J., Peter S.; m. Deborah Fiedler, Dec. 2, 1978; 1 dau., Jessica B. AB, Miami U., Oxford, Ohio, 1953; LL.M., U. Cin., 1958. Bar: Ohio 1958, N.Y. 1962. Staff atty. SEC, Washington, 1958-61; assoc. Cleary, Gottlieb, Steen & Hamilton, N.Y.C., 1961-67, ptnr., 1968-88, mng. ptnr., from 1988. Pres., chmn. bd. Fir Tree Internat. Fund Mem., bd. eds., Cincinnati Law Review, 1957-58; co-author: The Silent Partners— Institutional Investors and Corporate Control, 1965; contbr. articles to legal publs. Pres., bd. dirs. Quogue Assn. Inc., N.Y.; treas., bd. dirs. Group for the South Fork, Southampton, N.Y.; bd. appeals Village of Quogue. Served to capt. USAF, 1953-55. Mem. ABA, Assn. Bar City N.Y. (former mem. securities regulation and corp. law coms.) Clubs: River (N.Y.C.), India House (N.Y.C.). Died Jan. 29, 2003.

STINE, WILLIAM ROLAND (ROLAND STINE), state representative; b. Shelbyville, Inc., Sept. 7, 1940; married; 2 children. BA, MA, Ind. U. Tchr. Shelbyville Ctrl. Schs.; state rep. dist. 57 Ind. Ho. of Reps., Indpls., from 2002. Mem. Shelbyville City Coun., 1998—2002, pres., 2000—02. Mem.: Rotary Internat. Republican. Methodist. Died Apr. 23, 2003.

STINSON, GEORGE ARTHUR, lawyer, former steel company executive; b. Camden, Ark., Feb. 11, 1915; s. John McCollum and Alice (Loving) S.; m. Betty Millsop, May 31, 1947; children: Thomas, Lauretta, Peter, Joel. AB, Northwestern U., 1936; JD, Columbia U., 1939; LL.D., U. W.Va., Bethany Coll., Theil Coll., Salem Coll. Bar: N.Y. 1939. Partner Cleary, Gottlieb, Friendly & Hamilton, N.Y.C., 1951-61; spl. asst. to atty. gen., acting asst. atty. gen. tax div. Dept. Justice, 1947-48; v.p., sec. Nat. Steel Corp., Pitts., 1961-63, pres., 1963-75, bd. dirs., 1963-86, CEO, 1966-80, chmn., 1972-81. Dir. Diamond Home Svcs.; trustee emeritus Mut. Life Ins. Co. N.Y. Trustee emeritus U. Pitts.; mem. Presdl. Commn. on Internat. Trade and Investment Policy, 1970-71; chmn. U.S. Indsl. Payroll Savs. Com., 1976; trustee George C. Marshall Found. Served to lt. col. USAAF, 1941-45. Decorated Legion of Merit. Mem. Am. Iron and Steel Inst. (chmn. bd. 1969-71), Internat. Iron and Steel Inst. (bd. dirs., chmn. 1975-77), Am. Law Inst., Bus. Coun., Links Club (N.Y.C.), Duquesne Club (Pitts.), Phi Beta Kappa. Home: Tryon, NC. Died Nov. 19, 1999.

STIVER, WILLIAM EARL, retired government administrator; b. Madison, Ind., Mar. 30, 1921; s. John Virgil and Anna Lynne (Ryker) S.; m. Norma A. Cull, June 11, 1944; children: Vicki, Raymond, Gena, John. Student, Hanover Coll., 1947-49; BS, U. Calif., Berkeley, 1951, MBA, 1952. With Fed. Ser. Bur. Census, Commerce Dept., Suitland, Md., 1952-79, chief budget and finance div., 1963-73, dep. assoc. adminstr. Social and Econ. Stats. Adminstrn., 1973-75; spl. asst., assoc. dir. adminstrn. and field ops. Bur. of Census, 1975-77, electronic data processing staff coordinator, 1977-78, ret., 1979. Served with USA, 1942-45, 45-46. Recipient Silver medal Commerce Dept., 1969. Mem. Phi Beta Kappa, Beta Gamma Sigma. Home: Fort Washington, Md. Died July 2002.

STOBIE, LARRY JOSEPH, art educator; b. Spokane, Wash., Jan. 26, 1937; s. James Stobie. BFA, Wash. State U., 1962, MFA, 1966. Cert. tchr., Wash. Instr. art Pub. Sch. Dist. 59, Cusick, Wash., 1962-66, Wash. State U., Pullman, 1966-67; prof. art Nebr. Wesleyan U., Lincoln, 1967-69, Western Oreg. State Coll., Monmouth, from 1969; head dept. Western Oreg. State U., Monmouth, from 1986. Exhibited work in numerous one man shows. Home: Lewiston, Idaho. Deceased.

STOCKER, HAROLD SYDNEY, speech pathologist; b. Detroit, Dec. 8, 1916; s. Ben and Anna (Rosen) S.; m. Elaine Esther Finkelstein, July 26, 1942; children: Ronald Paul, Carol Patricia, Linda Ruth. DDS, U. Detroit, 1943; BA, Wayne State U., 1947, MA, 1963, PhD, 1970. Lic. dentist, Mich., speech pathologist, Tex., psychologist, Mich. Commd. ensign USNR, 1943, advanced through grades to comdr., 1963; pvt. practice dentistry Dearborn, Mich., 1946-76; prof. Henry Ford Community Coll., Dearborn, Mich., 1963-65, Wayne State U., Detroit, 1966-76, U. Detroit, 1967-75; instr. Tarrant County Community Coll., Ft. Worth, 1976-77; pvt. practice speech therapy Ft. Worth, from 1977. Ensign USN, 1943-46; comdr. USNR, 1946-63. Mem. ADA, APA, Am. Speech and Hearing Assn., Tex. Speech and Hearing, Tex. Assn. Counseling and Devel. Home: Fort Worth, Tex. Died Mar. 7, 2002.

STOCKHAM, THOMAS GREENWAY, JR., electrical engineering educator; b. Passaic, N.J., Dec. 22, 1933; s. Thomas Greenway and Dorothy (Post) S.; m. Martha Goodman, June 22, 1963; children: Thomas Greenway III, Carol H., John M., David W. SB, MIT, 1955, SM, 1957, ScD, 1959. Instr. elec. engring. MIT, 1957-59, asst. prof., 1959-66, mem. staff Lincoln Lab., 1966-68; assoc. prof. computer sci. U. Utah, Salt Lake City, 1968-70, prof., 1970-80; pres., chmn. Soundstream, Inc., Salt Lake City, 1975-82. Cons. in field. Contbr. articles on digital signal processing, digital sound recording to profl. jours. 1st lt. USAF, 1959-62. Recipient Alexander M. Poniatoff gold medal for tech. excellence, Utah Engr. of Yr. award, Utah Engrs. Council, 1986, Emmy award NATAS, 1988, Grammy award NARAS, 1993. Fellow IEEE Audio Engring Soc. (pres. 1982-83, Gold medal); mem. Assn. for Computing Machinery, Sigma Xi, Eta Kappa Nu, Tau Beta Pi. Republican. Developer tech. and equipment for digital mastering of sound. Home: Salt Lake City, Utah. Died Jan. 6, 2004.

STOFFA, MICHAEL, artist; b. Hlinne, Slovakia, Dec. 18, 1923; came to U.S., 1930; s. Michael and Anna (Hruska) S.; m. Esther Emily Mathiason, May 16, 1952 (div. Nov. 1979) children: Cathy Ann, Michael, Drew Mark, Susan L.E., John Hardvig; m. Dorothy J. Ramsey, July 23, 1980. Owner Michael Stoffa Studio & Gallery, Westfield, N.J., 1956-66, Rockport, Mass., from 1964. Author: Michael Stoffa, Artist and Storyteller, 1999. Art. Com. Rockport Libr., 1993. Named among Top Ten Vols. of the North Shore, 1990, Small Bus. Man of Yr. 1991 Cape Ann; recipient dedicated service award St. Paul Lutheran Ch., Gloucester, Mas., 1993. Mem. Rockport Art Assn. (gov. bd. 1993—, pres. 1985-89, Martha Moore award 1978), North Shore Art Assn. (bd. dirs. 1980—, disting. svc. award 1990), Salmagundi Club (8 awards 1978-91), Artists Fellowship, Burr Artists. Avocations: storytelling, research, writing. Home: Rockport, Mass. Died Dec. 12, 2001.

STOFFER, TERRY JAMES, advertising executive; b. Alexander, Iowa, May 28, 1946; s. Jacob John and Almeda Juanita (Roe) S.; m. Linda Rosburg, Apr. 11, 1966 (div. Mar. 1980); m. Catherine S. Jewell, Dec. 28, 1984 (div. Dec. 1990); 1 child, Alan J. BS in Journalism, Iowa State U., 1968, MS in Journalism, 1970. Instr. Iowa State U. Sch. Journalism, Ames, 1969-70; publs. mgr. Express Communications, West Des Moines, Iowa, 1970-72; sr. v.p. Creswell, Munsell, Fultz and Zirbel, Des Moines, from 1972. Mktg. adv. com. Iowa State U., 1991-93; advt. adv. bd. Drake U., 1993—. Mem. Nat. Adv. Bd. Iowa State U. Sch. Journalism, Ames, 1985-88; bd. dirs. Better Bus. Bur., Des Moines, 1983. Mem. Des Moines Advt. Club (v.p. 1974-75, Cliff DePuy award 1978), Advt. Profls. of Des Moines (pres. 1982-83, Ad Person of Yr. 1980), Am. Advt. Fedn. (nat. standards com. 1984-85). Republican. Methodist. Avocations: literature, cooking. Home: West Des Moines, Iowa. Deceased.

STOKES, WILLIAM LEE, writer, geologist; b. Hiawatha, Utah, Mar. 27, 1915; s. William Peace and Grace Elizabeth (Cox) S.; m. Betty Asenath Curtis, Sept. 7, 1939; children—Betty Lee Stokes Huff, Mary Susan Stokes Griffith (dec.), William Michael, Patricia Jane, Jennifer Joy (dec.). B.S., Brigham Young U., 1937, M.S., 1938; Ph.D., Princeton U., 1941. Geologist, U.S. Geol. Survey, western states, 1942-47; prof. geology U. Utah, Salt Lake City, 1947-82, dept. head, 1954-68; cons. U.S. AEC, Colo., Utah, 1952-55, Standard Oil of Calif., Utah, Nev., 1950-51. Author: Essentials of Earth History, 1960, 66, 73, 82; co-author: Introduction to Geology 1968, 78; The Genesis Answer, 1984; The Great Salt Lake, 1985; Scenes of the Plateau Lands, 1969—; co-author: Messages on Stone, 1981, Geology of Utah, 1986; Glossary of Selected Geologic Terms, 1955; articles profl. and tech. papers, ann. rev. articles. Fellow Geol. Soc. Am.; mem. Am. Assn. Petroleum Geologists, Soc. Econ. Paleontologists and Mineralogists, Am. Geophys. Union, AAAS, Soc. Vertebrate Paleontology, Utah Geol. Assn. (pres.). Mormon. Club: Explorers (N.Y.C.). Home: Salt Lake City, Utah.

STOKOE, WILLIAM CLARENCE, editor, consultant; b. Lancaster, N.H., July 21, 1919; s. William Clarence and Marie Cecelia (Stafford) S.; m. Ruth Adeline Palmeter Stokoe, Nov. 21, 1942; children: Helen Marie, James Stafford. AB, Cornell U., 1942, PhD, 1946; DLitt (hon.), Gallaudet U., 1989; DPhil (hon.), Copenhagen (Denmark) U., 1992; DEd (hon.), Madonna U., 1996. Asst. prof., assoc. prof. Wells Coll., Aurora, N.Y., 1946-55; prof., chmn. English dept. Gallaudet U., Washington, 1955-72, dir. linguistics rsch. lab., 1972-84; pub. Sign Lang. Studies Linstok Press, Silver Spring, Md., 1975-90; editor Sign Lang. Studies, Burtonsville, Md., from 1972. Adv. bd. CSLI Stanford, Calif., 1993—. Author: Sign Language Structure, 1960; co-editor: Dictionary of American Sign Language, 1965; co-author: Gesture and the Nature of Language, 1995. Mem. Am. Acad. Arts and Scis., St. Andrew's Soc. of Washington, Cosmos Club, Am. Anthropological Assn. Avocations: playing pibroch, home improvement. Died Apr. 4, 2000.

STONE, FRANZ THEODORE, retired fabricated metal products manufacturing executive; b. Columbus, Ohio, May 11, 1907; s. Julius Frederick and Edna (Andress) S.; m. Katherine Devereux Jones, Feb. 23, 1935 (dec.); children: Franz Theodore, Thomas Devereux Mackay, Raymond Courtney (dec.), Catherine Devereux Diebold. AB magna cum laude, Harvard U., 1929; hon. degrees, Canisius Coll., 1975, Ohio State U., 1976, Keuka Coll., 1999. Chmn. bd. Columbus McKinnon Corp., Amherst, N.Y., 1935-86. Chmn. emeritus Arts Council in Buffalo and Erie County, 1973-86; pres. Buffalo Philharmonic Orch. Soc., 1959-61, also life dir.; chmn. emeritus Studio Arena Theatre, Buffalo, 1968-86; Nat. Conf. of Christian and Jews Brother Sisterhood citation, 1986; First Arts award Arts Council and Greater Buffalo C. of C. Recipient Gold Key award Buffalo YMCA, 1966, Red Jacket award Buffalo & Erie County Hist. Soc., 1976, Disting. Citizen award SUNY, Buffalo, 1985, Conductor's award Buffalo Philharm. Orch., 1993. Mem. Buffalo Club, Buffalo Yacht Club, Saturn Club (Buffalo). Home: Buffalo, NY. Died Sept. 1, 2002.

STONE, JOHN FLOYD, soil physics researcher and educator; b. York, Nebr., Oct. 13, 1928; s. Harry Floyd and Anastasia (Klima) S.; m. Carol Ottilie Youngson, Aug. 2, 1953; children: Mary, Margaret, David, Jana. BS, U. Nebr., 1952; MS, Iowa State U., 1955, PhD, 1957. Lab. technician U. Nebr., 1944-53; from rsch. asst. to rsch. assoc. Iowa State U., 1953-57; from asst. to assoc. prof. Okla. State U., Stillwater, 1957-69, prof. soil physics, 1969-94; prof. emeritus, from 1994. Mem. adv. agrl. panel U.S. Dept. Def., 1977-78; mem. grant evaluation panel Water Quality Grant Program, USDA, 1989, Small. Bus. Initiative Rsch. Grant Program, 1990. Editor: Plant Modification for More Efficient Water Use, 1975, Plant Production and Management under Drought Conditions, 1983; contbr. chpts. to books, rsch. articles to profl. jours.; co-patentee nuclear apparatus for measuring water content of soil; co-discoverer Nova-Cygni, 1975. Commr. Stillwater City, 1974-75; mem. Stillwater Housing Appeals Bd., 1975-79; com. mem. troop 14 Boy Scouts Am., 1976-83, merit badge counselor, 1974—; del. to jurisdictional conf. United Meth. Ch., 1968, alt. del. to gen. conf., 1968. With USN, 1946-48 (WWII Victory medal). Grantee USDA, 1980, 83, 89, 90, 91, 92, NSF, 1961, U.S. Dept. Interior, 1968, 73, 79, 89, 91, Okla. Dept. Commerce, 1988, Okla. Coun. for Applied Sci. and Tech., Energy Efficient Irrigation, 1990. Fellow Am. Soc. Agronomy (editl. bd., assoc. editor Agronomy jour. 1982-85); mem. ASCE (com. on irrigation water requirements 1979-95, chmn. task com. on calibration and use of neutron moisture meters 1990-94, State-of-the-Art of Civil Engring. award 1992), Soil Sci. Soc. Am. (assoc. editor, mem. editl. bd. 1968-76 Soil Sci. Am. jour., com. on water resources 1964-73), Internat. Soil Sci. Soc., Am. Geophys. Union (vis. scientist lectr. 1972, mem. com. on the unsaturated zone of the hydrology sect. 1978-88, chmn. 1986-88), Sigma Xi, Am. Radio Relay League, Stillwater Amateur Radio Club. Democrat. Methodist. Avocations: photography, amateur astronomy, music, amateur radio. Home: Stillwater, Okla. Died Feb. 14, 2004; Stillwater, Fla..

STONE, PETER, playwright, scenarist; b. Los Angeles, Feb. 27, 1930; s. John and Hilda (Hess) S.; m. Mary O'Hanley, Feb. 17, 1961. BA, Bard Coll., 1951, DLitt, 1971; MFA, Yale U., 1953. Ind. stage and screen writer, 1961—2003. Author: (musical comedies) Kean, 1961, Skyscraper, 1965, 1776, 1969 (Tony award Best Musical Book 1969, N.Y. Drama Critics Circle award 1969, London Plays and Players award 1969, Drama Desk award Best Musical Book writer 1969), Two by Two, 1970, Sugar, 1972, Woman of the Year, 1981 (Tony award Best Musical Book 1981), My One and Only, 1983, Grand Hotel, 1989, The Will Rogers Follies, 1991 (Tony award Best Musical 1991, N.Y. Drama Critics Circle award Best New Musical 1991, Grammy award 1991), Titanic, 1997 (Tony award Best Musical Book 1997), 1776 revival, 1997, Annie Get Your Gun, 1999 (Tony award Best Musical Revival 1999, Grammy award 1999), Finian's Rainbow, 2000, (play) Full Circle, 1973, (films) Charade, 1963 (Writers Guild award Best Comedy Film 1964, Mystery Writers Am. award Best Mystery Film 1964), Father Goose, 1964 (Acad. award Best Original Screenplay 1964), Mirage, 1965, Arabesque, 1966, Secret War of Harry Frigg, 1968, Sweet Charity 1969, Skin Game, 1971, 1776, 1972 (Christopher award for Best Film), Taking of Pelham 123, 1974, Silver Bears, 1978, Who is Killing the Great Chefs of Europe?, 1978, Why Would I Lie?, 1980, Just Cause, 1995, (TV spl.) Androcles and the Lion, 1968; (TV episodes) Studio One, 1956, Brenner, 1959, Witness, 1961, Asphalt Jungle, 1961, The Defenders, 1961-62 (Emmy award 1962), The Benefactors, 1962, Espionage, 1963, Adam's Rib, 1973-74, Ivan the Terrible, 1976, Baby on Board, 1988, Grand Larceny. Mem. Dramatists Guild (coun.), Authors League, Writers Guild Am., Motion Picture Acad. Home: New York, NY. Died Apr. 26, 2003.

STONEKING, JERRY EDWARD, dean; b. Cin., July 12, 1942; s. Charles E. and Esther H. (Holmeyer) S.; m. Linda Kaye Parnell, Dec. 30, 1967; children: Jennifer, Jeffrey. BS in Engring. Mechanics cum laude, Ga. Inst. Tech., 1965; MS in Theoretical and Applied Mechanics, U. Ill., 1966, PhD in Theoretical and Applied Mechanics, 1969. Registered profl. engr., Tenn. Grad. student instr. theoretical and applied mechanics dept. U. Ill., Urbana, 1969-70; asst. prof. dept. civil and environ. engring. Clarkson U., Potsdam, N.Y., 1970-74; asst. prof. dept. civil engring. and mechanics U. S.C., Columbia, 1974-75; assoc. prof. dept. engring. sci. and mechanics U. Tenn., Knoxville, 1975-78, prof., 1978-92, Internat. Bus. Machines prof., 1981-84, head dept. engring. sci. and mechanics, 1983-92, interim dean coll. engring., 1992-93, dean, from 1993. Mem. various coms. U. Tenn., 1976—, mem. faculty senate, 1980-83, 94—, mem. Saturn core team, 1991—, mem. policy adv. bd., 1992—; cons., rschr. in field. Author: Hydraulics, 1975; editor: Developments in Theoretical & Applied Mechanics, 1980; reviewer Internat. Jour. Structures and Solids, Applied Mechanics Revs., Jour. Applied Mechanics, others; contbr. articles to profl. jours. Recipient Outstanding Teaching and Rsch. award IBM, 1981-84, Best Tech. Presentation award Tenn. Dental Assn., 1990; fellow NSF, 1965-69. Mem. ASME, ASCE, Am. Soc. Engring. Edn., Soc. Engring. Sci. (bd. dirs. 1990—), Southeastern Conf. Theoretical and Applied Mechanics (chmn. editorial com. 10th conf. 1979-80, organizer, conf. chmn. 10th conf. 1980, chmn. ops. com. 1987-88, mem. policy com. 1988—), Phi Kappa Phi, Sigma Xi, Tau Beta Pi. Avocations: golfing, fishing, house renovation, paddle ball. Home: Knoxville, Tenn. Died Nov. 16, 2001.

STONER, GERALD LEE, neurovirologist, medical researcher; b. Elizabethtown, Pa., Feb. 8, 1943; s. Andrew Kraybill and Esther (Longenecker) S.; m. Linda Elaine Buckwalter, Aug. 1, 1964 (dec. Oct. 1994); children: Anne Marie Stoner-Eby, Andrea E. AA, Hershey (Pa.) Jr. Coll., 1963; BA in Natural Sci., Eastern Mennonite Coll., Harrisonburg, Va., 1965; PhD in Biochemistry, Columbia U., 1974. Rsch. fellow Albert Einstein Coll. Medicine, Bronx, N.Y., 1974-76; rsch. scientist Armauer Hansen Rsch. Inst., Addis Ababa, Ethiopia, 1976-81; sr. staff fellow NIH, Bethesda, Md., 1981-88; chief neurotoxicology sect. Nat. Inst. Neurol. Disorders and Stroke, NIH, Bethesda, from 1988. Cons. WHO/IMMLEP Sci. Working Group, Geneva, 1977, 80, USPHS Hansen's Disease Rsch. Adv. Com., Carville, La., 1983-86. Co-editor: Human Polyomariruses, 2001; mem. editl. bd. Jour. Neurovirology, 1994—; contbr. articles to profl. jours. Bd. dirs. Internat. Cmty. Sch., Addis Ababa, 1978-81, Mennonite Devel. Rehab. Bd., Addis Ababa, 1978-81, Am. Leprosy Missions, Greenville, S.C., 1987-93. Mem.: AAAS, Am. Soc. Virology. Mennonite. Avocations: book collecting, gardening, travel. Home: Bainbridge, Pa. Died Nov. 28, 2002.

STONEROOK, ELEANOR RAE, librarian; b. Clarence, Iowa, Mar. 22, 1929; d. Orba Alvin and Erma Catherine S.; children: Franklin Port, Eleanor Rae. Grad. high sch., Clarence, 1946. Mem. Am. Legion Auxiliary #286 (past pres.). Republican. Methodist. Avocation: napkin collector. Home: Clarence, Iowa. Died Oct. 20, 2000.

STONIER, TOM, theoretical biologist, educator; b. Hamburg, Germany, Apr. 29, 1927; came to U.S., 1939; BA, Drew U., 1950; MS, Yale U., 1951, PhD, 1955. Jr. rsch. assoc. Brookhaven Nat. Lab., Upton, N.Y., 1952-54; post-doctoral fellow Rockefeller U., N.Y.C., 1954-57, rsch. assoc., 1957-62; assoc. prof. biology Manhattan Coll., N.Y.C., 1962-71, prof. biology, 1971-75; dir. Pacem/in Terris Inst., N.Y.C., 1971-75; prof., head sci. and soc. U. Bradford, U.K., 1975-90, prof. emeritus, from 1990. Chmn. Valiant Tech., London, 1985— . Author: Nuclear Disaster, 1964, The Wealth of Information, 1983, The Three Cs: Children, Computers and Communication, 1985, Information and the Internal Structure of the Universe, 1990, Beyond Information, 1992, Information and Meaning, 1997; contbr. numerous articles to profl. jours. Sec. Fedn. of Am. Scientists, Washington, 1967-68, mem. coun., 1965-68. With USNR, 1945-46. H.D. Hooker fellow Yale U., 1950-51, Damon Runyon Meml. fellow Rockefeller U., 1954-56, Inst. for Advanced Studies in Humanities fellow, Edinburgh U., 1989, Egremont Bd. of Health, 1995—. Fellow Royal Soc. of Arts (life); mem. AAAS, N.Y. Acad. Scis., Phi Beta Kappa, Sigma Xi. Died June 15, 1999.

STOOPS, CHARLES EMMET, chemical engineer, educator; b. Grove City, Pa., Dec. 17, 1914; s. Charles Emmet and Elizabeth (Burke) S.; m. Clarice Elizabeth Koehler, Mar. 13, 1943; children: Carol Elizabeth, David Charles, John Frederick. BChemE, Ohio State U., 1937; PhD in Chem. Engring., Purdue U., 1942. Registered profl. engr., Ohio. Plant and devel. engr. Oldbury Electrochem. Co., Niagara Falls, N.Y., 1941-42; asst. prof. chem. engring. Lehigh U., 1942-44; process engr. Publicker Alcohol Co., Phila., 1944; with Phillips Petroleum Co., Bartlesville, Okla., 1944-67, chief chem. engring. sect. nuclear divsn. Idaho Falls, Idaho, 1953-55, mgr. radiation chemistry sect., 1955-67; prof., head dept. chem. engring. Clemson Coll., 1947-48; with Idaho Nuclear Corp., Idaho Falls, 1969; assoc. prof. engring., 1967-70; prof. chem. engring., from 1970; chmn. chem. engring., 1969-72; acting chmn. chem. engring., 1980-82. Cons. in field. Contbr. articles to profl. jours. Fellow AAAS, AIChE, Am. Inst. Chemists (treas. Toledo sect. 1972-73, sec. 1973-74, vice chmn. 1974-75, chmn. 1975-76, mem. nominating com. nuclear divsn. 1975), Am. Chem. Soc., Am. Soc. Engring. Edn., Sigma Xi, Tau Beta Pi, Phi Kappa Phi, Phi Lambda Upsilon. Home: Portland, Oreg. Died Apr. 27, 2000.

STOPPANI, ANDRES OSCAR MANUEL, research center director, educator; b. Buenos Aires, Aug. 19, 1915; s. Oscar Carlos and Julia Severa (Bahia) S.; m. Antonia Emmy Delius, July 1, 1967. MD, U. Buenos Aires, 1941, PhD in Chemistry, 1945; postgrad., U. Liege, Belgium, 1947, Nat. Inst. Med. Rsch., London, 1953, U. Calif., Berkeley, 1954; PhD, U. Cambridge, Eng., 1953. Prof. biochemistry U. La Plata, Argentina, 1947-48; prof. biochemistry Sch. Medicine U. Buenos Aires, 1949-55, prof., dir. Inst. Biochemistry, Sch. Medicine, 1955-80, prof. emeritus, dir. dept. physiol. scis., 1970-80; bd. dirs. NRC, Argentina, 1963-66, 80-83; pres. Nat. Acad. Exact, Phys. and Natural Scis., Buenos Aires. Emeritus investigator NRC Argentina; hon. pres. Argentine Sci. Soc., 2001. Contbr. numerous articles to profl. jours. Recipient Weissman prize NRC, 1962, Campomar prize, 1970, Silver award Rotary, 1975, Bunge-Born prize, 1979, Am. States Orgn. Interam. Sci. prize, Bernardo A. Houssay, 1989, Platinum prize Konex Found., 1993, Nat. Sci. prize Argentina, 1993, award Hadassah Internat. Orgn., 1997; grantee Rockefeller Found., 1957-60, The Jane Coffin Childs Found. for Med. Rsch., 1961-63, USAF Office Sci. Rsch., 1969-71, WHO, 1977-82, Swedish Agy. for Rsch.

Cooperation with Developing Countries, 1988-95. Fellow Royal Soc. Medicine, Third World Acad. Scis. Trieste, Chilean Acad. Scis., Latin Am. Acad. Scis., Am. Acad. Clin. Biochemistry; mem. Royal Nat. Acad. Medicine (Spain), Royal Nat. Acad. Pharmacy (Spain), Argentine Assn. for Advancement of Sci., Argentine Soc. for Biochem. Rsch. (pres. 1970-71), Argentine Soc. Biology (pres. 1980-83), Argentine Soc. Protozoologists (pres. 1980-81), Am. Chem. Soc., Biochem. Soc. U.K., Soc. Gen. Microbiology U.K., N.Y. Acad. Scis., Am. Soc. Biochemistry and Molecular Biology, Oxygen Soc., Soc. for Free Radical Rsch., Internat. Soc. for Study of Xenobiotics, Nat. Acad. Exact, Phys. and Natural Scis., Nat. Acad. Medicine (pres. 1996), Buenos Aires Nat. Acad. Scis., Chilean Acad. Medicine (hon.), Chilean Acad. Scis. (hon.), Brazilian Acad. Scis. (corr.), Nat. Rsch. Coun. Argentina (hon. pres. 1996), Paraguay Acad. Medicine (hon.), Uruguay Nat. Acad. Medicine (corr.), Nitric Oxide Soc., Am. Soc. Cell Biology, Societé de Chimie Biologique, Co. Biologists Unltd. U.K., Am. Soc. Microbiology, Protein Soc., Soc. Biol. Inorganic Chemistry. Home: Buenos Aires, Argentina. Died Mar. 18, 2003.

STRADLING, LESLIE EDWARD, bishop; b. Reading, Eng., Feb. 11, 1908; s. Walter Herbert and Mary Louise (Collier) S.; M.A., Queen's Coll., Oxford U., 1930; student Westcott House, Cambridge U., 1932; D.C.L. (hon.), U. Lenoxville. Ordained priest Anglican Ch., 1934; curate, then vicar chs. in South London, 1933-45; bishop of Masasi, Tanzania, 1945-52, of S.W. Tanganyika, 1952-61, of Johannesburg, South Africa, 1961-74. Club: City and Civil Service (Cape Town, South Africa). Author: A Bishop on Safari, 1960; A Bishop at Prayer, 1970; Praying Now, 1976; Praying the Psalms, 1977. Deceased.

STRANARD, OSCAR DAMAS, Belgian government official; b. Gosselies, Belgium, Nov. 25, 1927; s. Rene Sylvain and Vergnon Marie Antoinette Stranard; m. Elisabeth Quinet, Dec. 22, 1956. Degree Ecole moyenne de Gosselies, Athénée Royal Charleroi, 1941; degree, 1945; hon. degree, U. Libre Brussels, 1951. Conseller Cour de Cassation, Brussels, 1978-90, pres., 1990-92, premier pres., from 1992; pres. Cour Benelux, Brussels, from 1995. With Belgian Armed Forces. Mem. Lions Club. Died June 18, 2001.

STRANDBERG, NEWTON DWIGHT, music educator, composer; b. River Falls, Wis., Jan. 3, 1921; s. Ernst David and Selma Ferdelphina (Ostrom) S. MusB in Edn., Northwestern U., 1942, MusM, 1947, MusD, 1956; DFA (hon.), North Park Coll., 1983. Prof. piano Denison U., Granville, Ohio, 1947-49; prof. piano, theory Samford U., Birmingham, Ala., 1950-67; prof. theory and composition Sam Houston State U., Huntsville, Tex., from 1967. Pres. Birmingham Chamber Music Soc., 1964-67; chmn. fine arts Birmingham Festival of Arts, 1962-65. Composer over 100 chamber, choral, organ, piano, vocal, wind, band and orchestral works, kinetic theater works including Picasso, 1967, Erika's Lullaby, 1972, There, 1980; compositions recorded on Opus One Records, also on Master Musicians Collective, Reading, Mass. Served with USN, 1942-46. Recipient Birmingham Symphony award, 1951. Mem. ASCAP, Am. Soc. Univ. Composers, Am. Music Ctr., Pi Kappa Lambda. Avocations: swimming, traveling. Home: Spring, Tex. Died Mar. 27, 2001.

STRAUS, ROGER W., JR., publishing company executive; b. N.Y.C., Jan. 3, 1917; s. Roger Williams and Gladys (Guggenheim) S.; m. Dorothea Liebmann, June 27, 1938; 1 son, Roger W. III. Student, Hamilton Coll., 1935-37; B.J., U. Mo., 1939, Litt.D. (hon.), 1976. Reporter Daily Reporter, White Plains, N.Y., 1936, feature writer, 1939-40; editorial writer, reporter Columbia Missourian, 1937-39; editor, pub. Asterisk, 1939; editorial asst. Current History, 1940, assoc. editor, 1940-45, Forum, 1940-45; pres. Book Ideas, Inc., 1943-46; founder Farrar, Straus & Co., Inc. (now Farrar, Straus & Giroux, Inc.), 1945; pres. Farrar, Straus & Giroux, Inc., N.Y.C., 198?—94. Chmn. adv. bd. Partisan Rev. mag., 1959-69 Co-editor: The Sixth Column, 1941, War Letters from Britain, 1941, The New Order, 1941; Chmn. publ. bd.: Am. Judaism mag, 1955-65. Vice pres. Fred L. Lavanburg Found., 1950-80, Daniel and Florence Guggenheim Found., 1960-76; bd. dirs. Harry Frank Guggenheim Found., Manhattanville Coll., 1970-76, John Simon Guggenheim Found.; fellow N.Y. Inst. for Humanities. Served to lt. USNR, 1941-45. Mem. P.E.N., Union Am. Hebrew Congregations (pub. com. 1955-65), Sigma Delta Chi. Clubs: Lotos, Westchester Country, Players. Home: New York, NY. Died May 24, 2004.

STREET, JAMES STEWART, geology educator, consultant; b. Chgo., July 26, 1934; s. Frank William and Letha M. (Frost) S.; m. Sarah Cunningham, Sept. 3, 1957; children: James S. Jr., Anne F., David M. AA, Wright Coll., Chgo., 1955; BS, U. Ill., 1958; MS, Syracuse U., 1963, PhD, 1966. Geologist Texaco, Inc., New Orleans, 1965-66; dir., N.Y. State Tech. Svc. Program in Geology St. Lawrence U., Canton, N.Y., 1966-70, assoc. prof., 1972-78, prof., from 1978, dept. chmn., 1976-81, 87-88, 1991, dir. acad. summerterm, 1986-87, James Henry Chapin prof. geology, from 1990. Vis. prof. geology U. S.C., Columbia, 1991—. Mem. Geol. Soc. Am., Internat. Assn. Quaternary Rsch., Am. Quaternary Assn., History of the Earth Scis. Soc., Empire State Pedologists Assn., Coun. on Undergrad. Rsch., Sigma Xi. Home: Canton, NY. Deceased.

STREICH, PAUL ROBERT, military officer; b. Kansas City, Kans., Dec. 22, 1928; s. Alferd Abraham and Ruth Eliza (Walker) S.; m. Jo Ann Oden, Apr. 3, 1951 (dec. Mar. 1988); children: Robert Christopher, Julie Ann. AS, Casper (Wyo.) Coll., 1948; BA, U. Colo., 1961, MBA, 1977; postgrad., Computer Inst. Anacostia, Va., 1969. Commd. ensign USN, 1948, advanced through grades to comdr., ret., 1975. Author: USN Plan for Photographic Reconnaissance, 1967, Command & Control Communications Plan, 1971. BD. dirs. Arthritis Found., Colorado Springs, Colo., 1982-85. Decorated Air medal. Fellow Explorers Club; mem. Navy League of U.S. (pres. Colo. chpt. 1989-99), Order of Daedalians. Republican. Methodist. Avocations: hydroponics, skiing, hunting. Home: Lake George, Colo. Died Aug. 18, 1999.

STREILEIN, JACOB WAYNE, research scientist; b. Johnstown, Pa., June 19, 1935; s. Jacob and Mina Alma (Krouse) S.; m. Joan Elaine Stein, June 15, 1957; children: Laura Anne, William Wayne, Robert Dietrich. BA in Chemistry, Gettysburg Coll., 1956; MD, U. Pa., 1960. Asst. prof., assoc. prof. genetics U. Pa. Sch. Medicine, Phila., 1965-71; prof. cell biology Southwestern Med. Sch., Dallas, 1971-84; prof., chair microbiology and immunology U. Miami, Fla., 1984-93; Charles L. Schepens prof. opthalmology, prof. dermatology Harvard Med. Sch., Boston, 1993—2004. Pres. Schepens Eye Rsch. Inst., Boston, 1993—2004; hon. prof. Univ. Coll., London, 2002—04. Capt. USAR, 1961-67. Recipient award Alcon Rsch. Inst., 1984, Merit award Nat. Eye Inst., 1990; Markle Found. scholar, 1967; named Outstanding Alumnus Gettysburg Coll., 2001. Mem. Assn. Rsch. in Vision and Ophthalmology (Procter award 1996), Am. Assn. Immunologists (chair pub. rels. 1988-93), Soc. Investigative Dermatology, Transplantation Soc. Achievements include elucidation of cellular and molecular basis of immune privilege in eye, genetic basis of effects of ultraviolet B light on cutaneous immunity, microenvironmental factor effects on tissue-restricted antigen presenting cells. Home: Beverly, Mass. Died Mar. 15, 2004.

STRICKLAND, THOMAS JOSEPH, artist; b. Keyport, N.J., Dec. 27, 1932; s. Charles Edward and Clementine Maria (Grasso) S.; m. Ann DeBaun Browne, Apr. 28, 1992. Student, Newark Sch. Fine and Indsl. Arts, 1951-53, Am. Art Sch., 1956-59, Nat. Acad. Sch. Fine Arts with Robert Philipp, 1957-59. Judge local and nat. art shows. Exhibited in one man shows at, Hollywood (Fla.) Art Mus., 1972-76, Elliott Mus., Stuart, Fla., 1974, others; exhibited in group shows at, Am. Artists Profl. League, N.Y.C., 1958, 61, 97, Parke-Bernet Galleries, N.Y.C., 1959, 61, 64, Exposition Intercontinentale, Monaco, 1966-68, Salon Rouge du Casino Dieppe, 1967, 7e Grand Prix Internat. de Peinture de la Cote d'Azur, Cannes, 1971, Am. Painters in Paris, 1975, La Fond Galleries, Pitts., 1997, 99, Conn. Pastel Soc., Wallingford, Conn., 1997, Audubon Artists Annual Exhbn., N.Y., 1997, 98, Sacramento Arts Ctr., 1998, Pastel Soc. of N.Mex., 1998, Ann. Fla. Art Ctr. Nat. 100, 1998, Degas Pastel Soc. of La., 1998; represented in permanent collections, St. Vincent Coll., Elliott Mus., Martin County Hist. Soc., Salem Coll., Winston-Salem, N.C., St. Hugh Catholic Ch., Fla.; (Recipient Digby Chandler prize Knickerbocker Artists 1965, 1st Place, Fine Arts League, La Junta, Colo. 1973, Blue Ribbon award Cape Coral Nat. Art Show 1973, 1st prize Hollywood Art Mus. 1973, Charles Hawthorne Meml. award Nat. Arts Club Exhbn. 1977, 2d Pl. award Pastel Soc. Oreg., 1997, Atlantic Papers Self Portrait Contest 1997 (winner), others; contbr. articles to profl. jours. and included in Best of Pastel, 1996, Portrait Inspirations, 1997. With AUS, 1953-55. Recipient 1st prize Internat. Juried Competition, Lafayette Art Assn., 1998, Atlantic Paper award Degas Pastel Soc., 1998. Mem. Pastel Soc. Am., Am. Artists Profl. League, Pastel Soc. S.W., Degas Pastel Soc., N.W. Pastel Soc. Roman Catholic. Home: Miami, Fla. Died Aug. 4, 1999.

STRICKLIN, NANCY A. English language educator, writer; b. Murfreesboro, Tenn., Nov. 19, 1946; d. Robert Howell and Ethel Virginia (Bowden) S. BA in English and Art History, U. Tenn., 1968, PhD, 1991; MA in English, Middle Tenn. State U., 1984. Secondary English tchr. Tullahoma (Tenn.) City Schs., 1969-81, 82-83; grad. teaching asst. Middle Tenn. State U., Murfreesboro, 1981-82, instr., 1985-87; grad. teaching. asst. U. Tenn., Knoxville, 1983-85, 87-91; asst. prof. English Pellissippi State Tech. C.C., Knoxville, from 1991. Adj. instr. Maryville (Tenn.) Coll., 1989. Author: A Comprehensive Index to Volumes 1 and 2 of E.L. Griggs's Collected Letters of Samuel Taylor Coleridge, 1991, The Trust, 1993. John B. Emperor fellow U. Tenn., 1990, John C. Hodges Competitive fellow, 1991. Mem. MLA, South Atlantic MLA, Phi Kappa Phi. Avocations: reading, needlepoint. Home: Maryville, Tenn. Deceased.

STRINGER, DANN POLLARD, executive search firm executive; b. Syracuse, N.Y., Nov. 24, 1938; s. Sydney Walter and Helen Claire (Dann) S.; children: Jonathan, Edward, Karen; m. Shawn Carrigan, May 14, 1994: stepchildren: Brendan, Kevin, Clare. BA, St. Lawrence U., 1961. Dist. mgr. Jamesbury Corp., Worchester, Mass., 1964-68; advance man The White House, Washington, 1969-71; dep. exec. dir. White House Com. on Exec. Interchange, Washington, 1968-71; sr. assoc. Korn/Ferry Internat., L.A., 1971-74; exec. v.p. Interface Group Ltd., Washington, 1975-80; pres. Corp. Rsch. & Communications Internat., Washington, 1980-87; sr. mgr., dir. KPMG Peat Marwick Exec. Search, Washington, 1987-90; sr. mng. dir. Foster Ptnrs., Inc. (KPMG Alliance), Washington, from 1990. Ptnr. Midcourt Realty, Manlius, N.Y., 1968—. Bd. dirs. Nat. Kidney Found. of Capital Area, Washington, 1990—, chmn., 1994-95; sr. advance man Reagan Campaign for Pres., 1975-76, 79-80. With U.S. Army N.G., 1960-65. Mem. Brit. Am. Bus. Assn. (bd. dirs.), Econs. Club of Washington. Republican. Avocations: yachting, skiing, tennis, fly fishing. Home: Silver Spring, Md. Died Apr. 6, 2002.

STROGATZ, IAN A. L. lawyer; b. Cin., 1948; BA, U. Pa., 1969, JD, 1972. Bar: Pa. 1972. Law clk. to Hon. Arlin M. Adams U.S. Ct. Appeals (3d cir.), 1972-73; former atty. Wolf, Block, Schorr and Solis-Cohen, Phila. Comment editor: U. Pa. Law Rev., 1971-72. Mem. Order of Coif. Died Apr. 3, 2004.

STROH, PETER WETHERILL, brewery executive; b. Detroit, Dec. 18, 1927; s. Gari Melchers and Suzanne (Suddards) S.; m. Nicole Elizabeth Fauquet-Lemaitre, June 30, 1964; children— Pierre Alexander, Frederic Charlton. B.A., Princeton U., 1951. Asst. to pres. Stroh Brewery Co., Detroit, 1952-65, v.p., 1965-66, dir. ops., 1966-68, pres., 1968-82, chmn., chief exec. officer, 1982—, also bd. dirs.; dir. NBD Bancorp., Inc.; chmn. Detroit Renaissance, Inc., Atlantic Salmon Fedn.; vice chmn. Detroit Econ. Growth Corp.; trustee New Detroit, Inc., Solomon Guggenheim Found. With USN, 1945-46. Mem. Nat. Audubon Soc. (bd. dirs.), Conservation Internat. (bd. dirs.), Econ. Alliance Mich. (bd. dirs.). Clubs: Detroit; Country of Detroit (Grosse Pointe Farms, Mich.), Grosse Pointe; Yondotega; Anglers of N.Y.; Island of Hobe Sound (Fla.). Home: Grosse Pointe, Mich. Died Sept. 17, 2002.

STUART, MARY, actress; b. Miami, Fla., July 4, 1926; d. Guy M. and Mary (Stuart) Houchins; m. Richard Krolik, Aug. 1, 1951 (div.); children: Cynthia, Jeffrey M.; m. Wolfgang Neumann, 1986. Student pub. schs., Tulsa. Appeared in leading role: Search For Tomorrow, NBC-TV, N.Y.C., 1951-86, continuing role as Meta in Guiding Light, 1996-2002; songwriter, singer, Columbia Records, 1956, Bell Records, 1973; author: (autobiography) Both of Me, 1980 (Lit. Guild selection); N.Y. chair, dir. "Book Pals" Screen Actors Guild Found., 1992. Mem. Actors Equity Assn., AFTRA, Screen Actors Guild, ASCAP. Episcopalian. Died Feb. 28, 2002.

STUBBLEFIELD, PAGE KINDRED, banker; b. Bloomington, Tex., Aug. 28, 1914; s. Edwin Page and Vinnye L. (Kindred) S.; m. Dorothea Mock, July 7, 1940; children— Edwin Mark, Bob Lynn. Student, Southwestern U., Georgetown, Tex., 1931; BBA, U. Tex., Austin, 1936. Mgr. Page Stubblefield Gen. Mdse., 1936-42; owner-operation P.K. Stubblefield Ins. Agy., 1946-51; asst. v.p. pub. relations Victoria (Tex.) Bank & Trust Co., 1951-52, v.p., 1952-58, sr. v.p., 1958-69, pres., 1969-81, chmn. bd., from 1977, chmn. bd. dirs., 1984-88; pres. Victoria Bankshares, Inc., 1974-84. Past chmn. bd. dirs. Victoria Bankshares, Inc.; past chmn. bd. dirs. Victoria Bank and Trust Co. Hon. mem. U. Tex. Centennial Commn. With fin. dept. USAAF, 1942-45. Mem.: Victoria Country Club, Plz. Club. Home: Victoria, Tex. Died 2004.

STUBBS, ROBERT SHERWOOD, II, lawyer; b. St. Louis, Nov. 11, 1922; s. Sherwood Obear and Marie Clifton (deVaux) S.; m. Laura Ann Cobb, June 26, 1943 (div. 1974); children: Robert S. III, Anna Lucille S. Smith; m. Kipling Louise McVay, Sept. 28, 1979. Student, Johns Hopkins U., 1939-41; AB, U. Ala., 1942; JD with distinction, George Washington U., 1949-52; postgrad., East Carolina U., 1959-62. Bar: Ala. 1952, D.C. 1952, Hawaii 1957, Ga. 1968, U.S. Dist. Ct. (no. dist.) Ga. 1973, U.S. Ct. Mil. Appeals 1953, US. Ct. Appeals (D.C. cir.) 1952, U.S. Ct. Appeals (5th cir.) 1973, U.S. Ct. Appeals (11th cir.) 1981, U.S. Supreme Ct 1961. Enlisted USMC, 1942, commd., 1943, advanced through grades to lt. col., 1959, ret., 1962; asst. prof. law Emory U., Atlanta, 1963-64, assoc. prof., 1964-65, prof., 1965-73, adj. prof. law, 1976-81; exec. asst. atty. gen. State of Ga., Atlanta, 1973-83; ptnr. McVay & Stubbs, Canton, Ga., from 1983. Instr. East Carolina Coll., 1959-61, Reinhardt Coll., 1981-83; bd. dirs. Legal Svcs. Corp., 1981-82. Author: Marriage and Divorce in Georgia, 1964, Georgia Law of Children, 1969, Criminal Practice and Procedure in Georgia 1863, 1971, Social Caseworker in Georgia Juvenile Courts, 1972, Georgia Appellate Court Jurisdiction, 1973, Powers and Limits of State Government, 1980, The Attorney General of Georgia, 1980, Under the Gun, 1966, The Plymouth Colony Connection, 1983, Cooking for Nice People, 1980; A Minister's Life, 1989, Pilgrim Families, 1994, New England Families, 1994, A Royal Ancestor, 1995, Harrington Ancestors, 1996, Nevens Ancestors, 1996, Obear Ancestors, 1997, Charlemagne, My Grandfather, 1997, Letters From the Far East, 1998, World War II Letters, 1998, China Letters, 1998; co-author: Governmental Ethics and Conflicts of Interest, 1980, rev. edit., 1988. Bd. dirs. Cherokee Family Violence Ctr., Canton, Ga., 1985-89, Rotary Club of Canton, 1985-88. Mem. VFW, SAR, Ga. Bar Assn., Blue Ridge Bar Assn., Canton-Cherokee Bar Assn., Am. Legion, Ga.'s Gridiron, Tudor and Stuart Soc., Marine Corps Assn. Ga. Lawyers, Soc. Mayflower Descs., Order of the Arrow, Order of Coif, Omicron Delta Kappa, Kappa Alpha, Pi Delta Epsilon, Phi Delta Phi. Republican. Methodist. Avocations: genealogy, travel. Home: Canton, Ga. Died Aug. 5, 2002.

STUCKEY, NATHAN WRIGHT, country music entertainer; b. Cass, Tex., Dec. 17; s. William Perry and Estelle (Graves) S.; m. Ann Monkhouse, Mar. 9, 1962. A. Communications, Arlington U. Country music entertainer, worldwide, from 1965. Composer: Waitin' in Your Welfare Line, 1966, Sweet Thang, 1967, Pop a Top, 1968. Mem. Am. Fedn. Musicians, AFTRA, Broadcast Music, Inc. Lodges: Masons. Baptist. Avocations: woodworking, gardening, cooking. Deceased.

STUMP, ROBERT LEE, congressman; b. Phoenix, Apr. 4, 1927; s. Jesse Patrick and Floy Bethany (Fields) S.; children: Karen, Bob, Bruce. BS in Agronomy, Ariz. State U., 1951. Mem. Ariz. State Ho. of Reps., 1959—67, Ariz. State Senate, 1967-76, pres., 1975-76; mem. U.S. Congress from 3d Ariz. dist., Washington, 1977—2002; vice chmn. nat. security com.; chmn. vets. affairs com., 1994—2002; chmn. armed svcs. com., 2001—02. With USN, 1943-46. Mem. Am. Legion, Ariz. Farm Bur. Republican. Seventh Day Adventist. Died June 20, 2003.

STURGE, MICHAEL DUDLEY, physicist, researcher; b. Bristol, Eng., May 25, 1931; came to U.S., 1961, naturalized 1991; s. Paul Dudley and Rachel (Graham) S.; m. Mary Balk, Aug. 21, 1956; children: David Mark, Thomas Graham, Peter Daniel, Benedict Paul. BA in Engring. and Physics, Gonville and Caius Coll., Cambridge, Eng., 1952; PhD in Physics, Cambridge U., 1957. Staff Mullard Rsch. Lab. (now Philips), Redhill, Eng., 1956-58; sr. rsch. fellow Royal Radar Establishment, Malvern, Eng., 1958-61; tech. staff Bell Labs., Murray Hill, N.J., 1961-83, Bellcore, Red Bank, N.J., 1984-86; prof. dept. physics Dartmouth Coll., Hanover, N.H., 1986-98, prof. emeritus, 1999—2003. Rsch. assoc. Stanford U., 1965, U. B.C., Vancouver, Can., 1969; vis. prof. Technion, Haifa, Israel, 1972, 76, 81, 85, Williams Coll., Williamstown, Mass., 1982, 84, Trinity Coll., Dublin, 1989, 93, 96, U. Fourier, Grenoble, France, 1989, 91, Hong Kong U. Sci. and Tech., 1999; exch. scientist Philips Rsch. Lab., Eindhoven, The Netherlands, 1973-74; vis. scholar U. Sheffield, Eng., 1996. Author: Statistical and Thermal Physics Fundamentals and Applications, 2003; contbr. over 130 papers in solid state physics to profl. jours.; co-editor: Excitons, 1982; editor: Jour. of Luminescence, 1984—90. Fellow Am. Phys. Soc.; mem. Am. Assn. Physics Tchrs. Home: Hanover, NH. Died July 13, 2003.

SUELFLOW, AUGUST ROBERT, historian, educator, archivist; b. Rockfield, Wis., Sept. 5, 1922; s. August Henry and Selma Hilda (Kressin) S.; m. Gladys I. Gierach, June 16, 1946; children: August Mark, Kathryn Lynn Du Bois. BA, Concordia Coll., Milw., 1942; BDiv, MDiv, Concordia Sem., St. Louis, 1946, fellow, 1947, STM, 1947; DivD, Concordia Sem., Springfield, Ill., 1967. Asst. curator Concordia Hist. Inst., St. Louis, 1946-48, dir., 1948-95, cons., 1995-97; guest lectr. Concordia Sem., St. Louis, 1952-69, 74-75, adj. prof., 1975—; asst. pastor Luther Meml. Ch., Richmond Heights, Mo., 1948-56, Mt. Olive, St. Louis, 1958-75; archivist Western Dist. Luth. Ch.-Mo. Synod, 1948-66, archivist Mo. Dist., 1966-87, 88-95; instr. Washington U., St. Louis, 1967-82. Inst. Mem. Am. Assn. Museums, Nat. Trust for Hist. Preservation, Soc. Am. Archivists, Orgn. Am. Historians, Western History Assn., Luth. Hist. Conf. Lutheran. Author: A Preliminary Guide to Church Records Depositories, 1969, Religious Archives: An Introduction, 1980, Heart of Missouri, 1954; cons., contbr. Luth. Cyclopedia, 1975; contbr. Moving Frontiers, 1964, Ency. of the Luth. Ch., 1965, The Luths. in N.Am., 1975, C.F.W. Walther: The American Luther, 1987; mng. editor Concordia Hist. Inst. Quar., 1950-95, assoc. editor., 1950—; Archives & History: Minutes and Reports, 1952-89; editor: Directory of Religious Hist. Depositories in America, 1963, Microfilm Index and Bibliography, vol. I, 1966, vol. II, 1978, Luth. Hist. Conf. Essays and Reports, 1964-92; series editor: Selected Writings of C.F.W. Walther, 6 vols., 1981; vol. editor, translator: Walther's Convention Essays, vol. III, 1981; sec., mem. editorial com. Concordia Jour., 1976-81; mem. editorial/adv. com. Luth. Higher Edn. in N.Am., 1980; mem. editorial com., contbr. Moving Frontiers, 1964. Deceased.

SULCER, FREDERICK DURHAM, advertising executive; b. Chgo., Aug. 28, 1932; s. Henry Durham and Charlotte (Thearle) S.; m. Dorothy Wright, May 2, 1953; children— Thomas W., Ginna M., David T. BA, U. Chgo., 1949, MBA, 1963. Reporter UP Assn., Chgo., 1945-46; reporter AP, 1947; with Needham, Harper & Steers Advt., Chgo., 1947-78, dir., 1965-78, sr. account dir., 1965-66, mem. exec. com., 1966-78, exec. v.p., 1967, dir. N.Y. div., 1967-78, pres. N.Y. div., 1974-75; chmn. bd. NH & S Internat., 1975-76; pres. Sulcer Communication Co., Inc., 1977-78; group exec., dir. Benton & Bowles (advt.), 1978-85; dir. bus. devel. D'Arcy Masius Benton & Bowles, advt., N.Y.C., 1985-90; vice-chmn. DDB Needham Worldwide, N.Y.C., 1990-95; founder, prin. The Persuasion Group, N.Y.C., from 1995. Schering-Plough disting. vis. prof. corp. comm. Fairleigh Dickinson U., Madison, N.J., 1993—. Served to capt. C.E. AUS, 1950-53. Mem. Am. Assn. Advt. Agys. (bd. govs, N.Y. chpt.), Internat. Advertisers Assn., Alpha Delta Phi. Died Jan. 18, 2004.

SULLIVAN, HAYWOOD COOPER, former professional baseball team executive; b. Donalsonville, Ga., Dec. 15, 1930; s. Ralph N. and Ruby L. (Cobia) S.; m. Patricia Ellen Peterson, Oct. 4, 1933; children: Marc, Kyle and Sharon (twins). Student, U. Fla., 1949-53. Player Boston Red Sox, Am. League, 1952, 55-60, Kansas City A's Am. League, 1961-63; mgr. minor leagues; mgr. Kansas City A's Am. League, 1965; v.p., player personnel Boston Red Sox, Am. League, 1965-77, co-owner, gen. ptnr., 1977—, co-owner, 1978-94. Served with U.S. Army, 1953-55. Named Exec. of Yr. Am. League, 1981 Democrat. Home: Naples, Fla. Died Feb. 12, 2003.

SUMMERSELL, FRANCES SHARPLEY, organization worker; b. Birmingham, Ala. Student, U. Montevallo, Peabody Coll.; LHD (hon.), U. Ala., 1996. Ptnr., artist, writer Assoc. Educators, from 1959. Home: Tuscaloosa, Ala. Died Jan. 15, 2003.

SUMNER, JAMES DUPRE, JR., lawyer, educator; b. Spartanburg, S.C., Nov. 30, 1919; s. James DuPre and Frances Grace (Harris) S.; m. Evvie Lucille Beach, Apr. 1, 1945 (dec.); children: Chery Erline (Mrs. Horacek), James DuPre III; m. Doris Kaiser Malloy, Oct. 20, 1972; children: John L. Malloy III, Mary Margaret Malloy, Kenneth S. Malloy, James M. Malloy. AB, Wofford Coll., 1941; LLB, U. Va., 1949; LLM, Yale U., 1952, JSD, 1955. Bar: Va. 1948, Calif. 1957. Practice law, Los Angeles, 1957—99; instr. law U. S.C., 1949-52; assoc. prof. UCLA, 1952-55, prof., 1955—89. Distinguished vis. prof. Instituto Luigi Sturzo, Rome, 1959; vis. prof. U. Tex., 1962, U. So. Calif., 1971; lectr. Calif. Bar Rev. Co-author: An Anatomy of Legal Education; contbr. articles to profl. jours. Lt. col. inf. AUS, 1941-46, ETO. Decorated Silver Star, Purple Heart with oak leaf cluster. Mem.: Bel Air Assn. (bd. dirs.), Rotary (pres. Westwood Village chpt.), Westwood Village Bar Assn. (pres.), Va. Bar Assn., Calif. Bar Assn., Sertoma (pres.), Westwood Village Sertome Club (pres.), Braemar Country Club, L.A. Country Club. Republican. Methodist. Died Apr. 1, 2003.

SUMNER, LORENE KNOWLES HART, retired medical/surgical and rehabilitation nurse; b. Telfair County, Ga., June 26, 1925; d. William Ira and Lola Amanda (Selph) Knowles; m. George Allen Hart, June 1, 1943 (dec. June 1953); children: Elizabeth Ann, George Allen, Charles Burnon; m. Joseph Rouss Sumner, Feb. 15, 1970; stepchildren: Joseph Rouss Jr., William Albert, Marvin Edwin, Charles Blaine (dec. Sept. 1972). Lic. Practical Nurse, Macon Area Vocat. Tech. Sch., 1968; cert. coronary care technician, Meml. Med. Ctr., Savannah, Ga., 1971; ADN, Mid. Ga. Coll., 1977; cert. in fetal monitoring, Coromoetric Med. Systems, Savannah, 1981. Lic. practical nurse, Ga.; RN, Ga.; cert. EMT, Ga. Nursing asst. Telfair County Hosp., McRae, Ga., 1953-66; practical nurse psychiat. unit College Street Hosp., Macon, Ga., 1968-70; obstet. supr. Dodge County Hosp., Eastman, Ga., 1980-81; staff nurse med.-surg. and drug rehab. units Carl Vinson VA Med. Ctr., Dublin, Ga., 1981-93, ret., 1993. Vol. nurse blood bank and cmty. disaster svcs. ARC, 1984—; vol. Salvation Army; mem. Siloam Bapt. Ch., Milan, Ga., 1940—. Mem. ANA, Ga. Nurses Assn., Order of Eastern Star. Home: Dublin, Ga. Deceased.

SUMPTER, SONJA KAY, elementary school educator; b. Weston, W.Va., Aug. 12, 1948; d. Glen A. and Sarah R. (White) Wade; m. Charles Fredrick Sumpter, Mar. 25, 1967; children: Lisa Marie Sumpter Pethtel, Charles Fredrick II. BS in Elem. Edn., Glenville (W.Va.) State Coll., 1984, MS in Edn., W.Va. Wesleyan Coll., 1993; postgrad., W.Va. U., 1994. Cert. tchr. elem. edn. 1-6, math. 5-8. Tchr. Weston (W.Va.) Jr. H.S., 1984-92, Robert Bland Mid. Sch., Weston, from 1992, team leader, 1992-94. Mem. Nat. Coun. Tchrs. Math., Order Ea. Star. Republican. Baptist. Avocations: singing, walking, macrame. Home: Weston, W.Va. Died Jan. 19, 1999.

SUNDERMAN, FREDERICK WILLIAM, SR., physician, educator, author, musician; b. Altoona, Pa., Oct. 23, 1898; s. William August and Elizabeth Catherine (Lehr) S.; m. Clara Louise Baily, June 2, 1925 (dec. 1972); children: Louise (dec.), F. William, Joel B. (dec.); m. Martha-Lee Taggart, May 3, 1980 (dec. Sept. 1998). BS, Gettysburg Coll., 1919, ScD (hon.), 1952; MD, U. Pa., 1923, MS, 1927, PhD, 1929; LittD, Beaver Coll., 2000. Diplomate Am. Bd. Internal Medicine, Am. Bd. Pathology (v.p. 1944-50 life trustee 1950—), Nat. Bd. Med. Examiners. Intern, then resident Pa. Hosp., 1923-25; assoc. rsch. med. U. Pa., Phila., 1925-48; assoc. in chem. divsn. William Pepper Lab. U. Pa. Hosp., Phila., 1929-48, physician, 1929-48; med. dir. Office of Sci. R & D, 1943-46; physician, hon. pathologist Pa. Hosp., from 1988; mem. faculty U. Pa. Sch. Medicine, Phila., 1925-47, assoc. prof. research medicine, also lectr.; acting head med. dept. Brookhaven Nat. Lab., Upton, N.Y., 1947-48; chief chem. div. William Pepper Lab. Clin. Medicine, U. Pa. Med. Sch., 1933-47; prof. clin. pathology, dir. Temple U. Lab. Clin. Medicine, 1947-48; med. dir. govt. explosives lab. Carnegie Inst. Tech. and Bur. Mines, 1943-46; head dept. clin. pathology Cleve. Clinic Found., 1948-49; dir. clin. research M.D. Anderson Hosp. Cancer Research, Houston, 1949-50; dir. clin. labs. Grady Meml. Hosp., Atlanta, 1949-51; prof. clin. medicine Emory U. Sch. Medicine, 1949-51; chief clin. pathology Communicable Disease Center, USPHS, 1950-51; med. adviser Rohm & Haas Co., 1947-71; med. cons. Redstone Arsenal, U.S. Army Ordnance Dept., Huntsville, Ala., 1947-49; cons. clin. pathology St. Joseph's Hosp., Tampa, Fla., 1965-66; attending physician Jefferson Hosp., Phila., 1951—, dir. div. metabolic research, clin. prof. medicine, 1951-67, clin. prof. medicine, 1951-74, hon. clin. prof. medicine, from 1975; dir. Inst. Clin. Sci., 1965—; prof. pathology Hahnemann U. Med. Coll., from 1970, co-chmn. dept. lab. medicine, 1970-75, prof. emeritus, 1989. Med. adviser and cons. bus. and industry, 1947—; dir. internat. seminars on clin. chemistry and pathology, 1947—; guest lectr. Beijing (People's Republic of China) Med. U., 1989. Author, editor 44 books on clin. chemistry and pathology; author: Our Madeira Heritage, 1979, Musical Notes of a Physician, 1982, Painting with Light, 1993, A Time to Remember, 1998; editor-in-chief Annals Clin. Lab. Sci., 1970—; mem. editl. bd. Am. Jour. Clin. Pathology, 1939-87, Am. Jour. Indsl. Medicine, 1979-85; cons. editor Am. Jour. Occupl. Medicine, 1979-85; also over 350 articles. Trustee Gettysburg Coll., 1967-89, chmn. bd. trustees, 1972-74, hon. life trustee, 1986—; bd. dirs. Mus. Fund Soc. Phila., 1938—, hon. life bd. dirs., 1993—; bd. dirs. Dwight D. Eisenhower Soc., 1984—, German Soc. Pa., 1986—, Geog. Soc. Phila., 1995; violin soloist Chautauqua Summer Series, Ea. U.S., 1919-20; guest soloist Concerto Soloists Pa., 1979, 83, 84, Pa. String Tchrs. Assn., Gettysburg, 1959, Westchester, 1962, 63, 67, 68, Trenton (N.J.) Tchrs. Coll. Orch., 1965; Internat. String Conf. soloist World Congress on Arts and Medicine, Carnegie Hall, N.Y.C., 1992; trustee Bermuda Biol. Sta. for Rsch., 1960, life trustee 1984. Recipient Naval Ordnance Devel. award, 1946, cert. appreciation War Dept., 1947, Honor medal Armed Forces Inst. Pathology, 1964; recipient Meritorious Svc. award, 1979, Honor award Latin Am. Assn. Clin. Biochemistry, 1976, Disting. Svc. award Am. Soc. Clin. Pathology-Coll. Am. Pathologists, 1988, Life-time Achievement award in clin. chemistry Joint Congresses of IX Congresso Nacional de la Sociedad Espanola de Quimica Clin., 2d Internat. Congress Therapeutic Drug Monitoring and Toxicology, and 4th Internat. Congress on Automation and New Tech., Spain, 1990, John Gunther Reinhold award Phila. Sect. Am. Assn. for Clin. Chemistry, 1991, Cert. of Honor N.J. sect., 1998, Jacob Ehrenzeller award Res. Assn. Pa. Hosp., 1993, Letter of Appreciation 100th Birthday Celebration Gettysburg Coll., 1998; named Disting. Alumnus Gettysburg Coll., 1963; Sunderman Seminar Rm. dedicated at Bermuda Biol. Sta. for Rsch., 1992, Letter of Appreciation from Bd. of Trustees for 100th Birthday, 1998, Little D. award Beaver Coll., 2000; 1st ann. F. William Sunderman award for Disting. Community Svc. and Excellence in a Chosen Field of Endeavor established by Rho Deuteron chpt. Phi Sigma Kappa, Gettysburg Coll; recipient Nat. Phi Sigma Kappa Disting. Alumnus award, 1995, Prime Time award Green Thumb, Inc., 1998, Union League Phila. Gold medal, 1998. Fellow ACP (life), Royal Soc. Medicine (hon., life), Royal Soc. Health Great Britain (life); mem. Am. Assn. History Medicine, Am. Diabetes Assn., AMA, Am. Soc. Clin. Investigation, Royal Soc. Health, AAUP, Endocrine Soc., Am. Assn. Biol. Chemistry, AAAS, Am. Chem. Soc., Internat. Union Pure and Applied Chemistry (nickel subcom. Commn. on Toxicology), Inst. Occupational Health (Finland), Outokumpu Oy (Finland), Am. Assn. Clin. Chemists (award for outstanding efforts in edn. and tng. 1981, John Gunther Reinhold award 1991), Coll. Am. Pathologists (founding gov., Pathologist of Yr. award 1962, Pres.'s Honor award 1984, Dist. Svc. award 1988, 50th Anniversary award 1997), Coll. Physicians (70 Yr. award 2000), Am. Soc. Clin. Pathology (pres. 1951, archives com. 1977—, intersoc. pathology coun. 1976—, interpathology soc. coun. 1976—, Ward Burdick award 1975, Continuing Edn. Distinguished Service award 1976), Assn. Clin. Scientists (pres. 1957-59, dir. edn. 1959—, diploma honor 1960, ann. goblet award 1964, Gold-headed cane 1974), Coll. Physicians of Phila. (sec. 1946-48, hon. pres. arts medicine sect. 1995, Disting. Service award 1980, 85, 90, 95), Knight of Order of St. Vincent of Portugal, Order of Merit (disting. svc. cross 1985), German Soc. Pa. (Bronze medal 1988, hon. dir. 1998), Am. Indsl. Hygiene Assn., Am. Occupational Medicine Assn., Med. Soc. Pa., Nat. Soc. Med. Research, Nat. Acad. Clin. Biochemistry, Pan Am. Med. Assn., Pa. Assn. Clin. Pathology (honors award 1997), Philadelphia County Med. Soc., Mus. Fund Soc. Phila. (hon. life), Soc. Toxicology, Brit. Assn. Clin. Biochemists (hon.), Soc. Pharm. and Environ. Pathologists (hon.), Internat. Union Pure and Applied Chemistry, Inst. Occupational Health Finland (nickel subcom. commn. toxicology), Phi Beta Kappa, Pa. Assn. Pathologists (Recognition award more than 50 yrs. contbns. to medicine and practice of pathology), Sigma Xi, Alpha Omega Alpha, Phi Sigma Kappa (1st annual F. William Sunderman award for Cmty. Svc Rho Deuteron chpt. Gettysburg Coll. 1995, Nat. Disting. Alumnus award grand chpt. 1995). Lutheran. Achievements include spl. symposium given in honor for lifetime achievement, Internat. Union Pure and Applied Chemistry, Finland, 1988. Home: Philadelphia, Pa. Died Mar. 9, 2003.

SUNIA, TAUESE TUAILEMAFUA PITA FITI, governor; b. Pago Pago, AS, Aug. 29, 1941; BA in Polit. Sci., U. Nebr.; M in Ednl. Adminstrn., U. Hawaii; DHL, Golden Gate U. Lt. gov. Ter. of Am. Samoa, Pago Pago, 1993—97, gov., 1997—2003. Democrat. Died Mar. 26, 2003.

SUPPLE, JEROME H. academic administrator; b. Boston, Apr. 27, 1936; m. Catherine Evans; 3 children. BS in Chemistry, Boston Coll., 1957, MS in Organic Chemistry, 1959; PhD in Organic Chemistry, U. New Hampshire, 1963. Asst. prof. chemistry SUNY Coll., Fredonia, 1964-69, assoc. prof., 1969-76, prof., 1976-78, acting dept. chair, 1975-76, assoc. dean for arts and scis., 1972-73, assoc. v.p. for acad. affairs, 1973-78, acting v.p. for acad. affairs, 1977, dean for gen. and spl. studies, 1977-78; assoc. provost for undergrad. edn. SUNY Cen. Adminstrn., 1974-75; prof. chemistry, v.p. for acad. affairs SUNY Coll., Plattsburgh, acting pres., 1978-89, on leave 1988-89, acting provost, v.p. for acad. affairs Postsdam, 1988-89; prof. chemistry, pres. S.W. Tex. State U., San Marcos, 1989—2002. Faculty fellow NSF, vis. rsch. faculty U. East Anglia, Norwich, Eng., 1970-71. Author books; contbr. numerous articles to profl. jours. Mem. Tex. Gov.'s total quality mgmt. steering com. Eastman Kodak rsch. fellow. Mem. AAAS, NCAA (pres. commn.), Am. Chem. Soc., Am. Assn. Higher Edn., Am. Assn. State Colls. and Univs. (bd. dirs.), Am. Coun. on Edn. (mem. commn. on govtl. rels.), So. Assn. Colls. and Schs. Commn. on Colls., Tex. Coun. on Econ. Edn. (bd. dirs.), Tex. Coun. Pub. Univ. Pres. and Chancellors (state affairs and exec. com.), Tex. Assn. Coll. Tchrs., Tex. Higher Edn. Master Plan Adv. Com., San Marcos C. of C. Econ. Devel. Coun., San Marcos Rotary, Golden Key, Sigma Xi (past pres. Fredonia club), Phi Eta Sigma (hon.), Omicron Delta Kappa (hon.). Home: San Marcos, Tex. Died Jan. 16, 2004.

SUSKIND, RAYMOND ROBERT, physician, educator; b. N.Y.C., Nov. 29, 1913; s. Alexander and Anna (Abramson) S.; m. Ida Blanche Richardson, Dec. 27, 1944; children: Raymond Robert, Stephen Alexander. AB, Columbia U., 1934; student medicine, Edinburgh, Scotland, 1938-39; MD, SUNY, Bklyn., 1943. Intern Cin. Gen. Hosp., 1944, resident in dermatology, 1944-46, 48-49; research fellow in indsl. health U. Cin., 1948-50; research asst. bacteriology N.Y. U., 1934-36; research asst. pharmacology, 1936-37; practice medicine specializing in dermatology, 1949-62; mem. faculty U. Cin., 1948-62, asso. prof. dermatology, 1952-62, dir. dermatol. research program Kettering Lab., 1948-62, Jacob G. Schmidlapp prof., chmn. dept. environ. health, dir. Kettering Lab., 1969-85, Jacob G. Schmidlapp prof. emeritus Inst. Environ. Health, 1985—, prof. medicine and dermatology, 1969-85, prof. emeritus medicine and dermatology, from 1985; attending physician U. Hosps., Cin., 1969-92; dir. environ. and occupational dermatology program Ctr. for Occupational Health, U. Cin. Hosp., Cin., 1985-88. Prof., head divsn. environ. medicine, prof. dermatology U. Oreg. Med. Sch., 1962-69; chmn. stds. adv. com. on cutaneous and eye hazards OSHA, 1978; Gehrmann lectr. Am. Acad. Occupl. Medicine, 1977; founding mem. certifying bd. Am. Bd. Toxicology, 1978-83; mem. nat. air quality adv. com. EPA, 1970-73; mem. com. on health related effects of herbicides VA, 1979-83; cons. on Agt. Orange studies; mem. panel on human health effects of stratospheric change NAS, 1977-85; trustee Dermatology Found., 1975-80; master, trustee Fernald Settlement Fund Program, Long Term Health Effects of Ionizing Radiation Exposure from Nuclear Fuel Processing Plant, 1989—; cons. Accreditation Coun. for Grad. Med. Edn.; advisor Sch. of Pub. Health, Mahidol U., Bangkok; vis. prof. dermatology Columbia U., 1996. Contbg. editor Am. Jour. Indsl. Medicine, 1979-89, now reviewer; mem. editorial bd. Annals Internal Medicine, 1983-86, Chemosphere, 1987-96; reviewer Archives Internal Medicine, Jour. AMA, Am. Jour. Pub. Health; contbr. articles to profl. jours., chpts. to books. Mem. Cin. Air Pollution Bd., 1972-76, chmn., 1974-75; bd. dirs. Cin. Chamber Music Soc., 1987-92. Served to capt. M.C. AUS, 1946-48. Recipient award Project Hope, 1984, Robert A. Kehoe award of merit Am. Acad. Occupational Medicine, 1987, Presdl. citation for outstanding contbns. to occupational medicine Am. Acad. Dermatology, 1988, Daniel Drake medal U. Cin., 1985, Disting. Alumni Achievement award SUNY Coll. Medicine, 1993; fellow U. Cin. Grad. Sch., 1971—. Fellow A.C.P.; mem AMA (adv. panel on toxicology council sci. affairs 1980-85), Am. Occupational Med. Assn. (chmn. dermatology com. and policy group 1958-66, dir. 1969-75, Health Achievement in Industry award 1977), Soc. Investigative Dermatology (dir., v.p., hon. mem. 1984—), Am. Acad. Dermatology (chmn. edn. com.), N.Y. Acad. Scis., Am. Indsl. Hygiene Assn., Soc. for Occupational and Environ. Health (councillor), AAAS, Am. Dermatol. Assn., Japanese Dermatol. Assn. (hon.), Chilean Dermatol. Soc. (hon.), Sigma Xi, Alpha Omega Alpha. Achievements include first description of inhibiting effect of ultraviolet radiation on allergic skin reactions; research on cutaneous toxicology, on effects of exposure to chlorinated dioxins, on effects of ionizing radiation on populations living in the vicinity of nuclear fuel processing plants. Died Nov. 29, 1913.

SUSSKIND, CHARLES, engineering educator, writer, publishing executive; b. Prague, Czech Republic; came to U.S., 1945, naturalized, 1946; s. Bruno Bronislav and Gertruda (Seger) S.; m. Teresa Gabriel, May 1, 1945; children: Pamela Susskind Pettler, Peter Gabriel, Amanda Frances. Student, City U., London, 1939-40; BS, Calif. Inst. Tech., 1948; M in Engring., Yale U., 1949, PhD, 1951. Rsch. asst. Yale U., 1949-51; rsch. assoc. Stanford U., 1951-55, lectr., asst. dir. microwave lab., 1953-55; faculty U. Calif., Berkeley, 1955:, prof., 1964-91, prof. emeritus, 1991–2004, asst. dean U. Calif. Coll. Engring., 1964-68; statewide adminstr. U. Calif., 1969-74. Vis. prof. U. London, 1961-62, U. Geneva, Switzerland, 1968-69; cons. EPA Sci. Adv. Bd., 1982-92; bd. dirs. San Francisco Press, Inc. Author: (with M. Chodorow) Fundamentals of Microwave Electronics, 1964; (with L. Schell) Exporting Technical Education, 1968, Understanding Technology, 1973, 74, 85 (transl. into Dutch, French, Italian, Korean, Spanish, Indian edit. in English), Twenty-Five Engineers and Inventors, 1976; (with F. Kurylo) Ferdinand Braun, 1981; (with M.E. Rowbottom) Electricity and Medicine: History of their Interaction, 1984, Janáček and Brod, 1985, Heinrich Hertz: A Short Life, 1995; editor: (with M. Hertz) Heinrich Hertz: Memoirs, Letters, Diaries, bilingual edit., 1977; editor-in-chief Ency. Electronics, 1962. With USAAF, 1942-45. Named to Hon. Order Ky. Cols. Fellow IEEE; mem. AAAS, Histor of Sci. Soc., Soc. for History of Tech., Instn. Elec. Engrs. (London), Sigma Xi (pres. Berkeley chpt. 1972-73), Tau Beta Pi. Died June 15, 2004.

SUSSMAN, CAROL, clinical social worker; b. N.Y.C., Jan. 30, 1927; d. Meyer and Anna (Roden) S. BA, U. Conn., 1949; MSS, Smith Coll., 1955. Diplomate Acad. Cert. Social Workers; lic. clin. social worker. Social worker Conn. Dept. Welfare, Hartford, 1949-53; psychiat. social worker dept. psychiatry Boston Univ. Med. Ctr., 1955-66; supr. Jewish Family and Child Svc., Boston, 1966-67; case worker, social worker Concord-Carlisle Regional High Sch., Concord, Mass., 1967-90; psychotherapist in pvt. practice Cambridge, Mass., from 1982. Contbr. articles to profl. jours. Mem. Nat. Assn. Social Workers (editorial and feature article writer for newsletter). Avocations: drawing, painting. Died Jan. 11, 2001.

SUTCLIFFE, ERIC, lawyer; b. Calif., Jan. 10, 1909; s. Thomas and Annie (Beare) S.; m. Joan Basché, Aug. 7, 1937; children: Victoria, Marcia, Thomas; m. Marie C. Paige, Nov. 1, 1975. AB, U. Calif., Berkeley, 1929, LLB, 1932. Bar: Calif. 1932. Mem. firm Orrick, Herrington & Sutcliffe, San Francisco, 1943-85, mng. ptnr., 1947-78. Trustee, treas., v.p. San Francisco Law Libr., 1974-88; founding fellow The Oakland Mus. of Calif.; bd. dirs. Merritt Peralta Found., 1988; past bd. dirs. Hong Kong Bank of Calif., Friends of U. Calif. Bot. Garden, sec. Fellow Am. Bar Found (life); mem. ABA (chmn state regulation securities com. 1960-65), San Francisco Bar Assn. (chmn. corp. law com., 1964-65), San Francisco C. of C. (past treas., dir.), State Bar Calif., Pacific Union Club, Bohemian Club, Phi Gamma Delta, Phi Delta Phi, Order of Coif. Home: Oakland, Calif. Died Oct. 9, 2003.

SUTHERLAND, DONALD JAMES, investment company executive; b. Teaneck, N.J., Jan. 2, 1931; s. Conrad James and LaVinia Marie (Peters) S.; m. Beatrice Wagstaff, June 8, 1957; children: Paige, Donald, Jr., Shelley, Julie; m. Denise Jackson, July 22, 1985; 1 child, Conor. AB, Princeton U., 1953; MBA, Harvard U., 1958; LHD (hon.), St..Michael's Coll., 1981. Regional sales mgr. Dahlstrom Corp., Jamestown, 1958-60; assoc. McKinsey & Co., N.Y.C., 1961-64; v.p. Laird, Inc., N.Y.C., 1965-67, New Court Securities Corp., N.Y.C., 1968-70; pres. Quincy Assocs., Inc., N.Y.C., 1970-75; pres., corp. gen. ptnr. Quincy Ptnrs., Glen Head, N.Y., from 1975. Chmn. bd. Crane Hoist Engrng. Corp., 1975-79, Am. Spring & Wire Splty. co., Inc., 1977-82, Muehlhausen Bros. Spring & Mfg. Co., Inc., 1977-82, Lewis Spring & Mfg. Co., Inc., 1979-82, Ohio Locomotive Crane Co., Inc., 1981-86, Water Products Co., 1988-89, Publix Shirt Co., L.P., 1979-91, Quincy Packaging Group, L.P., 1984-91, Will & Baumer, Inc., 1984-94, Quincy Spring Group, Inc., 1986-94, Quincy Techs., Inc., 1987—, PCI Group, Inc., 1987-93, Perfection Forms Corp., 1990-94, Tectron Tube Corp., 1991-95, The Lion Brewery Inc., 1993-99, Cavert Wire Co., Inc., 1994-98; chmn. bd., pres. Ala. Metal Products Co. Inc., 1976-77. Contbr. articles to profl. jours. Trustee Sheltering Arms Children's Svc., 1973-75, St. Michael's Coll., 1972—, Cancer Rsch. Inst., 1984-99, Joffrey Ballet, 1982-91, pres. 1985-87, Barry Goldwater Scholarship and Excellence in Edn. Found., 1991—, Hofstra U., 1992—; Villa I Tatti Coun., 1991—, The New Sch., 1992—, Muhlenberg Coll., 1992—, steering com. Human Rights Watch, Europe, 1996—; adv. bd. World Policy Inst., 1996—; Nassau County (N.Y.) Planning Commn., 1965-68, Internat. Coun. of World Monuments Fund, 1991—. Lt. (j.g.) USN, 1953-56. Mem. The Creek (gov. 1987—, treas. 1991-93), Cap and Gown (trustee 1981—), The Links, Beaver Dam Winter Sports Club, Econ. Club of N.Y.C. Democrat. Roman Catholic. Home: Glen Head, NY. Died Aug. 11, 2002.

SUTTER, RICHARD ANTHONY, physician; b. St. Louis, July 20, 1909; s. John Henry and Molly Louisa (Schuchman) S.; m. Elizabeth Henby, June 15, 1935; children— John Richard, Jane Elizabeth; Judith Sutter Hinrichs AB, Washington U., St. Louis, 1931, MD, 1935. Diplomate Am. Bd. of Preventive Medicine, Am. Bd. of Occupational Medicine. Intern St. Louis City Hosp., 1935-36; asst. to Otto Sutter, M.D., 1937; founder, med. dir. Sutter Clinic, St. Louis, 1947-84; mem. faculty Washington U. Sch. Medicine. Apptd. physician mem. nat. adv. com. on occupational safety and health OSHA, 1971-75; med. dir. St. Louis Internat. Airport, 1964-84, emeritus med. dir., 1988—; mem. Mo. Gov.'s Council on Occupational Health and Safety, Gov's Adv. Com. on Worker's Compensation, Com. on Vocat. Rehab.; cons. Barnes/Sutter Health Care, 1984— ; hon. cons. St. Mary's Hosp. East St. Louis, Ill., 1991—; mem. emeritus staff Barnes. Contbr. articles to med. publs. Bd. dirs. Downtown St. Louis, Inc. (hon. chmn. membership com., Leadership award 1994); past dir. Blue Cross/Blue Shield; mem. St. Louis Merc. Libr. Assn., Jefferson Nat. Expansion Commn., Commn. on Future of Washington U., St. Louis, mem. aviation com. Regional Commerce and Growth Assn. Served to lt. col. M.C., U.S. Army, 1941-46, ETO. Decorated Bronze Star; recipient Man of Yr. award St. Louis chpt. Beta Theta Pi, 1974; Alumni Achievement award Washington U. Med. Sch., 1985; Richard A. and Elizabeth H. Sutter chair Occupational, Indsl. and Environ. Medicine named in honor, Washington U. Sch. Medicine, 1993; Am. Lung Assn. honoree, 1997; inductee Celebration of the Century Hall of Fame, 1999. Fellow APHA, Am. Coll. Occupational and Environ. Medicine (Health Achievement in Industry award 1978), Am. Coll. Preventive Medicine, Am. Indsl. Hygiene Assn. (emeritus, mem. Internat. com. occupational health); mem. AMA (coun. on occupational health, coun. on aviation and space medicine), Mo. Med. Assn. (del.), St. Louis Met. Med. Soc. (hon., pres. 1947, Dr. Robert Schlueter award for Leadership 1994), Am. Assn. Ry. Surgeons (past pres.), Cen. States Soc. Ind. Medicine and Surgery (past pres.), Univ. Club, Old Warson Country Club, Washington U. Faculty Club, Eliot Soc. (founder, life), Yachting Club Am. (founder), Bradenton Country Club. Avocations: aviation, hunting, golf, fishing, estate management. Died Nov. 15, 1999.

SUTTLE, DORWIN WALLACE, federal judge; b. Knox County, Ind., July 16, 1906; s. William Sherman and Nancy Cordelia (Hungate) S.; m. Anne Elizabeth Barrett, Feb. 1, 1939 (dec.); children: Stephen Hungate, Nancy Joanna Suttle Walker (dec.); m. Lucile Cram Whitecotton, Aug. 21, 1956; stepchildren: Fred and Frank Whitecotton. JD, U. Tex., 1928. Bar: Tex., U.S. Supreme Ct. 1960. Practiced law, Uvalde, Tex., 1928-64; U.S. dist. judge Western Dist. Tex., 1964-2000, ret., 2000. Democrat. Methodist. Died Sept. 29, 2001.

SUTTON, WILLIS ANDERSON, JR., sociology educator; b. Atlanta, July 18, 1917; s. Willis Anderson and Louneal (Walton) S.; m. Dorothy Rebecca Drake, Dec. 22, 1941; children: Willis Anderson III, Franklin Drake, Sarah Sutton Haggard. Student, Young Harris Jr. Coll., 1934-36; BA, U. N.C., 1939, MA, 1941, PhD, 1952. Project dir. WPA, Ga., 1940-41; instr. Emory U., Atlanta, 1948-52; asst. prof. U. Ky., Lexington, 1952-58, asso. prof., 1959-68, prof. sociology, 1968-82, chmn. dept., 1976-82. Author: Village Level Workers and Their Work, 1962. Served to 2d lt. U.S. Army, 1941-45. Ford Found. fellow India, 1959-60 Mem. Am. Sociol. Assn., Soc. Study Social Problems, Soc. Study Symbolic Interaction, So. Sociol. Soc., North Central Sociol. Soc. Democrat. Presbyterian. Home: Lexington, Ky. Died Sept. 18, 2002.

SVEDA, MICHAEL, management and research consultant; b. West Ashford, Conn., Feb. 3, 1912; s. Michael and Dorothy (Druppa) S.; m. Martha Augusta Gaeth, Aug. 23, 1936; children: Sally Anne, Michael Max. BS, U. Toledo, 1934; PhD (Eli Lilly rsch. fellow), U. Ill., 1939. Tchr. chemistry U. Toledo, 1932-35, U. Ill., 1935-37; research, sales and product mgmt. positions E.I. du Pont de Nemours & Co., Inc., 1939-54; mgmt. counsel Wilmington, Del., 1955-59; dir. acad. sci. projects NSF, 1960-61; corp. assoc. dir. research FMC Corp., 1962-64; mgmt. and research counsel to academia, industry and govt., from 1965. Lectr. univs., 1961—, fed. govt., groups, 1965—; mem. adv. com. on creativity in scientists and engrs. Rensselaer Poly. Inst., 1965—. Numerous appearances on pub. and comml. TV and radio; patentee chems. and processes in polymers, pesticides, chem. intermediates; synthesizer, discoverer cyclamates, sweetening agts., 1937; deviser new concepts and patentee 3 dimensional models complex orgns., selection key personnel; new approach to diets, taking off human fat; new use Boolean algebra, theory of sets in people problems; active drive to have cyclamate sweeteners reinstated, 1973—. Named Outstanding Alumnus U. Toledo, 1954 Fellow AAAS (life); mem. Am. Chem. Soc., Sigma Xi, Phi Kappa Phi, Alpha Chi Sigma, Phi Lambda Upsilon. Died Aug. 10, 1999.

SWANSON, AUGUST GEORGE, physician, retired association executive; b. Kearney, Nebr., Aug. 25, 1925; s. Oscar Valderman and Elnora Wilhelmina Emma (Block) Swanson; m. Ellyn Constance Weinel, June 28, 1947; children: Eric, Rebecca, Margaret, Emilie, Jennifer, August. BA, Westminster Coll., Fulton, Mo., 1951; MD, Harvard U., 1949; DSc (hon.), U. Nebr., 1979. Intern King County Hosp., Seattle, 1949—50; resident in internal medicine U. Wash. Affiliated Hosp., 1953—55, neurology, 1955—57; resident in neurology Boston City Hosp., 1958; dir. pediatric neurology, then dir. divsn. neurology U. Wash. Med. Sch., Seattle, 1958—67, assoc. dean acad. affairs, 1967—71; v.p. acad. affairs Assn. Am. Med. Colls., Washington, 1971—89, v.p. grad. med. edn., exec. dir. nat. resident matching program, 1989—91; ret., 1991. Vis. fellow physiology Oxford (Eng.) U., 1963—64; cons. in field. Contbr. articles to profl. jours. With USNR, 1943—46, with USNR, 1950—53. Recipient Abraham Flexner award for distinguished svc. to medical edn., Assn. of Am. Medical Coll., 1992; scholar Markle scholar medicine, 1959—64. Mem.: Am. Neurol. Assn., Inst. Medicine NAS. Achievements include research in brain function, physician edn., med. manpower. Home: Seattle, Wash. Died Dec. 19, 2003.

SWARTZ, RANDALL WOLFE, biotechnology engineer; b. Phila., June 1, 1946; s. Bernard Henry and Mildred (Anton) S.; m. Paula Katherine Champion, Mar. 14, 1970; children: Mark Anton, David Wightman, Patricia Katherine. BS, Rennselaer Polytechnic, 1968, PhD, 1973. Rsch. investigator E.R. Squibb & Sons, 1973-74; sr. scientist, mgr. Eli Lilly & Co., Indpls., 1974-81; dir. biochem. div. Genetics Inst., inc., Boston, 1981-84; owner Swartz Assocs., Winchester, Mass., from 1984; dir. biotech. engring. Tufts U., Medford, Mass., from 1985. Cons. in field. Contbr. chpt. to book. Asst. scout master Princeton coun. Boy Scouts Am., N.J., 1973-74; den leader Winchester coun. Boy Scouts Am., 1986-89. NSF grantee, 1986. Mem. Soc. Indsl. Microbiologist, Am. Chem. Soc. (chairperson microbial and biochem. tech. div.), Sigma Xi. Episcopalian. Avocations: hiking, camping, sailing, reading, skiing. Home: Winchester, Mass. Died May 20, 2000.

SWARTZ, ROBERT JOEL, accountant, consultant; b. N.Y.C., Dec. 17, 1925; s. Arthur Nathan and Anne (Hutt) S.; m. Inez B. Nelson, May 20, 1956; children: Richard J., Barbara J., Andrew J. BA, NYU, 1948; MBA, Columbia U., 1950; JD, Bklyn. Law Sch., 1954. From jr. act. to mng. ptnr. Aronson & Oresman & Co., N.Y.C., 1950-73; ptnr. in charge of N.Y. office Clarence Raines & Co., N.Y.C., 1974-79; ptnr. Main Hurdman & Co., N.Y.C., 1979-87, KPMG, N.Y.C., 1987-91; v.p. Alco Capital Group Inc., N.Y.C., from 1991; ind. cons. N.J., from 1991; pres. 745 Svc. Corp., N.Y.C., from 1999; v.p. AlcoCadillac-N.J., from 1991. Bd. dirs. Bed Bath & Beyond, N.J., Std. Motor Products Inc. 1st lt. U.S. Army, 1943-46, PTO. Avocations: tennis, swimming, reading. Home: Fort Lee, NJ. Died July 24, 2001.

SWARTZ, RUSSELL BRUCE, real estate executive; b. Gt. Falls, Mont., May 28, 1915; s. Benjamin Harrison and Eleanor (Brusseau) S.; m. Maurine Lucy Mosier, Sept. 17, 1937 (div. 1963); children: Russell Bruce, Margaret Ann.; m.

Ritva Helena Perttula, Apr. 7, 1964; children: David Bruce, Lisa Ann, Michael Bruce. JD, U. Wash., 1941; MBA, Harvard U., 1947; LLD (hon.), U. Mont., 1987. Pres., chief exec. officer Russell B. Swartz and Assocs. Inc., Seattle, 1963-87; sec. Searle St. Estates Inc., Seattle, 1976-89; pres. Seattle-Swartz Inc., Seattle, from 1980, Rainier Comml. Carpet Co., Seattle, from 1980; pres., chief exec. officer Capital Resources Internat. Inc., Seattle, from 1987. Maj. USAF, 1940-45. Decorated DFC (3), Air medals (2), Combat Stars (5). Mem. Masons, VFW, Royal Order of Scotland. Republican. Mem. Lds Ch. Avocation: yachting. Home: Seattle, Wash. Deceased.

SWARTZ, SEYMORE BERNARD, dentist; b. Rochester, N.Y., Feb. 20, 1923; s. Samuel Raymond and Sarah (Migdalowitz) S.; m. Clarine Stierer, May 11, 1944; children: Richard, Michel, Ellen, Irving. Student, Wayne State U., 1940-41, W.Va. U., 1943, U. Detroit, 1941-43, DDS, 1950. Dentist, Southfield, Mich. Chief oral medicine, oral diagnosis Sinai Hosp., Detroit, 1978-90. 1st lt. U.S. Army, 1943-46. Fellow Am. Acad. Oral Medicine (pres. 1975-77); mem. ADA, Mich. Dental Assn., Alpha Omega, DAV, Jewish Vets. Avocations: photography, woodworking, art, music, fishing. Home: West Bloomfield, Mich. Died Aug. 21, 2000.

SWEETING, LINDA MARIE, chemist; b. Toronto, Ont., Can., Dec. 11, 1941; came to U.S., 1965, naturalized, 1979; d. Stanley H. and Mary (Robertson) S. BSc, U. Toronto, 1964, MA, 1965; PhD, UCLA, 1969. Asst. prof. chemistry Occidental Coll., L.A., 1969-70; asst. prof. chemistry Towson (Md.) State U., 1970-75, assoc. prof., 1975-85, prof., 1985—; guest worker NIH, 1976-77; program dir. chem. instrumentation NSF, 1981-82; vis. scholar Harvard U., 1984-85; contractor U.S. Army MRICD, 1991-93; vis. lectr. Johns Hopkins U., 1999—. Bd. dirs. Chamber Music Soc. Balt., 1985-91. Exec. com. Exptl. NMR. Conf. 1985-87, local arr. chair 1986. Mem. Md. Acad. Scis. (mem. sci. council 1975-83, 89-94), Assn. for Women in Sci. (treas. 1977-78, Woman of Yr. 1989), Am. Chem. Soc. (mem. women chemists Com. 1983-89), AAAS, Nature Conservancy, Sierra Club, Phi Lambda Upsilon, Sigma Xi (sec. TSU Club 1979-81, Towson chpt. pres. 1987-88, 91-92, 98-99, sec. 1995-98, 2001-02, mid-Atlantic nominating com. 1987-90, regional dir. 1988-89, nat. nominating com. 1991-94), Assn. for Practical and Profl. Ethics. Died Sept. 28, 2003.

SWEETMAN, LORETTA VINETTE, social worker; b. Niagara Falls, N.Y., Sept. 27, 1941; d. Vincent and Loretta Viola (Williams) Leone; m. George W. Sweetman, Sept. 14, 1967 (div. July 1972); children: Loretta, Mary, GiGi. AS, Claremore (Okla.) Jr. Coll., 1975; BS in Sociology, East Cen. State Coll., 1978; MSW, U. Okla., 1980. With Tulsa Dist. Office Corp Engrs., 1975; with practicum placement dept. VA Hosp., Muskogee, Okla., 1979-80, clin. social worker Sheridan, Wyo., from 1980, St. Joseph Hosp., Ponca City, Okla., 1980. Tchr. Sheridan Community Coll., 1983—; presenter seminars. Bd. dirs. Wyo. Health Care, Sheridan, 1982-85, Sr. Citizens Coord. Council, Sheridan, 1982-84, exec. bd. pres., 1984-87; Sheridan County Hospice rep. Nat. Hospice Mgrs., 1984-87; bd. pres., owner exec. ste. Edn., Conseling Svc., Sheridan. Named one of Women of the Yr. Sheridan chpt. Bus. and Profl. Women, 1982, one of Women of the Day Sheridan chpt. Bus. and Profl. Women, 1982. Mem. NAFE, Nat. Assn. Social Workers. Democrat. Roman Catholic. Home: Beaverton, Oreg. Died Jan. 8, 2001.

SWEETWOOD, HANNELORE MARGARETE, nursing educator; b. Germany, May 20, 1930; d. Paul and Anna (Frei) Liede; m. Milton Sweetwood, Aug. 30, 1953; children: Lori Ann, Paul Charles. Diploma, Jersey City Med. Ctr., 1953; BS, Monmouth Coll., 1976, MS, 1979; EdD, Columbia U. Tchrs. Coll., 1986. Adj. faculty Monmouth U., West Long Branch, N.J., from 1993. Ednl. cons., rschr. in field. Contbr. articles to profl. jours. Grantee Am. Heart Assn., 1974. Mem. AACN (Nurse of Yr. award Monmouth/Ocean chpt. 1982), Sigma Theta Tau (former pres. Lambda Delta chpt.). Home: Long Branch, NJ. Died Mar. 22, 2002.

SWEEZY, PAUL MARLOR, editor, publisher; b. N.Y.C., Apr. 10, 1910; s. Everett Benjamin and Caroline (Wilson) S.; m. Zirel Dowd, June 17, 1961; children by previous marriage: Samuel Everett, Elizabeth MacDougall, Martha Adams. BA, Harvard U., 1931, PhD, 1937; LittD (honoris causa), Jawaharlal Nehru U., 1983. With econs. dept. Harvard U., 1934-42; former editor Monthly Rev. Vis. prof. Cornell U., Stanford U., New Sch. Social Research, U. Calif., Davis, Yale U., Hosei U., Tokyo, U. Manchester, Eng.; lectr. Cambridge (Eng.) U., 1971; pres. Monthly Rev. Found., Inc. Author or editor: Monopoly and Competition in the English Coal Trade, 1950-1850, 1938, The Theory of Capitalist Development, 1942, Socialism, 1949, The Present as History, 1953; co-author: (with Leo Huberman) Cuba: Anatomy of a Revolution, 1960, (with Paul Baran) Monopoly Capital, 1966, (with Leo Huberman) Socialism in Cuba, 1969, (with Charles Bettelheim) On the Transition to Socialism, 1971, (with Harry Magdoff) The Dynamics of U.S. Capitalism, 1972, Modern Capitalism and Other Essays, 1972, (with Harry Magdoff) The End of Prosperity, 1977, Post Revolutionary Society, 1981, (with Harry Magdoff) The Deepening Crisis of U.S. Capitalism, 1981, Four Lectures on Marxism, 1981, (with Harry Magdoff) Stagnation and Financial Explosion, 1987, (with Harry Magdoff) The Irreversible Crisis, 1988. Served with AUS, 1942-46. Decorated Bronze Star; recipient David A. Wells prize, 1938. Home: Larchmont, NY. Died Feb. 28, 2004.

SWENSEN, EMMA LOU, elementary school educator; b. Milford, Utah, Nov. 3, 1933; d. Clarence Vernon and Ruby (Williams) Davis; m. Adolph LeRoy Swensen, Aug. 14, 1963 (widowed Apr. 8, 1988). BS, Brigham Young U., 1956. Cert. elem. tchr. K-8, Utah, Calif. Elem. sch. tchr. grades 3-4 San Diego City Schs., 1956-58, Provo (Utah) City Sch. Dist., 1958-63, tchr. grade 2, 4, 1967-99; tchr. grade 7 Fall River Jct. Unified Sch. Dist., Fall River Mills, Calif., 1963-64; tchr. grade 5 San Leandro (Calif.) Unified sch. Dist., 1964-67. Textbookn selection team Provo Sch. Dist., Utah, 1991-93. Singer Ladies Sextette, San Diego, 1957-58; chorus mem. Choraliers, Provo, Utah, 1987; mem. LDS Ch. Mem. Nat. Edn. Assn. (del. 1991), Utah Edn. Assn. (faculty rep. 1987, 91, del.), Delta Kappa Gamma (pres. 1976-78). Republican. Avocations: quilting, art, travel, gardening, reading. Home: Provo, Utah. Died July 6, 1999.

SWIFT, HEWSON HOYT, educator, biologist; b. Auburn, N.Y., Nov. 8, 1920; s. Arthur L., Jr. and Hildegarde (Hoyt) S.; m. Joan Woodcock, June 6, 1942; children: Deirdre Anne, Barbara Jean. AB, Swarthmore Coll., 1942; MS, State U. Iowa, 1945; PhD, Columbia U., 1950. Curator spiders U.S. Nat. Museum, Washington, 1945-46; lectr. zoology Columbia, 1948-49; mem. faculty U. Chgo., 1949—2004, prof. zoology, 1958-70, Distinguished Service prof. biology and pathology, 1971-77, chmn. dept. biology, 1972-77, George Wells Beadle Disting. Service prof. biology and pathology, 1977-84, former George Wells Beadle Disting. Service prof. dept. molecular genetics and cell biology and dept. pathology. Vis. prof. Harvard U., 1970-71; vis. sr. scientist CSIRO, Canberra, Australia, 1977-78; mem. cell biology study sect. NIH, 1958-62; mem. devel. adv. panel NSF, 1962-65; adv. panel etiology of cancer Am. Cancer Soc., 1965-70; mem. adv. panel Nat. Cancer Inst., 1972-75 Recipient Quantrell award for excellence in teaching U. Chgo., 1977; E.B. Wilson award for outstanding contbns. to cell biology, 1985. Fellow AAAS, Am. Acad. Arts and Scis., Nat. Acad. Scis. (chmn. sect. on cellular and developmental biology 1974-77); mem. Am. Soc. Cell Biology (pres. 1964, editorial bd. of Jour.), Histochem. Soc. (pres. 1973, editorial bd. jour.), Electron Microscope Soc. Am., Genetics Soc. Am., Nat. Acad. Scis. India (fgn. assoc.) Home: Chicago, Ill. Died Jan. 1, 2004.

SWIFT, JOEL, law educator; b. S.I., Apr. 24, 1939; s. Meyer Richard and Dorothy Jean (Levin) S.; m. Deborah L. Ballou, Aug. 11, 1984. BS, Wagner Coll., 1959; JD, U. Pa., 1962, LLM, 1979. Bar: N.Y. 1963, U.S. Dist. Ct. (so. and ea. dists.) N.Y. 1964. Law clk. Demou & Morris, N.Y.C., 1962-67; trial atty. Dept. Labor, N.Y.C., 1963-68; law sec. Supreme Ct. N.Y., N.Y.C., 1968-70; sr. trial atty. Hale & Russell, N.Y.C., 1970-71; gen. counsel SUNY, New Paltz, 1971-75; pvt. practice New Paltz, 1975-78; pub. defender Dutchess County N.Y., Poughkeepsie, 1977-78; prof. law No. Ill. U., DeKalb, from 1979. Vis. prof. law Fla. Coastal U., Jacksonville; assoc. dean No. Ill. U., DeKalb, 1990-92. Contbr. articles to profl. jours. Bd. dirs. Stagecoach Players, DeKalb, 1987. Grantee CBS Found., 1978-79, NEW, 1986. Fellow Am. Bar Found.; mem. Am. Inns of Ct. (exec. dir. 1993—). Avocations: theatre, music. Home: Fernandina Beach, Fla. Died Mar. 4, 2002.

SWINGLE, EDWARD R. marketing professional; Sr. v.p. worldwide mktg. AGCO Corp., Duluth, Ga., sr. v.p. sales and mktg. Ams. region, 1999—2002. Died Jan. 4, 2002.

SWOPE, CHARLES EVANS, bank president, lawyer; b. West Chester, Pa., June 16, 1930; s. Charles S. and Edna (McAllister) S.; m. Stephanie Swope; 1 child, Charles E. BS, Bucknell U., 1953; JD, Washington and Lee U., 1959; MS, Ind. Coll., 1966; attended Naval War Coll., Judge Adv. Gen. Sch., 1957; attended, Command and Staff Coll., 1969; D in Pub. Svc. (hon.), West Chester U., 1994. Assoc. Gawthorp & Greenwood, Attys., West Chester, Pa., 1960; pres., chmn. bd., sr. trust officer 1st Nat. Bank, Chester County, Pa., from 1965, also chmn. bd. dirs. Pres. Eachus Dairy Co., 1970-84; pres., bd. dirs. West Chester Corp.; bd. dirs. Madison Co., Penjerdel, Penn Mut. Ins. Co., dir. 1st Nat. Bank Chester County; pres. Automobile Assn. Chester County; lectr. corp. law. Pres. West Chester Civic Assn., 1964; co-chmn. Chester County Heart Assn. Dr., West Chester Cmty. Ctr. Bldg. Dr., 1970-90, 175th Anniversary West Chester, 200th Anniversary West Chester, co-chmn.; mem. Nat. Football Found. and Hall of Fame; dir. Chester County coun. Boy Scouts Am., 1961-97; bd. dirs. Chester County Svc.; pres. Swope Found. Trust; bd. dirs., pres. West Chester U. Found.; mem. Marine Corps Scholarship Fund; chmn. Bus. and Indsl. Coun. Chester County, pres., 1981; chmn. Easter Seal Soc. Chester County; mem. Com. to Restore Tun Tavern; trustee West Chester U., 1962-72, pres. bd. trustees, 1966-72; trustee Chester County Devel. Fund, Dr. Charles S. Swope Scholarshpi Fund, Hatfield Home; YMCA trustee Chester County Hosp. Corp. Maj. USMC, 1952-58, col. Res. Decorated Legion of Merit, Nat. Def. medal, Navy Commendation medal, Meritorious Svc. medal; recipient Coll. Football Centennial award, 1970; Congl. Medal of Merit, 1981; Disting. Eagle Scout award Boy Scouts Am., 1983; Legion of Hon. Gold medallion Chapel of Four Chaplains, 1998; named to Hall of Fame, West Chester U., 1997, West Chester H.S., 1999; recipient CEO of Yr. Chester County C. of C., 2000. Mem. ABA (life), VFW (life), Am. Bankers Assn., Pa. Bankers Assn. (chmn. legis. com. 1965, 70), U.S. Naval Inst., Assn. Univ. Trustees Pa., Am. Soc. Internat. Law, Chester County Bar Found. (v.p.), Greater West Chester C. of C. (pres. 1963), Marine Corps League Chester County (vice comdr. 1960-72), Freedoms Found., Am. Legion (life), Chester County Hist. Soc. (Founder's award), Mil. Order of the World Wars, Marine Corps Res. Officer Assn. (nat. pres. 1982-83, vice chmn. bd. dirs.), Marine Corps League, Pa. C. of C., Navy League U.S., Washington and Lee Law Sch. Assn., Bucknell Alumni Assn., West Chester U. Alumni Assn., Pa. Economy League, Brandywind Valley Assn., Maxwell Football Club, West Chester Club, Golf and Country Club, Union League Club (Phila), Applebrook Country club, Italian Social Club, Sky Top Club, Great Oaks Yacht and Country Club, Masons, Rotary (pres. West Chester, Pa. club 1968-69, Paul Harris fellow), Elks, Phi Alpha Delta, Phi Kappa Psi. Republican. Methodist (ofcl. bd.). Home: West Chester, Pa. Died Nov. 8, 2003.

SYLBERT, RICHARD, production designer, art director; b. N.Y.C., Apr. 16, 1928; V.p. prodn. Paramount Pictures, 1975-78; prodn. designer, TV art dir. Studio City, Calif. Art dir.: (films) Patterns, 1956, Wind Across the Everglades, 1958, The Fugitive Kind, 1960, Mad Dog Coll, 1961, Splendor in the Grass, 1961, Walk on the Wild Side, 1962, Lilith, 1964, The Pawnbroker, 1965, The Heartbreak Kid, 1972, (TV series) Inner Sanctum, 1951-53; prodn. designer: (films) Crowded Paradise, 1956, (with Paul Sylbert) Baby Doll, 1956, Edge of the City, 1957, (with P. Sylbert) A Face in the Crowd, 1957, Murder, Inc., 1960, The Young Doctors, 1961, The Connection, 1962, How to Murder Your Wife, 1965, Who's Afraid of Virginia Woolf?, 1966 (Academy award best art direction 1966), Grand Prix, 1966, The Graduate, 1967, Rosemary's Baby, 1968, The April Fools, 1969, Catch-22, 1970, Carnal Knowledge, 1971, Fat City, 1972, The Day of the Dolphin, 1973, Chinatown, 1974 (Academy award nomination best art direction 1974), The Fortune, 1975, Shampoo, 1975 (Academy award nomination best art direction 1975), Players, 1979, Reds, 1981 (Academy award nomination best art direction 1981), Frances, 1982, Partners, 1982, Breathless, 1983, The Cotton Club, 1984 (Academy award nomination best art direction 1984), Under the Cherry Moon, 1986, Shoot to Kill, 1988, Tequila Sunrise, 1988, Bonfire of the Vanities, 1990, Mobsters, 1991, Carlito's Way, 1993; prodn. designer, art dir.: (films) Long Day's Journey into Night, 1962, (with Phil Jeffries) The Manchurian Candidate, 1962, All the Way Home, 1963, Dick Tracy, 1990 (Academy award best art direction 1990), (TV movie) Last Hours Before Midnight, 1975; assoc. prodr.: (films) What's New Pussycat?, 1965; visual arts cons.: (films) The Illustrated Man, 1969; set designer: (theatre) The Prisoner of Second Avenue, 1971-74, A Big Killing in Little Saigon, 1996; The Prince of Tides, 1991; Ruby Cairo, 1993; Mulholland Falls (also actor), 1996; Blood and Wine, 1997; My Best Friends Wedding, 1997; Red Corner, 1997. Died Mar. 23, 2002.

SZAZ, ZOLTAN MICHAEL, association executive; b. Budapest, Hungary, Jan. 3, 1930; came to U.S., 1950; s. Geza and Magda (Nagy) S.; m. Jayne Anne Davis, Sept. 7, 1957 (div. Nov. 1995); children: Claire Anne, Anna Maria, Mary Carol, Christopher Michael; m. Elizabeth Susan Almassy, Nov. 11, 1995. BA cum laude, St. John's U., Collegeville, Minn., 1951; MA in History, Cath. U. Am., 1953, PhD in Polit. Sci., 1956. Instr, asst. prof. history St. John's U., Jamaica, N.Y., 1960-64; assoc. prof. polit. sci. Seton Hall U., South Orange, N.J., 1965-68, Troy (Ala.) State U., 1971-72; exec. v.p. Am. Fgn. Policy Inst., Washington, 1968-98, pres., from 1998, immigration cons., 1987-97, pres., from 1998; exec. v.p. Nat. Confedn. Am. Ethnic Groups, Washington, 1979-90, nat. sec., from 1990, pres., from 1998. Author: Germany's Eastern Frontiers, 1960, Die deutsche Ostgrenze, 1961, Southeast Asia, 1984, Erdely Vedelmeben (In Defense of Transylvania), 1996. Speechwriter on ethnic issues 1960 Nixon Campaign; founding mem. Rep. Nat. Heritage Group Coun., Washington, 1970; sec. Internat. Rels. Am. Hungarian Fedn., 1965-90; founding pres. U. Profs. for Acad. Order, 1970-71. Recipient Ellis Island Medal of Honor, N.Y. State Bicentennial Commn., 1986, Medal of Honor, Transylvanian World Fedn., São Paulo, Brazil, 1983, Little Cross of the Order of Merit, Republic of Hungary, 1998, Hungarian Am. Order Hon., 1999. Mem. World Affairs Coun., Internat. Studies Assn. Roman Catholic. Home: Vienna, Va. Died Mar. 8, 2001.

TABACHNICK, IRVING I. A. pharmacologist/toxicologist; b. N.Y.C., July 20, 1924; s. Jacob Monish and Muriel (Roshinski) T.; m. Barbara Tabachnick, Sept. 3, 1951; children: John Frederick, Joan Leslie. AB, Harvard Coll., 1948; PhD, Yale U., 1953. Dept. head biochemistry Schering-Plough, Bloomfield, N.J., 1961-65, dept. head physiology/biochemistry, 1965-68, assoc. dir. physiology/biochemistry, 1968-70, dir. physiology/biochemistry, 1970-72, dir. biology, 1973, sr. dir. biology, 1973-77, v.p. rsch., 1977-85; ret., from 1989; cons., from 1989. Sec., treas. Am. Soc. for Pharmacology and Exptl. Therapeutics, 1978-81; cons. Republic of France, 1979-85. Sect. editor ACS, Washington, 1962-65. With U.S. Army, 1943-46. Home: N Caldwell, NJ. Died May 24, 2002.

TABLER, WILLIAM BENJAMIN, architect; b Momence, Ill., Oct. 28, 1914; s. Clyde Lyeth and Frances Beatrice (Ridley) T.; m. Phyllis May Baker, June 12, 1937; children: William, Judith. BS cum laude, Harvard U., 1936, B.Arch., M.Arch., Harvard U., 1939. Architect specializing in hotels; prin. works include Hilton hotels in N.Y.C., Dallas, Pitts., San Francisco, Toronto, Rye Town, N.Y., Long Branch and Woodcliff Lake, N.J., Washington and Izmir, Turkey; Conrad Internat. Istanbul, Turkey; Intercontinental hotels in Lahore, Rawapindi, Jamaica, Ras Al Khaimah, Jeddah, Nairobi, Lusaka, Dacca, Amman, Karachi and Jerusalem; Marriott Bklyn. and Phila., Sheraton Universal City, New Orleans, Brussels and Sheraton Centre, Toronto; Meridien hotels in Colombo, Sri Lanka, Cairo and Heliopolis, Egypt and Jakarta, Indonesia, Othon Palace in Rio and Bahia;

Registry in Bloomington and Scottsdale; Grand Kempinski, Dallas; Hosts of Houston and Tampa; Sonesta Bermuda; Radisson Duluth, Lough Key, Ireland; New Otani L.A., Chosen, Korea; Stouffers, Chgo. and St. Louis; Bonaventure Montreal; Hanover, Woodstock and Princeton Inns; 15 Hospitality Motor Inns; also Harper and Stony Brook Coll. Dormitories; many others; former mem. bldg. constrn. adv. council N.Y.C. Bldg. Dept. Bd. dirs. Manhattan Eye, Ear and Throat Hosp., Community Hosp., Glen Cove. Served as lt. USNR, 1943-46, PTO. Recipient Horatio Alger award Am. Schs. and Colls. Assn., 1958; 1st prize for excellence in design Internat. Hotel, Queens C. of C., N.Y., 1958; Producers Council award, 1967 Fellow AIA (nat. chmn. bldg. codes com., pres. N.Y. chpt. 1967-68), ASCE; mem. Royal Inst. Brit. Architects, Bldg. Research Inst., N.Y. Bldg. Congress, NYU Hotel and Restaurant Soc., Am. Nat. Standards Inst. (exec. com. constrn. standards bd.), Nat. Fire Protection Assn. (chmn. sect. com. on residential occupancies, com. on safety to life), Ave. of Americas Assn. (bd. dirs.), Harvard Club (bd. mgrs., exec. com., chmn. house com.), Piping Rock Club. Clubs: Harvard (bd. mgrs., exec. com., chmn. house com. N.Y.C.). Home: Glen Head, NY. Died Feb. 3, 2004.

TAIT, JOHN CHARLES, Canadian government official; b. Montreal, Que., Can., Dec. 4, 1945; s. John Watterson and Eleanor (Raymond) T.; m. Sonia Plourde. BA, Princeton U., 1967, Oxford (Eng.) U., Eng., 1969; MA, Oxford (Eng.) U., 1995; BCL, McGill U., Montreal, 1972. Bar: Que. 1974. Asst. sec. Cabinet Privy Coun. Office, Can., 1978-81; asst. dep. minister Can. Dept. Indian Affairs, 1981-83, Can. Dept. Justice, 1983-86, dep. solicitor gen., 1986-88, dep. minister of justice, 1988-94; sr. advisor Privy Coun. Office, Ottawa, from 1994. Skelton-Clark fellow Queen's U., 1994-95. Sr. fellow Can. Ctr. for Mgmt. Devel., 1994-96; coord. of Security and Intelligence, Privy Coun. Office, 1996-98; Rhodes scholar, Eng., 1967. Mem. Can. Bar Assn. Avocation: sports. Home: Ottawa, Canada. Died Aug., 1999.

TALBERT, BOB, newspaper columnist; Columnist Detroit Free Press. Died Nov. 19, 1999.

TALONE, ROSALIE MURRAY, secondary school educator; b. Phila., Aug. 30, 1900; d. Patrick Joseph and Rosanna (Brady) Murray; m. Ferdinando Joseph Talone, Sept. 6, 1941. Student, Eastman U., Temple U., Columbia U.; cert. piano, Combs Coll. Music, Phila., 1927. Studied with Breithaupt Group, 1928, asst. to Am. rep., 1928-38; tchr. Phila.; pvt. tchr. Bryn Mawr, Pa., from 1941. Mem. Bryn Mawr Civic Assn., 1950—, Rosemont (Pa.) Villa Nova Assn., 1950—; pres. Women's Bd. Med. Coll. Pa., Phila., 1985-87; v.p. Matinee Musical Club Phila., 1985—, Phila. Orch. Opera Co. Recipient Outstanding Civic Svc. in Music award Chapel of Four Chaplains, Phila., 1977, Disting. Svc. award Pa. State Music Tchrs. Assn., 1970. Mem. Phila. Music Tchrs. (pres. 1963-73, pres. Forum 3 1946-49), Nat. Music Tchrs., Morning Musicals. Republican. Roman Catholic. Avocations: reading, gardening. Home: Bryn Mawr, Pa. Died Jan. 15, 1999.

TANNER, ROBERT HUGH, engineer, consultant; b. London, July 22, 1915; s. George John and Evelyn (Stratton) T.; m. Joan Margaret Garnham, July 6, 1940; children: Christopher John, Rosemary June, Peter Pinckney, David Stephen. BS in Engring., U. London, 1936, MS in Engring., 1962; LLD, Concordia U., 1989. From TV to rsch. engr. BBC, London, 1936-47; from engr. to dir. info. No. Electric Co., Ltd., Ottawa, Can., Ont., 1947-70; dir. info. Bell-No. Rsch., Ottawa, Can., Ont., 1970-72; pres. IEEE, N.Y.C., 1972; dir. indsl. rsch. Can. Dept. Comm., Ottawa, 1973-75; pvt. practice cons. engr. Naples, Fla., from 1975. Cons. in field. Inventor various patents. Maj. Brit. Army, 1939—45, ETO. Fellow IEEE (pres. 1972, McNaughton Gold medal 1974, Pratt award 1981, Award for Engring Professionalism, 1993), Acoustical Soc. Am., Engring. Inst. Can., Instn. of Elec. Engrs.; mem. Nat. Coun. Acoustical Cons. (bd. dirs. 1982-88). Episcopalian. Home: Naples, Fla. Died Nov. 2, 2002.

TANNER, WILLIAM FRANCIS, JR., geology educator; b. Milledgeville, Fla., Feb. 4, 1917; s. William Francis and Robbie Belle (Carter) T.; m. Julia Katherine Rigby, July 17, 1938; children: William Francis III, Bruce R., Julianne Tanner Talley. BA, Baylor U., 1937; MA, Tex. Tech U., 1939; PhD, U. Okla., 1953. Teaching asst. Tex. Tech U., Lubbock, 1937-39; oil editor Amarillo (Tex.) Times, 1939-41, mng. editor, 1945-46; asst. prof. geology Okla. Bapt. U., Shawnee, 1946-51; spl. instr. U. Okla., Norman, 1951-54; geologist Shell Oil Co., Denver, 1954; vis. prof. Fla. State U., Tallahassee, 1954, assoc. prof., 1956, prof., 1966, Regents prof., from 1974. Mem. exec. com. Tertiary-Quaternary Inst., Lincoln, Nebr., 1986-93. Author 2 books; editor Coastal Rsch., 1962—, Coastal Sedimentology Symposium Series, 1974—; contbr. over 350 articles to profl. jours. Bd. dirs. home mission bd. So. Bapt. Conv., Atlanta, 1985-93, mem. exec. com., 1989-92; mem. state bd. missions Fla. Bapt. Conv., Jacksonville, 1989—. With USNR, 1941-45. Avocations: photography, music, travel, linguistics. Home: Tallahassee, Fla. Died Apr. 9, 2000.

TAPLEY, DONALD FRASER, university official, physician, educator; b. Woodstock, N.B., Can., May 19, 1927; s. Roy Donald and Velma (Fraser) T.; m. Caroline Southall, Sept. 14, 1957; children: Katherine, Elizabeth, Sarah Tapley Bangs. BS, Acadia U., 1948; MD, U. Chgo., 1952. Intern Presbyn. Hosp., N.Y.C., 1952-53, asst. resident, 1953-54, asst. attending physician, 1957-64, assoc. attending physician, 1964-72, attending physician, from 1972. Life Ins. Research fund fellow dept. physiol. chemistry Johns Hopkins U., Balt., 1954-56; Jane Coffin Childs fellow dept. physiol. chemistry Oxford U., Eng., 1956-57; asst. prof. medicine Columbia U., 1956-64, assoc. prof., 1964-72, prof., 1972—, assoc. dean for faculty affairs Coll. Physicians and Surgeons, 1970-73, acting dean, 1973-74, dean, 1974-84, alumni prof., sr. dep. v.p., 1984—. Contbr. numerous articles to profl. publs.; assoc. editor Endocrinology Mag., 1963-68. Trustee Morris Jumel Mansion, The Riverkeeper, The Mary Imogene Bassett Hosp., Cooperstown, N.Y. Mem. Am. Soc. Clinical Investigation, Endocrine Soc., Am. Thyroid Assn., Harvey Soc., N.Y. Med. and Surg. Soc. Home: Palisades, NY. Died Dec. 16, 1999.

TAPLIN, FRANK E., JR., trustee education and arts institutions and associations; b. Cleve., June 22, 1915; s. Frank Elijah and Edith R. (Smith) T.; m. Ngaio I. Thornton, Sept. 3, 1943 (div. Mar. 1951); children: Caroline I. Taplin Ruschell, Jennifer Taplin Jerome, David F.; m. Margaret A. Eaton, Apr. 27, 1953; stepchildren: Jennifer A. Sichel Dickerman, Martha D. Sichel Kelly, Susan Sichel Panella. BA in History, Princeton U., 1937; MA in Jurisprudence (Rhodes scholar), Oxford U., 1939; JD, Yale U., 1941; MusD (hon.), Cleve. Inst. Music, 1981; DHL (hon.), Fordham U., 1984; Dr. Mus. Arts (hon.), Manhattan Sch. Music, 1984; LLD (hon.), Rider Coll., 1988. Bar: Ohio 1946. With firm Jones, Day Cockley & Reavis, Cleve., 1946-50; dir. NACCO Industries, Inc., 1946—97, trustee Environ. Def. Fund., 1990-2001; asst. to Sen. Taft in Ohio senatorial campaign, 1950; pvt. bus. investments Cleve., 1951-57; asst. to pres. Princeton U., 1957-59; chmn. bd. Scurry-Rainbow Oil, Ltd., 1954-74; trustee Inst. for Advanced Study, 1972-88; pres. Cleve. Inst. Music, 1952-56; trustee Cleve. Orch., 1946-57, pres., 1955-57, Nat. Council Met. Opera, 1961-64; dir. Met. Opera Assn., 1961-91, pres., chief exec. officer, 1977-84; hon. trustee Bradford (Mass.) Coll.; trustee Princeton (N.J.) Day Sch., 1966-72, Princeton Area United Community Fund, 1963-76; mem. Princeton U. Music Dept. Adv. Council, 1960-85, chmn., 1965-71; trustee Sarah Lawrence Coll., 1969-77, chmn., 1973-77, hon. trustee, 1977—; trustee Lincoln Center for Performing Arts, 1972-88, vice chmn., 1981-84; trustee, founding pres. Lincoln Center Chamber Music Soc., 1969-73; fellow Morgan Library; mem. council Friends Princeton Library; chmn. bd. Marlboro Sch. Music, 1964-70; trustee Woodrow Wilson Nat. Fellowship Found., 1972—93, Am. Schs. Oriental Rsch., 1970—75, Western Res. Hist. Soc., Cleve.; internat. bd. dirs. United World Colls., London, 1973-76; also chmn. United World Colls. (U.S. com.), 1973-75; bd. dirs. Am. Friends of Covent Garden and Royal Ballet, Friends of Aldeburgh Festival.; mem. vestry Trinity Ch., Princeton, 1984-87. Chmn. adv. coun. Princeton U. Environ. Inst., 1998-2003. Vice chmn. council of fellows Morgan Library, 1987-90. Served from ensign to lt. comdr. USNR, 1941-46. Decorated hon. mem. (mil. div.) Order Brit. Empire.; recipient Gold Medal award Nat. Inst. Social Scis., 1983, Disting. Service award Third St. Music Sch. Settlement, 1983 Mem. ABA, Assn. Am. Rhodes Scholars, Am. Philos. Soc., Am.-Scandinavian Found. (exec. trustee), Univ. Club (N.Y.C.), Century Assn. (N.Y.C., bd.mgmt. 1981-84), Springdale Golf Club, Nassau Club (Princeton), Pretty Brook Club (Princeton), Tavern Club (Cleve.). Home: Princeton, NJ. Died May 11, 2003.

TAPPER, DAVID, pediatric surgeon; b. Balt., Aug. 26, 1945; s. Herman A. and Sylvia Phyllis (Golomb) T.; m. Susan Irene Wagner, June 25, 1968; children: JoEllen, Erica, Jacalyn, Aaron. BS, U. Md., College Park, 1966; MD, U. Md., Balt., 1970. Intern and resident in surgery U. Calif. San Francisco Med. Ctr., 1970-73; pediatric surg. rsch. fellow Boston Children's Hosp., 1973-75; sr. and chief surg. resident U. Calif., San Francisco, 1975-77; sr. and chief pediatric surg. fellow Children's Hosp., Boston, 1977-79; asst. prof. surgery Harvard Med. Sch., Boston, 1979-83; surgeon-in-chief Children's Hosp. Med. Ctr., Seattle, from 1983; prof. surgery and pediatrics U. Wash., Seattle, from 1983, vice-chmn. dept. surgery, from 1986. Exec. com. Am. Bd. Surgery, Phila., 1996-98, chmn. surg. forum, 1998-2000. Maj. USAR, 1971-82. Fellow ACS; mem. Am. Surg Assn., Am. Pediatric Surgery Assn. (bd. govs. 1993-96, pres. 2001), Soc. Univ. Surgeons, Pacific Coast Surg. Soc. (councilor N.W. region 1999—), Halsted Surg. Soc., Seattle Surg. Soc. (pres. 1999). Jewish. Home: Mercer Island, Wash. Died July 23, 2002.

TAQUEY, CHARLES HENRI, writer, consultant; b. Paris; came to U.S., 1937, naturalized, 1942; s. Henri and Marguerite (Normand) T.; m. Ruth McVitty, Feb. 1, 1947 (dec. May 1994); children: Antony, Chantal Sanders. BS, U. Paris, 1929; Lauréat, Ecole Libre des Sciences Politiques, 1933; Licencié and Lauréat, D.E.S, Paris Law Sch., 1934. French Treasury rep., Paris, London, Berlin, N.Y.C., 1934-39; local currencies mgr. ECA, 1948-51; staff officer Exec. Office of Pres., 1952-57; fgn. service econ. officer Am. embassies Phnom-Penh, Cambodia, Tunis, Tunisia, Kingston, Jamaica; also detailed to Dept. Commerce as dep. dir. fgn. activities mgmt., 1957-70. Mgmt. cons., ecol. economist (internat. trade and resources recovery), 1970—; expert witness Internat. Trade Commn., Ways and Means Com. U.S. Ho. of Reps., GAO, fgn. govts. Author: German Financial Crisis, 1931, Richard Cobden, 1938, Trusts and Patents, 1946, Obstacles to Development in Indonesia, 1952, Fisheries in Cambodia, 1959, Against Full Employment, 1973, Democracy and Socialism, 1976, Transnational Corporations and the State, 1979, Beyond Free Trade, 1983, Free Trade, Morality of Nations, 1987. Served as lt., arty. French Army, 1940; lt., arty. AUS, 1942-46; capt. 1952. Mem. Consumers for World Trade Died Apr. 1, 1999.

TARADASH, DANIEL IRWIN, screenwriter; b. Louisville, Jan. 29, 1913; s. William Taradash and Elizabeth Sylvia Bornstein; m. Madeleine Forbes; children: Jan Elizabeth, Meg, William Brian. AB, Harvard U., 1933, LLB, 1936. Screenwriter: Knock On Any Door, 1949, Don't Bother to Knock, 1952, From Here to Eternity, 1953, Desiree, 1954, Picnic, 1956, Bell, Book and Candle, 1958, Hawaii, 1966, The Other Side of Midnight, 1977, and others; dir., screenwriter Storm Center, 1956; playwright: Red Gloves, 1948, There Was a Little Girl, 1960. Trustee Am. Film Inst., 1967-69, The Humanitas Prize, 1979—; panelist Nat. Endowment for the Arts, 1975-85. Served with U.S. Army, 1941-46. Page One award N.Y. Newspaper Guild, 1954, Prix du Chevalier de la Barre Cannes Film Festival, 1957. Mem. Acad. Motion Picture Arts and Scis. (bd. govs. 1964-74, 1990-93, v.p. 1968-70, pres. 1970-73; Acad. award 1953), Writers Guild of Am.-West (pres. 1977-79; Valentine Davies award 1971, Morgan Cox award 1988, Edmund H. North award 1991, Laurel award for Lifetime Screenwriting Achievement 1996), The Dramatists Guild, Delta Kappa Alpha. Democrat. Jewish. Avocations: stamp collecting, breeding and showing dalmatians. Home: Beverly Hills, Calif. Died Feb. 22, 2003.

TARAS, JOHN, ballet master, choreographer; b. N.Y.C., Apr. 18, 1919; s. Vassil and Varvara (Dohunyk) T. Student, NYU, Sch. Am. Ballet. Choreographer, repetiteur, dancer Ballet Theater, 1942-46; asst. regisseur Col. De Basil's Ballet Russes, 1947; ballet master, choreographer Grand Ballets De Marquis De Cuevas, 1948-59, N.Y.C. Ballet, 1959-84; ballet master Theatre National de L'Opera, Paris, France, 1969-70; assoc. dir. Am. Ballet Theatre, 1984-90. Dir. ballet Deutsche's Opera, Berlin, Germany, 1971-73. Decorated officer Order Arts and Letters (France), 1985. Home: New York, NY. Died Apr. 2, 2004.

TAUBER, LASZLO NANDOR, physician; b. Budapest, Hungary, Feb. 18, 1915; came to U.S., 1947; Grad. summa cum laude, Real Gymnasium, Budapest, 1932; MD, U. Budapest, 1938. Diplomate Hungarian Bd. Surgery, Am. Bd. Abdominal Surgery. Resident in gen. surgery U. Budapest Sch. Medicine, 1938-42, chief resident St. Elizabeth's Hosp., 1942-44; acting chief surgeon Internat. Red Cross Hosp., Budapest, 1944-45; adj. surgeon-in-chief Pest Izr. Hitkozseg Hosp. Budapest, 1945-46; asst. to Dr. H. Olivecrona Neurosurg. Clinic, Univ. Stockholm, 1946-47, post-grad. fellow, 1947-48; teaching fellow neurosurgery George Washington U. Med. Sch., Washington, 1948-50; mem. gen. surgery staff Capital Hill Hosp., 1949-78, Sibley Meml. Hosp., Washington, 1951-78, assoc. attending surgeon, 1960-66, Children's Hosp., 1951-78; clin. prof. surgery George Washington U. Med. Sch., Washington; mem. gen. surgery staff, dir. dept. surgery, med. dir., dir. med. edn. Jefferson Meml. Hosp., Alexandria, Va., from 1965. Contbr. articles to profl. jours. Past trustee Am. U., Washington; bd. visitors Boston U. Recipient Medal of Merit for heroic work during the Holocaust, Red Cross, Golden Plate award Am. Acad. Achievement, 1985, Maimoindes award Anti-Defamation League of B'nai B'rith, 1986. Fellow ACS, Internat. Coll. Surgeons, Southeastern Surg. Congress, Am. Soc. Abdominal Surgeons; mem. N.Y. Med. Soc. (life). Died July 28, 2002.

TAYER, DONALD S. lawyer; b. N.Y.C., Apr. 23, 1932; s. Nathan and Pearl Tayer; m. Joyce Hill, Sept. 5, 1954; children: Lisa, Marc. BA, Swarthmore Coll., 1953; LLB, Harvard U., 1956. Bar: N.Y. 1956, Calif. 1960, U.S. Dist. Ct. (no. dist.), Calif. 1960, U.S. Ct. Appeals (9th cir.) 1975, U.S. Supreme Ct. 1978. Atty. Port of N.Y. Authority, N.Y.C., 1956-59, AEC, Berkeley, Calif., 1959-60; ptnr. Beeson, Tayer, & Bodine, San Francisco, from 1960. Professorial lectr. Golden Gate U., San Francisco, 1975--. Mayor, mem. city coun. Ciy of Tiburon (Calif.), 1974-78; bd. dirs. Yerba Buena Gardens, San Francisco, 1985—, pres., 1989—; mem. San Francisco chpt. Am. Jewish Com., 1960—, chmn., 1978-81. Mem. ABA, Calif. Bar Assn., N.Y. Bar Assn., San Francisco Bar Assn., Tiburon Peninsula Club, Commonwealth Club. Democrat. Jewish. Home: Belvedere Tiburon, Calif. Died Oct. 26, 2001.

TAYLOR, BARBARA JO ANNE HARRIS, government official, civic and political worker; b. Providence, Sept. 09; d. Ross Cameron and Anita (Coia) Harris; m. Richard Powell Taylor, Dec. 19, 1959; 1 child, Douglas Howard. Student, Georgetown U., 1956-59, 62-63, BS cum laude, 1963. Adminstrv. asst. profl. devel. and welfare NEA, Washington, 1956-59; asst. to dir. Georgetown U., Washington, 1956-59; exec. asst. All Am. Conf. to Combat Communism, Washington, 1960; spl. legis. asst. mil. affairs to chmn. mil. R & D subcom. U.S. Senate Armed Svcs. Com., 1971-72; U.S. nat. commr. UNESCO, 1982—2002, mem. exec. com. U.S. nat. commn., 1983—2002, sr. advisor 22d gen. conf., 1983. Speaker in field. Contbr. articles to profl. jours. Del. numerous internat. confs.; U.S. commr. Nat. Commn. Librs. and Info. Sci., 1985-96, mem. various coms.; gen. chmn. George Bush for Pres. Md. State Steering Com., 1987-88; co-chmn. Md. del. Rep. Nat. Conv., 1988, 92; dep. chmn. Md. Victory '88, Bush-Quayle Campaign; mem. Nat. Fin. Com. Reagan for Pres., 1980, Reagan-Bush, 1984; state fin. chmn. Md. Rep. Party, 1980; mem. Nat. Rep. Club; mem. exec. bd. Salvation Army Aux., Washington, 1967-75, chmn. membership com., 1969-70, chmn. fund-raising com., 1968-69, mem. exec. com. of exec. bd., 1970-75, treas., mem. fin. com., 1970-71, v.p., 1971-72, historian, 1972-73, editor newsletter, 1968-69, chmn. nominating com., 1974-75, spl. awards. for exceptional vol. svc., 1969, 72; mem. exec. bd. Welcome to Washington Internat., 1969-74, bd. advisers, 1969-74, dir. workshop, 1969-74; exec. bd. Am.

Opera Sch. Soc., Washington, 1970-85, v.p., 1974-85; mem. Episc. Ch. Home for Aged Women's Aux., 1970-75, Episc. Ctr. for Emotionally Disturbed Children Women's Aux., 1970-75; exec. bd. St. David's Episc. Ch. Aux., 1970-72, 73-74; bd. dirs., treas. Spanish-Portuguese Study Group, 1970-72; mem. exec. bd. League Rep. Women D.C., 1964-67, 75-77, treas., 1964-67; former mem. nat. coun. Women's Nat. Rep. Club, N.Y.C., chmn. Washington-Md.-Va. legis. com., 1970-75; mem. Nat. Fedn. Rep. Women, 1964; mem. nat. fin. com. Reagan for Pres., 1979-80; mem. governing bd. Capital Speakers Club, 1973-75, chmn. by-laws com., 1973-74; mem. exec. bd. Nat. Vols. in Action, 1975-77; mem. adv. com. Rock Creek Found. Mental Health, 1982-87; mem. 50th anniversary com. Save the Children; mem. fund-raising com. Washington Choral Arts Soc., 1982-84; state fin. chmn. Reagan-Bush campaign Md. Rep. Com., 1980; Md. coord. Nat. Inaugural Com., 1981, 85; trustee Crossnore Sch., Inc., N.C., 1983—, vice chmn. bd; trustee Kate Duncan Smith DAR Sch., Grant, Ala., 1983-86, Tamassee (S.C.) DAR Sch., 1983-86; adviser Bacone Am. Indian Coll., Inc., Muscogee, Okla., 1983-88. Mem. ALA, Spl. Librs. Assn., Coun. on Libr. Resources (commn. on preservation and access), Am. Libr. Trustees Assn., Libr. Adminstrn. and Mgmt. Assn., Assn. Coll. and Rsch. Librs., Am. Antiquarian Soc., Internat. Platform Assn., Spanish-Portuguese Study Group, Nat. Lawyers' Wives, Nat. Capital Law League, Nat. Soc. DAR (chmn. nat. resolutions com. 1980-83, chmn. nat. Nat. Soc. DAR sch. com. 1983-86; state historian 1978-80, mem. state bd. mgmt. 1973—, Nat. Soc. DAR libr. gen., mem. exec. com. and nat. corp. bd. mgmt. 1986-89, chmn. nat. commemorative events com. 1992-95, 98-2001, Nat. Soc. DAR libr. centennial com. 1995-98), Nat. Soc. Children Am. Revolution (sr. nat. asst. registrar 1978-80, mem. sr. nat. bd. mgmt. 1978-80, sr. nat. exec. com. 1978-80), Nat. Assn. Parliamentarians, World Affairs Coun., League of Rep. Women, Md. Fedn. Rep. Women, Women's Nat. Republican Club, Nat. Fed. Rep. Women, Commn. on Preservation and Access, Lit. Vols. Am. (Washington Met. area affiliate), Exec. Women in Govt., Gen. Soc. Mayflower Descendants, Am. News Women's Club, Internat. Club, Capitol Hill Club, Univ. Club Washington, Washington Club, Congl. Country Club (Potomac, Md.). Home: Germantown, Md. Died Oct. 29, 2002.

TAYLOR, ELAINE CLAIRE NELSON, experimental psychologist; b. Meadville, Pa., Dec. 2, 1927; d. John David and Martha Margaret (Zurfluh) Nelson; m. John Edward Taylor, Sept. 10, 1949 (div. 1970); children: Jenny L., Jess N. BS, Pa. State U., 1949; MA, Bowling Green State U., 1951; PhD, State U. Iowa, 1954. Sr. scientist Human Resources Rsch. Orgn., Alexandria, Va., 1954-57, cons., 1960-63, sr. staff scientist, 1967-84; pvt. cons., Carmel Valley, Calif., 1984-91; cons. FMC Ordnance Engring., San Jose, Calif., 1977-80, RCA Edn. Programs, Cherry Hill, N.J., 1976; cons. McFann-Gray Assocs., Monterey, Calif., 1984-85, The Woodside Summit Group, Mountain View, Calif., 1984-85, The Nellie Thomas Inst., Monterey, 1984-90. Bd. dirs., sec. Cornerstone 2000 Literacy Alliance, 1993-95. U.S. Army Tng. Mgmt. Inst., Fort Eustis, Va., 1975-76, Calif. Dept. Mental Hygiene, Sacramento, 1972. Author tech. papers, book chpts. Sec. Property Owners' Assn., Carmel Valley, 1962-63; mem. adv. com. Monterey Peninsula Water Mgmt. Dist. (Calif.), 1984-87; mem. bd. dirs., sec. Carmel Valley Environ. Def. Fund, 1989-92. NIMH grantee, 1972-74. Fellow Am. Psychol. Assn. (pres. div. mil. psychology, 1978-79, sec.-treas. 1975-77, editor newsletter 1973-75); mem. Human Factors Soc., Sigma Xi. Democrat. Died July 18, 1998. Home: Carmel Valley, Calif.

TAYLOR, KENNETH J. diagnostic sonologist; b. Rochford, Essex, Eng., Mar. 8, 1939; s. William Albert and Florence (Soulsby) T.; m. Anne Bowen Simpkins, Apr. 8, 1964 (div. Nov. 1968); 1 child, Sally-Anne; m. Caroline Rix, May 17, 1975; children: Andrew, Ian. BSc, London U., 1961; MBBS, London U./Guys Hosp., Eng., 1964, PhD, 1972; MD, U. London, 1975; MA, FACP, Yale U., 1979. House surgeon Royal Surrey Hosp., Guildford, Eng., 1964-66; sr. house surgeon Guys Maudsley Hosp., London, 1966-67; jr. lectr. Guys Hosp. Med. Sch., London, 1967-70, lectr., 1970-72; sr. fellow Royal Marsden Hosp., Sutton, Surrey, Eng., 1973-75; assoc. prof. radiology Yale U., New Haven, 1975-77; assoc. Yale-New Haven Hosp., 1975—2003; med. dir. Yale New Haven Sch. for Ultrasonography, 1975—2003; assoc. prof. Yale U., New Haven, 1977-79, tenured prof., from 1979, prof. vascular surgery and ob-gyn., from 2000. Co-dir. Yale Ctr. for Ultrasonics and Sonics, New Haven, 1991—; dir. Yale Vascular Lab., 1992—; ad hoc adv. bd. NIH, Washington. Chmn. editl. bd. Clinics in Diagnostic Ultrasound, 1978-2000; co-editor: Doppler in Clinic Diagnosis, 1988, 2d edit., 1995, assoc. editor Radiology Jour., 1992-97; author: Atlas of Ultrasound, 1978-2001, 2d edit., 1984; cons. to editor Radiology Jour., 1997-2000; mem. editl. bd. Ultrasound Med. Biology, 1975-2003, Jour. Ultrasound Medicine, 1980-2001, 02-03, Clin. Ultrasound, Jour. Clin. Ultrasound. Bd. dirs. Friends of Hospice, New Haven, 1980. Lt. Royal Navy Res., 1962-65. Rsch. grantee Am. Cancer Soc., N.Y., 1976, 82, NIH Cancer Inst., Washington, 1988-89, 88-91. Fellow ACP, Am. Inst. Ultrasound Med. (bd. gov. 1978-82); mem. Radiol. Soc. N.Am. Achievements include pioneering applications for grey scale ultrasound, applications of Doppler ultrasound; ultrasonic contrast agents. Home: Guilford, Conn. Died Feb. 15, 2003.

TAYLOR, NELSON FEREBEE, law educator; b. Oxford, N.C., Jan. 24, 1921; s. Leonidas C. and Martha (Ferebee) T.; children— Louise Ferebee, Sarah Ellington, Martha Gregory. AB (Herbert Worth Jackson scholar), U. N.C., 1942; LL.B. cum laude, Harvard, 1949; AB (Rhodes scholar), Oxford (Eng.) U., 1951, MA, 1955; grad., Advanced Mgmt. Program, Harvard, 1956. Bar: N.C. 1949, N.Y. 1953. Asso. firm Arthur, Dry & Dole, N.Y.C., 1951-57; partner Arthur, Dry, Kalish, Taylor & Wood (and predecessor), 1958-70; asso. gen. counsel Uniroyal, Inc., N.Y.C., 1961-70; v.p. adminstrn. U. N.C., 1970-72; chancellor U. N.C. at Chapel Hill, 1972-80, prof. law, 1980-91. Served to lt. USNR, 1942-46. Decorated Bronze Star. Mem. N.C. State Bar, Phi Beta Kappa. Mem. P.E. Ch. Home: Chapel Hill, NC. Died Feb. 25, 2004.

TAYLOR, WILLIAM DAVIS, newspaperman; b. Boston, Apr. 2, 1908; s. William Osgood and Mary (Moseley) T.; m. Mary Hammond, 1931 (dec. 1947); children: William Osgood, Anna Taylor Freeman; m. Ann C. Macy, Nov. 1947; children: Thomas Macy, Margaret Moseley (Mrs. Richard Kane), Wendy Elizabeth (Mrs. William Patriquin), James Morgan. Student, Harvard U., 1927-31; LLD, Colby Coll., 1968, Framingham State Coll., 1983; D of Journalism, Suffolk U., 1974; D of Humane Services, Mass. Maritime Acad., 1975. With Globe Newspaper Co., 1931—94, treas., 1937-40, gen. mgr., 1940; pub. Boston Globe, 1955-94, also chmn. bd., 1963-94, retired, 1994; chmn. bd., dir. Affiliated Publs., Inc. Dir. Met-Sunday Newspapers, Inc., N.Y.C., Million Market Newspapers, Inc. Past chmn. bd. Am. Comml. Fish Expn., Inc.; mem. exec. bd. Boston council Boy Scouts Am.; bd. dirs. Am. Cancer Soc., Hurricane Island Outward Bound Sch.; bd. overseers Harvard, Vineyard Open Land Found.; past pres. USS Constitution Mus., Charlestown, Mass.; past pres. bd. trustees Noble and Greenough Sch., Dedham, Mass., Woods Hole Oceanographic Instn. Recipient Elijah Lovejoy award Colby Coll., 1975 Mem. Am. Newspaper Pubs. Assn. (past pres. and dir.), SEA (assoc. Woods Hole, Mass. chpt.). Home: Boston, Mass. Died Feb. 19, 2002.

TAYMOR, MELVIN L. obstetrician-gynecologist, endocrinologist; b. Brockton, Mass., Feb. 10, 1919; s. Aaron and Emma Bertle (Madfis) T.; m. Betty Bernstein, June 7, 1942; children: Michael, Laurie, Julie. BA, Johns Hopkins U., 1940; MD, Tufts U., 1943. Diplomate Am. Bd. Surgery. Resident in surgery Peter Bent Brigham Hosp., Boston, 1947-50, chief gynecology dept., 1971-76; USPH fellow Mass. Gen. Hosp., Boston, 1950-51; instr. ob-gyn. Boston U. Sch. Medicine, 1951-53; assoc. in surgery Harvard Med. Sch., Boston, 1955-60, asst. prof., then assoc. prof., 1960-82, prof. ob-gyn., from 1982; sr. obstetrician-gynecologist Brigham & Women's Hosp., Boston, from 1971; reproductive endocrinologist Lahey Clinic, Burlington, Mass., from 1991. Author: (textbooks) Management of Infertility, 1966, Infertility: A Guide for Clinicians, 1989; editor: (textbook) Program in Gynecology, 1970, 3d edit., 1986; contbr. over 190 articles to med. jours. Treas. Am. Fertility Soc., Birmingham, Ala., 1960-66. Lt. (j.g.) USN, 1944-45, PTO. Fellow ACOG; mem. Am. Ob-Gyn Soc., Am. Soc. Reproductive Medicine (treas.), Boston Obstetrical Soc. (sec. 1966-72), Soc. for Gynecol. Investigation, Endocrine Soc., Honolulu Ob-Gyn. Soc. (hon.), Pacific Coast Fertility Soc. (hon.). Avocations: gardening, tennis, sailing, skiing, classical music, painting. Home: Newton, Mass. Deceased.

TECLAFF, LUDWIK ANDRZEJ, law educator, consultant, author, lawyer; b. Czestochowa, Poland, Nov. 14, 1918; came to U.S., 1952, naturalized, 1958; s. Emil and Helena (Tarnowska) T.; m. Eileen Johnson, May 30, 1952. dec. Mag Iuris, Oxford (Eng.) U., 1944; MS, Columbia U., 1955; LLM, NYU, 1961, JSD, 1965. Attaché Polish Fgn. Ministry, London, 1943-46; consul in Ireland, Polish Govt. in London, 1946-52; student libr. Columbia U. Sch. Libr. Sci., 1953-54; libr. Bklyn. Pub. Libr., 1954-59; rsch. librar. Fordham U. Sch. Law, 1959-62, asst. prof. law, 1962-65, assoc. prof. law, 1965-68, prof. 1968-89, prof. emeritus, 1989—, dir. law libr., 1962-86; cons. in field. With Polish Army, 1940-43, France, Eng. Recipient Clyde Eagleton award in internat. law NYU, 1965. Mem. Am. Soc. Internat. Law, Internat. Law Assn., Am. Law Librs. Assn., Internat. Coun. Environ. Law, Internat. Water Law Assn. Roman Catholic. Author: The River Basin in History and Law, 1967; Abstraction and Use of Water, 1972; Legal and Institutional Responses to Growing Water Demand, 1978; Economic Roots of Oppression, 1984, Water Law in Historical Perspective, 1985; editor: (with Albert E Utton) International Environmental Law, 1974, Water in a Developing World, 1978, International Groundwater Law, 1981, Transboundary Resources Law, 1987; contbr. articles on water law, law of the sea and environ. law to law jours. Home: Saint Petersburg, Fla. Died May 29, 2003.

TEETER, ROBERT M. public opinion pollster; b. Mich., Feb. 5, 1939; s. Howard M. and Marion (Warner) T.; m. Elizabeth Carter, June 17, 1967; children: Katherine Carter, John Warner. AB, Albion Coll., 1961; MA, Mich. State U., 1964. Grad. asst., instr. Albion (Mich.) Coll., 1961-64; instr. Adrian (Mich.) Coll., 1964-66; with Market Opinion Rsch. Co., Detroit, 1967—79, exec. v.p., 1973-79. Former strategist, poll taker for Pres. George Bush; mem. adv. com. small and rural areas Census Bur. Author articles in field. Trustee Albion Coll. Mem. Nat. Assn. Polit. Pollsters, Am. Polit. Sci. Assn., Nat. Coun. Pub. Polls, Mich. C. of C. (bd. dirs.), Econ Club Detroit, Detroit Club. Republican. Presbyterian. Died June 13, 2004.

TEKEYAN, VARTAN, bishop; b. Adana, Turkey, Mar. 5, 1921; arrived in Lebanon, 1921; s. Avétis Tékéyan and Khatoon Demirjian. PhB, licenciate in theology, Gregorian U., Rome, 1942, D in Canon Law, 1947; philology diploma, St. Joseph U., Beirut, Lebanon, 1952. Ordained Armenian Catholic priest, 1944, consecrated bishop, 1973. Parish priest, Beirut, 1949-72. Mem., pres. Ecclesiastical Tribunal, Beirut, 1946-73; mem. Papal Commn. for the New Oriental Canon Law, Rome, 1974-89; pres. Supreme Ecclesiastical Armenian Cath. Tribunal, Episc. Conf. Iran; mem. Ecumenical Commn. Unity of Christians; founder Home for Aged Persons, 1980, Cultural Ctr., Tehran, 1987. Editor (polit. and religious weekly) Massis, 1953-73, (theol. monthly) Avetik, 1953-73; author 37 books; contbr. articles to profl. jours; dir. polyphonic choir, Beirut, 1953-73. Founder Beneficence Soc., Beirut, 1966. Died 1999.

TELLER, EDWARD, physicist; b. Budapest, Hungary, Jan. 15, 1908;, naturalized, 1941; s. Max and Ilona (Deutch) Teller; m. Augusta Harkanyi Teller, Feb. 26, 1934 (dec. 2000); children: Paul, Susan Wendy. Student, Inst. Tech., Karlsruhe, Germany, 1926—28, U. Munich, 1928; PhD, U. Leipzig, Germany, 1930; DSc (hon.), Yale U., 1954, U. Alaska, 1959, Fordham U., 1960, George Washington U., 1960, U. So. Calif., 1960, St. Louis U., 1960, Rochester Inst. Tech., 1962, PMC Colls., 1963, U. Detroit, 1964, Clemson U., 1966, Clarkson Coll., 1969; LLD (hon.), Boston Coll., 1961, Seattle U., 1961, U. Cin., 1962, U. Pitts., 1963, Pepperdine U., 1974, U. Md. at Heidelberg, 1977; DSc, LHD (hon.), Mt. Mary Coll., 1964; PhD (hon.), Tel Aviv U., 1972; D Natural Sci. (hon.), DeLaSalle U., Manila, 1981; D Med. Sci. (hon.), Med. U. S.C., 1983. Research assoc., Leipzig, 1929—31, Goettingen, Germany, 1931—33; Rockefeller fellow Copenhagen, 1934; lectr. U. London, 1934—35; prof. physics George Washington U., Washington, 1935—41, Columbia, 1941—42; physicist U. Chgo., 1942—43, Manhattan Engr. Dist., 1942—46, Los Alamos Sci. Lab., 1943—46; prof. physics U. Chgo., 1946—52, U. Calif., 1953—60, prof. physics-at-large, 1960—70, Univ. prof., 1970—75, Univ. prof. emeritus, chmn. dept. applied sci., 1963—66; asst. dir. Los Alamos Sci. Lab., 1949—52; cons. Livermore br. U. Calif. Radiation Lab., 1952—53; assoc. dir. Lawrence Livermore Lab., U. Calif., 1954—58, 1960—75; dir. Lawrence Livermore Radiation Lab., U. Calif., 1958—60; now dir. emeritus, cons. Lawrence Livermore Nat. Lab., U. Calif., Manhattan Dist. of Columbia, 1942—46; also Metall. and Lab. of Argonne Nat. Lab., U. Chgo., 1942—43, 1946—52, 1943—46, Radiation Lab., Livermore, Calif., 1952—75; sr. research fellow Hoover Instn. War, Revolution and Peace, Stanford U., from 1975. Mem. sci. adv. bd. USAF; bd. dirs. Assn. to the Unite the Democracies; past mem. gen. adv. com. AEC; former mem. Pres.'s Fgn. Intelligence Adv. Nat. Space Coun. Bd. Author (with Francis Owen Rice): The Structure of Matter, 1949; author: (with A.L. Latter) Our Nuclear Future, 1958; author: (with Allen Brown) The Legacy of Hiroshima, 1962; author: The Reluctant Revolutionary, 1964; author: (with G.W. Johnson, W.K. Talley, G.H. Higgins) The Constructive Uses of Nuclear Explosives, 1968; author: (with Segre, Kaplan and Schiff) Great Men of Physics, 1969; author: The Miracle of Freedom, 1972, Energy: A Plan for Action, 1975, Nuclear Energy in the Developing World, 1977, Energy from Heaven and The Earth, 1979, The Pursuit of Simplicity, 1980, Better a Shield than a Sword, 1987, Conversations on the Dark Secrets of Physics, 1991. Sponsor Atlantic Union, Atlantic Council U.S., Univ. Ctrs. for Rational Alternatives; mem. Com. to Unite Am., Inc.; bd. govs. Am. Acad. Achievement; bd. dirs. Def. Intelligence Sch., Naval War Coll., Fed. Union, Hertz Found., Am. Friends of Tel Aviv U. Named ARCS Man of Yr., 1980, Disting. Scientist, Nat. Sci. Devel. Bd., 1981; recipient Harrison medal, Am. Ordnance Assn., 1955, Joseph Priestley Meml. award, Dickinson Coll., 1957, Albert Einstein award, 1958, General Donovan Meml. award, 1959, Midwest Rsch. Inst. award, 1960, Rsch. Inst. Am. Living History award, 1960, Golden Plate award, Am. Acad. Achievement, 1961, Gold medal, 1982, Thomas E. White and Enrico Fermi awards, 1962, Robins award of Am., 1963, Leslie R. Groves Gold medal, 1974, Harvey prize in sci. and tech., Technion Inst., 1975, Albert Einstein award, 1977, Semmelweiss medal, 1977, Henry T. Heald award, Ill. Inst. Tech., 1978, Gold medal, Am. Coll. Nuc. Medicine, 1980, A.C. Eringen award, 1980, Paul Harris award, Rotary Found., 1980, Disting. Scientist, Phil-Am. Acad. Sci. and Engring., 1981, Lloyd Freeman Hunt Citizenship award, 1982, Nat. medal of Sci., 1983, Joseph Handleman prize, 1983, Sylvanus Thayer medal, 1986, Shelby Cullom Davis award, Ethics & Pub. Policy Assn., 1988, Presdl. Citizen medal, Pres. Reagan, 1989, Majorana Erice Scíenza Per La Pace award, 1990, Order of Banner with Rubies of the Republic of Hungary, 1990, Middle Cross with the star of the Order of Merit, Republic Hungary, 1994, Gold award, Dept. Energy, 2002, Presdl. Medal of Freedom, George W. Bush, 2003. Fellow: Am. Acad. Arts and Scis., Am. Phys. Soc., Hungarian Acad. Scis. (hon.), Am. Nuc. Soc.; mem.: NAS, Internat. Platform Assn., Soc. Engring. Scis., Am. Geophys. Union. Achievements include research in on chemical, molecular and nuclear physics, quantum mechanics, thermonuclear reactions, applications of nuclear energy, astrophysics, spectroscopy of polyatomic molecules, theory of atomic nuclei. Died Sept. 9, 2003.

TEMPLE, DOUGLAS, lawyer; b. DeWitt, N.Y., Sept. 20, 1919; s. Reuben E. and Susan P. (Purdy) T.; m. Carolyn Burrows, Aug. 5, 1948; children: Robert S., David T., Thomas J. BA, Syracuse U., 1941, LLB, 1944. Pvt. practice, East Syracuse, N.Y., 1944-93; ptnr. Temple and Temple, East Syracuse, N.Y., from 1993. Atty. East Syracuse-Minoa Sch. Dist., 1962—; village atty. East Syracuse, 1954-72. Home: De Witt, NY. Died Oct. 3, 2001.

TEMPLE, WICK, journalist; b. Little Rock, Oct. 24, 1937; s. Robert Wickliffe and Lorene (Bullard) T.; m. Margaret A. McCay, May 27, 1989; children: Wick III, Ellen Wallace,

Carol Halter, Shawn Temple. AA, Texarkana Coll., 1957; postgrad., U. Tex., 1958-59. Reporter, sports editor Texarkana (Tex.) Gazette-News, 1954-58; reporter Austin (Tex.) American-Statesman, 1958-59; reporter, news editor AP, Little Rock, 1959-65, corr. St. Louis, 1965-66, bur. chief Helena, Mont., 1966-68, Seattle, 1968-73, sports editor N.Y.C., 1973-80, mng. editor, 1980-85, dir. human resources, 1985-88, v.p., 1988, dir. newspaper membership, from 1988. Home: Millburn, NJ. Died Feb. 1, 2003; Livingston, N.J..

TEN BENSEL, ROBERT WILLIAM, pediatrician, educator; b. Atlanta, June 27, 1936; s. Harold William and Mildred Anna (Putney) ten B.; m. Myrna L. Olson, Aug. 8, 1958 (div. 1978); children: Kristin, David, Elizabeth, Charles, Sarah; m. Claire M. Chase, Aug. 15, 1987. BA, Dartmouth Coll., 1958; MD, Harvard U., 1961; MPH, U. Minn., 1974. Intern, then resident U. Minn., Mpls., 1961-63, from instr. to assoc. prof. pediatrics, 1964-74, prof. pediatrics and pub. health, from 1975. Cons. faculty Nat. Coun. Juvenile and Family Ct. Judges, Reno, Nev., 1977—. Lt. comdr. USN, 1965-67. Recipient Vincent de Francis award Am. Humane Soc., 1980, Outstanding Svc. award Nat. Coun. Juvenile and Family Ct. Judges, 1992. Fellow APA (Ray Helfer award 1992), Am. Acad. Pediatrics. Home: Saint Paul, Minn. Died Apr. 29, 2002.

TERASMAE, JAAN, geology educator; b. Estonia, May 28, 1926; s. Enn and Virge (Lepik) T.; m. Vaike Jurima, July 31, 1954. Phil. Cand., U. Uppsala, Swden, 1951; PhD, McMaster U., Can., 1955. Head palynology lab. Geol. Survey of Can., 1955-67, head paleoecology and geochronology sect., 1968; prof. dept. geology Brock U., St. Catharines, Ont., Can., 1968-91, prof. emeritus, from 1991, chmn. dept. geology, 1969-73, 75-76. Contbr. numerous articles to profl. jours. Fellow Geol. Assn. Can., Geol. Soc. Am., Royal Soc. Can.; mem. Am. Assn. Stratigraphic Palynologists, Am. Quaternary Assn., Arctic Inst. N.Am., Can. Assn. Palynologists (pres. 1984-85), Can. Quaternary Assn. (William A. Johnston medal 1990), Internat. Assn. Gt. Lakes Rsch., Internat. Glaciological Soc., Internat. Limnological Soc., Internat. Orgn. Palaeobotany, Tree-Ring Sooc., Royal Can. Geog. Soc. Lutheran. Avocation: photography. Deceased.

TERENZIO, PETER BERNARD, hospital administrator; b. N.Y.C., Mar. 6, 1916; s. Vincent and Marianna (Piantino) T.; m. Eileen Alma Mosher, May 29, 1941; children— Mary Ellen Alecci, Vincent, Nancy Britton, Peter Bernard. Student, Yale U., 1934-37; JD, U. Conn., 1940; M. Hosp. Adminstrn., Northwestern U., 1950. Bar: Conn. bar 1941. Practice in, New Haven, 1945-48; with standardization div. A.C.S., Chgo., 1948-49; adminstrv. resident Evanston (Ill.) Hosp., 1949-50; asst. dir. Roosevelt Hosp., N.Y.C., 1950-52, exec. v.p., dir., 1953-76, cons., 1976-81; pres. Hosp. Bur. Inc., Pleasantville, N.Y., 1977-81. Dir. Greenville (S.C.) Gen. Hosp., 1952-53; cons. to surgeon gen. USPHS, 1960-65, 66-69; to commr. Dept. Hosps., N.Y.C., 1961-68; prof. clin. dentistry community Sch. Dental and Oral Surgery, Columbia U., 1963-84; univ. lectr. pub. health and adminstrv. medicine; adj. prof. Pace U., 1978-82, New Sch. Social Research 1977-85; Mem. facilities planning com. Hosp. Rev. and Planning Council of So. N.Y., 1963-69; mem. vol. adv. staff N.Y. State Health and Mental Retardation, 1966-69 Adv. editorial bd., Hosp. and Health Services Adminstrn. Bd. dirs., exec. com. Asso. Hosp. Service N.Y., 1970-74, N.Y. Coll. Podiatry, 1971-73; bd. dirs. Blue Cross-Blue Shield Greater N.Y., 1974-78, Abacus, 1965-86, Dominican Sisters Home Health Agy., 1977-82, Health Services Improvement Fund, 1978-85; mem. exec. adv. bd. Hosp. Home Care Santa Ana, Calif., 1984-86; vol., assoc., Sr. Friendship Health Ctr., Naples, Fla., 1986-99, mem. adv. bd., 1992-99. Capt., Med. Adminstrn. Corps AUS, 1941-45. Fellow Am. Coll. Hosp. Execs. (gov. 1964-65, regent 2d dist. 1960-64, pres. 1966-67, chmn. bd. dirs.), Am. Pub. Health Assn.; mem. Am. Hosp. Assn. (ho. of dels. 1969-76, rep. Am. Blood Commn., trustee liaison com. podiatry), Hosp. Research and Devel. Inst., N.Y. Acad. Medicine, Pub. Health Assn. N.Y.C. (dir., v.p. 1973-74, pres. 1976-77), Roosevelt Hosp. Alumni Assn. (asso.), Hosp. Assn. N.Y. (pres. 1970-71), Middle Atlantic Hosp. Assembly (bd. govs.), Hosp. Adminstrs. Study Soc., Am. Bar Assn., Greater N.Y. Hosp. Assn. (pres. 1960), Hosp. Adminstrs. Club (pres. 1959), Hosp. Soc. (pres. 1965), Coquina Club of Naples, Inc. (sec., treas. 1984-86, pres. 1987-90). Roman Catholic. Died Aug. 12, 1999.

TERRIS, MILTON, physician, educator; b. N.Y.C., Apr. 22, 1915; s. Harry and Gussie (Dokshitski) T.; m. Rema Lapouse, Nov. 23, 1941 (dec. Aug. 1970); children— Andrew David, Eugene Charles (dec.); m. Lillian Long, Feb. 6, 1971. AB, Columbia, 1935; MD, N.Y.U., 1939; M.P.H., Johns Hopkins, 1944. Intern Harlem Hosp., N.Y.C., 1939-41; resident Bellevue Hosp., N.Y.C., 1941-42; practice medicine specializing in preventive medicine Buffalo, 1951-58, N.Y.C., 1960-80, South Burlington, Vt., 1980—; asst. dean post-grad. edn. Sch. Medicine, U. Buffalo, 1951-58, assoc., 1952-54, asst. prof., 1954-55, assoc. prof. preventive medicine, 1955-58; prof. epidemiology Sch. Medicine, Tulane U., 1958-60; head chronic disease unit dept. epidemiology Pub. Health Research Inst., N.Y.C., 1960-64; prof. preventive medicine N.Y. Med. Coll., 1964-80, chmn. dept. community and preventive medicine, 1968-80. Vis. prof. U. Toronto, 1984-93, U. Montreal, 1985—. Author: Goldberger on Pellagra, 1964, La Revolución Epidemiológica y la Medicina Social, 1980; Editor: Jour. Public Health Policy, 1980—. Recipient Abraham M. Lilienfeld award Am. Coll. Epidemiology. Fellow N.Y. Acad. Medicine, Am. Pub. Health Assn. (past pres.; Sedgwick Meml. award 1984); mem. Assn. Tchrs. Preventive Medicine (Duncan Clark award 1984; past pres.), Soc. Epidemiologic Research (past pres.), Nat. Assn. Pub. Health Policy (past pres.), Phi Beta Kappa, Alpha Omega Alpha, Delta Omega. Died Nov. 3, 2002.

TERRY, JOHN HART, retired utility company executive, congressman; b. Syracuse, N.Y., Nov. 14, 1924; s. Frank and Saydee (Hart) T.; m. Catherine Jean Taylor Phelan, Apr. 15, 1950; children: Catherine Jean (Mrs. Richard Thompson), Lynn Marie (Mrs. Robert Tacher), Susan Louise (Mrs. Stanley Germain), Mary Carole (Mrs. Stephen Brady). BA, U. Notre Dame, 1945; JD, Syracuse U., 1948. Bar: N.Y. bar 1950, D.C. bar 1972. Asst. to partner Smith & Sovik, 1948-59; asst. sec. to Gov. State of N.Y., 1959-61; sr. partner firm Smith, Sovik, Terry, Kendrick, McAuliffe & Schwarzer, 1961-73; sr. v.p., gen. counsel, sec. Niagara Mohawk Power Corp., Syracuse, 1973-87; counsel Hiscock & Barclay, Syracuse, 1987-94; atty. in pvt. practice, 1994-99; ret., 2000. Mem. N.Y. State Assembly, 1962-70, 92d Congress from 34th N.Y. Dist., 1971-73; presdl. elector, 1972. State chmn. United Services Orgn., 1964-73; past pres. John Timothy Smith Found.; Founder, dir. Bishop Foery Found., Inc.; dir. St. Joseph's Hosp. Council; past pres. Lourdes Camp; bd. dirs. N.Y. State Traffic Council; past nat. bd. dirs. Am. Cancer Soc.; mem. adv. council Syracuse U. Sch. Mgmt.; past pres. Cath. Youth Orgn.; bd. dirs. Syracuse Community Baseball Club. Served to 1st lt. AUS, 1943-46. Decorated Purple Heart, Bronze Star; named Man of Year Syracuse Jr. C. of C., 1958, Man of Yr. N.Y. State Jr. C. of C., 1959, Young Man of Yr. U. Notre Dame Club Cen. N.Y., 1959; recipient U. Notre Dame Exemplar award, 1997, Rev. Theodore Hesborgh Alumni award, 1997. Mem. ABA (utility law sect.), N.Y. State Bar Assn. (chmn. com. on public utility law), Onondaga County Bar Assn. (chmn. membership and legis. coms.), D.C. Bar Assn., County Officers Assn., Citizens Found., U. Notre Dame, Syracuse U. law assns., Am. Legion, VFW, DAV, 40 and 8, Mil. Order of Purple Heart, Bellevue Country Club, Capitol Hill Club (Washington), Vero Beach Country Club. Roman Catholic. Deceased.

TERRY, MORTON, academic administrator, physician; b. Utica, N.Y., Mar. 23, 1921; s. Isadore and Fanny (Brooks) T.; m. Geraldine Marie Rafferty, Oct. 31, 1948; children: Matthew, Jeffrey, Sheryl, Pamela. BA, Bklyn. Coll., 1942; DO, Phila. Coll. Osteo. Medicine, 1945, MS, 1950; postgrad., Am. Coll. Osteo. Internists, 1961. Diplomate Am. Osteo. Bd. Internal Medicine, Am. Osteo. Bd. Nuclear Medicine. Intern Osteo. Hosp. Phila., 1945-46, resident in internal medicine, 1946-48; internist, chmn. dept. internal medicine, exec. com. staff Biscayne (Fla.) Osteo. Hosp., 1953-60, chief staff, 1956-57; internist, chmn. dept. internal medicine Osteo. Gen. Hosp., 1960-75, chief staff, 1962-76; founder, former pres., Coll. Ostheopathic Medicine Southeastern U. Health Scis., North Miami Beach, Fla.; chancellor, health services div. Nova Southeastern U., Ft. Lauderdale, Fla., 1994—2004. Cons. internal medicine; bd. dirs. County Nat. Bank. Chmn. osteo. div. United Way Dade County, 1966-75; former mem. bd. dirs. Am. Heart Assn. Gereater Miami, del. state of Fla., 1975-77; bd. dirs. Comprehensive Health Planning Coun. Dade County, 1969-73, Health Systems Agy. South Fla., 1976-79, Dade County unit Am. Cancer Soc., 1974-76, Am. Osteo. Bd. Internal Medicine, 1971-73, South Fla. Scholarship and Awards Found, 1973-81, Boys Town Fla., 1958-71, Biscayne Osteo. Found., 1979-82, Southeastern Coll. Osteo. Medicine, 1979—. Recipient Recognition and Appreciation cert. City North Miami Beach, 1973, Outstanding Svc. award, Osteo. Profession and Community, 1973, Recognition and Appreciation cert. State of Fla., 1982, Leadership award Fla. chpt. Bklyn. Coll. Pharmacy, 1989, O. J. Snyder medal Disting. Alumnus Phila. Coll. Osteo. Medicine, 1990. Mem. Am. Coll. Osteo. Internists (bd. dirs., Disting. Svc. award 1981), Am. Assn. Colls. Osteo. Medicine (bd. dirs. 1979—), Am. Osteo. Assn. (life), Fla. Osteo. Med. Assn. (pres. 1961-62, hon. life), Dade County Osteo. Med. Assn. (pres. 1952-53), Sigma Sigma Phi (hon.). Died Jan. 11, 2004.

TERRY, ROGER HAROLD, minister, musician, composer, author, editor; b. Salisbury, NC, Feb. 3, 1925; s. Roger Harold and Marie (Kneeburg) T.; m. Martha Frye, June 30, 1948 (div. July 1973); children: Barbara (dec.), Ruth, Julia, Glenn; m. Kathryn Wagoner, Nov. 22, 1973. AB, Lenoir-Rhyne Coll., Hickory, N.C., 1945, D Sacred Music (hon.), 1973; BD, Lutheran Theological Southern Seminary, Columbia, S.C., 1948; MS in Theology, Union Theological Seminary, 1955. Asst. pastor St. John Luth. Ch., Salisbury, N.C., 1948-50; pastor Emanuel Luth. Ch., Ridgefield Park, N.J., 1950-53, St. Mark Luth. Ch., China Grove, N.C., 1953-59; worship/music editor Bd. Parish Edn. United Luth. Ch. in Am., 1959-62; worship/music editor div. for parish services Luth. Ch. in Am., Phila., 1963-77; pastor Peace Luth. Ch., Gibsonville, N.C., 1977-83, Macedonia Luth. Ch., Burlington, N.C., 1983-84, Nazareth Luth. Ch., Rural Hall, N.C., 1985-87; interim pastor Friedens Luth. Ch., Gibsonville, N.C., from 1991. Program dir. Lutheridge Sch. Music, Arden, N.C., 1956-72; pres. Council of Chs., Ridgefield Park, N.J., 1952-53; chaplain Internat. Order of St. Luke Physician, 1978—; interim pastor Messiah Luth. Ch., Burlington, N.C., 1997—; pastor emeritus Macedonia Luth. Ch., Burlington, 1997—. Author: Church School Hymnal for Children, 1964, Young Children Sing, 1967, Music Resource Book, 1967, Music in Christian Education, 1969, Sing! Hymnal for Youth and Adults, 1970, Children Sing, Books 1-3, 1972-77, Celebrate, 1974-77, (with others) Hymnal Companion to the Lutheran Book of Worship, 1981; editor: (quar. jour.) Soli Deo Gloria, 1992—; editor, author of numerous Luth. curriculum resources; contbr. articles to religious publs. Sec., bd. trustees Lowman Home for Aged, White Rock, S.C., 1957-59; vol. relief worker, fund raiser Hurricane Hugo victims, 1989-90; interim pastor Friedens Luth. Ch., Gibsonville, N.C., 1991-92. Mem. Forsyth Luth. Council. (pres. 1986-87), Am. Guild Organists (exec. com. 1985-86), Hymn Soc. Am. (pres. Phila. chpt. 1970-72). Clubs: Rotary. Republican. Avocations: organic gardening, small scale tree farming. Died Jan. 14, 2004.

TESTA, RICHARD JOSEPH, lawyer; b. Marlboro, Mass., Apr. 21, 1939; s. Joseph N. and Jeannette (Clement) T.; children: Jo-Anne, Richard J. Jr., Nancy, Susan, Karen. AB, Assumption Coll., 1959; LLB, Harvard U., 1962. Bar: Mass. 1962. Chmn. Testa, Hurwitz & Thibeault, Boston, from 1973. Mem. ABA. Roman Catholic. Home: Wayland, Mass. Died Dec. 2002.

THAYER, ROSEALYCE CULLEN, painter; b. Portland, Maine, July 1, 1928; d. Thomas Roswell and Helena (Murphy) Cullen; m. Edward P. Craig, II (dec.); children: Edward P., III, Thomas R., Peter A., Catherine C. (dec.); m. Charles V. Thayer, July 16, 1984; children: Charles W., David W. Diploma, Fryeburg Acad., Maine, 1946, Maine Coll. of Art, Portland, 1948, Westbrook Coll., 1948; BS, U. Maine, 1966; hon. degree, Maine Coll. Art, 2000. Dir. adult edn. S.D. Warren Co., Westbrook, Maine, 1961-73; art dir. SAD 55, Hiram, Maine, 1967-68; art tchr. North Yarmouth (Maine) Acad., 1961-64. Represented in permanent collections U.S., Can. and Mexico. Trained victim advocate; instrumental in obtaining legis. for Immediate Search Law for Missing Children and Handicapped Persons, Vt. 1985 (adopted by Tex. 1997); active advocate stalking laws, Conn., Vt.; active Victims' Advocates, Victim Compensation and Victims' Rights, Nat. Victim Assistance Orgn., Washington, 1984—, Parents of Murdered Children, Cin., 1985; mem. Nat. Mus. Women Arts, Washington, 1997. Recipient life mem. award The Giraffe Project, Langley, Wash., 1993. Avocation: family. Home: Springfield, Vt. Died Feb. 22, 2004.

THEIL, HENRI, economist, educator; b. Amsterdam, Netherlands, Oct. 31, 1924; s. Hendrik and Hermina (Siegmann) T.; m. Eleonore A.I. Goldschmidt, June 15, 1951. PhD in Econs., U. Amsterdam, 1951; LLD (hon.), U. Chgo., 1964; D honoris causa, Free U., Brussels, 1974, Erasmus U., Rotterdam, 1983; LLD (hon.), Hope Coll., 1985. Mem. staff Central Planning Bur. (The Hague), 1952-55; prof. econometrics Netherlands Sch. Econs., Rotterdam, 1953-66; vis. prof. econs. U. Chgo., 1955-56, 64, Stanford U., 1956, 59, Harvard U., 1960, U. So. Calif., 1979, 80, 81, U. Western Australia, 1982; dir. Econometric Inst. (Netherlands Sch. Econs.), 1956-66; prof. U. Chgo., 1965-81, dir. Center Math. Studies in Bus. and Econs., 1965-81; McKethan-Matherly prof. econometrics and decision scis. U. Fla., 1981-2000. Author: Linear Aggregation of Economic Relations, 1954, Economic Forecasts and Policy, 2d edit., 1961, Optimal Decision Rules for Government and Industry, 1964, Operations Research and Quantitative Economics, 1965, Applied Economic Forecasting, 1966, Economics and Information Theory, 1967, Principles of Econometrics, 1971, Statistical Decomposition Analysis with Applications in the Social and Administrative Sciences, 1972, Theory and Measurement of Consumer Demand, Vol. 1 1975, Vol. 2 1976, Introduction to Econometrics, 1978, The System-Wide Approach to Microeconomics, 1980, System-Wide Explorations in International Economics, Input-Output Analysis, and Marketing Research, 1980, International Consumption Comparisons, 1981, Exploiting Continuity, 1984, Applied Demand Analysis, 1987, International Evidence on Consumption Patterns, 1989, Contributions to Consumer Demand and Econometrics: Essays in Honour of Henri Theil, 1992, Henri Theil's Contributions to Economics and Econometrics, 1992, Studies in Global Econometrics, 1996, Recollections of My Years in Rotterdam (in Dutch), 1997, A Proposed Set of Nine Regions for the United States and the Inequality of Population Densities, 2000; editor Mathematical and Managerial Economics, 1964—; co-editor Series on Econometrics and Management Sciences, 1984—. Fellow Am. Acad. Arts and Scis., Royal Netherlands Acad. Scis., Am. Statis. Assn.; mem. Internat. Statis. Inst., Am. Econ. Assn., Ops. Research Soc. Am., Econometric Soc. (pres. 1961), Inst. Mgmt. Scis. (council 1961-64) Home: Saint Augustine, Fla. Deceased.

THIELSCH, HELMUT JOHN, engineering company executive; b. Berlin, Nov. 16, 1922; came to U.S., 1939, naturalized, 1954; s. Kurt and Anna-Sibylle T.; m. Margaret E. McKenna, Aug. 16, 1952; children: Barbara Anne, Donald Kurt, Deborah Lee, Helmut John. BS, Auburn U., 1943; postgrad., U. Mich., 1943-45, Lehigh U., 1948. Registered profl. engr., R.I., Mass., Maine, N.J., Ga., Calif. Research engr. Allis Chalmers Co., Milw., 1945-46; metall. engr. Black, Sivalls & Bryson, Inc., Kansas City, Mo., 1946-47; research engr. Lukens Steel Co., Coatsville, Pa., 1948-49; engr. Welding Research Council, N.Y.C., 1949-52; dir. research Eutectic Welding Alloys Co., N.Y.C., 1952-53; v.p., dir. research, devel. and engring. ITT Grinnell Corp., Providence, 1954-84; pres. Thielsch Engring., Inc., Providence, 1984—. Pres. HiTech Realty Assocs. Inc.; cons. on failure analysis to industry, public utilities, equipment builders, 1954—; lectr. at confs. on failures and failure prevention; mem. component tech. com. Argonne (Ill.) Nat. Lab.; bd. dirs. Goldline Controls, Inc. Author: Defects and Failures in Pressure Vessels and Piping, 1965; contbr. numerous articles to profl. publs.; patentee in field. Recipient Nat. Safety award, Nat. Bd. Boiler and Pessure Vessel Insps., 1990, John J. Tuohy Businessman of Yr. award, City of

Cranston, 2000, Bus. Leadership award, Providence Bus. News Orgn., 2002. Fellow: ASME, Am. Bd. Forensic Examiners, Am. Welding Soc. (Adams Lecture award 1982), Am. Soc. Nondestructive Testing, Am. Soc. Metals; mem.: NSPE, TAPPI, ASTM, ACS, NSPE (Freeman award 1985), Nat. Fire Protection Assn., Tech. Assn. Pulp and Paper Industry, Am. Soc. for Metals, Am. Mgmt. Assn., Nat. Assn. Corrosion Engrs., Am. Nuclear Soc., Am. Soc. Quality Control, Am. Water Works Assn., Sigma Xi. Home: Providence, RI. Died May 2, 2003.

THIGPEN, LYNNE, actress; b. Joliet, Ill., Dec. 22, 1948; Appeared in Broadway play Fences, Tintypes (Tony nomination), A Month of Sundays, Working, The Magic Show, An American Daughter (Tony award 1997); (off-Broadway) Boesman and Lena (Obie award), Balm in Gilead, Godspell; (regional) Having Our Say, Educating Rita, Fences (L.A. Drama Critics award); (nat. tour) St. Mark's Gospels; (film) Godspell, 1973, The Warriors, 1979, Tootsie, 1982, Running on Empty, 1988, Lean on Me, 1989, Bob Roberts, 1992, Article 99, 1992, The Paper, 1994, Naked in New York, 1994, Blankman, 1994, Just Cause, 1995, Bicentennial Man, 1999, Random Hearts, 1999, The Insider, 1999, Shaft, 2000, Novocaine, 2001, Anger Management, 2003; (TV series) L.A. Law, Thirtysomething, Law & Order, All My Children, The Cosby Show, Frank's Place, Roseanne, F.M. Television, Bear in the Big Blue House, Where in the World is Carmen San Diego? (Emmy nominations), The District; (TV movie) Rockabye, 1986, Fear Stalk, 1989, Separate But Equal, 1991, Cagney and Lacey: The View Through the Glass Ceiling, 1995, The Boys Next Door, 1996, Pretty Poison, 1996, A Mother's Instinct, 1996, Change of a Lifetime, 1998, Night Ride Home, 1999, An American Daughter, 2000. Died Mar. 12, 2003.

THIMM, ALFRED LOUIS, management educator; b. Vienna, Dec. 10, 1923; came to U.S., 1939, naturalized, 1943; s. Hartwig H. and Olga F. (Felsner) T.; m. Patricia Mullen, Dec. 18, 1954; children: Alfred Louis, Peter H. BA, NYU, 1948, MA, 1949, PhD, 1959. Asst. prof. econs. St. Lawrence U., Canton, N.Y., 1953-55; research fellow NYU, 1955-56; assoc. prof. Clarkson Coll., Potsdam, N.Y., 1956-59; mem. faculty Union Coll., Schenectady, 1960-81, prof. econs. and indsl. adminstrn., 1968-81, dir. Inst. Adminstrn. and Mgmt., 1968-80, dir. Ph.D. program in adminstrn. and engring. systems, 1980-81; dean, dir. Sch. Bus. U. Vt., Burlington, 1981-85, prof. mgmt., from 1981. Mgmt. cons., 1973-81; cons. in field; vis. prof. Wirtschafts U., Vienna, 1980, 85-86, 89, 92, 93, 94, 95, Inst. Entscheidungs und Organisationsforschung, U. Munich, 1972, 74-75, 90, 91. Author: Economists and Society: From Aquinas to Keynes, 1973, 81, Business Ideologies in the Reform-Progressive: 1880-1914, 1976, Entscheidungstheorie, 1977, The False Promise of Codetermination, 1980, America's Stake in European Telecommuncation Policies, 1992, 94; contbr. articles to profl. jours., monographs. Grantee NSF, 1959, 61; grantee Ford Found., summers 1960, 62; Fulbright rsch. scholar Austria, 1967-68, 92. Mem. Am. Econs. Assn., Am. Statis. Assn., Inst. Mgmt. Sci. Died Dec. 21, 2003.

THOM, RENÉ, mathematician; b. Montbéliard, Doubs, France, Sept. 2, 1923; B Elementary Math., Bescancon, 1940; B Philosophy, U. Lyon, 1941; student, Lycée Saint-Louis, Paris, 1942, Ecole Normale Supérieure, 1943; D, 1951. Tchr. U. Grenoble, 1953-54; faculty U. Strasbourg, 1954-63, prof., 1957-63; hon. prof. Inst des Hautes Etudes Scientifique, Bures-sur-Yvette, France, from 1964. Recipient Fields medal, 1958, Grand Prix Scientifique de la Ville de Paris, 1974. Mem. London Math. Soc. (hon.). Achievements include development of catastrophe theory, a mathematical threatment of continuous action producing a discontinuous result. Died Oct. 25, 2002.

THOMAS, ALEXANDER, psychiatrist; b. N.Y.C., Jan. 11, 1914; s. Herman and Rose T.; m. Stella Chess, June 28, 1938; children— Joan, Richard, Leonard, Kenneth. BS magna cum laude, Coll. City N.Y., 1932; MD, N.Y. U., 1936. Diplomate: Am. Bd. Psychiatry, 1948. Intern Mt. Sinai Hosp., N.Y.C., 1936-39; resident Bellevue Hosp., N.Y.C., 1946-48, dir. psychiat. div., 1968-78; attending psychiatrist U. Hosp., 1966—; prof. psychiatry N.Y. U. Med. Center, 1966—. Prin. investigator longitudinal study child devel., 1960— Author: (with others) Behavioral Individuality in Early Childhood, 1963, Your Child is a Person, 1965, Temperament and Behavior Disorders in Children; Racism and Psychiatry, 1972, Temperament and Development, 1977, Dynamics of Psychological Development, 1980, (with Stella Chess) Origins and Evolution of Behavior Disorders; contbr. (with others) articles to profl. jours. Served to capt USAAF, 1942-46. Fellow Am. Psychiat. Assn. (pres. N.Y. dist. br. 1973); mem. Phi Beta Kappa, Sigma Xi, Alpha Omega Alpha. Home: New York, NY. Died Jan. 29, 2003.

THOMAS, JAMES EGBERT, symphony orchestra administrator; b. Charleston, W.Va., Apr. 14, 1921; s. James E. Thomas and Ruth Maude Cloud; m. Ireene M. Tolbert, Feb. 28, 1944; children: James Edwin, Jeffrey Alan. BA, W.Va. Wesleyan Coll., 1946; MA, Ohio State U., 1949. Enlisted USAF, 1942, advanced through grades to maj., 1966, ret., 1973; supr. music Ashland (Ohio) City Schs., 1954-80; gen. mgr. Ashland Symphony Orch., from 1984. Chmn. govt. rels. Music Educators Nat. Conf., Reston, Va., 1978-80. Decorated Air medal with 2 oak leaf clusters. Mem. Ohio Music Edn. Assn. (pres. 1974-78; Disting. Svc. award 1981), Ashland City Club (sec. 1978—). Republican. Methodist. Avocations: golf, swimming. Home: Ashland, Ohio. Deceased.

THOMAS, JOYCE MOFFETT, secondary school educator; b. Hobart, Ind., July 29, 1935; d. Walter and Ruby (Stephenson) Moffett; m. John James Thomas, Oct. 18, 1958 (dec. Dec. 30, 1994); children: Amy Carrell, Sarah Smith. BA in English, Ind. U., 1971; MA in English, Purdue U., 1977. Tchr. Andrean H.S., Merrillville, Ind., from 1971. Instr. North Ctrl. Purdue U., Westville, Ind., 1989-93. Contbr. articles to various publs. Named Outstanding Chgo. Area Tchr., U. Chgo., 1984, Tchr. of Yr., Inland-Ryerson Fedn., 1989. Mem. Nat. Coun. Tchrs. English, Nat. Cath. Edn. Assn. Democrat. Episcopalian. Home: Edmond, Okla. Died May 16, 2000.

THOMAS, WILLIAM GERAINT, museum administrator; b. Columbo, Sri Lanka, June 27, 1931; came to U.S., 1941; s. Cecil James and Iris Katharine (Evans) T.; m. Maria Alcalde, Jan. 2, 1976; 1 child, Laura. BA, U. Calif., Berkeley, 1952. Reporter, editor San Francisco Chronicle, 1952-64; asst. to mayor City of San Francisco, 1964-66; chief cons. majority caucus Calif. State Assembly, Sacramento, 1966-68; adminstrv. asst. U.S. Congressman Phillip Burton, Washington, 1968-70; cons. interior com. U.S. Ho. of Reps., Washington, 1970-72; ptnr. Thomas & Iovino, San Francisco, 1972-78; asst. regional dir. Nat. Park Svc., San Francisco, 1978-89; supt. San Francisco Maritime NHP, 1989—2002; ret., 2002. Mem. Nat. Dem. Club; bd. dirs. Nat. Libery Ship Meml., 1978-80. Sgt. U.S. Army, 1952-54, Korea. Mem. Nat. Maritime Mus. Assn., Nat. Maritime Hist. Soc., Press Club of San Francisco (pres. 1973-74, Best News Story 1963). Episcopalian. Avocation: sailing. Home: San Francisco, Calif. Died Apr. 14, 2004.

THOMAS, WILLIAM RICHARD, real estate executive, consultant; b. Sayre, Pa., Feb. 1, 1928; s. Eli Elbert and Dorothy (Welty) T.; m. Dorothy Eileen Homan, Dec. 9, 1950; children: Patricia Anne, Scott Wynn, Randall Welty. Student, Paul Smiths Coll., 1948-49; BA, Mich. State Coll., 1952. Comml. sales engr. Consumers Power Co., Jackson and Grand Rapids, Mich., 1953-57; owner, pres. Bill Thomas Foods Inc., Traverse City, Mich., 1957-77; comml. real estate salesman Paul Scott Real Estate, Traverse City, 1977-79; comml. real estate broker Bill Thomas Real Estate, Traverse City, 1980-83; comml. real estate salesman Rauch, Weaver, Millsaps & Co., Inc., Ft. Lauderdale, 1981-82, Evin Welch & Co., Inc., Ft. Lauderdale, 1982-84; pvt. practice comml. real estate broker Margate, Fla., from 1984. Fee cons. Bill Thomas Foods Inc., 1965-79; real estate cons., Margate, 1980—. V.p., bd. dirs. Jr. C. of C., Traverse City, 1959-62; pres., bd. dirs. Grand Traverse YMCA, 1968-71. Served with U.S. Army, 1946-47, Korea. Mem. Nat. Assn. Realtors (cert., mem. comml. investment council of Realtors Nat. Mktg. Inst.), Fla. Assn. Realtors, Pompano Beach North Broward Bd. Realtors (Honor Soc. 1986). Lodges: Masons. Republican. Methodist. Deceased.

THOMASMA, DAVID CHARLES, humanities educator, academic administrator; b. Evergreen Park, Ill., Oct. 31, 1939; s. Charles W. and Rosemary (Olma) T.; divorced; children: Pieter Jon, Elizabeth (Lisa) Rose. BS, Aquinas Coll., Grand Rapids, 1961; BA, Aquinas Inst., 1963; MA, Ph.L., 1964; STB, Dominican House of Studies, 1965, Sacrae Theol. Licentiate, 1968; PhD, Cath. U. Am., 1972. Instr. Cath. U. of Am., Washington D.C., 1967-69; asst. prof. Christian Bros. Coll., 1969-73; dir. med. humanities U. Tenn. Ctr. Health Sci., 1973-81; prof., dir. med. humanities Loyola U. Chgo. Med. Ctr., from 1981. Pres. Chgo. Clin. Ethics Programs, 1988-89. Author 15 pub. books; contbr. numerous articles to profl. jours. Bd. dirs. Hospice of Memphis, Inc., 1979-81, Soc. of the right to Die, N.Y., 1987-90; mem. ethics adv. com. Am. Hosp. Assn., Chgo., 1986-90, Theology and Ethics adv. com. Cath. Health Assn., St. Louis, 1986-91. Sr. Fulbright fellow, 1984, Woodrow Wilson fellow, 1986—. Mem. Soc. for Health and Human Values Coun., Am. Acad. of Religion, Am. Philos. Assn., Am. Cath. Philos. Assn., Am. Geriatics Soc., Soc. for Bioethics Cons., Inst. of Medicine of Chgo. Democrat. Avocations: classical music, woodworking, swimming, hi-fidelity. Home: Elmhurst, Ill. Died Oct. 31, 1939.

THOMPSON, ROBERT ELLIOTT, columnist, writer; b. Los Angeles, June 28, 1921; s. Robert W. and Sadie (Berry) T.; m. Mary C. Mattern, Feb. 27, 1954; children: Robert Elliott, Monica Louise. AB, Ind. U., 1949. Reporter Ft. Wayne (Ind.) Jour.-Gazette, 1949-51, INS, 1951-58; press sec. John F. Kennedy's re-election campaign in, Mass., 1958; reporter N.Y. Daily News, 1959-62; White House corr. Los Angeles Times, 1962-66; chief Washington bur. Hearst Newspapers, 1966-68, nat. editor, 1968-74, columnist, 1978—2003; pub. Seattle Post-Intelligencer, 1974-78, chief Washington bur., 1978-89. Author: (with Hortense Myers) Robert Kennedy: the Brother Within, 1962. Mem. standing com. Corrs. House and Senate, 1960-62, chmn., 1961. Served with USNR, 1942-45. Mem. White House Corr. Assn. (pres. 1966-67), Seattle C. of C. (past trustee). Clubs: Nat. Press, Cosmos, Gridiron (Washington). Episcopalian. Died Nov. 18, 2003.

THOMPSON, WILLIAM BENBOW, JR., obstetrician, gynecologist, educator; b. Detroit, July 26, 1923; s. William Benbow and Ruth (Locke) T.; m. Constance Carter, July 30, 1947 (div. Feb. 1958); 1 child, William Benbow IV; m. Jane Gilliland, Mar. 12, 1958; children: Reese Ellison, Belinda Day. AB, U. So. Calif., 1947, MD, 1951. Diplomate Am. Bd. Ob-Gyn. Resident Gallinger Mun. Hosp., Washington, 1952-53, George Washington U. Hosp., Washington, 1953-55; asst. ob-gyn. La. State U., 1955-56; asst. clin. prof. UCLA, 1957-64; assoc. prof. U. Calif.-Irvine Sch. Med., Orange, 1964-92, dir. gynecology, 1977-92, prof. emeritus, from 1993, vice chmn. ob-gyn., 1978-89. Assoc. dean U. Calif.-Irvine Coll. Med., Irvine, 1969-73. Inventor: Thompson Retractor, 1976; Thompson Manipulator, 1977. Bd. dirs. Monarch Bay Assn. Laguna Niguel, Calif. 1969-77, Monarch Summitt II A ssn. 1981-83. With U.S. Army, 1942-44, PTO. Fellow ACS, Am. Coll. Ob-Gyn. (life), L.A. Ob-Gyn. Soc. (life); mem. Orange County Gynecology and Obstetrics Soc. (hon.), Capistrano Bay Yacht Club (commodore 1975), Internat. Order Blue Gavel, Dana West Yacht Club. Avocation: boating. Home: Jefferson City, Mo. Deceased.

THOMSON, ROBERT JAMES, natural gas distribution company executive; b. Detroit, Dec. 16, 1927; s. Harold E.J. and Irene L. (Silsbee) T.; m. Doris L. Mullen, Sept. 19, 1953; children— Gregory R., Susan C., Jeffrey S., Arthur J. AB, Mich. State U., 1951, MBA, 1967. CPA, Mich. Mgr. Arthur Andersen & Co., Detroit, 1951-58; v.p. Southeastern Mich. Gas Co., Port Huron, 1961-71, pres., 1971-84, pres., chief exec. officer, 1984-86; pres., CEO Southeastern Mich. Gas Enterprise, Inc., Pt. Huron, 1977-93, chmn. Port Huron, 1987-95. Bd. dirs. Mich. Nat. Bank-Port Huron, 1972-97. Trustee Cmty. Found. St. Clair County, 1972—, pres., 1981-83; bd. dirs. Indsl. Devel. Corp., Port Huron, 1972-86, pres. 1976-78; trustee Port Huron Hosp., 1981-90, vice chmn., 1985-90; bd. dirs. Blue Water Health Svcs. Corp., 1981—, vice chmn., 1981-93, chmn., 1993—; trustee Marwood Manor Nursing Home., 1987-99, chmn. 1996-99; vestryman Grace Episcopal Ch., Port Huron, 1990-93. With USN, 1946-47. Mem. Mich. C. of C. (bd. dirs. 1982-88), Mich. Utilities Assn. (bd. dirs., treas. 1983-85), Detroit Renaissance Club, Port Huron Golf Club, Port Huron Yacht Club, Mich. State U. Advanced Mgmt. Program Club, Port Huron/Marysville C. of C. (bd. dirs. 1973-75, v.p. 1975). Home: Fort Gratiot, Mich. Deceased.

THON, WILLIAM, artist; b. N.Y.C., Aug. 8, 1906; s. Felix Leo and Jane (Upham) T.; m. Helen Elizabeth Walters, June 3, 1929. Student, Art Students League, 1924-25; A.F.D., Bates Coll., 1957. Represented in nat. art exhibits at Corcoran Gallery Art, Washington, Art Inst. Chgo., Pa. Acad., Va. Mus., Toldeo Mus., Met. Mus., Nat. Acad., Carnegie Inst.; one-man show Farnsworth Mus., Rockland, Me.; included in permanent collections Swope Art Gallery, Terre Haute, Ind., Farnsworth Mus., Bloomington Art Assn., Ency. Brit., Toledo Mus., Am. Acad. Arts and Letters, Mus. of Ann Arbor, Mich., Met. Mus. Art, N.Y.C., Portland Mus. Art, U. Hawaii, Honolulu, Johnson's Wax Collection, Bklyn. Mus., Whitney Mus., Portland Mus., Oquenquet Mus., others.; artist-in-residence Am. Acad., Rome, 1956. Served with USNR, 1942-46. Recipient prize Salmagundi Club, 1941, Dana watercolor medal Pa. Acad., 1950, prize Bklyn. Mus., 1945, Prix de Rome, 1947, Maine State award, 1970, Florence and H. Samuel Slater Meml. award Adirondacks Nat. Exhibit, Arts Guild Old Forge, Inc., 1992, Pulsifer award, 1993, Hardware prize, 1995, Watercolor prize Old Forge, 1996. Mem. NAD (2d Altman prize for landscape 1951, 1st 1954, 67, Palmer Meml. prize 1944, Samuel F.B. Morse medal 1956, Altman prize for landscape 1961, Adolph and Clara Obrig prize 1965, Ranger Fund purchase award 1976, Ogden Pliessner Meml. prize 1988, William A. Patton prize 1991, Adolph and Clara Obrig award 1992), Nat. Inst. Arts and Letters (grantee 1951), Am. Watercolor Soc. (silver medal 1957, 67, Gordon Grant Meml. award 1963, gold medal of honor 1970, 79, Lena Newcastle Meml. award 1976, Caroline Stern award 1986), Audubon Artists (silver medal 1986, Lillian Judith Newman award 1992), Friendship Sloop Soc. Home: Portland, Maine. Deceased.

THORBECKE, G. JEANETTE, pathology educator; b. Nes/Ameland, The Netherlands, Aug. 2, 1929; came to U.S., 1957; d. Lubbertus D. Thorbecke and Johanna Reeder; m. Gerald Martin Hochwald, Sept. 30, 1957; children: Bertrand Martijn, Steven Norbert, Neal Leonard. MD, U. Groningen, The Netherlands, 1950, PhD, 1954. Lic. to practice medicine The Netherlands. Asst. prof. pathology NYU Sch. Medicine, N.Y.C., 1961-66, assoc. prof. pathology, 1966-70, prof. pathology, from 1970. Sci. cons. Schering-Plough Corp., Kenilworth, 1975-2000; counselor bd. sci. counselors Nat. Cancer Inst., Bethesda, Md., 1971-75, Nat. Inst. Allergy and Infectious Disease, Bethesda, 1979-84. Editor: The Biology of Aging and Development, 1975; author, editor: The Biology of Germinal Centers in Lymphoid Tissue, 1998; contbr. more than 425 articles to profl. jours. Mem. peer rev. panel Nat. Multiple Sclerosis Soc., N.Y.C., 1966-68, 86-88; mem. grant rev. com. State of N.J. Commn. on Cancer Rsch., Trenton, 1984-2000; mem. rev. panel Nat. Cancer Inst., Bethesda, 1985-87; mem. peer rev. com. Arthritis Found., 1996-98. Recipient Nat. Svc. citation Arthritis Found., 1998, Rose Hirschler award, 1999; scholar Fgn. Operation Mission to The Netherlands under Auspices of NAS, 1954-56; R01 grantee Nat. Inst. Allergy and Infectiuos Disease/Nat. Inst. Aging, 1963—, Nat. Cancer Inst., 1971—; rsch. grantee Multiple Sclerosis Soc., 1996—. Fellow N.Y. Acad. Scis.; mem. Royal Acad. Sci. of The Netherlands (corr.), Am. Assn. for Immunologists (pres. 1989-90, Disting. Svc. award 1991). Home: Douglaston, NY. Died Nov. 16, 2001.

THORBURN, JOHN THOMAS, III, marine engineer, consultant; b. Boston, May 23, 1920; s. John and Ellen Louise (Doddy) T.; m. Doris Louise Kenney, June 16, 1951; children: Debra, John IV. PhD in Marine Engring. and Naval Architecture, MIT, 1968. Pres. Thorburn Marine, Boston, 1943-92; pvt. pracitce cons. Boston, from 1992. Died May 2, 2002.

THORLAKSON BELL, ROSEMARY AHEARN, contract trauma nurse; b. Columbus, Ohio, July 12, 1947; d. Joseph Edmond and Elizabeth Sabrina (Morse) Ahearn; m.

Robert E. Thorlakson, Dec. 29, 1969 (div. Oct. 1972); children: AmySue Elizabeth, Stephen Robert; m. Gary Lee Bell, May 13, 1993. AAS in Nursing, Germanna C.C., 1975; BSN, U. Va., 1976, MEd, 1986, postgrad. Cert. BLS/ACLS instr., CCRN, CEN, TNCC instr., PALS, NALS, ATLS, C-EMT instr., first aid instr., water safety instr., breast self exam instr., cold water rescue and recovery; RN in 21 states. Night shift supr. emergency dept. Potomac Hosp., Woodbridge, Va., 1975-77; emergency rm. trauma and life flight nurse U. Va., Charlottesville, 1977-79; supr. emergency dept. Carbon County Meml. Hosp., Rawlins, Wyo., 1979-80; contract nurse, 1980-89 and from 91; supr. emergency dept. Minidoka Meml. Hosp., Rupert, Idaho, 1989-91. Cmty. educator Am. Heart Assn., N.Y., Va., Wyo, Idaho, 1972—, ARC, N.Y., Ky., Wyo., Idaho, 1972—; state steering com. State EMS, Idaho, 1990-91; with Med. Mission to VN, 1997. Contbr. articles to profl. jours. Former v.p. MADD, 1991-72; vol. ARC, Idaho, Ky., Va., 1975—, Spl. Olympics, Idaho, 1991—. Capt. U.S. Army, 1967-70. Mem. VFW (life), Vietnam Vets. of Am., Vietnams Womens' Assn., Am. Legion, Am. Vets, Women in Svc. to Am., Beta Sigma Phi Democrat. Roman Catholic. Avocations: reading, playing classical piano, conservation, golf, skiing. Home: Priest River, Idaho. Deceased.

THORN, GEORGE WIDMER, physician, educator; b. Buffalo, Jan. 15, 1906; s. George W. and Fanny R. (Widmer) T.; m. Doris Weston, June 30, 1931 (dec. Jan. 1984); 1 son, Weston Widmer; m. Claire Steinert, Dec. 28, 1985 (dec. Mar. 1990). Student, Coll. of Wooster, 1923-25; MD, U. Buffalo, 1929; MA (hon.), Harvard U., 1942, DSc (hon.), 1987, Temple U., 1951, Suffolk U., 1961, Coll. Wooster, 1963, N.Y. Med. Coll., 1972, Boston U., 1983; LLD (hon.), Dalhousie U., 1950; LLD, Queen's U., Can., 1954; DMed, Cath. U., Louvain, 1960; MD (hon.), U. Geneva, 1965; DSc (hon.), Med. Coll. of Ohio, Toledo, Rockefeller U., 1993, U. Buffalo, 1995. Diplomate Am. Bd. Internal Medicine. House officer Millard Fillmore Hosp., Buffalo, 1929-30; researcher dept. physiology U. Buffalo, 1930-31, asst. researcher dept. physiology and medicine, 1931-34; asst. prof. physiology Ohio State U., Columbus, 1935-36; asst. physician Johns Hopkins Hosp., Balt., 1937-39, assoc. prof. medicine, 1938-42, assoc. physician, 1939-42; mem. med. adv. bd. Howard Hughes Med. Inst., 1955-85, dir., res., 1956-78, chmn. med. adv. bd., 1975-85, mem. exec. com., 1977-84, pres., 1981-84, chmn. bd. trustees, 1984-90; physician-in-chief Peter Bent Brigham Hosp., Boston, 1942-72, physician-in-chief emeritus, 1972—2004; Samuel A. Levine prof. medicine Harvard U., Cambridge, 1967-72, Samuel A. Levine prof. emeritus, 1972—2004, Hersey prof. theory and practice physic emeritus, 1972—2004. Hugh J. Morgan vis. prof. Vanderbilt U., 1967; vis. prof. medicine Columbia Coll. Physicians and Surgeons, 1968, Cornell U. Med. Sch. and N.Y. Hosp., 1970; Wingate Johnson vis. prof. Bownman Gray Sch. Medicine Wake Forest U., 1972; cons. internist Boston Psychopathic Hosp., 1943-2004; mem. research and devel. adv. bd. Smith, Kline and French Labs., 1953-69; cons. Children's Med. Ctr., USPHA, U.S. Army Med. Services Grad. Sch.; mem. com. stress NRC; mem. Nat. Com. on Radiation, 1958-2004; mem. drug research bd. NRC-Nat. Acad. Scis., 1972; lectr.U. London, 1957; Jacobaeus lectr., Oslo, 1957; Maurice C. Pincoff lectr. U. Md. Sch. Medicine, 1958; Mellon lectr. U. Pitts., 1959; Banting Meml. lectr. Am. Diabetes Assn., 1959; 1st Lilly lectr. Royal Coll. Physicians, 1966, Soc. Mexicana de Nutricion y Endocrologia, Mexico, 1969; Thayer lectr. Johns Hopkins U., 1967; Billings lectr. AMA, 1968; John C. Leonard Med. lectr. Hartford Med. Soc., 1969; mem. corp. MIT, 1965-2004, Mus. Sci., 1979-2004; v.p. Whitaker Health Scis. Fund, Inc., 1974-92; bd. visitors Boston u. Sch. Medicine, 1979-2004; chmn. sci. adv. bd. Whitaker Found., 1979-93. Editor-in-chief Principles of Internal Medicine, 8th edit., 1974. Pres. Howard Hughes Med. Inst., Boston, 1981-84, chmn. bd. dirs. and trustee, 1984-2004. Rockefeller fellow in medicine, Harvard U., 1936 37, Johns Hopkins U. Sch. Medicine, 1938, Read Ellsworth fellow in medicine John Hopkins U. Sch. Medicine, 1938; recipient Chancellor's medal U. Buffalo, 1943, Osler oration Can. Med. Assn., 1949, U.S. Pharm. Mfrs. Assn. award 1950, Alvarenga award, 1951, Dr. Charles V. Chapin Meml. award 1956, Ann. Meml. award Buffalo Urol. Soc., 1958, Modern Medicine award, 1961, Oscar B. Hunter Meml. award Am. Therapeutic Soc., 1967, Robert H. Williams award Assn. Profs. of Medicine, 1972, George M. Kober medal Assn. Am. Physicians, 1976, Gold-Headed Can. Soc. award, 1976, Medical Times Physician of Excellence award, 1980, Hubert H. Humphrey Research Ctr. award Boston U., 1980, Gold medal Phi Lambda Kappa, 1981, Pub. Welfare medal Nat. Acad. Sci., 1997. Fellow Royal Coll. Physicians (London), ACP (master, John Phillips Meml. award 1955); mem. Am. Soc. Clin. Investigation (emeritus), AMA (gold medalist 1932, 39, George Minot award 1963), Assn. Am. Physicians (pres. 1970), Am. Physiol. Soc., Royal Soc. of Medicine (hon. mem. endocronology sect.), Endocrine Soc. (pres. 1962), Am. Clin. and Climatol. Assn. (pres.), Am. Acad. Arts and Scis., Royal Soc. Medicine (hon.), Royal Acad. of Medicine of Belgium, Interurban Clin. Club, John Hopkins Soc. Scholars, Aesculapian Club, Order of Hipolito of Peru (comdr. 1960), Sigma Xi, Nu Sigma Nu, Alpha Omega Alpha. Clubs: Harvard, Harvard Faculty; Country (Brookline); Essex County, St. Botolph, Tavern, Badminton & Tennis, Singing Beach (Manchester). Home: Beverly, Mass. Died June 26, 2004.

THROCKMORTON, JOAN HELEN, direct marketing consultant; b. Evanston, Ill., Apr. 11, 1931; d. Sydney L. and Anita H. (Pusheck) T.; m. Sheldon Burton Satin, June 26, 1982 (dec. Feb. 2002). BA with honors, Smith Coll., 1953. Mktg. exec. Lawrence Chait & Co., N.Y.C., 1965; mktg. exec. Cowles Communications, Inc., N.Y.C., 1968-69; founder, chief exec. officer Throckmorton Assocs., Inc., N.Y.C., 1970-83; pres. Joan Throckmorton, Inc., Pound Ridge, N.Y., from 1983. Lectr. in field; instr. Direct Mktg. Assn., Sch. Continuing Edn., NYU, N.Y.C., 1985; mem. corp. Culinary Inst. Am., 2000. Author: Winning Direct Response Advertising, 1986, 2d edit., 1996. Trustee Halle Ravine Com. Nature Conservancy, 2001; mem. expedition com. Outward Bound, 1980-83. Recipient Edward N. Mayer Jr. award, Direct Mktg. Edn. Found., 1996, Andi Emerson award John Caples Internat. Awards, Inc., 1996, E.F. Sisk award for vision Direct Mktg. Assn. Washington, 2001; named Direct Mktg. Women of the Yr., 1986; named to Direct Mktg. Assn.'s Hall of Fame, 1997. Mem. Women's Dir. Response Group (founding mem.), Dir. Mktg. Assn. (bd. dirs. 1971-77, exec. com. 1972-77, mem. long-range planning com. 1977-78), Women's Forum, Dir. Mktg. Idea Exchange, Dir. Mktg. Creative Guild (bd. dirs. 1984-85), Jr. League Mexico City, Jr. League N.Y.C., Phi Beta Kappa. Died Mar. 6, 2003.

THROP, GEORGE LAWRENCE, secondary education educator, mathematics educator; b. Greenville, Ohio, Jan. 17, 1942; s. Walter Ray and Virginia Maude (Carpenter) T.; m. Janet Irene Parker, June 26, 1966; children: Randall Jay, Laura Kay. BS in Edn., Ball State U., 1965, MA in Edn., 1969; postgrad., U. Ariz., 1975-85. Cert. prin. K-12, std. secondary tchr. 7-12 Ariz. C.C. Tchr. math./sci. Warren Twp. Schs., Indpls., 1966-69, Catalina Foothills Sch. Dist., Tucson, 1969-85; adminstrv. asst., tchr. Santa Cruz Valley Union H.S., Eloy, Ariz., 1985-88; asst. prin., at-risk dir. Somerton (Ariz.) Elem. Sch. Dist., 1988-90; assoc. prin. Creighton Elem. Sch. Dist., Phoenix, 1990-91; tchr. math. Phoenix Union H.S. Dist., from 1991. Asst. prof. math. U. Advancing Computer Tech., Phoenix, 1992—; evaluation cons. Sunnyside Unified Sch. Dist., Tucson, 1980; mem. evaluation team North Ctrl. Accrediting Assn., Marana, Ariz., 1988; mem. discipline task force Ariz. Dept. Edn., Phoenix, 1989-90; curriculum developer Phoenix Union H.S. Dist., 1994-99. Author: Integrated and Individualized Math/Science Curriculum, 1969-72; (handbook) Public Relations for Teachers, 1985 Sch. coord. United Way of Tucson, 1983; mem. Somerton Substance Abuse Task Force, 1988-90, Ariz. Humane Soc., Phoenix, 1991—; mem. exec. bd. Gov.'s Alliance Against Drugs, Phoenix, 1989-90. Recipient Mentor Program award Western Ariz. Area Health Edn. Ctr., Yuma, 1990; Dropout Prevention grantee Ariz. Dept. Edn., Somerton, 1988-90. Mem. ASCD, Catalina Foothills Edn. Assn. (pres. 1979-81), Phi Delta Kappa. Avocations: spectator sports, puzzles, computers, chess. Home: Glendale, Ariz. Died June 14, 2001.

THULIN, INGRID, actress, director, writer; b. Solleftea, Sweden, Jan. 27, 1929; d. Adam and Nana T.; m. Harry Schein, Sept. 15, 1956. Grad., Royal Dramatic Theatre Sch., Stockholm, 1951. Actress in numerous modern and classical plays Royal Dramatic Theatre, Stockholm, mcpl. theatres Malmo and Stockholm until 1962; actress Broadway, Italian stage, U.S. TV; films include: When Love Comes to the Village, 1950, Wild Strawberries, 1957; So Close to Life, 1958 (Best Actress, Cannes Internat. Film Festival); The Face, 1958; The Judge, 1960; The Four Horsemen of the Apocalypse, 1961; Winter Light, 1962; The Silence, 1963; La Guerre est Finie, 1968; The Damned, 1970; Cries and Whispers, 1973; A Handful of Love, 1974; La Cage, 1975; Cassandra Crossing, 1976; Agnes Will Die, 1977; One and One, 1978; Broken Skies, 1982; The Rehearsal, 1983; Il Corsario, La Casa del Sorriso, 1991; writer, dir. Swedish feature film Broken Skyes, 1983; dir. (short film) Devotion, Autobiography Somebody I Knew, 1992. Recipient numerous awards for acting excellence in theatre and films; named Best New Dir., Chgo. Film Festival, 1983. Died Jan. 7, 2004.

THURMOND, STROM, retired senator; b. Edgefield, S.C., Dec. 5, 1902; s. John William and Eleanor Gertrude (Strom) T.; m. Jean Crouch, Nov. 7, 1947 (dec. Jan. 1960); m. Nancy Moore, Dec. 22, 1968; children: Nancy Moore (dec.), J. Strom, Jr., Juliana Gertrude, Paul Reynolds, Essie Mae Washington-Williams. BS, Clemson Coll., 1923; 34 hon. degrees. Bar: S.C. 1930. Tchr. S.C. schs., 1923-29; city atty., county atty., supt. edn. Edgefield County, 1929-33; state senator, 1933-38; circuit judge, 1938-46; gov. of S.C., 1947-51; chmn. So. Govs. Conf., 1950; practiced in Alken, S.C., 1951-55; U.S. senator from S.C., 1954—2003; pres. pro tem, 1981-87, 1995—2001. Del. Nat. Democratic Conv., 1932, 36, 48, 52, 56, 60; chmn. S.C. dels., armed svcs. com.; mem. Judiciary VA com.; mem. Dem. Nat. Com., 1948; States Rights candidate for Pres. U.S., 1948; del. Nat. Republican Conv., 1968, 72, 76, 80, 84, 88, 92, 96. Bd. dirs. Ga.-Carolina council Boy Scouts Am. Served with AUS; attached to 82d Airborne Div. for D-Day invasion 1942-46, Europe; maj. gen. Res. Decorated Legion of Merit with oak leaf cluster, Bronze Star with V, Purple Heart, Croix de Guerre France; Cross of Order of Crown Belgium; others; recipient Congl. Medal Honor Soc. Nat. Patriots award, 1974, Presdl. Medal of Freedom, 1993. Mem. S.C. (past v.p.), ABA, Clemson Coll. Alumni Assn. (past pres.), also numerous def., vets., civic, fraternal and farm orgns. Republican. Baptist. Home: Aiken, SC. Died June 26, 2003.

TILLER, MICHAEL HEINRICH, environmental consultant; b. Huntsville, Ala., Feb. 1, 1953; s. Werner Gerhard and Ruth Lina (Urbanski) T.; m. Margaret Wilkinson, May 21, 1983. BS, Vanderbilt U., 1975; MBA, Pepperdine U., 1982; MS in Environ. Engring., U. So. Calif., 1984. Sr. staff engr. Woodward-Clyde Cons., Santa Ana, Calif., 1980-82; sr. environ. engr. Earth Tech. Corp., Long Beach, Calif., 1983-85; pres. environ. risk div. Tiller Cons. Group, Inc., Corona Del Mar, Calif., from 1985. Contbr. articles to profl. jours. Lt. USN, 1975-81. Mem. ASCE, Am. Indsl. Hygiene Assn. (full mem.), Soc. Risk Analysis, World Future Soc. (profl.), ASTM, Nat. Inst. Bldg. Scis. (asbestos task force 1985), Nat. Assn. Ins. Commnrs. (adv. com. environ. impairment liability ins. 1985), Newport Harbor C. of C. Avocations: chess, astromomy, swimming. Home: Saint Louis, Mo. Deceased.

TILLINGHAST, CHARLES CARPENTER, JR., aviation and financial consultant; b. Saxton's River, Vt., Jan. 30, 1911; s. Charles C. and Adelaide Barrows (Shaw) T.; m. Lisette Micoleau, Nov. 16, 1935; children: Charles Carpenter III, Elizabeth, Jane, Anne Shaw. Ph.B., Brown U., 1932; JD, Columbia U., 1935; L.H.D., S.D. Sch. Mines and Tech., 1959; LL.D., Franklin Coll., 1963, U. Redlands, 1964, Brown U., 1967, Drury Coll., 1967, William Jewell Coll., 1973. Bar: N.Y. bar 1935, Mich. 1943. Assoc. Hughes, Schurman & Dwight, 1935-37; dep. asst. dist. atty. N.Y. County, 1938-40; assoc. Hughes, Richards, Hubbard & Ewing, 1940-42; ptnr. Hughes, Hubbard, Blair & Reed (and predecessor firms), N.Y.C., 1942-57; v.p., dir. The Bendix Corp., Detroit, 1957-61; pres., chief exec. officer Trans World Airlines, Inc., 1961-69, chmn. bd., chief exec. officer, 1969-76, dir., 1961-81; dir., vice chmn. bd. White Weld & Co., Inc., 1977-78; mng. dir. Merrill Lynch White Weld Capital Markets Group, 1978-82. Bd. dirs. Henry Luce Found., Air Transport Assn., 1961-72, 74-75; mem. exec. com. Internat. Air Transport Assn., 1969-75. Bd. dirs. Cmty. Welfare Fund, Bronxville, 1951-53, pres., 1953; gov. Lawrence Hosp., Bronxville, 1955-59; trustee Brown U., 1954-61, 65-79, chancellor, 1968-79, fellow, 1979—; fellow Midwest Rsch. Inst., 1963-76, the Conf. Bd., 1965-76, People to People Program, 1961-70, Com. for Econ. Devel., 1967—; bd. visitors Sch. Law, Columbia U., 1962-92; bd. govs. John Carter Brown Libr., 1989-96. Mem. ABA, Assn. Bar City N.Y., Brown U. Club (N.Y.C.), Hope Club (R.I.), Sakonnet Golf Club. Home: Providence, RI. Deceased.

TIMBERG, SIGMUND, retired lawyer; b. Antwerp, Belgium, Mar. 5, 1911; came to U.S., 1916, naturalized, 1921; s. Arnold and Rose (Mahler) T.; m. Eleanor Ernst, Sept. 22, 1940; children: Thomas Arnold, Bernard Mahler, Rosamund and Richard Ernst (twins). AB, A.M., Columbia U., 1930, LL.B., 1933. Bar: N.Y. 1935, U.S. Supreme Ct. 1940, D.C. 1954. Sr. atty., solicitors' office Dept. Agr., 1933-35, chief, soil conservation sect., 1935-38; staff mem. Temporary Nat. Econ. Com., 1938-39; sr. atty. SEC, 1938-42; chief, property relations and indsl. orgn. div., reoccupation br. Bd. Econ. Warfare and Fgn. Econ. Adminstrn., 1942-44; spl. asst. to atty. gen., antitrust div. Dept. Justice, 1944-45, chief judgments and judgment enforcement sect., 1946-52; sec. UN Com. on Restrictive Bus. Practices, 1952-53; cons. UN, 1953-55, 62-64; pvt. law practice, 1954-88. Prof. law Georgetown U. Law School, 1952-54; faculty Parker Sch. Comparative Law, Columbia U., 1967-80; spl. counsel Senate Mil. Affairs Subcom. on Surplus Property Legislation, 1944; mem. Mission for Econ. Affairs, Am. Embassy, London, 1945; del. Anglo-Am. Telecommunications Conf., Bermuda, 1945, Geneva Copyright Conf., 1952; cons. Senate Patents Subcom., 1961, UN Patents Study, 1962-64, OAS, 1970; mem. adv. com. on fed. policy on indsl. innovation, patent and info. policy sub com., 1978-79, adv. com. on internat. investment, tech. and devel., 1979-85. Contbr. articles on antitrust, intellectual property and internat. law to legal periodicals. Mem. ABA, D.C. Bar Assn., Internat. Bar Assn., Internat. Law Assn., Am. Soc. Internat. Law, Washington Fgn. Law Soc., Am. Law Inst., Assn. Bar City N.Y., Copyright Soc. Am., Cosmos Club (Washington), Philosophy Club (Washington). Home: Washington, DC. Died Feb. 12, 2003.

TIMBERLAKE, MARSHALL, lawyer; b. Birmingham, Ala., July 25, 1939; s. Landon and Mary (Perry) T.; m. Rebecca Ann Griffin, Aug. 22, 1987; children: Sumner Timberlake Starling, Jane Ellison. BA, Washington and Lee U., 1961; JD, U. Ala., 1970. Bar: Ala. 1970, Ala. Supreme Ct. 1970, U.S. Dist. Ct. (no., so. and mid. dists.) Ala. 1970, U.S. Supreme Ct. 1976, U.S. Ct. Appeals (11th and 5th cirs.) 1981, U.S. Ct. Appeals (D.C. cir.) 1991. Assoc. Balch & Bingham Law Firm, Birmingham, 1970-76, ptnr., from 1976. Pres. Legal Aid Soc., Birmingham, 1980-81; chmn. Ala. Supreme Ct. Commn. on Dispute Resolution, 1994-96, commr., 1996—; trustee Ala. Dispute Resolution Found., 1995—, vice chmn., 1997—. Pres. Ala. Alcohol and Drug Abuse Coun., 1994-95, dir., 1989—; v.p. Assn. Atty. Mediators, 1994-97; co-chair Gov.'s Task Force on State Agy. Alternative Dispute Resolution, 1998—; bd. dirs. Partnership Assistance to the Homeless, 1998—, chmn. endowment fund com., 1999—. Capt. U.S. Army, 1962-66, Vietnam. Recipient Ann. award Dispute Resolution Inst., 1998; hon. fellow State Agy. ADR Program, 2001. Fellow Ala. Law Found.; mem. ABA, Ala. State Bar (chmn. corp. banking and bus. law sect. 1981-82, chmn. state bar task force on alternative dispute resolution 1992-94, State Bar Merit award 1995, co-chmn. state bar com. on ADR 1996-97, mem. state bar task force on jud. selection 1996-98), Birmingham Bar Assn. (mem. and co-chmn. grievance com. 1972-74, chmn. ethics com. 1975-76, chmn. unauthorized practice of law com. 1976-77, chmn. spl. projects com. 1994-95, co-chmn. com. on jud. and legal reform 1996-97, chmn. com. on jud. and legal reform 1997-98), Am. Arbitration Assn. (state adv. com.), Ala. Acad. Atty. Mediators (co-founder), Redstone Club (bd. govs. 1977 -78), Rotary (Birmingham chpt., chmn. civic club found. 1984), Beaux Arts Krewe, Mountain Brook Club. Republican. Presbyterian. Avocations: tennis, thoroughbred racing, photography. Home: Birmingham, Ala. Died Dec. 9, 2002.

TIMPTE, ROBERT NELSON, secondary school educator; b. Mpls., Dec. 4, 1925; s. Oscar William and Mildred Marie (Nelson) T. BS in Edn., U. Minn., 1949, postgrad., 1955-73; MA in History, U. Iowa, 1956. Jr. high english, social studies tchr. Bloomington (Minn.) Pub. Schs., 1955-63, secondary schs. social studies coord., 1963-65, K-12 social studies coord., 1965-73, jr. high sch. social studies tchr., 1973-85. Condr. insvc. in field. Editor curriculum guides and catalogs Bloomington K-12 Social Studies Guides, 1963-73, Human Rels. Guide: Inter and Intracultural Education, 1974; creator Realia (Material Culture Kits) Asia and Africa, 1966-73. Cons. Human Rights Commn., Bloomington, 1970—73; City Hall tour guide City of Bloomington, 1963—73; treas., bd. dirs. Hidden Village Townhomes, Golden Valley, Minn. India Inst. grant, 1966; recipient Omar Bonderud Human Rights award Bloomington Human Rights Commn., 1974, WCCO Radio Good Neighbor award, 1974. Mem. Am. Fedn. Tchrs., Minn. Ret. Tchrs. Assn., Minn. Coun. for Social Studies (treas., conv. arrangements chmn.). Democrat. Avocations: travel, the arts, american indian culture research. Home: Golden Valley, Minn. Died 2003.

TISCH, LAURENCE ALAN, diversified manufacturing and service executive; b. N.Y.C., Mar. 5, 1923; s. Al and Sadye (Brenner) T.; m. Wilma Stein, Oct. 31, 1948; children: Andrew, Daniel, James, Thomas. BSc cum laude, NYU, 1942; MA in Indsl. Engring, U. Pa., 1943; postgrad., Harvard Law Sch., 1946; LLD (hon.), Skidmore Coll., 1994. Pres. Tisch Hotels, Inc., N.Y.C., 1946-74; chmn. bd., co-CFO Loews Corp., N.Y.C., from 1960, now co-chmn.; CEO, chmn. CBS, N.Y.C., 1986—95. Chmn. bd. dirs. CNA Fin. Corp., Chgo.; bd. dirs. Bulova Corp. subs. Loews Corp., N.Y.C., ADP Corp., Petrie Stores Corp. Bd. dirs. United Jewish Appeal-Fedn.; chmn. bd. trustees NYU; trustee Met. Mus. Art, N.Y.C., N.Y. Pub. Libr. Mem. Coun. Fgn. Rels. Home: Rye, NY. Died Nov. 15, 2003.

TODD, BEN, lawyer; b. Tupelo, Miss., Mar. 27, 1944; s. James B. Sr. and Carma Francis (Robinson) T.; m. Janice Grissom, 1963 (div. 1964); 1 child, Sulynn, m. Carolyn Victoria Meason, Sept. 18, 1971; children: Amy, Brad. BBA, U. Miss., 1967; JD, Memphis State U., 1970. Bar: Miss. 1970, Tenn. 1970, U.S. Dist. Ct. Miss. 1976, U.S. Dist. Ct. Tenn. 1976, U.S. Supreme Ct. 1976. Assoc. Walter Buford, Memphis, 1970-73; sole practice Memphis, 1973-76 and from 86; sr. ptnr. Todd & Deal P.C., Memphis, 1976-86. Mem. men's com. Memphis Symphony, 1982-85; leadership mem. Boy Scouts Am., Memphis, 1984-86. Mem.Mem. ABA, Memphis Bar Assn., Shelby County Bar Assn., Assn. Trial Lawyers Am., N.Y. Trial Lawyers Assn., Tenn. Trial Lawyers Assn. (bd. of govs. 1974-84), Miss. Trial Lawyers Assn. Home: Coppell, Tex. Deceased.

TOLAND, JOHN WILLARD, historian, writer; b. La Crosse, Wis., June 29, 1912; s. Ralph and Helen Chandler (Snow) T.; m. Toshiko Matsumura, Mar. 12, 1960; 1 dau., Tamiko; children by previous marriage: Diana Toland Netzer, Marcia BA, Williams Coll., 1936; student, Yale Drama Sch., 1936-37; L.H.D., Williams Coll., 1968, U. Alaska, 1977, Western Conn. U., 1986. Mem. adv. council Nat. Archives. Author: Ships in the Sky, 1957, Battle: The Story of the Bulge, 1959, But Not in Shame, 1961 (Best Book Fgn. Affairs award Overseas Press Club), The Dillinger Days, 1963, The Flying Tigers, 1963, The Last 100 Days, 1966 (Best Book Fgn. Affairs citation Overseas Press Club), The Battle of the Bulge, 1966, The Rising Sun, 1970 (Van Wyck Brooks award for non-fiction, Best Book Fgn. Affairs award Overseas Press Club, Pulitzer prize for non-fiction), Adolf Hitler, 1976 (Best Book Fgn. Affairs award Overseas Press Club, Gold Medal Nat. Soc. Arts and Letters), Hitler, The Pictorial Documentary of His Life, 1978, No Man's Land, 1980 (Best Book Fgn. Affairs citation Overseas Press Club), Infamy, 1982, In Mortal Combat, 1991; (novels) Gods of War, 1985, Occupation, 1987, In Mortal Combat, 1991, Captured by History, 1997; author short stories. Served to capt. USAAF, 1942-46, 1947-49. Mem. Authors Guild, Accademia del Mediterraneo., Western Front Assn. (hon. v.p.) Home: Danbury, Conn. Died Jan. 4, 2004.

TOLLETT, KENNETH SCRUGS, education educator; b. Wash., July 14, 1931; s. Harrel E. and Hattie Mae (Scruggs) T.; m. Jacqueline Scott, June 1953 (div. 1974); children: Erica, Nicola; Queen Wiggs (div. June 1995); 1 child, Kenneth S. AB, U. Chgo., 1952, MA, 1958, JD, 1955. Bar: Tex. 1961, U.S. Dist. Ct. (no. dist.) Ill. 1955. Legal aide, atty. Sheriff Joseph Lohman Cook County, Chgo., 1955-57; acting dean, prof. Tex. So. U., Houston, 1958-62, dean Sch. Law, 1963-70; vis. fellow Ctr. for study of Dem. Instns., Santa Barbara, Calif., 1970, 71; dir. Inst. Study Ednl. Policy Howard U., Wash., 1974-85, disting. prof. higher edn., 1971—2003. Vis. prof. Sch. Law U. Colo., Boulder, 1970-71; cons., writer Pres. bd. advisors Hist. Black Colls. and U., Wash., 1992; dir., supr. prodn. ISEP various publs. Author: Affirmative Action: Sound Advocacy, Full Data and Debate Can Save it, 2000; contbr. articles to profl. jours. Recipient C. Francis Stodford award Nat. Bar Assn., 1968, U. Chgo. Alumni Assocs. Profl. Achievement award, 1972; grantee Howard U., 1971—. Mem. Am. Assn. U. Profs. (com. govt. rels. 1992, cons. com. minority edn. 1991-94), Nat. Coun. Educating Black Children, Senate Coun. Howard U. (faculty), Internat. Assn. Philosophy Law and Social Philosophy (Am. sect., 1972), Carnegie Commn. Future Higher Edn., Tex. Constl. Revision Commn., Supreme Ct. Hist. Soc. (program com. 1994). Avocations: reading, art appreciation, history, fitness. Home: Washington, DC. Died Sept. 22, 2003.

TOMBAUGH, RICHARD LEE, financial aid consultant; b. Warsaw, Ind., Aug. 16, 1938; s. Wayne Hurst and Trella Marie (Kuhn) Tombaugh; m. Phyllis Cook, 1960 (div. 1967); children: Brian, Bradley; m. C. Jeannie Bauridl, Apr. 10, 1976; children: Randall, Meagan. B of Phys. Edn., Purdue U., 1960, MS in Edn., 1961; postgrad. in higher edn., Mich. State U., 1965. Asst. unit mgr. residence halls U. Wis., Madison, 1961-63; head resident advisor Mich. State U., 1963-65; asst. dir. admissions, dir. student loans and fin. aid Purdue U., West Lafayette, Ind., 1965-72; from assoc. dir. to dir. fin. aid George Washington U., Washington, 1972-74; exec. sec. Nat. Assn. Student Fin. Aid Adminstrs., Washington, 1972-75; exec. dir. Nat. Inst. Fin. Aid Adminstrn., Washington, 1972-75; pres. Ednl. Methods, Inc., Denver and Washington, 1975-79; v.p. mktg. Sys. Rsch. Inc., Washington and L.A., 1979-80; dir. Student Fin. Assistance Tng. Program, Nat. Assn. Student Fin. Aid Adminstrs., others, 1980-82; sr. program analyst Advanced Tech., Inc., Reston, Va., 1983-84; coord. market devel., mgr. ednl. svcs. Nat. Computer Sys., Inc., Englewood, Colo., 1984-88; cons., dir. need analysis svcs., dir. mktg. CSX Comml. Svcs., Jacksonville, Fla., 1989-92; pres., CEO, Edn. Fin. Cons. Group, Jacksonville, from 1992. Columnist Greentree Gazette; contbr. articles to profl. publs. Scoutmaster Boy Scouts Am., 1956-60. Mem.: Fla. Assn. Student Fin. Aid Adminstrs., Midwest Assn. Student Fin. Aid Adminstrs. (Disting. Svc. award 1975), Nat. Assn. Student Fin. Aid Adminstrs. (nat. coun. 1968—70, 1970—75, Hall of Honor inductee, Disting. Svc. award 1975), Del./D.C./Md. Assn. Student Fin. Aid Adminstrs. (life). Home: Atlantic Beach, Fla. Died Dec. 26, 2002.

TONDEL, LYMAN MARK, JR., lawyer; b. July 19, 1912; s. Lyman Mark and Emma (Sweet) T.; m. Alice B. Jones, June 12, 1936; 1 son, Mark, III.; m. Jean Basch, Feb. 11, 1944; children: Marcia Jean Tondel Davis, Lawrence Chapman; m. Betty Capps, May 3, 1980. LLB, Harvard U., 1936; AB, U. Wash., 1933. Bar: N.Y. 1937, U.S. Supreme Ct. 1942, U.S. Ct. Appeals (2d and 3d cirs.) 1943, D.C. 1952, U.S. Dist. Ct. (so., eas. and no. dists.) N.Y., U.S. Ct. Appeals (4th cir.) 1974. Assoc. Root, Clark, Buckner and Ballantine, N.Y.C., 1936-42, 42-47; asst. to gen. counsel Bd. Investigation and Rsch. Under the Transp. Act., 1940, 42; asst. gen. counsel ASARCO, N.Y.C., 1947-51; asv. com., 1948-51; ptnr. Cleary, Gottlieb, Steen and Hamilton and predecessor firms, N.Y.C., 1951-82; counsel Cleary, Gottlieb, Steen and Hamilton, N.Y.C., from 1982. Lectr. NYU Sch. Law, 1931-51, Columbia U. Sch. of Law, 1982. Editor: The Hammarskjold Forum Series on the Role of Law in the Settlement of International Disputes, 1st 8 vols., 1962-66; contbr. articles and studies for profl. jours. and orgns. Former mem. adv. com. internat. law dept. State; chmn. adv. bd. Internat. and Comparative Law Ctr., Southwestern Legal Found., 1972-74. Fellow Inst. Jud. Adminstrn. (pres. 1976-78, exec. com.), Am. bar Found. (chmn. fellows 1977-78); mem. ABA (bd. govs. 1974-75, ho. of dels. 1946-48, 58-60, 62-79, 83, nat. chmn. Jr. Bar Conf. 1945-46, chmn. sect. internat. law 1951-53, chmn. commn. med. prof. liability, 1975-78, chmn. commn. legal problems of elderly 1979-85), Am. Law Inst. (coun. emeritus), N.y. State bar Assn. (pes. 1968-69), 2d Cir. Jud. Conf. (chmn. program and planning com. 1971-74), Southwestern Legal Found. (chmn. adv. bd. Internat. and Comparative Law Ctr. 1972-74, dir.), Assn. Bar City N.Y. (chmn. com. on profl. responsibility 1981-84). Episcopalian. Club: Century. Deceased.

TOOMEY, THOMAS MURRAY, lawyer; b. Washington, Dec. 9, 1923; s. Vincent L. and Catherine V. (McCann) T.; m. Grace Donohoe, June 22, 1948; children: Isabelle Marie Toomey Hessick, Helen Marie, Mary Louise, Thomas Murray. Student, Duke U., 1943-44, Catholic U. Am., 1942-43, 47-49, JD, 1949. Bar: D.C. 1949, Md. 1952. Sole practice, Washington and Md., 1949—. Bd. dirs. Allied Capital Corp, Washington, Chgo., Detroit, San Francisco, Atlanta, Frankfurt, Germany, Fed. Ctr. Plz. Corp., Nat. Capital Bank, Washington. Chmn. aviation and transp. coms. Met. Washington Bd. Trade, 1954-76, bd. dirs., 1962-77; chmn. dedication Dulles Internat. Airport, 1962; trustee Cath. U. Am., 1981—; founding trustee Heights Sch. Served to 1st lt. USMC, 1942-46, 50-52. Recipient Ann. Alumni Achievement award, Cath. U., 1977, Most. Disting. Alumnus award, St. John's Coll. H.S. D.C., 1994, 1st Bishop Thomas J. Shahan award, Cath. U., 2001. Mem. ABA, D.C. Bar Assn., Md. Bar Assn., Bar Assn. D.C., Am. Judicature Soc., Comml. Law League Am., Friendly Sons St. Patrick (pres. 1983), Sovereign Mil. Order of Malta (Fed. Assn. U.S.A.), Congl. Golf and Country Club, Kenwood Golf and Country Club, Univ. Club, Army and Navy Club (Washington), Tower Club, Lago Mar Beach Club (Ft. Lauderdale, Fla.). Home: Chevy Chase, Md. Died 2003.

TOOTHACKER, WILLIAM SANFORD, III, physics educator; b. Washington, Mar. 23, 1943; s. William Sanford Jr. and Grace (Nelson) T. BS, Purdue U., 1965; MA, Wayne State U., 1970; PhD, U. Mich., 1977. Rsch. asst. Edsel B. Ford Inst. for Med. Rsch., Detroit, 1966-72; instr. physics Wayne County C.C., Detroit, 1972-83; asst. prof. physics Pa. State U., Mont Alto, 1984-89, assoc. prof. physics, 1989-96, prof. physics, from 1996. Vis. lectr. The Open U., Eng., 1981-82; vis. scientist Fermi Nat. Lab., Chgo., 1990-91, Deutsches Elektronen-Synchrotron Lab., Germany, 1997-98. Reviewer Am. Jour. Physics, 1990—; contbr. more than 60 articles to profl. jours. Mem. Am. Phys. Soc., Am. Assn. Physics Tchrs. Home: Chambersburg, Pa. Died May 16, 2000.

TOPAZ, MURIEL, dance educator, author; b. Phila., May 7, 1932; d. Joseph Topaz and Rhea Rebecca Rosenbloom; m. Jacob Druckman, June 5, 1954; children: Karen Druckman Jeanneret, Daniel Druckman. Student, NYU, 1950-51; studies with Martha Graham, Antony Tudor, The Juilliard Sch., 1951-54; student, Dance Notation Bur., N.Y.C., 1954-56. Mem. faculty The Juilliard Sch., N.Y.C., 1959-70, dir. dance div., 1985-92; exec. dir. Dance Notation Bur., 1978-85; co-chmn. First Internat. Congress on Movement Notation Bur., Israel, 1984, 2d Internat. Congress, Hong Kong, 1990. Chmn. artistic com. Dance Notation Bur.; adjudicator Regional Dance/Am., Mid-States 1980, Pacific 1981, N.E. 1996. Author: Changes and New Developments in Labanotation, 1966, Intermediate Reading Studies, 1972, Choreography and Dance: The Notation Issue, 1988, Alvin Ailey, An American Visionary, 1995, Elementary Labanotation, A Study Guide, 1996; author: (with Hackney & Manno) Elementary Study Guide, 1970, Elementary Reading Studies, 1970, (with Edelson) Readings in Modern Dance, 1972, (with Everett) Guide to Performing Arts Programs, 1998; author, sr. editor Dance Mag.; exec. editor Choreography and Dance, Dance Studies; reconstructor: Lilac Garden (Milw. Ballet), Continuo (Paris Conservatory, N.C. Sch. Arts), Notator Moor's Pavane. Mem. May O'Donnell Hon. Com., 1979; chmn. dance panel N.Y. State Coun. on Arts, 1982-83; assessor Can. Coun., 1987; auditor NEA, 1989-97; chmn. Internat. Coun. Kinetography Laban, 1997—; panel chair Am. Dancing, Kennedy Ctr.; dance cons. Mass. Cultural Coun. Recipient fgn. travel grant Inst. Internat. Edn., 1967; Guggenheim fellow, 1997-98. Home: Milford, Conn. Died Apr. 28, 2003.

TOPHAM, DOUGLAS WILLIAM, writer, consultant; b. Hollywood, Calif. s. Ollie Austin and Harriet Winifred (Scott) T. BS, Stanford U., 1964, AM, 1965. Cert. secondary tchr., Calif. Tchr. The Principia, St. Louis, 1969-72; instr. Can. Coll., Redwood City, Calif., 1973-74; writer Varian Assocs., Palo Alto, Calif., 1977, Four-Phase Systems Inc., Cupertino, Calif., 1977-80, MicroPro Internat., San Rafael, Calif., 1980-81, Zentec Corp., Santa Clara, Calif., 1981-85; contract writer various cos., 1985-96, TeleVideo Systems Inc., Sunnyvale, Calif., 1988-89; freelance writer, cons. Santa Clara, 1989-96. Cons. ABC-TV, Burbank, Calif., 1974. Author: WordStar Training Guide, 1981, UNIX and XENIX, 1985 (Small Computer Club Book of Month 1985), Using WordStar, 1988, WordPerfect 5.0 with 5.1 Extensions, 1990, A DOS User's Guide to UNIX, 1990, First Book of UNIX, 1990 (Small Computer Club Book of Month 1992), A System V Guide to UNIX and XENIX, 1990, Up and Running with Q & A, 1991, Portable UNIX, 1992 (Small Computer Club Book of Month 1993). Bd. dirs. Las Brisas Condominium Assn., 1988-89, Christian Sci. Ch., 1988-89. Capt. USAF, 1965-69. Acad. scholar Stanford U., 1960-64. Mem. Authors Guild, Writers Connection, Nat. Writers Union. Avocations: tennis, swimming, bicycling, running. Deceased.

TOPLITZ, GEORGE NATHAN, lawyer; b. Winsted, Conn., June 13, 1936; s. Morris and Rose (Dolinsky) T.; m. Janet S. Strauss, July 30, 1961 (div.); children: Jill, Wendy, Anna; m. Kimilene A. Snead, Nov. 25, 1979. BA, U. Conn., 1958; LLB, Boston U., 1961. Bar: N.Y. 1964, U.S. Dist. Ct. (so. dist.) N.Y. 1968, U.S. Dist. Ct. (ea. dist.) N.Y. 1968, U.S. Ct. Appeals (2d cir.) 1986, U.S. Supreme Ct. 1987. Claims atty. Royal-Globe Ins. Co., surety dept., N.Y.C., 1963-65; surety atty. Transam. Inst. Co., N.Y.C., 1965-67; assoc. Max E. Greenberg, Cantor, Reiss, N.Y.C., 1967—, ptnr., 1974-88; ptnr. Max E. Greenberg, Cantor, Trager, Toplitz, 1988—; lectr. Am. Mgmt. Assn., 1974-76, Am. Assn. Cost Engrs., 1974-75, Sch. Continuing Edn. NYU, 1975; NW Ctr. Profl. Edn., 1988. With U.S. Army, 1961-63. Recipient Letter of Commendation for acting vol. spl. master Supreme Ct. N.Y., 1982, 84, 85, 86, 87, 88, 89, 90, Fed. mediator, U.S. Dist. Ct. (ea. dist.), N.Y., 1992. Mem. ABA, N.Y. State Bar Assn., N.Y. County Lawyers Assn., Assn. Trial Lawyers Am., Internat. Platform Assn. Home: Fort Lee, NJ. Died Mar. 13, 2002.

TOPPING, PETER, historian, educator; b. Milw., May 13, 1916; s. William P. and Anastasia (Makris) Topitzes; m. Eva V. Catafygiotu, June 20, 1951; 1 son, John Themis. BA, U. Wis., 1937, MA, 1938; postgrad., U. Cin., 1939-40; PhD, U. Pa., 1942. Instr. history U. Wis., 1943-44, Northwestern U., 1944-45; asst. prof. history U. Calif.-Santa Barbara, 1948-53; librarian Gennadeion Am. Sch. Classical Studies, Athens, Greece, 1953-60, mem. mng. com., 1961—; vis. assoc. prof. history, library cons. U. Pa., 1960-61; assoc. prof. history, later Greek studies U. Cin., 1961-64, prof., 1964-67, Charles Phelps Taft prof., 1967-78; fellow Grad. Sch., 1972—78; sr. research assoc. Dumbarton Oaks Rsch. Libr. and Collection, Washington, 1978-84; mem. bd. scholars Dumbarton Oaks Center for Byzantine Studies, 1972-74, mem. sr. fellows, 1979-86, hon. sr. research assoc., 1984—. Interpreting officer U.S. staff Allied Mission to Observe Greek Elections, 1946; mem. exec. com. Frank L. Weil Inst. in Religion and Humanities, 1964-78 Author: Feudal Institutions as Revealed in the Assizes of Romania, 1949, (with Jean Longnon) Documents sur le régime des terres dans la principauté de Moreé au XIVme siècle, 1969, Studies on Latin Greece A.D. 1205-1715, 1977; contbr. articles, revs. to hist. jours. Advanced fellow Belgian Am. Edn. Found., 1947-48; Fulbright sr. research awardee Greece, 1950-51; sr. fellow NEH, 1974-75 Mem. Am. Hist. Assn., Mediaeval Acad. Am., Soc. Byzantine Studies (Athens, Greece) (hon.), Modern Greek Studies Assn., Phi Beta Kappa. Democrat. Mem. Greek Orthodox Ch. Home: Mc Lean, Va. Died Oct. 21, 2003.

TORREBLANCA REYES, MAGIN, bishop; b. Huajuapan de Leon, Mexico, Aug. 19, 1929; Ordained priest Roman Cath. Ch., 1953; named titular bishop of Assava, 1973; bishop of Texcoco, 1978—. Died Jan. 10, 1998.

TORREY, ELLA KING, academic administrator; b. Bronxville, NY; Graduate, Yale U., 1980, U. Miss. Program officer for culture The Pew Charitable Trusts, 1995; founder, dir. Pew Fellowships in the Arts, 1985-91, 1985-91; pres. San Francisco Art Inst., 1995—2002. Founder, pres. Grantmakers in the Arts; panelist NEA, NEH; mem. Mayor's Cultural Adv. Coun. City of Phila.; art adv. com., adv. com. Art in City Hall; cons., adv. in field; curator Ctr. Study So. Culture, Miss., Whitney Mus., N.Y.C., Harvard Theater Collection, Cambridge, Mass., others; mem. profl. coms. Coun. on Founds. Bd. dirs. nat. Campaign Freedom of Expression. Died Apr. 30, 2003.

TOSE, LEONARD H. professional football team executive; b. Bridgeport, Pa., Mar. 6, 1915; s. Mike Tose. Grad., U. Notre Dame, 1937. With Tose Trucking Co., Bridgeport, from 1946, pres., from 1946. Pres. K & S Canning Co., Bridgeport; pres., owner Phila. Eagles, NFL team, 1969-1985; mem. mgmt. council NFL and NFL Films. Donor Phila. Sch. System Varsity Football Program, 1971. Died Apr. 15, 2003.

TOWNSEND, CHARLES DELMAR, editor; b. Holbrook, Mass., May 18, 1911; s. Leon Irving and Georgiana Maybre (Dorr) T.; m. Edna Caroline Waugh, Apr. 8, 1936 (dec. July 1989). BSME, Northea. U., Boston, 1934. Plant supt. S.K. Wellman Co., Cleve., 1944-46; chief indsl. engr. A.B. Chance Co., Centralia, Mo., 1946-49; owner, cons. Profl. Expediting, West Hartford, Conn., 1954-58; co-owner Chedwato Svc., Conn. and Vt., 1954-69, Aceto Bookmen, Middleboro, Mass., 1969-79, owner, editor, genealogist Sarasota, Fla., from 1979. Editor: Death Records of Ludlow, Vermont, 1995, Gravestone Inscriptions of Acworth, New Hampshire, 1996; compiler, editor: Some Cemetery Inscriptions, 1996. Mem. Nat. Geneal. Soc., New England Hist. Geneal. Soc., Sarasota Geneal. Soc. Avocation: genealogical research. Died May 13, 2002.

TOWNSEND, CHARLES EBY, retired obstetrician-gynecologist; b. Washington, Aug. 22, 1926; BA, George Washington U., 1948, MD, 1951. Intern Emer Hosp., Washington, 1951-52; resident Columbia Hosp. Women, Washington, 1952-55, with. Clin. assoc. prof. ob-gyn. Georgetown U., 1988-96. Mem. Am. Coll. Ob-gyn. Home: Washington, DC. Died Sept. 3, 2001.

TOWNSEND, JAMES ROGER, political science educator; b. Hastings, Nebr., Nov. 9, 1932; s. Lewis A. and Ruby (Nelson) T.; m. Lucile Peake, Dec. 27, 1960 (div. Aug. 1974); children: Matthew P., Michael N.; m. Sandra J. Perry, Sept. 20, 1981. BA, U. Omaha, 1953; MA, U. Calif., Berkeley, 1957, PhD, 1965. Asst. prof. polit. sci. U. Calif., Berkeley, 1964-68; assoc. prof. polit. sci. and East Asian studies U. Wash., Seattle, 1968-74, assoc. dir. comparative and fgn. area studies, 1972-75, prof., 1974—91. Vis. lectr. Chinese U. Hong Kong, 1966-67, Inst. Polit. Sci. U. Tübingen, Fed. Republic Germany, 1986; mem. Joint Com. Contemporary China Social Sci. Research Council, N.Y.C., 1970-74, Com. for Scholarly Communication with the People's Republic of China, Washington, 1976-78; former internat. adviser Internat. Asian Studies Program Chinese U. Hong Kong, external examiner dept. govt., 1983-85. Author: Political Participation in Communist China, 1967, The Revolutionization of Chinese Youth, 1967, Politics in China, 1974; author/editor: People's Republic of China: A Basic Handbook, 1979. Bd. dirs. Nat. Com. on U.C.-China Relations, N.Y.C., 1969-72; chmn. Seattle Regional China Council, Seattle, 1977-80. Served as cpl. U.S. Army, 1953-55, Korea. Fellow Ford Found., Hong Kong, 1961-63, Rockefeller Found., Hong Kong, 1966-67, Social Sci. Research Council, 1975-76, 82-83, Research Sch. Pacific Studies Austrialian Nat. U., Canberra, 1983. Mem. Am. Polit. Sci. Assn., Assn. Asian Studies, Asia Soc. (China council 1975-78). Home: Seattle, Wash. Died Jan. 17, 2004.

TRACHTENBERG, JUDITH, lawyer, educator; b. Newark, May 21, 1949; d. Bertram and Estelle (Meyers) T. Diplôme, McGill U., Montreal, Que., Can., 1970; BA in Math. and French, Rutgers U., 1971; MAT in French, Ind. U., 1973, JD, 1978. Bar: Ind. 1978, N.J. 1985, Pa., 1985. Various tchg. positions, 1973-76; assoc. Montgomery, Elsner, & Pardieck, Seymour, Ind., 1978-80; pvt. practice Columbus, Ind., 1980-82; mng. atty. Women's Legal Clinic, South Bend, Ind., 1982-84; v.p. Ctr. for Non-Profit Corps., Princeton, N.J., 1985-91; instr. Fairleigh Dickinson U. and Seton Hall U., Madison and South Orange, N.J., from 1990; pvt. practice Roosevelt, N.J., from 1991. Cons. Ctr. for Non-Profit Corps., North Brunswick, 1992—. Editor: (book chpt.) Bender's Federal Tax Service, 1992; mem. editl. bd. Non-Profit Sector Resource Institute, 1994—. Mem. charter class Leadership N.J., New Brunswick, 1986-87; sec., trustee Roosevelt Arts Project, 1988—; chair, trustee Mercer St. Friends Ctr., Trenton, N.J., 1991-97; treas., trustee Storytelling Arts, 1998—; sec., treas. Friends Ctr. Fund, 1998—; trustee N.J. Policy Perspective, 1999—, Fund for Roosevelt, 2000—; mem. numerous charitable orgns. Recipient Equal Justice medal Legal Svcs. of N.J., 1995. Home: Roosevelt, NJ. Died July 6, 2001.

TRAIL, MERVIN L. health facility administrator; b. Cumberland, Md., Dec. 2, 1933; s. Watson Daniel and Lelah Blanche (Deahl) T.; m. Edythe Marie Wenger, June 8, 1958; children: Shelby, Lisa, Kelly, Kristi. BA, Bridgewater Coll., 1955; MD, U. Md., 1959; PhD, U. New Orleans, 1994. Intern U.S. Naval Hosp., Portsmouth, Va., 1959-60; resident in otolaryngology, head and neck surgery Johns Hopkins Hosp., Balt., 1967-68; asst. prof., dir. clin. tng. dept. otorhinolaryngology U. New Orleans, 1968-70, assoc. prof., 1970-74, clin. prof., 1974-92, prof. dir., 1992-93, prof., chmn., 1993-94; dir. Stanley S. Scott Cancer Ctr., New Orleans, 1991-94; chancellor La. State U. Med. Ctr., New Orleans, from 1994. Bd. dirs. Drs. Hosp., Metairie, La., La. State U. Med. Ctr. Found., New Orelans Regional Med. Ctr. Contbr. articles to profl. jours. Pres. Greater New Orleans Tourist and Conv. Commn., 1987-88; co-chmn. media and hospitality com. Rep. Nat. Conv., New Orleans, 1988; chmn. exec. com. New Orleans Sports Found., 1988-94; pres. Ernest N. Morial Exhbn. Hall Authority, New Orleans, 1992-95. Lt. USN, 1959-63. Mem. Assn. Acad. Health Ctrs., Alpha Omega Alpha. Avocations: golf, travel. Home: Metairie, La. Died Jan. 3, 2001.

TRAJKOVSKI, BORIS, President of Macedonia; b. Strumica, Macedonia, June 25, 1956; m. Vilma Trajkovski; children: Sara, Stefan. LLM, U. St. Cyril and Methodius, 1980. Head legal dept. Sloboda, 1980—97; chief Cabinet Major Kisela Voda, Skopje, Macedonia, 1997—98; dep. min. fgn. affairs Rep. Macedonia, 1998—99, pres., 2000—04. Mem. Internat. Conf. Conflict Resolution, Atlanta; pres. Macedonian-Croatian Soc. Friendship; pres. ch. coun. United Meth. Ch. Died Feb. 26, 2004.

TREFILIO, ANN, medical/surgical nurse, educator; b. Bklyn., May 6, 1954; d. Pasquale and Jacqueline (Deodato) Spinelli; m. Alan Trefilio, Sept. 3, 1978; children: John, Bernadette. ADN, SUNY, Farmingdale, 1974; BSN, SUNY, Stony Brook, 1982. Staff nurse Community Hosp. Western Suffolk, Hauppauge, N.Y., from 1974. Charge nurse diabetic unit Community Hosp. Western Suffolk, Hauppauge, 1992-99, LPN instr. Ea. Suffolk Boces, 1995-99. Recipient Dr. Stein Meml. award Community Hosp. Western Suffolk, 1990. Avocations: fitness, class mother, quilling, eucharistic minister. Home: Port Jefferson Station, NY. Died Aug. 15, 1999.

TRENTON, JOHN WILLIAM, retired surgeon; b. Petersburg, W.Va., 1917; MD, U. Pa., 1942. Diplomate Am. Bd. Surgery. Intern USN Hosp., Bethesda, Md., 1942-43, resident Phila., 1948-50, 51-52. Fellow Am. Coll. Surgeons; mem. AMA. Home: Somerset, Pa. Died May 12, 1999.

TREVOR, BRONSON, economist; b. N.Y.C., Nov. 12, 1910; s. John Bond and Caroline Murray (Wilmerding) T.; A.B., Columbia Coll., 1931; m. Eleanor Darlington Fisher, Nov. 8, 1946; children— Eleanor, Bronson, Caroline. Own bus., 1931—; dir., asst. sec. Northwestern Terminal R.R., 1952-58; chmn. bd. Texinia Corp., 1959-92. Former dir. chmn. fin. com. Gen. Hosp. of Saranac Lake mem. Council for Agrl. and Chemurgic Research, Am. Forestry Assn. Mem. Republican County Com. of N.Y. County, 1937-39; leader in primary election campaigns N.Y. County, 1937, 38, 39 to free local Rep. party orgn. from leftwing affiliations. Served with U.S. Army, 1942, World War II. Mem. S.A.R., Soc. Colonial Wars. Clubs: Union, Knickerbocker, Racquet and Tennis, Piping Rock, Bath and Tennis. Author: (pamphlet) The United States Gold Purchase Program, 1941; also numerous articles on econ. subjects. Home: Paul Smiths, NY. Deceased.

TREVOR, LEIGH BARRY, lawyer; b. Galesburg, Ill., Aug. 29, 1934; s. Dean Spaulding and Jean Elizabeth (Barry) T.; m. Mary Witherell, Aug. 8, 1978; children: John W. Hoffman, Ann Kete, Stephen S., Julia B. Kramer, Elizabeth P. Grad., Phillips Acad., 1952; AB magna cum laude, Harvard U., 1956, LLB, 1962. Bar: Ohio 1963, U.S. Dist. Ct. D.C. 1970. Assoc. Jones, Day, Reavis & Pogue, Cleve., 1962-68, ptnr., from 1969, ptnr.-in-charge, 1990-93. Sec. Dix & Eaton, Inc., Cleve.; lectr. on hostile corp. takeovers, other corp. law topics. Contbr. articles to profl. jours. Trustee State Troopers of Ohio, 1985—; pres. Stakeholders in Am., Mpls., 1987-88; trustee Cleveland State U. Found., 1990-94, Gt. Lakes Theater Festival, 1991-94. Lt. (j.g.) USN, 1956-59. Fellow Ohio State Bar Found.; mem. Ohio State Bar Assn. (mem. tender offer subcom. 1982—, chmn. corp. law com. 1989-91, coun. of dels. 1991—), Cleve. Bar Assn., D.C. Bar Assn., Phi Beta Kappa. Republican. Episcopalian. Home: Cleveland, Ohio. Died Sept. 21, 1999.

TREVOR-ROPER, H(UGH) R(EDWALD) (BARON DACRE OF GLANTON), historian, author, educator; b. Jan. 15, 1914; s. Bertie William Edward and Kathleen (Davison) Trevor-Roper; m. Alexandra Howard-Johnston, 1954 (dec. Aug. 1997). Educated Charterhouse, Christ Ch., Oxford. Rsch. fellow Merton Coll., Oxford, 1937-39, student, Christ Ch., 1945-57, censor, 1947-52; Regius prof. modern history, fellow Oriel Coll. Oxford U., 1957-80; master of Peterhouse, Cambridge, Eng., 1980-87; dir. Times Newspapers Ltd., 1974-88. Author: Archbishop Laud, 1573-1645, 1940, The Last Days of Hitler, 1947, Hitler's Secret Conversations, 1941-44, 1953, The Gentry 1540-1640, 1953, Men and Events: Historical Essays, 1957, The Rise of Christian Europe, 1965, George Buchanan and the Ancient Scottish Constitution, 1966, Religion, the Reformation and Social Change, and Other Essays, 1967, The Philby Affair, 1968, The European Witch-Craze of the 16th and 17th Centuries, 1970, A Hidden Life: The Enigma of Sir Edmund Backhouse, 1976, Princes and Artists: Patronage and Ideology at Four Habsburg Courts, 1517-1633, 1976, Renaissance Essays 1985, Catholics, Anglicans and Puritans, 1987, From Counter-Reformation to Glorious Revolution, 1992; editor: The Bormann Letters, 1954, Gibbon, The Decline and Fall of the Roman Empire, 1963, Blitzkrieg to Defeat: Hitler's War Directives, 1939-1945, 1964, Essays in British History, 1964, The Age of Expansion: Europe and the World, 1559-1660, 1968, Macaulay, The History of England, 1968, Final Entries 1945: The Diaries of Joseph Goebbels, 1978. Died Jan. 26, 2003.

TRIAS-MONGE, JOSE, lawyer, former territory supreme court chief justice; b. San Juan, P.R., May 5, 1920; s. José and Belén Monge; m. Jane G. Trías(dec.), June 3, 1943; children: Jose Enrique, Peter James, Arturo Trías, m. Viola Orsini. BA, U. P.R., 1940; MA, Harvard U., 1943, LL.B., 1944; J.S.D., Yale U., 1947. Bar: P.R. 1945, U.S. Supreme Ct 1949. Teaching fellow Harvard U., 1943-44; practiced law San Juan, 1950-52, 57-74; atty. gen. P.R., 1953-57; chief justice Supreme Ct. P.R., San Juan, 1974-85; of counsel Trías, Acevedo & Otero, San Juan, 1989—2003. Mem. P.R. Constl. Conv., 1951-52, Inter-Am. Juridical Commn., OAS, 1966-67; pres. P.R. Acad. Legislation and Jurisprudence, 1985—2003; lectr. U. P.R., 1947-49 Author: El Sistema Judicial de Puerto Rico, 1978, La Crisis del Derecho en Puerto Rico, 1979, Historia Constitucional de Puerto Rico, Vol. I, 1980, Vol. II, 1981, Vol. III, 1982, Vol. IV, 1983, Vol. V, 1994; Sociedad, Derecho y Justicia, 1985, El Choque de Dos Culturas Juridicas en Puerto Rico, 1991, Puerto Rico: The Trials of the Oldest Colony in the World, 1997. Mem. nat. com. ACLU, 1958-74; v.p. Festival Casals, Inc., 1957-69, 73-74; trustee U. P.R., 1962-72. Mem. Bar Assn. P.R., ABA, Soc. de Legislation Comparée, French Acad. Comparative Law, Royal Acad. Spanish Lang. (life) Roman Catholic. Home: San Juan, PR. Died June 24, 2003.

TRIBBLE, DAGMAR HAGGSTROM (MRS. ELSTON J. TRIBBLE), artist; b. N.Y.C.; d. Olaf Albin and Ida (Sabini) Haggstrom; m. Elston J. Tribble, July 15, 1933; 1 child, Martha Watkins (Mrs. James Malcolm McKinnon). Student, Parsons Sch. Design, N.Y. and Paris, 1928, Art Students League, 1930-32, Farnsworth Sch. Painting, 1949-50. Tchr. fashion illustration Parsons Sch. Design, 1929-32; designer sportswear and beachwear Travelo Corp., N.Y.C., 1933-45; founder, pres. The Garden State Watercolor Soc., 1969—. One-woman shows at Beard Sch., Orange, N.J., Monmouth Coll., West Long Branch, The Present Day Club, Princeton, N.J., 1968, 71, 73-75, 77-78, 82, M.S. Kungsholm, 1971-74, M.S. Sagafjord, 1971, United Nat. Bank, Fenwood, N.J., 1972, others; exhibited in group shows at Cape Cod Art Assn., 1963, Knickerbocker Artists Ann. Exhbn., 1963, Westfield Art Assn. State Show, 1963-64, Hunterdon County Art Ctr. Ann., 1963-64, Catherine Lorillard Wolfe Art Show, 1964, Nat. Arts Club shows, Met. Mus. Art, Nat. Acad., N.Y.C., Am. Water Color Soc. anns., 1967—, Nat. Assn. Women Artists anns., 1967—, Nat. Assn. Women Artists Internat., Paris, 1969, Garden State Watercolor Soc. anns., 1970—, Am. Watercolor Soc. Ann. Traveling Exhbn., 1972, N.J. State Cultural Ctr., Trenton, 1977; represented in pvt. collections. Recipient Agnes B. Noyes award, 1962, Windsor Newton award, 1963, Captain's Barn award for Watercolor Westfield Art Assn. State Show, 1964, Steinback Co. award for watercolor Festival of Fine Art Exhbn., 1964, Am. Artist medal merit, Am. Watercolor Soc., 1965, Jane C. Stanley Meml. prize, Nat. Assn. Women Artists, 1966. Mem. Am. Watercolor Soc. (hon.), Garden State Watercolor Soc. (pres. 1970—; Squibb award 1973), Nat. Assn. Women Artists, Princeton Art Assn. (pres. 1968-69). Clubs: Nat. Arts (N.Y.C.), Salmagundi. Home: Princeton, NJ.

TRIFFIN, NICHOLAS, law librarian, law educator; b. Boston, May 30, 1942; s. Robert and Lois (Brandt) T.; m. Mary M. Bertolet, June 1, 1965 (div. June 1975); children: Amyk (dec.), A. Robert; m. Madeleine J. Wilken, May 30, 1981. BA cum laude, Yale U., 1965, JD, 1968; MLS, Rutgers U., 1978. Bar: N.Y. 1969, Conn. 1973, U.S. Dist. Ct. Conn. 1973, U.S. Ct. Appeals (2nd cir.) 1973, U.S. Tax Ct. 1974. Assoc. Willkie Farr & Gallagher, N.Y.C., 1968-70; dean students Johnson (Vt.) State Coll., 1970-72; assoc. Di Sesa & Evans, New Haven, 1972-76; head pub. services, instr. law U. Conn., W. Hartford, 1977-81; law library dir., assoc. prof. Hamline U., St. Paul, 1982-84; dir. law library Pace U., White Plains, N.Y., 1984-98, prof., from 1984. Bd. dirs. Hale Found.; bd. advisors Oceana Pub., Inc., 1987-95; chief info. svcs. Inst. Internat. Comml. Law, 1993-94, dir., 1994—; adj. prof. Hartford Coll., 1978-80; lectr. Peking U., summer 1997; vis. scholar Yale U. Law Sch., fall 1998. Author: Law Books Published, 1984-95, Law Books in Print, 5th edit., 1987, 6th edit., 1991, 7th edit., 1995, Law Books in Review, 1984-92, Drafting History of the Federal Rules of Criminal Procedure, 1991; columnist Law Libr. Jour., 1983-84. Justice of peace, Conn., 1976-78. Mem. Am. Assn. Law Librs. (chmn. reader svcs. spl. interest sect. 1982-83, chmn. legal history and rare books spl. interest sect. 1991-92, chmn. constn. and bylaws com. 1994-95), Westchester Acad. Libr. Dirs. Orgn., Inc. (v.p. 1990-91, pres. 1991-92, exec. bd. dirs. 1992-94), Law Libr. New Eng. (pres. 1981-82), Minn. Assn. Law Librs. (v.p. 1983-84), Westchester Libr. Assn. (exec. bd. 1990-91), Myositis Assn. Am., Mory's Club, Beta Phi Mu. Mem. Soc. Of Friends. Avocations: kayaking, rare books, opera. Home: Wilton, Conn. Deceased.

TRIMBLE, WANDA NELL, special education educator; b. Hico, Tex., Feb. 2, 1938; d. Mathew Clinton and Flora Mae (Patterson) Roberson; m. Tommy Wyane Trimble, July 19, 1958; children: John Olin, Tommy Wayne Jr., Mary Allene Trimble Messer, Zachary Taylor. BS in Bus. Adminstrn., Ea. Tex. State U., 1958; MEd, No. Tex. State U., 1971; cert., Tex. Western U., 1974-73. Cert. tchr., Tex. Tchr. 1st grade Huntsville (Ala.) Ind. Sch. Dist., 1963-64; tchr. 5th and 6th grades Everman (Tex.) Ind. Sch. Dist., 1965-66; tchr. 3d grade Weatherford (Tex.) Ind. Schs., 1968-71; tchr. 2d grade All Sts. Catholic Schs., Ft. Worth, 1971-72; substitute tchr. Ft. Worth Ind. Sch. Dist., 1972-73; elem. tchr. spl. edn. Lakeworth (Tex.) Ind. Schs., 1973-74; high sch. tcrh. spl. edn. Birdville (Tex.) Ind. Schs., from 1974. Sales person, supr. Sears Roebuck & Co., Ft. worth, 1977-90; distributor Amway, Ft. Worth, 1992—. Hostess Colters Barbecue, Ft. Worth, 1992—. Presdl. scholar, 1955. Mem. NEA, ASCD, Tex. Tchrs. Assn. (rep. 1978-92, sec. 1988-89, calender com. 1990-91, community com. 1991-93), Assn. English Tchrs., Assn. LLD, Nat. Bus. Edn. Assn., Birdville Tex. State Tchrs. Assn. Democrat. Avocations: cooking, sewing, rock collecting, reading, going to church. Home: Hico, Tex. Died Nov. 2, 2001.

TRINDADE, ARMANDO, archbishop; b. Goa, Oct. 25, 1927; arrived in Pakistan, 1927; s. Athanasius Crispin and Olinda (D'Souza) T. M in Philosophy, Papal U., Kandy, Sri Lanka, 1946, M in Theology, 1950; MA with honors, Oxford (Eng.) U., 1960; MA in Edn., U. Notre Dame, 1963; PhD in Edn., Stanford U., 1971. Consecrated bishop, 1973. Asst. prin., prin. in various schs., Pakistan, 1951-70; variouis pastoral assignments, 1951-73; bishop, 1973-93; archbishop, from 1994. Died July 31, 2000.

TRINKLE, J. KENT, medical educator; b. New Albany, Ind., July 6, 1934; MD, Ind. U., 1959. Intern Ohio State U. Hosp., Columbus, 1959-60, resident, 1960-61, U. Ky. Med. Ctr., Lexington, 1963-66; with Med. Ctr. Hosp., San Antonio; prof. U. Tex. Health Sci. Ctr. Deceased.

TRIPP, PAUL, actor, writer, lyricist; b. N.Y.C., Feb. 20, 1916; s. Benjamin and Esther (Stelzer) T.; m. Ruth Beatrice Enders, Aug. 8, 1943; children: Suzanne Tripp Jurmain, David Enders. BA, CCNY, 1933. Drama dir., social worker Christadora House, N.Y.C., 1935-42. Actor: (debut) Broadway Cyrano de Bergerac, 1936, (short film) Tubby the Tuba (Oscar award nomination 1947); creator, producer, star. Mr. I Magination, CBS-TV, 1949-53 (Peabody award 1950, Ohio State Ednl. Radio TV award 1951), On the Carousel, CBS-TV, 1954-59 (Emmy award 1956, Ohio State Ednl. TV Radio award 1955, 56, 57, 58), Birthday House, NBC-TV, 1963-68 (Emmy citation 1966);, featured actor over 100 TV shows, commls., 1968—; composer, lyricist children's record albums, 1945—; star (nat. tours) as Ben Franklin in 1776, 1970-71, Will Rogers USA, 1979; PBS Thomas Edison, 1980; author: The Strawman Who Smiled by Mistake, 1967—, Little Red Flower, 1969, The Tail That Went Looking, 1971, David, Ancient of Kings (symphonic soliloquy), 1981; author, lyricist: record, book, film short Tubby the Tuba, 1945 (Grammy Hall Fame 1982), film, 1983; creator, lyricist, star: perennial children's film classic Christmas That Almost Wasn't, 1966 (Grammy award 1966); star children's video cassette: Return of Halley's Comet, 1985; recs. (5 symphonies stories) Tubby the Tuba and His Friends (in Czechoslovakia), 1991. Served with Signal Corps, AUS, 1941-45; CBI. Mem. The Players. Home: New York, NY. Died Aug. 29, 2002.

TRISKA, JAN FRANCIS, retired political science educator; b. Prague, Czechoslovakia, Jan. 26, 1922; came to U.S., 1948, naturalized, 1955; s. Jan and Bozena (Kubiznak) T.; m. Carmel Lena Burastero, Aug. 26, 1951; children: Mark Lawrence, John William. JUD, Charles U., Prague, 1948; LLM, Yale U., 1950, JSD, 1952; PhD, Harvard U., 1957. Co-dir. Soviet treaties Hoover Instn., Stanford, Calif., 1956-58; lectr. dept. polit. sci. U. Calif., Berkeley, 1957-58; asst. prof. Cornell U., Ithaca, N.Y., 1958-60; assoc. prof. Stanford U., Calif., 1960-65, prof. polit. sci., 1965-89, assoc. chmn. dept., 1965-66, 68-69, 71-72, 74-75, prof. emeritus, from 1990. Cons. Inst. State and Law, Czech Acad. Scis., Prague, 1995—. Co-author: (with Slusser) The Theory, Law and Policy of Soviet Treaties, 1962; (with Finley) Soviet Foreign Policy, 1968; (with Cocks) Political Development and Political Change in Eastern Europe, 1977; (with Ike, North) The World of Superpowers, 1981, (with Gati) Blue Collar Workers in Eastern Europe, 1981, Dominant Powers and Subordinate States, 1986, The Great War's Forgotten Front, 1998 (Czech, German, Slovene & Italian edits.); mem. editl. bd. East European Quar. Comparative Politics, Internat. Jour. Sociology, Jour. Comparative Politics, Studies in Comparative Communism, Soviet Statutes and Decisions, Documents in Communist Affairs. Recipient Rsch. award Ford Found., 1963-68, Josef Hlavka Commemorative medal Czechoslovak Acad. Scis., 1992, M.A. Comenius 1592-1992 Meml. medal Czechoslovak Pedagogical Mus., Prague, 1991, medal of merit 1st class Pres. Vaclav Havel, 2002; fellow NSF, 1971-72, Sen. Fulbright fellow, 1973-74, Woodrow Wilson fellow Internat. Ctr. for Scholars, 1980-81. Mem. Am. Polit. Sci. Assn. (sec. pres. conf. on communist studies 1970-76), Assn. Advancement Slavic Studies (bd. dirs. 1975-83), Am. Soc. Internat. Law (exec. coun. 1964-67), Czechoslovak Soc. Arts and Scis. (pres. 1978-80, 90-92), Inst. for Human Scis. Vienna (acting for Commn. European Communities, Brussels, com. experts on transformation of nat. higher edn. and rsch. system in Ctrl. Europe, Brussels 1991—), Fly Fishers Club (Palo Alto, Calif.). Democrat. Home: Menlo Park, Calif. Died Feb. 20, 2003.

TROWBRIDGE, C. ROBERTSON, publishing executive; b. Salem, Mass., Mar. 31, 1932; s. Cornelius P. and Margaret M. (Laird) T.; m. Lorna Sagendorph, July 7, 1956; children: James, Cornelia, Beatrix, Philip. AB, Princeton U., 1954; LL.B., Harvard U., 1957; L.H.D. (hon.), Franklin Pierce Coll., 1976, Keene State Coll., 1979. Chmn. Yankee Pub., Inc., Dublin, NH, 1964—2003; mem. N.H. Senate, 1973-78, chmn. fin. Mem. N.H. Ho. of Reps., 1967-72; chmn. public works com.; dir. Granir Bank, Keene, N.H. Mem. exec. com. N.H. Citizen Task Force, 1969; trustee Phillips Exeter Acad., N.H. Lands, Soc. for Protection N.H. Forests; moderator Town of Dublin. Home: Dublin, NH. Died Sept. 8, 2003.

TRUDEAU, DONALD BENJAMIN, engineering services company executive; b. Cheboygan, Mich., Sept. 20, 1922; s. Benjamin Joseph and Phoebe T.; m. Pansy May Howey, Nov. 2, 1946. Student, Fla. State U., 1957, U. Omaha, 1959, U. Md., 1959; AS in Math. and Statis., Highline Jr. Coll., Seattle, 1963. Lic. profl. engr., Calif. Joined USAF USAF, 1941, advanced through grades to master sgt., 1950, ret., 1961; quality systems auditor, statis. engr. The Boeing Co.; pres. Donald B. Trudeau & Assocs., Federal Way, Wash., from 1985. Decorated DFC, Air medal. Sr. mem. Am Soc. for Quality Control (charter mem. customer/supplier div.); mem. Intertel, Mensa. Roman Catholic. Avocations: reading, fishing, travel. Deceased.

TRUE, WILLIAM WADSWORTH, physics educator; b. Rockland, Maine, Dec. 27, 1925; s. Elmer LaForest and Alice Annette (Wadsworth) T.; m. Sarah Elizabeth Goodwin, June 12, 1954; children: William G., Kenneth W., Anne E., Katherine M. BS, U. Maine, 1950; MS, U. R.I., 1952; PhD, Ind. U., 1957. Instr. Princeton (N.J.) U., 1957-60; asst. prof. physics U. Calif., Davis, 1960-64, assoc. prof. phsyics, 1964-69, prof. physics, from 1969. With USAAF, 1944-45. Fellow Am. Phys. Soc.; mem. Phi Kappa Phi, Sigma Xi. Home: Davis, Calif. Died Oct. 13, 2001.

TRUMAN, DAVID BICKNELL, political scientist, educator; b. Evanston, Ill., June 1, 1913; s. Malcolm George and Jane Mackintosh Truman; m. Elinor Griffenhagen, Feb. 4, 1939; 1 child, Edwin Malcolm. BA, Amherst Coll., 1935; MA, U. Chgo., 1936, PhD, 1939; LHD, Amherst Coll., 1974; LLD, Mt. Holyoke Coll., 1978. Instr. Bennington (Vt.) Coll., 1939-41, Cornell U., Ithaca, N.Y., 1941-43; lectr. Harvard U., Cambridge, Mass., 1946, 47; assoc. prof. Williams Coll., Williamstown, Mass., 1947-59; prof., dean, v.p., provost Columbia U., N.Y.C., 1969-78; prof., pres. emeritus Mt. Holyoke, 69-78. Vis. prof. Yale U., 1957-58. Author books, including The Governmental Process, 1951, 71. Trustee Amherst Coll., 1964-70, 20th Century Fund, N.Y., 1968-2003; trustee, pres. Russell Sage Found., N.Y., 1967-2003. Lt. (j.g.) USNR, 1943-47. Guggenheim fellow, 1962-63. Fellow Am. Acad. Arts and Letters; mem. Am. Philosophies Soc., Am. Polit. Sci. Assn. (pres. 1965), Student Loan Mktg. Assn. (dir. 1977-88), Social Sci. Rsch. Coun. (dir. 1951-88) Democrat. Home: Sarasota, Fla. Died Aug. 28, 2003.

TSAO, CHIA KUEI, retired mathematics educator, researcher; b. Hwai-Ju, Hopei, People's Republic China, Jan. 14, 1922; came to U.S., 1948; s. Hou-Tong and En-Yu (Shang) T.; m. Ying-Lan Wang, Dec. 19, 1952; children: Anna, Marilyn, John, Josephine. PhD, U. Oreg., 1952. Teaching asst. Fu-Jen U., Beijing, 1945-46; rsch. asst. U. Oreg., Eugene, 1948-51; instr. math. Wayne State U., Detroit, 1952-53, asst. prof., 1953-57, assoc. prof., 1957-63, prof., 1963-87, prof. emeritus, from 1987. Home: Manhattan Bch, Calif. Died Apr. 9, 2001.

TUCK, EDWARD HALLAM, lawyer; b. Brussels, June 27, 1927; s. William Hallam and Hilda (Bunge) T.; m. Liliane Solmsen, June 8, 1978; children by previous marriage— Edward, Jessica, Matthew BA, Princeton U., 1950; LL.B., Harvard Law Sch., 1953. Bar: N.Y. Assoc. Shearman & Sterling, N.Y.C., 1953-62, ptnr., 1962-86, of counsel, from 1986. Bd. dirs. The French-Am. Found.; bd. dirs. Comml. Bank. Bd. dirs. Belgian Am. Ednl. Found., The Drawing Ctr.; trustee French Inst. Alliance Francaise; chmn. bd. North County Sch., Inc., 1974-78, The Drawing Ctr., Gateway Citizens Com., 1972-74; pres. The Parks Council, 1970-74; chmn. N.Y. State Parks and Recreation Commn., City of N.Y., 1971-76. Served with USN, 1945-46 Mem. Assn. Bar City N.Y., Coun. on Fgn. Rels., Racquet and Tennis Club, The Brook Club, The Ivy Club, Pilgrims, Soc. of the Cin. Episcopalian. Home: New York, NY. Died Oct. 2, 2002.

TUCKER, FRANCIS CARLILE, medical missionary; b. Beidaihe, China, June 27, 1915; s. Francis Fisher and Emma Jane (Boose) T.; m. Emma Elizabeth Scott, June 14, 1941; children: Elizabeth Jane, Robert Francis, Jean Marilyn, Joan Eloise, John Frederick. AB, Oberlin (Ohio) Coll., 1937; MD, Harvard U., 1941. Diplomate Am. Bd. Pathology. Intern Roosevelt Hosp., N.Y.C., 1941-42, resident, 1942; asst. pathologist St. Luke's Hosp., Chgo., 1945-48; asst. prof. pathology U. S.D., Vermillion, 1948-50; pathologist, dir. lab. St. Luke's Meth. Hosp., Cedar Rapids, Iowa, 1950-58, Freeport (Ill.) Meml. Hosp., 1958-81; with Evangel. Alliance Mission (TEAM), Wheaton, Ill., 1981-92; med. missionary The Evangel. Alliance Mission (TEAM), Taitung, Taiwan, Republic of China, 1981-92. Coroner's physician counties of Stephenson, Jo Daviess, Ogle and Carroll, Ill., 1958-81. Maj. M.C. AUS, 1942-45, CBI, PTO. Decorated Bronze Star medal. Mem. Christian Med. and Dental Soc. Republican. Avocations: travel, reading, tennis, collecting chinese stamps, singing. Deceased.

TUCKER, WILLIAM FULTON, lawyer; b. Vaughn, N.Mex., Dec. 29, 1931; s. Albert Fulton and Kathryn T.; m. Bebe Davis, May 15, 1962; children: William F. Jr., Glenn Davis, Brent Bradley. BS, McMurry Coll., Abilene, Tex., 1953; JD, So. Meth. U., 1956. Asst. dist. atty. Dallas (Tex.) County, 1957-61; pvt. practice law Dallas, 1961-99. Home: Dallas, Tex. Died May 25, 1999.

TUNNESSEN, WALTER WILLIAM, JR., pediatrician; b. Hazleton, Pa., July 25, 1939; s. Walter William and Grace Louise (Schaller) T.; m. Nancy Louise Layton, Aug. 24, 1963; children: Walter William III, Anne L. BA, Lafayette Coll., Easton, Pa., 1961; MD, U. Pa., 1965. Diplomate Am. Bd. Pediat. (bd. dirs. 1993—). Resident Children's Hosp. of Phila., 1965-67; chief resident in pediatrics Hosp. U. Pa., Phila., 1967-68; instr., dir. newborn nurseries Hosp. U. Pa./U. Pa. Sch. Medicine, Phila., 1970-72; from asst. prof. to assoc. prof. pediatrics SUNY Health Sci. Ctr., Syracuse, 1972-81, prof. pediat., 1981, acting chair dept., 1985-86; assoc. prof. pediatrics and dermatology Johns Hopkins U. Sch. Medicine, Balt., 1986-90, dir. pediatric dermatology, dir. pediatric diagnostic clinic, 1986-90; assoc. chmn. for med. edn. Children's Hosp. of Phila., 1990-95; prof. pediatrics U. Pa. Sch. Medicine, Phila., 1990-95; sr. v.p. Am. Bd. Pediatrics, Chapel Hill, N.C., from 1995. Robert Wood Johnson clin. Scholar Yale U. Sch. Medicine, New Haven, 1978-79; mem. Nat. Bd. Med. Examiners, 1989-91; mem. sci. bd. Nat. Found. for Ectodermal Dysplasia, 1989-93; mem. adv. com. on tng. in primary care medicine and dentistry HHS Health Resources and Svcs. Adminstrn., 1999-2000. Author: Signs and Symptoms in Pediatrics, 1983, 2d edit., 1988, 3d edit., 1999; editor monthly jour. sects.; editl. bd. Contemporary Pediats., Advances in Pediats., Arch. Pediat. and Adolescent Medicine, 1990-2000. Capt. USAF, 1968-70. Mem. Am. Acad. Pediats. (sect. on dermatology exec. com. 1993-95, com. on pediat. workforce 1997—, com. on pediat. edn. 1999—), Soc. for Pediat. Dermatology (pres. 1988-89, bd. dirs.), Am. Pediat. Soc. Avocation: furniture refinishing. Home: Chapel Hill, NC. Deceased.

TURECK, ROSALYN, concert performer, author, editor, educator; b. Chgo., Dec. 14, 1914; d. Samuel and Mary (Lipson) T.; (w. 1964). Piano studies with Sophia Brilliant-Liven, Chgo., 1925-29; with Jan Chiapusso, 1929-31; harpsichord studies with Gavin Williamson, Chgo., 1931-32; piano studies with Olga Samaroff, N.Y.C., 1931-35, studies with Leon Theremin with 2 electronic instruments, 1931-32; BA cum laude, The Juilliard Sch. Music, 1935; MusD (hon.), Colby Coll., 1964, Roosevelt U., 1968, Wilson Coll., 1968, Oxford U., Eng., 1977, Music and Arts Inst., San Francisco, 1987. Mem. faculty Phila. Conservatory Music, 1935-42, Mannes Sch., N.Y.C., 1940-44, Juilliard Sch. Music, N.Y.C., 1943-55, Columbia U., N.Y.C., 1953-55; prof. music, lectr.; regents prof. U. Calif., San Diego, 1966, prof. music, 1966-74. Vis. prof. Washington U., St. Louis, 1963-64, U. Md., 1981-85, Yale U., 1991-93; vis. fellow St. Hilda's Coll., Oxford (Eng.) U., 1974, hon. life fellow, 1974-2003; vis. fellow Wolfson Coll., Oxford, 1975-2003; lectr. numerous ednl. instns., U.S., Eng., Spain, Denmark, Holland, Can., Israel, Brazil, Argentina, Chile; lectr. Royal Inst. Great Britain, 1993, 96, Boston U., 1993, 94, Smithsonian Instn., 1994, Rockefeller U., 1994, U. Calif., Santa Barbara, 1995, Hebrew U., Israel, Royal Inst. Gt. Britain, London, U. Southampton, Oxford U., 1993, 96, 97, Internat. Piano Found., Lake Como, Italy, 1993, 94, 95, 97, 99; 10th Internat. Congress Logic, Methodology and Philosophy Sci., 1995; founder Composers of Today, 1949-53; soc. for performance internat. contemporary music, founder, dir. Tureck Bach Players, London, 1957, N.Y.C., 1981; founder, dir. Internat. Bach Soc., Inst. for Bach Studies, 1968; founder, dir. Tureck Bach Inst., Inc., 1981, Symposia 1968-86, Tureck Bach Rsch. Found., Oxford, U.K., 1994, First and Second Ann. Symposium, Structure: Principles and Applications in the Sciences and Music and the Notion of Authenticity, 1996-97, Third Annual Symposium, on Structure and the Concept of Concept, Worcester Coll., Oxford Univ., 1998; Academia Bartolomeo Cristofori, Florence, 1993-97; recitals, lectr. Oxford U., 1996; Regents prof. UCLA, Santa Barbara, 1995; lectr. Royal Instn., London, 1996, Oxford U., 1996, 97, internat. Piano Found., Lake Como, Italy, 1993-97; with Second Internat. Symposium: Structure, Principles, and Applications in the Scis. and Music: The Notion of Authenticity, 1997, dir., Inst. for Advanced Mus. Studies, AUg., 1997, Dec., 1997, Aug., 1998, Aug., 1999. Debut solo recital, Chgo., 1924; soloist Ravinia Park, Chgo., 1926, 2 all-Bachrecitals, Chgo., 1930; N.Y.C. debut Carnegie Hall with Phila. Orch., 1936; series 6 all-Bach recitals, Town Hall, N.Y.C., 1937, ann. series 3 all-Bach recitals, N.Y.C., 1944-54, 1959-2003, ann. U.S.-Can. tours, 1937-2003; European debut Copenhagen, 1947; extensive ann. European tours; continuing ann. concert tours, recitals, master classes in Spain, Italy, Russia, Eng., Germany, U.S., 1995; world tours in Far East, India, Australia, Europe, 1971, S.Am., 1986, 87, 88, 89, 91, 92, Europe, Israel, Turkey, Spain, 1986-90, Argentina, Chile, 1989, 90, 91, 92, Casals Festival, 1991, European and U.S. tour, recitals and master classes, 1999; N.Y.C. series Met. Mus. Art and Carnegie Hall, 1969-2003; numerous solo recitals including N.Y.C., 1992, Mostly Mozart Festival, Lincoln Ctr., N.Y.C., 1994; appeared with leading orchs. U.S., Can., Europe, South Africa, S.Am., Israeli; condr., soloist Collegium Musicum, Copenhagen, 1957, London, Philharm. Orch., 1959, N.Y. Philharm., 1960, Glyndebourne Festival Tureck Bach Players, London, 1960-72, San Antonio Symphony, Okla. Symphony, 1962, Scottis Nat. Symphony, Edinburg, Glasgow, 1963, Israel Philharm., Tel Aviv, Haifa and Kol Israel orchs., 1963, Glyndebourne series: Tureck Bach Players, Carnegie Hall, N.Y.C., 1970, Kans. City Philharm., 1968, Washington Nat. Symphony, 1970, Madrid Chamber Orch., 1970, Israel Festival, Internat. Bach Soc. Orchs., 1967, 69, 70, Tureck Bach Players, Wales, 1976, Carnegie Hall, N.Y., 1975-86, St. Louis Symphony Orch., 1981; Bach festivals cities, Eng., Ireland, Spain, 1959-2003, Carnegie Hall Ann. Series, N.Y.C., 1975-2003; TV series Well-Tempered Clavier, Book I, Granada TV, Eng., 1961; BBC series Well-Tempered Clavier, Books I and 2, 1976; numerous TV appearances, U.S., 1961-2003, including Wm. F. Buckley's Firing Line, 1970, 85, 87, 89, Today Show, Camera Three, Bach recitals on piano, harpsichord, clavichord, antique and electronic instruments, 1963—; Tureck on Television, CBS, 1999, video concert Teatro Colon, Buenos Aires, 1992; recs. for HMV, Odeon, Decca, Columbia Masterworks, Everest, Allegro, Sony, Video Artists Internat., 1993-2003, R. Tureck Plays Bach, Goldberg Variations, Great Solo Works Vol. 1 and 2, Live at the Teatro Colon, Rosalyn Tureck: Live in St. Petersburg Videos: Live at the Teatro Colon Live in St. Petersburg, The R. Tureck Collection, vol. 1 The Young Firebrand, vol. 2 The Young Visionary, Tribute to a Keyboard Legend, vol. 3 Tribute to a Keyboard Legend, vol. 4 Rosalyn Tureck: Premiere Performances, vol. 5 Harpsichord Recital, Deutsche Grammophon Gesellschaft: Bach's Goldberg Variations, BWV 988 (CD-ROM), 1999, Philips Great Pianists of the Twentieth Century, J.S. Bach Clavierubung, books 1 and 2, Philips Great Pianists of The Twentieth Century, Rosalyn Tureck (series), J.S. Bach, Goldberg variation BWV 988 issue, 2000; author: Introduction to the Performance of Bach, 3 vols., 1960, Authenticity, 1994, J.S. Bach and Number, Symmetries and Other Relationships, Music and Mathematics, 1995, Cells, Functions and Relationships in Musical Structure and Performance-Proceedings of the Royal Instn., London, 1996; contbr. articles to various mags.; creator, editor jour. Interaction, 1997editor Bach-Sarabande, C minor, 1960, Tureck Bach Urtext Series: Italian Concerto, 1983, 2d edit., 1991, Lute Suite, E minor, 1984, C minor, 1985, Schirmer Music, Inc., Carl Fischer Paginini-Tureck: Moto Perpetuo, A. Scarlatti: Air and Gavotte; creator and editor, jour., Interaction, Proceedings of Symposia of Tureck Bach Rsch. Found., Oxford, U.K., 1997, J.S. Bach and Number, Symmetrics and other Relationships, Musical Authenticity, Is it a Legitamate Offspring of Janus, 1999; films: Fantasy and Fugue: Rosalyn Tureck Plays Bach, 1972, Rosalyn Tureck plays on Harpsichord and Organ, 1977, Joy of Bach, 1978, Camera 3: Bach on the Frontier of the Future, CBS film, Ephesus, Turkey, 1985. Decorated Officers Cross of the Order of Merit, Fed. Republic Germany, 1979; recipient 1st prize Greater Chgo. Piano Playing Tournament, 1928, 1st Town Hall Endowment award, 1937, Phi Beta award, 1946, 1st prize and Schubert Meml. Contest winner, 1935, Nat. Fedn. Music Clubs Competition winner, 1935, Musician of Yr., Music Tchrs. Nat. Assn., 1987; NEH grantee. Fellow Guildhall Sch. Music and Drama (hon.); mem. Royal Mus. Assn. London, Am. Musicological Soc., Inc. Soc. Musicians (London), Royal Philharmonic Soc. London, Sebastian Bach de Belgique (hon.), Am. Bach Soc., Oxford Soc. Clubs: Century (N.Y.C., Oxford and Cambridge, London), Bohemians (N.Y.C.) (hon.). Died July 17, 2003.

TURNER, LELAND S., JR., (LEE TURNER), civil engineer, consultant, former utilities executive; b. Dallas, Nov. 5, 1926; s. James A. and Fay Sims; m. Donetta Mae Johnson, Jan. 17, 1947. BCE, Tex. A&M U., 1948; JD, So. Meth. U., 1957. Engr. Dallas Power & Light Co., 1948, various exec. positions, pres., chief exec., 1967-76; dir. Tex. Utilities Co., 1967-82, exec. v.p., 1976-84; cons., 1984—96. Trustee Com. for Econ. Devel., Southwestern Med. Found.; past pres., bd. dirs. Dallas Citizens Coun.; former bd. dirs. So. Meth. U. Found. for Sci. and Engring.; past chmn. Children's Med. Ctr.; past chmn. United Way, YMCA, Community Coun. of Greater Dallas; past pres. Greater Dallas Ahead, Inc., Dallas Assembly. With U.S. Army, 1945-46. Mem. ABA, Am. Arbitration Assn., Tex. Profl. Engrs. Presbyterian. Deceased.

TURNER, SHIRLEY J. nurse, educator; b. Freeport, Ill., Mar. 15, 1929; d. Clifford Ernest and Dorothy Loraine (Kencke) Gartman; m. Paul Raymond Turner, Sept. 2, 1950; children: Rachel Hendrickson, Scott E. BA, Wheaton Coll., 1950; MA, U. Ariz., 1970, BSN, 1988, MSN, 1989. Staff devel. educator Handmaker Jewish Geriatric Ctr., Tucson; clin. instr. nursing U. Ariz., Tucson. Mem. ANA, Ariz. Nurses Assn., Sigma Theta Tau, Phi Kappa Phi, Golden Key. Home: Elgin, Ariz. Deceased.

TYLER, LEWIS ADAIR, not-for-profit organization executive; b. Long Beach, Calif., June 14, 1939; s. James Lewis and Martha Elizabeth (Adair) T. AB, U. Kans., 1963, MEd, 1968; PhD, Ind. U., 1978. Campus coord. basic scis. devel. program Ford Found./Kans. U., Lawrence, 1964-69; campus coord. Chile edn. reform project U.S. Agy. for Internat. Devel., Bloomington, Ind., 1969-73; regional dir. Latin Am. Scholarship Program of Am./Harvard U., Cambridge, Mass., 1973-83, exec. dir., 1983-97. Mem. svcs. com. TOEFL policy coun. Ednl. Testing Svc., Princeton, N.J., 1983-87; co-chmn. Alliance for Internat. Edn. and Cultural Exch., Washington, 1992-93; bd. dirs. NAFSA, Washington. Editor: Guide to Graduate Programs in Latin American Countries, 1981. Bd. dirs. New Erlich Theater, Boston, 1989-92. Home: Melrose, Mass. Died May 30, 2002.

TYLER, MARGO HILLS (MRS. CONVERSE TYLER), retired foundation communications executive, freelance writer; b. Salt Lake City, Sept. 4, 1921; d. Harold Haven and Mary Edith (Roberts) Hills; B.A., U. Utah, 1942; m. Converse Tyler, Sept. 30, 1950. Asst. city editor Salt Lake Telegram, Salt Lake City, 1942-45; adminstrv. asst. safety service ARC, Washington, 1945-55; dir. public relations Am. Cancer Soc., Washington, 1957-65, Am. Assn. Motor Vehicle Adminstrs., Washington, 1966-68; dir. public info. Coll. V.I., St. Thomas, 1968-70; asst. dir. communications div. Nat. 4-H Council. Washington, 1970-86, mng. editor 4-H Leader mag., 1983-86. Mem. adv. council nat. orgns. Corp. Public Broadcasting, Washington, 1971-77, exec. com., 1973-75, 77; co-founder Public Info. Assn. St. Thomas, V.I., 1969, sec., 1969. Mem. Public Relations Soc. Am. (chpt. bd. 1962-64, 1967, 72-73, 81, v.p. 1980), Mortar Bd., Nat. Press Club, Woman's Nat. Dem. Club, Phi Beta Kappa, Phi Kappa Phi, Delta Gamma. Died Jan. 1, 1999. Home: Silver Spring, Md.

TYNER, GEORGE S. ophthalmologist, educational administrator; b. Omaha, Oct. 9, 1916; s. George S. and Ethel (Holmquist) T.; m. Jean Walt, June 13, 1942; children—Holly Jean, Helen Tyner Thompson. BS, U. Nebr., 1940, MD, 1942; M. Med. Sci., U. Pa., 1952; postgrad., Tex. Tech. U., 1971-73. Diplomate: Am. Bd. Ophthalmology. Intern Phila. Gen. Hosp., 1942-43, resident in ophthalmology, 1947-48; research fellow, resident in ophthalmology Hosp. U. Pa., 1948-51, asst. instr., 1948-52; practice medicine specializing in ophthalmology Denver, 1952-61; with U. Colo., 1952-71, asst. clin. prof., 1952-61, chief glaucoma clinic, 1953-61, asso. prof. ophthalmology, 1964-71, asso. prof., preventive medicine, 1968-71, asso. dean, 1963-71; prof. ophthalmology Tex. Tech. U., Lubbock, 1971—, prof. preventive medicine and community health, 1973, prof. psychiatry, 1974, asso. dean adminstrn., 1971-72, chmn. dept. ophthalmology, 1971-74, asso. dean edn. and student affairs, 1973-74, dean Sch. Medicine, 1974-81, dean emeritus, 1981—. Contbr. articles to med. jours. Dir. Colo. chpt. Soc. Prevention of Blindness, 1961-66; bd. dirs., 1st v.p. Lubbock Council on Alcoholism, 1973-74; mem. Colo. State Bd. Basic Sci. Examiners, 1962-67. Served with USN, 1943-47. Fellow A.C.S.; mem. AMA, Colo. Med. Soc., Denver Med. Soc. (past pres.), Am. Assn. Ophthalmology (trustee 1961—), Colo. Ophthal. Soc. (past pres.), Assn. Univ. Profs. Ophthalmology, N.Y. Acad. Sci., Am. Acad. Ophthalmology and Otolaryngology, Tex. Med. Assn., AMA, Am. Med. Soc. on Alcoholism, Nat. Council on Alcoholism, Assn. Research in Vision and Ophthalmology, Sigma Xi, Alpha Omega Alpha. Home: Denver, Colo. Died Nov. 30, 1999.

TYRRELL, NANCY JANE, postmaster; b. Cass County, Nebr., Jan. 27, 1934; d. Byron Charles and Gaybelle Blanche (Siddens) Perkins; m. Roger Alan Tyrrell, Sept. 7, 1958; children: Suzanne Jean, Sandra Lynn, Sheila Rea, Amy Renee. BS, U. Nebr., 1958. Tchr. Norfolk (Nebr.) Pub. Schs., 1954-57; clk., carrier U.S. Postal Svc., Waverly, Nebr., 1980-87, postmaster Davey, Nebr., 1987-93, Greenwood, Nebr., 1993-99. Mem. Nat. Assn. Postmasters, League Postmasters, Order Odd Fellows-Rebekah Lodge 150. Methodist. Home: Omaha, Nebr. Died Apr. 29, 1999.

TYSON, HERBERT REX, appraiser; b. Cadillac, Mich., Mar. 1, 1922; s. Herbert Raymond and Mabel I. (Johnson) T.; Audrey Ann Wendell, Feb. 12, 1943; children: Kitrick Wendell, Scott Stafford, Tyler Raymond Tyson. Student, Cen. High Sch., 1940, U. Mich., 1961, student, 1962. Owner Tyson and Assocs. Appraisers, Flint, Mich., from 1946-. Chmn. Multiple Listing Svc., Flint 1963-64; chmn. land econs., cert. instr. Am. Right of Way, Mich. chpt. 7, 1975-76, edn. chmn. Region 5, 1975-79. Mem. Flint Metro. Planning Commn., Flint Bd. Realtors, Soc. Real Estate Appraisers (pres. 1972-73, cert. instr., Am. Inst. Banking (cert. instr.), VFW, Jr. C. of C. Presbyterian. Avocations: reading, golf. Deceased.

UDENFRIEND, SIDNEY, biochemist; b. N.Y.C., Apr. 5, 1918; s. Max and Esther (Tabak) U.; m. Shirley Frances Reidel, June 20, 1943; children: Aliza, Elliot. BS, Coll. City N.Y., 1939; MS, N.Y. U., 1942, PhD, 1948; D.Sc. honoris causa, N.Y. Med. Coll., 1974, Coll. Medicine and Dentistry of N.J., 1979, Mt. Sinai Sch. Medicine, City U. N.Y., 1981. Lab. asst. N.Y.C. Dept. Health, 1940-42; jr. chemist NYU Rsch. Svc., 1942-43, asst. chemist, 1943-44, research chemist, 1944-46; research asst. Med. Sch., 1946-47, instr., 1947-48, Washington U. Med. Sch., 1948-50; biochemist Nat. Heart Inst., Bethesda, Md., 1950-53, head sect. cellular pharmacology lab. chem. pharmacology, 1953-56, chief lab. clin. biochemistry, 1956-68; dir. Roche Inst. Molecular Biology, N.J., 1968-83, head lab. molecular neurobiology, 1983-96, dir. emeritus, 1983-96; dir. Dana Inst., Drew U., Madison, N.J., from 1996. Professorial lectr. George Washington U., 1962-69; adj. prof. human genetics and devel. dept. Columbia U., 1969-74; adj. prof. dept. biochemistry City U. N.Y., 1968-95; dept. pharmacology Emory U., 1976-78; adj. prof. biochemistry Cornell U. Med. Sch., 1982-95; mem. sci. adv. bd. Scripps Clinic and Research Found., 1974-78; mem. adv. com. to dir. NIH, 1976-78; mem. Sci. Adv. Com. for Cystic Fibrosis; mem. adv. council of sci. and engring. City U. N.Y., 1980—; mem. sci. adv. com. Mass. Gen. Hosp., 1980-84. Trustee Wistar Inst., 1968-71; mem. adv. bd. Weizmann Inst. Sci., 1978-79, bd. govs., 1979—. Recipient Cert. of Merit for studies on malignant carcinoid A.M.A., 1956, Arthur S. Flemming award, 1958; City of Hope research award, 1975; NIH fellow St. Mary's Hosp. Med. Sch., London, Eng., 1957; Harvey lectr., 1964; recipient Superior Service award Dept. HEW, 1965, Distinguished Service award, 1966; Gairdner Found. award, 1967; Heinrich Waelsch lectr. in neurosci., 1978; recipient Townsend Harris medal CCNY Alumni Assn., 1979; Rudolph Virchow gold medal, 1979; Chauncey Leake lectr. U. Calif., 1980 Fellow N.Y. Acad. Scis. (trustee 1978—); mem. NAS, AAAS, Am. Soc. Biol. Chemists, Am. Soc. Pharmacology and Exptl. Therapeutics (sec.), Soc. Exptl. Biology and Medicine, Am. Assn. Clin. Chemists (Van Slyke award 1967, Ames award 1969), Am. Chem. Soc. (Hillebrand award 1962, Torald Sollmann award 1975), Am. Acad. Arts and Scis., Japanese Pharmacol. Soc. (hon.), Japanese Biochem. Soc. (hon.), Czechoslovak Pharmacology Soc. (hon.), Congress Internat. Neuropsychopharmacologists (hon.), Instituto de Investigaciones Citológicas (corr.) (Spain), Phi Beta Kappa, Sigma Xi. Home: Atlanta, Ga. Died December 1999.

UITTI, KARL DAVID, language educator, educator; b. Calumet, Mich., Dec. 10, 1933; s. Karl Abram and Joy (Weidelman) U.; m. Maria Esther Clark, Feb. 15, 1953 (div. Feb. 1973, dec.); children: Maria Elisabeth, Karl Gerard (dec.); m. Michelle Alice Freeman, Mar. 13, 1974; children: David Charles, Jacob Christian. AB, U. Calif., Berkeley, 1952; AM, U. Calif., Berkley, 1952, PhD, 1959; postgrad., Nancy and Bordeaux U., 1952-54. From instr. to assoc. prof. Princeton U., 1959-68, class of 1936 preceptor, 1963-66, prof., 1968—2003, John N. Woodhull prof. modern langs., 1978—2003, chmn. dept. Romance langs., 1972-78. Vis. prof. Universidad de P.R., U. Pa., Queens Coll., U. Iowa, U. Wash., Rutgers U., UCLA, Johns Hopkins U., Ecole Normale Supérieure de Saint-Cloud, de Sévres, Paris, U. Warwick, England; corr. Romance Philology, 1970-85; NEH dir. summer seminars for coll. tchrs., 1983, 87, 94, cons., 1976-78, bd. dirs.; bd. dirs. Alumni Coll. Princeton U., Paris, Fontevraud, France; dir. Charrette Project, Princeton U. Author: The Concept of Self in the Symbolist Novel, 1961, La Passion littéraire de Remy de Gourmont, 1962, Linguistics and Literary Theory, 1969, Story, Myth and Celebration in Old French Narrative Poetry (1050-1200), 1973, (with A. Foulet) Chrétien de Troyes, Le Chevalier de la Charrette, 1989, Letteratura europea: dalle origini a Dante, 1993, Chrétien de Troyes, Le Chevalier au Lion, 1994, (with M.A. Freeman) Chrétien de Troyes Revisited, 1995; contbr. numerous articles and revs. to scholarly jours.; editor: Edward C. Armstrong Monographs on Medieval Literature; gen. editor The Charrette Project, 1997; mem. edit. bd. Romance Philology, 1980-98, French Forum; mem. adv. coun. Dictionary of the Middle Ages. Chmn. bd. elders Luth. Ch. of Messiah, Princeton, N.J., 1978-81. With AUS, 1954-56. Decorated officier des Palmes Académiques, France; Guggenheim fellow, 1964-65, sr. fellow Nat. Endowment for Humanities, 1974-75, vis. fellow All Souls Coll., Oxford (Eng.) U., 1975. Mem. MLA, Linguistic Soc. Am., Medieval Acad. Am. Société de linguistique romane, Phi Beta Kappa. Clubs: Codrington (Oxford, Eng.). Home: Princeton, NJ. Died Nov. 11, 2003.

UNDERWOOD, BERNARD EDWARD, retired religious organization administrator; b. Bluefield, W.Va., Oct. 26, 1925; s. W. B. and Annie Theresa (Bain) U.; m. Esther Parramore, Dec. 22, 1947; children: Paul, Karen, Pam. BA, Emmanuel Coll., Franklin Springs, Ga., 1947; MA, Marshall U., 1954. Lic. to ministry Pentecostal Holiness Ch., 1942; ordained, 1944. Mem. Pentecostal Holiness Youth Soc. bd. Va. conf. Pentecostal Holiness Ch., Kingsport, Tenn., 1946-53; Christian edn. dir. Pentecostal Holiness Ch., Va. Conf., 1951-60, asst. supt., 1958-64; supt. Va. conf. Pentecostal Holiness Ch., Roanoke, 1964-69, 74-78, exec. dir. world missions Oklahoma City, 1969-73, 77-89, vice chmn., 1981-89, gen. supt., 1989-97. Author: Gifts of the Spirit, 1967, Spiritual Gifts: Ministries and Manifestations, 1984, 16 New Testament Principles for World Evangelization, 1988; contbr. numerous articles to profl. jours. Phi Alpha Theta scholar, 1954. Mem. Nat. Assn. Evangelicals (mem. exec. com. 1989—), Pentecostal Fellowship N.Am. (pres. 1991—), Pentecostal Renewal Svcs. (chmn. 1987—), Evang. Fgn. Missions Assn. (bd. adminstrn. 1981—). Republican. Avocation: reading. Home: Royston, Ga. Deceased.

UNGAR, MANYA SHAYON, volunteer, education consultant; b. N.Y.C., May 30, 1928; d. Samuel and Ethel M. (Liese) Shayon; m. Harry Fireman Ungar, June 25, 1950; children: Paul Benedict, Michael Shayon. BA, Mills Coll., 1950. Cert. tutor LVA/UC adult learners2001. Actress TV and radio NBC, CBS, N.Y.C., 1950-58; founder, pres., bd. dirs. chpt. AFS, Scotch Plains-Fanwood, N.J., 1963-70; vol. project dir. handicapped cub scouts Boy Scouts Am., Plainfield, N.J., 1958-61; founder, co-dir. Summer Theater Workshop, Scotch Plains, 1967-78; legis. v.p. N.J. State PTA, 1977-79, pres., 1979-81; legis. v.p. Nat. PTA, Chgo., 1981-85, 1st v.p., 1985-87, pres., 1987-89. Mem. arts edn. adv. panel Nat. Endowment Arts, Washington, 1988-91, panel Nat. Inst. Work and Learning, 1988-91; adv. coun. Nat. Panel Drug Free Schs., Washington, 1989-91, edn. adv. bd. NBC, 1988-92, PBS, 1988-91, Scholastic, Inc., 1990-94; bd. dirs. Math. Sci. Edn. Bd., 1988-92. Trustee N.J. Children's Specialized Hosp., 1990—99, N.J. Pub. Edn. Inst., from 1987; mem. adv. coun. Natural Resources Def. Coun., Mothers and Others, 1999—99; mem. gography assessment adv. coun. Nat. Assessment Edn. Progress, 1991—92, mem. nat. oversite commn. on geog. stds., 1992—94; mem. N.J. Basic Skills Coun., 1990—94; chmn. N.J. Math. Coalition, from 1994; mem. accreditation com. APA, 1992—98; mem. tchr. programs adv. panel Ednl. Testing Svc., 1990—94; mem. external rev. com. CDC Preventing Rsik Behaviors in Adolescents, 1993; chmn. scholarship com. Fanwood-Scotch Plains Coll. Club, from 1997; mem. N.J. United for HIgher Stds., from 2000; mem. stds. rev. com. N.J. Dept. Edn., from 2001; bd. dirs. Washington Rock Girl Scout Coun., 1995—98, Literacy Vols. of Am., Union County, from 2001; bd. dirs., sec. SP-F Cmty. Sch. Adv. Commn., from 2000. Manya Shayon Ungar Scholarship and Scotch Plains H.S. Auditorium named in her honor, 1989; named Outstanding Citizen N.J. Jaycees, 1979, Scotch Plains Twp., 1989, 92, State of N.J., 1987, Bd. of Freeholders, 1987; named life mem. nat. PTA, 45 state PTAs. Mem.: LWV (chmn. voters svc. Westfield area 1991—95, N.J. fiscal policy and edn. coms. from 1998, SP-7 cmty. schs. adv. com. from 2000). Avocations: piano, acting, singing, recording talking books. Home: Scotch Plains, NJ. Died July 10, 2003.

UNITAS, JOHN CONSTANTINE, former restauranteur, former professional football player; b. Pitts., May 7, 1933; m. Sandra Unitas; children: Francis Joseph, Chad Elliott, Alicia Ann Paige; children by previous marriage: Janice, John Constantine, Robert, Christopher, Kenneth. Player Pitts. Steelers, 1955, Balt. Colts, 1956-72, San Diego Chargers, 1973-74; sports analyst CBS, 1975; former owner Johnny Unitas Golden Arm Restaurant, Balt.; owner, exec. v.p. Printed Circuit Bd. Mfg. Co., Balt., from 1984. Leading passer Nat. Football League Recipient Nat. Football League Man of Yr. award Vitalis Scholarship Fund, 1972; Gold medal award Pa. Broadcasters, 1972; elected to Profl. Football Hall of Fame, 1979; named Nat. Football League Most Valuable Player, 1957, 64, 67; Greatest Quarterback of All Time Nat. Football League 50th Anniversary Com.; player of decade A.P., 1970; named All Pro; player Pro Bowl, 1957-59, 64-65, 67 Super Bowl, 1969-70. Died Sept. 11, 2002.

UNRUG, RAPHAEL, geologist, educator, researcher, consultant; b. Krakow, Poland, Oct. 24, 1931; came to U.S., 1983; s. Wojciech Unrug and Jadwiga Jagninska; m. Sophia Unrug, Mar. 8, 1973; 1 child, Agnieszka. MSc in Geol. Engring., Sch. Mining and Metallurgy, Krakow, 1957, PhD in Geology, 1962, DSc in Geodynamics, 1968. Rsch. geologist, lectr., sr. lectr., assoc. prof., prof. Jagellonian U., 1957-79; prof., rsch. geologist U. Zambia Sch. Mines, Lusaka, 1980-83; cons. geologist Geoexplorer Internat. Inc., Denver, 1983-89; prof., chmn. dept. geol. scis. Wright State U., Dayton, Ohio, 1984-99; with Internat. Geol. Correlation Program, Punta Gorda, Fla. Sr. vis. sci. and prof. univs. Reading, Eng., Paris, Granada, Spain, U. Bologna, Italy, Sao Paulo, Brazil, Cape Town, South Africa, 1966-98; leader program 288 Internat. Union Geol. Sci. and UNESCO, 1990-98, co-leader program 440, 1998—; vis. hon. rsch. fellow Tectonic Spl. Rsch. Ctr., U. Western Australia, Perth, 2000—. Editor, co-author: Handbook of Sedimentology, 1976; contbr. over 200 articles to sci. jours. Grantee Swedish Agy. for Rsch. Cooperation, 1982, Wright State U., 1984-85, Internat. Union Geol. Scis. and UNESCO, 1990. Mem. Geol. Soc. Am., Am. Assn. Petroleum Geologists. Home: Punta Gorda, Fla. Deceased.

URIS, LEON MARCUS, author; b. Balt., Aug. 3, 1924; s. Wolf William and Anna (Blumberg) U.; m. Betty Katherine Beck, Jan. 5, 1945 (div. 1968); children: Karen Lynn, Mark Jay, Michael Cady; m. Margery Edwards, 1968 (dec. 1969); m. Jill Peabody, Feb. 15, 1970; 1 child, Rachael Jackson. Ed., Balt. City Coll.; hon. doctorate, U. Colo., 1976, Santa Clara U., 1977, Wittenberg U., 1980, Lincoln Coll., 1985. Author: Battle Cry, 1953, The Angry Hills, 1955, Exodus, 1957, Exodus Revisited,1959, Mila 18, 1960 (Calif. Literature Silver Medal award 1962), Armageddon, 1964 (Calif. Literature Gold Medal award 1965), Topaz, 1967, The Third Temple, 1967, QB VII, 1970, Ireland: A Terrible Beauty, 1975, Trinity, 1976, (with Jill Uris) Jerusalem, Song of Songs, 1981, The Haj, 1984, Mitla Pass, 1988, Redemption, 1995, A God in Ruins, 1999; screenwriter: (films) Battle Cry, 1954, Gunfight at the O.K. Corral, 1957; adaptor: (musical play) Ari, 1971. Served with USMCR, 1942-46. Recipient Daroff Meml. award, 1959, John F. Kennedy medal Irish/Am. Soc. of N.Y., 1977, Eire Soc. of Boston Gold medal, 1978, Jobotinsky medal State of Israel, 1980, Scopus award Hebrew U. of Jerusalem, 1981; Nat. Inst. Arts and Letters grantee, 1959; Hall fellow (with Jill Uris) Concord Academy, 1980. Died June 21, 2003.

USEEM, RUTH HILL, sociology educator; b. Hamilton, Ohio, May 31, 1915; d. William E. and Anna E. (Starlin) Hill; m. John Hearld Useem, June 6, 1940; children: Michael, Howard Sheldon, Bert. BA, Miami U., Oxford, Ohio, 1936; PhD, U. Wis., 1947. Asst. prof. Queens Coll., N.Y.C., 1942-43, 1944-45; rsch. cons. Mich. State U., East Lansing, 1951-52, instr., 1952-58, asst. prof., 1958-60, assoc. prof., 1960-70, prof. sociology and edn., 1970-85, prof. emerita, 1985—2003. Sr. fellow East-West Center, 1970 Author: (with J. Useem) The Western-Educated Man in India, 1955, (with F. Kempf) Psychology: Dynamics of Behavior in Nursing; contbr. articles to profl. jours. Disting. scholar Internat. Soc. Ednl., Cultural and Sci. Interchanges, 1979; recipient Excellence award Mich. State U. Faculty Women's Assn., 1979, award for Research in Internat. Ednl. Exchange, Council Internat. Ednl. Exchange, 1986; Edward W. Hazen Found. grantee India, 1952-53, 58; Edward W. Hazen Found. grantee Philippines, 1968-75; recipient Lee Founders' award for disting. career Soc. for Study of Social Problems, 1987, Pioneering Rsch. on Third Culture Kids award Global Nomads Internat., 1988. Mem. Am. Sociol. Assn. (council 1973-75, com. on coms. 1975-76, com. world sociology 1975-77, com. nominations 1979-81, liaison AAAS com. 1986-87), North Cen. Sociol. Assn. (council 1976-77, v.p./program chmn. 1977-78, pres. 1979-80, Disting. Profl. Service award 1984), Sociologists for Women in Soc., Soc. Internat. Edn., Tng. and Research (council 1978-81), Internat. Soc. Ednl., Cultural and Sci. Interchanges, Sociol. Research Assn., Mortar Bd.; fellow Am. Anthrop. Assn. Home: Merion Station, Pa. Died Sept. 10, 2003.

USSERY, HARRY MACRAE, investor, lawyer; b. Rockingham, N.C., Jan. 27, 1920; s. Robert Roy and Maggie Estelle (MacRae) U.; m. Olive Dual Simmons, Mar. 19, 1949. AA, Wake Forest U., 1947; JD, George Washington U., 1950. Bar: D.C. 1950. Assoc. firm Geiger & Harmel, Washington, 1950-52; ptnr. firm McNeill & Ussery, Washington, 1952-53; gen. counsel, dir. Harry R. Byers, Inc., Engring. and Constrn. Power Plants, Washington and Denver, 1953-59; procurement counsel Martin Marieta Corp., Denver, 1959-62; authorized agt. RCA, Camden N.J., 1962-69; staff counsel, mgr. internat. subcontract ops. Burns & Roe Constrn. Corp., Paramus, N.J., 1969-74; staff counsel Burns & Roe Indsl. Svcs. Corp., 1975-78; asst. to pres., Burns & Roe Svcs. Corp., Oradell, N.J., 1978-81; investor, Santa Fe, 1981—; broker Collector Cars, 1990—; founder, chmn. Assn. Mortgage Investors, Inc., 1983-86; chmn. Santa Fe Mortgage Investments, Inc., 1984-86; spl. city atty for annexations-contracts, Santa Fe, 1985-87; editor Investors Voice, 1983-86; chief moderator, dir., Dist. Roundtable, Sta. WWDC, Washington, 1950-53; cons., estate planning counsel Tom Lovell Trust, 1986—. Served with USAAF, 1941-45. Recipient Cmty. Chest campaign awards, 1951, 52. Mem. ABA, Am. Judicature Soc., Nat. Contract Mgmt. Assn., D.C. Bar Assn. (exec. coun. Jr. bar sect. 1954-56), George Washington U. Law Assn., Wake Forest U. Alumni Assn., Geneal. Soc. Santa Fe (state commr.), Council Scottish Clans Assns., St. Andrew's Soc., Clan MacRae Soc., Scottish Am. Mil. Soc., Sons Am. Revolution (pres. Santa Fe chpt. 1995-98, pres. N.Mex. Soc. 1997-98), Clan Donald and Assoc. Scots N.Mex., Delta Theta Phi. Republican. Presbyterian. Club: Santa Fe Vintage Car (pres., editor newsletter 1985-94). Author: The Origin of the Surname of Ussery, 1983 (founder-pres. The House of Usser, Internat., a Norman-Celtic family soc. 1993—); contbr. articles to various publs. and hist. socs. Died: Nov. 21, 1999.

USTINOV, SIR PETER ALEXANDER, actor, director, writer; b. London, Apr. 16, 1921; s. Iona and Nadia (Benois) U.; m. Isolda Denham, 1940 (div.); 1 child, Tamara; m. Suzanne Cloutier, Feb. 15, 1954 (div. 1971); children: Pavla, Igor, Andrea; m. Hélène du Lau d'Allemans, 1972. Student, Westminster Sch., London, Mr. Gibbs Prep. Sch., London Theatre Sch.; D.Mus. (hon.), Cleve. Inst. Music, 1967; LL.D. (hon.), U. Dundee, 1969, LaSalle Coll. of Phila., 1971, U. Ottawa, 1991; Litt.D. (hon.), U. Lancaster, 1972; Doctorate (hon.), U. Toronto, 1984, 95; LHD (hon.), Georgetown U., 1988; Doctorate (hon.), Free U. Brussels, 1995. Stage appearances include The Wood Demon, 1938, The Bishop of Limpopoland, 1939, Madame Liselotte Beethoven-Fink, 1939, White Cargo, Rookery Nook, Laburnum Grove, Pygmalion, 1939, First Night, 1940, Swinging the Gate, 1940, Fishing For Shadows, 1940, Hermione Gingold Revue, 1940, Diversion No. 1 Revue, 1940, Squaring the Circle, 1941, Crime and Punishment, 1946, Frenzy, 1948, Love in Albania, 1949, The Love of Four Colonels, 1951-52 (N.Y. Critics award, Donaldson award), Romanoff and Juliet, 1956 (Evening Standard drama award), Photo Finish, 1962, 63, The Unknown Soldier and His Wife, 1968, 73, Who's Who in Hell, 1974, King Lear, 1979, 80, Beethoven's Tenth, 1983, 83-84, 87-88; currently appearing worldwide in An Evening with Peter Ustinov; film appearances include One of Our Aircraft Is Missing, 1941, The Way Ahead, 1944, Private Angelo, 1949, Odette, 1950, Quo Vadis (Acad. award nomination for Best Supporting Actor), 1950, Hotel Sahara, 1952, Beau Brummel, 1953-54, The Egyptian, 1954, We're No Angels, 1955, Lola Montez, 1955, The Spies, 1955, An Angel Flew Over Brooklyn, 1955, I Girovaghi, 1955, The Sundowners, 1960, Spartacus, 1960-61 (Acad. award for Best Supporting Actor), Romanoff and Juliet, 1961, Billy Budd, 1962, Topkapi, 1963 (Acad. award for Best Supporting Actor), John Goldfarb, Please Come Home!, 1964, Blackbeard's Ghost, 1967, The Comedians, 1967, Hot Millions, 1968, Viva Max, 1969, Hammersmith Is Out, 1971, Big Truck and Poor Clare, 1971, One of Our Dinosaurs Is Missing, 1974, Logan's Run, 1975, Treasure of Matecumba, 1975, The Last Remake of Beau Geste, 1976, Purple Taxi, 1977, Death on the Nile, 1977, The Thief of Baghdad, 1978, Ashanti, 1979, Charlie Chan and the Curse of the Dragon Queen, 1980, Evil Under the Sun, 1981, Memed, My Hawk, 1982, Appointment With Death, 1988, The French Revolution, 1989, Lorenzo's Oil, 1992, The Phoenix and The Magic Carpet, 1993, Stiff Upper Lips, 1997, The Bachelor, 1999, The Will To Resist, 2002; dir.: (plays) Squaring the Circle, 1941, Love in Albania, 1949, No Sign of the Dove, 1952, A Fiddle at the Wedding, 1952, Romanoff and Juliet, 1956, Photo Finish, 1962, 64, Half Way Up the Tree, 1967, The Unknown Soldier and His Wife, 1968, 73, (operas) L'Heure Espagnole (Ravel), Covent Garden, 1962, Gianni Schicchi (Puccini), Covent Garden, 1962, Erwartung (Schoenberg), Covent Garden, 1962, The Magic Flute (Mozart), Hamburg Opera, 1968; dir., scenery and costume designer: Don Giovanni (Mozart), Edinburgh Festival, 1973; dir., producer, set and costume designer: Don Quichotte (Massenet), Paris Opera, 1973; dir., producer: The Brigands (Offenbach), The German Opera, Berlin, 1978; dir., writer libretto: The Marriage (Moussorgsky), Piccola Scala, 1981; dir.: Mavra and The Flood (Stravinsky), Piccola Scala, 1982, Katja Kabanowa (Janacek), Hamburg Opera, 1985, The Marriage of Figaro, Mozarteum and the Hamburg Opera, 1987, Jolanthe (Tchaikovsky) and Francesca da Rimini (Rachmaninoff), Dresden Opera, 1993, The Love of the Three Oranges (Prokofiev), Bolschoi, Moscow, 1997; appeared on radio, London (BBC), Germany, Belgium, Rome, Paris, N.Y.C., Hollywood; TV appearances include In All Directions (host, producer, co-star), BBC, History of Europe, BBC, Einstein's Universe, PBS and BBC, 1979, Barefoot in Athens (Emmy award), Storm in Summer (Emmy award), The American Revolution, CBS (George Peabody award), Omnibus (Emmy award), The Well Tempered Bach (Emmy award nomination), PBS, 1984, 13 at Dinner, CBS, 1985, Deadman's Folly, CBS, 1985, Peter Ustinov's Russia, 1985, Appointment with Death, 1987, Around the World in Eighty Days, NBC, 1988-89, Secret Identity of Jack the Ripper, 1989-90, Monet: Legacy of Light, 1990, Ustinov Aboard the Orient Express, 1991-92, Ustinov Meets Pavarotti, 1993, Inside the Vatican, 1994, The Old Curiosity Shop, 1995, Haydn Gala, 1995, Alice in Wonderland, 1999, Animal Farm (voice), 1999, Deutschlandspiel, 2000, Victoria & Albert, 2001, Salem Witch Trials, 2002, WinterSolstice, 2003; documentaries on Thailand and Hong Kong, 1995, an Evening with Sir Peter Ustinov, 1995, Russia Now, 1995, Paths of the Gods, 1996, Following the Equator, 1998, occasional political commentaries, BBC; recordings include Mock Mozart, The Grand Prix of Gibralter, Peter and the Wolf (directed by Herbert Von Karajan), Nutcracker Suite, The Soldier's Tale (Stravinsky) (with Jean Cocteau), Hary Janos (Kodaly), London Symphony Orch., The Little Prince (St. Exupéry), (narration) Grandpa, Babar and Father Christmas, The Old Man of Lochnagar, Grandpa, Peter Ustinov Reads the Orchestra; author: (plays) Fishing for Shadows, 1940, House of Regrets, 1942, Blow Your Own Trumpet, 1943, Beyond, 1943, The Banbury Nose, 1944, The Tragedy of Good Intentions, 1945, The Indifferent Shepherd, 1948, Frenzy, 1948, The Man in the Raincoat, 1949, The Moment of Truth, 1951, The Love of Four Colonels, 1951, High Balcony, 1952, No Sign of the Dove, 1953, Romanoff and Juliet, 1956, The Empty Chair, 1956, Paris Not So Gay, 1958, Photo Finish, 1962, The Life in My Hands, 1964, The Unknown Soldier and His Wife, 1967, Halfway Up the Tree, 1967, Who's Who in Hell, 1974, Overheard, 1981, Beethoven's Tenth, 1983, 87-88, others, (films) The Way Ahead (with Eric Ambler), 1942-43, School for Secrets, 1946, Vice Versa, 1947, Private Angelo, 1949, Romanoff and Juliet, 1961, Billy Budd (with DeWitt Bodeen), 1962-63, The Lady L (with Ira Wallach), 1964, Hot Millions (with Ira Wallach), 1968, Memed, My Hawk, 1982, (cartoon) We Were Only Human, 1960, (short stories) Add a Dash of Pity, 1960, Frontiers of the Sea, 1966, (novels) The Loser, 1961, Krumnagel, 1971, The Disinformer, 1989, The Old Man and Mr. Smith, 1991, (autobiography) Dear Me, 1977, My Russia, 1983, Ustinov in Russia, 1987, Ustinov at Large, 1991, Still at Large, 1993, Quotable Ustinov, 1995. Chancellor U. Durham, 1992; pres. World Federalist Movement, 1992. With Brit. Army, 1942-46. Decorated Comdr. Order of Brit. Empire, 1975, Commandeur des Arts et Lettres, 1985, Knight of the Realm, 1990; recipient Disting. Svc. award UNICEF, 1978, Prix de la Butte, 1978, Best Actor award Variety Club Gt. Britain, 1979, medal of Honor Charles U. (Prague), 1991, Britannia award, 1992, Critic's Circle award, 1993, German Cultural award, 1994, German Bambi, 1994, Internat. Child Survival award, 1995, Rudolph Valentino award, 1995, Norman Cousins Global Governance award, 1995, German Video prize for life-time achievement, 1997; named rector U. Dundee, 1971-73; elected to Acad. Fine Arts Paris, 1988. Died Mar. 28, 2004.

VACCARO, NICK DANTE, painter, educator; b. Youngstown, Ohio, Apr. 9, 1931; s. Frank and Carmela (Santoianni) V.; m. Luella Grace Ray, Feb. 18, 1955; 1 child, Nick Dante Jr. BA in Art, U. Wash., 1958; MA in Painting, U. Calif., Berkeley, 1960. Instr. drawing and painting art dept. U. Tex., Austin, 1960-61, asst. prof. Sch. Architecture, 1961-63; chmn. dept. art U. Kans., Lawrence, 1963-67, prof. art, from 1963. Vis. artist art dept. Pa. State U., College Park, Pa., 1970. One man show: Baker U., Baldwin, Ks., 1999; group exhibiton: Retrospective U. Kan., Lawrence, 1996. Staff sgt. USAF, 1951-55. Recipient Print purchase awards San Francisco Mus. Art, 1958, Dallas Mus. Fine Art, 1961, Montgomery (Ala.) Mus. Fine Art. Avocations: collecting, dance. Home: Lawrence, Kans. Died Jan. 2, 2002.

VAGLIANO, ALEXANDER MARINO, banker; b. Paris, Mar. 15, 1927; came to U.S., 1940, naturalized, 1945; s. Andre M. and Barbara (Allen) V.; children: Barbara A., Andre M., Justin C. Grad., St. Paul's Sch., Concord, N.H., 1944; BA, Harvard, 1949, LL.B. cum laude, 1952. Bar: N.Y. bar 1952. Asso. firm White & Case, N.Y.C., 1952-58; asst. treas. J.P. Morgan & Co., Inc., N.Y.C., 1959; v.p. Morgan Guaranty Trust Co., N.Y.C., 1959-62, 65-66, sr. v.p., 1968-76, exec. v.p., 1976-81; chief exec. officer Banca Vonwiller, Milan, Italy, 1967-68; chmn. Morgan Guaranty Internat. Finance Corp., 1976-81, J.P. Morgan Overseas Capital Corp., 1976-81; ptnr. Price Waterhouse and Ptnrs., 1983-85; chmn. Sunset Ridge Farm, Inc., from 1983, Michelin Fin. Corp., Greenville, S.C., 1985-98; chmn. bd. advisors Equity Linked Investors, N.Y.C., from 1985; pres. The N.Y. Farmers, 1992-94. Bd. dirs. Holographics, Inc., N.Y.; dir. office of capital devel. and fin. Near East and South Asia, AID, 1963-65; adviser Yale Econ. Growth Ctr., 1973-80, NYU Inst. French Studies, 1979-86; trustee Coun. for Excellence in Govt., 1990-93. Pres. Parks Council N.Y.C., 1971-73; bd. dirs. French Am. Found., N.Y.C., 1986-93; gov. The Atlantic Inst. Internt. Affairs, 1986-90; active Norfolk Ct. Zoning and Planning Commn. Served with AUS, 1945-47. Decorated Chevalier de l'Ordre des Arts et des Lettres. Mem. Coun. Fgn. Rels. Clubs: Brook (N.Y.C.); Travellers (Paris). Died Nov. 13, 2003.

VAGVOLGYI, JOSEPH, biology educator; b. Budapest, Hungary, Sept. 9, 1927; s. Joseph and Anna Vagvolgyi; m. Alice E. Anderson, 1970 (div. 1979); m. Maria Wagner, Jan. 28, 1984; 1 child, Pal. AB in biology geography, Univ. Budapest, 1950; MS in biology zoology, Harvard Univ., 1960, PhD in biology zoology, 1962. Rsch. assoc. Staten Island (N.Y.) Zoology Soc., 1973-83; scientific adv. Univ. Calif., Berkeley, Calif., 1976; postgrad. teaching fellow Harvard Univ., 1959-62; asst. prof. Univ. Fla., Gainesville, 1963-64; instr. Brooklyn (N.Y.) Coll., 1964-67; asst. prof. Coll. Staten Island, 1967-78, assoc. prof., from 1978. Asst. to curator Acad. Nat. Scis., Phila., 1956-58; curator Hungarian Nat. Mus., 1952-56; dep. to sec. Hungarian Nat. Acad. Scis., Budapest, 1951-52; asst. curator Xanthus Janos Mus., Hungary, 1950-51. Contbr. articles to profl. jours. Recipient

Rsch. award Hungarian Nat. Acad. Sci., 1955, 54. Mem. Am. Assn. Advancement of Sci. Democrat. Avocations: sports, classical music, politics. Home: Staten Island, NY. Died May 20, 2000.

VALLE, VICENTE, management consultant; b. Navarcles, Barcelona, Spain, May 8, 1926; came to U.S., 1944; s. Manuel and Carmen (Marti) V.; m. Maria Luisa Bencomo, Dec. 15, 1951; children: Carmen Alicia Valle Patel, Vicente Jr. SB, Harvard U., 1948. Mgr. human resources Exxon's Creole Petroleum Corp., Venezuela, 1948-61; asst. human resources mgr. internat. ops. Continental Oil Co. (Conoco), N.Y.C., 1961-64; mgr. human resources Exxon Corp. affiliates, Brazil, Argentina, 1964-72; dep. human resources mgr. Esso Inter-Am., Coral Gables, Fla., 1978-80; mem. compensation, orgn. and exec. devel. com. Exxon Corp., N.Y.C., 1978-80; corp. officer, sec. Esso Inter-Am., Inc., Rio de Janeiro and London, 1972-78, corp. officer, sec., mgr. human rels. Coral Gables, 1980-87; corp. officer, sec. Esso Africa, Rio de Janeiro and London, 1972-78; dir. ops. Internat. Exec. Svc. Corps, Stamford, Conn., Panama, Costa Rica, 1990-94; pres. Valle & Assocs., Inc., Longboat Key, Fla., from 1994. Vol. bus. advisor, cons. to various local firms throughout L.Am., Internat. Exec. Svc. Corps, 1987-94. Republican. Roman Catholic. Deceased.

VANCE, CLARENCE JOSEPH, insurance executive; b. Birmingham, Ala., July 2, 1913; s. Clarence Lucian and Edna Mae (Elum) V.; m. Mary Jean Burton, Jan. 19, 1939; children: Florence, Helen, Bingham, Clarence, Jr. BA in Journalism, Birmingham So. Coll., 1935; BS in Pharmacy, Samford U., 1938. Registered pharmacist, Ala. Advt. writer The Birmingham News, 1936; practice of pharmacy Drug Stores, Jasper, Birmingham, 1939-41; hosp. adminstr. South Highlands Hosp., Birmingham, 1946-57; sr. v.p. Blue Cross and Blue Shield Ala., Birmingham, 1957-78. Adj. prof. pharmacy Samford U., Birmingham, 1946-57; chmn. Birmingham Red Cross Blood Program, 1949-50. Author: History of Blue Cross and Blue Shield, 1978, Gadsden Baptist Hospital of Alabama, 1980; contbg. editor: So. Hosps. Mag., 1946-76. Chmn. sr. citizen coms. City of Pell City, Ala., 1986; inspector poll election ofcl., St. Clair County, 1990. With USNR, 1941-46. Fellow Am. Coll. Health Care Execs. (life), Ala. Soc. Health System Pharmacists (life); mem. Birmingham Com. of Fgn. Rels., Pine Harbor Golf and Racquet Club (pres., sec. 1980—). Episcopalian. Avocations: tenor soloist, golf, gardening, fishing. Home: Pell City, Ala. Died Mar. 23, 2001.

VANCE, SHIRLEY R. insurance company executive; b. Iaeger, W.Va., June 30, 1914; s. Frank Johnson and Florence (Murphy) V.; m. Rosemary Eugenia Spitzer, June 11, 1938; children: Johnson David, Pamela Vance Worley. Student, Marshall U., 1935. Cashier Bank of Iaeger, 1936-1950; prin. Vance Ins. Agy., Iaeger, 1950-66; v.p. Vance Ins. Agy. Inc., Iaeger, from 1974; field agt. W.Va. Tax Dept., Charleston, 1966-74. Pres. McDowell County (W.Va.) Bd. Edn., 1946-60. Mem. Profl. Ins. Agents of W.Va. Lodges: Odd Fellows (Noble Grand, 1936), Lions (local pres. 1959, 1981), Masons (treas. 1982—). Democrat. Methodist. Deceased.

VAN CLEVE, WILLIAM MOORE, lawyer; b. Mar. 17, 1929; s. William T Van Cleve and Catherine (Baldwin) Moore Van Cleve; m. Georgia Hess Dunbar, June 27, 1953; children: Peter Dunbar, Robert Baldwin, Sarah Van Cleve Van Doren, Emory Basford. Grad., Phillips Acad., 1946; AB in Econs., Princeton U., 1950; JD, Washington U., St. Louis, 1953, LLD (hon.), 2001. Bar: Mo. 1953. Assoc. Dunbar and Gaddy, St. Louis, 1955-58; ptnr. Bryan Cave LLP (and predecessor firm), St. Louis, 1958-2000, chmn., 1973-94, sr. counsel., from 2001. Bd. dirs. Emerson Electric Co. Trustee Washington U., 1983—, vice chmn. bd. trustees, 1988-93, 95-2000, chmn., 1993-95, mem. exec. com., 1985—; pres. Eliot Soc., 1982-86; chmn. Law Sch. Nat. Coun., 1986 93; commr. St. Louis Sci. Ctr., 1993-2000, bd. trustees, 2001—; bd. dirs., Parents As Tchrs. Nat. Ctr., 1991—, pres., 1997-2000. Mem. ABA, Bar Assn. Met. St. Louis, St. Louis County Bar Assn., Order of Coif (hon.). Clubs: Princeton (pres. 1974-75), Noonday (pres. 1985), St. Louis Country, Bogey (pres. 1990-91), Round Table (St. Louis). Democrat. Episcopalian. Home: Saint Louis, Mo. Died Feb. 28, 2003.

VANDIVER, ROBERT SANFORD, civic association executive; b. Barksdale Field, La., Apr. 2, 1937; s. William Marion and Mattie Katherine (Tiller) V.; m. Patricia Gail Kelly, Feb. 10, 1956; children: Cynthia Ann, Kathleen. AA, U. Md., 1973; BA, SUNY, Albany, 1975; MS, Golden Gate U., 1985, MPA, 1986. Enlisted U.S. Army, 1955, commd. lt., 1967, advanced through grades to maj., 1978; materiel mgr. Pima County Sheriff Dept., Tucson, 1979-81; task leader Computer Scis. Corp., Sierra Vista, Ariz., 1981-83, Mandex, Inc., Sierra Vista, 1983-86; project mgr. Planning Rsch. Corp., Sierra Vista, 1986-90; Boy Scout exec. Catalina Coun., Tucson, from 1990. Adj. faculty Cochise Coll., Sierra Vista, 1987-90, Golden Gate U., San Francisco, 1988-92; instr. Sch. Pub. Adminstrn., Ariz. State U., Tucson, 1988-92. Co-editor, South Vietnam Boy Scout Handbook, 1965. Vol. leader Boy Scouts Am., various locations, 1956-90. Decorated Legion of Merit, Bronze Star medal, Soldier's medal; recipient Silver Beaver award, Boy Scouts Am., 1977. Mem. Nat. Property Mgmt. Assn., Soc. Logistics Engrs., Am. Soc. Pub. Adminstrn., Co. Mil. Historians. Lutheran. Avocations: skiing, golf, history. Home: Tucson, Ariz. Deceased.

VAN EATON, ERROL HAY, career officer; b. Yakima, Wash., Sept. 9, 1947; s. Howard Hopkins and Jane Ann (Karr) van E.; m. P. Suzan Bandy, Oct. 25, 1969; children: Jason Lee, Joshua Hay. BS in Profl. Aeronautics, Embry-Riddle Aero. U., 1978; grad., U.S. Army War Coll., 1991. Cert. airline transport pilot. S-4 logistics officer 174th Gen. Support Group U.S. Army, Ft. Lawton, Wash., 1980-82, comdr. 324th Mil. Police Battalion, 1982-85, chief TMED, DCST 124th U.S. Army Res. Command, 1985-87, ADCS for Pers., 1987-88, comdr. 1397th Trans Terminal Unit, 1988-92; comdr. 540th Aviation Group Camp Murray, Tacoma, 1992-93, comdr. 66th Aviation Brigade (corps), 1993-99. Chief army aviation support facility 124th Army Res. Command, U.S. Army, Everett, Wash., 1972-84; supervisory aviation safety insp. FAA, Seattle, 1984-94, ret.; agt. for svc. Nat. Charter Network, Inc., Seattle, 1994-99; v.p. aviation ops. Global Safety Svcs., Inc., Fayetteville, Ga., 1994-99. Decorated 26 Air medals, 2 DFCs, Bronze star; Paul Harris fellow Rotary Internat. Mem. Internat. Soc. Air Safety Investigators, NG Assn., Res. Officers Assn. Avocation: piloting airships and hot air balloons. Home: Everett, Wash. Died Mar. 14, 1999.

VAN GORKOM, JEROME WILLIAM, financial executive; b. Denver, Aug. 6, 1917; s. A.G. and Elizabeth (Laux) Van G.; m. Betty Jean Alexander, June 27, 1942; children: Gayle, Lynne. BS, U. Ill., 1939, JD, 1941. Bar: Ill. 1941; C.P.A., 1950. Law assoc. Kix Miller, Baar & Morris, Chgo., 1945-47; accountant Arthur Andersen & Co., 1947-54, ptnr., 1954-56; treas., contr. Trans Union Corp., Chgo., from 1956, dir., 1957—, v.p., 1958-60, exec. v.p., 1960-63, pres., 1963-78, chmn. bd., 1978-82; under sec. Dept. State, 1982-83. Mng. dir. Chgo. Housing Authority, 1987-88. Chmn. bd. Lyric Opera of Chgo.; chmn. Chgo. Sch. Fin. Authority, 1980-89. With USNR, 1941-45. Mem.: Chicago, Mid America, Comml, Onwentsia, Pauma Valley Country. Home: Lake Forest, Ill. Deceased.

VANHOUTEN, RUTGER ARN, forester; b. Apeldoorn, Netherlands, July 15, 1944; came to U.S., 1962; s. Herman Johan and Rudolphine Johanna (Enger) vanH.; m. Katherine Rosalie Wafstet, Aug. 28, 1965; children: Joanne Marie, Karla Kay, Michael William. BA, U. Mont., 1969, MA, 1974. Forestry technician Clearwater Nat. Forest U.S. Forest Svc., Orofino, Idaho, 1973-78; forester, forest mgr. Nez Perce Tribe, Lapwai, Idaho, from 1979. Nez Perce del. to Intertribal Timber Coun., Warm Springs, Oreg.,1980-85, bd. dirs., 1985—; mem. People to People Ambassadors Tour, forestry, People's Republic China, 1986. Contbr. articles to profl. publs. Bd. dirs., Sch. Dist. 341, Lapwai, 1979-87, chmn., 1982-87. Mem. Soc. Am. Foresters (sec.-treas. Snake River chpt. 1982, vice chmn., 1983, chmn. 1984), Am. Forestry Assn. Avocations: stamp collecting/philately, photography. Home: Lapwai, Idaho. Deceased.

VAN SINDEREN, ALFRED WHITE, former telephone company executive; b. Bklyn., June 20, 1924; s. Adrian and Jean (White) Van S.; m. Suzanne Petersen, Apr. 21, 1962; children: Alexander, David Cabot, Sylvia Van Sinderen Abbate, Jean Van Sinderen Vashaw, Katherine Van Sinderen Tucker. BA, Yale U., 1945; MBA, Harvard U., 1947. With So. New Eng. Telephone Co., New Haven, 1947-85; v.p. So. New Eng. Telephone Co. (No. area), Hartford, Conn., 1962-65; v.p. ops. So. New Eng. Telephone Co., 1965-67, pres., 1967-82, chmn., chief exec. officer, 1982-84, chmn. bd., 1984-85; William H. Donaldson disting. faculty fellow Yale U. Sch. Mgmt., 1985-89. Past mem. adv. bd. Yale U. Sch. Orgn. and Mgmt.; mem. Yale Libr. Assocs.; past co-chmn. Gov. Conf. Human Rights, 1967; past bd. dirs. Conn. Econ. Devel. Corp., Hartford; bd. dirs., past chmn. Shirley Frank Found.; pres Found. for New Haven Green, Inc., 1986-91. With USNR, 1943-46. Recipient Charter Oak Leadership medal Hartford, 1965; Conn. Man of Yr. New Eng. Council, 1976; Human Relations award NCCJ, 1981 Mem. Quinnipiack Club (New Haven). Home: Woodbridge, Conn. Deceased.

VARCO, RICHARD LYNN, surgeon, educator; b. Fairview, Mont., Aug. 14, 1912; s. Lynn G. and Maurine V.; m. Louise Miller, June 4, 1940. M.B., U. Minn., 1936, MD, 1937, PhD, 1944. Diplomate: Am. Bd. Surgery, Am. Bd. Thoracic Surgery. Resident surgery U. Minn., to 1942, instr. dept. surgery, 1943-44, asst. prof., 1944-46, asso. prof., 1946-50, prof. surgery, 1950, Regents' prof., 1974-81, prof. emeritus, 1981—2004. Mem. Am. Bd. Med. Spltys. Fellow A.C.S. (1st v.p. 1976-77); mem. Am. Assn. Thoracic Surgery, Am. Fedn. Clin. Research, A.M.A., Am. Surg. Assn., Soc. Univ. Surgeons (pres. 1958), Soc. Exptl. Biology and Medicine, Soc. Vascular Surgery (pres. 1964), Am. Heart Assn., Sigma Xi. Died May 3, 2004.

VARNEDOE, JOHN KIRK TRAIN, art historian, educator; b. Savannah, Ga., Jan. 18, 1946; s. Samuel Lamartine and Lilla (Train) V.; m. Elyn Zimmerman. BA with honors, Williams Coll., 1967, DFA (hon.), 1994; MA, Stanford U., 1970, PhD, 1972; DFA (hon.), Pratt Inst., 1997. Asst. instr. art history Williams Coll., 1967-68; asst. prof. art history Stanford (Calif.) U., 1973-74; asst. prof. Columbia U., N.Y.C., 1974-80; assoc. prof. Inst. Fine Arts, NYU, N.Y.C., 1980-84, prof. fine arts, 1984-88; chief curator dept. painting and sculpture Mus. Modern Art, N.Y.C., 1989—2001; prof. Sch. Hist. Studies Inst. Advanced Study, Princeton, NJ, 2001—03. Vis. lectr. in law Columbia U. Law Sch., 1980-81; adj. curator dept. painting and sculpture Mus. Modern Art, 1985-88; mem. adv. bd. J. Paul Getty Program for Art on Film, 1985-87, Ctr. for Advanced Study in Visual Arts, 1990-93; mem. selection panel J. Paul Getty Postdoctoral Fellowships, 1985-88, J. Paul Getty Sr. Fellowships, 1988-90; Slade prof. art history Oxford (Eng.) U., 1992; lectr. in field. Author: The Drawings of Auguste Rodin, 1971, Vienna 1900, 1986, Gustave Caillebotte, 1987, Northern Light, 1988 (Henry Allen Moe prize 1983), A Fine Disregard--What Makes Modern Art Modern, 1990, High and Low: Modern Art and Popular Culture, 1990, Cy Twombly: A Retrospective, 1994, Jasper Johns: A Retrospective, 1996 ed. Jasper Johns: Writings, Sketchbook Notes, Interviews, 1996, Jackson Pollock, 1998; mem. editl. bd. The Art Bull., 1985-90; contbr. articles and revs. to profl. jours. Decorated knight The Royal Order of Donnebroge (Denmark), officer Order of Arts and Letters (France); David E. Finley fellow Nat. Gallery Art, 1970-73, NEH fellow, 1977-78, MacArthur Found. fellow, 1984-89; Rsch. grantee Columbia U., 1975, Travel grantee Am. Coun. Learned Socs. Fellow Am. Acad. Arts & Scis., NYU Soc. Fellows. Home. New York, NY. Died Aug. 14, 2003.

VASVARY, BRIGITTE, medical/surgical nurse; b. Bamburg, Ger., Apr. 15, 1947; d. C.W. and Martha (Schrodel) Dintleman. ASN, Dalton (Ga.) Jr. Coll., 1982. Staff nurse SNIV Emroy U. Hosp., Atlanta. Mem. Am. Assn. Critical Care Nurses, Phi Theta Kappa. Home: Tucker, Ga. Died Apr. 30, 2001.

VATERS, MARY, retired educator, academic organization executive; b. Boston; d. William and Agnes Strickland; m. Malcolm Vaters, July 10, 1942; children: Bonnie Vaters Whitney, Gary Vaters, Gale Vaters Donovan. Student, Harvard U.; BA in Psychology, U. Mass., 1996. Investigator Commonwealth of Mass., Registry of Motor Vehicles, Boston, 1955-70; tax examiner IRS, Andover, mass., 1970-86; CEO, owner Lakeside Sch. Day Care and Nursery, Wakefield, Mass., 1975-99; owner, CEO Tutorial Internat., Stoneham, Mass., from 1975. Mem. NEA, Nat. Assn. of Speakers of Am., Retired Fed. Employees Assn., Nat. Assn. Police Orgns., Mass. Tchrs. Assn., Harvard Faculty Club, Harvard U. Alumni Assn. Avocations: reading, walking, music, other languages. Home: Stoneham, Mass. Died June 8, 2002.

VAUGHN, RUFUS MAHLON, psychiatrist; b. Ensley, Ala., Oct. 31, 1924; s. Rufus Samuel and Anna Martina (Fink) V.; children: Stephen Andrew, Alexander. Student, U. Mich., 1942-43, 46-47; AB, Birmingham So. Coll., 1949; MD, Med. Coll. Ala., 1953. Diplomate Am. Bd. Psychiatry and Neurology, Am. Bd. Forensic Psychiatry. Intern USPHS Hosp., San Francisco, 1953-54; resident in psychiatry Ind. U. Hosp., Indpls., 1954-56, U. Calif. Hosp., L.A., 1956-57; dir. psychiatry Student Health Svc., U. Mass., Amherst, 1958-59; researcher Boston State Hosp., 1959-61; assoc. prof. psychiatry U. Fla., Gainesville, 1961-70; dir. Palm Beach County Mental Health Ctr., West Palm Beach, Fla., 1970-71; med. dir. Lake Hosp. and Clinic, Lake Worth, Fla., 1971-73; dir. tng., rsch. So. Fla. State Hosp., Hollywood, 1973-74, supt., 1974; chief Bur. Mental Hosp. Svcs., Fla. Div. Mental Health, Tallahassee, 1974-75; pvt. practice medicine specializing in forensic psychiatry West Palm Beach, 1975-87; sr. physician No. Fla. Evaluation and Treatment Ctr., Gainesville, 1982-89; clin. prof. psychiatry U. Miami, 1973-75; med. dir. USPHS Res., 1980—; clin. assoc. prof. psychiatry U. Fla., from 1983; med. dir. Mental Health Svcs. Inc., Gainesville, Fla., 1989-94, cons., from 1994. With USNR, 1943-46. Home: Palm Bay, Fla. Died Dec. 22, 1999.

VAZSONYI, BALINT, concert pianist, television producer, political philosopher, columnist; b. Budapest, Hungary, Mar. 7, 1936; came to U.S., 1959; s. Miklos and Hedvig (Felsner) V.; m. Barbara Whittington, Feb. 26, 1960; 1 child, Nicholas. Artist Diploma, Franz Liszt Acad., Budapest, 1956; MMus, Fla. State U., 1960; PhD, U. Budapest, 1982. Concert and recording career, worldwide, from 1948; prof. music Ind. U., Bloomington, 1978-84; pres. Telemusic, Inc., Bloomington, 1983-98; sr. fellow The Potomac Found., McLean, Va., from 1993; dean of music New World Sch. of the Arts, 1993-95; dir. Ctr. of the Am. Founding, from 1996. Tchr. master classes in piano Yale, Harvard, New Eng. Conservatory, Dartmouth Coll. Author: Erno Dohnanyi, 1971, 2002, The Battle for America's Soul, 1995, America's 30 Years War: Who Is Winning?, 1998; author, producer, presenter TV biographies Beethoven, 1983, Mozart, Schubert, 1986, Brahms, 1987; first chronological cycle of Beethoven Sonatas, N.Y., 1976. Hon. Cultural Counselor of the Republic of Hungary, 1993-95; decorated Officers' Cross Order of the Republic of Hungary, 1999; recipient Americanism award DAR, 2000, Hon. Citizen of Indpls., 2000, Key to City of Charleston, W.Va., 2000. Home: Washington, DC. Died Jan. 17, 2003.

VEATCH, KENNETH W. computer information systems educator; b. Quincy, Ill., Sept. 22, 1930; s. Gilbert Wade and Martha Olivia (Wilson) V.; children: Steven Wade, Gregory Wallace. BSBA, Cen. Mo. State U., 1952; postgrad, U. No. Colo., U. Tex. Cert. systems profl. Dep. dir. data automation USAF Acad., Colorado Springs, Colo., 1959-73; assoc. prof., CIS program coord. San Antonio Coll., from 1979. Mem. competency com. San Antonio Coll. Faculty Senate, curriculum review and evaluation com.; sponsor DPMA student chpt. Mem. DMPA. Deceased.

VELA, FILEMON B. federal judge; b. Harlingen, Tex., May 1, 1935; s. Roberto and Maria Luisa Cardenas V.; m. Blanca Sanchez, Jan. 28, 1962; children: Filemon, Rafael Eduardo, Sylvia Adriana. Student, Tex. Southmost Coll., 1954-56, U. Tex., 1956-57; JD, St. Mary's U., San Antonio, 1962. Bar: Tex. 1962. Mem. Vela & Vela, 1962-63; atty. Mexican-Am. Legal Def. Fund, 1962-75; pvt. practice law Brownsville, 1963-75; judge dist. 107, Tex. Dist. Ct., 1975-80; judge U.S. Dist. Ct. (so. dist.) Tex., Brownsville,

1980—2004; instr. Law Enforcement Coll. Presenter in field. City commr., Brownsville, 1971-73. Served with U.S. Army, 1957-59. Mem. State Bar Tex. Democrat. Died Apr. 13, 2004.

VELARDO, JOSEPH THOMAS, molecular biology and endocrinology educator; b. Newark, Jan. 27, 1923; s. Michael Arthur and Antoinette (I.) V.; m. Forresta M.-M. Power, Aug. 12, 1948 (dec. July 1976). AB, U. No. Colo., 1948; SM, Miami U., Oxford, Ohio, 1949; PhD, Harvard U., 1952. Rsch. fellow in biology and endocrinology Harvard U., Cambridge, Mass., 1952-53; rsch. assoc. in pathology, ob-gyn. and surgery Harvard U. Sch. Medicine, Boston, 1953-55; asst. in surgery Peter Bent Brigham and Women's Hosp., Boston, 1954-55; asst. prof. anatomy and endocrinology Sch. Medicine, Yale U., New Haven, 1955-61; prof. anatomy, chmn. dept. N.Y. Med. Coll., N.Y.C., 1961-62; cons. N.Y. Fertility Inst., 1961-62; dir. Inst. for Study Human Reprodn., Cleve., 1962-67; prof. biology John Carroll U., Cleve., 1962-67; mem. rsch. and edn. divs. St. Ann Ob-Gyn. Hosp., Cleve., 1962-67, head dept. rsch., 1964-67; prof. anatomy Stritch Sch. Medicine Loyola U., Chgo., 1967-88, chmn. dept. anatomy Stritch Sch. of Medicine, 1967-73; v.p. Universal Rsch. Systems, Warren, Ohio, from 1975; pres. University Rsch. Systems, Lombard, from 1979, Internat. Basic and Biol.-Biomed. Curricula, Lombard, Ill., from 1979. Course moderator laparoscopy Brazil-Israel Congress on Fertility and Sterility, Brazil Soc. of Human Reprodn., Rio de Janeiro, 1973; mem. curriculum com. Yale U. Sch. Medicine, 1956—61, dir. exptl. mammalian labs., 1956—61; organizer, chmn. symposia in field; initial charter founder, mem. U. Sacramento, 2003. Author: (with others) Annual Reviews Physiology, Reproduction, 1961, Histochemistry of Enzymes in the Female Genital System, 1963, The Ovary, 1963, The Ureter, 1967, rev. edit., 1981; editor, contbr.: Endocrinology of Reproduction, 1958, The Essentials of Human Reproduction, 1958; cons. editor, co-author: The Uterus, 1959; contbr. Progestational Substances, 1958, Trophoblast and Its Tumors, 1959, The Vagina, 1959, Hormonal Steroids, Biochemistry, Pharmacology and Therapeutics, 1964, Human Reproduction, 1973; co-editor, contbr.: Biology of Reproduction, Basic and Clinical Studies, 1973; contbr. articles to profl. jours.; live broadcasts on major radio and TV networks on subjects of bioscis., biomed. careers and biomed. subjects; co-author, co-dir. med. movie on human reprodn. The Soft Anvil; life history and research highlights chronicled in The Endocrinologist, vol II, 2001, Initial Charter Founder Member, University of Sacramento, 2003. Apptd. U.S. del. to Vatican, 1964; charter mem. U.S. Rep. Presdl. Task Force, 1988—; charter mem. U.S. Rep. Nat. Senatorial Com., 1988—, Rep. Nat. Com. Victory Team, 2003; mem. Rep. Senate Adv. Coun., 1997—; rep. U.S. Senate Inner Circle, 1988—, U.S. Rep. Senatorial Commn., 1991—. With USAAF, World War II, 1943-45. Decorated Presdl. Unit citation, 2 Bronze Stars; recipient award Lederle Med. Faculty Awards Com., 1955-58, Cert. of Achievement U.S. Rep. Nat. Senatorial Com., 1999; Disting. Alumni award, The William R. Ross award in sci., U. No. Colo., 1999; named hon. citizen City of Sao Paulo, Brazil, 1972; U.S. del. to Vatican, 1964. Fellow AAAS, N.Y. Acad. Scis. (co-organizer, chmn., consulting editor internat. symposium The Uterus), Gerontol. Soc., Pacific Coast Fertility Soc. (hon.); mem. French Nat. Soc. for Study of Sterility and Fertility (exec. hon. pres. IVth World Congress on Fertility and Sterility 1962), Am. Assn. Anatomists, Am. Soc. Zoologists, Soc. for Integrative and Comparative Biology (organizer symposium The Uterus), Am. Physiol. Soc. (vis. prof. 1962), Endocrine Soc., Soc. Endocrinology (Gt. Britain), Soc. Exptl. Biology and Medicine, Am. Soc. Study Sterility (Rubin award 1954), Internat. Fertility Assn., Pan Am. Assn. Anatomy (co-organizer symposium Reproduction 1972), Midwestern Soc. Anatomists (pres. 1973-74), Mexican Soc. Anatomy (hon.), Harvard Club, Sigma Xi, Kappa Delta Pi, Phi Sigma, Gamma Alpha, Alpha Epsilon Delta. Roman Catholic. Achievements include extensive original research and publications on the physiology and development of decidual tissue (experimental equivalent of the maternal portion of the placenta) in the rat; biological investigation of eighteen human adenohypophyses (anterior lobes of the human pituitary glands); induction of ovulation utilizing highly purified adenohypophyseal gonadotropic hormones in mammals; the pacemaker action of ovarian sex steroid hormones in reproductive processes; and the interaction of steroids in reproductive mechanisms. Home: Lombard, Ill. Died Oct. 5, 2003.

VELASCO SUAREZ, MANUEL, science academy executive; Pres. Acad. Nacional de Ciencias, Mexico City, Mexico. Died Dec. 2, 2002.

VELDE, JOHN ERNEST, JR., investment company executive; b. Pekin, Ill., June 15, 1917; s. John Ernest and Alga (Anderson) V.; m. Shirley Margaret Walker, July 29, 1940 (dec. 1969); 1 dau., Drew; m. Gail Patrick, Sept. 28, 1974 (dec. July 1980); m. Gretchen Swanson Pullen, Nov. 7, 1981. AB, U. Ill., 1938. Pres. Velde, Roelfs & Co., Pekin, 1955-60; dir. Herget Nat. Bank, 1948-75, Kroehler Mfg. Co., 1974-81; pres. Paisano Prodns., Inc., 1980-94, mng. ptnr., from 1994, The Gardner Partnership, from 1994. Trustee Pekin Pub. Library, 1948-69, Pekin Meml. Hosp., 1950-69, Everett McKinley Dirksen Rsch. Ctr., 1965-74, Am. Libr. Assn. Endowment, 1976-82, Joint Coun. Econ. Edn., 1977-83, Ctr. Am. Archeology, 1978-83, Western Heritage Mus., Omaha, 1994—; chmn. Am. Libr. Trustee Assn. Found., 1976; chmn. trustees, bd. dirs. Ctr. Ulcer Rsch. and Edn. Found., 1977-82; mem. bd. councilors Brain Rsch. Inst. UCLA, 1977-82; mem. Nat. Commn. on Libr. and Info. Sci., 1970-79; mem. adv. bd. on White House Conf. on Librs., 1976-80; bd. dirs. U. Ill. Found., 1977-83, Omaha Pub. Libr. Found., 1985-92, James Madison Coun. Libr. Congress, 1990—; vice chmn. U. Ill. Pres.' Coun., 1977-79, chmn., 1979-81, mem. fin. resources coun. steering com., 1976-78; mem. adv. coun. UCLA Grad. Sch. Libr. and Info. Sci., 1981-82; pres. Ill. Valley Library System, 1965-69; dir. Lakeview Ctr. for Arts and Scis., Peoria, Ill., 1962-73; mem. Nat. Book Com., 1969-74. Served as lt. (j.g.) USNR, World War II. Mem. Am. Libr. Trustee Assn. (regional v.p. 1970-72, chmn. internat. rels. com. 1973-76), Internat. Boy Scouts (Baden-Powell fellow 1987—), Kappa Sigma. Clubs: Chgo. Yacht, Internat. (Chgo.); California (Los Angeles); Outrigger Canoe (Honolulu); Thunderbird Country (Rancho Mirage, Calif.); Chaine des Rotisseurs, Chevaliers du Tastevin; Circumnavigators (N.Y.C.); Omaha, Omaha Country; Happy Hollow, Old Baldy (Saratoga, Wyo.), Eldorado Country (Indian Wells, Calif.). Home: Omaha, Nebr. Died Dec. 10, 2002.

VENTRY, PAUL GUERIN, physician, government official; b. Ossining, N.Y., Sept. 1, 1934; s. Victor and Catherine (Dillon) V.; m. Betty Anne Baildon, Aug. 20, 1960. BS, Manhattan Coll., 1957; MD, Syracuse U., 1962. Diplomate Am. Bd. Profl. Disability Cons., Am. Bd. Forensic Medicine. Commd. 1st lt. U.S. Army, 1962; advanced through grades to lt. col., 1971; intern Walter Reed Gen. Hosp., 1962-63; resident, physician Pres. Eisenhower and Gen. Douglas McArthur, 1963-66; chief med. outptatient clinic, 1971; allergy cons. Surgeon Gen., Europe, 1967-70; chief medicine 47th Mobile Army Surg. Hosp., 1968-70; retired, 1971; chief adult svcs. Montgomery County (Md.) Health Dept., 1972; spl. dep. sheriff Montgomery County, 1972—2003; med. dir. Goddard Space Flight Ctr., NASA, 1973; ptnr. Med. Assocs., Washington, 1974. Med. dir. Civilian Employees Health Svc., Dept. Def., Washington, Walter Reed Army Med. Ctr., Pentgon Drug & Alcohol Program, Dept. Def. Blood Donor Program, Def. Intelligence Agy., 1975-83; prin. med. cons., sr. med. officer to Office HEarings and Appeals, Social Security Adminstrn., Arlington, Va., 1983—; asst. clin. prof. medicine George Washington U., 1973-79; chief med. surg. cons., sr. med. officer in charge Social Security Adminstrn., 1983—; med. dir. Nat. Coun. Social Security Adminstrn. OHA, 1991, Am. Fedn. Govt. Employees #3615, 1991—, Nat. Coun. Social Security Employees, Am. Fed. Govt. Coun. 215; med. surg. cons. Wash. Hq. Svc. Dept. Def.; chief cons. med. surg. medicare fraud divsn. HHS Med. Dir. Contbr. articles to profl. jours. Immunology fellow, 1966, Allergy fellow, 1967. Fellow Am. Occupational Med. Assn., Am. Coll. Occupational and Environ. Medicine, Am. Acad. Disability Evaluating Physicians; mem. AMA, ACP, VFW, Fed. Physicians Assn. (treas.), Am. Pub. Health Assn., Am. Acad. Allergy, Royal Soc. Medicine, Brit. Allergy Soc., Am. Acad. Civil Svc. Physicians (treas.), Am. Coll. Physician Execs., Am. Bd. Forensic Examiners, Am. Legion, Assn. Mil. Surgeons, Mil. Dist. Washington Officers Assn., Nat. Fire Prevention Assn., Potomac C. of C., Washingtoin PErforming Arts Soc., D.C. Med. Soc., Montgomery County Med. Soc., Va. Med. Soc., Alpha Kappa Kappa. Home: Potomac, Md. Died Feb. 28, 2003.

VERMA, RAM SAGAR, geneticist, educator, author, administrator; b. Barabanki, India, Mar. 3, 1946; came to the U.S., 1972; s. Gaya Prasad and Late Moonga (Devi) V.; m. Shakuntala Devi, May 4, 1962; children: Harendra K., Narendra K. BSc, Agra U., India, 1965, MSc in Quantitative Genetics, 1967; PhD in Cytogenetics, U. Western Ont., London, Ont., Can., 1972; diploma clinical cytogenetics, The Royal Coll. Pathologists, London, 1984. Diplomate The Royal Coll of Pathologists, London; lic. dir. clin. Cytogenetics, N.Y.C. and N.Y. state. Rsch. and teaching asst. dept. plant scis. U. Western London, Ont., Can., 1967-73; postdoctoral rsch. assoc. cytogenetics U. Colo. Dept. of Pediatrics, Denver, 1973-76; instr. to prof. human cytogenetics dept. of medicine Health Sci. Ctr. SUNY, Bklyn., from 1976, prof. dept. anatomy and cell biology, from 1988. Chief cytogenetics div. hematology and cytogenetics Interfaith Med. Ctr. (formerly Jewish Hosp. and Med. Ctr. Bklyn.), 1980-86; chief div. genetics L.I. Coll. Hosp., Bklyn., 1986-97, dir. Inst. Mol. Biol. and Genetics, Bklyn, 1997-99; cons. WHO, Switzerland, 1982, Nat. Geog. Soc., Washington, 1982, Phototake, 1982-87; dir. Inst. Molecular Biol. Genetics, Bklyn., 1997—; mem. cytogenetic adv. com. Prenatal Diagnosis Lab. N.Y.C. Dept. Health, 1978-90, Genetic Task Force N.Y. State, N.Y.C., 1976—; reviewer grants Nat. and Internat. Health Agys. and Socs.; lectr. colls., univs. and profl. assns. Author: Heterochromatin: Molecular and Structural Aspects, 1988, The Genome, 1990, (with A. Babu) Human Chromosomes: Manual of Basic Techniques, 1989, Human Chromosomes: Principles and Techniques; editor-in-chief: Advances in Genome Biology, 1989; contbr. over 350 abstracts and presentations and over 375 articles to profl. publs. including Am. Jour. Ob.-Gyn., Blood, Jour. Med. Genetics, Japanese Jour, Human Genetics, Oncology, Cytobios, Am. Jour. Human Genetics, Am. Jour. clin. Oncology, Internat. Jour. Cancer, Chromosoma, Cytogenetics. Apptd. to Adv. Coun. to Asst. Commr. City of N.Y. Dept. Health, Bur. Lab. Svcs., 1988. Nat. Merit scholar Gov. India, 1964-67, 1965-67; rsch. scholar Nat. Rsch. Coun. Can. and U. Western Ont., 1967-72, also teaching assistantship, 1972-73; rsch. grantee N.Y. State Dept. Health, Albany, 1985, 85-86, Cancer Treatment Fund, Cornell Med. Coll., 1985-86, United Leukemia Fund, Cornell Med. Coll., 1985-86, 86-87, Nat. Cancer Inst. of Health, Md., 1985-86, 86-87, 97-88, 88-90, Nat. Cancer Inst., 1976-77, 77-78, 78-80. Fellow AAAS, Royal Coll. Pathologists London, Assn. Clin. Scientists, The Inst. of Biology, N.Y. Acad. Scis., N.Y. Acad. Medicine (assoc.); mem. Am. Assn. Clin. Rsch., Am. Fedn. Clin. Rsch., Am. Genetic Assn. (life), Am. Soc. Cell Biology, Am. Soc. Human Genetics (life), European Soc. Human Genetics, Fedn. Am. Scientists, Genetic Soc. Am., Genetic Soc. Can., Genetic Toxicology Assn., Internat. Assn. Human Biologists, Indian Soc. Human Genetics (life), Soc. Exptl. Biology and Medicine, Inst. Molecular Biology and Genetics (dir. 1997-2000). Achievements include research in differentiation of eukaryotic chromosomes with special interest on molecular aspects of structural organization of hetero-and euchromatin, cytological detection of cell damage using old and new classical methods of cytogenetics, application of animal models to understand the human genetic diseases, mechanisms of human cancer using DNA probes and blotting techniques, application of various banding techniques in basic and clinical cytogenetics, automation of human genome using computers. Home: Bayside, NY. Deceased.

VEST, PAUL JOE, educational media firm executive; b. Portsmouth, Ohio, Feb. 17, 1946; s. Eugene Orse and Garnet May (Eatherly) V. BA with honors, Lake Forest Coll., 1968. Research assoc. Inst. for Juvenile Research, Chgo., 1969-72; tchr. February Sch., Chgo., 1972-73; dir. student housing Naropa Inst., Boulder, Colo., 1973-74; mgr., dir. Market Street Theatre, Marion, Ill., 1975; media producer v.p. Clearvue Inc., Chgo., 1975-78; media producer, dir. mktg. Centre Productions Inc., Boulder, 1978-83, mng. dir., 1984-86; v.p. Clearvue Inc., Chgo., 1986-88, pres., from 1988. Bd. dirs. Isabella Film, Inc., Boulder. Assoc. producer (16mm film) Nicholas and the Baby, 1980 (1st runner up Nat. Coun. on Family Film Fest 1981); asst. dir. (16mm film) Concert In the Sky, 1982 (Red ribbon Am. Film Fest, 1983); co-writer, co-producer (16mm film) The Dream Forest, 1984; asst. producer (16mm film) The Lion's Roar, 1986; premiere performance of composition Requiem, Boulder, Colo., 1990, broadcast KVOD Radio, Denver, 1992-93; subject of video documentary Song of the Open Road. Mem. NOW, Chgo., 1987-89, Network 44, Chgo., 1989, area chmn.; vol. AIDS educator San Luis Valley Area Health Edn. Ctr., 1990-91. Mem. Am. Film and Video Assn., Phi Beta Kappa. Democrat. Buddhist. Avocations: composer, pianist. Home: Crestone, Colo. Deceased.

VICKERMAN, BARB, state legislator; m. Gerald Vickerman; four children. Minn. State Rep. Dist. 23A, from 1992; retail sales profl. Mem. health and human svc. com./fin. divsn., labor-mgmt. rels. com., regulated industry and engery com. Home: Redwood Falls, Minn. Died Dec. 22, 1997.

VIEIRA DE MELLO, SERGIO, international organization official; b. Rio de Janeiro, Brazil, Mar. 15, 1948; m. Annie Vieira de Mello; children: Adrien, Laurent. Licence, U. Paris, 1969, Maitrise, 1970, Doctorat in Philosophy, 1974, Doctorat d'Etat, 1985. Asst. editor, Secretariat UNHCR, Geneva, 1969—71; field officer, Dhaka East Pakistan/Bangladesh, 1971—72; assoc. programme officer South Sudan Ops. Khartoum, Juba, Sudan, 1973—74; programme officer, asst. rep. UNHCR Spl. Ops., Cyprus, 1974—75; dep. rep., rep. ad interim Maputo, Mozambique, 1975—77; regional rep. UNHCR, Northern Latin Am., Lima, Peru, 1978—80; sr. polit. adv UN Interim Force in Lebanon, Naqoura, Lebanon, 1981—83; dep. head, personnel svcs. UNHCR, Geneva, 1983—85, chef de cabinet of high commr. and sec., 1986—87, dir., regional bureau for Asia and Oceania, 1988—90, dir., divsn. external rels., 1990—93; head civil affairs UN Protection Force, Yugoslavia, 1994; dir. policy planning and ops. Exec. Office of High Commr., UNHCR, Geneva, 1995—96; asst. sec. gen., asst. high commr. for refugees UN, N.Y.C., 1996—97, under sec. gen for humanitarian affairs, 1998; spl. rep. for sec. gen. UN Transitional Admin. in Timor, 1999—2002; high commr. for human rights UN, Geneva, 2002—03, spl. repr. in Iraq Baghdad, 2003. Died Aug. 19, 2003.

VILLARD, OSWALD GARRISON, JR., engineer, educator; b. Dobbs Ferry, N.Y., Sept. 17, 1916; s. Oswald Garrison and Julia B. (Sandford) V.; m. Barbara S. Letts, June 27, 1942; children— Thomas Houghton, Barbara Suzanne, John Sandford. AB with honors, Yale U., 1938; E.E., Stanford U., 1943, PhD, 1949. Instr. elec. engring. Stanford, 1941-42, acting asst. prof., 1946-50, asst. prof., 1950-52, assoc. prof., 1952-55; prof. elec. engring Stanford U., 1955—; dir. Radioscience Lab., 1958-73; dir. ionospheric dynamics lab. Stanford Research Inst., 1970-72, sr. sci. adviser, 1972—. Spl. research asso. Radio Research Lab., Harvard, 1941-42, mem. sr. staff, 1944-46; mem. Air Force Sci. Adv. Bd., 1963-75, Naval Research Adv. Com., 1967-75, chmn., 1972-75; Dir. Flagg Fund, Inc., Calif. Microwave, Inc. Named Outstanding Young Bay Area Engr. Engrs. Joint Council, 1955; recipient Morris Liebmann Meml. prize Inst. Radio Engrs., 1957, Meritorious service medal Dept. Air Force, Fellow IEEE (life, Centennial medal), Am. Acad. Advancement Sci. (Sec. Def. medal for Outstanding Pub. Service 1987); mem. Nat. Acad. Scis., Nat. Acad. Engrng., Am. Acad. Arts and Scis., Internat. Sci. Radio Union. Home: San Mateo, Calif. Died Jan. 7, 2004.

VINCI, MARTIN F.P., III, lawyer; b. McKees Rocks, Pa., Dec. 3, 1954; s. Michael Anthony and Helen V. (Divecchio) V.; m. Janice Cianchetti, Dec. 1, 1979. BA, U. Pitts, 1976; JD, Duquesne U., 1979. Bar: Pa. 1979, U.S. Dist. Ct. (we. dist.) Pa. 1979, U.S. Ct. Appeals (3d cir.) 1981, U.S. Supreme Ct. 1988. Law clk. L. Tarasi & Assocs., Pitts., 1977-79; assoc. Tarasi & Tighe, Pitts., 1979-81; ptnr. Law Offices of Martin F.P. Vinci III, Coraopolis, Pa., 1981-87, Lewis, Vinci & Partel, Coraopolis, 1988-99. Jud. law clk. Allegheny County Ct., Pitts., 1982-99; gen. counsel Ohio River Land and Transp. Co., Pitts., 1986. Mem. ABA, Pa.

Bar Assn., Pa. Trial Lawyers Assn., Assn. Trial Lawyers Am., Am. Law Enforcement Officers, Italian Heritage Soc. Roman Catholic. Avocations: drummer, building musical instruments, hockey, computers. Home: Coraopolis, Pa. Died June 15, 1999.

VINING, PIERRE HERBERT, real estate consultant; b. Moira, N.Y., Nov. 20, 1924; s. Pierre James and Grace (Ramsdell) V.; m. Betty Jane Sanders, Mar. 14, 1949; 1 child, Pierre Grigsby. BA in Internat. Studies, George Washington U., 1966; MBA, Am. U., 1976. Accredited land cons. Realtors Land Inst.; gen. accredited appraiser Nat. Assn. Realtors; cert. gen. appraiser, Md. Dairy farmer, Dickinson Ctr., N.Y., 1935-41; enlisted USN, 1942, advanced through grades to O-6, ret., 1973; realtor Nat. Assn. Realtors, Md., from 1974; broker, owner Pierre Vining, Realtor, Dunkirk, Md., from 1978; pres., appraiser AA-CALV Appraisal Svc., Prince Frederick, Md., from 1991. Dir. Nat. Assn. Realtors, Chgo., 1986-96; pres. Md. Assn. Realtors, Annapolis, Md., 1992. Editor (newsletters) Chpt. Ideas, 1993-97, Catch (up on) 22, 1997-98. Lt. gov. Kiwanis Divsn. 22 Capital Dist., So. Md., 1997-98. Mem. So. Md. Assn. Realtors (pres. 1985, com. chair, Realtor of Yr. 1982), Anne Arundel Assn. Realtors (com. chair), Realtors Land Inst. (nat. pres. 1996, gov. 1985—, Farm and Land Realtor of Yr. Md., Del. and D.C. chpts. 1991). Died May 10, 2001.

VINOCUR, EDWARD WILLIAM, nursing home administrator; b. Cleve., Mar. 4, 1951; s. Harry and Goldie (Brown) V.; m. Debra Gilbert, Dec. 21, 1960; children: Jonathon Harry, Alicia Gilbert, Joel Gilbert. BA, Ohio State U., 1974; MPA, North Tex. State U., 1983, cert. in aging, 1984. Lic. nursing home adminstr. Exec. dir. student community projects, Columbus, Ohio, 1971-73; asst. adminstr. Heritage House, Columbus, 1974-77; exec. dir. Heritage Tower, Columbus, 1977-79; ops. adminstr. Heritage Village, Columbus, 1980-84; exec. dir. Menorah Manor, St. Petersburg, Fla., 1984-88, Montefiore Home, Cleve., from 1988; pres., COO Montefiore Found., Cleve., from 1995. Com. mem. Jewish Fedn. Pinellas County, Clearwater, Fla., 1984-88. Named one of Outstanding Young Men in Am., 1984. Mem. Am. Assn. Homes for Aging, Fla. Assn. Homes for Aging (mem. nursing home com. 1984-88), Ohio Assn. Homes for Aging (treas. 1982-83, v.p. 1983 84, bd. dirs. 1993—), North Am. Assn. Jewish Homes (Outstanding Young Exec. 1991), Gerontol. Assn., Nat. Coun. on Aging, Ohio State U. Alumni Assn., North Tex. State U. Alumni Assn. Avocations: reading, racquetball. Home: Columbus, Ohio. Died Sept. 10, 2000.

VITNER, SAUL, obstetrician, gynecologist; b. Atlanta, May 20, 1930; MD, Emory U., 1954. Diplomate Am. Bd. Ob-Gyn. Intern D.C. Gen. Hosp., Washington, 1954-55; resident St. Louis Maternity Hosp./Barnes Hosp., 1957-60; mem. staff Northside Hosp., Atlanta, St. Joseph Hosp., Atlanta; clin. asst. ob-gyn. Emory U. Sch. Medicine, Atlanta. Fellow Am. Coll. Ob-Gyn.; mem. AMA. Died June 4, 2001.

VOGEL, RONALD BRUCE, food products executive, real estate broker; b. Vancouver, Wash., Feb. 16, 1934; s. Joseph John and Thelma Mae (Karker) V.; m. Carol Vandecar, Mar. 16, 1958; children: Joseph S., Rhonda L., Theresa J., Denise R.; m. Donita Dawn Schneider, Aug. 8, 1970 (dec. June 1974); 1 child, Cynthia Dawn. BS in Chemistry, U. Wash., 1959. Glass maker Penberthy Instrument Co., Seattle, 1959-60; lab. technician Gt. Western Malting Co., Vancouver, 1960-62, chief chemist, 1962-67, mgr. corp. quality control, 1967-72, mgr. customer svcs., 1972-77, v.p. customer svcs., 1977-79, v.p. sales, 1979-84, gen. mgr., 1984-89, pres., CEO, 1989-95; ret. Gen. ptnr. Rou Vogel Family Partnership. Chmn. bd. dirs. Columbia Empire Jr. Achievement, Portland, Oreg., 1991-92. With U.S. Army, 1954-56. Recipient numerous awards. Mem. Master Brewers Assn. Am. (pres. 1996), Am. Malting Barley Assn. (chmn. 1984-86, 89-91), Vancouver C. of C. (chmn. 1991-93), Applied Phytologics, Inc. (bd. dirs.). Home: Washougal, Wash. Died Feb. 15, 2002.

VOGT, EVON ZARTMAN, JR., anthropologist, writer; b. Gallup, N.Mex., Aug. 20, 1918; s. Evon and Shirley (Bergman) V.; m. Catherine Christine Hiller, Sept. 4, 1941; children— Shirley Naneen (Mrs. Geza Teleki), Evon Zartman III, Eric Edwards, Charles Anthony. AB, U. Chgo., 1941, MA, 1946, PhD, 1948. Instr. Harvard U., 1948-50, asst. prof., 1950-55, assoc. prof., 1955-59, prof. anthropology, 1959-89, prof. emeritus, 1989—2004, former dir. Harvard Chiapas project, chmn. dept. anthropology, 1969-73, master Kirkland House, 1974-82; asst. curator Am. ethnology Harvard (Peabody Mus.), 1950-59, curator Middle Am. ethnology, 1960-89, hon. curator Middle Am. ethnology, 1990—2004. Vis. prof. U. Hawaii, 1972; Mem. div. anthropology and psychology NRC, 1955-57 Author: Navaho Veterans, 1951, Modern Homesteaders, 1955, (with W.A. Lessa) Reader in Comparative Religion, 1958, (with Ray Hyman) Water Witching U.S.A., 1959, 3d edit., 2000, Zinacantan: A Maya Community in The Highlands of Chiapas, 1969 (Harvard Press Faculty prize Sahagun prize 1969), The Zinacantecos of Mexico: A Modern Maya Way of Life, 1970, 2d edit. 1990, Tortillas for the Gods: A Symbolic Analysis of Zinacanteco Rituals, 1976, 2d edit., 1993, Fieldwork Among the Maya: Reflections on The Harvard Chiapas Project, 1994; editor: Desarrollo Cultural de Los Mayas, 1964, Los Zinacantecos, 1966, People of Rimrock, 1966, Handbook of Middle American Indians, vols. 7 and 8, 1969, Aerial Photography in Anthropological Field Research, 1974, (with Richard M. Leventhal) Prehistoric Settlement Patterns, 1983. Served from ensign to lt. USNR, 1942-46. Decorated Order Aztec Eagle Mexico; fellow Center for Advanced Study in Behavioral Sci., 1956-57 Fellow Am. Acad. Arts and Scis. (councilor 1974-78), Am. Anthrop. Assn. (exec. bd. 1958-60); mem. NAS (chmn. anthropology sect. 1981-84, class V behavioral and social scis. 1986-89), Am. Philos. Soc., Soc. Am. Archaeology, Royal Anthrop. Inst. Gt. Britain and Ireland, Am. Ethnological Soc., Tavern Club. Home: Cambridge, Mass. Died May 13, 2004.

VOLLMER, RICHARD WADE, federal judge; b. St. Louis, Mar. 7, 1926; s. Richard W. and Beatrice (Burke) V.; m. Marilyn S. Stikes, Sept. 17, 1949. Student, Springhill Coll., 1946-49; LLB, U. Ala., 1953. Bar: Ala. 1953, U.S. Dist. Ct. (so. dist.) Ala. 1956, U.S. Ct. Appeals (5th cir.) 1963, U.S. Ct. Appeals (11th cir.) 1983. Sr. judge U.S. Dist. Ct. (so. dist.) Ala., 1990—2003. Mem. Mobile Bar Assn. (pres. 1990), Rotary (Paul Harris fellow 1988). Roman Catholic. Died Mar. 20, 2003.

VON HEIMBURG, ROGER LYLE, surgeon; b. Chgo., Feb. 5, 1931; s. Franklin Dederick and Alice Julia (Zebuhr) von H.; m. Mary Ellen Janson, July 12, 1952; children: Mary Deborah, Donald Franklin. AB, Johns Hopkins U., 1951, MD, 1955; MS in Surgery, U. Minn., Rochester, 1964. Diplomate Am. Bd. Surgery. Intern Johns Hopkins Hosp., Balt., 1955-56; resident in surgery Mayo Clinic, Rochester, 1958-62, chief resident in surgery, 1962, asst. to staff in surgery, 1962-64; pvt. practice Green Bay, Wis., 1964-94; staff St. Vincent Hosp., Green Bay, 1964-94, Bellin Meml. Hosp., Green Bay, 1964-94; ret., 1994. Contbr. articles to profl. jours. Mem. state Bd. of Health Care Info., 1988-95. Lt. USNR, 1956-58. Fellow ACS; mem. State Med. Soc. Wis. (bd. dirs. 1980-89, vice-chmn. 1983-87, chmn. 1987-89, pres.-elect 1989-90, pres. 1990-91), Wis. Chpt. ACS (v.p. 1985-86, pres.-elect 1986-88, pres. 1988-90), Brown County Med. Soc. (pres. 1986), Wis. Surg. Soc. (coun. mem. 1987-90). Republican. Methodist. Avocations: piano, auto repair. Home: Green Bay, Wis. Died Sept. 22, 1999.

VOZELLA, VICTORIA WREN, elementary school educator; b. San Antonio, Oct. 10, 1951; d. John and Mary Agnes (Quinn) Thomas. BA, Our Lady of the Lake U., San Antonio, 1975; MS, U. Tex., San Antonio, 1991. Chpt. 1 tchr. Southside Ind. Sch Dist., San Antonio. Mem. Delta Kappa Gamma. Home: San Antonio, Tex. Deceased.

WADDINGHAM, JOHN ALFRED, artist, journalist; b. London, Eng., July 9, 1915; came to U.S., 1927, naturalized, 1943; s. Charles Alfred and Mary Elizabeth (Coles) W.; m. Joan Lee Larson, May 3, 1952; children: Mary Kathryn, Thomas Richard. Student, Coronado (Calif.) Sch. Fine Arts, 1953-54, Portland Art Mus., 1940-65, U. Portland, 1946-47; pupil, Rex Brandt, Eliot Ohara, George Post. Promotion art dir. Oreg. Jour., Portland, 1946-59; with The Oregonian, Portland, 1959-81, editl. art dir., 1959-81; tchr. watercolor Oreg. Soc. Artists, 1954-56; tchr. art Oreg. Sch. Arts and Crafts, 1981—, Portland C.C., Multnomah Athletic Club, Mittleman Jewish Cmty. Ctr. Represented by several galleries, Oreg. and Wash. One man shows include Art in the Gov.'s Office, Oreg. State Capitol, 1991 and more than 30 shows in the Northwest; rep. mus. rental collections, Portland Art Mus., Bush House, Salem, Ore., U. Oreg. Mus., Vincent Price collection, Ford Times collection, also Am. Watercolor Soc. Travelling Show; paintings included in Salmagundi Club, N.Y.C., UN Bldg., Watercolor, U.S.A. of Springfield, Mo., others; judge art events, 1946—; ofcl. artist, Kiwanis Internat. Conv., 1966; designed, dir. constrn. cast: concrete mural Genesis, St. Barnabas Episcopal Ch., Portland, 1960; spl. work drawings old Portland landmarks and houses; propr. John Waddingham Hand Prints, fine arts serigraphs and silk screen drawings, 1965—; featured artist: Am. Artist mag., Watercolor mag., Oreg. Painters, the First Hundred Years, (1859-1959), others. Artist mem. Portland Art Mus. With USAAF, 1942-46. Recipient gold medal Salone Internazionale dell' Umorismo, Italy, 1974, 76, 80; honored with a 45 yr. retrospective Assignment: The Artist as Journalist Oreg. Hist. Soc., 1991; winner Palme do Oro in three exhbns., Bordighera, Italy. Mem. Portland Art Dirs. Club (past pres.), N.W. Watercolor Soc., Am. Watercolor Soc. (hon. sustaining), Watercolor Soc. Oreg., Oreg. Soc. Artists (watercolor tchr.), Multnomah Athletic Club, Jewish Community Ctr., Univ. Oreg. Med. Sch., Art in the Mounts., Oreg. Old Time Fiddlers, Clan Macleay Bagpipe Band. Home: Portland, Oreg. Died Sept. 19, 2002.

WADE, ROBERT GEORGE, investment executive; b. Rockland, Mass., Aug. 9, 1900; s. William Ernest and Anna (Stockbridge) W.; m. Nelly Knowlton Milliken, Sept. 1, 1926 (dec. Jan. 1990); children: Robert George, Charles Milliken. BS, Bates Coll., 1923; postgrad., Harvard Bus. Sch., 1927-29. Asst. mgr. Guild of Boston Artists, 1930-32; ins. broker Hinckley Woods, Boston, 1932-43; registered rep. Frederick M. Swan & Co., Boston, 1943-45, W.E. Hutton & Co., Boston, 1945-49; owner Morton, Hall & Rounds, Inc., Lewiston, Maine, 1949-75; registered rep. Robert C. Carr & Co., Lewiston, 1975-83, Advest, Lewiston, 1983-86. Pres. Maine Ind. Telephone Assn., Portland, 1950-56, Maine Investment Dealers Assn., Portland, 1952-54. Mem. Maine Ho. of Reps., com. chair, 1955-56, asst. majority floor leader, 1957-58, majority floor leader, 1959-60. Pvt. U.S. Army, 1918. Republican. Congregationalist. Avocation: birdwatching. Home: Bonita Spgs, Fla. Died Mar. 19, 2000.

WADE, SUSAN LYNN, elementary school educator; b. Monroe, La., July 7, 1967; d. Aaron Gray and Katy June (Minor) W. BA in Elem. Edn., Northeast U., 1990. Sec., sales profl. Wade's Floor Co., Monroe, 1983-84, 84-85; asst. dance tchr. Tommie's Sch. of Dance, Monroe, 1984-85; sales assoc. Millers Outpost, Monroe, 1985-90; with Ouachita Parish Sch. System, Monroe, from 1990. Mem. Alpha Omicron Pi. Democrat. Roman Catholic. Avocations: dance, arts and crafts. Home: Monroe, La. Died Feb. 23, 2001.

WADSWORTH, MICHAEL A. former athletic director, former ambassador; b. Toronto, ON, Canada, 1943; Professional football player Toronto Argonauts, CFL, 1966-70; lawyer, 1971-81; amb. to Ireland Canadian Foreign Min., 1989-94; athletic dir. U. Notre Dame, 1995—2000. Home: Granger, Ind. Died Apr. 28, 2004.

WAGER, WALTER HERMAN, author, communications director; b. N.Y.C., Sept. 4, 1924; s. Max Louis and Jessie (Smith) W.; m. Sylvia Liebowitz Leonard, May 6, 1951 (div. May 1975); 1 child, Lisa Wendy; m. Winifred McIvor, June 4, 1975. BA, Columbia U., 1943; LLB, Harvard U., 1946; LLM, Northwestern U., 1949. Bar: N.Y. 1946. Spl. asst. to Israel dir. Civil Aviation, 1951-52; freelance writer N.Y.C., 1952-54; editor UN, N.Y.C., 1954-56; writer, prodr. NBC-TV, 1956; freelance TV and mag. writer N.Y.C., 1956-63; editor-in-chief Playbill mag., N.Y.C., 1963-66; editor Show mag., N.Y.C., 1965; cons. pub. rels. and editorial dept. ASCAP, N.Y.C., 1966-72, dir. pub. relations, 1972-78; cons. pub. relations Nat. Music Pub. Assn., N.Y.C., 1978-84; dir. communications Juilliard Sch., N.Y.C., 1985-86; counsel pub. relations Mann Music Ctr., Phila., 1986-87, Eugene O'Neill Theater Ctr., N.Y.C., 1987-89; dir. pub. info. U. Bridgeport, 1991-93. Tchr. Northwestern U., 1949, Columbia U., 1955-56, U. Bridgeport, 1994; spl. asst. to atty. gen. N.Y. State investigation hate lit. in elections, 1962; bd. dirs. Jazz Hall of Fame, 1975-77. Author: Death Hits the Jackpot, 1954, Operation Intrigue, 1956, I Spy, 1965, Masterstroke, 1966, Superkill, 1966, Wipeout, 1967, Countertrap, 1967, Death Twist, 1968, The Girl Who Split, 1969, Sledgehammer, 1970, Viper Three, 1971 (filmed as Twilights's Last Gleaming 1977), Swap, 1972, Telefon, 1975 (filmed in 1977), My Side-By King Kong, 1976, Time of Reckoning, 1977, Blue Leader, 1979, Blue Moon, 1980, Blue Murder, 1981, Designated Hitter, 1982, The Caribbeans, 1983, Otto's Boy, 1984, 58 The Wildcatters, 1986, 58 Minutes, 1987 (filmed as Die Hard 2, 1990), The Spirit Team, 1996, Tunnel, 2000, Kelly's People, 2002; (non-fiction) Camp Century, 1962, Playwrights Speak, 1967, (with Mel Tillis) Stutterin' Boy, 1984. Pres. Columbia Coll., class 1944. Fulbright fellow Sorbonne, Paris, 1949-50, Northwestern U. Law Sch. fellow, 1948-49. Mem.: Mystery Writers Am. (bd. dirs. 1988—94, 1997—2000, 2002—04), Writers Guild Am. Democrat. Jewish. Avocation: traveling. Died July 11, 2004.

WAGNER, CARRUTH JOHN, physician; b. Omaha, Sept. 4, 1916; s. Emil Conrad and Mabel May (Knapp) W. AB, Omaha U., 1938; B.Sc., U. Nebr., 1938, MD, 1941, D.Sc., 1966. Diplomate: Am. Bd. Sugery, Am. Bd. Orthopaedic Surgery. Intern U.S. Marine Hosp., Seattle, 1941-42; resident gen. surgery and orthopaedic surgery USPHS hosps., Shriners Hosp., Phila., 1943-46; med. dir. USPHS, 1952-62; chief orthopaedic service USPHS Hosp., San Francisco, 1946-51, S.I., N.Y., 1951-55, health mblzn., 1959-62; asst. surgeon gen. dep. chief div. hosps. UPHS, 1957-59; chief div. USPHS, 1962-65, USPHS (Indian Health), 1962-65; dir. Bur. Health Services, 1965-68; Washington rep. AMA, 1968-72; health services cons., 1972-79; dept. health services, 1979—. Contbr. articles to med. jours. Served with USCGR, World War II. Recipient Pfizer award, 1962; Meritorious award Am. Acad. Gen. Practice, 1965; Disting. Svc. medal, 1968, Calif. Dept. Health Svcs. Pub. Health Recognition award, 1995. Fellow A.C.S. (bd. govs.), Am. Soc. Surgery Hand, Am. Assn. Surgery Trauma, Am. Geriatrics Soc., Am. Acad. Orthopaedic Surgeons; mem. Nat. Assn. Sanitarians, Am. Pub. Health Assn. Sanitarians, Am. Pub. Health Assn., Washington Orthopaedic Club, Am. Legion, Alpha Omega Alpha. Clubs: Mason (Shriner). Lutheran. Home: Carmichael, Calif. Died Nov. 25, 2002.

WAGNER, FREDERICK BALTHAS, JR., historian, retired surgery educator; b. Phila., Jan. 18, 1916; s. Frederick Balthas and Gertrude Louise (Mattes) W.; m. Jean Lockwood, June 30, 1945; children: Frederick B. III, Theodore Walter. AB, U. Pa., 1937; MD, Thomas Jefferson U., 1941, LHD (hon.), 1996. Diplomate: Am. Bd. Surgery. Clin. prof. surgery Jefferson Med. Coll. Thomas Jefferson U., Phila., 1954-78, Grace Revere Osler prof. surgery, 1978-84, former historian. Author: Twilight Years of Lady Osler, 1985; editor: Thomas Jefferson University: Tradition and Heritage, 1989. Recipient Alumni Achievement award Jefferson Med. Coll., 1987. Fellow Phila. Acad. Surgery (pres. 1985-86), Coll. Physicians Phila.; mem. Meigs Med. Assn. (pres. 1989-91), Jefferson Alumni Assn. (pres. 1975), Union League Phila. Republican. Methodist. Home: Gladwyne, Pa. Died Jan. 23, 2004.

WAGNER, PETER EWING, physics and electrical engineering educator; b. Ann Arbor, Mich., July 4, 1929; s. Paul Clark and Charlotta Josephine (Ewing) W.; m. Caryl Jean Veon, June 23, 1951; children: Ann Frances, Stephen Charles. Student, Occidental Coll., 1946-48; AB with honors, U. Calif., Berkeley, 1950, PhD, 1956. Teaching rsch. asst. U. Calif., 1950-56; rsch. physicist Westinghouse Rsch. Labs., Pitts., 1956-59; assoc. prof. elec. engring. Johns Hopkins, 1960-65, prof., 1965-73; dir. Ctr. for Environ. and Estuarine Studies U. Md., 1973-80, prof., 1973-81. Vis. prof. physics U. Ala., Huntsville, 1980-81, prof., 1981; vice chancellor for acad. affairs, prof. physics U. Miss., 1981-84; provost, prof. physics and elec. engring. Utah State U., 1984-89; v.p. acad. affars and provost SUNY, Binghamton, 1989-92, prof. physics and elec. engring., 1989-99, prof.

emeritus, 1999—; spl. projects engr. State of Md., 1971-72; mem. Gov.'s Sci. Adv. Coun., 1973-77, Md. Power Plant Siting Adv. Com., 1972-80; cons. in field. Contbr. articles to profl. jours.; patentee in field. Trustee Chesapeake Rsch. Consortium, 1974-80, chmn. bd. trustees, 1979-80. Guggenheim fellow Oxford U., 1966-67 Mem. Nat. Assn. State Univs. and Land Grant Colls. (mem. coun. acad. affairs, mem. affirmative action com. 1986-89, chmn. nominating com. 1988-89, chmn. libr. commn. 1989-92), Ctr. Rsch. Librs. (bd. dirs. 1991-97, mem. budget and fin. com. 1991-93, vice chair 1992-93, chair 1993-94, chair nominating com. 1994-95), Sierra Club (chpt. chair conservation com. 2000—, mem. chpt. exec. com. 2000—), U. Calif. Berkeley Alumni Assn. (life), Blue Key, Gold Key, Phi Beta Kappa, Phi Beta Kappa Fellows (life, bd. dirs. 1995-2001), Sigma Xi (life), Phi Kappa Phi, Eta Kappa Nu. Home: Morro Bay, Calif. Died Nov. 29, 2003.

WAGONER, HOWARD EUGENE, agribusiness consultant, councilman; b. Colorado Springs, Colo., Oct. 17, 1925; s. Howard Eugene Sr. and Hazel Marie (Walbrand) W.; m. Donna Alta Welts, Aug. 29, 1948; children: Howard E. III, Victoria M., William A. BS, U. Maine, 1950; MS, Duke U., 1951. Irrigation supr. Oahu Sugar Co., Ltd., Waipahu, Hawaii, 1962-64, dir. of agr. rsch. and control, 1971-72, field supt., 1978-79; resident dir., asst. mgr. CAINSA/CASSA, Bella Union, Uruguay, 1964-68; gen. supt. CAIESA, Aguadulce, Panama, 1968-70; cons. P.R. Dept. Agr., San Juan, 1970-71; opns. mgr. Columbia River Farms, Paterson, Wash., 1972-78; pres., mgr. Amfac Tropical Products, Keaau, Hawaii, 1979-85; cons. Pacific Agromanagement Corp., Hermiston, Oreg., from 1985. Councilman City of Hermiston, 1986—; bd. dirs. Ea. Oreg. Assn. Counties, 1988—; chmn. Umatilla Rep. Cen. Com., 1986. With U.S. Navy, 1943-45, ATO, PTO. Mem. Inst. Food Tech., Soc. Am. Forester, Kiwanis, Sigma Xi. Episcopalian. Avocations: reading, walking, travel Home: Cedar Rapids, Iowa. Died Mar. 28, 2002.

WAKEFIELD, BENTON MCMILLIN, JR., banker; b. Monroe, La., Apr. 8, 1920; s. Benton McMillin and Adele (Rhodes) W.; m. Cindy Walton, May 19, 1951; children: Benton McMillin, III, Will Walton. BS in Commerce summa cum laude, Washington and Lee U., 1941; postgrad., Grad. Sch. Banking, U. Wis., 1949-51. Asst. v.p. First Nat. Bank Memphis, 1946-52; v.p. Ouachita Nat. Bank, Monroe, La., 1952-63; pres., CEO, bd. dirs. Merc. Nat. Bank Ind., Hammond, 1963-72; pres., CEO 1st Bank and Trust Co., South Bend, Ind., 1972-79, FBT Bancorp., 1972-79; chmn., CEO First Nat. Bank of Jefferson Parish, 1979-84; chmn., pres., CEO First Fin. Bank, New Orleans, 1984-88; prin. Bank and Thrift Cons. Group, New Orleans, from 1988. Dir. Eureka Homestead Soc., New Orleans, 1995—; cons., including trial expert testimony Fin. Litigation Support, 1988—; bd. dirs. 10 banks, Mich. and Ind., 1972-79, Carpetland U.S.A., Chgo.; mem. fin. adv. coun. Fed. Res. Bank Atlanta; mem. visitors com. Loyola U. Bus. Sch.; Chpt. 11 bankruptcy trustee Kirk Mfg. Inc. Bd. dirs. Econ. Devel. Com. New Orleans, Bur. Govt. Research, United Way. Served to lt. comdr. USNR, 1941-46. Mem. Am. Bankers Assn. (econ. policy com.), U.S. C. of C. (fin. com.), New Orleans Country Club, Bienville Club, Phi Beta Kappa, Sigma Alpha Epsilon, Omicron Delta Kappa, Beta Gamma Sigma, Rotary, Royal Soc. St. George, Huguenot Soc. Methodist. Home: New Orleans, La. Deceased.

WALBRIDGE, MARJORIE HOFER, community health nurse; b. Muskegon, Mich., May 5, 1916; d. John Franklin and Wauneta (Gates) Hofer; m. Howard Aikman Walbridge, Aug. 15, 1938; children: Jean, Mary. Diploma, St. Joseph's Mercy Hosp., Ann Arbor, Mich., 1936. RN, Mich. Night supr. St. Joseph's Mercy Hosp., Ann Arbor, 1936-38; staff nurse St. Joseph's Hosp., Kansas City, Mo., 1941-42. Nurse vol. ARC, Kansas City, Mo., 1938-99, mem. adv. com., 1976-99; nurse vol. Vis. Nurse Assn., Kansas City, 1977-99; nurse vol. Shepherd's Ctr. Internat., Kansas City, 1980-99, sec., 1990-99. Mem. Coalition on Elder Abuse, Kansas City, Mo., 1986-92; mem. Civic Health Found., Kansas City, 1984-92; nurse, mem. Nat. Health Screening Coun., Kansas City, 1984-90; leader, nurse Am. Youth Found., 1990-93. Recipient Eunice Shirley Vol. of Yr. award ARC, 1988, Disting. Alumni award Mercy Coll. of Detroit, 1990, Spl. Achievement award United Way, 1989, Outstanding Vol. award ARC, State of Mo., 1994. Mem. Mo. Soc. Profl. Engrs. Aux. (chmn. telephone com.), PEO. Republican. Avocations: travel, sewing, knitting, reading. Home: Kansas City, Mo. Died May 13, 1999

WALDBILLIG, GERALD WILLIAM, construction company executive; b. Albany, N.Y., Aug. 6, 1905; s. John B. and Katherine M. (Monman) W.; m. Frances D. McDonough, July 13, 1932; children: Susanna, Michael, Gretchen, Kirsten, Stephen. BSCE, Rensselaer Poly. Inst., 1925. Registered profl. engr., N.Y. State. Jr. engr. Horter Barrows Middlebrok, Boston, 1925-26, Conn. Middlebrook, Albany, N.Y., 1926-28; constrn. mgr. Duplex Constrn., Glens Falls, N.Y., 1928-29; engr.-in-charge Wells Bros., Chgo., 1929-30; pres. Waldbillig Constrn. Corp., Albany, from 1930. Trustee Home Savs. Bank, Albany, 1950-85. Trustee Oliver Dist. Sch., Slingerlands, N.Y., 1937, St. Mary's Roman Cath. Ch., albany, 1980—. Fellow ASCE; mem. Albany Bldrs. Exchange (pres. 1940), Bldg. Industry Employers Assn. N.Y. State (pres. 1953), Univ. Club, Ft. Orange Club (pres. 1956), Albany Country Club, Lake Placid Club, Knights of Malta. Roman Catholic. Avocation: farming. Home: Slingerlands, NY. Deceased.

WALDMAN, JAY CARL, judge; b. Pitts., Nov. 16, 1944; s. Milton and Dorothy (Florence) W.; m. Roberta Tex Landy, Aug. 28, 1969. B.S., U. Wis., 1966; J.D., U. Pa., 1969. Bar: Pa. 1970, D.C. 1976, U.S. Supreme Ct. 1976. Assoc., Rose, Schmidt, Dixon & Hasley, Pitts., 1970-71; asst. U.S. atty. western dist. Pa., Pitts., 1971-75; dep. asst. U.S. Atty. Gen., Washington, 1975-77; counsel Gov. of Pa., Harrisburg, 1978-86; sr. ptnr., Dilworth, Paxson, Kalish & Kauffman, Phila., 1986-88; judge U.S. Dist. Ct. (ea. dist.) Pa., 1988—. Dir. Thornburgh for Gov. campaign., Pa., 1977-78; commr. Pa. Convention Ctr. Authority, 1986-88. Fellow Am. Bar Found.; mem. ABA, Fed. Bar Assn., Union League Phila. Republican. Died May 30, 2003.

WALKER, CHARLES MONTGOMERY, lawyer; b. St. Louis, Sept. 30, 1915; s. Charles J. and Gertrude (Zoll) W.; m. Gertrude E. Acton, Apr. 30, 1943. AB, U. Mo., 1937, LL.B., 1939. Bar: Mo. 1939, Calif. 1941, D.C. 1977. Practiced in, L.A., from 1941; mem. Brady, Nossaman & Walker, 1941-62; ptnr. Paul, Hastings, Janofsky & Walker, 1962-75, 77-81, counsel, 1981—; asst. sec. treasury for tax policy Washington, 1975-77. Served with AUS, 1942-46. Decorated Bronze Star. Fellow Am. Bar Found., Am. Coll. Tax Counsel (bd. regents 1987-93), Am. Bar Retirement Assn. (bd. dirs., pres. 1986), Am. Tax Policy Inst. (pres. 1990-93); mem. ABA (chmn. taxation sect. 1979-80, coms.), L.A. Bar Assn., Am. Law Inst., State Bar Calif., Order of Coif, L.A. Country Club, Met. Club, Sigma Chi. Home: West Hollywood, Calif. Deceased.

WALKER, DOROTHY KEISTER, minister; b. Lock Haven, Pa., Sept. 24, 1920; d. Charles Lester and Eva Derr (Schuyler) K.; m. Dean E. Walker, May 28, 1962 (dec. 1988). BS in Elem. Edn., Lock Haven U., 1942; BD in Ch. History, MS in Religious Edn., Butler U., 1949; DD (hon.), Milligan Coll., 1962. Ordained to ministry Ch. of Christ, 1949. Asst. min. Fleming Garden Christian Ch., Indpls., 1946-49; with Jones-Keister Evang. Team, nat., 1949-59; dir., lectr. Mission to Women, nat., from 1959; elder Hopwood Christian Ch., Milligan Coll., Tenn., from 1985. Co-founder Emmanuel Sch. of Religion, Johnson City, Tenn.; asst. bd. mem. N.Am. Christian Conv., 1985-87; trustee Appalachian Christian Village, Johnson City, 1986—, European Evang. Soc., Tubingen, Germany, 1989—. Contbr. articles to religious jours. Mem. Phi Kappa, Theta Phi, Kappa Delta Pi. Died Aug. 1, 1999.

WALKER, ELIZABETH PRESCOTT, journalist; b. Detroit, Dec. 15, 1925; d. Joel Henry and Ruth Magdalen (Weber) Prescott; m. Richard Dilworth Walker, May 23, 1959; 1 child, Richard Dilworth. BA in English Lit., Western Coll. for Women, 1948. Cert. Nat. Book Critics Circle. Asst. editor bull. Sigma Gamma Assn., Detroit, 1955-60; reporter bull. Jr. League, Detroit, 1967-75; editor quarterly jour. Book Club Detroit, 1967-68; columnist The Hearing Eye AGBell Assn. Mich. Chpt., Detroit, 1985-89; book reviewer Biblio-chat The Alpena (Mich.) News, from 1991; book reviewer Biblio-file Grosse Pointe (Mich.) News, from 1991. Mem. Quota Internat. Iosco County (bd. dirs. 1995-97, Deaf Woman of the Yr. 1996), Sigma Gamma Assn. Republican. Episcopalian. Avocations: book collecting, pets, travel. Home: Greenbush, Mich. Died Nov. 10, 2001.

WALKER, HAROLD BLAKE, minister, writer; b. Denver, May 7, 1904; s. Herbert R. and Ethel G. (Blake) W.; m. Mary Alice Corder, Feb. 1, 1930; children— Herbert Elwood, Howard Deane, Timothy Blake. AB, U. Denver, 1925, DD, 1952; AM, Boston U., 1927; BD, McCormick Theol. Sem., 1932; postgrad., U. Chgo., 1933-34; DD, Emporia Coll., 1944, Hamilton Coll., 1949, U. Denver, 1952, Rocky Mountain Coll., 1971; LHD, Lake Forest U., 1959, Nat. Coll. Edn., 1970; STD, Northwestern U., 1970. Editor, writer A.P., Kansas City, 1927-30; ordained to ministry Presbyn. Ch., 1932; minister Fullerton-Covenant Ch., Chgo., 1932-36, First Ch., Utica, N.Y., 1936-42, Oklahoma City, 1942-47, 1st Presbyn. Ch., Evanston, Ill., 1947-69; columnist Splty. Salesman mag., 1954-67, Chgo. Tribune-N.Y. News syndicated columnist, 1954-81. Lectr. homiletics McCormick Theol. Sem.; lectr., bd. dirs. Harold Blake Walker chair pastoral theology; cons. W. Clement Stone Enterprises, 1970-74; sem. v.p. Bd. Fgn. Missions Presbyn. Ch. U.S.A.; Nat. Commn. Evangelism, 1946-47; dir. Presbyn. Tribune, 1943-55; mem. Presbyn. Commn. on Consolidation, 1957-58, Commn. on Ecumenical Mission Relations, 1958-61. Author: Going God's Way, 1946, Ladder of Light, 1951, Upper Room on Main Street, 1954, Power to Manage Yourself, 1955, (with wife) Venture of Faith, 1959, Heart of the Christian Year, 1962, Faith for Times of Tension, 1963, Thoughts to Live By, 1965, To Conquer Loneliness, 1966, Prayers to Live By, 1966, Memories to Live By, 1968, Inspirational Thoughts for Everyday, 1970, Days Demanding Courage, 1978, History of St. John's of Red Cross of Constantine, 1985, Caring Community, 1986; contbr. to religious publs. Bd. dirs. Nat. Presbyn. Ch. and Ctr., Washington; bd. dirs. McCormick Theol. Sem., pres., 1953-55, 57-71; bd. dirs. Ill. Masonic Med. Center, Chgo., Lake Forest Coll.; trustee Maryville Coll. Recipient DeMolay Legion of Honor; Freedoms Found. sermon prize, 1950, 55, 77; citations Protestant Fund. Greater Chgo., 1970; Chgo. Inst. Medicine Citizens fellow, 1987; citations Chgo. Friends of Lit., 1971, 79; Disting. Alumnus award McCormick Theol. Sem., 1979. Mem. Utica Council Chs. (pres. 1940), Am. Theol. Soc. Chgo. Cleric, Pi Kappa Alpha. Clubs: Univ. (Chgo.). Lodges: Masons (Chgo., Evanston) (Shriner, 33 deg., grand chaplain N.Y. 1940-41). Presbyterian. Home: Evanston, Ill. Died Nov. 4, 2002.

WALKER, JOHN DENLEY, foundation director, former government official; b. Petersburg, Va., July 15, 1921; s. John Otey and Evelyn Mildred (Denley) W.; m. Diana Taylor, Apr. 30, 1949 (div. 1980); children— Walker Diana, John Denley, Joseph Warren; m. Helen Hoogerwerff, Mar. 15, 1984; step children— Saskia Roskam, Hugo, Frederick BA, U. N.C.-Chapel Hill, 1944; postgrad., U. Pa., 1950-51. Superintendant N.J. Bell, 1946-48; asst. dir. labor div. ECA, Paris, France, 1948-50; mgmt. cons., 1951-53; fgn. service res. officer U.S. Govt., Paris, Malta, Israel, Australia, 1953-77; exec. dir. English Speaking Union of U.S., N.Y.C., 1978-87. Contbr. articles to profl. jours. Pres. Ctr. for Security Studies, 2001; bd. dirs. Am. Student Ctr., Paris, 1953—57. Lt. USN, 1942—45. Mem.: Pilgrims, Standrews (N.Y.C.); Univ. (Washington); Chevy Chase (Md.), Legion of Valor, Soc. Cin., Order of St. Johns of Jerusalem. Episcopalian. Home: Washington, DC. Died Oct. 1, 2002.

WALKER, KENNETH ROY, podiatrist; b. Guntersville, Ala., Mar. 19, 1958; s. Cecil Roy and Ethel Lee (Stewart) W.; m. Albertina Louise Cole, Mar. 25, 1989; children: Victor Kenneth, Lilena Marie. BS, Ala. A&M U., 1982; DPM, Ohio Coll. Podiatric Medicine, 1986. Sr. assoc. Kettering (Ohio) Podiatry Assn., 1988-92; owner Dayton (Ohio) Podiatry Assn., from 1992. Cons. VA, Dayton, 1994—; v.p. Latitude 30 degrees Shoe Corp., Kettering, 1994—; bd. dirs. Diabetes Assn. Dayton, chmn. spkrs. bur., 1994-96, treas. Illustrator: (book) Medical Emergencies, 3d edit., 1991; designer shoe last, 1992. Avocations: jet skiing, bass guitar. Home: Dayton, Ohio. Died May 1, 2002.

WALKER, RICHARD LOUIS, former ambassador, educator, author; b. Bellefonte, Pa., Apr. 13, 1922; s. Robert Shortlidge and Genevieve (Bible) W.; m. Celeno Claypole Kenly, Mar. 29, 1945; children: Geoffrey Kenly, Dorothy Anne, Stephen Bradley. BA, Drew U., 1944; cert. Chinese lang. and area, U. Pa., 1944; MA, Yale U., 1947, PhD, 1950; LLD (hon.), Coll. of Charleston, 1985, Drew U., 1986, The Citadel, 1990; D of Polit. Sci. (hon.), Seoul Nat. U., 1982; D. Pub. Svc., U. S.C., 1991. Asst. prof. history Yale U., 1950-57; prof. internat. studies U. S.C., 1957—2003, James F. Byrnes prof. internat. relations, 1959—2003, prof. emeritus, 1992—2003; U.S. amb. to Republic of Korea, 1981-86; amb.-in-residence U. S.C., 1986—2003. Vis. assoc. prof. Nat. Taiwan U., Taipei, China, 1954-55; vis. prof. U. Wash., 1959, 65; prof. polit. affairs Nat. War Coll., 1960-61; spl. rsch. internat. rels., Far East; lectr., cons. U.S. Govt., 1953-2003, Dept. Def., 1969-2003; rep. U.S. Dept. State, USIS, 1973-74; lectr. numerous confs., major U.S. govt. svc. schs. and univs. in Asia, Australia and Europe. Author: Western Language Periodicals on China, 1949, Multi-State System of Ancient China, 1953, China Under Communism, 1955, China and the West, 1956, The Continuing Struggle, 1958, Democracy Confronts Communism in World Affairs, 1965, Edward R. Stettmius, Jr., 1965, The China Danger, 1966, Ancient China, 1969, Prospects in the Pacific, 1972, Asia in Perspective, 1974, Ancient Japan, 1975, Korean Remembrances, 1998; contbr. articles to various symposium vols., learned jours. Bd. dirs. Nat. Com. U.S.-China Rels., 1968-94, U.S. Strategic Inst., 1977-2003, U. S.C. Ednl. Found., 1958-2003, Conf. on European Problems, 1967-2003. With AUS, 1942-46, PTO. Recipient Alumni Achievement award in arts Drew U., 1958; Disting. Service award Air U., 1970; Fgn. Service Inst. award, 1971; Armed Forces Staff Coll. award, 1978; Fulbright-Social Sci. Research Council research scholar Academia Sinica Republic China, 1965-66. Mem. Assn. Asian Studies, Am. Assn. for China Studies (v.p. 1994-95, nat. pres. 1995-97), Aurelian Honor Soc., Korea Soc., Forest Lake Club, Torch Club, Pi Gamma Mu, Omicron Delta Kappa. Episcopalian. Home: Columbia, SC. Died July 22, 2003.

WALKER, ROBERT MOWBRAY, physicist, researcher; b. Phila., Feb. 6, 1929; s. Robert and Margaret (Seivwright) W.; m. Alice J. Agedal, Sept. 2, 1951 (dec. Oct. 15, 2002); children: Eric, Mark; m. Ghislaine Crozaz, Aug. 24, 1973. BS in Physics, Union Coll., 1950, D.Sc., 1967; MS, Yale U., 1951, PhD, 1954; Dr honoris causa, Université de Clermont-Ferrand, 1975. Physicist Gen. Electric Research Lab., Schenectady, 1954-62, 63-66; McDonnell prof. physics Washington U., St. Louis, 1966—2002, prof. physics, from 2002; dir. McDonnell Center for Space Scis., St. Louis, 1975-99. Vis. prof. U. Paris, 1962—63; adj. prof. metallurgy Rensselaer Poly. Inst., 1958, adj. prof. physics, 1965—66; vis. prof. physics and geology Calif. Inst. Tech., 1972, Phys. Research Lab., Ahmedabad, India, 1981, Institut d'Astrophysique, Paris, 1981; vis. prof. Inst. D'Astrophysique Univ. Libre, Brussels, from 2001; nat. lectr. Sigma Xi, 1984—85; pres. Vols. for Internat. Tech. Assistance, 1960—62, 1965—66, founder, 1960; mem. Lunar Sample Analysis Planning Team, 1968—70; bd. dirs. Univs. Space Rsch. Assn., 1969—71; mem. Lunar Sample Rev. Bd., 1970—72; adv. com. Lunar Sci. Inst., 1972—75; mem. temporary nominating group in planetary scis. Nat. Acad. Scis., 1973—75, bd. on sci. and tech. for internat. devel., 1974—76, com. planetary and lunar exploration, 1977—80, mem. space sci. bd., 1979—82; mem. organizing com. Com. on Space Research-Internat. Astron. Union, Marseille, France, 1984; mem. task force on sci. uses of space sta. Solar System Exploration Com., 1985—86; mem. Antarctic Meteorite Working Group, 1985—92, NASA Planetary Geosci. Strategy Com., 1986—88, European Sci. Found. Sci. Orgn. Com., Workshop on Analysis of Samples from Solar System Bodies, 1990; chmn. Antarctic Meteorite Working Group, 1990—92; mem. cosmic dust allocation com. NASA, 1998; vis. com. dept. terrestial magnetism Carnegie Instn., 1998; vis. com. Max Planck fur Chemie, Mainz, Germany, 1998. Decorated officer de l'Ordre des

Palmes Academiques (France); recipient Disting. Svc. award Am. Nuclear Soc., 1964, Yale Engring. Assn. award for contbn. to basic and applied sci., 1966, Indsl. Rsch. awards, 1964, 65; Exceptional Sci. Achievement award NASA, 1970; E.O. Lawrence award AEC, 1971; Antarctic Svc. medal NSF, 1985; NSF fellow, 1962-63; Asteroid 1985 JWI named in his honor, 1999. Fellow AAAS, Am. Phys. Soc., Meteoritical Soc. (Leonard medal 1993), Am. Geophys. Union, Indian Inst. of Astrophycis (hon.); mem. NAS (mem. polar rsch. bd. com. 1995, J. Lawrence Smith medal 1991), Am. Astron. Soc., St. Louis Acad. Scis. (Peter Raven Lifetime Scientific Achievement award 1997); founder, first pres. Vol. Internat. Tech. Assistance (VITA), 1958. Achievements include research and publs. on cosmic rays, nuclear physics, geophysics, radiation effects in solids, particularly devel. solid state track detectors and their application to geophysics and nuclear physics problems; discovery of fossil particle tracks in terrestrial and extra-terrestrial materials and fission track method of dating; application of phys. scis. to art and archaeology; lab. studies of interplanetary dust and interstellar grains in primitive meteorites. Home: Saint Louis, Mo. Died Feb. 12, 2004.

WALKER, WALTER WILLARD, real estate and investments executive; b. Mpls., Dec. 4, 1911; s. Archie Dean and Bertha Willard (Hudson) W.; BA, Princeton U., 1935; MD, Harvard U., 1940; postgrad. U. Minn., 1942-48; m. Elva Mae Dawson, Dec. 16, 1939 (div. Oct. 1969); m. Elaine Barbatsis, Mar. 17, 1972; stepchildren: Nicholas K. Barbatsis, Marianna Barbatsis Priest, Becka Barbatsis Mourmouras, Christian Barbatsis Dayton. Teaching fellow pathology U. Minn., 1942-48; left medicine, went into bus., 1948; dir. Shasta Forest Co., Redding, Calif., 1951-71, treas., 1954-66, v.p., 1966-71; sec., dir. Barlow Realty Co., Mpls., 1954-67, pres., 1967-77, chmn., 1977-80, sec., 1980-83, v.p., 1983-88; ptnr. Barlow Assocs., 1988—; sec., bd. dir. Walker Pence Co., 1950-72; sec. Penwalk Investment Co., 1958-72, bd. dir., 1943-72; bd. dir. Craig-Hallum Corp., Mpls., 1954-92; adv. bd. Lincoln office Northwestern Nat. Bank, Mpls., 1957-74. Bd. dirs. T.B. Walker Found., 1953-76, v.p., 1954-76; bd. dirs. Minn. Opera Co., 1968-73, Archie D. and Bertha H. Walker Found., 1953—, Mpls. Found., 1962-79, Walker Art Ctr, 1954-76, United Fund, 1966-72; trustee Abbott-Northwestern Hosp., 1969-77; trustee Children's Health Ctr., Inc., 1968-73, treas., 1969-73; pres. Found. Services, 1967-73; bd. dirs., exec. com. Minn. Charities Review Council, 1965-74; mem. Hennepin County Capital Budgeting Task Force, 1973-74. Mem. Sigma Xi, Nu Sigma Nu, Mpls. Club, Princeton Club (N.Y.C.), U. Minn. Alumni Club. Methodist. Home: Minneapolis, Minn. Deceased.

WALKER, WARREN STANLEY, English educator; b. Bklyn., Mar. 19, 1921; s. Harold Stanley and Althea (Luscher) W.; m. Barbara Jeanne Kerlin, Dec. 9, 1943; children— Brian, Theresa. BA, SUNY-Albany, 1947, MA, 1948; PhD, Cornell U., 1951; LittD (hon.), Selcuk U., 1989. Prof., chmn. dept. English Blackburn Coll., Carlinville, Ill., 1951-59; prof., dean arts and scis. Parsons Coll., Fairfield, Iowa, 1959-64; Fulbright lectr. Am. lit. Ankara (Turkey) U., 1961-62; prof. English Tex. Tech U., Lubbock, 1964-86, Horn prof., 1972-86. Dir. Archive Turkish Oral Narrative, 1971; adv. council Tex. Cultural Alliance, 1975 Author: Nigerian Folktales, 1961, Twentieth-Century Short Story Explication, 14 vols., 1961-93, James Fenimore Cooper, 1962, Leatherstocking and the Critics, 1965, Tales Alive in Turkey, 1966, Archive of Turkish Oral Narrative: Catalogue 1, 1975, Catalogue 2, 1988, Catalogue 3, 1994, Catalogue 4, 1998, Plots and Characters in the Fiction of J.F. Cooper, 1978, A Bibliography of American Scholarship on Turkish Folklore and Ethnography, 1982, Turkish Games for Health and Recreation, 1983, The Book of Dede Korkut-A Turkish Epic, 1991, More Tales Alive in Turkey, 1992, A Turkish Folktale: The Art of Behçet Mahir, 1996; mem. editorial bd. Definitive Edit. Works of James Fenimore Cooper, 1968; bibliographer Studies in Short Fiction, 1973. Served with USAAF, 1943-45. Recipient Tex. Writers award, 1967; citation Turkish Ministry Edn., 1967, Turkish Ministry State, 1973; research grantee Am. Council Learned Socs., 1973, 79; Am. Philos. Soc., 1974, Tex. Tech U., 1971-74, 76, 83, Republic of Turkey, 1983, Inst. Turkish Studies, 1984 Mem. MLA, Am. Folklore Soc., Nat. Coun. Tchrs. English, Internat. Soc. Folk Narrative Rsch., Middle East Studies Assn., Tex. Assn. Middle East Scholars (exec. coun.), Turkish Studies Assn., Atatürk Supreme Coun. on Turkish Culture (hon.). Home: Lubbock, Tex. Died Nov. 22, 2002; Lubbock, TX.

WALKLET, JOHN JAMES, JR., publishing executive; b. Trenton, NJ, June 14, 1922; s. John James and Katherine Helen (Slamin) W.; m. Gretchen Crowell, Aug. 21, 1948; children: John III, Philip, Deborah, Preston, Richard, Colin, Keith, Christopher, Megan. BL in Journalism, Rutgers U., 1943. Reporter Montclair (N.J.) Times, 1943; prodn. editor Macmillan Pub. Co., N.Y.C., 1946-52, dir. mfg. sch. div., 1969-88, asst. v.p., 1982, v.p., 1983-88, cons., 1989, ret.; tech. writer Shell Chem. Corp., N.Y.C., 1952-54; dir. publs. Colonial Williamsburg, Williamsburg, Va., 1954-69. Cons. book prodn. U. Press of Va., Charlottesville, 1963-69. Author, designer: Adventure in Williamsburg, 1960 (So. Books Competition award), A Window on Williamsburg, 1966 (So. Books Competition award); designer: The Journal of John Harrower, 1963 (One of 50 Books of Yr. award Am. Inst. Graphic Arts). Pres. Kiwanis Club of Williamsburg, 1969; bd. dirs. Edenton-Chowan Kiwanis Club, 1996-97, v.p., 1998; cons. Va. Travel Coun., Richmond, 1960-69. Sgt. U.S. Army, 1943-46. Mem. Assn. Am. Pubs. (mfg. com. rep. Adv. Commn. Textbook Specifications 1980-84, vice chmn. mfg. com. 1984-86, chmn. mfg. com. 1986-88), Williamsburg Stirrup Club (bd. dirs. 1965-69), James Iredell Assn. (bd. dirs. Edenton soc. 1989-97). Republican. Roman Catholic. Avocations: reading, piano and organ, golf, fishing, spectator sports. Died Feb. 27, 2003.

WALLACH, RICHARD WINGARD, judge; b. N.Y.C., Sept. 16, 1927; s. Michael and Estelle H. (Hamburger) W.; m. Anne Tolstoi, Dec. 25, 1976. AB, Harvard U., 1949, LLB, 1952. Bar: N.Y. 1952, U.S. Dist. Ct. (so. and ea. dists.) N.Y. 1954, U.S. Tax Ct. 1959, U.S. Ct. Appeals (2d cir.) 1959, U.S. Supreme Ct. 1969. Judge N.Y.C. Civil Ct., 1970-76; justice N.Y. Supreme Ct., N.Y.C., 1976-85, assoc. justice appellate div., 1986—2003. Adj. prof. Fordham U. Law Sch., N.Y.C., 1975-81; mem. faculty Nat. Coll. Advocacy, Reno, Nev., 1976-2003. Mem. ABA (chmn. nat. conf. Chgo. chpt. 1976). Democrat. Jewish. Avocations: literature, tennis. Home: New York, NY. Died June 1, 2003.

WALLER, WILLIAM A. transportation executive; b. Fair Bluff, N.C., Jan. 9, 1931; s. William L. and Martha P. (Williamson) W. Student, U. N.C., Chapel Hill, 1952, U. N.C., Asheville, 1966-67, U. N.C., Greensboro, 1971, N.C. State U., 1963-64, Western Carolina U., 1971, Sandhill Community Coll., Southern Pines, N.C., 1973-74, Durham Tech. Coll., 1976-77, Duke U., 1979-83. Co. clk. Taylor Tobacco Co., Fair Bluff, 1953-54; bank teller UCB, Fairmont, N.C., 1956-59; bank br. mgr. N.C. Nat. Bank, Raleigh, 1959-64; fin. dir. Pines of Carolina Girl Scouts USA, Raleigh, 1964-65; right-of-way agt. N.C. Dept. Transp., Raleigh, from 1966. Editor: Internat. Right of Way Assn. Mag., 1981-83. With U.S. Army, 1954-56. Episcopalian. Avocations: golf, softball, handball, tennis, walking. Home: Raleigh, NC. Deceased.

WALOTSKY, RON, illustrator; b. Bklyn., Aug. 21, 1943; s. Joe and Rebecca (Cohen) W., divorced; 1 child, Lennon. Student, Sch. of Visual Arts, 1962-66. Illustrator Fantasy and Sci. Fiction Mag., Cornwall, Conn., from 1967, St. Martins Press, N.Y.C., from 1989, Avon Books, N.Y.C., from 1970, Doubleday Book and Music Club, N.Y.C., from 1980, TOR Books, N.Y.C., from 1980. Tchr. Sullivan County C.C., Hurleyville, N.Y., 1981-82, Daytona C.C., 2000—. One-man shows include Herst Gallery, Long Island, N.Y., 1967, Spectrum Gallery, N.Y.C., 1969, West Beth, N.Y.C., 1972, John O'Rourke Gallery, N.Y.C., 1977, Martin Mulinary Gallery, N.Y.C., 1987, The Pike St. Arts Ctr., Port Jervis, N.Y., 1990; exhibited in group shows at The Pendragon Gallery, L.A. and Annapolis, Md., 1986, Bryce Gallery, Phila., 1988, York Atrium, N.Y.C., 1989-90, Works of Wonder Gallery, Washington, 1992-99, Canton (Ohio) Art Gallery, 1996, Ormond Beach Art Mus., 1997-98, Butterfield Garage Gallery, 2000; author: Inner Visions, 2000. Recipient Frank R. Paul award, Kublacon, Nashville, Tenn., 1987, first prize Boscon, Boston, 1986; first prize I.S.D.C., 1988, first prize Lunacon, N.Y., 1988, 1st prize in painting Oasis, 1994; named guest artist U.S. Cultural Ctr., U.S. Embassy, Paris, France, 1979; given Key to City, New Orleans, 1994; Hugo Award nominee, 1996. Mem. Graphic Artist Guild, Assn. Sci. Fiction Artists. Home: Flagler Beach, Fla. Died July 29, 2002.

WALSH, GEORGE WILLIAM, engineering executive; b. Teton County, Idaho, Mar. 22, 1923; s. Raymond Eugene and Maude Ethel (Brack) W.; m. Catherine Mary Yunker, July 1, 1950; children: Dwight, Maureen, John. BSEE, U. Idaho, 1947; MEE, Rensselaer Poly. Inst., 1960. Registered profl. engr., N.Y. With GE, 1947-94, test engr., 1947-49, design engr. Pittsfield, Mass., 1949-50, power system engr. Schenectady, 1950-66, mgr. power system engring., 1966-85, mgr. power system cons. engring., 1985-93, cons., 1993-94; profl. cons. engr., from 1994. Contbr. numerous papers and articles relating to electric power system engring. to profl. publs. Recipient GE Power Systems Engring. awards for Outstanding Tech. Contbn., 1986, and Outstanding Profl. and Social Svcs., 1991. Fellow IEEE (life, Centennial medal 1984, Richard Harold Kaufmann field award for outstanding contbn. to indsl. engring. 1993); mem. IEEE Industry Applications Soc. (pres., mem. exec. bd., adminstrv. and tech. coms., Power Systems Achievement award 1980, Outstanding Achievement award 1990), IEEE Power Engring. Soc., Sigma Xi, Sigma Tau. Died Mar. 11, 2003.

WALSH, MICHAEL FRANCIS, education consultant, marketing research executive; b. Bell Harbor, N.Y., Dec. 5, 1947; s. Michael Francis and Patricia (Bratz) W.; m. Julia Ann Finn, Apr. 17, 1983; 1 child, Kelly Michelle. Student, U. Tex., Arlington, 1966-67, Coll. San Mateo, 1967-69; BA in Psychology, U. Calif., Santa Barbara, 1971; MS in Psychology, U. Wis., 1976. Cert. instr. community colls., Calif. Instr. Berlitz Sprachenschule, Munich, 1971-72; research asst. U. Wis., Madison, 1972-75; project dir. Ednl. Testing Service, Berkeley, Calif., 1976-82, dir. representation of western states, 1980-82; founder, pres. Walsh and Assocs., El Sobrante, Calif., from 1982. Mem. adv. bd. Internat. Trade Inst., Berkeley, 1983-88, chmn. funding com., 1986-88; cons. World Bank. Editor, contbg. author: Handbook for Proficiency Assessment, 1979; author: (state agy. reports) Evaluation of Artists in Social Institutions for California Arts Council, 1981, Evaluation of Creative Arts Computer Course, 1985, Humanists-in-Schools: Eight Years Later, 1986 (Joint Dissemination and Rev. Panel Nat. Dissemination Program award 1986), Conversations with Teacher Leaders: Their Reflections on Leadership, Equity, Mathematics Instruction, and other Topics, 1989, Feasibility Study of Assessment Approaches for Credentialing School Administrators in California, 1990, Teacher Leadership Development in Mathematics: An Evaluation of the California Mathematics Leadership Program, 1992, Evaluation of a Regional Partnership Training and Internship Program for School-site Counseling Teams, 1992. Commr. Richmond (Calif.) Arts Commn., 1988-91; rep. Sch. Site Coun., Valley View Sch., El Sobrante, Calif., 1992-94. Pres.'s Research grantee U. Calif., 1970. Mem. Am. Mktg. Assn. (exec.), Am. Coun. Arts, Am. Ednl. Rsch. Assn., Am. Evaluation Assn., Nat. Coun. Measurement Edn. Democrat. Roman Catholic. Avocations: traveling, hiking, gardening, cooking. Home: Alameda, Calif. Died Apr. 30, 1999.

WALTER, JAMES W. diversified manufacturing executive; b. Lewes, Del., 1922; m. Monica Saraw, 1946 (wid. 1982); children: James W., Robert; m. Constance Spoto, 1983. Ptnr. Walter Constrn. Co., 1948-55. Chmn. bd., dir. Walter Industries Inc. (formerly Jim Walter Corp.), Tampa, Fla., 1955—; bd. dirs. Gen. Telephone & Electronics Co., Contel Cellular, Inc., Anchor Glass Container Corp. With USN, 1942-46. Died 1/6/00.

WALTER, OTTO L. lawyer, accountant; b. Hof, Bavaria, Germany, Dec. 7, 1907; s. Hugo and Laura (Oberz) W.; m. Frances E. Doonan, Jan. 18, 1947. Abitur, Maxmilians Coll., Munich, 1925; referendar, Munich U., 1929; D of Laws magna cum laude, Erlangen U., 1930; JD, N.Y. Law Sch., 1954, LLD (hon.), 1984. Bar: German cts. 1932, N.Y. Bar 1955, European Community Bar 1979, U.S. Dist. Ct., U.S. Supreme Ct. Lawyer Ballin & Walter, Munich, Germany, 1932-33, Ackermann & Co., Munich, 1933-36; bookkeeper, accountant, controller various positions, N.Y.C., 1936-40; accountant O.L. Walter & Co., CPAs, N.Y.C., 1940-57; founder, now sr. counsel Walter, Conston, Alexander & Green, P.C., N.Y.C., from 1955. Ptnr. Weiss, Walter, Fischer-Zernin, Munich, 1993—; adj. prof. N.Y. Law Sch., 1963—. Author (with Debatin) Commentary to German American Tax Treaty (4 vols.); contbr. articles to profl. jours. Pres. Walter & Lorenz Found., N.Y.C.; v.p. Cosmopolitan Arts Found., N.Y.C. Recipient Officers Cross Verdienstkreuz 1st class, Fed. Republic Germany, Grand Cross of the Order of Merit. Mem. German Am. Law Assn. (founder, past pres.), Am. Inst. Contemporary German Studies (coun.), Am. Foreign Law Assn. (v.p.), Consular Law Assn. (dir.). Republican. Avocations: golf, piano. Home: New York, NY. Died Jan. 1912.

WALTERS, RAYMOND, JR., newspaper editor, author; b. Bethlehem, Pa., Aug. 23, 1912; s. Raymond and Elsie (Rosenberg) W. AB, Swarthmore Coll., 1933; postgrad., Princeton U., 1933-35; MA, Columbia U., 1937, PhD, 1942. Editorial staff Current History mag., 1937-39; editorial staff Saturday Rev., 1946-58, book rev. editor, 1948-58; editor Encore mag., 1946-48; editor, columnist N.Y. Times Book Rev., 1958-82. Mem. fiction jury Pulitzer Prize adv. bd., 1968 Author: Alexander James Dallas: Lawyer, Politician, Financier, 1943, Albert Gallatin: Jeffersonian Financier and Diplomat, 1957 (named One of Notable Books of Year, ALA), The Virginia Dynasty, 1965, Paperback Talk, 1985; Contbr. articles to profl. jours. Served with USAAF, 1942-46; hist. office hdqrs. USAAF, 1943-46. Mem. Am. Hist. Assn., Soc. Am. Historians. Episcopalian. Died Aug. 30, 2003.

WALTON, RUSSELL SPAREY, foundation administrator; b. Trenton, N.J., Nov. 28, 1921; s. Lewis Kirk and Edna Russell (Sparey) W.; m. Ila E. Lappe, Aug. 23, 1969. Student, King's Coll., 1938-39, DHL (hon.), 1991; student, Temple U., 1940-41. Mgr. publs. and pub. rels. Rexall Drug Co., L.A., 1946-49; mgr. advt. and pub. rels. Gladding McBean & Co., Glendale, Calif., 1949-51; editor, pub. San Bruno (Calif.) Herald, 1951-52; dir. pub. affairs West Divsn. Nat. Assn. Mfgrs., Palo Alto, Calif., 1952-62; exec. dir. United Rep. Calif., Los Altos, 1962-66; sec. program devel. Gov. Calif., Sacramento, 1967-71; columnist, radio commentator newspapers in Calif. and Midwest, 1971-74; mng. editor Third Century Pub., Washington, 1974-76; exec. dir. Plymouth Rock Found., Marlborough, N.H., from 1976. Author: One Nation Under God, 1978, Fundamentals for American Christians, 1979, Biblical Solutions to Contemporary Problems, 1984. Capt. U.S. Army Air Corps, 1941-46. Baptist. Home: Marlborough, NH. Died Oct. 1999.

WALTON, STEPHEN EDWARD, treasurer, entrepreneur; b. Jacksonville AFB, Ark., Apr. 10, 1971; s. Frank Joseph and Joanne Carol (Koski) W. AS Fin., Adirondack C.C., Queensbury, N.Y., 1993. Office mgr. CGM Corp., Glens Falls, N.Y., 1991-94; acct. Robert Half Internat., Ft. Lauderdale, Fla., 1994-95; treasury mgr. NAL Fin., Ft. Lauderdale, 1995-98; corp. treas. rep. SunTrust Bank, Ft. Lauderdale, from 1998. Owner, mgr. property svc., Ft. Lauderdale, 1997—. Mem. Treasury Mgmt. Assn. Democrat. Roman Catholic. Avocations: skin diving, travel, animals, showing afghan dogs. Home: Cambridge, Mass. Died Nov. 15, 2000.

WALTZ, JON RICHARD, lawyer, educator, author; b. Napoleon, Ohio, Oct. 11, 1929; s. Richard R. and Lenore (Tharp) W. BA with honors in Polit. Sci, Coll. Wooster, 1951; JD, Yale U., 1954. Bar: Ohio 1954, Ill. 1965. Assoc. Squire, Sanders & Dempsey, Cleve., 1954-64; chief prosecutor City of Willowick (Ohio), 1958-64; assoc. prof. law Northwestern U. Sch. Law, Chgo., 1964-65, prof. law, 1965-98, Edna B. and Ednyfed H. Williams prof. law emeritus, 1998—2004; instr. med. jurisprudence Northwestern Med. Sch., 1969-74. Book critic Washington Post, Chgo. Tribune, others; Disting. vis. prof. law Ill. Inst. Tech.-Chgo.-Kent Coll. Law, 1974; lectr. Author: The Federal Rules of Evidence—An Analysis, 1973, Criminal Evidence, 1975, Chinese lang. edits., 1994, 2000, Evidence: A Summary Analysis, 1976, Introduction to Criminal Evidence, 1991,

Chinese lang. edit., 1993; co-author: The Trial of Jack Ruby, 1965, Cases and Materials on Evidence, 1968, Principles of Evidence and Proof, 1968, Medical Jurisprudence, 1971, Cases and Materials on Law and Medicine, 1980, Evidence: Making the Record, 1981, Criminal Prosecution in the People's Republic of China and the United States of America: A Comparative Study, 1995; note and comment editor Yale Law Jour., 1953-54; mem. editorial adv. bd. Harcourt Brace Law Group,. 1978—; contbr. numerous articles to profl. jours. Mem. Ill. adv. com. U.S. Commn. on Civil Rights, 1971-74; mem. Ill. Criminal Justice System Policy and Planning Com., 1973-74, Ill. Jud. Inquiry Bd., 1980-88; mem. com. med. edn. AMA, 1982-83; mem. Gov.'s Task Force on Med. Malpractice, 1985; Capt. AUS, 1955-58. Decorated Commendation medal; recipient Disting. Svc. award Soc. Midland Authors, 1972, Disting. Alumni award Coll. Wooster, 1987. Mem. Assn. Am. Law Schs., Order of Coif, Phi Alpha Delta, Pi Sigma Alpha. Presbyterian. Home: Holland, Mich. Died Jan. 9, 2004.

WALZAK, MYRON PAUL, JR., urologist, educator; b. Cleve., Jan. 17, 1930; s. Myron Paul and Elizabeth Catherine (Rusnak) W.; m. Mary Christina Provan, Nov. 24, 1954; children— Kevin, Keith, Katherine, Christine, Myron Paul, Mary, Maura, Michael. MD, Yale U., 1955. Diplomate: Am. Bd. Urology. Intern Ohio State U. Hosp., Columbus, 1955-56; resident in surgery St. Alexis Hosp., Cleve., 1956-57, Yale-New Haven Hosp., New Haven, 1957-58; resident in urology N.Y. Hosp.-Cornell U., N.Y.C., 1958-62; asst. prof. urology U. Va., Charlottesville, 1964-69, asso. prof., 1969-71; prof., chmn. dept. urology Creighton U. Sch. Medicine, Omaha, 1971-81; prof., chmn. div. urology U. Conn. Sch. Medicine, Farmington, 1981—. Served with M.C. U.S. Army, 1962-64. Fellow Am. Acad. Pediatrics; mem. Assn. Am. Med. Colls., Soc. Univ. Urologists, A.C.S., AMA, Am. Urol. Assn. Died Jun. 23, 1999.

WANG, GUNG H. management consultant; b. Ningpo, Zhejiang, China, Feb. 3, 1909; s. Cheng V. and Zhao S. (Zhu) W.; m. Gladys Chen Wang, Sept. 10, 1938; children: Edward, Jo-Ann, Nancy, James. BA, U. Shanghai, China, 1928; MA, Tulane U., New Orleans, 1952; LLD (hon.), Loyola U., Chgo., 1989. Staff officer Mil. Fgn. Affairs, Nanking, China, 1928-30; vice cons. Consulate Gen. China, Chgo., 1930-38; cons. Consulate of China, New Orleans, 1938-50; counsul Chinese Am. Civic Coun., Chgo.; mng. dir. Chinatown Devel. Inc., Chgo., 1960-64; asst. dir. Chgo. Dwellings Assn., 1964-69; housing specialist Model Cities Program, Chgo., 1969-73; dir. Neighborhood Housing Svs., Dept. Human Svcs., 1973-76; owner G.H. Wang Assocs., Chgo., from 1976-. Sec. Chinese Del. UN Gen. Assembly, Lake Success, N.Y., 1946-47; alt. del. UN Temporary Commn. on Korea, Seoul and Paris, 1948; pres. Neighborhood Redevel. Assn. Inc., Chgo., 1972—; exec. dir. South Side Planning Bd., 1977; adminstr. fund for intercultural edn. NRAI, 1989—. Author: The Chinese Mind 1946, Kinsiskt Tankande, 1948; contbr. articles to profl. jours. 1948-51. Mem. Nat. Assn. Housing and Redevel. Ofcls., Am. Planning Assn., Rotary Club Chgo., Phi Sigma Alpha. Presbyterian. Avocation: writing. Home: Fitchburg, Wis. Deceased.

WANG, JAMES TING-SHUN, engineering educator and consultant; b. Cheng-Chiang, China, Feb. 8, 1931; came to U.S., 1955; s. Ta-Sui and Lang-Fang (Chang) W.; m. Elaine Woo, Sept. 7, 1963; children: Caroline Wei-Hwa, Sophia Wei-Min, Irene Wei-Wen. BSCE, Nat. Taiwan U., Taipei, 1954; MSCE, U. Kans., 1958; PhD, Purdue U., 1961. Instr. engring. mechanics U. Kans., Lawrence, 1955-58; rsch. asst., rsch. assoc. Purdue U., West Lafayette, Ind., 1958-61; asst. prof. engring. sci. and mechanics Ga. Inst. Tech., Atlanta, 1961-64, assoc. prof., 1964-70; aircraft devel. engr.-specialist Lockheed-Ga. Co., Marietta, 1966-67; prof. engring. sci. and mechanics Ga. Inst. Tech., 1970-86, prof. civil engring., from 1986. Vis. prof. Tech. U. Hannover, Germany, 1974-75; NSC vis. chair prof. Nat. Chung-Hsing U., Taichung, Taiwan, 1992-95, 97, 98; AvH vis. prof. U. Stuttgart, Germany, 1995; cons. Lockheed-Ga. Co., Marietta, 1966-70, 72, 76-87. Contbr. numerous articles to jours. and procs. Recipient Sr. U.S. Scientist award Alexander von Humboldt Found., Germany, 1974; Ford Found. residency awardee, 1966. Mem. ASCE (life), Am. Acad. Mechanics, Am. Soc. Engring. Edn., Sigma Xi, Tau Beta Pi, Phi Kappa Phi. Home: Atlanta, Ga. Died Sept. 24, 2000.

WARD, BENJAMIN, former police commissioner; b. Bklyn., Aug. 10, 1926; s. Edward and Loretta (Taylor) W.; m. Olivia Irene Tucker, May 30, 1956; children— Benjamin, Jacquelyn Ward Shepherd, Gregory, Margie Lewis, Mary I. AAS, Bklyn. Coll., 1957, BA, 1960; JD, Bklyn. Law Sch., 1965; LLD (hon.), St. Joseph's Coll., Bklyn., 1984, Pace U., 1988. Bar: N.Y., U.S. Dist. Ct. (so. and ea. dists.) N.Y. Commr. N.Y.C. Traffic Dept., 1972-74; dep. dir. Vera Inst. Justice, N.Y.C., 1974-75; commr. N.Y. State Dept. Correctional Services, 1975-78; police chief N.Y.C. Housing Authority, 1978-79; commr. N.Y.C. Dept. Correction, 1979-83, N.Y.C. Police Dept., 1984-89. Bd. dirs. Police Athletic League; mem. N.Y. State Crime Control Planning Bd.; adj. prof. Bklyn. Law Sch. Author: Improving Management in Criminal Justice, 1980; also papers Trustee St. Joseph's Coll.; commr. N.Y.C. Traffic Dept., 1973-74; bd. dirs. Nat. Inst. Against Prejudice & Violence. Served as sgt. U.S. Army, 1945-46. Recipient August Volmer award Am. Soc. Criminology, 1984 Mem. Police Mgmt. Assn., Police Exec. Research Forum, Internat. Assn. Chiefs Police, Nat. Inst. Policing (bd. dirs.), Nat. Orgn. Black Law Enforcement Execs. Roman Catholic. Avocation: gardening. Died June 10, 2002.

WARD, ROBERT JOSEPH, federal judge; b. N.Y.C., Jan. 31, 1926; s. Joseph G. and Honor V. (Hess) W.; m. Florence C. Maisel, Apr. 15, 1951 (dec. Mar. 1994); children: Laura Alice, Carolyn; m. Renée J. Sokolow, May 28, 1995. SB, Harvard Coll., 1945, LLB, 1949. Bar: N.Y. 1949. Practiced in, N.Y.C., 1949-51, 61-72; asst. dist. atty. N.Y. County, 1951-55; asst. U.S. atty. So. Dist. N.Y., 1956-61; judge U.S. Dist. Ct. (so. dist.) N.Y., 1972-91, sr. judge, 1991—2003. With USNR, 1944-46. Mem. N.Y. State Bar Assn., Assn. of Bar of City of N.Y., Fed. Bar Coun. Home: New York, NY. Died Aug. 5, 2003.

WARD, WILLIAM REED, composer, educator; b. Norton, Kans., May 20, 1918; s. Joseph Aloysius and Maude (Jones) W.; m. Elizabeth Jane Adam, Aug. 8, 1943; children— Claudia Christine, Joseph Andrew, John David. Mus.B., Mus.Edn.B., U. Kans., 1941; Mus.M., Eastman Sch. Music, 1942, PhD, 1954; student, Charles S. Skilton, L.E. Anderson, Robert Palmer, Bernard Rogers, Howard Hanson. Instr. music Colo. State U., 1942-44; asst. prof. music, head composition and theory curriculum Lawrence U., 1944-47; faculty San Francisco State U., 1947-88, head music dept., 1954-69, prof. music, 1959-99; asso. dean San Francisco State U. (Sch. Creative Arts), 1977-80. Lectr. panelist music Idyllwild Inst. Arts; Lectr. panelist music Cal. Music Tchrs. Assn., Choral Condrs. Guild Calif., Am. Guild Organists, Music Educators Nat. Conf., Music Tchrs. Nat. Assn. Choir dir., First Christian Ch., Ft. Collins, Colo., 1942-44, Meml. Presbyn. Ch., Appleton, Wis., 1944-47, First Bapt. Ch., Burlingame, Calif., 1949-63, United Meth. Ch., 1967-99; dir., Asian Arts Acad. and Music of Whole Earth Festival, San Francisco, 1978, World Arts Acad., San Francisco, 1979; compositions performed by Eastman-Rochester, Indpls., Oklahoma City, San Francisco symphony orchs., numerous others; composer: Lullaby for a Pinto Colt, 1941, A Vision of the World, 1955, Psalm 136, 1959, Fray Junipero Serra, The Great Walker; dramatic oratorio, 1960, Symphony 1, 1938, 2, 1947, 3, 1954, Variations on a Western Tune, 1948, Suite for Woodwind Quintet, 1954, A Psalm of Praise, 1964, The Crucufixion, 1971, Fun, Love, Joy, Trains, 1971, In Town Again, 1973, Arcs, 1973, O For A Thousand Tongues, 1973, They Shall Mount Up With Wings, 1980, Four Old American Songs of Merriment, 1994, Fantasia on St. Dunstan's Tune, 1996, others.; Author: Examples for the Study of Musical Style, rev. edit, 1970, American Bicentennial Song Book, 2 vols, 1975. Mem. City of Burlingame Beautification Commn., 1988-99; mem. artistic adv. com. Music at Kohl Mansion, 1987-99. Recipient Nat. Arrangers contest award, 1947. Mem. Assn. Univ. Composers, ASCAP, Music Tchrs. Nat. Assn., Music Educators Nat. Conf., Choral Condrs. Guild, AAUP. Home: Burlingame, Calif. Died Nov. 30, 1999.

WARFIELD, WILLIAM CAESAR, singer, actor, educator; b. West Helena, Ark., Jan. 22, 1920; s. Robert Elza and Bertha (McCamery) W.; m. Leontyne Price, Aug. 31, 1952 (div. Dec. 1972). MusB, Eastman Sch. Music, 1942; LLD (hon.), U. Ark., 1972; MusD (hon.), Lafayette Coll., 1978. Prof. music dept. U. Ill., Champaign, from 1974. Bd. dirs. N.Y. Coll. Music; also trustee; trustee Berkshire Boys Choir, 1966-70, Nat. Assn. Negro Musicians. Actor nat. co. Call Me Mister, 1946-47; Broadway plays include Regina, 1948-49; Town Hall debut, 1950, tour of, Australia, 1950; motion picture Showboat, 1951; toured with: govt. sponsored European prodn. Porgy and Bess; singing role of Porgy govt. sponsored European prodn., 1952, concerts, radio and TV appearances; Symphony soloist recitals, 1950—, concert tour for, Dept. State; as soloist with Phila. Orch. for its continental debut, 1955, tour, Africa, Nr. East, Europe, 1956, Asia, Australia, 1958, Cuba, 1959, Europe, 1966, recital, Brussels Fair, 1958; starred as De Lawd in: Green Pastures, NBC-TV, 1957, 59; star: N.Y.C. Opera revival Porgy and Bess, 1961, 64; also Vienna prodn., 1965-72; featured soloist, Casals Festival, P.R. and N.Y.C., 1962-63, Athens Festival, Greece, 1966; starred in: Richard Rodgers' prodn. Show Boat for, Music Theater of Lincoln Center, 1966; German lang. Show Boat for Vienna Volksoper, 1971-72; soloist (with Pablo Casals) German lang., Geneva, Switzerland, Pacem in Terris II Convocation, 1967; title role in: German lang. Mendelssohn's Elijah, 1969; presented by Central City Opera (Colo.) as: star prodn. Puccini opera Gianni Schicchi, 1972; performed concert, Carnegie Hall, 1975. Recipient hon. citation Eastman Sch. Music, 1954, Grammy award Nat. Acad. Rec. Arts and Scis., 1984. Mem. Actors Equity, Am. Guild Mus. Artists, Screen Actors Guild, AFTRA, NAACP (life), Phi Mu Alpha Sinfonia (life) Home: Chicago, Ill. Died Aug. 27, 2002.

WARNER, CECIL RANDOLPH, JR., lawyer; b. Ft. Smith, Ark., Jan. 13, 1929; s. Cecil Randolph and Reba (Cheeves) W.; m. Susan Curry, Dec. 10, 1955 (div. 1982); children: Susan Rutledge, Rebecca Jane, Cecil Randolph III, Matthew Holmes Preston, Katherine Mary; m. Barbara Ragsdale, May 26, 1983. BA magna cum laude, U. Ark., 1950; LL.B. magna cum laude, Harvard U., 1953, Sheldon fellow, 1953-54. Bar: Ark. 1953. Ptnr. Warner & Smith and predecessor firm, 1954-89; pres., CEO, Fairfield Communities Inc., Little Rock, 1973-81, chmn., CEO, 1981-85, chmn., pres., CEO, 1985-91, Environ. Systems Co., Little Rock, 1991-93; cons., 1993-95. Chmn. bd. Wortz Co., Poteau, Okla., 1993-97; instr. U. Ark. Sch. Law, 1954, 56; vice chmn. Ark. Constl. Revision Study Commn., 1967; v.p. 7th Ark. Constl. Conv., 1969-70. Scoutmaster troop 23 Boy Scouts Am., Fort Smith, 1955-58; commr. Ark. State Police Commn., 1970. Fellow Am. Bar Found., Ark. Bar Found.; mem. ABA, Ark. Bar Assn. (past chmn. exec. com., past chmn. young lawyers sect.), Pulaski County Bar Assn., Am. Law Inst., Fifty for the Future, Phi Beta Kappa, Phi Eta Sigma, Omicron Delta Kappa, Sigma Alpha Epsilon. Methodist. Home: Palm City, Fla. Died Aug. 29, 2001.

WARNER, HARRY BACKER, JR., retired journalist, freelance writer; b. Chambersburg, Pa., Dec. 19, 1922; s. Harry Backer, Sr. and Margaret Caroline (Klipp) W. Student, Hagerstown, Md. Reporter, editor, columnist Herald-Mail Co., Hagerstown, 1942-82; ret., 1982. Author: All Our Yesterdays, 1969, A Wealth of Fable, 1976; editor, author (amateur jour.) Horizons, 1939—. Com. mem. Community Action Coun., Hagerstown, Civic Music Assn., Hagerstown, Washington County Adult Edn., Hagerstown; mem. publicity com. Washington County United Fund, Hagerstown. Recipient Hugo award World Sci. Fiction Convs., 1968, 72, 93, Hist. Preservation award Washington County Commrs., 1980, First Fandom Hall of Fame award, 1995. Mem. Spectator Amateur Press Soc. (v.p. 1982-97), So. Fandom Pubs. Alliance. Republican. Lutheran. Avocations: science fiction fandom, classical music. Home: Hagerstown, Md. Died Feb. 17, 2003.

WARRIOR, ANNETTE, writer; b. Sasakwa, Okla., Feb. 20, 1958; d. Enrit Ben and Bessie Louise (Thurman) W. Home: Sasakwa, Okla. Died Feb. 8, 2002.

WARSHAW, JOSEPH BENNETT, dean, pediatrician; b. Miami Beach, Fla., July 17, 1936; s. Phillip Robert and Mona (Monashefsky) Warshaw; m. Cynthia Ann Stober, June 6, 1961; children: Deborah, Kathryn, Lawrence. BS, U. Fla., 1957; MD, Duke U., 1961; MS (hon.), Yale U., 1976; MD (hon.), Catholic U., Santiago, Chile; Josiah Macy Jr. faculty scholar, U. Oxford, 1979—80. Diplomate Am. Bd. Pediat., subsplty bd. in neonatal-perinatal medicine. Intern, resident in pediat. Strong Meml. Hosp., Rochester, NY, 1961—63; resident in pediat. Duke Hosp., Durham, NC, 1963—64; research assoc. NIH, 1964—66, Retina Found., Boston, 1966—68; assoc. in pediat. Harvard U., 1968—71, asst. prof. pediat., 1971—72, assoc. prof., 1972—73; assoc. prof. pediat. and ob-gyn Yale U. Sch. Medicine, New Haven, 1973—76, prof. pediat. and ob-gyn, 1976—82; prof., chmn. dept. pediat. U. Tex. Health Sci. Ctr., Dallas, 1982—87; chief staff Children's Med. Ctr., Dallas, 1982—87; chief pediat. Parkland Meml. Hosp., Dallas, 1982—87; prof., chmn. dept. pediat. Yale U. Sch. Medicine, New Haven, 1987—2000, dep. dean for clin. affairs, 1995—2000; dean Coll. Medicine U. Vt., Burlington, 2000—03. Physician-in-chief Children's Hosp. at Yale-New Haven Hosp., 1987—2000; mem. human embryology and devel. study sect. NIH, 1974—78; nat. adv. con. Nat. Inst. Child Health and Human Devel., 1987—91. Clin. rsch. adv. com. Nat. Found. March of Dimes, 1978—92; mem. rsch. com. United Cerebral Palsy, 1987—2000. Served USPHS, 1964—66. Fellow: Am. Acad. Pediat.; mem.: Conn. Acad. Sci. and Engring., Conn. Acad. Arts and Scis., Internat. Pediatric Rsch. Found. (chmn. bd. 1989—93), Assn. Am. Physicians, Soc. Pediatric Rsch. (pres. 1981—82), Soc. Devel. Biology, Am. Soc. Cell Biology, Am. Soc. Biol. Chemistry, Am. Soc. Clin. Investigation, Am. Pediatric Soc. (coun. mem. 1988—94), Inst. Medicine NAS. Home: Burlington, Vt. Died Dec. 29, 2003.

WARSHAW, LEON J(OSEPH), physician; b. N.Y.C., July 20, 1917; s. Samuel and Bessie (Olken) W.; m. Mona Glassman, Aug. 31, 1941; children: Peter M., David C. AB, Columbia U., 1938, MD, 1942. Diplomate Am. Bd. Internal Medicine, Am. Bd. Preventive Medicine (occupational medicine). Intern, house physician 1st med. div. Bellevue Hosp., N.Y.C., 1942-44, from clin. asst. vis. physician to asso. vis. physician, 1942-59; clin. asst., then adj. Beth Israel Hosp., N.Y.C., 1944-49, asso. attending physician, 1949-87, chief adult cardiac clinic, 1950-62; practice internal medicine N.Y.C., 1944-55; med. dir. and/or med. cons. various corps., 1944-69; with Equitable Life Assurance Soc., N.Y.C., 1967-80, v.p., chief med. dir., 1970-75, v.p., corp. med. dir., 1975-80; on leave as dep. dir. N.Y.C. Mayor's Office of Ops., 1978-80; clin. prof. environ. medicine NYU, 1980—. Cons. health care delivery, 1980—; exec. dir. N.Y. Bus. Group on Health, 1980-94; mem. N.Y. Gov.'s Health Adv. Coun., 1978-84, N.Y. State Adv. Coun. on Alcoholism Svcs., 1988-97, chmn., 1990-97; mem. faculty Columbia U. Coll. Physicians and Surgeons, 1944-60, NYU Med. Sch., 1945-47; chmn. bd. Equitable Environ. Health, Inc., Woodbury, N.Y., 1973-75, dir., 1975-78; trustee Ins. Med. Scientist Scholarship Fund, 1975-78; mem. adv. bd. Ctr. Productive Aging, N.Y. Ctr. for Policy on Aging; bd. dirs. Med. & Health Rsch. Assn.; mem. nat. adv. com. Pres.'s Com. Employment Handicapped, 1965-89; mem. Pres.'s Coun. Phys. Fitness and Sports, 1970-85; bd. sponsors Twin Cities Health Care Devel. Project, 1972-75; chmn. med. adv. com. Washington Bus. Group Health, 1977-79; mental health adv. bd. Cornell U., 1970-80; Sappington Meml. lectr. Indsl. Med. Assn.; dir. Health Sys. Agy. N.Y.C., 1987-93; Thackrah lect. Soc. Occupl. Medicine/Leeds U., 1988. Author: Malaria: Biography of a Killer, 1949, Managing Stress, 1979, The Heart in Industry, 1969, Enhancing the Health of the Public: The New York Academy of Medicine 1947-1997, 1998; assoc. editor: Encyclopedia on Occupational Health and Safety, 1994-98; contbr. articles to profl. jours.; mem. editorial bd. jours. Fellow Am. Coll. Occupl. & Environ. Medicine, Am. Coll. Cardiology, ACP, Am. Coll. Preventive Medicine, Am. Occupl. Medicine Assn. (past dir.), N.Y. Acad. Scis., Med. and Health Rsch. Assn. N.Y.C. (bd. dirs.), Soc. Occupl. Medicine (hon.); mem. AMA, N.Y. State, N.Y. County med. socs., Am. Arbitration Assn. (adv. health council 1972-80), Am. Heart Assn. (chmn. heart industry com. 1966-68, dir. 1969-73), Conf. Board, Nat. Safety Council (dir. 1972-74, v.p. research 1972-74), Greater N.Y.

Safety Council (1970), N.Y. C. of C., N.Y. Heart Assn. (dir. 1968-70, 76-82), Occupational Health Inst. (dir. 1970-87), N.Y. Acad. Medicine (chmn. sec. occupational medicine 1964-66), N.Y. Occupl. Med. Assn. (pres. 1965-67, exec. com. 1967-77), Occupl. Psychiatry Group, Alpha Omega Alpha, Beta Sigma Rho, Phi Delta Epsilon. Home: Ho Ho Kus, NJ. Deceased.

WASHBURN, ABBOTT MCCONNELL, government official; b. Duluth, Minn., Mar. 1, 1915; s. Abbott McConnell and Ruby Leslie (Frisk) W.; m. Mary Brennan, May 12, 1939 (div. 1959); children: Abbott Michael, Daniel Norton; m. Wanda Allender, Aug. 3, 1963; 1 dau., Julie. BA, Harvard, 1937. Mgr. dept. pub. services Gen. Mills, Inc., Mpls., 1937-52; exec. vice chmn. Crusade for Freedom, Inc. (nat. hdqrs.), N.Y.C., 1950-52; dir. orgn. Nat. Hdqrs. Citizens for Eisenhower, N.Y.C., 1952; corr. sec., mem. personal staff Gen. Eisenhower, Denver, N.Y.C., 1952; exec. sec. Pres.'s Com. on Internat. Information Activities., Washington, 1953; dep. to spl. asst. to Pres., 1953; dep. dir. USIA, 1954-61; v.p. internat. operations Carl Byoir & Assos., 1961-62; pres. Washburn, Stringer Assocs., Inc., Washington, Mexico City, 1962-69; dep. chmn. U.S. delegation Conf. on Definitive Arrangements for Internat. Telecommunications Satellite Orgn., 1969-70, chmn. with rank ambassador, 1970-71; cons. to dir. Office Telecommunications Policy, Exec. Office Pres., 1972-74; mem. Bd. for Internat. Broadcasting, 1974; commr. Fed. Communications Commn., 1974-82; chmn. U.S. del. with rank ambassador Internat. Telecommunication Union Radio Conf. on Direct-to-Home Satellite Broadcasting Western Hemisphere, 1982-83. Cons. Dept. State, 1984-88; dir. Metro Mobile Cellular Telephone Service, Inc., 1985-92, Lorimar-Telepictures, Inc., 1984-88; mem. bd. George Foster Peabody Awards, 1984-88; mem. Pres.' Task Force on U.S. Govt. Internat. Broadcasting, 1991; bd. dirs. Eisenhower World Affairs Inst., 1988—. Active World Freedom Bell project, Berlin, 1950. Served from ensign to lt. USNR, 1942-45. Recipient Distinguished Service medal USIA, 1960 Mem. Council on Fgn. Relations, Washington Inst. Fgn. Affairs. Clubs: National Press, DACOR (Washington). Home: Washington, DC. Died Dec. 11, 2003.

WASHINGTON, CHARLES EDWARD, secondary education educator, insurance executive; b. Little Rock, Nov. 27, 1933; s. David D. and Hazel M. Washington; BA, Philander Smith Coll., Little Rock, 1958; MEd, U. Okla., 1962; postgrad. U. So. Calif.; m. Ruby N. Jones, Sept. 4, 1956 (div. 1965); 1 child, Toni Regail. Tchr. public schs., Ft. Smith, Ark., 1958-60, Oklahoma City, 1960-69, L.A., 1969—; registered rep. ITT Hamilton Mgmt. Corp., 1963-70; fin. counselor Fin. Congeneric Corp., 1971-74, Am. Inst. Property and Liability Underwriters; spl. agt. Welsh & Assos., Ins. Svcs., Walnut, Calif., 1979—; sales mgr. Sun Belt Ins. Svcs., Walnut, 1982—; gen. agt. Alvo Ins. and Fin. Svcs., 1984—. Umpire Internat. Fedn. Amateur Softball Assn. Umpires, 1961-63. Mem. Crenshaw Christian Center. Served with USMC, 1951-54; Korea. Mem. NEA, Calif. Tchrs. Assn., United Tchrs. L.A., Ind. Ins. Assn. Calif., U. Okla. Alumni Assn. (class rep. 1964-67), Nat. Dunbar High Sch. Alumni Assn., Philander Smith Coll. Alumni Assn., Nat. Notary Assn., U.S. Coast Guard Aux., Omega Psi Phi. Democrat. Died Dec. 30, 2001.

WASHINGTON, WALTER, retired academic administrator; b. Hazlehurst, Miss., July 13, 1923; s. Kemp and Mable (Comous) W.; m. Carolyn Carter, July 31, 1949. BA, Tougaloo Coll., 1948, LLD (hon.), 1972; MS, Ind. U., 1952, LLD (hon.), 1983; Edn. Specialist, Peabody Coll., 1958; postgrad., Yale, 1953; EdD, U. So. Miss., 1969; postgrad., Harvard U., 1989; DSc (hon.), Purdue U., 1993. Tchr. Holtzclaw High Sch., Crystal Springs, Miss., 1948-49; asst. prin., tchr. Parrish High Sch., Hazlehurst, 1949-52; prin. Utica Jr. Coll. High Sch., Miss., 1951 54; dean Utica Jr. Coll., 1954-55, pres., 1957-69; prin. Sumner Hill High Sch., Clinton, Miss., 1955-57; pres. Alcorn (Miss.) State U., 1969-94, pres. emeritus, 1994-99. Past ptnr. Klinger Industries, Ltd.; bd. dirs. Miss. Power and Light. Pres. Nat. Pan-Hellenic Council, 1964-67, Nat. Alumni Council of United Negro Coll. Fund, 1959-60; past. mem. adv. council Miss. Vocational Edn. Program, Miss. Regional Med. Programs; mem. Miss. Econ. Council; mem. S.E. regional exec. com. Boy Scouts Am.; mem. exec. com. Andrew Jackson council; past mem. adv. council Miss. 4-H Clubs; bd. dirs. Miss. Mental Health Assn., Miss. Easter Seal Soc.; past bd. dirs. Miss. Heart Assn. Recipient Presdl. citation for outstanding leadership to Univ./Industry Cluster, 1980-81, Disting. Alumni award Vanderbilt-Peabody, 1991, George Washington Carver Lifetime Achievement award Tuskegee Inst., 1993; named to U. So. Miss. Alumni Hall of Fame, 1987; Walter Washington Bldgs. named in his honor, Utica Jr. Coll., 1969, U. So. Miss., 1993, Alcorn State U., 1994. Mem. NEA, ASCD, Am. Assn. Sch. Adminstrs. (So. Regional Edn. bd.), Nat. Assn. State Univs. and Land Grant Colls., So. Assn. Colls. Secondary Schs. (past bd. dirs., past chmn. secondary commn., past chmn. commn. on colls., past trustee), Miss. Educators Assn. (pres. 1964-65), Miss. Tchrs. Assn., Nat. Soc. for Study of Higher Edn., Tougaloo Nat. Alumni Assn. (pres. 1960), George Peabody Coll. Alumni Assn. (past v.p. exec. com., Disting. Alumni of Yr. 1991), John Dewey Soc., Delta Kappa Pi, Phi Delta Kappa, Alpha Kappa Mu, Alpha Phi Alpha (gen. pres. 1974-76). Home: Jackson, Miss. Died Dec. 1, 1999.

WASHINGTON, WALTER EDWARD, lawyer; b. Dawson, Ga., Apr. 15, 1915; s. William L. and Willie Mae (Thornton) Washington; m. Bennetta Bullock (dec. 1991); 1 child, Bennetta Jules Rosette; m. Mary Burke, 1994. AB, Howard U., 1938, JD, 1948; postgrad., Am. U., 1939—43; LL.D., Fisk U., Georgetown U., 1968, Cath. U., Boston U., 1969, George Washington U., Princeton, 1970, Lincoln U., 1984; L.H.D., Bishop Coll., 1970; JD, Washington Coll., Md., 1972, Ind. Central Coll., 1972, Boston Coll., 1972, Carnegie-Mellon U., 1973, Howard U., 1974, Trinity Coll., 1974, Colgate U., 1976. Bar: D.C. 1948, U.S. Supreme Ct. 1952. With Nat. Capital Housing Authority, Washington, 1941—66, exec. dir., 1961—66; chmn. N.Y.C. Housing Authority, 1966—67; apptd. mayor commr. Washington, 1967—75; elected mayor, 1975—79; former ptnr. Burns, Jackson, Summit, Rovins & Washington. Dir. Woodward & Lothrop, Inc., Nat. Permanent Fed. Savs. & Loan Assn., Dist.-Reality Title Ins. Corp. Mem. adv. bd. U.S. Conf. Mayors; vice chmn. human resources com. Nat. League of Cities; mem. ins. panel Nat. Adv. Commn. on Civil Disorders; v.p. United Cmty. Funds and Couns. Am.; trustee John F. Kennedy Ctr. for Performing Arts, Fed. City Coun.; bd. dirs. Washington Coun. Chs., Washington area Boy Scouts Am., United Planning Orgn., Big Bros. Am. Recipient Alumni award, Howard U., 1963, Career Svc. award, Nat. Civil Svc. League, 1965, Archdiocesan award, 1968, award, NCCJ, Nat. Bar Assn. award, Health and Welfare Coun. award, Disting. Svc. award, Howard U. Law Alumni Assn., 1974, award, Capitol Press Club, 1974, Silver Beaver award, Boy Scouts Am., 1973, Nat. Jewish Hosp. award for outstanding svc., 1973, Man of Yr. award, Greater Washington Bd. of Trade, 1983, Judge Egarton award, ACLU, 1984. Mem.: ABA, Washington Urban League (dir.), Nat. Lawyers Club (Washington), Internat. Club (bd. govs.), Cosmos Club, Federal City Club, Masons (32 degree), Order of Coif. Democrat. Home: Washington, DC. Died Oct. 27, 2003.

WASSERMAN, WALTER LEONARD, magnetics company executive; b. N.Y.C., Sept. 16, 1936; s. Soloman J. and Esther (Honigman) W.; m. Barbara Koenig, June 15, 1957 (div. 1973); children: Beth, Greg, Eli. BSEE, CUNY, 1957; MSEE, U. Pa., 1961, PhD in Bio Engring., 1964. Engring. supr. Hevey Mil. Electric GE, Syracuse, N.Y., 1958-60; engring. mgr. Philco Corp., Phila., 1960-65; v.p. bioengring. Hoffman-LaRoche, Nutley, N.J., 1965-67; pres. Health Tech. Corp., Moorestown, N.J., 1967-70; gen. mgr. Med. Data Systems, Dublin, Ireland, 1971-77; dir. mktg. El Scint (Israel), Inc., London, 1978-81; v.p. R&D Electro Biology, Inc., Parsippany, N.J., 1982-85; chief exec. officer Meditron Corp., Spring valley, N.Y., 1985-90, Modular Magnetics, New City, N.Y., from 1990. Bd. dirs. Interpore Internat., Inc., Irvine, Calif., Theradyne, Inc., Salt Lake City, TriDyne, Inc., Salt Lake City. Contbr. articles to profl. jours.; patentee in field. Mem. Pres.'s Commn. for Handicapped, 1964. Capt. USAF, 1964-66, Vietnam. Recipient Gold medal Am. Assn. Rehab. Medicine, 1964. Democrat. Jewish. Avocations: stamp collecting, antiques. Home: New City, NY. Died Mar. 2, 2000.

WATERMAN, BYRON OLNEY, minister; b. Johnston, R.I., Nov. 23, 1909; s. Walter Day and Fannie May (Sweet) W.; m. Marion Palmer Eddy, Aug. 24, 1934; children: Byron Eddy, Holden Tozer. AB, Brown U., 1932; BD, Andover-Newton Theol. Sch., 1934, MDiv, 1973. Ordained to ministry Am. Bapt. Chs., United Ch. of Christ, 1935. Asst. min. 1st Calvary Bapt. Ch., Lawrence, Mass., 1935-41; min. 1st Bapt. Ch., Plaistow, N.H., 1941-50, M. Vernon Larger Parish, Greene, R.I., 1950-94. Vis. chaplain R.I. Med. Ctr. Inst. Mental Health, 1953-71. Active Griswold (Conn.) Conservation Commn., 1971-97; violinist Conn. Coll. Orch., New London, 1967-89, Ea. Conn. Symphony Orch., New London, 1968-88, Nat. Sr. Symphony, Mystic (Conn.) and New London, 1989-95; vol. chaplain R.I. Hosp., Providence, 1986—; rep. chaplaincy com. United Ch. of Christ R.I. State Coun. of Chs., 1992-99; mem. ACLU, Planned Parenthood. Recipient citations R.I. Ho. of Reps., 1975, 90, citation R.I. Senate, 1990, Community Citizen award The Grange, 1990. Mem. Assn. Mental Health Chaplains, Am. Fedn. Musicians, Archeol. Soc. Am., Brown Faculty Club. Home: Jewett City, Conn. Died Mar. 25, 2003.

WATERS, GEORGE WILBUR, travel and financial company executive; b. North Madison, Ind., Jan. 9, 1916; s. George Wilbur and Nellie (Wray) W.; m. Pauline Wasson, Feb. 19, 1942; children: Diane, Lawrence, Mildred. BS, U. Ind., 1938; grad. sr. execs. program, MIT, 1956. Data processing sales rep. IBM, Cin., 1938-41; dir., pres. Mass. S.S. Lines, Boston, 1946-48; v.p., dir. Colonial Stores, Inc., Atlanta, 1949-61; v.p. Am. Express Co., N.Y.C., 1961-81, pres. travel related services, 1977-78, 79-80, exec. v.p., 1981, sr. adviser, 1981-86, also chmn. Office of Strategic Devel.; cons., 1981-87. Advisor/cons. Intec Systems, Inc., 1989—. Mem. Nat. Commn. on Electronic Fund Transfers, 1976-89; mem. dean's adv. coun. Ind. U. Sch. Bus.; mem. U.S. Senatorial Bus. Adv. Bd.; mem. adv. bd. GSA, 1982-85; chmn. fin. and property com., chmn. ch. corp., elder First Presbyn. Ch., Red Bank, N.J. Col. USAAF, 1941-45. Decorated Legion of Merit. Mem. Acad. Alumni Fellows of Ind. U. Sch. Bus. Clubs: Rumson (N.J.) Country. Republican. Presbyterian. Home: Fair Haven, NJ. Died Jan. 11, 2003.

WATSON, ARTHUR RICHARD, retired zoo director; b. Cleve., June 25, 1915; s. George Henry and Martha Helen (Rathensperger) W.; m. Ruth Eleanor Garland, Nov. 1939 (div. 1955); 1 child, Lois Ruth Watson Ferber; m. Marybeth Wiemer Anderson, Nov. 2, 1967. Student, Case Western Res. U., 1935-47. Asst. to dir. Cleve. Zoo, 1942-48; dir. Balt. Zoo, 1948-80; pres., owner Zoo Animals Inc., Balt., from 1980. Mem. collecting safaris to Africa for gorillas, 1954, for giraffes, 1966. Editor zoo sect. Parks And Recreation mag., 1952-53; host (TV shows) This is Your Zoo, 1949-59, 71-72, (radio show) The Balt. Zoo, 1966-76. Recipient Unsung Pub. Service award McCormick Spice Co., Balt., 1949, Hats Off award Order of DeMolay, Balt., 1956, commendation Am. Legion, Balt., 1958, citation U.S. Hall of Fame Soc., 1968, Pub. Service award Boy Scouts Am., Balt., 1976 Mem. Am. Assn. Zool. Parks and Aquariums, St. Georges Soc. of Balt., English Spoeaking Union. Democrat. Unitarian Universalist. Home: Baltimore, Md. Died Dec. 6, 1999.

WATSON, DEBORAH ROSZAK, quality engineer; b. Staunton, Va., Sept. 13, 1956; d. Walter Felix and Jean Viktoria (Wozniak) Roszak; m. Francis Marion Watson III, May 2, 1981; 1 stepchild, Leslie Cauvel. ASME, W.Va. Inst. Tech., 1977; BS in Mfg. Mgmt., Va. Commonwealth U., 1994. Sr. designer GE, Waynesboro, Va., 1977-78; from specialist to engr. B, project leader Philip Morris USA, Richmond, Va., 1978-90, quality engr., from 1990. V.p. programs Womens Resource Com., Richmond, 1986-87; quality assurance rep. Project BOB (Bldg. Our Bus.), Richmond, 1990-92. Mem. Lewis Ginter Bot. Garden, Fishing Bay Yacht Club, Golden Kay, Phi Kappa Phi. Avocations: sailing, snow skiing, reading, fishing, baking. Home: Hartfield, Va. Deceased.

WATTERSON, THOMAS BATCHELOR, investment executive; b. Cleve., July 11, 1938; s. William Herbert and Mercedes (Rendall) W.; m. Joyce Marie Grande, Sept. 27, 1968; children: Sean Anthony, William Grande. BA, William Coll., 1962. Loan officer Cleveland Trust Co., Cleve., 1962-65; v.p. Merrill, Turben and Co., Cleve., 1965-70, Prescott, Merrill Turben, Cleve., 1970-75; ptnr. Ball, Burge and Krause, Cleve., 1975-78; sr. ptnr. Prescott, Ball and Turben, Cleve., 1978-79; exec. v.p. McCloy, Watterson and Co., Cleve., 1974-79; spl. ltd. ptnr. Cowen and Co., Cleve., 1979-94. Trustee Univ. Sch., Cleve., 1988—, Greater Cleve. Garden Ctr., 1989-92; pres. men's coun. St. Paul's Episcopal Ch., Cleve., 1978-81; chmn. stewardship com. Cottonwood Hollow-Cleve. Natural History Mus. Mem. Nat. Assn. Security Dealers (regional bus. conduct com. 1989-92), Cleve. Bond Club (bd. govs. 1992—), Ohio Mcpl. Adv. Coun. (pres. bd. govs. 1972-74, 94-96), Univ. Sch. Alumni Assn. (pres. 1987), Williams Club. Republican. Episcopalian. Avocations: gardening, boating, stained glass windows. Home: Painesville, Ohio. Died Mar. 4, 2001.

WATTS, THOMAS SUMTER, judge; b. Statesville, N.C., Mar. 11, 1939; s. Atwell Edwin Jr. and Katharine Sumter (Cowan) W.; m. Marguerite "Peggy" Peters, Dec. 28, 1963; 1 child, Mary Katharine. AB History, Polit. Sci., Davidson Coll., 1961; LLB, Wake Forest U., 1964. Bar: N.C. 1964, U.S Dist. Ct. (ea. dist.) N.C. 1964. Assoc. Small & Small Attys., Elizabeth City, N.C., 1964-65; ptnr. Small, Small & Watts, Elizabeth City, 1966-70; prosecutor 1st Dist. State of N.C., Elizabeth City, 1970, asst. dist. atty., 1971-74, dist. atty., 1975-82; spl. judge Superior Ct. State of N.C., Elizabeth City, 1982-84, resident judge, from 1985. Mem. jud. forms com. Adminstrn. Office of Cts., Raleigh, N.C., 1985-89, mem. N.C. Pattern Jury Instrn. Com., Inst. of Govt., Chapel Hill, 1989—; pres. N.C. Dist. Attys. Assn., 1978-79. Bd. dirs. U.S. and N.C. Jaycees, 1969-71, legal counsel NC. chpt., 1968-69 (Disting. Svc. award Elizabeth City chpt. 1968, named among Five Outstanding Young Men of N.C. 1969). Mem. ABA, N.C. Bar Assn. (continuing legal edn. com. 1988—), 1st Jud. Dist. Bar Assn., N.C. Conf. Superior Ct. Judges, Rotary (pres. Elizabeth City Morning Club 1987-88). Democrat. Methodist. Avocation: amateur radio. Home: Elizabeth City, NC. Deceased.

WAYLAND, J(AMES) HAROLD, biomedical scientist, educator; b. Boise, Idaho, July 2, 1909; s. Charles William and Daisy (McConnell) W.; m. Virginia Jane Kartzke, June 24, 1933; children— Ann Marie Peters, Elizabeth Jane (Mrs. Paul T. Barber). BS, U. Idaho, 1931, D.Sc. (hon.), 1977; MS, Calif. Inst. Tech., 1935, PhD, 1937. Am. Scandinavian Found. fellow U. Copenhagen, 1937; asst. prof. physics U. Redlands, 1938-41; mil. research in mine warfare and torpedo devel., 1941-48; assoc. prof. applied mechanics Calif. Inst. Tech., Pasadena, 1949-57, prof., 1957-63, prof. engring. sci., 1963-79, prof. emeritus, 1979—. U.S. coordinator U.S.-Japan Coop. Seminars on Peripheral Circulation, 1967, 70; mem. cardiovascular and renal study sect. NIH, 1973-77; vis. prof. Shinshu U., Matsumoto, Japan, 1973, U. Limburg, Maastricht, The Netherlands, 1979, U. New South Wales, Australia, 1980, U. Heidelberg, 1982, U. of Tsukuba, Japan, 1987; Disting. vis. prof. U. Del., 1985. Contbr. articles to profl. publs., also books and articles on history of playing cards. Recipient Ordnance Devel. award U.S. Navy, 1945, Cert. of Recognition, NASA, 1975, Humboldt Sr. Scientist Rsch. award U. Heidelberg, 1982, 91, Malpighi prize, 1988; named to Alumni Hall of Fame, U. Idaho, 1990; Guggenheim fellow, 1953-54; rsch. grantee NIH, NSF, John A. Hartford Found., Kroc Found. Fellow AAAS (chmn. med. scis. sect. 1976), Am. Inst. Med. and Biol. Engring. (founding), Asian Union for Microcirculation (award 1997); mem. AAUP, Microcirculatory Soc. (pres. 1971-72, Landis award 1981), Am. Phys. Soc., Am. Physiol. Soc., European Microcirculatory Soc. (hon.), German Microcirculatory Soc. (hon.), Internat. Soc. Biorheology, Am. Heart Assn., Am. Inst. Archeology, Am. Soc. Enology and Viticulture, Playing Card Soc., Sigma Xi, Phi Beta Kappa, Sigma Tau. Clubs: Athenaeum. Democrat. Unitarian Universalist. Achievements include patents for scanning confocal microscopy; development of quantitative methods for measuring blood flow in microvessels and macromolecular diffusion in living tissues, of servo-microscope for maintaining focus on moving tissue. Home: Pasadena, Calif. Deceased.

WAYMAN, MORRIS, chemical engineering educator, consultant; b. Toronto, Can., Mar. 19, 1915; s. Harry and Martha (Alt) W.; m. Sara Gertrude Zadkin; children: Michael Lash, Thomas Ethan; m. Mary Chabot. BA, U. Toronto, 1936, MA, 1937, PhD, 1941. Registered profl. engr., Ont. Researcher Can. Internat. Paper Co., Hawkesbury, Ont., 1942-52; tech. dir. Columbia Cellulose Co., Prince Rupert, B.C., 1958-63; prof. chem. engring. U. Toronto, 1963-93, prof. forestry, 1973-93; pres. Morris Wayman, Ltd., Toronto, 1966—. Adj. prof. chem. engring. U. Alberta, 1993—; cons., Can., U.S., Brazil, Sweden, UN. Author: Guide for Planning Pulp and Paper Enterprises, 1973, Wealth and Welfare, 1978, Biotechnology of Biomass Conversion: fuels and chemicals from renewable resources, 1990; contbr. numerous articles to sci. jours.; patentee in field. Mem. Ont. Waste Mgmt. Adv. Bd., 1975-80, Edmonton Philharm Orch. Hon. fellow Innis Coll., Toronto, 1977 Fellow AAAS, Royal Soc. Can., Chem. Inst. Can.; mem. Can. Wood Chemistry Symposium (chmn. 1979-82), Sigma Xi Home: Laguna Hills, Calif. Deceased.

WAYNICK, VIRGINIA DANIEL, artist; b. Roxboro, N.C., Jan. 19, 1920; d. Hubert James Daniel and Anna Wilma Connally; m. James Fletcher Waynick, Oct. 6, 1945; children: Betty, Fletcher, Joan. One-woman shows include: Yanceyville Civic Ctr., Link Bros. Pharmacy, Golden Corral, Reidsville, Annie Penn Meml. Hosp., Rockingham County Govt. Ctr., Reidsville and Eden Pub. Librs., Penn Civic Ctr., Reidsville, Morehead Meml. Hosp. Recipient numerous art awards at shows and from Fine Arts Festival of Rockingham County, including the Fournier award for Best in Show. Mem. Women in the Arts of Washington, Greensboro Artists League, Danville Art League, High Point Art Guild, Associated Artists of Winston Salem, The Studio Group of Rockingham County, others. Home: Reidsville, NC. Died June 3, 2000.

WEATHERBEE, LINDA, insurance executive; b. Decatur, Ill., July 20, 1956; d. Carl and V. Lucile (Westwood) W. BA magna cum laude, James Millikin U., 1977; postgrad., Ill. State U., 1981-82. CLU, chartered fin. cons. Fin. analyst State Farm Life Ins., Bloomington, Ill., 1979-82, supr. Austin, Tex., 1982-86, asst. supt. Salem, Oreg., from 1986. Cellist Decatur Civic Orch., 1973-75; ch. pianist, 1975-77, youth advisor Cen. Ill, 1979-81; Rep. vol., Bloomington, 1982; tutor adult edn. program Chemeketa Community Coll., Salem, 1986, 87; tchr. high sch. religion course, Salem, 1987—. Fellow Life Mgmt. Inst.; mem. Adminstrv. Mgmt. Soc., Life Office mgmt. Assn., Williamette Soc. CLU and Chrtered Fin. Cons. (bd. dirs. 1987—), Am. Horse Show Assn., N.W. Horse Council (Oreg.), Am. Bus. Women's Assn. (Townlake chpter Austin, Tex. 1984-86), Nat. Assn. Female Execs., Phi Kappa Phi. Mem. LDS Church. Avocations: hunter/jumper horses, reading, dance, cake decorating, needlepoint. Home: Moraga, Calif. Deceased.

WEATHERS, MELBA ROSE, hospital utilization review coordinator; b. Ladonia, Tex., Mar. 31, 1940; d. E. Carl and Rosa Lee (Evans) W. BSN, Holy Family Coll., 1974; BS, Tex. Woman's U., 1989. Staff/charge nurse maternal and child health St. Paul Med. Ctr., Dallas, 1974-87; rev. coord. Tex. Med. Found., Austin, 1989-95; quality case mgr. Marshall (Tex.) Meml. Hosp., from 1995. Mem. Am. Health Info. Mgmt. Assn., VFW Ladies Aux. Roman Catholic. Avocation: collecting nursing memorabilia. Home: Katy, Tex. Died May 1, 2000.

WEBB, HOWARD WILLIAM, JR., retired humanities educator, university official; b. Dayton, Ohio, June 23, 1925; s. Howard William and Martha (Brown) W.; m. Joyce Moore Cooper, Nov. 20, 1947; children: Howard William (dec.), Amy Forrest, Sarah Winship. BA, Denison U., 1947; MA, State U. Iowa, 1950, PhD, 1953. Asst. prof. English Central Mo. State Coll., 1953-56, So. Ill. U., Carbondale, 1956-62, assoc. prof., 1962-67, prof., 1967-90, dir. grad. studies in English, 1961-67, acting chmn., 1968, chmn., 1968-72, acad. affairs officer on bd. trustees staff, 1974-79, system acad. officer on chancellor's staff, 1979-85, vice chancellor for acad. affairs, 1985-90; interim dir. SIU Press, 1993. Editor: Illinois Prose Writers: An Anthology, 1968; contbr. articles to profl. jours. With USNR, 1943-46. Mem. MLA, Melville Soc. Home: Carbondale, Ill. Died Jan. 27, 2003.

WEBB, ROSS ALLAN, historian, educator; b. Westchester, N.S., Can., July 22, 1923; came to U.S. 1929; s. William Oswald and Permilla Madge (Purdy) W.; m. Ruth evangeline Keil, June 19, 1954; children: Eric Seth, Alan George. BA with honors in history, Acadia U., Wolfville, N.S., 1949; MA in History, U. Pitts., 1951, PhD in History, 1956. Lectr. U. Pitts., 1950-56; asst./assoc. prof., dir. undergrad. studies in history U. Ky., Lexington, 1956-67; prof., chair dept. history Winthrop Coll., Rock Hill, S.C., 1967-68, prof. history, dean faculty, v.p. acad. affairs, 1968-75, prof. history, 1975-89, univ. historian, prof. emeritus, 1989—2003. Cons. in field; vis. prof. summer sch. Wesleyan U., 1966, Acadia U., 1951-64. Author: A Book of Remembrance, 1956, The Alaskan Boundary Dispute, 1779-1903, 1951, Benjamin Helm Bristow Border State Politician, 1969, Kentucky in the Reconstruction Era, 1978; contbr. articles to profl. jours., chpts. in books; contbr. to: Ency. of Southern History, 1979, Kentucky Governors, 1985, The Kentucky Ency., 1992; book reviewer scholarly jours. including The Am. Hist. Rev., Civil War History, The Register of the Kentucky Hist. Assn., Western Pennsylvania Hist. Mag. Mem. S.C. Commn. of Archives and History, 1967-69, York Tech. Edn. Commn., 1968-77; bd. trustees Diocese of Upper S.C.; priest Episcopal Ch. Am. Philos. Soc. grantee, 1977, S.C. Com. on Humanities grantee, 1984; recipient Algernon Sydney Sullivan award, Winthrop Coll., 1981. Mem. Am. Assn. Ret. Persons (S.C. state legis. com. chmn. 1991-93, former mem. nat. legis. coun.), So. Conf. Brit. Studies, So. Hist. Assn. (European sect.), Ky. Hist. Soc., Kiwanis (pres. 1980-81), Phi Beta Kappa, Omicron Delta Kappa, Phi Kappa Phi, Phi Alpha Theta. Avocations: music, travel, photography. Home: Rock Hill, SC. Died Nov. 21, 2003.

WEBER, MORTON M. microbial biochemist, educator; b. N.Y.C., May 26, 1922; s. Morris and Mollie (Scherer) W.; m. Phyllis Stern Levy, July 31, 1955; children— Stephen Abbott, Ethan Lenard. BS, Coll. City N.Y., 1949; Sc.D., Johns Hopkins, 1953. Instr. microbiology Sch. Medicine, Johns Hopkins, 1951-55; Am. Cancer Soc. fellow in biochemistry McCollum-Pratt Inst., 1953-56; instr. bacteriology and immunology Med. Sch., Harvard, 1956-59; asst. prof. Sch. Medicine, St. Louis U., 1959-61, assoc. prof., 1961-63, prof., 1963-99, chmn. dept. microbiology, 1964-87, chmn. emeritus, 1987-99, prof. emeritus, 1992-99. Vis. scientist microbiology unit U. Oxford (Eng.) Dept. Biochemistry, 1970-99; sr. mem. Linacre Coll. Oxford U., 1970-99; mem. microbial chemistry study sect. NIH, USPHS, 1969-73. Served with USAAF, 1942-46. Fellow AAAS, Am. Acad. Microbiology, Infectious Disease Soc. Am., Johns Hopkins Soc. Scholars; mem. Am. Soc. Biol. Chemists, Am. Soc. Microbiology (sec. physiology div. 1964-65, vice chmn. 1965-66, chmn. 1966-67), Soc. Gen. Microbiology, N.Y. Acad. Scis., St. Louis Biochemistry Group (pres. 1968-69), Phi Beta Kappa (hon.), Sigma Xi. Avocations: research in biochemistry of microorganisms, with emphasis on pathways and mechanisms of electron transport, enzymatic regulatory mechanisms, and mode of action of antimicrobial drugs and antibiotics. Home: Saint Louis, Mo. Died Sept. 4, 1999.

WEBER, NEAL ALBERT, retired biology educator; b. Towner, N.D., Dec. 14, 1908; s. Albert and Kathryn (Boom) W.; m. Jean Charlotte Jeffery, May 29, 1940; children: Nancy Beth, Cornelius Jeffery, Peter Albert. BA, U. N.D., 1930, MS, 1932; MA, Harvard U., 1933, PhD, 1935. Assoc. prof. biology U. N.D., Grand Forks, 1936-43, assoc. prof. biology Sch. Medicine, 1943-47; assoc. prof. biology Swarthmore (Pa.) Coll., 1947-57, prof. biology, 1958-74, Coll. Arts and Sci., Baghdad, Iraq, 1950-52; adj. prof. biology Fla. State U., Tallahassee, from 1974. Sci. attaché U.S. Dept. State, Buenos Aires, 1960-62; mem. polar rsch. team Nat. Acad. Sci., Washington, 1958-60; del. U.S. spl. commn. Internat. Coun. Sci. Unions, Australia, 1959. Author: Gardening Ants, 1972; contbg. author Insect Fungus Symbiosis, 1979, Social Insects, 1982; contbr. over 140 articles to profl. publs. ScD (hon.) U. N.D., 1958; grantee NSF, 1950s, 70s; recipient John F. Lewis prize Am. Philos. Soc., Phila., 1973. Mem. Cosmos Club Washington, Explorers Club N.Y. (1st chmn. Phila. chpt. 1947, recipient Phila. Explorers award 1974). Episcopalian. Home: Tallahassee, Fla. Died Jan. 21, 2001.

WEBSTER, RALPH TERRENCE, metallurgical engineer; b. Crookston, Minn., Nov. 24, 1922; s. Clifford and Elmira Kathleen (Johnson) W.; m. Eileen Mathilde Carrow, Aug. 9, 1947; children: Paul David, Kathleen Mary, Keith Clifford, Richard Terrence. BS, U. Nev., 1949. Registered profl. engr., Calif., Oreg. Metall. engr. U.S. Steel, Pitts., 1949-51; group leader U. Calif. Radiation Lab., Livermore, Calif., 1951-52; asst. chief metallurgist Rockwell Nordston Valve Co., Oakland, Calif., 1953-54; sr. engr. Westinghouse Atomic Power, Pitts., 1954-59; supr. engr. Aerojet Nucleonics, San Ramon, Calif., 1959-62; plant mgr. metals div. Stauffer Corp., Richmond, Calif., 1962-64; prin. metall. engr. Teledyne Wah Chang, Albany, Oreg., 1964-91; metall. cons., from 1991. Part time tchr. Linn Benton Community Coll., Albany, 1964—. Contbr. articles to profl. publs. Active Episc. Ch., Lebanon, Oreg., 1975-92. Sgt. U.S. Army, 1942-48; 1st lt. USAF, 1949-64. Fellow ASTM (award of merit 1981, 1st vice chmn. 1979—); mem. Am. Soc. Metals (chmn. com.), Am. Welding Soc. (chmn. com.), Nat. Assn. Corrosion Engring., ASME (chmn. com.). Democrat. Home: Scio, Oreg. Deceased.

WEDDIGE, EMIL ALBERT, lithographer, art educator; b. Sandwich, Ont., Can., Dec. 23, 1907; came to U.S., 1909; s. Carl Albert and Marie Emma (Boismier) W.; m. Juanita Gertrude Pardon, Aug. 18, 1919. BS (hon.), Ea. Mich. U., 1934, DFA (hon.), 1973; student, Art Students League, N.Y.C.; studies with Emil Ganso, Woodstock, N.Y.; M of Design, U. Mich., 1937; DFA (hon.), Ea. Mich. U., 1973; D (hon.), Cleary Coll., 1992. Tchr. Dearborn (Mich.) Pub. Schs., 1934-35; supr. art Dearborn Sch. System, 1935-37; from instr. to prof. art U. Mich., Ann Arbor, 1937-73, prof. emeritus, 1974; owner pvt. studio Paris, from 1949, Ann Arbor. Cons. to John Weiss, Detroit, 1969—, to Louis G. Basso, West Bloomfield Hills, Mich., 1980—. One-man shows include Fishy Whale Studio, 1975, Washtenaw C.C., Ann Arbor, Tokyo, Japan, others; exhibited in Paris, 1986-87, T'Marra Gallery, Japan, 1991, U. Mich. Mus. of Art, Tokyo, Japan, 1993; permanent collections at Met. Mus. Art, N.Y.C., Libr. of Congress, Washington, Bibliotheque Nationale, Paris, Nat. Gallery of Art, Washington, U.S. Embassies, Gene Stapleton Collection, Plymouth, Mich., others; retrospective Jean-Paul Shusser Gallery, U. Mich., Creag Gallery, Birmingham, Mich.; commd. by Parke Davis & Co., Chrysler Corp., Dow Chem. Co., United Nergo S. F.; designer Mich. Artain; contbr. articles to profl. jours. Pres. Izaack Walton League, Ann Arbor, 1945—; established scholarship in music U. Mich., scholarship in art East Mich. U. Recipient Philip and Ester Klein prize Am. Color Print Soc., 1965, Print award Libr. of Congress, 1951, Print of Yr. award The Print Club, Phila., 1957, Eugene Power award for art work done for United Negro Found., 1993, United Meml. Coll. Found. award, 1st Founders award USA Artrain, 1999, others. Mem. Internat. Soc. Appraisers, Mich. Water Color Soc. (founder, pres., charter organizer), Mich. Printmakers (founder, pres.), Ann Arbor Art Assn. (exhbn. dir. 1943-55). Republican. Congregationalist. Home: Ann Arbor, Mich. Deceased.

WEED, RONALD DE VERN, engineering consulting company executive; b. Indian Valley, Idaho, Sept. 1, 1931; s. David Clinton and Grace Elizabeth (Lavendar) W.; m. Doris Jean Hohener, Nov. 15, 1953; children: Geraldine Gayle, Thomas De Vern, Cheryl Ann. BSChemE, U. So. Calif., 1957; MS in Chem. Engring., U. Wash., 1962; LLB, La Salle U., Chgo., 1975; postgrad., Century U., Beverly Hills, Calif., from 1979. Registered profl. engr., Washington, Calif. Devel. engr. GE Co., Richland, Washington, 1957-65, Battelle N.W. Labs., Richland, 1965-68; oper. plant engr. NIPAK, Inc., Kerens, Tex., 1968-72; aux. systems task engr. Babcock & Wilcox Co., Lynchburg, Va., 1972-74; materials and welding engr. Bechtel Group Cos., San Francisco, 1974-85; cons. engr. Cygna Energy Svcs., Walnut Creek, Calif., 1985-91, with inter city fund Oakland, Calif., 1991-94; corrosion engr. Gen. Physics Corp., Oakland, from 1994; sr. environ. engr. Jacobs Engring. Group. Contbr. rsch. reports, papers and chpts. in books; patentee in field. With U.S. Army, 1951-53. Mem. Am. Inst. Chem. Engrs., Am. Welding Soc., Nat. Assn. Corrosion Engrs. (cert., sect. vice chmn. and chmn. 1962-68). Avocations: reading, photography, gardening. Deceased.

WEEKS, HARVEY, retired therapist; b. Buffalo, June 26, 1925; s. Harvey and Elizabeth Maria (Kimbell) W.; m. Joan Remley, June 27, 1948; children: Florence Jane Spangler, Deborah Joan Tessmann. BA in Gen. Studies, U. Colo., 1949; MSW, UCLA, 1965. Lic. clin. social worker and marriage, family, and child counselor, Calif. Counselor Family Service Assn., San Diego, 1967-69; dir. social work services Northside Psychiat. Hosp., Fresno, Calif., 1970-73; psychiat. social worker Fresno County Health Dept., 1973-78; mental health specialist Pacific County, Long Beach, Wash., 1982-88, ret., 1989. Instr. social work dept. Calif. State U., Fresno, 1972-73, 76-77. Served as cpl. U.S. Army, 1943-46. Died Apr. 1, 2002.

WEGMAN, MYRON EZRA, retired pediatrician, educator, consultant; b. Bklyn., July 23, 1908; s. Max and Nettie (Finkelstein) W.; m. Isabel Howe, July 4, 1936 (dec. Jan. 1997); children: Judith (Mrs. John A. Hirst) (dec.), David Howe, Jane (Mrs. David D. Dunatchik), Elizabeth Gooding (Mrs. Ralph A. Petersen) (dec.). AB, CCNY, 1928; MD cum laude, Yale U., 1932; MPH, Johns Hopkins U., 1938. Diplomate Am. Bd. Preventive Medicine, Am. Bd. Pediatrics (ofcl. examiner). Intern, asst. resident, resident in pediatrics New Haven Hosp., 1932-36; instr. pediatrics Yale U., 1933-36; state pediatrician Md. State Health Dept., 1936-41; asst. prof. child hygiene Sch. Tropical Medicine, San Juan, P.R., 1941-42; dir. rsch. and tng. in child health, dir. sch. health N.Y.C. Health Dept., 1942-46; instr. pediatrics and lectr. pub. health adminstrn. Johns Hopkins U., 1939-46; asst. prof. pediatrics and pub. health Cornell U., 1942-46; asst. prof. pub. health Columbia U., 1940-46; prof. pediatrics, head dept. La. State U., 1946-52; pediatrician-in-chief Charity Hosp., New Orleans, 1946-52; prof. pub. health Sch. Pub. Health, U. Mich., Ann Arbor, 1960-74, dean, 1960-74, dean emeritus, 1974; prof. pediatrics U. Mich. Med. Sch., 1961-78, prof. emeritus, 1978, chmn. div. health sci., 1970-74; John G. Searle prof. pub. health, 1974-78; emeritus, 1978. Chief divsn. edn. and tng. Pan-Am. San. Bur., Regional Office for Ams., WHO, 1952-56; sec.-gen. Pan-Am. San. Bur., WHO Regional Office, 1957-60; vis. prof. U. Malaya, 1974, Centro Universitario de Salud Publica, U. Autónoma Madrid, 1990—, U Cin., 1993; external examiner Nat. U. Singapore, 1983; cons. Internat. Sci. and Tech. Inst., 1986-2004, Sch. Pub. Health, Zaire, 1987, Schs. Pub. Health, Indonesia, 1988; coord. Mich.-Madrid Sch. Pub. Health collaboration, 1990-2004 Editor: Public Health in the People's Republic of China, 1973; mem. editl. bd. Revista Mexicana de Salud Publica, 1990-2004. Pres. Assn. Schs. Pub. Health, 1963—66, Comprehensive Health Planning Coun., S.E. Mich., 1970—74; trustee Pan-Am. Health and Edn. Found., 1970—85, 1986—92, 1994—2000, pres., 1984—85, chmn. devel. com., 1991—2000, v.p., 1996—2000; trustee Nat. San. Found., 1969—84, emeritus trustee, from 1984; pres. Physicians for Social Responsibility, Ann Arbor, 1987—92; mem. com. on carcinogenesis of pesticides NAS, 1977—79, com. on advanced study in China, 1978—82; chmn. Task Force in Nat. Immunization Policy HEW, 1975—76; adv. com. Kellogg Nat. Fellowship Program, from 1982; rsch. adv. com. Resources for Future, 1978—84; spl. cons. State U. System Fla., 1982—87; mem. com. on prevention ctrs. CDC, 1986—94. Recipient Man of Yr. award CCNY, 1955; Clifford G. Grulee award Am. Acad. Pediatrics, 1958; Townsend Harris medal CCNY, 1961; Brontman prize Am. Public Health Assn., 1967; Disting. Service award Mich. Public Health Assn., 1974; Walter P. Reuther award for disting. service United Auto Workers, 1974; Sedgwick medal Am. Pub. Health Assn., 1974; Outstanding Alumnus award Johns Hopkins Sch. Hygiene, 1982; Disting. Service award Delta Omega Soc., 1982; Spes Hominum award Nat. Sanitation Found., 1986, Disting. Alumnus award Yale U. Med. Sch., 1987; Spl. award Korean Soc. Preventive Medicine, 1989. Fellow AAAS, Royal Soc. Health (hon.); mem. Am. Pediatric Soc., Soc. Pediatric Rsch., Am. Acad. Pediatrics (E.H. Christopherson award 1997), Am. Assn. World Health (v.p. 1979-82, 85-88, pres. 1982-84), Am. Pub. Health Assn. (chmn. exec. bd. 1965-70, pres. 1971-72), Fedn. Assn. Schs. Health Professions (1st pres. 1968-70),

Soc. Exptl. Biol. and Medicine, Peruvian, Eduadorian, Argentinian Pediatric Socs. (hon.), P.R. Pub. Health Assn. (hon.), Cosmos Club (Washington), Sigma Xi, Alpha Omega Alpha, Delta Omega, Phi Kappa Phi, Phi Beta Kappa. Home: Ann Arbor, Mich. Died Apr. 14, 2004.

WEGNER, WALDO WILBERT, retirement community and health care facility executive; b. Clay County, Iowa, Jan. 17, 1913; BSCE, Iowa State U., 1935. Registered profl. engr., Iowa, Minn. CIRAS Iowa State U., Ames, 1963-78; civil engr. Stenberg Concrete, Ames, 1978-90; chmn. Green Hills Residents Assn., Ames, 1988-95. Capt. U.S. Navy Res., 1941-78. Mem. NSPE (v.p. 1935—), Iowa Engring. Soc. (pres. 1956, Herbert Hoover award 1994), Ctr. for Indsl. Rsch. and Svc. (founding dir.). Republican. Avocations: spectator sports, golf, fish. Died June 2, 2001.

WEIDMAN, JUDITH LYNNE, news service director; b. Savanna, Ill., Mar. 6, 1941; d. Arthur Henry and Mildred Marie (Doty) W. BA, DePauw U., 1963, LHD (hon.), 1986; M in Div., Duke U., 1966. Asst. editor United Meth. Publ. House, Nashville, 1966-68; spl. assignment reporter Kokomo (Ind.) Trubune, 1968-71; assoc. editor United Meth. Reporter, Dallas, 1971-74; assoc. gen. sec./interpretation United Meth. Bd. Higher Edn. and Ministry, Nashville, 1975-84; editor, dir. Religious News Service, N.Y.C., from 1984; gen. sec. United Methodist Comm., Nashville. Editor: Women Ministers, 1981, Make Plain the Vision, 1983, Christian Feminism, 1984, Women in Ministry. Elder No. Ill. Conf. United Meth. Ch.; mem. commn. communications Nat. Council Chs., 1985—, faith and order commn., 1982-84. Named one of Outstanding Young Women of Am.; recipient Best Reportage award Associated Ch. Press, 1967. Mem. United Meth. Communications, Asian Women's Inst., Nat. Council Chs. Communications, Ecumedia, United Meth. Assn. Communicators (Best Newsletter award 1986), Women In Communications, The Deadline Club, Religious Pub. Relations Council. Democrat. Avocations: swimming, reading. Died Dec. 2000.

WEIKART, DAVID POWELL, educational research foundation administrator; b. Youngstown, Ohio, Aug. 26, 1931; s. Hubert James and Catherine (Powell) W.; m. Phyllis Saxton, Aug. 24, 1957; children: Cynthia, Catherine, Jennifer, Gretchen. AB, Oberlin Coll., 1953, DSc (hon.), 1992; PhD, U. Mich., 1966. Cert. sch. psychologist, Mich. Dir. spl. svcs. Ypsilanti (Mich.) Pub. Schs., 1957-70; pres. High Scope Ednl. Rsch. Found., Ypsilanti, 1970-2000, pres. emeritus, 2001—03. Dir. High Scope Inst., 1991, Netherlands, 1995, Ireland, 1999, U.K. Author: Young Children in Action, 1979, Changed Lives, 1984, Challenging the Potential, 1992, Significant Benefits, 1993, Educating Young Children, 1995, 2d edit., 2002, Lasting Difference, 1997; editor: How Nations Serve Young Children, 1991, Families Speak, 1994, What Should Young Children Learn, 1999. Mem., Nat. Commn. on Children, 1990-93. 1st lt. USMC, 1953-55. Recipient Lela Rowland award Nat. Mental Health Assn., Washington, 1987. Mem. Nat. Assn. for Edn. of Young Children (Lifetime Achievement award 1999). Avocation: camping. Died Dec. 9, 2003.

WEINBERG, MARTIN HERBERT, retired psychiatrist; b. Bklyn., Sept. 3, 1923; s. Abe and Ida (Levine) W.; m. Elizabeth Carwardine, Sept. 20, 1951; children: Mark David, Sheila Ann, Keith Warren. BS, CCNY, 1947; licentiate, Royal Coll. Surgeons, Edinburgh, Royal Coll. Physicians, Royal Faculty Physicians and Surgeons, Glasgow. Diplomate: Am. Bd. Psychiatry and Neurology, certified mental hosp. adminstr. Intern Kings County Med. Center, Bklyn., 1952; resident psychiatry Essex County Overbrook Hosp., Cedar Grove, N.J., 1954-56; staff psychiatrist Ancora State Hosp., Hammonton, N.J., 1956, chief service, 1957, clin. dir., 1958 60, asst. med. dir., 1960-62, dep. med. dir., 1962-67; med. dir. Trenton Psychiat. Hosp., 1967-73; dir. div. mental health and hosps. N.J. Dept. Instns. and Agys., 1973-74; med. dir. Trenton Psychiat. Hosp., 1974-79; surveyor psychiat. programs Joint Commn. Accreditation of Hosps., 1979-80; asst. supt. clin. services Phila. State Hosp., 1980-81; individual practice medicine specializing in psychiatry, 1981-86; ret., 1986. Staff psychiatrist Woods Sch., Langhorne, Pa., to 1986; cons. N.J. Neuropsychiat. Inst., 1981-83, New Lisbon State Sch., to 1985. Fellow Am. Psychiat. Assn., AAAS; mem. N.J. Psychiat. Assn. (past pres.) Home: Trenton, NJ. Died Nov. 21, 2003.

WEINER, HERBERT, psychiatry educator; b. Vienna, Feb. 6, 1921; came to U.S., 1939; s. Ludwig and Hedwig Blanche (Monath) W.; m. Dora Bierer, Nov. 27, 1953; children: Timothy E., Richard A., Anthony P. AB magna cum laude, Harvard U., 1943; MD, Columbia U., 1946. Prof. psychiatry Albert Einstein Coll. Medicine, N.Y.C., 1966-82, chmn. dept. psychiatry Montefiore Hosp. Med. Ctr., 1969-82, prof. neurosci., 1974-82, Melitta Sperling lectr., 1982; chief behavioral medicine UCLA, 1982, dir. clin. research tng., dept. psychiatry, 1982, prof. psychiatry, 1982. Cons. VA Wadsworth Med. Ctr., Los Angeles, 1982, VA Med. Ctr., Sepulveda, Calif., 1982, VA Brentwood (Calif.) Med. Ctr., 1984. Author: Psychobiology and Human Disease, 1977, Brain, Behavior & Bodily Disease, 1981. Research grantee NIMH, 1976-86, John D. and Catherine T. MacArthur Found., 1983—. Fellow Am. Psychiat. Assn., N.Y. Acad. Medicine; mem. Acad. Behavioral Med. Research (founder, pres. 1983-84), Internat. Coll. Psychosomatic Medicine (founder, pres. 1983), Los Angeles Psychoanalystic Soc. and Instn. Home: Encino, Calif. Died Nov. 12, 2002.

WEINER, RICHARD S. healthcare administrator; b. Yonkers, N.Y., July 14, 1951; s. Joseph and Muriel (Zucker) W.; m. Kathryn, Aug. 25, 1985; children: Jason C., Rebecca E. BA, U. Del., 1976, MC, 1978, PhD, 1981. Nat. cert. counselor, crt. behavioral medicine, mediator; diplomate med. psychotherapy, profl. counseling; diplomate in pain mgmt. Exec. dir. Inst. Pain Mgmt., Ceres, 1983-90; assoc. dir. planning Meml. Hosp., Ceres, Calif., 1987-90; exec. dir. Am. Acad. Pain Mgmt., from 1988. Contbr. articles to profl. jours. Hon. citizen ambassador Med. Exch. Program to People's Republic China, coleader to Russia, Czechoslovakia, Hungary, Vietnam, Singapore, Thailand. Mem. Am. Pain Soc. (profl. edn. com.), Am. Mental Health Counseling (editorial rev. bd.). Home: Twain Harte, Calif. Died May 7, 2002.

WEINHOUSE, SIDNEY, biochemist, educator; b. Chgo., May 21, 1909; s. Harry and Dora (Cutler) Weinhouse; m. Sylvia Krawitz, Sept. 13, 1935 (dec. Aug. 1957); children: Doris Joan, James Lester, Barbara May; m. Adele Klein, Dec. 27, 1969. BS, U. Chgo., 1933, PhD, 1936; D.MS (hon.) (hon.), Med. Coll. Pa., 1973; D.Sc. (hon.) (hon.), Temple U., 1976, U. Chieti, Italy, 1979, Jefferson Med. Coll., 1983. Eli Lilly fellow U. Chgo., 1936—38, Coman fellow, 1939—41; staff OSRD, 1941—44; with Houdry Process Corp., 1944—47; biochem. research dir. Temple U. Research Inst., 1947—50, prof. chemistry, 1952—77; emeritus prof. biochemistry Temple U. Med. Sch., from 1977; emeritus prof. Jefferson Med. Coll., 1991; sr. scientist Lankenau Med. Research Ctr., from 1987. Head dept. metabolic chemistry Lankenau Hosp. Research Inst. and Inst. Cancer Research, 1950—57; chmn. div. biochemistry Inst. Cancer Research, 1957—61; assoc. dir. Fels Research Inst., Temple U. Med. Sch., Phila., 1961—64, dir., 1964—67; mem. bd. sci. advisers Inst. Environ. Health, NIH. Contbr.; editor: Jour. Cancer Research, 1969—79. Bd. dirs. Am. Cancer Soc. Mem.: NAS, Am. Assn. Cancer Research, Am. Soc. Biol. Chemists, Am. Chem. Soc. Home: Philadelphia, Pa. Died Feb. 9, 2001.

WEINSTEIN, IRWIN MARSHALL, internist, hematologist; b. Denver, Mar. 5, 1926; m. Judith Braun, 1951. Student, Dartmouth Coll., 1943—44, Williams Coll., 1944—45; MD, U. Colo., Denver, 1949. Diplomate Am. Bd. Internal Medicine. Intern Montefiore Hosp., N.Y.C., 1949—50, jr. asst. resident in medicine, 1950—51; sr. asst. resident in medicine U. Chgo., 1951—52, resident in medicine, 1952—53, instr. in medicine, 1953—54, asst. prof. medicine, 1954—55; vis. assoc. prof. medicine U. Calif. Ctr. for Health Scis., L.A., 1955—56, assoc. clin. prof., 1957—60, clin. prof., 1970—2002; hon. prof., 1996—2002; sect. chief in medicine, hematology sect. Wadsworth Gen. Hosp., VA Ctr., L.A., 1956—59; pvt. practice medicine specializing in hematology and internal medicine L.A., 1959—2002; mem. staff Cedars-Sinai Med. Ctr., L.A., 1959—2002, chief of med. staff, 1972—74, bd. govs., 1974—2002. Assoc. bd. govs. hematology subcom. Am. Bd. Internal Medicine; mem. staff U. Calif. Ctr. Health Scis., Wadsworth Gen. Hosp., VA Ctr.; vis. prof. Hadassah Med. Ctr., Jerusalem, 1967; adv. for health affairs to Hon. Alan Cranston, 1971—92; mem. com. on space biology and medicine Space Sci. Bd.; active UCLA Comprehensive Cancer Ctr. Contbr. articles to profl. publs.; editor (with Ernest Beutler): Mechanisms of Anemia, 1962. Recipient Pioneer in Medicine award, Cedars-Sinai Med. Ctr., 1997. Master: ACP (gov. So. Calif. region I 1989—93); fellow: Israel Med. Assn. (hon.); mem.: AAAS, Western Soc. Clin. Rsch., Royal Soc. Medicine, Reticulo-Endothelial Soc., N.Y. Acad. Sci., Inst. of Medicine NAS, L.A. Soc. Nuc. Medicine, L.A. Acad. Medicine, Internat. Soc. Internal Medicine, Internat. Soc. Hematology, Assn. Am. Med. Colls., Am. Soc. Internal Medicine, Am. Soc. Hematology (exec. com. 1974—78, chmn. com. on practice 1978—87, mem. conn. 1974—78), Am. Fedn. Clin. Rsch., Alpha Omega Alpha. Home: Beverly Hills, Calif. Died July 19, 2002.

WEINTRAUB, KARL JOACHIM, history educator; b. Darmstadt, Fed. Republic Germany, Dec. 31, 1924; came to U.S., 1948; s. Micha B. Weintraub and Elizabeth (Hammel) Anders; m. D. Kathryn Lamphiear, Mar. 16, 1957 (div. 1980); m. Katy O'Brien, Apr. 23, 1983. BA, U. Chgo., 1949, MA, 1952, PhD, 1957; LHD (hon.), Knox Coll., 1986. Bibliographer U. Chgo. Librs., 1953-60; instr. U. Chgo. Coll., 1954-57, asst. prof., 1957-63; assoc. prof. U. Chgo., 1963-70, prof., 1970—2004, Disting. Svc. prof., 1978—2004, dean humanities, 1973-83. Author: Visions of Culture, 1966, The Value of the Individual, 1978; contbr. articles to profl. jours. Trustee Knox Coll., Galesburg, Ill., Art Inst., Chgo.; bd. govs. Sch. of the Art Inst., Chgo.. Recipient Quantrell award for Excellence in Teaching, 1960, 86, E. Harris Harbison award Danforth Found., 1967, Amoco Teaching award, 1995. Fellow Am. Acad. Arts and Scis.; mem. Am. Hist. Assn., Quadrangle Club (pres. 1960s). Mem. Soc. Of Friends. Home: Chicago, Ill. Died Mar. 25, 2004.

WEIR, THOMAS CHARLES, banker; b. Sandwich, Ill., Oct. 18, 1933; s. Glendon V. and Eleanor (Hoge) W.; m. Angela Di Giovanni. Grad., Pacific Coast Banking Sch., U. Wash., 1966. Mgr. consumer loans Barnett Nat. Bank, Cocoa, Fla., 1955-58; with 1st Interstate Bank Ariz., 1958-79; head retail banking div. 1st Nat. Bank Ariz., various locations, 1974-79, exec. v.p., 1975-79; chmn., chief exec. officer Home Fed. Savs., Tucson, 1979-87; chmn. Ariz. Commerce Bank, 1987-88; pres. Tucson Resources, Inc., 1988-89; pres., chief exec. officer Tucson Electric Power Co., 1989-90; fin. cons. Tucson, from 1990; pres. WD Enterprises, Inc., from 1994, Dependable Personnel, Inc., from 1994. Bd. dirs. Apollo Group, Inc.; pres. Dependable Nurses, Inc., Phoenix, 1994-96. With AUS, 1953-55. Mem.: Tucson Country, White Mountain Country. Republican. Episcopalian. Died Feb. 5, 2003.

WEISBERG, GERARD MAXWELL, city official, former judge, educator; b. Bklyn., Aug. 1, 1925; s. Reuben and Florence (Narder) W.; m. Blanche Silber, Feb. 28, 1954; children: Bruce Adam, Andrea Murphy. BA magna cum laude, St. John's U., 1946; JD, Columbia U., 1948; LLM, Bklyn. Law Sch., 1966. Bar: N.Y. 1948. Gen. practice law specializing in labor rels., N.Y.C., 1948-62; dep. commr. Dept. Licenses City of N.Y., 1962-66, commr. Dep. Markets, 1966-68, commr. Dept. Consumer Affairs, 1968-69, judge Criminal Ct., 1969-77; judge Ct. Claims State of N.Y., 1977-95; justice N.Y. State Supreme Ct., 1979-94; civil svc. commr. City of N.Y., 1996—98. Guest lectr. times Farmingdale State C.C., Manhattan C.C.; adj. prof., adj. lectr. law Kingsborough C.C., 1974-92; adj. asso. prof., lectr. labor rels. NYU., 1977-82. Kings County chmn. Liberal Party N.Y. State, 1962-65. Recipient citations U.S. Treasury Dept., 1943, 2d Spanish Evang. Ch., 1957, Presbyn. Ch. of Crossroads, 1961, United Hebrew Immigrant Aid Soc., Ch. St. Ignatius Loyola, 1964, Fedn. Jewish Philanthropies, 1967; recipient H.F. Stone scholarship Columbia U., 1948. Mem. N.Y. State Trial Lawyers Assn., Bklyn. Bar Assn. Home: Manahawkin, NJ. Died May 17, 2003.

WEISENFELD, MILDRED (MRS. ALBERT G. MOSLER), research organization executive; b. Bklyn. d. David and Augusta (Kagen) W.; m. Albert G. Mosler, June 24, 1956. Student, Bklyn. Coll., 1939-42. Founder, exec. dir. Fight for Sight, Inc., N.Y.C., from 1959. Founder Nat. Coun. to COmbat Blindness, 1946; organizer eye rsch. testimony subcom. Com. Interstate and Fgn. Commerce, U.S. Ho. of Reps., 1949. Recipient Eleanor Roosevelt Community Svc. citation, 1954, Citizens Meritorious Svc. award Med. Soc. County N.Y., 1962, Spl. Honorary award Glaucoma Found., 1991; named 1st lay person to receive award Am. Acad. Ophthalmology, 1974. Mem. Assn. Rsch. Vision and Ophthalmology (hon., Ann. Mildred Weisenfeld Excellence in Ophthalmology award established in 1986). Home: New York, NY. Died Dec. 1997.

WEISS, CHARLES KARL, rabbi; b. McKeesport, Pa., June 1, 1933; s. Phillip and Ethel (Weiss) W.; m. Miriam Weiss, Feb. 15, 1955; children: Shimon, Sheina, Yehudah, Golda. Rabbi, 1955. Rabbi Young Israel of Pitts., from 1961. Exec. dir. Yeshiva Sch., Pitts., 1961-85; adminstr. Congregation Poale Zedeck, Pitts., 1985—. Mem. Rabbinical Coun. Am., RAbbinical Coun. Pa. Home: Pittsburgh, Pa. Died Mar. 29, 2000.

WEISS, DONALD L(OGAN), retired sports association executive; b. Aurora, Ill., Aug. 22, 1926; s. Harry H. and Esther (Cook) W.; m. Charlene Thomas, Aug. 23, 1947; children: Deborah Lynn Weiss Geline, Barbara Jane Weiss Juckett, Pamela Sue Weiss Van der Lee. Student, Cornell Coll., Mt. Vernon, Iowa, 1943, 46; B.J., U. Mo., 1949. Newsman AP, Huntington, W.Va., 1949-51, sports writer-editor N.Y.C., 1951-63; publs. editor, info. dir. U.S. Golf Assn., N.Y.C., 1963-65; dir. info. Nat. Football League, N.Y.C., 1965-68, dir. public relations, 1968-77, exec. dir., 1977-94. Author (with Charles Day): The Making of the Super Bowl, 2002; contbr. articles on golf and football to profl. publs. With submarine svc., USN, 1944-46. Recipient Journalistic Achievement awards Sigma Delta Chi, Kappa Tau Alpha, 1948-49, Trustees' award Ohio U., 1978, Nat. citation Nat. H.S. Athletic Coaches Assn., 1990, Pete Rozelle award New Orleans Touchdown Club, 2000, Leather Helmet awrd NFL Alumni ASsn., 2004. Methodist. Home: Ponte Vedra Beach, Fla. Died Sept. 14, 2003.

WEISS, EGON ARTHUR, retired library administrator; b. Vienna, June 7, 1919; Came to U.S., 1938; s. Arthur and Martha (Schrecker) W.; m. Renee Hansi Weiss, July 11, 1942; children— Helen Louise, Steven Arthur Student, Berea Coll., Ky., 1938-40; AB, Harvard U., 1947; MA, Boston U., 1949; MSL.S., Simmons Coll., Boston, 1951. Prof. asst. Brookline (Mass.) Pub. Library, 1949-51, br. dir., 1951-58; asst. dir. library U.S. Mil. Acad., West Point, N.Y., 1958-62, libr., dir. libr., 1962-87, libr. emeritus, 1987—2003. Libr. cons., 1987—; trustee Southeast N.Y. Libr. Rsch. Coun., Poughkeepsie, 1966—; mem. John Cotton Dana Com., N.Y.C., 1975-79; cons. Pergamon Press, McLean, Va., 1983—. Co-author: Catalog Military Science Coll., 4 vols., 1969; contbr. to Funk & Wagnalls Ency., 1965—; appraiser rare books and spl. collections. Chmn. Black Rock Forest Preservation Council, Cornwall, N.Y., 1981—; trustee Mus. Hudson Highlands, Cornwall-on-Hudson, N.Y., 1968; vice chmn. Citizens Adv. Com., Cornwall, 1963-64; pres. Friends of Cornwall (N.Y.) Pub. Libr., 1989—, chmn. gifts and bequests, 1984—; counsellor Friends of West Point Libr., 1987—; trustee David Libr. of Am. Revolution, Pa., 1986—; alt. del. The White House Conf. on Libr. and Info. Svcs., 1991. Served to lt. col. U.S. Army, 1942-46, ETO Mem. ALA (pres. armed forces sect. 1966), Spl. Libraries Assn. (chmn. mil. library div. 1970), Archons of Colophon, Res. Officers Assn. (pres. Orange County 1965—), Assn. U.S. Army (bd. govs. 1984—) Clubs: Harvard (v.p. schs. and scholarship) (Poughkeepsie, N.Y.). Lodges: Toastmasters (edn. v.p. Newburgh, N.Y. 1968), Masons. Avocations: reading, swimming, tennis, playing violin. Home: La Jolla, Calif. Died Sept. 5, 2003.

WEISS, HERBERT KLEMM, retired aeronautical engineer; b. Lawrence, Mass., June 22, 1917; s. Herbert Julius and Louise (Klemm) W.; m. Ethel Celesta Giltner, May 14, 1945 (dec.); children: Janet Elaine, Jack Klemm (dec.). BS,

MIT, 1937, MS, 1938. Engr. U.S. Army Arty. Bds., Ft. Monroe, Va, 1938-42, Camp Davis, N.C., 1942-44, Ft. Bliss, Tex., 1944-46; chief WPN Systems Lab., Ballistic Research Labs., Aberdeen Proving Grounds, Md, 1946-53; chief WPN systems analysis dept. Northrop Aircraft Corp., 1953-58; mgr. advanced systems devel. mil. systems planning aeronutronic div. Ford Motor Co., Newport Beach, Calif., 1958-61; group dir., plans devel. and analysis Aerospace Corp., El Segundo, Calif., 1961-65; sr. scientist Litton Industries, Van Nuys, Calif., 1965-82; cons. mil. systems analysis, 1982-90. Mem. Sci. Adv. Bd. USAF, 1959-63, sci. adv. panel U.S. Army, 1965-74, sci. adv. commn. Army Ball Research Labs., 1973-77; advisor Pres.'s Commn. Law Enforcement and Adminstrn. Justice, 1966; cons. Office Dir. Def., Research and Engring., 1954-64. Contbr. articles to profl. jours. Patentee in field Recipient Commendation for meritorious civilian service USAF, 1964, cert. appreciation U.S. Army, 1976. Fellow AAAS, AIAA (assoc.); mem. IEEE, Ops. Rsch. Soc. Am., Cosmos Club. Republican. Home: Palos Verdes Peninsula, Calif. Died 2004.

WEISS, HERMAN, lawyer; b. Crystal, N.D., June 4, 1921; s. Herman Otto and Anna Carolyn (Schulz) W.; m. Donna Marie Ovind, Sept. 4, 1943; children— Donald A., Robert M., Elizabeth Gunderson, Jean M. Melton. Student St. Olaf Coll., 1943; J.D., U. N.D., 1949. Bar: N.D. 1949, U.S. Dist. Ct. N.D., 1958, U.S. Ct. Appeals (8th cir.) 1959, U.S. Ct. Appeals (9th cir.) 1969. Sr. ptnr. Hjellum, Weiss, Nerison, Jukkala, Wright & Paulson, Jamestown, N.D., 1949—; asst. state's atty., 1949-50; city atty. Jamestown, 1959-74. Bd. dirs. Anne Carlsen Sch., Jamestown, 1959-86, pres., 1973-86; bd. dirs. Luth. Hosps. and Homes Soc., Fargo, N.D., 1963—, 2d vice chmn., 1975-84, chmn. bd., 1984-86. Served to lt. AC, USNR, 1942-45. Decorated D.F.C. with one star, Air medal with five stars. Fellow Am. Coll. Probate Counsel, Am. Bar Found.; mem. ABA, State Bar Assn. N.D. (pres. 1969-70), Stutsman County Bar Assn. (pres. 1953-54), 4th Jud. Dist. Bar Assn. (pres. 1961-63), Jamestown C. of C. (pres. 1965-66), Am. Legion (post comdr. 1952-53, dist. dep. 1953-54), VFW, Order of Coif, Phi Alpha Delta. Lutheran. Clubs: Jamestown Lions (pres. 1960-61), Lions, Masons, Jamestown Country. Home: Jamestown, ND. Deceased.

WEISS, THEODORE RUSSELL, poet, editor; b. Reading, Pa., Dec. 16, 1916; s. Nathan and Mollie T. (Weinberg) W.; m. Renée Karol, July 6, 1941. BA, Muhlenberg Coll., 1938, Litt.D. (hon.), 1968; MA, Columbia U., 1940, postgrad., 1940-41; Litt.D. (hon.), Bard Coll., 1973. Instr. English U. Md., 1941, U. N.C., 1942-44, Yale U., 1944-46; prof. English, Bard Coll., 1946-68; vis. prof. poetry MIT, 1961-62; resident fellow creative writing Princeton U., 1966-67, prof. English and creative writing, 1968-87, emeritus, William and Annie S. Paton prof. ancient and modern lit., 1977-87, emeritus. Fannie Hurst vis. prof. lit. Washington U., St. Louis, 1978; prof. English poetry Cooper Union, 1988; poet-in-residence Monash U., Melbourne, Australia, 1982; lectr. New Sch. Social Research, 1955-56, N.Y.C. YMHA, 1965-67; lectr. for USIS in various countries; guest Inst. for Advanced Study, Princeton, N.J., 1986-87, 87-88, Villa Serbelloni, Bellagio, Italy, 1989; guest lectr. Peking U., Shanghai U., People's Republic China, 1991. Editor, pub. Quar. Rev. Lit., 1943—2003; editor poetry series Princeton U. Press, 1974-78; mem. poetry bd. poetry series Wesleyan U. Press, 1964-70; juror in poetry for poetry series, Bollingen Com., 1965, Nat. Book Awards, 1967, 77; author: Selections from the Note-Books of G.M. Hopkins, 1945; author: The Breath of Clowns and Kings: Shakespeare's Early Comedies and Histories, 1971, The Man from Porlock, Selected Essays, 1982; (poems) The Catch, 1951; Outlanders, 1960, Gunsight, 1962, The Medium, 1965, The Last Day and the First, 1968, The World Before Us: Poems, 1950-70, 1970, Fireweeds, 1976, Views and Spectacles, Selected Poems, 1978, Views and Spectacles, New and Selected Shorter Poems, 1979, Recoveries, 1982, A Slow Fuse, 1984, Collected Poems, 1987, paper back edit., 1988, A Sum of Destructions, 1994, Selected Poems, 1995; also articles and recs. Recipient Wallace Stevens award, 1956, Creative Arts award Brandeis U., 1977, Shelley Meml. award Poetry Soc. Am., 1989, Lifetime Achievement award Pen/Nora Magid, 1997, Oscar Williams and Gene Derwood award, 1997; fellow Ford Found., 1953-54, Ingram Merrill Found., 1974-75, Guggenheim Found., 1986-87 hon. fellow Ezra Stiles Coll., Yale U.; grantee Nat. Found. Arts and Humanities, 1967-68; subject of films Living Poetry, 1988, Yes, With Lemon, 1996. Home: Princeton, NJ. Died Apr. 15, 2003.

WEISSENBERGER, CHARLOTTE, media consultant; b. Bridgeport, Conn., Mar. 26, 1941; d. George Francis and Margaret Beatrice (Kosc) Mrazik; m. William G. Weissenberger, Apr. 20, 1968. BS, U. Bridgeport, 1964. V.p., media dir. Hutchins/Y&R, Rochester, N.Y., 1970-76; v.p., assoc. media dir. J. Walter Thompson, Atlanta, 1976-78, N.Y.C., 1978-82, sr. v.p., media dir. San Francisco, 1986-91; dir. media svcs. Coca Cola, Atlanta, 1982-85; sr. v.p., media dir. The Bloom Agy., Dallas, 1985-86; prin. CMW Media, San Rafael, Calif., from 1991. Pres. Fairhills Homeowners Assn., 1992. Recipient Creative Media award Ad Week, 1987; named one of Women We Love in Advt., Esquire Mag., 1990. Avocation: international travel. Home: San Rafael, Calif. Deceased.

WEISSHAAR, MILTON LEON, minister; b. Chgo., Dec. 14, 1921; s. Samuel and Elizabeth (Herr) W.; m. Jean Garnet Edwards, June 1950 (div. 1973); children: Barbara Pino, Janet Brigham, James Weisshaar; m. Eleanor Louise Bell, May 26, 1973. AB, U. Chgo., 1949; MA, Northwestern U., Evanston, 1952; BD, Garrett Sem., 1952. Ordained to ministry United Meth. Ch., 1953. Min. Wesley Meth. Ch., Wausau, Wis., 1952-58, First Meth. Ch., Oconomowoc, Wis., 1958-64, Pacific Beach United Meth. Ch., San Diego, 1966-71; asst. min. First United Meth. Ch., Santa Monica, Calif., 1972-78; min. North Long Beach (Calif.) United Meth. Ch., 1979-83, Crescenta Valley United Meth. Ch., Montrose, Calif., 1983-88, Los Altos United Meth. Ch., Long Beach, Calif., from 1988. Author: Prayers for Worship, 1977. Republican. Home: Tustin, Calif. Died May 29, 2001.

WELCH, CHARLES SMITH, telecommunications executive; b. Cleve., Oct. 17, 1942; s. Bierce Wilghos and Evelyn (Smith) W.; m. Barbara Jean Hunt, June 19, 1965; children: Laura, Kristen, Kathryn. BBA, Ohio U., 1964; postgrad., U. Colo., 1968-69; MBA, Case Western Res. U., 1973. With yellow pages sales dept. Ohio Bell, Cleve., 1965-67, communications cons., 1967-72, sales mgr., 1972-80; dist. mgr. AT&T, Cleve., 1980-84, br. mgr., 1984-92, area mgr. inbound svcs., from 1992. Dir. Priority Mgmt., Cleve. Active Greater Cleve. Growth Assn., 1985-90; chmn. AT&T campaign United Way, Cleve., 1988-89; chmn. membership Christian Businessmen's Com. USA, Cleve., 1990; active Eagle Scout Assn. Greater Cleve. With U.S. Army, 1964-65, 68-69. Named Eagle Scout Boy Scouts Am., 1966. Mem. Rotary (vocat. svcs. chmn. Cleve. chpt. 1987-88, 89-90, 4-Way Test award 1989). Republican. Avocations: collecting baseball cards and stamps, golf, bible study. Home: Cleveland, Ohio. Deceased.

WELCH, ERNEST WENDELL, lawyer; b. Cottondale, Fla., Oct. 5, 1917; s. Ernest Columbus and Edna Beatrice (Wallace) W.; m. Helen Phillips, Feb. 28, 1948; children: Kevin M., Lisa W. BSBA, U. Fla., 1939, JD, 1941. Bar: Fla. 1941, U.S. Dist. Ct. (no. dist.) Fla. 1941, U.S. Ct. Appeals (5th cir.) 1961. Asst. atty. gen. Fla., 1946-48; sole practice, Panama City, Fla., 1948-49; ptnr. Isler & Welch et al, 1949-73, Welch, Bennett, Logue, Burke & Blue, P.A., 1975-78, Welch & Munroe, P.A., Tallahassee, 1978-88, of counsel, 1988—; mem. Fla. Bd. Bar Examiners, 1960-67, chmn., 1965-66; mem. bd. govs. Fla. Bar, 1953-56. Served with USAAF, 1942-46. Fellow Am. Coll. Trial Lawyers, Am. Coll. Probate Counsel; mem. ABA, Govs. Club, Tallahassee Exch. Club. Home: Orlando, Fla.

WELCH, HARRY SCOVILLE, lawyer, retired gas pipeline company executive; b. Hugo, Okla., Nov. 14, 1923; s. John Calvin and Gaynell (Potts) W.; m. Peggy Joyce Weis, Dec. 18, 1954; children— Marshall Porter, Gay, Harry Scoville, Mary Margaret, Anne. BBA, U. Tex. at Austin, 1947, LL.B., 1949. Bar: Tex. 1948. Atty. Am. Republics Corp., Houston, 1949-51; ptnr. Turner, White, Atwood, McLane & Francis, Dallas, 1951-59; exec. asst., then v.p. Tenneco Inc., Houston, 1959-73; v.p., gen. counsel Panhandle Ea. Corp., Houston, 1973-74, sr. v.p., gen. counsel, 1975-85; v.p., gen. counsel Tex. Ea. Corp., Houston, 1987-89. Mem. bd. adjustment Hunter's Creek Village, Tex., 1970-77, chmn., 1973-77; mem. adv. bd. Internat. Oil and Gas Ednl. Ctr., Southwestern Legal Found., Dallas, 1975-85; bd. dirs. Barrett Resources Corp. Served with USNR, 1943-46. Fellow Tex. Bar Found.; mem. Am., Houston Bar Assns., State Bar Tex., Phi Kappa Sigma, Phi Alpha Delta. Clubs: Ramada (Houston). Presbyterian. Home: Houston, Tex. Died May 1, 1999.

WELLES, MELINDA FASSETT, artist, educational psychologist; b. Palo Alto, Calif., Jan. 4, 1943; d. George Edward and Barbara Helena (Todd) W. Student, San Francisco Inst. Art, 1959-60, U. Oreg., 1960-62; BA in Fine Arts, UCLA, 1964, MA in Spl. Edn., 1971, PhD in Ednl. Psychology, 1976; student fine arts and illustration Art Ctr. Coll. Design, 1977-80. Cert. ednl. psychologist, Calif. Asst. prof. Calif. State U., Northridge, 1979-82, Pepperdine, U.C.L.A., 1979-82; assoc. prof. curriculum, teaching and spl. edn. U. So. Calif., L.A., 1980-89; prof. liberal studies Art Ctr. Coll. Design, 1978—; mem. acad. faculty Pasadena City Coll., 1973-79, Otis Coll. Art and Design, L.A., 1986—, UCLA Extension, 1980-84, Coll. Devel. Studies, L.A., 1978-87, El Camino C.C., Redondo Beach, Calif., 1982-86; cons. spl. edn.; pub. adminstrn. analyst UCLA Spl. Edn. Rsch. Program, 1973-76; exec. dir. Atwater Park Ctr. Disabled Children, L.A., 1976-78; coord. Pacific Oaks Coll. in svc. programs for L.A. Unified Schs., Pasadena, 1978-81; mem. Southwest Blue Book, The Blue Ribbon, Friends of Robinson Gardens, Freedom's Found. at Valley Forge, The Mannequins, Costume Coun. L.A. County Mus. of Art., Assistance League of So. Calif. Author: Calif. Dept. Edn. Tech. Reports, 1972-76; editor: Teaching Special Students in the Mainstream, 1981, Educating Special Learners, 1986, 88, Teaching Students with Learning Problems, 1988, Exceptional Children and Youth, 1989, Left Brain Right Brain, 1997; group shows include: San Francisco Inst. Art, 1960, U. Hawaii, 1978, Barnsdall Gallery, L.A., 1979, 80; represented in various pvt. collections. HEW fellow, 1971-72; grantee Calif. Dept. Edn., 1975-76, Calif. Dept. Health, 1978. Mem. Am. Psych. Assn., Calif. Learning Disabilities Assn., Am. Council Learning Disabilities, Calif. Scholarship Fedn. (life), Alpha Chi Omega. Died Jan. 10, 2000.

WELLS, DANIEL RUTH, physics educator; b. N.Y.C., May 2, 1921; s. Daniel R. and Charlotte T. (Danziger) W.; m. Mary E. O'Connell, 1944; children: Donna Mary, Christina Mary. BME, Cornell U., 1942; MS, NYU, 1953; PhD, Stevens Inst. Tech., 1963. Instrument rated comml. pilot. Aero. engr. Chance-Vought Aircraft, Stratford, Conn., 1942-43; aero. engr. Sunsdet Aircraft, N.Y.C., 1943; engr. Indsl. Tng. Co., N.Y.C., 1946-50; design engr. Republic Aircraft, L.I., N.Y., 1950-55; physicist Plasma Physics Lab. Princeton U., 1955-63; assoc. prof. physics U. Miami, Fla., 1963-66, prof. physics, 1966-92, prof. emeritus; nuclear physicist rsch. div. NYU, N.Y.C., 1952-53; assoc. prof. physics Seton Hall U., South Orange, N.J., 1962-63. Cons. U.S. Army Piccatiny (N.J.) Arsenal, 1968-70, Sandia Labs. (N.Mex.), 1972-73, various Fla. cos., 1973—. Contbr. numerous articles to profl. jours.; patentee in field. 1st. lt. U.S. Army Air Force, 1943-46. Recipient AFOSR (1964-73) and NSF (1973-78) grants for plasma rsch. Mem. Am. Phys. Soc., Sigma Xi, Theta Chi, Sigma Pi Sigma. Avocations: flying, boating, tennis, golf. Home: Miami, Fla. Died May 28, 2001.

WELLS, EDWARD PHILLIPS, radiologist; b. Hanover, N.H., Oct. 4, 1916; s. Harry Artemas and Madeleine Roberta (Lucky) W.; m. Barbara Mix, Jan. 25, 1941; children: James C., Phyllis L. Fahey, Lucinda W. Graves, Patricia Wells-Bogue, Kenneth R. BA, Dartmouth Coll., 1939; MD, NYU, 1942. Diplomate Am. Bd. Radiology. Intern rotating Mary Hitchcock Hosp., Hanover, N.H., 1942-43; maj. U.S. Army Med. Corps, 1943-46; resident in radiology Mary Hitchcock Hosp., Hanover, 1946-48; radiologist Rutland (Vt.) Hosp., 1949-51, North Shore Radiol. Assoc., Danvers, Mass., 1951-82; adj. radiologist Hitchcock Hosp., Hanover, 1982-90; intermittent radiologist V.A. Hosp., White River Junction, Vt., 1984-94. Named to U.S. Olympic Ski Team, 1940. Mem. AMA, New Eng. Med. Assn., Vt. Med. Assn., N.H. Med. Assn., Lake Mitchell Trout Club, Black Brook Salmon Club. Avocation: trout and salmon fishing. Home: Grantham, NH. Died June 6, 1999.

WELLS, HUGH ALBERT, retired judge; b. Shelby, N.C., June 8, 1922; s. Charles Hudson and Tonce Walker Wells; m. Virginia DiaFabilo, Feb. 3, 1945 (div. Aug. 1958); children: Kathleen Mary, Hugh A. Jr.; m. Anne Hubner, June 30, 1962; 1 child, Joseph Walker; stepchildren: Rawell C. Cloninger Jr., Debi Cloninger McDaniel, Stephanie Cloninger Stadler, Michael Charles, Beth Cloninger Mayo. LLB, U. N.C., 1952. Bar: N.C. 1952. Gen. law practice, Shelby, N.C., 1952-60, Atlanta, 1960-63, Raleigh, N.C., 1963-70; appt. N.C. Utilities Commn., 1969, 73-75; v.p. gen. coun. N.C. Elec. Inc., 1975-76; spl. counsel to joint utilities rev. com. N.C. Gen. Assembly, 1976-77; exec. dir. Pub. Staff N.C. Utilities Commn., 1977-79; judge N.C. Ct. Appeals, 1979-92; ret.; chmn. N.C. Utilities Commn., 1992-96; ret., 1996. Democrat. Methodist. Avocations: reading, music. Home: Shelby, NC. Deceased.

WELLSTONE, PAUL, senator; b. Arlington, Va., July 21, 1944; s. Leon and Minnie W.; m. Sheila Wellstone, 1963; children: David, Marcia, Mark. BA, U. N.C., 1965, PhD Polit. Sci., 1969. Tchr. Carleton Coll., Minn.; U.S. senator from Minn., from 1991. Mem. U.S. Senate coms. small bus., energy and natural resources, Indian affairs, labor and human resources, Senate Dem. policy com., chmn. subcom. rural economy and family farming; mem. com. fgn. rels., 1997-2003; mem. com. health, edn., labor & pensions, 1991-2003; ranking mem. fgn. rels. subcom. on Near Easter and South Asian affairs, health, education, labor and pensions subcom. on employment safety and tng. Author: How the Rural Poor Got Power, Powerline. Dir. Minn. Community Energy Program. Democrat. Died Oct. 25, 2002.

WENIG, MARY MOERS, law educator; b. N.Y.C. d. Robert and Celia Lewis (Kauffman) Moers; m. Jerome Wenig, Dec. 19, 1946 (dec. Oct. 1994); children: Margaret Moers Wenig, Michael M. Wenig. BA, Vassar Coll., 1946; JD, Columbia U., 1951. Bar: N.Y. 1952, U.S. Ct. Appeals (2d cir.) 1954, U.S. Dist. Ct. (so. dist.) N.Y. 1956, Conn. 1977. Assoc. Cahill, Gordon, Reindel & Ohl, N.Y.C., 1951-57; assoc. Greenbaum, Wolff & Ernst, N.Y.C., 1957-60, Skadden, Arps, Slate, Meagher & Flom, N.Y.C., 1960-71; asst. prof. sch. law St. John's U., N.Y.C., 1971-75, assoc. prof. sch. law, 1975-78; rsch. affiliate Yale Law Sch., New Haven, 1978-79; prof. sch. law U. Bridgeport, Conn., 1978-82, Charles A. Dana prof. law, 1982-92; prof. sch. law Quinnipiac U., Bridgeport, 1992-95, Hamden, from 1995. Cons. The Merrill Anderson Co., Stratford, Conn., 1982—, Conn. Permanent Commn. on Status of Women, 1978-79; vis. prof. sch. law Pace U., White Plains, N.Y., 1979; commr. State of Conn. Permanent Commn. on Status of Women, 1985-91; mem. Conn. Gen. Assembly's Adv. Commn. to Study the Uniform Marital Property Act., 1985-86; bd. dirs. Tax Analysts. Author: Tax Management Portfolio on Disclaimer, 1992; editor: PLI Tax Handbooks, 1978-86; co-editor: Bittker, Fundamentals of Federal Income Taxation, student edit., 1983; co-author: (with Douthwaite) Unmarried Couples and the Law, 1979; contbr. tax, estate planning, trust and estates and marital property articles to profl. jours.; editorial adv. bd. Estate Planning for the Elderly & Disabled, 1987-90, Community Property Jour., 1986-88, Estate Planning, 1975—, Estates, Gifts & Trusts Jour., 1976—; assoc. editor: Encyclopedia of Marriage and the Family, 1996. Mem. probate com. Conn. Law Revision Commn., 1985—, com. to study the probate system Conn. Probate Assembly, 1988-91, task force on the legal rights of women in marriage NOW, 1987-91; 2nd cir. rep. Fedn. of Women Lawyers Jud. Screening Panel, 1979; bd. govs. Radcliffe Club N.Y., 1975-77; mem. 1st selectman's com. on taxation relief for the elderly Town of Westport, 1974-75; pres. bd. dirs. Conn. Women's Ednl. and Legal Fund, Inc., 1975-79, bd. dirs., 1973-79. Named Salute to Women honoree Outstanding Women of Conn., Greater Bridgeport YWCA, 1990, Women in Leadership honoree New Haven YWCA, 1979, honoree U. Bridgeport Sch. Law Women's Law Assn., 1990; Harlan Fiske Stone scholar Columbia U. Sch. Law, 1949; recipient Award for Equality United Nations Assn.-USA of Conn., 1987; Summer Stipend grantee NEH, 1984, rsch. grantee Conn. Bar Found., 1980. Fellow Am. Coll. Trust & Estate Counsel (bd. regents 1985-91); mem. ABA (advisor to NCCUSL 1980-84, sect. coun. mem. 1970-72), Internat.

Acad. Estates & Trust Law (exec. coun. 1992-94), Conn. Bar Assn. (sects.' exec. coun., Disting. Svc. commendation 1977), Assn. Am. Law Schs., Assn. of Bar of City of N.Y., N.Y. State Bar Assn., Am. Law Inst., Am. Coll. Tax Counsel. Democrat. Jewish. Home: Brooklyn, NY. Died Jan. 18, 2003.

WENTWORTH, MICHAEL JUSTIN, curator; b. Detroit, June 15, 1938; s. Harold Arnold and Marian (Jones) W. MFA, U. Mich., 1962; PHD, Harvard U., 1976. Curator, acting dir. Smith Coll. Mus. Art, Northhampton, Mass., 1968—69; dir. Rose Art Mus., Brandies U., Waltham, Mass., 1970—74; assoc. prof. Wellesley Coll., Mass., 1976; curator Boston Athenaeum, Mass., from 1985. Author: Tissot: Catalogue Raisonné of Prints, 1976, James Tissot, 1984, Tissot, 1988, 50 Books in the Collection of the Boston Athenaeum, 1994, The Boston Library Society, 1995. Home: Boston, Mass. Died Sept. 3, 2002.

WENTZ, JANET MARIE, state legislator; b. McClusky, N.D., July 21, 1937; d. Charles G. and Martha (Schindler) Neff; m. Thomas Arthur Wentz, 1957; children: Elizabeth, Karin, Thomas. Student, Westmar Coll., 1955-57, U. Minn., 1960-62, Minot State Coll., 1967-70. Registered securities rep.; mem. from dist. 3 N.D. State Ho. of Reps., Bismarck, from 1975, vice chmn., then chmn. appropriations com., spkr., from 2003. Bd. dirs. Ind. Peace Gardens; mem. Commn. on Status of Women in N.D. United Meth. Ch., rep. N.D. Conf. Chs., 1973—; mem. Ct. Svc. Adminstrn. Com.; mem. N.D. Displaced Homemaker Program, Souris Valley Humane Soc. Mem. LWV, PEO, Orgn. Women Legislators, Nat. Assn. Securities Dealers, Minot C. of C. Died Sept. 15, 2003.

WENZEL, LEONARD ANDREW, engineering educator; b. Palo Alto, Calif., Jan. 21, 1923; s. Robert N. and Frances A. (Browne) W.; m. Mary E. Leathers, Oct. 21, 1944; children: Frances B., Alma L., Jesse R., Sara V.; m. Constance L. Houser, Jan. 1, 2000. BSChemE, Pa. State U., 1943; MSChemE, U. Mich., 1948, PhD in Chem. Engring., 1950. Registered profl. engr., Pa. Jr. rsch. engr. Phillips Petroleum Co., Bartlesville, Okla., 1943-44; jr. rsch. scientist Mellon Inst., Pitts., 1944; rsch. engr. Colgate-Palmolive, Jersey City, 1949-51; asst. prof. engring. Lehigh U., Bethlehem, Pa., 1951—56, assoc. prof., 1956-60, prof., 1960-88, chmn. dep. chem. engring., 1962-83, prof. emeritus, 1988—2003. Project dir. UNESCO, Bucaramanga, Colombia, 1969-70, cons. in chem. engring., Maracaibo, Venezuela,, 1970-73; cons. Air Products and Chems., Allentown, Pa., 1951-80, Exxon, Baytown, Tex., 1983-86; chief scientist Arencibia Techs., Inc., Allentown, 1987-93; former pres. L.A. Wenzel, Inc., Bethlehem; dir. of tech. Eco-Gen Techs., Inc., Bethlehem, 1993-96. Co-author: Principles of Unit Operations, 1960, Introduction to Chemical Engineering, 1961, Chemical Process Analysis: Mass and Energy Balances, 1987. Bd. dirs. South Bethlehem Neighborhood Ctr., Bethlehem Housing Authority, 1988-2002. Lt. (j.g.) USN, 1944-46, PTO. Fellow Am. Inst. Chem. Engrs.; mem. Am. Chem. Soc., Am. Soc. for Engring. Edn. Avocations: stamps, gardening, travel. Home: Bethlehem, Pa. Died Nov. 23, 2003.

WERLER, JOHN E. zoo director; b. Oldenburg, Germany, June 10, 1922; arrived in U.S., 1926; m. Ingrid Longstrom (dec. 2003). With Houston Zoo, 1956—92, Dir., 1963—92. Co-author (with James R. Dixon): Texas Snakes: Distribution, Identification, and Natural History, 1992. Died Mar. 21, 2004.

WERNER, WALTER AUGUST, retired ranger captain; b. Taylor, Tex., July 5, 1930; s. Walter August and Hannah Margaret (Walther) W.; m. Jeanne Francis Fannin, Aug. 16, 1952; children: Elizabeth Virginia Bailey, Robert Blake. Student, Daniel Baker Coll., Brownwood, Tex., 1949-50. Mem. Tex. Hwy. Patrol, Fredericksburg, 1951-66, Tex. Rangers, Navasota, 1966-70, sgt. San Antonio, 1970-74, capt. Lubbock, 1974-81, asst. chief criminal law enforcement Austin, 1981-85; police chief City of Navasota, 1986-89, City of Fredericksburg, 1989-98. Lt. col. U.S. Army, 1949-81, Tex. Nat. Guard. Named Outstanding Young Man of Gillespie County, Fredericksburg Jr. C. ofC., 1961; recipient Outstanding Svc. award C. of C., Fredericksburg, 1998. Republican. Presbyterian. Avocations: hunting, fishing, woodworking. Home: Navasota, Tex. Died Nov. 1, 2000.

WERNICK, SIDNEY WILLIAM, retired judge; b. Phila., Nov. 29, 1913; s. Abraham David and Sadie (Osteicher) W.; m. Charlotte Lucille Berman, Aug. 6, 1939; children: Judith Wernick Gilmore, Lawrence. BA, U. Pa., 1934, MA, 1935; PhD, Harvard U., 1937, LLB, 1940; LLD (hon.), U. Maine, 1974, Bowdoin Coll., 1981. Judge U.S. Supreme Ct., Maine. Home: Chevy Chase, Md. Deceased.

WERTZ, DOROTHY CORBETT, sociologist; b. Buffalo, May 18, 1937; d. William Joseph and Helen (Leggett) Corbett; m. Richard Wayne Wertz, Jan. 29, 1967. AB, Radcliffe Coll., 1958; postgrad., London Sch. Econ., 1959; MA, Harvard U., 1961, PhD, 1966. Instr. Bryn Mawr Coll., 1963-65; asst. prof. Boston Coll., 1966-68, Bridgewater (Mass.) State Coll., 1969-71; instr. Lowell (Mass.) Technol. Inst., 1971-72; asst. prof. U. Bridgeport, Conn., 1972-73; assoc. prof. U. New Haven, 1973-74, Suffolk U., Boston, 1975-81; NSF fellow Sch. of Pub. Health Boston U., Boston, 1981-84, assoc. rsch. prof. Sch. of Pub. Health, 1984-86, rsch. prof. Sch. of Pub. Health, from 1986; sr. scientist Shriver Ctr., Waltham, Mass., 1991—2000; rsch. prof. U. Mass. Med. Sch., Waltham, from 2000; sr. scientist Am. Soc. Law, Medicine and Ethics, Boston, from 2003. Cons., advisor Sci. Coun. Can., Ottawa, 1987-90, World Health Orgn., Geneva, 1993—; researcher, reviewer Royal Commn. on New Reproductive Techs., Ottawa, 1988-92; mem. sci. and industry adv. com. Genome Can., 2003--; cons. NIH, Bethesda, 1990-91. Author: Lying-In: A History of Childbirth in America, 1989, Ethics and Human Genetics, 1989, Guidelines on Ethical Issues in Medical Genetics and the Provision of Genetics Services, 1995; contbr. articles to profl. jours. Recipient Silver Gavel award ABA, 1991. Mem. APHA, Am. Soc. of Human Genetics (social issues com. 1991-94), European Soc. Human Genetics, Human Genome Orgn. (mem. ethics com. 1999—). Achievements include organization of worldwide surveys regarding ethical views. Home: Westport Point, Mass. Died Apr. 29, 2003.

WESCOE, W(ILLIAM) CLARKE, physician; b. Allentown, Pa., May 3, 1920; s. Charles H. and Hattie G. (Gilham) W.; m. Barbara Benton, Apr. 29, 1944; children: Barbara, William, David. BS, Muhlenberg Coll., 1941; ScD, 1957; MD, Cornell U., 1944. Intern N.Y. Hosp., 1944-45, resident, 1945-46; asst. prof. pharmacology Med. Coll., Cornell U., 1949-51; prof. pharmacology and exptl. medicine U. Kans. Med. Center, from 1951, dir., 1953-60; dean U. Kans. Med. Center (Sch. Medicine), 1952-60; chancellor U. Kan., 1960-69; v.p. med. affairs Sterling Drug Inc., N.Y.C., 1969-71, exec. v.p., 1971-72, vice chmn., 1972-74, chmn., 1974-85. Editor: Jour. Pharmacol. and Exptl. Therapeutics, 1953-57. Chmn. China Med. Bd. N.Y., N.Y.C., 1960-90; bd. dirs. N.Y. Stock Exch., 1986-92, Tinker Found., 1968-93, Minn. Opera, 1992-97; trustee emeritus Samuel Kress Found., Columbia U.; chmn. John Simon Guggenheim Meml. Found., 1983-91, Muhlenberg Coll. Markle scholar med. scis., 1949-54 Fellow ACP; mem. Am. Soc. Pharmacology and Exptl. Therapeutics, Phi Beta Kappa, Sigma Xi, Alpha omega Alpha, Alpha Tau Omega, Nu Sigma Nu. Home: Mequon, Wis. Died Feb. 29, 2004.

WESCOTT, ROGER WILLIAMS, anthropologist, educator; b. Phila., Apr. 28, 1925; s. Ralph Wesley and Marion (Sturges-Jones) W.; m. Hilja J. Brigadier, Apr. 11, 1964; children: Walter, Wayne. Grad., Phillips Exeter Acad., 1942; BA summa cum laude, Princeton U., 1945, MA, 1947, PhD, 1948; MLitt, Oxford U., 1953. Asst. prof. history and human relations Boston U. and Mass. Inst. Tech., 1953-57; assoc. prof. English and social sci., also dir. African lang. program Mich. State U., 1957-62; prof. anthropology and history So. Conn. State Coll., 1962-66; prof., chmn. anthropology and linguistics Drew U., Madison, N.J., 1966-91; Presdl. prof. Colo. Sch. Mines, 1980-81; first holder endowed Chair of Excellence in Humanities U. Tenn., 1988-89; shipboard lectr., from 1980. Fgn. lang. cons. U.S. Office Edn., 1961; pres. Sch. Living, Brookville, Ohio, 1962-65; exec. dir. Inst. Exploratory Edn., N.Y.C., 1963-66; Korzybski lectr. Inst. Gen. Semantics, N.Y.C., 1976; forensic linguist N.J. State Cts., 1982-83; host Other Views, N.J. Cable TV, Trenton, 1985-87; 1st v.p. World Bank Internat. Terms; dean distance learning program Mind Exploration Corp., Phoenix. Author: A Comparative Grammar of Albanian, 1955, Introductory Ibo, 1961, A Bini Grammar, 1963, An Outline of Anthropology, 1965, The Divine Animal, 1969, Language Origins, 1974, Visions, 1975, Sound and Sense, 1980, Language Families, 1986, Getting It Together, 1990, Predicting the Past An Exploration of Myth, Science, and Prehistory, Comparing Civilizations An Unconsensual View; also poems and articles; host, program dir. Other Views, N.J. Cable TV, 1985-87; co-author: Sorokin and Civilization, 1996. Rhodes scholar, 1948-50; Ford fellow, 1955-56; Am. Council Learned Socs. scholar, 1951-52 Fellow AAAS, Am. Anthrop. Assn., African Studies Assn.; mem. Acad. Ind. Scholars (life mem.), Assn. for Poetry Therapy, Internat. Soc. Comparative Study Civilizations (co-founder, pres. 1992—), Linguistic Assn. Can. and U.S. (pres. 1976-77), Internat. Linguistic Assn., Linguistic Soc. Am., Com. for Future, Soc. for Hist. Rsch. (v.p.), Internat. Orgn. for Unification Terminological Neologisms (1st v.p.), World Hist. Assn., Assn. for Study of Lang. in Prehistory (v.p., co-editor), Phi Beta Kappa. Home: Southbury, Conn. Deceased.

WESOLOWSKI, ADOLPH JOHN, electrical engineer; b. Chelsea, Mass., June 4, 1916; s. Joseph A. and Adamina (Ploharska) W.; B.S., Harvard U., 1938; postgrad. Pa. State U., 1958-59; M.S. in Engring., Ariz. State U., 1964; m. Eleanor Louise Currier, June 3, 1939 (div. 1967); children—Mary Eleanor (Mrs. Harold A. Downing), Eleanor Louise (Mrs. John Tennyson), Joseph Walter, Allen Joseph, Frank James, Steven Michael; m. Gabrielle Bourgon, 1968. Turbine engr. Gen. Electric Co., Lynn, Mass., 1938-41; field engr., Boston, 1941-45, motor design engr., Lynn, 1945-50, chief aircraft generator engr., Lynn, also Erie, Pa., 1950-59; sr. design engr. AiResearch Mfg. Co., Phoenix, 1959-66; project engr. Garrett Mfg. Ltd., Rexdale, Ont., Can., 1966-68, Leland Airborne Products, Vandalia, Ohio, 1968-70; chief engr. Dyna Corp., Dayton, Ohio, 1970-75; pres. World Wide Artifacts Inc., 1975—; cons. engr. electro-mech. design. Registered profl. engr., Mass. Mem. IEEE (chmn. aerospace energy conversion com. 1962-64), Internat. Aerospace Elec. Conf. (chmn. 1964), Phoenix C. of C., Greater Erie C. of C., Ohio Archaeol. Soc., Central States Archaeol. Soc., Artifact Soc. (founder). Club: Point of Pines Yacht (past fin. sec.) (Revere, Mass.). Patentee in field. Deceased, 1994. Home: Phoenix, Ariz.

WEST, ARTHUR JAMES, II, retired biologist, educator; b. Boston, Dec. 14, 1927; s. Arthur James and Lillian (Laming) W.; m. Carolyn Barbara Ross, June 4, 1948 (div. May 1972); children: Arthur James, Gregory Thomas, Donald Robert; m. Linda Jean Cummings, July 21, 1985 (div. Sept. 1993); children: Melissa Ida, Benjamin Cummings; m. Pamela Kay Yenco, Oct. 2, 1999. BS, Suffolk U., 1951, MA in Edn., 1956; MS, U. N.H., 1962, PhD in Zoology, 1964. Faculty Suffolk U., Boston, 1952-68, assoc. prof. biology, 1964-65, prof., 1965-68, co-chmn. biology, 1964-68; dean, prof. div. natural sci. New Eng. Coll., Henniker, N.H., 1968-70; prof., chmn. dept. biology Suffolk U., 1970-72, 78-88; assoc. program dir. Pre-coll. Edn. in Scis./NSF, 1972-73; prof. dept. biology Suffolk U., 1973-89, prof. emeritus, from 1989. Acad. v.p. for curriculum devel. U. San Juan Capistrano, 1992-93; owner, operator Subway of Farmington and Skowhegan, Maine, 1990-98, chmn. adv. coun. 1993-94, Art W. Enterprises Nev. Corp., 1997-2001; treas. Dahl Assocs., Inc., 1991-98, Lamb Assocs., Inc., 1990—; CEO, Mountain View Chocolate Shoppe, 2001—; dir. R.S. Friedman Cobscook Bay Lab., 1975-88; mem. exec. com. MIT/SEA Grant Consortium Program, 1979-85; asst. prof., chmn. biology Mass. Coll. Optometry, 1957-60; instr., chmn. sci. Emerson Coll., 1956-59; staff Norwich U., 1960; cons. Ginn & Co. Sci. Publs., 1967-70; hon. cons., parasitologist Akvapatologisk Lab., 1987; civil svc. examiner Mass. Dept. Natural Resources, 1965-72; bd. dirs. Life Enrichment Advancing People (LEAP), 1997—. Founding pres. Keltown Civic Assn., 1954; chmn. Woburn United Fund, 1958; mem. Woburn Sch. Com., 1955-60, chmn. 1957; chmn. Woburn YMCA, 1958, Woburn Rep. City Com., 1959, New Vineyard Town Com., 1990; vice-chmn. Franklin County Rep. Com.; mem. commn. on ocean mgmt. Mass. Served with USN, 1946-47, with Res., 1947-52. NSF grantee, 1968-71, 70-71, 75-82. Mem. Mass. Bay Marine Studies Consortium (pres. 1982-85), Mass. Marine Educators, Inc. (com. 1978-86), AAAS, Am. Inst. Biol. Scis., Nat. Marine Edn. Assn. (dir. 1976-78, pres. 1985-86), Ea. Star, Rotary, Masons, Sigma Xi (Suffolk U. club pres. 1972), Sigma Zeta, Phi Beta Chi (pres. 1951), Beta Beta Beta, Phi Sigma. Home: New Vineyard, Maine. Died June 30, 2002.

WEST, JOHN CARL, lawyer, former ambassador, former governor; b. Camden, S.C., Aug. 27, 1922; s. Shelton J. and Mattie (Ratterree) W.; m. Lois Rhame, Aug. 29, 1942; children: John Carl Jr., Douglas Allen, Shelton West Bosley. BA, The Citadel, 1942; LB magna cum laude, U. S.C., 1948; D (hon.), The Citadel, U. S.C., Davidson Coll., Presbyn. Coll., Francis Marion Coll., Wofford Coll., Coll. Charleston. Bar: S.C. 1947. Ptnr. West, Holland, Furman & Cooper, Camden, S.C., 1947-70; state senator Kershaw County State of S.C., 1954-66; lt. gov. State of S.C., 1966-70, gov., 1971-75; ptnr. West, Cooper, Bowen, Beard & Smoot, Camden, S.C., 1975-77; amb. to Saudi Arabia, 1977-81; sr. ptnr. West & West, P.A., Hilton Head Island, 1981-88. Disting. prof. Middle East Studies U. S.C., 1981-2004; of counsel McNair Law Firm, Hilton Head Island, S.C., 1988-92, Bethea, Jordan & Griffin, P.A., Hilton Head Island, S.C., 1993-2004. Maj. AUS, 1942-46. Decorated Army commendation medal; comdr. Order of Merit (West Germany); recipient Freedom award S.C. C. of C. Mem. Phi Beta Kappa. Democrat. Presbyterian. Died Mar. 21, 2004.

WEST, WILLIAM BEVERLEY, III, lawyer; b. Ft. Worth, Feb. 5, 1922; s. William Beverley Jr. and Ella Louise (Moore) W. BA, U. Tex., 1942, LL.B., 1948; Indsl. Adminstr., Harvard Grad. Sch. Bus. Adminstrn., 1943; LL.M., Columbia, 1949; grad., Command and Gen. Staff Sch. Bar: Tex. 1949. Practice in, Ft. Worth; asst. U.S. atty. No. Dist. Tex., 1953, 1st asst. U.S. atty., 1957-58, U.S. atty., 1958-61; exec. asst. to asst. atty. gen., lands div. Dept. Justice, 1961-63; ptnr. Clark, West, Keller, Butler & Ellis, Dallas, 1963-89, of counsel, from 1989. Mem. adv. bd. Southwestern Law Enforcement Inst., Dallas, 1959-82; mem. adv. com. on criminal rules U.S. Jud. Conf., 1973-77; mem. lawyers adv. com. U.S. Ct. Appeals, 5th Cir., 1985-87. Bd. dirs. prison ministry Kairos, Inc. of Tex., 1990-96, chmn., 1992; mem. nat. bd. Kairos Inc., 1991-96, sec., 1992-96; lay eucharistic min. Episc. Ch. Capt. AUS, 1942-46. Decorated Bronze Star. Fellow Tex. Bar Found., Southwestern Legal Found.; mem. ABA (chmn. sect. jud. adinstrn. 1970-71, ho. dels. 1971-74, sect. litigation, co-editor Antitrust Litigator 1988-92), Inst. Jud. Adminstrn. N.Y.C., Nat. Assn. Former U.S. Attys. (bd. dirs. 1990-93), Nat. Inst. for Trial Advocacy (dir. 1970-83), Fed. Bar Assn., Am. Judicature Soc., Ft. Worth Club, City Club (Dallas), Delta Tau Delta, Phi Alpha Delta, Pi Sigma Alpha. Home: Fort Worth, Tex. Died December 4, 1998.

WESTER, KEITH ALBERT, film and television recording engineer, real estate developer; b. Seattle, Feb. 21, 1940; s. Albert John and Evelyn Grayce (Nettell) W., m. Judith Elizabeth Jones, 1968 (div. Mar. 1974); 1 child, Wendy Elizabeth; m. Joan Marie Bursler, Feb. 2001. AA, Am. River Coll., Sacramento, 1959; BA, Calif. State U., L.A., 1962; MA, UCLA, 1965. Lic. multi-engine rated pilot. Prodn. asst. Sta. KCRA-TV, Sacramento, 1956; announcer Sta. KSFM, Sacramento, 1960; film editor, sound rec. technician Urie & Assocs., Hollywood, Calif., 1963-66; co-owner Steckler-Wester Film Prodns., Hollywood, 1966-70; owner Profl. Sound Recorders, Studio City, Calif., from 1970, Aerochar-ter, Studio City, from 1974, Wester Devel., Sun Valley, Coeur d'Alene, Idaho, from 1989, also Studio City, from 1989; majority stockholder Channel 58 TV, Coeur d'Alene/Spokane, 1993-99. Prodn. sound mixer: (films) Cradle to Grave, 2002, Carolina, 2001, Orange County, 2001, Princess Diaries, 2000, The Perfect Storm, 1999 (acad. award co-nominee for best sound 2001), Never Been Kissed, 1999, Runaway Bride, 1999, Armageddon, 1998 (Acad. award co-nominee 1999), Mouse Hunt, 1997, Air Force One, 1997 (Acad. award co-nominee for best sound 1998), Shadow Conspiracy, 1996, G.I. Jane, 1997, The Rock, 1996

(Acad. award co-nominee for best sound, 1997), Waterworld, 1995 (Acad. award co-nominee for best sound 1996), The Shadow, 1994, Wayne's World II, 1993, Coneheads, 1993, Body of Evidence, 1992, Indecent Proposal, 1992, School Ties, 1991, Frankie and Johnny, 1991, Another You, 1991, Thelma and Louise, 1990, Shattered, 1990, Desperate Hours, 1989, Joe vs. the Volcano, 1989, Black Rain, 1989 (Acad. award co-nominee 1990), Sea of Love, 1988, Real Men, 1985, Mask, 1984, Thief of Hearts, 1983, Young Doctors in Love, 1982, First Monday in October, 1981. Mem. NATAS (Emmy award An Early Frost 1986, Emmy nominations in 1982, 84, 85, 87), SAG, Acad. Motion Picture Arts and Scis., Brit. Acad. Film and TV Arts (award nomination for The Rock 1997, The Perfect Storm 2001), Cinema Audio Soc. (sec. 1985-91, Sound award 1987), Soc. Motion Picture and TV Engrs., Internat. Sound Technicians, Local 695, Assn. Film Craftsmen (sec. 1967-73, treas. 1973-76), Aircraft Owners and Pilots Assn. (Commemorative Air Force col.), Am. Radio Relay League (K6DGN). Home: Studio City, Calif. Died Nov. 1, 2002.

WESTON, COLE, photographer; b. L.A., Jan. 30, 1919; s. Edward and Flora (Chandler) W.; m. Dorothy Hermann, 1940 (div.); m. Helen Prosser, 1951 (div.); children: Ivor, Kim, Cara, Rhys; m. Margaret Woodward, 1963; 1 child, Matthew. Student, Cornish Sch., Seattle, 1937-40; studies with Edward Weston. With Lockheed Aircraft Corp., 1940-43; photographer Life mag., L.A., 1945-46; photog. studio asst. to Edward Weston Carmel, Calif., 1946-58; executor Edward Weston's estate, 1958; ind. photographer, 1958—2003. Founder Weston Trout Farm, Carrapata Canyon, Calif., 1949; stage dir. Forest Theatre, Carmel, 1951; founder Old Mill Stream Trout Farm at Knott's Farm, Buena Park, Calif., 1959; cultural dir. Sunset Ctr., Carmel, 1966-69; co-founder Three Generation Gallery, Carmel, 1981. Exhibited in group show at Focus Gallery (with Edward Weston), 1971, 73; one-man shows include Afterimage Gallery, Dallas, 1974, Halsted 831 Gallery, Birmingham, Mich., 1975, 77, Witkin Gallery, N.Y.C., 1976, Leiserowitz Gallery, Des Moines, 1978, Deja Vue Gallery, Toronto, Ont., Can., 1979, Susan Spiritus Gallery, Newport Beach, Calif., 1981, Maine Photog. Workshops, Rockport, 1982, Focus Gallery, San Francisco, 1985, Equivalents Gallery, Seattle, 1985, Daytona Beach (Fla.) Community Coll., 1986; represented in permanent collections Mus. Modern Art, N.Y.C., Internat. Mus. Photography, George Eastman House, Rochester, N.Y., Fogg Art Mus., Harvard U., Cambridge, Mass., Phla. Mus. Art, L.A. Mus. Art; author: Cole Weston: 18 Photographs, 1981. Ind. Progressive Party candidate for U.S. Congress, 1948. With USN, 1943-45. Died Apr. 20, 2003.

WETHERILL, PHYLLIS STEISS, writer, publisher; b. Ft. Wayne, Ind., Aug. 16, 1923; d. Fred Wilhelm and Myrta May (Flightner) Steiss; m. George West Wetherill, June 17, 1950; children: Rachel, George, Sarah. PhB, U. Chgo., 1947, MA, 1950. Lic. marriage, family and child therapist, Calif. Directing tchr. South Side Spl. Play Sch., Chgo., 1950-51; tchr. spl. edn. Montgomery County Schs., Rockville, Md., 1954-57; tchr. Calvery Luth. Sch., Silver Spring, Md., 1957-59; marriage, family and child therapist Am. Inst. Family Rels., L.A., 1960-68, assoc. dir. Child Guildance Clinic, 1964-68; marriage, family and child therapist in pvt. practice L.A., 1968-75; pub. Cookie Cutter Collectors Club Newsletter, L.A., also Washington, 1972-84; pub. newsletter Cookies, Washington, from 1984; ptnr. Elegant Bouquets. Author: Identifying Your Cookie Cutters, 1978, Encyclopedia of Cookie Shaping, 1981, Cookie Cutters and Cookie Molds, 1985, The Cookie Shapers Bible, 1994. Fellow Calif. Assn. Marriage and Family Therapists (pres. 1974-75); mem. Bead Soc. Washington, Needlechasers, Assn. for Gravestone Studies, Cookie Cutter Collectors Club (founder). Episcopalian. Deceased.

WETZEL, KARL H. computer programmer; b. Mineral Wells, Tex., Apr. 21, 1951; BA, Morningside Coll., 1973. Libertarian candidate for Clay County Commr., 1994, for U.S. House 6th Dist., Mo., 1996; treas. Mo. Libertarian Party, 1994—. Deceased.

WEXLER, NORMAN, playwright, screenwriter; b. New Bedford, Mass., Aug. 6, 1926; s. Harry and Sophia (Brisson) W.; children: Erica, Merin. Student, Harvard Coll., 1948. Prin. works include Joe, 1970, Serpico, 1973, Mandingo, 1975, Drum, 1976, Saturday Night Fever, 1977. Nat. Endowment for Arts grantee, 1970; recipient numerous awards including State Film award Yugoslavia, 1970, Stanley Drama award Wagner Coll., 1980, Acad. award Best Screen Play nominations for Joe and Saturday Night Fever, Writer's Guild nominations Best Screenplay for Joe. Mem. Dramatists Guild, Writers Guild (award for best screenplay 1973), Acad. Motion Picture Arts and Scis. Home: New Haven, Conn. Died Aug. 23, 1999.

WHIPPLE, DAVID DOTY, professional society administrator, deceased; b. Akron, Ohio, Dec. 26, 1923; s. Hugh Scott and Helene Eleanore (Doty) W.; m. Carolyn Terhune Decker, Feb. 28, 1953; children: Susan Casselman, Marc Evan, Tim Decker, Scott Adams Montgomery. BA, Dartmouth Coll., 1949; postgrad., Johns Hopkins U., 1949-50, The Nat. War Coll., Washington, 1966-67. From ops. officer to chief of various stations overseas CIA, Washington, 1950-85; officer for counterterrorism The Nat. Intelligence Coun., Washington, 1983-85; cons. internat. terrorism, 1985-89; exec. dir. Assn. Former Intelligence Officers, McLean, Va., 1989-97. Exec. v.p. Pagan Internat., Washington, 1987-89. Vol. Brit. 8th Army, 1944-45, Italy; sgt. U.S. Army, 1945-46, Italy, Philippines. Mem. Assn. Former Intelligence Officers (exec. dir. 1989-97), Nat. War Coll. Alumni Assn., CIA Retirees Assn. Home: Great Falls, Va. Died June 24, 2002.

WHITE, BARRY, musician, vocalist; b. Galveston, Tex., Sept. 12, 1944; s. Melvin and Sadie Marie Carter; m. Betty Smith (div.); 4 children; m. Glodean James, 1973 (div. 1988); 4 children. Album recs. I've Got So Much to Give, Stone Gon', 1973, Can't Get Enough, 1974, Just Another Way to Say I Love You, 1975, Barry White's Greatest Hits, 1975, Let the Music Play, Is This Whatcha Wont?, 1976, Barry White Sings for Someone You Love, 1977, The Man, 1978, The Message is Love, 1979, I Love to Sing the Songs I Sing, 1979, Barry White's Greatest Hits, Vol. 2, 1980, Sheet Music, 1980, Beware!, 1981, Change, 1982, Dedicated, 1983, The Right Night and Barry White, 1987, The Man is Back!, 1989, Put Me in Your Mix, 1992, Just for You (boxed set), 1992, The Icon is Love, Barry White's All-Time Greatest Hits, 1994, Staying Power, 1999, Ultimate Collection, 2000, Your Heart & Soul: The Love Album, 2000, Soul Seduction, 2001, condr. The Love Unlimited Orchestra, recs. Rhapsody in White, Together Brothers, White Gold, 1974, Music Maestro Please, 1975, My Sweet Summer Suite, 1976, My Musical Bouquet, 1978, Super Movie Themes, Just a Little Bit Different, 1979, Let 'em Dance, Welcome Aboard, 1981, Rise, 1983; author: Love Unlimited: Insights on Life & Love, 1999. Died July 4, 2003.

WHITE, FRANK, state banking commissioner; b. Texarkana, Tex., June 4, 1933; Student, Tex. A&M U., 1950-51; grad., U.S. Naval Acad., 1956. Commd. 2d lt. USAF, 1956, advanced through grades to capt., pilot, 1956-61, hon. discharge, 1961; acct. exec. Merrill Lynch, Pierce, Fenner and Smith, Inc., 1961-73; mem. mgmt. team Comml. Nat. Bank, Little Rock, 1973-75; dir. Ark. Indsl. Devel. Commn., 1975-77; pres., CEO, Capital Savs. and Loan Assn., 1977-80; gov. State of Ark., Little Rock, 1981-83; sr. v.p. fixed income divsn. Stephens Inc., 1983-85; sr. v.p. 1st Comml. Bank, Little Rock, 1988-98; bank commr. State of Ark., Little Rock, 1998—2003. Pres. Little Rock Jaycees, 1965-66, Little Rock Rotary Club, 1976-77; bd. dirs. Little Port Authority, 1977-82, Bapt. Health Found.; treas., bd. dirs. Ark. Children's Hosp., 1966-80; nat. bd. dirs. Family Ministry, Campus Crusade for Christ; gen. chmn. Pulaski County Campaign, United Way, 1993; treas. Little Rock Air Base Coun.; vice-chmn. Nat. Commn. Drunk Driving, 1983-84; mem. Commn. on Future of the South. Recipient Arkansan of Yr. award Ark. Easter Seals, 1998. Died May 21, 2003.

WHITE, JAMES EDWARD, geophysicist, educator; b. Cherokee, Tex., May 10, 1918; s. William Cleburne and Willie (Carter) W.; m. Courtenay Brumby, Feb. 1, 1941; children: Rebecca White Vanderslice, Peter McDuffie, Margaret Marie White Jamleson, Courtenay White Forte. BA, U. Tex., 1940, MA, 1946; PhD, MIT, 1949. Dir. Underwater Sound Lab., MIT, Cambridge, 1941-45; scientist Def. Research Lab., Austin, Tex., 1945-46; research assoc. MIT, 1946-49; group leader, field research lab. Mobil Oil Co., Dallas, 1949-55; mgr. physics dept. Denver Research Center, Marathon Oil Co., 1955-69; v.p. Globe Universal Scis., Midland, Tex., 1969-71; adj. prof. dept. geophysics Colo. Sch. Mines, Golden, 1972-73, C.H. Green prof., 1976-87, prof. emeritus, from 1986; L.A. Nelson prof. U. Tex., El Paso, 1973-76. Esso vis. prof. U. Sydney, Australia, 1975; vis. prof. MIT, 1982, U. Tex.-Austin, 1985, Macquarie U., Sydney, 1988; del. U.S.-USSR geophysics exch. Dept. State, 1965; mem. bd. Am. Geol. Inst., 1972; mem. space applications bd. NAE, 1972-77; NAS exch. scientist US-USSR, Zagreb, Yugoslavia, 1973-74; del. conf. on oil exploration China Geophys. Soc.-Soc. Exploration Geophysicists, 1981; cons. world bank Chinese U. Devel. Project II, 1987. Author: Seismic Waves: Radiation, Transmission, Attenuation, 1965, Underground Sound: Application of Seismic Waves, 1983, (with R.L. Sengbush) Production Seismology, 1987, Seismic Wave Propagation: Collected Works of J.E. White, 2000; editor: Vertical Seismic Profiling (E.I. Galperin), 1974; contbr. articles to profl. jours.; patentee in field. Recipient Halliburton award, 1987, Kapitsa Gold medal Russian Acad. Natural Scis., 1996. Fellow Acoustical Soc. Am.; mem. NAE, Soc. Exploration Geophysicists (hon., Maurice Ewing medal 1986), Cosmos Club, Sigma Xi. Unitarian Universalist. Died Jan. 30, 2003.

WHITE, JOHN GREVILLE, chemist, educator; b. Saltcoats, Ayrshire, Scotland, Mar. 27, 1922; came to U.S., 1947; s. Albert Greville and Minnie (Sayer) W.; m. Julia Theodora Adams, Aug. 28, 1953; children: Susan, David, Ian. BSc, Glasgow U., 1944, PhD, 1947. Asst. in chemistry Glasgow (Scotland) U., 1946-47; instr., asst. prof. Princeton (N.J.) U., 1947-55; tech. staff mem. RCA Labs., Princeton, 1956-66; prof. Chemistry Fordham U., N.Y.C., 1966-86, prof. emeritus, from 1987. Mem. Am. Crystallographic Assn. Home: Missoula, Mont. Died Aug. 22, 2001.

WHITE, LAURENS PARK, physician; b. St. Louis, Dec. 21, 1925; s. Park Jerauld and Maria (Bain) W.; m. Sylvia Wisotzky, 1950 (div. 1972); m. Annette Jeanne Marie Campbell, May 19, 1983; children; Sonia Pearson, Maria Southworth. Student, Westminster Coll., 1945; MD, Washington U., 1949. Diplomate Am. Bd. Internal Medicine, Am. Bd. Med. Oncology. Intern then resident Mass Gen. Hosp., Boston, 1949-51; resident U. Calif., San Francisco, 1951-53; fellow U. London, Bethesda, 1953-55; instr. Stanford Med. Sch., San Francisco, 1955-59; rschr. Children's Cancer Rsch. Found., Boston Mass., 1959-63; pvt. practice San Francisco, from 1963. Clin. profl. medicine U. Calif. Med. Sch., San Francisco, 1975; vice chief staff St. Luke's Hosp., San Francisco, 1994—. Editor: Enzymes in Blood, 1958, Care of Patients With Fatal Illness, 1969; contbr. articles to profl. jours. Mem. State of Calif. AIDS Adv. Com., Sacramento, 1988-90; co-chair AIDS Testing Sub Com., 1989-90. With USPHS, 1951-55. Recipient Leadership award San Francisco AIDS Found., 1989. Mem. Calif. Med. Assn. (pres. 1988, chmn. bd. trustees 1983-87), San Francisco Med. Soc. (pres. 1979), Internat. Work Group Death and Dying (sec. 1979), Internat. Work Group Death and Dying (sec. 1980-83), Health Outreach Team (bd. dirs. 1990—). Home: San Francisco, Calif. Died Aug. 25, 2000.

WHITE, NELSON HENRY, writer, publisher, realtor; b. Balt., Oct. 29, 1938; s. Thomas Robert and Edith Eyre W.; m. Sergei Saint-Germain, Aug. 29, 1972 (div. Dec. 30, 1992); m. Sheila Ann Emery White, Apr. 1, 1994. BA in History, U. Redlands, Calif., 1968; D in Divinity, Light of Truth Ch., Pasadena, Calif., 1971; D in Theology, Pasadena Inst., Pasadena, Calif., 1973. Teaching cert., Calif. 1969. Opr. Religious Supply and Book Store, Pasadena, Calif.; sr. calibration lab. technician NASA Ames Rsch. Ctr., Moffet Field, Calif., 1991-96; ret., 1996. Estate conservator Superior Ct., Martinez, Calif., 1997. Author over 130 books; contbr. articles to profl. jours. Deputy sheriff San Bernandino County, 1959-61; import specialist U.S. Customs Svc., Terminal Island, Calif., 1970; mem. Contra Costa County Sheriff's Posse, 2001--. Named Knight and officer Gross Priorat Österreck Templer Orden, Klagenfürt, Austria, 1989. Mem. Mensa, The Richmond Chor, Pro-Constitution Polit. Action Group. Avocations: private pilot, amateur radio, 4-wheel drive enthusiast, photography, camping, hiking. Home: El Sobrante, Calif. Deceased.

WHITE, PHYLLIS MARGARET, scriptwriter; b. Mobridge, S.D. d. Peter C. and Mildred Jessalyn (Hanstrom) Kremer; m. Robert White, Oct. 2, 1960; children: Lorry, Steven. Scriptwriter CBS Radio/TV, Chgo., 1946-48, CBS/NBC-TV, N.Y.C., 1953-59; freelance TV scriptwriter London, 1961-63, Hollywood, Calif., 1964-85; freelance dramatist Venice, Calif., from 1985. Tchr. writing Santa Monica (Calif.) Coll., 1980. Scriptwriter: (TV series) My Favorite Martian, 1965 66, Love Of Life, 1977, Guiding Light, 1978-79, As the World Turns, 1980-81, Search for Tomorrow, 1983, Rituals, 1985; co-writer (film) Hot Mikado, 1963; contbr. numerous travel articles to mags., newspapers. Recipient George Foster Peabody award, 1954, Emmy nomination Nat. Acad. TV Arts and Scis., 1978. Mem. Writers Guild Am. West (bd. dirs. 1975-78, v.p. 1978-80, Outstanding Script award 1979, 84). Died July 7, 2002.

WHITEHEAD, EDWIN C. entrepreneur; b. N.Y.C., June 1, 1919; s. Edwin C. and Lucille S. (Sternau) W.; m. Elizabeth A. Whitehead, 1969 (dec. 1983); children: John, Peter, Susan. DSc, U. Bridgeport, 1979; LHD, N.Y. Med. Coll., 1984. Founder Technicon Corp., Tarrytown, N.Y., 1939, pres., chmn., chief exec. officer, 1960-80; prin. Whitehead Assocs., Greenwich, Conn., from 1981; also ptnr. Whitehead/Sterling, Stamford, Conn. Recipient Sama award, Van Slyke award, Am. Acad. Achievement award. Achievements include patents in automation in clinical chemistry and autophoresis. Home: White Plains, NY. Deceased.

WHITLEY, CHARLES ORVILLE, Congressman; b. Siler City, N.C., Jan. 3, 1927; s. J.B. and Mamie G. (Goodwin) W.; m. Audrey Kornegay, June 11, 1949; children: Charles Orville, Martha, Sara. BA, Wake Forest U., 1948, LL.B., 1950. Bar: N.C. 1950. Sole practice law, Mt. Olive, 1950-60; town atty., 1951-56; adminstrv. asst. to Congressman David Henderson, 1961-76; mem. 95th-99th Congresses from 3d N.C. Dist., mem. Agr. com. Served with AUS, 1944-46. Mem.: Masons, Woodmen of World. Democrat. Baptist. Died Oct. 27, 2002.

WHITMORE, BEATRICE EILEEN, publishing company official; b. Harrisonburg, Va., Mar. 15, 1935; d. Everett Dulaney and Beatrice M. (Shorts) Ott; m. William Eugene Taylor, Sept. 30, 1955 (div. Mar. 1965); children: John David, Mark Wayne; m. Dale Wilford Whitmore, May 3, 1967; 1 child, Theresa Ann. High sch. grad., Harrisonburg. Clk. typist USAF Civil Service, Eglin AFB, Fla., 1956-58, Clark AFB, Phillipines, 1958-60, sec. Wright-Patterson AFB, Ohio, 1960-75, fire insp., 1975-85, sec.-treas. local F-88, 1977-83, pres. local F-88, 1983-85, pres. emeritus, from 1985; fed. staff rep. Internat. Assn. Fire Fighters, Washington, 1985-89; assn. sec. Nat. Coffee Svc. Assn., Fairfax, Va., 1989-90; sec. Nat. Assn. Rehab. Facilitiies, 1990-91; editorial asst. Army Times Pub. Co., Springfield, Va., from 1992. Cons. Q&D Cons. Svc., Inc., 1989-91. Leader, organizer Little Sparkies, Wright-Patterson AFB, 1976-79; den mother Boy Scouts Am., New Carlisle, Ohio, 1963-65; mem. Staff Reps. Union. Served with USAF, 1953-55. Mem. NAFE, Staff Reps. Union, Internat. Platform Assn., Job's Daus. Lodges: Job's Daughters. Avocations: crocheting, needlepoint, flowers, reading. Died Apr. 28, 2000.

WHITNEY, ROBERT MICHAEL, lawyer; b. Green Bay, Wis., Jan. 29, 1949; s. John Clarence and Helen (Mayer) W. Student, U. Wis., 1967-70, JD, 1974. Bar: Wis. 1974, U.S. Dist. Ct. (we. dist.) Wis. 1979, U.S. Ct. Appeals (7th cir.) 1980, U.S. Dist. Ct. (ea. dist.) Wis. 1984, U.S. Supreme Ct. 1990, U.S. Ct. Appeals (9th cir.) 1992. Legal counsel Wis. State Election Bd., Madison, 1976-78; ptnr. Walsh, Walsh, Sweeney & Whitney, S.C., Madison, 1979-86, Foley & Lardner, Madison, 1986-2000, Lawton & Cates SC, Madison, 2000—03. Counsel Dane County Advocates for Battered Women; instr. torts I, U. Wis. Labor Sch., 1996; adj. prof. U. Wis. Law Sch., 1996-97. Contbr. articles to profl. jours. Bd. dirs. Community TV, Inc., Madison, 1984-87, Transitional/Homeless Shelters. Mem. Assn. Trial Lawyers Am., Wis. Acad. Trial Lawyers, Wis. Bar Assn., Dane County Bar Assn., Rugby Club of Madison. Died Mar. 28, 2003.

WHITNEY, RUTH REINKE, magazine editor; b. July 23, 1928; d. Leonard G. and Helen (Diestler) Reinke; m. Daniel A. Whitney, Nov. 19, 1949; 1 child, Philip. BA, Northwestern U., 1949. Copywriter edn. dept. circulation div. Time, Inc., 1949—53; editor-in-chief Better Living mag., 1953—56; assoc. editor Seventeen mag., 1956—62, exec. editor, 1962—67; editor-in-chief Glamour mag., N.Y.C., 1967—98. Recipient Nat. Mag. award gen. excellence, 1991, Pub. Interest, 1992, Cosmetic Exec. Women Achiever award, 1993, Northwestern Alumni medal, 1995, Honor award, Women's City Club N.Y., Henry Johnson Fischer award, Mag. Pubs. Am., 1998, Columbia Journalism Sch. Disting. Svc. Hon. medal, U. Mo., 1997, Honoree Gala 11, Birmingham, So. Coll., 1993. Mem.: U.S. Info. Agy. (mag. and print com. 1989—93), Women in Media, Women in Comm. (Matrix award 1980), Am. Soc. Mag. Editors (pres. 1975—77, exec. com. 1989—92, Editors Hall of Fame 1996), Fashion Group, Alpha Chi Omega. Deceased.

WHITSELL, LEON JEFFERSON, psychiatrist, neurologist; b. Fernley, Nev., Sept. 6, 1914; s. Leon Otto and Betty Loren (McKaig) W.; m. Alice Jane Lawrence, Dec. 22, 1938; children— Leon Lawrence, George Edward, James Lawrence. A.B., Stanford U., 1935, M.D., 1939. Diplomate Am. Bd. Psychiatry and Neurology. Merril fellow in psychiatry Stanford Sch. Medicine, Calif., 1946-47; cons. psychiatrist U.S. Penitentiary, Alcatraz Island, Calif., 1947-63; practice medicine specializing in psychiatry and neurology, San Francisco, 1947—; asst. clin. prof. of medicine Stanford U., San Francisco, Palo Alto, 1947-62; attending physician, cons. in neurology VA Hosp., Martinez, Oakland, Calif., 1947-70; examiner for med. commn. Superior Court, San Francisco, 1952-54; asst. prof. to assoc. clin.l prof. U. Calif., San Francisco, 1962-84. Med. editor Internat. Trumpet Guild Publs., 1980—. Mem. sci. adv. bd. Orton Dyslexia Soc., 1976—. Served to lt. commdr. (j.g.) USNR, 1942-46, active duty med. corps. Fellow Am. Psychiat. Assn. (life), Am. Acad. Neurology; mem. San Francisco Neurol. Soc. (pres.), San Francisco Med. Soc., Calif. Med. Assn. (chmn. nervous and mental disease com. 1962). Republican. Clubs: Santa Cruz; San Francisco (pres.). Lodges: Masons, San Francisco Hofskapelle. Died Jan. 24, 2000. Home: San Francisco, Calif.

WHITTELSEY, SOUTHER, real estate corporation officer; b. Greenwich, Conn., July 30, 1910; s. Henry Newton and Myrtle (Souther) W.; m. Harriet Petra Nelson, Nov. 1, 1941; children: Henry Newton, Gale Harriet Sherman, Neil Leonard. Student, Phillip Acad., Andover, Md., Cheshire Acad., Yale U., 1934. Salesman Gen. Foods Corp., Cleve., 1932-36, Mfrs. Fabricators, Inc., Elyria, Ohio, 1936-39; pres., gen. mgr. H. Newton Whittelsey, Inc. Naval Architects & Marine Engrs., N.Y.C., 1939-72; prin. Gateway Properties Engrs. Realtors, Greenwich, Conn., from 1972. Chmn. Greenwich (Conn.) Bldg. Commn., 1945—; active many other Greenwich civic groups, 1939—. Mem. Nat. Assn. Realtors (cert. residential broker and comml. investments div.), Soc. Naval Architects and Marine Engrs., Am. Soc. Naval Engrs., Indian Harbor Yacht Club, Cleve. Yacht Club, Royal Ocean Raching Yacht Club, Storm Trisail Yacht Club, Propellor Club of U.S. Republican. Episcopalian. Avocations: sail yacht racing, skiing. Home: Greenwich, Conn. Deceased.

WHITTEMORE, NENA THAMES, college administrator; b. New Orleans, Apr. 17, 1939; d. William Mackentyre and Ida Bernice (Self) Thames; m. Alexander Douglas Whittemore Jr., Oct. 26, 1963 (div. 1979); 1 child, Alexander Douglas; m. Robert Aalbu Fliegel, Apr. 2, 1983. BA, Carleton Coll., Northfield, Mass., 1961; MA, CUNY, 1963, PhD, 1968. Cert. fund-raising exec. Teaching fellow Hunter Coll., N.Y.C., 1961-63, lectr., 1963-68; instr. Rutgers U., Newark, 1968-69; asst. prof. John Jay Coll., CUNY, 1969-75; dir. alumni affairs Carleton Coll., Northfield, Minn., 1976-82, sr. devel. officer, 1981-84; exec. dir. devel. Hollins Coll., Roanoke, Va., 1984-87; v.p. I.A. Bryant Coll., Smithfield, R.I., 1988-89, Flagler Coll., St. Augustine, Fla., from 1990. Cons. St. Andrews Episcopal Sch., Bethesda, 1990. Contbr. articles to profl. jours., chpts. to book. Bd. Nat. Conf. Christians and Jews, Roanoke, 1985-87; adv. coun. Bldg. Better Bds., United Way, 1987-89. Mem. Coun. for Advancement and Support of Edn. (regional bd. dirs. 1980, 87, 90), Nat. Soc. Fund Raising Execs. (Roanoke bd. dirs. 1985-87), Mortar Bd. Episcopalian. Avocations: tennis, hiking, canoeing. Deceased.

WIENER, ANNABELLE, United Nations official; b. N.Y.C., Aug. 2, 1922; d. Philip and Bertha (Wrubel) Kalbfeld; ed. Hunter Coll.; married, Jan. 1, 1941; children: Marilyn Grunewald, Marjorie Petit, Mark. Chmn. UN Dept. Pub. Info., Nongovtl. Orgns. Exec. Com., spl. adviser to sec. gen. Internat. Women's Year Conf.; mem. exec. bd. Nongovtl. Orgns. Com. on Disarmament UN, UN Dept. Pub. Info's NGO Exec. Com.; bd. dirs. World Fedn. UN Assns., also founder, dir. art and philatelic program; bd. dirs. N.Y. chpt. UN Assn.-USA; bd. dirs., chmn. UN Day Programme, So. N.Y. State Div., v.p. North Shore chpt.; mem. UN Dept. Pub. Info.'s Non-Govtl. Orgn. Exec. Com.; mem., bd. dir. Non-Govtl. Orgn. for UNICEF at UN Hdqrs. Recipient Diplomatic World Bull. award for Distinction in politics and diplomacy and svc. to high ideals of UN, 1989; apptd. dep. sec.-gen. World Fedn. UN Assns., 1991. Mem. Am. Fedn. Arts, Mus. Modern Art, Musee Nat. Message Biblique Marc Chagall, Am. Philatelic Soc., UN Philatelic Soc., UN Assn. U.S., UNO Philatelie, Fed. Republic Germany. Deceased.

WIENER, JERRY M. psychiatrist; b. Baytown, Tex., May 11, 1933; s. Isidore and Dora L. (Lerner) W.; m. Louise W. Weingarten, Apr. 12, 1964; children— Matthew, Ethan, Ross, Aaron. Student, Rice U., 1952; MD, Baylor U., 1956; tng. in psychoanalysis, Columbia U. Psychoanalytic Center, 1968. Resident in psychiatry Mayo Clinic, Rochester, Minn., 1957-61, Columbia U. Coll. Physicians and Surgeons, N.Y.C., 1961-62; dir. child and adolescent psychiatry St. Luke's Hosp., N.Y.C., 1962-71; dir. child psychiatry Emory U., Atlanta, 1971-75; chmn. dept. psychiatry Children's Hosp., Washington, 1976-77; prof., chmn. dept. psychiatry George Washington U., 1977-98; prof. emeritus. Mem. faculty Washington Psychoanalytic Inst. Editor: Textbook of Child and Adolescent Psychiatry, 1991, 96, Psychopharmacology in Childhood and Adolescence, 1977, Diagnosis and Psychopharmacology in Childhood and Adolescence, 1996; contbr. articles to profl. jours., chpts. to books. Fellow Am. Psychiat. Assn. (past pres.), Am. Coll. Psychiatrists; mem. Am. Assn. Chmn. Depts. Psychiatry (past pres.), Am. Psychiat. Press, Inc. (chmn. bd. dirs.), Am. Acad. Child and Adolescent Psychiatry (past pres.). Home: Chevy Chase, Md. Died Sept. 7, 2002.

WIKERD, PAUL HUBERT, chemical company executive; b. Lancaster, Pa., Sept. 14, 1947; s. Paul Huber and Loretta Mae (Hufford) W.; m. Marjorie Ann Roland, Oct. 25, 1947. BS in Chem. Engring., U. Pitts., 1970. Lic. AKC judge. Devel. engr. Western Elec., Lisle, Ill., 1970-73; engr. Buckbee-Mears Co., St. Paul, 1973-76, engring. mgr. Cortland, N.Y., 1976-80, tech. svcs. mgr., 1980-81, ops. mgr., 1981-82, gen. mgr., 1982-89, v.p., 1989-90, J.M. Murray Ctr., from 1990; v.p. worldwide sales and mktg. BMC Industries, N.Y.C., from 1991. Chair bd. dirs. J.M. Murray Ctr., Cortland. Bd. dirs. Baden-Powell coun. Boy Scouts Am., Dryden, 1983-87; exec. devel. U. Mich., 1990. Mem. Soc. Info. Display, Photo Chem. Machining Inst., Corland County C. of C. (bd. dirs. 1983-86), Basset Hound Club Am. (pres. 1991—). Republican. Avocations: showing and breeding basset hounds, tibetan spaniels. Home: Homer, NY. Deceased.

WILBUR, STEPHEN, internist, oncologist, hematologist, pathologist; b. Cheyenne, Wyo., Dec. 6, 1954; MD, U. Kans., 1980. Diplomate Am. Bd. Internal Medicine, Am. Bd. Oncology, Am. Bd. Hematology, Am. Bd. Pathology, Am. Bd. Anatomic Pathology, Am. Bd. Clin. Pathology. Resident in internal medicine St. Francis Hosp., Wichita, Kans., 1980-81; resident in pathology U. Kans. Sch. Medicine, Kansas City, 1981-85, resident in internal medicine, 1985-87, fellow in hematol. oncology, 1987-89, 89-90; mem. staff Royal C. Johnson VA Hosp., Sioux Falls, S.D. Mem. Am. Soc. Clin. Oncology, Am. Soc. Hematology. Home: Waite Park, Minn. Died 2003.

WILCOCK, JAMES WILLIAM, corporation executive, retired capital equipment manufacturing company executive; b. Dayton, Ohio, Sept. 2, 1917; s. Lewis Floyd and Blanche Irene (Conner) W.; m. Catherine Crosby, July 19, 1941; 1 child, Tod C. BS, U. Mich., 1938; postgrad., Ohio Wesleyan U., 1938-41. With 3M Co., 1948-52, Oliver Iron and Steel Co., 1952-56; mktg. mgr., then mgr. Sturtevant div. Westinghouse Elec. Corp., 1956-62; pvt. cons., 1962-65; with Joy Mfg. Co., Pitts., 1965—, sr. v.p., 1967, pres., chief exec. officer, 1967-76, chmn. bd., chief exec. officer, 1976-82, ret., 1982, chmn. exec. com., 1982-87; assoc. Kolberg, Kravis and Roberts Co., from 1983; chmn., pres., chief exec. officer Pace Industries, 1984-89; chmn., pres. Pace Industries, Inc., from 1989. Bd. dirs. Copperweld Corp., Michael Baker Corp.; chmn., bd. dirs. L.B. Foster Co., 1990—; chmn., CEO Monitor Group, Inc., 1991—; adj. prof. Grad. Bus. Sch. U. Pitts. Served as officer AUS, 1942-46. Mem.: Duquesne, Allegheny Country, John's Island, Rivers. Republican. Episcopalian. Home: Sewickley, Pa. Died September 16, 1998.

WILCOX, MICHAEL WING, lawyer; b. Buffalo, July 21, 1941; s. Paul Wing and Barbara Ann (Bauter) W.; m. Diane Rose Dell, June 18, 1966; children: Timothy, Katherine, Matthew. AB, UCLA, 1963; JD, Marquette U., 1966. Bar: Wis. 1966, U.S. Ct. Appeals (7th cir.) 1967. Law clk. to judge U.S. Ct. Appeals (7th cir.), Chgo., 1966-67; with Boardman, Suhr, Curry & Field, Madison, Wis., 1967-83; ptnr. Quarles & Brady, Madison, 1983-90, Stolper, Koritzinsky, Brewster & Neider, Madison, 1990-94, Stolper & Wilcox, Madison, from 1995. Lectr. in field. Author: (with others) Marital Property Law in Wisconsin, 1986. Fin. com. Meriter Found. Mem. ABA (chmn. marital property com. of real property probate and trust law sect. 1986-89), Wis. State Bar Assn. (chmn. taxation sect. 1983-84), Am. Coll. Trust and Estate Counsel, Rotary (pres. Madison West chpt. 1998-99), Blackhawk Country Club. Home: Madison, Wis. Died Nov. 4, 2002.

WILKE, CHARLES ROBERT, chemical engineer, educator; b. Dayton, Ohio, Feb. 4, 1917; s. Otto Alexander and Stella M. (Dodge) W.; m. Bernice Lucille Arnett (dec. 2003), June 19, 1946. B. Chem. Engring., U. Dayton, 1940; MS in Chemistry, State Coll. Wash., 1942; PhD in Chem. Engring, U. Wis., 1944. Assoc. engr. Union Oil Co. of Calif., 1944-45, cons., 1952-72; instr. chem. engring. Wash. State Coll., 1945-46, U. Calif. at Berkeley, 1946-47, asst. prof., 1947-51, asso. prof., 1951-53, prof., 1953-87, prof. emeritus, 1987—2003, chmn. dept. chem. engring., 1957—63, asst. to chancellor acad. affairs, 1967-69, former prin. investigator Lawrence Berkeley Lab.; former indsl. cons. Former chmn. bd. C.R. Wilke Internat. Corp.; cons. editor Reinhold Pub. Co., 1958-64; mem. Calif. Bd. Registration Civil and Profl. Engrs., 1964-72, pres., 1967-69 Contbr. articles to profl. jours. Recipient Colburn award, 1951, Walker award Am. Inst. Chem. Engrs., 1965, Disting. Service citation, U. Wis., 1976, Disting. Alumnus award, U. Dayton, 1984, Berkeley citation, U. Calif., 1988. Fellow AIChE (past chmn. No. Calif. sect., Founders award 1986); mem. NAE, Soc. Applied Bacteriology, Am. Chem. Soc., Am. Soc. Engring. Edn. (Chem. Engring. Lectr. award 1964), World Trade Club San Francisco, Sigma Xi, Tau Beta Pi. Home: El Cerrito, Calif. Died Oct. 2, 2003.

WILKENING, GEORGE MARTIN, environmental health scientist, researcher; b. N.Y.C., Dec. 31, 1923; s. George Herbert and Mary Veronica (Doyle) W.; m. Lorraine Morris Wilkening, Aug. 26, 1950; children: Karen, George, Robert, Heidi, Holly. BS, Queens Coll., N.Y.C., 1949; MS, Columbia U., N.Y.C., 1950. Cert. Am. Bd. Indsl. Hygiene, Va., Safety Profl., Ill. Environ. hygiene specialist Va. State Health Dept., Richmond, 1949-51; sr. environ. health specialist Exxon Corp., N.Y.C., 1952-63; dir. Environ. Health Ctr. AT&T Bell Labs. Inc., Murray Hill, N.J., 1963-90; sci. coord., acting exec. dir. Environ. and Occupational Health Scis. Inst., Piscathaway, N.J., 1990-91; exec. dir., 1991-94. Prof. Environ. Medicine N.Y.U., 1983—; asst. prof. Environ. and Occupational Scis. Inst., Piscataway, N.J., 1989—; dir. environ. Health Ctr. AT&T Labs., Murray Hill, N.J., 1963-90; v.p. Sci. and Toxicology, elextromagnetic Energy Policy Alliance, Washington, 1984-90. Author: Health Effects of Non-Curing Radiation, The Medical Clinics of North America Volts, 1990, Industrial Hygiene and Toxicology, 1990. Pres. Warren (N.J.) Bd. Health, 1964-68, Warren (N.J.) Bd. Edn., 1973-84; dir. N.J. State Industrial Safety Bd., Trenton, N.J., 1966-79, Safety and Health Standards Mgmt. Bd., N.Y.C., 1971-77. Capt. USAF, 1943-46. Mem. AAAS, Nat. Coun. on Radiation Protection and Measurements, Am. Bd. Industrial Hygiene, N.Y. Acad. Scis., Nat. telecommunications and Info. Adminstrn., World Health Orgn. Research interests include effects of chemical substances, acoustic energy and electromagnetic energy on human health and methods of their control; environmental impact of chemical, physical, and biological agents; relationships between the interdisciplinary research process, creative thinking and discovery. Home: Doylestown, Pa. Deceased.

WILKENSON, MILDRED BERYL, retired nursing educator; b. Grand Junction, Colo., Nov. 4, 1919; d. Irvin Columbus and Eula Ingaborg (Anderson) Baughman; m. John Lloyd Wilkenson, June 18, 1943; children: John Raymond, Anita Lea, David Earl, Daniel Allen, Susan Marie. AA, Mesa Jr. Coll., 1939; BSN, U. Colo., 1942; postgrad., Bapt. Bible Coll., 1949-50, Moody Bible Inst., 1950-51. RN, Colo. Mem. med. missionary team Evang. Alliance Mission, Zululand, Republic South Africa, 1951-55; staff nurse St. Mary's Hosp., Grand Junction, 1957, VA Hosp., Grand Junction, 1957-61, asst. chief evening nursing svc., 1961-64, assoc. chief nursing svc. for edn., 1964-76; supr. Liberty Bapt. Ch. Sch., Grand Junction, from 1986. Rating panelist inter-agy. bd. ch. sch. examiners U.S. Clv. Svcs. Commn., Washington, 1966. Rep. precinct chmn., Grand Junction, 1985-89, mem. Rep. Cen. Com., 1985-89; election judge, Grand Junction, 1990, 91, 92, 94. Mem. Nat. Assn. Ret. Fed. Employees (treas. 1987, historian 1992-95), Delta Kappa Gamma (internat. soc.). Avocations: painting, sewing, reading, bowling. Home: Grand Junction, Colo. Died July 4, 2000.

WILKIE, BRIAN FRANCIS, English educator; b. Bklyn., Mar. 30, 1929; s. James William and Mary Ellen (Devine) W.; m. Ann Allen Johnson, Aug. 8, 1957; children: John Michael, Brian Scott, Neil Thomas. BA, Columbia U., 1951; MA, U. Rochester, 1952; PhD, U. Wis., 1959. Asst. prof. English Dartmouth Coll., Hanover, N.H., 1959-63; assoc. prof. English U. Ill., Urbana, 1963-70, prof. English, 1970-85, U. Ark., Fayetteville, 1985—2003. Author: Romantic Poets and Epic Tradition, 1965, Blake's Thel and Oothoon, 1990; co-author: Blakes Four Zoas The Design of a Dream, 1978, (anthology) Literature of the Western World, 1984, 88, 92, 97, 2001. Cpl. U.S. Army, 1952-54. Mem. MLA (mem. exec. com. English Romantics div. 1973-78, del. assembly 1974-76). Avocations: piano, music, book collecting. Home: Fayetteville, Ark. Died Dec. 14, 2003.

WILLERDING, MARGARET FRANCES, mathematician, educator; b. St. Louis, Apr. 26, 1919; d. Herman J. and Mildred F. (Icenhower) W. AB, Harris Tchrs. Coll., 1940; MA, St. Louis U., 1943, PhD, 1947. Tchr. (Pub. Schs.), St. Louis, 1940-46; instr. math. Washington U., St. Louis, 1947-48; asst. prof. Harris Tchrs. Coll., St. Louis, 1948-56; mem. faculty San Diego State Coll., 1956—76, asso. prof., 1959-65, prof. math., 1966-76, prof. emeritus, 1976—2003. Author: Intermediate Algebra, 1969, Elementary Mathematics, 1971, College Algebra, 1971, College Algebra and Trigonometry, 1971, Arithmetic, 1968, Probability: The Science of Chance, 1969, Mathematics Around the Clock, 1969, Mathematical Concepts, 1967, From Fingers to Computers, 1969, Probability Primer, 1968, Mathematics: The Alphabet of Science, 1972, 74, 77, A First Course in College Mathematics, 1973, 77, 80, Mathematics Worktext, 1973, 77, Business and Consumer Mathematics for College Students, 1976, The Numbers Game, 1977. Mem. Nat. Council

Tchrs. Math., Assn. Tchrs. Sci. and Math., Am. Math. Soc., Math. Assn. Am., Greater San Diego Math. Council (dir. 1963-65), Sigma Xi, Pi Mu Epsilon. Home: La Mesa, Calif. Died Dec. 29, 2003.

WILLIAMS, SIR BERNARD ARTHUR OWEN, philosopher, educator; b.Westcliff, Essex, Eng., Sept. 21, 1929; s. O.P.D. and H.A. Williams; B.A., Balliol Coll., Oxford U., 1951, M.A., 1954, hon. fellow, 1984, fellow All Souls Coll., 1951-54, fellow New Coll., 1954-59. Vis. lectr. Univ. Coll., Ghana, 1958-59; lectr. philosophy Univ. Coll., London, 1959-64; prof. philosophy Bedford Coll., London, 1964-67; Knightbridge prof. philosophy Cambridge U., fellow King's Coll., 1967-79, provost, 1979-87, prof. philosophy, 1988-2003; vis. prof. Princeton U., 1963, Harvard U., 1973; U. Calif., Berkeley, 1986; vis. fellow Inst. Advanced Study, Australian Nat. U., 1969; sr. vis. fellow Princeton U., 1978; vis. prof. U. Calif., Berkeley, 1986. Mem. Public Schs. Commn., 1965-70, Royal Commn. Gambling, 1976-78; chmn. Com. Obscenity and Film Censorship, 1977-79; bd. dirs. English Nat. Opera. Named hon. fellow Balliol Coll., Oxford U. Fellow Brit. Acad.; mem. Am. Acad. Arts and Scis. (fgn. hon.). Author: Morality, 1972; Problems of the Self, 1973; A Critique of Utilitarianism, 1973; Descartes: The Project of Pure Enquiry, 1978; Moral Luck, 1981; Ethics and the Limits of Philosophy, 1985, Shame and Necessity, 1993, Making Sense of Humanity, 1995, Plato, 1998, Truth and Truthfulness, 2002; also articles. Co-editor: British Analytical Philosophy, 1966, Utilitarianism and Beyond, 1982. Died June 10, 2003.

WILLIAMS, CLEVELAND, muncipal or county official; BA in Psychology, M in Pub. Adminstrn., San Jose U. Recreation supr. City of San Jose, Calif., 1965-68; asst. to city mgr. City of Seaside, Calif., 1971-82; mgr. recreation svcs. Oakland (Calif.) Office Parks and Recreation, 1982-86; supt. parks and recreation Portland (Oreg.) Bur. Parks/Recreation, 1986-90; asst. dir. parks and recreation, dir. Oakland Office Parks and Recreation, 1990-96; dir. parks, recreation and cmty. svcs. City of Santa Ana, Calif., from 1996. Home: Santa Ana, Calif. Died Aug. 18, 2002.

WILLIAMS, FRED ALTON, JR., (AL WILLIAMS), business educator, college administrator; b. Paris, Tex., June 13, 1923; s. Fred Alton and Mary Catherine (Gilliland) W.; BBA, U. Tex., Austin, 1950; m. Patsy Ruth Williams, Dec. 17, 1954; children: Marilyn Williams Dixon, Carol Williams Huska. Ptnr. Williams Air Activities, Civilian Flight Sch., Sales & Service, Tyler, Tex., 1946-52; ptnr., v.p. Williams Marine Co., Tyler, Holiday Marina-Resort, Inc., Lake Tawakoni, Tex., 1952-65; recruiter Dallas Fashion Merchandising Coll., 1965-70; exec. dir. Tyler Comml. Coll., 1970-76; dir. fin. aid and secretarial studies Northwood Inst. Tex., Cedar Hill, 1976-91, dir. ops. and fin. aid, instr., 1979-91, ret., 1991; cons. in field; coord. workshops. Served with USAF, World War II; capt. Res. ret. Mem. Kappa Sigma. Baptist. Died Sept. 30, 1992. Home: Tyler, Tex.

WILLIAMS, GEORGE HOWARD, lawyer, association executive; b. Hempstead, N.Y., Feb. 12, 1918; s. George R. and Marcella (Hogan) W.; m. Mary Celeste Madden, Nov. 23, 1946; children— Mary Beth Williams Barritt, Stephen, Kevin, Jeanne Marie. AB, Hofstra Coll., 1939, LL.D. (hon.), 1969; JD, N.Y. U., 1946, LL.D. (hon.), 1969; postgrad., NYU, 1959. Bar: N.Y. 1946. Adminstrv. asst. to dean NYU Law Sch., N.Y.C., 1946-48, instr. law, 1948-50, asst. prof., 1950-52, assoc. prof., 1952-55, prof., 1956-62, v.p. univ. devel., 1962-66, exec. v.p. planning and devel., 1966-68; pres. Am. U., Washington, 1968-75; exec. v.p., dir. Am. Judicature Soc., Chgo., 1976-87. Author: (with A.T. Vanderbilt and L.L. Pelletier) Report on Liberal Adult Education, 1955; (with K. Sampson) Handbook for Judges, 1984 Bd. dirs. Nat. Ctr. Edn. Politics, 1948-58, trustee, 1958-65; trustee Hofstra U., 1961-64; chmn. bd. trustees Trinity Coll., Vt., 1978-86; bd. dirs. Ctr. for Conflict Resolution, 1988-2000, Univ. Support Svcs. Served to lt. col., inf. AUS, World War II. Decorated Legion of Merit, Silver Star. Mem. Am. Polit. Sci. Assn., ABA Assn. Bar City N.Y., Alpha Kappa Delta, Phi Delta Phi. Clubs: N.Y. U. (N.Y.C.); Nat. Lawyers (Washington). Home: Evanston, Ill. Died May 18, 2003.

WILLIAMS, HIRAM DRAPER, artist, educator; b. Indpls., Feb. 11, 1917; s. Earl Boring and Inez Mary (Draper) W.; m. Avonell Baumunk, July 7, 1941; children— Curtis Earl, Kim Avonell. BS, Pa. State U., 1950, M.Ed., 1951. Tchr. art U. So. Calif., 1953-54, UCLA, summer 1959, U. Tex., 1954-60; mem. faculty and pres's. coun. U. Fla., Gainesville, 1960—, Disting. Service prof., until 1982, prof. emeritus, 1982. Mem. chancellor's council U. Tex. System. Exhibited, Pa. Acad. Fine Arts anns., Whitney Mus. Am. Art bi-anns., Corcoran Gallery Bi-anns., U. Ill. bi-anns., Mus. Modern Art exhbns., also Nordness Gallery, N.Y.C.; represented in permanent exhbns., Mus. Modern Art, Wilmington Art Center, Whitney Mus. of Am. Art, N.Y.C., Sheldon Meml. Art Mus., Milw. Art Center, Guggenheim Mus., Smithsonian Inst., Harn Art Mus., U. Fla., Yale; also pvt. collections.; author: Notes for a Young Painter, 1963, rev., 1985; contbr. articles to mags. Served to capt. C.E. U.S. Army, World War II, ETO. Tex. Rsch. grantee, 1958; Guggenheim fellow, 1962-63; inducted into Fla. Artists Hall of Fame, 1994. Died Jan. 5, 2003.

WILLIAMS, LESLIE ANN, art historian, writer; b. Allentown, Pa., Dec. 15, 1941; d. Edgar Daniel and Merle Leslie (Williamson) Leibensperger; m. William H.A. Williams, June 27, 1964; children: Bill, Lavinia. BA, U. Pa. Coll. for Women, 1963; MA (hon.), U. Ireland, Dublin, 1971; PhD, Ind. U., Blomington, 1990. Lectr. Gesamt Hoch Schule Kassel, Kassel, Germany, 1972-74; curator Phoneix Art Mus., 1974-76; producer, writer Young & Rubicam, Bozell & Jacobs, Phoenix, 1977-80; officer Ariz. State Govt., Phoenix, 1980-81; grant writer, curator Ariz. State U., Phoenix, 1982-83; Kress fellow Samuel Kress Found., London, 1985-86; asst. dir. Collins Living Learning Ctr., Bloomington, Ind., 1986-87; vis. asst. prof. Ohio U., Athens, 1988-89; assoc. prof. U. Cin., from 1989, head humanities and social scis., from 1996. Consulting curator Handicapped Artists of Ariz., Phoenix, 1979. Author: A Bear in the Air, 1976, What's Behind That Tree, 1982, What is Work?, 1969; author, producer Infrared Reflectoraphy, 1984, Africans in Western Art, 1993. Pres. Ariz. Women's Caucus for Art, Phoenix, 1978; liaison officer McCluskey for Cong., Bloomington, Ind., 1986. Recipient Ariz. Humanities Coun. award NEH, 1981-83, IBM Multicultural Humanities, IBM, 1992, Lily Lecture prize Ind. U., Bloomington; fellow Samuel Kress Found., London, 1985-86. Mem. Medieval Acad. Ireland, Coll. Art Assn., Victorian Inst., Midwest Victorian Studies Assn., Midwestern Art History Soc., Sixteenth Century Studies Assn. Democrat. Avocations: science fiction, classical music, cats. Died Feb. 7, 2001.

WILLIAMS, RHYS, minister; b. San Francisco, Feb. 27, 1929; s. Albert Rhys and Lucita (Squier) W.; m. Eleanor Hoyle Barnhart, Sept. 22, 1956; children: Rhys Hoyle, Eleanor Pierce. AB, St. Lawrence U., 1951, BD, MDiv, 1953, DD, 1966; postgrad., Union Sem., summer 1956; LLD (hon.), Emerson Coll., 1962. Ordained to ministry Unitarian Ch., 1954. Min. Unitarian Ch., Charleston, SC, 1953-60, 1st and 2d Ch., Boston, 1960—2000, min. emeritus, 2000—03. Mem. faculty, field edn. supr. Harvard U., 1969—; Russell lectr. Tufts U., 1965, Minns lectr., 1986. Pres. Edward Everett Hale House, 1987—, Soc. of Cincinnati, State of N.H., 1986-89; v.p. Franklin Inst., 1960-99,, sec., 1990-96, trustee, 1999—; v.p. Benevolent Frat. Unitarian Universalist Chs., 1982-93; pres. Unitarian Universalist Urban Ministry, 1991-99, pres. emeritus, 1999—; sec. bd. trustees Emerson Coll., 1961-94, trustee, 1994-2002, trustee emeritus, 2002—; chaplain Gen. Soc. Cin., Washington, 1977—, Founders and Patriots of Mass., SR; chmn. Festival Fund, Inc., Am.-Soviet Cultural Exch., 1989-91; trustee Opera Co. Boston, 1970—; trustee Meadville Lombard Theol. Sch., Chgo., 1971-77, mem. ministerial fellowship com., 1961-69, chmn., 1968-69; fin. chmn. Ch. Larger Fellowship, 1968-86; bd. dirs. Peter Faneuil Housing Corp., AIDS Housing, 1995, clk. 1996—; trustee Franklin Square House, 1993—; chmn. Franklin Found., 1997; mem. pres. coun. U.U.A., 1999—, mem. adv. com. New Horizons - U.S.-Russia students. Mem. Unitarian Universalist Mins. Assn. (pres. 1968-70), Unitarian Hist. Soc. (pres. 1960-75), Evang. Missionary Soc. (pres. 1965-80, v.p. 1980—), Soc. for Propagation Gospel Among Indians and Others in N.Am. (v.p. 1975-99, pres. 1999—), Unitarian Svc. Pension Soc. (pres. 1973—), Soc. Ministerial Relief (pres. 1973—, mem. com. for ch. staff fin.), Mass. Hist. Soc., Colonial Soc. Mass., Union Club of Boston (2d v.p. 2002), Unitarian Universalist Assn., Beta Theta Pi (pres. New Eng. 1964-66). Died July 20, 2003.

WILLIAMS, WILLIAM ARNOLD, agronomy educator; b. Johnson City, NY, Aug. 2, 1922; s. William Truesdall and Nellie Viola (Tompkins) W.; m. Madeline Patricia Moore, Nov. 27, 1943; children— David, Kathleen, Andrew BS, Cornell U., 1947, MS, 1948, PhD, 1951. Prof. emeritus U. Calif., Davis, from 1993. Contbr. articles to profl. jours. Mem. Nat. Alliance for Mentally Ill. Served to lt. U.S. Army, 1943-46 Grantee NSF, 1965-82, Kellogg Found., 1963-67; Fulbright scholar, Australia, 1960, Rockefeller Found. scholar, Costa Rica, 1966 Fellow AAAS, Am. Soc. Agronomy, Crop Sci. Soc. Am.; mem. Soil Sci. Soc. Am., Soc. Range Mgmt., Am. Statis. Assn., Assn. for Tropical Biology, Fedn. Am. Scientists. Democrat. Died May 21, 2003.

WILLIAMS-ASHMAN, HOWARD GUY, biochemist, educator; b. London, Eng., Sept. 3, 1925; came to U.S., 1950, naturalized, 1962; s. Edward Harold and Violet Rosamund (Sturge) Williams-A.; m. Elisabeth Bächli, Jan. 25, 1959; children: Anne Clare, Christian, Charlotte, Geraldine. BA, U. Cambridge, 1946; PhD, U. London, 1949. Asst. prof. biochemistry U. Chgo., 1953-64; prof. U.Chgo., 1964—91; prof. pharmacology and exptl. therapeutics, also prof. reproductive biology Johns Hopkins Sch. Medicine, 1964-69; prof. biochemistry Ben May Inst., U. Chgo., 1969, Maurice Goldblatt prof., 1973-91, interim dir., 1983—86, prof. emeritus, 1991. Contbr. numerous articles in field to publs. Recipient Research Career award USPHS, 1962-64 Fellow Am. Acad. Arts and Scis. (Amory prize 1975); mem. Am. Soc. Biochemistry and Molecular Biology. Home: Chicago, Ill. Died May 24, 2004.

WILLIAMSON, JAMES GASTON, lawyer; b. Monticello, Ark., Jan. 22, 1914; s. Lamar and Lillian (Phillips) W.; m. Wrenetta Worthen, Nov. 27, 1940; children: James, George Gordon, Edith. BA, U. Ark., 1934; JD, U. Oxford, 1937, BLITT, 1938; PhD (hon.), Ark. Coll., 1977. Bar: Ark. 1935, N.Y. 1947. Assoc. Williamson & Williamson, Monticello, Ark., 1939-40, Cahill, Gordon, Zachry & Ohl, N.Y.C., 1946-47; ptnr. Rose Law Firm, Little Rock, 1948-86, of counsel, from 1987. Bd. dir. Worthen Banking Corp., Little Rock, 1964-88. Lt. col. U.S. Army, 1941-46: PTO; ETO. Rhodes scholar U. Ark., 1935. Fellow Am. Coll. Probate Counsel; mem. ABA, Ark. Bar Found. (pres. 1962-63), Ark. Bar Assn., Phi Beta Kappa. Home: Little Rock, Ark. Died June 30, 2002.

WILLIAMSON, MALCOLM BENJAMIN GRAHAM, composer, performer, writer, lecturer; b. Sydney, New South Wales, Australia, Nov. 21, 1931; s. Rev. George and Bessie (Wrigley) W.; m. Dolores Irene Daniel, Jan. 9, 1960; 3 children. Student, Barker Coll., Sydney, Sydney Conservatory of Music; MusD (hon.), Westminster Choir Coll., Princeton, N.J., 1970, U. Melbourne, 1982, U. Sydney, 1982; D of Univ. (hon.), Open U. of Great Britain, 1983. Asst. organist Farm St., London, 1955-58; organist St. Peter's Ch. Limehouse, London, 1958-60; lectr. in Music Cen. Sch. Speech and Drama, London, 1961-62; composer in residence Westminster Choir Coll., Princeton, N.J., 1970-71, Fla. State U., Tallahassee, 1975. Mem. exec. com. Composer's Guild of Great Britain, 1964; vis. prof. in music U. Strathclyde, Glasgow, Scotland, 1983-86; pianist and organist Africa, Australia, Asia, Can., Denmark, Europe, Finland, France, Scandinavia, U.K., U.S., Russia, Yugoslavia. Compositions include: (grand opera) Our Man in Havana, The Violins of Saint-Jacques, Lucky Peter's Journey; (chamber opera) English Eccentrics, The Happy Prince, The Musicians of Bremen; (film scores) The Brides of Dracula, Thunder in Heaven, title music and prologue to Watership Down, The Masks of Death; numerous ballet, orchestral, and choral compositions, concertos, chamber music, brass ensembles, piano and organ works, documentary film scores, others. Pres. Beauchamp Sinfonietta, 1972—, U. London choir, 1976—, Purbeck Festival of Music, 1976—, Royal Philharmonic Orch., 1977-82, Sing for Pleasure, 1977—, Finchley Childrens Music Group, 1991—; v.p. The Elgar Found., St. Michael's Singers, Nat. Music Coun. Great Britain, Nat. Youth Orch. Great Britain; patron numerous orgns. Named Master of the Queen's Music, 1975, Commdr. of Brit. Empire, 1976, Hon. Officer of Australian Order, 1987; hon. fellow Westminster Choir Coll., 1971; fellow Australian Nat. U., 1974-81, U. NSW, 1981. Mem. Birmingham Chamber Music Soc. (pres. 1975—), Brit. Soc. Music Therapy (pres. 1977—), Stevenage Music Soc. (pres. 1987—), Ditchling Choral Soc. (pres. 1989—). Avocation: literature. Died Mar. 2, 2003.

WILLS, OLIVE BOLINE, elementary school educator, educator; b. Augusta, Ga., May 10, 1928; d. Francis Ensey and Gazena (Visscher) Boline; m. James Wingfield Wills, Apr. 16, 1952; children: Anne Visscher, Deana Boline Wills Burgess, Ensey James. Student, U. Chgo., 1948; AB in Social Sci. and Edn., Ga. State Coll. for Women, 1949; student, Emory U., 1950. Cert. tchr., Ga. Teen-age program dir. YWCA, Charleston, S.C., 1949-50; dir. voluntary religious activities Ga. State Coll. for Women, Milledgeville, 1950-52; social studies tchr. Washington (Ga.) High Sch., 1952-53, Wilkes Acad., Washington, 1970-91; 5th grade language arts tchr. John Milledge Acad., Milledgeville, 1991-92; curator, callaway restoration City of Washington, from 1992. Program chmn. PTA, Washington, 1965-66, fund raising chmn., 1966-67, dist. chmn., 1968-69; baton twirling tchr. Ga. Music Educators Assn., Washington, 1975-88; chmn. Wilkes County ARC, Washington, 1982—; pres. Ga. State Coll. For Women Alumni Assn., Milledgeville, 1965-67, Starlight Garden Club, Washington, 1963; sec. Friends the Libr., Washington, 1990-91, Womens Club, Washington, 1964-65, 96-97; Sunday sch. tchr. First Bapt. Ch., Washington, 1952—, choir mem., 1965—. Recipient Clara Barton award ARC, Washington, 1989, Cert. Appreciation, 1965, 79, 89, 91; named one of Outstanding Secondary Tchrs. Am. Wilkes Acad., Washington, 1974, U.S. History Tchr. of Yr., DAR, Washington, 1983. Avocations: swimming, embroidery, reading, grandchildren. Home: Milledgeville, Ga. Died July 17, 2001.

WILSDORF, HEINZ G.F. engineering educator; D in Metallurgy, Göttingen U., Germany, 1947, postdoctoral fellow. Sr. rsch. Nat. Physical Lab, South Africa, Franklin Inst. Rsch. Labs., Phila.; dir. light metals ctr., dir. ctr. light metallic thermal structures U. Va., 1984-90. Author of 140 scientific publications. Recipient Va. laureate for Engring. and Applied Sci., 1992. Mem. ASM, APS, Va. Acad. Sci. Deceased.

WILSON, ALMA, former state supreme court justice; b. Pauls Valley, Okla. d. William R. and Anna L. (Schuppert) Bell; m. William A. Wilson, May 30, 1948 (dec. Mar. 1994); 1 child, Lee Anne. AB, U. Okla., 1939, JD, 1941, LLD (hon.), 1992. Bar: Okla. 1941. Law clk. fed. ct., Muskogee, Okla., 1941-43; pvt. practice Oklahoma City, 1943-47, Pauls Valley, 1948-69; judge Pauls Valley Mcpl. Ct., 1967-68; spl. judge Garvin & McLain Counties, Norman, Okla., 1969-75; dist. judge Cleveland County, Norman, Okla., 1975-79; justice Okla. Supreme Ct., Oklahoma City, from 1982, chief justice, 1995-96. Mem. alumni bd. dirs. U. Okla.; mem. Assistance League; trustee Univ.Okla. Meml. Union. Recipient Guy Brown award, 1974, Woman of Yr. award Norman Bus. and Profl. Women, 1975, Okla. Women's Hall of Fame award, 1983, Okla Hall of Fame, 1996, Pauls Valley Hall of Fame, 1997, Pioneer Woman award, 1985, Disting. Svc. Citation U. Okla., 1985. Mem. AAUW, Am. Judicature Soc., Garvin County Bar Assn. (past pres.), Okla. Bar Assn. (co-chmn. law and citizenship edn. com.), Okla. Trial Lawyers Assn. (Appellate Judge of Yr. 1986, 89), Luther Bohanon Am. Inns Ct. XXIII, Altrusa, Am. Legion Aux. Died July 27, 1999.

WILSON, ALMON CHAPMAN, surgeon, physician, retired naval officer; b. Hudson Falls, N.Y., July 13, 1924; s. Almon Chapman and Edith May (Truesdale) W.; m. Sofia M. "Kit" Bogdons, Jan. 24, 1945; 1 child, Geoffrey Peter. BA, Union Coll., Schenectady, 1946; MD, Albany Med. Coll., 1952; MS, George Washington U., 1969; student, Naval War Coll., Newport, R.I., 1968-69. Diplomate: Am. Bd. Surgery.

Served as enlisted man and officer U.S. Navy, 1943-46, lt. j.g., M.C., 1952, advanced through grades to rear adm., 1976; intern U.S. Naval Hosp., Bremerton, Wash., 1952-53; resident VA Hosp., Salt Lake City, 1954-58; chief of surgery Sta. Hosp. Naval Sta., Subic Bay, Philippines, 1959-61; staff surgeon Naval Hosp., San Diego, 1961-64, asst. chief surgery Chelsea, Mass., 1964-65; comdg. officer 3d Med. Bn., 3d Marine Div. Fleet Marine Force, Pacific, Vietnam, 1965-66; chief surgery Naval Hosp., Yososuka, Japan, 1966-68; assigned Naval War Coll., 1968-69; fleet med. officer, comdr. in chief U.S. Naval Forces, Europe; sr. med. officer Naval Activities London, 1969-71; dep. dir. planning div. Bur. Medicine and Surgery Navy Dept., Washington, 1971-72, dir. planning div., 1972-74; with additional duty as med. adv. to dep. chief naval ops. (logistics) and personal physician to chmn. Joint Chiefs of Staff, 1972-74; comdg. officer Naval Hosp., Great Lakes, Ill., 1974-76; asst. chief for material resources Bur. Medicine and Surgery Navy Dept., Washington, 1976-79; comdg. officer (Navy Health Scis. Edn. and Tng. Command), 1979-80; the med. officer U.S. Marine Corps., 1980-81, project mgr. Fleet Hosp. Programs, 1981-82; dir. Resources Div., 1982-83; dep. dir. naval medicine, dep. surgeon gen. Dept. Navy, 1983-84; ret., 1984. Mem. grad. med. edn. adv. com. Dept. Def. Decorated Legion of Merit with gold V (2 stars), Meritorious Service medal, Joint Service Commendation medal. Fellow ACS (gov.); mem. Assn. Mil. Surgeons U.S. Home: Alexandria, Va. Died June 30, 2003.

WILSON, GEORGE MCCONNELL, religious organization executive; b. Churchs Ferry, N.D., Oct. 19, 1913; s. Clarence McNair and Mary Belle (McConnell) W.; m. Helen Josephine Bjorck, Sept. 3, 1940; children: Jean Elizabeth (Mrs. Ralph Bertram Greener), Judith (Mrs. Larry Grimes), Janet (Mrs. Steve Hanks). Student, N.D. State Sch. of Sci., 1932-33, U. Minn., 1936, Northwestern Coll., 1933-37; Litt. D. (hon.) Houghton Coll., 1962; LL.D. (hon.) Gordon Coll., 1969. Owner, mgr. Wilson Press & NW Book & Bible House, Mpls., 1940-50; asst. to pres., bus. mgr. Northwestern Coll., Mpls., 1947-50; bus. mgr., sec.-treas. Billy Graham Evangelistic Assn., Mpls., 1950—, exec. v.p., 1962-87; pres. World Wide Publs., Mpls., 1970-88; bd. dirs. Billy Graham Evangelistic Assn., Eng., Australia, Can., France, Ger., Hong Kong, U.S.; pres., founder Evang. Coun. for Fin. Accountability, Washington; Sec. Christian Broadcasting Assn., Honolulu, Global Concern, Montrose, Calif.; treas. Blue Ridge Broadcasting Corp., Black Mountain, N.C.; asst. treas. World Wide Pictures, Burbank, Calif.; v.p., bd. dirs. Bank of Mpls. and Trust Co., chmn. bd., 1985—. Author: 20 Years Under God, 1971. Compiler: Words of Wisdom, 1967. Mng. editor Decision mag. Bd. dirs. Children's Heart Fund, Mpls., pres., 1980-83; chmn. bd. Prison Fellowship, Washington; bd. dirs. Mail Users Coun., chmn. 1969; bd. dirs. Laubach Literacy Found., 1963-67, Youth for Christ U.S.A., Wheaton, Ill., Northwestern Coll., Roseville, Minn., Community Coll. Mpls.; founder, dir. Mpls. Youth for Christ; v.p., chmn. exec. com. Tyndale Theol. Sem.; pres. Tom Tipton Ministries. Named Layman of Yr., Nat. Assn. Evangelicals, Tyndale Theol. Sem., World Opportunities Internat., Mgr. of the Yr., Christian Ministries Mgmt. Assn., 1988; apptd. Pres.'s Com. on Mental Retardation, 1988; recipient Managerial Achievement award Adminstrv. Mgmt. Soc., Award of Distinction, Direct Mail Advertising Assn., 1980, William W. Holes Direct Mail award, 1973, Disting. Service award Greater Mpls. C. of C., 1972, Disting. Service award City of Mpls., 1977, Exec. of Yr. award Mpls. Gopher Chpt. Nat. Secs. Assn., 1979, Good Neighbor award Sta. WCCO, Mpls., 1983, 87, Appreciation award Downtown Coun. of Mpls.; George Wilson Day proclaimed in Minnesota by Gov., and Mpls. by Mayor. Mem. Mpls. Press Club, Direct Mail Mktg. Assn., Adminstrv. Mgmt. Soc., Nat. Religious Broadcasters (named Outstanding Christian Mgmt. 1988), Bus. and Profl. award Religious Heritage of Am., 1990, Religious Pub. Relations Coun., Nat. Soc. Fund Raisers, Presdl. Roundtable, Rep. Congrl. Leadership Coun., Rep. Sen. Inner Circle, U.S. Sen. Bus. Adv. Bd., Loring-Nicollet Community Council, Citizens League Mpls., Independent-Republicans of Minn. Elephant Club. Baptist. Clubs: Decathlon, Mpls. Athletic, Six O'clock. Lodge: Kiwanis (bd. dirs. Kiwanis Found., Disting. Svc. to the Community award Downton club 1989, Dist. Minnesotan award 1992). Home: Minneapolis, Minn.

WILSON, JAMES BARKER, lawyer, writer; b. Visalia, Calif., Jan. 29, 1926; s. John Fleming and Helen Mae (Barker) W.; m. Joanne Bailey, Apr. 27, 1956. BA, U. Wash., 1948, JD, 1950. Bar: Wash. 1950, U.S. Supreme Ct. 1955. Asst. atty. gen. Wash. State Atty. Gen., Seattle, 1951-52; prin. Harlow, Ringold & Wilson, Seattle, 1953-63; asst. atty. gen. U. Wash., Seattle, 1963-65, sr. asst. atty. gen., 1965-89; gen. counsel U. Wash., 1965-89; pres. Intourex, Inc. 1988-92. Contbr. chpts. to books, articles to profl. jours. Democrat candidate for U.S. Congress, 1st Dist., Wash., 1956; del. Dem. Nat. Conv., 1952, 60; pres. bd. trustees Group Health Credit Union, 1954-61; v.p. Group Health Co-op, Seattle, 1963-64; bd. dirs. Henry Gallery, U. Wash., 1972-80, Allied Arts of Seattle, 1973-75; pres. Pacific Basin Council, 1988-92; arbitrator Wash. State Superior Ct., 1995-96; mem. bd. supervisors Seattle YMCA, 1995-96. Served with USAAF, 1944-45. Mem. ABA, Wash. State Bar Assn., Seattle-King County Bar Assn., Nat. Assn. Coll. and Univ. Attys. (bd. dirs. 1972-73, 75-82, pres. 1979-80, cert. of merit 1980, life mem. 1990), Phi Alpha Delta, Theta Chi. Died Oct. 14, 1996. Home: Seattle, Wash.

WILSON, JOHN LONG, physician; b. Sturgis, Ky., Feb. 9, 1914; s. Clarence Herbert and Anna Opie (Long) W.; m. Janice Lee Schwensen; children: Rosser, Wyndham, John, Burgess, Damaris. BA, Vanderbilt U., 1935; MD, Harvard U., 1939. Diplomate Am. Bd. Surgery, Am. Bd. Thoracic Surgery. Intern, asst. resident in surgery Mass. Gen. Hosp., Boston, 1939-42, resident in surgery, 1947-49; sr. resident in surgery U.S. Naval Hosp., Chelsea, Mass., 1946-47; clin. instr. surgery Stanford U. Sch. Medicine, 1949-52; asst. prof. surgery Washington U. Sch. Medicine, 1952-53; assoc. clin. prof. surgery U. Calif. Sch. Medicine, San Francisco, 1958-60; chief surg. svc. U.S. VA Hosp., San Francisco, 1958-60; prof., chmn. dept. surgery Am. U., Beirut, Lebanon, 1953-68, dean Faculties of Med. Scis., 1966-68; prof. surgery Stanford U. Sch. Medicine, from 1968, acting dean, 1970-71, assoc. dean, 1968-70 and from 71. Author: Handbook of Surgery, 5 edits., 1960-73; contbr. chpts. to books, articles to profl. jours. Served to lt. comdr. M.C., U.S. Navy, 1942-47. Mem. AMA, ACS, Am. Assn. for Thoracic Surgery, Internat. Soc. Surgery, Samson Thoracic Surg. Soc., Santa Clara County Med. Soc., San Francisco Surg. Soc., Pacific Coast Surg. Soc. Died Apr. 5, 2001.

WILSON, JOHN STEUART, author, critic; b. Elizabeth, N.J., Jan. 6, 1913; s. Wylie G. and Alice (Niven) W.; m. Susan Barnes, Jan. 2, 1950 (dec. Feb. 1981); children: Gordon Barnes, Duncan Hoke; m. Mary Morris Schmidt, Oct. 18, 1983. AB, Wesleyan U., Middletown, Conn., 1935; MS, Columbia Sch. Journalism, 1942. Promotion, product devel. Vick Chem. Co., N.Y.C., 1935-41; entertainment editor, sports editor, columnist PM, N.Y.C., 1942-49; New York editor Down Beat mag., N.Y.C., 1948-50; editor Common Council for Am. Unity, N.Y.C., 1951-52; jazz critic N.Y. Times, 1952-90, High Fidelity Mag., 1952-90, Video Rev., 1980-90. Author: The Collector's Jazz: Traditional and Swing, 1958, The Collector's Jazz: Modern, 1959, Jazz: The Transition Years, 1966; Producer, commentator: The World of Jazz, radio sta. WQXR, N.Y.C., 1954-70, Jazz Today, Voice of America, 1971-89, Manhattan Jazz Hour, Am. Pub. Radio, 1985-86, John Wilson's Classic Jazz, WQXR, N.Y.C., 1986-90. Died Aug. 27, 2002.

WILSON, JUDY VANTREASE, publishing executive; b. Old Hickory, Tenn., Apr. 8, 1939; d. Luther Benjamin and Ethel (Shepherd) Vantrease; m. Robert Roland Wilson, May 4, 1968; children: Robert Roland Jr., Hilary Shepherd. BA, Smith Coll., 1961. Project mgr. Ency. Britannica, Palo Alto, Calif., 1961-62; prodn. mgr. AICPA, N.Y.C., 1962-63; successively editorial asst., assoc. editor, editor, mgr. programmed instrn., editor profl. group, pub. John Wiley & Sons, N.Y.C., 1963-85; v.p., gen. mgr. Macmillan Pub. Co., N.Y.C., 1985-88, pres., gen. mgr., 1988-94; pres. Wilson & Assocs., 1995-96; pres., pub. Orchard Books, N.Y.C., 1996—2001. Named to Acad. Women Achievers, YWCA, 1983. Mem. Women in Comm., Assn. Booksellers for Children, Soc. Childrens Book Writers, Am. Assn. Pubs. (exec. coun. 1979-82, childrens pub. com. 1988-93, gen. pub. divsn. coun. 1993-94, mem. exec. trade com. 1996-2001). Home: Brooklyn, NY. Died Mar. 14, 2003.

WILSON, PHYLLIS COLLINS, educator, counselor, psychotherapist; b. Wallingford, Vt., June 16, 1907; d. Orvis K. and May Antonie (Burditt) Collins; m. Stanley K. Wilson Jr., Aug. 10, 1932; 1 child, Phyllis Ruth. AB in Romance Langs., Radcliffe Coll., 1928; MA in English, Columbia U., 1936, EdD in Counseling Psychology, 1942. Lic. psychologist, N.Y. Tchr. English, Bd. of Edn., North Andover, Mass., 1927, Cohasset, Mass., 1927-28; Latin and English libr. Wykeham Rise, Washington, Conn., 1928; tchr. English jr. high sch. Bd. Edn., South Orange, N.J., 1928-30; tchr. English sr. high sch. Horace Mann Sch., Columbia U. T.C., N.Y.C., 1930-33; cons. psychologist Bedford and Hartsdale Bd. Edn., N.Y., 1942-43; guidance counselor Bd. Edn., Hasbrouck Heights, N.J., 1942-43; dir., prin. Bd. Higher Edn., N.Y.C., 1952-77; dir. 2 yr. post-master's degree program Queen's Coll., CUNY, 1952-77; asst. prof. to prof. guidance counselors; pvt. practice in psychotherapy, 1951-80. Fellow Am. Bd. Profl Psychology (cert.); mem. Am. Acad. Counseling Psychology (founding). Avocations: travel, walking, theater. Home: Hanover, NH. Died Apr. 13, 2000.

WILSON, ROBERT NEAL, sociologist, educator; b. Syracuse, N.Y., Nov. 15, 1924; s. Robert Marchant and May Eloise (Neal) W.; m. Arleene Eleanor Smith, Aug. 21, 1948 (div. 1973); children— Lynda Lee, Deborah Eloise; m. Joan Wallace, Aug. 1, 1973 BA, Union Coll., 1948; PhD, Harvard U., 1952. Research assoc. Cornell U., Ithaca, N.Y., 1951-53; staff Social Sci. Research Council, Washington, 1953-56; lectr. Harvard U., Cambridge, Mass., 1957-60; assoc. prof. Yale U., New Haven, 1960-63; prof. sociology U. N.C., Chapel Hill., 1963—. Trustee Easter Seal Research Found., Chgo., 1966-72; cons. NIMH, Washington, 1968-72, Nat. Inst. Child Health and Human Devel., Washington, 1970-77; reviewer NEH, Washington, 1977— Author: Man Made Plain, 1958, Sociology of Health, 1970, The Writer as Social Seer, 1979, Experiencing Creativity, 1986; author, editor: The Arts in Soc., 1964. Served to sgt. U.S. Army, 1943-46, ETO Ctr. for Advanced Study Behavioral Scis. fellow, 1956-57; Fulbright scholar, 1975 Fellow Am. Sociol. Assn., Am. Pub. Health Assn., So. Sociol. Soc. Democrat. Episcopalian. Avocation: poetry. Died Dec. 20, 2002.

WILSON, SLOAN, writer, educator; b. Norwalk, Conn., May 8, 1920; s. Albert F. and Ruth (Danenhower) Wilson; m. Elise Pickhardt, Feb. 4, 1941 (div.); children: Lisa, Rebecca, David Sloan; m. Betty Stephens; 1 child, Jessica. Grad., Fla. Adirondack Sch., 1938; AB, Harvard, 1942; LHD (hon.), Rollins Coll., 1982. Writer, contbr. New Yorker and other mags.; with Providence Jour., 1946-47, Time, Inc., 1947-49, Nat. Citizens Commn. for Pub. Schs., 1949-53; dir. info. svcs., asst. prof. English Buffalo U., 1953-55; asst. dir. White House Conf. on Edn., 1955-56; lectr. creative writing NYU, 1961—62; Disting. writer-in-residence Rollins Coll., Winter Park, Fla., 1981-82; dir. Winter Park Artists Workshop, 1983-85; cons. Philip Crosby Assocs., Winter Park, 1984-87. Lectr. Va. Commonwealth U., 1990. Author: (novels) Voyage To Somewhere, 1946, The Man in the Gray Flannel Suit, 1955, A Summer Place, 1958, A Sense of Values, 1960, Georgie Winthrop, 1962, Janus Island, 1966, Away From It All, 1969, All The Best People, 1970, What Shall We Wear to This Party?, 1976, Small Town, 1978, Ice Brothers, 1979, Greatest Crime, 1980, Pacific Interlude, 1982, The Man in the Gray Flannel Suit II, 1983. Served to lt. USCGR, World War II. Died May 25, 2003.

WILZIG, SIGGI BERT, banker; b. Krojanke, Germany, Mar. 11, 1926; came to U.S., 1947, naturalized, 1956; s. Isidor and Sophie (Sommerfeld) W.; m. Naomi Barbara Sisselman, Dec. 31, 1953; children: Ivan, Sherry, Alan. Student high sch., Berlin; LL.D. (hon.), Hofstra U., 1983. Unskilled worker, salesman, 1947-54; gen. mgr. Nieswand & Son, Newark, 1954-58; dir., exec. v.p. Bronze & Granite Memorials, Inc., Clifton, N.J., 1958-65; pres., chief exec. officer Wilshire Oil Co., Tex., N.Y.C., 1965-80; dir. Trust Co. N.J., Jersey City, 1968—, vice chmn., 1970-71, chmn. bd., chief exec. officer, 1971—, pres., 1974—. Lectr. U.S. Mil. Acad., 1975; Mem. Jersey City Fiscal Adv. Bd., 1974 Mem. nat. campaign cabinet State of Israel Bonds; chmn. banking div. No. N.J. region; trustee Daus. of Miriam Center for Aged, Clifton; dir. trustees, fellow N. Cardozo Sch. Law Yeshiva U.; bd. dirs. Jewish Hosp. and Rehab. Center of N.J., L.I. Heart Inst., N.J. Banking Adv. Bd., Passaic County Econ. Devel. Commn.; mem. adv. bd. President's Commn. on Holocaust, 1978; mem. U. S. Holocaust Meml. Council, 1980—; Nazi forced laborer 1941-42; in Auschwitz concentration camp, 1943-45, Mauthausen concentration camp, 1945 Recipient Prime Minister's medal State of Israel, 1975; Disting. Service award Yeshiva U., 1977; Hadassah Myrtle Wreath award, 1981; Univ. medal Hofstra U., 1985, Medal of Honor Ellis Island, 1998; established Siggi B. Wilzig Disting. professorship, also Ctr. of Banking Law, Hofstra U. Sch. Law, 1985 Mem. Passaic C. of C. (dir.), Jersey City C. of C., dir.), B'nai B'rith., Odd Fellow. Jewish (trustee congregation). Club: Marco Polo (N.Y.C.). Home: Fort Lee, NJ. Died Jan. 7, 2003.

WINANT, ETHEL WALD, broadcasting executive; b. Worcester, Mass., Aug. 5, 1922; d. William and Janice (Woolson) Wald; children: William, Scott, Bruce. BA, U. Calif., Berkeley; MTA, Whittier Coll. Dir. casting Talen Assocs., N.Y.C., 1953-56; assoc. producer Playhouse '90, CBS, Hollywood, Calif., 1956-60; assoc. producer All Fall Down, MGM, Calif., 1960-61; producer Gt. Adventure, CBS, Hollywood, 1961-62; v.p. talent, dir. program devel. CBS, Hollywood, 1962-75; exec. producer Best of Families, PBS, N.Y.C., 1975-77; former v.p. talent NBC, Burbank, Calif., v.p. mini-series and novels for TV, 1979; former sr. v.p. Metromedia Producers Co.; former mem. adv. bd. Ctr. for Advanced Film Studies, Am. Film Inst., Procter & Gamble Gt. Am. Women; cons. in field. Exec. producer: (TV movie) A Time to Triumph, 1985. Mem. Pres.'s Commn. for Women; mem. Calif. Arts Council; mem. speakers bur. Braille Inst.; bd. dirs. Circle Reperatory Theatre. Recipient Disting. Alumni award Calif. Community Colls., 1981, Life Achievement award Casting Soc. Am., 1987; named TV Woman of Yr., Conf. Personal Mgrs., 1974. Mem. Nat. Acad. TV Arts and Scis. (exec. com. 1981—, bd. govs., Emmy award 1960), John Tracy Clinic, Women in Film (Crystal award 1979), Hollywood Radio and TV Soc. (bd. dirs., former sec.). Home: Beverly Hills, Calif. Died Nov. 29, 2003.

WINDSOR, JAMES THOMAS, JR., printing company executive, newspaper publisher; b. Blakely, Ga., July 30, 1924; s. James Thomas and Mary Alice (Blitch) W. Student, Emory Jr. Coll., Valdosta, Ga., 1941-42, Cardiff (Wales) U., 1945-46; BA, Emory U., 1947. Insp./scientist U.S. Argl. Rsch. Adminstrn., San Augustine, Tex., 1948; pres. J.T. Windsor & Co., McRae, Ga., 1949-65; v.p. McRae Industries, Inc., 1963-64; pers. dir. Sunbeam Corp., McRae, 1965-71; editor, pub. The Laurens County News, 1973-74; editor, publisher The Soperton (Ga.) News, from 1971, The Wheeler County Eagle, Alamo, Ga., from 1975, The Montgomery Monitor, Mt. Vernon, Ga., from 1987; pres. The Mulberry Bush, Inc., Soperton, 1985-89, Suburban Printing Corp., Higgston, Ga., from 1972. Editor: Blueprint for Progress, 1963 (Washington Model award), also cookbooks and hist. books; area newspaper columnist, 1971—. Mayor City of McRae, 1962-70; adminstr. Telfair County, McRae, 1965; pres. Telfair Redevel. Corp., 1963-64; former coun. bd. dirs. Boy Scouts Am., Macon, Ga.; bd. dirs. Million Pines Festival, Soperton, 1973-87, Ga. Mcpl. Assn., Atlanta, 1963-66; dir. Eastman (Ga.) Planning and Devel. Commn., 1965-70; supt. sch. McRae Meth. Ch., 1951-71; active Eagle Scouts Am. With AUS, 1943-46, ETO. Recipient 20 yrs. perfect attendance award McRae Meth. Ch. Sch. Mem. Ga. Press Assn. (numerous awards 1972—), Nat. Newspaper Assn., Montgomery County C. of C., Soperton-Treutlen C. of C., Telfair County C. of C. (pres.), Wheeler county C. of C., Jaycees (editor jour. 1959, 1st place Jour. in Nation award, Rebel Corps col. 1991—, One of 5 Ga. Outstanding Young Men award 1961), VFW, Am. Legion (post comdr. 1957-58), Treutlen County Sportsman Club, McRae Rotary Club (pres.), Toastmasters, Lions (pres. Soperton 1975-76, 15 yrs. perfect attendance award). Avocations: photography, reading, walking, writing, graphic arts. Home: Soperton, Ga. Died May 19, 2002.

WINDSTEIN, KENNETH ALFRED, lawyer; b. Pitts., Dec. 11, 1955; s. Alfred M. and Dorothy E. (Kaczmarek) W.; stepmother, Marleen (Spitler) Windstein; m. Elizabeth A. Natti, Oct. 18, 1980; 1 child, Kenneth Zane. BA in Polit. Sci. magna cum laude, Indiana U. Pa., 1976; JD, Syracuse U., 1978. Bar: N.Y. 1979, W.Va. 1980, U.S. Dist. Ct. (no. dist.) N.Y. 1982, U.S. Dist. Ct. (we. dist.) N.Y. 1988, U.S. Claims Ct. 1985, U.S. Ct. Appeals (2d cir.) 1998. Atty. Legal Aid Soc., Charleston, W.va., 1979-81; assoc. O'Hara and O'Hara, Liverpool, N.Y., 1981-84; pvt. practice Syracuse, 1984-88; asst. county atty. Ontario County Atty's Office, Canandaigua, N.Y., from 1988; town justice South Bristol, N.Y., from 1998. Instr. Finger Lakes Law Enforcement Acad., Canandaigua, 1988—. 1st v.p. Ctr. N.Y. Lupus Found., Syracuse, 1985-87. Mem. Ontario County Bar Assn., N.Y. State Bar Assn. (ho. of dels. 1992-96). Avocations: harness racing, chess, camping. Home: Naples, NY. Died Aug. 6, 2000.

WINFIELD, PAUL EDWARD, actor; b. L.A., May 22, 1941; Student, U. Portland, 1957-59, Stanford U., 1959, L.A. City Coll., 1959-63, UCLA, 1962-64. Artist-in-residence Stanford U., 1964-65, U. Hawaii, 1965, U. Calif., Santa Barbara, 1970-71 Films include Gordons War, 1973, Huckleberry Finn, 1974, Conrack, 1974, Guess Who's Minding the Mint, 1969, Sounder, 1972 (Acad. Award nomination 1973), Hustle, 1975, Twilights Last Gleaming, 1976, A Hero Ain't Nothing But A Sandwich, 1978, Carbon Copy, 1981, White Dog, 1981, Star Trek II, 1982, Mike's Murder, 1982, On the Run, 1982, The Terminator, 1985, Blue City, 1986, Death Before Dishonor, 1987, The Serpent and the Rainbow, 1988, Presumed Innocent, 1990, Cliff Hanger, 1993, Dennis the Menace (The Movie), 1993, Kingdom of The Blind, 1994, The Mike Tyson Story, 1994, Fluke, 1994, Original Gangsters, 1995, Mars Attacks, 1995, Strategic Command, 1997, Built to Last, 1997, Teen Angel, 1997, Knockout, 1998, Relax...It's Just Sex, 1998, Assignment Berlin, 1998, Strange Justice, 1999, Catfish in Black Bean Sauce, 1999, Second to Die, 2001others; TV appearances include Green Eyes, 1976, All Deliberate Speed, 1976, King, 1978 (Emmy nomination), Backstairs at the White House, 1979, The Blue and the Gray, 1982, Star Trek: Next Generation, 1992, Batman Beyond, 1999, Crossing Jordan, 2001; guest star: TV appearances include Roots II (Emmy nomination), Angel City, 1980, Sisters, 1981, Sophisticated Gents, 1981, Go Tell It on the Mountain, 1983, Queen (miniseries), 1993, Scarlett (miniseries), 1994, Picket Fences, 1994 (Guest Actor in a Drama Emmy award), Touched By An Angel, 1995, Secrets of the Rose Garden, 1995; theatrical appearances include Checkmates, 1988, nat. tour A Few Good Men, 1992, Othello, Guthrie Theatre, 1993. Recipient Trailblazer award, NAACP, 2001. Died Mar. 7, 2004.

WINFREE, ARTHUR TAYLOR, biologist, educator; b. St. Petersburg, Fla., May 15, 1942; s. Charles Van and Dorothy Rose (Scheb) W.; m. Ji-Yun Yang, June 18, 1983; children: Rachael, Erik from previous marriage. B of Engring. Physics, Cornell U., 1965; PhD in Biology, Princeton U., 1970. Lic. pvt. pilot. Asst. prof. theoretical biology U. Chgo., 1969-72; assoc. prof. biology Purdue U., West Lafayette, Ind., 1972-79, prof., 1979-86; prof. ecology and evolutionary biology U. Ariz., Tucson, 1986-88, Regents' prof., from 1989. Pres., dir. rsch. Inst. Natural Philosophy, Inc., 1979-88; Aisenstadt chair applied math. U. Montreal, 2000. Author: The Geometry of Biological Time, 1980, 2d ed., 2001, When Time Breaks Down, 1986, The Timing of Biological Clocks, 1987. Recipient Career Devel. award NIH, 1973-78, The Einthoven award Einthoven Found. and Netherlands Royal Acad. Scis., 1989, Norbert Wiener prize Am. Math. Soc. and Soc. Ind. Applied Maths., 2000-2004; NSF grantee, 1966—; MacArthur fellow, 1984-89, John Simon Guggenheim Meml. fellow, 1982. Home: Tucson, Ariz. Died Nov. 5, 2002.

WINFREY, JOE CRAWFORD, financial planner; b. Somerset, Ky., Oct. 19, 1929; s. Joe Gibson and Beatrice (Gossett) W.; m. Barbara Jane Knowles, Apr. 11, 1952; children: Richard Joel, Reid David. BA, So. Ill. U., 1955. CLU. Dist. exec. Boy Scouts Am., Princeton, Ill., 1955-58, Jackson, Mich., 1958-60; agt. Mass. Mut. Life, Jackson, 1960-66, Nat. Life of Vt., Jackson, 1966-68, gen. agt. Battle Creek, Mich., 1968-76, agt., from 1976. Fin. cons. Winfrey, Boling & Assoc., Battle Creek, 1986—; registered fin. planner IARFP Inc., Battle Creek, 1988; adj. faculty Olivet (Mich.) Coll., 1980—. Pres. local coun. Boy Scouts Am., 1971-73; 2d v.p. Goodwill Industries, 1988. Recipient Silver Beaver award Boy Scouts Am., 1973. Mem. Exch. Club (pres. 1981—), Life Ins. Assn. (pres. 1977-78), Nat. Assn. Security Dealers (rep. 1966—, class 7), Internat. Assn. Registered Fin. Planners, Riverside Country Club. Republican. Avocation: fishing. Home: Battle Creek, Mich. Deceased.

WINGER, RALPH O. lawyer; b. Keokuk, Iowa, July 8, 1919; s. Ralph O. and Mary Ellen (Lee) W.; m. Irene L. Sutton, Apr. 5, 1941 (dec.); children: Ralph O. (dec.), Allen, Louise, Robert. BA, State U. Iowa, 1940; LLB, Harvard U., 1947. Bar: N.Y. 1948. Assoc. Cahill Gordon & Reindel and predecessor firms, N.Y.C., 1947-60, ptnr., 1960-91, sr. counsel, from 1992. Lt. USNR, 1942-46, PTO. Mem. ABA, N.Y. State Bar Assn. (chmn. tax sect. 1973-74, ho. of dels. 1974-75), Bay Terrace Country Club (N.Y.). Republican. Home: Flushing, NY. Died Sept. 25, 2003.

WINKS, ROBIN WILLIAM, history educator; b. West Lafayette, Ind., Dec. 5, 1930; s. Evert McKinley and Jewell (Sampson) W.; m. Avril Flockton, Sept. 27, 1952; children:

Honor Leigh, Eliot Myles. BA magna cum laude, U. Colo., 1952, MA, 1953; PhD with distinction, Johns Hopkins U., 1957; MA (hon.), Yale U., 1967; DLitt (hon.), U. Nebr., 1976, U. Colo., 1987; MA (hon.), Oxford U., 1992; DPhil, Westminster Coll., 1995. From instr. to Randolph W. Townsend prof. history Yale U., New Haven, 1957—2003, dir. office of spl. projects and founds., 1974-76, master Berkeley Coll., 1977-90, chair Can. studies, 1985-99. Eastman prof. Oxford U., 1992-93, chair studies in environment, 1993-96, Harmsworth prof. Oxford U., 1999-2000; chair dept. history Yale U., 1996-99. Author: Canada and the U.S., 1960, The Cold War, 1964, Historiography of the British Empire-Commonwealth, 1966, History of Malaysia, 1967, Age of Imperialism, 1969, Pastmasters, 1969; The Historian as Detective, 1969, A Forty-Year Minuet, 1970, The Blacks in Canada, 1971, Slavery, 1972, An American's Guide to Britain, 1977, Other Voices, Other Views, 1978, Relevance of Canadian History, 1979, Western Civilization, 1979, Detective Fiction, 1980, Modus Operandi, 1982, History of Civilization, 1984, Cloak and Gown, 1987, Asia in Western Fiction, 1990, Frederick Billings, 1991, The Imperial Revolution, 1994, Laurance S. Rockefeller, Catalyst for Conservation, 1997, Mystery and Suspense Writers, 1998, Oxford History British Empire: Historiography, 1999, To Stimulate to Some Action, 2001. Cultural attache U.S. Embassy, London, 1969-71; chair Nat. Park System Adv. Bd., Washington, 1981-83, bicentennial com. for Internat. Confs. of Americanists Dept. State, 1974-77. Smith-Mundt prof. U. Malaya, 1962; Inst. Commonwealth Studies at U. London fellow, 1966-67; Guggenheimn fellow, 1976-77; grantee Social Sci. Rsch. Coun., 1959, 75; Resident scholar Sch. Am. Rsch., 1985, 91, 94. Fellow Royal Hist. Soc., Explorers Club; mem. Am. Hist. Assn., Can. Hist. Assn., Royal Commonwealth Soc. (life), Yale Club (N.Y.C.), Athenaeum, Spl. Forces Club. Home: Northford, Conn. Died Apr. 7, 2003.

WINN, WASHINGTON CARLYLE, retired obstetrician; b. Va., Apr. 20, 1910; MD, Med. Coll. Va., 1935. Diplomate Am. Coll. Obstetrics & Gynecology. Intern Med. Coll. Va. Hosp., Richmond, 1935 36, resident in ob/gyn, 1938-40. Fellow Am. Coll. Obstetrics & Gynecology; mem. AMA, So. Med. Assn. Home: Richmond, Va. Died May 30, 1999.

WINNER, THOMAS GUSTAV, Slavic and comparative literature, poetry educator; b. Prague, Czechoslovakia, May 4, 1917; came to U.S., 1939, naturalized, 1950; s. Julius and Franziska (Grünhutová) Wiener; m. Irene Portis, Sept. 25, 1942; children: Ellen, Lucy Franziska. Student, Charles U., Prague, 1936-38, U. Lille, France, 1936; BA, Harvard U., 1942, MA, 1943; PhD, Columbia U., 1950; MA (hon.), Brown U., 1966; PhD (hon.), Masaryk U., 1995. With OWI, 1943-46; vis. fellow Johns Hopkins, 1947-48; from instr. Russian to asso. prof. Duke, 1948-58; asso. prof., then prof. Slavic langs. and lits. U. Mich., 1958-65; prof. Slavic langs. and comparative lit. Brown U., 1965-82, chmn. dept. Slavic langs., 1968-72, prof. emeritus, 1982—2004; dir. Center for Research in Semiotics, 1977-83; dir. Program in Semiotic Studies Boston U., 1984—2004. Fulbright lectr. Sorbonne, Paris, 1956-57, Ruhr Univ., Bochum, Fed. Republic Germany, 1989; exchange prof. U. Warsaw, 1972-73, U. Zagreb, spring 1973; mem. seminar theory lit. Columbia, 1968—Author: Oral Art and Literature of the Kazakhs of Russian Central Asia, 1958, Chekhov and his Prose, 1965; editor: Brown U. Slavic Reprints; editor Am. Jour. Semiotics, 1980-85; spl. interests Russian lit., Czech lit., semiotics and poetics. Ford Found. sr. fellow, 1951-52, NEH sr. fellow, 1972, 92-93; Rockefeller grantee, 1977, IREX grantee, 1972, 78, 79, 90, 92, Fulbright-Hayes, 1973; recipient Josef Dobrovsky medal Acad. Scis. Czech Republic, 1997, Jubilee medal Charles U., Prague. Mem. MLA, Am. Com. Slavists, Internat. Assn. for Semiotic Studies, Semiotics Soc. Am. (pres. 1977-78), Czech Semiotic Soc. (hon.), Prague Linguistic Cir. (hon.), Am. Soc. Tchrs. Slavic and East European Langs., Czechoslovak Soc. for Arts and Scis. (v.p. 1982-85), Comparative Lit. Assn., Internat. Assn. Slavists, Am. Assn. Advancement of Slavic Studies, Karel Teige Soc. (Czech Republic), F.X. Salda Soc. (Czech Republic). Died Apr. 20, 2004.

WINSLOW, ANNE, retired foundation executive; b. Brookline, Mass., Mar. 29, 1908; d. Charles Edward Amory and Anne Fuller (Rogers) W. BA, Vassar Coll., Pughkeepsie, N.Y., 1930. Mem. staff Group Health Coop., N.Y.C., 1940-43; editor Carnegie Endowment for Internat., N.Y.C., 1947-55, editor-in-chief, 1953-70, program officer, 1969-72; fellow UN Inst. for Tng. and Rsch., N.Y.C., 1977, ret., 1977. Program chmn. seminar-faculty Columbia U., N.Y.C., 1955—; officer Conf. Consultative NGO's, N.Y. and Geneva, 1952-60; chmn. NGO coms. Internat. Human Rights, N.Y., 1967-68. Co-author: Social Justice for Women; ccontbr. articles to profl. jours. Lt. U.S. Army, 1943-46, Eng., France, Fed. Republic Germany. Mem. Internat. Orgn., Internat. Studies Assn., Can. Inst. Internat. Affairs, Assn. Former Internat. Civil Servants, Cosmopolitan Club (fgn. visitors com. N.Y. chpt. 1988—). Democrat. Avocations: reading, gardening. Home: New York, NY. Died 1999.

WINTER, WILLIAM DAVID, psychologist; b. N.Y.C., Apr. 16, 1927; s. Harry P. and Lillian (Sokol) W.; m. Louise Morrison, May 2, 1954 (dec. Dec. 12, 1984); children: Linda, Susan, Daniel; m. Amal-Sedky, Nov. 27, 1988. PhD, U. Mich., 1953. Lic. psychologist, Calif. Psychiat. social worker U.S. Army, Ft. Belvoir, Vt., 1946-48; psychol. intern VA, Ft. Custer, Detroit, 1948-52; instr. U. Mich., Ann Arbor, 1952-54; chief psychologist Milw. County Health Ctr., Wauwatosa, Wis., 1954-56; coord. therapy Shady Grove Boys Ranch, Middleton, Calif., 1953-66; prin. investigator

NIMH, San Jose, Calif., 1962-64; vis. prof. U. Kans., Lawrence, 1968-69; cons. Stanford Rsch. Inst., Palo Alto, Calif., 1969-84; asst. prof. to prof. emeritus San Jose State U., 1956-83; psychologist Foothill Psychol. Ctr., Los Gatos, Calif., from 1983. Sr. field assessment officer Peace Corps, San Jose, 1967; lectr. in field; bd. dirs. Zonta Children's Ctr., San Jose, 1969-84. Co-author: Research in Family Interaction, 1969; contbr. articles to profl. jours. Mem. Arab-Am. Leadership Coun., Washington, 1990—. Pvt. U.S. Army. Fellow APA, Soc. for Personality Assessment. Democrat. Jewish. Avocations: nature, walking, music, art. Home: Seattle, Wash. Deceased.

WINTERS, JANET LEWIS, writer; b. Chgo., Aug. 17, 1899; d. Edwin Herbert and Elizabeth (Taylor) Lewis; m. Yvor Winters, June 22, 1926; children: Joanna, Daniel. PhB, U. Chgo., 1920. Writer from 1934. Vis. lectr. Stanford U., Palo Alto, Calif., 1969-70, U. Calif., Berkeley, winter 1979; vis. artist Dierassi Found., Woodside, Calif., Yaddo, Saratoga Springs, N.Y., 1979. Author: (novels) Invasion, 1932, The Wife of Martin Guerre, 1941, The Trial of Sören Quist, 1947, The Ghost of Monsieur Scarron, 1959, also 3 books of poetry and 5 librettos. Guggenheim fellow, France, 1951. Mem. NAACP. Avocation: gardening. Home: Davis, Calif. Died 1998.

WINTERS, RALPH E. film editor; b. Toronto, 1909; Films include The Penalty, 1941, The People vs. Dr. Kildare, 1941, Mr. and Mrs. North, 1942, Kid Glove Killer, 1942, The Affairs of Martha, 1942, Eyes in the NIght, 1942, Dr. Gillespie's New Assistant, 1942, The Youngest Profession, 1943, Young Ideas, 1943, Cry 'Havoc', 1943, Gaslight, 1944, The Thin Man Goes Home, 1945, Our Vines Have Tender Grapes, 1945, Boys' Ranch, 1946, The Romance of Rosy Ridge, 1947, Killer McCoy, 1947, Tenth Avenue Angel, 1948, Hills of Home, 1948, Little Women, 1949, Any Number Can Play, 1949, On the Town, 1949, King Solomon's Mines, 1950, Quo Vadis (Acad. award nomination), 1951, The Story of Three Loves, 1953, Young Bess, 1953, Kiss Me Kate, 1953, Executive Suite, 1954, Seven Brides for Seven Brothers (Acad. award nomination), 1954, Jupiter's Darling, 1955, Love Me or Leave Me, 1955, Tribute to a Bad Man, 1956, High Society, 1956, Man on Fire, 1957, Jailhouse Rock, 1957, The Sheepman, 1958, Ben-Hur (Acad. award), 1959, Butterfield 8, 1960, Ada, 1961 Dime with a Halo, 1963, Soldier in the Rain, 1963, The Pink Panther, 1963, A Shot in the Dark, 1964, The Great Race (Acad. award nomination), 1965, What Did You Do in the War, Daddy?, 1966, Fitzwilly, 1967, How to Succeed in Business Without Really Trying, 1967, The Party, 1968, The Thomas Crown Affair, 1968, Gaily, Gaily, 1969, The Hawaiians, 1970, Kotch (Acad. award nomination), 1971, The Carey Treatment, 1972, Avati!, 1972, The Outfit, 1974, Spike's Gang, 1974, The Front Page, 1974, Mr. Majestyk, 1974, King Kong, 1976, Orca, 1977, 10, 1979, The American Success Company, 1980, S.O.B., 1981, Victor Victoria, 1982, Curse of the Pink Panther, 1983, The Man Who Loved Women, 1983, Micki + Maude, 1984, Big Trouble, 1986, Let's Get Harry, 1986, Cutthroat Island, 1995; TV Films: The Entertainer, 1976, The Other Side of Hell, 1978, Trouble Shooters: Trapped Beneath the Earth, 1993, Lily in Winter, 1994; TV Series: Combat!, 1962; Author: Some Cutting Remarks: 70 Years a Film Editor, 2001. Died Feb. 26, 2004.

WISDOM, WILLIAM RUSSELL, radiologist; b. Bedford, Iowa, 1922; s. Franklin Dale and Chloe (Huey) W.; m. Veronica Morrissey, Jan. 9, 1948; children: Deborah, William R. Jr., Franklin D. II, Stephanie, Sarah. MD, U. Iowa, 1947. Diplomate Am. Bd. Radiology. Intern St. Vincent's Hosp., L.A., 1947-48; resident in radiology Groover-Christie-Merritt, Washington, 1949-50; with U.S. Naval Hosp., Phila., 1950-51, USN Dept. Dispensary, Washington, 1951-52, U.S. Naval Hosp., San Diego, 1952-53; fellow in radiation oncology Soiland Cancer Found., L.A., 1953-54. Staff physician L.A. Tumor Inst., 1954-55; head radiation oncology St. Mary Hosp., Long Beach, Calif., 1955-62; head dept. radiology Little Company of Mary Hosp., Torrance, Calif., 1962-77; asst. clin. prof. U. Calif. Irvine Coll. Medicine, 1963-67. Lt. USNR, 1951-53. Fellow Royal Med. Soc., Am. Coll. Radiology; mem. AMA, Am. Roentgen Ray Soc., Radiol. Soc. N.Am. Republican. Roman Catholic. Home: Palos Verdes Estates, Calif. Died Jan. 23, 2003.

WISE, JOHN S. retired surgeon; b. Madison Barracks, N.Y., 1914; MD, U. Pa., 1941. Diplomate Am. Bd. Surgery. Mem. staff Mercer Med. Ctr., Trenton, N.J. Fellow ACS. Died Oct. 24, 1999.

WISH, MARY ELIZABETH, business development professional, consultant; b. Weymouth, Mass., Sept. 14, 1964; d. John J. Jr. and Rita J. McLaughlin; m. James Alan Wish, Mar. 6, 1993; 1 child, Alan Joseph. BS, Worcester (Mass.) Poly. Inst., 1986. Program mgr. Digital Equipment Corp., Maynard, Mass., 1985-94; sr. process cons. New. Eng. Bus. Svcs., Inc., Groton, Mass., 1994-97; dir. Profl. Devel. Group, Framingham, Mass., from 1997. Pres., cons. Ops. Improvement Co., Hudson, Mass., 1993—. Author: The Manufacturer's Re-engineering Guide: How to Use Time as Your Competetive Weapon, 1995. Treas. Bolton (Mass.) Hist. Soc., 1990-92. Mem. Am. Mgmt. Assn. (instr.), Assn. for Mfg. Excellence, Epsilon Upsilon Pi. Republican. Roman Catholic. Avocation: painting. Died Nov. 27, 2001.

WISNIEWSKI, DAVID, author juvenile prose; b. Eng. m. Donna Wisniewski; children: Ariana, Alexander. Trained as circus clown with Ringling Bros. & Barnum and Bailey Circus, 1973, 74; circus clown Circus Vargas, Calif., 1975; co-founder Clarion Shadow Theatre, Bowie, Md., from

1980. Author, illustrator: The Warrior and the Wiseman, 1989, Elfwyn's Saga, 1990, Rain Player, 1991, Sundiata: Lion King of Mali, 1992, The Wave of the Sea-Wolf, 1994, Golem, 1996 (Caldecott award 1997), Worlds of Shadow: Teaching with Shadow Puppetry, 1997, The Secret Knowledge of Grown-Ups, 1998, Tough Cookie, 1999; illustrator: Ducky, 1997, Workshop, 1999, I'll Play With You, 2000, Master Man, 2000, Halloweenies, 2002, Sumo Mouse, 2002. Henson Found. grantee; recipient citation of excellence UNIMA, 1997. Died Sept. 11, 2002.

WISSNER, GARY CHARLES, motion picture art director, production designer; b. N.Y.C., Feb. 9, 1964; s. Sidney and Penina (Gologor) W.; m. Tambre Hemstreet, Nov. 13, 1993. BFA, NYU, 1986. Scenic artist Cape Code Melody Tent, Hyannas, Mass., 1983; prodn. technician Imero Fiorentino Assocs., N.Y.C., 1984-86; asst. scenic designer Radio City Music Hall, N.Y.C., 1986; art dir. MTV Networks, N.Y.C., 1987-88; asst. art dir. Country Music Awards, L.A., 1987; asst. art dir. TV show Young and the Restless, L.A., 1987; asst. art dir. Patty Hearst Atlantic Entertainment, L.A., 1987. Art dir.: (commls.) Chrysler, Laser Tag, Michelob, (theme parks/indsls.) Tomorrowland, 1990, Korean World Expo, 1991, AT&T Futurecom, 1993, (TV) Road to Daytona (MTV segment), 1987, Superbowl in San Diego (MTV spl.), 1988, Family of Spies (CBS mini-series), 1989, In Living Color, 1991, (feature films) Teenage Mutant Ninja Turtles, 1989, Another 48 Hours, 1990, Hoffa, 1992, Wyatt Earp, 1993, Junior, 1994, Seven, 1995; prodn. designer: (comml.) Balance Health Foods, 1993, (television) Millenium, 1996, (feature film) Stephen King's Graveyard Shift, 1990, Last Man Standing, 1995, Steel, 1996, I Know What You Did Last Summer, 1997, Eight Millimeter, 1998; asst. art dir. feature films Warlock, 1988, The Abyss, 1988. Mem. Acad. Motion Picture Arts and Scis. (voting mem.), Soc. Motion Picture Art Dirs. (bd. dirs.), United Scenic Artists (voting mem.). Avocations: computers, sculpture, sports, fitness. Home: Los Angeles, Calif. Deceased.

WIST, PAUL GABRIEL, retired accountant; b. Balt., July 25, 1929; s. George John and Regina Marie (Ward) W.; m. Mary Lee Vaeth, Oct. 23, 1954; children: Paul Gabriel, Timothy V., Matthew W., Ami A. ABA, U. Balt., 1951. CPA; cert. fin. planner. Assoc. C.W. Amos & Co., Balt., 1952-56, ptnr., 1956-69, mng. ptnr., 1969-85, sr. ptnr., 1985-91, ret., 1991. Bd. dirs. Md. Blue Cross, 1965-73, Assoc. Cath. Charities, 1976-88, pres. 1985-88; mem. adv. bd. St. Joseph Hosp., 1964-88, Stella Maris Hospice, 1969-73; trustee Cardinal Shehan Ctr. for Aging, 1977-97, Marian House, Inc., 1982-89, McAuley Inst., Inc., 1987-93, St. Joseph Hosp. Found., 1988-95; trustee Am. Inst. CPAs Benevolent Fund, 1977-83, pres. 1980-83; bd. visitors U. Balt., 1984-88, 94-97, trustee ednl. found., 1984-97; trustee Children's Fund, Inc., 1986-95, pres., 1987-95; trustee New Cathedral Cemetery, 1994—, pres. 1996—; trustee Cherry Hill Town Ctr., Inc., 1997—, pres. 1997—; trustee Stella Maris, Inc., 1997-99. With USNR, 1948-49. Recipient Cardinal Gibbons medal, 1973, Papal medal, 1982, U. Balt. Disting. Svc. award, 1990; named Alumnus of Yr. U. Balt., 1982, Disting. Alumnus award Mt. St. Joseph H.S., 1999. Mem. AICPAs (coun. 1974-75, 77-80), Md. Assn. CPAs (pres. 1975-76, Pub. Svc. award 1990), Fin. Planners Assn., Internat. Exec. Svc. Corps (vol. svc. Guatemala, Poland, Egypt, Lithuania, Russia, Republic of Georgia), Towson (Md.) Golf and Country Club, Rotary (pres. 1986-87). Roman Catholic. Home: Baltimore, Md. Deceased.

WITHERSPOON, FREDDA LILLY, educator; b. Houston; d. Fred D. and Vanita E. (Meredith) Lilly; AB, Bishop Coll.; MSW, Washington U., St. Louis, MA in Guidance and Counseling, MA in Ednl. Psychology, PhD, St. Louis U., 1965; m. Robert L. Witherspoon; children: Robert L., Vanita. Social worker, supr. St. Louis City Welfare Office, Homer G. Phillips Hosp.; tchr. English, guidance counselor St. Louis Pub. Schs.; prof. student personnel services Forest Park Community Coll., St. Louis, 1965—; cons. Ednl. Testing Service, Princeton, N.J., Head Start program, 1965-68; counseling cons. St. Louis Job Corps Center for Women, 1966-68. V.p. St. Louis chpt. NAACP, 1969-83, pres. Mo. Conf., 1973-84, also organizer Forest Park young adult coun., also bd. dirs.; mem. Challenge of 70's Crime Commn., 1970-75; mem. adv. coun., Central Inst. for Deaf, 1970-78; mem. exec. bd. Mayor's St. Louis Ambassadors; mem. Mayor's Coun. Youth, 1970-75; dir. teens fund drive March of Dimes, 1960-72, Lily Day drive for Crippled Children, 1966-72; mem. speakers bur. United Way, 1969-82; bd. dirs. children's services City of St. Louis; exec. bd. Mo. Heart Assn.; bd. dirs. United Negro Coll. Fund; bd. dirs. Social Health Assn., Conservatory Assn. Schs. for Arts, St. Louis Heart Assn., Girl Scouts; pres. St. Louis Met. YWCA, 1978-79, bd. dirs.; bd. dirs. St. Louis Urban League, vice chmn., 1977-81; organizer Jr. Annie Malone Service Guild; active St. Louis Ambassadors, Jr. League Community Adv. Bd., St. Louis, Salvation Army Adv. Coun. Named Woman of Year, Greyhound Bus Corp., 1967, St. Louis Argus, 1968, Nat. Outstanding Woman, Iota Phi Lambda, 1970; named Outstanding Woman of Achievement, Globe Dem., 1970, Outstanding Educator of Am., 1971, Nat. Top Lady Distinction, 1974; recipient Negro History award, 1971; George Washington Carver award, 1976; Health and Welfare Council award, 1975; Vol. of Yr. award United Negro Coll. Fund.; Continental Socs. award, 1984; Mo. State Dr. M.L. King award, 1991. Mem. NAACP (life; Nat. Outstanding Youth Adv. 1977, numerous awards 1977—), Am. Assn. for Counseling and Devel., AAUP (pres. 1975-81), AAUW, Am. Vocational Guidance Assn., Assn. Measurement and Evaluation in Guidance, Nat. Assn. Jr. Colls., Nat. Faculty Assn. Jr. Colls., LWV, Nat. Coun. Negro Women (life), Mo. Assn. Social Welfare, Jack and Jill, Nat. Bar Assn. (Gertrude Rush award 1992), Mound City Bench and Bar Spouses (founder, pres. 1946-49), Nat. Assn. Women Lawyers, Nat. Assn. Bench and Bar Spouses (founder, pres.), Top Ladies of Distinction (organizer Met. St. Louis chpt. founder), Metro St. Louis Inter-Alumni Coun. of UNCF (founder), Continental Socs. (founder Met. St. Louis chpts.), The Links, Inc. (Gateway chpt.), Urban League Guild, Coalition of 100 Black Women (founder, pres. 1984-91), Kappa Delta Pi, Iota Phi Lambda (nat. pres. 1977-81), Sigma Gamma Rho, Pi Lambda Theta, Phi Delta Kappa, Kappa Delta Pi. Died Aug. 14, 1996. Home: Herndon, Va.

WITTMANN, OTTO, museum executive; b. Kansas City, Mo., Sept. 1, 1911; s. Otto and Beatrice Knox (Billingsley) W.; m. Margaret Carlisle Hill, June 9, 1945 (dec. July 1997); children: William Hill, John Carlisle. Student, Country Day Sch., Kansas City; AB, Harvard U., 1933; postgrad., 1937-38, postgrad. Carnegie scholar, summer 1937; LLD, U. Toledo; DFA, Hillsdale Coll., Bowling Green State U., U. Mich., Kenyon Coll., Skidmore Coll. Curator prints Nelson Gallery Art, Kansas City, 1933-37; instr. history of art Emerson Sch., Boston, 1937-38; curator Hyde Collection, Glens Falls, N.Y., 1938-41; instr. history of art Skidmore Coll., Saratoga Springs, N.Y., 1938-41; asst. dir. Portland (Oreg.) Mus. Art, 1941; assoc. dir. Toledo Mus. Art, 1946-59, trustee, 1958—, dir., 1959-76, dir. emeritus, from 1977. V.p., cons., art advisor, 1977—; trustee, cons. Los Angeles County Mus. Art, 1977-78; vice chmn., trustee, cons. J. Paul Getty Trust, 1977—; organizer exhbns. art activities Am. museums USIA, 1953-55; editl. cons. Gazette des Beaux Arts; vice chmn. Nat. Collection Fine Arts Commn.; bd. dirs. Toledo Trust Co.; cons. Clark Art Inst., 1990—. Editl. chmn. Toledo Mus. Catalogue of European Paintings and Guide to Collections; writer numerous museum catalogues, profl. articles. Founding mem. Nat. Coun. Arts; mem. mus. panel NEH; chmn. adv. panel Nat. Found. Arts and Humanities; mem. art adv. panel IRS; mem. nat. arts accessions com. U.S. embassies; mem. U.S.-ICOM Nat. Com.; former sec. gen. com. pour Musées du Verre, ICOM; founding mem. Ohio Arts Coun.; sponsor Nat. Trust Sch., Attingham, Shropshire, Eng. Maj. AUS, USAAF, OSS, 1941-46. Decorated officer Legion of Honor, France, officer Order Orange Nassau, Netherlands, comdr. Arts and Letters France; comdr. Order of Merit Italy). Fellow Museums Assn. (Eng.); mem. Intermus. Conservation Assn. (pres. 1955-56, trustee), Harvard Soc. Contemporary Art (co-dir. 1931-33), Assn. Art Mus. Dirs. (pres. 1961-62, 71-72), Am. Assn. Museums (former v.p., Disting. Service to Mus. award 1987), Coll. Art Assn., Archeol. Inst. Am., Internat. Inst. for Conservation of Hist. and Artistic Works, Soc. Archtl. Historians, Verien der Freunde Antiker Kunst, Am. Soc. French Legion Honneur, Alliance Francaise de Toledo (trustee), Phi Kappa Phi. Episcopalian (vestryman). Clubs: Traveller's (London); Century Assn. (N.Y.C.); Toledo, Harvard (pres. 1956-57), Rotary (pres. 1963-64). Home: Montecito, Calif. Deceased.

WOHL, RONALD GENE, lawyer; b. N.Y.C., Dec. 10, 1934; s. Arthur and Bernice (Deutch) W.; m. Linda Susan Meltsner, May 2, 1965; children: Allison Brooke Wohl George, Arthur Evan, Amanda Kate. AB, Syracuse U., 1956, LLB, 1961; LLM, Bklyn. Law Sch., 1967. Bar: N.Y. 1962, U.S. Dist. Ct. (so. and ea. dists.) N.Y. 1963, U.S. Ct. Appeals (2d cir.) 1964, U.S. Supreme Ct. 1965, U.S. Dist. Ct. (no. dist.) N.Y. 1977, U. S. Dist. Ct. Conn. 1980, U.S. Tax Ct. 1986. Law clk. to judge Jacob Mishler U.S. Dist. Ct. (ea. dist.) N.Y., 1963-64; assoc. Edward Gettinger & Peter Gettinger, N.Y.C., 1962-63, 68-70; asst. U.S. atty. U.S. Dept. of Justice, N.Y.C., 1964-68; ptnr. Squadron, Gartenberg, Ellenoff & Pleasant, N.Y.C., 1970-71; pvt. practice N.Y.C., 1971-74; ptnr. Ferster, Bruckman, Wohl, Most & Rothman, LLP, N.Y.C., 1974-96, sr. counsel, 1997-98, Goetz, Fitzpatrick, Most & Bruckman LLP, from 1999. Trustee Roslyn (N.Y.) Union Free Sch. Dist., 1981-93. Mem. N.Y. Bar Assn., N.Y. Dist. Attys. Assn., Assn. of Bar of City of N.Y., Nassau County Bar, Soc. of Med. Jurisprudence. Avocation: photography. Home: Roslyn, NY. Died Feb. 16, 2003.

WOLD, JEFFREY WAYNE, psychiatrist; b. Sioux Falls, S.D., Oct. 27, 1947; s. Roger DeWayne and Rhoda Marion (Paulsness) W.; m. Mary Elizabeth Johnson, July 19, 1969; children: Ian David, Leif Eric. BA, Augustana Coll., 1969; BS, U. S.D., 1973; MD, Tufts U., 1975. Diplomate Am. Bd. Psychiatry and Neurology. Intern Hosp. St. Raphael, New Haven, Conn., 1975-76; resident in psychiatry Yale U., New Haven, Conn., 1976-79; Medication adminstr., staff psychiatrist Austen Riggs Ctr., Stockbridge, Mass., from 1982. Instr. psychiatry Yale U., New Haven, 1981-84, Harvard U., Cambridge, 1983—. Co-author: The Facilitating Environment, IUP, 1989. Chmn. bd. trustees First Congregational Ch. Stockbridge, Mass., 1988—. With U.S. Army, 1969-71. Mem. Am. Psychiat. Assn., U.S. Cycling Fedn. Democrat. Mem. United Ch. Christ. Avocations: bicycle racing, skiing, tennis, baseball coaching, golf, gardening. Home: Morris, Conn. Deceased.

WOLFE, CAMERON WITHGOT, SR., federal judge; b. San Francisco, Aug. 14, 1910; s. Frederick Lee and Edythe (Turnor) W.; m. Jean Brown, Aug. 15, 1936; children: Cameron Jr., Bruce McLaren, Robert Reese. AB, Stanford U., 1931; LLB, U. Calif., Berkeley, 1934. Bar: Calif. 1934, U.S. Dist. Ct. (no. dist.) Calif. 1934, U.S. Ct. Appeals (9th cir.) 1934. Dep. dist. atty. Alameda County, Oakland, Calif., 1936-42; ptnr. Feruhoff & Wolfe, Oakland, 1946-75; bankruptcy judge U.S. Cts., Oakland, 1975-93. Adj. prof. U. Calif., Berkeley, 1946-51. Lt. commdr. USN, 1942-46. Mem. Nat. Conf. Bankruptcy Judges, Calif. State Bar Assn., Alameda County Bar Assn., Phi Beta Kappa. Avocations: teaching, gardening, golf, boating. Home: Piedmont, Calif. Died Dec. 19, 2002.

WOLFSON, MURRAY, economics educator; b. N.Y.C., Sept. 14, 1927; s. William and Bertha (Finkelstein) W.; m. Betty Ann Goessel, July 21, 1950; children: Paul G., Susan D., Deborah R. BS, CCNY, 1948; MS, U. Wis., 1951, PhD, 1964; postgrad., Marquette U., 1958-59. Cert. secondary tchr., Wis., Mich. Tchr. math. Montrose (Mich.) High Sch., 1959-61; instr. econs. Thornton Jr. Coll., Harvey, Ill., 1961-63; prof. Oreg. State U., Corvallis, 1963-86, Calif. State U., Fullerton, from 1986. Vis. prof. numerous univs., including Ahamdu Bello U., Zaria, Nigeria, U. Canterbury, Christchurch, New Zealand, U. Wis., Milw., Marquette U., Milw., U. Durham, Eng., U. Oreg., U. So. Calif., Haifa (Israel) U., U. Adelaide, Australia; Fulbright specialist lectr., Japan, 1976-77, Tokyo U., Hitotsubashi U., Waseda U., Keio U.; docent Groningen U., The Netherlands; vis. fellow history of ideas unit Australian Nat. U., Sofia U., 1993-94; adj. prof. U. Calif., Irvine, 1986—; others. Author: A Reappraisal of Marxian Economics, 1968, (transl. into Japanese and Portuguese), Karl Marx, 1971, Spanish transl., 1977, A Textbook of Economics: Structure, Activities, Issues, 1978, Marx: Economist, Philosopher, Jew, 1982, Japanese transl., 1987, Economic Activities: Microeconomics, 1989, rev. edit., 1991, Essays on the Cold War, 1992, Computer Laboratory Manual, 1997, (with Vincent Buranelli) In the Long Run We Are All Dead, A Macroeconomics Murder Mystery, 1983, 2d edit., 1989; editor: The Political Economy of War and Peace, 1998; also numerous articles. Adv. bd. Yale U. Civic Edn. Project. With USN, 1945-46. Scholar N.Y. Bd. Regents, 1943; staff devel. fellow Oreg. State U., 1976; travel grantee Am. Coun. Learned Socs., 1979; recipient 1st nat. prize for excellence in teachng coll. econs. Joint Coun. on Econ. Edn., 1970. Mem. AAUP (chpt. pres. 1983-84), Am. Econ. Assn., Hist. of Econs. Soc., Peace Sci. Soc., Def. Econs. Assn., Western Econs. Assn., Peace Sci. Soc. (pres.). Avocations: gardening, music, drawing. Home: Laguna Hills, Calif. Died Feb. 3, 2002.

WOLINS, JOSEPH, artist; b. Atlantic City, Mar. 26, 1915; s. Morris and Rebecca (Katerinska) W.; m. Selma Lazaar, Dec. 7, 1957; children: Richard Lazaar, David Lazaar, John Wolins, Sarah Wolins. Student, Nat. Acad. Design, 1931-35. Painter with Fed. art projects, 1934-41; pvt. classes, 1961—. One-man shows include Contemporary Arts Gallery, N.Y.C., Bodley Gallery, N.Y.C., Silvermine Guild, Norwalk, Conn., Slater Mus., Norwich, Conn., Agra Gallery, Washington; exhibited in group shows at Everson Mus., Syracuse, N.Y., World's Fair, N.Y.C., 1939, J.B. Neumann Gallery, N.Y.C., Toledo Mus., Corcoran Art Gallery, U. Ill. Mus., Pa. Acad. Fine Art, Whitney Mus., Sao Paolo Mus. Modern Art, Norfolk (Va.) Mus., Smithsonian Instn., Butler Art Inst., Youngstown, Ohio, Met. Mus. Art, N.Y.C.; represented in permanent collections Met. Mus. Art, Norfolk Mus., Albert Gallery at St. Joseph's (Mo.) U., Ball State Mus. Art, Muncia, Ind., Fiske U. Art Gallery, Mobile, Mus. in Ein Horod, Israel, Butler Art Inst., Nat. Mus. Am. Art, Washington, Slater Mem. Mus., Norwich, Conn., Wichita (Kans.) Art Mus., Everson Mus. of Art, Syracuse, New Brit. Mus. Art, Conn., Boca Raton Art Mus., Fla., also pvt. collections. Grantee Mark Rothko Found., 1971; recipient Painting award Audubon Artists, 1976, Painting award Nat. Inst. Arts and Letters, 1976, Painting award Am. Soc. Contemporary Artists, 1976 Mem. Audubon Artists, Am. Soc. Contemporary Artists. Deceased.

WONG, MELVIN, dance educator; b. Oakland, Calif. s. Tom and Louise (Lee) W.; m. Betty Jean Erickson (div.); m. Constance Kreemer, Aug. 14, 1984. BA, San Francisco State U., 1965; postgrad., UCLA, 1967-68; MFA, Mills Coll., Oakland, Calif., 1967. Dance tchr. Profl. Dance Classes, N.Y.C., 1975-87; tchr. Am. Dance Festival, New London, Conn., 1975-77 summers; dancer Merce Cunningham Dance Co., N.Y.C., 1968-72; lectr. Cornell U., Ithaca, N.Y., 1972-74; artistic dir. The Mel Wong Dance Co., N.Y.C., 1975—2003; asst. prof., lectr. SUNY, Purchase, 1974-87; artistic dir. U. Colo., Boulder, 1988—2003; prof., Dept. Theater Arts, U. Calif., Santa Cruz, 1989—2003. Guest artist Ariz. State U., Tempe, 1985-86, Hong Kong Acad. Performing Arts, 1987-88; dance panelist Asian Pacific Dance Alliance, Hong Kong, 1988; choreographer for TV, Centro Assocs., Hong Kong, 1988; keynote panelist Congress on Research in Dance, Hartford, 1984. Choreographer dances, Blue Mesa, 1987, Buddha Meets Einstein, 1985, Future Antiquities, 1984, Scenario on a Bridge, 1983. With USN, 1958-60. Guggenheim Found. choreographic fellow, 1983-84; N.Y. State Council on Arts dance co. grantee, 1986-87; Nat. Endowment for Arts choreographic fellow 1981-82, 86-87. Mem. Dance Theatre Workshop. Democrat. Avocations: running, hiking, swimming, camping. Home: Santa Cruz, Calif. Died July 16, 2003.

WOOD, FREDERICK HARRISON, dean, educator; b. LaPorte, Ind., July 2, 1936; s. Frederick Harrison Sr. and Margaret (Gross) W.; m. Betty Blanton, Nov. 28, 1987; children: Andrew, Mark Ayers, Christopher, Kristin Ayers. BA, Western Mich. U., 1958, MA, 1962; postgrad., U. Mich., 1959-60; EdD, U. Mo., 1966. Prin. intern Columbia (Mo.) Pub. Schs., 1965-66; asst. prof. U. Mo., Columbia, 1966-68; dir. secondary edn. Ferguson (Mo.) Florissant Sch. Dist., 1966-69, asst. supt., 1969-70; assoc. prof. U. Nebr., Lincoln, 1970-74, prof., 1975-76; dept. head Pa. State U., University Park, 1976-85; dean Coll. Edn. U. Okla., Norman, 1985-95, prof., from 1995. Contbr. numerous articles to profl. jours. Mem. Am. Ednl. Rsch. Assn., Assn. for

Supervision and Curriculum Devel., Nat. Staff Devel. Coun., Okla. Assn. for Supervision and Curriculum Devel., Okla. Assn. Col. Tchr. Educators, Coun. Profs. of Curriculum, Coun. Profs. of Instructional Supervision. Episcopalian. Home: Norman, Okla. Died Jan. 26, 2002.

WOODBURN, MARY STUART, education educator; b. Franklin, Va., June 5, 1941; d. Stuart Holland and Mary Hazel (Bryant) Jenkins; m. Robert James Woodburn, June 4, 1967; children: Robert James II, Tammy Lee Woodburn West, Robert Stuart. BS, Madison Coll., Harrisonburg, Va., 1962; MEd, U. Va., 1966, EdD, 1979. Elem. tchr. Portsmouth (Va.) City Schs., 1962-63, Lexington (Va.) Pub. Schs., 1963-64, Colonial Heights (Va.) Pub Schs., 1964-66; prof. edn. Longwood Coll., Farmwood, Va., from 1966, developer literacy and acad. retention programs, 1987-89. Ednl. cons. to over 500 sch. dists., 1966—; mem. adj. faculty U. Va., Charlottesville, 1971-78; testing supr. Ednl. Testing Svc., Trenton, N.J., 1967—; vis. prof. Dalhousie U., Halifax, N.S., Can., summers 1969-71, Jyvaskyla U., Finland, 1987; dir. adopt-a-sch. project Va. Dept. Edn., Richmond, 1988-90; developer instructional materials Va. Hwy. Dept., Richmond, 1987-90. Contbr. articles to profl. jours. Advisor Paralyzed Vets. Am., Richmond, 1988-89; vol. Am. Cancer Soc., Leukemia Soc.; writer, vol. ESL programs for schs. and communities. Recipient Meritorious Achievement award Longwood Coll.; scholar Delta Kappa Gamma, 1978; grantee Longwood Coll. Mem. ASCD, Internat. Reading Assn., New Horizons for Learning, Phi Delta Kappa, Sigma Sigma Sigma. Methodist. Avocations: reading, cooking, writing, basketball, music. Home: Chesterfield, Va. Deceased.

WOODRUFF, NEIL PARKER, agricultural engineer; b. Clyde, Kans., July 25, 1919; s. Charles Scott and Myra (Christian) W.; m. Dorothy Adele Russ, June 15, 1952; children: Timothy C., Thomas S. BS, Kans. State U., 1949, MS, 1953; postgrad., Iowa State U., 1959. Agrl. engr. Agrl. Research Service, Dept. Agr., Manhattan, Kans., 1949-63, research leader, 1963-75; cons. engr. Manhattan, 1975-77; civil engr. Kans. Dept. Transp., Topeka, 1977-79; prof., mem. grad. faculty Kans. State U., civil engr. facilities planning, 1979-84. Mem. sci. exchange team to, Soviet Union, 1974; with W/PT Cons., 1984—. Contbr. articles to tech. jours. and books. Fellow Am. Soc. Agrl. Engrs. (Hancor Soil Water Engring. award 1975); mem. Sigma Xi, Gamma Sigma Delta. Died Nov. 10, 2003.

WOOLDRIDGE, HELENE, association administrator; b. May 29, 1913; d. Reuben R. and Georgia (Cart) Detweiler; married; children: Dean Jr., Anna Lou Wooldridge Eklof, James Allen. BS, U. So. Calif., 1935. Co-founder Achievement Rewards for Coll. Scientist, L.A. Vol. Planned Parenthood Common Cause; pub. broadcasting booster Sta. KCET. Mem. AAUW, LWV, Alpha Gamma Delta. Avocations: charities, reading, writing, current events. Home: Santa Barbara, Calif. Died Nov. 29, 2001.

WOOLF, HARRY, historian, educator; b. N.Y.C., Aug. 12, 1923; s. Abraham and Anna (Frankman) W.; children: Susan Deborah, Alan, Aaron, Sara Anna. BS, U. Chgo., 1948, MA, 1949; PhD, Cornell U., 1955; DSc (hon.), Whitman Coll., 1979, Am. U., 1982; LHD (hon)., Johns Hopkins U., 1983, St. Lawrence U., 1986. Instr. physics Boston U., 1953-55; instr. history Brandeis U., 1954-55; asst. prof. history U. Wash., 1955-58, assoc. prof., 1958-59, prof. history of sci., 1959-61; Willis K. Shepard prof. history of sci. Johns Hopkins U., 1961-76, chmn. dept. history of sci., 1961-72, provost, 1972-76; dir. Inst. for Advanced Study, Princeton, N.J., 1976-87, prof., 1987-94, prof. emeritus, from 1994; trustee Cluster C Funds Merrill Lynch, 1982-95. Mem. adv. coun. Sch. Advanced Internat. Studies, Washington, 1973-76; adv. bd. Smithsonian Rsch. awards, 1975-79; trustee Assoc. Univs., Inc., Brookhaven Nat. Labs., 1972-82; mem. vis. com. student affairs MIT, 1973-77, mem. corp. vis. com. dept. linguistics and philosophy, 1977-83, mem. corp. vis. com. dept. physics, 1979-85; mem. Nat. Adv. Child Health and Human Devel. Coun. NIH, 1977-80; mem. vis. com. Rsch. Ctr. for Lang. Scis., Ind. U., 1977-80; com. visitors Vanderbilt Grad. Sch., Nashville, 1977-79; adv. coun. dept. philosophy Princeton U., 1980-84, adv. coun. dept. comparative lit., 1982-94; mem. sci. adv. bd. Alexander von Humboldt-Stiftung, 1985-98; mem. nat. adv. bd. Ill. Math. and Sci. Acad., 1986—; mem. adv. com. Pew Neurosci. Program, 1986-91; mem. adv. panel WGBH, NOVA, 1979—; bd. dirs. Westmark Internat., 1987-92; mem. adv. coun. NSF, 1984-89; pres., chmn. bd. dirs. Johns Hopkins Program Internat. Edn. Gynecology and Obstetrics, Inc., 1973-76, trustee 1976—; pres. Bankers Trust/Alex. Brown Flag Funds, 1997—. Author: Transits of Venus, 1959, 81, Quantification, 1961, Science as a Cultural Force, 1964, Some Strangeness in the Proportion, 1980, The Analytic Spirit, 1981; contbr. articles, revs. to profl. publs.; editor: Isis Internat., rev. devoted to history of sci. and its cultural influences, 1958-64; series editor The Sources of Sci., 1964-93; assoc. editor: Dictionary of Scientific Biography, 1970-80; editorial bd. Interdisciplinary Sci. Revs, 1975—; editorial adv. bd. The Writings of Albert Einstein, 1977—. Trustee Hampshire Coll., Amherst, Mass., 1977-79, Winterthur Mus., 1978-83, Reed Coll., 1992-97, Family Health Internat., 1992—, Dibner Inst. for the History of Sci. and Tech., 1992-98, Advanced Tech. Labs., 1992-98, Spacelabs Med., Inc., 1992-98; bd. govs. Tel-Aviv U., 1977-92; trustee-at-large Univs. Rsch. Assn., Inc., 1978-89, chmn. bd., 1979-89; mem. adv. coun. John F. Kennedy Inst. for Handicapped Children, 1979-87; mem. Internat. Rsch. and Exchs. Bd., 1980-94; chmn. MX Missile basing adv. panel Office Tech. Assessment U.S. Congress, 1980-81; trustee Rockefeller Found., 1984-94; dir.-at-large Am. Cancer Soc., 1982-86; mem. sci. adv. bd. Wissenschaftskolleg zu Berlin, 1981-87; mem. adv. bd. Stanford Humanities Ctr., 1981-87; bd. dirs. W. Alton Jones Cell Sci. Ctr., 1982-85. NSF sr. postdoctoral fellow, Europe, 1961-62. Fellow AAAS (v.p. 1960, sci. program com. 1991—), Royal Astron. Soc., Acad. Internat. d'Histoire des Scis.; mem. History of Sci. Soc., Am. Philos. Soc., Coun. on Fgn. Rels., Am. Acad. Arts and Scis. (com. on publs. 1989-93), Phi Beta Kappa, Sigma Xi, Phi Alpha Theta. Home: Princeton, NJ. Died Jan. 6, 2003.

WORLEY, JAMES SAMUEL, economist, educator; b. Birmingham, Ala., Apr. 16, 1926; s. Arthur R. and Katherine (Gill) W.; m. Rosemary Nichols, Dec. 19, 1947; children—Paul N., Marian G., Susan P., James Samuel. BA, Vanderbilt U., 1949, MA, 1950; PhD, Princeton, 1959. Instr. Wofford Coll., 1950-51, asst. prof., 1951-53; instr. Princeton, 1955-57; asst. prof. econs. Vanderbilt U., Nashville, 1958-62, asso. prof., 1962-67, prof. econs. and bus. adminstrn., 1967—88, prof. emeritus, 1988—2003, dir. grad. program in econ. devel., 1963—88, asso. provost of univ., 1968-71, chmn. dept. econs. and bus. adminstrn., 1971-74, adjunct prof., Owen Grad. Sch. Mgmt., 1976—79. Served with AUS, 1944-46, ETO. Mem. Am., So. econ. assns., Phi Beta Kappa. Died July 26, 2003.

WRIGHT, GARLAND (JAMES GARLAND WRIGHT), artistic director; b. Midland, Tex., Apr. 18, 1946; s. Joe Bailey and Flora Gladys (Milstead) W. BFA, So. Meth. U., 1969; LittD (hon.), St. John's U., 1991. Freelance dir., from 1970; assoc. dir. Am. Shakespeare Theatre, Stratford, Conn., 1970-73; artistic dir. Lion Theatre Co., N.Y.C., 1974-77; assoc. artistic dir. The Guthrie Theater, Mpls., 1980-83; artistic assoc. Arena Stage, Washington, 1985-86; artistic dir. The Guthrie Theater, 1986-96; mem. drama faculty Juilliard Sch., N.Y.C., from 1996. Adj. prof. U. Minn., Mpls., 1987—. Dir. (plays) Vanities, 1976, "K"Impressions of KAFKA'S The Trial, 1977 (Obie award), Imaginary Invalid, 1982, Moliere's The Misanthrope, 1984, Happy End & Good Person of Sechuan, 1984, 85, Don Juan, 1985 (Denver Critics award), On The Verge, 1986 (Obie award), Cherry Orchard, 1986 (Denver Critics award), Richard III, 1987, Hamlet, 1988, History Cycle: Richard II, Henry IV & Henry V, 1990, The Clytemnestra Project (Iphegenia in Aulis, Agamemnon, Electra), 1992, The Seagull, 1992. Co-founder Arts over AIDS, Mpls., 1988—; bd. dirs. Theater Communications Group, N.Y.C., 1986-88; panel mem. N.E.A Profl. Theaters Co., Washington, 1990—. Winston Churchill fellow English Speaking Union, Eng., 1972. Democrat. Avocation: gardening. Home: Wayzata, Minn. Died 1998.

WRIGHT, GILBERT LAWRENCE, surgeon; b. Chgo., Jan. 29, 1915; MD, U. Ill., 1941. Diplomate Am. Bd. Surgery. Intern St. Louis City Hosp., 1940-41; resident in gen. surgery Mo. Pacific Hosp., St. Louis, 1941-44; asst. clin. prof. emeritus surgery U. Utah. Fellow ACS; mem. AMA, NWSCRS, SWSC. Home: Salt Lake City, Utah. Died Oct. 30, 2001.

WRIGHT, JERRY SMITH, lawyer; b. Houston, Oct. 18, 1942; s. Ethridge R. and Betsy S. Wright; children: Shannon Leigh, Daniel Ethridge. BBA, Lamar U., 1965; JD, U. Tex., 1969. Bar: Tex. 1968, U.S. Dist. Ct. (so. dist.) Tex. 1971, (ea. dist.) Tex. 1988, U.S. Ct. Appeals (5th cir.) 1985, U.S. Supreme Ct. 1985, U.S. Ct. Fed. Claims 1991. V.p., trust officer 1st Republic Bank, Houston, 1969-78, 1st City Nat. Bank, Beaumont, Tex., 1978-83; pvt. practice Beaumont, 1983-87; gen. atty. Entergy Svcs., Inc., Beaumont, from 1987. Mem. S.E. Tex. Estate Planning Coun. Mem. Beaumont Knife & Fork Club (pres.), Lions(pres. Beaumont 1983). Baptist. Home: Beaumont, Tex. Died Dec. 24, 2001.

WRIGLEY, ELIZABETH SPRINGER (MRS. OLIVER K. WRIGLEY), foundation executive; b. Pitts., Oct. 4, 1915; d. Charles Woodward and Sarah Maria (Roberts) Springer; BA U. Pitts., 1935; BS, Carnegie Inst. Tech., 1936; m. Oliver Kenneth Wrigley, June 16, 1936 (dec. July 1978). Procedure analyst U.S. Steel Corp., Pitts., 1941-43; rsch. asst. The Francis Bacon Found., Inc., Los Angeles, 1944, exec., 1945-50, trustee, 1950—, dir. rsch., 1951-53, pres., 1954—, dir. Francis Bacon Libr.; mem. adv. coun. Shakespeare Authorship Roundtable, Santa Monica, Calif.; mem. regional Fine Arts adv. coun. Calif. State Poly. U., Pomona. Mem. ALA, Calif. Libr. Assn., Renaissance Soc. Am., Modern Humanities Rsch. Assn., Cryptogram Assn., Alpha Delta Pi. Presbyn. Mem. Order Eastern Star, Damascus Shrine. Editor: The Skeleton Text of the Shakespeare Folio L.A. (by W.C. Arensberg), 1952. Compiler: Short Title Catalogue Numbers in the Library of the Francis Bacon Foundation, 1958; Wing Numbers in the Library of the Francis Bacon Foundation, 1959; Supplement To Francis Bacon Library Holdings in the STC of English Books, 1967; (with David W. Davies) A Concordance to the Essays of Francis Bacon, 1973., Died April 26, 1997. Home: Claremont, Calif.

WRIGLEY, WILLIAM, corporation executive; b. Chgo., Jan. 21, 1933; s. Philip Knight and Helen Blanche (Atwater) W.; m. Alison Hunter, June 1, 1957 (div. 1969); children: Alison Elizabeth, Philip Knight, William Jr.; m. Julie Burns, Nov. 28, 1981. Grad., Deerfield Acad., 1950; BA, Yale, 1954. With Wm. Wrigley Jr. Co., Chgo., 1956—99, v.p., 1960-61, pres., CEO, 1961—99, also bd. dirs. Mem. Wm. Wrigley Jr. Co. Found.; bd. dirs. Texaco Inc.; bd. dirs., exec. com., chmn. Santa Catalina Island Co.; chmn., bd. dirs., mem. corp. issues com, mem. nominating com. Am. Home Products Corp.; dir. Grocery Mfrs. Am. Benefactor, mem. Santa Catalina Island Conservancy; trustee. CEO adv. bd., mem. devel. com. U. So. Calif. Lt. (j.g.) USNR, 1954-56, lt. comdr. Res., 1956-77. Home: Lake Geneva, Wis. Died Mar. 8, 1999.

WU CHENG-CHUNG, JOHN BAPTIST CARDINAL, bishop; b. Ng Wah County, Kwangtung, China, Mar. 26, 1925; s. Wu Shing Sing and Mary Chow. Degrees in philosophy and theology, South China Regional Sem., Hong Kong; D Canon Law summa cum laude, Pontifical U., Rome, 1956. Ordained priest Roman Cath. Ch., 1952; ordained bishop, 1975. Priest Cath. Ch., Hong Kong, 1952-53; pastor parishes N.Y.C., Boston, Chgo., 1956-57, 1957-75; bishop of Hong Kong, from 1975; cardinal, from 1988. Mem. (apptd.) Congregation for Evangelization of Peoples, Pontifical Coun. Interreligious Dialogue, Pontifical Coun. Culture, Pontifical Coun. Social Communications. Died Sept. 23, 2002; St. Michael's Catholic Cemetary, Happy Valley.

WUCHTER, MICHAEL DAVID, pastor; b. Atlantic City, Feb. 16, 1946; s. Robert Zimmerman and Eleanor Joyce (Freed) W.; m. Shirley Ann Dyer, Aug. 16, 1969; children: Andrew, J. Kirsten. BA, Wittenberg U., 1968; M of Div., The Luth. Theol. Sem., 1972; D of Ministry, Princeton Theol. Sem., 1983. Ordained to ministry Luth. Ch., 1972. Pastor Resurrection Luth. Ch., Hamilton Sq., N.J., 1972-79; pastor to the univ. Wittenberg U., Springfield, Ohio, from 1979. Pres. Trenton (N.J.) Campus Ministry, 1974-79; chaplain Lakeside (Ohio) Luth. Conf., 1980; chaplain to 75th anniversary conf. Luth. Ednl. Conf. N.Am., Washington, 1985; participant summer seminar Fulbright-Hays Faculty Devel., New Delhi, 1984; bd. dirs. Clrk Co. Children's Trust Fund. Author: (study guide) Disarmament in a Nuclear Age, 1983, (contbg.) In Praise of Preaching, 1984, Religions of India and Human Values, 1985; author numerous book revs. Pres., co-founder The Nottingham Recreation Ctr. for the Physically Ltd., Mercer County, N.J., 1979; bd. dirs. Springfield Pastoral Counseling Ctr., 1983, Specialized Ministries Council, Springfield, 1985, Springfield Peace Sch., 1988; bd. dirs. community adv. bd. Teen Suicide Prevention Project, Springfield, 1985, chmn., 1988. Fulbright-Hay Faculty Devel. Program grantee, 1984. Mem. Am. Acad. Religion, Nat. Assn. Coll. and Univ. Chaplains, Luth. Coll. Chaplains Assn. Democrat. Home: Duluth, Minn. Died Aug. 5, 2000.

WYMAN, THOMAS H. food products executive; b. 1930; Bachelors, Amherst Coll., 1951. With Nestle, Switzerland, 1961-63, Polaroid, Cambridge, Mass., 1963-75, sr. v.p., gen. mgr., 1972-75; with Green Giant Co., Mpls., 1975-79; vice chmn. Pillsbury Co., Mpls., 1979-80; with CBS Inc., N.Y.C., 1980-83, chmn., 1983; chmn., pres. United Biscuits (Holdings) U.S., Ltd.; UB Investments US Inc., Elmhurst, Ill., from 1992. Died Jan. 8, 2003.

WYNN, EARLY, retired baseball player; b. Hartford, Ala., Jan. 6, 1920; Pitcher Washington Senators, 1939-49, Cleve. Indians, 1949-58, 63, coach, 1964-66; pitcher Chgo. White Sox, 1958-63; coach Minn. Twins, 1967-69. Recipient Cy Young award, 1959; named to Baseball Hall of Fame, 1972. Achievements include selected to Am. League All-Star Team, 1955-60. Home: Venice, Fla. Died Apr. 4, 1999.

YAHR, MELVIN DAVID, physician; b. N.Y.C., Nov. 18, 1917; s. Isaac and Sarah (Reigelhaupt) Y.; m. Felice Turtz, May 9, 1948; children— Carol, Nina, Laura, Barbara Anne. AB, N.Y. U., 1939, MD, 1943. Diplomate: Am. Bd. Psychiatry and Neurology (pres.). Intern Lenox Hill Hosp., N.Y.C., 1943-44; resident Lenox Hill Hosp., also Montefiore Hosp., Bronx, N.Y., 1947-48; staff Columbia, 1948-73, asso. prof. clin. neurology, 1957-62, prof. neurology, 1962-70, H.H. Merritt prof. neurology, 1970-73, asst. dean grad. medicine, 1959-67, assoc. dean, 1967-73. Asst. neurologist N.Y. Neurol. Inst., 1948-53, assoc. attending neurologist, 1953-60, attending neurologist, 1960-73; Goldschmidt prof. neurology, chmn. dept. neurology Mt. Sinai Med. Center, 1973-92; former Aidekman Family Prof. Neurological Rsch.; exec. dir. Parkinson's Disease Found., 1957-73; panel neurologist N.Y.C. Bd. Edn., 1958-59; mem. com. evalutation drugs in neurology NIH, 1959-60, panel mem. neurol. study sect., 1959-80; mem. com. revisions U.S. Pharmacopea. Assoc. editor: Internat. Jour. Neurology; former editor-in-chief Jour. Neural Transmission; Archives Neurology, 1964-89. Fellow Am. Acad. Neurology, N.Y. Acad. Medicine, Harvey Soc.; mem. A.M.A. (chmn. com. neurol. disorders in industry), Am. Neurol. Assn. (sec.-treas. 1959-68, pres. 1969), Assn. Research Nervous and Mental Disease, N.Y. State Neurol. Soc., New York County Med. Soc., Am. Epilepsy Soc., Eastern Assn. Electroencephalographers. Home: Scarsdale, NY. Died Jan. 1, 2004.

YAMAJI, KEIZO, industry executive; b. Dec. 26, 1927; PhD, Tokyo U., 1951. Pres. Canon Inc., Tokyo, 1989-93, vice chmn., 1993-95. Chmn. bd. dirs. Nihon Tetra Pak K.K., Toyko; hon. advisor Canon, Inc. Decorated Medal of Honor with purple ribbon. Avocation: traveling. Died Dec. 26, 2003.

YANG, CHARLES CHAO-FU, mechanical engineering educator; b. Taichung, Taiwan, July 4, 1932; s. Tue-King and Nie (Chen) Y.; m. Shon H. Yu, Dec. 21, 1963; children: Robert, Paul. BSME, Nat. Taiwan U., Taipei, 1957; MS in Solid Mechanics, Yale U., 1967; PhD in Mechanics, Rensselaer Poly. Inst., 1970. Registered profl. engr., Calif. Sr. engr. GE, Schenectady, 1970-74, cons. on Japanese rels., 1970-80, sr. engr., acting mgr. Sunnyvale, Calif., 1974-84; v.p. fin. Silicon Svcs., Inc., Santa Clara, Calif., 1984; contr. Dielectric Semicondr., Inc., San Jose, Calif., 1985; Asian regional mgr. Gemini Rsch. Corp., Fremont, Calif., 1985-86; mgr. Chinese ops. Briggs & Stratton Corp., Milw., 1986-89; cons. Collaborative Engring. Svc., Cupertino, Calif., 1989-91; prof. mech. engring., chmn. dept. Chinese Culture U., Taipei, from 1991. Vice chmn. bd. Chinese Joint Venture, Chong Qing, 1989; engring. cons. Briggs-Pu Yi Engine Co., Chong Qing, China, 1986-89. Contbr. articles to profl. jours. Pres. Capitol dist. N.Y. Taiwanese Assn. Am., Albany, 1973, San Francisco Bay area, San Jose, 1974, v.p., Houston, 1978; pres. Taiwanese Alliance for Interculture, Sunnyvale, 1977. 2d lt. Taiwan Air Force, 1957-59. Mem. ASME, Chinese Soc. Mech. Engrs. (com. acad.-indsl. rels. 1990—), Chinese Engrs. Assn. Mem. U.S. Democratic Party. Avocations: public relations, political commentary. Home: Taipei, Taiwan. Died Mar. 4, 2002.

YANNUZZI, ROLAND A. social security administration district manager; b. Bronx, N.Y., Aug. 5, 1925; s. Thomas Leo and Jennie (DaMare) Y.; m. Florence Helen Konior, Sept. 3, 1951; children: Roland Victor, Debra Ann Bader, Patrice Mary Davidson. BA in Psychology, Hunter Coll., 1952; MA in Psychology, CCNY, 1955; Cert. of Psychology, Am. Inst. Psychoanalysis, 1973. Claims rep. Social Security Adminstrn., Bklyn., 1954-58, asst. ops. supr., 1958-60, ops. supr. White Plains, N.Y., 1960-67, asst. dist. mgr. Spring Valley, N.Y., 1967-68, Bronx, N.Y., 1968-71; tchr. English part time George Washington H.S., N.Y.C., 1964-82, clin. psychologist, 1974-82; dist. mgr. Social Security Adminstrn., Nanuet, N.Y., 1971-77, Hackensack, N.J., 1977-93. Columnist in field; contbr. articles to newspapers. Chmn. adv. com. Office on Aging, New City, N.Y., 1972-77, Helen Hayes Exhibit on Social Security, Nanuet, 1973; union negotiator Social Security Adminstrn., 1977-93; chmn. legis. com. Bergen County, N.J., 1979-93; seminar conductor Social Security Coll., Paramus, N.J., 1991-92; vol. English Tutor Tagaste Monaster, Suffern, N.Y., 1994-95. Sgt. U.S. Army, 1943-46. Recipient award for improving Social Security Adminstrn., 1992. Mem. Social Security Mgmt. Assn. (exec. v.p. 1970-72, pres. 1972-74, founding editor newsletter 1985-93, Award for editing newsletter 1992), Fed. Employees Retirement Assn. Republican. Roman Catholic. Avocations: cultivate roses, grafting various species of fruit trees. Home: New Windsor, NY. Deceased.

YARGER, FREDERICK LYNN, physics educator; b. Lindsey, Ohio, Mar. 8, 1925; s. Sherman Washington and Burdena (Lynn) Y.; m. Mary Jean Petersen, Aug. 21, 1948; children: Frederick Daniel, Peter David. BS in Physics, Capital U., Columbus, Ohio, 1950; MS in Physics, Ohio State U., 1953, PhD in Physics, 1960. Staff mem. Los Alamos (N.Mex.) Sci. Lab., 1953-55, 56; grad. asst. Ohio State U., Columbus, 1955-56, rsch. asst., 1958-60; sr. rsch. engr. N.Am. Aviation, Inc., Columbus, 1956-58; scientist Nat. Bur. Stds., Boulder, Colo., 1960-63; scientist specialist EG&G, Inc., Las Vegas, Nev., 1963-65; sr. rsch. physicist Falcon Rsch. & Devel. Co., Denver, 1965-66; prof. physics N.Mex. Highlands U., Las Vegas, from 1966. Vis. rsch. prof. Instituto de Fisica, UNAM, Ciudad Mexico, Mexico, 1968-98; vis. staff mem. Los Alamos Nat. Lab., 1971-93. Officer, vol. Las Vegas Fire Dept., Co. No. 1, Las Vegas, 1971-91; instr. First Aid, ARC, Las Vegas, 1971-90. With USN, 1943-47. Named Outstanding Educator, Outstanding Educators Am., N.Mex. Highlands U., 1971, Svc. to Sci. Fairs, N.E. N.Mex. Sci. & Engring. Fair, Las Vegas, 1967—. Mem. Am. Phys. Soc., Optical Soc. Am., N.Mex. Acad. Sci., Sigma Xi. Lutheran. Avocations: mountain climbing, skiing, travel. Home: Corrales, N.Mex. Deceased.

YODER, HATTEN SCHUYLER, JR., petrologist; b. Cleve., Mar. 20, 1921; s. Hatten Schuyler and Elizabeth Katherine (Knieling) Y.; m. Elizabeth Marie Bruffey, Aug. 1, 1959 (dec.); children: Hatten Schuyler III (dec.), Karen Marianne Yoder Wallace. AA, U. Chgo., 1940, SB, 1941; postgrad., U. Minn., 1941; PhD, Mass. Inst. Tech., 1948; PhD (hon.), U. Paris VI, 1981; DEngring. (hon.), Colo. Sch. of Mines, 1995. Petrologist Geophys. Lab., Carnegie Instn., Washington, 1948-71, dir., 1971-86, dir. emeritus, from 1986; cons. Los Alamos (N.Mex.) Nat. Lab., from 1972, chmn. external adv. com. earth & environ. scis. divsn., 1991-97. Author: Generation of Basaltic Magma, 1976, Planned Invasion of Japan, 1945, The Siberian Weather Advantage, 1997; editor: The Evolution of the Igneous Rocks: Fiftieth Anniversary Perspectives, 1979; co-editor: Geochemical Transport and Kinetics, 1974; co-editor Jour. of Petrology, 1959-69; assoc. editor Am. Jour. Sci, 1972-90; mem. editl. bd. Earth Scis. History, 1993-2000; contbr. articles to profl. jours. Trustee The Cutler Trust, 1992—; bd. advisors Coll. of Democracy of the Nat. Grad. U., founders com. 1985, exec. com./sec.-treas. 1995-2003. Lt. comdr. USNR, 1942-58. Naval Expedition to Siberia, 1945-46. Recipient Bicentennial medal Columbia U., 1954, A.G. Werner medal German Mineral Soc., 1972, Cert. of Recognition for Svc. in Cold War 1945-1991, U.S. Dept. Def., Profl. Achievement award U. Chgo. Club Washington, 2000; named to Disting. Alumni Hall of Fame, Lakewood (Ohio) H.S., 1990; mineral yoderite named in his honor, Yoder Symposium named in his honor, 2001. Fellow Geol. Soc. Am. (coun. 1966-68, A.L. Day medal 1962, History Geology award 1998), Geol. Soc. London (hon. Wollaston medal 1979), Geol. Soc. South Africa (du Toit lectr. 1987), World Innovation Found. (hon.), Am. Acad. Arts and Scis., Mineral. Soc. Am. (coun. 1962-64, 69-73, pres. 1971-72, MSA award 1954, Roebling medal 1992), Am. Geophys. Union (pres. volcanology, geochemistry and petrology sect. 1962-64); mem. NAS (chmn. geology sect. 1973-76, A.L. Day prize and lectr. 1972), Mineral Soc. London (hon., Hallimond lectr. 1979), Geol. Soc. Finland, Russian Mineral Soc. (hon.), Geochem. Soc. (organizer, founding mem., coun. 1956-58, spl. publ. 1 named in his honor 1987), Am. Chem. Soc., Mineral Assn. Can., Washington Acad. Sci., Geol. Soc. Washington, Chem. Soc. Washington, French Soc. Mineralogy and Crystallography (hon.), Am. Philos. Soc. (coun. 1983-85, 94—), Pub. Mems. Assn. of Fgn. Svc. (bd. dirs. 1993-96, 97—, v.p. 1994, 98-2000, 2003—, treas. 2000-2002), History of Earth Scis. Soc. (pres. 1995-96), History of Sci. Soc. (Forum lectr. 1998), SAR, Sigma Xi, Phi Delta Theta (Golden Legion award). Deceased.

YOKICH, STEPHEN PHILLIP, labor union administrator; b. Detroit, Aug. 20, 1935; m. Tekla Baumgartner. Trades apprentice Heidrich Tool and Die Co., Oak Park, Mich., 1956; region 1 staff UAW, 1969-77, dir. region 1, 1977, dir. agrl. implement dept., 1980-83, dir. organizing dept., 1983-89, v.p., 1989-95, pres., from 1995. Chair UAW Nat. Cmty. Action Program; v.p., mem. exec. coun. AFL-CIO, 1995. Active Dem. Nat. Com., Mich. Dem. Party State Ctrl. Com.; del. Dem. Nat. Conv.; bd. mem., mem. steering com. Econ. Alliance Mich., Mich. Blue Cross-Blue Shield, Mich. Cancer Found., Father Clement Kern Found.; founder Cmty. Caring Program, 1993; co-chair Cmty. Caring Program for Children. With USAF, 1952-56. Recipient Arab Am. of the Yr. award Arab Cmty. Ctr. for Econ. and Social Svcs., Dearborn, Mich., 1995; co-recipient Chmns. award for vehicle quality improvement J.D. Power and Assocs., 1998. Mem. NAACP, Coalition Labor Union Women. Avocations: hunting, golfing, fishing. Died 2002.

YORK, RICHARD TRAVIS, art dealer; b. Nashville, Oct. 22, 1950; s. James Samuel and Jeane (Townes) Y. BA, Vanderbilt U., 1972. Dir. Am. art Hammer Galleries, N.Y.C., 1974-76; in charge Am. dept. M. Knoedler & Co., N.Y.C., 1976-77; assoc. Hirschl & Adler Galleries, N.Y.C., 1977-81; dir., owner Richard York Gallery, N.Y.C., 1981—2003. Mem. adv. bd. Nat. Acad. Design, N.Y.C. Author: (exhbn. catalogs) American Folk Art, 1977, The Eye of Steiglitz, 1978 (Arlis award), Buildings Architecture in American Modernism, 1980, Ellen Day Hale, 1981 (Arlis award), The Natural Image: Plant Forms in American Modernism, 1982, An American Gallery, 1986, vols. I & II, 1987, III & IV, 1988, V, 1989, VI, 1990, VII, 1992, VIII, 1997, Charles G. Shaw: Abstractions of the Thirties, 1987, Will Henry Stevens: A Modernist's Response to Nature, 1987, Joseph Stella: The Tropics, 1988, Joseph Goldyne: Twenty Years of Work, 1992, American Paintings from the Collection of James H. Ricau, 1993, Modernism at the Salons of America, 1922-1936, 1995, California: One-hundred Forty Years of Art Produced in the State, 1996, Passion and Reverence—Joseph Stella and Nature, 1998, John Marin: The 291 Years, 1998, John Marin, The Painted Frame, 2000, Lockwood de Forest: Plein-Air Oil Sketches, 2001, Movement: Marin, 2001, Paintings by Walter Beck, 2002, John Graham's Renaissance and Revolution, 2002, No Record So True: The Wildflower Photographs of Edwin Hale Lincoln (1848-1938), 2002. Mem. art adv. com. Colby Coll., 1990-94; mem. art adv. panel IRS, 1991-97; mem. steering com. Direct Effect for AIDS Rsch., Rockefeller U., 1997-2003; mem. Am. fellows Whitney Mus. Am. Art, N.Y.C.; mem. dirs. cir. Nat. Gallery Art, Washington, 2002-2003; mem. nat. adv. coun. Boise Art Mus., 2002-2003. Mem.: William Cullen Bryant Fellows, Pa. Acad. Art (adv. com. from 1998), Art Dealers Assn. Am. (bd. dirs. 1992—95, v.p. 1997—2000, art show com. 1997—2001, chmn. membership com. 1998—2001), Nat. Arts Club, Met. Mus. of Art N.Y.C., Lotos Club (art com. from 2000), Ky. Cols. Home: New York, NY. Died Apr. 2, 2003.

YOUNES, NADIA, United Nations official; b. Cairo, June 13, 1946; BA, Cairo U., 1966; MA, NYU, 1973. With UN, 1970—2003; dep. spokesperson to the sec. gen. UN, 1988—93; chief of protocol Exec. Office Sec.- Gen., UN, N.Y.C., 1996—2002; spokesperson for Bernard Kouchner UN, 1999—2001, chief of staff to Sergio Vieria de Mello, 2003. Died Aug. 18, 2003.

YOUNG, EDMOND GROVE, consultant; b. Govans, Md., Oct. 29, 1917; s. Robert E. Lee and Lottie Gertrude (Grove) Y.; m. Jean Elizabeth Auwetter, Sept. 14, 1946; children: Stephen Edmond, Janet Louise Russell, Timothy Alan. BS, U. Md., 1938, PhD, 1943. Chemist Sharples Chems., Wyandotte, Mich., 1943-44; rsch. chemist E.I. DuPont de Nemours & Co., Wilmington, Del., 1944-48, tech. sales rep., 1948-50, mgr. propellant sales, 1950-52, mgr. sales devel., 1952-57, mgr. devel. confs., 1957-68, from mgr. devel. confs., govt. liaison to mgr. bus. devel., 1968-82; cons. NASA, Washington, 1983-85, Jet Propulsion Lab., Pasadena, Calif., 1985-88, U. Del., Newark, from 1988. Chmn. East Greenwich Bd. Zoning Adjustment, Clarksboro, N.J., 1974-92. Recipient Silver Medal for Outstanding Svc., Am. Def. Preparedness Assn., 1984. Fellow AAAS; mem. Am. Chem. Soc., Comml. Devel. Assn., Soc. of the Sigma Xi, Phi Kappa Phi, Alpha Chi Sigma. Republican. Methodist. Avocations: american history, mass transit history, stamp collecting/philately. Died Apr. 19, 2002.

YOUNG, JOHN BYRON, retired lawyer; b. Bakersfield, Calif., Aug. 10, 1913; s. Lewis James and Gertrude Lorraine (Clark) Y.; m. Helen Beryl Stone, Dec. 26, 1937; children: Sally Jean, Patricia Helen, Lucia Robin. BA, UCLA, 1934; LLB, U. Calif., Berkeley, 1937; student, U. Chgo., 1943. Pvt. practice law Hargreaves & Young, later Young Wooldridge, Bakersfield, 1937-40; dep. county counsel County of Kern, Bakersfield, 1940-42; dep. rationing atty. U.S. OPA, Bakersfield and Fresno, Calif., 1942; ptnr. firm Young Wooldridge and predecessors, Bakersfield, 1946-78, assoc. law firm, 1978-91. Bd. dirs., legal counsel Kern County Water Assn., Bakersfield, 1953-76. Mem., chmn. Kern County Com. Sch. Dist. Orgn., Bakersfield, 1950s and 60s; mem. Estate Planning Coun. of Bakersfield, 1960-76, pres., 1965-66. Capt. JAGC, U.S. Army, 1943-46. Mem. Kern County Bar Assn. (prs. 1948, Bench and Bar award 1978). Home: Del Mar, Calif. Died Jan. 27, 2003.

YOUNG, MORRIS NATHAN, ophthalmologist, writer; b. Lawrence, Mass., July 20, 1909; s. Charles Michael and Ida (Davis) Y.; children: Cheryl Lesley Deknatel, Charles Chesley. BS, MIT, 1930; MA, Harvard U., 1931; MD, Columbia U., 1935; PhD, U. San Marino, 1998. Diplomate Am. Bd. Ophthalmology. Intern Queens (N.Y.) Gen. Hosp., 1935-37; resident in ophthalmology Harlem Eye and Ear Hosp., N.Y.C., 1938-40; pvt. practice in ophthalmology N.Y.C., from 1945. Med. advisor N.Y.C. Dir. Selective Svs. Sys., N.Y.C. Dept. Health; asst. ophthalmologist NYU Univ. Hosp., 1947-61; cons. Beth Israel Hosp., 1972-93, hon., 1994, St. Vincent's Hosp. and Med. Ctr., N.Y.C., 1978—; dir. emeritus ophthalmology N.Y. Downtown Hosp.; v.p. Life Music, Inc.; pres. Denton & Haskins Corp. Author: Presto Prestige, 1929, Hobby Magic, 1950, Houdini on Magic, 1953, Bibliography of Memory, 1961, Houdini's Fabulous Magic, 1961, How to Develop an Exceptional Memory, 1962, How to Read Faster and Remember More, 1965, A Complete Guide to Science Fair Competition, 1972, Radio Music Live, 1999, Original Magicol and Indices, Vols. 1-3, 1998; editor MAGICOL mag., 1949-52; contbr. articles to profl. jours. Bd. dirs. Houdini Hist. Ctr., Houdini Mus., Las Vegas; mem. exec. bd. Houdini Picture Corp.; hon. cons. Libr. Congress. Col. USAR, 1930-69, ret. Mem. AMA, ASCAP, Am. Assn. Ophthalmology, Am. Acad. Ophthalmology (life), N.Y. State Med. Soc., Pan Am. Med. Assn., Queens Gen. Hosp. Alumni Assn., Res. Officers Assn., Ret. Officers Assn., Soc. of Mil. Ophthalmologists, Glaucoma Found. (adv. bd.), Chinatown Lions Club (hon.), Lawrence Unitcd Lodge, Nat. Sojourners (pres. Manhattan chpt., trustee Knickerbocker chpt.), Heroes of '76, Soc. Am. Magicians (hon.), Internat. Brotherhood Magicians, Magic Collectors Assn. (founding), N.Eng. Magic Collectors Assn. (hon.), Mil. Order of World Wars (surgeon 1997—), Order of Lafayette (surgeon gen. 1998—), Magic Cir. (Inner Magic Cir.), Harvard Magic Club (hon.), Soc. of Osiris (hon. mem.). Died Nov. 13, 2002.

YOUNG, ROBERT GORDON, artist; b. Utica, N.Y., Jan. 23, 1929; s. Arnold Oscar and Elsie Mae (Payne) Y.; m. Bernice Ann Sitnik, June 24, 1954; children: John Stanley, Peter Gordon, Paul Robert. Student, Atlantic Ctr. for the Arts, Fla. Sch. Arts, S.W. State Tchrs. Coll., Tex.; BS in Art Edn., Buffalo State Tchrs. Coll., N.Y., 1951; AS in Art, Fla. Sch. of the Arts, Palatka, 1980; student, Procter, Munson, Williams Inst., N.Y. One-man shows include U. West Fla., Ft. Walton Beach, 1993, Art and Asian Soc., Ft. Walton Beach, 1993, Traveling Show-The Secret War in Laos, 1988-90, Brest Gallery, Jacksonville, Fla., Internat. Sanibel Symposium, Palm Coast, Fla., Fla. Sch. Arts mus., Fla., others; juried shows include Fla. Sch. Arts Gallery, Palatka, Fla., Soc. Four Arts, Palm Beach, Boca Raton Art Ctr., Fla., St. Augustine Art Gallery, Fla., others; represented in permanent collections including Permanent Collection State of Fla., Shin-Kai-Ju-Sha guild collection, Lithonia Internat. Corp., others. Mem. Fla. Artist Group Inc., Fla. Pastel Soc., Fla. Watercolor Soc. Deceased.

YOUNG, VERNON ROBERT, nutrition, biochemistry educator; b. Rhyl, Wales, Nov. 15, 1937; arrived in U.S., 1961; married, 1966; 5 children. BS, U. Reading, Eng., 1959; diploma in agr., Cambridge U., Eng., 1960; PhD in Nutrition, U. Calif., Davis, 1965; MD (hon.), Uppsala U., Sweden, 1997. Lectr. nutritional biochemistry MIT, Cambridge, Mass., 1965—66, asst. prof. physiology chemistry, 1966—72, assoc. prof., 1972—76, prof. nutritional biochemistry, 1976—2004. Program mgmt. human nutrition competitive rsch. grants program USDA, 1980—81; assoc. program dir. MIT Clin. Rsch. Ctr., Cambridge, Mass., 1985—87; biochemist dept. surgery Mass. Gen. Hosp. and Harvard Med. Sch., Boston, 1987—2004; sr. vis. scientist USDA Human Nutrition Ctr. Aging, Tufts U., 1988—2004. Recipient Danone prize, French Med. Found., 1987, Rank prize in Nutrition, 1989, Bristol-Myers Squibbs/Mead Johnson award of Nutrition, 1995. Mem.: NAS, Am.Chem. Soc., Gerontology Soc. Am., Nutrition Soc., Am. Soc. Clin. Nutrition (McCollum award 1987), Am. Soc. Nutritional Sci., Inst. Medicine NAS (Mead Johnson award 1973, Borden award 1982). Died Mar. 30, 2004.

YOUNG, WILLIAM THOMPSON, soft drink company executive; b. Lexington, Ky., Feb. 15, 1918; s. Willis Samuel and Margaret (Thompson) Y.; m. Lucy Hilton Maddox, Apr. 16, 1945; children— William Thompson, Lucy Meade. BS in Mech. Engring. with high distinction, U. Ky., 1939. With Bailey Meter Co., Cleve., 1939-41; pres. W.T. Young Foods, Lexington, 1946-55; gen. mgr. W.T. Young Foods (subs. Procter & Gamble Co.), 1955-57; chmn. bd. Royal Crown Cos., Inc., Atlanta, W.T. Young Storage Co., Lexington, 1957—. Dir. First Security Nat. Bank & Trust Co., Lexington, Ky.-Am. Water Co.; chmn. bd. Transylvania U., Lexington. Bd. dirs. Humana Inc. Served to capt. AUS, 1941-45. Mem. Sigma Alpha Epsilon. Clubs: Rotary, Optimists (past pres. Lexington chpt.). Presbyterian. Home: Lexington, Ky. Died Jan. 12, 2004.

YOUNGER, GEORGE (KENNETH HOTSON) (BARON YOUNGER OF PRESTWICK), former government official, bank executive; b. Stirling, Scotland, Sept. 22, 1931; s. Viscount Younger of Leckie and Evelyn Margaret McClure; m. Diana Rhona, 1954; children: James, Joanna, Charles, Andrew. Grad. with honors in Modern History,

Oxford U. Dir., George Younger & Son Ltd., 1958-68, J.G. Thomson & Co. Ltd., Leith, 1962-66, Maclachlans Ltd., 1968-70, Tennant Caledonian Breweries Ltd., 1977-79; M.P. for Ayr, 1964-92; Scottish Conservative whip, 1965-67; Parliamentary under-sec. state for devel. Scottish Office, 1970-74; minister of state for def., 1974, sec. of state for Scotland, 1979-86; sec. state for def., 1986-89; chmn. Conservative Party in Scotland, 1974-75; pres. Nat. Union Conservative and Unionist Asssn., 1987-88; bd. dirs., chmn. various Murray Internat. Trusts PLC, 1993—; chmn. bd. Royal Bank of Scotland plc, 1989—, Royal Bank of Scotland Group plc, 1989—, Siemens Plessey Electronic Systems Ltd., 1990—, BCH Property Ltd., 1991—, Scottish Partnership in Electronics for Effective Distbn. Ltd., 1992—; bd. trustees Royal Armorie; bd. dirs. Banco Santander, SA., 1991, Scotish Equitable Holdings Ltd., 1993, Scotish Equitable Policy Holders Trust Ltd., 1993, Scotish Equitable plc, 1993, Fleming Mercantile Investment Trust PLC, 1994; chmn. PIK Holdings Ltd., 1991, Quality Scotland Fond. Ltd., 1992, Quality Scotland Edn. Trust, 1992, Edinburgh Festival Theatre Trust, 1991; pres. Royal Highland & Agrl. Soc., 1990; chancellor Napier U., 1993. Served with Argyll and Sutherland Highlanders Regular and Territorial Army, 1950-65. Recipient Terr. Decoration. Mem. Royal Co. of Archers (brigadier, dep. lt. Stirlingshire 1968—). Club: Caledonian (London). Died Jan. 26, 2003.

YU, YI-YUAN, mechanical engineering educator; b. Tienjin, China, Jan. 29, 1923; came to U.S., 1947, naturalized, 1962; s. Tsi-Chi and Hsiao-Kung (Wang) Y.; m. Eileen Hsiu-Yung Wu, June 14, 1952; children: Yolanda, Lisa. BS, Tienjin U., 1944; MS, Northwestern U., 1950, PhD, 1951. Prof. mech. engring. (Poly Inst. Bklyn.), 1957-66; cons. engr. GE Space Divsn., Valley Forge, Pa., 1966-70; Disting. prof. aero. engring. (Wichita State U.), 1972-75; mgr. components and analysis Rockwell Internat., Rocketdyne, Canoga Park, Calif., 1975-79, exec. engr. Energy Systems, 1979-81; dean engring. N.J. Inst. Tech., Newark, 1981-85, prof. mech. engring., 1981-93, prof. emeritus, from 1993, rsch. prof., 1996-98. Vis. prof. Cambridge U., 1960; advisor Middle East Tech. U., Ankara, Turkey, 1966; lectr. Gen. Electric Co., 1963-73; mem. ad hoc com. on dynamic analysis USN, 1968-69; cons. internat. adv. panel Chinese U. Devel. Project, 1983, David W. Taylor Naval Ship Rsch. and Devel. Ctr., 1987-88; cons. Atty. Gen.'s Office State N.J., 1982-84. Contbr. Handbook of Engineering Mechanics, 1962; author: Vibrations of Elastic Plates, 1997. Guggenheim fellow, 1959-60; Air Force Office Sci. Rsch. grantee, 1956-66; NASA grantee, 1967-69, 74-75 Fellow AIAA (assoc.), ASME (life); mem. Am. Soc. Engring. Edn., Am. Soc. for Composites, Am. Acad. Mechanics (chmn. com. mech. edn. 1993-94), Sigma Xi, Phi Kappa Phi, Pi Tau Sigma, Tau Beta Pi. Presbyterian. Home: Essex Fells, NJ. Died May 7, 2004.

YUKER, HAROLD ELWOOD, psychologist, educator; b. Newark, N.J., Apr. 15, 1924; s. Hyman and Sadie (Glucksman) Y. BA, U. Newark, 1944; MA, New Sch. Social Research, 1950; PhD, N.Y. U., 1954. Research asst. Columbia U. Bur. Applied Social Research, 1947-48; mem. faculty dept. psychology Hofstra U., Hempstead, N.Y., 1948—, prof., 1964-83, Mervyn Livingston Schloss prof., 1983—; dir. Ctr. for Study of Higher Edn., 1965-75, interim provost, 1973-74, provost, dean of faculties, 1976-81, dir. Ctr. for Study of Attitudes toward Persons with Disabilities, 1982—. Dir. research Human Resources Found., 1956-63, research cons., 1963-81 Author: A Guide to Statistical Calculations, 1958, The Measurement of Attitudes Toward Disabled Persons, 1966, Faculty Workload: Research, Theory, and Interpretation, 1985; editor: Attitudes Toward Disabled Persons, 1987; contbr. articles to profl. jours. Mem. Am. Psychol. Assn., Soc. for Study of Social Issues, AAAS. Home: Bellmore, NY. Died August 1997.

YUN, SUK KOO, physics educator, academic administrator; b. Seoul, Korea, Nov. 10, 1930; came to U.S., 1955; s. Il Sun and Margaret (Cho) Y.; m. July 20, 1957; children: Stephen T., Elise H., Christina A. BS in Physics, Seoul Nat. U., 1955; MS in Physics, U. Chgo., 1957; PhD in Physics, Boston U., 1967. Instr. Clarkson U., Potsdam, N.Y., 1959-63; rsch. assoc. Syracuse (N.Y.) U., 1967-69; from asst. prof. to prof. Saginaw Valley State U., University Center, Mich., from 1969, chmn. natural sci. dept., 1972-74, chmn. physics dept., from 1977; hon. rsch. fellow Harvard U., Cambridge, Mass., 1975-76. Vis. scientist Fermi Nat. Accelerator Lab., Batavia, Ill., 1978-82, MIT, Cambridge, Mass., 1980, 84, 85-89, U. Mich., Ann Arbor, 1974-75; cons. Syracuse, summer, 1977. Author: Lab. Manual for General Physics, 1971, A Vision of Beauty in Order, 1972; editor: Readings in the Interaction of Science Society, 1973. Grantee NSF, Frederick Gardner Cottrell, Saginaw Valley State U. scholar, 1988; recipient E.L. Warrick award for excellence in rsch., 1987, Disting. Faculty award State of Mich., 1988. Mem. Am. Phys. Soc., Assn. Korean Physicists in Am. (pres. Washington 1991-92), Korean Scientists and Engrs. in Am. (councilor 1984-86), Sigma Xi. Methodist. Home: Midland, Mich. Deceased.

ZABALETA, NICANOR, harpist; b. San Sebastian, Guipuzcoa, Spain, Jan. 7, 1907; s. Pedro Zabaleta and Isabel Zala S.; m. Graciela Torres, Feb. 22, 1952; children: Pedro, Estella. Grad., Madrid Royal Conservatory, 1920. Harpist in numerous concerts worldwide, various music festivals including those in West Berlin, Lucerne, France, Edinburgh, Scotland, Osaka, Japan, Paris, Prague, Venice, Italy; producer numerous records including (with Y. Menuhin) Music for Violin and Harp, (with the Madrid Nat. Orch.) Concierto de Aranjuez, (with the Berlin Philhamonic and the Vienna Philharmonic) Mozart's Flute and Harp Concerto, (with English Chamber Orch) Bach/Handel Concertos, (solo) Bach Program, Spanish Harp Music from the 16th to the 18th Centuries, others; publ. Six Variations Faciles Sur Un Theme Suisse Pour la Harpe ou le Forte Piano, 1959, Dussek-Sonata for Harp in C minor, 1959, 16th to 18th Century Spanish Harp Music, 1959. Home: San Sebastian, Spain. Died: Mar. 31, 1993.

ZACHARIAS, RITA TIMMONS, real estate agent; b. Dagsboro, Del., Jan. 31, 1934; d. William Edgar and Ethel Mae (Burton) Timmons; m. Jerrold Matthew Zacharias, Aug. 14, 1954; children: Jerrold Matthew, Dana Timmons, David Stuart. BA, U. Del., 1955. Cert. Residential Specialist, Grad. Realtor's Inst., Women's Coun. Realtors, assoc. broker. Assoc. broker Rucker Enterprises/Realtors, Arlington, Va., from 1976. Chmn. adminstrv. bd. Dulin United Meth. Ch., 1990—; mem. Dulin United Meth. Women, past pres.; chmn. Personal Support Network Assn. Retarded Citizens No. Va. Mem. NAT, Va. Assn. Realtors, No. Va. Assn. Realtors (chmn. 1990—), Multiple Listing Svc. Com. Avocations: reading, crossword puzzles, music. Home: Falls Church, Va. Deceased.

ZAK, JOHN MICHAEL, retired agronomy educator; b. Sunderland, Mass., May 12, 1914; s. John William and Mary (Swaluk) Z.; m. Ruth Symonds, May 5, 1945; children: Karen Elizabeth Zak Benbury, John Merrill, Richard Paul, Rebecca Louise. BS, U. Mass., 1936, MS, 1938. Agronomy U. Mass., Amherst, 1938-84; ret., 1984. Co-founder Mohawk Trout Hatchery, Sunderland. 1960-84. Author pamphlets and bulls. in field, including Establishment and Management of Roadside Vegetative Cover in Massachusetts, 1967, Handbooks I and II: A Plant Material's Manual, 1976, Roadside Vegetative Cover for Critical and Eroded Areas, 1976, Massachusetts Roadside Development Researcher, 1977. Grantee Fed. Highway Adminstrn., 1969-80. Mem. Cushman Investment Club (v.p. 1985, pres. 1999), Masons, Sigma Xi, Alpha Tau Gamma. Avocations: beekeeping, fishing, hunting, gardening. Home: Amherst, Mass. Died 1999.

ZALLINGER, RUDOLPH FRANZ, artist, educator; b. Irkutsk, Siberia, Nov. 12, 1919; came to U.S., 1924; s. Franz Xavier and Marie (Koncheravich) Z.; m. Jean Farquharson Day, Sept. 27, 1941; children: Peter Franz, Kristina, Lisa Day. BFA, Yale U., 1942, MFA, 1971; D Fine Art, U. New Haven, 1980. Instr. painting Yale Sch. Fine Arts, New Haven, 1942-47, asst. prof. painting, 1948-50; artist-in-residence Yale Peabody Mus./Yale U., New Haven, 1953-95; faculty Hartford Art Sch. U. Hartford, West Hartford, Conn., 1961-72, prof. drawing and painting, 1972-89, prof. emeritus, 1989-95. Fellow Davenport Coll., Yale U., 1964-95, vis. prof., 1989-95; bd. dirs. Paier Coll. Art, Hamden, Conn.; adv. com. Sanford Low Meml. Collection Am. Illustration, New Britain (Conn.) Mus. Am. Art. Solo exhbns. include Mystic (Conn.) Seaport Galleries, 1967, Ctr. Gallery, New Haven Jewish Community Ctr., 1975, New Britain Mus. Am. Art, 1979, Dorsky Galleries, N.Y.C., 1981, GE Corp. Hdqrs., Fairfield, Conn., 1981, Davenport Coll., Yale U., 1989, Hartford Art Sch., 1992, Saguaro Gallery, Park City, Utah, 1994; retrospective Paul Mellon Arts Ctr. Gallery Choate Sch., Wallingford, Conn., 1993; group exhbns. include N.Y. Hist. Soc., 1976, Cleve. Art Inst., 1977, Joseloff Gallery, U. Hartford, 1964-89; represented in permanent collections Seattle Art Mus., New Britain Mus. Am. Art, N.Y. Times Dist. Hdqrs., Atlanta, Yeshiva U., Tel Aviv, numerous others and pvt. collections. Bd. dirs. Conn. Hospice, 1982, vice-chmn., 1988, co-chmn., 1990-95. Winner Pulitzer award for painting, 1949; recipient Addison Emery Verrill medal Yale U., 1980, Rudolph F. Zallinger fellowship, 1989; recipient James and Frances Bent award for creativity U. Hartford, 1988. Mem. Nat. Soc. Mural Painters, Conn. Acad. Arts and Scis., Puget Sound Group Northwest Painters, New Haven Paint and Clay Club (bd. dirs., past pres.). Avocations: piano, tennis. Home: Branford, Conn. Deceased.

ZAMPANO, ROBERT CARMINE, federal judge; b. New Haven, Mar. 18, 1929; s. Anthony N. and Marie (Fusco) Z.; m. Dorothea Mea Gilbride, Nov. 23, 1950; children: Deborah Lee, Robert Anthony. BA, Yale U., 1951, LL.B., 1954. Bar: Conn. 1954. Law clk. to U.S. dist. judge Conn., 1954-55; with Thompson, Weir & MacDonald, New Haven, 1955-57, Zampano & Mager, East Haven, 1959-61; judge East Haven, 1959-60; counsel, 1956-61; exec. sec. rev. div. Superior Ct. Conn., 1956-61; U.S. dist. atty. Conn., 1961-64; judge U.S. Dist. Ct., 1964—77, sr. judge, 1977—94; pvt. practice Conn., 1994—2004. Co-chmn. bar sect. New Haven United Fund, 1956-57; commr. Quinnipiac council Boy Scouts Am., 1953; pres. East Haven 175th Anniversary Comm., 1960; chmn. East Haven Democratic party, 1956-61; bd. dirs. New Haven ARC, Community Health Care Plan, 1978-79, East Haven Community Ctr.; bd. govs. U. New Haven; trustee Gunnery Sch., 1966-76, Hamden Hall Country Day Sch., 1966-76; mem. adv. bd. Conn. Mental Health Ctr., 1969-74, New Haven Regional Ctr. for Mentally Retarded, 1966-73. Mem. Am., New Haven County bar assns., Am. Justinian Soc. Jurists (dir.) Clubs: K.C; Melebus (New Haven), Yale (New Haven) (dir. 1960-63), Amity (New Haven) (sec. 1961). Home: East Haven, Conn. Died Jan. 12, 2004.

ZANE, ARNIE, performing company executive, choreographer; b. Bronx, N.Y., 1948; Student, SUNY, Binghamton. Co-founder, with Lois Welk Am. Dance Asylum, Binghamton, 1973—82; co-founder, choreographer Bill T. Jones/Arnie Zane Dance Co., N.Y.C., 1982—88. Choreographer (ballets) Blauvelt Mountain, 1980 (co-recipient German Critics award with Bill T. Jones, 1980), How to Walk an Elephant, 1985 (N.Y. Dance and Performance "Bessie" award, 1985). Fellow Creative Artists Public Svc. fellow in Photography, 1973, Creative Artists Public Svc. fellow in Choreography, 1981, in Choreography, N.E.A., 1983, 1984. Died 1988.

ZATUCHNI, JACOB, internal medicine educator; b. Phila., Oct. 8, 1920; AB in Chemistry, Temple U., 1941, MD, 1944. Cert. cardiovascular diseases Am. Bd. Internal Medicine. Intern Jewish Hosp., Phila., 1944-45; resident diseases of the chest Eagleville (Pa.) Sanatorium, 1945-47; resident internal medicine Temple U. Hosp., Phila., 1947-50; internist Temple U. Sch. Medicine, Phila., 1950; instr. medicine Temple U. Sch. Medicine and Hosp., Phila., 1950-54, asst. prof. medicine, 1954-58, assoc. prof. medicine, 1958-61, chief cardiac clinic B, 1959-60, prof. clin. medicine, 1962-66, prof. medicine, 1966-87, prof. emeritus, from 1987. Clin. asst. medicine Episcopal Hosp., 1950-53, assoc. in medicine, 1953-59, teaching chief medicine, 1959-67, head sect. cardiovascular disease, 1967-82, dir. dept. medicine, 1974-82, head heart sta., 1982-87, attending physician, 1982-87; sr. diagnostician Pa. Hosp., 1987—, dir. clin. svcs. cardiovascular sect., 1987—; clin. prof. medicine U. Pa. Sch. Medicine, 1988—. Author: Notes on Physical Diagnosis, 1964; contbr. articles to profl. jours. Fellow ACP, Am. Coll. Chest Physicians, Am. Coll. Cardiology; mem. AMA, Am. Heart Assn. (fellow coun. clin. cardiology), Phila. Coll. Physicians, N.Y. Acad. Scis., Am. Fedn. for Clin. Rsch., Heart Assn. Southeastern Pa. (bd. govs.), Am. Phoracic Soc., Pa. Med. Soc., Philadelphia County Med. Soc. (standing com. on med. edn., standing com. med. econs., standing com. profl. rels. and grievances), So. Med. Assn., Am. Soc. Nuclear Medicine, Am. Soc. Echocardiography, Pyramid Honor Soc., Sigma Xi, Alpha Omega Alpha. Home: Bala Cynwyd, Pa. Died Oct. 6, 2001.

ZATZKIN, HERBERT R. retired radiologist; b. N.Y., 1915; s. Rudolph Jacob and Anna (Bogart) Z.; m. Florence R. Kaplan, Jan. 24, 1944; children: Jay, Charles, Anne. BA, NYU, 1936; MD, U. Louisville, 1940. Diplomate Am. Bd. Radiology. Intern St. Peters Gen. Hosp., New Brunswick, N.J., 1940-41; resident in roentgenology U. Mich. Hosp., Ann Arbor, 1946-48; chmn. dept. radiology Nassau County Pub. Gen. Hosp., East Meadow, N.Y., 1949-69. Assoc. clin. prof. radiology Med. U. S.C., Charleston, 1982-85. Author: Roentgen Diagnosis of Trauma, 1963. Fellow Am. Coll. Radiology; mem. AMA, Am. Roentgen Ray Soc. Home: Johns Island, SC. Died Jul. 10, 1999.

ZAVIN, THEODORA, music industry executive; b. N.Y.C., Jan. 29, 1922; m. Benjamin Zavin, June 17, 1945 (dec. 1981); children: Jonathan, Joshua. AB, Hunter Coll., 1941; LLB, Columbia U., 1943. Bar: N.Y. 1944. Assoc. George Z. Medalie, N.Y.C., 1943-44, Greenbaum, Wolfe and Ernst, N.Y.C., 1944-50; house counsel Broadcast Music Inc., N.Y.C., 1952-57, asst. v.p., 1957-65, v.p., 1965-68, sr. v.p., 1968—2001. Pres. BMI Found., Inc., 1984-2004 Author: (with Harriet F. Pilpel) Your Marriage and The Law, 1952, rev. edit., 1964, Rights and Writers, 1960. Co-chmn. United Jewish Appeal, 1963-87 (Music Exec. Yr. 1976). Mem. Copyright Soc. U.S. (pres. 1986-88), ABA, Columbia Law Sch. Alumni Fedn. (bd. dirs. 1988-91), N.Y. State Bar Assn. (1994 Ann. award). Democrat. Avocations: reading, cooking. Home: New York, NY. Died June 21, 2004.

ZECCA, JOHN ANDREW, retired association executive; b. Bklyn., June 18, 1914; s. Joseph and Elvira (Orsi) Z.; m. Jean Ann Scott, June 27, 1964; 1 son, John Andrew. Student, Heffley Queensboro Coll., Ridgewood, N.Y., 1931, N.Y. U., 1933-36. Auditor ASCE, 1936-50, comptroller, 1950-60; registered rep. Goodbody & Co., 1960-61; pvt. cons. practice, 1961-64; sec., gen. mgr. United Engring. Trustees, 1965-81; trustee Engring. Index, Inc., 1967-81; sec. Engring. Found., 1965-81. John Fritz Medal Bd. Award, 1965-81; Daniel Guggenheim Medal Bd. Award, 1965-81 Mem. East Side Assn., ASCE, Council Engring. and Sci. Soc. Execs., Am. Soc. Assn. Execs. Home: Suffern, NY. Died May 14, 1999.

ZELNIK, REGINALD ELY, education educator, researcher; b. N.Y.C., May 8, 1936; s. Simon Bernard and Salomea (Czysz) Z.; m. Elaine Rosebery, 1956; children: Pamela, Michael David. BA, Princeton U., 1956; MA, Stanford U., 1961, PhD, 1966. Lectr. dept. history Ind. U., Bloomington, 1963-64; from acting asst. prof. to assoc. prof. dept. history U. Calif., Berkeley, 1964-76, prof., from 1976, chmn. dept. history, 1994—97, vice chmn. for grad. affairs, 2003—04. Chmn. Joint Com. on the Soviet Union and its Successor States, 1993-95. Author: Labor and Society in Tsarist Russia, 1971, Law and Disorder on the Narova River, 1995; editor, translator: A Radical Worker in Tsarist Russia: The Autobiography of Semen Kanatchikov, 1986 (Babra award 1987); editor: Workers and Intelligentsia in Late Imperial Russia, 1999; co-editor: The Free Speech Movement: Reflections on Berkeley in the 1960s, 2002; mem. editl. bd. Jour. Social History, 1968—, Kritika, 2000—; Am. Hist. Rev., Slavic Rev., Jour. Modern History; bd. dirs. NCEEER; contbr. articles to profl. jours. Bd. dirs. Mental Health Assn. Alameda County, Calif. Lt. (j.g.) USN, 1957-59. Fulbright fellow U. Vienna, 1956-57, Guggenheim fellow, 1971-72, Ctr. for Study & Behavior Scis. fellow, 1989-90; grantee NEH, Ford Found. Mem. Am. Hist. Assn., Am. Assn. for Advancement Slavic Studies. Democrat. Jewish. Avocations: reading, music, conversation, travel. Home: Berkeley, Calif. Died May 17, 2004.

ZEVON, WARREN, singer, songwriter; b. Chgo., Jan. 24, 1947; m. Crystal Zevon (div.); 1 child, Ariel; 1 child from previous marriage, Jordan. Folksinger, writer commls., pianist with Everly Bros., 1970-73; albums include Wanted Dead or Alive, 1969, Warren Zevon, 1976, Excitable Boy, 1978 (gold record), Bad Luck Streak in Dancing School, 1980, Stand in the Fire, 1980, The Envoy, 1982, Sentimental Hygiene, 1987, Transverse City, 1989, (with Hindu Love Gods) Hindu Love Gods, 1990, Mr. Bad Example, 1991, Learning to Flinch, 1993, A Quiet Normal Life (the best of Warren Zevon), 1993, Mutineer, 1995, I'll Sleep When I'm Dead: The Warren Zevon Anthology, 1996, Life'll Kill Ya, 2000, My Ride's Here, 2002, Genius: The Best of Warren Zevon, 2002, The Wind, 2003; composer: When Johnny Strikes up the Band, Hasten Down the Wind, Werewolves of London, Poor Poor Pitiful Me, Play It All Night Long, Roland the Headless Thompson Gunner. Died Sept. 7, 2003.

ZICK, LEONARD OTTO, accountant, manufacturing executive, consultant; b. St. Joseph, Mich., Jan. 16, 1905; s. Otto J. and Hannah (Heyn) Z.; m. Anna Essig, June 27, 1925 (dec. May 1976); children: Rowene Neidow Zick, Arlene (Mrs. Thomas Anton), Constance Mae (Mrs. Hilary Snell), Shirley Ann (Mrs. John Vander Ley) (dec.); m. Genevieve Evans, Nov. 3, 1977 (dec. Nov. 1996); m. Vera H. Helscher, Dec. 6, 1997. Student, Western State U., Kalamazoo, Mich. Sr. ptnr. Zick, Campbell & Rose Accts. (and predecessor firms), South Bend, Ind., 1928-48; sec., treas. C.M. Hall Lamp Co., Detroit, 1948-51, pres., 1951-54; chmn. bd., 1954-56; pres., treas., dir. Allen Electric & Equipment Co. (now Allen Group, Inc.), Kalamazoo, 1957-61; fin. v.p., treas., dir., chmn. bd. Crampton Mfg. Co., 1961-63; mgr. corp. fin. dept. Manley, Bennett, McDonald & Co., Detroit, 1963-68; mgr. Leonard O. Zick & Assocs., Holland, Mich., 1968-88. Contbg. editor: Cost Accountants Hand Book. Former mem. Mich. Rep. Cen. Com.; trustee YMCA Found., Clearwater, Fla., Richard E. Byrd Polar Ctr., Boston; vice chmn. Army-Navy Munitions Bd., 1941-42, asst. to vice chmn. War Prodn. Bd., 1941-43; chmn. bd. Greater Holland United Fund. Mem. Inst. Mgmt. Accts. (past nat. v.p., dir.), Mich. Self Insurers Assn. (past pres.), Fin. Execs. Inst., Stuart Cameron McLeod Soc. (past pres.), Union League (Chgo.), Soc. Automotive Engrs. (chmn. lighting com.), Rotary (Paul Harris fellow), Holland Country Club. Lutheran. Home: Holland, Mich. Died Feb. 4, 2003.

ZIEGLER, RONALD LOUIS, former association and government official, writer; b. Covington, Ky., May 12, 1939; s. Louis Daniel and Ruby (Parsons) Z.; m. Nancy Lee Plessinger, July 30, 1960; children: Cynthia Lee Charas, Laurie Michelle Albright. Student, Xavier U., 1957-58; BS, U. So. Calif., 1961; DSc (hon.), Mass. Coll. Pharmacy, 1989, L.I. U., 1993. With Procter & Gamble Distbg. Co., 1961; account rep. J. Walter Thompson Co., 1962-68; press dir. Calif. Rep. Central Com., 1961-62; press aide to Richard Nixon in Calif. gubernatorial campaign, 1962; press aide staff Richard Nixon, 1968-69; press sec. to Pres. Nixon, 1969-74, asst. to, 1973-74; mng. dir., sr. v.p. internat. services Syska and Hennessy, Inc., Washington, 1975-80; pres. Nat. Assn. Truck Stop Operators, Alexandria, Va., 1980-87; pres., CEO, Nat. Assn. Chain Drug Stores, Alexandria, 1987-98; ret., now writer, from 1998. Mem. nat. adv. bd. U. Okla.; adv. coun. Pharm. Found. U. Tex. Writer on current and polit. events. Bd. dirs. Nat. Coun. on Patient Info. and Edn., Nat. Conf. on Pharm. Assns., Richard Nixon Libr. and Birthplace. Mem. Am. Soc. Assn. Execs., Nat. Retail Fedn. (bd. dirs.), Pharmacists Against Drug Abuse, Assn. White House Press Secs., Nat. Orgn. Rare Disorders, Sigma Chi Alumni. Home: Alexandria, Va. Died Feb. 10, 2003.

ZIFF, PAUL, philosophy educator; b. N.Y.C., Oct. 22, 1920; m. Loredana Vanzetto; 3 children. BFA, Cornell U., 1949, PhD, 1951. Instr. philosophy U. Mich., Ann Arbor, 1952-53; from instr. to asst. prof. Harvard U., Cambridge, Mass., 1953-59; from asst. prof. to assoc. prof. U. Pa., 1959-63; prof. U. Wis., 1964-68, U. Ill., Chgo., 1968-70; Kenan prof. U. N.C., Chapel Hill, 1970-88, prof. emeritus, from 1988; chmn. bd. dirs. Chapel Hill Ctr. Linguistic Rsch. Cons. in field. Contbr. articles to profl. jours. Paul Ziff chair installed in his honor U. N.C., 1994; festschrift Language, Mind and Art pub. in his honor, 1994; grantee Rockefeller Found., spring 1955, Guggenheim Found., Rome, 1962-63. Died Jan. 9, 2003.

ZIKAKIS, JOHN P. life scientist, biochemist, nutritionist, educator; b. Piraeus, Greece; came to U.S., 1958; s. Philip J. and Salome J. (Moshou) Z.; m. Kiki K. Matrozos, Aug. 29, 1958; 1 child, Salome J. Assoc. engr., Pythagoras Coll., Piraeus, 1956; BA, U. Del., 1965, MS, 1967, PhD, 1970. Third merchant marine engr. Onassis Shipping Enterprises, Ltd., London, 1956-58; lab. asst. DuPont de Nemours and Co., Newark, Del., 1959-61; rsch. asst. U. Del., Newark, 1965-70, asst. prof. animal sci. dept., 1970-75, assoc. prof. animal sci. dept., 1975-81, prof. animal sci. dept., coll. marine studies, 1981-89; acad. indust. cons., from 1986; prof. food sci. U. Del., Newark, 1987-89, prof. emeritus, 1989; v.p. United Chitotechnologies, Inc., Newark, 1989-93; chief scientist, marine resource specialist Biopolymer Engring., Inc., St. Paul, from 1997, also bd. dirs. Cons. U. Thessaloniki, Greece, 1972-80; vis. prof. U. Panama, 1984-85, sci. advisor, 1985-89; sci. advisor Govt. of Greece, 1972-74; organizer nat. and internat. sci. confs. and symposia. Author: Chitin, Chitosan and Related Enzymes, 1984, Advances in Chitin and Chitosan, 1992; mem. editorial bd. Jour. Agr. Food Chemistry, 1983-86; contbr. over 125 articles to profl. jours. Patentee in field. Trustee Riverside Hosp., Wilmington, Del., 1977-84; pres. bd. dirs. Maison Grande Condominium Assn., Inc., Miami Beach, Fla., 1990-92; bd. dirs. Holy Trinity Greek Orthodox Ch., Wilmington, 1971-73; pres. bd. govs. Commondore Condominium Assn., Ft. Lauderdale, Fla., 1993-94. 1st lt. Greek Air Force, 1952-56. Sr. Fulbright scholar, U. Panama, 1984-85; recipient Gold medal and cert. U. Patra, 1973, cert. recognition, commendation for excellence in rsch., edn., pub. svc. Pres. of U. Del., 1977. Mem. AAAS, Am. Chem. Soc. (historian div. agrl. and food chemistry 1980-84, chmn. pub. rels. com. 1980-85, chmn. disting. svc. award com. 1987-88, cofounder, editor div. agrl. and food chemistry membership directory 1980-86, chmn. div. agrl. and food chemistry 1986-87, Disting. Svc. award 1991), N.Y. Acad. Scis., Del. Acad. Sci., Inst. Food Technologists, Am. Inst. Biol. Sci., Am. Chitosci. Soc. (co-founder, trustee, pres. 1989—), Am. Dairy Sci. Assn., Sigma Xi. Avocations: tennis, sailing, swimming, gymnastics, travel. Home: Fort Lauderdale, Fla. Died Oct. 5, 2003.

ZIMMERMAN, BRUCE R. medical association administrator, medical educator; b. N.Y.C., May 23, 1942; MD, U. Minn., 1967. Diplomate Am. Bd. Internal Medicine, Am. Bd. Endocrinology. Intern Parkland Meml. Hosp., Dallas, 1967-68; resident in internal medicine Mayo Grad. Sch., Rochestern, Minn., 1968-69, 72-74, resident in endocrinology, 1974-76; prof. internal medicine Mayo Med. Sch., Rochester, from 1996; pres. Am. Diabetes Assn., Alexandria, Va., 1999-2000. Past vice-chair divsn. endocrinology, chair coordinating com., mem. clin. practice com. Mayo Clinic, Rochester; past mem., chair diabetes steering com. Minn. Dept. Health. Past assoc. editor, mem. editl. bd. Diabetes Care; past mem. editl. bd. Diabetes Spectrum; editor in chief: Medical Management of Type 2 Diabetes, 4th edit.; contbg. editor: Medical Management of Type 1 Diabetes, 3rd edit. Recipient Leadership award Roche Diabetes Disease Mgmt., 2000. Mem. AAAS, ADA (Banting award 2000), AMA, AFCR, AACE, Soc. Endocrinologists, Am. Diabetes Assn. (past chair publs. policy com. and profl. practice com., past bd. dirs. and numerous coms. and task forces, Outstanding Physician Clinician in Diabetes award 1997). Deceased.

ZIMMERMAN, DONALD LEE, media executive; b. Covington, Ohio, Aug. 8, 1935; s. Leslie Loy and Wauneta Waveline (Gephardt) Z.; m. Judith Anne Kelly; children: Sandra Lynne, Susan Elaine, Stacey Carol. BFA, Ohio U., 1957; postgrad., Ind. U., 1974. Photographer Cromer Photos, Covington, 1957-58; studio mgr. Krider Studios, Inc., Lawrenceburg, Ind., 1958-62; photographer Alderman Studios, High Point, N.C., 1962-67; dir. photographers, v.p. Format, Indpls., 1967-76; pres. Foto-Graphics, Inc., Indpls., 1976-92, Zimmerman & Assocs., from 1992. Co-chmn. mini marathon com. 500 Festival Assocs., Indpls., 1988. Mem. Profl. Photographers Am. (cert. profl. photographer, master of photography), Am. Soc. Profl. Photographers, Masons. Home: Indianapolis, Ind. Died June 25, 2000.

ZIMMERMAN, EVERETT LEE, English educator, academic administrator; b. Lancaster, Pa., Dec. 9, 1936; s. Amos Wanner and Anna (Sensenig) Z.; m. Muriel Laden, Apr. 28, 1963, children: Andrew, Daniel. BA, Bob Jones U., 1958; MA, Temple U., 1961, PhD, 1966. Lectr. Temple U., Phila., 1961-62; instr. Rutgers U., Camden, N.J., 1962-66, asst. prof., 1966-69, U. Calif., Santa Barbara, 1969-72, assoc. prof., 1972-80, prof. English, 1980—2003, dean, 1988-89, provost, 1997—2001. Author: Defoe and the Novel, 1975, Swift's Narrative Satires, 1983, The Boundaries of Fiction, 1996; also articles. Dem. committeeman, Phila., 1965-66. Jr. Faculty fellow, 1971, Humanities Inst. fellow, 1975 U. Calif.; NEH grantee, 1986; Guggenheim fellow, 1989-90. Mem. MLA, Am. Soc. 18th Century Studies. Home: Santa Barbara, Calif. Died Sept. 22, 2003.

ZIMMERMANN, WARREN, former foreign service officer; b. Phila., Nov. 16, 1934; s. Albert Walter and Barbara (Shoemaker) Z.; m. Corinne Roosevelt Robinson Chubb, Apr. 18, 1959; children: Corinne Alsop, Warren Jr., Elizabeth Zimmermann Metcalfe. BA, Yale U., 1956; BA/MA, Cambridge U., Eng., 1958. Joined Office Fgn. Svc., 1961; consular and polit. officer Am. Embassy, Caracas, Venezuela, 1962-64; student Serbo-Croation lang. Fgn. Svc. Inst., 1964-65; polit. officer Am. Embassy, Belgrade, Yugoslavia, 1965-68; Soviet policy analyst Bur. Intelligence & Rsch., Dept. State, 1968-70; speechwriter to sec. of state Dept. State, Washington, 1970-73; student Russian lang. Fgn. Svc. Inst., Dept. State, 1973; dep. chief, polit. sect. Am. Embassy, Moscow, 1973-75; spl. asst. policy planning Bur. European Affairs, Dept. State, 1975-77; counselor polit. affairs Am Embassy, Paris, 1977-80; dep. chmn. U.S. del. Madrid Conf. Security and Cooperation in Europe, 1980-81; dep. chief mission Am. Embassy, Moscow, 1981-84; dep. U.S. del. with rank of amb. negotiations on nuclear/space arms race with Soviet Union, Geneva, 1985-86; chmn. U.S. del. with rank of amb. Vienna meeting Conf. on Security and Cooperation in Europe, 1986-89; amb. to Yugoslavia, 1989-92; dir. Bur. Refugee Programs Dept. State, Washington, 1992-94; sr. fellow Rand Corp., 1994. Sr. fellow Rand, 1994, sr. cons., 1995—; former disting. fellow New Sch. Social Rsch.; professorial lectr. Johns Hopkins Sch. Advanced Internat. Studies, 1994-96; disting. fellow Sch. Pub. Affairs, U. Md., 1995; Kathryn and Shelby Cullom Davis prof. columbia U., 1996-2000; vis. fellow coun. Fgn. Rels., N.Y.C., 1984-85; chief U.S. del. negotiations Hotline Upgrade Agreement with Soviet Union, 1983-84; Carnegie tchg. fellow Yale U., 1958-59. Author: Origins of a Catastrophe: Yugoslavia and Its Destroyers, 1996, First Great Triumph: How Five Americans Made Their Country A World Power, 2004. With U.S. Army, 1959. Mem. Coun. Fgn. Rels., Internat. Inst. Strategic Studies, Am. Acad. of Diplomacy. Democrat. Avocations: history, tennis, skiing, fishing. Home: Great Falls, Va. Died Feb. 3, 2004.

ZINDEL, PAUL, author; b. S.I., N.Y., May 15, 1936; s. Paul and Betty (Frank) Z.; m. Bonnie Hildebrand, Oct. 25, 1973; children: David Jack, Lizabeth Claire. BS, Wagner Coll., 1958, MS, 1959, HHD (hon.), 1971. Chemistry tchr. Tottenville High Sch., S.I., N.Y., 1959-69; playwright-in-residence Alley Theatre, Houston, 1967. Author: (plays) Dimensions of Peacocks, 1959, Euthanasia and the Endless Hearts, 1960, A Dream of Swallows, 1964, The Effect of Gamma Rays On Man-In-The-Moon Marigolds, 1965 (Obie award 1970, N.Y. Drama Critics Circle award 1970, Variety award 1970, Pulitzer Prize in drama 1971, N.Y. Critics award 1971, Vernon Rice Drama Desk award 1971), And Miss Reardon Drinks A Little, 1967 (L.A. Drama Critics award 1968), Let Me Hear You Whisper, 1973, The Secret Affairs of Mildred Wild, 1973, The Ladies Should Be in Bed, 1973, Ladies at the Alamo, 1977, A Destiny with Half Moon Street, 1983, Amulets Against the Dragon Forces, 1989; (screenplays) Up The Sandbox, 1972, Mame, 1973, Maria's Lovers, 1985, Runaway Train, 1986; (TV movies) The Effect of Gamma Rays on Man-In-The-Moon Marigolds, 1966, Let Me Hear You Whisper, 1974, Alice in Wonderland, 1985, Babes in Toyland, 1986, A Connecticut Yankee in King Arthur's Court, 1989; (novels for teenagers) The Pigman, 1968, My Darling, My Hamburger, 1969, I Never Loved Your Mind, 1970, I Love My Mother, 1975, Pardon Me, You're Stepping on My Eyeball, 1976, Confessions of a Teen-Age Baboon, 1977, The Undertaker's Gone Bananas, 1978, (with Bonnie Zindel) A Star for the Latecomer, 1980, The Pigman's Legacy, 1980 (ALA Best Books for Young Adults Selection 1981), The Girl Who Wanted a Boy, 1981, (with Crescent Dragonwagon) To Take a Dare, 1982, Compromising Positions, 1982, Harry and Hortense at Hormone High, 1984, When A Darkness Falls, 1984, The Amazing and Death-Defying Diary of Eugene Dingman, 1987, A Begonia for Miss Applebaum, 1989, The Pigman and Me, 1991, David and Della, 1993, Attack of the Killer Fishsticks, 1993, Fright Party!, 1993, Fifth Grade Safari, 1993, City Safari, 1994, One Hundred Percent Laugh Riot, 1994, Loch, 1994, The Doom Stone, 1995, Reef of Death, 1997, Amulets Against the Dragon Forces, 1998, The Pigman: With Connections, 1998, Raptor, 1998, Rats, 1999, Every 17 Minutes the Crowd Goes Crazy!, 2000, The Gadget, 2001, Night of the Bat, 2001, The Scream Museum, 2001, The Surfing Corpse, 2001, The E-Mail Murders, 2001, The Lethal Gorilla, 2001, The Square Root of Murder, 2001, Death on the Amazon, 2002, The Gourmet Zombie, 2002, The Phantom of 86th Street, 2002, The Houdini Whodunit, 2002, Death by CD, 2003, The Pretrified Parrot, 2003. Ford Found. grantee, 1967. Died Mar. 27, 2003.

ZINKIN, VIVIAN, retired humanities educator; b. Lakewood, N.J., Apr. 12, 1911; d. Isaac and Golda (Sachs) Z. BS, Rutgers U., 1935; MA, NYU, 1940; PhD, Columbia U., 1960. Cert. tchr., N.J. Tchr. Newark Elem. Sch., 1930-59; prof. English Glassboro State Tchrs. Coll., 1959-75. Mem. MLA. Home: Lakewood, NJ. Died July 29, 2001.

ZOGHBY, GUY ANTHONY, lawyer; b. Mobile, Ala., Sept. 30, 1934; s. Herbert Michael and Laurice (Haik) Z.; m. Verna Madelyn Antoine, Mar. 2, 1957 (dissolved); children: Guy Anthony II, Madelyn A., Gregory M.; m. Judy-ann EcKberg, Jan. 2, 1976. AB in English, Spring Hill Coll., 1955; JD, U. Cin., 1963; cert., U.S. Army JAG Sch., 1964. Bar: Ohio 1963, Ala. 1965, Calif. 1978, Pa. 1988. Advanced through grades to capt. U.S. Army, 1963, various assignments, 1955-63; dep. staff JAG 11th Air Assault Div., Ft. Benning, Ga., 1963-64, 1st Cav. Div., 1964-65; atty. office of v.p. and gen. counsel IBM, Armonk, N.Y., 1965-67, staff atty., 1967-69, sr. atty., 1969-71, regional counsel Bethesda, Md., 1972-73, corp. staff counsel London, 1973-77, div. counsel Armonk, N.Y., 1977-80, mng. atty., 1980-83, group counsel, from 1983; v.p., gen. counsel PPG Industries Inc., Pitts., 1987-93, sr. v.p., gen. counsel, 1994-97; now mediator, arbitrator, Pitts., from 1997. Lectr. profl. seminars; co-chmn. corp. counsel com. Nat. Ctr. for St. Cts., 1998—. Editor U. Cin. Law Rev., 1962-63. Bd. dirs. Allegheny ARC, 1989—, Am. Judicature Soc., 1988—, pres., 1993-95; bd. dirs. Pitts. Civic Light Opera, 1992—, Am. Arbitration Assn., 1996—; mem. Am. Law Inst., 1992—, The Duquesne Club, 1988; bd. visitors U. Cin. Coll. Law, 1986—; exec. com. Ctr. for Pub. Resource, 1994—. Decorated Commendation medal with one oak leaf cluster; recipient Lawrence Maxwell prize U. Cin. Mem. Am. Corp. Counsel Assn. (cir. 1982—, exec. com. 1982-88, chmn. 1987—), Assn. Gen. Counsel, Order of Coif. Roman Catholic. Deceased.

ZOHN, HARRY, author, educator; b. Vienna, Nov. 21, 1923; came to U.S., 1940, naturalized, 1945; s. Abraham Leon and Adele (Awin) Z.; m. Judith Ann Gorfinkle, Sept. 3, 1962; children: Steven David, Marjorie Eve. BA, Suffolk U., Boston, 1946; MA in Edn., Clark U., 1947; AM, Harvard U., 1949, PhD, 1952; LittD (hon.), Suffolk U., 1976. Credit investigator Credit Bur. Greater Boston, 1941-46; tchg. fellow in German Harvard U., 1947-51; mem. faculty Brandeis U., 1951-96, prof. German, 1967-96, chmn. dept. Germanic and Slavic langs., 1967-77, 87-90, chmn. Sch. Humanities coun., 1978-79, chmn. grad. program in lit. studies, 1981-84, prof. German emeritus, from 1996. Exec. dir. Goethe Soc. New England, 1963-68. Author: Wiener Juden in der deutschen Literatur, 1964, Karl Kraus, 1971, German edit., 1990, Jüdisches Erbe in der österreichischen Literatur, 1986, Amerikanische "Thirty-Eighters" aus Wien als doppelte Kulturträger, 1994, Austriaca and Judaica, 1995, Karl Kraus and the Critics, 1997, Schüttelreime, 1997;

editor: Liber Amicorum Friderike Zweig, 1952, Wie sie es sehen, 1952, Schachnovelle, 1960, Men of Dialogue, 1969, Der farbenvolle Untergang, 1970, Greatness Revisited, 1971, Deutschland, Deutschland über alles, 1972, The Saints of Qumran, 1977, Germany?, Germany!, 1990, Aus dem Tagebuch eines Emigranten, 1992, A Peter Fabrizius Reader, 1994, Die Stimme des Wortes, 1998; transl. books by Theodor Herzl, Kurt Tucholsky, Karl Kraus, Jacob Burckhardt, Walter Benjamin, Gershom Scholem, Alex Bein, André Kaminski, Fritz Molden, Manès Sperber, Hermann Langbein, others; mem. editl. bd. Modern Austrian Lit., Cross Currents; gen. editor (series) Austrian Culture. Mem. adv. com. fgn. langs. Commonwealth Mass., 1961-64; trustee Suffolk U., 1978-81, 83—. Decorated officer's cross Order Merit (Fed. Republic Germany) 1960; Cross of Honor for Sci. and Art (Republic of Austria) 1984; Gold Medal of Honor, City of Vienna, 1994; recipient Art prize Wolfgang Altendorf Cultural Found., 1991, Ring of HOnor, City of Vienna. Mem. Am. Assn. Tchrs. German (pres. Mass. chpt. 1954-59), Am. PEN Ctr., Austro-Am. Assn. Boston (chmn. bd. dirs. 1965—), Internat. Stefan Zweig Soc. (v.p. 1957-90), Internat. Arthur Schnitzler Assn. (v.p. 1978—), Austrian PEN Club, Internat. Franz Werfel Soc. (chmn. bd. dirs. 1995—), PEN Ctr. German-Speaking Writers Abroad, New Eng. MLA (past sec.-treas., chmn. Mass. chpt., bd. dirs.). Home: Newton, Mass. Deceased.

ZOLL, JEFFERY MARK, lawyer; b. Evergreen Park, Ill., Sept. 25, 1954; s. Frank Earl and Earline Ruth (Abadie) Z. AB cum laude, U. Ill., 1975, JD, 1978. Bar: Ill. 1978; CPA, Ill. Tax mgr. Touche Ross and Co., Chgo., 1978-85, Arthur Andersen and Co., Chgo., from 1985. Mem. ABA, Chgo. Bar Assn., Am. Inst. CPA's, Phi Beta Kappa. Home: Chicago, Ill. Deceased.

ZOPPO, CIRO ELLIOTT, retired political science educator, consultant; b. Caserta, Campania, Italy, Aug. 21, 1923; came to U.S., 1936, naturalized, 1943; s. Romualdo and Romilda (Veccia) Z.; m. Rosemary Pampalone, June 25, 1949; children: Adriana, Gian. BA, Montclair State U., 1948; MA, Columbia U., 1959, PhD, 1963. Rschr. Rand Corp., Santa Monica, Calif., 1960-63, 66-68, cons., 1968-83; rsch. assoc. Ctr. for Internat. Affairs, Harvard U., Cambridge, Mass., 1963-66; assoc. dir. Security Studies Project, UCLA, 1968-70; prof. polit. sci. UCLA, 1969-91, prof. emeritus, from 1991. Author, editor: Geopolitics: Classical and Nuclear, 1985, Nordic Security and 21st Century, 1992; contbr. articles to profl. publs. Assoc. rsch. coun Inst. Civil-Mils., Toulouse, France, 1982-87; mem. World Affairs Coun., L.A., 1995—; acad. assoc. Atlantic Coun. U.S., Washington, 1986. Lt. U.S. Army, 1943-45, ETO. Decorated Bronze star; grantee Ford Found., 1970-75, U.S. Dept. State, 1972, UCLA, 1976—. Mem. Internat. Inst. Strategic Studies (London), Istituto Affari Internazionali (Rome), Istituto Cuestiones Internacionales (Spain). Avocations: painting, languages, travel. Home: Los Angeles, Calif. Deceased.

ZORNOW, WILLIAM FRANK, historian, educator; b. Cleve., Aug. 13, 1920; s. William Frederick Emil and Viola (Schulz) Z. AB, Western Res. U., 1942, A.M., 1944, PhD, 1952. Vice pres., treas. Glenville Coal & Supply Co., Real Value Coal Corp., Zornow Coal Corp., 1941-45; dep. clk. Probate Ct., Cuyahoga County, Ohio, 1941-43; prodn. planning engr. Hickok Elec. Instrument Co., Cleve., 1943-46; teaching asst. Western Res. U., 1944-47; instr. U. Akron, 1946-47, Case Inst. Tech., 1947-50, Washburn U., 1950-51; lectr. Cleve. Coll., 1948-49; asst. prof. Kans. State U., 1951-58; asst. prof. history Kent (Ohio) State U., 1958-61, asso. prof., 1961-66, prof. history, 1966—. Perpetual hon. fellow Harry S. Truman Libr. Inst., Independence, Mo.; collection corr. Berkshire Loan and Fin. Co., Painesville (Ohio) Security Credit Acceptance Corp., Mentor, Ohio, 1951-60; cons. Karl E. Mundt Library, Dakota State Coll., Madison, S.D.; presenter 1st coll. arts and scis. faculty lecture series Kent State U., 1962. Author: Lincoln and the Party Divided, 1954, rev. edit., 1972, Kansas: A History of the Jayhawk State, 1957, America at Mid-Century, 1959, The Many Faces of Lincoln, 1997; author: (with others) Abraham Lincoln: A New Portrait, 1959, Kansas: The First Century, 1956, The Many Faces of Lincoln, 1997; contbr. articles to encys. and profl. jours.; editor: Shawnee County (Kans.) Hist. Bull., 1950-51; abstractor: America: History and Life: Historical Abstracts, 1964—. Mem. Dir.'s Circle Cleve. Mus. Art, 1989—, Cleve. Clin. Found., 1992—, Soc. Fellows. Faculty rsch. grantee Kans. State U., 1955-57, Kent State U., 1960-64. Mem. AAAS, AAUP, N.Y. Acad. Scis., Soc. Fellow of Cleve. Clinic Found., Am. Acad. Polit. and Social Sci., Am. Assn. State and Local History (award of merit 1958), Am. Hist. Assn., Orgn. Am. historians, Ohio Acad. History (chmn. awards com.), Ohio Hist. Soc. (libr. adv. com. 1969—), Ohio Soc. N.Y., Ctr. Study of Presidency, Acad. Polit. Sci., Lincoln Fellowship of Wis., Sierra Club San Francisco, Delta Tau Delta (4-star coun. 1992—), Pi Gamma Mu, Phi Alpha Theta, Phi Delta Kappa. Home: Mentor, Ohio. Died Dec. 16, 2003.

ZOUNGRANA, PAUL CARDINAL, archbishop; b. Ouagadougou, Burkina Faso, Sept. 3, 1917. Ordained priest Roman Cath. Ch., 1942; archbishop of Ouagadougou, 1960, now archbishop emeritus; elevated to Sacred Coll. Cardinals, 1965; titular ch. St. Camillus de Lellis; former pres. adminstrn. coun. La Fondation Jean-Paul II Pour Le Sahel, hon. life pres. Former mem. Congregation Evangelization of Peoples, Congregation Culte divisi et sacrements, CongregationInst. vie consacrée et societés de vie apostolique, Conseil Pontifical Pastorale des Services de Santé, The Cardinals Coun. for Adminstrv. and Econ. Problems of St. Siege (former mem. Group of 15 Cardinals)., Died 2000.

ZWEMER, FRANK LANUS, retired surgeon; b. Cleve., Dec. 11, 1928; BA, Hope Coll.; MD, Ohio State U., 1954. Diplomate Am. Bd. Surgery. Intern, then resident in gen. surgery Cleve. Met. Gen. Hosp., 1954-61, fellow, 1959-61; surgeon, supr. Scudder Meml. Hosp., Ranipet, N. Arcot, Tamil Nadu, India, 1961-70; chief surgery Phoenix Indian Med. Ctr., 1971-91; sr. clin. surgery USPHS, 1989-91; ret. Fellow ACS; mem. AMA, Commd. Officers Assn. of US-PHS, Alpha Omega Alpha. Home: San Marcos, Calif. Died Feb. 11, 2001.

ZWERIN, CHARLOTTE MITCHELL, freelance/self-employed film producer; b. Detroit, Aug. 15, 1931; d. Charles and Margaret (Oliphant) Mitchell; m. Michael Zwerin, Dec. 16, 1959 (div. 1964). BA, Wayne State, 1952. Film editor CBS News, N.Y.C., 1956-61, NBC News, N.Y.C., 1962; dir. Sta. WGBH, Boston, 1964, Maysles Film Inc., N.Y.C., 1965, 70, 76, 86; producer, dir. Maysles Film, Inc., N.Y.C., 1987; dir. Cort Prodns., N.Y.C., 1982-84, Zwerin Films, Inc., N.Y.C., 1984; producer NBC News, N.Y.C., 1985. Dir.: (films) Robert Frost (Acad. Award 1963), Gimme Shelter, 1970, Running Fence (Blue Ribbon Ednl. Film Library Assn), Arshile Gorky (Blue Ribbon Ednl. Film Library Assn 1983), Thelonious Monk: Straight, No Chaser, Music for the Movies, Toru Takemitsu; dir., writer: Isamu Noguchi, The Sculpture of Spaces. NEA grantee, 1990. Mem. Dirs. Guild, Internat. Alliance Theatrical Stage Employees, Writers Guild Am. Home: New York, NY. Died Jan. 22, 2004.

ZYTKOW, JAN MIKOLAJ, computer science educator; b. Warsaw, Sept. 9, 1944; came to U.S., 1982; s. Swiatozar Mikolaj and Maria (Szeruda) Z.; m. Malgorzata Krzywińska, Oct. 14, 1972; children: Nikola, Ania, Andrzej, Michael. MS in Philosophy, 1970, PhD in Philosophy Sci., 1972, habilitation docent, 1979. Asst. prof. U. Warsaw, 1972-80, assoc. prof., 1981-82; vis. prof. Carnegie-Mellon U., Pitts., 1982-84; assoc. prof. Wichita (Kans.) State U., 1984-87, prof., 1987-97, computer sci. chmn., 1996-97; prof. U. N.C., Charlotte, from 1997. Author: (with others) Scientific Discovery, 1987; contbr. articles to profl. jours. Mem. Am. Assn. Artificial Intelligence, Philosophy Sci. Assn. Lutheran. Died Jan. 16, 2001.